AA

Th
Hotel
Guide

CREDITS

39th edition September 2005 First published by the Automobile Association as the Hotel and Restaurant Guide, 1967 The contents of this publication are believed correct at the time of printing. Nevertheless, the publishers cannot be held responsible for any errors or omissions or for any changes in the details given in this guide or for the consequences of any reliance on the information provided by the same. This does not affect your statutory rights. Assessments of AA inspected establishments are based on the experience of the Hotel and Restaurant Inspectors on the occasion(s) of their visit(s) and therefore descriptions given in this guide necessarily contain an element of subjective opinion which may not reflect or dictate a reader's own opinion on another occasion. See page 6 for a clear explanation of how, based on our Inspectors' inspection experiences, establishments are graded. If the meal or meals experienced by an Inspector or Inspectors during an inspection fall between award levels the restaurant concerned may be awarded the lower of any award levels considered applicable. The AA strives to ensure accuracy of the information in this guide at the time of printing. Due to the constantly evolving nature of the subject matter the information is subject to change. The AA will gratefully receive any advice from our readers of any necessary updated information. Please contact:

Advertising Sales Department: advertisingsales@theAA.com
Editorial Department: lifestyleguides@theAA.com
AA Hotel Scheme Enquiries: 01256 844455

Cover photographs courtesy of: Hand Picked Hotels (l) (Norton House Hotel & Restaurant) (m) Buxted Park CHH photography by Piet Johnson (r) Gordon Cartwright

Typesetting and colour repro by Microset Graphics Ltd, Basingstoke, Hampshire

Printed and bound in Spain by Printer Industria Grafica Barcelona

Directory compiled by the AA Hotel Services Department and generated from the AA establishment database.

www.theAA.com

Published by AA Publishing, a trading name of Automobile Association Developments Limited, whose registered office is Fanum House, Basing View, Basingstoke, Hampshire RG21 4EA. Registered number 1878835

A CIP catalogue record for this book is available from the British Library

ISBN-10: 0-7495-4621-2

ISBN-13: 978-0-7495-4621-2

A02438

CONTENTS

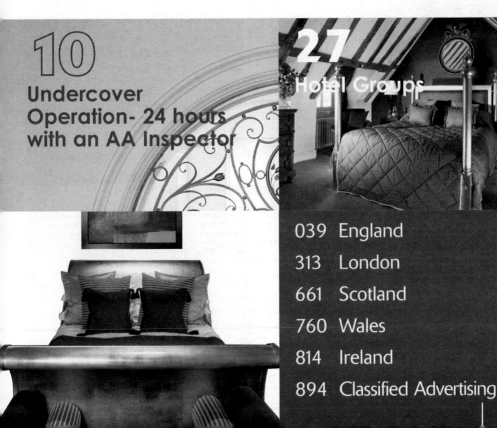

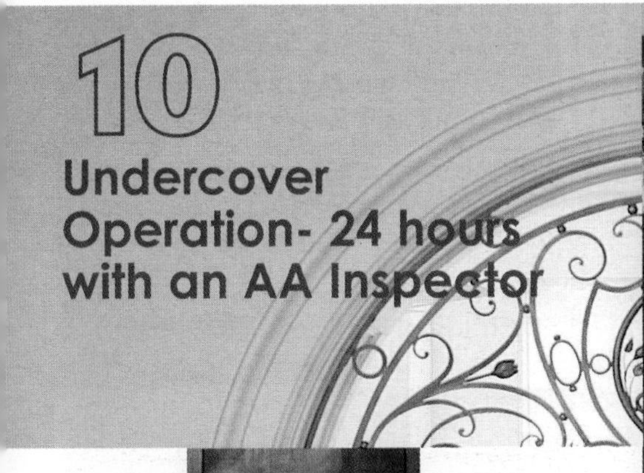

Welcome to the Guide

This Guide brings you the widest choice of accommodation across the length and breadth of Britain and Ireland. All the hotels featured have been assessed under quality standards agreed between the national rating bodies, enabling you to make your choice with confidence. Each AA rated hotel is given a classification that is based on an overnight 'mystery guest' visit by one of our own highly qualified inspectors.

How does the AA Assess a Hotel?

Any hotel applying for AA recognition receives an annual unannounced visit to check standards. The hotels with full entries in this guide have all paid an annual fee for AA inspection, recognition and rating. AA inspectors pay as a guest for their inspection visit, they do not accept free hospitality of any kind. Although AA inspectors do not stay overnight at Travel Accommodation or Associate Hotels (see page 7) they call in annually to verify standards and procedures.

Quality Assessment Score - making hotel choice easier

AA inspectors supplement their report with an additional quality assessment of everything the hotel offers, including hospitality, based on what they experience as the 'mystery guest'. This results in an overall Quality Assessment Score. This Score offers a comparison of quality within each star classification. Readers can see at a glance that a hotel with a percentage score of 69 offers a higher quality experience than one with the same star classification but a percentage score of 59. To gain AA recognition in the first place, a hotel must achieve a minimum quality score of 50 per cent.

AA Top Hotels in Britain and Ireland

Each year we select the best hotels in each rating. These are recognised as the AA s Top Hotels. These hotels stand out as the very best in the British Isles, regardless of style. Top Hotels can be identified by their Red Stars.

AA Awards 2005-2006

Every year we present a range of awards to the finest AA-inspected and rated hotels from England, Scotland, Ireland and Wales. The Hotel of the Year Award is our ultimate accolade and is awarded to those hotels that are recognised as outstanding examples in their field. Often innovative, the winning hotels always set high standards in hotel keeping. The hotels are listed on pages 8-9.

FEEDBACK

We welcome your feedback about the hotels included and about the guide itself. You can write to us at AA Lifestyle Guides, Fanum House, Basingstoke RG21 4EA or e-mail us at: lifestyleguides@theAA.com.

Please note, however, that if you have a complaint to make during a visit, we strongly recommend that you discuss the matter with the hotel management there and then so that they have a chance to put things right before your visit is spoilt. The AA does not undertake to arbitrate between you and the hotel management, or to obtain compensation or engage in correspondence.

HINTS ON BOOKING YOUR STAY

It's always worth booking as early as possible, particularly for the peak holiday period from the beginning of June to the end of September. Bear in mind that Easter and other public holidays may be busy too and in some parts of Scotland, the ski season is a peak holiday period. Some hotels will ask for a deposit or full payment in advance, especially for one-night bookings, and not all hotels will take advance bookings for bed and breakfast, overnight or short stays. Some will not make reservations from mid week. Some hotels charge half-board (bed, breakfast and dinner) whether you eat the meals or not, while others may only accept full-board bookings. Once a booking is confirmed, let the hotel know at once if you are unable to keep your reservation. If the hotel cannot re-let your room you may be liable to pay about two-thirds of the room price (a deposit will count towards this payment). In Britain a legally binding contract is made when you accept an offer of accommodation, either in writing or by telephone, and illness is not accepted as a release from this contract. You are advised to take out insurance against possible cancellation, for example AA Single Trip Insurance (telephone 0800 085 7240 or consult the AA website www.theAA.com for details).

BOOKING ONLINE

Booking a place to stay can be a time-consuming process, so why not search quickly and easily online for a place that best suits your needs. Simply visit www.theAA.com/hotels to search from around 8,000 quality rated hotels and B&Bs in Great Britain and Ireland. Then contact the establishment direct by clicking the 'Make a booking' button.

Website Addresses

Web Site addresses are included where they have been supplied and specified by the respective establishment. Such Web Sites are not under the control of The Automobile Association Developments Limited and as such The Automobile Association Developments Limited has no control over them and will not accept any responsibility or liability in respect of any and all matters whatsoever relating to such Web Sites including access, content, material and functionality. By including the addresses of third party Web Sites the AA does not intend to solicit business or offer any security to any person in any country, directly or indirectly.

AA Star Classification

All hotels recognised by the AA should :

- have high standards of cleanliness
- keep proper records of booking
- give prompt and professional service to guests assist with luggage on request accept and deliver messages
- provide a designated area for breakfast and dinner, with drinks available in a bar or lounge
- provide an early morning call on request
- have good quality furniture and fittings
- provide adequate heating and lighting
- undertake proper maintenance

A guide to some of the general expectations for each star classification is as follows:

★ One Star

- Polite, courteous staff providing a relatively informal yet competent style of service, available during the day and evening to receive guests
- At least one designated eating area open to residents for breakfast
- If dinner is offered it should be on at least five days a week, with last orders no later than 6.30pm
- Television in lounge or bedroom
- Majority of rooms en suite, bath or shower room available at all times

★★ Two Star

As for one star, plus

- At least one restaurant or dining room open to residents for breakfast (and for dinner at least five days a week)
- Last orders for dinner no earlier than 7pm
- Television in bedroom
- En suite or private bath or shower and WC

★★★ Three Star

- Management and staff smartly and professionally presented and usually uniformed
- A dedicated receptionist on duty at peak times
- At least one restaurant or dining room open to residents and non-residents for breakfast and dinner whenever the hotel is open
- Last orders for dinner no earlier than 8pm
- Remote-control television, direct-dial telephone
- En suite bath or shower and WC.

★★★★ Four Star

- A formal, professional staffing structure with smartly presented, uniformed staff anticipating and responding to your needs or requests. Usually spacious, well-appointed public areas
- Reception staffed 24 hours by well-trained staff
- Express checkout facilities where appropriate
- Porterage available on request
- Night porter available
- At least one restaurant open to residents and non-residents for breakfast and dinner seven days per week, and lunch to be available in a designated eating area
- Last orders for dinner no earlier than 9pm
- En suite bath with fixed overhead shower, WC

★★★★★ Five Star

- Luxurious accommodation and public areas with a range of extra facilities. First time guests shown to their bedroom
- Multilingual service
- Guest accounts well explained and presented
- Porterage offered
- Guests greeted at hotel entrance, full concierge service provided
- At least one restaurant open to residents and non-residents for all meals seven days per week
- Last orders for dinner no earlier than 10pm
- High-quality menu and wine list
- Evening turn-down service. Remote-control television, direct-dial telephone at bedside and desk, a range of luxury toiletries, bath sheets and robes. En suite bath with fixed overhead shower, WC

★ Top Hotels Each year we select the best hotels in each rating. These are recognised as the AA's Top Hotels. These hotels stand out as the very best in the British Isles, regardless of style. Top Hotels can be identified by their Red Stars.

Other Categories of Accommodation

TOWN HOUSE ACCOMMODATION

These individual city or town-centre properties provide a high degree of personal service and privacy. They concentrate on luxuriously furnished bedrooms and suites, rather than public rooms or formal dining rooms. Town house accommodation may have some restaurant provision but if not, a high standard of room service will be offered. All fall within the four or five star classification, though no Quality Assessment Score is shown.

COUNTRY HOUSE HOTELS

These offer a relaxed, informal atmosphere, with an emphasis on personal welcome. They are usually, but not always, in a secluded or rural setting and should offer peace and quiet regardless of location.

RESTAURANTS WITH ROOMS

A restaurant which also offers accommodation. The focus is on the food, and most have 12 bedrooms or less. No star rating is shown but bedrooms reflect at least the level of quality associated with two stars.

TRAVEL ACCOMMODATION

This classification indicates budget or lodge accommodation, usually in purpose-built units close to main roads and motorways and in town and city centres.

U HOTELS WITH AN UNCONFIRMED STAR CLASSIFICATION

A small number of hotels in the guide have a 'U' symbol. These had not had their star classification confirmed at the time of going to print.*

A ASSOCIATE ENTRIES

These are establishments that have been inspected and rated by the national rating bodies in Britain and Northern Ireland. They are rated with stars ★ although some of the bodies use a slightly different set of criteria. Associate Hotels have paid to belong to the AA Associate Hotels Scheme and therefore receive a limited entry in the guide. Descriptions of these hotels can be found on the AA website.

AA Rosette Awards

Out of the many thousands of restaurants in the UK, the AA identifies some 1,800 as the best. The following is an outline of what to expect from restaurants with AA Rosette Awards. For a more detailed explanation of Rosette criteria please see www.theAA.com

Excellent local restaurants serving food prepared with care, understanding and skill, using good quality ingredients.

The best local restaurants, which aim for and achieve higher standards, better consistency and where a greater precision is apparent in the cooking. There will be obvious attention to the selection of quality ingredients.

Outstanding restaurants that demand recognition well beyond their local area.

Amongst the very best restaurants in the British Isles, where the cooking demands national recognition.

The finest restaurants in the British Isles, where the cooking stands comparison with the best in the world.

O HOTELS WITH NO STAR CLASSIFICATION

Hotels preceded by the 'O' symbol were not open at the time of going to print but are due to open during the year.*

***Check the AA website www.theAA.com for current information and ratings.**

AA Hotel of the Year

Hotel of the Year is the AA's most prestigious award. One hotel from each country - England, Scotland, Wales and Ireland - is chosen as a winner.

Winner for England

Calcot Manor

Tetbury, Gloucestershire

★★★ ®®®

p560

Winner for Scotland

Glenapp Castle

Ballantrae,
South Ayrshire

★★★ ֍֍֍

p670

Winner for Wales

Castle Hotel

Conwy,
Conwy

★★★ ֍֍

p780

Winner for
Republic of Ireland

Dromoland Castle

Newmarket-on-Fergus,
County Clare

★★★★★ ֍֍

p854

NOVOTEL

Hotel Group of the Year Award

This award reflects the hotel group which has demonstrated an outstanding commitment to improving and developing their portfolio of hotels, whilst maintaining a high level of consistency throughout the group

Feature

Undercover Operation – 24 Hours with an AA Hotel Inspector

by Denise Laing

ARE THEY THE GUESTS FROM HELL? HOTEL STAFF MIGHT BE FORGIVEN FOR THINKING SO, AND LABEL THEM AS THE FUSSIEST, MOST DEMANDING CUSTOMERS THEY EVER HAVE TO DEAL WITH. THEIR INEXPLICABLE DESIRE TO EAT NON-STOP FROM THE MOMENT THEY CHECK IN TO THE POINT OF DEPARTURE CAN MAKE THEM SEEM LIKE GLUTTONS. THEIR REQUESTS FOR HELP: "WHERE IS THE LIGHT SWITCH IN THE BATHROOM?", "HOW DO I OPEN THE MINIBAR?"; THEIR NEED FOR INFORMATION DESPITE CLEAR DETAILS IN THE HOTEL LITERATURE AND MENUS PROVIDED IN THE BEDROOMS: "DO YOU DO ROOM SERVICE?", "WHAT IS THE TOMATO SOUP MADE FROM?"; THEIR APPARENT DISSATISFACTION: "CAN I HAVE AN EXTRA BLANKET/PILLOW/HEATER"?, AND SEEMING HELPLESSNESS: "WOULD YOU RECOMMEND A SANDWICH FILLING?" CAN GIVE THE IMPRESSION OF SOMEONE DECIDEDLY OUT OF THEIR COMFORT ZONE. BUT THE IMPRESSION IS A WHOLLY INACCURATE ONE. FOR IN ORDER THAT YOU AND I MIGHT SAFELY ASSUME THAT OUR HOTEL VISITS WILL PROVIDE EXACTLY WHAT WE EXPECT AND PAY FOR, THESE GUINEA PIGS TRY THEM OUT FIRST ON OUR BEHALF. WHEN I ACCOMPANIED AN AA INSPECTOR RECENTLY ON AN OVERNIGHT VISIT TO A FOUR-STAR LONDON HOTEL, I WAS IN FOR PLENTY OF SURPRISES.

The endless questions are all geared towards finding out how helpful are the staff, how responsive they are to requests for assistance, how much product knowledge they have, how proactive they are in terms of selling their hotel's services, and how good the services themselves are. To test all of these the hotel inspector has to

appear a little eccentric, and just a touch unworldly. But it is all part of the job of going undercover to highlight and praise strengths, and expose and eliminate weaknesses. How their requests for assistance are dealt with, and by whom, will be carefully noted. Come the debrief the next day with the hotel owner or manager, the winners and the losers will be identified individually by name. Their performances will be analysed, and ways in which the hotel's hospitality, services and customer care can be improved will be suggested. The AA hotel inspector is not trying to catch anyone out or shame them, but is working with the hotel to make it the best it can be. This can be a highly productive partnership.

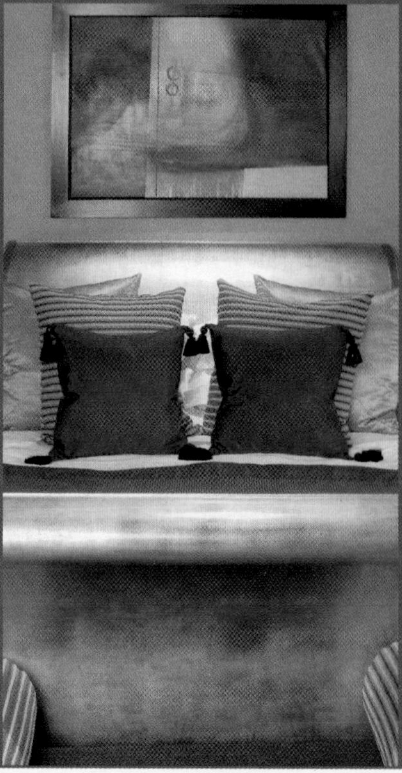

AA inspectors are adept at concealing their identities when they book a hotel room, and hotels are equally practised and skilled at spotting them. It's a game that both sides need to win, though the practice works best when the inspector stays incognito. It can quickly become clear when they have been identified, even if indications can be strangely contrary. On the one hand the presence of a hotel inspector can cause owners and staff to freeze, and appear cold and ill at ease. The inspector can even be ignored to the point of rudeness, for fear of staff appearing to give them preferential treatment.

On the other hand, the staff can fawn embarrassingly over the inspector à la Basil Fawlty, paying a sycophantic homage that other guests are blatantly denied. The 'recognised' inspector in both of these scenarios must behave as if they have noticed nothing untoward, and following the next morning's debrief can adjust the hospitality scoring according to what they are told. As we went through the procedure of checking in, trying out the services and ordering food, I kept my eyes peeled to see if we had been spotted, but it didn't look like it, a hunch borne out next day.

Eating goes hand in hand with the job of inspecting hotels, and the first task after check in is to order something from room service. Typically this will be soup, since it can be easily disposed of if the inspector has already had lunch, which they probably have! Here it is not so much the food as the service that is being considered, though obviously the food has to be decent. The questions that have to be asked are: Does it arrive when promised? Are trays removed promptly afterwards? Did the kitchen recommend something in addition to the requested item? Could they explain what a dish consisted of, or give assurance that it didn't contain any allergens if asked? My inspector duly ordered the daily special soup, and was persuaded to add on a plate of designer chips, a good sign that the hotel staff were actively selling products.

Tea is the next item on the agenda, and where a hotel serves the fully Monty, some of this must be sampled. Again, this is less about the actual food than the whole afternoon tea 'experience', and our hotel pulled this off magnificently. Staff seemed to outnumber patrons, though every table was taken, and tea (properly made from tea leaves) was poured for us by smiling waiters (full marks). We were asked several times if everything was all right, and it was indeed. The inspector made a valiant attempt to nibble on a scone and a tiny piece of poppy seed cake, and managed two cups of Earl Grey. I felt uninhibitedly greedy, and tucked in. So far so good.

Back in my mentor's room (similar to mine but with a few key differences) I was shown around and had the pros and cons pointed out. Too few lights by far, and none over the bed, was an immediate issue.

continued

The AA guidelines require there to be a minimum of 160 combined watts for a single room, and 220 watts for a double, but heavy lampshades can cast a gloomy shadow even where the right wattage is provided. Business guests hoping to work in their room, or anyone wanting to read comfortably knows how irritating this can be. The bathroom was well equipped but small, and at the debrief next morning we were assured that all rooms were being gradually upgraded to meet four star expectations. The carpet was a slightly worn but expensive one that was standing up well to the strains placed on it, and so was the well-upholstered armchair. Scuffs on the wall where suitcases had been carelessly banged, and even a hair in the bath tub, were noted. Dust was satisfyingly absent, even on the top of the TV cabinet and on the curtain rail. Throughout these visits, everything is recorded on the inspector's laptop; the previous report is summoned up, and the current one is filled out.

When the visit is over, the computer adds up the final scores, and sums up a particular establishment's place in the pecking order. The inspector checks to see that this agrees with his/her mental view, and any necessary adjustments are made.

I was instructed to make a bit of a mess in my room before going down to dinner, to see if the turndown maid cleared it up. It went against the grain to drop wet towels on the floor, scrumple up the outer bed coverings, and leave my newspaper scattered on the desk, but when I returned later everything was immaculate again, and my bed had been turned down for the night. Even the bin had been emptied. Later, after a heavy dinner, I had to test room service again by ordering some juice and a sandwich. First, I followed instructions and engaged in a lengthy discussion over the telephone about what exactly was on offer, concealing my embarrassment at having the room service menu open beside me. A delightful young man soon appeared with my order, smilingly setting my tray down and uncovering my food. He asked if I needed anything else, and then disappeared swiftly without the awkward hesitation you get when a tip is required but your expenses won't cover it. He returned within the hour for the tray as agreed, the sandwich now stashed away for my lunch the following day.

It was all slick and considerate, and I could pass on a good report next morning. But soon I genuinely needed help again. Taking a bottle of mineral water from the minibar for the night ahead, I found I couldn't get the cap off, though my knuckles went white in the attempt and I nearly passed out from exertion. I had to admit defeat. It took several tries before the room service person understood that I was actually, really asking someone to come to my room to undo a screw top on a bottle, but they did come, they solved the problem, and they left again after a nice little joke at my expense.

I was coming to realise that a hotel can only be as good as its most junior staff, and these were making a very positive impression.

The inspector and I met again for breakfast in the dining room. The low-key space of the night before when we dined was now thronging with people, but we were spotted at the entrance and found a table. Breakfast was a superb selection of fresh fruits, pastries and cereals, cooked items, cold cuts and cheeses. Yet even this feast could be bettered, and we were treated to fresh fruit salad and perfectly cooked scrambled eggs, both made to order. I kept forgetting why I was there and enthusing over the scrumptious fare, but my inspector never lost concentration, and her eyes were everywhere, though discreetly. Breakfast for her was a job, not an enjoyable meal. She noticed who was doing what, whether any tables were being neglected, and in particular the girl who checked our coffee and toast several times, and seamlessly brought replacements; this person was highly praised later to her manager.

At the checkout desk, the inspector called for separate hotels bills but a combined restaurant bill to go on different credit cards, a complicated procedure that was conducted smoothly. At last her unusual name, not used during the booking procedure, was recognised and word quickly spread among the staff that the AA inspector was in town. It was too late for them to improve on anything, and it was unnecessary. Over a relaxed cup of coffee the manager was informed that his hotel was performing at an exceptional level, and his well-trained team of staff were of excellent calibre. He knew it anyway, but the praise was appreciated. The inspector now processed her visit, pointing out where improvements could be made to increase the hotel's standing. Recommending the restaurant to guests on arrival and offering to book a table was suggested, and instantly taken up. The question of the room lighting was brought up, and would be considered. The staff who had been singled out would be commended.

Before we disappeared into our separate taxis I asked the inspector where she was off to next. She was going to grab a sandwich before heading off for an overnight visit to a two diamond B&B in Kent, and a few 'drop-in' visits to similar places nearby. From the truly sublime to the more modest then, but it was all in a day's work.

How to use the Guide

1 — ANYTOWN, Anyshire Map 4 SU46

2 — ★★★★ 71% The Example Hotel
Any Road XX1 11XX
☎ 0022 001122 0022 001122
e-mail: sendto@isp.co.uk www.theexamplehotel.co.uk

3 — ***Dir:*** *2m north of Any Town - Any Road signed turn left at Business Park.*

4 — 

A purpose-built hotel with a well equipped leisure and conference centre in a separate, linked building. Bedrooms are generously planned to give working space and adequate power points and lighting. Reception rooms consist of a bar lounge and carvery-style dining room.

5 — **ROOMS:** 50 en suite (6 fmly) (5GF) s fr £68; d fr £125 (incl. bkfst) **LB**

6 — **FACILITIES: Spa** STV air con. Squash Snooker Gym Sauna **CONF:** BC Thtr 80 Class 30 Board 40 **PARKING:** 30 — 7

8 — **NOTES:** No children 14 yrs No credit cards accepted in restaurant Civ Wed 80

1 Towns Towns are listed alphabetically within each country section: England, Channel Islands, Isle of Man, Scotland, Wales, Ireland. The administrative county or region follows the town name. Towns on islands are listed under the island (e.g. Wight, Isle of). The map reference gives the map page number, then the National Grid Reference. Read the first figure horizontally and the second figure vertically within the lettered square.

2 Hotel name This is preceded by the Star Rating, Quality Assessment Score (see page 4) and Rosette Award, followed by the address, phone/fax numbers and e-mail address where applicable. Please note that e-mail addresses are believed correct at the time of printing but may change during the currency of the guide. Hotels are listed in star and Quality Assessment Score order within each location. If the hotel name is in *italic type* the information that follows has not been confirmed by the hotel management for 2006. A company or consortium name or logo may appear (hotel groups are listed on pages 27-33); for those with a central reservation number, specify the name and location of your chosen hotel when booking.

3 Directions Brief directions are given to the hotel.

4 Photograph Establishments may choose to include a photograph with their entry.

5 Rooms The first figure shows the number of en suite letting bedrooms, or total number of bedrooms, then the number with en suite or family facilities. Bedrooms in an annexe or extension are only noted if they are at least equivalent in quality to those in the main building, but facilities and prices may differ. In some hotels all bedrooms are in an annexe or extension. Prices (per room per night) are provided by hoteliers in good faith and are indications not firm quotations. Some hotels only accept cheques if notice is given and a cheque card produced. Not all hotels take travellers cheques. LB indicates that the hotel offers special leisure breaks; these may be activity-based breaks or 'two nights for the price of one' type offers.

6 Facilities **Colour TV** is provided in all bedrooms unless otherwise indicated. Where **entertainment** appears, weekly live entertainment should be available at least once a week all year. Some hotels provide entertainment only in summer or on special occasions; check when booking.
Leisure facilities are as stated.
Child facilities may include: baby intercom, babysitting service, playroom, playground, laundry, drying/ironing facilities, cots, high chairs, special meals. In some hotels children can sleep in parents' rooms at no extra cost; check all details when booking.

7 Parking
Shows number of spaces available for guests' use. May include covered, charged spaces.

8 Notes Although many hotels allow dogs, some breeds may be forbidden and dogs may be excluded from areas of the hotel, especially the dining room. It is essential to check when booking. However guide dogs for the blind and assist dogs should be accepted, but once again please check when booking.

No children A minimum age may be given, e.g. 'No children 4 yrs'. If neither 'ch fac' (see FACILITIES) nor 'no children' appears, the hotel accepts children but may not offer special facilities such as high chairs; check before booking if you have very young children. **RS** Some hotels have a restricted service during quieter months, when some of the listed facilities are not available; ask when booking. **Civ Wed** indicates that the hotel is licensed for civil weddings.

As most hotels now accepted credit or debit card we have only indicated where an establishment does not accept any cards for payment. Credit cards may be subject to a surcharge; check when booking if this is how you intend to pay.

Key to Symbols & Abbreviations

★ Black Stars
Star Classification (see page 6)

★ Red Stars
Indicate the AA's Top Hotels in Britain & Ireland.

Rosettes
Rosette Awards (see page 7)

DIFFERENT ACCOMMODATION CATEGORIES
see page 7 for explanation of the following...

Country House Hotel

Town House Accommodation

Restaurant with Rooms

Travel Accommodation

○ Hotel due to open during the currency of the guide

U Star rating not yet confirmed

A Associate Entries

ROOMS

fmly – Family rooms (and number)

GF – Ground floor rooms (and number)

No smoking

s – Single room

d – Double room

fr – from

incl. bkfst – Breakfast included

LB – Special leisure breaks available

Bedroom restrictions are stated, e.g, no smoking in 15 bedrooms

FACILITIES

STV – Satellite television

air con – Air conditioning

Indoor swimming pool

Heated indoor swimming pool

Outdoor swimming pool

Heated outdoor swimming pool

Entertainment

ch fac – Special facilities for children

Xmas – Special programme for Christmas/ New Year

Leisure facilities are as stated, e.g, Squash, Snooker, Spa

Tennis

croquet

golf course

CONF – Conference facilities

BC – Business centre available

Thtr – Seats theatre style (and number)

Class – Seats classroom style (and number)

Board – Seats boardroom style (and number)

Del – Typical overnight delegate rate

NOTES

No dogs allowed in bedrooms (guide dogs for the blind and assist dogs may be accepted)

No children –indicates that children cannot be accommodated

RS – Restricted opening, e.g, RS Jan-Mar, closed Xmas/New Year

Civ Wed – Licensed for civil weddings (and maximum number of guests for ceremony)

Other restrictions as stated, e.g, No smoking in restaurant

For more detailed information on AA classifications and ratings see page 6

Assessed and announced annually, the AA's Top Hotel Awards recognise the very best hotels in Britain and Ireland. A Top Hotel will offer consistently outstanding levels of quality, comfort, cleanliness and customer care

Central London

KNIGHTS-
BRIDGE

Regent's
Park

Hyde Park

MARYLEBONE

BLOOMSBURY

MAYFAIR

STRAND

WESTMINSTER

LAMBETH

Thames

146
148
151
143 149 152 147 Inverness
145 125 Aberdeen
144 Fort William
150 155 126
128 156 157
129 127 139,140,141
164 154 137 138
163 136
142 130 Edinburgh
Glasgow 131,132,133
153 161 158
162 160
159 134
Stranraer 135
Belfast Newcastle
upon Tyne
13
Carlisle Middlesbrough
17 18 37 38
16 119
15 19,20,21,22, 115
Kendal 23,24
14 118 117
114 116 120,121
York
Leeds Kingston
upon Hull
185 58
184 Galway 181,182 183
189 Dublin
175 Liverpool Manchester
176 Limerick 192 Sheffield Lincoln
Holyhead 168,169,170
190 167 6 25
Rosslare 171 166
193 172 Nottingham
187,188 191 57 82 81
186 180 165 88 Birmingham 87 83
178 179 Cork 177 Aberystwyth 113 108 85 Cambridge 84 Norwich
Carmarthen 173 54 109 43 97
174 Cardiff 44 40 48 1 39
Gloucester 41,42 45 Oxford 4 Colchester
47 46 86 5 LONDON
112 3 2 98 Maidstone
Bristol 110 52 99 105
92 111 89,90 Guildford 107 100 56
94 53 106 104 102 Dover
Barnstaple 91 96 93 Southampton 51 49 103 101 Brighton
27 95 35 34 36 50 55
26 30 Exeter 31
32 28,29 33
8 9 Weymouth
10 Plymouth
Penzance
Isles of Scilly 12
7 11

The Channel Islands
122,
123,
124

© Automobile Association Developments Limited 2005

Top Hotel Regional Index

The number shown against each hotel in the index corresponds with the number given on the Top Hotel map. Hotels are listed in country and county order, showing their star classification, rosettes and telephone number.

ENGLAND

BEDFORDSHIRE
1 FLITWICK
★★★ ◉◉
Menzies Flitwick Manor
☎ 01525 712242

BERKSHIRE
2 MAIDENHEAD
★★★★ ◉◉◉
Fredrick's Hotel
☎ 01628 581000

3 NEWBURY
★★★★★ ◉◉◉◉
The Vineyard at Stockcross
☎ 01635 528770

BUCKINGHAMSHIRE
4 AYLESBURY
★★★★ ◉◉◉
Hartwell House
☎ 01296 747444

5 TAPLOW
★★★★★ ◉◉◉
Cliveden
☎ 01628 668561

CHESHIRE
6 CHESTER
★★★★★ ◉◉◉
The Chester Grosvenor & Spa
☎ 01244 324024

CORNWALL & ISLES OF SCILLY
7 BRYHER
★★★ ◉◉◉
Hell Bay
☎ 01720 422947

8 FOWEY
★★ ◉◉
Marina Hotel
☎ 01726 833315

9 LISKEARD
★★ ◉◉◉
Well House Hotel
☎ 01579 342001

10 PORTSCATHO
★★ ◉◉◉
Driftwood
☎ 01872 580644

11 ST MARTIN'S
★★★ ◉◉◉
St Martin's on the Isle
☎ 01720 422090

12 TRESCO
★★★ ◉◉
The Island Hotel
☎ 01720 422883

CUMBRIA
13 BRAMPTON
★★★ ◉◉
Farlam Hall Hotel
☎ 016977 46234

14 GRANGE-OVER-SANDS
★ ◉
Clare House
☎ 015395 33026

15 GRASMERE
★ ◉
White Moss House
☎ 015394 35295

16 HOWTOWN
★★★ ◉◉
Sharrow Bay Country House
☎ 017684 86301

17 KESWICK
★ ◉◉
Swinside Lodge
☎ 017687 72948

18 WATERMILLOCK
★★★ ◉◉◉
Rampsbeck Country House Hotel
☎ 017684 86442

19 WINDERMERE
★★★ ◉◉◉
Gilpin Lodge Country House Hotel & Restaurant
☎ 015394 88818

20 WINDERMERE
★★★ ◉◉◉
Holbeck Ghyll Country House Hotel
☎ 015394 32375

21 WINDERMERE
★★ ◉
Lindeth Fell Country House Hotel
☎ 015394 43286

22 WINDERMERE
★★★ ◉◉
Linthwaite House Hotel
☎ 015394 88600

23 WINDERMERE
★★ ◉◉
Miller Howe
☎ 015394 42536

24 WINDERMERE
★★★
The Samling *
☎ 015394 31922

DERBYSHIRE
25 BASLOW
★★ ◉◉◉
Fischer's Baslow Hall
☎ 01246 583259

DEVON
26 ASHWATER
★★ ◉◉
Blagdon Manor Hotel & Restaurant
☎ 01409 211224

27 BURRINGTON
★★★ ◉◉
Northcote Manor
☎ 01769 560501

28 CHAGFORD
★★★ ◉◉◉◉
Gidleigh Park
☎ 01647 432367

29 CHAGFORD
★★ ◉◉
Mill End Hotel
☎ 01647 432282

30 HONITON
★★★ ◉◉
Combe House Hotel & Restaurant - Gittisham
☎ 01404 540400

31 KINGSBRIDGE
★★★ ◉◉
Buckland-Tout-Saints
☎ 01548 853055

32 LEWDOWN
★★★ ◉◉◉
Lewtrenchard Manor
☎ 01566 783256

33 TORQUAY
★★★ ◉◉
Orestone Manor Hotel
☎ 01803 328098

*(Hotels marked with an asterisk * had not had their Rosette rating confirmed at the time of going to press. See the AA website www.theAA.com for current information.)*

DORSET

34	EVERSHOT ★★★★ ❁❁❁	Summer Lodge Country House Hotel Restaurant & Spa ☎ 01935 482000
35	GILLINGHAM ★★★ ❁❁❁	Stock Hill Country House ☎ 01747 823626
36	POOLE ★★★ ❁❁	Mansion House Hotel ☎ 01202 685666

CO DURHAM

37	ROMALDKIRK ★★ ❁❁	Rose & Crown Hotel ☎ 01833 650213
38	SEAHAM ★★★★ ❁❁❁	Seaham Hall Hotel ☎ 0191 516 1400

ESSEX

39	DEDHAM ★★★ ❁❁	Maison Talbooth ☎ 01206 322367

GLOUCESTERSHIRE

40	BUCKLAND ★★★ ❁❁❁	Buckland Manor ☎ 01386 852626
41	CHELTENHAM ★★★ ❁❁❁	The Greenway ☎ 01242 862352
42	CHELTENHAM ★★★ ❁❁	Hotel on the Park ☎ 01242 518898
43	CHIPPING CAMPDEN ★★★ ❁❁	Cotswold House ☎ 01386 840330
44	CORSE LAWN ★★★ ❁❁	Corse Lawn House Hotel ☎ 01452 780479

45	LOWER SLAUGHTER ★★★ ❁❁	Lower Slaughter Manor ☎ 01451 820456
46	TETBURY ★★★ ❁❁	Calcot Manor ☎ 01666 890391
47	THORNBURY ★★★ ❁❁	Thornbury Castle ☎ 01454 281182
48	UPPER SLAUGHTER ★★★ ❁❁❁	Lords of the Manor ☎ 01451 820243

HAMPSHIRE

49	BEAULIEU ★★★ ❁❁	Montagu Arms ☎ 01590 612324
50	MILFORD ON SEA ★★★ ❁❁	Westover Hall Hotel ☎ 01590 643044
51	NEW MILTON ★★★★★ ❁❁❁	Chewton Glen Hotel ☎ 01425 275341
52	ROTHERWICK ★★★★ ❁	Tylney Hall Hotel ☎ 01256 764881
53	WINCHESTER ★★★★ ❁❁	Lainston House Hotel ☎ 01962 863588

HEREFORDSHIRE

54	HEREFORD ★★★ ❁❁❁	Castle House Hotel ☎ 01432 356321

ISLE OF WIGHT

55	YARMOUTH ★★★ ❁❁❁	George Hotel ☎ 01983 760331

KENT

56	LENHAM ★★★★ ❁❁	Chilston Park ☎ 01622 859803

LEICESTERSHIRE

57	MELTON MOWBRAY ★★★★ ❁❁	Stapleford Park ☎ 01572 787522

LINCOLNSHIRE

58	WINTERINGHAM ⌂ ❁❁❁❁❁	Winteringham Fields ☎ 01724 733096

LONDON

59	LONDON E14 ★★★★★ ❁	Four Seasons Hotel Canary Wharf ☎ 020 7510 1999
60	LONDON EC2 ★★★★★ ❁❁❁	Great Eastern Hotel ☎ 020 7618 5000
61	LONDON NW1 ★★★★★ ❁	The Landmark London ☎ 020 7631 8000
62	LONDON SW1 ★★★★★ ❁❁❁❁❁	The Berkeley ☎ 020 7235 6000
63	LONDON SW1 ★★★★★ ❁❁	The Carlton Tower Hotel ☎ 020 7235 1234
64	LONDON SW1 ★★★★★ ❁❁	The Goring ☎ 020 7396 9000
65	LONDON SW1 ★★★★ ❁❁❁	The Halkin Hotel ☎ 020 7333 1000
66	LONDON SW1 ★★★★★ ❁❁	The Lanesborough ☎ 020 7259 5599
67	LONDON SW1 ★★★★★ ❁❁❁❁❁	Mandarin Oriental Hyde Park ☎ 020 7235 2000
68	LONDON SW1 ★★★★★ ⌂	No 41 ☎ 020 7300 0041
69	LONDON SW1 ★★★★ ❁❁	The Stafford ☎ 020 7493 0111
70	LONDON SW3 ★★★★★ ⌂ ❁❁❁❁	The Capital ☎ 020 7589 5171
71	LONDON W1 ★★★★★ ⌂ ❁	Athenaeum Hotel & Apartments ☎ 020 7499 3464
72	LONDON W1 ★★★★★ ❁❁❁	Claridge's ☎ 020 7629 8860
73	LONDON W1 ★★★★★ ❁❁❁	The Connaught ☎ 020 7499 7070
74	LONDON W1 ★★★★★ ❁❁	The Dorchester ☎ 020 7629 8888
75	LONDON W1 ★★★★★ ❁	Four Seasons Hotel London ☎ 020 7499 0888
76	LONDON W1 ★★★★★ ❁❁	The Ritz ☎ 020 7493 8181

77 LONDON W8 — Royal Garden Hotel
★★★★★ ✿✿✿ — ☎ 020 7937 8000

78 LONDON W8 — Milestone Hotel & Apartments
★★★★★ ⌂ ✿ — ☎ 020 7917 1000

79 LONDON WC2 — One Aldwych
★★★★★ ✿✿ — ☎ 020 7300 1000

80 LONDON WC2 — The Savoy
★★★★★ ✿✿✿ — ☎ 020 7836 4343

NORFOLK

81 BLAKENEY — Morston Hall
★★ ✿✿✿ — ☎ 01263 741041

82 GRIMSTON — Congham Hall Country House Hotel
★★★ ✿✿ — ☎ 01485 600250

83 NORTH WALSHAM — Beechwood Hotel
★★ ✿✿ — ☎ 01692 403231

84 NORWICH — The Old Rectory
★★ ✿✿ — ☎ 01603 700772

NORTHAMPTONSHIRE

85 DAVENTRY — Fawsley Hall
★★★★ ✿✿✿ — ☎ 01327 892000

OXFORDSHIRE

86 GREAT MILTON — Le Manoir Aux Quat' Saisons
★★★★ ✿✿✿✿✿ — ☎ 01844 278881

RUTLAND

87 OAKHAM — Hambleton Hall
★★★ ✿✿✿✿ — ☎ 01572 756991

SHROPSHIRE

88 WORFIELD — Old Vicarage Hotel
★★★ ✿✿✿ — ☎ 01746 716497

SOMERSET

89 BATH — The Bath Priory *
★★★★ — ☎ 01225 331922

90 BATH — The Queensberry Hotel
★★★ ✿✿ — ☎ 01225 447928

91 DULVERTON — Ashwick House Hotel
★★ ✿ — ☎ 01398 323868

92 PORLOCK — The Oaks Hotel
★★ ✿ — ☎ 01643 862265

93 SHEPTON MALLET — Charlton House
★★★ ✿✿✿ — ☎ 01749 342008

94 TAUNTON — Castle Hotel
★★★ ✿✿✿ — ☎ 01823 272671

95 WELLINGTON — Bindon Country House Hotel & Restaurant
★★★ ✿✿ — ☎ 01823 400070

96 YEOVIL — Little Barwick House
★ ✿✿✿ — ☎ 01935 423902

SUFFOLK

97 HINTLESHAM — Hintlesham Hall Hotel
★★★★ ✿✿✿ — ☎ 01473 652334

SURREY

98 BAGSHOT — Pennyhill Park Hotel & The Spa
★★★★★ ✿✿✿ — ☎ 01276 471774

99 HORLEY — Langshott Manor
★★★ ✿✿ — ☎ 01293 786680

SUSSEX, EAST

100 FOREST ROW — Ashdown Park Hotel and Country Club
★★★★ ✿✿ — ☎ 01342 824988

101 NEWICK — Newick Park Hotel & Country Estate
★★★ ✿✿ — ☎ 01825 723633

102 UCKFIELD — Horsted Place
★★★ ✿✿ — ☎ 01825 750581

SUSSEX, WEST

103 AMBERLEY — Amberley Castle
★★★ ✿✿ — ☎ 01798 831992

104 CUCKFIELD — Ockenden Manor
★★★ ✿✿✿ — ☎ 01444 416111

105 EAST GRINSTEAD — Gravetye Manor Hotel
★★★ ✿✿✿ — ☎ 01342 810567

106 LOWER BEEDING — South Lodge Hotel
★★★★ ✿✿✿ — ☎ 01403 891711

107 TURNERS HILL — Alexander House Hotel
★★★ ✿✿ — ☎ 01342 714914

WARWICKSHIRE

108 ROYAL LEAMINGTON SPA — Mallory Court Hotel
★★★ ✿✿✿ — ☎ 01926 330214

WEST MIDLANDS

109 HOCKLEY HEATH — Nuthurst Grange Country House & Restaurant *
★★★ — ☎ 01564 783972

WILTSHIRE

110 CASTLE COMBE — Manor House Hotel & Golf Club
★★★★ ✿✿ — ☎ 01249 782206

111 COLERNE — Lucknam Park
★★★★ ✿✿✿ — ☎ 01225 742777

112 MALMESBURY — Whatley Manor
★★★★ ✿✿✿ — ☎ 01666 822888

WORCESTERSHIRE

113 CHADDESLEY CORBETT — Brockencote Hall Country House Hotel
★★★ ✿✿ — ☎ 01562 777876

YORKSHIRE, NORTH

114 BOLTON ABBEY — The Devonshire Arms Country House Hotel
★★★ ✿✿✿ — ☎ 01756 710441

115 CRATHORNE — Crathorne Hall Hotel
★★★★ ✿✿ — ☎ 01642 700398

116 HARROGATE — Rudding Park Hotel & Golf
★★★★ ✿✿ — ☎ 01423 871350

117 MASHAM — Swinton Park
★★★★ ✿✿✿ — ☎ 01765 680900

118 RAMSGILL ◎◎◎ — Yorke Arms ☎ 01423 755243

119 YARM ★★★ ◎◎ — Judges Country House Hotel ☎ 01642 789000

120 YORK ★★★ ◎◎ — The Grange Hotel ☎ 01904 644744

121 YORK ★★★ ◎◎◎ — Middlethorpe Hall & Spa ☎ 01904 641241

CHANNEL ISLANDS

JERSEY

122 ROZEL ★★★ ◎◎ — Château la Chaire ☎ 01534 863354

123 ST BRELADE ★★★★ ◎◎◎ — The Atlantic Hotel ☎ 01534 744101

124 ST SAVIOUR ★★★★ ◎◎◎ — Longueville Manor Hotel ☎ 01534 725501

SCOTLAND

ABERDEENSHIRE

125 BALLATER ★★★ ◎◎◎ — Darroch Learg Hotel ☎ 013397 55443

ANGUS

126 GLAMIS ★★★ ◎◎◎ — Castleton House Hotel ☎ 01307 840340

ARGYLL & BUTE

127 ERISKA ★★★★ ◎◎◎ — Isle of Eriska ☎ 01631 720371

128 PORT APPIN ★★★ ◎◎◎ — Airds Hotel ☎ 01631 730236

129 TOBERMORY ★★ ◎◎ — Highland Cottage ☎ 01688 302030

CITY OF EDINBURGH

130 EDINBURGH ★★★★ ◎◎ — Channings ☎ 0131 332 3232

131 EDINBURGH ★★★★ ◎ — The Howard Hotel ☎ 0131 557 3500

132 EDINBURGH ★★★★ ◎◎ — Prestonfield ☎ 0131 225 7800

133 EDINBURGH ★★★★★ ◎◎ — The Scotsman ☎ 0131 556 5565

DUMFRIES & GALLOWAY

134 NEWTON STEWART ★★★ ◎◎ — Kirroughtree House ☎ 01671 402141

135 PORTPATRICK ◎◎◎ — Knockinaam Lodge ☎ 01776 810471

EAST LOTHIAN

136 GULLANE ★★★ ◎◎ — Greywalls Hotel ☎ 01620 842144

FIFE

137 MARKINCH ★★★★ ◎◎ — Balbirnie House ☎ 01592 610066

138 PEAT INN ★★ ◎◎◎ — The Peat Inn ☎ 01334 840206

139 ST ANDREWS ★★★★★ ◎◎◎ — The Old Course Hotel Golf Resort & Spa ☎ 01334 474371

140 ST ANDREWS ★★★ ◎◎ — Rufflets Country House & Garden Restaurant ☎ 01334 472594

141 ST ANDREWS ★★★ ◎◎ — St Andrews Golf Hotel ☎ 01334 472611

CITY OF GLASGOW

142 GLASGOW ★★★★ ◎◎ — One Devonshire Gardens Hotel ☎ 0141 339 2001

HIGHLAND

143 COLBOST ◎◎◎ — The Three Chimneys & The House Over-By ☎ 01470 511258

144 FORT WILLIAM ★★★★ ◎◎◎ — Inverlochy Castle Hotel ☎ 01397 702177

145 KINGUSSIE ◎◎◎ — The Cross ☎ 01540 661166

146 LOCHINVER ★★★ ◎ — Inver Lodge Hotel ☎ 01571 844496

147 NAIRN ★★ ◎◎◎ — Boath House ☎ 01667 454896

148 POOLEWE ★★★ ◎◎ — Pool House Hotel ☎ 01445 781272

149 SHIELDAIG ★ ◎◎ — Tigh an Eilean ☎ 01520 755251

150 STRONTIAN ★★ ◎◎ — Kilcamb Lodge Hotel ☎ 01967 402257

151 TAIN ★★ ◎◎ — The Glenmorangie Highland Home at Cadbole ☎ 01862 871671

152 TORRIDON ★★★ ◎◎ — Loch Torridon Country House Hotel ☎ 01445 791242

NORTH AYRSHIRE

153 BRODICK ★★ ◎◎ — Kilmichael Country House Hotel ☎ 01770 302219

PERTH & KINROSS

154 AUCHTERARDER ★★★★★ ◎◎◎◎ — The Gleneagles Hotel ☎ 01764 662231

155 BLAIRGOWRIE ★★★ ◎◎ — Kinloch House Hotel ☎ 01250 884237

156 DUNKELD ★★★ ◎◎◎ — Kinnaird ☎ 01796 482440

157 KINCLAVEN ★★★ ◎◎ — Ballathie House Hotel ☎ 01250 883268

SCOTTISH BORDERS

No.	Town	Rating	Hotel	Telephone
158	PEEBLES	★★★ ◉◉	Cringletie House	☎ 01721 725750

SOUTH AYRSHIRE

No.	Town	Rating	Hotel	Telephone
159	BALLANTRAE	★★★ ◉◉◉	Glenapp Castle	☎ 01465 831212
160	MAYBOLE	★★ ◉	Ladyburn	☎ 01655 740585
161	TROON	★★★ ◉◉◉	Lochgreen House	☎ 01292 313343
162	TURNBERRY	★★★★★ ◉◉	Westin Turnberry Resort	☎ 01655 331000

STIRLING

No.	Town	Rating	Hotel	Telephone
163	DUNBLANE	★★★ ◉◉	Cromlix House Hotel	☎ 01786 822125
164	STRATHYRE	★ ◉◉	Creagan House	☎ 01877 384638

WALES

CEREDIGION

No.	Town	Rating	Hotel	Telephone
165	EGLWYSFACH	★★★ ◉◉◉◉	Ynyshir Hall	☎ 01654 781209

CONWY

No.	Town	Rating	Hotel	Telephone
166	BETWS-Y-COED	★★ ◉◉◉	Tan-y-Foel Country House	☎ 01690 710507
167	CONWY	★★ ◉◉◉	The Old Rectory Country House	☎ 01492 580611
168	LLANDUDNO	★★★★ ◉◉◉	Bodysgallen Hall Hotel	☎ 01492 584466
169	LLANDUDNO	★★★★ ⌂ ◉	Osborne House	☎ 01492 860330
170	LLANDUDNO	★★ ◉◉	St Tudno Hotel and Restaurant	☎ 01492 874411

GWYNEDD

No.	Town	Rating	Hotel	Telephone
171	CAERNARFON	★★★ ◉◉	Seiont Manor	☎ 01286 673366
172	TALSARNAU	★★ ◉◉	Maes y Neuadd Country House Hotel	☎ 01766 780200

POWYS

No.	Town	Rating	Hotel	Telephone
173	LLANGAMMARCH WELLS	★★★ ◉◉	Lake Country House Hotel	☎ 01591 620202

SWANSEA

No.	Town	Rating	Hotel	Telephone
174	REYNOLDSTON	★★★ ◉◉	Fairyhill	☎ 01792 390139

REPUBLIC OF IRELAND

CLARE

No.	Town	Rating	Hotel	Telephone
175	BALLYVAUGHAN	★★★ ◉◉	Gregans Castle	☎ 065 7077005
176	NEWMARKET-ON-FERGUS	★★★★★ ◉◉	Dromoland Castle Hotel	☎ 061 368144

CORK

No.	Town	Rating	Hotel	Telephone
177	BALLYCOTTON	★★★ ◉◉	Bay View Hotel	☎ 021 4646746
178	BALLYLICKEY	★★★ ◉◉	Sea View House Hotel	☎ 027 50073
179	CORK	★★★★ ◉◉	Hayfield Manor	☎ 021 4845900
180	MALLOW	★★★ ◉◉◉	Longueville House Hotel	☎ 022 47156

DUBLIN

No.	Town	Rating	Hotel	Telephone
181	DUBLIN	★★★★ ◉◉	The Clarence	☎ 01 4070800
182	DUBLIN	★★★★★ ◉◉◉◉	The Merrion Hotel	☎ 01 6030600
183	PORTMARNOCK	★★★★ ◉◉	Portmarnock Hotel & Golf Links	☎ 01 8460611

GALWAY

No.	Town	Rating	Hotel	Telephone
184	CASHEL	★★★ ◉◉	Cashel House Hotel	☎ 095 31001
185	RECESS	★★★ ◉	Lough Inagh Lodge Hotel	☎ 095 34706

KERRY

No.	Town	Rating	Hotel	Telephone
186	KENMARE	★★★★ ◉◉◉	Sheen Falls Lodge	☎ 064 41600
187	KILLARNEY	★★★★★ ◉	Aghadoe Heights Hotel	☎ 064 31766
188	KILLARNEY	★★★★★ ◉◉	Killarney Park Hotel	☎ 064 35555

KILDARE

No.	Town	Rating	Hotel	Telephone
189	STRAFFAN	★★★★★ ◉◉◉	The K Club	☎ 01 6017200

KILKENNY

No.	Town	Rating	Hotel	Telephone
190	THOMASTOWN	★★★★ ◉◉	Mount Juliet Conrad Hotel	☎ 056 777 3000

WATERFORD

No.	Town	Rating	Hotel	Telephone
191	WATERFORD	★★★★ ◉◉	Waterford Castle Hotel	☎ 051 878203

WEXFORD

No.	Town	Rating	Hotel	Telephone
192	GOREY	★★★ ◉◉◉	Marlfield House Hotel	☎ 055 21124
193	ROSSLARE	★★★★ ◉◉	Kelly's Resort Hotel	☎ 053 32114

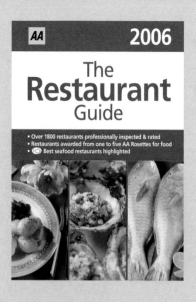

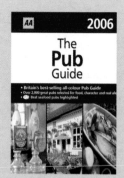

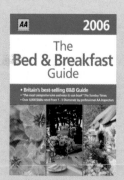

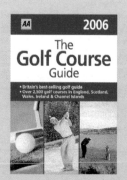

Useful Information

Prices The AA encourages the use of the Hotel Industry Voluntary Code of Booking Practice, which aims to ensure that guests know how much they will have to pay and what services and facilities that includes, before entering a financially binding agreement. If the price has not previously been confirmed in writing, guests should be given a card stipulating the total obligatory charge when they register at reception.

The Tourism (Sleeping Accommodation Price Display) Order of 1977 compels hotels, travel accommodation, guest houses, farmhouses, inns and self-catering accommodation with four or more letting bedrooms, to display in entrance halls the minimum and maximum for one or two persons but they may vary without warning.

FACILITIES FOR DISABLED GUESTS

The final stage (Part III) of the Disability Discrimination Act (access to Goods and Services) came into force in October 2004. This means that service providers may have to consider making permanent physical adjustments to their premises. For further information, see the government website www.disability.gov.uk/dda. We indicate in entries if an establishment has ground floor rooms, and if a hotel tells us that they have disabled facilities this is included in the description. The establishments in this guide should all be aware of their responsibilities under the Act. We recommend that you always telephone in advance to ensure that the establishment you have chosen has appropriate facilities.

Useful websites:
www.disability.gov.uk/dda
www.holidaycare.org.uk
www.tripscope.org.uk

Licensing laws differ in England, Wales, Scotland, the Republic of Ireland, the Isle of Man, the Isles of Scilly and the Channel Islands. Public houses are generally open from mid morning to early afternoon, and from about 6 or 7pm until 11pm, although closing times may be earlier or later and some pubs are open all afternoon. Unless otherwise stated, establishments listed are licensed. Hotel residents can obtain alcoholic drinks at all times, if the licensee is prepared to serve them. Non-residents eating at the hotel restaurant can have drinks with meals. Children under 14 may be excluded from bars where no food is served. Those under 18 may not purchase or consume alcoholic drinks. Club license means that drinks are served to club members only, 48 hours must lapse between joining and ordering.

The Fire Precautions Act does not apply to the Channel Islands, Republic of Ireland, or the Isle of Man, which have their own rules. As far as we are aware, all hotels listed in Great Britain have applied for and not been refused a fire certificate.

For information on Ireland see page 814

Bank and Public Holidays 2006

New Year's Day 1st January
New Year's Holiday 2nd January (Scotland)
Good Friday 14th April
Easter Monday 17th April
May Day Bank Holiday 1st May
Spring Bank Holiday 29th May
August Holiday 1st August (Scotland)
Late Summer Holiday 28th August
Christmas Day 25th December
Boxing Day 26th December

Hotel Groups Information

The following hotel groups have at least four hotels and 400 rooms or are part of an internationally significant brand with a central reservations number.

	Company Statement	Central Reservations Contact Number
APEX HOTELS	A small group of predominately 4 star hotels based hotels based primarily in Edinburgh with a new opening planned in London.	Apex Hotels 0845 3650000 www.apexhotels.co.uk
bespoke HOTELS	A small group of personally managed three and four star hotels in leisure locations.	Bespoke 01454 322 977 (Head Office) www.bespokehotels.com
Best Western	Britain's largest consortia group has around 300 independently owned and managed hotels, modern and traditional, in the two, three and four star markets. Many have leisure facilities and many have rosette awards.	Best Western 08457 73 73 73 www.bestwestern.co.uk
Best Western PREMIER	Are selected for their beautiful settings, range of facilities and enhanced levels of service. There are currently 4 Best Western Great Britain hotels that have achieved Premier status.	Best Western Premier 08457 73 73 73 www.bestwestern.co.uk
Bewley's EST 1840 BEWLEY'S HOTELS	A privately owned group of high quality, contemporary three star hotels in key locations in the UK and Ireland	Bewley's Hotels 0845 234 59 59 www.BewleysHotels.com
PRB Brend Hotels	A privately owned group of 11 three and four star hotels in Devon and Cornwall	Brend 01271 34 44 96 www.brendhotels.co.uk
BRITISH TRUST HOTELS	A division of North British Trust Group, comprising of a selection of three star hotels, providing accommodation throughout Scotland and the north of England	British Trust 0870 0507711 www.british-trust-hotels.com
CRERAR HOTELS	A division of North British Trust Group, representing the group's flagship hotels, providing accommodation throughout Scotland and the north of England	Crerar Hotels 0870 0507711 www.crerarhotels.com
Campanile	French owned company, Campanile has 17 properties in the UK offering modern accommodation for the budget market	Campanile 0208 3261500 www.envergure.fr
Comfort Quality Sleep Inn Clarion CHOICE HOTELS EUROPE	Offers mainly three brands in the UK: Quality Hotels in the three star market, Comfort Inns at two star and Sleep Inns in the travel accommodation market	Choice 0800 44 44 44 www.choicehotelseurope.com
CLASSIC BRITISH	A consortium of independent hotels at the four star and high-quality three star level, categorised by quality and style, and marketed under the Classic British Hotels hallmark	Classic British 0845 0707090 www.classicbritishhotels.com
COPTHORNE	Part of the Millennium and Copthorne group, comprising 11 four star hotels in primary provincial locations and London	Copthorne 0800 41 47 41 www.millenniumhotels.com
corus hotels	A large group of three star hotels ranging from rural to city centre locations across the UK.	Corus UK 0845 300 2000 www.corushotels.com
COURTYARD Marriott	There are 11 hotels in the UK, part of the international brand of modern three star hotels	Courtyard by Marriott 0800 221 222 0800 699 996
DAYS INN	Quality modern budget accommodation at motorway services	Days Inn Good www.welcomebreak.co.uk

	Company Statement	Central Reservations Contact Number
DE VERE HOTELS Hotels of character, run with pride	Comprises 21 four and five star hotels, which specialise in leisure, golf and conferences	De Vere 0870 606 3606 www.devereonline.co.uk
EXCLUSIVE	A small privately owned group of luxury five and four star hotels all located in the South of England	Exclusive 01276 471774 www.exclusivehotels.co.uk
folio Hotels	A newly developed small group of 3 and 4 star hotels.	Folio Hotels (020 89402247) www.foliohotels.co.uk
Forestdale Hotels	A privately owned group of 18 three star hotels across the UK	Forestdale 0808 144 9494 www.forestdale.com
FOUR PILLARS HOTELS	Half a dozen three and four star hotels based in the Oxfordshire area	Four Pillars 0800 374692 www.four-pillars.co.uk
FURLONG	A small group of personally managed three and four star hotels in leisure locations, business facilities	Furlong 01454 322 977 (Head Office) www.furlonghotels.co.uk
GRANGE HOTELS	A collection of privately owned hotels, seven located in central London and one in Bracknell, Berkshire	Grange Hotels 020 7233 7888 www.grangehotels.co.uk
GRESHAM HOTELS	Part of the Ryan Hotels group, Gresham is a collection of four star properties, conveniently located in city centre locations in the Republic of Ireland	Gresham Hotels 00 353 1 7966 (Head Office)
HandPICKED HOTELS	A group of 15 three and four star, high quality country house hotels, with a real emphasis on quality food	Handpicked Hotels 0845 458 0901 www.handpicked.co.uk
Hotel du Vin & Bistro	A group of six four star town house properties predominantly located in the south of England	Hotel Du Vin 01962 850676 (Head Office) www.hotelduvin.com
ibis	A growing chain of modern travel accommodation with properties across the UK	Ibis 0870 609 0963 www.ibishotel.com
THE INDEPENDENTS HOTEL ASSOCIATION	A consortium of independently owned, mainly two and three star hotels across Britain	Independents 0800 88 55 44
Innkeeper's Lodge	Travel accommodation from Bass Leisure Retail, featuring comfortable rooms and complimentary breakfast	Innkeepers Lodges 0870 243 0500 www.innkeeperslodge.com
INTER·CONTINENTAL. HOTELS AND RESORTS	This internationally renowned group is primarily represented in the UK with two five star hotels in central London	Inter-Continental 0800 0289 387
IRELAND'S BLUE BOOK	Ireland's Blue Book is a unique association comprising Ireland's most gracious Country Manor Houses, Castles and Restaurants.	Ireland's Blue Book 00 353 1 676 9914
IRISH COUNTRY HOTELS	Friendly and informal in style, Irish Country Hotels is a collection of 30 individual family owned and run hotels, located throughout the country	Irish Country Hotels 00 353 1 295 8900
JURYS DOYLE HOTELS	This Irish company has a range of three and four star hotels in the UK and the Republic of Ireland	Jury's Doyle 0870 9072222 (Group Information) www.jurysdoyle.com
Leisureplex	A group of 14 two star hotels located in the 'Best of British' seaside resorts	Leisureplex 08451 305666 (Head Office) www.alfatravel.co.uk
MACDONALD HOTELS & RESORTS	A large group of predominately four-star hotels, traditional and modern in style, located across the UK	Macdonald 0871 522 8417 www.macdonald-hotels.co.uk

A family of four can stay here for under £50.
I think someone at Premier Travel Inn deserves a very big hug.
Really nice rooms from £46.95 a night
premier travel inn
Good night, after night, after night...
Go to premiertravelinn.com or call 08708 503 765
Room rate correct at 29/04/05. May be subject to change. Calls charged at national rate.

Company Statement	Central Reservations Contact Number
A growing brand of three star city centre hotels, all rated over 70%	Malmaison 0207 479 9512 (Head Office) www.malmaison.com
Located throughout Northern and Southern Ireland, Manor House Hotels is an independent group comprising Georgian manors, country houses, shooting lodges, castles and four star guest houses	Manor House 00 353 1 295 8900 08705 300 200
This international brand offers four star hotels in primary locations. Most are modern and have leisure facilities; some have a focus on golf	Marriott 0800 221 222 0800 699 996 www.marriott.co.uk
A quality independent group of four star hotels with leisure facilities in primary locations across England	Marston 0845 1300 700 www.marstonhotels.com
Newly formed hotel group representing the prestigious London 5 Star hotels of The Berkeley, Claridge's and The Connaught	Maybourne Hotels 020 7107 8800 (Head Office) www.maybourne.com
A portfolio of four star hotels located throughout the UK	Menzies 0845 600 3013 www.menzies-hotels.co.uk
Part of the Millennium and Copthorne group, comprising six high-quality four star hotels, mainly in central London	Millennium 0800 41 47 41 www.millenniumhotels.com
Part of French group Accor, Novotel provides mainly modern three star hotels in key locations throughout the UK	Novotel 020 8283 4500 www.novotel.com
A large collection of former coaching inns, mainly in the two and three star markets	Old English Inns & Hotels 0800 917 3085 www.oldenglish.co.uk
A group of predominately four-star hotels, many with leisure facilities	Paramount 0500 342 543 www.paramount-hotels.co.uk
A Europe based group increasing its presence within the UK through quality four-star hotels in primary locations	Park Plaza Hotels 020 70344807 www.parkplaza.com
A group of mainly three star hotels located across the UK	Peel Hotels 0207 2661100 www.peelhotel.com
The largest budget group in the UK offering high quality, modern accommodation in key locations throughout the UK. Every Premier Travel Inn is located adjacent to a family restaurant and bar	Premier Travel Inn 0870 242 8000 www.premiertravelinn.com
A consortium of privately owned British hotels, often in the country house style	Pride of Britain 0870 6093012 www.prideofbritainhotels.com
A small expanding group of 4 star hotels currently represented by 5 hotels situated in prime city centre locations	Principal 0870 2427474 www.principal-hotels.com
A newly formed hotel group currently represented by five 4 star hotels across the UK	Quintessential 0113 289 8989 www.quintessential-hotels.co.uk
This high-quality London-based group offers mainly four star hotels in key locations throughout the capital	Radisson Edwardian 020 8757 7900 www.radissonedwardian.com
A recognised international brand increasing its presence in the UK, offering high-quality four star hotels in key locations	Radisson SAS 0800 374411 www.radisson.com

Company Statement	Central Reservations Contact Number
A large hotel group with good coverage throughout the UK represented through 3 brands- Ramada Plaza, Ramada Jarvis and Ramada Resort	Ramada Jarvis 08457 30 30 40 www.ramadajarvis.co.uk
A unique collection of prestigious four and five star central London hotels, providing luxurious surroundings and attentive service	Red Carnation 0845 634 2665 www.redcarnationhotels.com
An international consortium of rural, privately owned hotels, mainly in the country house style	Relais et Chateaux 00 800 2000 00 02 www.relaischateaux.com
One of the Marriott brands, Renaissance is a collection of individual hotels offering comfortable guest rooms, quality cuisine and good levels of service	Renaissance 0800 181 737
Small group of luxury hotels spread across Europe, owned by Sir Rocco Forte. Represented in the UK by 4 hotels all situated in major city locations	Rocco Forte Hotels 0870 460 6040 www.roccofortehotels.com
A consortium of independent Scottish hotels, in the three and four star market	Scotland's Hotels of Distinction 01333 360 888
Is represented in the UK by a small number of four and five star hotels in London and Scotland	Sheraton 0800 35 35 35
A small group of mostly four star hotels many of which many feature spa facilities	Shire 01282 414141 (Head Office) www.shirehotels.com
Part of an international consortium of mainly privately owned hotels, often in the country house style	Small Luxury Hotels of the World 00800 525 48000 www.slh.com
A new brand from choice hotels representing a small group of hotels in the Midlands and Northern England	Stop Inn 0800 44 44 44 www.choicehotelseurope.com
A consortium of independently owned mainly two and three star hotels across Britain	The Circle 0845 345 1965 www.circlehotels.co.uk
The Tower Hotel Group has quality hotels in Ireland offering accommodation in convenient locations.	Tower Hotel Group 353 (0)1 428 2400
Good-quality, modern, budget accommodation across the UK. Almost every lodge has an adjacent family restaurant, often a Little Chef, Harry Ramsden's or Burger King	Travelodge 08700 850 950 www.travelodge.co.uk
With over 90 properties across Europe, this brand is starting to grow its presence in the UK currently represented by Tulip Inn's in Manchester and Glasgow.	Tulip Inn 01765 658911 www.tulipinn.co.uk
A privately owned collection of country house hotels, all individual in style and based predominately in the south of England	Von Essen 01761 241631 www.vonessenhotels.co.uk
Good-quality, modern, budget accommodation at motorway services	Welcome Break www.welcomebreak.co.uk
A small group of individual character hotels, located in countryside settings and in the historic towns of Windsor and Eton	Wrens Hotels 01753 838850 (Head Office) www.wrensgroup.com

ONLY AT CAMPANILE & KYRIAD HOTELS-RESTAURANTS

18 LOCATIONS ACROSS THE UK

395 Hotels-Restaurants Campanile & 210 Hotels-Restaurants Kyriad in Europe

FREE CAR PARK

Campanile GLASGOW

Recently opened on the SECC Site

106 bedrooms, 5 conference rooms, Café-Bistro restaurant

Campanile LEICESTER

Recently opened in Leicester City Center

93 bedrooms, 3 conference rooms, Café Bistro restaurant

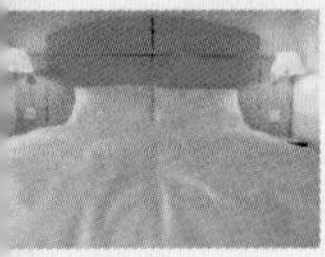

SPECIAL WEEKEND RATE FROM

ALL EN-SUITE ROOMS
FOR 1, 2 OR 3 PEOPLE
(FRI-SAT-SUN)

£ 35*

CENTRAL RESERVATION

Tel.: 0207 519 50 45
www.campanile.com

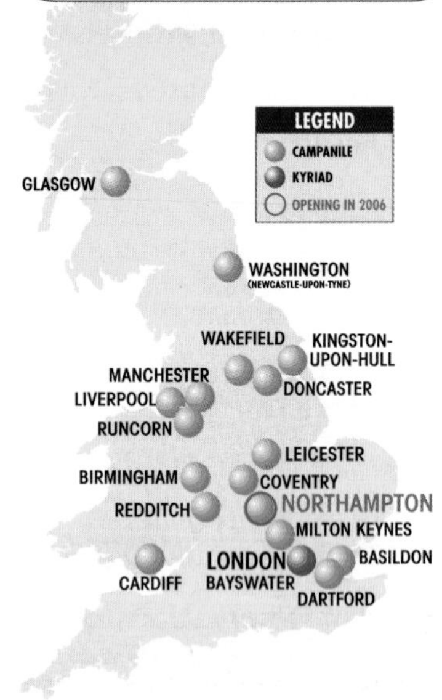

ENJOY A MEAL AT OUR CAFÉ BISTRO RESTAURANTS

- FOOD SERVED ALL DAY**
- 2 COURSE-MENU AT £ 10**
- FULL ENGLISH PLUS CONTINENTAL BREAKFAST: £ 5.95***

FUNCTIONAL AND COMFORTABLE CONFERENCE ROOMS**

- DAY DELEGATE RATE: £21.50
- COMPLIMENTARY USE OF TV, VIDEO, OHP, 2 COURSE LUNCH, 2 BREAKS WITH REFRESHMENTS

*Offer subject to availability in participating hotels.
This discount is not applicable with any other promotional offers.

**Available only at Campanile hotels.

***Prices subject to change without notice.

England

Hotel of the Year for England

Calcot Manor

Tetbury, Gloucestershire

★★★

A

ABBERLEY, Worcestershire Map 10 SO76

★★★74% ◎◎
The Elms Hotel & Restaurant
Stockton Rd WR6 6AT
☎ 01299 896666 🖷 01299 896804
e-mail: info@theelmshotel.co.uk
web: www.vonessenhotels.co.uk
Dir: *on A443 2m beyond Great Witley*

Surrounded by its own well manicured grounds, this imposing Queen Anne mansion dates back to 1710 and offers a sophisticated and relaxed ambience throughout. The spacious public rooms and generously proportioned bedrooms have much elegance and charm. The restaurant overlooks the gardens and serves imaginative and memorable dishes.
ROOMS: 16 en suite 5 annexe en suite (1 fmly) (3 GF) **FACILITIES:** Xmas **CONF:** Thtr 70 Class 30 Board 30 Del from £135 **PARKING:** 50 **NOTES:** in restaurant Civ Wed 70

ABBOT'S SALFORD, Warwickshire Map 10 SP05

★★★72% ◎ **Salford Hall**
WR11 5UT
☎ 01386 871300 & 0800 212671
🖷 01386 871301
e-mail: reception@salfordhall.co.uk
web: www.salfordhall.co.uk
Dir: *A46 take road signed Salford Priors, Abbot's Salford & Harvington. Hotel 1.5m on left*

Built in 1470 as a retreat for the Abbot of Evesham, this impressive building retains many original features. Bedrooms have their own individual character and most offer a view of the attractive gardens. Oak-panelling, period tapestries, open fires and fresh flowers grace the public areas, while leisure facilities include a snooker room, tennis court, solarium and sauna.
ROOMS: 14 en suite 19 annexe en suite (4 GF) in 4 bedrooms s £75-£140; d £110-£150 (incl. bkfst) **LB** **FACILITIES:** STV Snooker Sauna Solarium Xmas **CONF:** Thtr 50 Class 35 Board 25 Del from £140 **PARKING:** 51 **NOTES:** in restaurant Closed 24-30 Dec Civ Wed 80

See advert under STRATFORD-UPON-AVON

ABINGDON, Oxfordshire Map 05 SU49

★★★66% **Abingdon Four Pillars Hotel**
Marcham Rd OX14 1TZ
☎ 0800 374 692 & 01235 553456
🖷 01235 554117
e-mail: abingdon@four-pillars.co.uk
web: www.four-pillars.co.uk
Dir: *A34 at junct with A415, in Abingdon, turn right at rdbt, hotel on right*
On the outskirts of Abingdon, this busy commercial hotel is well located for access to major roads. Bedrooms are comfortable and well equipped with extras such as satellite TV and trouser presses. All day refreshments are offered in the lounge and conservatory.
ROOMS: 62 en suite (7 fmly) (31 GF) in 40 bedrooms s £58-£108; d £76-£134 (incl. bkfst) **LB** **FACILITIES:** STV Xmas **CONF:** Thtr 140 Class 80 Board 48 Del £145 **PARKING:** 85 **NOTES:** in restaurant Civ Wed 100

★★64% **Crown & Thistle**
18 Bridge St OX14 3HS
☎ 01235 522556 🖷 01235 553281
e-mail: reception@crownandthistle.com
Dir: *follow A415 towards Dorchester into town centre*
This popular former coaching inn enjoys an enviable position close to the town centre and the river. Diners can choose between Stocks bar, which retains the air of a local pub, and the more formal but equally friendly restaurant. Bedrooms, located in the original building, are full of character and include some four-poster and family rooms.
ROOMS: 19 en suite (3 fmly) s £65-£75; d £75-£100 **LB** **FACILITIES:** STV Pool table Xmas **CONF:** Thtr 12 Class 8 Board 12 **PARKING:** 35 **NOTES:** in restaurant

Premier Travel Inn Abingdon
Marcham Rd OX14 1AD
☎ 08701 977014 🖷 01235 554149
web: www.premiertravelinn.com
Dir: *On A415 0.5 m from Abingdon town centre. Approx. 0.5m from the A34 at the Abingdon South junct*
High quality, modern budget accommodation ideal for both families and business travellers. Spacious, en suite bedrooms feature bath and shower, satellite TV and many have telephones and modem points. The adjacent family restaurant features a wide and varied menu. For further details consult the Hotel Groups page.
ROOMS: 25 en suite s £49.95; d £49.95

ACCRINGTON, Lancashire Map 18 SD72

★★★★62% **Dunkenhalgh Hotel & Spa**
Blackburn Rd, Clayton-le-Moors BB5 5JP
☎ 01254 303400 & 303407 🖷 01254 872230
e-mail: dunkenhalgh@macdonald-hotels.co.uk
web: www.macdonald-hotels.co.uk
Dir: *adjacent to M65 junct 7*
Set in its own grounds just off the M65, this fine mansion is undergoing extensive refurbishment. Conference and banqueting facilities attract the wedding and corporate market, whilst a new leisure complex will appeal to mixed markets. Bedrooms come in a variety of styles, sizes and standards, some out with the main hotel building.
ROOMS: 61 en suite 119 annexe en suite (50 fmly) in 140 bedrooms s £70-£120; d £70-£120 **LB** **FACILITIES: Spa** STV Sauna Solarium Gym Jacuzzi Thermal suite, Beauty spa, Dance studio Xmas **CONF:** Thtr 400 Class 250 Board 100 Del from £135 **SERVICES:** Lift **PARKING:** 400 **NOTES:** in restaurant Civ Wed 400

★★★67% Sparth House Hotel
Whalley Rd, Clayton Le Moors BB5 5RP
☎ 01254 872263 Fax 01254 872263
e-mail: mail.sparth@btinternet.com
Dir: *A6185 to Clitheroe along Dunkenhalgh Way, right at lights onto A678, left at next lights, A680 to Whalley. Hotel on left after 2 sets of lights*

This 18th-century listed building nestles in three acres of well-tended gardens. Bedrooms offer a choice of styles from the cosy modern rooms ideal for business guests, to the spacious classical rooms - including one with furnishings from one of the great cruise liners. Public rooms feature a panelled restaurant and plush lounge bar.
ROOMS: 16 en suite (3 fmly) ⊗ in 2 bedrooms s £65-£85; d £75-£99 (incl. bkfst) **LB** **CONF:** Thtr 160 Class 50 Board 40 Del from £85 **PARKING:** 50 **NOTES:** ⊗ in restaurant Civ Wed 150

ACLE, Norfolk — Map 13 TG41

Travelodge Great Yarmouth
NR13 3BE
☎ 08700 850 950 Fax 01493 751970
web: www.travelodge.co.uk
Dir: *junct of A47 & Acle bypass*
Travelodge offers good quality, good value, modern accommodation. Ideal for families, the spacious, en suite bedrooms include remote-control TV, tea and coffee-making facilities and comfortable beds. Meals can be taken at the nearby family restaurant. For further details consult the Hotel Groups page.
ROOMS: 40 en suite s fr £26; d fr £26

ALCESTER, Warwickshire — Map 10 SP05

★★★67% Kings Court
Kings Coughton B49 5QQ
☎ 01789 763111 Fax 01789 400242
e-mail: info@kingscourthotel.co.uk
Dir: *1m N on A435*
This privately-owned hotel dates back to Tudor times and the bedrooms in the original house have oak beams. Most guests are accommodated in the well-appointed modern wings. The bar and restaurant have undergone complete refurbishment and offer very good cooking from interesting menus. The hotel is licensed to hold civil ceremonies and the pretty garden is ideal for summer weddings.
ROOMS: 4 en suite 37 annexe en suite (3 fmly) (22 GF) ⊗ in 15 bedrooms s £42-£73; d £76-£90 (incl. bkfst) **LB** **CONF:** Thtr 100 Class 60 Board 40 Del from £104 **PARKING:** 120 **NOTES:** Closed 24-30 Dec Civ Wed 100

Travelodge Stratford Alcester
Oversley Mill Roundabout B49 6AA
☎ 08700 850 950 Fax 01789 766987
web: www.travelodge.co.uk
Dir: *at junct A46/A435*
Travelodge offers good quality, good value, modern accommodation. Ideal for families, the spacious, en suite bedrooms include remote-control TV, tea and coffee-making facilities and comfortable beds. Meals can be taken at the nearby family restaurant. For further details consult the Hotel Groups page.
ROOMS: 66 en suite s fr £26; d fr £26

ALDEBURGH, Suffolk — Map 13 TM45

★★★78% Wentworth
Wentworth Rd IP15 5BD
☎ 01728 452312 Fax 01728 454343
e-mail: stay@wentworth-aldeburgh.co.uk
web: www.wentworth-aldeburgh.com
Dir: *off A12 onto A1094, 6m to Aldeburgh, with church on left & left at bottom of hill*
A delightful privately owned hotel overlooking the beach and sea beyond. The attractive, well-maintained public rooms include three stylish lounges as well as a bar and elegant restaurant. Bedrooms are smartly decorated with co-ordinated fabrics and have many

continued on p42

ALDEBURGH, continued

thoughtful touches; some rooms have superb sea views. Several very spacious Mediterranean-style rooms are located across the road.

Wentworth Hotel, Aldeburgh

ROOMS: 28 en suite 7 annexe en suite (5 GF) ⊗ in all bedrooms s £63-£115; d £102-£158 (incl. bkfst & dinner) **LB** **FACILITIES:** STV Xmas **CONF:** Thtr 15 Class 12 Board 12 Del from £119 **PARKING:** 30 **NOTES:** ⊗ in restaurant

See advert on page 41

★★★77% ⊛⊛ The Brudenell

The Parade IP15 5BU
☎ 01728 452071 📠 01728 454082
e-mail: info@brudenellhotel.co.uk
Dir: *A12/A1094, on reaching town, turn right at junct into High St. Hotel on seafront adjoining Fort Green car park*

Situated at the far end of the town centre just a step away from the beach, this hotel has a contemporary appearance, enhanced by subtle lighting and quality soft furnishings. Many of the bedrooms have superb sea views; they include deluxe rooms with king-sized beds and superior rooms suitable for families.
ROOMS: 42 en suite (15 fmly) ⊗ in all bedrooms s £65-£104; d £102-£208 (incl. bkfst) **LB** **FACILITIES:** STV Xmas **SERVICES:** Lift **PARKING:** 20 **NOTES:** ⊗ in restaurant

★★★77% ⊛ White Lion

Market Cross Place IP15 5BJ
☎ 01728 452720 📠 01728 452986
e-mail: whitelionaldeburgh@btinternet.com
web: www.whitelion.co.uk
Dir: *follow signs to Aldeburgh & town centre. At x-rds turn left*

A popular 15th-century hotel situated at the quiet end of town overlooking the sea. Bedrooms are pleasantly decorated and thoughtfully equipped, many rooms have lovely sea views. Public areas include two lounges and an elegant restaurant, where locally-caught fish and seafood are served. There is also a modern brasserie.

continued

ROOMS: 38 en suite (1 fmly) ⊗ in 19 bedrooms s £50-£120; d £90-£184 (incl. bkfst) **LB** **FACILITIES:** STV Xmas **CONF:** Thtr 120 Class 50 Board 50 Del from £99 **PARKING:** 15 **NOTES:** ⊗ in restaurant Civ Wed 100

ALDERLEY EDGE, Cheshire

Map 16 SJ87

★★★77% ⊛⊛ Alderley Edge

Macclesfield Rd SK9 7BJ
☎ 01625 583033 📠 01625 586343
e-mail: sales@alderleyedgehotel.com
web: www.alderleyedgehotel.com
Dir: *off A34 in Alderley Edge onto B5087 towards Macclesfield. Hotel 200yds on right*

This well-furnished hotel, with its charming grounds, was originally a country house built for one of the region's cotton kings. The bedrooms and suites are attractively furnished, offering excellent quality and comfort. The welcoming bar and adjacent lounge lead into the split-level conservatory restaurant; imaginative, memorable food and friendly attentive service are highlights of any visit.
ROOMS: 52 en suite (6 GF) ⊗ in 19 bedrooms s £130-£250; d £150-£400 **LB** **FACILITIES:** STV ♫ Xmas **CONF:** Thtr 90 Class 40 Board 30 Del £165 **SERVICES:** Lift **PARKING:** 90 **NOTES:** ✗ ⊗ in restaurant Civ Wed 90

⌂ Innkeeper's Lodge Alderley Edge

5-9 Wilmslow Rd SK9 7NZ
☎ 01625 599959 📠 01625 599432
web: www.innkeeperslodge.com
Dir: *M56 junct 6, S on A538. Right at traffic lights towards Alderley Edge. Lodge on left, after 2nd rdbt*

A growing concept in the travel accommodation market. Smart rooms meet essential business requirements but also have home comforts. Dining options include all-day menus plus the added advantage of breakfast, which is included in the room price. For further details consult the Hotel Groups page.
ROOMS: 10 en suite s £49.95-£59.95; d £49.95-£59.95

Premier Travel Inn Alderley Edge

Congleton Rd, Alderley Edge SK9 7AA

☎ 0870 9906498 🖹 0870 9906499

web: www.premiertravelinn.com

Dir: *From N, exit M56 junct 6 onto A538 towards Wilmslow or from S, exit M6 junct 17, follow A534 to Congleton.Then take A34 to Alderley Edge*

High quality, modern budget accommodation ideal for both families and business travellers. Spacious, en suite bedrooms feature bath and shower, satellite TV and many have telephones and modem points. The adjacent family restaurant features a wide and varied menu. For further details consult the Hotel Groups page.

ROOMS: 37 en suite s £47.95-£50.95; d £47.95-£50.95 **CONF:** Thtr 20

> If you wish to use a particular credit card or debit card please check with the hotel that they are happy to accept it

ALDERMINSTER, Warwickshire — Map 10 SP24

★★★★78% Ettington Park

CV37 8BU

☎ 01789 450123 🖹 01789 450472

e-mail: ettingtonpark@handpicked.co.uk

web: www.handpicked.co.uk

Dir: *off A3400, 5m S of Stratford, just outside Alderminster*

Ettington Park offers the peaceful charm of Shakespeare country, with easy access to the motorway and road network. Bedrooms boast views over either the delightful manicured grounds or the formal gardens and chapel. All are spacious and individually designed with comfort in mind. Public rooms include a period

continued

drawing room, oak-panelled dining room and contemporary meeting rooms and leisure centre.

ROOMS: 28 en suite 20 annexe en suite (5 fmly) (10 GF) ⊗ in 5 bedrooms s £126-£200; d £147-£210 (incl. bkfst) **FACILITIES: Spa** STV Fishing Sauna Spa bath, Clay pigeon shooting, Archery, Health & Beauty treatments ♫ Xmas **CONF:** Thtr 90 Class 48 Board 48 Del from £185 **SERVICES:** Lift **PARKING:** 150 **NOTES:** ⊗ in restaurant Civ Wed 96

See advert on this page

> Late for dinner? Quality standards mean that last orders for dinner vary according to star rating and should be no earlier than: ★★ 7.00pm ★★★ 8:00pm ★★★★ 9:00pm ★★★★★ 10:00pm

ALDERSHOT, Hampshire Map 05 SU85

★★★66% **Potters International**
1 Fleet Rd GU11 2ET
☎ 01252 344000 ▤ 01252 311611
e-mail: reservations@pottersinthotel.com
Dir: access via A325 & A321 towards Fleet
This modern hotel is located within easy reach of Aldershot.
Extensive air-conditioned public areas include ample lounge areas,
a pub and a more formal restaurant; there are also conference
rooms and a very good leisure club. Bedrooms mostly spacious,
are well equipped and have been attractively decorated and
furnished.
ROOMS: 100 en suite (6 fmly) (8 GF) ⊗ in 10 bedrooms s £90; d £110
(incl. bkfst) **FACILITIES:** STV ⊡ supervised Sauna Solarium Gym
Jacuzzi **CONF:** Thtr 400 Del £165 **SERVICES:** Lift **PARKING:** 120
NOTES: ✗ ⊗ in restaurant

⌂ **Premier Travel Inn Aldershot**
7 Wellington Av GU11 1SQ
☎ 08701 977015 ▤ 01252 344073
web: www.premiertravelinn.com
Dir: Exit M3 (J4), join A331 then A325 through Farnborough, past airfield,
over roundabout. Inn ahead
High quality, modern budget accommodation ideal for both
families and business travellers. Spacious, en suite bedrooms
feature bath and shower, satellite TV and many have telephones
and modem points. The adjacent family restaurant features a wide
and varied menu. For further details consult the Hotel Groups page.
ROOMS: 60 en suite s £49.95-£52.95; d £49.95-£52.95

ALDWARK, North Yorkshire Map 19 SE46

★★★★77% ⊛⊛ **Aldwark Manor**
YO61 1UF
☎ 01347 838146 ▤ 01347 838867
e-mail: aldwark@marstonhotels.com
web: www.marstonhotels.com
Dir: A1/A59 towards Green Hammerton, then B6265 Little Ouseburn.
Follow signs for Aldwark Bridge/Manor. A19 through Linton-on-Ouse

Mature parkland forms the impressive backdrop for this rambling
19th-century mansion, with the River Ure flowing gently through
the hotel's own 18-hole golf course. Bedrooms vary; the
main-house rooms are traditional and those in the extension are
modern in design. Impressive conference and banqueting facilities
and a stylish, very well equipped leisure club are available.
ROOMS: 60 en suite (2 fmly) s £129-£229; d £166-£266 (incl. bkfst) **LB**
FACILITIES: Spa STV ⊡ ⅄ 18 Fishing Sauna Solarium Gym Putt
green Jacuzzi Health & beauty Xmas **CONF:** Thtr 240 Class 100 Board
80 Del from £195 **SERVICES:** Lift **PARKING:** 150 **NOTES:** ✗ ⊗ in
restaurant Civ Wed 140

ALFRETON, Derbyshire Map 16 SK45

⌂ **Travelodge**
Old Swanwick Colliery Rd DE55 1HJ
☎ 08700 850 950 ▤ 01773 520040
web: www.travelodge.co.uk
Dir: 3m from M1 junct 28, at A38 & A61 junct
Travelodge offers good quality, good value, modern
accommodation. Ideal for families, the spacious, en suite
bedrooms include remote-control TV, tea and coffee-making
facilities and comfortable beds. Meals can be taken at the nearby
family restaurant. For further details consult the Hotel Groups page.
ROOMS: 60 en suite s fr £26; d fr £26

ALFRISTON, East Sussex Map 06 TQ50

★★★71% **Deans Place**
Seaford Rd BN26 5TW
☎ 01323 870248 ▤ 01323 870918
e-mail: mail@deansplacehotel.co.uk
Dir: off A27 signed Alfriston & Drusillas Zoo Park. Continue S through
village
Situated on the southern fringe of the village, this friendly hotel is
set in attractive gardens. Bedrooms vary in size and are well
appointed with good facilities. A wide range of food is offered
including an extensive bar menu and a fine dining option in
Harcourt's Restaurant.
ROOMS: 36 en suite (3 fmly) (8 GF) ⊗ in 16 bedrooms s £65-£105;
d £80-£145 (incl. bkfst) **LB FACILITIES:** STV ⤳ ⅃⚘ Putt green Boules
♫ Xmas **CONF:** Thtr 200 Class 100 Board 60 Del from £130
PARKING: 100 **NOTES:** ⊗ in restaurant Civ Wed 150

★★★69% **The Star Inn**
BN26 5TA
☎ 01323 870495 ▤ 01323 870922
web: www.star-inn-alfriston.com
Dir: 2m off A27 at Drusillas rdbt
Located in a sleepy town on the edge of the South Downs this
14th-century inn provides smart accommodation. Whilst some
rooms retain original features, the majority are contemporary in
style and design. Public areas maintain the original charm and
character of the house including open fires and flagstones.
ROOMS: 37 en suite (12 GF) ⊗ in 18 bedrooms s £34-£64; d £68-£148
(incl. bkfst) **LB FACILITIES:** Xmas **CONF:** Thtr 30 Class 15 Del from
£100 **PARKING:** 40 **NOTES:** ⊗ in restaurant

ALMONDSBURY, Gloucestershire Map 04 ST68

★★★★71% ⊛ **Aztec Hotel & Spa**
Aztec West Business Park BS32 4TS
☎ 01454 201090 ▤ 01454 201593
e-mail: aztec@shirehotels.com
web: www.shirehotels.com
(For full entry see Bristol)

ALNWICK, Northumberland Map 21 NU11
See also Embleton

★★★59% **White Swan**
Bondgate Within NE66 1TD
☎ 01665 602109 ▤ 01665 510400
e-mail: info.whiteswan@classiclodges.co.uk
Dir: from A1 follow town centre signs. Hotel in town centre near
Bondgate Tower
This former coaching inn is situated in the centre of the town.
Bedrooms are modern, while public areas include the Atlantic
continued

Suite, which features original wooden panelling and fittings from the sister ship of the *SS Titanic*.

ROOMS: 56 en suite (5 fmly) (11 GF) ⊗ in 35 bedrooms s £60-£90; d £90-£180 (incl. bkfst) **LB** **FACILITIES:** Xmas **CONF:** Thtr 150 Class 50 Board 40 **PARKING:** 25 **NOTES:** ⊗ in restaurant Civ Wed 150

ALSAGER, Cheshire — Map 15 SJ75

★★★69% Manor House

Audley Rd ST7 2QQ
☎ 01270 884000 01270 882483
e-mail: mhres@compasshotels.co.uk
Dir: *M6 junct 16/A500 toward Stoke. After 0.5m take 1st slip road to Alsager. Left at top & continue, hotel on left approaching village*

Developed around an old farmhouse, the original oak beams are still very much a feature in the hotel bars and restaurant. Modernised and extended over the years, the hotel today is well geared towards the needs of the modern traveller. Some of the main features include a range of conference rooms, a lovely patio garden and an indoor swimming pool.

ROOMS: 57 en suite (4 fmly) (21 GF) ⊗ in 31 bedrooms s £68-£98; d £92-£120 (incl. bkfst) **LB** **FACILITIES:** STV supervised Jacuzzi **CONF:** Thtr 200 Class 108 Board 82 Del from £120 **PARKING:** 150 **NOTES:** ⊗ in restaurant RS Sat & Sun Civ Wed 150

ALSTON, Cumbria — Map 18 NY74

★★78% *Lovelady Shield Country House*

CA9 3LF
☎ 01434 381203 & 381305 01434 381515
e-mail: enquiries@lovelady.co.uk
Dir: *2m E, signed off A689 at junct with B6294*

Located in the heart of the Pennines close to England's highest market town, this delightful country house is set in three acres of landscaped gardens. Accommodation is provided in stylish, thoughtfully equipped bedrooms. Carefully prepared meals are served in the elegant dining room and there is a choice of appealing lounges with log fires lit in the cooler months.

ROOMS: 10 en suite (1 fmly) **CONF:** Class 12 Board 12 **PARKING:** 20 **NOTES:** ⊗ in restaurant Civ Wed 100

★★73% *Nent Hall Country House Hotel*

CA9 3LQ
☎ 01434 381584 01434 382668
web: www.nenthall.com
Dir: *from Alston proceed up main cobbled street. Turn left at top onto A689, Hotel is 2m on right*

Enthusiastic new owners have considerably upgraded this delightful old house that stands in well-kept gardens. Warm and friendly hospitality is provided, with well-appointed and comfortable accommodation, some rooms being on the ground floor and others being suitable for families. There are two comfortable lounges and a pleasant bar serving bar meals and light snacks as well a more formal dining room.

ROOMS: 18 en suite (2 fmly) (9 GF) ⊗ in all bedrooms **CONF:** Thtr 50 Class 50 Board 50 **PARKING:** 100 **NOTES:** ⊗ in restaurant Civ Wed 200

ALTON, Hampshire — Map 05 SU73

★★★72% Alton Grange

London Rd GU34 4EG
☎ 01420 86565 01420 541346
e-mail: info@altongrange.co.uk
web: www.altongrange.co.uk
Dir: *from A31 right at rdbt signed Alton/Holybourne/Bordon B3004. Hotel 300yds on left*

A friendly family owned hotel, conveniently located on the outskirts of this market town and set in two acres of lovingly tended gardens. The individually styled bedrooms, including three suites, are all thoughtfully equipped. Diners can choose between the more formal Truffles Restaurant or relaxed Muffins Brasserie.The attractive public areas include a function suite.

ROOMS: 26 en suite 4 annexe en suite (4 fmly) (7 GF) ⊗ in 6 bedrooms s £85-£105; d £105-£115 (incl. bkfst) **FACILITIES:** STV Hot air ballooning **CONF:** BC Thtr 80 Class 30 Board 40 Del from £145 **PARKING:** 48 **NOTES:** No children 3yrs ⊗ in restaurant Closed 24 Dec-2 Jan Civ Wed 100

ALTON, continued

★★★66% **Alton House**
Normandy St GU34 1DW
☎ 01420 80033 📠 01420 89222
e-mail: mail@altonhouse.com
web: www.altonhousehotel.com
Dir: *off A31, close to railway station*
Conveniently located on the edge of the town, this popular hotel offers comfortably furnished and well-equipped bedrooms. The restaurant serves an extensive menu with daily specials with more informal meals served within the bar. Attractive rear gardens are a plus, along with an outdoor pool and tennis court.
ROOMS: 39 en suite (3 fmly) (3 GF) ⊗ in 2 bedrooms s £89-£99; d £94-£99 **LB** **FACILITIES:** STV ⩚ 🎾 Snooker Xmas **CONF:** BC Thtr 170 Class 80 Board 50 Del from £99 **PARKING:** 94 **NOTES:** 🐕 Closed 25-26 Dec RS 27-29 Dec Civ Wed 70

ALTRINCHAM, Greater Manchester — Map 15 SJ78

★★★68% **Cresta Court**
Church St WA14 4DP
☎ 0161 927 7272 📠 0161 929 6548
e-mail: paul.hindley@cresta-court.co.uk
web: www.cresta-court.co.uk
This modern hotel enjoys a prime location on the A56, close to the station and town centre shops and amenities. Bedrooms vary in style from spacious four-posters to smaller, traditionally furnished rooms. Public areas include a choice of bars, a small gym, beauty salon and extensive function and conference facilities.
ROOMS: 136 en suite (8 fmly) ⊗ in 80 bedrooms s £75-£105; d £150-£210 **LB** **FACILITIES:** STV 🎾 Gym Beauty salon/fitness & cardiovascular training room Xmas **CONF:** BC Thtr 350 Class 200 Board 150 Del from £130 **SERVICES:** Lift **PARKING:** 200 **NOTES:** ⊗ in restaurant Civ Wed 300

★★★66% **Quality Hotel Altrincham**
Langham Rd, Bowdon WA14 2HT
☎ 0161 928 7121 📠 0161 927 7560
e-mail: enquiries@hotels-altrincham.com
web: www.choicehotelseurope.com
Dir: *M6 junct 19 to airport, join A556, over M56 rdbt onto A56, right at traffic lights onto B5161. Hotel 1m on right*
This popular hotel is located within easy reach of the motorways and airport. It provides comfortable and well-equipped bedrooms. The public areas consist of the modern Café Continental, the main restaurant which offers modern cuisine, and a leisure club. A range of conference rooms is also available.
ROOMS: 91 en suite (6 fmly) (13 GF) ⊗ in 30 bedrooms s £55-£125; d £80-£130 **LB** **FACILITIES: Spa** STV ⛆ supervised Sauna Solarium Gym Beauty treatments Xmas **CONF:** Thtr 165 Class 60 Board 48 **PARKING:** 160 **NOTES:** ⊗ in restaurant Civ Wed 150

⌂ **Premier Travel Inn Altrincham North**
Manchester Rd WA14 4PH
☎ 0870 9906580 📠 0870 9906581
web: www.premiertravelinn.com
Dir: *From N, exit M60 junct 7, follow A56 towards Altrincham. From S, exit M6 junct 19, take A556 then A56 towards Sale*
High quality, modern budget accommodation ideal for both families and business travellers. Spacious, en suite bedrooms feature bath and shower, satellite TV and many have telephones and modem points. The adjacent family restaurant features a wide and varied menu. For further details consult the Hotel Groups page.
ROOMS: 46 en suite s £46.95-£48.95; d £46.95-£48.95

⌂ **Premier Travel Inn Altrincham South**
Manchester Rd, West Timperley WA14 5NH
☎ 0870 9906330 📠 0870 9906631
web: www.premiertravelinn.com
Dir: *2m from Altrincham. From N, exit M60 junct 7, take A56 towards Altrincham. From S, exit M6 junct 19. Follow A556 then A56 towards Sale.*
High quality, modern budget accommodation ideal for both families and business travellers. Spacious, en suite bedrooms feature bath and shower, satellite TV and many have telephones and modem points. The adjacent family restaurant features a wide and varied menu. For further details consult the Hotel Groups page.
ROOMS: 48 en suite s £46.95-£48.95; d £46.95-£48.95 **CONF:** Thtr 50

ALVELEY, Shropshire — Map 10 SO78

★★★★66% ***Mill Hotel & Restaurant***
WV15 6HL
☎ 01746 780437 📠 01746 780850
e-mail: enquiries@themillalveley.fsnet.co.uk
web: www.themill-hotel.co.uk
Dir: *Midway between Kidderminster & Bridgnorth, turn off A442 signposted Enville & Turley Green*

Built around a 17th-century water mill, with the original water wheel still on display, this extended and renovated hotel is set in eight acres of landscaped grounds. Bedrooms are pleasant, well equipped and include some superior rooms, which have sitting areas. There are also some rooms with four-poster beds. The restaurant provides carefully prepared dishes and there are extensive wedding and function facilities.
ROOMS: 41 en suite (3 fmly) ⊗ in 18 bedrooms **FACILITIES:** STV Gym **CONF:** Thtr 220 Class 150 Board 80 **SERVICES:** Lift **PARKING:** 200 **NOTES:** 🐕 ⊗ in restaurant Civ Wed 200

ALVESTON, Gloucestershire — Map 04 ST68

★★★76% **Alveston House**
Davids Ln BS35 2LA
☎ 01454 415050 📠 01454 415425
e-mail: info@alvestonhousehotel.co.uk
web: www.alvestonhousehotel.co.uk
Dir: *M5 junct 14 from N or junct 16 from S, on A38*
In a quiet area with easy access to the city and a short drive from both the M4 and M5, this smartly presented hotel provides an impressive combination of good service, friendly hospitality and a relaxed atmosphere. Bedrooms are well equipped and comfortable for business or leisure use. The restaurant offers carefully prepared fresh food, and a pleasant bar and conservatory are the newest additions.
ROOMS: 30 en suite (1 fmly) (6 GF) ⊗ in 27 bedrooms s £75-£99; d £95-£115 (incl. bkfst) **LB** **FACILITIES:** STV **CONF:** Thtr 85 Class 48 Board 50 Del from £135 **PARKING:** 75 **NOTES:** ⊗ in restaurant Civ Wed 75

See advert under BRISTOL

Premier Travel Inn Bristol (Alveston)
Thornbury Rd BS35 3LL
☎ 0870 9906496 📠 0870 9906497
web: www.premiertravelinn.com
Dir: *Just off M5. From N, exit at junct 14 onto A38 towards Bristol. From S, exit at junct 16 take A38 towards Gloucester*
High quality, modern budget accommodation ideal for both families and business travellers. Spacious, en suite bedrooms feature bath and shower, satellite TV and many have telephones and modem points. The adjacent family restaurant features a wide and varied menu. For further details consult the Hotel Groups page.
ROOMS: 74 en suite s £46.95-£49.95; d £46.95-£49.95 **CONF:** Thtr 70 Class 40 Board 40

AMBERLEY, Gloucestershire Map 04 SO80

★★71% ***The Amberley Inn***
Culver Hill GL5 5AF
☎ 01453 872565 📠 01453 872738
e-mail: theamberley@zoom.co.uk web: www.theamberley.co.uk
Dir: *on A46*
On a hillside at the edge of the common, this traditional Cotswold inn extends an equally warm welcome to visitors and locals. Most bedrooms have been upgraded and offer high standards of comfort and quality. Front-facing rooms boast wonderful views of the Woodchester Valley. Public areas include a choice of bars and the attractive restaurant, where excellent local produce is used in impressive dishes.
ROOMS: 14 rms (9 en suite) (1 fmly) **CONF:** BC Thtr 20 Class 14 Board 14 **PARKING:** 14 **NOTES:** ⊗ in restaurant

AMBERLEY, West Sussex Map 06 TQ01

Top Hotel

★★★ **Amberley Castle**
BN18 9LT
☎ 01798 831992 📠 01798 831998
e-mail: info@amberleycastle.co.uk
web: www.amberleycastle.co.uk
Dir: *SW of village, off B2139 between Storrington and Bury Hill*
This partly ruined castle, is now a superb luxury hotel, that has been run with great passion and dedication by the Cummings family for over fifteen years. It is a treasure trove of historical interest, featuring an impressive gatehouse, portcullis and immaculate gardens. Bedrooms are charming and individually decorated; some even have direct access to the battlements and ramparts. The antique-filled day rooms are the ideal place to relax with a book or to take tea. Dining is a treat and the accomplished cooking is served in elegant surroundings.
ROOMS: 14 en suite 5 annexe en suite (7 GF) **FACILITIES:** 18 Putt green Jacuzzi Xmas **CONF:** Thtr 55 Class 12 Board 30 Del from £275 **PARKING:** 50 **NOTES:** No children 12yrs ⊗ in restaurant Civ Wed 55

AMBLESIDE, Cumbria Map 18 NY30
See also Elterwater

Town House

★★★★ **Waterhead**
Lake Rd LA22 0ER
☎ 015394 32566 📠 015394 31255
e-mail: waterhead@elhmail.co.uk
web: www.elh.co.uk/hotels/waterhead.htm
Dir: *A591 into Ambleside, hotel opposite Waterhead Pier*
With an enviable location opposite the bay, this well-established hotel offers contemporary and comfortable accommodation with some innovative features, including CD/DVD players and internet access. There is a fine bar with a garden terrace overlooking the lake and a stylish restaurant serving classical cuisine with a modern twist. Staff are very attentive and friendly. Guests have full use of the Low Wood Hotel leisure facilities nearby.
ROOMS: 41 en suite (3 fmly) (7 GF) ⊗ in 29 bedrooms s £80-£135; d £160-£220 (incl. bkfst) **LB** **FACILITIES:** STV Use of nearby sister hotels sport/beauty facilities Xmas **CONF:** Thtr 40 Class 30 Board 26 Del £129.25 **PARKING:** 43 **NOTES:** ⊗ in restaurant

★★★78% **Rothay Manor**
Rothay Bridge LA22 0EH
☎ 015394 33605 📠 015394 33607
e-mail: hotel@rothaymanor.co.uk
web: www.rothaymanor.co.uk
Dir: *In Ambleside follow signs for Coniston (A593). Hotel 0.25 mile SW of Ambleside opposite rugby pitch*

The former home of a Liverpool merchant, this attractive listed building, built in Regency style, is a short walk from both the town centre and Lake Windermere. Spacious bedrooms, including suites, family rooms and rooms with balconies, are very comfortably equipped and finished to a high standard. Public
continued on p48

AMBLESIDE, continued

areas include a choice of lounges, a spacious restaurant and conference facilities.
ROOMS: 17 en suite 2 annexe en suite (7 fmly) (3 GF) ⊗ in all bedrooms s £70-£120; d £125-£195 (incl. bkfst) **LB FACILITIES:** Nearby leisure centre free to guests, free fishing permit available Xmas **CONF:** Thtr 22 Board 18 Del from £145 **PARKING:** 45 **NOTES:** ⊗ in restaurant Closed 3-26 Jan

See advert on opposite page

★★★75% Regent
Waterhead Bay LA22 0ES
☎ 015394 32254 015394 31474
e-mail: info@regentlakes.co.uk
Dir: *1m S on A591*

This attractive holiday hotel, situated close to Waterhead Bay, offers a warm welcome. Bedrooms come in a variety of styles, including three suites and five bedrooms in the garden wing. There is a modern swimming pool and the restaurant offers a fine dining experience in a tasteful contemporary setting.
ROOMS: 30 en suite (7 fmly) ⊗ in all bedrooms s £60-£80; d £100-£140 (incl. bkfst) **LB FACILITIES:** Xmas **PARKING:** 39 **NOTES:** ⊗ in restaurant Closed 19-27 Dec

★★★71% Ambleside Salutation Hotel
Lake Rd LA22 9BX
☎ 015394 32244 015394 34157
e-mail: enquiries@hotelambleside.uk.com
web: www.hotelslakedistrict.com
Dir: *A591 to Ambleside, onto one-way system down Wansfell Rd into Compston Rd. Right at lights back into village*

A former coaching inn, this hotel has been welcoming guests since the 1600s. Bedrooms vary in size and all are tastefully appointed and thoughtfully equipped; many boast balconies and delightful views. Bright public areas include an attractive restaurant and there is also a choice of spacious lounges.
ROOMS: 38 en suite 4 annexe en suite (4 fmly) ⊗ in 15 bedrooms s £46.50-£103; d £93-£136 (incl. bkfst) **LB FACILITIES:** STV Sauna Gym Jacuzzi Use of pool at sister hotel Xmas **CONF:** Thtr 100 Class 40 Board 16 Del from £95 **PARKING:** 50 **NOTES:** ⊗ in restaurant

See advert on opposite page

★★★68% Skelwith Bridge
Skelwith Bridge LA22 9NJ
☎ 015394 32115 015394 34254
e-mail: skelwithbr@aol.com
web: www.skelwithbridgehotel.co.uk
Dir: *2.5m W on A593 at junct with B5343 to Langdale*
This delightful 17th-century inn is peacefully located at the heart of the Lake District National Park. It offers high standards of comfort and friendly service. Bedrooms include rooms with four-poster beds, and are tastefully appointed and thoughtfully equipped. Spacious public areas include a choice of lounges and bars and the elegant Bridge restaurant overlooks the stunning Lakeland fells.
ROOMS: 21 en suite 6 annexe en suite (2 fmly) ⊗ in 21 bedrooms s £40-£60; d £70-£110 (incl. bkfst) **LB FACILITIES:** Xmas **PARKING:** 60 **NOTES:** ⊗ in restaurant

★★67% Queens
Market Place LA22 9BU
☎ 015394 32206 015394 32721
e-mail: enquiries@queenshotelambleside.com
Dir: *A591 to Ambleside, follow town centre signs on one-way system. Right lane at traffic lights, hotel on right.*
Situated in the heart of the village, this traditional Lakeland stone-clad hotel offers good tourist facilities. The bar meal operation, along with a good range of real ales, makes this a popular venue throughout the year. Bedrooms vary in size and have all the expected features.
ROOMS: 26 en suite (5 fmly) s £31-£47; d £62-£108 (incl. bkfst) **FACILITIES:** STV Xmas **PARKING:** 6 **NOTES:** ⊗ in restaurant

AMERSHAM, Buckinghamshire Map 06 SU99

★★★69% The Crown
High St HP7 0DH
☎ 0870 400 8103 01494 431283
Combining the charm of a bygone era with the modern conveniences expected by today's traveller, this 16th-century coaching inn is a great base for antique shopping and walks in the Chilterns. One claim to fame is that the hotel was featured in the film '*Four Weddings and a Funeral*'. Bedrooms are a strength, all are individually styled and some feature original hand-painted murals.
ROOMS: 19 en suite 18 annexe en suite (10 GF) ⊗ in 21 bedrooms s fr £110; d £125-£195 **LB FACILITIES:** STV Xmas **CONF:** Thtr 30 Board 18 Del from £175 **PARKING:** 30 **NOTES:** ⊗ in restaurant Civ Wed 40

AMESBURY, Wiltshire Map 05 SU14

★★62% *Antrobus Arms*
15 Church St SP4 7EU
☎ 01980 623163 01980 622112
e-mail: enquiries@antrobusarmshotel.co.uk
Dir: *A303 rdbt through one-way system. Turn left at T-junct & hotel on left*
Claiming to be the nearest hotel to Stonehenge, The Antrobus Arms offers individually furnished bedrooms, some of which overlook the walled Victorian garden at the rear of the property. With a history dating back to the 17th century, the place has plenty of character, and public rooms reflect the elegance of the

continued

past. Bar meals are available as an alternative to dining in the main restaurant.

ROOMS: 16 en suite (2 fmly) **FACILITIES:** STV ✂ **CONF:** Thtr 40 Class 40 Board 20 **PARKING:** 15 **NOTES:** ⊗ in restaurant

⌂ Travelodge

Countess Services SP4 7AS
☎ 08700 850 950 📠 01980 625273
web: www.travelodge.co.uk
Dir: *at junct A345 & A303 eastbound*

Travelodge offers good quality, good value, modern accommodation. Ideal for families, the spacious, en suite bedrooms include remote-control TV, tea and coffee-making facilities and comfortable beds. Meals can be taken at the nearby family restaurant. For further details consult the Hotel Groups page.
ROOMS: 48 en suite s fr £26; d fr £26

ANDOVER, Hampshire — Map 05 SU34

★★★73% ◎◎ Esseborne Manor

Hurstbourne Tarrant SP11 0ER
☎ 01264 736444 📠 01264 736725
e-mail: info@esseborne-manor.co.uk
Dir: *halfway between Andover & Newbury on A343, just 1m N of Hurstbourne Tarrant*

Set in two acres of well-tended gardens, this attractive manor house is surrounded by the open countryside of the North Wessex Downs. Bedrooms are delightfully individual and are split between the main house, an adjoining courtyard and separate garden cottage. A wonderfully relaxed atmosphere pervades throughout, with public rooms combining elegance with comfort.
ROOMS: 11 en suite 9 annexe en suite (2 fmly) (6 GF) ⊗ in 6 bedrooms s £95-£130; d £125-£180 (incl. bkfst) **LB** **FACILITIES:** STV ✂ Gym ♫ **CONF:** Thtr 60 Class 40 Board 30 Del from £140 **PARKING:** 50 **NOTES:** ⊗ in restaurant Civ Wed 100

Bad hair day?
Hairdryers in all rooms three stars and above

ANDOVER, continued

★★★62% Quality Hotel Andover

Micheldever Rd SP11 6LA
☎ 01264 369111 📠 01264 369000
e-mail: andover@quality-hotels.co.uk
Dir: *off A303 at A3093. 1st rdbt take 1st exit, 2nd rdbt take 1st exit. Turn left immediately before BP petrol station, then left again*
Located on the outskirts of the town, this hotel is popular with business guests. Bedrooms offer some smart new rooms, and public areas consist of a cosy lounge, a hotel bar and a traditional style restaurant serving a range of meals. There is also a large conference suite available.
ROOMS: 13 en suite 36 annexe en suite (13 GF) ⊗ in 21 bedrooms s fr £72; d fr £82 (incl. bkfst) **LB** **FACILITIES:** STV Xmas **CONF:** Thtr 180 Class 60 Board 60 Del from £99 **PARKING:** 100 **NOTES:** ✗ ⊗ in restaurant Civ Wed 85

ANSTY, Warwickshire — Map 11 SP48

★★★★69% Ansty Hall

Main Rd CV7 9HZ
☎ 024 7661 2222 📠 024 7660 2155
e-mail: ansty@macdonald-hotels.co.uk
web: www.macdonald-hotels.co.uk
Dir: *M6 junct 2 onto B4065 signed 'Ansty'. Hotel 1.5m on left*
Dating back to 1678, this Grade II listed Georgian house is set within eight acres of attractive grounds and woodland. The hotel enjoys the best of both worlds with its central, yet tranquil location. Spacious bedrooms feature a traditional decorative style and a range of extras. Rooms are divided between the main house and the more recently built annexe.
ROOMS: 23 en suite 39 annexe en suite (4 fmly) (22 GF) ⊗ in 55 bedrooms s £110; d £120 (incl. bkfst) **LB** **FACILITIES:** STV Xmas **CONF:** Thtr 200 Class 60 Board 60 Del from £150 **SERVICES:** Lift **PARKING:** 150 **NOTES:** ⊗ in restaurant Civ Wed 100

APPLEBY-IN-WESTMORLAND, Cumbria — Map 18 NY62

★★★78% ®® Appleby Manor Country House

Roman Rd CA16 6JB
☎ 017683 51571 📠 017683 52888
e-mail: reception@applebymanor.co.uk
web: www.applebymanor.co.uk
Dir: *M6 junct 40/A66 towards Brough. Take Appleby turn, then immediately right. Continue for 0.5m*

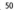

This imposing country mansion is set in extensive grounds amid fabulous Cumbrian scenery. The Dunbobbin family and their experienced staff ensure a warm welcome and attentive service. Bedrooms, including a number with patios, vary in style, with the garden rooms now refurbished. The bar offers a wide range of malt whiskies and the restaurant serves carefully prepared meals.
ROOMS: 23 en suite 7 annexe en suite (9 fmly) ⊗ in 23 bedrooms s £85-£110; d £120-£170 (incl. bkfst) **LB** **FACILITIES:** STV Sauna Solarium Putt green Jacuzzi Steam room, Table tennis, Pool table ch fac **CONF:** Thtr 38 Class 25 Board 28 Del from £110 **PARKING:** 53 **NOTES:** ⊗ in restaurant Closed 24-26 Dec

See advert on opposite page

ARNCLIFFE, North Yorkshire — Map 18 SD97

★★77% ®® Amerdale House

BD23 5QE
☎ 01756 770250 📠 01756 770266
Dir: *left at Threshfield-Kettlewell road 0.5m past Kilnsey Crag*
This former manor house enjoys a peaceful, idyllic location with wonderful views of the dale and fells from every room. Spacious, inviting public areas are tastefully furnished and have real fires in winter. A daily-changing imaginative menu and impressive wine list are offered in the elegant dining room. Bedrooms are beautifully decorated and elegantly furnished.
ROOMS: 10 en suite 1 annexe en suite (3 fmly) s £99-£103; d £168-£176 (incl. bkfst & dinner) **LB** **PARKING:** 30 **NOTES:** ✗ ⊗ in restaurant Closed mid Nov-mid Mar

ARUNDEL, West Sussex — Map 06 TQ00

★★★69% Norfolk Arms

High St BN18 9AD
☎ 01903 882101 📠 01903 884275
e-mail: norfolk.arms@forestdale.com
web: www.forestdale.com
Built by the 10th Duke of Norfolk, this Georgian coaching inn enjoys a superb setting beneath the battlements of Arundel Castle. Bedrooms come in a variety of sizes and styles, all are well equipped. Public areas include two bars, a comfortable lounge, a traditional English restaurant and a range of meeting rooms.
ROOMS: 21 en suite 13 annexe en suite (4 fmly) (8 GF) ⊗ in 6 bedrooms s £75-£95; d £120-£130 (incl. bkfst) **LB** **FACILITIES:** Xmas **CONF:** Thtr 100 Class 40 Board 40 Del from £125 **PARKING:** 34 **NOTES:** ⊗ in restaurant Civ Wed 60

★★65% Comfort Inn

Crossbush BN17 7QQ
☎ 01903 840840 📠 01903 849849
e-mail: admin@gb642.u-net.com
Dir: *A27/A284, 1st right into services*
This modern, purpose-built hotel provides a good base for exploring the nearby historic town. Good access to local road networks and a range of meeting rooms, all air conditioned, make this an ideal venue for business guests. Bedrooms are spacious, smartly decorated and well equipped.
ROOMS: 53 en suite (25 GF) ⊗ in 39 bedrooms s £55-£70; d £65-£120 (incl. bkfst) **LB** **FACILITIES:** STV Xmas **CONF:** BC Thtr 30 Class 30 Board 30 Del from £65 **PARKING:** 53 **NOTES:** ⊗ in restaurant

Premier Travel Inn Arundel

Crossbush Ln BN18 9PQ
☎ 08701 977016 📠 01903 884381
web: www.premiertravelinn.com
Dir: *1m E of Arundel at junct of A27/A284*
High quality, modern budget accommodation ideal for both families and business travellers. Spacious, en suite bedrooms feature bath and shower, satellite TV and many have telephones and modem points. The adjacent family restaurant features a wide and varied menu. For further details consult the Hotel Groups page.
ROOMS: 30 en suite s £49.95; d £49.95 **CONF:** Thtr 50 Board 26

ASCOT, Berkshire

Map 06 SU96

★★★★71%
The Royal Berkshire Ramada Plaza
RAMADA

London Rd, Sunninghill SL5 0PP
☎ 01344 623322 🖷 01344 627100
e-mail: sales.royalberkshire@ramadajarvis.co.uk
web: www.ramadajarvis.co.uk
Dir: *A30 towards Bagshot, right opposite Wentworth Club onto A329, continue for 2m, hotel entrance on right*

Once occupied by the Churchill family, this delightful Queen Anne house is set in 14 acres of attractive gardens on the edge of Ascot. Public areas include a comfortable lounge bar, an attractive restaurant that overlooks the rear gardens and extensive conference facilities. The main house has been skilfully extended to offer smart, well-equipped bedrooms.

ROOMS: 63 en suite (8 fmly) (8 GF) ⊗ in 25 bedrooms s £154-£215; d £154-£215 **FACILITIES:** STV Putt green Xmas **CONF:** Thtr 100 Class 60 Board 45 Del from £265 **PARKING:** 150 **NOTES:** ⊗ in restaurant Civ Wed 90

★★★★66% The Berystede
MACDONALD HOTELS & RESORTS

Bagshot Rd, Sunninghill SL5 9JH
☎ 0870 400 8111 🖷 01344 872301
e-mail: general.berystede@macdonald-hotels.co.uk
web: www.macdonald-hotels.co.uk
Dir: *A30/B3020 (Windmill Pub). Continue 1.25m to hotel on left just before junct with A330*

This impressive Victorian mansion, close to Ascot Racecourse, is set in nine acres of wooded grounds. Spacious bedrooms have comfortable armchairs and internet facilities. There is a cosy bar and fine traditional restaurant, which overlooks the heated outdoor swimming pool and gardens. An excellent range of modern meeting rooms is available.

ROOMS: 125 en suite (61 fmly) (33 GF) ⊗ in 109 bedrooms s £80-£170; d £100-£200 **LB** **FACILITIES:** STV Putt green Leisure complex from April 2006 Xmas **CONF:** BC Thtr 150 Class 90 Board 70 Del from £185 **SERVICES:** Lift **PARKING:** 150 **NOTES:** ⊗ in restaurant Civ Wed 140

★★69% Highclere
19 Kings Rd, Sunninghill SL5 9AD
☎ 01344 625220 🖷 01344 872528
e-mail: info@highclerehotel.com
web: www.highclerehotel.com
Dir: *opp Sunninghill Post Office*

This privately owned establishment is situated in a quiet residential area, 10 minutes from Windsor and the M3. Modest bedrooms are attractively decorated and well equipped. A cosy bar is available adjacent to the comfortable conservatory lounge. Dinner is available in the Villa Moura Portuguese restaurant.

ROOMS: 11 en suite (1 fmly) (2 GF) ⊗ in 7 bedrooms s £80-£90; d £90-£100 (incl. bkfst) **CONF:** Thtr 15 Class 15 Del from £120 **PARKING:** 11 **NOTES:** ⊗ in restaurant

★★66% *Brockenhurst*
Brockenhurst Rd SL5 9HA
☎ 01344 621912 🖷 01344 873252
e-mail: info@brockenhurst.com
Dir: *on A330*

Located within easy reach of the famous racecourse, Windsor Castle and other local attractions, this attractive Edwardian house offers comfortable accommodation. Bedrooms are mostly spacious with a range of thoughtful extras. Relaxed and friendly service is provided in the cosy bar and restaurant, both of which overlook the charming grounds.

ROOMS: 12 en suite 5 annexe en suite (2 fmly) (2 GF) **FACILITIES:** STV **CONF:** Thtr 50 Class 25 Board 30 **PARKING:** 32 **NOTES:** ⊗ in restaurant

♫ Entertainment

ASHBOURNE, Derbyshire — Map 10 SK14

See also Thorpe

★★★75% Callow Hall

Mappleton Rd DE6 2AA
Tel 01335 300900 Fax 01335 300512
e-mail: reservations@callowhall.demon.co.uk
Dir: *A515 through Ashbourne towards Buxton, left at Bowling Green pub, then 1st right*

This delightful, creeper-clad, early Victorian house, set on a 44-acre estate, enjoys views over Bentley Brook and the Dove Valley. The atmosphere is relaxed and welcoming, and some of the spacious bedrooms in the main house have comfortable sitting areas. Public rooms feature high ceilings, ornate plasterwork and antique furniture. There is a good range of dishes available from both the fixed-price, daily changing menu and the carte.
ROOMS: 16 en suite (2 fmly) (2 GF) in 8 bedrooms s £95-£120; d £135-£200 (incl. bkfst) **LB** **FACILITIES:** Fishing Cycle hire nearby (Tissington Trail) Riding nearby Golf course within 2m **CONF:** BC Thtr 30 Board 16 Del £155 **PARKING:** 21 **NOTES:** in restaurant Closed 25-26 Dec RS Sun

See advert on opposite page

★★★67% *Hanover International Hotel & Club*

Derby Rd DE6 1XH
Tel 01335 346666 Fax 01335 346549
e-mail: rso@hanover-international.com
web: www.hanover-international.com
Dir: *A52 to Ashbourne, at rdbt turn right to Airfield Ind Est, hotel 400yds on right*
This modern, purpose-built hotel is just a short drive from the town on the Derby road. It offers comfortable, well-equipped bedrooms, some of which are especially designed for visitors with disabilities. The indoor leisure facilities, which include a good-sized swimming pool and sauna, are an added attraction.
ROOMS: 50 en suite (5 fmly) in 10 bedrooms **FACILITIES:** STV supervised Sauna Steam room, Fitness room **CONF:** Thtr 200 Class 100 Board 80 **SERVICES:** Lift **PARKING:** 130 **NOTES:** in restaurant Civ Wed 200

★★64% The Dog & Partridge Country Inn

Swinscoe DE6 2HS
Tel 01335 343183 Fax 01335 342742
e-mail: info@dogandpartridge.co.uk
web: www.dogandpartridge.co.uk
Dir: *A52 towards Leek, hotel 4m on left*
This 17th-century inn is situated in the hamlet of Swinscoe, within easy reach of Alton Towers. Bedroom have direct access and are sited within the hotel's grounds. Well-presented self-catering family suites are also available. Meals are served every evening until late and can be enjoyed either in the bar, the conservatory or on an outdoor terrace weather permitting.
ROOMS: 25 en suite (15 fmly) s £40-£80; d £80-£100 (incl. bkfst) **LB** **FACILITIES:** Fishing Xmas **CONF:** Thtr 20 Class 15 Board 18 **PARKING:** 115 **NOTES:** in restaurant

ASHBURTON, Devon — Map 03 SX77

★★★74% Holne Chase

Two Bridges Rd TQ13 7NS
Tel 01364 631471 Fax 01364 631453
e-mail: info@holne-chase.co.uk
web: www.holne-chase.co.uk
Dir: *3m N on unclass Two Bridges/Tavistock road*

This former hunting lodge is peacefully situated in a secluded position, with sweeping lawns leading to the river and panoramic views of the moor. Bedrooms are attractively and individually furnished, and there are a number of split-level suites available. Good quality local produce features on the daily-changing menu.
ROOMS: 10 en suite 7 annexe en suite (9 fmly) (1 GF) s £115-£125; d £150-£210 (incl. bkfst) **LB** **FACILITIES:** Fishing Riding Putt green Fly fishing, Riding, Beauty treatments for people and dogs Xmas **CONF:** Thtr 40 Class 60 Board 60 Del £150 **PARKING:** 40 **NOTES:** in restaurant Civ Wed 60

ASHBY-DE-LA-ZOUCH, Leicestershire — Map 11 SK31

⌂ Premier Travel Inn Ashby de la Zouch

Flagstaff Island, Flagstaff Park LE65 1DS
Tel 08701 977281 Fax 01530 561211
web: www.premiertravelinn.com
Dir: *Exit M1 junct 23A, follow signs for A42 (M42) to Tamworth & Birmingham. Inn off rdbt at A42 junct 13*
High quality, modern budget accommodation ideal for both families and business travellers. Spacious, en suite bedrooms feature bath and shower, satellite TV and many have telephones and modem points. The adjacent family restaurant features a wide and varied menu. For further details consult the Hotel Groups page.
ROOMS: 40 en suite s £46.95-£48.95; d £46.95-£48.95

ASHFORD, Kent — Map 07 TR04

★★★★74% Eastwell Manor

Eastwell Park, Boughton Lees TN25 4HR
Tel 01233 213000 Fax 01233 635530
e-mail: enquiries@eastwellmanor.co.uk
Dir: *on A251, 200yds on left when entering Boughton Aluph*
Set in 62 acres of landscaped grounds, this lovely hotel dates back to the Norman Conquest and boasts a number of interesting features, including carved wood-panelled rooms and huge baronial stone fireplaces. Accommodation is divided between the manor house and the courtyard mews cottages. The luxury

continued on p54

Callow Hall

Country House Hotel

AA ★★★ Hotel

Good Food Guide Main Entry

Mappleton, Ashbourne, Derbyshire DE6 2AA
Tel 01335 300900 Fax 01335 300512
e-mail enquiries@callowhall.co.uk www.callowhall.co.uk

THE IZAAK WALTON HOTEL

Dovedale, Ashbourne, Derbys DE6 2AY
Tel: +44 (0) 1335 350 555 Fax: +44 (0) 1335 350 539
Email: reception@izaakwaltonhotel.com
Website: www.izaakwaltonhotel.com

The Izaak Walton Hotel is a picturesque 17th century farmhouse nestled in the heart of the Derbyshire Peak District. We offer a warm welcome, comfort and tranquility with views of outstanding natural beauty. With cosy lounges and attractive country house décor we are able to offer a tailor-made conference service and we are also the perfect setting for weddings. Our 34 en-suite bedrooms mostly have breathtaking views of the Peaks. Savour the imaginative and classical cuisine in our Haddon Restaurant with its extensive menu and carefully selected wine list or relax in the informal surroundings of the Dovedale Bar. We are also able to offer excellent fishing on our own two-mile stretch of the River Dove.

See Thorpe for more details.

The Peveril of the Peak

Thorpe, Dovedale, Ashbourne,
Derbyshire DE6 2AW
Tel: 01335 350396
frontdesk@peverilofthepeak.co.uk
www.peverilofthepeak.co.uk

The Hotel, originally the local vicarage, is situated in eleven acres of beautiful, landscaped grounds with views of the Dovedale valley. The Hotel name is taken from the historical novel of the same name by Sir Walter Scott. The hotel is ideally situated for visiting the surrounding wealth of places of interest to visit. Afterwards complete your day by dining in the restaurant, which opens out on the garden and provides award-winning food using the freshest ingredient. Then relax in one of the 46 spacious bedrooms all well equipped, some ground floor rooms have their own patio with wooden chairs and tables. The Peveril Of The Peak can also help when planning weddings or conferences, to ensure a smooth and successful event.

ASHFORD, continued

Pavilion Spa in the grounds has an all-day brasserie, whilst fine dining in the main restaurant is a highlight of any stay.
ROOMS: 23 en suite 39 annexe en suite (2 fmly) ⊗ in 4 bedrooms s £160-£355; d £190-£395 (incl. bkfst) **LB** **FACILITIES: Spa** STV Sauna Solarium Gym Putt green Jacuzzi Boules, & Beauty spa Xmas **CONF:** Thtr 200 Class 60 Board 48 Del from £230 **SERVICES:** Lift **PARKING:** 200 **NOTES:** ⊗ in restaurant Civ Wed 250

★★★★69% Ashford International
Simone Weil Av TN24 8UX
☎ 01233 219988 01233 647743
e-mail: info@ashfordinthotel.com
Dir: *off M20 junct 9, 3rd exit for Ashford/Canterbury. Left at 1st rdbt, hotel 200mtrs on left.*

Ideally situated just off the M20 and its links to the channel tunnel and ferry terminal. Public areas feature a superb mall housing a range of boutiques and eating places, including a popular brasserie, the Alhambra Restaurant and Florentine Bar. The spacious bedrooms are pleasantly furnished and equipped with modern facilities.
ROOMS: 177 en suite (4 fmly) ⊗ in 151 bedrooms s £70-£115; d £70-£115 **LB** **FACILITIES:** Sauna Solarium Gym Jacuzzi Xmas **CONF:** BC Thtr 400 Class 160 Del from £37 **SERVICES:** Lift **PARKING:** 400 **NOTES:** ⊗ in restaurant Closed 24-27 Dec Civ Wed 150

Premier Travel Inn Ashford Central
Hall Av, Orbital Park, Sevington TN24 0GN
☎ 08701 977305 01233 500742
web: www.premiertravelinn.com
Dir: *M20 junct 10. Southbound take 4th exit at rdbt. Northbound take 1st exit/ A2070 for Brenzett. Inn at next rdbt on right*
High quality, modern budget accommodation ideal for both families and business travellers. Spacious, en suite bedrooms feature bath and shower, satellite TV and many have telephones and modem points. The adjacent family restaurant features a wide and varied menu. For further details consult the Hotel Groups page.
ROOMS: 60 en suite s £49.95; d £49.95

Premier Travel Inn Ashford North
Maidstone Rd, Hothfield Common TN26 1AP
☎ 08701 977018 01233 713945
web: www.premiertravelinn.com
Dir: *on A20, between Ashford & Charing, close to M20 junct 8/9*
High quality, modern budget accommodation ideal for both families and business travellers. Spacious, en suite bedrooms feature bath and shower, satellite TV and many have telephones and modem points. The adjacent family restaurant features a wide and varied menu. For further details consult the Hotel Groups page.
ROOMS: 60 en suite s £46.95-£49.95; d £46.95-£49.95

Travelodge
Eureka Leisure Park TN25 4BN
☎ 08700 850 950 01233 622676
web: www.travelodge.co.uk
Dir: *M20 junct 9, take 1st exit on left*
Travelodge offers good quality, good value, modern accommodation. Ideal for families, the spacious, en suite bedrooms include remote-control TV, tea and coffee-making facilities and comfortable beds. Meals can be taken at the nearby family restaurant. For further details consult the Hotel Groups page.
ROOMS: 67 en suite s fr £26; d fr £26

ASHFORD-IN-THE-WATER, Derbyshire Map 16 SK16

★★★82% Riverside House
Fennel St DE45 1QF
☎ 01629 814275 01629 812873
e-mail: riversidehouse@enta.net
Dir: *turn right off A6 Bakewell/Buxton road 2m from Bakewell, hotel at end of main street*
This delightful and welcoming hotel, with outstanding service, is becoming a popular destination for its high quality accommodation and fine dining. Partly dating back to 1630, the hotel enjoys a peaceful location by the River Wye. Individually styled bedrooms are thoughtfully equipped and the smart public rooms include a bright conservatory, an oak-panelled lounge with inglenook fireplace, a drawing room and two dining rooms.
ROOMS: 15 en suite (4 GF) ⊗ in all bedrooms s £100-£140; d £135-£150 (incl. bkfst) **LB** **FACILITIES:** STV Xmas **CONF:** BC Thtr 15 Class 15 Board 15 Del from £190 **PARKING:** 40 **NOTES:** No children 16yrs ⊗ in restaurant Civ Wed 32

ASHWATER, Devon Map 03 SX39

Top Hotel

★★ Blagdon Manor Hotel & Restaurant
EX21 5DF
☎ 01409 211224 01409 211634
e-mail: stay@blagdon.com
web: www.blagdon.com
Dir: *Take A388 N of Launceston towards Holsworthy. Approx 2m N of Chapman's Well take 2nd right for Ashwater. Next right beside Blagdon Lodge, hotel 0.25m*
Located on the borders of Devon and Cornwall, this small and friendly hotel offers a charming home-from-home atmosphere. The tranquillity of the secluded setting, the character and charm of the house and its unhurried pace ensures calm and relaxation. High levels of service, personal touches and thoughtful extras are all part of a stay here. Steve
continued

Morey cooks with passion and his dependence on only the finest of local ingredients speaks volumes.
ROOMS: 7 en suite ⊘ in all bedrooms s fr £80; d fr £110 (incl. bkfst) **FACILITIES:** Boules, giant chess/draughts ch fac **PARKING:** 10 **NOTES:** No children 12yrs ⊘ in restaurant Closed 2wks Jan/Feb & 2wks Oct/Nov

ASPLEY GUISE, Bedfordshire — Map 11 SP93

★★★69% Moore Place

The Square MK17 8DW
☎ 01908 282000 📠 01908 281888
e-mail: manager@mooreplace.com
web: www.mooreplace.co.uk
Dir: *M1 junct 13, take A507 signed Aspley Guise & Woburn Sands. Hotel on left side of village square*

This impressive Georgian house, set in delightful gardens in the village centre, is very conveniently located for the M1. Bedrooms do vary in size, but consideration has been given to guest comfort, with many thoughtful extras provided. There is a wide range of meeting rooms and private dining options.
ROOMS: 37 en suite 27 annexe en suite (16 GF) ⊘ in 43 bedrooms s £63-£119; d £84-£220 (incl. bkfst) **LB** **FACILITIES:** Xmas **CONF:** Thtr 40 Class 24 Board 20 **PARKING:** 70 **NOTES:** ⊘ in restaurant Civ Wed 80

ASTON CLINTON, Buckinghamshire — Map 05 SP81

Innkeeper's Lodge Aylesbury East

London Rd HP22 5HP
☎ 01296 632777 📠 01296 632685
web: www.innkeeperslodge.com
Dir: *on A41 in Aston Clinton, between Aylesbury & Tring*

A growing concept in the travel accommodation market. Smart rooms meet essential business requirements but also have home comforts. Dining options include all-day menus plus the added advantage of breakfast, which is included in the room price. For further details consult the Hotel Groups page.
ROOMS: 11 en suite s £49.95-£65; d £49.95-£65

ATHERSTONE, Warwickshire — Map 10 SP39

★★71% Chapel House

Friar's Gate CV9 1EY
☎ 01827 718949 📠 01827 717702
e-mail: info@chapelhousehotel.co.uk
Dir: *turn off A5, follow signs to town centre, half way up Long St turn right into Church St. Hotel is on right of church*

Sitting next to the church this 18th-century town house offers excellent hospitality and service while the cooking, using much local produce, is very notable. Bedrooms are well equipped and lounges are extensive; there is also a delightful walled garden for guests to use.
ROOMS: 12 en suite ⊘ in all bedrooms s £65-£70; d £95 (incl. bkfst) **CONF:** Board 24 **NOTES:** ⊘ in restaurant Closed 26 Aug-4 Sep & 24 Dec-1 Jan

Popped the question? Hotels with Civ wed in their entry are licensed for civil wedding ceremonies. Maximum numbers for the ceremony only are shown e.g. Civ wed 120

AXMINSTER, Devon — Map 04 SY29

See also Colyford

★★★74% Fairwater Head Country House Hotel

Hawkchurch EX13 5TX
☎ 01297 678349 📠 01297 678459
e-mail: info@fairwaterheadhotel.co.uk
web: www.fairwaterheadhotel.co.uk
Dir: *off B3165, Crewkerne to Lyme Regis road. Hotel signposted to Hawkchurch*

Under new ownership, this well-managed hotel is peacefully located in the countryside and has attractive gardens and stunning views. The proprietors and staff provide a friendly and attentive service in a relaxing environment. Bedrooms are individually decorated, spacious and comfortable, and guests can enjoy best quality local ingredients cooked with great care.
ROOMS: 14 en suite 7 annexe en suite (9 GF) ⊘ in all bedrooms s £75-£100; d £130-£200 (incl. bkfst & dinner) **LB** **FACILITIES:** Xmas **CONF:** BC Thtr 30 Class 20 Board 20 Del from £100 **PARKING:** 25 **NOTES:** No children 6yrs ⊘ in restaurant

AYLESBURY, Buckinghamshire — Map 11 SP81

Top Hotel

★★★★ Hartwell House Hotel, Restaurant & Spa

Oxford Rd HP17 8NL
☎ 01296 747444 📠 01296 747450
e-mail: info@hartwell-house.com
web: www.hartwell-house.com
Dir: *from S - M40 junct 7, A329 to Thame, then A418 towards Aylesbury. After 6m, through Stone, hotel on left. From N - M40 junct 9 for Bicester. A41 to Aylesbury, A418 to Oxford for 2m. Hotel on right*

This beautiful, historic house is set in 90 acres of unspoilt parkland. The grand public rooms are truly magnificent, and feature many fine works of art. The service standards are very high, being attentive and traditional without stuffiness. There is an elegant, award-winning restaurant, where carefully prepared dishes use the best local produce. Bedrooms, many with high ceilings, are spacious, elegant and very comfortable. Most are in the main house, but some including suites, are in the nearby, renovated coach-house, which also houses a fine spa.
ROOMS: 30 en suite 16 annexe en suite (10 GF) ⊘ in 12 bedrooms s fr £165; d fr £270 (incl. bkfst) **LB** **FACILITIES:** **Spa** STV supervised Sauna Solarium Gym Jacuzzi Treatment rooms & Steam rooms Xmas **CONF:** BC Thtr 100 Class 40 Board 40 Del from £255 **SERVICES:** Lift **PARKING:** 91 **NOTES:** No children 8yrs ⊘ in restaurant Civ Wed 60

AYLESBURY, continued

⌂ Innkeeper's Lodge Aylesbury South

40 Main St, Weston Turville HP22 5RW
☎ 01296 613131 & 0870 243 0500 📠 01296 616902
web: www.innkeeperslodge.com
Dir: *M25 junct 20/A41(Hemel Hempstead). Continue for 12m to Aston Clinton. Left onto B4544 to Weston Turville, lodge on left*
A growing concept in the travel accommodation market. Smart rooms meet essential business requirements but also have home comforts. Dining options include all-day menus plus the added advantage of breakfast, which is included in the room price. For further details consult the Hotel Groups page.
ROOMS: 16 en suite s £46.95-£62; d £46.95-£62

⌂ Premier Travel Inn Aylesbury

Buckingham Rd HP19 9QL
☎ 08701 977019 📠 01206 330432
web: www.premiertravelinn.com
Dir: *N from Aylesbury centre on A413, Inn 1m on left, adjacent to rdbt*
High quality, modern budget accommodation ideal for both families and business travellers. Spacious, en suite bedrooms feature bath and shower, satellite TV and many have telephones and modem points. The adjacent family restaurant features a wide and varied menu. For further details consult the Hotel Groups page.
ROOMS: 64 en suite s £46.95-£49.95; d £46.95-£49.95

AYSGARTH, North Yorkshire — Map 19 SE08

★★69% *The George & Dragon Inn*

DL8 3AD
☎ 01969 663358 📠 01969 663773
e-mail: info@georgeanddragonaysgarth.co.uk
This 17th-century coaching inn offers spacious, comfortably appointed rooms. Popular with walkers, the cosy bar has a real fire and a good selection of local beers. The beamed restaurant serves hearty breakfasts and interesting meals using fresh local produce. Service is very friendly and attentive.
ROOMS: 7 en suite (2 fmly) **PARKING:** 35 **NOTES:** ⊘ in restaurant

BABBACOMBE See Torquay

BAGINTON, Warwickshire — Map 11 SP37

★★70% *Old Mill*

Mill Hill CV8 3AH
☎ 024 7630 2241 📠 024 7630 7070
Dir: *in village 0.25m from junct A45 & A46*
Enjoying a peaceful riverside location, yet within easy reach of the motorway networks, the Old Mill has been furnished to a high standard. Public areas include the popular Chef & Brewer bar and restaurant, with a pleasant patio for summer evenings. Spacious bedrooms are smartly appointed and well equipped.
ROOMS: 28 en suite (6 fmly) **CONF:** Class 16 Board 20 **PARKING:** 200
NOTES: ✗

○ Hotel due to open in late 2005 or 2006
U Star rating not confirmed

Indoor Swimming pool
Indoor Swimming pool (heated)
Outdoor Swimming pool
Outdoor Swimming pool (heated)

BAGSHOT, Surrey — Map 06 SU96

Top Hotel

★★★★★ ◎◎◎

Pennyhill Park Hotel & The Spa

London Rd GU19 5EU
☎ 01276 471774 📠 01276 473217
e-mail: enquiries@pennyhillpark.co.uk
web: www.exclusivehotels.co.uk
Dir: *on A30 between Bagshot & Camberley opposite Texaco garage*
This delightful country-house hotel set in 120-acre grounds provides every modern comfort. The stylish bedrooms are individually designed and have impressive bathrooms. The award-winning Latymer Restaurant is among the range of dining options and there is a choice of lounges and bars. Leisure facilities include a jogging trail, a golf course and a state-of-the-art spa with a thermal sequencing experience, ozone treated swimming and hydrotherapy pools along with a comprehensive range of therapies and treatments.
ROOMS: 26 en suite 97 annexe en suite (6 fmly) (26 GF) ⊘ in 20 bedrooms d fr £205 **LB FACILITIES: Spa** STV 9 Fishing Snooker Sauna Gym Jacuzzi Archery, Clay shooting, Plunge pool, Turkish Steam Rm, Volleyball, ♫ Xmas **CONF:** BC Thtr 160 Class 80 Board 60 Del from £350 **SERVICES:** Lift
PARKING: 500 **NOTES:** ⊘ in restaurant Civ Wed 160

⌂ Premier Travel Inn Bagshot

1 London Rd GU19 5HR
☎ 08701 977021 📠 01276 451357
web: www.premiertravelinn.com
Dir: *on A30, 0.25m from Bagshot*
High quality, modern budget accommodation ideal for both families and business travellers. Spacious, en suite bedrooms feature bath and shower, satellite TV and many have telephones and modem points. The adjacent family restaurant features a wide and varied menu. For further details consult the Hotel Groups page.
ROOMS: 40 en suite s £49.95-£52.95; d £49.95-£52.95

BAINBRIDGE, North Yorkshire — Map 18 SD99

★★67% *Rose & Crown*

DL8 3EE
☎ 01969 650225 📠 01969 650735
e-mail: info@theprideofwensleydale.com
Dir: *on A684 between Hawes & Leyburn*
This traditional coaching inn, overlooking the village green, is full of character. Bedrooms are appropriately furnished and comfortably equipped. There are two well-stocked bars, one very popular with locals, both offering an interesting range of dishes. Finer dining is served in the restaurant and a cosy residents' lounge is also provided.
ROOMS: 12 rms (11 en suite) (1 fmly) ⊘ in 2 bedrooms **CONF:** Class 30 Board 30 **PARKING:** 65 **NOTES:** ⊘ in restaurant

BAKEWELL, Derbyshire — Map 16 SK26

★★★68% Rutland Arms
The Square DE45 1BT
☎ 01629 812812 📠 01629 812309
e-mail: rutland@bakewell.demon.co.uk
Dir: *M1 junct 28 to Matlock, A6 to Bakewell. Hotel in town centre*

This 19th-century hotel lies at the very centre of Bakewell and offers a wide range of quality accommodation. The friendly staff are attentive and welcoming, and The Four Seasons candlelit restaurant offers interesting fine dining in elegant surroundings.
ROOMS: 18 en suite 17 annexe en suite (2 fmly) ⊘ in 12 bedrooms
FACILITIES: Xmas **CONF:** Thtr 100 Class 60 Board 40 **PARKING:** 25
NOTES: ⊘ in restaurant

★★70% Monsal Head Hotel
Monsal Head DE45 1NL
☎ 01629 640250 📠 01629 640815
e-mail: christine@monsalhead.com
web: www.monsalhead.com
Dir: *A6 from Bakewell to Buxton. After 2m turn into Ashford-in-the-Water, take B6465 for 1m*
Popular with walkers, this friendly hotel commands one of the most splendid views in the Peak Park, overlooking Monsal Dale and the walking path along the disused railway line. Bedrooms are well equipped, and four have superb views down the valley. Imaginative food is served in either an attractive modern restaurant or separate original pub, which also offers a range of fine wines and real ales.
ROOMS: 7 en suite (1 fmly) s £45-£55; d £50-£100 (incl. bkfst) **LB**
FACILITIES: ♫ Xmas **CONF:** BC Thtr 60 Class 30 Board 30 Del from £95 **PARKING:** 20 **NOTES:** ⊘ in restaurant Closed 25 Dec

BALDOCK, Hertfordshire — Map 12 TL23

Sleep Inn Baldock
Baldock Services (A1M/A507), Radwell SG7 5TR
☎ 01462 832900 📠 01462 832901
e-mail: enquiries@hotels-baldock.com
web: www.hotels-baldock.com
Dir: *400yds E of A1(M) junct 10 & A507*
This modern, purpose built accommodation offers smartly appointed, well-equipped bedrooms, with good power showers. There is a choice of adjacent food outlets where guests may enjoy breakfast, snacks and meals.
ROOMS: 62 en suite

Travelodge
Great North Rd, Hinxworth SG7 5EX
☎ 08700 850 950 📠 01462 835329
web: www.travelodge.co.uk
Dir: *on A1, southbound*
Travelodge offers good quality, good value, modern

continued

accommodation. Ideal for families, the spacious, en suite bedrooms include remote-control TV, tea and coffee-making facilities and comfortable beds. Meals can be taken at the nearby family restaurant. For further details consult the Hotel Groups page.
ROOMS: 40 en suite s fr £26; d fr £26

BALSALL COMMON, West Midlands — Map 10 SP27

★★★★67% Nailcote Hall
Nailcote Ln, Berkswell CV7 7DE
☎ 024 7646 6174 📠 024 7647 0720
e-mail: info@nailcotehall.co.uk
web: www.nailcotehall.co.uk
Dir: *on B4101*

This 17th-century house, set in 15 acres of grounds, boasts a 9-hole championship golf course and Roman bath-style swimming pool amongst its many facilities. Rooms are spacious and elegantly furnished. Dinner may be taken in the fine dining restaurant

continued on p58

BALSALL COMMON, continued

where smart casual dress is required, or the less formal Rick's Cafe & Bar.

ROOMS: 21 en suite 19 annexe en suite (2 fmly) (15 GF) ⊗ in 30 bedrooms s £90-£175; d £99-£190 (incl. bkfst) **LB** **FACILITIES: Spa** supervised 9 Snooker Solarium Gym Putt green Jacuzzi Xmas **CONF:** Thtr 140 Class 80 Board 44 Del from £165 **SERVICES:** Lift **PARKING:** 200 **NOTES:** ⊗ in restaurant Civ Wed 120

See advert under SOLIHULL

★★★68% Haigs

Kenilworth Rd CV7 7EL
☎ 01676 533004 01676 535132
e-mail: info@haigsemail.co.uk
Dir: *on A452 4m N of Kenilworth & 6m S of M6 junct 4. 5m S of M42 junct 6. 8m N of M40 junct 15*

This hotel, set in residential surroundings, offers a warm welcome, highly attentive service and good food. The comfortable bedrooms are decorated in an attractive, homely style, and facilities include a lounge bar and a meeting room. It is well positioned for Birmingham NEC and just 5 miles from the M6.

ROOMS: 23 en suite (5 GF) ⊗ in 8 bedrooms **CONF:** Thtr 25 Board 16 Del from £140 **PARKING:** 23 **NOTES:** ⊗ in restaurant Closed 26 Dec-3 Jan & Etr RS Mon-Sat & Sun Lunch

Premier Travel Inn Balsall Common (Near NEC)

premier travel inn

Kenilworth Rd CV7 7EX
☎ 08701 977022 01676 535929
web: www.premiertravelinn.com
Dir: *M42 junct 6, A45 towards Coventry for 0.5m, then A452 towards Leamington, Inn 3m on right*

High quality, modern budget accommodation ideal for both families and business travellers. Spacious, en suite bedrooms feature bath and shower, satellite TV and many have telephones and modem points. The adjacent family restaurant features a wide and varied menu. For further details consult the Hotel Groups page.

ROOMS: 42 en suite s £47.95-£50.95; d £47.95-£50.95

BAMBURGH, Northumberland — Map 21 NU13

★★★72% Waren House

Waren Mill NE70 7EE
☎ 01668 214581 01668 214484
e-mail: enquiries@warenhousehotel.co.uk
web: www.warenhousehotel.co.uk
Dir: *2m E of A1 turn onto B1342 to Waren Mill, at T-junct turn right, hotel 100yds on right.*

This delightful Georgian mansion is set in six acres of woodland and offers a welcoming atmosphere and views of the coastline. The individually designed bedrooms, including suites, are themed in differing styles, and many have large bathrooms. Good, home-cooked food is served in the elegant dining room. A comfortable lounge and library are also available.

ROOMS: 13 en suite (1 GF) ⊗ in all bedrooms s £79-£115; d £98-£175 (incl. bkfst) **LB** **FACILITIES:** ch fac Xmas **CONF:** Class 24 Board 24 Del from £98 **PARKING:** 20 **NOTES:** No children 14yrs ⊗ in restaurant

★★70% *Victoria*

Front St NE69 7BP
☎ 01668 214431 01668 214404
e-mail: enquiries@victoriahotel.net
web: www.victoriahotel.net
Dir: *off A1, N of Alnwick onto B1342, near Belford & follow signs to Bamburgh. Hotel in centre of Bamburgh opposite village green*

Overlooking the village green, this hotel offers an interesting blend of traditional and modern. Both the pub bar and a residents'-diners' bar lounge are relaxing venues throughout the day and evening, while the brasserie, with its conservatory roof, provides a contemporary dinner menu. Bedrooms, some refurbished, come in a variety of styles and sizes.

ROOMS: 29 en suite (2 fmly) (2 GF) ⊗ in 18 bedrooms **FACILITIES:** ch fac **CONF:** Thtr 50 Class 30 Board 20 **NOTES:** ⊗ in restaurant Closed 8-23 Jan Civ Wed 50

★★69% *The Lord Crewe*

Front St NE69 7BL
☎ 01668 214243 01668 214273
e-mail: lordcrewebamburgh@tiscali.co.uk
Dir: *just below the castle*

Located in the heart of the village in the shadow of impressive Bamburgh Castle, this hotel has been developed from an old inn. Public areas include a choice of lounges, a cosy bar and a smart modern restaurant. Bedrooms offer good levels of equipment.

ROOMS: 18 rms (17 en suite) **PARKING:** 20 **NOTES:** No children 5yrs ⊗ in restaurant Closed Dec/Jan

U Star rating not confirmed

BAMFORD, Derbyshire Map 16 SK28

★★72% *Yorkshire Bridge Inn*

Ashopton Rd, Hope Valley S33 0AZ
☎ 01433 651361 Fax 01433 651361
e-mail: mr@ybridge.force9.co.uk
web: www.yorkshire-bridge.co.uk
Dir: *A57 Sheffield/Glossop road, at Ladybower Reservoir take A6013 Bamford road, inn 1m on right*

A well-established country inn, ideally located beside Ladybower Dam and within reach of the Peak District's many beauty spots. The hotel offers a wide range of excellent dishes in both the bar and dining area, along with a good selection of real ales. Bedrooms are attractively furnished, comfortable and well equipped.
ROOMS: 14 en suite (3 fmly) (4 GF) ⊗ in 10 bedrooms **CONF:** Class 12 **PARKING:** 40 **NOTES:** ⊗ in restaurant

BANBURY, Oxfordshire Map 11 SP44

★★★71% Banbury House

Oxford Rd OX16 9AH
☎ 01295 259361 Fax 01295 270954
e-mail: sales@banburyhouse.co.uk
web: www.banburyhouse.co.uk
Dir: *approx 200yds from Banbury Cross on A423 towards Oxford*
Within easy reach of the Banbury Cross, this attractive Georgian property offers smart, comfortable accommodation in individually decorated and furnished bedrooms. New contemporary rooms and a spacious suite are particularly stylish. The public areas include a spacious foyer lounge and a contemporary bar and restaurant, both offering a good choice of menus. Staff are particularly friendly and helpful.
ROOMS: 64 en suite (4 fmly) (8 GF) ⊗ in 24 bedrooms s £115; d £140 **LB** **FACILITIES:** STV **CONF:** Thtr 70 Class 35 Board 28 Del £145 **PARKING:** 60 **NOTES:** ✈ ⊗ in restaurant Closed 24 Dec-1 Jan

★★★71% Whately Hall

Banbury Cross OX16 0AN
☎ 0870 400 8104 Fax 01295 271736
e-mail: whatelyhall@macdonald-hotels.co.uk
web: www.macdonald-hotels.co.uk
Dir: *M40 junct 11, straight over 2 rdbts, left at 3rd, 0.25m to Banbury Cross, hotel on right*
Dating back to 1677, this historic inn boasts many original features such as stone passages, priests' holes and a fine wooden staircase. Spacious public areas include the oak-panelled restaurant, which overlooks the attractive well-tended gardens, a choice of lounges and a traditional bar. Smartly appointed bedrooms vary in size and style but all are thoughtfully equipped.
ROOMS: 69 en suite (3 fmly) ⊗ in 41 bedrooms s £60-£112; d £112-£187 (incl. bkfst) **LB** **FACILITIES:** STV ♫ Xmas **CONF:** Thtr 150 Class 80 Board 40 Del from £145 **SERVICES:** Lift **PARKING:** 80 **NOTES:** ⊗ in restaurant Civ Wed 100

★★★69% Wroxton House

Wroxton St Mary OX15 6QB
☎ 01295 730777 Fax 01295 730800
e-mail: reservations@wroxtonhousehotel.com
Dir: *A422 from Banbury, 2.5m to Wroxton, hotel on right entering village*
Dating in parts from 1647, this partially thatched hotel is set just off the main road. Bedrooms, which have either been created out of converted cottages or are situated in a more modern wing, are comfortable and well equipped. The public areas are open plan and consist of a reception lounge and a bar, and the low-beamed Inglenook Restaurant offering a peaceful atmosphere for dining.
ROOMS: 32 en suite (1 fmly) (7 GF) ⊗ in 15 bedrooms s £60-£100; d £60-£150 (incl. bkfst) **LB** **FACILITIES:** STV Xmas **CONF:** Thtr 45 Class 20 Board 25 Del from £110 **PARKING:** 50 **NOTES:** ⊗ in restaurant Civ Wed 60

★★70% Cromwell Lodge Hotel

North Bar OX16 0TB
☎ 01295 259781 Fax 01295 276619
e-mail: 6434@greeneking.co.uk
web: www.oldenglish.co.uk
Dir: *M40 junct 11, B4662 to Banbury, left at 3rd rdbt. Follow road to traffic lights, straight over, hotel on left.*
Enjoying a central location, this character 17th-century property has been stylishly refurbished. Diners have a choice between the contemporary lounge bar leading onto the delightful walled garden and patio and the smart, modern restaurant. The comfortable bedrooms are furnished and equipped to a high standard and include a number of spacious suites.
ROOMS: 23 en suite (3 GF) ⊗ in all bedrooms s £70; d £95 (incl. bkfst) **LB** **FACILITIES:** STV Xmas **CONF:** Thtr 30 Class 20 Board 25 **PARKING:** 30 **NOTES:** ✈ ⊗ in restaurant

⌂ Premier Travel Inn Banbury

Warwick Rd, Warmington OX17 1JJ
☎ 0870 9906512 Fax 0870 9906513
web: www.premiertravelinn.com
Dir: *5m from Banbury. From N, M40 junct 12 onto B4100 towards Warmington. From S, exit M40 junct 11 onto A423. Take A442, right at B4100*
High quality, modern budget accommodation ideal for both families and business travellers. Spacious, en suite bedrooms feature bath and shower, satellite TV and many have telephones and modem points. The adjacent family restaurant features a wide and varied menu. For further details consult the Hotel Groups page.
ROOMS: 39 en suite s £47.95-£50.95; d £47.95-£50.95

BARFORD, Warwickshire Map 10 SP26

★★★68% The Glebe at Barford

Church St CV35 8BS
☎ 01926 624218 Fax 01926 624625
e-mail: sales@glebehotel.co.uk
Dir: *M40 junct 15/A429 Barford/Wellesbourne. At mini island turn left, hotel 500mtrs on right*
The giant Lebanese cedar tree in front of this hotel was ancient even in 1820, when the original rectory was built. Public rooms within the house include a lounge bar and the aptly named Cedars Conservatory Restaurant which offers interesting cuisine. Individually appointed bedrooms are tastefully decorated in soft pastel fabrics, with coronet, tented ceiling or four-poster style beds.
ROOMS: 39 en suite (3 fmly) (4 GF) s £105; d £125 (incl. bkfst) **LB** **FACILITIES:** STV Indoor pool Sauna Solarium Gym Jacuzzi Beauty salon Xmas **CONF:** Thtr 120 Class 60 Board 60 Del £159 **SERVICES:** Lift **PARKING:** 60 **NOTES:** ⊗ in restaurant Civ Wed 70

♫ Entertainment

BARKING, Greater London
See LONDON SECTION plan 1 H4

⇧ *Hotel Ibis*

Highbridge Rd IG11 7BA
☎ 020 8477 4100 📠 020 8477 4101
e-mail: H2042@accor-hotels.com
Dir: *exit Barking on A406*
Modern, budget hotel offering comfortable accommodation in bright and practical bedrooms. Breakfast is self-service and dinner is available in the restaurant. For further details, consult the Hotel Groups page.
ROOMS: 86 en suite

⇧ Premier Travel Inn Barking

Highbridge Rd IG11 7BA
☎ 0870 9906318 📠 0870 9906319
web: www.premiertravelinn.com
Dir: *1.5m from Barking. Exit M25 after Dartford Tunnel at junct 30. Follow A13, signed to London City & Docklands, onto A406 North Circular*
High quality, modern budget accommodation ideal for both families and business travellers. Spacious, en suite bedrooms feature bath and shower, satellite TV and many have telephones and modem points. The adjacent family restaurant features a wide and varied menu. For further details consult the Hotel Groups page.
ROOMS: 88 en suite s £55.95-£59.95; d £55.95-£59.95

BARLBOROUGH, Derbyshire — Map 16 SK47

⇧ *Hotel Ibis Sheffield South*

Tallys End, Chesterfield Rd S43 4TX
☎ 01246 813222 📠 01246 813444
e-mail: H3157@accor-hotels.com
Dir: *M1 junct 30. Towards A619, right at rdbt towards Chesterfield. Hotel immediately left*
Modern, budget hotel offering comfortable accommodation in bright and practical bedrooms. Breakfast is self-service and dinner is available in the restaurant. For further details, consult the Hotel Groups page.
ROOMS: 86 en suite **CONF:** Thtr 35 Class 18 Board 18

BARNARD CASTLE, Co Durham — Map 19 NZ01

★★★76% ® The Morritt Arms Hotel & Restaurant

Greta Bridge DL12 9SE
☎ 01833 627232 📠 01833 627392
e-mail: relax@themorritt.co.uk
web: www.themorritt.co.uk
Dir: *turn off A1 at Scotch Corner onto A66 towards Penrith. Greta Bridge 9m on left*
Set off the main road at Greta Bridge, this 17th-century former coaching house provides comfortable public rooms full of character. The bar, with its interesting Dickensian mural, is very much focused on food, but in addition a fine-dining experience is offered in the oak-panelled restaurant. Bedrooms come in individual styles and varying sizes. The attentive service is noteworthy.
ROOMS: 23 en suite (3 fmly) ⊗ in 17 bedrooms s £65-£95; d £90-£130 (incl. bkfst) **LB** **FACILITIES:** Xmas **CONF:** Thtr 200 Class 60 Board 50 Del from £119.50 **PARKING:** 40 **NOTES:** ⊗ in restaurant Civ Wed 200

A ★★★ Jersey Farm Country Hotel

Darlington Rd DL12 8TA
☎ 01833 638223 📠 01833 631988
e-mail: enquiries@jerseyfarm.co.uk
web: www.jerseyfarm.co.uk
Dir: *On A67 1m E of Barnard Castle*
ROOMS: 20 rms (11 en suite) (6 fmly) (9 GF) s £68-£80; d £94-£120 (incl. bkfst) **LB** **FACILITIES:** STV Pool table Xmas **CONF:** Thtr 200 Class 80 Board 60 Del from £65 **PARKING:** 202 **NOTES:** ⊗ in restaurant RS Mondays

BARNBY MOOR, Nottinghamshire — Map 16 SK68

★★★67% ® Ye Olde Bell Hotel

DN22 8QS
☎ 01777 705121 📠 01777 860424
e-mail: yeoldebell@crerarhotels.com
web: www.crerarhotels.com
Dir: *on A638 midway between Retford and Bawtry*

Formerly a posting house on the London to York mail coach route, this charming inn has been welcoming guests for more than three centuries. Public rooms include the very smart, oak-panelled 1650 restaurant, a choice of lounges and an informal bar. Bedrooms vary in size and some overlook the attractive and well-kept gardens.
ROOMS: 51 en suite (12 fmly) ⊗ in 21 bedrooms s £55-£80; d £79-£125 (incl. bkfst) **LB** **FACILITIES:** ♫ Xmas **CONF:** Thtr 250 Class 50 Board 40 Del from £70 **PARKING:** 100 **NOTES:** ⊗ in restaurant Civ Wed 250

BARNHAM BROOM, Norfolk — Map 13 TG00

★★★75% Barnham Broom Hotel, Golf & Country Club

NR9 4DD
☎ 01603 759393 759522 📠 01603 758224
e-mail: enquiry@barnhambroomhotel.co.uk
web: www.barnham-broom.co.uk
Dir: *From A11 onto A47 towards Swaffham, follow brown tourist signs*
Situated in a peaceful rural location just a short drive from Norwich. Bedrooms are tastefully furnished in a contemporary style and equipped with a range of useful extras. The informal Sports bar serves a range of snacks and meals throughout the day, or guests may choose from the carte menu in the more formal

continued

Flints Restaurant. The hotel also has extensive leisure, conference and banqueting facilities.

ROOMS: 52 en suite (8 fmly) (6 GF) ⊗ in 37 bedrooms s £112; d £137 (incl. bkfst) **LB** **FACILITIES:** STV ⛆ ⛳ 36 Squash Sauna Solarium Gym Putt green Aerobics/yoga/pilates, pool table, 6ft projection screen **CONF:** Thtr 180 Class 90 Board 70 Del £140 **PARKING:** 200 **NOTES:** ⊗ in restaurant Civ Wed 120

BARNSDALE BAR SERVICE AREA (A1), North Yorkshire — Map 16 SE51

Travelodge Pontefract Barnsdale
Wentbridge WF8 3QQ
☎ 08700 850 950 📠 01977 620711
web: www.travelodge.co.uk
Dir: *on A1, southbound*
Travelodge offers good quality, good value, modern accommodation. Ideal for families, the spacious, en suite bedrooms include remote-control TV, tea and coffee-making facilities and comfortable beds. Meals can be taken at the nearby family restaurant. For further details consult the Hotel Groups page.
ROOMS: 56 en suite s fr £26; d fr £26

BARNSLEY, South Yorkshire — Map 16 SE30
See also Tankersley

★★★★75% Tankersley Manor
Church Ln S75 3DQ
☎ 01226 744700 📠 01226 745405
e-mail: tankersley@marstonhotels.com
web: www.marstonhotels.com
(For full entry see Tankersley)

★★★75% Ardsley House
Doncaster Rd, Ardsley S71 5EH
☎ 01226 309955 📠 01226 205374
e-mail: ardsley.house@forestdale.com
web: www.forestdale.com
Dir: *on A635, 0.75m from Stairfoot rdbt*
Quietly situated on the Barnsley to Doncaster road, this hotel has many regular customers. Comfortable and well-equipped bedrooms, excellent leisure facilities including a gym and pool, and good conference facilities are just some of the attractions here. Public rooms include a choice of bars and a busy restaurant.
ROOMS: 75 en suite (12 fmly) (14 GF) ⊗ in 50 bedrooms s £100-£120; d £130-£140 (incl. bkfst) **LB** **FACILITIES:** STV ⛆ supervised Sauna Solarium Gym Jacuzzi Beauty Spa ♫ Xmas **CONF:** Thtr 350 Class 250 Board 40 Del from £130 **PARKING:** 200 **NOTES:** Civ Wed

⊗ No smoking

New Country Inns-Barnsley
Elmhirst Ln, Dodworth S75 4LS
☎ 01226 786188 📠 01226 786199
e-mail: reception@newcountryinns.com
Dir: *1m from M1 junct 37, follow A628 towards Manchester*
At the time of going to press, the star classification for this hotel was not confirmed. Please refer to the AA internet site www.theAA.com for current information.
ROOMS: 41 en suite (10 fmly) ⊗ in all bedrooms s £50; d £50 **FACILITIES:** ♫ **CONF:** Thtr 250 **SERVICES:** Lift **PARKING:** 130 **NOTES:** Civ Wed 230

Premier Travel Inn Barnsley
Meadow Gate, Dearne Valley, Wombwell S73 0UN
☎ 08701 977024 📠 01226 273810
web: www.premiertravelinn.com
Dir: *M1 junct 36, eastbound. Take A6195 (A635) to Doncaster for 5 miles. Inn is adjacent to rdbt*
High quality, modern budget accommodation ideal for both families and business travellers. Spacious, en suite bedrooms feature bath and shower, satellite TV and many have telephones and modem points. The adjacent family restaurant features a wide and varied menu. For further details consult the Hotel Groups page.
ROOMS: 41 en suite s £53.95-£57.95; d £53.95-£57.95

Travelodge
School St S70 3PE
☎ 08700 850 950 📠 01226 298799
web: www.travelodge.co.uk
Dir: *at Stairfoot rdbt A633/A635*
Travelodge offers good quality, good value, modern accommodation. Ideal for families, the spacious, en suite bedrooms include remote-control TV, tea and coffee-making facilities and comfortable beds. Meals can be taken at the nearby family restaurant. For further details consult the Hotel Groups page.
ROOMS: 32 en suite s fr £26; d fr £26

BARNSTAPLE, Devon — Map 03 SS53

★★★★72% The Imperial
Taw Vale Pde EX32 8NB
☎ 01271 345861 📠 01271 324448
e-mail: info@brend-imperial.co.uk
web: www.brend-hotels.co.uk
Dir: *M5 junct 27/A361 to Barnstaple. Follow town centre signs, passing Tesco. Straight on at next 2 rdbts. Hotel on right*

This smart and attractive hotel is pleasantly located at the centre of Barnstaple and overlooks the river. The staff are friendly and offer attentive service. The comfortable bedrooms are in a range of sizes, some with balconies and many overlooking the river.
continued on p62

BARNSTAPLE, continued

Afternoon tea is available in the newly refurbished lounge and the cuisine is appetising and freshly prepared.
ROOMS: 63 en suite (7 fmly) (4 GF) s £80-£130; d £90-£150 **LB**
FACILITIES: STV leisure facilities at sister hotel Xmas **CONF:** Thtr 60 Class 40 Board 30 **SERVICES:** Lift **PARKING:** 80 **NOTES:** in restaurant

See advert on opposite page

★★★75% Barnstaple Hotel
Braunton Rd EX31 1LE
☎ 01271 376221 01271 324101
e-mail: info@barnstaplehotel.co.uk
web: www.brend-hotels.co.uk
Dir: *outskirts of Barnstaple on A361*
This well-established hotel enjoys a convenient location on the edge of town. Bedrooms are spacious and well equipped, many with access to a balcony overlooking the outdoor pool and garden. A wide choice is offered from various menus based on local produce. There is an extensive range of leisure and conference facilities.
ROOMS: 60 en suite (3 fmly) (17 GF) s £60-£85; d £70-£95 **LB**
FACILITIES: Spa STV supervised supervised Snooker Sauna Solarium Gym ch fac Xmas **CONF:** BC Thtr 250 **PARKING:** 250
NOTES: in restaurant Civ Wed 100

★★★73% Royal & Fortescue
Boutport St EX31 1HG
☎ 01271 342289 01271 340102
e-mail: info@royalfortescue.co.uk
web: www.brend-hotels.co.uk
Dir: *A361 along Barbican Rd signed town centre, turn right into Queen St & left onto Boutport St, hotel on left*
Formerly a coaching inn, this friendly and convivial hotel is conveniently located in the centre of town. Bedrooms vary in size and all are decorated and furnished to a consistently high standard. In addition to the formal restaurant, guests can take snacks in the popular coffee shop or dine more informally in 'The Bank', a bistro and café bar.
ROOMS: 50 en suite (5 fmly) (3 GF) s £55-£65; d £65-£75 **LB**
FACILITIES: STV ♫ Xmas **CONF:** Thtr 25 Class 25 Board 25
SERVICES: Lift **PARKING:** 40 **NOTES:** in restaurant

★★★70% Park
Taw Vale EX32 9AE
☎ 01271 372166 01271 323157
e-mail: info@parkhotel.co.uk
web: www.brend-hotels.co.uk
Dir: *opposite Rock Park, 0.5m from town centre*
Enjoying views across the park and in easy walking distance of the town centre, this modern hotel offers a choice of bedrooms in both the main building and the Garden Court, just across the car park. Public rooms are open-plan in style and the friendly staff offer attentive service in a relaxed atmosphere.
ROOMS: 25 en suite 17 annexe en suite (7 fmly) (5 GF) s £60-£70; d £70-£80 **LB** **FACILITIES:** STV ♫ Xmas **PARKING:** 80 **NOTES:** in restaurant Civ Wed 100

Premier Travel Inn Barnstaple
Eastern Av, Whiddon Dr EX32 8RY
☎ 08701 977025 01271 377710
web: www.premiertravelinn.com
Dir: *adjacent to North Devon Link Rd at junct with A39*
High quality, modern budget accommodation ideal for both families and business travellers. Spacious, en suite bedrooms feature bath and shower, satellite TV and many have telephones and modem points. The adjacent family restaurant features a wide and varied menu. For further details consult the Hotel Groups page.
ROOMS: 40 en suite s £49.95; d £49.95

BARROW-IN-FURNESS, Cumbria
Map 18 SD26

★★★71% Clarence House Country Hotel & Restaurant
Skelgate LA15 8BQ
☎ 01229 462508 01229 467177
e-mail: info@clarencehouse-hotel.co.uk
web: www.clarencehouse-hotel.co.uk
This hotel is peacefully located in its own ornamental grounds with unrestricted countryside views. Bedrooms are individually themed with rooms in the main hotel being particularly stylish and comfortable. The public rooms are spacious and also furnished to a high standard. The popular conservatory restaurant offers well prepared dishes from extensive menus. There is a delightful barn conversion that is ideal for weddings.
ROOMS: 7 en suite 12 annexe en suite (1 fmly) (5 GF) in 11 bedrooms s fr £79; d fr £105 (incl. bkfst) **LB** **FACILITIES:** Jacuzzi ♫ Xmas **CONF:** Thtr 100 Class 40 Board 15 Del from £110 **PARKING:** 40
NOTES: in restaurant Civ Wed 100

★★★69% *Clarke's Hotel & Brasserie*
Rampside LA13 0PX
☎ 01229 820303 01229 430954
e-mail: clarkeshotel@lineone.net
Dir: *A590 to Ulverston then A5087, take coastal road for 8m, turn left at rdbt into Rampside*
This smart, well-maintained hotel enjoys a peaceful location on the south Cumbrian coastline, overlooking Morecambe Bay. The tastefully appointed bedrooms come in a variety of sizes and are thoughtfully equipped for the business guest. Inviting public areas include an open-plan bar and brasserie offering freshly prepared food throughout the day.
ROOMS: 14 en suite (1 fmly) in 3 bedrooms **FACILITIES:** STV ♫
PARKING: 50 **NOTES:** in restaurant

★★64% Lisdoonie
307/309 Abbey Rd LA14 5LF
☎ 01229 827312 01229 820944
e-mail: lisdoonie@aol.com
Dir: *on A590, at 1st set of lights in town (Strawberry pub on left) continue for 100yds, hotel on right*
This friendly hotel is conveniently located for access to the centre of the town and is popular with commercial visitors. The comfortable bedrooms are well equipped, and vary in size and style. There are two comfortable lounges, one with a bar and restaurant adjacent. There is also a large function suite.
ROOMS: 12 en suite (2 fmly) **CONF:** Class 255 **PARKING:** 30
NOTES: Closed Xmas & New Year

Travelodge Barrow-in-Furness
Cockden Villas, Walney Rd LA14 5UG
☎ 08700 850950 01229 827129
web: www.travelodge.co.uk
Dir: *Just off A590, south of Hawcoat.*
Travelodge offers good quality, good value, modern accommodation. Ideal for families, the spacious, en suite bedrooms include remote-control TV, tea and coffee-making facilities and comfortable beds. Meals can be taken at the nearby family restaurant. For further details consult the Hotel Groups page.
ROOMS: 40 en suite s fr £26; d fr £26

BARTON, Lancashire Map 18 SD53

★★★74% Barton Grange
Garstang Rd PR3 5AA
☎ 01772 862551 📠 01772 861267
e-mail: stay@bartongrangehotel.com
web: www.bartongrangehotel.com
Dir: *M6 junct 32, follow signs to Garstang (A6) for 2.5 miles. Hotel on right*

Situated close to the M6, this modern, stylish hotel benefits from extensive public areas that include an award-winning garden centre, spa and leisure facilities. Comfortable, well-appointed bedrooms include four-poster and family rooms, as well as attractive rooms in an adjacent cottage. The unique Walled Garden restaurant offers all-day dining and refreshments.
ROOMS: 43 en suite 8 annexe en suite (4 fmly) (4 GF) ⊗ in 28 bedrooms s £50-£85; d £60-£95 **LB** **FACILITIES:** STV ⛉ Sauna Gym Jacuzzi Garden Centre within the grounds, pool table, bar billiards Xmas **CONF:** BC Thtr 300 Class 100 Board 80 Del from £120 **SERVICES:** Lift **PARKING:** 250 **NOTES:** ✗ ⊗ in restaurant Civ Wed 120

BARTON MILLS, Suffolk Map 12 TL77

⌂ Travelodge
Fiveways IP28 6AE
☎ 08700 850 950 📠 01638 717675
web: www.travelodge.co.uk
Dir: *on A11 at Fiveways rdbt*
Travelodge offers good quality, good value, modern accommodation. Ideal for families, the spacious, en suite bedrooms include remote-control TV, tea and coffee-making facilities and comfortable beds. Meals can be taken at the nearby family restaurant. For further details consult the Hotel Groups page.
ROOMS: 40 en suite s fr £26; d fr £26

BARTON STACEY, Hampshire Map 05 SU44

⌂ Travelodge
SO21 3NP
☎ 08700 850 950 📠 01264 720260
web: www.travelodge.co.uk
Dir: *on A303 westbound*
Travelodge offers good quality, good value, modern accommodation. Ideal for families, the spacious, en suite bedrooms include remote-control TV, tea and coffee-making facilities and comfortable beds. Meals can be taken at the nearby family restaurant. For further details consult the Hotel Groups page.
ROOMS: 20 en suite s fr £26; d fr £26

BARTON-UNDER-NEEDWOOD, Staffordshire Map 10 SK11

⌂ Travelodge Burton-upon-Trent
DE13 8EG
☎ 08700 850 950 📠 01283 716343
web: www.travelodge.co.uk
Dir: *on A38, northbound*
Travelodge offers good quality, good value, modern accommodation. Ideal for families, the spacious, en suite bedrooms include remote-control TV, tea and coffee-making facilities and comfortable beds. Meals can be taken at the nearby family restaurant. For further details consult the Hotel Groups page.
ROOMS: 20 en suite s fr £26; d fr £26

⌂ Travelodge Burton (South)
Rykneld St DE13 8EH
☎ 08700 850 950 📠 01283 716784
web: www.travelodge.co.uk
Dir: *on A38, southbound*
Travelodge offers good quality, good value, modern accommodation. Ideal for families, the spacious, en suite bedrooms include remote-control TV, tea and coffee-making facilities and comfortable beds. Meals can be taken at the nearby family restaurant. For further details consult the Hotel Groups page.
ROOMS: 40 en suite s fr £26; d fr £26

BARTON-UPON-HUMBER, Lincolnshire Map 17 TA02

★★★72% Reeds Hotel

Westfield Lakes, Far Ings Rd DN18 5RG
☎ 01652 632313 🖷 01652 636361
e-mail: info@reedshotel.co.uk
Dir: *A15 rdbt take 2nd exit (Humber Bridge) & exit at Barton-upon-Humber, left at rdbt. In 200yds right at hotel sign, down hill & hotel at junct*

This hotel is situated in a quiet wildlife sanctuary, with splendid views of the Humber Bridge. Public rooms include an attractive restaurant, an all-day brasserie and a foyer lounge. Bedroom sizes vary; all are well equipped and well presented, and service is both friendly and helpful.
ROOMS: 31 en suite (2 fmly) ⊗ in all bedrooms s £85; d £98 (incl. bkfst) **LB** **FACILITIES: Spa** STV Xmas **CONF:** Thtr 300 Class 200 Board 70 Del from £105 **SERVICES:** Lift **PARKING:** 100 **NOTES:** ✗ ⊗ in restaurant Civ Wed 300

BASILDON, Essex Map 06 TQ78

★★★68% Chichester

Old London Rd, Wickford SS11 8UE
☎ 01268 560555 🖷 01268 560580
e-mail: reception@chichester-hotel.com
web: www.chichester-hotel.com
Dir: *off A129*
This friendly hotel, set in landscaped gardens and surrounded by farmland, has been owned by the same family for over 25 years. Spacious bedrooms are located around an attractive courtyard; each is pleasantly decorated and equipped with useful extras. A range of menus is offered in the smart restaurant with more informal fare served in the bar.
ROOMS: 2 en suite 32 annexe en suite (4 fmly) (16 GF) ⊗ in 26 bedrooms s £49-£58; d £60-£68 **LB** **FACILITIES:** STV **PARKING:** 150 **NOTES:** ✗ ⊗ in restaurant

⌂ *Campanile*

Pipps Hill, Southend Arterial Rd SS14 3AE
☎ 01268 530810 🖷 01268 286710
e-mail: basildon@envergure.co.uk
web: www.envergure.fr
Dir: *M25 junct 29 Basildon exit., back under A127, then left at rdbt*
This modern building offers accommodation in smart, well-equipped bedrooms, all with en suite bathrooms.

continued

Refreshments may be taken at the informal Bistro. For further details consult the Hotel Groups page.

ROOMS: 97 annexe en suite **CONF:** Thtr 35 Class 18 Board 24

⌂ Premier Travel Inn Basildon (East Mayne)

Felmores, East Mayne SS13 1BW
☎ 08701 977026 🖷 01268 530092
web: www.premiertravelinn.com
Dir: *M25 junct 29/A127 towards Southend, then A132 towards Basildon*
High quality, modern budget accommodation ideal for both families and business travellers. Spacious, en suite bedrooms feature bath and shower, satellite TV and many have telephones and modem points. The adjacent family restaurant features a wide and varied menu. For further details consult the Hotel Groups page.
ROOMS: 32 en suite s £47.95-£50.95; d £47.95-£50.95

⌂ Premier Travel Inn Basildon (Festival Park)

Festival Leisure Park, Pipps Hill Rd South, off Cranes Farm Rd SS14 3WB
☎ 0870 9906598 🖷 0870 9906599
web: www.premiertravelinn.com
Dir: *9m from M25 junct 29. Follow A127 towards Basildon. Hotel 4m outside Basildon just off A1235*
High quality, modern budget accommodation ideal for both families and business travellers. Spacious, en suite bedrooms feature bath and shower, satellite TV and many have telephones and modem points. The adjacent family restaurant features a wide and varied menu. For further details consult the Hotel Groups page.
ROOMS: 64 en suite s £49.95-£52.95; d £49.95-£52.95 **CONF:** Thtr 20 Class 20 Board 12

⌂ Premier Travel Inn Basildon South

High Rd, Fobbing, Stanford le Hope SS17 9NR
☎ 08701 977027 🖷 01268 581752
web: www.premiertravelinn.com
Dir: *From M25 junct 30/31 take A13 towards Southend. Follow A13 for approx 10 miles then at Five Bells rdbt turn right onto Fobbing High Rd for hotel on left*
High quality, modern budget accommodation ideal for both families and business travellers. Spacious, en suite bedrooms feature bath and shower, satellite TV and many have telephones and modem points. The adjacent family restaurant features a wide and varied menu. For further details consult the Hotel Groups page.
ROOMS: 60 en suite s £49.95-£52.95; d £49.95-£52.95 **CONF:** Thtr 40

⌂ Travelodge Basildon

Festival Leisure Park, Festival Way SS14 3WB
☎ 08700 850 950 ▤ 01268 186559
web: www.travelodge.co.uk

Dir: M25 junct 29, A127 follow signs Basildon town centre, onto A176 signed Festival Leisure Park

Travelodge offers good quality, good value, modern accommodation. Ideal for families, the spacious, en suite bedrooms include remote-control TV, tea and coffee-making facilities and comfortable beds. Meals can be taken at the nearby family restaurant. For further details consult the Hotel Groups page.
ROOMS: 60 en suite s fr £26; d fr £26

BASINGSTOKE, Hampshire Map 05 SU65
See also North Waltham, Odiham & Stratfield Turgis

★★★★ ◉◉ ⬥ Tylney Hall Hotel

RG27 9AZ
☎ 01256 764881 ▤ 01256 768141
e-mail: sales@tylneyhall.com
web: www.tylneyhall.com
(For full entry see Rotherwick)

★★★★73% The Hampshire Centrecourt

Centre Dr, Chineham RG24 8FY
☎ 01256 319700 ▤ 01256 319730
e-mail: hampshirec@marstonhotels.com
web: www.marstonhotels.com

Dir: off A33 (Reading road) behind Chineham Shopping Centre via Great Binfields Rd

Having completed a multi-million pound transformation, this hotel now boasts a range of smart, comfortable and stylish bedrooms and leisure facilities unrivalled locally. Facilities include indoor and outdoor tennis courts, two swimming pools, a gym and a number of treatment rooms.
ROOMS: 90 en suite (6 fmly) ⊗ in 25 bedrooms s fr £140; d fr £166 (incl. bkfst) **LB FACILITIES: Spa** STV ▣ ◞ Sauna Solarium Gym Jacuzzi Steam room Beauty salon Xmas **CONF:** Thtr 220 Class 130 Board 60 Del from £189 **SERVICES:** Lift **PARKING:** 200 **NOTES:** ✖ ⊗ in restaurant Civ Wed 220

★★★★70% ◉ Apollo

Aldermaston Roundabout RG24 9NU
☎ 01256 796700 ▤ 01256 796701
e-mail: admin@apollo-hotels.co.uk
web: www.apollohotels.com

Dir: M3 junct 6. Follow ringroad N, exit A340 (Aldermaston). Hotel on rdbt, 5th exit into Popley Way for access

This modern hotel provides well-equipped accommodation and spacious public areas, appealing to both the leisure and business

continued

guest. Facilities include a smartly appointed leisure club, a business centre, along with a good choice of formal and informal eating in two restaurants - Vespers is the fine dining option.
ROOMS: 125 en suite ⊗ in 100 bedrooms s £155-£160; d £180-£200 **LB FACILITIES: Spa** STV ▣ **FACILITIES:** ▣ supervised Sauna Solarium Gym Jacuzzi Xmas **CONF:** BC Thtr 255 Class 196 Board 30 Del from £160 **SERVICES:** Lift air con **PARKING:** 200 **NOTES:** ✖

★★★★68% Basingstoke Country Hotel

Scures Hill, Nately Scures, Hook RG27 9JS
☎ 01256 764161 ▤ 01256 768341
e-mail: basreception@paramount-hotels.co.uk
web: www.paramount-hotels.co.uk

Dir: M3 junct 5, A287 towards Newnham. Left at lights. Hotel 200mtrs on right

This modern hotel is popular with both business and leisure guests. Comfortable bedrooms are well equipped and include a number of spacious executive rooms. Guests have a choice of dining in the formal restaurant, or for lighter meals and snacks there is a relaxing café or a smart bar. Extensive conference and leisure facilities complete the picture.
ROOMS: 100 en suite (14 fmly) (26 GF) ⊗ in 45 bedrooms s £47-£192.95; d £94-£205.90 (incl. bkfst) **FACILITIES:** STV ▣ Sauna Solarium Gym Jacuzzi Xmas **CONF:** Thtr 220 Class 100 Board 80 Del from £150 **SERVICES:** Lift air con **PARKING:** 200 **NOTES:** ⊗ in restaurant RS 24 Dec-2 Jan Civ Wed 90

★★★72% Romans

Little London Rd RG7 2PN
☎ 0118 970 0421 ▤ 0118 970 0691
e-mail: romanhotel@hotmail.com
(For full entry see Silchester and advert on page 67)

★★★63% Red Lion

24 London St RG21 7NY
☎ 01256 328525 ▤ 01256 844056
e-mail: redlion.enquiries@zolahotels.com

Dir: M3 junct 6 to Black Dam rdbt. 2nd exit onto Ringway East (A339). Take slip road signed town centre onto Churchill Way East (A3010). At rdbt take 1st exit onto Timberlake Rd, leads into New Rd. After pedestrian lights, right into Red Lion Lane

Centrally located in the town, the Red Lion is an ideal choice for business guests. Bedrooms are mostly spacious and include non-smoking rooms, interconnecting rooms and rooms with four-poster beds. Public areas comprise an attractive lounge and restaurant, and a popular bar. Other facilities include a selection of function and conference rooms.
ROOMS: 59 en suite (2 fmly) ⊗ in 16 bedrooms s £55-£120; d £75-£150 (incl. bkfst) **LB FACILITIES:** STV Xmas **CONF:** Thtr 80 Class 40 Board 20 Del from £110 **SERVICES:** Lift **PARKING:** 62 **NOTES:** ⊗ in restaurant

BASINGSTOKE, continued

Premier Travel Inn Basingstoke Central
Basingstoke Leisure Park, Worting Rd RG22 6PG
☎ 08701 977028 📠 01256 819329
web: www.premiertravelinn.com
Dir: *M3 junct 6 follow signs for Leisure Park*
High quality, modern budget accommodation ideal for both families and business travellers. Spacious, en suite bedrooms feature bath and shower, satellite TV and many have telephones and modem points. The adjacent family restaurant features a wide and varied menu. For further details consult the Hotel Groups page.
ROOMS: 71 en suite s £49.95-£52.95; d £49.95-£52.95

Travelodge
Stag and Hounds, Winchester Rd RG22 6HN
☎ 08700 850 950 📠 01256 843566
web: www.travelodge.co.uk
Dir: *Off A30, S of town centre*
Travelodge offers good quality, good value, modern accommodation. Ideal for families, the spacious, en suite bedrooms include remote-control TV, tea and coffee-making facilities and comfortable beds. Meals can be taken at the nearby family restaurant. For further details consult the Hotel Groups page.
ROOMS: 44 en suite s fr £26; d fr £26

BASLOW, Derbyshire Map 16 SK27

★★★77% Cavendish
DE45 1SP
☎ 01246 582311 📠 01246 582312
e-mail: info@cavendish-hotel.net
web: www.cavendish-hotel.net
Dir: *M1 junct 29/A617 W to Chesterfield & A619 to Baslow. Hotel in village centre, off main road*
This stylish property, dating back to the 18th century, is delightfully situated on the edge of the Chatsworth Estate. Elegantly appointed bedrooms offer a host of thoughtful amenities, while comfortable public areas are furnished with period pieces and paintings. Guests have a choice of dining in the informal conservatory Garden Room or the elegant Gallery Restaurant.
ROOMS: 24 en suite (3 fmly) (2 GF) in 10 bedrooms s £108-£146; d £142-£182 **LB** **FACILITIES:** STV Fishing Putt green Xmas **CONF:** Thtr 25 Class 8 Board 18 Del from £200 **PARKING:** 50 **NOTES:** in restaurant

Top Hotel

★★ Fischer's Baslow Hall
Calver Rd DE45 1RR
☎ 01246 583259 📠 01246 583818
e-mail: m.s@fischers-baslowhall.co.uk
web: www.fischers-baslowhall.co.uk
Dir: *on A623 between Baslow & Calver*
Located at the end of a chestnut tree-lined drive on the edge of the Chatsworth Estate, this beautiful Derbyshire manor house offers sumptuous accommodation and facilities. Staff provide very friendly and personally attentive hospitality and service. There are two styles of bedroom available: traditional, individually-themed rooms in the main house and spacious, more contemporary-styled rooms with Italian marble bathrooms in the Garden House. The cuisine is extremely memorable and the highlight of any stay.

ROOMS: 6 en suite 5 annexe en suite (4 GF) in all bedrooms s £100-£130; d £140-£180 (incl. bkfst) **LB** **CONF:** Thtr 40 Board 18 Del from £125 **PARKING:** 40 **NOTES:** in restaurant Closed 25-26 Dec Civ Wed 40

BASSENTHWAITE, Cumbria Map 18 NY23

★★★★72% Armathwaite Hall
CA12 4RE
☎ 017687 76551 📠 017687 76220
e-mail: reservations@armathwaite-hall.com
web: www.armathwaite-hall.com
Dir: *M6 junct 40/A66 to Keswick rdbt then A591 signed Carlisle. 8m to Castle Inn junct, turn left. Hotel 300yds*

Enjoying fine views over Bassenthwaite Lake, this impressive mansion, dating from the 17th century, is peacefully situated amid 400 acres of deer park. Comfortably furnished bedrooms are complemented by a choice of public rooms featuring splendid wood panelling and roaring log fires in the cooler months. The indoor and outdoor leisure facilities are also an added attraction.
ROOMS: 43 en suite (4 fmly) (8 GF) s £78-£125; d fr £156 (incl. bkfst) **LB** **FACILITIES: Spa** STV supervised Fishing Snooker Sauna Solarium Gym Putt green Jacuzzi Archery, Beauty salon, Clayshooting, Quad bikes, Falconry, Mountain Bikes Xmas **CONF:** Thtr 80 Class 50 Board 60 Del from £135 **SERVICES:** Lift **PARKING:** 100 **NOTES:** in restaurant Civ Wed 80

See advert under KESWICK

★★★75% The Pheasant
CA13 9YE
☎ 017687 76234 📠 017687 76002
e-mail: info@the-pheasant.co.uk
web: www.the-pheasant.co.uk
Dir: *Midway between Keswick & Cockermouth, signed from A66*
Enjoying a rural setting, within well tended gardens, on the

continued

western side of Bassenthwaite Lake, this 500-year-old, friendly, inn is steeped in tradition. The attractive oak panelled bar has seen few changes in recent years and features log fires and a great selection of malt whisky. The individually decorated bedrooms are stylish and thoughtfully equipped.

ROOMS: 13 en suite 2 annexe en suite (2 GF) ⊗ in all bedrooms s £67-£87; d £120-£144 (incl. bkfst) **LB** **FACILITIES:** Xmas **PARKING:** 40 **NOTES:** No children 12yrs ⊗ in restaurant Closed 25-Dec

★★★61% The Castle Inn Hotel
CA12 4RG
☎ 017687 76401 🖹 017687 76604
e-mail: reservations.castleinn@foliohotels.co.uk
web: www.foliohotels.co.uk
Dir: *leave A66 at Keswick, onto A591 towards Carlisle, pass Bassenthwaite village on right & hotel 6m on left*

Located to the north of the lake and enjoying distant views of the hills, this hotel stands in extensive grounds and gardens. It has a

continued

wide range of indoor and outdoor leisure facilities, spacious public areas, and a selection of rooms for conferences and functions. Bedrooms are well equipped and come in a variety of styles and sizes.

ROOMS: 48 en suite (7 fmly) (4 GF) **FACILITIES:** STV supervised Sauna Solarium Gym Putt green Jacuzzi Table tennis Xmas **CONF:** BC Thtr 120 Class 60 Board 60 **PARKING:** 100 **NOTES:** ⊗ in restaurant Civ Wed 120

BATH, Somerset — Map 04 ST76

See also Colerne & Hinton Charterhouse

★★★★★73% ⊛⊛⊛ The Royal Crescent
16 Royal Crescent BA1 2LS
☎ 01225 823333 🖹 01225 339401
e-mail: info@royalcrescent.co.uk
web: www.vonessenhotels.co.uk
Dir: *from A4, right at traffic lights. 2nd left onto Bennett St. Continue into The Circus, 2nd exit onto Brock St*

John Wood's masterpiece of fine Georgian architecture provides the setting for this elegant hotel in the centre of the world famous Royal Crescent. Spacious, air-conditioned bedrooms are individually designed and furnished with antiques. Delightful central grounds lead to a second house, which is home to further rooms, the award-winning Pimpernel's restaurant and the Bath House which offers therapies and treatments.

ROOMS: 45 en suite (8 fmly) ⊗ in 8 bedrooms d £220-£850 (incl. bkfst) **LB** **FACILITIES:** STV Sauna Gym 1920s river launch, Outdoor heated plunge pool Xmas **CONF:** Thtr 50 Class 25 Board 24 Del from £235 **SERVICES:** Lift air con **PARKING:** 27 **NOTES:** ⊗ in restaurant Civ Wed 50

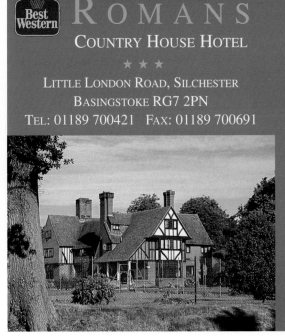

BATH, continued

★★★★★69% The Bath Spa
Sydney Rd BA2 6JF
☎ 0870 400 8222 01225 444006
e-mail: sales@bathspahotel.com
web: www.macdonald-hotels.co.uk
Dir: *M4 junct 18/A46 for Bath/A4 city centre. Left onto A36 at 1st traffic lights. Right at lights after pedestrian crossing then left into Sydney Place. Hotel 200yds on right*

A delightful Georgian mansion set amidst seven acres of pretty landscaped grounds, just a short walk from the many and varied delights of the city centre. A timeless elegance pervades the gracious public areas and bedrooms. Facilities include a popular leisure club, a choice of dining options and a number of meeting rooms.
ROOMS: 104 en suite (3 fmly) (17 GF) in 76 bedrooms s £175-£275; d £250-£360 (incl. bkfst) **LB** **FACILITIES:** STV supervised Sauna Gym Jacuzzi Beauty treatment, Hair salon Xmas **CONF:** Thtr 120 Class 100 Board 50 Del from £189 **SERVICES:** Lift **PARKING:** 156 **NOTES:** in restaurant Civ Wed 120

Top Hotel

★★★★ Bath Priory
Weston Rd BA1 2XT
☎ 01225 331922 01225 448276
e-mail: mail@thebathpriory.co.uk
web: www.thebathpriory.co.uk
Dir: *adjacent to Victoria Park*
Set in delightful walled gardens, this attractive Georgian house provides peace and tranquillity overlooking the city. An extensive display of pictures and fine art create a charming atmosphere throughout the sumptuously furnished public rooms. Cuisine is accomplished with excellently sourced ingredients and flavours, complemented by an impressive wine list. Bedrooms, including some suites in an adjacent building, are well proportioned and offer the many thoughtful touches expected in an establishment of this quality.
At the time of going to press the rosette award had not been finalised due to a change of chef.
ROOMS: 28 en suite (6 fmly) (1 GF) in all bedrooms s fr £200; d fr £245 (incl. bkfst) **LB** **FACILITIES:** STV Sauna Solarium Gym Jacuzzi Holistic beauty therapy and treatments Xmas **CONF:** BC Thtr 60 Class 30 Board 30 Del £225 **PARKING:** 40 **NOTES:** in restaurant Civ Wed 60

★★★★71% Combe Grove Manor Hotel & Country Club
Brassknocker Hill, Monkton Combe BA2 7HS
☎ 01225 834644 01225 834961
e-mail: info@combegrovemanor.com
web: www.furlonghotels.co.uk
Dir: *M4 junct 18/A46 to city centre, then signs for University & American Museum. Hotel 2m past University on left*

The friendly proprietors ensure guests have a comfortable stay at this pleasant house, which is convenient for both coast and countryside. The cosy bar has an open fire in winter, and the bedrooms are pleasantly appointed and attractively decorated. A hearty Cornish breakfast, including a vegetarian option, is served in the dining room.
ROOMS: 9 en suite 33 annexe en suite (11 fmly) (11 GF) s £130-£350; d £130-£350 (incl. bkfst) **LB** **FACILITIES: Spa** STV supervised supervised 5 Squash Sauna Solarium Gym Putt green Jacuzzi Aerobics, Beauty salon, Jogging trail, Indoor tennis ch fac **CONF:** Thtr 120 Class 50 Board 40 Del £155 **PARKING:** 150 **NOTES:** in restaurant Civ Wed 50

Bad hair day?
Hairdryers in all rooms three stars and above

Town House

★★★★ The Windsor Hotel
69 Great Pulteney St BA2 4DL
☎ 01225 422100 01225 422550
e-mail: sales@bathwindsorhotel.com
web: www.bathwindsorhotel.com
Dir: *M4 junct 18/A4. Turn left onto A36, after 500yds turn right at mini rdbt. 2nd left into Great Pulteney Street*
This delightful Grade I listed, terraced Georgian town house is a short walk from the town centre. It has been refurbished to the highest standard and sumptuously furnished with antique pieces. The restaurant has Japanese decor and offers a choice of either sukiyaki or shabu shabu; fresh ingredients are

continued

cooked at the table. The Windsor is a non-smoking establishment.

ROOMS: 14 en suite (3 fmly) ⊗ in all bedrooms s £85-£115; d £135-£195 (incl. bkfst) **LB** **FACILITIES:** STV **CONF:** Thtr 16 Class 14 Board 16 Del £145 **PARKING:** 15 **NOTES:** ✖ No children 12yrs ⊗ in restaurant Closed Xmas wk

See advert on this page

★★★★66% Menzies Waterside

Rossiter Rd, Widcombe Basin BA2 4JP
☎ 01225 338855 🖷 01225 428941
e-mail: waterside@menzies-hotels.co.uk
web: www.menzies-hotels.co.uk
Dir: *M4 junct 18, follow signs to Bath City Centre. At 3rd lights turn left into A36 Widcombe Parade, right into Rossiter Rd.*

In a quiet location within walking distance of the main town and train station, this hotel is a popular leisure break destination. Now refurbished, the bedrooms are compact but well designed with comfortable seating. The brasserie serves contemporary cuisine in air-conditioned surroundings overlooking the canal.

ROOMS: 107 en suite 6 annexe en suite ⊗ in 67 bedrooms s £140; d £140 **LB** **FACILITIES:** Xmas **CONF:** Thtr 120 Class 70 Board 60 Del £155 **SERVICES:** Lift **PARKING:** 80 **NOTES:** ⊗ in restaurant Civ Wed

Top Hotel

★★★ ◎◎ Queensberry

Russel St BA1 2QF
☎ 01225 447928 🖷 01225 446065
e-mail: reservations@thequeensberry.co.uk
web: www.thequeensberry.co.uk
Dir: *100mtrs from the Assembly Rooms*

This charming family-run hotel, situated in a quiet residential street near the city centre, consists of four delightful townhouses. The spacious bedrooms offer deep armchairs, marble bathrooms and a range of modern comforts. Sumptuously furnished sitting rooms add to The

continued

Queensberry's appeal and allow access to the very attractive and peaceful walled gardens. The Olive Tree is a stylish restaurant that combines Georgian opulence with contemporary simplicity. Innovative menus are based on best quality ingredients and competent cooking. Valet parking proves a useful service.

ROOMS: 29 en suite s £85-£295; d £85-£295 **LB** **CONF:** Thtr 35 Board 25 Del from £175 **SERVICES:** Lift **PARKING:** 9 **NOTES:** ✖ ⊗ in restaurant

★★★73% Cliffe

Cliffe Dr, Crowe Hill, Limpley Stoke BA2 7FY
☎ 01225 723226 🖷 01225 723871
e-mail: cliffe@bestwestern.co.uk
Dir: *A36 S from Bath, at A36/B3108 lights left toward Bradford-on-Avon, 0.5m. Turn right before bridge through village, hotel on right*

With stunning countryside views, this attractive country house is

continued on p70

BATH, continued

just a short drive from the City of Bath. Bedrooms vary in size and style but are well equipped; several are particularly spacious and a number of rooms are on the ground floor. The restaurant overlooks the well-tended garden and offers a tempting selection of carefully prepared dishes.
ROOMS: 8 en suite 3 annexe en suite (2 fmly) (4 GF) ⊗ in 5 bedrooms s £97-£120; d fr £118 (incl. bkfst) **LB** **FACILITIES:** STV peaceful gardens Xmas **CONF:** Thtr 20 Class 15 Board 10 Del from £142.50 **PARKING:** 20 **NOTES:** ⊗ in restaurant

See advert on opposite page

★★★72% The Francis

Queen Square BA1 2HH
☎ 0870 400 8223 📠 01225 319715
e-mail: francis@macdonald-hotels.co.uk
web: www.macdonald-hotels.co.uk
Dir: *M4 junct 18/A46 to Bath junct. Take 3rd exit onto A4. Right fork into George St, sharp left into Gay St onto Queen Sq, hotel on left*

Overlooking Queen Square in the centre of the city, this elegant Georgian hotel is situated within walking distance of Bath's many attractions. Public rooms provide a variety of environments where guests can eat, drink and relax - from the informal café-bar to the traditional lounge and more formal restaurant. Bedrooms now have air conditioning.
ROOMS: 95 en suite (16 fmly) ⊗ in 41 bedrooms s £105-£115; d £150-£170 (incl. bkfst) **LB** **FACILITIES:** STV ♫ Xmas **CONF:** Thtr 80 Class 40 Board 30 Del from £110 **SERVICES:** Lift **PARKING:** 42 **NOTES:** ⊗ in restaurant

★★★70% Pratts

South Pde BA2 4AB
☎ 01225 460441 📠 01225 448807
e-mail: pratts@forestdale.com
web: www.forestdale.com
Dir: *A46 into city centre. Left at 1st lights (Curfew Pub), right at next rdbt. 2nd exit at next rdbt, right at lights, left at next rdbt, 1st left into South Pde*
Part of a Georgian terrace, this long-established and popular hotel stands close to the city centre. Public rooms and bedrooms have undergone a refurbishment programme and all decor has been chosen to complement the Georgian surroundings. The ground-floor day rooms include two lounges, a writing room and a very comfortable restaurant.
ROOMS: 46 en suite (2 fmly) ⊗ in 8 bedrooms s £85-£115; d £130-£150 (incl. bkfst) **LB** **FACILITIES:** Xmas **CONF:** Thtr 50 Class 12 Board 30 Del from £125 **SERVICES:** Lift **NOTES:** ⊗ in restaurant Civ Wed

AA Rosette Award for culinary excellence

★★★66% The Abbey Hotel

North Pde BA1 1LF
☎ 0845 130 2556 01225 461603
📠 0870 950 2443
e-mail: ahres@compasshotels.co.uk
Dir: *close to the Abbey in city centre*
Originally built for a wealthy merchant in the 1740s and forming part of a handsome Georgian terrace, this welcoming hotel is situated in the heart of the city. The thoughtfully equipped bedrooms vary in size and style. Public areas include a smart lounge bar and although the restaurant is available, many guests have dinner in the lounge or choose from extensive room service menu.
ROOMS: 60 en suite (4 fmly) (2 GF) ⊗ in 22 bedrooms s £69-£96; d £79-£145 (incl. bkfst) **LB** **FACILITIES:** STV Bath Leisure Centre 200m **SERVICES:** Lift **NOTES:** ⊗ in restaurant Closed 23-27 Dec

★★75% Haringtons

8-10 Queen St BA1 1HE
☎ 01225 461728 & 445883 📠 01225 444804
e-mail: post@haringtonshotel.co.uk
web: www.haringtonshotel.co.uk
Dir: *A4 to George St & turn into Milsom St. 1st right into Quiet St & 1st left into Queen St*
Dating back to the 18th century this hotel, set in the heart of the city, has been completely refurbished to provide all modern facilities and comforts. The café-bar is open throughout the day for light meals and refreshments. A warm welcome is assured from the proprietors and staff, making this a delightful place to stay.
ROOMS: 13 en suite (2 fmly) ⊗ in all bedrooms s £68-£108; d £88-£128 (incl. bkfst) **FACILITIES:** STV Xmas **PARKING:** 15 **NOTES:** ⊗ in restaurant

★★70% Old Malt House

Radford, Timsbury BA2 0QF
☎ 01761 470106 📠 01761 472726
e-mail: hotel@oldmalthouse.co.uk
web: www.oldmalthouse.co.uk
Dir: *A367 towards Radstock for 1m pass Park & Ride, right onto B3115 towards Tunley/Timsbury. At sharp bend straight ahead & hotel 2nd left*
This privately owned, personally run and friendly hotel provides an ideal base for exploring the many attractions the area has to offer. Formerly a brewery malt house, it is peacefully located within easy reach of Bath. Bedrooms are well equipped and include some thoughtful touches. A varied choice of home-cooked meals is served in the pleasant restaurant.
ROOMS: 11 en suite (1 fmly) (2 GF) ⊗ in all bedrooms s £60; d £68-£78 (incl. bkfst) **LB** **PARKING:** 25 **NOTES:** ⊗ in restaurant Closed Xmas/New Yr

★★70% Wentworth House Hotel

106 Bloomfield Rd BA2 2AP
☎ 01225 339193 📠 01225 310460
e-mail: stay@wentworthhouse.co.uk
web: www.wentworthhouse.co.uk
Dir: *A367 Radstock/Shepton Mallet signs to small shopping area, 'The Bear' pub on right. Take 2nd turning past pub. Hotel on right*
This small personally managed hotel on the outskirts of Bath offers a delightful homely atmosphere, comfortable accommodation and delicious home-cooked dishes from a varied menu. Many bedrooms have four-poster beds and two have conservatory lounges. There is an outdoor swimming pool and a hot tub in the garden from where stunning views across the city can be enjoyed.
ROOMS: 18 en suite (2 fmly) (9 GF) ⊗ in 5 bedrooms s £60-£80; d £60-£110 (incl. bkfst) **LB** **FACILITIES:** **Spa** Jacuzzi **PARKING:** 18 **NOTES:** No children 7yrs ⊗ in restaurant

★★69% Avondale Hotel & Waterside Restaurant
London Rd East, Bathford BA1 7RB
☎ 01225 859847 852207 🖷 01225 859847
Dir: *A46/A4 junct follow signs Chippenham/Batheaston/Bathford. Continue through Batheaston, hotel on right just before large rdbt*
The peaceful riverside location of this hotel is convenient for the city, and easily accessible from all major transport links. Bedrooms are well equipped and comfortable, and some have balconies overlooking the extensive gardens. The restaurant is memorable for its many interesting architectural features as well as its varied menu, which includes vegetarian options.
ROOMS: 15 rms (13 en suite) (3 fmly) s £49-£65; d £69-£85 (incl. bkfst) **LB** **FACILITIES:** Fishing Boating, Fishing ch fac **CONF:** Thtr 90 Class 60 Board 40 Del from £78 **PARKING:** 60

⌂ Travelodge Bath (Royal Oak)
York Buildings, George St BA1 2EB
☎ 08700 850 950 🖷 01225 442061
web: www.travelodge.co.uk
Dir: *at corner of George St (A4) & Broad St*
Travelodge offers good quality, good value, modern accommodation. Ideal for families, the spacious, en suite bedrooms include remote-control TV, tea and coffee-making facilities and comfortable beds. Meals can be taken at the nearby family restaurant. For further details consult the Hotel Groups page.
ROOMS: 66 en suite s fr £26; d fr £26

BATLEY, West Yorkshire — Map 19 SE22

★★70% Alder House
Towngate Rd, Healey Ln WF17 7HR
☎ 01924 444777 🖷 01924 442644
e-mail: info@alderhousehotel.co.uk
web: www.alderhousehotel.co.uk
Dir: *M62 junct 27/A62. After 2m turn left into Whitelee Rd, left at next junct. Left into Healey Ln & after 0.25m hotel on left*
An attractive Georgian house tucked away in leafy grounds. Bedrooms are pleasantly furnished and contain many comfortable extras. There is an intimate dining room offering a selection of interesting dishes, as well as a bar with a separate lounge area. The service and hospitality are both caring and friendly.
ROOMS: 20 en suite (1 fmly) (2 GF) ⊗ in 3 bedrooms s £50-£61; d £62-£120 (incl. bkfst) **LB** **FACILITIES:** STV **CONF:** BC Thtr 80 Class 40 Board 35 Del £90 **PARKING:** 52 **NOTES:** ⊗ in restaurant Civ Wed 80

Town House Hotel
Country House Hotel
Travel Accommodation

BATTLE, East Sussex — Map 07 TQ71

★★★76% ⊛⊛ Powder Mills
Powdermill Ln TN33 0SP
☎ 01424 775511 🖷 01424 774540
e-mail: powdc@aol.com
web: www.powdermillshotel.com
Dir: *pass Abbey on A2100. 1st right, hotel 1m on right*
A delightful 18th-century country house hotel set amidst 150 acres of landscaped grounds with lakes and woodland. The individually decorated bedrooms are tastefully furnished and thoughtfully equipped, some rooms have sun terraces with lovely views over

continued

the lake. Public rooms include a cosy lounge bar, music room, drawing room, library, restaurant and conservatory.

Powder Mills

ROOMS: 30 en suite 10 annexe en suite (3 GF) **FACILITIES:** STV Fishing Jogging trails & woodland walks ♫ Xmas **CONF:** Thtr 250 Class 50 Board 16 Del from £145 **PARKING:** 101 **NOTES:** ⊗ in restaurant Civ Wed 100

★★★70% Brickwall Hotel
The Green, Sedlescombe TN33 0QA
☎ 01424 870253 & 870339 🖷 01424 870785
e-mail: info@brickwallhotel.com
Dir: *off A21 on B2244 at top of Sedlescombe Green*
A well-maintained Tudor house situated in the heart of this pretty village and overlooking the green. The spacious public rooms feature a lovely wood-panelled restaurant with a wealth of oak beams, a choice of lounges and a smart bar. Bedrooms are

continued on p72

BATTLE, continued

pleasantly decorated, have co-ordinated soft furnishings and all the usual facilities.
ROOMS: 25 en suite (2 fmly) (17 GF) ⊗ in 9 bedrooms s £60-£65; d £42-£48 (incl. bkfst) **LB** **FACILITIES:** STV Xmas **CONF:** Thtr 30 Class 40 Board 30 **PARKING:** 50 **NOTES:** ⊗ in restaurant

BAWTRY, South Yorkshire Map 16 SK69

U The Crown
High St DN10 6JW
☎ 01302 710341 01302 711798
e-mail: events@thecrownhotel-bawtry.co.uk
Dir: *A614 to Bawtry. Hotel is on left of High St*
At the time of going to press, the star classification for this hotel was not confirmed. Please refer to the AA internet site www.theAA.com for current information.
ROOMS: 65 en suite (6 fmly) (20 GF) ⊗ in 57 bedrooms s fr £85; d fr £105 (incl. bkfst) **CONF:** Thtr 200 Class 90 Board 50 Del from £135 **PARKING:** 35 **NOTES:** ⊗ in restaurant Civ Wed 120

BEACONSFIELD, Buckinghamshire Map 06 SU99

Innkeeper's Lodge Beaconsfield
Aylesbury End HP9 1LW
☎ 01494 671211 01494 685042
web: www.innkeeperslodge.com
Dir: *M40 junct 2 turn left at next two rdbts. Pub on rdbt*
A growing concept in the travel accommodation market. Smart rooms meet essential business requirements but also have home comforts. Dining options include all-day menus plus the added advantage of breakfast, which is included in the room price. For further details consult the Hotel Groups page.
ROOMS: 32 en suite s £49.95-£79.95; d £49.95-£79.95

BEAMINSTER, Dorset Map 04 ST40

★★★72% Bridge House
3 Prout Bridge DT8 3AY
☎ 01308 862200 01308 863700
e-mail: enquiries@bridge-house.co.uk
web: www.bridge-house.co.uk
Dir: *off A3066, 100yds from Town Square*

Dating back to the 13th century, this property offers friendly and attentive service. Bedrooms are tastefully furnished and decorated; those in the main house are generally more spacious than those in the adjacent coach house. Smartly presented public areas include the Georgian dining room, cosy bar and adjacent lounge, together with a breakfast room overlooking the attractive garden.
ROOMS: 9 en suite 5 annexe en suite (1 fmly) (5 GF) s £57-£98; d £108-£142 (incl. bkfst) **LB** **FACILITIES:** Xmas **CONF:** BC Thtr 24 Class 14 Board 10 Del £145 **PARKING:** 20 **NOTES:** ⊗ in restaurant Closed 30-31 Dec RS Mon-Tue (winter)

BEAMISH, Co Durham Map 19 NZ25

★★★69% Beamish Park
Beamish Burn Rd NE16 5EG
☎ 01207 230666 01207 281260
e-mail: reception@beamish-park-hotel.co.uk
web: www.beamish-park-hotel.co.uk
Dir: *A1(M)/A692 towards Consett, then A6076 towards Stanley. Hotel on left behind Causey Arch Inn*
The Metro Centre, Beamish Museum and south Tyneside are all within striking distance of this modern hotel, set in open countryside alongside its own golf course and floodlit range. Bedrooms, some with their own patios, provide a diverse mix of styles and sizes. The conservatory bistro offers a modern menu.
ROOMS: 47 en suite (7 fmly) ⊗ in 20 bedrooms s £47.50-£75; d £69.50-£85 **FACILITIES:** STV 9 Putt green 20 bay floodlit golf driving range. Golf tuition by PGA professional **CONF:** Thtr 50 Class 20 Board 30 Del from £75 **PARKING:** 100

BEAULIEU, Hampshire Map 05 SU30

Top Hotel

★★★ Montagu Arms
Palace Ln SO42 7ZL
☎ 01590 612324 & 0845 123 5613 01590 612188
e-mail: reservations@montaguarmshotel.co.uk
web: www.montaguarmshotel.co.uk
Dir: *M27 junct 2, turn left at rdbt, follow signs for Beaulieu. Continue to Dibden Purlieu, then right at rdbt. Hotel on left*
Surrounded by the glorious scenery of the New Forest, this lovely hotel manages to achieve the impression of almost total seclusion, though it is within easy reach of the major towns in the area. Bedrooms, all named after types of tree, are individually decorated and come with a range of thoughtful extras. Public rooms include a cosy lounge, an adjoining conservatory and a choice of two dining options, the informal Monty's or the stylish Terrace Restaurant.
ROOMS: 23 en suite (3 fmly) ⊗ in all bedrooms s fr £125; d fr £180 (incl. bkfst) **LB** **FACILITIES:** Use of spa in Brockenhurst Xmas **CONF:** Thtr 50 Class 16 Board 26 **PARKING:** 86 **NOTES:** ⊗ in restaurant Civ Wed 50

See advert on opposite page

★★★75% Master Builders House Hotel
SO42 7XB
☎ 01590 616253 01590 616297
e-mail: res@themasterbuilders.co.uk
web: www.themasterbuilders.co.uk
Dir: *M27 junct 2, follow Beaulieu signs. At T-junct left onto B3056, 1st left to Bucklers Hard. Hotel 2m on left before village entrance*
The name of the hotel is a testament to the master shipbuilder

continued

Henry Adams who once owned the property. A full list of the famous ships built in the village can be found in the Yachtsman's Bar. The Riverside Restaurant and many of the individually styled bedrooms enjoy views over the Beaulieu River. For those guests wishing to travel to the Isle of Wight, the hotel also has its own boat.
ROOMS: 8 en suite 17 annexe en suite (2 fmly) (8 GF) ⊗ in 19 bedrooms s £135-£155; d £180-£265 (incl. bkfst) **LB** **FACILITIES:** STV Sailing on Beaulieu River, mountain biking Xmas **CONF:** Thtr 50 Class 18 Board 25 Del from £155 **PARKING:** 70 **NOTES:** Civ Wed 60

★★★67% ® **Beaulieu**
Beaulieu Rd SO42 7YQ
☎ 023 8029 3344 023 8029 2729
e-mail: beaulieu@newforesthotels.co.uk
web: www.newforesthotels.co.uk
Dir: *M27 junct 1/A337 towards Lyndhurst. Left at lights in Lyndhurst, through village, turn right onto B3056, continue for 3m.*
Conveniently located in the heart of the New Forest and close to Beaulieu Road railway station, this popular, small hotel provides an ideal base for exploring the surrounding area. Facilities include an indoor swimming pool, an outdoor children's play area and an adjoining pub. A daily changing menu is offered in the restaurant. The hotel will be closed from September 2005 to May 2006 for refurbishment.
ROOMS: 15 en suite 3 annexe en suite (2 fmly) s £70-£82.50; d £110-£135 (incl. bkfst) **LB** **FACILITIES:** Steam room Xmas **CONF:** Thtr 60 Class 40 Board 30 Del from £90 **PARKING:** 60 **NOTES:** ⊗ in restaurant Civ Wed 60

BEBINGTON, Merseyside — Map 15 SJ38

Travelodge Wirral
New Chester Rd CH62 9AQ
☎ 08700 850 950 0151 327 2489
web: www.travelodge.co.uk
Dir: *on A41, northbound off M53 junct 5*
Travelodge offers good quality, good value, modern accommodation. Ideal for families, the spacious, en suite bedrooms include remote-control TV, tea and coffee-making facilities and comfortable beds. Meals can be taken at the nearby family restaurant. For further details consult the Hotel Groups page.
ROOMS: 31 en suite s fr £26; d fr £26

BECKENHAM, Greater London
See LONDON SECTION plan 1 G1

Innkeeper's Lodge Beckenham
422 Upper Elmers End Rd BR3 3HQ
☎ 020 8650 2233
web: www.innkeeperslodge.com
Dir: *From M25 junct 6 Croydon, take A232 for Shirley. At West Wickham take A214 opposite Eden Park Station*
A growing concept in the travel accommodation market. Smart rooms meet essential business requirements but also have home comforts. Dining options include all-day menus plus the added advantage of breakfast, which is included in the room price. For further details consult the Hotel Groups page.
ROOMS: 24 en suite s £55-£65; d £55-£65

BECKINGTON, Somerset — Map 04 ST85

★★63% ***Woolpack Inn***
BA3 6SP
☎ 01373 831244 01373 831223
web: www.oldenglish.co.uk
Dir: *on A36*
This charming coaching inn dates back to the 16th century and
continued

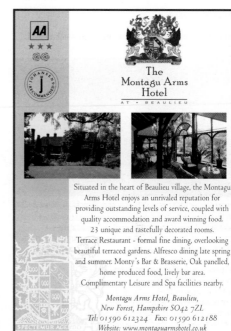

retains many original features including flagstone floors, open fireplaces and exposed beams. There is a cosy lounge and a choice of places to eat: the bar for light snacks and for more substantial meals the Oak Room or the Garden Room, which leads onto a pleasant inner courtyard.
ROOMS: 12 en suite ⊗ in 1 bedroom **FACILITIES:** STV **CONF:** Thtr 30 Class 20 Board 20 **PARKING:** 16 **NOTES:** No children 5yrs

Travelodge
BA11 6SF
☎ 08700 850 950 01373 830251
web: www.travelodge.co.uk
Dir: *at junct of A36/A361*
Travelodge offers good quality, good value, modern accommodation. Ideal for families, the spacious, en suite bedrooms include remote-control TV, tea and coffee-making facilities and comfortable beds. Meals can be taken at the nearby family restaurant. For further details consult the Hotel Groups page.
ROOMS: 40 en suite s fr £26; d fr £26

BEDFORD, Bedfordshire — Map 12 TL04

★★★73% ®® **Woodlands Manor**
Green Ln, Clapham MK41 6EP
☎ 01234 363281 01234 272390
e-mail: reception@woodlandsmanorhotel.com
web: www.signaturegroup.co.uk
Dir: *A6 towards Kettering. Clapham 1st village N of town centre. On entering village 1st right into Green Lane, Manor 200mtrs on right*
Sitting in acres of well-tended grounds, this Victorian manor offers a warm welcome. Bedrooms are spacious and well appointed providing a variety of thoughtful extras. Traditional public areas
continued on p74

BEDFORD, continued

include a cosy bar and restaurant where award-winning food is served.

Woodlands Manor, Bedford

ROOMS: 30 en suite 3 annexe en suite (4 fmly) (10 GF) ⊗ in 6 bedrooms s fr £85; d £95-£105 (incl. bkfst) **LB** **FACILITIES:** STV Xmas **CONF:** Thtr 80 Class 40 Board 40 Del from £135 **PARKING:** 100 **NOTES:** ⊗ in restaurant Civ Wed 90

★★★65% Bedford Moat House

2 St Mary's St MK42 9NE
☎ 01234 799988 🖷 01234 799902
e-mail: reservations.bedford@moathousehotels.com
Dir: *M1 junct 13, follow A421, then A6 to town centre. Hotel on bank of River Ouse*

A few minutes' walk from the town centre, this business hotel stands on the south bank of the Great Ouse. Everything is colourful and comfortable and the public rooms look out over the river. Bedrooms are well equipped and the hotel has good conference and leisure facilities.

ROOMS: 120 en suite ⊗ in 72 bedrooms **FACILITIES:** STV Sauna Solarium Gym **CONF:** BC Thtr 400 Class 120 Board 30 Del from £80 **SERVICES:** Lift **PARKING:** 99 **NOTES:** ⊗ in restaurant Civ Wed 120

★★★64% Corus hotel Bedford

Cardington Rd MK44 3SA
☎ 0870 609 6108 🖷 01234 273102
e-mail: bedford@corushotels.com
web: www.corushotels.com
Dir: *From M1 junct 13, A421, approx 10m to A603 Sandy/Bedford exit, hotel on right at 2nd rdbt*

A tranquil location on the outskirts of Bedford, friendly staff and well-equipped bedrooms are the main attractions here. Cosy day rooms and two informal bars add to the appeal, while large windows in the restaurant make the most of the view over the river. The original barn now houses the conference and function suite.

ROOMS: 48 en suite (20 GF) ⊗ in 27 bedrooms s £45-£103; d £60-£115 (incl. bkfst) **LB** **FACILITIES:** STV Free use of local leisure centre (1mile) **CONF:** Thtr 120 Class 40 Board 40 **PARKING:** 90 **NOTES:** ⊗ in restaurant Civ Wed 90

⌂ Innkeeper's Lodge Bedford

403 Goldington Rd MK41 0DS
☎ 0870 243 0500 & 01234 272707
🖷 01234 343926
web: www.innkeeperslodge.com
Dir: *on A428*

A growing concept in the travel accommodation market. Smart rooms meet essential business requirements but also have home comforts. Dining options include all-day menus plus the added advantage of breakfast, which is included in the room price. For further details consult the Hotel Groups page.

ROOMS: 47 en suite s £45-£49.95; d £45-£49.95 **CONF:** Thtr 25 Class 25 Board 20

⌂ Premier Travel Inn Bedford

Priory Country Park, Barkers Ln MK41 9DJ
☎ 08701 977030 🖷 01234 325697
web: www.premiertravelinn.com
Dir: *M1 junct 13/A421/A6 towards Bedford then A428 signed Cambridge. Cross River Ouse & right at next rdbt, follow signs for Priory Country Park*

High quality, modern budget accommodation ideal for both families and business travellers. Spacious, en suite bedrooms feature bath and shower, satellite TV and many have telephones and modem points. The adjacent family restaurant features a wide and varied menu. For further details consult the Hotel Groups page.

ROOMS: 32 en suite s £47.95-£50.95; d £47.95-£50.95

⌂ Travelodge Bedford

Saturn Heights, Brickhill Dr MK41 7PH
☎ 08700 850950 🖷 01234 270908
web: www.travelodge.co.uk
Dir: *From M1 into Bedford via A421 and A6. Follow A5141 to Manton Lane.*

Travelodge offers good quality, good value, modern accommodation. Ideal for families, the spacious, en suite bedrooms include remote-control TV, tea and coffee-making facilities and comfortable beds. Meals can be taken at the nearby family restaurant. For further details consult the Hotel Groups page.

ROOMS: 51 en suite s fr £26; d fr £26

⌂ Travelodge Bedford East

Black Cat Roundabout MK44 3OT
☎ 08700 850 950
web: www.travelodge.co.uk
Dir: *A1 N'bound at Black Cat rdbt at junct with A421*

Travelodge offers good quality, good value, modern accommodation. Ideal for families, the spacious, en suite bedrooms include remote-control TV, tea and coffee-making facilities and comfortable beds. Meals can be taken at the nearby family restaurant. For further details consult the Hotel Groups page.

ROOMS: 40 en suite s fr £26; d fr £26

BELFORD, Northumberland

Map 21 NU13

★★67% *Blue Bell*

Market Place NE70 7NE
☎ 01668 213543 🖷 01668 213787
e-mail: bluebel@globalnet.co.uk
web: www.bluebellhotel.com
Dir: *centre of village on left of St Mary's Church*

Formerly a coaching inn, this popular and long established hotel is

continued

located in the village square. Currently undergoing refurbishment, it offers a choice of superior and standard bedrooms all in classical style. Well-prepared meals can be enjoyed in the restaurant and in addition to the bar there is a comfortable lounge in which to relax.
ROOMS: 17 en suite (1 fmly) (1 GF) **FACILITIES:** Riding ⛳ Putt green **PARKING:** 16 **NOTES:** ⊘ in restaurant

⌂ *Purdy Lodge*
Adderstone Services NE70 7JU
THE INDEPENDENTS
☎ 01668 213000 ⎙ 01668 213131
e-mail: james@purdylodge.co.uk
web: www.purdylodge.co.uk
Dir: *turn off A1 onto B1341 then immediately left*
Situated on the A1, this family-owned lodge provides quiet bedrooms that look out over fields towards Bamburgh Castle. Food is readily available in the attractive restaurant, the smart 24-hour café, or the cosy lounge bar.
ROOMS: 20 en suite **CONF:** Thtr 40 Class 30 Board 20

BELLINGHAM, Northumberland — Map 21 NY88

★★69% *Riverdale Hall*
NE48 2JT
THE INDEPENDENTS
☎ 01434 220254 ⎙ 01434 220457
e-mail: iben@riverdalehall.demon.co.uk
web: www.riverdalehall.demon.co.uk
Dir: *turn off B6320, after bridge, hotel on left*
This hotel dates from 1866 and is located outside the village. It boasts its own cricket square and football pitch, and fishing on the Tyne. The well-equipped bedrooms are spacious and some have balconies. Meals are available in the bar or stylish restaurant, where local produce and Thai specialities feature on the menus.
ROOMS: 20 en suite (11 fmly) (3 GF) **FACILITIES:** ⛶ Fishing Sauna ⛳ Putt green Cricket field ch fac **CONF:** Thtr 60 Class 40 Board 40 **PARKING:** 60 **NOTES:** ⊘ in restaurant

BELPER, Derbyshire — Map 11 SK34

★★★70% Makeney Hall Hotel
Makeney, Milford DE56 0RS
folio Hotels
☎ 01332 842999 ⎙ 01332 842777
e-mail: makeneyhall@foliohotels.co.uk
web: www.foliohotels.co.uk/makeneyhall
Dir: *off A6 at Milford, signed Makeney. Hotel 0.25m on left*
This restored Victorian mansion stands in six acres of landscaped gardens and grounds above the River Derwent. Bedrooms vary in style and are generally very spacious. They are divided between the main house and the ground-floor courtyard. Comfortable public rooms include a lounge, bar and spacious restaurant with views of the gardens.
ROOMS: 27 en suite 18 annexe en suite (8 fmly) ⊘ in 15 bedrooms s £89-£149; d £89-£149 **LB** **FACILITIES:** STV Xmas **CONF:** Thtr 180 Class 80 Board 50 Del £135 **SERVICES:** Lift **PARKING:** 150 **NOTES:** ⊘ in restaurant Civ Wed 150

★★★63% The Lion Hotel & Restaurant
Bridge St DE56 1AX
☎ 01773 824033 ⎙ 01773 828393
e-mail: enquiries@lionhotel.uk.com
Dir: *8m NW of Derby, hotel on A6*
Situated in the centre of town and on the border of the Peak District, this 18th-century hotel provides an ideal base for exploring the many local attractions. The tastefully decorated bedrooms are well equipped and the public rooms include an attractive restaurant and two cosy bars; a modern function suite also proves popular.

ROOMS: 22 en suite (3 fmly) ⊘ in 7 bedrooms s £60-£70; d fr £85 (incl. bkfst) **FACILITIES:** STV Xmas **CONF:** Thtr 110 Class 60 Board 50 Del from £100 **PARKING:** 30 **NOTES:** 🐕 ⊘ in restaurant Civ Wed 90

BELTON, Lincolnshire — Map 11 SK93

★★★★75% De Vere Belton Woods
NG32 2LN
DE VERE HOTELS
☎ 01476 593200 ⎙ 01476 574547
e-mail: belton.woods@devere-hotels.com
web: www.devereonline.co.uk
Dir: *A1 to Gonerby Moor Services. B1174 towards Great Gonerby. At top of hill turn left towards Manthorpe/Belton. At T-junct turn left onto A607. Hotel 0.25m on left*
Beautifully located amidst 475 acres of picturesque countryside, this is a destination venue for lovers of sport, especially golf, as well as providing a relaxing executive retreat for seminars. Comfortable and well-equipped accommodation complements the elegant and spacious public areas, which include a good choice of drinking and dining options.
ROOMS: 136 en suite (136 fmly) (68 GF) ⊘ in 117 bedrooms **FACILITIES: Spa** STV ⛶ ⛳ 45 🎾 Fishing Squash Snooker Sauna Solarium Gym ⛳ Putt green Jacuzzi Outdoor activity centre - quad biking, laser shooting etc ♫ ch fac **CONF:** Thtr 245 Class 180 Board 80 **SERVICES:** Lift **PARKING:** 350 **NOTES:** ⊘ in restaurant Civ Wed 80

BEMBRIDGE See Wight, Isle of

BERKELEY, Gloucestershire — Map 04 ST69

★★66% The Old School House Hotel
34 Canonbury St GL13 9BG
☎ 01453 811711 ⎙ 01453 511761
e-mail: oldschoolhouse@btopenworld.com
Dir: *0.5m off A38 next to Berkeley Castle. Follow tourist signs*
Situated just 10 minutes from the M5, this unique hotel is a conversion of a chapel and schoolhouse. Many original features have been retained. Bedrooms, all of a generous size, have extensive modern facilities, and public areas include a drawing room and dining room, both with crackling log fires in winter. The cooking is accomplished.
ROOMS: 10 rms (8 en suite) (1 fmly) (2 GF) ⊘ in all bedrooms s £58-£60; d £75 (incl. bkfst) **LB** **CONF:** Class 12 Board 12 Del £95 **PARKING:** 12 **NOTES:** ⊘ in restaurant Closed 23-26 Dec

> Packed in a hurry? Ironing facilities should be available at all star levels, either in the rooms or on request

B

BERKELEY ROAD, Gloucestershire Map 04 SO70

★★★65% Prince of Wales
Berkeley Rd GL13 9HD
☎ 01453 810474 📠 01453 511370
e-mail: enquiries@theprinceofwaleshotel.com
Dir: *on A38, 6m S of M5 junct 13/6m N of junct 14*
Handily situated by the A38, this smartly presented hotel is convenient for major road networks. Bedrooms are generally a good size with a range of facilities. The public bar is popular with both residents and locals alike, whilst the restaurant menu features a selection of Italian dishes.
ROOMS: 43 en suite (2 fmly) (15 GF) ⊗ in 20 bedrooms s £52-£73; d £62-£83 (incl. bkfst) **LB** **FACILITIES:** STV **CONF:** Thtr 200 Class 60 Board 60 Del from £92 **PARKING:** 150 **NOTES:** ⊗ in restaurant Civ Wed 100

BERWICK-UPON-TWEED, Northumberland Map 21 NT95

★★★70% Marshall Meadows Country House
TD15 1UT
☎ 01289 331133 📠 01289 331438
e-mail: stay@marshallmeadows.co.uk
web: www.marshallmeadows.co.uk
Dir: *signed directly off A1, 300yds from Scottish Border*

This stylish Georgian mansion is set in wooded grounds flanked by farmland and has convenient access to the A1. A popular venue for weddings and conferences, it offers comfortable and well-equipped bedrooms. Public rooms include a cosy bar, a relaxing lounge and a two-tier restaurant, that serves imaginative dishes.
ROOMS: 19 en suite (1 fmly) ⊗ in 12 bedrooms s £85; d £115 (incl. bkfst) **LB** **FACILITIES:** ♫ Petanque Xmas **CONF:** Thtr 200 Class 120 Board 40 Del from £105 **PARKING:** 87 **NOTES:** ⊗ in restaurant Closed 15-27 Dec Civ Wed 200

★★★64% *King's Arms*
43 Hide Hill TD15 1EJ
☎ 01289 307454 📠 01289 308867
e-mail: kingsarms.berwick@virgin.net
web: www.kings-arms-hotel.com
Dir: *from A1 follow town centre signs. Hotel behind Guild Hall, on left of Hide Hill*
A hotel of contrasting styles, this former coaching inn boasts a bar and restaurant that are contemporary and trendy with menus to match. By contrast bedrooms are set on traditional lines but most are a good size.
ROOMS: 35 en suite (3 fmly) ⊗ in 20 bedrooms **CONF:** Thtr 200 Class 100 Board 50 **NOTES:** ⊗ in restaurant Closed 24 Dec-14 Jan Civ Wed 150

★★66% Queens Head
Sandgate TD15 1EP
☎ 01289 307852 📠 01289 307858
e-mail: queensheadhotel@berwickontweed.fsbusiness.co.uk
Dir: *A1 towards centre & Town Hall, along High St. Turn right at bottom to Hide Hill, located next to cinema*
This small hotel is situated in the town centre close to the old walls of this former garrison town. An impressive choice of tasty freshly prepared dishes from a daily-changing blackboard menu is served in the smart reception lounge or dining room. The bright stylish bedrooms are furnished in pine and are well equipped.
ROOMS: 6 en suite (5 fmly) ⊗ in all bedrooms s £53; d £75 (incl. bkfst) **NOTES:** No dogs ⊗ in restaurant

⌂ Travelodge (Berwick-upon-Tweed)
Loaning Meadow, North Rd
☎ 08700 850 950 📠 01289 306555
web: www.travelodge.co.uk
Dir: *Follow A1 signed to Berwick to rdbt with A1167*
Travelodge offers good quality, good value, modern accommodation. Ideal for families, the spacious, en suite bedrooms include remote-control TV, tea and coffee-making facilities and comfortable beds. Meals can be taken at the nearby family restaurant. For further details consult the Hotel Groups page.
ROOMS: 40 en suite s fr £26; d fr £26

BEVERLEY, East Riding of Yorkshire Map 17 TA03

★★★69% ⊛⊛ Tickton Grange
Tickton HU17 9SH
☎ 01964 543666 📠 01964 542556
e-mail: info@ticktongrange.co.uk
Dir: *3m NE on A1035*
A charming Georgian country house situated in four acres of private grounds and attractive gardens. Bedrooms are individual, and redecorated to a high specification. Pre-dinner drinks may be enjoyed in the comfortable library lounge, prior to enjoying fine, modern British cooking in the restaurant. The hotel has excellent facilities for both weddings and business conferences.
ROOMS: 17 en suite (2 fmly) (4 GF) ⊗ in all bedrooms s £60-£80; d £80-£120 **LB** **CONF:** Thtr 200 Class 100 Board 80 Del from £101 **PARKING:** 90 **NOTES:** No dogs ⊗ in restaurant RS 25-29 Dec Civ Wed 200

★★★67% Lairgate Hotel
30/32 Lairgate HU17 8EP
☎ 01482 882141 📠 01482 861067
Dir: *A63 towards town centre. Hotel 220yds on left (follow one-way system)*
Located just off the Market Square, this pleasing Georgian hotel has now been refurbished to offer stylish accommodation. Bedrooms are elegant and well equipped, and public rooms include a comfortable lounge, a lounge bar, and restaurant with a popular sun terrace.
ROOMS: 16 en suite (1 fmly) (2 GF) ⊗ in 13 bedrooms s £70; d £90-£105 (incl. bkfst) **LB** **CONF:** Thtr 50 Board 20 **PARKING:** 16 **NOTES:** No dogs ⊗ in restaurant Civ Wed 80

★★★65% *The Beverley Arms Hotel*
North Bar Within HU17 8DD
☎ 0870 609 6149 📠 01482 870907
e-mail: beverleyarms@corushotels.com
web: www.corushotels.com
Dir: *opposite St Marys Church. Left lane at lights just before North Bar. Hotel 100yds on left. Car park at rear*
This hotel has historic links to the highwayman Dick Turpin, and

continued

today features the spacious, flagstone Shires Lounge, which includes the bar and several cosy sitting areas with a lounge menu. The attractively appointed restaurant also offers careful and friendly service. Bedrooms are equipped with modern comforts and there are good parking facilities.

ROOMS: 56 en suite (4 fmly) ⊗ in 41 bedrooms **CONF:** Thtr 80 Class 40 Board 30 **SERVICES:** Lift **PARKING:** 50 **NOTES:** ⊗ in restaurant

★★74% Manor House

Northlands, Walkington HU17 8RT
☎ 01482 881645 01482 866501
e-mail: info@walkingtonmanorhouse.co.uk
web: www.walkingtonmanorhouse.co.uk
Dir: *from M62 junct 38 follow 'Walkington' signs. 4m SW off B1230. Through Walkington village, left at lights. Left at 1st x-roads. Approx 400yds hotel on left*

This delightful country-house hotel is set in well-tended gardens surrounded by open countryside. The spacious bedrooms have been attractively decorated and thoughtfully equipped. Public rooms include a conservatory restaurant and a very inviting lounge. A good range of dishes is available from two menus, with an emphasis on fresh and local produce.

ROOMS: 6 en suite 1 annexe en suite (1 fmly) (1 GF) s £75-£85; d £95-£115 **FACILITIES:** **CONF:** Thtr 24 Class 16 Board 16 Del from £120 **PARKING:** 40 **NOTES:** ⊗ in restaurant Closed 25 Dec-4 Jan RS Sun Civ Wed 40

BEWDLEY, Worcestershire — Map 10 SO77

★★65% Black Boy

Kidderminster Rd DY12 1AG
☎ 01299 402119 01299 402119
e-mail: rc@midnet.co.uk
web: www.blackboyhotel.co.uk
Dir: *follow town centre signs*

This privately-owned and personally-run 18th-century inn stands close to both the River Severn and the centre of this lovely old town. A good range of food is served in both the cosy restaurant and bar. The accommodation, which has private, rather than en suite bathrooms, includes a two-bedroom unit that is located in a separate house, making it ideal for families. The Severn Valley Steam Railway is nearby.

ROOMS: 8 en suite (2 fmly) **CONF:** Thtr 20 Class 20 Board 20 **PARKING:** 28 **NOTES:** ⊗ in restaurant

U Ramada Hotel & Resort Kidderminster

RAMADA HOTEL & RESORT

Habberley Rd DY12 1LJ
☎ 01299 406400 01299 400921
e-mail: sales.kidderminster@ramadajarvis.co.uk
Dir: *A456 towards Kidderminster to ring road, follow signs to Bewdley. Pass Safari Park then exit A456 Bewdley Town Centre, take sharp right after 200yds onto B4190, hotel is 400yds on right.*

This Victorian hotel is set in 20 acres of attractive countryside and

continued

is in easy reach of both the M5 and M42. Bedrooms are comfortably appointed for both business and leisure guests.

ROOMS: 44 en suite (9 fmly) (17 GF) ⊗ in 20 bedrooms s £82-£99; d £82-£99 **FACILITIES:** STV supervised Sauna Solarium Gym Jacuzzi **CONF:** Thtr 450 Class 150 Board 80 Del from £145 **PARKING:** 150 **NOTES:** ⊗ in restaurant Civ Wed 200

BEXLEY, Greater London — Map 06 TQ47

★★★★67% *Bexleyheath Marriott Hotel*

Marriott HOTELS & RESORTS

1 Broadway DA6 7JZ
☎ 0870 400 7245 0870 400 7345
e-mail: bexleyheath@marriotthotels.co.uk
web: www.marriott.co.uk
Dir: *M25 junct 2/A2 towards London. Exit at Black Prince junct onto A220, signed Bexleyheath. Left at 2nd set of lights into hotel*

Well positioned for access to major road networks, this large, modern hotel offers spacious, air-conditioned bedrooms with a comprehensive range of extra facilities. Planters Bar is a popular venue for pre-dinner drinks and traditional English fare is served in the Copper Restaurant. The hotel also boasts a well-equipped leisure centre.

ROOMS: 142 en suite (16 fmly) ⊗ in 53 bedrooms **FACILITIES: Spa** STV supervised Solarium Gym Steam room, health & beauty **CONF:** Thtr 250 Class 120 Board 34 **SERVICES:** Lift air con **PARKING:** 77 **NOTES:** Civ Wed 40

BIBURY, Gloucestershire — Map 05 SP10

★★★78% Swan

CLASSIC BRITISH

GL7 5NW
☎ 01285 740695 01285 740473
e-mail: info@swanhotel.co.uk
web: www.swanhotel.co.uk
Dir: *9m S of Burford A40 on B4425, 6M N of Cirencester A4179 on B4425*

The Swan Hotel, built in the 17th-century as a coaching inn, is set in peaceful, picturesque and beautiful surroundings. It now provides well-equipped and smartly presented accommodation, and public areas that are comfortable and elegant. There is a choice of dining options to suit all tastes.

ROOMS: 18 en suite (1 fmly) ⊗ in all bedrooms d £140-£300 (incl. bkfst) **LB** **FACILITIES: Spa** Fishing Swan sanctuary, Beauty rooms Xmas **CONF:** Thtr 48 Class 10 Board 20 Del £155 **SERVICES:** Lift **PARKING:** 22 **NOTES:** ⊗ in restaurant Civ Wed 48

★★★74% *Bibury Court*

GL7 5NT
☎ 01285 740337 01285 740660
e-mail: info@biburycourt.com
web: www.biburycourt.com
Dir: *on B4425 beside the River Coln, behind St Marys Church*

Dating back to Tudor times, this elegant manor is the perfect antidote to the hustle and bustle of the modern world. Spacious public areas have abundant charm and character, while bedrooms offer solid quality and contemporary comforts. Seasonal produce is used to good effect in carefully prepared dishes served by a friendly team of helpful staff.

ROOMS: 18 en suite (3 fmly) (1 GF) **FACILITIES:** Fishing **CONF:** Board 12 **PARKING:** 100 **NOTES:** ⊗ in restaurant Civ Wed 32

Late for dinner? Quality standards mean that last orders for dinner vary according to star rating and should be no earlier than: ★★ 7.00pm ★★★ 8:00pm ★★★★ 9:00pm ★★★★★ 10:00pm

BICESTER, Oxfordshire Map 11 SP52

★★★69%
Bignell Park Hotel & Restaurant
Chesterton OX26 1UE
☎ 01869 326550 🖹 01869 322729
e-mail: enq@bignellparkhotel.co.uk
Dir: *M40 junct 9/A41 to Bicester, over 1st & 2nd rdbts, left at mini-rdbt, follow signs to Witney A4095. Hotel 0.5m*
Dating from the 16th century, Bignell Park combines charm and character with modern facilities. Situated in the peaceful village of Chesterton, the hotel is ideally placed for Bicester Village Retail Outlet, the M40 and the City of Oxford. The oak-beamed restaurant provides a unique ambience in which to enjoy modern food and traditional favourites, complemented by fine wines.
ROOMS: 23 en suite (1 fmly) (5 GF) **FACILITIES:** STV Xmas **CONF:** Thtr 40 Class 16 Board 22 Del from £135 **PARKING:** 40 **NOTES:** ⊗ in restaurant Civ Wed 40

Travelodge (Cherwell Valley)
Moto Service Area, Northampton Rd, Ardley OX6 9RD
☎ 08700 850 950 🖹 01869 346390
web: www.travelodge.co.uk
Dir: *M40 junct 10*
Travelodge offers good quality, good value, modern accommodation. Ideal for families, the spacious, en suite bedrooms include remote-control TV, tea and coffee-making facilities and comfortable beds. Meals can be taken at the nearby family restaurant. For further details consult the Hotel Groups page.
ROOMS: 98 en suite s fr £26; d fr £26 **CONF:** Thtr 40 Class 20 Board 20

BIDEFORD, Devon Map 03 SS42

★★★70%
Royal
Barnstaple St EX39 4AE
☎ 01237 472005 🖹 01237 478957
e-mail: info@royalbideford.co.uk
web: www.brend-hotels.co.uk
Dir: *at eastern end of Bideford Bridge*
A quiet and relaxing hotel, the Royal is set near the riverbank within five minutes' walk of the busy town centre and quay. Well-maintained public areas are bright and retain much of the charm and style of its 16th-century origins, particularly in the wood-panelled Kingsley Suite. Bedrooms are well equipped and comfortable. Both dinner and lounge snacks are appetising.
ROOMS: 32 en suite (3 fmly) (2 GF) s £60-£80; d £70-£100 **LB** **FACILITIES:** STV ♫ Xmas **CONF:** Thtr 100 Class 100 Board 100 **SERVICES:** Lift **PARKING:** 70 **NOTES:** Civ Wed

★★74%
Yeoldon Country House
Durrant Ln, Northam EX39 2RL
☎ 01237 474400 🖹 01237 476618
e-mail: yeoldonhouse@aol.com
web: www.yeoldonhousehotel.co.uk
Dir: *A39 from Barnstaple over River Torridge Bridge. At rdbt turn right onto A386 towards Northam, then 3rd right into Durrant Ln*
In a tranquil location with superb views over the River Torridge and attractive grounds, the Yeoldon is a charming Victorian house. Bedrooms are individually decorated, some have balconies with breathtaking views and all are well equipped. The public rooms are full of character with many interesting features and artefacts.

continued

Dinner offers a daily-changing menu using fresh local produce in imaginative dishes.

ROOMS: 10 en suite ⊗ in all bedrooms s £65-£75; d £100-£125 (incl. bkfst) **LB** **PARKING:** 20 **NOTES:** ⊗ in restaurant Closed 24-27 Dec

BIDFORD-ON-AVON, Warwickshire Map 10 SP15

★★★63%
Bidford Grange
Stratford Rd B50 4LY
☎ 01789 490319 🖹 01789 490998
e-mail: info@bidfordgrange.com
Dir: *M42 junct 3 towards Studley & Alcester along bypass onto B439, through Bidford-on-Avon. Hotel on right*
This pleasant hotel is situated by a golf course and is within easy driving distance of Stratford-upon-Avon. Staff are polite and friendly and there are two bars and a spacious dining room serving well-produced food.
ROOMS: 32 en suite 6 annexe en suite (10 GF) ⊗ in 10 bedrooms **FACILITIES:** STV ⛳ 18 Fishing Snooker Putt green Xmas **CONF:** Thtr 140 Class 60 Board 35 Del from £75 **PARKING:** 100 **NOTES:** Civ Wed 100

BIGBURY-ON-SEA, Devon Map 03 SX64

★★73%
Henley
TQ7 4AR
☎ 01548 810240 🖹 01548 810240
e-mail: enquiries@thehenleyhotel.co.uk
Dir: *through Bigbury, past Golf Centre into Bigbury-on-Sea. Hotel on left as road slopes towards shore*
Built in Edwardian times and complete with its own private cliff path to a sandy beach, this small hotel boasts stunning views from an elevated position. The Henley has an unhurried atmosphere which, when combined with its understated style, makes it a peaceful retreat and perfect for relaxation. The menu offers innovative dishes cooked with care using local produce.
ROOMS: 6 en suite (1 fmly) ⊗ in all bedrooms s £45-£58; d £96-£110 (incl. bkfst) **LB** **PARKING:** 9 **NOTES:** No children ⊗ in restaurant Closed Nov-Mar

BILBROUGH, North Yorkshire Map 16 SE54

Premier Travel Inn York South West
Bilborough Top, Colton YO23 3PP
☎ 0870 238 3317 🖹 01937 835934
web: www.premiertravelinn.com
Dir: *on A64 between Tadcaster & York*
High quality, modern budget accommodation ideal for both families and business travellers. Spacious, en suite bedrooms feature bath and shower, satellite TV and many have telephones and modem points. The adjacent family restaurant features a wide and varied menu. For further details consult the Hotel Groups page.
ROOMS: 59 en suite s £51.95; d £51.95 **CONF:** Thtr 20 Board 12

⇧ Travelodge York
Tadcaster LS24 8EG
☎ 08700 850 950 📠 0870 1911685
web: www.travelodge.co.uk
Dir: *on A64 eastbound*
Travelodge offers good quality, good value, modern accommodation. Ideal for families, the spacious, en suite bedrooms include remote-control TV, tea and coffee-making facilities and comfortable beds. Meals can be taken at the nearby family restaurant. For further details consult the Hotel Groups page.
ROOMS: 62 en suite s fr £26; d fr £26

BILLINGHAM See Stockton-on-Tees

BILSBORROW, Lancashire Map 18 SD53

⇧ Premier Travel Inn Preston North
Garstang Rd PR3 0RN
☎ 0870 9906410 📠 0870 9906411
web: www.premiertravelinn.com
Dir: *4m from M6 junct 32 on A6 towards Garstang. 7m from Preston*
High quality, modern budget accommodation ideal for both families and business travellers. Spacious, en suite bedrooms feature bath and shower, satellite TV and many have telephones and modem points. The adjacent family restaurant features a wide and varied menu. For further details consult the Hotel Groups page.
ROOMS: 40 en suite s £46.95-£48.95; d £46.95-£48.95

BINFIELD, Berkshire Map 05 SU87

⇧ Travelodge Bracknell
London Rd RG12 4AA
☎ 08700 850 950 📠 01344 485940
web: www.travelodge.co.uk
Dir: *M4 junct 10 (Bracknell) take 1st exit towards Binfield B3408*
Travelodge offers good quality, good value, modern accommodation. Ideal for families, the spacious, en suite bedrooms include remote-control TV, tea and coffee-making facilities and comfortable beds. Meals can be taken at the nearby family restaurant. For further details consult the Hotel Groups page.
ROOMS: 35 en suite s fr £26; d fr £26

BINGLEY, West Yorkshire Map 19 SE13

U Ramada Bradford/Bingley
Bradford Rd BD16 1TU
☎ 01274 567123 📠 01274 551331
e-mail: sales.bradford@ramadajarvis.co.uk
web: www.ramadajarvis.co.uk
Dir: *From M62 junct 26 onto M606, at rdbt follow signs for A650 Skipton/Keighley, hotel is 2m out of Shipley.*
This large hotel is set in private landscaped grounds with many rooms enjoying views of the Aire Valley. Bedrooms are comfortably appointed for both business and leisure guests.
ROOMS: 103 en suite (5 fmly) (2 GF) ⊘ in 55 bedrooms s £69-£89; d £69-£89 **FACILITIES:** STV Xmas **CONF:** Thtr 350 Class 200 Board 30 Del from £130 **SERVICES:** Lift **PARKING:** 300 **NOTES:** ✈ ⊘ in restaurant Civ Wed 300

⇧ Premier Travel Inn Bradford North (Bingley)
Off Bradford Rd BD20 5NH
☎ 08701 977038 📠 01274 551692
web: www.premiertravelinn.com
Dir: *M62 junct 27 follow signs for A650, then to Bingley Main Street. At next rdbt straight on 50 mtrs on left*
High quality, modern budget accommodation ideal for both families and business travellers. Spacious, en suite bedrooms feature bath and shower, satellite TV and many have telephones and modem points. The adjacent family restaurant features a wide and varied menu. For further details consult the Hotel Groups page.
ROOMS: 40 en suite s £46.95-£48.95; d £46.95-£48.95

BIRCHANGER GREEN MOTORWAY SERVICE AREA (M11), Essex Map 06 TL52

⇧ Days Inn Stansted
Birchanger Green, Bishop Stortford CM23 5QZ
☎ 01279 656477 📠 01279 656590
e-mail: birchanger.hotel@welcomebreak.co.uk
web: www.welcomebreak.co.uk
Dir: *M11 junct 8*
This modern building offers accommodation in smart, spacious and well-equipped bedrooms, suitable for families and business travellers, and all with en suite bathrooms. Continental breakfast is available and other refreshments may be taken at the nearby family restaurant. For further details see the Hotel Groups page.
ROOMS: 60 en suite s £69-£99; d £69-£99

BIRCH MOTORWAY SERVICE AREA (M62), Greater Manchester Map 16 SD80

⇧ Travelodge Manchester North (Eastbound)
M62 Service Area East Bound OL10 2HQ
☎ 08700 850 950 📠 0161 655 3716
web: www.travelodge.co.uk
Dir: *Between junct 18 & 19 on M62 eastbound*
Travelodge offers good quality, good value, modern accommodation. Ideal for families, the spacious, en suite bedrooms include remote-control TV, tea and coffee-making facilities and comfortable beds. Meals can be taken at the nearby family restaurant. For further details consult the Hotel Groups page.
ROOMS: 55 en suite s fr £26; d fr £26

⇧ Travelodge Manchester North (Westbound)
M62 Service Area West Bound OL10 2HQ
☎ 08700 850 950 📠 0161 655 6422
web: www.travelodge.co.uk
Dir: *Between junct 18 & 19 on M62 westbound*
Travelodge offers good quality, good value, modern accommodation. Ideal for families, the spacious, en suite bedrooms include remote-control TV, tea and coffee-making facilities and comfortable beds. Meals can be taken at the nearby family restaurant. For further details consult the Hotel Groups page.
ROOMS: 35 en suite s fr £26; d fr £26

We have indicated only the hotels that don't accept credit or debit cards

BIRKENHEAD, Merseyside Map 15 SJ38

★★★68% Riverhill
Talbot Rd, Prenton CH43 2HJ
☎ 0151 653 3773 📠 0151 653 7162
e-mail: reception@theriverhill.co.uk
Dir: *1m from M53 junct 3, along A552. Turn left onto B5151 at lights hotel 0.5m on right*
Pretty lawns and gardens provide the setting for this friendly hotel, conveniently situated about a mile from the M53. Attractively furnished, well-equipped bedrooms include ground-floor, family, and four-poster rooms. Business meetings and weddings can be

continued on p80

BIRKENHEAD, continued

catered for. A wide choice of dishes is available in the restaurant, overlooking the garden.

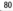

Riverhill, Birkenhead

ROOMS: 15 en suite (1 fmly) s £59.75-£69.75; d £69.75-£75 **LB** **FACILITIES:** STV Free use of local leisure facilities **CONF:** Thtr 50 Class 30 Board 52 **PARKING:** 32 **NOTES:** Civ Wed 40

Premier Travel Inn Wirral (Greasby)

Greasby Rd CH49 2PP
☎ 0870 9906588 0870 9906589
web: www.premiertravelinn.com
Dir: *9m from Liverpool city centre. 2m from M53 junct 2. Just off B5139*
High quality, modern budget accommodation ideal for both families and business travellers. Spacious, en suite bedrooms feature bath and shower, satellite TV and many have telephones and modem points. The adjacent family restaurant features a wide and varied menu. For further details consult the Hotel Groups page.
ROOMS: 30 en suite s £46.95-£48.95; d £46.95-£48.95

BIRMINGHAM, West Midlands Map 10 SP08
See also Bromsgrove, Lea Marston, Oldbury & Sutton Coldfield

Town House

★★★★ Hotel Du Vin & Bistro

25 Church St B3 2NR
☎ 0121 200 0600 0121 236 0889
e-mail: info@birmingham.hotelduvin.com
web: www.hotelduvin.com
Dir: *M6 junct 6/A38(M) to city centre, over flyover. Keep left & exit at St Chads Circus signed Jewellery Quarter. At traffic lights & rdbt take 1st exit, follow signs for Colmore Row, opposite Cathedral. Right into Church St, across Berwick St. Hotel on right*
The former Birmingham Eye Hospital has undergone a dramatic transformation, with the Victorian structure now housing a chic, sophisticated hotel. Stylish, high-ceilinged rooms, all with a wine theme, are luxuriously appointed and feature stunning bathrooms, sumptuous duvets and Egyptian cotton sheets. The Bistro offers relaxed dining and a top-notch wine list, while other attractions include a champagne bar, a cigar and wine boutique and a health club.
ROOMS: 66 en suite s £125-£350; d £125-£350 **FACILITIES:** STV Snooker Sauna Solarium Gym Pool table Treatment rooms Xmas **CONF:** Thtr 80 Class 40 Board 40 **SERVICES:** Lift air con **NOTES:** in restaurant Civ Wed 60

GF indicates the number of bedrooms at ground level

★★★★71%

Birmingham Marriott Hotel

12 Hagley Rd, Five Ways B16 8SJ
☎ 0121 452 1144 0121 456 3442
e-mail: pascal.demarchi@whitbread.com
web: www.marriott.co.uk
Situated in the suburb of Edgbaston, this Edwardian hotel is a prominent landmark on the outskirts of the city centre. Air-conditioned bedrooms are decorated in a comfortable, modern style and provide a comprehensive range of extra facilities. Public rooms include the contemporary, brasserie-style West 12 Bar and Restaurant.
ROOMS: 104 en suite in 60 bedrooms s fr £98 **LB** **FACILITIES: Spa** STV Solarium Gym Jacuzzi Beauty salon, Steam room Xmas **CONF:** Thtr 80 Board 35 Del from £140 **SERVICES:** Lift air con **PARKING:** 50 **NOTES:** Civ Wed 60

★★★★70% The Burlington

Burlington Arcade, 126 New St B2 4JQ
☎ 0121 643 9191 0121 628 5005
e-mail: mail@burlingtonhotel.com
web: www.macdonald-hotels.co.uk
Dir: *M6 junct 6, follow signs for city centre, then onto A38*
The Burlington's original Victorian grandeur - marble and iron staircases, high ceilings - has been blended together with modern facilities. Bedrooms are equipped to a good standard and public areas include a stylish bar and coffee lounge. The Berlioz Restaurant specialises in innovative dishes using fresh produce.
ROOMS: 112 en suite (6 fmly) in 49 bedrooms s £130-£140; d £150-£170 (incl. bkfst) **LB** **FACILITIES: Spa** STV Sauna Gym Jacuzzi Xmas **CONF:** Thtr 400 Class 175 Del from £99 **SERVICES:** Lift air con **NOTES:** Closed 25 Dec - 26 Dec Civ Wed 320

★★★★67%

Copthorne Hotel Birmingham

Paradise Circus B3 3HJ
☎ 0121 200 2727 0121 200 1197
e-mail: reservations.birmingham@mill-cop.com
web: www.copthorne.com/birmingham
Dir: *M6 junct 6, city centre A38(M). After Queensway Tunnel emerge left, follow International Convention Centre signs . Paradise Circus island - follow right lane - hotel in centre.*
This hotel is one of the few establishments in the city that benefits from its own car park. Bedrooms are spacious and come in a choice of styles, all with excellent facilities. Guests can enjoy a variety of dining options, including the contemporary menu in Goldies Brasserie.
ROOMS: 212 en suite in 108 bedrooms s £160-£180; d £180 **LB** **FACILITIES:** STV supervised Sauna Solarium Gym Jacuzzi Xmas **CONF:** BC Thtr 200 Class 120 Board 30 Del from £145 **SERVICES:** Lift **PARKING:** 88 **NOTES:**

★★★76% *Malmaison Birmingham*

1 Wharfside St, The Mailbox B1 1RD
☎ 0121 246 5000 0121 246 5002
e-mail: birmingham@malmaison.com
web: www.malmaison.com
Dir: *M6 junct 6, follow A38 towards B'ham, hotel within The Mailbox, signed from A38*
The 'Mailbox' development, of which this stylish and contemporary hotel is a part, incorporates the very best in fashionable shopping, an array of restaurants and ample parking. Air-conditioned bedrooms are stylishly decorated and feature a great range of facilities. Public rooms include a stylish bar and brasserie which are already proving a hit with guests and locals alike.
ROOMS: 189 en suite in 132 bedrooms **FACILITIES: Spa** STV Sauna Gym Jacuzzi **CONF:** Thtr 40 Class 24 Board 24 **SERVICES:** Lift air con

★★★70% The Westley
80-90 Westley Rd, Acocks Green B27 7UJ
☎ 0121 706 4312 🖷 0121 706 2824
e-mail: reservations@westley-hotel.co.uk
web: www.westley-hotel.co.uk
Dir: *A41 signed Birmingham on Solihull by-pass, continue to Acocks Green. At rdbt, 2nd exit B4146 Westley Rd. Hotel 200yds on left*

Set in the city suburbs and conveniently located for the N.E.C. and airport, this friendly hotel provides well-equipped, smartly presented bedrooms. In addition to the main restaurant, there is also a lively bar and brasserie together with a large function room.
ROOMS: 26 en suite 11 annexe en suite (1 fmly) ⊗ in 15 bedrooms s £75-£130; d £88.50-£130 (incl. bkfst) **LB** **FACILITIES:** STV ♫ **CONF:** Thtr 200 Class 80 Board 50 Del from £100 **PARKING:** 150 **NOTES:** ⊗ in restaurant Civ Wed 200

★★★67% Novotel Birmingham Centre
70 Broad St B1 2HT
☎ 0121 643 2000 🖷 0121 643 9796
e-mail: h1077@accor-hotels.com
web: www.novotel.com
This large, modern, purpose-built hotel benefits from an excellent city centre location, with the bonus of secure parking. Bedrooms are spacious, modern and well equipped for business users. Four rooms have facilities for less able guests. Public areas include the Garden Brasserie, function rooms and a fitness room.
Novotel - AA Hotel Group of the Year 2005-6.
ROOMS: 148 en suite (148 fmly) ⊗ in 98 bedrooms s £65-£140; d £75-£150 (incl. bkfst) **LB** **FACILITIES:** STV Sauna Gym Jacuzzi **CONF:** Thtr 300 Class 120 Board 90 Del from £100 **SERVICES:** Lift air con **PARKING:** 53 **NOTES:** ⊗ in restaurant

The vast majority of establishments in this guide accept credit and debit cards. We indicate those that don't take any

★★★65% Corus hotel Birmingham South
Redditch Rd, Hopwood B48 7AL
☎ 0870 609 6119 🖷 0121 445 6163
e-mail: birminghamsouth@corushotels.com
web: www.corushotels.com
Dir: *M42 junct 2 towards Birmingham on A441. At rdbt turn right and follow A441 for 1m. Hotel on right*
In a quiet location on the outskirts of the city, yet close to the M42, this hotel offers a number of meeting and conference rooms. The bedrooms are generally spacious, well equipped and

continued on p82

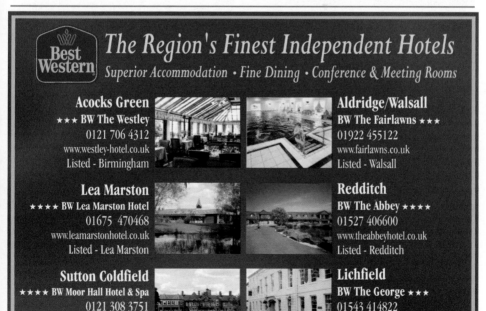

BIRMINGHAM, continued

comfortable. A spacious bar offers carvery lunches and dinner is served in the adjacent restaurant.

Corus hotel, Birmingham South

ROOMS: 58 en suite (2 fmly) ⊗ in 28 bedrooms s £49-£93; d £49-£93 **LB FACILITIES:** STV **CONF:** Thtr 220 Class 120 Board 80 Del from £99 **PARKING:** 200 **NOTES:** ⊗ in restaurant Civ Wed 120

★★★64% Jurys Inn Birmingham

245 Broad St B1 2HQ
☎ 0121 626 0626 & 606 9000 📠 0121 626 0627
e-mail: jurysinn_birmingham@jurysdoyle.com
web: www.jurysdoyle.com
Dir: *on A456 in city centre*

This large hotel is ideally located in the centre of the city and offers extensive conference facilities. Bedrooms are spacious and modern in design and the restaurant is designed for efficiency, offering a buffet-style operation.

ROOMS: 445 en suite (336 fmly) ⊗ in 325 bedrooms s £79-£155 **FACILITIES:** STV **CONF:** Thtr 280 Class 144 Board 44 Del from £120 **SERVICES:** Lift air con **PARKING:** 230 **NOTES:** 🐕 ⊗ in restaurant Closed 24-26 Dec

★★★63% Great Barr Hotel & Conference Centre

Pear Tree Dr, Newton Rd, Great Barr B43 6HS
☎ 0121 357 1141 📠 0121 357 7557
e-mail: sales@thegreatbarrhotel.com
web: www.thegreatbarrhotel.com
Dir: *M6 junct 7, at Scott Arms x-rds turn right towards West Bromwich (A4010) Newton Rd. Hotel 1m from Scotts Arms, on right*

This busy hotel, situated in a residential area, is particularly popular with business people. Bedrooms are well equipped and modern in style. There is a wide range of meeting rooms, a traditional oak-panelled bar and formal restaurant.

ROOMS: 105 en suite (6 fmly) ⊗ in 50 bedrooms s £45-£69; d £65-£85 **LB FACILITIES:** STV Xmas **CONF:** Thtr 200 Class 90 Board 60 Del from £90 **PARKING:** 200 **NOTES:** 🐕 RS BH (restaurant may be closed) Civ Wed 200

★★★63% The Plough & Harrow Hotel

135 Hagley Rd B16 8LS
☎ 0870 609 6118 📠 0121 454 1868
e-mail: ploughandharrow@corushotels.com
web: www.corushotels.com
Dir: *from the city, A456 (Hagley Road). Hotel on right after rdbt*

This well-established hotel is approximately a mile west of the city centre, with a relaxed and friendly atmosphere. Bedrooms come in a variety of styles and sizes and the attractive garden restaurant offers a good selection of freshly prepared dishes. Free parking for residents is a bonus.

ROOMS: 44 en suite (5 fmly) (11 GF) ⊗ in 22 bedrooms s £99-£130; d £99-£130 **LB FACILITIES:** STV **CONF:** Thtr 70 Class 35 Board 35 Del from £110 **PARKING:** 90 **NOTES:** ⊗ in restaurant Civ Wed 100

★★72% Copperfield House

60 Upland Rd, Selly Park B29 7JS
☎ 0121 472 8344 📠 0121 415 5655
e-mail: info@copperfieldhousehotel.fsnet.co.uk
Dir: *M6 junct 6/A38 through city centre. After tunnels, right at lights into Belgrave Middleway. Right at rdbt onto A441. At Selly Park Tavern, right into Upland Rd*

A delightful Victorian hotel, situated in a leafy suburb, close to the BBC's Pebble Mill Studios and within easy reach of the city centre. Accommodation is smartly presented and well-equipped; the executive rooms are particularly spacious. A tasteful lounge with honesty bar, carefully prepared, seasonally-inspired food and a well-chosen wine list add to the attractions.

ROOMS: 17 en suite (1 fmly) (2 GF) s £45-£75; d £60-£100 (incl. bkfst) **LB CONF:** BC **PARKING:** 11 **NOTES:** ⊗ in restaurant Closed 24 Dec - 2 Jan

★★70% Norwood

87-89 Bunbury Rd, Northfield B31 2ET
☎ 0121 411 2202 📠 0121 477 7447
e-mail: norwoodhotel@aol.com
Dir: *left on A38 at Grosvenor shopping centre, 5m S of city centre*

This comfortable, small hotel provides a friendly personal service and individually appointed accommodation; each bedroom is well equipped and there are several executive rooms available. Public rooms include the contemporary lounge bar, and an attractive dining room where carefully prepared home-cooking is served.

ROOMS: 18 en suite s £35-£70; d £50-£80 **LB CONF:** Thtr 40 Class 24 Board 20 **PARKING:** 11 **NOTES:** 🐕 Closed 23 Dec-2 Jan

★★66% Fountain Court

339-343 Fountain Court Hotel B17 8NH
☎ 0121 429 1754 📠 0121 429 1209
e-mail: info@fountain-court.co.uk
Dir: *on A456, towards Birmingham, 3 miles from M5 junct 3*

This family-owned hotel is on the A456, near to the M5 and a short drive from the city centre. A warm welcome is assured and day

continued

rooms include comfortable lounges and a cottage-style dining room, the setting for home cooked dinners and comprehensive breakfasts.
ROOMS: 23 en suite (4 fmly) (3 GF) s £45; d £65 (incl. bkfst)
PARKING: 20 **NOTES:** ⊘ in restaurant

★★64% Astoria
311 Hagley Rd B16 9LQ
☎ 0121 454 0795 📠 0121 456 3537
e-mail: reservations@astoriahotel.uk.com
Dir: *on A456 2m from city centre*
This Victorian property stands between the city centre and the M5 motorway. Personally run, it provides simple yet spacious accommodation that includes some family and ground floor rooms. There is a choice of lounges and a homely bar. The traditionally furnished dining room serves a selection of grill-orientated dishes.
ROOMS: 26 en suite (6 fmly) (5 GF) ⊘ in 2 bedrooms s £40-£49; d £55-£63 (incl. bkfst) **FACILITIES:** STV **CONF:** BC **PARKING:** 27
NOTES: ✗ ⊘ in restaurant

U Comfort Inn Birmingham City Centre
Station St B5 4DY
☎ 0121 643 1134
e-mail: comfort.inn2talk.com
Dir: *M6 junct 6. A38 city centre, Queensway ring road to Holloway Head/Smallbridge Queensway, left into hill street and 1st right.*
At the time of going to press, the star classification for this hotel was not confirmed. Please refer to the AA internet site www.theAA.com for current information.
ROOMS: 40 en suite (3 fmly) ⊘ in 18 bedrooms s £50-£75; d £50-£85 (incl. bkfst) **CONF:** Thtr 50 Class 25 Board 30 **SERVICES:** Lift
NOTES: ✗ Closed 25th & 26th December

U Days Hotel Birmingham
160 Wharfside St, The Mailbox B1 1RL
☎ 0121 643 9344 📠 0121 643 2044
e-mail: reservations.mailbox@dayshotel.co.uk
At the time of going to press, the star classification for this hotel was not confirmed. Please refer to the AA internet site www.theAA.com for current information.
ROOMS: 90 en suite **FACILITIES:** STV **CONF:** Thtr 90 Board 52 Del from £127.95 **PARKING:** 50 **NOTES:** ✗

⌂ *Campanile*
Aston Locks, Chester St B6 4BE
☎ 0121 359 3330 📠 0121 359 1223
e-mail: birmingham@envergure.co.uk
web: www.envergure.fr
Dir: *next to rdbt at junct of A4540/A38*

This modern building offers accommodation in smart, well-equipped bedrooms, all with en suite bathrooms. Refreshments may be taken at the informal Bistro. For further details consult the Hotel Groups page.
ROOMS: 109 en suite **CONF:** Thtr 150 Class 80 Board 55

⌂ *Hotel Ibis Birmingham Holloway*
55 Irving St B1 1DH
☎ 0121 622 4925 📠 0121 622 4195
e-mail: h2092@accor-hotels.com
Dir: *150yds from Dome Night Club, just off Bristol Street*
Modern, budget hotel offering comfortable accommodation in bright and practical bedrooms. Breakfast is self-service and dinner is available in the restaurant. For further details, consult the Hotel Groups page.
ROOMS: 51 en suite

⌂ *Hotel Ibis Birmingham Bordesley*
1 Bordesley Park Rd, Bordesley B10 0PD
☎ 0121 506 2600 📠 0121 506 2610
e-mail: H2178@accor-hotels.com
Modern, budget hotel offering comfortable accommodation in bright and practical bedrooms. Breakfast is self-service and dinner is available in the restaurant. For further details, consult the Hotel Groups page.
ROOMS: 87 en suite

⌂ *Hotel Ibis Birmingham Centre*
Arcadian Centre, Ladywell Walk B5 4ST
☎ 0121 622 6010 📠 0121 622 6020
e-mail: h1459@accor-hotels.com
Dir: *Follow signs to city centre from all motorways. Then follow 'Markets Area' or 'Indoor Market' signs. Hotel next to market.*
Modern, budget hotel offering comfortable accommodation in bright and practical bedrooms. Breakfast is self-service and dinner is available in the restaurant. For further details, consult the Hotel Groups page.
ROOMS: 159 en suite **CONF:** BC Thtr 100 Class 60 Board 40

⌂ Innkeeper's Lodge Birmingham West
563 Hagley Rd West, Quinton B32 1HP
☎ 0870 243 0500 & 0121 423 3895
web: www.innkeeperslodge.com
Dir: *M5 junct 3/A456 westbound. On opposite side of dual carriageway, accessed a short distance from rdbt*
A growing concept in the travel accommodation market. Smart rooms meet essential business requirements but also have home comforts. Dining options include all-day menus plus the added advantage of breakfast, which is included in the room price. For further details consult the Hotel Groups page.
ROOMS: 24 en suite s £45-£52.50; d £45-£52.50

⌂ Premier Travel Inn Birmingham Broad Street
20 Bridge St B1 2JH
☎ 08701 977031 📠 0121 633 4779
web: www.premiertravelinn.com
Dir: *From M6/M5/M42 follow signs for city centre. Bridge St off A456 (Broad Street). Turn left in front of Hyatt Hotel, Inn on right*
High quality, modern budget accommodation ideal for both families and business travellers. Spacious, en suite bedrooms feature bath and shower, satellite TV and many have telephones and modem points. The adjacent family restaurant features a wide and varied menu. For further details consult the Hotel Groups page.
ROOMS: 53 en suite

Popped the question? Hotels with Civ wed in their entry are licensed for civil wedding ceremonies. Maximum numbers for the ceremony only are shown e.g. Civ wed 120

BIRMINGHAM, continued

⇧ Premier Travel Inn Birmingham Central East
Richard St, Aston, Waterlinks B7 4AA
☎ 0870 238 3312 🖷 0121 333 6490
web: www.premiertravelinn.com
Dir: *On ring road A4540 at junct with A38(M). From M6 junct 6 take 2nd exit off A38(M), ring road, left at island, 1st left*
High quality, modern budget accommodation ideal for both families and business travellers. Spacious, en suite bedrooms feature bath and shower, satellite TV and many have telephones and modem points. The adjacent family restaurant features a wide and varied menu. For further details consult the Hotel Groups page.
ROOMS: 60 en suite s £49.95-£52.95; d £49.95-£52.95 **CONF:** Thtr 14

⇧ Premier Travel Inn Birmingham South
Birmingham Great Park, Ashbrook Drive, Parkway, Rubery B45 9FP
☎ 0870 9906538 🖷 0870 9906539
web: www.premiertravelinn.com
Dir: *M5 junct 4 onto A38 towards Birmingham. Left into Birmingham Great Park. Hotel behind superstore*
High quality, modern budget accommodation ideal for both families and business travellers. Spacious, en suite bedrooms feature bath and shower, satellite TV and many have telephones and modem points. The adjacent family restaurant features a wide and varied menu. For further details consult the Hotel Groups page.
ROOMS: 62 en suite s £47.95-£50.95; d £47.95-£50.95 **CONF:** Board 12

⇧ Premier Travel Inn Broad Street (Fiveways)
80 Broad St B15 1AU
☎ 0870 9906404 🖷 0870 9906405
web: www.premiertravelinn.com
Dir: *Exit M6 junct 6 onto A38 Aston Expressway. Follow city centre, ICC & NIA signs, onto Broad St. Right at lights, 2nd left at rdbt. Hotel on left*
High quality, modern budget accommodation ideal for both families and business travellers. Spacious, en suite bedrooms feature bath and shower, satellite TV and many have telephones and modem points. The adjacent family restaurant features a wide and varied menu. For further details consult the Hotel Groups page.
ROOMS: 60 en suite s £55.95-£57.95; d £55.95-£57.95 **CONF:** Thtr 60

⇧ Travelodge (Birmingham Central)
230 Broad St B15 1AY
☎ 08700 850 950 🖷 0121 644 5251
web: www.travelodge.co.uk
Dir: *lodge on left corner of Broad St/Granville St*
Travelodge offers good quality, good value, modern accommodation. Ideal for families, the spacious, en suite bedrooms include remote-control TV, tea and coffee-making facilities and comfortable beds. Meals can be taken at the nearby family restaurant. For further details consult the Hotel Groups page.
ROOMS: 136 en suite s fr £26; d fr £26

⇧ Travelodge (Birmingham East)
A45 Coventry Rd, Acocks Green, Yardley B26 1DS
☎ 08700 850 950 🖷 0121 764 5882
web: www.travelodge.co.uk
Dir: *on A45 approx 5m from M42 junct 6*
Travelodge offers good quality, good value, modern accommodation. Ideal for families, the spacious, en suite bedrooms include remote-control TV, tea and coffee-making facilities and comfortable beds. Meals can be taken at the nearby family restaurant. For further details consult the Hotel Groups page.
ROOMS: 40 en suite s fr £26; d fr £26

BIRMINGHAM AIRPORT, West Midlands Map 10 SP08

★★★68% Novotel Birmingham Airport
B26 3QL
☎ 0121 782 7000 0121 782 4111
🖷 0121 782 0445
e-mail: H1158@accor.com
web: www.novotel.com
Dir: *M42 junct 6/A45 to Birmingham, signed to airport. Hotel opposite main terminal*
This large, purpose-built hotel is located opposite the main passenger terminal. Bedrooms are spacious, modern in style and well equipped, including Playstations to keep the children busy. Two rooms have facilities for less able guests. The Garden Brasserie is open from noon until midnight, the bar is open 24 hours and a full room service is available.
Novotel - AA Hotel Group of the Year 2005-6.
ROOMS: 195 en suite (31 fmly) ⊗ in 159 bedrooms s £129-£154; d £139-£164 (incl. bkfst) **FACILITIES:** STV **CONF:** BC Thtr 35 Class 20 Board 22 Del from £149 **SERVICES:** Lift air con

BIRMINGHAM (NATIONAL EXHIBITION CENTRE), West Midlands Map 10 SP18

★★★★74%
Crowne Plaza Birmingham NEC
National Exhibition Centre, Pendigo Way B40 1PS
☎ 0870 400 9160 🖷 0121 781 4321
e-mail: sales@cpbirminghamnec.com
web: www.birminghamnec.crowneplaza.com
Dir: *M42 junct 6, follow signs for NEC, take 2nd exit on left, South Way for hotel entrance 50mtrs on right*
Within walking distance of the NEC, this hotel has many attributes including the bar and restaurant facilities. The restaurant is run by celebrity chef Brian Turner, and the bar is affiliated to the 606 jazz club in Chelsea. The air-conditioned bedrooms have duvet-covered beds and well designed workstations. The leisure facilities include a gym and sauna.
ROOMS: 242 en suite ⊗ in 190 bedrooms s £85-£275; d £85-£275 **LB** **FACILITIES:** STV Sauna Solarium Gym **CONF:** BC Thtr 192 Class 114 Board 52 Del from £120 **SERVICES:** Lift air con **PARKING:** 180 **NOTES:** ✈ ⊗ in restaurant Civ Wed 70

★★★★68% Moor Hall Hotel & Spa
Moor Hall Dr, Four Oaks B75 6LN
☎ 0121 308 3751 🖷 0121 308 8974
e-mail: mail@moorhallhotel.co.uk
web: www.moorhallhotel.co.uk
(For full entry see Sutton Coldfield)

★★★★67% ❀❀ Nailcote Hall
Nailcote Ln, Berkswell CV7 7DE
☎ 024 7646 6174 🖷 024 7647 0720
e-mail: info@nailcotehall.co.uk
web: www.nailcotehall.co.uk
(For full entry see Balsall Common)

★★★69% Arden Hotel & Leisure Club
Coventry Rd, Bickenhill B92 0EH
☎ 01675 443221 🖷 01675 445604
e-mail: enquiries@ardenhotel.co.uk
Dir: *M42 junct 6/A45 towards Birmingham. Hotel 0.25m on right, just off Birmingham International railway island*
This smart hotel neighbouring the NEC offers modern rooms and well-equipped leisure facilities. After dinner in the formal

continued

restaurant, the place to relax is the spacious lounge area. A buffet breakfast is served in the bright and airy Meeting Place.
ROOMS: 216 en suite (6 fmly) (6 GF) ⊗ in 105 bedrooms
s £65-£114.75; d £75-£154.50 (incl. bkfst) **FACILITIES:** STV ⊡
supervised Snooker Sauna Solarium Gym Jacuzzi Steamroom ♫ Xmas
CONF: Thtr 200 Class 40 Board 60 **SERVICES:** Lift **PARKING:** 300
NOTES: ⊗ in restaurant RS 25 Dec Civ Wed 100

See advert on this page

★★★68% ◉ **Haigs**
Kenilworth Rd CV7 7EL
☎ 01676 533004 ▤ 01676 535132
e-mail: info@haigsemail.co.uk
(For full entry see Balsall Common)

★★67% **Heath Lodge**
117 Coleshill Rd, Marston Green B37 7HT
☎ 0121 779 2218 ▤ 0121 770 5648
e-mail: reception@heathlodgehotel.freeserve.co.uk
Dir: M6 junct 4/A446 towards N Coleshill. After 0.5m turn left into Coleshill Heath Rd, signed to Marston Green. Hotel on right
This privately-owned and personally-run hotel is ideally located for visitors to the NEC and Birmingham Airport. Hospitality and service standards are high and while some bedrooms are compact, all are well equipped and suitably comfortable. Public areas include a bar, a lounge and a dining room which overlooks the garden.
ROOMS: 17 rms (16 en suite) (1 fmly) s £49-£59; d £69-£77 (incl. bkfst)
CONF: Thtr 20 Class 16 Board 14 **PARKING:** 22 **NOTES:** ⊗ in restaurant

⌂**Premier Travel Inn**
Birmingham NEC/ Airport
Bickenhill Parkway, Northway, National Exhibition
Centre B40 1QA
☎ 0870 9906326 ▤ 0870 9906327
web: www.premiertravelinn.com
Dir: From M6 junct 4 onto A446 towards Warwick, left in 0.5m signed NEC. 2nd exit at rdbt. At next rdbt take 2nd exit onto Bickenhill Parkway, follow Birmingham Airport signs. At next rdbt take 1st exit to hotel
High quality, modern budget accommodation ideal for both families and business travellers. Spacious, en suite bedrooms feature bath and shower, satellite TV and many have telephones and modem points. The adjacent family restaurant features a wide and varied menu. For further details consult the Hotel Groups page.
ROOMS: 199 en suite s £57.95; d £57.95 **CONF:** Class 12

Early start?
Hotels at all star levels should provide
in-room alarm clocks and/or alarm clocks

AA 2006
The **Pub** Guide

Over 2,200 pubs hand-picked for their great food and authentic character.

www.theAA.com AA

BISHOP'S STORTFORD, Hertfordshire Map 06 TL42

★★★★71% ◉◉ **Down Hall Country House**
Hatfield Heath CM22 7AS
☎ 01279 731441 ▤ 01279 730416
e-mail: reservations@downhall.co.uk
Dir: A1060, at Hatfield Heath keep left. Right into lane opp Hunters Meet, left at end
This imposing Victorian country-house hotel, set amidst 100 acres of mature grounds, is handy for Stansted Airport. Bedrooms are generally quite spacious; each one is pleasantly decorated and equipped with modern facilities. Public rooms include a choice of restaurants, a cocktail bar, two lounges and leisure facilities.

ROOMS: 99 en suite ⊗ in 81 bedrooms s £60-£140 (incl. bkfst) **LB**
FACILITIES: STV ⊡ ⚲ Snooker Sauna ⚑ Putt green Jacuzzi Giant chess, Whirlpool Xmas **CONF:** BC Thtr 200 Class 140 Board 68
SERVICES: Lift **PARKING:** 150 **NOTES:** ✠ ⊗ in restaurant
Civ Wed 120

BISHOPSTEIGNTON, Devon Map 03 SX97

★★65% Cockhaven Manor Hotel
Cockhaven Rd TQ14 9RF
☎ 01626 775252 📠 01626 775572
e-mail: cockhaven.manor@virgin.net
web: www.cockhavenmanor.com
Dir: *M5/A380 towards Torquay, then A381 towards Teignmouth. Left at Metro Motors. Hotel 500yds on left*
A friendly, family-run inn that dates back to the 16th century. Bedrooms are well equipped and many enjoy views across the beautiful Teign estuary. A choice of dining options is offered, and traditional and interesting dishes along with locally caught fish are popular with visitors and locals alike.
ROOMS: 12 en suite (2 fmly) ⊗ in 10 bedrooms s £35-£45; d £55-£65 (incl. bkfst) **LB** **FACILITIES:** Petanque **CONF:** BC Thtr 50 Class 50 Board 30 Del from £47.50 **PARKING:** 50 **NOTES:** ⊗ in restaurant RS 25-26 Dec

BLACKBURN, Lancashire Map 18 SD62
See also Langho

★★★★66% Clarion Hotel & Suites Foxfields
Whalley Rd, Billington BB7 9HY
☎ 01254 822556 📠 01254 824613
e-mail: enquiries@hotels-blackburn.com
web: www.hotels-blackburn.com
Dir: *off A59 at signpost for Billington/Whalley & hotel 0.5m on right*
This modern, stylish hotel is easily accessible from major road networks. Bedrooms are comfortable and spacious, and include some suites and others with separate dressing areas. Facilities include a good-sized swimming pool, a small gym and conference suites. The traditional restaurant serves creative cuisine.
ROOMS: 44 en suite (27 fmly) (21 GF) ⊗ in 17 bedrooms s £89-£115; d £99-£125 (incl. bkfst) **LB** **FACILITIES:** STV Sauna Gym Steam room ♫ Xmas **CONF:** Thtr 180 Class 60 Board 60 Del from £125 **PARKING:** 170 **NOTES:** ⊗ in restaurant Civ Wed 120

★★78% Millstone at Mellor
Church Ln, Mellor BB2 7JR
☎ 01254 813333 📠 01254 812628
e-mail: info@millstonehotel.com
web: www.shirehotels.com
Dir: *3m NW off A59*
Once a coaching inn, the Millstone is situated in a village just outside the town. The hotel provides a very high standard of accommodation, professional and friendly service and good food. Bedrooms, some in an adjacent house, are comfortable and generally spacious, and all are very well equipped. A room for less able guests is also available.
ROOMS: 17 en suite 6 annexe en suite (5 fmly) (8 GF) ⊗ in 10 bedrooms s £72-£102; d £94-£122 (incl. bkfst) **LB** **FACILITIES:** STV Xmas **CONF:** Thtr 25 Class 15 Board 16 **PARKING:** 40 **NOTES:** ⊗ in restaurant Civ Wed 60

Premier Travel Inn Blackburn North West
Myerscough Rd, Balderstone BB2 7LE
☎ 0870 9906388 📠 0870 9906389
web: www.premiertravelinn.com
Dir: *On A59 opp British Aerospace. Exit at M6 junct 3 take A59 to Clitheroe*
High quality, modern budget accommodation ideal for both families and business travellers. Spacious, en suite bedrooms feature bath and shower, satellite TV and many have telephones and modem points. The adjacent family restaurant features a wide and varied menu. For further details consult the Hotel Groups page.
ROOMS: 20 en suite s £46.95-£48.95; d £46.95-£48.95 **CONF:** Board 12

BLACKPOOL, Lancashire Map 18 SD33

★★★★68% *De Vere Herons' Reach*
East Park Dr FY3 8LL
☎ 01253 838866 📠 01253 798800
e-mail: reservations.herons@devere-hotels.com
web: www.devereonline.co.uk
Dir: *M6 junct 32/M55 junct 4/A583. At 4th lights turn right into South Park Drive for 0.25m, right at mini-rdbt onto East Park Dr, hotel 0.25m on right*
Set in over 200 acres of grounds, this hotel is popular with both business and leisure guests. The pleasure beach is a few minutes' walk from the hotel, and the Lake District and Trough of Bowland are an hour away. Extensive indoor and outdoor leisure facilities include an 18-hole championship golf course. Bedrooms include a number of suites and smart, well-appointed clubrooms.
ROOMS: 172 en suite ⊗ in 70 bedrooms **FACILITIES:** STV supervised 18 Squash Snooker Sauna Solarium Gym Putt green Jacuzzi Aerobic studio, Beauty room, Spinning Studio **CONF:** BC Thtr 650 Class 250 Board 70 **SERVICES:** Lift **PARKING:** 500 **NOTES:** ⊗ in restaurant Civ Wed 650

★★★★65% Imperial
North Promenade FY1 2HB
☎ 01253 623971 📠 01253 751784
e-mail: imperialblackpool@paramount-hotels.co.uk
web: www.paramount-hotels.co.uk
Dir: *M55 junct 2, take A583 North Shore, follow signs to North Promenade. Hotel on seafront, north of tower.*
Enjoying a prime seafront location, this grand Victorian hotel offers smartly appointed, well-equipped bedrooms and spacious, elegant public areas. Facilities include a smart leisure club; a comfortable lounge, the No.10 bar and an attractive split level restaurant that overlooks the seafront. Conferences and functions are extremely well catered for.
ROOMS: 180 en suite (9 fmly) ⊗ in 80 bedrooms s £59-£155; d £118-£155 **LB** **FACILITIES:** STV supervised Sauna Solarium Gym Jacuzzi Xmas **CONF:** Thtr 600 Class 240 Board 128 Del £169 **SERVICES:** Lift **PARKING:** 150 **NOTES:** ⊗ in restaurant Civ Wed 200

★★★70% Carousel
663-671 New South Prom FY4 1RN
☎ 01253 402642 📠 01253 341100
e-mail: carousel@sleepwellhotels.com
Dir: *from M55 follow signs to airport, pass airport to lights. Turn right, hotel 100yds on right*
This friendly seafront hotel, close to the Pleasure Beach, has undergone a complete refurbishment and offers smart, contemporary accommodation. Bedrooms are comfortably appointed and have a modern, stylish feel to them. An airy restaurant and a spacious bar/lounge both overlook the Promenade. The hotel has smart conference/meeting facilities and its own car park.
ROOMS: 92 en suite (7 fmly) ⊗ in 28 bedrooms s £68; d £88 (incl. bkfst) **LB** **FACILITIES:** STV ♫ Xmas **CONF:** Thtr 100 Class 30 Board 40 Del £120 **SERVICES:** Lift **PARKING:** 46 **NOTES:** ⊗ in restaurant Civ Wed 150

★★★68% Carlton
282-286 North Promenade FY1 2EZ
☎ 01253 628966 📠 01253 752587
e-mail: info@carltonhotelblackpool.co.uk
web: www.carltonhotelblackpool.co.uk
Dir: *M6 junct 32/M55 follow signs for North Shore. Between Blackpool Tower & Gynn Sq*
Enjoying a prime seafront location, this hotel has been extensively

continued

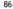

refurbished throughout. Bedrooms are brightly appointed and modern in style. Public areas include an open-plan dining room and lounge bar, and a spacious additional bar where lunches are served. Functions are well catered for and ample parking is available.

ROOMS: 58 en suite ⊗ in 20 bedrooms s £40-£70; d £60-£110 (incl. bkfst) **LB** **FACILITIES:** STV Xmas **CONF:** Thtr 90 Class 40 Board 40 Del from £100 **SERVICES:** Lift **PARKING:** 43 **NOTES:** ✗ ⊗ in restaurant Civ Wed 80

See advert on this page

★★70% Hotel Sheraton
54-62 Queens Promenade FY2 9RP
☎ 01253 352723 📠 01253 595499
e-mail: email@hotelsheraton.co.uk
web: www.hotelsheraton.co.uk
Dir: *1m N from Blackpool Tower on promenade towards Fleetwood*

This family-owned and run hotel is situated at the quieter, northern end of the promenade. Public areas include a choice of spacious lounges with sea views, a large function suite where popular dancing and cabaret evenings are held, and a heated indoor swimming pool. The smartly appointed bedrooms come in a range of sizes and styles.
ROOMS: 104 en suite (45 fmly) s £35-£70; d £50-£120 (incl. bkfst & dinner) **LB** **FACILITIES:** 🏊 Sauna Table Tennis Darts ♫ Xmas **CONF:** Thtr 200 Class 100 Board 150 **SERVICES:** Lift **PARKING:** 20 **NOTES:** ✗ ⊗ in restaurant

★★66% Headlands
611-613 South Promenade FY4 1NJ
☎ 01253 341179 📠 01253 342657
e-mail: headlands@blackpool.net
Dir: *M55 & filter left, right at rdbt to Promenade, turn right & hotel 0.5m on right*
This friendly, family owned hotel stands on the South Promenade, close to the Pleasure Beach and many of the town's major attractions. Bedrooms are traditionally furnished, many enjoying sea views. There is a choice of lounges and live entertainment is provided regularly. Home cooked food is served in the panelled dining room.
ROOMS: 41 en suite (10 fmly) s £36.50-£47; d £73-£94 (incl. bkfst) **LB** **FACILITIES:** Snooker Solarium Darts Games Room Pool Snooker ♫ Xmas **SERVICES:** Lift **PARKING:** 46 **NOTES:** ⊗ in restaurant Closed 2-15 Jan

★★65% Belgrave Madison
270-274 Queens Promenade FY2 9HD
☎ 01253 351570 📠 01253 500698
This family-run hotel, now under new ownership, enjoys a seafront location at the quieter end of town. Thoughtfully equipped bedrooms vary in size and include family and four-poster rooms. Spacious public areas include a choice of lounges with views over the promenade, a bar lounge where guests can enjoy live entertainment and a bright restaurant.
ROOMS: 43 en suite (10 fmly) s £27-£37; d £50-£70 (incl. bkfst) **LB** **FACILITIES:** Xmas **SERVICES:** Lift **PARKING:** 32 **NOTES:** ✗ ⊗ in restaurant

★★65% Warwick
603-609 New South Promenade FY4 1NG
☎ 01253 342192 📠 01253 405776
Dir: *M55 junct 4/A5230 for South Shore then right on A584, Promenade South*
Located on the renovated South Promenade and close to pleasure beach, this friendly family hotel has been extensive refurbished to provide a range of thoughtfully furnished bedrooms with modern bathrooms. Spacious public areas include an attractive dining room, choice of bars and an indoor swimming pool.
ROOMS: 51 en suite (11 fmly) ⊗ in all bedrooms s £43-£55; d £86-£110 (incl. bkfst & dinner) **LB** **FACILITIES:** 🏊 ♫ Xmas **CONF:** Thtr 50 Class 24 Board 30 Del from £49 **SERVICES:** Lift **PARKING:** 24 **NOTES:** ✗ ⊗ in restaurant Closed Jan RS Feb

BLACKPOOL, continued

The Southdown Hotel
567 New South Promenade FY4 1NF
☎ 01253 345964 🖹 01253 345964
e-mail: info@southdownhotel.co.uk
Dir: *Follow signs to Stargate, right at lights, hotel on right.*
At the time of going to press, the star classification for this hotel was not confirmed. Please refer to the AA internet site www.theAA.com for current information.
ROOMS: 30 en suite (6 fmly) (1 GF) ⊗ in 10 bedrooms s £18-£35; d £36-£70 (incl. bkfst) LB **FACILITIES:** Xmas **CONF:** Del from £30 **PARKING:** 25 **NOTES:**

Premier Travel Inn Blackpool Airport
Squires Gare Ln FY4 2QS
☎ 08701 977034 🖹 01253 362413
web: www.premiertravelinn.com
Dir: *M55 junct 4/A5230 & turn left at 1st rdbt towards airport. Inn is just before Squires Gate railway station*
High quality, modern budget accommodation ideal for both families and business travellers. Spacious, en suite bedrooms feature bath and shower, satellite TV and many have telephones and modem points. The adjacent family restaurant features a wide and varied menu. For further details consult the Hotel Groups page.
ROOMS: 39 en suite s £49.95; d £49.95 **CONF:** Thtr 15 Board 8

Premier Travel Inn Blackpool (Bispham)
Devonshire Rd, Bispham FY2 0AR
☎ 08701 977033 🖹 01253 590498
web: www.premiertravelinn.com
Dir: *M55 junct 4 right onto A583. At 5th set of lights turn right (Whitegate Drive) for approx. 4-5 miles onto Devonshire Rd (A587)*
High quality, modern budget accommodation ideal for both families and business travellers. Spacious, en suite bedrooms feature bath and shower, satellite TV and many have telephones and modem points. The adjacent family restaurant features a wide and varied menu. For further details consult the Hotel Groups page.
ROOMS: 39 en suite s £48.95; d £48.95 **CONF:** Thtr 50 Board 20

Premier Travel Inn Blackpool East
Whitehills Park, Preston New Rd FY4 5NZ
☎ 0870 9906608 🖹 0870 9906609
web: www.premiertravelinn.com
Dir: *Just off M55 junct 4. Take 1st left off rdbt. Inn on right*
High quality, modern budget accommodation ideal for both families and business travellers. Spacious, en suite bedrooms feature bath and shower, satellite TV and many have telephones and modem points. The adjacent family restaurant features a wide and varied menu. For further details consult the Hotel Groups page.
ROOMS: 81 en suite s £49.95-£52.95; d £49.95-£52.95

Premier Travel Inn Blackpool South
Yeadon Way, South Shore FY1 6BF
☎ 08701 977032 🖹 01253 343805
web: www.premiertravelinn.com
Dir: *M55, follow signs for central car park/coach area. Located next to Total garage*
High quality, modern budget accommodation ideal for both families and business travellers. Spacious, en suite bedrooms feature bath and shower, satellite TV and many have telephones and modem points. The adjacent family restaurant features a wide and varied menu. For further details consult the Hotel Groups page.
ROOMS: 79 en suite s £49.95-£52.95; d £49.95-£52.95 **CONF:** Thtr 40

BLAKENEY, Norfolk Map 13 TG04

★★★75% The Blakeney
The Quay NR25 7NE
☎ 01263 740797 🖹 01263 740795
e-mail: reception@blakeney-hotel.co.uk
web: www.blakeney-hotel.co.uk
Dir: *off A149 coast road, 8m W of Sheringham*
A traditional privately owned hotel situated on the quayside with superb views across the estuary and the salt marshes to Blakeney Point. Public rooms feature an elegant restaurant, ground floor lounge, bar and a further first-floor sun lounge overlooking the harbour. Bedrooms are smartly decorated and equipped with modern facilities, some have lovely sea views.
ROOMS: 48 en suite 16 annexe en suite (23 fmly) (16 GF) ⊗ in all bedrooms s £82-£130; d £164-£260 (incl. bkfst & dinner) LB **FACILITIES:** Spa Snooker Sauna Gym Jacuzzi Table tennis Xmas **CONF:** Thtr 200 Class 100 Board 100 Del from £110 **SERVICES:** Lift **PARKING:** 60 **NOTES:** ⊗ in restaurant

Top Hotel

★★ Morston Hall
Morston, Holt NR25 7AA
☎ 01263 741041 🖹 01263 740419
e-mail: reception@morstonhall.com
web: www.morstonhall.com
Dir: *1m W of Blakeney on A149 Kings Lynn/Cromer Rd coastal road*
This delightful 17th-century country-house hotel enjoys a tranquil setting amid well-tended gardens. The comfortable public rooms offer a choice of attractive lounges and a sunny conservatory, while the elegant dining room is a perfect setting to enjoy Galton Blackiston's award-winning cuisine. The spacious bedrooms are individually decorated and stylishly furnished with modern opulence.
ROOMS: 7 en suite (1 GF) s £135-£150; d £220-£260 (incl. bkfst & dinner) LB **PARKING:** 40 **NOTES:** ⊗ in restaurant Closed 1 Jan-2 Feb & 2 days Xmas

★★73% The Pheasant
Coast Rd, Kelling NR25 7EG
☎ 01263 588382 🖹 01263 588101
e-mail: enquiries@pheasanthotelnorfolk.co.uk
Dir: *on A419 coast road, mid-way between Sheringham & Blakeney*
Popular hotel ideally situated on the main road amidst landscaped grounds. Bedrooms are split between the main house and a modern wing of spacious rooms to the rear of the property. Public rooms include a busy lounge bar, a residents' lounge and a large restaurant where a wide-ranging selection of appetising dishes is served.
ROOMS: 30 en suite (1 fmly) (24 GF) ⊗ in all bedrooms s £55-£65; d £90-£100 (incl. bkfst) LB **FACILITIES:** Xmas **CONF:** Thtr 80 Class 50 Board 50 Del from £105 **PARKING:** 80 **NOTES:** ⊗ in restaurant

★★69% Blakeney Manor
The Quay, Blakeney NR25 7ND
☎ 01263 740376 🖷 01263 741116
e-mail: reception@blakeneymanor.co.uk
Dir: *exit A149 at Blakeney towards Blakeney Quay. Hotel at end of quay between Mariner's Hill & Friary Hills*

An attractive Norfolk flint building overlooking Blakeney Marshes and within easy walking distance of the quayside. The bedrooms have been sympathetically converted from flint-faced barns and are located in courtyards adjacent to the main building. The spacious public rooms include a choice of lounges, a conservatory, popular bar and a large restaurant offering an interesting choice of dishes.

ROOMS: 7 en suite 28 annexe en suite (26 GF) s fr £45; d fr £88 (incl. bkfst) **LB** **FACILITIES:** Xmas **PARKING:** 40 **NOTES:** No children 14yrs ⊗ in restaurant

BLANCHLAND, Northumberland
Map 18 NY95

★★70% Lord Crewe Arms
DH8 9SP
☎ 01434 675251 🖷 01434 675337
e-mail: lord@crewearms.freeserve.co.uk
web: www.lordcrewehotel.com
Dir: *10m S of Hexham via B6306*

Adjacent to Blanchland Abbey, many rooms in this historic, hotel date from medieval times. Public areas feature flagstone floors, vaulted ceilings and original inglenook fireplace. Bedrooms, some housed in what was the village's second hotel, are well equipped and retain a period style. Bar meals are popular and there is an elegant restaurant.

ROOMS: 9 en suite 10 annexe en suite (2 fmly) **FACILITIES:** Xmas **CONF:** Thtr 20 Class 16 Board 16 Del £85 **NOTES:** Civ Wed 65

BLANDFORD FORUM, Dorset
Map 04 ST80

★★★71% Crown
West St DT11 7AJ
☎ 01258 456626 🖷 01258 451084
e-mail: thecrownhotel@blandforddorset.freeserve.co.uk
Dir: *100mtrs from town bridge*

Efficient and friendly service is provided at this attractive, former coaching inn. The well-equipped, stylish bedrooms are very comfortable and have been refurbished to a high standard. A choice of menus is offered in the panelled dining room, while in the bar an extensive range of meals is served in a less formal atmosphere.

ROOMS: 32 en suite (2 fmly) ⊗ in 27 bedrooms s £78-£88; d £99 (incl. bkfst) **LB** **FACILITIES:** STV **CONF:** BC Thtr 250 Class 200 Board 60 Del £110 **SERVICES:** Lift **PARKING:** 144 **NOTES:** Closed 25-28 Dec Civ Wed 150

BLETCHINGDON, Oxfordshire
Map 11 SP51

★★★62% The Oxfordshire Inn
Heathfield Village OX5 3DX
☎ 01869 351444 🖷 01869 351555
e-mail: staff@oxfordshireinn.co.uk
web: www.oxfordshireinn.co.uk

Located a short drive from major road networks this newly refurbished property sits in a tranquil rural location. Annexed accommodation varies in size but all is finished to a good decorative standard. Home-cooked meals are available either in the bar or extensive restaurant.

ROOMS: 16 en suite (1 fmly) (8 GF) ⊗ in all bedrooms s £49-£69; d £69-£89 (incl. bkfst) **FACILITIES:** STV **CONF:** BC Thtr 140 Class 80 Board 30 Del from £75 **PARKING:** 50

BLOCKLEY, Gloucestershire
Map 10 SP13

A ★★★ Crown Inn & Hotel
High St GL56 9EX
☎ 01386 700245 🖷 01386 700247
e-mail: info@crown-inn-blockley.co.uk

ROOMS: 22 en suite 2 annexe en suite (7 fmly) (8 GF) s £59.95-£80; d £90-£130 (incl. bkfst) **LB** **FACILITIES:** Xmas **CONF:** Thtr 50 Class 36 Board 20 Del from £115 **PARKING:** 30 **NOTES:** ⊗ in restaurant

BLYTH, Nottinghamshire
Map 16 SK68

★★★70% Charnwood
Sheffield Rd S81 8HF
☎ 01909 591610 🖷 01909 591429
e-mail: charnwood@bestwestern.co.uk
web: www.bw-charnwoodhotel.com
Dir: *A614 into Blyth village, right past church onto A634 Sheffield road. Hotel 0.5m on right past humpback bridge*

A peaceful rural setting, surrounded by attractive views and gardens, this hotel offers a range of carefully prepared meals and

continued on p90

BLYTH, continued

snacks in either the formal restaurant, or the comfortable lounge bar. Bedrooms are comfortably furnished and attractively decorated. Service is friendly and attentive.
ROOMS: 34 en suite (1 fmly) ⊗ in 16 bedrooms s £65-£80; d £77.50-£120 (incl. bkfst) **LB** **FACILITIES:** STV Mini-gym **CONF:** Thtr 135 Class 60 Board 45 Del £110.95 **PARKING:** 70 **NOTES:** ⊗ in restaurant Civ Wed 110

⌂ Travelodge
Hilltop Roundabout S81 8HG
☎ 08700 850 950 📠 01909 591831
web: www.travelodge.co.uk
Dir: *at junct of A1(M)/A614*
Travelodge offers good quality, good value, modern accommodation. Ideal for families, the spacious, en suite bedrooms include remote-control TV, tea and coffee-making facilities and comfortable beds. Meals can be taken at the nearby family restaurant. For further details consult the Hotel Groups page.
ROOMS: 38 en suite s fr £26; d fr £26

BODMIN, Cornwall & Isles of Scilly — Map 02 SX06

★★75% Trehellas House Hotel & Restaurant
Washaway PL30 3AD
☎ 01208 72700 & 74499 📠 01208 73336
e-mail: enquiries@trehellashouse.co.uk
web: www.trehellashouse.co.uk
Dir: *take A389 from Bodmin towards Wadebridge. Hotel on right. 0.5m beyond road to Camelford*
This 18th-century former posting inn retains many original features, with contemporary additions, and offers comfortable accommodation. Bedrooms are located in the main house and adjacent coach house; all provide the same high standards. An interesting choice of cuisine is offered in the impressive slate-floored restaurant, with an emphasis on locally sourced produce.
ROOMS: 4 en suite 7 annexe en suite (2 fmly) (5 GF) ⊗ in all bedrooms s £65-£95; d £90-£170 (incl. bkfst) **LB** **FACILITIES:** **CONF:** Thtr 12 Board 12 Del from £99.50 **PARKING:** 30 **NOTES:** No children 10yrs ⊗ in restaurant Closed 24-31 Dec

★★70% Westberry
Rhind St PL31 2EL
☎ 01208 72772 📠 01208 72212
e-mail: westberry@btconnect.com
web: www.westberryhotel.net
Dir: *on ring road off A30 & A38. St Petroc's Church on right, at mini rdbt turn right. Hotel on right*

This popular hotel is conveniently located for both Bodmin town centre and the A30. Bedrooms, including a four-poster room, are comfortably furnished and well equipped. A spacious bar lounge and a billiard room are also provided, and the restaurant serves a variety of dishes, ranging from bar snacks to a more extensive carte menu.
ROOMS: 12 en suite 8 annexe en suite (1 fmly) (6 GF) ⊗ in 11 bedrooms s £48-£68; d £58-£78 (incl. bkfst) **LB** **FACILITIES:** STV Snooker Gym Full sized snooker table **CONF:** BC Thtr 100 Class 80 Board 80 Del from £80 **PARKING:** 30 **NOTES:** ⊗ in restaurant

⌂ Premier Travel Inn Bodmin
Launceston Rd PL31 2AR
☎ 08701 977107 📠 08701 977705
web: www.premiertravelinn.com
Dir: *1m N of town on A389. From A30 S/bound exit onto A389, Inn 0.5m on right. N/bound exit onto A38, follow A389 signs. At T-junct turn left*
High quality, modern budget accommodation ideal for both families and business travellers. Spacious, en suite bedrooms feature bath and shower, satellite TV and many have telephones and modem points. The adjacent family restaurant features a wide and varied menu. For further details consult the Hotel Groups page.
ROOMS: 44 en suite s £49.95; d £49.95

BOGNOR REGIS, West Sussex — Map 06 SZ99

★★★64% *The Inglenook*
255 Pagham Rd, Nyetimber PO21 3QB
☎ 01243 262495 & 265411 📠 01243 262668
e-mail: reception@the-inglenook.com
Dir: *A27 to Vinnetrow Rd left at Walnut Tree 2.5m on right*

This 16th-century inn retains much of its original character, including exposed beams throughout. Bedrooms are individually decorated and vary in size. There is a cosy lounge, a well-kept garden and a bar (complete with a parrot and two cats) that offers a popular evening menu and convivial atmosphere. The restaurant, overlooking the garden, also serves enjoyable cuisine.
ROOMS: 18 en suite (1 fmly) (2 GF) ⊗ in all bedrooms **FACILITIES:** STV **CONF:** BC Thtr 100 Class 50 Board 50 **PARKING:** 35 **NOTES:** ⊗ in restaurant Civ Wed 80

TV dinner?
Room service at three stars and above

Town House Hotel
Country House Hotel
⌂ Travel Accommodation

★★71% Beachcroft
Clyde Rd, Felpham Village PO22 7AH
☎ 01243 827142 🖹 01243 863500
e-mail: reservations@beachcroft-hotel.co.uk
web: www.beachcroft-hotel.co.uk
Dir: *off A259 at Butlins rdbt into Felpham Village. In 800mtrs right into Sea Rd then 2nd left into Clyde Rd*

This popular family-run hotel overlooks a secluded part of the seafront. Bedrooms are bright and spacious with a good range of facilities; and leisure facilities include a heated indoor swimming pool. Diners may choose from the varied choice of the traditional restaurant menus or the more informal cosy bar.

ROOMS: 35 en suite (4 fmly) (6 GF) s £50-£78; d £60-£106 (incl. bkfst) **LB** **FACILITIES:** STV 🏊 **CONF:** Thtr 60 Class 30 Board 30 Del from £71.50 **PARKING:** 27 **NOTES:** 🐕 ⊗ in restaurant

🅰 ★★ The Royal
The Esplanade PO21 1SZ
☎ 01243 864665 🖹 863175
Dir: *opposite Bognor Pier, 300yds from town centre*

ROOMS: 22 en suite (3 fmly) s £35-£45; d £60-£70 (incl. bkfst) **LB** **FACILITIES:** Xmas **CONF:** Thtr 60 Class 30 Board 30 **SERVICES:** Lift

⌂ Premier Travel Inn Bognor Regis
Shripney Rd PO22 9PA
☎ 0870 9906434 🖹 0870 9906435
web: www.premiertravelinn.com
Dir: *From A27 take Bognor Regis exit at rdbt junct of A29. Continue approx 4m. Inn on left*

High quality, modern budget accommodation ideal for both families and business travellers. Spacious, en suite bedrooms feature bath and shower, satellite TV and many have telephones and modem points. The adjacent family restaurant features a wide and varied menu. For further details consult the Hotel Groups page.

ROOMS: 24 en suite s £51.95; d £51.95 **CONF:** Thtr 80 Class 40 Board 30

BOLTON, Greater Manchester
Map 15 SD70

★★★★71% Last Drop Village Hotel & Spa
The Last Drop Village & Hotel, Bromley Cross BL7 9PZ
☎ 01204 591131 🖹 01204 304122 & 598824
e-mail: lastdrop@macdonald-hotels.co.uk
web: www.macdonald-hotels.co.uk
Dir: *3m N of Bolton off B5472*

Built along the lines of a small self-contained village, this resort complex includes a variety of shops, a pub, a steak house, a bakery and a tearoom. Bedrooms are varied, including cottage-style accommodation set around a delightful courtyard. A dazzling, fully equipped spa and extensive conference facilities make this an ideal business and leisure destination.

ROOMS: 118 en suite 10 annexe en suite (72 fmly) (36 GF) ⊗ in 60 bedrooms s £79-£94; d £98-£128 (incl. bkfst) **LB** **FACILITIES: Spa** STV 🏊 supervised 🎾 Gym Jacuzzi Craft shops, Thermal suite ♫ Xmas **CONF:** Thtr 700 Class 300 Board 95 Del from £125 **SERVICES:** Lift **PARKING:** 400 **NOTES:** ⊗ in restaurant Civ Wed 500

★★★71% Egerton House
Blackburn Rd, Egerton BL7 9SB
☎ 01204 307171 🖹 01204 593030
e-mail: reservation@egertonhouse-hotel.co.uk
web: www.egertonhouse-hotel.co.uk
Dir: *from M61 take A666 (Bolton Rd), pass Asda on right. Hotel 500yds on right*

Peace and relaxation come as standard at this popular hotel, nestling in acres of well-tended woodland gardens. The location offers the best of both worlds, close to the city of Manchester and the natural beauty of the West Pennine Moors. Public rooms and many guest bedrooms enjoy delightful garden views.

ROOMS: 32 en suite (7 fmly) ⊗ in 20 bedrooms s £65-£95; d £80-£98 (incl. bkfst) **FACILITIES:** STV Complimentary use of nearby leisure club Xmas **CONF:** Thtr 150 Class 90 Board 60 Del from £120 **PARKING:** 120 **NOTES:** 🐕 ⊗ in restaurant Civ Wed 200

🅤 Ramada Bolton
Manchester Rd, Blackrod BL6 5RU
☎ 01942 814598 🖹 01942 816026
e-mail: sales.bolton@ramadajarvis.co.uk
web: www.ramadajarvis.co.uk
Dir: *Exit M61 junct 6 and follow signs for Blackrod A6027. After 200yds turn right onto A6 signed Chorley. Hotel is 0.5m on the right.*

This modern hotel enjoys easy access to the M61, M62, M60 and M6. Bedrooms are comfortably appointed for both business and leisure guests.

ROOMS: 91 en suite (6 fmly) (12 GF) ⊗ in 76 bedrooms s £79-£105; d £79-£105 **FACILITIES:** STV 🏊 supervised Sauna Solarium Gym Jacuzzi Xmas **CONF:** Thtr 250 Class 100 Board 40 Del from £140 **SERVICES:** Lift **PARKING:** 300 **NOTES:** ⊗ in restaurant Civ Wed 100

BOLTON, continued

⇧ Premier Travel Inn Bolton

991 Chorley New Rd, Horwich BL6 4BA
☎ 08701 977282 🖷 01204 692585
web: www.premiertravelinn.com
Dir: *M61 junct 6 follow dual carriageway to Bolton/Horwich with Reebok Stadium on left, continue & Inn on the 2nd rdbt*
High quality, modern budget accommodation ideal for both families and business travellers. Spacious, en suite bedrooms feature bath and shower, satellite TV and many have telephones and modem points. The adjacent family restaurant features a wide and varied menu. For further details consult the Hotel Groups page.
ROOMS: 40 en suite s £46.95-£49.95; d £46.95-£49.95

⇧ Travelodge Bolton West

Bolton West Service Area, Horwich BL6 5UZ
☎ 08700 850 950 🖷 01204 668585
web: www.travelodge.co.uk
Dir: *between junct 6 & 7 of M61*
Travelodge offers good quality, good value, modern accommodation. Ideal for families, the spacious, en suite bedrooms include remote-control TV, tea and coffee-making facilities and comfortable beds. Meals can be taken at the nearby family restaurant. For further details consult the Hotel Groups page.
ROOMS: 32 en suite s fr £26; d fr £26 **CONF:** Thtr 60 Class 60 Board 30

BOLTON ABBEY, North Yorkshire Map 19 SE05

Top Hotel

★★★ ®®® The Devonshire Arms Country House

BD23 6AJ
☎ 01756 710441 & 718111 🖷 01756 710564
e-mail: reservations@thedevonshirearms.co.uk
web: www.devonshirehotels.co.uk
Dir: *on B6160, 250yds N of junct with A59*
With stunning views of the Wharfedale countryside, this beautiful hotel, owned by the Duke and Duchess of Devonshire, dates back to the 17th century. Bedrooms are elegantly furnished; those in the old part of the house are particularly spacious, complete with four-posters and fine antiques. The sitting rooms are delightfully cosy with log fires, and dedicated staff deliver service with a blend of friendliness and professionalism. The Burlington Restaurant offers highly accomplished, award-winning cuisine, while the brasserie provides a lighter alternative.
ROOMS: 40 en suite (17 GF) ⊘ in 30 bedrooms s £160-£380; d £220-£380 (incl. bkfst) **LB** **FACILITIES: Spa** STV supervised Fishing Sauna Solarium Gym Putt green Jacuzzi Classic cars, Falconry, Laser pigeon shooting. Xmas **CONF:** BC Thtr 90 Class 80 Board 30 **PARKING:** 150 **NOTES:** ⊘ in restaurant Civ Wed 90

BONCHURCH See Wight, Isle of

BOOTLE, Merseyside Map 15 SJ39

⇧ Premier Travel Inn Liverpool North

Northern Perimiter Rd, Bootle L30 7PT
☎ 08701 977158 🖷 0151 520 1842
web: www.premiertravelinn.com
Dir: *on A5207, off A5036, 0.25m from end of M58/M57*
High quality, modern budget accommodation ideal for both families and business travellers. Spacious, en suite bedrooms feature bath and shower, satellite TV and many have telephones and modem points. The adjacent family restaurant features a wide and varied menu. For further details consult the Hotel Groups page.
ROOMS: 63 en suite s £46.95-£48.95; d £46.95-£48.95 **CONF:** Thtr 50

BOREHAMWOOD, Hertfordshire Map 06 TQ19

⇧ Innkeeper's Lodge Borehamwood

Studio Way WD6 5JY
☎ 020 8905 1455 🖷 020 8236 9822
web: www.innkeeperslodge.com
Dir: *M25 junct 23/A1(M) signed to London. Follow signs to Borehamwood after double rdbt turn into Studio Way*
A growing concept in the travel accommodation market. Smart rooms meet essential business requirements but also have home comforts. Dining options include all-day menus plus the added advantage of breakfast, which is included in the room price. For further details consult the Hotel Groups page.
ROOMS: 55 en suite s £49.95-£62; d £49.95-£62 **CONF:** Thtr 38 Class 20 Board 20

BOROUGHBRIDGE, North Yorkshire Map 19 SE36

★★★69% Crown

Horsefair YO51 9LB
☎ 01423 322328 🖷 01423 324512
e-mail: sales@crownboroughbridge.co.uk
web: www.crownboroughbridge.co.uk
Dir: *A1(M) junct 48. Hotel 1m towards town centre at T-junct*
Situated in the centre of town but convenient for the A1, The Crown provides a full leisure complex, conference rooms and a secure car park. Bedrooms are well appointed. A wide range of well-prepared dishes can be taken in both the restaurant and bar.
ROOMS: 37 en suite (3 fmly) (2 GF) ⊘ in all bedrooms s £75-£95; d £99-£130 (incl. bkfst) **LB** **FACILITIES:** STV supervised Sauna Solarium Gym Jacuzzi Xmas **CONF:** Thtr 150 Class 80 Board 80 Del from £120 **SERVICES:** Lift **PARKING:** 60 **NOTES:** ⊘ in restaurant Civ Wed 120

BORROWDALE, Cumbria Map 18 NY21
See also Keswick & Rosthwaite

★★★76% ® Borrowdale Gates Country House

CA12 5UQ
☎ 017687 77204 🖷 017687 77254
e-mail: hotel@borrowdale-gates.com
web: www.borrowdale-gates.com
Dir: *From A66 follow B5289 for approx 4m. Turn right over bridge, hotel 0.25m beyond village.*
Now under new ownership, this attractive, well-maintained and friendly hotel enjoys an idyllic, peaceful, woodland location in the middle of the Borrowdale Valley. Inviting public rooms include a choice of lounges and a smart restaurant, enjoying stunning views.

continued

Bedrooms come in a variety of styles and sizes, including superior rooms that are particularly thoughtfully equipped.

ROOMS: 29 en suite (10 GF) s £69.50-£107; d £123-£198 (incl. bkfst & dinner) **LB** **FACILITIES:** STV Xmas **NOTES:** No children 12yrs ⊗ in restaurant Closed 3-6 Jan

See advert under KESWICK

★★★70% Borrowdale

CA12 5UY
☎ 017687 77224 77338
e-mail: theborrowdalehotel@yahoo.com
Dir: *3 miles from Keswick, on B5289 at S end of Lake Derwentwater*

Situated in the beautiful Borrowdale Valley overlooking Derwent Water, this traditional hotel has been family-run for over 30 years. Extensive public areas include a choice of lounges, a stylish dining room, and a lounge bar, plus a conservatory. There are a wide variety of bedroom sizes and styles; some rooms are rather spacious, including two at the rear that are particularly suitable for less able guests.

ROOMS: 34 en suite 2 annexe en suite (9 fmly) (2 GF) s £80; d £150-£190 (incl. bkfst & dinner) **LB** **FACILITIES:** Free use of nearby Health Club Xmas **PARKING:** 100 **NOTES:** ⊗ in restaurant

★★★70% *Leathes Head*

CA12 5UY
☎ 017687 77247 017687 77363
e-mail: enq@leatheshead.co.uk
Dir: *3.5m out of Keswick on Borrowdale Rd (B5289) hotel on left 0.25m before Grange Bridge.*

Located within well-tended gardens in the picturesque Borrowdale Valley, this personally run hotel offers a haven of calm and tranquillity. There are three comfortable lounge areas and an elegant restaurant serving interesting meals. The well appointed bedrooms are mostly spacious with many enjoying splendid views of towering fells and rolling countryside.

ROOMS: 12 en suite (2 fmly) (3 GF) ⊗ in all bedrooms **PARKING:** 16 **NOTES:** No children 9yrs ⊗ in restaurant Closed mid Nov-Xmas & 3 Jan-mid Feb

★★★70% Lodore Falls Hotel

CA12 5UX
☎ 017687 77285 017687 77343
e-mail: info@lodorefallshotel.co.uk
Dir: *M6 junct 40 take A66 to Keswick, then B5289 to Borrowdale. Hotel on left*

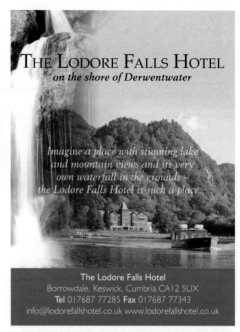

This impressive hotel has an enviable location overlooking Derwentwater. Bedrooms are comfortably equipped and are presently being upgraded; the finished rooms are tastefully styled, many with lake views or views to the fells. The dining room, bar and lounge areas are all very comfortable, a choice of indoor and outdoor leisure facilities are available.

ROOMS: 71 en suite (11 fmly) ⊗ in 14 bedrooms s £67-£99; d £122-£164 (incl. bkfst) **LB** **FACILITIES:** **Spa** STV supervised supervised Fishing Squash Sauna Solarium Gym Xmas **CONF:** Thtr 200 Class 90 Board 45 Del from £120 **SERVICES:** Lift **PARKING:** 91 **NOTES:** ⊗ in restaurant Civ Wed 130

See advert on this page

BORROWDALE, continued

★70% Royal Oak
CA12 5XB
☎ 017687 77214 📠 017687 77214
e-mail: info@royaloakhotel.co.uk
web: www.royaloakhotel.co.uk
Dir: *6m S of Keswick on B5289 in centre of Rosthwaite*
Set in a village in one of Lakeland's most picturesque valleys, this family-run hotel offers friendly and obliging service. There is a variety of accommodation styles, with particularly impressive rooms being located in a converted barn across the courtyard and backed by a stream. Family rooms are available. The cosy bar is for residents and diners only. A set home-cooked dinner is served at 7pm.
ROOMS: 11 rms (8 en suite) 4 annexe en suite (6 fmly) s £35-£58; d £72-£104 (incl. breakfast & dinner) **LB** **FACILITIES:** no TV in bdrms **PARKING:** 15 **NOTES:** ⊗ in restaurant Closed 5-19 Jan & 7-27 Dec

BOSCASTLE, Cornwall & Isles of Scilly Map 02 SX09

★★73% ⊚ The Bottreaux Hotel and Restaurant
PL35 0BG
☎ 01840 250231 📠 01840 250170
e-mail: info@boscastlecornwall.co.uk
web: www.boscastlecornwall.co.uk
Built some 200 years ago, this hotel is just a short walk from the picturesque harbour. Refurbishment has resulted in a stylish establishment where guests are genuinely welcomed. Bedrooms are light and airy, the doubles featuring wonderful 6ft, teak beds. The bar is a convivial venue for a drink and perusal of the imaginative menu, which makes good use of local produce.
ROOMS: 9 en suite ⊗ in all bedrooms s £50-£75; d £65-£90 (incl. dinner) **LB** **FACILITIES:** Xmas **PARKING:** 10 **NOTES:** ✗ No children 10yrs ⊗ in restaurant

★★68% The Wellington Hotel
The Harbour PL35 0AQ
☎ 01840 250202 📠 01840 250621
e-mail: info@boscastle-wellington.com
web: www.boscastle-wellington.com
Dir: *A30/A395, right at Davidstow, signed to Boscastle*
Affectionately known as 'The Welly', this 16th-century coaching inn has an abundance of charm and character. The Long Bar is a popular watering hole for both visitors and locals alike. Bedrooms come in varying sizes, including the spacious Tower rooms; all are comfy and suitably equipped. There is a bar menu and, in the restaurant, a daily-changing carte.
ROOMS: 15 en suite (1 fmly) s £38-£45; d £76-£90 (incl. bkfst) **LB** **FACILITIES:** ♫ Xmas **CONF:** Thtr 20 Class 6 Board 24 Del from £80 **PARKING:** 20 **NOTES:** ✗ ⊗ in restaurant

BOSHAM, West Sussex Map 05 SU80

★★★76% ⊚ The Millstream
Bosham Ln PO18 8HL
☎ 01243 573234 📠 01243 573459
e-mail: info@millstream-hotel.co.uk
Dir: *4m W of Chichester on A259, left at Bosham rdbt. After 1m right at T-junct signed to church & quay. Hotel 0.5m on right*
Lying in the idyllic village of Bosham, this attractive hotel provides comfortable, well-equipped and tastefully decorated bedrooms. Many guests regularly return here for the relaxed atmosphere created by the notably efficient and friendly staff. Public rooms include a cocktail bar, opening out onto the garden, and a pleasant restaurant where varied and freshly prepared cuisine can be enjoyed.

ROOMS: 33 en suite 2 annexe en suite (2 fmly) (9 GF) ⊗ in all bedrooms s £85-£95; d £135-£155 (incl. bkfst) **LB** **FACILITIES:** Bridge breaks ♫ Xmas **CONF:** Thtr 45 Class 20 Board 20 Del from £99 **PARKING:** 44 **NOTES:** ✗ ⊗ in restaurant Civ Wed 92

See advert under CHICHESTER

BOSTON, Lincolnshire Map 12 TF34

⌂ Premier Travel Inn Boston
Wainfleet Rd PE21 9RW
☎ 08701 977035 📠 01205 310908
web: www.premiertravelinn.com
Dir: *A52, 300yds E of junct with A16 Boston/Grimsby road. (Nearest landmark is Pilgrim Hospital)*
High quality, modern budget accommodation ideal for both families and business travellers. Spacious, en suite bedrooms feature bath and shower, satellite TV and many have telephones and modem points. The adjacent family restaurant features a wide and varied menu. For further details consult the Hotel Groups page.
ROOMS: 34 en suite s £48.95-£49.95; d £48.95-£49.95 **CONF:** Thtr 12 Board 8

BOTLEY, Hampshire Map 05 SU51

★★★★69%
Botley Park Hotel Golf & Country Club
Winchester Rd, Boorley Green SO32 2UA
☎ 01489 780888 📠 01489 789242
e-mail: botleypark@macdonald-hotels.co.uk
web: www.macdonald-hotels.co.uk
Dir: *A334 towards Botley, left at 1st rdbt past M&S, continue over next 4 mini-rdbts, at 3rd rdbt follow hotel signs*

This modern and spacious hotel sits peacefully in the midst of its own 176 acres parkland golf course. Bedrooms are comfortably appointed with a good range of extras and an extensive range of

continued

leisure facilities is on offer. Attractive public areas include a relaxing restaurant and the more informal Swing and Divot Bar.
ROOMS: 100 en suite (34 GF) ⊘ in 52 bedrooms **FACILITIES:** STV 18 Squash Sauna Solarium Gym Jacuzzi Aerobics studio, Beauty salon, Golf driving range ch fac **CONF:** Thtr 240 Class 100 Board 60 **PARKING:** 250 **NOTES:** ⊘ in restaurant Civ Wed 200

BOURNEMOUTH, Dorset Map 05 SZ19
See also Christchurch & Ferndown

★★★★75%
Bournemouth Highcliff Marriott
St Michaels Rd, West Cliff BH2 5DU
☎ 01202 557702 01202 292734
e-mail: reservations.bournemouth@marriotthotels.co.uk
web: www.marriott.co.uk
Dir: *A338 through Bournemouth. Follow BIC signs to West Cliff Rd. 2nd right into St Michaels Rd. Hotel at end of road on left*
Originally built as a row of coastguard cottages, this establishment has expanded over the years into a very elegant and charming hotel. Impeccably maintained throughout, many of the bedrooms have sea views. An excellent range of leisure, business and conference facilities are offered, as well as private dining and banqueting rooms. The hotel also has direct access to the Bournemouth International Centre.
ROOMS: 141 en suite 19 annexe en suite (26 fmly) ⊘ in 65 bedrooms s £110-£150; d £125-£165 (incl. bkfst) **LB FACILITIES:** STV Sauna Solarium Gym Putt green Jacuzzi Beautician **CONF:** Thtr 350 Class 180 Board 90 **SERVICES:** Lift air con **PARKING:** 80 **NOTES:** ⊘ in restaurant Civ Wed 250

★★★★74% Menzies East Cliff Court
East Overcliff Dr BH1 3AN
☎ 01202 554545 01202 557456
e-mail: eastcliff@menzies-hotels.co.uk
web: www.menzies-hotels.co.uk
Dir: *From M3/M27 approach Bournemouth on A338 (leads onto Wessex Way), follow signs to East Cliff, hotel on seafront*
Enjoying panoramic views across the bay, extensive refurbishment at this popular hotel has had impressive results. Bedrooms, modern and contemporary in style, have been appointed to a very high standard, with many benefiting from balconies and sea views. Stylish public areas include a range of inviting lounges, a spacious restaurant and a selection of conference rooms.
ROOMS: 67 en suite (10 fmly) s £120; d £140 (incl. bkfst) **LB FACILITIES:** STV Leisure facilities at nearby hotel Xmas **CONF:** Thtr 200 Class 40 Board 45 Del £160 **SERVICES:** Lift **PARKING:** 70 **NOTES:** ⊘ in restaurant Civ Wed

★★★★72% *De Vere Royal Bath*
Bath Rd BH1 2EW
☎ 01202 555555 01202 554158
e-mail: royalbath@devere-hotels.com
web: www.devereonline.co.uk
Dir: *A338 follow signs for pier & beaches. Hotel on Bath Rd just before Lansdowne rdbt and Pier*
Overlooking the bay, this well-established seafront hotel is surrounded by beautifully kept gardens. Public rooms, which include lounges, a choice of restaurants and indoor leisure facilities, are of a scale and style befitting the golden era in which the hotel was built. Local attractions include the motor museum at Beaulieu and the Oceanarium. Valet parking is provided for a small charge.

ROOMS: 140 en suite (16 fmly) (5 GF) **FACILITIES: Spa** STV supervised Sauna Solarium Gym Jacuzzi Beauty salon, Hairdressing **CONF:** Thtr 400 Class 220 Board 100 **SERVICES:** Lift **PARKING:** 70 **NOTES:** ⊘ in restaurant Civ Wed 200

★★★★70% Menzies Carlton
East Overcliff BH1 3DN
☎ 01202 552011 01202 299573
e-mail: carlton@menzies-hotels.co.uk
web: www.menzies-hotels.co.uk
Dir: *From M3/M27, approach Bournemouth on A338 (leads on to Wessex Way), follow signs to the East Cliff, hotel on seafront*
Enjoying a prime location on the East Cliff, and with views of the Isle of Wight and Dorset coastline, the Carlton has attractive gardens and pool area. Conference and banqueting facilities are varied. Most of the spacious bedrooms enjoy sea views and all are well equipped. Guests can enjoy an interesting range of carefully prepared dishes in Fredericks restaurant.
ROOMS: 73 en suite ⊘ in 20 bedrooms s £135; d £160 (incl. bkfst) **LB FACILITIES:** STV Sauna Solarium Gym Jacuzzi Spa pool Xmas **CONF:** Thtr 140 Class 90 Board 45 Del £160 **SERVICES:** Lift **PARKING:** 90 **NOTES:** ⊘ in restaurant Civ Wed

★★★76% Chine
Boscombe Spa Rd BH5 1AX
☎ 01202 396234 01202 391737
e-mail: reservations@chinehotel.co.uk
web: www.chinehotel.co.uk
Dir: *Follow BIC signs, A338/Wessex Way to St Pauls rdbt. 1st exit - St Pauls Rd to next rdbt, 2nd exit signed Eastcliff/Boscombe/Southbourne. Next rdbt, 1st exit into Christchurch Rd. After 2nd lights, right into Boscombe Spa Rd*

Benefiting from superb views this popular hotel is set in delightful gardens with private access to the seafront and beach. The excellent range of facilities includes an indoor and outdoor pool, a small leisure centre and a selection of meeting rooms. The

continued on p96

BOURNEMOUTH, continued

spacious bedrooms, some with balconies, are well appointed and thoughtfully equipped.
ROOMS: 65 en suite 22 annexe en suite (13 fmly) ⊗ in 14 bedrooms s £75-£95; d £150-£190 (incl. bkfst) **LB FACILITIES: Spa** STV ☒ supervised ⚓ supervised Sauna Solarium Gym ♫ Putt green Jacuzzi Games room, Outdoor & indoor childrens play area ch fac Xmas
CONF: Thtr 140 Class 70 Board 40 Del from £125 **SERVICES:** Lift
PARKING: 50 **NOTES:** ✗ ⊗ in restaurant Civ Wed 120

See advert under POOLE and on opposite page

★★★74% ⊛ *Langtry Manor - Lovenest of a King*
Derby Rd, East Cliff BH1 3QB
☎ 01202 553887 ◳ 01202 290115
e-mail: lillie@langtrymanor.com
web: www.langtrymanor.co.uk
Dir: *A31/A338, 1st rdbt by rail station turn left. Over next rdbt, 1st left into Knyveton Rd. Hotel opposite*

Retaining a stately air, this property was originally built in 1877 by Edward VII for his mistress Lillie Langtry. The individually furnished and decorated bedrooms include several with four-poster beds. Enjoyable cuisine is served in the magnificent dining hall, complete with several large Tudor tapestries. There is an Edwardian banquet on Saturday evenings.
ROOMS: 12 en suite 8 annexe en suite (2 fmly) (3 GF) ⊗ in 4 bedrooms
FACILITIES: STV Free use of local health club ♫ **CONF:** Thtr 100 Class 60 Board 40 **PARKING:** 30 **NOTES:** ⊗ in restaurant Civ Wed 100

★★★73% Elstead
Knyveton Rd BH1 3QP
☎ 01202 293071 ◳ 01202 293827
e-mail: info@the-elstead.co.uk
web: www.the-elstead.co.uk
Dir: *A338 Wessex Way to St Pauls rdbt, left & left again*
Ideal as a base for both business and leisure travellers, this popular hotel is conveniently located for the town centre, seafront and BIC. An impressive range of facilities is offered, including meeting rooms, an indoor leisure centre and comfortable lounges. Most bedrooms have been refurbished to a high standard.
ROOMS: 50 en suite (15 fmly) ⊗ in 30 bedrooms s £59.50-£76.50; d £97-£127 (incl. bkfst) **LB FACILITIES: Spa** STV ☒ supervised Snooker Sauna Gym Steam room, Pool Table, Xmas **CONF:** BC Thtr 80 Class 60 Board 40 Del from £85 **SERVICES:** Lift **PARKING:** 40
NOTES: ⊗ in restaurant

CLASSIC BRITISH

★★★73% Hermitage
Exeter Rd BH2 5AH
☎ 01202 557363 ◳ 01202 559173
e-mail: info@hermitage-hotel.co.uk
Dir: *A338 Ringwood, left at St. Pauls rdbt, follow signs for BIC and pier. Across bridge, hotel entrance on right*
Occupying an impressive position overlooking the seafront, at the

continued

heart of Bournemouth's town centre, the Hermitage offers friendly and attentive service. The majority of the smart bedrooms are comfortably appointed and all are very well equipped; many rooms have sea views. The wood-panelled lounge provides an elegant and tranquil area, as does the restaurant where well-prepared and interesting dishes are served.
ROOMS: 63 en suite 11 annexe en suite (9 fmly) (7 GF) ⊗ in 65 bedrooms s £54-£105; d £108-£140 (incl. bkfst) **LB FACILITIES:** Xmas
CONF: Thtr 180 Class 60 Board 60 **SERVICES:** Lift **PARKING:** 58
NOTES: ✗ ⊗ in restaurant

★★★72% *Durley Hall*
Durley Chine Rd, West Cliff BH2 5JS
☎ 01202 751000 ◳ 01202 757585
e-mail: Sales@durleyhall.co.uk
web: www.durleyhall.co.uk
Dir: *A338 follow signs to West Cliff & BIC*
This attractive, conveniently situated hotel offers a friendly atmosphere and attentive service. In addition to a diverse range of business and conference facilities, guests have access to extensive leisure, beauty and therapy treatments. The smart bedrooms are well designed, comfortable and suited to business and leisure guests alike. A candlelit dinner dance is normally held on Saturdays.
ROOMS: 66 en suite 11 annexe en suite (27 fmly) **FACILITIES: Spa** STV ☒ Sauna Solarium Gym Jacuzzi Beauty therapist Table tennis Hydro Therapy, aromatherapy ♫ **CONF:** Thtr 200 Class 80 Board 35 **SERVICES:** Lift **PARKING:** 150 **NOTES:** ✗ ⊗ in restaurant Civ Wed

★★★72% The Riviera
Burnaby Rd, Alum Chine BH4 8JF
☎ 01202 763653 ◳ 01202 768422
e-mail: info@rivierabournemouth.co.uk
web: www.rivierabournemouth.co.uk
Dir: *A338, follow signs to Alum Chine*
Part of the Calotels group, this hotel offers a range of comfortable, well-furnished bedrooms and bathrooms. Welcoming staff provide efficient service delivered in a friendly manner. In addition to a spacious lounge with regular entertainment, there is an indoor and an outdoor pool.
ROOMS: 69 en suite 4 annexe en suite (25 fmly) (11 GF) s £35-£65; d £70-£150 (incl. bkfst) **LB FACILITIES:** ☒ ⚓ Sauna Jacuzzi Games room ♫ Xmas **CONF:** Thtr 180 Class 120 Board 50 Del from £65 **SERVICES:** Lift **PARKING:** 45 **NOTES:** ⊗ in restaurant Civ Wed 100

★★★71% The Connaught
West Hill Rd, West Cliff BH2 5PH
☎ 01202 298020 ◳ 01202 298028
e-mail: sales@theconnaught.co.uk
web: www.theconnaught.co.uk
Dir: *follow Town Centre West & BIC signs*
Conveniently located on the West Cliff, close to the BIC, beaches and town centre, this privately-owned hotel offers well equipped, neatly decorated rooms, some with balconies. The hotel boasts a very well equipped leisure complex with a large pool and snooker table and gym. Breakfast and dinner offer imaginative dishes made with quality local ingredients.
ROOMS: 56 en suite (13 fmly) ⊗ in 21 bedrooms s £44-£68; d £88-£158 (incl. bkfst) **LB FACILITIES: Spa** STV ☒ supervised ⚓ supervised Sauna Solarium Gym Jacuzzi Cardio-vascular suite, Pool table, Beauty therapy salon, Hairdresser Xmas **CONF:** Thtr 200 Class 40 Board 60 Del from £85 **SERVICES:** Lift **PARKING:** 45 **NOTES:** ⊗ in restaurant

Best Western

See advert on opposite page

⊗ No smoking

★★★71% *Hotel Miramar*

East Overcliff Dr, East Cliff BH1 3AL
☎ 01202 556581 ▤ 01202 291242
e-mail: sales@miramar-bournemouth.com
web: www.miramar-bournemouth.com
Dir: *Wessex Way rdbt turn into St Pauls Rd, right at next rdbt. 3rd exit at next rdbt, 2nd exit at next rdbt into Grove Rd. Hotel car park on right*
Conveniently located on the East Cliff, this Edwardian hotel enjoys glorious sea views. The Miramar was a favoured destination of Tolkien, who often stayed here. Friendly staff and a relaxing environment are keynotes, and the bedrooms are comfortable and well equipped. Spacious public areas and a choice of lounges complete the experience.
ROOMS: 43 en suite (6 fmly) ⊗ in 10 bedrooms **FACILITIES:** STV ♫ **CONF:** Thtr 200 Class 50 Board 50 **SERVICES:** Lift **PARKING:** 80 **NOTES:** ⊗ in restaurant Civ Wed 110

B

BOURNEMOUTH, continued

★★★71% Piccadilly
25 Bath Rd BH1 2NN
☎ 01202 552559 & 298024 ▤ 01202 298235
e-mail: enquiries@hotelpiccadilly.co.uk
Dir: *From A338 take 1st exit rdbt, signed East Cliff. 3rd exit at next rdbt signed Lansdowne, 3rd exit at next rdbt into Bath Rd*

This hotel, under new ownership, offers a friendly welcome to guests, many of whom return on a regular basis, particularly for the superb ballroom dancing facilities and short breaks. Bedrooms are smartly decorated, well maintained and comfortable. Dining in the attractive restaurant is always popular and dishes are freshly prepared and appetising.
ROOMS: 45 en suite (2 fmly) (5 GF) s £65-£75; d £95-£110 (incl. bkfst) **LB** **FACILITIES:** Xmas **SERVICES:** Lift **PARKING:** 35 **NOTES:** ✈ ⊗ in restaurant

★★★71% Suncliff
29 East Overcliff Dr BH1 3AG
☎ 01202 291711 ▤ 01202 293788
e-mail: info@suncliffbournemouth.co.uk
web: www.suncliffbournemouth.co.uk
Dir: *A338 to B'mouth. 1st left at rdbt into St Pauls Rd, follow signs East Cliff*
Enjoying splendid views from the East Cliff and catering mainly for leisure guests, this friendly hotel provides a range of facilities and services. The Bedrooms are well equipped and comfortable, and many have sea views. Public areas include a large conservatory, an attractive bar and pleasant lounges.
ROOMS: 94 en suite (29 fmly) (13 GF) s £40-£80; d £80-£160 (incl. bkfst) **LB** **FACILITIES:** ⛆ Squash Snooker Sauna Solarium Gym Jacuzzi Table tennis ♫ Xmas **CONF:** Thtr 100 Class 70 Board 60 Del from £65 **SERVICES:** Lift **PARKING:** 60 **NOTES:** ⊗ in restaurant Civ Wed 100

★★★71% Wessex
West Cliff Rd BH2 5EU
☎ 01202 551911 ▤ 01202 297354
e-mail: wessex@forestdale.com
web: www.forestdale.com
Dir: *Follow M27/A35 or A338 from Dorchester & A347 N*
Centrally located and handy for the beach, the Wessex is a popular, relaxing hotel. Bedrooms vary in size and include premier rooms; all are comfortable, and equipped with a range of modern amenities. There are excellent leisure facilities, ample function rooms and an open-plan bar and lounge.
ROOMS: 109 en suite (22 fmly) ⊗ in 3 bedrooms s £75-£95; d £120-£150 (incl. bkfst) **LB** **FACILITIES:** STV ⛆ ⛆ Snooker Sauna Solarium Gym Table tennis Xmas **CONF:** Thtr 400 Class 160 Board 160 Del from £125 **SERVICES:** Lift **PARKING:** 160 **NOTES:** ⊗ in restaurant Civ Wed 100

★★★70% Anglo Swiss
16 Gervis Rd BH1 3EQ
☎ 01202 554794 ▤ 01202 299615
e-mail: reservations@angloswisshotel.com
Dir: *M27 junct 1, A31 onto A338 to Bournemouth follow signs for East Cliff and seafront. Over 2 rdbts into Gervis Rd, Hotel on right*

Located on the East Cliff, just a short walk from the seafront and local shops and amenities, this privately owned hotel has benefited from a ground floor refurbishment. Public areas are now contemporary in style and facilities include a small health club and spacious function rooms. Bedrooms are comfortable.
ROOMS: 56 en suite 8 annexe en suite (22 fmly) (8 GF) ⊗ in 27 bedrooms s £50-£65; d £75-£125 (incl. bkfst) **LB** **FACILITIES:** STV ⛆ supervised Sauna Gym Jacuzzi Xmas **CONF:** Thtr 100 Class 60 Board 40 Del from £90 **SERVICES:** Lift **PARKING:** 80 **NOTES:** ⊗ in restaurant Civ Wed 120

★★★70% East Anglia
6 Poole Rd BH2 5QX
☎ 01202 765163 ▤ 01202 752949
e-mail: info@eastangliahotel.com
web: www.eastangliahotel.com
Dir: *A338 at Bournemouth West rdbt. Follow signs for BIC & West Cliff. At next rdbt right into Poole Rd. Hotel on right*
This privately owned and well-managed hotel provides modern accommodation, including ground-floor bedrooms. The friendly team of staff offers a warm welcome and attentive service. Public areas include a number of function and conference rooms, ample lounges and an air-conditioned restaurant. There is also an outdoor swimming pool.
ROOMS: 45 en suite 25 annexe en suite (18 fmly) (10 GF) ⊗ in 23 bedrooms s £57-£61; d £114-£122 (incl. bkfst) **LB** **FACILITIES: Spa** STV ⛆ Sauna American Pool Room Xmas **CONF:** Thtr 150 Class 75 Board 60 Del from £75 **SERVICES:** Lift **PARKING:** 70 **NOTES:** ✈ ⊗ in restaurant

★★★70% The Montague Hotel
Durley Rd South, West Cliff BH2 5JH
☎ 01202 551074 ▤ 01202 553948
e-mail: enquiries@montaguehotel.co.uk
web: www.montaguehotel.co.uk
Dir: *A31/A338 to Bournemouth turn left into Cambridge Rd at Bournemouth West rdbt, take 2nd exit at next rdbt into Durley Chine Rd. Next rdbt take 2nd exit. Hotel on right*
With its convenient location a short walk from the attractions of the town centre and beaches, this hotel has a busy leisure trade, especially at weekends. The well-equipped bedrooms are especially attractive having now been refurbished. Guests can unwind on the terrace or in the relaxing bar. Dinner features appetising dishes made with fresh local produce.
ROOMS: 32 en suite (9 fmly) (10 GF) ⊗ in 6 bedrooms s £33-£45; d £56-£130 (incl. bkfst) **LB** **FACILITIES:** STV ⛆ supervised Xmas **CONF:** Thtr 60 Class 12 Board 30 Del £70 **SERVICES:** Lift **PARKING:** 50 **NOTES:** ✈ ⊗ in restaurant

★★★69% Carrington House

31 Knyveton Rd BH1 3QQ
☎ 01202 369988 📠 01202 292221
e-mail: carrington.house@forestdale.com
web: www.forestdale.com
Dir: *A338 at St Paul's rdbt, continue 200mtrs & turn left into Knyveton Rd. Hotel 400mtrs on right*
This hotel occupies a prominent position on a tree-lined avenue and is a short walk from the seafront. Bedrooms are generally spacious, comfortable and usefully equipped. In addition to the hotel's bar and restaurant there are extensive conference facilities and a leisure complex.
ROOMS: 145 en suite (42 fmly) ⊗ in 40 bedrooms s £75-£95; d £120-£140 (incl. bkfst) **FACILITIES:** STV Snooker Gym Purpose built children s play area Xmas **CONF:** Thtr 500 Class 260 Board 80 Del from £125 **SERVICES:** Lift **PARKING:** 100 **NOTES:** ⊗ in restaurant

★★★69% *Hotel Collingwood*

11 Priory Rd, West Cliff BH2 5DF
☎ 01202 557575 📠 01202 293219
e-mail: info@hotel-collingwood.co.uk
web: www.hotel-collingwood.co.uk
Dir: *A338 left at West Cliff sign, over 1st rdbt and left at 2nd rdbt. Hotel 500yds on left*
This privately owned and managed hotel is situated close to the BIC. Bedrooms are airy, with the emphasis on comfort. An excellent range of leisure facilities is available and the public areas are spacious and welcoming. Pinks Restaurant offers carefully prepared cuisine and a fixed-price, five-course dinner.
ROOMS: 53 en suite (16 fmly) (6 GF) ⊗ in 6 bedrooms
FACILITIES: STV Snooker Sauna Solarium Gym Jacuzzi Mini gym, Steam room, Games room ♫ **SERVICES:** Lift **PARKING:** 55 **NOTES:** ⊗ in restaurant Closed First 2 weeks of Jan.

★★★69% Royal Exeter

Exeter Rd BH2 5AG
☎ 01202 438000 📠 01202 297963
e-mail: enquiries@royalexeterhotel.com
web: www.royalexeterhotel.com
Dir: *opposite Bournemouth International Centre*

Ideally located opposite the Bournemouth International Centre, and convenient for the beach and town centre, this busy hotel caters for both business and leisure guests. New and extensive refurbishment of the public areas has resulted in a smart, modern and open-plan lounge bar and restaurant together with an exciting adjoining bar complex.
ROOMS: 54 en suite (13 fmly) s £45-£90; d £80-£150 (incl. bkfst) **LB**
FACILITIES: Spa STV Sauna Gym Xmas **CONF:** Thtr 100 Class 40 Board 40 Del from £82 **SERVICES:** Lift **PARKING:** 50 **NOTES:** 🚫

★★★68% Cliffeside

East Overcliff Dr BH1 3AQ
☎ 01202 555724 📠 01202 314534
e-mail: cliffeside@bluemermaidhotels.com
Dir: *M27/A338 approx 7m, then 1st rdbt left into East Cliff*
Benefiting from an elevated position on the seafront and just a short walk to town, it's no wonder that this friendly hotel has many returning guests. Bedrooms and public areas are attractively appointed, many with sea views. The newly refurbished Atlantic Restaurant offers guests a fixed-price menu.
ROOMS: 62 en suite (10 fmly) s £39-£69; d £69-£99 (incl. bkfst) **LB**
FACILITIES: Table tennis Xmas **CONF:** Thtr 180 Class 140 Board 60 Del from £75 **SERVICES:** Lift **PARKING:** 45 **NOTES:** ⊗ in restaurant

★★★68% Marsham Court

Russell Cotes Rd, East Cliff BH1 3AB
☎ 01202 552111 📠 01202 294744
e-mail: reservations@marshamcourt.com
web: www.marshamcourt.com
Dir: *From Wessex Way take Bournemouth East exit at St Pauls rdbt. Over station rdbt. Follow ringroad, over St Swithuns rdbt. Left with church on left over Meyrick rdbt. Left at St Peters rdbt. Hotel on left*

This hotel is set in attractive gardens with splendid views over the sea and town, and is very accessible and convenient for the town and BIC. Bedrooms vary in size, are comfortably appointed and some have sea views. There is a well-stocked bar, lounge areas, terrace and pool, as well as impressive conference rooms.
ROOMS: 87 en suite (15 fmly) ⊗ in all bedrooms s £59-£89; d £98-£118 (incl. bkfst) **LB** **FACILITIES:** STV Pool table Xmas
CONF: Thtr 200 Class 100 Board 80 Del from £89 **SERVICES:** Lift
PARKING: 100 **NOTES:** 🚫 ⊗ in restaurant Civ Wed 200

★★★68% Queens

Meyrick Rd, East Cliff BH1 3DL
☎ 01202 554415 📠 01202 294810
e-mail: queens@bluemermaidhotels.com
Dir: *A338 St Paul's rdbt take Holdenhurst Rd. 2nd exit at Lansdown rdbt onto Meyrick Rd*
This attractive hotel enjoys a good location near the seafront and is popular for conferences and functions. Public areas include a bar, lounge and a large restaurant. Leisure facilities include indoor pool and small gym. Bedrooms vary in size and style, many have sea views.
ROOMS: 109 en suite (15 fmly) ⊗ in 40 bedrooms s £67-£85; d £99-£125 (incl. bkfst) **LB** **FACILITIES: Spa** Snooker Sauna Solarium Gym Jacuzzi Beauty salon, Games Room, Snooker table ♫ Xmas **CONF:** Thtr 220 Class 120 Board 50 Del from £82.50
SERVICES: Lift **PARKING:** 80 **NOTES:** ⊗ in restaurant

BOURNEMOUTH, continued

★★★67% *Belvedere*

Bath Rd BH1 2EU
☎ 01202 297556 & 293336 🖷 01202 294699
e-mail: enquiries@belvedere-hotel.co.uk
web: www.belvedere-hotel.co.uk
Dir: *from A338 with railway station and Asda on left. At rdbt 1st left then 3rd exit at next 2 rdbts. Hotel on Bath Hill after 4th rdbt*

Close to the town centre and the seafront, this friendly, family-run hotel offers spacious public areas and comfortable bedrooms. The lively bar and attractive restaurant are both popular with locals, and there are meeting rooms which provide an ideal location for conferences or functions.

ROOMS: 100 en suite (20 fmly) **FACILITIES: Spa** STV Sauna Solarium Gym Jacuzzi ♫ **CONF:** Thtr 120 Class 60 Board 50 **SERVICES:** Lift **PARKING:** 90 **NOTES:** in restaurant

★★★67% Heathlands Hotel

12 Grove Rd, East Cliff BH1 3AY
☎ 01202 553336 🖷 01202 555937
e-mail: info@heathlandshotel.com
web: www.heathlandshotel.com
Dir: *A338 St Pauls rdbt 1st exit to East Cliff, 3rd exit at next rdbt to Holdenhurst Rd, 2nd exit off Lansdowne rdbt into Meyrick Rd. Left into Gervis Rd. Hotel on right*

This is a large hotel on the East Cliff that is popular with many groups and for conferences. The public areas are bright and spacious. There is a coffee shop, open all day, a leisure centre and regular live entertainment is provided for guests.

ROOMS: 115 en suite (16 fmly) (11 GF) in 15 bedrooms s £49-£63; d £98-£146 (incl. bkfst) **LB** **FACILITIES:** STV Sauna Gym Jacuzzi Health suite ♫ Xmas **CONF:** Thtr 270 Class 102 Board 54 Del from £80 **SERVICES:** Lift **PARKING:** 100 **NOTES:** in restaurant Civ Wed 90

★★★67% Trouville

Priory Rd BH2 5DH
☎ 01202 552262 🖷 01202 293324
e-mail: trouville@bluemermaidhotels.com
Dir: *A338 onto A35, follow signs for BIC*

Located near Bournemouth International Centre, the seafront and shops, the hotel has the advantage of indoor leisure facilities and a large car park. Bedrooms are generally a good size with comfortable furnishings; there are plenty of family rooms here. The air-conditioned restaurant offers a daily changing menu.

ROOMS: 77 en suite (21 fmly) s £59-£89; d £84-£129 (incl. bkfst) **LB** **FACILITIES:** Sauna Solarium Gym Jacuzzi ♫ Xmas **CONF:** Thtr 100 Class 45 Board 50 Del from £79 **SERVICES:** Lift **PARKING:** 55 **NOTES:** in restaurant

★★★66% Bay View Court

35 East Overcliff Dr BH1 3AH
☎ 01202 294449 🖷 01202 292883
e-mail: enquiry@bayviewcourt.co.uk
Dir: *on A338 left at St Pauls rdbt. Over St Swithuns rdbt. Bear left onto Manor Rd, 1st right, next right*

This relaxed and friendly hotel enjoys far-reaching sea views from many of the public areas and bedrooms. Bedrooms vary in size and are attractively furnished. There is a choice of south facing lounges and, for the more energetic, an indoor swimming pool. Live entertainment is provided during the evenings.

ROOMS: 64 en suite (11 fmly) (5 GF) s £49-£62; d £98-£124 (incl. bkfst & dinner) **LB** **FACILITIES: Spa** STV Snooker Jacuzzi Steam room ♫ Xmas **CONF:** Thtr 170 Class 85 Board 50 Del from £50 **SERVICES:** Lift **PARKING:** 58 **NOTES:** in restaurant

★★★66% Hinton Firs

Manor Rd, East Cliff BH1 3ET
☎ 01202 555409 🖷 01202 299607
e-mail: reservations@hintonfirshotel.co.uk
Dir: *A338 turn W at St Paul's rdbt, over next 2 rdbts then fork left to side of church. Hotel on next corner*

This hotel is conveniently located on East Cliff, just a short stroll from the sea. Guests are offered leisure facilities including indoor pool and sauna. There is also a spacious lounge, bar and restaurant in which to relax. The well-appointed bedrooms are light and airy.

ROOMS: 46 en suite 6 annexe en suite (12 fmly) (6 GF) s £59-£64; d £98-£106 (incl. bkfst & dinner) **LB** **FACILITIES: Spa** Sauna Games room ♫ Xmas **CONF:** Thtr 50 Class 40 Board 30 **SERVICES:** Lift **PARKING:** 40 **NOTES:** in restaurant

★★★66% Quality Hotel Bournemouth

47 Gervis Rd, East Cliff BH1 3DD
☎ 01202 316316 🖷 01202 316999
e-mail: reservations@qualityhotelbournemouth.com
web: www.qualityhotelbournemouth.com
Dir: *A338 left at rdbt, right at next rdbt. Take 2nd exit at next rdbt into Meyrick Rd. Then at next rdbt right into Gervis Rd. Hotel on left*

The hotel was once the home of Tony Hancock and is situated a short walk form the East Cliff. Guests can enjoy the terrace, garden and the indoor heated swimming pool. A lounge menu is available through the day. Bedrooms are comfortable and well equipped; some are newly updated.

ROOMS: 57 en suite (11 fmly) (2 GF) in 22 bedrooms s £46-£60; d £92-£120 (incl. bkfst & dinner) **LB** **FACILITIES:** Sauna Gym Gym privately run prebooking necessary Xmas **CONF:** Thtr 70 Class 60 Board 35 Del from £70 **SERVICES:** Lift **PARKING:** 36 **NOTES:** in restaurant

★★★65% Cumberland
East Overcliff Dr BH1 3AF
☎ 01202 290722 📠 01202 311394
e-mail: cumberland@bluemermaidhotels.com
Many of the well-equipped and attractively decorated bedrooms at this hotel benefit from sea views and balconies. The lounges and restaurant are spacious and comfortable. The restaurant offers a daily-changing, fixed-price menu. Guests may use the leisure club at the sister hotel, The Queens.
ROOMS: 102 en suite (12 fmly) s £59-£89; d £99-£139 (incl. bkfst) LB **FACILITIES:** Free membership of nearby Leisure Club in sister hotel Xmas **CONF:** Thtr 120 Class 70 Board 45 Del from £82.50 **SERVICES:** Lift **PARKING:** 51 **NOTES:** in restaurant Civ Wed 100

★★★63% Burley Court
Bath Rd BH1 2NP
☎ 01202 552824 & 556704 📠 01202 298514
e-mail: info@burleycourthotel.co.uk
Dir: *leave A338 at St Pauls rdbt, take 3rd exit at next rdbt into Holdenhurst Rd. 3rd exit at next rdbt into Bath Rd, over crossing, 1st left*
Located on Bournemouth's West Cliff, this well-established hotel is easily located and convenient for the town and beaches. Bedrooms, many now refurbished, are pleasantly furnished and decorated in bright colours. A daily-changing menu is served in the spacious dining room.
ROOMS: 38 en suite (8 fmly) (4 GF) in 20 bedrooms s £34-£47; d £68-£94 (incl. bkfst) LB **FACILITIES:** Xmas **CONF:** Thtr 30 Class 15 Board 15 **SERVICES:** Lift **PARKING:** 35 **NOTES:** in restaurant Closed 30 Dec-14 Jan

★★★63% *Ocean View Hotel*
East Overcliff Dr BH1 3AR
☎ 01202 558057 📠 01202 556285
e-mail: enquiry@oceanview.uk.com
Splendid sea views can be enjoyed from all of the public rooms at this popular East Cliff hotel. Bedrooms vary in size, and all are light, airy and well equipped. A comfortable bar/lounge offers an informal alternative to the drawing room, whilst the spacious restaurant offers a fixed-price menu every evening.
ROOMS: 52 rms (51 en suite) (13 fmly) **FACILITIES:** Indoor leisure suite at Bayview Court Hotel (sister hotel) ♫ ch fac **CONF:** Thtr 120 Class 100 Board 30 **SERVICES:** Lift **PARKING:** 39 **NOTES:** in restaurant Civ Wed 100

★★73% New Westcliff
27-29 Chine Crescent, West Cliff BH2 5LB
☎ 01202 551926 & 551062 📠 01202 315377
e-mail: reservations@newwestcliffhotel.co.uk
Dir: *off Wessex Way at signs for Westcliff and BIC. Over Poole Road rdbt, continue along Durley Chine Rd, hotel 0.5m right*
A warm welcome awaits guests at this privately owned hotel. The bedrooms are of different sizes and are attractively decorated and well equipped. There is a lovely garden and a bowling green as well as three lounges. All-weather leisure facilities, including a small cinema, are a definite plus.
ROOMS: 55 en suite (16 fmly) (3 GF) in 45 bedrooms s £36-£50; d £72-£100 (incl. bkfst) LB **FACILITIES:** Sauna Solarium Jacuzzi Cinema, Bowling Green, Ballroom ♫ Xmas **SERVICES:** Lift **PARKING:** 70 **NOTES:** in restaurant

U Star rating not confirmed

★★71% Arlington
Exeter Park Rd BH2 5BD
☎ 01202 552879 & 553012 📠 01202 298317
e-mail: enquiries@arlingtonbournemouth.co.uk
web: www.arlingtonbournemouth.co.uk
Dir: *follow BIC signs through Priory Rd, onto rdbt and exit at Royal Exeter Hotel sign. Hotel along Exeter Park Rd*
Well-equipped bedrooms and comfortable accommodation along with friendly hospitality are offered at this privately owned and run hotel. Conveniently located, midway between the square and the pier and ideally situated for the BIC, the Arlington has direct access to the flower gardens, which are overlooked from the hotel's lounge and terrace bar.
ROOMS: 27 en suite 1 annexe en suite (6 fmly) s £36.50-£43.50; d £73-£87 (incl. bkfst) LB **FACILITIES:** STV Xmas **SERVICES:** Lift **PARKING:** 21 **NOTES:** No children 2yrs in restaurant Closed 4-15 Jan

★★69% Durley Grange
6 Durley Rd, West Cliff BH2 5JL
☎ 01202 554473 📠 01202 293774
e-mail: reservations@durleygrange.com
Dir: *A338/St Michaels rdbt. Over next rdbt, 1st left into Sommerville Rd & right into Durley Rd*
Located in a quiet area, with some parking, the town and beaches are all in walking distance of this welcoming and friendly hotel. Bedrooms are brightly decorated, comfortable and well equipped. There is an indoor pool and sauna for year-round use. Enjoyable meals are served in the newly decorated dining room.
ROOMS: 51 en suite (8 fmly) (4 GF) s £36-£49; d £72-£98 (incl. bkfst) LB **FACILITIES: Spa** Sauna Solarium ♫ Xmas **SERVICES:** Lift **PARKING:** 35 **NOTES:** in restaurant

★★68% Sun Court
32 West Hill Rd BH2 5PH
☎ 01202 551343 📠 01202 316747
e-mail: sales@theconnaught.co.uk
Dir: *from A338 follow signs to West Cliff. First exit off St Michaels rdbt. 1st right into West Hill Road*
Located on the West Cliff, this hotel is well placed to offer convenient access to the town centre and seafront attractions. Bedrooms come in a range of sizes, some have sun lounges and there are also some family rooms. Public areas include an airy restaurant, a residents' lounge and a friendly bar where live entertainment is laid on for guests' enjoyment.
ROOMS: 33 en suite (7 fmly) s £35-£60; d £70-£120 (incl. bkfst & dinner) **FACILITIES:** STV Use of leisure facilities at nearby hotel ♫ Xmas **SERVICES:** Lift **PARKING:** 28 **NOTES:** in restaurant

★★68% Whitehall
Exeter Park Rd BH2 5AX
☎ 01202 554682 📠 01202 292637
e-mail: reservations@thewhitehallhotel.co.uk
web: www.thewhitehallhotel.co.uk
Dir: *follow BIC signs then turn into Exeter Park Rd off Exeter Rd*
This friendly hotel enjoys an elevated position overlooking the park and is also close to the town centre and seafront. The spacious public areas include a choice of lounges, a cosy bar and a well-presented restaurant. The bedrooms are spread over three floors and are inviting and well equipped.
ROOMS: 46 en suite (5 fmly) (3 GF) in 20 bedrooms s £36-£48; d £72-£96 (incl. bkfst) LB **FACILITIES:** ♫ Xmas **CONF:** Thtr 70 Class 40 Board 32 **SERVICES:** Lift **PARKING:** 25 **NOTES:** in restaurant

BOURNEMOUTH, continued

★★67% Bourne Hall Hotel
14 Priory Rd, West Cliff BH2 5DN
☎ 01202 299715 🖷 01202 552669
e-mail: info@bournehall.co.uk
web: www.bournehall.co.uk
Dir: *M27/A31 from Ringwood into Bournemouth on A338, Wessex Way. Follow signs to BIC, onto West Cliff. Hotel on right*
A friendly, comfortable hotel conveniently located close to the BIC and seafront. Bedrooms are well equipped; some rooms are located on the ground floor and some have sea views. There is a spacious lounge, and two bars and a meeting area are provided.
ROOMS: 48 en suite (9 fmly) (5 GF) ⊗ in all bedrooms
FACILITIES: STV ♫ Xmas **CONF:** Thtr 130 Class 60 Board 40 Del from £55 **SERVICES:** Lift **PARKING:** 35 **NOTES:** ⊗ in restaurant

★★67% *Mansfield*
West Cliff Gardens BH2 5HL
☎ 01202 552659 🖷 01202 297115
e-mail: mail@bournemouthhotel.net
Dir: *from A338 follow signs for West Cliff, over 2 rdbts via Cambridge & Durley Chine Rd*
A friendly hotel located in a quiet crescent on the West Cliff. Only a short stroll away from the sandy beaches and the many shops and attractions, this is an ideal base for visitors. Perfect as a business base during the week, it will also suit people trying to get 'away from it all' at the weekend.
ROOMS: 29 en suite (3 fmly) (2 GF) ⊗ in 4 bedrooms **PARKING:** 12
NOTES: ✗ ⊗ in restaurant

★★66% Ullswater
West Cliff Gardens BH2 5HW
☎ 01202 555181 🖷 01202 317896
e-mail: enq@ullswater.uk.com
web: www.ullswater.uk.com
Dir: *In Bournemouth follow signs to West Cliff. Hotel just off Westcliff Rd*
Conveniently situated close to the city centre and seafront, this pleasant hotel offers comfortable accommodation and attracts a loyal following. Bedrooms are generously equipped and offer a range of sizes, and the lounge and dining room are spacious and smartly appointed. There is a good choice of dishes on the daily-changing menu.
ROOMS: 42 en suite (8 fmly) (2 GF) s £31-£39; d £62-£78 (incl. bkfst) **LB** **FACILITIES:** Snooker Table tennis ♫ Xmas **CONF:** Thtr 40 Class 30 Board 24 Del from £65 **SERVICES:** Lift **PARKING:** 10 **NOTES:** ⊗ in restaurant

★★65% Fircroft
4 Owls Rd BH5 1AE
☎ 01202 309771 🖷 01202 395644
e-mail: info@fircrofthotel.co.uk
web: www.fircrofthotel.co.uk
Dir: *off A338 signed Boscombe Pier. Hotel 400yds from pier close to Christchurch Rd*
This friendly hotel is located close to Boscombe pier. Offering a range of comfortable lounges and meeting facilities, the hotel is popular with tour and dance groups. In addition, entertainment is provided most nights throughout the year. All of the bedrooms are comfortable and well equipped.
ROOMS: 51 en suite (20 fmly) s £30-£36; d £60-£72 (incl. bkfst) **LB** **FACILITIES:** Sauna Solarium Gym Jacuzzi Sports at health club owned by hotel Xmas **CONF:** Thtr 200 Class 100 Board 40 **SERVICES:** Lift **PARKING:** 50 **NOTES:** ⊗ in restaurant

★★64% Aaron Croham Hurst
9 Durley Rd South, West Cliff BH2 5JH
☎ 01202 552353 🖷 01202 311484
e-mail: crohamhurst.reception@aaron-hotels.com
This friendly hotel is popular with individuals and coach parties alike and is conveniently located for the beach and town centre. Bedrooms come in a variety of sizes and styles and all are well equipped. The lounge is also the venue for regular evening entertainment and the restaurant offers traditional home-cooked meals.
ROOMS: 41 en suite (11 fmly) (8 GF) s £25-£50; d £50-£100 (incl. bkfst & dinner) **LB** **FACILITIES:** STV Free use of indoor pool, sauna & jacuzzi at sister hotel, 5 mins walk away ♫ Xmas **SERVICES:** Lift **PARKING:** 28 **NOTES:** ✗ ⊗ in restaurant

★★64% Cliff Court
15 Westcliff Rd BH2 5EX
☎ 01202 555994 🖷 01202 780954
e-mail: info@cliffcourthotel.com
Dir: *A338 Wessex Way into Cambridge Rd. Follow Durley Chine Rd into West Cliff Rd*
This friendly hotel enjoys easy access to the main approach roads and the seafront, which is only a few minutes' walk away. It is popular with tour groups, and boasts a spacious dining room, a bar and small lounge. The comfortable bedrooms make best use of the available space.
ROOMS: 40 en suite (4 fmly) s £28-£50; d £60-£110 (incl. bkfst) **LB** **FACILITIES:** STV ♫ Xmas **SERVICES:** Lift **PARKING:** 31 **NOTES:** ⊗ in restaurant

★★63% Aaron Diplomat Hotel
6/8 Durley Chine Rd, West Cliff BH2 5JY
☎ 01202 555025 🖷 01202 559019
e-mail: diplomat.reception@aaron-hotels.com
web: www.aaron-hotels.com
Dir: *follow town centre/West Cliff sign. Over St Michaels rdbt, hotel on left*
The Diplomat is ideally placed to benefit from all of the town's attractions. Bedrooms have all the expected amenities and are decorated in warm colours. The refurbished bar area now provides guests with a range of dining options in addition to the main restaurant menu. Entertainment is provided most evenings throughout the year.
ROOMS: 58 en suite (8 fmly) (3 GF) s £25-£50; d £50-£100 (incl. bkfst & dinner) **LB** **FACILITIES:** STV Free use of indoor pool, sauna & jacuzzi at sister hotel, 5mins walk away ♫ Xmas **SERVICES:** Lift **PARKING:** 40 **NOTES:** ✗ ⊗ in restaurant

★★63% *Devon Towers*
58-62 St Michael's Rd, West Cliff BH2 5ED
Leisureplex
☎ 01202 553863 🖷 01202 315265
e-mail: devontowers.bournemouth@alfatravel.co.uk
web: www.alfatravel.co.uk
Dir: *A338 into Bournemouth, follow signs for BIC. Left into St. Michaels Rd at top of hill. Hotel 100mtrs on left*
Located in a quiet road within walking distance of the West Cliff and central shops, this hotel appeals to the budget leisure market. The four-course menus offer plenty of choice and entertainment is featured on most evenings. The bar and lobby area offer plenty of space for relaxing.
ROOMS: 54 en suite (6 GF) **FACILITIES:** ♫ **SERVICES:** Lift **PARKING:** 6 **NOTES:** ✗ ⊗ in restaurant Closed Jan-mid Feb ex Xmas RS Nov, Feb & Mar

★★60% Aaron Westleigh
26 Westhill Rd, Westcliff BH2 5PG
☎ 01202 786678 🖹 01202 786670
e-mail: westleigh.reception@aaron-hotels.com
Dir: *On A338 to Cambridge Rd rdbt turn left, at next rdbt left then right. Hotel is halfway down on the right.*
Within walking distance of the town centre and the beach, this hotel offers value for money and attracts numerous groups of guests. The spacious South African themed bar opens on to the rear terrace, where BBQs are held on summer evenings. Guests enjoy relaxing in the separate lounge.
ROOMS: 28 en suite (6 fmly) (7 GF) s £25-£50; d £50-£100 (incl. bkfst & dinner) **LB** **FACILITIES:** STV Sauna Jacuzzi ♫ Xmas **SERVICES:** Lift **PARKING:** 20 **NOTES:** in restaurant

Innkeeper's Lodge Bournemouth
Cooper Dean Roundabout, Castle Ln East BH7 7DP
☎ 01202 390837 🖹 01202 390378
web: www.innkeeperslodge.com
Dir: *A338 Bournemouth spur road, follow until exit signed Bournemouth Hospital. Hotel on corner next to hospital*
A growing concept in the travel accommodation market. Smart rooms meet essential business requirements but also have home comforts. Dining options include all-day menus plus the added advantage of breakfast, which is included in the room price. For further details consult the Hotel Groups page.
ROOMS: 28 en suite s £59.95; d £59.95 **CONF:** Thtr 30 Class 22 Board 18

Travelodge Bournemouth Central
43 Christchurch Rd BH1 3NS
☎ 08700 850950
web: www.travelodge.co.uk
Dir: *From city centre N along Deansgate. At junct with Blackfriars Street and St. Mary's Gate turn left over bridge. Travelodge is on right.*
Travelodge offers good quality, good value, modern accommodation. Ideal for families, the spacious, en suite bedrooms include remote-control TV, tea and coffee-making facilities and comfortable beds. Meals can be taken at the nearby family restaurant. For further details consult the Hotel Groups page.
ROOMS: 107 en suite (incl. bkfst) s fr £26; d fr £26

BOURTON-ON-THE-WATER, Gloucestershire — Map 10 SP12

★★79% *Dial House*
The Chestnuts, High St GL54 2AN
☎ 01451 822244 🖹 01451 810126
e-mail: info@dialhousehotel.com
web: www.dialhousehotel.com
Dir: *off A429, 0.5m to village centre*

Tucked away in the centre of this beguiling village, this mellow Cotswold-stone hotel which dates back to 1698, combines the character of original features with modern comforts. In the summer guests can enjoy delightful gardens, and in winter log fires and comfy sofas ensure relaxation. Two intimate dining rooms provide the setting for quality cuisine, while bedrooms, including some with four-posters, are stylishly furnished and well equipped.
ROOMS: 13 en suite (7 GF) in all bedrooms **FACILITIES:** Putt green **CONF:** Class 15 Board 15 **PARKING:** 20 **NOTES:** No children 10 yrs in restaurant

BOVEY TRACEY, Devon — Map 03 SX87

★★71% Coombe Cross
Coombe Ln TQ13 9EY
☎ 01626 832476 🖹 01626 835298
e-mail: info@coombecross.co.uk
web: www.coombecross.co.uk
Dir: *A38 signed Bovey Tracey & town centre, along High St, up hill 400yds beyond Parish Church. Hotel on left*

With delightful views over Dartmoor, this peaceful hotel is set in well-tended gardens on the edge of the town. Bedrooms are well equipped and offer ample comfort, whilst public areas include a choice of lounges and a range of leisure and fitness facilities. At dinner, carefully prepared dishes are served in the spacious dining room.
ROOMS: 23 en suite (1 fmly) (2 GF) in all bedrooms s £44-£52; d £58-£74 (incl. bkfst) **LB** **FACILITIES: Spa** Sauna Solarium Gym Table tennis **CONF:** Thtr 80 Class 30 Board 30 Del £80.50 **PARKING:** 20 **NOTES:** in restaurant Closed 24 Dec-1 Jan

BOWNESS ON WINDERMERE See Windermere

BOXWORTH, Cambridgeshire — Map 12 TL36

Sleep Inn Cambridge
Cambridge Services A14 CB3 8WU
☎ 01954 268400 🖹 01954 268419
e-mail: enquiries@hotels-cambridge.com
web: www.hotels-cambridge.com
Dir: *A14 junct 28 6m N of Cambridge. 8m S of Huntington*
This modern, purpose built accommodation offers smartly appointed, well-equipped bedrooms, with good power showers. There is a choice of adjacent food outlets where guests may enjoy breakfast, snacks and meals.
ROOMS: 82 en suite

Late for dinner? Quality standards mean that last orders for dinner vary according to star rating and should be no earlier than: ★★ 7.00pm ★★★ 8:00pm ★★★★ 9:00pm ★★★★★ 10:00pm

BRACKNELL, Berkshire
Map 05 SU86

See also Crowthorne

★★★★73% ❀❀ Coppid Beech
John Nike Way RG12 8TF
☎ 01344 303333 🖷 01344 301200
e-mail: welcome@coppid-beech-hotel.co.uk
web: www.coppidbeech.com
Dir: *M4 junct 10 take Wokingham/Bracknell onto A329. In 2m take B3408 to Binfield at rdbt. Hotel 200yds on right*

This chalet-style complex offers extensive facilities and includes a ski-slope, ice rink, nightclub, health club and Bier Keller. Bedrooms offer a range of suites and standard rooms, all of which are impressively equipped. A choice of dining is offered and a full bistro menu is available in the Keller. For more formal dining Rowan's restaurant provides award-winning cuisine.

ROOMS: 205 en suite (6 fmly) ⊗ in 138 bedrooms s £75-£275; d £85-£295 (incl. bkfst) **LB** **FACILITIES: Spa** STV supervised Sauna Solarium Gym Jacuzzi Dry ski slope, Ice rink ♫ Xmas **CONF:** BC Thtr 400 Class 240 Board 24 Del from £150 **SERVICES:** Lift **PARKING:** 350 **NOTES:** Civ Wed 120

★★★★69% *Grange Bracknell*
Charles Square RG12 1DF
☎ 01344 474000 🖷 01344 474125
e-mail: bracknell@grangehotels.com
web: www.grangehotels.co.uk

Just a few years ago the former Honeywell Offices opened their doors as an impressive Four Star hotel. Lighting is used to impressive effect both inside and outside to create a modern environment that is both comfortable and stylish. Public rooms include the Callela Bar, Ascot Green Restaurant, a fitness suite and a range of interconnecting conference and banqueting rooms. Air-conditioned bedrooms are spacious and come equipped with a host of extras.

ROOMS: 120 en suite (6 fmly) ⊗ in 60 bedrooms **FACILITIES:** STV Gym **CONF:** Thtr 200 Class 120 Board 80 **SERVICES:** Lift air con **PARKING:** 111 **NOTES:** 🐕̸

★★★71% Stirrups Country House
Maidens Green RG42 6LD
☎ 01344 882284 🖷 01344 882300
e-mail: reception@stirrupshotel.co.uk
web: www.stirrupshotel.co.uk
Dir: *3m N on B3022 towards Windsor*

Situated in a peaceful location between Maidenhead, Bracknell and Windsor, this hotel has high standards of comfort in the bedrooms, with newer rooms boasting a small sitting room area. There is a popular bar, a restaurant, function rooms and delightful grounds.

ROOMS: 30 en suite (4 fmly) (2 GF) ⊗ in 20 bedrooms s £90-£135; d £95-£180 **LB** **FACILITIES:** STV **CONF:** Thtr 100 Class 50 Board 40 Del from £140 **SERVICES:** Lift **PARKING:** 100 **NOTES:** 🐕̸ ⊗ in restaurant Civ Wed 100

⌂ Premier Travel Inn Bracknell
Arlington Square, Wokingham Rd RG42 1NA
☎ 08701 977036 🖷 01344 319526
web: www.premiertravelinn.com
Dir: *M4 (J10) A329(M) Bracknell to lights. 1st left, 3rd exit rdbt by Safeway to town centre. Left at rdbt, left at next rdbt. Inn on left.*

High quality, modern budget accommodation ideal for both families and business travellers. Spacious, en suite bedrooms feature bath and shower, satellite TV and many have telephones and modem points. The adjacent family restaurant features a wide and varied menu. For further details consult the Hotel Groups page.

ROOMS: 60 en suite s £57.95-£59.95; d £57.95-£59.95

BRADFORD, West Yorkshire
Map 19 SE13

See also Gomersal & Shipley

★★★70% Midland Hotel
Forster Square BD1 4HU
☎ 01274 735735 🖷 01274 720003
e-mail: info@midland-hotel-bradford.com
web: www.peelhotel.com
Dir: *A6177/ A641/A6181. Past St Georges Hall to Eastbrook Well rdbt. Take 1st exit along Petergate to Forster Sq, left to Cheapside. Hotel on right*

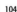

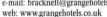

Ideally situated in the heart of the city, this grand Victorian hotel provides modern, very well equipped accommodation and comfortable, spacious day rooms. Ample parking is available in what used to be the city's railway station, and a passage dating from Victorian times linking the hotel to the old platform can still be used today.

ROOMS: 90 en suite (4 fmly) ⊗ in 40 bedrooms s £86-£106; d £96-£120 (incl. bkfst) **FACILITIES:** STV Free use of local health club ♫ Xmas **CONF:** BC Thtr 450 Class 150 Board 100 Del from £120 **SERVICES:** Lift **PARKING:** 50 **NOTES:** Civ Wed 400

★★★69% Best Western Guide Post Hotel
Common Rd, Low Moor BD12 0ST
☎ 01274 607866 🖷 01274 671085
e-mail: sales@guideposthotel.net
web: www.guideposthotel.net
Dir: *take M606, then signed*

Situated south of the city, this hotel offers attractively furnished, comfortable bedrooms. The restaurant offers an extensive range of food using fresh, local produce; lighter snack meals are served in the bar. There is also a choice of well-equipped meeting and function rooms.

ROOMS: 43 en suite (3 fmly) (14 GF) ⊗ in 8 bedrooms s £55-£80; d £65-£90 (incl. bkfst) **FACILITIES:** STV **CONF:** BC Thtr 120 Class 80 Board 60 Del £105 **PARKING:** 10 **NOTES:** ⊗ in restaurant Civ Wed 100

★★★68% *Courtyard by Marriott Leeds/Bradford*
The Pastures, Tong Ln BD4 0RP
☎ 0870 400 7218 🖷 0870 400 7318
web: www.kewgreen.co.uk
Dir: *M62 junct 27/A650 towards Bradford. 3rd rdbt, take 3rd exit to Tong Village & Pudsey. Left into Tong Lane. Hotel 0.5m on right*

Built onto an elegant, 19th-century former vicarage, this modern, stylish hotel has been sympathetically designed to complement its Victorian heritage. The hotel is particularly well located for both Leeds and Bradford and the local motorway networks. The well-equipped bedrooms are furnished and decorated to a high standard.

ROOMS: 53 en suite (8 fmly) (11 GF) ⊗ in 31 bedrooms **FACILITIES:** STV Gym **CONF:** Thtr 200 Class 150 Board 100 **SERVICES:** Lift **PARKING:** 230 **NOTES:** 🐕̸ Civ Wed 100

★★★67% Cedar Court Hotel
Mayo Av, Off Rooley Ln BD5 8HZ
☎ 01274 406606 🖷 01274 406600
e-mail: sales@cedarcourtbradford.co.uk
Dir: *M62 junct 26/M606. At end take 3rd exit off rdbt onto A6177 towards Bradford. Take 1st sharp right at lights*

This modern attractive hotel, now under new ownership, is conveniently located just off the motorway and close to the city centre and the airport. The hotel boasts extensive function and conference facilities, a well-equipped leisure club and an elegant restaurant. Bedrooms are comfortably appointed for both business and leisure guests.
ROOMS: 131 en suite (7 fmly) (25 GF) ⊗ in 75 bedrooms **FACILITIES:** STV supervised Sauna Solarium Gym Jacuzzi Pool table Xmas **CONF:** BC Thtr 800 Class 300 Board 150 **SERVICES:** Lift **PARKING:** 300 **NOTES:** Civ Wed 800

★★★63% Novotel Bradford
6 Roydsdale Way BD4 6SA
☎ 01274 683683 🖷 01274 651342
e-mail: h0510@accor-hotels.com
web: www.novotel.com
Dir: *M606 junct 2, exit to Euroway Trading Estate turn right at traffic lights at bottom of slip road, take 2nd right onto Roydsdale Way*
This purpose-built hotel is in a good location for access to the motorway. It provides spacious bedrooms that are comfortably equipped. Open-plan day rooms include a stylish bar, and a lounge that leads into the Garden Brasserie. Several function rooms are also available.
Novotel - AA Hotel Group of the Year 2005-6.
ROOMS: 119 en suite (37 fmly) (9 GF) ⊗ in 69 bedrooms s £65; d £65 **LB FACILITIES:** STV Xmas **CONF:** Thtr 300 Class 100 Board 100 Del £119 **SERVICES:** Lift **PARKING:** 200 **NOTES:** Civ Wed 200

⌂ Premier Travel Inn Leeds/Bradford (South)
Wakefield Rd, Drighlington BD11 1EA
☎ 08701 977152 🖷 0113 287 9115
web: www.premiertravelinn.com
Dir: *on Drighlington bypass, adjacent to M62 J27. A650 to Bradford then right to Drighlington, right and Inn on left*
High quality, modern budget accommodation ideal for both families and business travellers. Spacious, en suite bedrooms feature bath and shower, satellite TV and many have telephones and modem points. The adjacent family restaurant features a wide and varied menu. For further details consult the Hotel Groups page.
ROOMS: 42 en suite s £46.95-£49.95; d £46.95-£49.95

The vast majority of establishments in this guide accept credit and debit cards. We indicate those that don't take any

BRADFORD-ON-AVON, Wiltshire — Map 04 ST86

★★★76% Woolley Grange
Woolley Green BA15 1TX
☎ 01225 864705 🖷 01225 864059
e-mail: info@woolleygrange.com
web: www.luxuryfamilyhotels.com
Dir: *Turn off A4 onto B3109. Bradford Leigh, left at crossroads, hotel 0.5m on right at Woolley Green*

This splendid Cotswold manor house is set in beautiful countryside. Children are made especially welcome; there is a trained nanny on duty in the nursery. Bedrooms and public areas are charmingly furnished and decorated in true country-house style, with many thoughtful touches and luxurious extras. The hotel offers a varied and well-balanced menu selection, including ingredients from the hotel's own garden.
ROOMS: 14 en suite 12 annexe en suite (8 fmly) s £170-£315; d £265-£375 (incl. bkfst & dinner) **LB FACILITIES:** Putt green Badminton, Beauty treatments, Cycling, Football, Games room ch fac Xmas **CONF:** Thtr 35 Class 12 Board 22 Del from £175 **PARKING:** 40 **NOTES:** ⊗ in restaurant

★★★70% *Leigh Park Hotel*
Leigh Park West BA15 2RA
☎ 01225 864885 🖷 01225 862315
e-mail: info@leighparkhotel.eclipse.co.uk
Dir: *A363 Bath/Frome road. Take B3105 signed Holt/Woolley Green. Hotel 0.25m on right on x-roads of B3105/B3109. N side of Bradford-on-Avon*
Enjoying splendid countryside views, this relaxing Georgian hotel is set in five acres of well-tended grounds, complete with a vineyard. Combining charm and character with modern facilities, the hotel is equally well suited to business and leisure travellers. The restaurant serves dishes cooked to order, using home-grown fruit and vegetables, and wine from the vineyard.
ROOMS: 22 en suite (4 fmly) (7 GF) ⊗ in 14 bedrooms **CONF:** Thtr 120 Class 60 Board 60 **PARKING:** 80 **NOTES:** ⊗ in restaurant Civ Wed 120

BRAINTREE, Essex — Map 07 TL72

★★★65% *White Hart*
Bocking End CM7 9AB
☎ 01376 321401 🖷 01376 552628
web: www.oldenglish.co.uk
Dir: *off A120 towards town centre. Hotel at junct B1256 & Bocking Causeway*
This 18th-century former coaching inn is conveniently located in the heart of the bustling town centre. The public rooms include a large lounge bar, restaurant and meeting rooms. The pleasantly decorated, well-equipped bedrooms provide a good level of comfort throughout.
ROOMS: 31 en suite (8 fmly) ⊗ in 21 bedrooms **FACILITIES:** STV **CONF:** Thtr 40 Class 16 Board 24 **PARKING:** 52 **NOTES:** ⊗ in restaurant

BRAINTREE, continued

Premier Travel Inn Braintree
Cressing Rd, Galley's Corner CM7 8GG
☎ 08701 977039 01376 555087
web: www.premiertravelinn.com
Dir: *on A120 bypass at Braintree junction of Cressing Rd & Galley's Corner*
High quality, modern budget accommodation ideal for both families and business travellers. Spacious, en suite bedrooms feature bath and shower, satellite TV and many have telephones and modem points. The adjacent family restaurant features a wide and varied menu. For further details consult the Hotel Groups page.
ROOMS: 40 en suite s £47.95-£50.95; d £47.95-£50.95

BRAITHWAITE, Cumbria Map 18 NY22

★★75% The Cottage in the Wood
Whinlatter Pass CA12 5TW
☎ 017687 78409 017687 78064
e-mail: info@thecottageinthewood.co.uk
Dir: *A66 for Cockermouth & Keswick. After Keswick, turn off for Braithwaite & Lorton via Whinlatter Pass (B5292). Hotel at top of Whinlatter Pass*
This charming little hotel sits amid wooded hills with striking views of Skiddaw, and is in a convenient location for Keswick. The professional owners provide excellent hospitality in a relaxed manner and offer a freshly prepared dinner from a set menu that includes a vegetarian choice. There is a cosy lounge and a small bar. The bedrooms are individually decorated, and the superior rooms include many useful extras.
ROOMS: 10 en suite (1 fmly) (1 GF) in all bedrooms s £50; d £70-£100 (incl. bkfst) **LB** **FACILITIES:** Xmas **PARKING:** 15 **NOTES:** No children 7yrs in restaurant Closed Jan-mid Feb RS Mon eve

BRAMHALL, Greater Manchester Map 16 SJ88

★★★61% The County Hotel
Bramhall Ln South SK7 2EB
☎ 0870 609 6148 0161 440 8071
web: www.corushotels.com/countymanchester
Dir: *A34 by-pass to Bramhall. In Bramhall village at rdbt turn R, continue under bridge. Hotel 100yds on right.*
This hotel is situated in a quiet residential area on the edge of Bramhall, within easy reach of the airport and Cheadle shopping centre. Bedrooms are well equipped and include a number of ground floor rooms. Public areas include an open plan lounge restaurant and the traditional Shires Pub.
ROOMS: 65 en suite (3 fmly) (20 GF) in 20 bedrooms s £40-£80; d £59-£80 **LB** **FACILITIES:** Xmas **CONF:** Thtr 200 Class 80 Board 60 Del from £80 **PARKING:** 120 **NOTES:** in restaurant Civ Wed 100

BRAMPTON, Cambridgeshire Map 12 TL27

★★70% The Grange
115 High St PE28 4RA
☎ 01480 459516 01480 459391
e-mail: nsteiger@grangehotelbrampton.com
web: www.grangehotelbrampton.com
Dir: *A1(M)/A14 towards Cambridge. After 0.5m take B1514 (racecourse) towards Huntingdon. After mini rdbt turn right into Grove Ln, hotel opp T-junct at bottom of road*
Located on the high street in the quiet village of Brampton, this historic building offers smart bedrooms; the newly refurbished ones are particularly attractive in their design. Imaginative cuisine is served in both the light and airy restaurant and in the more informal and inviting bar area. Guests have access to a comfortable lounge and service is both friendly and attentive.

ROOMS: 7 en suite in all bedrooms s £65-£75; d £85-£95 (incl. bkfst) **CONF:** Thtr 30 Class 15 Board 36 **PARKING:** 20 **NOTES:** in restaurant RS 29 Dec-5 Jan Civ Wed 40

Premier Travel Inn Huntingdon
Brampton Hut PE28 4NQ
☎ 08701 977139 01480 811298
web: www.premiertravelinn.com
Dir: *junct of A1/A14. (From north do not use junct 14 but take next main exit for Huntingdon & Brampton). Access via services*
High quality, modern budget accommodation ideal for both families and business travellers. Spacious, en suite bedrooms feature bath and shower, satellite TV and many have telephones and modem points. The adjacent family restaurant features a wide and varied menu. For further details consult the Hotel Groups page.
ROOMS: 80 en suite s £46.95-£49.95; d £46.95-£49.95 **CONF:** Thtr 25

BRAMPTON, Cumbria Map 21 NY56

Top Hotel

★★★ Farlam Hall
CA8 2NG
☎ 016977 46234 016977 46683
e-mail: farlam@relaischateaux.com
web: www.farlamhall.co.uk
Dir: *On A689 (Brampton to Alston). Hotel 2m on left, not in Farlam village*
This delightful family-run country house dates back to 1428. Steeped in history, the hotel is set in beautifully landscaped Victorian gardens complete with an ornamental lake and stream. Lovingly restored over many years, it now provides the highest standards of comfort and hospitality. Gracious public

continued

rooms invite relaxation, whilst every thought has gone into the beautiful bedrooms, many of which are simply stunning.
ROOMS: 11 en suite 1 annexe en suite (2 GF) ⊘ in all bedrooms s £140-£160; d £260-£300 (incl. bkfst & dinner) **LB** **FACILITIES:** ♫ **CONF:** Thtr 12 Class 12 Board 12 Del from £169.50 **PARKING:** 35 **NOTES:** No children 5yrs ⊘ in restaurant Closed 24-30 Dec

BRANCASTER STAITHE, Norfolk Map 13 TF74

★★76% ❀ White Horse
PE31 8BY
☎ 01485 210262 🖷 01485 210930
e-mail: reception@whitehorsebrancaster.co.uk
web: www.whitehorsebrancaster.co.uk
Dir: *on A149 coast road midway between Hunstanton & Wells-next-the-Sea*
A charming hotel on the north Norfolk coast with contemporary bedrooms in two wings, some featuring an interesting cobbled fascia. Each room is attractively decorated and thoughtfully equipped. There is a large bar and a lounge area leading through to the conservatory restaurant, with stunning tidal marshland views across to Scolt Head Island.
ROOMS: 7 en suite 8 annexe en suite (5 fmly) (8 GF) s £75-£95; d £110-£140 (incl. bkfst) **LB** **FACILITIES:** Bar billiards Xmas **PARKING:** 60 **NOTES:** ⊘ in restaurant

Bad hair day?
Hairdryers in all rooms three stars and above

BRANDESBURTON, East Riding of Yorkshire Map 17 TA14

★★69% Burton Lodge
YO25 8RU
☎ 01964 542847 🖷 01964 544771
e-mail: email@burtonlodge.fsnet.co.uk
Dir: *7m from Beverley off A165, adjoining Hainsworth Park Golf Club*
A tennis court, sports play area and extensive lawn are features of this friendly hotel, which is situated on a golf course. Rooms are modern and there is a comfortable lounge, while the spacious restaurant serves tasty home cooking.
ROOMS: 7 en suite 2 annexe en suite (3 fmly) (2 GF) ⊘ in 5 bedrooms s £38-£42; d £57-£60 (incl. bkfst) **LB** **FACILITIES:** ⛳ 18 🎾 Putt green Pitch and putt **CONF:** Class 20 **PARKING:** 15 **NOTES:** ⊘ in restaurant

BRANDON, Suffolk Map 13 TL78

★★66% *Brandon House*
High St IP27 0AX
☎ 01842 810171 🖷 01842 814859
Dir: *In town centre left at traffic lights into High St. Hotel 400yds on right after small bridge over River Ouse*
An 18th-century, red brick manor house set in landscaped gardens a short walk from the town centre. The pleasantly decorated, well-maintained bedrooms are thoughtfully equipped and come in a variety of styles. Public rooms include a comfortable lounge bar, the Conifers English Restaurant and a more relaxed bistro.
ROOMS: 15 en suite (3 fmly) **FACILITIES:** STV **CONF:** Thtr 70 Class 25 Board 20 **PARKING:** 40 **NOTES:** ⊘ in restaurant Closed 25-26 Dec & 1 Jan

B

BRANDON, Warwickshire · Map 11 SP47

★★★67% Brandon Hall
Main St CV8 3FW

MACDONALD
HOTELS & RESORTS

☎ 0870 400 8105 📠 024 7654 4909
e-mail: general.brandonhall@
macdonald-hotels.co.uk
web: www.macdonald-hotels.co.uk
Dir: *A45 towards Coventry S. After Peugeot-Citroen garage on left, at island take 5th exit to M1 South/London (back onto A45). After 200yds, immediately after Texaco garage, left into Brandon Ln, hotel after 2.5m*
Set within 17 acres of well-tended lawns and woodland, this former shooting lodge is located within easy reach of both Coventry and Rugby. Public rooms are stylishly decorated and fairly modern in style, bedrooms are more traditional. Leisure facilities include a pitch-and-putt course and squash courts.
ROOMS: 60 en suite 60 annexe en suite (7 fmly) (80 GF) ⊗ in 65 bedrooms **FACILITIES:** Spa STV ❐ supervised Sauna Solarium Gym ♨ Steam room. Xmas **CONF:** Thtr 280 Class 120 Board 80
SERVICES: Lift **PARKING:** 200 **NOTES:** ⊗ in restaurant Civ Wed 80

BRANDS HATCH, Kent · Map 06 TQ56

★★★★74% ◉◉ Brandshatch Place
Brands Hatch Rd, Fawkham DA3 8NQ

Hand PICKED HOTELS

☎ 01474 875000 📠 01474 879652
e-mail: brandshatchplace@handpicked.co.uk
web: www.handpicked.co.uk
Dir: *M25 junct 3/A20 West Kingsdown. Left at paddock entrance/Fawkham Green sign. 3rd left signed Fawkham Rd. Hotel 500mtrs on right*

This charming 18th-century Georgian country house is close to the famous racing circuit. Public areas have been completely transformed and include a range of stylish and elegant rooms. Bedrooms have also been upgraded to a very high standard, offering impressive facilities and levels of comfort and quality. The hotel also features a comprehensive leisure club with substantial crèche facilities.
ROOMS: 26 en suite 12 annexe en suite (1 fmly) ⊗ in 10 bedrooms s £150; d £180 (incl. bkfst) **LB** **FACILITIES:** Spa STV ❐ ❑ Squash Snooker Sauna Solarium Gym ♨ Jacuzzi Use of health/leisure club Xmas **CONF:** Thtr 120 Class 60 Board 50 Del £215 **SERVICES:** Lift
PARKING: 100 **NOTES:** ⊗ in restaurant Civ Wed 80

See advert on page 107

BRANKSOME See Poole

BRANSCOMBE, Devon · Map 04 SY18

★★70% ◉ The Masons Arms
EX12 3DJ
☎ 01297 680300 📠 01297 680500
e-mail: reception@masonsarms.co.uk
Dir: *off A3052 towards Branscombe, hotel in valley at bottom of hill*
This delightful 14th-century village inn, now under new ownership, is just half a mile from the sea. Bedrooms in the thatched annexed cottages, with their own patios with seating, tend to be more spacious; those in the inn reflect much period charm as do the bars and public areas. An extensive selection of dishes, which includes many local specialities, is offered. The Waterfall Restaurant offers a more formal dining option.
ROOMS: 6 rms (4 en suite) 16 annexe en suite (2 fmly) (1 GF) s £35-£130; d £50-£150 (incl. bkfst) **LB** **FACILITIES:** Xmas
PARKING: 43 **NOTES:** ⊗ in restaurant

BRAY, Berkshire · Map 06 SU97

★★★★64% ◉ Monkey Island
Old Mill Ln SL6 2EE
☎ 01628 623400 📠 01628 784732
e-mail: info@monkeyisland.co.uk
Dir: *M4 junct 8/9/A308 signed Windsor. 1st left into Bray, 1st right into Old Mill Lane, opp Crown pub*
This hotel is charmingly set on an island in the Thames, yet is within easy reach of major routes. Access is by footbridge or boat, but there is a large car park nearby. The hotel comprises two buildings, one for accommodation and the other for dining and drinking. Ample grounds are beautifully maintained and provide a peaceful haven for wildlife.
ROOMS: 26 en suite (1 fmly) (12 GF) **FACILITIES:** STV Fishing ♨ Boating ♫ **CONF:** Thtr 120 Class 70 Board 50 **PARKING:** 100
NOTES: ✈ ⊗ in restaurant Civ Wed

BREADSALL, Derbyshire · Map 11 SK33

★★★★67% ◉ Marriott Breadsall Priory Hotel, Country Club
Moor Rd DE7 6DL

Marriott.
HOTELS & RESORTS

☎ 01332 832235 📠 01332 833509
web: www.marriott.co.uk
Dir: *A52 to Derby, then signs to Chesterfield. Right at 1st rdbt, left at next. Follow A608 to Heanor Rd, after 3m left then left again*

This extended mansion house is set in 400 acres of parkland and well-tended gardens. The smart bedrooms are mostly contained in the modern wing. There is a vibrant café-bar, a more formal restaurant and a large room-service menu. The extensive leisure
continued

facilities, including a golf course and swimming pool, are an asset. Dinner in the Priory Restaurant is a highlight.
ROOMS: 12 en suite 100 annexe en suite (35 fmly) ⊗ in 69 bedrooms
FACILITIES: STV ⛳ 18 Sauna Solarium Gym Putt green Jacuzzi Health, beauty & hair salon, dance studio **CONF:** Thtr 120 Class 50 Board 36
SERVICES: Lift **PARKING:** 300 **NOTES:** ⊗ in restaurant Civ Wed 100

BRENTFORD, Greater London
See LONDON plan 1 C3

Premier Travel Inn London Kew
52 High St TW8 0BB
☎ 0870 9906304 🖷 0870 9906305
web: www.premiertravelinn.com
***Dir:** At junct of A4 (M4), A205 & A406, Chiswick rdbt, take A205 towards Kew & Brentford. 200yds right fork onto A315 (High St), for 0.5m. Hotel on left*
High quality, modern budget accommodation ideal for both families and business travellers. Spacious, en suite bedrooms feature bath and shower, satellite TV and many have telephones and modem points. The adjacent family restaurant features a wide and varied menu. For further details consult the Hotel Groups page.
ROOMS: 141 en suite s £59.95-£69.95; d £59.95-£69.95

Travelodge (London Kew Bridge)
North Rd, High St TW8 0BO
☎ 08700 850 950 🖷 0208 758 1190
web: www.travelodge.co.uk
Travelodge offers good quality, good value, modern accommodation. Ideal for families, the spacious, en suite bedrooms include remote-control TV, tea and coffee-making facilities and comfortable beds. Meals can be taken at the nearby family restaurant. For further details consult the Hotel Groups page.
ROOMS: 111 en suite s fr £26; d fr £26

BRENT KNOLL, Somerset Map 04 ST35

★★72% Woodlands Country House
Hill Ln TA9 4DF
☎ 01278 760232 🖷 01278 769090
e-mail: info@woodlands-hotel.co.uk
web: www.woodlands-hotel.co.uk
***Dir:** A38 take 1st left into village, then 5th right & 1st left, follow brown tourist information signs*

With glorious countryside views, this family-run hotel is set in four acres of wooded parkland and offers a relaxed and peaceful environment. The attractively co-ordinated bedrooms are comfortable and very well equipped. Guests are welcome to use the outdoor pool and enjoy the terrace seating. Imaginative dishes make up the daily-changing dinner menu.
ROOMS: 9 en suite (1 fmly) (1 GF) ⊗ in all bedrooms s £70-£95; d £100-£135 (incl. bkfst) **LB FACILITIES:** Xmas **CONF:** Thtr 30 Class 20 Board 30 Del from £99 **PARKING:** 16 **NOTES:** ⊗ in restaurant RS Sun Civ Wed 65
See advert under WESTON-SUPER-MARE

★★68% Battleborough Grange Country Hotel
Bristol Rd - A38 TA9 4HJ
☎ 01278 760208 🖷 01278 761950
e-mail: info@battleboroughgrangehotel.co.uk
***Dir:** M5 junct 22, right at rdbt onto A38 past garden centre on right, hotel 500yds on left*

Conveniently located, this popular hotel is surrounded by mellow Somerset countryside. Bedrooms are well equipped and some have superb views of the Iron Age fort of Brent Knoll. In the conservatory restaurant, both fixed-price and carte menus are offered. Relax in the convivial bar after a busy day either working or exploring the area's many attractions. Extensive function facilities are also provided.
ROOMS: 21 en suite (1 fmly) (2 GF) s £57-£65; d £77-£139 (incl. bkfst) **LB CONF:** Thtr 85 Class 40 Board 40 Del from £80 **PARKING:** 60 **NOTES:** ⊗ in restaurant Closed 26 Dec - 1 Jan Civ Wed 90

U Star rating not confirmed

B

BRENTWOOD, Essex

Map 06 TQ59

★★★★73% Marygreen Manor
London Rd CM14 4NR
☎ 01277 225252 01277 262809
e-mail: info@marygreenmanor.co.uk
web: www.marygreenmanor.co.uk
Dir: *M25 junct 28, onto A1023 over 2 sets of lights, hotel on left*
A 16th-century house which was built in 1535 by Robert Wright, who named the house his 'Manor of Mary Green' after his young bride. Public rooms exude character and have a wealth of original features that include exposed beams, carved panelling and the impressive Tudors restaurant. Bedrooms are tastefully decorated and thoughtfully equipped.
ROOMS: 4 en suite 40 annexe en suite (35 GF) in 24 bedrooms s £135-£197; d £150-£240 **FACILITIES:** STV **CONF:** Thtr 60 Class 20 Board 25 Del £205 **PARKING:** 100 **NOTES:** in restaurant Civ Wed 60

See advert on page 109

★★★71% Weald Park Hotel, Golf & Country Club
Coxtie Green Rd, South Weald CM14 5RJ
☎ 01277 375101 01277 374888
e-mail: info@wealdpark.net
Dir: *M25 junct 28 Brentwood, left at 1st traffic lights. Left at T-junct, follow winding road for 1.5m. 2nd turn on right, hotel is 1m on right*
Expect a warm welcome at this family-run hotel situated close to the M25 and M11 that creates easy links to London or Stansted Airport. The spacious, tastefully appointed and well-equipped bedrooms are situated in attractive courtyard-style blocks adjacent to the main building. Public rooms include a first-floor bar, a residents' lounge and a stylish restaurant.
ROOMS: 32 annexe en suite (2 fmly) (25 GF) s £75-£120; d £75-£135 (incl. bkfst) **LB** **FACILITIES:** 18 Fishing Putt green **CONF:** Thtr 80 Class 40 Board 20 **PARKING:** 180 **NOTES:** in restaurant

BRIDGNORTH, Shropshire

Map 10 SO79

See also Alveley

★★★★66% *Mill Hotel & Restaurant*
WV15 6HL
☎ 01746 780437 01746 780850
e-mail: enquiries@themillalveley.fsnet.co.uk
web: www.themill-hotel.co.uk
(For full entry see Alveley)

★★★ Old Vicarage Hotel and Restaurant
Worfield WV15 5JZ
☎ 01746 716497 01746 716552
e-mail: admin@the-old-vicarage.demon.co.uk
web: www.oldvicarageworfield.com
(For full entry see Worfield)

★★67% Parlors Hall
Mill St WV15 5AL
☎ 01746 761931 01746 767058
e-mail: info@parlorshallhotel.co.uk
Dir: *from A454, right & right again in 200yds*
Parlors Hall has been a hotel since 1929 and retains many original features, such as oak panelling and magnificent fireplaces. Named after the family who lived here between 1419 and 1539, the property now features well-equipped bedrooms, some with four-poster beds, a restaurant and charming bar.
ROOMS: 15 en suite (2 fmly) **FACILITIES:** Xmas **CONF:** Thtr 50 Class 25 Board 25 **PARKING:** 24 **NOTES:**

See advert on opposite page

★★61% Falcon Hotel
Saint John St, Lowtown WV15 6AG
☎ 01746 763134 01746 765401
e-mail: enquiries@thefalconhotel.co.uk
web: www.thefalconhotel.co.uk
Dir: *A442 Telford to Kidderminster road. Follow Bridgnorth town centre signs. Hotel 100yds on left before bridge over River Severn*
This 17th-century former coaching inn stands near the River Severn in the Lowtown area of Bridgnorth, and offers comfortable bedrooms which are equipped to modern standards. A good selection of dishes is served in the open-plan bar with its beamed restaurant.
ROOMS: 12 en suite (4 fmly) in 5 bedrooms **CONF:** Thtr 40 Class 20 Board 25 **PARKING:** 100

BRIDGWATER, Somerset

Map 04 ST23

See also Holford

★★★72% *Walnut Tree Hotel*
North Petherton TA6 6QA
☎ 01278 662255 01278 663946
e-mail: sales@walnuttreehotel.com
web: www.walnuttreehotel.com
Dir: *on A38, 1m S of M5 junct 24*

Popular with business and leisure guests, this 18th-century former coaching inn is located within easy reach of the M5. Smartly decorated bedrooms are well furnished and equipped with a range of facilities. An extensive selection of dishes is offered and guests can dine in either the restaurant, bistro area or bar.
ROOMS: 33 en suite (5 fmly) (13 GF) in 7 bedrooms **FACILITIES:** STV ♫ ch fac **CONF:** Thtr 120 Class 76 Board 70 **PARKING:** 70 **NOTES:** in restaurant Civ Wed 50

★★70% Apple Tree
Keenthorne TA5 1HZ
☎ 01278 733238 01278 732693
e-mail: reservations@appletreehotel.com
web: www.appletreehotel.com
(For full entry see Nether Stowey)

Premier Travel Inn Bridgwater
Express Park, Bristol Rd TA6 4RR
☎ 0870 242 3344 0870 241 9000
web: www.premiertravelinn.com
High quality, modern budget accommodation ideal for both families and business travellers. Spacious, en suite bedrooms feature bath and shower, satellite TV and many have telephones and modem points. The adjacent family restaurant features a wide and varied menu. For further details consult the Hotel Groups page.
ROOMS: 40 en suite s £49.95; d £49.95

♫ Entertainment

⌂ Travelodge Bridgwater
Huntsworth Business Park
☎ 08700 850950 🖷 01278 450 432
web: www.travelodge.co.uk
Dir: *Exit M5 at junct 24 A38 towards Bridgwater. Follow signs for Services. Travelodge is located within the Service Area.*
Travelodge offers good quality, good value, modern accommodation. Ideal for families, the spacious, en suite bedrooms include remote-control TV, tea and coffee-making facilities and comfortable beds. Meals can be taken at the nearby family restaurant. For further details consult the Hotel Groups page.
ROOMS: 29 en suite s fr £26; d fr £26

BRIDLINGTON, East Riding of Yorkshire — Map 17 TA16

★★★70% Revelstoke
1-3 Flamborough Rd YO15 2HU
☎ 01262 672362 🖷 01262 672362
e-mail: info@revelstokehotel.co.uk
web: www.revelstokehotel.co.uk
Dir: *B1255 Flamborough Head road, 0.5m right at mini rdbt to junct of Promenade & Flamborough Rd. Hotel opp Holy Trinity Church*

Family owned and run, this friendly hotel is close to both the town centre and the North Bay seafront and is a popular choice. Bedrooms are well equipped and very comfortable. Public areas include the well-furnished lounge bar where informal bar meals can be taken and the attractive dining room for a more formal dining atmosphere.
ROOMS: 26 en suite (6 fmly) s £49; d £78-£88 **LB** **FACILITIES:** STV ♫ Xmas **CONF:** BC Thtr 250 Class 200 Board 100 **PARKING:** 14
NOTES: ✈ ⊗ in restaurant RS 25-28 Dec Civ Wed 200
See advert on this page

Popped the question? Hotels with Civ wed in their entry are licensed for civil wedding ceremonies. Maximum numbers for the ceremony only are shown e.g. Civ wed 120

★★★68% *Expanse*
North Marine Dr YO15 2LS
☎ 01262 675347 🖷 01262 604928
e-mail: expanse@brid.demon.co.uk
web: www.expanse.co.uk
Dir: *follow North Beach signs, pass under railway arch for North Marine Drive. Hotel at bottom of hill*
This traditional seaside hotel overlooks the bay and has been in the same family's ownership for many years. Service is relaxed and friendly and the modern bedrooms are well equipped.
continued on p112

BRIDLINGTON, continued

Comfortable public areas include a conference suite, a choice of bars and an inviting lounge.

Expanse, Bridlington

ROOMS: 48 en suite (4 fmly) ⊗ in 12 bedrooms **FACILITIES:** STV ♫ **CONF:** Thtr 180 Class 50 Board 50 **SERVICES:** Lift **PARKING:** 23 **NOTES:** ✗ ⊗ in restaurant Civ Wed

See advert on opposite page

BRIDPORT, Dorset — Map 04 SY49

★★★65% Haddon House

West Bay DT6 4EL

☎ 01308 423626 & 425323 📠 01308 427348

Dir: *at Crown Inn rdbt take B3157 West Bay Rd, hotel 0.5m on right at mini-rdbt*

This attractive, creeper-clad hotel offers good standards of accommodation and is situated a few minutes' walk from the seafront and the quay. A friendly and relaxed style of service is provided. An extensive range of dishes, from lighter bar snacks to main meals, is on offer in the Tudor-style restaurant.

ROOMS: 12 en suite (2 fmly) (1 GF) ⊗ in all bedrooms **FACILITIES:** Xmas **CONF:** Thtr 40 Class 20 Board 26 **PARKING:** 44 **NOTES:** ✗ ⊗ in restaurant

★66% Bridge House

115 East St DT6 3LB

☎ 01308 423371 📠 01308 459573

e-mail: info@bridgehousebridport.co.uk

Dir: *follow signs to town centre from A35 rdbt, hotel 200mtrs on right*

A short stroll from the town centre, this 18th-century Grade II listed property has undergone a major refurbishment. The well-equipped bedrooms vary in size. In addition to the main lounge, there is a small bar-lounge and a separate breakfast room. An interesting range of home-cooked meals is provided in the restaurant.

ROOMS: 10 en suite (3 fmly) ⊗ in 5 bedrooms s fr £49; d fr £73 (incl. bkfst) **PARKING:** 13 **NOTES:** ⊗ in restaurant

BRIGG, Lincolnshire — Map 17 TA00

★★66% The Red Lion Inn at Redbourne

Main Rd, Redbourne DN21 4QR

☎ 01652 648302 📠 01652 648900

e-mail: enquiries@redlion.org

web: www.redlion.org

Dir: *from M180 junct 4 take A15. After 4m left at mini-rdbt, follow signs left to Redbourne. Hotel 1st building on left in village*

Dating back to the 17th century, this former coaching inn overlooks the village green and holds a key to the historic fire station that is adjacent. Newly restored, the inn has pleasantly furnished bedrooms and a wholesome range of food is available either in the modern bar or air-conditioned dining room. There is a warm and friendly atmosphere.

ROOMS: 11 en suite (2 fmly) ⊗ in 2 bedrooms s £40-£60; d £65-£90 (incl. bkfst) **LB** **CONF:** Thtr 35 Class 35 Board 35 **PARKING:** 30 **NOTES:** ⊗ in restaurant

BRIGHOUSE, West Yorkshire — Map 16 SE12

⌂ Premier Travel Inn Huddersfield North

Wakefield Rd HD6 4HA

☎ 0870 9906360 📠 0870 9906361

web: www.premiertravelinn.com

Dir: *Exit M62 junct 25, follow A644 Huddersfield, Dewsbury & Wakefield signs. Inn 500mtrs up hill on right*

High quality, modern budget accommodation ideal for both families and business travellers. Spacious, en suite bedrooms feature bath and shower, satellite TV and many have telephones and modem points. The adjacent family restaurant features a wide and varied menu. For further details consult the Hotel Groups page.

ROOMS: 71 en suite s £46.95-£48.95; d £46.95-£48.95

BRIGHTON & HOVE, East Sussex — Map 06 TQ30

★★★★★68% *De Vere Grand Brighton*

King's Rd BN1 2FW

☎ 01273 224300 📠 01273 224321

e-mail: reservations@grandbrighton.co.uk

web: www.devereonline.co.uk

Dir: *on seafront between piers, next to Brighton Centre*

Dating back to the mid 19th century, this landmark seafront hotel, with its eye-catching white façade and intricate balconies, is as grand as the name suggests. Bedrooms include a number of deluxe sea view rooms, some with balconies, and suites, also with sea views. The hotel is perhaps best known for its extensive conference and banqueting facilities; there is also a well-equipped leisure centre and an impressive conservatory adjoining the bar.

ROOMS: 200 en suite (60 fmly) **FACILITIES: Spa** STV supervised Sauna Solarium Gym Jacuzzi Hairdresser, Tropicarium, beauty salon & treatment rooms ♫ **CONF:** Thtr 800 Class 420 Board 50 **SERVICES:** Lift **PARKING:** 70 **NOTES:** Civ Wed 800

Town House

★★★★ 🏵 🏠 **Hotel Du Vin Brighton**
2-6 Ship St BN1 1AD
☎ 01273 718588 📠 01273 718599
e-mail: info@brighton.hotelduvin.com
web: www.hotelduvin.com

Hotel du Vin & Bistro

Dir: *A23 from London, signs to seafront/city centre. Right at seafront, right up Middle St follow road in U shape to Ship St*

This tastefully converted mock-Tudor building occupies a convenient location in a quiet side street close to the seafront. The individually designed bedrooms have a wine theme, and all are comprehensively equipped. Public areas offer a spacious split-level bar, an atmospheric and locally popular restaurant, plus useful private dining and meeting facilities.

ROOMS: 37 en suite (5 GF) d £130-£140 **FACILITIES:** STV Snooker Xmas **CONF:** Thtr 30 Board 22 Del £195 **SERVICES:** air con **PARKING:** 10 **NOTES:** 🚫🐕 🚭 in restaurant

If you wish to use a particular credit card or debit card please check with the hotel that they are happy to accept it

Indoor Swimming pool
Indoor Swimming pool (heated)
Outdoor Swimming pool
Outdoor Swimming pool (heated)

B

BRIGHTON & HOVE, continued

Town House

★★★★ ⊛ ⌂ **Alias Hotel Seattle**
The Strand, Brighton Marina BN2 5WA
☎ 01273 679799 🖷 01273 679899
e-mail: info@aliasseattle.com
web: www.aliashotels.com
Dir: *Follow signs to seafront. Hotel in Marina 1m E of Palace Pier*
This smart, modern hotel enjoys a prime position overlooking Brighton Marina and has much to offer guests whether on business or leisure. The chic saloon lounge and trendy Black and White bar both have balconies with sea views, while the spacious, atmospheric Café Paradise offers cuisine with a Mediterranean theme.
ROOMS: 71 en suite d fr £100 **LB** **FACILITIES:** STV Special rates for hotel guests at nearby David Lloyd Leisure Centre **CONF:** Thtr 120 Class 50 Board 70 Del from £169 **SERVICES:** Lift **NOTES:** ⊘ in restaurant Civ Wed 100

See advert on page 113

Town House

★★★★ ⌂ ***The Royal Pavilion Townhouse***
12A Regency Square BN1 2FG
☎ 01273 722123 🖷 01273 722293
e-mail: info@rpthotel.co.uk
An elegant Regency townhouse on four floors enjoying close proximity to the West Pier and seafront. The spacious and individually themed bedrooms are comprehensively equipped and those on the front of the building offer views over the square. There is a comfortable bar and attractive Italian-style restaurant. Parking is available in the NCP car park opposite.
ROOMS: 8 en suite ⊘ in 3 bedrooms **FACILITIES:** STV **CONF:** Thtr 12 Board 12 **NOTES:** ✗ No children 21yrs

★★★★66% **Old Ship**
King's Rd BN1 1NR
☎ 01273 329001 🖷 01273 820718
e-mail: oldship@paramount-hotels.co.uk
web: www.paramount-hotels.co.uk
Dir: *A23 to seafront, right at rdbt along Kings Rd. Hotel 200yds on right*
The Old Ship enjoys a stunning seafront location and offers guests elegant surroundings to relax in. Bedrooms are well designed, with modern facilities ensuring comfort. Many original features have been retained, including the oak-panelled bar. Facilities include a variety of conference rooms and a car park.
ROOMS: 152 en suite (10 fmly) ⊘ in 15 bedrooms s £89-£165; d £178-£200 (incl. bkfst) **LB** **FACILITIES:** Xmas **CONF:** Thtr 300 Class 100 Board 60 Del from £120 **SERVICES:** Lift **PARKING:** 40 **NOTES:** ✗ Civ Wed 150

★★★68% ***Imperial***
First Av BN3 2GU
☎ 01273 777320 🖷 01273 777310
e-mail: info@imperial-hove.com
web: www.imperial-hove.com
Dir: *M23 to Brighton seafront, right at rdbt to Hove, 1.5m to First Avenue turn right*

Located within minutes of the seafront, this Regency property is constantly being improved and upgraded. A good range of conference suites complement the comfortable public rooms, which include a lounge, a smart bar area and an attractive restaurant. Bedrooms are generally of comfortable proportions, well appointed and with a good range of facilities.
ROOMS: 76 en suite (4 fmly) ⊘ in 10 bedrooms **CONF:** BC Thtr 110 Class 30 Board 34 **SERVICES:** Lift **NOTES:** ✗ ⊘ in restaurant

★★★67% **Brighton Hotel**
143/145 King's Rd BN1 2PQ
☎ 01273 820555 🖷 01273 821555
e-mail: brighton.hotel@btconnect.com
web: www.bw-brightonhotel.co.uk
Dir: *signs to Brighton Pier, turn right & hotel 100yds past West Pier*

This friendly, family-run hotel is well placed in a prime seafront location that is close to the historic West Pier. All of the bedrooms are bright, comfortably appointed and well equipped, and public rooms have been fully refurbished. The parking facilities, though limited, are a real bonus in this area of the town.
ROOMS: 52 en suite s £60-£95; d £110-£240 (incl. bkfst) **LB** **FACILITIES:** STV **CONF:** Thtr 130 Class 35 Board 35 Del from £99 **SERVICES:** Lift **PARKING:** 12 **NOTES:** ✗ ⊘ in restaurant

★★★67% **The Granville**
124 King's Rd BN1 2FA
☎ 01273 326302 🖷 01273 728294
e-mail: granville@brighton.co.uk
web: www.granvillehotel.co.uk
Dir: *opposite West Pier*
This stylish hotel is located on Brighton's busy seafront. Bedrooms

continued

are carefully furnished and decorated with great style. A trendy cocktail bar and restaurant is located in the cellar with street access and a cosy terrace for warmer months.
ROOMS: 24 en suite (2 fmly) (1 GF) ⊗ in all bedrooms s £65-£105; d £85-£185 (incl. bkfst) **LB** **FACILITIES:** Jacuzzi **CONF:** BC Thtr 50 Class 30 Board 30 Del from £85 **SERVICES:** Lift **PARKING:** 3

★★★66% Princes Marine

153 Kingsway BN3 4GR
☎ 01273 207660 🖷 01273 325913
e-mail: princesmarine@bestwestern.co.uk
Dir: *right at Brighton Pier, follow seafront for 2m. Hotel 200yds from King Alfred leisure centre*

This friendly hotel enjoys a seafront location and offers spacious, comfortable bedrooms equipped with a good range of facilities. There is a cosy restaurant, bar and useful meeting room and limited parking at the rear.
ROOMS: 48 en suite (4 fmly) ⊗ in 24 bedrooms s £45-£65; d £70-£140 (incl. bkfst) **LB** **FACILITIES:** Xmas **CONF:** BC Thtr 80 Class 40 Board 40 **SERVICES:** Lift **PARKING:** 30

★★★64% The Courtlands

15-27 The Drive BN3 3JE
☎ 01273 731055 🖷 01273 328295
e-mail: info@courtlandshotel.com
Dir: *At A23/ A27 Junct. 1st exit to Hove, 2nd exit at rdbt, right at 1st junct and left at shops. Straight on at junct. Hotel on left*

This hotel is within walking distance of the seafront and has its own small car park. The majority of bedrooms are newly decorated and have smart bathrooms. Guests have the use of a comfortable lounge, a light and spacious restaurant; service is both friendly and attentive.
ROOMS: 60 en suite 7 annexe en suite (8 fmly) ⊗ in 20 bedrooms s £45-£67.50; d £85-£115 **LB** **FACILITIES:** Xmas **CONF:** Thtr 60 Class 20 Board 30 Del from £75 **SERVICES:** Lift **PARKING:** 24
NOTES: ⊗ in restaurant

★★★64% Quality Hotel Brighton

West St BN1 2RQ
☎ 01273 220033 🖷 01273 778000
e-mail: enquiries@hotels-brighton.com
web: www.choicehotelseurope.com
Dir: *A23 into Brighton, then town centre/seafront signs. A259 to Hove & Worthing. Hotel next to Brighton Centre*
Conveniently located for the seafront and close to the town centre, this purpose-built hotel offers modern and well-equipped bedrooms. Public areas include a spacious, open-plan lounge bar area with a feature staircase. A choice of restaurants serves a wide selection of dishes.
ROOMS: 138 en suite (2 fmly) ⊗ in 60 bedrooms **CONF:** Thtr 200 Class 80 Board 60 **SERVICES:** Lift **NOTES:** ⊗ in restaurant

★★63% Preston Park Hotel

216 Preston Rd BN1 6UU
☎ 01273 507853 🖷 01273 540039
e-mail: manager@prestonparkhotel.co.uk
This hotel enjoys a convenient roadside location on the outskirts of Brighton. Bedrooms are modern and are well provisioned for both the leisure and business guest. Freshly prepared meals are offered in the spacious bar or the more intimate and relaxing restaurant.
ROOMS: 33 en suite (4 fmly) ⊗ in 20 bedrooms s £55-£105; d £69-£125 (incl. bkfst) **LB** **FACILITIES:** supervised Sauna Gym Xmas **CONF:** Thtr 100 Class 60 Board 60 Del from £110 **PARKING:** 60
NOTES: ⊗ in restaurant Civ Wed 80

BRIGHTON & HOVE, continued

Lansdowne Place

Lansdowne Place BN3 1HQ
☎ 01273 736266 📠 01273 729802
e-mail: bookings@lansdowneplace.co.uk
web: www.lansdowneplace.co.uk
Dir: *A23 to seafront. Right at Brighton Pier, along seafront, right at Lansdowne Place*

At the time of going to press, the star classification for this hotel was not confirmed. Please refer to the AA internet site www.theAA.com for current information.
ROOMS: 84 en suite (3 fmly) ⊗ in all bedrooms s fr £70; d £130-£225 **FACILITIES: Spa** STV Sauna Gym Xmas **CONF:** BC Thtr 200 Class 60 Board 30 Del £159 **SERVICES:** Lift **PARKING:** 16 **NOTES:** ✗ ⊗ in restaurant Civ Wed

See advert on opposite page

Ramada Brighton

149 Kings Rd BN1 2PP
☎ 01273 738201 📠 01273 821752
e-mail: sales.brighton@ramadajarvis.co.uk
web: www.ramadajarvis.co.uk
Dir: *Take A23, follow seafront signs, turn right at Palace Pier rdbt. Hotel is on right, just after West Pier.*
This Regency-style hotel enjoys a prime seafront location along the Kings Road. Bedrooms are comfortably appointed for both business and leisure guests.
ROOMS: 121 en suite (2 fmly) ⊗ in 75 bedrooms s £95-£119; d £95-£119 **FACILITIES: Spa** STV Sauna Solarium Xmas **CONF:** Thtr 180 Class 60 Board 60 Del from £149 **SERVICES:** Lift **PARKING:** 41 **NOTES:** ✗ ⊗ in restaurant Civ Wed 150

Innkeeper's Lodge Brighton

London Rd, Patcham BN1 8YQ
☎ 01273 552886
web: www.innkeeperslodge.com
A growing concept in the travel accommodation market. Smart rooms meet essential business requirements but also have home comforts. Dining options include all-day menus plus the added advantage of breakfast, which is included in the room price. For further details consult the Hotel Groups page.
ROOMS: 18 rms s £59; d £59

> Late for dinner? Quality standards mean that last orders for dinner vary according to star rating and should be no earlier than:
> ★★ 7.00pm ★★★ 8:00pm ★★★★ 9:00pm ★★★★★ 10:00pm

Premier Travel Inn Brighton City Centre

144 North St BN1 1RE
☎ 0870 9906340 📠 0870 9906341
web: www.premiertravelinn.com
Dir: *From A23 follow signs for city centre. Right at lights nr Royal Pavilion, then take road ahead on left (runs adjacent to Pavilion) onto Church St, 1st left onto New Rd leading North St*
High quality, modern budget accommodation ideal for both families and business travellers. Spacious, en suite bedrooms feature bath and shower, satellite TV and many have telephones and modem points. The adjacent family restaurant features a wide and varied menu. For further details consult the Hotel Groups page.
ROOMS: 160 en suite s £57.95-£64.95; d £57.95-£64.95

Travelodge Brighton Central

Preston Rd BN1 6AU
☎ 08700 850 950 📠 01273 554917
web: www.travelodge.co.uk
Dir: *south on A23 follow signs for Brighton town centre. Lodge on right*
Travelodge offers good quality, good value, modern accommodation. Ideal for families, the spacious, en suite bedrooms include remote-control TV, tea and coffee-making facilities and comfortable beds. Meals can be taken at the nearby family restaurant. For further details consult the Hotel Groups page.
ROOMS: 94 en suite s fr £26; d fr £26

BRISTOL, Bristol — Map 04 ST57

★★★★ 74% ®®®

Bristol Marriott Royal Hotel

College Green BS1 5TA
☎ 0117 925 5100 📠 0117 925 1515
e-mail: bristol.royal@marriotthotels.co.uk
web: www.marriott.co.uk
Dir: *next to cathedral*
A truly stunning hotel located in the centre of the city, next to the cathedral. Public areas are particularly impressive with luxurious lounges and a leisure club. Dining options include the more informal Terrace and the newly opened Michael Caines restaurant, adjacent to the champagne bar. The spacious bedrooms have the benefit of air conditioning, comfortable armchairs and marbled bathrooms.
ROOMS: 242 en suite ⊗ in 163 bedrooms s £85-£155; d £130-£155 (incl. bkfst) **LB FACILITIES:** STV Sauna Solarium Gym Jacuzzi Xmas **CONF:** BC Thtr 300 Class 80 Board 84 Del from £160 **SERVICES:** Lift air con **PARKING:** 200 **NOTES:** ✗ ⊗ in restaurant Civ Wed 200

Town House

★★★★ ® Hotel du Vin & Bistro

The Sugar House, Narrow Lewins Mead BS1 2NU
☎ 0117 925 5577 📠 0117 925 1199
e-mail: info@bristol.hotelduvin.com
web: www.hotelduvin.com
Dir: *A4 follow city centre signs. 400yds pass Rupert St NCP on right. Hotel on opposite carriageway*
A member of one of Britain's most innovative and expanding hotel groups extends the high standards for which the chain is renowned. The hotel is housed in a Grade II listed, converted 18th-century sugar refinery. Bedrooms are exceptionally well designed and the hotel provides great facilities with a modern minimalist feel. The bistro offers an excellent menu.
ROOMS: 40 en suite s £130-£330; d £130-£330 **FACILITIES:** STV Snooker Xmas **CONF:** Thtr 50 Class 25 Board 26 **SERVICES:** Lift **PARKING:** 33 **NOTES:** ✗ ⊗ in restaurant

★★★★71% Aztec Hotel & Spa
Aztec West Business Park BS32 4TS
☎ 01454 201090 🖹 01454 201593
e-mail: aztec@shirehotels.com
web: www.shirehotels.com
Dir: *access via M5 junct 16 & M4*

SHIRE HOTELS

Situated close to Cribbs Causeway shopping centre and major motorway links, this stylish hotel offers comfortable, very well-equipped bedrooms. Built in a Nordic style, public rooms boast log fires and vaulted ceilings. Leisure facilities include a popular gym and good size pool. The new-look Quarterjacks restaurant offers relaxed informal dining with a focus on simply prepared, quality regional foods.

ROOMS: 128 en suite (6 fmly) (29 GF) ⊘ in 84 bedrooms s £90-£164; d £130-£184 (incl. bkfst) **LB FACILITIES:** STV supervised Squash Sauna Solarium Gym Jacuzzi Steam room, Health & beauty, Childrens splash pool Xmas **CONF:** BC Thtr 200 Class 120 Board 36 Del from £169 **SERVICES:** Lift air con **PARKING:** 240 **NOTES:** ⊘ in restaurant Civ Wed 120

★★★★69% Bristol Marriott City Centre
Lower Castle St BS1 3AD
☎ 0870 400 7210 🖹 0870 400 7310
web: www.marriott.co.uk
Dir: *M32 follow signs to Broadmead, take slip road to large rdbt, take 3rd exit. Hotel on right*

Marriott HOTELS & RESORTS

Situated at the foot of the picturesque Castle Park, this mainly business-orientated hotel is well placed for the city centre. Executive and de-luxe bedrooms have high speed internet access.

continued on p118

BRISTOL, continued

In addition to a coffee bar and lounge menu, the Mediterrano restaurant offers an interesting selection of well-prepared dishes.

Bristol Marriott City Centre, Bristol

ROOMS: 301 en suite (135 fmly) ⊗ in 232 bedrooms **FACILITIES:** **Spa** STV supervised Sauna Solarium Gym Jacuzzi Steam room **CONF:** BC Thtr 600 Class 280 Board 40 Del from £135 **SERVICES:** Lift air con **NOTES:** ⊗ in restaurant Civ Wed

★★★★68% The Brigstow

5-7 Welsh Back BS1 4SP
☎ 0117 929 1030 📠 0117 929 2030
e-mail: brigstow@fullers.co.uk
Dir: *Follow signs to City Centre. Turn left into Baldwin St, 2nd right into Queen Charlotte St. NCP on left*

In a prime position, with its own river frontage, this handsome purpose-built hotel is designed and finished with care taken in every detail. The shopping centre and theatres are within easy walking distance. Bedrooms are stylish and extremely well equipped, including plasma TV screens in the bathrooms. There is an integrated state-of-the-art conference and meeting centre, and a smart restaurant and bar overlooking the harbour. Guests have complimentary use of a squash and health club plus free internet access.
ROOMS: 116 en suite ⊗ in 78 bedrooms s £95-£169; d £95-£169 **LB** **FACILITIES:** STV Complimentary access to squash & health club nearby **CONF:** BC Thtr 60 Class 30 Board 36 Del £175 **SERVICES:** Lift air con **NOTES:** RS 24 Dec-5 Jan Civ Wed 50

★★★★65% Jurys Bristol Hotel

JURYS DOYLE HOTELS

Prince St BS1 4QF
☎ 0117 923 0333 📠 0117 923 0300
e-mail: bristol_hotel@jurysdoyle.com
web: www.jurysdoyle.com
Dir: *from Temple Meads right at 1st rdbt into Victoria St. At Bristol Bridge lights left into Baldwin St, 2nd left into Marsh St, right at rdbt*
This modern hotel enjoys an excellent location near Bristol's Millennium Project. Bedrooms vary in size and are well appointed with a range of facilities. There is a choice of eating options, including a Quayside restaurant and adjoining inn. Extensive conference facilities are also available.
ROOMS: 192 en suite (17 fmly) ⊗ in 53 bedrooms s £84-£150; d £94-£150 **LB** **FACILITIES:** STV Complimentary use of local gym 2mins walk from hotel. ♫ Xmas **CONF:** Thtr 400 Class 160 Board 80 Del from £150 **SERVICES:** Lift **PARKING:** 400 **NOTES:** ⊗ in restaurant

★★★★65% Novotel Bristol Centre

NOVOTEL

Victoria St BS1 6HY
☎ 0117 976 9988 📠 0117 925 5040
e-mail: h5622@accor.com
web: www.novotel.com
Dir: *at end of M32 follow signs for Temple Meads station to rdbt. Final exit, hotel immediately on right*
A major transformation at this city centre hotel has seen the introduction of the latest Novotel 'Novation' style bedroom with unique swivel desk, air-conditioning and a host of extras. The hotel is convenient for the mainline railway station and also has its own car park. Novotel - AA Hotel Group of the Year 2005-6.
ROOMS: 131 en suite (20 fmly) ⊗ in 119 bedrooms s £130; d £130 **LB** **FACILITIES:** STV Solarium Gym **CONF:** Thtr 230 Class 70 Board 35 Del £173 **SERVICES:** Lift **PARKING:** 120 **NOTES:** ⊗ in restaurant

★★★70% ® Arno's Manor

Forestdale Hotels

470 Bath Rd, Arno's Vale BS4 3HQ
☎ 0117 971 1461 📠 0117 971 5507
e-mail: arnos.manor@forestdale.com
web: www.forestdale.com
Once the home of a wealthy merchant, this historic 18th-century building is now a comfortable hotel and offers spacious, well-appointed bedrooms with plenty of workspace. The lounge was once the chapel and has many original features, while meals are taken in the atmospheric, conservatory-style restaurant.
ROOMS: 73 en suite (1 fmly) (7 GF) s £100-£120; d £130-£140 (incl. bkfst) **LB** **FACILITIES:** STV Xmas **CONF:** Thtr 150 Class 60 Board 40 Del from £135 **SERVICES:** Lift **PARKING:** 200 **NOTES:** ⊗ in restaurant Civ Wed 100

★★★68% Berkeley Square

15 Berkeley Square, Clifton BS8 1HB
☎ 0117 925 4000 📠 0117 925 2970
e-mail: berkeleysquare@bestwestern.co.uk
Dir: *M32 follow Clifton signs. 1st left at traffic lights by Nills Memorial Tower (University) into Berkeley Sq*
Set in a peaceful square close to the university, art gallery and Clifton village, this smart, elegant Georgian hotel has modern, tastefully decorated bedrooms that include many welcome extras. There is a busy bar in the basement, and the restaurant features dishes with a contemporary European feel to match the surroundings.
ROOMS: 43 en suite (4 GF) ⊗ in 30 bedrooms s £64-£139; d £105-£155 (incl. bkfst) **LB** **FACILITIES:** STV use of local gym and swimming pool 5.00 day pass **SERVICES:** Lift **PARKING:** 20 **NOTES:** ⊗ in restaurant

★★★68% ® City Inn Bristol

Temple Way BS1 6BF
☎ 0117 925 1001 📠 0117 907 4116
e-mail: bristol.reservations@cityinn.com
This popular hotel offers spacious, contemporary public areas and bedrooms, and is situated within walking distance of the city centre and railway station. The young team of staff are well motivated and friendly. The City Café offers an interesting

continued

selection of carefully prepared, quality ingredients and the adjacent bar serves coffee and tea throughout the day.
ROOMS: 167 en suite (3 GF) ⊗ in 134 bedrooms s £65-£129; d £65-£129 **LB** **FACILITIES:** STV Gym **CONF:** Thtr 45 Class 22 Board 24 Del from £199 **SERVICES:** Lift air con **PARKING:** 45 **NOTES:** ⊗ in restaurant

★★★68% *Corus hotel Bristol*
Beggar Bush Ln, Failand BS8 3TG
☎ 0870 609 6144 ■ 01275 392104
e-mail: reservations.redwoodlodge@corushotels.com
web: www.corushotels.com
Dir: *M5 junct 19, A369 for 3m then right at traffic lights. Hotel 1m on left*

Situated close to the suspension bridge, this popular hotel offers guests a peaceful location combined with excellent leisure facilities, including a cinema, gym, squash, badminton and tennis courts, plus indoor and outdoor pools. Bedrooms have plenty of amenities and are well suited to the business guest.
ROOMS: 112 en suite (1 fmly) (52 GF) ⊗ in 81 bedrooms **FACILITIES:** STV Squash Sauna Solarium Gym 175 seater Cinema, Aerobics/Dance studios, Badminton courts **CONF:** BC Thtr 175 Class 80 Board 40 **PARKING:** 1000 **NOTES:** ⊗ in restaurant Civ Wed 200

★★★66% The Avon Gorge
Sion Hill, Clifton BS8 4LD
☎ 0117 973 8955 & 906 4655 ■ 0117 923 8125
e-mail: info@avongorge-hotel-bristol.com
web: www.peelhotel.com
Dir: *M5 junct 19, follow signs for Clifton Toll, over suspension bridge, 1st right into Sion Hill*

Overlooking Avon Gorge and Brunel's famous suspension bridge, this popular hotel offers rooms with glorious views. Bedrooms are very well equipped and have extras such as ceiling fans. Public areas include a traditional restaurant and a popular modern bar and brasserie, both overlooking a large outdoor terraced area.
ROOMS: 76 en suite (9 fmly) ⊗ in 53 bedrooms s £115-£130; d £135-£160 **FACILITIES:** STV Xmas **CONF:** Thtr 100 Class 50 Board 30 Del from £120 **SERVICES:** Lift **NOTES:** ⊗ in restaurant Civ Wed 100

★★74% Best Western Victoria Square
Victoria Square, Clifton BS8 4EW
☎ 0117 973 9058 ■ 0117 970 6929
e-mail: victoriasquare@btopenworld.com
web: www.vicsquare.com
Dir: *M5 junct 19, follow Clifton signs. Over suspension bridge, right into Clifton Down Rd. Left at mini rdbt into Merchants Rd then into Victoria Sq*

Situated with convenient access to the heart of Clifton and the city centre, these two former Victorian houses have undergone a refurbishment programme throughout. Bedrooms are generally spacious, all are well equipped with a range of useful extras such as modem points for internet access. A pleasant conference room and small rear car park are also on hand.
ROOMS: 21 en suite 19 annexe en suite (5 fmly) (2 GF) ⊗ in 30 bedrooms s £65-£95; d £75-£105 (incl. bkfst) **FACILITIES:** STV **CONF:** Thtr 30 Class 20 Board 20 **PARKING:** 14 **NOTES:** ⊗ in restaurant Closed 22 Dec-2 Jan

★★70% *Clifton*
St Pauls Rd, Clifton BS8 1LX
☎ 0117 973 6882 ■ 0117 974 1082
e-mail: clifton@cliftonhotels.com
web: www.cliftonhotels.com/clifton
Dir: *M32 follow Bristol/Clifton signs, along Park St. Left at lights into St Pauls Rd*
This popular hotel offers very well equipped bedrooms and relaxed, friendly service. There is a welcoming lounge by the reception, and in summer months drinks and meals can be enjoyed on the terrace. Racks Bar and Restaurant offers an interesting selection of modern dishes in informal surroundings. Some street parking is possible although for a small charge, secure garage parking is available.
ROOMS: 59 en suite (2 fmly) ⊗ in 28 bedrooms **FACILITIES:** STV **SERVICES:** Lift **PARKING:** 20

★★68% The Bowl Inn
16 Church Rd, Lower Almondsbury BS32 4DT
☎ 01454 612757 ■ 01454 619910
e-mail: reception@thebowlinn.co.uk
web: www.thebowlinn.co.uk
Dir: *M5 junct 16 onto Gloucester road, N for 500yds. Turn left into Over Lane, turn right by Garden Centre. Hotel next to church on right*
With easy access to the motorway network, this popular 16th-century village inn offers all the comforts of modern life. Each bedroom has been individually furnished to complement the

continued on p120

BRISTOL, continued

many original features. Dining options include an extensive bar menu with cask ales, and a more intimate restaurant.

The Bowl Inn, Bristol

ROOMS: 11 rms (2 en suite) 2 annexe en suite (1 GF) ⊗ in 4 bedrooms s £44.50-£87; d £71-£97.50 **LB** **FACILITIES:** STV **CONF:** Thtr 30 Class 20 Board 24 **PARKING:** 30 **NOTES:** RS 25-Dec

★★68% Rodney Hotel

4 Rodney Place, Clifton BS8 4HY
☎ 0117 973 5422 🖷 0117 946 7092
e-mail: rodney@cliftonhotels.com
Dir: *off Clifton Down Rd*

With easy access from the M5, this attractive, listed building in Clifton is conveniently close to the city centre. The individually decorated bedrooms provide a useful range of extra facilities for the business traveller and the refurbished public areas include a smart new bar and restaurant.

ROOMS: 31 en suite (2 GF) ⊗ in 10 bedrooms s £54-£77; d £84 (incl. bkfst) **FACILITIES:** STV **CONF:** Thtr 30 Class 20 Board 20 Del from £105 **PARKING:** 10 **NOTES:** ⊗ in restaurant Closed 22 Dec-3 Jan RS Sun

★★64% Westbourne

THE INDEPENDENTS

40-44 St Pauls Rd, Clifton BS8 1LR
☎ 0117 973 4214 🖷 0117 974 3552
e-mail: westbournehotel@bristol8.fsworld.co.uk
web: www.westbournehotel-bristol.co.uk
Dir: *M32/A4018 along Park St to Triangle, then Whiteladies Rd. Turn left at 1st lights opposite the BBC onto St Pauls Rd. Hotel 200yds on right*

This privately owned hotel is situated in the heart of Clifton and is popular with business guests during the week. It offers comfortable, well-equipped bedrooms. Freddie's Bar and Restaurant provide a choice of eating options, and in the summer guests can enjoy a drink on the terrace.

ROOMS: 29 en suite (7 fmly) (1 GF) ⊗ in 1 bedroom s £50-£61; d fr £75 (incl. bkfst) **PARKING:** 9 **NOTES:** 🐕︎

U Henbury Lodge

Station Rd, Henbury BS10 7QQ
☎ 0117 950 2615 🖷 0117 950 9532
e-mail: contactus@henburylodgehotel.com
web: www.henburylodgehotel.com
Dir: *M5 junct 17/A4018 towards city centre, 3rd rdbt right into Crow Ln. At end turn right & hotel 200mtrs on right*

At the time of going to press, the star classification for this hotel was not confirmed. Please refer to the AA internet site www.theAA.com for current information.

ROOMS: 12 en suite 9 annexe en suite (4 fmly) (6 GF) ⊗ in all bedrooms d £57-£102 (incl. bkfst) **LB** **FACILITIES:** STV Sauna Solarium **CONF:** Thtr 32 Class 20 Board 20 **PARKING:** 24 **NOTES:** ⊗ in restaurant

U Ramada Grange

RAMADA

Northwoods, Winterbourne BS36 1RP
☎ 01454 777333 🖷 01454 777447
e-mail: sales.grange@ramadajarvis.co.uk
web: www.ramadajarvis.co.uk
Dir: *Take A38 towards Filton/Bristol. At rdbt take 1st exit into Bradlet Stoke Way, at lights take 1st left into Woodlands Lane, at 2nd rdbt turn left into Tench Lane. After 1m turn left at T-junct, hotel is 200yds on left.*

This well presented country-house hotel which dates back to 1851, is set in 18 acres of attractive woodland. Bedrooms are comfortably appointed for both business and leisure guests.

ROOMS: 68 en suite (6 fmly) (22 GF) ⊗ in 51 bedrooms s £92-£125; d £92-£125 **FACILITIES: Spa** STV supervised Sauna Solarium Gym Jacuzzi Xmas **CONF:** Thtr 150 Class 72 Board 76 Del from £150 **PARKING:** 150 **NOTES:** ⊗ in restaurant Civ Wed 80

U Ramada Plaza Bristol

RAMADA PLAZA

Redcliffe Way BS1 6NJ
☎ 0117 926 0041 🖷 0117 925 5054
e-mail: sales.plazabristol@ramadajarvis.co.uk
Dir: *adjacent to St Mary Redcliffe church and 400yds from Temple Meads BR station*

This large modern hotel is situated in the heart of the city centre. Bedrooms are comfortably appointed for both business and leisure guests.

ROOMS: 201 en suite (4 fmly) ⊗ in 173 bedrooms s £99-£135; d £99-£135 **FACILITIES:** STV supervised Sauna Xmas **CONF:** Thtr 350 Class 200 Board 40 Del from £159 **SERVICES:** Lift air con **PARKING:** 150 **NOTES:** 🐕︎ ⊗ in restaurant Civ Wed 250

Premier Travel Inn Bristol City Centre

premier travel inn

Haymarket BS1 3LR
☎ 0870 238 3307 🖷 0117 9100619
web: www.premiertravelinn.com
Dir: *M4 junct 19/M32 towards city centre. Through 2 sets of lights, at 3rd set, turn right. To rdbt, take 2nd exit. Inn on left.*

High quality, modern budget accommodation ideal for both

continued

families and business travellers. Spacious, en suite bedrooms feature bath and shower, satellite TV and many have telephones and modem points. The adjacent family restaurant features a wide and varied menu. For further details consult the Hotel Groups page.
ROOMS: 224 en suite s £53.95-£57.95; d £53.95-£57.95

Premier Travel Inn Bristol East

200/202 Westerleigh Rd, Emersons Green BS16 7AN
☎ 08701 977042 🖹 0117 956 4644
web: www.premiertravelinn.com
Dir: *From M4 junct 19 onto M32 junct 1, turn left onto A4174 (Avon Ring Rd). Inn on 3rd rdbt*
High quality, modern budget accommodation ideal for both families and business travellers. Spacious, en suite bedrooms feature bath and shower, satellite TV and many have telephones and modem points. The adjacent family restaurant features a wide and varied menu. For further details consult the Hotel Groups page.
ROOMS: 40 en suite s £52.95; d £52.95 **CONF:** Thtr 26 Board 17

Premier Travel Inn Bristol (Filton)

Shield Retail Park, Gloucester Rd North, Filton BS34 7BR
☎ 0870 9906456 🖹 0870 9906457
web: www.premiertravelinn.com
Dir: *Exit M5 junct 16, towards A38 signed Filton/Patchway. Pass airport & Royal Mail on right. Left at 2nd rdbt, then 1st left into retail park*
High quality, modern budget accommodation ideal for both families and business travellers. Spacious, en suite bedrooms feature bath and shower, satellite TV and many have telephones and modem points. The adjacent family restaurant features a wide and varied menu. For further details consult the Hotel Groups page.
ROOMS: 60 en suite s £49.95-£52.95; d £49.95-£52.95 **CONF:** Board 12

Premier Travel Inn Bristol (King Street)

Llandoger Trow, Kings St BS1 4ER
☎ 0870 9906424 🖹 0870 9906425
web: www.premiertravelinn.com
Dir: *A38 into city centre. Left onto B4053 Baldwin St. Right into Queen Charlotte St, follow one-way system, bear right at river. Inn on right*
High quality, modern budget accommodation ideal for both families and business travellers. Spacious, en suite bedrooms feature bath and shower, satellite TV and many have telephones and modem points. The adjacent family restaurant features a wide and varied menu. For further details consult the Hotel Groups page.
ROOMS: 60 en suite s £57.95; d £57.95

Premier Travel Inn Bristol North West

Cribbs Causeway, Catbrain Ln BS10 7TQ
☎ 0870 9906570 🖹 0870 9906571
web: www.premiertravelinn.com
Dir: *Exit M5 junct 17 onto A4018. 1st left at rdbt into Lysander Rd. Right into Catbrain Hill which leads into Catbrain Ln*
High quality, modern budget accommodation ideal for both families and business travellers. Spacious, en suite bedrooms feature bath and shower, satellite TV and many have telephones and modem points. The adjacent family restaurant features a wide and varied menu. For further details consult the Hotel Groups page.
ROOMS: 106 en suite s £53.95-£57.95; d £53.95-£57.95

> Packed in a hurry? Ironing facilities should be available at all star levels, either in the rooms or on request

Premier Travel Inn Bristol South

Hengrove Leisure Park, Hengrove Way BS14 0HR
☎ 08701 977043 🖹 01275 834721
web: www.premiertravelinn.com
Dir: *From city centre take A37 to Wells & Shepton Mallet. Right onto A4174. Inn at 3rd traffic lights*
High quality, modern budget accommodation ideal for both families and business travellers. Spacious, en suite bedrooms feature bath and shower, satellite TV and many have telephones and modem points. The adjacent family restaurant features a wide and varied menu. For further details consult the Hotel Groups page.
ROOMS: 40 en suite s £46.95-£49.95; d £46.95-£49.95

Travelodge (Bristol Central)

Anchor Rd, Harbourside BS1 5TT
☎ 08700 850 950 🖹 0117 9255149
web: www.travelodge.co.uk
Dir: *on Anchor Road (A4) on left*

Travelodge offers good quality, good value, modern accommodation. Ideal for families, the spacious, en suite bedrooms include remote-control TV, tea and coffee-making facilities and comfortable beds. Meals can be taken at the nearby family restaurant. For further details consult the Hotel Groups page.
ROOMS: 119 en suite s fr £26; d fr £26

Travelodge (Bristol Cribbs Causeway)

Cribbs Causeway BS10 7TL
☎ 08700 850 950 🖹 0117 950 1530
web: www.travelodge.co.uk
Dir: *A4018, off M5 junct 17*
Travelodge offers good quality, good value, modern accommodation. Ideal for families, the spacious, en suite bedrooms include remote-control TV, tea and coffee-making facilities and comfortable beds. Meals can be taken at the nearby family restaurant. For further details consult the Hotel Groups page.
ROOMS: 56 en suite s fr £26; d fr £26

BRIXHAM, Devon
Map 03 SX95

★★★70% Quayside

41-49 King St TQ5 9TJ
☎ 01803 855751 🖹 01803 882733
e-mail: reservations@quaysidehotel.co.uk
web: www.quaysidehotel.co.uk
Dir: *A380, at 2nd rdbt at Kinkerswell towards Brixham on A3022. Hotel overlooks harbour*
With views over the harbour and bay, this hotel was formerly six cottages. The owners and their team of local staff provide friendly and attentive service. Public rooms retain a certain cosiness and intimacy, and include the lounge, residents' bar and Ernie Lister's

continued on p122

BRIXHAM, continued

public bar. Freshly-landed fish features on menus in the well-appointed restaurant.

Quayside, Brixham

ROOMS: 29 en suite (2 fmly) ⊗ in 6 bedrooms s £55-£100; d £80-£130 (incl. bkfst) **LB** **FACILITIES:** ♫ Xmas **CONF:** Thtr 25 Class 18 Board 18 **PARKING:** 30 **NOTES:** ⊗ in restaurant

★★★67% Berry Head

Berry Head Rd TQ5 9AJ
☎ 01803 853225 📠 01803 882084
e-mail: stay@berryheadhotel.com
Dir: *Turn left at town hall to harbour. Right past statue, sharp left. Leave marina, 1m, hotel on left*

From its stunning cliff-top location, this imposing property that dates back to 1809 has spectacular views across Torbay. Public areas include two comfortable lounges, an outdoor terrace, a swimming pool, together with a bar serving a range of popular dishes. Many of the bedrooms have the benefit of the splendid sea views.

ROOMS: 32 en suite (7 fmly) s £48-£80; d £96-£160 (incl. bkfst) **LB** **FACILITIES: Spa** Jacuzzi Petanque Sailing Deep sea fishing ♫ Xmas **CONF:** BC Thtr 300 Class 250 Board 40 **PARKING:** 200 **NOTES:** ⊗ in restaurant Civ Wed 200

See advert on opposite page

BROADSTAIRS, Kent — Map 07 TR36

★★★68% Royal Albion

Albion St CT10 1AN
☎ 01843 868071 📠 01843 861509
e-mail: enquiries@albionbroadstairs.co.uk
web: www.albionbroadstairs.co.uk
Dir: *follow signs for seafront and town centre*

Situated on the seafront in the heart of this bustling town centre overlooking the beach. Bedrooms are smartly decorated and equipped with a good range of useful facilities; many rooms have superb views of the sea. Public areas include Ballards coffee lounge, a sun terrace a lounge bar and Marchesi's restaurant.

ROOMS: 19 en suite (3 fmly) ⊗ in 4 bedrooms s £60-£100; d £100-£170 (incl. bkfst) **LB** **FACILITIES:** STV ♫ **CONF:** Thtr 30 Class 20 Board 20 **PARKING:** 21 **NOTES:** ✗ ⊗ in restaurant

⌂ Town House Hotel
Country House Hotel
Travel Accommodation

BROADWAY, Worcestershire — Map 10 SP03

See also Buckland

★★★79% ◎◎ Dormy House

Willersey Hill WR12 7LF
☎ 01386 852711 📠 01386 858636
e-mail: reservations@dormyhouse.co.uk.
web: www.dormyhouse.co.uk
Dir: *2m E off A44, top of Fish Hill, turn for Saintbury/Picnic area. After 0.5m fork left and hotel on left*

A converted 17th-century farmhouse set in extensive grounds and with stunning views over Broadway. Some rooms are in a collection of honey-coloured stone cottages; some have four-poster beds. Furnishings are tasteful throughout, with some stylish contemporary touches. The best traditions have been retained - real fires, comfortable sofas and afternoon teas.

ROOMS: 25 en suite 22 annexe en suite (3 fmly) s £115-£155; d £155-£205 (incl. bkfst) **LB** **FACILITIES:** STV Sauna Gym Putt green Games room, nature & jogging trail **CONF:** Thtr 170 Class 100 Board 25 Del £185 **PARKING:** 80 **NOTES:** ⊗ in restaurant Closed 25-26 Dec Civ Wed 170

See advert on opposite page

★★★68% Broadway

The Green, High St WR12 7AA
☎ 01386 852401 📠 01386 853879
e-mail: info@broadwayhotel.info
Dir: *From N exit M5 junct 7, then take A44. After Evesham follow signs to Broadway. From London M40 junct 8, follow A40 to A44. Follow signs to Evesham, then Broadway*

A half-timbered Cotswold stone property, built in the 15th century as a retreat for the Abbots of Pershore. Following refurbishment the hotel now combines modern, attractive decor with original charm and character. Bedrooms are tastefully furnished and well equipped while public rooms include a relaxing lounge, cosy bar and charming restaurant.

ROOMS: 20 en suite (1 fmly) ⊗ in all bedrooms s £90-£125; d £130-£205 (incl. bkfst) **LB** **FACILITIES:** Xmas **CONF:** Thtr 20 Board 12 Del £130 **PARKING:** 20 **NOTES:** ⊗ in restaurant Civ Wed 50

Restaurant with Rooms

◎◎ Russell's

20 High St WR12 7DT
☎ 01386 853555 📠 01386 853555
e-mail: info@russellsofbroadway.com
Dir: *on high street opposite village green*

Situated in the centre of a picturesque Cotswold village this restaurant with rooms is a great base for exploring local attractions. Bedrooms, each with their own character, boast superb quality, air conditioning and a wide range of extras for guests. Cuisine is a real draw with freshly prepared local produce used with skill.

ROOMS: 4 en suite (4 fmly) ⊗ in all bedrooms s £95-£160; d £95-£160 (incl. bkfst) **FACILITIES:** STV **SERVICES:** air con **PARKING:** 16 **NOTES:** ⊗ in restaurant

Late for dinner? Quality standards mean that last orders for dinner vary according to star rating and should be no earlier than: ★★ 7.00pm ★★★ 8:00pm ★★★★ 9:00pm ★★★★★ 10:00pm

BROCKENHURST, Hampshire Map 05 SU30

★★★★77% ❀❀ Rhinefield House

Rhinefield Rd SO42 7QB

☎ 01590 622922 🖷 01590 622800

e-mail: rhinefieldhouse@handpicked.co.uk

web: www.handpicked.co.uk

Dir: *A35 towards Chistchurch. 3m from Lyndhurst turn left to Rhinefield*

This splendid 19th-century mock-Elizabethan mansion is set in 40 acres of beautifully landscaped gardens. Bedrooms are spacious and great consideration is given to guest comfort. The open-plan lounge and bar overlook an ornamental pond and the elegant restaurant is impressive with antique features.

ROOMS: 34 en suite ⊗ in 30 bedrooms s £175-£275; d £210-£310 (incl. bkfst) **LB** **FACILITIES:** STV Xmas **CONF:** Thtr 120 Class 50 Board 35 Del from £195 **PARKING:** 100 **NOTES:** ⊗ in restaurant Civ Wed

See advert on opposite page

★★★★71% ❀❀ Careys Manor

New Forest SO42 7RH

☎ 01590 623551 & 08707 512305 🖷 08707 512306

e-mail: stay@careysmanor.com

web: www.careysmanor.com

Dir: *M27 J3, then M271, then A35 to Lyndhurst. Then A337 towards Brockenhurst. Hotel on left after 30mph sign.*

This smart property offers a host of facilities that include the Oriental-style spa and leisure suite with an excellent range of unusual treatments, three very contrasting restaurants that offer a choice of Thai, French or modern British cuisine. Many of the spacious and well appointed bedrooms have balconies overlooking the gardens. Extensive function and conference facilities are also available.

ROOMS: 18 en suite 62 annexe en suite (32 GF) ⊗ in 28 bedrooms s £119-£210; d £148-£210 (incl. bkfst) **LB** **FACILITIES: Spa** STV supervised Sauna Gym Jacuzzi Steam room, Beauty therapists, treatment rooms, hydrotherapy pool Xmas **CONF:** Thtr 120 Class 70 Board 40 Del from £150 **SERVICES:** Lift **PARKING:** 180 **NOTES:** ⊗ in restaurant Civ Wed 100

★★★75% ❀❀ Balmer Lawn

Lyndhurst Rd SO42 7ZB

☎ 01590 623116 🖷 01590 623864

e-mail: info@balmerlawnhotel.com

Dir: *A337 towards Lymington, hotel on left behind village cricket green*

Situated in the heart of the New Forest, this imposing house provides comfortable public rooms and a good range of bedrooms. A selection of carefully prepared and enjoyable dishes is offered in the spacious restaurant whilst extensive function and leisure facilities make this a popular conference venue.

ROOMS: 55 en suite (6 fmly) ⊗ in all bedrooms s £100-£115; d £125-£135 (incl. bkfst) **LB** **FACILITIES: Spa** Squash Sauna Gym Jacuzzi Modems in bedrooms. Play stations in family rooms ♫ Xmas **CONF:** BC Thtr 150 Class 76 Board 48 Del from £146.90 **SERVICES:** Lift **PARKING:** 100 **NOTES:** ⊗ in restaurant Civ Wed 120

See advert on opposite page

★★★73% ❀❀ New Park Manor

Lyndhurst Rd SO42 7QH

☎ 01590 623467 🖷 01590 622268

e-mail: info@newparkmanor.co.uk

web: www.vonessenhotels.co.uk

Dir: *M27 junct 1, A337 to Lyndhurst & Brockenhurst. Hotel 1.5m on right*

Once the favoured hunting lodge of King Charles II, this well presented hotel enjoys a peaceful setting in the New Forest and comes complete with an equestrian centre and a new spa. Bedrooms have now been refurbished and are divided between the old house and a purpose-built wing.

ROOMS: 24 en suite (6 fmly) ⊗ in all bedrooms **FACILITIES:** Riding Mountain biking Xmas **CONF:** Thtr 120 Class 52 Board 60 **PARKING:** 70 **NOTES:** ⊗ in restaurant Civ Wed 142

★★★68% Forest Park

Rhinefield Rd SO42 7ZG

☎ 01590 622844 🖷 01590 623948

e-mail: forest.park@forestdale.com

web: www.forestdale.com

Dir: *A337 to Brockenhurst turn into Meerut Rd, follow road through Waters Green. Right at t-junct into Rhinefield Rd*

A friendly hotel offering good facilities for both adults and children. A heated pool, riding, children's meal times and a quiet location in the forest are just a few of the advantages here. The well-equipped, comfortable bedrooms vary in size and style, and a choice of lounge and bar areas is available.

ROOMS: 38 en suite (2 fmly) (7 GF) ⊗ in 2 bedrooms s £85-£110; d £120-£140 (incl. bkfst) **LB** **FACILITIES:** Riding Sauna Xmas **CONF:** Thtr 50 Class 20 Board 24 Del from £125 **PARKING:** 80 **NOTES:** ⊗ in restaurant Civ Wed 50

❀ AA Rosette Award for culinary excellence

★★76% Cloud
Meerut Rd SO42 7TD
☎ 01590 622165 🖷 01590 622818
e-mail: enquiries@cloudhotel.co.uk
web: www.cloudhotel.co.uk
Dir: *1st right off A337, follow tourist signs*
This charming hotel enjoys a peaceful location on the edge of the village. The bedrooms are bright and comfortable with pine furnishings and smart en suite facilities. Public rooms include a selection of cosy lounges, a delightful garden and a restaurant specialising in home-cooked wholesome English food.
ROOMS: 18 en suite (1 fmly) (2 GF) s £72; d £110-£144 (incl. bkfst) **LB FACILITIES:** Xmas **CONF:** Thtr 40 Class 12 Board 12 Del from £110 **PARKING:** 20 **NOTES:** No children 8yrs ⊘ in restaurant Closed 28 Dec - 10 Jan

Packed in a hurry? Ironing facilities should be available at all star levels, either in the rooms or on request

★★66% Watersplash
The Rise SO42 7ZP
☎ 01590 622344 🖷 01590 624047
e-mail: bookings@watersplash.co.uk
web: www.watersplash.co.uk
Dir: *M3 junct 13/M27 junct 1/A337 S through Lyndhurst to Brockenhurst. Through Brockenhurst, The Rise on left, hotel on left*
This popular, welcoming Victorian hotel has been in the same family for 40 years. Upgraded bedrooms have co-ordinated decor and good facilities. The restaurant overlooks the neatly tended
continued on p126

BROCKENHURST, continued

garden and there is also a comfortably furnished lounge, separate bar and an outdoor pool.

Watersplash, Brockenhurst

ROOMS: 23 en suite (6 fmly) s £49-£70; d £82-£126 (incl. bkfst) **LB**
FACILITIES: ⚡ ch fac Xmas **CONF:** Thtr 80 Class 20 Board 20
PARKING: 29 **NOTES:** ⊗ in restaurant

🅤 ⊛⊛⊛ Le Poussin @ Whitley Ridge Country House Hotel

Beaulieu Rd SO42 7QL
☎ 01590 622354 ▤ 01590 622856
e-mail: whitleyridge@lepoussin.co.uk
web: www.whitleyridge.co.uk
Dir: *At Brockenhurst onto B3055 Beaulieu Road. 1m on left up private road.*
At the time of going to press, the star classification for this hotel was not confirmed. Please refer to the AA internet site www.theAA.com for current information.
ROOMS: 14 en suite 4 annexe en suite (2 GF) ⊗ in all bedrooms
s £65-£75; d £95-£195 (incl. bkfst) **LB FACILITIES:** ⚡ Xmas **CONF:** BC
Thtr 35 Class 20 Board 20 **PARKING:** 40 **NOTES:** ⊗ in restaurant
Civ Wed 50

BROMBOROUGH, Merseyside
Map 15 SJ38

⌂ Premier Travel Inn Wirral (Bromborough)

High St, Bromborough Cross CH62 7EZ
☎ 08701 977273 ▤ 0151 344 0443
web: www.premiertravelinn.com
Dir: *on A41 New Chester Road, 2m from M53 junct 5*
High quality, modern budget accommodation ideal for both families and business travellers. Spacious, en suite bedrooms feature bath and shower, satellite TV and many have telephones and modem points. The adjacent family restaurant features a wide and varied menu. For further details consult the Hotel Groups page.
ROOMS: 32 en suite s & d £46.95-£48.95 **CONF:** Thtr 80 Board 35

BROME, Suffolk
Map 13 TM17

★★★71% ⊛ Brome Grange

IP23 8AP
☎ 01379 870456 ▤ 01379 870921
e-mail: bromegrange@fastnet.co.uk
web: www.bromegrange.com
Dir: *A12 take A140, turn off towards Norwich, hotel on right*
Expect a warm welcome at this charming inn, which is situated on the A140 between Diss and Ipswich. Bedrooms are situated around a large courtyard to the rear of the property; each one is pleasantly decorated and thoughtfully equipped. Public rooms
continued

include a smartly appointed restaurant, a lounge bar and banqueting suite.

ROOMS: 19 annexe en suite (4 fmly) (19 GF) ⊗ in all bedrooms
s £50-£65; d £65-£85 (incl. bkfst) **FACILITIES:** Xmas **CONF:** Thtr 80 Class
30 Board 30 **PARKING:** 70 **NOTES:** ✘ ⊗ in restaurant Civ Wed 75

BROMLEY, Greater London
See LONDON SECTION plan 1 G1

★★★71% Bromley Court

Bromley Hill BR1 4JD
☎ 020 8461 8600 ▤ 020 8460 0899
e-mail: info@bromleycourthotel.co.uk
web: www.bw-bromleycourthotel.co.uk
Dir: *N of Bromley off A21. Hotel opposite garage*
This grand mansion is set in three acres of grounds. Bedrooms are appointed to a good standard, each well designed and thoughtfully equipped. The contemporary-style restaurant offers a good choice of meals. Extensive facilities include a leisure club and a good range of meeting rooms.
ROOMS: 114 en suite (4 fmly) ⊗ in 50 bedrooms s £85-£109;
d £95-£120 (incl. bkfst) **LB FACILITIES:** Spa STV Sauna Gym Jacuzzi
CONF: Thtr 150 Class 80 Board 45 Del from £130 **SERVICES:** Lift
PARKING: 100 **NOTES:** ⊗ in restaurant Civ Wed 55

BROMSGROVE, Worcestershire
Map 10 SO97

★★★★66% ⊛ The Bromsgrove Hotel

Kidderminster Rd B61 9AB
☎ 01527 576600 ▤ 01527 878981
Dir: *on A448, 1m W of town centre*
Public areas in this striking building have a Mediterranean theme with white-washed walls, a courtyard garden and plenty of natural light. Bedrooms are in a variety of styles; some are more compact than others but all offer an excellent working environment for the business guest.
ROOMS: 114 en suite (17 fmly) (34 GF) ⊗ in 77 bedrooms s £45-£135;
d £90-£150 **LB FACILITIES:** Spa STV ⚡ Snooker Sauna Solarium Gym
Jacuzzi Xmas **CONF:** BC Thtr 200 Class 140 Board 30 Del from £85
SERVICES: Lift **PARKING:** 250 **NOTES:** ✘ ⊗ in restaurant Civ Wed 200

⊗ No smoking

Popped the question? Hotels with Civ wed in their entry are licensed for civil wedding ceremonies. Maximum numbers for the ceremony only are shown e.g. Civ wed 120

☆ Innkeeper's Lodge Bromsgrove
462 Birmingham Rd, Marlbrook B61 0HR
☎ 01527 878060
web: www.innkeeperslodge.com
Dir: on A38 0.5m between M5 & M42
A growing concept in the travel accommodation market. Smart rooms meet essential business requirements but also have home comforts. Dining options include all-day menus plus the added advantage of breakfast, which is included in the room price. For further details consult the Hotel Groups page.
ROOMS: 29 en suite s £45-£49.95; d £45-£49.95

☆ Premier Travel Inn Bromsgrove Central
Birmingham Rd B61 0BA
☎ 08701 977 044 ▤ 01527 834719
web: www.premiertravelinn.com
High quality, modern budget accommodation ideal for both families and business travellers. Spacious, en suite bedrooms feature bath and shower, satellite TV and many have telephones and modem points. The adjacent family restaurant features a wide and varied menu. For further details consult the Hotel Groups page.
ROOMS: 74 en suite s £46.95-£49.95; d £46.95-£49.95

☆ Premier Travel Inn Bromsgrove South
Worcester Rd, Upton Warren B61 7ET
☎ 0870 9906408 ▤ 0870 9906409
web: www.premiertravelinn.com
Dir: 1.2m from M5 junct 5 towards Bromsgrove on A38. From M42 junct 1 follow A38 south, crossing over A448
High quality, modern budget accommodation ideal for both families and business travellers. Spacious, en suite bedrooms feature bath and shower, satellite TV and many have telephones and modem points. The adjacent family restaurant features a wide and varied menu. For further details consult the Hotel Groups page.
ROOMS: 27 en suite s £46.95-£49.95 d £46.95-£49.95 **CONF:** Board 10

BROOK (NEAR CADNAM), Hampshire Map 05 SU21

★★★67% ◉ Bell Inn
SO43 7HE
☎ 023 8081 2214 ▤ 023 8081 3958
e-mail: bell@bramshaw.co.uk
web: www.bramshaw.co.uk
Dir: M27 junct 1 onto B3079, hotel 1.5m on right

The Bell Inn is part of the Bramshaw Golf Club and has tailored its style to suit this market, but it is also an ideal base for visiting the New Forest. Bedrooms are comfortable and attractively furnished, and the public areas, particularly the welcoming bar, have a cosy and friendly atmosphere.
ROOMS: 25 en suite (8 GF) ⊗ in 11 bedrooms s £65-£90; d £90-£110 (incl. bkfst) **LB** **FACILITIES:** ⌁ 54 Putt green Xmas **CONF:** Thtr 50 Class 20 Board 30 Del from £85 **PARKING:** 150 **NOTES:** ⚕ ⊗ in restaurant

BROXTON, Cheshire Map 15 SJ45

★★★★72% *De Vere Carden Park*
Carden Park CH3 9DQ
☎ 01829 731000 ▤ 01829 731599
e-mail: reservations.carden@devere-hotels.com
web: www.devereonline.co.uk
Dir: M56 junct 15/M53 Chester. Take A41 for Whitchurch for approx 8m. At Broxton rdbt right onto A534 Wrexham. Hotel 1.5m on left
This impressive Cheshire estate dates back to the 17th-century and consists of 750 acres of mature parkland. The hotel offers a choice of dining options along with superb leisure facilities that include golf courses, a fully equipped gym, a swimming pool and popular spa. Spacious, thoughtfully equipped bedrooms were about to undergo a stylish, contemporary themed refurbishment at the time of the last inspection.
ROOMS: 113 en suite 79 annexe en suite (24 fmly) ⊗ in 134 bedrooms **FACILITIES:** Spa STV ▤ supervised ⌁ 45 ⚲ Snooker Sauna Solarium Gym ♨ Putt green Jacuzzi Archery, Quadbikes, Off road driving, Mountain biking, Walking trails **CONF:** BC Thtr 400 Class 240 Board 125 **SERVICES:** Lift **PARKING:** 500 **NOTES:** ⚕ ⊗ in restaurant Civ Wed 375

BRYHER See Scilly, Isles of

Britains best-selling Golf Course Guide featuring over 2,500 courses.

www.theAA.com

AA

BUCKINGHAM, Buckinghamshire Map 11 SP63

★★★★65% ◉◉ *Villiers*
3 Castle St MK18 1BS
☎ 01280 822444 ▤ 01280 822113
e-mail: villiers@villiers-hotels.demon.co.uk

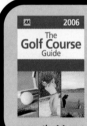

Guests can enjoy a town centre location with a high degree of comfort at this 400-year-old former coaching inn. Relaxing public areas feature flagstone floors, oak panelling and real fires whilst

continued on p128

BUCKINGHAM, continued

bedrooms are modern, spacious and equipped to a high level. Diners can unwind in the atmospheric Swan and Castle bar before taking dinner in the award-winning Henry's restaurant.
ROOMS: 46 en suite (43 fmly) **FACILITIES:** STV Free membership of nearby private leisure club ♫ **CONF:** Thtr 250 Class 120 Board 80 **SERVICES:** Lift **PARKING:** 53 **NOTES:** Civ Wed 150

See advert on opposite page

★★★65%
Best Western Buckingham Beales
Buckingham Ring Rd MK18 1RY
☎ 01280 822622 01280 823074
e-mail: buckingham@bealeshotels.co.uk
Dir: *M1 junct 13/14 follow signs to Buckingham-A422/A421. M40 exit junct 9/10 follow signs Buckingham. Hotel on ring road*
A purpose-built hotel, which offers spacious rooms with well-designed working spaces for business travellers. There are also extensive conference facilities. The open-plan restaurant and bar offers a good range of dishes, and the well-equipped leisure suite is popular with guests.
ROOMS: 70 en suite (6 fmly) in 24 bedrooms s £65-£98; d £90-£120 (incl. bkfst) **LB** **FACILITIES:** STV Sauna Solarium Gym Jacuzzi Beauty treatment, Massage Xmas **CONF:** BC Thtr 160 Class 90 Board 30 Del from £140 **PARKING:** 120 **NOTES:** in restaurant Civ Wed 120

Travelodge Buckingham
A421 Bypass MK18 1SH
☎ 08700 850950 01280 815 136
web: www.travelodge.co.uk
Dir: *M1 junct 38/39. Travelodge can be found on both the northbound and southbound carriageways of the M1.*
Travelodge offers good quality, good value, modern accommodation. Ideal for families, the spacious, en suite bedrooms include remote-control TV, tea and coffee-making facilities and comfortable beds. Meals can be taken at the nearby family restaurant. For further details consult the Hotel Groups page.
ROOMS: 45 en suite s fr £26; d fr £26

BUCKLAND (NEAR BROADWAY), Gloucestershire — Map 10 SP03

Top Hotel

★★★ **Buckland Manor**
WR12 7LY
☎ 01386 852626 01386 853557
e-mail: info@bucklandmanor.co.uk
web: www.vonessenhotels.co.uk
Dir: *off B4632 Broadway to Winchcombe Road*
A grand 13th-century manor house surrounded by well-kept and beautiful gardens. Everything here is geared to encourage rest and relaxation. Spacious bedrooms and public areas are furnished with high quality pieces and decorated in keeping with the style of the manor. Crackling log fires warm the wonderful lounges. The cuisine continues to impress, with high quality produce skilfully used.
ROOMS: 13 en suite (2 fmly) (4 GF) s £225-£410; d £235-£420 (incl. bkfst) **LB** **FACILITIES:** STV Putt green Xmas **PARKING:** 30 **NOTES:** No children 12yrs in restaurant

BUDE, Cornwall & Isles of Scilly — Map 02 SS20

★★★72% **Falcon**
Breakwater Rd EX23 8SD
☎ 01288 352005 01288 356359
e-mail: reception@falconhotel.com
web: www.falconhotel.com
Dir: *off A39 into Bude, then Widemouth Bay. Hotel on right over canal bridge*

Dating back to 1798, this long-established hotel boasts delightful walled gardens, ideal for afternoon teas. Bedrooms all offer high standards of comfort and quality, with a four-poster room available complete with spa bath. A choice of menus is offered in the elegant restaurant or the friendly bar, and there is an impressive function room.
ROOMS: 27 en suite (7 fmly) in all bedrooms s £50-£65; d £100-£110 (incl. bkfst) **LB** **FACILITIES:** STV Mini gym **CONF:** BC Thtr 200 Class 50 Board 50 **PARKING:** 40 **NOTES:** in restaurant RS 25-Dec Civ Wed 160

★★★69% **Hartland**
Hartland Ter EX23 8JY
☎ 01288 355661 01288 355664
e-mail: hartlandhotel@aol.com
Dir: *off A39 to Bude, follow town centre signs. Left into Hartland Terrace opposite Boots the chemist. Hotel at seaward end of road*

Enjoying a pleasantly quiet yet convenient location, the Hartland

continued

has excellent sea views. A popular stay for those wishing to tour the area and also with families, this hotel offers entertainment on many evenings throughout the year. Bedrooms are comfortable and offer a range of sizes. The public areas are smart, and in the dining room a pleasant fixed-price menu is available.
ROOMS: 28 en suite (2 fmly) ⊗ in 9 bedrooms s £49-£60; d £86-£100 (incl. bkfst) **LB** **FACILITIES:** ♫ ch fac Xmas **SERVICES:** Lift **PARKING:** 30 **NOTES:** ⊗ in restaurant Closed mid Nov-Etr (ex Xmas & New Year) No credit cards accepted

★★★68% Camelot

Downs View EX23 8RE
☎ 01288 352361 📠 01288 355470
e-mail: stay@camelot-hotel.co.uk
web: www.camelot-hotel.co.uk
Dir: *off A39 into town centre, onto one-way system, left lane, bottom of hill on left*

This friendly and welcoming Edwardian property offers a range of facilities including a smart and comfortable conservatory bar and lounge, a games room and Hawkers restaurant, which offers skilful cooking using much local produce. Bedrooms are light and airy, with high standards of housekeeping and maintenance.
ROOMS: 24 en suite (2 fmly) (7 GF) ⊗ in 21 bedrooms s £43-£65; d £86-£96 (incl. bkfst) **LB** **FACILITIES:** Darts Pool table Table tennis **PARKING:** 21 **NOTES:** ⊗ in restaurant

★★69% Penarvor

Crooklets Beach EX23 8NE
☎ 01288 352036 📠 01288 355027
e-mail: hotel.penarvor@boltblue.com
Dir: *From A39 towards Bude for 1.5m. At 2nd rdbt right, pass shops. Top of hill left signed Crooklets Beach*
Adjacent to the golf course and overlooking Crooklets Beach, this family owned hotel benefits from a relaxed and friendly atmosphere. Bedrooms vary in size and are all equipped to a similar standard. An interesting selection of dishes, using fresh local produce, is available in the restaurant; bar meals are also provided.
ROOMS: 16 en suite (6 fmly) ⊗ in all bedrooms s £30-£50; d £60-£80 (incl. bkfst) **LB** **PARKING:** 20 **NOTES:** ⊗ in restaurant

U Atlantic House

Summerleaze Crescent EX23 8HJ
☎ 01288 352451 📠 01288 356666
e-mail: enq@atlantichousehotel.co.uk
Dir: *M5 junct 31, follow A30 to by-pass in Okehampton. Follow signs to Bude via Halwill & Holsworthy*
At the time of going to press, the star classification for this hotel was not confirmed. Please refer to the AA internet site www.theAA.com for current information.
ROOMS: 16 rms (15 en suite) (5 fmly) ⊗ in all bedrooms s £28-£72; d £50-£72 (incl. bkfst) **LB** **FACILITIES:** Instructor led outdoor pursuits. Games room with pool table, darts ch fac Xmas **PARKING:** 7 **NOTES:** ⊗ in restaurant

BUNGAY, Suffolk — Map 13 TM38

★★65% Kings Head

2 Market Place NR35 1AW
☎ 01986 893583 📠 01986 893583
e-mail: info@kingsheadhotel.biz
Dir: *Off A143 to town centre. Hotel in town centre*
This 18th-century coaching inn is situated in the heart of town, amid a range of antique shops. The spacious bedrooms are furnished with pine pieces and have a good range of useful extras; one room has a superb four-poster bed. Public rooms include a restaurant, the Duke of Wellington lounge bar and Oddfellows bar.
ROOMS: 12 en suite (1 fmly) ⊗ in 4 bedrooms s £45; d £59.50-£75 (incl. bkfst) **LB** **FACILITIES:** ♫ **CONF:** Thtr 100 Class 50 Board 30 **PARKING:** 29 **NOTES:** ⊗ in restaurant

BURFORD, Oxfordshire — Map 05 SP21

★★★75% The Lamb Inn

Sheep St OX18 4LR
☎ 01993 823155 📠 01993 822228
e-mail: info@lambinn-burford.co.uk
Dir: *Turn off A40 into Burford, downhill, take 1st left into Sheep St, hotel last on right*
A stone's throw from the centre of a quintessential Cotswold town, this delightful old inn (now under new ownership) possesses an abundance of character and charm. The bedrooms retain many original features and there is a selection of comfortable lounges with flagstone floors and log fires,

continued on p130

B

BURFORD, continued

together with an atmospheric bar to relax in. The elegant restaurant offers carefully cooked meals that use the best of ingredients.
ROOMS: 15 en suite (1 fmly) (3 GF) ⊗ in all bedrooms s £115; d £130-£225 (incl. bkfst) **LB** **FACILITIES:** Xmas **PARKING:** 15
NOTES: ⊗ in restaurant

★★★73% ❀ The Bay Tree Hotel

CLASSIC BRITISH

12-14 Sheep St OX18 4LW
☎ 01993 822791 📠 01993 823008
e-mail: info@baytreehotel.info
Dir: *M40 junct 8 or M5 junct 11, then A40 to Burford. Or M4 junct 15, then A419 then A361 to Burford. From High St turn into Sheep St. Hotel is on right.*
History and modern innovations sit happily side by side at this delightful old inn, situated near the town centre. Bedrooms are tastefully furnished using the original features to good effect and some have four-poster and half-tester beds. Public areas consist of a character bar, a sophisticated airy restaurant, a selection of meeting rooms and an attractive walled garden.
ROOMS: 8 en suite 13 annexe en suite (2 fmly) ⊗ in all bedrooms s £119-£165; d £165-£300 (incl. bkfst) **LB** **FACILITIES:** ♫ Xmas **CONF:** Thtr 40 Class 12 Board 25 Del from £155 **PARKING:** 50
NOTES: ⊗ in restaurant Civ Wed 60

★★★68% Cotswold Gateway

Cheltenham Rd OX18 4HX
☎ 01993 822695 📠 01993 823600
e-mail: cotswold.gateway@dial.pipex.com
web: www.cotswold-gateway.co.uk
Dir: *Hotel on rdbt at A40 Oxford/Cheltenham at junct with A361*

Ideally suited for both business and leisure guests, The Cotswold Gateway Hotel is prominently situated on the A40 and yet only a short walk away from Burford. The tastefully decorated bedrooms include two four-poster rooms. Diners have an extensive choice of popular dishes and the option of eating in the character bar, the coffee shop or in the more formal restaurant.
ROOMS: 13 en suite 8 annexe en suite (2 fmly) ⊗ in all bedrooms s £75-£85; d £90-£140 (incl. bkfst) **LB** **FACILITIES:** Xmas **CONF:** Thtr 40 Class 20 Board 24 **PARKING:** 60 **NOTES:** ✗ ⊗ in restaurant

★★67% The Inn For All Seasons

THE INDEPENDENTS

The Barringtons OX18 4TN
☎ 01451 844324 📠 01451 844375
e-mail: sharp@innforallseasons.com
web: www.innforallseasons.com
Dir: *3m W of Burford on A40 towards Cheltenham*
This 16th-century coaching inn is conveniently near to Burford. Bedrooms are comfortable and steadily being upgraded, and public areas retain a feeling of period charm with original fireplaces and oak beams. A good selection of bar meals is

continued

available at lunchtime, while the evening menu includes an appetising selection of fresh fish.

ROOMS: 9 en suite 1 annexe en suite (2 fmly) (1 GF) s £56-£59; d £96-£99 (incl. bkfst) **LB** **FACILITIES:** STV Clay pigeon shooting ch fac Xmas **CONF:** Thtr 25 Class 30 Board 30 Del from £125 **PARKING:** 62

★★64% Golden Pheasant

91 High St OX18 4QA
☎ 01993 823223 📠 01993 822621
Dir: *M40 junct 8, follow signs A40 Cheltenham into Burford*
This attractive old inn is set on Burford's main street and dates, in part, back to the 16th century. Bedrooms can be compact and are well furnished with attractive fabrics, period furniture and many thoughtful extras. Both the bar and restaurant are full of character and serves a wide selection of meals.
ROOMS: 11 rms (10 en suite) (1 fmly) s £60-£75; d £85-£110 (incl. bkfst) **LB** **FACILITIES:** Xmas **PARKING:** 12 **NOTES:** ⊗ in restaurant

⌂ Travelodge (Cotswolds)

Travelodge

Bury Barn OX8 4JF
☎ 08700 850 950 📠 01993 822699
web: www.travelodge.co.uk
Dir: *A40/A361*
Travelodge offers good quality, good value, modern accommodation. Ideal for families, the spacious, en suite bedrooms include remote-control TV, tea and coffee-making facilities and comfortable beds. Meals can be taken at the nearby family restaurant. For further details consult the Hotel Groups page.
ROOMS: 40 en suite s fr £26; d fr £26

BURLEY, Hampshire Map 05 SU20

★★★71% Burley Manor

Forestdale Hotels

Ringwood Rd BH24 4BS
☎ 01425 403522 📠 01425 403227
e-mail: burley.manor@forestdale.com
web: www.forestdale.com
Dir: *leave A31 at Burley sign, hotel 3m on left*
Set in extensive grounds, this 18th-century mansion house enjoys a relaxed ambience and a peaceful setting. Half of the well-equipped, comfortable bedrooms, including several with four-posters, are located in the main house. The remainder, many with balconies, are in the adjacent converted stable block overlooking the outdoor pool. Cosy public rooms benefit from log fires in winter.
ROOMS: 21 en suite 17 annexe en suite (3 fmly) (17 GF) ⊗ in 4 bedrooms s fr £120; d £130-£150 (incl. bkfst) **LB** **FACILITIES:** ⛱ Fishing Riding ♫ Xmas **CONF:** Thtr 60 Class 40 Board 40 Del from £140 **PARKING:** 60 **NOTES:** ⊗ in restaurant Civ Wed 70

★★★67% ◎ *Moorhill House*
BH24 4AH
☎ 01425 403285 🖷 01425 403715
e-mail: moorhill@newforesthotels.co.uk
web: www.newforesthotels.co.uk
Dir: *M27, A31, follow signs to Burley village, through village, up hill, turn right opposite school and cricket grounds*

Situated deep in the heart of the New Forest and formerly a grand gentleman's residence, this charming hotel offers a relaxed and friendly environment. Bedrooms, of varying sizes, are smartly decorated. A range of facilities is provided and guests can relax by walking around the extensive grounds. Both dinner and breakfast offer a choice of interesting and freshly prepared dishes.

ROOMS: 31 en suite (13 fmly) (3 GF) **FACILITIES:** Sauna Gym Putt green badminton (Apr-Sep) **CONF:** Thtr 120 Class 60 Board 65 **PARKING:** 50 **NOTES:** in restaurant Civ Wed 80

BURNHAM, Buckinghamshire — Map 06 SU98

★★★72% *Grovefield*
Taplow Common Rd SL1 8LP
☎ 01628 603131 🖷 01628 668078
e-mail: gm.grovefield@classiclodges.co.uk
Dir: *From M4 left on A4 towards Maidenhead. Next rdbt turn right under railway bridge. Straight over mini rdbt, garage on right. Continue for 1.5m, hotel on right*

Set in its own spacious grounds, the Grovefield is conveniently located for Heathrow Airport as well as the industrial centres of Slough and Maidenhead. Accommodation is spacious and well presented and most rooms have views over the attractive gardens. Public areas include a range of meeting rooms, comfortable bar/lounge area and Hamilton's restaurant.

ROOMS: 40 en suite (5 fmly) (7 GF) in 24 bedrooms **FACILITIES:** STV Fishing Putt green **CONF:** Thtr 180 Class 80 Board 80 **SERVICES:** Lift **PARKING:** 155 **NOTES:** in restaurant Civ Wed 200

★★★65% *Burnham Beeches Hotel*
Grove Rd SL1 8DP
☎ 0870 609 6124 🖷 01628 603994
e-mail: burnhambeeches@corushotels.com
web: www.corushotels.com
Dir: *A355 towards Slough. Left at 2 mini-rdbts, left at next mini-rdbt. Grove Rd 1st on right*

Set in attractive mature grounds on the fringes of woodland, this extended Georgian manor house has spacious and comfortable well-equipped bedrooms. Public rooms include a cosy lounge/bar offering all-day snacks and an elegant wood-panelled restaurant that serves interesting cuisine; there are also conference facilities, a fitness centre and pool.

ROOMS: 82 en suite (19 fmly) (9 GF) in 30 bedrooms **FACILITIES: Spa** STV Snooker Sauna Gym Jacuzzi **CONF:** Thtr 180 Class 100 Board 60 **SERVICES:** Lift **PARKING:** 200 **NOTES:** in restaurant Civ Wed 120

BURNHAM MARKET, Norfolk — Map 13 TF84

★★77% ◎◎ Hoste Arms
The Green PE31 8HD
☎ 01328 738777 🖷 01328 730103
e-mail: reception@hostearms.co.uk
web: www.hostearms.co.uk
Dir: *signed on B1155, 5m W of Wells-next-the-Sea*

Stylish, privately owned inn situated in the heart of this bustling village close to the north Norfolk coast. The extensive public rooms feature a range of dining areas that include a conservatory with plush furniture, a sunny patio and a traditional pub. The tastefully furnished, thoughtfully equipped bedrooms are generally very spacious and offer a high degree of comfort.

ROOMS: 36 en suite (1 fmly) (7 GF) s £82-£248; d £114-£248 (incl. bkfst) **LB** **FACILITIES:** Xmas **CONF:** BC Thtr 25 Board 16 Del from £145 **PARKING:** 45

B

BURNLEY, Lancashire Map 18 SD83

★★★74% Oaks

Colne Rd, Reedley BB10 2LF
☎ 01282 414141 🖹 01282 433401
e-mail: oaks@shirehotels.com
web: www.shirehotels.com
Dir: *M65 junct 12. Follow signs to Burnley. At B&Q mini rdbt left, right at rdbt, right onto A682. Hotel 1m on left*

The friendly team here provide super hospitality in this former Victorian coffee merchant's house. The hotel offers traditional public areas and modern, well-equipped bedrooms that come in a variety of styles and sizes. A well-equipped leisure club is available on site. The attractive, peaceful location and impressive function facilities makes this a popular wedding venue.

ROOMS: 50 en suite (10 fmly) ⊗ in 31 bedrooms s £87-£119; d £104-£139 (incl. bkfst) **LB** **FACILITIES:** STV supervised Sauna Solarium Gym Jacuzzi Steam room Xmas **CONF:** Thtr 120 Class 48 Board 60 Del from £127 **PARKING:** 110 **NOTES:** ⊗ in restaurant Civ Wed 100

★★★70% Rosehill House

Rosehill Av BB11 2PW
☎ 01282 453931 🖹 01282 455628
e-mail: rhhotel@provider.co.uk
Dir: *0.5m S of Burnley town centre, off A682*

This fine Grade II listed building stands its own leafy grounds in a quiet area of town. There are two restaurants (one a tapas bar) and a comfortable lounge bar. All rooms are tastefully fitted and comfortably equipped, in addition to the standard accommodation; two loft conversions and a former coach house also offer a range of individual stylish bedrooms.

ROOMS: 34 en suite (3 fmly) (4 GF) ⊗ in 10 bedrooms s £50-£65; d £60-£75 (incl. bkfst) **LB** **FACILITIES:** STV Snooker **CONF:** BC Thtr 50 Class 30 Board 30 **PARKING:** 52 **NOTES:** ⊗ in restaurant Civ Wed 90

★★★68% Sparrow Hawk

Church St BB11 2DN
☎ 01282 421551 🖹 01282 456506
e-mail: enquiries@sparrowhawkhotel.co.uk
web: www.sparrowhawkhotel.co.uk
Dir: *M65 junct 10, 5th exit at traffic island (Cavalry Way). Left at next island, right lane along Westway, right at lights. Take 2nd exit from rdbt , 2nd exit at next rdbt. Hotel 300yds on right*

A warm welcome awaits guests at this centrally located grand Victorian hotel, which is handy for key local attractions. Well-equipped bedrooms vary in size and include a number of stylishly refurbished rooms. Public areas include the bright Mediterranean-style Smithies Café Bar, Farriers Restaurant and a traditional bar serving speciality ales.

ROOMS: 35 en suite (1 fmly) ⊗ in 9 bedrooms s £46-£55; d £53-£62 (incl. bkfst) **LB** **FACILITIES:** STV ♫ Xmas **CONF:** Thtr 80 Class 50 Board 40 Del from £49.50 **PARKING:** 20 **NOTES:** ⊗ in restaurant

Premier Travel Inn Burnley

Queen Victoria Rd BB10 3EF
☎ 08701 977045 🖹 01282 448431
web: www.premiertravelinn.com
Dir: *M65 junct 12 take 5th exit at rdbt, 1st exit at rdbt, keep in right lane at lights, next rdbt, 2nd exit then 3rd at next rdbt, under bridge turn left before football ground*

High quality, modern budget accommodation ideal for both families and business travellers. Spacious, en suite bedrooms feature bath and shower, satellite TV and many have telephones and modem points. The adjacent family restaurant features a wide and varied menu. For further details consult the Hotel Groups page.

ROOMS: 40 en suite s £46.95-£48.95; d £46.95-£48.95

Travelodge

Cavalry Barracks, Barracks Rd BB11 4AS
☎ 08700 850 950 🖹 01282 416039
web: www.travelodge.co.uk
Dir: *at junct of A671/A679*

Travelodge offers good quality, good value, modern accommodation. Ideal for families, the spacious, en suite bedrooms include remote-control TV, tea and coffee-making facilities and comfortable beds. Meals can be taken at the nearby family restaurant. For further details consult the Hotel Groups page.

ROOMS: 32 en suite s fr £26; d fr £26

BURNSALL, North Yorkshire Map 19 SE06

★★72% Red Lion Hotel

By the Bridge BD23 6BU
☎ 01756 720204 🖹 01756 720292
e-mail: redlion@daelnet.co.uk
web: www.redlion.co.uk
Dir: *on B6160 between Grassington and Bolton Abbey*

This delightful 16th-century Dales inn stands adjacent to a five-arch bridge over the scenic River Wharfe. Stylish, comfortable bedrooms are all individually decorated and well equipped. Public areas include a tasteful lounge and a traditional oak-panelled bar. The elegant restaurant makes good use of fresh local ingredients, and breakfasts are memorable. Guests are free to fish in the hotel's own stretch of water.

ROOMS: 11 en suite 4 annexe en suite (2 fmly) (2 GF) s £60-£100; d £180-£200 (incl. bkfst & dinner) **LB** **FACILITIES:** Fishing Xmas **CONF:** Thtr 30 Class 10 Board 20 Del from £100 **PARKING:** 80 **NOTES:** ⊗ in restaurant Civ Wed 50

BURRINGTON (NEAR PORTSMOUTH ARMS STATION), Devon Map 03 SS61

Top Hotel

★★★ Northcote Manor

EX37 9LZ
☎ 01769 560501 🖹 01769 560770
e-mail: rest@northcotemanor.co.uk
web: www.northcotemanor.co.uk
Dir: *off A377 opposite Portsmouth Arms, into hotel drive. NB.Do not enter Burrington village*

A warm and friendly welcome is assured at this beautiful country-house hotel. Built in 1716, the house sits in 20 acres of grounds and woodlands. Guests can enjoy wonderful views over the Taw River Valley whilst relaxing in the delightful environment created by the attentive staff. An elegant restaurant is a highlight of any stay with the finest of local

continued

produce used in well-prepared dishes. Bedrooms, including some suites, are individually styled, spacious and well appointed.

ROOMS: 11 en suite s £99-£170; d £150-£250 (incl. bkfst) **LB** **FACILITIES:** STV Xmas **CONF:** Thtr 20 Class 20 Board 20 Del £120 **PARKING:** 30 **NOTES:** ⊗ in restaurant Civ Wed 80

BURTON MOTORWAY SERVICE AREA (M6), Cumbria — Map 18 SD57

Travelodge
Burton in Kendal LA6 1JF
☎ 08700 850 950 Fax 01524 784014
web: www.travelodge.co.uk
Dir: *between M6 junct 35/36 northbound*
Travelodge offers good quality, good value, modern accommodation. Ideal for families, the spacious, en suite bedrooms include remote-control TV, tea and coffee-making facilities and comfortable beds. Meals can be taken at the nearby family restaurant. For further details consult the Hotel Groups page.
ROOMS: 47 en suite s fr £26; d fr £26

BURTON UPON TRENT, Staffordshire — Map 10 SK22

★★72% Riverside
Riverside Dr, Branston DE14 3EP
☎ 01283 511234 Fax 01283 511441
e-mail: riverside.branston@oldenglishinns.co.uk
web: www.oldenglish.co.uk
Dir: *follow signs for Branston on A5121 until small humped bridge, over bridge and right turn into Warren Lane. 2nd left into Riverside Drive*
With its quiet residential location and well-kept terraced garden stretching down to the River Trent, this hotel has all the ingredients for a relaxing stay. Many of the tables in the Garden Room restaurant have views over the garden. Bedrooms are tastefully furnished and decorated and provide a good range of extras.
ROOMS: 22 en suite (10 GF) ⊗ in all bedrooms s £60-£80; d £80-£90 (incl. bkfst) **LB** **FACILITIES:** STV Fishing Xmas **CONF:** Thtr 120 Class 60 Board 30 Del £120 **PARKING:** 200 **NOTES:** ⊗ in restaurant Civ Wed 120

U Ramada Newton Park
DE15 0SS
☎ 01283 703568 Fax 01283 703214
e-mail: sales.newtonpark@ramadajarvis.co.uk
web: www.ramadajarvis.co.uk
Set in well tended gardens, this country-house hotel is a popular venue for conferences and meetings. Bedrooms are comfortably appointed for both business and leisure guests.
ROOMS: 50 en suite (5 fmly) (7 GF) s £89-£115; d £89-£115 **FACILITIES:** Xmas **CONF:** Thtr 100 Class 75 Board 60 Del from £150 **SERVICES:** Lift **PARKING:** 120 **NOTES:** ⊗ in restaurant Civ Wed 70

BURTONWOOD MOTORWAY SERVICE AREA (M62), Cheshire — Map 15 SJ59

Welome Lodge Burtonwood
Burtonwood Services (M62), Great Sankey WA5 3AX
☎ 01925 710376 Fax 01925 710378
e-mail: burtonwood.hotel@welcomebreak.co.uk
web: www.welcomebreak.co.uk
Dir: *between M62 junct 7 & 9*
This modern building offers accommodation in smart, spacious and well-equipped bedrooms, suitable for families and business travellers, and all with en suite bathrooms. Refreshments may be taken at the nearby family restaurant. For further details consult the Hotel Groups page.
ROOMS: 39 en suite s £35-£45; d £35-£45 **CONF:** Board 8

BURWARDSLEY, Cheshire — Map 15 SJ55

★★70% Pheasant Inn
Higher Burwardsley CH3 9PF
☎ 01829 770434 Fax 01829 771097
e-mail: info@thepheasantinn.co.uk
web: www.thepheasantinn.co.uk
Dir: *from A41, left to Tattenhall, right at 1st junct and left at 2nd to Higher Burwardsley. At post office left, hotel signed*
This delightful 300-year-old inn sits high on the Peckforton Hills and enjoys spectacular views over the Cheshire plain. Well-equipped, comfortable bedrooms are housed in an adjacent converted barn. Creative dishes are served either in the stylish

continued on p134

BURWARDSLEY, continued

restaurant or in the traditional, beamed bar. Real fires are lit in the winter months.
ROOMS: 2 en suite 8 annexe en suite (2 fmly) (3 GF) ⊘ in all bedrooms s fr £65; d fr £80 (incl. bkfst) **LB** **FACILITIES:** Xmas **CONF:** Thtr 15 Board 10 Del from £127 **PARKING:** 80 **NOTES:** 🐕 ⊘ in restaurant

BURY, Greater Manchester — Map 15 SD81

★★★66% Bolholt Country Park

Walshaw Rd BL8 1PU
☎ 0161 762 4000 📠 0161 762 4100
e-mail: reservations@bolholt.co.uk
Dir: *M60 junct 17 for Whitefield, A56 to Bury for 4m. Follow signs for A58 to Bolton. Take 3rd lane at car showroom signed Tottington. Left at pub, left again*
This former mill owner's house is located in attractive parkland and secluded gardens just a short walk from the town centre. Bedrooms are comfortable and modern, whilst an impressive leisure club boasts two swimming pools, extensive fitness facilities and a fashionable café-bar. Wide ranging conference and banqueting facilities are available and the setting is ideal for weddings.
ROOMS: 65 en suite (13 fmly) ⊘ in 14 bedrooms s £74-£84; d £74-£84 (incl. bkfst) **FACILITIES:** STV 🏊 supervised Fishing Squash Sauna Solarium Gym Jacuzzi Fitness & leisure centre Xmas **CONF:** Thtr 300 Class 120 Board 40 Del from £109 **PARKING:** 300 **NOTES:** 🐕 ⊘ in restaurant Civ Wed 200

BURY ST EDMUNDS, Suffolk — Map 13 TL86

★★★77% ❀❀ Angel

Angel Hill IP33 1LT
☎ 01284 714000 📠 01284 714001
e-mail: staying@theangel.co.uk
Dir: *from A134, left at rdbt into Northgate St. Continue to T-junct with traffic lights, right into Mustow St, left into Angel Hill, hotel on right*
Impressive building situated just a short walk from the town centre. One of the Angel's more notable guests over the last 400 years was Charles Dickens who is reputed to have written part of the *Pickwick Papers* whilst in residence. The hotel offers a range of individually designed bedrooms that includes a selection of four-poster rooms and a suite.
ROOMS: 76 en suite (7 fmly) (7 GF) ⊘ in 14 bedrooms s £120-£185; d £130-£195 (incl. bkfst) **LB** **FACILITIES:** STV Xmas **CONF:** BC Thtr 120 Class 20 Board 30 **SERVICES:** Lift **PARKING:** 20 **NOTES:** ⊘ in restaurant Civ Wed 100

★★★75% ❀ Ravenwood Hall

Rougham IP30 9JA
☎ 01359 270345 📠 01359 270788
e-mail: enquiries@ravenwoodhall.co.uk
Dir: *3m E off A14*
Delightful 15th-century property set in seven acres of woodland and landscaped gardens. The building has many original features including carved timbers and inglenook fireplaces. The spacious bedrooms are attractively decorated, tastefully furnished with well-chosen pieces and equipped with many thoughtful touches. Public rooms include an elegant restaurant and a smart lounge bar with an open fire.
ROOMS: 7 en suite 7 annexe en suite (5 GF) ⊘ in all bedrooms s £85-£115; d £110-£165 (incl. bkfst) **LB** **FACILITIES:** 🏊 supervised Riding 🎾 Shooting & fishing ch fac Xmas **CONF:** Thtr 150 Class 80 Board 40 Del from £150.35 **PARKING:** 150 **NOTES:** ⊘ in restaurant Civ Wed 130

★★★74% ❀❀ The Priory

Tollgate IP32 6EH
☎ 01284 766181 📠 01284 767604
e-mail: reservations@prioryhotel.co.uk
Dir: *from A14 take Bury St Edmunds W slip road. Follow signs to Brandon. At mini-rdbt turn right. Hotel 0.5m on left*
An 18th-century Grade II listed building set in landscaped grounds on the outskirts of town. The attractively decorated, tastefully furnished and thoughtfully equipped bedrooms are split between the main house and garden wings, and have their own patios. Public rooms feature a smart restaurant, a conservatory dining room and a lounge bar.
ROOMS: 9 en suite 30 annexe en suite (1 fmly) (30 GF) ⊘ in 15 bedrooms s £89-£99; d £120-£140 (incl. bkfst) **LB** **FACILITIES:** Xmas **CONF:** Thtr 40 Class 20 Board 20 Del from £135 **PARKING:** 60 **NOTES:** ⊘ in restaurant

BUTTERMERE, Cumbria — Map 18 NY11

★★★70% *Bridge*

CA13 9UZ
☎ 017687 70252 📠 70215
e-mail: enquiries@bridge-hotel.com
web: www.bridge-hotel.com
Dir: *A66 around town centre, off at Braithwaite. Over Newlands Pass. Follow Buttermere signs. Hotel in village*

Enjoying a tranquil setting in a dramatic valley close to Buttermere, this long-established hotel has undergone impressive refurbishment. The bedrooms are tastefully appointed and have stylish bathrooms, and the comfortable public areas include a delightful lounge, attractive dining room and lively bar popular with walkers.
ROOMS: 21 en suite ⊘ in 15 bedrooms **FACILITIES:** no TV in bdrms ch fac **CONF:** Board 10 **PARKING:** 40 **NOTES:** ⊘ in restaurant

BUXTON, Derbyshire — Map 16 SK07

★★★★66% Palace Hotel

Palace Rd SK17 6AG
☎ 01298 22001 📠 01298 72131
e-mail: palace@paramount-hotels.co.uk
web: www.paramount-hotels.co.uk
Dir: *M6 junct 20, follow M56/M60 signs to Stockport then A6 to Buxton, hotel adjacent to railway station*
This impressive Victorian hotel is located on the hill overlooking the town. Public areas are traditional and elegant in style, including chandeliers and decorative ceilings. The bedrooms are spacious and equipped with modern facilities, and The Dovedale restaurant provides modern British cuisine.
ROOMS: 122 en suite (20 fmly) ⊘ in 80 bedrooms s £110; d £130 (incl. bkfst) **LB** **FACILITIES:** STV 🏊 supervised Snooker Sauna Solarium Gym Beauty and hairdressing facilities Xmas **CONF:** BC Thtr 300 Class 125 Board 80 Del £145 **SERVICES:** Lift **PARKING:** 200 **NOTES:** ⊘ in restaurant Civ Wed 100

★★★77% Best Western Lee Wood
The Park SK17 6TQ
☎ 01298 23002 🖷 01298 23228
e-mail: leewoodhotel@btinternet.com
web: www.leewoodhotel.co.uk
Dir: *NE on A5004, 300mtrs beyond Devonshire Royal Hospital*
This elegant Georgian hotel offers high standards of comfort and hospitality. Individually furnished bedrooms are generally spacious, with all of the expected modern conveniences. There is a choice of two comfortable lounges and a conservatory restaurant. Quality cooking is a feature of the hotel, as is good service and fine hospitality.
ROOMS: 35 en suite 5 annexe en suite (4 fmly) ⊘ in 25 bedrooms s £55-£95; d £85-£140 (incl. bkfst) **LB** **FACILITIES:** STV Xmas **CONF:** BC Thtr 120 Class 65 Board 40 Del from £110 **SERVICES:** Lift **PARKING:** 50 **NOTES:** ⊘ in restaurant Civ Wed 120

★★★68% Buckingham Hotel
1 Burlington Rd SK17 9AS
☎ 01298 70481 🖷 01298 72186
e-mail: frontdesk@buckinghamhotel.co.uk
web: www.buckinghamhotel.co.uk
Dir: *follow tourist signs for Pavilion Gardens Car Park. Hotel opposite car park at junct of St Johns (A53) & Burlington Rd*
The Buckingham is close to the Pavilion Gardens and offers pleasant, modern public areas. These include Ramsay's Bar, serving bar meals and real ales, and the popular carvery, serving grills and other dishes. Bedrooms, many now refurbished, are spacious and comfortable; many overlook the Gardens. Walls throughout are adorned with photographs of film stars.
ROOMS: 37 en suite (13 fmly) ⊘ in 27 bedrooms s £45-£75; d £90-£105 (incl. bkfst) **LB** **FACILITIES:** STV **CONF:** Thtr 75 Class 20 Board 16 Del from £75 **SERVICES:** Lift **PARKING:** 35 **NOTES:** ⊘ in restaurant Closed Christmas/New Year Civ Wed 85

★★61% Portland Hotel & Park Restaurant
32 St John's Rd SK17 6XQ
☎ 01298 22462 🖷 01298 27464
e-mail: robert@portland-hotel.freeserve.co.uk
Dir: *on A53 opposite the Pavilion & Gardens*

This privately owned and personally run hotel is situated near the famous opera house and the Pavilion Gardens. Facilities include a comfortable lounge and an open-plan bar & restaurant area with an adjacent conservatory. An extensive refurbishment is planned.
ROOMS: 22 en suite (3 fmly) ⊘ in 3 bedrooms **CONF:** Thtr 50 Class 30 Board 25 **PARKING:** 18 **NOTES:** ⊘ in restaurant

Early start?
Hotels at all star levels should provide in-room alarm clocks and/or alarm clocks

CADNAM, Hampshire
Map 05 SU31

★★★69% Bartley Lodge
Lyndhurst Rd SO40 2NR
☎ 023 8081 2248 🖷 023 8081 2075
e-mail: bartley@newforesthotels.co.uk
web: www.newforesthotels.co.uk
Dir: *M27 junct 1 at 1st rdbt 1st exit, at 2nd rdbt 3rd exit onto A337. Hotel sign on left*
This 18th-century former hunting lodge is very quietly situated, yet is just minutes from the M27. Bedrooms vary in size and all are well equipped. There is a selection of small lounge areas, a cosy bar and an indoor pool, together with a small fitness suite. The Crystal dining room offers a tempting choice of well prepared dishes.
ROOMS: 31 en suite (12 fmly) (2 GF) **FACILITIES:** Sauna Gym **CONF:** Thtr 120 Class 60 Board 60 **PARKING:** 60 **NOTES:** ⊘ in restaurant Civ Wed 80

See advert on this page

CALNE, Wiltshire
Map 04 ST97

★★★68% Lansdowne Strand
The Strand SN11 0EH
☎ 01249 812488 🖷 01249 815323
e-mail: reservations@lansdownestrand.co.uk
web: www.lansdownestrand.co.uk
Dir: *off A4, in town centre*
In the centre of the market town, this 16th-century, former coaching inn still retains many period features. Individually decorated bedrooms vary in size. There are two friendly bars; one offers a wide selection of ales and a cosy fire to sit by. An interesting

continued on p136

CALNE, continued

menu and choice of wines is available in the brasserie-style restaurant.
ROOMS: 21 en suite 5 annexe en suite (3 fmly) ⊗ in 19 bedrooms s £85-£89; d £95-£102 (incl. bkfst) **LB FACILITIES:** STV Complimentary use of nearby leisure centre Xmas **CONF:** Thtr 90 Class 28 Board 30 Del from £80 **PARKING:** 21

CAMBERLEY, Surrey Map 06 SU86

★★★72% ⊛ **Frimley Hall Hotel & Spa**
Lime Av GU15 2BG
☎ 0870 400 8224 🖹 01276 691253
e-mail: salesfrimleyhall@macdonald-hotels.co.uk
web: www.macdonald-hotels.co.uk
Dir: M3 junct 3, A321 follow Bagshot signs. Through lights, left onto A30 signed Camberley/Basingstoke. To rdbt, 2nd exit onto A325, take 5th right

Classic English elegance in the heart of rural Surrey, this ivy-clad Victorian manor house is set in two acres of immaculate grounds. With continued investment in the hotel, both bedrooms and public areas are looking particularly smart and feature a modern, yet timeless, decorative theme.
ROOMS: 96 en suite (4 fmly) ⊗ in 60 bedrooms s £105-£165; d £130-£190 (incl. bkfst) **LB FACILITIES:** Spa STV 🏊 supervised Sauna Gym ⛳ Putt green Beauty treatment rooms ♫ Xmas **CONF:** Thtr 250 Class 100 Board 60 Del from £200 **SERVICES:** air con **PARKING:** 100 **NOTES:** ⊗ in restaurant Civ Wed 220

★★★64% *Lakeside International*
Wharf Rd, Frimley Green GU16 6JR
☎ 01252 838000 🖹 01252 837857
Dir: off A321 at mini-rdbt turn into Wharf Rd, Lakeside complex on right
This hotel, geared towards the business market, enjoys a lakeside location with noteworthy views. Bedrooms are modern, comfortable and with a range of facilities. Public areas are spacious and include a residents' lounge, bar and games room, a smart restaurant and an established health and leisure club. Bedrooms are modern, comfortable with a range of facilities.
ROOMS: 98 en suite (1 fmly) ⊗ in 18 bedrooms **FACILITIES:** STV 🏊 Squash Snooker Sauna Solarium Gym Jacuzzi **CONF:** Thtr 120 Class 100 Board 40 **SERVICES:** Lift **PARKING:** 250 **NOTES:** ✗ ⊗ in restaurant Civ Wed 100

⇧ **Premier Travel Inn Camberley**
221 Yorktown Rd, College Town GU47 0RT
☎ 08701 977047 🖹 01582 842811
web: www.premiertravelinn.com
Dir: M3 junct 4 follow A331 to Camberley. At large rdbt, exit to A321 towards Bracknell. At 3rd set of traffic lights, Inn on left
High quality, modern budget accommodation ideal for both families and business travellers. Spacious, en suite bedrooms
continued

feature bath and shower, satellite TV and many have telephones and modem points. The adjacent family restaurant features a wide and varied menu. For further details consult the Hotel Groups page.
ROOMS: 40 en suite s £49.95-£55.95; d £49.95-£55.95

CAMBORNE, Cornwall & Isles of Scilly Map 02 SW64

★★★66% **Tyacks**
27 Commercial St TR14 8LD
☎ 01209 612424 🖹 01209 612435
e-mail: tyack@smallandfriendy.co.uk
Dir: W on A30 past A3047 junct & turn off at Camborne West junct. Left & left again at rdbt, follow town centre signs. Hotel on left
This 18th-century former coaching inn has spacious, well-furnished public areas which include a smart lounge and bar, a popular public bar and a restaurant serving fixed-price and carte menus. The comfortable bedrooms are attractively decorated and well equipped; two have separate sitting areas.
ROOMS: 15 en suite (2 fmly) ⊗ in 4 bedrooms s £50; d £75 (incl. bkfst) **LB FACILITIES:** STV 6x6 sports entertainment screen ♫ Xmas **CONF:** Class 35 **PARKING:** 27 **NOTES:** ⊗ in restaurant

CAMBOURNE, Cambridgeshire Map 12 TL35

★★★★75% ⊛ **The Cambridge Belfry**
Back St CB3 6BW
☎ 01954 714600 🖹 01954 714610
e-mail: cambridge@marstonhotels.com
web: www.marstonhotels.com
Dir: M11 junct 13 take A428 to Bedford, follow signs to Cambourne. Leave at Cambourne keeping left. Left at rdbt. Hotel on the left.

The latest addition to the Marston Hotels portfolio, this exciting new hotel is located at the gateway to Cambourne Village & Business Park. Contemporary in style throughout, the hotel boasts two eating options, state-of-the-art leisure facilities and extensive conference and banqueting rooms. Original artwork takes guests on a guided tour of Cambridge, along the River Cam.
ROOMS: 120 en suite (30 GF) ⊗ in 105 bedrooms s fr £149; d fr £178 (incl. bkfst) **LB FACILITIES:** Spa STV 🏊 ✂ Sauna Solarium Gym Jacuzzi Xmas **CONF:** Thtr 258 Class 104 Board 72 Del from £219 **SERVICES:** Lift **PARKING:** 260 **NOTES:** ✗ ⊗ in restaurant Civ Wed 160

CAMBRIDGE, Cambridgeshire Map 12 TL45

★★★★75% ⊛⊛ **Hotel Felix**
Whitehouse Ln CB3 0LX
☎ 01223 277977 🖹 01223 277973
e-mail: help@hotelfelix.co.uk
web: www.hotelfelix.co.uk
Dir: N on A1307 (Huntingdon road) turn right at The Travellers Rest into Whitehouse Lane
A beautiful Victorian mansion set amidst three acres of landscaped
continued

gardens, this property was originally built in 1852 for a surgeon from the famous Addenbrookes Hospital. The contemporary-style bedrooms have carefully chosen furniture and many thoughtful touches, whilst public rooms feature an open-plan bar, the adjacent Graffiti restaurant and a small quiet lounge.

ROOMS: 52 en suite (5 fmly) (26 GF) ⊗ in 22 bedrooms s £85-£132; d £110-£163 (incl. bkfst) **LB** **FACILITIES:** STV Xmas **CONF:** Thtr 60 Class 36 Board 34 Del £185 **SERVICES:** Lift **PARKING:** 90 **NOTES:** ⊗ in restaurant Civ Wed 180

★★★★68% *De Vere University Arms*

Regent St CB2 1AD

☎ 01223 351241 🖷 01223 273037

e-mail: dua.sales@devere-hotels.com

web: www.devereonline.co.uk

Dir: *M11 junct 11, follow city centre signs for 3m. Right at 2nd mini rdbt, left at lights into Regent St. Hotel 600yds on right*

Built as a post house in 1834, the University Arms has an enviable position in the very heart of the city, overlooking Parker's Piece. Public rooms include an elegant domed lounge, a smart restaurant, a bar and lounge overlooking the park. Conference and banqueting rooms are extensive, many with oak panelling. Given the hotel's central location parking is a bonus.

ROOMS: 120 en suite (2 fmly) ⊗ in 83 bedrooms **FACILITIES:** STV Reduced rate at local fitness centre Play Stations and pay movies in all rooms **CONF:** Thtr 300 Class 150 Board 80 **SERVICES:** Lift **PARKING:** 88 **NOTES:** ⊗ in restaurant Civ Wed 120

★★★76% 🏵 Cambridge Quy Mill Hotel

Newmarket Rd CB5 9AG

☎ 01223 293383 🖷 01223 293770

e-mail: cambridgequy@bestwestern.co.uk

Dir: *off A14 at junct E of Cambridge onto B1102 for 50yds.*

Set in open countryside, this 19th-century former watermill is convenient for Cambridge. Bedroom styles differ, yet each room is smartly appointed and brightly decorated. Well-designed public areas include several spacious bar/lounges, with a choice of casual and formal eating areas; service is both friendly and helpful. A new leisure club with state-of-the-art equipment is an impressive addition to the hotel.

continued

ROOMS: 23 en suite 18 annexe en suite (2 fmly) (18 GF) ⊗ in 18 bedrooms s £90-£140; d £98-£190 **LB** **FACILITIES:** STV supervised Sauna Gym Jacuzzi Clay pigeon shooting by prior booking subject to availability **CONF:** Thtr 80 Class 30 Board 24 Del £155 **PARKING:** 90 **NOTES:** Closed 24-30 Dec RS 31-Dec Civ Wed 80

★★★71% Gonville

Gonville Place CB1 1LY

☎ 01223 366611 & 221111 🖷 01223 315470

e-mail: all@gonvillehotel.co.uk

web: www.gonvillehotel.co.uk

Dir: *M11 junct 11, on A1309 follow city centre signs. At 2nd mini rdbt right into Lensfield Rd, over junct with traffic lights. Hotel 25yds on right*

This hotel is situated on the inner ring road, a short walk across the green from the city centre. Well established, with regular guests and very experienced staff, the Gonville is popular for its relaxing, informal atmosphere. The air-conditioned public areas are cheerfully furnished, now enhanced by the creation of a new lounge bar and brasserie; bedrooms are well appointed and appealing.

ROOMS: 103 en suite (1 fmly) (5 GF) ⊗ in 38 bedrooms s £89-£150; d £99-£160 **LB** **FACILITIES:** Arrangement with gym/swimming pool **CONF:** BC Thtr 200 Class 100 Board 50 Del from £125 **SERVICES:** Lift **PARKING:** 80 **NOTES:** ⊗ in restaurant

★★★68% Sorrento

190-196 Cherry Hinton Rd CB1 7AN

☎ 01223 243533 🖷 01223 213463

e-mail: info@sorrentohotel.com

web: www.sorrentohotel.com

Dir: *M11 junct 11 towards Cambridge on B1309, 2nd set lights right into Long Road. 1st set lights left into Hills Road. 1st set lights right into Cherry Hinton Rd*

Friendly, family run hotel situated close to the city centre. Although the bedrooms vary in size and style, they are all are pleasantly decorated and equipped with many thoughtful extras. Public rooms have an Italian feel with superb marble flooring throughout; they include a smart lounge bar, attractive restaurant and a huge conservatory.

ROOMS: 30 en suite (4 fmly) (8 GF) ⊗ in 20 bedrooms **FACILITIES:** STV Xmas **CONF:** Thtr 60 Class 35 Board 35 **PARKING:** 40 **NOTES:** ⊗ in restaurant

★★★67% Royal Cambridge

Trumpington St CB2 1PY

☎ 01223 351631 🖷 01223 352972

e-mail: royal.cambridge@forestdale.com

web: www.forestdale.com

Dir: *M11 junct 11, signed city centre. 1st mini rdbt left into Fen Causeway. Hotel 1st right*

This impressive Georgian hotel enjoys a central location. Bedrooms are well equipped and comfortable, and include the new superior bedrooms/apartments. Public areas are traditionally decorated to a good standard; the elegant restaurant is a popular choice and the lounge/bar serves evening snacks. Parking and conferencing are added benefits.

ROOMS: 57 en suite (9 fmly) ⊗ in 28 bedrooms s £120-£145; d £155-£165 (incl. bkfst) **LB** **FACILITIES:** STV Xmas **CONF:** Thtr 120 Class 40 Board 40 Del from £140 **SERVICES:** Lift **PARKING:** 80 **NOTES:** ⊗ in restaurant Civ Wed 100

We have indicated only the hotels that don't accept credit or debit cards

C

CAMBRIDGE, continued

★★75% Arundel House
Chesterton Rd CB4 3AN
☎ 01223 367701 🖷 01223 367721
e-mail: info@arundelhousehotels.co.uk
web: www.arundelhousehotels.co.uk
Dir: *city centre on A1303*

Overlooking the River Cam and enjoying views over open parkland, this popular smart hotel was originally a row of Victorian townhouses. Bedrooms are attractive and have a special character. The smart public areas feature a conservatory for informal snacks, a spacious bar and an elegant restaurant for serious dining; the restaurant, now redesigned in a warm colour scheme, offers a modern dining experience.
ROOMS: 81 en suite 22 annexe en suite (7 fmly) (14 GF) ⊗ in all bedrooms s £75-£95; d £95-£120 (incl. bkfst) **LB** **CONF:** Thtr 50 Class 34 Board 32 Del from £125 **PARKING:** 70 **NOTES:** ✗ ⊗ in restaurant Closed 25-26 Dec

★★71% Centennial
63-71 Hills Rd CB2 1PG
☎ 01223 314652 🖷 01223 315443
e-mail: reception@centennialhotel.co.uk
Dir: *M11 junct 11 take A1309 to Cambridge. Right onto Brooklands Ave to end. Left, hotel 100yds on right*
This friendly hotel is convenient for the railway station and town centre. Well-presented public areas include a welcoming lounge, and a relaxing bar and restaurant on the lower-ground level. Bedrooms are generally spacious, well maintained and thoughtfully equipped with a good range of facilities; several rooms are available on the ground floor.
ROOMS: 39 en suite (1 fmly) (7 GF) ⊗ in 26 bedrooms s £70-£80; d £88-£96 (incl. bkfst) **LB** **CONF:** Thtr 25 Class 25 Board 25 **PARKING:** 30 **NOTES:** ✗ ⊗ in restaurant Closed 23 Dec-1 Jan
See advert on opposite page

⌂ Travelodge (Cambridge)
Cambridge Leisure Park, Clifton Way CB1 7DY
☎ 0122 3241066
web: www.travelodge.co.uk
Travelodge offers good quality, good value, modern accommodation. Ideal for families, the spacious, en suite bedrooms include remote-control TV, tea and coffee-making facilities and comfortable beds. Meals can be taken at the nearby family restaurant. For further details consult the Hotel Groups page.
ROOMS: 120 rms s fr £26; d fr £26

⊗ No smoking

⌂ Travelodge (Cambridge South)
Fourwentways CB8 6AP
☎ 08700 850 950 🖷 01223 839479
web: www.travelodge.co.uk
Dir: *adjacent to Little Chef at junct A11/A1307, 5m S of Cambridge*
Travelodge offers good quality, good value, modern accommodation. Ideal for families, the spacious, en suite bedrooms include remote-control TV, tea and coffee-making facilities and comfortable beds. Meals can be taken at the nearby family restaurant. For further details consult the Hotel Groups page.
ROOMS: 40 en suite s fr £26; d fr £26

CAMELFORD, Cornwall & Isles of Scilly — Map 02 SX18

★★★66% Bowood Park Hotel & Golf Course
Lanteglos PL32 9RF
☎ 01840 213017 🖷 01840 212622
e-mail: golf@bowoodpark.com
web: www.bowoodpark.com
Dir: *A39 W through Camelford, 0.5m, turn right for Tintagel/Boscastle, 1st left after garage*
Situated in wonderfully picturesque countryside, this hotel provides much for golfers and non-golfers alike. Spacious bedrooms are comfortable and some have private patios and wonderful views over the course. Salmon and trout fishing is available on the River Camel and the hotel's treatment room is just the place for a relaxing massage or beauty treatment.
ROOMS: 31 en suite (3 fmly) ⊗ in 12 bedrooms s £59-£89; d £78-£118 (incl. bkfst) **LB** **FACILITIES:** ⛳ 18 Fishing Putt green Massage, Sports therapy Xmas **CONF:** BC Thtr 130 Class 100 Board 100 Del from £80 **PARKING:** 100 **NOTES:** ✗ ⊗ in restaurant
See advert on Inside Front Cover

CANNOCK, Staffordshire — Map 10 SJ91

★★★64% The Roman Way Hotel
Watling St, Hatherton WS11 1SH
☎ 0870 609 6125 🖷 01543 502749
e-mail: romanway@corushotels.com
web: www.corushotels.com
Dir: *M6 junct 11/12, take A5 towards Telford. Hotel 100yds*

Named after the Roman road on which it stands, this modern hotel provides a good standard of accommodation. Doric columns and marble floors feature in the reception area, and Nero's Restaurant and Gilpin's Lounge provide options for formal or informal eating.
ROOMS: 56 en suite (17 fmly) (23 GF) ⊗ in 23 bedrooms s £55-£79; d £55-£79 **LB** **FACILITIES:** STV Xmas **CONF:** BC Thtr 150 Class 100 Board 50 Del from £95 **PARKING:** 150 **NOTES:** ⊗ in restaurant Civ Wed 150

⌂ Premier Travel Inn Cannock
Watling St WS11 1SJ
☎ 08701 977048 🖷 01543 466130
web: www.premiertravelinn.com
Dir: *on at junct of A5/A460, 2m from M6 junct 11/12*
High quality, modern budget accommodation ideal for both families and business travellers. Spacious, en suite bedrooms feature bath and shower, satellite TV and many have telephones and modem points. The adjacent family restaurant features a wide and varied menu. For further details consult the Hotel Groups page.
ROOMS: 60 en suite s £46.95-£49.95; d £46.95-£49.95 **CONF:** Thtr 80 Board 40

CANTERBURY, Kent
Map 07 TR15

★★★★66% *The County Hotel*
High St CT1 2RX
☎ 01227 766266 🖷 01227 451512
e-mail: enquiries@thecountryhotel-canterbury.co.uk
Dir: *M2, junct 7. Follow Canterbury signs onto ringroad. At Wincheap rdbt turn into city. Left into Rosemary Ln, into Stour St. Hotel at end*
This historic hotel has cellars dating back to the 12th century. It offers warm hospitality and comfortable accommodation in the heart of the city. Bedrooms are individually decorated and tastefully furnished, while public areas include tea rooms offering traditional cream teas and Sully's Restaurant, where the emphasis is on fine dining.
ROOMS: 74 en suite (9 fmly) ⊗ in 33 bedrooms **FACILITIES:** STV **CONF:** BC Thtr 120 Class 80 Board 60 **SERVICES:** Lift **PARKING:** 62 **NOTES:** ⊗ in restaurant Civ Wed 100

★★★72% Abbots Barton
New Dover Rd CT1 3DU
☎ 01227 760341 🖷 01227 785442
e-mail: sales@abbotsbartonhotel.com
Dir: *Turn off A2 onto A2050 at bridge, S of Canterbury. Hotel is 0.75m past Old Gate Inn on left*
With nearly two acres of landscaped gardens, the Abbots Barton has the feel of a country-house hotel, but is still easily accessible from the city centre and major routes. The spacious accommodation is well equipped and the public areas include The Cathedral Room with conference facilities for 150 people. The Fountain Restaurant serves imaginative food, and the bar overlooks the pretty gardens.
ROOMS: 50 en suite (2 fmly) (6 GF) ⊗ in 27 bedrooms s £83-£103; d £101-£133 **LB** **FACILITIES:** STV Xmas **CONF:** Thtr 150 Class 80 Board 60 Del from £140 **SERVICES:** Lift **PARKING:** 80 **NOTES:** ⊗ in restaurant Civ Wed 100

★★★67% The Falstaff Hotel
8-10 St Dunstan's St CT2 8AF
☎ 0870 609 6102 🖷 01227 463525
e-mail: thefalstaff@corushotels.com
Dir: *In city take 2nd rdbt into St Peters Place, hotel is opposite Westgate, turn right then immediately left for car park*
Located next to the Westgate Tower, the hotel (now under new ownership) offers easy access to the city centre and motorway network. Many original 16th-century features are still present in this historic coaching inn, especially in the cosy lounge and bar. Bedrooms are split between the newer annexe and the rooms in the main building which have individual character.
ROOMS: 25 en suite 22 annexe en suite (1 fmly) (14 GF) ⊗ in 27 bedrooms **FACILITIES:** STV Xmas **PARKING:** 34 **NOTES:** ⊗ in restaurant

★★70% Bow Window Inn
50 High St, Littlebourne CT3 1ST
☎ 01227 721264 🖷 01227 721250
Dir: *from Canterbury take A257 to Sandwich. From E of Canterbury to Littebourne hotel at bottom of hill on left*
A country cottage offering friendly hospitality and comfortable accommodation. Bedrooms are furnished to suit the style of the house and are all well equipped. Public areas are cosy with exposed beams providing character, especially within the restaurant, which provides an interesting menu.
ROOMS: 11 annexe en suite (1 fmly) (1 GF) **PARKING:** 10 **NOTES:** ⊗ in restaurant

Late for dinner? Quality standards mean that last orders for dinner vary according to star rating and should be no earlier than:
★★ 7.00pm ★★★ 8:00pm ★★★★ 9:00pm ★★★★★ 10:00pm

★★64% *Victoria*
59 London Rd CT2 8JY
☎ 01227 459333 🖷 01227 781552
e-mail: manager@vichotel.fsnet.co.uk
Dir: *M2/A2 onto A2052, hotel on left off 1st rdbt*
Just 15 minutes' walk from the city, the hotel is away from the hustle and bustle of the centre, yet within sight of the cathedral. Bedrooms vary in size and shape, and all are attractively

continued on p140

CANTERBURY, continued

decorated with an excellent range of facilities. Public areas include a busy bar and carvery restaurant.

Victoria, Canterbury

ROOMS: 34 en suite (12 fmly) ⊗ in 4 bedrooms **CONF:** Thtr 20 Class 20 Board 20 **PARKING:** 70 **NOTES:** ✗

⌂ Innkeeper's Lodge Canterbury
162 New Dover Rd CT1 3EL
☎ 01227 829951 📠 01227 829952
web: www.innkeeperslodge.com
Dir: M2 junct 7, A2 left at junct for Rough Common onto A2050. At 2nd rdbt follow signs for Dover (A2), lodge on right
A growing concept in the travel accommodation market. Smart rooms meet essential business requirements but also have home comforts. Dining options include all-day menus plus the added advantage of breakfast, which is included in the room price. For further details consult the Hotel Groups page.
ROOMS: 9 en suite s £55; d £55

⌂ Travelodge (Canterbury West)
A2 Gate Services, Dunkirk ME13 9LN
☎ 08700 850 950 📠 01227 752781
web: www.travelodge.co.uk
Dir: 5m W on A2 northbound
Travelodge offers good quality, good value, modern accommodation. Ideal for families, the spacious, en suite bedrooms include remote-control TV, tea and coffee-making facilities and comfortable beds. Meals can be taken at the nearby family restaurant. For further details consult the Hotel Groups page.
ROOMS: 40 en suite s fr £26; d fr £26

CARBIS BAY See St Ives

CARCROFT, South Yorkshire Map 16 SE50

⌂ Travelodge Doncaster
Great North Rd DN6 9LF
☎ 08700 850 950 📠 0870 1911631
web: www.travelodge.co.uk
Dir: on A1 northbound
Travelodge offers good quality, good value, modern accommodation. Ideal for families, the spacious, en suite bedrooms include remote-control TV, tea and coffee-making facilities and comfortable beds. Meals can be taken at the nearby family restaurant. For further details consult the Hotel Groups page.
ROOMS: 40 en suite s fr £26; d fr £26

GF indicates the number of bedrooms
at ground level

CARLISLE, Cumbria Map 18 NY35
See also Brampton

★★★71% **Crown**
Wetheral CA4 8ES
☎ 01228 561888 📠 01228 561637 & 564184
e-mail: info@crownhotelwetheral.co.uk
web: www.crownhotelwetheral.co.uk
Dir: M6 junct 42 take B6263 to Wetheral, right at village shop, car park at rear of hotel

Set in the attractive village of Wetheral and with landscaped gardens to the rear, this hotel is well suited to both business and leisure guests. Rooms vary in size and style and include two apartments in an adjacent house ideal for long stays. A choice of dining options is available, with the popular Waltons Bar an informal alternative to the main restaurant.
ROOMS: 49 en suite 2 annexe en suite (10 fmly) (3 GF) ⊗ in 30 bedrooms s £70-£110; d £100-£135 (incl. bkfst) **LB FACILITIES:** Spa STV ⌨ supervised Squash Sauna Solarium Gym Jacuzzi Children's splash pool Steam room Beauty facilities Xmas **CONF:** BC Thtr 175 Class 90 Board 50 Del from £115 **PARKING:** 80 **NOTES:** ⊗ in restaurant Civ Wed 120

★★★69% **Cumbria Park**
32 Scotland Rd, Stanwix CA3 9DG
☎ 01228 522887 📠 01228 514796
e-mail: enquiries@cumbriaparkhotel.co.uk
web: www.cumbriaparkhotel.co.uk
Dir: M6 junct 44, 1.5 miles on main road into Carlisle on left
Just minutes from the M6, this privately owned hotel, with its own feature garden, is also convenient for the city centre. Well-equipped bedrooms come in a variety of sizes, and several have four-poster or tester beds and whirlpool baths. Conferences and functions are well catered for with a wide choice of meeting rooms and suites.
ROOMS: 47 en suite (3 fmly) (7 GF) ⊗ in 13 bedrooms s £75-£95; d £98-£125 (incl. bkfst) **LB FACILITIES:** STV Sauna Solarium Gym Jacuzzi Steam room **CONF:** Thtr 120 Class 50 Board 35 Del from £105 **SERVICES:** Lift **PARKING:** 51 **NOTES:** ✗ Closed 25-26 Dec

★★★66% **Lakes Court**
Court Square CA1 1QY
☎ 01228 531951 📠 01228 547799
e-mail: reservations@lakescourthotel.co.uk
Dir: M6 junct 43, to city centre, then follow road to left & railway station
This Victorian building is located in the heart of the city centre, adjacent to the railway station. The bedrooms, including a four-poster room, are modern in style and mostly spacious. There are extensive conference facilities and a secure car park. A comfortable bar serves light meals and a wide range of drinks.
ROOMS: 70 en suite (3 fmly) ⊗ in 19 bedrooms s £50-£70; d £60-£90 (incl. bkfst) **LB FACILITIES:** STV Xmas **CONF:** BC Thtr 175 Class 60 Board 60 Del from £99.50 **SERVICES:** Lift **PARKING:** 20 **NOTES:** ⊗ in restaurant Civ Wed 170

★★★61% The Crown & Mitre
4 English St CA3 8HZ
☎ 01228 525491 📠 01228 514553
e-mail: info@crownandmitre-hotel-carlisle.com
web: www.peelhotel.com
Dir: *A6 to city centre, pass station & Woolworths on left. Right into Blackfriars St. Rear entrance at end*

Located in the heart of the city, this Edwardian hotel is close to the cathedral and a few minutes' walk from the castle. Hotel bedrooms vary in size and style from smart executive rooms to more functional standard rooms. Public rooms include the lovely bar with its feature stained glass windows and a comfortable lounge area.
ROOMS: 74 en suite 20 annexe en suite (4 fmly) ⊗ in 10 bedrooms s £69-£95; d £89-£135 (incl. bkfst) **LB** **FACILITIES:** STV 🏊 Jacuzzi Xmas **CONF:** Thtr 400 Class 250 Board 50 Del from £110 **SERVICES:** Lift **PARKING:** 42

⌂ *Hotel Ibis Carlisle*
Portlands, Botchergate CA1 1RP
☎ 01228 518000 📠 01228 518010
e-mail: H3443@accor-hotels.com
Dir: *M6 junct 42/43 follow signs for city centre. Hotel on Botchergate*
Modern, budget hotel offering comfortable accommodation in bright and practical bedrooms. Breakfast is self-service and dinner is available in the restaurant. For further details, consult the Hotel Groups page.
ROOMS: 102 en suite

⌂ Premier Travel Inn Carlisle (Central)
Warwick Rd CA1 2WF
☎ 08701 977053 📠 01228 534096
web: www.premiertravelinn.com
Dir: *M6 junct 43, on A69*
High quality, modern budget accommodation ideal for both families and business travellers. Spacious, en suite bedrooms feature bath and shower, satellite TV and many have telephones and modem points. The adjacent family restaurant features a wide and varied menu. For further details consult the Hotel Groups page.
ROOMS: 44 en suite s £52.95; d £52.95

⌂ Premier Travel Inn Carlisle North
Kingstown Rd CA3 0AT
☎ 0870 9906502 📠 0870 9906503
web: www.premiertravelinn.com
Dir: *1m from M6 junct 44, on A7 towards Carlisle, on left*
High quality, modern budget accommodation ideal for both families and business travellers. Spacious, en suite bedrooms feature bath and shower, satellite TV and many have telephones and modem points. The adjacent family restaurant features a wide and varied menu. For further details consult the Hotel Groups page.
ROOMS: 49 en suite s £52.95; d £52.95 **CONF:** Board 12

⌂ Premier Travel Inn Carlisle South
Carleton CA4 0AD
☎ 08701 977054 📠 01228 633313
web: www.premiertravelinn.com
Dir: *just off J42 on M6 south of Carlisle*
High quality, modern budget accommodation ideal for both families and business travellers. Spacious, en suite bedrooms feature bath and shower, satellite TV and many have telephones and modem points. The adjacent family restaurant features a wide and varied menu. For further details consult the Hotel Groups page.
ROOMS: 40 en suite s £46.95-£48.95; d £46.95-£48.95 **CONF:** Thtr 50 Class 50

⌂ Travelodge (Carlisle North)
A74 Southbound, Todhills CA6 4HA
☎ 08700 850 950 📠 01228 674335
web: www.travelodge.co.uk
Dir: *S'bound carriageway of A74 (M)*
Travelodge offers good quality, good value, modern accommodation. Ideal for families, the spacious, en suite bedrooms include remote-control TV, tea and coffee-making facilities and comfortable beds. Meals can be taken at the nearby family restaurant. For further details consult the Hotel Groups page.
ROOMS: 40 en suite s fr £26; d fr £26

CARNFORTH, Lancashire — Map 18 SD47

★★65% Royal Station
Market St LA5 9BT
☎ 01524 732033 & 733636 📠 01524 720267
e-mail: royalstation@mitchellshotels.co.uk
Dir: *M6 junct 35 onto A6 signed Carnforth. After 1m at x-rds in town centre right into Market St. Hotel opposite railway station*
This commercial hotel enjoys a town centre location close to the railway station. Bedrooms are well equipped and comfortably furnished. A good range of tasty good value meals can be taken in either the bright attractive lounge bar or the restaurant.
ROOMS: 13 en suite (1 fmly) s £36-£42; d £44-£58 **LB** **CONF:** Thtr 130 Class 80 Board 80 Del from £55 **PARKING:** 4 **NOTES:** ⊗ in restaurant

CARTMEL, Cumbria — Map 18 SD37

★★77% ⊛ ⚑ Aynsome Manor
LA11 6HH
☎ 015395 36653 📠 015395 36016
e-mail: info@aynsomemanorhotel.co.uk
Dir: *M6 junct 36, A590 signed Barrow-in-Furness towards Cartmel. Left at end of road, hotel before village*

Dating back to the early 16th century in parts, this manor house overlooks the fells and the nearby Priory. Spacious bedrooms, including some courtyard rooms, are comfortably furnished.
continued on p142

CARTMEL, continued

Dinner in the elegant restaurant features local produce whenever possible and there is a choice of lounges to relax in afterwards.
ROOMS: 10 en suite 2 annexe en suite (2 fmly) s £70-£93; d £126-£160 (incl. bkfst & dinner) **LB** **PARKING:** 20 **NOTES:** ⊗ in restaurant Closed 2-31 Jan RS Sun

C

CASTLE ASHBY, Northamptonshire Map 11 SP85

★★74% Falcon

NN7 1LF
☎ 01604 696200 01604 696673
e-mail: falcon.castleashby@oldenglishinns.co.uk
web: www.oldenglish.co.uk
Dir: *off A428*

Set in the heart of a peaceful village, this family-run hotel consists of a main house and two neighbouring cottages. Bedrooms are all individually decorated and provide a wealth of thoughtful extras. Character public rooms, in the main house, include a first-floor sitting area, a choice of bars and a pretty restaurant serving good quality cuisine.
ROOMS: 5 en suite 11 annexe en suite (1 fmly) ⊗ in 3 bedrooms **FACILITIES:** STV **CONF:** Thtr 50 Class 30 Board 25 **PARKING:** 75 **NOTES:** Civ Wed 60

CASTLE COMBE, Wiltshire Map 04 ST87

Top Hotel

★★★★ Manor House

SN14 7HR
☎ 01249 782206 01249 782159
e-mail: enquiries@manor-housecc.co.uk
web: www.exclusivehotels.co.uk
Dir: *M4 junct 17 follow Chippenham signs onto A420 Bristol, then right onto B4039. Through village, right after crossing bridge*
This hotel is situated in a secluded valley near the village, where there have been no new buildings for 300 years. There are 365 acres of grounds to enjoy, complete with an Italian garden and 18-hole golf course. Bedrooms are both in the main house and in a row of stone cottages, have been superbly furnished, and public rooms include a number of cosy lounges with roaring fires. Service is a pleasing blend of professionalism and friendliness, while food focuses on top quality local produce.
ROOMS: 22 en suite 26 annexe en suite (8 fmly) (12 GF) s £150-£600; d £180-£600 (incl. bkfst) **LB** **FACILITIES:** STV 18 Fishing Sauna Putt green Jogging track, croquet lawn Xmas **CONF:** BC Thtr 70 Class 70 Board 30 Del from £185 **PARKING:** 100 **NOTES:** ⊗ in restaurant Civ Wed 110

★★71% Castle Inn

SN14 7HN
☎ 01249 783030 01249 782315
e-mail: enquiries@castle-inn.info
Dir: *M4 junct 17, follow signs to racing circuit, through Upper Castle Combe. Left into Lower Village. Hotel at bottom of hill on right*

This charming 12th-century hostelry is set in the market place of this historic village. Bedrooms, including many with old beams, are individually decorated and offer a host of thoughtful extras. Guests can choose from a varied and tempting menu focusing on fresh ingredients, served either in the smart restaurant or in the more informal surroundings of the bar.
ROOMS: 11 en suite ⊗ in all bedrooms s £60-£75; d £100-£165 (incl. bkfst) **LB** **FACILITIES:** Xmas **CONF:** Thtr 20 Class 20 Board 20 **NOTES:** ⊗ in restaurant

CASTLE DONINGTON See Nottingham East Midlands Airport

CASTLEFORD, West Yorkshire Map 16 SE42

Premier Travel Inn Castleford

Pioneer Way WF10 5TG
☎ 0870 9906592 0870 9906593
web: www.premiertravelinn.com
Dir: *Just off A655. From M62 junct 31 take A655 towards Castleford, right at 1st lights, then left*
High quality, modern budget accommodation ideal for both families and business travellers. Spacious, en suite bedrooms feature bath and shower, satellite TV and many have telephones and modem points. The adjacent family restaurant features a wide and varied menu. For further details consult the Hotel Groups page.
ROOMS: 62 en suite s £46.95-£48.95; d £46.95-£48.95 **CONF:** Thtr 20 Class 8 Board 10

We have indicated only the hotels that don't accept credit or debit cards

CASTLETON, Derbyshire Map 16 SK18

Innkeeper's Lodge Castleton
Castle St S33 8WG
☎ 01433 620578 Fax 01433 622902
web: www.innkeeperslodge.com
Dir: *on A6187, in the centre of the village*
A growing concept in the travel accommodation market. Smart rooms meet essential business requirements but also have home comforts. Dining options include all-day menus plus the added advantage of breakfast, which is included in the room price. For further details consult the Hotel Groups page.
ROOMS: 6 en suite 6 annexe en suite s £59.95-£69.95; d £59.95-£69.95

CHADDESLEY CORBETT, Worcestershire Map 10 SO87

Top Hotel

★★★ Brockencote Hall Country House
DY10 4PY
☎ 01562 777876 Fax 01562 777872
e-mail: info@brockencotehall.com
web: www.brockencotehall.com
Dir: *0.5m W, off A448, opposite St Cassians Church*
Glorious countryside extends all around this magnificent mansion, and grazing sheep can be seen from the conservatory. Not surprisingly, relaxation comes high on the list of priorities here. Despite its very English location the hotel's owner actually hails from Alsace and the atmosphere is very much that of a provincial French château. The chef too is French (from Brittany) and the chandeliered dining room is a popular venue for the accomplished modern French cuisine.
ROOMS: 17 en suite (2 fmly) (5 GF) s £89-£140; d £116-£180 (incl. bkfst) **LB** **FACILITIES:** STV Reflexology /aromatherapy Xmas **CONF:** Thtr 30 Class 20 Board 20 Del from £42 **SERVICES:** Lift **PARKING:** 45 **NOTES:** in restaurant Civ Wed 60

CHAGFORD, Devon Map 03 SX78

Top Hotel

★★★ Gidleigh Park
TQ13 8HH
☎ 01647 432367 Fax 01647 432574
e-mail: gidleighpark@gidleigh.co.uk
web: www.gidleigh.com
Dir: *from Chagford, right at Lloyds Bank into Mill St. After 150yds fork right, follow lane 2m to end*
Set in 45 acres of well-tended grounds and gardens this world-renowned establishment is a delight. Individually styled

continued

bedrooms are beautifully furnished some with separate seating areas and many enjoying panoramic views of the grounds and countryside beyond. Public areas are spacious featuring antique furniture and beautiful flower arrangements. Facilities include a putting course, bowling, croquet and tennis courts. The cuisine is a highlight of any stay with an accompanying wine list that is a testament to the dedication the establishment has for high quality.

ROOMS: 12 en suite 3 annexe en suite s £275-£495; d £440-£600 (incl. bkfst & dinner) **LB** **FACILITIES:** STV Fishing Putt green Bowls **CONF:** Board 22 Del from £300 **PARKING:** 25 **NOTES:** in restaurant Closed 12 days Jan

Top Hotel

★★ Mill End
Dartmoor National Park TQ13 8JN
☎ 01647 432282 Fax 01647 433106
e-mail: info@millendhotel.com
Dir: *from A30 at Whiddon Down follow A382 to Moretonhampstead. After 3.5m hump back bridge at Sandy Park, hotel on right by river*
In an attractive location, Mill End, an 18th-century working water mill sits by the River Teign that offers six miles of angling. The atmosphere is akin to a family home where guests are encouraged to relax and enjoy the peace and informality. Bedrooms are available in a range of sizes and all are stylishly decorated and thoughtfully equipped. Dining is certainly a highlight of a stay here; the menus offer exciting dishes featuring local produce.
ROOMS: 15 en suite (3 GF) in all bedrooms s £80-£110; d £110-£150 (incl. bkfst) **LB** **FACILITIES:** Fishing Xmas **CONF:** Thtr 40 Class 20 Board 30 **PARKING:** 29 **NOTES:** in restaurant

AA Rosette Award for culinary excellence

CHAGFORD, continued

★★68% **Three Crowns Hotel**
High St TQ13 8AJ
☎ 01647 433444 ▤ 01647 433117
e-mail: threecrowns@msn.com
web: www.chagford-accom.co.uk
Dir: exit A30 at Whiddon Down. Hotel in town centre opposite church

This 13th-century inn is located in the heart of the village. Exposed beams, mullioned windows and open fires are all part of the charm which is evident throughout. There is a range of comfortable bedrooms; several with four-poster beds. A choice of bars is available along with a pleasant lounge and separate dining room.
ROOMS: 17 en suite (1 fmly) ⊗ in 8 bedrooms s £55-£74; d £55-£74 (incl. bkfst) **LB FACILITIES:** STV Pool table in bar Xmas **CONF:** Thtr 90 Board 90 **PARKING:** 20 **NOTES:** ⊗ in restaurant

CHARD, Somerset Map 04 ST30

★★★70% **Lordleaze**
Henderson Dr, Forton Rd TA20 2HW
☎ 01460 61066 ▤ 01460 66468
e-mail: enquiries@lordleazehotel.fsnet.co.uk
web: www.lordleazehotel.co.uk
Dir: from Chard take A358, at St Mary's Church turn left to Forton & Winsham on B3162. Follow signs to hotel

The hotel is quietly located close to the Devon, Dorset and Somerset borders. All bedrooms, including some newly added, are well equipped and comfortable. The friendly lounge bar has a wood-burning stove and a tempting bar meal selection. The conservatory restaurant offers more formal carte dining.
ROOMS: 25 en suite (2 fmly) (7 GF) ⊗ in 21 bedrooms s £58-£65; d £80-£90 (incl. bkfst) **LB FACILITIES:** Xmas **CONF:** Thtr 180 Class 60 Board 40 Del £100 **PARKING:** 55 **NOTES:** ⊗ in restaurant Civ Wed 100

CHARLBURY, Oxfordshire Map 11 SP31

★★67% ◉ **The Bell**
Church St OX7 3PP
☎ 01608 810278 ▤ 01608 811447
e-mail: reservationsatthebell@msn.com
web: www.bellhotel-charlbury.co.uk
Dir: from Oxford take A34 towards Woodstock, 2nd turn off B4437 towards Charlbury. In village, 2nd on left, hotel opposite St Mary's Church

This mellow Cotswold-stone inn dates back to the 16th century, when it was home to Customs & Excise, and sits close to the town centre. Popular with locals, the bar has an enjoyable and relaxed atmosphere and comes complete with flagstone floors and log fires. The well-equipped bedrooms are situated in the main building and the adjacent converted barn.
ROOMS: 7 en suite 4 annexe en suite (3 fmly) ⊗ in all bedrooms s fr £69; d fr £85 (incl. bkfst) **LB FACILITIES:** Xmas **CONF:** Thtr 60 Class 60 Board 30 **PARKING:** 40 **NOTES:** ⊗ in restaurant

CHARMOUTH, Dorset Map 04 SY39

★★74% **White House**
2 Hillside, The Street DT6 6PJ
☎ 01297 560411 ▤ 01297 560702
e-mail: ian@whitehousehotel.com
Dir: off A35 signed Charmouth. Hotel opposite church halfway up hill

Famed for its fossils and cliff-top walks, the interesting beach at Charmouth is within walking distance of this charming Regency property. Comfortable accommodation is provided at this friendly, small hotel, where individually styled bedrooms are equipped with modern facilities. In the evening, imaginative cuisine using fresh, local produce is served in the attractive restaurant.
ROOMS: 6 en suite 1 annexe en suite (7 fmly) (2 GF) ⊗ in all bedrooms s £75-£130; d £100-£180 (incl. bkfst) **LB CONF:** Thtr 20 Class 20 Board 18 Del from £85 **PARKING:** 9 **NOTES:** No children 14yrs ⊗ in restaurant Closed Jan RS Feb, Nov & Dec

CHARNOCK RICHARD MOTORWAY SERVICE AREA (M6), Lancashire — Map 15 SD51

Welcome Lodge Charnock Richard
Welcome Break Service Area PR7 5LR
☎ 01257 791746 Fax 01257 793596
e-mail: charnockhotel@welcomebreak.co.uk
web: www.welcomebreak.co.uk
Dir: *between junct 27 & 28 of M6 N'bound. 500yds from Camelot Theme Park via Mill Lane*
This modern building offers accommodation in smart, spacious and well-equipped bedrooms, suitable for families and business travellers, and all with en suite bathrooms. Refreshments may be taken at the nearby family restaurant. For further details consult the Hotel Groups page.
ROOMS: 100 en suite s £35-£50; d £35-£50 **CONF:** Thtr 40 Class 16 Board 24

CHATHAM, Kent — Map 07 TQ76

★★★★74%
Bridgewood Manor Hotel
Bridgewood Roundabout, Walderslade Woods ME5 9AX
☎ 01634 201333 Fax 01634 201330
e-mail: bridgewoodmanor@marstonhotels.com
web: www.marstonhotels.com
Dir: *adjacent to Bridgewood rdbt on A229. Take 3rd exit signed Walderslade and Lordswood. Hotel 50mtrs on left*

A modern, purpose-built hotel situated on the outskirts of Rochester. Bedrooms are pleasantly decorated, comfortably furnished and equipped with many thoughtful touches. The hotel has an excellent range of leisure and conference facilities. Guests can dine in the informal Terrace Bistro or experience fine dining in the more formal Squires restaurant, where the service is both attentive and friendly.
ROOMS: 100 en suite (12 fmly) ⊗ in 63 bedrooms s fr £129; d fr £166 (incl. bkfst) **LB FACILITIES: Spa** STV Snooker Sauna Solarium Gym Putt green Jacuzzi Beauty treatments Xmas **CONF:** Thtr 200 Class 110 Board 80 Del from £175 **SERVICES:** Lift **PARKING:** 170 **NOTES:** ⊗ in restaurant Civ Wed 130

CHEADLE, Greater Manchester — Map 16 SJ88

Premier Travel Inn Manchester (Cheadle)
Royal Crescent SK8 3FE
☎ 08701 977172 Fax 0161 491 5886
web: www.premiertravelinn.com
Dir: *off Cheadle Royal rdbt off A34 behind TGI Friday's*
High quality, modern budget accommodation ideal for both families and business travellers. Spacious, en suite bedrooms feature bath and shower, satellite TV and many have telephones and modem points. The adjacent family restaurant features a wide and varied menu. For further details consult the Hotel Groups page.
ROOMS: 40 en suite s £52.95; d £52.95 **CONF:** Thtr 30

CHELMSFORD, Essex — Map 06 TL70

★★★72% ***Atlantic***
New St CM1 1PP
☎ 01245 268168 Fax 01245 268169
e-mail: info@atlantichotel.co.uk
Ideally situated just a short walk from the railway station with its quick links to London, this modern, purpose-built hotel has contemporary-style bedrooms equipped with modern facilities. The open-plan public areas include the popular New Street Brasserie, a lounge bar and a conservatory.
ROOMS: 59 en suite (3 fmly) (27 GF) ⊗ in 49 bedrooms **FACILITIES:** STV Sauna Solarium Gym Steam room ♫ **CONF:** Thtr 15 Board 10 **SERVICES:** air con **PARKING:** 60 **NOTES:** Closed 24 Dec-2 Jan

★★★72% **Pontlands Park Country Hotel**
West Hanningfield Rd, Great Baddow CM2 8HR
☎ 01245 476444 Fax 01245 478393
e-mail: sales@pontlandsparkhotel.co.uk
web: www.pontlandsparkhotel.co.uk
Dir: *A12/A130/A1114 to Chelmsford. 1st exit at rdbt, 1st slip road on left. Left towards Gt Baddow, 1st left into West Hanningfield Rd. Hotel 400yds on left*
A Victorian country-house hotel in a peaceful rural setting amidst attractive landscaped grounds. The stylishly furnished bedrooms are generally quite spacious; each is individually decorated and equipped with modern facilities. The elegant public rooms include a tastefully furnished sitting room, a cosy lounge bar, smart conservatory restaurant and an intimate dining room.
ROOMS: 36 en suite (10 fmly) (12 GF) ⊗ in 9 bedrooms s £105-£125; d £130-£170 **LB FACILITIES: Spa** STV Sauna Gym Jacuzzi Beauty Room **CONF:** Thtr 100 Class 20 Board 22 Del from £150 **PARKING:** 100 **NOTES:** ⊗ in restaurant Closed 24 Dec-3 Jan (ex 31 Dec) Civ Wed 100

★★★71% **County Hotel, Bar & Restaurant**
Rainsford Rd CM1 2PZ
☎ 01245 455700 Fax 01245 492762
e-mail: kloftus@countyhotelgroup.co.uk
web: www.countyhotelgroup.co.uk
Dir: *from town centre, past rail and bus station. Hotel 300yds left beyond lights*
Expect a friendly welcome at this popular hotel, which is ideally situated within easy walking distance of the railway station, bus depot and town centre. Public areas include a smart new restaurant and the plushly furnished wine bar. The hotel also has a range of meeting rooms and banqueting facilities.
ROOMS: 54 en suite (1 GF) ⊗ in 30 bedrooms s £60-£95; d £80-£100 (incl. bkfst) **LB FACILITIES:** STV Xmas **CONF:** Thtr 200 Class 84 Board 64 Del £140 **SERVICES:** Lift **PARKING:** 80 **NOTES:** ⊗ in restaurant Closed 27-30 Dec Civ Wed 80

★★★68% ***Ivy Hill***
Writtle Rd, Margaretting CM4 0EH
☎ 01277 353040 Fax 01277 355038
e-mail: sales@ivyhillhotel.co.uk
web: www.ivyhillhotel.co.uk
Dir: *at top of slip road, off A12*
This smartly appointed hotel is ideally situated, just off the A12. The spacious bedrooms are tastefully decorated, have

continued on p146

CHELMSFORD, continued

co-ordinated fabrics and all the usual facilities. Public rooms include a choice of lounges, a cosy bar, a smart conservatory and the Ivy restaurant, as well as a range of conference and banqueting facilities.
ROOMS: 33 en suite (5 fmly) (11 GF) **FACILITIES:** STV ⚓ ↘ **CONF:** BC Thtr 80 Class 60 Board 20 **PARKING:** 60 **NOTES:** ✗ ⊗ in restaurant Civ Wed 100

⌂ Premier Travel Inn Chelmsford (Borehamwood)

Main Rd, Boreham CM3 3HJ
☎ 0870 9906394 📠 0870 9906395
web: www.premiertravelinn.com
Dir: *From M25 junct 28, follow A12 to Colchester then B1137 to Boreham*
High quality, modern budget accommodation ideal for both families and business travellers. Spacious, en suite bedrooms feature bath and shower, satellite TV and many have telephones and modem points. The adjacent family restaurant features a wide and varied menu. For further details consult the Hotel Groups page.
ROOMS: 78 en suite s £49.95-£52.95; d £49.95-£52.95

⌂ Premier Travel Inn Chelmsford (Springfield)

Chelmsford Service Area, Colchester Rd, Springfield CM2 5PY
☎ 0870 238 3310 📠 01245 464010
web: www.premiertravelinn.com
Dir: *on A12 junct 19, Chelmsford bypass, signed Chelmsford Service Area. 2nd service area from A12 on M25*
High quality, modern budget accommodation ideal for both families and business travellers. Spacious, en suite bedrooms feature bath and shower, satellite TV and many have telephones and modem points. The adjacent family restaurant features a wide and varied menu. For further details consult the Hotel Groups page.
ROOMS: 61 en suite s £49.95-£52.95; d £49.95-£52.95

CHELTENHAM, Gloucestershire — Map 10 SO92

★★★★72% The Queen's

The Promenade GL50 1NN
☎ 0870 400 8107 📠 01242 224145
e-mail: general.queens@macdonald-hotels.co.uk
web: www.macdonald-hotels.co.uk
Dir: *follow town centre signs. Left at Montpellier Walk rdbt. Entrance 500mtrs right*
With its spectacular position at the top of the main promenade, this landmark hotel is an ideal base from which to explore the charms of this Regency spa town and the Cotswolds. Bedrooms are very comfortable and include two beautiful four-poster rooms. Smart public rooms include the popular Gold Cup bar and a choice of dining options.
ROOMS: 79 en suite ⊗ in 70 bedrooms s £95-£155; d £105-£155 (incl. bkfst) **LB** **FACILITIES:** STV Xmas **CONF:** Thtr 100 Class 60 Board 40 Del from £120 **SERVICES:** Lift air con **PARKING:** 80 **NOTES:** ⊗ in restaurant Civ Wed 100

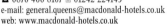

♫ Entertainment

Packed in a hurry? Ironing facilities should be available at all star levels, either in the rooms or on request

Town House

★★★★ ◎ ⌂ Alias Hotel Kandinsky

Bayshill Rd, Montpellier GL50 3AS
☎ 01242 527788 📠 01242 226412
e-mail: info@aliaskandinsky.com
Dir: *M5 junct 11, A40 to town centre. Right at 2nd rdbt. 2nd exit at 3rd rdbt into Bayshill Rd. Hotel on corner of Bayshill/Parabola Rds*
A large Regency villa successfully blending modern comfort with quirky eclectic decoration. Stylish bedrooms vary in size and have additional facilities such as CD/video players. There are several lounges, a conservatory, and the bright Café Paradiso restaurant. Hidden in the cellars is U-bahn, a wonderful 1950's style cocktail bar.
ROOMS: 48 en suite (3 fmly) (5 GF) ⊗ in 4 bedrooms s £70-£75; d £70-£99 **LB** **FACILITIES:** STV Access to local pool & gym, free of charge to guests Xmas **CONF:** Board 20 Del from £150 **SERVICES:** Lift **PARKING:** 32 **NOTES:** ✗ ⊗ in restaurant

See advert on opposite page

★★★★65% Cheltenham Park

Cirencester Rd, Charlton Kings GL53 8EA
☎ 01242 222021 📠 01242 254880
e-mail: cheltenhamparkreservations@paramount-hotels.co.uk
web: www.paramount-hotels.co.uk
Dir: *on A435, 2m SE of Cheltenham near Lilley Brook Golf Course*
Located south of Cheltenham, this attractive Georgian hotel is set in its own landscaped gardens, adjacent to Lilley Brook Golf Course. All of the bedrooms are spacious and well equipped and the hotel has an impressive leisure club and extensive meeting facilities. The Lakeside restaurant serves carefully prepared cuisine.
ROOMS: 33 en suite 110 annexe en suite (2 fmly) ⊗ in 67 bedrooms s £125; d £145 **LB** **FACILITIES:** STV ⛆ supervised Sauna Solarium Gym Jacuzzi Beauty treatment rooms Xmas **CONF:** BC Thtr 350 Class 180 Board 110 Del £161 **PARKING:** 170 **NOTES:** ⊗ in restaurant Civ Wed 100

Top Hotel

★★★ ◎◎◎ The Greenway

Shurdington GL51 4UG
☎ 01242 862352 📠 01242 862780
e-mail: greenway@btconnect.com
web: www.vonessenhotels.co.uk
Dir: *2.5m SW on A46*
This hotel, with a wealth of history, is peacefully located in a delightful setting close to the A46 and the M5. Within easy reach of the many attractions of the Cotswolds, as well as the

continued

interesting town of Cheltenham, The Greenway certainly offers something special. The attractive dining room overlooks the sunken garden and is the venue for exciting food, proudly served by dedicated and attentive staff.

ROOMS: 11 en suite 10 annexe en suite (1 fmly) (4 GF) ⊗ in 10 bedrooms s £99-£159; d £150-£280 (incl. bkfst) **LB**
FACILITIES: ♨ Clay pigeon shooting, Horse riding, Mountain biking, Beauty treatment Xmas **CONF:** Thtr 40 Class 25 Board 18 Del from £205 **PARKING:** 50 **NOTES:** ⊗ in restaurant Civ Wed 45

Top Hotel

★★★ ◉◉ **Hotel on the Park**
38 Evesham Rd GL52 2AH
☎ 01242 518898 ▤ 01242 511526
e-mail: stay@hotelonthepark.com
web: www.hotelonthepark.com
Dir: opposite Pittville Park. Join one-way system, off A435 towards Evesham
The Hotel on the Park is a wonderfully different hotel with style, originality and flair throughout. Bedrooms have tremendous character and exceptional comfort. Similar comments apply to public areas, comprising the elegant drawing room, library and Parkers, a modern brasserie, serving relaxed and enjoyable cuisine looking across the park.
ROOMS: 12 en suite ⊗ in all bedrooms s £99-£169; d £114-£184
LB FACILITIES: STV **CONF:** Board 18 Del from £54.75
PARKING: 8 **NOTES:** ✕ No children 8yrs ⊗ in restaurant

Late for dinner? Quality standards mean that last orders for dinner vary according to star rating and should be no earlier than:
★★ 7.00pm ★★★ 8:00pm ★★★★ 9:00pm
★★★★★ 10:00pm

★★★72% ◉ **George Hotel**
St Georges Rd GL50 3DZ
☎ 01242 235751 ▤ 01242 224359
e-mail: hotel@stayatthegeorge.co.uk
web: www.stayatthegeorge.co.uk
Dir: M5 junct 11 follow town centre signs. At 1st lights left into Gloucester Rd, past rail station over mini-rdbt. At lights right into St Georges Rd. Hotel 0.75m on left

Just a short stroll from the town centre, this genuinely friendly hotel is privately owned and occupies part of an elegant Regency terrace. Standard and superior bedrooms are well equipped and tastefully furnished. There are two dining options - the modern and lively Monty's brasserie and the stylish and contemporary Seafood Restaurant. A new chic designer bar occupies the basement.
ROOMS: 38 en suite (1 GF) ⊗ in 30 bedrooms s £55-£85; d £90-£105 (incl. bkfst) **LB FACILITIES:** STV Complimentary membership of local health club **CONF:** Board 24 Del £137.50 **PARKING:** 30 **NOTES:** ✕ ⊗ in restaurant RS 24-26 Dec

CHELTENHAM, continued

★★★70% Charlton Kings
London Rd, Charlton Kings GL52 6UU
☎ 01242 231061 📠 01242 241900
e-mail: enquires@charltonkingshotel.co.uk
web: www.charltonkingshotel.co.uk
Dir: *entering Cheltenham from Oxford on A40, 1st on left*

Conveniently located on the outskirts of Cheltenham, the Charlton Kings is an attractive and friendly hotel providing comfortable, modern accommodation. The neatly presented bedrooms are well equipped with tasteful furnishings and contemporary comforts. The popular and stylish restaurant serves a variety of dishes for all tastes from a menu based on quality ingredients.
ROOMS: 13 en suite (1 fmly) (4 GF) ⊗ in 11 bedrooms s £65-£85; d £98-£125 (incl. bkfst) **LB** **FACILITIES:** STV **PARKING:** 26 **NOTES:** ⊗ in restaurant

★★★68% Carlton
Parabola Rd GL50 3AQ
☎ 01242 514453 📠 01242 226487
e-mail: enquiries@thecarltonhotel.co.uk
web: www.thecarltonhotel.co.uk
Dir: *Follow signs to town centre, at Town Hall straight on through 2 sets of lights, turn left, then 1st right.*
This well-presented family owned and run Regency property is situated just a short walk from the town centre. Bedrooms are located both in the main hotel and also within an annexe building, where rooms are larger and more luxurious. Other features include a choice of bars, lounge and conference facilities.
ROOMS: 62 en suite 13 annexe en suite (2 fmly) (4 GF) ⊗ in 15 bedrooms s £48-£85; d £93-£110 (incl. bkfst) **LB** **FACILITIES:** STV Xmas **CONF:** Thtr 200 Class 150 Board 100 Del from £95 **SERVICES:** Lift **PARKING:** 85 **NOTES:** ⊗ in restaurant

★★★65% *Royal George*
Birdlip GL4 8JH
OLD ENGLISH INNS
☎ 01452 862506 📠 01452 862277
e-mail: 6503@greeneking.co.uk
web: www.oldenglish.co.uk
Dir: *on B4070, off A417*
This attractive 18th-century Cotswold building has been sympathetically converted and extended into a pleasant hotel. Bedrooms are spacious and comfortably furnished with modern facilities. The public areas have been designed around a traditional English pub with the bar leading on to a terrace overlooking extensive lawns.
ROOMS: 34 en suite (2 fmly) (12 GF) ⊗ in 22 bedrooms **FACILITIES:** ♫ **CONF:** Thtr 90 Board 45 **PARKING:** 120 **NOTES:** ⊗ in restaurant Civ Wed 80

★★★63% The Prestbury House Hotel & Oaks Restaurant
The Burgage, Prestbury GL52 3DN
☎ 01242 529533 📠 01242 227076
e-mail: enquiries@prestburyhouse.co.uk
web: www.prestburyhouse.co.uk
Dir: *1m NE of Cheltenham. Follow all signs for racecourse. From racecourse follow Prestbury signs. Hotel 2nd left, 500mtrs from racecourse*

This hotel retains much of its Georgian charm and is ideally situated for the town centre and racecourse. Well-equipped, spacious accommodation is offered in the main house and converted coach house. An interesting range of dishes is offered in 'Oaks', the hotel's elegant, oak-panelled restaurant. The owners also run a management training company, and team-building activities are sometimes held here.
ROOMS: 7 en suite 8 annexe en suite (3 GF) ⊗ in 16 bedrooms s £60-£92; d £60-£110 (incl. bkfst) **LB** **FACILITIES:** STV Riding Gym Putt green Archery, Bike hire, Trim Trail, Hill Walking, Petanque Xmas **CONF:** BC Thtr 65 Class 30 Board 25 Del from £80 **PARKING:** 40 **NOTES:** ⊗ in restaurant Civ Wed 60

★★★62% *Hotel De La Bere*
Southam GL52 3NH
☎ 01242 545454 📠 01242 236016
e-mail: delabere@corushotels.com
web: www.corushotels.com/delabere
Dir: *M5 junct 10 into Cheltenham, left at first rdbt on B road for 3m crossing A435 to B4632. Turn right hotel on right.*

This elegant 15th-century building is situated to the north of town, overlooking the famous racecourse. There is a tangible sense of history here with many original features retained. Bedrooms are split between the main house and the courtyard, all of which offer ample comfort and plenty of character. Leisure facilities, including a heated outdoor pool, are available.
ROOMS: 33 en suite 24 annexe en suite (3 fmly) (10 GF) ⊗ in 28 bedrooms **FACILITIES:** Squash Sauna Solarium Gym **CONF:** Thtr 100 Class 60 Board 40 **PARKING:** 125 **NOTES:** ⊗ in restaurant Civ Wed 100

★★★62% Quality Hotel Cheltenham
Gloucester Rd GL51 0ST
☎ 01452 713226 📠 01452 857590
e-mail: info@qualitycheltenham.com
Dir: *M5 junct 11 onto A40 to Cheltenham. Left at rdbt, hotel 1m on left*
This hotel is situated on the edge of town and provides comfortable and modern accommodation. The lounge bar and the restaurant are attractively presented and a number of function rooms are also available. Friendly service and helpful staff ensure a pleasant stay.
ROOMS: 49 en suite (4 fmly) ⊗ in 13 bedrooms s £39-£69; d £39-£69 **LB** **FACILITIES:** STV pool table bar games ♫ **CONF:** Thtr 180 Class 80 Board 45 Del from £99 **PARKING:** 150 **NOTES:** ⊗ in restaurant RS 12-16 Mar & 10-12 Nov Civ Wed 150

★★68% Cotswold Grange
Pittville Circus Rd GL52 2QH
☎ 01242 515119 📠 01242 241537
e-mail: paul@cotswoldgrange.co.uk
Dir: *from town centre, follow Prestbury signs. Right at 1st rdbt, hotel 200yds on left*
Built from Cotswold limestone, this attractive Georgian property retains many impressive architectural features. Situated conveniently close to the centre of Cheltenham, this long-established, family-run hotel offers well-equipped and comfortable accommodation. The convivial bar is a popular venue, and additional facilities include a spacious restaurant, cosy lounge and ample parking.
ROOMS: 25 en suite (4 fmly) s fr £55; d fr £80 (incl. bkfst) **CONF:** Thtr 20 Class 15 Board 15 Del from £85 **PARKING:** 20 **NOTES:** ⊗ in restaurant Closed 24 Dec-5 Jan RS Sat & Sun evening (food by arrangement)

★★66% North Hall
Pittville Circus Rd GL52 2PZ
☎ 01242 520589 📠 01242 261953
e-mail: northhallhotel@btinternet.com
web: www.northhallhotel.co.uk
Dir: *from Cheltenham town centre, follow Pittville signs. At Pittville Circus take 1st left into Pittville Circus Rd. Hotel on right*

This three-storey Victorian house is conveniently located in a quiet residential area, within easy reach of the town centre and racecourse. Bedrooms are individually designed and offer ample comfort and quality with a range of extra facilities. A brasserie-style menu is served in the elegant surroundings of the restaurant, and there is also a bar/lounge with convivial atmosphere.
ROOMS: 20 en suite (2 fmly) ⊗ in 8 bedrooms s £45-£65; d £75-£95 (incl. bkfst) **LB** **FACILITIES:** STV Xmas **CONF:** Thtr 40 Class 25 Board 15 **PARKING:** 25 **NOTES:** ⊗ in restaurant

⌂ Premier Travel Inn Cheltenham Central
374 Gloucester Rd GL51 7AY
☎ 08701 977056 📠 01242 260042
web: www.premiertravelinn.com
Dir: *M5 junct 11 onto A40 (Cheltenham). Follow dual carriageway to end, straight at 1st rdbt, turn right at 2nd*
High quality, modern budget accommodation ideal for both families and business travellers. Spacious, en suite bedrooms feature bath and shower, satellite TV and many have telephones and modem points. The adjacent family restaurant features a wide and varied menu. For further details consult the Hotel Groups page.
ROOMS: 40 en suite s £49.95; d £49.95

⌂ Premier Travel Inn Cheltenham West
Tewkesbury Rd, Uckington GL51 9SL
☎ 08701 977055 📠 01242 244887
web: www.premiertravelinn.com
Dir: *opposite Sainsbury's & Homebase on A4019, 2 miles from junct 10 (S'bound exit only) and 3 miles from junct 11 (both exits) of M5*
High quality, modern budget accommodation ideal for both families and business travellers. Spacious, en suite bedrooms feature bath and shower, satellite TV and many have telephones and modem points. The adjacent family restaurant features a wide and varied menu. For further details consult the Hotel Groups page.
ROOMS: 40 en suite s £49.95; d £49.95 **CONF:** Thtr 30 Class 30

⌂ Travelodge Cheltenham
Golden Valley Roundabout, Hatherley Ln GL51 6PN
☎ 08700 850 950 📠 01242 241 748
web: www.travelodge.co.uk
Dir: *M5 junct 11 follow signs for Cheltenham. Travelodge at 1st rdbt.*
Travelodge offers good quality, good value, modern accommodation. Ideal for families, the spacious, en suite bedrooms include remote-control TV, tea and coffee-making facilities and comfortable beds. Meals can be taken at the nearby family restaurant. For further details consult the Hotel Groups page.
ROOMS: 106 en suite s fr £26; d fr £26

CHENIES, Buckinghamshire — Map 06 TQ09

★★★71% The Bedford Arms Hotel
WD3 6EQ
☎ 01923 283301 📠 01923 284825
e-mail: contact@bedfordarms.co.uk
web: www.bedfordarms.co.uk
Dir: *M25 junct 18, then A404, follow signs for Amersham, approx 2.5m*
This attractive, 19th-century country inn enjoys a peaceful rural setting. Comfortable bedrooms are decorated in traditional style and feature a range of thoughtful extras. Each room is named after a relation of the Duke of Bedford, whose family has an historic association with the hotel. There are two bars, a lounge and a cosy, wood-panelled restaurant.
ROOMS: 10 en suite 8 annexe en suite (2 fmly) (8 GF) ⊗ in 6 bedrooms s £60-£110; d £95-£150 (incl. bkfst) **FACILITIES:** STV **CONF:** Thtr 50 Class 16 Board 24 Del from £150 **PARKING:** 60 **NOTES:** ⊗ in restaurant Civ Wed 55

> Popped the question? Hotels with Civ wed in their entry are licensed for civil wedding ceremonies. Maximum numbers for the ceremony only are shown e.g. Civ wed 120

CHESSINGTON, Greater London Map 06 TQ16

Premier Travel Inn Chessington
Leatherhead Rd KT9 2NE
☎ 08701 977057 🖷 01372 720889
web: www.premiertravelinn.com
Dir: *From M25 junct 9 towards Kingston on A243, for approx 2 miles. Inn is next to Chessington World of Adventures*
High quality, modern budget accommodation ideal for both families and business travellers. Spacious, en suite bedrooms feature bath and shower, satellite TV and many have telephones and modem points. The adjacent family restaurant features a wide and varied menu. For further details consult the Hotel Groups page.
ROOMS: 42 en suite s £59.95-£62.95; d £59.95-£62.95

CHESTER, Cheshire Map 15 SJ46
See also Puddington

Top Hotel

★★★★★ ⊛⊛⊛
The Chester Grosvenor & Spa
Eastgate CH1 1LT
☎ 01244 324024 🖷 01244 313246
e-mail: hotel@chestergrosvenor.com
Dir: *off M56 for M53, then A56. Follow signs for city centre hotels*
Located within the Roman walls of the city, this Grade II listed, half-timbered building is the essence of Englishness. Furnished with fine fabrics and queen or king-size beds, the suites and bedrooms are of the highest standard, each designed with guest comfort as a priority. The art deco La Brasserie (awarded one AA rosette) is bustling, and the fine dining restaurant, The Arkle (with three AA rosettes) offers creative cuisine with flair and style. A luxury spa & small fitness centre are also available.
ROOMS: 80 en suite (7 fmly) ⊗ in all bedrooms d £180-£881.25 **LB** **FACILITIES: Spa** STV Sauna Solarium Gym Membership of nearby Country Club ♫ **CONF:** BC Thtr 250 Class 120 Board 48 Del from £225 **SERVICES:** Lift air con **NOTES:** ✗ ⊗ in restaurant Closed 25-26 Dec RS 27-30 Dec & 1-20 Jan Civ Wed 100

See advert on opposite page

★★★★72% *De Vere Carden Park*
Carden Park CH3 9DQ
☎ 01829 731000 🖷 01829 731599
e-mail: reservations.carden@devere-hotels.com
web: www.devereonline.co.uk
(For full entry see Broxton)

Bad hair day?
Hairdryers in all rooms three stars and above

★★★★70% ⊛ *Mollington Banastre*
Parkgate Rd CH1 6NN
☎ 01244 851471 🖷 01244 851165
e-mail: events.mollington@arcadianhotels.co.uk
Dir: *M56 junct 16 at rdbt left for Chester on A540. Hotel 2m on right*
Set in its own attractive grounds, this hotel remains popular with both the business and the leisure markets. The bedrooms, which come in various styles, are well equipped and comfortable. Stylish, open-plan public areas include a comfortable bar and lounge, the Garden Room restaurant and a comprehensive leisure club.
ROOMS: 63 en suite (7 fmly) ⊗ in 40 bedrooms **FACILITIES:** STV Squash Sauna Solarium Gym Jacuzzi Hairdressing Health & beauty salon ♫ **CONF:** BC Thtr 260 Class 60 Board 50 **SERVICES:** Lift **PARKING:** 200 **NOTES:** ⊗ in restaurant Civ Wed 150

See advert on page 153

★★★★66% The Queen Hotel
City Rd CH1 3AH
☎ 01244 305000 🖷 01244 318483
e-mail: queenhotel@feathers.uk.com
web: www.feathers.uk.com
Dir: *follow signs for railway station, hotel opposite*
This hotel is ideally located opposite the railway station and just a couple minutes' walk from the city. Public areas include a new restaurant, small gym, waiting room bar, separate lounge and Roman-themed gardens. Bedrooms are generally spacious; all have been refurbished and reflect the hotel's Victorian heritage.
ROOMS: 129 en suite (6 fmly) (10 GF) ⊗ in 59 bedrooms s £119; d £129 (incl. bkfst) **LB** **FACILITIES:** STV Gym Xmas **CONF:** BC Thtr 400 Class 150 Board 60 Del from £120 **SERVICES:** Lift **PARKING:** 100 **NOTES:** ✗ ⊗ in restaurant Civ Wed 250

★★★76% ⊛ *Rowton Hall Country House Hotel*
Whitchurch Rd, Rowton CH3 6AD
☎ 01244 335262 🖷 01244 335464
e-mail: rowtonhall@rowtonhall.co.uk
web: www.rowtonhallhotel.co.uk
Dir: *2m SE of Chester at Rowton off A41 towards Whitchurch*
This delightful Georgian manor house set in mature grounds retains many original features such as a superb carved staircase and several eye-catching fireplaces. Bedrooms vary in style and all have been stylishly fitted and have impressive en suites. Public areas include a smart leisure centre, extensive function facilities and a striking restaurant that serves imaginative dishes.
ROOMS: 38 en suite (4 fmly) (8 GF) **FACILITIES:** STV Sauna Solarium Gym Jacuzzi ch fac **CONF:** Thtr 170 Class 48 Board 50 **PARKING:** 120 **NOTES:** ✗ ⊗ in restaurant Civ Wed 120

★★★74% Grosvenor Pulford
Wrexham Rd, Pulford CH4 9DG
☎ 01244 570560 🖷 01244 570809
e-mail: enquiries@grosvenorpulfordhotel.co.uk
web: www.grosvenorpulfordhotel.co.uk
Dir: *M53/A55 at junct signed A483, Chester and Wrexham, North Wales. Onto B5445, hotel 2m on right*
Set in rural surroundings, this modern, stylish hotel features a magnificent leisure club with a large Roman-style swimming pool. Among the bedrooms available are several executive suites and others containing spiral staircases leading to the bedroom sections. A brasserie restaurant and bar provide a wide range of imaginative dishes in a relaxed atmosphere.
ROOMS: 73 en suite (6 fmly) (21 GF) ⊗ in 10 bedrooms **FACILITIES: Spa** STV Snooker Sauna Solarium Gym Jacuzzi Hairdressing & Beauty salon, coffee bar Xmas **CONF:** Thtr 200 Class 100 Board 50 **PARKING:** 200 **NOTES:** ⊗ in restaurant

See advert on page 153

CHESTER, continued

★★★69% Westminster

City Rd CH1 3AF
☎ 01244 317341 🖷 01244 325369
e-mail: westminsterhotel@bestwestern.co.uk
web: www.feathers.uk.com
Dir: *A56 3m to city centre, left signed rail station. Hotel opposite station, on right*

Situated close to the railway station and city centre, the Westminster is an old, established hotel which has been extensively upgraded. It has an attractive Tudor-style exterior, while bedrooms are brightly decorated with a modern theme. No smoking bedrooms and family rooms are both available. There is a choice of bars and lounges, and the large dining room serves a good range of dishes.
ROOMS: 75 en suite (5 fmly) (6 GF) ⊗ in 35 bedrooms s £55-£75; d £80-£125 (incl. bkfst) **LB** **FACILITIES:** STV Free gym facilities at sister hotel ♫ Xmas **CONF:** Thtr 150 Class 60 Board 40 **SERVICES:** Lift **PARKING:** 50 **NOTES:** ✗ ⊗ in restaurant Civ Wed 100

★★★68% *Mill*

Milton St CH1 3NF
☎ 01244 350035 🖷 01244 345635
e-mail: reservations@millhotel.com
web: www.millhotel.com
Dir: *M53 junct 12, onto A56, left at 2nd rdt (A5268), then 1st left and 2nd left*

This hotel is a stylish conversion of an old corn mill and enjoys an idyllic canalside location next to the inner ring road and close to the city centre. The bedrooms offer varying styles, and public rooms are spacious and comfortable. There are several dining options and dinner is often served on a large boat that cruises Chester's canal system between courses. A well-equipped leisure centre is also provided.
ROOMS: 80 en suite 49 annexe en suite (57 fmly) ⊗ in 51 bedrooms **FACILITIES: Spa** STV Indoor Swimming pool (heated) supervised Sauna Solarium Gym Jacuzzi Steam room, hairdressing, nails, beauty treatments, fitness classes ♫ **CONF:** Thtr 40 Class 27 Board 28 **SERVICES:** Lift **PARKING:** 120 **NOTES:** ✗

★★★66% *Blossoms*

St John St CH1 1HL
☎ 0870 400 8108 🖷 01244 346433
e-mail: general.blossoms@macdonald-hotels.co.uk
web: www.macdonald-hotels.co.uk
Dir: *in city centre, follow signs for Eastgate and City Centre Hotels, continue through pedestrianised zone, hotel on the left*
For those seeking to explore this charming, medieval walled city, the central location of this elegant hotel is ideal. The public areas retain much of their Victorian charm. Occasionally, piano music at dinner adds to the intimate atmosphere.
ROOMS: 64 en suite (3 fmly) ⊗ in 43 bedrooms **FACILITIES:** STV Free use of local health club ♫ **CONF:** Thtr 80 Class 60 Board 60 **SERVICES:** Lift **NOTES:** ⊗ in restaurant Civ Wed

★★★62% Hoole Hall Hotel

Warrington Rd, Hoole Village CH2 3PD
☎ 0870 609 6126 01244 408800
🖷 01244 320251
e-mail: hoolehall@corushotels.com
web: www.corushotels.com
Dir: *M53 junct 12, A56 for 0.5m towards city centre, hotel 500yds on left*

Situated in extensive gardens on the outskirts of the city, part of this hotel dates back to the 18th century. It is now much extended and modernised, with smart, well-equipped bedrooms. Meetings, banquets and conferences are well catered for and ample car parking space is available.
ROOMS: 97 en suite (4 fmly) (33 GF) ⊗ in 78 bedrooms s £75-£100; d £75-£100 **LB** **FACILITIES:** STV Xmas **CONF:** Thtr 160 Class 40 Board 50 Del from £99 **SERVICES:** Lift **PARKING:** 200 **NOTES:** ⊗ in restaurant Civ Wed 140

Indoor Swimming pool
Indoor Swimming pool (heated)
Outdoor Swimming pool
Outdoor Swimming pool (heated)

★★70% Curzon

52/54 Hough Green CH4 8JQ
☎ 01244 678581 🖷 01244 680866
e-mail: curzon.chester@virgin.net
web: www.curzonhotel.co.uk
Dir: *at junct of A55/A483 follow sign for Chester, 3rd rdbt, 2nd exit (A5104). Hotel 500yds on right*
This smart period property is located in a residential suburb, close to the racecourse and just a short walk from the city centre. Spacious bedrooms are comfortable, well equipped and include

continued on p154

THE GROSVENOR PULFORD HOTEL

Wrexham Road, Pulford, Chester CH4 9DG
Tel: 01244 570560 Fax: 01244 570809
Email: enquiries@grosvenorpulfordhotel.co.uk
www.grosvenorpulfordhotel.co.uk

18 metre Swimming Pool – Whirlpool – Aromatherapy Steam Room – Sauna – Solarium – Fully equipped Gymnasium – Hair and Beauty Salon – Snooker Room – Tennis Court. 73 en-suite bedrooms with all the modern conveniences. Award winning restaurant Ciro's Brasserie open daily serving Mediterranean style cuisine.
All day coffee bar overlooking courtyard. Bar snacks and Sunday Carvery luncheon. Conference and Banqueting facilities for between 10 and 250 delegates – Wedding receptions our speciality. Leisure break packages available
Golf course adjacent to hotel

Ideally located only five minutes from Chester city centre

Mollington Banastre Hotel

Mollington Banastre, Parkgate Road, Chester, CH1 6NN
Tel: 01244 851 471 Fax: 01244 851 165
Email phateley@mollingtonbanastre.com
www.mollingtonbanastrehotel.com

Mollington Banastre is set in beautiful grounds and gardens and is an ideal base for experiencing the historic city of Chester. The hotel is renowned for genuine hospitality which reflects the high quality of service and accommodation offered to guests.

There is a choice of dining at the hotel, our newly refurbished Garden Room restaurant, or the informal Brasserie in the Health and Leisure Club. The facilities in the Health and Leisure Club include a heated pool, fully equipped gym, spa bath, sauna and beauty spa.

AA ★★

The Curzon Hotel

A warm welcome and excellent cuisine await you at the Curzon Hotel . . .

Family owned and managed
Lounge Bar and Superb Restaurant
Sixteen Individual Guest Bedrooms
Four Poster Suites
Special Breaks and Themed Weekends
Walking distance to Chester
Private Parking

. . . we look forward to welcoming you soon

52-54 Hough Green · Chester
Cheshire · CH4 8JQ
Email: curzon.chester@virgin.net
www.curzonhotel.co.uk
Tel: 01244 678581 · Fax: 01244 680866

CROSS LANES
HOTEL & BRASSERIE

Cross Lanes, Bangor Road
Marchwiel, Wrexham, LL13 0TF
Tel: 01978 780555 Fax: 01978 780568
Website: www.crosslanes.co.uk
Email: guestservices@crosslanes.co.uk

Best Western

AA ★★★

Three-star country hotel, set in acres of beautiful grounds. Ideally located for Chester, plus the castles, gardens and scenic hills of North Wales. Enjoy quality food cooked simply with fresh ingredients in Kagan's Brasserie (AA Rosette). Situated three miles from Wrexham on the A525 between Marchwiel and Bangor-on-Dee.

For further information see Wrexham, Wales section.

CHESTER, continued

family and four-poster rooms. The atmosphere is friendly and the dinner menu offers a creative choice of freshly prepared dishes.

Curzon, Chester

ROOMS: 16 en suite (7 fmly) (1 GF) ⊗ in 12 bedrooms s £60-£80; d £80-£110 (incl. bkfst) **LB PARKING:** 20 **NOTES:** ✗ ⊗ in restaurant Closed 20 Dec-6 Jan

See advert on page 153

★★70% Dene
95 Hoole Rd CH2 3ND
☎ 01244 321165 📄 01244 350277
e-mail: info@denehotel.com
web: www.denehotel.com
Dir: M53 junct 12 take A56 towards Chester. Hotel 1m from M53 next to Alexander Park
This friendly hotel is now part of a small privately owned group and is located close to both the city centre and M53. The bedrooms are very well equipped and many are on ground-floor level. Family rooms and interconnecting rooms are also available. In addition to bar meals, an interesting choice of dishes is offered in the welcoming Castra Brasserie, which is also very popular with locals.
ROOMS: 44 en suite 8 annexe en suite (5 fmly) (20 GF) ⊗ in 16 bedrooms s £40-£62; d £45-£100 (incl. bkfst) **LB FACILITIES:** STV Pool table **CONF:** Thtr 30 Class 12 Board 16 Del from £80 **PARKING:** 55 **NOTES:** ⊗ in restaurant

★★70% The Gateway To Wales
Welsh Rd, Sealand, Deeside CH5 2HX
☎ 01244 830332 📄 01244 836190
e-mail: mikesudbury@gatewaytowaleshotel.co.uk
web: www.gatewaytowaleshotel.co.uk
Dir: 4m NW via A548 towards Sealand and Queensferry
This modern hotel enjoys an ideal location offering easy access to Chester, the Wirral and North Wales. Bedrooms are stylish and comfortably appointed, as is the Louis XVI lounge bar. Meals are served in a modern pub/restaurant just opposite and the hotel benefits from extensive parking and well-equipped leisure facilities.
ROOMS: 39 en suite (18 GF) ⊗ in 20 bedrooms **FACILITIES:** ➴ Sauna Solarium Gym Jacuzzi Use of Indoor Bowls & Snooker Club **CONF:** Thtr 150 Class 50 Board 50 **SERVICES:** Lift **PARKING:** 60 **NOTES:** ✗ ⊗ in restaurant

★★68% Brookside
Brook Ln CH2 2AN
☎ 01244 381943 & 01244 390898 📄 01244 651910
e-mail: info@brookside-hotel.co.uk
Dir: from city centre take A5116 towards Birkenhead/Ellesmere Port. Right at mini-rdbt into Brook Lane. Hotel 200yds on left. From M53 take A56 then A41, left into Plas Newton Lane, right into Brook Lane, hotel on right
This hotel is conveniently located in a residential area just north of
continued

the city centre. The attractive public areas consist of a foyer lounge, a small bar and a split-level restaurant. Homely bedrooms are thoughtfully furnished and some feature four-poster beds.
ROOMS: 26 en suite (9 fmly) (4 GF) s £40-£46; d £58-£78 (incl. bkfst) **LB CONF:** Class 20 Board 12 **PARKING:** 20 **NOTES:** ✗ ⊗ in restaurant Closed 20 Dec-3 Jan

⒰ Ramada Chester
Whitchurch Rd, Christleton CH3 5QL
☎ 01244 332121 📄 01244 335287
e-mail: sales.chester@ramadajarvis.co.uk
web: www.ramadajarvis.co.uk
Dir: Take A41 towards Newport, through Whitchurch, hotel on left
ⓇRAMADA
Just a short drive from Chester city centre this large hotel is a popular venue for conferences and meetings. Bedrooms are comfortably appointed for both business and leisure guests.
ROOMS: 126 en suite (6 fmly) (58 GF) ⊗ in 66 bedrooms **FACILITIES:** STV ➴ Sauna Gym Jacuzzi Xmas **CONF:** Thtr 230 Class 140 Board 100 Del from £145 **SERVICES:** Lift **PARKING:** 160 **NOTES:** ✗ ⊗ in restaurant Civ Wed 180

⌂ Comfort Inn Chester
74 Hoole Rd, Hoole CH2 3NK
☎ 01244 327542 📄 01244 344889
e-mail: comfortinn@chestergb.u.net.com
Comfort
Dir: 1m from town centre on A56, on right, back from main road
This modern building offers accommodation in smart, spacious and well equipped bedrooms, all with en suite bathrooms. Refreshments may be taken at the nearby family restaurant. For further details and the Comfort Inn phone number, consult the Hotel Groups page under 'Choice'.
ROOMS: 26 en suite 5 annexe en suite **CONF:** Thtr 40 Class 18 Board 18

⌂ Innkeeper's Lodge Chester
Whitchurch Rd CH3 6AE
☎ 01244 332200 📄 01244 336415
web: www.innkeeperslodge.com
Inn keeper's Lodge
Dir: on A41. 1m outside Chester towards Whitchurch
A growing concept in the travel accommodation market. Smart rooms meet essential business requirements but also have home comforts. Dining options include all-day menus plus the added advantage of breakfast, which is included in the room price. For further details consult the Hotel Groups page.
ROOMS: 5 en suite 9 annexe en suite s £55-£58; d £55-£58

⌂ Innkeeper's Lodge Chester Northeast
Warrington Rd, Mickle Trafford CH2 4EX
☎ 01244 301391 📄 01244 302002
web: www.innkeeperslodge.com
Inn keeper's Lodge
Dir: M53 junct 12, onto A56 signed Helsby, hotel 0.25m on right
A growing concept in the travel accommodation market. Smart rooms meet essential business requirements but also have home comforts. Dining options include all-day menus plus the added advantage of breakfast, which is included in the room price. For further details consult the Hotel Groups page.
ROOMS: 36 en suite s £49.95-£55; d £49.95-£55 **CONF:** Thtr 20 Class 12 Board 20

⌂ Premier Travel Inn Chester Central
Caldy Valley Rd CH3 5QJ
☎ 08701 977058 📄 01244 403687
web: www.premiertravelinn.com
premier travel inn
Dir: Exit M53 junct 12 onto A56 (signed Chester). Onto A41 (signed Whitchurch) onto Caldy Valley Rd for Inn on right.
High quality, modern budget accommodation ideal for both families and business travellers. Spacious, en suite bedrooms
continued

feature bath and shower, satellite TV and many have telephones and modem points. The adjacent family restaurant features a wide and varied menu. For further details consult the Hotel Groups page.
ROOMS: 70 en suite s £52.95; d £52.95 **CONF:** Class 20

Premier Travel Inn Chester Central (North)
76 Liverpool Rd CH2 1AU
☎ 0870 9906470 Fax 0870 9906471
web: www.premiertravelinn.com
Dir: *Exit M53 junct 12. At 1st rdbt right for A56. At 2nd rdbt right signed A41 to Chester Zoo. At 1st lights left into Heath Rd leading into Mill Ln. Under small rail bridge. Inn at end on right*
High quality, modern budget accommodation ideal for both families and business travellers. Spacious, en suite bedrooms feature bath and shower, satellite TV and many have telephones and modem points. The adjacent family restaurant features a wide and varied menu. For further details consult the Hotel Groups page.
ROOMS: 31 en suite s £52.95; d £52.95 **CONF:** Class 17

CHESTERFIELD, Derbyshire — Map 16 SK37
See also Renishaw

★★★65% *Sandpiper*
Sheffield Rd, Sheepbridge S41 9EH
☎ 01246 450550 Fax 01246 452805
e-mail: sales.sandpiper@virgin.net
web: www.sandpiperhotel.co.uk
Dir: *M1 junct 29, A617 to Chesterfield then A61 to Sheffield. 1st exit take Dronfield Rd. Hotel 0.5m on left*
Conveniently situated for both the A61 and M1 and providing a good touring base, being just three miles from Chesterfield, this modern hotel offers comfortable and well-furnished bedrooms. Public areas are situated in a separate building across the car park, and include a cosy bar and open plan restaurant, serving a range of interesting and popular dishes.
ROOMS: 46 en suite (8 fmly) (18 GF) ⊗ in 32 bedrooms
FACILITIES: STV **CONF:** Thtr 100 Class 35 Board 35 **SERVICES:** Lift
PARKING: 120 **NOTES:** ⊗ in restaurant Civ Wed 90

★★★65% Sitwell Arms
Station Rd S21 3WF
☎ 01246 435226 & 01246 437327 Fax 01246 433915
e-mail: sitwellarms@renishaw79.fsnet.co.uk
(For full entry see Renishaw)

Hotel Ibis Chesterfield
Lordsmill St S41 7RW
☎ 01246 221333 Fax 01246 221444
e-mail: H3160@accor-hotels.com
Dir: *M1 junct 29, take A617 to Chesterfield. 2nd exit at 1st rdbt. Hotel situated on right at 2nd rdbt.*
Modern, budget hotel offering comfortable accommodation in bright and practical bedrooms. Breakfast is self-service and dinner is available in the restaurant. For further details, consult the Hotel Groups page.
ROOMS: 86 en suite **CONF:** Thtr 30 Class 16 Board 20

Premier Travel Inn Chesterfield
Tapton Lock Hill, Off Rotherway S41 7NJ
☎ 08701 977060 Fax 01246 560707
web: www.premiertravelinn.com
Dir: *adjacent to Tesco, A61 and A619 rdbt, 1m N of city centre*
High quality, modern budget accommodation ideal for both families and business travellers. Spacious, en suite bedrooms
continued

feature bath and shower, satellite TV and many have telephones and modem points. The adjacent family restaurant features a wide and varied menu. For further details consult the Hotel Groups page.
ROOMS: 60 en suite s £46.95-£48.95; d £46.95-£48.95 **CONF:** Thtr 25

Travelodge
Brimmington Rd, Inner Ring Rd, Wittington Moor S41 9BE
☎ 08700 850 950 Fax 01246 455411
web: www.travelodge.co.uk
Dir: *on A61, N of town centre*
Travelodge offers good quality, good value, modern accommodation. Ideal for families, the spacious, en suite bedrooms include remote-control TV, tea and coffee-making facilities and comfortable beds. Meals can be taken at the nearby family restaurant. For further details consult the Hotel Groups page.
ROOMS: 20 en suite s fr £26; d fr £26

CHESTER-LE-STREET, Co Durham — Map 19 NZ25

Innkeeper's Lodge Durham North
Church Mouse, Great North Rd, Chester Moor DH2 3RJ
☎ 0191 389 2628
web: www.innkeeperslodge.com
Dir: *A1(M) junct 63, take A167 S Durham/Chester-Le-Street. Straight on at 3 rdbts, Inn on left*
A growing concept in the travel accommodation market. Smart rooms meet essential business requirements but also have home comforts. Dining options include all-day menus plus the added advantage of breakfast, which is included in the room price. For further details consult the Hotel Groups page.
ROOMS: 21 en suite s £49.95-£55; d £49.95-£55

CHESTER MOTORWAY SERVICE AREA (M56), Cheshire — Map 15 SJ47

Premier Travel Inn Chester East
Junction 14 M56, Chester East Service Area, Elton CH2 4QZ
☎ 08701 977059 Fax 01928 726721
web: www.premiertravelinn.com
Dir: *M56 junct 14/A5117 junct*
High quality, modern budget accommodation ideal for both families and business travellers. Spacious, en suite bedrooms feature bath and shower, satellite TV and many have telephones and modem points. The adjacent family restaurant features a wide and varied menu. For further details consult the Hotel Groups page.
ROOMS: 40 en suite s £46.95-£48.95; d £46.95-£48.95 **CONF:** Thtr 20

CHICHESTER, West Sussex — Map 05 SU80

★★★★73% ®® *Marriott Goodwood Park Hotel & Country Club*
PO18 0QB
☎ 0870 400 7225 Fax 0870 400 7325
e-mail: reservations.goodwood@marriotthotels.co.uk
web: www.marriott.co.uk
(For full entry see Goodwood)

★★★76% ® The Millstream
Bosham Ln PO18 8HL
☎ 01243 573234 Fax 01243 573459
e-mail: info@millstream-hotel.co.uk
(For full entry see Bosham. See advert on p157)

CHICHESTER, continued

★★★70% Crouchers Country Hotel & Restaurant

Birdham Rd PO20 7EH
☎ 01243 784995 01243 539797
e-mail: crouchers@btconnect.com
Dir: *off A27 to A286, 1.5m from Chichester centre opposite Black Horse pub*
This friendly, family-run hotel is situated in open countryside and just a short drive from the harbour. The comfortable and well-equipped rooms include some in a separate barn and coach house and the open-plan public areas have pleasant views.
ROOMS: 18 en suite (1 fmly) (12 GF) in 9 bedrooms s £65-£95; d £85-£120 (incl. bkfst) **LB** **FACILITIES:** STV Xmas **CONF:** BC Thtr 80 Class 80 Board 50 Del from £95 **PARKING:** 70 **NOTES:** in restaurant

See advert on opposite page

★★★63% The Ship Hotel

North St PO19 1NH
☎ 01243 778000 01243 788000
e-mail: booking.shiphotel@eldridge-pope.co.uk
web: www.shiphotel.com
Dir: *from A27, onto inner ring road to Northgate. At large Northgate rdbt left into North St, hotel on left*
This well-presented former Georgian hotel has a prime position at the top of North Street. The bar and brasserie offer a contemporary lively venue for refreshments and meals, with cocktails and a wine list to tempt. The hotel is in a good location for the Festival Theatre, so pre- and post-performance dinner offers are popular.
ROOMS: 36 en suite (2 fmly) in all bedrooms **FACILITIES:** STV Xmas **CONF:** Thtr 70 Class 35 Board 30 **SERVICES:** Lift **PARKING:** 35

★★58% Suffolk House

THE INDEPENDENTS

3 East Row PO19 1PD
☎ 01243 778899 01243 787282
e-mail: admin@suffolkhousehotel.co.uk
Dir: *right off East St into Little London, follow into East Row, hotel on left*
This former Georgian residence is situated in a quiet side street, yet only a few minutes' walk from the town centre. Bedrooms vary in shape and size and offer a good level of comfort and facilities. There is also a small bar area, a pleasant patio and a peaceful dining room. Telephone beforehand for advice on parking.
ROOMS: 11 en suite (2 fmly) (4 GF) in 5 bedrooms s £49-£59; d £89-£150 (incl. bkfst) **LB** **CONF:** Thtr 25 Class 12 Board 16 Del £205 **NOTES:** in restaurant

U Ramada Chichester

RAMADA

Westhampnett PO19 4UL
☎ 01243 786351 01243 782371
e-mail: sales.chichester@ramadajarvis.co.uk
web: www.ramadajarvis.co.uk
Dir: *Take A27 towards Portsmouth/Chichester. At Portfield rdbt take 3rd exit towards Goodwood, at next rdbt take 2nd exit, hotel is on left.*
This modern hotel is conveniently located on the outskirts of the town. Bedrooms are comfortably appointed for both business and leisure guests.
ROOMS: 77 en suite (1 fmly) (41 GF) in 50 bedrooms s £85-£140; d £85-£140 **FACILITIES: Spa** STV supervised Sauna Solarium Jacuzzi Xmas **CONF:** Thtr 370 Class 120 Board 80 Del from £135 **PARKING:** 150 **NOTES:** in restaurant Civ Wed 200

Town House Hotel
Country House Hotel
Travel Accommodation

Premier Travel Inn Chichester

premier travel inn

Chichester Gate Leisure Park, Terminus Rd PO19 8EL
☎ 0870 9906578 0870 9906579
web: www.premiertravelinn.com
Dir: *Exit A27 at Stockbridge rdbt towards city centre. Follow Terminus Road Industrial Estate signs. Left at 1st lights then left again at next lights into Chichester Gate Leisure Park. Inn on right*
High quality, modern budget accommodation ideal for both families and business travellers. Spacious, en suite bedrooms feature bath and shower, satellite TV and many have telephones and modem points. The adjacent family restaurant features a wide and varied menu. For further details consult the Hotel Groups page.
ROOMS: 83 en suite s £49.95-£52.95; d £49.95-£52.95

CHIDDINGFOLD, Surrey — Map 06 SU93

Restaurant with Rooms

The Swan Inn

Petworth Rd GU8 4TY
☎ 01428 682073 01428 683259
e-mail: the-swan-inn@btconnect.com
web: www.swaninnandrestaurant.co.uk
This charming inn, with its deceptively traditional façade, has been lovingly renovated internally in a contemporary style. Spacious bedrooms are well appointed with extensive modern facilities. The bar and restaurant are a highlight, where a wide range of homemade fare is on offer. The wine list and range of guest ales are noteworthy.
ROOMS: 11 rms (10 en suite) (1 fmly) in 9 bedrooms s £65-£160; d £70-£160 (incl. bkfst) **FACILITIES:** Xmas **SERVICES:** air con **PARKING:** 40 **NOTES:** in restaurant

CHIDEOCK, Dorset — Map 04 SY49

★★71% Chideock House

Main St DT6 6JN
☎ 01297 489242 01297 489184
e-mail: aa@chideockhousehotel.com
web: www.chideockhousehotel.com
Dir: *on A35 between Lyme Regis and Bridport, in centre of Chideock*
This delightful, partly thatched house dates back to the 15th century and retains many original features, such as beams and fireplaces. Relaxed and quietly attentive, the service is genuinely friendly and welcoming. Lots of thoughtful extras are provided in the bedrooms. An interesting and innovative menu featuring local produce is served in the comfortable restaurant.
ROOMS: 9 rms (8 en suite) (1 fmly) s £60-£85; d £70-£90 (incl. bkfst) **LB** **FACILITIES:** Xmas **PARKING:** 15 **NOTES:** No children 12yrs in restaurant Closed 4 Jan-Feb RS 3 Jan-5 Feb

CHIEVELEY, Berkshire — Map 05 SU47

Restaurant with Rooms

The Crab at Chieveley

Wantage Rd RG20 8UE
☎ 01635 247550 01635 247440
e-mail: info@crabatchieveley.com
Dir: *M4 junct 13 N A34 to Oxford. 1st left to Chieveley after Red Lion. Left at school road. After 1.5m at T-junct turn right. Hotel at top of hill*
The individually themed bedrooms at this former pub have been appointed to a very high standard and include a full range of modern amenities. Ground floor rooms have a small private patio area complete with a hot tub. The restaurant is divided into a

continued

modern brasserie area with a bar and a more formal dining area. Both offer an extensive and award-winning range of dishes and specialise in fish and seafood.
ROOMS: 10 en suite (6 GF) ⊗ in all bedrooms s £90-£130; d £110-£170 (incl. bkfst) **LB** **FACILITIES:** STV Sauna Gym Jacuzzi Hot Tub Xmas **CONF:** Thtr 20 Class 20 Board 20 Del from £150 **PARKING:** 80 **NOTES:** ⊗ in restaurant Civ Wed 120

CHILDER THORNTON, Cheshire — Map 15 SJ37

⌂ Premier Travel Inn Wirral Childer Thornton
New Chester Rd CH66 1QW
☎ 08701 977275 Fax 0151 347 1401
web: www.premiertravelinn.com
Dir: *On A41, near M53 junct 5 towards Chester. Inn is on the right, same entrance as Burleydam Garden Centre*
High quality, modern budget accommodation ideal for both families and business travellers. Spacious, en suite bedrooms feature bath and shower, satellite TV and many have telephones and modem points. The adjacent family restaurant features a wide and varied menu. For further details consult the Hotel Groups page.
ROOMS: 31 en suite s £46.95-£48.95; d £46.95-£48.95 **CONF:** Thtr 20

CHIPPENHAM, Wiltshire — Map 04 ST97

★★★71% Angel Hotel
Market Place SN15 3HD
☎ 01249 652615 Fax 01249 443210
e-mail: reception@angelhotelchippenham.co.uk
web: www.angelhotelchippenham.co.uk
Dir: *follow tourist signs for Bowood House. Under railway arch, follow 'Borough Parade Parking' signs. Hotel next to car park*
These impressive buildings make up a smart, comfortable hotel. The well-equipped bedrooms vary, from those in the main house where character is the key, to the smart executive-style, courtyard rooms. The lounge and restaurant are bright and modern where in addition to the imaginative carte, an all-day menu is served.
ROOMS: 15 en suite 35 annexe en suite (3 fmly) (12 GF) ⊗ in 29 bedrooms s £73-£108.25; d £88-£129 (incl. bkfst) **LB** **FACILITIES:** STV Gym **CONF:** Thtr 100 Class 50 Board 50 Del from £140 **PARKING:** 50

★★★70% Stanton Manor Country House
SN14 6DQ
☎ 01666 837552 & 0870 890 02880 Fax 01666 837022
e-mail: reception@stantonmanor.co.uk
web: www.stantonmanor.co.uk
(For full entry see Stanton St Quintin)

⌂ Premier Travel Inn Chippenham
Cepen Park, West Cepen Way SN14 6UZ
☎ 08701 977061 Fax 01249 461359
web: www.premiertravelinn.com
Dir: *M4 junct 17, take A350 towards Chippenham. Inn is at 1st main rdbt at gateway to Chippenham*
High quality, modern budget accommodation ideal for both families and business travellers. Spacious, en suite bedrooms feature bath and shower, satellite TV and many have telephones and modem points. The adjacent family restaurant features a wide and varied menu. For further details consult the Hotel Groups page.
ROOMS: 79 en suite s £46.95-£49.95; d £46.95-£49.95

○ Hotel due to open in late 2005 or 2006
U Star rating not confirmed

CHIPPERFIELD, Hertfordshire — Map 06 TL00

★★72% *The Two Brewers*
The Common WD4 9BS
☎ 01923 265266 ⎙ 01923 261884
e-mail: twobrewers.hotel@spiritgroup.com
web: www.twobrewers.com
Dir: *left in centre of village overlooking common*

This 16th-century inn retains much of its old-world charm while providing modern comforts and amenities. The spacious bedrooms are tastefully furnished and decorated, offering a comprehensive range of in-room facilities. The bar, popular with locals, is the focal point of the hotel, which serves enjoyable pub-style meals.
ROOMS: 20 en suite ⊗ in 10 bedrooms **FACILITIES:** STV **CONF:** Board 15 **PARKING:** 25 **NOTES:** ✗

CHIPPING CAMPDEN, Gloucestershire — Map 10 SP13

Top Hotel

★★★ ◎◎ Cotswold House
The Square GL55 6AN
☎ 01386 840330 ⎙ 01386 840310
e-mail: reception@cotswoldhouse.com
web: www.cotswoldhouse.com
Dir: *A44 take B4081 to Chipping Campden. Right at T-junct into High St. House in The Square*
Relaxation is inevitable at this mellow Cotswold stone house, set in the centre of the town. Bedrooms, including spacious suites in the courtyard, are impressively individual and offer a beguiling blend of style, quality and comfort. The restaurant is a stunning venue to sample accomplished and imaginative cuisine, with local produce utilised wherever possible. Alternatively, Hicks Brasserie and Bar provides a more informal dining experience.
ROOMS: 29 en suite (1 fmly) (5 GF) ⊗ in 18 bedrooms s £120-£130; d £205-£265 (incl. bkfst) **LB** **FACILITIES:** STV Gym Access to local Sports Centre Xmas **CONF:** BC Thtr 90 Class 50 Board 30 Del from £225 **PARKING:** 28 **NOTES:** ⊗ in restaurant Civ Wed 90

★★★72% ◎ Three Ways House
Mickleton GL55 6SB
☎ 01386 438429 ⎙ 01386 438118
e-mail: reception@puddingclub.com
Dir: *in centre of Mickleton, on B4632 Stratford-upon-Avon to Broadway road*

Built in 1870, this charming hotel has welcomed guests for over 100 years and is home to the world famous Pudding Club, formed in 1985 to promote traditional English puddings. Individuality is a hallmark here, as reflected in a number of bedrooms, which have been styled according to a pudding theme. Public areas are stylish and include the air-conditioned restaurant, lounges and meeting rooms.
ROOMS: 48 en suite (7 fmly) (14 GF) s £75-£89; d £120-£175 (incl. bkfst) **LB** **FACILITIES:** ♫ Xmas **CONF:** Thtr 100 Class 40 Board 35 Del from £150 **SERVICES:** Lift **PARKING:** 37 **NOTES:** ⊗ in restaurant Civ Wed 100

★★★68% Noel Arms
CLASSIC BRITISH
High St GL55 6AT
☎ 01386 840317 ⎙ 01386 841136
e-mail: reception@noelarmshotel.com
web: www.noelarmshotel.com
Dir: *off A44 onto B4081 to Chipping Campden, 1st right down hill into town. Hotel on right opposite Market Hall*

This historic 14th-century hotel has a wealth of character and charm, and retains some of its original features. Bedrooms are very individual in style, but all have high levels of comfort and interesting interior design. Such distinctiveness is also evident throughout the public areas, which include the popular bar, conservatory lounge and attractive restaurant.
ROOMS: 26 en suite (1 fmly) (6 GF) s fr £90; d fr £125 (incl. bkfst) **LB** **FACILITIES:** Xmas **CONF:** BC Thtr 60 Class 35 Board 35 Del from £140 **PARKING:** 26 **NOTES:** ⊗ in restaurant Civ Wed 50

Early start?
Hotels at all star levels should provide in-room alarm clocks and/or alarm clocks

CHIPPING NORTON, Oxfordshire   Map 10 SP32

★★★67% Crown & Cushion

23 High St OX7 5AD
☎ 01608 642533 📠 01608 642926
e-mail: alan@thecrownandcushion.com
Dir: *west end of Market Place. Hotel is on right opposite TIC*

A former coaching inn with the ambience of a past age but with the comforts of today. Guests can enjoy the popular and welcoming bar, the more formal restaurant and the indoor leisure facilities. Bedrooms are situated in the main building or the courtyard and offer a variety of sizes and styles.
ROOMS: 40 en suite (5 fmly) (5 GF) ⊘ in 10 bedrooms s £64-£100; d £75-£160 (incl. bkfst) **LB** **FACILITIES:** supervised Squash Gym Xmas **CONF:** BC Thtr 180 Class 120 Board 80 Del from £135 **PARKING:** 45 **NOTES:** ⊘ in restaurant

CHITTLEHAMHOLT, Devon   Map 03 SS62

★★★67% Highbullen

EX37 9HD
☎ 01769 540561 📠 01769 540492
e-mail: highbullen@sosi.net
Dir: *M5 junct 27 onto A361 to South Molton, then B3226 Crediton Rd. After 5.2m turn right to Chittlehamholt. Hotel 0.5m beyond village*
Set in magnificent parkland with extensive views and an 18-hole golf course, Highbullen also offers a magnificent leisure facility with its own brasserie restaurant. The bedrooms, situated in the main house and in converted out buildings, are spacious and comfortable. A more formal dinner option is served in the restaurant, which looks out over the impressive country views.
ROOMS: 12 en suite 25 annexe en suite **FACILITIES:** 18 Fishing Squash Snooker Sauna Solarium Gym Putt green Hairdressing Beauty Massage **CONF:** Board 20 **PARKING:** 60 **NOTES:** No children 8yrs ⊘ in restaurant Civ Wed

CHORLEY, Lancashire   Map 15 SD51

★★★68% *Park Hall*

Park Hall Rd, Charnock Richard PR7 5LP
☎ 01257 455000 📠 01257 451838
e-mail: conference@parkhall-hotel.co.uk
web: www.parkhall-hotel.co.uk
Dir: *between Preston & Wigan, signed from M6 junct 27 N'bound & junct 28 S'bound, or from M61 junct 8*
The popular Camelot Theme Park is just a short stroll across the grounds from this hotel, which focuses on the leisure and corporate/conference markets. Conveniently located for the motorway network, this idyllic country retreat is shared between

continued

the main hotel and The Village, a series of chalet/bungalows. The Cadbury and Bassett rooms with special themed furnishings will be a real hit with the kids.
ROOMS: 56 en suite 84 annexe en suite (52 fmly) (84 GF) ⊘ in 34 bedrooms **FACILITIES: Spa** STV supervised Sauna Solarium Gym Jacuzzi Steam room, air-conditioned Gymnasium **CONF:** Thtr 700 Class 240 Board 40 **SERVICES:** Lift **PARKING:** 2600 **NOTES:** ⊘ in restaurant Civ Wed 150

See advert under PRESTON

Premier Travel Inn Chorley

Malthouse Farm, Moss Ln, Whittle le Woods PR6 8AB
☎ 0870 9906376 📠 0870 9906377
e-mail: malthousefarm20@hotmail.com
web: www.premiertravelinn.com
Dir: *M61 junct 8 onto A674 (Wheelton), 400yds on left into Moss Ln*
High quality, modern budget accommodation ideal for both families and business travellers. Spacious, en suite bedrooms feature bath and shower, satellite TV and many have telephones and modem points. The adjacent family restaurant features a wide and varied menu. For further details consult the Hotel Groups page.
ROOMS: 81 en suite s £46.95-£48.95; d £46.95-£48.95 **CONF:** Board 15

Premier Travel Inn Chorley South

Bolton Rd PR7 4AB
☎ 0870 9906604 📠 0870 9906605
web: www.premiertravelinn.com
Dir: *From N, exit M61 junct 8 onto A6 to Chorley. From S, exit M6 junct 27 follow Standish signs. Left onto A5106 to Chorley then A6 towards Preston. Inn 0.5m on right*
High quality, modern budget accommodation ideal for both families and business travellers. Spacious, en suite bedrooms feature bath and shower, satellite TV and many have telephones and modem points. The adjacent family restaurant features a wide and varied menu. For further details consult the Hotel Groups page.
ROOMS: 29 en suite s £46.95-£48.95; d £46.95-£48.95 **CONF:** Board 12

Travelodge Preston Chorley

Preston Rd, Clayton-le-Woods PR6 7JB
☎ 08700 850 950 📠 01772 311963
web: www.travelodge.co.uk
Dir: *from M6 junct 28 take B5256 for 2m, next to Halfway House pub*
Travelodge offers good quality, good value, modern accommodation. Ideal for families, the spacious, en suite bedrooms include remote-control TV, tea and coffee-making facilities and comfortable beds. Meals can be taken at the nearby family restaurant. For further details consult the Hotel Groups page.
ROOMS: 40 en suite s fr £26; d fr £26

C

CHRISTCHURCH, Dorset

Map 05 SZ19

★★★74% ◎ Waterford Lodge

87 Bure Ln, Friars Cliff BH23 4DN
☎ 01425 272948 & 278801 ▯ 01425 279130
e-mail: waterford@bestwestern.co.uk
web: www.waterfordlodge.com
Dir: *A35 take A337 towards Highcliffe. Right signed Mudeford. Hotel 0.5m*

Peacefully located within easy reach of Christchurch, this welcoming hotel is popular with business guests as well as holidaymakers. It offers attractive, spacious and well-equipped bedrooms, a comfortable bar lounge overlooking the gardens and a pleasant restaurant serving carefully prepared, award-winning cuisine.
ROOMS: 18 en suite (2 fmly) (3 GF) ⊗ in 15 bedrooms s £80-£100; d £95-£120 (incl. bkfst) **LB FACILITIES:** STV Xmas **CONF:** Thtr 100 Class 48 Board 36 Del from £100 **PARKING:** 38 **NOTES:** ✗ No children 7yrs ⊗ in restaurant

★★★72% ◎ The Avonmouth

95 Mudeford BH23 3NT
☎ 01202 483434 ▯ 01202 479004
e-mail: enquiries@avonmouth-hotel.co.uk
web: www.avonmouth-hotel co.uk
Dir: *A35 to Christchurch onto A337 to Highcliffe. Right at rdbt, hotel 1.5m*

In a superb location alongside Mudeford Quay, this friendly hotel offers a variety of bedrooms including smart garden rooms with their own small patios. Several bedrooms in the main house overlook the quay and have private balconies. Modern facilities and decor enhance the overall comfort. Enjoyable cuisine is served in Quays Restaurant.
ROOMS: 26 en suite 14 annexe en suite (7 fmly) (14 GF) ⊗ in 20 bedrooms s £65-£85; d £130-£150 (incl. bkfst) **LB FACILITIES:** STV ⛳ ♫ Xmas **CONF:** Thtr 70 Class 20 Board 24 Del from £100 **PARKING:** 80 **NOTES:** ✗ ⊗ in restaurant Civ Wed 60

⌂ Premier Travel Inn Christchurch East

Somerford Rd BH23 3QG
☎ 08701 977062 ▯ 01202 474939
web: www.premiertravelinn.com
Dir: *from M27 take A337 to Lyndhurst, then A35 to Christchurch. On B3059 rdbt towards Somerford*
High quality, modern budget accommodation ideal for both families and business travellers. Spacious, en suite bedrooms feature bath and shower, satellite TV and many have telephones and modem points. The adjacent family restaurant features a wide and varied menu. For further details consult the Hotel Groups page.
ROOMS: 70 en suite s £49.95; d £49.95

⌂ Premier Travel Inn Christchurch West

Barrack Rd BH23 2BN
☎ 08701 977063 ▯ 01202 483453
web: www.premiertravelinn.com
Dir: *from A338 take A3060 towards Christchurch. Turn left onto A35. Inn on right*
High quality, modern budget accommodation ideal for both families and business travellers. Spacious, en suite bedrooms feature bath and shower, satellite TV and many have telephones and modem points. The adjacent family restaurant features a wide and varied menu. For further details consult the Hotel Groups page.
ROOMS: 42 en suite s £49.95; d £49.95

CHURCH STRETTON, Shropshire

Map 15 SO49

★★★67% ◎ Stretton Hall Hotel

All Stretton SY6 6HG
☎ 01694 723224 0845 1668404
▯ 01694 724365
e-mail: aa@strettonhall.co.uk
Dir: *from Shrewsbury, on A49, right onto B4370 signed All Stretton. Hotel 1m on left opposite The Yew Tree pub*
This fine 18th-century country house stands in spacious gardens. Original oak panelling features throughout the lounge bar, lounge and halls. Bedrooms are traditionally furnished and have modern facilities. Family and four-poster rooms are available and the restaurant has been tastefully refurbished.
ROOMS: 12 en suite (1 fmly) s £50-£65; d £80-£150 (incl. bkfst) **LB FACILITIES:** Xmas **CONF:** BC Thtr 70 Class 24 Board 18 Del from £90 **PARKING:** 70 **NOTES:** ⊗ in restaurant Civ Wed 60

U Star rating not confirmed

★★65% Longmynd Hotel

Cunnery Rd SY6 6AG
☎ 01694 722244 ⎙ 01694 722718
e-mail: info@longmynd.co.uk
Dir: *A49 into town centre along Sandford Ave, left at Lloyds TSB, over mini-rdbt, 1st right into Cunnery Rd up hill, hotel at top on left*

This family-run hotel overlooks this country town and the views from many of the rooms are breathtaking. Bedrooms are generally spacious, comfortable and well equipped. Facilities include a range of comfortable lounges and the hotel is set in attractive grounds and gardens.

ROOMS: 50 en suite (8 fmly) ⊗ in all bedrooms s £40-£65; d £80-£130 (incl. bkfst) **LB** **FACILITIES:** Sauna Putt green Pitch and putt course Xmas **CONF:** Thtr 100 Class 50 Board 40 Del from £75 **SERVICES:** Lift **PARKING:** 100 **NOTES:** ⊗ in restaurant Civ Wed 100

CHURT, Surrey — Map 05 SU83

★★★73% Frensham Pond Hotel

Bacon Ln GU10 2QB
☎ 01252 795161 ⎙ 01252 792631
e-mail: info@frenshampondhotel.co.uk
web: www.frenshampondhotel.co.uk
Dir: *A3 onto A287. 4m left at 'Beware Horses' sign. Hotel 0.25m*

This 15th-century house occupies a superb location on the edge of Frensham Pond. Bedrooms are mostly spacious and there are also some pleasant garden suites available. Public areas are light and well-appointed and a good range of leisure facilities is offered, including a squash court.

ROOMS: 39 en suite 12 annexe en suite ⊗ in 21 bedrooms s £80-£140; d £80-£175 (incl. bkfst) **LB** **FACILITIES:** STV supervised Squash Sauna Solarium Gym Jacuzzi Steam room Xmas **CONF:** Thtr 120 Class 45 Board 40 Del from £95 **PARKING:** 120 **NOTES:** ⊗ in restaurant Civ Wed 130

See advert under FARNHAM

CIRENCESTER, Gloucestershire — Map 05 SP00

★★★70% Stratton House

Gloucester Rd GL7 2LE
☎ 01285 651761 ⎙ 01285 640024
e-mail: stratton.house@forestdale.com
web: www.forestdale.com
Dir: *M4 junct 15, A419 to Cirencester. Hotel on left on A417 or M5 junct 11 to Cheltenham onto B4070 to A417. Hotel on right*

This attractive 17th-century manor house is quietly situated about half a mile from the town centre. Bedrooms are well presented, and spacious premier rooms are available. The comfortable drawing rooms and restaurant have views over well-tended gardens: the perfect place to enjoy pre-dinner drinks on a summer evening.

ROOMS: 41 en suite (10 GF) ⊗ in 19 bedrooms s £85-£110; d £125-£140 (incl. bkfst) **LB** **FACILITIES:** Xmas **CONF:** Thtr 150 Class 50 Board 40 Del from £125 **PARKING:** 100 **NOTES:** ⊗ in restaurant Civ Wed

★★★66% The Crown of Crucis

Ampney Crucis GL7 5RS
☎ 01285 851806 ⎙ 01285 851735
e-mail: info@thecrownofcrucis.co.uk
web: www.thecrownofcrucis.co.uk
Dir: *A417 to Fairford, hotel 2.5m on left*

This delightful hotel consists of two buildings; one a 16th-century coaching inn, which now houses the bar and restaurant, and a more modern bedroom block which surrounds a courtyard. Rooms are attractively appointed and offer modern facilities; the restaurant serves a range of imaginative dishes.

ROOMS: 25 en suite (2 fmly) (13 GF) ⊗ in 21 bedrooms s £60-£73; d £75-£99 (incl. bkfst) **LB** **FACILITIES:** Free membership of local leisure centre **CONF:** Thtr 80 Class 40 Board 25 Del from £99 **PARKING:** 82 **NOTES:** ⊗ in restaurant RS 25-26 Dec & 1 Jan Civ Wed 50

★★★66% Fleece Hotel

Market Place GL7 2NZ
☎ 01285 658507 ⎙ 01285 651017
e-mail: relax@fleecehotel.co.uk
web: www.fleecehotel.co.uk
Dir: *A417/A419 Burford rd junct, follow signs for town centre. Right at lights into 'The Waterloo', hotel car park 250yds on left*

This old town-centre coaching inn, which dates back to the Tudor period, retains many original features such as flagstone floors and oak beams. Well-equipped bedrooms vary in size and shape, all offering good levels of comfort and plenty of character. The bar lounge is a popular venue for morning coffee, and the stylish restaurant offers a range of dishes in an informal and convivial atmosphere.

ROOMS: 28 en suite (3 fmly) (4 GF) ⊗ in 20 bedrooms s £49.50-£110; d £79-£119 (incl. bkfst) **LB** **FACILITIES:** Local gym 100yds from hotel provides discount for hotel guests. Xmas **PARKING:** 10 **NOTES:** ⊗ in restaurant

GF indicates the number of bedrooms at ground level

CIRENCESTER, continued

★★ Corinium Hotel
12 Gloucester St GL7 2DG
☎ 01285 659711 📠 01285 885807
e-mail: info@coriniumhotel.co.uk
web: www.coriniumhotel.com
Dir: *from lights on A417 into Spitalgate Ln, hotel car park 50mtrs on right*
ROOMS: 15 en suite (2 fmly) (2 GF) ⊗ in 12 bedrooms s £55-£75; d £79-£105 (incl. bkfst) **LB** **FACILITIES:** Xmas **PARKING:** 30 **NOTES:** ⊗ in restaurant

⌂ Travelodge
Hare Bushes, Burford Rd GL7 5DS
☎ 08700 850 950 📠 01285 655290
web: www.travelodge.co.uk
Dir: *M5 junct 12, take A417 to Swindon. Lodge a A417/A429 junct*
Travelodge offers good quality, good value, modern accommodation. Ideal for families, the spacious, en suite bedrooms include remote-control TV, tea and coffee-making facilities and comfortable beds. Meals can be taken at the nearby family restaurant. For further details consult the Hotel Groups page.
ROOMS: 43 en suite s fr £26; d fr £26

CLACKET LANE MOTORWAY SERVICE AREA (M25), Surrey
Map 06 TQ45

⌂ Premier Travel Inn Westerham (Clacket Lane)
TN16 2ER
☎ 08701 977265 📠 01959 561311
web: www.premiertravelinn.com
Dir: *M25 between junct 5 & 6*
High quality, modern budget accommodation ideal for both families and business travellers. Spacious, en suite bedrooms feature bath and shower, satellite TV and many have telephones and modem points. The adjacent family restaurant features a wide and varied menu. For further details consult the Hotel Groups page.
ROOMS: 58 en suite s £53.95-£57.95; d £53.95-£57.95 **CONF:** Thtr 50 Board 30

CLACTON-ON-SEA, Essex
Map 07 TM11
See also Weeley

★★67% Esplanade Hotel
27-29 Marine Pde East CO15 1UU
☎ 01255 220450 📠 01255 221800
e-mail: mjs@esplanadehoteluk.com
web: www.esplanadehoteluk.com
Dir: *from A133 to Clacton-on-Sea, follow seafront signs. At seafront turn right and hotel on right in 50yds*
Situated in a prominent position on the seafront overlooking the pier and just a short walk from the town centre. Bedrooms vary in size and style and are pleasantly decorated and well equipped; some rooms have lovely sea views. Public rooms include a comfortable lounge bar and Coasters Restaurant.
ROOMS: 29 en suite (2 fmly) s £35-£40; d £60-£65 (incl. bkfst) **LB** **FACILITIES:** Xmas **CONF:** BC Thtr 80 Class 50 Board 50 **PARKING:** 13 **NOTES:** ✗ ⊗ in restaurant Civ Wed 85

> Destination dining!
> This symbol indicates a Restaurant with Rooms

★73% Chudleigh
13 Agate Rd, Marine Pde West CO15 1RA
☎ 01255 425407 📠 01255 470280
e-mail: reception@chudleighhotel.com
Dir: *follow town centre, seafront and pier signs. Right at seafront,after traffic lights at the pier, right into Agate Rd*
Expect a warm welcome from the caring hosts at this small, privately owned hotel. It is situated just off the seafront and within easy walking distance of the town centre and pier. Bedrooms are generally quite spacious; each is attractively decorated and equipped with many thoughtful touches. Public rooms include a cosy lounge and a smart dining room in which freshly prepared breakfasts are served.
ROOMS: 10 en suite (2 fmly) (2 GF) ⊗ in 3 bedrooms s £39.50-£45; d £55-£60 (incl. bkfst) **LB** **PARKING:** 7 **NOTES:** ⊗ in restaurant RS Oct-Mar

⌂ Days Inn Clacton-on-Sea
8 Marine Pde West CO15 1RD
☎ 01255 422716 📠 01255 426354
e-mail: enquirires@daysinnclacton.com
Dir: *from marine parade turn right at seafront. Hotel just after pier*
This modern building offers accommodation in smart, spacious and well-equipped bedrooms, suitable for families and business travellers, and all with en suite bathrooms. Continental breakfast is available and other refreshments may be taken at the nearby family restaurant. For further details consult the Hotel Groups page.
ROOMS: 50 en suite **CONF:** Thtr 250 Class 50 Board 50

CLAVERDON, Warwickshire
Map 10 SP16

★★★★74% Ardencote Manor Hotel, Country Club & Spa
Lye Green Rd CV35 8LS
☎ 01926 843111 📠 01926 842646
e-mail: hotel@ardencote.com
web: www.ardencote.com
Dir: *in Claverdon centre, follow Shrewley signs off A4189. Hotel 0.5m on right*

Originally built as a gentleman's residence around 1860, this hotel is set in 45 acres of landscaped grounds. Public rooms include a choice of lounge areas, a cocktail bar and conservatory breakfast room. Main meals are served in the Lodge, a separate building that sits on the lake. An extensive range of leisure and conference facilities is provided and bedrooms are smartly decorated and tastefully furnished.
ROOMS: 75 en suite (5 fmly) (11 GF) ⊗ in 50 bedrooms s fr £105; d £150-£225 (incl. bkfst) **LB** **FACILITIES:** **Spa** STV 9 Squash Sauna Solarium Gym Putt green Jacuzzi Ardencote Spa Xmas **CONF:** Thtr 200 Class 100 Board 50 Del from £115 **SERVICES:** Lift air con **PARKING:** 150 **NOTES:** ✗ ⊗ in restaurant Civ Wed 150
See advert under WARWICK

CLEARWELL, Gloucestershire Map 04 SO50

★★74% Tudor Farmhouse Hotel & Restaurant
High St GL16 8JS
☎ 01594 833046 01594 837093
e-mail: info@tudorfarmhousehotel.co.uk
web: www.tudorfarmhousehotel.co.uk
Dir: *off A4136 onto B4228, through Coleford, turn right into Clearwell, hotel on right just before War Memorial Cross*

Dating from the 13th century, this idyllic former farmhouse retains a host of original features including exposed stonework, oak beams, wall panelling and wonderful inglenook fireplaces. Bedrooms have great individuality and style and are located either within the main house, or in converted buildings within the grounds. Creative menus offer quality cuisine, served in the intimate, candlelit restaurant.
ROOMS: 6 en suite 16 annexe en suite (2 fmly) (7 GF) in 19 bedrooms s £55-£85; d £60-£150 (incl. bkfst) **LB FACILITIES:** STV **CONF:** Thtr 30 Class 20 Board 12 Del from £80 **PARKING:** 30 **NOTES:** in restaurant Closed 24-27 Dec

CLEATOR, Cumbria Map 18 NY01

★★★70% Ennerdale Country House
CA23 3DT
☎ 01946 813907 01946 815260
e-mail: ennerdale@bestwestern.co.uk
web: www.feathers.uk.com
Dir: *A5086 to Egremont, approx 12m to Cleator Moor. A5086 for 1m to Cleator*
This fine Grade II listed building lies on the edge of the village and is backed by landscaped gardens. Impressive bedrooms, including split-level suites and four-poster rooms, are richly furnished, smartly decorated and offer an amazing array of facilities. Attractive public areas include an elegant restaurant, an inviting lounge and an American theme bar which offers a good range of bar meals.
ROOMS: 30 en suite (4 fmly) in 4 bedrooms **FACILITIES:** STV Xmas **CONF:** Thtr 150 Class 100 Board 40 **PARKING:** 65 **NOTES:** in restaurant

CLECKHEATON, West Yorkshire Map 19 SE12

★★★64% The Whitcliffe
Prospect Rd BD19 3HD
☎ 01274 873022 01274 870376
e-mail: info@thewhitcliffehotel.co.uk
Dir: *M62 junct 26, follow A638 to Dewsbury, over 1st lights, right into Mount St, to T-junct, right then 1st left*
This popular commercial hotel offers comfortable, well-equipped accommodation. Spacious public areas provide a variety of amenities, including several meeting rooms, two attractive bars, and the popular Flickers Brasserie.

continued

ROOMS: 35 en suite 6 annexe en suite (3 fmly) (6 GF) in 17 bedrooms s £49; d £65 (incl. bkfst) **LB FACILITIES:** STV **CONF:** Thtr 120 Class 60 Board 40 **PARKING:** 150 **NOTES:** in restaurant Civ Wed 80

Premier Travel Inn Bradford South
Whitehall Rd BD19 6HG
☎ 08701 977037 01274 855901
web: www.premiertravelinn.com
Dir: *on A58 at intersection with M62 & M606*
High quality, modern budget accommodation ideal for both families and business travellers. Spacious, en suite bedrooms feature bath and shower, satellite TV and many have telephones and modem points. The adjacent family restaurant features a wide and varied menu. For further details consult the Hotel Groups page.
ROOMS: 40 en suite s £46.95-£49.95; d £46.95-£49.95

CLEETHORPES, Lincolnshire Map 17 TA30

★★★69% Kingsway
Kingsway DN35 0AE
☎ 01472 601122 0871 236 0671
e-mail: reception@kingsway-hotel.com
web: www.kingsway-hotel.com
Dir: *leave A180 at Grimsby, to Cleethorpes seafront. Hotel at Kingsway and Queen Parade junct (A1098)*
This seafront hotel has been in the same family for four generations and continues to provide traditional comfort and friendly service. The lounges are comfortable and good food is served in the pleasant dining room. Most of the bedrooms are comfortably proportioned, and all are bright and pleasantly furnished.
ROOMS: 49 en suite in 15 bedrooms s £53-£82; d £88-£97 (incl. bkfst) **LB FACILITIES:** STV **CONF:** Thtr 22 Board 18 Del from £102 **SERVICES:** Lift **PARKING:** 50 **NOTES:** No children 5yrs in restaurant Closed 25-26 Dec

CLEVEDON, Somerset Map 04 ST47

★★★67% Walton Park
Wellington Ter BS21 7BL
☎ 01275 874253 01275 343577
e-mail: waltonpark@aol.com
Dir: *M5 junct 20, signs for seafront. Stay on coast road, past pier into Wellington Terrace, hotel on left*
Quietly located with spectacular views across the Bristol Channel to Wales, this popular Victorian hotel offers a relaxed atmosphere. Bedrooms are well decorated and equipped to meet the demands of both business and leisure guests. In the comfortable restaurant,

continued on p164

CLEVEDON, continued

a high standard of home-cooked food is served and lighter meals are available in the convivial bar at lunchtime.
ROOMS: 40 en suite (4 fmly) ⊗ in 23 bedrooms s £50-£83; d £85-£105 (incl. bkfst) **LB** **FACILITIES:** STV **CONF:** Thtr 120 Class 80 Board 80 Del from £95 **SERVICES:** Lift **PARKING:** 50 **NOTES:** Civ Wed 150

CLIMPING, West Sussex — Map 06 SU90

★★★78% ⊛⊛
Bailiffscourt Hotel & Health Spa
Climping St BN17 5RW
☎ 01903 723511 ⎙ 01903 718987
e-mail: bailiffscourt@hshotels.co.uk
web: www.hshotels.co.uk
Dir: *exit A259 at Climping, follow Climping Beach signs. Hotel 0.5m on right*

This delightful 'medieval manor' dating back only to the 1920s has the appearance of having been in existence for centuries. Bedrooms vary from atmospheric feature rooms with log fires, oak beams and four-poster beds to spacious stylish, contemporary rooms located in the grounds. Classic European cooking is a highlight, whilst a stylish Spa and a choice of cosy lounges, with log fires, complete the package.
ROOMS: 9 en suite 30 annexe en suite (25 fmly) (16 GF) s £175-£410; d £195-£460 (incl. bkfst) **LB** **FACILITIES: Spa** STV supervised supervised Sauna Gym Jacuzzi Xmas **CONF:** Thtr 40 Class 20 Board 26 Del from £165 **PARKING:** 100 **NOTES:** ⊗ in restaurant Civ Wed 60

CLITHEROE, Lancashire — Map 18 SD74

★★70% Shireburn Arms
Whalley Rd, Hurst Green BB7 9QJ
☎ 01254 826518 ⎙ 01254 826208
e-mail: sales@shireburnarmshotel.com
web: www.shireburnarmshotel.com
Dir: *A59 to Clitheroe, left at lights to Ribchester, follow Hurst Green signs. Hotel on B6243 at entrance to Hurst Green village*
This long established, family-owned hotel dates back to the 17th century and enjoys panoramic views over the Ribble Valley. Rooms are individually designed and thoughtfully equipped. The lounge bar offers a selection of real ales, and the spacious restaurant, opening onto an attractive patio and garden, offers home-cooked food.
ROOMS: 18 en suite (3 fmly) ⊗ in 3 bedrooms s £50-£70; d £70-£100 (incl. bkfst) **LB** **FACILITIES:** Xmas **CONF:** Thtr 100 Class 50 Board 50 Del £80 **PARKING:** 71 **NOTES:** ⊗ in restaurant Civ Wed 100

⊗ No smoking

U Eaves Hall Country Hotel
Eaves Hall Ln, West Bradford BB7 3JG
☎ 01200 425271 & 0845 345 3427 ⎙ 01200 425131
e-mail: eaves.hall@csma.uk.com
At the time of going to press, the star classification for this hotel was not confirmed. Please refer to the AA internet site www.theAA.com for current information.
ROOMS: 34 en suite 2 annexe en suite ⊗ in all bedrooms s £60-£78; d £88-£143 (incl. bkfst) **FACILITIES:** Fishing Snooker Gym Putt green Bowling Green Pitch & putt Xmas **SERVICES:** Lift **PARKING:** 40 **NOTES:** ⊗ in restaurant Civ Wed

CLOVELLY, Devon — Map 03 SS32

★★70% New Inn
High St EX39 5TQ
☎ 01237 431303 ⎙ 01237 431636
e-mail: newinn@clovelly.co.uk
Dir: *at Clovelly Cross, off A39 onto B3237. Follow down hill for 1.5m. Right at sign 'All vehicles for Clovelly'*

Famed for its cobbled descent to the harbour, this fascinating fishing village is a traffic-free zone. Consequently, luggage is conveyed by sledge or donkey to this much-photographed hotel (now under new ownership). Carefully renovated bedrooms and public areas are smartly presented with quality, locally-made furnishings. Meals may be taken in the elegant restaurant or the popular Upalong bar.
ROOMS: 8 en suite (2 fmly) s £40-£44.50; d £80-£89 (incl. bkfst) **LB** **FACILITIES:** Xmas **NOTES:** ⊗ in restaurant

★★70% *Red Lion Hotel*
The Quay EX39 5TF
☎ 01237 431237 ⎙ 01237 431044
e-mail: redlion@clovelly.co.uk
web: www.clovelly.co.uk
Dir: *turn off A39 at Clovelly Cross onto B3237. To bottom of hill and take 1st left by white rails to harbour*

Idyllic is the only way to describe the harbour-side setting of this
continued

charming 18th-century inn (now under new ownership), where the historic fishing village forms a spectacular backdrop. Bedrooms are stylish and enjoy delightful views. The inn's relaxed atmosphere is conducive to switching off from the pressures of life, even if the harbour comes alive with the activities of the local fishermen during the day.
ROOMS: 11 en suite (2 fmly) **FACILITIES:** Tennis can be arranged **PARKING:** 11 **NOTES:** ✗ ⊗ in restaurant

See advert on this page

COALVILLE, Leicestershire

★★62% Charnwood Arms Hotel
Beveridge Ln, Bardon Hill LE67 1TB
☎ 01530 813644 🖷 01530 815425
e-mail: charnwoodarm.barronhill@nhg.uk
Dir: *M1 junct 22, on A511 towards Coalville at 2nd rdbt. Stay left & hotel on right*
This popular inn, now under new ownership, is conveniently located only a few minutes' drive from the M1. Public areas include a spacious open-plan lounge bar and restaurant offering a selection of cask ales and serving food throughout the day. The extremely well equipped bedrooms are situated around a courtyard.
ROOMS: 34 en suite ⊗ in 5 bedrooms **CONF:** Thtr 200 Class 80 Board 80 **PARKING:** 200 **NOTES:** ✗ Civ Wed 100

COBHAM, Surrey — Map 06 TQ16

⌂ Premier Travel Inn Cobham
Portsmouth Rd, Fairmile KT11 1BW
premier travel inn
☎ 0870 9906358 🖷 0870 9906359
web: www.premiertravelinn.com
Dir: *M25 junct 10, A3 towards London, onto A245 towards Cobham. In Cobham town centre left onto A307 Portsmouth Rd. Hotel on left*
High quality, modern budget accommodation ideal for both families and business travellers. Spacious, en suite bedrooms feature bath and shower, satellite TV and many have telephones and modem points. The adjacent family restaurant features a wide and varied menu. For further details consult the Hotel Groups page.
ROOMS: 48 en suite s £59.95-£62.95; d £59.95-£62.95 **CONF:** Board 12

COCKERMOUTH, Cumbria — Map 18 NY13

★★★76% ⊛ The Trout
Crown St CA13 0EJ
☎ 01900 823591 🖷 01900 827514
e-mail: enquiries@trouthotel.co.uk
web: www.trouthotel.co.uk
Dir: *next to Wordsworth House*
Dating back to 1670, this privately owned hotel has an enviable setting on the banks of the River Derwent. The well-equipped bedrooms, some contained in a new wing overlooking the river, are mostly spacious and comfortable. The new Terrace Bar and Bistro, serving food all day, has a sheltered patio area. There is also a cosy bar, a choice of lounge areas and an attractive, traditional-style dining room that offers a good choice of set-price and carte dishes.
ROOMS: 43 en suite (4 fmly) (15 GF) ⊗ in 12 bedrooms s £90-£109; d £109-£149 (incl. bkfst) **LB** **FACILITIES:** STV Fishing Xmas **CONF:** Thtr 25 Class 20 Board 20 Del from £135 **PARKING:** 40 **NOTES:** ⊗ in restaurant Civ Wed 60

⌂ *Shepherds Hotel*
Lakeland Sheep & Wool Centre, Egremont Rd CA13 0QX
☎ 01900 822673 🖷 01900 822673
e-mail: reception@shepherdshotel.co.uk
web: www.shepherdshotel.co.uk
Dir: *At junct of A66 and A5086 S of Cockermouth, entrance off A5086, 200mtrs off rdbt*
This hotel is modern in style and offers thoughtfully equipped accommodation. The property also houses the Lakeland Sheep and Wool Centre, with live sheep shows from Easter to mid November. A restaurant serving a wide variety of meals and snacks is open all day.
ROOMS: 13 en suite **CONF:** BC Thtr 200 Class 10 Board 10

COGGESHALL, Essex — Map 07 TL82

★★★70% *White Hart*
Market End CO6 1NH
OLD ENGLISH INNS
☎ 01376 561654 🖷 01376 561789
e-mail: 6529@greeneking.co.uk
web: www.oldenglish.co.uk
Dir: *from A12 through Kelvedon & onto B1024 to Coggeshall*
This cosy inn is located in the centre of the town. Bedrooms vary in size and all offer good quality and comfort with extras such as CD players, fruit and mineral water. Public areas are heavily beamed with a popular bar serving a varied menu, a large restaurant with an Italian menu and cosy residents' lounge.
ROOMS: 18 en suite (1 fmly) **FACILITIES:** STV ♫ ch fac **CONF:** Thtr 30 Class 10 Board 22 **PARKING:** 47

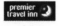

COLCHESTER, Essex — Map 13 TL92
See also Earls Colne

★★★★73% Five Lakes Resort
Colchester Rd CM9 8HX
☎ 01621 868888 🖷 01621 869696
e-mail: enquiries@fivelakes.co.uk
web: www.fivelakes.co.uk
(For full entry see Tolleshunt Knights)

★★★ ⓖⓖ🡇 Maison Talbooth
Stratford Rd CO7 6HN
☎ 01206 322367 🖷 01206 322752
e-mail: maison@milsomhotels.co.uk
web: www.milsomhotels.com
(For full entry see Dedham)

★★★74% ⓖⓖ The Rose & Crown
East St CO1 2TZ
☎ 01206 866677 🖷 01206 866616
e-mail: info@rose-and-crown.com
web: www.rose-and-crown.com
Dir: from A12 follow Rollerworld signs, hotel by level crossing
This delightful coaching inn is situated close to the shops and is full of charm. The character public areas feature a wealth of exposed beams and timbered walls, and The Oak Room restaurant offers an interesting concept - French and Indian fusion cuisine. Although the bedrooms vary in size and style all are pleasantly decorated and equipped with many thoughtful extras.
ROOMS: 38 en suite (3 fmly) (12 GF) ⊗ in 17 bedrooms s fr £59; d fr £69 (incl. bkfst) **FACILITIES:** STV Pay for Movie channels Internet/email each room **CONF:** Thtr 100 Class 50 Board 45 Del from £135 **PARKING:** 50 **NOTES:** ✗ ⊗ in restaurant

★★★71% George Hotel
116 High St CO1 1TD
☎ 01206 578494 🖷 01206 761732
e-mail: colcgeorge@aol.com
Dir: 200yds beyond Town Hall on High St
A 15th-century coaching inn, now under new ownership, situated in the centre of this bustling town. Bedrooms are pleasantly decorated, have co-ordinated fabrics and generally offer a good levels of comfort. Many of the rooms have original features such as exposed beams. An interesting choice of dishes and daily-changing specials is served in the smart restaurant, alternatively bar snacks are available in the lounge.
ROOMS: 47 en suite ⊗ in 32 bedrooms s £60-£100; d £80-£110 **FACILITIES:** STV **CONF:** Thtr 70 Class 30 Board 40 Del £129.95 **PARKING:** 40 **NOTES:** ⊗ in restaurant

We have indicated only the hotels that
don't accept credit or debit cards

★★★70%
The Stoke by Nayland Club Hotel
Keepers Ln, Leavenheath CO6 4PZ
☎ 01206 262836 🖷 01206 263356
e-mail: sales@stokebynaylandclub.co.uk
web: www.stokebynaylandclub.co.uk
Dir: off A134 at Leavenheath onto B1068, hotel 0.75m on right
Situated on the edge of Dedham Vale, in 300 acres of undulating countryside with lakes and two golf courses. The spacious bedrooms are attractively decorated and equipped with modern facilities, including ISDN lines. Public rooms include the Spikes bar,
continued

a conservatory, a lounge, a smart restaurant, conference and banqueting suites and a superb leisure complex.

ROOMS: 30 en suite (4 fmly) (15 GF) ⊗ in 22 bedrooms **FACILITIES:** Spa STV ⊠ supervised ⛳ 36 Fishing Squash Snooker Sauna Solarium Gym Putt green Jacuzzi Health/beauty salon, Driving range **CONF:** Thtr 500 Class 200 Board 36 **SERVICES:** Lift **PARKING:** 300 **NOTES:** ✗ ⊗ in restaurant Civ Wed 200

★★★69% ⓖ milsoms
Stratford Rd, Dedham CO7 6HW
☎ 01206 322795 🖷 01206 323689
e-mail: milsoms@milsomhotels.com
web: www.milsomhotels.com
(For full entry see Dedham)

⌂ Premier Travel Inn Colchester
Ipswich Rd CO4 9WP
☎ 08701 977065 🖷 01206 751327
web: www.premiertravelinn.com
Dir: take A120 (A1232) junct off A12, follow A1232 towards Colchester, Inn on right
High quality, modern budget accommodation ideal for both families and business travellers. Spacious, en suite bedrooms feature bath and shower, satellite TV and many have telephones and modem points. The adjacent family restaurant features a wide and varied menu. For further details consult the Hotel Groups page.
ROOMS: 40 en suite s £47.95-£50.95; d £47.95-£50.95

COLEFORD, Gloucestershire — Map 04 SO51

★★★68% The Speech House
GL16 7EL
☎ 01594 822607 🖷 01594 823658
e-mail: relax@thespeechhouse.co.uk
web: www.thespeechhouse.co.uk
Dir: on B4226 between Cinderford and Coleford

Dating back to 1676, this former hunting lodge is tucked away in the Forest of Dean. Bedrooms, some with four-poster beds,
continued

combine modern amenities with period charm; they include some stylish, impressive new rooms in the courtyard. The beamed restaurant serves good, imaginative food, whilst additional features include a mini gym, aqua spa and conference facilities. **ROOMS:** 15 en suite 22 annexe en suite (4 fmly) (12 GF) ⊗ in 6 bedrooms **FACILITIES:** ♨ 18 Sauna Solarium Gym Jacuzzi Beauty Salon Xmas **CONF:** BC Thtr 50 Class 30 Board 30 Del from £120 **PARKING:** 70 **NOTES:** ⊗ in restaurant Civ Wed 70

★★64% The Angel Hotel
Market Place GL16 8AE
☎ 01594 833113 ▤ 01594 832413
Dir: access to hotel via A48 or A40
This friendly 17th-century coaching inn is centrally located and provides an excellent base for exploring the area. All bedrooms are spacious, well equipped and suitable for both business and leisure guests. Additional features include a choice of bars, that all have a relaxing atmosphere, a good range of real ales and wholesome cuisine.
ROOMS: 9 en suite (1 fmly) s £39-£45; d £65-£85 (incl. bkfst)
FACILITIES: STV ♫ **PARKING:** 9

COLERNE, Wiltshire Map 04 ST87

Top Hotel

★★★★ ◉◉◉ ♨ Lucknam Park
SN14 8AZ
☎ 01225 742777 ▤ 01225 743536
e-mail: reservations@lucknampark.co.uk
web: www.lucknampark.co.uk
Dir: M4 junct 17, A350 to Chippenham, then A420 to Bristol for 3m. At Ford village, left to Colerne, 3m right at x-rds. Entrance on right
Guests may well feel a theatrical sense of arrival when approaching this Palladian mansion along its magnificent mile-long avenue of beech and lime trees. Surrounded by 500 acres of parkland and beautiful gardens, this fine hotel offers a wealth of choices ranging from enjoying pampering treatments to taking vigorous exercise. Elegant bedrooms and suites are split between the main building and adjacent courtyard. Dining options range from the informal Pavilion Restaurant, to the formal, and very accomplished, main restaurant.
ROOMS: 23 en suite 18 annexe en suite (16 GF) s £235-£800; d £235-£800 **LB FACILITIES:** Spa STV ⌗ ९ Riding Snooker Sauna Gym ♨ Jacuzzi Whirlpool, Beauty & hair salon, Steam room, Cross country course, Mountain bikes ♫ Xmas **CONF:** BC Thtr 60 Class 24 Board 24 Del from £260 **PARKING:** 70 **NOTES:** ✘ ⊗ in restaurant Civ Wed 60

COLESHILL, Warwickshire Map 10 SP28

★★★65% Grimstock Country House
Gilson Rd, Gilson B46 1LJ
☎ 01675 462121 & 462161 ▤ 01675 467646
e-mail: enquiries@grimstockhotel.co.uk
Dir: off A446 at rdbt onto B4117 to Gilson, hotel 100yds on right
This privately owned hotel is convenient for Birmingham International Airport and the NEC, and benefits from a peaceful rural setting. Bedrooms are spacious and comfortable. Public rooms include two restaurants, a wood-panelled bar, good conference facilities and a gym featuring the latest cardiovascular equipment.
ROOMS: 44 en suite (1 fmly) (13 GF) s £60-£95; d £70-£109 (incl. bkfst) **LB FACILITIES:** STV Solarium Gym Xmas **CONF:** Thtr 100 Class 60 Board 50 Del from £120 **PARKING:** 100 **NOTES:** ⊗ in restaurant Civ Wed 90

⌂ Innkeeper's Lodge Birmingham Coleshill
High St B46 3BL
☎ 01675 462212
web: www.innkeeperslodge.com
A growing concept in the travel accommodation market. Smart rooms meet essential business requirements but also have home comforts. Dining options include all-day menus plus the added advantage of breakfast, which is included in the room price. For further details consult the Hotel Groups page.
ROOMS: 32 rms

COLN ST ALDWYNS, Gloucestershire Map 05 SP10

★★72% ◉◉ The New Inn At Coln
GL7 5AN
☎ 01285 750651 ▤ 01285 750657
e-mail: stay@new-inn.co.uk
web: www.new-inn.co.uk
Dir: 8m E of Cirencester, between Bibury and Fairford
Set in the heart of the Coln Valley, this quintessential Cotswold inn has been welcoming weary travellers since the reign of Elizabeth I. The bedrooms are very cosy, while crackling log fires, flagstone floors, wooden beams and genuine hospitality make for a beguiling atmosphere. An excellent bar menu is available. Aperitifs can be savoured in the lounge, whilst perusing the interesting range of dishes on the restaurant menu.
ROOMS: 8 en suite 6 annexe en suite (1 GF) **FACILITIES:** Fishing **CONF:** Thtr 20 Board 12 **PARKING:** 22 **NOTES:** No children 10 yrs ⊗ in restaurant

COLSTERWORTH, Lincolnshire Map 11 SK92

⌂ Travelodge Grantham Colsterworth
NG35 5JR
☎ 08700 850 950 ▤ 01476 860680
web: www.travelodge.co.uk
Dir: on A1/A151 s'bound at junct with A151/B676
Travelodge offers good quality, good value, modern accommodation. Ideal for families, the spacious, en suite bedrooms include remote-control TV, tea and coffee-making facilities and comfortable beds. Meals can be taken at the nearby family restaurant. For further details consult the Hotel Groups page.
ROOMS: 31 en suite s fr £26; d fr £26

COLYFORD, Devon Map 04 SY29

★★77% ◉ **Swallows Eaves**
EX24 6QJ
☎ 01297 553184 ▤ 01297 553574
e-mail: swallows-eaves@hotmail.com
Dir: *on A3052 between Lyme Regis and Sidmouth, in village centre, opposite post office store*
This delightful hotel has gained a well-deserved reputation for excellent standards of service, food and hospitality; many guests return year after year. Bedrooms combine comfort with quality, each individually styled and equipped with many thoughtful extras. The restaurant serves a daily menu of carefully prepared dishes, making good use of fresh local ingredients. Safe, on-site parking is an added bonus.
ROOMS: 8 en suite (1 GF) ◉ in all bedrooms s £47-£53; d £78-£106 (incl. bkfst) **LB FACILITIES:** Free use of nearby Swimming Club
PARKING: 10 **NOTES:** ✖ No children 14yrs ◉ in restaurant RS Nov-Feb

CONSETT, Co Durham Map 19 NZ15

★★★68% Derwent Manor
Allensford DH8 9BB
☎ 01207 592000 ▤ 01207 502472
e-mail: info@derwent-manor-hotel.com
web: www.derwent-manor-hotel.com
Dir: *from A1(M) junct 58 onto A68 (Darlington to Corbridge road). Hotel 11m on left*
This hotel, built in the style of a manor house, is set in open grounds overlooking the River Derwent. Spacious bedrooms, including a number of suites, are comfortably equipped. A popular wedding venue, there are also extensive conference facilities and an impressive leisure suite. The Grouse & Claret bar serves a wide range of drinks and light meals, and Guinevere's restaurant offers the fine dining option.
ROOMS: 48 en suite (3 fmly) ◉ in 26 bedrooms s £69-£99; d £79-£115 (incl. bkfst) **LB FACILITIES:** STV ⌇ supervised Sauna Gym Jacuzzi Xmas **CONF:** Thtr 300 Class 200 Board 80 Del from £95 **SERVICES:** Lift
PARKING: 150 **NOTES:** ◉ in restaurant Civ Wed 300

CONSTANTINE, Cornwall & Isles of Scilly Map 02 SW72

★★70% ◉ **Trengilly Wartha Inn**
Nancenoy TR11 5RP
☎ 01326 340332 ▤ 01326 341121
e-mail: reception@trengilly.co.uk
Dir: *A39 to Falmouth. At rdbt by Asda in Penryn, signed to Constantine then Gweek. Hotel signed on left in 1m*
The charm and tranquillity of this character inn, which is located close to the Helford River, provides a welcoming environment. Interesting cuisine based on local produce, fine wines, hand-pulled ales and an impressive selection of malts are offered along with comfortable bedrooms and pleasant public rooms.
ROOMS: 6 en suite 2 annexe en suite (2 fmly) ◉ in 2 bedrooms s £49; d £78 (incl. bkfst) **LB PARKING:** 50 **NOTES:** ◉ in restaurant RS 25 Dec (b fast only) 31 Dec

THE CIRCLE
Selected Individual Hotels
GREAT BRITAIN

CONSTANTINE BAY, Cornwall & Isles of Scilly Map 02 SW87

★★★★69% ◉ **Treglos**
PL28 8JH
☎ 01841 520727 ▤ 01841 521163
e-mail: stay@treglos-hotel.com
web: www.tregloshotel.com
Dir: *right at Constantine Bay stores, hotel 50yds on left*
Owned by the Barlow family for over 30 years, this hotel has a
continued

tradition of high standards. The genuine welcome, choice of comfortable lounges, indoor pool and children's play facilities entice guests back year after year. Bedrooms vary in size; those with sea views are always popular. The restaurant continues to provide imaginative menus incorporating seasonal local produce.
ROOMS: 42 en suite (12 fmly) (1 GF) ◉ in all bedrooms s £72-£97; d £144-£193 (incl. bkfst & dinner) **LB FACILITIES:** ⌇ ⌂ 18 Snooker ⌲ Putt green Jacuzzi Converted 'boat house' for table tennis **SERVICES:** Lift
PARKING: 58 **NOTES:** ◉ in restaurant Closed 30 Nov-1 Mar

COOKHAM DEAN, Berkshire Map 05 SU88

Restaurant with Rooms

🏠 ◉◉ **The Inn on the Green**
The Old Cricket Common SL6 9NZ
☎ 01628 482638 ▤ 01628 487474
e-mail: reception@theinnonthegreen.com
Dir: *A404 towards Marlow High St. Cross suspension bridge towards Bisham. 1st left into Quarry Wood Rd, right Hills Lane, right at Memorial Cross*

This charming English country inn enjoys a peaceful location in a beautiful rural Berkshire village. Individually designed stylish bedrooms, some located round a delightful courtyard, retain many original features and are equipped with lots of thoughtful extras. Imaginative, noteworthy food is served in the attractive wood-panelled dining room.
ROOMS: 9 en suite (4 GF) s £60-£90; d £90-£195 (incl. bkfst) **LB FACILITIES:** Spa STV Jacuzzi Xmas **CONF:** BC Thtr 30 Class 30 Board 30 Del from £185 **PARKING:** 50 **NOTES:** ✖ RS Sun

COPTHORNE See Gatwick Airport

CORFE CASTLE, Dorset Map 04 SY98

★★★77% ◉◉ **Mortons House**
49 East St BH20 5EE
☎ 01929 480988 ▤ 01929 480820
e-mail: stay@mortonshouse.co.uk
web: www.mortonshouse.co.uk
Dir: *on A351 between Wareham & Swanage*
Set in delightful gardens and grounds with excellent views of Corfe Castle, this impressive building dates back to Tudor times. The oak-panelled drawing room has a roaring log fire and an interesting range of enjoyable cuisine is available in the well-appointed dining room. Bedrooms, many with views of the castle, are comfortable and well equipped.
ROOMS: 14 en suite 5 annexe en suite (2 fmly) (5 GF) ◉ in all bedrooms s £75-£145; d £126-£145 (incl. bkfst) **LB FACILITIES:** Jacuzzi Xmas **CONF:** BC Thtr 45 Class 45 Board 20 Del from £115 **PARKING:** 40 **NOTES:** ✖ ◉ in restaurant Civ Wed 60

🎵 Entertainment

CORNHILL-ON-TWEED, Northumberland Map 21 NT83

★★★76% ◉◉≗ Tillmouth Park Country House
TD12 4UU
☎ 01890 882255 📠 01890 882540
e-mail: reception@tillmouthpark.force9.co.uk
web: www.tillmouthpark.com
Dir: off A1(M) at East Ord rdbt at Berwick-upon-Tweed. Take A698 to Cornhill and Coldstream. Hotel 9m on left

An imposing mansion set in landscaped grounds by the River Till. Gracious public rooms include a stunning galleried lounge with drawing room off. The quietly elegant dining room overlooks the gardens, whilst lunches and early dinners are available in the bistro. Bedrooms retain a traditional character and include several magnificent master rooms.
ROOMS: 12 en suite 2 annexe en suite (1 fmly) s £60-£140; d £120-£180 (incl. bkfst) LB **FACILITIES:** STV ♬ 3/4 snooker table, Game shooting, fishing Xmas **CONF:** Thtr 50 Class 20 Board 20 Del from £125 **PARKING:** 50 **NOTES:** ⊗ in restaurant Civ Wed 50

CORSE LAWN, Gloucestershire Map 10 SO83

Top Hotel

★★★ ◉◉ Corse Lawn House
GL19 4LZ
☎ 01452 780479 & 780771 📠 01452 780840
e-mail: enquiries@corselawn.com
web: www.corselawn.com
Dir: on B4211 5m SW of Tewkesbury
This gracious Grade II listed Queen Anne house has been home to the Hine family since 1978. Aided by an enthusiastic and committed team, the family still presides over all aspects, creating a relaxed and wonderfully comforting environment. Bedrooms offer a reassuring mix of comfort and quality.
continued

Impressive cuisine is based upon excellent produce, much of it locally sourced.
ROOMS: 19 en suite (2 fmly) (5 GF) s £87.50; d £135-£170 (incl. bkfst) LB **FACILITIES:** STV ⬚ ♣ ♬ Badminton Croquet Table tennis **CONF:** Thtr 50 Class 30 Board 25 Del from £140 **PARKING:** 62 **NOTES:** ⊗ in restaurant Closed 24-26 Dec Civ Wed 70

See advert under TEWKESBURY

COVENTRY, West Midlands Map 10 SP37
See also Brandon, Meriden & Nuneaton

★★★72% ◉ Brooklands Grange Hotel & Restaurant
Holyhead Rd CV5 8HX
☎ 024 7660 1601 📠 024 7660 1277
e-mail: info@brooklands-grange.co.uk
web: www.brooklands-grange.co.uk
Dir: exit A45 at city centre rdbt. At next rdbt take A4114. Hotel 100yds on left
Behind the Jacobean façade of Brooklands Grange is a well run modern and comfortable business hotel. Well-appointed bedrooms are thoughtfully equipped for corporate guests and a smartly appointed four-poster bedroom has now been created. The food continues to be worthy of note, with the emphasis on contemporary, well-flavoured dishes.
ROOMS: 31 en suite (3 fmly) (11 GF) ⊗ in 25 bedrooms s £60-£105; d £70-£135 (incl. bkfst) LB **CONF:** BC Thtr 20 Class 10 Board 14 Del £130 **PARKING:** 52 **NOTES:** ⊗ in restaurant Closed 26-28 Dec & 1-2 Jan

★★★71%
Courtyard by Marriott Coventry
London Rd, Ryton on Dunsmore CV8 3DY
☎ 0870 400 7216 📠 0870 400 7316
e-mail: meetings.coventry@courtyardhotels.co.uk
web: www.kewgreen.co.uk
Dir: M6 junct 2, take A46 towards Warwick, then A45 London at Coventry Airport
Located on the outskirts of the city, this modern hotel appeals to both business and leisure guests. A range of meeting rooms along with convenient access to the road networks makes this an ideal business venue, while the hotel's proximity to a number of attractions also makes it an excellent base for a weekend of sightseeing. The public areas and accommodation are smartly presented and the spacious bedrooms are particularly well equipped for corporate guests.
ROOMS: 51 en suite (2 fmly) (22 GF) ⊗ in 25 bedrooms s fr £98; d fr £106 LB **FACILITIES:** STV Gym Xmas **CONF:** Thtr 300 Class 100 Board 24 Del from £140 **PARKING:** 120 **NOTES:** ✖ ⊗ in restaurant Civ Wed 116

★★★68% The Chace
London Rd, Toll Bar End CV3 4EQ
☎ 0870 609 6130 📠 024 7630 1816
e-mail: chacehotel@corushotels.com
web: www.corushotels.com
Dir: A45 or A46 follow to Toll Bar Roundabout / Coventry Airport, take B4116 to Willenhall, over mini-rdbt, hotel on left
A former doctor's mansion, the main building retains many of its original Victorian features, including public rooms with high ceilings, stained glass windows, oak panelling and an impressive
continued on p170

COVENTRY, continued

staircase; there is also a patio and well-kept gardens. Bedroom styles and sizes vary somewhat; most are bright and modern.

The Chace, Coventry

ROOMS: 66 en suite (23 fmly) (24 GF) ⊗ in 34 bedrooms s £50-£86; d £60-£96 **LB** **FACILITIES:** STV Pool Table, Free use of nearby leisure centre Xmas **CONF:** Thtr 65 Class 40 Board 36 Del from £90 **PARKING:** 120 **NOTES:** ⊗ in restaurant Civ Wed 60

★★★68% Menzies Leofric

Broadgate CV1 1LZ
☎ 024 7622 1371 📠 024 7655 1352
e-mail: leofric@menzies-hotels.co.uk
web: www.menzies-hotels.co.uk

Dir: *junct 9 off Coventry ring road, follow signs to West Orchards Car Park, situated to rear of hotel*

Right in the centre of the city, this hotel has the advantage of preferred parking rates in the nearby multi-storey car park, and that most rooms have a quiet outlook. Bedrooms are well lit and comfortable with good business facilities. Contemporary public areas include two bars, a brasserie, plus a hairdresser.

ROOMS: 94 en suite (5 fmly) ⊗ in 20 bedrooms s £115; d £125 **LB** **FACILITIES:** STV Xmas **CONF:** Thtr 600 Class 200 Board 60 Del £125 **SERVICES:** Lift **NOTES:** ⊗ in restaurant Civ Wed

★★★66% *Best Western Hylands*

Warwick Rd CV3 6AU
☎ 024 7650 1600 📠 024 7650 1027
e-mail: hylands@bestwestern.co.uk

Dir: *on A429, 500yds from junct 6 of town centre ring road, opposite Memorial Park*

This hotel is convenient for the station and the city centre and overlooks an attractive park. Bedroom styles vary, yet each room is well equipped; the most recent additions are smartly decorated and modern, with bold colour schemes. Public rooms offer an open-plan lounge bar and Restaurant 153.

ROOMS: 61 en suite ⊗ in 54 bedrooms **FACILITIES:** STV **CONF:** Thtr 60 Class 40 Board 30 **PARKING:** 60 **NOTES:**

★★★64% Novotel Coventry

Wilsons Ln CV6 6HL
☎ 024 7636 5000 📠 024 7636 2422
e-mail: h0506@accor-hotels.com
web: www.novotel.com

Dir: *M6 junct 3. Follow signs for B4113 towards Longford and Bedworth. 3rd exit on large rdbt*

A modern hotel, convenient for Birmingham, Coventry and the motorway network, offering spacious, well-equipped accommodation. The bright brasserie offers extended dining hours, or alternatively there is an extensive room-service menu. Family rooms and a play area make this a child-friendly hotel, and there is also a selection of meeting rooms.

Novotel - AA Hotel Group of the Year 2005-6.

ROOMS: 98 en suite (15 fmly) ⊗ in 70 bedrooms **FACILITIES:** Petanque, Pool table **CONF:** Thtr 200 Class 100 Board 40 **SERVICES:** Lift **PARKING:** 120 **NOTES:** ⊗ in restaurant

★★★61% Allesley

Birmingham Rd, Allesley Village CV5 9GP
☎ 024 7640 3272 📠 024 7640 5190
e-mail: info@allesleyhotel.com

Dir: *from A45 take A4114 towards Coventry city, take 1st left onto Birmingham Rd, hotel on left*

This purpose built hotel, now under new ownership, provides well-equipped bedrooms suited to the corporate guest. Public rooms are split over two levels and include a spacious reception foyer, a large restaurant and a lounge bar. Extensive conference and function facilities are available and prove popular.

ROOMS: 75 en suite 15 annexe en suite (2 fmly) ⊗ in 45 bedrooms s £39-£89; d £39-£89 **LB** **CONF:** BC Thtr 450 Class 150 Board 80 Del from £99 **SERVICES:** Lift **PARKING:** 500 **NOTES:** ⊗ in restaurant Civ Wed 300

U Quality Hotel Coventry NEC

Birmingham Rd, Allesley CV5 9BA
☎ 024 7640 3835 📠 024 7640 3081
e-mail: enquiries@hotels-coventry.com

Dir: *A45 onto A4114 towards Allesley Village. Follow brown signs for hotel*

At the time of going to press, the star classification for this hotel was not confirmed. Please refer to the AA internet site www.theAA.com for current information.

ROOMS: 80 rms (48 en suite) (4 fmly) (24 GF) ⊗ in 42 bedrooms s £50-£120; d £60-£140 **FACILITIES:** STV Sauna **CONF:** Thtr 180 Class 70 Board 40 Del from £80 **PARKING:** 150 **NOTES:** ⊗ in restaurant Civ Wed 140

> Late for dinner? Quality standards mean that last orders for dinner vary according to star rating and should be no earlier than: ★★ 7.00pm ★★★ 8:00pm ★★★★ 9:00pm ★★★★★ 10:00pm

⌂ *Hotel Campanile*

4 Wigston Rd, Walsgrave CV2 2SD
☎ 024 7662 2311 📠 024 7660 2362
e-mail: coventry@envergure.co.uk
web: www.envergure.fr

Dir: *M6 exit 2, 2nd rdbt turn right*

This modern building offers accommodation in smart, well-equipped bedrooms, all with en suite bathrooms.

continued

Refreshments may be taken at the informal Bistro. For further details consult the Hotel Groups page.

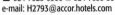

ROOMS: 47 en suite **CONF:** Thtr 35 Class 18 Board 24

⌂ *Hotel Ibis Coventry Centre*

Mill Ln, St John's Ringway CV1 2LN
☎ 024 7625 0500 📠 024 7655 3548
e-mail: H2793@accor.hotels.com
Dir: *from M45 junct 17 to Coventry. Follow City Centre/Ring Road signs for Birmingham. A45 to Coventry, then A4114 signed to Jaguar Assembly Plant. At inner ring road towards ring road S. Off exit 5 for Mill Lane*
Modern, budget hotel offering comfortable accommodation in bright and practical bedrooms. Breakfast is self-service and dinner is available in the restaurant. For further details, consult the Hotel Groups page.
ROOMS: 89 en suite

⌂ *Hotel Ibis Coventry South*

Abbey Rd, Whitley CV3 4BJ
☎ 024 7663 9922 📠 024 7630 6898
e-mail: H2094@accor-hotels.com
Dir: *signed from A46/A423 rdbt. Take A423 towards A45. Follow signs for Esporta Health Club and Jaguar Engineering Plant*
Modern, budget hotel offering comfortable accommodation in bright and practical bedrooms. Breakfast is self-service and dinner is available in the restaurant. For further details, consult the Hotel Groups page.
ROOMS: 51 en suite **CONF:** BC Thtr 20 Class 20

⌂ Innkeeper's Lodge Coventry

Brinklow Rd, Binley CV3 2DS
☎ 0870 2430500
web: www.innkeeperslodge.com
A growing concept in the travel accommodation market. Smart rooms meet essential business requirements but also have home comforts. Dining options include all-day menus plus the added advantage of breakfast, which is included in the room price. For further details consult the Hotel Groups page.
ROOMS: 40 rms s fr £55; d fr £55

⌂ Innkeeper's Lodge Meriden

Main Rd, Meriden CV7 7NN
☎ 01676 523798 📠 01676 531922
web: www.innkeeperslodge.com
Dir: *just off A45 between Coventry & Birmingham on B4102. Lodge on left down hill from Meriden Village Green*
A growing concept in the travel accommodation market. Smart rooms meet essential business requirements but also have home comforts. Dining options include all-day menus plus the added advantage of breakfast, which is included in the room price. For further details consult the Hotel Groups page.
ROOMS: 13 (9 en suite) s £49.95-£59.95; d £49.95-£59.95

⌂ Premier Travel Inn Coventry

Rugby Rd, Binley Woods CV3 2TA
☎ 08701 977066 📠 024 7643 1178
web: www.premiertravelinn.com
Dir: *from M6 junct 2 follow signs Warwick (A46 & M40). Follow "All traffic" signs, under bridge onto A46. Left at 1st rbt to Binley. Inn on right at next rbt*
High quality, modern budget accommodation ideal for both families and business travellers. Spacious, en suite bedrooms feature bath and shower, satellite TV and many have telephones and modem points. The adjacent family restaurant features a wide and varied menu. For further details consult the Hotel Groups page.
ROOMS: 75 en suite s £47.95-£50.95; d £47.95-£50.95 **CONF:** Thtr 25 Board 18

⌂ Premier Travel Inn Coventry East

Combe Fields Rd, Ansty CV7 9JP
☎ 0870 9906472 📠 0870 9906473
web: www.premiertravelinn.com
Dir: *M6 junct 2 onto B4065 towards Ansty. After village right onto B4029 signed Brinklow. Right into Coombe Fields Rd, Inn on right*
High quality, modern budget accommodation ideal for both families and business travellers. Spacious, en suite bedrooms feature bath and shower, satellite TV and many have telephones and modem points. The adjacent family restaurant features a wide and varied menu. For further details consult the Hotel Groups page.
ROOMS: 28 en suite s £47.95-£50.95; d £47.95-£50.95 **CONF:** Thtr 12 Class 14 Board 14

COWES See Wight, Isle of

U Star rating not confirmed

CRAMLINGTON, Northumberland Map 21 NZ27

⇧ Innkeeper's Lodge Cramlington

Blagdon Ln NE23 8AU
☎ 01670 736111 📠 01670 715709
web: www.innkeeperslodge.com
Dir: from A1, exit for A19. At rdbt, left onto A1068, lodge at junct of Blagdon Lane and Fisher Lane

A growing concept in the travel accommodation market. Smart rooms meet essential business requirements but also have home comforts. Dining options include all-day menus plus the added advantage of breakfast, which is included in the room price. For further details consult the Hotel Groups page.

ROOMS: 18 en suite s £49.95-£58; d £49.95-£58 **CONF:** Board 24

⇧ Premier Travel Inn Newcastle (Cramlington)

Moor Farm Roundabout, off Front St NE23 7QA
☎ 08701 977188 📠 0191 250 2216
web: www.premiertravelinn.com
Dir: at rdbt on junction of A19/A189 S of Cramlington

High quality, modern budget accommodation ideal for both families and business travellers. Spacious, en suite bedrooms feature bath and shower, satellite TV and many have telephones and modem points. The adjacent family restaurant features a wide and varied menu. For further details consult the Hotel Groups page.

ROOMS: 40 en suite s £49.95; d £49.95

CRANBROOK, Kent

★★71% ⊛ The George Hotel

Stone St TN17 3HE
☎ 01580 713348 📠 01580 715532
e-mail: reservations@thegeorgehotelkent.co.uk
web: www.thegeorgehotelkent.co.uk
Dir: off A21 to Goudhurst & Cranbrook. At large rdbt, right into Cranbrook

This delightful 13th-century coaching inn is located in the heart of this bustling town centre. Bedrooms have a wealth of original features and include some with four-poster beds. Public rooms include a smart lounge bar, a cosy wine bar and a restaurant, where imaginative freshly prepared dishes are served.

ROOMS: 8 en suite (2 fmly) ⊛ in all bedrooms s £60-£80; d £90-£125 (incl. bkfst) **FACILITIES:** STV **CONF:** Board 20 **PARKING:** 10 **NOTES:** ✗ ⊛ in restaurant

CRANTOCK, Cornwall & Isles of Scilly Map 02 SW76

★★★71% Crantock Bay

West Pentire TR8 5SE
☎ 01637 830229 📠 01637 831111
e-mail: stay@crantockbayhotel.co.uk
web: www.crantockbayhotel.co.uk
Dir: at Newquay A3075 to Redruth. After 500yds right towards Crantock, follow signs to West Pentire

This family-run hotel has spectacular sea views and a tradition of friendly and attentive service. With direct access to the beach from its four acres of grounds, and its extensive leisure facilities, the hotel is a great place for family guests. There are separate

continued

lounges, a spacious bar and enjoyable cuisine is served in the dining room.

ROOMS: 33 en suite (3 fmly) (10 GF) s £55-£90; d £110-£180 (incl. bkfst & dinner) **LB FACILITIES:** ⊠ ⊶ Sauna Gym 🏌 Putt green Jacuzzi Hotel leads on to sandy beach ch fac Xmas **CONF:** Thtr 60 Class 30 Board 30 Del from £89 **PARKING:** 40 **NOTES:** ⊛ in restaurant Closed 2 wks Nov & Jan RS Dec & Feb

CRATHORNE, North Yorkshire Map 19 NZ40

Top Hotel

★★★★ ⊛⊛🏆 Crathorne Hall

TS15 0AR
☎ 01642 700398 📠 01642 700814
e-mail: crathorne-cro@handpicked.co.uk
web: www.handpicked.co.uk
Dir: off A19, take slip road signed Teesside Airport and Kirklevington, then right signed Crathorne to hotel

This splendid Edwardian hall sits in its own landscaped grounds and enjoys fine views of the Leven Valley and rolling Cleveland Hills. Both the impressively equipped bedrooms and the delightful public areas offer sumptuous levels of comfort, with elegant antique furnishings that complement the hotel's architectural style. Conference and banqueting facilities are available.

ROOMS: 37 en suite (4 fmly) ⊛ in 15 bedrooms s fr £120; d fr £180 (incl. bkfst & dinner) **LB FACILITIES:** STV 🏃 Jogging track, Clay pigeon shooting Xmas **CONF:** Thtr 120 Class 80 Board 60 Del from £145 **PARKING:** 88 **NOTES:** ⊛ in restaurant Civ Wed 120

See advert on opposite page

CRAWLEY See Gatwick Airport

CREWE, Cheshire Map 15 SJ75

★★★★75% ❀ Crewe Hall
Weston Rd CW1 6UZ
☎ 01270 253333 📠 01270 253322
e-mail: crewehall@marstonhotels.com
web: www.marstonhotels.com
Dir: *M6 junct 16 follow A500 to Crewe. Last exit at rdbt onto A5020. 1st exit next rdbt to Crewe. Crewe Hall 150yds on right*

Standing in 500 acres of mature grounds, this historic hall dates back to the 17th century. It retains an elaborate interior with Victorian-style architecture. Bedrooms are spacious, well equipped and comfortable - traditionally styled rooms in the main hall and modern suites in the west wing. Guests have a choice of formal dining in the elegant Ranulph restaurant or the more relaxed atmosphere of the modern Brasserie.
ROOMS: 26 en suite 39 annexe en suite (5 fmly) (17 GF) ⊗ in 40 bedrooms s fr £183; d fr £233 (incl. bkfst) **LB FACILITIES:** STV Full size football pitch Xmas **CONF:** Thtr 260 Class 110 Board 100 Del from £199 **SERVICES:** Lift **PARKING:** 140 **NOTES:** ⊗ in restaurant Civ Wed 200

★★★72% ❀ Hunters Lodge
Sydney Rd, Sydney CW1 5LU
☎ 01270 583440 📠 01270 500553
e-mail: info@hunterslodge.co.uk
web: www.hunterslodge.co.uk
Dir: *1m from Crewe station, off A534*
Dating back to the 18th century, this family-run hotel has been extended and modernised. Accommodation, mainly located in adjacent well-equipped bedroom wings, includes family and four-poster rooms. Imaginative dishes are served in the spacious restaurant, and the popular bar also offers a choice of tempting meals. Service throughout is friendly and efficient.
ROOMS: 57 en suite (4 fmly) (31 GF) ⊗ in 31 bedrooms s £75-£103; d £99-£121 (incl. bkfst) **FACILITIES:** STV Gym **CONF:** Thtr 160 Class 100 Board 80 Del from £113.50 **PARKING:** 240 **NOTES:** ⊗ in restaurant RS Sunday Civ Wed 130

★★63% White Lion
Weston CW2 5NA
☎ 01270 587011 & 500303 📠 01270 500303
e-mail: whitelion.inn@landmarkinns.co.uk
Dir: *M6 junct 16, A500 signed Crewe/Nantwich/Chester. 2nd rdbt right into Weston village. Hotel in centre on left*
Once a Tudor farmhouse, this privately owned hotel provides
continued on p174

CREWE, continued

comfortable, modern accommodation, yet retains much of its old charm. Dining choices include The White Lion Restaurant and its adjoining cocktail lounge; a selection of bar snacks is also available in the oak-beamed lounge bar.
ROOMS: 16 en suite (2 fmly) (7 GF) s £48-£58; d £58-£68 (incl. bkfst) **LB FACILITIES:** Crown Green bowling Xmas **CONF:** Thtr 50 Class 28 Board 20 **PARKING:** 100 **NOTES:** ⊗ in restaurant Civ Wed 65

Premier Travel Inn Crewe
Coppenhall Ln, Woolstanwood CW2 8SD
☎ 08701 977068 🖷 01270 256316
web: www.premiertravelinn.com
Dir: *at junct of A530 & A532, 9m from M6 junct 16 N'bound*
High quality, modern budget accommodation ideal for both families and business travellers. Spacious, en suite bedrooms feature bath and shower, satellite TV and many have telephones and modem points. The adjacent family restaurant features a wide and varied menu. For further details consult the Hotel Groups page.
ROOMS: 41 en suite s £46.95-£49.95; d £46.95-£49.95

Travelodge
Alsager Rd, Barthomley CW2 5PT
☎ 08700 850 950 🖷 01270 883157
web: www.travelodge.co.uk
Dir: *M6 junct 16, A500 between Nantwich & Stoke-on-Trent*
Travelodge offers good quality, good value, modern accommodation. Ideal for families, the spacious, en suite bedrooms include remote-control TV, tea and coffee-making facilities and comfortable beds. Meals can be taken at the nearby family restaurant. For further details consult the Hotel Groups page.
ROOMS: 42 en suite s fr £26; d fr £26

CRICK, Northamptonshire — Map 11 SP57

Hotel Ibis Rugby East
Parklands NN6 7EX
☎ 01788 824331 🖷 01788 824332
e-mail: H3588@accor-hotels.com
Dir: *M1 junct 18/A428*
Modern, budget hotel offering comfortable accommodation in bright and practical bedrooms. Breakfast is self-service and dinner is available in the restaurant. For further details, consult the Hotel Groups page.
ROOMS: 111 en suite **CONF:** BC Thtr 30 Class 16 Board 18

If you wish to use a particular credit card or debit card please check with the hotel that they are happy to accept it

CRICKLADE, Wiltshire — Map 05 SU09

★★★72% Cricklade Hotel
Common Hill SN6 6HA
☎ 01793 750751 🖷 01793 751767
e-mail: reception@crickladehotel.co.uk
web: www.crickladehotel.co.uk
Dir: *off A419 onto B4040. Turn left at clock tower. Right at rdbt. Hotel 0.5m up hill on left*
A haven of peace and tranquillity with spectacular views, this hotel is surrounded by over 30 acres of beautiful countryside. Bedrooms vary in size and style; those in the main building offer high levels of comfort and quality. There is an elegant lounge and dining room, and a Victorian-style conservatory that runs the full length of the building.

ROOMS: 25 en suite 21 annexe en suite (1 fmly) ⊗ in all bedrooms s £112-£118; d £152-£155 (incl. bkfst) **LB FACILITIES:** STV ⛳ 9 Snooker Solarium Gym Jacuzzi Aromatherapy Beautician, Golf professional ♫ Xmas **CONF:** Thtr 80 Class 60 Board 30 Del £155 **PARKING:** 100 **NOTES:** No children 14yrs ⊗ in restaurant Closed 25-26 Dec Civ Wed 120

See advert under SWINDON

CROMER, Norfolk — Map 13 TG24

★★★74% Sea Marge
16 High St NR27 0AB
☎ 01263 579579 🖷 01263 579524
e-mail: info@mackenziehotels.com
Dir: *A140 from Norwich until A149 to Cromer. Take B1159 to Overstrand. Hotel in village centre*

An elegant Grade II listed Edwardian mansion perched on the cliff top amidst pretty landscaped gardens which lead down to the beach. Bedrooms are tastefully decorated and thoughtfully equipped, many have superb sea views. Public rooms offer a wide choice of areas in which to relax, including Frazer's restaurant and a smart lounge bar.
ROOMS: 17 en suite ⊗ in all bedrooms s £75-£110; d fr £110 (incl. bkfst) **LB FACILITIES:** Xmas **CONF:** Thtr 50 Class 40 Board 24 Del from £115 **SERVICES:** Lift **PARKING:** 50 **NOTES:** ⊗ in restaurant

★★★63% The Cliftonville
NR27 9AS
☎ 01263 512543 🖷 01263 515700
e-mail: reservations@cliftonvillehotel.co.uk
web: www.cliftonvillehotel.co.uk
Dir: *From A149 (coastal road), 500yd from town centre, northbound*
An imposing Edwardian hotel situated on the main coast road with stunning views of the sea. Public rooms feature a magnificent staircase, minstrels' gallery, coffee shop, lounge bar, a further residents' lounge, Boltons Bistro and an additional restaurant. The

continued

bedrooms, for the most part spacious, are pleasantly decorated and have lovely sea views.

ROOMS: 30 en suite (5 fmly) ⊗ in 14 bedrooms s £45-£62; d £90-£124 (incl. bkfst) **LB** **FACILITIES:** Xmas **CONF:** Thtr 150 Class 100 Board 60 Del from £65 **SERVICES:** Lift **PARKING:** 20 **NOTES:** ⊗ in restaurant

★★73% Red Lion

Brook St NR27 9HD
☎ 01263 514964 🖷 01263 512834
e-mail: enquiries@yeolderedlionhotel.co.uk
web: www.yeolderedlionhotel.co.uk
Dir: *from town centre 1st left after church*

Victorian property situated in an elevated position overlooking the beach and sea beyond. The smartly appointed public areas include a billiard room, lounge bar, a popular restaurant, a sunny conservatory and a first floor residents' lounge with superb views of the sea. The spacious bedrooms are tastefully decorated, with co-ordinated soft furnishings and many thoughtful touches.

ROOMS: 12 en suite (1 fmly) s £60; d £100 (incl. bkfst) **LB** **FACILITIES:** Snooker Sauna Discount for local leisure centre **CONF:** Thtr 100 Class 50 Board 60 **PARKING:** 12 **NOTES:** 🐕 ⊗ in restaurant Closed Xmas Day

★★63% *Hotel de Paris*

Leisureplex

High St NR27 9HG
☎ 01263 513141 🖷 01263 515217
e-mail: deparis.cromer@alfatravel.co.uk
web: www.alfatravel.co.uk
Dir: *enter Cromer on A140 Norwich Rd. Left at lights onto Mount St. 2nd traffic lights right into Prince of Wales Rd. 2nd right into New St leading into High St*

An imposing, traditional-style resort hotel, situated in a prominent position overlooking the pier and beach. The bedrooms are pleasantly decorated and equipped with a good range of useful extras; many rooms have lovely sea views. The spacious public areas include a large lounge bar, restaurant, games room and a further lounge.

ROOMS: 56 en suite (5 fmly) **FACILITIES:** Games room ♫ **SERVICES:** Lift **PARKING:** 14 **NOTES:** 🐕 ⊗ in restaurant Closed Dec-Feb RS Mar & Nov

A ★★ Virginia Court Hotel

Cliff Av NR27 0AN
☎ 01263 512398 🖷 01263 515529
e-mail: virginiacourt.hotel@virgin.net
Dir: *from Norwich follow A140, turn onto Cliff Ave, take 2nd right. From King's Lynn follow A148 to Cromer, turn left onto Overstrand Rd, then 1st right onto Cliff Ave*

ROOMS: 25 en suite (2 fmly) (3 GF) ⊗ in all bedrooms s £45-£65; d £70-£130 (incl. bkfst) **LB** **FACILITIES:** STV 🎾 Xmas **PARKING:** 20 **NOTES:** 🐕 ⊗ in restaurant

CROOKLANDS, Cumbria — Map 18 SD58

★★★65% Crooklands

LA7 7NW
☎ 015395 67432 🖷 015395 67525
e-mail: reception@crooklands.com
web: www.crooklands.com
Dir: *M6 junct 36 onto A65. Left at rdbt, Hotel 1.5m on right past garage*

Although only a stone's throw from the M6, this hotel enjoys a peaceful rural location. Housed in a converted 200-year-old farmhouse, the restaurant retains many original features such as the beams and stone walls. Bedrooms are a mix of modern and traditional and vary in size. The hotel is a popular staging post for both leisure and corporate guests travelling between England and Scotland.

ROOMS: 30 en suite ⊗ in 26 bedrooms s £48-£62; d £48-£62 **LB** **CONF:** Thtr 80 Class 50 Board 40 Del from £110 **PARKING:** 80 **NOTES:** 🐕 ⊗ in restaurant Closed 24-26 Dec

CROSTHWAITE, Cumbria — Map 18 SD49

★★★61% Damson Dene

LA8 8JE
☎ 015395 68676 🖷 015395 68227
e-mail: info@damsondene.co.uk
web: www.damsondene.co.uk
Dir: *M6 junct 36, A590 signed Barrow-in-Furness, 5m right onto A5074. Hotel on right in 5m*

A short drive from Lake Windermere, this hotel enjoys a tranquil and scenic setting. Bedrooms include a number with four-poster beds and jacuzzi baths. The spacious restaurant serves a daily-changing menu, with much of the produce coming from the hotel's own kitchen garden. Real fires warm the lounge and there is a games room and cosy bar.

ROOMS: 37 en suite (4 fmly) (9 GF) ⊗ in 29 bedrooms s £59-£79; d £78-£118 (incl. bkfst) **LB** **FACILITIES: Spa** 🏊 Squash Sauna Solarium Gym Jacuzzi Beauty salon Xmas **CONF:** Thtr 140 Class 60 Board 40 Del from £84.50 **PARKING:** 45 **NOTES:** ⊗ in restaurant Civ Wed 120

CROWTHORNE, Berkshire — Map 05 SU86

★★★69% Corus hotel Bracknell

corus hotels

Duke's Ride RG45 6DW
☎ 0870 609 6111 🖷 01344 778913
e-mail: reservations.bracknell@corushotels.com
web: www.corushotels.com
Dir: *M3 junct 4, A331 to Camberley, follow signs to Sandhurst/Crowthorne A3095, left B3348, hotel past 2nd rdbt*

Situated in a quiet location but convenient for both the M3 and M4, this hotel attracts a high proportion of business guests. The modern bedrooms, which include interconnecting pairs of rooms,

continued on p176

CROWTHORNE, continued

are attractively appointed and well maintained. Public areas include a pleasant brasserie-style restaurant and a bar area.

Corus hotel Bracknell, Crowthorne

ROOMS: 79 en suite ⊗ in 43 bedrooms **FACILITIES:** STV Discounts at local leisure facilities Xmas **CONF:** Thtr 50 Class 20 Board 24 **PARKING:** 96 **NOTES:** ⊗ in restaurant Civ Wed 40

★★70% Dial House

62 Dukes Ride RG45 6DL
☎ 01344 776941 ℻ 01344 777191
e-mail: stay@thedialhouse.com
web: www.thedialhouse.com
Dir: *A3095/B3348 towards Crowthorne*

Located close to the station, this friendly hotel is particularly suitable for guests who require good connections into London. Bedrooms are comfortable - all being en suite and some with baths. The welcoming bar and restaurant offers residents a home-from-home atmosphere together with interesting and competent cooking.

ROOMS: 19 en suite (2 fmly) (5 GF) ⊗ in all bedrooms s £55-£90; d £69-£120 (incl. bkfst) **FACILITIES:** STV Complimentary entry to Wellington Country Club Xmas **CONF:** BC Thtr 16 Class 10 Board 12 Del from £115 **PARKING:** 20 **NOTES:** ✈ ⊗ in restaurant

CROYDON, Greater London

Map 06 TQ36

★★★★75% ֎֎ Coulsdon Manor

Coulsdon Court Rd, Coulsdon CR5 2LL
☎ 020 8668 0414 ℻ 020 8668 3118
Dir: *A23 right into Stoats Nest Road. Hotel top of hill on left*

This delightful Victorian manor house is peacefully set amidst 140 acres of landscaped parkland, complete with its own professional 18-hole golf course. Bedrooms are spacious and comfortable, whilst public areas include a choice of lounges and an elegant restaurant serving carefully prepared, imaginative food.

ROOMS: 35 en suite ⊗ in 13 bedrooms s £115-£149; d £138-£186 (incl. bkfst) **LB FACILITIES:** STV ⛳ 18 Squash Sauna Solarium Gym Putt green Racketball, aerobic studio **CONF:** Thtr 180 Class 90 Board 70 **SERVICES:** Lift **PARKING:** 200 **NOTES:** ✈ ⊗ in restaurant Civ Wed 60

> Popped the question? Hotels with Civ wed in their entry are licensed for civil wedding ceremonies. Maximum numbers for the ceremony only are shown e.g. Civ wed 120

★★★★67% Selsdon Park Hotel & Golf Course

Addington Rd, Sanderstead CR2 8YA
☎ 020 8657 8811 ℻ 020 8651 6171
e-mail: sales.selsdonpark@principal-hotels.com
web: www.principal-hotels.com
Dir: *3m SE of Croydon, off A2022*

Surrounded by 200 acres of mature parkland with its own 18-hole golf course, this imposing Jacobean mansion is less than 20 minutes from central London. The hotel's impressive range of conference rooms, along with the spectacular views of the North Downs' countryside make this a popular venue for both weddings and meetings. The leisure facilities are impressive.

ROOMS: 204 en suite (12 fmly) (12 GF) **FACILITIES: Spa** STV supervised ⛳ 18 Squash Sauna Solarium Gym Putt green boules, Jogging track, croquet ♫ Xmas **CONF:** BC Thtr 350 Class 220 Board 60 Del from £149 **SERVICES:** Lift **PARKING:** 300 **NOTES:** ✈ ⊗ in restaurant Civ Wed 120

★★★69% Aerodrome

Purley Way CR9 4LT
☎ 020 8710 9000 & 8680 1999
℻ 020 8681 6438
e-mail: info@aerodrome-hotel.co.uk
Dir: *Follow A23 Central London. Hotel on left next to Airport House*

The Croydon Aerodrome was the world's first international airport and the starting point for Amy Johnson's record-breaking flight to Darwin. The hotel has benefited from substantial investment in recent years. Bedrooms feature a smart, modern design and up-to-date facilities, including broadband internet access. Public areas include two restaurants, two bars and conference facilities.

ROOMS: 84 en suite ⊗ in 44 bedrooms s £60-£111; d £80-£141 (incl. bkfst) **LB FACILITIES:** Complimentary pass to nearby health club Xmas **CONF:** Thtr 100 Class 50 Board 40 Del from £125 **PARKING:** 200 **NOTES:** ✈ Civ Wed 100

★★★66% Jurys Inn

Wellesley Rd CR0 9XY
☎ 020 8448 6000 ℻ 020 8448 6111
e-mail: jurysinncroydon@jurysdoyle.com
web: www.jurysdoyle.com
Dir: *Off A212, in town centre adjacent to Whitgift Centre*

This modern hotel, located in the town centre, has spacious bedrooms with air conditioning. The contemporary public areas include a choice of eating options and a busy state-of-the-art conference centre.

ROOMS: 240 en suite (168 fmly) ⊗ in 140 bedrooms s £59-£85; d £59-£85 **FACILITIES:** STV **CONF:** BC Thtr 100 Class 50 Board 40 Del from £99 **SERVICES:** Lift air con **NOTES:** ✈ Closed 24-28 Dec

★★67% South Park Hotel
3-5 South Park Hill Rd, South Croydon CR2 7DY
☎ 020 8688 5644 ⎙ 020 8760 0861
e-mail: reception@southparkhotel.co.uk
web: www.southparkhotel.co.uk
Dir: *Follow A235 to town centre. At Coombe Rd lights turn right (A212) towards Addington 0.5m to rdbt take 3rd exit into South Park Hill Rd, hotel on left*
This intimate hotel has easy access to rail and road networks with some off-street parking available. Attractively decorated bedrooms vary in size and offer a good range of in-room facilities. Public areas consist of an informal bar, a lounge with large sofas and a delightful garden.
ROOMS: 21 en suite (2 fmly) ⊗ in 8 bedrooms s £60-£66; d £76-£85 (incl. bkfst) **PARKING:** 15 **NOTES:** ✗ ⊗ in restaurant

⌂ Innkeeper's Lodge Croydon South
415 Brighton Rd CR2 6EJ
☎ 020 8680 4559 ⎙ 020 8649 9802
web: www.innkeeperslodge.com
Dir: *M23 junct 7/ A23 or M25 junct 6/A22. At Purley take A235 Brighton Rd, N towards South Croydon, for 1m. Lodge on right.*
A growing concept in the travel accommodation market. Smart rooms meet essential business requirements but also have home comforts. Dining options include all-day menus plus the added advantage of breakfast, which is included in the room price. For further details consult the Hotel Groups page.
ROOMS: 30 en suite s £49.95-£62; d £49.95-£62

⌂ Premier Travel Inn Croydon East
104 Coombe Rd CR0 5RB
☎ 08701 977069 ⎙ 020 8686 6439
web: www.premiertravelinn.com
Dir: *M25 junct 7, A23 to Purley, then follow A235 to Croydon. Pass Tree House pub on left. Turn right at lights, onto A212*
High quality, modern budget accommodation ideal for both families and business travellers. Spacious, en suite bedrooms feature bath and shower, satellite TV and many have telephones and modem points. The adjacent family restaurant features a wide and varied menu. For further details consult the Hotel Groups page.
ROOMS: 39 en suite s £59.95-£62.95; d £59.95-£62.95

⌂ Premier Travel Inn Croydon West
The Colonnades Leisure Park, 619 Purley Way CR0 4RQ
☎ 0870 9906554 ⎙ 0870 9906555
web: www.premiertravelinn.com
Dir: *From N, exit M1, M25, then follow A23 towards Croydon. From S, hotel 8m from M25 junct 7 on A23 towards Purley Way, close to junct of Waddon Way*
High quality, modern budget accommodation ideal for both families and business travellers. Spacious, en suite bedrooms feature bath and shower, satellite TV and many have telephones and modem points. The adjacent family restaurant features a wide and varied menu. For further details consult the Hotel Groups page.
ROOMS: 82 en suite s £59.95-£62.95; d £59.95-£62.95 **CONF:** Thtr 120

AA Rosette Award for culinary excellence

The vast majority of establishments in this guide accept credit and debit cards. We indicate those that don't take any

CUCKFIELD, West Sussex — Map 06 TQ32

Top Hotel

★★★ ❀❀❀ Ockenden Manor
Ockenden Ln RH17 5LD
☎ 01444 416111 ⎙ 01444 415549
e-mail: reservations@ockenden-manor.com
Dir: *from N, at end of M23 onto A23 towards Brighton. 4.5m left onto B2115 towards Haywards Heath. Cuckfield 3m. Ockendon Lane off High St. Hotel at end*
This charming 16th-century hotel enjoys fine views of the South Downs. Bedrooms offer high standards of accommodation, some with historic features. Public rooms, retaining much of the original character, include an elegant sitting room with all the elements for a relaxing afternoon in front of the fire. Imaginative, noteworthy cuisine is a highlight to any stay.
ROOMS: 22 en suite (4 fmly) (4 GF) s £108-£175; d £155-£325 (incl. bkfst) **LB** **FACILITIES:** STV Xmas **CONF:** Thtr 50 Class 20 Board 26 Del from £205 **PARKING:** 43 **NOTES:** ⊗ in restaurant Civ Wed 75

★★73% Hilton Park Hotel
Tylers Green RH17 5EG
☎ 01444 454555 ⎙ 01444 457222
e-mail: hiltonpark@janus-systems.com
web: www.janus-systems.com/hiltonpark.htm
Dir: *halfway between Cuckfield and Haywards Heath on A272*
Situated between the delightful village of Cuckfield and Haywards Heath, this charming Victorian country house is set in three acres of grounds. The comfortable bedrooms are tastefully decorated and equipped with an excellent range of facilities. In addition to an elegant drawing room, the public rooms include a contemporary bar and restaurant and two conference rooms.
ROOMS: 11 en suite (2 fmly) s £75-£80; d £105-£115 (incl. bkfst) **LB** **FACILITIES:** STV ch fac **CONF:** Thtr 30 Board 20 Del from £150 **PARKING:** 50 **NOTES:** ✗ ⊗ in restaurant

CULLOMPTON, Devon — Map 03 ST00

★★★70% Padbrook Park
EX15 1RU
☎ 01884 38286 ⎙ 01884 34359
e-mail: info@padbrookpark.co.uk
Dir: *1m from M5 junct 28*
Opened in early summer 2005, this purpose built hotel is part of a golf and leisure complex and is located one mile from the M5. Set in 100 acres of parkland/golf course, this hotel has a friendly, relaxed atmosphere and a modern, contemporary feel.
ROOMS: 40 en suite (4 fmly) (11 GF) ⊗ in 26 bedrooms s £60; d £90 (incl. bkfst) **LB** **FACILITIES:** ⛳ 9 Fishing Gym Putt green 3 rink bowling centre ♫ Xmas **CONF:** Thtr 200 Class 40 Board 30 Del from £87 **SERVICES:** Lift **NOTES:** ✗ ⊗ in restaurant Civ Wed 200

DARLINGTON, Co Durham Map 19 NZ21
See also Tees-Side Airport

★★★75% Headlam Hall
Headlam, Gainford DL2 3HA
☎ 01325 730238 01325 730790
e-mail: admin@headlamhall.co.uk
web: www.headlamhall.co.uk
Dir: *2m N of A67 between Piercebridge and Gainford*
This impressive Jacobean hall lies in farmland north-east of Piercebridge which now includes a 9-hole golf course. The main house retains many historical features, including flagstone floors and a pillared hall. Bedrooms are well proportioned and traditionally styled. A converted coach house contains the more modern rooms, as well as a conference and leisure centre.
ROOMS: 19 en suite 15 annexe en suite (4 fmly) (10 GF) in all bedrooms s £80-£120; d £100-£140 (incl. bkfst) **LB** **FACILITIES:** STV 9 Fishing Sauna Gym Putt green **CONF:** Thtr 150 Class 40 Board 40 Del from £115 **PARKING:** 60 **NOTES:** in restaurant Closed 24-25 Dec Civ Wed 150

★★★73% Hall Garth Golf & Country Club
Coatham Mundeville DL1 3LU
☎ 01325 300400 01325 310083
e-mail: hallgarth@corushotels.com
web: www.corushotels.com
Dir: *A1(M) junct 59, A167 towards Darlington. After 600yds left at top of hill, hotel on right*

Peacefully situated in grounds that includes a golf course, this hotel is just a few minutes from the motorway network. The well-equipped bedrooms come in various styles, with the trendy modern rooms worth asking for. Public rooms include relaxing lounges, a fine-dining restaurant and a separate pub. The extensive leisure and conference facilities are an important focus here.
ROOMS: 40 en suite 11 annexe en suite (5 fmly) in 31 bedrooms s £98-£118; d £98-£118 **LB** **FACILITIES:** STV 9 Sauna Solarium Gym Putt green Jacuzzi Steam room Beauty Salon Xmas **CONF:** Thtr 300 Class 120 Board 80 Del from £100 **PARKING:** 150 **NOTES:** in restaurant Civ Wed 170

★★★69% The Croft
Croft-on-Tees DL2 2ST
☎ 01325 720319 01325 721252
e-mail: enquiries@croft-hotel.co.uk
Dir: *from Darlington take A167 Northallerton road. Hotel 3m S*
Set in the village of Croft, this hotel has undergone significant upgrading. Smart well-equipped accommodation features a series of themed bedrooms reflecting different eras and countries around the world. The impressive Raffles Restaurant sports a colonial style and offers with a contemporary brasserie menu.

ROOMS: 20 en suite (2 fmly) in all bedrooms s £100-£175; d £100-£175 (incl. bkfst) **LB** **FACILITIES:** STV Snooker Sauna Gym Xmas **CONF:** Thtr 200 Class 120 Board 50 Del from £140 **PARKING:** 60 **NOTES:** in restaurant Civ Wed 150

★★★68% Walworth Castle Hotel
Walworth DL2 2LY
☎ 01325 485470 01325 462257
e-mail: enquiries@walworthcastle.co.uk
web: www.walworthcastle.co.uk
Dir: *A1(M) junct 58 follow signs to Corbridge. Left at rdbt, left at The Dog pub. Hotel on left after 1m*
This 12th-century castle is privately owned and has been tastefully converted. Accommodation is offered in a range of styles, including an impressive suite and more compact rooms in an adjoining wing. Dinner can be taken in the fine dining Hansards Restaurant or the more relaxed Farmer's Bar. A popular venue for conferences and weddings.
ROOMS: 20 en suite 14 annexe en suite (4 fmly) in 6 bedrooms s £85-£150; d £95-£195 (incl. bkfst) **LB** **FACILITIES:** Xmas **CONF:** BC Thtr 150 Class 100 Board 80 Del from £95 **PARKING:** 100 **NOTES:** in restaurant

★★★64% The Blackwell Grange Hotel
Blackwell Grange DL3 8QH
☎ 0870 609 6121 & 01325 509955
01325 380899
e-mail: blackwellgrange@corushotels.com
web: www.corushotels.com
Dir: *on A167, 1.5m from central ring road*

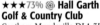

A popular venue for the corporate and wedding market, this fine period mansion is peacefully situated in its own grounds yet convenient for the motorway network. The pick of the bedrooms

continued

are in a courtyard building or the impressive feature rooms in the original house. Standard rooms are practical though well equipped.
ROOMS: 99 en suite 11 annexe en suite (3 fmly) (36 GF) ⊗ in 51 bedrooms s £89-£109; d £89-£109 **LB** **FACILITIES: Spa** STV Sauna Solarium Gym Jacuzzi Beauty room Xmas **CONF:** Thtr 300 Class 110 Board 50 Del from £110 **SERVICES:** Lift **PARKING:** 250 **NOTES:** ⊗ in restaurant Civ Wed 200

Premier Travel Inn Darlington

Morton Park Way, Morton Park DL1 4PJ
☎ 08701 977300 01325 373341
web: www.premiertravelinn.com
High quality, modern budget accommodation ideal for both families and business travellers. Spacious, en suite bedrooms feature bath and shower, satellite TV and many have telephones and modem points. The adjacent family restaurant features a wide and varied menu. For further details consult the Hotel Groups page.
ROOMS: 58 en suite s £46.95-£48.95; d £46.95-£48.95

DARRINGTON, West Yorkshire — Map 16 SE42

Premier Travel Inn Pontefract South

Great North Rd WF8 3BL
☎ 0870 9906386 0870 9906387
web: www.premiertravelinn.com
Dir: *Just off A1, 2m south of A1/M62 junct*
High quality, modern budget accommodation ideal for both families and business travellers. Spacious, en suite bedrooms feature bath and shower, satellite TV and many have telephones and modem points. The adjacent family restaurant features a wide and varied menu. For further details consult the Hotel Groups page.
ROOMS: 28 en suite s £46.95-£48.95; d £46.95-£48.95 **CONF:** Thtr 10 Class 10 Board 10

DARTFORD, Kent — Map 06 TQ57

★★★★75% Rowhill Grange Hotel & Spa

DA2 7QH
☎ 01322 615136 01322 615137
e-mail: admin@rowhillgrange.co.uk
web: www.rowhillgrange.co.uk
Dir: *M25 junct 3 take B2173 to Swanley, then B258 to Hextable*

Set within nine acres of mature woodland, including a Victorian walled garden, the hotel enjoys a tranquil setting, yet remains accessible to road networks. Bedrooms are stylishly and individually decorated, many have four-poster or sleigh beds. The hotel features a smart, conservatory restaurant and a more informal brasserie.
ROOMS: 38 en suite (3 fmly) (3 GF) ⊗ in all bedrooms s £155-£270; d £180-£330 (incl. bkfst) **LB** **FACILITIES: Spa** STV Sauna Solarium Gym Jacuzzi Beauty treatment, Hair salon, Aerobic studio, Japanese Therapy pool Xmas **CONF:** Thtr 160 Class 64 Board 34 Del from £165 **SERVICES:** Lift **PARKING:** 150 **NOTES:** ⊗ in restaurant Civ Wed 150

Campanile

1 Clipper Boulevard West,
Crossways Business Park DA2 6QN
☎ 01322 278925 01322 278948
e-mail: dartford@envergure.co.uk
web: www.envergure.fr
Dir: *follow signs for Ferry Terminal from Dartford Bridge*

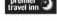

This modern building offers accommodation in smart, well-equipped bedrooms, all with en suite bathrooms. Refreshments may be taken at the informal Bistro. For further details consult the Hotel Groups page.
ROOMS: 125 en suite s £38.95-£50.95; d £38.95-£50.95 **CONF:** Thtr 50 Class 20 Board 40 Del £75

TV dinner?
Room service at three stars and above

DARTFORD, continued

Travelodge
Charles St, Greenhithe DA9 9AP
☎ 08700 850 950 🖷 01322 387854
web: www.travelodge.co.uk
Dir: *M25 junct 1a, take A206 towards Gravesend*
Travelodge offers good quality, good value, modern accommodation. Ideal for families, the spacious, en suite bedrooms include remote-control TV, tea and coffee-making facilities and comfortable beds. Meals can be taken at the nearby family restaurant. For further details consult the Hotel Groups page.
ROOMS: 65 en suite s fr £26; d fr £26

DARTMOUTH, Devon — Map 03 SX85

★★★74% Royal Castle
11 The Quay TQ6 9PS
☎ 01803 833033 🖷 01803 835445
e-mail: enquiry@royalcastle.co.uk
web: www.royalcastle.co.uk
Dir: *in centre of town, overlooking Inner Harbour*

At the edge of the harbour, this imposing 17th-century former coaching inn is filled with charm and character. Bedrooms are well equipped and comfortable; many have harbour views. A choice of quiet seating areas is offered in addition to both the traditional and contemporary bars. A variety of eating options is available, including the main restaurant which features accomplished cuisine and has lovely views.
ROOMS: 25 en suite (4 fmly) ⊗ in all bedrooms s £75-£85; d £165-£195 **LB** **FACILITIES:** STV Xmas **CONF:** Thtr 70 Class 40 Board 40 **PARKING:** 17 **NOTES:** ⊗ in restaurant Civ Wed 60

★★★73% The Dart Marina
Sandquay TQ6 9PH
☎ 01803 832 580 🖷 01803 835040
e-mail: info@dartmarinahotel.com
web: www.dartmarinahotel.com
Dir: *A3122 from Totnes to Dartmouth. Follow road which becomes College Way, before Higher Ferry. Hotel sharp left in Sandquay Rd*
Situated in an idyllic position by the marina, with direct access to the water and stunning views of the Dart Estuary. Bedrooms, or cabins as they are referred to, have a nautical theme and are named after famous ships, sailors and shipbuilders. Stylish and comfortable public areas enable guests to take full advantage of the waterside location.
ROOMS: 45 en suite 4 annexe en suite (4 fmly) (4 GF) ⊗ in all bedrooms s £79.50-£126.50; d £129-£173 (incl. bkfst) **LB**
FACILITIES: Spa Solarium Gym Jacuzzi Beauty treatments, Canoeing, Sailing Xmas **SERVICES:** Lift **PARKING:** 50 **NOTES:** ⊗ in restaurant Civ Wed 40

See advert on opposite page

★★★68% Stoke Lodge
Stoke Fleming TQ6 0RA
☎ 01803 770523 🖷 01803 770851
e-mail: mail@stokelodge.co.uk
web: www.stokelodge.co.uk
Dir: *2m S A379*
This family-run hotel continues to attract returning guests and is set in three acres of gardens and grounds with lovely views across to the sea. A range of leisure facilities is offered including both indoor and outdoor pools, along with a choice of comfortable lounges. Bedrooms are pleasantly appointed. The restaurant offers a choice of menus and an impressive wine list.
ROOMS: 25 en suite (5 fmly) s £58-£70; d £87-£112 (incl. bkfst) **LB**
FACILITIES: Spa Snooker Sauna Putt green Table tennis, Pool table Xmas **CONF:** Thtr 80 Class 60 Board 30 **PARKING:** 50
NOTES: ⊗ in restaurant

DARWEN, Lancashire — Map 15 SD62

Premier Travel Inn Blackburn South
Oakenhurst Farm, Eccleslink Rd BB3 0SN
☎ 08701 977 187 🖷 08701 977701
web: www.premiertravelinn.com
Dir: *directly off M6 junct 4, near Blackburn*
High quality, modern budget accommodation ideal for both families and business travellers. Spacious, en suite bedrooms feature bath and shower, satellite TV and many have telephones and modem points. The adjacent family restaurant features a wide and varied menu. For further details consult the Hotel Groups page.
ROOMS: 41 en suite s £46.95-£48.95; d £46.95-£48.95

Travelodge Blackburn
Darwen Motorway services BB3 0AT
☎ 08700 850 950 🖷 01254 776058
web: www.travelodge.co.uk
Travelodge offers good quality, good value, modern accommodation. Ideal for families, the spacious, en suite bedrooms include remote-control TV, tea and coffee-making facilities and comfortable beds. Meals can be taken at the nearby family restaurant. For further details consult the Hotel Groups page.
ROOMS: s fr £26; d fr £26

○ Hotel due to open in late 2005 or 2006
U Star rating not confirmed

DAVENTRY, Northamptonshire — Map 11 SP56

Top Hotel

★★★★ Fawsley Hall
Fawsley NN11 3BA
☎ 01327 892000 🖷 01327 892001
e-mail: reservations@fawsleyhall.com
web: www.fawsleyhall.com
Dir: *From A361 turn at 'Fawsley Hall' sign. Follow single track for 1.5m until reaching iron gates*
Dating back to the 15th century, this delightful hotel is peacefully located in beautiful gardens designed by 'Capability' Brown. Spacious, individually designed bedrooms and stylish public areas are beautifully furnished with antique and period pieces. Afternoon tea is served in the impressive Great Hall with its sumptuous deep cushioned sofas and real

continued

fires. Dinner in Knightly Restaurant offers imaginative cuisine with Mediterranean influences.

ROOMS: 43 en suite (2 GF) s £145-£155; d £185-£425 (incl. bkfst) **LB** **FACILITIES: Spa** STV Sauna Gym Putt green Jacuzzi Health & Beauty treatment rooms Xmas **CONF:** Thtr 100 Class 45 Board 45 Del from £210 **PARKING:** 100 **NOTES:** in restaurant Civ Wed 100

★★★★63% The Daventry Hotel

PARAMOUNT GROUP OF HOTELS

Sedgemoor Way NN11 5SG
☎ 01327 307000 01327 706313
e-mail: daventry@paramount-hotels.co.uk
web: www.paramount-hotels.co.uk
Dir: *N of Daventry on A361 Ring Road*

This modern, striking hotel overlooking Drayton Water boasts spacious public areas that include a good range of banqueting, meeting and leisure facilities. It is a popular venue for conferences. Bedrooms all have double beds and excellent showers.

ROOMS: 138 en suite in 100 bedrooms s £90-£170; d £105-£180 **LB** **FACILITIES: Spa** STV supervised Sauna Solarium Gym Jacuzzi Steam room Health & beauty salon Xmas **CONF:** BC Thtr 600 Class 200 Board 30 Del from £120 **SERVICES:** Lift **PARKING:** 350 **NOTES:** in restaurant Civ Wed 250

DAWLISH, Devon — Map 03 SX97

★★★71% Langstone Cliff

THE INDEPENDENTS HOTEL ASSOCIATION

Dawlish Warren EX7 0NA
☎ 01626 868000 01626 868006
e-mail: reception@langstone-hotel.co.uk
web: www.langstone-hotel.co.uk
Dir: *1.5m NE off A379 Exeter road to Dawlish Warren*

A family owned and run hotel, the Langstone Cliff offers a range of leisure, conference and function facilities. Bedrooms, many with sea views and balconies, are spacious, comfortable and well equipped. There are a number of attractive lounges and a well stocked bar. Dinner is served, often carvery style, in the restaurant.

ROOMS: 62 en suite 4 annexe en suite (52 fmly) (10 GF) s £62-£74; d £106-£140 (incl. bkfst) **LB** **FACILITIES:** STV Snooker Gym Table tennis, Golf practice area, Hair and beauty salon ch fac Xmas **CONF:** Thtr 400 Class 200 Board 80 Del from £95 **SERVICES:** Lift **PARKING:** 200 **NOTES:** Civ Wed 400

DEAL, Kent — Map 07 TR35

★★★72% Dunkerleys Hotel & Restaurant

19 Beach St CT14 7AH
☎ 01304 375016 01304 380187
e-mail: dunkerleysofdeal@btinternet.com
web: www.dunkerleys.co.uk
Dir: *from M20 or M2 follow signs for A258 Deal. Hotel close to Pier*

This hotel is situated on the seafront and is centrally located.

continued

Bedrooms are furnished to a high standard with a good range of amenities. The restaurant and bar are attractively decorated and menus make the best use of local ingredients with a strong emphasis on seafood. Service throughout is friendly and attentive.

ROOMS: 16 en suite (2 fmly) s fr £65; d fr £100 (incl. bkfst) **LB** **FACILITIES:** STV Xmas **NOTES:** in restaurant RS Mon morning

DEBENHAM, Suffolk — Map 13 TM16

Restaurant with Rooms

The Angel Inn

5 High St IP14 6QL
☎ 01728 860954 01728 861854
e-mail: d.given@btconnect.com
Dir: *A14 junct 51, 2m A140 right for Stonhams, follow Debenham signs, approx 3m*

Expect a warm welcome at this charming inn, set in the heart of this peaceful village. Public rooms include a cosy lounge bar and a comfortable restaurant with pine furniture. Bedrooms are generally quite spacious; each one is simply decorated, tastefully furnished and equipped with modern facilities.

ROOMS: 3 en suite (1 fmly) in all bedrooms s £40-£50; d £60-£70 (incl. bkfst) **FACILITIES:** Xmas **CONF:** Thtr 30 Class 30 Board 30 Del from £40 **PARKING:** 14 **NOTES:** in restaurant

Late for dinner? Quality standards mean that last orders for dinner vary according to star rating and should be no earlier than:
★★ 7.00pm ★★★ 8:00pm ★★★★ 9:00pm
★★★★★ 10:00pm

DEDDINGTON, Oxfordshire — Map 11 SP43

★★★70% Deddington Arms

Horsefair OX15 0SH
☎ 0800 3287031 01869 338364
01869 337010
e-mail: deddarms@oxfordshire-hotels.co.uk
web: www.deddington-arms-hotel.co.uk
Dir: *From S – M40 junct 10 signed Northampton onto A43. 1st rdbt left to Aynho and left to Deddington. From N – M40 junct 11 to Banbury. Through Banbury to hospital and Adderbury on A4260, then to Deddington*

This charming and friendly old inn is conveniently located off the Market Square. The well-equipped bedrooms are comfortably appointed and either situated in the main building or a purpose built courtyard wing. The bar is full of character and the delightful restaurant enjoys well-deserved local popularity.
ROOMS: 27 en suite (4 fmly) (9 GF) in 7 bedrooms s £85-£99; d £95-£120 (incl. bkfst) **LB FACILITIES:** STV Many facilities avaliable locally Xmas **CONF:** Thtr 40 Class 20 Board 25 Del £135 **PARKING:** 36 **NOTES:** in restaurant

★★★68% Holcombe Hotel & Restaurant

High St OX15 0SL
☎ 01869 338274 01869 337010
e-mail: holcombe@oxfordshire-hotels.co.uk
web: www.holcombe-hotel.co.uk
Dir: *on A4260 (Banbury to Oxford road). From M40 junct 11 follow Adderbury signs, then Deddington. From M40 junct 10 take B4100 to Aynho, then B4031 to Deddington*

This hotel enjoys a convenient roadside location, within easy reach of the village centre. Public areas include the stylish Peppers bar and an eye-catching restaurant serving pasta, pizzas and other specialities; in the warmer months the gardens offer a peaceful place in which to relax. Bedrooms are traditional in design with many thoughtful touches.
ROOMS: 17 en suite (3 fmly) in 4 bedrooms s £85-£99; d £95-£120 (incl. bkfst) **LB FACILITIES:** Xmas **CONF:** Thtr 25 Class 15 Board 18 Del £135 **PARKING:** 40 **NOTES:** in restaurant

DEDHAM, Essex — Map 13 TM03

Top Hotel

★★★ Maison Talbooth

Stratford Rd CO7 6HN
☎ 01206 322367 01206 322752
e-mail: maison@milsomhotels.co.uk
web: www.milsomhotels.com
Dir: *A12 towards Ipswich, 1st turning signed Dedham, follow road until left bend, take right turn. Hotel 1m on right*

A Victorian country house hotel situated in a peaceful rural location amidst pretty landscaped grounds overlooking the Stour River valley. Public areas include a comfortable drawing room where guests may take afternoon tea or snacks. Residents are chauffeured to the popular Le Talbooth Restaurant just a mile away for dinner. The spacious bedrooms are individually decorated, tastefully furnished, have lovely co-ordinated fabrics and many thoughtful touches. Hospitality is warm and friendly and quality service is to be expected.
ROOMS: 10 en suite (1 fmly) (5 GF) s £120-£180; d £165-£275 (incl. bkfst) **LB FACILITIES:** STV Jacuzzi Garden chess, croquet Xmas **CONF:** Thtr 30 Class 20 Board 16 Del £170 **PARKING:** 20 **NOTES:** Civ Wed 50

★★★69% milsoms

Stratford Rd, Dedham CO7 6HW
☎ 01206 322795 01206 323689
e-mail: milsoms@milsomhotels.com
web: www.milsomhotels.com
Dir: *6m N of Colchester off A12, turn off to Stratford St Mary/Dedham. Turn right over A12 hotel on left*

Situated in the Dedham Vale, an Area of Outstanding Natural Beauty, this is the perfect base to explore the countryside on the Essex/Suffolk border. Milsoms is styled along the lines of a contemporary 'gastro bar' combining good food served in an

continued

informal atmosphere, with stylish and well-appointed accommodation.
ROOMS: 15 en suite (3 fmly) (4 GF) ⊗ in all bedrooms s fr £75; d fr £95 **FACILITIES:** STV ♫ Xmas **CONF:** Board 14 Del from £140 **PARKING:** 70

DERBY, Derbyshire — Map 11 SK33

★★★★74% ⓖ **Menzies Mickleover Court**
Etwall Rd, Mickleover DE3 0XX
☎ 01332 521234 🖷 01332 521238

e-mail: mickleovercourt@menzies-hotels.co.uk
web: www.menzies-hotels.co.uk
Dir: Take A50 towards Derby, leave at junct 5 and follow A516 towards Derby, take exit signed Mickleover
Located close to Derby, this large, modern hotel is well suited for both conference and leisure guests. Bedrooms are spacious, with some traditional rooms and some more contemporary in style. A choice of two restaurants, a superb indoor leisure centre and excellent conference and leisure facilities are popular with both residents and visitors.
ROOMS: 99 en suite (20 fmly) ⊗ in 45 bedrooms s £150; d £150 **LB**
FACILITIES: STV ☞ Sauna Solarium Gym Jacuzzi Beauty salon, Steam room Xmas **CONF:** Thtr 200 Class 80 Board 40 Del £145
SERVICES: Lift air con **PARKING:** 270 **NOTES:** ✗ ⊗ in restaurant Civ Wed

★★★★67% ⓖ *Marriott Breadsall Priory Hotel, Country Club*
Moor Rd DE7 6DL
☎ 01332 832235 🖷 01332 833509
web: www.marriott.co.uk
(For full entry see Breadsall)

Marriott.
HOTELS & RESORTS

★★★76% **Midland**
Midland Rd DE1 2SQ
☎ 01332 345894 🖷 01332 293522
e-mail: sales@midland-derby.co.uk
web: www.midland-derby.co.uk
Dir: opposite Derby railway station

This early Victorian hotel situated opposite Derby Midland Station provides very comfortable accommodation. The executive rooms are ideal for business travellers, equipped with writing desks and fax/computer points. Public rooms include a comfortable lounge and a popular restaurant. Service is skilled, attentive and friendly. There is also a walled garden and private car parking.
ROOMS: 100 en suite ⊗ in 75 bedrooms s £64-£123; d £64-£133 **LB**
FACILITIES: ♫ **CONF:** Thtr 150 Class 50 Board 40 Del from £115
SERVICES: Lift **PARKING:** 90 **NOTES:** ✗ ⊗ in restaurant Closed 24-26 Dec & 1 Jan Civ Wed 150

See advert on this page

DERBY, continued

★★★68% Aston Court Hotel & Conference Centre
Midland Rd DE1 2SL
☎ 01332 342716 🖹 01332 293503
e-mail: astoncourtderby@hotelres.co.uk
Dir: *Midland Road opposite entrance of the Derby Railway Station*
Situated just a few minutes from the city centre and opposite the station, this hotel benefited from a massive refurbishment. Bedrooms are very smart, and executive rooms are available. Public rooms provide comfort and contemporary surroundings in which to relax. The Cavendish Restaurant offers traditional cuisine.
ROOMS: 55 en suite (5 fmly) (6 GF) ⊗ in 36 bedrooms
FACILITIES: STV More facilities available at a nearby health club ♫ Xmas
CONF: BC Thtr 250 Class 90 Board 65 Del from £124.50
SERVICES: Lift **PARKING:** 70 **NOTES:** ⊗ in restaurant

★★★67% Littleover Lodge
222 Rykneld Rd, Littleover DE23 7AN
☎ 01332 510161 🖹 01332 514010
e-mail: enquiries@littleoverlodge.co.uk
web: www.littleoverlodge.co.uk
Dir: *A38 towards Derby approx 1m on left slip lane signed Littleover/Mickleover/Findon, take 2nd exit off island marked Littleover 0.25m on right*
Situated in a rural location this friendly hotel offers modern bedrooms with direct access from the car park. Two styles of dining are available - an informal carvery operation which is very popular locally, and a more formal restaurant experience at both lunch and dinner every day.
ROOMS: 16 en suite (3 fmly) (8 GF) s £55-£80; d £55-£90 (incl. bkfst) **LB** **FACILITIES:** STV ♫ Xmas **PARKING:** 75 **NOTES:** ⊗ in restaurant
See advert on page 183

★★★65% Hotel Ristorante La Gondola
220 Osmaston Rd DE23 8JX
☎ 01332 332895 🖹 01332 384512
e-mail: service@la-gondola.co.uk
web: www.la-gondola.co.uk
Dir: *on A514 towards Melbourne*
Imaginatively designed and well-equipped bedrooms, including a spacious family suite, are offered at this conveniently located Georgian house. Situated between the inner and outer ring roads and close to the General Hospital. There are two small comfortable lounges, a well-established Italian restaurant and conference and banqueting rooms are available.
ROOMS: 20 rms (19 en suite) (7 fmly) (4 GF) s £64.50-£69.50; d £69.50-£77.50 (incl. bkfst) **LB** **FACILITIES:** STV Xmas **CONF:** BC Thtr 120 Class 60 Board 100 Del from £103 **PARKING:** 70 **NOTES:** ✗

★★★63% International
288 Burton Rd DE23 6AD
☎ 01332 369321 🖹 01332 294430
e-mail: internationalhotel.derby@virgin.net
Dir: *0.5m from city centre on A5250*
Within easy reach of the city centre, this hotel offers comfortable, modern public rooms. An extensive range of dishes is served in the pleasant restaurant. There is a wide range of bedroom sizes and styles, and each room is very well equipped; some suites are also available, and parking is a bonus.
ROOMS: 41 en suite 21 annexe en suite (4 fmly) ⊗ in 28 bedrooms s £48.50-£87; d £55-£96 (incl. bkfst) **LB** **FACILITIES:** STV ♫ Xmas **CONF:** Thtr 100 Class 40 Board 40 Del from £102 **SERVICES:** Lift **PARKING:** 100 **NOTES:** Civ Wed 100

♫ Entertainment

⌂ *Days Hotel Derby*
Derbyshire C C Ground, Pentagon Roundabout, Nottingham Rd DE21 6DA
☎ 01332 363600 🖹 01332 200630
e-mail: derby@kewgreen.co.uk
web: www.dayshotelderby.com
Dir: *M1 junct 25, take A52 towards Derby. At Pentagon rdbt take 4th exit and turn into cricket club*
This modern building offers accommodation in smart, spacious and well-equipped bedrooms, suitable for families and business travellers, and all with en suite bathrooms. Continental breakfast is available and other refreshments may be taken at the nearby family restaurant. For further details consult the Hotel Groups page.
ROOMS: 100 en suite **CONF:** Thtr 50 Class 25 Board 18

⌂ *European Inn*
Midland Rd DE1 2SL
☎ 01332 292000 🖹 01332 293940
e-mail: admin@euro-derby.co.uk
web: www.euro-derby.co.uk
Dir: *City centre, 200yds from railway station*
Excellent value accommodation is provided at this modern lodge. Bedrooms are well appointed and equipped with modern facilities. Shops form part of the complex and include an Italian pizza restaurant. A good choice of English breakfast is served buffet-style in the breakfast room; takeaway meals can also be eaten here.
ROOMS: 88 en suite **CONF:** Thtr 60 Class 30 Board 25

⌂ Innkeeper's Lodge Derby
Nottingham Rd, Chaddesdon DE21 6LZ
☎ 0870 243 0500 & 01332 662504
🖹 01332 673306
web: www.innkeeperslodge.com
Dir: *from M1 junct 25 take A52 towards Derby, take exit signed Spondon & Chaddesden, at rdbt take exit signed Chaddesden pass Asda store, 1m at lights right into car park*
A growing concept in the travel accommodation market. Smart rooms meet essential business requirements but also have home comforts. Dining options include all-day menus plus the added advantage of breakfast, which is included in the room price. For further details consult the Hotel Groups page.
ROOMS: 29 en suite s £48-£52; d £48-£52

⌂ Premier Travel Inn Derby East
The Wyvern Business Park, Chaddesden Sidings DE21 6BF
☎ 0870 238 3313 🖹 01332 667827
web: www.premiertravelinn.com
Dir: *From M1 junct 25 follow A52 to Derby. After 6.5m take exit for Wyvern/Pride Park. 1st exit at rdbt (A52 Nottingham), straight over next rdbt. Inn on left*
High quality, modern budget accommodation ideal for both families and business travellers. Spacious, en suite bedrooms feature bath and shower, satellite TV and many have telephones and modem points. The adjacent family restaurant features a wide and varied menu. For further details consult the Hotel Groups page.
ROOMS: 82 en suite s £49.95-£52.95; d £49.95-£52.95

⌂ Premier Travel Inn Derby North West
95 Ashbourne Rd, Mackworth DE22 4LZ
☎ 0870 9906606 🖹 0870 9906607
web: www.premiertravelinn.com
Dir: *Exit M1 junct 25 onto A52 towards Derby. At Pentagon Island straight ahead towards city centre. Follow A52/Ashbourne signs into Mackworth*
High quality, modern budget accommodation ideal for both
continued

families and business travellers. Spacious, en suite bedrooms feature bath and shower, satellite TV and many have telephones and modem points. The adjacent family restaurant features a wide and varied menu. For further details consult the Hotel Groups page.
ROOMS: 22 en suite s £49.95-£52.95; d £49.95-£52.95

⇧ Premier Travel Inn Derby South

Foresters Leisure Park, Osmaston Park Rd
DE23 8AG
☎ 0870 9906306 🖷 0870 9906307
web: www.premiertravelinn.com
Dir: *On A5111 in Derby. Exit M1 junct 24 onto A6 to Derby. Left onto A5111 ring road for 2m*
High quality, modern budget accommodation ideal for both families and business travellers. Spacious, en suite bedrooms feature bath and shower, satellite TV and many have telephones and modem points. The adjacent family restaurant features a wide and varied menu. For further details consult the Hotel Groups page.
ROOMS: 27 en suite s £49.95-£52.95; d £49.95-£52.95

⇧ Premier Travel Inn Derby West

Uttoxeter New Rd, Manor Park Way DE22 3HN
☎ 08701 977072 🖷 01332 207506
web: www.premiertravelinn.com
Dir: *M1 junct 25 take A38 W towards Burton-upon-Trent. Left at island (city hospital), right at lights, 3rd exit (15m)*
High quality, modern budget accommodation ideal for both families and business travellers. Spacious, en suite bedrooms feature bath and shower, satellite TV and many have telephones and modem points. The adjacent family restaurant features a wide and varied menu. For further details consult the Hotel Groups page.
ROOMS: 43 en suite s £47.95-£50.95; d £47.95-£50.95 **CONF:** Thtr 15

⇧ Travelodge

Kingsway, Rowditch DE22 3NN
☎ 08700 850 950 🖷 01332 367255
web: www.travelodge.co.uk
Dir: *A38 Derby north, exit at ringroad, A5111. Lodge 0.25m on left*
Travelodge offers good quality, good value, modern accommodation. Ideal for families, the spacious, en suite bedrooms include remote-control TV, tea and coffee-making facilities and comfortable beds. Meals can be taken at the nearby family restaurant. For further details consult the Hotel Groups page.
ROOMS: 40 en suite s fr £26; d fr £26

DERBY SERVICE AREA (A50), Derbyshire — Map 11 SK42

⇧ Days Inn Donnington

Welcome Break Services DE72 2WW
☎ 01332 799666 🖷 01332 794166
e-mail: donnington.hotel@welcomebreak.co.uk
web: www.welcomebreak.co.uk
Dir: *M1 junct 24/24a, onto A50 towards Stoke/Derby. Hotel between juncts 1 & 2*
This modern building offers accommodation in smart, spacious and well-equipped bedrooms, suitable for families and business travellers, and all with en suite bathrooms. Continental breakfast is available and other refreshments may be taken at the nearby family restaurant. For further details see the Hotel Groups page.
ROOMS: 47 en suite s £45-£60; d £45-£60 **CONF:** Thtr 10 Class 10 Board 10

> We have indicated only the hotels that don't accept credit or debit cards

DEREHAM, Norfolk — Map 13 TF91

★★70% George

Swaffham Rd NR19 2AZ
☎ 01362 696801 🖷 01362 695711
Dir: *From A47 follow signs for Dereham, on High St to the memorial, hotel on left*
Delightful old Inn situated in the heart of this bustling market town and ideally placed for touring Norfolk. The spacious bedrooms are pleasantly decorated, furnished with pine pieces and have many thoughtful touches. Public rooms include a smart restaurant, a stylish lounge with leather sofas, a conservatory dining room and a large lounge bar.
ROOMS: 8 en suite (2 fmly) s £45-£60; d £65-£80 (incl. bkfst) **LB**
PARKING: 50 **NOTES:** ✗ ⊗ in restaurant Closed 26 Dec

DEVIZES, Wiltshire — Map 04 SU06

★★★64% *Bear*

Market Place SN10 1HS
☎ 01380 722444 🖷 01380 722450
e-mail: info@thebearhotel.net
web: www.thebearhotel.net
Dir: *in town centre*
Set in the market place of this small Wiltshire town, this attractive hotel has a popular local following. The individually furnished and decorated bedrooms vary in size. The attractive lounge offers a quiet area for residents to enjoy afternoon tea. Homemade cakes are available throughout the day and the restaurant serves enjoyable meals.
ROOMS: 24 en suite (5 fmly) ⊗ in all bedrooms **FACILITIES:** Solarium **CONF:** Thtr 100 Class 60 Board 60 **SERVICES:** Lift **NOTES:** ⊗ in restaurant Closed 25-26 Dec

DEWSBURY, West Yorkshire — Map 16 SE22

★★★67% Heath Cottage Hotel & Restaurant

Wakefield Rd WF12 8ET
☎ 01924 465399 🖷 01924 459405
e-mail: bookings@heathcottage.co.uk
web: www.heathcottage.co.uk
Dir: *M1 junct 40/A638 for 2.5m towards Dewsbury. Hotel before traffic lights, opposite Earlsheaton Cemetery*

Standing in an acre of grounds, Heath Cottage is just two and a half miles from the M1. It has extensive parking and the service is friendly and professional. All the bedrooms are modern and well appointed and some are in a converted stable building. The lounge bar and restaurant are air conditioned.
ROOMS: 22 en suite 6 annexe en suite (3 fmly) (2 GF) ⊗ in 18 bedrooms s £52-£63; d £68-£74 (incl. bkfst) **LB** **FACILITIES:** Xmas **CONF:** Thtr 80 Class 50 Board 30 **PARKING:** 80 **NOTES:** ✗ ⊗ in restaurant Civ Wed 90

DEWSBURY, continued

★★★66% Healds Hall
Leeds Rd, Liversedge WF15 6JA
☎ 01924 409112 01924 401895
e-mail: enquire@healdshall.co.uk
web: www.healdshall.co.uk
Dir: *on A62 between Leeds and Huddersfield. 50yds on left after Swan Pub traffic lights*

This 18th-century house in the heart of West Yorkshire offers comfortable and well-equipped accommodation and excellent hospitality. The hotel has earned a good local reputation for the quality of its food and offers a choice of casual or more formal dining styles, with a wide range of dishes on the various menus.
ROOMS: 24 en suite (3 fmly) (3 GF) in 4 bedrooms s £40-£61; d £60-£75 (incl. bkfst) **LB** **CONF:** Thtr 100 Class 60 Board 80 Del from £90 **PARKING:** 90 **NOTES:** in restaurant Closed New Years Day and BH Mondays Civ Wed 100

DIDCOT, Oxfordshire Map 05 SU59

Premier Travel Inn Didcot
Milton Interchange, Milton OX14 4DP
☎ 08701 977073 01235 820465
web: www.premiertravelinn.com
Dir: *on A4130 at junct with A34*
High quality, modern budget accommodation ideal for both families and business travellers. Spacious, en suite bedrooms feature bath and shower, satellite TV and many have telephones and modem points. The adjacent family restaurant features a wide and varied menu. For further details consult the Hotel Groups page.
ROOMS: 60 en suite s £46.95-£49.95; d £46.95-£49.95

DIDSBURY, Greater Manchester Map 16 SJ89

Travelodge Manchester South
Kingsway M20 5PG
☎ 08700 850 950 0161 448 0399
web: www.travelodge.co.uk
Dir: *M60 junct 4, follow A34 towards Didsbury. Lodge at Parswood Leisure Park*
Travelodge offers good quality, good value, modern accommodation. Ideal for families, the spacious, en suite bedrooms include remote-control TV, tea and coffee-making facilities and comfortable beds. Meals can be taken at the nearby family restaurant. For further details consult the Hotel Groups page.
ROOMS: 62 en suite s fr £26; d fr £26

Packed in a hurry? Ironing facilities should be available at all star levels, either in the rooms or on request

DONCASTER, South Yorkshire Map 16 SE50

★★★★70% Mount Pleasant
Great North Rd DN11 0HW
☎ 01302 868696 & 868219 01302 865130
e-mail: reception@mountpleasant.co.uk
web: www.bw-mountpleasant.co.uk
(For full entry see Rossington)

★★★69% Regent
Regent Square DN1 2DS
☎ 01302 364180 01302 322331
e-mail: admin@theregenthotel.co.uk
web: www.theregenthotel.co.uk
Dir: *on corner of A630 & A638, 1m from racecourse*
This town centre hotel overlooks a delightful small square. Public rooms include a newly extended and modern style bar and the delightful restaurant, where an interesting range of dishes is offered. Service is friendly and attentive. Most bedrooms have been furnished in a modern style with contemporary colour schemes.
ROOMS: 52 en suite (6 fmly) (8 GF) s £60-£95; d £75-£100 (incl. bkfst) **LB** **FACILITIES:** STV ♫ **CONF:** Thtr 150 Class 50 Board 40 Del from £125 **SERVICES:** Lift **PARKING:** 20 **NOTES:** in restaurant Closed New Years Day Xmas Day RS Bank Hols Civ Wed 100

★★★68% Danum
High St DN1 1DN
☎ 01302 342261 01302 329034
e-mail: info@danumhotel.com
web: www.danumhotel.co.uk
Dir: *M18 junct 3, A6182 to Doncaster. Over rdbt, right at next. Right at 'give way' sign, left at mini rdbt, hotel ahead*
Situated in the centre of the town, this Edwardian hotel offers spacious public rooms together with soundly equipped accommodation. A pleasant restaurant on the first floor serves quality dinners, and especially negotiated rates at a local leisure centre are offered.
ROOMS: 66 en suite (5 fmly) in 12 bedrooms s £55-£75; d £70-£105 (incl. bkfst) **LB** **FACILITIES:** STV Jacuzzi special rates with Cannons health club ♫ Xmas **CONF:** Thtr 350 Class 160 Board 100 Del from £94 **SERVICES:** Lift **PARKING:** 36 **NOTES:** Civ Wed 250

★★★63% Grand St Leger
Bennetthorpe DN2 6AX
☎ 01302 364111 01302 329865
e-mail: sales@grandstleger.com
web: www.grandstleger.com
Dir: *follow Doncaster Racecourse signs, at Racecourse rdbt hotel on corner*
This friendly hotel is located next to the racecourse and is only ten minutes' walk from the town centre. There is a cheerful bar-lounge and an elegant restaurant offering an extensive choice of dishes. The bedrooms are comfortable and thoughtfully equipped.
ROOMS: 20 en suite in all bedrooms s £50-£70; d £65-£85 (incl. bkfst) **LB** **CONF:** Thtr 80 Class 50 Board 50 Del from £120 **PARKING:** 28 **NOTES:** in restaurant RS Xmas Day (open for lunch only) Civ Wed 60

Campanile
Doncaster Leisure Park, Bawtry Rd DN4 7PD
☎ 01302 370770 01302 370813
e-mail: doncaster@envergure.co.uk
web: www.envergure.fr
Dir: *follow signs to Doncaster Leisure Centre, left at rdbt before Dome complex*
This modern building offers accommodation in smart, well-equipped bedrooms, all with en suite bathrooms. Refreshments

continued

may be taken at the informal Bistro. For further details consult the Hotel Groups page.

ROOMS: 50 en suite **CONF:** Thtr 35 Class 18 Board 24 Del £70

⌂ Innkeeper's Lodge Doncaster
Bawtry Rd, Bessacarr DN4 7BS
☎ 01302 370037
web: www.innkeeperslodge.com
A growing concept in the travel accommodation market. Smart rooms meet essential business requirements but also have home comforts. Dining options include all-day menus plus the added advantage of breakfast, which is included in the room price. For further details consult the Hotel Groups page.
ROOMS: 24 rms s £45-£49.95; d £45-£49.95 **CONF:** Thtr 40 Class 30 Board 20

⌂ Premier Travel Inn Doncaster
Wilmington Dr, Doncaster Carr DN4 5PJ
☎ 08701 977074 🖷 01302 364811
web: www.premiertravelinn.com
***Dir:** off A6182 near junct with access road to M18 junct 3*
High quality, modern budget accommodation ideal for both families and business travellers. Spacious, en suite bedrooms feature bath and shower, satellite TV and many have telephones and modem points. The adjacent family restaurant features a wide and varied menu. For further details consult the Hotel Groups page.
ROOMS: 42 en suite s £49.95; d £49.95 **CONF:** Class 32

⌂ Travelodge (Doncaster North)
DN8 5GS
☎ 08700 850 950 🖷 01302 845469
web: www.travelodge.co.uk
***Dir:** M18 junct 5/M180*
Travelodge offers good quality, good value, modern accommodation. Ideal for families, the spacious, en suite bedrooms include remote-control TV, tea and coffee-making facilities and comfortable beds. Meals can be taken at the nearby family restaurant. For further details consult the Hotel Groups page.
ROOMS: 39 en suite s fr £26; d fr £26

DONNINGTON See Telford

DORCHESTER, Dorset — Map 04 SY69

★★★66% The Wessex Royale
High West St DT1 1UP
☎ 01305 262660 🖷 01305 251941
e-mail: info@wessex-royale-hotel.com
web: www.wessex-royale-hotel.com
This centrally situated Georgian townhouse dates from 1756 but has been sympathetically refurbished to combine its historic charm with modern comforts. Durberville's Restaurant is a relaxed

continued

location for enjoying innovative food, and the hotel offers the benefit of limited courtyard parking and a smart conservatory ideal for functions.
ROOMS: 25 en suite 2 annexe en suite (2 fmly) ⊘ in 10 bedrooms s £75-£115; d £95-£149 (incl. bkfst) **FACILITIES:** STV **CONF:** Thtr 80 Class 40 Board 40 **PARKING:** 12 **NOTES:** ✗ ⊘ in restaurant

DORCHESTER (ON THAMES), Oxfordshire — Map 05 SU59

★★★71% ❀❀ White Hart
High St OX10 7HN
☎ 01865 340074 🖷 01865 341082
e-mail: whitehart@oxfordshire-hotels.co.uk
web: www.oxfordshire-hotels.co.uk
***Dir:** M40 junct 6, take B4009 through Watlington & Benson to A4074. Follow signs to Dorchester. Hotel on right*

Period charm and character are plentiful throughout this 17th-century coaching inn, which is situated in the heart of a picturesque village. The spacious bedrooms are individually decorated and thoughtfully equipped. Public rooms include a cosy bar, a choice of lounges and an atmospheric restaurant, complete with vaulted timber ceiling.
ROOMS: 22 en suite 4 annexe en suite (2 fmly) (9 GF) ⊘ in 6 bedrooms s £85-£105; d £115-£135 (incl. bkfst) **LB** **FACILITIES:** STV Xmas **CONF:** BC Thtr 30 Class 20 Board 18 Del from £135 **PARKING:** 36 **NOTES:** ✗

★★★64% ❀ George
25 High St OX10 7HH
☎ 01865 340404 🖷 01865 341620
e-mail: thegeorgehotel@fsmail.net
***Dir:** M40 junct 6 onto B4009 through Watlington & Benson. Take A4074 at BP petrol station, follow signs to Dorchester. Hotel on left*

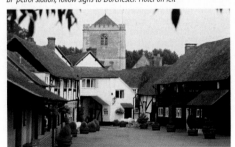

Full of character and charm, this quintessential coaching inn stands beside Dorchester Abbey and dates back to the 15th century. The bedrooms are decorated in keeping with the style of the building, and are divided between the main house and the

continued on p188

courtyard. Meals can be taken either in the lively, atmospheric bar or in the intimate restaurant.
ROOMS: 9 en suite 8 annexe en suite (1 fmly) ⊗ in 4 bedrooms s £60-£70; d £75-£120 (incl. bkfst) **LB CONF:** Thtr 40 Class 36 Board 24 Del from £120 **PARKING:** 75 **NOTES:** ⊗ in restaurant

DORKING, Surrey Map 06 TQ14

D

★★★★70% ⊛ **The Burford Bridge**
Burford Bridge, Box Hill RH5 6BX
☎ 0870 400 8283 🖷 01306 880386
e-mail: burfordbridge@macdonald-hotels.co.uk
web: www.macdonald-hotels.co.uk
Dir: M25 junct 9 follow Dorking signs on A24. Hotel on left

Steeped in history, this hotel was reputedly where Lord Nelson and Lady Hamilton met for the last time, and it is said that the landscape around the hotel has inspired poets. The hotel has benefited from refurbishment throughout, creating a more contemporary feel. The grounds, running down to the River Mole, are extensive, and there are good transport links to major centres, including London.
ROOMS: 57 en suite (14 fmly) (8 GF) ⊗ in 37 bedrooms s £110-£170; d £120-£180 **LB FACILITIES:** STV ⛳ ♪♪ Putt green ♫ Xmas **CONF:** Thtr 300 Class 100 Board 60 Del from £150 **PARKING:** 140 **NOTES:** ⊗ in restaurant Civ Wed 200

★★★68% **The White Horse**
High St RH4 1BE
☎ 0870 400 8282 🖷 01306 887241
e-mail: whitehorsedorking@
macdonald-hotels.co.uk
web: www.macdonald-hotels.co.uk
Dir: M25 junct 9 take A24 S towards Dorking. Hotel in centre of town
The hotel was first established as an inn in 1750, although parts of the building date back as far as the 15th century. Its town centre location and Dickensian charm have long made this a popular destination for travellers. Character features include beamed ceilings, open fires and four-poster beds.
ROOMS: 37 en suite 41 annexe en suite (2 fmly) (5 GF) ⊗ in 59 bedrooms **FACILITIES:** STV Xmas **CONF:** Thtr 50 Class 30 Board 30 **PARKING:** 73 **NOTES:** ⊗ in restaurant

★★★61% **Gatton Manor Hotel Golf & Country Club**
Standon Ln RH5 5PQ
☎ 01306 627555 🖷 01306 627713
e-mail: gattonmanor@enterprise.net
(For full entry see Ockley)

⇧ **Travelodge**
Reigate Rd RH4 1QB
☎ 08700 850 950 🖷 01306 741673
web: www.travelodge.co.uk
Dir: 0.5m E of Dorking, on A25
Travelodge offers good quality, good value, modern accommodation. Ideal for families, the spacious, en suite bedrooms include remote-control TV, tea and coffee-making facilities and comfortable beds. Meals can be taken at the nearby family restaurant. For further details consult the Hotel Groups page.
ROOMS: 55 en suite s fr £26; d fr £26

DORRIDGE, West Midlands Map 10 SP17

Restaurant with Rooms

♨ ⊛⊛ **The Forest**
25 Station Approach B93 8JA
☎ 01564 772120 🖷 01564 732680
e-mail: info@forest-hotel.com
web: www.forest-hotel.com
Dir: M42 junct 5, follow A4141 for 2m. After Knowle village turn right signed Dorridge in 1.5m. Left before rail bridge, hotel 200yds
This well-established restaurant with rooms is situated in the heart of Dorridge village, 30 minutes from both Stratford-upon-Avon and the Cotswolds. Rooms are very well equipped with modern facilities. Food is served in a choice of bars or in the restaurant, and there is also a function room.
ROOMS: 12 en suite ⊗ in all bedrooms s £92.50-£130; d £97.50-£140 (incl. bkfst) **CONF:** Thtr 100 Class 60 Board 40 Del from £120 **PARKING:** 50 **NOTES:** ✘ ⊗ in restaurant RS Sun eve Civ Wed 75

DOVER, Kent Map 07 TR34

★★★75% ⊛⊛ **Wallett's Court Country House Hotel & Spa**
West Cliffe, St Margarets-at-Cliffe CT15 6EW
☎ 01304 852424 & 0800 0351628 🖷 01304 853430
e-mail: wc@wallettscourt.com
Dir: from Dover take A258 towards Deal. 1st right to St Margarets-at-Cliffe & West Cliffe, 1m on right opposite West Cliffe church
Lovely Jacobean manor situated in a peaceful location on the outskirts of town. Bedrooms in the original house are traditionally furnished whereas the rooms in the courtyard buildings are more modern; all are equipped to a high standard. Public rooms include a smart bar, a lounge and a restaurant that utilises local organic produce.
ROOMS: 3 en suite 13 annexe en suite (2 fmly) (7 GF) s £99-£119; d £119-£159 (incl. bkfst) **LB FACILITIES:** Spa ⛲ ☂ Sauna Solarium Gym ♪♪ Putt green Jacuzzi Treatment suite, aromatherapy massage, golf pitching range, beauty therapy **CONF:** BC Thtr 25 Class 25 Board 16 Del from £169 **PARKING:** 30 **NOTES:** ✘ ⊗ in restaurant Closed 24-26 Dec

★★★71% **Best Western Churchill Hotel and Health Club**
Dover Waterfront CT17 9BP
☎ 01304 203633 🖷 01304 216320
e-mail: enquiries@churchill-hotel.com
web: www.bw-churchillhotel.co.uk
Dir: A20 follow signs for Hoverport, left onto seafront, hotel 800yds along
Attractive terraced waterfront hotel overlooking the harbour. The hotel offers a wide range of facilities including meeting rooms, health club, a hairdresser and beauty treatments. Some of the tastefully decorated bedrooms have balconies and many of the

continued

rooms have superb sea views. Public rooms include a large, open-plan lounge bar and a smart Bistro restaurant.

ROOMS: 81 en suite (5 fmly) ⊗ in 12 bedrooms **FACILITIES:** STV Sauna Solarium Gym Health Club, Hair & Beauty Salons Xmas **CONF:** Thtr 110 Class 60 Board 50 **SERVICES:** Lift **PARKING:** 32 **NOTES:** ✗ ⊗ in restaurant Civ Wed 100

★★★69% The Mildmay
78 Folkestone Rd CT17 9SF
☎ 01304 204278 🖷 01304 215342
e-mail: themildmayhotel@btopenworld.com
Dir: *on B2011 Dover to London road, 300yds from Dover Priory Railway Station*
This friendly, family-run hotel is ideally placed for the town centre, railway station and ferry terminal. The spacious bedrooms are pleasantly decorated and thoughtfully equipped with modern facilities. Public rooms include a large open-plan lounge bar with plush seating and a smartly appointed restaurant.
ROOMS: 21 en suite (3 fmly) (2 GF) ⊗ in 7 bedrooms s £50-£60; d £60-£80 (incl. bkfst) **PARKING:** 20 **NOTES:** ✗ ⊗ in restaurant

★★★69% Ramada Hotel Dover
Singledge Ln, Whitfield CT16 3EL
☎ 01304 821230 🖷 01304 825576
e-mail: reservations@ramadadover.co.uk
web: www.ramadadover.co.uk
Dir: *from M20 follow signs to A2 towards Canterbury. Turn right after Whitfield rdbt. From A2 towards Dover, turn left before Whitfield rdbt*
Modern purpose-built hotel situated in a quiet location between Dover and Canterbury, close to the ferry port and seaside. The open-plan public areas are contemporary in style; they include a lounge, a bar and the Bleriot's restaurant. The stylish bedrooms are simply decorated, have co-ordinated soft furnishings and many thoughtful extras.
ROOMS: 68 en suite (19 fmly) (68 GF) ⊗ in 56 bedrooms s £56-£115; d £56-£115 **FACILITIES:** STV Gym Xmas **CONF:** BC Thtr 60 Class 18 Board 20 Del from £105 **PARKING:** 80 **NOTES:** ✗ ⊗ in restaurant Civ Wed 45

⌂ Premier Travel Inn Dover Central
Marine Court, Marine Pde CT16 1LW
☎ 0870 9906516 🖷 0870 9906517
web: www.premiertravelinn.com
Dir: *In town centre adjacent to ferry terminal. Exit M20 junct 13 onto A20 for 8.2m*
High quality, modern budget accommodation ideal for both families and business travellers. Spacious, en suite bedrooms feature bath and shower, satellite TV and many have telephones and modem points. The adjacent family restaurant features a wide and varied menu. For further details consult the Hotel Groups page.
ROOMS: 100 en suite s £52.95; d £52.95

⌂ Premier Travel Inn Dover East
Jubilee Way, Guston Wood CT15 5FD
☎ 08701 977075 🖷 01304 240614
web: www.premiertravelinn.com
Dir: *on rdbt of A2 & A258*
High quality, modern budget accommodation ideal for both families and business travellers. Spacious, en suite bedrooms feature bath and shower, satellite TV and many have telephones and modem points. The adjacent family restaurant features a wide and varied menu. For further details consult the Hotel Groups page.
ROOMS: 40 en suite s £47.95-£50.95; d £47.95-£50.95

⌂ Premier Travel Inn Dover (West)
Folkestone Rd CT15 7AB
☎ 08701 977076 🖷 01304 214504
web: www.premiertravelinn.com
Dir: *M20 then A20 to Dover. Through tunnel, take 2nd exit onto B2011. Take 1st left at rbt . Inn is on the left, after 1 mile*
High quality, modern budget accommodation ideal for both families and business travellers. Spacious, en suite bedrooms feature bath and shower, satellite TV and many have telephones and modem points. The adjacent family restaurant features a wide and varied menu. For further details consult the Hotel Groups page.
ROOMS: 64 en suite s £46.95-£48.95; d £46.95-£48.95

DOWNHAM MARKET, Norfolk — Map 12 TF60

★★72% Castle
High St PE38 9HF
☎ 01366 384311 🖷 01366 384311
e-mail: howards@castle-hotel.com
Dir: *M11 take A10 for Ely into Downham Market, hotel opposite traffic lights, on corner of High St in town*
This popular coaching inn is situated close to the centre of town and has been welcoming guests for over 300 years. Well maintained public areas include a cosy lounge bar and two smartly appointed restaurants. Inviting bedrooms, some with four-poster beds, are attractively decorated, thoughtfully equipped, and have bright, modern decor.
ROOMS: 12 en suite s £65-£80; d £85-£99 (incl. bkfst) **LB** **FACILITIES:** Xmas **CONF:** Thtr 60 Class 30 Board 40 **PARKING:** 26 **NOTES:** ⊗ in restaurant

DRIFFIELD (GREAT), East Riding of Yorkshire — Map 17 TA05

★★★73% Bell
46 Market Place YO25 6AN
☎ 01377 256661 🖷 01377 253228
e-mail: bell@bestwestern.co.uk
Dir: *from A164, right at lights. Car park 50yds on left behind black railings*
This 250-year-old hotel incorporates the old corn exchange and the old town hall. It is furnished with antique and period pieces, and contains many items of local historical interest. The bedrooms vary in size, but all offer modern facilities and some have their own sitting rooms. The hotel has a relaxed and very friendly atmosphere. A newly refurbished spa provides a superb range of facilities and treatments.
ROOMS: 16 en suite (3 GF) ⊗ in 11 bedrooms s £78-£88; d £98-£108 (incl. bkfst) **LB** **FACILITIES: Spa** Squash Snooker Sauna Solarium Gym Jacuzzi Masseur, Hairdressing, Chiropody ♫ **CONF:** Thtr 150 Class 100 Board 40 **SERVICES:** Lift **PARKING:** 18 **NOTES:** ✗ No children 16yrs ⊗ in restaurant

⊗ No smoking

D

DROITWICH, Worcestershire
Map 10 SO86

★★★★67% *Château Impney*
WR9 0BN
☎ 01905 774411 📠 01905 772371
e-mail: chateau@impney.demon.co.uk
Dir: *on A38, 1m from M5 junct 5 towards Droitwich/Worcester*
Overlooking 120 acres of beautiful parkland, this elegant and imposing French-style château dates back to the 1800s. All bedrooms are furnished and equipped to modern standards, and come in a variety of sizes. The hotel has excellent conference, function, exhibition and leisure facilities.
ROOMS: 67 en suite 53 annexe en suite (10 fmly) **FACILITIES:** Sauna Solarium Gym 55 acres of parkland **CONF:** Thtr 1000 Class 550 Board 160 **SERVICES:** Lift **PARKING:** 1000 **NOTES:** ⊘ in restaurant Closed Xmas

★★★★65% *Raven*
Victoria Square WR9 8DQ
☎ 01905 772224 📠 01905 797100
e-mail: sales@ravenhotel.demon.co.uk
Dir: *in town centre on A38, 1.5m from M5 junct 5 towards Droitwich/Worcester*
Situated in the heart of the spa town, close to the Brine Baths, this timber-framed property dates back to the early 16th century. Considerably extended over the years, it provides comfortable, well-equipped accommodation. Public areas have a gentleman's club feel with leather sofas in the lounge and a relaxing bar, while the dessert trolley takes pride of place in the restaurant.
ROOMS: 72 en suite (1 fmly) **CONF:** Thtr 150 Class 70 Board 40 **SERVICES:** Lift **PARKING:** 250 **NOTES:** ⊘ in restaurant Closed Xmas

Travelodge
Rashwood Hill WR9 8DA
☎ 08700 850 950 📠 01527 861807
web: www.travelodge.co.uk
Dir: *0.5m W of M5 junct 5*
Travelodge offers good quality, good value, modern accommodation. Ideal for families, the spacious, en suite bedrooms include remote-control TV, tea and coffee-making facilities and comfortable beds. Meals can be taken at the nearby family restaurant. For further details consult the Hotel Groups page.
ROOMS: 32 en suite s fr £26; d fr £26

DUDLEY, West Midlands
Map 10 SO99
See also Himley

★★★★68% Copthorne Hotel Merry Hill-Dudley
The Waterfront, Level St, Brierley Hill DY5 1UR
☎ 01384 482882 📠 01384 482773
e-mail: apearson@mill-cop.com
web: www.copthorne.com/dudley
Dir: *follow signs for Merry Hill Centre*
The hotel enjoys a waterfront aspect and is close to the Merry Hill shopping mall. Polished marble floors, rich fabrics and striking interior design are features of the stylish public areas. Bedrooms are spacious and some have Connoisseur status, which includes the use of a private lounge. A modern leisure centre with pool occupies the lower level.
ROOMS: 138 en suite (14 fmly) ⊘ in 90 bedrooms s £70-£95; d £80-£105 **LB** **FACILITIES:** STV supervised Sauna Solarium Gym Jacuzzi Aerobics Beauty/massage therapists **CONF:** BC Thtr 570 Class 240 Board 60 Del from £135 **SERVICES:** Lift **PARKING:** 100 **NOTES:** Civ Wed 400

★★★63% Ward Arms
Birmingham Rd DY1 4RN
☎ 01384 458070 📠 01384 457502
e-mail: reservations@wardarms.co.uk
Dir: *M5 junct 2. 1st left at rdbt, 3rd exit at 2nd rdbt then1st exit at 3rd rdbt. Hotel on A4123, 200yds on left*
This busy and popular modern hotel is within easy reach of the M5, in the heart of the Black Country. The bedrooms are well equipped, and some are on ground floor. Public areas include the traditionally furnished conservatory restaurant and bar, where freshly prepared dishes are served.
ROOMS: 72 en suite (36 GF) ⊘ in 48 bedrooms s £75; d £75 **LB** **FACILITIES:** STV **CONF:** Thtr 140 Class 80 Board 60 Del £105 **PARKING:** 100 **NOTES:** ⊘ in restaurant Civ Wed 120

Travelodge Birmingham Dudley
Dudley Rd, Brierley Hill DY5 1LQ
☎ 08700 850 950 📠 0870 1911563
web: www.travelodge.co.uk
Dir: *3m W of Dudley, on A461*
Travelodge offers good quality, good value, modern accommodation. Ideal for families, the spacious, en suite bedrooms include remote-control TV, tea and coffee-making facilities and comfortable beds. Meals can be taken at the nearby family restaurant. For further details consult the Hotel Groups page.
ROOMS: 32 en suite s fr £26; d fr £26

DULVERTON, Somerset
Map 03 SS92

Top Hotel

★★ Ashwick House
TA22 9QD
☎ 01398 323868 📠 01398 323868
e-mail: ashwickhouse@talk21.com
Dir: *in Dulverton left at post office, 3m NW on B3223, over 2 cattlegrids, signed on left*
A small yet inviting Edwardian hotel, set on the edge of Exmoor in six beautiful acres above the breathtaking valley of the River Barle. Exuding a quintessential country-house atmosphere, the public areas include a galleried hall with a welcoming log fire, and stylish lounges, which boast deep sofas. Bedrooms are spacious, comfortable and are equipped with a host of thoughtful touches. Each evening a set menu, based on the finest local ingredients (with a choice of starter and dessert) is served.
ROOMS: 6 en suite ⊘ in 1 bedroom s fr £85; d fr £150 (incl. bkfst & dinner) **LB** **FACILITIES:** Solarium Xmas **PARKING:** 27 **NOTES:** No children 8yrs ⊘ in restaurant No credit cards accepted

★★63% Lion
Bank Square TA22 9BU
☎ 01398 323444 🖷 01398 323980
e-mail: jeffeveritt@tiscali.co.uk
Dir: *from A361 at Tiverton rdbt onto A396. Left at Exbridge onto B3223. Over bridge in Dulverton, hotel in Bank Sq*
Old-fashioned hospitality is always evident at this charming, traditional inn in the centre of Dulverton, an ideal base from which to explore Exmoor National Park. The bar is popular with locals and visitors alike, offering a variety of local real ales and quality meals. A pleasant dining room provides a quieter, non-smoking option.
ROOMS: 13 en suite (2 fmly) ⊗ in 2 bedrooms **FACILITIES:** Xmas **PARKING:** 6 **NOTES:** ⊗ in restaurant

DUMBLETON, Gloucestershire — Map 10 SP03

★★★64% Dumbleton Hall
WR11 7TS
☎ 01386 881240 🖷 01386 882142
e-mail: dh@pofr.co.uk
Dir: *M5 junct 8 follow A46 for Evesham. 5m S of Evesham take right signed Dumbleton. Hotel is set back at S end of village.*
Originally constructed in the 16th century, the existing building, set in 19 acres of landscaped gardens and parklands, was rebuilt in the mid-18th century. Spacious public rooms make this an ideal venture for weddings and conferences, or a hideaway retreat, and the location an ideal touring base. Panoramic views of the Vale of Evesham can be seen from every window.
ROOMS: 34 en suite (6 fmly) ⊗ in 20 bedrooms s £90; d £140 (incl. bkfst) **LB** **FACILITIES:** ♫ Xmas **CONF:** Thtr 100 Class 60 Board 60 Del £145 **SERVICES:** Lift **PARKING:** 60 **NOTES:** ⊗ in restaurant

DUNCHURCH, Warwickshire — Map 11 SP47

⌂ Travelodge Rugby
London Rd, Thurlaston CV23 9LG
☎ 08700 850 950 🖷 01788 521538
web: www.travelodge.co.uk
Dir: *4m S of Rugby, on A45, westbound*
Travelodge offers good quality, good value, modern accommodation. Ideal for families, the spacious, en suite bedrooms include remote-control TV, tea and coffee-making facilities and comfortable beds. Meals can be taken at the nearby family restaurant. For further details consult the Hotel Groups page.
ROOMS: 40 en suite s fr £26; d fr £26

DUNSTABLE, Bedfordshire — Map 11 TL02

★★★63% Old Palace Lodge
Church St LU5 4RT
☎ 01582 662201 🖷 01582 696422
e-mail: reservations@mgmhotels.co.uk
Dir: *M1 junct 11 take A505. Hotel 2m on right opposite Priory church*
This hotel is steeped in history and has with many original features in the public areas still prominent. Its central location and easy access to local communication links makes it an ideal for corporate guests. Bedrooms, which are spacious and well equipped, are found in a more newly added extension.
ROOMS: 68 en suite (12 fmly) (21 GF) ⊗ in 33 bedrooms s £47-£99; d £58-£109 **FACILITIES:** STV Full leisure facilities provided off site with local fitness centre Xmas **CONF:** BC Thtr 60 Class 40 Board 40 Del from £94 **SERVICES:** Lift **PARKING:** 50 **NOTES:** Civ Wed 70

⌂ Premier Travel Inn Dunstable/Luton
350 Luton Rd LU5 4LL
☎ 08701 977083 🖷 01582 664114
web: www.premiertravelinn.com
Dir: *on A505. From M1 junct 11 follow signs to Dunstable. At first rdbt turn right. Inn on left*
High quality, modern budget accommodation ideal for both families and business travellers. Spacious, en suite bedrooms feature bath and shower, satellite TV and many have telephones and modem points. The adjacent family restaurant features a wide and varied menu. For further details consult the Hotel Groups page.
ROOMS: 42 en suite s £47.95-£50.95; d £47.95-£50.95

⌂ Premier Travel Inn Dunstable South
Watling St, Kensworth LU6 3QP
☎ 08701 977082 🖷 01582 842811
web: www.premiertravelinn.com
Dir: *M1 junct 9 towards Dunstable on A5, Inn on right past Packhorse pub*
High quality, modern budget accommodation ideal for both families and business travellers. Spacious, en suite bedrooms feature bath and shower, satellite TV and many have telephones and modem points. The adjacent family restaurant features a wide and varied menu. For further details consult the Hotel Groups page.
ROOMS: 40 en suite

⌂ Travelodge
Watling St LU7 9LZ
☎ 08700 850 950 🖷 01525 211177
web: www.travelodge.co.uk
Dir: *M1 junct 12, take A5120 to Toddington. Then 1st right through Tebworth, right onto A5*
Travelodge offers good quality, good value, modern accommodation. Ideal for families, the spacious, en suite bedrooms include remote-control TV, tea and coffee-making facilities and comfortable beds. Meals can be taken at the nearby family restaurant. For further details consult the Hotel Groups page.
ROOMS: 28 en suite s fr £26; d fr £26

DUNSTER, Somerset — Map 03 SS94

★★★71% ❀ The Luttrell Arms Hotel
High St TA24 6SG
☎ 01643 821555 🖷 01643 821567
e-mail: info@luttrellarms.fsnet.co.uk
web: www.bhere.co.uk/luttrell/main.htm
Dir: *A39/A396 S toward Tiverton. Hotel on left opposite Yarn Market*

Occupying an enviable position on the High Street, this 15th-century hotel looks up to the town's famous castle. Beautifully decorated in a contemporary style, high levels of

continued on p192

DUNSTER, continued

comfort can be found throughout. The warm and friendly staff provide attentive service in a relaxed atmosphere.
ROOMS: 28 en suite (3 fmly) ⊗ in all bedrooms s £64-£94; d £89-£140 (incl. bkfst) **LB** **FACILITIES:** Exmoor safaris, Historic tours, Walking tours Xmas **CONF:** Thtr 35 Class 20 Board 20 Del from £135 **NOTES:** ⊗ in restaurant

A ★★★ Yarn Market Hotel
25-33 High St TA24 6SF
☎ 01643 821425 🖷 01643 821475
e-mail: yarnmarket.hotel@virgin.net
web: www.yarnmarkethotel.co.uk
Dir: *M5 junct 23, follow A39. Hotel in centre of village*
ROOMS: 15 en suite 5 annexe en suite (3 fmly) ⊗ in all bedrooms s £45-£55; d £70-£100 (incl. bkfst) **LB** **FACILITIES:** Xmas **CONF:** Thtr 60 Class 30 Board 25 **PARKING:** 4 **NOTES:** ⊗ in restaurant

DURHAM, Co Durham — Map 19 NZ24

★★★★72%
Durham Marriott Hotel, Royal County
Old Elvet DH1 3JN
☎ 0191 386 6821 🖷 0191 386 0704
e-mail: durhamroyal.marriott@whitbread.com
web: www.marriott.co.uk
Dir: *from A1(M) junct 62, then A690 to Durham, over 1st rdbt, left at 2nd rdbt left at lights, hotel on left*

In a wonderful position on the banks of the River Wear, the hotel's central location makes it ideal for visiting the attractions of this historic city. The building was developed from a series of Jacobean town houses (once owned by the Bowes-Lyon family, ancestors of the late Queen Mother). Today the hotel offers up-to-date, air-conditioned bedrooms, a choice of restaurants and lounge areas, gym and swimming pool.
ROOMS: 142 en suite 8 annexe en suite (10 fmly) (15 GF) ⊗ in 111 bedrooms s £135-£150; d £145-£160 (incl. bkfst) **LB** **FACILITIES: Spa** STV supervised Sauna Solarium Gym Jacuzzi Turkish steamroom Plungepool, sanarium, tropical fun shower **CONF:** Thtr 120 Class 50 Board 50 Del from £125 **SERVICES:** Lift **PARKING:** 76 **NOTES:** ⊗ in restaurant Civ Wed 70

★★★74%
Whitworth Hall Country Park Hotel
MEAR DL16 7QX
☎ 01388 811772 🖷 01388 818669
e-mail: enquiries@whitworthhall.co.uk
(For full entry see Spennymoor)

★★★72% Ramside Hall
Carrville DH1 1TD
☎ 0191 386 5282 🖷 0191 386 0399
e-mail: mail@ramsidehallhotel.co.uk
web: www.ramsidehallhotel.co.uk
Dir: *from A1(M) junct 62 take A690 to Sunderland. 200mtrs after railway bridge turn right*

With its proximity to the motorway and delightful parkland setting, Ramside Hall combines the best of both worlds - convenience and tranquillity. The hotel boasts 27 holes of golf, a choice of lounges, two eating options and two bars. Bedrooms are furnished and decorated to a very high standard and include two very impressive presidential suites.
ROOMS: 80 en suite (10 fmly) (28 GF) ⊗ in 36 bedrooms s £122; d £142 (incl. bkfst) **LB** **FACILITIES:** STV ⛳ 27 Snooker Sauna Putt green Steam room Golf academy Driving Range ♫ **CONF:** BC Thtr 400 Class 160 Board 40 Del £157.50 **SERVICES:** Lift **PARKING:** 500 **NOTES:** ⊗ in restaurant Civ Wed 400

See advert on opposite page

★★★66% Bowburn Hall
Bowburn DH6 5NH
☎ 0191 377 0311 🖷 0191 377 3459
e-mail: onfo@bowburnhallhotel.co.uk
Dir: *towards Bowburn. Right at Cooperage Pub, then 0.5m to junct signed Durham. Hotel on left*
A former country mansion, this hotel lies in five acres of grounds in a residential area, but within easy reach of the A1. The spacious lounge bar and conservatory overlook the gardens and are comfortable and popular venues for both bar and restaurant meals. Bedrooms are not large but are very smartly presented and well equipped.
ROOMS: 19 en suite **FACILITIES:** STV **CONF:** Thtr 150 Class 80 Board 30 Del from £85 **PARKING:** 100 **NOTES:** RS 24-26 Dec & 1 Jan Civ Wed 120

⌂ Premier Travel Inn Durham East
Broomside Park, Belmont Industrial Estate
DH1 1GG
☎ 08701 977084 🖷 0191 370 6501
web: www.premiertravelinn.com
Dir: *from A1(M) junct 62 take A690 west towards Durham. 1st exit, after 1m turn left. Inn on left*
High quality, modern budget accommodation ideal for both families and business travellers. Spacious, en suite bedrooms feature bath and shower, satellite TV and many have telephones and modem points. The adjacent family restaurant features a wide and varied menu. For further details consult the Hotel Groups page.
ROOMS: 40 en suite s £52.95; d £52.95

⇧ Premier Travel Inn Durham North
Adj Arnison Retail Centre, Pity Me DH1 5GB
☎ 08701 977086 📠 0191 383 1166
web: www.premiertravelinn.com
Dir: *A1 junct 63, then A167 to Durham. Over 5 rbts and turn left at 6th rbt. Inn is on the right after 200 yds*
High quality, modern budget accommodation ideal for both families and business travellers. Spacious, en suite bedrooms feature bath and shower, satellite TV and many have telephones and modem points. The adjacent family restaurant features a wide and varied menu. For further details consult the Hotel Groups page.
ROOMS: 60 en suite s £46.95-£49.95; d £46.95-£49.95

⇧ Travelodge Durham
Station Rd, Gilesgate DH1 1LJ
☎ 08700 850 950 📠 0191 386 5461
web: www.travelodge.co.uk
Dir: *A1(M) junct 62 onto A690 towards Durham, 1st rdbt, 1st left into Station Rd*
Travelodge offers good quality, good value, modern accommodation. Ideal for families, the spacious, en suite bedrooms include remote-control TV, tea and coffee-making facilities and comfortable beds. Meals can be taken at the nearby family restaurant. For further details consult the Hotel Groups page.
ROOMS: 57 en suite s fr £26; d fr £26

DURHAM SERVICE AREA (A1(M)), Co Durham Map 19 NZ33

⇧ Premier Travel Inn Durham South
Motorway Service Area, Tursdale Rd, Bowburn DH6 5NP
☎ 08701 977087 📠 0191 377 8722
web: www.premiertravelinn.com
Dir: *A1(M) junct 61& A177 Bowburn junction*
High quality, modern budget accommodation ideal for both families and business travellers. Spacious, en suite bedrooms feature bath and shower, satellite TV and many have telephones and modem points. The adjacent family restaurant features a wide and varied menu. For further details consult the Hotel Groups page.
ROOMS: 38 en suite s £46.95-£48.95; d £46.95-£48.95 **CONF:** Thtr 1 Board 10

DUXFORD, Cambridgeshire Map 12 TL44

★★★74% ⊛⊛ *Duxford Lodge*
Ickleton Rd CB2 4RT
☎ 01223 836444 📠 01223 832271
e-mail: admin@duxfordlodgehotel.co.uk
web: www.duxfordlodgehotel.co.uk
Dir: *M11 junct 10, onto A505 to Duxford. 1st right at T- junct. Hotel on left*

A warm welcome is assured at this attractive red-brick hotel in the heart of a delightful village. Public areas include a cosy relaxing

continued on p194

DUXFORD, continued

bar, separate lounge, and an attractive restaurant, where an excellent and imaginative menu is offered. The bedrooms are well appointed, comfortable and smartly furnished.
ROOMS: 11 en suite 4 annexe en suite (2 fmly) **FACILITIES:** ♫ **CONF:** Thtr 30 Class 20 Board 20 **PARKING:** 34 **NOTES:** ⊗ in restaurant Closed 26-30 Dec

See advert on page 193

D

EARLS COLNE, Essex — Map 13 TL82
See also Colchester

★★★79% @@ de Vere Arms
53 High St CO6 2PB
☎ 01787 223353 🖷 01787 223365
e-mail: dining@deverearms.com
web: www.deverearms.com

Situated in the picturesque countryside of the Colne Valley, this former inn has been transformed into a very stylish small hotel and fine dining restaurant. The open-plan reception/lounge and all the bedrooms have been enhanced in an energetic modern fashion with hand-painted murals and original art, without compromising guest comfort.
ROOMS: 9 en suite (1 fmly) (1 GF) ⊗ in all bedrooms s £65-£95; d £95-£165 (incl. bkfst) **FACILITIES:** Xmas **CONF:** Thtr 40 Board 20 **PARKING:** 12 **NOTES:** ✗ ⊗ in restaurant

EASINGWOLD, North Yorkshire — Map 19 SE56

★★72% George
Market Place YO61 3AD
☎ 01347 821698 🖷 01347 823448
e-mail: info@the-george-hotel.co.uk
web: www.the-george-hotel.co.uk
Dir: *off A19 midway between York & Thirsk, in Market Place*

THE CIRCLE
Selected Individual Hotels
GREAT BRITAIN

A friendly welcome awaits at this former coaching inn that faces the Georgian market square. Bedrooms are very comfortably furnished and well equipped, and the mews rooms have their own external access. An extensive range of well-produced food is available both in the bar and restaurant. There are two comfortable lounges and complimentary use of a local fitness centre.
ROOMS: 15 en suite (2 fmly) ⊗ in all bedrooms s £75; d £95 (incl. bkfst) **LB** **FACILITIES:** Complimentry use of local fitness centre Xmas **CONF:** Board 12 Del from £80 **PARKING:** 10 **NOTES:** ✗ ⊗ in restaurant

If you wish to use a particular credit card or debit card please check with the hotel that they are happy to accept it

EAST AYTON, North Yorkshire — Map 17 SE98

★★★65% East Ayton Lodge Country House
Moor Ln, Forge Valley YO13 9EW
☎ 01723 864227 🖷 01723 862680
e-mail: ealodgehtl@cix.co.uk
Dir: *400yds off A170*

Set in three acres of grounds close to the River Derwent and discreetly situated in a quiet lane on the edge of the forest, this hotel is constructed around two cottages, the original buildings on the site. Bedrooms are well equipped and those on the courtyard are particularly spacious; public rooms include a large conservatory. A good range of food is available.
ROOMS: 10 en suite 20 annexe en suite (5 fmly) (10 GF) ⊗ in 9 bedrooms s £55-£82; d £85-£140 (incl. bkfst) **FACILITIES:** STV Xmas **CONF:** Thtr 50 Board 30 Del from £50 **PARKING:** 70 **NOTES:** ⊗ in restaurant

EASTBOURNE, East Sussex — Map 06 TV69
See also Wilmington

★★★★★73% @@ Grand
King Edward's Pde BN21 4EQ
☎ 01323 412345 🖷 01323 412233
e-mail: reservations@grandeastbourne.com
Dir: *on seafront W of Eastbourne, 1m from railway station*

This famous Victorian hotel offers high standards of service and hospitality. The extensive public rooms feature a magnificent Great Hall, with marble columns and high ceilings, where guests can relax and enjoy afternoon tea. The spacious bedrooms provide high levels of comfort and some rooms have balconies with stunning sea views. There is a choice of restaurants and bars as well as superb leisure facilities.
ROOMS: 152 en suite (20 fmly) s £135; d £165 (incl. bkfst) **LB** **FACILITIES:** **Spa** supervised supervised Snooker Sauna Solarium Gym Putt green Jacuzzi Hairdressing, Beauty therapy ♫ ch fac Xmas **CONF:** BC Thtr 350 Class 200 Board 40 Del £245 **SERVICES:** Lift **PARKING:** 60 **NOTES:** ⊗ in restaurant Civ Wed 300

★★★74% Lansdowne

King Edward's Pde BN21 4EE
☎ 01323 725174 📠 01323 739721
e-mail: reception@lansdowne-hotel.co.uk
web: www.bw-lansdownehotel.co.uk
Dir: *hotel at W end of seafront (B2103) facing Western Lawns*

Enjoying an enviable position at the quieter end of the parade, this hotel overlooks the Western Lawns and Wish Tower and is just a few minutes' walk from many of the town's attractions. Public rooms include a variety of lounges, a range of meeting rooms and games rooms. Bedrooms are attractively decorated and many offer sea views.
ROOMS: 101 en suite (9 fmly) ⊘ in 25 bedrooms s £47-£75; d £94-£135 (incl. bkfst) **LB** **FACILITIES:** STV Snooker Table tennis, Pool table Xmas **CONF:** Thtr 100 Class 40 Board 40 Del from £75 **SERVICES:** Lift **PARKING:** 22 **NOTES:** ⊘ in restaurant Closed 2-12 Jan Civ Wed 60

See advert on this page

★★★73% Hydro

Mount Rd BN20 7HZ
☎ 01323 720643 📠 01323 641167
e-mail: Sales@hydrohotel.com
Dir: *from pier/seafront, right along Grand Parade. At Grand Hotel follow Hydro Hotel sign. Up South Cliff 200yds*

This well-managed and popular hotel enjoys an elevated position with views of attractive gardens and the sea beyond. The spacious bedrooms are attractive and well-equipped. In addition to the comfortable lounges, guests also have access to fitness facilities and a hairdressing salon. Service is both professional and efficient throughout.
ROOMS: 84 rms (83 en suite) (3 fmly) (3 GF) ⊘ in 36 bedrooms s £45-£73; d £90-£146 (incl. bkfst) **LB** **FACILITIES:** STV Gym Putt green Beauty room, Hairdressing salon Xmas **CONF:** Thtr 140 Class 90 Board 40 Del from £89.50 **SERVICES:** Lift **PARKING:** 40 **NOTES:** ⊘ in restaurant RS 24-28 & 30-31 Dec Civ Wed 120

★★★66% York House

14-22 Royal Pde BN22 7AP
☎ 01323 412918 📠 01323 646238
e-mail: frontdesk@yorkhousehotel.co.uk
web: www.yorkhousehotel.co.uk
Dir: *A27 to Eastbourne. On seafront 0.25m E of pier*
With a prime location on the seafront many rooms enjoy wonderful panoramic views. Bedrooms vary in size but are comfortably and practically fitted. Public areas include a spacious lobby, cosy bar, games room and indoor swimming pool. The only parking available is on the street in front of the hotel.
ROOMS: 87 en suite (15 fmly) (5 GF) ⊘ in 30 bedrooms **FACILITIES:** STV ♫ Xmas **CONF:** Thtr 100 Class 40 Board 24 Del £150 **SERVICES:** Lift **NOTES:** ⊘ in restaurant Civ Wed 50

U Star rating not confirmed

★★★63% Chatsworth

Grand Pde BN21 3YR
☎ 01323 411016 📠 01323 643270
e-mail: stay@chatsworth-hotel.com
web: www.chatsworth-hotel.com
Dir: *M23 then A27 to Polegate. A2270 into Eastbourne, follow seafront & signs. Hotel is in centre of seafront near pier*
Within minutes of the town centre and pier, this attractive Edwardian hotel is located on the seafront. Service is friendly and helpful throughout the public areas, which consist of the Dukes

continued on p196

EASTBOURNE, continued

Bar, a cosy lounge and the Devonshire Restaurant. Bedrooms, many with sea views, are traditional in style and have a range of facilities.

Chatsworth Hotel, Eastbourne

ROOMS: 47 en suite (2 fmly) ⊗ in 10 bedrooms s £55-£70; d £80-£120 (incl. bkfst) **LB** **FACILITIES:** STV ♫ Xmas **CONF:** Thtr 100 Class 60 Board 40 Del from £112.50 **SERVICES:** Lift **NOTES:** ⊗ in restaurant Civ Wed 140

See advert on opposite page

★★★63% Quality Hotel Langham

Royal Pde BN22 7AH
☎ 01323 731451 🖷 01323 646623
e-mail: info@langhamhotel.co.uk
web: www.langhamhotel.co.uk
Dir: *In Eastbourne, follow seafront signs. Hotel 0.5m E of pier*
This popular hotel is situated in a prominent position with superb views of the sea and pier. Bedrooms are pleasantly decorated and equipped with modern facilities. The spacious public rooms include a terrace restaurant, business lounge area and Grand Parade bar.
ROOMS: 85 en suite (4 fmly) (2 GF) ⊗ in 22 bedrooms s £45-£60; d £85-£105 (incl. bkfst) **LB** **FACILITIES:** Temporary membership of Sovereign Club pools & gym Xmas **CONF:** Thtr 80 Class 40 Board 24 Del from £85 **SERVICES:** Lift **PARKING:** 4 **NOTES:** ⊗ in restaurant Civ Wed 110

★★71% New Wilmington

25 Compton St BN21 4DU
☎ 01323 721219 🖷 01323 746255
e-mail: info@new-wilmington-hotel.co.uk
web: www.new-wilmington-hotel.co.uk
Dir: *A22 to Eastbourne seafront. Right along promenade to Wish Tower. Right, then left at end of road, hotel 2nd on left*
This friendly, family-run hotel is conveniently located close to the seafront, the Congress Theatre and Winter Gardens. Public rooms are well presented and include a cosy bar, small comfortable non-smoking lounge and a spacious restaurant. Bedrooms are comfortably appointed and tastefully decorated; family and superior bedrooms are available.
ROOMS: 40 en suite (14 fmly) (3 GF) s £50-£57; d £90-£111 (incl. bkfst & dinner) **LB** **FACILITIES:** ♫ Xmas **SERVICES:** Lift **PARKING:** 2 **NOTES:** ✖ ⊗ in restaurant Closed 3 Jan - mid-Feb

★★68% Farrar's Hotel

Wilmington Gardens BN21 4JN
☎ 01323 723737 🖷 01323 732902
Dir: *off seafront by Wish Tower, hotel opposite Congress Theatre*
Situated opposite the Congress Theatre, this hotel is just a short walk from both the seafront and Devonshire Park. Bedrooms are comfortably furnished and pleasantly decorated. Public areas are smartly appointed and include a cosy bar, a separate lounge and an attractive downstairs dining room.
ROOMS: 45 en suite (4 fmly) **FACILITIES:** Xmas **CONF:** Thtr 80 **SERVICES:** Lift **PARKING:** 35 **NOTES:** ⊗ in restaurant Closed Jan

★★66% Alexandra

King Edwards Pde BN21 4DR
☎ 01323 720131 🖷 01323 417769
e-mail: alexandrahotel@mistral.co.uk
web: http://alexandrahotel.eastbourne.biz
Dir: *situated on seafront at junct of Carlisle Rd and King Edward Parade*
Located at the West end of the town, opposite the Wishing Tower, this hotel boasts panoramic views of the sea from many rooms. Bedrooms vary in size but are comfortable with good facilities for guests. A warm welcome is guaranteed at this long-standing family run establishment.
ROOMS: 38 en suite (2 fmly) (3 GF) s £28-£40; d £56-£80 (incl. bkfst) **FACILITIES:** Xmas **SERVICES:** Lift **NOTES:** ⊗ in restaurant Closed Jan & Feb RS Mar

★★65% Afton

1-8 Cavendish Place BN21 3EJ
☎ 01323 733162 🖷 01323 645720
e-mail: info@aftonhotel.com
This friendly family run hotel takes its name from a river in the proprietor's home county. Ideally located in the centre of this town, opposite the pier and close to the shopping centre. Bedrooms vary in size but are all comfortable and well co-ordinated.
ROOMS: 56 en suite (4 fmly) (4 GF) ⊗ in all bedrooms s £30-£45; d £60-£90 (incl. bkfst & dinner) **LB** **FACILITIES:** ♫ Xmas **CONF:** Del from £45 **SERVICES:** Lift **NOTES:** ⊗ in restaurant Closed Feb RS Jan

★★63% *Queens Hotel*

Marine Pde BN21 3DY
☎ 01323 722822 🖷 01323 731056
e-mail: queens.eastbourne@alfatravel.co.uk
web: www.alfatravel.co.uk
Dir: *proceed to seafront, hotel opposite pier on left*
Popular with tour groups, this long-established hotel enjoys a central, prominent seafront location overlooking the pier. Spacious public areas include a choice of lounges, and regular entertainment is also provided. Bedrooms are suitably appointed and equipped.
ROOMS: 122 en suite (1 fmly) **FACILITIES:** Snooker ♫ **CONF:** Thtr 100 Class 56 Board 40 **SERVICES:** Lift **PARKING:** 50 **NOTES:** ✖ ⊗ in restaurant Closed Jan RS Nov, Feb-Mar

★★62% Oban

King Edward's Pde BN21 4DS
☎ 01323 731581 🖷 01323 721994
e-mail: info@oban-hotel.co.uk
Dir: *opposite Wish Tower on seafront*

Situated on the seafront overlooking the Wishing Tower this

continued

privately owned hotel provides a friendly welcome. Bedrooms vary in size and are pleasantly decorated; some of bedrooms and bathrooms have now been upgraded to a good modern standard. Public areas include a smartly decorated large open-plan lounge bar area with a small terrace. Enjoyable meals are served in the lower ground-floor dining room.
ROOMS: 31 en suite (2 fmly) (4 GF) s £28-£40; d £56-£80 (incl. bkfst) **LB FACILITIES:** ♫ Xmas **SERVICES:** Lift **NOTES:** ⊗ in restaurant

★★62% West Rocks
Grand Pde BN21 4DL
☎ 01323 725217 📠 01323 720421
e-mail: westrockshotel@btinternet.com
Dir: *western end of seafront*
Ideally located near to the pier and bandstand, this hotel is only a short walk from the town centre. Bedrooms vary in size, with many offering a stunning sea views. Guests have the choice of two comfortable lounges and a bar.
ROOMS: 47 rms (45 en suite) (8 fmly) (6 GF) **FACILITIES:** ♫ Xmas **CONF:** BC Thtr 20 Class 12 Board 12 **SERVICES:** Lift **NOTES:** ✗ ⊗ in restaurant Closed 3 Jan -20 Feb

⌂ Innkeeper's Lodge Eastbourne
Highfield Park, Willingdon Drove BN23 8AL
☎ 01323 507222
web: www.innkeeperslodge.com
A growing concept in the travel accommodation market. Smart rooms meet essential business requirements but also have home comforts. Dining options include all-day menus plus the added advantage of breakfast, which is included in the room price. For further details consult the Hotel Groups page.
ROOMS: 42 rms s £52; d £52

⌂ Premier Travel Inn Eastbourne
Willingdon Dr BN23 8AL
☎ 08701 977089 📠 01323 767379
web: www.premiertravelinn.com
Dir: *A22, towards Eastbourne. At next rbt left. Inn on the left*
High quality, modern budget accommodation ideal for both families and business travellers. Spacious, en suite bedrooms feature bath and shower, satellite TV and many have telephones and modem points. The adjacent family restaurant features a wide and varied menu. For further details consult the Hotel Groups page.
ROOMS: 47 en suite s £49.95; d £49.95

EAST GRINSTEAD, West Sussex — Map 06 TQ33

Top Hotel

★★★ ⊛⊛⊛ Gravetye Manor
RH19 4LJ
☎ 01342 810567 📠 01342 810080
e-mail: info@gravetyemanor.co.uk
web: www.gravetyemanor.co.uk
Dir: *B2028 to Haywards Heath. 1m after Turners Hill fork left towards Sharpthorne, immediate 1st left into Vowels Lane*
This beautiful Elizabethan mansion was built in 1598 and enjoys a tranquil setting. It was one of the first country-house hotels and remains a shining example in its class. There are several day rooms, each with oak panelling, fresh flowers and open fires that offer guests a relaxing atmosphere. Bedrooms are decorated in traditional English style, furnished with antiques and with many thoughtful extras. The cuisine is excellent and makes full use of home grown fruit and vegetables. Guests should make a point of exploring the outstanding gardens.
ROOMS: 18 en suite s £100-£150; d £150-£325 **FACILITIES:** Fishing **CONF:** Del from £235 **PARKING:** 35 **NOTES:** ✗ No children 7yrs ⊗ in restaurant RS 25 Dec Civ Wed 45

⌂ Premier Travel Inn East Grinstead
London Rd, Felbridge RH19 2QR
☎ 08701 977088 📠 01342 326187
web: www.premiertravelinn.com
Dir: *at junction of A22 & A264 south from M25 junct 6*
High quality, modern budget accommodation ideal for both families and business travellers. Spacious, en suite bedrooms feature bath and shower, satellite TV and many have telephones and modem points. The adjacent family restaurant features a wide and varied menu. For further details consult the Hotel Groups page.
ROOMS: 41 en suite s £47.95-£50.95; d £47.95-£50.95

GF indicates the number of bedrooms at ground level

EAST HORNDON, Essex Map 06 TQ68

⌂ Travelodge Brentwood

CM13 3LL

☎ 08700 850 950 ▤ 01277 810819

web: www.travelodge.co.uk

Dir: on A127, eastbound, 4m off M25 junct 29

Travelodge offers good quality, good value, modern accommodation. Ideal for families, the spacious, en suite bedrooms include remote-control TV, tea and coffee-making facilities and comfortable beds. Meals can be taken at the nearby family restaurant. For further details consult the Hotel Groups page.

ROOMS: 45 en suite s fr £26; d fr £26

EAST HORSLEY, Surrey Map 06 TQ05

⊞ Ramada Guildford/Leatherhead

Guildford Rd KT24 6TB ®RAMADA.

☎ 01483 280500 ▤ 01483 284222

e-mail: sales.guildford@ramadajarvis.co.uk

web: www.ramadajarvis.co.uk

Dir: A25 towards Leatherhead/Dorking. Pass West Horsley, hotel 0.5m on left.

With easy access to the M25 the hotel's 19th-century oak beamed exterior conceals a wide range of modern facilities. Bedrooms are comfortably appointed for both business and leisure guests.

ROOMS: 87 en suite (11 fmly) (20 GF) ⊗ in 46 bedrooms s £99-£119; d £99-£119 **FACILITIES:** STV Xmas **CONF:** Thtr 170 Class 70 Board 66 Del from £190 **SERVICES:** Lift **PARKING:** 110 **NOTES:** ⊗ in restaurant Civ Wed 180

EASTLEIGH, Hampshire Map 05 SU41

ⓐ ★★★ Concorde Club & Hotel

Stoneham Ln SO50 9HQ

☎ 023 8065 1478 & 8061 3989 ▤ 023 8065 1479

e-mail: hotel@theconcordeclub.com

web: www.theconcordeclub.com

Dir: M27 junct 5, at rdbt follow Chandlers Ford signs, hotel 500yds on right

ROOMS: 35 en suite (18 GF) ⊗ in 26 bedrooms s £65-£90; d £80-£120 (incl. bkfst) **FACILITIES:** STV Fishing Fishing available with prior notice & chargeable daily ♫ **CONF:** Thtr 200 Class 50 Board 40 **SERVICES:** Lift air con **PARKING:** 250 **NOTES:** No children 18yrs ⊗ in restaurant Closed 24-26 Dec

⌂ Premier Travel Inn Eastleigh

Leigh Rd SO50 9YX

☎ 08701 977090 ▤ 023 8062 9048

web: www.premiertravelinn.com

Dir: adjacent to M3 junct 13, near Eastleigh on A335

High quality, modern budget accommodation ideal for families and business travellers. Spacious, en suite bedrooms feature bath and shower, satellite TV and many have telephones and modem points. The adjacent family restaurant features a wide and varied menu. For further details consult the Hotel Groups page.

ROOMS: 60 en suite s £50.95; d £50.95

⌂ Travelodge Southampton Eastleigh

Twyford Rd SO50 4LF

☎ 08700 850 950 ▤ 023 8061 6813

web: www.travelodge.co.uk

Dir: M3 junct 12 on A335 Eastleigh & Boyatt Wood to next rdbt, take 2nd exit signed Eastleigh town centre

Travelodge offers good quality, good value, modern accommodation. Ideal for families, the spacious, en suite

continued

bedrooms include remote-control TV, tea and coffee-making facilities and comfortable beds. Meals can be taken at the nearby family restaurant. For further details consult the Hotel Groups page.

ROOMS: 32 en suite s fr £26; d fr £26

EDGWARE, Greater London

See LONDON SECTION plan 1 C6

⌂ Premier Travel Inn London Edgware

435 Burnt Oak Broadway HA8 5AQ

☎ 0870 9906522 ▤ 0870 9906523

web: www.premiertravelinn.com

Dir: M1 junct 4 take A41 then A5 towards Edgware. 3m. Inn opposite Peugeot dealership

High quality, modern budget accommodation ideal for both families and business travellers. Spacious, en suite bedrooms feature bath and shower, satellite TV and many have telephones and modem points. The adjacent family restaurant features a wide and varied menu. For further details consult the Hotel Groups page.

ROOMS: 111 en suite s £59.95; d £59.95

EGHAM, Surrey Map 06 TQ07

★★★★74% *Runnymede Hotel & Spa*

Windsor Rd TW20 0AG

☎ 01784 436171 ▤ 01784 436340

e-mail: info@runnymedehotel.com

web: www.runnymedehotel.com

Dir: M25 junct 13, onto A308 towards Windsor

Enjoying a peaceful location beside the River Thames, this large modern hotel attracts a largely business clientele during the week. Extensive function suites are available, together with spacious lounges and practically laid out bedrooms. At weekends, leisure visitors come to enjoy impressive spa facilities and regular dinner dances in the airy restaurant overlooking the river.

ROOMS: 180 en suite (19 fmly) ⊗ in 116 bedrooms **FACILITIES:** STV ⚲ ⚲ Snooker Sauna Solarium Gym ♫ Putt green Jacuzzi Beauty Salon Dance studio Hairdressers ♫ **CONF:** BC Thtr 300 Class 250 Board 76 **SERVICES:** Lift air con **PARKING:** 280 **NOTES:** ✱ RS Restaurant closed Sat lunch/Sun dinner Civ Wed 150

See advert under WINDSOR

ELLESMERE PORT, Cheshire Map 15 SJ47

★★★69% Quality Hotel Chester

Berwick Rd, Little Sutton CH66 4PS

☎ 0151 339 5121 ▤ 0151 339 3214

e-mail: enquiries@quality-hotels-chester.com

web: www.choicehotelseurope.com

Dir: M53 junct 5 left at rdbt. At 2nd lights right onto A550 over hump-back bridge, left into Berwick Rd. Hotel 1m on left

This modern hotel is conveniently located for access to Chester, the

continued

M53 and the many attractions of the area. The well-equipped accommodation includes bedrooms on ground-floor level and no-smoking rooms, and facilities include a leisure complex and versatile banqueting and conference suites. Staff are friendly and keen to please.
ROOMS: 75 en suite (10 fmly) (23 GF) ⊘ in 30 bedrooms **FACILITIES:** STV ⛆ Sauna Gym Steam room Exercise equipment ♫ **CONF:** Thtr 300 Class 150 Board 50 **PARKING:** 150 **NOTES:** ⊘ in restaurant Civ Wed 200

★★63% Woodcote Hotel & Restaurant

3 Hooton Rd CH66 1QU
☎ 0151 327 1542 🖷 0151 328 1328
e-mail: thewoodcotehotel@lineone.net
Dir: *M53 junct 5, take A41 towards Chester, 1st lights right to Willaston. Hotel 300yds on left*
This popular commercial hotel offers generally spacious bedrooms, some of which are located in a separate building, adjacent to the pretty garden. Public areas include a bar and restaurant serving a range of popular, reasonably priced dishes and a separate breakfast room. Staff are friendly and helpful.
ROOMS: 10 en suite 11 annexe en suite (1 fmly) (6 GF) s £35-£40; d £40-£50 **FACILITIES:** ♫ **CONF:** Thtr 90 Class 50 Board 48 **PARKING:** 35 **NOTES:** ✖ RS Sun

ELSTREE, Hertfordshire Map 06 TQ19

★★★67% Corus hotel Elstree

Barnet Ln WD6 3RE
☎ 0870 609 6151 🖷 020 8207 3668
e-mail: edgwarebury@corushotels.com
web: www.corushotels.com
Dir: *M1 junct 5 follow A41 to Harrow, left onto A411 into Elstree. Through x-rds into Barnet Ln, hotel on right*

Sitting in ten acres of landscaped gardens this hotel is full of charm and character, with a Tudor-style façade and interiors of a traditional design. The oak-panelled bar, with two large fireplaces and the stately Cavendish restaurant enjoy wonderful views over the gardens and the city lights beyond.
ROOMS: 47 en suite (1 fmly) ⊘ in 19 bedrooms s £45-£99; d £55-£99 **LB** **FACILITIES:** STV Xmas **CONF:** Thtr 80 Class 50 Board 10 Del from £130 ,**PARKING:** 100 **NOTES:** ⊘ in restaurant Civ Wed 70

ELTERWATER, Cumbria Map 18 NY30

★★★76% Langdale Hotel & Country Club

LA22 9JD
☎ 01539 437302 🖷 01539 437694
e-mail: info@langdale.co.uk
web: www.langdale.co.uk/accomm/frhotel.htm
Dir: *into Langdale, hotel part of private estate on left*
Founded on the site of an abandoned 19th-century gunpowder works, this modern hotel is set in 35 acres of woodland and waterways. Comfortable bedrooms, many with spa baths, vary in size. Extensive public areas include a choice of stylish restaurants, conference and leisure facilities and an elegant bar with an interesting selection of snuff. There is also a traditional pub run by the hotel just along the main road.
ROOMS: 5 en suite 52 annexe en suite (8 fmly) (17 GF) ⊘ in all bedrooms s £95-£230; d £70-£205 (incl. bkfst) **LB** **FACILITIES: Spa** STV ⛆ supervised ✂ Fishing Squash Sauna Solarium Gym Jacuzzi Steam room Hair & beauty salon Cycle hire ch fac Xmas **CONF:** Thtr 80 Class 40 Board 35 **PARKING:** 65 **NOTES:** ✖ ⊘ in restaurant

★★70% New Dungeon Ghyll

Langdale LA22 9JX
☎ 015394 37213 🖷 015394 37666
e-mail: enquiries@dungeon-ghyll.com
web: www.dungeon-ghyll.com
Dir: *from Ambleside follow A593 towards Coniston for 3m, at Skelwith Bridge right onto B5343 towards 'The Langdales'*

This friendly hotel enjoys a tranquil, idyllic position at the head of the valley. Bedrooms vary in size and style; the refurbished rooms are brightly decorated and smartly furnished. Bar meals are served all day, and dinner can be enjoyed in the restaurant overlooking the landscaped gardens; there is also a cosy lounge/bar.
ROOMS: 20 en suite (1 fmly) (3 GF) ⊘ in all bedrooms s £59; d £98 (incl. bkfst) **LB** **FACILITIES:** Xmas **CONF:** Del £108 **PARKING:** 30 **NOTES:** ⊘ in restaurant

ELY, Cambridgeshire Map 12 TL58

★★★67% Lamb

2 Lynn Rd CB7 4EJ
☎ 01353 663574 🖷 01353 662023
e-mail: lamb.ely@oldenglishinns.co.uk
web: www.oldenglish.co.uk
Dir: *from A10 into Ely, hotel in town centre*
This 15th-century former coaching inn is situated in the heart of this popular market town. The hotel offers a combination of light, modern and traditional public rooms, whilst the bedrooms provide contemporary standards of accommodation. Food is available throughout the hotel, the same menu provided within the bar and restaurant areas.
ROOMS: 31 en suite (6 fmly) ⊘ in 24 bedrooms s £50-£70; d £75-£95 (incl. bkfst) **LB** **FACILITIES:** STV Xmas **CONF:** Thtr 100 Class 40 Board 70 Del £95 **PARKING:** 20 **NOTES:** ⊘ in restaurant

> Popped the question? Hotels with Civ wed in their entry are licensed for civil wedding ceremonies. Maximum numbers for the ceremony only are shown e.g. Civ wed 120

ELY, continued

⌂ Travelodge
Witchford Rd CB6 3NN
☎ 08700 850 950 🖷 01353 668499
web: www.travelodge.co.uk
Dir: *at rdbt A10/A142*
Travelodge offers good quality, good value, modern accommodation. Ideal for families, the spacious, en suite bedrooms include remote-control TV, tea and coffee-making facilities and comfortable beds. Meals can be taken at the nearby family restaurant. For further details consult the Hotel Groups page.
ROOMS: 39 en suite s fr £26; d fr £26

E

EMBLETON, Northumberland — Map 21 NU22

★★71% Dunstanburgh Castle Hotel
NE66 3UN
☎ 01665 576111 🖷 01665 576203
e-mail: stay@dunstanburghcastlehotel.co.uk
web: www.dunstanburghcastlehotel.co.uk
Dir: *from A1, take B1340 to Denwick past Rennington & Masons Arms. Next right signed Embleton and into village*

The focal point of the village, this friendly family-run hotel has a dining room and grill room offering different menus. There is also a cosy bar and two lounges. In addition to the main bedrooms, a small courtyard conversion gives three stunning suites each with a lounge and galleried bedroom above.
ROOMS: 20 en suite (4 fmly) ⊘ in all bedrooms **PARKING:** 16
NOTES: ⊘ in restaurant Closed Nov-Feb

EMPINGHAM, Rutland — Map 11 SK90

★★68% The White Horse Inn
Main St LE15 8PS
☎ 01780 460221 🖷 01780 460521
e-mail: info@whitehorserutland.co.uk
web: www.whitehorserutland.co.uk
Dir: *on A606, Oakham to Stamford road*
This attractive stone-built inn, offering bright, comfortable accommodation, is conveniently located just minutes from the A1. Bedrooms in the main building are spacious and include a number of family rooms. Public areas include a well-stocked bar, a bistro and restaurant where a wide range of meals is served.
ROOMS: 4 en suite 9 annexe en suite (3 fmly) (5 GF) ⊘ in 4 bedrooms s £50; d £65-£80 (incl. bkfst) **LB** **CONF:** Thtr 50 Class 40 Board 30 Del from £65 **PARKING:** 60 **NOTES:** ⊘ in restaurant

EMSWORTH, Hampshire — Map 05 SU70

★★★69% Brookfield
Havant Rd PO10 7LF
☎ 01243 373363 🖷 01243 376342
e-mail: bookings@brookfieldhotel.co.uk
Dir: *From A27 onto A259 towards Emsworth. Hotel 0.5m on left*
This well-established family-run hotel has spacious public areas with popular conference and banqueting facilities. Bedrooms are in a modern style, and comfortably furnished. The popular Hermitage Restaurant offers a seasonally changing menu and an interesting wine list.
ROOMS: 40 en suite (4 fmly) (13 GF) ⊘ in 20 bedrooms s £70-£80; d £90-£120 (incl. bkfst) **LB** **FACILITIES:** STV **CONF:** Thtr 100 Class 60 Board 40 Del from £120 **PARKING:** 80 **NOTES:** ✗ Closed 24 Dec-2 Jan

Restaurant with Rooms

◎◎◎ 36 on the Quay
47 South St PO10 7EG
☎ 01243 375592 372257
Occupying a prime position with far reaching views over the estuary, this 16th-century house is the scene for some accomplished and exciting cuisine. As would be expected the elegant restaurant occupies centre stage with peaceful pastel shades, local art and crisp napery together with glimpses of the bustling harbour outside. The contemporary bedrooms offer style, comfort and thoughtful extras.
ROOMS: 5 en suite **PARKING:** 6 **NOTES:** ⊘ in restaurant Closed 3wks Jan, 1wk Oct

⌂ Travelodge Chichester (West)
PO10 7RB
☎ 08700 850 950 🖷 01243 370877
web: www.travelodge.co.uk
Dir: *eastbound carriageway of A27*
Travelodge offers good quality, good value, modern accommodation. Ideal for families, the spacious, en suite bedrooms include remote-control TV, tea and coffee-making facilities and comfortable beds. Meals can be taken at the nearby family restaurant. For further details consult the Hotel Groups page.
ROOMS: 36 en suite s fr £26; d fr £26

ENFIELD, Greater London — Map 06 TQ39

★★★75% ◎ Royal Chace
The Ridgeway EN2 8AR
☎ 020 8884 8181 🖷 020 8884 8150
e-mail: enquiries@royalchacehotel.co.uk
Dir: *M25 junct 24 take A1005 towards Enfield. Hotel 3m on right*
This professionally run, privately owned hotel enjoys a peaceful location with open fields to the rear. Public rooms are smartly appointed; the first floor Chace Brasserie is particularly appealing with its warm colour schemes and friendly service. Bedrooms are well presented and thoughtfully equipped.
ROOMS: 92 en suite (2 fmly) (32 GF) ⊘ in 34 bedrooms s £99; d £115 (incl. bkfst) **FACILITIES:** STV Free access to local leisure centre **CONF:** Thtr 250 Class 100 Board 40 Del from £155 **PARKING:** 200 **NOTES:** ✗ ⊘ in restaurant Closed 24-30 Dec RS Restaurant closed lunchtime/Sun eve Civ Wed 220

★★60% *Enfield*
52 Rowantree Rd EN2 8PW
☎ 020 8366 3511 🖷 020 8366 2432
e-mail: admin@enfieldhotel.com
Dir: *M25 junct 24 follow signs for A1005 towards Enfield. Hospital on L, across mini- rdbt, 3rd left into Bycullah Rd, 2nd left into Rowantree Rd*
This old house is situated in a quiet residential area, close to the centre of Enfield. Comfortable accommodation is provided in the thoughtfully equipped bedrooms, which include ground floor and family rooms. Public areas include a cosy bar and lounge, conference and function rooms and a smart restaurant.
ROOMS: 34 en suite (2 fmly) **FACILITIES:** STV **CONF:** Thtr 70 Class 20 Board 25 **PARKING:** 19 **NOTES:** ✗ ⊘ in restaurant Civ Wed 65

⌂ Premier Travel Inn Enfield
Innova Park, Mollison Av EN3 7XY
☎ 0870 238 3306 🖷 01992 707070
web: www.premiertravelinn.com
Dir: *M25 junct 25, A10 to London, left onto Bullsmoor Lane/Mollison Avenue. Over rbt, right at lights into Innova Science Park.*
High quality, modern budget accommodation ideal for both families and business travellers. Spacious, en suite bedrooms feature bath and shower, satellite TV and many have telephones and modem points. The adjacent family restaurant features a wide and varied menu. For further details consult the Hotel Groups page.
ROOMS: 159 en suite s £53.95-£59.95; d £53.95-£59.95 **CONF:** Thtr 60 Board 26

EPSOM, Surrey
Map 06 TQ26

★★★73% ⊛⊛ Chalk Lane Hotel
Chalk Ln, Woodcote End KT18 7BB
☎ 01372 721179 🖷 01372 727878
e-mail: smcgregor@chalklanehotel.com
web: www.chalklanehotel.com
Dir: *from M25 junct 9 onto A24 to Epsom. Right at lights by BP garage. Left into Avenue Rd, right into Worple Rd. Left at T-junct & hotel on right*

This delightful, deceptively spacious, privately owned hotel is only a ten minute' walk from the racecourse. Staff are committed to providing a professional service and a warm and caring atmosphere. Bedrooms are mostly spacious, attractively furnished and thoughtfully equipped, while the smartly appointed restaurant offers an imaginative selection of dishes.
ROOMS: 22 en suite (1 fmly) ⊘ in all bedrooms s £85 (incl. bkfst) **FACILITIES:** STV Complimentary membership at local health club **CONF:** Thtr 140 Class 40 Board 30 Del £175 **PARKING:** 60 **NOTES:** ⊘ in restaurant

⌂ Premier Travel Inn Epsom Central
2-4 St Margarets Dr, Off Dorking Rd KT18 7LB
☎ 08701 977096 🖷 01372 739761
web: www.premiertravelinn.com
Dir: *M25 junct 9, A24 towards Epsom, Inn on left, just before town centre*
High quality, modern budget accommodation ideal for both families and business travellers. Spacious, en suite bedrooms feature bath and shower, satellite TV and many have telephones and modem points. The adjacent family restaurant features a wide and varied menu. For further details consult the Hotel Groups page.
ROOMS: 40 en suite s £59.95-£62.95; d £59.95-£62.95 **CONF:** Thtr 40

⌂ Premier Travel Inn Epsom North
272 Kingston Rd, Ewell KT19 0SH
☎ 0870 9906466 🖷 0870 9906467
web: www.premiertravelinn.com
Dir: *Exit M25 junct 8 onto A217 towards Sutton. Take A240 towards Ewell. At Beggars Hill rdbt take 2nd exit into Kingston Rd*
High quality, modern budget accommodation ideal for both families and business travellers. Spacious, en suite bedrooms feature bath and shower, satellite TV and many have telephones and modem points. The adjacent family restaurant features a wide and varied menu. For further details consult the Hotel Groups page.
ROOMS: 29 en suite s £59.95-£62.95; d £59.95-£62.95

ESCRICK, North Yorkshire
Map 16 SE64

★★★73% ⊛ Parsonage Country House
York Rd YO19 6LF
☎ 01904 728111 🖷 01904 728151
e-mail: reservations@parsonagehotel.co.uk
web: www.parsonagehotel.co.uk
Dir: *From A64 take A19 Selby. Follow to Escrick . Hotel on right of St Helens Church*

This 19th-century, former parsonage, has been lovingly restored and extended to provide delightful accommodation, set in well-tended gardens. Bedrooms are smartly appointed and well equipped both for business and leisure guests. Spacious public areas include an elegant restaurant, excellent meeting and conference facilities and a choice of attractive lounges.
ROOMS: 12 en suite 36 annexe en suite (4 fmly) (6 GF) ⊘ in 30 bedrooms s £75-£95; d £95-£140 (incl. bkfst) **LB** **FACILITIES:** STV Able to book tee times al local courses. Xmas **CONF:** Thtr 160 Class 80 Board 50 Del from £125 **SERVICES:** Lift **PARKING:** 100 **NOTES:** ✗ ⊘ in restaurant Civ Wed 160

See advert under YORK

ESKDALE GREEN, Cumbria Map 18 NY10

★★69% Bower House Inn
CA19 1TD
☎ 019467 23244 📠 019467 23308
e-mail: Info@bowerhouseinn.freeserve.co.uk
web: www.bowerhouseinn.co.uk
Dir: *4m off A595 0.5m W of Eskdale Green*

This former farmhouse enjoys a countryside location with delightful mountain views and offers true peace and relaxation. The traditional bar and formal restaurant, where a good range of dishes is served, reflect the coaching inn origins of the house. There are ten attractive bedrooms in a converted barn plus those in both the original house and the Garden Cottage.
ROOMS: 10 en suite 19 annexe en suite (2 fmly) (9 GF) s £45-£58; d £74-£84 (incl. bkfst) **LB** **FACILITIES:** STV Xmas **CONF:** Thtr 40 Class 20 Board 30 Del £98 **PARKING:** 60 **NOTES:** ⊗ in restaurant Civ Wed 40

EVERSHOT, Dorset Map 04 ST50

Top Hotel

★★★★ ◎◎◎ Summer Lodge Country House Hotel, Restaurant & Spa
DT2 0JR
☎ 01935 482000 📠 01935 482040
e-mail: summer@relaischateaux.com
Dir: *1m W of A37 halfway between Dorchester and Yeovil*
This picturesque hotel is situated in the heart of Dorset and is the ideal retreat for getting away from it all. Try to arrive for afternoon tea or try out the new spa and swimming pool. Bedrooms, all been refurbished to a very high standard, are individually designed and come with a wealth of facilities. Delightful public areas include a sumptuous lounge complete with an open fire and the elegant restaurant where the cuisine continues to be a high point of any stay.
ROOMS: 10 en suite 14 annexe en suite (6 fmly) (5 GF) ⊗ in 10 bedrooms s £152-£490; d £185-£513 (incl. bkfst) **FACILITIES: Spa** STV Sauna Solarium Gym Jacuzzi Xmas **CONF:** Thtr 24 Class 16 Board 16 Del from £255 **SERVICES:** air con **PARKING:** 41 **NOTES:** ⊗ in restaurant Civ Wed 30

EVESHAM, Worcestershire Map 10 SP04

★★★★75% ◎◎ *Wood Norton Hall*
Wood Norton WR11 4YB
☎ 01386 425780 📠 01386 425781
e-mail: info@wnhall.co.uk
web: www.bespokehotels.com
Dir: *2m from Evesham on A44, after Chadbury*
Once the home to the House of Orleans, with stunning views of the Vale of Evesham, oak-panelled public areas and luxurious bedrooms are situated in the main house. The adjoining stable conversion has smaller and more modest bedrooms, but all are thoughtfully furnished and have a wealth of extras. The restaurant offers carefully prepared dishes with a local and international flavour.
ROOMS: 15 en suite 30 annexe en suite (6 fmly) (14 GF) ⊗ in 30 bedrooms **FACILITIES:** STV Fishing Squash Gym Indoor sports hall - badminton, 5-a-side football etc **CONF:** BC Thtr 70 Class 30 Board 32 **PARKING:** 300 **NOTES:** ⊗ in restaurant Civ Wed 72

★★★77% ◎ The Evesham
Coopers Ln, Off Waterside WR11 1DA
☎ 01386 765566 & 0800 716969 (Res) 📠 01386 765443
e-mail: reception@eveshamhotel.com
web: www.eveshamhotel.com
Dir: *Coopers Lane is off road by River Avon*
Dating from 1540 and set in extensive grounds, this delightful hotel has well-equipped accommodation that includes a selection of quirkily themed rooms (Alice in Wonderland, Egyptian, and Aquarium which has a tropical fish tank in the bathroom). A reputation for food is well deserved, with a particularly strong choice for vegetarians. Children are welcome.
ROOMS: 39 en suite 1 annexe en suite (3 fmly) (11 GF) ⊗ in 20 bedrooms s £74-£87; d £118 (incl. bkfst) **LB** **FACILITIES:** Putt green ch fac **CONF:** Thtr 12 Class 12 Board 12 **PARKING:** 50 **NOTES:** ⊗ in restaurant Closed 25 - 26 Dec

★★★70% Northwick Hotel
Waterside WR11 1BT
☎ 01386 40322 📠 01386 41070
e-mail: enquiries@northwickhotel.co.uk
Dir: *off A46 onto A44 over traffic lights and right at next set onto B4035. Past hospital, hotel on right opposite river*

Standing by the River Avon, this former coaching inn is within easy

continued

walking distance of the centre of Evesham. Bedrooms are tastefully decorated and well equipped, with one specially adapted for less able guests. The public areas offer a choice of bars, meeting rooms and a restaurant.
ROOMS: 29 en suite (4 fmly) (1 GF) ⊗ in all bedrooms
FACILITIES: STV **CONF:** Thtr 240 Class 150 Board 80 Del from £110
PARKING: 85 **NOTES:** ⊗ in restaurant Civ Wed 60

★★★64% Dumbleton Hall
WR11 7TS
☎ 01386 881240 01386 882142
e-mail: dh@pofr.co.uk
(For full entry see Dumbleton)

★★73% Riverside
The Parks, Offenham Rd WR11 8JP
☎ 01386 446200 01386 49755
e-mail: info@theparksoffenham.freeserve.co.uk
web: www.river-side-hotel.co.uk
Dir: *from A46 follow signs for Offenham, right onto B4510. Hotel 0.5m on left on private drive*

A secluded hotel offering personal attention and service that stands in three acres of gardens sloping down to the River Avon. The lounge, restaurant and many of the comfortable bedrooms overlook the river. Cooking remains one of the hotel's strong points, with a menu of imaginative dishes based on high-quality produce.
ROOMS: 10 rms (7 en suite) (5 GF) **FACILITIES:** Fishing **CONF:** BC
PARKING: 30 **NOTES:** ⊗ in restaurant Closed 1-15 Jan

Premier Travel Inn Evesham
Evesham Country Park, A46 Trunk Rd WR11 4TP
☎ 08701 977 288 01386 444301
web: www.premiertravelinn.com
High quality, modern budget accommodation ideal for both families and business travellers. Spacious, en suite bedrooms feature bath and shower, satellite TV and many have telephones and modem points. The adjacent family restaurant features a wide and varied menu. For further details consult the Hotel Groups page.
ROOMS: 40 en suite s £49.95; d £49.95

EWEN, Gloucestershire — Map 04 SU09

★★67% *Wild Duck Inn*
Drakes Island GL7 6BY
☎ 01285 770310 01285 770924
e-mail: wduckinn@aol.com
web: www.thewildduckinn.co.uk
Dir: *from Cirencester take A429. At Kemble left to Ewen*
This bustling, ever-popular inn dates back to the early 16th century and is full of character. Bedrooms vary in style and are well equipped and tastefully furnished. Open fires, old beams and rustic pine tables add to the charm in the bar and restaurant, where the cooking has earned a loyal following.
ROOMS: 11 en suite **FACILITIES:** Discounted leisure facilities within 3m
PARKING: 50 **NOTES:** RS 25 Dec

EXETER, Devon — Map 03 SX99

Town House

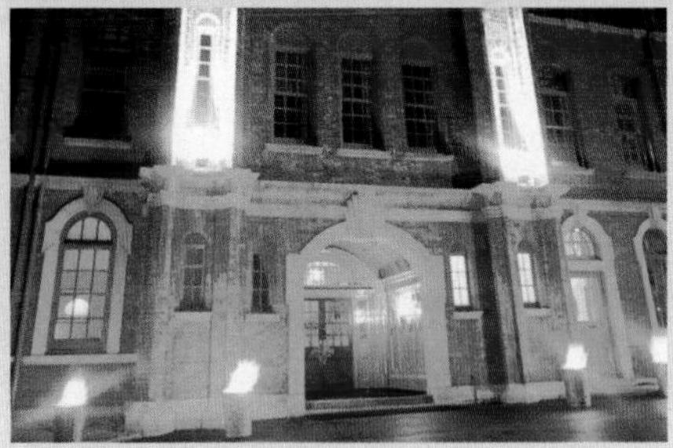

★★★★ Hotel Barcelona
Magdalen St EX2 4HY
☎ 01392 281000 01392 281001
e-mail: info@aliasbarcelona.com
web: www.aliasbarcelona.com
Dir: *from A30 Okehampton follow city centre signs. At Exe Bridges rdbt right for city centre, up hill, on at lights. Hotel on right*
Situated within walking distance of the city centre, Hotel Barcelona was formerly an eye hospital and has been totally transformed to provide stylish accommodation with a glamorous atmosphere. Public areas include Café Paradiso, an informal eatery with a varied menu, a night club, a range of meeting rooms and a delightful garden terrace ideal for alfresco dining.
ROOMS: 46 en suite ⊗ in 3 bedrooms s £85-£120; d £99-£120 **LB**
FACILITIES: STV ♫ **CONF:** Thtr 65 Class 18 Board 22 Del from £140 **SERVICES:** Lift **PARKING:** 35 **NOTES:** ⊗ in restaurant

See advert on page 205

★★★★68% *The Southgate*
Southernhay East EX1 1QF
☎ 0870 400 8333 01392 413549
e-mail: southgate@macdonald-hotels.co.uk
web: www.macdonald-hotels.co.uk
Dir: *M5 junct 30, 3rd exit (Exeter), 2nd left towards city centre, 3rd exit at next rdbt, hotel 2m on right*
Centrally located and with excellent parking, The Southgate offers a diverse range of leisure and business facilities. Public areas are smart and spacious with comfortable seating in the bar and lounge; there is also a pleasant terrace. A range of bedroom sizes is available and all are well equipped with modern facilities.
ROOMS: 110 en suite (6 fmly) (13 GF) ⊗ in 55 bedrooms
FACILITIES: Spa STV supervised Sauna Solarium Gym **CONF:** Thtr 150 Class 70 Board 50 **SERVICES:** Lift **PARKING:** 115 **NOTES:** ⊗ in restaurant RS Sat (restaurant closed for lunch) Civ Wed 80

★★★73% Devon
Exeter Bypass, Matford EX2 8XU
☎ 01392 259268 01392 413142
e-mail: info@devonhotel.co.uk
web: www.brend-hotels.co.uk
Dir: *M5 junct 30 follow Marsh Barton Ind Est signs on A379. Hotel on A38 rdbt*
Within easy access of the city centre, the M5 and the city's

continued on p204

EXETER, continued

business parks, this smart Georgian hotel offers modern, comfortable accommodation. The Carriages Bar and Brasserie is popular with guests and locals alike, offering a wide range of dishes as well as a carvery at both lunch and dinner. Service is friendly and attentive, and extensive meeting and business facilities are available.
ROOMS: 41 annexe en suite (3 fmly) (11 GF) s £65-£85; d £75-£85 **LB** **FACILITIES:** STV Xmas **CONF:** Thtr 150 Class 150 Board 150 **PARKING:** 250 **NOTES:** ⊘ in restaurant Civ Wed 100

★★★72%
Lord Haldon Country House
THE INDEPENDENTS

Dunchideock EX6 7YF
☎ 01392 832483 📠 01392 833765
e-mail: enquiries@lordhaldonhotel.co.uk
web: www.lordhaldonhotel.co.uk
Dir: *M5 junct 31or A30 signed to Ide, 2.5m through village. Left after phone box. 0.5m left after stone bridge*

Set amidst rural tranquillity, this attractive country house goes from strength to strength. Guests are assured of a warm welcome from the resident owners and the well-equipped bedrooms are comfortable, many with stunning views. The daily-changing menu features skilfully cooked dishes with most of the produce sourced locally.
ROOMS: 19 en suite (3 fmly) ⊘ in 10 bedrooms s £65; d £85-£110 (incl. bkfst) **LB** **FACILITIES:** Xmas **CONF:** Thtr 300 Class 150 Board 60 Del from £110 **PARKING:** 120 **NOTES:** ⊘ in restaurant Civ Wed 120

See advert on opposite page

★★★72% St Olaves Court Restaurant & Hotel
Mary Arches St EX4 3AZ
☎ 01392 217736 📠 01392 413054
e-mail: info@olaves.co.uk
web: www.olaves.co.uk
Dir: *city centre, signed to Mary Arches Car Park. Hotel entrance opposite car park entrance*

Only a short stroll from the cathedral and city centre and set in an attractive walled garden, St Olaves seems to be a country house in its almost hidden location. Bedrooms are comfortably furnished and full of character.
ROOMS: 15 en suite (2 fmly) (1 GF) ⊘ in all bedrooms s £75-£115; d £85-£155 (incl. bkfst) **LB** **FACILITIES:** Xmas **CONF:** Thtr 80 Class 60 Board 35 Del from £135 **PARKING:** 18 **NOTES:** ⊘ in restaurant Civ Wed 65

★★★71% Barton Cross Hotel & Restaurant
Huxham, Stoke Canon EX5 4EJ
☎ 01392 841245 📠 01392 841942
e-mail: bartonxhuxham@aol.com
Dir: *0.5m off A396 at Stoke Canon, 3m N of Exeter*

17th-century charm combined with 21st-century luxury perfectly sums up the appeal of this lovely country hotel. The bedrooms are spacious, tastefully decorated and well maintained. Public areas include the cosy first-floor lounge and the lounge/bar with its warming log fire. The restaurant offers a seasonally changing menu of consistently enjoyable cuisine.
ROOMS: 9 en suite (2 fmly) (2 GF) ⊘ in 2 bedrooms s £69-£75; d £98-£110 (incl. bkfst) **LB** **FACILITIES:** STV Xmas **CONF:** Thtr 20 Class 20 Board 20 **PARKING:** 35 **NOTES:** ⊘ in restaurant

See advert on opposite page

★★★70% Queens Court
6-8 Bystock Ter EX4 4HY
☎ 01392 272709 📠 01392 491390
e-mail: enquiries@queenscourt-hotel.co.uk
web: www.queenscourt-hotel.co.uk
Dir: *from city centre 'Clock Tower' rdbt, left at lights (Hele Rd) 1st left (Queens Terrace), hotel next on right*

Quietly located within walking distance of the city centre, this privately owned hotel occupies listed early Victorian premises and provides friendly hospitality. The smart public areas and bedrooms are tastefully furnished in contemporary style. Rooms are available for conferences, meetings and other functions. The bright and

continued

attractive Olive Tree restaurant offers an interesting selection of dishes.
ROOMS: 18 en suite (3 fmly) ⊗ in all bedrooms s £69-£105; d £85-£147 (incl. dinner) **LB** **FACILITIES:** STV Xmas **CONF:** Thtr 60 Class 30 Board 30 Del £130 **SERVICES:** Lift **NOTES:** ✈ ⊗ in restaurant RS Restaurant closed 25-30 Dec

★★★66% Gipsy Hill
Gipsy Hill Ln, Monkerton EX1 3RN
☎ 01392 465252 📠 01392 464302
e-mail: stay@gipsyhillhotel.co.uk
web: www.gipsyhillhotel.co.uk
Dir: *M5 junct 29 towards Exeter. Turn right at 1st rdbt and right again at next rdbt. Hotel 0.5m on right*
Located on the edge of the city, with easy access to the M5 and the airport, this popular hotel is set in attractive, well-tended gardens and boasts far-reaching country views. The hotel offers a range of conference and function rooms, comfortable bedrooms and modern facilities. An intimate bar and lounge are next to the elegant restaurant.
ROOMS: 20 en suite 17 annexe en suite (3 fmly) (12 GF) ⊗ in 11 bedrooms s £55-£75; d £60-£120 (incl. bkfst) **LB** **FACILITIES:** Xmas **CONF:** Thtr 100 Class 40 Board 30 Del from £100 **PARKING:** 60 **NOTES:** ✈ ⊗ in restaurant Civ Wed 60

Town House Hotel
Country House Hotel
Travel Accommodation

EXETER, continued

★★★64% Buckerell Lodge Hotel
Topsham Rd EX2 4SQ
☎ 01392 221111 📠 01392 491111
e-mail: buckerelllodge@foliohotels.co.uk
web: www.foliohotels.co.uk/buckerelllodge

folio
Hotels

Dir: M5 junct 30 follow city centre signs, hotel on Topsham Rd, 0.5m from Exeter
Although situated outside the city centre, this hotel is easily accessed by car or public transport. Accommodation is comfortable, fairly spacious and generally quiet. Public areas include a popular bar and restaurant and a variety of function rooms, and there is an attractive, extensive garden for guests to enjoy.
ROOMS: 53 en suite (2 fmly) ⊗ in 26 bedrooms s £87; d £92 **LB**
FACILITIES: STV **CONF:** Thtr 80 Class 40 Board 40 Del £120
PARKING: 60 **NOTES:** ✘ ⊗ in restaurant Civ Wed 50

U ◉◉ The Royal Clarence Hotel
Cathedral Yard EX1 1HD
☎ 01392 319955 📠 01392 439423
e-mail: reservations@royalclarencehotel.co.uk
web: www.royalclarencehotel.co.uk
Dir: M5 junct 30 towards A379. Follow city centre signs. Hotel opposite cathedral behind High St

As this guide went to press, the Royal Clarence was shortly to become the first Abode Hotel - a new group of individual, mid-size boutique hotels. The restaurant continues to offer award-winning food under the direction of the highly acclaimed chef Michael Caines, who is joint owner of the new venture. Please refer to the AA internet site www.theAA.com for current information.
ROOMS: 53 en suite (4 fmly) ⊗ in all bedrooms s £115-£185; d £115-£185 **LB FACILITIES:** STV Gym Beauty Therapy ♪ Xmas
CONF: BC Thtr 100 Class 50 Board 50 **SERVICES:** Lift air con
PARKING: 15 **NOTES:** ✘ ⊗ in restaurant Civ Wed 50

⟰ Innkeeper's Lodge Exeter East
Clyst St George EX3 0QJ
☎ 01392 876121 📠 01392 872022
web: www.innkeeperslodge.com
Dir: M5 junct 30, A376 towards Exmouth. Right at 1st rdbt, straight over 2nd rdbt, at 3rd rdbt turn into Bridge Hill, lodge on right
A growing concept in the travel accommodation market. Smart rooms meet essential business requirements but also have home comforts. Dining options include all-day menus plus the added advantage of breakfast, which is included in the room price. For further details consult the Hotel Groups page.
ROOMS: 13 en suite s £55; d £55 **CONF:** Thtr 75 Class 45 Board 30

⟰ Premier Travel Inn Exeter
398 Topsham Rd EX2 6HE
☎ 08701 977097 📠 01392 876174
web: www.premiertravelinn.com

premier travel inn

Dir: 2m from M5 junct 30/A30 junct 29. Follow signs for Exeter & Dawlish (A379). On dual carriageway take 2nd slip road on left at Countess Wear rdbt. Inn next to Beefeater
High quality, modern budget accommodation ideal for both families and business travellers. Spacious, en suite bedrooms feature bath and shower, satellite TV and many have telephones and modem points. The adjacent family restaurant features a wide and varied menu. For further details consult the Hotel Groups page.
ROOMS: 44 en suite s £52.95; d £52.95

⟰ Travelodge
Moor Ln, Sandygate EX2 7HF
☎ 08700 850 950 📠 01392 410406
web: www.travelodge.co.uk

Travelodge

Dir: M5 junct 30
Travelodge offers good quality, good value, modern accommodation. Ideal for families, the spacious, en suite bedrooms include remote-control TV, tea and coffee-making facilities and comfortable beds. Meals can be taken at the nearby family restaurant. For further details consult the Hotel Groups page.
ROOMS: 102 en suite s fr £26; d fr £26 **CONF:** Thtr 80 Class 18 Board 25

EXFORD, Somerset Map 03 SS83

★★★70% ◉◉ Crown
TA24 7PP
☎ 01643 831554 📠 01643 831665
e-mail: info@crownhotelexmoor.co.uk
web: www.crownhotelexmoor.co.uk
Dir: M5 junct 25, follow Taunton signs. Take A358 out of Taunton, then B3224 via Wheddon Cross into Exford

Guest comfort is certainly the hallmark here. Afternoon tea is served in the lounge beside a roaring fire and tempting menus in the bar and restaurant are all part of the charm of this delightful old coaching inn that specialises in breaks for shooting and other country sports. Bedrooms retain a traditional style yet offer a range of modern comforts and facilities, many with views of this pretty moorland village.
ROOMS: 17 en suite ⊗ in 3 bedrooms s £65-£68; d fr £99 (incl. bkfst)
LB FACILITIES: Fishing Riding Shooting, Riding Xmas **CONF:** BC
PARKING: 30 **NOTES:** ⊗ in restaurant

Bad hair day?
Hairdryers in all rooms three stars and above

EXMOUTH, Devon
Map 03 SY08

★★★71% Royal Beacon
The Beacon EX8 2AF
☎ 01395 264886 Fax 01395 268890
e-mail: reception@royalbeaconhotel.co.uk
web: www.royalbeaconhotel.co.uk
Dir: *From M5 take A376 and Marine Way. Follow seafront signs. On Imperial Rd turn left at T-junct then 1st right. Hotel 100yds on left*
This elegant Georgian property sits in an elevated position overlooking the town and has fine views of the estuary towards the sea. Bedrooms are individually styled and many have sea views. Public areas include a well stocked bar, a cosy lounge, an impressive function suite and a restaurant where freshly prepared and enjoyable cuisine is offered.
ROOMS: 30 en suite (2 fmly) ⊗ in 15 bedrooms s £48-£77; d £85-£110 (incl. bkfst) **LB** **FACILITIES:** STV ♫ Xmas **CONF:** Thtr 160 Class 100 Board 60 Del from £105 **SERVICES:** Lift **PARKING:** 16 **NOTES:** ⊗ in restaurant Civ Wed 160

★★74% Barn
Foxholes Hill, Marine Dr EX8 2DF
☎ 01395 224411 Fax 01395 225445
e-mail: Info@barnhotel.co.uk
Dir: *M5 junct 30 take A376 to Exmouth, then signs to seafront. At rdbt last exit into Foxholes Hill. Hotel on right*
This unique Grade II listed property is quietly situated just a couple of minutes' walk from the beach. Views across the bay from the elegant public areas and most of the bedrooms are breathtaking. Akin to that of a country house hotel, the atmosphere here is relaxed and hospitable.
ROOMS: 11 en suite (4 fmly) ⊗ in all bedrooms s £30-£47; d £60-£94 (incl. bkfst) **LB** **FACILITIES:** Putt green **CONF:** Class 40 Board 20 **PARKING:** 24 **NOTES:** No dogs ⊗ in restaurant Closed 23 Dec-10 Jan

★★66% Manor Hotel
The Beacon EX8 2AG
☎ 01395 272549 & 274477 Fax 01395 225519
e-mail: post@manorexmouth.co.uk
Dir: *M5 junct 30 take A376 to Exmouth. Hotel 300yds from seafront overlooking Manor Gardens*
Conveniently located for easy access to the town centre and with views overlooking the sea, this friendly hotel offers traditional values of hospitality and service, drawing guests back year after year. The well-equipped bedrooms vary in style and size; many have far-reaching views. The fixed-price menu offers a varied selection of dishes.
ROOMS: 39 en suite (3 fmly) ⊗ in 6 bedrooms s £35-£40; d £60-£80 (incl. bkfst) **LB** **FACILITIES:** Xmas **CONF:** Thtr 100 Class 60 Board 60 Del from £35 **SERVICES:** Lift **PARKING:** 15 **NOTES:** No dogs ⊗ in restaurant

★★63% *Cavendish Hotel*
11 Morton Crescent, The Esplanade EX8 1BE
☎ 01395 272528 Fax 01395 269361
e-mail: cavendish.exmouth@alfatravel.co.uk
web: www.alfatravel.co.uk
Dir: *follow seafront signs, hotel in centre of large crescent*
Situated on the seafront, this terraced hotel attracts many groups from around the country. With fine views out to sea, the hotel is within walking distance of the town centre. The bedrooms are neatly presented; front facing rooms are always popular. Entertainment is provided on some evenings during the summer.
ROOMS: 72 en suite (3 fmly) (19 GF) **FACILITIES:** Snooker ♫ **CONF:** Thtr 30 Board 12 **SERVICES:** Lift **PARKING:** 25 **NOTES:** No dogs ⊗ in restaurant Closed Dec-Jan ex Xmas RS Nov & Mar

FAIRFORD, Gloucestershire
Map 05 SP10

★★66% Bull Hotel
The Market Place GL7 4AA
☎ 01285 712535 & 712217 Fax 01285 713782
e-mail: info@thebullhotelfairford.co.uk
Dir: *on A417 in market square adjacent to post office*
Located in a picturesque Cotswold market town, this family-run inn's history dates back to the 15th century and still retains much period character and charm. A wide range of meals can be enjoyed within the popular bar or alternatively in the bistro restaurant. Bedrooms are all individual in style with a number overlooking the square.
ROOMS: 22 rms (20 en suite) 4 annexe en suite (4 fmly) s £50-£80; d £80-£110 (incl. bkfst) **LB** **FACILITIES:** Fishing Cycle hire **CONF:** Thtr 60 Class 40 Board 40 Del from £83 **PARKING:** 10 **NOTES:** ⊗ in restaurant

See advert on this page

FALFIELD, Gloucestershire
Map 04 ST69

U Bristol Inn
Bristol Rd GL12 8DL
☎ 01454 260502 Fax 01454 261821
e-mail: info@bristolinn.co.uk
Dir: *M5 junct 14 follow sign to Dursley. Right at A38 junct, hotel 200yds on right*
At the time of going to press, the star classification for this hotel

continued on p208

FALFIELD, continued

was not confirmed. Please refer to the AA internet site www.theAA.com for current information.

Bristol Inn, Falfield

ROOMS: 46 en suite (18 GF) ⊗ in 40 bedrooms s £65-£70; d £70-£77.50 (incl. bkfst) **FACILITIES:** STV ⛳ 18 Putt green **CONF:** BC Thtr 200 Class 60 Board 50 Del from £117 **PARKING:** 107 **NOTES:** ✗ ⊗ in restaurant Civ Wed 140

FALMOUTH, Cornwall & Isles of Scilly Map 02 SW83
See also Mawnan Smith

★★★★72% Royal Duchy
Cliff Rd TR11 4NX
☎ 01326 313042 📠 01326 319420
e-mail: info@royalduchy.com
web: www.brend-hotels.co.uk
Dir: *on Cliff Rd, along Falmouth seafront*

Looking out over the sea and towards Pendennis Castle, this hotel provides a friendly environment. The comfortable lounge and cocktail bar are well appointed, and leisure facilities and meeting rooms are also available. The restaurant serves carefully prepared dishes and bedrooms vary in size and aspect, with many rooms having sea views.
ROOMS: 43 en suite (6 fmly) (1 GF) s £70-£100; d £130-£260 (incl. bkfst) **LB** **FACILITIES: Spa** STV Sauna Table tennis ♫ ch fac Xmas **CONF:** Thtr 50 Class 50 Board 50 **SERVICES:** Lift **PARKING:** 50 **NOTES:** ✗ ⊗ in restaurant Civ Wed 100

See advert on opposite page

★★★76% Penmere Manor
Mongleath Rd TR11 4PN
☎ 01326 211411 📠 01326 317588
e-mail: reservations@penmere.co.uk
web: www.penmeremanorhotel.co.uk
Dir: *right off A39 at Hillhead rdbt, over double mini rdbt. After 0.75m left into Mongleath Rd*

Set in five acres on the outskirts of Falmouth, this family-owned hotel provides friendly service and a range of facilities. A choice of freshly prepared dishes is served in either the bar or in the more formal Bolitho's Restaurant. A wide range of bedrooms is available - the spacious garden-wing rooms are furnished and equipped to a particularly high standard.

ROOMS: 37 en suite (12 fmly) (13 GF) ⊗ in all bedrooms s £49-£77; d £98-£154 (incl. bkfst) **LB** **FACILITIES: Spa** STV Sauna Gym Jacuzzi Beauty treatment room, Croquet **CONF:** Thtr 60 Class 20 Board 30 Del from £90 **PARKING:** 50 **NOTES:** ✗ ⊗ in restaurant Closed 23-26 Dec Civ Wed 70

See advert on opposite page

★★★73% *Falmouth Beach Resort Hotel*
Gyllyngvase Beach, Seafront TR11 4NA
☎ 01326 310500 📠 01326 319147
e-mail: info@falmouthbeachhotel.co.uk
web: www.falmouthbeachhotel.co.uk
Dir: *A39 to Falmouth, follow seafront signs.*

Enjoying wonderful views, this popular hotel is situated opposite the beach and within easy walking distance of Falmouth's attractions and port. A friendly atmosphere is maintained and guests have a good choice of leisure and fitness, entertainment and dining options. Bedrooms, many with balconies and sea views, are well equipped and comfortable.
ROOMS: 116 en suite 7 annexe en suite (20 fmly) (4 GF) ⊗ in 94 bedrooms **FACILITIES: Spa** STV supervised Sauna Solarium Gym Jacuzzi Steam room ♫ **CONF:** Thtr 300 Class 200 Board 250 **SERVICES:** Lift **PARKING:** 88 **NOTES:** ⊗ in restaurant Civ Wed 120

See advert on opposite page

★★★73% The Greenbank
Harbourside TR11 2SR
☎ 01326 312440 📠 01326 211362
e-mail: sales@greenbank-hotel.com
web: www.greenbank-hotel.com
Dir: *500yds past Falmouth Marina on Penryn River*

Located by the marina, and with its own private quay dating from the 17th century, this smart hotel has a strong maritime theme throughout. Set at the water's edge, the lounge, restaurant and

continued on p210

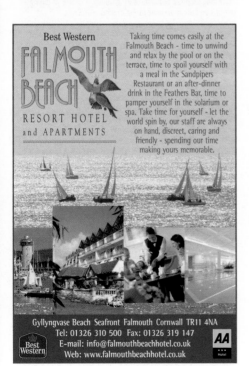

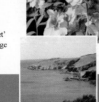

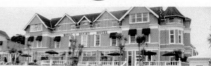

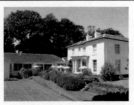

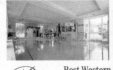

many bedrooms benefit from having harbour views. The restaurant provides a choice of interesting and enjoyable dishes.

The Greenbank, Falmouth

ROOMS: 60 en suite (4 fmly) ⊗ in 30 bedrooms s £65-£100; d £105-£185 (incl. bkfst) **LB FACILITIES:** Private beach **CONF:** Thtr 60 Class 45 Board 20 **SERVICES:** Lift **PARKING:** 68 **NOTES:** ⊗ in restaurant Civ Wed 100

★★★71% Green Lawns
Western Ter TR11 4QJ
☎ 01326 312734 📠 01326 211427
e-mail: info@greenlawnshotel.com
web: www.greenlawnshotel.com
Dir: on A39

THE INDEPENDENTS

This attractive property enjoys a convenient location close to the town centre and within easy reach of the sea. Spacious public areas include inviting lounges, an elegant restaurant, conference and meeting facilities and a leisure centre. Bedrooms vary in size and style but all are well equipped and comfortable. The friendly service is noteworthy.
ROOMS: 39 en suite (8 fmly) (11 GF) ⊗ in 24 bedrooms s £55-£110; d £110-£170 (incl. bkfst) **LB FACILITIES:** ⌨ ♋ Squash Sauna Solarium Gym Jacuzzi Swimming pool cameras **CONF:** Thtr 200 Class 80 Board 100 Del from £95 **PARKING:** 69 **NOTES:** ⊗ in restaurant Closed 24-30 Dec Civ Wed 50

★★★70% ◉ St Michaels of Falmouth
Gyllyngvase Beach, Seafront TR11 4NB
☎ 01326 312707 📠 01326 211772
e-mail: info@stmichaelshotel.co.uk
Dir: A39 into Falmouth, follow beach signs, at 2nd mini-rdbt into Pennance Rd. Take 2nd left & 2nd left again
Overlooking the bay, this establishment has an excellent location. The contemporary public areas include comfortable lounges and leisure facilities and there are attractive gardens. The Flying Fish bistro and the hotel's main restaurant, Oyster Bay, offer enjoyable
continued

dining. Bedrooms are well equipped and available in a range of sizes.

ROOMS: 54 en suite 8 annexe en suite (7 fmly) (12 GF) ⊗ in 15 bedrooms s £36-£64; d £42-£70 (incl. bkfst) **LB FACILITIES:** ⌨ Sauna Solarium Gym ♨ Jacuzzi Xmas **CONF:** Thtr 200 Class 150 Board 50 Del from £80 **PARKING:** 30 **NOTES:** ✻ ⊗ in restaurant Civ Wed 80
See advert on opposite page

★★★69% Falmouth
Castle Beach TR11 4NZ
☎ 01326 312671 & 0800 0193121 📠 01326 319533
e-mail: info@falmouthhotel.com
web: www.falmouthhotel.com
Dir: take A30 to Truro then A390 to Falmouth. Follow signs for beaches, hotel on seafront near Pendennis Castle
This spectacular beachfront Victorian property affords wonderful sea views from many of its comfortable bedrooms, some of which have their own balconies. Spacious public areas include a number of inviting lounges, beautiful leafy grounds, a choice of dining options and an impressive range of leisure facilities.
ROOMS: 69 en suite 34 annexe en suite (13 fmly) s £47-£55; d £84-£147 **LB FACILITIES:** STV ⌨ supervised Snooker Sauna Solarium Gym Putt green Jacuzzi Beauty Salon **CONF:** Thtr 250 Class 150 Board 100 Del from £75 **SERVICES:** Lift **PARKING:** 175 **NOTES:** ⊗ in restaurant Closed 24 Dec-2 Jan Civ Wed 250
See advert on opposite page

★★★66% Penmorvah Manor
Budock Water TR11 5ED
☎ 01326 250277 📠 01326 250509
e-mail: reception@penmorvah.co.uk
web: www.penmorvah.co.uk
Dir: A39 to Hillhead rdbt, take 2nd exit. Right at Falmouth Football Club, through Budock and hotel opposite Penjerrick Gardens

Situated within two miles of central Falmouth, this extended Victorian manor house is a peaceful hideaway, set in six acres of private woodland and gardens. Penmorvah is well positioned for visiting the local gardens, and offers many garden-tour breaks.
continued

Dinner features locally sourced, quality ingredients such as Cornish cheeses, meat, fish and game.
ROOMS: 27 en suite (1 fmly) (10 GF) ⊗ in all bedrooms s £65; d £100 (incl. bkfst) **LB** **FACILITIES:** Xmas **CONF:** Thtr 250 Class 100 Board 56 Del from £95 **PARKING:** 150 **NOTES:** ⊗ in restaurant Closed 31 Dec-31 Jan Civ Wed 120

★★77% Crill Manor

Maen Valley, Budock Water TR11 5BL
☎ 01326 211880 📠 01326 211229
e-mail: info@crillmanor.com
Dir: *A39 Truro towards Falmouth, then right for Mawnan Smith/ Budock Water. Over double mini rdbt. Through village to 40mph sign then left*

Set in a secluded Area of Outstanding Natural Beauty, this delightful hotel, now under new ownership, offers friendly and attentive service. Bedrooms are well equipped and attractively decorated. The open plan, split-level lounge and bar area overlooks the gardens. The Four Seasons Restaurant offers a daily-changing menu and enjoyable dining.
ROOMS: 14 en suite (2 GF) ⊗ in all bedrooms s £49-£69; d £98-£138 (incl. bkfst & dinner) **LB** **FACILITIES:** Xmas **PARKING:** 20 **NOTES:** 🐕 No children 14yrs ⊗ in restaurant Closed 1 Nov-1 Feb RS 22-29 Dec

★★69% Hotel Anacapri

Gyllyngvase Rd TR11 4DJ
☎ 01326 311454 📠 01326 311454
e-mail: anacapri@btconnect.com
web: www.hotelanacapri.co.uk
Dir: *A39 Truro to Falmouth, straight on at lights, 2 rdbts straight on. 5th right into Gyllyngvase Road, hotel on right*
In an elevated position, overlooking Gyllyngvase Beach and Falmouth Bay beyond, this family run establishment extends a warm welcome to all. Bedrooms all share similar standards of comfort and quality and the majority have sea views. Public areas include a convivial bar, a lounge and the smart restaurant, where carefully prepared and very enjoyable cuisine is on offer.
ROOMS: 16 en suite (1 fmly) ⊗ in 8 bedrooms s £30-£50; d £50-£160 (incl. bkfst) **LB** **PARKING:** 20 **NOTES:** 🐕 No children 8yrs ⊗ in restaurant RS Except Xmas 20-28 Dec

★★68% Park Grove

THE INDEPENDENTS

Kimberley Park Rd TR11 2DD
☎ 01326 313276 📠 01326 211926
e-mail: reception@parkgrovehotel.com
web: www.parkgrovehotel.com
Dir: *off A39 at lights by Riders Garage towards harbour. Hotel 400yds on left opposite park*
Within walking distance of the town centre, this friendly family-run hotel is situated in a pleasant residential area opposite Kimberley Park. Comfortable accommodation is provided and public areas

continued on p212

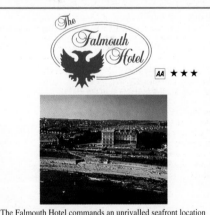

FALMOUTH, continued

include a relaxing and stylish lounge and a well-spaced dining room and bar. Bedrooms are also comfortable and well equipped. **ROOMS:** 17 en suite (6 fmly) s £35-£78; d £61-£88 (incl. bkfst) **LB PARKING:** 25 **NOTES:** ✻ ⊘ in restaurant Closed Dec-Feb

★★67% Broadmead
66/68 Kimberley Park Rd TR11 2DD
☎ 01326 315704 🖹 01326 311048
e-mail: mail@broadmeadhotel.fsnet.co.uk
Dir: A39 from Truro to Falmouth, at lights turn left into Kimberley Park Rd, hotel 200 yds on left
Conveniently located, with views across the park and within easy walking distance of the beaches and town centre, this pleasant hotel, under new ownership, has smart and comfortable accommodation. Bedrooms are well equipped and attractively decorated. A choice of lounges is available and, in the dining room, menus offer freshly prepared home-cooked dishes. **ROOMS:** 12 en suite (2 fmly) (2 GF) ⊘ in all bedrooms s £31-£35; d £60-£70 (incl. bkfst) **LB PARKING:** 8 **NOTES:** ✻ ⊘ in restaurant

THE CIRCLE
Selected Individual Hotels
GREAT BRITAIN

★★67% Rosslyn
110 Kimberley Park Rd TR11 2JJ
☎ 01326 312699 & 315373 🖹 01326 312699
e-mail: mail@rosslynhotel.co.uk
web: www.rosslynhotel.co.uk
Dir: on A39 towards Falmouth, to Hillend rdbt, turn right and over next mini rdbt. At 2nd mini rdbt left into Trescobeas Rd. Hotel on left past hospital
A relaxed and friendly atmosphere is maintained at this family-run hotel. Situated on the northern edge of Falmouth, the Rosslyn is easily located and is suitable for both business and leisure guests. A comfortable lounge overlooks the well-tended garden, and enjoyable freshly prepared dinners are offered in the restaurant. **ROOMS:** 27 en suite (3 fmly) (6 GF) ⊘ in all bedrooms s £25-£35; d £50-£70 (incl. bkfst) **LB FACILITIES:** Table tennis Pool table Computer in lounge Internet access Xmas **CONF:** BC Class 60 Board 20 **PARKING:** 22 **NOTES:** ⊘ in restaurant

★★64% Membly Hall
Sea Front, Cliff Rd TR11 4NT
☎ 01326 312869 & 311115 🖹 01326 211751
e-mail: memblyhallhotel@btopenworld.com
Dir: A39 to Falmouth. Follow seafront and beaches sign.

Located conveniently on the seafront and enjoying splendid views, this family-run hotel offers friendly service. Bedrooms are pleasantly spacious and well equipped. Carefully prepared and enjoyable meals are served in the spacious dining room. Live
continued

entertainment is provided on some evenings in the attractive lounge bar area, and there is also a sun room.
ROOMS: 37 en suite (3 fmly) s £38-£46; d £76-£92 (incl. bkfst & dinner) **LB FACILITIES: Spa** STV Riding Sauna Putt green Indoor short bowls, Table tennis, Pool table ♫ **CONF:** Thtr 150 Class 130 Board 60 **SERVICES:** Lift **PARKING:** 30 **NOTES:** ✻ ⊘ in restaurant Closed Xmas week RS Dec-Jan No credit cards accepted

★★63% *Madeira Hotel*
Cliff Rd TR11 4NY
☎ 01326 313531 🖹 01326 319143
e-mail: madeira.falmouth@alfatravel.co.uk
web: www.alfatravel.co.uk
Dir: A39 (Truro to Falmouth), follow tourist signs 'Hotels' to seafront
This popular hotel offers splendid sea views and a pleasantly convenient location, which is close to the town. Extensive sun lounges are popular haunts in which to enjoy the views, whilst additional facilities include an oak panelled cocktail bar. Bedrooms, many with sea views, are available in a range of sizes. **ROOMS:** 50 en suite (8 fmly) (7 GF) **FACILITIES:** ♫ **SERVICES:** Lift **PARKING:** 11 **NOTES:** ✻ ⊘ in restaurant Closed Dec-Feb RS Nov & Mar

Leisureplex

FAREHAM, Hampshire Map 05 SU50

★★★★73% ◉ Solent
Rookery Av, Whiteley PO15 7AJ
☎ 01489 880000 🖹 01489 880007
e-mail: solent@shirehotels.com
web: www.shirehotels.com
Dir: M27 junct 9, hotel on Solent Business Park
Although close to the M27, this smart, purpose-built hotel enjoys a peaceful location. Bedrooms are very spacious and well-appointed. There is a well-equipped leisure centre and spa, and the lounge, bar and restaurant feature beams and log fires throughout. **ROOMS:** 111 en suite (9 fmly) (20 GF) ⊘ in 83 bedrooms s £88-£150; d £126-£170 (incl. bkfst) **LB FACILITIES:** STV ⛴ supervised ⚲ Sauna Solarium Gym Jacuzzi Steam room, Childrens splash pool, activity studio, Spa treatments from Mar 2006 Xmas **CONF:** BC Thtr 250 Class 120 Board 80 Del from £160 **SERVICES:** Lift **PARKING:** 200 **NOTES:** ✻ ⊘ in restaurant Civ Wed 160

SHIRE
HOTELS

★★★66% ◉ Lysses House
51 High St PO16 7BQ
☎ 01329 822622 🖹 01329 822762
e-mail: lysses@lysses.co.uk
web: www.lysses.co.uk
Dir: M27 junct 11 stay in left lane. At rdbt 3rd exit into East St & follow into High St. Hotel at top on right
This attractive Georgian hotel is situated on the edge of the town in a quiet location and provides spacious and well-equipped accommodation. There are conference facilities, a lounge bar serving a range of snacks and the Richmond Restaurant that serves both accomplished and imaginative cuisine. **ROOMS:** 21 en suite (7 GF) ⊘ in 14 bedrooms s £55-£60; d £80 (incl. bkfst) **CONF:** Thtr 95 Class 42 Board 28 Del from £124 **SERVICES:** Lift **PARKING:** 30 **NOTES:** ✻ ⊘ in restaurant Closed 25 Dec-1 Jan RS Dec & BHs Civ Wed 100

> **Early start?**
> Hotels at all star levels should provide
> in-room alarm clocks and/or alarm clocks

Premier Travel Inn Fareham
Southampton Rd, Park Gate SO31 6AF
☎ 08701 977100 📠 01489 577238
web: www.premiertravelinn.com
Dir: *on 2nd rdbt off M27 junct 9, signed A27 Fareham*
High quality, modern budget accommodation ideal for both families and business travellers. Spacious, en suite bedrooms feature bath and shower, satellite TV and many have telephones and modem points. The adjacent family restaurant features a wide and varied menu. For further details consult the Hotel Groups page.
ROOMS: 41 en suite s £50.95; d £50.95

FARINGDON, Oxfordshire — Map 05 SU29

★★★70% Sudbury House Hotel & Conference Centre
London St SN7 8AA
☎ 01367 241272 📠 01367 242346
e-mail: stay@sudburyhouse.co.uk
web: www.sudburyhouse.co.uk
Dir: *off A420, signed Folly Hill*

Sudbury House lies between Oxford and Swindon. Bedrooms are attractive, decorated in warm colour schemes, spacious and well equipped. Dining options include the restaurant, bar and a comprehensive room service menu. In addition to pleasant grounds, conference facilities, a small fitness room and private dining rooms are also available.
ROOMS: 49 en suite (2 fmly) (10 GF) ⊘ in 28 bedrooms s £85-£95; d £95-£105 (incl. bkfst) **LB FACILITIES:** STV Gym Putt green Pitch & Putt, Badminton, Boules Xmas **CONF:** Thtr 100 Class 30 Board 34 Del from £135 **SERVICES:** Lift **PARKING:** 100 **NOTES:** ⊘ in restaurant

See advert on this page

FARNBOROUGH, Hampshire — Map 05 SU85

★★★65% Falcon
68 Farnborough Rd GU14 6TH
☎ 01252 545378 📠 01252 522539
e-mail: hotel@falconfarnborough.com
web: www.falconfarnborough.com
Dir: *A325 off M3, pass Farnborough Gate Retail Park. Left at next rdbt & straight at next 2 rdbts. Hotel on left at junct of aircraft esplanade & A325*
This well-presented hotel is conveniently located for business guests. Modern bedrooms are practically furnished and equipped with a useful range of extras. Public areas include the conservatory restaurant offering a range of contemporary and traditional fare. Aircraft enthusiasts are well catered for as there is an aeronautical centre adjacent.
ROOMS: 30 en suite (1 fmly) (3 GF) ⊘ in 25 bedrooms s £55-£95; d £65-£110 (incl. bkfst) **FACILITIES:** STV Xmas **CONF:** Thtr 25 Class 8 Board 16 Del from £105 **PARKING:** 25 **NOTES:** ⊘ in restaurant RS 23 Dec - 4 Jan Civ Wed 50

FARNBOROUGH, continued

Premier Travel Inn Farnborough

Ively Rd, Southwood GU14 0JP
☎ 08701 977101 01252 546427
web: www.premiertravelinn.com
Dir: *From M3 junct 4a, join A327 to Farnborough. Inn on left at 5th rbt (Monkey Puzzle roundabout)*
High quality, modern budget accommodation ideal for both families and business travellers. Spacious, en suite bedrooms feature bath and shower, satellite TV and many have telephones and modem points. The adjacent family restaurant features a wide and varied menu. For further details consult the Hotel Groups page.
ROOMS: 62 en suite s £49.95-£52.95; d £49.95-£52.95

FARNHAM, Surrey Map 05 SU84

★★★73% Frensham Pond Hotel

Bacon Ln GU10 2QB
☎ 01252 795161 01252 792631
e-mail: info@frenshampondhotel.co.uk
web: www.frenshampondhotel.co.uk
(For full entry see Churt and advert on page 213)

★★★72% Bishop's Table

27 West St GU9 7DR
☎ 01252 710222 01252 733494
e-mail: welcome@bishopstable.com
web: www.bishopstable.com
Dir: *from M3 junct 4 take A331 or from A3 take A31and follow town centre signs. Hotel next to library*

This family-run Georgian townhouse hotel is in the centre of Farnham and offers comfortable accommodation and friendly, attentive service. Each bedroom is individual in style and some are situated in a restored coach house. Public areas include a cosy bar and an elegant restaurant.
ROOMS: 9 en suite 8 annexe en suite (6 GF) in 5 bedrooms s £95-£105; d fr £115 **LB** **FACILITIES:** free use of nearby gym **CONF:** BC Thtr 26 Class 10 Board 20 Del from £165 **NOTES:** No children 16yrs in restaurant Closed 25 Dec-3 Jan RS Closed for lunch Mon

★★★68% The Bush

The Borough GU9 7NN
☎ 0870 400 8225 01252 715237
01252 733530
e-mail: gm.bush@macdonald-hotels.co.uk
web: www.macdonald-hotels.co.uk
Dir: *M3 junct 4, A31, follow signs for town centre. At East St. traffic lights turn left, hotel on right.*
Dating back to the 17th century, this extended coaching inn is attractively presented and has a courtyard and a lawned garden. The bedrooms are well appointed, with quality fabrics and good facilities. The public areas include the panelled Oak Lounge, a smart cocktail bar and a conference facility, developed in an adjoining building.

ROOMS: 83 en suite (3 fmly) (22 GF) in 60 bedrooms s £109-£160; d £119-£170 (incl. bkfst) **LB** **FACILITIES:** Xmas **CONF:** Thtr 140 Class 80 Board 30 **PARKING:** 70 **NOTES:** in restaurant Civ Wed 90

★★★62% Farnham House

Alton Rd GU10 5ER
☎ 01252 716908 01252 722583
e-mail: mail@farnhamhousehotel.com
web: www.hollybournehotels.com
Dir: *1m from town, off A31 Alton road*
Popular for conferences and weddings, Farnham House is surrounded by five acres of grounds. The architecture is part Tudor, part baronial in style, and features an oak-panelled bar with an inglenook fireplace. Most bedrooms enjoy countryside views, and a tennis court and swimming pool are peacefully set in the tranquil gardens.
ROOMS: 25 en suite (1 fmly) in 7 bedrooms **FACILITIES:** STV **CONF:** Thtr 55 Class 14 Board 25 Del from £99 **PARKING:** 75 **NOTES:** RS 25 & 26 Dec Civ Wed 74

FAVERSHAM, Kent Map 07 TR06

Travelodge Canterbury North

Thanet Way ME13 9EL
☎ 08700 850 950 01227 281135
web: www.travelodge.co.uk
Dir: *M2 from junct 7, A299 to Ramsgate. Lodge 4m on left*
Travelodge offers good quality, good value, modern accommodation. Ideal for families, the spacious, en suite bedrooms include remote-control TV, tea and coffee-making facilities and comfortable beds. Meals can be taken at the nearby family restaurant. For further details consult the Hotel Groups page.
ROOMS: 40 en suite s fr £26; d fr £26

FEERING, Essex Map 07 TL82

Travelodge (Colchester)

A12 London Rd Northbound CO5 9EL
☎ 08700 850 950 01376 572848
web: www.travelodge.co.uk
Dir: *northbound carriageway of A12, 0.5m N of Kelvedon*
Travelodge offers good quality, good value, modern accommodation. Ideal for families, the spacious, en suite bedrooms include remote-control TV, tea and coffee-making facilities and comfortable beds. Meals can be taken at the nearby family restaurant. For further details consult the Hotel Groups page.
ROOMS: 39 en suite s fr £26; d fr £26

No smoking

FELIXSTOWE, Suffolk — Map 13 TM33

★★★72% Elizabeth Orwell
Hamilton Rd IP11 7DX
☎ 01394 285511 🖹 01394 670687
e-mail: elizabeth.orwell@elizabethhotels.co.uk
Dir: *from A14 over Dock rdbt and next rdbt. At 3rd rdbt 4th exit to Beatrice Ave. At end of road hotel over rdbt*

Imposing Victorian building situated just a short walk from the town centre. The pleasantly decorated, well-equipped bedrooms come in a variety of styles and feature several large, superior rooms. The public areas are superbly appointed and offer a wealth of charm and character; they include two bars, a choice of lounges, an informal buttery and the spacious Westerfield's restaurant.
ROOMS: 60 en suite (8 fmly) ⊘ in 15 bedrooms s £45-£85; d £90-£150 (incl. bkfst) **LB** **FACILITIES:** STV ♫ Xmas **CONF:** Thtr 200 Class 100 Board 60 Del £127 **SERVICES:** Lift **PARKING:** 70 **NOTES:** ⊘ in restaurant Civ Wed 200

★★65% Marlborough
Sea Front IP11 2BJ
☎ 01394 285621 🖹 01394 670724
e-mail: hsm@marlborough-hotel-felix.com
web: www.marlborough-hotel-felix.com
Dir: *from A14 follow Docks signs. Over Dock rdbt, railway crossing and traffic lights. Left at T-junct and hotel 400mtrs on left*
Situated on the seafront, overlooking the beach and just a short stroll from the pier and town centre. This traditional resort hotel offers a good range of facilities including the smart Rattan Restaurant, Flying Boat Bar and L'Aperitif lounge. The pleasantly decorated bedrooms come in a variety of styles; some have lovely sea views.
ROOMS: 49 en suite ⊘ in 3 bedrooms s £52-£70; d £65-£85 (incl. bkfst) **LB** **FACILITIES:** STV Pool table Xmas **CONF:** Thtr 80 Class 60 Board 40 Del £70 **SERVICES:** Lift **PARKING:** 16 **NOTES:** ✈ ⊘ in restaurant

FENNY BENTLEY, Derbyshire — Map 16 SK14

★★68% Leatherbritches Bentley Brook Inn
DE6 1LF
☎ 01335 350278 🖹 01335 350422
e-mail: all@bentleybrookinn.co.uk
web: www.bentleybrookinn.co.uk
Dir: *2m N of Ashbourne at junct of A515 & B5056, entrance off B5056*
This popular family-owned inn is located within the Peak District National Park, just north of Ashbourne. It is a charming building with an attractive terrace, sweeping lawns, and nursery gardens. A well-appointed family restaurant dominates the ground floor, where a wide range of dishes is available all day. The character *continued* bar serves beer from its own micro-brewery. Bedrooms vary in styles and sizes, but all are well equipped.

ROOMS: 9 en suite 1 annexe rms ⊘ in 1 bedroom s £52.50; d £76 (incl. bkfst) **LB** **FACILITIES:** Fishing Brewery tour Xmas **CONF:** Thtr 28 Class 28 Board 18 Del from £85 **PARKING:** 100 **NOTES:** ⊘ in restaurant

FENSTANTON, Cambridgeshire — Map 12 TL36

⇧ Travelodge Huntingdon
PE18 9LP
☎ 08700 850 950 🖹 01954 230919
web: www.travelodge.co.uk
Dir: *4m SE of Huntingdon, on A14 eastbound*
Travelodge offers good quality, good value, modern accommodation. Ideal for families, the spacious, en suite bedrooms include remote-control TV, tea and coffee-making facilities and comfortable beds. Meals can be taken at the nearby family restaurant. For further details consult the Hotel Groups page.
ROOMS: 40 en suite s fr £26; d fr £26

FERNDOWN, Dorset — Map 05 SU00

⇧ Premier Travel Inn Bournemouth/ Ferndown
Ringwood Rd, Tricketts Cross BH22 9BB
☎ 08701 977102 🖹 01202 897794
web: www.premiertravelinn.com
Dir: *off A348 just before Tricketts Cross rdbt*
High quality, modern budget accommodation ideal for both families and business travellers. Spacious, en suite bedrooms feature bath and shower, satellite TV and many have telephones and modem points. The adjacent family restaurant features a wide and varied menu. For further details consult the Hotel Groups page.
ROOMS: 32 en suite s £55.95; d £55.95 **CONF:** Thtr 20

FERRYBRIDGE SERVICE AREA (M62/A1), West Yorkshire — Map 16 SE42

⇧ Travelodge Pontefract Ferrybridge
WF11 0AF
☎ 08700 850 950 🖹 01977 622509
web: www.travelodge.co.uk
Dir: *M62 junct 33*
Travelodge offers good quality, good value, modern accommodation. Ideal for families, the spacious, en suite bedrooms include remote-control TV, tea and coffee-making facilities and comfortable beds. Meals can be taken at the nearby family restaurant. For further details consult the Hotel Groups page.
ROOMS: 36 en suite s fr £26; d fr £26

FILEY, North Yorkshire　　　Map 17 TA18

★★75% Downcliffe House
6 The Beach YO14 9LA
☎ 01723 513310 ▤ 01723 512659
e-mail: info@downcliffehouse.co.uk
Dir: A165/A1039 into Filey, through town centre along Cargate Hill & turn right. Hotel 200yds along seafront
This very friendly hotel is set right on the seafront and the inviting public areas include a cosy bar and an attractive restaurant serving an excellent range of freshly prepared meals. Furnished throughout to a high standard, the bedrooms are smart and well equipped; some are very spacious and enjoy panoramic sea views.
ROOMS: 12 en suite (5 fmly) ⊗ in all bedrooms s £48; d £96-£130 (incl. bkfst) **LB FACILITIES:** Xmas **PARKING:** 6 **NOTES:** ⊗ in restaurant RS Jan

FIR TREE, Co Durham　　　Map 19 NZ13

★★★66% Helme Park Hall Hotel
DL13 4NW
☎ 01388 730970 ▤ 01388 731799
e-mail: enquiries@helmeparkhotel.co.uk
web: www.helmeparkhotel.co.uk
Dir: 1m N of A689/A68 rdbt between Darlington & Corbridge
Dating back to the 13th century, this welcoming hotel boasts superb panoramic views up the Wear Valley. The bedrooms are comfortably equipped and furnished. The cosy lounge bar is extremely popular for its comprehensive selection of bar meals, and the restaurant offers both table d'hote and carte menus.
ROOMS: 13 en suite (1 fmly) ⊗ in 5 bedrooms s £54; d £90 (incl. bkfst) **LB FACILITIES:** STV Xmas **CONF:** BC Thtr 150 Class 80 Board 80 Del from £99 **PARKING:** 70 **NOTES:** ⊗ in restaurant Civ Wed 100

FIVE OAKS, West Sussex　　　Map 06 TQ02

⌂ Travelodge Billingshurst
Staines St RH14 9AE
☎ 08700 850 950 ▤ 01403 782711
web: www.travelodge.co.uk
Dir: on A29, northbound, 1m N of Billingshurst
Travelodge offers good quality, good value, modern accommodation. Ideal for families, the spacious, en suite bedrooms include remote-control TV, tea and coffee-making facilities and comfortable beds. Meals can be taken at the nearby family restaurant. For further details consult the Hotel Groups page.
ROOMS: 26 en suite s fr £26; d fr £26

FLAMBOROUGH, East Riding of Yorkshire　　　Map 17 TA27

★★72% North Star
North Marine Dr YO15 1BL
☎ 01262 850379 ▤ 01262 850379
web: www.puffinsatflamborough.co.uk
Dir: follow signs for North Landing. Hotel 100yds from sea
Standing close to the North Landing of Flamborough Head, this family-run hotel overlooks delightful countryside. It provides excellent accommodation and hospitality, together with a very popular bar. A good range of well-produced food is available in both the bar and the dining room.
ROOMS: 7 en suite **PARKING:** 30 **NOTES:** ✖ ⊗ in restaurant Closed Xmas & 2wks Nov & Jan

> **U** Star rating not confirmed

FLEET, Hampshire　　　Map 05 SU85

★★★63% Lismoyne
Church Rd GU51 4NE
☎ 01252 628555 ▤ 01252 811761
e-mail: info@lismoynehotel.com
web: www.lismoynehotel.com
Dir: M3 junct 4a. B3013, over railway bridge to town centre. Through lights, take 4th right. Hotel 0.25m on left
Set in extensive grounds, this attractive hotel is located close to the town centre. Public rooms include a comfortable lounge and pleasant bar with a conservatory overlooking the garden, and a traditional restaurant. Accommodation is divided between the bedrooms in the original building and those in the modern extension; styles vary but all rooms are well equipped.
ROOMS: 62 en suite (3 fmly) (19 GF) ⊗ in 18 bedrooms s £40-£125; d £50-£150 (incl. bkfst) **LB FACILITIES:** STV Gym Xmas **CONF:** Thtr 170 Class 92 Board 80 Del from £110 **PARKING:** 150 **NOTES:** ✖ ⊗ in restaurant Civ Wed 100

⌂ Innkeeper's Lodge Fleet
Cove Rd GU51 2SH
☎ 01252 774600
web: www.innkeeperslodge.com
Dir: M3, junct 4a
A growing concept in the travel accommodation market. Smart rooms meet essential business requirements but also have home comforts. Dining options include all-day menus plus the added advantage of breakfast, which is included in the room price. For further details consult the Hotel Groups page.
ROOMS: 40 en suite s £49.95-£68; d £49.95-£68

FLEET MOTORWAY SERVICE AREA (M3),　　　Map 05 SU75
Hampshire

⌂ Days Inn Fleet
Fleet Services GU51 1AA
☎ 01252 815587 ▤ 01252 815587
e-mail: fleethotel@welcomebreak.co.uk
web: www.welcomebreak.co.uk
Dir: between junct 4a & 5 southbound on M3
This modern building offers accommodation in smart, spacious and well-equipped bedrooms, suitable for families and business travellers, and all with en suite bathrooms. Continental breakfast is available and other refreshments may be taken at the nearby family restaurant. For further details see the Hotel Groups page.
ROOMS: 58 en suite **CONF:** Board 10

FLITWICK, Bedfordshire　　　Map 11 TL03

Top Hotel

★★★ ◉◉ Menzies Flitwick Manor
Church Rd MK45 1AE
☎ 01525 712242 ▤ 01525 718753
e-mail: flitwick@menzies-hotels.co.uk
web: www.menzies-hotels.co.uk
Dir: M1 junct 12, follow signs for Flitwick, turn left into Church Rd, hotel on left
With its picturesque setting in acres of gardens and parkland, yet only minutes by car from the motorway, this lovely Georgian house combines the best of both worlds - accessible and peaceful. Bedrooms are individually decorated and furnished with period pieces; some are air conditioned. Cosy

continued

and intimate, the lounge and restaurant help give the hotel a home-from-home feel, which makes it popular with many guests.

ROOMS: 17 en suite s £140-£160; d £170-£195 **LB** **FACILITIES:** Putt green Xmas **CONF:** Thtr 40 Class 30 Board 24 Del £210 **PARKING:** 50 **NOTES:** in restaurant Civ Wed

FLORE, Northamptonshire Map 11 SP66

★★★72%
Courtyard by Marriott Daventry
High St NN7 4LP
☎ 01327 349022 01327 349017
e-mail: res.ntwcourtyard@kewgreen.co.uk
web: www.kewgreen.co.uk
Dir: *M1 junct 16 onto A45 towards Daventry. Hotel 1m on right between Upper Heyford and Flore*
Just off the M1 in rural surroundings, this modern hotel is particularly suited to the business guest. Professional staff provide a warm welcome and helpful service throughout. The public areas comprise a lounge bar and restaurant, and the bedrooms provide smart decor, plenty of workspace and a good range of facilities.
ROOMS: 53 en suite (7 fmly) in 34 bedrooms s £47-£94; d £64-£101 (incl. bkfst) **LB** **FACILITIES:** STV Gym **CONF:** Thtr 80 Class 40 Board 40 Del from £130 **PARKING:** 120 **NOTES:** in restaurant Civ Wed 100

FOLKESTONE, Kent Map 07 TR23

★★★70% **Clifton**
The Leas CT20 2EB
☎ 01303 851231 01303 223949
e-mail: reservations@thecliftonhotel.com
Dir: *M20 junct 13, 0.25m W of town centre on A259*

This privately-owned Victorian-style hotel occupies a prime location, looking out across the English Channel. The bedrooms are all comfortably appointed and most have views of the sea.

continued

Public areas include a comfortable, traditionally furnished lounge, a popular bar serving a good range of beers and several well-appointed conference rooms.
ROOMS: 80 en suite (5 fmly) in 31 bedrooms s £57-£71; d £72-£92 **LB** **FACILITIES:** STV Games room Xmas **CONF:** Thtr 80 Class 36 Board 32 Del from £105 **SERVICES:** Lift **NOTES:** in restaurant

See advert on this page

★★★63% **Quality Hotel Burlington**
Earls Av CT20 2HR
☎ 01303 255301 01303 251301
e-mail: sales@theburlingtonhotel.com
Situated close to the beach in a peaceful side road just a short walk from the town centre. The extensive public rooms include a choice of lounges, the Bay Tree restaurant and a large cocktail bar. Bedrooms are pleasantly decorated and equipped with modern facilities; some rooms have lovely sea views.
ROOMS: 62 en suite (6 fmly) (5 GF) in 24 bedrooms s fr £56; d fr £68 **LB** **FACILITIES:** Riding Putt green Jacuzzi Preferential rates at Open Health Club next door Xmas **CONF:** Thtr 240 Class 100 Board 80 **SERVICES:** Lift **PARKING:** 20 **NOTES:** in restaurant Civ Wed 120

Premier Travel Inn Folkestone
Cherry Garden Ln CT19 4AP
☎ 08701 977103 01303 273641
web: www.premiertravelinn.com
Dir: *M20 junct 13. At 1st rdbt turn right, at 2nd rdbt turn right signed Folkestone A20. At traffic lights turn right, Inn is on the right.*
High quality, modern budget accommodation ideal for both families and business travellers. Spacious, en suite bedrooms feature bath and shower, satellite TV and many have telephones and modem points. The adjacent family restaurant features a wide and varied menu. For further details consult the Hotel Groups page.
ROOMS: 79 en suite s £48.95; d £48.95

FONTWELL, West Sussex Map 06 SU90

⟳ Travelodge Bognor Regis
BN18 0SB
☎ 08700 850 950 ▤ 01243 543973
web: www.travelodge.co.uk

Dir: on A27/A29 rdbt
Travelodge offers good quality, good value, modern accommodation. Ideal for families, the spacious, en suite bedrooms include remote-control TV, tea and coffee-making facilities and comfortable beds. Meals can be taken at the nearby family restaurant. For further details consult the Hotel Groups page.
ROOMS: 63 en suite s fr £26; d fr £26

FORDINGBRIDGE, Hampshire Map 05 SU11

F

★★72% ◉ Ashburn Hotel & Restaurant
Station Rd SP6 1JP
☎ 01425 652060 ▤ 01425 652150
e-mail: ashburn@mistral.co.uk
web: www.ashburn.mistral.co.uk
Dir: from Fordingbridge High St, follow Damerham signs. Pass police and fire stations, hotel 400yds on left
This friendly family-run hotel, situated in an elevated position on the edge of the village, is surrounded by beautiful countryside. Bedrooms, some in the original house and others in a purpose built extension, are comfortable and well equipped. There is a smart function room, a spacious bar, a cosy lounge and a wonderful garden. A good choice is offered at dinner and dishes are carefully prepared.
ROOMS: 20 en suite (3 fmly) ⊗ in 10 bedrooms **FACILITIES:** ch fac Xmas **CONF:** Thtr 130 Class 80 Board 40 **PARKING:** 60 **NOTES:** ⊗ in restaurant RS 24-29 Dec, 1-5 Jan Civ Wed 180

FOREST ROW, East Sussex Map 06 TQ43

Top Hotel

★★★★ ◉◉ Ashdown Park Hotel and Country Club

Wych Cross RH18 5JR
☎ 01342 824988 ▤ 01342 826206
e-mail: reservations@ashdownpark.com
web: www.ashdownpark.com
Dir: A264 to East Grinstead, then A22 to Eastbourne, 2m S of Forest Row at Wych Cross traffic lights. Left to Hartfield, hotel on right 0.75m
Magnificent country house hotel set in attractive landscaped grounds, overlooking 186 acres of parkland in the heart of Ashdown Forest. The stylish bedrooms are full of character; each one individually decorated and tastefully furnished to provide guests with an excellent degree of comfort. Public areas include a chapel, which has been converted into a
continued

conference room, a leisure club, a golf course and the Anderida Restaurant.
ROOMS: 106 en suite (16 GF) ⊗ in 49 bedrooms s £135-£335; d £165-£365 (incl. bkfst) LB **FACILITIES:** Spa STV 🏊 ♨ 👙 18 🎯 Snooker Sauna Solarium Gym 🏑 Putt green Jacuzzi Beauty/Hair salon, Aerobics, Treatment room, Mountain bike hire, Steam room Xmas **CONF:** BC Thtr 170 Class 80 Board 40 Del from £235 **SERVICES:** Lift **PARKING:** 200 **NOTES:** ✖ ⊗ in restaurant Civ Wed 150

FORMBY, Merseyside Map 15 SD30

★★★66% *Tree Tops Country House Restaurant & Hotel*
Southport Old Rd L37 0AB
☎ 01704 572430 ▤ 01704 572430
Dir: off A565 Southport to Liverpool road

This country house residence boasts an attractive restaurant where good food is served by an attentive staff. Rooms are in delightful lodges situated in five acres of wooded grounds. The hotel is adjacent to a fabulous golf course, near to beaches and all the local amenities.
ROOMS: 11 annexe en suite (3 fmly) (11 GF) **FACILITIES:** 🎣 **CONF:** Thtr 200 Class 80 Board 40 **PARKING:** 100 **NOTES:** ✖ ⊗ in restaurant Civ Wed 75

FORTON MOTORWAY Map 18 SD55
SERVICE AREA (M6), Lancashire

⟳ Travelodge Lancaster Forton
White Carr Ln, Bay Horse LA2 9DU
☎ 08700 850 950 ▤ 01524 791703
web: www.travelodge.co.uk
Dir: between junct 32 & 33 of M6
Travelodge offers good quality, good value, modern accommodation. Ideal for families, the spacious, en suite bedrooms include remote-control TV, tea and coffee-making facilities and comfortable beds. Meals can be taken at the nearby family restaurant. For further details consult the Hotel Groups page.
ROOMS: 53 en suite s fr £26; d fr £26

FOUR MARKS, Hampshire Map 05 SU63

⟳ Travelodge Alton
156 Winchester Rd GU34 5HZ
☎ 08700 850 950 ▤ 01420 562659
web: www.travelodge.co.uk
Dir: 5m S of Alton on A31 n'bound
Travelodge offers good quality, good value, modern accommodation. Ideal for families, the spacious, en suite bedrooms include remote-control TV, tea and coffee-making
continued

facilities and comfortable beds. Meals can be taken at the nearby family restaurant. For further details consult the Hotel Groups page.
ROOMS: 31 en suite s fr £26; d fr £26

FOWEY, Cornwall & Isles of Scilly — Map 02 SX15

★★★77% Fowey Hall

Hanson Dr PL23 1ET
☎ 01726 833866 Fax 01726 834100
e-mail: info@foweyhall.com
Dir: *in Fowey, cross mini rdbt into town centre. Pass school on right, after 400mtrs right into Hanson Drive*

Built in 1899, this listed mansion looks out on to the English Channel. The imaginatively designed bedrooms offer charm, individuality and sumptuous comfort, while beautifully appointed public rooms include the wood-panelled dining room where accomplished cuisine is served. Enjoying glorious views, the well-kept grounds have a covered pool and sunbathing area.
ROOMS: 16 en suite 8 annexe en suite (18 fmly) s £135-£415; d £150-£450 (incl. bkfst & dinner) **LB** **FACILITIES:** STV supervised Childrens play area, Table tennis, Bicycle hire ch fac Xmas **CONF:** Thtr 30 Class 20 Board 20 **PARKING:** 40 **NOTES:** in restaurant Civ Wed 50

See advert on opposite page

★★★73% The Fowey Hotel

Best Western

The Esplanade PL23 1HX
☎ 01726 832551 Fax 01726 832125
e-mail: fowey@richardsonhotels.co.uk
web: www.richardsonhotels.co.uk
Dir: *M5 take A30 to Okehampton, continue to Bodmin. Then B3269 to Fowey for 1m, on right bend left junct then right into Dagands Rd. Hotel 200mtrs on left*

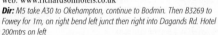

This attractive hotel stands proudly above the estuary, with marvellous views of the river from the public areas and the majority of the bedrooms. High standards are evident throughout, augmented by a relaxed and welcoming atmosphere. There is a

continued on p220

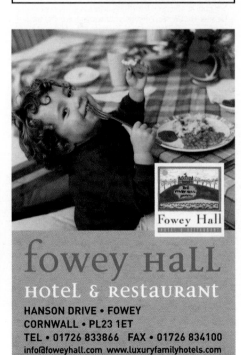

FOWEY, continued

spacious bar, elegant restaurant and smart drawing room. Imaginative dinners make good use of quality local ingredients.
ROOMS: 37 en suite (1 fmly) ⊗ in 3 bedrooms s £79-£149; d £98-£238 (incl. bkfst & dinner) **LB** **FACILITIES:** Fishing Xmas **CONF:** Thtr 100 Class 60 Board 20 **SERVICES:** Lift **PARKING:** 18 **NOTES:** ⊗ in restaurant

Top Hotel

★★ Marina
Esplanade PL23 1HY
☎ 01726 833315 🖷 01726 832779
e-mail: marina.hotel@dial.pipex.com
web: www.themarinahotel.co.uk
Dir: *into town down Lostwithiel St, near bottom of hill, right into Esplanade*
Built in 1815 as a seaside retreat, the Marina has much style, and from its setting on the water's edge has glorious views of the river and the sea. Bedrooms, some with balconies, are spacious and comfortable - not forgetting the addition of a host of thoughtful touches that are provided. Skilled cuisine, using the freshest local produce, including fish landed nearby, is the hallmark of the waterside restaurant.
ROOMS: 13 en suite (1 fmly) ⊗ in all bedrooms s £65-£100; d £100-£200 (incl. bkfst) **LB** **FACILITIES:** Fishing Sailing Xmas **PARKING:** 13 **NOTES:** ⊗ in restaurant Civ Wed 55

U The Old Quay House Hotel
28 Fore St PL23 1AQ
☎ 01726 833302 🖷 01726 833668
e-mail: info@theoldquayhouse.com
Dir: *M5 junct 31 onto A30 to Bodmin. Then A389 through town and take B3269 to Fowey*
At the time of going to press, the star classification for this hotel was not confirmed. Please refer to the AA internet site www.theAA.com for current information.
ROOMS: 12 en suite ⊗ in all bedrooms s £120-£190; d £150-£190 (incl. bkfst) **LB** **FACILITIES:** STV **NOTES:** ✈ No children 12yrs ⊗ in restaurant

FRADDON, Cornwall & Isles of Scilly — Map 02 SW95

⌂ Premier Travel Inn Newquay
Penhale TR9 6NA
☎ 08701 977194 🖷 01726 860641
web: www.premiertravelinn.com
Dir: *on A30 2m S of Indian Queens*
High quality, modern budget accommodation ideal for both families and business travellers. Spacious, en suite bedrooms feature bath and shower, satellite TV and many have telephones and modem points. The adjacent family restaurant features a wide and varied menu. For further details consult the Hotel Groups page.
ROOMS: 40 en suite s £49.95; d £49.95

FRANKBY, Merseyside — Map 15 SJ28

★★★★ Hillbark
Royden Park CH48 1NP
☎ 0151 625 2400 🖷 0151 625 4040
e-mail: enquiries@hillbarkhotel.co.uk
Originally built in 1891 on Bidston Hill, this Elizabethan-style mansion was actually moved to its current site, brick by brick, in 1931. The house now sits within a 250-acre woodland estate and enjoys delightful views towards the River Dee and the North Wales hills. Bedrooms are luxuriously furnished and well equipped whilst elegant days rooms are richly styled with a wealth of historical features. The lavish Yellow Room provides a delightful venue in which to enjoy skilfully prepared dishes.
ROOMS: 20 en suite (1 fmly) ⊗ in all bedrooms s £150-£330; d £165-£345 (incl. bkfst) **FACILITIES:** STV Putt green Jacuzzi ♫ Xmas **CONF:** BC Thtr 750 Class 250 Board 100 Del from £200 **SERVICES:** Lift **PARKING:** 143 **NOTES:** ✈ ⊗ in restaurant Civ Wed 160

FRANKLEY MOTORWAY SERVICE AREA (M5), West Midlands — Map 10 SO98

⌂ Travelodge Birmingham South
Illey Ln, Frankley Motorway Service Area, Frankley B32 4AR
☎ 08700 850 950 🖷 0121 501 2880
web: www.travelodge.co.uk
Dir: *between juncts 3 and 4 on s'bound carriageway of M5*
Travelodge offers good quality, good value, modern accommodation. Ideal for families, the spacious, en suite bedrooms include remote-control TV, tea and coffee-making facilities and comfortable beds. Meals can be taken at the nearby family restaurant. For further details consult the Hotel Groups page.
ROOMS: 62 en suite s fr £26; d fr £26

FRESHWATER See Wight, Isle of

FRIMLEY, Surrey — Map 05 SU85

⌂ Innkeeper's Lodge Frimley
114 Portsmouth Rd GU15 1HS
☎ 01276 691939 🖷 01276 605900
web: www.innkeeperslodge.com
Dir: *M3 junct 4/ A321 for Frimley take A325 (towards A30 Bagshot), over 1st rdbt past Frimley Park Hospital, straight over 2nd rdbt into Portsmouth Rd. Lodge 500mtrs on left.*
A growing concept in the travel accommodation market. Smart rooms meet essential business requirements but also have home comforts. Dining options include all-day menus plus the added advantage of breakfast, which is included in the room price. For further details consult the Hotel Groups page.
ROOMS: 43 en suite s £49.95-£79.95; d £49.95-£79.95 **CONF:** Thtr 40 Class 20 Board 20

FRITTON, Norfolk — Map 13 TG40

★★★73% Caldecott Hall Golf & Leisure
Caldecott Hall, Beccles Rd NR31 9EY
☎ 01493 488488 🖷 01493 488561
e-mail: hotel@caldecotthall.co.uk
web: www.caldecotthall.co.uk
Dir: *On A143 Beccles to Great Yarmouth road, 4m from Great Yarmouth*
This hotel enjoys an ideal situation in its own attractive landscaped

continued

grounds that include an 18-hole golf course (plus an interesting par 3 course), fishing lakes and the Redwings Horse sanctuary. The individually decorated bedrooms are spacious, and equipped with many thoughtful touches. Public rooms include a smart sitting room, a lounge bar, restaurant, clubhouse and smart new leisure complex.
ROOMS: 8 en suite (6 fmly) ⊗ in all bedrooms s £75; d £85-£110 **LB** **FACILITIES: Spa** supervised 18 Gym Putt green Jacuzzi Driving range Pitch & Putt **CONF:** Thtr 100 Class 80 Board 20 **PARKING:** 100 **NOTES:** ⊗ in restaurant

FRODSHAM, Cheshire Map 15 SJ57

★★★70% Forest Hill Hotel & Leisure Complex
Overton Hill WA6 6HH
☎ 01928 735255 01928 735517
e-mail: info@foresthillshotel.com
Dir: *at Frodsham turn onto B5151. After 1m right into Manley Rd, right into Simons Ln after 0.5m. Hotel 0.5m past Frodsham golf course*
This modern, purpose-built hotel is set high up on Overton Hill, so offering panoramic views. There is a range of spacious, well-equipped bedrooms, including executive rooms. Guests have a choice of bars and there is a tasteful split-level restaurant, as well as conference facilities and a very well equipped leisure suite and gym.
ROOMS: 58 en suite (4 fmly) ⊗ in 26 bedrooms s £55-£90; d £70-£130 **LB** **FACILITIES:** STV Snooker Sauna Solarium Gym Jacuzzi Nightclub, Dance studio, Aerobics/pilates ♫ Xmas **CONF:** Thtr 200 Class 80 Board 70 Del from £100 **PARKING:** 350 **NOTES:** ⊗ in restaurant Civ Wed 200

FROME, Somerset Map 04 ST74

★★★66% *Mendip House*
Bath Rd BA11 2HP
☎ 01373 463223 01373 463990
e-mail: latonamlh@aol.com
Dir: *on Bath side of Frome, on B3090, opp Frome College*
Located on the edge of town, this welcoming hotel is set in attractive grounds. Bedrooms, some on the ground floor, enjoy glorious country views over the Mendip Hills. Relaxed and friendly service can be enjoyed in the bar, on the outdoor terrace and in the comfortable restaurant.
ROOMS: 40 en suite (3 fmly) (20 GF) **FACILITIES:** STV **CONF:** Thtr 80 Class 40 Board 40 **PARKING:** 80 **NOTES:** ⊗ in restaurant Civ Wed 85

★★65% *The George at Nunney*
11 Church St BA11 4LW
☎ 01373 836458 01373 836565
e-mail: georgenunneyhotel@barbox.net
(For full entry see Nunney)

GARFORTH, West Yorkshire Map 16 SE43

★★★73% Milford
A1 Great North Rd, Peckfield LS25 5LQ
☎ 01977 681800 01977 681245
e-mail: enquiries@mlh.co.uk
web: www.mlh.co.uk
Dir: *On A63, 1.5m W of A1 & 4.5m E of M1 junct 46*
This friendly, family owned and run hotel conveniently situated on the A1, provides comfortable modern accommodation. Bedrooms, which are air conditioned, are all particularly spacious and comfortable and have been well insulated against traffic noise.
continued

Public areas include a stylish lounge area and the contemporary Watermill Restaurant and Bar which features a working waterwheel.

ROOMS: 46 en suite (10 fmly) (14 GF) ⊗ in 19 bedrooms s £75-£125; d £75-£125 **LB** **FACILITIES:** STV Xmas **CONF:** Thtr 70 Class 35 Board 30 Del from £115 **SERVICES:** air con **PARKING:** 80
See advert under LEEDS

GARSTANG, Lancashire Map 18 SD44

★★★70% Garstang Country Hotel & Golf Club
Garstang Rd, Bowgreave PR3 1YE
☎ 01995 600100 01995 600950
e-mail: reception@ghgc.co.uk
web: www.garstanghotelandgolf.co.uk
Dir: *M6 junct 32 take 1st right after Rogers Esso garage on A6 onto B6430. Continue for 1m and hotel on left*

This smart, purpose-built hotel enjoys a peaceful location alongside its own 18-hole golf course. Comfortable and spacious bedrooms are well equipped for both business and leisure guests, whilst inviting public areas include a choice of bars - one serving food - and a restaurant.
ROOMS: 32 en suite (16 GF) ⊗ in 20 bedrooms s £60-£75; d £80-£96 (incl. bkfst) **LB** **FACILITIES:** STV 18 Golf driving range **CONF:** Thtr 200 Class 100 Board 80 Del from £85 **SERVICES:** Lift **PARKING:** 172 **NOTES:** ⊗ in restaurant Civ Wed 250

★★★66% Pickerings
Garstang Rd, Catterall PR3 0HD
☎ 01995 600999 01995 602100
e-mail: info@pickeringshotel.com
Dir: *from S M6 junct 32 onto M55 exit junct 1& take A6 N, after Esso garage right onto B6430 then right after bus shelter*
This appealing and welcoming hotel, now under new ownership, dates back to the 17th century and nestles in carefully tended grounds that feature a well-equipped children's play area. Bedrooms are spacious and include several smart four-poster
continued on p222

GARSTANG, continued

rooms. Public areas include an inviting bar lounge, two elegant dining rooms and a purpose-built conference suite.
ROOMS: 12 en suite (1 fmly) s £50-£70; d £70-£140 (incl. bkfst) **LB** **FACILITIES:** STV ch fac Xmas **CONF:** BC Thtr 150 Class 80 Board 50 Del from £70 **PARKING:** 40 **NOTES:** ✈ ⊗ in restaurant Civ Wed 150

GATESHEAD, Tyne & Wear — Map 21 NZ26
See also Beamish & Whickham

★★★★68%
Newcastle Marriott Hotel MetroCentre
MetroCentre NE11 9XF
☎ 0191 493 2233 🖷 0191 493 2030
e-mail: reservations.newcastle@marriotthotels.co.uk
web: www.marriott.co.uk
Dir: *from N leave A1 at MetroCentre exit, take 'Other Routes'. From S leave A1 at MetroCentre exit and turn right.*

Set just off the A1 and on the doorstep of the popular Metro shopping, this stylish purpose-built hotel provides modern amenities including a leisure centre, conference facilities and an informal stylish restaurant offering a range of dining styles. All bedrooms are smartly laid out and thoughtfully equipped and suit the business traveller and the leisure guest.
ROOMS: 150 en suite (145 fmly) ⊗ in 90 bedrooms s fr £115; d fr £115 **LB** **FACILITIES:** STV supervised Sauna Solarium Gym Jacuzzi Health & beauty clinic Dance studio Hairdressers Xmas **CONF:** BC Thtr 400 Class 147 Board 12 **SERVICES:** Lift air con **PARKING:** 300 **NOTES:** ✈ ⊗ in restaurant Civ Wed 100

★★★71% ❀❀ **Eslington Villa**
8 Station Rd, Low Fell NE9 6DR
☎ 0191 487 6017 & 420 0666 🖷 0191 420 0667
e-mail: admin@eslingtonvilla.fsnet.co.uk
Dir: *off A1 onto Team Valley Trading Est. Right at 2nd rdbt along Eastern Av then left past Belle Vue Motors, hotel on left*

Set in a residential area, this smart hotel marries a bright contemporary approach to the period style of a fine Victorian villa. The overall ambience is relaxed and inviting. Chunky sofas grace the cocktail lounge, while tempting dishes can be enjoyed in either the classical dining room or modern conservatory overlooking the Team Valley.
ROOMS: 17 en suite (2 fmly) (3 GF) s £70; d £80 (incl. bkfst) **CONF:** Thtr 36 Class 30 Board 25 Del from £110 **PARKING:** 15 **NOTES:** ✈ ⊗ in restaurant Closed 25-26 Dec RS Sun/BHs (restricted restaurant service)

⌂ Premier Travel Inn Gateshead
Derwent Haugh Rd, Swalwell NE16 3BL
☎ 08701 977283 🖷 0191 414 5032
web: www.premiertravelinn.com
Dir: *accessed from the A1/A694 junct 1m N of the Metro Centre*
High quality, modern budget accommodation ideal for both families and business travellers. Spacious, en suite bedrooms feature bath and shower, satellite TV and many have telephones and modem points. The adjacent family restaurant features a wide and varied menu. For further details consult the Hotel Groups page.
ROOMS: 40 en suite s £49.95; d £49.95

⌂ Premier Travel Inn Newcastle South
Lobley Hill Rd NE11 9NA
☎ 0870 9906590 🖷 0870 9906591
web: www.premiertravelinn.com
Dir: *Just off A1, on A692, 2m from Angel of the North. 3m from Metro Centre*
High quality, modern budget accommodation ideal for both families and business travellers. Spacious, en suite bedrooms feature bath and shower, satellite TV and many have telephones and modem points. The adjacent family restaurant features a wide and varied menu. For further details consult the Hotel Groups page.
ROOMS: 40 en suite s £49.95; d £49.95

⌂ Travelodge Gateshead
Clasper Way, Swalwell NE16 3BE
☎ 08700 850 950
web: www.travelodge.co.uk
Dir: *From S - Follow A1 at the 2nd junct after the Metro Centre junct, signed Consett/Blaydon A694. Follow signs for the A694/695 and then A1114 (Metro Centre). Lodge is 0.25m from A1, oppoiste to TGI Friday's.*
Travelodge offers good quality, good value, modern accommodation. Ideal for families, the spacious, en suite bedrooms include remote-control TV, tea and coffee-making facilities and comfortable beds. Meals can be taken at the nearby family restaurant. For further details consult the Hotel Groups page.
ROOMS: 60 en suite s fr £26; d fr £26

GATWICK AIRPORT (LONDON), West Sussex — Map 06 TQ24
See also Dorking, East Grinstead & Reigate

★★★★70% ❀
Copthorne Hotel London Gatwick
Copthorne Way RH10 3PG
☎ 01342 348800 & 348888 🖷 01342 348833
e-mail: coplgw@mill-cop.com
web: www.copthorne.com/gatwick
Dir: *on A264, 2m E of A264/B2036 rdbt*
Situated in a tranquil position, the Copthorne is set in 100 acres of wooded, landscaped gardens containing jogging tracks, a putting green and a petanque pit. The sprawling building is built around a 16th-century farmhouse and has comfortable, well-maintained

continued

bedrooms. In addition to the main restaurant, dining options include an inn or the more formal, award-winning restaurant.
ROOMS: 227 en suite (10 fmly) in 136 bedrooms s £77-£175; d £87-£175 (incl. bkfst) **LB FACILITIES: Spa** STV Squash Sauna Solarium Gym Jacuzzi Petanque pit, Aerobic studio **CONF:** BC Thtr 135 Class 60 Board 40 Del from £145 **SERVICES:** Lift **PARKING:** 300 **NOTES:** Civ Wed 100

★★★★70% Le Meridien London Gatwick

North Terminal RH6 0PH
☎ 01293 567070 01293 567739
e-mail: reservations.gatwick@lemeridien.com
Dir: *M23 junct 9, follow to 2nd rdbt. Hotel large white building straight ahead*
One of the closest hotels to the airport, this modern, purpose-built hotel is located only minutes from the terminals. Bedrooms are contemporary and all are air-conditioned. Guests have a choice of eating options including a French-style café, brasserie and oriental restaurant.
ROOMS: 500 en suite (18 fmly) in 283 bedrooms s £105-£212; d £105-£212 **FACILITIES:** STV Sauna Solarium Gym **CONF:** BC Thtr 300 Class 200 Board 120 **SERVICES:** Lift air con **PARKING:** 120 **NOTES:**

★★★★66% Copthorne Hotel and Resort Effingham Park

COPTHORNE

West Park Rd RH10 3EU
☎ 01342 714994 01342 716039
e-mail: sales.effingham@mill-cop.com
web: www.millenniumhotels.com
Dir: *M23 junct 10, take A264 towards East Grinstead. Over rdbt and at 2nd rdbt left onto B2028. Effingham Park on right*
A former stately home, set in 40 acres of grounds, this hotel is popular for conference and weekend functions. The main restaurant is an open-plan, Mediterranean-themed brasserie, and snacks are also available in the bar. Bedrooms are spacious and well equipped. Facilities include an 18-hole golf course and a leisure club.
ROOMS: 122 en suite (6 fmly) in 74 bedrooms **FACILITIES:** STV 9 Sauna Solarium Gym Putt green Jacuzzi Aerobic studio Bowls Croquet Xmas **CONF:** Thtr 600 Class 250 Board 30 **SERVICES:** Lift **PARKING:** 500 **NOTES:** in restaurant Civ Wed

Top Hotel

★★★ Langshott Manor

Langshott Ln RH6 9LN
☎ 01293 786680 01293 783905
e-mail: admin@langshottmanor.com
Dir: *from A23 take Ladbroke Rd, off Chequers rdbt to Langshott, after 0.75m hotel on right*
Charming timber-framed Tudor house set amidst beautifully landscaped grounds on the outskirts of town. The stylish public areas feature a choice of plushly furnished lounges with polished oak panelling, exposed beams and log fires. The individually decorated bedrooms combine the most up-to-date modern comforts with flair, individuality and traditional elegance. The Mulberry restaurant overlooks a picturesque pond and offers an imaginative menu.
ROOMS: 14 en suite 8 annexe en suite in all bedrooms s £150-£210; d £190-£330 (incl. bkfst) **LB FACILITIES:** STV Xmas **CONF:** Thtr 40 Class 20 Board 22 Del £215 **PARKING:** 25 **NOTES:** in restaurant

★★★73% Stanhill Court

Stanhill Rd, Charlwood RH6 0EP
☎ 01293 862166 01293 862773
e-mail: enquiries@stanhillcourthotel.co.uk
web: www.stanhillcourthotel.co.uk
Dir: *N of Charlwood towards Newdigate*

This hotel dates back to 1881 and enjoys a secluded location in 35
continued on p224

GATWICK AIRPORT (LONDON), continued

acres of well-tended grounds with views over the Downs. Bedrooms are individually furnished and decorated, and many have four-poster beds. Public areas include a library, a bright Spanish-style bar and a traditional wood-panelled restaurant. Extensive and varied function facilities make this a popular wedding venue.
ROOMS: 15 en suite (3 fmly) ⊗ in 3 bedrooms **FACILITIES:** STV Fishing Putt green **CONF:** Thtr 250 Class 100 Board 60 **PARKING:** 110 **NOTES:** ⊗ in restaurant Civ Wed 140

★★★64% Gatwick Worth Hotel

Crabbet Park, Turners Hill Rd, Worth RH10 4ST
☎ 01293 884806 01293 882444
e-mail: reception@gatwickworthhotel.com
web: www.gatwickworthhotel.com
Dir: *M23 junct 10, left to A264. At 1st rdbt right signed to Maidenbower. 1st left into Old Hollow Rd, follow to end. At T-junct right. Hotel 200yds right*
This purpose-built hotel is ideally placed for access to Gatwick Airport. The bedrooms are spacious and suitably appointed with good facilities. Public areas consist of a light and airy bar area and a brasserie-style restaurant offering good value meals. Guests have use of the superb leisure club next door.
ROOMS: 118 en suite (9 fmly) (56 GF) ⊗ in 57 bedrooms **FACILITIES: Spa** supervised Riding Sauna Solarium Gym Jacuzzi Cannon's fitness centre adjacent to hotel. **CONF:** Thtr 200 Class 100 Board 60 Del from £110 **PARKING:** 150 **NOTES:** ⊗ in restaurant Civ Wed 150

★★★62% Gatwick Moat House

Longbridge Roundabout, Gatwick RH6 0AB
☎ 01293 899988 01293 785991
e-mail: csm.gatwick@moathousehotels.com
Dir: *A217, left at Esso Garage*
Ideally situated for both terminals, this hotel provides a shuttle service to the airport twice an hour. Conference facilities are provided in one of the air-conditioned modern function rooms, which have the bonus of a café break out area. Bedrooms are practically furnished and all have access to satellite TV and movies.
ROOMS: 124 en suite (8 fmly) ⊗ in 62 bedrooms **FACILITIES:** STV Gym **CONF:** BC Thtr 30 Class 15 Board 15 Del from £110 **SERVICES:** Lift **PARKING:** 130 **NOTES:** ⊗ in restaurant

U Ramada Plaza Gatwick

Tinsley Ln South, Three Bridges RH10 8XH
☎ 01293 561186 01293 561169
e-mail: sales.plazagatwick@ramadajarvis.co.uk
Dir: *From M23 junct 10, follow A2011 to Crawley. Hotel is at 1st rdbt on left.*
This modern, purpose built hotel is just four miles from the airport with easy access to the M23. Bedrooms are comfortably appointed for both business and leisure guests.
ROOMS: 151 en suite (31 fmly) ⊗ in all bedrooms s £99-£130; d £99-£130 **FACILITIES: Spa** STV supervised Sauna Solarium Gym Jacuzzi **CONF:** Thtr 200 Class 110 Board 40 Del from £149 **SERVICES:** Lift air con **PARKING:** 150 **NOTES:** ⊗ in restaurant Civ Wed 200

Hotel Ibis London Gatwick

London Rd, County Oak RH11 0PF
☎ 01293 590300 01293 590310
e-mail: H1889@accor-hotels.com
Dir: *M23 junct 10, take A2011 to Crawley. At rdbt 3rd exit, at next rdbt A23 London Rd towards Gatwick. Adjacent to Manor Industrial Est*
Modern, budget hotel offering comfortable accommodation in bright and practical bedrooms. Breakfast is self-service and dinner is available in the restaurant. For further details, consult the Hotel Groups page.
ROOMS: 141 en suite

Premier Travel Inn Crawley (Pound Hill)

Balcombe Rd RH10 3NL
☎ 08701 977067 01293 873034
web: www.premiertravelinn.com
Dir: *On B2036 south towards Crawley from M23 junct 10*
High quality, modern budget accommodation ideal for both families and business travellers. Spacious, en suite bedrooms feature bath and shower, satellite TV and many have telephones and modem points. The adjacent family restaurant features a wide and varied menu. For further details consult the Hotel Groups page.
ROOMS: 41 en suite s £47.95-£50.95; d £47.95-£50.95

Premier Travel Inn Gatwick Airport South

London Rd, Lowfield Heath RH10 9ST
☎ 0870 9906354 0870 9906355
web: www.premiertravelinn.com
Dir: *Near airport on A23. From M23 junct 9a towards North Terminal rdbt then follow A23 Crawley signs. 2m*
High quality, modern budget accommodation ideal for both families and business travellers. Spacious, en suite bedrooms feature bath and shower, satellite TV and many have telephones and modem points. The adjacent family restaurant features a wide and varied menu. For further details consult the Hotel Groups page.
ROOMS: 102 en suite s £53.95-£57.95; d £53.95-£57.95 **CONF:** Thtr 200 Class 100 Board 80

Premier Travel Inn Gatwick/Crawley East

Crawley Av, Gossops Green RH10 8BA
☎ 0870 9906546 0870 9906547
web: www.premiertravelinn.com
Dir: *2m from M23/5m from Gatwick Airport. Exit M23 junct 11 onto A23 towards Crawley & Gatwick Airport*
High quality, modern budget accommodation ideal for both families and business travellers. Spacious, en suite bedrooms feature bath and shower, satellite TV and many have telephones and modem points. The adjacent family restaurant features a wide and varied menu. For further details consult the Hotel Groups page.
ROOMS: 83 en suite s £50.95-£53.95; d £50.95-£53.95

Premier Travel Inn Gatwick/Crawley South

Goffs Park Rd RH11 8AX
☎ 0870 9906390 0870 9906391
web: www.premiertravelinn.com
Dir: *Exit M23 junct 11 onto A23 towards Crawley. At 2nd rdbt take 3rd exit for town centre, then 2nd right into Goffs Park Rd*
High quality, modern budget accommodation ideal for both families and business travellers. Spacious, en suite bedrooms feature bath and shower, satellite TV and many have telephones and modem points. The adjacent family restaurant features a wide and varied menu. For further details consult the Hotel Groups page.
ROOMS: 57 en suite s £50.95-£53.95; d £50.95-£53.95 **CONF:** Thtr 120 Class 70 Board 40

Premier Travel Inn London Gatwick Airport

North Terminal, Longbridge Way RH6 0NX
☎ 0870 238 3305 01293 568278
web: www.premiertravelinn.com
Dir: *M23 junct 9/9A towards North Terminal, at rdbt take 3rd exit, Inn on right*
High quality, modern budget accommodation ideal for both families and business travellers. Spacious, en suite bedrooms

continued

feature bath and shower, satellite TV and many have telephones and modem points. The adjacent family restaurant features a wide and varied menu. For further details consult the Hotel Groups page.
ROOMS: 219 en suite s £53.95-£57.95; d £53.95-£57.95

Travelodge Gatwick Airport

Church Rd, Lowfield Heath RH11 0PQ
☎ 08700 850 950 📠 01293 535369
web: www.travelodge.co.uk
Dir: *M23 junct 10, follow signs for Crawley, take A23 to Gatwick*
Travelodge offers good quality, good value, modern accommodation. Ideal for families, the spacious, en suite bedrooms include remote-control TV, tea and coffee-making facilities and comfortable beds. Meals can be taken at the nearby family restaurant. For further details consult the Hotel Groups page.
ROOMS: 186 en suite s fr £26; d fr £26 **CONF:** Thtr 60 Class 25 Board 25

GERRARDS CROSS, Buckinghamshire — Map 06 TQ08

★★★69% *Bull*

Oxford Rd SL9 7PA
☎ 01753 885995 📠 01753 885504
e-mail: bull@sarova.co.uk
web: www.sarova.co.uk/sarova/hotelcollection/bull
Dir: *M40 junct 2 follow Beaconsfield on A355. After 0.5m 2nd exit at rdbt signed A40 Gerrards Cross for 2m. The Bull on right*
This 17th-century inn has been sympathetically extended and tastefully furnished to provide smart, well-equipped accommodation including a number of spacious state rooms. There is an elegant cocktail bar and restaurant, and the popular Jack Shrimpton bar offers snacks and informal bar meals. Attractive gardens and a good range of function rooms make this a popular wedding venue.
ROOMS: 123 en suite (3 fmly) (20 GF) ⊗ in 74 bedrooms
FACILITIES: STV Leisure facilities available nearby **CONF:** Thtr 150 Class 60 Board 50 **SERVICES:** Lift **PARKING:** 200 **NOTES:** ✗ ⊗ in restaurant Civ Wed

★★71% *Ethorpe*

Packhorse Rd SL9 8HY
☎ 01753 882039 📠 01753 887012
e-mail: ethorpe.hotel@thespiritgroup.com
web: www.ethorpehotel.com
Dir: *M40 junct 2 for Beaconsfield. At island right onto A40 to Gerrards Cross. At lights left into Packhouse Rd. Hotel at end on left*

This attractive hotel is located in the centre of town, within easy reach of the motorway network and Heathrow Airport. Stylish bedrooms are particularly thoughtfully equipped and all boast spacious well-appointed en suite bathrooms. Meals are served all day in the popular informal 'Chef and Brewer' restaurant and bar.
ROOMS: 32 en suite (3 fmly) (11 GF) ⊗ in 25 bedrooms
FACILITIES: STV **CONF:** Thtr 40 Class 30 Board 22 **SERVICES:** air con
PARKING: 80 **NOTES:** ✗

GILLINGHAM, Dorset — Map 04 ST82

Top Hotel

★★★ ⊛⊛⊛ Stock Hill Country House

Stock Hill SP8 5NR
☎ 01747 823626 📠 01747 825628
e-mail: reception@stockhillhouse.co.uk
web: www.stockhillhouse.co.uk
Dir: *3m E on B3081, off A303*
Set in eleven acres, Stock Hill House has an impressive beech-lined driveway and beautiful gardens. The luxurious bedrooms, tastefully furnished with antiques, combine high standards of comfort with modern facilities. Public rooms are delightful in every way with sumptuous fabrics and furnishings. The complete tranquillity makes taking tea in front of fires a very enjoyable experience. Accomplished cooking based on top-quality local ingredients shows strong Austrian influences. Nita and Peter Hauser and their team are clearly dedicated to their guests' enjoyment of this lovely small hotel.
ROOMS: 6 en suite 3 annexe en suite (3 GF) s £135-£165; d £240-£300 (incl. bkfst & dinner) **LB** **FACILITIES:** Sauna Bird watching, croquet Xmas **CONF:** Thtr 12 **PARKING:** 20
NOTES: ✗ No children 7yrs ⊗ in restaurant

GILLINGHAM, Kent — Map 07 TQ76

Premier Travel Inn Gillingham, Kent

Will Adams Way ME8 6BY
☎ 08701 977105 📠 01634 261232
web: www.premiertravelinn.com
Dir: *From M2 junct 4 turn left along A278 to A2. Turn left at Tesco & Inn is left at next rdbt*
High quality, modern budget accommodation ideal for both families and business travellers. Spacious, en suite bedrooms feature bath and shower, satellite TV and many have telephones and modem points. The adjacent family restaurant features a wide and varied menu. For further details consult the Hotel Groups page.
ROOMS: 45 en suite s £49.95; d £49.95 **CONF:** Thtr 20

Travelodge Medway

Medway Motorway Service Area, Rainham ME8 8PQ
☎ 08700 850 950 📠 01634 263187
web: www.travelodge.co.uk
Dir: *between junct 4 & 5 of M2 westbound*
Travelodge offers good quality, good value, modern accommodation. Ideal for families, the spacious, en suite bedrooms include remote-control TV, tea and coffee-making facilities and comfortable beds. Meals can be taken at the nearby family restaurant. For further details consult the Hotel Groups page.
ROOMS: 58 en suite s fr £26; d fr £26

G

GLENRIDDING, Cumbria
Map 18 NY31

★★★76% The Inn on the Lake
Lake Ullswater, Glenridding CA11 0PE
☎ 01768 482444 📠 01768 482303
e-mail: info@innonthelakeullswater.co.uk
web: www.innonthelakeullswater.com
Dir: *M6 junct 40, then A66 to Keswick. At rdbt take A592 to Ullswater Lake. Along lake to Glenridding. Hotel on left on entering village*

In a picturesque lakeside setting, this restored Victorian hotel is a popular leisure destination as well as catering for weddings and conferences. Superb views may be enjoyed the bedrooms and from the garden terrace where afternoon teas are served during warmer months. There is a popular pub in the grounds and moorings for yachts are available to guests. Sailing tuition can be arranged.
ROOMS: 46 en suite (6 fmly) (2 GF) ⊗ in 15 bedrooms
FACILITIES: STV ⚓ 9 ⚲ Fishing Sauna Solarium Gym ⛳ Putt green Jacuzzi Sailing, 9 hole pitch and putt, Bowls Xmas **CONF:** BC Thtr 120 Class 60 Board 40 Del from £99 **SERVICES:** Lift **PARKING:** 200
NOTES: ⊗ in restaurant Civ Wed 100

See advert on opposite page

★★★70% Glenridding
CA11 0PB
☎ 01768 482228 📠 482555
e-mail: glenridding@bestwestern.co.uk
Dir: *Northbound M6 exit 36, A591 Windermere then A592 14 miles. Southbound M6 exit 40, A592 for 13 miles*
This friendly hotel benefits from a picturesque location in the centre of the village. Many of the bedrooms have fine views of the lake and fells. Public areas are extensive and include a choice of restaurants and bars, a coffee shop including a cyber café, and smart leisure facilities.
ROOMS: 36 en suite (9 fmly) ⊗ in all bedrooms s £85-£90; d £110-£130 (incl. bkfst) **LB** **FACILITIES:** STV ⚲ Sauna Jacuzzi Billiards 3/4 Snooker table Table tennis Xmas **CONF:** Thtr 30 Class 30 Board 20 Del from £110 **SERVICES:** Lift **PARKING:** 38 **NOTES:** ⊗ in restaurant Civ Wed 80

GLOSSOP, Derbyshire
Map 16 SK09

★★78% Wind in the Willows
Derbyshire Level SK13 7PT
☎ 01457 868001 📠 01457 853354
e-mail: info@windinthewillows.co.uk
Dir: *1m E of Glossop on A57, turn right opp Royal Oak, hotel 400yds on right*
A warm and relaxed atmosphere prevails at this small and very comfortable hotel. The bedrooms are well furnished, each offering many thoughtful extras and some executive rooms are available.

continued

Public areas include two comfortable lounges, a dining room, and a modern meeting room with views over the extensive grounds.

ROOMS: 12 en suite ⊗ in all bedrooms s £88-£105; d £120-£145 (incl. bkfst) **LB** **FACILITIES:** Fishing **CONF:** Thtr 40 Class 12 Board 16 Del from £135 **PARKING:** 16 **NOTES:** No dogs No children 10yrs ⊗ in restaurant

GLOUCESTER, Gloucestershire
Map 10 SO81

★★★74% ® Hatton Court
Upton Hill, Upton St Leonards GL4 8DE
☎ 01452 617412 📠 01452 612945
e-mail: res@hatton-court.co.uk
web: www.hatton-hotels.co.uk
Dir: *leave Gloucester on B4073 Painswick Rd. Hotel at top of hill on right*
Built in the style of a 17th-century Cotswold manor house, and set in seven acres of well-kept gardens this hotel is popular with both business and leisure guests. It stands at the top of Upton Hill and commands truly spectacular views of the Severn Valley. Bedrooms are comfortable and tastefully furnished with many extra facilities. The elegant Carringtons Restaurant offers a varied choice of menus, and there is also a traditionally furnished bar and foyer lounge.
ROOMS: 17 en suite 28 annexe en suite ⊗ in all bedrooms s £85-£175; d £100-£195 (incl. bkfst) **LB** **FACILITIES:** STV Sauna Gym ⛳ Jacuzzi Xmas **CONF:** Thtr 60 Class 30 Board 30 Del from £115 **PARKING:** 80
NOTES: ⊗ in restaurant Civ Wed 75

★★★70% Hatherley Manor
Down Hatherley Ln GL2 9QA
☎ 01452 730217 📠 01452 731032
e-mail: hatherleymanor@macdonaldhotels.co.uk
web: www.macdonald-hotels.co.uk
Dir: *off A38 onto Down Hatherley Lane, signed. Hotel 600yds on left*

Within easy striking distance of the M5, Gloucester, Cheltenham and the Cotswolds, this stylish 17th-century manor remains popular with both business and leisure guests. Bedrooms have undergone a substantial refurbishment and all offer contemporary comforts. A range of meeting and function rooms is available.
ROOMS: 52 en suite ⊗ in 41 bedrooms s £50-£100; d £80-£120 (incl. bkfst) **LB** **FACILITIES:** Xmas **CONF:** Thtr 300 Class 90 Board 75 Del from £110 **PARKING:** 250 **NOTES:** ⊗ in restaurant Civ Wed 300

Ⓤ Ramada Bowden Hall

Bondend Ln, Upton St Leonards GL4 8ED
☎ 01452 614121 📠 01452 611885
e-mail: sales.bowdenhall@ramadajarvis.co.uk
web: www.ramadajarvis.co.uk
Dir: *B4073 to Kings Head PH, turn left, through village, turn right at x-rds into Bondend Rd, 1st left into Bondend Lane, hotel at end of lane.*
This well presented country house hotel is set in attractive gardens and conveniently located on the outskirts of town close to the M5. Bedrooms are comfortably appointed for both business and leisure guests.
ROOMS: 72 en suite (21 fmly) (7 GF) ⊗ in 54 bedrooms s £85-£145; d £85-£145 **FACILITIES:** STV supervised Sauna Jacuzzi Xmas **CONF:** Thtr 120 Class 70 Board 30 Del from £145 **PARKING:** 150 **NOTES:** ⊗ in restaurant Civ Wed 80

Ⓤ Ramada Hotel & Resort Gloucester

Matson Ln, Robinswood Hill GL4 6EA
☎ 01452 525653 📠 01452 307212
e-mail: sales.gloucester@ramadajarvis.co.uk
Dir: *Hotel opposite ski centre.*
Conveniently located close to the M5, this large hotel is set in 240 acres of grounds. Bedrooms are comfortably appointed for both business and leisure guests.
ROOMS: 107 en suite (7 fmly) (22 GF) ⊗ in 34 bedrooms s £82-£142; d £82-£142 **FACILITIES: Spa** STV supervised ⛳ 18 Squash Sauna Solarium Gym Putt green Jacuzzi **CONF:** Thtr 180 Class 120 Board 60 Del from £140 **PARKING:** 350 **NOTES:** ⊗ in restaurant Civ Wed 150

⌂ Premier Travel Inn Gloucester East (Barnwood)

Barnwood GL4 3HR
☎ 0870 9906322 📠 0870 9906323
web: www.premiertravelinn.com
Dir: *Exit M5 junct 11 onto A40 towards Gloucester. At 1st rdbt take A417 towards Cirencester, at next rdbt take 4th exit*
High quality, modern budget accommodation ideal for both families and business travellers. Spacious, en suite bedrooms feature bath and shower, satellite TV and many have telephones and modem points. The adjacent family restaurant features a wide and varied menu. For further details consult the Hotel Groups page.
ROOMS: 83 en suite s £49.95-£52.95; d £49.95-£52.95

⌂ Premier Travel Inn Gloucester (Longford)

Tewkesbury Rd, Longford GL2 9BE
☎ 08701 977115 📠 01452 300924
web: www.premiertravelinn.com
Dir: *10 minutes from M5 junct 11, follow A40 to Gloucester, A40 to Ross, Inn on A38*
High quality, modern budget accommodation ideal for both families and business travellers. Spacious, en suite bedrooms feature bath and shower, satellite TV and many have telephones and modem points. The adjacent family restaurant features a wide and varied menu. For further details consult the Hotel Groups page.
ROOMS: 60 en suite s £46.95-£49.95; d £46.95-£49.95 **CONF:** Thtr 40

⌂ Premier Travel Inn Gloucester North

Tewkesbury Rd, Twigworth GL2 9PG
☎ 0870 9906560 📠 0870 9906561
web: www.premiertravelinn.com
Dir: *2m from Gloucester. Exit M5 junct 11, A40 towards Gloucester, then A38 towards Tewkesbury*
High quality, modern budget accommodation ideal for both families and business travellers. Spacious, en suite bedrooms *continued*

feature bath and shower, satellite TV and many have telephones and modem points. The adjacent family restaurant features a wide and varied menu. For further details consult the Hotel Groups page.
ROOMS: 52 en suite s £46.95-£49.95; d £46.95-£49.95

⌂ Premier Travel Inn Gloucester (Witcombe)

Witcombe GL3 4SS
☎ 08701 977116 📠 01452 864926
web: www.premiertravelinn.com
Dir: *M5 junct 11A follow A417 (Cirencester) at 1st exit turn right onto A46 towards Stroud/Witcombe. Left at next rdbt by Crosshands PH*
High quality, modern budget accommodation ideal for both families and business travellers. Spacious, en suite bedrooms feature bath and shower, satellite TV and many have telephones and modem points. The adjacent family restaurant features a wide and varied menu. For further details consult the Hotel Groups page.
ROOMS: 39 en suite s £46.95-£49.95; d £46.95-£49.95

GODALMING, Surrey — Map 06 SU94

⌂ Innkeeper's Lodge Godalming

Ockford Rd GU7 1RH
☎ 01483 419997 📠 01483 410852
web: www.innkeeperslodge.com
Dir: *Turn off A3/Milford at petrol station turn left onto A3100 through Milford under railway bridge. Lodge on rdbt on right*
A growing concept in the travel accommodation market. Smart rooms meet essential business requirements but also have home comforts. Dining options include all-day menus plus the added advantage of breakfast, which is included in the room price. For further details consult the Hotel Groups page.
ROOMS: 19 rms s £49.95-£79.95; d £49.95-£79.95

GOMERSAL, West Yorkshire
Map 19 SE22

★★★71% Gomersal Park
Moor Ln BD19 4LJ
☎ 01274 869386 📠 01274 861042
e-mail: enquiries@gomersalparkhotel.com
Dir: *A62 to Huddersfield. At junct with A65, by Greyhound Pub right, after 1m take 1st right after Oakwell Hall*
Constructed around a 19th-century house, this stylish, modern hotel enjoys a peaceful location and pleasant grounds. Deep sofas ensure comfort in the open-plan lounge and imaginative meals are served in the popular Brasserie 101. The well-equipped bedrooms provide high quality and comfort. Extensive public areas include a well-equipped leisure complex and pool, and a wide variety of air-conditioned conference rooms.
ROOMS: 100 en suite (3 fmly) (32 GF) ⊘ in 80 bedrooms s £99-£225; d £99-£225 (incl. bkfst) **LB FACILITIES:** STV supervised Sauna Solarium Gym Jacuzzi Xmas **CONF:** Thtr 250 Class 130 Board 60 Del £135 **SERVICES:** Lift **PARKING:** 150 **NOTES:** ⊘ in restaurant Closed 26-30 Dec Civ Wed 200

★★65% Gomersal Lodge
Spen Ln BD19 4PJ
☎ 01274 861111 📠 01274 861111
e-mail: enquiries@gomersallodge.co.uk
Dir: *M62 junct 27, A62 towards Huddersfield. Right at Greyhound Pub, hotel 1m on right*
Gomersal Lodge sits in five acres of landscaped grounds and attractive gardens. This 19th-century house offers well-furnished bedrooms together with a cosy bar. The elegant restaurant is noted for its flexible, contemporary menu, and is popular as a venue for weddings.
ROOMS: 9 en suite (1 fmly) ⊘ in 4 bedrooms s fr £55; d fr £63 (incl. bkfst) **CONF:** Thtr 20 Class 12 Board 12 **PARKING:** 70 **NOTES:** ⊘ in restaurant

GOODRICH, Herefordshire
Map 10 SO51

★★71% *Ye Hostelrie*
HR9 6HX
☎ 01600 890241 📠 01600 890838
e-mail: info@ye-hostelrie.co.uk
Dir: *1m off A40, between Ross-on-Wye and Monmouth, 100yds from Goodrich Castle*

Parts of this unusual building are reputed to date back to 1625. It is privately owned and personally run, and considerable improvements to both the accommodation and the public areas have been made in recent years. Facilities include a function room, a pleasant garden and a patio area. The hotel is very popular for the extensive range of food on offer.
ROOMS: 7 en suite (1 fmly) **CONF:** Thtr 80 Class 60 Board 20 **PARKING:** 25 **NOTES:** ⊘ in restaurant

GOODRINGTON See Paignton

GOODWOOD, West Sussex
Map 06 SU81

★★★★73% *Marriott Goodwood Park Hotel & Country Club*
PO18 0QB
☎ 0870 400 7225 📠 0870 400 7325
e-mail: reservations.goodwood@marriotthotels.co.uk
web: www.marriott.co.uk
Dir: *off A285, 3m NE of Chichester*
Set in the middle of the 12,000 acre Goodwood Estate, this attractive hotel boasts extensive indoor and outdoor leisure facilities, along with a range of meeting rooms and conference and banqueting facilities. Bedrooms are furnished to a consistently high standard. Public rooms include the Richmond Restaurant and a smart cocktail bar, which reflects motor-racing heritage at Goodwood.
ROOMS: 94 en suite ⊘ in 54 bedrooms **FACILITIES:** STV supervised 18 Sauna Solarium Gym Putt green Jacuzzi Beauty salons **CONF:** BC Thtr 150 Class 60 Board 50 **PARKING:** 350 **NOTES:** ⊘ in restaurant Civ Wed 120

GOOLE, East Riding of Yorkshire
Map 17 SE72

Premier Travel Inn Goole
Rawcliffe Rd, Airmyn DN14 8JS
☎ 08701 977 031 📠 0121 633 4779
web: www.premiertravelinn.com
Dir: *Leave M62 at junct 36, onto A614 signed Rawcliffe. Inn immediately on left.*
High quality, modern budget accommodation ideal for both families and business travellers. Spacious, en suite bedrooms feature bath and shower, satellite TV and many have telephones and modem points. The adjacent family restaurant features a wide and varied menu. For further details consult the Hotel Groups page.
ROOMS: 79 en suite s £55.95-£57.95; d £55.95-£57.95 **CONF:** Board 12

GORDANO SERVICE AREA (M5), Somerset
Map 04 ST57

Days Inn Bristol West
BS20 7XG
☎ 01275 373709 & 373624 📠 01275 374104
e-mail: gordano.hotel@welcomebreak.co.uk
web: www.welcomebreak.co.uk
Dir: *M5 junct 19, follow signs for Gordano services*
This modern building offers accommodation in smart, spacious and well-equipped bedrooms, suitable for families and business travellers, and all with en suite bathrooms. Continental breakfast is available and other refreshments may be taken at the nearby family restaurant. For further details see the Hotel Groups page.
ROOMS: 60 en suite s £49-£60; d £49-£60 **CONF:** Board 10

GORLESTON ON SEA, Norfolk
Map 13 TG50

★★64% The Pier
Harbourmouth, South Pier NR31 6PL
☎ 01493 662631 📠 01493 440263
e-mail: info@pierhotelgorleston.co.uk
Dir: *From A143 turn left Shrublands then onto Church Lane, continue to Baker St, right onto Pier Plain, left onto Pier Walk then right onto Quay Rd*
This family run small hotel sits adjacent to the harbour wall, with splendid views along the sandy beach. Refurbished public rooms

continued

include a popular bar and a pleasant restaurant, both offering home cooked food options.
ROOMS: 19 en suite (1 fmly) ⊗ in 1 bedroom s £40-£45; d £60-£125 (incl. bkfst) **LB** **FACILITIES:** STV Xmas **CONF:** Thtr 90 Class 120 Board 120 Del from £53.50 **SERVICES:** air con **PARKING:** 30 **NOTES:** ⊗ in restaurant Civ Wed 140

GRANGE-OVER-SANDS, Cumbria Map 18 SD47

★★★75% Netherwood
Lindale Rd LA11 6ET
☎ 015395 32552 📠 34121
e-mail: blawith@aol.com
Dir: *on B5277 before station*
This imposing hotel stands in terraced grounds and enjoys fine views of Morecambe Bay. Though a popular conference and wedding venue, good levels of hospitality and service ensure all guests are well looked after. Bedrooms vary in size but all are well furnished and decorated, and have smart modern bathrooms. Magnificent woodwork is a feature of the public areas.
ROOMS: 32 en suite (5 fmly) ⊗ in 18 bedrooms s £70-£90; d £140-£180 (incl. bkfst) **LB** **FACILITIES: Spa** supervised Solarium Gym Jacuzzi Beauty salon, Steam room **CONF:** BC Thtr 150 Class 30 Board 40 Del from £105 **SERVICES:** Lift **PARKING:** 100 **NOTES:** ⊗ in restaurant Civ Wed 180

★★★67% *Graythwaite Manor*
Fernhill Rd LA11 7JE
☎ 015395 32001 & 33755 📠 015395 35549
e-mail: enquiries@graythwaitemanor.co.uk
Dir: *B5277 through Grange, Fernhill Rd opposite fire station behind small traffic island, hotel 1st left*
This well established hotel is set in very well tended gardens, complete with sub-tropical plants, and offers a delightful outlook over Morecambe Bay. Public areas include an Orangery, a number of comfortable lounges and an elegant restaurant. The comfortable bedrooms, which vary in size, are traditional in style.
ROOMS: 21 en suite (2 fmly) **FACILITIES:** Putt green **CONF:** Thtr 50 Class 30 Board 20 **SERVICES:** Lift **PARKING:** 32 **NOTES:** ⊗ in restaurant

★★70% Hampsfell House
Hampsfell Rd LA11 6BG
☎ 015395 32567 📠 015395 35995
e-mail: hampsfellhotel@msn.com
web: www.hampsfellhotel.com
Dir: *M6 junct 36 take A590 signed Barrow-in-Furness. At junct with B5277, follow to Grange-over-Sands signs. Left at rdbt into Main St, 2nd rdbt right and right at x-rds. At Hampsfell Rd left*
Dating back to 1800, this family-run hotel is peacefully set in two acres of private grounds yet is just minutes' walk from the town centre. Bedrooms are smartly decorated and well maintained. The two cosy and comfortable lounges, where guests can enjoy pre-dinner drinks, share a central bar. Comprehensive and imaginative dinners are taken in an attractive dining room.
ROOMS: 9 en suite (1 fmly) (1 GF) ⊗ in 6 bedrooms s £40-£53; d £80-£106 (incl. bkfst) **LB** **FACILITIES:** Xmas **PARKING:** 12 **NOTES:** No children 5yrs ⊗ in restaurant

The vast majority of establishments in this guide accept credit and debit cards. We indicate those that don't take any

Top Hotel

★ Clare House
Park Rd LA11 7HQ
☎ 015395 33026 & 34253 📠 015395 34310
e-mail: info@clarehousehotel.co.uk
web: www.clarehousehotel.co.uk
Dir: *off A590 onto B5277, through Lindale into Grange, keep left, hotel 0.5m on left past Crown Hill and St Paul's Church*
A warm, genuine welcome awaits guests at this delightful, family-run hotel. Nestling in its own secluded gardens, it provides a relaxed haven in which to enjoy the panoramic views across Morecambe Bay. Bedrooms and public areas are comfortable and attractively furnished. Skilfully prepared dinners and hearty breakfasts are served in the elegant dining room.
ROOMS: 19 rms (18 en suite) (1 fmly) (2 GF) s £70; d £140 (incl. bkfst & dinner) **LB** **FACILITIES:** Putt green **PARKING:** 18 **NOTES:** ⊗ in restaurant Closed Dec-Mar RS 10-30 Nov

U Cumbria Grand
LA11 6EN
☎ 015395 32331 📠 015395 34534
e-mail: salescumbria@strathmorehotels.com
Dir: *M6 junct 36. Follow A590 and signs for Grange-over-Sands*
At the time of going to press, the star classification for this hotel was not confirmed. Please refer to the AA internet site www.theAA.com for current information.
ROOMS: 122 en suite (10 fmly) s £65-£75; d £100-£130 (incl. bkfst) **FACILITIES:** STV Snooker Putt green Pool table Putting Table tennis Darts **SERVICES:** Lift **PARKING:** 75 **NOTES:** ⊗ in restaurant

GRANTHAM, Lincolnshire Map 11 SK93

★★★74% Angel & Royal
High St NG31 6PN
☎ 01476 565816 📠 01476 567149
e-mail: enquiries@angelandroyal.co.uk
web: www.angelandroyal.co.uk
Dir: *Follow signs to town centre. Hotel on left, continue past taking 1st left after Marks & Spencers & 1st left again. Car park 200yds on right*
This former coaching inn in the centre of town claims to be one of the oldest in the country and retains many original features. The accommodation is varied in size and is stylish and comfortable. The bar offers over 200 whiskies and the brasserie provides a modern selection of dishes. Additionally, the historic King's Room restaurant is open at weekends.
ROOMS: 29 en suite (1 GF) ⊗ in 26 bedrooms s £65-£85; d £110-£120 (incl. bkfst) **LB** **FACILITIES:** STV **CONF:** Thtr 30 Class 30 Board 30 Del from £129 **PARKING:** 70 **NOTES:** ⊗ in restaurant

GRANTHAM, continued

★★★70% **Grantham Marriott**
Swingbridge Rd NG31 7XT
Marriott
HOTELS & RESORTS
☎ 01476 593000 ▤ 01476 592592
e-mail: neil.shears@whitbread.com
web: www.marriott.co.uk
Dir: off A1 at junct Grantham/Melton Mowbray onto A607. From N 1st exit at mini rdbt, hotel on right. From S at T-junct, right to Grantham under A1. Left to hotel
This smart, modern hotel is a convenient base from which to explore the countryside. Hotel bedrooms are spacious, tastefully decorated and have a wide range of extras. Public rooms, which extend into a pretty courtyard in the summer, include a serviced lounge, function rooms and a small leisure club with pool and fitness room.
ROOMS: 90 en suite (44 GF) ⊗ in 68 bedrooms s £99-£109; d £109-£119 (incl. bkfst) **LB FACILITIES: Spa** STV ▣ supervised Sauna Solarium Gym Jacuzzi Steam room Xmas **CONF:** Thtr 200 Class 90 Board 50 Del £155 **PARKING:** 150 **NOTES:** ✗ ⊗ in restaurant Civ Wed 80

★★★70% **Kings**
North Pde NG31 8AU
Best Western
☎ 01476 590800 ▤ 01476 577072
e-mail: kings@bestwestern.co.uk
Dir: off A1 at rdbt N end of Grantham onto B1174, follow road for 2m. Hotel on left by bridge
A friendly atmosphere exists within this extended Georgian house. Bedrooms are attractively decorated and furnished in modern light oak. Dining options include the formal Victorian restaurant and the popular Orangery, which also operates as a coffee shop and breakfast room; a lounge bar and a comfortable open-plan foyer lounge are also available.
ROOMS: 21 en suite (3 fmly) ⊗ in 9 bedrooms s £58-£64; d £68-£74 (incl. bkfst) **LB FACILITIES:** STV **CONF:** BC Thtr 100 Class 50 Board 40 Del from £102 **PARKING:** 36 **NOTES:** ⊗ in restaurant Closed 25-26 Dec

⌂ **Travelodge Grantham North**
Grantham Service Area, Grantham North,
Gonerby Moor NG32 2AB
Travelodge
☎ 08700 850 950 ▤ 01476 577500
web: www.travelodge.co.uk
Dir: 4m N on A1
Travelodge offers good quality, good value, modern accommodation. Ideal for families, the spacious, en suite bedrooms include remote-control TV, tea and coffee-making facilities and comfortable beds. Meals can be taken at the nearby family restaurant. For further details consult the Hotel Groups page.
ROOMS: 39 en suite s fr £26; d fr £26

GRASMERE, Cumbria
Map 18 NY30

★★★★71% ◉◉ **Wordsworth**
LA22 9SW
☎ 015394 35592 ▤ 015394 35765
e-mail: enquiry@wordsworth-grasmere.co.uk
web: www.grasmere-hotels.co.uk
Dir: centre of village adjacent to St Oswald's Church
This traditional hotel, named after the famous poet who is buried in the adjacent churchyard, is set in well-tended gardens against a backdrop of towering fells. Bedrooms, varying in size and style, are complemented by a choice of comfortable lounge areas. To complete the package there are comprehensive leisure facilities,
continued

and diners have a choice between the popular pub and the more formal Prelude restaurant.

ROOMS: 37 en suite (3 fmly) s £120-£200; d £190-£300 (incl. bkfst & dinner) **LB FACILITIES:** STV ▣ Sauna Solarium Gym ♨ Jacuzzi ♫ Xmas **CONF:** BC Thtr 100 Class 50 Board 40 Del from £142.50 **SERVICES:** Lift **PARKING:** 60 **NOTES:** ✗ ⊗ in restaurant Civ Wed 100
See advert on opposite page

★★★73% *Gold Rill Country House*
Red Bank Rd LA22 9PU
☎ 015394 35486 ▤ 015394 35486
e-mail: enquiries@gold-rill.com
web: www.gold-rill.com
Dir: turn off A591 into village centre, turn into road opposite St Oswald's Church. Hotel 300yds on left

This popular hotel enjoys a fine location on the edge of the village with spectacular views of the lake and surrounding fells. Attractive bedrooms, some with balconies, are tastefully decorated and many have separate, comfortable seating areas. The hotel boasts a private pier, an outdoor heated pool and a putting green. Public areas include a well-appointed restaurant and choice of lounges.
ROOMS: 25 en suite 6 annexe en suite (2 fmly) **FACILITIES:** STV ⌇ Putt green **PARKING:** 35 **NOTES:** ✗ ⊗ in restaurant Closed mid Dec-mid Jan (open New Year)

★★★73% ◉◉ *Rothay Garden*
Broadgate LA22 9RJ
☎ 015394 35334 ▤ 015394 35723
e-mail: stay@rothay-garden.com
web: www.rothay-garden.com
Dir: off A591, opposite Swan Hotel, into Grasmere, 300yds on left
Located on the northern approach to this unspoilt Cumbrian village, this hotel offers comfortable bedrooms, including some with four-posters and whirlpool baths. There is a choice of relaxing
continued

lounges, a cosy cocktail bar and an attractive conservatory restaurant, which looks out across the garden towards the fells.

ROOMS: 25 en suite (2 fmly) (6 GF) ⊗ in 6 bedrooms
FACILITIES: STV Fishing Jacuzzi use of local leisure club **PARKING:** 38
NOTES: ⊗ in restaurant

★★★72% Grasmere Red Lion

Red Lion Square LA22 9SS
☎ 015394 35456 🖷 015394 35579
e-mail: enquiries@hotelgrasmere.uk.com
web: www.hotelslakedistrict.com
Dir: *off A591, signed Grasmere Village, hotel in centre of village*

This modernised and extended 18th-century coaching inn, located in the heart of the village, offers spacious well-equipped rooms and a number of meeting and conference facilities. The Lamb Inn offers a range of pub meals to complement the more formal Courtyard restaurant. The spacious and comfortable lounge area is ideal for relaxing and for the more energetic there is a pool and gym.
ROOMS: 47 en suite (4 fmly) ⊗ in 22 bedrooms s £48-£114.50; d £96-£159 (incl. bkfst) **FACILITIES:** STV supervised Sauna Gym Jacuzzi Hairdressing Guests may borrow a permit to fish the local angling assoc. waters Xmas **CONF:** Thtr 60 Class 30 Board 30 Del from £100 **SERVICES:** Lift **PARKING:** 38 **NOTES:** ⊗ in restaurant

See advert on this page

★★★72% Prince of Wales Hotel

Keswick Rd LA22 9PR
☎ 0870 333 9135 🖷 0870 333 9235
e-mail: cwatts@princeofwalesgrasmere.com
Dir: *N - A51 Grasmere. 1st hotel on left opposite Dove Cottage. S - follow signs for Ambleside. Last hotel on right.*

This large hotel stands in its own gardens leading to the lake, and many of the bedrooms have fine views over the surrounding fells. Bedrooms are comfortably furnished and include a stylish suite, complete with a four-poster bed. Service is friendly and the choice

continued on p232

GRASMERE, continued

of meals, from a selection of restaurant and bar menus, should suit most tastes.

Prince of Wales Hotel, Grasmere

ROOMS: 71 en suite (8 fmly) ⊗ in 58 bedrooms s £60-£80; d £80-£140 (incl. bkfst) **LB** **FACILITIES:** STV Fishing Xmas **CONF:** Thtr 110 Class 60 Board 40 Del from £95 **PARKING:** 60 **NOTES:** ⊗ in restaurant Civ Wed 120

★★★71% *The Swan*

LA22 9RF

☎ 0870 400 8132 📠 015394 35741

e-mail: swangrasmere@macdonald-hotels.co.uk

web: www.macdonald-hotels.co.uk

Dir: *M6 junct 36, A591 towards Kendal, A590 to Keswick through Ambleside. The Swan on right on entering the village*

Close to Dove Cottage and occupying a prominent position on the edge of the village, this 300-year-old inn is mentioned in Wordsworth's poem '*The Waggoner*'. Attractive public areas are spacious and comfortable, and bedrooms are equally stylish with some having CD players. A good range of bar meals is available, while the elegant restaurant offers more formal dining.

ROOMS: 38 en suite (1 fmly) (28 GF) ⊗ in 14 bedrooms **CONF:** Thtr 30 Class 24 Board 16 **PARKING:** 45 **NOTES:** ⊗ in restaurant Civ Wed 58

★★75% ® Grasmere

Broadgate LA22 9TA

☎ 015394 35277 📠 35277

e-mail: enquiries@grasmerehotel.co.uk

web: www.grasmerehotel.co.uk

Dir: *A591 north from Ambleside, 2nd left into Grasmere town centre. Follow road over humpback bridge, past playing field. Hotel on left*

Attentive and hospitable service contribute to the atmosphere at this family-run hotel, set in secluded gardens by the River Rothay. There are two inviting lounges (one with residents' bar) and an attractive dining room looking onto the garden. The thoughtfully prepared dinner menu makes good use of fresh ingredients. Pine furniture is featured in most bedrooms, along with some welcome personal touches.

ROOMS: 13 en suite (2 GF) ⊗ in all bedrooms s £50-£70; d £90-£140 (incl. bkfst & dinner) **LB** **FACILITIES:** Full leisure facilities at nearby country club, Free fishing permit available Xmas **PARKING:** 14 **NOTES:** No children 9yrs ⊗ in restaurant Closed 3 Jan-early Feb

★★73% *Oak Bank*

Broadgate LA22 9TA

☎ 015394 35217 📠 35685

e-mail: info@lakedistricthotel.co.uk

Dir: *on right in village centre*

This privately owned and personally run hotel provides well-equipped accommodation, including a bedroom on ground floor level and a four-poster room. Public areas include a choice of comfortable lounges with welcoming log fires when the weather is cold. There is a pleasant bar and an attractive restaurant with a conservatory extension overlooking the garden.

continued

ROOMS: 15 en suite (1 fmly) (1 GF) ⊗ in all bedrooms **FACILITIES:** Jacuzzi **PARKING:** 11 **NOTES:** ⊗ in restaurant Closed 6-20 Jan

Top Hotel

★ ® White Moss House

Rydal Water LA22 9SE

☎ 015394 35295 📠 015394 35516

e-mail: sue@whitemoss.com

web: www.whitemoss.com

Dir: *on A591, 1m S of Grasmere*

This traditional Lakeland house was once bought by Wordsworth for his son. It benefits from a central location and has a loyal following. The individually styled bedrooms are comfortable and thoughtfully equipped. There is also a two-room suite in a cottage on the hillside above the hotel. The five-course set dinner makes good use of the quality local ingredients. Afternoon tea and pre-dinner drinks are served in the inviting lounge.

ROOMS: 5 en suite 2 annexe en suite s fr £94; d £154-£198 (incl. bkfst & dinner) **LB** **FACILITIES:** Free use local leisure club, Free fishing at local waters, walking **PARKING:** 10 **NOTES:** ⊗ in restaurant Closed Dec-Jan RS Sun

GRASSINGTON, North Yorkshire Map 19 SE06

★★67% Grassington House

5 The Square BD23 5AQ

☎ 01756 752406 📠 01756 752135

e-mail: info@grassingtonhousehotel.co.uk

web: www.grassingtonhousehotel.co.uk

Dir: *B6265 from Skipton, on right side of village square*

Looking over the cobbled square of a quaint village, this historic hotel skilfully combines the smart provision of spacious, stylish bedrooms with the flair, character, great beer and food of one of the region's finest inns. Extensive menus provide something for everyone with contemporary ideas served alongside real classics: The steak and kidney pudding is unforgettable! Staff throughout are genuinely friendly and keen to please.

ROOMS: 9 en suite (2 fmly) ⊗ in all bedrooms s £31.50-£40; d £63 (incl. bkfst) **LB** **FACILITIES:** Xmas **PARKING:** 20 **NOTES:** ⊗ in restaurant

Destination dining!
This symbol indicates a Restaurant with Rooms

GRAVESEND, Kent Map 06 TQ67

★★★72% *Manor Hotel*

Hever Court Rd DA12 5UQ
☎ 01474 353100 🖷 01474 354978
e-mail: manor@bestwestern.co.uk
Dir: *at junct of A2 Gravesend East turn off*

Conveniently located just off the A2, this hotel is ideal for local attractions, such as Bluewater shopping village. Attractively decorated bedrooms are spacious and fitted with numerous facilities. A bar and smart restaurant are available along with an impressive health club with swimming pool, sauna and gym.

ROOMS: 59 en suite (3 fmly) ⊗ in 37 bedrooms **FACILITIES:** STV supervised Sauna Solarium Gym **CONF:** BC Thtr 200 Class 100 Board 25 **PARKING:** 100 **NOTES:** ⊗ in restaurant

Premier Travel Inn Gravesend

Wrotham Rd DA11 7LF
☎ 08701 977118 🖷 01474 323776
web: www.premiertravelinn.com
Dir: *1m from A2 on A227 towards Gravesend town centre*

High quality, modern budget accommodation ideal for both families and business travellers. Spacious, en suite bedrooms feature bath and shower, satellite TV and many have telephones and modem points. The adjacent family restaurant features a wide and varied menu. For further details consult the Hotel Groups page.

ROOMS: 36 en suite s £49.95-£52.95; d £49.95-£52.95 **CONF:** Thtr 40 Board 20

TV dinner?
Room service at three stars and above

Premier Travel Inn Gravesend South

Hevercourt Rd, Singlewell DA12 5UQ
☎ 0870 9906352 🖷 0870 9906353
web: www.premiertravelinn.com
Dir: *Just off A2 towards Rochester & Channel Tunnel. Turn at Singlewell Services Rd*

High quality, modern budget accommodation ideal for both families and business travellers. Spacious, en suite bedrooms feature bath and shower, satellite TV and many have telephones and modem points. The adjacent family restaurant features a wide and varied menu. For further details consult the Hotel Groups page.

ROOMS: 31 en suite s £49.95-£52.95; d £49.95-£52.95

GRAYS, Essex Map 06 TQ67

★★★67% Lakeside Moat House

High Rd, North Stifford RM16 5UE
☎ 01708 719988 🖷 01375 390426
e-mail: reservations.lakeside@moathousehotels.com
Dir: *M25 junct 30/31, follow A13 towards Brentwood/Southend, A1012 (Grays), hotel is 1st exit on rdbt.*

Sitting in six acres of grounds, this extended Georgian manor house is well located for access to motorways and local business parks. The mostly spacious bedrooms provide a good range of facilities. Public areas include a sports bar and a restaurant where guests can enjoy live music at weekends. A flexible and extensive range of meeting rooms and conference suites is available alongside a dedicated business centre.

ROOMS: 97 en suite (32 GF) ⊗ in 48 bedrooms s £49-£99; d £49-£99 **FACILITIES:** STV **CONF:** BC Thtr 445 Class 134 Board 185 Del from £99 **SERVICES:** Lift **PARKING:** 150 **NOTES:** ⊗ in restaurant Civ Wed 100

GREAT CHESTERFORD, Essex — Map 12 TL54

★★★69% ⊛ The Crown House
CB10 1NY
☎ 01799 530515 ▤ 01799 530683
e-mail: stay@thecrownhouse.com
web: www.thecrownhouse.com
Dir: *from N exit M11 at junct 9, from S junct 10, follow signs for Saffron Walden & then Great Chesterford (B1383)*
This Georgian coaching inn, situated in a peaceful village close to the M11, has been sympathetically restored and retains much original character. The bedrooms are well equipped and individually decorated; some rooms have delightful four-poster beds. Public rooms include an attractive lounge bar, an elegant oak-panelled restaurant and an airy conservatory.
ROOMS: 8 en suite 14 annexe en suite (2 fmly) (5 GF) s £65-£110; d £85-£145 (incl. bkfst) **LB** **CONF:** Thtr 40 Class 12 Board 16
PARKING: 30 **NOTES:** ⊗ in restaurant Civ Wed 60
See advert on page 233

GREAT DUNMOW, Essex — Map 06 TL62

Restaurant with Rooms

🏠 ⊛⊛ Starr Restaurant with Rooms
Market Place CM6 1AX
☎ 01371 874321 ▤ 01371 876337
e-mail: starrrestaurant@btinternet.com
Dir: *M11 junct 8, onto A120. After 7m, left into Great Dunmow, then left. Hotel in town centre*

A 15th-century, former coaching inn situated in the heart of this charming Essex village. It is well known locally for its quality food, which is served in the elegantly appointed beamed restaurant and conservatory. The spacious bedrooms are in a converted stable block adjacent to the main building, each one is individually decorated and tastefully furnished.
ROOMS: 8 annexe en suite s £80-£95; d £120-£145 (incl. bkfst)
CONF: BC Thtr 36 Board 16 Del from £67.50 **PARKING:** 16 **NOTES:** ⊗ in restaurant Closed 26-31 Dec

GREAT MILTON, Oxfordshire — Map 05 SP60

Top Hotel

★★★★ ⊛⊛⊛⊛⊛ 🏆 Le Manoir Aux Quat' Saisons
Church Rd OX44 7PD
☎ 01844 278881 ▤ 01844 278847
e-mail: lemanoir@blanc.co.uk
web: www.manoir.com
Dir: *from A329 2nd right to Great Milton Manor, hotel 200yds on right*
Set in beautiful grounds and gardens that produce many of the organic ingredients for the kitchens, this renowned hotel epitomises luxury and truly remarkable cooking. Bedrooms are individually styled and are either in the main house or in the garden courtyard. All offer the highest levels of comfort and quality, have magnificent marble bathrooms and are equipped with a host of thoughtful extra touches. Stylish public areas feature wonderful artwork and include the centrepiece at Le Manoir, the conservatory restaurant.
ROOMS: 9 en suite 23 annexe en suite s £275-£1250; d £275-£1250 (incl. bkfst) **LB** **FACILITIES:** STV 🏊 Cookery School, Water Gardens Xmas **CONF:** Thtr 24 Board 20 **PARKING:** 60
NOTES: ✗ ⊗ in restaurant Civ Wed 50

GREAT YARMOUTH, Norfolk — Map 13 TG50
See also Gorleton on Sea

★★★71% ⊛ Imperial
North Dr NR30 1EQ
☎ 01493 842000 ▤ 01493 852229
e-mail: imperial@scs-datacom.co.uk
web: www.imperialhotel.co.uk
Dir: *follow signs to seafront and turn left. Hotel opposite tennis courts*
Friendly, family-run hotel situated at the quieter end of the seafront within easy walking distance of the town. Bedrooms are attractively decorated with co-ordinated soft furnishings and equipped with modern facilities; many rooms have superb sea views. Public areas offer a good level of comfort and include the smart Savoie Lounge Bar and the Rambouillet Restaurant.
ROOMS: 39 en suite (4 fmly) ⊗ in 32 bedrooms s £55-£78; d £60-£92 (incl. bkfst) **LB** **FACILITIES:** STV Xmas **CONF:** Thtr 140 Class 40 Board 30 Del from £80 **SERVICES:** Lift **PARKING:** 50 **NOTES:** ⊗ in restaurant Civ Wed 140

★★★68% Regency Dolphin
Albert Square NR30 3JH
☎ 01493 855070 ▤ 01493 853798
e-mail: info@regencydolphinhotel.co.uk
web: www.regencydolphinhotel.co.uk
Dir: *from seafront at pier into Kimberley Ter. Left in Albert Sq.*
Large privately owned hotel situated in the quieter end of town,
continued

THE INDEPENDENTS

just off the seafront and within easy walking distance of the town centre. The pleasantly decorated bedrooms are generally quite spacious and well equipped. Public rooms include a comfortable lounge, a bar and intimate restaurant. The hotel also has an outdoor swimming pool.

ROOMS: 47 en suite (5 fmly) (2 GF) ⊗ in 9 bedrooms s £60-£120; d £90-£120 (incl. bkfst) **LB FACILITIES:** STV ⚹ Xmas **CONF:** Thtr 120 Class 50 Board 30 Del from £82.50 **PARKING:** 19 **NOTES:** ⊗ in restaurant Civ Wed 120

★★★66% Star
Hall Quay NR30 1HG
☎ 01493 842294 ▤ 01493 330215
e-mail: star.hotel@elizabethhotels.co.uk
Dir: from Norwich on A47 over 1st rdbt. At 2nd rdbt 3rd exit. Hotel on left
The unusual façade of this 17th-century property makes it one of the town's most striking buildings. It overlooks the quay and is just a short walk from the town centre. The smartly appointed public rooms include a choice of bars, a restaurant and a tastefully furnished lounge. Bedrooms are pleasantly decorated and equipped with modern facilities.

ROOMS: 40 en suite (1 fmly) ⊗ in 13 bedrooms s £50-£65; d £70-£85 (incl. bkfst) **LB FACILITIES:** STV Discount for the marina leisure centre pool, gym Xmas **CONF:** Thtr 75 Class 30 Board 30 Del from £80 **SERVICES:** Lift **PARKING:** 20 **NOTES:** ✗ ⊗ in restaurant Civ Wed 70

★★72% The Arden Court Hotel
93-94 North Denes Rd NR30 4LW
☎ 01493 855310 ▤ 01493 843413
e-mail: barry@ardencourthotel.freeserve.co.uk
web: www.ardencourt-hotel.co.uk
Dir: At seafront left along North Dr. At boating lake left along Beaconsfield Rd. At mini rdbt right into North Denes Rd.
Friendly, family-run hotel situated in a residential area just a short walk from the seafront. The individually decorated bedrooms are smartly furnished and equipped with a good range of useful extras. Public rooms are attractively presented; they include a smart lounge bar and a restaurant serving an interesting choice of dishes.

ROOMS: 14 en suite (2 GF) ⊗ in all bedrooms s £30-£50 (incl. bkfst) **LB FACILITIES:** ♬ Xmas **CONF:** BC **PARKING:** 10 **NOTES:** ✗ ⊗ in restaurant

★★70% Furzedown
19-20 North Dr NR30 4EW
☎ 01493 844138 ▤ 01493 844138
e-mail: Paul@furzedownhotel.co.uk
web: www.furzedownhotel.co.uk
Dir: at end of A47 or A12, towards seafront, left, hotel opposite Waterways

Friendly family-run hotel situated at the northern end of the seafront overlooking the beach and Venetian Waterways. Bedrooms are pleasantly decorated and equipped with a good
continued

range of useful extras; many have superb sea views. The stylish public areas include a comfortable lounge bar, a smartly appointed restaurant and a cosy TV room.

ROOMS: 24 rms (20 en suite) (11 fmly) **FACILITIES:** STV **CONF:** Thtr 75 Class 80 Board 40 Del from £69 **PARKING:** 15 **NOTES:** ⊗ in restaurant

★★69% Burlington Palm Court Hotel
11 North Dr NR30 1EG
☎ 01493 844568 & 842095 ▤ 01493 331848
e-mail: enquiries@burlington-hotel.co.uk
web: www.burlington-hotel.co.uk
Dir: A12 to seafront, left at Britannia Pier. Hotel near tennis courts
This privately-owned hotel is situated at the quiet end of the resort, overlooking the sea. Bedrooms come in a variety of sizes and styles; they are pleasantly decorated and well equipped, and many have lovely sea views. The spacious public rooms include a range of seating areas, a choice of dining rooms and two bars.

ROOMS: 70 en suite (9 fmly) ⊗ in 14 bedrooms **FACILITIES:** Spa STV ▣ Jacuzzi Turkish steam room ♬ **CONF:** Thtr 120 Class 60 Board 30 **SERVICES:** Lift **PARKING:** 70 **NOTES:** ✗ ⊗ in restaurant Closed Jan-Feb RS Dec-Feb (group bookings only)

★★63% New Beach Hotel
67 Marine Pde NR30 2EJ
☎ 01493 332300 ▤ 01493 331880
e-mail: newbeach.gtyarmouth@alfatravel.co.uk
web: www.alfatravel.co.uk

Leisureplex

Dir: Follow signs to seafront. Hotel facing Britannia Pier
This Victorian building is centrally located on the seafront, overlooking Britannia Pier and the sandy beach. Bedrooms are pleasantly decorated and equipped with modern facilities; many have lovely sea views. Dinner is taken in the restaurant which doubles as the ballroom, and guests can also relax in the bar or sunny lounge.

ROOMS: 75 en suite (3 fmly) **FACILITIES:** ♬ **SERVICES:** Lift **NOTES:** ✗ ⊗ in restaurant Closed Dec-Feb RS Nov & Mar

GREENFORD, Greater London
See LONDON SECTION plan 1 B4

★★★67% The Bridge
Western Av UB6 8ST
☎ 020 8566 6246 ▤ 020 8566 6140
e-mail: bridgehotel@youngs.co.uk
Dir: Turn off A40 before flyover onto A4127 towards Greenford, hotel on roundabout
A popular venue for business guests this hotel is ideally located for accessing central London, just off the A40. Spacious bedrooms offer good levels of comfort and a range of useful facilities. Public areas include a popular public bar, a bistro-style restaurant and conference and meeting facilities. The hotel benefits from its own spacious car park.

ROOMS: 68 en suite (4 fmly) ⊗ in 44 bedrooms **FACILITIES:** STV Arrangement with local leisure centre **CONF:** Thtr 120 Class 60 Board 60 **SERVICES:** Lift air con **PARKING:** 68 **NOTES:** ✗ ⊗ in restaurant

⌂ Premier Travel Inn Greenford, Middlesex
Western Av UB6 8TE
☎ 08701 977119 ▤ 020 8998 8823
web: www.premiertravelinn.com

premier travel inn

Dir: From the Western Avenue (A40), Eastbound, exit Perivale. Turn right, then at 2nd lights turn left. Inn is opposite Hoover Building
High quality, modern budget accommodation ideal for both
continued on p236

G

GREENFORD, continued

families and business travellers. Spacious, en suite bedrooms feature bath and shower, satellite TV and many have telephones and modem points. The adjacent family restaurant features a wide and varied menu. For further details consult the Hotel Groups page.
ROOMS: 39 en suite s £59.95-£62.95; d £59.95-£62.95

GREETHAM, Rutland

U Greetham Valley
Wood Ln LE15 7NP
☎ 01780 460444 01780 460623
e-mail: info@gvgc.co.uk
At the time of going to press, the star classification for this hotel was not confirmed. Please refer to the AA internet site www.theAA.com for current information.
ROOMS: 35 en suite (17 GF) ⊗ in all bedrooms s £52.50-£60; d £52.50-£60 **LB** **FACILITIES: Spa** STV 36 Fishing Solarium Putt green 4x4 course Off road training course Archery centre ch fac Xmas **CONF:** Thtr 200 Class 150 Board 80 Del from £95 **SERVICES:** Lift **PARKING:** 300 **NOTES:** ⊗ in restaurant Civ Wed 200

GRIMSBY, Lincolnshire Map 17 TA21

★★★66% Beeches
42 Waltham Rd, Scartho DN33 2LX
☎ 01472 278830 01472 752880
e-mail: joeramsden@freeuk.com
web: www.thebeecheshotel.com
In the suburb of Scartho, not far from the town centre, this contemporary hotel offers good modern accommodation and pleasing public rooms. Bedrooms are inviting and well equipped with a thoughtful range of facilities. There is a popular brasserie and a comfortable lounge bar; quality, interesting food is on offer.
ROOMS: 18 en suite (4 GF) ⊗ in all bedrooms s £49-£70; d £54-£85 (incl. bkfst) **LB** **CONF:** Class 40 **SERVICES:** Lift **PARKING:** 70 **NOTES:** ⊗ in restaurant Closed 25 Dec-1st wk Jan

★★★66% Hotel Elizabeth
Littlecoates Rd DN34 4LX
☎ 01472 240024 & 0870 1162716 01472 241354
e-mail: elizabeth.grimsby@elizabethhotels.co.uk
web: www.elizabethhotels.co.uk
Dir: *A1136 signed Greatcoates, 1st rdbt left, 2nd rdbt right. Hotel on right in 200mtrs*
Bedrooms at this pleasantly situated hotel are equipped with modern comforts and many have large windows and balconies overlooking the adjoining golf course. The popular restaurant shares the same tranquil view. There is a large banqueting suite, smaller meeting and conference rooms, and extensive parking which makes this an ideal business centre.
ROOMS: 52 en suite (4 fmly) ⊗ in 27 bedrooms s £65-£75; d £85 (incl. bkfst) **LB** **FACILITIES:** STV Xmas **CONF:** Thtr 300 Class 100 Board 60 Del from £89 **SERVICES:** Lift **PARKING:** 200 **NOTES:** ⊗ in restaurant Civ Wed 100

Premier Travel Inn Grimsby
Europa Park, Appian Way, Off Gilbey Rd DN31 2UT
☎ 08701 977121 01472 241648
web: www.premiertravelinn.com
Dir: *From M180 junct 5, A180 towards town centre. At 1st rdbt take 2nd exit. Take 1st left, then left at mini-rbt onto Appian Way*
High quality, modern budget accommodation ideal for both families and business travellers. Spacious, en suite bedrooms feature bath and shower, satellite TV and many have telephones and modem points. The adjacent family restaurant features a wide and varied menu. For further details consult the Hotel Groups page.
ROOMS: 40 en suite s £46.95-£49.95; d £46.95-£49.95

GRIMSTON, Norfolk Map 12 TF72

Top Hotel

★★★ Congham Hall Country House Hotel
Lynn Rd PE32 1AH
☎ 01485 600250 01485 601191
e-mail: info@conghamhallhotel.co.uk
web: www.vonessenhotels.co.uk
Dir: *at A149-A148 junct, NE of King's Lynn, take A148 towards Fakenham for 100yds. Right to Grimston, hotel 2.5m on left*
Elegant 18th-century Georgian manor set amid 30 acres of mature landscaped grounds and surrounded by parkland. The inviting public rooms provide a range of tastefully furnished areas in which to sit and relax. Imaginative cuisine is served in the Orangery Restaurant, which has an intimate atmosphere and panoramic views of the gardens. The bedrooms are tastefully furnished with period pieces, have modern facilities and many thoughtful touches.
ROOMS: 14 en suite ⊗ in all bedrooms **FACILITIES:** Putt green ch fac **CONF:** Thtr 50 Class 20 Board 30 **PARKING:** 50 **NOTES:** ⊗ in restaurant Civ Wed 100

GRINDLEFORD, Derbyshire Map 16 SK27

★★★65% Maynard Arms
Main Rd S32 2HE
☎ 01433 630321 01433 630445
e-mail: info@maynardarms.co.uk
web: www.maynardarms.co.uk
Dir: *from Sheffield take A625 to Castleton. Left into Grindleford on B6521. After Fox House hotel on left*
A delightful country hotel set in attractive gardens with fine views. Bedrooms are very practically furnished and decorated; some have separate sitting rooms. A residents' lounge is situated on the first floor, with superb rural views, and the restaurant overlooks the gardens. Bar food is available at both lunch and dinner.
ROOMS: 10 en suite s £75-£95; d £85-£105 (incl. bkfst) **LB** **FACILITIES:** STV Xmas **CONF:** BC Thtr 140 Class 80 Board 40 Del from £130 **PARKING:** 80 **NOTES:** ⊗ in restaurant Civ Wed 120

Indoor Swimming pool
Indoor Swimming pool (heated)
Outdoor Swimming pool
Outdoor Swimming pool (heated)

continued

GUILDFORD, Surrey Map 06 SU94

★★★69% The Manor
Newlands Corner GU4 8SE
☎ 01483 222624 📠 01483 211389
e-mail: mail@hollybournehotels.com
web: www.hollybournehotels.com
Dir: *3.5m on A25 to Dorking*
Set peacefully in its own grounds, this conveniently located hotel is a popular choice for weddings and conferences. The well-appointed public areas include a selection of meeting rooms, a choice of bars and a newly added spa and leisure facility. Bedrooms, which are mostly modern, are tastefully furnished and have a good range of facilities.
ROOMS: 50 en suite (4 fmly) ⊗ in 4 bedrooms s £98-£108; d £98-£108 **LB** **FACILITIES:** STV Sauna Solarium Gym Jacuzzi Steam room, dance studio **CONF:** Thtr 150 Class 50 Board 50 Del from £150 **PARKING:** 100 **NOTES:** ⊗ in restaurant Civ Wed 120

Premier Travel Inn Guildford
Parkway GU1 1UP
☎ 08701 977122 📠 01483 450678
web: www.premiertravelinn.com
Dir: *From M25 junct 10 follow signs to Portsmouth (A3). Turn off signed Guildford centre/Leisure Centre (A322/A320/A25). Left and Inn on left*
High quality, modern budget accommodation ideal for both families and business travellers. Spacious, en suite bedrooms feature bath and shower, satellite TV and many have telephones and modem points. The adjacent family restaurant features a wide and varied menu. For further details consult the Hotel Groups page.
ROOMS: 87 en suite s £57.95-£59.95; d £57.95-£59.95 **CONF:** Thtr 45 Board 25

Travelodge Guildford
Woodbridge Rd GU1 4QD
☎ 08700 850 890
web: www.travelodge.co.uk
Dir: *In town centre adjacent to Friary Shopping Centre and bus station.*
Travelodge offers good quality, good value, modern accommodation. Ideal for families, the spacious, en suite bedrooms include remote-control TV, tea and coffee-making facilities and comfortable beds. Meals can be taken at the nearby family restaurant. For further details consult the Hotel Groups page.
ROOMS: 152 en suite (incl. bkfst) s fr £26; d fr £26

GUISBOROUGH, North Yorkshire Map 19 NZ61

★★★★72% *Gisborough Hall*
Whitby Ln TS14 6PT
☎ 0870 400 8191 📠 01287 610844
e-mail: general.gisboroughhall@macdonald-hotels.co.uk
web: www.macdonald-hotels.co.uk
Dir: *A171, follow signs for Whitby until Waterfall rdbt then into Whitby Lane, hotel 500yds on right*
Dating back to the mid-19th century, this elegant establishment has been carefully refurbished and extended to provide a pleasing combination of original features and modern facilities. Bedrooms, including four-poster and family rooms, are richly furnished, while there is a choice of welcoming lounges with log fires. Imaginative fare is served in Tockett's restaurant.
ROOMS: 71 en suite (2 fmly) (12 GF) ⊗ in 37 bedrooms
FACILITIES: STV Sauna Revival zone-2 beauty treatment zones
CONF: BC Thtr 400 Class 150 Board 32 **SERVICES:** Lift air con
PARKING: 400 **NOTES:** ⊗ in restaurant Civ Wed

Restaurant with Rooms

Pinchinthorpe Hall
Pinchinthorpe TS14 8HG
☎ 01287 630200 📠 01287 632000
e-mail: nyb@pinchinthorpe.freeserve.co.uk
web: www.pinchinthorpehall.co.uk
Dir: *Between Guisborough and Great Ayton on A173.*
An elegant 17th-century country manor house that has stylish bedrooms, each very individually and tastefully decorated and with many thoughtful extras. The Brewhouse Bistro serves interesting dishes using home grown and local produce, and offers caring and attentive service.
ROOMS: 6 en suite ⊗ in all bedrooms s £85-£105; d £130-£170 **LB**
FACILITIES: Fishing Riding Xmas **CONF:** Thtr 50 Class 20 Board 24 Del from £75 **PARKING:** 110 **NOTES:** ⊗ in restaurant Civ Wed 80

Premier Travel Inn Middlesbrough South
Middlesbrough Rd, Upsall TS14 6RW
☎ 0870 9906540 📠 0870 9906541
web: www.premiertravelinn.com
Dir: *Off A171 towards Whitby*
High quality, modern budget accommodation ideal for both families and business travellers. Spacious, en suite bedrooms feature bath and shower, satellite TV and many have telephones and modem points. The adjacent family restaurant features a wide and varied menu. For further details consult the Hotel Groups page.
ROOMS: 20 en suite s £46.95-£48.95; d £46.95-£48.95

GULWORTHY, Devon Map 03 SX47

★★★75% Horn of Plenty
PL19 8JD
☎ 01822 832528 📠 01822 832528
e-mail: enquiries@thehornofplenty.co.uk
web: www.thehornofplenty.co.uk
Dir: *from Tavistock take A390 W for 3m. Right at Gulworthy Cross. After 400yds turn left and after 400yds hotel on right*

With stunning views over the Tamar Valley, The Horn of Plenty maintains its reputation as one of Britain's best country-house hotels. The bedrooms are well equipped and have many

continued on p238

GULWORTHY, continued

thoughtful extras; some, more simply decorated, are in adjacent converted cottages. Cuisine here is also impressive and local produce provides interesting and memorable dining.
ROOMS: 4 en suite 6 annexe en suite (3 fmly) (4 GF) ⊗ in all bedrooms s £110-£220; d £120-£230 (incl. bkfst) **LB** **FACILITIES:** Xmas **CONF:** BC Thtr 36 Class 20 Board 16 Del from £150 **PARKING:** 25 **NOTES:** ⊗ in restaurant Closed 24-26 Dec Civ Wed 80

HACKNESS, North Yorkshire — Map 17 SE99

★★★68% *Hackness Grange Country House*
North York National Park YO13 0JW
☎ 01723 882345 📠 01723 882391
e-mail: admin@englishrosehotels.co.uk
Dir: *A64 to Scarborough, then A171 to Whitby and Scalby. Follow Hackness and Forge Valley National Park signs, through Hackness village on left*
Close to Scarborough, and set in the North Yorkshire Moors National Park, Hackness Grange is surrounded by well-tended gardens. Comfortable bedrooms have views of the open countryside; those in the cottages are ideally suited to families, and the courtyard rooms include facilities for the less able. Lounges and the restaurant are spacious and relaxing.
ROOMS: 33 en suite (5 fmly) (8 GF) **FACILITIES:** 9 hole pitch & putt **CONF:** Thtr 20 Board 14 **PARKING:** 60 **NOTES:** ⊗ in restaurant
See advert under SCARBOROUGH

HADLEY WOOD, Greater London — Map 06 TQ29

★★★★73% West Lodge Park
Cockfosters Rd EN4 0PY
☎ 020 8216 3900 📠 020 8216 3937
e-mail: westlodgepark@bealeshotels.co.uk
Dir: *on A111, 1m S of M25 junct 24*
An impressive country-house hotel set in mature parkland and gardens, yet only 12 miles from central London. Bedrooms are individually decorated and offer comprehensive in-room facilities; superior annexed rooms have air conditioning and exclusive access to an outdoor patio. The Cedar Restaurant provides a good choice of interesting dishes. Informal dining and afternoon teas are also readily available.
ROOMS: 46 en suite 13 annexe en suite (1 fmly) (11 GF) ⊗ in 23 bedrooms s £110-£160; d £150-£250 **LB** **FACILITIES:** STV Putt green Massage, Manicure, Free use of nearby leisure club ♫ Xmas **CONF:** Thtr 70 Class 30 Board 30 Del from £192 **SERVICES:** Lift **PARKING:** 200 **NOTES:** ⊗ in restaurant RS Saturday Civ Wed 60

HAGLEY, Worcestershire — Map 10 SO98

Premier Travel Inn Hagley
Birmingham Rd DY9 9JS
☎ 08701 977123 📠 01562 884416
web: www.premiertravelinn.com
Dir: *5m off M5 junct 3 on opposite side of A456 dual carriageway towards Kidderminster*
High quality, modern budget accommodation ideal for both families and business travellers. Spacious, en suite bedrooms feature bath and shower, satellite TV and many have telephones and modem points. The adjacent family restaurant features a wide and varied menu. For further details consult the Hotel Groups page.
ROOMS: 40 en suite s £46.95-£49.95; d £46.95-£49.95 **CONF:** Thtr 20 Board 18

♫ Entertainment

HAILSHAM, East Sussex — Map 06 TQ50

★★★66% Boship Farm
Lower Dicker BN27 4AT
☎ 01323 844826 📠 01323 843945
e-mail: boship.farm@forestdale.com
web: www.forestdale.com
Dir: *on A22 at Boship rdbt, junct of A22, A267 and A271*
Dating back to 1652, a lovely old farmhouse forms the hub of this hotel, which is set in 17 acres of well-tended grounds. Guests have the use of an all-weather tennis court, an outdoor pool and a croquet lawn. Bedrooms are smartly appointed and well-equipped; most have views across open fields and countryside.
ROOMS: 47 annexe en suite (5 fmly) (21 GF) ⊗ in 17 bedrooms s £70-£85; d £115-£135 (incl. bkfst) **LB** **FACILITIES:** Sauna Jacuzzi Xmas **CONF:** Thtr 175 Class 40 Board 46 Del from £125 **PARKING:** 100 **NOTES:** ⊗ in restaurant

★★71% The Olde Forge Hotel & Restaurant
Magham Down BN27 1PN
☎ 01323 842893 📠 01323 842893
e-mail: theoldeforgehotel@tesco.net
Dir: *off Boship rdbt on A271 to Bexhill & Herstmonceux. 3m on left*
In the heart of the countryside, this family-run hotel offers a friendly welcome and an informal atmosphere. The bedrooms are attractively decorated with thoughtful extras. The restaurant, with its timbered beams and log fires, was a forge in the 16th century and has a good local reputation for its cuisine and service.
ROOMS: 7 en suite ⊗ in all bedrooms s fr £48; d fr £70 (incl. bkfst) **LB** **PARKING:** 11 **NOTES:** ⊗ in restaurant

Travelodge Hellingly Eastbourne
Boship Roundabout, Hellingly BN27 4DT
☎ 08700 850 950 📠 01323 844556
web: www.travelodge.co.uk
Dir: *on A22 at Boship rdbt*
Travelodge offers good quality, good value, modern accommodation. Ideal for families, the spacious, en suite bedrooms include remote-control TV, tea and coffee-making facilities and comfortable beds. Meals can be taken at the nearby family restaurant. For further details consult the Hotel Groups page.
ROOMS: 58 en suite s fr £26; d fr £26

HALIFAX, West Yorkshire — Map 19 SE02

★★★75% Holdsworth House
Holdsworth HX2 9TG
☎ 01422 240024 📠 01422 245174
e-mail: info@holdsworthhouse.co.uk
web: www.holdsworthhouse.co.uk
Dir: *from town centre take A629 Keighley Road. Right at garage up Shay Ln after 1.5m. Hotel on right after 1m*

This delightful 17th-century Jacobean manor house is set in
continued

well-tended gardens and offers individually decorated, thoughtfully equipped bedrooms. Public rooms, adorned with beautiful paintings and antique pieces, include a choice of inviting lounges and superb conference and function facilities. Dinner provides the highlight of any stay and is served in the elegant restaurant, by friendly, attentive staff.
ROOMS: 40 en suite (2 fmly) (15 GF) s £98-£140; d £130-£175 (incl. bkfst) **LB** **FACILITIES:** STV **CONF:** Thtr 150 Class 75 Board 50 Del £135 **PARKING:** 60 **NOTES:** ⊗ in restaurant Civ Wed 120

★★★63% Imperial Crown Hotel

42/46 Horton St HX1 1QE
☎ 0870 609 6114 📠 01422 349866
e-mail: imperialcrown@corushotels.com
web: www.corushotels.com
Dir: *opposite railway station & Eureka Children's Museum*

This friendly hotel enjoys a central location and in addition to the main accommodation there are 15 smart, contemporary rooms in a building opposite. The Wallis Simpson Restaurant and Bar are packed with interesting memorabilia and extensive conference and banqueting facilities are available.
ROOMS: 41 en suite 15 annexe en suite (3 fmly) ⊗ in 22 bedrooms **FACILITIES:** Complimentary use of Workout Warehouse gym, opposite the hotel **CONF:** Thtr 150 Class 120 Board 70 Del from £90 **PARKING:** 63 **NOTES:** ✈ ⊗ in restaurant Civ Wed 150

⌂ Premier Travel Inn Halifax

Salterhebble Hill, Huddersfield Rd HX3 0QT
☎ 0870 9906308 📠 0870 9906309
web: www.premiertravelinn.com
Dir: *Just off M62 junct 24 on A629 towards Halifax*
High quality, modern budget accommodation ideal for both families and business travellers. Spacious, en suite bedrooms feature bath and shower, satellite TV and many have telephones and modem points. The adjacent family restaurant features a wide and varied menu. For further details consult the Hotel Groups page.
ROOMS: 31 en suite s £46.95-£48.95; d £46.95-£48.95 **CONF:** Thtr 30

⌂ Travelodge (Halifax Central)

Dean Clough Park HX3 5AY
☎ 08700 850 950 📠 01422 362669
web: www.travelodge.co.uk
Dir: *M62 junct 24, take A629, follow signs for town centre, then brown tourist signs for Dean Clough Mills*
Travelodge offers good quality, good value, modern accommodation. Ideal for families, the spacious, en suite bedrooms include remote-control TV, tea and coffee-making facilities and comfortable beds. Meals can be taken at the nearby family restaurant. For further details consult the Hotel Groups page.
ROOMS: 52 en suite s fr £26; d fr £26

HAMPTON COURT, Greater London
See LONDON SECTION plan 1 B1

★★★★62% The Carlton Mitre

Hampton Court Rd KT8 9BN
☎ 020 8979 9988 📠 020 8979 9777
e-mail: mitre@carltonhotels.co.uk
Dir: *M3 junct 1 follow signs to Sunbury & Hampton Court Palace. At Hampton Court Palace rdbt right and hotel on right*
This hotel, dating back in parts to 1655, enjoys an enviable setting on the banks of the River Thames opposite Hampton Court Palace. The riverside restaurant and Edge bar/brasserie command wonderful views. Bedrooms are generally spacious with excellent facilities. Parking is limited.
ROOMS: 36 en suite (2 fmly) ⊗ in 20 bedrooms s £125-£180; d £125-£180 (incl. bkfst) **LB** **FACILITIES:** STV Xmas **CONF:** BC Thtr 120 Class 60 Board 40 Del from £190 **SERVICES:** Lift **PARKING:** 13 **NOTES:** ✈ ⊗ in restaurant Civ Wed 100

★★★66% Liongate

Hampton Court Rd KT8 9DD
☎ 020 8977 8121 📠 020 8943 4029
e-mail: events@dhillonhotels.co.uk
Dir: *M25 junct 12/M3 towards London. M3 junct 1, follow A308 at mini-rdbt turn left. Hotel opposite Hampton Court Palace gates*
Dating back to 1721 this hotel enjoys a wonderful location opposite the Lion Gate entrance to Hampton Court and beside the gate into Bushy Park. Despite its history it boasts rooms with plenty of contemporary style. Public areas are all open-plan and feature a modern European restaurant.
ROOMS: 14 en suite 18 annexe en suite (2 fmly) (12 GF) ⊗ in 5 bedrooms **FACILITIES:** Xmas **CONF:** Thtr 60 Class 50 Board 35 **PARKING:** 30 **NOTES:** ✈

HANDFORTH See Manchester Airport

HARLOW, Essex
Map 06 TL41

★★★65% *Corus hotel Harlow*

Mulberry Green, Old Harlow CM17 0ET
☎ 0870 609 6146 📠 01279 626113
web: www.corushotels.com
Dir: *M11 junct 7 onto A414. Right at 4th rdbt then left into Mulberry Green, hotel on left*

This popular coaching inn, dating back to the 14th century, is situated just a short drive from the town centre. The busy lounge bar is an enjoyable place for a drink, and there is also a trendy brasserie-style restaurant offering both carte and daily-changing menus. Modern, well-equipped bedrooms are located to the rear of the property.
ROOMS: 55 annexe en suite (14 GF) ⊗ in 27 bedrooms **CONF:** Thtr 60 Class 26 Board 30 **PARKING:** 75 **NOTES:** ⊗ in restaurant

HARLOW, continued

Premier Travel Inn Harlow
Cambridge Rd CM20 2EP
☎ 08701 977125 ☐ 01279 452169
web: www.premiertravelinn.com
Dir: *M11 junct 7. Off A414 on Sawbridgeworth to Bishop's Stortford rd (A1184)*
High quality, modern budget accommodation ideal for both families and business travellers. Spacious, en suite bedrooms feature bath and shower, satellite TV and many have telephones and modem points. The adjacent family restaurant features a wide and varied menu. For further details consult the Hotel Groups page.
ROOMS: 61 en suite s £52.95; d £52.95

Travelodge Harlow
Burnt Mill CM20 2JE
☎ 08700 850950 ☐ 01279 437 349
web: www.travelodge.co.uk
Dir: *From M11 junct 7 follow A414 E towards Hertford. Lodge on left.*
Travelodge offers good quality, good value, modern accommodation. Ideal for families, the spacious, en suite bedrooms include remote-control TV, tea and coffee-making facilities and comfortable beds. Meals can be taken at the nearby family restaurant. For further details consult the Hotel Groups page.
ROOMS: 90 en suite s fr £26; d fr £26

Travelodge Harlow East (Stansted)
A414 Eastbound, Tylers Green, North Weald CM16 6BJ
☎ 08700 850 950 ☐ 01992 523276
web: www.travelodge.co.uk
Dir: *M11 junct 7, take A414 towards Chelmsford, after 2nd rdbt on left*
Travelodge offers good quality, good value, modern accommodation. Ideal for families, the spacious, en suite bedrooms include remote-control TV, tea and coffee-making facilities and comfortable beds. Meals can be taken at the nearby family restaurant. For further details consult the Hotel Groups page.
ROOMS: 60 en suite s fr £26; d fr £26

HAROME See Helmsley

HARPENDEN, Hertfordshire — Map 06 TL11

★★★67% *Corus hotel Harpenden*
18 Southdown Rd AL5 1PE
☎ 01582 449955 ☐ 01582 769858
e-mail: harpendenhouse@corushotels.com
web: www.corushotels.com
Dir: *M1 junct 10 left at rdbt. Next rdbt right onto A1081 to Harpenden. Over mini rdbt, through town centre and over next mini rdbt. Next rdbt left, hotel 200yds on left*

This attractive Grade II listed Georgian building overlooks East Common. The hotel gardens are particularly attractive and the public areas are stylishly decorated, including the restaurant that has an impressively decorated ceiling. Some of the bedrooms and a large suite are located in the original house but most of the accommodation is in the annexe.
ROOMS: 17 en suite 59 annexe en suite (13 fmly) (2 GF) ⊘ in 49 bedrooms **FACILITIES:** STV Complimentary use of local leisure centre **CONF:** BC Thtr 150 Class 60 Board 60 **PARKING:** 80 **NOTES:** ✗ ⊘ in restaurant RS wknds & BH's Civ Wed 120

HARROGATE, North Yorkshire — Map 19 SE35
See also Knaresborough

Top Hotel

★★★★ ◎◎ Rudding Park Hotel & Golf
Rudding Park, Follifoot HG3 1JH
☎ 01423 871350 ☐ 01423 872286
e-mail: sales@ruddingpark.com
web: www.ruddingpark.com
Dir: *from A61 at rdbt with A658 take York exit and follow signs to Rudding Park*
In the heart of 200-year-old landscaped parkland, this modern hotel is elegant and stylish. Bedrooms, including two luxurious suites, are smartly presented and thoughtfully equipped. Carefully prepared meals are served in the Clocktower, with its striking, contemporary decor. A spacious bar and comfortable lounges are also available. There is an adjoining 18-hole, par 72 golf course and an 18-bay floodlit, covered driving range.
ROOMS: 49 en suite (10 GF) ⊘ in 39 bedrooms s £140-£320; d £170-£320 (incl. bkfst) **LB** **FACILITIES:** STV ⛳ 18 Putt green Driving range Jogging trail Membership of local gym Xmas **CONF:** BC Thtr 300 Class 150 Board 36 Del £190 **SERVICES:** Lift **PARKING:** 150 **NOTES:** ⊘ in restaurant Civ Wed 300

Town House

★★★★ ◎ *Hotel du Vin & Bistro*
Prospect Place HG1 1LB
☎ 01423 856800 ☐ 01423 856801
e-mail: info@harrogate.hotelduvin.com
web: www.hotelduvin.com
Dir: *Enter town centre & stay in right lane, pass West Park Church on right. Hotel on right*
The latest Hotel du Vin is a marvellous new town house overlooking the Stray. The spacious, open-plan lobby has seating, a bar and the reception desk. Hidden downstairs is a cosy snug cellar. The French-influenced Bistro offers high quality cooking and a great choice of wines. Bedrooms face

continued

front and back, are smart and modern, and have excellent 'deluge' showers.
ROOMS: 43 en suite (2 GF) **FACILITIES:** STV Snooker Gym **CONF:** Thtr 50 Board 20 **SERVICES:** Lift **PARKING:** 30 **NOTES:** ✗ Civ Wed 90

★★★★70% The Majestic
Ripon Rd HG1 2HU
☎ 01423 700300 🖷 01423 521332
e-mail: majestic@paramount-hotels.co.uk
web: www.paramount-hotels.co.uk
Dir: *from M1 onto A1(M) at Wetherby. Take A661 to Harrogate. Hotel in town centre adjacent to Royal Hall*

PARAMOUNT GROUP OF HOTELS

Popular for conferences and functions, this grand Victorian hotel is set in 12 acres of landscaped grounds and is centrally located within walking distance of the town centre and benefits from spacious public areas. The bedrooms are comfortably equipped; these come in a variety of sizes and include several spacious suites.
ROOMS: 156 en suite (9 fmly) ⊘ in 86 bedrooms s £120-£130; d £140-£170 **LB** **FACILITIES:** STV supervised Snooker Sauna Solarium Gym Jacuzzi Golf practice net Xmas **CONF:** BC Thtr 500 Class 250 Board 70 Del from £150 **SERVICES:** Lift **PARKING:** 250 **NOTES:** ⊘ in restaurant Civ Wed 200

★★★★61% Cedar Court
Queens Buildings, Park Pde HG1 5AH
☎ 01423 858585 & 858595(res)
🖷 01423 504950
e-mail: cedarcourt@bestwestern.co.uk
web: www.cedarcourthotels.co.uk
Dir: *from A1(M) follow signs to Harrogate on A661 past Sainsburys. At rdbt left onto A6040. Hotel right after church*

Best Western

This Grade II listed building was Harrogate's first hotel and enjoys a peaceful location in landscaped grounds, close to the town centre. It provides spacious, well-equipped accommodation. Public areas include a Brasserie style restaurant, a gym and an open-plan lounge and bar. Functions and conferences are particularly well catered for.
ROOMS: 100 en suite (8 fmly) (7 GF) ⊘ in 75 bedrooms s £65-£135; d £90-£150 (incl. bkfst) **LB** **FACILITIES:** STV Gym Xmas **CONF:** BC Thtr 320 Class 90 Board 80 Del from £138 **SERVICES:** Lift **PARKING:** 150 **NOTES:** ✗ ⊘ in restaurant Civ Wed 70

★★★79% ◎◎ The Boar's Head Hotel
Ripley Castle Estate HG3 3AY
☎ 01423 771888 🖷 01423 771509
e-mail: reservations@boarsheadripley.co.uk
Dir: *on A61 Harrogate to Ripon road. Hotel in centre of Ripley Village*
Part of the Ripley Castle estate, this delightful and popular hotel is renowned for its warm hospitality and as a dining destination. Bedrooms offer many comforts, and the luxurious day rooms

continued

feature works of art from the nearby castle. A new addition this year is the superb range of banqueting suites in the castle.

The Boar's Head Hotel

ROOMS: 19 en suite 6 annexe en suite (2 fmly) ⊘ in 15 bedrooms s £105-£125; d £125-£150 (incl. bkfst) **LB** **FACILITIES:** Fishing Clay pigeon shooting ♫ Xmas **CONF:** BC Thtr 150 Class 80 Board 150 Del from £155 **PARKING:** 50 **NOTES:** ⊘ in restaurant Civ Wed 120

★★★74% *Grants*
3-13 Swan Rd HG1 2SS
☎ 01423 560666 🖷 01423 502550
e-mail: enquiries@grantshotel-harrogate.com
web: www.grantshotel-harrogate.com
Dir: *off A61*
A long established, family-run hotel with an attractive flower bedecked patio. The smartly presented, well-equipped bedrooms include some with four-poster beds. A comfortable lounge bar with plenty of interesting old photographs, and imaginative food

continued on p242

HARROGATE, continued

in the colourful Chimney Pots Bistro, are just some of the features at this friendly hotel.

Grants, Harrogate

ROOMS: 42 en suite (2 fmly) **FACILITIES:** STV Use of local Health & Leisure Club **CONF:** Thtr 70 Class 20 Board 30 **SERVICES:** Lift **PARKING:** 26 **NOTES:** ⊗ in restaurant

★★★70% The Yorkshire

Prospect Place HG1 1LA

CRERAR HOTELS

☎ 01423 565071 🖷 01423 500082
e-mail: theyorkshire@crerarhotels.com
web: www.crerarhotels.com
Dir: *follow A61 into town centre. Hotel opposite Betty's Tea Rooms*

Occupying an imposing Victorian building The Yorkshire Hotel is a smart, contemporary town-centre venue. There are two relaxing lounges, an 'upstairs' restaurant with lovely views and the modern HG1 Bar Brasserie that serves snack meals. All bedrooms are smart and well appointed.

ROOMS: 80 en suite (4 fmly) ⊗ in 52 bedrooms s £135; d £225 (incl. bkfst) **LB** **FACILITIES:** Xmas **CONF:** Thtr 150 Class 80 Board 60 Del £130 **SERVICES:** Lift **PARKING:** 35 **NOTES:** ✈ ⊗ in restaurant Civ Wed 100

★★★67% Studley

Swan Rd HG1 2SE
☎ 01423 560425 🖷 01423 530967
e-mail: info@studleyhotel.co.uk
web: www.studleyhotel.co.uk
Dir: *Swan Rd adjacent to Valley Gardens and opp Mercer Gallery*

This friendly well-established hotel, close to the town centre and Valley Gardens, is renowned for its Orchid Restaurant, which provides a dynamic and authentic approach to Pacific Rim and Asian cuisine. Bedrooms come in a variety of styles and sizes, whilst the bar lounge provides a relaxing ambience for guests.

ROOMS: 36 en suite (1 fmly) ⊗ in 6 bedrooms s fr £70; d fr £94 (incl. bkfst) **LB** **FACILITIES:** STV Free use of local Health & Spa Club **CONF:** Thtr 15 Class 15 Board 12 **SERVICES:** Lift **PARKING:** 15 **NOTES:** ⊗ in restaurant

★★★60% *The Crown*

Crown Place HG1 2RZ
☎ 01423 567755 🖷 01423 502284
e-mail: thecrown@corushotels.com
web: www.corushotels.com/thecrown
Dir: *A61 to Harrogate down Parliament St to traffic lights by Royal Hall. Left to Valley Gardens and 1st left to rdbt. Hotel on right*

Centrally situated, this hotel has been welcoming guests for some 250 years. Bedrooms are mixed both in standard and size, but have good facilities such as a movie channel and modem links. Public areas reflect a bygone era - tall ceilings with columns and plenty of space.

ROOMS: 121 en suite (8 fmly) ⊗ in 61 bedrooms **FACILITIES:** free use of local sports club **CONF:** Thtr 400 Class 200 Board 80 **SERVICES:** Lift **PARKING:** 25 **NOTES:** ⊗ in restaurant Civ Wed

★★74% Ascot House

53 Kings Rd HG1 5HJ
☎ 01423 531005 🖷 01423 503523
e-mail: admin@ascothouse.com
web: www.ascothouse.com
Dir: *follow signs for Town Centre/Conference & Exhibition Centre into Kings Rd, hotel on left after park*

This late-Victorian house has been tastefully transformed into a friendly and meticulously maintained hotel. Situated a short distance from the International Conference Centre, it provides comfortable and extremely well-appointed bedrooms, an inviting lounge bar and a dining room offering an interesting choice at dinner.

ROOMS: 19 en suite (2 fmly) (5 GF) ⊗ in all bedrooms s £61-£73; d £90-£115 (incl. bkfst) **LB** **FACILITIES:** Xmas **CONF:** Thtr 80 Class 36 Board 36 Del from £109 **PARKING:** 14 **NOTES:** ⊗ in restaurant Closed 22 Jan-5 Feb Civ Wed 80

Restaurant with Rooms

Harrogate Brasserie Hotel & Bar

28-30 Cheltenham Pde HG1 1DB

THE INDEPENDENTS

☎ 01423 505041 🖷 01423 722300
e-mail: info@brasserie.co.uk
web: www.brasserie.co.uk
Dir: *on A61 town centre behind theatre*

This town centre restaurant with rooms is distinctly continental in style. The brasserie covers three cosy dining areas richly decorated and adorned with artefacts. Live jazz is featured on Wednesday, Friday and Sunday nights. The individual bedrooms have period collectibles; many rooms have DVD players and all have lots to read.

ROOMS: 17 en suite (3 fmly) s fr £55; d fr £85 (incl. bkfst) **LB** **FACILITIES:** ♫ ch fac Xmas **PARKING:** 12 **NOTES:** Closed 26 & 31 Dec

AA Rosette Award for culinary excellence

⌂ Innkeeper's Lodge Harrogate West

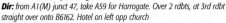

Otley Rd, Beckwith Knowle HG3 1PR
☎ 01423 533091 📠 01423 533092
web: www.innkeeperslodge.com
Dir: *from A1(M) junct 47, take A59 for Harrogate. Over 2 rdbts, at 3rd rdbt straight over onto B6162. Hotel on left opp church*
A growing concept in the travel accommodation market. Smart rooms meet essential business requirements but also have home comforts. Dining options include all-day menus plus the added advantage of breakfast, which is included in the room price. For further details consult the Hotel Groups page.
ROOMS: 11 en suite s £55; d £55 **CONF:** Thtr 30 Class 30 Board 30

⌂ Premier Travel Inn Harrogate

Hornbeam Park Ave, Hornbeam Park HG2 8RA
☎ 08701 977 126 📠 01423 878581
web: www.premiertravelinn.com
Dir: *A1(M) junct 46 west then A661 to Harrogate. After 2m left at The Woodlands lights. Hornbeam Park Avenue 1.5m on left*
High quality, modern budget accommodation ideal for both families and business travellers. Spacious, en suite bedrooms feature bath and shower, satellite TV and many have telephones and modem points. The adjacent family restaurant features a wide and varied menu. For further details consult the Hotel Groups page.
ROOMS: 50 en suite s £52.95; d £52.95

⌂ Travelodge (Harrogate)

The Gubbel HG1 2RF
☎ 0870 1911737 📠 01423562734
web: www.travelodge.co.uk
Travelodge offers good quality, good value, modern accommodation. Ideal for families, the spacious, en suite bedrooms include remote-control TV, tea and coffee-making facilities and comfortable beds. Meals can be taken at the nearby family restaurant. For further details consult the Hotel Groups page.
ROOMS: 46 en suite s fr £26; d fr £26

HARROW, Greater London

See LONDON SECTION plan 1 B5

★★★68% Best Western Cumberland

1 St Johns Rd HA1 2EF
☎ 020 8863 4111 📠 020 8861 5668
e-mail: reservations@cumberlandhotel.co.uk
web: www.cumberlandhotel.co.uk
Dir: *from A404 or A409 into Gayton Rd, then into Lyon Rd. Hotel at end*

Situated within walking distance of the town centre, this hotel is ideally located for all local attractions and amenities. Bedrooms provide good levels of comfort and are practically equipped to meet the requirements of all travellers. Impressive public areas include a restaurant and bar, both serving a good variety of fresh food.
ROOMS: 31 en suite 53 annexe en suite (5 fmly) (15 GF) ⊘ in 51 bedrooms s £60-£98; d £75-£110 (incl. bkfst) **FACILITIES:** STV Sauna Gym Xmas **CONF:** Thtr 130 Class 70 Board 62 Del from £105 **PARKING:** 67 **NOTES:** ✂ ⊘ in restaurant

Late for dinner? Quality standards mean that last orders for dinner vary according to star rating and should be no earlier than:
★★ 7.00pm ★★★ 8:00pm ★★★★ 9:00pm ★★★★★ 10:00pm

continued

HARROW, continued

★★★68% Quality Harrow Hotel

12-22 Pinner Rd HA1 4HZ
☎ 020 8427 3435 🖹 020 8861 1370
e-mail: info@harrowhotel.co.uk
web: www.harrowhotel.co.uk
Dir: *off rdbt on A404 at junct with A312*

This privately owned hotel offers a great variety of accommodation to suit all needs. At the top of the range are the air-conditioned executive rooms and suites. These have hi-tech facilities including MD/CD, interactive TV and multiple phone lines. Public areas comprise a bar, conservatory lounge, meeting rooms and a smart restaurant.
ROOMS: 79 en suite (4 fmly) (17 GF) ⊗ in 48 bedrooms s £70-£98; d £80-£150 (incl. bkfst) **FACILITIES:** STV **CONF:** Thtr 160 Class 60 Board 60 Del from £140 **SERVICES:** Lift **PARKING:** 70 **NOTES:** ⊗ in restaurant RS Xmas (limited service) Civ Wed 80
See advert on opposite page

★★59% *The Lindal*

2 Hindes Rd HA1 1SJ
☎ 020 8863 3164 🖹 020 8427 5435
Dir: *Turn off M40 or M1 towards Harrow, hotel is off A409, opposite Tesco*
This family-run hotel is conveniently located for the local shopping centre and provides good transport links to the centre of London. Bedrooms are modern and attractively furnished. Day rooms consist of a combined bar-lounge area and dining room.
ROOMS: 24 en suite (3 fmly) ⊗ in 9 bedrooms **PARKING:** 21 **NOTES:** ✗ No children 6yrs ⊗ in restaurant

HARROW WEALD, Greater London
LONDON SECTION plan 1 B6

★★★68% ❀❀ Grim's Dyke

Old Redding HA3 6SH
☎ 020 8385 3100 🖹 020 8954 4560
e-mail: enquiries@grimsdyke.com
web: www.grimsdyke.com
Dir: *Turn off A410 onto A409 North towards Bushey, at top of hill traffic lights turn left into Old Redding*
Once home to Sir William Gilbert, this Grade II mansion contains many references to well-known Gilbert and Sullivan productions. The house is set in over 40 acres of beautiful parkland and gardens. Rooms in the main house are elegant and traditional, while those in the adjacent lodge are aimed more at the business guest.
ROOMS: 9 en suite 37 annexe en suite (17 GF) ⊗ in 26 bedrooms s £85-£95; d £100 (incl. bkfst) **LB** **FACILITIES:** STV Putt green Gilbert ans Sullivan opera dinner fortnightly. ♫ **CONF:** BC Thtr 100 Class 80 Board 32 Del £160 **PARKING:** 97 **NOTES:** ⊗ in restaurant Closed 25-30 Dec RS 24-26 Dec Civ Wed 90

HARTINGTON, Derbyshire — Map 16 SK16

★★ *Biggin Hall*

SK17 0DH
☎ 01298 84451 🖹 01298 84681
e-mail: enquiries@bigginhall.co.uk
web: www.bigginhall.co.uk
Dir: *0.5m off A515 midway between Ashbourne and Buxton*
ROOMS: 20 en suite (4 fmly) (4 GF) ⊗ in 3 bedrooms **CONF:** Thtr 20 Class 20 Board 20 **PARKING:** 25 **NOTES:** No children 12yrs ⊗ in restaurant
See advert on opposite page

HARTLEBURY, Worcestershire — Map 10 SO87

Travelodge

Shorthill Nurseries DY13 9SH
☎ 08700 850 950 🖹 01299 251774
web: www.travelodge.co.uk
Dir: *A449 southbound*
Travelodge offers good quality, good value, modern accommodation. Ideal for families, the spacious, en suite bedrooms include remote-control TV, tea and coffee-making facilities and comfortable beds. Meals can be taken at the nearby family restaurant. For further details consult the Hotel Groups page.
ROOMS: 32 en suite s fr £26; d fr £26

HARTLEPOOL, Co Durham — Map 19 NZ53

Premier Travel Inn Hartlepool

Maritme Av, Hartlepool Marina TS24 0XZ
☎ 08701 977127 🖹 01429 233105
web: www.premiertravelinn.com
Dir: *approx 1m from A689/A179 link road on marina*
High quality, modern budget accommodation ideal for both families and business travellers. Spacious, en suite bedrooms feature bath and shower, satellite TV and many have telephones and modem points. The adjacent family restaurant features a wide and varied menu. For further details consult the Hotel Groups page.
ROOMS: 40 en suite s £46.95-£48.95; d £46.95-£48.95

HARTLEY WINTNEY, Hampshire — Map 05 SU75

★★★68% Elvetham

RG27 8AR
☎ 01252 844871 🖹 01252 844161
e-mail: enq@theelvetham.co.uk
web: www.theelvetham.co.uk
Dir: *M3 junct 4A W, junct 5 E or junct 11 N of M4. Hotel signed from A323 between Hartley Wintney & Fleet.*
A spectacular 19th-century mansion set in 35 acres of grounds with an arboretum. All bedrooms are individually styled and many have views of the manicured gardens. A popular venue for weddings and conferences, the hotel lends itself to team building events and outdoor pursuits.
ROOMS: 41 en suite 29 annexe en suite (7 GF) s £95-£110; d £130 (incl. bkfst) **FACILITIES:** STV Squash Sauna Gym Putt green Jacuzzi Volleyball, Badminton and Boules **CONF:** BC Thtr 110 Class 80 Board 48 Del from £185 **PARKING:** 200 **NOTES:** ⊗ in restaurant Closed 24 Dec-1 Jan Civ Wed 100

Destination dining!
This symbol indicates a Restaurant with Rooms

HARTSHEAD MOOR MOTORWAY SERVICE AREA (M62), West Yorkshire
Map 19 SE12

Days Inn Bradford
Hartshead Moor Service Area, Clifton HD6 4JX
☎ 01274 851706 📠 01274 855169
e-mail: hartsheadmoor.hotel@welcomebreak.co.uk
web: www.welcomebreak.co.uk
Dir: *M62 between junct 25 and 26*

This modern building offers accommodation in smart, spacious and well-equipped bedrooms, suitable for families and business travellers, and all with en suite bathrooms. Continental breakfast is available and other refreshments may be taken at the nearby family restaurant. For further details see the Hotel Groups page.
ROOMS: 38 en suite s £45-£55; d £45-£55 **CONF:** Board 10

HARWICH, Essex
Map 13 TM23

★★★74% The Pier at Harwich
The Quay CO12 3HH
☎ 01255 241212 📠 01255 551922
e-mail: pier@milsomhotels.com
web: www.milsomhotels.com
Dir: *from A12, take A120 to Quay. Hotel opposite lifeboat station*

This hotel is situated on the quay, overlooking the ports of Harwich and Felixstowe. The bedrooms are tastefully decorated, thoughtfully equipped and furnished in a contemporary style; many rooms have superb sea views. Public rooms include an informal bistro, the Harbour restaurant, a smart lounge bar and a plush residents' lounge.
ROOMS: 7 en suite 7 annexe en suite (5 fmly) (1 GF) s £70-£82.50; d £95-£170 (incl. bkfst) **LB** **FACILITIES:** STV Xmas **CONF:** Thtr 50 Class 50 Board 24 Del from £140 **PARKING:** 10 **NOTES:** in restaurant Civ Wed 50

The vast majority of establishments in this guide accept credit and debit cards. We indicate those that don't take any

★★68% Cliff
Marine Pde, Dovercourt CO12 3RE
☎ 01255 503345 & 507373 📠 01255 240358
e-mail: reception@thecliffhotelharwich.fsnet.co.uk
web: www.thecliffhotelharwich.co.uk
Dir: *A120 to Parkeston rdbt, take road to Dovercourt, on seafront after Dovercourt town centre*

Conveniently situated on the seafront close to the railway station and ferry terminal. Public rooms are smartly appointed and include the Shade Bar, a comfortable lounge, a restaurant and the Marine Bar with views of Dovercourt Bay. The pleasantly

continued on p246

HARWICH, continued

decorated bedrooms have co-ordinated soft furnishings and modern facilities; many have sea views.

Cliff, Harwich

ROOMS: 26 en suite (3 fmly) ⊗ in 1 bedroom s £55-£60; d £65-£70 (incl. bkfst) **LB** **FACILITIES:** STV Jacuzzi ♫ **CONF:** Thtr 200 Class 150 Board 40 Del £66.50 **PARKING:** 50 **NOTES:** ✗ RS Xmas & New Year

★★68% Hotel Continental

28/29 Marine Pde, Dovercourt CO12 3RG

THE INDEPENDENTS

☎ 01255 551298 🖷 01255 551698

e-mail: hotconti@btconnect.com

web: www.hotelcontinental-harwich.co.uk

Dir: *off A120 at Ramsay rdbt onto B1352 to pedestrian crossing and Co-op store on right, turn right into Fronks Rd*

Privately owned hotel situated on the seafront within easy reach of the ferry terminals and town centre. Bedrooms are pleasantly decorated, well equipped and have many innovative features; some rooms also have lovely sea views. Public rooms include a popular lounge bar, a restaurant and a non-smoking lounge.

ROOMS: 14 en suite (2 fmly) ⊗ in 2 bedrooms s £40-£85; d £75-£110 (incl. bkfst) **FACILITIES:** STV Jacuzzi **CONF:** Thtr 10 Del from £65 **PARKING:** 4 **NOTES:** ✗ ⊗ in restaurant

See advert on opposite page

HASLEMERE, Surrey — Map 06 SU93

★★★★71% ®® Lythe Hill Hotel and Spa

Petworth Rd GU27 3BQ

☎ 01428 651251 🖷 01428 644131

e-mail: lythe@lythehill.co.uk

web: www.lythehill.co.uk

Dir: *left from Haslemere High St onto B2131. Lythe Hill 1.25m on right*

This privately owned hotel sits in 30 acres of attractive parkland with lakes, complete with roaming geese. The hotel has been described as a hamlet of character buildings, each furnished in a style that complements the age of the property; the oldest one

continued

dating back to 1475. Cuisine in the adjacent 'Auberge de France' offers interesting, quality dishes, whilst breakfast is served in the hotel dining room. The bedrooms are split between a number of 15th-century buildings and vary in size. The stylish, Spa includes a 16-metre swimming pool.

ROOMS: 41 en suite (8 fmly) (18 GF) s £160-£350; d £160-£350 **LB** **FACILITIES: Spa** STV Fishing Sauna Solarium Gym Jacuzzi Boules Games Room, Giant Draughts Xmas **CONF:** Thtr 60 Class 40 Board 30 Del from £155 **PARKING:** 200 **NOTES:** ⊗ in restaurant Civ Wed 128

★★★66% Georgian House Hotel

High St GU27 2JY

☎ 01428 656644 🖷 01428 645600

e-mail: mail@georgianhousehotel.com

web: www.georgianhousehotel.com

Dir: *A3 onto A287, then A286. Past station, hotel on left on High St*

An attractive and imposing Georgian building, situated on the high street. Bedrooms in the old wing offer the most character with oak beams and four-poster beds, but all rooms are spacious and well furnished. Public areas include a bar and brasserie, while the leisure centre boasts an indoor pool and jacuzzi.

ROOMS: 51 en suite (7 GF) ⊗ in 15 bedrooms s £79-£85; d £79-£85 **LB** **FACILITIES:** STV supervised Sauna Solarium Gym Jacuzzi Beauty treatments **CONF:** Thtr 150 Class 50 Board 30 Del from £99 **SERVICES:** Lift **PARKING:** 50 **NOTES:** ✗ Civ Wed 100

HASTINGS & ST LEONARDS, East Sussex — Map 07 TQ80

★★★70% Beauport Park

Battle Rd TN38 8EA

☎ 01424 851222 🖷 01424 852465

e-mail: reservations@beauportprkhotel.co.uk

web: www.beauportparkhotel.co.uk

Dir: *3m N off A2100*

Elegant Georgian manor house set in 40 acres of mature gardens on the outskirts of Hastings. The individually decorated bedrooms are tastefully furnished and thoughtfully equipped with modern facilities. Public rooms convey much of the original character and feature a large conservatory, a lounge bar, a restaurant and a further lounge, as well as conference and banqueting rooms.

ROOMS: 25 en suite (2 fmly) ⊗ in 11 bedrooms s £95; d £140 (incl. bkfst) **LB** **FACILITIES:** STV supervised 18 Riding Sauna Gym Putt green Jacuzzi Country walks around estate ♫ ch fac Xmas **CONF:** Thtr 70 Class 25 Board 30 Del from £120 **PARKING:** 60 **NOTES:** ⊗ in restaurant Civ Wed 70

See advert on opposite page

If you wish to use a particular credit card or debit card please check with the hotel that they are happy to accept it

★★★68% High Beech
Battle Rd TN37 7BS
☎ 01424 851383 📠 01424 854265
e-mail: highbeech@barbox.net
Dir: *400yds from A2100 between Hastings and Battle*

A privately owned hotel situated between the historic towns of Hastings and Battle in a woodland setting. The generously proportioned bedrooms are pleasantly decorated and thoughtfully equipped. Public rooms include St. Patricks Bar, which also doubles as the lounge area, and the elegant Wedgwood Restaurant where an interesting and varied menu is served.
ROOMS: 17 en suite (4 fmly) ⊘ in all bedrooms **FACILITIES:** STV **CONF:** BC Thtr 250 Class 60 Board 50 **PARKING:** 60 **NOTES:** ✗ ⊘ in restaurant

See advert on this page

GF indicates the number of bedrooms at ground level

HASTINGS & ST LEONARDS, continued

★★★67% *Cinque Ports Hotel*

Bohemia Rd TN34 1ET
☎ 01424 439222 🖷 01424 437277
e-mail: enquiries@cinqueportshotel.co.uk
web: www.cinqueportshotel.co.uk
Dir: *A21 into Hastings. Police HQ and courts on left, hotel next left before ambulance HQ*

This modern hotel enjoys a central location and is close to the coast. Features of the public areas include old flagstone floors, oriental rugs, hanging tapestries, beams and open fireplaces. Bedrooms are well equipped and offer a good degree of comfort throughout.
ROOMS: 40 en suite (8 fmly) ⊘ in 6 bedrooms **FACILITIES:** STV free m/ship at next door leisure centre **CONF:** Thtr 250 Class 150 Board 120 **PARKING:** 80 **NOTES:** ⊘ in restaurant

★★★66% Royal Victoria

Marina, St Leonards-on-Sea TN38 0BD
☎ 01424 445544 🖷 01424 721995
e-mail: reception@royalvichotel.co.uk
web: www.royalvichotel.co.uk
Dir: *on A259 seafront road 1m W of Hastings pier*

This imposing 18th-century property is situated in a prominent position overlooking the sea. A superb marble staircase leads up from the lobby to the main public areas on the first floor, which has panoramic views of the sea. The spacious bedrooms are pleasantly decorated and well equipped, and include duplex and family suites.
ROOMS: 50 en suite (15 fmly) s £70-£110; d £80-£150 (incl. bkfst) **LB** **FACILITIES:** Xmas **CONF:** Thtr 100 Class 40 Board 40 Del from £90 **SERVICES:** Lift **PARKING:** 6 **NOTES:** ⊘ in restaurant Civ Wed 50

> Popped the question? Hotels with Civ wed in their entry are licensed for civil wedding ceremonies. Maximum numbers for the ceremony only are shown e.g. Civ wed 120

★★71% ❀ Chatsworth

Carlisle Pde TN34 1JG
☎ 01424 720188 🖷 01424 445865
e-mail: mail@chatsworthhotel.com
Dir: *A21 to town centre. At seafront turn right before next set of lights.*

Enjoying a central position on the seafront, close to the pier, this much-improved hotel is a short walk from the old town and within easy reach of the county's many attractions. Bedrooms are smartly decorated, equipped with a range of extras and many rooms enjoy splendid sea views. Guests can also enjoy an exciting Indian meal in the newly decorated, contemporary restaurant.
ROOMS: 52 en suite (5 fmly) ⊘ in 37 bedrooms s £45-£65; d £65-£90 **LB** **FACILITIES:** STV Xmas **CONF:** Thtr 40 Class 20 Board 20 **SERVICES:** Lift **PARKING:** 8 **NOTES:** ⊘ in restaurant

See advert on opposite page

⌂ Premier Travel Inn Hastings

1 John Macadam Way, St Leonards on Sea TN37 7DB
☎ 08701 977128 🖷 01424 756911
web: www.premiertravelinn.com
Dir: *into Hastings on A21 London rd, Inn on right after junct with A2100 Battle road*
High quality, modern budget accommodation ideal for both families and business travellers. Spacious, en suite bedrooms feature bath and shower, satellite TV and many have telephones and modem points. The adjacent family restaurant features a wide and varied menu. For further details consult the Hotel Groups page.
ROOMS: 44 en suite s £49.95; d £49.95

HATFIELD, Hertfordshire — Map 06 TL20

★★★★68% Beales

Comet Way AL10 9NG
☎ 01707 288500 🖷 01707 256282
e-mail: hatfield@bealeshotels.co.uk
web: www.bealeshotels.co.uk
Dir: *On A1001 opposite Galleria Shopping Mall - follow signs for Galleria*

The Beales Hotel has undergone a multi-million pound re-build to

continued

create a stunning modern, contemporary property. Within easy access of the M25, its striking exterior incorporates giant glass panels and cedar wood slats. Bedrooms continue the contemporary feel with luxurious beds, flat screen televisions and smart bathrooms. Public areas include a small bar and attractive restaurant, which opens throughout the day. A selection of meeting rooms and ample parking are available.
ROOMS: 53 en suite (21 GF) ⊗ in 32 bedrooms s £90-£150; d £80-£150 **LB** **FACILITIES:** STV Use of nearby leisure club ♫ Xmas **CONF:** Thtr 300 Class 80 Board 60 Del £165 **SERVICES:** Lift **PARKING:** 126 **NOTES:** ✗ ⊗ in restaurant Civ Wed 90

★★★71% Bush Hall
Mill Green AL9 5NT
☎ 01707 271251 🖷 01707 272289
e-mail: enquiries@bush-hall.com
Dir: *From A1(M) junct 4 take 2nd left at rdbt onto A414 signed Hertford & Welwyn Garden City. Left at rdbt, take A1000. Hotel on left*

Standing in delightful grounds with a river running through it, this hotel boasts extensive facilities. Outdoor enthusiasts can enjoy a range of activities including go-karting and clay pigeon shooting. Bedrooms and public areas are comfortable and tastefully decorated. Kipling's restaurant continues to offer a wide range freshly prepared dishes using quality produce; service is both professional and friendly.
ROOMS: 25 en suite (2 fmly) (8 GF) s £79.50-£125; d £99.50-£185 **FACILITIES:** Clay pigeon shooting, archery, quad bikes and karting - pre booked only **CONF:** Thtr 150 Class 70 Board 50 Del £155 **PARKING:** 100 **NOTES:** ✗ Closed 26 Dec-3 Jan Civ Wed 160

★★★65% Quality Hotel Hatfield
Roehyde Way AL10 9AF
☎ 01707 275701 🖷 01707 266033
e-mail: enquiries@hotels-hatfield.com
web: www.choicehotelseurope.com
Dir: *M25 junct 23 take A1(M) northbound to junct 2. At rdbt take exit left, hotel 0.5m on right*
The well-equipped rooms at this hotel feature extras such as trouser presses and modem access. Executive rooms are very spacious. Room service is 24 hour, or guests may dine in the bar or main restaurant, where service is informal and friendly.
ROOMS: 76 en suite (14 fmly) (39 GF) ⊗ in 39 bedrooms s £110-£130; d £120-£140 **LB** **FACILITIES:** STV Xmas **CONF:** Thtr 120 Class 60 Board 50 **PARKING:** 120 **NOTES:** ⊗ in restaurant

Premier Travel Inn Hatfield
Comet Way, Lemsford Rd AL10 0DZ
☎ 08701 977129 🖷 01707 256054
web: www.premiertravelinn.com
Dir: *From A1(M) junct 4, follow A1001 towards Hatfield. At next rdbt take 2nd exit & 1st road on right*
High quality, modern budget accommodation ideal for both

continued

families and business travellers. Spacious, en suite bedrooms feature bath and shower, satellite TV and many have telephones and modem points. The adjacent family restaurant features a wide and varied menu. For further details consult the Hotel Groups page.
ROOMS: 40 en suite s £52.95; d £52.95

U Ramada Hatfield
301 St Albans Rd West AL10 9RH
☎ 01707 265411 🖷 01707 265019
e-mail: sales.hatfield@ramadajarvis.co.uk
web: www.ramadajarvis.co.uk
Dir: *From A1 (M) junct 3, take 2nd exit at rdbt signed Hatfield onto Comet Way. Hotel 0.5m on left.*
This large hotel is a themed art deco Grade II listed building and retains many of its original 1930's features. Bedrooms are comfortably appointed for both business and leisure guests.
ROOMS: 120 en suite (2 fmly) (65 GF) ⊗ in 100 bedrooms s £105-£125; d £105-£125 **FACILITIES:** STV Xmas **CONF:** Thtr 120 Class 40 Board 45 Del from £160 **PARKING:** 150 **NOTES:** ⊗ in restaurant Civ Wed 85

HATHERSAGE, Derbyshire — Map 16 SK28

★★★73% The George at Hathersage
Main Rd S32 1BB
☎ 01433 650436 & 0845 456 0581
🖷 01433 650099
e-mail: info@george-hotel.net
web: www.george-hotel.net
Dir: *in village centre on A6187 SW of Sheffield*
The George is a relaxing 500-year-old hostelry in the heart of this picturesque town. The beamed bar lounge has great character and

continued on p250

HATHERSAGE, continued

traditional comfort, and the restaurant is light, modern and with spacious original artworks. Upstairs the decor is simpler with lots of light hues; the split-level and four-poster rooms are especially appealing. Quality cooking is a key feature of the hotel.
ROOMS: 21 en suite (2 fmly) (2 GF) ⊗ in 4 bedrooms s £80-£144; d £112-£165 (incl. bkfst) **LB** **FACILITIES:** Xmas **CONF:** Thtr 80 Class 20 Board 36 Del £139 **PARKING:** 40 **NOTES:** ✗ ⊗ in restaurant Civ Wed 50

HAVANT, Hampshire — Map 05 SU70

Premier Travel Inn Havant, Portsmouth

65 Bedhampton Hill, Bedhampton PO9 3JN
☎ 08701 977130 📠 023 9245 3471
web: www.premiertravelinn.com
Dir: *on rdbt just off A3(M) to Bedhampton*
High quality, modern budget accommodation ideal for both families and business travellers. Spacious, en suite bedrooms feature bath and shower, satellite TV and many have telephones and modem points. The adjacent family restaurant features a wide and varied menu. For further details consult the Hotel Groups page.
ROOMS: 36 en suite s £51.95; d £51.95

HAWES, North Yorkshire — Map 18 SD88

★★73% *Simonstone Hall*

Simonstone DL8 3LY
☎ 01969 667255 📠 01969 667741
e-mail: hotel@simonstonehall.demon.co.uk
web: www.simonstonehall.co.uk
Dir: *1.5m N on road signed to Muker and Buttertubs*
This former hunting lodge provides professional, friendly service and a relaxed atmosphere. There is an inviting drawing room, stylish fine, dining restaurant – a bar and a conservatory. The generally spacious bedrooms are elegantly finished to reflect the style of the house, and many offer spectacular views of the countryside.
ROOMS: 18 en suite (10 fmly) (2 GF) ⊗ in all bedrooms **FACILITIES:** ch fac **CONF:** Thtr 50 Class 20 Board 20 **PARKING:** 40 **NOTES:** ⊗ in restaurant Civ Wed

HAWKSHEAD (NEAR AMBLESIDE), Cumbria — Map 18 SD39

★★70% ◎ Queen's Head

Main St LA22 0NS
☎ 015394 36271 📠 015394 36722
e-mail: enquiries@queensheadhotel.co.uk
web: www.queensheadhotel.co.uk
Dir: *M6 junct 36, then A590 to Newby Bridge. Over rdbt, 1st right for 8m into Hawkshead*

This 16th-century inn features a wood-panelled bar with low, oak-beamed ceilings and an open log fire. Substantial, carefully prepared meals are served in the bar and in the pretty dining room. The bedrooms, three of which are in an adjacent cottage, are attractively furnished and include some four-poster rooms.
ROOMS: 11 rms (9 en suite) 3 annexe en suite (2 fmly) (2 GF) ⊗ in all bedrooms s £50-£65; d £90-£110 (incl. bkfst) **LB** **FACILITIES:** Xmas **NOTES:** ✗ ⊗ in restaurant

See advert on opposite page

HAWORTH, West Yorkshire — Map 19 SE03

★★71% Old White Lion

Main St BD22 8DU
☎ 01535 642313 📠 01535 646222
e-mail: enquiries@oldwhitelionhotel.com
Dir: *from A629 onto B6142, hotel 0.5m past Haworth Station, at top of cobbled main street leading to Tourist Info Centre*

Prominently situated at the top of the old cobbled street in this popular village, this hotel is steeped in history. There is a small oak-panelled residents' lounge and a choice of cosy bars, serving a range of meals. More formal dining is available in the popular restaurant. Comfortably furnished bedrooms are well equipped and vary in size and style.
ROOMS: 15 en suite (3 fmly) s £50-£60; d £69.50-£79.50 (incl. bkfst) **LB** **FACILITIES:** STV Xmas **CONF:** Thtr 90 Class 20 Board 38 **PARKING:** 10 **NOTES:** ✗

Restaurant with Rooms

◎ Weavers Bar Restaurant with Rooms

13-17 West Ln BD22 8DU
☎ 01535 643822 📠 01535 644832
e-mail: weaversinhaworth@aol.com
web: www.weaversmallhotel.co.uk
Dir: *A629/B6142 towards Haworth, Stanbury and Colne. At top of village pass Brontë Weaving Shed on right. Left after 100yds to Parsonage car park*
Centrally located on the cobbled main street, this family-owned restaurant provides well-equipped, stylish and comfortable accommodation. Each of the three rooms is en suite and have many thoughtful extras. The kitchen serves both modern and traditional dishes with flair and creativity.
ROOMS: 3 en suite s £55; d £80-£85 (incl. bkfst) **NOTES:** ✗ ⊗ in restaurant RS Sun/Mon

HAYDOCK, Merseyside — Map 15 SJ59

Premier Travel Inn Haydock

Yew Tree Way, Golborne WA3 3JD
☎ 08701 977131 📠 01942 296100
web: www.premiertravelinn.com
Dir: *M6 junct 23, take A580 towards Manchester. Approx 2m passing over one major rdbt. Inn on left*
High quality, modern budget accommodation ideal for both

continued

families and business travellers. Spacious, en suite bedrooms feature bath and shower, satellite TV and many have telephones and modem points. The adjacent family restaurant features a wide and varied menu. For further details consult the Hotel Groups page.
ROOMS: 60 en suite s £46.95-£48.95; d £46.95-£48.95

⌂ Travelodge
Piele Rd WA11 0JZ
☎ 08700 850 950 📠 01942 272067
web: www.travelodge.co.uk
Dir: *1m W of M6 junct 23, on A580 westbound*
Travelodge offers good quality, good value, modern accommodation. Ideal for families, the spacious, en suite bedrooms include remote-control TV, tea and coffee-making facilities and comfortable beds. Meals can be taken at the nearby family restaurant. For further details consult the Hotel Groups page.
ROOMS: 62 en suite s fr £26; d fr £26

HAYLE, Cornwall & Isles of Scilly — Map 02 SW53

⌂ Premier Travel Inn Hayle
Carwin Rise TR27 4PN
☎ 08701 977133 📠 01736 759514
web: www.premiertravelinn.com
Dir: *on A30 at Loggans Moor rdbt, take 1st exit on left, Carwin Rise, Inn on right*
High quality, modern budget accommodation ideal for both families and business travellers. Spacious, en suite bedrooms feature bath and shower, satellite TV and many have telephones and modem points. The adjacent family restaurant features a wide and varied menu. For further details consult the Hotel Groups page.
ROOMS: 40 en suite s £49.95; d £49.95

HAYTOR VALE, Devon — Map 03 SX77

★★75% ❁ Rock Inn
TQ13 9XP
☎ 01364 661305 & 661465 📠 01364 661242
e-mail: inn@rock-inn.co.uk
Dir: *off A38 onto A382 to Bovey Tracey, after 0.5m turn left onto B3387 to Haytor*
Dating back to the 1750s, this former coaching inn is in a pretty hamlet on the edge of Dartmoor. Each named after a Grand National winner, the individually decorated bedrooms have some nice extra touches. Bars are full of character, with flagstone floors and old beams and offer a wide range of dishes, cooked with imagination and flair.
ROOMS: 9 en suite (2 fmly) ⊗ in 2 bedrooms s £66; d £76 (incl. bkfst) **LB FACILITIES:** STV **PARKING:** 20 **NOTES:** ✖ ⊗ in restaurant

HAYWARDS HEATH, West Sussex — Map 06 TQ32

★★★69% The Birch Hotel
Lewes Rd RH17 7SF
☎ 01444 451565 📠 01444 440109
e-mail: info@birchhotel.co.uk
Dir: *on A272 opposite Princess Royal Hospital and behind Shell Garage*
Originally the home of an eminent Harley Street surgeon, this attractive Victorian property has been extended to combine modern facilities with the charm of its original period. Public rooms include the conservatory-style Pavilion Restaurant, along with an open-plan lounge and brasserie style bar serving a range of snacks.
ROOMS: 51 en suite (3 fmly) (12 GF) ⊗ in 23 bedrooms s £65-£95; d £85-£105 (incl. bkfst) **FACILITIES:** STV **CONF:** Thtr 60 Class 30 Board 26 Del £130 **PARKING:** 60 **NOTES:** ✖ ⊗ in restaurant Civ Wed 60

HEATHROW AIRPORT (LONDON), Greater London
See LONDON SECTION plan 1 A3
See also Slough & Staines

★★★★76% ❁ Crowne Plaza London - Heathrow
Stockley Rd UB7 9NA
☎ 0870 400 9140 📠 01895 445122
e-mail: reservations.cplhr@ichotelsgroup.com
web: www.london-heathrow.crowneplaza.com
Dir: *M4 junct 4 follow signs to Uxbridge on A408, hotel 400yds on left*
This hotel is conveniently located for access to Heathrow Airport and the motorway network. Excellent facilities include versatile conference and meeting rooms, golfing and a spa and leisure complex. Guests have the choice of two bars, both serving food, and two restaurants. Air-conditioned bedrooms are furnished and decorated to a high standard and feature a comprehensive range of extra facilities.
ROOMS: 458 en suite (237 fmly) (35 GF) ⊗ in 370 bedrooms **FACILITIES:** STV 🏊 supervised ⛳ 9 Sauna Solarium Gym Jacuzzi Beauty room **CONF:** BC Thtr 200 Class 120 Board 75 **SERVICES:** Lift air con **PARKING:** 410 **NOTES:** ✖

★★★★73% London Heathrow Marriott Hotel
Bath Rd UB3 5AN
☎ 0870 4007250
web: www.marriott.co.uk
Dir: *M4 junct 4, follow Terminal 1 2 & 3 signs via M4 and Heathrow Airport. Left at rdbt signed A4/London. Hotel 0.5m left through 2 sets of traffic lights*
This smart, modern hotel, with its striking design, meets all the

continued on p252

HEATHROW AIRPORT (LONDON), continued

expectations of a successful airport hotel. The light and airy atrium offers several eating and drinking options, each with a different theme. Spacious bedrooms are appointed to a good standard with an excellent range of facilities, and there are some indoor leisure facilities.
ROOMS: 393 en suite (143 fmly) ⊗ in 305 bedrooms s £182-£198; d £182-£198 **FACILITIES:** STV supervised Sauna Solarium Gym Jacuzzi Steam Room Xmas **CONF:** BC Thtr 550 Class 220 Board 65 Del from £180 **SERVICES:** Lift air con **PARKING:** 270 **NOTES:** Civ Wed 112

★★★★72% **Sheraton Skyline**
Bath Rd UB3 5BP
☎ 020 8759 2535 020 8750 9150
e-mail: res268_skyline@sheraton.com
web: www.starwood.com
Dir: *M4 junct 4 for Heathrow, follow Terminal 1, 2 & 3 signs. Before airport entrance take slip road to left for 0.25m signed A4 Central London*
Within easy reach of all terminals this hotel offers well appointed bedrooms featuring air conditioning. Bedrooms provide excellent levels of quality and comfort. The extensive, contemporary public areas are light and spacious, and include a wide range of eating and drinking options, function rooms and a gym.
ROOMS: 350 en suite (10 fmly) ⊗ in 311 bedrooms s £128-£293.75 **LB** **FACILITIES:** STV Gym Pool table Xmas **CONF:** BC Thtr 500 Class 325 Board 100 Del from £195 **SERVICES:** Lift air con **PARKING:** 320 **NOTES:** RS Xmas & New Year Civ Wed 200

★★★★70%
Slough/Windsor Marriott Hotel
Ditton Rd, Langley SL3 8PT
☎ 0870 400 7244 0870 400 7344
e-mail: conferenceandevents.sloughwindsor@marriotthotels.co.uk
web: www.marriott.co.uk
Dir: *M4 junct 5, follow 'Langley' signs and left at lights into Ditton Rd*
Ideally located for access to Heathrow and the M4, this smart hotel offers a wide range of facilities. The well-appointed leisure centre includes a spa, gym and pool. Extensive conference facilities, a bar offering 24hr snacks and light meals and a restaurant with a wide ranging cuisine are also available. Spacious bedrooms are well equipped for both leisure and business guests.
ROOMS: 382 en suite (120 fmly) (96 GF) ⊗ in 267 bedrooms s £145-£165; d £145-£165 **FACILITIES:** STV supervised Sauna Solarium Gym **CONF:** Thtr 400 Class 220 Board 42 Del from £150 **SERVICES:** Lift air con **PARKING:** 550 **NOTES:** ⊗ in restaurant

★★★★67%
The Renaissance London Heathrow Hotel
Bath Rd TW6 2AQ
☎ 020 8897 6363 020 8897 1113
e-mail: lhrrenaissance@aol.com
web: www.renaissancehotels.com
Dir: *M4 junct 4 follow spur road towards airport, take 2nd left. At rdbt take 2nd exit signed 'Renaissance Hotel'. Hotel next to Customs House*
Located right on the perimeter of the airport, this hotel commands superb views over the runways. The smart bedrooms are fully soundproofed and equipped with air conditioning, each is well suited to meet the needs of today's business travellers. The hotel boasts extensive conference facilities, and is a very popular venue for air travellers and conference organisers.

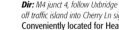

ROOMS: 649 en suite (59 GF) ⊗ in 468 bedrooms s £117; d £117 **LB** **FACILITIES:** STV Sauna Solarium Gym Steam Room Fitness Studio Massage treatment Personal trainer, studio classes Xmas **CONF:** BC Thtr 400 Class 300 Board 60 Del from £169 **SERVICES:** Lift air con **PARKING:** 700 **NOTES:** ⊗ in restaurant Civ Wed 100

★★★★66% **Park Inn Heathrow**
Bath Rd, West Drayton UB7 0DU
☎ 020 8759 6611 020 8759 3421
e-mail: info.heathrow@rezidorparkinn.com
web: www.heathrow.parkinn.co.uk
Dir: *adjacent to M4 spur at junct with A4 exit 4*
Conveniently located for the airport, this busy, corporate hotel is one of the largest in the area. There is an extensive range of facilities including two bars, modern conference rooms, indoor leisure club and extensive car parking. Bedrooms vary in size; the executive rooms are particularly impressive.
ROOMS: 880 en suite (43 fmly) (90 GF) ⊗ in 563 bedrooms s £119-£149; d £119-£149 **LB** **FACILITIES:** STV supervised Sauna Solarium Gym Jacuzzi Xmas **CONF:** BC Thtr 220 Class 140 Board 60 Del from £150 **SERVICES:** Lift air con **PARKING:** 500 **NOTES:** Civ Wed 200

★★★69% **Jury's Inn Heathrow**
Eastern Perimeter Rd, Hatton Cross TW6 2SR
☎ 020 8266 4664 020 8266 4665
e-mail: jurysinnheathrow@jurysdoyle.com
web: www.jurysdoyle.com
Dir: *200mtrs E of Hatton Cross station*
This modern hotel is located near Heathrow Airport and has good motorway access. Bedrooms provide good guest comfort and in-room facilities are ideal for both leisure and business markets. Public areas include a number of meeting rooms, a small shop, a restaurant and popular bar.
ROOMS: 364 en suite (305 fmly) ⊗ in 260 bedrooms s £59-£89; d £59-£89 **FACILITIES:** STV **CONF:** BC Thtr 45 Class 20 Board 24 Del from £135 **SERVICES:** Lift air con **PARKING:** 125 **NOTES:**

★★★69% **Novotel London Heathrow**
Cherry Ln UB7 9HB
☎ 01895 431431 01895 431221
e-mail: H1551@accor-hotels.com
web: www.novotel.com
Dir: *M4 junct 4, follow Uxbridge signs on A408. Keep left and take 2nd exit off traffic island into Cherry Ln signed West Drayton. Hotel on left*
Conveniently located for Heathrow and the motorway network, this modern hotel provides comfortable accommodation. The large, airy indoor atrium creates a real sense of space in public areas, which include a bar, meeting rooms, fitness centre and

continued

swimming pool. Hotel holds a Safer Car Park award for its security measures. Novotel - AA Hotel Group of the Year 2005-6.
ROOMS: 178 en suite (33 fmly) (10 GF) ⊗ in 140 bedrooms s £119; d £119 **LB** **FACILITIES:** STV Gym **CONF:** BC Thtr 250 Class 100 Board 90 Del £185 **SERVICES:** Lift **PARKING:** 100

★★★67% Comfort Inn Heathrow
Shepiston Ln UB3 1LP
☎ 020 8573 6162 📠 020 8848 1057
e-mail: info@comfortheathrow.com
Dir: *M4 junct 4, follow directions to Hayes & Shepiston Lane, hotel approx 1m next to fire station*
This hotel is located a little way from the airport, and guests may prefer its quieter position. There is a frequent bus service, which runs to and from the hotel throughout the day. Bedrooms are well equipped and many have the benefit of air conditioning.
ROOMS: 184 en suite (7 fmly) (50 GF) ⊗ in 80 bedrooms s £42-£125; d £42-£125 **LB** **FACILITIES:** STV Gym **CONF:** Thtr 150 Class 72 Board 90 Del from £99 **SERVICES:** Lift **PARKING:** 120 **NOTES:** ⊗ in restaurant Civ Wed 90

★★★66% Best Western Master Robert
366 Great West Rd TW5 0BD
☎ 020 8570 6261 📠 020 8569 4016
e-mail: stay@masterrobert.co.uk
web: www.masterrobert.co.uk
Dir: *M4 junct 3 take A312, follow airport signs. At 1st rdbt take 1st exit. 100yds straight onto 2nd rdbt then turn left. Hotel on left by 2nd lights*
A well-known landmark on the Great West Road, this hotel is conveniently located near to Heathrow and the area's business community. Bedrooms are set in motel-style buildings behind the main hotel; most are spacious with good facilities. There is residents' lounge bar, a restaurant and a popular pub.
ROOMS: 96 annexe en suite (22 fmly) (40 GF) ⊗ in 50 bedrooms s £55-£99; d £69.50-£114 **LB** **FACILITIES:** STV Putt green Local health club nearby **CONF:** Thtr 150 Class 60 Board 40 Del from £125 **PARKING:** 200 **NOTES:** ⊗ in restaurant Civ Wed 80

U Radisson Edwardian
Bath Rd UB3 5AW
☎ 020 8759 6311 📠 020 8759 4559
e-mail: resreh@radisson.com
web: www.radissonedwardian.com
At the time of going to press, the star classification for this hotel was not confirmed. Please refer to the AA internet site www.theAA.com for current information.
ROOMS: 459 en suite (83 GF) ⊗ in 132 bedrooms s £115-£234; d £115-£258 **LB** **FACILITIES:** **Spa** STV Sauna Solarium Gym Jacuzzi Massage, Hairdressing Xmas **CONF:** BC Thtr 700 Class 300 Board 60 Del from £160 **SERVICES:** Lift air con **PARKING:** 550 **NOTES:** Civ Wed 368

U Ramada Heathrow
Bath Rd TW5 9QE
☎ 020 8897 2121 📠 020 8897 7014
e-mail: sales.heathrow@ramadajarvis.co.uk
web: www.ramadajarvis.co.uk
Dir: *From M4 junct 4 follow signs for Heathrow Airport, take A4 sliproad prior to airport tunnel. Follow signs for Central London for 2m, hotel is on left.*
This well presented hotel is conveniently located just two miles from Heathrow. Bedrooms are comfortably appointed for both business and leisure guests.
ROOMS: 56 en suite (8 GF) ⊗ in 49 bedrooms **CONF:** Thtr 100 Class 30 Board 40 Del from £145 **SERVICES:** Lift **PARKING:** 85

Hotel Ibis Heathrow
112/114 Bath Rd UB3 5AL
☎ 020 8759 4888 📠 020 8564 7894
e-mail: H0794@accor-hotels.com
Dir: *follow Heathrow Terminals 1, 2 & 3 signs, then onto spur road, exit at sign for A4 Central London. Hotel 0.5m on left*
Modern, budget hotel offering comfortable accommodation in bright and practical bedrooms. Breakfast is self-service and dinner is available in the restaurant. For further details, consult the Hotel Groups page.
ROOMS: 347 en suite **CONF:** BC

Premier Travel Inn London Heathrow (M4/J4)
Shepiston Ln, Heathrow Airport UB3 1RW
☎ 0870 9906612 📠 0870 9906613
web: www.premiertravelinn.com
Dir: *From M4 junct 4 take 3rd exit off rdbt. Hotel on right*
High quality, modern budget accommodation ideal for both families and business travellers. Spacious, en suite bedrooms feature bath and shower, satellite TV and many have telephones and modem points. The adjacent family restaurant features a wide and varied menu. For further details consult the Hotel Groups page.
ROOMS: 133 en suite s £52.95-£74.95; d £52.95-£74.95

Premier Travel Inn Hayes, Heathrow
362 Uxbridge Rd UB4 0HF
☎ 08701 977132 📠 020 8569 1204
web: www.premiertravelinn.com
Dir: *M4 junct 3 follow A312 north, straight across next rdbt onto dual carriageway, at A4020 junct turn left, Inn is 100yds on the right*
High quality, modern budget accommodation ideal for both families and business travellers. Spacious, en suite bedrooms feature bath and shower, satellite TV and many have telephones and modem points. The adjacent family restaurant features a wide and varied menu. For further details consult the Hotel Groups page.
ROOMS: 62 en suite s £51.95-£59.95; d £51.95-£59.95

Premier Travel Inn London Heathrow
362 Uxbridge Rd UB4 0HF
☎ 08701 977 132 📠 020 8569 1204
web: www.premiertravelinn.com
High quality, modern budget accommodation ideal for both families and business travellers. Spacious, en suite bedrooms feature bath and shower, satellite TV and many have telephones and modem points. The adjacent family restaurant features a wide and varied menu. For further details consult the Hotel Groups page.
ROOMS: 590 en suite

Premier Travel Inn London Heathrow (Bath Rd)
Bath Rd TW6 2AB
☎ 0870 6075 075 📠 0870 241 9000
web: www.premiertravelinn.com
Dir: *from M4 junct 4 follow signs for Heathrow Terminals 1, 2 & 3. Turn left onto Bath Rd signed A4/London. Inn on right after 0.5 mile*
High quality, modern budget accommodation ideal for both families and business travellers. Spacious, en suite bedrooms feature bath and shower, satellite TV and many have telephones and modem points. The adjacent family restaurant features a wide and varied menu. For further details consult the Hotel Groups page.
ROOMS: 590 en suite s £52.95-£74.95; d £52.95-£74.95

⊗ No smoking

H

HELLIDON, Northamptonshire — Map 11 SP55

★★★★76% ⊛ Hellidon Lakes
NN11 6GG
☎ 01327 262550 ⎙ 01327 262559
e-mail: hellidon@marstonhotels.com
web: www.marstonhotels.com
Dir: *signed, off A361 between Daventry and Banbury*

Some 220 acres of beautiful countryside, which include 27 holes of golf and 12 lakes, combine to form a rather spectacular backdrop to this impressive hotel. Bedroom styles vary, from ultra smart, modern rooms through to those in the original wing that offer superb views. There is an extensive range of facilities available from meeting rooms to swimming pool, gymnasium and ten-pin bowling - golfers of all levels can try some of the world's most challenging courses on the indoor golf simulator.
ROOMS: 110 en suite ⊗ in 72 bedrooms s fr £129; d fr £166 (incl. bkfst) **LB FACILITIES: Spa** STV 27 Solarium Gym Putt green Beauty therapist, Indoor smartgolf, 4 lane 10 pin bowling, Steam room Xmas **CONF:** Thtr 300 Class 150 Board 80 Del from £205 **SERVICES:** Lift **PARKING:** 150 **NOTES:** ⊗ in restaurant Civ Wed 220

HELMSLEY, North Yorkshire — Map 19 SE68

★★★77% ⊛ Feversham Arms
1 High St YO62 5AG
☎ 01439 770766 ⎙ 01439 770346
e-mail: stay@fevershamarmshotel.com
web: www.fevershamarmshotel.com
Dir: *A168 'Thirsk' from A1 then A170 or A64 'York' from A1 to York North, then B1363 to Helmsley. Hotel 125mtrs from Market Place*
A friendly welcome is guaranteed at this establishment. There is a snug bar and stylish but cosy lounges in which to relax. The bedrooms are comfortable and furnished to a high standard with many useful extras including DVDs and CDs. There is a comprehensively equipped leisure centre and pleasant grounds with a pool and tennis court.
ROOMS: 19 en suite (4 GF) ⊗ in all bedrooms s £130-£200; d £140-£210 (incl. bkfst) **LB FACILITIES:** STV Xmas **CONF:** Thtr 35 Class 20 Board 24 Del from £155 **PARKING:** 50 **NOTES:** ⊗ in restaurant Civ Wed 50

See advert on opposite page

★★★75% The Black Swan
Market Place YO62 5BJ
☎ 0870 400 8112 ⎙ 01439 770174
e-mail: blackswan@macdonald-hotels.co.uk
web: www.macdonald-hotels.co.uk
Dir: *A170 towards Scarborough into Helmsley. Hotel at top of Market Place*
The exterior of this former coaching inn is a blend of Elizabethan, Georgian and Tudor and inside there are warm, welcoming interiors with candlelight, oak beams and open fireplaces. There are six guest lounges and plenty of cosy nooks for quiet conversation. The hotel also has comfortable, individually decorated bedrooms and a popular restaurant.
ROOMS: 45 en suite (4 fmly) ⊗ in all bedrooms s £80-£160; d £140-£200 (incl. bkfst & dinner) **LB FACILITIES:** ch fac Xmas **CONF:** Thtr 50 Class 18 Board 24 Del from £135 **PARKING:** 60 **NOTES:** ⊗ in restaurant

★★★71% Pheasant
Harome YO62 5JG
☎ 01439 771241 ⎙ 01439 771744
Dir: *2.5m SE, leave A170 after 0.25m. Right signed Harome for further 2m*
Guests can expect a family welcome at this hotel, which has spacious, comfortable bedrooms and enjoys a delightful setting next to the village pond. The beamed, flagstoned bar leads into the charming lounge and conservatory dining room, where very enjoyable English food is served. A separate building contains the swimming pool. The hotel offers dinner-inclusive tariffs, and has many regulars.
ROOMS: 12 en suite 2 annexe en suite (1 GF) s £73-£79; d £146-£158 (incl. bkfst & dinner) **LB FACILITIES:** STV **PARKING:** 20 **NOTES:** No children 12yrs ⊗ in restaurant Closed Xmas & Jan-Feb

★★68% Crown
Market Square YO62 5BJ
☎ 01439 770297 ⎙ 01439 771595
Dir: *on A170*
A 16th-century inn, now under new ownership, with plenty of character standing in the market square. Bedrooms are comfortable and thoughtfully equipped. Public areas are pleasantly traditional and include cosy bars and a dining room serving wholesome dishes in generous portions.
ROOMS: 12 en suite (1 fmly) (1 GF) **FACILITIES:** Xmas **PARKING:** 20

HELSTON, Cornwall & Isles of Scilly — Map 02 SW62

★★69% The Gwealdues
Falmouth Rd TR13 8JX
☎ 01326 572808 ⎙ 01326 561388
e-mail: gwealdueshotel@btinternet.com
Dir: *from Truro/Falmouth on A394. Hotel on approach into Helston*

The family-run Gwealdues is a friendly establishment located just outside Helston. Bedrooms are comfortable and well maintained, and some have balconies. A major attraction here is the Thai restaurant (although European dishes are also available) that has a great local following. For yachting enthusiasts, a 42-foot motor sailing yacht can be hired.
ROOMS: 18 en suite (2 fmly) (1 GF) ⊗ in 5 bedrooms s £45; d £65 (incl. bkfst) **LB FACILITIES:** Sailing on own yacht Xmas **CONF:** Thtr 70 Class 50 Board 50 **PARKING:** 50 **NOTES:** ⊗ in restaurant

HEMEL HEMPSTEAD, Hertfordshire Map 06 TL00

★★★67% The Bobsleigh Inn

Hempstead Rd, Bovingdon HP3 0DS
☎ 01442 833276 📠 01442 832471
e-mail: bobsleigh@macdonald-hotels.co.uk
web: www.macdonald-hotels.co.uk
Dir: *turn left after Hemel Hempstead station onto B4505 towards Chesham and follow into Bovingdon, hotel on left*

Located just outside the town, the hotel enjoys a pleasant rural setting, yet is within easy reach of local transport links and the motorway network. Bedrooms vary in size; all are modern in style. There is an open-plan lobby and bar area and an attractive dining room with views over the garden.
ROOMS: 30 en suite 15 annexe en suite (8 fmly) (29 GF) ⊗ in 39 bedrooms s £50-£95; d £90-£140 (incl. bkfst) **LB** **FACILITIES:** STV **CONF:** Thtr 150 Class 50 Board 40 Del from £110 **PARKING:** 60 **NOTES:** ⊗ in restaurant Civ Wed 100

U Ramada Hemel Hempstead

Hemel Hempstead Rd, Redbourn AL3 7AF
☎ 01582 792105 📠 01582 792001
e-mail: sales.hemel@ramadajarvis.co.uk
web: www.ramadajarvis.co.uk
Dir: *From M1 junct 9 follow signs for Hemel Hempstead and St Albans for 3m, straight across 2 rdbts onto B487 signed Hemel Hempstead, hotel is on the right.*
With easy access to both the M1 and M25 motorways, this well presented hotel is set in six acres of landscaped gardens. Bedrooms are comfortably appointed for both business and leisure guests.
ROOMS: 137 en suite (4 fmly) (67 GF) ⊗ in 105 bedrooms s £92-£119; d £92-£119 **FACILITIES:** STV Xmas **CONF:** Thtr 75 Class 30 Board 30 Del from £150 **SERVICES:** Lift **PARKING:** 150 **NOTES:** ⊗ in restaurant Civ Wed 120

Town House Hotel
Country House Hotel
Travel Accommodation

U The Watermill

London Rd, Bourne End HP1 2RJ
☎ 01442 349955 📠 01442 866130
e-mail: info@hotelwatermill.co.uk
Dir: *from M25 & M1 follow signs to Aylesbury on A41, then A4251 to Bourne End. Hotel 0.25m on right*
At the time of going to press, the star classification for this hotel

continued

was not confirmed. Please refer to the AA internet site www.theAA.com for current information.

The Watermill

ROOMS: 8 en suite 67 annexe en suite (9 fmly) (35 GF) ⊗ in 45 bedrooms s £55-£115; d £55-£115 **LB** **FACILITIES:** STV Xmas **CONF:** BC Thtr 100 Class 60 Board 50 Del from £130 **PARKING:** 100 **NOTES:** ⊗ in restaurant Civ Wed 100

Premier Travel Inn Hemel Hempstead (West)

Stoney Ln, Bourne End Services HP1 2SB
☎ 0870 238 3309 📠 01442 879149
web: www.premiertravelinn.com
Dir: *from M25 junct 20 (A41) exit at services. From M1 junct 8, follow A414, then A41, exit at services*
High quality, modern budget accommodation ideal for both

continued on p256

HEMEL HEMPSTEAD, continued

families and business travellers. Spacious, en suite bedrooms feature bath and shower, satellite TV and many have telephones and modem points. The adjacent family restaurant features a wide and varied menu. For further details consult the Hotel Groups page.
ROOMS: 61 en suite s £49.95-£52.95; d £49.95-£52.95

Travelodge
Wolsey House, Wolsey Rd HP2 4SS
☎ 08700 850 950 🖷 01442 266887
web: www.travelodge.co.uk
***Dir:** M1 junct 8 into city centre, 5th rdbt turn back towards M1, take 1st left*
Travelodge offers good quality, good value, modern accommodation. Ideal for families, the spacious, en suite bedrooms include remote-control TV, tea and coffee-making facilities and comfortable beds. Meals can be taken at the nearby family restaurant. For further details consult the Hotel Groups page.
ROOMS: 53 en suite s fr £26; d fr £26

HENLEY-IN-ARDEN, Warwickshire — Map 10 SP16

★★63% Henley
Tanworth Ln B95 5RA
☎ 01564 794551 🖷 01564 795044
e-mail: reception@henleyhotel.co.uk
***Dir:** Follow A3400 towards Henley-in-Arden*
This modern hotel is located just outside Henley-in-Arden and is well situated for access to major road networks. Bedrooms vary in style and all are thoughtfully equipped. The establishment is popular with local organisations and benefits from good car parking. It holds a licence for civil weddings.
ROOMS: 32 en suite (2 fmly) (14 GF) ⊗ in 19 bedrooms
FACILITIES: STV **CONF:** BC Thtr 80 Class 50 Board 24 **PARKING:** 40
NOTES: ⊗ in restaurant

HENLEY-ON-THAMES, Oxfordshire — Map 05 SU78

Restaurant with Rooms

◎◎ *The White Hart Hotel*
High St, Nettlebed RG9 5DD
☎ 01491 641245 🖷 01491 649018
e-mail: info@whitehartnettlebed.com
***Dir:** on A4130 3.5m from Henley-on-Thames towards Oxford*

This pleasant restaurant with rooms, now under new ownership, is a popular venue. The combination of traditional and contemporary within such a relaxed atmosphere creates unique surroundings in which to enjoy the attentive service. Bedrooms, many of which have their own access from the inner courtyard are equipped with a host of modern comforts and thoughtful extras.
continued

A wide selection of dishes can be enjoyed in either the bar or the restaurant.
ROOMS: 6 en suite 6 annexe en suite (3 fmly) (3 GF) ⊗ in all bedrooms **CONF:** BC Thtr 30 Class 30 Board 20 **PARKING:** 50
NOTES: 🐕

The Catherine Wheel Hotel
7-15 Hart St RG9 2AR
☎ 01491 848484 🖷 01491 413409
e-mail: henleylodge@jdwetherspoon.co.uk
***Dir:** M4 junct 8/9, A404, A1430. Over Henley Bridge. Hotel on right*
Conveniently situated near to the town centre and river, this popular establishment, although traditional in appearance, is very smart and modern. A comprehensive selection of meals is offered in the extensive bar whilst bedrooms are spacious, well presented and filled with useful extras.
ROOMS: 30 en suite **CONF:** Thtr 50 Class 40 Board 40

U Hotel Du Vin
New St RG9 2BP
☎ 01582 792105 🖷 01582 792001
e-mail: info@henley.hotelduvin.com
web: www.hotelduvin.com
***Dir:** M4 junct 8/9, A404(M). 2m, onto A4130 to Henley. Over bridge to 1st lights. Right into Hart Street. Right again into New Street*
At the time of going to press the star classification for this hotel was not confirmed. Please refer to the AA internet site www.theAA.com for current information.
ROOMS: 43 en suite

HEREFORD, Herefordshire — Map 10 SO54
See also Leominster & Much Birch

Top Hotel

★★★ ◎◎◎ Castle House
Castle St HR1 2NW
☎ 01432 356321 🖷 01432 365909
e-mail: info@castlehse.co.uk
web: www.castlehse.co.uk
***Dir:** city centre; near cathedral. Follow signs to City Centre East. At junct of Commercial Rd and Union St, follow Castle House hotel signs.*
Enjoying a prime city centre location and overlooking the castle moat, this delightful Victorian mansion is the epitome of elegance and sophistication. The character bedrooms are equipped with every luxury to ensure a memorable stay and are complemented perfectly by the well-proportioned and restful lounge and bar. The experience is completed by award-winning cuisine in the topiary-style restaurant.
ROOMS: 15 en suite s £113; d £200-£245 (incl. bkfst) LB
FACILITIES: STV Xmas **SERVICES:** Lift **PARKING:** 15 **NOTES:** ⊗ in restaurant

See advert on opposite page

★★★69% Belmont Lodge & Golf Course
Belmont HR2 9SA
☎ 01432 352666 📠 01432 358090
e-mail: info@belmont-hereford.co.uk
web: www.belmont-hereford.co.uk
Dir: *off A465 into Ruckhall Ln. Hotel on right in 0.5m*

This impressive complex is based around Belmont House, a Grade II listed building that dates back to 1788. It is surrounded by its own golf course and commands delightful views over the River Wye and surrounding countryside. Bedrooms, in a modern lodge, are comfortable and well equipped while the smart restaurant and bar, in the main house, offer an excellent choice of food.
ROOMS: 30 en suite (4 fmly) (15 GF) ⊗ in 15 bedrooms s £58-£65; d £64-£73 (incl. bkfst) **LB** **FACILITIES:** ⛳ 18 Fishing Putt green Games room with Pool Table Xmas **CONF:** Thtr 50 Class 25 Board 25 **PARKING:** 150 **NOTES:** ⊗ in restaurant

HEREFORD, continued

★★★67% Three Counties Hotel
Belmont Rd HR2 7BP
☎ 01432 299955 📠 01432 275114
e-mail: enquiries@threecountieshotel.co.uk
web: www.threecountieshotel.co.uk
Dir: *on A465 Abergavenny Rd*
A mile west of the city centre, this large, privately owned, modern complex has well-equipped, spacious bedrooms, many of which are located in separate single-storey buildings around the extensive car park. There is a spacious, comfortable lounge, a traditional bar and an attractive restaurant.
ROOMS: 28 en suite 32 annexe en suite (4 fmly) (14 GF) ⊗ in 23 bedrooms s £55-£71.50; d £72-£92 (incl. bkfst) **LB** **FACILITIES:** STV **CONF:** Thtr 350 Class 154 Board 80 Del from £85 **PARKING:** 250 **NOTES:** Civ Wed 250

See advert on page 257

Restaurant with Rooms

Ancient Camp Inn
Ruckhall, Eaton Bishop HR2 9QX
☎ 01981 250449
e-mail: reservations@theancientcampinn.co.uk
Dir: *From A465 follow Ruckhall sign, after bridge follow Inn sign*
Named after the nearby Iron Age fort, this engaging establishment has all the right ingredients; great location, great food and great hosts. From its elevated position, it offers stunning views of the River Wye. Excellent seasonal produce is used to great effect in simple and memorable dishes. Bedrooms offer ample comfort, with those at the front benefiting from that wonderful view!
ROOMS: 5 en suite ⊗ in all bedrooms s £60-£90; d £70-£90 (incl. bkfst) **FACILITIES:** Fishing **PARKING:** 20 **NOTES:** No dogs No children 14yrs ⊗ in restaurant Closed 3 wks Feb

Premier Travel Inn Hereford
Holmer Rd, Holmer HR4 9RS
☎ 08701 977134 📠 01432 343003
web: www.premiertravelinn.com
Dir: *from N M5 junct 7, follow A4103 to Worcester. M50 junct 4 take A49 Leominster road Inn 800yds on left*
High quality, modern budget accommodation ideal for both families and business travellers. Spacious, en suite bedrooms feature bath and shower, satellite TV and many have telephones and modem points. The adjacent family restaurant features a wide and varied menu. For further details consult the Hotel Groups page.
ROOMS: 60 en suite s £46.95-£49.95; d £46.95-£49.95 **CONF:** Thtr 20 Board 24

HESTON MOTORWAY SERVICE AREA (M4), Greater London
See LONDON SECTION plan 1 B3

Travelodge (Eastbound)
Phoenix Way TW5 9NB
☎ 08700 850 950 📠 020 8580 2028
web: www.travelodge.co.uk
Dir: *M4 junct 2 & 3 westbound*
Travelodge offers good quality, good value, modern accommodation. Ideal for families, the spacious, en suite bedrooms include remote-control TV, tea and coffee-making facilities and comfortable beds. Meals can be taken at the nearby family restaurant. For further details consult the Hotel Groups page.
ROOMS: 66 en suite s fr £26; d fr £26

♫ Entertainment

Travelodge (Westbound)
Cranford Ln TW5 9NB
☎ 08700 850 950 📠 0208 580 2006
web: www.travelodge.co.uk
Dir: *M4 junct 2 & 3 eastbound*

Travelodge offers good quality, good value, modern accommodation. Ideal for families, the spacious, en suite bedrooms include remote-control TV, tea and coffee-making facilities and comfortable beds. Meals can be taken at the nearby family restaurant. For further details consult the Hotel Groups page.
ROOMS: 145 en suite s fr £26; d fr £26

HESWALL, Merseyside — Map 15 SJ28

Premier Travel Inn Wirral (Heswall)
Chester Rd, Gayton CH60 3SD
☎ 08701 977274 📠 0151 342 8983
web: www.premiertravelinn.com
Dir: *M53 junct 4 follow A5137 signed Heswall for 3m & turn left at next rdbt, Inn on left*
High quality, modern budget accommodation ideal for both families and business travellers. Spacious, en suite bedrooms feature bath and shower, satellite TV and many have telephones and modem points. The adjacent family restaurant features a wide and varied menu. For further details consult the Hotel Groups page.
ROOMS: 37 en suite s £46.95-£48.95; d £46.95-£48.95

HETHERSETT, Norfolk — Map 13 TG10

★★★76% Park Farm
NR9 3DL
☎ 01603 810264 📠 01603 812104
e-mail: enq@parkfarm-hotel.co.uk
web: www.parkfarm-hotel.co.uk
Dir: *5m S of Norwich, off A11 on B1172*

Elegant Georgian farmhouse set in landscaped grounds surrounded by open countryside. The property has been owned and run by the Gowing family since 1958. Bedrooms are

continued

pleasantly decorated and tastefully furnished; some rooms have patio doors with a sun terrace. Public rooms include a stylish conservatory, a lounge bar, a smart restaurant and superb leisure facilities.
ROOMS: 3 en suite 39 annexe en suite (15 fmly) (22 GF) ⊗ in 15 bedrooms s £95-£125; d £122-£175 (incl. bkfst) **LB FACILITIES:** ➁ supervised Sauna Solarium Gym Jacuzzi Beauty salon, Hairdressing Xmas **CONF:** Thtr 120 Class 50 Board 50 Del from £137 **PARKING:** 150 **NOTES:** ✕ ⊗ in restaurant Civ Wed 100

See advert on this page

HETTON, North Yorkshire Map 18 SD95

Restaurant with Rooms

🏨 ⊛⊛ **The Angel Inn**
BD23 6LT
☎ 01756 730263 📠 01756 730363
e-mail: info@angelhetton.co.uk
web: www.angelhetton.co.uk
Dir: *Turn off A59 onto B6265 for Grassington. In Rylstone turn left at sign for Hetton*
Individually furnished studios and suites bring together contemporary and traditional style in a tastefully converted Dale's Barn, opposite the Angel Inn. All are stylish and very comfortable, and feature many thoughtful extras. The barn also houses a wine cave available to guests for private wine tasting. Tantalising dishes are served at the inn itself.
ROOMS: 5 annexe en suite (1 GF) ⊗ in all bedrooms s £120-£170; d £120-£170 (incl. bkfst) **LB PARKING:** 40 **NOTES:** ⊗ in restaurant Closed 1 wk Jan Civ Wed 40

HEXHAM, Northumberland Map 21 NY96

★★★★73% **Langley Castle**
Langley on Tyne NE47 5LU
☎ 01434 688888 📠 01434 684019
e-mail: manager@langleycastle.com
web: www.langleycastle.com
Dir: *from A69 S on A686 for 2m. Castle on right*

Langley is a magnificent 14th-century fortified castle, set in ten acres of parkland. There is a restaurant, a comfortable drawing room and a cosy bar. Bedrooms are furnished with period pieces and most feature window seats; and restored buildings in the grounds have been converted into very comfortable 'Castle View' rooms.
ROOMS: 8 en suite 10 annexe en suite (4 fmly) (5 GF) s £99-£175; d £115-£230 (incl. bkfst) **LB FACILITIES:** STV Xmas **CONF:** Thtr 120 Class 60 Board 40 Del from £155 **PARKING:** 70 **NOTES:** ✕ ⊗ in restaurant Civ Wed 120

⬛ AA ★★★
Park Farm
COUNTRY HOTEL & LEISURE

• 42 individual en-suite rooms • Four-poster rooms with spa baths • Fully Licensed Bar & Restaurant • Six Conference Rooms • Wedding Receptions a speciality • Attractive Landscaped Gardens

Superb Leisure Facilities including -
• Indoor Swimming Pool • Jacuzzi • Steam Room, Sauna and Solarium • Fully-equipped Gymnasium • Beauty and Hairdressing Salon

See also listing under Hethersett.

Park Farm Hotel
Hethersett, Norwich NR9 3DL
Tel: 01603 810264 Fax: 01603 812104
Email: enq@parkfarm-hotel.co.uk
www.parkfarm-hotel.co.uk

★★★★72% ⊛ **De Vere Slaley Hall**
Slaley NE47 0BX DE VERE ● HOTELS
☎ 01434 673350 📠 01434 673962
e-mail: slaley.hall@devere-hotels.com
web: www.devereonline.co.uk
Dir: *A1 from S to A68 link road follow signs for Slaley Hall*
One thousand acres of Northumbrian forest and parkland, two championship golf courses and indoor leisure facilities can all be found here. Spacious bedrooms are fully air-conditioned and equipped with a range of extras. Public rooms include a number of lounges, conference and banqueting rooms, the informal Golf Clubhouse restaurant and the impressive main restaurant.
ROOMS: 139 en suite (22 fmly) ⊗ in 101 bedrooms **FACILITIES:** Spa STV ➁ supervised ⛳ 18 Sauna Solarium Gym Jacuzzi Quad bikes, Archery, Clay pigeon shoot, 4x4 driving, Creche **CONF:** Thtr 300 Class 220 Board 150 **SERVICES:** Lift air con **PARKING:** 500 **NOTES:** ⊗ in restaurant Civ Wed 250

★★★68% **Beaumont**
Beaumont St NE46 3LT [Best Western]
☎ 01434 602331 📠 01434 606184
e-mail: reservations@beaumonthotel.eclipse.co.uk
Dir: *A69 towards Hexham town centre*
In a region steeped in history, this hotel is located in the centre of the popular county town, overlooking the park and 6th-century abbey. The hotel has two bars, a comfortable reception lounge and a first-floor restaurant; bedrooms are stylish and comfortably equipped.
ROOMS: 25 en suite (3 fmly) ⊗ in all bedrooms **FACILITIES:** STV Snooker Solarium **CONF:** Thtr 100 Class 60 Board 40 Del from £80 **SERVICES:** Lift **PARKING:** 16 **NOTES:** ✕ ⊗ in restaurant Closed 25-26 Dec

HEXHAM, continued

★★66% The County Hotel & Restaurant
Priestpopple NE46 1PS
☎ 01434 603601
e-mail: reception@thecounthexham.co.uk
Dir: *off A69 at Hexham, follow signs for General Hospital. Hotel at top of hill*
Centrally located in the popular market town. The resident owners provide caring and personal service. Bedrooms are comfortably equipped. Dining options are the County Restaurant and Bottles bistro - both offer an interesting selection of freshly prepared dishes that utilise local produce.
ROOMS: 7 en suite (1 fmly) ⊗ in 2 bedrooms s £42.50-£45; d £65-£70 (incl. bkfst) **NOTES:** ⊗ in restaurant

HICKSTEAD, West Sussex — Map 06 TQ22

★★★62% The Hickstead Hotel
Jobs Ln, Bolney RH17 5NZ
☎ 01444 248023 Fax 01444 245280
e-mail: gm.hickstead@macdonald-hotels.co.uk
Dir: *M23 South, take A2300 exit (Burgess Hill), 1st left, next right, hotel is 100yds on left*
In the heart of West Sussex, this hotel is located not far from the main London to Brighton road. The hotel's proximity to the local business park and its accessibility to a number of local attractions make it popular with both business and leisure guests who can make use of the indoor leisure centre.
ROOMS: 49 en suite (4 fmly) (24 GF) ⊗ in 34 bedrooms **FACILITIES: Spa** STV supervised Fishing Sauna Gym Jacuzzi **CONF:** BC Thtr 80 Class 60 Board 50 **PARKING:** 100 **NOTES:** ⊗ in restaurant Civ Wed 80

Travelodge
Jobs Ln RH17 5NX
☎ 08700 850 950 Fax 01444 881377
web: www.travelodge.co.uk
Dir: *A23 southbound*
Travelodge offers good quality, good value, modern accommodation. Ideal for families, the spacious, en suite bedrooms include remote-control TV, tea and coffee-making facilities and comfortable beds. Meals can be taken at the nearby family restaurant. For further details consult the Hotel Groups page.
ROOMS: 55 en suite s fr £26; d fr £26

> Packed in a hurry? Ironing facilities should be available at all star levels, either in the rooms or on request

HIGHAM, Derbyshire — Map 16 SK35

★★★67% Santo's Higham Farm Hotel
Main Rd DE55 6EH
☎ 01773 833812 Fax 01773 520525
e-mail: reception@santoshighamfarm.demon.co.uk
web: www.santoshighamfarm.co.uk
Dir: *M1 junct 28 take A38 towards Derby, then A61 towards Chesterfield. Then B6013 towards Belper, hotel 300yds on right*
With panoramic views across the rolling Amber Valley, this 15th-century crook barn and farmhouse now has an Italian Wing and an International Wing of themed bedrooms. Freshly prepared dishes, especially fish, are available in Guiseppe's restaurant, and in summer barbecues are held in the Rose Garden. An ideal romantic hideaway.

ROOMS: 28 en suite (2 fmly) (7 GF) ⊗ in all bedrooms s £79-£100; d £99-£120 (incl. bkfst) **LB** **FACILITIES:** STV Xmas **CONF:** Thtr 100 Class 40 Board 34 Del from £98 **PARKING:** 100 **NOTES:** ⊗ in restaurant Civ Wed 100

HIGHBRIDGE, Somerset — Map 04 ST34

★★67% Sundowner
74 Main Rd, West Huntspill TA9 3QU
☎ 01278 784766 Fax 01278 794133
e-mail: runnalls@msn.com
Dir: *from M5 junct 23, 3m N on A38*
Friendly service and an informal atmosphere are just two of the highlights of this small hotel. The open-plan lounge/bar is a comfortable area in which to relax after a busy day exploring the area or working in the locality. An extensive menu, featuring freshly cooked, imaginative dishes, is offered in the popular restaurant.
ROOMS: 8 en suite (1 fmly) s £40-£45; d £55-£60 (incl. bkfst) **CONF:** Thtr 40 Board 24 Del £65 **PARKING:** 18 **NOTES:** ⊗ in restaurant Closed 26-31 Dec & 1 Jan RS 25-Dec

A ★★ Laburnum House Lodge
Sloway Ln, West Huntspill TA9 3RJ
☎ 01278 781830 Fax 01278 781612
e-mail: laburnumhh@aol.com
web: www.laburnumhh.co.uk
Dir: *M5 junct 22. W on A38 approx 5m, right at Crossways Inn. 300yds & left into Sloway Ln, 300yds to hotel*
ROOMS: 60 annexe en suite (10 fmly) (60 GF) ⊗ in 30 bedrooms s £58-£84; d £64-£84 (incl. bkfst) **LB** **FACILITIES:** Fishing Sauna Solarium Clay pigeon shooting, Water-ski park, Go cart Xmas **CONF:** BC Thtr 140 Class 60 Board 40 **PARKING:** 100 **NOTES:** ⊗ in restaurant

HIGH WYCOMBE, Buckinghamshire — Map 05 SU89
See also Stokenchurch

★★★70% Ambassador Court
145 West Wycombe Rd HP12 3AB
☎ 01494 461818 Fax 01494 461919
e-mail: ach@fardellhotels.com
web: www.fardellhotels.com/ambassadorcourt
Dir: *M4 junct 4/A404 to A40 west towards Aylesbury. Hotel 0.5m on left next to petrol station*
A small privately owned hotel, now under new ownership, that is handily situated close to the M40 midway between London and Oxford. Bedrooms are pleasantly decorated and suitably well equipped for business or leisure travellers. Public rooms are

continued

contemporary in style and include a lounge with leather sofas, a cosy bar and Fusions restaurant.
ROOMS: 18 en suite (2 fmly) (1 GF) ⊗ in all bedrooms
FACILITIES: STV Xmas **CONF:** Thtr 30 Class 18 Board 16 Del from £125
PARKING: 18 **NOTES:** ✗ ⊗ in restaurant

⌂ Premier Travel Inn High Wycombe

Thanestead Farm, London Rd, Loudwater HP10 9YL
☎ 08701 977135 ▯ 01494 446855
web: www.premiertravelinn.com
Dir: *On A40 near M40 junct 3, 3m from High Wycombe. From M40 (West), exit junct 2. Follow signs to High Wycombe via Beaconsfield*
High quality, modern budget accommodation ideal for both families and business travellers. Spacious, en suite bedrooms feature bath and shower, satellite TV and many have telephones and modem points. The adjacent family restaurant features a wide and varied menu. For further details consult the Hotel Groups page.
ROOMS: 81 en suite s £52.95; d £52.95 **CONF:** Class 24 Board 24

HILLINGTON, Norfolk — Map 12 TF72

★★66% Ffolkes Arms

Lynn Rd PE31 6BJ
☎ 01485 600210 ▯ 01485 601196
e-mail: ffolkespub@aol.com
Dir: *on A149 at Knights Hill rdbt, right onto A148 towards Cromer. Hotel in 6m*
A popular 17th-century former coaching inn, situated close to the Norfolk coastline and within easy reach of King's Lynn. Facilities include a bar, restaurant and lounge area. Bedrooms are in an annexe adjacent to the main building; each one is pleasantly appointed and well equipped. The hotel also has a function suite and social club.
ROOMS: 20 annexe en suite (2 fmly) ⊗ in all bedrooms
FACILITIES: Xmas **CONF:** BC Thtr 200 Class 60 Board 50 Del £70
PARKING: 200 **NOTES:** ✗ ⊗ in restaurant

HILTON PARK MOTORWAY SERVICE AREA (M6), West Midlands — Map 10 SJ90

⌂ Travelodge Birmingham North

Hilton Park Services (M6), Essington WV11 2AT
☎ 08700 850 950 ▯ 01922 701967
web: www.travelodge.co.uk
Dir: *M6 between junct 10a & 11 southbound*
Travelodge offers good quality, good value, modern accommodation. Ideal for families, the spacious, en suite bedrooms include remote-control TV, tea and coffee-making facilities and comfortable beds. Meals can be taken at the nearby family restaurant. For further details consult the Hotel Groups page.
ROOMS: 63 en suite s fr £26; d fr £26

HIMLEY, Staffordshire — Map 10 SO89

★★★64% The Himley Country Hotel

School Rd DY3 4LG
☎ 0870 609 6112 ▯ 01902 896668
e-mail: himleycountryhotel@corushotels.com
web: www.corushotels.com
Dir: *leave A449 into School Rd at lights by Dudley Arms*
This modern hotel has been tastefully built around a 19th-century village schoolhouse. Bedrooms are well equipped and many are quite spacious. Day rooms include a stylish conservatory restaurant where wide-ranging menus and traditional buffet roasts are offered.

ROOMS: 73 en suite (1 fmly) ⊗ in 38 bedrooms s £75; d £75 **LB**
FACILITIES: STV Xmas **CONF:** Thtr 150 Class 80 Board 50 Del £105
PARKING: 100 **NOTES:** ⊗ in restaurant Civ Wed 100

★★67% *Himley House Hotel*

Stourbridge Rd DY3 4LD
☎ 01902 892468 ▯ 01902 892604
e-mail: himleyhouse@hotmail.com
web: www.himleyhousehotel.com
Dir: *on A449 N of Stourbridge*

Dating back to the 17th century, and formerly the lodge for nearby Himley Hall, this hotel offers well-equipped and comfortable accommodation. The comfortable bedrooms of varying sizes are located both in the main house and separate buildings nearby, and the busy restaurant offers a wide selection of dishes.
ROOMS: 24 en suite (2 fmly) **FACILITIES:** ch fac **CONF:** Thtr 50 Class 30 Board 22 **PARKING:** 162 **NOTES:** ✗

HINCKLEY, Leicestershire — Map 11 SP49

★★★★74% ✿✿ Sketchley Grange

Sketchley Ln, Burbage LE10 3HU
☎ 01455 251133 ▯ 01455 631384
e-mail: info@sketchleygrange.co.uk
web: www.sketchleygrange.co.uk
Dir: *SE of town, off A5/M69 junct 1, take B4109 to Hinckley. Left at 2nd rdbt. 1st right onto Sketchley Lane*
Close to motorway connections, this hotel is peacefully set in its own grounds, and enjoys open country views. Extensive leisure facilities include a stylish health and leisure spa with a crèche. Modern meeting facilities, a choice of bars, and two dining

continued on p262

HINCKLEY, continued

options, together with comfortable bedrooms furnished with many extras, make this a special hotel.
ROOMS: 52 en suite (9 fmly) (1 GF) ⊗ in 15 bedrooms s £50-£121; d £50-£142 (incl. bkfst) **LB** **FACILITIES: Spa** STV supervised Sauna Solarium Gym Jacuzzi Steam room, Hairdressing, Creche, Beauty therapy **CONF:** BC Thtr 300 Class 150 Board 30 Del from £130 **SERVICES:** Lift **PARKING:** 200 **NOTES:** ⊗ in restaurant Civ Wed 300

See advert under LEICESTER

★★★★62% Hinckley Island Hotel

Watling St (A5) LE10 3JA
☎ 01455 631122 01455 634536
e-mail: hinckleyisland@paramount-hotels.co.uk
web: www.paramount-hotels.co.uk

PARAMOUNT GROUP OF HOTELS

Dir: *on A5, S of junct 1 on M69*

A large hotel offering good facilities for conference and business guests. Bedrooms are spacious with the Club Floors providing high levels of comfort, such as leather seating at good-sized desks. The Brasserie and Conservatory restaurants are the eating options and there are also extensive leisure facilities in the Bodysense health club.
ROOMS: 350 en suite (156 fmly) ⊗ in 200 bedrooms **FACILITIES: Spa** STV supervised Snooker Sauna Solarium Gym Putt green Jacuzzi Steam room **CONF:** BC Thtr 400 Class 180 Board 38 Del £160 **SERVICES:** Lift air con **PARKING:** 600 **NOTES:** ⊗ in restaurant Civ Wed 350

★★74% Kings Hotel & Restaurant

13/19 Mount Rd LE10 1AD
☎ 01455 637193 01455 636201
e-mail: info@kings-hotel.net

Dir: *follow A447 signed to Hinckley. Under railway bridge, right at rdbt. 1st road left opposite railway station, then 3rd right*

A friendly atmosphere exists within this privately owned and managed hotel, which is situated in a quiet road within easy walking distance of the town centre and station. Bedrooms are tastefully decorated. The public rooms include a residents' lounge, a lounge-bar with striking Chinese-style wallpaper and a large restaurant.
ROOMS: 7 en suite ⊗ in all bedrooms **FACILITIES: Spa** STV **CONF:** Thtr 30 Class 40 Board 20 Del from £100 **PARKING:** 20 **NOTES:** No children 10yrs ⊗ in restaurant

Indoor Swimming pool
Indoor Swimming pool (heated)
Outdoor Swimming pool
Outdoor Swimming pool (heated)

HINTLESHAM, Suffolk — Map 13 TM04

Top Hotel

★★★★ Hintlesham Hall

George St IP8 3NS
☎ 01473 652334 01473 652463
e-mail: reservations@hintleshamhall.com
web: www.hintleshamhall.com

Dir: *4m W of Ipswich on A1071 to Hadleigh & Sudbury*

Hospitality and service are key features at this imposing Grade I listed country-house hotel, situated in 175 acres of grounds and landscaped gardens. Individually decorated bedrooms offer a high degree of comfort; each one is tastefully furnished and equipped with many thoughtful touches. The spacious public rooms include a series of comfortable lounges and an elegant restaurant, which serves fine classical cuisine.
ROOMS: 33 en suite (10 GF) s £155-£300; d £175-£390 (incl. bkfst & dinner) **LB** **FACILITIES: Spa** 18 Sauna Gym Putt green Jacuzzi Health & Beauty services Clay pigeon shooting Xmas **CONF:** BC Thtr 80 Class 50 Board 32 Del from £205 **PARKING:** 60 **NOTES:** ⊗ in restaurant Civ Wed 110

HINTON CHARTERHOUSE, Somerset — Map 04 ST75

★★★73% Homewood Park

BA2 7TB
☎ 01225 723731 01225 723820
e-mail: info@homewoodpark.co.uk
web: www.vonessenhotels.co.uk

Dir: *6m SE of Bath on A36, turn left at 2nd sign for Freshford*

Homewood Park, an unassuming yet stylish Georgian house set in delightful grounds, offers relaxed surroundings and maintains high standards of quality and comfort throughout. Bedrooms, all individually decorated, include thoughtful extras to ensure a

continued

comfortable stay. The hotel has a reputation for excellent cuisine - offering an imaginative interpretation of classical dishes.
ROOMS: 19 en suite (3 fmly) (2 GF) in all bedrooms s fr £120; d £155-£275 (incl. bkfst) **LB** **FACILITIES:** STV Fishing, hunting & horseriding on request Xmas **CONF:** Thtr 40 Class 30 Board 25 Del from £165 **PARKING:** 30 **NOTES:** in restaurant Civ Wed 50

HITCHIN, Hertfordshire Map 12 TL12

★★67% Firs
83 Bedford Rd SG5 2TY
01462 422322 01462 432051
e-mail: info@firshotel.co.uk
web: www.firshotel.co.uk
Dir: *from M1 junct 10 take A505 or A1 junct 8 onto A602 to Hitchin. Follow signs to Bedford on A600. Hotel 1m on left, next to Shell petrol station*
This family-run hotel is situated on the northern edge of town and caters for business as well as leisure guests. Well-equipped bedrooms vary in size and style, the majority have been tastefully refurbished boasting smartly appointed bathrooms. The restaurant offers a range of homemade Italian style dishes.
ROOMS: 29 en suite (3 fmly) (9 GF) in 16 bedrooms s £55-£60; d £68-£80 (incl. bkfst) **CONF:** Thtr 30 Class 24 Board 20 Del from £95 **PARKING:** 30 **NOTES:** in restaurant

HOCKLEY HEATH, West Midlands Map 10 SP17

Top Hotel

★★★ Nuthurst Grange Country House & Restaurant
Nuthurst Grange Ln B94 5NL
01564 783972 01564 783919
e-mail: info@nuthurst-grange.com
Dir: *off A3400, 0.5m south of Hockley Heath*
The approach to this period country house (now under new ownership) is a stunning avenue drive, and the hotel benefits from several acres of well-tended gardens and mature grounds and views over rolling countryside. Public areas include restful lounges, meeting rooms and a sunny restaurant. At the time of going to press the kitchen brigade had just changed but award-winning chef Stuart Nicholson remains in charge; the British and French cuisine is complemented by very attentive, professional restaurant service. The spacious bedrooms and bathrooms offer considerable luxury and comfort.
ROOMS: 15 en suite (15 fmly) (2 GF) s £129-£139; d £165-£195 (incl. bkfst) **LB** **FACILITIES:** STV Helipad **CONF:** BC Thtr 100 Class 50 Board 45 Del from £179 **PARKING:** 86 **NOTES:** in restaurant Closed 1 wk Xmas Civ Wed 70

Premier Travel Inn Solihull (Hockley Heath)
Stratford Rd, Hockley Heath B94 6NX
08701 977230 01564 783197
web: www.premiertravelinn.com
Dir: *on A3400, 2m S of M42 junct 4*
High quality, modern budget accommodation ideal for both families and business travellers. Spacious, en suite bedrooms feature bath and shower, satellite TV and many have telephones and modem points. The adjacent family restaurant features a wide and varied menu. For further details consult the Hotel Groups page.
ROOMS: 55 en suite s £49.95-£52.95; d £49.95-£52.95 **CONF:** Thtr 25

HODNET, Shropshire Map 15 SJ62

★★65% Bear
TF9 3NH
01630 685214 685788 01630 685787
e-mail: info@bearhotel.org.uk
Dir: *junct of A53 & A442 in village*
This 16th-century former coaching inn provides bedrooms equipped with all modern comforts. The public areas have a wealth of charm and character, enhanced by features such as exposed beams. There is a large baronial-style function room and medieval banquets are something of a speciality here.
ROOMS: 6 en suite 2 annexe en suite (2 fmly) s £49.50-£55; d £65-£100 (incl. bkfst) **CONF:** Thtr 60 Class 40 Board 30 Del £99.50 **PARKING:** 70 **NOTES:** Civ Wed 100

HOLCOMBE, Somerset Map 04 ST64

★★71% *The Ring O' Roses*
Stratton Rd BA3 5EB
01761 232478 01761 233737
e-mail: ringorosesholcombe@tesco.net
Dir: *A367 to Stratton on The Fosse, take hidden left turn opposite Downside Abbey, signed Holcombe. Next right, hotel 1.5m on left*
With views of Downside Abbey in the distance, this inn dates back to the 16th century. The attentive owners and pleasant staff create a friendly and relaxed atmosphere. Bedrooms are individually furnished and very comfortable. Real ales are served in the bar, which is open-plan with the attractive split-level restaurant.
ROOMS: 8 en suite in all bedrooms **CONF:** Thtr 40 Class 40 Board 14 **PARKING:** 35 **NOTES:** in restaurant

If you wish to use a particular credit card or debit card please check with the hotel that they are happy to accept it

HOLFORD, Somerset Map 04 ST14

★★76% Combe House
TA5 1RZ
01278 741382 01278 741322
e-mail: enquiries@combehouse.co.uk
web: www.combehouse.co.uk
Dir: *from A39 W left in Holford then left at T-junct. Left at fork, 0.25m to Holford Combe*
Once a tannery, this 17th-century longhouse is peacefully situated in lovely grounds, and provides an ideal retreat for walking in the Quantock Hills. Bedrooms are traditional in style and the public

continued on p264

HOLFORD, continued

rooms include a choice of sitting areas. There is a focus on home cooking in the dining room.

Combe House Hotel, Holford

ROOMS: 17 rms (16 en suite) (3 fmly) (1 GF) ⊗ in 16 bedrooms s £50-£57.50; d £100-£115 (incl. bkfst) **LB** **FACILITIES:** STV Sauna Gym Xmas **PARKING:** 33 **NOTES:** ⊗ in restaurant

HOLKHAM, Norfolk Map 13 TF84

★★74% The Victoria at Holkham

Park Rd NR23 1RG
☎ 01328 711008 01328 711009
e-mail: victoria@holkham.co.uk
web: www.victoriaatholkham.co.uk
Dir: *A149, 2m W of Wells-next-the-Sea*

A Grade II listed property built from local flintstone ideally situated on the North Norfolk coast road and forming part of the Holkham estate. Decor is very much influenced by the local landscape: the stylish bedrooms are individually decorated and tastefully furnished with pieces specially made for the hotel in India. The brasserie-style restaurant serves an interesting choice of dishes.
ROOMS: 9 en suite 1 annexe en suite (2 fmly) (1 GF) ⊗ in all bedrooms s £90-£130; d £110-£175 (incl. bkfst) **LB** **FACILITIES:** STV Fishing Shooting on Holkham Estate, Bird watching reserve nearby Xmas **CONF:** Thtr 12 Class 40 Board 30 **PARKING:** 30 **NOTES:** ⊗ in restaurant Civ Wed 70

HOLLINGBOURNE, Kent Map 07 TQ85

Ramada Hotel & Resort Maidstone

Ashford Rd ME17 1RE
☎ 01622 631163 01622 735290
e-mail: sales.maidstone@ramadajarvis.co.uk
Dir: *M20 junct 8 follow signs for Leeds Castle. At 3rd rdbt turn right*
This large well presented hotel offering extensive conference facilities is set in acres of landscaped gardens yet is within easy reach of the M20. Bedrooms are comfortably appointed for both business and leisure guests.
ROOMS: 126 en suite (4 fmly) ⊗ in 85 bedrooms s £82-£109; d £82-£109 **FACILITIES: Spa** supervised Fishing Sauna Solarium Gym Jacuzzi Pitch&Put, Archery, Clay Pigeon Shooting, Air Rifle Shooting Xmas **CONF:** Thtr 650 Class 200 Board 48 Del from £140 **SERVICES:** Lift **PARKING:** 500 **NOTES:** ⊗ in restaurant Civ Wed 120

HOLMES CHAPEL, Cheshire Map 15 SJ76

★★★67% Ye Olde Vicarage

Knutsford Rd CW4 8EF
☎ 01477 532041 01477 535728
e-mail: yeoldevicarage@harlequinhotels.co.uk
web: www.cheshire-hotels.com
Dir: *on A50, 1m from M6 junct 18*
This attractive hotel is located just to the north of the village and enjoys a rural setting. Bedrooms are very well equipped and include several styles. Public rooms are comfortable and good choice of dishes are provided in the attractive restaurant
ROOMS: 25 en suite 4 annexe en suite (3 fmly) (12 GF) ⊗ in all bedrooms s £52.50-£80; d £65-£105 (incl. bkfst) **LB** **FACILITIES:** STV Xmas **CONF:** Thtr 36 Class 10 Board 30 Del from £115 **PARKING:** 52 **NOTES:** ⊗ in restaurant Civ Wed 80

★★★63% Holly Lodge Hotel & Truffles Restaurant

70 London Rd CW4 7AS
☎ 01477 537033 01477 535823
e-mail: sales@hollylodgehotel.co.uk
web: www.hollylodgehotel.co.uk
Dir: *A50/A54 x-rds, 1m from M6 junct 18*
Situated close to the centre of Holmes Chapel, this hotel caters for both business and leisure guests. Accommodation varies in style, with particularly comfortable, bright modern bedrooms located in an adjacent cottage. A carefully prepared menu is served in Truffles Restaurant, and there are also several function rooms available.
ROOMS: 17 en suite 25 annexe en suite (3 fmly) (8 GF) ⊗ in 16 bedrooms s £55-£95; d £75-£135 (incl. bkfst) **LB** **FACILITIES:** STV Discounted rates with local gym Xmas **CONF:** Thtr 120 Class 60 Board 60 Del from £100 **PARKING:** 90 **NOTES:** ⊗ in restaurant Civ Wed 120

HOLMFIRTH, West Yorkshire Map 16 SE10

★★67% Old Bridge

HD9 7DA
☎ 01484 681212 01484 687978
e-mail: oldbridgehotel@enterprise.net
web: www.oldbridgehotel.com
Dir: *at traffic lights on A6024/A635 in centre of Holmfirth, turn into Victoria St, left after bank and shops to hotel*
Located centrally in the town that became famous for BBC's *'The Last of the Summer Wine'*, and with ample parking, this stone-built hotel offers well-equipped, stylishly refurbished bedrooms and a variety of spacious public rooms. There is a wide range of food available in both the attractive restaurant and the cosy bars.
ROOMS: 20 en suite s £55; d £65 (incl. bkfst) **CONF:** Thtr 80 Class 50 Board 40 **PARKING:** 30 **NOTES:**

Late for dinner? Quality standards mean that last orders for dinner vary according to star rating and should be no earlier than: ★★ 7.00pm ★★★ 8:00pm ★★★★ 9:00pm ★★★★★ 10:00pm

HOLSWORTHY, Devon Map 03 SS30

★★73% ♨ Court Barn Country House
Clawton EX22 6PS
☎ 01409 271219 📠 01409 271309
e-mail: courtbarnhotel@talk21.com
web: www.hotels-devon.com
Dir: 2.5m S of Holsworthy off A388 Tamerton Rd next to Clawton Church
This engaging, family-run Victorian country house is set in five acres of attractive grounds, including a 9-hole putting course and croquet lawn. Comfortable bedrooms are individually furnished, and there are two relaxing lounges. A four-course dinner featuring fresh, local produce is served in the spacious restaurant, and leisurely breakfasts are taken overlooking the garden.
ROOMS: 8 rms (7 en suite) (1 fmly) ⊗ in all bedrooms s £40-£60; d £70-£90 (incl. bkfst) **LB FACILITIES:** ९ ♨ Putt green Badminton Xmas **CONF:** BC Thtr 25 Board 8 Del from £115 **PARKING:** 13 **NOTES:** ⊗ in restaurant

HONILEY, Warwickshire Map 10 SP27

★★★66% Corus hotel Warwick
Meer End Rd CV8 1NP
☎ 0870 609 6142 📠 01926 484474
e-mail: warwick@corushotels.com
web: www.corushotels.com
Dir: M40 junct 15, A46 then A4177 to Solihull. Right at 1st main rdbt, hotel 2m on left

Incorporating an inn with 16th-century origins, this busy hotel provides brightly decorated and open-plan public areas. The spacious bedrooms are comfortably appointed and well equipped for both business and leisure guests. A good choice of meals and snacks is readily available in the contemporary Boot Inn and Bistro.
ROOMS: 62 en suite (2 fmly) (14 GF) ⊗ in 44 bedrooms s £49-£99; d £49-£99 **FACILITIES:** STV Xmas **CONF:** Thtr 200 Class 80 Board 40 Del from £110 **SERVICES:** Lift **PARKING:** 250 **NOTES:** ⊗ in restaurant Civ Wed 160

HONITON, Devon Map 04 ST10

Top Hotel

★★★ ◉◉◉ ♨ Combe House Hotel & Restaurant - Gittisham
Gittisham EX14 3AD
☎ 01404 540400 📠 01404 46004
e-mail: stay@thishotel.com web: www.thishotel.com
Dir: off A30 1m S of Honiton, follow Gittisham Heathpark signs
Standing proudly in an elevated position, this Elizabethan mansion enjoys uninterrupted views over acres of its own woodland, meadow and pasture. Bedrooms are a blend of comfort and quality with relaxation being the ultimate objective. A range of atmospheric public rooms retain all the charm and history of the old house. Dining is equally impressive - a skilled kitchen brigade maximises the best of local and home-grown produce, augmented by excellent wines. Private dining is available in the magnificently restored old kitchen.
ROOMS: 15 en suite s fr £128; d £148-£320 (incl. bkfst) **LB FACILITIES:** Fishing ♨ Jacuzzi Xmas **CONF:** BC Thtr 60 Class 40 Board 26 Del from £162 **PARKING:** 51 **NOTES:** ⊗ in restaurant Civ Wed 80

★★71% Home Farm
Wilmington EX14 9JR
☎ 01404 831278 📠 01404 831411
e-mail: homefarmhotel@breathemail.net
web: www.homefarmhotel.co.uk
Dir: 3m E of Honiton on A35 in village of Wilmington
Set in well-tended gardens, this thatched former farmhouse is now a comfortable hotel. Many of the original features have been retained with the cobbled courtyard and farm implements attractively displayed. A range of interesting dishes is offered either in the bar or in the more intimate restaurant. Bedrooms, some with private gardens, are well equipped and comfortably furnished.
ROOMS: 8 en suite 5 annexe en suite (4 fmly) (6 GF) ⊗ in all bedrooms s £45-£55; d £65-£95 (incl. bkfst) **LB FACILITIES:** Xmas **PARKING:** 20 **NOTES:** ⊗ in restaurant

★★68% *Monkton Court*
Monkton EX14 9QH
☎ 01404 42309 📠 01404 46861
e-mail: yeotelsmonkton@aol.com
Dir: 2m E of Honiton on A30 towards Ilminster, opposite Monkton Church
Set in five acres of grounds, this attractive 17th-century manor house retains much of its historical character. Friendly staff provide attentive service. A comfortable lounge and pleasant bar with crackling log fire are available. Cuisine offers a good choice of imaginative dishes.
ROOMS: 6 en suite (1 fmly) **CONF:** Thtr 50 Class 25 Board 25 **PARKING:** 40 **NOTES:** ✖ ⊗ in restaurant Closed Xmas & New Year

HOOK, Hampshire
Map 05 SU75
See also Hartley Wintney

★★74% Hook House
London Rd RG27 9EQ
☎ 01256 762630 01256 760232
e-mail: reception@hookhousehotel.co.uk
Dir: *1m E of Hook on A30*
Several acres of landscaped grounds and a relaxing environment are provided at this friendly, small hotel. Bedrooms are well equipped, and some are located in an adjacent building. Public areas include two lounges and a dining room overlooking the gardens. Popular for weddings at weekends.
ROOMS: 13 en suite 9 annexe en suite (4 GF) s £80-£90; d £100 (incl. bkfst) **CONF:** Thtr 40 Class 20 Board 20 **PARKING:** 20 **NOTES:** in restaurant Closed Xmas Civ Wed 50

HOPE, Derbyshire
Map 16 SK18

★★★70% Losehill House
Edale Rd S33 6RF
☎ 01433 621219 01433 622501
e-mail: info@losehillhouse.co.uk
web: www.losehillhouse.co.uk
Dir: *A6187 into Hope, turn opp church into Edale Rd. 0.5m, take left fork & follow signs to hotel*
Standing in a peaceful location, this hotel offers very well equipped bedrooms and a comfortable lounge with spectacular views. Staff are friendly and helpful, and quality cooking is served in the pleasant restaurant.
ROOMS: 18 en suite 4 annexe en suite (3 fmly) (4 GF) in all bedrooms s fr £65; d £85-£150 (incl. bkfst) **FACILITIES: Spa** Sauna Jacuzzi Outdoor Hot Tub Xmas **CONF:** Thtr 25 Class 25 Board 16 Del from £95 **SERVICES:** Lift **PARKING:** 25 **NOTES:** in restaurant

HOPE COVE, Devon
Map 03 SX63

★★71% Lantern Lodge
TQ7 3HE
☎ 01548 561280 01548 561736
e-mail: lanternlodge@hopecove.wanadoo.co.uk
web: www.lantern-lodge.co.uk
Dir: *right off A381 Kingsbridge to Salcombe road. 1st right after passing Hope Cove sign then 1st left along Grand View Rd*
This attractive hotel, close to the South Devon coastal path, benefits from a friendly team of loyal staff. Bedrooms are well furnished and some have balconies. An imaginative range of home cooked meals is available. There is a choice of lounges and a pretty garden with putting green. The indoor pool has large doors opening directly on to the garden.
ROOMS: 14 en suite (1 fmly) (1 GF) s £66-£90; d £110-£150 (incl. bkfst & dinner) **LB** **FACILITIES:** Sauna Putt green Multi-gym **PARKING:** 15 **NOTES:** No children 12yrs in restaurant Closed Dec-Feb

★★70% Cottage
TQ7 3HJ
☎ 01548 561555 01548 561455
e-mail: info@hopecove.com
web: www.hopecove.com
Dir: *from Kingsbridge on A381 to Salcombe. 2nd right at Marlborough, left*
Glorious sunsets can be seen over the attractive bay from this popular hotel. Friendly and attentive service from the staff and

continued

management mean many guests return here. Bedrooms, many with sea views and some with balconies, are well equipped. The restaurant offers an enjoyable dining experience.
ROOMS: 35 rms (26 en suite) (5 fmly) (7 GF) s £54-£79.50; d £88-£139 (incl. bkfst & dinner) **LB** **FACILITIES:** Table Tennis Xmas **CONF:** Thtr 50 Class 20 Board 24 **PARKING:** 50 **NOTES:** in restaurant Closed early Jan - early Feb

HORLEY – Hotels are listed under Gatwick Airport
Map 06 TQ24

HORNCASTLE, Lincolnshire
Map 17 TF26

★★71% Admiral Rodney
North St LN9 5DX
☎ 01507 523131 01507 523104
e-mail: reception@admiralrodney.com
web: www.admiralrodney.com
Dir: *off A153 - Louth to Horncastle*
Enjoying a prime location in the centre of town, this smart hotel offers a high standard of accommodation. Bedrooms are well appointed and thoughtfully equipped for both business and leisure guests. Public areas include the Rodney public bar and an open-plan restaurant and lounge bar.
ROOMS: 31 en suite (3 fmly) (7 GF) in 17 bedrooms s £52-£60; d £74-£90 (incl. bkfst) **LB** **FACILITIES:** STV Xmas **CONF:** Thtr 140 Class 60 Board 50 Del £77 **SERVICES:** Lift **PARKING:** 60 **NOTES:**

HORNING, Norfolk
Map 13 TG31
See also Wroxham

★★★68% *Petersfield House*
Lower St NR12 8PF
☎ 01692 630741 01692 630745
e-mail: reception@petersfieldhotel.co.uk
web: www.petersfieldhotel.co.uk
Dir: *A1062 from Wroxham, 2.5m right into Horning. Hotel on left*
Charming property dating back to the 1920s situated amid pretty landscaped grounds in the heart of this delightful riverside village. Bedrooms vary in size and style, each one is comfortably furnished and thoughtfully equipped; many rooms have lovely garden views. Public areas include a large lounge, a bar and a restaurant.
ROOMS: 17 en suite (1 fmly) (3 GF) **FACILITIES:** Fishing Putt green Private moorings Boating ♫ **CONF:** Thtr 100 Class 100 Board 50 **PARKING:** 70 **NOTES:** in restaurant Closed Jan Civ Wed 90

HORNS CROSS, Devon
Map 03 SS32

★★★67% Hoops
The Hoops EX39 5DL
☎ 01237 451222 01237 451247
e-mail: sales@hoopsinn.co.uk
web: www.hoopsinn.co.uk
Dir: *M5 junct 27 follow Barnstaple signs. A39, by-passing Bideford, towards Bude. Hotel in dip just outside Horns Cross*
The Hoops with its whitewashed walls, thatched roof and real fires has been welcoming guests for many centuries. Bedrooms offer plenty of character and include a number that have four-poster or half-tester beds. Guests have the private use of a quiet lounge and

continued

a pleasant seating area in the delightful rear garden. A fine selection of home-cooked meals can be taken in the bar or restaurant.

ROOMS: 4 en suite 9 annexe en suite (1 GF) ⊗ in 9 bedrooms s £60-£110; d £90-£180 (incl. bkfst) **LB** **FACILITIES:** Jacuzzi **CONF:** BC **PARKING:** 66 **NOTES:** ⊗ in restaurant Closed 25 Dec

HORRINGER, Suffolk Map 13 TL86

★★★★77% @@ The Ickworth

IP29 5QE
☎ 01284 735350 🖷 01284 736300
e-mail: ickwoth@luxuryfamilyhotels.com
Dir: *from A14 take 1st exit for Bury St Edmunds, follow brown signs for Ickworth House, 4th exit at rdbt, to staggered x-rds. T-junct, left into village, almost immediately right into Ickworth Estate*

Gifted to the National Trust in 1956 this stunning property is in part a luxurious hotel that combines the glorious design and atmosphere of the past with a reputation for making children very welcome. The staff are friendly and easy going, there is a children's den, horses and bikes to ride and wonderful 'Capability' Brown gardens to roam in – certainly a winning formula, especially for visiting families. Quality produce and technical skill are behind the inspiring food here.
ROOMS: 27 en suite 11 annexe en suite (35 fmly) (4 GF) ⊗ in all bedrooms s £180-£580; d £180-£580 (incl. bkfst & dinner) **LB** **FACILITIES: Spa** STV Riding Childrens creche, massage, manicures, aromatherapy ch fac Xmas **CONF:** Thtr 35 Class 30 Board 20 **SERVICES:** Lift **PARKING:** 40 **NOTES:** ⊗ in restaurant

HORSHAM, West Sussex Map 06 TQ13

★★★★ @@@ South Lodge

Brighton Rd RH13 6PS
☎ 01403 891711 🖷 01403 891766
e-mail: enquiries@southlodgehotel.co.uk
web: www.exclusivehotels.co.uk
(For full entry see Lower Beeding)

Premier Travel Inn Horsham

57 North St RH12 1RB
☎ 08701 977136 🖷 01403 270797
web: www.premiertravelinn.com
Dir: *opposite railway station, 5m from M23 junct 11*
High quality, modern budget accommodation ideal for both families and business travellers. Spacious, en suite bedrooms feature bath and shower, satellite TV and many have telephones and modem points. The adjacent family restaurant features a wide and varied menu. For further details consult the Hotel Groups page.
ROOMS: 40 en suite s £47.95-£50.95; d £47.95-£50.95

HORTON, Northamptonshire Map 11 SP85

★★78% @@ The New French Partridge

Newport Pagnell Rd NN7 2AP
☎ 01604 870033 🖷 01604 870032
e-mail: info@newfrenchpartridge.co.uk
Set in private grounds within the rural village of Horton, a short drive from Northampton, this unique and historic Manor House offers superb accommodation and good food. Accomplished cooking is served within the restaurant, whilst a friendly team provide an attentive service within the day rooms which include small lounge areas and a character cellar bar. Individually appointed bedrooms are attractively presented and extremely well equipped, well suited to both corporate and leisure guests.
ROOMS: 10 en suite ⊗ in all bedrooms s £140; d £140-£250 (incl. bkfst) **LB** **FACILITIES:** Xmas **CONF:** Thtr 50 Class 40 Board 25 **PARKING:** 30 **NOTES:** ⊗ in restaurant Civ Wed 70

HORWICH, Greater Manchester Map 15 SD61

★★★★72% @@ *De Vere White's*

De Havilland Way BL6 6SF
☎ 01204 667788 🖷 01204 673721
e-mail: whites@devere-hotels.com
web: www.devereonline.co.uk
Dir: *M61 junct 6. 3rd right from slip road rdbt onto A6027 Mansell Way. Follow visitors car park A for hotel*
Fully integrated within the Reebok Stadium, home of Bolton Wanderers FC, this modern hotel is a popular venue for business and conferences. Bedrooms are contemporary in style and equipped with a range of extras; many offer views of the pitch. The hotel has two eating options - a fine dining restaurant and informal brasserie. It also boasts a fully equipped indoor leisure centre and spacious bar/lounge area.
ROOMS: 125 en suite (1 fmly) ⊗ in 99 bedrooms **FACILITIES: Spa** STV Sauna Solarium Gym Jacuzzi Steam room, Beauty salon **CONF:** Thtr 1690 Class 1080 Board 72 **SERVICES:** Lift **PARKING:** 2750 **NOTES:** ⊗ in restaurant Civ Wed 1000

HOUGHTON-LE-SPRING, Tyne & Wear Map 19 NZ34

★★67% *Chilton Lodge*

Black Boy Rd, Chilton Moor, Fencehouses DH4 6LX
☎ 0191 385 2694 🖷 0191 385 6762
Dir: *A1(M) junct 62, onto A690 to Sunderland. Left at Rainton Bridge and Fencehouses sign, cross rdbt and 1st left*
This country pub and hotel has been extended from the original farm cottages. Bedrooms are modern and comfortable and some rooms are particularly spacious. This hotel is popular for weddings
continued on p268

HOUGHTON-LE-SPRING, continued

and functions; there is also a well stocked bar, and a wide range of dishes is served in the Orangery and restaurant.

Chilton Lodge, Houghton-Le-Spring

ROOMS: 25 en suite (7 fmly) ⊗ in 7 bedrooms **FACILITIES:** STV Horse riding ♫ **CONF:** Thtr 60 Class 50 Board 30 **PARKING:** 100 **NOTES:** ✗

HOUNSLOW Hotels are listed under Heathrow Airport

HOVE See Brighton & Hove

HOVINGHAM, North Yorkshire Map 19 SE67

★★★68% ◎ Worsley Arms
High St YO62 4LA
☎ 01653 628234 ▯ 01653 628130
e-mail: worsleyarms@aol.com
Dir: *from S take A64, signed York, towards Malton. At dual carriageway left to Hovingham. At Slingsby left, then 2m. Hotel on main street*
Overlooking the village green, this hotel has relaxing and attractive lounges with welcoming open fires. Bedrooms are also comfortable and several are contained in cottages across the green. The restaurant provides interesting quality cooking, with less formal dining in the Cricketers' Bar and Bistro to the rear.
ROOMS: 12 en suite 8 annexe en suite (2 fmly) (4 GF) ⊗ in all bedrooms s £60-£85; d £70-£125 (incl. bkfst) **LB** **FACILITIES:** ♀ Squash Shooting Xmas **CONF:** BC Thtr 40 Class 40 Board 20 **PARKING:** 25 **NOTES:** ⊗ in restaurant Civ Wed 75
See advert on opposite page and under YORK

HOWTOWN (NEAR POOLEY BRIDGE), Cumbria Map 18 NY41

Top Hotel

★★★ ◎◎
Sharrow Bay Country House
Sharrow Bay CA10 2LZ
☎ 017684 86301 & 86483
▯ 017684 486349
e-mail: info@sharrowbay.co.uk
web: www.vonessenhotels.co.uk
Dir: *at Pooley Bridge right fork by church to Howtown. At x-rds right and follow Lakeside Rd for 2m*
Enjoying breathtaking views and an idyllic location on the shores of Lake Ullswater, Sharrow Bay is often described as the first country-house hotel. Individually styled bedrooms, all with a host of thoughtful extras, are situated either in the main house, in delightful buildings in the grounds or at Bank House - an Elizabethan farmhouse complete with lounges and breakfast room. Opulently furnished public areas include a choice of inviting lounges and two elegant dining rooms.

ROOMS: 8 en suite 14 annexe en suite (5 GF) s fr £160; d £340-£470 (incl. bkfst & dinner) **LB** **FACILITIES:** Xmas **CONF:** Thtr 30 Class 15 Board 20 **PARKING:** 35 **NOTES:** ✗ No children 13yrs ⊗ in restaurant Civ Wed 30

HOYLAKE, Merseyside Map 15 SJ28

★★★66% *Kings Gap Court*
CH47 1HE
☎ 0151 632 2073 ▯ 0151 632 0247
e-mail: kingsgapcourt@aol.com
web: www.kingsgapcourt.co.uk
In the reign of William III 'Hoyle Lake' was an army staging post from where the invasion of Ireland was launched in 1690, and the 'Kings Gap' area commemorates this time. The lake no longer exists but the hotel that has adopted the name enjoys a peaceful residential location just a short walk from glorious sandy beaches. Modern bedrooms are stylish and comfortable whilst the bright and spacious day rooms include a popular bar and a conservatory restaurant.
ROOMS: 30 en suite (4 fmly) (7 GF) ⊗ in 15 bedrooms **CONF:** Thtr 150 Class 100 Board 32 **PARKING:** 60 **NOTES:** ⊗ in restaurant

HUCKNALL, Nottinghamshire Map 16 SK54

⌂ Premier Travel Inn Nottingham North West
Nottingham Rd NG15 7PY
☎ 0870 9906518 ▯ 0870 9906519
web: www.premiertravelinn.com
Dir: *A611/A6002 straight over 2 rdbts. Inn 500yds on right.*
High quality, modern budget accommodation ideal for both families and business travellers. Spacious, en suite bedrooms feature bath and shower, satellite TV and many have telephones and modem points. The adjacent family restaurant features a wide and varied menu. For further details consult the Hotel Groups page.
ROOMS: 35 en suite s £47.95-£50.95; d £47.95-£50.95 **CONF:** Thtr 80

HUDDERSFIELD, West Yorkshire Map 16 SE11

★★★★61% Cedar Court
Ainley Top HD3 3RH
☎ 01422 375431 ▯ 01422 314050
e-mail: huddersfield@cedarcourthotels.co.uk
web: www.cedarcourthotels.co.uk
Dir: *500yds from M62 junct 24*
Sitting adjacent to the M62, this hotel is an ideal location for business travellers or for those touring West Yorkshire. Bedrooms
continued

are spacious and comfortable and there is a busy lounge with snacks available all day, as well as a modern restaurant and a fully equipped leisure centre. There are extensive meeting and banqueting facilities.
ROOMS: 114 en suite (6 fmly) (10 GF) ⊗ in 70 bedrooms s £68-£138; d £75-£160 (incl. bkfst) **LB** **FACILITIES:** supervised Sauna Solarium Gym Jacuzzi Steam room **CONF:** BC Thtr 500 Class 150 Board 100 Del from £90 **SERVICES:** Lift **PARKING:** 250 **NOTES:** Civ Wed 400

★★★69% Bagden Hall

Wakefield Rd, Scissett HD8 9LE
☎ 01484 865330 01484 861001
e-mail: info@bagdenhallhotel.co.uk
web: www.bagdenhallhotel.co.uk
Dir: *on A636, between Scissett and Denby Dale*

This elegant mansion house with wonderful views over the valley boasts its own nine-hole golf course. Comfortable bedrooms include classical feature rooms in the main house and new contemporary rooms in a separate building. Guests can dine in the all-day Mediterranean bistro or the more formal elegant restaurant. An airy, stylish conference suite and beautiful grounds make this a popular wedding destination.
ROOMS: 16 en suite (3 fmly) (10 GF) s £65; d £95-£130 (incl. bkfst) **FACILITIES:** STV ⛳ 9 Putt green **CONF:** Thtr 180 Class 120 Board 50 Del £110 **PARKING:** 96 **NOTES:** ✈ ⊗ in restaurant Civ Wed 150

★★★67% The Old Golf House Hotel

corus hotels

New Hey Rd, Outlane HD3 3YP
☎ 0870 609 6128 01422 372694
e-mail: oldgolfhouse@corushotels.com
web: www.corushotels.com
Dir: *M62 junct 23 (eastbound only), or junct 24. Follow A640 to Rochdale. Hotel on A640*

Situated close to the M62, this traditionally styled hotel offers bedrooms which are equipped to a high, modern standard. A wide choice of dishes is served in the restaurant, and lighter meals are

continued

available in the lounge bar. The hotel, with lovely grounds, is a popular venue for weddings.
ROOMS: 52 en suite (4 fmly) (19 GF) ⊗ in 30 bedrooms s £45-£65; d £45-£65 **LB** **FACILITIES:** STV Putt green **CONF:** Thtr 70 Class 35 Board 30 Del from £85 **PARKING:** 100 **NOTES:** ⊗ in restaurant Civ Wed 90

★★★66% Pennine Manor

Best Western

Nettleton Hill Rd, Scapegoat Hill HD7 4NH
☎ 01484 642368 01484 642866
e-mail: penninemanor@bestwestern.co.uk
Dir: *M62 junct 24, signed for Rochdale (A640) - Outlane Village, left after Highlander pub, hotel signed*

Set high in The Pennines, this attractive stone-built hotel enjoys magnificent panoramic views. Bedrooms are thoughtfully equipped and many have benefited from a stylish contemporary refurbishment. There is a popular bar and restaurant offering a good

continued on p270

HUDDERSFIELD, continued

selection of snacks and meals. The modern function facilities make this a popular venue for both weddings and business meetings.
ROOMS: 30 en suite (4 fmly) (15 GF) ⊗ in 22 bedrooms s £55-£73; d £68-£83 (incl. bkfst) **LB** **FACILITIES:** STV **CONF:** BC Thtr 132 Class 56 Board 40 Del from £100 **PARKING:** 115 **NOTES:** ✗ ⊗ in restaurant Civ Wed 100

⌂ Premier Travel Inn Huddersfield West

New Hey Rd, Ainley Top HD2 2EA
☎ 0870 9906488 🖷 0870 9906489
web: www.premiertravelinn.com
Dir: *Just off M62 junct 24. From M62 take Brighouse exit from rdbt (A643). 1st left into Grimescar Rd, right into New Hey Rd*
High quality, modern budget accommodation ideal for both families and business travellers. Spacious, en suite bedrooms feature bath and shower, satellite TV and many have telephones and modem points. The adjacent family restaurant features a wide and varied menu. For further details consult the Hotel Groups page.
ROOMS: 40 en suite s £46.95-£48.95; d £46.95-£48.95

⌂ Travelodge

Leeds Rd, Mirfield WF14 0BY
☎ 08700 850 950 🖷 01924 489921
web: www.travelodge.co.uk
Dir: *M62 junct 25, follow A62 across 2 rdbts. Lodge on right*
Travelodge offers good quality, good value, modern accommodation. Ideal for families, the spacious, en suite bedrooms include remote-control TV, tea and coffee-making facilities and comfortable beds. Meals can be taken at the nearby family restaurant. For further details consult the Hotel Groups page.
ROOMS: 27 en suite s fr £26; d fr £26

HUNMANBY, North Yorkshire Map 17 TA07

★★69% Wrangham House Hotel

10 Stonegate YO14 0NS
☎ 01723 891333 🖷 01723 892973
e-mail: staciedevos@aol.com
Dir: *A64 onto A1039 to Filey. Right onto Hunmanby Rd, hotel behind All Saints Church*

This former Georgian vicarage is only a few minutes' drive from lovely sandy beaches, and stands in beautiful wooded gardens next to the village church. This well-furnished hotel has individually styled bedrooms, a comfortable sitting room and cosy bar. The spacious dining room offers a good selection of well produced dishes.
ROOMS: 8 en suite 4 annexe en suite (1 fmly) (2 GF) ⊗ in all bedrooms s £40-£60; d £75-£90 (incl. bkfst) **LB** **FACILITIES:** Xmas **CONF:** Thtr 50 Class 20 Board 20 Del from £85 **PARKING:** 20 **NOTES:** ⊗ in restaurant Civ Wed 46

HUNSTANTON, Norfolk Map 12 TF64

★★★69% Le Strange Arms

Golf Course Rd, Old Hunstanton PE36 6JJ
☎ 01485 534411 🖷 01485 534724
e-mail: reception@lestrangearms.co.uk
Dir: *off A149 1m N of Hunstanton. Left at sharp right bend by pitch & putt course*

Impressive hotel with superb views from the wide lawns down to the sandy beach and across The Wash. Bedrooms in the main house have period furnishings whereas the rooms in the wing are more contemporary in style. Public rooms include a comfortable lounge bar and an attractive restaurant, where an interesting choice of dishes is served.
ROOMS: 36 en suite (4 fmly) ⊗ in 6 bedrooms s £70-£75; d £110-£125 (incl. bkfst) **LB** **FACILITIES:** STV Snooker Xmas **CONF:** BC Thtr 180 Class 150 Board 50 **PARKING:** 80 **NOTES:** ⊗ in restaurant Civ Wed 70

★★74% Caley Hall

Old Hunstanton Rd PE36 6HH
☎ 01485 533486 🖷 01485 533348
e-mail: mail@caleyhallhotel.co.uk
Dir: *1m from Hunstanton, on A149*

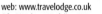

Situated just off the A149 in Old Hunstanton and within easy walking distance of the seafront. The tastefully decorated bedrooms are in a series of converted outbuildings; each is smartly furnished and thoughtfully equipped. Public rooms feature a large open-plan lounge/bar with plush leather seating, and a restaurant offering an interesting choice of dishes.
ROOMS: 40 en suite (20 fmly) (30 GF) ⊗ in all bedrooms s £39-£65; d £70-£99 (incl. bkfst) **LB** **FACILITIES:** STV **PARKING:** 80 **NOTES:** ⊗ in restaurant Closed 18 Dec-20 Jan

Early start?
Hotels at all star levels should provide in-room alarm clocks and/or alarm clocks

HUNSTRETE, Somerset Map 04 ST66

★★★79% Hunstrete House
BS39 4NS
☎ 01761 490490 01761 490732
e-mail: reception@hunstretehouse.co.uk
web: www.hunstretehouse.co.uk
Dir: *from Bath take A4 to Bristol. At Globe Inn rdbt 2nd left onto A368 to Wells. 1m after Marksbury turn right for Hunstrete village. Hotel next left*
This delightful Georgian house enjoys a stunning setting in 92 acres of deer park and woodland on the edge of the Mendip Hills. Elegant bedrooms in the main building and coach house are both spacious and comfortable. Public areas feature antiques, paintings and fine china. The restaurant enjoys a well-deserved reputation for fine food and utilises much home-grown produce.
ROOMS: 25 en suite (2 fmly) (8 GF) in 14 bedrooms s £135-£145; d £170-£180 (incl. bkfst) **LB FACILITIES:** STV Xmas **CONF:** Thtr 50 Class 40 Board 30 Del from £175 **PARKING:** 50 **NOTES:** in restaurant Civ Wed 50

HUNTINGDON, Cambridgeshire Map 12 TL27

★★★★71% Huntingdon Marriott Hotel
Kingfisher Way, Hinchingbrooke Business Park PE29 6FL
☎ 01480 446000 01480 451111
e-mail: reservations.huntingdon@whitbread.com
web: www.marriott.co.uk
Dir: *1m from Huntington centre on A14, close to Brampton racecourse*
With its excellent road links, this modern, purpose-built hotel is a popular venue for conferences and business meetings, and is convenient for Huntingdon, Cambridge and racing at Newmarket. Bedrooms are spacious and offer every modern comfort, including air conditioning. Leisure facilities are also impressive.
ROOMS: 150 en suite (45 GF) in 60 bedrooms s fr £110; d fr £110 **LB FACILITIES: Spa** STV supervised Sauna Solarium Gym Jacuzzi Xmas **CONF:** Thtr 300 Class 150 Board 100 Del from £145 **SERVICES:** Lift air con **PARKING:** 250 **NOTES:** in restaurant Civ Wed 300

★★★78% The Old Bridge
1 High St PE29 3TQ
☎ 01480 424300 01480 411017
e-mail: oldbridge@huntsbridge.co.uk
web: www.huntsbridge.com
Dir: *from A14 or A1 follow Huntingdon signs. Hotel visible from inner ring road*
An imposing 18th-century building on the ring road close to shops and amenities. This charming hotel offers superb accommodation with good modern facilities. Guests can choose from the same menu whether dining in the open-plan terrace, decorated with murals or the more formal restaurant with its bold colour scheme and panelled walls (now with a good fixed-price option). The stylish and individually decorated bedrooms include many useful extras. The hotel also has a particularly good business centre with secretarial services.
ROOMS: 24 en suite (2 fmly) (2 GF) s £95-£125; d £125-£180 (incl. bkfst) **LB FACILITIES:** STV Fishing Private mooring for boats Xmas **CONF:** BC Thtr 50 Class 20 Board 24 Del from £175 **SERVICES:** air con **PARKING:** 50 **NOTES:** in restaurant Civ Wed 100

AA Rosette Award for culinary excellence

HYDE, Cheshire Map 16 SJ99

Premier Travel Inn Manchester (Mottram)
Stockport Rd, Mottram SK14 3AU
☎ 0870 9906334 0870 9906335
web: www.premiertravelinn.com
Dir: *At end of M67 between A57 & A560*
High quality, modern budget accommodation ideal for both families and business travellers. Spacious, en suite bedrooms feature bath and shower, satellite TV and many have telephones and modem points. The adjacent family restaurant features a wide and varied menu. For further details consult the Hotel Groups page.
ROOMS: 83 en suite s £46.95-£48.95; d £46.95-£48.95

HYTHE, Kent Map 07 TR13

★★★★77% The Hythe Imperial
Princes Pde CT21 6AE
☎ 01303 267441 01303 264610
e-mail: hytheimperial@marstonhotels.com
web: www.marstonhotels.com
Dir: *M20, junct 11 onto A261. In Hythe follow Folkestone signs. Right into Twiss Rd to hotel*

Enjoying a seafront setting in a historic town, this lovely hotel is surrounded by 50 acres of golf course and beautiful gardens. Well-kept bedrooms are spacious and many enjoy views of the grounds or sea. Guests have a whole host of facilities on hand during their stay, including indoor and outdoor leisure facilities, a beauty salon and a choice of dining.
ROOMS: 100 en suite (5 fmly) in 38 bedrooms s fr £108; d fr £166 (incl. bkfst) **LB FACILITIES:** STV 9 Squash Snooker Sauna Solarium Gym Putt green Jacuzzi Beauty salon, Fitness assessments Xmas **CONF:** Thtr 220 Class 100 Board 50 Del from £185 **SERVICES:** Lift **PARKING:** 200 **NOTES:** in restaurant Civ Wed 220

★★★65% Stade Court
West Pde CT21 6DT
☎ 01303 268263 01303 261803
e-mail: stadecourt@bestwestern.co.uk
Dir: *M20 junct 11 onto A261*
This privately owned hotel is built on the site of a landing place, or 'stade', and is located on the seafront in this historic Cinque Port. Many of its well-maintained bedrooms enjoy splendid sea views and some of these have additional seating areas. Guests can also enjoy the well-tended garden in warmer months and sit and watch the world go by!
ROOMS: 42 en suite (5 fmly) in 16 bedrooms s £40-£77; d £50-£111 (incl. bkfst) **LB FACILITIES:** STV Xmas **CONF:** BC Thtr 40 Class 20 Board 30 Del from £85 **SERVICES:** Lift **PARKING:** 11 **NOTES:** in restaurant

ILFORD, Greater London
See LONDON SECTION plan 1 H5

⬆ Premier Travel Inn Ilford
Redbridge Ln East IG4 5BG
☎ 08701 977140 ▤ 020 8550 6214
web: www.premiertravelinn.com
Dir: M11 (signed London East/A12 Chelmsford) follow A12 Chelmsford
signs, Inn on left at bottom of slip road
High quality, modern budget accommodation ideal for both
families and business travellers. Spacious, en suite bedrooms
feature bath and shower, satellite TV and many have telephones
and modem points. The adjacent family restaurant features a wide
and varied menu. For further details consult the Hotel Groups page.
ROOMS: 44 en suite s £59.95; d £59.95 **CONF:** Thtr 30

⬆ Travelodge London (Ilford Central)
Clements Rd IG1 1BA
☎ 08700 850 950 ▤ 020 8553 2920
web: www.travelodge.co.uk
Dir: M25 junct 28, A12 to Hackney, at A406, left A118 for Ilford/Romford,
left before cinema complex
Travelodge offers good quality, good value, modern
accommodation. Ideal for families, the spacious, en suite
bedrooms include remote-control TV, tea and coffee-making
facilities and comfortable beds. Meals can be taken at the nearby
family restaurant. For further details consult the Hotel Groups page.
ROOMS: 91 en suite s fr £26; d fr £26

⬆ Travelodge London (Ilford North)
Beehive Ln, Gants Hill IG4 5DR
☎ 08700 850 950 ▤ 020 8551 1712
web: www.travelodge.co.uk
Dir: Off A12 on B192 adjacent Beehive Pub
Travelodge offers good quality, good value, modern
accommodation. Ideal for families, the spacious, en suite
bedrooms include remote-control TV, tea and coffee-making
facilities and comfortable beds. Meals can be taken at the nearby
family restaurant. For further details consult the Hotel Groups page.
ROOMS: 32 en suite s fr £26; d fr £26

ILFRACOMBE, Devon Map 03 SS54

★★71% Elmfield
Torrs Park EX34 8AZ
☎ 01271 863377 ▤ 01271 866828
e-mail: ann@elmfieldhotelilfracombe.co.uk
web: www.elmfieldhotelilfracombe.co.uk
Dir: A361 to Ilfracombe. Left at 1st lights, left at 2nd lights. After 10yds left,
hotel near top of hill on left
Set in attractive grounds and with good parking, this Victorian
property maintains much of its charm and enjoys views over the
town towards the sea. Bedrooms are well equipped and spacious.
The friendly proprietor and staff provide attentive service and
carefully prepared, home-cooked cuisine. Public areas include a
cosy bar, a small games room and comfortable lounge.
ROOMS: 11 en suite 2 annexe en suite (3 GF) ⊗ in 5 bedrooms
s £45-£50; d £90-£100 (incl. bkfst & dinner) **LB** **FACILITIES:** Sauna
Solarium Gym Jacuzzi Pool table Xmas **PARKING:** 14 **NOTES:** ✗ No
children 8yrs ⊗ in restaurant Closed Nov-mid Mar (ex Xmas)

See advert on opposite page

★★68% Ilfracombe Carlton
Runnacleave Rd EX34 8AR
☎ 01271 862446 & 863711 ▤ 01271 865379
e-mail: enquiries@ilfracombecarlton.co.uk
web: www.ilfracombecarlton.co.uk
Dir: A361 to Ilfracombe, left at traffic lights, left at lights. Follow signs
'Tunnels, Beaches'

Situated in the town and just a short walk from the theatre and
harbour, this well-maintained hotel has a loyal following. The
public areas include two lounges and a bar with an entertainment
area. The comfortable bedrooms are attractively decorated and
well equipped. A short set-price menu is offered in the bright and
airy dining room.
ROOMS: 48 en suite (8 fmly) (6 GF) ⊗ in 24 bedrooms s £32.50-£35;
d £65-£70 (incl. bkfst) **LB** **FACILITIES:** ♫ Xmas **SERVICES:** Lift
PARKING: 25 **NOTES:** ✗ ⊗ in restaurant RS Feb

★★64% *Imperial Hotel*
Wilder Rd EX34 9AL Leisureplex
☎ 01271 862536 ▤ 01271 862571
e-mail: imperial.ilfracombe@alfatravel.co.uk
web: www.alfatravel.co.uk
Dir: hotel opposite Landmark Theatre
This popular hotel is just a short walk from the shops and
harbour, overlooking gardens and the sea. Public areas include
the spacious sun lounge where guests can relax and enjoy the
excellent views. Comfortable bedrooms are well equipped with
several having the added bonus of sea views.
ROOMS: 104 en suite (6 fmly) **FACILITIES:** ♫ **SERVICES:** Lift
PARKING: 10 **NOTES:** ✗ ⊗ in restaurant Closed Dec-Feb RS Mar & Nov

★★59% Palm Court
Wilder Rd EX34 9AS
☎ 01271 866644 ▤ 01271 863581
e-mail: contactholiday@palmcourt-hotel.co.uk
Dir: A361 to Ilfracombe, then follow signs to seafront
The Palm Court Hotel is very popular with groups and is within
level walking distance of the harbour. Bedrooms are neatly
presented and are all of a similar standard. Entertainment is
provided in the bar/ballroom on certain evenings during the
season, and short mat bowls can be played in another large area.
ROOMS: 50 en suite (20 fmly) (3 GF) ⊗ in 25 bedrooms s fr £31;
d fr £54 (incl. bkfst) **LB** **FACILITIES:** Pool table, Short mat bowls, Skittles
♫ Xmas **SERVICES:** Lift **PARKING:** 16 **NOTES:** ✗ ⊗ in restaurant
Closed 3-26 Jan

ILKLEY, West Yorkshire Map 19 SE14

★★★76% Rombalds
11 West View, Wells Rd LS29 9JG
☎ 01943 603201 📠 01943 816586
e-mail: reception@rombalds.demon.co.uk
web: www.rombalds.co.uk
Dir: *A65 from Leeds. Left at 3rd main lights, follow Ilkley Moor signs. Right at HSBC Bank onto Wells Rd. Hotel 600yds on left*

This elegantly furnished Georgian townhouse is located in a peaceful terrace between the town and the moors. Delightful day rooms include a choice of comfortable lounges and an attractive restaurant which provides a relaxed venue in which to sample the skilfully prepared, imaginative meals. The bedrooms are tastefully furnished, well-equipped and include several spacious suites.
ROOMS: 15 en suite (4 fmly) ⊗ in 9 bedrooms s £55-£99.50; d £80-£119 (incl. bkfst) **LB FACILITIES:** STV Xmas **CONF:** Thtr 70 Class 40 Board 25 Del from £82.50 **PARKING:** 28 **NOTES:** ⊗ in restaurant Closed 28 Dec-2 Jan Civ Wed 70

★★★66% *The Crescent*
Brook St LS29 8DG
☎ 01943 600012 📠 01943 601513
e-mail: creschot@dialstart.net
Dir: *at junct of Leeds Rd (A65) & Brook St*
This newly refurbished hotel is located in the heart of Ilkley, yet is convenient for major travel networks and the stunning Yorkshire countryside. Spacious bedrooms, including a honeymoon suite with its fabulous bathroom, offer pleasing decor and facilities. The restaurant serves a variety of interesting dishes.
ROOMS: 21 en suite (3 fmly) ⊗ in all bedrooms **FACILITIES:** STV ♫ **CONF:** Thtr 100 Class 60 Board 40 **SERVICES:** Lift **PARKING:** 10 **NOTES:** ⊗ in restaurant

Town House Hotel
Country House Hotel
Travel Accommodation

★★★64% The Craiglands
Cowpasture Rd LS29 8RQ
☎ 01943 430001 📠 01943 430002
e-mail: reservations@craiglands.co.uk
web: www.craiglands.co.uk
Dir: *off A65 into Ilkley. Left at T-junct. Past rail station, fork right into Cowpasture Rd. Hotel opp school*
This grand Victorian hotel is ideally situated close to the town centre. Spacious public areas and a good range of services are ideal for business or leisure. Extensive conference facilities are available along with an elegant restaurant and traditionally styled bar and lounge. Bedrooms, varying in size and style, are comfortably furnished and well equipped.

The Craiglands, Ilkley

ROOMS: 60 en suite (6 fmly) ⊗ in 19 bedrooms
FACILITIES: Complimentary use of local fitness centre Xmas **CONF:** Thtr 500 Class 200 Board 100 **SERVICES:** Lift **PARKING:** 200 **NOTES:** 🐕✕ Civ Wed 500

Innkeeper's Lodge Ilkley
Hangingstone Rd LS29 8BT
☎ 01943 607335 📠 01943 604712
web: www.innkeeperslodge.com
Dir: *A65 at station right into Cowpasture Rd. Lodge 0.75m*
A growing concept in the travel accommodation market. Smart rooms meet essential business requirements but also have home comforts. Dining options include all-day menus plus the added advantage of breakfast, which is included in the room price. For further details consult the Hotel Groups page.
ROOMS: 16 en suite s £52-£55; d £52-£55

ILMINSTER, Somerset
Map 04 ST31

★★★68% Shrubbery
TA19 9AR
☎ 01460 52108 📠 01460 53660
e-mail: stuart@shrubberyhotel.com
Dir: *0.5m from A303 towards Ilminster town centre*
Set in attractive terraced gardens, the Shrubbery is a well established hotel in this small town. Bedrooms are well equipped and bright, they include three ground-floor rooms. Bar meals or full meals are available in the bar, lounges and restaurant. Additional facilities include a range of function rooms and a heated outdoor pool.
ROOMS: 16 en suite (3 fmly) s £89-£95; d £116-£126 (incl. bkfst) **LB** **FACILITIES:** STV Xmas **CONF:** BC Thtr 250 Class 120 Board 80 Del from £120 **PARKING:** 100 **NOTES:** in restaurant Civ Wed 200

Travelodge
Southfields Roundabout, Horton Cross TA19 9PT
☎ 08700 850 950 📠 01460 53748
web: www.travelodge.co.uk
Dir: *on A303/A358 atjunct with Ilminster bypass*
Travelodge offers good quality, good value, modern accommodation. Ideal for families, the spacious, en suite bedrooms include remote-control TV, tea and coffee-making facilities and comfortable beds. Meals can be taken at the nearby family restaurant. For further details consult the Hotel Groups page.
ROOMS: 32 en suite s fr £26; d fr £26

ILSINGTON, Devon
Map 03 SX77

★★★75% The Ilsington Country House
Ilsington Village TQ13 9RR
☎ 01364 661452 📠 01364 661307
e-mail: hotel@ilsington.co.uk
web: www.ilsington.co.uk
Dir: *M5 onto A38 to Plymouth. Exit at Bovey Tracey. 3rd exit from rdbt to 'Ilsington', then 1st right. Hotel 5m by Post Office*

Peacefully situated with far-reaching views, this friendly family owned hotel occupies an elevated position on the southern slopes of Dartmoor. Bedrooms, some on the ground floor, are individually furnished. Local fish, meat and game feature on the daily-changing innovative menus. On site leisure facilities, meeting rooms and extensive gardens are also available.
ROOMS: 25 en suite (2 fmly) (8 GF) in 5 bedrooms s £80-£86; d £120-£126 (incl. bkfst) **LB** **FACILITIES: Spa** supervised Sauna Gym Jacuzzi Xmas **CONF:** Thtr 40 Class 30 Board 20 Del from £125 **SERVICES:** Lift **PARKING:** 100 **NOTES:** in restaurant

INSTOW, Devon
Map 03 SS43

★★★74% Commodore
Marine Pde EX39 4JN
☎ 01271 860347 📠 01271 861233
e-mail: admin@the-commodore.co.uk
web: www.commodore-instow.co.uk
Dir: *M5 junct 27 follow N Devon link road to Bideford. Right before bridge, hotel 3m from bridge*

Maintaining its links with the local maritime and rural communities, The Commodore provides a comfortable and interesting place to stay. Situated at the mouth of the Tor and Torridge estuaries and overlooking the sandy beach, the hotel offers well equipped bedrooms, many with balconies and five ground floor suites especially suited to less able visitors. Guests have the option of eating in the restaurant, less formally in the Quarterdeck bar or on the terrace in the warmer months.
ROOMS: 20 en suite (5 GF) in 25 bedrooms s £68-£100; d £98-£172 (incl. bkfst & dinner) **LB** **FACILITIES:** Xmas **PARKING:** 200 **NOTES:** in restaurant

IPSWICH, Suffolk
Map 13 TM14

★★★★ Hintlesham Hall
George St IP8 3NS
☎ 01473 652334 📠 01473 652463
e-mail: reservations@hintleshamhall.com
web: www.hintleshamhall.com
(For full entry see Hintlesham)

Town House

★★★★ Salthouse Harbour
No 1 Neptune Quay IP4 1AS
☎ 01473 226789 📠 01473 226927
e-mail: staying@salthouseharbour.co.uk
Overlooking Ipswich quays this hotel offers accommodation that is a clever mix of contemporary style and original features. Spacious bedrooms provide luxurious comfort with good facilities. Two air-conditioned suites with stunning views are available. Award-winning food is served in the busy ground-floor brassiere.
ROOMS: 43 en suite (4 fmly) in 35 bedrooms s £100-£125; d £130-£135 (incl. bkfst) **LB** **FACILITIES:** STV **CONF:** Board 24 Del from £170 **SERVICES:** Lift **PARKING:** 30 **NOTES:** in restaurant Civ Wed 70

★★★71% Courtyard by Marriott Ipswich
The Havens, Ransomes Europark IP3 9SJ
☎ 01473 272244 🖹 01473 272484
e-mail: res.ipscourtyard@kewgreen.co.uk
web: www.kewgreen.co.uk
Dir: *off A14 Ipswich Bypass at 1st junct after Orwell Bridge signed Ransomes Europark. Hotel faces slip road*

Conveniently situated within easy striking distance of the town centre and major road networks, this modern and well-maintained hotel offers stylish accommodation with attractive, spacious bedrooms. The open-plan public rooms include a restaurant, a bar and a suite of conference rooms. Guests also have the use of a small fitness studio.
ROOMS: 60 en suite (14 fmly) (30 GF) ⊗ in 44 bedrooms s £54-£98; d £76-£107 (incl. bkfst) **LB** **FACILITIES:** STV Gym Xmas **CONF:** Thtr 160 Class 70 Board 55 Del from £135 **SERVICES:** Lift **PARKING:** 150
NOTES: ✗ Civ Wed 100

★★★68% *Claydon Country House*
16-18 Ipswich Rd, Claydon IP6 0AR
☎ 01473 830382 🖹 01473 832476
e-mail: kayshotels@aol.com
Dir: *from A14, NW of Ipswich. After 4m take Great Blakenham Rd, B1113 to Claydon, hotel on left*

Delightful hotel situated just off the A14 within easy driving distance of the town centre. The pleasantly decorated bedrooms are thoughtfully equipped and one room has a lovely four-poster bed. An interesting choice of freshly prepared dishes is available in the smart restaurant, and guests have the use of a relaxing lounge bar.
ROOMS: 19 en suite (2 fmly) (5 GF) ⊗ in 10 bedrooms
FACILITIES: STV **CONF:** Thtr 120 Class 60 Board 55 **PARKING:** 60
NOTES: ✗ ⊗ in restaurant Civ Wed 75

★★★67% Hotel Elizabeth
Old London Rd, Copdock IP8 3JD
☎ 01473 209988 🖹 01473 730801
e-mail: pauline.dable@elizabethhotels.co.uk
Dir: *close to A12/A14 junct, S of Ipswich. Exit A12 at Washbrook and Copdock sign. Hotel on A12, 1m on left*

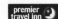

A purpose-built hotel situated on the outskirts of the town centre, and close to the major road networks. The spacious bedrooms are pleasantly decorated and equipped with all the usual facilities. The open-plan public areas include a smart restaurant, a bar and a comfortable lounge, as well as leisure facilities.
ROOMS: 76 en suite (51 fmly) (23 GF) ⊗ in 60 bedrooms s fr £82.50; d fr £82.50 **LB** **FACILITIES:** Sauna Gym Jacuzzi Xmas **CONF:** BC Thtr 400 Class 200 Board 40 **SERVICES:** Lift **PARKING:** 280
NOTES: ✗ ⊗ in restaurant Civ Wed 90

★★★65% Novotel Ipswich
Greyfriars Rd IP1 1UP
☎ 01473 232400 🖹 01473 232414
e-mail: h0995@accor-hotels.com
web: www.novotel.com
Dir: *from A14 towards Felixstowe. Left onto A137, follow for 2m into town centre. Hotel on double rdbt by Stoke Bridge*
Situated in the centre of town, this modern, red-brick hotel is close to shops, bars and restaurants. The open-plan public areas include a Mediterranean-style restaurant and a bar with a small games area. Bedrooms are well designed and simply decorated; three are suitable for less mobile guests.
Novotel - AA Hotel Group of the Year 2005-6.
ROOMS: 100 en suite (6 fmly) ⊗ in 76 bedrooms **FACILITIES:** STV Pool table, Complimentary use of gym, sauna, jacuzzi **CONF:** BC Thtr 180 Class 75 Board 45 Del from £105 **SERVICES:** Lift air con **PARKING:** 50

⌂ Premier Travel Inn Ipswich North
Paper Mill Ln, Claydon IP6 0BE
☎ 0870 238 3311 🖹 01473 833127
e-mail: ipswich.mti@whitbread.com
web: www.premiertravelinn.com
Dir: *on A14 NW of Ipswich at Great Blakenham/Claydon/RAF Wattisham junct, at rdbt take exit into Papermill Ln, Inn on left*
High quality, modern budget accommodation ideal for both families and business travellers. Spacious, en suite bedrooms feature bath and shower, satellite TV and many have telephones and modem points. The adjacent family restaurant features a wide and varied menu. For further details consult the Hotel Groups page.
ROOMS: 59 en suite s £46.95-£48.95; d £46.95-£48.95

IPSWICH, Suffolk Map 13 TM14

⌂ Premier Travel Inn Ipswich South

Bourne Hill, Wherstead IP2 8ND
☎ 08701 977143 🖷 01473 692283
web: www.premiertravelinn.com
Dir: *From A14 follow signs for Ipswich Central A137 and then Ipswich Central & Docks. At bottom of hill take 2nd exit off rdbt. Inn on right*
High quality, modern budget accommodation ideal for both families and business travellers. Spacious, en suite bedrooms feature bath and shower, satellite TV and many have telephones and modem points. The adjacent family restaurant features a wide and varied menu. For further details consult the Hotel Groups page.
ROOMS: 40 en suite s £46.95-£48.95; d £46.95-£48.95 **CONF:** Thtr 30 Board 20

⌂ Travelodge (Ipswich Capel)

Capel St Mary IP9 2JP
☎ 08700 850 950 🖷 0870 1911542
web: www.travelodge.co.uk
Dir: *5m S on A12*
Travelodge offers good quality, good value, modern accommodation. Ideal for families, the spacious, en suite bedrooms include remote-control TV, tea and coffee-making facilities and comfortable beds. Meals can be taken at the nearby family restaurant. For further details consult the Hotel Groups page.
ROOMS: 32 en suite s fr £26; d fr £26

ISLE OF Places incorporating the words 'Isle of' or 'Isle' will be found under the actual name - eg Isle of Wight is listed under Wight, Isle of.

IVYBRIDGE, Devon Map 03 SX65

★★64% *Sportsmans Inn Hotel & Restaurant*

Exeter Rd PL21 0BQ
☎ 01752 892280 🖷 01752 690714
e-mail: info@thesportsmansinn.co.uk
Dir: *off A38 at Ivybridge. Through town, hotel on main road*
This friendly and deservedly popular inn continues to enjoy a healthy trade from both locals and visitors, who are attracted to the wide choice of good-value meals and snacks that are available in its open-plan bar and restaurant. Bedrooms are well equipped and include both a ground-floor room and an impressive four-poster.
ROOMS: 14 en suite **FACILITIES:** ♫ **PARKING:** 50 **NOTES:** ⋈ RS 25 Dec

KEGWORTH See Nottingham East Midlands Airport

KEIGHLEY, West Yorkshire Map 19 SE04

★★67% Dalesgate

406 Skipton Rd, Utley BD20 6HP
☎ 01535 664930 🖷 01535 611253
e-mail: stephen.e.atha@btinternet.com
Dir: *In town centre follow A629 over rdbt. Right after 0.75m into St. John's Rd. 1st right into hotel car park*
Originally the residence of a local chapel minister, this modern, well-established hotel provides well-equipped, comfortable bedrooms. The hotel also boasts a cosy bar and pleasant restaurant, serving an imaginative range of dishes. A large car park is provided to the rear.
ROOMS: 20 en suite (2 fmly) (3 GF) s £35-£40; d £50-£60 (incl. bkfst) **LB** **PARKING:** 25 **NOTES:** ⊗ in restaurant RS 22 Dec-4 Jan

⌂ Innkeeper's Lodge Keighley

Bradford Rd BD21 4BB
☎ 01535 610611
web: www.innkeeperslodge.com
Dir: *From M606 rdbt take A6177, at next rdbt A641 & A650 towards Keighley. Lodge on 2nd rdbt*
A growing concept in the travel accommodation market. Smart rooms meet essential business requirements but also have home comforts. Dining options include all-day menus plus the added advantage of breakfast, which is included in the room price. For further details consult the Hotel Groups page.
ROOMS: 43 en suite s £45; d £45

KENDAL, Cumbria Map 18 SD59
See also Crooklands

★★★77% ⊛⊛ The Castle Green Hotel in Kendal

LA9 6BH
☎ 01539 734000 🖷 01539 735522
e-mail: reception@castlegreen.co.uk
web: www.castlegreen.co.uk
Dir: *M6 junct 36, towards Kendal. Right at 1st lights, left at rdbt to "K" Village then right for 0.75m to hotel at T- junct*
This smart, modern hotel enjoys a peaceful location and is conveniently situated for access to both the town centre and the M6. Stylish bedrooms are thoughtfully equipped for both the business and leisure guest. The Greenhouse Restaurant provides imaginative dishes; alternatively Alexander's pub serves food all day. The hotel has a fully equipped business centre.
ROOMS: 100 en suite (3 fmly) (25 GF) ⊗ in 59 bedrooms s £69-£89; d £78-£118 (incl. bkfst) **LB** **FACILITIES:** STV 🏊 Solarium Gym Steam Room, Aerobics, Yoga, Beauty Salon ♫ **CONF:** BC Thtr 350 Class 120 Board 100 Del from £125 **SERVICES:** Lift **PARKING:** 200 **NOTES:** ⋈ ⊗ in restaurant Civ Wed 250

★★★60% Riverside Hotel Kendal

Beezon Rd, Stramongate Bridge LA9 4BZ
☎ 01539 734861 🖷 01539 734863
e-mail: info@riversidekendal.co.uk
Dir: *M6 junct 36 Sedburgh, Kendal 7 miles, left at end of Ann St, 1st right onto Beelow Rd, hotel on left*

Centrally located in this market town, and enjoying a peaceful riverside location, this 17th-century former tannery provides a suitable base for both business travellers and tourists. The comfortable bedrooms are well equipped, and open-plan day rooms include the attractive restaurant and bar. Conference facilities are available, and at the last inspection the new Sanctuary leisure club was about to open.
ROOMS: 47 en suite (18 fmly) (10 GF) ⊗ in 20 bedrooms s £65-£85; d £78-£98 (incl. bkfst) **LB** **FACILITIES:** **Spa** STV 🏊 supervised Sauna Solarium Gym Jacuzzi Beauty Salon Xmas **CONF:** Board 90 Del from £95 **SERVICES:** Lift **PARKING:** 60 **NOTES:** ⊗ in restaurant Civ Wed 120

KENILWORTH, Warwickshire Map 10 SP27

★★★★64% Chesford Grange
Chesford Bridge CV8 2LD
☎ 01926 859331 📠 01926 859272
e-mail: chesfordgrangereservations@quintessential-hotels.co.uk
web: www.quintessential-hotels.co.uk
Dir: *0.5m SE of junct A46/A452. At rdbt turn right signed Leamington Spa. After 250yds at x-rds turn right and hotel on left*
This much-extended hotel set in 17 acres of private grounds is well situated for Birmingham International Airport, the NEC and major routes. Bedrooms range from traditional style to contemporary Art + Tech rooms featuring state-of-the-art technology. Public areas include a leisure club and extensive conference and banqueting facilities.
ROOMS: 209 en suite (20 fmly) (43 GF) ⊗ in 146 bedrooms s £95-£170; d £105-£190 (incl. bkfst) **FACILITIES: Spa** supervised Solarium Gym Jacuzzi Xmas **CONF:** BC Thtr 710 Class 350 Board 50 Del from £165 **SERVICES:** Lift **PARKING:** 500 **NOTES:** ⊗ in restaurant Civ Wed 700

★★★★62% De Montfort
Abbey End CV8 1ED
☎ 01926 855944 📠 01926 857830
e-mail: demontfort@macdonald-hotels.co.uk
web: www.macdonald-hotels.co.uk
Dir: *from A46 take A452 towards Leamington. At rdbt left to Kenilworth town centre, along high street. Hotel at top opposite clock tower*
Situated in the centre of town, in the heart of Shakespeare country, this popular business hotel is well located for access to the major commercial centres of the Midlands. Public areas include a range of meeting and function rooms, a comfortable lounge/bar area and a traditional restaurant.
ROOMS: 108 en suite (15 fmly) ⊗ in 55 bedrooms s £50-£160; d £70-£180 (incl. bkfst) **LB** **FACILITIES:** STV Free use of nearby pool and gym Xmas **CONF:** Thtr 300 Class 100 Board 40 **SERVICES:** Lift **PARKING:** 65 **NOTES:** ⊗ in restaurant Civ Wed 116

★★★76% *Peacock*
149 Warwick Rd CV8 1HY
☎ 01926 851156 & 864500 📠 01926 864644
e-mail: reservations@peacockhotel.com
Dir: *A46/A452 signed to Kenilworth. Hotel in 0.25m on right after St John's Church*
Conveniently located for the town centre, the Peacock offers a peaceful retreat and service is delivered in a most professional manner by friendly staff. Vibrant colour schemes run through pleasing public rooms and the attractive accommodation is complemented by two dining options: the Malabar room, offering modern European dining, and the Coconut Lagoon serving Southern Indian dishes.
ROOMS: 23 en suite 6 annexe en suite (5 fmly) (10 GF) ⊗ in 18 bedrooms **FACILITIES:** STV **CONF:** BC Thtr 90 Class 50 Board 50 **PARKING:** 30 **NOTES:** 🐕 Civ Wed 90

KENTON, Greater London
See LONDON SECTION plan 1 C5

Premier Travel Inn Harrow
Kenton Rd HA3 8AT
☎ 08701 977146 📠 020 8909 1604
web: www.premiertravelinn.com
Dir: *M1 junct 5 follow signs to Harrow & Kenton. Between Harrow & Wembley on A4006 opposite Kenton Railway Station*
High quality, modern budget accommodation ideal for both families and business travellers. Spacious, en suite bedrooms feature bath and shower, satellite TV and many have telephones and modem points. The adjacent family restaurant features a wide and varied menu. For further details consult the Hotel Groups page.
ROOMS: 70 en suite s £57.95-£59.95; d £57.95-£59.95 **CONF:** Class 50

KESWICK, Cumbria Map 18 NY22

★★★77% Derwentwater
Portinscale CA12 5RE
☎ 017687 72538 📠 017687 71002
e-mail: info@derwentwater-hotel.co.uk
web: www.derwentwater-hotel.co.uk
Dir: *off A66 turn into Portinscale and through village then as road turns right take left turn as signed*

This is a popular and friendly holiday hotel with gardens that stretch down to the shores of Derwentwater. It offers a wide range of bedrooms, all thoughtfully equipped and some with good views of the lake. Inviting public areas include a conservatory lounge and shop.
ROOMS: 46 en suite (1 fmly) (2 GF) s £70-£200; d £140-£200 (incl. bkfst) **LB** **FACILITIES:** Fishing Putt green Access to local leisure facilities ♫ Xmas **CONF:** Thtr 20 Class 10 Board 14 **SERVICES:** Lift **PARKING:** 60 **NOTES:** ⊗ in restaurant
See advert on page 279

★★★75% Dale Head Hall Lakeside
Lake Thirlmere CA12 4TN
☎ 017687 72478 📠 017687 71070
e-mail: onthelakeside@daleheadhall.co.uk
Dir: *between Keswick and Grasmere. Off A591 onto private drive*

Formerly the summer residence of the Mayor of Manchester, the main house dates from the mid 16th century and has a spectacular lakeside location within well tended gardens. Dinner is served in the atmospheric beamed restaurant and features the best local produce. Bedrooms are spacious. This establishment is under new ownership.
ROOMS: 12 en suite (1 fmly) ⊗ in all bedrooms s £72.50-£77.50; d £95-£105 (incl. bkfst) **LB** **FACILITIES:** no TV in bdrms Fishing Xmas **PARKING:** 31 **NOTES:** 🐕 ⊗ in restaurant Closed 31 Dec-31 Jan
See advert on page 279

KESWICK, continued

★★★69% Keswick Country House

Station Rd CA12 4NQ
☎ 0845 458 4333 🖷 01253 754222
e-mail: reservations@choice-hotels.co.uk
web: www.thekeswickhotel.co.uk
Dir: *M6 junct 40/A66 , 1st slip road into Keswick, then follow signs for leisure pool.*

This impressive Victorian hotel is set amid landscaped gardens. Eight superior bedrooms have been created in the Station Wing, which is accessed through the Victorian conservatory. Main house rooms are comfortably modern in style and offer a good range of amenities. Public areas include a well-stocked bar, a spacious and relaxing lounge, and an attractive restaurant.

ROOMS: 74 en suite (6 fmly) (4 GF) s £44-£110; d £88-£220 (incl. bkfst & dinner) **FACILITIES:** STV Snooker ⛳ Putt green Leisure facilities close by. Xmas **CONF:** Thtr 110 Class 70 Board 60 Del from £95 **SERVICES:** Lift **PARKING:** 70 **NOTES:** 🐕 ⊗ in restaurant Civ Wed 100

★★★67% Skiddaw

Main St CA12 5BN
☎ 017687 72071 🖷 017687 74850
e-mail: info@skiddawhotel.co.uk
web: www.skiddawhotel.co.uk
Dir: *A66 to Keswick follow signs for town centre. Hotel in Market Square*

This privately owned hotel is centrally located overlooking Market Square. The smartly furnished bedrooms include some family suites and a room with a four-poster bed. Facilities include an attractive and spacious restaurant, a lounge bar, a quiet lounge for residents and two conference/function rooms.

ROOMS: 40 en suite (7 fmly) ⊗ in 10 bedrooms s fr £55; d fr £110 (incl. bkfst) **LB** **FACILITIES:** STV Sauna Use of pool at nearby sister hotel Xmas **CONF:** Thtr 70 Class 60 Board 40 Del from £90 **SERVICES:** Lift **PARKING:** 22 **NOTES:** 🐕 ⊗ in restaurant Civ Wed 90

See advert on opposite page

> Late for dinner? Quality standards mean that last orders for dinner vary according to star rating and should be no earlier than: ★★ 7.00pm ★★★ 8:00pm ★★★★ 9:00pm ★★★★★ 10:00pm

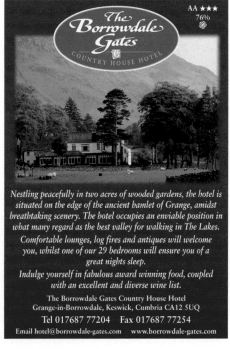

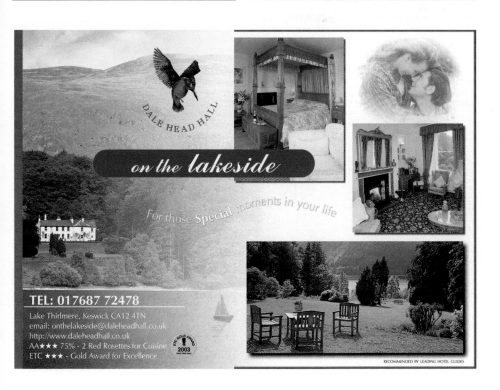

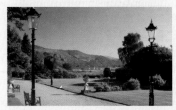

KESWICK, continued

★★77% Highfield
The Heads CA12 5ER
☎ 017687 72508 017687 80634
e-mail: info@highfieldkeswick.co.uk
web: www.highfieldkeswick.co.uk
Dir: *M6 junct 40, take A66 2nd exit at rdbt. Left following road to T- junct. Left again and right at mini rdbt. Then turn 4th right*
This friendly hotel close to the centre of town offers stunning views of Skiddaw, Cats Bells and Derwent Water. Elegant bedrooms, many of them spacious, are thoughtfully equipped. Newly redecorated public areas include a choice of comfortable lounges and a traditional restaurant, where imaginative, modern cuisine is served.
ROOMS: 19 en suite (2 fmly) (2 GF) in all bedrooms s £75-£95; d £100-£150 (incl. bkfst & dinner) **LB** **FACILITIES:** Xmas **CONF:** BC **PARKING:** 20 **NOTES:** in restaurant Closed Jan

★★76% Lyzzick Hall Country House
Under Skiddaw CA12 4PY
☎ 017687 72277 017687 72278
e-mail: lyzzickhall@btconnect.com
web: www.lyzzickhall.co.uk
Dir: *M6 junct 40 onto A66 to Keswick. Do not enter town, keep on Keswick by-pass. At rdbt 3rd exit onto A591 to Carlisle. Hotel 1.5m on right*
This delightful privately-owned and personally run hotel stands in lovely landscaped gardens in the foothills of Skiddaw and enjoys fabulous views across the valley. Bedrooms are smartly appointed and thoughtfully equipped. Public areas include two spacious lounges, a small bar and an attractive restaurant offering a wide range of international cuisine. Staff are delightful and nothing is too much trouble.
ROOMS: 30 en suite 1 annexe en suite (3 fmly) **FACILITIES:** Sauna Jacuzzi ch fac **CONF:** Board 15 **PARKING:** 40 **NOTES:** in restaurant Closed 24-26 Dec & mid Jan-mid Feb

★★75% Lairbeck
Vicarage Hill CA12 5QB
☎ 017687 73373 017687 73144
e-mail: aa@lairbeckhotel-keswick.co.uk
Dir: *A66 to rdbt with A591. Left then right onto Vicarage Hill, hotel 150yds*

This impeccably maintained, fine Victorian country house is situated close to the town in peacefully secluded, attractive gardens. There is a welcoming residents' bar and a formal dining room in which a range of freshly prepared dishes are served each day. Bedrooms, which include rooms on ground floor level, are individually styled and well equipped.
ROOMS: 14 en suite (1 fmly) (2 GF) in all bedrooms s £40-£46; d £80-£96 (incl. bkfst) **LB** **PARKING:** 15 **NOTES:** No children 5yrs in restaurant Closed Mid Nov-Mid Mar

Top Hotel

★ Swinside Lodge
Grange Rd, Newlands CA12 5UE
☎ 017687 72948 017687 73312
e-mail: info@swinsidelodge-hotel.co.uk
Dir: *off A66 left at Portinscale. Follow road to Grange for 2m ignoring signs to Swinside & Newlands Valley*
No visit to the Lake District is complete without a stay at this delightful country house. Superb hospitality and attentive services are the key to this popular hotel. Bedrooms are cosy, comfortable and thoughtfully equipped and the elegantly furnished lounges are an ideal place to relax before dinner. The four-course set dinner menu is creative and well prepared and provides superb value for money.
ROOMS: 7 en suite & 1 with private bathroom in all bedrooms s £112-£120; d £200-£240 (incl. bkfst & dinner) **LB** **FACILITIES:** Boules Xmas **CONF:** BC **PARKING:** 12 **NOTES:** No children 12yrs in restaurant

KETTERING, Northamptonshire — Map 11 SP87

★★★★76% Kettering Park
Kettering Parkway NN15 6XT
☎ 01536 416666 01536 416171
e-mail: kpark@shirehotels.com
web: www.shirehotels.com
Dir: *off A14 junct 9, on Kettering Venture Park*
A modern, stylish hotel providing a warm welcome and spacious, well-equipped and meticulously maintained bedrooms. Guests can choose from a menu of classical and contemporary dishes in the restaurant, alternatively light meals are served in the bar area. The wide-ranging leisure facilities are impressive. The creation of a new Conference Café concept will further enhance the already strong conference facilities.
ROOMS: 119 en suite (28 fmly) (20 GF) in 80 bedrooms s £90-£149; d £130-£169 (incl. bkfst) **LB** **FACILITIES:** STV supervised Sauna Solarium Gym Jacuzzi Steam rooms, Childrens splash pool, Activity studio Xmas **CONF:** BC Thtr 260 Class 120 Board 40 Del from £179 **SERVICES:** Lift air con **PARKING:** 200 **NOTES:** in restaurant Civ Wed 150

Premier Travel Inn Kettering
Rothwell Rd NN16 8XF
☎ 08701 977147 01536 415020
web: www.premiertravelinn.com
Dir: *on A14, off junct 7*
High quality, modern budget accommodation ideal for both families and business travellers. Spacious, en suite bedrooms feature bath and shower, satellite TV and many have telephones and modem points. The adjacent family restaurant features a wide and varied menu. For further details consult the Hotel Groups page.
ROOMS: 39 en suite s £46.95-£48.95; d £46.95-£48.95 **CONF:** Thtr 15

Travelodge
On the A14 (Westbound) NN14 1WR
☎ 08700 850 950
web: www.travelodge.co.uk
Dir: *M6 junct 1 or M1 junct 19, take A14, 0.5m past A43 junct*
Travelodge offers good quality, good value, modern accommodation. Ideal for families, the spacious, en suite bedrooms include remote-control TV, tea and coffee-making facilities and comfortable beds. Meals can be taken at the nearby family restaurant. For further details consult the Hotel Groups page.
ROOMS: 40 en suite s fr £26; d fr £26

KIDDERMINSTER, Worcestershire — Map 10 SO87
See also Stourport-on-Severn

★★★★68% Stone Manor
Stone DY10 4PJ
☎ 01562 777555 Fax 01562 777834
e-mail: enquiries@stonemanorhotel.co.uk
Dir: *2.5m from Kidderminster on A448, on right*
This converted, much extended former manor house stands in 25 acres of impressive grounds and gardens. The well-equipped accommodation includes rooms with four-poster beds and some luxuriously appointed annexe bedrooms. The hotel is a popular venue for wedding receptions.
ROOMS: 52 en suite 5 annexe en suite (7 GF) ⊗ in 11 bedrooms s £95-£150; d £95-£150 **FACILITIES:** STV Putt green Pool Table **CONF:** Thtr 150 Class 48 Board 60 Del £150 **PARKING:** 400 **NOTES:** ⊗ in restaurant Civ Wed 150

★★★67% Gainsborough House
Bewdley Hill DY11 6BS
☎ 01562 820041 Fax 01562 66179
e-mail: reservations@gainsboroughhotel.co.uk
web: www.gainsborough-hotel.co.uk
Dir: *on A456. At hospital, over lights, hotel 200yds on right*
This listed Georgian property is situated on the edge of the town. The no-smoking bedrooms are well equipped and comfortable. Additional features include a bar lounge, a restaurant with a carvery and also a carte menu, a lounge and attractive function rooms.
ROOMS: 43 en suite (8 fmly) ⊗ in 12 bedrooms s £50-£70; d £60-£90 (incl. bkfst) **LB** **FACILITIES:** Solarium & beauty salon Xmas **CONF:** Thtr 250 Class 80 Board 60 **PARKING:** 130 **NOTES:** ⊗ in restaurant Civ Wed 200

★★★66% The Granary Hotel & Restaurant
Heath Ln, Shenstone DY10 4BS
☎ 01562 777535 Fax 01562 777722
e-mail: info@granary-hotel.co.uk web: www.granary-hotel.co.uk
Dir: *on A450, 0.5m from junct with A448*

This modern hotel offers spacious, well-equipped accommodation with many rooms enjoying views towards Great Witley and the Amberley Hills. There is an attractive modern restaurant and a carvery is available at weekends. There are also extensive conference facilities and the hotel is popular as a wedding venue.
ROOMS: 18 en suite (1 fmly) (18 GF) ⊗ in 9 bedrooms s £70-£90; d £85-£140 (incl. bkfst) **LB** **CONF:** Thtr 200 Class 80 Board 70 **PARKING:** 96 **NOTES:** ⊗ in restaurant Closed 24-26 Dec

KILLINGTON LAKE MOTORWAY SERVICE AREA (M6), Cumbria — Map 18 SD59

Premier Travel Inn Kendal (Killington Lake)
Killington Lake, Motorway Service Area, Killington LA8 0NW
☎ 08701 977145 Fax 01539 621660
web: www.premiertravelinn.com
Dir: *From M6 junct 37 Southbound, Inn 1 mile south. From M6 northbound, exit J37 and rejoin southbound. Take access road to Inn*
High quality, modern budget accommodation ideal for both families and business travellers. Spacious, en suite bedrooms feature bath and shower, satellite TV and many have telephones and modem points. The adjacent family restaurant features a wide and varied menu. For further details consult the Hotel Groups page.
ROOMS: 36 en suite s £48.95; d £48.95 **CONF:** Thtr 10

KINGHAM, Oxfordshire — Map 10 SP22

★★★72% Mill House Hotel & Restaurant
OX7 6UH
☎ 01608 658188 Fax 01608 658492
e-mail: stay@millhousehotel.co.uk
web: www.millhousehotel.co.uk
Dir: *off A44 onto B4450. Hotel indicated by tourist sign*

This Cotswold-stone, former mill house has been carefully converted into a comfortable and attractive hotel, that is set in well-kept grounds bordered by its own trout stream. Bedrooms are comfortable and provide thoughtfully equipped accommodation. There is a peaceful lounge and bar and an atmospheric restaurant where imaginative, skilful cooking is a highlight of any stay.
ROOMS: 21 en suite 2 annexe en suite (1 fmly) (7 GF) s £85-£95; d £115-£175 (incl. bkfst & dinner) **LB** **FACILITIES:** STV Fishing Xmas **CONF:** BC Thtr 70 Class 24 Board 20 Del from £145 **PARKING:** 62 **NOTES:** ⊗ in restaurant Civ Wed 80

Indoor Swimming pool
Indoor Swimming pool (heated)
Outdoor Swimming pool
Outdoor Swimming pool (heated)

KINGSBRIDGE, Devon Map 03 SX74

Top Hotel

★★★ ◎◎ **Buckland-Tout-Saints**
Goveton TQ7 2DS
☎ 01548 853055 📠 01548 856261
e-mail: buckland@tout-saints.co.uk
web: www.tout-saints.co.uk
Dir: *off A381 Totnes/Kingsbridge road to Goveton. Left into Goveton, up hill to St Peter's Church. Hotel 2nd right after church*

It's well worth navigating the winding country lanes to find this delightful Queen Anne manor house that has been host to many famous guests over the years. Set in seven acres of gardens and grounds the hotel is a peaceful retreat. Bedrooms are tastefully furnished and attractively decorated, most of them enjoying views of the gardens. Local produce is used with care and imagination in the restaurant. The large function room opens on to the terrace and is a popular choice for weddings.

ROOMS: 12 en suite (1 fmly) ⊗ in 1 bedroom s £65-£120; d £130-£300 (incl. bkfst) **LB** **FACILITIES:** ♫ Putt green Petanque pitch Xmas **CONF:** Thtr 125 Class 40 Board 40 Del from £120 **PARKING:** 42 **NOTES:** ⊗ in restaurant Closed 3 wks Jan Civ Wed 90

KINGSGATE, Kent Map 07 TR37

★★★70% ***The Fayreness***
Marine Dr CT10 3LG
☎ 01843 868641 📠 01843 608750
e-mail: fayreness@thorleytaverns.com
web: www.fayreness.com
Dir: *A28 onto B2051 which becomes B2052. Pass Holy Trinity Church on right and '19th Hole' public house. Next left, down Kingsgate Ave, hotel at end on left*

Situated on the cliff tops overlooking the English Channel, just a few steps from a sandy beach and adjacent to the North Foreland Golf Club. The spacious bedrooms are tastefully furnished with many thoughtful touches; some rooms have stunning sea views. Public rooms include a large open-plan lounge/bar, a function room, dining room and conservatory restaurant.

ROOMS: 29 en suite ⊗ in 17 bedrooms **FACILITIES:** STV **CONF:** Thtr 50 Class 28 Board 36 **PARKING:** 70 **NOTES:** ⊗ in restaurant Civ Wed 80

See advert under BROADSTAIRS

KINGS LANGLEY, Hertfordshire Map 06 TL00

⌂ **Premier Travel Inn Kings Langley**
Hempstead Rd WD4 8BR
☎ 0870 9906372 📠 0870 9906373
web: www.premiertravelinn.com
Dir: *1m from M25 junct 20 on A4251 after Kings Langley*

High quality, modern budget accommodation ideal for both families and business travellers. Spacious, en suite bedrooms feature bath and shower, satellite TV and many have telephones and modem points. The adjacent family restaurant features a wide and varied menu. For further details consult the Hotel Groups page.

ROOMS: 60 en suite s £55.95-£59.95; d £55.95-£59.95

KING'S LYNN, Norfolk Map 12 TF62

★★★ ◎◎ ***Congham Hall Country House Hotel***
Lynn Rd PE32 1AH
☎ 01485 600250 📠 01485 601191
e-mail: info@conghamhallhotel.co.uk
web: www.vonessenhotels.co.uk
(For full entry see Grimston)

★★★70% **Knights Hill**
Knights Hill Village, South Wootton PE30 3HQ
☎ 01553 675566 📠 01553 675568
e-mail: reception@knightshill.co.uk
Dir: *junct A148/A149*

Knights Hill is a hotel village complex, set on a 16th-century site, conveniently located for main road access on the outskirts of the town. Smartly decorated and well-equipped bedrooms are situated in extensions to the original hunting lodge. The main house is full of historic charm, combined with modern conference, banqueting and indoor leisure facilities. Public rooms also include a choice of dining options in the Garden Restaurant and the Farmers Arms pub.

ROOMS: 55 en suite 18 annexe en suite (45 GF) ⊗ in 51 bedrooms s £68-£110; d £84-£125 **LB** **FACILITIES:** STV 🏊 🎾 Sauna Gym ♫ Jacuzzi Heli-pad Xmas **CONF:** Thtr 200 Class 150 Board 30 Del £130 **PARKING:** 350 **NOTES:** 🐕 ⊗ in restaurant Civ Wed 90

★★70% **Stuart House**
35 Goodwins Rd PE30 5QX
☎ 01553 772169 📠 01553 774788
e-mail: reception@stuarthousehotel.co.uk
web: www.stuart-house-hotel.co.uk
Dir: *at A47/A10/A149 rdbt take signs to King's Lynn town centre. Under Southgate Arch, right into Guanock Ter and right Goodwins Rd*

This privately-owned hotel is situated in a peaceful residential area, yet is just a short walk from the town centre. Bedrooms come in a variety of styles and sizes; all rooms are pleasantly appointed and well equipped. There is a choice of dining options with informal dining in the bar and a daily-changing menu in the elegant restaurant.

ROOMS: 18 en suite (2 fmly) ⊗ in 4 bedrooms s £64; d £85-£130 **LB** **FACILITIES:** Jacuzzi ♫ **CONF:** BC Thtr 50 Class 30 Board 20 **PARKING:** 30 **NOTES:** 🐕 ⊗ in restaurant RS 25-26 Dec & 1 Jan

★★68% *Grange*
Willow Park, South Wootton Ln PE30 3BP
☎ 01553 673777 & 671222 📠 01553 673777
e-mail: info@thegrangehotelkingslynn.co.uk
Dir: *A148 towards King's Lynn for 1.5m. At traffic lights left into Wootton Rd, 400yds on right South Wootton Ln. Hotel 1st on left*
Expect a warm welcome at this Edwardian house, which is situated in a quiet residential area amid its own grounds. Public rooms include an entrance hall, smart lounge bar and a cosy restaurant. The spacious bedrooms are pleasantly decorated, with some located in an adjacent wing, and are equipped with many thoughtful touches.
ROOMS: 5 en suite 4 annexe en suite (2 fmly) **CONF:** Thtr 20 Class 15 Board 12 **PARKING:** 15 **NOTES:** ⊗ in restaurant

★★65% *Russet House*
53 Goodwins Rd PE30 5PE
☎ 01553 773098 📠 01553 773098
e-mail: stewart@russethousehotel100.freeserve.co.uk
Dir: *follow town centre signs along Hardwick Rd. Right at rdbt before Southgates into Vancouver Av. Hotel on left*
A friendly and relaxed atmosphere exists at this detached property, that dates back to 1890 and is situated just a short walk from the River Ouse and town centre. Public rooms offer a good choice of areas to relax in, including a cosy bar, restaurant and a lounge with an open fire. Bedrooms are pleasantly decorated with co-ordinated soft furnishings and many useful extras.
ROOMS: 13 en suite (2 fmly) ⊗ in 1 bedroom **PARKING:** 20 **NOTES:** ⊗ in restaurant

See advert on this page

⌂ Premier Travel Inn King's Lynn
Freebridge Farm PE34 3LJ
☎ 08701 977149 📠 01553 775827
web: www.premiertravelinn.com
Dir: *junct of A47 & A17*
High quality, modern budget accommodation ideal for both families and business travellers. Spacious, en suite bedrooms feature bath and shower, satellite TV and many have telephones and modem points. The adjacent family restaurant features a wide and varied menu. For further details consult the Hotel Groups page.
ROOMS: 40 en suite s £48.95; d £48.95

KINGSTON UPON HULL, East Riding of Yorkshire
Map 17 TA02
See also Little Weighton

★★★73% ❀❀ Willerby Manor
Well Ln HU10 6ER
☎ 01482 652616 📠 01482 653901
e-mail: willerbymanor@bestwestern.co.uk
web: www.willerbymanor.co.uk
(For full entry see Willerby)

★★★70% Portland
Paragon St HU1 3JP
☎ 01482 326462 📠 01482 213460
e-mail: info@portland-hotel.co.uk
web: www.portland-hull.com
Dir: *M62 onto A63, to 1st main rdbt. Left at 2nd lights and over x-rds. Right at next junct onto Carr Ln, follow one-way system*
A modern hotel situated in the city centre providing a good range of accommodation. Most of the public rooms are on the first floor and include the Windows Restaurant and Bar/Lounge. In addition, the Bay Tree Café, at street level, is open during the day and evening. Staff are friendly and helpful and take care of car parking.

Portland

ROOMS: 126 en suite (4 fmly) ⊗ in 70 bedrooms s £68-£150; d £68-£150 **FACILITIES:** STV Complimentary use of nearby health & fitness centre Xmas **CONF:** BC Thtr 220 Class 100 Board 50 Del from £120 **SERVICES:** Lift **PARKING:** 12 **NOTES:** ⊗ in restaurant

★★★67% Quality Hotel Royal Hull
170 Ferensway HU1 3UF
☎ 01482 325087 📠 01482 323172
e-mail: enquiries@hotel-hull.com
web: www.choicehotelseurope.com
Dir: *From M62 take A63 to Hull. Over flyover, left at 2nd lights signed Railway Station. Hotel on left at 2nd lights*
A former Victorian railway hotel modernised in recent years. Bedrooms are well equipped and include a number of premier rooms. A spacious lounge provides an ideal setting for light meals,

continued on p284

KINGSTON UPON HULL, continued

drinks and relaxation. There are extensive banqueting and conference facilities, as well as an adjacent leisure club.
ROOMS: 155 en suite (6 fmly) ⊘ in 85 bedrooms s £45-£103; d £50-£112 **LB** **FACILITIES:** Sauna Solarium Gym Jacuzzi Steamroom Xmas **CONF:** Thtr 450 Class 150 Board 105 Del from £80 **SERVICES:** Lift **PARKING:** 130 **NOTES:** Civ Wed 450

★★★66% *Elizabeth Hotel Hull*
Ferriby High Rd HU14 3LG
☎ 01482 645212 🖷 01482 643332
e-mail: elizabeth.hull@elizabethhotels.co.uk
web: www.elizabethhotels.co.uk
(For full entry see North Ferriby)

★★66% *The Rowley Manor*
Rowley Rd HU20 3XR
☎ 01482 848248 🖷 01482 849900
e-mail: info@rowleymanor.com
(For full entry see Little Weighton)

★★60% Stop Inn Hull
11 Anlaby Rd HU1 2PJ
☎ 01482 323299 🖷 01482 214730
e-mail: hull@stop-inns.com
web: www.stop-inns.com/hull
Dir: *M62 to A63, over flyover, left at lights, hotel 500yds on left*
An unpretentious hotel situated in the centre of the city with well-equipped and generally spacious bedrooms. Staff are friendly, and whilst there is no formal restaurant a limited range of dishes is served in the lounge bar during the evening. Free parking is available.
ROOMS: 59 en suite (5 fmly) ⊘ in 29 bedrooms s £46-£59; d £52-£64 (incl. bkfst) **LB** **FACILITIES:** leisure facilities at sister hotel Xmas **CONF:** Thtr 140 Class 80 Board 45 Del from £75 **SERVICES:** Lift **PARKING:** 100 **NOTES:** ⊘ in restaurant

⇧ *Campanile*
Beverley Rd, Freetown Way HU2 9AN
☎ 01482 325530 🖷 01482 587538
e-mail: hull@envergure.co.uk
web: www.envergure.fr
Dir: *From M62 join A63 to Hull, pass Humber Bridge on right. Over flyover, follow railway station signs onto A1079. Hotel at bottom of Ferensway*

This modern building offers accommodation in smart, well-equipped bedrooms, all with en suite bathrooms. Refreshments may be taken at the informal Bistro. For further details consult the Hotel Groups page.
ROOMS: 47 annexe en suite **CONF:** Thtr 35 Class 18 Board 24

U Star rating not confirmed

⇧ *Hotel Ibis Hull*
Osborne St HU1 2NL
☎ 01482 387500 🖷 01482 385510
e-mail: h3479-gm@accor-hotels.com
Dir: *M62/A63 straight across at rdbt, follow signs for Princes Quay onto Myton St. Hotel on corner of Osborne St & Ferensway*
Modern, budget hotel offering comfortable accommodation in bright and practical bedrooms. Breakfast is self-service and dinner is available in the restaurant. For further details, consult the Hotel Groups page.
ROOMS: 106 en suite

⇧ Premier Travel Inn Hull North
Kingswood Park, Ennerdale HU7 4HS
☎ 08701 977137 🖷 01482 820300
web: www.premiertravelinn.com
Dir: *N of Hull, Ennerdale link road in Kingswood Park. A63 to city centre, then A1079 north, right onto A1033, hotel on 2nd rdbt*
High quality, modern budget accommodation ideal for both families and business travellers. Spacious, en suite bedrooms feature bath and shower, satellite TV and many have telephones and modem points. The adjacent family restaurant features a wide and varied menu. For further details consult the Hotel Groups page.
ROOMS: 42 en suite s £46.95-£49.95; d £46.95-£49.95

⇧ Premier Travel Inn Hull West
Ferriby Rd, Hessle HU13 0JA
☎ 08701 977138 🖷 01482 645285
web: www.premiertravelinn.com
Dir: *From A63 take exit for A164/A15 to Humber Bridge, Beverley & Hessle Viewpoint. Inn on 1st rdbt*
High quality, modern budget accommodation ideal for both families and business travellers. Spacious, en suite bedrooms feature bath and shower, satellite TV and many have telephones and modem points. The adjacent family restaurant features a wide and varied menu. For further details consult the Hotel Groups page.
ROOMS: 40 en suite s £46.95-£49.95; d £46.95-£49.95

⇧ Travelodge Hull
Beacon Service Area HU15 1RZ
☎ 08700 850 950 🖷 01430 424455
web: www.travelodge.co.uk
(For full entry see South Cave)

KINGSTON UPON THAMES, Greater London
See LONDON SECTION plan 1 C1

⇧ Travelodge London Kingston
21-23 London Rd KT2 6ND
☎ 08700 850 950 🖷 0208 546 5904
web: www.travelodge.co.uk
Travelodge offers good quality, good value, modern accommodation. Ideal for families, the spacious, en suite bedrooms include remote-control TV, tea and coffee-making facilities and comfortable beds. Meals can be taken at the nearby family restaurant. For further details consult the Hotel Groups page.
ROOMS: 72 en suite s fr £26; d fr £26

KINGSWINFORD, West Midlands
Map 10 SO88

⇧ Innkeeper's Lodge Kingswinford
Swindon Rd DY6 9XA
☎ 01384 295254 & 270066 🖷 01384 287959
web: www.innkeeperslodge.com
Dir: *A491 into Kingswinford, at x-rds lights, turn onto A4101 towards Kidderminster along 'Summerhill'. At 1st set of lights, hotel on right*
A growing concept in the travel accommodation market. Smart

continued

rooms meet essential business requirements but also have home comforts. Dining options include all-day menus plus the added advantage of breakfast, which is included in the room price. For further details consult the Hotel Groups page.
ROOMS: 22 en suite s £45-£52.50; d £45-£52.50

⇧ Premier Travel Inn Dudley (Kingswinford)

Dudley Rd DY6 8WT
☎ 08701 977303 📠 01384 402736
web: www.premiertravelinn.com
Dir: *A4123 to Dudley, A461 following signs for Russell's Hall Hospital. On A4101 to Kingswinford, Inn is opposite Pensnett Trading Estate*
High quality, modern budget accommodation ideal for both families and business travellers. Spacious, en suite bedrooms feature bath and shower, satellite TV and many have telephones and modem points. The adjacent family restaurant features a wide and varied menu. For further details consult the Hotel Groups page.
ROOMS: 43 en suite s £47.95-£50.95; d £47.95-£50.95 **CONF:** Thtr 30 Board 20

KINGTON, Herefordshire — Map 09 SO25

★★★68% Burton

Mill St HR5 3BQ
☎ 01544 230323 📠 01544 239023
e-mail: burton@hotelherefordshire.co.uk
Dir: *rdbt at A44/A411 junct take road signed Town Centre*
Situated in the town centre, this friendly, privately-owned hotel offers spacious, pleasantly proportioned and well equipped bedrooms. Smartly presented public areas include a lounge bar, newly completed swimming pool and leisure facilities. An attractive restaurant where carefully prepared cuisine can also be enjoyed. There are function and meeting facilities available in a purpose-built, modern wing.
ROOMS: 16 en suite (5 fmly) ⊘ in 2 bedrooms s £44-£54; d £75-£85 (incl. bkfst) **LB** **FACILITIES:** Xmas **CONF:** BC Thtr 150 Class 100 Board 20 Del from £75 **PARKING:** 50 **NOTES:** ⊘ in restaurant Civ Wed 120

KIRBY MUXLOE, Leicestershire — Map 11 SK50

★★63% *Castle Hotel & Restaurant*

Main St LE9 2AP
☎ 0116 239 5337 📠 0116 238 7868
e-mail: thecastle.kirbymuxloe@snr.co.uk
Dir: *M1 junct 21A northbound, follow signs for Kirby Muxloe*

This attractive, creeper-clad former farmhouse dates back to the 16th century, when it was built using stone and timbers taken from the nearby castle. The property features inglenook fireplaces and exposed timbers and open-plan public rooms include a

continued

lounge bar and restaurant with a non-smoking area. Bedrooms vary in size and style, and all are pleasantly decorated.
ROOMS: 22 en suite (3 fmly) **CONF:** Thtr 150 Class 100 Board 100
NOTES: ✈ Civ Wed 100

KIRKBURTON, West Yorkshire — Map 16 SE11

⇧ Innkeeper's Lodge Huddersfield

36a Penistone Rd HD8 0PQ
☎ 01484 602101 📠 01484 603938
web: www.innkeeperslodge.com
Dir: *from A62 Huddersfield ring road onto A629 towards Wakefield*
A growing concept in the travel accommodation market. Smart rooms meet essential business requirements but also have home comforts. Dining options include all-day menus plus the added advantage of breakfast, which is included in the room price. For further details consult the Hotel Groups page.
ROOMS: 20 en suite 3 annexe en suite **CONF:** Thtr 30 Board 20 s £45-£48; d £45-£48

KIRKBY LONSDALE, Cumbria — Map 18 SD67

★★68% ◎ *The Whoop Hall*

Burrow with Burrow LA6 2HP
☎ 015242 71284 📠 015242 72154
e-mail: info@whoophall.co.uk
Dir: *on A65 1m SE of Kirkby Lonsdale*

This popular inn combines traditional charm with modern facilities, that includes a very well-equipped leisure complex. Bedrooms, some with four-poster beds, and some housed in converted barns, are being upgraded to a smart stylish standard. A fire warms the bar on chillier days and an interesting choice of dishes is available in the bar and galleried restaurant throughout the day and evening.
ROOMS: 24 rms (23 en suite) (4 fmly) (2 GF) **FACILITIES: Spa** supervised Snooker Sauna Solarium Gym Jacuzzi Beauty salon ♫ **CONF:** Thtr 169 Class 72 Board 56 **PARKING:** 100 **NOTES:** ⊘ in restaurant Civ Wed 120

KIRKBYMOORSIDE, North Yorkshire — Map 19 SE68

★★67% George & Dragon Hotel

17 Market Place YO62 6AA
☎ 01751 433334 📠 01751 432933
e-mail: reception@georgeanddragon.net
Dir: *off A170 between Thirsk and Scarborough, in centre of market town*
Set in the market square, this coaching inn dates from the 17th century. With its blazing fire in season and its sporting theme the pub offers a cosy and welcoming atmosphere. A wide range of hearty dishes is offered from both the menu and a specials board. Spacious bedrooms are individually furnished and housed in the quiet courtyard buildings.
ROOMS: 12 en suite 7 annexe en suite (2 fmly) (3 GF) s £54-£59; d £89-£109 (incl. bkfst) **LB** **FACILITIES:** Xmas **PARKING:** 20
NOTES: ⊘ in restaurant

KIRKHAM, Lancashire Map 18 SD43

Premier Travel Inn Blackpool (Kirkham)
Fleetwood Rd, Greenhalgh PR4 3HE
☎ 0870 9906636 📠 0870 9906637
web: www.premiertravelinn.com
Dir: *Exit M6 junct 32, take M55 to Blackpool. Inn just off junct 3 towards Kirkham, left of rdbt*
High quality, modern budget accommodation ideal for both families and business travellers. Spacious, en suite bedrooms feature bath and shower, satellite TV and many have telephones and modem points. The adjacent family restaurant features a wide and varied menu. For further details consult the Hotel Groups page.
ROOMS: 28 en suite s £48.95; d £48.95

KNARESBOROUGH, North Yorkshire Map 19 SE35

★★★70% **Dower House**
Bond End HG5 9AL
☎ 01423 863302 📠 01423 867665
e-mail: enquiries@bwdowerhouse.co.uk
web: www.bwdowerhouse.co.uk
Dir: *A1(M) onto A59 Harrogate road. Through Knaresborough, hotel on right after traffic lights at end of high street*
This attractive 15th-century house stands in pleasant gardens on the edge of the town. Features such as welcoming real fires enhance its charm and character. Restaurant 48 has a relaxed and comfortable atmosphere and overlooks the garden. There is a cosy bar and comfortable non-smoking lounge. Other facilities include two function rooms and a popular health and leisure club, which has its own lounge bar.
ROOMS: 28 en suite 3 annexe en suite (2 fmly) (3 GF) in 27 bedrooms s £60-£120; d £115-£140 (incl. bkfst) **LB** **FACILITIES:** supervised Sauna Gym Jacuzzi Xmas **CONF:** Thtr 65 Class 35 Board 36 Del from £120 **PARKING:** 100 **NOTES:** in restaurant Civ Wed 70

★★★70% **General Tarleton Inn**
Boroughbridge Rd, Ferrensby HG5 0PZ
☎ 01423 340284 📠 01423 340288
e-mail: gti@generaltarleton.co.uk
web: www.generaltarleton.co.uk
Dir: *A1(M) junct 48 at Boroughbridge, take A6055 to Knaresborough. Inn 4m on right*
Food is a real feature here with skilfully prepared meals served in the restaurant, traditional bar and modern conservatory. Accommodation is provided in brightly decorated and airy rooms, and the bathrooms are thoughtfully equipped. Enjoying a country location, yet close to the A1 (M), ensures the hotel remains popular with both business and leisure guests.
ROOMS: 14 en suite (7 GF) in 11 bedrooms s £85-£108; d £97-£120 (incl. bkfst) **LB** **CONF:** Thtr 40 Class 35 Board 20 Del from £140 **PARKING:** 40 **NOTES:** in restaurant

Innkeeper's Lodge Harrogate East
Wetherby Rd, Plompton HG5 8LY
☎ 01423 797979 📠 01423 887276
web: www.innkeeperslodge.com
Dir: *turn off A658 onto A661 towards Harrogate, lodge on left*
A growing concept in the travel accommodation market. Smart rooms meet essential business requirements but also have home comforts. Dining options include all-day menus plus the added advantage of breakfast, which is included in the room price. For further details consult the Hotel Groups page.
ROOMS: 11 en suite s £55; d £55

KNOWLE, West Midlands Map 10 SP17

Innkeeper's Lodge Knowle
Warwick Rd, Knowle B93 0EE
☎ 01564 771177 📠 01564 730862
web: www.innkeeperslodge.com
Dir: *on A41*
A growing concept in the travel accommodation market. Smart rooms meet essential business requirements but also have home comforts. Dining options include all-day menus plus the added advantage of breakfast, which is included in the room price. For further details consult the Hotel Groups page.
ROOMS: 13 en suite s £48-£59; d £48-£59

KNOWL HILL, Berkshire Map 05 SU87

A ★★★ **Bird in Hand Country Inn**
Bath Rd RG10 9UP
☎ 01628 826622 & 822781 📠 01628 826748
e-mail: sthebirdinhand@aol.com
web: www.birdinhand.co.uk
Dir: *on A4 between Maidenhead & Reading*
ROOMS: 15 en suite (1 fmly) (6 GF) s £70-£90; d £80-£100 (incl. bkfst) **LB** **CONF:** Thtr 50 Class 40 Board 50 Del from £150 **PARKING:** 80 **NOTES:** in restaurant

KNUTSFORD, Cheshire Map 15 SJ77

★★★★73% **Cottons Hotel & Spa**
Manchester Rd WA16 0SU
☎ 01565 650333 📠 01565 755351
e-mail: cottons@shirehotels.com
web: www.shirehotels.com
Dir: *on A50 1m from M6 junct 19*
The superb leisure facilities and quiet location are great attractions at this hotel, which is just a short distance from Manchester Airport. Bedrooms are smartly appointed in various styles and executive rooms have very good working areas. The hotel now has more spacious lounge areas and an improved leisure centre.
ROOMS: 109 en suite (4 fmly) (38 GF) in 80 bedrooms s £90-£165; d £130-£185 (incl. bkfst) **LB** **FACILITIES: Spa** STV supervised Sauna Solarium Gym Jacuzzi Spa treatment rooms, Steam room, Relaxation area Xmas **CONF:** BC Thtr 200 Class 120 Board 30 Del from £165 **SERVICES:** Lift **PARKING:** 180 **NOTES:** in restaurant Civ Wed 120

★★★★70% ***Mere Court Hotel & Conference Centre***
Warrington Rd, Mere WA16 0RW
☎ 01565 831000 📠 01565 831001
e-mail: sales@merecourt.co.uk
web: www.merecourt.co.uk
Dir: *A50 Knutsford-Warrington road. 1m W of junct with A556 on right*

This is a smart and attractive hotel, set in extensive, well-tended

continued

gardens. The elegant and spacious bedrooms are all individually styled and offer a host of thoughtful extras. Conference facilities are particularly impressive and there is a large, self contained, conservatory function suite. Dining is available in the fine dining Arboreum Restaurant.
ROOMS: 34 en suite (24 fmly) (12 GF) ⊗ in 5 bedrooms
FACILITIES: STV **CONF:** Thtr 100 Class 60 Board 35 **SERVICES:** Lift
PARKING: 150 **NOTES:** ✗ ⊗ in restaurant Civ Wed 120

See advert on this page

★★★69% Cottage Restaurant & Lodge
London Rd, Allostock WA16 9LU
☎ 01565 722470 ℻ 01565 722749
web: www.thecottageknutsford.co.uk
Dir: *M6 junct 18/19 onto A50, Hotel between Holmes Chapel & Knutsford*
This well presented family run hotel enjoys a peaceful location on the A50 between Knutsford and Holmes Chapel. Smart, spacious lodge-style bedrooms complement an attractive open-plan restaurant and bar lounge. Bedrooms are thoughtfully equipped and offer good levels of comfort. Conference and meeting facilities, as well as ample parking, are available.
ROOMS: 12 en suite (6 GF) ⊗ in 8 bedrooms s £45-£69; d £60-£85 (incl. bkfst) **FACILITIES:** STV **CONF:** Thtr 40 Class 20 Board 24 Del from £80 **PARKING:** 40 **NOTES:** ✗ ⊗ in restaurant Closed New Years Day

★★76% The Longview Hotel & Restaurant
55 Manchester Rd WA16 0LX
☎ 01565 632119 ℻ 01565 652402
e-mail: enquiries@longviewhotel.com
web: www.longviewhotel.com
Dir: *M6 junct 19 take A556 W towards Chester. Left at lights onto A5033, 1.5m to rdbt then left. Hotel 200yds on right*
This friendly Victorian hotel offers high standards of hospitality and service. Attractive public areas include a cellar bar and foyer lounge area. The restaurant has a traditional feel and offers an imaginative selection of dishes. Bedrooms, some located in a superb renovation of nearby houses, are individually styled and offer a good range of thoughtful amenities, including broadband internet access.
ROOMS: 13 en suite 19 annexe en suite (1 fmly) (5 GF) s £55-£118; d £75-£140 (incl. bkfst) **LB** **FACILITIES:** Jacuzzi **PARKING:** 20
NOTES: ⊗ in restaurant Civ Wed

⌂ Premier Travel Inn Knutsford North
Bucklow Hill WA16 6RD
☎ 0870 9906428 ℻ 0870 9906429
web: www.premiertravelinn.com
Dir: *Exit M6 junct 19 onto A556 towards Manchester Airport/Stockport*
High quality, modern budget accommodation ideal for both families and business travellers. Spacious, en suite bedrooms feature bath and shower, satellite TV and many have telephones and modem points. The adjacent family restaurant features a wide and varied menu. For further details consult the Hotel Groups page.
ROOMS: 66 en suite s £47.95-£50.95; d £47.95-£50.95 **CONF:** Thtr 60 Board 30

⌂ Premier Travel Inn Knutsford North West
Warrington Rd, Hoo Green, Mere WA16 0PZ
☎ 0870 9906482 ℻ 0870 9906483
web: www.premiertravelinn.com
Dir: *Exit M6 junct 19, follow A556 to Manchester signs. At 1st lights left onto A50 towards Warrington. Hotel 1m on right*
High quality, modern budget accommodation ideal for both families and business travellers. Spacious, en suite bedrooms

continued

feature bath and shower, satellite TV and many have telephones and modem points. The adjacent family restaurant features a wide and varied menu. For further details consult the Hotel Groups page.
ROOMS: 28 en suite s £47.95-£50.95; d £47.95-£50.95

⌂ Travelodge
Chester Rd, Tabley WA16 0PP
☎ 08700 850 950 ℻ 01565 652187
web: www.travelodge.co.uk
Dir: *on A556, N'bound just E M6 junct 19*
Travelodge offers good quality, good value, modern accommodation. Ideal for families, the spacious, en suite bedrooms include remote-control TV, tea and coffee-making facilities and comfortable beds. Meals can be taken at the nearby family restaurant. For further details consult the Hotel Groups page.
ROOMS: 32 en suite s fr £26; d fr £26

KNUTSFORD MOTORWAY SERVICE AREA (M6), Cheshire
Map 15 SJ77

⌂ Travelodge
Granada Services, M6 junct 18/19 WA1 0TL
☎ 08700 850 950
web: www.travelodge.co.uk
Dir: *between junct 18 & 19 of M6 northbound*
Travelodge offers good quality, good value, modern accommodation. Ideal for families, the spacious, en suite bedrooms include remote-control TV, tea and coffee-making facilities and comfortable beds. Meals can be taken at the nearby family restaurant. For further details consult the Hotel Groups page.
ROOMS: 54 en suite s fr £26; d fr £26

LANCASTER, Lancashire Map 18 SD46

★★★★72% Lancaster House

Green Ln, Ellel LA1 4GJ
☎ 01524 844822 01524 844766
e-mail: lancaster@elhmail.co.uk
web: www.elh.co.uk/hotels/lancaster
Dir: *M6 junct 33 N towards Lancaster. Through Galgate and into Green Ln. Hotel before university on right*

This modern hotel enjoys a rural setting south of the city and close to the university. The attractive open-plan reception and lounge boasts traditional flagstone floors and a roaring log fire in colder months. Bedrooms are spacious with 19 new rooms being especially well equipped for business guests. Public areas have been extended to create larger leisure facilities, a new function room and more space in Sandemans lounge bar. Staff are friendly and keen to please.
ROOMS: 99 en suite (29 fmly) (44 GF) in 79 bedrooms s £89-£129; d £89-£145 **LB** **FACILITIES: Spa** STV supervised Sauna Solarium Gym Jacuzzi Beauty salon, Outside hot tub Xmas **CONF:** BC Thtr 170 Class 60 Board 48 Del from £94 **PARKING:** 120 **NOTES:** in restaurant Civ Wed 100

See advert on opposite page

Premier Travel Inn Lancaster

Lancaster Business Park, Caton Rd LA1 3PE
☎ 0870 977 290 01524 384801
web: www.premiertravelinn.com
High quality, modern budget accommodation ideal for both families and business travellers. Spacious, en suite bedrooms feature bath and shower, satellite TV and many have telephones and modem points. The adjacent family restaurant features a wide and varied menu. For further details consult the Hotel Groups page.
ROOMS: 60 en suite s £48.95; d £48.95

LANDFORD, Wiltshire Map 05 SU21

★★68% New Forest Lodge Hotel

Southampton Rd SP5 2ED
☎ 01794 390999 01794 390066
e-mail: reservations@newforestlodge.co.uk
web: www.newforestlodge.co.uk
Dir: *M27 junct 2, take A36 towards Salisbury, hotel 5m on left. From Salisbury A36 towards Southampton, hotel 9m on right.*
Set between Salisbury and Southampton, this is an ideal location for those visiting the area either for business or pleasure. Accommodation is self-contained and purpose built with bedrooms offering high standards of comfort and quality. Food is available in the adjacent Keepers Inn, where accomplished, contemporary cuisine is served in a convivial atmosphere.
ROOMS: 14 en suite (6 fmly) (6 GF) in all bedrooms s £55-£65; d £65-£75 (incl. bkfst) **LB** **PARKING:** 36 **NOTES:** in restaurant

LAND'S END, Cornwall & Isles of Scilly Map 02 SW32

See also Sennen

★★★64% The Land's End Hotel

TR19 7AA
☎ 01736 871844 01736 871599
e-mail: reservations@landsendhotel.wanado.co.uk
web: www.landsendhotel.co.uk
Dir: *from Penzance take A30 and follow Land's End signs. After Sennen 1m to Land's End*
This famous location provides a most impressive setting for this attractive hotel. Bedrooms, many with stunning views of the Atlantic, are pleasantly decorated and comfortable. A relaxing lounge and attractive bar are provided and in the Longships restaurant, fresh local produce and fish dishes are a speciality.
ROOMS: 33 en suite (2 fmly) s £50-£92; d £80-£164 (incl. bkfst) **LB** **FACILITIES:** Free entry Lands End visitor centre Xmas **CONF:** BC Thtr 200 Class 100 Board 50 **PARKING:** 1000 **NOTES:** in restaurant Civ Wed 110

LANGAR, Nottinghamshire Map 11 SK73

★★★74% Langar Hall

NG13 9HG
☎ 01949 860559 01949 861045
e-mail: langarhall-hotel@ndirect.co.uk
web: www.langarhall.com
Dir: *via Bingham from A52 or Cropwell Bishop from A46, both signed. Hotel behind church.*
This delightful hotel enjoys a picturesque rural location, yet is only a short drive from Nottingham. Individually styled bedrooms are furnished with fine period pieces and benefit from some thoughtful extras. There is a choice of lounges, warmed by real fires, and a snug little bar. Imaginative food is served in a pillared dining room and the garden conservatory.
ROOMS: 12 en suite (1 fmly) in all bedrooms s £65-£98; d £90-£185 **LB** **FACILITIES:** Fishing ch fac **CONF:** BC Thtr 20 Class 20 Board 20 Del £165 **PARKING:** 20 **NOTES:** in restaurant Civ Wed 40

LANGHO, Lancashire Map 18 SD73

★★70% The Avenue

Brockhall Village BB6 8AY
☎ 01254 244811 01254 244812
e-mail: bookingenquiries@theavenuehotel.co.uk
Dir: *Turn off A59 by Northcote Manor, follow for 1m. Turn right then 1st left into Brockhall Village*
One the Ribble Valley's newest hotels, The Avenue offers a modern and relaxed atmosphere throughout. Bedrooms are especially good being very well equipped and delightfully furnished. A wide range of dishes is available in the café bar/restaurant and good conference facilities are also on offer.
ROOMS: 21 en suite (9 fmly) (11 GF) in 11 bedrooms s fr £50; d fr £50 **FACILITIES:** STV **CONF:** Thtr 30 Class 30 Board 30 Del from £72 **PARKING:** 30 **NOTES:** Closed 24-25 Dec

Restaurant with Rooms

Northcote Manor

Northcote Rd BB6 8BE
☎ 01254 240555 01254 246568
e-mail: sales@northcotemanor.com
web: www.northcotemanor.com
Dir: *M6 junct 31, 9m to Northcote. Follow Clitheroe (A59) signs, hotel on left before rdbt*
Northcote Manor is a gastronomic haven where many guests

continued

return to sample the delights of its famous kitchen, which has twice in the past produced the Young Chef of the Year. Excellent cooking includes much of Lancashire's finest fare. Drinks can be enjoyed in the comfortable, elegantly furnished lounges and bar. Bedrooms have been individually furnished and thoughtfully equipped.
ROOMS: 14 en suite (4 GF) s £110-£145; d £140-£175 (incl. bkfst) **LB**
FACILITIES: STV Clay and game shooting, Blackburn Rovers tickets can be purchased by the hotel Xmas **CONF:** BC Thtr 40 Class 20 Board 26
PARKING: 50 **NOTES:** in restaurant Closed 25 Dec, 1 Jan & most BH Mondays Civ Wed 40

LANGTOFT, East Riding of Yorkshire Map 17 TA06

★★72% Old Mill Hotel & Restaurant
Mill Ln YO25 3BQ
☎ 01377 267284 & 07910 071641 01377 267383
e-mail: enquiries@oldbigglesmill.co.uk
Dir: *A64 eastbound, right at Staxton Hill traffic lights, through Foxholes village. Straight across at rdbt then 1st right*

Standing in the open countryside of the Wolds, this modern hotel has been very well furnished throughout. Bedrooms are thoughtfully equipped, and there is a popular bar/lounge where a good range of well produced food is available. There is also a charming restaurant that is popular with locals.
ROOMS: 9 en suite in 6 bedrooms s £45; d £65 (incl. bkfst) **LB**
CONF: BC Thtr 20 Class 16 Board 18 Del from £80 **PARKING:** 25
NOTES: No children 14yrs in restaurant

LASTINGHAM, North Yorkshire Map 19 SE79

★★★74% Lastingham Grange
YO62 6TH
☎ 01751 417345 & 417402 01751 417358
e-mail: lastinghamgrange@aol.com
Dir: *2m E on A170 to Scarborough, onto Lastingham. In village left uphill towards Moors. Hotel on right*

A warm welcome and sincere hospitality have been the hallmarks

continued

of this hotel for over 50 years. Antique furniture abounds, and the lounge and the dining room both look out onto the terrace and sunken rose garden below. There is a large play area for older children and the moorland views are breathtaking.
ROOMS: 12 en suite (2 fmly) s £99-£102; d £189-£195 (incl. bkfst) **LB**
FACILITIES: Large adventure playground ch fac **PARKING:** 30
NOTES: in restaurant Closed Dec-Feb

LAUNCESTON, Cornwall & Isles of Scilly Map 03 SX38
See also Lifton

★★65% Eagle House
Castle St PL15 8BA
☎ 01566 772036 01566 772036
e-mail: eaglehousehotel@aol.com
Dir: *from Launceston on Holsworthy Rd follow brown signs for hotel*
Next to the castle, this elegant Georgian house dates back to 1767 and is within walking distance of all local amenities. Many of the bedrooms have wonderful views over the Cornish countryside. A fixed-price menu is served in the restaurant, and on Sunday evenings a more modest menu is available.
ROOMS: 14 en suite (1 fmly) s fr £36; d £60-£72 (incl. bkfst) **LB**
FACILITIES: STV **CONF:** Thtr 190 Class 190 Board 190 **PARKING:** 100
NOTES: Civ Wed 190

Late for dinner? Quality standards mean that last orders for dinner vary according to star rating and should be no earlier than: ★★ 7.00pm ★★★ 8:00pm ★★★★ 9:00pm ★★★★★ 10:00pm

LAVENHAM, Suffolk
Map 13 TL94

★★★★75% ®® The Swan
High St CO10 9QA
☎ 01787 247477 🖷 01787 248286
e-mail: info@theswanatlavenham.co.uk
Dir: *from either A12 or A14 onto A134 turn onto B1071 to Lavenham*

A delightful collection of listed buildings dating back to the 14th century, lovingly restored to retain their original charm. Public rooms include comfortable lounge areas, a charming rustic bar, an informal brasserie and a fine-dining restaurant. Bedrooms are tastefully furnished and equipped with many thoughtful touches. The friendly staff are helpful, attentive and offer professional service.
ROOMS: 51 en suite (4 fmly) (12 GF) ⊗ in 8 bedrooms s £90-£100; d £140-£220 (incl. bkfst) **LB** **FACILITIES:** STV Xmas **CONF:** Thtr 60 Class 25 Board 25 Del from £140 **PARKING:** 62 **NOTES:** ⊗ in restaurant Civ Wed 90

★★72% ® Angel
Market Place CO10 9QZ
☎ 01787 247388 🖷 01787 248344
e-mail: angellav@aol.com
web: www.theangelhotel-lavenham.co.uk
Dir: *from A14 take Bury East and Sudbury turn off onto A143. After 4m take A1141 to Lavenham, Angel off high street*
Delightful 15th-century inn situated in the heart of this historic medieval town overlooking the market place. The Angel is well known for its cuisine and offers an imaginative menu based on fresh ingredients. Public rooms include a spacious first-floor lounge and an open plan bar/dining area. Bedrooms are tastefully furnished, attractively decorated and thoughtfully equipped.
ROOMS: 8 en suite (1 fmly) (1 GF) ⊗ in all bedrooms s fr £55; d fr £80 (incl. bkfst) **LB** **FACILITIES:** Use of Lavenham Tennis Club facilities ♫ **PARKING:** 5 **NOTES:** ✈ ⊗ in restaurant Closed 25-26 Dec

LEA MARSTON, Warwickshire
Map 10 SP29

★★★★67% Lea Marston Hotel & Leisure Complex
Best Western
Haunch Ln B76 0BY
☎ 01675 470468 🖷 01675 470871
e-mail: info@leamarstonhotel.co.uk
Dir: *M42 junct 9, take A4097 to Kingsbury. Hotel signed 1.5m on right*
Excellent access to the motorway network and a good range of sports facilities make this hotel a popular choice for conferences and leisure breaks. Bedrooms are mostly set around an attractive quadrangle and are generously equipped. Diners can choose

continued

between the popular Sportsman's Lounge Bar and the elegant Adderley Restaurant.

ROOMS: 80 en suite (4 fmly) (46 GF) ⊗ in 74 bedrooms s £70-£147; d £90-£168 (incl. bkfst) **LB** **FACILITIES:** **Spa** STV ⛆ ⛳ 9 ✂ Sauna Solarium Gym Putt green Jacuzzi Golf driving range, Beauty Salon, Childrens play area, Golf simulator Xmas **CONF:** Thtr 140 Class 50 Board 30 Del from £120 **SERVICES:** Lift **PARKING:** 220 **NOTES:** ✈ ⊗ in restaurant Civ Wed 100

LEAMINGTON SPA (ROYAL), Warwickshire
Map 10 SP36

Top Hotel

★★★ ®®® Mallory Court
Harbury Ln, Bishop's Tachbrook CV33 9QB
☎ 01926 330214 🖷 01926 451714
e-mail: reception@mallory.co.uk
web: www.mallory.co.uk
Dir: *2m S off B4087 towards Harbury*
Relais & Châteaux
With its tranquil rural setting, this elegant Lutyens-style country house is an idyllic retreat. Set in ten acres of landscaped gardens with immaculate lawns it offers two sumptuous lounges, a drawing room, conservatory and an elegant restaurant that all provide ample opportunity for relaxation and indulgence. Bedrooms in the main house are really luxurious, each individual in style, beautifully decorated and most with wonderful views. Those in the Knights Suite are more contemporary and have their own access via a smart conference and banqueting facility, where a brasserie operation is also being developed. Simon Haigh heads up a team of expert chefs producing dishes that continue to delight.
ROOMS: 18 en suite 11 annexe en suite (1 fmly) (4 GF) s £125-£260; d £135-£305 (incl. bkfst) **LB** **FACILITIES:** STV ⛆ ✂ ⛳ Use of nearby club facilities Xmas **CONF:** Thtr 200 Class 160 Board 50 Del from £175 **SERVICES:** Lift **PARKING:** 80 **NOTES:** No children 9yrs ⊗ in restaurant Civ Wed 160

★★★70% Courtyard by Marriott Leamington Spa

Olympus Av, Tachbrook Park CV34 6RJ
☎ 01926 425522 Fax 01926 881322
e-mail: res.lspcourtyard@kewgreen.co.uk
web: www.kewgreen.co.uk
Dir: *From M40 junct 13 (northbound exit) or M40 junct 14 (southbound exit) follow signs for Leamington A452*

Just a short distance from both Warwick and Leamington Spa, this modern hotel is conveniently situated for local businesses and tourist attractions. Bedrooms are furnished and decorated to a high standard providing a comprehensive range of extras. A friendly and helpful team efficiently delivers a professional service.

ROOMS: 91 en suite (14 fmly) (13 GF) No smoking in 48 bedrooms **FACILITIES:** STV Gym Xmas **CONF:** Thtr 70 Class 30 Board 40 **SERVICES:** Lift **PARKING:** 150 **NOTES:** No smoking in restaurant

★★★65% Angel

143 Regent St CV32 4NZ
☎ 01926 881296 Fax 01926 313853
e-mail: angelhotel143@hotmail.com
web: www.angelhotelleamington.co.uk
Dir: *in town centre at junct of Regent St and Holly Walk*

This centrally located hotel is divided in two parts - the original inn and a more modern extension. Public rooms include a comfortable foyer lounge area, a smart restaurant and an informal bar. Bedrooms are individual in style, and, whether modern or traditional, all have the expected facilities.

ROOMS: 48 en suite (3 fmly) s £60-£80; d £80-£120 (incl. bkfst) **LB** **FACILITIES:** STV Xmas **CONF:** Thtr 70 Class 40 Board 40 Del from £100 **SERVICES:** Lift **PARKING:** 38 **NOTES:** No smoking in restaurant

★★★65% Falstaff

16-20 Warwick New Rd CV32 5JQ
☎ 01926 312044 Fax 01926 450574
e-mail: falstaff@meridianleisure.com
web: www.meridianleisure.com
Dir: *M40 junct 13 or 14 follow signs for Leamington Spa. Over 4 rdbts then under bridge. Left into Princes Drive, then right at mini rdbt*

Bedrooms at this hotel come in a variety of sizes and styles and are well equipped, with many thoughtful extras. Snacks can be taken in the relaxing lounge bar, and an interesting selection of English and continental dishes is offered in the restaurant; 24-hour room service is also available. Conference and banqueting facilities are extensive.

ROOMS: 63 en suite (2 fmly) (16 GF) No smoking in 28 bedrooms s £60-£85; d £70-£100 (incl. bkfst) **LB** **FACILITIES:** Arrangement with local Health Club Xmas **CONF:** Thtr 70 Class 30 Board 30 Del from £110 **PARKING:** 50 **NOTES:** No smoking in restaurant Civ Wed 50

See advert on this page

LEAMINGTON SPA (ROYAL), continued

★★★65% Royal Leamington Hotel

64 Upper Holly Walk CV32 4JL
☎ 01926 883777 🖹 01926 330467
e-mail: royal@meridianleisure.com
Dir: *off A46 onto A452, left onto Clarendon Ave, then right into Clarendon St, then left, hotel on left*

This Victorian town house is situated near the thriving shopping centre of Leamington Spa, yet retains the relaxed and peaceful feel of yesteryear. Bedrooms are individually appointed and well equipped; public areas are full of character and include a traditional residents' lounge. Guests can dine in the atmospheric brasserie, or choose from the room service menu.
ROOMS: 32 en suite (3 GF) ⊗ in 10 bedrooms s £60-£80; d £80-£100 (incl. bkfst) **LB** **FACILITIES:** STV Xmas **CONF:** Thtr 40 Class 20 Board 20 Del from £125 **PARKING:** 20 **NOTES:** ⊗ in restaurant Civ Wed 60

See advert on page 291

⌂ Travelodge (Leamington Spa)

The Parade CV32 4AT
☎ 08700 850950 🖹 01926 432 473
web: www.travelodge.co.uk
Dir: *A425 follow town centre signs. Lodge off B4087*
Travelodge offers good quality, good value, modern accommodation. Ideal for families, the spacious, en suite bedrooms include remote-control TV, tea and coffee-making facilities and comfortable beds. Meals can be taken at the nearby family restaurant. For further details consult the Hotel Groups page.
ROOMS: 54 en suite (incl. bkfst) s fr £26; d fr £26

We have indicated only the hotels that don't accept credit or debit cards

LEATHERHEAD, Surrey — Map 06 TQ15

★★66% Bookham Grange

Little Bookham Common, Bookham KT23 3HS
☎ 01372 452742 🖹 01372 450080
e-mail: bookhamgrange@easynet.co.uk
web: www.bookham-grange.co.uk
Dir: *off A246 at Bookham High Street onto Church Rd, 1st right after Bookham railway station*
This attractive family-run hotel is situated in over two acres of landscaped grounds with extensive parking. Spacious bedrooms are individually decorated and well equipped. Public areas include

continued

extensive banqueting facilities and a beamed bar. This is a popular wedding venue.

ROOMS: 27 en suite (3 fmly) s £75-£85; d £95 (incl. bkfst) **LB**
FACILITIES: Xmas **CONF:** Thtr 80 Class 24 Board 24 Del from £117.50
PARKING: 60 **NOTES:** ⊗ in restaurant Civ Wed 90

⌂ Travelodge (Leatherhead)

The Swan Centre, High St KT22 8AA
☎ 0870 191 1748 🖹 01372 386577
web: www.travelodge.co.uk
Travelodge offers good quality, good value, modern accommodation. Ideal for families, the spacious, en suite bedrooms include remote-control TV, tea and coffee-making facilities and comfortable beds. Meals can be taken at the nearby family restaurant. For further details consult the Hotel Groups page.
ROOMS: 91 en suite s fr £26; d fr £26

LEDBURY, Herefordshire — Map 10 SO73

★★★74% ❀ Feathers

High St HR8 1DS
☎ 01531 635266 🖹 01531 638955
e-mail: mary@feathers-ledbury.co.uk
web: www.feathersledbury.co.uk
Dir: *S from Worcester on A449, E from Hereford on A438, N from Gloucester on A417. Hotel in High St*

Guests will be greeted with much old-fashioned charm at this historic timber-framed hostelry, situated in the middle of town. The comfortably equipped bedrooms are authentically and tastefully decorated, and well-prepared meals can be enjoyed in Fuggles Brasserie with its adjoining bar. Facilities include a leisure centre and a function suite.
ROOMS: 19 en suite (2 fmly) ⊗ in 2 bedrooms s £74.50-£99.50; d £99.50-£175 (incl. bkfst) **FACILITIES:** STV Sauna Solarium Gym Jacuzzi Steam room Xmas **CONF:** Thtr 140 Class 80 Board 40 Del £130
PARKING: 30 **NOTES:** Civ Wed 100

★★74% ⊛ The Verzon
Hereford Rd, Trumpet HR8 2PZ
☎ 01531 670381 🖷 01531 670830
e-mail: info@theverzon.co.uk
web: www.theverzon.co.uk
Dir: *2m W of Ledbury on A438*

Dating back to 1790, this delightful country house stands in extensive gardens commanding far reaching views over the Malvern Hills. The newly renovated public rooms blend original features with contemporary designs to create a stunning effect, and the atmosphere is one of chic elegance. Individually styled bedrooms offer superior quality and a host of thoughtful touches. A range of innovative dishes can be enjoyed in the brasserie bar.
ROOMS: 8 en suite (1 fmly) ⊗ in all bedrooms s £60-£80; d £70-£130 (incl. bkfst) **LB** **CONF:** Thtr 70 Class 40 Board 25 Del from £50
PARKING: 60 **NOTES:** ✈ ⊗ in restaurant

LEEDS, West Yorkshire
Map 19 SE23
See also Gomersal & Shipley

★★★★★64% ⊛ *De Vere Oulton Hall*
Rothwell Ln, Oulton LS26 8HN
☎ 0113 282 1000 🖷 0113 282 8066
e-mail: oulton.hall@devere-hotels.com
web: www.devereonline.co.uk
Dir: *2m from M62 junct 30 on left, or 1m from M1 junct 44. Follow Castleford and Pontefract signs on A639*
Surrounded by the beautiful Yorkshire Dales, yet within 15 minutes of the city centre, this elegant 19th-century house really does offer the best of both worlds. Impressive features of the hotel include the formal gardens, which have been faithfully restored to their original design, and the galleried Great Hall. The hotel also offers a choice of dining options and golfers can book preferential tee times at the adjacent golf club.
ROOMS: 152 en suite ⊗ in 144 bedrooms **FACILITIES:** STV supervised Sauna Solarium Gym Jacuzzi Beauty therapy Aerobics, spa treatments **CONF:** Thtr 350 Class 150 Board 40 **SERVICES:** Lift
PARKING: 260 **NOTES:** ⊗ in restaurant

★★★★77% ⊛ The Thorpe Park Hotel
Century Way, Thorpe Park LS15 8ZB
☎ 0113 264 1000 🖷 0113 264 1010
e-mail: thorpepark@shirehotels.com
web: www.shirehotels.com
Dir: *M1 junct 46 left at top of slip road, then right at rdbt into Thorpe Park*
Conveniently close to the M1, this newly built hotel offers bedrooms that are modern in both style and facilities. The terrace and courtyard offer all-day casual dining and refreshments, and

continued

the restaurant features a Mediterranean- themed menu. There is also a state-of-the-art spa and leisure facility.
ROOMS: 123 en suite (31 GF) ⊗ in 80 bedrooms s £90-£155; d £130-£175 (incl. bkfst) **LB** **FACILITIES: Spa** STV supervised Sauna Solarium Gym Jacuzzi Steam room, Activity studio, 6 spa treatment rooms Xmas **CONF:** BC Thtr 200 Class 100 Board 50 Del from £170 **SERVICES:** Lift air con **PARKING:** 200 **NOTES:** ✈ ⊗ in restaurant Civ Wed 150

Town House

★★★★ ⊛⊛ Haley's Hotel & Restaurant
Shire Oak Rd, Headingley LS6 2DE
☎ 0113 278 4446 🖷 0113 275 3342
e-mail: info@haleys.co.uk
web: www.haleys.co.uk
Dir: *from city centre follow signs to University on A660. After 1.5m right in Headingley between HSBC and Starbucks*
Only ten minutes from the city centre yet this hotel has a real country house feel to it. The bedrooms offer tasteful decor, some with interesting period furnishings. The modern restaurant is decorated with contemporary works of art (all for sale) and is the setting for imaginative meals. There is a choice of comfortable lounges.
ROOMS: 22 en suite 6 annexe en suite (3 fmly) (2 GF) ⊗ in 10 bedrooms s £85-£125; d £120-£160 (incl. bkfst) **LB**
FACILITIES: STV **CONF:** Thtr 40 Class 20 Board 25 Del from £120
PARKING: 29 **NOTES:** ✈ ⊗ in restaurant Closed 26-30 Dec RS Sun evening & Mon-Sat lunch Civ Wed 100

See advert on this page

LEEDS, continued

Town House

★★★★ 🏠 Radisson SAS Leeds
No 1 The Light, The Headrow LS1 8TL
☎ 0113 236 6000 📠 0113 236 6100
e-mail: annettejung@radissonsas.com
web: www.radisson.com
Dir: *follow city centre 'loop' up Park Row, straight at lights onto Cockeridge St, hotel on left*
Situated in the shopping complex known as 'The Light', the hotel occupies a converted building that was formerly the headquarters of the Leeds Permanent Building Society. Three styles of decor have been used in the bedrooms: Art Deco, Hi Tech and Italian. All rooms are air conditioned, with excellent business facilities. The lobby bar area serves substantial meals and is ideal for relaxation. Public parking is available, contact the hotel for details.
ROOMS: 147 en suite ⊘ in 130 bedrooms **FACILITIES:** STV Access to Esporta Health Club Xmas **CONF:** BC Thtr 60 Class 28 Board 24 Del £185 **SERVICES:** Lift air con **NOTES:** 🐕

★★★★69% Leeds Marriott Hotel
4 Trevelyan Square, Boar Ln LS1 6ET
☎ 0113 236 6366 📠 0113 236 6367
web: www.marriott.co.uk
Dir: *M621/M1 junct 3. Follow signs for city centre on A653. Stay in right lane. Energis building on left, right and follow signs to hotel*
With a charming courtyard setting in the heart of the city, this modern, elegant hotel provides the perfect base for shopping and sightseeing. Air-conditioned bedrooms are tastefully decorated and offer good workspace. Public areas include an informal bar, lobby lounge area and Georgetown Colonial Malaysian restaurants.
ROOMS: 244 en suite ⊘ in 194 bedrooms s £50-£240; d £50-£240 **LB**
FACILITIES: STV 🏊 supervised Sauna Solarium Gym Jacuzzi Subsidised use of NCP car park **CONF:** BC Thtr 280 Class 120 Board 80 Del from £145 **SERVICES:** Lift air con **NOTES:** 🐕 Civ Wed 300

★★★★68% Park Plaza Leeds
Boar Ln LS1 5NS
☎ 0113 380 4000 📠 0113 380 4100
e-mail: pplinfo@parkplazahotels.co.uk
web: www.parkplaza.com
Dir: *Follow signs for Leeds city centre*
Chic, stylish, ultra modern, city-centre hotel located just opposite City Square. Chino Latino, located on the first floor, is a fusion Far East and modern Japanese restaurant with a Latino bar. Stylish, air conditioned bedrooms are spacious and have a range of modern facilities, including high-speed internet connection.
ROOMS: 186 en suite ⊘ in 96 bedrooms s £60-£160; d £60-£160 **LB**
FACILITIES: Gym **CONF:** BC Thtr 160 Class 70 Board 40 Del from £135
SERVICES: Lift air con **NOTES:** 🐕 Closed 24 Dec-27 Dec

★★★★68% Queens
City Square LS1 1PL
☎ 0113 243 1323 📠 0113 242 5154
e-mail: queensreservations@quintessential-hotels.co.uk
web: www.quintessential-hotels.co.uk
Dir: *M621 junct 3. Follow signs for City Centre, under railway bridge. Left at 2nd lights, hotel on left.*
A legacy from the golden age of railways, this grand Victorian hotel has retained much of its original splendour and is located in the very heart of the city. Public rooms include the spacious bar, a range of function rooms and the restaurant.

continued

ROOMS: 217 en suite (25 fmly) ⊘ in 157 bedrooms s £140; d £140
FACILITIES: STV Free access to local gym **CONF:** BC Thtr 600 Class 255 Board 80 Del £165 **SERVICES:** Lift **PARKING:** 70 **NOTES:** Civ Wed 600

★★★★66% *Hotel Metropole*
King St LS1 2HQ
☎ 0113 245 0841 📠 0113 242 5156
e-mail: metropole.sales@principal-hotels.com
web: www.principal-hotels.com
Dir: *from M1, M62 and M621 follow city centre signs. Take A65 into Wellington St. At 1st traffic island right into King St, hotel on right*
Said to be the best example of this type of building in the city, this splendid terracotta-fronted hotel is centrally located and convenient for the railway station. Having undergone a major refurbishment the hotel takes on a whole new aspect, yet still retains all its character of old.
ROOMS: 118 en suite ⊘ in 98 bedrooms **FACILITIES:** STV **CONF:** BC Thtr 250 Class 100 Board 80 **SERVICES:** Lift **PARKING:** 40 **NOTES:** 🐕 ⊘ in restaurant RS 24 Dec-1 Jan Civ Wed 200

★★★78% ❁ *Malmaison Hotel*
Sovereign Quay LS1 1DQ
☎ 0113 398 1000 📠 0113 398 1002
e-mail: leeds@malmaison.com
web: www.malmaison.com
Dir: *M621/M1 junct 3, to city centre. At KPMG building, right into Sovereign St*
Close to the waterfront, this stylish property offers striking bedrooms with CD players and air conditioning. The popular bar and brasserie feature vaulted ceilings, intimate lighting and offer a choice of a full three-course meal or a substantial snack. Service is both willing and friendly.
ROOMS: 100 en suite ⊘ in 70 bedrooms **FACILITIES:** STV Gym
CONF: Thtr 40 Class 20 Board 28 **SERVICES:** Lift air con **NOTES:** 🐕

★★★77% ❁❁ Hazlewood Castle
Paradise Ln, Hazlewood LS24 9NJ
☎ 01937 535353 📠 01937 530630
e-mail: info@hazlewood-castle.co.uk
(For full entry see Tadcaster)

★★★73% Milford Hotel
A1 Great North Rd, Peckfield LS25 5LQ
☎ 01977 681800 📠 01977 681245
e-mail: enquiries@mlh.co.uk
web: www.mlh.co.uk
(For full entry see Garforth and advert on opposite page)

★★★72% Novotel Leeds Centre
4 Whitehall, Whitehall Quay LS1 4HR
☎ 0113 242 6446 Fax 0113 242 6445
e-mail: H3270@accor-hotels.com
web: www.novotel.com
Dir: *exit M621 junct 3, follow signs to train station. Turn into Aire St and left at lights*
With a minimalist style, this contemporary hotel provides a quality, value-for-money experience close to the city centre. Spacious, air-conditioned bedrooms are provided, whilst public areas offer deep leather sofas and an eye-catching water feature in reception. Light snacks are provided in the airy bar and the restaurant doubles as a bistro.
Novotel - AA Hotel Group of the Year 2005-6.
ROOMS: 195 en suite (50 fmly) ⊗ in 159 bedrooms s £59-£119; d £59-£119 **LB** **FACILITIES:** STV Sauna Gym Play station computers in rooms & play area Steam room Xmas **CONF:** Thtr 80 Class 50 Board 50 **SERVICES:** Lift air con **PARKING:** 70 **NOTES:** Civ Wed 70

★★★70% The Merrion
Merrion Centre LS2 8NH
☎ 0113 243 9191 Fax 0113 242 3527
e-mail: themerrion@brook-hotels.co.uk
Dir: *from M1, M62 and A61 onto city loop road to junct 7*
This smart modern hotel benefits from a city centre location. Bedrooms are smartly appointed and thoughtfully equipped for both business and leisure guests. Public areas include a comfortable lounge and a pleasing restaurant with an adjacent bar. There is direct access to a car park via a walkway.
ROOMS: 109 en suite ⊗ in 48 bedrooms s £49-£95; d £55-£115 **LB** **FACILITIES:** STV Discount at local leisure centre Xmas **CONF:** Thtr 80 Class 25 Board 25 Del from £105 **SERVICES:** Lift **NOTES:** ⊗ in restaurant

★★★69% Chevin Country Park Hotel
Yorkgate LS21 3NU
☎ 01943 467818 Fax 01943 850335
e-mail: reception@chevinhotel.com
(For full entry see Otley)

★★★68% Bewley's Hotel Leeds
City Walk, Sweet St LS11 9AT
☎ 0113 234 2340 Fax 0113 234 2349
e-mail: leeds@BewleysHotels.com
web: www.bewleyshotels.com/leeds_index.htm
Dir: *M621 junct 3, at 2nd lights. Left onto Sweet St right & right again*

Located on the edge of the city centre, this new hotel has the added advantage of secure underground car parking. Bedrooms are spacious and comfortable. Downstairs, the light and airy bar lounge leads into a brasserie where a wide selection of popular dishes is offered. High quality meeting rooms are also available.
ROOMS: 334 en suite (99 fmly) ⊗ in 246 bedrooms s £69; d £69 **FACILITIES:** STV **CONF:** BC Board 18 Del from £129 **SERVICES:** Lift **PARKING:** 160 **NOTES:** Closed 24-26 Dec

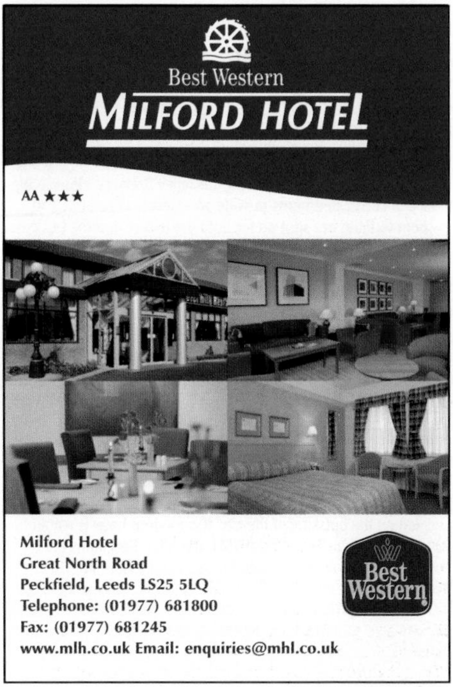

Best Western
MILFORD HOTEL
AA ★★★
Milford Hotel
Great North Road
Peckfield, Leeds LS25 5LQ
Telephone: (01977) 681800
Fax: (01977) 681245
www.mlh.co.uk Email: enquiries@mhl.co.uk
Best Western

★★★68% Golden Lion
2 Lower Briggate LS1 4AE
☎ 0113 243 6454 Fax 0113 242 9327
e-mail: info@goldenlion-hotel-leeds.com
web: www.peelhotel.com
Dir: *M621 junct 3. Keep in right lane. Follow until road splits into 4 lanes. Keep right. Right at lights. (Asda House on left). Left at lights. Over bridge, turn left, hotel opposite. Parking 150mtrs further on*

This smartly presented hotel is set in a Victorian building on the south side of the city. The well-equipped bedrooms offer a choice of standard or executive grades. Staff are friendly and helpful, ensuring a warm and welcoming atmosphere. Free overnight parking is provided in a 24-hour car park close-by the hotel.
ROOMS: 89 en suite (5 fmly) ⊗ in 46 bedrooms s £95-£110; d £105-£140 **FACILITIES:** STV Xmas **CONF:** Thtr 120 Class 45 Board 40 Del £140 **SERVICES:** Lift **PARKING:** 2 **NOTES:** ⊗ in restaurant

♫ Entertainment

LEEDS, continued

★★★68% Jurys Inn Leeds

Kendell St, Brewery Place, Brewery Wharf LS10 1NE
☎ 0113 283 8800 🖹 0113 283 8888
e-mail: info@jurysdoyle.com
web: www.jurysdoyle.com
This modern hotel is located near the Tetley Brewery, close to the centre of Leeds. Bedrooms provide good levels of comfort and in-room facilities are spot on for both the leisure and the business markets. Public areas include a number of meeting rooms, a restaurant and a popular bar.
ROOMS: 248 en suite ⊗ in 200 bedrooms s £69-£99; d £69-£99 **FACILITIES:** STV **CONF:** Thtr 60 Class 50 Board 25 Del from £115 **SERVICES:** Lift air con **NOTES:** ✖ ⊗ in restaurant

U Ramada Leeds North

Ring Rd, Seacroft LS14 5QF
☎ 0113 273 2323 🖹 0113 232 3018
e-mail: sales.leedsnorth@ramadajarvis.co.uk
web: www.ramadajarvis.co.uk
Dir: *From M1 junct 46 towards Leeds/Airport. Follow A6120 across several rdbts to Crossgates. Hotel 1m on right - need to double back at next rdbt.*
Located on the outskirts of the city, this modern hotel is within easy reach of the city centre, A1/M1 and M62. Bedrooms are comfortably appointed for both business and leisure guests.
ROOMS: 105 en suite (12 fmly) (21 GF) ⊗ in 73 bedrooms s £75-£95; d £75-£95 **FACILITIES:** STV Xmas **CONF:** Thtr 340 Class 200 Board 40 Del from £125 **SERVICES:** Lift **PARKING:** 150 **NOTES:** ⊗ in restaurant Civ Wed 250

U Ramada Leeds Parkway

Otley Rd LS16 8AG
☎ 0113 269 9000 🖹 0113 267 4410
e-mail: sales.leeds@ramadajarvis.co.uk
web: www.ramadajarvis.co.uk
Dir: *From A1 take A58 towards Leeds, then right onto A6120. At A660 turn right towards Airport/Skipton. Hotel is 2m on right.*
This large hotel is situated next to Golden Acre Park and Nature Reserve. Bedrooms are comfortably appointed for both business and leisure guests.
ROOMS: 118 en suite (2 fmly) (2 GF) ⊗ in 69 bedrooms s £89-£110; d £89-£110 **FACILITIES: Spa** STV supervised Sauna Solarium Gym Xmas **CONF:** Thtr 300 Class 120 Board 80 Del from £150 **SERVICES:** Lift **PARKING:** 250 **NOTES:** ⊗ in restaurant Civ Wed 100

⌂ Hotel Ibis Leeds

Marlborough St LS1 4PB
☎ 0113 220 4100 🖹 0113 220 4110
e-mail: H3652@accor.com
Dir: *3rd exit at A58 (M). Slip-road to Wellington St. A58/West St turn left to Marlborough St*
Modern, budget hotel offering comfortable accommodation in bright and practical bedrooms. Breakfast is self-service and dinner is available in the restaurant. For further details, consult the Hotel Groups page.
ROOMS: 168 en suite

⌂ Innkeeper's Lodge Leeds South

Bruntcliffe Rd, Morley LS27 0LY
☎ 0113 253 3115 🖹 0113 253 9365
web: www.innkeeperslodge.com
Dir: *M62 junct 27 take A650 towards Morley. On junct of A650 and A643*
A growing concept in the travel accommodation market. Smart rooms meet essential business requirements but also have home comforts. Dining options include all-day menus plus the added advantage of breakfast, which is included in the room price. For further details consult the Hotel Groups page.
ROOMS: 32 en suite s £45-£57; d £45-£57

⌂ Premier Travel Inn Leeds City Centre

Citygate, Wellington St LS3 1LW
☎ 08701 977150 🖹 0113 242 8105
web: www.premiertravelinn.com
Dir: *on junct of A65 & A58*
High quality, modern budget accommodation ideal for both families and business travellers. Spacious, en suite bedrooms feature bath and shower, satellite TV and many have telephones and modem points. The adjacent family restaurant features a wide and varied menu. For further details consult the Hotel Groups page.
ROOMS: 139 en suite s £53.95-£57.95; d £53.95-£57.95 **CONF:** Class 16 Board 16

⌂ Premier Travel Inn Leeds City West

City West One Office Park, Gelderd Rd LS12 6LX
☎ 0870 9906448 🖹 0870 9906449
web: www.premiertravelinn.com
Dir: *Exit M621 junct 1 take ring road towards Leeds. At 1st lights right into Gelderd Rd, right at rdbt*
High quality, modern budget accommodation ideal for both families and business travellers. Spacious, en suite bedrooms feature bath and shower, satellite TV and many have telephones and modem points. The adjacent family restaurant features a wide and varied menu. For further details consult the Hotel Groups page.
ROOMS: 126 en suite s £49.95-£52.95; d £49.95-£52.95 **CONF:** Thtr 12 Class 12 Board 12

⌂ Premier Travel Inn Leeds East

Selby Rd, Whitkirk LS15 7AY
☎ 08701 977151 🖹 0113 232 6195
web: www.premiertravelinn.com
Dir: *M1 junct 46 towards Leeds. At 2nd rdbt follow Temple Newsam signs. Inn 500mtrs on right.*
High quality, modern budget accommodation ideal for both families and business travellers. Spacious, en suite bedrooms feature bath and shower, satellite TV and many have telephones and modem points. The adjacent family restaurant features a wide and varied menu. For further details consult the Hotel Groups page.
ROOMS: 87 en suite s £46.95-£49.95; d £46.95-£49.95

⌂ Travelodge Leeds (Central)

Blaydes Court, Blaydes Yard, off Swinegate LS1 4AD
☎ 08700 850 950 🖹 0113 246 0076
web: www.travelodge.co.uk
Dir: *Exit M62 at M621 to city centre, right before Hilton Hotel into Sovereign St*

Travelodge offers good quality, good value, modern

continued

accommodation. Ideal for families, the spacious, en suite bedrooms include remote-control TV, tea and coffee-making facilities and comfortable beds. Meals can be taken at the nearby family restaurant. For further details consult the Hotel Groups page.
ROOMS: 100 en suite s fr £26; d fr £26

⌂ Travelodge Leeds (East)
Stile Hill Way, Colton LS15 9JA
☎ 08700 850 950 🖷 0113 264 8839
web: www.travelodge.co.uk
Dir: *M1 junct 46*

Travelodge offers good quality, good value, modern accommodation. Ideal for families, the spacious, en suite bedrooms include remote-control TV, tea and coffee-making facilities and comfortable beds. Meals can be taken at the nearby family restaurant. For further details consult the Hotel Groups page.
ROOMS: 60 en suite s fr £26; d fr £26

LEEDS/BRADFORD AIRPORT, West Yorkshire — Map 19 SE23

⌂ Premier Travel Inn Leeds/Bradford Airport
Victoria Av, Yeadon LS19 7AW
☎ 08701 977153 🖷 0113 202 9383
web: www.premiertravelinn.com
Dir: *on A658, near Leeds/Bradford Airport*
High quality, modern budget accommodation ideal for both families and business travellers. Spacious, en suite bedrooms feature bath and shower, satellite TV and many have telephones and modem points. The adjacent family restaurant features a wide and varied menu. For further details consult the Hotel Groups page.
ROOMS: 40 en suite s £52.95; d £52.95 **CONF:** Thtr 12

⌂ Travelodge (Leeds Bradford Airport)
White House Ln LS19 7TZ
☎ 0113 250 3996 🖷 0113 250 6842
web: www.travelodge.co.uk
Travelodge offers good quality, good value, modern accommodation. Ideal for families, the spacious, en suite bedrooms include remote-control TV, tea and coffee-making facilities and comfortable beds. Meals can be taken at the nearby family restaurant. For further details consult the Hotel Groups page.
ROOMS: 48 en suite s £26-£50; d £26-£50

LEEK, Staffordshire — Map 16 SJ95

★★★62% *Hotel Rudyard*
Lake Rd, Rudyard ST13 8RN
☎ 01538 306208 🖷 01538 306208
This large stone-built Victorian property is set in extensive wooded grounds in the centre of Rudyard village. It provides modern and well-equipped accommodation and a room with a four-poster bed

continued

is also available. There is a function room, a large carvery restaurant and a traditionally furnished bar.
ROOMS: 15 en suite (2 fmly) ⊗ in 2 bedrooms **CONF:** Thtr 80 Class 60 Board 40 **PARKING:** 100 **NOTES:** ⊗ in restaurant

★★70% ® Three Horseshoes Inn & Restaurant
Buxton Rd, Blackshaw Moor ST13 8TW
☎ 01538 300296 🖷 01538 300320
web: www.threeshoesinn.co.uk
Dir: *2m N of Leek on A53*

A family owned hostelry in spacious grounds that include a beer garden and children's play area. The non-smoking bedrooms are tastefully appointed and furnished in keeping with the character of the hotel. Public areas include a choice of bars and eating options - the Bistro is open only for dinner. New for 2006 is an extension of 20 additional quality bedrooms and a small spa.
ROOMS: 6 en suite ⊗ in all bedrooms **CONF:** Thtr 60 Class 50 Board 25 **PARKING:** 80 **NOTES:** ✗ ⊗ in restaurant Closed 24 Dec-1 Jan

Restaurant with Rooms

® Number 64
64 St Edwards St ST13 5DL
☎ 01538 381900 🖷 01538 370918
e-mail: enquiries@number64.com
web: www.number64.com
Dir: *in town centre near junct of A520 & A53, at bottom of hill*
This listed Georgian building, located in the centre of the town, is devoted to food but also offers spacious and comfortably furnished bedrooms. There is also an evening wine bar, two speciality food shops and a coffee lounge, whilst an imaginative menu is offered in the main restaurant.
ROOMS: 3 en suite ⊗ in all bedrooms s fr £65; d fr £75 (incl. bkfst) **CONF:** Board 14 **NOTES:** ✗ ⊗ in restaurant Civ Wed 50

LEEMING BAR, North Yorkshire — Map 19 SE28

★★62% The White Rose
Bedale Rd DL7 9AY
☎ 01677 422707 🖷 01677 425123
e-mail: john@whiterosehotel.co.uk
Dir: *turn off A1 onto A684 and turn left towards Northallerton. Hotel 0.25m on left*
Conveniently situated just minutes from the A1, this commercial hotel boasts pleasant, well-equipped bedrooms contained in a modern block to the rear. Good-value meals are offered in either the traditional bar or attractive dining room.
ROOMS: 18 en suite (2 fmly) (1 GF) s £49; d £63 (incl. bkfst) **LB** **CONF:** BC **PARKING:** 50 **NOTES:** ⊗ in restaurant

LEICESTER, Leicestershire Map 11 SK50
See also Rothley

★★★74% ⊛ Belmont House

De Montfort St LE1 7GR
☎ 0116 254 4773 📠 0116 247 0804
e-mail: info@belmonthotel.co.uk
web: www.belmonthotel.co.uk
Dir: *from A6, take 1st right after rail station. Hotel 200yds on left*

This well established hotel has been welcoming guests under the same family ownership for over 70 years. It is conveniently situated within easy walking distance of the railway station and city centre though sits in a quiet leafy residential area. Extensive public rooms are smartly appointed and include the informal Bowie's Bistro, formal dining in the Cherry Restaurant and a relaxed atmosphere in Jamie's Bar.
ROOMS: 77 en suite (7 fmly) ⊘ in 57 bedrooms s £70-£135; d £90-£140 (incl. bkfst) **LB** **FACILITIES:** STV Gym **CONF:** Thtr 175 Class 75 Board 65 Del from £135 **SERVICES:** Lift **PARKING:** 75 **NOTES:** ⊘ in restaurant Closed 25-26 Dec Civ Wed 120

★★★70% Leicester Stage Hotel

Leicester Rd, Wigston LE18 1JW
☎ 0116 288 6161 📠 0116 257 3900
e-mail: reservations@stagehotel.co.uk
web: www.stagehotel.co.uk
Dir: *M69/M1 junct 21, ring road S to Leicester. Follow Oadby & Wigston signs, right onto A5199 towards Northampton. Hotel on left*

This striking, purpose-built, glass-fronted building is situated to the south of the city centre. Bedrooms vary in style and include executive rooms and four-poster bridal suites. Open-plan public areas include a lounge bar, restaurant and a further seating area in the entrance hall. Staff are friendly and nothing is too much trouble. Ample parking is an added bonus.
ROOMS: 77 en suite (10 fmly) (39 GF) ⊘ in 30 bedrooms s £79-£99; d £89-£109 (incl. bkfst) **LB** **FACILITIES:** STV ⛆ Sauna Gym Jacuzzi Steam room Xmas **CONF:** Thtr 500 Class 320 Board 120 Del from £120 **PARKING:** 200 **NOTES:** ✗ ⊘ in restaurant Civ Wed

★★★68% *Corus hotel Leicester*

Enderby Rd, Blaby LE8 4GD
☎ 0116 278 7898 & 0870 609 6106
📠 0116 278 1974
e-mail: corushotelleicester@corushotels.co.uk
web: www.corushotels.com
Dir: *M1 junct 21, A5460 to Leicester. 4th exit at 1st rdbt, ahead at 2nd, left at 3rd. Follow signs to Blaby, over 4th rdbt. Hotel on left*

Situated in a quiet location on the outskirts of the city, yet remaining convenient for the adjacent link road. Public areas include a bar brasserie, Hunters Restaurant, various meeting rooms and an extensive gym and indoor pool. Bedrooms are comfortably appointed and generally quite spacious, and many are decorated to very high standards.
ROOMS: 48 en suite (5 fmly) ⊘ in 30 bedrooms **FACILITIES: Spa** STV ⛆ Sauna Solarium Gym Steam room **CONF:** Thtr 70 Class 30 Board 36 **PARKING:** 110 **NOTES:** ⊘ in restaurant Civ Wed 60

★★★68% Regency

360 London Rd LE2 2PL
☎ 0116 270 9634 📠 0116 270 1375
e-mail: info@the-regency-hotel.com
web: www.the-regency-hotel.com
Dir: *on A6, 1.5m from city centre*

This friendly hotel is located on the edge of town and provides smart accommodation, suitable for both business and leisure guests. Dining options include an airy conservatory brasserie and a formal restaurant. A relaxing lounge and bar are also available, along with good conference and banqueting facilities. Bedrooms vary in size and style and include some spacious and stylishly appointed rooms.
ROOMS: 32 en suite (4 fmly) s £40-£55; d £56-£70 (incl. bkfst) **FACILITIES:** STV Xmas **CONF:** Thtr 50 Class 50 Board 25 Del from £92 **PARKING:** 40 **NOTES:** ✗ ⊘ in restaurant

⊘ No smoking

Ramada Leicester
Granby St LE1 6ES
☎ 0116 255 5599 Fax 0116 254 4736
e-mail: sales.leicester@ramadajarvis.co.uk
web: www.ramadajarvis.co.uk
Dir: *Take A5460 into city. Follow signs for Leicester Central Station. Granby Street is left off St. George's Way (A594).*

Built in 1898, this Victorian hotel is set in the heart of the city centre. Bedrooms are comfortably appointed for both business and leisure guests.

ROOMS: 104 en suite (4 fmly) no smoking in 80 bedrooms s £90-£110; d £90-£110 **FACILITIES:** STV Xmas **CONF:** Thtr 450 Class 180 Board 35 Del from £145 **SERVICES:** Lift **PARKING:** 120 **NOTES:** no smoking in restaurant Civ Wed 60

Campanile Leicester
St Matthew's Way, 1 Bedford St North LE1 3JE
☎ 0116 261 6600 Fax 0116 261 6601
e-mail: leicester@evergure.co.uk
web: www.envergure.fr
Dir: *A5460. Right at end of road, left at rdbt on A594. Follow Vaughan Way, Burleys Way then St. Matthews Way. Hotel on left.*

This modern building offers accommodation in smart, well-equipped bedrooms, all with en suite bathrooms. Refreshments may be taken at the informal Bistro. For further details consult the Hotel Groups page.

ROOMS: 93 en suite **CONF:** Thtr 50 Class 30 Board 25

Days Inn Leicester Central
14-17 Abbey St LE1 3TE
☎ 0116 251 0666 & 0870 033 9633
Fax 0870 033 9634
e-mail: stephen.hughes@daysinn.co.uk

This modern building offers accommodation in smart, spacious and well-equipped bedrooms, suitable for families and business travellers, and all with en suite bathrooms. Continental breakfast is available and other refreshments may be taken at the nearby family restaurant. For further details consult the Hotel Groups page.

ROOMS: 71 en suite **CONF:** Thtr 150 Class 100 Board 40

Hotel Ibis
St Georges Way, Constitution Hill LE1 1PL
☎ 0116 248 7200 Fax 0116 262 0880
e-mail: H3061@accor-hotels.com
Dir: *From M1/M69 J21, follow town centre signs, central ring road (A594)/railway station, hotel opposite the Leicester Mercury.*

Modern, budget hotel offering comfortable accommodation in bright and practical bedrooms. Breakfast is self-service and dinner is available in the restaurant. For further details, consult the Hotel Groups page.

ROOMS: 94 en suite

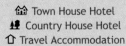

Innkeeper's Lodge Leicester
Hinckley Rd LE3 3PG
☎ 0116 238 7878
web: www.innkeeperslodge.com

A growing concept in the travel accommodation market. Smart rooms meet essential business requirements but also have home comforts. Dining options include all-day menus plus the added advantage of breakfast, which is included in the room price. For further details consult the Hotel Groups page.

ROOMS: 31 rms s £49.95-£55; d £49.95-£55

Premier Travel Inn Leicester Central
Heathley Park, Groby Rd LE3 9QE
☎ 0870 9906398 Fax 0870 9906399
web: www.premiertravelinn.com
Dir: *Off A50, city centre side of County Hall & Glenfield General Hospital*

High quality, modern budget accommodation ideal for both families and business travellers. Spacious, en suite bedrooms feature bath and shower, satellite TV and many have telephones and modem points. The adjacent family restaurant features a wide and varied menu. For further details consult the Hotel Groups page.

ROOMS: 72 en suite s £49.95-£52.95; d £49.95-£52.95 **CONF:** Thtr 10 Class 10 Board 10

Town House Hotel
Country House Hotel
Travel Accommodation

LEICESTER, continued

⌂ Premier Travel Inn Leicester (Forest East)

Hinckley Rd, Leicester Forest East LE3 3GD
☎ 08701 977155 🖹 0116 239 3429
web: www.premiertravelinn.com
Dir: *M1 junct 21 onto A5460. At major junct (Holiday Inn on right), left into Braunstone Lane. After 2m ; left onto A47 towards Hinkley. 400yds on left*
High quality, modern budget accommodation ideal for both families and business travellers. Spacious, en suite bedrooms feature bath and shower, satellite TV and many have telephones and modem points. The adjacent family restaurant features a wide and varied menu. For further details consult the Hotel Groups page.
ROOMS: 40 en suite s £47.95-£50.95; d £47.95-£50.95 **CONF:** Thtr 50 Board 25

⌂ Premier Travel Inn Leicester North West

Leicester Rd, Glenfield LE3 8HB
☎ 0870 9906520 🖹 0870 9906521
web: www.premiertravelinn.com
Dir: *Off A50, just before County Hall and Glenfield General Hospital. Into County Hall on left.*
High quality, modern budget accommodation ideal for both families and business travellers. Spacious, en suite bedrooms feature bath and shower, satellite TV and many have telephones and modem points. The adjacent family restaurant features a wide and varied menu. For further details consult the Hotel Groups page.
ROOMS: 43 en suite s £49.95-£52.95; d £49.95-£52.95 **CONF:** Thtr 25 Class 20 Board 20

⌂ Premier Travel Inn Leicester South (Oadby)

Glen Rise, Oadby LE2 4RG
☎ 0870 9906452 🖹 0870 9906453
web: www.premiertravelinn.com
Dir: *From M1 junct 21 A563 signed South. Right at Leicester racecourse. Follow Market Harborough signs. Dual carriageway, straight on at rdbt. Into single lane, Inn on right*
High quality, modern budget accommodation ideal for both families and business travellers. Spacious, en suite bedrooms feature bath and shower, satellite TV and many have telephones and modem points. The adjacent family restaurant features a wide and varied menu. For further details consult the Hotel Groups page.
ROOMS: 30 en suite s £47.95-£50.95; d £47.95-£50.95 **CONF:** Thtr 10 Class 8 Board 10

⌂ Premier Travel Inn Leicester (Thorpe Astley)

Meridian Business Park, Meridian Way, Braunstone LE19 1LU
☎ 08701 977154 🖹 0116 282 7486
web: www.premiertravelinn.com
Dir: *M1 junct 21 follow signs for A563 (outer ring road) W to Thorpe Astley. Slip road past Texaco garage, Inn on left.*
High quality, modern budget accommodation ideal for both families and business travellers. Spacious, en suite bedrooms feature bath and shower, satellite TV and many have telephones and modem points. The adjacent family restaurant features a wide and varied menu. For further details consult the Hotel Groups page.
ROOMS: 51 en suite s £47.95-£50.95; d £47.95-£50.95 **CONF:** Class 20 Board 20

○ Hotel due to open in late 2005 or 2006
U Star rating not confirmed

⌂ Travelodge (Leicester)

Vaughan Way LE1 4NN
☎ 0870 1911755 🖹 0116 251 0560
web: www.travelodge.co.uk
Travelodge offers good quality, good value, modern accommodation. Ideal for families, the spacious, en suite bedrooms include remote-control TV, tea and coffee-making facilities and comfortable beds. Meals can be taken at the nearby family restaurant. For further details consult the Hotel Groups page.
ROOMS: 95 en suite s fr £26; d fr £26

LEICESTER FOREST MOTORWAY SERVICE AREA (M1), Leicestershire — Map 11 SK50

⌂ Days Inn Leicester

Leicester Forest East, Junction 21 M1 LE3 3GB
☎ 0116 239 0534 🖹 0116 239 0546
e-mail: leicester.hotel@welcomebreak.co.uk
web: www.welcomebreak.co.uk
Dir: *on M1 northbound between junct 21 & 21A*
This modern building offers accommodation in smart, spacious and well-equipped bedrooms, suitable for families and business travellers, and all with en suite bathrooms. Continental breakfast is available and other refreshments may be taken at the nearby family restaurant. For further details see the Hotel Groups page.
ROOMS: 92 en suite s £45-£60; d £45-£60 **CONF:** Board 10

LEIGH DELAMERE MOTORWAY SERVICE AREA (M4), Wiltshire — Map 04 ST87

⌂ Travelodge Chippenham (Eastbound)

SN14 6LB
☎ 08700 850 950 🖹 01666 837112
web: www.travelodge.co.uk
Dir: *between juncts 17 & 18 on M4*
Travelodge offers good quality, good value, modern accommodation. Ideal for families, the spacious, en suite bedrooms include remote-control TV, tea and coffee-making facilities and comfortable beds. Meals can be taken at the nearby family restaurant. For further details consult the Hotel Groups page.
ROOMS: 69 en suite s fr £26; d fr £26

⌂ Travelodge Chippenham (Westbound)

Service Area SN14 6LB
☎ 08700 850 950 🖹 01666 838529
web: www.travelodge.co.uk
Dir: *between juncts 17 & 18 on M4*
Travelodge offers good quality, good value, modern accommodation. Ideal for families, the spacious, en suite bedrooms include remote-control TV, tea and coffee-making facilities and comfortable beds. Meals can be taken at the nearby family restaurant. For further details consult the Hotel Groups page.
ROOMS: 31 en suite s fr £26; d fr £26

LENHAM, Kent — Map 07 TQ85

Top Hotel

★★★★ ◎◎ *Chilston Park*

Sandway ME17 2BE
☎ 01622 859803 🖹 01622 858588
e-mail: chilstonpark-cro@handpicked.co.uk
web: www.handpicked.co.uk
Dir: *from A20 into Lenham village, turn right onto High St, pass railway station on right, 1st left, over crossroads, hotel 0.25 mile on left*
This elegant Grade I listed country house is set in 23 acres of

continued

immaculately landscaped gardens and parkland. An impressive collection of original paintings and antiques creates a unique feel to the property. The sunken Venetian-style restaurant serves modern British food, with French influences. Bedrooms are individual in design; some have four-poster beds and many have garden views.

ROOMS: 30 en suite 23 annexe en suite (2 fmly) (3 GF) **FACILITIES:** STV Fishing **CONF:** Thtr 100 Class 40 Board 40 **SERVICES:** Lift **PARKING:** 100 **NOTES:** ⊗ in restaurant Civ Wed 80

See advert on this page

TV dinner?
Room service at three stars and above

LEOMINSTER, Herefordshire — Map 10 SO45

★★★66% Talbot

West St HR6 8EP
☎ 01568 616347 Fax 01568 614880
e-mail: talbot@bestwestern.co.uk
Dir: *from A49, A44 or A4112, hotel in centre of town*

This charming former coaching inn is located in the town centre and offers an ideal base from which to explore this delightful area. Public areas feature original beams and antique furniture, and include an atmospheric bar and elegant restaurant. Bedrooms are comfortably furnished and equipped. There are also facilities available for private functions and conferences.

ROOMS: 20 en suite (3 fmly) ⊗ in 15 bedrooms s £55-£67; d £68-£82 **LB FACILITIES:** Xmas **CONF:** Thtr 130 Class 25 Board 28 Del from £90 **PARKING:** 22 **NOTES:** ⊗ in restaurant RS 25-Dec

LEOMINSTER, continued

★★66% ❀ Royal Oak
South St HR6 8JA
☎ 01568 612610 🖷 01568 612710
e-mail: reservations@theroyaloakhotel.net
web: www.theroyaloakhotel.net
Dir: *0.25m from railway station*
This privately owned hotel is conveniently located in the town centre. New owners here have already introduced many positive changes including the delightful new Déjà Vu restaurant. The charm and character of the traditional inn have been maintained in other public areas including the welcoming bar. Bedrooms are generally spacious and, at the last inspection, about to undergo complete refurbishment.
ROOMS: 17 en suite (1 fmly) s £45-£50; d £59-£66 (incl. bkfst) **LB**
FACILITIES: Xmas **CONF:** Thtr 140 Class 100 Board 70 Del from £89.50
PARKING: 15 **NOTES:** ⊘ in restaurant

LEWDOWN, Devon Map 03 SX48

Top Hotel

★★★ ❀❀❀ Lewtrenchard Manor
EX20 4PN
☎ 01566 783256 & 783222
🖷 01566 783332
e-mail: info@lewtrenchard.co.uk
web: www.vonessenhotels.co.uk
Dir: *A30 from Exeter to Plymouth/Tavistock road. At T-junct turn right, then left onto old A30 Lewdown road. After 6m left signed Lewtrenchard*
This Jacobean mansion was built in the 1600s, with many interesting architectural features, and is surrounded by its own idyllic grounds in a quiet valley close to the northern edge of Dartmoor. Public rooms include a fine gallery, as well as magnificent carvings and oak panelling. Meals can be taken in the dining room where imaginative and carefully prepared dishes are served using the best of Devon produce. Bedrooms are comfortably furnished and spacious.
ROOMS: 14 en suite (2 fmly) (3 GF) ⊘ in all bedrooms s £95-£120; d £150-£250 (incl. bkfst) **LB** **FACILITIES:** Fishing ♫ Clay pigeon shooting Xmas **CONF:** Thtr 50 Class 40 Board 20 Del from £175 **PARKING:** 50 **NOTES:** ⊘ in restaurant Civ Wed 100

See advert on opposite page

LEWES, East Sussex Map 06 TQ41

★★★ ❀❀ Newick Park Hotel & Country Estate
BN8 4SB
☎ 01825 723633 🖷 01825 723969
e-mail: bookings@newickpark.co.uk
web: www.newickpark.co.uk
(For full entry see Newick and advert on opposite page)

★★★75% ❀❀ *Shelleys Hotel*
High St BN7 1XS
☎ 01273 472361 🖷 01273 483152
e-mail: info@shelleys-hotel-lewes.com
web: www.shelleys-hotel.com
Dir: *A23 to Brighton onto A27 to Lewes. At 1st rdbt left for town centre, after x-rds hotel on left*
This elegant hotel enjoys a central location and is steeped in history, with previous owners including the Earl of Dorset. Nowadays Shelleys boasts beautifully appointed bedrooms, furnished and decorated in a traditional style. The elegant restaurant overlooks the enclosed garden and serves good food using local produce.
ROOMS: 19 en suite (2 fmly) ⊘ in 4 bedrooms **FACILITIES:** STV ♫
CONF: Thtr 50 Class 24 Board 28 **PARKING:** 25 **NOTES:** ⊘ in restaurant Civ Wed 50

LEYBOURNE, Kent Map 06 TQ65

⌂ Premier Travel Inn Maidstone (Leybourne)
Castle Way ME19 5TR
☎ 08701 977170 🖷 01732 844474
web: www.premiertravelinn.com
Dir: *M20 junct 4, take A228, Inn on left*
High quality, modern budget accommodation ideal for both families and business travellers. Spacious, en suite bedrooms feature bath and shower, satellite TV and many have telephones and modem points. The adjacent family restaurant features a wide and varied menu. For further details consult the Hotel Groups page.
ROOMS: 40 en suite s £46.95-£49.95; d £46.95-£49.95

LEYBURN, North Yorkshire Map 19 SE19

★64% Golden Lion
Market Place DL8 5AS
☎ 01969 622161 🖷 01969 623836
e-mail: AnneGoldenLion@aol.com
web: www.thegoldenlion.co.uk
Dir: *on A684 in market square*
Dating back to 1765, this traditional inn overlooks the cobbled market square where weekly markets still take place. Bedrooms, including some family rooms, offer appropriate levels of comfort. The restaurant, with murals depicting scenes from the Dales, offers a good range of meals. Food can also be enjoyed in the cosy bar, a popular meeting place for local people.
ROOMS: 15 rms (14 en suite) (5 fmly) s £26-£34; d £52-£68 (incl. bkfst)
LB **SERVICES:** Lift **NOTES:** ⊘ in restaurant Closed 25 & 26 Dec

LEYLAND, Lancashire Map 15 SD52

★★★67% *Leyland*

Leyland Way PR5 2JX
☎ 01772 422922 🖷 01772 622282
e-mail: leylandhotel@feathers.uk.com
web: www.feathers.uk.com
Dir: *M6 junct 28 turn left at end of slip road, hotel 100mtrs on left*

This purpose-built hotel enjoys a convenient location, just off the M6, within easy reach of Preston and Blackpool. Spacious public areas have benefited from a stylish refurbishment by the hotel's new owners, as have several bedrooms. Amenities include extensive conference and banqueting facilities as well as a smart leisure club.

ROOMS: 93 en suite (6 fmly) (31 GF) ⊗ in 30 bedrooms
FACILITIES: Spa supervised Sauna Solarium Jacuzzi ch fac
CONF: BC Thtr 500 Class 250 Board 250 **PARKING:** 150 **NOTES:** ⊗ in restaurant Civ Wed 200

LICHFIELD, Staffordshire Map 10 SK10

★★★★77% Swinfen Hall
Swinfen WS14 9RE
☎ 01543 481494 01543 480341
e-mail: info@swinfenhallhotel.co.uk
web: www.swinfenhallhotel.co.uk
Dir: *set back from A38 2.5m outside Lichfield, towards Birmingham*

Dating from 1757, this lavishly decorated mansion has been painstakingly restored by the present owners. Public rooms are particularly stylish, with intricately carved ceilings and impressive oil portraits. Rooms on the first floor boast period features and tall sash windows; those on the second floor (the former servants' quarters) are smaller and more contemporary by comparison. Service within the award-winning restaurant is both professional and attentive.
ROOMS: 19 en suite s £120-£195; d £140-£245 (incl. bkfst) **FACILITIES:** STV Fishing 100 acres of parkland with 45 acres private deer park **CONF:** Thtr 96 Class 50 Board 120 Del from £160 **PARKING:** 80 **NOTES:** in restaurant Civ Wed 120

★★★68% The George
12-14 Bird St WS13 6PR
☎ 01543 414822 01543 415817
e-mail: mail@thegeorgelichfield.co.uk
web: www.thegeorgelichfield.co.uk
Dir: *from Bowling Green Island on A461 take Lichfield exit. Left at next island into Swan Road as road bears left turn right for Hotel straight ahead*

Situated in the city centre, this privately owned hotel provides good quality, well-equipped accommodation, which includes a room with a four-poster bed. Facilities here include a large ballroom, plus several other rooms for meetings and functions.
ROOMS: 45 en suite (5 fmly) in 28 bedrooms s £54-£120; d £64-£130 (incl. bkfst) **LB** **CONF:** Thtr 110 Class 60 Board 40 Del from £125 **SERVICES:** Lift **PARKING:** 45 **NOTES:** in restaurant Civ Wed 100

★★★68% Little Barrow
62 Beacon St WS13 7AR
☎ 01543 414500 01543 415734
e-mail: reservations@tlbh.co.uk
web: www.tlbh.co.uk
Conveniently situated for the cathedral and the city, this friendly hotel provides well-equipped accommodation. The cosy lounge bar, popular with locals and visitors alike, has a good range of drinks and a choice of bar meals. More formal dining is offered in the pleasant restaurant. Service is relaxed and attentive.
ROOMS: 32 en suite (2 fmly) in 8 bedrooms s £50-£69; d £68-£80 (incl. bkfst) **LB** **FACILITIES:** Xmas **CONF:** BC Thtr 150 Class 100 Board 80 Del from £105 **PARKING:** 60 **NOTES:** in restaurant Civ Wed 120

★★64% Olde Corner House
Walsall Rd, Muckley Corner WS14 0BG
☎ 01543 372182 01543 372211
e-mail: philip@emerton.fsbusiness.co.uk
Dir: *at junct of A5 & A461*
Well located on the A5 this family owned and run hotel offers modern bedrooms and friendly and attentive service. A good range of good value food is available either in the bar or restaurant.
ROOMS: 23 en suite (1 fmly) (5 GF) in 12 bedrooms s fr £50; d fr £65 (incl. bkfst) **LB** **PARKING:** 60

★★62% *Angel Croft*
Beacon St WS13 7AA
☎ 01543 258737 01543 415605
Dir: *opposite west gate entrance to Cathedral*
This traditional, family-run, Georgian hotel is close to the cathedral and city centre. A comfortable lounge leads into a pleasantly appointed dining room; there is also a cosy bar on the lower ground floor. Bedrooms vary and most are spacious, particularly those in the adjacent Westgate House.
ROOMS: 10 rms (8 en suite) 8 annexe en suite (1 fmly) **CONF:** Thtr 30 Board 20 **PARKING:** 60 **NOTES:** in restaurant Closed 25 & 26 Dec RS Sun evenings

Innkeeper's Lodge Lichfield
Stafford Rd WS13 8JB
☎ 01543 415789 01543 420752
web: www.innkeeperslodge.com
Dir: *on A51, 0.75m outside city centre*
A growing concept in the travel accommodation market. Smart rooms meet essential business requirements but also have home comforts. Dining options include all-day menus plus the added advantage of breakfast, which is included in the room price. For further details consult the Hotel Groups page.
ROOMS: 10 en suite s £48-£59.95; d £48-£59.95

Premier Travel Inn Lichfield
Rykneld St, Fradley WS13 8RD
☎ 0870 9906438 0870 9906439
web: www.premiertravelinn.com
Dir: *From N, M6 junct 15, A500/A50 to Uttoxeter. A50 onto A38 to Lichfield. Hotel on left past petrol station. From S, M42 junct 9, A446, A38 to Lichfield, then Fradley signs. Do not exit at Fradley Park*
High quality, modern budget accommodation ideal for both families and business travellers. Spacious, en suite bedrooms feature bath and shower, satellite TV and many have telephones and modem points. The adjacent family restaurant features a wide and varied menu. For further details consult the Hotel Groups page.
ROOMS: 30 en suite s £46.95-£49.95; d £46.95-£49.95 **CONF:** Thtr 40

LIFTON, Devon
Map 03 SX38

★★★77% (2 rosettes) Arundell Arms
PL16 0AA
☎ 01566 784666 Fax 01566 784494
e-mail: reservations@arundellarms.com
Dir: *1m off A30 in Lifton*

This former coaching inn, boasting a long history, sits in the heart of a quiet Devon village. It is internationally famous for its country pursuits such as winter shooting and angling. Bedrooms, many refurbished, offer individual style and comfort. Public areas are full of character and offer a relaxed atmosphere. Award-winning cuisine is a celebration of local produce.
ROOMS: 21 en suite (4 GF) s fr £95; d £150-£180 (incl. bkfst) **LB** **FACILITIES:** STV Fishing Skittle alley, 3 acre lake, Shooting in Winter, Fly fishing school **CONF:** Thtr 100 Class 30 Board 40 Del from £143 **PARKING:** 70 **NOTES:** ⊘ in restaurant Closed 3 days Xmas Civ Wed 80

Restaurant with Rooms

(guest house) (rosette) Tinhay Mill Guest House and Restaurant
Tinhay PL16 0AJ
☎ 01566 784201 Fax 01566 784201
e-mail: tinhay.mill@talk21.com
web: www.tinhaymillrestaurant.co.uk
Dir: *A30/A388, approach Lifton, restaurant at bottom of village on right*
Former mill cottages dating from the 15th century, this is now a delightful restaurant-with-rooms of much character and charm. Beams and open fireplaces set the scene, with everything geared to ensure a relaxed and comfortable stay. Bedrooms are spacious and well-equipped, with many thoughtful extras. Cuisine is taken seriously here, with the best of local produce used.
ROOMS: 3 en suite s £45-£50; d £65-£72 (incl. bkfst) **LB** **FACILITIES:** Xmas **PARKING:** 18 **NOTES:** 🐕 no dogs No children 12yrs ⊘ in restaurant

LIMPLEY STOKE, Wiltshire
Map 04 ST76

★★★66% Limpley Stoke
BA2 7FZ
☎ 01225 723333 Fax 01225 722406
e-mail: latonalsh@aol.com
Dir: *4.5m S of Bath on A36 left at lights on viaduct, take next right, just before bridge into Lower Stoke. Hotel opposite Hope Pole Inn*
This quietly located former Georgian mansion is on the outskirts of Bath in a peaceful village setting; easily accessible from the M4. Attentive levels of service and friendly hospitality are to be found throughout the hotel. Bedrooms come in various shapes and sizes and some enjoy memorable views over the valley below.
ROOMS: 60 en suite (8 fmly) ⊘ in 10 bedrooms s £75-£99; d £89-£110 (incl. bkfst) **LB** **FACILITIES:** ♫ Xmas **CONF:** Thtr 120 Class 40 Board 30 Del from £105 **SERVICES:** Lift **PARKING:** 90 **NOTES:** ⊘ in restaurant Civ Wed 120

LINCOLN, Lincolnshire
Map 17 SK97

★★★73%
The Bentley Hotel & Leisure Club
Newark Rd, South Hykeham LN6 9NH
☎ 01522 878000 Fax 01522 878001
e-mail: infothebentleyhotel@btconnect.com
web: www.thebentleyhotel.uk.com
Dir: *from A1 take A46 E towards Lincoln for 10m. Over 1st rdbt on Lincoln Bypass to hotel 50yds on left*

This modern hotel offers bright, attractive accommodation with a stylish leisure suite including a large pool with access for the less able. The bedrooms are spacious and well equipped with air conditioning. This hotel is especially noteworthy for its special facilities and the care given to less able guests.
ROOMS: 80 en suite (5 fmly) (26 GF) ⊘ in 50 bedrooms s £80-£90; d £95-£130 (incl. bkfst) **LB** **FACILITIES:** STV (indoor pool) Sauna Gym Jacuzzi Beauty salon, Steam Room Xmas **CONF:** Thtr 300 Class 150 Board 30 Del from £110 **SERVICES:** Lift **PARKING:** 140 **NOTES:** 🐕 no dogs ⊘ in restaurant Civ Wed 120

★★★71% (rosette) Branston Hall
Branston Park, Branston LN4 1PD
☎ 01522 793305 Fax 01522 790734
e-mail: info@branstonhall.com
web: www.branstonhall.com
Dir: *5 min drive from Lincoln on B1188*

Many original features have been retained in this country house, which sits in beautiful grounds complete with a lake. There is an elegant restaurant, a spacious bar and a beautiful lounge in addition to impressive conference and leisure facilities. Individually styled bedrooms vary in size and include several with four-poster beds.
ROOMS: 43 en suite 7 annexe en suite (3 fmly) (4 GF) ⊘ in 6 bedrooms s £70-£90; d £99-£164.50 (incl. bkfst) **LB** **FACILITIES: Spa** STV (indoor pool) Sauna Gym Jacuzzi Jogging circuit Xmas **CONF:** Thtr 200 Class 54 Board 40 Del £100 **SERVICES:** Lift **PARKING:** 100 **NOTES:** 🐕 no dogs ⊘ in restaurant Civ Wed 160

LINCOLN, continued

★★★70% Courtyard by Marriott Lincoln

Brayford Wharf North LN1 1YW
☎ 01522 544244 ▤ 01522 560805
e-mail: res.lincourtyard@kewgreen.co.uk
web: www.kewgreen.co.uk
Dir: *From A46 onto A57 to Lincoln Central. Left at lights, right, take next right onto Lucy Tower St then right onto Brayford Wharf North for hotel on right*

A short walk away from the city centre, this smart hotel has an idyllic waterfront location overlooking Brayford Pool. Bedrooms are spacious and comfortably appointed, with many extra facilities. Public areas are focused around a galleried restaurant that overlooks the spacious lounge bar.
ROOMS: 97 en suite (9 GF) ⊗ in 57 bedrooms s £69-£98; d £96-£120 (incl. bkfst) **LB** **FACILITIES:** STV Fitness Room Xmas **CONF:** Thtr 30 Class 20 Board 20 Del from £95 **SERVICES:** Lift air con **PARKING:** 100 **NOTES:** 🐕 ⊗ in restaurant

★★★70% Washingborough Hall

Church Hill, Washingborough LN4 1BE
☎ 01522 790340 ▤ 01522 792936
e-mail: enquiries@washingboroughhallhotel.com
web: www.washingboroughhallhotel.com
Dir: *on B1190 into Washingborough. Right at rdbt, hotel 500yds on left*

This Georgian manor stands on the edge of the quiet village of Washingborough among attractive gardens, with an outdoor swimming pool available in the summer. Public rooms are pleasantly furnished and comfortable, whilst the restaurant offers interesting menus. Bedrooms are individually designed, and most have views out over the grounds and countryside.
ROOMS: 14 en suite (1 fmly) ⊗ in all bedrooms s £65-£90; d £90-£135 (incl. bkfst) **FACILITIES:** 🏊 supervised 🎾 Xmas **CONF:** Thtr 50 Class 25 Board 25 Del from £95 **PARKING:** 50 **NOTES:** 🐕 ⊗ in restaurant Civ Wed 50

★★★68% The Lincoln

Eastgate LN2 1PN
☎ 01522 520348 ▤ 01522 051080
e-mail: sales@thelincolnhotel.com
web: www.thelincolnhotel.com
Dir: *adjacent to cathedral*
This privately owned modern hotel enjoys superb uninterrupted views of Lincoln Cathedral. There are ruins of the Roman wall and Eastgate in the grounds. Bedrooms have been refurbished in a contemporary style with up-to-the-minute facilities. An airy restaurant and bar, plus a comfortable lounge are provided, in addition to substantial conference and meeting facilities. Good hospitality is notable here.
ROOMS: 72 en suite (4 fmly) ⊗ in 46 bedrooms s £79-£89; d £89-£109 (incl. bkfst) **LB** **CONF:** BC Thtr 100 Class 50 Board 40 Del from £99 **SERVICES:** Lift **PARKING:** 110 **NOTES:** 🐕 ⊗ in restaurant Civ Wed 100

★★★66% The White Hart

Bailgate LN1 3AR
☎ 01522 526222 ▤ 01522 531798
e-mail: info@whitehart-lincoln.co.uk
web: www.whitehart-lincoln.co.uk
Dir: *turn off A46 (right) at island onto B1226, through Newport Arch. Hotel 0.5m on left as road bends left*

Lying in the shadow of Lincoln's magnificent cathedral, this hotel is perfectly positioned for exploring the shops and sights of this medieval city. The attractive bedrooms are furnished and decorated in a traditional style and many have views of the cathedral. Given the hotel's central location, parking is a real benefit.
ROOMS: 48 en suite (10 fmly) ⊗ in 23 bedrooms **FACILITIES:** STV **CONF:** Thtr 160 Board 103 **SERVICES:** Lift **NOTES:** ⊗ in restaurant Civ Wed

★★73% Hillcrest

15 Lindum Ter LN2 5RT
☎ 01522 510182 ▤ 01522 538009
e-mail: reservations@hillcrest-hotel.com
web: www.hillcrest-hotel.com
Dir: *from A15 Wragby Rd and Lindum Rd, turn into Upper Lindum St at sign. Left at bottom for hotel 200mtrs on right*
The hospitality offered by Jenny Bennett and her staff is one of the strengths the Hillcrest, which sits in a quiet residential location just a seven minute' walk from the cathedral and city shops. Well-equipped bedrooms come in a variety of sizes, and the pleasant conservatory/dining room, with views over the park, offers a good range of freshly prepared food. A computer room is available for residents.
ROOMS: 14 en suite (5 fmly) (6 GF) ⊗ in 6 bedrooms s £56-£78; d £85-£95 (incl. bkfst) **LB** **CONF:** Thtr 20 Class 16 Board 12 Del from £112 **PARKING:** 8 **NOTES:** ⊗ in restaurant Closed 23 Dec-3 Jan

See advert on opposite page

★★72% Castle

Westgate LN1 3AS
☎ 01522 538801 📠 01522 575457
e-mail: aa@castlehotel.net
web: www.castlehotel.net
Dir: *follow signs for Historic Lincoln. Hotel at NE corner of castle*

Located in the heart of historic Lincoln, this privately owned and run hotel has been carefully restored to offer comfortable, attractive, well-appointed accommodation. Bedrooms are thoughtfully equipped, particularly the deluxe rooms and the spacious Lincoln Suite. Specialising in traditional fayre, Knights Restaurant has an interesting medieval theme.
ROOMS: 16 en suite 3 annexe en suite (5 GF) ⊗ in 12 bedrooms s £67-£100; d £89-£160 (incl. bkfst) **LB** **CONF:** Thtr 20 Class 40 Board 30 **PARKING:** 20 **NOTES:** No children 8yrs ⊗ in restaurant RS Evening of Dec 25-26

★★66% Tower Hotel

38 Westgate LN1 3BD
☎ 01522 529999 📠 01522 560596
e-mail: tower.hotel@btclick.com
Dir: *from A46 follow signs to Lincoln N then to Bailgate area. Through arch and 2nd left*

This hotel faces the Norman castle wall and is in a very convenient location for the city. The relaxed and friendly atmosphere is one of the strengths here. Public rooms are smartly appointed and include a modern lounge bar, a separate, quieter lounge and a stylish brasserie dining area; food is also readily available in the bar.
ROOMS: 14 en suite (1 fmly) ⊗ in 2 bedrooms s £62-£72; d £80-£90 (incl. bkfst) **LB** **CONF:** Thtr 24 Class 24 Board 16 Del from £72.50 **PARKING:** 6 **NOTES:** ⊗ in restaurant Closed 24 Dec-26 Dec & 1Jan

Indoor Swimming pool
Indoor Swimming pool (heated)
Outdoor Swimming pool
Outdoor Swimming pool (heated)

⌂ *Hotel Ibis Lincoln*

Runcorn Rd (A46), off Whisby Rd LN6 3QZ
☎ 01522 698333 📠 01522 698444
e-mail: H3161@accor-hotels.com
Dir: *off A46 ring road onto Whisby Rd. 1st turning on left*
Modern, budget hotel offering comfortable accommodation in bright and practical bedrooms. Breakfast is self-service and dinner is available in the restaurant. For further details, consult the Hotel Groups page.
ROOMS: 86 en suite **CONF:** Thtr 35 Class 12 Board 20

⌂ Premier Travel Inn Lincoln

Lincoln Rd, Canwick Hill LN4 2RF
☎ 08701 977156 📠 01522 542521
web: www.premiertravelinn.com
Dir: *Approx 1 mile south of city centre at the junction of B1188 to Branston and B1131 to Brakebridge Heath*
High quality, modern budget accommodation ideal for both families and business travellers. Spacious, en suite bedrooms feature bath and shower, satellite TV and many have telephones and modem points. The adjacent family restaurant features a wide and varied menu. For further details consult the Hotel Groups page.
ROOMS: 40 en suite s £49.95; d £49.95

Late for dinner? Quality standards mean that last orders for dinner vary according to star rating and should be no earlier than:
★★ 7.00pm ★★★ 8:00pm ★★★★ 9:00pm ★★★★★ 10:00pm

LINCOLN, continued

Travelodge
Thorpe on the Hill LN6 9AJ
☎ 08700 850 950 Fax 01522 697213
web: www.travelodge.co.uk
Dir: *on A46 Newark/Lincoln rdbt*
Travelodge offers good quality, good value, modern accommodation. Ideal for families, the spacious, en suite bedrooms include remote-control TV, tea and coffee-making facilities and comfortable beds. Meals can be taken at the nearby family restaurant. For further details consult the Hotel Groups page.
ROOMS: 32 en suite s fr £26; d fr £26

LIPHOOK, Hampshire Map 05 SU83

★★★75% **_Old Thorns Hotel, Golf & Country Club_**
Griggs Green GU30 7PE
☎ 01428 724555 Fax 01428 725036
e-mail: info@oldthorns.com
web: www.oldthorns.com
Dir: *A3 Guildford to Portsmouth road. Griggs Green exit S of Liphook*

This smartly presented hotel offers a range of leisure facilities, including a golf course, indoor pool, sauna, solarium and fitness room. The bedrooms are spacious, and equipped with good facilities. There is a choice of eating options: the Japanese Nippon Kan Restaurant or the Greenview, which enjoys views over the golf course.
ROOMS: 29 en suite 4 annexe rms (3 en suite) (2 fmly) (14 GF) in 9 bedrooms **FACILITIES:** STV 18 Sauna Solarium Gym Putt green Steam room, Beauty treatment rooms **CONF:** Thtr 100 Class 50 Board 30 **PARKING:** 80 **NOTES:** Civ Wed 77

Travelodge
GU30 7TT
☎ 08700 850 950 Fax 01428 727619
web: www.travelodge.co.uk
Dir: *on n'bound carriageway of A3, 1m from Griggs Green exit at Shell services*
Travelodge offers good quality, good value, modern accommodation. Ideal for families, the spacious, en suite bedrooms include remote-control TV, tea and coffee-making facilities and comfortable beds. Meals can be taken at the nearby family restaurant. For further details consult the Hotel Groups page.
ROOMS: 40 en suite s fr £26; d fr £26

Popped the question? Hotels with Civ wed in their entry are licensed for civil wedding ceremonies. Maximum numbers for the ceremony only are shown e.g. Civ wed 120

LISKEARD, Cornwall & Isles of Scilly Map 02 SX26

Top Hotel

★★ **Well House**
St Keyne PL14 4RN
☎ 01579 342001 Fax 01579 343891
e-mail: enquiries@wellhouse.co.uk
web: www.wellhouse.co.uk
Dir: *from Liskeard on A38 take B3254 to St Keyne (3 miles). At church fork left and hotel 0.5m*
Tucked away in an attractive valley and set in impressive grounds, Well House enjoys a tranquil setting. Friendly staff provide attentive yet relaxed service and add to the elegant atmosphere of the house. The comfortable lounge offers deep cushioned sofas and an open fire and in the intimate bar an extensive choice of wines and drinks is available. The accomplished cuisine features carefully sourced ingredients from local suppliers resulting in enjoyable dining.
ROOMS: 9 en suite (1 fmly) s £80-£110; d £125-£180 (incl. bkfst) LB **FACILITIES:** Xmas **PARKING:** 30 **NOTES:** in restaurant Closed 2 wks in Jan

LITTLE LANGDALE, Cumbria Map 18 NY30

★★69% **Three Shires Inn**
LA22 9NZ
☎ 015394 37215 Fax 015394 37127
e-mail: enquiry@threeshiresinn.co.uk
web: www.threeshiresinn.co.uk
Dir: *off A593, 2.5m from Ambleside at 2nd junct signed Langdales & Wrynose Pass. 1st left after 0.5m, hotel in 1m*
Enjoying an outstanding rural location, this family-run inn was built in 1872. The brightly decorated bedrooms are individual in style and many offer panoramic views. The attractive lounge features a roaring fire in the cooler months and there is a traditional style bar with a great selection of local ales. Meals can be taken in either the bar or cosy restaurant.
ROOMS: 10 en suite (1 fmly) in all bedrooms s £37-£68; d £74-£100 (incl. bkfst) LB **PARKING:** 21 **NOTES:** in restaurant Closed Xmas RS Dec & Jan

LITTLE WEIGHTON, East Riding of Yorkshire Map 17 SE93

★★66% **_The Rowley Manor_**
Rowley Rd HU20 3XR
☎ 01482 848248 Fax 01482 849900
e-mail: info@rowleymanor.com
Dir: *leave A63 at South Cave/Market Weighton exit. Into South Cave, right into Beverley Rd at clock tower, and follow signs for Rowley*
Rowley Manor is a Georgian country house and former vicarage set in rural gardens and parkland. Bedrooms are traditionally

continued

decorated and furnished with period pieces; many rooms have panoramic views, and some are particularly spacious. The public rooms include a magnificent pine-panelled study, and the gardens feature a croquet lawn.
ROOMS: 16 en suite (2 fmly) **FACILITIES:** ch fac **CONF:** Thtr 110 Class 48 Board 50 **PARKING:** 100 **NOTES:** ⊗ in restaurant Civ Wed 110

LIVERPOOL, Merseyside Map 15 SJ39

★★★★73%
Radisson SAS Hotel Liverpool
107 Old Hall St L3 9BD
☎ 0151 966 1500 🖷 0151 966 1501
e-mail: info.liverpool@radissonsas.com
web: www.radisson.com
Dir: *Follow signs for Liverpool City Centre & Albert Dock. Turn right onto Old Hall St. from the main Leeds St dual carriageway.*

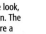

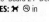

This smart, new hotel enjoys an enviable location on the city's waterfront. The stylish bedrooms are designed in two eye-catching schemes, Ocean and Urban and are particularly well equipped; junior suites and business rooms offer additional choices. Public areas include extensive conference and leisure facilities, the trendy White Bar and Filini Restaurant, serving imaginative, accomplished Italian cuisine.
ROOMS: 204 en suite ⊗ in 131 bedrooms s £99-£135; d £99-£135 LB **FACILITIES:** STV Sauna Solarium Gym Jacuzzi **CONF:** BC Thtr 130 Class 70 Board 44 Del from £160 **SERVICES:** Lift air con **NOTES:** ⊗ in restaurant Civ Wed 130

★★★★70% **Thornton Hall Hotel and Health Club**
Neston Rd CH63 1JF
☎ 0151 336 3938 🖷 0151 336 7864
e-mail: reservations@thorntonhallhotel.com
web: www.thorntonhallhotel.com
(For full entry see Thornton Hough)

★★★★69%
Liverpool Marriott Hotel City Centre
1 Queen Square L1 1RH
☎ 0151 476 8000 🖷 0151 474 5000
e-mail: liverpool.city@marriotthotels.co.uk
web: www.marriott.co.uk
Dir: *from city centre follow signs for Queen Sq Parking. Hotel adjacent*
An impressive modern hotel located in the heart of the city. The elegant public rooms include a ground-floor café bar, and a cocktail bar and stylish Oliver's Restaurant on the first floor. The hotel also boasts a well-equipped, indoor leisure health club with pool. Bedrooms are stylishly appointed and benefit from a host of extra facilities.
ROOMS: 146 en suite (29 fmly) ⊗ in 120 bedrooms **FACILITIES:** STV Sauna Solarium Gym Jacuzzi Xmas **CONF:** Thtr 300 Class 90 Board 30 **SERVICES:** Lift air con **PARKING:** 158 **NOTES:** ⊗ in restaurant Civ Wed 150

★★★★68%
Liverpool Marriott Hotel South
Speke Aerodrome L24 8QD
☎ 0870 4007269 🖷 0151 494 5053
e-mail: liverpool.south@marriotthotels.co.uk
web: www.marriott.co.uk
Dir: *M62 junct 6, take Knowsley Expressway towards Speke. At end of Expressway right onto A561 towards Liverpool. Continue for approx 4 miles, hotel on left just after Estuary Commerce Park*
Previously Liverpool airport, this hotel has a distinctive look, reflected by its art deco architecture and interior design. The spacious bedrooms are fully air-conditioned and feature a comprehensive range of facilities. Feature rooms include the presidential suite in the base of the old control tower.
ROOMS: 164 en suite (50 fmly) (46 GF) ⊗ in 100 bedrooms s £99-£285; d £99-£285 LB **FACILITIES: Spa** STV supervised Squash Sauna Solarium Gym Jacuzzi Selected use of David Lloyd Leisure Centre adjacent to hotel **CONF:** Thtr 280 Class 120 Board 24 Del from £115 **SERVICES:** Lift air con **PARKING:** 200 **NOTES:** ⊗ in restaurant Civ Wed 100

★★★68% **The Royal**
Marine Ter, Waterloo L22 5PR
☎ 0151 928 2332 🖷 0151 949 0320
e-mail: enquiries@liverpool-royalhotel.co.uk
web: www.liverpool-royalhotel.co.uk
Dir: *6.5m NW of city centre, left off A565 Liverpool to Southport road at monument. Hotel at bottom of road*
Dating back to 1815, this Grade II listed hotel is situated on the outskirts of the city, beside the Marine Gardens. Bedrooms are smartly appointed and some feature four-poster beds and spa baths. Spacious public areas enjoy splendid views and include an elegant restaurant, an attractive bar lounge and a conservatory.
ROOMS: 25 en suite (5 fmly) ⊗ in 1 bedroom s £50-£75; d £85-£95 (incl. bkfst) **FACILITIES:** STV **CONF:** Thtr 100 Class 70 Board 40 **PARKING:** 25 **NOTES:** ⊗ in restaurant

★★★67% **Alicia**
3 Aigburth Dr, Sefton Park L17 3AA
☎ 0151 727 4411 🖷 0151 727 6752
e-mail: aliciahotel@feathers.uk.com
web: www.feathers.uk.com
This stylish and friendly hotel overlooks Sefton Park and is just a few minutes' drive from both the city centre and John Lennon Airport. Bedrooms are well equipped and comfortable. Day rooms include a striking modern restaurant and bar. Extensive, stylish function facilities make this a popular wedding venue.
ROOMS: 41 en suite (8 fmly) ⊗ in 16 bedrooms s fr £55; d £65-£200 (incl. bkfst) LB **FACILITIES:** STV Xmas **CONF:** Thtr 120 Class 80 Board 40 Del from £110 **SERVICES:** Lift **PARKING:** 40 **NOTES:** ⊗ in restaurant Civ Wed 120

U **Hope Street Hotel**
40 Hope St L1 9DA
☎ 0151 709 3000 🖷 0151 709 2454
e-mail: sleep@hopestreethotel.co.uk
Dir: *on entering follow signs for Cathedrals and Universities*
At the time of going to press, the star classification for this hotel was not confirmed. Please refer to the AA internet site www.theAA.com for current information.
ROOMS: 48 en suite (10 fmly) ⊗ in 32 bedrooms s £125-£315; d £125-£315 **FACILITIES:** STV Xmas **CONF:** Thtr 45 Class 45 Board 20 **SERVICES:** Lift **NOTES:** ⊗ in restaurant

TV dinner?
Room service at three stars and above

LIVERPOOL, continued

⌂ Campanile
Chaloner St, Queens Dock L3 4AJ
☎ 0151 709 8104 📠 0151 709 8725
e-mail: liverpool@campanile-hotels.com
web: www.envergure.fr
Dir: *follow tourist signs marked Albert Dock. Hotel on waterfront*

This modern building offers accommodation in smart, well-equipped bedrooms, all with en suite bathrooms. Refreshments may be taken at the informal Bistro. For further details consult the Hotel Groups page.
ROOMS: 100 en suite s £47-£60; d £47-£60 **CONF:** Thtr 20 Class 18 Board 16 Del from £75

⌂ *Hotel Ibis Liverpool*
27 Wapping L1 8LY
☎ 0151 706 9800 📠 0151 706 9810
e-mail: H3140@accor-hotels.com
Dir: *M62 follow signs for Albert Dock. Hotel entrance by Dock*
Modern, budget hotel offering comfortable accommodation in bright and practical bedrooms. Breakfast is self-service and dinner is available in the restaurant. For further details, consult the Hotel Groups page.
ROOMS: 127 en suite

⌂ Innkeeper's Lodge Liverpool North
502 Queen's Dr, Stoneycroft L13 0AS
☎ 0151 254 2271 📠 0151 254 2394
web: www.innkeeperslodge.com
Dir: *from M62 take A5080 N towards Bootle Docks. Continue at lights at junct with A57. Hotel on left in Queen's Drive*
A growing concept in the travel accommodation market. Smart rooms meet essential business requirements but also have home comforts. Dining options include all-day menus plus the added advantage of breakfast, which is included in the room price. For further details consult the Hotel Groups page.
ROOMS: 21 annexe en suite s £49.95; d £49.95

⌂ Innkeeper's Lodge Liverpool South
531 Aigburth Rd L19 9DN
☎ 0151 494 1032 📠 0151 494 3345
web: www.innkeeperslodge.com
Dir: *on A56, opposite Liverpool cricket ground*
A growing concept in the travel accommodation market. Smart rooms meet essential business requirements but also have home comforts. Dining options include all-day menus plus the added advantage of breakfast, which is included in the room price. For further details consult the Hotel Groups page.
ROOMS: 32 en suite s £49.95; d £49.95 **CONF:** Thtr 18 Class 20 Board 12

⌂ Premier Travel Inn Liverpool (Aintree)
1 Ormskirk Rd, Aintree L9 5AS
☎ 08701 977157 📠 0151 525 8696
web: www.premiertravelinn.com
Dir: *M58/57 then follow A59 to Liverpool. Past Aintree Retail Park, left at lights into Aintree Racecourse. Inn on left*
High quality, modern budget accommodation ideal for both families and business travellers. Spacious, en suite bedrooms feature bath and shower, satellite TV and many have telephones and modem points. The adjacent family restaurant features a wide and varied menu. For further details consult the Hotel Groups page.
ROOMS: 40 en suite s £46.95-£48.95; d £46.95-£48.95 **CONF:** Thtr 10

⌂ Premier Travel Inn Liverpool Albert Dock
East Britannia Building, Albert Dock L3 4AD
☎ 0870 9906432 📠 0870 9906433
web: www.premiertravelinn.com
Dir: *just off A5036. In city centre, follow brown signs for Albert Dock & Beatles Story. Inn by Beatles Story*
High quality, modern budget accommodation ideal for both families and business travellers. Spacious, en suite bedrooms feature bath and shower, satellite TV and many have telephones and modem points. The adjacent family restaurant features a wide and varied menu. For further details consult the Hotel Groups page.
ROOMS: 130 en suite s £52.95-£55.95; d £52.95-£55.95

⌂ Premier Travel Inn Liverpool City Centre
Vernon St L2 2AY
☎ 0870 238 3323 📠 0870 241 9000
web: www.premiertravelinn.com
Dir: *from M62 follow Liverpool City Centre and Birkenhead Tunnel signs. At rdbt take 3rd exit onto Dale St then right into Vernon St. Inn on left*
High quality, modern budget accommodation ideal for both families and business travellers. Spacious, en suite bedrooms feature bath and shower, satellite TV and many have telephones and modem points. The adjacent family restaurant features a wide and varied menu. For further details consult the Hotel Groups page.
ROOMS: 165 en suite s £52.95-£55.95; d £52.95-£55.95

⌂ Premier Travel Inn Liverpool (Roby)
Roby Rd, Huyton L36 4HD
☎ 0870 9906596 📠 0870 9906597
web: www.premiertravelinn.com
Dir: *Just off M62 junct 5 on A5080*
High quality, modern budget accommodation ideal for both families and business travellers. Spacious, en suite bedrooms feature bath and shower, satellite TV and many have telephones and modem points. The adjacent family restaurant features a wide and varied menu. For further details consult the Hotel Groups page.
ROOMS: 53 en suite s £46.95-£48.95; d £46.95-£48.95 **CONF:** Thtr 25 Class 15 Board 22

⌂ Premier Travel Inn Liverpool (Tarbock)
Wilson Rd, Tarbock L36 6AD
☎ 08701 977159 📠 0151 480 9361
web: www.premiertravelinn.com
Dir: *at junct M62/M57. M62 junct 6 take A5080 Huyton then 1st right into Wilson Rd*
High quality, modern budget accommodation ideal for both families and business travellers. Spacious, en suite bedrooms feature bath and shower, satellite TV and many have telephones and modem points. The adjacent family restaurant features a wide and varied menu. For further details consult the Hotel Groups page.
ROOMS: 40 en suite s £46.95-£48.95; d £46.95-£48.95

⇧ Premier Travel Inn Liverpool (West Derby)

Queens Dr, West Derby L13 0DL
☎ 08701 977160 📠 0151 220 7610
web: www.premiertravelinn.com
Dir: *At end of M62 turn right under flyover onto A5058 (following signs to football stadium). Inn is 1.5 m on left, just past Esso garage*
High quality, modern budget accommodation ideal for both families and business travellers. Spacious, en suite bedrooms feature bath and shower, satellite TV and many have telephones and modem points. The adjacent family restaurant features a wide and varied menu. For further details consult the Hotel Groups page.
ROOMS: 84 en suite s £46.95-£48.95; d £46.95-£48.95

⇧ Travelodge (Liverpool Central)

25 Haymarket L1 6ER
☎ 08700 850 950 📠 0151 227 5838
web: www.travelodge.co.uk
Travelodge offers good quality, good value, modern accommodation. Ideal for families, the spacious, en suite bedrooms include remote-control TV, tea and coffee-making facilities and comfortable beds. Meals can be taken at the nearby family restaurant. For further details consult the Hotel Groups page.
ROOMS: 105 en suite s fr £26; d fr £26

⇧ Travelodge (Liverpool South)

Brunswick Dock, Sefton St L3 4BH
☎ 08700 850 950 📠 0151 707 7769
web: www.travelodge.co.uk
Travelodge offers good quality, good value, modern accommodation. Ideal for families, the spacious, en suite bedrooms include remote-control TV, tea and coffee-making facilities and comfortable beds. Meals can be taken at the nearby family restaurant. For further details consult the Hotel Groups page.
ROOMS: 31 en suite s fr £26; d fr £26

LIZARD, THE, Cornwall & Isles of Scilly — Map 02 SW71

★★★68% ***Housel Bay***

Housel Cove TR12 7PG
☎ 01326 290417 & 290917 📠 01326 290359
e-mail: info@houselbay.com
web: www.houselbay.com
Dir: *A39 or A394 to Helston, then A3083. At Lizard sign turn left, at school left and down lane to hotel*
This long-established hotel has stunning views across the Western Approaches, equally enjoyable from the lounge and many of the bedrooms. Most bedrooms have high standards of comfort with modern facilities. Enjoyable cuisine is available in the stylish dining room, after which guests might enjoy a stroll to the end of the garden which leads directly onto the Cornwall coastal path.
ROOMS: 20 en suite (1 fmly) ⊘ in 10 bedrooms **FACILITIES:** STV
CONF: Thtr 20 Class 16 Board 12 **SERVICES:** Lift **PARKING:** 37
NOTES: ✈ ⊘ in restaurant RS Winter

LOCKINGTON Hotels are listed under Nottingham East Midlands Airport

LOLWORTH, Cambridgeshire — Map 12 TL36

⇧ Travelodge

Huntingdon Rd CB3 8DR
☎ 08700 850 950 📠 01954 781335
web: www.travelodge.co.uk
Dir: *on A14 northbound, 3m N of M11 junct 14*
Travelodge offers good quality, good value, modern accommodation. Ideal for families, the spacious, en suite bedrooms include remote-control TV, tea and coffee-making facilities and comfortable beds. Meals can be taken at the nearby family restaurant. For further details consult the Hotel Groups page.
ROOMS: 36 en suite s fr £26; d fr £26

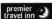

R

S

T

V

W

London Plan 1
0 1 2 miles
0 1 2 3 kilometres
Central London Congestion Charging Zone
Northwood
Harrow Weald
Stanmore
Edgware
Mill Hill
Highwood Hill
Finchley
Church End
Pinner
Wealdstone
HARROW
Kenton
Kingsbury
Queensbury
Colindale
Burnt Oak
Belmont
Hendon
West Hendon
Brent Cross
Hampstead Garden Suburb
Golders Green
Eastcote
Eastcote Village
Ruislip
South Ruislip
Ickenham
Rayners Lane
North Harrow
Harrow on the Hill
South Harrow
Preston
North Wembley
WEMBLEY
Neasden
Cricklewood
Willesden
Willesden Green
Kilburn
Sudbury
Northolt Aerodrome
North Hillingdon
Northolt
Perivale
Alperton
Stonebridge
Harlesden
Kensal Green
Park Royal
North Acton
Greenford
Hillingdon
Hayes End
Yeading
Wood End
Southall
Hanwell
EALING
Acton
East Acton
North Kensington
Notting Hill
Shepherds Bush
KENSINGTON
Hayes
Norwood Green
Heston Motorway Service Area
Heston
OSTERLEY PARK
Chiswick
HAMMERSMITH
Kew
West Brompton
FULHAM
Brentford
KEW GARDENS
Barnes
Mortlake
East Sheen
Putney
Cranford
HEATHROW AIRPORT
HOUNSLOW
Isleworth
RICHMOND
Hatton
Roehampton
East Bedfont
Whitton
Twickenham
Petersham
RICHMOND PARK
Feltham
Lower Feltham
Ham
WIMBLEDON COMMON
WIMBLEDON
Felthamhill
Hanworth
Hampton Hill
Teddington
BUSHY PARK
Hampton
Hampton Wick
KINGSTON UPON THAMES
Norbiton
New Malden
Raynes Park
Morden
Charlton
Sunbury
Littleton
West Molesey
Hampton Court
HAMPTON COURT PARK
East Molesey
Berrylands
Motspur Park
Shepperton
Walton-on-Thames
Queen Elizabeth II Reservoir
Thames Ditton
Surbiton
Long Ditton
Tolworth
Old Malden
Worcester Park
A B C D
1 2 3 4 5 6

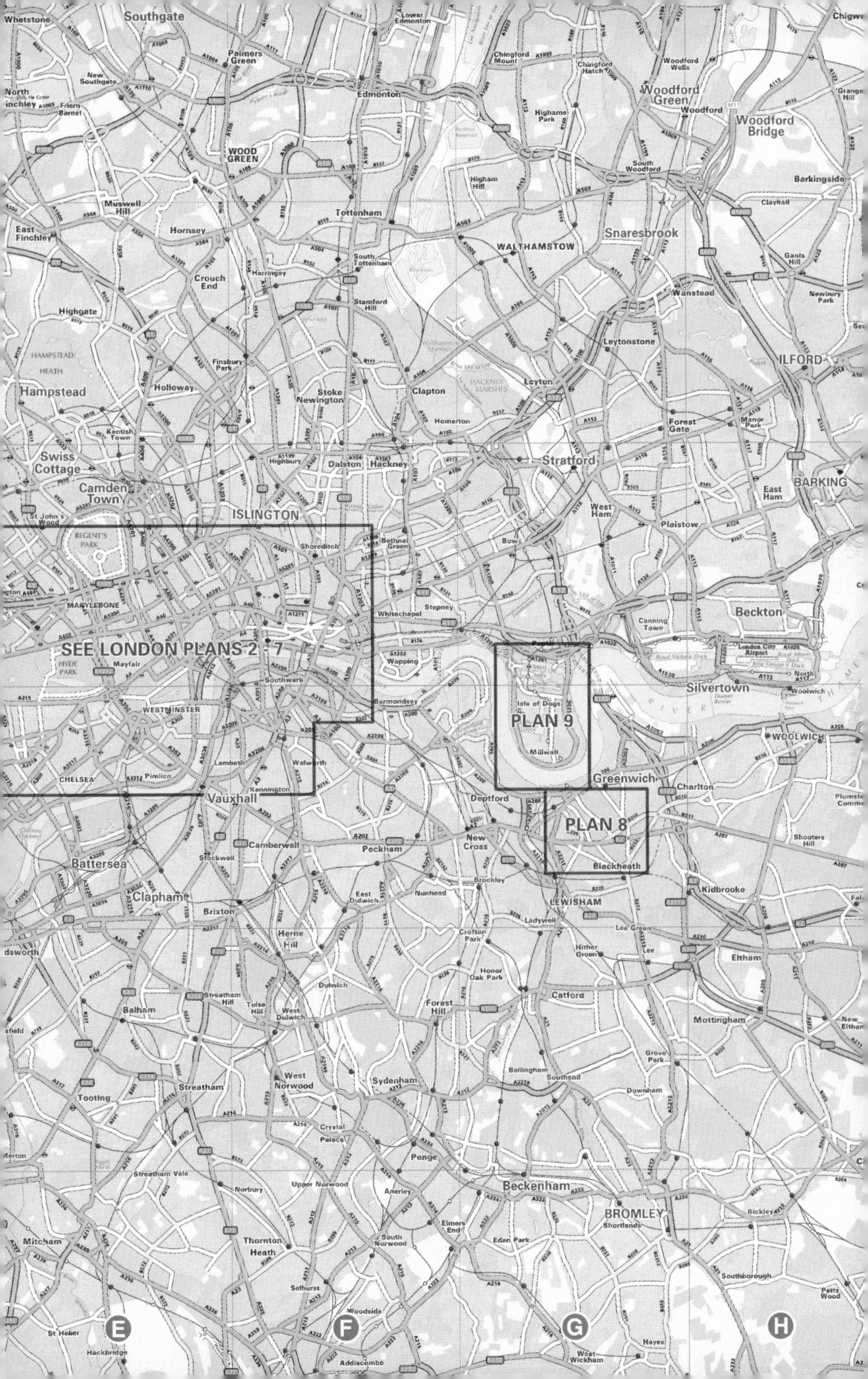

Whetstone
Southgate
Lower Edmonton
Chingford Mount
Chingford Hatch
Woodford Wells
Chigwell
Palmers Green
New Southgate
North Finchley
Friern Barnet
Edmonton
Woodford Green
Woodford
Grange Hill
Woodford Bridge
Highams Park
WOOD GREEN
South Woodford
Higham Hill
Barkingside
Muswell Hill
Tottenham
Clayhall
East Finchley
Hornsey
Snaresbrook
WALTHAMSTOW
South Tottenham
Gants Hill
Crouch End
Harringay
Wanstead
Newbury Park
Stamford Hill
Highgate
HAMPSTEAD HEATH
Leytonstone
Finsbury Park
ILFORD
Hampstead
Holloway
Stoke Newington
Clapton
HACKNEY MARSHES
Leyton
Homerton
Kentish Town
Forest Gate
Manor Park
Swiss Cottage
Highbury
Dalston
Hackney
Stratford
Camden Town
BARKING
East Ham
ISLINGTON
West Ham
St John's Wood
Plaistow
REGENT'S PARK
Shoreditch
Bethnal Green
Bow
MARYLEBONE
Stepney
Whitechapel
Beckton
Canning Town
Poplar
SEE LONDON PLANS 2–7
HYDE PARK
Mayfair
Wapping
London City Airport
Royal Victoria Dock
Royal Albert Dock
King George V Dock
North Woolwich
Southwark
Isle of Dogs
Silvertown
Thames Barrier
WESTMINSTER
Bermondsey
PLAN 9
RIVER THAMES
Millwall
WOOLWICH
Lambeth
Walworth
CHELSEA
Pimlico
Kennington
Vauxhall
Greenwich
Charlton
Deptford
Plumstead Common
PLAN 8
New Cross
Camberwell
Peckham
Shooters Hill
Battersea
Stockwell
Blackheath
Brockley
Nunhead
Kidbrooke
Clapham
Brixton
East Dulwich
LEWISHAM
Ladywell
Lee Green
Herne Hill
Crofton Park
Hither Green
Lee
Eltham
Wandsworth
Honor Oak Park
Dulwich
Streatham Hill
Catford
Balham
Tulse Hill
West Dulwich
Forest Hill
Mottingham
New Eltham
Grove Park
Bellingham
Southend
West Norwood
Sydenham
Streatham
Downham
Tooting
Crystal Palace
Merton
Penge
Streatham Vale
Norbury
Upper Norwood
Beckenham
Anerley
BROMLEY
Bickley
Shortlands
Mitcham
Elmers End
South Norwood
Thornton Heath
Eden Park
Southborough
Petts Wood
Selhurst
Woodside
St Helier
E
F
G
H
Hayes
Hackbridge
Addiscombe
West Wickham

London Plan 2
0 220 440 yards
0 100 200 300 400 metres
A
B
C
D
1
2
3
4
5
6
Maida Vale
Paddington Recreation Ground
Maida Vale Station
Middlesex CCC (Lord's Cricket Ground)
Lord's Tour & MCC Museum
Maida Vale Hospital
BBC Studios
Warwick Avenue Station
Little Venice
Westbourne Green
Royal Oak Station
PADDINGTON
Paddington Station
St Marys Hospital
Delmere Hotel
Best Western Paddington Court Hotel and Suites
The Royal Park
Bayswater
Berjaya Eden Park
Royal Lancaster Hotel
The Gresham Hyde Park
Corus hotel Hyde Park
Pembridge Court Hotel
Ramada Hyde Park
The Abbey Court
Notting Hill Gate Stn
Queensway Station
Bayswater Stn
Lancaster Gate Station
Kensington Gardens
MAIDA VALE
KILBURN PARK ROAD
SHIRLAND ROAD
HARROW ROAD
WESTWAY
A40
ST JOHN'S WOOD ROAD
GROVE END ROAD
CLIFTON GARDENS
EDGWARE ROAD
WARWICK AV
BISHOP'S BRIDGE ROAD
WESTBOURNE GROVE
QUEENSWAY
PORCHESTER RD
CHEPSTOW ROAD
PEMBRIDGE VILLAS
PEMBRIDGE RD
NOTTING HL GATE
BAYSWATER ROAD
EASTBOURNE TERRACE
CRAVEN ROAD
PRAED STREET
SUSSEX GARDENS
KENSINGTON
PALACE GDNS TER
4

E
F
G
H
Regent's Park
Regent's Park
London Central Mosque
London Business School
Queen Mary's Garden
Inner Circle
Outer Circle
Chester Road
Cumberland Gate
Clarence Gate
Royal Academy of Music
York Bridge
Park Square
Regent's Park Stn
Great Portland St Stn
Madame Tussaud's & The London Planetarium
Baker Street Stn
Marylebone Station
Lisson Grove
MARYLEBONE
Mayfair
Hyde Park
Speakers Corner
Marble Arch Station
Bond Street Stn
Edgware Road Stn
Emb of USA
MARYLEBONE ROAD
PARK ROAD
BAKER ST
GLOUCESTER PLACE
DORSET SQ
EDGWARE ROAD
OXFORD ST
WIGMORE STREET
PORTLAND PL
NEW BOND STREET
PARK LANE
BAYSWATER ROAD
CUMBERLAND GATE
ALBANY STREET
Ramada Marylebone
Dorset Square Hotel
The Landmark London
Sherlock Holmes Hotel
The Langham
Jurys Clifton-Ford Hotel
The Mandeville
London Marriott Hotel Marble Arch
Radisson SAS Portman Hotel
Hyatt Regency London, The Churchill
Montcalm - Hotel Nikko London
Mostyn Hotel
Radisson Edwardian Sussex Hotel
Radisson Edwardian Berkshire Hotel
London Marriott Hotel Park Lane
London Marriott Hotel, Grosvenor Square
Claridge's
Millennium Hotel London - Mayfair
The Connaught
Le Meridien Grosvenor House
The Westbury Hotel
Chesterfield Mayfair
The Washington Mayfair Hotel
The Dorchester
Meliá White House Regents Park
3
4
Congestion Charging Zone boundary

London Plan 3
0 220 440 yards
0 100 200 300 400 metres
A
B
C
D
Regent's Park
Somers Town
King's Cross Station
St Pancras Station
British Library
Euston Station
Premier Travel Inn (London King's Cross)
Travelodge (London King's Cross)
Novotel London Euston
Premier Travel Inn (London Euston)
Hotel Ibis London Euston
St Pancras
Meliá White House Regents Park
Radisson Edwardian Grafton Hotel
University College London
Holiday Inn Bloomsbury
The Hotel Russell
Coram's Fields Playground
National Hosp for Sick Children (Great Ormond St)
Bloomsbury
Grange Fitzrovia
Grange Langham Court
The Montague on the Gardens
Grange Blooms Hotel
Grange Whitehall
British Museum
The Bonnington in Bloomsbury
Grange Holborn Hotel
Radisson Edwardian Kenilworth Hotel
Radisson Edwardian Marlborough Hotel
Jurys Great Russell Street
Renaissance London Chancery Court
The Berners Hotel
Kingsway Hall
St Giles
Middlesex Hosp
Radisson Edwardian Mountbatten Hotel
Travelodge (London Covent Garden)
Royal Opera House
Soho
Best Western Shaftesbury Hotel
China Town
One Aldwych
Courtauld Institute Somerset House
The Westbury Hotel
Strand
Strand Palace Hotel
The Savoy
Radisson Edwardian Hampshire Hotel
Le Meridien Piccadilly
Brown's
Royal Academy of Arts
22 Jermyn Street Townhouse
Radisson Edwardian Pastoria Hotel
National Gallery
National Portrait Gal
Trafalgar Square
Radisson Edwardian May Fair Hotel
De Vere Cavendish St James's London
Sofitel St James London
The Ritz
The Stafford
Admiralty Arch
Old Admiralty
Charing Cross Stn
Embankment Station
Queen Elizabeth Golden Jubilee Bridge
Victoria Embankment Gardens
EUSTON ROAD
OXFORD STREET
REGENT STREET
PICCADILLY
PALL MALL
STRAND
KINGSWAY
CHARING CROSS RD
TOTTENHAM COURT RD
SHAFTESBURY AV
HIGH HOLBORN
2
5

Congestion Charging Zone boundary
E
F
G
H
6
5
4
3
2
1
7
9
5
PENTONVILLE ROAD
A501
CITY ROAD
A1
A7
WAKLEY STREET
JOHN ST
ST JOHN ST
GOSWELL ROAD
KING'S CROSS RD
PENTON RISE
FINSBURY
Travelodge (London Farringdon)
Travelodge (London Islington)
Jurys Inn London
Myddelton Square
Chadwell St
Amwell St
Lloyd Baker St
Margery Street
Wharton St
Great Percy Street
ROSEBERY AVENUE
A401
FARRINGDON ROAD
CALTHORPE STREET
Mount Pleasant (Postal Sorting Office)
Clerkenwell
CLERKENWELL ROAD
A5201
B502
LEVER STREET
OLD STREET
St Luke's
The City University
Spencer Street
Percival St
Moorfields Eye Hospital
BATH STREET
BUNHILL ROW
B144
SHEPHERDESS WALK
Wenlock St
Nile Street
Central Street
Malmaison Charterhouse Square
Farringdon Station
Barbican Station
The Barbican
BEECH ST (BELOW)
A1 ALDERSGATE ST
CHISWELL
LONDON WALL
A1211
Moorgate Stn
Central London Mkts
St Bartholomews Hospital
Chancery Lane Stn
HIGH HOLBORN
HOLBORN
Holborn
HOLBORN CIRCUS
A40
HOLBORN VIAD
NEWGATE ST
THEOBALD'S ROAD
Gray's Inn
Lincoln's Inn
CHANCERY LA
HATTON GARDEN
FETTER LA
NEW FETTER LA
B521
A201
FARRINGDON STREET
SHOE LANE
Royal Courts of Justice
London School of Economics
FLEET ST
A4
STRAND
ALDWYCH
Inns of Court and Chancery
Stock Exchange
St Paul's Station
St Paul's Cathedral
Paternoster Square
Guildhall
Cheapside
Poultry
Bank Stn
Mansion House Station
City Thameslink Station
Ludgate Hill
Cannon St
Cannon Street Stn
Queen Victoria St
UPPER THAMES ST
NEW BRIDGE STREET
Blackfriars Station
Blackfriars Stn
VICTORIA EMB
EMBANKMENT
Temple Stn
Swissôtel The Howard, London
Kings College London
CITY OF LONDON
River Thames
Millennium Bridge
Southwark Bridge
SOUTHWARK BRIDGE ROAD
QUEEN ST PLACE
Blackfriars Bridge
Waterloo Bridge
Entrance to Strand Underpass (northbound only)
WATERLOO BRIDGE
A301
Oxo Tower Wharf
Shakespeare's Globe Theatre
Bankside
Tate Modern
The London Television Centre (LWT)
Royal National Theatre
National Film Theatre
Upper Ground
STAMFORD ST
A3200
SOUTHWARK ST
BLACKFRIARS RD
Hopton St
Holland Street
Sumner St
Premier Travel Inn (London Southwark)
Mercure London City Bankside
Novotel London City South
Southwark Cath
Thames Path

London Plan 4
Pembridge Sq
Pembridge
Pembridge Rd
B415
6
The Abbey Court
Notting Hill Gate Stn
Notting Hl Gate
A402
Queensway Station
Orme Sq Gate
Black Lion Gate
Porchester Gate
2
Bayswater Road
The Gresham Hyde Park
Lancaster Gate
Corus hotel Hyde Park
Marlborough Gate
Kensington Gardens
The Broad Walk
Round Pond
Kensington Palace
Palace Green
Kensington Church St
Palace Gdns Ter
B405
Vicarage Ga
A4204
Campden Hill Rd
Kensington Pl
Edge St
Peel St
Campden Street
Bedford Gardens
Sheffield Terrace
Airlie Gdns
5
Tor Gdns
Gloucester Walk
Camden Hl
Hornton St
Holland St
Duchess of Bedford's Wk
Phillimore Gardens
Kensington & Chelsea Town Hall
York House Place
Lancer Square
Royal Garden Hotel
Albert Memorial
Alexandra Gate
West Carriage Drive
Kensington Road
Hyde Park Gate
Kensington Gore
Milestone Hotel & Apartments
Baglioni
Kensington House Hotel
Palace Ga
De Vere Gdns
Royal College of Art
Royal Geographical Soc
Royal Albert Hall
Prince Consort Road
Princes Gdns
Royal College of Music
Imperial College
Science Museum
Exhibition Rd
4
Kensington High St
High Street Kensington Stn
Young Street
Derry St
Wright's Lane
A315
Phillimore Walk
Essex Vls
Allen St
Copthorne Tara Hotel London Kensington
Cottesmore Gdns
Victoria Road
Launceston Pl
Gloucester Road
Queen's Gate
Queen's Ga Ms
Hyde Park Gate
Canning Pl
St Alban's Gv
Eldon Road
KENSINGTON
Kynance Ms
Cornwall Gdns
Elvaston Pl
Imperial College Rd
RCA
Natural History Museum
Earth Galleries
Victoria Albert M
B316
Earl's Court Rd
Abingdon Villas
Scarsdale Villas
Stratford Rd
Lexham Gardens
Pembroke Square
Pembroke Road
3
Grange Strathmore
Radisson Edwardian Vanderbilt Hotel
Cromwell Road
A4
Thurloe Pl
Cromwell Hospital
London Marriott Kensington
Pennant Ms
A3220
Logan Place
Comfort Inn Kensington
Premier Travel Inn (London Kensington)
Gloucester Rd Stn
Millennium Bailey's Hotel London Kensington
Millennium Gloucester Hotel London Kensington
Harrington Rd
Stanhope Gdns
South Kensington Station
Harrington Hall
Jurys Kensington Hotel
Onslow Sq
Onslow Gdns
B304
Courtfield Gardens
Collingham Rd
Barkston Gdns
Burns Hotel
K+K Hotel George
Earl's Court
Earl's Court Station
Nevern Sq
20 Nevern Square
2
Warwick Road
Philbeach Gardens
The Bentley Kempinski
South Kensington
The Cranley Hotel
Old Brompton Road
A3218
Wetherby Gdns
Bolton Gdns
Bramham Gdns
Penywern Rd
Earl's Ct Square
The Boltons
Cresswell Place
Drayton Gardens
Roland Gardens
Cranley Gardens
Onslow Gardens
Fulham Road
A308
CHEL
Earl's Court Exhibition Centre
Redcliffe Gardens
Finborough Road
Coleherne Rd
Redcliffe Sq
Tregunter Road
Cathcart Rd
Hollywood Rd
Elm Park Gdns
Old Church Street
Mulberry Walk
The Vale
Beaufort St
Callow Street
1
West Brompton Station
Hotel Ibis London Earl's Court
A
West Brompton
B
C
D
Chelsea & Westminster
A3217
Lillie Rd
Seagrave Rd
Tamworth

Hyde Park
The Serpentine
Serpentine Road
South Carriage Drive
Knightsbridge
Mayfair
Belgravia
Brompton
Le Meridien Grosvenor House
Millennium Hotel London - Mayfair
The Connaught
Chesterfield Mayfair
The Washington Mayfair Hotel
The Dorchester
Athenaeum Hotel & Apartments
Four Seasons Hotel London
InterContinental London
Apsley House, The Wellington Museum
Hyde Park Corner Stn
Queen Mother Gate
Albert Gate
Mandarin Oriental Hyde Park
Sheraton Park Tower
The Berkeley
The Lanesborough
Basil Street Hotel
The Capital
Millennium Hotel London Knightsbridge
Knightsbridge Stn
Harrods Store
The Lowndes Hotel
The Carlton Tower Hotel
The Halkin Hotel
Sheraton Belgravia
Parkes Townhouse Hotel
The Beaufort
The Draycott
Brompton Oratory
Buckingham Palace
Buckingham Palace Gardens
The Royal Mews
Constitution Hill
The Goring
Victoria Station
Victoria Coach Station
Sloane Sq Stn
Duke of York's HQ
Burtons Court
Royal Hospital Museum
Royal Hospital Chelsea
Chelsea Barracks
National Army Museum
Chelsea Physic Garden
Chelsea Bridge
Grosvenor Bridge
Green Park
KENSINGTON ROAD
KNIGHTSBRIDGE
BROMPTON ROAD
SLOANE STREET
KING'S ROAD
PIMLICO ROAD
CHELSEA BRIDGE ROAD
EBURY BRIDGE ROAD
BUCKINGHAM PALACE ROAD
GROSVENOR PLACE
PARK LANE
ROYAL HOSPITAL ROAD
EMBANKMENT
Congestion Charging Zone boundary
0 220 440 yards
0 100 200 300 400 metres
E
F
G
H
2
5

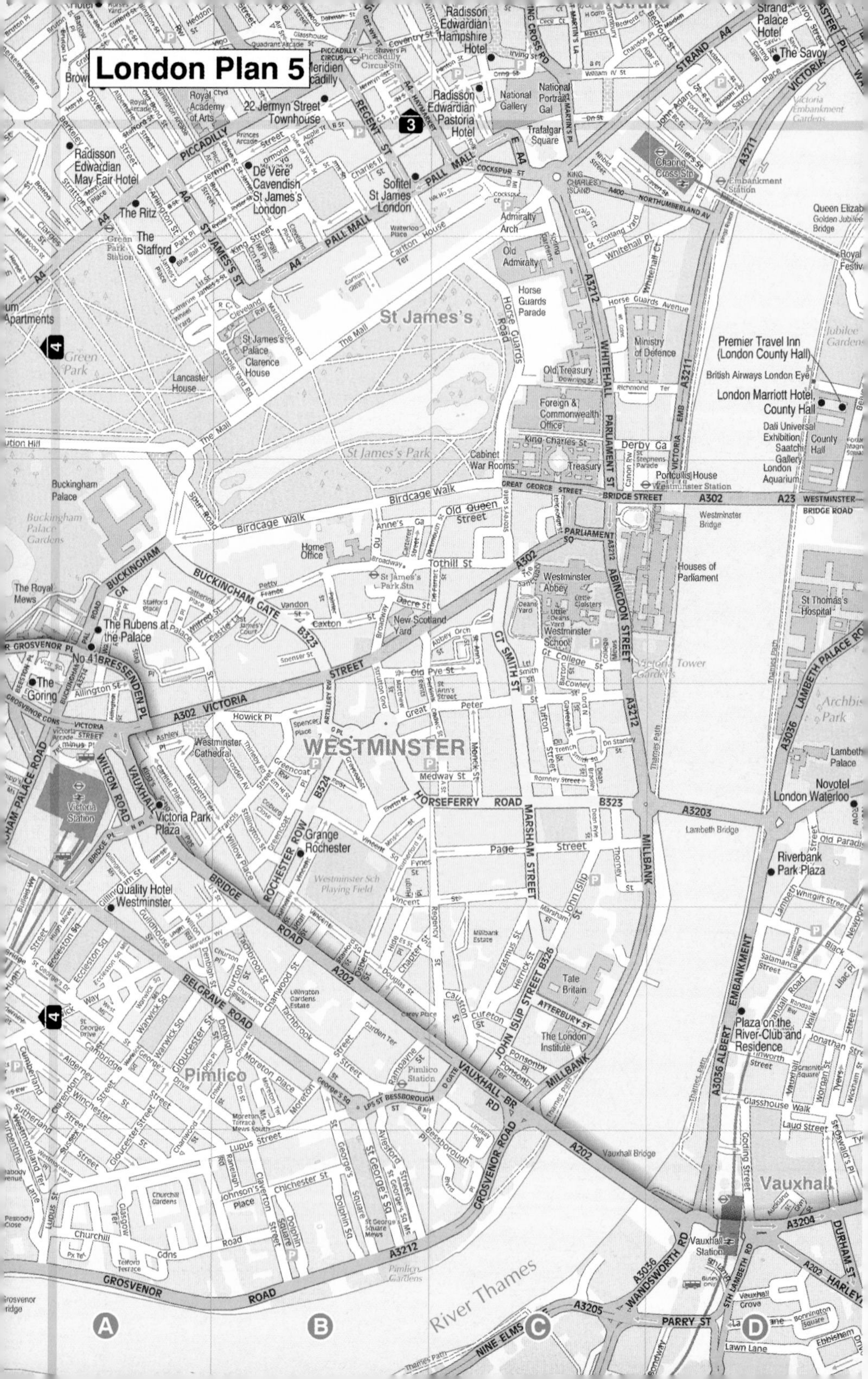

London Plan 5
Piccadilly Circus
Piccadilly Circus Stn
Meridien Piccadilly
Radisson Edwardian Hampshire Hotel
Royal Academy of Arts
22 Jermyn Street Townhouse
Radisson Edwardian Pastoria Hotel
National Gallery
National Portrait Gal
Trafalgar Square
Strand Palace Hotel
The Savoy
STRAND
Victoria Embankment Gardens
Charing Cross Stn
Embankment Station
NORTHUMBERLAND AV
Queen Elizabeth Golden Jubilee Bridge
Royal Festival
Radisson Edwardian May Fair Hotel
PICCADILLY
De Vere Cavendish St James's London
Sofitel St James London
PALL MALL
COCKSPUR ST
KING CHARLES I ISLAND
The Ritz
The Stafford
Green Park Station
ST JAMES'S ST
Carlton House Ter
Admiralty Arch
Old Admiralty
Horse Guards Parade
Horse Guards Road
Horse Guards Avenue
WHITEHALL
Ministry of Defence
St James's
The Mall
St James's Palace
Clarence House
Lancaster House
Green Park
Old Treasury
Foreign & Commonwealth Office
King Charles St
Premier Travel Inn (London County Hall)
British Airways London Eye
London Marriott Hotel, County Hall
Dali Universal Exhibition
Saatchi Gallery
London Aquarium
County Hall
Jubilee Gardens
Buckingham Palace
Buckingham Palace Gardens
St James's Park
Cabinet War Rooms
Treasury
Derby Ga
Portcullis House
Westminster Station
PARLIAMENT ST
VICTORIA EMB
GREAT GEORGE STREET
BRIDGE STREET
WESTMINSTER BRIDGE ROAD
Westminster Bridge
Birdcage Walk
Old Queen Street
Home Office
Tothill St
PARLIAMENT SQ
Houses of Parliament
St Thomas's Hospital
The Royal Mews
BUCKINGHAM GATE
Petty France
St James's Park Stn
Westminster Abbey
Westminster School
Victoria Tower Gardens
ABINGDON STREET
LAMBETH PALACE RD
Archbishop's Park
The Rubens at the Palace
No 41
BRESSENDEN PL
New Scotland Yard
Caxton St
VICTORIA STREET
GT SMITH ST
Lambeth Palace
The Goring
Westminster Cathedral
WESTMINSTER
Novotel London Waterloo
Victoria Station
VAUXHALL BRIDGE ROAD
WILTON ROAD
Victoria Park Plaza
HORSEFERRY ROAD
Lambeth Bridge
Grange Rochester
ROCHESTER ROW
MARSHAM STREET
Page Street
MILLBANK
Riverbank Park Plaza
Quality Hotel Westminster
Westminster Sch Playing Field
Millbank Estate
ALBERT EMBANKMENT
Tate Britain
ATTERBURY ST
BELGRAVE ROAD
Lillington Gardens Estate
The London Institute
Plaza on the River-Club and Residence
Pimlico
Pimlico Station
BESSBOROUGH ST
VAUXHALL BR RD
Glasshouse Walk
Vauxhall Bridge
Vauxhall
Vauxhall Station
GROSVENOR ROAD
Churchill Gdns
Pimlico Gardens
River Thames
WANDSWORTH RD
NINE ELMS
PARRY ST
STH LAMBETH RD
HARLEYFORD
DURHAM ST
A
B
C
D

CITY OF LONDON
River Thames
Millennium Bridge
Blackfriars Bridge
Southwark Bridge
Waterloo Bridge
Entrance to Strand Underpass (northbound only)
Oxo Tower Wharf
Shakespeare's Globe Theatre
Tate Modern
The London Television Centre (LWT)
Royal National Theatre
National Film Theatre
IMAX Cinema
Shell Centre
International Rail Terminal
Waterloo Station
Waterloo East Stn
Southwark Station
Lambeth North Stn
Borough Stn
Elephant and Castle Stn
Elephant and Castle Stn
Kennington Station
Premier Travel Inn (London Southwark)
Mercure London City Bankside
Novotel London City South
St GEORGES CIRCUS
South Bank University
Imperial War Museum
Geraldine Mary Harmsworth Park
London Coll of Printing
LAMBETH
Newington
The Borough
Newington Gardens
Surrey Cricket Ground (The Oval)
STAMFORD ST
SOUTHWARK STREET
UNION STREET
THE CUT
BLACKFRIARS ROAD
WATERLOO ROAD
BOROUGH ROAD
WESTMINSTER BR RD
LAMBETH ROAD
ST GEORGE'S RD
LONDON ROAD
NEWINGTON BUTTS
NEWINGTON CSWY
NEW KENT ROAD
KENNINGTON ROAD
KENNINGTON PARK ROAD
KENNINGTON LANE
WALWORTH ROAD
SOUTHWARK BRIDGE ROAD
BOROUGH HIGH ST
GREAT DOVER ST
A3200
A201
A301
A23
A3
A302
A3202
A3204
A215
B300
6
5
4
3
2
1
E
F
G
H
Congestion Charging Zone boundary
0 220 440 yards
0 100 200 300 400 metres

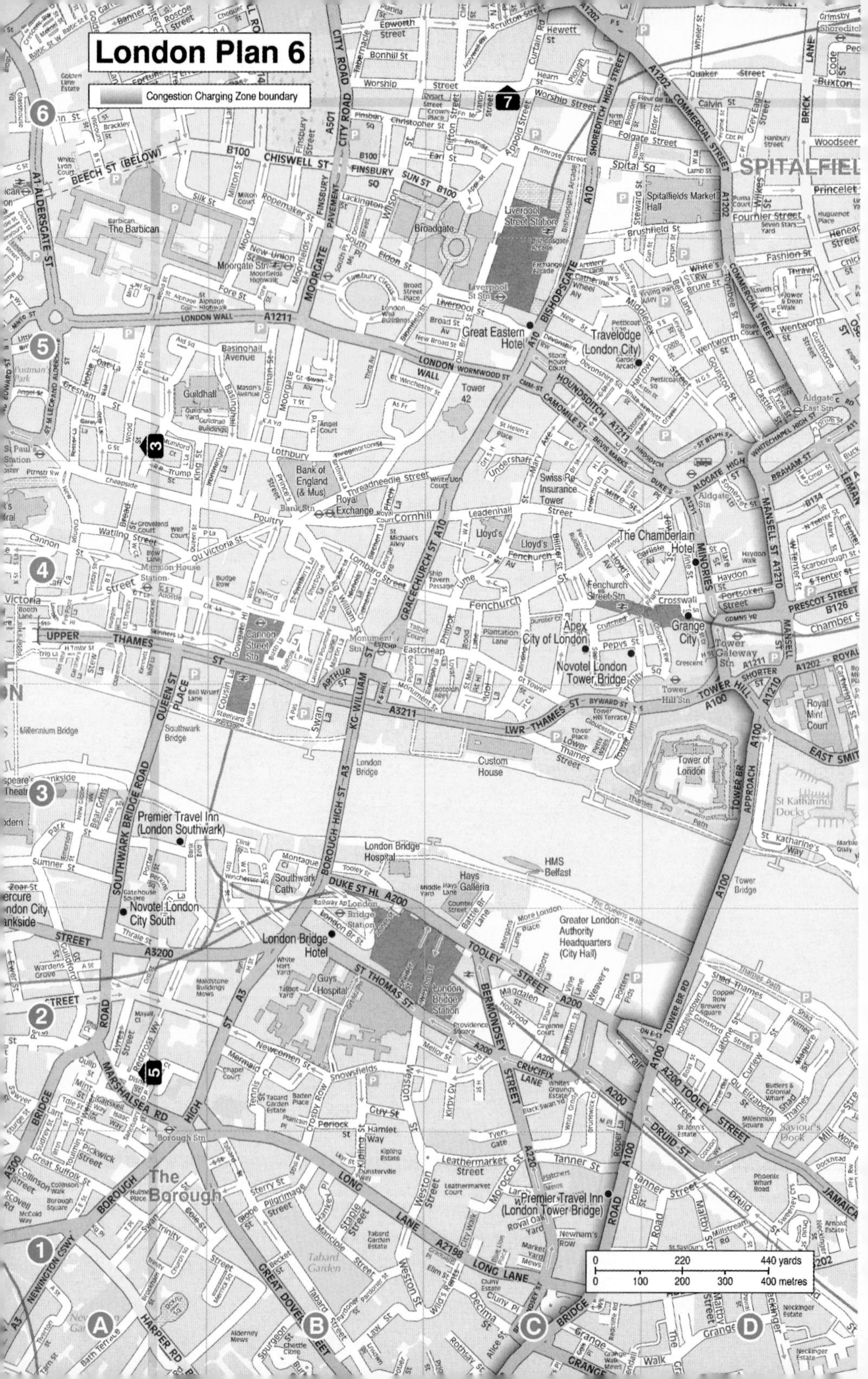
London Plan 6
Congestion Charging Zone boundary
SPITALFIELDS
The Barbican
Barbican
Moorgate Stn
Liverpool Street Station
Liverpool St Stn
Broadgate
Finsbury Circus
Great Eastern Hotel
Travelodge (London City)
Spitalfields Market Hall
Tower 42
Guildhall
Bank of England (& Mus)
Royal Exchange
Bank Stn
Swiss Re Insurance Tower
Lloyd's
The Chamberlain Hotel
Fenchurch Street Stn
Apex City of London
Novotel London Tower Bridge
Grange City
Aldgate Stn
Aldgate East Stn
Tower Gateway Stn
Tower Hill Stn
Tower of London
Royal Mint Court
St Katharine Docks
Mansion House Station
Cannon Street Stn
Monument Stn
Custom House
London Bridge
Millennium Bridge
Southwark Bridge
Premier Travel Inn (London Southwark)
Southwark Cath
London Bridge Hospital
HMS Belfast
Hays Galleria
Tower Bridge
Greater London Authority Headquarters (City Hall)
London Bridge Station
London Bridge Hotel
Guys Hospital
Novotel London City South
Borough Stn
The Borough
Premier Travel Inn (London Tower Bridge)
Tabard Garden
LONDON WALL
UPPER THAMES ST
LWR THAMES ST
TOWER HILL
TOOLEY STREET
LONG LANE
BOROUGH HIGH ST
SOUTHWARK BRIDGE ROAD
GREAT DOVER STREET
BERMONDSEY STREET
TOWER BR RD
COMMERCIAL STREET
BISHOPSGATE
MOORGATE
CITY ROAD
SHOREDITCH HIGH STREET
CHISWELL ST
BEECH ST (BELOW)
A1 ALDERSGATE ST
0 220 440 yards
0 100 200 300 400 metres
A B C D
1 2 3 4 5 6

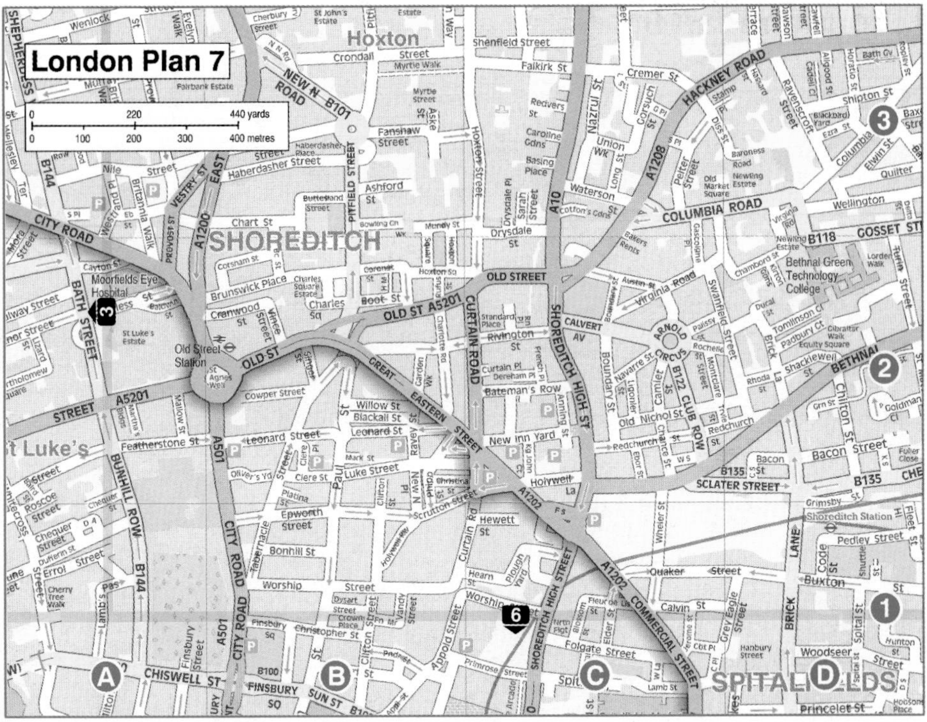
London Plan 7
0 220 440 yards
0 100 200 300 400 metres
Hoxton
SHOREDITCH
St Luke's
SPITALFIELDS
CITY ROAD
OLD ST
OLD STREET
GREAT EASTERN STREET
CURTAIN ROAD
SHOREDITCH HIGH ST
HACKNEY ROAD
COLUMBIA ROAD
COMMERCIAL STREET
BUNHILL ROW
BATH STREET
NEW N ROAD
PITFIELD STREET
Hoxton Street
Haberdasher Street
Fanshaw Street
Shenfield Street
Falkirk St
Cremer St
Crondall Street
Moorfields Eye Hospital
Old Street Station
Shoreditch Station
Bethnal Green Technology College
ARNOLD CIRCUS
Virginia Road
Calvert AV
Rivington St
Leonard Street
Featherstone St
Worship Street
Christopher St
Quaker Street
Buxton St
Pedley Street
Hanbury Street
Folgate Street
Princelet St
CHISWELL ST
FINSBURY SQ
SUN ST
SCLATER STREET
BRICK LANE
Bacon Street
Holywell La
Redchurch St
Old Nichol St
Swanfield Street
Wellington
Gosset St
Quilter
Shipton St
A1200
A5201
A501
A1202
A10
A1208
B101
B144
B100
B118
B122
B135
A
B
C
D
1
2
3
6

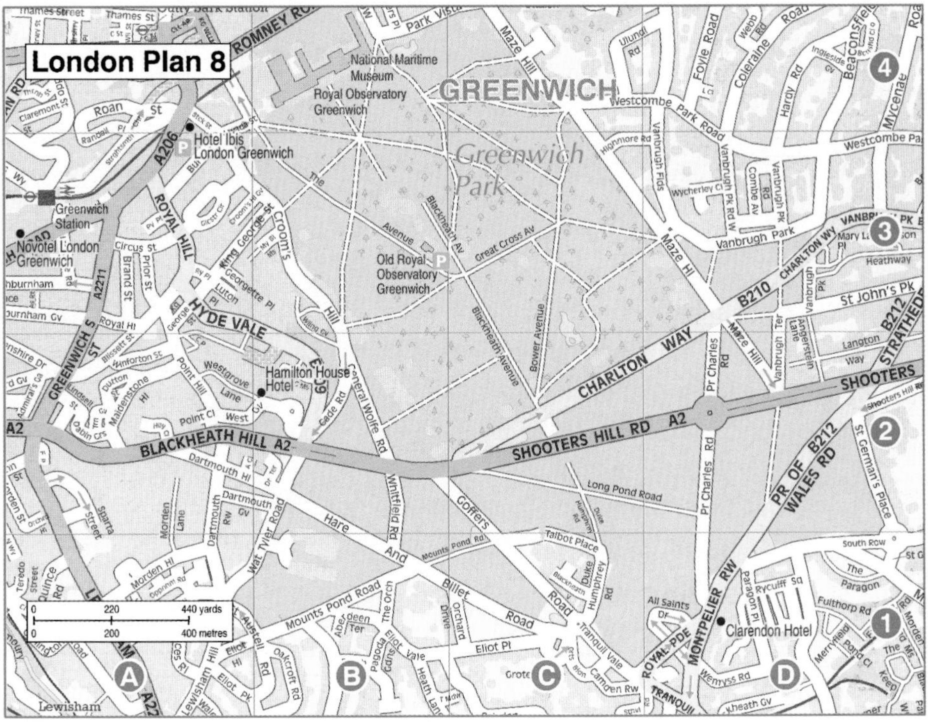
London Plan 8
GREENWICH
Greenwich Park
National Maritime Museum
Royal Observatory Greenwich
Old Royal Observatory Greenwich
Hotel Ibis London Greenwich
Novotel London Greenwich
Greenwich Station
Hamilton House Hotel
Clarendon Hotel
ROMNEY RD
ROYAL HILL
HYDE VALE
GREENWICH S ST
BLACKHEATH HILL A2
SHOOTERS HILL RD A2
CHARLTON WAY
SHOOTERS
PR OF WALES RD
MONTPELIER RW
ROYAL PDE
Maze Hill
Westcombe Park Road
Vanbrugh Park
St John's Pk
Great Cross AV
Blackheath Avenue
Bower Avenue
General Wolfe Rd
Croom's Hill
Long Pond Road
Hare And Billet Road
Goffers Road
Mounts Pond Road
Dartmouth Hl
Point Hill
Westgrove Lane
Pr Charles Rd
Lewisham
A206
A2211
B210
B212
0 220 440 yards
0 200 400 metres
A
B
C
D
1
2
3
4

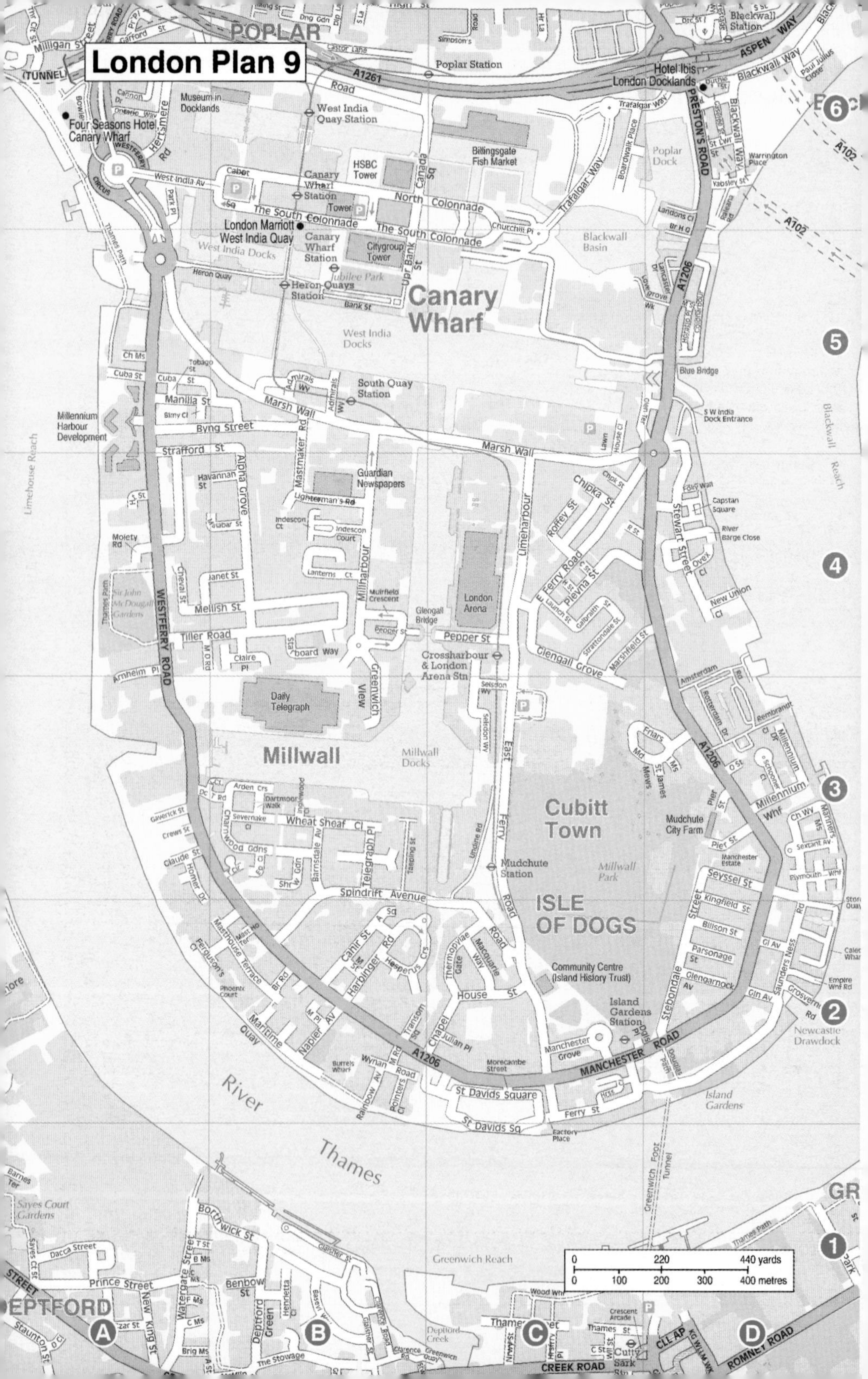
London Plan 9
POPLAR
Poplar Station
West India Quay Station
Museum in Docklands
Four Seasons Hotel Canary Wharf
Hotel Ibis London Docklands
Blackwall Station
Billingsgate Fish Market
HSBC Tower
Canary Wharf Station
Canary Wharf Tower
London Marriott West India Quay
Citygroup Tower
Heron Quays Station
Jubilee Park
West India Docks
Canary Wharf
Poplar Dock
Blackwall Basin
Blue Bridge
S W India Dock Entrance
South Quay Station
Millennium Harbour Development
Guardian Newspapers
London Arena
Glengall Bridge
Crossharbour & London Arena Stn
Daily Telegraph
Millwall
Millwall Docks
Cubitt Town
Mudchute City Farm
Mudchute Station
Millwall Park
ISLE OF DOGS
Community Centre (Island History Trust)
Island Gardens Station
Island Gardens
Newcastle Drawdock
Sir John McDougall Gardens
Limehouse Reach
Blackwall Reach
River Thames
Greenwich Reach
Greenwich Foot Tunnel
Sayes Court Gardens
DEPTFORD
Deptford Creek
Cutty Sark Stn
A1261
A1206
A102
WESTFERRY ROAD
MANCHESTER ROAD
PRESTON'S ROAD
ASPEN WAY
CREEK ROAD
ROMNEY ROAD
Marsh Wall
North Colonnade
The South Colonnade
East Ferry Road
Limeharbour
Millharbour
Spindrift Avenue
Prince Street
Watergate Street
New King St
Borthwick St
Thames Path
0 220 440 yards
0 100 200 300 400 metres
1
2
3
4
5
6
A
B
C
D

LONDON Greater London Plans 1-9, pages 316-328. (Small scale maps 6 & 7 at back of book.) Hotels are listed below in postal district order, commencing East, then North, South and West, with a brief indication of the area covered. Detailed plans 2-9 show the locations of AA-appointed hotels within the Central London postal districts. If you do not know the postal district of the hotel you want, please refer to the index preceding the street plans for the entry and map pages. The plan reference for each AA-appointed hotel also appears within its directory entry.

E1 STEPNEY AND EAST OF THE TOWER OF LONDON

⌂ Travelodge (London City)

1 Harrow Place E1 7DB plan 6 C5
☎ 08700 850 950 🖷 020 7626 1105
web: www.travelodge.co.uk

Travelodge offers good quality, good value, modern accommodation. Ideal for families, the spacious, en suite bedrooms include remote-control TV, tea and coffee-making facilities and comfortable beds. Meals can be taken at the nearby family restaurant. For further details consult the Hotel Groups page.

ROOMS: 142 en suite s fr £26; d fr £26

GF indicates the number of bedrooms at ground level

E6 BECKTON

See LONDON plan 1 H4

⌂ Premier Travel Inn London Beckton

1 Woolwich Manor Way, Beckton E6 4NT
☎ 08701 977029 🖷 020 7511 4214
web: www.premiertravelinn.com

Dir: *from A13 take A117, Woolwich Manor Way, towards City Airport, on left after 1st rdbt*

High quality, modern budget accommodation ideal for both families and business travellers. Spacious, en suite bedrooms feature bath and shower, satellite TV and many have telephones and modem points. The adjacent family restaurant features a wide and varied menu. For further details consult the Hotel Groups page.

ROOMS: 90 en suite s £53.95-£59.95; d £53.95-£59.95

E11 SNARESBROOK

See LONDON plan 1 G5

⌂ Innkeeper's Lodge Snaresbrook

37 Hollybush Hill, Snaresbrook E11 1PE
☎ 020 8989 7618
web: www.innkeeperslodge.com

A growing concept in the travel accommodation market. Smart rooms meet essential business requirements but also have home comforts. Dining options include all-day menus plus the added advantage of breakfast, which is included in the room price. For further details consult the Hotel Groups page.

ROOMS: 24 en suite s £58; d £58

London

E14 CANARY WHARF & LIMEHOUSE
See also LONDON plan 1 G3

Top Hotel

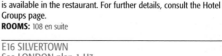

★★★★★ ⊛ **Four Seasons Hotel Canary Wharf**
Westferry Circus, Canary Wharf E14 8RS plan 9 A6
☎ 020 7510 1999 📠 020 7510 1998
e-mail: res.canarywharf@fourseasons.com
web: www.fourseasons.com/canarywharf
Dir: *From A13 follow signs to Canary Wharf, Isle of Dogs and Westferry Circus. Hotel off 3rd exit of Westferry Circus rdbt*
With superb views over the London skyline, this stylish modern hotel enjoys a delightful riverside location. Spacious contemporary bedrooms are particularly thoughtfully equipped. Public areas include the Italian Quadrato Bar and Restaurant, an impressive business centre and gym. Guests also have complimentary use of the impressive Holmes Place health club and spa. Welcoming staff provide exemplary levels of service and hospitality.
ROOMS: 142 en suite ⊗ in 120 bedrooms s £364-£423; d £388-£447 **FACILITIES: Spa** STV supervised Sauna Solarium Gym Jacuzzi ♫ Xmas **CONF:** BC Thtr 200 Class 120 Board 56 **SERVICES:** Lift air con **PARKING:** 29 **NOTES:** Civ Wed 200

★★★★★68% ⊛
London Marriott West India Quay
22 Hertsmere Rd, Canary Wharf E14 4ED plan 9 B6
☎ 020 7093 1000 📠 020 7093 1001
web: www.marriott.co.uk
Dir: *Turn off Aspen Way at Hertsmere Rd. Hotel directly opposite. Adjacent to Canary Wharf*
This spectacular new skyscraper with curved glass façade is located at the heart of the docklands, adjacent to Canary Wharf and overlooking the water of West India Quay. The style of the hotel is modern, but not pretentiously trendy. White glazed tile floors, eye-catching floral displays and occasional bold bursts of colour give warmth to the public areas. Bedrooms, many of which overlook the quay, provide every modern convenience, including broadband access and air-conditioning. Curve Restaurant offers good quality American-influenced cooking.
ROOMS: 301 en suite (21 fmly) ⊗ in 228 bedrooms **FACILITIES:** STV Sauna Solarium Gym **CONF:** BC Thtr 300 Class 120 Board 27 **SERVICES:** Lift air con **NOTES:** ⊗ in restaurant Civ Wed 290

Town House Hotel
Country House Hotel
⇧ Travel Accommodation

⇧ ***Hotel Ibis London Docklands***
1 Baffin Way E14 9PE plan 9 D6
☎ 020 7517 1100 📠 020 7987 5916
e-mail: H2177@accor-hotels.com
Dir: *from Tower Bridge follow City Airport and Royal Docks signs, exit for 'Isle of Dogs'. Hotel on 1st left opposite McDonalds*
Modern, budget hotel offering comfortable accommodation in bright and practical bedrooms. Breakfast is self-service and dinner is available in the restaurant. For further details, consult the Hotel Groups page.
ROOMS: 87 en suite

⇧ **Travelodge (London Dockland)**
Coriander Av, East India Dock Rd E14 2AA
☎ 08700 850 950 📠 020 7515 9178
web: www.travelodge.co.uk
Dir: *on A13 at East India Dock Rd*
Travelodge offers good quality, good value, modern accommodation. Ideal for families, the spacious, en suite bedrooms include remote-control TV, tea and coffee-making facilities and comfortable beds. Meals can be taken at the nearby family restaurant. For further details consult the Hotel Groups page.
ROOMS: 232 en suite s £26-£60; d £26-£60

E15 STRATFORD
See LONDON plan 1 G4

⇧ ***Hotel Ibis London Stratford***
1A Romford Rd, Stratford E15 4LJ
☎ 020 8536 3700 📠 020 8519 5161
e-mail: H3099@accor-hotels.com
Modern, budget hotel offering comfortable accommodation in bright and practical bedrooms. Breakfast is self-service and dinner is available in the restaurant. For further details, consult the Hotel Groups page.
ROOMS: 108 en suite

E16 SILVERTOWN
See LONDON plan 1 H3

★★★★70% **Novotel London ExCel**
7 Western Gateway, Royal Victoria Docks E16 1AA
☎ 020 7540 9700 📠 020 7540 9710
e-mail: H3656@accor-hotels.com
web: www.novotel.com
Dir: *M25 junct 30. A13 towards 'City', off at Canning Town. Follow signs to 'ExCel West'. Hotel next door*
This hotel is situated adjacent to the ExCel exhibition centre and overlooks the Royal Victoria Dock. Design throughout the hotel is contemporary and stylish. Public rooms include a range of meeting rooms, a modern coffee station, indoor leisure facilities and a smart bar and restaurant, both with a terrace overlooking the dock. Bedrooms feature modern decor, a bath and separate shower and an extensive range of extras.
Novotel - AA Hotel Group of the Year 2005-6.
ROOMS: 257 en suite (203 fmly) ⊗ in 183 bedrooms s fr £135; d fr £155 **LB FACILITIES:** STV Sauna Gym Steam room, relaxation room with massage bed. Xmas **CONF:** Thtr 70 Class 55 Board 30 Del from £185 **SERVICES:** Lift air con **PARKING:** 80 **NOTES:** Civ Wed

⇧ ***Hotel Ibis London ExCel***
9 Western Gateway, Royal Victoria Docks E16 1AB
☎ 020 7055 2300 📠 020 7055 2310
e-mail: H3655@accor-hotels.com
Dir: *M25 then A13 to London, City Airport, ExCel East*
Modern, budget hotel offering comfortable accommodation in

continued

bright and practical bedrooms. Breakfast is self-service and dinner is available in the restaurant. For further details, consult the Hotel Groups page.
ROOMS: 278 en suite

⇧ Premier Travel Inn London Docklands (ExCeL)

Royal Victoria Dock E16 1SL
☎ 0870 238 3322 ⎙ 020 7540 2250
web: www.premiertravelinn.com
Dir: *on ExCel East. Follow A13 onto A1020. At the Connaught rdbt take 2nd exit into Connaught Road. Inn is on the right.*
High quality, modern budget accommodation ideal for both families and business travellers. Spacious, en suite bedrooms feature bath and shower, satellite TV and many have telephones and modem points. The adjacent family restaurant features a wide and varied menu. For further details consult the Hotel Groups page.
ROOMS: 202 en suite s £59.95-£72.95; d £59.95-£72.95

EC1 CITY OF LONDON

★★★74% ◎
Malmaison Charterhouse Square

18-21 Charterhouse Square, Clerkenwell
EC1M 6AH plan 3 G4
☎ 020 7012 3700 ⎙ 020 7012 3702
e-mail: london@malmaison.com
web: www.malmaison.com
Dir: *Exit Barbican Station turn left, take 1st left.*
Situated in a leafy and peaceful square Malmaison Charterhouse maintains the same focus on quality service and food as the other hotels in the group. The bedrooms, stylishly decorated in calming tones have all the expected facilities including power showers, CD players and internet access. The brasserie and bar at the hotel's centre has a buzzing atmosphere and traditional French cuisine.
ROOMS: 97 en suite (5 GF) ⊘ in 79 bedrooms **FACILITIES:** STV Gym **CONF:** Thtr 30 Board 16 **SERVICES:** Lift air con **NOTES:** ✗

EC2

Top Hotel

★★★★★ ◎◎◎ ***Great Eastern Hotel***
Liverpool St EC2M 7QN plan 6 C5
☎ 020 7618 5000 ⎙ 020 7618 5001
e-mail: sales@great-eastern-hotel.co.uk
web: www.great-eastern-hotel.co.uk
The largest hotel in the city, the Great Eastern is adjacent to Liverpool Street station. Design-led bedrooms are stylish and
continued

come complete with all the extras you could need. The impressive array of restaurants includes the elegant Aurora offering fine dining, Fishmarket with its champagne bar, Terminus offering all-day meals and snacks and a Miyabi, a Japanese restaurant. The basement gym offers a range of treatments and personal trainers are available.
ROOMS: 267 en suite ⊘ in 74 bedrooms **FACILITIES:** STV Gym steam room **CONF:** Thtr 200 Class 120 **SERVICES:** Lift air con **NOTES:** Civ Wed

EC3 CHEAPSIDE

★★★★★68% ***The Grange City***
Coopers Row EC3 2BQ plan 6 D4
☎ 020 7863 3700 ⎙ 020 7863 3701
e-mail: city@grangehotels.com
web: www.grangehotels.co.uk
Dir: *M4 E into A4 E, to Piccadilly, onto Trafalgar Sq, B308 to Victoria Embankment, follow river, just before Tower Hill. Coopers Row on left*
This modern hotel enjoys a prime city location overlooking the Tower of London and Tower Bridge. Spacious, air-conditioned bedrooms have been appointed to a high standard and are extensively equipped. Public areas include an impressive leisure club. Guests can choose from a variety of eating options, including the Forum, which offers Italian fare, a more informal brasserie, or Koto 2, a Japanese sushi and noodle bar.
ROOMS: 254 en suite ⊘ in 120 bedrooms **FACILITIES: Spa** STV Sauna Gym Jacuzzi Virtual golf simulator. **CONF:** BC Thtr 800 Class 400 Board 200 **SERVICES:** Lift air con

Town House

★★★★ ⌂ **The Chamberlain**
130-135 Minories EC3N 1NU plan 6 D4
☎ 020 7680 1500 ⎙ 020 7702 2500
e-mail: thechamberlain@fullers.co.uk
web: www.thechamberlainhotel.com
Dir: *M25 junct 30. Then A13 W towards London. Follow into Aldgate, left after bus station. Hotel halfway down Minories.*
This smart hotel is ideally situated for the City, Tower Bridge, Aldgate and Tower Gateway Tube Stations. Impressive bedrooms are stylish, well equipped and comfortable, while the modern bathrooms are fitted with TVs to watch while you soak in the bath. Informal day rooms include a popular pub, a lounge and an attractive split-level dining room.
ROOMS: 64 en suite ⊘ in 49 bedrooms s £195-£235; d £195-£235 LB **FACILITIES:** STV Discounted leisure facilities for hotel guests nearby **CONF:** Thtr 50 Class 20 Board 25 **SERVICES:** Lift air con **NOTES:** ✗ ⊘ in restaurant Closed 24 Dec-2 Jan (TBC)

London

EC3 CHEAPSIDE, continued

★★★72% Novotel London Tower Bridge
10 Pepys St EC3N 2NR plan 6 C4
☎ 020 7265 6000 🖷 020 7265 6060
e-mail: H3107@accor.com
web: www.novotel.com
Located near the Tower of London, this smart hotel is convenient for Docklands, the City, Heathrow and London City airports. Bedrooms are spacious, modern, and offer a great range of facilities, including air conditioning. There is a smart bar and restaurant, a small gym and extensive meeting and conference facilities. Novotel - AA Hotel Group of the Year 2005-6.
ROOMS: 203 en suite (77 fmly) (56 GF) ⊗ in 174 bedrooms s £169-£184; d £139-£204 **LB** **FACILITIES:** STV Sauna Gym Steam Room **CONF:** Thtr 100 Class 56 Board 18 Del £240 **SERVICES:** Lift air con

U Apex City of London
No 1 Seething Ln EC3N 4AX plan 6 C4
☎ 0845 365 0000 🖷 0131 666 5128
e-mail: www.londonsales@apexhotels.co.uk
At the time of going to press, the star classification for this hotel was not confirmed. Please refer to the AA internet site www.theAA.com for current information.
ROOMS: 130 en suite ⊗ in 108 bedrooms s £269-£387; d £269-£387 **LB** **FACILITIES:** STV Sauna Gym **CONF:** Thtr 70 Class 35 Board 32 **SERVICES:** Lift air con **NOTES:** ✗ ⊗ in restaurant

London

N1 ISLINGTON

★★★65% *Jurys Inn Islington*
60 Pentonville Rd, Islington N1 9LA plan 3 E6
☎ 020 7282 5500 🖷 020 7282 5511
e-mail: london_inn@jurysdoyle.com
web: www.jurysdoyle.com
Dir: *from A1 right onto A501, right again onto Pentonville Rd*
This modern hotel offers spacious bedrooms with good facilities, and provides guests with a choice of comfortable public areas. There is an Irish pub serving snacks and a popular restaurant serving a daily-changing menu.
ROOMS: 229 en suite (116 fmly) ⊗ in 135 bedrooms **FACILITIES:** STV **CONF:** Thtr 50 Class 24 Board 28 **SERVICES:** Lift air con **NOTES:** ✗ Closed 24-27 Dec

⌂ Premier Travel Inn London Kings Cross
York Way, Kings Cross N1 9AA plan 3 D6
☎ 0870 9906414 🖷 0870 9906415
web: www.premiertravelinn.com
Dir: *Exit M25 junct 16 onto M40 (which becomes A40). Follow City signs, exit at Euston Rd follow one-way system to York Way*
High quality, modern budget accommodation ideal for both families and business travellers. Spacious, en suite bedrooms feature bath and shower, satellite TV and many have telephones and modem points. The adjacent family restaurant features a wide and varied menu. For further details consult the Hotel Groups page.
ROOMS: 278 en suite s £74.95-£82.95; d £74.95-£82.95

N14 SOUTHGATE
See LONDON SECTION plan 1 E6

⌂ Innkeeper's Lodge Southgate
22 The Green, Southgate N14 6EN
☎ 020 8447 8022 🖷 020 8447 8022
web: www.innkeeperslodge.com
Dir: *take A111 from junct 24, 3m to rdbt for A1004, turn right into High Street, hotel at next rdbt*
A growing concept in the travel accommodation market. Smart rooms meet essential business requirements but also have home comforts. Dining options include all-day menus plus the added advantage of breakfast, which is included in the room price. For further details consult the Hotel Groups page.
ROOMS: 19 en suite s £59.95; d £59.95

NW1 REGENT'S PARK

Top Hotel

★★★★★ ⊛ The Landmark London
222 Marylebone Rd NW1 6JQ plan 2 F4
☎ 020 7631 8000 🖷 020 7631 8080
e-mail: reservations@thelandmark.co.uk
web: www.landmarklondon.co.uk
Dir: *adjacent to Marylebone Station and near Paddington Station*
Once one of the last truly grand railway hotels, The Landmark boasts a number of stunning features, the most spectacular being the naturally lit central atrium forming the focal point. When it comes to eating and drinking there are a number of choices, including the Cellars bar for cocktails and upmarket bar meals. The Winter Garden restaurant has the centre stage in the atrium and is a great place to watch the world go by. Refurbished air-conditioned bedrooms are luxurious and have large, stylish bathrooms.
ROOMS: 299 en suite (60 fmly) ⊗ in 179 bedrooms **FACILITIES: Spa** STV Sauna Gym Jacuzzi Beauty treatments and massages ♫ Xmas **CONF:** BC Thtr 380 Class 224 Board 50 **SERVICES:** Lift air con **PARKING:** 80 **NOTES:** ✗ Civ Wed 300

Town House

★★★★ ⌂ *Dorset Square Hotel*
39-40 Dorset Square NW1 6QN plan 2 F4
☎ 020 7723 7874 🖷 020 7724 3328
e-mail: info@dorsetsquare.co.uk
Dir: *M40 onto A40 (Euston Rd). Left lane off flyover. Turn left onto Gloucester Place. Hotel 1st left*
This delightfully restored Regency townhouse enjoys a prime location close to Hyde Park, Regents Park and all of central London's attractions. Stylish bedrooms are individually themed and extremely well equipped for both business and leisure guests. Elegant public areas include the popular Potting Shed Restaurant and Bar as well as an inviting sumptuous lounge. Service is personalised and attentive.
ROOMS: 37 en suite (2 fmly) (4 GF) **FACILITIES:** STV ♫ **CONF:** Thtr 12 Board 10 **SERVICES:** Lift air con **NOTES:** ✗

Packed in a hurry? Ironing facilities should be available at all star levels, either in the rooms or on request

★★★★74% Meliá White House Regents Park
Albany St, Regents Park NW1 3UP plan 3 A5
☎ 020 7391 3000 🖷 020 7388 0091
e-mail: melia.white.house@solmelia.com
Dir: *opposite Gt Portland St underground station*
Owned by the Spanish 'Sol' company, this impressive art deco building is located opposite Great Portland Street tube station. Public areas offer a high degree of comfort and include a fine dining restaurant and a more informal brasserie. Stylish bedrooms come in a variety of sizes, but all offer high levels of comfort and are well equipped.
ROOMS: 582 en suite (1 fmly) ⊘ in 166 bedrooms **FACILITIES:** STV Sauna Gym Xmas **CONF:** BC Thtr 120 Class 45 Board 40 Del from £190 **SERVICES:** Lift air con **PARKING:** 7 **NOTES:** 🐕

★★★★69% Holiday Inn Camden Lock
30 Jamestown Rd, Camden Lock NW1 7BY
☎ 020 7485 4343 🖷 020 7485 4344
e-mail: sales@holidayinncamden.co.uk
Dir: *from Camden tube station take left fork. Jamestown Rd 2nd on left*
In the heart of Camden this smart modern hotel actually has rooms, which overlook the Camden Lock. Bedrooms are spacious and well equipped, whilst the light and airy first-floor restaurant offers delicious and innovative Mediterranean dishes. A small but well equipped gym is located on the ground floor, as are a good selection of meeting rooms.
ROOMS: 130 en suite ⊘ in 65 bedrooms s £125; d £125 **LB** **FACILITIES:** STV Gym **CONF:** BC Thtr 200 Class 80 Board 40 Del from £180 **SERVICES:** Lift air con **NOTES:** 🐕 ⊘ in restaurant

★★★★67% ◎ Novotel London Euston
100-110 Euston Rd NW1 2AJ plan 3 C5
☎ 020 7666 9000 🖷 020 7766 9100
e-mail: H5309@accor.com
web: www.novotel.com
Dir: *between St Pancras & Euston stations*
This hotel enjoys a central location adjacent to the British Library and close to some of London's main transport hubs. The style is modern and contemporary throughout. Bedrooms are spacious, very well equipped and many have views over the city. Open-plan public areas include a leisure suite and extensive conference facilities including the Shaw Theatre.
Novotel - AA Hotel Group of the Year 2005-6.
ROOMS: 312 en suite (36 fmly) ⊘ in 246 bedrooms s £89-£160; d £89-£160 **FACILITIES:** STV Sauna Gym Steam room Xmas **CONF:** BC Thtr 446 Class 220 Board 80 Del from £212 **SERVICES:** Lift air con **NOTES:** 🐕 ⊘ in restaurant

U Ramada Marylebone
Harewood Row NW1 6SE plan 2 E4
☎ 020 7262 2707 🖷 020 7262 2975
e-mail: sales.marylebone@ramadajarvis.co.uk
web: www.ramadajarvis.co.uk
Dir: *From M40 onto A40 and over Paddington flyover onto Marylebone Rd, left into Lison Gr and 1st left into Harewood Row.*
This modern hotel is conveniently located to both Marylebone station and Baker Street. Bedrooms are comfortably appointed for both business and leisure guests.
ROOMS: 92 en suite ⊘ in 76 bedrooms s £99-£135; d £99-£135 **FACILITIES:** STV **SERVICES:** Lift **NOTES:** 🐕 ⊘ in restaurant

⊘ No smoking

⌂ *Hotel Ibis London Euston*
3 Cardington St NW1 2LW plan 3 B5
☎ 020 7388 7777 🖷 020 7388 0001
e-mail: H0921@accor-hotels.com
Dir: *from Euston Rd or station, right to Melton St leading to Cardington St*
Modern, budget hotel offering comfortable accommodation in bright and practical bedrooms. Breakfast is self-service and dinner is available in the restaurant. For further details, consult the Hotel Groups page.
ROOMS: 380 en suite **CONF:** BC Thtr 100 Class 40 Board 30

NW2 BRENT CROSS & CRICKLEWOOD
See LONDON plan 1 D5

★★★★72% Crown Moran
142-152 Cricklewood Broadway, Cricklewood NW2 3ED
☎ 020 8452 4175 🖷 020 8452 0952
e-mail: crownres@moranhotels.com
web: www.crownmoranhotel.co.uk
Dir: *M1 junct 1 follow signs onto North Circular (W) A406. Junct with A5 (Staples corner). At rdbt take 1st exit onto A5 to Cricklewood*

This striking hotel is connected by an impressive glass atrium to the popular Crown Pub. Features include excellent function and conference facilities, a leisure club, a choice of stylish lounges and bars and a contemporary restaurant. The air-conditioned bedrooms are appointed to a high standard and include a number of trendy suites.
ROOMS: 116 en suite (8 fmly) (20 GF) ⊘ in 60 bedrooms s £95-£180; d £105-£190 (incl. bkfst) **LB** **FACILITIES:** STV Sauna Gym Jacuzzi ♫ **CONF:** Thtr 120 Class 60 Board 60 Del from £170 **SERVICES:** Lift air con **PARKING:** 41 **NOTES:** 🐕 Closed 25-26 Dec Civ Wed 100

NW3 HAMPSTEAD AND SWISS COTTAGE
See LONDON plan 1 E5/E4

★★★★73%
London Marriott Hotel Regents Park
128 King Henry's Rd NW3 3ST
☎ 0870 400 7240 🖷 0870 400 7340
web: www.marriott.co.uk
Dir: *200yds off Finchley Rd on A41*
Situated in a quieter part of town and close to the tube station, this hotel offers guests comfortably appointed, air-conditioned accommodation which meet the needs of today's business traveller. The open-plan ground floor contains all the main facilities including a well-equipped leisure centre with indoor pool.
ROOMS: 303 en suite ⊘ in 130 bedrooms **FACILITIES:** STV Sauna Solarium Gym Hair & Beauty salon, Steam room ♫ **CONF:** Thtr 440 Class 150 Board 175 **SERVICES:** Lift air con **PARKING:** 150 **NOTES:** 🐕 Civ Wed 300

London

NW6 MAIDA VALE
See LONDON plan 1 D4

★★★★70% London Marriott Maida Vale

Plaza Pde, Maida Vale NW6 5RP
☎ 020 7543 6000 🖷 020 7543 2100
e-mail: marriottmaidavale@btinternet.com
web: www.marriott.co.uk
Dir: *From M1, A406 W, A5 south, through Kilburn, hotel left*

This smart, modern hotel is conveniently located just north of central London. Air-conditioned bedrooms are tastefully decorated and provide a range of extras. The hotel also boasts extensive function facilities as well as a smart indoor leisure centre, which has a swimming pool, gym and health and beauty salon.

ROOMS: 238 en suite (6 fmly) ⊗ in 110 bedrooms s £110-£160; d £110-£160 **LB** **FACILITIES:** STV 🏊 supervised Sauna Solarium Gym Hair & beauty salons Xmas **CONF:** BC Thtr 200 Class 90 Board 40 Del from £170 **SERVICES:** Lift air con **PARKING:** 30 **NOTES:** ✗

SE1 SOUTHWARK AND WATERLOO

★★★★★67% London Marriott Hotel County Hall

Westminster Bridge Rd, County Hall SE1 7PB
plan 5 D5
☎ 020 7928 5200 🖷 020 7928 5300
e-mail: salesadmin.countyhall@marriotthotels.co.uk
web: www.marriott.co.uk
Dir: *on Thames South Bank, between Westminster Bridge & London Eye*

This impressive building enjoys an enviable position on the south bank of the Thames, adjacent to the London Eye. Public areas have a traditional elegance and the crescent-shaped restaurant offers fine views of Westminster. All bedrooms are smartly laid out and thoughtfully equipped with the business traveller in mind.

ROOMS: 200 en suite (60 fmly) ⊗ in 147 bedrooms **FACILITIES: Spa** STV 🏊 Sauna Solarium Gym Jacuzzi Health & beauty spa ♫ Xmas **CONF:** BC Thtr 80 Class 40 Board 30 Del from £220 **SERVICES:** Lift air con **PARKING:** 70 **NOTES:** ✗ Civ Wed 80

★★★★68% Novotel London City South

Southwark Bridge Rd SE1 9HH plan 5 H5
☎ 020 7089 0400 🖷 020 7089 0410
e-mail: H3269@accor.com web: www.novotel.com
Dir: *junct at Thrale St*

First in a new generation of Novotels, this hotel is contemporary in design with smart, modern bedrooms and spacious public rooms. There are a number of options for guests wanting to unwind, including treatments such as reflexology and immersion therapy, while a gym is available for the more energetic. Novotel - AA Hotel Group of the Year 2005-6.

ROOMS: 182 en suite (139 fmly) ⊗ in 158 bedrooms s £160; d £180 **LB** **FACILITIES:** STV Sauna Gym **CONF:** Thtr 100 Class 40 Board 35 Del £225 **SERVICES:** Lift air con **PARKING:** 80

★★★★66% London Bridge Hotel

8-18 London Bridge St SE1 9SG plan 6 B2
☎ 020 7855 2200 🖷 020 7855 2233
e-mail: sales@london-bridge-hotel.co.uk
web: www.london-bridge-hotel.co.uk
Dir: *Access through London Bridge Station (bus/taxi yard), into London Bridge St (one-way). Hotel on left, 50yds from station*

This elegant independently owned hotel enjoys a prime location on the edge of the city, adjacent to London Bridge station. Smartly appointed, well-equipped bedrooms include a number of spacious deluxe rooms and suites. Compact yet sophisticated public areas include a selection of conference and meeting rooms, Georgetown Asian restaurant and a well-equipped gym.

ROOMS: 138 en suite (12 fmly) ⊗ in 108 bedrooms s £99-£195; d £99-£195 **LB** **FACILITIES:** STV Sauna Solarium Gym Arrangement with local club for swimming pool **CONF:** Thtr 100 Class 40 Board 40 Del £266 **SERVICES:** Lift air con **NOTES:** ✗

★★★71% Mercure London City Bankside

71-79 Southwark St SE1 0JA plan 5 G5
☎ 020 7902 0800 🖷 020 7902 0810
e-mail: H2814@accor.com
Dir: *A200 to London Bridge. Left into Southwark St. Hotel 2 mins by car from station*

This smart, contemporary hotel forms part of the rejuvenation of the South Bank. With the City of London just over the river and a number of tourist attractions within easy reach, the hotel is well located for business and leisure visitors alike. Facilities include spacious air-cooled bedrooms, a modern bar and the stylish Loft Restaurant.

ROOMS: 144 en suite (24 fmly) (5 GF) ⊗ in 115 bedrooms s £79-£145; d £99-£175 **LB** **FACILITIES:** STV Gym **CONF:** Thtr 60 Class 40 Board 30 Del from £189 **SERVICES:** Lift air con **PARKING:** 3

★★★68% *Novotel London Waterloo*

113 Lambeth Rd SE1 7LS plan 5 D3
☎ 020 7793 1010 🖷 020 7793 0202
e-mail: h1785@accor-hotels.com
web: www.novotel.com
Dir: *opposite Houses of Parliament on S bank of River Thames, off Lambeth Bridge, opposite Lambeth Palace*

This hotel has an excellent location with Lambeth Palace, the Houses of Parliament and Waterloo Station all within a short walk. Bedrooms are spacious and air conditioned, a number of rooms have been designed for less able guests. The open-plan public areas include the Garden Brasserie, the Flag and Whistle Pub and children's play area. Novotel - AA Hotel Group of the Year 2005-6.

ROOMS: 187 en suite (80 fmly) ⊗ in 158 bedrooms **FACILITIES:** Sauna Gym Steam room Fitness room **CONF:** Thtr 40 Class 24 Board 24 **SERVICES:** Lift **PARKING:** 40

♫ Entertainment

U Plaza on the River - Club and Residence

Park Plaza
Hotels & Resorts

18 Albert Embankment SE1 7TJ plan 5 D2
☎ 020 7769 2525 📠 020 7769 2524
e-mail: info@plazaontheriver.co.uk
web: www.parkplaza.com
Dir: From Houses of Parliament turn onto Millbank, at rdbt left onto Lambeth Bridge. At rdbt take 3rd right onto Albert Embankment.
At the time of going to press, the star classification for this hotel was not confirmed. Please refer to the AA internet site www.theAA.com for current information.
ROOMS: 66 en suite (11 fmly) s £200-£595; d £200-£595 **LB**
FACILITIES: Spa STV ⬚ supervised Sauna Solarium Gym Jacuzzi Xmas **CONF:** BC Thtr 530 Class 405 Board 40 Del from £220
SERVICES: Lift air con **PARKING:** 120 **NOTES:** ✗ ⊛ in restaurant Civ Wed

U Riverbank Park Plaza

Park Plaza
Hotels & Resorts

Albert Embankment SE1 7SP plan 5 D3
☎ 020 7769 9872
e-mail: rppres@parkplazahotels.co.uk
web: www.parkplaza.com
Dir: From Houses of Parliament turn onto Millbank, at rdbt left onto Lambeth Bridge. At rdbt take third exit onto Albert Embankment.
At the time of going to press, the star classification for this hotel was not confirmed. Please refer to the AA internet site www.theAA.com for current information.
ROOMS: 394 en suite ⊛ in 315 bedrooms **FACILITIES: Spa** STV ⬚ supervised Solarium Gym Jacuzzi Cardio machines, weights, exercise mats and stretch balls ♫ **CONF:** Thtr 530 Class 405 Board 40
SERVICES: Lift air con **PARKING:** 120 **NOTES:** ✗ ⊛ in restaurant Civ Wed

⌂ Premier Travel Inn London County Hall

Belvedere Rd SE1 7PB plan 5 D5

premier travel inn

☎ 0870 238 3300 📠 020 7902 1619
web: www.premiertravelinn.com
Dir: in County Hall building, next to London Eye
High quality, modern budget accommodation ideal for both families and business travellers. Spacious, en suite bedrooms feature bath and shower, satellite TV and many have telephones and modem points. The adjacent family restaurant features a wide and varied menu. For further details consult the Hotel Groups page.
ROOMS: 313 en suite s £84.95-£86.95; d £84.95-£86.95

⌂ Premier Travel Inn London Southwark

Anchor, Bankside, 34 Park St SE1 9EF plan 6 A3

premier travel inn

☎ 0870 9906402 📠 0870 9906403
web: www.premiertravelinn.com
Dir: From A3200 into Southwark Bridge Rd (A300), 1st left into Sumner St, right into Park St. From S, M3 (then A3) follow Central London signs
High quality, modern budget accommodation ideal for both families and business travellers. Spacious, en suite bedrooms feature bath and shower, satellite TV and many have telephones and modem points. The adjacent family restaurant features a wide and varied menu. For further details consult the Hotel Groups page.
ROOMS: 56 en suite s £82.95; d £82.95 **CONF:** Thtr 22 Board 22

Early start?
Hotels at all star levels should provide in-room alarm clocks and/or alarm clocks

⌂ Premier Travel Inn London Tower Bridge

Tower Bridge Rd SE1 3LP plan 6 C1

premier travel inn

☎ 0870 238 3303 📠 020 7940 3719
web: www.premiertravelinn.com
Dir: South of Tower Bridge
High quality, modern budget accommodation ideal for both families and business travellers. Spacious, en suite bedrooms feature bath and shower, satellite TV and many have telephones and modem points. The adjacent family restaurant features a wide and varied menu. For further details consult the Hotel Groups page.
ROOMS: 195 en suite s £72.95-£79.95; d £72.95-£79.95

SE3 BLACKHEATH

★★69% Clarendon

8-16 Montpelier Row, Blackheath SE3 0RW

THE INDEPENDENTS

plan 8 D1
☎ 020 8318 4321 📠 020 8318 4378
e-mail: relax@clarendonhotel.com
web: www.clarendonhotel.com
Dir: off A2 at Blackheath junct. Hotel on left before village

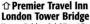

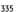

Overlooking the heath, this impressive Georgian hotel offers well-equipped, attractive accommodation. A number of suites are also available. Spacious public areas include a choice of bars, a restaurant and meeting and conference facilities. The hotel has its own car park and guests have use of local leisure facilities.
ROOMS: 181 en suite (3 fmly) (5 GF) ⊛ in 22 bedrooms s £80-£95; d £90-£100 (incl. bkfst) **LB FACILITIES:** STV ♫ Xmas **CONF:** BC Thtr 120 Class 40 Board 50 Del from £127 **SERVICES:** Lift **PARKING:** 80 **NOTES:** ⊛ in restaurant Civ Wed 60

SE10 GREENWICH

★★★★69% Novotel London Greenwich

173-185 Greenwich High Rd SE10 8JA plan 8 A3

NOVOTEL

☎ 020 8312 6800 📠 020 8312 6810
e-mail: H3476@accor.com
web: www.novotel.com
Dir: next to Greenwich Station
This new, purpose-built hotel is conveniently located for rail and DLR stations, as well as major attractions such as the Royal Maritime Museum and the Royal Observatory. Air-conditioned bedrooms are spacious and equipped with a host of extras, and public areas include a small gym, contemporary lounge bar and restaurant. Novotel - AA Hotel Group of the Year 2005-6.
ROOMS: 151 en suite (34 fmly) ⊛ in 115 bedrooms s £89-£185; d £89-£195 **LB FACILITIES:** STV Gym Steam room **CONF:** Thtr 92 Class 40 Board 32 Del from £159 **SERVICES:** Lift air con **PARKING:** 30

London

SE10 GREENWICH, continued

★★72% Hamilton House

14 West Grove, Greenwich SE10 8QT plan 8 B2
☎ 020 8694 9899 Fax 020 8694 2370
e-mail: reception@hamiltonhousehotel.co.uk
web: www.hamiltonhousehotel.co.uk
Dir: *from Blackheath Common on A2 towards Central London, 2nd right after Blackheath Tea Hut into Hyde Vale. West Grove next left*
This small Georgian hotel boasts true style and character, along with some impressive views of the Docklands. Elegant bedrooms are individually designed and equipped with a host of thoughtful extras, including CD players. The restaurant is bright and offers creative cooking. The bar area opens out onto an attractive garden with seating. This hotel is very popular as a wedding venue.
ROOMS: 9 en suite (8 fmly) (1 GF) ⊗ in 4 bedrooms s fr £100; d £120-£150 (incl. bkfst) **LB** **FACILITIES:** STV Xmas **CONF:** Thtr 50 Class 22 Board 22 **NOTES:** ⊗ in restaurant Civ Wed 104

⌂ *Hotel Ibis London Greenwich*

30 Stockwell St, Greenwich SE10 9JN plan 8 A4
☎ 020 8305 1177 Fax 020 8858 7139
e-mail: H0975@accor-hotels.com
Dir: *from Waterloo Bridge, Elephant & Castle, A2 to Greenwich.*
Modern, budget hotel offering comfortable accommodation in bright and practical bedrooms. Breakfast is self-service and dinner is available in the restaurant. For further details, consult the Hotel Groups page.
ROOMS: 82 en suite

London

SW1 WESTMINSTER

Top Hotel

★★★★★ @@@@@ The Berkeley

Wilton Place, Knightsbridge SW1X 7RL plan 4 G4
☎ 020 7235 6000 Fax 020 7235 4330
e-mail: info@the-berkeley.co.uk
Dir: *300mtrs along Knightsbridge from Hyde Park Corner*
This stylish hotel, just off Knightsbridge, boasts an excellent range of bedrooms; each furnished with care and a host of thoughtful extras. Newer rooms feature trendy, spacious glass and marble bathrooms and some of the private suites have their own private roof terrace. The striking Blue Bar enhances the reception rooms, all adorned with magnificent flower arrangements. The health spa offers a range of treatment rooms and includes a stunning open-air, roof-top pool. Two renowned, award-winning restaurants provide complete contrast of styles - a modern upscale New York style café, the Boxwood, and the stunning French cuisine at Pétrus.
ROOMS: 214 en suite ⊗ in 188 bedrooms **FACILITIES: Spa** STV Indoor pool supervised Sauna Solarium Gym Beauty/therapy treatments **CONF:** BC Thtr 250 Class 80 Board 52 **SERVICES:** Lift air con **PARKING:** 50 **NOTES:** No dogs Civ Wed 160

Top Hotel

★★★★★ @@@@@ Mandarin Oriental Hyde Park

66 Knightsbridge SW1X 7LA plan 4 F4
☎ 020 7235 2000 Fax 020 7235 2001
e-mail: molon-reservations@mohg.com
web: www.mandarinoriental.com/london
Dir: *Harrods on right, hotel 0.5m on left opp Harvey Nichols*
Situated in fashionable Knightsbridge and overlooking Hyde Park, this landmark hotel is a popular venue for highfliers and the young and fashionable. Bedrooms, many of which have park views, are appointed to the highest standards with luxurious features such as the finest Irish linen and goose down pillows. Guests have a choice of dining options, from the brasserie-style, all-day dining Park Restaurant to the chic, award-winning Foliage Restaurant. The Mandarin Bar also serves light snacks and cocktails. The stylish spa is a destination in its own right and offers a range of innovative treatments.
ROOMS: 200 en suite ⊗ in 106 bedrooms **FACILITIES: Spa** STV Sauna Gym Jacuzzi Fitness centre, steam room, relaxation area, sanarium ♫ Xmas **CONF:** BC Thtr 250 Class 120 Board 60 **SERVICES:** Lift air con **PARKING:** 13 **NOTES:** No dogs Civ Wed 220

Top Hotel

★★★★★ @@ The Carlton Tower

Cadogan Place SW1X 9PY plan 4 F4
☎ 020 7235 1234 Fax 020 7235 9129
e-mail: contact@carltontower.com
web: www.carltontower.com
Dir: *A4 towards Knightsbridge, turn right onto Sloane St. Hotel on left before Cadogan Place*
This impressive hotel enjoys an enviable position in the heart of Knightsbridge, overlooking Cadogan Gardens. Bedrooms vary in size and style and include a number of suites, many with wonderful views of the city. Leisure facilities include a glass-roofed swimming pool, a well-equipped gym and a

continued

number of treatment rooms. Dining options Grissini London and the famous Rib Room and Oyster Bar.

ROOMS: 220 en suite (60 fmly) ⊗ in 116 bedrooms **FACILITIES: Spa** STV supervised Sauna Gym Jacuzzi Massage and Spa treatments ♫ **CONF:** BC Thtr 400 Class 250 Board 30 **SERVICES:** Lift air con **PARKING:** 50 **NOTES:** Civ Wed 400

See advert on this page

Top Hotel

★★★★★ The Goring

Beeston Place, Grosvenor Gardens SW1W 0JW plan 4 H3
☎ 020 7396 9000 020 7834 4393
e-mail: reception@goringhotel.co.uk
web: www.goringhotel.co.uk
Dir: *off Lower Grosvenor Place, just prior to Royal Mews*

Situated in central London, this icon of British hospitality is within walking distance of the Royal Parks and principal shopping areas. The well-equipped bedrooms are furnished in a traditional style and boast high levels of comfort and quality. Stylish reception rooms include the garden bar and the drawing room, both popular for afternoon tea and cocktails. The restaurant menu has a classic repertoire but also enjoys a well-deserved reputation for its contemporary British cuisine.
ROOMS: 72 en suite (9 fmly) s £212-£247; d £259-£311 **LB** **FACILITIES:** STV Free membership of nearby Health Club ♫ Xmas **CONF:** BC Thtr 60 Class 30 Board 30 **SERVICES:** Lift air con **PARKING:** 8 **NOTES:** Civ Wed 50

Top Hotel

★★★★★ The Lanesborough

Hyde Park Corner SW1X 7TA plan 4 G5
☎ 020 7259 5599 020 7259 5606
e-mail: info@lanesborough.co.uk
Dir: *follow signs to central London and Hyde Park Corner*

Occupying an enviable position on Hyde Park Corner, this elegant hotel offers the highest international standards of comfort, quality and security, much appreciated by the loyal clientele. Stylish bedrooms reflect the historic nature of the property, offering high levels of comfort and a superb range of complimentary facilities including internet access, DVDs and CDs. Services are equally impressive with your own personal butler ensuring individual attention. The conservatory restaurant is in demand for meals, superb afternoon teas and Sunday Brunch. The Spa Studio has many original treatments to soothe and pamper.

ROOMS: 95 en suite (5 GF) ⊗ in 24 bedrooms **FACILITIES: Spa** STV Gym Fitness studio ♫ Xmas **CONF:** Thtr 80 Class 55 Board 40 **SERVICES:** Lift air con **PARKING:** 38 **NOTES:** Civ Wed 80

AA Rosette Award for culinary excellence

London

SW1 WESTMINSTER, continued

Top Town House

★★★★★ No 41
41 Buckingham Palace Rd SW1W 0PS plan 5 A4
☎ 020 7300 0041 020 7300 0141
e-mail: book41@rchmail.com
web: www.redcarnationhotels.com
Dir: *opp Buckingham Palace Mews entrance.*
Small, intimate and very private, this stunning town house is located opposite the Royal Mews and ideally positioned for London's theatres, shops and tourist attractions. Decorated in stylish black and white, bedrooms successfully combine comfort with state-of-the-art technology. Attentive personal service and a host of thoughtful extra touches make this town house really special.
ROOMS: 18 en suite s fr £295; d fr £295 (incl. bkfst) **LB** **FACILITIES:** STV use of 2 health clubs **CONF:** BC Board 12 Del from £470 **SERVICES:** Lift air con

★★★★★71%

Sheraton Park Tower
101 Knightsbridge SW1X 7RN plan 4 F4
☎ 020 7235 8050 020 7235 8231
e-mail: 00412.central.london.reservations@sheraton.com
web: www.starwood.com
Dir: *next to Harvey Nichols*
Superbly located for some of London's most fashionable stores, this modern hotel offers some stunning views over the city. Bedrooms combine a high degree of comfort with up-to-date decor and a super range of extras; the suites are particularly impressive. The hotel offers the intimate Knightsbridge lounge, the more formal Piano Bar and extensive conference and banqueting facilities. Restaurant One-O-One is renowned for its seafood.
ROOMS: 280 en suite (280 fmly) in 116 bedrooms s fr £380 **FACILITIES:** STV Gym Fitness room ♫ **CONF:** BC Thtr 120 Class 60 Board 26 **SERVICES:** Lift air con **PARKING:** 67 **NOTES:**

★★★★★71%

Sofitel St James London
6 Waterloo Place SW1Y 4AN plan 5 B6
☎ 020 7747 2222 020 7747 2210
e-mail: H3144@accor.com
Dir: *On corner of Pall Mall & Waterloo Place*
Located in the exclusive area of St James, this Grade II listed, former bank is convenient for most of the city's attractions, theatres and the financial district. The modern bedrooms are equipped to a high standard, whilst more traditional public areas,
continued
including the Brasserie Roux and the Rose Lounge, provide a taste of classical charm.
ROOMS: 186 en suite in 97 bedrooms s £153-£1410; d £153-£1410 **FACILITIES:** STV Gym Steam rooms, Treatment rooms ♫ Xmas **CONF:** BC Thtr 180 Class 110 Board 60 **SERVICES:** Lift air con **NOTES:** Civ Wed 140

Town House

★★★★★ ***22 Jermyn Street***
St James's SW1Y 6HL plan 3 B1
☎ 020 7734 2353 020 7734 0750
e-mail: office@22jermyn.com
web: www.22jermyn.com
Dir: *A4 into Piccadilly, right into Duke St and left into King St. Through St James' Sq to Charles II St. Left into Regent St and left again*
This attractive townhouse enjoys an enviable location close to Piccadilly, Regent Street and the fashionable St James's area. Smartly appointed accommodation mainly consists of spacious suites with a few smaller studios. All are thoughtfully equipped with mini-bar, satellite TV, video recorder and fax/modem lines. 24-hour room service is available and breakfast is served in guest bedrooms.
ROOMS: 18 en suite (13 fmly) **FACILITIES:** STV Membership of nearby Health Club ch fac **CONF:** BC Thtr 15 Class 15 Board 10 **SERVICES:** Lift air con **NOTES:** in restaurant

Top Hotel

★★★★ **The Halkin Hotel**
Halkin St, Belgravia SW1X 7DJ plan 4 G4
☎ 020 7333 1000 020 7333 1100
e-mail: res@halkin.como.bz
Dir: *hotel between Belgrave Sq & Grosvenor Place. Via Chapel St into Headfort Place and left into Halkin St*
This smart, contemporary hotel enjoys an enviable and peaceful position just a short stroll from both Hyde Park and from the designer shops of Knightsbridge. Service is attentive, friendly and very personalised. The stylish bedrooms and suites are equipped to the highest standard with smart, marble bathrooms and every conceivable extra. Public areas include an airy bar lounge and the famous Thai restaurant, Nahm.
ROOMS: 41 en suite in 9 bedrooms s £280-£820; d £280-£820 **LB** **FACILITIES:** STV **CONF:** Thtr 36 Class 15 Board 22 **SERVICES:** Lift air con **NOTES:**

♫ Entertainment

Top Hotel

★★★★ ®® **The Stafford**
16-18 St James's Place SW1A 1NJ plan 5 A5
☎ 020 7493 0111 🖷 020 7493 7121
e-mail: info@thestaffordhotel.co.uk
web: www.thestaffordhotel.co.uk
Dir: *off Pall Mall into St James's St. 2nd left into St James's Place*
Tucked away in a quiet corner of St James's, this lovely boutique hotel retains an air of understated luxury. The American Bar is a fabulous venue in its own right, festooned with an eccentric array of celebrity photos, caps and ties. Afternoon tea is a long established tradition here. From the pristine, tastefully decorated and air-conditioned bedrooms, to the highly professional, yet friendly service, this exclusive hotel is keeping the highest standards.
ROOMS: 81 en suite (6 GF) ⊗ in 73 bedrooms s £253-£700; d £265-£700 **LB** **FACILITIES:** STV Membership of Fitness Club available Xmas **CONF:** Thtr 40 Board 24 **SERVICES:** Lift air con **NOTES:** 🐕 ⊗ in restaurant Civ Wed 44

★★★★76% ® **The Rubens at the Palace**
39 Buckingham Palace Rd SW1W 0PS plan 5 A4
☎ 020 7834 6600 🖷 020 7233 6037
e-mail: bookrb@rchmail.com
web: www.redcarnationhotels.com
Dir: *opposite Royal Mews, 100mtrs away from Buckingham Palace*
This hotel enjoys an enviable location next to Buckingham Palace. Stylish, air-conditioned bedrooms include the pinstripe-walled Saville Row rooms, which follow a tailoring theme, and the opulent Royal rooms, named after different monarchs. Public rooms include the Library fine dining restaurant and a comfortable stylish cocktail bar and lounge. The team here pride themselves on their warmth and friendliness.
ROOMS: 172 en suite ⊗ in 127 bedrooms s fr £190; d fr £245 **LB** **FACILITIES:** STV Health clubs locally ♫ Xmas **CONF:** Thtr 90 Class 40 Board 30 Del from £230 **SERVICES:** Lift air con **NOTES:** ⊗ in restaurant

★★★★74% ®®® **Millennium Hotel London Knightsbridge**
17 Sloane St, Knightsbridge SW1X 9NU plan 4 F4
☎ 020 7235 4377 🖷 020 7235 3705
e-mail: knightsbridge.reservations@mill.cop.com
web: www.millenniumhotels.com
Dir: *from Knightsbridge tube station towards Sloane St. Hotel 70mtrs on right*
This fashionable hotel boasts an enviable location in Knightsbridge's chic shopping district. Air-conditioned, thoughtfully equipped bedrooms are complemented by a popular lobby lounge and the much-acclaimed Mju Restaurant and Bar. Cuisine *continued*
is French with Asian influences. Lighter meals may be taken in the new Tangerine bar. (Valet parking is available if pre-booked.)
ROOMS: 222 en suite ⊗ in 86 bedrooms s £128-£247; d £153-£270 **LB** **FACILITIES:** STV **CONF:** BC Thtr 120 Class 80 Board 50 Del from £245 **SERVICES:** Lift air con **PARKING:** 7 **NOTES:** 🐕 ⊗ in restaurant

★★★★72% **Victoria Park Plaza**
239 Vauxhall Bridge Rd SW1V 1EQ plan 5 A3
☎ 020 7769 9999 🖷 020 7769 9998
e-mail: info@victoriaparkplaza.com
web: www.parkplaza.com
Dir: *turn right out of Victoria Station. Hotel 1 min away*

This smart modern hotel close to Victoria station is well located for all of central London's major attractions. Air-conditioned bedrooms are tastefully appointed and thoughtfully equipped for both business and leisure guests. Airy, stylish public areas include an elegant bar and restaurant, a popular coffee bar and extensive conference facilities complete with a business centre.
ROOMS: 299 en suite ⊗ in 116 bedrooms s £128-£265; d £128-£265 **FACILITIES:** STV Sauna Gym ♫ **CONF:** BC Thtr 500 Class 240 Board 120 **SERVICES:** Lift air con **PARKING:** 42 **NOTES:** 🐕 Civ Wed 500

★★★★71%
De Vere Cavendish St James's London
81 Jermyn St SW1Y 6JF plan 5 B6
☎ 020 7930 2111 🖷 020 7839 2125
e-mail: cavendish.reservations@devere-hotels.com
web: www.devereonline.co.uk
Dir: *from Marble Arch along Park Ln to Hyde Park Corner. Left to Piccadilly, past Ritz and right down Dukes St. Behind Fortnum and Mason*
This smart, stylish hotel enjoys an enviable location in the prestigious St James's area, minutes' walk from Green Park and Piccadilly. Bedrooms have a fresh, contemporary feel and include a number of spacious executive rooms, studios and suites. Elegant public areas include a spacious first-floor lounge, the popular Aslan Restaurant and well-appointed conference and function facilities.
ROOMS: 230 rms (229 en suite) ⊗ in 36 bedrooms **FACILITIES:** STV ch fac **CONF:** BC Thtr 80 Class 50 Board 35 **SERVICES:** Lift air con **PARKING:** 60 **NOTES:** 🐕

★★★★71% **Sheraton Belgravia**
20 Chesham Place SW1X 8HQ plan 4 G3
☎ 020 7235 6040 🖷 020 7259 6243
e-mail: reservations.sheratonbelgravia@sheraton.com
web: www.starwood.com
Dir: *A4 Brompton Rd into Central London. After Brompton Oratory right into Beauchamp Pl. Follow into Pont St, cross Sloane St & hotel on corner*
This smart, boutique style hotel is situated in the heart of Belgravia, just a short walk from the shops of Knightsbridge, Kings Road and Sloane Street. Bedrooms are well equipped for both business and leisure guests and include a number of spacious
continued on p340

London

SW1 WESTMINSTER, continued

executive rooms and suites. Bijou public areas include a stylish lounge where all day snacks are available and Mulberry's restaurant offering a more formal option.
ROOMS: 89 en suite (16 fmly) ⊗ in 37 bedrooms s £142.50-£320; d £142.50-£320 **FACILITIES:** STV comp membership to local health spa ♫ **CONF:** BC Thtr 35 Class 14 Board 20 **SERVICES:** Lift air con **NOTES:** ✗

Town House

★★★★ The Lowndes
21 Lowndes St SW1X 9ES plan 4 F4
☎ 020 7823 1234 020 7235 1154
e-mail: contact@lowndeshotel.com
Dir: *M4 onto A4 into London. Left from Brompton Rd into Sloane St. Left into Pont St and Lowndes St next left. Hotel on right*
This friendly and popular hotel enjoys an enviable location within walking distance of Harrods, Harvey Nichols and the designer shops of Sloane Street. Bedrooms are smartly appointed, well equipped and some boast spacious balconies; a number of junior suites are also available. Bijou public areas include a brasserie restaurant, lounge and meeting room.
ROOMS: 78 en suite ⊗ in 31 bedrooms d fr £265 (incl. bkfst) **LB** **FACILITIES:** STV Use of facilities at Carlton Tower Hotel **CONF:** Thtr 25 Class 8 Board 18 **SERVICES:** Lift air con **NOTES:** ✗

Town House

★★★★ *Grange Rochester*
69 Vincent Square SW1P 2PA plan 5 B3
☎ 020 7828 6611 020 7233 6724
e-mail: rochester@grangehotels.com
web: www.grangehotels.co.uk
Overlooking leafy Vincent Square, this boutique-style hotel is well located for access to London's finest shopping, theatres and tourist attractions. Stylish bedrooms are quiet and well equipped, but do vary in size. Some rooms have balconies with views over the square. The compact public rooms are elegant and offer all day dining and drinking options.
ROOMS: 76 en suite (6 fmly) ⊗ in 30 bedrooms **FACILITIES:** STV **CONF:** Thtr 45 Class 35 Board 35 **SERVICES:** Lift **NOTES:** ✗

★★★66% Quality Hotel Westminster
82-83 Eccleston Square SW1V 1PS plan 5 A2
☎ 020 7834 8042 020 7630 8942
e-mail: enquiries@hotels-westminster.com
web: www.choicehotelseurope.com
Dir: *from Victoria Station, right into Wilton Rd, 3rd right into Gillingham St, hotel 150mtrs*
Situated close to Victoria, this hotel provides a good base for exploring London. Bedrooms vary in size and style and include a number of spacious premier rooms along with several stylishly refurbished contemporary rooms. Public areas include a bar/lounge, a range of conference rooms and the Connaughts Brasserie, which provides a good range of meals.
ROOMS: 107 en suite (8 fmly) ⊗ in 62 bedrooms s £129-£149; d £145-£185 **LB** **FACILITIES:** STV **CONF:** Thtr 150 Class 60 Board 40 Del from £165 **SERVICES:** Lift air con **NOTES:** ✗ ⊗ in restaurant

AA Rosette Award for culinary excellence

SW3 CHELSEA, BROMPTON

Top Town House

★★★★★ ⓇⓇⓇⓇ Capital
Basil St, Knightsbridge SW3 1AT plan 4 F4
☎ 020 7589 5171 020 7225 0011
e-mail: reservations@capitalhotel.co.uk
Dir: *20yds from Harrods*
Personal service is assured at this small, family-owned hotel set in the heart of Knightsbridge. Beautifully designed bedrooms come in a number of styles; all rooms feature antique furniture, marble bathroom and a thoughtful range of extras. Dinner is a highlight of any visit; Eric Chavot and his committed brigade continue to cook to a consistently high standard. Cocktails are a speciality in the delightful, stylish bar, whilst afternoon tea in the elegant, bijou lounge is a must.
ROOMS: 49 en suite ⊗ in 24 bedrooms s £170-£195; d £210-£275 **LB** **FACILITIES:** STV **CONF:** BC Thtr 30 Board 12 **SERVICES:** Lift air con **PARKING:** 15 **NOTES:** ✗ ⊗ in restaurant

Town House

★★★★★ The Draycott
26 Cadogan Gardens SW3 2RP plan 4 F2
☎ 020 7730 6466 020 7730 0236
e-mail: reservations@draycotthotel.com
web: www.draycotthotel.com
Dir: *From Sloane Sq station towards Peter Jones, keep to left. At Kings Rd. take first right Cadogan Gdns, 2nd right, hotel on left.*
Enjoying a prime location just yards from Sloane Square, this town house provides an ideal base in one of the most fashionable areas of London. Many regular guests regard this as their London residence and staff pride themselves on their hospitality. Beautifully appointed bedrooms include a number of very spacious suites and all are equipped to a high standard. Attractive day rooms, furnished with antique and

continued

period pieces, include a choice of lounges, one with access to a lovely sheltered garden.
ROOMS: 35 en suite (9 fmly) (2 GF) ⊗ in 30 bedrooms s £141-£176; d £179-£230 **FACILITIES:** STV Beauty treatment, Massage **CONF:** Thtr 20 Class 12 Board 12 Del from £300 **SERVICES:** Lift air con **NOTES:** ⊗ in restaurant

Town House

★★★★ The Beaufort

33 Beaufort Gardens SW3 1PP plan 4 F3
☎ 020 7584 5252 020 7589 2834
e-mail: reservations@thebeaufort.co.uk
web: www.thebeaufort.co.uk
Dir: *100yds past Harrods on left of Brompton Rd*

This friendly, attractive town house enjoys a peaceful location in a tree-lined cul-de-sac just minutes' walk from Knightsbridge. Air-conditioned bedrooms are thoughtfully equipped with chocolates, fruit, fresh flowers, videos, CD players and free internet and movie channel access. Guests are offered complimentary drinks and afternoon tea, served in the attractive drawing room. A good continental breakfast is served in guests' rooms.
ROOMS: 29 en suite (3 GF) ⊗ in 12 bedrooms s £135-£185; d £185-£360 (incl. cont bkfst) **FACILITIES:** STV **CONF:** BC Thtr 20 Class 12 Board 12 Del from £249 **SERVICES:** Lift air con **NOTES:** ✈ ⊗ in restaurant

Town House

★★★★ Parkes

41 Beaufort Gardens, Knightsbridge SW3 1PW plan 4 E4
☎ 020 7581 9944 020 7581 1999
e-mail: reception@parkeshotel.com
web: www.parkeshotel.com
Dir: *off Brompton Rd, 100yds from Harrods*

This sophisticated and friendly hotel is located in a tree-lined square in the heart of fashionable Knightsbridge. Stylish

continued

bedrooms and spacious suites with kitchens are beautifully appointed and equipped with every conceivable extra including UK/US modems and sockets, wireless ADSL and mini-bars. Whilst there is no hotel restaurant, a wide range of dishes from local eateries can be delivered to your room.
ROOMS: 33 en suite (16 fmly) (4 GF) s £229-£488; d £282-£488 **FACILITIES:** STV arrangement with nearby gym **CONF:** Board 12 **SERVICES:** Lift air con **NOTES:** ✈ ⊗ in restaurant

★★★73% Basil Street

Basil St, Knightsbridge SW3 1AH plan 4 F4
☎ 020 7581 3311 020 7581 3693
e-mail: info@thebasil.com
web: www.thebasil.com
Dir: *M4 & A4 Brompton Rd, right before Harrods. Left into Basil St and hotel on left*

An elegant, classic British hotel located in the heart of this shoppers' paradise. The public rooms are full of character with antiques, parquet floors, fine paintings and tapestries, and service is professional and efficient. Bedrooms are in keeping with the original style of the property with the addition of up-to-date facilities.
ROOMS: 80 en suite (4 fmly) ⊗ in 40 bedrooms s £137-£170; d £197-£241 **LB** **FACILITIES:** STV ♫ Xmas **CONF:** BC Thtr 30 Class 16 Board 20 Del £231 **SERVICES:** Lift **NOTES:** ✈

SW4 CLAPHAM

See LONDON plan 1 E3

★★★68% The Windmill on The Common

Southside, Clapham Common SW4 9DE
☎ 020 8673 4578 020 8675 1486
e-mail: windmillhotel@youngs.co.uk

This popular hotel is located on the edge of Clapham Common and dates back to 1729. The lively pub bar, with its outdoor seating, makes it a favourite venue in the summer months. The smart air-conditioned bedrooms are spacious, comfortable and well equipped for business guests.
ROOMS: 29 en suite (12 GF) ⊗ in 21 bedrooms s £99; d £115 (incl. bkfst) **LB** **FACILITIES:** STV **CONF:** Thtr 40 Class 25 Board 20 **SERVICES:** air con **PARKING:** 16 **NOTES:** ✈ ⊗ in restaurant

SW5 EARL'S COURT

Map 06 TQ27

★★★★72% London Marriott Kensington

Marriott HOTELS & RESORTS

Cromwell Rd SW5 0TH plan 4 B3
☎ 020 7973 1000 020 7370 1685
e-mail: kensington.marriott@marriotthotels.co.uk
web: www.marriott.co.uk
Dir: *on A4, opposite Cromwell Rd Hospital*

This stylish contemporary hotel features a stunning glass exterior

continued on p342

London

SW5 EARL'S COURT, continued

and a seven-storey atrium lobby. Fully air conditioned throughout, the hotel has elegant design combined with a great range of facilities, including indoor leisure, a range of conference rooms and parking. Smart bedrooms offer a host of extras including the very latest communications technology.
ROOMS: 216 en suite (39 fmly) **FACILITIES:** STV Sauna Gym Jacuzzi **CONF:** BC Thtr 200 Class 100 Board 60 Del from £200 **SERVICES:** Lift air con **PARKING:** 20 **NOTES:** ⊗ in restaurant Civ Wed 50

The vast majority of establishments in this guide accept credit and debit cards. We indicate those that don't take any

Town House

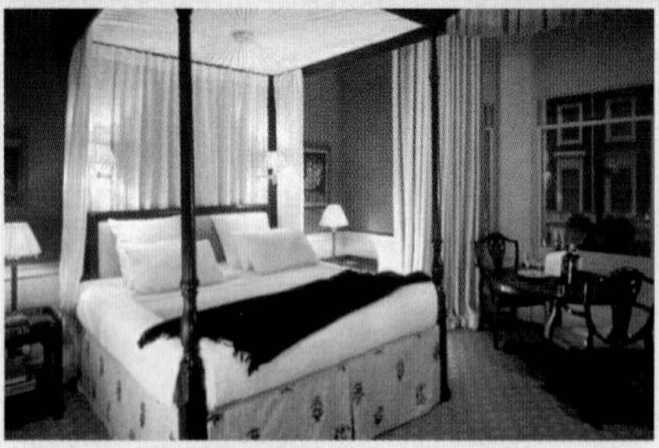

★★★★ The Cranley

10 Bina Gardens, South Kensington SW5 0LA plan 4 C2
☎ 020 7373 0123 020 7373 9497
e-mail: info@thecranley.com
web: www.thecranley.com
Dir: *down Gloucester Rd towards Old Brompton Rd. 3rd right after station into Hereford Sq, then 3rd left into Bina Gardens*
This elegant Victorian town house is set in a quiet residential area of South Kensington where a friendly welcome awaits guests. The bedrooms, including a number of suites, have all undergone a stylish refurbishment and feature antique pieces and many thoughtful extras. Breakfast is continental and served in guest bedrooms.
ROOMS: 39 en suite (4 GF) s £141-£205; d £164.50-£246 (incl. bkfst) **LB** **FACILITIES:** STV **SERVICES:** Lift air con **NOTES:** ⊗ in restaurant

Town House

★★★★ Twenty Nevern Square

20 Nevern Square, Earls Court SW5 9PD plan 4 A2
☎ 020 7565 9555 & 020 7370 4934 020 7565 9444
e-mail: hotel@twentynevernsquare.co.uk
web: www.twentynevernsquare.co.uk
Dir: *from station take Warwick Rd exit, right, 2nd right into Nevern Sq. Hotel 30yds on right*
This small, smart town house is discreetly located in Nevern Square and is ideally situated for both Earls Court and Olympia. The stylish bedrooms, which vary in shape and size, are appointed to a high standard and well equipped. Public areas include a delightful lounge and Café Twenty where breakfast and dinner are served.

ROOMS: 20 en suite (3 GF) ⊗ in 10 bedrooms s £79-£110; d £89-£170 (incl. cont bkfst) **FACILITIES:** STV Arrangements for day membership at Cannons Leisure Centre **CONF:** BC **SERVICES:** Lift **PARKING:** 4 **NOTES:** ⊗ in restaurant

★★★69% K + K Hotel George

1-15 Templeton Place, Earl's Court SW5 9NB plan 4 A2
☎ 020 7598 8700 020 7370 2285
e-mail: hotelgeorge@kkhotels.co.uk
web: www.kkhotels.com/george
Dir: *A3220 Earls Court Rd, right onto Trebouir Rd, right onto Templeton Place*
This smart hotel enjoys a central location, just a few minutes' walk from Earls Court and with easy access to London's central attractions. Smart public areas include a bar/bistro, a stylish restaurant that overlooks the attractive rear garden, an executive lounge and meeting facilities. Bedrooms are particularly well equipped with a host of useful extras including free, high-speed internet access.
ROOMS: 154 en suite (12 fmly) (8 GF) ⊗ in 120 bedrooms s £175; d £210 (incl. bkfst) **LB** **FACILITIES:** STV **CONF:** BC Thtr 25 Class 14 Board 15 Del from £153 **SERVICES:** Lift air con **PARKING:** 32 **NOTES:** ⊗ in restaurant

★★★66% *Burns*

18-26 Barkston Gardens, Kensingston SW5 0EN plan 4 B2
☎ 020 7373 3151 020 7370 4090
e-mail: burnshotel@vienna-group.co.uk
Dir: *Off A4, right to Earls Court Rd (A3220), 2nd left. Hotel in Barkston Gardens, 2nd left past Earls Court underground station.*
This friendly Victorian hotel overlooks a leafy garden in a quiet residential area not far from the Earls Court underground and exhibition centres. Bedrooms are attractively appointed and include duvets and modern facilities. Public areas, although not extensive, are stylish.
ROOMS: 105 en suite (10 fmly) ⊗ in 38 bedrooms **FACILITIES:** STV **SERVICES:** Lift **NOTES:** ⊗ in restaurant

Comfort Inn Kensington

22-32 West Cromwell Rd, Kensington SW5 9QJ plan 4 A3
☎ 020 7373 3300 020 7835 2040
e-mail: enquiries@hotels-kensington.com
web: www.hotels-kensington.com
Dir: *on N side of West Cromwell Rd, between juncts of Cromwell Rd, Earls Court Rd & Warwick Rd*
This modern building offers accommodation in smart, spacious and well equipped bedrooms, all with en suite bathrooms. Refreshments may be taken at the nearby family restaurant. For further details and the Comfort Inn phone number, consult the Hotel Groups page under 'Choice'.
ROOMS: 125 en suite **CONF:** Thtr 80 Class 60 Board 30

London

⌂ Premier Travel Inn London Kensington
11 Knaresborough Place, Kensington SW5 0TJ
plan 4 B2
☎ 0870 238 3304 📠 020 7370 9292
web: www.premiertravelinn.com
Dir: *Just off the A4 Cromwell Road, 2 minutes from Earls Court Underground Station*
High quality, modern budget accommodation ideal for both families and business travellers. Spacious, en suite bedrooms feature bath and shower, satellite TV and many have telephones and modem points. The adjacent family restaurant features a wide and varied menu. For further details consult the Hotel Groups page.
ROOMS: 183 en suite s £72.95-£79.95; d £72.95-£79.95

SW6 FULHAM
See LONDON plan 1 D3/E3

★★★★71% *Chelsea Village*
Stamford Bridge, Fulham Rd SW6 1HS
☎ 020 7565 1400 📠 020 7565 1450
e-mail: reservation@chelseavillage.co.uk
This stylish, eye-catching hotel forms a part of the ambitious development of Chelsea Football Club and is situated adjacent to the ground. Public areas are extensive and feature a wide range of facilities including two restaurants and bars; the Chelsea Club is one of London's premier health and beauty spas. Air-conditioned bedrooms are spacious and well equipped.
ROOMS: 291 en suite (64 fmly) ⊘ in 138 bedrooms **FACILITIES: Spa** STV supervised Sauna Solarium Gym Jacuzzi **CONF:** BC Thtr 300 Class 250 Board 50 **SERVICES:** Lift air con **PARKING:** 290 **NOTES:** Civ Wed 50

★★★68% Jurys Inn Chelsea
Imperial Rd, Imperial Wharf SW6 2GA
☎ 020 7411 2200 📠 020 7411 2444
e-mail: info@jurysdoyle.com
web: www.jurysdoyle.com
This modern hotel is located in Chelesa close to the Wharf. Bedrooms provide good guest comfort and in-room facilities are ideal for both leisure and business markets. There is even one floor designed by Laura Ashley. Public areas include a number of meeting rooms, a restaurant and a popular bar.
ROOMS: 172 en suite (172 fmly) ⊘ in 29 bedrooms s £89; d £89 **FACILITIES:** STV Xmas **CONF:** Thtr 15 Board 10 Del £110 **SERVICES:** Lift air con **NOTES:** ⊘ in restaurant Closed 24-26 Dec

★★★63% Hotel Ibis London Earls Court
47 Lillie Rd SW6 1UD plan 4 A1
☎ 020 7610 0880 📠 020 7381 0215
e-mail: h5623@accor.com
web: www.ibishotels.com
Dir: *A4/A315, at Olympia Exhibition Centre, turn right into North End Rd. Continue to mini rdbt turn left into Lillie Rd, hotel on right*
Situated opposite the Earls Court Exhibition Centre, this large, modern hotel is popular with business and leisure guests. Bedrooms are comfortable and well equipped. There is a café bar open all day and a restaurant that serves evening meals. There are also extensive conference facilities and an underground car park.
ROOMS: 502 en suite (20 fmly) ⊘ in 240 bedrooms s £70-£80; d £70-£80 **FACILITIES:** STV Health club and gym nearby **CONF:** BC Thtr 1200 Class 700 Board 100 Del £150 **SERVICES:** Lift **PARKING:** 130 **NOTES:** ⊘ in restaurant

Destination dining!
This symbol indicates a Restaurant with Rooms

⌂ Premier Travel Inn London Putney Bridge
3 Putney Bridge Approach SW6 3JD
☎ 0870 238 3302 📠 020 7471 8315
web: www.premiertravelinn.com
Dir: *north bank of River Thames by Putney Bridge*
High quality, modern budget accommodation ideal for both families and business travellers. Spacious, en suite bedrooms feature bath and shower, satellite TV and many have telephones and modem points. The adjacent family restaurant features a wide and varied menu. For further details consult the Hotel Groups page.
ROOMS: 154 en suite s £69.95-£79.95; d £69.95-£79.95

SW7 SOUTH KENSINGTON

★★★★★76% The Bentley Kempinski
27-33 Harrington Gardens SW7 4JX plan 4 C2
☎ 020 7244 5555 📠 020 7244 5566
e-mail: info@thebentley-hotel.com
web: www.thebentley-hotel.com
Dir: *S of A4 into Knightsbridge at junct with Gloucester Rd, right, 2nd right turn, hotel on left just after mini-rdbt*

This hotel, discreetly located in the heart of Kensington, features lavish opulence throughout the public areas. Spacious air-conditioned bedrooms are equally luxurious, whilst marble clad bathrooms offer jacuzzi baths and walk-in showers. Public areas include the Peridot where breakfast and lunch are served, a cosy cigar den and the cocktail bar, Malachite. The fine dining restaurant, 1880, which is open for dinner, provides excellent contemporary cuisine and highly professional service.
ROOMS: 64 en suite ⊘ in 11 bedrooms s £295-£4700; d £295-£4700 **FACILITIES: Spa** STV Sauna Gym Jacuzzi Traditional Turkish Hamam ♫ Xmas **CONF:** Thtr 70 Class 60 Board 50 Del from £425 **SERVICES:** Lift air con **NOTES:** ⊘ in restaurant

Town House

★★★★★ Baglioni
60 Hyde Park Gate, Kensington Rd, Kensington SW7 5BB
plan 4 C2
☎ 020 7368 5700 📠 020 7368 5701
e-mail: info@baglionihotellondon.com
A centrally located hotel in the heart of Kensington. This highly impressive property offers superb accommodation, predominately suites, which feature espresso machines, interactive plasma TV screens and a host of other fine touches. Service is both professional and friendly, and includes butlers for the rooms. Public areas include the small Caroli Health Club, a trendy basement bar and the main open-plan bar, lounge and award-winning Brunello restaurant
ROOMS: 88 en suite (16 fmly) ⊘ in all bedrooms s £247-£353; d £494-£706 **FACILITIES:** STV Sauna Gym Jacuzzi Xmas **CONF:** BC Thtr 60 Class 60 Board 60 **SERVICES:** Lift air con **NOTES:**

SW7 SOUTH KENSINGTON, continued

★★★★73% Millennium Gloucester Hotel London Kensington

MILLENNIUM HOTELS AND RESORTS

4-18 Harrington Gardens SW7 4LH plan 4 C2
☎ 020 7373 6030 🖷 020 7373 0409
e-mail: sales.gloucester@mill-cop.com
web: www.millenniumhotels.com
Dir: *opposite Gloucester Rd underground station*

This spacious, stylish hotel is centrally located, close to The Victoria and Albert Museum and minutes walk from Gloucester Road tube station. Air-conditioned bedrooms are furnished in a variety of contemporary styles and Clubrooms benefit from a dedicated club lounge with complimentary breakfast and snacks. A wide range of eating options includes Singaporean and Mediterranean cuisine.

ROOMS: 610 en suite (6 fmly) ⊘ in 439 bedrooms s £250; d £250 **LB** **FACILITIES:** STV Gym **CONF:** BC Thtr 500 Class 280 Board 40 Del £380 **SERVICES:** Lift air con **PARKING:** 110 **NOTES:** ✗

★★★★72% ❀ Harrington Hall

5-25 Harrington Gardens SW7 4JW plan 4 C2
☎ 020 7396 9696 🖷 020 7396 9090
e-mail: sales@harringtonhall.co.uk
web: www.harringtonhall.co.uk
Dir: *towards Knightsbridge into Gloucester Rd. 2nd right into Harrington Gdns and hotel on left*

This classic Victorian façade conceals a modern, elegant hotel. Bedrooms are spacious, comfortable, well equipped and air conditioned. The hotel has a multi-gym and extensive meeting rooms. The busy ground floor lounge and bar offers all day refreshments and is a popular meeting venue.

ROOMS: 200 en suite ⊘ in 132 bedrooms s £120-£185; d £120-£195 **LB** **FACILITIES:** STV Sauna Gym Xmas **CONF:** BC Thtr 200 Class 80 Board 25 Del from £215 **SERVICES:** Lift air con **NOTES:** ✗

★★★★71% ❀ Radisson Edwardian Vanderbilt

Radisson EDWARDIAN

68-86 Cromwell Rd SW7 5BT plan 4 C3
☎ 020 7761 9000 🖷 020 7761 9001
e-mail: resvand@radisson.com
web: www.radissonedwardian.com
Dir: *A4 into central London on Cromwell Rd. Hotel on left at junct of Gloucester Rd & Cromwell Rd*

Located in South Kensington close to many features and attractions. The hotel offers the ideal base for exploring London. Once home to the Vanderbilt family the hotel retains many of its original features including stunning artwork and fireplaces. Bedrooms have a warm classic ambiance with rich décor and marble bathrooms.

ROOMS: 215 en suite (18 fmly) (28 GF) ⊘ in 113 bedrooms **FACILITIES:** Fitness room Business centre, Valet Laundry Service & Valet Parking on request. **CONF:** BC Thtr 100 Class 56 Board 40 **SERVICES:** Lift air con **NOTES:** ✗ No children

★★★★70% Jurys Kensington Hotel

JURYS DOYLE HOTELS

109-113 Queensgate, South Kensington SW7 5LR plan 4 D2
☎ 020 7589 6300 🖷 020 7581 1492
e-mail: Kensington@jurysdoyle.com
web: www.jurysdoyle.com
Dir: *From A4 take Cromwell Rd, turn right at V&A Museum onto Queensgate, hotel at end on left*

This beautiful building has been carefully refurbished and offers an excellent location for visitors to London. Smartly appointed public areas include an open-plan lobby/bar, Copplestones restaurant with adjoining library lounge and the lively Kavanagh's bar. Bedrooms vary in size and are well equipped and have modern colour themes.

ROOMS: 173 annexe en suite (10 fmly) ⊘ in 130 bedrooms s £89-£199; d £89-£240 (incl. bkfst) **FACILITIES:** STV Health Club facilities available locally at discounted rate ♫ Xmas **CONF:** Thtr 90 Class 45 Board 35 Del from £175 **SERVICES:** Lift air con **NOTES:** ✗ ⊘ in restaurant

★★★★69% Millennium Baileys Hotel London Kensington

MILLENNIUM HOTELS AND RESORTS

140 Gloucester Rd SW7 4QH plan 4 C3
☎ 020 7373 6000 🖷 020 7370 3760
e-mail: reservations@mill-cop.com
web: www.millenniumhotels.com
Dir: *A4, turn right at Cromwell Hospital into Knaresborough Place, follow to Courtfield Rd to corner of Gloucester Rd, hotel opposite underground*

This elegant hotel has a townhouse feel to it and enjoys a prime location opposite Gloucester Road tube station. Air-conditioned bedrooms are smartly appointed and thoughtfully equipped, particularly the club rooms which have DVD players. Public areas include a stylish contemporary restaurant and bar. Guests may also use the facilities at its adjacent, larger sister hotel.

ROOMS: 212 en suite ⊘ in 120 bedrooms **FACILITIES:** STV Gym **CONF:** Thtr 20 Class 18 Board 12 Del from £175 **SERVICES:** Lift air con **PARKING:** 70 **NOTES:** ✗

★★★65% *Grange Strathmore*

41 Queens Gate Gardens SW7 5NB plan 4 C3
☎ 020 7584 0512 🖷 020 7584 0246
e-mail: strathmore@grangehotels.com
web: www.grangehotels.co.uk
Dir: *M4 E into Kensington, left into Queens Gate Gardens.*

Formerly the residence of the Earl of Strathmore, this elegant property retains many of its original features. Bedrooms, which vary in shape and size, are appointed to a high standard. Public areas include a selection of meeting rooms, Glamis lounge bar and the chandeliered Earls restaurant.

ROOMS: 77 en suite (10 fmly) ⊘ in 40 bedrooms **FACILITIES:** STV **CONF:** Thtr 60 Class 25 Board 26 **SERVICES:** Lift

SW10 WEST BROMPTON

See LONDON plan 1 D/E3

★★★★★69% Conrad London

Chelsea Harbour SW10 0XG
☎ 020 7823 3000 🖷 020 7351 6525
e-mail: londoninfo@conradhotels.com
web: www.conradhotels.com
Dir: *A4 to Earls Court Rd S towards river. Right into Kings Rd, left down Lots Rd. Chelsea Harbour in front*

Against the picturesque backdrop of Chelsea Harbour's small marina, this modern hotel offers spacious, comfortable accommodation. All rooms are suites which are superbly equipped, many enjoy splendid views of the marina. In addition, there are also several luxurious penthouse suites. Public areas

continued

London

include a modern bar and restaurant, excellent leisure facilities and extensive meeting and function rooms.
ROOMS: 160 en suite (39 fmly) ⊗ in 110 bedrooms **FACILITIES:** STV Sauna Solarium Gym Conrad Health Club with beauty treatments ♫ Xmas **CONF:** Thtr 280 Class 120 Board 50 **SERVICES:** Lift air con **PARKING:** 17 **NOTES:** Civ Wed 200

SW11 BATTERSEA
See LONDON plan 1 E3

Travelodge (London Battersea)
200 York Rd, Battersea SW11 3SA
☎ 08700 850 950 📠 020 7978 5898
web: www.travelodge.co.uk
Dir: *from Wandsworth Bridge southern rdbt, take A3205 (York Rd) towards Battersea. 0.5m on left*
Travelodge offers good quality, good value, modern accommodation. Ideal for families, the spacious, en suite bedrooms include remote-control TV, tea and coffee-making facilities and comfortable beds. Meals can be taken at the nearby family restaurant. For further details consult the Hotel Groups page.
ROOMS: 87 en suite s fr £26; d fr £26

SW19 WIMBLEDON
See LONDON plan 1 D1

W1 WEST END

Top Hotel

★★★★★ ◎◎◎ ***Claridge's***
Brook St W1A 2JQ plan 2 H2
☎ 020 7629 8860 📠 020 7499 2210
e-mail: info@claridges.co.uk
Dir: *Take 1st turn after Green Park underground station to Berkeley Sq & 4th exit into Davies St. Take 3rd turn right into Brook St*
Once renowned as the resort of kings and princes, Claridge's today continues to set the standards by which other hotels are judged. The sumptuous, air-conditioned bedrooms are elegantly themed to reflect the Victorian or art deco architecture of the building. Gordon Ramsay at Claridge's has fast become one of London's most popular dining venues, while the stylish cocktail bar is proving to be equally well supported by residents and non-residents alike. Service throughout is punctilious and thoroughly professional.
ROOMS: 203 en suite (144 fmly) ⊗ in 34 bedrooms
FACILITIES: STV Gym Beauty & health treatments. Use of sister hotel swimming pool ♫ **CONF:** Thtr 250 Class 130 Board 60
SERVICES: Lift air con **NOTES:** 🐕 Civ Wed 200

We have indicated only the hotels that don't accept credit or debit cards

Top Hotel

★★★★★ ◎◎◎ **Connaught**
Carlos Place W1K 2AL plan 2 G1
☎ 020 7499 7070 📠 020 7495 3262
e-mail: info@the-connaught.co.uk
Dir: *between Grosvenor Sq and Berkeley Sq in Mayfair*
Smaller than some of the major London hotels, The Connaught offers guests a more intimate atmosphere. Couple this with exemplary standards of service and its easy to see why people return time after time. To ensure that every guest is pampered, butlers and valets respond at the touch of a button and nothing is too much trouble. Dining is now in the hands of Angela Hartnett, a protégé of Gordon Ramsay, and the restaurant menu has more than a hint of Italian about it.
ROOMS: 92 en suite **LB** **FACILITIES:** STV Gym Fitness studio, Health club facilities at sister hotels **CONF:** Board 18 **SERVICES:** Lift air con **NOTES:** 🐕

Top Hotel

★★★★★ ◎◎ **The Dorchester**
Park Ln W1A 2HJ plan 4 G6
☎ 020 7629 8888 📠 020 7409 0114
e-mail: reservations@dorchesterhotel.com
Dir: *halfway along Park Ln between Hyde Park Corner & Marble Arch*
One of London's finest hotels, The Dorchester is sumptuously decorated. The spacious bedrooms and suites are beautifully appointed and feature fabulous marble bathrooms. Leading off from the foyer, The Promenade is the perfect setting for afternoon tea or drinks. In the evenings guests can relax to the sound of live jazz in the bar, and enjoy a cocktail or an Italian meal. Further dining options include the classic Dorchester Grill and a sophisticated new Chinese restaurant, China Tang, due to open at the time of going to press.
ROOMS: 250 en suite ⊗ in 34 bedrooms s £351.52-£460; d £424-£600 **LB** **FACILITIES: Spa** STV Sauna Solarium Gym Jacuzzi The Dorchester Spa Health club ♫ Xmas **CONF:** BC Thtr 500 Class 300 Board 42 **SERVICES:** Lift air con **PARKING:** 21 **NOTES:** 🐕 Civ Wed 500

London

Top Hotel

★★★★★ @@ **The Ritz**
150 Piccadilly W1J 9BR plan 5 A6
☎ 020 7493 8181 📠 020 7493 2687
e-mail: enquire@theritzlondon.com
web: www.theritzlondon.com
Dir: *from Hyde Park Corner E on Piccadilly. Hotel on right after Green Park*
This renowned, stylish hotel offers guests the ultimate in sophistication whilst still managing to retain all of its former historical glory. Bedrooms and suites are exquisitely furnished in Louis XVI style, with fine marble bathrooms and every imaginable comfort. Elegant reception rooms include the Palm Court with its legendary afternoon teas, the beautiful fashionable Rivoli Bar and the sumptuous Ritz Restaurant, complete with gold chandeliers and extraordinary trompe-l'oeil decoration.
ROOMS: 133 en suite ◎ in 36 bedrooms s £365; d £435-£2235
LB FACILITIES: STV Gym ♬ Xmas **CONF:** Thtr 60 Class 25 Board 32 **SERVICES:** Lift air con **NOTES:** ✖ Civ Wed 70

Top Town House

★★★★★ @ 🏠 **Athenaeum**
116 Piccadilly W1J 7BJ plan 4 H5
☎ 020 7499 3464 📠 020 7493 1860
e-mail: info@athenaeumhotel.com
web: www.athenaeumhotel.com
Dir: *on Piccadilly, overlooking Green Park*
With a discreet address in the heart of Mayfair, this well-loved hotel has become a favourite with many guests over the years for its efficient service and caring hospitality. Bedrooms are equipped to the highest standard with several enjoying elevated views over Green Park. A row of Edwardian town houses immediately adjacent to the hotel offer a range of
continued

spacious and well-appointed apartments. Public rooms include Bullochs Restaurant and the Windsor Lounge; a cosy cocktail bar specialising in its range of malt whiskies.
ROOMS: 157 en suite ◎ in 58 bedrooms d £199-£650 **LB**
FACILITIES: Spa STV Sauna Gym Jacuzzi Steam rooms, spa treatments, hair dressing salon Xmas **CONF:** BC Thtr 55 Class 35 Board 36 **SERVICES:** Lift air con **NOTES:** ✖ Civ Wed 80

Top Hotel

★★★★★ @ **Four Seasons Hotel London**
Hamilton Place, Park Ln W1A 1AZ plan 4 G5
☎ 020 7499 0888 📠 020 7493 1895
e-mail: fsh.london@fourseasons.com
Dir: *from Piccadilly into Old Park Ln. Then Hamilton Place*
This long-established popular hotel is discreetly located near Hyde Park Corner, in the heart of Mayfair. It successfully combines modern efficiencies with traditional luxury. Guest care is consistently of the highest order, even down to the smallest detail of the personalised wake-up call. The bedrooms are elegant and spacious, and the unique conservatory rooms are particularly special. Spacious public areas include extensive conference and banqueting facilities, Lane's bar and fine-dining restaurant and an elegant lounge where wonderful afternoon teas are served.
ROOMS: 219 en suite ◎ in 96 bedrooms s £376-£1880;
d £440-£2703 **LB FACILITIES:** STV Gym ♬ Xmas **CONF:** BC Thtr 400 Class 200 Board 70 **SERVICES:** Lift air con **PARKING:** 72 **NOTES:** Civ Wed 180

★★★★★72% @@
InterContinental London
1 Hamilton Place, Hyde Park Corner W1J 7QY INTER·CONTINENTAL.
plan 4 G5 HOTELS AND RESORTS
☎ 020 7409 3131 📠 020 7493 3476
e-mail: london@interconti.com
Dir: *at Hyde Park Corner, on corner of Park Lane and Piccadilly*
A well-known and well-loved landmark on Hyde Park Corner. At the time of going to press we were informed that the hotel was due to close in October 2005 for a complete refurbishment. Please refer to the AA internet site www.theAA.com for current information.
ROOMS: 451 en suite ◎ in 312 bedrooms s fr £376; d fr £376
FACILITIES: STV Sauna Gym Jacuzzi Beauty treatments, Health Club, Horse riding, Crazy golf, Tennis courts nearby ♬ Xmas **CONF:** BC Thtr 750 Class 340 Board 62 **SERVICES:** Lift air con **PARKING:** 100 **NOTES:** ✖ Civ Wed 750

> TV dinner?
> Room service at three stars and above

★★★★★71% @@@ Hyatt Regency London - The Churchill
30 Portman Square W1A 4ZX plan 2 F2
☎ 020 7486 5800 020 7486 1255
e-mail: london.churchill@hyattintl.com
Dir: *from Marble Arch rdbt, follow signs for Oxford Circus onto Oxford St. Left turn after 2nd lights onto Portman St. Hotel on left*

This smart hotel enjoys a central location overlooking Portman Square. Excellent conference, hairdressing and beauty facilities and a fitness room make this the ideal choice for both corporate and leisure guests. Two floors of executive club bedrooms benefit from a host of facilities and extras. The Montagu restaurant has a buzzing atmosphere, while Locanda Locatelli showcases the enormous talents of Giorgio Locatelli in its fine Italian cuisine.
ROOMS: 445 en suite in 156 bedrooms s £125-£290; d £125-£290 **LB FACILITIES:** STV Sauna Gym Jogging track Xmas **CONF:** BC Thtr 250 Class 160 Board 68 **SERVICES:** Lift air con **PARKING:** 48 **NOTES:** Civ Wed 250

★★★★★69% Langham Hotel
1c Portland Place W1B 1JA plan 2 H4
☎ 020 7636 1000 020 7323 2340
e-mail: lon.info@langhamhotels.com
Dir: *N of Oxford Circus, left opposite All Souls Church*
Originally opened in 1865, this elegant hotel is now part of Langham Hotels International and enjoys a central location ideal for both theatreland and principal shopping areas. Bedrooms offer a choice of styles from traditional through to modern, all comfortably appointed with a full range of amenities. Public areas include the elegant Palm Court ideal for afternoon tea, Memories restaurant and an extensive health club complete with a 16-metre pool. At the time of inspection the hotel was due to embark on a multi-million pound refurbishment.
ROOMS: 427 en suite (5 fmly) d fr £255 **FACILITIES: Spa** STV Sauna Solarium Gym Jacuzzi Xmas **CONF:** BC Thtr 775 Class 442 Board 312 Del from £295 **SERVICES:** Lift air con **NOTES:** in restaurant Civ Wed 300

★★★★★68%
London Marriott Hotel Park Lane
140 Park Ln W1K 7AA plan 2 F2
☎ 020 7493 7000 020 7493 8333
e-mail: mhrs.parklane@marriotthotels.com
web: www.marriott.co.uk
Dir: *From Hyde Park Corner left on Park Ln onto A4202, 0.8m. At Marble Arch onto Park Ln. Take 1st left onto North Row. Hotel on left*
This modern and stylish hotel is situated in a prominent position in the heart of central London. Bedrooms are all superbly appointed and air conditioned. Public rooms include a popular lounge/bar, and there are wonderful leisure facilities and an executive lounge.
ROOMS: 157 en suite in 95 bedrooms d £311.37-£358.37 **LB FACILITIES:** STV Gym Steam Room Xmas **CONF:** BC Thtr 72 Class 33 Board 42 **SERVICES:** Lift air con **NOTES:** in restaurant

★★★★★67% @@ Le Meridien Piccadilly
21 Piccadilly W1J 0BH plan 3 B1
☎ 0870 400 8400 & 020 7734 8000 020 7437 3574
e-mail: lmpiccres@lemeridien.com
Dir: *100mtrs from Piccadilly Circus*
This landmark hotel enjoys a prime central location on the doorstep of Piccadilly, Regent Street, Soho and theatreland. Thoughtfully equipped bedrooms vary in size and style and include some stylish and spacious suites. The hotel boasts a contemporary airy Terrace Restaurant and the palatial Oak Room lounge where a pianist accompanies afternoon teas.
ROOMS: 266 en suite (19 fmly) in 87 bedrooms s £193-£229; d £193-£264 **FACILITIES:** STV Squash Sauna Gym Jacuzzi Xmas **CONF:** BC Thtr 250 Class 160 Board 80 **SERVICES:** Lift air con **NOTES:** Civ Wed 120

★★★★★65% Grosvenor House
Park Ln W1A 3AA plan 2 G1
☎ 020 7499 6363 & 7399 8400 020 7493 3341
e-mail: grosvenor.house@marriotthotels.com
web: www.grosvenor-house.co.uk
Dir: *Marble Arch, halfway down Park Ln*
This internationally renowned hotel, overlooking Hyde Park, has first class amenities for both business and leisure guests, along with spacious surroundings. The Grosvenor House epitomises the fine hotel culture and history of London. The property also boasts some of the finest function facilities in London. At the time of going to press, the hotel was embarking on major redevelopment. Please refer to our website (www.theAA.com) for the latest information.
ROOMS: 446 en suite in 236 bedrooms s £210-£258; d £210-£258 **LB FACILITIES: Spa** STV supervised Sauna Solarium Gym Jacuzzi Health & Fitness centre/Beauty salon Xmas **CONF:** BC Thtr 1770 Class 800 Board 34 **SERVICES:** Lift air con **PARKING:** 80 **NOTES:** Civ Wed 1500

★★★★★63%
Radisson Edwardian May Fair Hotel
Stratton St W1J 8LL plan 5 A6
☎ 020 7629 7777 020 7629 1459
e-mail: mayfair@interconti.com
web: www.radissonedwardian.com
Dir: *from Hyde Park Corner or Piccadilly left onto Stratton St*
Situated in the heart of Mayfair with easy access to Piccadilly Circus, Bond Street, Knightsbridge, Green Park and Buckingham Palace. This prestigious hotel is undergoing a complete refurbishment programme. Redevelopment of all public areas, bedrooms, restaurants and conference rooms, should ensure its position as one of London's finest hotels. The new May Fair bar and the Health Spa have already opened their doors.
ROOMS: 289 en suite (14 fmly) in 148 bedrooms **FACILITIES:** STV Sauna Solarium Gym **CONF:** Thtr 292 Class 108 Board 60 **SERVICES:** Lift air con **NOTES:** Civ Wed 250

★★★★77% @ The Westbury
Bond St W1S 2YF plan 3 A2
☎ 020 7629 7755 020 7495 1163
e-mail: reservations@westburymayfair.com
Dir: *from Oxford Circus S down Regent St, right onto Conduit St, hotel at junct of Conduit St & Bond St*
A well-known favourite with an international clientele, the Westbury is located at the heart of London's finest shopping district and provides a calm atmosphere away from the hubbub. The standards of accommodation are high throughout. Reception rooms offer a good choice for both relaxing and eating; the stylish

continued on p348

London

W1 WEST END, continued

restaurant and popular Polo Bar were undergoing an impressive refurbishment programme at the time of this inspection.
ROOMS: 247 en suite ⊗ in 150 bedrooms s £310; d £310 (incl. bkfst) **LB** **FACILITIES:** STV Gym Fitness centre, Business centre ♫ Xmas **CONF:** BC Thtr 120 Class 55 Board 35 Del £265 **SERVICES:** Lift air con **PARKING:** 8

See advert on opposite page

★★★★74% ◎ Chesterfield Mayfair
35 Charles St, Mayfair W1J 5EB plan 4 H6
☎ 020 7491 2622 🖷 020 7491 4793
e-mail: bookch@rchmail.com
web: www.redcarnationhotels.com
Dir: *From Hyde Park corner along Piccadilly, left into Half Moon St. At end left and 1st right into Queens St, then right into Charles St*
Quiet elegance and an atmosphere of exclusivity characterise this stylish Mayfair hotel where attentive, friendly service is a highlight. Bedrooms have been decorated in a variety of contemporary styles, some with fabric walls; all are extremely thoughtfully equipped and boast marble-clad bathrooms with heated floors and mirrors. Bedrooms and public areas are air conditioned.
ROOMS: 110 en suite (7 fmly) ⊗ in 52 bedrooms s £99-£225; d £119-£295 **LB** **FACILITIES:** STV ♫ Xmas **CONF:** Thtr 100 Class 45 Board 45 Del from £195 **SERVICES:** Lift air con **NOTES:** Civ Wed 120

★★★★74% ◎◎ The Montcalm-Hotel Nikko London
Great Cumberland Place W1H 7TW plan 2 F2
☎ 020 7402 4288 🖷 020 7724 9180
e-mail: reservations@montcalm.co.uk
web: www.montcalm.co.uk
Dir: *2 mins' walk N from Marble Arch station*

Ideally located on a secluded crescent close to Marble Arch, this charming Georgian property is named after the Marquis de Montcalm. Japanese-owned, the hotel offers extremely comfortable accommodation, ranging from standard to duplex 'junior' and penthouse suites. Staff are thoughtful and the stylish restaurant has a reputation for creative, modern cooking. Restaurant prices include a half bottle of wine per person. Lunch is particularly good value for money.
ROOMS: 120 en suite (4 fmly) ⊗ in 58 bedrooms s fr £270.25; d fr £293.75 (incl. bkfst) **LB** **FACILITIES:** STV **CONF:** Thtr 80 Class 36 Board 36 Del from £250 **SERVICES:** Lift air con **PARKING:** 10 **NOTES:** ✗

Packed in a hurry? Ironing facilities should be available at all star levels, either in the rooms or on request

★★★★73% London Marriott Hotel Marble Arch
134 George St W1H 5DN plan 2 F3
☎ 020 7723 1277 🖷 020 7402 0666
e-mail: salesadmin.marblearch@marriotthotels.co.uk
web: www.marriott.co.uk
Dir: *from Marble Arch turn into Edgware Rd, then 4th right into George St. Left into Forset St for entrance*
Conveniently situated just off the Edgeware Road and close to the Oxford Street shops, this modern hotel offers smart, well-equipped, air-conditioned bedrooms. Public areas are stylish, if a little compact, and include a smart indoor leisure club, bar and restaurant. Secure underground parking is also available.
ROOMS: 240 en suite (100 fmly) ⊗ in 167 bedrooms **FACILITIES:** STV supervised Sauna Solarium Gym Jacuzzi Beauty parlour & Sun beds Xmas **CONF:** Thtr 150 Class 75 Board 80 **SERVICES:** Lift air con **PARKING:** 80 **NOTES:** ✗ ⊗ in restaurant

★★★★73% Radisson Edwardian Berkshire
350 Oxford St W1N 0BY plan 2 H2
☎ 020 7629 7474 🖷 020 7629 8156
e-mail: resberk@radisson.com
web: www.radissonedwardian.com
Dir: *opposite Bond St Underground. Entrance on Marylebone Lane.*
A friendly atmosphere prevails at this elegant hotel, centrally located next to Oxford Street's major department stores. Public areas have a boutique feel and include a contemporary bar, smart restaurant and a selection of meeting and conference rooms. Well-equipped bedrooms vary in size, but all are stylishly decorated.
ROOMS: 147 en suite (10 fmly) ⊗ in 99 bedrooms **FACILITIES:** STV Valet Laundry & Parking services on request **CONF:** BC Thtr 40 Class 16 Board 16 **SERVICES:** Lift air con **NOTES:** ✗ No children

★★★★73% The Washington Mayfair Hotel
5-7 Curzon St, Mayfair W1J 5HE plan 4 H6
☎ 020 7499 7000 🖷 020 7495 6172
e-mail: sales@washington-mayfair.co.uk
web: www.washington-mayfair.co.uk
Dir: *from Green Park station take Piccadilly exit and turn right. Take 4th street on right into Curzon St.*
Situated in the heart of Mayfair, this stylish independently owned hotel offers a very high standard of accommodation. Personalised, friendly service is noteworthy. Bedrooms are attractively furnished and provide high levels of comfort. The hotel is also a popular venue for afternoon tea and refreshments, served in the marbled and wood-panelled lounge.
ROOMS: 171 en suite ⊗ in 94 bedrooms s £253-£470; d £253-£470 **LB** **FACILITIES:** STV Gym ♫ Xmas **CONF:** BC Thtr 110 Class 40 Board 36 Del from £250 **SERVICES:** Lift air con **NOTES:** ✗

★★★★72% ◎◎ *London Marriott Hotel Grosvenor Square*
Grosvenor Square W1K 6JP plan 2 G2
☎ 020 7493 1232 🖷 020 7491 3201
e-mail: businesscentre@londonmarriott.co.uk
web: www.marriott.co.uk
Dir: *M4 E to Cromwell Rd through Knightsbridge to Hyde Park Corner. Park Lane right at Brook Gate onto Upper Brook St to Grosvenor Sq*
Situated adjacent to Grosvenor Square in the heart of Mayfair, this hotel combines the best of a relatively peaceful setting with convenient access to the city, West End and some of the most exclusive shopping in London. Bedrooms and public areas are

continued

London

furnished and decorated to a high standard and retain the traditional elegance for which the area is known.
ROOMS: 221 en suite (26 fmly) ⊗ in 120 bedrooms **FACILITIES:** STV Gym Exercise & fitness centre **CONF:** BC Thtr 900 Class 500 Board 120 **SERVICES:** Lift air con **PARKING:** 80 **NOTES:** ✖ Civ Wed

Town House

★★★★ *Grange Fitzrovia*
20-28 Bolsover St W1W 5NB plan 3 A4
☎ 020 7467 7000 020 7636 5085
e-mail: fitzrovia@grangehotels.com
web: www.grangehotels.co.uk
Situated in a quiet side street, this charming central London townhouse hotel is just minutes away from the theatres of the West End and the shops of Oxford and Street Bond Street. Guest bedrooms, accessed via panoramic glass lifts, are generally spacious and offer an excellent range of facilities. Public rooms feature a non-smoking lounge and an elegant lounge bar.
ROOMS: 88 en suite ⊗ in 40 bedrooms **FACILITIES:** STV **CONF:** Thtr 100 Class 45 Board 40 **SERVICES:** Lift **NOTES:** ✖

★★★★71% Jurys Clifton-Ford
47 Welbeck St W1M 8DN plan 2 G3
☎ 020 7486 6600 020 7486 7492
e-mail: cliftonford@jurysdoyle.com
web: www.jurysdoyle.com
Dir: *from Portland Place, turn into New Cavendish St. Welbeck St last turning on left*
This well kept hotel enjoys a central location just 5 minutes' walk from Oxford Street and fashionable Bond Street. Bedrooms vary in space and style and include a number of penthouse apartments with balconies. Public areas include an excellent leisure club with a good-sized swimming pool, extensive conference facilities and a spacious lounge, bar and restaurant.
ROOMS: 256 en suite (7 fmly) ⊗ in 130 bedrooms s £91-£235; d £91-£235 **LB** **FACILITIES:** STV Sauna Solarium Gym Jacuzzi Leisure club Health/beauty treatments Dance studio **CONF:** Thtr 120 Class 70 Board 40 Del £250 **SERVICES:** Lift air con **NOTES:** ✖ ⊗ in restaurant

★★★★71% *The Mandeville*
Mandeville Place W1U 2BE plan 2 G3
☎ 020 7935 5599 020 7935 9588
e-mail: info@mandeville.co.uk
web: www.mandeville.co.uk
Dir: *off Oxford Street and Wigmore St near Bond St underground station*
With a full refurbishment completed, this hotel is now a stylish and attractive establishment with a very contemporary feel. Bedrooms have state-of-the-art TVs and very comfortable beds. One of the suites has a patio with views over London. The cocktail bar is already proving to be a popular attraction.
ROOMS: 155 en suite ⊗ in 30 bedrooms **FACILITIES:** STV **CONF:** Thtr 35 Class 20 Board 20 **SERVICES:** Lift air con **NOTES:** ✖

★★★★71% Millennium Hotel London Mayfair
Grosvenor Square W1K 2HP plan 2 G1
☎ 020 7629 9400 020 7629 7736
e-mail: sales.mayfair@mill-cop.com
web: www.millenniumhotels.com
Dir: *on S side of Grosvenor Square - near Park Lane and Oxford St.*
This hotel benefits from a prestigious location in the heart of Mayfair, close to Bond Street. Smart bedrooms are generally

continued

spacious and club-floor rooms have use of their own lounge with complimentary refreshments. A choice of bars and dining options include the stylish Brian Turner Restaurant offering classic British food. Conference facilities along with a fitness room complete the picture.
ROOMS: 348 en suite ⊗ in 265 bedrooms s £170-£229; d £206-£323 **LB** **FACILITIES:** STV Gym ♫ ch fac Xmas **CONF:** BC Thtr 450 Class 250 Board 70 Del from £240 **SERVICES:** Lift air con **NOTES:** ✖ Civ Wed 250

★★★★71% Sherlock Holmes
108 Baker St W1U 6LJ plan 2 F4
☎ 020 7486 6161 020 7958 5211
e-mail: info@sherlockholmeshotel.com
web: www.parkplaza.com
Dir: *from Marylebone Flyover onto Marylebone Rd and at Baker St turn right for hotel on left*
Chic and modern, this boutique-style hotel is conveniently located close to a number of London underground lines and railway stations. Public rooms include a popular bar, sited just inside the main entrance, and Sherlock's Grill, where the mesquite-wood burning stove is a feature of the cooking. The hotel also has an indoor health suite and a relaxing lounge.
ROOMS: 119 en suite (20 fmly) ⊗ in 60 bedrooms s £133-£225; d £133-£225 (incl. bkfst) **FACILITIES:** **Spa** STV Sauna Gym Xmas **CONF:** Thtr 50 Class 40 Board 30 Del from £235 **SERVICES:** Lift air con **NOTES:** ✖ ⊗ in restaurant Civ Wed 50

Early start?
Hotels at all star levels should provide in-room alarm clocks and/or alarm clocks

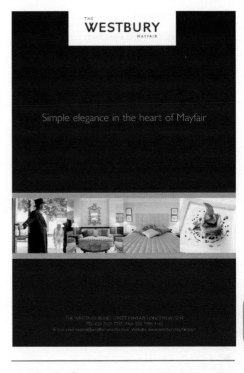

W1 WEST END, continued

★★★★70% ***Radisson SAS Portman***
22 Portman Square W1H 7BG plan 2 F3
☎ 020 7208 6000 🖹 020 7208 6001
e-mail: sales.london@radissonsas.com
web: www.radisson.com
Dir: *100mtrs N of Oxford St and 500mtrs E of Edgware Rd*
This smart, popular hotel enjoys a prime location a short stroll from Oxford Street and close to all the city's major attractions. The spacious, well-equipped bedrooms are themed ranging from Oriental through to classical and contemporary Italian decor. Public areas include extensive conference facilities, a bar and a smart restaurant.
ROOMS: 272 en suite (93 fmly) ⊗ in 129 bedrooms **FACILITIES:** STV Sauna Solarium Gym ♫ **CONF:** BC Thtr 600 Class 280 Board 70 **SERVICES:** Lift air con **PARKING:** 400 **NOTES:** ✈ Civ Wed

★★★★67% **The Berners Hotel**
Berners St W1A 3BE plan 3 B3
☎ 020 7666 2000 🖹 020 7666 2001
e-mail: berners@berners.co.uk
web: www.thebernershotel.co.uk
In the heart of London's West End, adjacent to Oxford Street, this traditional hotel has an elegant atmosphere. Marble columns and ornately carved ceilings are features of the luxurious lounge, a popular venue for afternoon tea. The elegant restaurant has an airy feel to it. Bedrooms are equipped with modern facilities and the clubrooms are particularly stylish.
ROOMS: 216 en suite ⊗ in 100 bedrooms s £110-£190; d £135-£235 **FACILITIES:** STV **CONF:** BC Thtr 160 Class 80 Board 40 Del from £230 **SERVICES:** Lift **NOTES:** ✈ Civ Wed 70

★★★★67%
Radisson Edwardian Grafton Hotel
130 Tottenham Court Rd W1T 5AY plan 3 B4
☎ 020 7388 4131 🖹 020 7387 7394
e-mail: resgraf@radisson.com
web: www.radissonedwardian.com
Dir: *along Euston Rd, onto Tottenham Court Rd. Past Warren St underground station*
Ongoing investment and a commitment to providing excellent levels of hospitality and service sees The Grafton going from strength to strength. Inside the mood is welcoming and calm with its designer furniture and original artwork. Public areas are smart and a popular meeting venue. Bedrooms come in a variety of sizes; and are beautifully decorated, with marble bathrooms. The hotel is well placed next to Warren Street tube station.
ROOMS: 330 en suite (23 fmly) ⊗ in 55 bedrooms s £90-£140; d £90-£140 **FACILITIES:** STV Fitness room. Valet Laundey & Parking services on request. Xmas **CONF:** BC Thtr 100 Class 50 Board 30 Del from £180 **SERVICES:** Lift air con **NOTES:** ✈ No children 16yrs ⊗ in restaurant

Town House

★★★★ **Best Western Premier Shaftesbury**
65 - 73 Shaftesbury Av, Piccadilly W1V 6EX
plan 3 B2
☎ 020 7871 6000
e-mail: reservations@shaftesburyhotel.co.uk
Dir: *from Piccadilly Circus 300yds up Shaftesbury Ave, at junct with Dean Street*
This smart town house enjoys a central location just minutes' walk from Covent Garden, in the heart of London's Theatreland. Bedrooms are stylishly appointed with a host of extra facilities and include a number of suites and four-poster rooms. A gym and small meeting room are available and guests may charge food taken in the adjacent restaurant to their hotel bill.
ROOMS: 67 en suite (2 fmly) ⊗ in 28 bedrooms **FACILITIES:** STV Gym **CONF:** BC Board 12 **SERVICES:** Lift air con **NOTES:** ✈ ⊗ in restaurant

★★★68% ꕥꕥ **Mostyn**
4 Bryanston St W1H 7BY plan 2 F2
☎ 0871 437 0044 🖹 0871 437 0280
e-mail: info@mostynhotel.co.uk
web: www.mostynhotel.co.uk
Dir: *A40(M) Marylebone Rd, close to Marble Arch and Bond St underground*

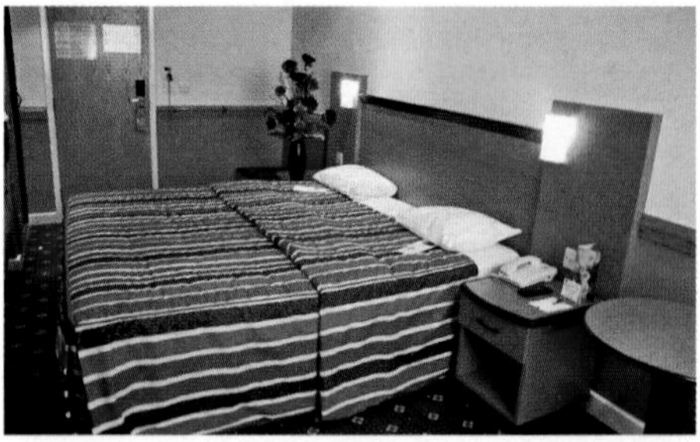

The Mostyn enjoys an enviable location, just off Oxford Street, in the heart of the West End. Originally built as a residence for Lady Back, a lady-in-waiting at the court of George II, the hotel retains many original features. Well-equipped, modern bedrooms have air conditioning, and public rooms include a stylish open-plan lounge and cocktail bar. Innovative Indian cooking is served in the restaurant.
ROOMS: 121 en suite (15 fmly) ⊗ in 54 bedrooms s £105-£145; d £145-£175 **FACILITIES:** STV **CONF:** BC Thtr 130 Class 70 Board 50 Del from £165 **SERVICES:** Lift air con **NOTES:** ✈

See advert on opposite page

★★★66% ***Grange Langham Court***
31-35 Langham St W1W 6BU plan 3 A3
☎ 020 7436 6622 🖹 020 7436 2303
e-mail: langhamcourt@grangehotels.com
web: www.grangehotels.co.uk
Dir: *just off Regents St*
Situated in a quiet, secluded street between Regents Park and Oxford Circus, this hotel has an elegant tiled façade. Formerly a nursing home, it now provides compact and well-equipped accommodation. Public areas include a wine bar serving snacks and light meals, a comfortable lounge and a basement dining room.
ROOMS: 58 en suite ⊗ in 20 bedrooms **FACILITIES:** STV **CONF:** Thtr 80 Class 35 Board 35 **SERVICES:** Lift **NOTES:** ✈

U ***Brown's***
Albemarle St, Mayfair W1S 4BP plan 3 A1
☎ 020 7493 6020 🖹 020 7493 9381
e-mail: brownshotel@brownshotel.com
web: www.roccofortehotels.com
At the time of going to press, the star classification for this hotel was not confirmed. Please refer to the AA internet site www.theAA.com for current information.
ROOMS: 118 en suite **NOTES:** ✈ Closed for refurbishment until Autumn 2005

U *Radisson Edwardian Sussex*

19-25 Granville Place W1H 6PA plan 2 G2
☎ 020 7408 0130 📠 020 7493 2070
e-mail: ressuss@radisson.com
web: www.radissonedwardian.com
Dir: *off Oxford St. Turn left to Portman St. Then right into Granville Place*
At the time of going to press, the star classification for this hotel was not confirmed. Please refer to the AA internet site www.theAA.com for current information.
ROOMS: 101 en suite (12 fmly) ⊗ in 70 bedrooms **FACILITIES:** Gym **CONF:** BC Board 10 **SERVICES:** Lift air con **NOTES:** ✗

W2 BAYSWATER, PADDINGTON

★★★★76% ❀ Royal Lancaster

Lancaster Ter W2 2TY plan 2 D2
☎ 020 7262 6737 📠 020 7724 3191
e-mail: book@royallancaster.com
web: www.royallancaster.com
Dir: *adjacent to Lancaster Gate Underground Station*
This smart hotel has an excellent range of public facilities, including impressive conference rooms, 24-hour business centre and car park. The rosette awarded Nipa Thai is among a choice of drinking and eating options that also includes the new Island Restaurant. Bedrooms are modern and well equipped, with upper floors enjoying stunning views across London.
ROOMS: 416 en suite (11 fmly) ⊗ in 111 bedrooms s £290-£378; d £290-£378 (incl. bkfst & dinner) **LB** **FACILITIES:** STV ♫ Xmas **CONF:** BC Thtr 1400 Class 650 Board 40 Del from £240 **SERVICES:** Lift air con **PARKING:** 70 **NOTES:** ✗

Town House

★★★★ ⌂ *The Abbey Court*

20 Pembridge Gardens, Kensington W2 4DU plan 2 A1
☎ 020 7221 7518 📠 020 7792 0858
e-mail: info@abbeycourthotel.co.uk
web: www.abbeycourthotel.co.uk
Dir: *2mins from Notting Hill Gate Underground station*
Situated in Notting Hill and close to Kensington, this five-storey Victorian town house stands in a quiet side road. Rooms are individually decorated and have marble bathrooms with jacuzzi baths. Room service is available for light snacks and full English breakfasts can be enjoyed in the conservatory.
ROOMS: 22 en suite (1 fmly) (3 GF) ⊗ in 10 bedrooms **FACILITIES: Spa** STV ch fac **CONF:** BC Board 10 **NOTES:** ✗

Town House

★★★★ ⌂ Pembridge Court

34 Pembridge Gardens W2 4DX plan 2 A1
☎ 020 7229 9977 📠 020 7727 4982
e-mail: reservations@pemct.co.uk
web: www.pemct.co.uk
Dir: *off Bayswater Rd at Notting Hill Gate by underground station*
This attractive Victorian town house is in a residential street near the Portobello Market and Notting Hill Gate tube. Individually styled bedrooms are generally spacious and most are air conditioned. Public areas include two spacious lounges, a small conference room and an airy breakfast room. The hotel features a collection of antique clothing and fans.
ROOMS: 20 en suite (4 fmly) (5 GF) s £125-£165; d £160-£195 (incl. bkfst) **FACILITIES:** STV Membership of local Health Club **CONF:** BC Board 12 **SERVICES:** Lift air con **PARKING:** 2 **NOTES:** ⊗ in restaurant RS 24 Dec-1 Jan

Town House

★★★★ ⌂ Royal Park

3 Westbourne Ter, Lancaster Gate, Hyde Park W2 3UL plan 2 D2
☎ 020 7479 6600 📠 020 7479 6601
e-mail: info@theroyalpark.com
web: www.theroyalpark.com
Close to Lancaster Gate and minutes' walk from Hyde Park, this delightful hotel has been created from three Grade II listed town houses dating back to 1842. Stylish, comfortable bedrooms and suites are thoughtfully equipped for both leisure and business guests and most boast half-tester or four-poster beds. Complimentary afternoon tea, champagne and canapés are served in the elegant drawing rooms and 24-hour room service is available.
ROOMS: 48 en suite (7 GF) ⊗ in 15 bedrooms s £182.12-£346.62; d £223.25-£346.62 **LB** **FACILITIES:** STV **CONF:** Thtr 10 Class 10 Board 10 **SERVICES:** Lift air con **PARKING:** 10 **NOTES:** ✗

★★★72% Corus hotel Hyde Park

1-7 Lancaster Gate W2 3LG plan 2 D2
☎ 0870 609 6161 📠 020 7724 8666
e-mail: londonhydepark@corushotels.com
web: www.corushotels.com
Dir: *200yds from Lancaster Gate underground. 0.25m from Paddington Station*
Centrally located adjacent to Hyde Park and a short walk from Marble Arch, this smart hotel offers accommodation that includes a number of spacious executive rooms and suites, now fitted out with modern colour schemes and a useful range of facilities; some

continued on p352

London

W2 BAYSWATER, PADDINGTON, continued

have air conditioning. Open-plan public areas include a popular restaurant and bar.

Corus hotel Hyde Park

ROOMS: 390 en suite (10 fmly) (12 GF) ⊗ in 285 bedrooms **CONF:** BC Thtr 25 Class 16 Board 18 Del £170 **SERVICES:** Lift **NOTES:** ✗ ⊗ in restaurant

★★★67% Best Western Paddington Court Hotel & Suites

27 Devonshire Ter W2 3DP plan 2 C2
☎ 020 7745 1200 📠 020 7745 1221
e-mail: info@paddingtoncourt.com
web: www.paddingtoncourt.com
Dir: *from A40 take exit before Paddington flyover, follow signs to Paddington Station. Devonshire Terrace is off Craven Rd*

This hotel is a short walk from Hyde Park and Kensington Gardens, offering easy access to the West End. Bedrooms vary in size and style, but all are smartly appointed and thoughtfully equipped; spacious suites are located in an adjacent property. Guests can relax in the stylish lounge or the smart bar, adjacent to the lower ground-floor restaurant.

ROOMS: 165 en suite 35 annexe en suite (43 fmly) (33 GF) ⊗ in 106 bedrooms s £130; d £150 **FACILITIES:** STV **SERVICES:** Lift **NOTES:** ✗ ⊗ in restaurant

★★71% Delmere

130 Sussex Gardens, Hyde Park W2 1UB
plan 2 D2
☎ 020 7706 3344 📠 020 7262 1863
e-mail: delmerehotel@compuserve.com
Dir: *M25 take A40 to London, exit at Paddington. Along Westbourne Terrace and into Sussex Gdns*

This friendly, privately owned hotel is situated within walking distance of Paddington Station, Hyde Park and Marble Arch. The smartly presented bedrooms are extremely well equipped and include some ground floor rooms. A small bar, a comfortable, elegant lounge and an Italian style restaurant complete the picture.

ROOMS: 36 en suite (6 GF) ⊗ in 10 bedrooms s £88-£109; d £109-£145 (incl. cont bkfst) **LB** **FACILITIES:** STV **SERVICES:** Lift **PARKING:** 2 **NOTES:** ✗

U Ramada Hyde Park

150 Bayswater Rd W2 4RT plan 2 B1
☎ 020 7229 1212 📠 020 7229 2623
e-mail: sales.hydepark@ramadajarvis.co.uk
web: www.ramadajarvis.co.uk
Dir: *From Hammersmith flyover turn left into Warwick Rd, at Kensington High St turn right, continue to Kensington Church St, left, onto T-junct, right into Bayswater Rd. Hotel 0.25m on left.*

This large hotel overlooks Kensington Gardens and is ideal for the West End, Oxford Street and Paddington. Bedrooms are comfortably appointed for both business and leisure guests.

ROOMS: 213 en suite (5 fmly) (12 GF) ⊗ in 180 bedrooms s £109-£140; d £109-£140 **FACILITIES:** STV ch fac **CONF:** Thtr 140 Class 80 Board 35 Del from £195 **SERVICES:** Lift **PARKING:** 39 **NOTES:** ✗ ⊗ in restaurant

---

W3 ACTON
See LONDON plan 1 C3

⌂ Travelodge (London Park Royal)

A40 Western Ave, Acton W3 0TE
☎ 08700 850 950 📠 020 8752 1134
web: www.travelodge.co.uk
Dir: *off A40 Western Ave eastbound*

Travelodge offers good quality, good value, modern accommodation. Ideal for families, the spacious, en suite bedrooms include remote-control TV, tea and coffee-making facilities and comfortable beds. Meals can be taken at the nearby family restaurant. For further details consult the Hotel Groups page.

ROOMS: 64 en suite s fr £26; d fr £26

W5 EALING
See LONDON SECTION plan 1 C4

U Ramada Ealing

Ealing Common W5 3HN plan 1 C4
☎ 020 8896 8400 📠 020 8992 7082
e-mail: sales.ealing@ramadajarvis.co.uk
web: www.ramadajarvis.co.uk
Dir: *at the junction of North Circular A406 with Uxbridge Road A4020*

This large modern, comfortable hotel is conveniently located a few minutes' walk from Ealing Common underground and has easy access to the M40. Bedrooms are comfortably appointed for both business and leisure guests.

ROOMS: 189 en suite (20 fmly) (44 GF) ⊗ in 114 bedrooms s £99-£140; d £99-£140 **FACILITIES:** STV Xmas **CONF:** Thtr 200 Class 110 Board 80 Del from £170 **SERVICES:** Lift **PARKING:** 150 **NOTES:** ✗ ⊗ in restaurant Civ Wed 180

W6 HAMMERSMITH
See LONDON plan 1 D3

★★★72% Novotel London West

1 Shortlands W6 8DR
☎ 020 8741 1555 📠 020 8741 2120
e-mail: H0737@accor-hotels.com
web: www.novotel.com
Dir: *M4 (A4) & A316 junct at Hogarth rdbt. Along Great West Rd, left for Hammersmith before flyover. On Hammersmith Bridge Rd to rdbt, take 5th exit. 1st left into Shortlands, 1st left to hotel main entrance*

Situated between Heathrow Airport and the West End, this

continued

substantial, purpose-built hotel is a popular base for both business and leisure travellers. Spacious, air-conditioned bedrooms boast a good range of extras and many have additional beds, making them suitable for families. The hotel also has its own paying car park and boasts one of the largest convention centres in Europe. Novotel - AA Hotel Group of the Year 2005-6.
ROOMS: 629 en suite (148 fmly) ⊗ in 473 bedrooms s fr £150; d fr £170 **FACILITIES:** STV Snooker Gym **CONF:** BC Thtr 1000 Class 525 Board 200 **SERVICES:** Lift air con **PARKING:** 240 **NOTES:** Civ Wed 1400

★★★63% Vencourt
255 King St, Hammersmith W6 9LU
☎ 020 8563 8855 🖷 020 8563 9988
e-mail: reservations@vencourthotel.com
Dir: *Central London on A4 to Hammersmith, follow A315 towards Chiswick*
This modern hotel provides good-value accommodation with city views from the higher floors. The hotel has open-plan public areas, including a lounge bar, where snacks are served all day, and an airy restaurant for more substantial meals. Smart, well-equipped conference and meeting facilities are also available.
ROOMS: 120 en suite (25 fmly) ⊗ in 18 bedrooms s £93-£113; d £103-£113 **LB** **FACILITIES:** STV Xmas **CONF:** BC Thtr 170 Class 86 Board 46 Del from £125 **SERVICES:** Lift **PARKING:** 27 **NOTES:** ⊗ in restaurant

W8 KENSINGTON

Top Hotel

★★★★★ ❀❀❀ Royal Garden Hotel
2-24 Kensington High St W8 4PT plan 4 B5
☎ 020 7937 8000 🖷 020 7361 1991
e-mail: sales@royalgardenhotel.co.uk
web: www.royalgardenhotel.co.uk
Dir: *next to Kensington Palace*
Situated in fashionable Kensington, this well-known landmark hotel is just a short walk from the Albert Hall and London's smart shops. Bedrooms are of contemporary design, equipped with many up-to-date facilities. Many are large and have views over the park. The hotel's popular eating and drinking options are varied; among them is the hotel's showcase restaurant, The Tenth, which offers fantastic views over the city and the park.
ROOMS: 396 en suite (19 fmly) ⊗ in 164 bedrooms s fr £318; d £388-£453 **FACILITIES:** **Spa** STV Sauna Gym Health & fitness centre ♫ Xmas **CONF:** BC Thtr 550 Class 260 Board 80 **SERVICES:** Lift air con **PARKING:** 160 **NOTES:** ✈ Civ Wed 400

○ Hotel due to open in late 2005 or 2006
U Star rating not confirmed

Top Town House

★★★★★ ❀ 🏠 Milestone Hotel & Apartments
Red Carnation HOTELS
1 Kensington Court W8 5DL plan 4 B4
☎ 020 7917 1000 🖷 020 7917 1010
e-mail: guestservicesms@rchmail.com
web: www.redcarnationhotels.com
Dir: *M4 into Central London. Into Warwick Rd, then right into Kensington High St. Hotel 400yds past Kensington underground*
This delightful, stylish town house enjoys a wonderful location opposite Kensington Palace; just minutes' walk from the elegant shops. Individually themed bedrooms include a selection of stunning suites and are equipped with every conceivable extra. Public areas include the luxurious Park lounge, where afternoon tea is served, a delightful panelled bar, a sumptuous restaurant and a small gym and resistance pool.
ROOMS: 57 en suite (3 fmly) (2 GF) ⊗ in 22 bedrooms d £300-£810 **LB** **FACILITIES:** STV Gym Jacuzzi Health Club ♫ Xmas **CONF:** Thtr 50 Class 20 Board 20 **SERVICES:** Lift air con **NOTES:** ⊗ in restaurant Civ Wed 30

Town House

★★★★ 🏠 Kensington House
15-16 Prince of Wales Ter W8 5PQ plan 4 B4
☎ 020 7937 2345 🖷 020 7368 6700
e-mail: sales@kenhouse.com web: www.kenhouse.com
Dir: *off Kensington High St, opposite Kensington Palace*
This beautiful, elegantly restored 19th-century property is conveniently located just off Kensington High Street and is convenient for the park, The Royal Albert Hall and most of the major attractions. Bedrooms vary in size but all are stylish, comfortable and thoughtfully equipped – many have air conditioning. Tiger Bar provides an airy, informal setting for light snacks, meals and refreshments all day.
ROOMS: 41 en suite (2 fmly) (3 GF) ⊗ in 30 bedrooms s £99-£150; d £130-£175 (incl. bkfst) **LB** **FACILITIES:** STV Arrangement with local health club **CONF:** BC **SERVICES:** Lift **NOTES:** ✈

★★★★64% Copthorne Tara Hotel London Kensington
COPTHORNE
Scarsdale Place, Wrights Ln W8 5SR plan 4 B4
☎ 020 7937 7211 🖷 020 7937 7100
e-mail: sales.tara@mill-cop.com
web: www.copthornetara.com
Dir: *off Kensington High Street*
One of the city's larger hotels, the Tara is ideally located for Kensington High Street's stylish shops and tube station. Smart public areas include Café Mozart, a stylish Brasserie and bar and extensive conference and meeting facilities. Bedrooms include

continued on p354

W8 KENSINGTON, continued

several well-equipped rooms for less mobile guests in addition to a number of Connoisseur rooms that include use of a club lounge with many complimentary facilities.
ROOMS: 834 en suite (3 fmly) ⊗ in 634 bedrooms s £70-£225; d £70-£225 **LB** **FACILITIES:** STV Xmas **CONF:** BC Thtr 280 Class 160 Board 90 Del from £179 **SERVICES:** Lift air con **PARKING:** 65 **NOTES:** ✗

WC1 BLOOMSBURY, HOLBORN

★★★★★74% Renaissance Chancery Court London
252 High Holborn WC1V 7EN plan 3 D3
☎ 020 7829 9888 020 7829 9889
e-mail: sales.chancerycourt@renaissancehotels.com
web: www.renaissancechancerycourt.com
Dir: *A4 along Piccadilly onto Shaftesbury Av. Into High Holborn, hotel on right*

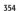

This is a grand place with splendid public areas, decorated from top to bottom in rare marble. Craftsmen have meticulously restored the sweeping staircases, archways and stately rooms of the 1914 building. The result is a spacious, relaxed hotel offering everything from stylish, luxuriously appointed bedrooms to a health club and state-of-the-art meeting rooms. Pearl restaurant has offers sophisticated cuisine.
ROOMS: 356 en suite ⊗ in 280 bedrooms d fr £276 **LB**
FACILITIES: Spa STV Sauna Gym Jacuzzi Spa treatments by ESPA
CONF: BC Thtr 435 Class 234 Board 40 **SERVICES:** Lift air con
PARKING: 4 **NOTES:** ✗ ⊗ in restaurant Civ Wed 260

★★★★74% *Grange Holborn*
50-60 Southampton Row WC1B 4AR plan 3 D4
☎ 020 7242 1800 020 7242 0057
e-mail: holborn@grangehotels.com
web: www.grangehotels.co.uk
This smart hotel is centrally located, close to Oxford Street and Covent Garden. The elegantly furnished, spacious bedrooms offer high levels of comfort and are equipped with every conceivable extra. Public areas include a smart leisure centre, a choice of restaurants and extensive meeting and function facilities.
ROOMS: 200 en suite (10 fmly) ⊗ in 100 bedrooms **FACILITIES:** STV Sauna Gym **CONF:** Thtr 220 Class 120 Board 80 **SERVICES:** Lift air con **NOTES:** ✗

★★★★73% Jurys Great Russell Street
16-22 Great Russell St WC1B 3NN plan 3 C3
☎ 020 7347 1000 020 7347 1001
e-mail: great_russell@jurysdoyle.com
web: www.jurysdoyle.com
Dir: *A40 onto A400, Gower St then south to Bedford Sq. Turn right, then first left to end of road*
On the doorstep of Covent Garden, Oxford Street and the West End, this impressive building, designed by the renowned Sir Edwin Lutyens in the 1930s, retains many original features. Bedrooms are attractively appointed and benefit from an excellent range of facilities. Public areas include a grand reception lounge, an elegant bar and restaurant and extensive conference facilities.
ROOMS: 170 en suite (5 GF) ⊗ in 153 bedrooms s £235; d £235 **LB** **FACILITIES:** STV Xmas **CONF:** BC Thtr 300 Class 180 Board 60 Del £280 **SERVICES:** Lift air con **NOTES:** ✗ ⊗ in restaurant

★★★★72% The Montague on the Gardens
15 Montague St, Bloomsbury WC1B 5BJ
plan 3 C4
☎ 020 7637 1001 020 7637 2516
e-mail: bookmt@rchmail.com web: www.redcarnationhotels.com
Dir: *just off Russell Square*
This stylish hotel is situated right next to the British Museum. A special feature is the alfresco terrace overlooking a delightful garden. Other public rooms include the Blue Door Bistro and Chef's Table, a bar, a lounge and a conservatory where traditional afternoon teas are served. The bedrooms are beautifully appointed and range from split-level suites to more compact rooms.
ROOMS: 99 en suite (18 GF) ⊗ in 47 bedrooms s £159-£211; d £176-£246 **LB** **FACILITIES:** STV Sauna Gym Jacuzzi ♫ ch fac Xmas **CONF:** Thtr 120 Class 50 Board 50 Del from £195 **SERVICES:** Lift air con **NOTES:** ⊗ in restaurant Civ Wed 90

★★★★71% Radisson Edwardian Kenilworth
Great Russell St WC1B 3LB plan 3 C3
☎ 020 7637 3477 020 7631 3133
e-mail: reskeni@radisson.com web: www.radissonedwardian.com
Dir: *past Oxford St and down New Oxford St. Turn into Bloomsbury St*
Ideally located for London's Theatreland, the City and the West End, this stylish hotel is popular with both business and leisure travellers. Air-conditioned bedrooms feature elegant and modern decor, and come with a range of thoughtful extras. Public rooms include a range of meeting rooms, a small gym and an open-plan bar and restaurant.
ROOMS: 186 en suite (15 fmly) ⊗ in 139 bedrooms **FACILITIES:** STV Fitness room, Valet Laundry & Parking service on request. Xmas
CONF: BC Thtr 120 Class 50 Board 35 Del from £204 **SERVICES:** Lift air con **NOTES:** ✗ No children

★★★★71% Radisson Edwardian Marlborough
Bloomsbury St WC1B 3QD plan 3 C3
☎ 020 7636 5601 020 7636 0532
e-mail: resmarl@radisson.com
web: www.radissonedwardian.com
Dir: *past Oxford St, down New Oxford St and turn into Bloomsbury St*
Within sight of the British Museum, this smart modern hotel is ideal for cultural visits to London. The theatre district is five minutes' walk away. Bedrooms are generally spacious with plenty of comfort, and public areas feature a number of interesting works of art. There are two bars and the modern Glass Restaurant. Guests can use the fitness room at the Radisson Edwardian Kenilworth Hotel located opposite.
ROOMS: 173 en suite (3 fmly) ⊗ in 82 bedrooms **FACILITIES:** Valet Laundry & Parking Services on request. Fitness room at Kenilwoth Hotel. Xmas **CONF:** BC Thtr 300 Class 150 Board 70 Del from £204
SERVICES: Lift **NOTES:** ✗ No children

★★★★67% The Hotel Russell
Russell Square WC1B 5BE plan 3 C4
☎ 020 7837 6470 020 7837 2857
web: www.principal-hotels.com
Dir: *from A501 into Woburn Place. Hotel 500mtrs on left*
This landmark Grade II, Victorian hotel is located on Russell

continued

London

Square, within walking distance of the West End and theatre district. Many bedrooms are stylish and state-of-the-art and others are more traditional. Spacious public areas include the impressive foyer with its restored mosaic floor, a choice of lounges and an elegant restaurant.
ROOMS: 373 en suite ⊗ in 192 bedrooms s £185; d £215
FACILITIES: STV **CONF:** BC Thtr 450 Class 200 Board 75 Del £250
SERVICES: Lift air con **NOTES:** ✗ ⊗ in restaurant Civ Wed 800

Town House

★★★★ *Grange Whitehall*
2-5 Montague St WC1B 5BP plan 3 C3
☎ 020 7580 2224 ⎙ 020 7580 5554
e-mail: whitehall@grangehotel.com
web: www.grangehotels.co.uk
This elegant, small hotel is well located, close to the city's financial district and to the theatres of the West End. Smart bedrooms are decorated to a very high standard and many have views over the delightful landscaped rear gardens. Public areas include an elegant and cosy restaurant and a popular bar and lounge as well as conference facilities.
ROOMS: 56 en suite (2 fmly) (3 GF) ⊗ in 20 bedrooms
FACILITIES: STV **CONF:** Thtr 90 Class 45 Board 45 **SERVICES:** Lift air con

★★★★66% Holiday Inn Kings Cross/Bloomsbury
1 Kings Cross Rd WC1X 9HX plan 3 E5
☎ 020 7833 3900 ⎙ 020 7917 6163
e-mail: sales@holidayinnlondon.com
Dir: *0.5m from Kings Cross Station on corner of King Cross Rd and Calthorpe St*
Conveniently located for Kings Cross station and the City, this modern hotel offers smart, spacious air-conditioned accommodation with a wide range of facilities. The hotel offers a choice of restaurants including one serving Indian cuisine, versatile meeting rooms, a bar and a well-equipped fitness centre.
ROOMS: 405 en suite (163 fmly) ⊗ in 160 bedrooms s £190; d £190-£210 **LB** **FACILITIES:** STV supervised Sauna Solarium Gym Jacuzzi **CONF:** BC Thtr 220 Class 120 Board 30 Del from £195
SERVICES: Lift air con **PARKING:** 12 **NOTES:** ✗

Town House

★★★★ *Grange Blooms*
7 Montague St WC1B 5BP plan 3 C4
☎ 020 7323 1717 ⎙ 020 7636 6498
e-mail: blooms@grangehotels.com
web: www.grangehotels.co.uk
Dir: *off Russell Square, behind Brirish Museum*
Conveniently located for London's theatre district and the British Museum, this elegant townhouse is part of an 18th century terrace. The bedrooms feature Regency-style decor; bedrooms at the rear of the hotel are quieter. Public rooms include a cosy lounge, garden terrace, breakfast room and small cocktail bar, all featuring antiques and paintings.
ROOMS: 26 en suite ⊗ in 12 bedrooms **FACILITIES:** STV Patio garden **CONF:** Thtr 20 Class 10 Board 18 **SERVICES:** Lift
NOTES: ✗ Civ Wed 20

Packed in a hurry? Ironing facilities should be available at all star levels, either in the rooms or on request

★★★72% *Bonnington Hotel, London*
92 Southampton Row WC1B 4BH plan 3 D4
☎ 020 7242 2828 ⎙ 020 7831 9170
e-mail: sales@bonnington.com
web: www.bonnington.com
Dir: *M40 Euston Rd. Opposite station turn into Upper Woburn Place past Russell Sq into Southampton Row. Hotel on left*

This smart hotel is centrally located close to the city, the British Museum and Covent Garden. Spacious public areas include the Malt Bar, an airy restaurant and a comfortable lobby lounge. Bedrooms are well equipped and include a number of superb executive rooms and suites. A good range of conference and meeting rooms is available.
ROOMS: 247 en suite (4 fmly) ⊗ in 87 bedrooms **FACILITIES:** STV Fitness room **CONF:** BC Thtr 250 Class 80 Board 50 **SERVICES:** Lift air con **NOTES:** ✗

⇧ Travelodge (London Farringdon)
10-42 Kings Cross Rd WC1X 9QN plan 3 E6
☎ 0870 1911774 ⎙ 020 7837 3776
web: www.travelodge.co.uk
Travelodge offers good quality, good value, modern accommodation. Ideal for families, the spacious, en suite bedrooms include remote-control TV, tea and coffee-making facilities and comfortable beds. Meals can be taken at the nearby family restaurant. For further details consult the Hotel Groups page.
ROOMS: 211 en suite s £26-£102; d £26-£113 **CONF:** Thtr 50 Class 18 Board 30

⇧ Travelodge (London Islington)
100 Kings Cross Rd WC1X 9DT plan 3 E5
☎ 0870 1911773 ⎙ 020 7833 0798
web: www.travelodge.co.uk
Travelodge offers good quality, good value, modern accommodation. Ideal for families, the spacious, en suite bedrooms include remote-control TV, tea and coffee-making facilities and comfortable beds. Meals can be taken at the nearby family restaurant. For further details consult the Hotel Groups page.
ROOMS: 351 en suite s £26-£110; d £26-£125 **CONF:** Thtr 170 Class 60 Board 50

⇧ Premier Travel Inn London Euston
1 Dukes Rd WC1H 9PJ plan 3 C5
☎ 0870 238 3301 ⎙ 020 7554 3419
web: www.premiertravelinn.com
Dir: *on corner of Euston Road (south side) Duke's Road, between Kings Cross/St Pancras & Euston stations. Inn is a blue building*
High quality, modern budget accommodation ideal for both families and business travellers. Spacious, en suite bedrooms feature bath and shower, satellite TV and many have telephones and modem points. The adjacent family restaurant features a wide and varied menu. For further details consult the Hotel Groups page.
ROOMS: 220 en suite s £74.95-£82.95; d £74.95-£82.95

London

WC1 BLOOMSBURY, continued

⌂ Travelodge (London Kings Cross)
Willing House, Grays Inn Rd, Kings Cross
WC1 8BH plan 3 D6
☎ 08700 850 950 🖷 020 7278 7396
web: www.travelodge.co.uk
Travelodge offers good quality, good value, modern accommodation. Ideal for families, the spacious, en suite bedrooms include remote-control TV, tea and coffee-making facilities and comfortable beds. Meals can be taken at the nearby family restaurant. For further details consult the Hotel Groups page.
ROOMS: 140 en suite s fr £26; d fr £26

WC2 SOHO, STRAND

Top Hotel

★★★★★ ◎◎◎ ***The Savoy***
Strand WC2R 0EU plan 3 D1
☎ 020 7836 4343 🖷 020 7240 6040
e-mail: info@the-savoy.co.uk
Dir: *halfway along The Strand between Trafalgar Sq and Aldwych*
There is a feeling of great anticipation on arrival at this internationally renowned hotel. Services flow smoothly and bedrooms offer excellent levels of comfort; many have fine views along the river. The choice of dining areas presents a predicament - whether to opt for Marcus Wareing's menu at the Grill or the more informal 'La Banquette'. No visit would be complete without experiencing afternoon tea in the Thames Foyer or a cocktail in the American Bar.
ROOMS: 263 en suite (6 fmly) ⊗ in 55 bedrooms
FACILITIES: STV Sauna Gym Health & beauty treatments ♫
CONF: Thtr 500 Class 200 Board 32 **SERVICES:** Lift air con
PARKING: 65 **NOTES:** ✖ Civ Wed 300

Top Hotel

★★★★★ ◎◎ **One Aldwych**
1 Aldwych WC2B 4RH plan 3 D2
☎ 020 7300 1000 🖷 020 7300 1001
e-mail: reservations@onealdwych.com
web: www.onealdwych.com
Dir: *at Aldwych & The Strand junct near Waterloo Bridge*
Regarded by many as the most contemporary address in the West End, One Aldwych is best known for its chic yet comfortable style and innovative, thought-provoking decor. There are a whole host of interesting features including a therapeutic pool with underwater music, the dramatic 'amber city' mural in the double height Axis restaurant and the contemporary lobby bar where the Martini cocktail is a speciality. Bedrooms are no less stylish and feature giant pillows, down duvets and TVs you can watch whilst relaxing in the bath.

ROOMS: 105 en suite ⊗ in 60 bedrooms s £210-£476; d £210-£476
LB FACILITIES: STV Sauna Gym Steam room, 3 Treatment rooms ♫ Xmas **CONF:** BC Thtr 50 Board 50 **SERVICES:** Lift air con **NOTES:** ✖ Civ Wed 50

★★★★★65% ◎◎ **Swissôtel The Howard, London**
Temple Place WC2R 2PR plan 3 E2
☎ 020 7836 3555 🖷 020 7379 4547
e-mail: ask-us-london@swissotel.com
web: www.swissotel-london.com
Dir: *From E turn off Aldwych, keep left of church (in centre of road). Turn left into Surrey St. Hotel at end*

This smart hotel enjoys wonderful views across London's historic skyline from its riverside location. The Eurostar terminal, Covent Garden and Theatreland are all within easy reach. The air-conditioned bedrooms offer a host of extra facilities. The restaurant, Jaan is a blend of modern French and Asian influences. The bar opens onto a delightful garden offering alfresco dining whenever the weather permits.
ROOMS: 189 en suite ⊗ in 159 bedrooms s £351-£693; d £351-£693
LB FACILITIES: STV Special rates for guests at health club ♫ Xmas
CONF: BC Thtr 120 Class 60 Board 60 **SERVICES:** Lift air con
PARKING: 30 **NOTES:** ✖ Civ Wed 120

★★★★★64%
Radisson Edwardian Hampshire Hotel
31 Leicester Square WC2H 7LH plan 3 C1
☎ 020 7839 9399 🖷 020 7930 8122
e-mail: reshamp@radisson.com
web: www.radissonedwardian.com
Dir: *from Charing Cross Rd turn into Cranbourn St at Leicester Sq. Left at end, hotel at bottom of square*
Located in the very heart of London's West End, most of the capital's top entertainment venues are within easy reach. The elegant public areas include the Apex Bar and Restaurant, with its

continued

London

beautiful wood panelling, and a small but smart gym. The Crescent Bar, adjacent to the hotel, with its vaulted alcoves, is an intimate venue for drinks. Air-conditioned bedrooms are smartly decorated and feature triple glazing and thoughtful extras.
ROOMS: 124 en suite (5 fmly) ⊗ in 93 bedrooms s £180-£250; d £180-£250 **FACILITIES:** STV Gym Fitness room, Valet Laundry & Parking services on request. **CONF:** Thtr 100 Class 48 Board 35 **SERVICES:** Lift air con **NOTES:** ✈

★★★★74%
Radisson Edwardian Mountbatten
Monmouth St, Seven Dials, Covent Garden WC2H 9HD plan 3 C2
☎ 020 7836 4300 📠 020 7240 3540
e-mail: resmoun@radisson.com
web: www.radissonedwardian.com
Dir: *off Shaftesbury Av, on corner of Seven Dials rdbt*
Located in the heart of Theatreland and close to Covent Garden, this smart hotel is named after Lord Mountbatten. The hotels 151 air-conditioned bedrooms are thoughtfully equipped for comfort and pleasure with stylish furniture, designer fabrics and the latest technology. Public areas include the popular Dial Bar and Restaurant, as well as a fitness room, conference and meeting facilities.
ROOMS: 151 en suite ⊗ in 104 bedrooms **FACILITIES:** STV Fitness room, Valet Laundry & Parking services on request. Xmas **CONF:** BC Thtr 90 Class 45 Board 32 **SERVICES:** Lift air con **NOTES:** ✈

★★★★72% ⊛ *Kingsway Hall*
Great Queen St, Covent Garden WC2B 5BZ plan 3 D3
☎ 020 7309 0909 📠 020 7309 9696
e-mail: enquiries@kingswayhall.co.uk
web: www.kingswayhall.co.uk
Dir: *from Holborn underground station follow Kingsway towards Aldwych. At 1st lights right. Hotel 50mtrs on left*
Conveniently situated close to Covent Garden, this stylish modern hotel offers very comfortable accommodation. Smart, air-conditioned bedrooms have been well designed and feature many extra facilities. The stylish compact lounge bar is available for drinks and lighter meals along with the Harlequin restaurant for more formal dining. There is a gym in the basement.
ROOMS: 170 en suite ⊗ in 125 bedrooms **FACILITIES:** STV Gym Jacuzzi Steam room **CONF:** BC Thtr 150 Class 90 Board 50 **SERVICES:** Lift air con **NOTES:** ✈

★★★69% Strand Palace
372 The Strand WC2R 0JJ plan 3 D2
☎ 020 7836 8080 & 0870 400 8702 📠 020 7836 2077
e-mail: reservations@strandpalacehotel.co.uk
Dir: *From Trafalgar Square, on A4 to Charing Cross, 150mtrs, hotel on left.*

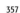

At the heart of Theatreland, this vast hotel is ideal for visiting many of the capital's attractions. The bedrooms vary in style and include Club rooms with enhanced facilities and exclusive use of the Club

continued

lounge as well as bright contemporary rooms. The extensive public areas include four eateries and a popular cocktail bar.
ROOMS: 785 en suite ⊗ in 500 bedrooms s £60-£150; d £80-£180 **LB** **FACILITIES:** STV Xmas **CONF:** BC Thtr 200 Class 90 Board 40 Del from £150 **SERVICES:** Lift **NOTES:** ✈ ⊗ in restaurant

U Radisson Edwardian Pastoria Hotel
3-6 Saint Martins St WC2H 7HL plan 3 C1
☎ 020 7930 8641 & 020 7451 0227(res)
📠 020 7451 0191
e-mail: reshamp@radisson.com
web: www.radissonedwardian.com
Dir: *from Whitcomb St into Panton St. St Martins St off Leicester Sq*
At the time of going to press, the star classification for this hotel was not confirmed. Please refer to the AA internet site www.theAA.com for current information.
ROOMS: 58 en suite ⊗ in 38 bedrooms **FACILITIES:** STV Gym **CONF:** BC **SERVICES:** Lift **NOTES:** ✈

⌂ Travelodge (London Covent Garden)
10 Drury Ln, High Holborn WC2B 5RE plan 3 D2
☎ 08700 850 950 📠 01376 572 724
web: www.travelodge.co.uk
Dir: *on High Holborn off Drury Lane.*
Travelodge offers good quality, good value, modern accommodation. Ideal for families, the spacious, en suite bedrooms include remote-control TV, tea and coffee-making facilities and comfortable beds. Meals can be taken at the nearby family restaurant. For further details consult the Hotel Groups page.
ROOMS: 163 en suite s fr £46; d fr £46 **CONF:** Thtr 100 Class 40 Board 30

LONDON AIRPORTS See under Gatwick & Heathrow

LONDON GATEWAY MOTORWAY SERVICE AREA (M1) See LONDON plan1 C6

★★★66% Days Hotel London Gateway
Welcome Break Service Area NW7 3HB
☎ 020 8906 7000 📠 020 8906 7011
e-mail: lgw.hotel@welcomebreak.co.uk
web: www.welcomebreak.co.uk
Dir: *on M1 between junct 2/4 northbound & southbound*
This modern hotel is the flagship of the Days Inn brand and occupies a prime location on the outskirts of London at London Gateway Services. Bedrooms have a contemporary feel, are spacious and well equipped. Public rooms are airy and include an open-plan restaurant and bar/lounge along with a range of meeting rooms. Ample parking is a bonus.
ROOMS: 200 en suite (190 fmly) (80 GF) ⊗ in 162 bedrooms s £49-£85; d £49-£85 **LB** **FACILITIES:** STV **CONF:** Thtr 70 Class 30 Board 50 **SERVICES:** Lift air con **PARKING:** 160 **NOTES:** ⊗ in restaurant

---

LONDON COLNEY, Hertfordshire — Map 06 TL10

⌂ Innkeeper's Lodge St Albans
1 Barnet Rd AL2 1BL
☎ 01727 823698 📠 01727 820902
web: www.innkeeperslodge.com
Dir: *clockwise from Heathrow on M25 towards Harlow, exit at junct 22 stay in left lane, at rdbt take 1st left to London Colney. Straight over rdbt. Lodge is 450yds on right*
A growing concept in the travel accommodation market. Smart rooms meet essential business requirements but also have home comforts. Dining options include all-day menus plus the added advantage of breakfast, which is included in the room price. For further details consult the Hotel Groups page.
ROOMS: 13 s £49-£59; d £49-£59

LONG EATON, Derbyshire Map 11 SK43

★★★66% Novotel Nottingham/Derby

Bostock Ln NG10 4EP
☎ 0115 946 5111 📠 0115 946 5900
e-mail: H0507@accor-hotels.com
web: www.novotel.com
Dir: *M1 junct 25 onto B6002 to Long Eaton. Hotel 400yds on left*
In close proximity to the M1, this purpose-built hotel has much to offer. All bedrooms are spacious, have sofa beds and provide exceptional desk space. Public rooms include a bright brasserie, which is open all day and provides extended dining until midnight, and a comprehensive range of meeting rooms.
Novotel - AA Hotel Group of the Year 2005-6.
ROOMS: 108 en suite (40 fmly) (20 GF) ⊗ in 66 bedrooms s £75-£97; d £75-£97 **LB** **FACILITIES:** STV **CONF:** Thtr 250 Class 100 Board 100 Del from £130 **SERVICES:** Lift **PARKING:** 220

★★60% Europa

20-22 Derby Rd NG10 1LW
☎ 0115 972 8481 📠 0115 849 6313
e-mail: k.riley3@ntlworld.com
Dir: *on A6005, in centre of Long Eaton. 1.5m from M1 junct 25 & A52*
Convenient for the town centre and the M1, this commercial hotel offers suitably furnished bedrooms. In addition to the restaurant, where Chinese cooking is offered, light refreshments are available throughout the day in the conservatory.
ROOMS: 15 en suite (2 fmly) (3 GF) ⊗ in 3 bedrooms s £40-£45; d £55 (incl. bkfst) **CONF:** Thtr 35 Class 35 Board 28 **PARKING:** 24
NOTES: ⊗ in restaurant Closed 25-28 Dec

U Ramada Nottingham

Bostock Ln NG10 4EP
☎ 0115 946 0000 📠 0115 946 0726
e-mail: sales.nottingham@ramadajarvis.co.uk
web: www.ramadajarvis.co.uk
Dir: *0.25m from M1 junct 25*
Conveniently located between Nottingham and Derby, this large modern hotel is set just off the M1. Bedrooms are comfortably appointed for both business and leisure guests.
ROOMS: 99 en suite (10 fmly) (40 GF) ⊗ in 70 bedrooms s £75-£89; d £75-£89 **FACILITIES:** STV Xmas **CONF:** Thtr 75 Class 30 Board 24 Del from £118 **PARKING:** 200 **NOTES:** ⊗ in restaurant

LONGHORSLEY, Northumberland Map 21 NZ19

★★★74% ⊛⊛ *Linden Hall*

NE65 8XF
☎ 01670 500000 📠 01670 500001
e-mail: stay@lindenhall.co.uk
web: www.macdonald-hotels.co.uk
Dir: *Northbound A1 exit A697 towards Coldstream. 1m N of Longhorsley*
This impressive Georgian mansion lies in 400 acres of parkland and offers extensive indoor and outdoor leisure facilities including a golf course. Elegant public rooms include an imposing entrance hall, drawing room and cocktail bar. The Dobson restaurant provides a fine dining experience, or guests can eat in the more informal Linden Tree pub which is located in the grounds.
ROOMS: 50 en suite (4 fmly) (20 GF) ⊗ in 21 bedrooms
FACILITIES: Spa STV Snooker Sauna Solarium Gym Putt green Jacuzzi Own golf course Hard tennis court ch fac **CONF:** Thtr 300 Class 100 Board 30 **SERVICES:** Lift **PARKING:** 260 **NOTES:** ⊗ in restaurant Civ Wed 120

See advert on opposite page

LONG MELFORD, Suffolk Map 13 TL84

★★★75% ⊛ The Black Lion

Church Walk, The Green CO10 9DN
☎ 01787 312356 📠 01787 374557
e-mail: enquiries@blacklionhotel.net
Dir: *at junct of A134/A1092*
This charming 15th-century hotel is situated on the edge of this bustling town overlooking the green. Bedrooms are generally spacious and each is attractively decorated, tastefully furnished and equipped with useful extras. An interesting range of dishes is served in the lounge bar or guests may choose to dine in the more formal restaurant.
ROOMS: 10 en suite (3 fmly) ⊗ in all bedrooms s £88-£110; d £120-£376 (incl. bkfst) **LB** **FACILITIES:** Board games Xmas
CONF: Thtr 50 Class 28 Board 28 Del from £115 **PARKING:** 10
NOTES: ⊗ in restaurant

★★★73% *The Bull*

Hall St CO10 9JG
☎ 01787 378494 📠 01787 880307
e-mail: 6420@greeneking.co.uk
web: www.oldenglish.co.uk
Dir: *3m N of Sudbury on A134*
The public areas of this delightful 14th-century property feature a wealth of charm and character, including exposed beams, carvings, heraldic markings and huge open fireplaces. Bedrooms are smartly decorated, thoughtfully equipped and retain many original features. Snacks or light lunches are served in the bar, or guests can choose to dine in the more formal restaurant.
ROOMS: 25 en suite (3 fmly) ⊗ in 11 bedrooms **CONF:** Thtr 60 Class 30 Board 35 **PARKING:** 30 **NOTES:** ⊗ in restaurant Civ Wed 100

LONG SUTTON, Lincolnshire Map 12 TF42

⌂ Travelodge Kings Lynn

Wisbech Rd PE12 9AG
☎ 08700 850 950 📠 01406 362230
web: www.travelodge.co.uk
Dir: *on junct A17/A1101 rdbt*
Travelodge offers good quality, good value, modern accommodation. Ideal for families, the spacious, en suite bedrooms include remote-control TV, tea and coffee-making facilities and comfortable beds. Meals can be taken at the nearby family restaurant. For further details consult the Hotel Groups page.
ROOMS: 40 en suite s fr £26; d fr £26

LOOE, Cornwall & Isles of Scilly Map 02 SX25

See also Portwrinkle

★★★66% Hannafore Point

Marine Dr, West Looe PL13 2DG
☎ 01503 263273 📠 01503 263272
e-mail: stay@hannaforepointhotel.com
Dir: *A38, left onto A385 to Looe. Over bridge left. Hotel 0.5m on left*
With panoramic coastal views embracing St George's Island around to Rame Head, this popular hotel provides a warm welcome. The wonderful views can be enjoyed from the spacious restaurant and bar, an excellent backdrop for dinners and breakfasts. Additional facilities include a heated indoor pool, squash court and gym.
ROOMS: 37 en suite (5 fmly) s £48-£66; d £96-£160 (incl. bkfst) **LB**
FACILITIES: Spa Squash Sauna Solarium Gym Jacuzzi Tennis/bowls 200yds away Xmas **CONF:** BC Thtr 120 Class 80 Board 40 Del from £65 **SERVICES:** Lift **PARKING:** 32 **NOTES:** ⊗ in restaurant Civ Wed 150

See advert on opposite page

★★76% Fieldhead

Portuan Rd, Hannafore PL13 2DR

THE INDEPENDENTS

☎ 01503 262689 📠 01503 264114

e-mail: enquiries@fieldheadhotel.co.uk

web: www.fieldheadhotel.co.uk

Dir: *in Looe over bridge, turn left, signed Hannafore. Past waterside church, up hill to seafront. 1st right, right again into Portuan Rd*

Overlooking the bay, this engaging hotel has a relaxing atmosphere. Bedrooms are furnished with care and many have sea views. Smartly presented public areas include a convivial bar and restaurant, and outside there is a palm-filled garden with a secluded patio and swimming pool. The fixed-price menu changes daily and features quality local produce.

ROOMS: 16 en suite (2 fmly) (2 GF) s £30-£50; d £60-£100 (incl. bkfst) **LB FACILITIES:** supervised **PARKING:** 15 **NOTES:** ⊗ in restaurant Closed Xmas

See advert on this page

LOOE, continued

★★64% Rivercroft Hotel
Station Rd PL13 1HL
☎ 01503 262251 📠 01503 265494
e-mail: rivercroft.hotel@virgin.net
web: www.rivercrofthotel.co.uk
Dir: *from A38 take B387 to Looe. Hotel on left near bridge*
Standing high above the river, this family-run hotel is conveniently located, just a short walk from the town centre and beach. Bedrooms are comfortably furnished and well equipped, and many enjoy wonderful views. A carte menu is offered in the Croft Restaurant, or alternatively, meals can be enjoyed in the convivial atmosphere of the bar.
ROOMS: 15 en suite (8 fmly) s £29-£35; d £29-£74 (incl. bkfst) **LB**
FACILITIES: Xmas **NOTES:** 🐕 ⊗ in restaurant

LOSTWITHIEL, Cornwall & Isles of Scilly — Map 02 SX15

★★★69% Restormel Lodge Hotel
Castle Hill PL22 0DD
☎ 01208 872223 📠 01208 873568
e-mail: restlodge@aol.com
web: www.restormelhotel.co.uk
Dir: *on A390 in Lostwithiel*

A short drive from the Eden Project, this popular hotel offers a friendly welcome to all visitors and is ideally situated for exploring the area. The original building houses the bar, restaurant and lounges, with some original features adding to the character. Bedrooms are comfortably furnished, with a number overlooking the secluded outdoor pool.
ROOMS: 24 en suite 12 annexe en suite (2 fmly) (9 GF) ⊗ in 28 bedrooms s £50-£75; d £75-£120 (incl. bkfst) **LB** **FACILITIES:** Outdoor pool Xmas **CONF:** Thtr 50 Class 10 Board 15 **PARKING:** 40 **NOTES:** ⊗ in restaurant

★★★65% Lostwithiel Hotel Golf & Country Club
Lower Polscoe PL22 0HQ
☎ 01208 873550 📠 01208 873479
e-mail: info@golf-hotel.co.uk
web: www.golf-hotel.co.uk
Dir: *off A38 at Dobwalls onto A390. In Lostwithiel right and hotel signed*
This rural hotel is based around its own golf club and other leisure activities. The main building offers guests a choice of eating options, including all-day snacks in the popular Sports Bar. The bedrooms are in separate buildings, attractively designed to feature beams and stone.

continued

ROOMS: 27 en suite (2 fmly) (17 GF) ⊗ in 16 bedrooms s £32-£50; d £64-£100 (incl. bkfst) **LB** **FACILITIES:** Indoor pool (heated) Golf 18 Snooker Gym Putt green Undercover floodlit driving range, Indoor golf simulator Xmas
CONF: Thtr 120 Class 60 Board 40 Del from £70 **PARKING:** 120
NOTES: ⊗ in restaurant Civ Wed 120

LOUGHBOROUGH, Leicestershire — Map 11 SK51

★★★★70% ®® Quorn Country Hotel
Charnwood House, 66 Leicester Rd LE12 8BB
☎ 01509 415050 📠 01509 415557
e-mail: reservations@quorncountryhotel.co.uk
(For full entry see Quorn and advert on opposite page)

★★★65% The Quality Hotel & Suites Loughborough
New Ashby Rd LE11 4EX
☎ 01509 211800 📠 01509 211868
e-mail: enquiries@hotels-loughborough.com
web: www.choicehotelseurope.com
Dir: *M1 junct 23 take A512 towards Loughborough. Hotel 1m on left*
Close to the motorway network, this popular, modern hotel offers comfortable, well-equipped accommodation. All the bedrooms have a spacious work area, and some have small lounges and kitchenettes. It is an ideal hotel for a long stay or for families. Open-plan public rooms include a lounge area, bar and carvery restaurant.
ROOMS: 94 en suite (12 fmly) (47 GF) ⊗ in 71 bedrooms s fr £105; d fr £125 **LB** **FACILITIES:** STV Indoor pool Sauna Solarium Gym Jacuzzi Xmas
CONF: Thtr 225 Class 120 Board 80 Del from £150 **PARKING:** 160
NOTES: ⊗ in restaurant Civ Wed 150

Indoor Swimming pool
Indoor Swimming pool (heated)
Outdoor Swimming pool
Outdoor Swimming pool (heated)

LOUTH, Lincolnshire Map 17 TF38

★★★73% Brackenborough Arms Hotel
Cordeaux Corner, Brackenborough LN11 0SZ
☎ 01507 609169 🖷 01507 609413
e-mail: ashley@brackenborough.co.uk
Dir: *off A16 2m N of Louth*
Set amid well tended gardens and patios, this hotel offers attractive bedrooms, each individually decorated with co-ordinated furnishings and many extras. Tippler's Retreat lounge bar offers informal dining; the more formal Signature Restaurant provides dishes using the best of local produce.
ROOMS: 24 en suite (1 fmly) (6 GF) ⊘ in 6 bedrooms s £59-£64; d £72-£77 (incl. bkfst) **LB FACILITIES:** STV Xmas **CONF:** Thtr 34 Class 24 Board 30 **PARKING:** 91 **NOTES:** 🐕⃠ ⊘ in restaurant Closed 25-26 Dec Civ Wed 34

★★★70% Kenwick Park
CLASSIC BRITISH
Kenwick Park Estate LN11 8NR
☎ 01507 608806 🖷 01507 608027
e-mail: enquiries@kenwick-park.co.uk
web: www.kenwick-park.co.uk
Dir: *A16 from Grimsby, then A157 Mablethorpe/Manby Rd. Hotel 400mtrs down hill on right*

This elegant Georgian house is situated on the 320-acre Kenwick Park estate, overlooking its own golf course. Bedrooms are spacious, comfortable and provide modern facilities. Public areas include a restaurant and a conservatory bar, which overlook the grounds. There is also an extensive leisure centre and state-of-the-art conference and banqueting facilities.
ROOMS: 29 en suite 5 annexe en suite (10 fmly) ⊘ in 11 bedrooms s £75-£115; d £85-£130 (incl. bkfst) **LB FACILITIES: Spa** STV 🏊 supervised ⛳ 18 🎾 Squash Sauna Solarium Gym Putt green Jacuzzi Health & Beauty Centre Xmas **CONF:** Thtr 250 Class 40 Board 90 Del from £100 **PARKING:** 100 **NOTES:** ⊘ in restaurant Civ Wed 200

Late for dinner? Quality standards mean that last orders for dinner vary according to star rating and should be no earlier than: ★★ 7.00pm ★★★ 8:00pm ★★★★ 9:00pm ★★★★★ 10:00pm

★★★69% Beaumont
66 Victoria Rd LN11 0BX
☎ 01507 605005 🖷 01507 607768
e-mail: beaumonthotel@aol.com

This smart, family-run hotel enjoys a quiet location, within easy reach of the town centre. Bedrooms are spacious and individually designed. Public areas include a smart restaurant with a strong Italian influence and an inviting lounge bar with comfortable deep sofas and open fires. Weddings and functions are also catered for.
ROOMS: 16 en suite (2 fmly) (6 GF) s £55-£68; d £80-£130 (incl. bkfst) **CONF:** Thtr 70 Class 50 Board 46 **SERVICES:** Lift **PARKING:** 70 **NOTES:** ⊘ in restaurant RS Sun

LOWER BEEDING, West Sussex Map 06 TQ22

Top Hotel

★★★★ South Lodge
Brighton Rd RH13 6PS
☎ 01403 891711 🖷 01403 891766
e-mail: enquiries@southlodgehotel.co.uk
web: www.exclusivehotels.co.uk
Dir: *on A23 left onto B2110. Turn right through Handcross to A281 junct. Turn left and hotel on right*
This impeccably presented 19th-century lodge with stunning views of the rolling South Downs is an ideal retreat. The traditional, award-winning restaurant offers memorable, seasonal dishes, and the elegant lounge is popular for afternoon teas. Bedrooms are individually designed with character and quality throughout. Leisure and conference facilities are impressive.
ROOMS: 45 en suite (4 fmly) (7 GF) s £99-£195; d £99-£195 **LB** **FACILITIES:** STV 18 Gym Putt green Can organise riding, shooting, fishing & quad biking Xmas **CONF:** BC Thtr 160 Class 60 Board 50 **SERVICES:** Lift **PARKING:** 100 **NOTES:** in restaurant Civ Wed 120

★★★65% Cisswood House
Sandygate Ln RH13 6NF
☎ 0871 871 3242 🖷 0871 871 3243
e-mail: cisswood.house@pageant.co.uk
Dir: *Turn off A23 at Handcross, follow signs for Lower Beeding, turn right at Plough Pub. Hotel 0.5m on right*

Convenient for the M23, this house is set in beautifully maintained gardens. Bedrooms are spacious and well presented, some with whirlpool baths. Public areas include the Pageant Health Club with swimming pool, hairdresser, gym and treatment rooms. The attractive function rooms make this a popular venue for weddings and conferences.
ROOMS: 51 en suite in 6 bedrooms **FACILITIES:** STV supervised Sauna Solarium Gym Jacuzzi Health & beauty salon, Hairdressing Xmas **CONF:** Thtr 200 Class 70 Board 70 **PARKING:** 60 **NOTES:** in restaurant Civ Wed 160

LOWER SLAUGHTER, Gloucestershire Map 10 SP12

Top Hotel

★★★ Lower Slaughter Manor
GL54 2HP
☎ 01451 820456 🖷 01451 822150
e-mail: info@lowerslaughterter.co.uk
web: www.vonessenhotels.co.uk
Dir: *off A429 signed "The Slaughters". Manor 0.5m on right on entering village*
There is a timeless elegance about this wonderful manor, which dates back to the 17th century. Its imposing presence makes it very much the centrepiece of this famous Cotswold village. Inside, the levels of comfort and quality are immediately evident, with crackling log fires warming the many sumptuous lounges. The hotel's dining room is an elegant creation that suitably complements the excellent cuisine on offer. Spacious and tastefully furnished bedrooms are either in the main building or in the adjacent coach house.
ROOMS: 11 en suite 5 annexe en suite s £175-£225; d £235-£345 (incl. bkfst & dinner) **FACILITIES:** Xmas **CONF:** Thtr 36 Class 20 Board 18 Del from £165 **PARKING:** 30 **NOTES:** No children 12yrs in restaurant

★★★75% Washbourne Court
GL54 2HS
☎ 01451 822143 🖷 01451 821045
e-mail: info@washbournecourt.co.uk
web: www.vonessenhotels.co.uk
Dir: *off A429 at signpost 'The Slaughters', between Stow-on-the-Wold and Bourton-on-the-Water. Hotel in centre of village*

Beamed ceilings, log fires and flagstone floors are some of the attractive features of this part 17th-century hotel, set in four acres of immaculate grounds beside the River Eye. Smartly decorated bedrooms are in the main house and self-contained cottages, many offering lovely views. The riverside terrace is popular during

continued

summer months, whilst the elegant dining room serves an interesting menu and a comprehensive wine list.
ROOMS: 15 en suite 13 annexe en suite s £90-£110; d £110-£130 (incl. bkfst) **LB** **FACILITIES:** Xmas **CONF:** Thtr 70 Class 40 Board 30 Del from £110 **PARKING:** 40 **NOTES:** ⊗ in restaurant Civ Wed 60

LOWESTOFT, Suffolk — Map 13 TM59

★★★77% ◎◎ Ivy House Country Hotel

Ivy Ln, Beccles Rd, Oulton Broad NR33 8HY
☎ 01502 501353 & 588144 🖷 01502 501539
e-mail: aa@ivyhousefarm.co.uk
web: www.ivyhousecountryhotel.co.uk
Dir: *on A146 SW of Oulton Broad turn into Ivy Ln beside Esso petrol station. Over railway bridge and follow private driveway*

Delightful, family-run hotel set in three acres of mature landscaped grounds just a short walk from Oulton Broad. Public rooms include an 18th-century thatched barn restaurant where an interesting choice of dishes is served. The attractively decorated bedrooms are housed in garden wings, and many have lovely views of the grounds and countryside beyond.
ROOMS: 19 annexe en suite (1 fmly) (17 GF) ⊗ in 6 bedrooms s £89-£109; d £119-£155 (incl. bkfst) **LB** **FACILITIES:** Reduced rates at neighbouring leisure club **CONF:** Thtr 55 Board 22 Del from £130 **PARKING:** 50 **NOTES:** ⊗ in restaurant Closed 23 Dec-6 Jan 2006

★★★69% *Hotel Hatfield*

The Esplanade NR33 0QP
☎ 01502 565337 🖷 01502 511885
e-mail: hotelhatfield@elizabethhotels.co.uk
Dir: *from town centre follow 'South Beach' signs on A12 Ipswich road. Hotel 200yds on left*

Ideally situated overlooking the sea, this hotel is in a prominent position on the esplanade. Bedrooms are pleasantly decorated and thoughtfully equipped and some have superb sea views. The spacious public rooms include a popular lounge bar, a cocktail bar and the Shoreline restaurant where an interesting choice of dishes is served.
continued
ROOMS: 33 en suite (1 fmly) ⊗ in 7 bedrooms **FACILITIES:** STV **CONF:** Thtr 100 Class 50 Board 40 **SERVICES:** Lift **PARKING:** 26 **NOTES:** Civ Wed 200

★★★69% *Hotel Victoria*

Kirkley Cliff NR33 0BZ
☎ 01502 574433 🖷 01502 501529
e-mail: info@hotelvictoria.freeserve.co.uk
Dir: *A12 to seafront on one-way system signed A12 Ipswich. Hotel on seafront just beyond the Thatched Cottage*
Attractive Victorian building situated on the esplanade overlooking the sea and has direct access to the beach. Bedrooms are pleasantly decorated and thoughtfully equipped; many rooms have sea views. Public rooms include modern conference and banqueting facilities, a choice of lounges, a comfortable bar and a restaurant, which overlooks the pretty garden.
ROOMS: 24 en suite (4 fmly) **FACILITIES:** STV ⺀ ♫ **CONF:** Thtr 200 Class 150 Board 50 **SERVICES:** Lift **PARKING:** 45 **NOTES:** ✖ Civ Wed 200

⌂ Premier Travel Inn Lowestoft

249 Yarmouth Rd NR32 4AA
☎ 08701 977165 🖷 01502 581223
web: www.premiertravelinn.com
Dir: *on A12, 2m N of Lowestoft*
High quality, modern budget accommodation ideal for both families and business travellers. Spacious, en suite bedrooms feature bath and shower, satellite TV and many have telephones and modem points. The adjacent family restaurant features a wide and varied menu. For further details consult the Hotel Groups page.
ROOMS: 40 en suite s £48.95; d £48.95

LOWESWATER, Cumbria — Map 18 NY12

★★69% Grange Country House

CA13 0SU
☎ 01946 861211 & 861570
e-mail: gchloweswater@hotmail.com
Dir: *left off A5086 for Mockerkin, through village. After 2m left for Loweswater Lake. Hotel at bottom of hill on left*
This delightful country hotel is set in a quiet valley at the north-western end of Loweswater and continues to prove popular with guests seeking peace and quiet. It has a friendly and relaxed atmosphere, and the cosy public areas include a small bar, a residents' lounge and an attractive dining room. The bedrooms are well equipped and comfortable.
ROOMS: 8 en suite (2 fmly) (1 GF) s £35-£50; d £70-£100 (incl. bkfst) **FACILITIES:** National Trust boats & fishing Xmas **CONF:** Thtr 25 Class 25 Board 25 **PARKING:** 22 **NOTES:** ⊗ in restaurant RS Jan-Feb No credit cards accepted

LOXTON, Somerset — Map 04 ST35

★★★67% Webbington

BS26 2XA
☎ 01934 750100 🖷 01934 750020
e-mail: webbington@latonahotels.co.uk
Despite being clearly visible from the M5 motorway, this popular hotel is situated in the countryside and has splendid views from many bedrooms and public areas. The hotel is well suited to a wide range of guests, from business to leisure to families, and offers a
continued on p364

LOXTON, continued

warm welcome to all. Facilities include an indoor swimming pool, tennis courts, cardio-gym and varied conference rooms.
ROOMS: 59 en suite (2 fmly) ⊘ in 10 bedrooms s £40-£65; d £75-£100 (incl. bkfst) **LB** **FACILITIES:** 🏊 🎾 Sauna Solarium Gym Beauty treatments Cardiovascular suite Steam Room Xmas **CONF:** Thtr 1000 Class 600 Del from £115 **PARKING:** 450 **NOTES:** 🐕 ⊘ in restaurant Civ Wed 500

LUDLOW, Shropshire
Map 10 SO57

★★★75% 🏵🏵🏵 Overton Grange Country House
Old Hereford Rd SY8 4AD
☎ 01584 873500 🖷 01584 873524
e-mail: info@overtongrangehotel.com
web: www.overtongrangehotel.com
Dir: *off A49 at B4361 to Ludlow. Hotel 200yds on left*
Overton Grange is a traditional country-house hotel offering stylish, comfortable bedrooms, and high standards of guest care. Food is an important element on offer here; the restaurant serves classically based, award-winning French-style cuisine, using locally sourced produce where possible. Meeting and conference rooms are available.
ROOMS: 14 en suite ⊘ in all bedrooms s £85-£190; d £130-£190 (incl. bkfst) **LB** **FACILITIES:** ♫ Xmas **CONF:** BC Thtr 100 Class 40 Board 20 Del from £150 **PARKING:** 50 **NOTES:** ⊘ in restaurant Civ Wed 60

★★★72% 🏵🏵 Dinham Hall
By the Castle SY8 1EJ
☎ 01584 876464 🖷 01584 876019
e-mail: info@dinhamhall.co.uk
web: www.dinhamhall.co.uk
Dir: *opposite the castle*
Built in 1792, this lovely old house stands in attractive gardens immediately opposite Ludlow Castle. It has a well-deserved reputation for warm hospitality and fine cuisine. Well-equipped bedrooms include two in a converted cottage and some with four-poster beds. The comfortable public rooms are elegantly appointed.
ROOMS: 11 en suite 2 annexe en suite (3 fmly) (1 GF) s £95-£210; d £140-£240 (incl. bkfst) **LB** **FACILITIES:** Xmas **CONF:** Thtr 80 Class 50 Board 26 Del from £135 **PARKING:** 16 **NOTES:** ⊘ in restaurant Civ Wed 150

★★★67% 🏵 Feathers
The Bull Ring SY8 1AA
☎ 01584 875261 🖷 01584 876030
e-mail: feathers.ludlow@btconnect.com
web: www.feathersatludlow.co.uk
Dir: *from A49 and follow town centre signs to centre of Ludlow. Hotel on left*

Famous for the carved woodwork outside and in, this picturesque 17th-century hotel is one of the town's best-known landmarks and is in an excellent location. Bedrooms are traditional in style and decor. Public areas have retained much of the traditional charm; the first-floor lounge is particularly stunning.
ROOMS: 40 en suite (3 fmly) ⊘ in 19 bedrooms s £75-£80; d £95-£105 (incl. bkfst) **LB** **FACILITIES:** Xmas **CONF:** Thtr 80 Class 40 Board 40 Del from £120 **SERVICES:** Lift **PARKING:** 33 **NOTES:** ⊘ in restaurant Civ Wed 25

★★68% Cliffe
Dinham SY8 2JE
☎ 01584 872063 🖷 01584 873991
e-mail: thecliffehotel@hotmail.com
Dir: *in town centre. Turn left at castle gates to Dinham, follow road over bridge. Take right fork, hotel 200yds on left*
Built in the 19th century and standing in extensive grounds and gardens, this privately owned and personally run hotel is quietly located close to the castle and the river. It provides well-equipped accommodation, and facilities include a lounge bar, a pleasant restaurant and a patio overlooking the garden.
ROOMS: 9 en suite (2 fmly) ⊘ in all bedrooms s £40-£50; d £60-£80 (incl. bkfst) **LB** **PARKING:** 22 **NOTES:** ⊘ in restaurant

⌂ Travelodge
Woofferton SY8 4AL
☎ 08700 850 950 🖷 01584 711695
web: www.travelodge.co.uk
Dir: *on A49 at junct A456/B4362*
Travelodge offers good quality, good value, modern accommodation. Ideal for families, the spacious, en suite bedrooms include remote-control TV, tea and coffee-making facilities and comfortable beds. Meals can be taken at the nearby family restaurant. For further details consult the Hotel Groups page.
ROOMS: 32 en suite s fr £26; d fr £26

LULWORTH COVE See West Lulworth

LUMBY, North Yorkshire
Map 16 SE43

U Quality Hotel Leeds Selby Fork
LS25 5LF
☎ 01977 682761 🖷 01977 685462
e-mail: info@qualityhotelleeds.co.uk
Dir: *A1M junct 42/A63 signed Selby, hotel on A63 on left*
At the time of going to press, the star classification for this hotel was not confirmed. Please refer to the AA internet site www.theAA.com for current information.
ROOMS: 97 en suite (18 fmly) (56 GF) ⊘ in 57 bedrooms s £40-£85; d £40-£95 **FACILITIES:** 🏊 🎾 Sauna Gym Xmas **CONF:** Thtr 160 Class 60 Board 40 Del from £85 **PARKING:** 230 **NOTES:** Civ Wed 60

♫ Entertainment

LUTON, Bedfordshire
Map 06 TL02

★★★66% Hotel St Lawrence
40A Guildford St LU1 2PA
☎ 01582 482119 🖷 01582 482818
e-mail: reservations@hotelstlawrence.co.uk
web: www.hotelstlawrence.co.uk
Dir: *M1 junct 10a & follow signs to town centre, after university take left fork at mini rdbt. Hotel 70yds on right*
This former Victorian hotel enjoys a central location and smart public areas, which include a modern restaurant and a welcoming bar. Bedrooms come in a variety of styles and sizes and continue

continued

to benefit from an ongoing programme of refurbishment. Parking is available in the multi-storey opposite.

ROOMS: 28 en suite ⊗ in 4 bedrooms s £70-£80; d £80-£90 (incl. bkfst) **LB** **FACILITIES:** Use of local fitness centre & snooker club **NOTES:** ✗ ⊗ in restaurant RS 25 Dec- 1 Jan

★★★60% *The Chiltern Hotel*

Waller Av LU4 9RU
☎ 0870 609 6120 ⎙ 01582 581859
e-mail: thechiltern@corushotels.com
web: www.corushotels.com/thechiltern
Dir: *M1 junct 11 take A505 to Luton past 2 sets of lights. Over rdbt, left at lights, hotel on right*

Conveniently close to the M1, this hotel is geared towards the business guest. It has a range of conference and meeting rooms. Bedrooms offer good levels of comfort. There is an air-conditioned restaurant and ample parking.
ROOMS: 91 en suite (6 fmly) ⊗ in 63 bedrooms **CONF:** Thtr 180 Class 120 Board 30 **SERVICES:** Lift **PARKING:** 150 **NOTES:** ⊗ in restaurant

⌂ Travelodge

641 Dunstable Rd LU4 8RQ
☎ 08700 850 950 ⎙ 01582 490065
web: www.travelodge.co.uk
Dir: *M1 junct 11 towards Luton, lodge on right in 100yds*

Travelodge offers good quality, good value, modern accommodation. Ideal for families, the spacious, en suite bedrooms include remote-control TV, tea and coffee-making facilities and comfortable beds. Meals can be taken at the nearby family restaurant. For further details consult the Hotel Groups page.
ROOMS: 140 en suite s fr £26; d fr £26 **CONF:** Thtr 80 Class 40 Board 30

LUTON AIRPORT, Bedfordshire — Map 06 TL12

⌂ *Hotel Ibis Luton*

Spittlesea Rd LU2 9NH
☎ 01582 424488 ⎙ 01582 455511
e-mail: H1040@accor-hotels.com
Dir: *M1 junct 10 follow Luton Airport signs. Hotel 600mtrs from airport*

Modern, budget hotel offering comfortable accommodation in bright and practical bedrooms. Breakfast is self-service and dinner is available in the restaurant. For further details, consult the Hotel Groups page.
ROOMS: 98 en suite **CONF:** Thtr 114 Class 64 Board 80

⌂ Premier Travel Inn Luton Airport

Osbourne Rd LU1 3HJ
☎ 08701 977166 ⎙ 01582 421900
web: www.premiertravelinn.com
Dir: *M1 junct 10 follow signs for Luton on A1081, at 3rd rdbt turn left onto Gypsy Lane, turn left at next rdbt*

High quality, modern budget accommodation ideal for both

continued

families and business travellers. Spacious, en suite bedrooms feature bath and shower, satellite TV and many have telephones and modem points. The adjacent family restaurant features a wide and varied menu. For further details consult the Hotel Groups page.
ROOMS: 129 en suite s £53.95-£59.95; d £53.95-£59.95 **CONF:** Thtr 70 Board 50

LYME REGIS, Dorset — Map 04 SY39

See also Colyford

★★★71% ❀ Alexandra

Pound St DT7 3HZ
☎ 01297 442010 ⎙ 01297 443229
e-mail: enquiries@hotelalexandra.co.uk
web: www.lymeregis.co.uk
Dir: *from A30 , A35, then onto A358, A3052 to Lyme Regis*

This welcoming, family-run hotel is Grade II listed and dates back to 1735. Public areas are spacious and comfortable, with ample seating areas to relax, unwind and enjoy the magnificent views. The elegant restaurant offers imaginative, innovative dishes. Bedrooms vary in size and shape, decorated with pretty chintz fabrics and attractive furniture.
ROOMS: 25 en suite 1 annexe en suite (8 fmly) (3 GF) s £55; d £96-£140 (incl. bkfst) **LB** **PARKING:** 18 **NOTES:** ⊗ in restaurant Closed Xmas & Jan

★★77% ❀ Swallows Eaves

EX24 6QJ
☎ 01297 553184 ⎙ 01297 553574
e-mail: swallows-eaves@hotmail.com
(For full entry see Colyford)

★★74% ❀ Mariners Hotel

Silver St DT7 3HS
☎ 01297 442753 ⎙ 01297 442431
e-mail: marinershotel@btopenworld.com
Dir: *W of town on A3052, right on B3070*

This small, friendly hotel has period character and charm and a relaxed atmosphere. The individually decorated bedrooms are comfortable; some rooms benefit from stunning views over the town to the sea. A beamed bar and choice of lounge is provided for guests, while in the restaurant carefully prepared meals use fresh ingredients, with locally caught fish a highlight on the menus.
ROOMS: 12 en suite ⊗ in all bedrooms s £37-£43; d £73-£86 (incl. bkfst) **FACILITIES:** Xmas **PARKING:** 20 **NOTES:** No children 7yrs ⊗ in restaurant Closed 27 Dec-31 Jan

★★73% ❀❀ Dower House

Rousdon DT7 3RB
☎ 01297 21047 ⎙ 01297 24748
e-mail: info@dhhotel.com
web: www.dhhotel.com
(For full entry see Rousdon, Devon)

LYME REGIS, continued

★★68% **Royal Lion**
Broad St DT7 3QF
☎ 01297 445622 🖷 01297 445859
e-mail: reception@royallionhotel.fsnet.co.uk
web: www.royallionhotel.com
Dir: *From W on A35, take A3052 or from E take B3165 to Lyme Regis. Hotel in centre of town, opp The Fossil Shop. Car park at rear*
This 17th-century, former coaching inn is full of character and charm, and is situated a short walk from the seafront. Bedrooms vary in size; those in the newer wing are more spacious and some have balconies, sea views or a private terrace. In addition to the elegant dining room and guest lounges, a heated pool, small gym and snooker table are available.
ROOMS: 29 en suite (11 fmly) ⊗ in 18 bedrooms s £43-£57; d £86-£114 (incl. bkfst) **LB** **FACILITIES: Spa** Snooker Gym Jacuzzi Games room Pool table Table tennis Xmas **CONF:** Thtr 50 Class 20 Board 20 **PARKING:** 30 **NOTES:** ⊗ in restaurant

LYMINGTON, Hampshire — Map 05 SZ39

★★★77% ***Passford House***
Mount Pleasant Ln SO41 8LS
☎ 01590 682398 🖷 01590 683494
e-mail: sales@passfordhousehotel.co.uk
web: www.passfordhousehotel.co.uk
Dir: *from A337 at Lymington over mini rdbt. 1st right at Tollhouse pub, then after 1m right into Mount Pleasant Lane*
A peaceful hotel set in attractive grounds on the edge of town. Bedrooms vary in size but all are comfortably furnished and well equipped. Extensive public areas include lounges, a smartly appointed restaurant and bar, and leisure facilities. A friendly and well-motivated team provides attentive service.
ROOMS: 49 en suite 2 annexe en suite (2 fmly) (10 GF) ⊗ in 10 bedrooms **FACILITIES: Spa** Sauna Gym Putt green Petanque, Table tennis, Helipad, pool table **CONF:** Thtr 80 Class 30 Board 30 **PARKING:** 100 **NOTES:** No children 8yrs ⊗ in restaurant

★★★72% **Elmers Court Hotel & Resort**
South Baddesley Rd SO41 5ZB
☎ 01590 676011 🖷 01590 679780
e-mail: elmerscourt@macdonald-hotels.co.uk
web: www.macdonald-hotels.co.uk
Dir: *M27 junct 1, through Lyndhurst, Brockenhurst & Lymington, hotel 200yds right after Lymington ferry terminal*

Originally known as The Elms, this Tudor-gabled manor house dates back to the 1820s. Ideally located at the edge of the New Forest and overlooking The Solent with views towards the Isle of Wight, the hotel offers suites and self-catering accommodation, along with well-appointed leisure facilities.
ROOMS: 42 annexe en suite (8 fmly) (22 GF) ⊗ in 16 bedrooms s £55-£145; d £85-£240 (incl. bkfst) **LB** **FACILITIES: Spa** supervised supervised Squash Sauna Solarium Gym Putt green Jacuzzi Beauty treatment rooms, , Steam room, Aerobics classes Xmas **CONF:** Thtr 100 Class 40 Board 40 Del from £130 **PARKING:** 100 **NOTES:** ⊗ in restaurant Civ Wed 100

★★★71% **Stanwell House**
14-15 High St SO41 9AA
☎ 01590 677123 🖷 01590 677756
e-mail: sales@stanwellhousehotel.co.uk
web: www.stanwellhousehotel.co.uk
Dir: *A337 to town centre, on right of High St, before descent to quay*
Centrally situated, this stylish hotel offers friendly and attentive service. Bedrooms are comfortable and very well equipped; some rooms in the older part of the building are particularly interesting and some have four-poster beds. The award-winning cuisine provides interesting, freshly prepared dishes.
ROOMS: 29 en suite (1 fmly) ⊗ in 10 bedrooms s £85-£160; d £110-£160 (incl. bkfst) **LB** **CONF:** Thtr 30 Class 20 Board 22 Del from £125 **NOTES:** ⊗ in restaurant Civ Wed 60

★★71% **The Mill at Gordleton**
Silver St, Hordle SO41 6DJ
☎ 01590 682219 🖷 01590 683073
e-mail: info@themillatgordleton.co.uk
Dir: *M27 junct 1 towards Lyndhurst to Lymington A337, turn right to Hordle at Tollhouse Inn, 1.5m to Mill*

A delightful 17th-century water mill located on the banks of the River Avon. The restaurant takes full advantage of the hotel's position and serves an extensive range of dishes at lunch and dinner. The picturesque gardens are popular for alfresco dining during the warmer months and the attractive bedrooms are equipped with whirlpool baths.
ROOMS: 9 en suite ⊗ in 8 bedrooms s £85-£120; d £120-£175 (incl. bkfst) **FACILITIES:** Fishing **PARKING:** 60 **NOTES:** ⊗ in restaurant Closed 25-26 Dec RS Sun

LYMM, Cheshire — Map 15 SJ68

★★★68% **Lymm Hotel**
Whitbarrow Rd WA13 9AQ
☎ 01925 752233 🖷 01925 756035
e-mail: general.lymm@macdonald-hotels.co.uk
web: www.macdonald-hotels.co.uk
Dir: *take M6 to B5158 to Lymm. Left at junct, right at mini rdbt, left into Brookfield Rd and 3rd left into Whitbarrow Rd*
In a peaceful residential area, this hotel benefits from both its quiet setting and its convenient access to local motorway networks. The hotel offers comfortable bedrooms equipped for both the business

continued

and leisure guest. Public areas include an attractive bar and an elegant restaurant. There is extensive parking.
ROOMS: 14 en suite 48 annexe en suite (5 fmly) (4 GF) ⊗ in 34 bedrooms s £60-£90; d £65-£110 (incl. bkfst) **LB FACILITIES:** STV Xmas **CONF:** BC Thtr 220 Class 140 Board 100 Del from £100 **PARKING:** 120 **NOTES:** ⊗ in restaurant Civ Wed 120

⌂ Travelodge
Granada Services A50, Cliffe Ln WA13 0SP
☎ 08700 850 950 📠 01925 759341
web: www.travelodge.co.uk
Dir: *A50, intersection of M6 junct 20 & M56 junct 9*
Travelodge offers good quality, good value, modern accommodation. Ideal for families, the spacious, en suite bedrooms include remote-control TV, tea and coffee-making facilities and comfortable beds. Meals can be taken at the nearby family restaurant. For further details consult the Hotel Groups page.
ROOMS: 61 en suite s fr £26; d fr £26

LYMPSHAM, Somerset Map 04 ST35

★★69% ***Batch Country Hotel***
Batch Ln BS24 0EX
☎ 01934 750371 📠 01934 750501
web: www.batchcountryhotel.co.uk
Dir: *M5 junct 22, take last exit on rdbt signed A370 to Weston-Super-Mare. 3.5m left into Lympsham. 1m, sign at end of road*

THE CIRCLE
Selected Individual Hotels
GREAT BRITAIN

Rurally situated between Weston-Super-Mare and Burnham-on-Sea, this former farmhouse offers a relaxed, friendly and peaceful environment. The comfortable bedrooms have views to the Mendip and Quantock Hills. Spacious lounges overlook the extensive gardens and the function room is very popular for wedding ceremonies. Meals are served in the beamed dining room.
ROOMS: 10 en suite (6 fmly) (1 GF) ⊗ in 2 bedrooms
FACILITIES: Fishing **CONF:** Thtr 80 Class 60 Board 100 **PARKING:** 80
NOTES: ⊗ in restaurant Closed 25-26 Dec Civ Wed 120

See advert under WESTON-SUPER-MARE

LYNDHURST, Hampshire Map 05 SU30

★★★70% Crown
High St SO43 7NF
☎ 023 8028 2922 📠 023 8028 2751
e-mail: reception@crownhotel-lyndhurst.co.uk
web: www.crownhotel-lyndhurst.co.uk
Dir: *in centre of village, opposite church*
The Crown, with its stone mullioned windows, panelled rooms and elegant period decor evokes the style of an Edwardian English country house. Bedrooms are generally a good size and offer a useful range of facilities. Public areas have style and comfort and

continued on p368

LYNDHURST, continued

include a choice of function and meeting rooms. The pleasant garden and terrace are havens of peace and tranquillity.

Crown, Lyndhurst

ROOMS: 39 en suite (8 fmly) ⊗ in 23 bedrooms s £72-£102; d £115-£145 (incl. bkfst) **LB** **FACILITIES:** STV Xmas **CONF:** Thtr 70 Class 30 Board 45 Del from £115 **SERVICES:** Lift **PARKING:** 60 **NOTES:** ⊗ in restaurant Civ Wed 70

★★★70% Lyndhurst Park

High St SO43 7NL
☎ 023 8028 3923 ⎙ 023 8028 3019
e-mail: lyndhurst.park@forestdale.com
web: www.forestdale.com
Dir: *M27 junct 1-3 to A35 to Lyndhurst. Hotel at bottom of High St*
Although it is just by the High Street, the hotel is afforded seclusion from the town due to its five acres of mature grounds. The comfortable bedrooms include home-from-home touches such as ducks in the bath! The stunning new bar offers a stylish setting for a snack whilst the restaurant provides a more formal dining venue.
ROOMS: 59 en suite (3 fmly) ⊗ in 10 bedrooms s £85-£105; d £115-£135 (incl. bkfst) **LB** **FACILITIES:** STV Snooker Sauna Table tennis Xmas **CONF:** Thtr 300 Class 120 Board 80 Del from £125 **SERVICES:** Lift **PARKING:** 100 **NOTES:** ⊗ in restaurant Civ Wed

★★★67% Bell Inn

SO43 7HE
☎ 023 8081 2214 ⎙ 023 8081 3958
e-mail: bell@bramshaw.co.uk
web: www.bramshaw.co.uk
(For full entry see Brook (Near Cadnam))

★★★67% Forest Lodge

Pikes Hill, Romsey Rd SO43 7AS
☎ 023 8028 3677 ⎙ 023 8028 2940
e-mail: forest@newforesthotels.co.uk
web: www.newforesthotels.co.uk
Dir: *M27 junct 1, A337 towards Lyndhurst. In village, with police station & courts on right, take 1st right into Pikes Hill*
Situated on the edge of Lyndhurst, this hotel is set well back from the main road. Bedrooms are on different floors and a number are well suited for family use. The indoor pool, with delightful murals, is a real bonus.
ROOMS: 28 en suite (7 fmly) (6 GF) ⊗ in 5 bedrooms s £70-£82.50; d £110-£135 (incl. bkfst) **LB** **FACILITIES:** Sauna Gym Xmas **CONF:** Thtr 120 Class 70 Board 60 Del from £90 **PARKING:** 50 **NOTES:** ⊗ in restaurant Civ Wed 60

★★68% Ormonde House

Southampton Rd SO43 7BT
☎ 023 8028 2806 ⎙ 023 8028 2004
e-mail: enquiries@ormondehouse.co.uk
web: www.ormondehouse.co.uk
Dir: *800yds E of Lyndhurst on A35 to Southampton*
Set back from the main road on the edge of Lyndhurst, this welcoming hotel combines an efficient mix of relaxed hospitality and attentive service. Bedrooms, including some on the ground floor, are well furnished and equipped. Larger suites with kitchen facilities are also available. Home-cooked dinners offer a range of carefully presented fresh ingredients.
ROOMS: 19 en suite 4 annexe en suite (1 fmly) (6 GF) ⊗ in all bedrooms **FACILITIES: Spa** STV **PARKING:** 26 **NOTES:** ⊗ in restaurant Closed Xmas wk

★71% Knightwood Lodge

Southampton Rd SO43 7BU
☎ 023 8028 2502 ⎙ 023 8028 3730
e-mail: jackie4r@aol.com
web: www.knightwoodlodge.co.uk
Dir: *exit M27 junct 1 follow A337 to Lyndhurst. Left at traffic lights in village onto A35 towards Southampton. Hotel 0.25m on left*
This friendly, family-run hotel is situated on the outskirts of Lyndhurst. Comfortable bedrooms are modern in style and well equipped with many useful extras. The hotel offers an excellent range of facilities including a swimming pool, a Jacuzzi and a small gym area.
ROOMS: 15 en suite 4 annexe en suite (2 fmly) (5 GF) s £35-£50; d £70-£100 (incl. bkfst) **LB** **FACILITIES:** STV Sauna Gym Jacuzzi Steam room **PARKING:** 15 **NOTES:** ⊗ in restaurant

Travelodge (New Forest)

A31 Westbound SO43 7GN
☎ 08700 850 950 ⎙ 02380 811544
web: www.travelodge.co.uk
Dir: *M27 w'bound becomes A31, on left after Rufus Stone sign*
Travelodge offers good quality, good value, modern accommodation. Ideal for families, the spacious, en suite bedrooms include remote-control TV, tea and coffee-making facilities and comfortable beds. Meals can be taken at the nearby family restaurant. For further details consult the Hotel Groups page.
ROOMS: 32 en suite s fr £26; d fr £26

LYNMOUTH, Devon

Map 03 SS74

See also Lynton

★★★65% Tors

EX35 6NA
☎ 01598 753236 ⎙ 01598 752544
e-mail: torshotel@torslynmouth.co.uk
web: www.torslynmouth.co.uk
Dir: *adjacent to A39 on Countisbury Hill just before entering Lynmouth from Minehead*
In an elevated position overlooking Lynmouth Bay, this friendly hotel is set in five acres of woodland. The majority of the bedrooms benefit from the superb views, as do the public areas; which are generous and well presented. Both fixed-price and short carte menus are offered in the restaurant.
ROOMS: 31 en suite (6 fmly) ⊗ in 1 bedroom s £70-£180; d £100-£220 (incl. bkfst) **LB** **FACILITIES:** Table tennis, Pool table ch fac Xmas **CONF:** Thtr 60 Class 40 Board 25 Del from £65 **SERVICES:** Lift **PARKING:** 40 **NOTES:** ⊗ in restaurant Closed 4-31 Jan RS Feb (wknds only)

★★73% ❀❀ Rising Sun
Harbourside EX35 6EG
☎ 01598 753223 🖷 01598 753480
e-mail: reception@risingsunlynmouth.co.uk
web: www.risingsunlynmouth.co.uk
Dir: *M5 junct 23 to Minehead. A39 to Lynmouth, hotel on harbour*

This delightful thatched inn that sits on the harbour front, and was once a smugglers' inn. Popular with locals and hotel guests alike, there is the option of eating in either the convivial bar or the restaurant; a comfortable, quiet lounge is also available. Bedrooms, located in the inn or adjoining cottages, are all individually designed and have modern facilities.
ROOMS: 16 en suite (1 fmly) (1 GF) ⊗ in all bedrooms **NOTES:** ⊗ in restaurant

★★68% Bath
Sea Front EX35 6EL
☎ 01598 752238 🖷 01598 753894
e-mail: bathhotel@torslynmouth.co.uk
Dir: *M5 junct 25, follow A39 to Minehead then Porlock and Lynmouth*
This well-established, friendly hotel is situated near the harbour and offers lovely views from the attractive, sea-facing bedrooms and is an excellent starting point for scenic walks. There are two lounges and a sun lounge, and the restaurant menu makes good use of fresh produce and local fish.
ROOMS: 22 en suite (9 fmly) ⊗ in 1 bedroom s £40-£55; d £64-£130 (incl. bkfst) **LB** **PARKING:** 12 **NOTES:** ⊗ in restaurant Closed Jan & Dec RS Feb-Mar and Nov

LYNTON, Devon — Map 03 SS74
See also Lynmouth

★★★68% ❀ Lynton Cottage
North Walk EX35 6ED
☎ 01598 752342 🖷 01598 752597
e-mail: enquiries@lynton-cottage.co.uk
web: www.lynton-cottage.co.uk
Dir: *M25 junct 23 A39 to Lynmouth then Lynton, hotel 100mtrs on right*

Magnificent views can be enjoyed from this peaceful hideaway,
continued
which stands some 500 feet above the sea. Bedrooms vary in size and most have scenic views, whilst public areas, such as the cosy Victorian-style bar, provide a relaxing environment. In Sanford's Restaurant, a short carte offers a balanced selection of tempting dishes.
ROOMS: 15 en suite (2 fmly) (1 GF) ⊗ in all bedrooms s £59-£105; d £84-£150 (incl. bkfst) **LB** **CONF:** BC Thtr 34 Class 24 Board 24 Del from £95 **PARKING:** 17 **NOTES:** ⊗ in restaurant Closed Dec-Jan

★★72% Seawood
North Walk EX35 6HJ
☎ 01598 752272 🖷 01598 752272
e-mail: seawoodhotel@aol.com
Dir: *turn right at St. Mary's Church in Lynton High St for hotel, 2nd on left*
Tucked away in a quiet area and spectacularly situated 400 feet above the seashore, the Seawood enjoys magnificent views, and is set in delightful grounds. Bedrooms, many with sea views and some with four-poster beds, are comfortable and well equipped. At dinner, the daily-changing menu provides freshly prepared and appetising dishes.
ROOMS: 12 en suite ⊗ in all bedrooms s £32-£37.50; d £64-£85 (incl. bkfst) **PARKING:** 12 **NOTES:** No children 10yrs ⊗ in restaurant Closed Dec-Feb

★★70% ❀ Chough's Nest
North Walk EX35 6HJ
☎ 01598 753315 🖷 01598 753315
e-mail: relax@choughsnesthotel.co.uk
Dir: *on Lynton High St. Turn at St. Marys Church, hotel 0.5m on left*
Lying on the south-west coastal path, this charming hotel can claim to have one of the most spectacular views around. Bedrooms offer ample comfort and quality, the majority looking out to sea. The dining room, also with the wonderful outlook, is a lovely setting in which to enjoy carefully cooked food in a convivial atmosphere.
ROOMS: 9 en suite (2 fmly) ⊗ in all bedrooms s £45-£52; d £60-£92 (incl. bkfst) **LB** **PARKING:** 9 **NOTES:** ✗ No children 8yrs ⊗ in restaurant Closed 6 Jan-4 Feb

LYTHAM ST ANNES, Lancashire — Map 18 SD32

★★★★70% ❀ Clifton Arms Hotel
West Beach, Lytham FY8 5QJ
☎ 01253 739898 🖷 01253 730657
e-mail: welcome@cliftonarms-lytham.com
web: www.cliftonarm-lytham.com
Dir: *on A584 along seafront*

This well-established hotel occupies a prime position overlooking Lytham Green and the Ribble estuary beyond. Bedrooms vary in size and style but most have now been refurbished to a high standard; front-facing rooms are particularly spacious and enjoy
continued on p370

L

LYTHAM ST ANNES, continued

splendid views. There is an elegant restaurant, a stylish open-plan lounge and cocktail bar as well as function and conference facilities.
ROOMS: 48 en suite (2 fmly) ⊗ in 44 bedrooms s £100-£130; d £125-£155 (incl. bkfst) **LB** **FACILITIES:** STV Xmas **CONF:** Thtr 200 Class 100 Board 60 Del from £139 **SERVICES:** Lift **PARKING:** 50 **NOTES:** ⊗ in restaurant Civ Wed 100

See advert on opposite page

★★★69% Bedford
307-311 Clifton Dr South FY8 1HN
☎ 01253 724636 🖷 01253 729244
e-mail: reservations@bedford-hotel.com
web: www.bedford-hotel.com
Dir: *from M55 follow signs for airport to last lights. Left through 2 sets of lights. Hotel 300yds on left*
This popular family-run hotel, close to the town centre and the seafront, has been stylishly extended. Bedrooms vary in size and style and include family and four-poster rooms. Newer bedrooms are particularly elegant and tastefully appointed. Spacious public areas include a choice of lounges, a coffee shop, fitness facilities and an impressive function suite.
ROOMS: 45 en suite (10 fmly) (6 GF) ⊗ in all bedrooms s £50; d £74-£100 (incl. bkfst) **LB** **FACILITIES:** STV Gym Xmas **CONF:** Thtr 200 Class 140 Board 60 Del £82.50 **SERVICES:** Lift **PARKING:** 25 **NOTES:** ✈ ⊗ in restaurant Civ Wed 200

L

★★★69% Chadwick
South Promenade FY8 1NP
THE INDEPENDENTS
☎ 01253 720061 🖷 01253 714455
e-mail: sales@thechadwickhotel.com
web: www.thechadwickhotel.com
Dir: *M6 junct 32 take M55 to Blackpool then A5230 to South Shore. Follow signs for St Annes*
This popular, comfortable and traditional hotel enjoys a seafront location. Bedrooms vary in size and style, but all are very thoughtfully equipped; those at the front boast panoramic sea views. Public rooms are spacious and comfortably furnished and the smart bar is stocked with some 200 malt whiskies. The hotel has a well-equipped, air-conditioned gym and indoor pool.
ROOMS: 75 en suite (28 fmly) (13 GF) s £46-£50; d £64-£78 (incl. bkfst) **LB** **FACILITIES:** **Spa** STV 🏊 Sauna Solarium Gym Jacuzzi Turkish bath Games room Soft play adventure area ♫ ch fac Xmas **CONF:** Thtr 72 Class 24 Board 28 Del from £65 **SERVICES:** Lift **PARKING:** 40 **NOTES:** ✈ ⊗ in restaurant

See advert on opposite page

⊗ No smoking

★★★64% Glendower
North Promenade FY8 2NQ
Best Western
☎ 01253 723241 🖷 01253 640069
e-mail: glendowerhotel@bestwestern.co.uk
web: www.theglendowerhotel.co.uk
Dir: *M55 follow airport signs. Left at Promenade to St Annes. Hotel 500yds from pier*
Located on the seafront and with easy access to the town centre, this popular, friendly hotel offers comfortably furnished, well-equipped accommodation. Bedrooms vary in size and style and include four-poster rooms and very popular family suites.

continued

Public areas feature a choice of smart, comfortable lounges, a bright and modern leisure club and function facilities.

ROOMS: 60 en suite (17 fmly) ⊗ in 12 bedrooms s £54-£69; d £88-£118 (incl. bkfst) **LB** **FACILITIES:** **Spa** STV 🏊 supervised Snooker Sauna Solarium Gym Jacuzzi Childrens playroom Xmas **CONF:** Thtr 150 Class 120 Board 40 Del from £95 **SERVICES:** Lift **PARKING:** 45 **NOTES:** ⊗ in restaurant

★★70% Lindum
63-67 South Promenade FY8 1LZ
☎ 01253 721534 722516 🖷 01253 721364
e-mail: info@lindumhotel.co.uk
web: www.lindumhotel.co.uk
Dir: *from M55 follow A5230 & signs for Blackpool Airport. After airport, left at lights to St Annes, right at lights in town centre. 1st left onto seafront. Hotel 250yds on left*

The same family has run this friendly and popular seafront hotel for over 40 years. Well-equipped bedrooms are generally spacious and some enjoy superb coastal views. Extensive, stylish public areas include a choice of lounges and a popular health suite. The open-plan restaurant offers a good choice of well-cooked dishes at breakfast and dinner.
ROOMS: 76 en suite (25 fmly) ⊗ in all bedrooms s £30-£45; d £50-£75 (incl. bkfst) **LB** **FACILITIES:** Sauna Solarium Jacuzzi Xmas **CONF:** Thtr 80 Class 30 Board 25 Del from £50 **SERVICES:** Lift air con **PARKING:** 20 **NOTES:** ⊗ in restaurant

U Grand
South Promenade FY8 1NB
☎ 01253 721288 🖷 01253 714459
e-mail: book@the-grand.co.uk
web: www.the-grand.co.uk
Dir: *M6 junct 32 take M55 to Blackpool then A5230 to South Shore. Follow signs for St Annes*
At the time of going to press, the star classification for this hotel

continued

was not confirmed. Please refer to the AA internet site www.theAA.com for current information.

ROOMS: 55 en suite (4 GF) ⊘ in all bedrooms s £75-£125; d £80-£160 (incl. bkfst) **LB** **FACILITIES: Spa** STV supervised Sauna Solarium Gym Jacuzzi Xmas **CONF:** Thtr 160 Class 80 Board 30 Del from £145 **SERVICES:** Lift **PARKING:** 75 **NOTES:** ⊘ in restaurant Closed 24-26 Dec Civ Wed 150

Premier Travel Inn Lytham St Annes

Church Rd FY8 5LH
☎ 0870 9906548 📠 0870 9906549
web: www.premiertravelinn.com

Dir: *M55/A584 coast road. Follow station signs. Church Rd just behind Lytham Station*

High quality, modern budget accommodation ideal for both families and business travellers. Spacious, en suite bedrooms feature bath and shower, satellite TV and many have telephones and modem points. The adjacent family restaurant features a wide and varied menu. For further details consult the Hotel Groups page.

ROOMS: 22 en suite s £48.95; d £48.95

MACCLESFIELD, Cheshire — Map 16 SJ97

★★★★68%

Shrigley Hall Hotel Golf & Country Club

Shrigley Park, Pott Shrigley SK10 5SB
☎ 01625 575757 📠 01625 573323
e-mail: shrigleyhall@paramount-hotels.co.uk
web: www.paramount-hotels.co.uk

Dir: *off A523 at Legh Arms towards Pott Shrigley. Hotel 2m on left before village*

Originally built in 1825, Shrigley Hall is an impressive hotel set in 262 acres of mature parkland and provides stunning views of the countryside. Features include a championship golf course. There is a wide choice of bedroom size and style. The public areas are spacious, combining traditional and contemporary decor, and include a well-equipped gym.

ROOMS: 150 en suite (8 fmly) ⊘ in 28 bedrooms s £140; d £180 **LB** **FACILITIES:** STV supervised 18 Fishing Sauna Solarium Gym Putt green Jacuzzi Beauty salon, tydro centre, Swimming pool supervised Xmas **CONF:** BC Thtr 280 Class 140 Board 50 Del £185 **SERVICES:** Lift **PARKING:** 300 **NOTES:** ⊘ in restaurant Civ Wed 150

★★★70% *Best Western Hollin Hall*

Jackson Ln, Kerridge, Bollington SK10 5BG
☎ 01625 573246 📠 01625 574791
e-mail: sales@hollinhallhotel.com

Dir: *off A523, 2m along B5090*

Set in the peaceful Cheshire countryside, this hotel is convenient for Manchester Airport (courtesy transport available). The main building has an impressive carved staircase, high ceilings and a

continued on p372

MACCLESFIELD, continued

bar lounge. Modern cooking is provided in the Orangey conservatory and both a gym and sauna are available. Attractively furnished accommodation is situated in a modern extension.
ROOMS: 54 en suite (2 fmly) ⊗ in 36 bedrooms **FACILITIES:** STV Sauna Gym Free use neighbouring Leisure Club & Golf Course **CONF:** Thtr 120 Class 50 Board 50 **PARKING:** 200 **NOTES:** ✗ ⊗ in restaurant Civ Wed 100

⌂ Premier Travel Inn Macclesfield North

Tytherington Business Park, Springwood Way, Tytherington SK10 2XA
☎ 08701 977167 ▤ 01625 422874
web: www.premiertravelinn.com
Dir: *on A523 Tytherington Business Park*
High quality, modern budget accommodation ideal for both families and business travellers. Spacious, en suite bedrooms feature bath and shower, satellite TV and many have telephones and modem points. The adjacent family restaurant features a wide and varied menu. For further details consult the Hotel Groups page.
ROOMS: 40 en suite s £46.95-£48.95; d £46.95-£48.95 **CONF:** Thtr 20

⌂ Premier Travel Inn Macclesfield South West

Congleton Rd, Gawsworth SK11 7XD
☎ 0870 9906412 ▤ 0870 9906413
web: www.premiertravelinn.com
Dir: *2m from Macclesfield. Exit M6 junct 17. Follow A534 to Congleton, then A536 towards Macclesfield to Gawsworth. Hotel on left*
High quality, modern budget accommodation ideal for both families and business travellers. Spacious, en suite bedrooms feature bath and shower, satellite TV and many have telephones and modem points. The adjacent family restaurant features a wide and varied menu. For further details consult the Hotel Groups page.
ROOMS: 28 en suite s £46.95-£48.95; d £46.95-£48.95 **CONF:** Thtr 10 Board 10

⌂ Travelodge Macclesfield

London Rd South SK12 4NA
☎ 08700 850 950 ▤ 01625 875292
web: www.travelodge.co.uk
Dir: *on A523*
Travelodge offers good quality, good value, modern accommodation. Ideal for families, the spacious, en suite bedrooms include remote-control TV, tea and coffee-making facilities and comfortable beds. Meals can be taken at the nearby family restaurant. For further details consult the Hotel Groups page.
ROOMS: 32 en suite s fr £26; d fr £26

MAIDENCOMBE See Torquay

MAIDENHEAD, Berkshire Map 06 SU88
See also Bray

Top Hotel

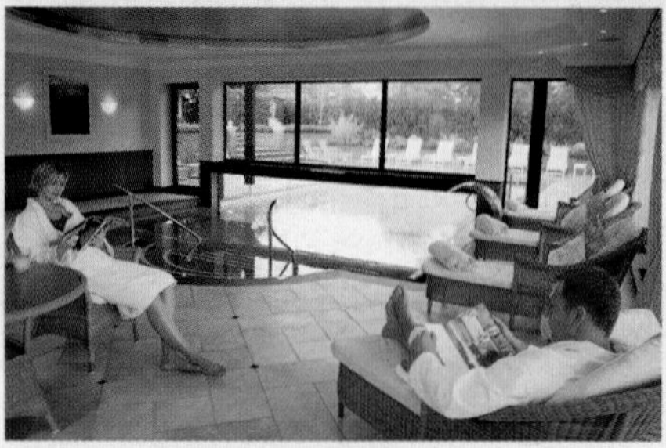

★★★★ ◎◎◎ Fredrick's Hotel Restaurant Spa

Shoppenhangers Rd SL6 2PZ
☎ 01628 581000 ▤ 01628 771054
e-mail: reservations@fredricks-hotel.co.uk
web: www.fredricks-hotel.co.uk
Dir: *M4 junct 8/9 onto A404(M) to Maidenhead West and Henley. 1st exit 9a to White Waltham. Left into Shoppenhangers Rd to Maidenhead, hotel on right*
Just 30 minutes from London, this delightful hotel enjoys a peaceful location yet is within easy reach of the M4 and only 20 minutes' drive from Wentworth and Sunningdale golf courses. The spacious bedrooms are all comfortably furnished and very well equipped. An enthusiastic team of staff ensure friendly and efficient service. Imaginative cuisine is a highlight, as is the newly completed luxurious spa offering the ultimate in relaxation and well being.
ROOMS: 34 en suite (11 GF) s £215-£235; d £285-£310 (incl. bkfst) **LB FACILITIES: Spa** STV supervised supervised Sauna Gym Jacuzzi Treatment rooms, hydrotherapy, Oriental steam room, Dead Sea flotation room **CONF:** BC Thtr 120 Class 80 Board 60 Del from £295 **SERVICES:** air con **PARKING:** 90 **NOTES:** ✗ ⊗ in restaurant Closed 24 Dec-3 Jan Civ Wed 120

★★ 69% Elva Lodge

Castle Hill SL6 4AD
☎ 01628 622948 ▤ 01628 778954
e-mail: reservations@elvalodgehotel.co.uk
web: www.elvalodgehotel.co.uk
Dir: *A4 from Maidenhead towards Reading. Hotel at top of hill on left*

Within easy reach of the town centre, this family-run hotel offers a warm welcome and friendly service. Bedrooms are pleasantly decorated and equipped with thoughtful extras. Spacious public

continued

areas include a smart, stylish lounge, a bar, and the Lion's Brassiere which offers a wide range of popular dishes.
ROOMS: 26 rms (23 en suite) (1 fmly) (5 GF) ⊗ in 6 bedrooms s £50-£95; d £70-£108 (incl. bkfst) **FACILITIES:** Reduced rates at local Leisure Centre **CONF:** Thtr 50 Class 30 Board 30 **PARKING:** 32 **NOTES:** ⊗ in restaurant Closed 24-30 Dec Civ Wed 60

U Ramada Ye Olde Bell

Hurley SL6 5LX
☎ 01628 825881 01628 825939
e-mail: sales.yeoldebell@ramadajarvis.co.uk
web: www.ramadajarvis.co.uk
Dir: *Take A4130 to Hurley & Henley, after 1m turn right signed Hurley village only, hotel 800yds on right.*
With easy access to the M4 and M40 this establishment dates back to 1135 and is reputed to be the oldest inn in England. Bedrooms are comfortably appointed for both business and leisure guests.
ROOMS: 47 en suite (6 fmly) (19 GF) ⊗ in 35 bedrooms s £109-£149; d £109-£149 **FACILITIES:** STV Xmas **CONF:** Thtr 130 Class 60 Board 52 Del from £195 **PARKING:** 90 **NOTES:** ⊗ in restaurant Civ Wed 120

MAIDSTONE, Kent — Map 07 TQ75

★★★★70% Marriott Tudor Park Hotel & Country Club

Ashford Rd, Bearsted ME14 4NQ
☎ 01622 734334 01622 735360
e-mail: salesadmin.tudorpark@marriotthotels.co.uk
web: www.marriott.co.uk
Dir: *M20 junct 8 to Lenham. Right at rdbt towards Bearsted and Maidstone on A20. Hotel 1m on left*
This fine country hotel provides good levels of comfort. Guests can dine in the main restaurant, Fairviews, which offers a range of modern, eclectic dishes, or in the more relaxed environment of the Long Weekend Brasserie. Take time to enjoy the excellent range of leisure options, such as playing golf, a workout, a swim, or pamper yourself in the beauty salon.
ROOMS: 120 en suite (48 fmly) (60 GF) ⊗ in 65 bedrooms **FACILITIES: Spa** STV 18 Sauna Solarium Gym Putt green Driving range, Beauty salon, Steam room Xmas **CONF:** Thtr 250 Class 100 Board 60 **SERVICES:** Lift **PARKING:** 250 **NOTES:** ⊗ in restaurant

★★★69% Russell

136 Boxley Rd ME14 2AE
☎ 01622 692221 01622 762084
e-mail: res@therussellhotel.com
Since its days as a Carmelite convent, this Victorian building has been extended and modernised. Set in attractive grounds and offering a range of function rooms, the hotel is a popular venue for weddings and conferences. The well-maintained bedrooms feature pleasing, modern decor.
ROOMS: 42 en suite (2 fmly) ⊗ in 20 bedrooms s £65-£95; d £85-£125 (incl. bkfst) **LB** **FACILITIES:** All residents allowed to use facilities at David Lloyd Health & Fitness Centre Xmas **CONF:** Thtr 300 Class 100 Board 70 Del from £125 **SERVICES:** air con **PARKING:** 100 **NOTES:** ⊗ in restaurant Civ Wed 250

★★★67% *Larkfield Priory*

London Rd, Larkfield ME20 6HJ
☎ 01732 846858 01732 846786
e-mail: larkfieldpriory@corushotels.com
web: www.corushotels.com/larkfieldpriory
Dir: *M20 junct 4 take A228 to West Malling. At lights left signed to Maidstone on A20, after 1m hotel on left*
This 18th-century building, now under new ownership, is conveniently located just a short drive from the motorway with

continued

links to both Dover and the Channel Tunnel. Bedrooms are brightly decorated and thoughtfully equipped. Public rooms include a spacious lounge, a welcoming bar and a smart dining room where an interesting choice of dishes is available.
ROOMS: 52 en suite (9 GF) ⊗ in 24 bedrooms **CONF:** Thtr 80 Class 36 Board 30 **PARKING:** 80 **NOTES:** ⊗ in restaurant

★★70% Grange Moor

St Michael's Rd ME16 8BS
☎ 01622 677623 01622 678246
e-mail: reservations@grangemoor.co.uk
Dir: *Town centre, towards A26 Tonbridge Rd. Hotel 0.25m on left, just after Church*
Expect a warm welcome at this friendly, privately owned hotel, which is ideally situated, within easy walking distance of the town centre. Bedrooms have almost all been refurbished and are smartly appointed and comfortable. Public areas include a popular bar, a popular restaurant and a small residents' lounge.
ROOMS: 38 en suite 12 annexe en suite (6 fmly) (5 GF) ⊗ in 21 bedrooms s £45-£52; d £60-£62 (incl. bkfst) **LB** **CONF:** Thtr 120 Class 60 Board 40 Del from £85 **PARKING:** 60 **NOTES:** Closed 26-30 Dec Civ Wed 80

Innkeeper's Lodge Maidstone

Sandling Rd ME14 2RF
☎ 01622 692212 01622 679265
web: www.innkeeperslodge.com
Dir: *M20 junct 6, S onto A229 towards Maidstone. At 3rd rdbt, turn left and left again*
A growing concept in the travel accommodation market. Smart rooms meet essential business requirements but also have home comforts. Dining options include all-day menus plus the added advantage of breakfast, which is included in the room price. For further details consult the Hotel Groups page.
ROOMS: 12 en suite s £57-£65; d £57-£65

Premier Travel Inn Maidstone (Allington)

London Rd ME16 0HG
☎ 08701 977168 01622 672469
web: www.premiertravelinn.com
Dir: *M20 junct 5, 0.5m on London Rd towards Maidstone*
High quality, modern budget accommodation ideal for both families and business travellers. Spacious, en suite bedrooms feature bath and shower, satellite TV and many have telephones and modem points. The adjacent family restaurant features a wide and varied menu. For further details consult the Hotel Groups page.
ROOMS: 40 en suite s £52.95; d £52.95 **CONF:** Thtr 45 Board 30

Premier Travel Inn Maidstone (Sandling)

Allington Lock, Sandling ME14 3AS
☎ 08701 977308 01622 715159
web: www.premiertravelinn.com
Dir: *M20 junct 6 follow sign for Museum of Kent Life*
High quality, modern budget accommodation ideal for both families and business travellers. Spacious, en suite bedrooms feature bath and shower, satellite TV and many have telephones and modem points. The adjacent family restaurant features a wide and varied menu. For further details consult the Hotel Groups page.
ROOMS: 40 en suite s £52.95; d £52.95

> Destination dining!
> This symbol indicates a Restaurant with Rooms

MAIDSTONE MOTORWAY SERVICE AREA (M20), Kent — Map 07 TQ85

⌂ Premier Travel Inn Maidstone (Hollingbourne)

ME17 1SS
☎ 08701 977169 🖷 01622 739535
web: www.premiertravelinn.com
Dir: *M20 junct 8*
High quality, modern budget accommodation ideal for both families and business travellers. Spacious, en suite bedrooms feature bath and shower, satellite TV and many have telephones and modem points. The adjacent family restaurant features a wide and varied menu. For further details consult the Hotel Groups page.
ROOMS: 58 en suite s £46.95-£49.95; d £46.95-£49.95 **CONF:** Thtr 30 Board 18

MALDON See Tolleshunt Knights

MALHAM, North Yorkshire — Map 18 SD96

★★68% The Buck Inn

BD23 4DA
☎ 01729 830317 🖷 01729 830670
e-mail: thebuckinn@ukonline.co.uk
Dir: *from Skipton take A65 to Gargrave. 7m to Malham. Hotel in centre*
Situated in the centre of a popular village, this attractive inn is full of character and offers a very friendly welcome. Bedrooms are individual, some with four-poster beds; all are comfortable and well equipped. Imaginative menus offer a good choice of homemade dishes. A wide range of real ales and malt whiskies are served in the two cosy bars.
ROOMS: 10 en suite (3 fmly) s £35-£50; d £60-£85 (incl. bkfst) **LB** **FACILITIES:** Riding Xmas **CONF:** Class 1 Board 1 **PARKING:** 25 **NOTES:** ✗ ⊗ in restaurant Civ Wed 100

MALMESBURY, Wiltshire — Map 04 ST98

Top Hotel

★★★★ ⊛⊛⊛ Whatley Manor

Easton Grey SN16 0RB
☎ 01666 822888 🖷 01666 826120
e-mail: reservations@whatleymanor.com
web: www.whatleymanor.com
Dir: *M4 junct 17 to Malmesbury, left at T-junct, left at next T-junct onto B4040, hotel 2m on left*
Sitting in 12 acres of beautiful Wiltshire countryside, this impressive country house has been lovingly renovated to provide the most luxurious surroundings. Spacious bedrooms, most with views over the attractive gardens, are individually decorated with splendid features. Two restaurants are available: Le Mazot, a Swiss-style brasserie and The Dining Room that serves classical French cuisine with a contemporary twist. The magnificent Aquarius Spa is a must on any visit offering an unforgettable experience.
ROOMS: 23 en suite (4 GF) ⊗ in 6 bedrooms s £275-£850; d £275-£850 (incl. bkfst) **LB** **FACILITIES: Spa** STV Fishing Sauna Solarium Gym Jacuzzi Cinema, hydro pool Xmas **CONF:** BC Thtr 40 Class 20 Board 25 Del from £265 **SERVICES:** Lift **PARKING:** 100 **NOTES:** No children 12yrs ⊗ in restaurant Civ Wed 120

★★★77% ⊛⊛ Old Bell

Abbey Row SN16 0AG
☎ 01666 822344 🖷 01666 825145
e-mail: info@oldbellhotel.com
web: www.oldbellhotel.com
Dir: *M4 junct 11, follow A429 north. Left at first rdbt. Left at T-junct. Hotel next to Abbey*
Dating back to 1220, the Old Bell is reputed to be the oldest purpose-built hotel in England. Bedrooms, now refurbished, vary in size and style; those in the main house are traditionally furnished with antiques, while the newer bedrooms have a contemporary feel. Guests have a choice of comfortable sitting areas and dining options.
ROOMS: 16 en suite 15 annexe en suite (7 GF) ⊗ in all bedrooms s fr £85; d fr £125 (incl. bkfst) **LB** **FACILITIES:** STV Aromatherapy massages Xmas **CONF:** Thtr 50 Class 22 Board 25 Del from £150 **PARKING:** 31 **NOTES:** ✗ ⊗ in restaurant Civ Wed 80

★★★76% ⊛⊛ The Old Rectory Country House Hotel

SN16 9EP
☎ 01666 577194 🖷 01666 577853
e-mail: office@oldrectorycrudwell.co.uk
Dir: *M4 junct 17. Follow A429 to Cirencester, right opposite Plough pub in Crudwell. Hotel next to church*
A former rectory, this beautiful house (now under new ownership), with its Victorian walled garden, offers a feeling of peace and seclusion. Individually decorated bedrooms offer comfort coupled with a host of thoughtful touches for guests' enjoyment. The highlight is the wood-panelled restaurant where local produce forms the basis of well-prepared dishes.
ROOMS: 12 en suite (1 fmly) ⊗ in all bedrooms s £75-£105; d £88-£145 (incl. bkfst) **LB** **FACILITIES:** ♫ Xmas **CONF:** Thtr 40 Class 20 Board 20 Del from £125 **PARKING:** 50 **NOTES:** ⊗ in restaurant Civ Wed 60

★★74% ⊛ Mayfield House

Crudwell SN16 9EW
☎ 01666 577409 🖷 01666 577977
e-mail: reception@mayfieldhousehotel.co.uk
web: www.mayfieldhousehotel.co.uk
Dir: *3m N on A429 from Malmesbury*
Guests are assured of a warm welcome at this charming hotel, on the edge of the Cotswolds. The bedrooms are equipped with modern facilities; some ground-floor rooms are available and others are situated in adjacent cottages. An imaginative menu is served in the renovated restaurant overlooking the attractive gardens. Additionally, there is a foyer lounge and a bar offering a wide range of popular dishes.
ROOMS: 21 en suite 3 annexe en suite (2 fmly) ⊗ in 8 bedrooms s £72; d £95 (incl. bkfst) **LB** **FACILITIES:** Xmas **CONF:** Thtr 40 Class 30 Board 25 **PARKING:** 50 **NOTES:** ⊗ in restaurant
See advert on opposite page

MALTON, North Yorkshire

Map 19 SE77

★★★73% *Burythorpe House*
Burythorpe YO17 9LB
☎ 01653 658200 01653 658204
e-mail: reception@burythorpehousehotel.com
web: www.burythorpehousehotel.com
Dir: *4m S of Malton, outside Burythorpe and 4m from A64 (York to Scarborough)*

This charming house offers spacious and individually furnished bedrooms. Five rooms are situated in a rear courtyard, two of which are equipped for less able guests, and all benefit from small kitchen areas. Comfortable, spacious lounge areas are provided along with an impressive oak-panelled dining room where interesting, freshly prepared meals are served; meals are also available in the conservatory.

ROOMS: 11 en suite 5 annexe en suite (2 fmly) (5 GF) in all bedrooms **FACILITIES:** Snooker Sauna Solarium Gym **PARKING:** 40 **NOTES:** in restaurant Civ Wed

★★63% Green Man
15 Market St YO17 7LY
☎ 01653 600370 01653 696006
e-mail: greenman@englishrosehotels.co.uk
Dir: *from A64 follow signs to Malton town centre. Left into Market St, hotel on left*

This friendly hotel set in the centre of town includes an inviting reception lounge where a log fire burns in winter. There is also a cosy bar, and dining takes place in the traditional restaurant at the rear. Bedrooms vary in size and are thoughtfully equipped.

ROOMS: 24 en suite (4 fmly) **FACILITIES:** Xmas **CONF:** Thtr 120 Class 20 Board 40 Del from £95 **PARKING:** 40 **NOTES:** in restaurant

★★63% *Talbot*
Yorkersgate YO17 7AJ
☎ 01653 694031 01653 693355
e-mail: sales@englishrosehotels.co.uk
Dir: *off A64 towards Malton. Hotel on right*

Situated close to the centre of town this long-established, creeper-covered hotel looks out towards the River Derwent and open countryside. Bedroom sizes vary, but all are comfortable. The public rooms are traditional and elegantly furnished and include a bar plus a separate lounge.

ROOMS: 31 en suite (3 fmly) **CONF:** Thtr 50 Board 20 **PARKING:** 30 **NOTES:** in restaurant

Indoor Swimming pool
Indoor Swimming pool (heated)
Outdoor Swimming pool
Outdoor Swimming pool (heated)

MALVERN, Worcestershire

Map 10 SO74

★★★74% Colwall Park
Walwyn Rd, Colwall WR13 6QG
☎ 01684 540000 01684 540847
e-mail: hotel@colwall.com
web: www.colwall.com
Dir: *Between Malvern & Ledbury in centre of Colwall on B4218*

Standing in extensive gardens, this hotel was purpose built in the early 20th century to serve the local racetrack. Today the proprietors and loyal staff provide high levels of hospitality and service. The Seasons restaurant has a well-deserved reputation for

continued on p376

MALVERN, continued

its cuisine. Bedrooms are tastefully appointed and public areas help to create a fine country-house atmosphere.

Colwall Park, Malvern

ROOMS: 22 en suite (1 fmly) ⊗ in all bedrooms s £70-£85; d £115-£135 (incl. bkfst) **LB** **FACILITIES:** STV Boules Xmas **CONF:** Thtr 150 Class 80 Board 50 Del £140 **PARKING:** 40 **NOTES:** ⊗ in restaurant

See advert on page 375

★★★74% Cottage in the Wood

Holywell Rd, Malvern Wells WR14 4LG
☎ 01684 575859 Fax 01684 560662
e-mail: reception@cottageinthewood.co.uk
web: www.cottageinthewood.co.uk
Dir: *3m S of Great Malvern off A449, 500yds N of B4209 junct, on opposite side of road*

Sitting high up on a wooded hillside, this delightful, family-run hotel boasts lovely views over the Severn Valley. The bedrooms are divided between the main house, Beech Cottage and the Pinnacles. Public rooms are elegantly styled and feature real fires, a variety of seating and fresh flowers.
ROOMS: 8 en suite 23 annexe en suite (10 GF) ⊗ in 11 bedrooms s £79-£105; d £99-£175 (incl. bkfst) **LB** **FACILITIES:** STV Direct access to Malvern Hills Xmas **CONF:** Thtr 20 Board 14 Del from £145 **PARKING:** 40 **NOTES:** ⊗ in restaurant

See advert on opposite page

★★★73% Foley Arms

14 Worcester Rd WR14 4QS
☎ 01684 573397 Fax 01684 569665
e-mail: reservations@foleyarmshotel.com
web: www.foleyarmshotel.co.uk
Dir: *M5 junct 8 N or junct 7 S or M50 junct 1 to Great Malvern on A449*
With spectacular views of the Severn Valley, this hotel provides attentive, friendly service. Reputed to be the oldest hotel in Malvern, it is situated in the heart of town. The bedrooms are comfortable and tastefully decorated with period furnishings and modern facilities. Public areas include Elgar's Restaurant, a popular bar and a choice of comfortable lounges.

ROOMS: 28 en suite (2 fmly) ⊗ in 5 bedrooms **FACILITIES:** STV Free use leisure centre pool, gym, solarium & sauna 5mins walk Xmas **CONF:** Thtr 150 Class 40 Board 45 Del from £130 **PARKING:** 64 **NOTES:** ⊗ in restaurant Civ Wed 100

See advert on opposite page

★★76% Holdfast Cottage

Marlbank Rd, Little Malvern WR13 6NA
☎ 01684 310288 Fax 01684 311117
e-mail: enquiries@holdfast-cottage.co.uk
Dir: *on A4104 midway between Welland and Upper Welland*
This charming, wisteria-covered hotel, now under new ownership, lies in attractive grounds at the foot of the Malvern Hills. The public areas offer all the comforts of a country retreat - log fire in the lounge, a cosy bar and an elegant dining room. The bedrooms include many thoughtful touches. The regularly changing menu features fresh local produce, and ice cream and breads are made on the premises.
ROOMS: 8 en suite (1 fmly) ⊗ in all bedrooms s £50-£66; d £84-£98 **LB** **FACILITIES:** Walking, bird watching Xmas **CONF:** Class 30 Board 30 **PARKING:** 20 **NOTES:** ⊗ in restaurant Civ Wed 35

★★71% Cotford

51 Graham Rd WR14 2HU
☎ 01684 572427 Fax 01684 572952
e-mail: reservations@cotfordhotel.co.uk
web: www.cotfordhotel.co.uk
Dir: *from Worcester follow signs to Malvern on A449. Left into Graham Rd signed town centre, hotel on right*

This delightful house, built in 1851, reputedly for the Bishop of Worcester, stands in attractive gardens with stunning views of the Malverns. Rooms have been authentically renovated, retaining

continued

many original features, and include all the expected comforts. Food, service and hospitality are major strengths.
ROOMS: 15 en suite (4 fmly) (1 GF) ⊗ in all bedrooms s £55-£75; d £80-£100 (incl. bkfst) **LB** **FACILITIES:** STV complimentary use of leisure centre in centre of Malvern **CONF:** Thtr 26 Class 26 Del from £82 **PARKING:** 18 **NOTES:** ⊗ in restaurant

★★71% The Malvern Hills Hotel

Wynds Point WR13 6DW
☎ 01684 540690 🖷 01684 540327
e-mail: malhilhotl@aol.com
web: www.malvernhillshotel.co.uk
Dir: *4m S, at junct of A449 with B4232*

This 19th-century hostelry is situated to the west of Malvern, opposite the British Camp, which was fortified and occupied by the Ancient Britons. Bedrooms are well equipped and facilities include a choice of bars and a sun terrace from which customers can view spectacular sunsets. The hotel is popular with walkers as well as business guests.
ROOMS: 14 en suite (1 fmly) (2 GF) ⊗ in 12 bedrooms s £50-£65; d £85-£110 (incl. bkfst) **LB** **FACILITIES:** STV Xmas **CONF:** Thtr 40 Class 24 Board 30 Del from £70 **PARKING:** 30 **NOTES:** ⊗ in restaurant

★★67% Great Malvern

Graham Rd WR14 2HN
☎ 01684 563411 🖷 01684 560514
e-mail: sutton@great-malvern-hotel.co.uk
web: www.great-malvern-hotel.co.uk
Dir: *from Worcester on A449, left beyond fire station into Graham Rd. Hotel at end of road on right*

This is a privately-owned and personally-run town centre hotel, situated close to many cultural and scenic attractions. Popular with business people, theatregoers and leisure travellers, the hotel offers well-equipped and comfortable accommodation, a busy bar, a lounge and a meeting room.
ROOMS: 14 rms (13 en suite) (1 fmly) **CONF:** Thtr 60 Class 20 Board 30 **SERVICES:** Lift **PARKING:** 9 **NOTES:** ✗

Early start?
Hotels at all star levels should provide in-room alarm clocks and/or alarm clocks

★★67% Mount Pleasant

Belle Vue Ter WR14 4PZ
☎ 01684 561837 🖷 01684 569968
e-mail: reception@mountpleasanthotel.co.uk
web: www.mountpleasanthotel.co.uk
Dir: *on A449, in central Malvern by crossroads opposite Priory Church*

This is an attractive Georgian house in the centre of Great Malvern, that from its elevated position, overlooks the picturesque Severn Valley and Priory Church. Over the last few years there

continued on p378

MALVERN, continued

have been many changes to both the public areas and bedrooms including the creation of the smart Spring Bar & Brasserie.

Mount Pleasant, Malvern

ROOMS: 14 en suite (1 fmly) s £40-£68; d £88-£98 (incl. bkfst) **LB**
FACILITIES: Xmas **CONF:** Thtr 90 Class 40 Board 50 **PARKING:** 20
NOTES: ✘

MANCHESTER, Greater Manchester Map 16 SJ89
See also Manchester Airport & Sale

★★★★★70% ⊛ **The Lowry Hotel**
50 Dearmans Place, Chapel Wharf, Salford
M3 5LH
☎ 0161 827 4000 ▤ 0161 827 4001
e-mail: enquiries@thelowryhotel.com
web: www.roccofortehotels.com

ROCCO FORTE
HOTELS

Dir: M6 junct 19, A556 & M56 follow signs for Manchester. A5103 for 4.5m. At rdbt take A57(M) to lights & turn right onto Water St. Left to New Quay St/Trinity Way. At 1st lights turn right onto Chapel St to Hotel
This modern, contemporary hotel, set beside the River Irwell in the centre of the city, offers spacious bedrooms equipped to meet the needs of business and leisure visitors alike. Many of the rooms look out over the river, as do the sumptuous suites. The River Room restaurant produces good brasserie cooking. Extensive business and function facilities are available, together with a spa to provide extra pampering.
ROOMS: 165 en suite (7 fmly) ⊛ in 90 bedrooms s £205-£1150; d £230-£1150 **LB FACILITIES:** Spa STV Sauna Gym Spa facilities & swimming available offsite ♫ Xmas **CONF:** BC Thtr 400 Class 250 Board 60 Del from £220 **SERVICES:** Lift air con **PARKING:** 100 **NOTES:** ✘ Civ Wed 400

See advert under Preliminary Section

★★★★71% ⊛⊛ **Midland**
Peter St M60 2DS
☎ 0161 236 3333 ▤ 0161 932 4100
web: www.quintessential-hotels.co.uk

ⒽⓄⓉⒺⓁⓈ

Dir: M602 junct 3 then follow signs for the G-Mex. Hotel is directly opposite G-Mex
Edwardian-style decor and friendly service are both noteworthy at this hotel. Bedrooms have loads of space; most are fairly quiet as they face into the centre of the hotel. The Octagon lounge and bar is a popular meeting spot for tea or pre-dinner drinks. The three restaurants are the modern Trafford, the bright and simple Nico Central and the classical cuisine of the award-winning French.
ROOMS: 303 en suite (62 fmly) ⊛ in 170 bedrooms s fr £115; d fr £115 (incl. bkfst) **FACILITIES:** STV ⊠ Squash Sauna Solarium Gym Jacuzzi Haird/beauty salon **CONF:** BC Thtr 500 Class 300 Board 120 Del from £150 **SERVICES:** Lift air con **NOTES:** Civ Wed 500

Town House

★★★★ ⊛ 🏠 **Alias Hotel Rossetti**
107 Piccadilly M1 2DB
☎ 0161 247 7744 ▤ 0161 247 7747
e-mail: info@aliashotels.com
Used as a textile headquarters in Victorian times, this impressive building has been transformed to offer stylish accommodation. Bedrooms feature CD/DVD players and combine modern comfort with quirky eclectic decor. Unique 50's style 'diners' are situated on each floor affording complimentary beverages, fresh fruit and cereals. Café Paradiso offers fresh Mediterranean food, while the basement has an exclusive club environment.
ROOMS: 61 en suite ⊗ in 47 bedrooms s £110-£265; d £110-£265 **FACILITIES:** STV ♫ Xmas **CONF:** Thtr 50 Class 20 Board 20 **SERVICES:** Lift **NOTES:** ⊗ in restaurant

See advert on opposite page

★★★★69% ⊛ **Marriott Worsley Park Hotel & Country Club**
Worsley Park, Worsley M28 2QT
☎ 0161 975 2000 ▤ 0161 799 6341
e-mail: salesadmin.worsleypark@marriotthotels.co.uk
web: www.marriott.co.uk

Marriott
HOTELS & RESORTS

Dir: M60 junct 13, over 1st rdbt and take A575. Hotel 400yds on left

This smart, modern hotel is set in impressive grounds with a championship golf course. Bedrooms are comfortably appointed and well equipped for both leisure and business guests. Public areas include extensive leisure and conference facilities, an all-day bistro and an elegant restaurant offering imaginative cuisine.
ROOMS: 158 en suite (5 fmly) (50 GF) ⊗ in 116 bedrooms **FACILITIES:** STV ⊠ ↧ 18 Sauna Solarium Gym Putt green Jacuzzi Steam room Health & Beauty salon Xmas **CONF:** Thtr 250 Class 150 Board 100 **SERVICES:** Lift **PARKING:** 400 **NOTES:** ✘ ⊗ in restaurant Civ Wed 200

★★★★68%
Copthorne Hotel Manchester
COPTHORNE
Clippers Quay, Salford Quays M50 3SN
☎ 0161 873 7321 📠 0161 877 8112
e-mail: roomsales.manchester@mill-cop.com
web: www.copthorne.com/manchester
Dir: *from M602 follow signs for Salford Quays & Trafford Park on A5063. Hotel 0.75m on right*
This smart hotel enjoys a convenient location on the redeveloped Salford Quays close to Old Trafford, The Lowry Centre and The Imperial War Museum. Bedrooms are comfortably appointed and well equipped for both business and leisure guests. A choice of dining options includes Chandlers Restaurant that serves accomplished food.
ROOMS: 166 en suite (6 fmly) ⊗ in 118 bedrooms s £160-£190; d £160-£190 **LB FACILITIES:** STV **CONF:** Thtr 150 Class 70 Board 70 Del £170 **SERVICES:** Lift **PARKING:** 120 **NOTES:** 🐕 ⊗ in restaurant

★★★★68% ***Marriott Manchester Victoria & Albert***
Marriott HOTELS & RESORTS
Water St M3 4JQ
☎ 0161 832 1188 📠 0161 834 2484
web: www.marriott.co.uk/manva
Dir: *M602 to A57 through lights on Regent Rd. Pass Sainsbury's, left at lights onto ring road, right at lights into Water St.*
This uniquely converted warehouse is located on the banks of the River Irwell, adjacant to the famous Granada Studios. Many of the hotel's individually styled and tastefully decorated bedrooms are themed around productions from the local studios. Interior features include original exposed brick walls and iron pillars.
ROOMS: 158 en suite (2 fmly) ⊗ in 90 bedrooms **FACILITIES:** STV Complimentary use of Livingwell Health Club **CONF:** BC Thtr 250 Class 120 Board 72 **SERVICES:** Lift air con **PARKING:** 120 **NOTES:** 🐕 Civ Wed 200

★★★★68% ***The Palace***
PRINCIPAL HOTELS
Oxford St M60 7HA
☎ 0161 288 1111 📠 0161 288 2222
web: www.principal-hotels.com
Dir: *opposite Oxford Rd Railway Station*
Formerly the offices of the Refuge Life Assurance Company, this impressive neo-Gothic building occupies a central location. There is a vast lobby, spacious open-plan bar lounge and restaurant, and extensive conference and function facilities. Bedrooms vary in size and style but are all spacious and well equipped.
ROOMS: 252 en suite (59 fmly) ⊗ in 30 bedrooms **FACILITIES:** STV ♫ **CONF:** Thtr 1000 Class 450 Board 100 **SERVICES:** Lift **NOTES:** 🐕 ⊗ in restaurant Civ Wed 100

★★★★68% **Renaissance Manchester**
RENAISSANCE HOTELS
Blackfriars St M3 2EQ
☎ 0161 831 6000 📠 0161 835 3077
e-mail: rhi.manbr.sales@renaissancehotels.com
web: www.renaissancehotels.com
Dir: *Follow signs to Deansgate, turn left onto Blackfriars St at 2nd set of lights after Kendals, hotel on right*
This smart hotel enjoys a central location just off Deansgate, within easy walking distance of The Arena and the city's many shops and attractions. Stylish, well-equipped bedrooms are extremely comfortable and those on higher floors offer wonderful views. Public areas include an elegant bar and restaurant and an impressive newly refurbished conference and banqueting suite.
ROOMS: 200 en suite ⊗ in 153 bedrooms s £95-£179; d £110-£179 **FACILITIES:** STV Complimentary leisure facilities nearby **CONF:** BC Thtr 400 Class 300 Board 100 Del from £160 **SERVICES:** Lift air con **PARKING:** 80 **NOTES:** 🐕 ⊗ in restaurant Civ Wed 100

M

MANCHESTER, continued

★★★76% *Malmaison*

Piccadilly M1 3AQ

☎ 0161 278 1000 🖺 0161 278 1002

e-mail: manchester@malmaison.com

web: www.malmaison.com

Dir: follow city centre signs, then signs to Piccadilly station. Hotel opposite station, at bottom of station approach

Stylish and chic, the Malmaison offers the very best of contemporary hotel keeping in a relaxed and comfortable environment. The hotel offers a range of bright meeting rooms, health spa with gym and treatment rooms, as well as the ever popular bar and French-style brasserie. Air-conditioned bedrooms combine style and comfort and provide a range of extras.

ROOMS: 167 en suite **FACILITIES:** Spa STV Sauna Solarium Gym Jacuzzi **CONF:** Thtr 80 Class 48 Board 30 **SERVICES:** Lift air con **NOTES:** ✖

★★★73% ◉◉ *Golden Tulip Manchester*

Waters Reach, Trafford Park M17 1WS

☎ 0161 873 8899 🖺 0161 872 6556

e-mail: info@goldentulipmanchester.com

Dir: from A56 turn onto Sir Matt Busby Way past Manchester United Stadium to traffic lights. Hotel on right

Situated opposite Old Trafford football stadium and within easy reach of the airport and motorway network, this modern establishment is the official hotel of Manchester United FC. The stylish rooms are spacious and comfortable and include mini-bars and CD players. The Waters Reach Restaurant and Bar is a fashionable and popular venue in which to enjoy modern British cooking.

ROOMS: 160 en suite (37 fmly) (8 GF) ◉ in 70 bedrooms **FACILITIES:** STV **CONF:** BC Thtr 160 Class 100 Board 60 **SERVICES:** Lift **PARKING:** 160 **NOTES:** ✖

★★★69% Princess on Portland

101 Portland St M1 6DF

☎ 0161 236 5122 🖺 0161 236 4468

e-mail: reception@princessonportland.co.uk

Dir: From Piccadilly Station, along Piccadilly. Left on Portland St, hotel at junct to Princess St

Situated in the heart of the city centre, this former Victorian silk warehouse has been transformed. Open plan public areas are modern, contemporary in style and include a split-level brasserie offering an interesting selection of freshly prepared dishes. Smartly presented bedrooms are comfortably furnished and have modern facilities.

ROOMS: 85 en suite (7 fmly) ◉ in 51 bedrooms **FACILITIES:** STV **CONF:** Thtr 25 Class 15 Board 18 **SERVICES:** Lift **NOTES:** ✖ ◉ in restaurant

See advert on page 379

★★★68% Novotel Manchester Centre

21 Dickinson St M1 4LX

☎ 0161 235 2200 🖺 0161 235 2210

e-mail: H3145@accor.com

web: www.novotel.com

Dir: from Oxford St into Portland St, left into Dickinson St. Hotel on right

This smart, modern property enjoys a central location convenient for theatres, shops and Manchester's business district. Spacious bedrooms are thoughtfully equipped and brightly decorated. Open plan, contemporary public areas include an all-day restaurant and

continued

a stylish bar. Extensive conference and meeting facilities are also available. Novotel - AA Hotel Group of the Year 2005-6.

ROOMS: 164 en suite (60 fmly) ◉ in 123 bedrooms s £59-£169; d £59-£169 **LB FACILITIES:** STV Sauna Gym Steam room **CONF:** BC Thtr 90 Class 50 Board 36 Del from £139 **SERVICES:** Lift air con

★★★68% Willow Bank Hotel

340-342 Wilmslow Rd, Fallowfield M14 6AF

☎ 0161 224 0461 🖺 0161 257 2561

e-mail: gm-willowbank@feathers.uk.com

web: www.feathers.uk.com

Dir: From M60 junct 5 on to A5103, turn left on to B5093. Hotel 2.5m on left

This popular hotel is conveniently located three miles from the city centre, close to the universities. Bedrooms vary in style; some are traditionally furnished; all are well equipped, and the newer rooms benefit from CD players and Playstations. Spacious, elegant public areas include a bar, restaurant, and meeting rooms.

ROOMS: 117 en suite (4 fmly) ◉ in 30 bedrooms s £46-£65; d £69-£140 (incl. bkfst) **LB FACILITIES:** STV Xmas **CONF:** BC Thtr 125 Class 60 Board 70 Del from £110 **PARKING:** 100 **NOTES:** ✖ ◉ in restaurant Civ Wed 125

★★★66% Days Hotel Manchester City

Weston Building, Sackville St M1 3BB

☎ 0161 955 8400 🖺 0161 955 8050

e-mail: weston@umist.ac.uk

web: www.meeting.co.uk

Dir: on Sackville St between Whitworth St & Mancunian Way

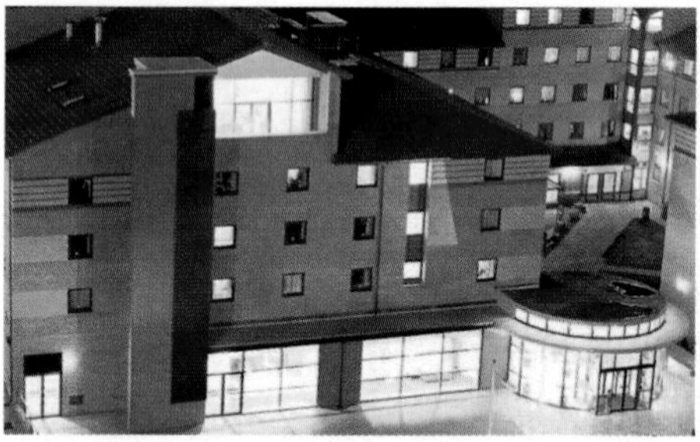

This state-of-the-art conference centre is conveniently located at the heart of the UMIST university buildings. Bedrooms are comfortable and equipped with a range of business-friendly facilities, including a high-speed internet connection. Public areas comprise a stylish bar and a spacious restaurant, as well as flexible meeting room provision.

ROOMS: 117 en suite (2 fmly) ◉ in 90 bedrooms s £40-£65; d £45-£75 **FACILITIES:** STV **CONF:** Thtr 300 Class 100 Board 40 Del from £127.45 **SERVICES:** Lift **PARKING:** 700 **NOTES:** ✖ ◉ in restaurant Closed 23 Dec-3 Jan

★★★65% *Old Rectory Hotel*

Meadow Ln, Haughton Green, Denton M34 7GD

☎ 0161 336 7516 🖺 0161 320 3212

e-mail: reservations@oldrectoryhotelmanchester.co.uk

This former Victorian rectory, peacefully set around an enclosed garden, is only a short drive from Manchester's city centre. Modern bedrooms are generally spacious and well appointed. Public rooms include a bar, an attractive and popular restaurant

continued

and a mini-gym. Pleasant banqueting facilities make this a popular wedding venue.

ROOMS: 30 en suite 6 annexe en suite (1 fmly) (12 GF) ⊗ in 12 bedrooms **FACILITIES:** STV Gym **CONF:** Thtr 100 Class 45 Board 50 **PARKING:** 50 **NOTES:** ⊗ in restaurant Civ Wed 90

★★★63% Jury's Inn Manchester

56 Great Bridgewater St M1 5LE

☎ 0161 953 8888 🖷 0161 953 9090

e-mail: manchester_inn@jurysdoyle.com

web: www.jurysdoyle.com

Dir: *In city centre next to G-Mex centre and Bridgewater Hall*

Enjoying a prime city centre location, Jury's Inn offers good-value, air-conditioned accommodation, ideal for both business travellers and families. Public areas include a smart, spacious lobby, the Inn Pub and Arches Restaurant. There are several convenient car parks with special rates available.

ROOMS: 265 en suite (11 fmly) (16 GF) ⊗ in 230 bedrooms **FACILITIES:** STV **CONF:** Thtr 50 Class 25 Board 25 **SERVICES:** Lift air con **NOTES:** 🐕

★★★63% *Novotel Manchester West*

Worsley Brow M28 2YA

☎ 0161 799 3535 🖷 0161 703 8207

e-mail: H0907@accor-hotels.com

web: www.novotel.com

(For full entry see Worsley)

★★63% Monton House

116-118 Monton Rd, Eccles M30 9HG

☎ 0161 789 7811 🖷 0161 787 7609

e-mail: hotel@montonhousehotel.co.uk

web: www.montonhousehotel.co.uk

Dir: *M602 junct 2 onto A576, 2nd left onto B5229 (Half Edge Ln) right onto Monton Rd, pass garage on left, hotel 100yds on right*

A modern, purpose built hotel conveniently situated for the motorway network, airport and city centre. The bedrooms are well equipped and the brightly furnished restaurant offers an imaginative choice at dinner and dishes served provide excellent value for money.

ROOMS: 62 en suite (2 fmly) (1 GF) ⊗ in 30 bedrooms s £35-£95; d £35-£95 **FACILITIES:** STV **CONF:** BC Thtr 150 Class 50 Board 50 Del from £85 **SERVICES:** Lift **PARKING:** 100 **NOTES:** 🐕 Civ Wed 100

U Quality Hotel Mancester - Central Park

888 Oldham Rd M40 2AG

☎ 0161 277 6910 🖷 0161 277 6929

web: www.choicehotelseurope.com

At the time of going to press, the star classification for this hotel was not confirmed. Please refer to the AA internet site www.theAA.com for current information.

ROOMS: 83 rms s fr £36; d fr £72 (incl. bkfst)

⌂ Campanile

55 Ordsall Ln, Salford M5 4RS

☎ 0161 833 1845 🖷 0161 833 1847

e-mail: manchester@campanile-hotels.com

web: www.envergure.fr

Dir: *M602 to Manchester, then A57. After large rdbt with Sainsbury's on left, left at next traffic lights. Hotel on right*

This modern building offers accommodation in smart, well-equipped bedrooms, all with en suite bathrooms. Refreshments may be taken at the informal Bistro. For further details consult the Hotel Groups page.

ROOMS: 104 en suite s £49.95-£65; d £49.95-£65 **CONF:** Thtr 50 Class 40 Board 30 Del from £85

If you wish to use a particular credit card or debit card please check with the hotel that they are happy to accept it

MANCHESTER, continued

⇧ *Diamond Lodge*
Hyde Rd, Belle Vue M18 7BA
☎ 0161 231 0770 ▯ 0161 231 0660
web: www.diamondlodge.co uk
Dir: *On A57 Manchester E, 2.5m W of M60 junct 24, Manchester orbital*

Offering very good value for money, this modern lodge provides comfortable accommodation near the city centre, motorway networks and football stadiums. Bright and airy, open-plan day rooms include a lounge and a brasserie-style dining room where complimentary continental breakfasts are served. An evening menu is also available.
ROOMS: 85 en suite **CONF:** Thtr 30 Class 15 Board 20

See advert on page 381

M

⇧ *Hotel Ibis Manchester (Charles Street)*
Charles St, Princess St M1 7DL
☎ 0161 272 5000 ▯ 0161 272 5010
e-mail: H3143@accor-hotels.com
Dir: *M62, M602 towards Manchester Centre, follow signs to UMIST(A34)*
Modern, budget hotel offering comfortable accommodation in bright and practical bedrooms. Breakfast is self-service and dinner is available in the restaurant. For further details, consult the Hotel Groups page.
ROOMS: 126 en suite

⇧ *Hotel Ibis Manchester City Centre*
96 Portland St M1 4GY
☎ 0161 234 0600 ▯ 0161 234 0610
e-mail: H3142@accor-hotels.com
Dir: *In city centre, between Princess St & Oxford St. 10min walk from Piccadilly*
Modern, budget hotel offering comfortable accommodation in bright and practical bedrooms. Breakfast is self-service and dinner is available in the restaurant. For further details, consult the Hotel Groups page.
ROOMS: 127 en suite

⇧ Premier Travel Inn Manchester City Centre
Oxford St M1 4WB
☎ 0870 238 3315 ▯ 01823 322054
web: www.premiertravelinn.com
Dir: *M6 junct 19 take 3rd exit onto A556. Join M56, exit junct 3 (A5103) to Medlock St, turn right into Whitworth St, then left into Oxford St & right into Portland St.*
High quality, modern budget accommodation ideal for both families and business travellers. Spacious, en suite bedrooms feature bath and shower, satellite TV and many have telephones and modem points. The adjacent family restaurant features a wide and varied menu. For further details consult the Hotel Groups page.
ROOMS: 226 en suite s £55.95; d £55.95

⇧ Premier Travel Inn Manchester City Centre (MEN Arena)
North Tower, Victoria Bridge St, Salford M3 5AS
☎ 0870 9906366 ▯ 0870 9906367
web: www.premiertravelinn.com
Dir: *Follow M602 to city centre, then A57(M) towards GMEX. 2nd exit, follow A56 city centre sign. Left before MEN arena onto A6, 1st left*
High quality, modern budget accommodation ideal for both families and business travellers. Spacious, en suite bedrooms feature bath and shower, satellite TV and many have telephones and modem points. The adjacent family restaurant features a wide and varied menu. For further details consult the Hotel Groups page.
ROOMS: 170 en suite s £55.95; d £55.95

⇧ Premier Travel Inn Manchester (Deansgate)
Gaythorne, River St M15 5FJ
☎ 0870 9906504 ▯ 0870 9906505
web: www.premiertravelinn.com
Dir: *Exit M60 junct 24 onto A57(M) Mancunian Way towards city centre. Inn adjacent A57(M) on A5103 Medlock St*
High quality, modern budget accommodation ideal for both families and business travellers. Spacious, en suite bedrooms feature bath and shower, satellite TV and many have telephones and modem points. The adjacent family restaurant features a wide and varied menu. For further details consult the Hotel Groups page.
ROOMS: 200 en suite s £54.95; d £54.95

⇧ Premier Travel Inn Manchester (Denton)
Alphington Dr, Manchester Rd South, Denton M34 3SH
☎ 08701 977173 ▯ 0161 337 9652
web: www.premiertravelinn.com
Dir: *M60 junct 24 onto A57 signed Denton. 1st right at lights, right at next lights, Inn on left*
High quality, modern budget accommodation ideal for both families and business travellers. Spacious, en suite bedrooms feature bath and shower, satellite TV and many have telephones and modem points. The adjacent family restaurant features a wide and varied menu. For further details consult the Hotel Groups page.
ROOMS: 40 en suite s £47.95-£50.95; d £47.95-£50.95

⇧ Premier Travel Inn Manchester (GMEX)
Bishopsgate, 7-11 Lower Mosley St M2 3DW
☎ 0870 9906444 ▯ 0870 9906445
web: www.premiertravelinn.com
Dir: *Follow M56 to end, onto A5103 towards Manchester city centre. Right Inn on left in Lower Mosley St*
High quality, modern budget accommodation ideal for both families and business travellers. Spacious, en suite bedrooms feature bath and shower, satellite TV and many have telephones and modem points. The adjacent family restaurant features a wide and varied menu. For further details consult the Hotel Groups page.
ROOMS: 147 en suite s £55.95; d £55.95 **CONF:** Thtr 60

⇧ Premier Travel Inn Manchester (Heaton Park)
Middleton Rd, Crumpsall M8 6NB
☎ 08701 977174 ▯ 0161 740 9142
web: www.premiertravelinn.com
Dir: *off M60 junct 19, ring road east. Take A576 to Manchester through 2 sets of lights. Inn on left*
High quality, modern budget accommodation ideal for both families and business travellers. Spacious, en suite bedrooms feature bath and shower, satellite TV and many have telephones

continued

and modem points. The adjacent family restaurant features a wide and varied menu. For further details consult the Hotel Groups page.
ROOMS: 45 en suite s £47.95-£50.95; d £47.95-£50.95 **CONF:** Thtr 15

Premier Travel Inn Manchester (Salford)
Basin 8 The Quays, Salford Quays M50 3SQ
☎ 08701 977176 🖹 0161 876 0094
web: www.premiertravelinn.com
Dir: *From M602 junct 3 take A5063 on Salford Quays, 1m from Manchester United's stadium.*
High quality, modern budget accommodation ideal for both families and business travellers. Spacious, en suite bedrooms feature bath and shower, satellite TV and many have telephones and modem points. The adjacent family restaurant features a wide and varied menu. For further details consult the Hotel Groups page.
ROOMS: 52 en suite s £52.95; d £52.95

Premier Travel Inn Manchester (Trafford Cntr)
Wilderspool Wood, Trafford Centre, Urmston M17 8WW
☎ 08701 977307 🖹 0161 747 4763
web: www.premiertravelinn.com
Dir: *M60 junct 10 on W side of Manchester*
High quality, modern budget accommodation ideal for both families and business travellers. Spacious, en suite bedrooms feature bath and shower, satellite TV and many have telephones and modem points. The adjacent family restaurant features a wide and varied menu. For further details consult the Hotel Groups page.
ROOMS: 60 en suite s £52.95; d £52.95 **CONF:** Thtr 12

Premier Travel Inn Manchester (West Didsbury)
Princess Parkway, Chorlton M21 7QS
☎ 08701 977 309 🖹 08701 977703
web: www.premiertravelinn.com
Dir: *From M60 junct 5, to Manchester on A5103, Princess Parkway. Inn is approx 1 m on left*
High quality, modern budget accommodation ideal for both families and business travellers. Spacious, en suite bedrooms feature bath and shower, satellite TV and many have telephones and modem points. The adjacent family restaurant features a wide and varied menu. For further details consult the Hotel Groups page.
ROOMS: 78 en suite s £47.95-£50.95; d £47.95-£50.95

Travelodge Anocats
22 Great Ancoats St, Ancoats M4 5AZ
☎ 08700 850950 🖹 0161 235 8631
web: www.travelodge.co.uk
Dir: *M60 junct 11 to A57, take 5th exit off rdbt. Follow M60, M602 junct 3. Follow signs for A62 to Lodge.*
Travelodge offers good quality, good value, modern accommodation. Ideal for families, the spacious, en suite bedrooms include remote-control TV, tea and coffee-making facilities and comfortable beds. Meals can be taken at the nearby family restaurant. For further details consult the Hotel Groups page.
ROOMS: 117 en suite s fr £26; d fr £26

> Popped the question? Hotels with Civ wed in their entry are licensed for civil wedding ceremonies. Maximum numbers for the ceremony only are shown e.g. Civ wed 120

Travelodge Ashton Under Lyne
Lapwing Ln, Audenshaw M34 5QL
☎ 08700 850 950
web: www.travelodge.co.uk
Dir: *From N - Follow M60 to junct 23, turn right onto A635, then 1st right onto Lord Sheldon Way. Lodge entrance is on left.*
From S - Exit junct 23 on M60, left onto Moss Way then at lights left on to Manchester Road, right onto Lord Sheldon Way, Travelodge is on left.
Travelodge offers good quality, good value, modern accommodation. Ideal for families, the spacious, en suite bedrooms include remote-control TV, tea and coffee-making facilities and comfortable beds. Meals can be taken at the nearby family restaurant. For further details consult the Hotel Groups page.
ROOMS: 62 en suite s fr £26; d fr £26

Travelodge (Manchester Central)
Townbury House, 11 Blackfriars St M3 5AL
☎ 08700 850 950 🖹 0161 839 5181
web: www.travelodge.co.uk
Dir: *N on Deansgate, junct of Blackfriars St & St Mary Gate, turn left over bridge*
Travelodge offers good quality, good value, modern accommodation. Ideal for families, the spacious, en suite bedrooms include remote-control TV, tea and coffee-making facilities and comfortable beds. Meals can be taken at the nearby family restaurant. For further details consult the Hotel Groups page.
ROOMS: 181 en suite s fr £26; d fr £26

Travelodge Sportcity
Hyde Rd, Birch St, West Gorton M12 5NT
☎ 08700 850 950
web: www.travelodge.co.uk
Dir: *M60 junct 24, follow A57 towards city centre for 2m, hotel on right*
Travelodge offers good quality, good value, modern accommodation. Ideal for families, the spacious, en suite bedrooms include remote-control TV, tea and coffee-making facilities and comfortable beds. Meals can be taken at the nearby family restaurant. For further details consult the Hotel Groups page.
ROOMS: 90 en suite s fr £26; d fr £26 **CONF:** Thtr 100 Class 50 Board 50

Tulip Inn
Old Park Ln M17 8PG
☎ 0161 755 3355 🖹 0161 755 3344
e-mail: info@tulipinnmanchester.co.uk
web: www.tulipinnmanchester.co.uk
Dir: *From Manchester M60 Orbital, take junct 10 towards the Trafford Centre*
ROOMS: 121 en suite **CONF:** Thtr 30 Board 30

MANCHESTER AIRPORT, Greater Manchester Map 15 SJ88
See also Altrincham

★★★★ 70% Radisson SAS Hotel Manchester Airport
Chicago Av M90 3RA
☎ 0161 490 5000 🖹 0161 490 5095
e-mail: sales.airport.manchester@radissonsas.com
web: www.radisson.com
Dir: *M56 junct 5, follow signs for Terminal 2. At rdbt 2nd left and follow signs for railway station. Hotel next to station*
This modern hotel is strategically integrated into the airport's terminal system so all three terminals can be accessed quickly by covered, moving walkways. Facilities are excellent and include a well-equipped gym and indoor pool. Bedrooms are air-conditioned, thoughtfully equipped and come in a variety of decorative themes: Maritime, Oriental, Scandinavian and Italian.
continued on p384

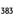

MANCHESTER AIRPORT, continued

Super views of the runway can be enjoyed in the 'Phileas Fogg' restaurant where a creative international menu is carefully prepared with flair and skill.

Radisson SAS Hotel, Manchester Airport

ROOMS: 360 en suite (27 fmly) ⊗ in 280 bedrooms s £120-£145; d £120-£145 **LB FACILITIES:** STV ⊠ Sauna Solarium Gym Health & beauty treatments **CONF:** BC Thtr 350 Class 180 Board 50 Del from £195 **SERVICES:** Lift air con **PARKING:** 250 **NOTES:** ✗ Civ Wed 230

★★★★69% Manchester Airport Marriott
Hale Rd, Hale Barns WA15 8XW
☎ 0161 904 0301 🖷 0161 980 1787
e-mail: manchesterairportmarriott@
whitbread.com
web: www.marriott.co.uk

With good airport links and convenient access to the thriving city, this sprawling modern hotel is a popular destination. The hotel offers extensive leisure and business facilities, a choice of eating and drinking options and ample car parking. Bedrooms are situated around a courtyard and offer a comprehensive range of facilities.
ROOMS: 215 en suite (22 fmly) ⊗ in 160 bedrooms s £105-£135; d £105-£135 **LB FACILITIES:** Spa STV ⊠ supervised Sauna Solarium Gym Jacuzzi **CONF:** BC Thtr 160 Class 70 Board 50 Del from £135 **SERVICES:** Lift **PARKING:** 400 **NOTES:** ✗ ⊗ in restaurant Civ Wed 110

★★★★68% ⊚⊚ Stanneylands
Stanneylands Rd SK9 4EY
☎ 01625 525225 🖷 01625 537282
e-mail: reservations@stanneylandshotel.co.uk
Dir: from M56 for Airport turn off, follow signs to Wilmslow. Left into Station Rd, onto Stanneylands Rd. Hotel on right

This traditional hotel has undergone a sympathetic refurbishment of the well-equipped bedrooms and delightful, comfortable day rooms. The cuisine on offer in the restaurant is of a high standard
continued

and ranges from traditional favourites to more imaginative contemporary dishes. Staff throughout are friendly and obliging.
ROOMS: 31 en suite (2 fmly) (10 GF) ⊗ in 10 bedrooms s £63-£105; d £85-£120 **LB FACILITIES:** STV **CONF:** BC Thtr 120 Class 50 Board 40 Del from £140 **PARKING:** 80 **NOTES:** ✗ Civ Wed 100

See advert on opposite page

★★★72% ⊚ Etrop Grange
Thorley Ln M90 4EG
☎ 0870 609 6123 🖷 0161 499 0790
e-mail: etropgrange@corushotels.com
web: www.corushotels.com
Dir: M56 junct 5 follow signs for Terminal 2, on slip road to rdbt take 1st exit. Immediately left and hotel 400yds

This Georgian country-house style hotel is close to Terminal 2 but one would never know once inside. Stylish, comfortable bedrooms provide modern comforts and good business facilities. Comfortable, elegant day rooms include the Coach House Restaurant that serves creative dishes. Complimentary chauffeured transport is available for guests using the airport.
ROOMS: 64 en suite (10 GF) ⊗ in 35 bedrooms s £59-£149; d £59-£199 **LB FACILITIES:** STV **CONF:** Thtr 80 Class 35 Board 35 Del from £145 **PARKING:** 80 **NOTES:** ⊗ in restaurant RS 25-26 Dec Civ Wed 90

★★★67% Belfry House
Stanley Rd SK9 3LD
☎ 0161 437 0511 🖷 0161 499 0597
e-mail: office@belfryhousehotel.co.uk
web: www.belfryhousehotel.co.uk
Dir: off A34, 4m S of junct 3 M60

This popular hotel, set in its own grounds, enjoys a convenient position close to Manchester Airport and the local motorway network. Extensive public areas include leisure and conference facilities and an elegant, contemporary restaurant. Bedrooms are traditionally furnished and overlook the attractive gardens.
ROOMS: 81 en suite (8 fmly) (12 GF) ⊗ in 69 bedrooms s £50-£94; d £60-£104 **LB FACILITIES:** Spa STV ⊠ Sauna Solarium Gym Jacuzzi ♫ **CONF:** Thtr 300 Class 120 Board 50 Del from £100 **SERVICES:** Lift **PARKING:** 150 **NOTES:** ✗ Civ Wed 120

★★★67% Bewley's Hotel Manchester Airport
Outwood Ln M90 4HL
☎ 0161 498 0333 🖷 0161 498 0222
e-mail: man@bewleyshotels.com
web: www.bewleyshotels.com/man_index.asp
Dir: at Manchester Airport. Follow signs to Manchester Airport Terminal 3. Hotel on left on Terminal 3 rdbt.

Located adjacent to the airport this modern, stylish hotel provides an ideal stop-off for air travellers and business guests alike. All bedrooms are spacious and well equipped and include a wing of
continued

superior rooms. Open-plan day rooms continue the contemporary theme.

ROOMS: 365 en suite (111 fmly) (30 GF) ⊗ in 307 bedrooms s £69; d £69 **FACILITIES:** STV **CONF:** Thtr 72 Class 40 Board 40 Del £129 **SERVICES:** Lift **PARKING:** 200 **NOTES:** 🐕̸

Premier Travel Inn Manchester Airport

premier travel inn

Finney Ln, Heald Green SK8 3QH
☎ 08701 977178 📠 0161 437 4910
web: www.premiertravelinn.com
Dir: *M56 junct 5 follow signs to Terminal 1, at rdbt take 2nd exit, at next rdbt follow signs for Cheadle. At lights turn left, then right at next lights*

High quality, modern budget accommodation ideal for both families and business travellers. Spacious, en suite bedrooms feature bath and shower, satellite TV and many have telephones and modem points. The adjacent family restaurant features a wide and varied menu. For further details consult the Hotel Groups page.
ROOMS: 66 en suite s £53.95-£55.95; d £53.95-£55.95

Premier Travel Inn Manchester Airport East

premier travel inn

30 Wilmslow Rd SK9 3EW
☎ 0870 9906602 📠 0870 9906603
web: www.premiertravelinn.com
Dir: *4m from Manchester Airport. Exit M56 junct 6 follow A538 towards Wilmslow. At main junct into town centre, bear left. 2m, hotel at top of hill on right just after Wilmslow Garden Centre*

High quality, modern budget accommodation ideal for both families and business travellers. Spacious, en suite bedrooms feature bath and shower, satellite TV and many have telephones and modem points. The adjacent family restaurant features a wide and varied menu. For further details consult the Hotel Groups page.
ROOMS: 35 en suite s £53.95-£55.95; d £53.95-£55.95

MANSFIELD, Nottinghamshire Map 16 SK56

★★68% Pine Lodge

281-283 Nottingham Rd NG18 4SE
☎ 01623 622308 📠 01623 656819
e-mail: enquiries@pinelodge-hotel.co.uk
web: www.pinelodge-hotel.co.uk
Dir: *on A60 Nottingham to Mansfield road, hotel is 1m S of Mansfield*

Located on the edge of Mansfield, this hotel offers welcoming and personal service to its guests - many return time and again. The public rooms include a comfortable lounge bar, a cosy restaurant and a choice of meeting and function rooms. Bedrooms are thoughtfully equipped, and are carefully maintained; a bedroom suite is also available.
ROOMS: 20 en suite (2 fmly) ⊗ in all bedrooms s £45-£60; d £65-£80 (incl. bkfst) **LB** **FACILITIES:** STV Sauna **CONF:** Thtr 50 Class 30 Board 35 **PARKING:** 40 **NOTES:** 🐕̸ ⊗ in restaurant Closed 25-26 Dec

★★65% Portland Hall

THE INDEPENDENTS

Carr Bank Park, Windmill Ln NG18 2AL
☎ 01623 452525 📠 01623 452550
e-mail: enquiries@portlandhallhotel.co.uk
web: www.portlandhallhotel.co.uk
Dir: *from town centre take A60 to Worksop for 100yds then right at pelican crossing into Nursery St, Carr Bank Park 50yds on right*

A former Georgian mansion, overlooking 15 acres of renovated parklands, the house retains some fine features, with original plasterwork and friezes in the cosy lounge bar and around the domed skylight over the spiral stairs. The attractive restaurant proves popular, offering a flexible choice of carvery or menu options; service is skilled and attentive.
ROOMS: 10 en suite (1 fmly) ⊗ in 5 bedrooms s £47-£50; d £60-£65 (incl. bkfst) **FACILITIES:** ⚲ Bowls Green Xmas **CONF:** Thtr 60 Class 30 Board 20 **PARKING:** 80 **NOTES:** ⊗ in restaurant Civ Wed 66

MARAZION, Cornwall & Isles of Scilly Map 02 SW53

★★77% ❀ Mount Haven Hotel & St Michaels Restaurant

Turnpike Rd TR17 0DQ
☎ 01736 710249 📠 01736 711658
e-mail: reception@mounthaven.co.uk
web: www.mounthaven.co.uk
Dir: *From A30 towards Penzance. At rdbt take exit for Helston onto A394. Next rdbt right into Marazion, hotel on left*

Art and style abound at this delightfully located hotel where exceptional views can be enjoyed - sunrises and sunsets can be particularly splendid. Bedrooms, many with balconies, are comfortably appointed. Fresh seafood and local produce are simply treated to produce interesting menus and enjoyable dining.

continued on p386

MARAZION, continued

A range of holistic therapies is available. Service is attentive and friendly and a relaxing and enchanting environment has been created throughout.

Mount Haven Hotel, Marazion

ROOMS: 18 en suite (2 fmly) (6 GF) ⊗ in all bedrooms s £60-£82; d £84-£150 (incl. bkfst) **LB** **FACILITIES: Spa** Aromatherapy reflexology, massage & reiki **CONF:** Thtr 50 Class 30 **PARKING:** 30 **NOTES:** ✈ ⊗ in restaurant Closed 20 Dec-5 Feb

★★70% Godolphin Arms

TR17 0EN
☎ 01736 710202 🖷 01736 710171
e-mail: enquiries@godolphinarms.co.uk
web: www.godolphinarms.co.uk
Dir: *from A30 follow Marazion signs for 1m to hotel. At end of the causeway to St Michael's Mount*

This 170-year-old waterside hotel is in a prime location with stunning views of St Michael's Mount – a backdrop for the restaurant and lounge bar. Bedrooms are colourful, comfortable and spacious. A choice of menu is offered in the main restaurant and the Gig Bar, all with an emphasis on local seafood.
ROOMS: 10 rms (9 en suite) (2 fmly) (2 GF) s £45-£75; d £70-£130 (incl. bkfst) **LB** **FACILITIES:** STV Direct access to large beach **PARKING:** 48 **NOTES:** ⊗ in restaurant Closed 24 & 25 Dec

MARCH, Cambridgeshire — Map 12 TL49

★★62% Olde Griffin

High St PE15 9JS
☎ 01354 652517 🖷 01354 650086
e-mail: griffhotel@aol.com
Dir: *on A141/142 N of Ely and off A47 E of Peterborough towards Norwich*
Overlooking the town square, this former coaching inn dates back to the 16th century, and retains many period features. Bedrooms vary in size and style and all are appropriately equipped and furnished.
continued

Meals are available in the lounge and bar areas, and there is a restaurant for more formal dining on a Friday and Saturday.

ROOMS: 21 rms (20 en suite) (1 fmly) s £45; d £59.50 (incl. bkfst) **CONF:** Thtr 100 Class 50 Board 36 **PARKING:** 50 **NOTES:** ⊗ in restaurant

MARGATE, Kent — Map 07 TR37

U ★★★ *Smiths Court*

Eastern Esplanade, Cliftonville CT9 2HL
☎ 01843 222310 🖷 01843 222312
e-mail: info@courthotels.com
Dir: *from clocktower on seafront take left fork on A28 for approx 1m. Hotel on right Eastern Esplanade at junct with Godwin Rd.*
ROOMS: 40 en suite (6 fmly) (6 GF) ⊗ in 10 bedrooms
FACILITIES: Gym ♫ ch fac **CONF:** Thtr 80 Class 50 Board 80
SERVICES: Lift **PARKING:** 15 **NOTES:** ⊗ in restaurant

⌂ Premier Travel Inn Margate

Station Green, Marine Ter CT9 5AF
☎ 08701 977182 🖷 01843 221101
web: www.premiertravelinn.com
Dir: *M2 follow A299 then A28 to Margate seafront. Inn adjacent to Margate station, facing sea*
High quality, modern budget accommodation ideal for both families and business travellers. Spacious, en suite bedrooms feature bath and shower, satellite TV and many have telephones and modem points. The adjacent family restaurant features a wide and varied menu. For further details consult the Hotel Groups page.
ROOMS: 44 en suite s £48.95; d £48.95

MARKET DRAYTON, Shropshire — Map 15 SJ63

★★★72% ⊛ Goldstone Hall

Goldstone TF9 2NA
☎ 01630 661202 🖷 01630 661585
e-mail: enquiries@goldstonehall.com
web: www.goldstonehall.com
Dir: *4m S of Market Drayton off A529 signed Goldstone Hall Gdns. 4m N of Newport signed from A41*
Situated in extensive grounds, this charming period property is a family-run hotel. It provides traditionally furnished, well-equipped accommodation, with some more contemporary artistic touches. Public rooms are extensive and include a choice of lounges, a snooker room and a conservatory. The hotel has a well-deserved reputation for good food.
ROOMS: 11 en suite (2 GF) s £78-£95; d £105-£140 (incl. bkfst) **LB**
FACILITIES: STV Snooker **CONF:** BC Thtr 50 Class 30 Board 30 Del from £110 **PARKING:** 60 **NOTES:** ✈ ⊗ in restaurant Civ Wed 70

U Star rating not confirmed

★★70% Rosehill Manor
Rosehill, Ternhill TF9 2JF
☎ 01630 638532 📠 01630 637008
Dir: *from rdbt at Ternhill A53 S towards Newport. Hotel 2m on right*
Parts of this charming old house, which stands in mature gardens, date back to the 16th century. Privately owned and personally run, it provides well-equipped accommodation including family rooms. Public areas comprise a pleasant restaurant serving award-winning cuisine, a bar and a comfortable lounge. There is also a conservatory, which is available for functions.
ROOMS: 8 en suite (2 fmly) s fr £52.50; d fr £75 (incl. bkfst)
FACILITIES: ♫ **CONF:** Thtr 100 Class 60 Board 40 **PARKING:** 80
NOTES: ⊗ in restaurant Civ Wed 100

MARKET HARBOROUGH, Leicestershire — Map 11 SP78
See also Marston Trussell

★★★70% Three Swans
21 High St LE16 7NJ
☎ 01858 466644 📠 01858 433101
e-mail: sales@threeswans.co.uk
web: www.threeswans.co.uk
Dir: *M1 junct 20 take A4304 to Market Harborough. Through town centre on A6 from Leicester, hotel on right*

Public areas in this former coaching inn include an elegant fine dining restaurant and cocktail bar, a smart foyer lounge and popular public bar areas. Bedroom styles and sizes vary, all are very well appointed and equipped and those in the wing are particularly impressive, offering high quality spacious accommodation.
ROOMS: 18 en suite 43 annexe en suite (8 fmly) (12 GF) ⊗ in 44 bedrooms s £78-£89; d £89-£95 (incl. bkfst) **LB FACILITIES:** STV Xmas **CONF:** Thtr 200 Class 120 Board 120 Del from £120 **SERVICES:** Lift **PARKING:** 100 **NOTES:** ⊗ in restaurant Civ Wed 140

MARKFIELD, Leicestershire — Map 11 SK40

Travelodge Leicester Markfield
Littleshaw Ln LE6 0PP
☎ 08700 850 950 📠 01530 244580
web: www.travelodge.co.uk
Dir: *on A50 from M1 junct 22*
Travelodge offers good quality, good value, modern accommodation. Ideal for families, the spacious, en suite bedrooms include remote-control TV, tea and coffee-making facilities and comfortable beds. Meals can be taken at the nearby family restaurant. For further details consult the Hotel Groups page.
ROOMS: 60 en suite s fr £26; d fr £26

MARKHAM MOOR, Nottinghamshire — Map 17 SK77

Travelodge Retford
DN22 0QU
☎ 08700 850 950 📠 01777 838091
web: www.travelodge.co.uk
Dir: *on A1 at junct with A57 northbound*
Travelodge offers good quality, good value, modern accommodation. Ideal for families, the spacious, en suite bedrooms include remote-control TV, tea and coffee-making facilities and comfortable beds. Meals can be taken at the nearby family restaurant. For further details consult the Hotel Groups page.
ROOMS: 40 en suite s fr £26; d fr £26

MARKINGTON, North Yorkshire — Map 19 SE26

★★★77% Hob Green
HG3 3PJ
☎ 01423 770031 📠 01423 771589
e-mail: info@hobgreen.com
web: www.hobgreen.com
Dir: *from A61, 4m N of Harrogate, left at Wormald Green, follow hotel signs*

This hospitable country house is set in delightful gardens amidst rolling countryside midway between Harrogate and Ripon. The inviting lounges boast open fires in season and there is an elegant restaurant with a small private dining room. The individual bedrooms are very comfortable and come with a host of thoughtful extras.
ROOMS: 12 en suite (1 fmly) ⊗ in all bedrooms s £90-£95; d £110-£115 **LB FACILITIES:** STV ♫ ch fac Xmas **CONF:** Thtr 15 Class 10 Board 10 Del from £125 **PARKING:** 40 **NOTES:** ⊗ in restaurant Civ Wed 35
See advert under HARROGATE

MARLBOROUGH, Wiltshire — Map 05 SU16

★★★64% *The Castle & Ball*
High St SN8 1LZ
☎ 01672 515201 📠 01672 515895
web: www.oldenglish.co.uk
Dir: *A338 and A4 to Marlborough*
This traditional coaching inn in the town centre offers bedrooms in a contemporary style that are very well equipped. Open-plan public areas include a comfortable bar/lounge area and a smartly appointed restaurant, which serves food all day. Meeting rooms and parking are also available.
ROOMS: 34 en suite (1 fmly) ⊗ in 13 bedrooms **FACILITIES:** STV **CONF:** Thtr 45 Class 20 Board 30 **PARKING:** 48 **NOTES:** ⊗ in restaurant

MARLOW, Buckinghamshire — Map 05 SU88

★★★★77% ⊛⊛
Danesfield House Hotel & Spa
Henley Rd SL7 2EY
☎ 01628 891010 🖷 01628 890408
e-mail: sales@danesfieldhouse.co.uk
web: www.danesfieldhouse.co.uk
Dir: *2m from Marlow on A4155 towards Henley*

Set in 65 acres of elevated grounds just 45 minutes from central London and 30 minutes from Heathrow, this hotel enjoys spectacular views across the River Thames. Impressive public rooms include the cathedral-like Great Hall, the panelled Oak Room Restaurant and The Orangery, a less formal option for dining. Some bedrooms have balconies and stunning views.
ROOMS: 87 en suite (3 fmly) (27 GF) ⊘ in 5 bedrooms s £175-£355; d £220-£355 (incl. bkfst) **LB** **FACILITIES: Spa** STV Snooker Sauna Solarium Gym Putt green Jacuzzi Jogging trail, Steam room, Hydrotherapy room, Treatment rooms Xmas **CONF:** Thtr 100 Class 60 Board 50 Del from £285 **SERVICES:** Lift **PARKING:** 100 **NOTES:** ⊘ in restaurant Civ Wed 100

See advert on opposite page

★★★★71% ⊛⊛⊛ **The Compleat Angler**
Marlow Bridge SL7 1RG
☎ 0870 400 8100 🖷 01628 486388
e-mail: compleatangler@macdonald-hotels.co.uk
web: www.macdonald-hotels.co.uk
Dir: *M4 junct 8/9, A404 to rdbt, Bisham exit, 1m to Marlow Bridge, hotel on right*

This well-established hotel enjoys a wonderful setting overlooking the River Thames and the Marlow weir. Bedrooms, which differ in size and style, are all individually decorated and comfortable. Dining choices include a cosy bar, informal brasserie-style restaurant and the award-winning Riverside restaurant.
ROOMS: 64 en suite (6 GF) ⊘ in 22 bedrooms s £240-£290; d £240-£485 **LB** **FACILITIES:** STV Fishing Boating, Fly fishing and course fishing ♫ Xmas **CONF:** Thtr 120 Class 65 Board 36 Del £270 **SERVICES:** Lift **PARKING:** 60 **NOTES:** ⊘ in restaurant Civ Wed 120

See advert on opposite page

MARSDEN, West Yorkshire — Map 16 SE01

★★73% ⊛ **Hey Green Country House**
Waters Rd HD7 6NG
☎ 01484 844235 🖷 01484 847605
e-mail: info@heygreen.com
web: www.heygreen.com
Dir: *off A62 1m outside village, towards Manchester.*

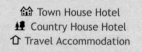

This delightful Victorian property is set in extensive landscaped gardens, close to the restored Huddersfield Canal and The Standedge Visitor Centre. Spacious bedrooms are stylishly designed, thoughtfully equipped and boast smart, modern en suite bathrooms. A contemporary brasserie offers imaginative dishes. The beautiful conservatory and function suite make this a popular venue for weddings.
ROOMS: 12 en suite ⊘ in 10 bedrooms s £55-£90; d £90-£150 (incl. bkfst) **LB** **FACILITIES:** Xmas **CONF:** Thtr 100 Class 80 Board 30 Del from £120 **PARKING:** 70 **NOTES:** ⊘ in restaurant RS 2-3 Jan Civ Wed 120

MARSTON MORETAINE, Bedfordshire — Map 11 SP94

⌂ **Travelodge Bedford South West**
Beancroft Rd Junction MK43 0PZ
☎ 08700 850 950 🖷 01234 766755
web: www.travelodge.co.uk
Dir: *on A421, northbound*
Travelodge offers good quality, good value, modern accommodation. Ideal for families, the spacious, en suite bedrooms include remote-control TV, tea and coffee-making facilities and comfortable beds. Meals can be taken at the nearby family restaurant. For further details consult the Hotel Groups page.
ROOMS: 54 en suite s fr £26; d fr £26

Town House Hotel
Country House Hotel
Travel Accommodation

MARSTON TRUSSELL, Northamptonshire — Map 11 SP68

★★72% ⊛ **The Sun Inn**
Main St LE16 9TY
☎ 01858 465531 🖷 01858 433155
e-mail: manager@suninn.com
Dir: *M1 junct 20 take A4304, right to Marston Trussell*
This pleasant inn successfully combines a mixture of modern facilities and accommodation with the classical traditions of the rural English inn. Bedrooms are comfortably furnished and tastefully appointed and offer a host of thoughtful facilities. Public

continued

areas consist of two elegant dining areas and a bar with open log fires. Service is both friendly and attentive.

ROOMS: 20 en suite (1 fmly) (10 GF) ⊗ in 10 bedrooms s £59; d £69 (incl. bkfst) **LB** **FACILITIES:** Rambling trails Xmas **CONF:** BC Thtr 60 Class 40 Board 28 **PARKING:** 60 **NOTES:** ⊁

MARTINHOE, Devon Map 03 SS64

★★75% The Old Rectory

EX31 4QT
☎ 01598 763368 ▤ 01598 763567
e-mail: reception@oldrectoryhotel.co.uk
web: www.oldrectoryhotel.co.uk
Dir: *M5 junct 27 onto A361, right onto A399 Blackmoor Gate and right onto A39 bypass Parracombe. 2nd left to Martinhoe and follow signs*

Originally built in the 1800s for the local rector, this peaceful hideaway is an ideal base for exploring Exmoor and is just 500 yards from the coastal footpath. In addition to the comfortable lounges, guests can relax in the vinery, overlooking the delightful gardens. Interesting menus are served in the spacious dining room. The bedrooms are tastefully decorated and a self-catering cottage is also available.
ROOMS: 9 en suite (2 GF) ⊗ in all bedrooms s £82-£119; d £134-£198 (incl. bkfst & dinner) **LB** **PARKING:** 9 **NOTES:** ⊁ No children 14yrs ⊗ in restaurant Closed Nov-Feb RS Mar

★★74% Heddon's Gate Hotel

Heddon's Mouth EX31 4PZ
☎ 01598 763481
e-mail: hotel@heddonsgate.co.uk
web: www.heddonsgate.co.uk
Dir: *A39 towards Lynton, left after 4m towards Martinhoe, left towards Hunters Inn, over x-rds, 1st right after Mannacott*
Re-launched in 2005, this hotel is superbly located on the slopes of the Heddon Valley, hidden at the end of a quarter mile private drive. Guests are assured of a warm and friendly welcome, with a complimentary, traditional afternoon tea served daily between 4-5pm. The individually furnished and decorated

continued on p390

MARTINHOE, continued

bedrooms are well equipped, the greater majority benefiting from the superb view. Dinner, served each evening, is described as an occasion, and features the best of local produce.

Heddon's Gate Hotel, Martinhoe

ROOMS: 11 en suite ⊗ in all bedrooms s £62-£80.40; d £124-£160.80 (incl. bkfst & dinner) **LB** **FACILITIES:** ♫ Xmas **PARKING:** 11 **NOTES:** No children 16yrs ⊗ in restaurant Closed Telephone for dates

MARTOCK, Somerset Map 04 ST41

★★★72% **The Hollies**
Bower Hinton TA12 6LG
☎ 01935 822232 01935 822249
e-mail: info@thehollieshotel.com
web: www.thehollieshotel.com
Dir: *on B3165 S of town centre off A303, take Bower Hinton slip road & follow hotel signs*

Within easy access of the A303, the bar and restaurant of this popular venue are housed in an attractive 17th-century farmhouse. Bar meals are available in addition to the interesting main menu. The spacious, well-equipped bedrooms are located to the rear of the property in a purpose-built wing and include both suites and mini-suites.

ROOMS: 33 annexe en suite (2 fmly) (30 GF) ⊗ in 10 bedrooms s £72-£120; d £82-£140 (incl. bkfst) **LB** **FACILITIES:** STV **CONF:** BC Thtr 150 Class 80 Board 60 Del from £97 **PARKING:** 80 **NOTES:** ⊗ in restaurant RS Xmas & New Year

♫ Entertainment

MASHAM, North Yorkshire Map 19 SE28

Top Hotel

★★★★ ◎◎◎ **Swinton Park**
HG4 4JH
☎ 01765 680900 01765 680901
e-mail: enquiries@swintonpark.com
web: www.swintonpark.com
Dir: *A1 onto B6267 to Masham. Follow signs through town centre & turn right onto Swinton Terrace. 1m past GC over bridge, up hill. Hotel is on right*

Extended during the Victorian and Edwardian eras, the original part of this welcoming castle dates from the 17th century. Bedrooms are luxuriously furnished and come with a host of thoughtful extras. Samuel's restaurant (built by the current owner's great-great-great grandfather) is very elegant and serves imaginative dishes using local produce, much being sourced from the Swinton estate itself.

ROOMS: 30 en suite (4 fmly) ⊗ in all bedrooms d £140-£350 (incl. bkfst) **LB** **FACILITIES: Spa** STV ⛳ 9 Fishing Riding Snooker Sauna Gym ♫ Putt green Jacuzzi Shooting, Falconry, Pony Trekking, cookery school ch fac Xmas **CONF:** Thtr 120 Class 60 Board 40 Del £170 **SERVICES:** Lift **PARKING:** 50 **NOTES:** ⊗ in restaurant Civ Wed 120

★★65% **The Kings Head**
Market Place HG4 4EF
☎ 01765 689295 01765 689070
e-mail: kings.head.6395@thespiritgroup.com
Dir: *from A1 take the B6268 to Masham - follow the Market Place signs*

This historic, stone-built hotel, with its uneven floors, beamed bars and attractive window boxes, looks out over the large Market Square. Guests have the option of either bedrooms in the main building which are elegantly furnished, or the more contemporary rooms newly converted at the rear of the property; all rooms are thoughtfully equipped. Public areas are traditional and include a popular bar and smartly appointed restaurant.

ROOMS: 13 en suite 11 annexe en suite (3 fmly) (9 GF) ⊗ in all bedrooms s £50-£55; d £65-£85 **CONF:** Thtr 40 Class 24 Board 30 **PARKING:** 3 **NOTES:** ⊗ in restaurant Civ Wed 40

MATFEN, Northumberland Map 21 NZ07

★★★★76% ◎◎ **Matfen Hall**
NE20 0RH
☎ 01661 886500 855708 01661 886055
e-mail: info@matfenhall.com
web: www.matfenhall.com
Dir: *off A69 to B6318. Hotel just before village*

This fine mansion lies in landscaped parkland overlooking its own golf course. Bedrooms are a blend of contemporary and traditional, but all are very comfortable and well equipped. Impressive public rooms include a splendid drawing room and the elegant Library and

continued

Print Room Restaurant, as well as a conservatory bar and very stylish spa, leisure and conference facilities.
ROOMS: 53 en suite (11 fmly) ⊗ in 42 bedrooms s £125-£190; d £150-£245 (incl. bkfst) **LB FACILITIES: Spa** STV supervised 18 Sauna Solarium Gym Putt green Jacuzzi Xmas **CONF:** Thtr 120 Class 46 Board 40 Del £170 **SERVICES:** Lift **PARKING:** 150 **NOTES:** ⊗ in restaurant Civ Wed 120

See advert under NEWCASTLE UPON TYNE

MATLOCK, Derbyshire Map 16 SK35

★★★77% Riber Hall
DE4 5JU
☎ 01629 582795 01629 580475
e-mail: info@riber-hall.co.uk
web: www.riber-hall.co.uk
Dir: *1m off A615 at Tansley*

This beautiful Elizabethan manor house enjoys an idyllic location in charming grounds overlooking Matlock. Beautifully furnished, thoughtfully equipped bedrooms, many with oak four-poster beds, are situated round a delightful courtyard with its own fountain. Tastefully appointed public rooms are furnished with period and antique pieces and an impressive wine list complements the imaginative, award-winning cuisine.
ROOMS: 3 en suite 11 annexe en suite (7 GF) ⊗ in 4 bedrooms s £97-£112; d £136-£182 (incl. bkfst) **LB FACILITIES:** STV **CONF:** Thtr 20 Class 20 Board 20 Del from £148 **PARKING:** 50 **NOTES:** No children 10yrs ⊗ in restaurant Closed 25-Dec RS 25-Dec Civ Wed 50

★★75% The Red House Country Hotel
Old Rd, Darley Dale DE4 2ER
☎ 01629 734854 01629 734885
e-mail: enquiries@TheRedHouseCountryHotel.co.uk
web: www.theredhousecountryhotel.co.uk
Dir: *off A6 onto Old Rd signed Carriage Museum, 2.5m N of Matlock*

A peaceful country hotel set in delightful Victorian gardens. Rich colour schemes are used to excellent effect throughout. The well-equipped bedrooms include three ground floor rooms in the adjacent coach house. A comfortable lounge with delightful rural views is available for refreshments and pre-dinner drinks; service is friendly and attentive.
ROOMS: 7 en suite 3 annexe en suite (3 GF) ⊗ in all bedrooms s £60-£70; d £95 (incl. bkfst) **LB CONF:** Thtr 30 Class 24 Board 24 **PARKING:** 12 **NOTES:** No children 12yrs ⊗ in restaurant Closed 2-15 Jan

MAWGAN PORTH, Cornwall & Isles of Scilly Map 02 SW86

★★★★67% Bedruthan Steps Hotel
TR8 4BU
☎ 01637 860555 860860 01637 860714
e-mail: office@bedruthan.com
Dir: *from A39/A30 follow signs to Newquay Airport. Right at T-junct, past airport, to Mawgan Porth. Hotel on left at top of hill*

With stunning views over Mawgan Porth Bay from the public rooms and the majority of the bedrooms, this child-friendly hotel has undergone extensive upgrading. Children's clubs for various ages are provided in addition to children's dining areas and appropriate meals and times. A homage to architecture of the 1970s, with a modern, comfortable, contemporary feel, this hotel is adding conference facilities. In the spacious restaurants, an imaginative fixed-price menu is offered; a short carte is available Tuesdays-Saturday.
ROOMS: 90 en suite 9 annexe en suite (60 fmly) (1 GF) ⊗ in all bedrooms s £67-£106; d £134-£264 (incl. bkfst & dinner) **LB FACILITIES: Spa** Snooker Sauna Gym Jacuzzi Jungle tumble ball pool ch fac Xmas **CONF:** BC Thtr 200 Class 100 Board 40 Del from £80 **SERVICES:** Lift **PARKING:** 100 **NOTES:** ⊗ in restaurant Civ Wed 150

The vast majority of establishments in this guide accept credit and debit cards. We indicate those that don't take any

MAWNAN SMITH, Cornwall & Isles of Scilly Map 02 SW72

★★★★73% Budock Vean-The Hotel on the River
TR11 5LG
☎ 01326 252100 & 0800 833927 01326 250892
e-mail: relax@budockvean.co.uk
web: www.budockvean.co.uk
Dir: *from A39 follow tourist signs to Trebah Gardens. 0.5m to hotel*
Set in 65 acres of attractive, well-tended grounds, this peaceful hotel offers an impressive range of facilities. Convenient for visiting the Helford River Estuary and many local gardens, or simply as a tranquil setting for a leisure break, Bedrooms are

continued on p392

MAWNAN SMITH, continued

spacious and offer a choice of styles; some overlook the grounds and golf course.

Budock Vean, Mawnan Smith

ROOMS: 57 en suite (2 fmly) ⊗ in 6 bedrooms s £68-£112; d £136-£224 (incl. bkfst & dinner) **LB** **FACILITIES:** STV ⛾ ⛳ 9 Fishing Snooker Putt green Natural health spa, private motor boat & foreshore ♫ Xmas **CONF:** Thtr 60 Class 40 Board 30 **SERVICES:** Lift **PARKING:** 100 **NOTES:** ⊗ in restaurant Closed 3 wks Jan Civ Wed 65

★★★79% ⊛ Meudon

TR11 5HT
☎ 01326 250541 📠 01326 250543
e-mail: wecare@meudon.co.uk web: www.meudon.co.uk
Dir: *from Truro A39 towards Falmouth at Hillhead rdbt, follow signs to Maenporth Beach. Hotel on left 1m after beach*

This charming late Victorian mansion, with its friendly hospitality, attentive service and impressive nine acres of gardens, which lead down to a private beach, provides a relaxing place to stay. Bedrooms are comfortable and spacious and cuisine features the best of local Cornish produce served in the conservatory restaurant.

ROOMS: 29 en suite (2 fmly) (15 GF) s £60-£115; d £120-£230 (incl. bkfst & dinner) **LB** **FACILITIES:** Fishing Riding Private beach, Hair salon, Yacht for skippered charter, sub-tropical gardens Xmas **CONF:** Thtr 30 Class 20 Board 15 Del from £25 **SERVICES:** Lift **PARKING:** 52 **NOTES:** ⊗ in restaurant Closed Jan

See advert under FALMOUTH

★★★69% ⊛ *Trelawne*

TR11 5HS
☎ 01326 250226 📠 01326 250909
e-mail: info@trelawnehotel.co.uk
Dir: *A39 to Falmouth, right at Hillhead rdbt signed Maenporth. Past beach, up hill and hotel on left*

This hotel is surrounded by attractive lawns and gardens, and enjoys superb coastal views. An informal atmosphere prevails, and many guests return year after year. Bedrooms, many with sea views, are of varying sizes, but all are well equipped. Dinner features quality local produce used in imaginative dishes.

ROOMS: 14 en suite (2 fmly) (4 GF) **FACILITIES:** ⛾ ch fac **PARKING:** 20 **NOTES:** ⊗ in restaurant Closed 23 Dec-12 Feb

See advert on opposite page

MEDBOURNE, Leicestershire — Map 11 SP89

Restaurant with Rooms

⊛⊛ The Horse & Trumpet

Old Green LE16 8DX
☎ 01858 565000 📠 01858 565551
e-mail: info@horseandtrumpet.com
Dir: *in village centre, opposite church*

Tucked away behind the village bowling green, this carefully restored, thatched former farmhouse and pub now offers fine dining and quality accommodation. The golden stone building houses three intimate dining areas, where imaginative meals are offered. Smartly appointed and comfortably furnished bedrooms are located in a barn conversion to the rear of the main building.

ROOMS: 4 annexe en suite (2 GF) ⊗ in all bedrooms s £75; d £150 (incl. bkfst) **NOTES:** No children 5yrs

MELKSHAM, Wiltshire — Map 04 ST96

★★72% Shaw Country

Bath Rd, Shaw SN12 8EF
☎ 01225 702836 & 790321 📠 01225 790275
e-mail: info@shawcountryhotel.co.uk
web: www.shawcountryhotel.co.uk
Dir: *1m from Melksham, 9m from Bath on A365*

Located within easy reach of both Bath and the M4, this relaxed and friendly hotel sits in its own gardens with a newly developed patio area ideal for enjoying a cool drink during warm summer months. The house boasts some very well-appointed bedrooms, a comfortable lounge and bar and the Mulberry Restaurant, where a wide selection of innovative dishes make up both carte and set menus.

ROOMS: 13 en suite (2 fmly) s £50-£74; d £70-£90 (incl. bkfst) **LB** **FACILITIES:** Jacuzzi **CONF:** Thtr 30 Class 20 Board 15 **PARKING:** 30 **NOTES:** ⊗ in restaurant Closed 26-27 Dec & 1 Jan

MELTON MOWBRAY, Leicestershire — Map 11 SK71

Top Hotel

★★★★ ⊛⊛ *Stapleford Park*

Stapleford LE14 2EF
☎ 01572 787522 📠 01572 787651
e-mail: reservations@stapleford.co.uk
web: www.staplefordpark.com
Dir: *1m SW of B676, 4m E of Melton Mowbray and 9m W of Colsterworth*

This stunning mansion, dating back to the 14th century, sits in

continued

over 500 acres of beautiful grounds. Spacious, sumptuous public rooms include a choice of lounges and an elegant restaurant; an additional brasserie-style restaurant is located in the new golf complex. The hotel also boasts a spa with health and beauty treatments and gym, a golf course, horse-riding and many other country pursuits. Bedrooms are individually styled and furnished to a high standard. Attentive service is delivered with a relaxed yet professional style. Dinner, in the impressive dining room, is a highlight of any stay.

ROOMS: 44 en suite 8 annexe en suite ⊗ in 44 bedrooms **FACILITIES:** STV 18 Fishing Riding Sauna Solarium Gym Putt green Jacuzzi Archery, Croquet, Falconry, Horse Riding, Petanque, Shooting ♫ **CONF:** BC Thtr 200 Class 140 Board 80 **SERVICES:** Lift **PARKING:** 120 **NOTES:** ⊗ in restaurant Civ Wed 200

♫ Entertainment

MELTON MOWBRAY, continued

★★★73% Sysonby Knoll

Asfordby Rd LE13 0HP
☎ 01664 563563 📠 01664 410364
e-mail: reception@sysonby.com
web: www.sysonby.com
Dir: *0.5m from town centre beside A6006*
This well-established hotel is on the edge of town and set within attractive gardens. A friendly and relaxed atmosphere prevails and many returning guests have become friends. Bedrooms, including superior rooms in an annexe, are generally spacious and thoughtfully equipped. A choice of lounges, a cosy bar and a smart restaurant offers carefully prepared meals.
ROOMS: 23 en suite 7 annexe en suite (1 fmly) (7 GF) ⊗ in 6 bedrooms s £61-£79; d £73-£99 (incl. bkfst) **LB** **FACILITIES:** STV Fishing **CONF:** Thtr 50 Class 25 Board 34 **PARKING:** 48 **NOTES:** ⊗ in restaurant Closed 25 Dec-1 Jan

See advert on page 393

★★★68% *Quorn Lodge*

46 Asfordby Rd LE13 0HR
☎ 01664 566660 & 562590 📠 01664 480660
e-mail: quornlodge@aol.com
web: www.quornlodge.co.uk
Dir: *from town centre take A6006. Hotel 300yds from junct of A606/A607 on right*
Centrally located, this smart privately owned and managed hotel offers a comfortable and welcoming atmosphere. Bedrooms are individually decorated and thoughtfully designed. The public rooms consist of a bright restaurant overlooking the garden, a cosy lounge bar and a modern function suite. High standards are maintained throughout and extensive parking is a bonus.
ROOMS: 19 en suite (2 fmly) (3 GF) ⊗ in 13 bedrooms **FACILITIES:** STV **CONF:** Thtr 90 Class 60 Board 85 **PARKING:** 33 **NOTES:** ⊗ in restaurant Closed 26 Dec-2 Jan

M

MEMBURY MOTORWAY SERVICE AREA (M4), Berkshire — Map 05 SU37

Days Inn Membury

Membury Service Area RG17 7TZ
☎ 01488 72336 📠 01488 72336
e-mail: membury.hotel@welcomebreak.co.uk
web: www.welcomebreak.co.uk
Dir: *M4 between junct 14 & 15*
This modern building offers accommodation in smart, spacious and well-equipped bedrooms, suitable for families and business travellers, and all with en suite bathrooms. Continental breakfast is available and other refreshments may be taken at the nearby family restaurant. For further details see the Hotel Groups page.
ROOMS: 38 en suite s £35-£55; d £35-£55 **CONF:** BC Board 10

MERIDEN, West Midlands — Map 10 SP28

★★★★73% Marriott Forest of Arden Hotel & Country Club

Maxstoke Ln CV7 7HR
☎ 0870 400 7272 📠 0870 400 7372
web: www.marriott.co.uk
Dir: *M42 junct 6 onto A45 towards Coventry, over Stonebridge flyover. After 0.75m left into Shepherds Ln. Hotel 1.5m on left*
The ancient oaks, rolling hills and natural lakes of the 10,000 acre Forest of Arden estate provide an idyllic backdrop for this modern hotel and country club. The hotel boasts an excellent range of leisure facilities and is regarded as one of the finest golfing destinations in the UK. Bedrooms provide every modern convenience and a full range of facilities.
ROOMS: 214 en suite (4 fmly) (65 GF) ⊗ in 135 bedrooms s £149-£199; d £149-£199 **LB** **FACILITIES: Spa** STV supervised 18 Fishing Sauna Gym Putt green Jacuzzi Health & Beauty salon, Floodlit golf academy Xmas **CONF:** Thtr 300 Class 180 Board 40 **SERVICES:** Lift air con **PARKING:** 300 **NOTES:** ⊗ in restaurant Civ Wed 160

★★★71% Manor

Main Rd CV7 7NH
☎ 01676 522735 📠 01676 522186
e-mail: reservations@manorhotelmeriden.co.uk
web: www.manorhotelmeriden.co.uk
Dir: *M42 junct 6 take A45 towards Coventry then A452, signed Leamington. At rdbt join B4102, signed Meriden, for hotel on left.*
A sympathetically extended Georgian manor in the heart of a sleepy village is just a few minutes away from the M6, M42 and National Exhibition Centre. The Regency Restaurant offers modern dishes, while the Triumph Buttery serves lighter meals and snacks. Bedroom styles vary considerably; the Executive rooms and those in the Princess Diana wing are smart and well equipped.
ROOMS: 110 en suite (20 GF) ⊗ in 54 bedrooms s £67-£145; d £87-£180 (incl. bkfst) **LB** **CONF:** Thtr 250 Class 150 Board 60 Del from £85 **SERVICES:** Lift **PARKING:** 200 **NOTES:** ⊗ in restaurant RS 24 Dec-2 Jan Civ Wed 150

★★★64% Strawberry Bank

Main Rd CV7 7NF
☎ 01676 522117 📠 01676 523804
e-mail: enquiries@strawberrybank.co.uk
Dir: *M42 junct 6/A45 towards Coventry for approx 1.5m. Just prior to Little Chef turn left signed Meriden. Right over flyover to island, then left to Meriden Island, 3.5m from NEC, airport & rail station*
This modern hotel enjoys a convenient position for both the airport and the exhibition centre. Bedrooms are well equipped and a good range of dishes is available in the spacious restaurant. Gardens are well kept and extensive.
ROOMS: 47 en suite (18 GF) ⊗ in all bedrooms s £60-£95; d £80-£115 (incl. bkfst) **FACILITIES:** STV **CONF:** Thtr 180 Class 50 Board 60 Del from £120 **PARKING:** 200 **NOTES:** ⊗ in restaurant RS Sun pm, Sat & Mon am Civ Wed 63

MEVAGISSEY, Cornwall & Isles of Scilly — Map 02 SX04

★★71% Tremarne

Polkirt PL26 6UL
☎ 01726 842213 📠 01726 843420
e-mail: info@tremarne-hotel.co.uk
web: www.tremarne-hotel.co.uk
Dir: *from A390 at St Austell take B3273 to Mevagissey. Follow Portmellon signs through Mevagissey, at top of Polkirt Hill turn right*
A relaxing, family-run hotel ideal for those exploring this beautiful area or visiting the nearby Eden Project. Many of the bedrooms have views across the countryside to the sea beyond. The friendly team of staff makes every effort to ensure a comfortable and enjoyable stay. Public areas include a bar, a well-appointed restaurant and a comfortable lounge.
ROOMS: 13 en suite (2 fmly) ⊗ in all bedrooms s £30-£35; d £37.50-£50 (incl. bkfst) **LB** **FACILITIES:** **PARKING:** 13 **NOTES:** No children 5yrs ⊗ in restaurant Closed Dec-Jan

AA Rosette Award for culinary excellence

MEXBOROUGH, South Yorkshire Map 16 SE40

★★64% Pastures
Pastures Rd S64 0JJ
☎ 01709 577707 📠 01709 577795
e-mail: info@pastureshotel.co.uk
web: www.pastureshotel.co.uk
Dir: *0.5m from town centre on A6023, left by ATS Tyres, signed Denaby Ings & Cadeby. Hotel on right*
This hotel has a modern, purpose-built block of bedrooms and a separate lodge where food is served. It is in a rural setting beside a working canal and convenient for the Earth Centre, Doncaster, or the Dearne Valley with its nature reserves and leisure centre. Bedrooms are quiet, comfortable and equipped with many modern facilities.
ROOMS: 29 en suite (6 fmly) (14 GF) ⊗ in 21 bedrooms s £47.50-£52.50; d £47.50-£57.50 **FACILITIES:** STV **CONF:** Thtr 250 Class 170 Board 100 Del from £79 **SERVICES:** Lift **PARKING:** 155 **NOTES:** ✗ Civ Wed 200

MICHAEL WOOD MOTORWAY SERVICE AREA (M5), Gloucestershire Map 04 ST79

⌂ Days Inn Michael Wood
Michael Wood Service Area, Lower Wick GL11 6DD
☎ 01454 261513 📠 01454 269150
e-mail: michaelwood.hotel@welcomebreak.co.uk
web: www.welcomebreak.co.uk
Dir: *M5 northbound between junct 13 and 14*
This modern building offers accommodation in smart, spacious and well-equipped bedrooms, suitable for families and business travellers, and all with en suite bathrooms. Continental breakfast is available and other refreshments may be taken at the nearby family restaurant. For further details see the Hotel Groups page.
ROOMS: 38 en suite s £45-£55; d £45-£55 **CONF:** Board 10

MIDDLESBROUGH, North Yorkshire Map 19 NZ41

U The Highfield Hotel
335 Marton Rd TS4 2PA
☎ 01642 817638 📠 01642 821219
e-mail: info@thehighfieldhotel.co.uk
Dir: *A172 to Stokesley, right at rdbt, straight on at mini rdbt. Left at next rdbt onto A172 Marton Rd, hotel 150yds on right*
At the time of going to press, the star classification for this hotel was not confirmed. Please refer to the AA internet site www.theAA.com for current information.
ROOMS: 23 en suite (2 fmly) ⊗ in 10 bedrooms s £55-£75; d £65-£95 **LB FACILITIES:** STV **CONF:** Thtr 170 Class 100 Board 65 Del from £100 **PARKING:** 100 **NOTES:** ✗ ⊗ in restaurant Civ Wed 180

MIDDLETON, Greater Manchester Map 16 SD80

⌂ Premier Travel Inn Manchester (Middleton)
818 Manchester Old Rd, Rhodes M24 4RF
☎ 0870 9906406 📠 0870 9906407
web: www.premiertravelinn.com
Dir: *At M60/M62 junct 18 follow Manchester/Middleton signs. Exit M60 junct 19 take A576 towards Middleton*
High quality, modern budget accommodation ideal for both families and business travellers. Spacious, en suite bedrooms feature bath and shower, satellite TV and many have telephones and modem points. The adjacent family restaurant features a wide and varied menu. For further details consult the Hotel Groups page.
ROOMS: 42 en suite s £47.95-£50.95; d £47.95-£50.95 **CONF:** Thtr 60 Class 60

MIDDLETON-IN-TEESDALE, Co Durham Map 18 NY92

★★62% The Teesdale Hotel
Market Place DL12 0QG
☎ 01833 640264 📠 01833 640651
e-mail: john@falconerO.wanadoo.co.uk
Dir: *follow signs to Barnard Castle then to Teesdale on B6278 towards Highforce*
Located in the heart of the popular village, this family-run hotel offers a relaxed and friendly atmosphere. Bedrooms come in a variety of sizes, but all are comfortably equipped. There is a well-stocked lounge bar that is also popular with the locals and meals are available in the lounge bar or the restaurant.
ROOMS: 14 en suite (1 fmly) ⊗ in all bedrooms s fr £42.50; d fr £65 (incl. bkfst) **LB FACILITIES:** Xmas **PARKING:** 20 **NOTES:** ⊗ in restaurant

MIDDLETON STONEY, Oxfordshire Map 11 SP52

★★72% Jersey Arms
OX25 4AD
☎ 01869 343234 📠 01869 343565
e-mail: jerseyarms@bestwestern.co.uk
web: www.jerseyarms.co.uk
Dir: *on B430 10m N of Oxford, between junct 9 & 10 of M40*
With a history dating back to the 13th century, the Jersey Arms combines old-fashioned charm with contemporary style and elegance. The individually designed bedrooms are well equipped and comfortable. The lounge has an open fire, and the smartly refurbished spacious restaurant provides a calm atmosphere in which to enjoy the hotel's popular cuisine.
ROOMS: 6 en suite 14 annexe en suite (3 fmly) (9 GF) ⊗ in 6 bedrooms s £88-£99; d £98-£135 (incl. bkfst) **LB FACILITIES:** Xmas **CONF:** Board 20 Del from £130 **PARKING:** 55 **NOTES:** ✗ ⊗ in restaurant

M

MIDDLEWICH, Cheshire Map 15 SJ76

⌂ Travelodge
M6 Junction 18, A54 CW10 0JB
☎ 08700 850 950 📠 01606 738229
web: www.travelodge.co.uk
Dir: *A54 westbound off M6 junct 18*
Travelodge offers good quality, good value, modern accommodation. Ideal for families, the spacious, en suite bedrooms include remote-control TV, tea and coffee-making facilities and comfortable beds. Meals can be taken at the nearby family restaurant. For further details consult the Hotel Groups page.
ROOMS: 32 en suite s fr £26; d fr £26

MIDHURST, West Sussex Map 06 SU82

★★★73% ®® Spread Eagle Hotel and Health Spa
South St GU29 9NH
☎ 01730 816911 📠 01730 815668
e-mail: spreadeagle@hshotels.co.uk
web: www.hshotels.co.uk/spread/spreadeagle-main.htm
Dir: *from M25 junct 10 follow A3 S, exit A3 at Milford and follow A286 to Midhurst. Hotel adjacent to Market Square on South Street*
Offering accommodation since 1430, this historic property is full of character, evident in its sloping floors and inglenook fireplaces. Individually styled bedrooms provide modern comforts; those in the main house have oak panelling and include some spacious

continued on p396

MIDHURST, continued

feature rooms. The hotel also boasts a well-equipped spa and noteworthy food in the oak beamed restaurant.

Spread Eagle Hotel, Midhurst

ROOMS: 35 en suite 4 annexe en suite (8 GF) ⊗ in 6 bedrooms s £119-£194; d £138-£228 (incl. bkfst) **LB** **FACILITIES: Spa** STV Sauna Gym Jacuzzi Health & beauty treatment rooms Steam room Fitness trainer Xmas **CONF:** Thtr 80 Class 40 Board 34 Del from £128 **PARKING:** 75 **NOTES:** ⊗ in restaurant Civ Wed 80

★★★72% The Angel
North St GU29 9DN
☎ 01730 812421 01730 815928
e-mail: info@theangelmidhurst.co.uk
web: www.theangelmidhurst.co.uk
Dir: *on S side of A272 in centre of Midhurst*

Dating back to the 15th century, this charming hotel offers a relaxed homely atmosphere. Bedrooms are individually decorated with some, including a room for less able guests, situated in an adjacent annexe. Public areas boast a cosy bar complete with log fire, Gabrial's, a fine-dining restaurant and Halo, a contemporary brasserie.

ROOMS: 24 en suite 4 annexe en suite (2 GF) ⊗ in all bedrooms s £50-£80; d £150 (incl. bkfst) **LB** **FACILITIES:** STV ♫ Xmas **CONF:** Thtr 70 Class 40 Board 30 Del from £125 **PARKING:** 75 **NOTES:** ⊗ in restaurant Civ Wed 100

★★★69% Southdowns Country
Dumpford Ln, Trotton GU31 5JN
☎ 01730 821521 01730 821790
e-mail: reception@southdownshotel.com
web: www.southdownshotel.com
Dir: *on A272, after town turn left at Keepers Arms*

Best Western

Ideal for a relaxing break, this private hotel enjoys a secluded location with views over the Sussex countryside. It is a popular choice for weddings, due to its setting and spacious public areas. Some of the comfortable bedrooms overlook the grounds. Meals are available in the bar and in the more formal restaurant that offers dishes based on local produce.

ROOMS: 22 en suite (2 fmly) (2 GF) ⊗ in 12 bedrooms s £50-£180; d £60-£200 (incl. bkfst) **LB** **FACILITIES:** Sauna Xmas **CONF:** Thtr 100 Class 30 Board 30 Del from £85 **PARKING:** 70 **NOTES:** No children 10yrs ⊗ in restaurant Civ Wed 100

See advert under PETERSFIELD

Popped the question? Hotels with Civ wed in their entry are licensed for civil wedding ceremonies. Maximum numbers for the ceremony only are shown e.g. Civ wed 120

MIDSOMER NORTON, Somerset — Map 04 ST65

★★★72% Centurion
Charlton Ln BA3 4BD
☎ 01761 417711 01761 418357
e-mail: enquiries@centurionhotel.co.uk
web: www.centurionhotel.com
Dir: *off A367, 10m S of Bath*

This privately owned, purpose built hotel incorporates the adjacent Fosseway Country Club with its 9-hole golf course and other extensive leisure amenities. Bedrooms on ground floor level, including two for less able guests, are available, as are family bedded rooms. All bedrooms are non-smoking. Public areas include a choice of bars, an attractive lounge and a range of meeting/function rooms.

ROOMS: 44 en suite (4 fmly) (18 GF) ⊗ in all bedrooms s £70-£75; d £95-£115 (incl. bkfst) **LB** **FACILITIES: Spa** STV 9 Sauna Gym Jacuzzi Bowling green Sports field **CONF:** Thtr 180 Class 70 Board 50 Del from £120 **PARKING:** 100 **NOTES:** ⊗ in restaurant Closed 24 Dec-1 Jan Civ Wed 100

U The Moody Goose at The Old Priory
Church Square BA3 2HX
☎ 01761 416784 & 01761 410846 01761 417851
e-mail: info@theoldpriory.co.uk
Dir: *A362 for 1m left to Midsomer Norton High St to traffic lights turn right to small rdbt by St John's Church turn right then ahead for hotel*

At the time of going to press, the star classification for this hotel was not confirmed. Please refer to the AA internet site www.theAA.com for current information.

ROOMS: 7 en suite (2 fmly) ⊗ in all bedrooms s £75-£90; d £100-£135 (incl. bkfst) **CONF:** Thtr 20 Class 6 Board 12 **PARKING:** 14 **NOTES:** ⊗ in restaurant RS Sun

MILDENHALL, Suffolk — Map 12 TL77

★★★73% Riverside
Mill St IP28 7DP
☎ 01638 717274 01638 715997
e-mail: bookings@riverside-hotel.net
Dir: *from A11 at Fiveways rdbt take A1101 in Mildenhall Town. Left at mini rdbt along High St. Hotel last building on left before bridge*

THE CIRCLE Selected Individual Hotels GREAT BRITAIN

An 18th-century red brick building situated in the heart of this charming town centre on the banks of the River Lark. Public rooms include a smart restaurant, which overlooks the river and the attractive gardens to the rear. The smartly decorated bedrooms have co-ordinated soft furnishings and many thoughtful touches.

ROOMS: 17 en suite 6 annexe en suite (4 fmly) (4 GF) s £69.50-£125; d £95-£150 (incl. bkfst) **LB** **FACILITIES:** Fishing Rowing boat hire ♫ Xmas **CONF:** BC Thtr 150 Class 60 Board 40 **SERVICES:** Lift **PARKING:** 50 **NOTES:** Civ Wed 120

★★★68% The Smoke House
Beck Row IP28 8DH
☎ 01638 713223 📠 01638 712202
e-mail: enquiries@smoke-house.co.uk
web: www.smoke-house.co.uk
Dir: *A1101 into Mildenhall, follow Beck Row signs. Hotel after mini rdbt through Beck Row on right*

An extended inn situated just a short drive from the town centre and ideally placed for touring the Suffolk countryside. Public areas have been sympathetically restored and retain much of their original character. The spacious bedrooms are attractively decorated and well equipped. Facilities include a shopping mall.
ROOMS: 94 en suite 2 annexe en suite (96 GF) ⊗ in 20 bedrooms s £60-£98; d £85-£140 (incl. bkfst) **LB FACILITIES:** ♫ Xmas **CONF:** Thtr 120 Class 80 Board 50 Del £100 **PARKING:** 100 **NOTES:** ✈ ⊗ in restaurant

See advert on this page

MILFORD ON SEA, Hampshire

Map 05 SZ29

Top Hotel

★★★ ◎◎ Westover Hall
Park Ln SO41 0PT
☎ 01590 643044 📠 01590 644490
e-mail: info@westoverhallhotel.com
web: www.westoverhallhotel.com
Dir: *M3 & M27 W onto A337 to Lymington. Follow signs to Milford-on-Sea onto B3058. Hotel outside village centre towards cliff*

Just a few moments' walk from the beach and boasting uninterrupted views across Christchurch Bay to the Isle of Wight in the distance, this late-Victorian mansion offers a relaxed, informal and friendly atmosphere together with efficient standards of hospitality and service. Each of the bedrooms has been decorated with flair and style. Architectural delights include dramatic stained-glass windows, extensive oak panelling and a galleried entrance hall. The cuisine is prepared with much care and attention to detail.
ROOMS: 12 en suite (1 fmly) ⊗ in all bedrooms **FACILITIES:** Beach Hut Xmas **CONF:** Thtr 35 Class 20 Board 20 **PARKING:** 50 **NOTES:** No children 5yrs ⊗ in restaurant Civ Wed 50

See advert under LYMINGTON

★★★72% ◎ South Lawn
Lymington Rd SO41 0RF
☎ 01590 643911 📠 01590 644820
e-mail: enquiries@southlawn.co.uk
Dir: *off A337 at Everton onto B3058 to Milford-on-Sea. Hotel 0.5m on left*

Peacefully located, this former dower house, now under new ownership, offers attentive and friendly service. The hotel is situated in four acres of well-tended grounds and is close to the sea. Bedrooms are spacious, include welcome extras and are attractively decorated; many enjoying delightful views over the

continued on p398

MILFORD ON SEA, continued

garden. The bright dining room serves a varied range of carefully prepared local produce.
ROOMS: 24 en suite (3 GF) ⊗ in all bedrooms s £60-£85; d £100-£170 (incl. bkfst & dinner) **LB** **FACILITIES:** Xmas **CONF:** BC Thtr 120 Class 60 Board 60 Del from £95 **PARKING:** 60 **NOTES:** No dogs No children 7yrs ⊗ in restaurant Closed 3-17 Jan Civ Wed 120

See advert under LYMINGTON

MILTON COMMON, Oxfordshire — Map 05 SP60

★★★★77% The Oxford Belfry

OX9 2JW
☎ 01844 279381 Fax 01844 279624
e-mail: oxfordbelfry@marstonhotels.com
web: www.marstonhotels.com
Dir: *M40 junct 7 onto A329 to Thame. Left onto A40 by Three Pigeons pub. Hotel 300yds on right*

This modern hotel has a relatively rural location and enjoys lovely views of the countryside to the rear. The hotel is built around two very attractive courtyards and has a number of lounges and conference rooms, as well as indoor leisure facilities and outdoor tennis courts. Bedrooms are large and feature a range of extras.
ROOMS: 130 en suite (10 fmly) ⊗ in 72 bedrooms s fr £129; d fr £166 (incl. bkfst) **LB** **FACILITIES:** STV Sauna Solarium Gym Xmas **CONF:** Thtr 300 Class 180 Board 100 Del from £205 **SERVICES:** Lift **PARKING:** 250 **NOTES:** No dogs ⊗ in restaurant Civ Wed 110

MILTON KEYNES, Buckinghamshire — Map 11 SP83

See also Aspley Guise & Flitwick

★★★70% Novotel Milton Keynes

Saxon St, Layburn Court, Heelands MK13 7RA
☎ 01908 322212 Fax 01908 322235
e-mail: H3272@accor-hotels.com
web: www.novotel.com
Dir: *M1 junct 14, follow Childsway signs towards city centre. Turn right into Saxon Way, continue straight across all rdbts hotel on left*
Contemporary in style, this purpose-built hotel is situated on the outskirts of the town, just a few minutes' drive from the centre and mainline railway station. Bedrooms provide ample workspace and a good range of facilities for the modern traveller, and public rooms include a children's play area and indoor leisure centre. Novotel - AA Hotel Group of the Year 2005-6.
ROOMS: 124 en suite (40 fmly) (40 GF) ⊗ in 105 bedrooms s fr £129; d fr £129 **LB** **FACILITIES:** STV Sauna Gym Steam bath **CONF:** Thtr 120 Class 75 Board 40 Del £169 **SERVICES:** Lift **PARKING:** 130 **NOTES:** Civ Wed 100

★★★70% Parkside

Newport Rd, Woughton on the Green MK6 3LR
☎ 01908 661919 Fax 01908 676186
e-mail: parkside@macdonald-hotels.co.uk
web: www.macdonald-hotels.co.uk

Situated in five acres of landscaped grounds in a peaceful village setting, this hotel is only five minutes' drive from the centre of town. Bedrooms are divided between executive rooms in the main house and standard rooms in the adjacent coach house. Public rooms include a range of meeting rooms, Lanes restaurant and Strollers bar.
ROOMS: 49 rms (38 en suite) (1 fmly) (19 GF) ⊗ in 15 bedrooms s £105-£135; d £115-£145 **FACILITIES:** STV Discounted entry to local health & fitness club Xmas **CONF:** Thtr 110 Class 60 Board 50 Del from £125 **PARKING:** 75 **NOTES:** ⊗ in restaurant Civ Wed 120

★★★69% Courtyard by Marriott Milton Keynes

London Rd, Newport Pagnell MK16 0JA
☎ 01908 613688 Fax 01908 617335
e-mail: events.mkcourtyard@kewgreen.co.uk
web: www.kewgreen.co.uk
Dir: *M1 junct 14, follow signs for A509 (Newport Pagnell), hotel 0.5m on right*

Ideally situated for access to the M1 motorway, town centre and local attractions, this former Georgian coach house enjoys a pleasant and peaceful rural location. The bedrooms are comfortable and well appointed. Public rooms include a small fitness room, modern bar and conservatory restaurant overlooking the courtyard.
ROOMS: 53 en suite (9 fmly) (22 GF) ⊗ in 36 bedrooms s £72-£134; d £72-£152 (incl. bkfst) **LB** **FACILITIES:** STV Gym Xmas **CONF:** Thtr 200 Class 90 Board 50 Del £145 **PARKING:** 160 **NOTES:** No dogs ⊗ in restaurant Civ Wed 120

★★★65% **Quality Hotel & Suites Milton Keynes**
Monks Way, Two Mile Ash MK8 8LY
☎ 01908 561666 🖷 01908 568303
e-mail: enquiries@hotels-milton-keynes.com
web: www.choicehotelseurope.com
Dir: *junct of A5/A422*
Bedrooms at this purpose-built hotel are particularly well-equipped many with air conditioning being added. There are also a number of suites with fax machines and kitchenettes. Eating options include an all-day room and lounge service in addition to the restaurant.
ROOMS: 88 en suite (15 fmly) ⊗ in 44 bedrooms s £59.50-£79.50; d £177-£137 **LB** **FACILITIES:** STV ⛆ supervised Sauna Solarium Gym Jacuzzi Steam room, Whirlpool spa **CONF:** BC Thtr 120 Class 50 Board 50 Del from £95 **SERVICES:** air con **PARKING:** 200 **NOTES:** ✗ ⊗ in restaurant Civ Wed 100

★★70% **Different Drummer**
94 High St, Stony Stratford MK11 1AH
☎ 01908 564733 🖷 01908 260646
e-mail: info@hoteldifferentdrummer.co.uk
web: www.hoteldifferentdrummer.co.uk

This attractive hotel located on the high street in historic Stony Stratford offers a genuine welcome to its guests. The oak-panelled restaurant is a popular dining venue and offers an Italian-style menu. Bedrooms are generally spacious and well equipped. A contemporary bar has now been added, and provides a further dining option.
ROOMS: 19 en suite 4 annexe en suite (1 fmly) (3 GF) ⊗ in 15 bedrooms s £49-£110; d £77-£140 (incl. bkfst) **FACILITIES:** STV **PARKING:** 4 **NOTES:** ✗

★★68% **Swan Revived**
High St, Newport Pagnell MK16 8AR
☎ 01908 610565 🖷 01908 210995
e-mail: swanrevived@btinternet.com
web: www.swanrevived.co.uk
Dir: *M1 junct 14 onto A509 then B526 into Newport Pagnell for 2m. Hotel on High St*
Once a coaching inn, this hotel dates from 17th century, occupying a prime location in the centre of town. Well-appointed bedrooms are mostly spacious, individually styled and have good levels of comfort. Public areas include a popular bar and a restaurant offering a variety of freshly prepared dishes.

ROOMS: 42 en suite (2 fmly) s £50-£84; d £68-£98 (incl. bkfst) **LB** **FACILITIES:** STV **CONF:** Thtr 70 Class 30 Board 28 Del from £75 **SERVICES:** Lift **PARKING:** 18 **NOTES:** ⊗ in restaurant RS 25 Dec-1 Jan Civ Wed 65

⌂ **Campanile**
40 Penn Rd, Fenny Stratford, Bletchley MK2 2AU
☎ 01908 649819 🖷 01908 649818
e-mail: mk@campanile-hotels.com
web: www.envergure.fr
Dir: *M1 junct 14, follow A4146 to A5. Southbound on A5. 4th exit at 1st rdbt to Fenny Stratford. Hotel 500yds on left*

This modern building offers accommodation in smart, well-equipped bedrooms, all with en suite bathrooms. Refreshments may be taken at the informal Bistro. For further details consult the Hotel Groups page.
ROOMS: 80 en suite s £38.50-£100 **CONF:** Thtr 35 Class 40 Board 35 Del from £85

⌂ **Innkeeper's Lodge Milton Keynes**
Burchard Crescent, Shenley Church End MK5 6HQ
☎ 01908 505467
web: www.innkeeperslodge.com
A growing concept in the travel accommodation market. Smart rooms meet essential business requirements but also have home comforts. Dining options include all-day menus plus the added advantage of breakfast, which is included in the room price. For further details consult the Hotel Groups page.
ROOMS: 50 en suite s £45-£69.95; d £45-£69.95 **CONF:** Thtr 100 Class 40 Board 60

MILTON KEYNES, continued

⇧ Premier Travel Inn Milton Keynes Central

Secklow Gate West MK9 3BZ
☎ 08701 977184 🖹 01908 607481
web: www.premiertravelinn.com
Dir: *from M1 junct 14 follow H6 route over 6 rdbts, at 7th (called Sth Secklow) turn right, Inn on left*
High quality, modern budget accommodation ideal for both families and business travellers. Spacious, en suite bedrooms feature bath and shower, satellite TV and many have telephones and modem points. The adjacent family restaurant features a wide and varied menu. For further details consult the Hotel Groups page.
ROOMS: 38 en suite s £55.95-£57.95; d £55.95-£57.95 **CONF:** Thtr 16

⇧ Premier Travel Inn Milton Keynes Central (SW)

Shirwell Crescent, Furzton MK4 1GA
☎ 0870 9906396 🖹 0870 9906397
web: www.premiertravelinn.com
Dir: *Exit M1 junct 14 take A509 to Milton Keynes. Straight over 8 rdbts, at 9th (North Grafton) turn left onto V6. Right at next onto H7. Over The Bowl rdbt and hotel on left*
High quality, modern budget accommodation ideal for both families and business travellers. Spacious, en suite bedrooms feature bath and shower, satellite TV and many have telephones and modem points. The adjacent family restaurant features a wide and varied menu. For further details consult the Hotel Groups page.
ROOMS: 120 en suite s £53.95-£57.95; d £53.95-£57.95 **CONF:** Thtr 10 Class 10 Board 10

M

⇧ Premier Travel Inn Milton Keynes East

Willen Lake, Brickhill St MK15 9HQ
☎ 08701 977185 🖹 01908 678561
web: www.premiertravelinn.com
Dir: *M1 junct 14 follow H6 Childsway. Turn right at 3rd rdbt into Brickhill St. Right at 1st mini rdbt, Inn 1st left*
High quality, modern budget accommodation ideal for both families and business travellers. Spacious, en suite bedrooms feature bath and shower, satellite TV and many have telephones and modem points. The adjacent family restaurant features a wide and varied menu. For further details consult the Hotel Groups page.
ROOMS: 41 en suite s £47.95-£50.95; d £47.95-£50.95

⇧ Premier Travel Inn Milton Keynes South

Bletcham Way, Caldecotte MK7 8HP
☎ 0870 9906558 🖹 0870 9906559
web: www.premiertravelinn.com
Dir: *Exit M1 junct 14. Right towards Milton Keynes on H6 Childs Way. Straight over 2 rdbts. Left at 3rd onto V10 Brickhill St. Straight over 5 rdbts, at 6th turn right onto H10 Bletcham Way*
High quality, modern budget accommodation ideal for both families and business travellers. Spacious, en suite bedrooms feature bath and shower, satellite TV and many have telephones and modem points. The adjacent family restaurant features a wide and varied menu. For further details consult the Hotel Groups page.
ROOMS: 40 en suite s £47.95-£50.95; d £47.95-£50.95 **CONF:** Board 10

⇧ Travelodge

109 Grafton Gate MK9 1AL
☎ 08700 850 950 🖹 01908 241737
web: www.travelodge.co.uk
Dir: *M1 junct 14 to city centre, H6 Childs Ways to junct V6 Grafton Gate, on right after rail station*
Travelodge offers good quality, good value, modern accommodation. Ideal for families, the spacious, en suite bedrooms include remote-control TV, tea and coffee-making facilities and comfortable beds. Meals can be taken at the nearby family restaurant. For further details consult the Hotel Groups page.
ROOMS: 80 en suite s fr £26; d fr £26

⇧ Travelodge Milton Keynes North (Old Stratford)

Old Stratford Roundabout MK19 6AQ
☎ 08700 850 950 🖹 01908 260802
web: www.travelodge.co.uk
Travelodge offers good quality, good value, modern accommodation. Ideal for families, the spacious, en suite bedrooms include remote-control TV, tea and coffee-making facilities and comfortable beds. Meals can be taken at the nearby family restaurant. For further details consult the Hotel Groups page.
ROOMS: 33 en suite s fr £26; d fr £26

MINEHEAD, Somerset — Map 03 SS94

★★★64% Northfield

Northfield Rd TA24 5PU
☎ 01643 705155 & 0845 1302678
🖹 01643 707715
e-mail: reservations@northfield-hotel.co.uk
web: www.northfield-hotel.co.uk
Dir: *M5 junct 23, follow A38 to Bridgwater and join A39 to Minehead*
Located conveniently close to the town centre and the seafront, this hotel is set in delightfully maintained gardens and has a loyal following. A range of comfortable sitting rooms and leisure facilities, including an indoor, heated pool is provided. A fixed-price menu is served every evening in the oak-panelled dining room. The attractively co-ordinated bedrooms vary in size and are equipped to a good standard.
ROOMS: 28 en suite (7 fmly) s £55-£84; d £110-£160 (incl. bkfst & dinner) **LB** **FACILITIES:** STV Gym Putt green Jacuzzi Steam room Xmas **CONF:** BC Thtr 70 Class 45 Board 30 Del from £60
SERVICES: Lift **PARKING:** 44 **NOTES:** ⊗ in restaurant

★★78% Channel House

Church Path TA24 5QG
☎ 01643 703229 🖹 01643 708925
e-mail: channel.house@virgin.net
web: www.channelhouse.co.uk
Dir: *from A39 right at rdbt to seafront, then left onto promenade. 1st right, 1st left to Blenheim Gdns and 1st right into Northfield Rd*

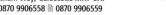

This charming, well-run hotel offers relaxing and tranquil surroundings, yet is only a short walk from the town centre. The South West coastal path starts from the hotel's 2-acre gardens. Many of the exceptionally well-equipped bedrooms benefit from wonderful views. The dining room is the venue for imaginative

continued

menus using the best of local produce. The hotel is totally non-smoking.
ROOMS: 8 en suite (1 fmly) ⊗ in all bedrooms s £83-£96; d £136-£162 (incl. bkfst & dinner) **LB** **FACILITIES:** Xmas **SERVICES:** air con **PARKING:** 10 **NOTES:** ✗ No children 15yrs ⊗ in restaurant Closed 5 Nov-18 Mar

See advert on this page

★★76% Alcombe House
Bircham Rd, Alcombe TA24 6BG
☎ 01643 705130 📠 01643 705130
e-mail: alcombe.house@virgin.net
web: www.alcombehouse.co.uk
Located midway between Minehead and Dunster in an ideal situation on the coastal fringe of the Exmoor National Park, this Grade II listed Georgian hotel offers a delightful combination of efficient service and genuine hospitality delivered by the very welcoming resident proprietors. Public areas include a comfortable lounge and a candlelit dining room where an enjoyable range of carefully prepared local produce is offered from a daily-changing menu.
ROOMS: 7 en suite ⊗ in all bedrooms s £40; d £60 (incl. bkfst) **LB** **FACILITIES:** Xmas **PARKING:** 9 **NOTES:** No children 15yrs ⊗ in restaurant Closed 8 Nov-18 Mar

MONK FRYSTON, North Yorkshire — Map 16 SE52

★★★74% Monk Fryston Hall
LS25 5DU
☎ 01977 682369 📠 01977 683544
e-mail: reception@monkfryston-hotel.co.uk
web: www.monkfrystonhotel.co.uk
Dir: *A1/A63 junct towards Selby. Left side in centre of Monk Fryston*
This delightful 16th-century mansion house enjoys a peaceful location in 30 acres of grounds, yet is only minutes' drive from the A1. Many original features have been retained and the public rooms are furnished with antique and period pieces. Bedrooms are individually styled and thoughtfully equipped for both business and leisure guests.
ROOMS: 29 en suite (2 fmly) (5 GF) ⊗ in 20 bedrooms s £95-£105; d £120-£175 (incl. bkfst) **LB** **FACILITIES:** STV Xmas **CONF:** Thtr 50 Class 20 Board 20 Del from £140 **PARKING:** 80 **NOTES:** ⊗ in restaurant Civ Wed 58

MORCOTT, Rutland — Map 11 SK90

⌂ Travelodge Uppingham
Uppingham LE15 8SA
☎ 08700 850 950 📠 01572 747719
web: www.travelodge.co.uk
Dir: *on A47, eastbound*
Travelodge offers good quality, good value, modern accommodation. Ideal for families, the spacious, en suite bedrooms include remote-control TV, tea and coffee-making facilities and comfortable beds. Meals can be taken at the nearby family restaurant. For further details consult the Hotel Groups page.
ROOMS: 40 en suite s fr £26; d fr £26

MORDEN, Greater London
See LONDON SECTION plan 1 D1

⌂ Travelodge London Wimbledon
Epsom Rd SM4 5PH
☎ 08700 850 950 📠 020 8640 8227
web: www.travelodge.co.uk
Dir: *on A24*
Travelodge offers good quality, good value, modern

continued

accommodation. Ideal for families, the spacious, en suite bedrooms include remote-control TV, tea and coffee-making facilities and comfortable beds. Meals can be taken at the nearby family restaurant. For further details consult the Hotel Groups page.
ROOMS: 32 en suite s fr £26; d fr £26

MORECAMBE, Lancashire — Map 18 SD46

★★★65% Clarendon
76 Marine Rd West, West End Promenade LA4 4EP
☎ 01524 410180 📠 01524 421616
e-mail: clarendon@mitchellshotels.co.uk
Dir: *M6 junct 34 follow Morecambe signs. At rdbt with 'The Shrimp' on corner 1st exit to Westgate, follow to seafront. Right at traffic lights, hotel 3rd block along*
A seafront hotel that is well maintained throughout, offering bright and cheerful public areas and smartly appointed bedrooms all with fully tiled bathrooms.
ROOMS: 29 en suite (4 fmly) ⊗ in 10 bedrooms s £60; d £90 (incl. bkfst) **LB** **FACILITIES:** Xmas **CONF:** Thtr 90 Class 40 Board 40 Del from £75 **SERVICES:** Lift **PARKING:** 22 **NOTES:** ⊗ in restaurant Civ Wed 60

★★★63% Elms
Bare Village LA4 6DD
☎ 01524 411501 📠 01524 831979
Dir: *Exit M6 junct 34. Follow signs to Morecambe to large rdbt. 4th exit into Hall Drive which becomes Bare Lane. Follow over railway crossing. Hotel 200yds on right.*
This long-established hotel lies just off the North Promenade and is popular with business and leisure guests. Public rooms include a

continued on p402

MORECAMBE, continued

spacious lounge bar, a classical style restaurant, function facilities and a pub in the grounds.
ROOMS: 39 en suite (3 fmly) ⊗ in 180 bedrooms s £45-£55; d £70-£80 (incl. bkfst) **LB** **FACILITIES:** STV Xmas **CONF:** Thtr 200 Class 72 Board 60 Del from £75 **SERVICES:** Lift **PARKING:** 80 **NOTES:** ⊗ in restaurant Civ Wed 90

MORETON, Merseyside — Map 15 SJ28

★★★69% Leasowe Castle

Leasowe Rd CH46 3RF
☎ 0151 606 9191 📠 0151 678 5551
e-mail: reservations@leasowecastle.com
web: www.leasowecastle.com
Dir: *M53 junct 1, 1st exit from rdbt, the take A551. Hotel 0.75m on right*
Located adjacent to Leasowe Golf Course and within easy reach of Liverpool, Chester and all of the Wirral's attractions, this historic hotel dates back to 1592. Bedrooms are smartly appointed and well equipped, many enjoying ocean views. Public areas retain many original features. Weddings and functions are well catered for.
ROOMS: 47 en suite (3 fmly) ⊗ in 3 bedrooms s £65-£85; d £75-£175 (incl. bkfst) **LB** **FACILITIES:** STV Sauna Gym Water sports, Sea Fishing, Sailing, Health club (mid Apr 2004) Xmas **CONF:** Thtr 400 Class 200 Board 80 Del from £99 **SERVICES:** Lift **PARKING:** 200 **NOTES:** ⊗ in restaurant Civ Wed 250

MORETONHAMPSTEAD, Devon — Map 03 SX78

M

★★★★★70% Bovey Castle

TQ13 8RE
☎ 01647 445000 📠 01647 440961
e-mail: enquiries@boveycastle.com
web: www.boveycastle.com
Dir: *2m from Moretonhampstead towards Princetown on B3212*
Set within 270 acres of magnificent grounds and with stunning views of the surrounding Dartmoor countryside, this Jacobean-style mansion offers a range of country pursuits ranging from angling to a championship golf course. Bedrooms are particularly spacious and many enjoy superb views. Following an extensive refurbishment the Castle has been returned to its art deco inspired glory.
ROOMS: 60 en suite 5 annexe en suite (5 fmly) (3 GF) ⊗ in all bedrooms s £175-£1762; d £212-£1762 **FACILITIES: Spa** STV 18 Fishing Riding Snooker Sauna Gym Putt green Jacuzzi clay pigeon shooting, archery, fly-fishing ♫ ch fac Xmas **CONF:** BC Thtr 120 Class 84 Board 48 Del from £290 **SERVICES:** Lift **PARKING:** 150 **NOTES:** ⊗ in restaurant Civ Wed 100

★★★67% The White Hart Hotel

The Square TQ13 8NF
☎ 01647 441340 📠 01647 441341
e-mail: whitehart1600@aol.com
Dir: *A30 towards Oakhampton. At Widdon Down take A382 for Mortonhampstead*
Dating back to the 1700s, this former coaching inn is located on the edge of Dartmoor. A relaxed and friendly atmosphere prevails, with the young staff providing an effective level of service. Comfortable bedrooms that have a contemporary feel, are well equipped. Guests have the choice of dining in either the restaurant or more informally in the bar. An added bonus for guests, is the use of Bovey Castle's golf and leisure facilities.
ROOMS: 20 en suite ⊗ in all bedrooms s £45-£55; d £70-£90 (incl. bkfst) **LB** **FACILITIES:** ♫ **CONF:** Thtr 60 Class 30 Board 30 Del from £95 **NOTES:** ⊗ in restaurant Civ Wed 50

MORETON-IN-MARSH, Gloucestershire — Map 10 SP23

★★★79% Manor House

CLASSIC BRITISH

High St GL56 0LJ
☎ 01608 650501 📠 01608 651481
e-mail: info@manorhousehotel.info
Dir: *off A429 at south end of town. Take East St off High St, hotel car park 3rd on right*
Dating back to the 16th century, this charming Cotswold coaching inn retains much of its original character with stone walls, impressive fireplaces and a relaxed, country-house atmosphere. Bedrooms vary in size and reflect the individuality of the building; all are well equipped and some are particularly opulent. Comfortable public areas include the newly refurbished Mulberry Restaurant where dinner should not be missed.
ROOMS: 35 en suite 3 annexe en suite (3 fmly) ⊗ in all bedrooms s £115-£180; d £135-£255 (incl. bkfst) **LB** **FACILITIES:** Putt green Xmas **CONF:** Thtr 120 Class 48 Board 54 Del £150 **SERVICES:** Lift **PARKING:** 24 **NOTES:** ⊗ in restaurant Civ Wed 120

★★★70% Redesdale Arms

High St GL56 0AW
☎ 01608 650308 📠 01608 651843
e-mail: info@redesdalearms.co.uk
Dir: *on A429, 1km from train station*
This fine old inn has played a central role in this town for centuries. Traditional features combine successfully with contemporary comforts. Bedrooms are split between the main building and the former stables, but all have high standards of comfort. Guests can choose to dine either in the stylish restaurant or conservatory.
ROOMS: 8 en suite 10 annexe en suite (2 fmly) (5 GF) ⊗ in all bedrooms s £60-£85; d £65-£120 (incl. bkfst) **FACILITIES:** STV Xmas **PARKING:** 14 **NOTES:** ⊗ in restaurant

★★63% *White Hart Royal*

OLD ENGLISH INNS

High St GL56 0BA
☎ 01608 650731 📠 01608 650880
web: www.oldenglish.co.uk
Dir: *on A429 in town centre*
This Cotswold coaching inn dates back to the 17th century and once provided a hiding place for Charles I. Much of the original character has been retained with flagstone floors, a cobbled entrance hall and a feature fireplace. Bedrooms are brightly decorated and comfortably appointed.
ROOMS: 19 en suite (2 fmly) **FACILITIES:** STV **CONF:** Thtr 80 **PARKING:** 20 **NOTES:** ⊗ in restaurant

MORLEY, Derbyshire

U The Morley Hayes Hotel

Main Rd DE7 6DG
☎ 01332 780480 📠 01332 781094
e-mail: hotel@morleyhayes.com
Dir: *4m N of Derby on A608*
At the time of going to press, the star classification for this hotel was not confirmed. Please refer to the AA internet site www.theAA.com for current information.
ROOMS: 32 en suite (4 fmly) (15 GF) ⊗ in all bedrooms s £105-£210; d £120-£225 (incl. bkfst) **FACILITIES:** STV **CONF:** Thtr 165 Class 130 Board 122 Del £145 **SERVICES:** Lift air con **PARKING:** 245 **NOTES:** ⊗ in restaurant Civ Wed 90

GF indicates the number of bedrooms at ground level

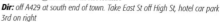

MORLEY, West Yorkshire Map 19 SE22

★★67% The Old Vicarage
Bruntcliffe Rd LS27 0JZ
☎ 0113 253 2174 📠 0113 253 3549
e-mail: oldvicmorley@aol.com
web: www.oldvicaragehotel.co.uk
Dir: *M62 junct 27, A650 towards Wakefield. Hotel on left adjacent to St Andrews Church*
A warm welcome awaits guests at this extended Victorian vicarage. The bedrooms are split between the main house and modern extension - all offer a range of extra facilities. There is a cosy lounge with honesty bar and hearty meals are served in the pleasant dining room. Private parking is provided.
ROOMS: 22 en suite (1 fmly) (2 GF) ⊗ in 15 bedrooms s £34-£54.50; d £55-£62 (incl. bkfst) **PARKING:** 22 **NOTES:** ✈ ⊗ in restaurant

MORPETH, Northumberland Map 21 NZ18

★★★74% ❀❀ *Linden Hall*
NE65 8XF
☎ 01670 500000 📠 01670 500001
e-mail: stay@lindenhall.co.uk
web: www.macdonald-hotels.co.uk
(For full entry see Longhorsley)

MOUSEHOLE, Cornwall & Isles of Scilly Map 02 SW42

★★73% ❀ Old Coastguard Hotel
The Parade TR19 6PR
☎ 01736 731222 📠 01736 731720
e-mail: bookings@oldcoastguardhotel.co.uk
web: www.oldcoastguardhotel.co.uk
Dir: *A30 to Penzance, coast road to Newlyn then Mousehole. 1st building on left on entering village*

A place to relax and unwind. The views are magnificent and the staff are friendly and provide good service. Bedrooms are bright and stylish; some have sea views and balconies. Guests can dine in the restaurant, or in summer months, alfresco on the terrace, and fish is fresh from the nearby Newlyn markets.
ROOMS: 14 en suite 7 annexe en suite (2 fmly) s £35-£80; d £80-£100 (incl. bkfst) **LB** **FACILITIES:** Sub-tropical garden Xmas **PARKING:** 12 **NOTES:** ✈ ⊗ in restaurant

> Late for dinner? Quality standards mean that last orders for dinner vary according to star rating and should be no earlier than: ★★ 7.00pm ★★★ 8:00pm ★★★★ 9:00pm ★★★★★ 10:00pm

Restaurant with Rooms

❀❀ *The Cornish Range Restaurant with Rooms*
6 Chapel St TR19 6BD
☎ 01736 731488
e-mail: info@cornishrange.co.uk
web: www.cornishrange.co.uk
Dir: *Follow coast road through Newlyn into Mousehole. Along harbour past Ship Inn, turn sharp right, then left . Restaurant on right*
This charming restaurant with rooms is a memorable place to eat and stay. Comfortable, stylish rooms, with delightful Cornish handmade furnishings, and attentive, friendly service create a relaxing environment. Interesting and accurate cuisine relies heavily on local freshly landed fish and shellfish, as well as local meat and poultry and the freshest fruit and vegetables.
ROOMS: 3 en suite **NOTES:** Closed Mon & Tue in winter and 26 Dec & 1 Jan

MUCH BIRCH, Herefordshire Map 10 SO53

★★★66% Pilgrim
Ross Rd HR2 8HJ
☎ 01981 540742 📠 01981 540620
e-mail: stay@pilgrimhotel.co.uk
web: www.pilgrimhotel.co.uk
Dir: *on A49 6m from Ross-on-Wye, 5m from Hereford*
This much-extended former rectory is set back from the A49 and has sweeping views over the surrounding countryside. The extensive grounds contain a pitch and putt course. Privately owned and personally run, it provides accommodation that includes ground floor and four-poster rooms. Public areas comprise of a restful lounge, a traditionally furnished restaurant and a pleasant bar.
ROOMS: 20 en suite (3 fmly) (8 GF) ⊗ in 12 bedrooms s £65-£85; d £80-£130 (incl. bkfst) **LB** **FACILITIES:** ⛳ 3 ✂ ⛳ Pitch & putt, Badminton Xmas **CONF:** Thtr 45 Class 45 Board 25 Del £99 **PARKING:** 42 **NOTES:** ⊗ in restaurant

MUCH WENLOCK, Shropshire Map 10 SO69

★★★72% ❀ *Raven*
Barrow St TF13 6EN
☎ 01952 727251 📠 01952 728416
e-mail: enquiry@ravenhotel.com
web: www.ravenhotel.com
Dir: *M54 junct 4 or 5, take A442 S, then A4169 to Much Wenlock*
This town centre hotel is spread across several historic buildings with a 17th-century coaching inn at its centre. Accommodation is well furnished and equipped to offer modern comfort, with some ground floor rooms. Public areas feature an interesting collection of prints and memorabilia connected with the modern-day Olympic Games, the idea for which was interestingly born in Much Wenlock.
ROOMS: 8 en suite 7 annexe en suite **FACILITIES:** STV Beauty salon **CONF:** Thtr 16 Board 16 **PARKING:** 30 **NOTES:** ✈ ⊗ in restaurant

★★65% Gaskell Arms
Bourton Rd TF13 6AQ
☎ 01952 727212 📠 01952 728505
e-mail: maxine@gaskellarms.co.uk
web: www.gaskellarms.co.uk
Dir: *from M6 turn off at junct 10A onto M54. Take junct 4 off M54 follow signs for Ironbridge/ Much Wenlock*
This 17th-century former coaching inn has exposed beams and log fires in the public areas. In addition to the lounge bar and restaurant, featuring a wide range of meals and snacks, there is a small bar that proves popular with locals. Well-maintained

continued on p404

MUCH WENLOCK, continued

bedrooms, which vary in size, are attractively furnished. Family rooms and bedrooms on ground floor level are both available.

Gaskell Arms, Much Wenlock

ROOMS: 16 rms (14 en suite) (3 fmly) (5 GF) ⊗ in 5 bedrooms s £55-£65; d £75-£95 (incl. bkfst) **LB** **FACILITIES:** Walking, horse riding **PARKING:** 41 **NOTES:** ⊗ in restaurant

---

MUDEFORD See Christchurch

MULLION, Cornwall & Isles of Scilly — Map 02 SW61

★★★71% Polurrian

TR12 7EN
☎ 01326 240421 📠 01326 240083
e-mail: relax@polurrianhotel.com
Dir: *A30 onto A3076 to Truro. Follow signs for Helston on A39 then A394 to The Lizard and Mullion*

This long-established hotel (now under new ownership) is set in 12 acres of landscaped gardens, 300 feet above the sea. The spectacular views over Polurrian Cove will remain long in the memory, along with the wonderful sunsets. Public areas are spacious and comfortable, and the bedrooms are individually styled. There is a well-equipped leisure centre.

ROOMS: 39 en suite (22 fmly) s £80-£180; d £130-£280 (incl. bkfst & dinner) **LB** **FACILITIES:** STV Squash Snooker Sauna Solarium Gym Putt green Jacuzzi Cricket net Whirlpool Mountain bikes Surfing Body boarding Xmas **CONF:** Thtr 100 Class 60 Board 30 Del from £80 **PARKING:** 80 **NOTES:** ⊗ in restaurant Civ Wed 100

See advert on opposite page

★★★70% Mullion Cove Hotel

TR12 7EP
☎ 01326 240328 📠 01326 240998
e-mail: mullion.cove@btinternet.com web: www.mullioncove.com
Dir: *from Helston follow signs to The Lizard, right at Mullion Holiday Park. Through village, left for Cove. Then right and hotel on top of hill*

Built at the turn of the last century and set high above the working harbour of Mullion, this hotel has spectacular views, and seaward facing rooms are always popular. The stylish restaurant offers some carefully prepared dishes using local produce. After dinner guests might like to relax in one of the elegant lounges.

ROOMS: 30 en suite (7 fmly) (3 GF) s £77-£212; d £96-£300 (incl. bkfst & dinner) **LB** **FACILITIES:** Sauna Solarium Beauty treatments Xmas **PARKING:** 60 **NOTES:** ⊗ in restaurant

---

MUNDESLEY, Norfolk — Map 13 TG33

★★68% Manor Hotel

Beach Rd NR11 8BG
☎ 01263 720309 📠 01263 721731
e-mail: manormundesley@aol.com
web: www.northnorfolk.co.uk/mundesleymanor
Dir: *B1150 Norwich-North Walsham, then follow coastal route & Mundesley signs*

An imposing Victorian property situated in an elevated position with superb views of the sea. The hotel has been owned and run by the same family for over 30 years. The spacious public rooms offer a choice of bars, two lounges, a conservatory, and traditional restaurant as well as the Bar Victoriana. The comfortable bedrooms are smartly decorated; many rooms taking full of advantage of the sea views.

ROOMS: 22 en suite 4 annexe en suite (3 fmly) (1 GF) ⊗ in 8 bedrooms s £50-£60; d £74-£90 (incl. bkfst) **LB** **FACILITIES:** Table Tennis, Pool table ♫ Xmas **CONF:** Thtr 20 Class 20 Board 15 Del from £38 **PARKING:** 40 **NOTES:** ⊗ in restaurant Closed 2-18 Jan

---

NAILSWORTH, Gloucestershire — Map 04 ST89

★★71% Egypt Mill

GL6 0AE
☎ 01453 833449 📠 01453 839919
e-mail: reception@egyptmill.com
Dir: *on A46, midway between Cheltenham and Bath*

Millstones and working waterwheels have been incorporated in the innovative design of this 17th-century former corn mill. Well-equipped bedrooms are located in two adjacent buildings and are tastefully furnished. Facilities include the stylish cellar bar and convivial bistro, where accomplished cuisine is proving very popular. During the summer, the riverside patios and gardens are great places to enjoy a drink.

ROOMS: 10 en suite 17 annexe en suite (2 fmly) (2 GF) ⊗ in 20 bedrooms s £60-£70; d £75-£90 (incl. bkfst) **LB** **FACILITIES:** STV Boules pitch Xmas **CONF:** Thtr 100 Class 80 Board 80 Del from £99.50 **PARKING:** 80 **NOTES:** ⊗ in restaurant Civ Wed 120

> If you wish to use a particular credit card or debit card please check with the hotel that they are happy to accept it

NANTWICH, Cheshire Map 15 SJ65

★★★★74% ⊛⊛ Rookery Hall
Main Rd, Worleston CW5 6DQ
☎ 01270 610016 🖷 01270 626027
e-mail: rookeryhall-cro@handpicked.co.uk
web: www.handpicked.co.uk
Dir: *B5074 off 4th rdbt, on Nantwich by-pass. Hotel 1.5m on right*

HandPICKED HOTELS

This fine 19th-century mansion is set in 38 acres of gardens, pasture and parkland. Bedrooms are spacious and appointed to a high standard. The public areas are particularly stylish and include a salon with enormous sofas. Many of the bedrooms provide a dazzling array of extras.
ROOMS: 30 en suite 16 annexe en suite (6 GF) s £130-£230; d £150-£250 **LB** **FACILITIES:** STV Fishing ♫ Xmas **CONF:** Thtr 90 Class 40 Board 40 Del from £170 **SERVICES:** Lift **PARKING:** 100 **NOTES:** ⊗ in restaurant Civ Wed 66

See advert on this page

NANTWICH, continued

★★70% Crown
High St CW5 5AS
☎ 01270 625283 🖷 01270 628047
e-mail: info@crown-hotel.net
Dir: *A52 to Nantwich, hotel in centre of town*
Ideally set in the heart of this historic and delightful market town, The Crown has been offering hospitality for centuries. It has an abundance of original features and the well-equipped bedrooms retain an old world charm. There is also a bar with live entertainment throughout the week and diners can enjoy Italian food in the atmospheric brasserie.
ROOMS: 18 en suite (2 fmly) ⊗ in 2 bedrooms s fr £69.50; d fr £79.50 **LB** **FACILITIES:** Putt green ♫ **CONF:** Thtr 200 Class 150 Board 70 **PARKING:** 18 **NOTES:** Civ Wed 140

⇧ Premier Travel Inn Nantwich
221 Crewe Rd CW5 6NE
☎ 0870 9906418 🖷 0870 9906419
web: www.premiertravelinn.com
Dir: *Exit M6 junct 16, A500 signed Nantwich & Chester. At 1st rdbt take 2nd exit, approx 4m. At 3rd rdbt, take 3rd exit signed A500 to Chester, at 4th left onto A534 towards Nantwich. Hotel approx 100yds on right*
High quality, modern budget accommodation ideal for both families and business travellers. Spacious, en suite bedrooms feature bath and shower, satellite TV and many have telephones and modem points. The adjacent family restaurant features a wide and varied menu. For further details consult the Hotel Groups page.
ROOMS: 37 en suite s £50.95; d £50.95

NEEDHAM MARKET, Suffolk — Map 13 TM05

⇧ Travelodge Ipswich Beacon
Beacon Hill IP6 8LP
☎ 08700 850 950 🖷 01449 721640
web: www.travelodge.co.uk
Dir: *A14/A140*
Travelodge offers good quality, good value, modern accommodation. Ideal for families, the spacious, en suite bedrooms include remote-control TV, tea and coffee-making facilities and comfortable beds. Meals can be taken at the nearby family restaurant. For further details consult the Hotel Groups page.
ROOMS: 40 en suite s fr £26; d fr £26

NETHER STOWEY, Somerset — Map 04 ST13

★★70% Apple Tree
Keenthorne TA5 1HZ
☎ 01278 733238 🖷 01278 732693
e-mail: reservations@appletreehotel.com
web: www.appletreehotel.com
Dir: *from Bridgwater follow A39 towards Minehead, Hotel on left 2m past Cannington*
Parts of this cottage-style property, convenient for the coast and the M5, date back some 340 years. Bedrooms vary in character and style and some overlook the garden. The friendly owners and their staff make every effort to ensure an enjoyable stay. Public areas include an attractive conservatory restaurant, a bar and a library lounge.
ROOMS: 15 en suite (2 fmly) (5 GF) ⊗ in 7 bedrooms s £56; d £70-£80 (incl. bkfst) **LB** **CONF:** BC Thtr 25 Class 12 Board 14 **PARKING:** 40 **NOTES:** 🐕 ⊗ in restaurant

NETHER WASDALE, Cumbria — Map 18 NY10

★★76% ® Low Wood Hall Hotel & Restaurant
CA20 1ET
☎ 019467 26100 🖷 019467 26111
e-mail: enquiries@lowwoodhall.co.uk
Dir: *A590/A595 towards Barrow-Whitehaven, through village of Gosforth, follow signs for Nether Wasdale*
This delightful country hotel, now under new ownership, is peacefully set in five acres of wooded gardens overlooking the village and valley. There are two lovely lounges and both are stocked with plenty to read and have roaring fires in season. Stylish interior designs blend well with the classical architecture. The carefully prepared meals are a highlight.
ROOMS: 6 rms (5 en suite) 6 annexe en suite (4 GF) ⊗ in all bedrooms s £50-£80; d £70-£100 (incl. bkfst) **FACILITIES:** STV **CONF:** BC Thtr 30 Class 30 Board 20 **PARKING:** 15 **NOTES:** 🐕 No children 12yrs ⊗ in restaurant Civ Wed 40

NEW ALRESFORD, Hampshire — Map 05 SU53

★★65% Swan
11 West St SO24 9AD
☎ 01962 732302 & 734427 🖷 01962 735274
e-mail: swanhotel@btinternet.com
Dir: *off A31 onto B3047*
This former coaching inn dates back to the 18th century and remains a busy and popular destination for travellers and locals. Bedrooms are in the main building and the more modern wing. The lounge bar and adjacent restaurant are open all day; for more traditional dining there is another restaurant which overlooks the busy village street.
ROOMS: 11 rms (10 en suite) 12 annexe en suite (3 fmly) **CONF:** Thtr 90 Class 60 Board 40 **PARKING:** 75 **NOTES:** 🐕 ⊗ in restaurant RS 25-26 Dec

See advert on opposite page

NEWARK-ON-TRENT, Nottinghamshire — Map 17 SK75

★★★71% The Grange Hotel
73 London Rd NG24 1RZ
☎ 01636 703399 🖷 01636 702328
e-mail: info@grangenewark.co.uk
web: www.grangenewark.co.uk
Dir: *from A1 follow signs to town centre. At castle rdbt follow signs to Balderton. Over 2 sets of lights. Hotel 0.25m on left*
Expect a warm welcome at this family-run hotel, situated just a short walk from the town. Bedrooms are attractively decorated with co-ordinated soft furnishings and equipped with many thoughtful extras. Public rooms include the Potters bar, Cutlers restaurant and a residents' lounge. In the summer guests can enjoy the pretty terrace garden.
ROOMS: 10 en suite 9 annexe en suite (1 fmly) ⊗ in 15 bedrooms s £67-£95; d £90-£140 (incl. bkfst) **LB** **PARKING:** 17 **NOTES:** 🐕 ⊗ in restaurant

> Popped the question? Hotels with Civ wed in their entry are licensed for civil wedding ceremonies. Maximum numbers for the ceremony only are shown e.g. Civ wed 120

⌂ Premier Travel Inn Newark
Lincoln Rd NG24 2DB
☎ 08701 977186 🖷 01636 605135
web: www.premiertravelinn.com
Dir: *at intersection of A1/A46/A17, follow B6166 signs*
High quality, modern budget accommodation ideal for both families and business travellers. Spacious, en suite bedrooms feature bath and shower, satellite TV and many have telephones and modem points. The adjacent family restaurant features a wide and varied menu. For further details consult the Hotel Groups page.
ROOMS: 40 en suite s £48.95; d £48.95

NEWBURY, Berkshire Map 05 SU46

Top Hotel

★★★★★ ⊛⊛⊛⊛
The Vineyard at Stockcross
Stockcross RG20 8JU
☎ 01635 528770 🖷 01635 528398
e-mail: general@the-vineyard.co.uk
web: www.the-vineyard.co.uk
Dir: *from M4 take A34 towards Newbury, exit at 3rd junct for Speen. Right at rdbt then right again at 2nd rdbt.*
A haven of style in the Berkshire countryside, this hotel prides itself on a superb art collection, which can be seen throughout the building. Bedrooms come in a variety of styles - many of them split-level suites that are exceptionally well equipped. Comfortable lounges lead into the stylish restaurant, which serves award-winning, imaginative and precise cooking, complemented by an equally impressive selection of wines from California and around the world. The welcome is warm and sincere, the service professional yet relaxed.
ROOMS: 49 en suite (15 GF) ⊗ in 10 bedrooms s fr £212; d £212-£787.25 (incl. bkfst) **LB** **FACILITIES: Spa** STV Sauna Gym Jacuzzi Treatment rooms ♫ Xmas **CONF:** BC Thtr 100 Class 50 Board 30 Del from £320 **SERVICES:** Lift air con **PARKING:** 100 **NOTES:** ⊗ in restaurant Civ Wed 100

★★★★77% ⊛⊛ **Donnington Valley**
Old Oxford Rd, Donnington RG14 3AG
☎ 01635 551199 🖷 01635 551123
e-mail: general@donningtonvalley.co.uk
web: www.donningtonvalley.co.uk
Dir: *M4 junct 13, take A34 southbound, take exit signed 'Donnington Hotels' towards Donnington. Hotel 2m on right*
This friendly hotel stands on its own 18-hole golf course and provides excellent accommodation. The striking modern building houses well-equipped meeting rooms and public areas that are furnished to a high standard. The WinePress restaurant offers

continued on p408

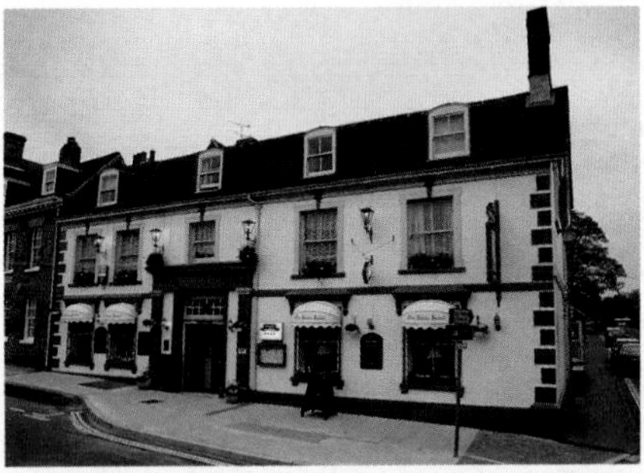

NEWBURY, continued

imaginative food and a comprehensive choice of wines in comfortable surroundings; service is attentive and friendly.
ROOMS: 58 en suite (11 fmly) (18 GF) ⊗ in 30 bedrooms s fr £160; d £200-£240 **LB** **FACILITIES:** STV ⛳ 18 Putt green Leisure fac available at sister hotel, The Vineyard 2miles away ♫ Xmas **CONF:** BC Thtr 140 Class 60 Board 40 **SERVICES:** Lift **PARKING:** 160 **NOTES:** ✗ Civ Wed 90

★★★★75% ⊛ Regency Park Hotel
Bowling Green Rd, Thatcham RG18 3RP
☎ 01635 871555 ▯ 01635 871571
e-mail: info@regencyparkhotel.co.uk
web: www.regencyparkhotel.co.uk
Dir: *from Newbury take A4 signed Thatcham & Reading. 2nd rdbt exit signed Cold Ash. Hotel 1m on left*

Following extensive redevelopment, this hotel boasts roomy bedrooms, a state-of-the-art leisure club with beauty treatment salon and extensive business facilities. The smart, spacious, contemporary public areas are a relaxing environment to while away the day and the Watermark restaurant provides imaginative, award-winning cuisine.
ROOMS: 109 en suite (7 fmly) (9 GF) ⊗ in 84 bedrooms s £95-£165; d £115-£295 (incl. bkfst) **LB** **FACILITIES: Spa** STV ⛆ Sauna Solarium Gym Jacuzzi 4 Health & Beauty treatment rooms Xmas **CONF:** BC Thtr 200 Class 80 Board 70 Del from £155 **SERVICES:** Lift **PARKING:** 160 **NOTES:** ✗ ⊗ in restaurant Civ Wed 100

See advert on page 407

★★★63% The Chequers Hotel
6-8 Oxford St RG14 1JB
☎ 01635 38000 0870 609 6141 ▯ 01635 37170
e-mail: thechequers@corushotels.com
web: www.corushotels.com
Dir: *off A34 at Newbury follow town centre signs. 2nd mini rdbt right, hotel on right*

In an enviable town centre location with parking, this hotel offers traditional public areas that include a lounge bar and pleasant restaurant. Bedrooms come in a variety sizes and outlook; most are in the original buildings but some are in modern wings. All have good facilities and offer good levels of comfort.
ROOMS: 46 en suite 11 annexe en suite (3 fmly) (6 GF) ⊗ in 41 bedrooms s £116; d £116-£131 **LB** **FACILITIES:** STV Xmas **CONF:** Thtr 100 Class 60 Board 40 Del from £125 **PARKING:** 60 **NOTES:** ✗ ⊗ in restaurant Civ Wed 70

U Newbury Manor Hotel
London Rd RG14 2BY
☎ 01635 528838 ▯ 01635 523406
e-mail: enquiries@newbury-manor-hotel.co.uk
Dir: *from Newbury follow A4 towards Thatcham. 300yds after rdbt for Newbury Business Park. Hotel on right*
At the time of going to press, the star classification for this hotel was not confirmed. Please refer to the AA internet site www.theAA.com for current information.
ROOMS: 33 en suite (22 fmly) (12 GF) s £160-£230; d £170-£240 (incl. bkfst) **LB** **FACILITIES:** STV Fishing ♫ ch fac **CONF:** Thtr 80 Class 32 Board 40 Del from £180 **NOTES:** ⊗ in restaurant Civ Wed 85

U Ramada Hotel & Resort Elcot Park
RG20 8NJ
☎ 01488 658100 ▯ 01488 658288
e-mail: sales.elcotpark@ramadajarvis.co.uk
Dir: *Take A4 towards Hungerford, hotel is on right after The Halfway Inn.*
Conveniently located to both the A4 and M4 this country-house hotel is set in 16 acres of woodland. Public areas include the Orangery restaurant, leisure club and a range of conference rooms.
ROOMS: 70 en suite (10 fmly) (26 GF) ⊗ in 48 bedrooms s £95-£130; d £95-£130 **FACILITIES: Spa** STV ⛆ supervised Sauna Solarium Gym ♫ Putt green Xmas **CONF:** Thtr 90 Class 48 Board 50 Del from £160 **PARKING:** 120 **NOTES:** ⊗ in restaurant Civ Wed 150

⌂ Premier Travel Inn Newbury
Bath Rd, Midgham RG7 5UX
☎ 0870 9906556 ▯ 0870 9906557
web: www.premiertravelinn.com
Dir: *Exit M4 junct 12, A4 towards Newbury. Hotel 7m on right*
High quality, modern budget accommodation ideal for both families and business travellers. Spacious, en suite bedrooms feature bath and shower, satellite TV and many have telephones and modem points. The adjacent family restaurant features a wide and varied menu. For further details consult the Hotel Groups page.
ROOMS: 49 en suite s £53.95-£57.95; d £53.95-£57.95 **CONF:** Thtr 10 Board 10

⌂ Travelodge (Newbury Chieveley)
Chieveley, Oxford Rd RG18 9XX
☎ 08700 850 950 ▯ 01635 247886
web: www.travelodge.co.uk
Dir: *on A34, off M4 junct 13*
Travelodge offers good quality, good value, modern accommodation. Ideal for families, the spacious, en suite bedrooms include remote-control TV, tea and coffee-making facilities and comfortable beds. Meals can be taken at the nearby family restaurant. For further details consult the Hotel Groups page.
ROOMS: 127 en suite s fr £26; d fr £26

⌂ Travelodge Newbury South
Tot Hill Services (A34), Newbury by-pass RG20 9ED
☎ 08700 850 950 ▯ 01635 278169
web: www.travelodge.co.uk
Dir: *Tot Hill Services on A34*
Travelodge offers good quality, good value, modern

continued

accommodation. Ideal for families, the spacious, en suite bedrooms include remote-control TV, tea and coffee-making facilities and comfortable beds. Meals can be taken at the nearby family restaurant. For further details consult the Hotel Groups page.
ROOMS: 52 en suite (incl. bkfst) s fr £26; d fr £26

NEWBY BRIDGE, Cumbria Map 18 SD38

★★★★77% ◉◉ Lakeside Hotel Lake Windermere
Lakeside LA12 8AT
☎ 015395 30001 ▤ 015395 31699
e-mail: sales@lakesidehotel.co.uk
web: www.lakesidehotel.co.uk
Dir: M6 junct 36 join A590 to Barrow, take signs to Newby Bridge. Right over bridge, hotel 1m on right or follow Lakeside Steamers signs from junct 36

This impressive hotel has an enviable location on the southern edge of Lake Windermere. Bedrooms are tastefully and individually styled, many with patios and wonderful lake views. Spacious lounges and a choice of restaurants are available. There is now a state-of-the-art luxury spa complex with spa treatments available.
ROOMS: 76 en suite (7 fmly) (8 GF) ◉ in 34 bedrooms s £160-£380; d £200-£390 (incl. bkfst) **LB FACILITIES: Spa** STV ☜ Fishing Sauna Gym ♨ Jacuzzi Private jetty, Rowing boats ♫ Xmas **CONF:** Thtr 100 Class 50 Board 40 Del from £140 **SERVICES:** Lift **PARKING:** 200 **NOTES:** ✖ ◉ in restaurant Civ Wed 80

★★★★74% ◉ Swan
LA12 8NB
☎ 015395 31681 ▤ 015395 31917
e-mail: enquiries@swanhotel.com
web: www.swanhotel.com
Dir: M6 junct 36 follow A590 signed Barrow for 16m. Hotel on right of old 5-arch bridge, at Newby Bridge

Set among 14 acres of gardens and lakeside pathways with mooring for 80 boats, this hotel stands on the River Leven at the south end of Lake Windermere. Bedrooms are comfortable, spacious and
continued

thoughtfully equipped. Public areas include a choice of lounges and restaurants, a traditional bar and impressive spa facilities.
ROOMS: 55 en suite (4 fmly) (14 GF) ◉ in 16 bedrooms
FACILITIES: Spa STV ☜ supervised Fishing Sauna Solarium Gym Steam Room **CONF:** Thtr 120 Class 40 Board 40 **SERVICES:** Lift
PARKING: 100 **NOTES:** ✖ ◉ in restaurant Civ Wed 80

★★★67% Whitewater
The Lakeland Village LA12 8PX
☎ 015395 31133 ▤ 015395 31881
e-mail: enquiries@whitewater-hotel.co.uk
web: www.whitewater-hotel.co.uk
Dir: M6 junct 36 follow signs for A590 Barrow, 1m through Newby Bridge. Right at sign for Lakeland Village, hotel on left

This tasteful conversion of an old mill on the River Leven is close to the southern end of Lake Windermere. Bedrooms, many with lovely river views, are spacious and comfortable. Public areas include a luxurious, well-equipped spa, squash courts, and a choice of dining options. Mountain bikes are available. The Fisherman's bar hosts regular jazz nights that are popular with locals.
ROOMS: 35 en suite (10 fmly) (2 GF) ◉ in 10 bedrooms s £97-£130; d £130-£195 (incl. bkfst) **LB FACILITIES: Spa** STV ☜ supervised ♋ Squash Sauna Solarium Gym Putt green Jacuzzi Beauty treatment Table tennis Steam room Golf driving range ♫ Xmas **CONF:** Thtr 80 Class 32 Board 40 Del from £135 **SERVICES:** Lift **PARKING:** 50 **NOTES:** ✖ ◉ in restaurant Civ Wed 110

NEWCASTLE-UNDER-LYME, Staffordshire Map 10 SJ84

★★60% Stop Inn Newcastle-under-Lyme
Liverpool Rd, Cross Heath ST5 9DX
☎ 01782 717000 ▤ 01782 713669
e-mail: enquiries@
hotels-newcastle-under-lyme.com
web: www.hotels-newcastle-under-lyme.com
Dir: M6 junct 16 onto A500 to Stoke-on-Trent. Take A34 to Newcastle-under-Lyme, hotel on right after 1.5m
Some of the well-equipped bedrooms at this purpose-built hotel are in a separate block at the rear. There is a large lounge bar with a pool table and the restaurant offers a good range of food.
ROOMS: 43 rms (42 en suite) 24 annexe en suite (13 fmly) (23 GF) ◉ in 31 bedrooms s £45-£66; d £50-£66 **LB FACILITIES:** STV Xmas **CONF:** Thtr 150 Class 80 Board 80 Del £87 **PARKING:** 160 **NOTES:** ◉ in restaurant

🏠 Town House Hotel
🏛 Country House Hotel
⬆ Travel Accommodation

NEWCASTLE-UNDER-LYME, continued

Premier Travel Inn Newcastle-under-Lyme
Talke Rd, Chesterton ST5 7AH
☎ 08701 977191 🖷 01782 578901
web: www.premiertravelinn.com
Dir: *M6 junct 16 - follow A500 for approx. 3.5 miles. Take A34 towards Newcastle-under-Lyme. Inn 0.5 mile on the right*
High quality, modern budget accommodation ideal for both families and business travellers. Spacious, en suite bedrooms feature bath and shower, satellite TV and many have telephones and modem points. The adjacent family restaurant features a wide and varied menu. For further details consult the Hotel Groups page.
ROOMS: 58 en suite s £49.95; d £49.95

NEWCASTLE UPON TYNE, Tyne & Wear Map 21 NZ26
See also Seaton Burn & Whickham

★★★★76% **Vermont**
Castle Garth NE1 1RQ
☎ 0191 233 1010 🖷 0191 233 1234
e-mail: info@vermont-hotel.co.uk
web: www.vermont-hotel.com
Dir: *city centre by high level bridge and Castle Keep*

Adjacent to the castle and close to the buzzing quayside area, this imposing hotel enjoys fine views of the Tyne Bridge. Thoughtfully equipped bedrooms offer a variety of styles, including grand suites. The elegant reception lounge and adjoining bar invite relaxation, while the Bridge restaurant is the focus for dining.
ROOMS: 101 en suite (12 fmly) ⊘ in 79 bedrooms s £120-£185; d £120-£185 **LB** **FACILITIES:** STV Solarium Gym Xmas **CONF:** BC Thtr 200 Class 60 Board 30 Del from £180 **SERVICES:** Lift **PARKING:** 100 **NOTES:** Civ Wed 120

★★★★74%
Newcastle Marriott Hotel Gosforth Park
High Gosforth Park, Gosforth NE3 5HN
☎ 0191 236 4111 🖷 0191 236 8192
web: www.marriott.co.uk
Dir: *onto A1056 to Killingworth and Wideopen. 3rd exit to Gosforth Park, hotel ahead*
Set within its own grounds, this modern hotel offers extensive conference and banqueting facilities, along with indoor and outdoor leisure and a choice of formal and informal dining. Many of the air-conditioned bedrooms have views over the park; executive rooms feature extras such as CD players. The hotel is conveniently located for the by-pass, airport and racecourse.
ROOMS: 178 en suite (30 fmly) ⊘ in 115 bedrooms s fr £115; d fr £115 **LB** **FACILITIES:** **Spa** STV supervised Squash Sauna Solarium Gym Jacuzzi Trim & jogging trail in hotel grounds ♫ **CONF:** BC Thtr 750 Class 280 Board 50 Del from £115 **SERVICES:** Lift air con **PARKING:** 340 **NOTES:** RS Xmas & New year Civ Wed 300

★★★★71% **Copthorne Hotel Newcastle**
The Close, Quayside NE1 3RT
☎ 0191 222 0333 🖷 0191 230 1111
e-mail: sales@newcastle.mill-cop.com
web: www.copthorne.com/newcastle
Dir: *follow signs to Newcastle city centre. Take B1600 Quayside exit, hotel on right*
Set on the banks of the River Tyne close to the city centre, this stylish purpose-built hotel provides modern amenities including a leisure centre, conference facilities and a choice of restaurants for dinner. Bedrooms overlook the river and there is a floor of 'Connoisseur' rooms with their exclusive lounge and business support services.
ROOMS: 156 en suite ⊘ in 85 bedrooms **FACILITIES:** **Spa** STV Sauna Solarium Gym Jacuzzi Steam room, Beauty treatment room, fitness studio Xmas **CONF:** Thtr 200 Class 85 Board 50 **SERVICES:** Lift air con **PARKING:** 180 **NOTES:** Civ Wed 150

★★★★68%
Newcastle Marriott Hotel MetroCentre
MetroCentre NE11 9XF
☎ 0191 493 2233 🖷 0191 493 2030
e-mail: reservations.newcastle@marriotthotels.co.uk
web: www.marriott.co.uk
(For full entry see Gateshead)

★★★★65% **Menzies Silverlink Park**
Silverlink, Coast Rd NE28 9HP
☎ 0191 202 9955 🖷 0191 263 4172
e-mail: silverlinkpark@menzies-hotels.co.uk
web: www.menzies-hotels.co.uk
Dir: *Through the Tyne Tunnel follow signs for A19 Morpeth and then signs for Silverlink. At 1st rdbt 3rd exit and at 2nd rdbt take 1st exit.*
A modern hotel located close to the Tyne Tunnel and major businesses in the area. Public areas are well proportioned and inviting, with pride of place going to the Waves health and leisure club. Bedrooms meet the needs of the business guest, and it is worth asking for one of the larger Club rooms.
ROOMS: 122 en suite (4 fmly) ⊘ in 60 bedrooms s £120; d £120 **LB** **FACILITIES:** Sauna Solarium Gym Jacuzzi Xmas **CONF:** Thtr 400 Class 200 Board 40 Del £145 **SERVICES:** Lift **PARKING:** 226 **NOTES:** ⊘ in restaurant Civ Wed

★★★78% **Malmaison**
Quayside NE1 3DX
☎ 0191 245 5000 🖷 0191 245 4545
e-mail: newcastle@malmaison.com
web: www.malmaison.com
Dir: *follow signs for Newcastle City Centre, then for Quayside/Law Courts. Hotel 100yds past Law Courts*
Overlooking the river and the Millennium Bridge, the hotel has a prime position in the up-and-coming redeveloped quayside district. Bedrooms have striking decor, CD players, mini-bars and a number of individual, welcoming touches. Food and drink are an integral part of the operation here, with a stylish brasserie-style restaurant and café bar.
ROOMS: 120 en suite (10 fmly) ⊘ in 22 bedrooms s £135-£250; d £135-£250 **LB** **FACILITIES:** STV Sauna Gym Xmas **CONF:** Board 18 Del from £165 **SERVICES:** Lift air con **PARKING:** 50

★★★71% **Eslington Villa**
8 Station Rd, Low Fell NE9 6DR
☎ 0191 487 6017 & 420 0666 🖷 0191 420 0667
e-mail: admin@eslingtonvilla.fsnet.co.uk
(For full entry see Gateshead)

N

★★★68%
The Caledonian Hotel, Newcastle
64 Osborne Rd, Jesmond NE2 2AT
☎ 0191 281 7881 📠 0191 281 6241
e-mail: info@caledonian-hotel-newcastle.com
web: www.peelhotel.com
Dir: *from A1 follow signs to Newcastle City, cross Tyne Bridge to Tynemouth. Left at traffic lights at Osborne Rd, hotel on right*

This hotel is located in the Jesmond area of the city, popular for its vibrant nightlife. Bedrooms are comfortable and well-equipped for business guests. Public area include the trendy Billabong Bar and Bistro, which serves food all day, and also on the terrace where a cosmopolitan atmosphere prevails.
ROOMS: 89 en suite (6 fmly) (7 GF) ⊗ in 32 bedrooms s £65-£105; d £80-£130 **LB FACILITIES:** STV Xmas **CONF:** Thtr 100 Class 50 Board 50 Del from £95 **SERVICES:** Lift **PARKING:** 35 **NOTES:** ✗ Civ Wed 70

★★★68% **Jurys Inn Newcastle**
St James Gate, Scotswood Rd NE4 7JH
☎ 0191 201 4400 📠 0191 201 4411
e-mail: jurysinnnewcastle@jurysdoyle.com
web: www.jurysdoyle.com
Lying west of the city centre, this modern, stylish hotel is easily accessible from major road networks. Bedrooms provide good guest comfort and in-room facilities are suited for both leisure and business markets. Public areas include a number of meeting rooms and a popular bar and restaurant.
ROOMS: 274 en suite ⊗ in 215 bedrooms **CONF:** BC Thtr 90 Class 50 Board 45 **SERVICES:** Lift **NOTES:** ✗ Closed 24-26 Dec

★★★67% **George Washington County Hotel**
Stone Cellar Rd, High Usworth NE37 1PH
☎ 0191 402 9988 📠 0191 415 1166
e-mail: reservations@georgewashington.co.uk
web: www.georgewashington.co.uk
(For full entry see Washington)

★★★67% ***Novotel Newcastle***
Ponteland Rd, Kenton NE3 3HZ
☎ 0191 214 0303 📠 0191 214 0633
e-mail: H1118@accor-hotels.com
web: www.novotel.com
Dir: *off A1(M) airport junct onto A696, take Kingston Park exit*
This modern well-proportioned hotel lies just off the bypass and is within easy reach of the airport and city centre. Bedrooms are spacious with a range of extras. The Garden Brasserie offers a flexible dining option and is open until late. There is also a small leisure centre for the more energetic.
Novotel - AA Hotel Group of the Year 2005-6.
ROOMS: 126 en suite (56 fmly) ⊗ in 82 bedrooms **FACILITIES:** STV Sauna Gym **CONF:** Thtr 200 Class 90 Board 40 **SERVICES:** Lift **PARKING:** 260 **NOTES:** Civ Wed 200

★★★66% ***New Kent Hotel***
127 Osborne Rd NE2 2TB
☎ 0191 281 7711 📠 0191 281 3369
e-mail: newkenthotel@hotmail.com
Dir: *beside B1600, opposite St Georges Church*
This popular business hotel offers relaxed service and typical Geordie hospitality. The bright modern bedrooms are well equipped and the modern bar is an ideal meeting place. A range of generous, good value dishes is served in the restaurant, which doubles as a wedding venue.
ROOMS: 32 en suite (4 fmly) **FACILITIES:** STV **CONF:** Thtr 60 Class 30 Board 40 **PARKING:** 22 **NOTES:** ⊗ in restaurant Civ Wed 90

★★★64%
Quality Hotel Newcastle upon Tyne
Newgate St NE1 5SX
☎ 0191 232 5025 📠 0191 232 8428
e-mail: enquiries@hotels-newcastle-upon-tyne.com
web: www.choicehotelseurope.com
Dir: *A1(M) take A184 Gateshead and Newcastle centre, follow A6082. Cross Redheugh Bridge take right lane, right at 3rd set of lights, then immediate right on to Fenkle St. Car park behind Old Assembly Rooms*
Benefiting from a city centre location and a secure rooftop car park, this hotel is popular with business travellers. Accommodation is provided in compact yet thoughtfully equipped bedrooms. The rooftop restaurant and lounge give fine views over the city.
ROOMS: 93 en suite (4 fmly) ⊗ in 42 bedrooms s £75-£100; d £90-£115 **LB FACILITIES:** STV Xmas **CONF:** Thtr 100 Class 40 Board 40 Del from £100 **SERVICES:** Lift **PARKING:** 120 **NOTES:** ⊗ in restaurant

NEWCASTLE UPON TYNE, continued

★★63% Cairn

97/103 Osborne Rd, Jesmond NE2 2TJ
☎ 0191 281 1358 🖷 0191 281 9031
e-mail: info@cairnnewcastle.com

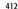

A smart modern reception hall welcomes guests to this commercial hotel in the village suburb of Jesmond. Bedrooms are well-equipped. There is a lively bar and a bright colourful restaurant.
ROOMS: 50 en suite (2 fmly) **FACILITIES:** STV Xmas **CONF:** Thtr 150 Class 110 Board 100 Del from £72.50 **PARKING:** 22

★65% Hadrian Lodge Hotel

Hadrian Rd, Wallsend NE28 6HH
☎ 0191 262 7733 & 08081 086892 🖷 0191 263 0714
e-mail: info@hadrianlodgehotel.co.uk
web: www.hadrianlodgehotel.co.uk
Dir: *from Newcastle city centre follow signs for Tyne Tunnel and Wallsend. Then follow A187 to Wallsend and Newcastle. Hotel opposite Hadrian Rd Metro station*
Mainly a business hotel, Hadrian Lodge lies on the north side of the River Tyne and takes its name from the nearby Roman remains. It offers well-equipped bedrooms of mixed sizes many being large and comfortable. A wide range of dishes is served in the spacious bar and restaurant area.
ROOMS: 25 en suite (1 fmly) ⊘ in 8 bedrooms s £42-£59; d £65 (incl. bkfst) **CONF:** BC **PARKING:** 60 **NOTES:** ✗ ⊘ in restaurant

U Jesmond Dene House

Jesmond Dene Rd NE2 2EY
☎ 0191 212 3000 🖷 0191 212 3001
e-mail: info@jesmonddenehouse.co.uk
web: www.jesmonddenehouse.co.uk
Dir: *A167 N to A184. Right, then right again along Jesmond Dene Rd, hotel on left*
At the time of going to press, the star classification for this hotel was not confirmed. Please refer to the AA internet site www.theAA.com for current information.
ROOMS: 32 en suite 8 annexe en suite (1 fmly) (4 GF) ⊘ in all bedrooms s £115-£270; d £115-£270 **FACILITIES:** STV Xmas **CONF:** Thtr 125 Class 80 Board 44 Del £245 **SERVICES:** Lift **PARKING:** 50 **NOTES:** ✗ ⊘ in restaurant

⌂ Innkeeper's Lodge Newcastle

Kenton Bank NE3 3TY
☎ 0191 214 0877 🖷 0191 214 1922
web: www.innkeeperslodge.com
Dir: *from A1(M), exit A696/B6918. At 1st rdbt, take B6918 (Kingston Park), 2nd rdbt turn right. Lodge on left*
A growing concept in the travel accommodation market. Smart rooms meet essential business requirements but also have home comforts. Dining options include all-day menus plus the added advantage of breakfast, which is included in the room price. For further details consult the Hotel Groups page.
ROOMS: 30 en suite s £49.95-£58; d £49.95-£58 **CONF:** Thtr 40 Class 25 Board 20

⌂ Premier Travel Inn Newcastle City Centre

City Rd, Quayside NE1 2AN
☎ 0870 238 3318 🖷 0191 232 6557
web: www.premiertravelinn.com
Dir: *at corner of City Rd (A186) & Crawhall Rd*
High quality, modern budget accommodation ideal for both families and business travellers. Spacious, en suite bedrooms feature bath and shower, satellite TV and many have telephones and modem points. The adjacent family restaurant features a wide and varied menu. For further details consult the Hotel Groups page.
ROOMS: 81 en suite s £52.95-£59.95; d £52.95-£59.95 **CONF:** Thtr 15 Board 12

⌂ Premier Travel Inn Newcastle (Holystone)

Holystone Roundabout NE27 0DA
☎ 08701 977189 🖷 0191 259 9509
web: www.premiertravelinn.com
Dir: *3m N of Tyne Tunnel, adjacent to A19. Take A191 signed Gosforth/Whitley Bay*
High quality, modern budget accommodation ideal for both families and business travellers. Spacious, en suite bedrooms feature bath and shower, satellite TV and many have telephones and modem points. The adjacent family restaurant features a wide and varied menu. For further details consult the Hotel Groups page.
ROOMS: 40 en suite s £49.95; d £49.95

⌂ Premier Travel Inn Newcastle (Quayside)

The Quayside NE1 3DW
☎ 0870 9906530 🖷 0870 9906531
web: www.premiertravelinn.com
Dir: *From N, follow A1, A167, A186 Walker & Wallsend. From S, follow A1, A184, A189 to city centre. Onto B1600 Quayside. Hotel by Tyne Bridge*
High quality, modern budget accommodation ideal for both families and business travellers. Spacious, en suite bedrooms feature bath and shower, satellite TV and many have telephones and modem points. The adjacent family restaurant features a wide and varied menu. For further details consult the Hotel Groups page.
ROOMS: 150 en suite s £59.95; d £59.95 **CONF:** Thtr 30 Class 30 Board 30

⌂ Travelodge (Newcastle Central)

Forster St NE1 2NH
☎ 08700 850 950 🖷 0191 261 7105
web: www.travelodge.co.uk
Dir: *from A1 or A194 (M) to city centre, over Tyne Bridge, right into Melbourne St, right into Forster St*
Travelodge offers good quality, good value, modern accommodation. Ideal for families, the spacious, en suite bedrooms include remote-control TV, tea and coffee-making facilities and comfortable beds. Meals can be taken at the nearby family restaurant. For further details consult the Hotel Groups page.
ROOMS: 120 en suite s fr £26; d fr £26

We have indicated only the hotels that don't accept credit or debit cards

NEWCASTLE UPON TYNE AIRPORT, Tyne & Wear
Map 21 NZ17

⌂ Premier Travel Inn Newcastle Airport
Newcastle Int. Airport, Ponteland Rd, Prestwick NE20 9DB
☎ 08701 977190 🖨 01661 824940
web: www.premiertravelinn.com
Dir: situated immediately adjacent to the main entrance to airport
High quality, modern budget accommodation ideal for both families and business travellers. Spacious, en suite bedrooms feature bath and shower, satellite TV and many have telephones and modem points. The adjacent family restaurant features a wide and varied menu. For further details consult the Hotel Groups page.
ROOMS: 86 en suite s £53.95; d £53.95 **CONF:** Thtr 20

⌂ Premier Travel Inn Newcastle Airport (South)
Callerton Ln Ends, Woolsington NE13 8DF
☎ 0870 9906338 🖨 0870 9906339
web: www.premiertravelinn.com
Dir: Just off A696 on B6918, 0.3m from airport. 4m from city centre
High quality, modern budget accommodation ideal for both families and business travellers. Spacious, en suite bedrooms feature bath and shower, satellite TV and many have telephones and modem points. The adjacent family restaurant features a wide and varied menu. For further details consult the Hotel Groups page.
ROOMS: 42 en suite 10 annexe en suite s £53.95; d £53.95 **CONF:** Thtr 60 Class 20 Board 26

NEWENT, Gloucestershire
Map 10 SO72

Restaurant with Rooms

🏠 ⊛ Three Choirs Vineyards
GL18 1LS
☎ 01531 890223 🖨 01531 890877
e-mail: info@threechoirs.com
web: www.threechoirs.com
Dir: on B4215 North of Newent, follow brown tourist signs

This thriving vineyard continues to go from strength to strength. The restaurant, which overlooks the 100-acre estate, enjoys a popular following. Spacious, high quality bedrooms are equipped with many extras and each opens on to a private patio area, from where wonderful views can be enjoyed.
ROOMS: 8 annexe en suite (2 fmly) (8 GF) ⊛ in all bedrooms s £75-£105; d £95-£105 (incl. bkfst) **LB FACILITIES:** Wine tasting, 75 acres of vineyards, guided & self guided tours **CONF:** Thtr 20 Class 15 Board 20 Del from £125 **PARKING:** 8 **NOTES:** ✗ ⊛ in restaurant Closed 24-26 Dec Civ Wed 20

♫ Entertainment

NEWHAVEN, East Sussex
Map 06 TQ40

⌂ Premier Travel Inn Newhaven
The Drove, Avis Rd BN9 0AG
☎ 08701 977192 🖨 01273 612359
web: www.premiertravelinn.com
Dir: from A26 (New Rd) through Drove Industrial Estate, left turn after underpass. On same complex as Sainsburys, A259
High quality, modern budget accommodation ideal for both families and business travellers. Spacious, en suite bedrooms feature bath and shower, satellite TV and many have telephones and modem points. The adjacent family restaurant features a wide and varied menu. For further details consult the Hotel Groups page.
ROOMS: 40 en suite s £51.95; d £51.95

NEWICK, East Sussex
Map 06 TQ42

Top Hotel

★★★ ⊛⊛ Newick Park Hotel & Country Estate
BN8 4SB
☎ 01825 723633 🖨 01825 723969
e-mail: bookings@newickpark.co.uk
web: www.newickpark.co.uk
Dir: S off A272 in Newick between Haywards Heath and Uckfield. Pass church, left at junct and hotel 0.25m on right
Delightful Grade II listed Georgian country house set amid 250 acres of Sussex parkland and landscaped gardens. The spacious, individually decorated bedrooms are tastefully furnished, thoughtfully equipped and have superb views of the grounds; many rooms have huge American king-size beds. The comfortable public rooms include a study, a sitting room, lounge bar and an elegant restaurant.
ROOMS: 13 en suite 3 annexe en suite (5 fmly) (1 GF) ⊛ in all bedrooms s fr £125; d fr £165 (incl. bkfst) **LB FACILITIES:** STV ↘ ⊛ Fishing ♬ Badminton, Tank driving, Quad biking, Clay pigeon shooting Xmas **CONF:** Thtr 80 Class 40 Board 40 Del from £185 **PARKING:** 52 **NOTES:** ⊛ in restaurant Civ Wed 100

See advert under LEWES

NEWMARKET, Suffolk
Map 12 TL66

★★★★71% ⊛ Bedford Lodge
Bury Rd CB8 7BX
☎ 01638 663175 🖨 01638 667391
e-mail: info@bedfordlodgehotel.co.uk
Dir: from town centre take Bury St Edmunds road , hotel 0.5m on left
Imposing 18th-century Georgian hunting lodge set in three acres of secluded landscaped gardens. Public rooms feature the elegant Orangery restaurant, a smart lounge bar and a small lounge. The hotel also features superb leisure facilities and self-contained

continued on p414

conference and banqueting suites. Contemporary bedrooms have a light, airy feel; each room tastefully furnished and well equipped.

Bedford Lodge, Newmarket

ROOMS: 55 en suite (3 fmly) (16 GF) ◎ in 39 bedrooms s £120-£250; d £160-£250 (incl. bkfst) **LB FACILITIES:** STV ☜ Sauna Solarium Gym Jacuzzi Steam room & beauty salon Xmas **CONF:** Thtr 200 Class 80 Board 60 Del from £155 **SERVICES:** Lift **PARKING:** 120 **NOTES:** ✖ ◎ in restaurant Civ Wed 150

★★★74% ◉ Swynford Paddocks Hotel
CB8 0UE
☎ 01638 570234 ▤ 01638 570283
e-mail: info@swynfordpaddocks.com
(For full entry see Six Mile Bottom)

★★★69% Heath Court
Moulton Rd CB8 8DY
☎ 01638 667171 ▤ 01638 666533
e-mail: quality@heathcourthotel.com
Best Western

Dir: leave A14 at Newmarket and Ely exit on A142. Follow town centre signs over mini rdbt. At clocktower left into Moulton Rd
Modern red brick hotel situated close to Newmarket Heath and perfectly placed for the town centre. Public rooms include a choice of dining options - informal meals can be taken in the lounge bar or a modern carte menu is offered in the restaurant. Bedrooms are mostly spacious, each smartly presented and a number have air conditioning.
ROOMS: 41 en suite (2 fmly) ◎ in 19 bedrooms s £81-£97; d £91-£200 (incl. bkfst) **LB FACILITIES:** STV Health & beauty salon **CONF:** Thtr 150 Class 40 Board 40 Del from £115 **SERVICES:** Lift **PARKING:** 60 **NOTES:** Civ Wed 50

NEW MILTON, Hampshire Map 05 SZ29

Top Hotel

★★★★★ ◉◉◉ ♨ Chewton Glen
Christchurch Rd BH25 5QS
☎ 01425 275341 ▤ 01425 272310
e-mail: reservations@chewtonglen.com
web: www.chewtonglen.com
RELAIS & CHATEAUX

Dir: A35 from Lyndhurst for 10m, left at staggered junct. Follow tourist sign for hotel through Walkford, take 2nd left
This outstanding hotel has been at the forefront of British hotel-keeping for many years. Once past the wrought iron entrance gates, guests are transported into a world of luxury. Log fires and afternoon tea are part of the tradition here, and lounges enjoy fine views over sweeping croquet lawns. Most
continued

bedrooms are very spacious, with private patios or balconies. Dining is a treat, and the extensive wine lists are essential reading for the enthusiast. The spa and leisure facilities are among the best in the country.

ROOMS: 58 en suite (9 GF) s £205-£435; d £205-£775 **LB FACILITIES: Spa** STV ☜ ☜ ♨ 9 ♋ Snooker Sauna Gym ℗ Putt green Hydrotherapy spa, Hot tub, Dance studio, Cycling and jogging trail ♫ Xmas **CONF:** BC Thtr 150 Class 70 Board 40 Del £350 **SERVICES:** air con **PARKING:** 100 **NOTES:** ✖ No children 5yrs ◎ in restaurant Civ Wed 140

See advert on opposite page

NEWPORT See Wight, Isle of

NEWPORT, Shropshire Map 15 SJ71

★★68% *Royal Victoria*
St Mary's St TF10 7AB
☎ 01952 820331 ▤ 01952 820209
e-mail: info@royal-victoria.co.uk
THE INDEPENDENTS

Dir: off A41 at 2nd Newport by-pass rdbt towards town centre. Right at 1st traffic lights, hotel 150mtrs on left
This town-centre hotel stands behind St Nicholas' Church. Dating from Georgian times, it derives its name from a visit made by Princess Victoria in 1832. The hotel provides well-equipped, modern accommodation. Facilities available to guests include an attractively appointed restaurant, a choice of bars and a large function/conference suite.
ROOMS: 24 rms (2 fmly) ◎ in 6 bedrooms **CONF:** Thtr 150 Board 90 **PARKING:** 70 **NOTES:** ◎ in restaurant

NEWPORT PAGNELL MOTORWAY Map 11 SP84
SERVICE AREA (M1), Buckinghamshire

⇧ Welcome Lodge Newport Pagnell
Newport Pagnell MK16 8DS
☎ 01908 610878 ▤ 01908 216539
e-mail: newport.hotel@welcomebreak.co.uk
web: www.welcomebreak.co.uk
Welcome Break

Dir: M1 junct 14-15. In service area - follow signs to Barrier Lodge
This modern building offers accommodation in smart, spacious and well-equipped bedrooms, suitable for families and business travellers, and all with en suite bathrooms. Refreshments may be taken at the nearby family restaurant. For further details consult the Hotel Groups page.
ROOMS: 90 en suite s £45-£60; d £45-£60 **CONF:** Thtr 40 Class 12 Board 16

○ Hotel due to open in late 2005 or 2006
ⓤ Star rating not confirmed

NEWQUAY, Cornwall & Isles of Scilly Map 02 SW86

★★★★69% Headland

Fistral Beach TR7 1EW
☎ 01637 872211 🖷 01637 872212
e-mail: office@headlandhotel.co.uk
web: www.headlandhotel.co.uk
Dir: *off A30 onto A392 at Indian Queens, approaching Newquay follow signs for Fistral Beach, hotel adjacent*

This Victorian hotel enjoys a stunning location overlooking the sea on three sides, so views can be enjoyed from most of the windows. Bedrooms are comfortable and spacious. Grand public areas, with impressive floral displays, include various lounges and dining options.
ROOMS: 104 en suite (40 fmly) s £76-£122; d £82-£289 (incl. bkfst) **LB** **FACILITIES: Spa** STV 9 Snooker Sauna Putt green Children's outdoor play area, Harry Potter playroom, Surf school ♫ ch fac Xmas **CONF:** Thtr 250 Class 120 Board 40 Del from £100 **SERVICES:** Lift **PARKING:** 400 **NOTES:** No smoking in restaurant Closed 23-27 Dec Civ Wed 200

★★★70% *Hotel Bristol*

Narrowcliff TR7 2PQ
☎ 01637 875181 🖷 01637 879347
e-mail: info@hotelbristol.co.uk
web: www.hotelbristol.co.uk
Dir: *off A30 onto A392, then onto A3058. Hotel 2.5m on left*

This hotel is conveniently situated and many of the bedrooms enjoy fine sea views. Staff are friendly and provide a professional and attentive service. There is a range of comfortable lounges, ideal for relaxing prior to eating in the elegant dining room. There are also leisure and conference facilities.
ROOMS: 74 en suite (23 fmly) **FACILITIES:** STV Snooker Sauna Solarium Table tennis ch fac **CONF:** Thtr 200 Class 80 Board 20 **SERVICES:** Lift **PARKING:** 105 **NOTES:** No smoking in restaurant

See advert on opposite page

★★★70% Trebarwith

Trebarwith Crescent TR7 1BZ
☎ 01637 872288 🖷 01637 875431
e-mail: trebahotel@aol.com web: www.trebarwith-hotel.co.uk
Dir: *from A3058 to Mount Wise Rd. 3rd right down Marcus Hill, across East St into Trebarwith Cres. Hotel at end*

With breathtaking views of the rugged coastline and a path leading to the beach, this friendly, family-run hotel is set in its own grounds close to the town centre. The public rooms include a lounge, ballroom, restaurant and cinema. The comfortable bedrooms include four-poster and family rooms, and many benefit from the sea views.
ROOMS: 41 en suite (8 fmly) (1 GF) s £35-£60; d £70-£120 (incl. bkfst) **LB** **FACILITIES: Spa** Fishing Snooker Sauna Solarium Jacuzzi Video theatre Games room ♫ **CONF:** Thtr 45 **PARKING:** 41 **NOTES:** No smoking in restaurant Closed Nov-5 Apr

See advert on opposite page

★★★69% Esplanade Hotel

Esplanade Rd, Pentire TR7 1PS
☎ 01637 873333 🖷 01637 851413
e-mail: info@newquay-hotels.co.uk
web: www.newquay-hotels.co.uk
Dir: *from A30 take A392 at Indian Queens towards Newquay, follow to rdbt and take left to Pentire, then right fork to beach*

Overlooking the rolling breakers at Fistral Beach, this family-owned hotel offers a friendly welcome. There is a choice of bedroom sizes; all have modern facilities and the most popular rooms benefit from stunning sea views. There are a number of bars, a continental-style coffee shop and the more formal Ocean View Restaurant.
ROOMS: 92 en suite (44 fmly) No smoking in 5 bedrooms s £25-£60; d £50-£120 (incl. bkfst & dinner) **LB** **FACILITIES: Spa** STV Sauna Solarium Jacuzzi Table tennis ♫ ch fac Xmas **CONF:** Thtr 300 Class 180 Board 150 Del from £20 **SERVICES:** Lift **PARKING:** 40 **NOTES:** No smoking in restaurant

★★★67% Barrowfield

Hilgrove Rd TR7 2QY
☎ 01637 878878 🖷 01637 879490
e-mail: booking@barrowfield.prestel.co.uk
web: www.cranstar.co.uk
Dir: *A3058 to Newquay towards Quintrell Downs. Right at rdbt into town, left at Texaco garage*

Offering a pleasant range of facilities and spacious public rooms, this popular hotel is ideally situated and offers friendly and attentive service. Bedrooms, some with sea views and balconies, are well appointed and comfortable. Public areas include an elegant restaurant, spacious foyer lounge, attractive coffee shop and an intimate piano bar.
ROOMS: 81 en suite (18 fmly) s £49-£55; d £98-£144 (incl. bkfst & dinner) **LB** **FACILITIES: Spa** STV Snooker Sauna Jacuzzi Pool room, Snooker room ♫ Xmas **CONF:** Thtr 250 Class 150 Board 90 **SERVICES:** Lift **PARKING:** 37 **NOTES:** No smoking in restaurant Civ Wed 60

★★★66% Hotel California
Pentire Crescent TR7 1PU
☎ 01637 879292 872798 📠 01637 875611
e-mail: info@hotel-california.co.uk
web: www.hotel-california.co.uk
Dir: *A392 to Newquay, follow signs for Pentire Hotels & Guest Houses*

This hotel is tucked away in a delightful location, close to Fistral Beach and adjacent to the River Gannel. Many rooms have views across the river towards the sea, and some have balconies. There is an impressive range of leisure facilities, including indoor and outdoor pools, and ten-pin bowling. Cuisine is enjoyable and menus offer a range of interesting dishes.
ROOMS: 70 en suite (27 fmly) (13 GF) s £32-£50; d £65-£100 (incl. bkfst & dinner) **LB** **FACILITIES: Spa** Squash Snooker Sauna Solarium ♫ Xmas **CONF:** Thtr 100 Class 100 Board 30 Del from £40 **SERVICES:** Lift **PARKING:** 66 **NOTES:** ⊘ in restaurant Civ Wed 150

NEWQUAY, continued

★★★66% *Hotel Riviera*

Lusty Glaze Rd TR7 3AA
☎ 01637 874251 🖷 01637 850823
e-mail: hotelriviera@btconnect.com
Dir: *approaching Newquay from Porth right at The Barrowfields. Hotel on right*

This popular cliff-top hotel enjoys panoramic views across the gardens to the sea beyond. Bedrooms vary in size and style, and many have sea views. Comfortable lounges are provided for rest and relaxation; the more energetic may wish to use the squash court or heated outdoor pool. There is also a range of conference and function facilities.

ROOMS: 48 en suite (6 fmly) **FACILITIES:** supervised Squash Sauna ♫ **CONF:** Thtr 200 Class 150 Board 50 **SERVICES:** Lift **PARKING:** 80 **NOTES:** ⊗ in restaurant Civ Wed

See advert on page 417

★★★61% Kilbirnie

Narrowcliff TR7 2RS
☎ 01637 875155 🖷 01637 850769
e-mail: info@kilbirniehotel.co.uk
web: www.kilbirniehotel.co.uk
Dir: *on A392*

With delightful views over the Barrowfields and the sea, this privately run hotel offers an impressive range of facilities. The reception rooms are spacious and comfortable, and during summer months feature a programme of entertainment. Bedrooms vary in size and style and some enjoy fine sea views.

ROOMS: 66 en suite (3 fmly) (8 GF) s £30-£40; d £60-£80 (incl. bkfst) **LB** **FACILITIES:** Snooker Sauna Solarium Gym Jacuzzi Fitness room, hair salon Xmas **CONF:** BC Thtr 100 Class 50 Board 50 Del from £60 **SERVICES:** Lift air con **PARKING:** 48 **NOTES:** ⊗ in restaurant

See advert on opposite page

N

★★72% Whipsiderry

Trevelgue Rd, Porth TR7 3LY
☎ 01637 874777 876066 🖷 01637 874777
e-mail: info@whipsiderry.co.uk
Dir: *right onto Padstow road (B3276) out of Newquay, in 0.5m right at Trevelgue Rd*

Quietly located, overlooking Porth Beach, this friendly hotel offers bedrooms in a variety of sizes and styles, many with superb views. A daily-changing menu offers interesting and well-cooked dishes with the emphasis on fresh, local produce. An outdoor pool is available, and at dusk guests may be able to enjoy badger-watching in the attractive grounds.

ROOMS: 20 rms (19 en suite) (5 fmly) (3 GF) ⊗ in 15 bedrooms s £49-£62; d £49-£62 (incl. bkfst & dinner) **LB** **FACILITIES:** Sauna American pool ♫ Xmas **PARKING:** 30 **NOTES:** ⊗ in restaurant Closed Nov-Etr (ex Xmas)

★★71% Porth Veor Manor

Porth Way, Porth Bay TR7 3LW
☎ 01637 873274 🖷 01637 851690
e-mail: booking@porthveor.co.uk
Dir: *200yds from junct A3058/B3276, on B3276 towards Padstow*

A relaxed and friendly atmosphere is maintained at this pleasant, family-run hotel, which is set in a quiet area. The hotel overlooks Porth Beach to which it has direct access from its two-acre grounds. Bedrooms are decorated in different styles and all are pleasantly spacious. A daily changing set price menu is served in the dining room.

ROOMS: 22 en suite (7 fmly) (3 GF) ⊗ in 6 bedrooms s £45-£52; d £85-£99 (incl. bkfst) **LB** **FACILITIES:** Sauna Gym Putt green Xmas **CONF:** BC Thtr 36 Class 24 Board 24 Del from £67.95 **PARKING:** 40 **NOTES:** ⊗ in restaurant RS Nov-Feb

★★69% Philema

1 Esplanade Rd, Pentire TR7 1PY
☎ 01637 872571 🖷 01637 873188
e-mail: info@philema.co.uk
Dir: *from A30 follow A392 then signs for Fistral Beach. Hotel on junction Esplanade Rd & Pentire Ave*

With excellent views over Fistral Beach, the Philema provides a relaxed and friendly family environment. Extensive leisure facilities are available, including the heated indoor pool, which overlooks the garden. Many rooms have wonderful views and all are comfortably furnished. The attractive dining room offers a range of home-cooked dishes.

ROOMS: 32 en suite (27 fmly) s £25-£42; d £50-£84 (incl. bkfst & dinner) **FACILITIES: Spa** STV Snooker Sauna Solarium Jacuzzi pool table, games machine ♫ Xmas **PARKING:** 40 **NOTES:** ⊗ in restaurant Closed 2 Jan-2 Feb

★★64% *Trenance Hotel*

The Crescent TR7 1DF
☎ 01637 873159 🖷 01637 850008
e-mail: reception@trenancehotel.co.uk

Set close to the town's many attractions, yet quietly located, this popular and friendly hotel overlooks the harbour. Bedrooms, some with large bay windows and sea views, are well equipped and comfortable. Entertainment is provided most evenings and guests can relax in the lounge, bar or games room.

ROOMS: 57 en suite (4 fmly) **FACILITIES:** pool table ♫ **SERVICES:** Lift **PARKING:** 20 **NOTES:** ⊗ in restaurant

★★63% *Eliot*

Leisureplex

Edgcumbe Av TR7 2NH
☎ 01637 878177 🖷 01637 852053
e-mail: eliot.newquay@alfatravel.co.uk
web: www.alfatravel.co.uk
Dir: *A30 onto A392 towards Quintrell Downs. Right at rdbt onto A3058. 4m to Newquay, left at amusements onto Edgcumbe Av. Hotel on left*

Located in a quiet residential area just a short walk from the beaches and the varied attractions of the town, this long-established hotel offers comfortable accommodation. Entertainment is provided most nights throughout the season and guests can relax in the spacious public areas.

ROOMS: 76 en suite (10 fmly) **FACILITIES:** Sauna Jacuzzi Pool table, Table tennis ♫ ch fac **SERVICES:** Lift **PARKING:** 20 **NOTES:** ⊗ in restaurant Closed Dec-Jan RS Nov & Feb-Mar

---

NEWTON ABBOT, Devon — Map 03 SX87

See also Ilsington

★★★70% Passage House

Hackney Ln, Kingsteignton TQ12 3QH
☎ 01626 355515 🖷 01626 363336
e-mail: hotel@passagehousegroup.co.uk
Dir: *leave A380 for A381 and follow racecourse signs*

With memorable views of the Teign Estuary, this popular hotel provides spacious, well-equipped bedrooms. An impressive range of leisure and meeting facilities is offered and a conservatory provides a pleasant extension to the bar and lounge. A choice of

continued

eating options is available, either in the main restaurant, or the adjacent Passage House Inn for less formal dining.
ROOMS: 38 en suite (32 fmly) (6 GF) ⊗ in 9 bedrooms s £75-£85; d £88-£98 (incl. bkfst) **LB** **FACILITIES: Spa** STV supervised Sauna Solarium Gym **CONF:** BC Thtr 120 Class 50 Board 40 Del from £95 **SERVICES:** Lift **PARKING:** 300 **NOTES:** ⊗ in restaurant RS 24-27 Dec

★★68% Queens

Queen St TQ12 2EZ
☎ 01626 363133 🖷 01626 354106
e-mail: reservations@queenshotel-southwest.co.uk
Dir: *M5 onto A380, follow signs for railway station. Hotel opposite station*
Pleasantly and conveniently located close to the railway station and racecourse, this hotel continues to be a popular venue for both business people and tourists. Bedrooms are pleasantly appointed and well equipped. The lounge bar provides light meals and specials, whilst a more extensive menu is available in the restaurant.
ROOMS: 20 en suite (3 fmly) ⊗ in 8 bedrooms s £50-£70; d £70-£100 (incl. bkfst) **LB** **CONF:** Thtr 100 Class 36 Board 36 Del from £97 **PARKING:** 6 **NOTES:** ⊗ in restaurant RS 24 Dec-2 Jan

NEWTON AYCLIFFE, Co Durham — Map 19 NZ22

Premier Travel Inn Durham (Newton Aycliffe)

Great North Rd DL5 6JG
☎ 08701 977085 🖷 01325 324910
web: www.premiertravelinn.com
Dir: *on A167 east of Newton Aycliffe, 3 miles from A1(M)*
High quality, modern budget accommodation ideal for both families and business travellers. Spacious, en suite bedrooms

continued

feature bath and shower, satellite TV and many have telephones and modem points. The adjacent family restaurant features a wide and varied menu. For further details consult the Hotel Groups page.
ROOMS: 44 en suite s £46.95-£48.95; d £46.95-£48.95

NEWTON-LE-WILLOWS, Merseyside — Map 15 SJ59

★★65% Kirkfield Hotel

2/4 Church St WA12 9SU
☎ 01925 228196 🖷 01925 291540
e-mail: enquiries@kirkfieldhotel.co.uk
Dir: *on A49 Newton-le-Willows opposite St Peter's Church*
A conveniently located hotel situated directly opposite the church, where parking is available. The hotel is family run and offers comfortable accommodation. A table d'hôte menu is available, or there are options for lighter dining in the bar area. Guests receive a friendly welcome and an informal atmosphere prevails.
ROOMS: 17 en suite (3 fmly) ⊗ in 10 bedrooms s £35; d £52 (incl. bkfst) **LB** **CONF:** Thtr 70 Class 60 Board 20 **PARKING:** 50

NORTHALLERTON, North Yorkshire — Map 19 SE39

★★★68% Solberge Hall

Newby Wiske DL7 9ER
☎ 01609 779191 🖷 01609 780472
e-mail: reservations@solbergehall.co.uk
Dir: *W of Northallerton on A684. Signed from x-roads 0.5m from town*
This Grade II listed Georgian country house is set in 16 acres of parkland and commands panoramic views over open countryside. Spacious bedrooms, some with four-poster beds, vary in style. Public areas include a comfortable lounge bar and an elegant

continued on p420

N

NORTHALLERTON, continued

drawing room. The restaurant offers an interesting range of carefully prepared dishes.
ROOMS: 24 en suite (2 fmly) (5 GF) ⊗ in 20 bedrooms s £75; d £120 (incl. bkfst) **LB** **FACILITIES:** STV ♫ Xmas **CONF:** Thtr 100 Class 20 Board 40 Del from £88 **PARKING:** 100 **NOTES:** ⊗ in restaurant Civ Wed 100

Restaurant with Rooms

The Three Tuns
9 South End, Osmotherley DL6 3BN
☎ 01609 883301 01609 883988
Dir: *turn off A19 signed Northallerton/Osmotherley. Turn at junction signed Osmotherley at Kings Head Hotel. Follow road into village, inn straight ahead*
Situated in the popular village of Osmotherley, this restaurant with rooms (now under new ownership) is full of character. Bedrooms, set above the bar and in an adjoining building, vary in size but are stylishly furnished in pine and well equipped. The restaurant offers an imaginative menu of wholesome modern British dishes.
ROOMS: 7 en suite (1 fmly) (1 GF) ⊗ in all bedrooms **PARKING:** 6 **NOTES:** ⊗ in restaurant

NORTHAMPTON, Northamptonshire Map 11 SP76
See also Flore

★★★★70% Northampton Marriott Hotel
Marriott HOTELS & RESORTS
Eagle Dr NN4 7HW
☎ 01604 768700 01604 769011
e-mail: northampton@marriotthotels.co.uk
web: www.marriott.co.uk
Dir: *M1 junct 15, follow signs to Delapre Golf Course, hotel on right*
Located on the outskirts of town, close to major road networks, this modern hotel caters to a cross section of guests. A self-contained management centre makes this a popular conference venue, and its spacious and well-designed bedrooms cater for business travellers especially well. The hotel's proximity to a number of attractions makes this a good base to explore the area.
ROOMS: 120 en suite (10 fmly) (52 GF) ⊗ in 82 bedrooms s £125; d £135 (incl. bkfst) **LB** **FACILITIES: Spa** STV supervised Sauna Solarium Gym Jacuzzi Steam room, beauty treatment room Xmas **CONF:** BC Thtr 250 Class 72 Board 30 Del from £135 **SERVICES:** air con **PARKING:** 187 **NOTES:** ⊗ in restaurant Civ Wed 180

★★★71%
Courtyard by Marriott Northampton
Bedford Rd NN4 7YF
☎ 0870 400 7214 0870 400 7314
e-mail: res.ntncourtyard@kewgreen.co.uk
web: www.kewgreen.co.uk
Dir: *M1 junct 15 onto A508 towards Northampton. Follow A45 towards Wellingborough for 2m then A428 towards Bedford, hotel on left*
With its convenient location on the eastern edge of town and easy access to transport links, this modern hotel is particularly popular with business travellers. Accommodation is spacious, practical, and includes a good range of extras. Open-plan public areas help to create an informal atmosphere and the staff are genuinely friendly.
ROOMS: 104 en suite (50 fmly) (27 GF) ⊗ in 91 bedrooms **FACILITIES:** STV Gym **CONF:** Thtr 60 Class 40 Board 40 **SERVICES:** Lift air con **PARKING:** 156 **NOTES:** ⊗ in restaurant

TV dinner?
Room service at three stars and above

★★★65% Northampton Moat House
Silver St NN1 2TA
☎ 01604 739988 01604 230614
e-mail: csm.northampton@moathousehotels.com
Dir: *M1 junct 15 to A508 to A45 to town centre, turn into Gas St and hotel is on the right*
This busy city centre hotel offers comfortable, well equipped bedrooms. With its manned business centre, extensive function rooms and leisure facilities it is the ideal venue for a relaxing stay whether as a business or leisure guest. Service in both the traditional bar and the modern restaurant is informal.
ROOMS: 145 en suite s fr £108; d fr £130 **FACILITIES:** STV supervised Sauna Solarium Gym Jacuzzi Steam room **CONF:** Thtr 500 Class 300 Board 40 Del from £100 **SERVICES:** Lift **PARKING:** 160 **NOTES:** ⊗ in restaurant Civ Wed 600

★★★65% *Quality Hotel Northampton*
Ashley Way, Weston Favell NN3 3EA
☎ 01604 739955 01604 415023
e-mail: enquiries@hotels-northampton.com
web: www.choicehotelseurope.com
Dir: *leave A45 at junct with A43 towards Weston Favell. After 0.5m left to town centre. Left at top of slip road, hotel signed off A4500*
On the edge of town, this hotel offers well-equipped accommodation in an older-style building and a more modern block. Public rooms are attractive and include an air-conditioned lounge area, an attractively furnished flag-stoned conservatory restaurant and a number of versatile meeting rooms.
ROOMS: 33 en suite 38 annexe en suite (5 fmly) (19 GF) ⊗ in 45 bedrooms **FACILITIES:** STV Can purchase passes to use at nearby leisure centre **CONF:** Thtr 180 Class 160 Board 60 **SERVICES:** Lift **PARKING:** 120 **NOTES:** ⊗ in restaurant Civ Wed 140

U *Lime Trees*
8 Langham Place, Barrack Rd NN2 6AA
☎ 01604 632188 01604 233012
e-mail: manager@limetreeshotel.co.uk
web: www.limetreeshotel.co.uk
Dir: *from city centre 0.5m N on A508 towards Leicester near racecourse park and cathedral*
At the time of going to press, the star classification for this hotel was not confirmed. Please refer to the AA internet site www.theAA.com for current information.
ROOMS: 20 rms (10 en suite) 7 annexe rms (3 fmly) (4 GF) ⊗ in 6 bedrooms **CONF:** Thtr 50 Class 30 Board 30 **PARKING:** 25 **NOTES:** ⊗ in restaurant Closed 24 Dec-3Jan

Hotel Ibis Northampton
Sol Central, Marefair NN1 1SR
☎ 01604 608900 01604 608910
e-mail: H3657@accor-hotels.com
Dir: *M1 junct 15/15a & towards city centre railway station*
Modern, budget hotel offering comfortable accommodation in bright and practical bedrooms. Breakfast is self-service and dinner is available in the restaurant. For further details, consult the Hotel Groups page. **ROOMS:** 151 en suite

Innkeeper's Lodge Northampton East
Talavera Way, Round Spinney NN3 8RN
☎ 01604 494241 01604 673701
web: www.innkeeperslodge.com
Dir: *M1 junct 15a, N on A43. Right at rdbt, pass 2 further rdbts. At 3rd rdbt, A45 N until exit for A43, continue to Round Spinney rdbt and Talavera Way*
A growing concept in the travel accommodation market. Smart rooms meet essential business requirements but also have home comforts. Dining options include all-day menus plus the added

continued

advantage of breakfast, which is included in the room price. For further details consult the Hotel Groups page.
ROOMS: 31 en suite s £45-£55; d £45-£55 **CONF:** Thtr 36 Class 24 Board 28

⌂ Innkeeper's Lodge Northampton South
London Rd, Wootton NN4 0TG
☎ 01604 769676 📠 01604 677981
web: www.innkeeperslodge.com
Dir: *M1 junct 15 take A508, towards Northampton. Pass under flyover, exit left immediately & turn right at rdbt into London Rd. Lodge on right.*
A growing concept in the travel accommodation market. Smart rooms meet essential business requirements but also have home comforts. Dining options include all-day menus plus the added advantage of breakfast, which is included in the room price. For further details consult the Hotel Groups page.
ROOMS: 51 en suite s £45-£55; d £45-£55 **CONF:** Thtr 100 Board 40

⌂ Premier Travel Inn Northampton East (Great Billing/A45)
Crow Ln, Great Billing NN3 9DA
☎ 0870 9906510 📠 0870 9906511
web: www.premiertravelinn.com
Dir: *5m from M1 junct 15. A508 to A45 then follow Billing Aquadrom signs*
High quality, modern budget accommodation ideal for both families and business travellers. Spacious, en suite bedrooms feature bath and shower, satellite TV and many have telephones and modem points. The adjacent family restaurant features a wide and varied menu. For further details consult the Hotel Groups page.
ROOMS: 60 en suite s £49.95-£52.95; d £49.95-£52.95 **CONF:** Thtr 10 Board 10

⌂ Premier Travel Inn Northampton East (Houghton/A428)
The Lakes, Bedford Rd NN4 7YD
☎ 08701 977196 📠 01604 621935
web: www.premiertravelinn.com
Dir: *M1 junct 15 A508 (A45) to Northampton. A428. At rdbt 4th exit (signed Bedford). Left at next rdbt. Inn on right*
High quality, modern budget accommodation ideal for both families and business travellers. Spacious, en suite bedrooms feature bath and shower, satellite TV and many have telephones and modem points. The adjacent family restaurant features a wide and varied menu. For further details consult the Hotel Groups page.
ROOMS: 44 en suite s £46.95-£49.95; d £46.95-£49.95

⌂ Premier Travel Inn Northampton South
Newport Pagnell Rd West, Wootton NN4 7JJ
☎ 0870 9906426 📠 0870 9906427
web: www.premiertravelinn.com
Dir: *Exit M1 junct 15 onto A508 towards Northampton. Exit at junct with A45. At rdbt take B526. Hotel on right*
High quality, modern budget accommodation ideal for both families and business travellers. Spacious, en suite bedrooms feature bath and shower, satellite TV and many have telephones and modem points. The adjacent family restaurant features a wide and varied menu. For further details consult the Hotel Groups page.
ROOMS: 39 en suite s £46.95-£49.95; d £46.95-£49.95 **CONF:** Thtr 75 Class 48 Board 30

⌂ Premier Travel Inn Northampton West (Harpole)
Harpole Turn, Weedon Rd, Harpole NN7 4DD
☎ 08701 977195 📠 01604 831807
web: www.premiertravelinn.com
Dir: *From M1 junct 16, take A45 to Northampton. After 1 mile turn left into Harpole Turn. Inn is on left*
High quality, modern budget accommodation ideal for both families and business travellers. Spacious, en suite bedrooms feature bath and shower, satellite TV and many have telephones and modem points. The adjacent family restaurant features a wide and varied menu. For further details consult the Hotel Groups page.
ROOMS: 51 en suite s £46.95-£49.95; d £46.95-£49.95 **CONF:** Thtr 40 Board 30

⌂ Travelodge
Upton Way NN5 6EG
☎ 08700 850 950 📠 01604 758395
web: www.travelodge.co.uk
Dir: *A45, towards M1 junct 16*
Travelodge offers good quality, good value, modern accommodation. Ideal for families, the spacious, en suite bedrooms include remote-control TV, tea and coffee-making facilities and comfortable beds. Meals can be taken at the nearby family restaurant. For further details consult the Hotel Groups page.
ROOMS: 62 en suite s fr £26; d fr £26

NORTH FERRIBY, East Riding of Yorkshire — Map 17 SE92

★★★66% *Elizabeth Hotel Hull*
Ferriby High Rd HU14 3LG
☎ 01482 645212 📠 01482 643332
e-mail: elizabeth.hull@elizabethhotels.co.uk
web: www.elizabethhotels.co.uk
Dir: *M62 onto A63 to Hull. Exit for Humber Bridge. At rdbt follow Leeds signs then signs for North Ferriby. Hotel 0.5m on left*
A modern, purpose built hotel that enjoys spectacular views of the Humber Bridge. Bedrooms are comfortable and well equipped. Public areas are spacious and both the restaurant and lounge bar look out over the river. There is a children's play area at the rear.
ROOMS: 95 en suite (6 fmly) (17 GF) ⊗ in 77 bedrooms
FACILITIES: STV Nearly full size pool table **CONF:** Thtr 200 Class 85 Board 86 **PARKING:** 140 **NOTES:** Civ Wed 70

NORTH KILWORTH, Leicestershire — Map 11 SP68

★★★★73% @@ Kilworth House
Lutterworth Rd LE17 6JE
☎ 01858 880058 📠 01858 880349
e-mail: info@kilworthhouse.co.uk
web: www.kilworthhouse.co.uk
Dir: *A4304 towards Market Harborough, after Walcote, hotel 1.5m on right*

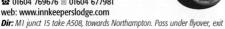

A restored Victorian country house located in 38 acres of private grounds. The gracious public areas feature many period pieces and original artworks. Bedrooms are very comfortable and well equipped, and the large Orangery is now used for informal dining while an opulent restaurant has a more formal air.
ROOMS: 44 en suite (2 fmly) (13 GF) ⊗ in 41 bedrooms s £135-£235; d £155-£255 **LB** **FACILITIES:** STV Fishing Gym Beauty therapy rooms Xmas **CONF:** Thtr 80 Class 30 Board 30 Del from £180
SERVICES: Lift **PARKING:** 140 **NOTES:** ⊗ in restaurant Civ Wed 100

NORTH MUSKHAM, Nottinghamshire Map 17 SK75

Travelodge (Newark)
NG23 6HT
☎ 08700 850 950 🖷 01636 703635
web: www.travelodge.co.uk
Dir: *4m N, on A1 southbound*
Travelodge offers good quality, good value, modern accommodation. Ideal for families, the spacious, en suite bedrooms include remote-control TV, tea and coffee-making facilities and comfortable beds. Meals can be taken at the nearby family restaurant. For further details consult the Hotel Groups page.
ROOMS: 30 en suite s fr £26; d fr £26

NORTHOLT, Greater London
See LONDON SECTION plan 1 B4

Innkeeper's Lodge Northolt
Mandeville Rd UB5 4LU
☎ 020 8422 2050
web: www.innkeeperslodge.com
Dir: *A40 at the Target roundabout*
A growing concept in the travel accommodation market. Smart rooms meet essential business requirements but also have home comforts. Dining options include all-day menus plus the added advantage of breakfast, which is included in the room price. For further details consult the Hotel Groups page.
ROOMS: 21 en suite s £59.95-£69; d £59.95-£69

NORTH WALSHAM, Norfolk Map 13 TG23

★★★68% Scarborough Hill Country House
Old Yarmouth Rd NR28 9NA
☎ 01692 402151 🖷 01692 406686
e-mail: scarboroughhill@nascr.net
Dir: *From Norwich B1150, straight through lights, across mini rdbt, right at next rdbt, hotel 1m on right*

Delightful country-house hotel situated on the outskirts of town in a peaceful location amidst landscaped grounds. Public rooms include a smart lounge bar with plush sofas, an intimate dining room and a large conservatory. Bedrooms are generally quite spacious; each one is tastefully furnished and thoughtfully equipped.
ROOMS: 8 en suite (2 fmly) ⊗ in 6 bedrooms s £55-£58; d £80-£85 (incl. bkfst) **LB** **CONF:** Thtr 120 Class 80 Board 60 Del from £95 **PARKING:** 80 **NOTES:** ✗ ⊗ in restaurant

Popped the question? Hotels with Civ wed in their entry are licensed for civil wedding ceremonies. Maximum numbers for the ceremony only are shown e.g. Civ wed 120

Top Hotel

★★ ◎◎ Beechwood
Cromer Rd NR28 0HD
☎ 01692 403231 🖷 01692 407284
e-mail: enquiries@beechwood-hotel.co.uk
web: www.beechwood-hotel.co.uk
Dir: *B1150 from Norwich. At North Walsham left at 1st lights, then right at next*
Expect a warm welcome at this elegant 18th-century house, situated just a short walk from the town centre. The individually styled bedrooms are tastefully furnished with well-chosen antique pieces, attractive co-ordinated soft fabrics and many thoughtful touches. The spacious public areas include a lounge bar with plush furnishings, a further lounge and a smartly appointed restaurant.
ROOMS: 17 en suite (4 GF) ⊗ in all bedrooms s fr £70; d £90-£160 (incl. bkfst) **LB** **FACILITIES:** **CONF:** Thtr 20 Class 20 Board 20 Del from £120 **PARKING:** 20 **NOTES:** No children 10yrs ⊗ in restaurant

NORTH WALTHAM, Hampshire Map 05 SU54

Premier Travel Inn Basingstoke South
RG25 2BB
☎ 0870 9906476 🖷 0870 9906477
web: www.premiertravelinn.com
Dir: *On A30 just off M3 junct 7. Turn left signed North Waltham, Popham & Kings Worthy. Hotel 2m on right, before A303*
High quality, modern budget accommodation ideal for both families and business travellers. Spacious, en suite bedrooms feature bath and shower, satellite TV and many have telephones and modem points. The adjacent family restaurant features a wide and varied menu. For further details consult the Hotel Groups page.
ROOMS: 28 en suite s £49.95-£52.95; d £49.95-£52.95 **CONF:** Thtr 80 Class 30 Board 35

NORTHWICH, Cheshire Map 15 SJ67

★★★64% The Floatel, Northwich
London Rd CW9 5HD
☎ 01606 44443 🖷 01606 42596
e-mail: enquiries@hotels-northwich.com
web: www.hotels-northwich.com
Dir: *M6 junct 19, follow A556 for 4m, take right turn & follow signs for town centre*
A first in the UK, this floating hotel has been built on the River Weaver in the town centre and is a very successful concept. The bedrooms are modern and well equipped, and there is a pleasant restaurant which overlooks the river.
ROOMS: 60 en suite (2 fmly) ⊗ in 30 bedrooms s £79-£85; d £89-£99 **LB** **FACILITIES:** STV Xmas **CONF:** Thtr 80 Class 40 Board 30 Del from £95 **SERVICES:** Lift **PARKING:** 110 **NOTES:** ⊗ in restaurant Civ Wed 80

★★64% Hartford Hall
School Ln, Hartford CW8 1PW
☎ 01606 780320 ⎙ 01606 782285
Dir: *in village of Hartford, between Northwich & Chester signed off A556*
Set in four acres of gardens and grounds on the edge of the village of Hartford, this 17th-century manor house offers well-equipped accommodation, including no-smoking and family bedrooms. Public areas are characteristic of the period and include the heavily beamed Nunn's Room, where civil weddings and other functions are held.
ROOMS: 20 en suite (4 fmly) (8 GF) ⊗ in 13 bedrooms **FACILITIES:** STV Games room **CONF:** Thtr 80 Class 50 Board 30 **PARKING:** 50 **NOTES:** ⊗ in restaurant RS 25-Dec Civ Wed 70

⌂ Premier Travel Inn Northwich
520 Chester Rd, Sandiway CW8 2DN
☎ 0870 9906494 ⎙ 0870 9906495
web: www.premiertravelinn.com
Dir: *11m from M6 junct 19, on A556 towards Chester*
High quality, modern budget accommodation ideal for both families and business travellers. Spacious, en suite bedrooms feature bath and shower, satellite TV and many have telephones and modem points. The adjacent family restaurant features a wide and varied menu. For further details consult the Hotel Groups page.
ROOMS: 52 en suite s £47.95-£50.95; d £47.95-£50.95 **CONF:** Thtr 65

⌂ Premier Travel Inn Northwich South
London Rd, Leftwich CW9 8EG
☎ 0870 9906362 ⎙ 0870 9906363
web: www.premiertravelinn.com
Dir: *Just off M6 junct 19 follow A556 to Chester. Right at sign for Northwich & Davenham*
High quality, modern budget accommodation ideal for both families and business travellers. Spacious, en suite bedrooms feature bath and shower, satellite TV and many have telephones and modem points. The adjacent family restaurant features a wide and varied menu. For further details consult the Hotel Groups page.
ROOMS: 32 en suite s £47.95-£50.95; d £47.95-£50.95 **CONF:** Thtr 15 Class 15 Board 15

NORTHWOLD, Norfolk — Map 13 TL79

★★66% Comfort Inn Thetford
Thetford Rd IP26 5LQ
☎ 01366 728888 ⎙ 01366 727121
e-mail: enquiries@hotels-thetford.com
web: www.hotels-thetford.com
Dir: *W of Mundford on A134*
A modern purpose-built hotel in a rural setting just off the main road. The generously proportioned bedrooms are situated in courtyard style wings; each room is pleasantly decorated and well equipped. Dinner and breakfast are served in the beamed Woodland Inn, which combines the roles of country pub and hotel restaurant.
ROOMS: 34 en suite (12 fmly) (18 GF) ⊗ in 17 bedrooms s £45-£95; d £55-£110 **LB** **FACILITIES:** STV Xmas **CONF:** Thtr 150 Class 55 Board 60 Del from £74.50 **PARKING:** 250 **NOTES:** ⊗ in restaurant Civ Wed 95

Late for dinner? Quality standards mean that last orders for dinner vary according to star rating and should be no earlier than: ★★ 7.00pm ★★★ 8:00pm ★★★★ 9:00pm ★★★★★ 10:00pm

NORTON, Shropshire — Map 10 SJ70

★★76% ®® Hundred House Hotel
Bridgnorth Rd TF11 9EE
☎ 01952 730353 ⎙ 01952 730355
e-mail: reservations@hundredhouse.co.uk
web: www.hundredhouse.co.uk
Dir: *midway between Telford and Bridgnorth on A442. In centre of Norton*
Primarily Georgian, but with parts dating back to the 14th century, this friendly family owned and run hotel offers individually styled, well-equipped bedrooms which have period furniture and attractive soft furnishings. Public areas include cosy bars and intimate dining areas where memorable meals are served. There is now an attractive conference centre in the old barn.
ROOMS: 10 en suite (4 fmly) s £69-£85 (incl. bkfst) **LB** **FACILITIES:** Xmas **CONF:** Thtr 80 Class 30 Board 32 Del from £115 **PARKING:** 45 **NOTES:** Closed 25 & 26 Dec nights RS Sun evenings

NORTON CANES MOTORWAY SERVICE AREA (M6 TOLL), Staffordshire — Map 10 SK00

⌂ Premier Travel Inn Birmingham North (M6 Toll)
Norton Canes MSA, M6 Toll Rd, North Canes WS11 9UX
☎ 08701 977070 ⎙ 08701 977 700
web: www.premiertravelinn.com
Dir: *at motorway service area between junct 6/7 of M6 toll road. Access from both sides via barrier and from A5*
High quality, modern budget accommodation ideal for both families and business travellers. Spacious, en suite bedrooms feature bath and shower, satellite TV and many have telephones and modem points. The adjacent family restaurant features a wide and varied menu. For further details consult the Hotel Groups page.
ROOMS: 40 en suite s £46.95-£48.95; d £46.95-£48.95

NORWICH, Norfolk — Map 13 TG20

★★★★75% ® Marriott Sprowston Manor Hotel & Country Club
Sprowston Park, Wroxham Rd, Sprowston NR7 8RP
☎ 01603 410871 ⎙ 01603 423911
e-mail: sprowston.manor@marriotthotels.co.uk
web: www.marriott.co.uk
Dir: *From A11/A47, 2m NE on A115 (Wroxham Rd). Follow signs to Sprowston Park*
Surrounded by open parkland, this imposing property is set in attractively landscaped grounds and is just a short drive from the city centre. Bedrooms are spacious and feature a variety of decorative styles. The hotel also has extensive conference, banqueting and leisure facilities. Other public rooms include a variety of seating areas and the elegant Manor Restaurant.
ROOMS: 94 en suite (3 fmly) (5 GF) ⊗ in 61 bedrooms **FACILITIES:** **Spa** STV supervised 18 Sauna Solarium Gym Putt green **CONF:** Thtr 120 Class 50 Board 50 **SERVICES:** Lift **PARKING:** 150 **NOTES:** ⊗ in restaurant Civ Wed 110

★★★★70% ® De Vere Dunston Hall
Ipswich Rd NR14 8PQ
☎ 01508 470444 ⎙ 01508 471499
e-mail: dhreception@devere-hotels.com
web: www.devereonline.co.uk
Dir: *from A47, take A140 Ipswich road, hotel off road on left after 0.25m*
Imposing Grade II listed building set amidst 170 acres of landscaped grounds just a short drive from the city centre. The

continued on p424

NORWICH, continued

spacious bedrooms are smartly decorated, tastefully furnished and equipped to a high standard. The attractively appointed public rooms offer a wide choice of areas in which to relax and the hotel also boasts a superb range of leisure facilities including an 18-hole PGA golf course, floodlit tennis courts and a football pitch.
ROOMS: 130 en suite (15 fmly) (15 GF) ⊗ in 112 bedrooms **FACILITIES: Spa** STV ⛳ 18 Snooker Sauna Solarium Gym Putt green Jacuzzi Floodlit Driving Range **CONF:** Thtr 300 Class 140 Board 80 **SERVICES:** Lift **PARKING:** 500 **NOTES:** ⊗ in restaurant Civ Wed 90

★★★75% Annesley House
6 Newmarket Rd NR2 2LA
☎ 01603 624553 📠 01603 621577
e-mail: annesleyhouse@bestwestern.co.uk
Dir: *on A11 0.5m before city centre*
Delightful Georgian property situated amid three acres of landscaped gardens close to the city centre. Bedrooms are split between three separate houses, two of which are linked by a glass walkway; they are attractively decorated, tastefully furnished and equipped with many useful extras. Public rooms include a comfortable lounge/bar and a smart conservatory restaurant, which overlooks the gardens.
ROOMS: 18 en suite 8 annexe en suite (3 fmly) (7 GF) ⊗ in 22 bedrooms s £82; d £96.50 (incl. bkfst) **LB FACILITIES:** STV **CONF:** Thtr 16 Board 16 Del £125 **PARKING:** 25 **NOTES:** ⊗ in restaurant Closed 24-27 & 30-31 Dec

★★★75% Barnham Broom Hotel, Golf & Country Club
NR9 4DD
☎ 01603 759393 759522 📠 01603 758224
e-mail: enquiry@barnhambroomhotel.co.uk
web: www.barnham-broom.co.uk
(For full entry see Barnham Broom)

★★★71% Beeches Hotel & Victorian Gardens
2-6 Earlham Rd NR2 3DB
☎ 01603 621167 📠 01603 620151
e-mail: reception@beeches.co.uk
web: www.beeches.co.uk
Dir: *W of city centre on B1108, next to St Johns Cathedral, off inner ring road*
Ideally situated just a short walk from the city centre, and set amidst landscaped grounds that include a lovely sunken Victorian garden, this hotel is under new ownership. The bedrooms are in three separate buildings; each room is tastefully decorated and equipped with many thoughtful touches. Public rooms include a smart lounge bar, a bistro-style restaurant and a residents' lounge.
ROOMS: 41 en suite (30 GF) ⊗ in all bedrooms s £64-£74; d £95-£105 (incl. bkfst) **FACILITIES:** Xmas **PARKING:** 50 **NOTES:** No children 12yrs ⊗ in restaurant

★★★68% The George Hotel
10 Arlington Ln, Newmarket Rd NR2 2DA
☎ 01603 617841 📠 01603 663708
e-mail: reservations@georgehotel.co.uk
Dir: *on A11 follow city centre signs, Newmarket Rd towards centre. Hotel on left*
Ideally situated just a few minutes' walk from the shops and well placed for guests wishing to explore the many sights of this historic city. The hotel occupies three adjacent buildings; the restaurant, bar and most bedrooms are located in the main building, while the adjacent cottages have been converted into comfortable and modern guest bedrooms.

ROOMS: 38 en suite 5 annexe en suite (4 fmly) (19 GF) ⊗ in 12 bedrooms s £63-£77; d £87-£97 (incl. bkfst) **LB FACILITIES:** Xmas **CONF:** Thtr 70 Class 30 Board 30 Del from £99 **PARKING:** 40 **NOTES:** ⊗ in restaurant

★★★68% The Georgian House
32-34 Unthank Rd NR2 2RB
☎ 01603 615655 📠 01603 765689
e-mail: reception@georgian-hotel.co.uk
Dir: *from city centre follow Roman Catholic Cathedral signs, hotel off inner ring road*
Located within easy walking distance of the historic centre of Norwich, this independent hotel offers individually appointed bedrooms and public areas. Interesting cuisine is served within the Goodwins restaurant by a friendly and helpful staff; a small bar and separate lounge are also available to guests.
ROOMS: 27 en suite 1 annexe en suite (3 fmly) (10 GF) ⊗ in 23 bedrooms s fr £68; d £85-£130 (incl. bkfst) **LB FACILITIES:** STV Xmas **PARKING:** 30 **NOTES:** ⊗ in restaurant
See advert on opposite page

★★★68% Quality Hotel Norwich
2 Barnard Rd, Bowthorpe NR5 9JB
☎ 01603 741161 📠 01603 741500
e-mail: enquiries@hotels-norwich.com
web: www.choicehotelseurope.com
Dir: *A1074 to Norwich & Cromer. Hotel off A47 southern bypass, 4m from city centre*
Modern hotel situated on the west side of the city, four miles from the centre. The spacious bedrooms are pleasantly decorated and equipped with up-to-date facilities. Public areas include a carvery restaurant, bar and lounge. The hotel offers conference and banqueting facilities, as well as a leisure centre.
ROOMS: 80 en suite (13 fmly) (40 GF) ⊗ in 40 bedrooms s £95-£105; d £105-£115 **LB FACILITIES:** STV Sauna Solarium Gym Jacuzzi Steamroom Xmas **CONF:** Thtr 200 Class 80 Board 60 Del from £95 **PARKING:** 200 **NOTES:** ⊗ in restaurant Civ Wed 75

★★★67% The Maids Head Hotel
Tombland NR3 1LB
☎ 0870 609 6110 📠 01603 613688
e-mail: maidshead@corushotels.com
web: www.corushotels.com
Dir: *follow city centre signs past Norwich Castle. 3rd turning after castle into Upper King St, hotel opposite Norman Cathedral*
Imposing 13th-century building situated close to the impressive Norman cathedral, the Anglian TV studios and within easy walking distance of the city centre. The bedrooms are pleasantly decorated and thoughtfully equipped; some rooms have original oak beams.
continued

The spacious public rooms include a Jacobean bar, a range of seating areas and the Courtyard restaurant.

ROOMS: 84 en suite (7 fmly) ⊗ in 52 bedrooms s £98; d £118 **LB**
FACILITIES: Xmas **CONF:** Thtr 150 Class 80 Board 40 Del £135
SERVICES: Lift **PARKING:** 70 **NOTES:** ⊗ in restaurant Civ Wed 100

Top Hotel

★★ ◉◉ **The Old Rectory**
103 Yarmouth Rd, Thorpe St Andrew NR7 0HF
☎ 01603 700772 ▤ 01603 300772
e-mail: enquiries@oldrectorynorwich.com
web: www.oldrectorynorwich.com
Dir: from A47 southern bypass onto A1042 towards Norwich N and E.
Left at mini rdbt onto A1242. After 0.3m through lights and hotel
100mtrs on right
This delightful Grade II listed Georgian property is ideally located in a peaceful area overlooking the River Yare, just a few minutes' drive from the city centre. Spacious bedrooms are individually designed with carefully chosen soft fabrics, plush furniture and many thoughtful touches; many of the rooms overlook the swimming pool and landscaped gardens. Accomplished cooking is offered via a interesting daily-changing menu, which features skilfully prepared local produce.
ROOMS: 5 en suite 3 annexe en suite ⊗ in all bedrooms
s £74-£90; d £99.50-£120 (incl. bkfst) **LB FACILITIES:** STV ⚲
CONF: Thtr 25 Class 18 Board 16 **PARKING:** 15 **NOTES:** ✖ ⊗ in
restaurant Closed 21 Dec-4 Jan

★★74% ◉ **Stower Grange**
School Rd, Drayton NR8 6EF
☎ 01603 860210 ▤ 01603 860464
e-mail: enquiries@stowergrange.co.uk
web: www.stowergrange.co.uk
Dir: Norwich ring road N to Asda supermarket. Take A1067 Fakenham Rd
at Drayton village, right at traffic lights along School Rd. Hotel 150yds on right
A 17th-century, ivy-clad property situated in a peaceful residential area just a short drive from the city centre and airport. The
continued

The Georgian House Hotel
32 - 34 Unthank Road, Norwich NR2 2RB
T: 01603 615655 F: 01603 765689
www.georgian-hotel.co.uk
reception@georgian-hotel.co.uk

Situated in the heart of Norwich, just a short walk from the city centre.

Two Georgian town houses tastefully refurbished offering a high standard of accommodation.

Set in beautiful landscaped gardens.

Licensed restaurant and comfortable bar.

Ample free car parking. AA ★★★ 68% ◉

individually decorated bedrooms are generally quite spacious; each one is individually decorated, tastefully furnished and equipped with many thoughtful touches. Public rooms include a smart open-plan lounge bar and an elegant restaurant.

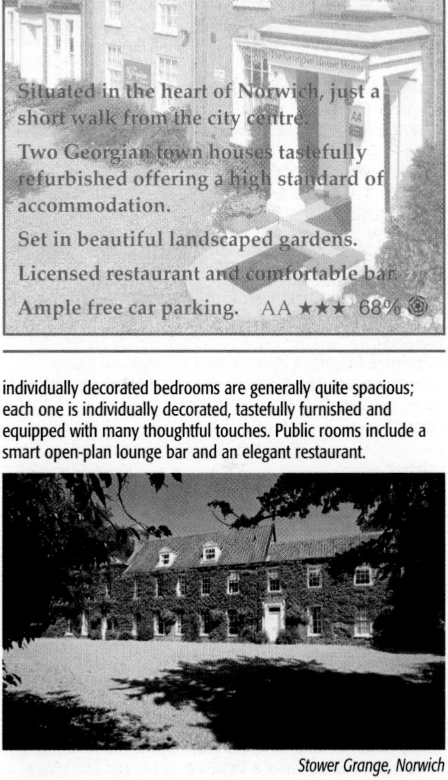

Stower Grange, Norwich

ROOMS: 11 en suite (1 fmly) s £67.50; d £89-£125 (incl. bkfst)
FACILITIES: ◉ **CONF:** Thtr 100 Class 45 Board 30 **PARKING:** 40
NOTES: ⊗ in restaurant Civ Wed 100

★★70% **The Old Rectory**
North Walsham Rd, Crostwick NR12 7BG
☎ 01603 738513 ▤ 01603 738712
e-mail: info@oldrectorycrostwick.com
web: www.oldrectorycrostwick.com
Dir: left off Norwich ring road onto B1150. Hotel 4m on left
Attractive family-run hotel situated on the outskirts of the city centre. Public rooms feature a superb hexagonal conservatory style dining room, which overlooks the pretty gardens, and guests
continued on p426

NORWICH, continued

have the use of a smart lounge as well as a cosy bar and private dining room. Bedrooms are attractively decorated and well equipped.

The Old Rectory, Norwich

ROOMS: 13 en suite (8 fmly) (13 GF) ⊗ in 5 bedrooms s £48; d £65 (incl. bkfst) **FACILITIES:** ⛳ **CONF:** Thtr 110 Class 80 Board 50 **PARKING:** 100 **NOTES:** ⊗ in restaurant Civ Wed 150

★★67% Wensum Valley Hotel Golf & Country Club

Beech Av, Taverham NR8 6HP
☎ 01603 261012 🖷 01603 261664
e-mail: enqs@wensumvalley.co.uk
Dir: *Turn left off A1067 Norwich to Fakenham road at Taverham into Beech Avenue. Hotel entrance on right next to High School*
Family-run hotel set amid 240 acres of lovely countryside just a short distance from the city centre. The modern, purpose-built bedrooms are generally spacious and thoughtfully equipped. Public rooms include a choice of bars, a lounge and a large restaurant overlooking the green. The hotel has superb golf and leisure facilities.
ROOMS: 84 en suite (12 fmly) (32 GF) ⊗ in all bedrooms s £46-£56; d £94 (incl. bkfst) **LB** **FACILITIES:** supervised ⛳ 36 Fishing Snooker Sauna Solarium Gym Putt green Jacuzzi Beauty therapy Golf driving range Hairdressing salon ♫ Xmas **CONF:** Thtr 200 Board 30 Del from £20 **PARKING:** 250 **NOTES:** ✱ ⊗ in restaurant Civ Wed 100

★★64% ◎ Cumberland

212-216 Thorpe Rd NR1 1TJ
☎ 01603 434550 🖷 01603 433355
e-mail: cumberland@paston.co.uk
web: www.cumberlandhotel.com
Dir: *Hotel accessed from A47, then A1242 (past Norwich City FC)*
This hotel, now under new ownership, is situated just a short drive from the railway station and city centre. Bedrooms are pleasantly decorated and thoughtfully equipped. An interesting choice of freshly prepared dishes is served in the Cape Dutch restaurant and guests also have the use of a smart lounge bar and cosy sitting room.
ROOMS: 22 en suite 4 annexe en suite (3 fmly) (6 GF) ⊗ in 10 bedrooms s £45-£59; d £59-£69 (incl. bkfst) **LB** **CONF:** Thtr 90 Class 30 Board 40 **PARKING:** 50 **NOTES:** ✱ ⊗ in restaurant Closed 26-31 Dec

U Ramada Norwich

RAMADA

121-131 Boundary Rd NR3 2BA
☎ 01603 787260 🖷 01603 400466
e-mail: sales.norwich@ramadajarvis.co.uk
web: www.ramadajarvis.co.uk
Dir: *approx 2m from airport on A140 Norwich ring road.*
Conveniently located on the city's outer ring road, this large hotel is a popular venue for both conferences and meetings. Bedrooms are comfortably appointed for both business and leisure guests.
ROOMS: 107 en suite (8 fmly) (22 GF) ⊗ in 75 bedrooms s £82-£109; d £82-£109 **FACILITIES:** STV supervised Sauna Gym Jacuzzi Xmas **CONF:** Thtr 300 Class 150 Board 50 Del from £130 **PARKING:** 230 **NOTES:** ✱ ⊗ in restaurant Civ Wed 50

⌂ Premier Travel Inn Norwich Airport

premier travel inn

Holt Rd, Norwich Airport NR6 6JA
☎ 08701 977 291 🖷 01603 428641
web: www.premiertravelinn.com
High quality, modern budget accommodation ideal for both families and business travellers. Spacious, en suite bedrooms feature bath and shower, satellite TV and many have telephones and modem points. The adjacent family restaurant features a wide and varied menu. For further details consult the Hotel Groups page.
ROOMS: 40 en suite s £49.95-£52.95; d £49.95-£52.95

⌂ Premier Travel Inn Norwich (Showground)

premier travel inn

Longwater Interchange, Dereham Rd, New Costessey NR5 0TL
☎ 08701 977197 🖷 01603 741219
web: www.premiertravelinn.com
Dir: *Follow brown tourist signs for Royal Norfolk Showground on A47 and A1074. Inn opposite showground*
High quality, modern budget accommodation ideal for both families and business travellers. Spacious, en suite bedrooms feature bath and shower, satellite TV and many have telephones and modem points. The adjacent family restaurant features a wide and varied menu. For further details consult the Hotel Groups page.
ROOMS: 40 en suite s £49.95; d £49.95

⌂ Premier Travel Inn Norwich South East

premier travel inn

Broadland Business Park, Old Chapel Way NR7 0WG
☎ 08701 977198 🖷 01603 307617
web: www.premiertravelinn.com
Dir: *A47 onto A1042, 3m E of city centre*
High quality, modern budget accommodation ideal for both families and business travellers. Spacious, en suite bedrooms feature bath and shower, satellite TV and many have telephones and modem points. The adjacent family restaurant features a wide and varied menu. For further details consult the Hotel Groups page.
ROOMS: 60 en suite s £46.95-£49.95; d £46.95-£49.95 **CONF:** Thtr 20 Board 14

⌂ Travelodge

Travelodge

Thickthorn Service Area, Norwich Southern Bypass NR9 3AU
☎ 08700 850 950 🖷 0870 191 1704
web: www.travelodge.co.uk
Dir: *at A11/A47 junct*
Travelodge offers good quality, good value, modern accommodation. Ideal for families, the spacious, en suite bedrooms include remote-control TV, tea and coffee-making facilities and comfortable beds. Meals can be taken at the nearby family restaurant. For further details consult the Hotel Groups page.
ROOMS: 62 en suite s fr £26; d fr £26

Town House Hotel
Country House Hotel
⌂ Travel Accommodation

NOTTINGHAM, Nottinghamshire Map 11 SK53
See also Langar

Town House

★★★★ Hart's
Standard Hill, Park Row NG1 6FN
☎ 0115 988 1900 0115 947 7600
e-mail: ask@hartshotel.co.uk
web: www.hartsnottingham.co.uk
Dir: *at junct of Park Row & Rope Walk, close to city centre*
This outstanding modern building stands on the site of the ramparts of the medieval castle, overlooking the city. Many of the bedrooms enjoy splendid views. Rooms are well appointed and stylish, while the Park Bar is the focal point of the public areas; service is professional and caring. Fine dining is offered at nearby Hart's Restaurant. Secure parking and private gardens are an added bonus.
ROOMS: 32 en suite (1 fmly) (5 GF) ⊗ in all bedrooms s £120-£245; d £120-£245 **LB FACILITIES:** STV Gym Small, unsupervised exercise room Xmas **CONF:** Thtr 80 Class 75 Board 33 Del from £185 **SERVICES:** Lift **PARKING:** 21 **NOTES:** ⊗ in restaurant

Town House

★★★★ Lace Market
29-31 High Pavement NG1 1HE
☎ 0115 852 3232 0115 852 3223
e-mail: stay@lacemarkethotel.co.uk
web: www.lacemarkethotel.co.uk
Dir: *follow tourist signs for Galleries of Justice which is opposite hotel*
This smart town house, a conversion of two Georgian houses, is located in the trendy Lace Market area of the city. Smart public areas, including the stylish and very popular Merchants Restaurant and Saints Bar, are complemented by the 'Cock and Hoop', a traditional pub offering real ales and fine wines. Accommodation is stylish and contemporary and includes spacious superior rooms and split-level suites; are all thoughtfully equipped with a host of extras including CD players and mini bars.
ROOMS: 42 en suite ⊗ in all bedrooms s £90-£112; d £112-£229 **LB FACILITIES:** STV Complimentary use of nearby health club, including indoor pool. **CONF:** Thtr 35 Class 35 Board 20 Del from £150 **SERVICES:** Lift **NOTES:** ⊗ in restaurant

★★★★66% **Park Plaza Nottingham**
41 Maid Marian Way NG1 6GD
☎ 0115 947 7200 0115 947 7300
e-mail: info@parkplazanottingham.com
web: www.parkplaza.com
Dir: *A6200 Derby Road onto Wollaton St. 2nd exit onto Maid Marian Way. Hotel on left*
This ultra modern hotel is located in the centre of the city within walking distance of retail, commercial and tourist attractions. Bedrooms are spacious and comfortable, with many extras, including laptop safes, high-speed telephone lines and air-conditioning. Service is discreetly attentive in the Foyer lounge and the Chino Latino restaurant, where fusion cooking is a feature.
ROOMS: 178 en suite (10 fmly) ⊗ in 126 bedrooms s £75-£145; d £75-£145 **FACILITIES:** STV Gym Complimentary fitness suite Xmas **CONF:** BC Thtr 175 Class 100 Board 54 Del from £135 **SERVICES:** Lift air con **NOTES:** RS 24-27 Dec

★★★67% **Rutland Square Hotel**
St James St NG1 6FJ
☎ 0115 941 1114 0115 941 0014
e-mail: rutland.square@forestdale.com
web: www.forestdale.com
Dir: *enter city and follow signs to castle. Hotel on right 50yds beyond castle*
An enviable location in the heart of the city adjacent to the castle makes this hotel a popular choice with both leisure and business travellers. Behind its mock Regency façade the hotel is modern and comfortable with good business facilities. Bedrooms come in a variety of styles with the Premier rooms offering a host of thoughtful extras. Public rooms include the informal Terrace Bar and Restaurant and Woods Restaurant.
ROOMS: 87 en suite (3 fmly) ⊗ in 38 bedrooms s £85-£105; d £120-£130 (incl. bkfst) **LB FACILITIES:** STV Discounted day passes to near by gym Xmas **CONF:** Thtr 200 Class 70 Board 45 Del from £130 **SERVICES:** Lift **NOTES:** ⊗ in restaurant Civ Wed

★★★67% **Westminster Hotel**
312 Mansfield Rd, Carrington NG5 2EF
☎ 0115 955 5000 0115 955 5005
e-mail: mail@westminster-hotel.co.uk
web: www.westminster-hotel.co.uk
Dir: *on A60 1m N of town centre*

This smart hotel is conveniently located close to the city centre,
continued on p428

NOTTINGHAM, continued

and offers well-appointed accommodation, suitably equipped for both business and leisure guests. Spacious superior rooms are particularly impressive. Public areas include a lounge bar, restaurant and range of meeting and function rooms.
ROOMS: 73 en suite (9 GF) ⊗ in 40 bedrooms s £38-£95; d £70-£110 (incl. bkfst) **LB** **FACILITIES:** STV **CONF:** Thtr 60 Class 30 Board 30 Del £107 **SERVICES:** Lift **PARKING:** 66 **NOTES:** ⊗ in restaurant Closed 25 Dec-2 Jan

See advert on opposite page

★★★66% Bestwood Lodge

Bestwood Country Park, Arnold NG5 8NE
☎ 0115 920 3011 📠 0115 964 9678
e-mail: bestwoodlodge@btconnect.com
web: www.bestwoodlodge.co.uk
Dir: *3m N off A60. Left at traffic lights into Oxclose Ln, right at next lights into Queens Bower Rd. 1st right and keep right at fork in road*

A Victorian hunting lodge in 700 acres of parkland, the stunning architecture includes Gothic features and high vaulted ceilings. Bedrooms include all modern comforts, suitable for both business and leisure guests, and a popular restaurant serves an extensive menu.
ROOMS: 39 en suite (5 fmly) ⊗ in 5 bedrooms s fr £40; d £80-£150 (incl. bkfst) **LB** **FACILITIES:** Riding Guided walks ch fac Xmas **CONF:** Thtr 200 Class 65 Board 50 Del from £99 **PARKING:** 120 **NOTES:** ⊗ in restaurant RS 25 Dec & 1 Jan

See advert on opposite page

★★★65% Comfort Hotel Nottingham

George St NG1 3BP
☎ 0115 947 5641 📠 0115 948 3292
e-mail: enquiries@comfort-hotels-nottingham.com
web: www.comfort-hotels-nottingham.com
Dir: *M1 junct 24, follow City Centre signs. George Street turn left, hotel at end on left*
Situated in heart of the city, this hotel dates back to the late 17th century. Smartly appointed, compact public areas include a bar lounge, where all-day snacks are served, and a brightly decorated restaurant. Parking is available at a multi-storey, a short walk from the hotel. The bedrooms are very comfortable and thoughtfully equipped, well suited for both business and leisure guests.
ROOMS: 70 en suite (7 fmly) ⊗ in 45 bedrooms **FACILITIES:** STV Xmas **CONF:** Thtr 150 Class 100 Board 60 **SERVICES:** Lift **NOTES:** ⊗ in restaurant

Destination dining!
This symbol indicates a Restaurant with Rooms

★★★62% The Strathdon

Derby Rd, City Centre NG1 5FT
☎ 0115 941 8501 📠 0115 948 3725
e-mail: info@strathdon-hotel-nottingham.com
web: www.peelhotel.com
Dir: *on one-way system on Wollaton St, keep right next right to hotel*

This city-centre hotel has modern facilities and is very convenient for all city attractions. A popular themed bar includes large-screen TV and serves an extensive range of popular fresh food, while more formal dining is available in Bobbins Restaurant. Bedrooms are modern and comprehensively equipped.
ROOMS: 68 en suite (4 fmly) ⊗ in 46 bedrooms **FACILITIES:** STV **CONF:** Thtr 150 Class 60 Board 40 **SERVICES:** Lift

★★★62% Swans Hotel & Restaurant

84-90 Radcliffe Rd, West Bridgford NG2 5HH
☎ 0115 981 4042 📠 0115 945 5745
e-mail: enquiries@swanshotel.co.uk
web: www.swanshotel.co.uk
Dir: *on A6011, approached from A60 or A52 close to Trent Bridge*
This privately owned hotel is located on the outskirts of the city, conveniently placed for the various sports stadiums. Bedrooms vary in size, but are all equipped to meet the needs of both business and leisure visitors. An interesting range of dishes is served in either the cosy bar or, more formally, in the restaurant.
ROOMS: 30 en suite (3 fmly) (1 GF) ⊗ in all bedrooms s £45-£60; d £65-£75 (incl. bkfst) **LB** **FACILITIES:** STV **CONF:** Thtr 50 Class 10 Board 24 Del from £70 **SERVICES:** Lift **PARKING:** 31 **NOTES:** ⊗ in restaurant Closed 24-28 Dec

Restaurant with Rooms

Restaurant Sat Bains with Rooms

Trentside, Lenton Ln NG7 2SA
☎ 0115 986 6566 📠 0115 986 0343
e-mail: info@restaurantsatbains.net
web: www.restaurantsatbains.net
Dir: *M1 junct 24 take A453 Nottingham S. Over River Trent in central lane to rdbt. Left then left again towards river. Hotel on left after bend*
This small hotel, a sympathetic conversion of Victorian farm buildings, is situated on the riverside. The bedrooms are attractively presented with quality soft furnishings and antique/period furniture; suites and four-poster bedrooms are available. Public rooms are contemporary, and the delightful restaurant complements the cuisine on offer. At the time of going to press the rosette award had not been confirmed.
ROOMS: 8 en suite ⊗ in all bedrooms s fr £114; d fr £129 (incl. bkfst) **FACILITIES:** STV **PARKING:** 22 **NOTES:** ⊗ in restaurant Closed 1st 2 wks Jan, mid 2 wks Aug, Rest closed Sun & Mon

U *Jury's Inn Nottingham*
London Rd NG2 3AB
☎ 0870 907 2222
web: www.jurysdoyle.com
At the time of going to press, the star classification for this hotel was not confirmed. Please refer to the AA internet site www.theAA.com for current information.
ROOMS: 250 en suite **NOTES:** Due to open October 2005

Citilodge
Wollaton St NG1 5FW
☎ 0115 912 8000 Fax 0115 912 8080
e-mail: mail@citilodge.co.uk
web: www.citilodge.co.uk
Dir: *From M1 junct 26, follow A610 into city centre. Hotel opposite Royal Centre on Wollaton St*
This city centre lodge offers superior accommodation along with a good range of bar and food options. Conferencing is a strength, with a range of quality meeting rooms and an impressive 100-seater tiered lecture theatre. Bedrooms are spacious and light with an excellent range of facilities including air conditioning and free Broadband access. A separate Citinet internet room is available.
ROOMS: 90 en suite **CONF:** Thtr 100 Class 25 Board 30

Innkeeper's Lodge Nottingham
Derby Rd, Wollaton Vale NG8 2NR
☎ 0115 922 1691
web: www.innkeeperslodge.com
Dir: *M1 junct 25, take A52 to Nottingham. At 3rd rdbt, left into Wollaton Vale, right across central reservation into car park*
A growing concept in the travel accommodation market. Smart rooms meet essential business requirements but also have home

continued on p430

NOTTINGHAM, continued

comforts. Dining options include all-day menus plus the added advantage of breakfast, which is included in the room price. For further details consult the Hotel Groups page.
ROOMS: 34 en suite s £59.95; d £59.95 **CONF:** Thtr 105 Class 62 Board 70

Premier Travel Inn Nottingham City Centre (London Road)

Island Site, London Rd NG2 4UU
☎ 0870 9906574 📠 0870 9906575
web: www.premiertravelinn.com
Dir: *Exit M1 junct 25, A52 into city centre. Then follow signs for A60 to Loughborough. Hotel next to BBC building*
High quality, modern budget accommodation ideal for both families and business travellers. Spacious, en suite bedrooms feature bath and shower, satellite TV and many have telephones and modem points. The adjacent family restaurant features a wide and varied menu. For further details consult the Hotel Groups page.
ROOMS: 87 en suite s £55.95; d £55.95

Premier Travel Inn Nottingham City Centre (Goldsmith Street)

Goldsmith St NG1 5LT
☎ 0870 238 3314 📠 0115 908 1388
web: www.premiertravelinn.com
Dir: *A610 to City Centre. Follow signs for Nottingham Trent University into Talbot Street. Take 1st left into Clarendon Street and at lights turn right for Inn on right.*
High quality, modern budget accommodation ideal for both families and business travellers. Spacious, en suite bedrooms feature bath and shower, satellite TV and many have telephones and modem points. The adjacent family restaurant features a wide and varied menu. For further details consult the Hotel Groups page.
ROOMS: 161 en suite s £55.95; d £55.95

Premier Travel Inn Nottingham City South

Castle Marina Park, Castle Bridge Rd NG7 1GX
☎ 08701 977199 📠 0115 958 2362
web: www.premiertravelinn.com
Dir: *0.5m from Nottingham city centre, follow signs for Castle Marina*
High quality, modern budget accommodation ideal for both families and business travellers. Spacious, en suite bedrooms feature bath and shower, satellite TV and many have telephones and modem points. The adjacent family restaurant features a wide and varied menu. For further details consult the Hotel Groups page.
ROOMS: 38 en suite s £55.95; d £55.95

Premier Travel Inn Nottingham North

101 Mansfield Rd, Daybrook NG5 6BH
☎ 0870 9906328 📠 0870 9906329
web: www.premiertravelinn.com
Dir: *Exit M1 junct 26, A610 towards Nottingham. Left onto A6514. Left onto A60 towards Mansfield. Hotel 0.25m on left*
High quality, modern budget accommodation ideal for both families and business travellers. Spacious, en suite bedrooms feature bath and shower, satellite TV and many have telephones and modem points. The adjacent family restaurant features a wide and varied menu. For further details consult the Hotel Groups page.
ROOMS: 64 en suite s £47.95-£50.95; d £47.95-£50.95 **CONF:** Thtr 50 Class 50

No smoking

Premier Travel Inn Nottingham South

Loughborough Rd, Ruddington NG11 6LS
☎ 0870 9906422 📠 0870 9906423
web: www.premiertravelinn.com
Dir: *Exit M1 junct 24, follow signs for A453 to Nottingham, then A52 to Grantham. Hotel at 1st rdbt on left*
High quality, modern budget accommodation ideal for both families and business travellers. Spacious, en suite bedrooms feature bath and shower, satellite TV and many have telephones and modem points. The adjacent family restaurant features a wide and varied menu. For further details consult the Hotel Groups page.
ROOMS: 42 en suite s £47.95-£50.95; d £47.95-£50.95

Premier Travel Inn Nottingham West

The Phoenix Centre, Millennium Way West NG8 6AS
☎ 08701 977200 📠 0115 977 0113
web: www.premiertravelinn.com
Dir: *M1 junct 26, 1m on A610 towards Nottingham*
High quality, modern budget accommodation ideal for both families and business travellers. Spacious, en suite bedrooms feature bath and shower, satellite TV and many have telephones and modem points. The adjacent family restaurant features a wide and varied menu. For further details consult the Hotel Groups page.
ROOMS: 86 en suite s £47.95-£50.95; d £47.95-£50.95

Travelodge (Nottingham Riverside)

Riverside Retail Park NG2 1RT
☎ 08700 850 950 📠 0115 986 0467
web: www.travelodge.co.uk
Dir: *M1 junct 21, follow signs for A453, on Riverside Retail Park*
Travelodge offers good quality, good value, modern accommodation. Ideal for families, the spacious, en suite bedrooms include remote-control TV, tea and coffee-making facilities and comfortable beds. Meals can be taken at the nearby family restaurant. For further details consult the Hotel Groups page.
ROOMS: 61 en suite s fr £26; d fr £26

NOTTINGHAM EAST MIDLANDS AIRPORT, Leicestershire Map 11 SK42

★★★★74%

The Priest House on the River

Kings Mills, Castle Donington DE74 2RR
☎ 01332 810649 📠 01332 811141
web: www.handpicked.co.uk
Dir: *M1 junct 24, onto A50, take 1st slip road signed Castle Donington. Right at lights, hotel in 2m*

A historic hotel peacefully situated in a picturesque riverside setting. Public areas include a fine-dining restaurant, a modern brasserie and conference rooms. Bedrooms are situated in both

continued

the main building and converted cottages, and the executive rooms feature state-of-the-art technology.
ROOMS: 24 en suite 18 annexe en suite (5 fmly) (16 GF)
FACILITIES: Spa STV Fishing **CONF:** Thtr 120 Class 40 Board 40
PARKING: 200 **NOTES:** ✗ ⊗ in restaurant Civ Wed 100

See advert on this page

★★★76% ⓖ
Best Western Yew Lodge Hotel
Packington Hill, Kegworth DE74 2DF
☎ 01509 672518 🖨 01509 674730
e-mail: info@yewlodgehotel.co.uk
web: www.yewlodgehotel.co.uk
Dir: M1 junct 24. Follow signs to Loughborough & Kegworth on A6. At bottom of hill, 1st right, after 400yds lodge on right

This smart, family-owned hotel is close to both the motorway and airport, yet is peacefully located. Modern bedrooms and public areas are thoughtfully appointed. The restaurant serves interesting *continued*

dishes, while lounge service and extensive conference facilities are available. A very well equipped spa and leisure centre is now open.
ROOMS: 98 en suite (22 fmly) ⊗ in 74 bedrooms s £53-£100;
d £74-£120 (incl. bkfst) **LB FACILITIES:** Spa STV ⚲ Sauna Solarium
Gym Jacuzzi Beauty therapy suite, foot spas **CONF:** Thtr 330 Class 150
Board 84 Del from £109 **SERVICES:** Lift **PARKING:** 180 **NOTES:** ⊗ in restaurant Civ Wed 130

★★★68% **Donington Manor**
High St, Castle Donington DE74 2PP
☎ 01332 810253 🖨 01332 850330
e-mail: enquiries@doningtonmanorhotel.co.uk
web: www.doningtonmanorhotel.co.uk
Dir: 1m into village on B5430, left at traffic lights

Near the village centre, this refined Georgian building offers high standards of hospitality and a professional service. Many of the original architectural features have been preserved; the elegant
continued on p432

NOTTINGHAM EAST MIDLANDS AIRPORT, continued

dining room is particularly appealing. Bedrooms are individually designed, and the newer suites are especially comfortable and well equipped.
ROOMS: 26 en suite 6 annexe en suite (2 fmly) (4 GF) s £75; d £80-£85 (incl. bkfst) **LB** **FACILITIES:** STV **CONF:** Thtr 120 Class 60 Board 40 Del £115 **PARKING:** 40 **NOTES:** in restaurant Closed 24-30 Dec Civ Wed 100

★★63% Tudor Hotel & Restaurant
Bond Gate DE74 2NR
☎ 01332 810875 01332 850883
e-mail: reservations@thetudorhotel.com
web: www.thetudorhotel.com
Dir: *M1 junct 24, A50 Castle Donington. 2m from Donington Park & North East Midlands Airport*
This Tudor-style hotel is close to Donington racetrack and East Midlands Airport. Bedrooms have been tastefully furnished and are comfortable and well equipped. A fully equipped suite complete with lounge is also available. Downstairs there is a large restaurant offering a wide range of traditional dishes, a character bar and a beer garden. Free wireless broadband is available and bar meals can be ordered all day.
ROOMS: 10 en suite (2 fmly) in all bedrooms s £43; d £59 (incl. bkfst) **LB** **FACILITIES:** STV Xmas **CONF:** BC Thtr 30 Class 30 Board 30 **PARKING:** 60 **NOTES:** in restaurant

Travelodge Donnington Park
Castle Donington DE74 2TN
☎ 08700 850 950 01509 673494
web: www.travelodge.co.uk
Dir: *M1 junct 23a follow signs for A453*
Travelodge offers good quality, good value, modern accommodation. Ideal for families, the spacious, en suite bedrooms include remote-control TV, tea and coffee-making facilities and comfortable beds. Meals can be taken at the nearby family restaurant. For further details consult the Hotel Groups page.
ROOMS: 80 en suite s fr £26; d fr £26

N

NUNEATON, Warwickshire Map 11 SP39

★★★66% *Weston Hall*
Weston Ln, Bulkington CV12 9RU
☎ 024 7631 2989 024 7664 0846
e-mail: info@westonhallhotel.co.uk
Dir: *M6 junct 2 follow B4065 through Ansty. Left in Shilton, follow Nuneaton signs out of Bulkington, turn into Weston Ln at 30mph sign*
This Grade II listed hotel, whose origins date back to the reign of Elizabeth I, sits within seven acres of peaceful grounds. The original three-gabled building retains many original features, such as the carved wooden fireplace situated in the library. Friendly service is provided; and bedrooms, that vary in size, are thoughtfully equipped.
ROOMS: 40 en suite (1 fmly) in 8 bedrooms **FACILITIES: Spa** Fishing Sauna Gym Jacuzzi Steam room **CONF:** BC Thtr 200 Class 100 Board 60 **PARKING:** 300 **NOTES:** in restaurant Civ Wed 200
See advert under COVENTRY

Premier Travel Inn Nuneaton/Coventry
Coventry Rd CV10 7PJ
☎ 08701 977201 024 7632 7156
web: www.premiertravelinn.com
Dir: *M6 junct 3 follow A444 towards Nuneaton. Inn on the right just off Griff rdbt towards Bedworth on B4113*
High quality, modern budget accommodation ideal for both families and business travellers. Spacious, en suite bedrooms feature bath and shower, satellite TV and many have telephones and modem points. The adjacent family restaurant features a wide and varied menu. For further details consult the Hotel Groups page.
ROOMS: 48 en suite s £46.95-£48.95; d £46.95-£48.95 **CONF:** Thtr 25

Travelodge
St Nicholas Park Dr CV11 6EN
☎ 08700 850 950 0870 1911594
web: www.travelodge.co.uk
Dir: *on A47*
Travelodge offers good quality, good value, modern accommodation. Ideal for families, the spacious, en suite bedrooms include remote-control TV, tea and coffee-making facilities and comfortable beds. Meals can be taken at the nearby family restaurant. For further details consult the Hotel Groups page.
ROOMS: 28 en suite s fr £26; d fr £26

Travelodge Bedworth
Bedworth CV10 7TF
☎ 08700 850 950 024 7638 2541
web: www.travelodge.co.uk
Dir: *on A444*
Travelodge offers good quality, good value, modern accommodation. Ideal for families, the spacious, en suite bedrooms include remote-control TV, tea and coffee-making facilities and comfortable beds. Meals can be taken at the nearby family restaurant. For further details consult the Hotel Groups page.
ROOMS: 40 en suite s fr £26; d fr £26

NUNNEY, Somerset Map 04 ST74

★★65% *The George at Nunney*
11 Church St BA11 4LW
☎ 01373 836458 01373 836565
e-mail: georgenunneyhotel@barbox.net
Dir: *0.5m N off A361 Frome to Shepton Mallet road*
Situated in the centre of Nunney, opposite the castle, The George dates back to the 17th century. Guests may choose from an extensive range of bar meals or a selection of dishes offered in the more intimate restaurant. Bedrooms vary in size, have plenty of character and offer a very good selection of extras.
ROOMS: 9 rms (8 en suite) (2 fmly) in 2 bedrooms **PARKING:** 30 **NOTES:**

OAKHAM, Rutland Map 11 SK80

Top Hotel

★★★ Hambleton Hall
Hambleton LE15 8TH
☎ 01572 756991 01572 724721
e-mail: hotel@hambletonhall.com
web: www.hambletonhall.com
Dir: *3m E off A606*
Spectacular views and tranquillity come as standard at this delightful country house, with its delightful gardens overlooking Rutland Water. The bedrooms are stylish and individually decorated and equipped with a range of thoughtful extras. Day rooms include a cosy bar and a sumptuous drawing room, both featuring open fires. The elegant restaurant serves skilfully prepared, award-winning
continued

cuisine with menus highlighting locally sourced, seasonal produce - some grown in the hotels' own grounds.

ROOMS: 15 en suite 2 annexe en suite ⊗ in 2 bedrooms s £165-£355; d £190-£355 (incl. bkfst) **FACILITIES:** STV Private access to lake Xmas **CONF:** Thtr 40 Board 24 Del £250 **SERVICES:** Lift **PARKING:** 40 **NOTES:** ⊗ in restaurant Civ Wed 64

★★★75% Barnsdale Lodge

The Avenue, Rutland Water, North Shore LE15 8AH
☎ 01572 724678 01572 724961
e-mail: enquiries@barnsdalelodge.co.uk
web: www.barnsdalelodge.co.uk
Dir: *off A1 onto A606. Hotel 5m on right, 2m E of Oakham*

A popular and interesting hotel converted from a farmstead and overlooking Rutland Water. The public areas are dominated by a very successful food operation with a good range of appealing meals on offer for either formal or informal dining. Bedrooms are comfortably appointed with excellent beds and period furnishings, enhanced by contemporary soft furnishings and thoughtful extras.
ROOMS: 45 en suite (2 fmly) (15 GF) ⊗ in all bedrooms s £75; d £99.50-£120 (incl. bkfst) **LB FACILITIES:** STV Fishing Shooting Archery Golf Riding arranged Xmas **CONF:** BC Thtr 330 Class 120 Board 76 **PARKING:** 200 **NOTES:** ⊗ in restaurant Civ Wed 200

★★★71% Barnsdale Hall

Barnsdale LE15 8AB
☎ 01572 757901 01572 756235
e-mail: reservations@barnsdalehotel.co.uk
web: www.barnsdalehotel.com
Dir: *from A1 take A606 to Oakham, through Erpingham and Whitwell. After 1m hotel on left*
Overlooking Rutland Water, this complex is set in attractive grounds leading to the water's edge. Public rooms offer a good choice of modern dining options and extensive leisure facilities; customer care is a particular strength. Spacious modern bedrooms have been refurbished and are equipped with many thoughtful extras; most are in adjacent buildings and many have a balcony.

ROOMS: 9 en suite 56 annexe en suite (9 fmly) (17 GF) ⊗ in 61 bedrooms s £65-£140; d £75-£180 (incl. bkfst) **LB FACILITIES: Spa** STV supervised Squash Snooker Sauna Solarium Gym Putt green Jacuzzi Boule, Bowls, Crazy Golf, Pitch & Putt, Soccer Pitch Xmas **CONF:** Thtr 200 Class 70 Board 42 Del from £115 **SERVICES:** Lift **PARKING:** 100 **NOTES:** ⊗ in restaurant Civ Wed 110

★★66% Admiral Hornblower

64 High St LE15 6AS
☎ 01572 723004 01572 722325
e-mail: enquiries@thehornblowerhotel.co.uk
Dir: *in town centre*
This sympathetically restored 17th-century farmhouse in the heart of Oakham is now an exceedingly popular small hotel offering tastefully appointed accommodation, good food and a lively bar. Bedrooms are individually appointed, furnished in country style and retain much of their original character. Public rooms are dominated by three dining areas with open fires and the main focal point is the bar.
ROOMS: 10 en suite (3 fmly) (2 GF) ⊗ in all bedrooms **CONF:** Del from £50 **PARKING:** 5 **NOTES:** ⊗ in restaurant

O

OCKLEY, Surrey — Map 06 TQ14

★★★61% Gatton Manor Hotel Golf & Country Club

Standon Ln RH5 5PQ
☎ 01306 627555 01306 627713
e-mail: gattonmanor@enterprise.net
Dir: *off A29 at Ockley turn into Cat Hill Ln. Hotel signed 2m on right*
Gatton Manor, now under new ownership, enjoys a peaceful setting in private grounds. It is a popular golf and country club, with an 18-hole professional course and offers a range of comfortable, modern bedrooms. The public areas include the main club bar, a small restaurant and an attractive drawing room.
ROOMS: 18 en suite (2 fmly) ⊗ in 6 bedrooms s fr £60; d fr £69 (incl. bkfst) **LB FACILITIES:** STV 18 Fishing Sauna Solarium Gym Putt green **CONF:** Thtr 50 Class 40 Board 30 Del from £99.50 **PARKING:** 250 **NOTES:** ⊗ in restaurant Civ Wed 50

ODIHAM, Hampshire — Map 05 SU75

★★74% George

High St RG29 1LP
☎ 01256 702081 01256 704213
e-mail: reception@georgehotelodiham.com
web: www.georgehotelodiham.com
Dir: *M3 junct 5 follow signs to Alton and Odiham. Through North Warnborough into Odiham left at top of hill, hotel on left*
The George is over 450 years old and is a fine example of an old

continued on p434

ODIHAM, continued

English inn. Bedrooms come in a number of styles; the older part of the property has old beams and period features, whilst the newer rooms have a contemporary feel. Guests can dine in the all-day café bar and bistro or the popular restaurant.

George, Odiham

ROOMS: 19 en suite 9 annexe en suite (1 fmly) (6 GF) ⊗ in 14 bedrooms s £60-£85; d £80-£115 (incl. bkfst) **LB** **FACILITIES:** STV **CONF:** Thtr 30 Class 10 Board 26 Del £125 **PARKING:** 20 **NOTES:** Closed 24-26 Dec

OKEHAMPTON, Devon — Map 03 SX59

★★67% *White Hart*

Fore St EX20 1HD
☎ 01837 52730 & 54514 📠 01837 53979
e-mail: whitehart.oke@btopenworld.com
Dir: *in town centre, adjacent to lights, car park at rear of hotel*

Dating back to the 17th century, the White Hart offers modern facilities. Bedrooms are well equipped and spacious and some have four-poster beds. A range of bar meals is offered or more relaxed dining may be taken in the Courtney restaurant. Guests can relax in the lounge or choice of bars, as well as a traditional skittles and games room.

ROOMS: 19 en suite (2 fmly) ⊗ in 8 bedrooms **FACILITIES:** Games room Skittle alley **CONF:** Thtr 100 Class 80 Board 40 **PARKING:** 20 **NOTES:** ✗

See advert on opposite page

★★66% Ashbury

Higher Maddaford, Southcott EX20 4NL
☎ 01837 55453 📠 01837 55468
Dir: *off A30 at Sourton Cross onto A386. Left onto A3079 to Bude at Fowley Cross. After 1m right to Ashbury. Hotel 0.5m on right*

Now boasting four courses and a clubhouse with lounge, bar and dining facilitites, The Ashbury is a golfer's paradise. The majority of the well-equipped bedrooms are located in the farmhouse and courtyard-style development around the putting green. Guests can enjoy the many on-site leisure facilities or join the activities available at the adjacent sister hotel.

ROOMS: 69 en suite 30 annexe en suite (54 fmly) (29 GF) s £48-£82; d £92-£157 (incl. bkfst) **LB** **FACILITIES:** 72 Fishing Snooker Sauna Solarium Putt green Jacuzzi Driving range, Indoor bowls, Ten-pin bowling, Outdoor chess, Golf simulator Xmas **PARKING:** 150 **NOTES:** ✗ ⊗ in restaurant

★★66% Manor House Hotel

Fowley Cross EX20 4NA
☎ 01837 53053 📠 01837 55027
web: www.manorhousehotel.co.uk
Dir: *off A30 at Sourton Cross flyover, right onto A386. Hotel 1.5m on right*

Enjoying views to Dartmoor in the distance, this hotel is set within 17 acres of grounds and is located close to the A30. An impressive range of facilities, including golf at the adjacent sister hotel, is available at this friendly establishment, which specialises in short breaks. Bedrooms, many located on the ground floor, are comfortable and well equipped.

ROOMS: 180 en suite (77 fmly) (96 GF) s £55-£90; d £105-£171 (incl. bkfst) **LB** **FACILITIES: Spa** Squash Snooker Sauna Gym Putt green Jacuzzi Craft centre, Indoor bowls, Shooting range, Laser clay pigeon shooting, Aerobics Xmas **PARKING:** 200 **NOTES:** ✗ ⊗ in restaurant

See advert on opposite page

Travelodge (Okehampton East)

Whiddon Down EX20 2QT
☎ 08700 850 950 📠 01647 231626
web: www.travelodge.co.uk
Dir: *at Merrymeet rdbt on A30/A382*

Travelodge offers good quality, good value, modern accommodation. Ideal for families, the spacious, en suite bedrooms include remote-control TV, tea and coffee-making facilities and comfortable beds. Meals can be taken at the nearby family restaurant. For further details consult the Hotel Groups page.

ROOMS: 40 en suite s fr £26; d fr £26

OLDBURY, West Midlands — Map 10 SO98

Premier Travel Inn Oldbury

Wolverhampton Rd B69 2BH
☎ 08701 977202 📠 0121 552 1012
web: www.premiertravelinn.com
Dir: *M5 junct 2, take A4123 towards Wolverhampton, hotel 0.75m on left*

High quality, modern budget accommodation ideal for both families and business travellers. Spacious, en suite bedrooms feature bath and shower, satellite TV and many have telephones and modem points. The adjacent family restaurant features a wide and varied menu. For further details consult the Hotel Groups page.

ROOMS: 40 en suite s £47.95-£50.95; d £47.95-£50.95

Travelodge

Wolverhampton Rd B69 2BH
☎ 08700 850 950 📠 0121 552 2967
web: www.travelodge.co.uk
Dir: *on A4123, northbound off M5 junct 2*

Travelodge offers good quality, good value, modern accommodation. Ideal for families, the spacious, en suite bedrooms include remote-control TV, tea and coffee-making facilities and comfortable beds. Meals can be taken at the nearby family restaurant. For further details consult the Hotel Groups page.

ROOMS: 33 en suite s fr £26; d fr £26

OLDHAM, Greater Manchester — Map 16 SD90

★★★★64% Menzies Avant

Windsor Rd, Manchester St OL8 4AS
☎ 0161 627 5500 📠 0161 627 5896
e-mail: avant@menzies-hotels.co.uk
web: www.menzies-hotels.co.uk
Dir: *M60 junct 22, onto A62 into Oldham, right after petrol station.*

The Avant is a contemporary landmark building only a few minutes from the M60 and features an extensive leisure complex including fitness studios, a gym and a good-sized pool. Accommodation is smart, comfortable and spacious. The public areas, which include a brasserie and comfortable lounge bar area are located on the lower ground floor.

ROOMS: 103 en suite (2 fmly) ⊗ in 16 bedrooms s £99; d £120 **LB** **FACILITIES:** STV Sauna Solarium Gym Jacuzzi Xmas **CONF:** Thtr 250 Class 120 Board 60 Del £135 **SERVICES:** Lift **PARKING:** 120 **NOTES:** ⊗ in restaurant Civ Wed

★★★73% Hotel Smokies Park
Ashton Rd, Bardsley OL8 3HX
☎ 0161 785 5000 🖷 0161 785 5010
e-mail: sales@smokies.co.uk
web: www.smokies.co.uk
Dir: *on A627 between Oldham and Ashton-under-Lyne*

This modern, stylish hotel offers smart, comfortable bedrooms and suites. A wide range of Italian and English dishes is offered in the Mediterranean-style restaurant and there is a welcoming lounge bar with live entertainment at weekends. A small but well equipped fitness centre is available for use by residents only. Residents also gain free admission to the hotel's nightclub.

ROOMS: 73 en suite (2 fmly) (22 GF) ⊗ in 36 bedrooms s £65-£130; d £65-£150 (incl. bkfst) **LB** **FACILITIES:** STV Sauna Solarium Gym Night club Cabaret lounge **CONF:** BC Thtr 200 Class 100 Board 40 Del from £115 **SERVICES:** Lift **PARKING:** 120 **NOTES:** ✈ RS 25 Dec-3 Jan Civ Wed 120

★★★65% La Pergola
Rochdale Rd, Denshaw OL3 5UE
☎ 01457 871040 🖷 01457 873804
e-mail: reception@lapergola.freeserve.co.uk
web: www.hotel-restaurant-uk.com
Dir: *M62 junct 21, right at rdbt onto A640, under motorway, left at Wagon & Horses public house. Hotel 500yds on left*

Situated in open moorland and convenient for the M62, this friendly, family-owned and run hotel offers comfortable and well-equipped bedrooms. There is a good range of food available either in the bar or restaurant, and a comfortable lounge in which to relax.

ROOMS: 26 en suite (4 fmly) ⊗ in 14 bedrooms s £53; d £61-£66 (incl. bkfst) **LB** **FACILITIES:** Xmas **CONF:** Thtr 150 Board 25 Del from £83.50 **PARKING:** 75 **NOTES:** ⊗ in restaurant Closed 26 Dec, 1 Jan & BH Mons

OLDHAM, continued

⌂ Innkeeper's Lodge Oldham

Burnley Ln, Chadderton OL1 2QS
☎ 0161 6273883
web: www.innkeeperslodge.com

A growing concept in the travel accommodation market. Smart rooms meet essential business requirements but also have home comforts. Dining options include all-day menus plus the added advantage of breakfast, which is included in the room price. For further details consult the Hotel Groups page.

ROOMS: 30 en suite s £45-£49.95; d £45-£49.95

⌂ Premier Travel Inn Oldham Central

Westwood Park, Chadderton Way OL1 2PH
☎ 08701 977292 🖷 08701 977702
web: www.premiertravelinn.com
Dir: From M62 junct 20, take A627M to Oldham. Inn is on A627, opposite B&Q Depot

High quality, modern budget accommodation ideal for both families and business travellers. Spacious, en suite bedrooms feature bath and shower, satellite TV and many have telephones and modem points. The adjacent family restaurant features a wide and varied menu. For further details consult the Hotel Groups page.

ROOMS: 40 en suite s £47.95-£50.95; d £47.95-£50.95

⌂ Premier Travel Inn Oldham (Chadderton)

The Broadway OL9 8DW
☎ 08701 977203 🖷 0161 682 7974
web: www.premiertravelinn.com
Dir: M60 ringroad (anticlockwise) junct 21, signed Manchester City Centre. A663, 400yds on left

High quality, modern budget accommodation ideal for both families and business travellers. Spacious, en suite bedrooms feature bath and shower, satellite TV and many have telephones and modem points. The adjacent family restaurant features a wide and varied menu. For further details consult the Hotel Groups page.

ROOMS: 40 en suite s £47.95-£50.95; d £47.95-£50.95

⌂ Travelodge

432 Broadway, Chadderton OL9 8AU
☎ 08700 850 950 🖷 0161 681 9021
web: www.travelodge.co.uk

Travelodge offers good quality, good value, modern accommodation. Ideal for families, the spacious, en suite bedrooms include remote-control TV, tea and coffee-making facilities and comfortable beds. Meals can be taken at the nearby family restaurant. For further details consult the Hotel Groups page.

ROOMS: 50 en suite s fr £26; d fr £26

ORFORD, Suffolk Map 13 TM45

★★78% ◉◉ The Crown & Castle

IP12 2LJ
☎ 01394 450205
e-mail: info@crownandcastle.co.uk
web: www.crownandcastle.co.uk
Dir: turn right from B1084 on entering village, towards castle

Adjacent to a Norman castle keep, this delightful inn has been transformed in recent years. Bedrooms are light, airy and contemporary. Some of those in the main building have great views and those in a purpose-built garden wing are more spacious and have patios. The restaurant, with polished tables and local

continued

artwork, has an informal atmosphere and features a breezy, high quality menu.

ROOMS: 7 en suite 11 annexe en suite (1 fmly) (11 GF) ⊗ in all bedrooms s £72-£130; d £90-£130 (incl. bkfst) **LB CONF:** Board 10 **PARKING:** 20 **NOTES:** ⊗ in restaurant Closed 19-22 Dec & 3-4 Jan

ORMSKIRK, Lancashire Map 15 SD40

★★★66% Beaufort

High Ln, Burscough L40 7SN
☎ 01704 892655 🖷 01704 895135
e-mail: info@beaufort.uk.com
web: www.beaufort.uk.com
Dir: M58 junct 3 follow signs for Ormskirk 7m. Hotel between Ormskirk and Burscough on A59

This is a privately owned and personally run, modern hotel with pleasing public areas, including an open-plan lounge bar and restaurant. Conference and banqueting facilities are also available. There is a wide choice of food available, served throughout the day.

ROOMS: 20 en suite **FACILITIES:** STV Free use of sister Hotel's (Stutelea Hotel, Southport) facilities **CONF:** Thtr 120 Class 32 Board 30 **PARKING:** 109 **NOTES:** ✄ ⊗ in restaurant Civ Wed 150

OSWESTRY, Shropshire Map 15 SJ22

★★★76% ◉◉ Pen-y-Dyffryn Hall Country Hotel

Rhydycroesau SY10 7JD
☎ 01691 653700 🖷 01691 650066
e-mail: stay@peny.co.uk
Dir: from A5 into Oswestry town centre. Follow signs to Llansilin on B4580, hotel 3m W of Oswestry before Rhydycroesau village

Peacefully situated in five acres of grounds, this charming old house dates back to around 1840, when it was built as a rectory. The tastefully appointed public rooms have real fires during cold weather, and accommodation includes several mini-cottages, each with their own patio. The hotel has a well deserved reputation for its food and attentive, friendly service.

ROOMS: 8 en suite 4 annexe en suite (1 fmly) (1 GF) ⊗ in all bedrooms s £82-£98; d £110-£148 (incl. bkfst) **LB FACILITIES:** Jacuzzi Country walks **PARKING:** 14 **NOTES:** No children 3yrs ⊗ in restaurant Closed 18 Dec-20 Jan

★★★72% ◉◉ Wynnstay

Church St SY11 2SZ
☎ 01691 655261 🖷 01691 670606
e-mail: info@wynnstayhotel.com
web: www.wynnstayhotel.com
Dir: B4083 to town, fork left at Honda Garage and right at traffic lights. Hotel opposite church

This Georgian property was once a coaching inn and posting house and surrounds a unique 200-year-old Crown Bowling Green. Elegant public areas include a health, leisure and beauty

continued

centre, which is housed in the former coach house. Well-equipped bedrooms are individually styled and include several suites, four-poster rooms and a self-catering apartment. The Four Seasons Restaurant has a well-deserved reputation for its food; bar meals are also available.

ROOMS: 29 en suite (4 fmly) ⊗ in 14 bedrooms s £60-£80; d £70-£100 **LB FACILITIES: Spa** STV Sauna Solarium Gym Jacuzzi Crown green bowling Beauty suite **CONF:** Thtr 290 Class 150 Board 50 Del from £88 **PARKING:** 70 **NOTES:** ⊗ in restaurant Civ Wed 90

See advert on this page

Lion Quays Hotel

Moreton, Nr Weston Rhyn SY11 3EN
☎ 01691 684300 Fax 01691 684313
e-mail: sales@lionquays.co.uk

At the time of going to press, the star classification for this hotel

continued

was not confirmed. Please refer to the AA internet site www.theAA.com for current information.

ROOMS: 82 en suite (3 fmly) (25 GF) ⊗ in 72 bedrooms s £75-£95; d £95-£105 (incl. bkfst) **FACILITIES:** STV Xmas **CONF:** Thtr 450 Class 200 Board 150 Del from £110 **SERVICES:** Lift air con **PARKING:** 150 **NOTES:** Civ Wed 300

Travelodge

Mile End Service Area SY11 4JA
☎ 08700 850 950 Fax 0870 191 1596
web: www.travelodge.co.uk

Dir: *at junct of A5/A483*

Travelodge offers good quality, good value, modern accommodation. Ideal for families, the spacious, en suite bedrooms include remote-control TV, tea and coffee-making facilities and comfortable beds. Meals can be taken at the nearby family restaurant. For further details consult the Hotel Groups page.

ROOMS: 40 en suite s fr £26; d fr £26

OTLEY, West Yorkshire

Map 19 SE24

★★★69% Chevin Country Park Hotel

Yorkgate LS21 3NU
☎ 01943 467818 Fax 01943 850335
e-mail: reception@chevinhotel.com

Dir: *From Leeds/Bradford Airport rdbt take A658 N, towards Harrogate, for 0.75m to 1st traffic lights. Turn left, then 2nd left onto 'Yorkgate'. Hotel 0.5m on left*

This hotel, peacefully situated in its own woodland yet conveniently located for major road links and the airport, offers comfortable accommodation. Rooms are split between the original main log building and chalet-style accommodation, situated in the

continued on p438

OTLEY, continued

extensive grounds. Public areas are spacious and well equipped. The split-level restaurant provides views over the small lake. Leisure facilities are also available.

Chevin Country Park Hotel, Otley

ROOMS: 19 en suite 30 annexe en suite (7 fmly) (45 GF) ⊗ in 30 bedrooms s £99-£135; d £110-£210 (incl. bkfst) **LB** **FACILITIES:** STV Fishing Sauna Solarium Gym Jacuzzi Mountain bikes, Jogging trails Xmas **CONF:** BC Thtr 120 Class 90 Board 50 Del £142 **PARKING:** 100 **NOTES:** ⊗ in restaurant Civ Wed 120

OTTERBURN, Northumberland — Map 21 NY89

★★★65% The Otterburn Tower Hotel

NE19 1NS
☎ 01830 520620 📠 01830 521504
e-mail: sales@otterburntower.com
web: www.otterburntower.com
Dir: *in village, on A696 (Newcastle to Edinburgh road)*

Built by the cousin of William the Conqueror, this mansion is set in its own grounds. The hotel is steeped in history - Sir Walter Scott stayed here in 1812. Bedrooms come in a variety of sizes and some have huge ornamental fireplaces. Though furnished in period style, they are equipped with all modern amenities. The restaurant features 16th-century oak panelling.

ROOMS: 18 en suite (2 fmly) (2 GF) ⊗ in all bedrooms s £65-£100; d £130-£190 (incl. bkfst) **LB** **FACILITIES:** STV Fishing ch fac Xmas **CONF:** Thtr 120 Class 40 Board 40 Del from £125 **PARKING:** 70 **NOTES:** ⊗ in restaurant Civ Wed 250

★★68% Percy Arms

NE19 1NR
☎ 01830 520261 📠 01830 520567
e-mail: percyarmshotel@yahoo.co.uk
Dir: *centre of Otterburn on A696*

This former coaching inn lies in the centre of the village, with good access to the Northumberland countryside. The welcoming public areas boast real fires in the cooler months. A very good range of dishes are offered in either the restaurant or cosy bar/bistro. Bedrooms are cheerfully decorated and thoughtfully equipped.

ROOMS: 27 en suite (2 fmly) (3 GF) ⊗ in 2 bedrooms s £45-£68; d £70-£100 (incl. bkfst) **LB** **FACILITIES:** STV Fishing Xmas **CONF:** Thtr 70 Class 40 Board 50 Del from £77.50 **PARKING:** 74 **NOTES:** ⊗ in restaurant Civ Wed 80

Indoor Swimming pool
Indoor Swimming pool (heated)
Outdoor Swimming pool
Outdoor Swimming pool (heated)

OTTERSHAW, Surrey — Map 06 TQ06

★★★★71% Foxhills Club & Resort

Stonehill Rd KT16 0EL
☎ 01932 872050 📠 01932 874762
e-mail: reservations@foxhills.co.uk
Dir: *A320 to Woking from M25. 2nd rdbt last exit into Chobham Rd. Right into Foxhills Rd, right at T-junct, then left into Stonehill Rd*

This hotel enjoys a peaceful setting in extensive grounds, not far from the M25 and Heathrow. Spacious well-appointed bedrooms are provided in an annexe, a short walk from the main house (an additional 26 rooms will be available from Spring 2006). Golf, tennis, three pools and impressive indoor leisure facilities are on offer. Two styles of restaurant are available.

ROOMS: 42 en suite (3 fmly) (25 GF) s £175-£300; d £175-£300 **LB** **FACILITIES:** STV 45 Squash Sauna Solarium Gym Putt green Boules, Childrens adventure playground, country pursuits, off-roadcourse, Snooker ch fac Xmas **CONF:** Thtr 100 Class 52 Board 56 Del from £200 **PARKING:** 500 **NOTES:** Civ Wed 75

OTTERY ST MARY, Devon — Map 03 SY19

★★70% Tumbling Weir Hotel

Canaan Way EX11 1AQ
☎ 01404 812752 📠 01404 812752
e-mail: reception@tumblingweirhotel.com
web: www.tumblingweir-hotel.co.uk
Dir: *off A30 take B3177 into Ottery St Mary, hotel signed off Mill St*

Quietly located between the River Otter and its millstream and set in well-tended gardens, this family-run hotel offers friendly and attentive service. Bedrooms are attractively presented and equipped with modern comforts. In the dining room, where a selection of carefully prepared dishes makes up the carte menu, beams and subtle lighting help to create an intimate atmosphere.

ROOMS: 10 en suite (1 fmly) ⊗ in all bedrooms s £50-£55; d £80-£88 (incl. bkfst) **LB** **FACILITIES:** **CONF:** Thtr 90 Class 60 Board 50 Del from £90 **PARKING:** 10 **NOTES:** ⊗ in restaurant Closed 26 Dec - 10 Jan Civ Wed 80

OWER, Hampshire — Map 05 SU31

★★70% Mortimer Arms

Romsey Rd SO51 6AF
☎ 023 8081 4379 📠 023 8081 2548
e-mail: info@mortimerarms.co.uk
Dir: *M27 junct 2 follow signs to Paultons Park. Hotel at entrance*

Located at the entrance of Paultons Park, this is ideally situated for access to the M27 and to the New Forest, so will suit leisure guests and business travellers alike. Bedrooms have now been refurbished to a high standard, and all have DVD players. Enjoyable meals are available in the relaxed, informal dining area.

ROOMS: 14 en suite (3 fmly) (2 GF) ⊗ in all bedrooms s £60; d £90 (incl. bkfst) **LB** **FACILITIES:** STV Xmas **CONF:** BC Thtr 80 Class 60 Board 50 **PARKING:** 64 **NOTES:** ⊗ in restaurant

OXFORD, Oxfordshire Map 05 SP50
See also Milton Common

★★★★ ◉◉◉◉◉ ⊞
Le Manoir Aux Quat' Saisons
Church Rd OX44 7PD
☎ 01844 278881 ▤ 01844 278847
e-mail: lemanoir@blanc.co.uk
web: www.manoir.com
(For full entry see Great Milton)

RELAIS & CHATEAUX.

Town House

★★★★ ◉ ⌂ **The Old Bank Hotel**
92-94 High St OX1 4BN
☎ 01865 799599 ▤ 01865 799598
e-mail: info@oldbank-hotel.co.uk
web: www.oxford-hotels-restaurants.co.uk
Dir: city centre to Magdalen Bridge, into High St, hotel 50yds on left
Located close to the city centre and colleges this former bank
benefits from an excellent location. An eclectic collection of
modern pictures and photographs many by well-known
artists, can be seen here. Bedrooms are smart with air
conditioning and excellent business facilities. Public areas
include the vibrant all-day Quod Bar and Restaurant. The
hotel also has a resident lounge and its own car park.
ROOMS: 42 en suite (10 fmly) (1 GF) s £150; d £165-£240
FACILITIES: STV Discounts with various leisure facilities **CONF:** Thtr
20 Class 20 Board 14 Del £205 **SERVICES:** Lift air con
PARKING: 40 **NOTES:** ✈ Closed 25-27 Dec

★★★★71% ◉ **The Randolph**
Beaumont St OX1 2LN
☎ 0870 400 8200 ▤ 01865 791678
e-mail: randolph@macdonald-hotels.co.uk
web: www.macdonald-hotels.co.uk

█ MACDONALD
HOTELS & RESORTS

*Dir: M40 junct 8, A40 towards Oxford. Follow signs to City Centre, leads to
St Giles, hotel on right*
Superbly located near the centre of town, The Randolph boasts
impressive neo-Gothic architecture and tasteful decor. The
spacious, traditional restaurant complete with picture windows,
are ideal places to watch the world go by, and enjoy freshly
prepared, modern dishes. Bedrooms are classical in style and
include an impressive new wing, which have been appointed to a
high standard. Parking is a real bonus.
ROOMS: 150 en suite ⊗ in 121 bedrooms s £110-£130; d £140-£160 **LB**
FACILITIES: Spa STV Sauna Gym Treatment rooms Xmas **CONF:** Thtr
300 Class 130 Board 60 Del from £135 **SERVICES:** Lift **PARKING:** 50
NOTES: ⊗ in restaurant Civ Wed 120

Town House

★★★★ ⌂ **Old Parsonage**
1 Banbury Rd OX2 6NN
☎ 01865 310210 ▤ 01865 311262
e-mail: info@oldparsonage-hotel.co.uk
web: www.oxford-hotels-restaurants.co.uk/op.html
*Dir: from Oxford ring road to city centre via Summertown. Hotel last
building on right next to St Giles Church before city centre*
Dating back in parts to the 16th century, this stylish hotel
offers great character and charm and is conveniently located
at the northern edge of the city centre. Individually styled
bedrooms are attractively furnished and particularly well
appointed. The focal point of the operation is the busy all-day
continued

bar restaurant, whilst the small garden areas and terraces are
popular in summer months.

ROOMS: 30 en suite (4 fmly) (10 GF) ⊗ in all bedrooms
FACILITIES: STV Complimentary use of punt and house bikes ♫
Xmas **CONF:** Board 20 **SERVICES:** air con **PARKING:** 16
NOTES: ⊗ in restaurant Civ Wed 20

★★★★70% **The Oxford Hotel**
Godstow Rd, Wolvercote Roundabout OX2 8AL
☎ 01865 489952 ▤ 01865 310259
e-mail: oxford@paramount-hotels.co.uk
web: www.paramount-hotels.co.uk

PARAMOUNT
GROUP OF HOTELS

Dir: adjacent to A34/A40, 2m from city centre
Conveniently located on the northern edge of the city centre, this
purpose-built hotel offers bedrooms that are bright, modern and
well equipped. Guests can eat in the 'Medio' restaurant or try the
Cappuccino bar menu. The hotel offers impressive conference,
business and leisure facilities.
ROOMS: 168 en suite (13 fmly) (89 GF) ⊗ in 140 bedrooms
FACILITIES: STV ⊞ Squash Sauna Solarium Gym Steam room Xmas
CONF: BC Thtr 300 Class 150 Board 60 Del from £145 **SERVICES:** Lift
PARKING: 250 **NOTES:** ⊗ in restaurant

★★★★69% ◉ **Cotswold Lodge**
66a Banbury Rd OX2 6JP
☎ 01865 512121 ▤ 01865 512490
e-mail: info@cotswoldlodgehotel.co.uk
web: www.cotswoldlodgehotel.co.uk

CLASSIC
BRITISH

*Dir: off A40 Oxford ring road onto A4165 Banbury Rd. Signed city centre
and Summertown. Hotel 2m on left*

This family-run Victorian property is located close to the centre of
Oxford and offers smart, comfortable accommodation. Stylish
bedrooms and suites are attractively presented and some have
balconies. The public areas have an elegant country-house feel.
continued on p440

OXFORD, continued

The hotel is popular with business guests and caters for conferences and banquets.
ROOMS: 49 en suite (8 GF) ⊗ in 40 bedrooms s £95-£125; d £120-£175 (incl. bkfst) **FACILITIES:** STV Discount at local gymnasium available to residents **CONF:** Thtr 100 Class 42 Board 34 Del from £120 **PARKING:** 40 **NOTES:** ⊗ in restaurant

★★★★67%
Oxford Spires Four Pillars Hotel
Abingdon Rd OX1 4PS
☎ 0800 374 692 & 01865 324324
01865 324325
e-mail: spires@four-pillars.co.uk
web: www.four-pillars.co.uk
Dir: *M40 junct 8 towards Oxford. Left at rdbt towards Cowley. Straight over next 2 rdbts. At next rdbt follow City Centre signs. Hotel 1m on right*
This purpose-built hotel is surrounded by extensive parkland, yet is only a short walk from the city centre. Bedrooms are attractively furnished, well equipped and include several apartments. Smartly appointed public areas include a spacious restaurant, open plan bar/lounge, leisure club and extensive conference facilities.
ROOMS: 115 en suite (8 fmly) ⊗ in 44 bedrooms s £79-£162; d £92-£209 (incl. bkfst) **LB** **FACILITIES:** STV Sauna Gym Jacuzzi Beauty, games, steam rooms ♫ Xmas **CONF:** BC Thtr 266 Class 96 Board 76 Del £179 **SERVICES:** Lift **PARKING:** 95 **NOTES:** ⊗ in restaurant Civ Wed 140

★★★★66%
Oxford Thames Four Pillars Hotel
Henley Rd, Sandford-on-Thames OX4 4GX
☎ 0800 374 692 & 01865 334444
01865 334400
e-mail: thames@four-pillars.co.uk
web: www.four-pillars.co.uk
Dir: *M40 junct 8. To Oxford follow ring road. Left at rdbt towards Cowley. At rdbt with lights take Left exit to Littlemore, the hotel approx 1m on right*

The main house of this hotel is built from local, yellow stone. The spacious and traditional River Restaurant has superb views over the hotel's own boat, moored on the river. The gardens can be enjoyed from the patios or balconies in the newer bedroom wings. Public rooms include a beamed bar and lounge area with minstrels' gallery.
ROOMS: 60 en suite (4 fmly) (24 GF) ⊗ in 35 bedrooms s £79-£162; d £92-£209 (incl. bkfst) **LB** **FACILITIES:** STV Sauna Gym Jacuzzi Steam room ♫ Xmas **CONF:** BC Thtr 160 Class 80 Board 60 Del £189 **PARKING:** 120 **NOTES:** Civ Wed 120

Early start?
Hotels at all star levels should provide in-room alarm clocks and/or alarm clocks

★★★70% **Weston Manor Hotel**
OX25 3QL
☎ 01869 350621 01869 350901
e-mail: reception@westonmanor.co.uk
web: www.westonmanor.co.uk
(For full entry see Weston-on-the-Green)

★★★69% **Eastgate**
73 High St OX1 4BE
☎ 0870 400 8201 & 01865 248332
01865 791681
e-mail: sales.eastgate@macdonald-hotels.co.uk
web: www.macdonald-hotels.co.uk
Dir: *A40 follow signs to Headington & Oxford city centre, over Magdalen Bridge, stay in left lane, left into Merton St, entrance to car park on left*
Just a short stroll from the city centre, this hotel, as its name suggests, occupies the site of the city's medieval East Gate and boasts its own car park. Bedrooms have undergone a contemporary refurbishment and all are appointed and equipped to a high standard. Stylish public areas include the new all-day Town House Brasserie and Bar.
ROOMS: 63 en suite (3 fmly) ⊗ in 30 bedrooms s £85-£110; d £120-£160 (incl. bkfst) **LB** **FACILITIES:** STV Xmas **CONF:** Board 16 Del from £130 **SERVICES:** Lift **PARKING:** 40 **NOTES:** ⊗ in restaurant

★★★68% **Fallowfields Country House Hotel**
Faringdon Rd, Kingston Bagpuize, Southmoor OX13 5BH
☎ 01865 820416 01865 821275
e-mail: stay@fallowfields.com
web: www.fallowfields.com
Dir: *from A420, take A415 towards Abingdon for 100yds. Right at mini rdbt, through Kingston Bagpuize, Southmoor and Longworth, follow signs*
With a history stretching back over 300 years, this spacious, comfortable hotel provides friendly, old-fashioned service. The thoughtfully equipped bedrooms are very much of this century and are decorated with skill. Public areas include an elegant drawing room and a charming conservatory restaurant where the hotel's own seasonal produce is served.
ROOMS: 10 en suite (2 fmly) ⊗ in all bedrooms **FACILITIES:** STV Falconry **CONF:** Thtr 60 Board 20 Del from £185 **PARKING:** 81 **NOTES:** ⊗ in restaurant Closed 24-26 Dec

★★★68% **Hawkwell House**
Church Way, Iffley Village OX4 4DZ
☎ 01865 749988 01865 748525
e-mail: reservations@hawkwellhouse.co.uk
web: www.bespokehotels.com
Dir: *A34 follow signs to Cowley. At Littlemore rdbt take A4158 exit onto Iffley Rd. After traffic lights left to Iffley*

Set in a peaceful residential location, Hawkwell House is just a few minutes' drive from the Oxford ring road. The spacious rooms are modern, attractively decorated and well equipped. Public areas

continued

are tastefully appointed and the conservatory-style restaurant offers an interesting choice of dishes. The hotel also has a range of conference and function facilities.
ROOMS: 66 en suite (10 fmly) (4 GF) ⊗ in 55 bedrooms s £84-£99; d £120-£135 (incl. bkfst) **LB** **FACILITIES:** STV ♫ Xmas **CONF:** Thtr 200 Class 100 Board 80 Del from £145 **SERVICES:** Lift **PARKING:** 85 **NOTES:** ✖ ⊗ in restaurant Civ Wed 150

★★★66% Linton Lodge

11-13 Linton Rd OX2 6UJ
☎ 01865 553461 🖷 01865 553691
e-mail: sales@lintonlodge.com
Dir: *to Oxford city centre, along Banbury Rd. After 0.5m right into Linton Rd. Hotel opposite St Andrews Church*

Located in a residential area, this hotel is within walking distance of the town centre. Bedrooms are modern, well equipped and comfortable. The restaurant has a library theme, and the bar overlooks extensive lawned gardens to the rear of the hotel.
ROOMS: 71 en suite (2 fmly) ⊗ in 40 bedrooms **FACILITIES:** STV ♫ Putt green **CONF:** Thtr 120 Class 50 Board 40 **SERVICES:** Lift **PARKING:** 40 **NOTES:** ✖ ⊗ in restaurant Civ Wed 120

See advert on this page

★★★66% Westwood Country

Hinksey Hill, Boars Hill OX1 5BG
☎ 01865 735408 🖷 01865 736536
e-mail: reservations@westwoodhotel.co.uk
web: www.westwoodhotel.co.uk
Dir: *off Oxford ring road at Hinksey Hill junct. Towards Boars Hill & Wootton. At top of hill road bends to left. Hotel on right*

This Edwardian country-house hotel is prominently set in terraced landscaped gardens and is within easy reach of the city centre by car. The hotel is modern in style, with very comfortable, well-equipped and tastefully decorated bedrooms. Public areas include a contemporary bar, a cosy lounge, and a restaurant looking out over the gardens.
ROOMS: 23 en suite (4 fmly) (6 GF) s £55-£75; d £99-£120 (incl. bkfst) **FACILITIES:** ♫ **CONF:** Thtr 60 Class 36 Board 35 Del from £135 **PARKING:** 60 **NOTES:** ⊗ in restaurant Civ Wed 130

★★67% Victoria

180 Abingdon Rd OX1 4RA
☎ 01865 724536 🖷 01865 794909
e-mail: victoriahotel@aol.com
Dir: *from M40/A40 take Eastern bypass and A4144 into city*
Located within easy reach of Oxford city centre and the motorway networks, this hotel offers a warm welcome. Bedrooms are comfortable, well maintained and furnished to a high standard. A conservatory bar and large dining room are ideal places to relax.
ROOMS: 15 en suite 5 annexe en suite (1 fmly) (4 GF) ⊗ in 15 bedrooms **CONF:** Board 20 **PARKING:** 20 **NOTES:** ⊗ in restaurant

★★66% Manor House

250 Iffley Rd OX4 1SE
☎ 01865 727627 🖷 01865 200478
Dir: *on A4158 1m from city centre*
This conveniently situated, family run hotel is easily accessible from the city centre and all major road links. The hotel provides informal but friendly and attentive service with evening meals and bar service available. The comfortably furnished bedrooms are well equipped and all have en suite facilities. The private parking is an asset.
ROOMS: 8 en suite (2 fmly) ⊗ in all bedrooms **PARKING:** 6 **NOTES:** ✖ Closed 20 Dec-20 Jan

★★65% The Balkan Lodge Hotel

315 Iffley Rd OX4 4AG
☎ 01865 244524 🖷 01865 251090
e-mail: balkanlodge@aol.co.uk
Dir: *from M40/A40 take eastern bypass, into city on A4158*
Conveniently located for the city centre and the ring road, this family operated hotel offers a comfortable stay. Bedrooms are attractive and well equipped; one has a four-poster bed and

continued on p442

OXFORD, continued

Jacuzzi bath. Public areas include a lounge, bar and restaurant. A large private car park is located to the rear of the building.
ROOMS: 13 en suite ⊘ in all bedrooms **FACILITIES:** STV **NOTES:** ⊘ in restaurant

U Express by Holiday Inn Oxford-Kassam Stadium

Grenoble Rd OX4 4XP
☎ 01865 780888 🖷 01865 780999
e-mail: reservations@expressoxford.com
Dir: *M40 junct 8 onto A40 for 4m. Left at Mcdonalds onto A4142. After 3.5m left onto A4074, take 1st exit signed Science Park & Kassam Stadium*
At the time of going to press, the star classification for this hotel was not confirmed. Please refer to the AA internet site www.theAA.com for current information.
ROOMS: 162 en suite (131 fmly) ⊘ in 127 bedrooms s £45-£89; d £45-£89 (incl. cont bkfst) **LB** **FACILITIES:** STV Use of health club 10 mins walk away **SERVICES:** Lift **PARKING:** 100 **NOTES:** ✗ ⊘ in restaurant

○ Malmaison Oxford

New Road OX1 1LD
☎ 0845 365 4247 (central reservations)
NOTES: Due to open in October 2005

⇧ Premier Travel Inn Oxford

Oxford Business Park, Garsington Rd OX4 2JZ
☎ 08701 977204 🖷 01865 775887
web: www.premiertravelinn.com
Dir: *just off A4142 at junct with B480, opposite BMW Works*
High quality, modern budget accommodation ideal for both families and business travellers. Spacious, en suite bedrooms feature bath and shower, satellite TV and many have telephones and modem points. The adjacent family restaurant features a wide and varied menu. For further details consult the Hotel Groups page.
ROOMS: 120 en suite s £57.95-£62.95; d £57.95-£62.95

⇧ Travelodge

Peartree Roundabout, Woodstock Rd OX2 8JZ
☎ 08700 850 950 🖷 01865 513474
web: www.travelodge.co.uk
Dir: *at junct of A34/A44*
Travelodge offers good quality, good value, modern accommodation. Ideal for families, the spacious, en suite bedrooms include remote-control TV, tea and coffee-making facilities and comfortable beds. Meals can be taken at the nearby family restaurant. For further details consult the Hotel Groups page.
ROOMS: 150 en suite s fr £26; d fr £26 **CONF:** Thtr 300 Class 150 Board 60

⇧ Travelodge (Oxford East)

London Rd, Wheatley OX33 1JH
☎ 08700 850 950 🖷 01865 875905
web: www.travelodge.co.uk
Dir: *off A40 next to The Harvester on outskirts of Wheatley*
Travelodge offers good quality, good value, modern accommodation. Ideal for families, the spacious, en suite bedrooms include remote-control TV, tea and coffee-making facilities and comfortable beds. Meals can be taken at the nearby family restaurant. For further details consult the Hotel Groups page.
ROOMS: 36 en suite s fr £26; d fr £26

♫ Entertainment

OXFORD MOTORWAY SERVICE AREA (M40), Oxfordshire — Map 05 SP60

⇧ Days Inn Oxford

M40 junction 8A, Waterstock OX33 1LJ
☎ 01865 877000 🖷 01865 877016
e-mail: oxford.hotel@welcomebreak.co.uk
web: www.welcomebreak.co.uk
Dir: *M40 junct 8a, Welcome Break service area.*
This modern building offers accommodation in smart, spacious and well-equipped bedrooms, suitable for families and business travellers, and all with en suite bathrooms. Continental breakfast is available and other refreshments may be taken at the nearby family restaurant. For further details see the Hotel Groups page.
ROOMS: 59 en suite s £54-£60; d £54-£60

PADSTOW, Cornwall & Isles of Scilly — Map 02 SW97
See also Constantine Bay

★★★70% ❀ The Metropole

Station Rd PL28 8DB
☎ 01841 532486 🖷 01841 532867
e-mail: info@the-metropole.co.uk
web: www.richardsonhotels.co.uk
Dir: *M5/A30 pass Launceston, turn off & follow signs for Wadebridge & N Cornwall. Take A39 & follow signs for Padstow*

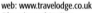

This long-established hotel first opened its doors to guests back in 1904 and there is still an air of the sophistication and elegance of a bygone age. Bedrooms are soundly appointed and well equipped and dining options include the informal Met Café Bar and the main restaurant, with enjoyable cuisine and wonderful views over the Camel estuary.
ROOMS: 50 en suite (3 fmly) (2 GF) ⊘ in 10 bedrooms s £69-£85; d £69-£85 (incl. bkfst & dinner) **LB** **FACILITIES:** Swimming pool open Jul & Aug only Xmas **SERVICES:** Lift **PARKING:** 36 **NOTES:** ⊘ in restaurant

★★★65% ❀ Old Custom House Inn

South Quay PL28 8BL
☎ 01841 532359 🖷 01841 533372
e-mail: oldcustomhouse@smallandfriendly.co.uk
Dir: *A359 from Wadebridge, take 2nd right. In Padstow follow road round bend to bottom of hill. Hotel on left*
Situated by the harbour, this charming inn continues to be a popular choice for locals and visitors alike. The lively bar serves real ales and good bar meals. Pescadou's restaurant provides a stylish and convivial venue for imaginative dishes that place the emphasis on locally caught fish. A wide selection of beauty treatments is available in the hotel's Lavender Room.
ROOMS: 24 en suite (8 fmly) ⊘ in all bedrooms s £82-£95; d £100-£170 (incl. bkfst) **LB** **FACILITIES:** STV **NOTES:** ✗ ⊘ in restaurant

★★67% **The Old Ship Hotel**
Mill Square PL28 8AE
☎ 01841 532357 ▤ 01841 533211
e-mail: stay@oldshiphotel-padstow.co.uk
web: www.oldshiphotel-padstow.co.uk
Dir: from M5 take A30 to Bodmin then A389 to Padstow, follow brown
tourist signs to car park
This attractive inn is situated in the heart of the old town's quaint
and winding streets, just a short walk from the harbour. A warm
welcome is assured, accommodation is pleasant and comfortable,
and public areas offer plenty of character. Freshly caught fish
features on both the bar and restaurant menus.
ROOMS: 14 en suite (4 fmly) ⊗ in all bedrooms s £35-£54; d £70-£108
(incl. bkfst) **LB FACILITIES:** STV ♫ Xmas **PARKING:** 20 **NOTES:** ⊗ in
restaurant

Restaurant with Rooms

🏠 ◉◉◉ **The Seafood Restaurant**
Riverside PL28 8BY
☎ 01841 532700 ▤ 01841 532942
e-mail: reservations@rickstein.com
Dir: A38 towards Newquay, then A389 towards Padstow. After 3m, right at
T-junct, follow signs for Padstow town centre. Restaurant on left
Rick Stein's Seafood Restaurant enjoys an enviable reputation for
the freshness and quality of its cuisine, and it is no surprise to
discover that such high standards are repeated in the
accommodation here. Each of the bedrooms is spacious and
comfortable, complete with fine quality fixtures and fittings.
Additional rooms, also luxuriously appointed, are housed close by
in St. Edmunds.
ROOMS: 14 en suite 19 annexe en suite (7 fmly) (3 GF) d £85-£245
(incl. bkfst) **LB FACILITIES:** STV Cookery schl. either non-residtl/residtl
variety of cours childn, fish, dessts, **PARKING:** 22 **NOTES:** Closed 1 May
& 24-26 Dec

PAIGNTON, Devon Map 03 SX86

★★★71% **Redcliffe**
Marine Dr TQ3 2NL
☎ 01803 526397 ▤ 01803 528030
e-mail: redclfe@aol.com
Dir: on seafront at Torquay end of Paignton Green
Set on the edge of the sea in three acres of well-tended grounds,
this popular hotel enjoys uninterrupted views across Tor Bay.
Offering a diverse range of facilities, including leisure, business
and beauty treatments, the Redcliffe is suitable for leisure or
business guests. Bedrooms are pleasantly appointed and
comfortably furnished, whilst public areas offer ample space for
rest and relaxation.
ROOMS: 67 en suite (8 fmly) (2 GF) s £55-£60; d £110-£120 (incl.
bkfst) **FACILITIES:** Spa STV ☜ supervised ☜ Fishing Sauna Solarium
Gym Putt green Jacuzzi Table tennis, Carpet Bowls Xmas **CONF:** Thtr
150 Class 50 Board 50 **SERVICES:** Lift **PARKING:** 80 **NOTES:** ✖ ⊗
in restaurant Civ Wed 150

★★71% **Dainton**
95 Dartmouth Rd, Goodrington TQ4 6NA
☎ 01803 550067 ▤ 01803 666339
e-mail: enquiries@daintonhotel.com
Dir: on A379 at Goodrington. Pass zoo entrance, right onto Penwill Way.
At bottom of road right into Dartmouth Rd. Hotel 0.25m on left
Located in a convenient position close to the beaches and Leisure
Park, the Dainton provides a friendly and welcoming place to stay.
Bedrooms are well equipped and brightly decorated. Service is
continued

TORBAY HOLIDAY MOTEL
★ ★

The ideal centre for touring South Devon
Open all year

All rooms en suite with colour TV (inc SKY), radio,
telephone and tea/coffee facilities
• Indoor and outdoor pools • Solarium • Sauna
• Mini-Gym • Launderette • Crazy golf
• Restaurant • Bar • Shop • Ample parking
• 35-acre picnic area •

Also studio apartments and family suites available

**Brochure from: Dept AA, Torbay Holiday Motel
Totnes Road, Paignton, Devon TQ4 7PP
Tel: 01803 558226 Website: www.thm.co.uk
E-mail: enquiries@thm.co.uk**

attentive, particularly in Christie's restaurant, which has an
extensive menu with vegetarian options.
ROOMS: 10 en suite (1 fmly) (2 GF) ⊗ in all bedrooms s £37-£50;
d £65-£100 (incl. bkfst) **LB FACILITIES:** Xmas **PARKING:** 20
NOTES: ✖ ⊗ in restaurant

★★68% **Sea Verge Hotel**
21 Marine Dr TQ3 2NJ
☎ 01803 557795
Dir: on seafront
With the added benefit of dedicated owners, this family-run hotel
is conveniently situated close to the seafront and Preston Green.
Several of the light and airy bedrooms have balconies, with views
over Torbay. Spacious public areas include a comfortable lounge
with adjacent sunroom, a cosy bar and dining room.
ROOMS: 10 en suite (1 fmly) ⊗ in 4 bedrooms d £40-£50 (incl. bkfst) **LB
PARKING:** 14 **NOTES:** ✖ No children 9yrs ⊗ in restaurant Closed Dec-Feb
No credit cards accepted

★★67% **Torbay Holiday Motel**
Totnes Rd TQ4 7PP
☎ 01803 558226 ▤ 01803 663375
e-mail: enquiries@thm.co.uk
Dir: on A385 Totnes to Paignton road, 2.5m from Paignton
Situated between Paignton and Totnes, this small complex offers
purpose built leisure facilities, self-catering apartments and motel
accommodation. The spacious bedrooms are comfortable and well
co-ordinated. There are two restaurants and traditional dining is
offered throughout.
ROOMS: 16 en suite (16 fmly) (8 GF) s £36-£41; d £54-£64 (incl. bkfst)
LB FACILITIES: STV ☜ ☜ Sauna Solarium Gym Putt green Crazy
golf, Adventure playground **PARKING:** 150 **NOTES:** RS 24-31 Dec
See advert on this page

PAIGNTON, continued

A ★★ *Summerhill*
Braeside Rd TQ4 6BX
☎ 01803 558101 📠 01803 558101
e-mail: info@summerhillhotel.co.uk
web: www.summerhillhotel.co.uk
Dir: *with harbour on left, follow for 600yds*
ROOMS: 26 en suite (9 fmly) (4 GF) ⊗ in all bedrooms
FACILITIES: Free membership to nearby leisure centre. ch fac
SERVICES: Lift **PARKING:** 40 **NOTES:** ✗ ⊗ in restaurant

★69% Britney
29 Esplanade Rd TQ4 6BL
☎ 01803 557820 📠 01803 551285
Dir: *on seafront by pier*
In an impressive location on the seafront, this pleasant hotel offers comfortable accommodation. The hotel is family run and the proprietors are friendly and attentive. Bedrooms, some facing the sea and some with balconies, are available in a range of sizes. A lively bar is provided, as well as a quieter lounge and sunroom.
ROOMS: 20 en suite (2 fmly) ⊗ in 3 bedrooms s £28; d £28 (incl. bkfst) **LB** **FACILITIES:** Xmas **SERVICES:** Lift **PARKING:** 8 **NOTES:** ⊗ in restaurant Closed 01/10/2005-Etr RS Xmas

PAINSWICK, Gloucestershire Map 04 SO81

★★★77% ®® Painswick Hotel and Restaurant
Kemps Ln GL6 6YB
☎ 01452 812160 📠 01452 814059
e-mail: reservations@painswickhotel.com
web: www.painswickhotel.com
Dir: *off A46 in centre of village by church. Hotel off 2nd road behind church off Tibbiwell Lane*

Dating back to 1790, this former rectory is situated in the heart of one of the Cotswolds' most enchanting villages. Attentive hospitality and service are key features. The day rooms house antiques and interesting artwork, contributing to a sense of timeless elegance. All bedrooms differ, while reflecting similar high standards. Accomplished cuisine and a serious choice of wine are served in the oak-panelled restaurant.
ROOMS: 19 en suite (2 fmly) (6 GF) s £125-£160; d £195-£275 (incl. bkfst & dinner) **LB** **FACILITIES:** Xmas **CONF:** Thtr 50 Class 15 Board 26 Del £150 **PARKING:** 20 **NOTES:** ⊗ in restaurant Civ Wed 80

See advert on opposite page

U Star rating not confirmed

Bad hair day?
Hairdryers in all rooms three stars and above

PANGBOURNE, Berkshire Map 05 SU67

★★★72% ®®
The Copper Inn Hotel and Restaurant
RG8 7AR
☎ 0118 984 2244 📠 0118 984 5542
e-mail: reservations@copper-inn.co.uk
web: www.copper-inn.co.uk
Dir: *M4 junct 12 take A4 W then A340 to Pangbourne. Hotel next to church at junct of A329 & A340*
This 19th-century coaching inn is in the heart of a quaint Berkshire village. Public rooms include a popular and lively bar, a quiet lounge and lovely restaurant where service is friendly and efficient. Well-equipped bedrooms, many of which overlook the secluded rear gardens, are comfortably appointed and individually decorated.
ROOMS: 14 en suite 8 annexe en suite (1 fmly) (4 GF) ⊗ in all bedrooms s £90-£110; d £100-£145 **LB** **FACILITIES:** STV Xmas **CONF:** BC Thtr 60 Class 24 Board 30 Del from £142 **PARKING:** 20 **NOTES:** ⊗ in restaurant Civ Wed 70

★★★64% *George Hotel*
The Square RG8 7AJ
☎ 0118 984 2237 📠 0118 984 4354
e-mail: info@georgehotelpangbourne.co.uk
Dir: *M4 junct 12 towards Newbury. Right at 2nd rdbt onto A340, 3m to Pangbourne. Right at rdbt, hotel 50yds on left*
Occupying a site where an inn has stood since 1295, The George offers modern facilities. Bedrooms are thoughtfully appointed and comfortable, a number are specially equipped for families. The 'Kidsden' rooms have computers and playstations and considering the hotel's location, just 20 minutes from Legoland, this is a popular venue for families. Dinner is available with an Italian theme in Mia Bene Restaurant.
ROOMS: 24 en suite (6 fmly) ⊗ in 12 bedrooms **FACILITIES:** STV **CONF:** Thtr 60 Class 25 Board 20 **PARKING:** 30

PARKHAM, Devon Map 03 SS32

★★★72% ® Penhaven Country House
Rectory Ln EX39 5PL
☎ 01237 451388 & 451711 📠 01237 451878
e-mail: reservations@penhaven.co.uk
web: www.penhaven.co.uk
Dir: *off A39 at Horns Cross, follow signs to Parkham, 2nd left after church into Rectory Lane*
The countryside is very much at the heart of this establishment and lucky guests can spot tame badgers most evenings in the lovely grounds. The tranquillity of the location and the friendliness of the staff combine to create a truly relaxing place to stay. Bedrooms are spacious and well equipped; some are located in the cottage annexe and two are on the ground floor. Dinners feature fresh, local produce and vegetarians are especially welcome.
ROOMS: 12 en suite s £86-£92; d £172-£184 (incl. bkfst & dinner) **LB** **FACILITIES:** 9 acres of woodland trail Xmas **PARKING:** 50 **NOTES:** No children 10yrs ⊗ in restaurant

PATTERDALE, Cumbria Map 18 NY31

★★64% *Patterdale*
CA11 0NN
☎ 0845 458 4333 & 017684 82231 📠 01253 754222
e-mail: reservations@choice-hotels.co.uk
Dir: *M6 junct 40, take A592 towards Ullswater, then 10m up Lakeside Rd to Patterdale*
Patterdale is a real tourist destination and this hotel enjoys

continued

delightful views of the valley and fells, being located at the southern end of Ullswater. Bedrooms vary in style; some are brightly decorated with a modern feel. In busier periods accommodation is let for a minimum period of two nights.
ROOMS: 57 en suite (16 fmly) **FACILITIES:** Fishing Free bike hire ch fac **SERVICES:** Lift **PARKING:** 30 **NOTES:** in restaurant

PATTINGHAM, Staffordshire Map 10 SO89

★★★68% Patshull Park Hotel Golf & Country Club

Patshull Park WV6 7HR
☎ 01902 700100 01902 700874
e-mail: sales@patshull-park.co.uk
web: www.patshull-park.co.uk
Dir: *1.5m W of Pattingham, at church take Patshull Rd, hotel 1.5m on right*

There has been a manor house here since before the Norman Conquest; the present house dates back to the 1730s and is now a comfortably appointed hotel. Sitting within 280 acres of parkland (with good golf and fishing) this hotel has a range of modern leisure and conference facilities. Public rooms include a lounge bar, coffee shop and restaurant with delightful views out over the lake. Bedrooms are well appointed and thoughtfully equipped; most have good views.
ROOMS: 49 en suite (15 fmly) (16 GF) in all bedrooms s £85-£119; d £95-£159 (incl. bkfst) **LB** **FACILITIES: Spa** STV supervised 18 Fishing Sauna Solarium Gym Putt green Jacuzzi Beauty therapist, Pool table, Cardio suite Xmas **CONF:** BC Thtr 160 Class 75 Board 44 Del from £99 **PARKING:** 200 **NOTES:** in restaurant RS 24-26 Dec Civ Wed 100

See advert under WOLVERHAMPTON

If you wish to use a particular credit card or debit card please check with the hotel that they are happy to accept it

PEASLAKE, Surrey Map 06 TQ04

★★★69% Hurtwood Inn Hotel

Walking Bottom GU5 9RR
☎ 01306 730851 01306 731390
e-mail: sales@hurtwoodinnhotel.com
web: www.hurtwoodinnhotel.com
Dir: *off A25 at Gomshall opposite Jet Filling Station towards Peaslake. After 2.5m turn right at village shop, hotel in village centre*
With its tranquil location this hotel makes an ideal base for exploring the attractions of the area. The brightly decorated bedrooms are well appointed, and some have views over the gardens. Public areas include a new restaurant, a private dining

continued

room and a bar/bistro where drinks by the open fire can be enjoyed. 'Oscars' is the setting to enjoy award-winning meals.

Hurtwood Inn Hotel, Peaslake

ROOMS: 15 en suite 6 annexe en suite (6 fmly) (6 GF) in 5 bedrooms s £65; d £75-£90 **LB** **CONF:** Thtr 40 Class 15 Board 20 Del from £126.95 **PARKING:** 22 **NOTES:** in restaurant

PEASMARSH, East Sussex Map 07 TQ82

★★★76% Flackley Ash

TN31 6YH
☎ 01797 230651 01797 230510
e-mail: enquiries@flackleyashhotel.co.uk
web: www.flackleyashhotel.co.uk
Dir: *A21 onto A268 to Newenden, A268 to Rye. Hotel on left*
Five acres of beautifully kept grounds are the lovely backdrop to this elegant Georgian country house. The hotel is superbly situated for exploring the many local attractions, including the ancient

continued on p446

PEASMARSH, continued

Cinque Port of Rye, just a short drive away. The pleasantly decorated bedrooms have co-ordinated fabrics and many thoughtful touches.

Flackley Ash, Peasmarsh

ROOMS: 45 en suite (5 fmly) s £87-£112; d £132-£182 (incl. bkfst) **LB** **FACILITIES: Spa** STV supervised Sauna Gym Putt green Jacuzzi Beauty salon Xmas **CONF:** BC Thtr 100 Class 60 Board 40 Del £125 **PARKING:** 80 **NOTES:** in restaurant Civ Wed 100

PENDLEBURY, Greater Manchester Map 15 SD70

Premier Travel Inn Manchester (Swinton)

219 Bolton Rd M27 8TG
☎ 0870 9906528 0870 9906529
web: www.premiertravelinn.com
Dir: *Exit M60 junct 13 towards A572, at rdbt take 3rd exit towards Swinton. At next take A572. 2m right onto A580. At 2nd lights take A666 Kearsley, then 1st left at rdbt. Pass fire station on right, take 1st right*

High quality, modern budget accommodation ideal for both families and business travellers. Spacious, en suite bedrooms feature bath and shower, satellite TV and many have telephones and modem points. The adjacent family restaurant features a wide and varied menu. For further details consult the Hotel Groups page.

ROOMS: 31 en suite s £47.95-£50.95; d £47.95-£50.95

PENKRIDGE, Staffordshire Map 10 SJ91

★★★66% Quality Hotel Stafford

Pinfold Ln ST19 5QP
☎ 01785 712459 01785 715532
e-mail: enquiries@hotels-stafford.com
web: www.choicehotelseurope.com
Dir: *M6 junct 12 onto A5 towards Telford. Right at 1st rdbt onto A449, 2m into Penkridge, left just beyond Ford Garage, opposite White Hart*

Just a few minutes' drive from the M6, this hotel is pleasantly located down a country lane. Bedrooms are comfortable with a good range of facilities. Public areas are neatly appointed with conference rooms and a leisure club. The Choices Restaurant serves popular meals to its guests.

ROOMS: 47 en suite (2 fmly) (6 GF) in 25 bedrooms **FACILITIES:** STV supervised Squash Sauna Solarium Gym Xmas **CONF:** Thtr 300 Class 120 Board 60 **PARKING:** 175 **NOTES:** in restaurant Civ Wed 200

The vast majority of establishments in this guide accept credit and debit cards. We indicate those that don't take any

PENRITH, Cumbria Map 18 NY53
See also Shap & Temple Sowerby

★★★★75% North Lakes Hotel & Spa

Ullswater Rd CA11 8QT
☎ 01768 868111 01768 868291
e-mail: nlakes@shirehotels.com
web: www.shirehotels.com
Dir: *M6 junct 40 at junct with A66*

With a great location, it's no wonder that this modern hotel is perpetually busy. Amenities include a good range of meeting and function rooms and excellent health and leisure facilities including a full spa. Themed public areas have a contemporary, Scandinavian country style and offer plenty of space and comfort. High standards of service are provided by a friendly team of staff.

ROOMS: 84 en suite (6 fmly) (22 GF) in 57 bedrooms s £87-£127; d £124-£147 (incl. bkfst) **LB** **FACILITIES: Spa** STV supervised Sauna Solarium Gym Jacuzzi Childrens pool, Steam room Xmas **CONF:** BC Thtr 200 Class 140 Board 24 Del from £150 **SERVICES:** Lift **PARKING:** 150 **NOTES:** in restaurant Civ Wed 200

★★★79% Temple Sowerby House Hotel & Restaurant

CA10 1RZ
☎ 017683 61578 017683 61958
e-mail: stay@templesowerby.com
web: www.templesowerby.com
(For full entry see Temple Sowerby)

★★★72% Westmorland Hotel

Westmorland Place, Orton CA10 3SB
☎ 015396 24351 015396 24354
e-mail: sales@westmorlandhotel.com
web: www.westmorlandhotel.com
(For full entry see Tebay)

★★★68% The George

Devonshire St CA11 7SU
☎ 01768 862696 01768 868223
e-mail: info@georgehotelpenrith.co.uk
web: www.georgehotelpenrith.co.uk
Dir: *M6 junct 40, 1m to town centre. From A6/A66 to Penrith*

This inviting and popular, long-standing hotel, that can trace its history back some 300 years, has been extended and upgraded. The spacious public areas retain a timeless sense of charm and include a choice of lounge areas where morning coffees and afternoon teas can be enjoyed.

ROOMS: 32 en suite (3 fmly) in 24 bedrooms s £49-£88; d £90-£148 (incl. bkfst) **LB** **FACILITIES:** STV Free use of local pool and gym Xmas **CONF:** Thtr 120 Class 60 Board 40 Del from £75 **PARKING:** 34 **NOTES:** in restaurant Civ Wed 120

See advert on opposite page

★★70% Edenhall Country Hotel
Edenhall CA11 8SX
☎ 01768 881454 📠 01768 881266
e-mail: info@edenhallhotel.co.uk
Dir: *take A686 from Penrith to Alston. Hotel signed on right in 3m*
Located in a peaceful hamlet yet convenient for the M6, this hotel is popular with business guests. Bedrooms and public areas continue to be upgraded; the comfortable lounge bar serving an attractive range of meals. Carefully prepared and well-presented dinners are served in the dining room that overlooks the well-tended gardens.
ROOMS: 17 en suite 8 annexe rms (7 en suite) (3 fmly) (7 GF) s £40-£60; d £65-£80 (incl. bkfst) **LB** **FACILITIES:** STV Jacuzzi Xmas **CONF:** Thtr 50 Class 30 Board 30 Del from £90 **PARKING:** 60 **NOTES:** ⊘ in restaurant Civ Wed 60

★★67% Brantwood Country Hotel
Stainton CA11 0EP
☎ 01768 862748 📠 01768 890164
e-mail: brantwood2@aol.com
Dir: *M6 junct 40, A66. Left in 0.5m then right signed Stainton. Left at x-roads. Hotel on left*

Located in a peaceful village this family-run hotel enjoys an open outlook to the rear. The traditional bedrooms are individual and cheerful in colour with all the expected facilities. Hearty meals are served in both the bar and restaurant and there is a separate conservatory-style residents' lounge.
ROOMS: 7 en suite (3 fmly) ⊘ in 5 bedrooms s £46-£51; d £68 (incl. bkfst) **LB** **FACILITIES:** Xmas **CONF:** Thtr 60 Class 30 Board 30 Del from £85 **PARKING:** 35 **NOTES:** ⊘ in restaurant Closed 25-28 Dec

Travelodge
Redhills CA11 0DT
☎ 08700 850 950 📠 01768 866958
web: www.travelodge.co.uk
Dir: *on A66, 0.25m from M6 junct 40*
Travelodge offers good quality, good value, modern accommodation. Ideal for families, the spacious, en suite bedrooms include remote-control TV, tea and coffee-making facilities and comfortable beds. Meals can be taken at the nearby family restaurant. For further details consult the Hotel Groups page.
ROOMS: 54 en suite s fr £26; d fr £26

PENSILVA, Cornwall & Isles of Scilly Map 03 SX27

★★66% *Wheal Tor Country Hotel*
Caradon Hill PL14 5PJ
☎ 01579 362281 📠 01579 363401
e-mail: enquiries@whealtorhotel.co.uk
web: www.whealtorhotel.co.uk
Wheal Tor has splendid views over Bodmin Moor and is set well away from the road, yet convenient for business and leisure

continued

guests alike. The proprietors provide friendly hospitality. The hotel and its 'Restaurant des Hauteurs' prove popular with locals.
ROOMS: 7 en suite (1 fmly) ⊘ in all bedrooms **FACILITIES:** **CONF:** **PARKING:** 50 **NOTES:** ⊘ in restaurant

PENZANCE, Cornwall & Isles of Scilly Map 02 SW43

★★★76% Mount Prospect
Britons Hill TR18 3AE
☎ 01736 363117 📠 01736 350970
e-mail: enquiries@hotelpenzance.com
web: www.hotelpenzance.com
Dir: *from A30 pass heliport on right, left at next rdbt for town centre. 3rd right and hotel on right*
This Edwardian house has been tastefully redesigned, focusing on the contemporary Bay Restaurant. Style is not only limited to the rooms, but is also apparent in the cuisine that is based upon fresh Cornish produce. Bedrooms have also been appointed to modern standards and are particularly well equipped; many have views across Mounts Bay.
ROOMS: 24 en suite (2 fmly) (2 GF) ⊘ in 20 bedrooms s £60-£80; d £110-£130 (incl. bkfst) **LB** **FACILITIES:** STV Xmas **CONF:** Thtr 80 Class 50 Board 25 **PARKING:** 14 **NOTES:** ⊘ in restaurant RS Nov-Apr

★★★66% Queen's
The Promenade TR18 4HG
☎ 01736 362371 📠 01736 350033
e-mail: enquiries@queens-hotel.com
web: www.queens-hotel.com
Dir: *A30 to Penzance, follow signs for seafront pass harbour and into promenade, hotel 0.5m on right*
With views across Mounts Bay towards Newlyn, this impressive

continued on p448

PENZANCE, continued

Victorian hotel has a long and distinguished history. Comfortable public areas are filled with interesting pictures and artefacts, and in the dining room guests can choose from the daily-changing menu. Bedrooms, many with sea views, are of varying style and size.
ROOMS: 70 en suite (10 fmly) **FACILITIES:** STV Yoga weekends Xmas **CONF:** Thtr 200 Class 100 Board 80 **SERVICES:** Lift **PARKING:** 50 **NOTES:** ⊗ in restaurant Civ Wed 250

See advert on opposite page

PETERBOROUGH, Cambridgeshire Map 12 TL19

★★★★65% Peterborough Marriott
Peterborough Business Park, Lynchwood PE2 6GB
☎ 01733 371111 🖷 01733 236725
e-mail: reservations.peterborough@marriotthotels.co.uk
web: www.marriott.co.uk
Dir: *opp East of England Showground. From A1 off at Alwalton Showground, Chesterton. Left at T-junct. Hotel on left at next rdbt*
Just a few minutes' drive from the heart of the city, this modern hotel is located in the village of Alwalton, birthplace of Sir Frederick Henry Royce and the Rolls Royce motorcar. Air-conditioned bedrooms are spacious and well designed for business use. Public rooms include the Garden Lounge, Cocktail Bar, Laurels Restaurant and leisure club.
ROOMS: 163 en suite (7 fmly) (74 GF) ⊗ in 125 bedrooms s £105; d £105 (incl. bkfst) **LB** **FACILITIES: Spa** STV Sauna Solarium Gym Putt green Jacuzzi Beauty therapist Hairdressing Xmas **CONF:** Thtr 300 Class 160 Board 45 **SERVICES:** air con **PARKING:** 175 **NOTES:** ⊗ in restaurant Civ Wed 80

★★★73% ⊛ Bell Inn
Great North Rd PE7 3RA
☎ 01733 241066 & 242626 🖷 01733 245173
e-mail: reception@thebellstilton.co.uk
web: www.thebellstilton.co.uk
(For full entry see Stilton)

★★★71% Bull
Westgate PE1 1RB
☎ 01733 561364 🖷 01733 557304
e-mail: info@bull-hotel-peterborough.com
web: www.peelhotel.com
Dir: *off A1, follow city centre signs. Hotel opp Queensgate shopping centre. Car park on Broadway next to Library*

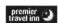

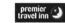

This pleasant city-centre hotel offers well-equipped, modern accommodation, which includes several wings of deluxe bedrooms. Public rooms include a popular bar and a brasserie-style restaurant serving a flexible range of dishes, with further

continued

informal dining available in the lounge. There is a good range of meeting rooms and conference facilities.
ROOMS: 118 en suite (3 fmly) ⊗ in 40 bedrooms s £95-£115; d £115-£125 (incl. bkfst) **LB** **FACILITIES:** STV Xmas **CONF:** Thtr 200 Class 80 Board 60 Del from £140 **PARKING:** 100 **NOTES:** ⊗ in restaurant Civ Wed 200

★★★68% ⊛ Best Western Orton Hall
Orton Longueville PE2 7DN
☎ 01733 391111 🖷 01733 231912
e-mail: reception@ortonhall.co.uk
Dir: *off A605 E opposite Orton Mere*
Set in 20 acres of woodland, this impressive country house has spacious and relaxing public areas. The many original features create a unique atmosphere, evident in The Great Room and in the Huntly Restaurant with its 17th-century oak panelling. The Ramblewood Inn, across the courtyard from the main hotel, offers an alternative, informal dining and bar option.
ROOMS: 65 en suite (2 fmly) (15 GF) ⊗ in 42 bedrooms s £65-£110; d £85-£150 **LB** **FACILITIES:** STV Three quarter size snooker table Xmas **CONF:** Thtr 120 Class 48 Board 42 Del from £140 **PARKING:** 200 **NOTES:** ⊗ in restaurant Civ Wed 90

⌂ Premier Travel Inn Peterborough(Ferry Meadow)
Ham Ln, Orton Meadows, Nene Park PE2 5UU
☎ 08701 977205 🖷 01733 391055
web: www.premiertravelinn.com
Dir: *From south, A1(M) junct 16, A15 through Yaxley. Left at rdbt. From north, A1 junct 17, A1139 junct 3 right to Yaxley. Right at 2nd rdbt*
High quality, modern budget accommodation ideal for both families and business travellers. Spacious, en suite bedrooms feature bath and shower, satellite TV and many have telephones and modem points. The adjacent family restaurant features a wide and varied menu. For further details consult the Hotel Groups page.
ROOMS: 40 en suite s £46.95-£48.95; d £46.95-£48.95 **CONF:** Thtr 24 Board 24

⌂ Premier Travel Inn Peterborough (Hampton)
4 Ashbourne Rd, Off London Rd, Hampton PE7 8BT
☎ 08701 977206 🖷 01733 391055
web: www.premiertravelinn.com
Dir: *South: A1(M) junct 16, follow A15 through Yaxley. Inn on left at 1st rdbt. North: A1(M) junct 17 follow A1139, 2nd exit junct 3 follow signs for Yaxley. Inn on right at 2nd rdbt.*
High quality, modern budget accommodation ideal for both families and business travellers. Spacious, en suite bedrooms feature bath and shower, satellite TV and many have telephones and modem points. The adjacent family restaurant features a wide and varied menu. For further details consult the Hotel Groups page.
ROOMS: 80 en suite s £46.95-£48.95; d £46.95-£48.95

⌂ *Sleep Inn Peterborough*
Peterborough Services, Great North Rd, Haddon PE7 3UQ
☎ 01733 396850 🖷 01733 396869
e-mail: enquiries@hotels-peterborough.co.uk
web: www.hotels-peterborough.com
Dir: *A1(M) junct 17 take A605 towards Northampton. Hotel 100mtrs on left*
This modern, purpose built accommodation offers smartly appointed, well-equipped bedrooms, with good power showers. There is a choice of adjacent food outlets where guests may enjoy breakfast, snacks and meals.
ROOMS: 82 en suite

⌂ Travelodge Alwalton
Great North Rd, Alwalton PE7 3UR
☎ 08700 850 950 📠 01733 231109
web: www.travelodge.co.uk
Dir: *on A1, southbound*
Travelodge offers good quality, good value, modern accommodation. Ideal for families, the spacious, en suite bedrooms include remote-control TV, tea and coffee-making facilities and comfortable beds. Meals can be taken at the nearby family restaurant. For further details consult the Hotel Groups page.
ROOMS: 32 en suite s fr £26; d fr £26

⌂ Travelodge Peterborough
Crowlands Rd PE6 7SZ
☎ 08700 850 950 📠 01733 223199
web: www.travelodge.co.uk
Dir: *junct of A47/A1073*
Travelodge offers good quality, good value, modern accommodation. Ideal for families, the spacious, en suite bedrooms include remote-control TV, tea and coffee-making facilities and comfortable beds. Meals can be taken at the nearby family restaurant. For further details consult the Hotel Groups page.
ROOMS: 42 en suite s fr £26; d fr £26

PETERLEE, Co Durham — Map 19 NZ44

★★69% Hardwicke Hall Manor
Hesleden TS27 4PA
☎ 01429 836326 📠 01429 837676
Dir: *NE on B1281, off A19 at sign for Durham and Blackhall*
This country mansion house nestles in pleasant gardens and is full of character, providing an ideal venue for secluded weddings or meetings. All bedrooms are individual in design and each is spacious, comfortable and very well equipped. Good value meals are presented in a variety of public areas, and real fires are a very welcoming in cooler months.
ROOMS: 15 en suite (2 fmly) s £58-£68; d £68-£78 (incl. bkfst) **LB** **CONF:** Thtr 60 Board 20 **PARKING:** 100 **NOTES:** ⊗ in restaurant Civ Wed 100

PETERSFIELD, Hampshire — Map 05 SU72

★★71% ⊛ Langrish House
Langrish GU32 1RN
☎ 01730 266941 📠 01730 260543
e-mail: frontdesk@langrishhouse.co.uk
web: www.langrishhouse.co.uk
Dir: *off A3 onto A272 towards Winchester. Hotel signed, 3m on left*
Located in an idyllic country location just outside Petersfield, this family home dates back to the 17th century. Rooms offer good levels of comfort with beautiful views over the countryside. The public areas consist of a small cosy restaurant, a bar in the vaults, and conference and banqueting rooms that are popular for weddings. Staff throughout are friendly and nothing is too much trouble.
ROOMS: 13 en suite (1 fmly) (3 GF) ⊗ in all bedrooms s £72-£90; d £104.40-£140 (incl. bkfst) **LB** **FACILITIES:** Fishing Xmas **CONF:** Thtr 60 Class 18 Board 25 Del from £85 **PARKING:** 80 **NOTES:** ⊗ in restaurant Civ Wed 60

> Popped the question? Hotels with Civ wed in their entry are licensed for civil wedding ceremonies. Maximum numbers for the ceremony only are shown e.g. Civ wed 120

PICKERING, North Yorkshire Map 19 SE78

★★★72% **Forest & Vale**
Malton Rd YO18 7DL
☎ 01751 472722 🖷 01751 472972
e-mail: forestvale@bestwestern.co.uk
web: www.bw-forestandvalehotel.co.uk
Dir: *on A169 between York and Pickering at rdbt on outskirts of Pickering*

This lovely 18th-century hotel is an excellent base from which to explore the North Yorkshire Moors, one of England's most beautiful retreats. A robust maintenance programme means that the hotel is particularly well kept, inside and out. Bedrooms vary in size and include some spacious 'superior' rooms, including one with a four-poster bed.
ROOMS: 18 en suite 5 annexe en suite (7 fmly) (5 GF) ⊗ in 10 bedrooms s £74-£94; d £99-£160 (incl. bkfst) **LB** **CONF:** Thtr 120 Class 50 Board 30 Del from £123 **PARKING:** 70 **NOTES:** 🐕 ⊗ in restaurant Civ Wed 90

★★76% ◎ **White Swan Inn**
Market Place YO18 7AA
☎ 01751 472288 🖷 01751 475554
e-mail: welcome@white-swan.co.uk
web: www.white-swan.co.uk
Dir: *between church and steam railway station*
This 16th-century coaching inn offers well-equipped, very comfortable bedrooms, including a suite. Service is friendly and attentive and the standard of cuisine high, in both the attractive restaurant and the cosy bar and lounge where log fires burn in the cooler months. A comprehensive wine list specialises in many fine vintages. A private dining room is also available.
ROOMS: 21 en suite (3 fmly) ⊗ in 12 bedrooms s £80-£120; d £139-£219 (incl. bkfst) **LB** **FACILITIES:** STV Xmas **CONF:** Thtr 20 Class 14 Board 24 Del from £80 **PARKING:** 35 **NOTES:** ⊗ in restaurant

★★73% ◎ ***Fox & Hounds Country Inn***
Main St, Sinnington YO62 6SQ
☎ 01751 431577 🖷 01751 432791
e-mail: foxhoundsinn@easynet.co.uk
web: www.thefoxandhoundsinn.co.uk
Dir: *3m W of Pickering, off A170*
This attractive inn lies in the quiet village of Sinnington just off the main road. It offers attractive, well-equipped bedrooms together with a cosy residents' lounge. The restaurant provides a good selection of modern British dishes; there is also a good range of bar meals. Service throughout is very friendly and attentive.

ROOMS: 10 en suite (4 GF) ⊗ in all bedrooms **PARKING:** 40
NOTES: ⊗ in restaurant

★★66% **Old Manse**
19 Middleton Rd YO18 8AL
☎ 01751 476484 🖷 01751 477124
e-mail: the_old_manse@btopenworld.com
Dir: *A169, left at rdbt. through lights, 1st right into Potter Hill. Follow road to left. From A170 left at 'local traffic only' sign*

A peacefully located house standing in mature grounds close to the town centre. It offers a combined dining room and lounge area and comfortable bedrooms that are also well equipped. Expect good hospitality from the resident owners.
ROOMS: 10 en suite (2 fmly) (2 GF) ⊗ in all bedrooms
FACILITIES: Xmas **CONF:** Thtr 20 Class 12 Board 10 **PARKING:** 12
NOTES: ⊗ in restaurant

PICKHILL, North Yorkshire Map 19 SE38

★★70% **Nags Head Country Inn**
YO7 4JG
☎ 01845 567391 & 567570 🖷 01845 567212
e-mail: reservations@nagsheadpickhill.freeserve.co.uk
web: www.nagsheadpickhill.co.uk
Dir: *4m SE of Leeming Bar, 1.25m E of A1*
Convenient for the A1, this 200-year-old country inn offers superb hospitality, and an extensive range of food either in the bar or the attractive Library Restaurant. The bars offer an extensive range of

continued

handpicked wines and are full of character featuring country sport memorabilia in particular. Bedrooms are well equipped.

ROOMS: 8 en suite 7 annexe en suite (1 fmly) s £45-£65; d £70-£90 (incl. bkfst) **LB** **FACILITIES:** Putt green Quoits pitch, Petanque **CONF:** BC Thtr 36 Class 18 Board 24 Del from £75 **PARKING:** 50 **NOTES:** ⊗ in restaurant

PINNER, Greater London
See LONDON SECTION plan 1 A5

★★70% Tudor Lodge

50 Field End Rd, Eastcote HA5 2QN
☎ 020 8429 0585 🖷 020 8429 0117
e-mail: tudorlodge@meridianleisure.com
web: www.meridianleisure.com
Dir: *off A40 at Swakeleys rdbt to Ickenham, onto A312 to Harrow. Left at Northholt Station to Eastcote*

This friendly hotel, set in its own grounds, is convenient for Heathrow Airport and many local golf courses. Bedrooms vary in style and size but all are well equipped, with some suitable for families. A good range of bar snacks is offered as an alternative to the main restaurant.
ROOMS: 24 en suite 22 annexe en suite (9 fmly) (17 GF) ⊗ in 6 bedrooms s £59-£89; d £69-£94 (incl. bkfst) **LB** **FACILITIES:** STV Xmas **CONF:** Thtr 60 Class 20 Board 26 Del from £80 **PARKING:** 30 **NOTES:** ⊗ in restaurant

See advert on this page

PLYMOUTH, Devon Map 03 SX45
See also St Mellion

★★★★62% Copthorne Hotel Plymouth

COPTHORNE

Armada Way PL1 1AR
☎ 01752 224161 🖷 01752 670688
e-mail: sales.plymouth@mill-cop.com
web: www.copthorne.com/plymouth
Dir: *from M5 follow A38 to Plymouth city centre. Follow ferryport signs over 2 rdbts. Hotel on 1st exit left before 4th rdbt*
Located right in the city centre, this hotel possesses extensive

continued

conference facilities and parking. Suites, Connoisseur and Classic rooms are available; all are spacious and well equipped. Public areas are spread over two floors and include Bentley's brasserie and bar and a small leisure centre with a pool and gym.
ROOMS: 135 en suite (29 fmly) ⊗ in 93 bedrooms s £140-£160; d £150-£170 **LB** **FACILITIES:** STV supervised Gym Steam room **CONF:** Thtr 140 Class 60 Board 60 Del from £135 **SERVICES:** Lift **PARKING:** 50 **NOTES:** ⊗ in restaurant Civ Wed 65

A ★★★★ Kitley House Hotel

Kitley Estate, Yealmpton PL8 2NW
☎ 01752 881555 🖷 01752 881667
e-mail: sales@kitleyhousehotel.com
web: www.kitleyhousehotel.com
Dir: *from Plymouth take A379 to Kingsbridge. Hotel on right after Brixton and before Yealmpton*
ROOMS: 19 en suite (9 fmly) (1 GF) ⊗ in 12 bedrooms s £79-£99; d £89-£119 (incl. bkfst) **LB** **FACILITIES:** STV Fishing Beauty salon Xmas **CONF:** BC Thtr 70 Class 40 Board 35 Del from £125 **PARKING:** 100 **NOTES:** ⊗ in restaurant

★★★71% Elfordleigh Hotel Golf Leisure

Colebrook, Plympton PL7 5EB
☎ 01752 336428 🖷 01752 344581
e-mail: reception@elfordleigh.co.uk
Dir: *Leave A38 at city centre exit, at Marsh Mills/Sainsbury's rdbt take Plympton road. At 4th lights left into Larkham Ln, at end right then left into Crossway. At end left into The Moors, hotel 1m*
Located in the beautiful Plym Valley, this well-established hotel is set in attractive wooded countryside. Bedrooms, many with lovely views, are spacious and comfortable. There is an excellent range of leisure facilities including an 18-hole golf course. A choice of

continued on p452

PLYMOUTH, continued

dining options is available, a friendly brasserie or the more formal restaurant.
ROOMS: 34 en suite (2 fmly) (7 GF) ⊗ in 9 bedrooms s £65-£95; d £75-£145 (incl. bkfst) **LB** **FACILITIES: Spa** supervised 18 Fishing Squash Sauna Solarium Gym Putt green Jacuzzi Hairdresser, Beautician, Dance/Aerobics studio, 5 aside football pitch (hard) ch fac Xmas **CONF:** Thtr 200 Class 120 Board 50 Del from £115 **SERVICES:** Lift **PARKING:** 200 **NOTES:** ⊗ in restaurant Civ Wed 200

★★★69% Duke of Cornwall

Millbay Rd PL1 3LG
☎ 01752 275850 01752 275854
e-mail: info@thedukeofcornwallhotel.com
web: www.thedukeofcornwallhotel.com
Dir: *follow city centre, then Plymouth Pavilions Conference & Leisure Centre signs past hotel*

An historic landmark, this city centre hotel is conveniently located. The spacious public areas include a popular bar, comfortable lounge and multi functional ballroom. Bedrooms, many with far reaching views, are individually styled and comfortably appointed. A range of dining options include bar meals, or the more formal atmosphere in the elegant dining room.
ROOMS: 71 en suite (6 fmly) ⊗ in 20 bedrooms s £90-£150; d £110-£175 (incl. bkfst) **LB** **FACILITIES:** STV ch fac Xmas **CONF:** Thtr 300 Class 125 Board 84 Del from £140 **SERVICES:** Lift **PARKING:** 50 **NOTES:** ⊗ in restaurant Closed 24 Dec-1st Mon in Jan Civ Wed 300

★★★68% Invicta

11-12 Osborne Place, Lockyer St, The Hoe PL1 2PU
☎ 01752 664997 01752 664994
e-mail: info@invictahotel.co.uk
web: www.invictahotel.co.uk
Dir: *A38 to Plymouth, follow city centre signs, then Hoe Park signs. Hotel opposite park entrance*
Just a short stroll from the city centre, this elegant Victorian establishment stands opposite the famous bowling green. The atmosphere is relaxed and friendly and bedrooms are neatly presented, well-equipped and attractively decorated. Dining options include bar meals or the more formal setting of the dining room.
ROOMS: 23 en suite (6 fmly) (1 GF) s £55-£70; d £65-£100 (incl. bkfst) **LB** **FACILITIES:** Xmas **CONF:** BC Board 45 Del from £80 **PARKING:** 14 **NOTES:** ⊗ in restaurant

★★★68% New Continental

Millbay Rd PL1 3LD
☎ 01752 220782 01752 227013
e-mail: newconti@aol.com
web: www.newcontinental.co.uk
Dir: *A38, follow city centre signs for Continental Ferryport. Hotel before ferryport & next to Plymouth Pavilions Conference Centre*
Within easy reach of the city centre and The Hoe, this privately owned hotel continues to offer high standards of service and hospitality. A variety of bedroom sizes and styles are available, all with the same levels of equipment and comfort. The hotel is a popular choice for conferences and functions.
ROOMS: 99 en suite (20 fmly) ⊗ in 28 bedrooms s fr £46; d fr £92 (incl. bkfst) **LB** **FACILITIES:** STV supervised Sauna Solarium Gym Steam Room Beautician **CONF:** Thtr 350 Class 100 Board 70 Del £120 **SERVICES:** Lift **PARKING:** 100 **NOTES:** Closed 24 Dec-2 Jan Civ Wed 110

★★★66% Novotel Plymouth

Marsh Mills PL6 8NH
☎ 01752 221422 01752 223922
e-mail: h0508@accor.com
web: www.novotel.com
Dir: *Exit A38 at Marsh Mills, follow Plympton signs, hotel on left*
Conveniently located on the outskirts of the city, close to Marsh Mills roundabout, this modern hotel offers good value accommodation. All rooms are spacious and designed with flexibility for family use. Public areas are open-plan with meals available throughout the day in either the Garden Brasserie, the bar, or from room service. Novotel - AA Hotel Group of the Year 2005-6.
ROOMS: 100 en suite (17 fmly) (18 GF) ⊗ in 80 bedrooms s £49-£65; d £49-£65 **LB** **FACILITIES:** STV Xmas **CONF:** Thtr 300 Class 120 Board 100 Del £90 **SERVICES:** Lift **PARKING:** 140

★★73% Langdon Court

Down Thomas PL9 0DY
☎ 01752 862358 01752 863428
e-mail: enquiries@langdoncourt.co.uk
Dir: *follow HMS Cambridge signs from Elburton and tourist signs on A379*

This magnificent Grade II listed Tudor manor, set in seven acres of lush countryside, has a direct path leading to the beach at Wembury and coastal footpaths. Bedrooms all enjoy countryside views while public areas include a stylishly updated bar and brasserie restaurant, where the contemporary menu incorporates local produce with excellent seafood.
ROOMS: 18 en suite (4 fmly) ⊗ in all bedrooms s £75-£90; d £120-£150 (incl. bkfst) **LB** **CONF:** Thtr 60 Board 20 Del from £125 **PARKING:** 100 **NOTES:** ⊗ in restaurant Civ Wed 75

★★71% Victoria Court

62/64 North Rd East PL4 6AL
☎ 01752 668133 01752 668133
e-mail: victoria.court@btinternet.com
web: www.victoriacourthotel.co.uk
Dir: *from A38 follow city centre signs, past railway station. Follow North Road E for 200yds and hotel on left*
Situated within walking distance of the city centre and railway station, this long-established, family-run hotel offers impeccably presented accommodation. The public areas retain the Victorian character of the building and include a comfortable lounge, bar

continued

and dining area. The attractively decorated bedrooms are well maintained with modern facilities.
ROOMS: 13 en suite (4 fmly) **PARKING:** 6 **NOTES:** ⊗ in restaurant Closed 22 Dec-1 Jan

★★70% Drake

1 & 2 Windsor Villas, Lockyer St, The Hoe PL1 2QD
☎ 01752 229730 📠 01752 255092
e-mail: reception@drakehotel.net
Dir: *follow city centre signs, left at Theatre Royal, last left and 1st right*

THE CIRCLE Selected Individual Hotels GREAT BRITAIN

Handily placed for access to the city centre and the historic Hoe, this popular hotel was originally two adjoining Victorian houses. Bedrooms are neatly presented, and public areas include a lounge, bar and elegant dining room. The convenient location, with its own parking, make this an ideal choice for business and leisure guests alike.
ROOMS: 35 rms (3 fmly) **PARKING:** 26 **NOTES:** ⊗ in restaurant Closed 24 Dec-3 Jan

★★65% *Camelot*

5 Elliot St, The Hoe PL1 2PP
☎ 01752 221255 & 669667 📠 01752 603660
e-mail: camelot@hotelplymouth.fsnet.co.uk
Dir: *from A38 follow city centre signs, then signs to The Hoe. Into Citadel Road, then onto Elliot Street*
Just a short walk from The Hoe, the Barbican and the city centre, this is a convenient choice for visitors to this historic naval city. The friendly, small hotel provides comfortable accommodation, with bedrooms varying in size and style. The convivial bar is a popular meeting point and additional facilities include a TV lounge and function room.
ROOMS: 18 en suite (5 fmly) ⊗ in 3 bedrooms **NOTES:** ⊗ in restaurant

> The vast majority of establishments in this guide accept credit and debit cards. We indicate those that don't take any

★★63% The Moorland

Wotter, Shaugh Prior PL7 5HP
☎ 01752 839228 📠 01752 839153
e-mail: enquiries@moorlandhotel.com
Dir: *From A38 take Lee Mill exit. Through underpass turn right then left, 6m through Cornwood to Wotter*
Situated on the southern slopes of the Dartmoor National Park, this family-run hotel offers a warm welcome to visitors. Bedrooms are soundly appointed and all have pleasant views. The convivial bar is popular with both visitors and locals. A range of menus is available in either the bar or attractive restaurant.

ROOMS: 18 en suite (2 fmly) ⊗ in 4 bedrooms s £35-£49; d £54-£60 (incl. bkfst) **LB FACILITIES:** Games room, secure field available for guests' horses. **CONF:** BC Thtr 65 Class 22 Board 20 Del from £68.50 **PARKING:** 40 **NOTES:** ⊗ in restaurant

★62% Grosvenor Park

114-116 North Rd East PL4 6AH
☎ 01752 229312 📠 01752 252777
e-mail: gphotel@grosvenorparkhotel.co.uk
Dir: *turn off A38 onto A374, follow signs to railway station. At rdbt after Drake Circus turn right in North Road East*
Conveniently located for the railway station and the city centre, this small hotel provides friendly and attentive service. Facilities include a small bar and a comfortable lounge. Dinner is availabe for groups only, however a range of snacks is served in the lounge or bar. Traditional breakfasts provide a satisfying start to the day.
ROOMS: 16 rms (11 en suite) (1 GF) ⊗ in all bedrooms **PARKING:** 6 **NOTES:** No children 12yrs ⊗ in restaurant Closed 19 Dec-5 Jan

⌂ *Hotel Ibis*

Marsh Mills, Longbridge Rd, Forder Valley PL6 8LD
☎ 01752 601087 📠 01752 223213
e-mail: H2093@accor-hotels.com
Dir: *A38 to Plymouth, 1st exit after flyover towards Estover, Leigham and Parkway Industrial Est. At rdbt, hotel on 4th exit*
Modern, budget hotel offering comfortable accommodation in bright and practical bedrooms. Breakfast is self-service and dinner is available in the restaurant. For further details, consult the Hotel Groups page.
ROOMS: 52 en suite

⌂ Innkeeper's Lodge Plymouth

8-9 Howeson Ln PL6 1ZZ
☎ 01752 783585
web: www.innkeeperslodge.com
A growing concept in the travel accommodation market. Smart rooms meet essential business requirements but also have home comforts. Dining options include all-day menus plus the added advantage of breakfast, which is included in the room price. For further details consult the Hotel Groups page.
ROOMS: 75 rms s £55; d £55

⌂ Premier Travel Inn Plymouth City Centre (Lockyers Quay)

Lockyers Quay, Coxside PL4 0DX
☎ 08701 977207 📠 01752 663872
web: www.premiertravelinn.com
Dir: *A38 Marsh Mills rdbt then A374 into Plymouth. Follow signs for Coxside & National Marine Aquarium*
High quality, modern budget accommodation ideal for both

continued on p454

P

PLYMOUTH, continued

families and business travellers. Spacious, en suite bedrooms feature bath and shower, satellite TV and many have telephones and modem points. The adjacent family restaurant features a wide and varied menu. For further details consult the Hotel Groups page.
ROOMS: 60 en suite s £55.95-£59.95; d £55.95-£59.95 **CONF:** Thtr 25 Board 20

Premier Travel Inn Plymouth City Centre

Sutton Rd, Shepherds Wharf PL4 0HX
☎ 0870 9906458 🖷 0870 9906459
web: www.premiertravelinn.com
Dir: *Follow signs for Plymouth city centre (A374) from Marsh Mills rdbt. After road splits, follow Barbican & Coxside signs. Pass Leisure Park, turn right at lights. Hotel 50yds along Sutton Rd*
High quality, modern budget accommodation ideal for both families and business travellers. Spacious, en suite bedrooms feature bath and shower, satellite TV and many have telephones and modem points. The adjacent family restaurant features a wide and varied menu. For further details consult the Hotel Groups page.
ROOMS: 107 en suite s £55.95-£59.95; d £55.95-£59.95 **CONF:** Thtr 20

Premier Travel Inn Plymouth East

300 Plymouth Rd, Crabtree, Marsh Mills PL3 6RW
☎ 08701 977208 🖷 01752 600112
web: www.premiertravelinn.com
Dir: *From E: Exit A38 Marsh Mill junction. Straight across rdbt, exit slip road 100mtrs on left. From W: Plympton junction A38, at rdbt exit slip road next to A38 Liskeard*
High quality, modern budget accommodation ideal for both families and business travellers. Spacious, en suite bedrooms feature bath and shower, satellite TV and many have telephones and modem points. The adjacent family restaurant features a wide and varied menu. For further details consult the Hotel Groups page.
ROOMS: 40 en suite s £51.95; d £51.95 **CONF:** Thtr 50 Board 30

Travelodge

Derry's Cross PL1 2SW
☎ 08700 850 950
web: www.travelodge.co.uk
Travelodge offers good quality, good value, modern accommodation. Ideal for families, the spacious, en suite bedrooms include remote-control TV, tea and coffee-making facilities and comfortable beds. Meals can be taken at the nearby family restaurant. For further details consult the Hotel Groups page.
ROOMS: 96 en suite s fr £26; d fr £26

POCKLINGTON, East Riding of Yorkshire — Map 17 SE84

★★ 63% Feathers

56 Market Place YO42 2AH
☎ 01759 303155 🖷 01759 304382
e-mail: info@thefeathers-hotel.co.uk
Dir: *from York, B1246 signed Pocklington. Hotel just off A1079*
This is busy, traditional inn has been sympathetically modernised to provide comfortable, well-equipped and spacious accommodation. Public areas are smartly presented and enjoyable meals are served in the bar and the conservatory restaurant. A wide choice of dishes makes excellent use of local and seasonal produce.
ROOMS: 10 en suite 6 annexe en suite (1 fmly) (10 GF) ⊗ in 4 bedrooms s fr £47; d fr £52 (incl. bkfst) **LB** **FACILITIES:** ♫ **CONF:** Thtr 20 Class 8 Board 12 **PARKING:** 46 **NOTES:** ✗

PODIMORE, Somerset — Map 04 ST52

Travelodge Yeovil

BA22 8JG
☎ 08700 850 950 🖷 01935 840074
web: www.travelodge.co.uk
Dir: *on A303, near junct with A37*
Travelodge offers good quality, good value, modern accommodation. Ideal for families, the spacious, en suite bedrooms include remote-control TV, tea and coffee-making facilities and comfortable beds. Meals can be taken at the nearby family restaurant. For further details consult the Hotel Groups page.
ROOMS: 41 en suite s fr £26; d fr £26

POLPERRO, Cornwall & Isles of Scilly — Map 02 SX25

★★★ 76% ®®® Talland Bay

PL13 2JB
☎ 01503 272667 🖷 01503 272940
e-mail: reception@tallandbayhotel.co.uk
web: www.tallandbayhotel.co.uk
Dir: *signed from x-rds on A387 Looe to Polperro road*
The hotel has the benefit of being sited in its own extensive gardens which run down almost to the cliff's edge. The atmosphere is warm and friendly throughout and the bedrooms have a number of styles, some are with sea views and balconies. The team in the kitchen are certainly putting Talland Bay on the map in terms of innovative and accomplished cooking.
ROOMS: 20 en suite 3 annexe en suite (4 fmly) (6 GF) ⊗ in 3 bedrooms **FACILITIES:** STV Putt green **PARKING:** 23 **NOTES:** ⊗ in restaurant

POLZEATH, Cornwall & Isles of Scilly — Map 02 SW97

A ★★ Seascape

Dunder Hill PL27 6SX
☎ 01208 863638 & 07968 010644 🖷 01208 862940
e-mail: information@seascapehotel.co.uk
web: www.seascapehotel.co.uk
Dir: *M5 from Exeter/A30 towards Launceston. Onto A395 & A39. From A39 take B3314 to Polzeath & follow signs to hotel*
ROOMS: 12 en suite 3 annexe en suite (9 GF) ⊗ in 2 bedrooms s £48-£132; d £76-£132 (incl. bkfst) **CONF:** BC **PARKING:** 20 **NOTES:** No children 12yrs ⊗ in restaurant Closed Nov-Feb

> Packed in a hurry? Ironing facilities should be available at all star levels, either in the rooms or on request

PONTEFRACT, West Yorkshire — Map 16 SE42

★★★ 74% ® Wentbridge House

Wentbridge WF8 3JJ
☎ 01977 620444 🖷 01977 620148
e-mail: info@wentbridgehouse.co.uk
web: www.wentbridgehouse.co.uk
Dir: *0.5m off A1 & 4m S of M62 junct 33 onto A1 south*
This well-established hotel sits in 20 acres of landscaped gardens, offering spacious, well-equipped bedrooms and a choice of dining styles. Service in the Fleur de Lys restaurant is polished and

continued

friendly, and a varied menu offers a good choice of interesting dishes. The Brasserie offers a more relaxed style of dining.

ROOMS: 14 en suite 4 annexe en suite (4 GF) s £75-£110; d £95-£140 (incl. bkfst) **LB** **CONF:** Thtr 130 Class 100 Board 60 Del from £100 **PARKING:** 100 **NOTES:** ✖ Closed 25 Dec-evening only Civ Wed 130

★★★65% Rogerthorpe Manor

Thorpe Ln, Badsworth WF9 1AB
☎ 01977 643839 📄 01977 641571
e-mail: ops@rogerthorpemanor.co.uk

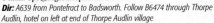

Dir: *A639 from Pontefract to Badsworth. Follow B6474 through Thorpe Audlin, hotel on left at end of Thorpe Audlin village*
This Jacobean manor house is situated in extensive grounds and lovely gardens, within easy access of road networks. Bedrooms vary between the old house with their inherent charm, and the more modern rooms in the extensions. A choice of dining styles, real ales, civil weddings, modern conference facilities and ample parking are all offered.
ROOMS: 23 en suite (4 fmly) ⊗ in 6 bedrooms s £50-£100; d £75-£140 (incl. bkfst) **FACILITIES:** STV Xmas **CONF:** Thtr 250 Class 80 Board 50 Del from £110 **PARKING:** 150 **NOTES:** ✖ ⊗ in restaurant Civ Wed 200

⇧ Premier Travel Inn Pontefract North

Pontefract Rd, Knottingley WF11 0BU
☎ 08701 977209 📄 01977 607954
web: www.premiertravelinn.com
Dir: *From M62 junct 33 onto A1 North. Take A645 Pontefract. Follow road to T-junct, right towards Pontefract. Inn on right*
High quality, modern budget accommodation ideal for both families and business travellers. Spacious, en suite bedrooms feature bath and shower, satellite TV and many have telephones and modem points. The adjacent family restaurant features a wide and varied menu. For further details consult the Hotel Groups page.
ROOMS: 40 en suite s £46.95-£48.95; d £46.95-£48.95

POOLE, Dorset Map 04 SZ09

★★★★76% ◉◉ Haven

Banks Rd, Sandbanks BH13 7QL
☎ 01202 707333 📄 01202 708796
e-mail: reservations@havenhotel.co.uk
web: www.havenhotel.co.uk
Dir: *B3965 towards Poole Bay, left onto the Peninsula. Hotel 1.5m on left next to Swanage Toll Ferry point*
Enjoying an enviable location at the water's edge with views of Poole Bay, this well established hotel was also the site for the world's first wireless transmission. A friendly team of staff provide good levels of customer care through the range of stylish and comfortable lounge and bar areas. Bedrooms vary in size and

continued

style; many have balconies and wonderful sea views. Leisure facilities are noteworthy.

ROOMS: 78 en suite (4 fmly) **FACILITIES: Spa** STV ▣ ⚘ ☞ Sauna Solarium Gym Jacuzzi Steam room, Hair salon, Health & Beauty suite ♫ ch fac **CONF:** BC Thtr 160 Class 70 Board 50 **SERVICES:** Lift **PARKING:** 160 **NOTES:** ✖ ⊗ in restaurant Civ Wed 100

★★★★73% ◉◉ Harbour Heights

73 Haven Rd, Sandbanks BH13 7PS
☎ 01202 707272 📄 01202 708594
e-mail: enquiries@harbourheights.net
web: www.fjbhotels.co.uk
Dir: *Follow signs for Sandbanks, hotel on left after Canford Cliffs*

The unassuming appearance of this hotel belies a wealth of innovation, quality and style. The contemporary bedrooms combine state-of-the-art facilities with traditional comforts. The smart public areas include the Harbar brasserie, popular bars and sitting areas where picture windows accentuate panoramic views of Poole Harbour. The sun deck is the perfect setting for watching the cross-channel ferries come and go.
ROOMS: 38 en suite (2 fmly) ⊗ in all bedrooms **FACILITIES:** STV Spa bath in all rooms **CONF:** BC Thtr 70 Class 36 Board 22 **SERVICES:** Lift air con **PARKING:** 50 **NOTES:** ✖ ⊗ in restaurant Civ Wed 120

POOLE, continued

Top Hotel

★★★ ◎◎ **Mansion House**
Thames St BH15 1JN
☎ 01202 685666 📠 01202 665709
e-mail: enquiries@themansionhouse.co.uk
web: www.themansionhouse.co.uk
Dir: *A31 to Poole, follow channel ferry signs. Left at Poole bridge onto Poole Quay, 1st left into Thames St. Hotel opposite St James Church*
This sophisticated hotel offers friendly hospitality and award-winning cuisine, equalled only by its relaxing charm and elegance. The comfortably furnished bedrooms are very well equipped with many thoughtful touches. Ideal for business or pleasure, the Mansion House is tucked away off the Old Quay, with the added bonus of parking.
ROOMS: 32 en suite (2 fmly) (2 GF) ⊗ in 12 bedrooms s £75-£95; d £130-£145 (incl. bkfst) **LB** **FACILITIES:** STV Facilities available locally Watersports, Use of local fitness club Xmas **CONF:** Thtr 40 Class 18 Board 20 Del from £140 **PARKING:** 46 **NOTES:** ✈ ⊗ in restaurant Civ Wed 35

P

★★★75% ◎ **Sandbanks**
15 Banks Rd, Sandbanks BH13 7PS
☎ 01202 707377 📠 01202 708885
e-mail: reservations@sandbankshotel.co.uk
web: www.sandbankshotel.co.uk
Dir: *A338 from Bournemouth onto Wessex Way, to Liverpool Victoria rdbt. Left and take 2nd exit onto B3965. Hotel on left*

Set on the delightful Sandbanks Peninsula, this large and popular hotel has direct access to a blue flag beach and stunning views across Poole Harbour. Most of the spacious bedrooms have sea views, and there is an extensive range of leisure facilities, which now include a state-of-the-art crèche.
ROOMS: 110 en suite (31 fmly) (4 GF) ⊗ in 40 bedrooms s £60-£110; d £120-£220 (incl. bkfst) **LB** **FACILITIES:** STV supervised Sauna Solarium Gym Jacuzzi Sailing, Mntn bikes, kids play area, massage room ♫ ch fac Xmas **CONF:** BC Thtr 150 Class 40 Board 25 Del from £100 **SERVICES:** Lift **PARKING:** 120 **NOTES:** ✈ ⊗ in restaurant Civ Wed 70

★★★66% **Arndale Court**
62/66 Wimborne Rd BH15 2BY
☎ 01202 683746 📠 01202 668838
e-mail: info@arndalecourthotel.com
web: www.arndalecourthotel.com
Dir: *on A349 close to town centre, opp Poole Stadium*

Ideally situated for the town centre and ferry terminal, this is a small, privately owned hotel. Bedrooms are well equipped, pleasantly spacious and comfortable. Particularly well suited to business guests, this hotel has a pleasant range of stylish public areas and good parking.
ROOMS: 39 en suite (7 fmly) (14 GF) ⊗ in 12 bedrooms s £67-£74; d £80-£90 (incl. bkfst) **FACILITIES:** STV **CONF:** Thtr 50 Class 35 Board 35 Del from £70 **PARKING:** 40 **NOTES:** ⊗ in restaurant

★★★64% **Salterns Harbourside**
38 Salterns Way, Lilliput BH14 8JR
☎ 01202 707321 📠 01202 707488
e-mail: reception@saltersharbourside.com
web: www.salternsharbourside.com
Dir: *in Poole follow B3369 Sandbanks road. 1m at Lilliput shops turn into Salterns Way by Barclays Bank*
Located next to the marina with superb views across to Brownsea Island, this modernised hotel used to be the headquarters for the flying boats in World War II and was later a yacht club. Bedrooms are spacious and some have private balconies, whilst the busy bar and restaurant both enjoy harbour views.
ROOMS: 20 en suite (4 fmly) ⊗ in 3 bedrooms s £60-£120; d £70-£130 (incl. bkfst) **LB** **FACILITIES:** Xmas **CONF:** Thtr 100 Class 50 Board 30 Del from £120 **PARKING:** 80 **NOTES:** ✈ ⊗ in restaurant Civ Wed 120

⌂ **Premier Travel Inn Poole Centre (Holes Bay)**
Holes Bay Rd BH15 2BD
☎ 08701 977210 📠 01202 661497
web: www.premiertravelinn.com
Dir: *follow Poole Channel Ferry signs, hotel S of A35/A349 on A350 dual carriageway*
High quality, modern budget accommodation ideal for both families and business travellers. Spacious, en suite bedrooms feature bath and shower, satellite TV and many have telephones and modem points. The adjacent family restaurant features a wide and varied menu. For further details consult the Hotel Groups page.
ROOMS: 62 en suite s £55.95; d £55.95

⌂ **Premier Travel Inn Poole North**
Cabot Ln BH17 7DA
☎ 0870 9906332 📠 0870 6606333
web: www.premiertravelinn.com
Dir: *Exit M3 follow signs for M27 (Southampton). M27 becomes A31 towards Bournemouth. Follow Poole/Channel Ferries signs. At Darby's Corner rdbt take 2nd exit. At 2nd lights turn right into Cabot Ln. Hotel on right*
High quality, modern budget accommodation ideal for both

continued

families and business travellers. Spacious, en suite bedrooms feature bath and shower, satellite TV and many have telephones and modem points. The adjacent family restaurant features a wide and varied menu. For further details consult the Hotel Groups page.
ROOMS: 126 en suite s £55.95; d £55.95

PORLOCK, Somerset Map 03 SS84

Top Hotel

★★ ⊛ The Oaks
TA24 8ES
☎ 01643 862265 📠 01643 863131
e-mail: info@oakshotel.co.uk
A relaxing atmosphere is found at this charming Edwardian house, located near to the setting of R D Blackmore's novel *Lorna Doone.* Quietly located and set in attractive grounds, the hotel enjoys elevated views across the village towards the sea. Bedrooms are thoughtfully furnished and comfortable, and the public rooms include a charming bar and a peaceful drawing room. In the dining room, guests can choose from the daily-changing menu, which features fresh, quality local produce.
ROOMS: 8 en suite ⊗ in all bedrooms s £102; d £165 (incl. bkfst & dinner) **LB** **FACILITIES:** Xmas **PARKING:** 12 **NOTES:** No children 8yrs ⊗ in restaurant Closed Nov-Mar (excl. Xmas & New Year)

Restaurant with Rooms

⊛⊛⊛ Andrews on the Weir
Porlock Weir TA24 8PB
☎ 01643 863300 📠 01643 863311
e-mail: information@andrewsontheweir.co.uk
web: www.andrewsontheweir.co.uk
Dir: *A39 from Minehead to Porlock, through village, 1st right signed Harbour (Porlock Weir) for 1.5m*

Enjoying a delightful location overlooking Porlock Bay, Andrews on the Weir is decorated in country-house style. Individually

continued

furnished bedrooms are spacious and comfortable; one has a four-poster bed. During colder months, a log fire creates a cosy atmosphere in the sitting room/bar. There is a choice of imaginative, innovative dishes available in the restaurant - Andrew Dixon is a very accomplished chef.
ROOMS: 5 en suite ⊗ in all bedrooms s £70-£130; d £85-£160 **LB** **FACILITIES:** Xmas **PARKING:** 6 **NOTES:** No children 12yrs ⊗ in restaurant Closed Jan & Mon, Tue

PORT GAVERNE, Cornwall & Isles of Scilly Map 02 SX08

★★68% Port Gaverne
PL29 3SQ
☎ 01208 880244 📠 01208 880151
Dir: *signed from B3314*
In a quiet seaside port half a mile from the old fishing village of Port Isaac, this hotel has a romantic feel, retaining its flagged floors, beamed ceilings and steep stairways. Bedrooms are available in a range of sizes. Local produce often features on the hotel menus, which include bar meals.
ROOMS: 14 en suite (4 fmly) s £39-£69; d £79-£99 (incl. bkfst) **LB** **PARKING:** 30 **NOTES:** ⊗ in restaurant

PORTISHEAD, Somerset Map 04 ST47

⇧ Premier Travel Inn Portishead
Wyndham Way BS20 7GA
☎ 08701 977212 📠 01275 846534
web: www.premiertravelinn.com
Dir: *From M5 junct 19 follow A369 towards Portishead. Across 1st rdbt. Inn on next rdbt.*
High quality, modern budget accommodation ideal for both families and business travellers. Spacious, en suite bedrooms feature bath and shower, satellite TV and many have telephones and modem points. The adjacent family restaurant features a wide and varied menu. For further details consult the Hotel Groups page.
ROOMS: 40 en suite s £49.95; d £49.95

PORTLOE, Cornwall & Isles of Scilly Map 02 SW93

★★★74% ⊛ The Lugger
TR2 5RD
☎ 01872 501322 📠 01872 501691
e-mail: office@luggerhotel.com
Dir: *M5/A30 or A38; turn off A390 St. Austell/Truro to Tregony B3287. A3078 St Mawes; 2m left Veryan; left Portloe.*
This delightful hotel enjoys a unique location adjacent to the slipway of the harbour. Bedrooms are appealing and well-equipped, while day rooms include a comfortable lounge and a contemporary-style restaurant that enjoys superb views. In warmer months a sun terrace overlooking the harbour proves a popular place.
ROOMS: 21 en suite s £120-£257; d £180-£415 (incl. bkfst & dinner) **LB** **FACILITIES:** STV Full spa treatments Xmas **PARKING:** 21 **NOTES:** No children 12yrs ⊗ in restaurant

⊛ AA Rosette Award for culinary excellence

TV dinner?
Room service at three stars and above

PORTSCATHO, Cornwall & Isles of Scilly Map 02 SW83

★★★76% Rosevine

TR2 5EW
☎ 01872 580206 01872 580230
e-mail: info@rosevinehotels.co.uk web: www.rosevine.co.uk
Dir: *from St Austell take A390 for Truro. Left onto B3287 to Tregony. Then A3078 through Ruan High Lanes. Hotel 3rd left*
Located on the coast, this family run hotel benefits from magnificent sea views and has beautifully tended gardens. The hotel also boasts its own beach at the head of the Roseland peninsula. The spacious bedrooms feature traditional decor and welcoming extras such as fresh fruit and mineral water; most have sea views and some have balconies. Public rooms include a cosy bar, spacious lounges and a large restaurant featuring fresh seafood dishes.
ROOMS: 11 en suite 6 annexe en suite (7 fmly) (3 GF) s £86-£143; d £172-£256 (incl. bkfst) **LB** **FACILITIES:** Table tennis Childrens playroom ♫ **PARKING:** 20 **NOTES:** in restaurant Closed Dec-8 Feb

Top Hotel

★★ Driftwood

Rosevine TR2 5EW
☎ 01872 580644 01872 580801
e-mail: info@driftwoodhotel.co.uk
Dir: *A390 towards St. Mawes. On A3078 turn left to Rosevine at Trewithian*
Poised on the cliffside with panoramic views this contemporary hotel has a peaceful and secluded location. A warm welcome is guaranteed here where professional standards of service are provided in an effortless and relaxed manner. Cuisine is a feature of any stay with quality local produce used with in a sympathetic and highly skilled manner. The extremely comfortable and elegant bedrooms are decorated in soft shades reminiscent of the seashore. The style is uncluttered. There is a sheltered terraced garden with a large deck with steamer chairs for sunbathing.
ROOMS: 14 en suite 1 annexe en suite (3 fmly) (1 GF) in all bedrooms s £120-£150; d £160-£200 (incl. bkfst)
FACILITIES: Private Beach Xmas **PARKING:** 30 **NOTES:** in restaurant Closed 3-31 Jan RS Xmas

PORTSMOUTH, Hampshire Map 05 SU60

★★★★65% Portsmouth Marriott Hotel

Southampton Rd PO6 4SH
☎ 0870 400 7285 0870 400 7385
e-mail: reservations.portsmouth@marriotthotels.com
web: www.marriott.co.uk
Dir: *M27 junct 12 keep left and hotel on left*
Close to the motorway and ferry port, this hotel is well suited to business trade. The comfortable and well laid-out bedrooms provide a comprehensive range of facilities including up-to-date workstations. The leisure club offers a pool, a gym, and a health and beauty salon.

ROOMS: 174 en suite (77 fmly) in 130 bedrooms **FACILITIES:** STV supervised Sauna Solarium Gym Jacuzzi Exercise studio, Beauty salon Xmas **CONF:** Thtr 350 Class 180 Board 30 **SERVICES:** Lift air con **PARKING:** 250 **NOTES:** Civ Wed 100

★★★70% Royal Beach

South Pde, Southsea PO4 0RN
☎ 023 9273 1281 023 9281 7572
e-mail: enquiries@royalbeachhotel.co.uk
web: www.royalbeachhotel.co.uk
Dir: *M27 to M275, follow signs to seafront. Hotel on seafront*

A refurbishment, still ongoing, has transformed this former Victorian seafront hotel into a smart and comfortable venue suitable for leisure and business guests alike. Bedrooms and public areas are well presented and generally spacious, and the smart new Coast bar is an ideal venue for a relaxing drink.
ROOMS: 124 en suite (18 fmly) in 72 bedrooms s £55-£95; d £75-£185 (incl. bkfst) **LB** **FACILITIES:** STV ♫ Xmas **CONF:** Thtr 280 Class 180 Board 40 Del from £109.95 **SERVICES:** Lift **PARKING:** 50 **NOTES:** in restaurant

See advert on opposite page

★★★66% Innlodge Hotel

Burrfields Rd PO3 5HH
☎ 023 9265 0510 023 9269 3458
e-mail: Innlodge@greeneking.co.uk
web: www.oldenglish.co.uk
Dir: *A3(M)/M27 onto A27. Take Southsea exit and follow A2030. 3rd traffic lights right into Burrfields Rd. Hotel 2nd car park on left*
Located on the eastern fringe of the city, this purpose-built hotel is conveniently located for all major routes. The modern bedrooms are spacious and well equipped. Guests have two eating options:

continued

the contemporary styled 'Lounge' restaurant and the Farmhouse Inn. The hotel also boasts a large covered children's play area.
ROOMS: 74 en suite (6 fmly) (33 GF) ⊗ in 39 bedrooms s £60-£80; d £60-£80 **FACILITIES:** STV Indoor fun factory & outdoor kids play area, Pool tables **CONF:** BC Thtr 150 Class 64 Board 40 **PARKING:** 200
NOTES: ✗ ⊗ in restaurant

★★72% *The Beaufort Hotel*
71 Festing Rd, Southsea PO4 0NQ
☎ 023 9282 3707 📠 023 9287 0270
e-mail: enq@beauforthotel.co.uk
Dir: *follow seafront signs. Left at South Parade Pier, then 4th on left*
This intimate hotel is located within easy reach of the seafront and the city centre and is ideal for accessing both local attractions and amenities. Individually decorated bedrooms are generally spacious providing good levels of comfort. Public areas include a pleasant lounge and cosy bar.
ROOMS: 20 en suite (2 fmly) (7 GF) ⊗ in 7 bedrooms
FACILITIES: STV **PARKING:** 7 **NOTES:** ✗ ⊗ in restaurant

★★72% Seacrest
11/12 South Pde, Southsea PO5 2JB
☎ 023 9273 3192 📠 023 9283 2523
e-mail: seacrest@boltblue.com
web: www.seacresthotel.co.uk
Dir: *from M27/M275 follow signs for seafront, Pyramids and Sea Life Centre. Hotel opposite Rock Gardens and Pyramids*

In a premier seafront location, this smart hotel provides the ideal base for exploring the town. Bedrooms, many benefiting from sea views, are decorated to a high standard with good facilities. Guests can relax in either the south-facing lounge, furnished with large leather sofas, or the adjacent bar; there is also a cosy dining room popular with residents.
ROOMS: 28 en suite (3 fmly) ⊗ in 20 bedrooms s £42-£60; d £55-£95 (incl. bkfst) **LB** **FACILITIES:** STV **SERVICES:** Lift **PARKING:** 12
NOTES: ⊗ in restaurant

⌂ *Hotel Ibis*
Winston Churchill Av PO1 2LX
☎ 023 9264 0000 📠 023 9264 1000
e-mail: h1461@accor-hotels.com
Dir: *M27 junct 2 onto M275. Follow signs for city centre then Sealife Centre and then Guildhall. Right at rdbt into Winston Churchill Ave*
Modern, budget hotel offering comfortable accommodation in bright and practical bedrooms. Breakfast is self-service and dinner is available in the restaurant. For further details, consult the Hotel Groups page.
ROOMS: 144 en suite **CONF:** Thtr 45 Class 24 Board 24

⌂ Innkeeper's Lodge Portsmouth
Copnor Rd, Hilsea PO3 5HS
☎ 0870 243 0500 & 023 9265 4645
web: www.innkeeperslodge.com
Dir: *From A27 take A2030. Right at lights, over 3 rbdts into Norway Road. Inn on A288*
A growing concept in the travel accommodation market. Smart rooms meet essential business requirements but also have home comforts. Dining options include all-day menus plus the added advantage of breakfast, which is included in the room price. For further details consult the Hotel Groups page.
ROOMS: 33 en suite s £49.95-£55; d £49.95-£55

⌂ Premier Travel Inn Portsmouth
Southampton Rd, North Harbour, Cosham PO6 4SA
☎ 08701 977213 📠 023 9232 4895
web: www.premiertravelinn.com
Dir: *on A27, close to M27 junct 12*
High quality, modern budget accommodation ideal for both families and business travellers. Spacious, en suite bedrooms feature bath and shower, satellite TV and many have telephones and modem points. The adjacent family restaurant features a wide and varied menu. For further details consult the Hotel Groups page.
ROOMS: 64 en suite s £51.95; d £51.95 **CONF:** Thtr 25

♫ Entertainment

PORTSMOUTH, continued

Premier Travel Inn Southsea
Long Curtain Rd, Clarence Pier, Southsea PO5 3AA
☎ 08701 977236 📠 023 9273 3048
web: www.premiertravelinn.com
Dir: *Pier Rd leads to Clarence Pier. Inn next to amusement park and Isle of Wight hovercraft*
High quality, modern budget accommodation ideal for both families and business travellers. Spacious, en suite bedrooms feature bath and shower, satellite TV and many have telephones and modem points. The adjacent family restaurant features a wide and varied menu. For further details consult the Hotel Groups page.
ROOMS: 40 en suite s £52.95; d £52.95

Travelodge
Kingston Crescent, North End PO2 8AB
☎ 08700 850 950 📠 02392 639121
web: www.travelodge.co.uk
Dir: *M275 towards north end, Rudmore rdbt turn left into Kingston Crescent*

Travelodge offers good quality, good value, modern accommodation. Ideal for families, the spacious, en suite bedrooms include remote-control TV, tea and coffee-making facilities and comfortable beds. Meals can be taken at the nearby family restaurant. For further details consult the Hotel Groups page.
ROOMS: 78 en suite s fr £26; d fr £26

PORTWRINKLE, Cornwall & Isles of Scilly Map 03 SX35
See also Looe

★★★68% Whitsand Bay Hotel & Golf Club
PL11 3BU
☎ 01503 230276 📠 01503 230329
e-mail: whitsandbayhotel@btconnect.com
web: www.whitsandbayhotel.co.uk
Dir: *A38 from Exeter over River Tamar, left at Trerulefoot rdbt onto A374 to Crafthole/Portwrinkle. Follow hotel signs*

An imposing Victorian stone building with oak panelling, stained-glass windows and a sweeping staircase. Bedrooms include family rooms and a suite with a balcony, many have superb sea views. Facilities include an 18-hole cliff-top golf course and indoor swimming pool. The fixed-price menu offers an interesting selection of dishes.
ROOMS: 32 en suite (7 fmly) in 10 bedrooms **FACILITIES:** 18 Sauna Solarium Gym Putt green Games room, Lounge with wide screen TV ♫ Xmas **CONF:** BC **PARKING:** 60 **NOTES:** in restaurant

POTTERS BAR, Hertfordshire Map 06 TL20

★★★★66% Ponsbourne Park Hotel
SG13 8QZ
☎ 01707 876191 & 879277 📠 01707 875190
e-mail: reservations@ponsbournepark.co.uk
web: www.ponsbournepark.co.uk

Set within 200 acres of quiet parkland, this 17th-century country house offers contemporary accommodation and public rooms, along with a flexible range of leisure and conference facilities. Smart modern bedrooms are located in the main house and adjacent annexe; each room is well equipped, but typically main house rooms are more spacious.
ROOMS: 23 en suite 28 annexe en suite (8 fmly) (10 GF) s £108-£165; d £108-£165 (incl. bkfst) **LB** **FACILITIES:** 9 Gym Xmas **CONF:** Thtr 100 Class 40 Board 40 Del £155 **PARKING:** 125 **NOTES:** in restaurant Civ Wed 94

PRESTBURY, Cheshire Map 16 SJ87

Town House

★★★★ White House Manor
New Rd SK10 4HP
☎ 01625 829376 📠 01625 828627
e-mail: info@thewhitehouse.uk.com
web: www.thewhitehouse.uk.com
Dir: *on A538 Macclesfield road*
This stylish Georgian house, situated in attractive gardens on
continued

the edge of the village, offers luxurious, individually styled bedrooms, many with four-poster beds. Meals can be ordered from the room service menu whilst delicious breakfasts are served in the bright conservatory. The White House restaurant, under the same ownership, is just a short walk away but guests can be driven there if needed.
ROOMS: 11 en suite (2 GF) ⊗ in all bedrooms s £45-£110; d £80-£130 **FACILITIES:** STV Jacuzzi Xmas **CONF:** Thtr 60 Class 40 Board 26 Del from £135 **PARKING:** 11 **NOTES:** ✖ No children 10yrs Closed 24-26 Dec

★★★68% Bridge

The Village SK10 4DQ
☎ 01625 829326 🖷 01625 827557
e-mail: reception@bridge-hotel.co.uk
web: www.bridge-hotel.co.uk
***Dir:** off A538 through village. Hotel next to church*

Dating in parts from the 17th century, this delightful, stylish hotel stands between the River Bollin and the ancient church. The cocktail bar is the ideal place to relax before enjoying a meal in the Bridge Restaurant. A wide range of bedroom styles is available in both the original building and the modern extension.
ROOMS: 23 en suite (1 fmly) ⊗ in all bedrooms s £45-£87; d £87-£90 (incl. bkfst) **LB** **FACILITIES:** STV ♫ **CONF:** Thtr 100 Class 56 Board 48 Del from £115 **PARKING:** 52 **NOTES:** ✖ Civ Wed 100

PRESTON, Lancashire Map 18 SD52

See also Garstang

★★★★68% Preston Marriott Hotel

Garstang Rd, Broughton PR3 5JB
☎ 01772 864087 🖷 01772 861728
e-mail: reservations.preston@marriotthotels.co.uk
web: www.marriott.co.uk
***Dir:** M6 junct 32 onto M55 junct 1, follow A6 towards Garstang. Hotel 0.5m on right*

Exuding a country-club atmosphere this stylish hotel enjoys good

continued

links to both the city centre and motorway network. There are two dining options and the extensive leisure facilities ensure that there is plenty to do. The bedrooms are smartly decorated and equipped with a comprehensive range of extras.
ROOMS: 149 en suite (40 fmly) (63 GF) ⊗ in 93 bedrooms s £70-£118; d £80-£128 (incl. bkfst) **LB** **FACILITIES: Spa** STV supervised Sauna Solarium Gym Jacuzzi Steam room, Beauty salon/hairdressing **CONF:** BC Thtr 220 Class 100 Board 70 Del from £120 **SERVICES:** Lift air con **PARKING:** 250 **NOTES:** ✖ ⊗ in restaurant Civ Wed 180

★★★74% Barton Grange

Garstang Rd PR3 5AA
☎ 01772 862551 🖷 01772 861267
e-mail: stay@bartongrangehotel.com
web: www.bartongrangehotel.com
(For full entry see Barton)

★★★72% ⊛ *Pines*

570 Preston Rd, Clayton-Le-Woods PR6 7ED
☎ 01772 338551 🖷 01772 629002
e-mail: mail@thepineshotel.co.uk
***Dir:** on A6, 1m S of M6 junct 29*
This unique and stylish hotel sits in four acres of mature grounds just a short drive from the motorway network. Elegant bedrooms are individually designed and offer high levels of comfort and facilities. Day rooms include a smart bar and Haworths brasserie, while extensive function rooms make this hotel a popular venue for weddings.
ROOMS: 37 en suite (12 fmly) (14 GF) ⊗ in 21 bedrooms **FACILITIES:** STV ♫ **CONF:** BC Thtr 200 Class 150 Board 60 **PARKING:** 120 **NOTES:** ✖ Closed 26 Dec Civ Wed 150

PRESTON, continued

★★★67% *Tickled Trout*
Preston New Rd, Samlesbury PR5 0UJ
☎ 01772 877671 🖹 01772 877463
e-mail: tickledtrout@macdonald-hotels.co.uk
web: www.macdonald-hotels.co.uk
Dir: *close to M6 junct 31*
On the banks of the River Ribble, this hotel is conveniently located for the motorway, making it a popular venue for both business and leisure guests. Smartly appointed bedrooms are all tastefully decorated and equipped with a thoughtful range of extras. The hotel boasts a stylish wing of newly built meeting rooms and plans were afoot at the time of inspection to add substantial leisure and function facilities.
ROOMS: 102 en suite (6 fmly) ⊗ in 43 bedrooms **FACILITIES:** STV Fishing ♫ **CONF:** BC Thtr 120 Class 60 Board 50 **SERVICES:** Lift **PARKING:** 240 **NOTES:** ⊗ in restaurant Civ Wed 100

★★★66% Novotel Preston
Reedfield Place, Walton Summit PR5 8AA
☎ 01772 313331 🖹 01772 627868
e-mail: H0838@accor-hotels.com
web: www.novotel.com
Dir: *M6 junct 29, M61 junct 9, then A6 Chorley Road. Hotel next to Bamber Bridge rdbt*
The hotel is well located just off main motorway networks. Bedrooms are spacious and feature ample desk space and additional bed space making them ideal for families or business travellers. Flexible dining is a feature with the Garden Brassiere, open throughout the day until midnight. The hotel also boasts an outdoor pool and children's play area.
Novotel - AA Hotel Group of the Year 2005-6.
ROOMS: 95 en suite (22 fmly) ⊗ in 49 bedrooms s £62; d £62 **LB** **FACILITIES:** STV supervised **CONF:** BC Thtr 180 Class 80 Board 52 Del from £95 **SERVICES:** Lift **PARKING:** 140 **NOTES:** ⊗ in restaurant

★★70% Haighton Manor
Haighton Green Ln, Haighton PR2 5SQ
☎ 01772 663170 🖹 01772 663171
e-mail: info@haightonmanor.net
web: www.haightonmanor.net
Dir: *Off A6 onto Durton Rd, or from M6 junct 32 right at rdbt & right onto Durton Rd. Right at end into Haighton Lane. Hotel 2m on left*
Located in sleepy, rolling countryside just ten minutes to the east of city, this impressive hotel is ideally situated for both the business and leisure guest. External appearances are deceptive, for once inside, this 17th-century manor house has ultra-modern bedrooms (including modem points)and stylishly fashioned day rooms providing a wonderful fusion of ancient and modern. Wide-ranging creative menus can be sampled in the candlelit restaurant. This hotel is a popular wedding venue.
ROOMS: 8 en suite (1 fmly) ⊗ in all bedrooms s £50-£70; d £70-£100 (incl. bkfst) **LB** **FACILITIES:** STV **CONF:** BC **PARKING:** 70 **NOTES:** ✈ ⊗ in restaurant Civ Wed 55

★★63% *Claremont*
516 Blackpool Rd, Ashton-on-Ribble PR2 1HY
☎ 01772 729738 🖹 01772 726274
Dir: *M6 junct 31 onto A59 towards Preston. Right at hilltop rdbt onto A583. Hotel on right past pub and over bridge*
This family run hotel offers a relaxed and informal atmosphere for its mainly business clientele. Bedrooms are comfortable and well equipped, whilst public areas include a cosy bar lounge and adjacent dining room offering a modest choice of good value home-cooked dishes.
ROOMS: 10 en suite **CONF:** Thtr 85 Class 45 Board 50 **PARKING:** 27 **NOTES:** ✈

⌂ *Hotel Ibis*
Garstang Rd, Broughton PR3 5JE
☎ 01772 861800 🖹 01772 861900
e-mail: H3162@accor-hotels.com
Dir: *M6 junct 32, then M55 junct 1. Left lane onto A6. Left at slip road, left again at mini-rdbt. 2nd turn, hotel on right past pub*
Modern, budget hotel offering comfortable accommodation in bright and practical bedrooms. Breakfast is self-service and dinner is available in the restaurant. For further details, consult the Hotel Groups page.
ROOMS: 82 en suite **CONF:** Thtr 30 Class 20 Board 20

⌂ Premier Travel Inn Preston East
Bluebell Way, Preston East Link Rd, Fulwood PR2 5PZ
☎ 08701 977215 🖹 01772 651619
web: www.premiertravelinn.com
Dir: *M6 junct 31A left at rdbt, follow ring road under motorway & Inn on left. No junction for southbound traffic so take junct 31 & join motorway northbound, take exit off junct 31A*
High quality, modern budget accommodation ideal for both families and business travellers. Spacious, en suite bedrooms feature bath and shower, satellite TV and many have telephones and modem points. The adjacent family restaurant features a wide and varied menu. For further details consult the Hotel Groups page.
ROOMS: 65 en suite s £46.95-£48.95; d £46.95-£48.95 **CONF:** Thtr 20

⌂ Premier Travel Inn Preston South
Lostock Ln, Bamber Bridge PR5 6BA
☎ 0870 9906462 🖹 0870 9906463
web: www.premiertravelinn.com
Dir: *Off M65 junct 1 (0.5m from M6 junct 29) close to rdbt of A582 & A6*
High quality, modern budget accommodation ideal for both families and business travellers. Spacious, en suite bedrooms feature bath and shower, satellite TV and many have telephones and modem points. The adjacent family restaurant features a wide and varied menu. For further details consult the Hotel Groups page.
ROOMS: 40 en suite s £49.95-£52.95; d £49.95-£52.95 **CONF:** Thtr 30 Board 30

⌂ Premier Travel Inn Preston West
Blackpool Rd, Lea PR4 0XB
☎ 08701 977214 🖹 01772 729971
web: www.premiertravelinn.com
Dir: *off A583, opposite Texaco garage.*
High quality, modern budget accommodation ideal for both families and business travellers. Spacious, en suite bedrooms feature bath and shower, satellite TV and many have telephones and modem points. The adjacent family restaurant features a wide and varied menu. For further details consult the Hotel Groups page.
ROOMS: 38 en suite s £46.95-£48.95; d £46.95-£48.95

PRESTWICH, Greater Manchester
Map 15 SD80

U Fairways Lodge & Leisure Club
George St, (Off Bury New Road) M25 9WS
☎ 0161 798 8905 🖹 0161 773 5562
e-mail: info@fairwayslodge.co.uk
Dir: *Exit M60 junct 17. Follow A56 for 1.5m, turn right into George St, hotel in cul-de-sac*
At the time of going to press, the star classification for this hotel was not confirmed. Please refer to the AA internet site www.theAA.com for current information.
ROOMS: 40 en suite (19 GF) ⊗ in 25 bedrooms s £50-£74; d £60-£89 (incl. bkfst) **LB** **FACILITIES:** STV Squash Sauna Solarium Gym Jacuzzi ♫ Xmas **CONF:** Thtr 100 Class 120 Del from £90 **PARKING:** 80 **NOTES:** ✈ ⊗ in restaurant Civ Wed 50

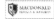

⇧ Premier Travel Inn Manchester (Prestwich)

Bury New Rd M25 3AJ
☎ 08701 977175 Fax 0161 773 8099
web: www.premiertravelinn.com
Dir: *M60 junct 17, on A56*
High quality, modern budget accommodation ideal for both families and business travellers. Spacious, en suite bedrooms feature bath and shower, satellite TV and many have telephones and modem points. The adjacent family restaurant features a wide and varied menu. For further details consult the Hotel Groups page.
ROOMS: 60 en suite s £47.95-£50.95; d £47.95-£50.95

PUDDINGTON, Cheshire — Map 15 SJ37

★★★★ 70% Craxton Wood

Parkgate Rd, Ledsham CH66 9PB
☎ 0151 347 4000 Fax 0151 347 4040
e-mail: craxton@macdonald-hotels.co.uk
web: www.macdonald-hotels.co.uk
Dir: *from M6 take M56 towards N Wales, then A5117 then A540 to Hoylake. Hotel 200yds past lights*

Set in extensive grounds, this hotel offers a variety of bedroom styles; the modern rooms are particularly comfortable. The nicely furnished restaurant overlooks the grounds and offers a wide choice of dishes, whilst full leisure facilities and a choice of function suites completes the package.
ROOMS: 72 en suite (8 fmly) (30 GF) ⊗ in all bedrooms s £75-£95; d £110-£180 (incl. bkfst) **LB** **FACILITIES:** STV Sauna Solarium Gym Beauty spa Xmas **CONF:** Thtr 400 Class 200 Board 160 Del from £125 **SERVICES:** Lift **PARKING:** 220 **NOTES:** ⊗ in restaurant Civ Wed 350

⇧ Premier Travel Inn Wirral (Two Mills)

Parkgate Rd, Two Mills CH66 9PD
☎ 0870 9906564 Fax 0870 9906565
web: www.premiertravelinn.com
Dir: *5m from M56 junct 16 & M53 junct 5. On x-rds of A550 & A540*
High quality, modern budget accommodation ideal for both families and business travellers. Spacious, en suite bedrooms feature bath and shower, satellite TV and many have telephones and modem points. The adjacent family restaurant features a wide and varied menu. For further details consult the Hotel Groups page.
ROOMS: 31 en suite s £46.95-£48.95; d £46.95-£48.95

PUDSEY, West Yorkshire — Map 19 SE23

⇧ Travelodge Bradford

1 Mid Point, Dick Ln BD3 8QD
☎ 08700 850 950 Fax 01274 665436
web: www.travelodge.co.uk
Dir: *M62 junct 26 (M606), take A6177 towards Leeds, A647, 2m on left*
Travelodge offers good quality, good value, modern accommodation. Ideal for families, the spacious, en suite bedrooms include remote-control TV, tea and coffee-making facilities and comfortable beds. Meals can be taken at the nearby family restaurant. For further details consult the Hotel Groups page.
ROOMS: 48 en suite s fr £26; d fr £26

PURFLEET, Essex — Map 06 TQ57

⇧ Premier Travel Inn

High St RM19 1QA
☎ 08701 977216 Fax 01708 860852
web: www.premiertravelinn.com
Dir: *from Dartford Tunnel follow signs Dagenham (A13), at rdbt take 1st exit to Purfleet (A1090)*
High quality, modern budget accommodation ideal for both families and business travellers. Spacious, en suite bedrooms feature bath and shower, satellite TV and many have telephones and modem points. The adjacent family restaurant features a wide and varied menu. For further details consult the Hotel Groups page.
ROOMS: 30 en suite

PURTON, Wiltshire — Map 05 SU08

★★★ 78% The Pear Tree at Purton

Church End SN5 4ED
☎ 01793 772100 Fax 01793 772369
e-mail: stay@peartreepurton.co.uk
Dir: *M4 junct 16 follow signs to Purton, at Spar shop turn right. Hotel 0.25m on left*
Charming 15th-century former vicarage set amidst pretty landscaped gardens in a peaceful location. The resident proprietors and staff provide efficient, dedicated service and friendly hospitality. The spacious bedrooms are individually decorated and have a good range of thoughtful extras such as fresh flowers and sherry. Fresh ingredients feature on the menus at both lunch and dinner.
ROOMS: 17 en suite (2 fmly) (6 GF) d £110-£140 (incl. bkfst) **LB** **FACILITIES: Spa** STV ch fac **CONF:** Thtr 70 Class 30 Board 30 Del £170 **PARKING:** 60 **NOTES:** ⊗ in restaurant Closed 26-30 Dec Civ Wed 50

QUORN, Leicestershire — Map 11 SK51

★★★★ 70% Quorn Country

Charnwood House, 66 Leicester Rd LE12 8BB
☎ 01509 415050 Fax 01509 415557
e-mail: reservations@quorncountryhotel.co.uk
Dir: *M1 junct 23 onto A512 into Loughborough. Follow A6 signs. At 1st rdbt towards Quorn, through lights, hotel 500yds from 2nd rdbt*

Professional service is one of the key strengths of this pleasing hotel, which sits beside the river in four acres of landscaped gardens and grounds. The smart modern conference centre and

continued on p464

QUORN, continued

function suites have proved to be a great success for both corporate functions and weddings. Public rooms include a smart, newly refurbished lounge and bar, whilst guests have the choice from two dining options: the formal Shires restaurant and the informal conservatory-style Orangery.
ROOMS: 30 en suite (2 fmly) (9 GF) ⊗ in 19 bedrooms s £84-£110; d £95-£125 **LB** **FACILITIES:** STV Fishing **CONF:** BC Thtr 300 Class 162 Board 40 Del from £135 **SERVICES:** Lift **PARKING:** 100 **NOTES:** ✗ Civ Wed 200

See advert under LOUGHBOROUGH

RADLETT, Hertfordshire — Map 06 TL10

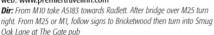

Premier Travel Inn St Albans/Bricketwood
Smug Oak Ln AL2 3PN
☎ 08701 977040 📠 01727 873289
web: www.premiertravelinn.com
Dir: *From M10 take A5183 towards Radlett. After bridge over M25 turn right. From M25 or M1, follow signs to Bricketwood then turn into Smug Oak Lane at The Gate pub*
High quality, modern budget accommodation ideal for both families and business travellers. Spacious, en suite bedrooms feature bath and shower, satellite TV and many have telephones and modem points. The adjacent family restaurant features a wide and varied menu. For further details consult the Hotel Groups page.
ROOMS: 56 en suite s £55.95-£57.95; d £55.95-£57.95

RAINHAM, Greater London — Map 06 TQ58

Premier Travel Inn Rainham
New Rd, Wennington RM13 9ED
☎ 08701 977217 📠 01708 634821
web: www.premiertravelinn.com
Dir: *M25 junct 30/31 - follow A13 for Dagenham/Rainham, then A1306 for Wennington, Aveley, Rainham. Inn 0.5 mile on right.*
High quality, modern budget accommodation ideal for both families and business travellers. Spacious, en suite bedrooms feature bath and shower, satellite TV and many have telephones and modem points. The adjacent family restaurant features a wide and varied menu. For further details consult the Hotel Groups page.
ROOMS: 60 en suite s £53.95-£57.95; d £53.95-£57.95

RAINHILL, Merseyside — Map 15 SJ49

Premier Travel Inn Liverpool (Rainhill)
804 Warrington Rd, Rainhill L35 6PE
☎ 0870 9906446 📠 0870 9906447
web: www.premiertravelinn.com
Dir: *Just off M62 junct 7, A57 towards Rainhill*
High quality, modern budget accommodation ideal for both families and business travellers. Spacious, en suite bedrooms feature bath and shower, satellite TV and many have telephones and modem points. The adjacent family restaurant features a wide and varied menu. For further details consult the Hotel Groups page.
ROOMS: 34 en suite s £46.95-£48.95; d £46.95-£48.95 **CONF:** Thtr 20

> Late for dinner? Quality standards mean that last orders for dinner vary according to star rating and should be no earlier than:
> ★★ 7.00pm ★★★ 8:00pm ★★★★ 9:00pm ★★★★★ 10:00pm

RAMSBOTTOM, Greater Manchester — Map 15 SD71

★★★62% Old Mill
Springwood BL0 9DS
☎ 01706 822991 📠 01706 822291
e-mail: reservations@oldmill-uk.com
Dir: *from M66 junct 4 follow A56 towards Rawtenstall. 1st left into Bridge Street. Over railway crossing, at lights straight over into Carr Street. 2nd left into Springwood, to end of road. Right to hotel*
Extended from an original water mill, this friendly hotel enjoys fine views over the town and Rossendale Valley. Bedrooms have attractive floral furnishings and inter-connecting family rooms are available. In addition to a comfortable bar and beamed restaurant, a well-equipped leisure centre is available to guests during their stay.
ROOMS: 29 en suite (6 fmly) s £51-£59; d £67-£74 (incl. bkfst) **LB** **FACILITIES:** STV Sauna Solarium Gym Jacuzzi Steam Room **CONF:** Thtr 70 Class 30 Board 20 Del £99 **PARKING:** 50 **NOTES:** ✗ ⊗ in restaurant Civ Wed 60

RAMSGATE, Kent — Map 07 TR36

★★★63% Comfort Inn Ramsgate
Victoria Pde, East Cliff CT11 8DT
☎ 01843 592345 📠 01843 580157
e-mail: reservations@sancluhotel.co.uk
Dir: *From M2 take A299 signed Ramsgate, B2054 to Victoria Parade*
This Victorian hotel stands on the seafront, close to the ferry and the town. Bedrooms, some with balconies, are generously sized and well equipped. Meals are served both in the bar lounge and in the restaurant.
ROOMS: 44 en suite (5 fmly) ⊗ in 22 bedrooms s £50-£80; d £80-£120 (incl. bkfst) **LB** **FACILITIES:** STV Xmas **CONF:** Thtr 130 Class 30 Board 60 Del from £80 **SERVICES:** Lift **PARKING:** 10 **NOTES:** ✗ ⊗ in restaurant

RAMSGILL, North Yorkshire — Map 19 SE17

Top Restaurant with Rooms

Yorke Arms
HG3 5RL
☎ 01423 755243 📠 01423 755330
e-mail: enquiries@yorke-arms.co.uk
web: www.yorke-arms.co.uk
Dir: *off B6265 at Pateley Bridge at Nidderdale filling station onto Low Wath road, signed to Ramsgill. Continue 4.5m*
Dominating the tiny hamlet, this ivy-clad former hunting lodge overlooks the village green in picturesque Nidderdale and a warm and welcoming atmosphere prevails throughout. Flagstone floors lead through to the cosy bar, and beams and open fires grace the two delightful dining rooms where excellent cuisine is matched by caring and attentive service.

continued

Bedrooms, now refurbished to a high standard, offer a full range of modern amenities.
ROOMS: 13 en suite 1 annexe en suite (2 fmly) (5 GF) ⊗ in 13 bedrooms s £120-£150; d £240-£340 (incl. bkfst & dinner) **LB**
FACILITIES: shooting, mountain biking, walking, bird watching Xmas
CONF: Class 20 Board 10 Del from £150 **PARKING:** 20
NOTES: ⊗ in restaurant RS Sun

RANGEWORTHY, Gloucestershire — Map 04 ST68

★★72% Rangeworthy Court
Church Ln, Wotton Rd BS37 7ND
☎ 01454 228347 📠 01454 228945
e-mail: hotel@rangeworthy.demon.co.uk
web: www.rangeworthy.demon.co.uk
Dir: *signposted off B4058*

This welcoming manor house hotel is peacefully located in its own grounds, and is within easy reach of the motorway network. The character bedrooms come in a variety of sizes and there is a choice of comfortable lounges to relax in. The candlelit restaurant offers a varied and interesting menu.
ROOMS: 13 en suite (4 fmly) ⊗ in 3 bedrooms s fr £82; d fr £100 (incl. bkfst) **FACILITIES:** Boules **CONF:** BC Thtr 22 Class 14 Board 16 **PARKING:** 40 **NOTES:** ⊗ in restaurant

RAVENSCAR, North Yorkshire — Map 19 NZ90

★★★67% Raven Hall Country House
YO13 0ET
☎ 01723 870353 📠 01723 870072
e-mail: enquiries@ravenhall.co.uk
Dir: *from Scarborough take A171 Whitby road. Take right turn in Cloughton to Ravenscar*

This impressive cliff top mansion enjoys breathtaking views over Robin Hood's Bay. Extensive well-kept grounds include tennis courts, putting green, swimming pools and historic battlements. The bedrooms vary in size but all are comfortably equipped, many offer panoramic views. Public rooms are extensive while the restaurant enjoys fine views over the bay.
ROOMS: 52 en suite (20 fmly) (5 GF) ⊗ in 2 bedrooms s £64.50-£102.50; d £79-£155 (incl. cont bkfst & dinner) **LB**
FACILITIES: supervised 9 Sauna Gym Putt green Bowls, Table tennis Xmas **CONF:** Thtr 100 Class 80 Board 40 Del from £85
SERVICES: Lift **PARKING:** 200 **NOTES:** Civ Wed 100

See advert under SCARBOROUGH

We have indicated only the hotels that don't accept credit or debit cards

RAVENSTONEDALE, Cumbria — Map 18 NY70

★★66% The Fat Lamb
Crossbank CA17 4LL
☎ 015396 23242 📠 015396 23285
e-mail: fatlamb@cumbria.com
Dir: *on A683, between Kirkby Stephen and Sedbergh*

Open fires and solid stone walls are a feature of this 17th-century inn, set on its own nature reserve. There is a choice of dining options with an extensive menu available in the traditional bar or a more formal dining experience in the restaurant. Bedrooms are bright and cheerful and include family rooms and easily accessible rooms for guests with limited mobility.
ROOMS: 12 en suite (4 fmly) ⊗ in all bedrooms s £44-£50; d £72-£80 (incl. bkfst) **LB** **FACILITIES:** Fishing Private 5 acre nature reserve Xmas
PARKING: 60 **NOTES:** ⊗ in restaurant

READING, Berkshire — Map 05 SU77
See also Swallowfield

★★★★75% ®® Millennium Madejski Hotel Reading
Madejski Stadium RG2 0FL
☎ 0118 925 3500 📠 0118 925 3501
e-mail: sales.reading@mill-cop.com
web: www.millenniumhotels.com
Dir: *M4 junct 11 onto A33, follow signs for Madejski Stadium Complex*

A stylish hotel, that features an atrium lobby with specially commissioned water sculpture, is part of the Madejski stadium complex, home to both Reading Football and London Irish Rugby teams. Bedrooms are appointed with spacious workstations and plenty of amenities; there is also a choice of suites and a club floor with its own lounge. The hotel also has an award-winning, fine dining restaurant.
ROOMS: 140 en suite (4 fmly) ⊗ in 92 bedrooms **FACILITIES:** Spa STV supervised Sauna Solarium Gym Jacuzzi **CONF:** Board 12 Del from £199 **SERVICES:** Lift air con **PARKING:** 150 **NOTES:** ⊗ in restaurant RS Xmas & New Yr

★★★★68% Renaissance Hotel Reading
Oxford Rd RG1 7RH
☎ 0118 958 6222 📠 0118 959 7842
e-mail: rhi.lhrlr.dos@renaissancehotels.com
web: www.marriott.co.uk/lhrlr

Situated in the heart of the town, this long-established hotel is well positioned for both business travellers and shoppers. Air-conditioned bedrooms feature a host of extras especially for the business guest including high-speed internet access. Public areas include a refurbished leisure area, a variety of meeting rooms and a business centre. Free parking is available in the adjoining multi-storey.
ROOMS: 196 en suite (67 fmly) ⊗ in 160 bedrooms s £85-£157; d £85-£157 (incl. bkfst) **LB** **FACILITIES:** STV supervised Sauna Solarium Gym Jacuzzi **CONF:** BC Thtr 220 Class 130 Board 60 Del from £169 **SERVICES:** Lift air con **PARKING:** 70 **NOTES:** Civ Wed 140

★★★71% Courtyard by Marriott Reading
Bath Rd, Padworth RG7 5HT
☎ 0870 400 7234 📠 0870 400 7334
web: www.kewgreen.co.uk
Dir: *M4 junct 12 onto A4 towards Newbury. Hotel 3.5m on left, after petrol station*

This purpose-built hotel combines the benefits of a peaceful rural location with the accessibility afforded by good road links. Modern

continued on p466

R

READING, continued

comforts include air-conditioned bedrooms and rooms with easy access for less mobile guests. A feature of the hotel is its pretty courtyard garden, which can be seen from the restaurant.
ROOMS: 50 en suite (25 GF) ⊗ in 45 bedrooms s £56-£150; d £72-£160 (incl. bkfst) **LB** **FACILITIES:** STV Gym Fitness room Xmas **CONF:** Thtr 200 Class 70 Board 80 Del from £125 **SERVICES:** air con **PARKING:** 200 **NOTES:** ⊗ in restaurant Civ Wed 100

★★★70% Calcot Hotel
98 Bath Rd, Calcot RG31 7QN
☎ 0118 941 6423 📠 0118 945 1223
e-mail: enquiries@calcothotel.co.uk
web: www.calcothotel.co.uk
Dir: *M4 junct 12 onto A4 towards Reading, hotel in 0.5m on N side of A4*
This hotel is conveniently located in a residential area just off the motorway. Bedrooms are well equipped with good business facilities, such as data ports and good workspace. There are attractive public rooms and function suites and the informal restaurant offers enjoyable food in welcoming surroundings.
ROOMS: 78 en suite (2 fmly) ⊗ in 60 bedrooms s £48-£130; d £65-£140 **FACILITIES:** STV ♫ **CONF:** Thtr 120 Class 35 Board 35 Del from £141 **PARKING:** 130 **NOTES:** ✈ ⊗ in restaurant Closed 25-27 Dec Civ Wed 60

★★★66% Kirtons Farm Hotel
Pingewood RG30 3UN
☎ 0118 950 0885 📠 0118 939 1996
Dir: *A33 towards Basingstoke. At Three Mile Cross rdbt right signed Burghfield. After 300mtrs 2nd right, over M4, through lights, hotel on left*
Enjoying a secluded and rural setting and yet just a few minutes south of Reading, this modern hotel been built around a man-made lake which is occasionally used for water sports. Bedrooms are generally spacious with good facilities, and most have balconies overlooking the lake and wildlife. Public areas include Brasserie 209 and a well-equipped leisure centre.
ROOMS: 81 en suite (23 fmly) ⊗ in 57 bedrooms s £40-£180; d £40-£200 (incl. bkfst) **LB** **FACILITIES: Spa** STV Squash Snooker Sauna Solarium Gym Jacuzzi Watersports , Team building ch fac Xmas **CONF:** BC Thtr 110 Class 50 Board 45 Del from £130 **SERVICES:** Lift **PARKING:** 250 **NOTES:** ✈ ⊗ in restaurant Civ Wed 80

★★★66% Quality Hotel Reading
648-654 Oxford Rd RG30 1EH
☎ 0118 950 0541 📠 0118 956 7220
e-mail: info@qualityreading.co.uk
Dir: *M4 junct 11, follow A33 bypass towards town centre, then A329 towards Pangbourne, follow signs for Oxford Rd*
Close to the city centre this modern, purpose-built hotel is a popular choice with business guests. Bedrooms are generally spacious and offer a good range of facilities. Guests have a choice of eating lighter meals and snacks in the bar lounge or a more formal menu is offered in the spacious restaurant. The hotel benefits from conference facilities and ample parking.
ROOMS: 96 en suite (15 fmly) ⊗ in 39 bedrooms s £42-£105; d £42-£105 **LB** **FACILITIES:** STV **CONF:** BC Thtr 100 Class 50 Board 40 Del from £99 **SERVICES:** Lift **PARKING:** 60 **NOTES:** ✈ ⊗ in restaurant

★★68% The Mill House
Old Basingstoke Rd, Swallowfield RG7 1PY
☎ 0118 988 3124 📠 0118 988 5550
e-mail: info@themillhousehotel.co.uk
(For full entry see Swallowfield)

Premier Travel Inn Reading South
Grazeley Green Rd RG7 1LS
☎ 0870 9906454 📠 0870 9906455
web: www.premiertravelinn.com
Dir: *Exit M4 junct 11 signed A33 towards Basingstoke. At rdbt take exit towards Burghfield & Mortimer. 3rd right into Grazeley Green. Under rail bridge turn left. Hotel on left*
High quality, modern budget accommodation ideal for both families and business travellers. Spacious, en suite bedrooms feature bath and shower, satellite TV and many have telephones and modem points. The adjacent family restaurant features a wide and varied menu. For further details consult the Hotel Groups page.
ROOMS: 32 en suite s £53.95-£57.95; d £53.95-£57.95 **CONF:** Class 8 Board 8

Travelodge
387 Basingstoke Rd RG2 0JE
☎ 08700 850 950 📠 0118 975 1303
web: www.travelodge.co.uk
Dir: *M4 junct 11, onto A33 to Reading, right onto B3031, 1m on right*
Travelodge offers good quality, good value, modern accommodation. Ideal for families, the spacious, en suite bedrooms include remote-control TV, tea and coffee-making facilities and comfortable beds. Meals can be taken at the nearby family restaurant. For further details consult the Hotel Groups page.
ROOMS: 36 en suite s fr £26; d fr £26

Travelodge (Reading Central)
Oxford Rd RG1 7LT
☎ 08700 850 950 📠 0118 950 3257
web: www.travelodge.co.uk
Dir: *M4 junct 11, A33 towards Reading, follow signs for A329 (Oxford road)*
Travelodge offers good quality, good value, modern accommodation. Ideal for families, the spacious, en suite bedrooms include remote-control TV, tea and coffee-making facilities and comfortable beds. Meals can be taken at the nearby family restaurant. For further details consult the Hotel Groups page.
ROOMS: 80 en suite s fr £26; d fr £26

Travelodge Reading M4 (Eastbound)
Burghfield RG30 3UQ
☎ 08700 850 950 📠 0118 959 2045
web: www.travelodge.co.uk
Travelodge offers good quality, good value, modern accommodation. Ideal for families, the spacious, en suite bedrooms include remote-control TV, tea and coffee-making facilities and comfortable beds. Meals can be taken at the nearby family restaurant. For further details consult the Hotel Groups page.
ROOMS: 86 en suite s fr £26; d fr £26 **CONF:** Thtr 20 Class 20 Board 20

Travelodge Reading M4 (Westbound)
Burghfield RG30 3UQ
☎ 08700 850 950 📠 0118 958 2350
web: www.travelodge.co.uk
Dir: *M4 between junct 11 & 12 westbound*
Travelodge offers good quality, good value, modern accommodation. Ideal for families, the spacious, en suite bedrooms include remote-control TV, tea and coffee-making facilities and comfortable beds. Meals can be taken at the nearby family restaurant. For further details consult the Hotel Groups page.
ROOMS: 102 en suite s fr £26; d fr £26

GF indicates the number of bedrooms at ground level

REDDITCH, Worcestershire
Map 10 SP06

★★★★67%
The Abbey Hotel Golf & Country Club
Hither Green Ln, Dagnell End Rd, Bordesley
B98 9BE
☎ 01527 406600 📠 01527 406514
e-mail: info@theabbeyhotel.co.uk
Dir: *M42 junct 2 take A441 to Redditch. End of carriageway turn left (A441), Dagnell End Rd on left. Hotel 600yds on right*

With its convenient access to the motorway and its proximity to local attractions, this modern hotel is popular with both business and leisure travellers. Bedrooms are well equipped and attractively decorated; the executive corner rooms are especially spacious. Hotel facilities include an 18-hole golf course, pro shop, large indoor pool and extensive conference facilities.
ROOMS: 72 en suite (2 fmly) (30 GF) ⊗ in 30 bedrooms s £75-£125; d £95-£145 (incl. bkfst) **LB FACILITIES:** STV 18 Fishing Sauna Solarium Gym Putt green Jacuzzi Beauty Salon, Golf driving range Xmas **CONF:** Thtr 150 Class 60 Board 30 Del from £120 **SERVICES:** Lift **PARKING:** 170 **NOTES:** ⊗ in restaurant Civ Wed 100

★★★63% Quality Hotel Redditch
Pool Bank, Southcrest B97 4JS
☎ 01527 541511 📠 01527 402600
e-mail: enquiries@hotels-redditch.com
web: www.choicehotelseurope.com
Dir: *Follow Redditch signs onto A441. In Redditch follow signs for all other Redditch Districts until Southcrest signed, then follow hotel signs*
Originally a manor house, this hotel enjoys a peaceful location in extensive wooded grounds. Bedrooms vary in size and style, but all are well appointed and equipped. Both the restaurant and bar/conservatory overlook the attractive, sloping gardens, with views stretching across to the Vale of Evesham.
ROOMS: 73 en suite (20 fmly) (22 GF) ⊗ in 35 bedrooms s £50-£92; d £70-£102 **LB FACILITIES:** STV Xmas **CONF:** Thtr 100 Class 45 Board 50 Del from £99 **PARKING:** 100 **NOTES:** ⊗ in restaurant Civ Wed 70

★★64% *Montville*
101 Mount Pleasant, Southcrest B97 4JE
☎ 01527 544411 📠 01527 544341
e-mail: sales@montvillehotel.co.uk
web: www.montvillehotel.co.uk
Dir: *M42 junct 2 then A441 Alvechurch. Redditch Ringway onto Mount Pleasant, hotel on left*
Situated less than half a mile from the town centre, this is a small, friendly, privately owned hotel (now under new ownership), that is suitable for both business and leisure guests. Rooms vary in size and style, and all have the necessary comforts. A well-stocked bar, a homely lounge and an interesting dining room complete the picture.
ROOMS: 14 en suite (1 fmly) (1 GF) **PARKING:** 8 **NOTES:**

Campanile
Far Moor Ln, Winyates Green B98 0SD
☎ 01527 510710 📠 01527 517269
e-mail: redditch@envergure.co.uk
web: www.envergure.fr
Dir: *A435 towards Redditch, then A4023 to Redditch and Bromsgrove*

This modern building offers accommodation in smart, well-equipped bedrooms, all with en suite bathrooms. Refreshments may be taken at the informal Bistro. For further details consult the Hotel Groups page.
ROOMS: 46 annexe en suite **CONF:** Thtr 35 Class 18 Board 20

Premier Travel Inn Redditch
Birchfield Rd B97 6PX
☎ 0870 9906392 📠 0870 9906393
web: www.premiertravelinn.com
Dir: *Exit M5 junct 4, A38 towards Bromsgrove. At rdbt take A448 to Redditch. 1st exit for Webheath. At next rdbt take 3rd exit then 1st right*
High quality, modern budget accommodation ideal for both families and business travellers. Spacious, en suite bedrooms feature bath and shower, satellite TV and many have telephones and modem points. The adjacent family restaurant features a wide and varied menu. For further details consult the Hotel Groups page.
ROOMS: 33 en suite s £46.95-£49.95; d £46.95-£49.95 **CONF:** Thtr 150

REDHILL, Surrey
Map 06 TQ25

★★★★73% Nutfield Priory
Nutfield RH1 4EL
☎ 01737 824400 📠 01737 824410
e-mail: nutfieldpriory@handpicked.co.uk
web: www.handpicked.co.uk
Dir: *M25 junct 6, follow Redhill signs via Godstone on A25. Hotel 1m on left after Nutfield Village. Or M25 junct 8 follow A25 through Reigate, Redhill & Godstone. Hotel on right 1.5m after railway bridge*

This Victorian country house dates back to 1872 and is set in 40 acres of grounds with stunning views over the Surrey countryside.
continued on p468

R

REDHILL, continued

Bedrooms are individually decorated and equipped with an excellent range of facilities. Public areas include the impressive grand hall, Cloisters restaurant, the library, and a cosy lounge bar area.
ROOMS: 60 en suite (4 fmly) ⊗ in 24 bedrooms s £160-£300; d £185-£300 **LB** **FACILITIES: Spa** STV Squash Sauna Solarium Gym Jacuzzi Steam room Beauty therapy Aerobic & Step classes Xmas **CONF:** Thtr 80 Class 45 Board 40 Del from £205 **SERVICES:** Lift air con **PARKING:** 130 **NOTES:** ⊗ in restaurant Civ Wed 80

See advert on opposite page

Innkeeper's Lodge Redhill
2 Redstone Hill RH1 4BL
☎ 01737 768434 01737 770742
web: www.innkeeperslodge.com
Dir: *M25 junct 8, follow signs for Redhill (A25). At railway station, left towards Godstone, Inn on right*
A growing concept in the travel accommodation market. Smart rooms meet essential business requirements but also have home comforts. Dining options include all-day menus plus the added advantage of breakfast, which is included in the room price. For further details consult the Hotel Groups page.
ROOMS: 37 en suite s £45-£69.95; d £45-£69.95 **CONF:** Thtr 50 Class 20 Board 24

Premier Travel Inn Redhill
Brighton Rd, Salfords RH1 5BT
☎ 08701 977218 01737 778099
web: www.premiertravelinn.com
Dir: *on A23 , 2m south of Redhill and 3m north of Gatwick Airport*
High quality, modern budget accommodation ideal for both families and business travellers. Spacious, en suite bedrooms feature bath and shower, satellite TV and many have telephones and modem points. The adjacent family restaurant features a wide and varied menu. For further details consult the Hotel Groups page.
ROOMS: 48 en suite s £47.95-£50.95; d £47.95-£50.95 **CONF:** Thtr 35

REDRUTH, Cornwall & Isles of Scilly — Map 02 SW64

R

★★★70% Penventon Park
TR15 1TE
☎ 01209 203000 01209 203001
e-mail: hello@penventon.com
web: www.penventon.com
Dir: *off A30 at Redruth. Follow signs for Redruth West, hotel 1m S*

Set in attractive parkland, this Georgian mansion is ideal for either the business or leisure guest. Bedrooms include 20 Garden Suites. Cuisine offers a wide choice and specialises in Italian, French, British and Cornish dishes. Leisure facilities include a fitness suite and health spa as well as function rooms and bars.
ROOMS: 68 en suite (3 fmly) (25 GF) ⊗ in 6 bedrooms s £35-£84; d £68-£116 (incl. bkfst) **LB** **FACILITIES: Spa** supervised Sauna Solarium Gym Jacuzzi Leisure spa Masseuse Steam bath Pool table, beautician ♫ Xmas **CONF:** Thtr 200 Class 100 Board 60 Del from £86 **PARKING:** 100 **NOTES:** ⊗ in restaurant Civ Wed 150

★★66% Crossroads Lodge
Scorrier TR16 5BP
☎ 01209 820551 01209 820392
e-mail: crossroads@hotelstruro.com
web: www.hotelstruro.com/crossroads
Dir: *turn off A30 onto A3047 towards Scorrier*
Situated on an historic stanary site and conveniently located just off the A30, the Crossroads Lodge has a smart appearance with attractive flower baskets. Bedrooms are soundly furnished and include executive and family rooms. Public areas include an attractive dining room, a quiet lounge and a lively bar. Conference, banqueting and business facilities are also available.
ROOMS: 36 en suite (2 fmly) (8 GF) ⊗ in 8 bedrooms s £48-£59; d £66-£74 (incl. bkfst) **LB** **FACILITIES:** STV **CONF:** BC Thtr 150 Class 80 Board 60 **SERVICES:** Lift **PARKING:** 140 **NOTES:** ⊗ in restaurant

REDWORTH, Co Durham — Map 19 NZ22

★★★★70% *Redworth Hall Hotel*
DL5 6NL
☎ 01388 770600 01388 770654
e-mail: redworthhall@paramount-hotels.co.uk
web: www.paramount-hotels.co.uk
Dir: *from A1(M) junct 58 take A68 signed 'Corbridge'. Follow hotel signs*

This imposing Georgian building includes a health club with state-of-the-art equipment and impressive conference facilities making this a popular destination for business travellers. There are several spacious lounges and two restaurants: the relaxed Conservatory and the intimate 1744 fine-dining option.
ROOMS: 100 en suite (8 fmly) ⊗ in 45 bedrooms **FACILITIES:** STV Sauna Solarium Gym Jacuzzi Bodysense Health & Beauty Club ♫ **CONF:** Thtr 300 Class 150 Board 100 **SERVICES:** Lift **PARKING:** 300 **NOTES:** Civ Wed

REIGATE, Surrey — Map 06 TQ25

★★★67% Reigate Manor Hotel
Reigate Hill RH2 9PF
☎ 01737 240125 01737 223883
e-mail: hotel@reigatemanor.co.uk
web: www.reigatemanor.co.uk
Dir: *on A217, 1m S of junct 8 on M25*
On the slopes of Reigate Hill, the hotel is ideally located for access to the town and for motorway links. A range of public rooms is

continued

provided along with a variety of function rooms. Bedrooms are either traditional in style in the old house or of contemporary design in the wing.
ROOMS: 50 en suite (1 fmly) ⊗ in all bedrooms s £75-£105; d £85-£115 (incl. bkfst) **FACILITIES:** STV **CONF:** Thtr 200 Class 80 Board 50 Del from £120 **PARKING:** 130 **NOTES:** ⊗ in restaurant Civ Wed 200

RENISHAW, Derbyshire — Map 16 SK47

★★★65% Sitwell Arms
Station Rd S21 3WF
☎ 01246 435226 & 01246 437327 📠 01246 433915
e-mail: sitwellarms@renishaw79.fsnet.co.uk
Dir: *on A6135 to Sheffield, W of M1 junct 30*

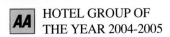

This stone-built hotel, parts of which date back to the 18th century, is conveniently situated close to the M1. The hotel has now opened a new leisure facility, and offers good value

continued

accommodation. Bedrooms are of a comfortable size and include modern facilities. There are extensive bars and a restaurant with a wide range of meals and snacks.
ROOMS: 29 en suite (8 fmly) (9 GF) ⊗ in 10 bedrooms s £38-£70; d £55-£80 (incl. bkfst) **LB** **FACILITIES:** STV Gym Fitness studio, Hair & Beauty Salon Xmas **CONF:** BC Thtr 160 Class 60 Board 60 **SERVICES:** Lift **PARKING:** 150 **NOTES:** ⊗ in restaurant Civ Wed 150

See advert under SHEFFIELD

RETFORD (EAST), Nottinghamshire — Map 17 SK78

★★★64% The West Retford Hotel
24 North Rd DN22 7XG
☎ 0870 609 6162 01777 706333 📠 01777 709951
web: www.corushotels.com/westretford
Dir: *From A1 take A620 to Ranby/Retford. Left at rdbt into North Rd (A638). Hotel on right*
Set in attractive grounds close to the town centre, this 18th-century manor house offers a good range of well-equipped meeting facilities. The spacious, well laid out bedrooms and suites are located in separate buildings; the Garden Cottage rooms are particularly pleasing.
ROOMS: 62 annexe en suite (37 fmly) (34 GF) ⊗ in 36 bedrooms s £65-£110; d £65-£110 **LB** **FACILITIES:** STV **CONF:** Thtr 150 Class 40 Board 43 Del from £90 **PARKING:** 100 **NOTES:** ⊗ in restaurant Civ Wed 120

○ Hotel due to open in late 2005 or 2006
U Star rating not confirmed

RICHMOND, North Yorkshire Map 19 NZ10

★★★66% King's Head
Market Place DL10 4HS
☎ 01748 850220 📠 01748 850635
e-mail: res@kingsheadrichmond.co.uk
web: www.kingsheadrichmond.com
Dir: *leave A1 or A66 at Scotch Corner & take A6108 to Richmond. Follow signs to town centre*

Centrally located in the historic market square, this hotel is a converted coaching inn. Bedrooms are comfortably furnished. Guests can relax in the elegant lounge, furnished with deep sofas. Afternoon tea is served in the lounge/bar along with good selection of light meals, and the first-floor restaurant offers a varied choice of more formal but relaxed dining together with views over the square.
ROOMS: 26 en suite 4 annexe en suite s £65-£85; d £95-£132 (incl. bkfst) **LB** **FACILITIES:** Riding Walking, Cycling Xmas **CONF:** BC Thtr 250 Class 150 Board 100 Del from £90 **PARKING:** 25 **NOTES:** ⊘ in restaurant Civ Wed 150

★★69% Frenchgate
59-61 Frenchgate DL10 7AE
☎ 01748 822087 📠 01748 823596
e-mail: info@frenchgatehotel.com
web: www.frenchgatehotel.com
Dir: *A1 into Richmond, on A6108 past War Memorial on left at traffic lights. 1st left into Lile Close and into car park*
A friendly welcome is offered at this elegant Georgian townhouse that sits on a quiet cobbled street. Bedrooms are comfortably equipped. Public areas offer an interesting blend of traditional and modern and include an upstairs lounge with a feature fireplace crafted by the famous 'Mouseman'. Carefully cooked contemporary dishes are served in the stylish restaurant that also features local artwork.
ROOMS: 8 en suite (1 fmly) (1 GF) ⊘ in all bedrooms s £58-£78; d £88-£108 (incl. bkfst) **LB** **FACILITIES:** Xmas **CONF:** Thtr 20 Class 20 Board 20 **PARKING:** 12 **NOTES:** ✗ ⊘ in restaurant

See advert on opposite page

RICHMOND (UPON THAMES), Greater London
See LONDON SECTION plan 1 C2

★★★★69% The Richmond Gate Hotel
Richmond Hill TW10 6RP
☎ 020 8940 0061 📠 020 8332 0354
e-mail: richmondgate@foliohotels.co.uk
web: www.foliohotels.co.uk/richmondgate
Dir: *from Richmond to top of Richmond Hill. Hotel on left opposite Star & Garter home at Richmond Gate exit*
A stylish Georgian hotel, sitting at the top of Richmond Hill and opposite the gates to Richmond Park. Bedrooms are equipped to a very high standard and include luxury doubles and spacious suites. Dinner in the Park Restaurant features bold, contemporary cooking and is the highlight of any visit.
ROOMS: 68 en suite ⊘ in 35 bedrooms s £140-£220; d £150-£230 (incl. bkfst) **LB** **FACILITIES:** **Spa** STV Sauna Solarium Gym Jacuzzi Health & beauty suite Steam room **CONF:** Thtr 50 Class 20 Board 30 Del from £220 **PARKING:** 50 **NOTES:** ✗ ⊘ in restaurant Civ Wed 70

★★★★66% The Petersham
Nightingale Ln TW10 6UZ
☎ 020 8940 7471 📠 020 8939 1098
e-mail: enq@petershamhotel.co.uk
web: www.petershamhotel.co.uk
Dir: *From Richmond Bridge rdbt (A316) follow Ham & Petersham signs. Hotel in Nightingale Lane (small turning on left off Petersham Rd)*

Managed by the same family for over 25 years, this attractive hotel is sited on a hill overlooking water meadows and a sweep of the River Thames. Bedrooms and suites are comfortably furnished, whilst public areas combine elegance and some fine architectural features. High quality produce is used to provide enjoyable meals in the restaurant which looks out over the river.
ROOMS: 61 en suite (4 fmly) (3 GF) s fr £110; d fr £170 (incl. bkfst) **LB** **FACILITIES:** STV Xmas **CONF:** BC Thtr 35 Board 25 Del from £235 **SERVICES:** Lift **PARKING:** 50 **NOTES:** ✗ Civ Wed 40

★★★69% Richmond Hill
Richmond Hill TW10 6RW
☎ 020 8940 2247 📠 020 8940 5424
e-mail: res.richmondhill@foliohotels.co.uk
web: www.foliohotels.com
Dir: *top of Richmond Hill on B321*
This attractive Georgian Manor built on Richmond Hill enjoys elevated views of the Thames. The town and the park are within easy walking distance. Bedrooms vary in size and style, all are comfortable and of modern design. The stylish, well-designed health club with large pool is shared with sister hotel the Richmond Gate.
ROOMS: 138 en suite (2 fmly) ⊘ in 48 bedrooms s £90-£145; d £120-£145 **LB** **FACILITIES:** **Spa** STV supervised Sauna Solarium Gym Jacuzzi Steam room Health & beauty suite **CONF:** Thtr 180 Class 100 Board 50 Del from £145 **SERVICES:** Lift **PARKING:** 150 **NOTES:** Civ Wed 150

★★★63% Bingham Hotel
61-63 Petersham Rd TW10 6UT
☎ 020 8940 0902 📠 020 8948 8737
e-mail: reservations@binghamhotel.co.uk
Dir: *on A307*
This Georgian building overlooks The Thames and is within walking distance of the town centre. Bedrooms vary in size and style and comfortable public rooms enjoy views of the pretty

continued

garden and river. Diners can choose from a selection of meals from light snacks to three-course dinners.

ROOMS: 23 en suite (2 fmly) s £70-£100; d £100-£160 (incl. bkfst) **LB**
FACILITIES: Gym Xmas **CONF:** Thtr 60 Class 40 Board 25 Del £195
PARKING: 12 **NOTES:** ✺ Civ Wed 40

RICKMANSWORTH, Hertfordshire Map 06 TQ09

★★★★★74% ◉◉◉ *The Grove*
Chandler's Cross WD3 4TG
☎ 01923 807807 📠 01923 221008
e-mail: info@thegrove.co.uk
web: www.thegrove.co.uk
Dir: From M25 follow A411 signs towards Watford. Hotel entrance on right.
From M1 follow brown hotel signs

Set in 300 acres of rolling grounds, much of which is golf course, the hotel combines its historic character with cutting edge modern design. The spacious bedrooms feature the latest in temperature control, flat-screen TV and lighting technology, and many have balconies. Suites in the original mansion are particularly stunning. Championship golf, a world-class spa and three dining options are just a few of the treasures to sample here. A crèche is a new addition.
ROOMS: 227 en suite (31 fmly) (35 GF) ⊗ in 144 bedrooms
FACILITIES: Spa STV ⊡ ⌔ 18 ✑ Fishing Sauna Solarium Gym ♨
Putt green Jacuzzi 12 Treatment rooms, cycling, kids club ♬ ch fac
CONF: BC Thtr 500 Class 300 Board 80 **SERVICES:** Lift air con
PARKING: 400 **NOTES:** ✺ Civ Wed

RINGWOOD, Hampshire Map 05 SU10

★★★67%♨ Tyrrells Ford Country House
Avon BH23 7BH
☎ 01425 672646 📠 01425 672262
e-mail: tyrrellsford@aol.com
web: www.tyrrellsfordhotel.com
Dir: off A31 to Ringwood. Follow B3347 and hotel 3m S on left at Avon
Set in the New Forest, this delightful family-run hotel has much to
continued

The Frenchgate Restaurant & Hotel is the result of the remodelling of a delightful Georgian gentleman's residence that dates back to the mid 18th century. We are located in the heart of old Frenchgate, one of Richmond's quietest and most beautiful cobbled streets, a short walk from the famous market square, Norman castle, Georgian theatre and many delights of Richmond.

Stylish dining, private parties, gardens & en suite rooms with some of the finest food, service and hospitality around. Fully licensed.

Dinner 7.00pm - 9.30pm Lunch 12.00pm - 2.30pm
Teas, coffees - All day

59-61 FRENCHGATE • RICHMOND • N. YORKSHIRE • DL10 7AE
T +44(0)1748 822087 F +44(0)1748 823596
E info@frenchgatehotel.com

offer. Most bedrooms have views over the open country. Diners may eat in the formal restaurant, or sample the wide range of bar meals, all prepared using fresh local produce. The Gallery lounge offers guests a peaceful area in which to relax.
ROOMS: 16 en suite s £70-£85; d £150-£180 (incl. bkfst) **LB**
FACILITIES: arrangement with local David Lloyd Fitness Club. Xmas
CONF: Thtr 40 Class 20 Board 20 **PARKING:** 100 **NOTES:** ✺ ⊗ in
restaurant Civ Wed 60

★★64% Candlesticks Inn
136 Christchurch Rd BH24 3AP
☎ 01425 472587 📠 01425 471600
e-mail: info@hotelnewforest.co.uk
web: www.hotelnewforest.co.uk
Dir: from M27/A31, take B3347 to Christchurch. Hotel on right 0.5m from flyover
This attractive, thatched 15th-century inn is close to the town centre. The cottage-style bedrooms are contained in a modern adjacent lodge and include ground floor rooms together with a bedroom equipped for less able guests. Snacks can be taken in a bright conservatory bar lounge and there is also an atmospheric restaurant for more formal meals.
ROOMS: 8 en suite (1 fmly) (4 GF) s £49-£78; d £68-£78 (incl. bkfst)
LB PARKING: 45 **NOTES:** ✺ No children 2yrs Closed 23 Dec-9 Jan

⌂ Travelodge
St Leonards BH24 2NR
☎ 08700 850 950 📠 01425 475941
web: www.travelodge.co.uk
Dir: Off A31 eastbound
Travelodge offers good quality, good value, modern accommodation. Ideal for families, the spacious, en suite
continued on p472

RINGWOOD, continued

bedrooms include remote-control TV, tea and coffee-making facilities and comfortable beds. Meals can be taken at the nearby family restaurant. For further details consult the Hotel Groups page.
ROOMS: s fr £26; d fr £26

RIPLEY, Derbyshire — Map 16 SK35

★★64% Moss Cottage
Nottingham Rd DE5 3JT
☎ 01773 742555 🖷 01773 741063
e-mail: mosshotel@aol.com
web: www.mosscottage.net
Dir: *M1 junct 26, A610 to Ripley. Hotel approx 4m from M1*

This busy roadside inn is popular for its value-for-money food and now has a modern bedroom block to the rear. Bedrooms are well equipped and spacious and staff are friendly.
ROOMS: 14 en suite (4 fmly) (6 GF) ⊗ in 6 bedrooms s £46.95; d £46.95 **FACILITIES:** cycling, golf, outdoor pursuits. **CONF:** BC Thtr 60 Class 40 Board 30 **PARKING:** 60 **NOTES:** ✗ ⊗ in restaurant

RIPON, North Yorkshire — Map 19 SE37

★★★69% Ripon Spa
Park St HG4 2BU
☎ 01765 602172 🖷 01765 690770
e-mail: spahotel@bronco.co.uk
web: www.riponspa.com
Dir: *From A61 follow signs for B6265 towards Fountains Abbey. Hotel on left after hospital*

This privately owned hotel is set in extensive and attractive gardens just a short walk from the city centre. Newly refurbished bedrooms are well equipped to meet the needs of leisure and business travellers alike, while the comfortable lounges are complemented by the convivial atmosphere of the Turf bar.
ROOMS: 40 en suite (5 fmly) (4 GF) ⊗ in 8 bedrooms s £95-£120; d £105-£130 (incl. bkfst) **LB** **FACILITIES:** STV ♫ Free use of local gym-approx 1m away Xmas **CONF:** Thtr 150 Class 35 Board 40 Del from £110 **SERVICES:** Lift **PARKING:** 60 **NOTES:** ⊗ in restaurant Civ Wed 150

See advert under HARROGATE

★★★68% ⊛ The Old Deanery
Minster Rd HG4 1QS
☎ 01765 600003 🖷 01765 600027
e-mail: reception@theolddeanery.co.uk
web: www.theolddeanery.co.uk
Dir: *From A168 take B6265 to Ripon for 5m. Straight over rdbt, over bridge and right at rdbt, hotel on left.*
In the shadow of the Cathedral, and close to the Market Square, this sensitive restoration of one of the town's oldest buildings now offers modern comfortable facilities and carefully prepared cuisine. Many original features are still evident among the minimalist decor schemes and staff are helpful and friendly.
ROOMS: 11 en suite ⊗ in all bedrooms s £85-£100; d £100-£125 (incl. bkfst) **FACILITIES: Spa** STV ⚲ Fishing Squash Riding Snooker Sauna Solarium Gym ♫ Jacuzzi **CONF:** BC Thtr 40 Class 12 Board 22 Del from £130 **PARKING:** 20 **NOTES:** ⊗ in restaurant RS 25 Dec Civ Wed 50

★★63% *Unicorn*
Market Place HG4 1BP
☎ 01765 602202 🖷 01765 690734
e-mail: info@unicorn-hotel.co.uk
web: www.unicorn-hotel.co.uk
Dir: *on SE corner of Market Place, 4m from A1 on A61*
Centrally located in the ancient market place, this traditional inn dates back 500 years to when it was a coaching house. The busy pub and attractive restaurant feature a wide selection of good-value dishes. Bedrooms are comfortable of mixed styles and all offer the expected amenities.
ROOMS: 33 en suite (4 fmly) **FACILITIES:** ♫ **CONF:** Thtr 60 Class 10 Board 26 **PARKING:** 20 **NOTES:** ⊗ in restaurant Closed 24-25 Dec

ROCHDALE, Greater Manchester — Map 16 SD81

★★★★62% Norton Grange
Manchester Rd, Castleton OL11 2XZ
☎ 01706 630788 🖷 01706 649313
e-mail: nortongrange@macdonald-hotels.co.uk
web: www.macdonald-hotels.co.uk
Dir: *M62 junct 20, follow signs for A664 Castleton. Right at next 2 rbts for hotel 0.5m on left*

Standing in nine acres of grounds and mature gardens, this Victorian house provides comfort in elegant surroundings. The

continued

R

well-equipped bedrooms provide a host of extras for both the business and leisure guest. Public areas include the Pickwick bistro and bar and a smart restaurant, both offering a good choice of dishes.
ROOMS: 51 en suite (14 fmly) (8 GF) ⊗ in 45 bedrooms s £70-£95; d £80-£115 (incl. bkfst) **LB** **FACILITIES:** STV Complimentary use of leisure centre Xmas **CONF:** Thtr 220 Class 120 Board 70 Del from £105 **SERVICES:** Lift **PARKING:** 150 **NOTES:** ⊗ in restaurant Civ Wed 150

Premier Travel Inn Rochdale

Newhey Rd, Milnrow OL16 4JF
☎ 08701 977219 📠 01706 299074
web: www.premiertravelinn.com
Dir: *M62 junct 21 at rdbt, right towards Shaw, under motorway bridge & take 1st left*
High quality, modern budget accommodation ideal for both families and business travellers. Spacious, en suite bedrooms feature bath and shower, satellite TV and many have telephones and modem points. The adjacent family restaurant features a wide and varied menu. For further details consult the Hotel Groups page.
ROOMS: 40 en suite s £46.95-£49.95; d £46.95-£49.95 **CONF:** Thtr 25 Board 12

ROMALDKIRK, Co Durham — Map 19 NY92

Top Hotel

★★ ◎◎ Rose & Crown

DL12 9EB
☎ 01833 650213 📠 01833 650828
e-mail: hotel@rose-and-crown.co.uk
web: www.rose-and-crown.co.uk
Dir: *6m NW from Barnard Castle on B6277*
This charming country inn is located in the heart of the village, overlooking fine fell scenery. Attractively furnished bedrooms, including suites, are split between the main house and the rear courtyard. There is a cosy bar, warmed by log fires, and a welcoming restaurant. Good local produce features extensively on the menu. Service is both friendly and attentive.
ROOMS: 7 en suite 5 annexe en suite (1 fmly) ⊗ in all bedrooms s £75-£90; d £126-£140 (incl. bkfst) **LB** **FACILITIES:** STV **PARKING:** 20 **NOTES:** ⊗ in restaurant Closed 24-26 Dec

ROMFORD, Greater London — Map 06 TQ58

Premier Travel Inn Romford Central

Mercury Gardens RM1 3EN
☎ 08701 977220 📠 01708 760456
web: www.premiertravelinn.com
Dir: *M25 junct 28, take A12 to Gallows Corner. A118 to next rbt, turn left*
High quality, modern budget accommodation ideal for both families and business travellers. Spacious, en suite bedrooms feature bath and shower, satellite TV and many have telephones and modem points. The adjacent family restaurant features a wide and varied menu. For further details consult the Hotel Groups page.
ROOMS: 64 en suite s £57.95-£59.95; d £57.95-£59.95

Premier Travel Inn Romford West

Whalebone Ln North, Chadwell Heath RM6 6QU
☎ 0870 9906450 📠 0870 9906451
web: www.premiertravelinn.com
Dir: *6m from M25 junct 28 on A12 at junct with A1112*
High quality, modern budget accommodation ideal for both families and business travellers. Spacious, en suite bedrooms feature bath and shower, satellite TV and many have telephones and modem points. The adjacent family restaurant features a wide and varied menu. For further details consult the Hotel Groups page.
ROOMS: 40 en suite s £57.95-£59.95; d £57.95-£59.95 **CONF:** Thtr 50

ROMSEY, Hampshire — Map 05 SU32

★★★68% Corus hotel Romsey

Winchester Rd, Ampfield SO51 9ZF
☎ 0870 609 6155 📠 023 8025 1359
e-mail: romsey@corushotels.com
web: www.corushotels.com
Dir: *M3 junct 12 follow Chandler's Ford signs. 2nd exit at 3rd rdbt and follow signs for Ampfield, over x-rds and hotel on left after 1m*

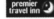

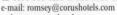

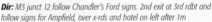

This distinctive thatched hotel retains many of its original features. A convenient location for access to Winchester and the M3, modern accommodation and spacious public areas are offered. The pub and restaurant offers an interesting range of dishes to suit a variety of tastes.
ROOMS: 54 en suite (29 GF) ⊗ in 40 bedrooms s £45-£103.75; d £90-£115.50 (incl. bkfst) **LB** **FACILITIES:** STV Pool table Xmas **CONF:** Thtr 120 Class 40 Board 40 Del from £99 **SERVICES:** Lift **PARKING:** 150 **NOTES:** ⊗ in restaurant Civ Wed 100

R

ROMSEY, continued

⌂ Premier Travel Inn Southampton West

Romsey Rd, Ower SO51 6ZJ
☎ 0870 9906350 🖷 0870 9906351
web: www.premiertravelinn.com
Dir: *Just off M27 junct 2. Take A36 towards Salisbury. Follow brown tourist signs 'Vine Inn'*
High quality, modern budget accommodation ideal for both families and business travellers. Spacious, en suite bedrooms feature bath and shower, satellite TV and many have telephones and modem points. The adjacent family restaurant features a wide and varied menu. For further details consult the Hotel Groups page.
ROOMS: 67 en suite s £47.95-£50.95; d £47.95-£50.95 **CONF:** Thtr 150 Class 80 Board 60

ROSEDALE ABBEY, North Yorkshire — Map 19 SE79

★★★69% Blacksmith's Country Inn

Hartoft End YO18 8EN
☎ 01751 417331 🖷 01751 417167
e-mail: office@blacksmithsinn.co.uk
web: www.blacksmithsinn-rosedale.co.uk
Dir: *off A170 in village of Wrelton, N to Hartoft*

Set amongst the wooded valleys and hillsides of the Yorkshire Moors, this charming hotel offers a choice of popular bars and intimate, cosy lounges, and retains the friendly atmosphere of a country inn. Food is available either in the bars or the spacious restaurant, while bedrooms vary in size all equipped to comfortable modern standards.
ROOMS: 19 en suite (2 fmly) (4 GF) ⊗ in all bedrooms s £35-£60; d £80-£110 (incl. bkfst) **LB** **FACILITIES:** Fishing Xmas **PARKING:** 100 **NOTES:** ⊗ in restaurant RS Oct-Mar

★★72% Milburn Arms

YO18 8RA
☎ 01751 417312 🖷 01751 417541
e-mail: info@milburnarms.co.uk

This attractive inn dates back to the 16th century and enjoys an idyllic, peaceful location in this scenic village. Bedrooms, some of which are located in an adjacent stone block, are spacious, comfortable and smartly appointed. Guests can enjoy carefully prepared food either in the traditional bar or in the elegant restaurant.
ROOMS: 5 en suite 8 annexe en suite (3 fmly) (4 GF) ⊗ in all bedrooms s £48-£60; d fr £80 (incl. bkfst) **LB** **FACILITIES:** Xmas **CONF:** Thtr 50 Class 20 Board 20 **PARKING:** 10 **NOTES:** ⊗ in restaurant Civ Wed 100

ROSSINGTON, South Yorkshire — Map 16 SK69

★★★★70% ⚘ Mount Pleasant

Great North Rd DN11 0HW
☎ 01302 868696 & 868219 🖷 01302 865130
e-mail: reception@mountpleasant.co.uk
web: www.bw-mountpleasant.co.uk
Dir: *on A638 Great North Rd between Bawtry and Doncaster*
This charming 18th-century house stands in 100 acres of wooded parkland. The spacious bedrooms have been thoughtfully equipped and pleasantly furnished; the premier bedrooms being particularly comfortable. Public rooms include an elegant restaurant and a very comfortable bar lounge. The hotel has extensive conference facilities and a licence for civil weddings.
ROOMS: 57 en suite (12 fmly) (28 GF) ⊗ in 56 bedrooms s £48-£109; d £96-£135 (incl. bkfst) **LB** **FACILITIES:** STV Gym Beauty Therapy **CONF:** BC Thtr 200 Class 70 Board 70 Del £145 **PARKING:** 100 **NOTES:** ✗ ⊗ in restaurant Closed 25-Dec RS 24-Dec Civ Wed 150

ROSS-ON-WYE, Herefordshire — Map 10 SO52
See also Goodrich

★★★74% Pengethley Manor

Pengethley Park HR9 6LL
☎ 01989 730211 🖷 01989 730238
e-mail: reservations@pengethleymanor.co.uk
web: www.pengethleymanor.co.uk
Dir: *4m N on A49 Hereford road, from Ross-on-Wye*

This fine Georgian mansion is set in extensive grounds with two vineyards and glorious views. The accommodation is tastefully appointed and there is a wide variety of bedroom styles, all similarly well equipped. The elegant public rooms are furnished in a style sympathetic to the character of the house.
ROOMS: 11 en suite 14 annexe en suite (3 fmly) (4 GF) s £75-£115; d £120-£160 (incl. bkfst) **LB** **FACILITIES:** ⛳ 9 Golf improvement course, walks accessible from hotel Xmas **CONF:** Thtr 70 Class 25 Board 28 Del from £105 **PARKING:** 70 **NOTES:** ⊗ in restaurant Civ Wed 90

> Packed in a hurry? Ironing facilities should be available at all star levels, either in the rooms or on request

★★★72% Chase

Gloucester Rd HR9 5LH

☎ 01989 763161 & 760644 01989 768330

e-mail: res@chasehotel.co.uk

web: www.chasehotel.co.uk

Dir: *M50 junct 4, 1st left exit towards rdbt, left at rdbt towards A40. Right at 2nd rdbt towards Ross-on-Wye town centre, hotel 0.5m on left*

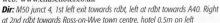

This attractive Georgian mansion sits in its own landscaped grounds and is only a short walk from the town centre. Bedrooms, including two four-poster rooms, vary in size and character, with the majority having been refurbished to impressive standards. There is also a light and spacious bar and the newly refurbished Harry's restaurant offering an excellent selection of enjoyable dishes.

ROOMS: 36 en suite (1 fmly) ⊗ in 15 bedrooms s £79-£99; d £95-£135 (incl. bkfst) **LB** **FACILITIES:** STV Xmas **CONF:** Thtr 300 Class 100 Board 80 Del £135 **PARKING:** 150 **NOTES:** ⊗ in restaurant Closed 26-30 Dec Civ Wed 300

★★★68% Pencraig Court

Pencraig HR9 6HR

☎ 01989 770306 01989 770040

e-mail: info@pencraig-court.co.uk

web: www.pencraig-court.co.uk

Dir: *off A40, into Pencraig 4m S of Ross-on-Wye*

Impressive views of the River Wye to Ross-on-Wye beyond, set the scene for a relaxing stay at this former Georgian mansion. The proprietors are on hand to ensure personal attention and service, while the bedrooms evoke a traditional feel and include a room with a four-poster bed. The country-house ambience is carried through in the choice of lounges and the elegant restaurant.

ROOMS: 11 en suite (1 fmly) ⊗ in 6 bedrooms s £50-£54; d £84-£92 (incl. bkfst) **LB** **FACILITIES:** Fishing **PARKING:** 20 **NOTES:** ⊗ in restaurant

★★★66% The Royal

Palace Pound HR9 5HZ

OLD ENGLISH INNS

☎ 01989 565105 01989 768058

e-mail: 6504@greeneking.co.uk

web: www.oldenglish.co.uk

Dir: *at end of M50 take A40 'Monmouth'. At 3rd rdbt, left to Ross, over bridge and take road signed 'The Royal Hotel' after left bend*

Close to the town centre, this imposing hotel enjoys panoramic views from its prominent hilltop position. Reputedly visited by Charles Dickens in 1867, the establishment has been sympathetically furnished to combine the ambience of a bygone era with the comforts of today. In addition to the lounge and elegant restaurant, there are function rooms and an attractive garden.

ROOMS: 42 en suite (1 fmly) ⊗ in all bedrooms s £75-£85; d £100-£140 (incl. bkfst) **LB** **FACILITIES:** Xmas **CONF:** Thtr 85 Class 20 Board 28 Del from £100 **PARKING:** 44 **NOTES:** ⊗ in restaurant Civ Wed 75

★★78% Wilton Court Hotel

Wilton Ln HR9 6AQ

☎ 01989 562569 01989 768460

e-mail: info@wiltoncourthotel.com

web: www.wiltoncourthotel.com

Dir: *M50 junct 4 onto A40 towards Monmouth at 3rd rdbt turn left signed Ross then take 1st right, hotel on right facing river*

Dating back to the 16th century, this hotel has great charm and a wealth of character. Standing on the banks of the River Wye and just a short walk from the town centre, there is a genuinely relaxed, friendly and unhurried atmosphere here. Bedrooms are tastefully furnished and well equipped, while public areas include a comfortable lounge, traditional bar and pleasant restaurant with a conservatory extension overlooking the garden.

ROOMS: 10 en suite (1 fmly) ⊗ in all bedrooms s £65-£105; d £85-£125 (incl. bkfst) **LB** **FACILITIES:** Fishing Boule Xmas **CONF:** Thtr 40 Class 25 Board 25 **PARKING:** 24 **NOTES:** ⊗ in restaurant

★★73% Glewstone Court

Glewstone HR9 6AW

☎ 01989 770367 01989 770282

e-mail: glewstone@aol.com

Dir: *from Ross Market Place take A40/A49 Monmouth/Hereford, over Wilton Bridge to rdbt, turn left onto A40 to Monmouth, after 1m turn right for Glewstone*

This charming hotel enjoys an elevated position with views over Ross-on-Wye, and is set in well-tended gardens. Informal service is delivered with great enthusiasm by Bill Reeve-Tucker, whilst the kitchen is the domain of Christine Reeve-Tucker who offers an extensive menu of well executed dishes. Bedrooms come in a variety of sizes and are tastefully furnished and well equipped.

ROOMS: 8 en suite (2 fmly) s £68-£87; d £104-£120 (incl. bkfst) **LB** **FACILITIES:** **CONF:** Thtr 18 Board 12 **PARKING:** 25 **NOTES:** ⊗ in restaurant Closed 25-27 Dec

ROSS-ON-WYE, continued

★★71% Castle Lodge Hotel
Wilton HR9 6AD
☎ 01989 562234 📠 01989 768322
e-mail: info@castlelodge.co.uk
Dir: *on rdbt at junct of A40/A49, 0.5m from centre of Ross-on-Wye*
This friendly hotel dates back to the 16th century and offers a convenient base on the outskirts of the town. Bedrooms are well equipped and comfortably furnished, while diners can choose between a good selection of bar meals and a varied restaurant menu, which features a wide range of fresh seafood.
ROOMS: 10 en suite (3 fmly) s £46; d £53 **LB** **CONF:** Thtr 100 Class 80 Board 60 **PARKING:** 40

★★67% *Orles Barn*
THE CIRCLE Selected Individual Hotels GREAT BRITAIN
Wilton HR9 6AE
☎ 01989 562155 📠 01989 768470
e-mail: orles.barn@clara.net
web: www.orles.barn.clara.net
Dir: *off junct A40/A49*
This privately owned and personally run hotel stands in extensive gardens. All of the bedrooms are well maintained and thoughtfully equipped. The owners' South African heritage is reflected in the restaurant menu. Extra facilities include an outdoor heated swimming pool.
ROOMS: 8 en suite (1 fmly) ⊗ in 2 bedrooms **FACILITIES:** Fishing Golf chipping parctice facility **CONF:** Board 16 **PARKING:** 20 **NOTES:** ⊗ in restaurant RS Nov-Jan

★★66% Chasedale
Walford Rd HR9 5PQ
☎ 01989 562423 & 01989 565801 📠 01989 567900
e-mail: chasedale@supanet.com
web: www.chasedale.co.uk
Dir: *from Ross-on-Wye town centre, S on B4234, hotel 0.5m on left*
This large, mid-Victorian property is situated on the south-west outskirts of the town. Privately owned and personally run, it provides spacious, well-proportioned public areas and extensive grounds. The accommodation is well equipped and includes ground floor and family rooms, whilst the restaurant offers a wide selection of wholesome food.
ROOMS: 10 en suite (2 fmly) (1 GF) ⊗ in 1 bedroom s £35-£38; d £70-£76 (incl. bkfst) **LB** **FACILITIES:** Xmas **CONF:** Thtr 40 Class 30 Board 25 **PARKING:** 14 **NOTES:** ⊗ in restaurant

★★65% King's Head
8 High St HR9 5HL
☎ 01989 763174 📠 01989 769578
e-mail: enquiries@kingshead.co.uk
Dir: *in town centre*

The King's Head, now under new ownership, dates back to the 14th century and has a wealth of charm and character. Bedrooms are well equipped and include both four-poster and family rooms. The restaurant doubles as a coffee shop during the day and is a popular venue with locals. There is also a very pleasant bar and comfortable lounge.
ROOMS: 15 en suite ⊗ in 4 bedrooms s £53.50; d £90 (incl. bkfst) **LB** **PARKING:** 13

Premier Travel Inn Ross-on-Wye
premier travel inn
Ledbury Rd HR9 7QJ
☎ 08701 977221 📠 01989 566124
web: www.premiertravelinn.com
Dir: *1m from town centre on M50 rdbt*
High quality, modern budget accommodation ideal for both families and business travellers. Spacious, en suite bedrooms feature bath and shower, satellite TV and many have telephones and modem points. The adjacent family restaurant features a wide and varied menu. For further details consult the Hotel Groups page.
ROOMS: 43 en suite s £49.95; d £49.95

ROSTHWAITE, Cumbria — Map 18 NY21
See also Borrowdale

★★68% Scafell
CA12 5XB
☎ 017687 77208 📠 017687 77280
e-mail: info@scafell.co.uk
Dir: *6m S of Keswick on B5289*

This friendly hotel is popular with walkers and enjoys a peaceful location. Bedrooms vary in style from traditional to modern, and are all well equipped and neatly decorated. Public areas include a residents' cocktail bar, lounge and spacious restaurant as well as the popular Riverside Inn pub, offering all-day dining in summer months.
ROOMS: 24 en suite (2 fmly) (8 GF) s £70.50; d £141 (incl. bkfst & dinner) **LB** **FACILITIES:** Guided walks Xmas **PARKING:** 50 **NOTES:** ⊗ in restaurant Civ Wed 75

ROTHERHAM, South Yorkshire — Map 16 SK49

★★★★64% Hellaby Hall
Old Hellaby Ln, Hellaby S66 8SN
☎ 01709 702701 📠 01709 700979
e-mail: reservations@hellabyhallhotel.co.uk
web: www.hellabyhallhotel.co.uk
Dir: *1m off M18 junct 1, onto A631 towards Maltby, in village of Hellaby*
This 17th-century house was built to a Flemish design with high, beamed ceilings, and staircases which lead off to private meeting rooms and a series of oak-panelled lounges. Bedrooms are elegant and well equipped and guests can dine in the formal Attic

continued

R

Restaurant. There are extensive leisure facilities and conference areas, and the hotel holds a licence for civil weddings.

ROOMS: 90 en suite (4 fmly) (28 GF) ⊗ in 71 bedrooms s £45-£99; d £79-£115 (incl. bkfst) **LB** **FACILITIES: Spa** STV supervised Sauna Solarium Gym Beauty room Xmas **CONF:** Thtr 500 Class 300 Board 150 **SERVICES:** Lift **PARKING:** 250 **NOTES:** ⊗ in restaurant Civ Wed 200

See advert on this page

★★★73% Consort

Brampton Rd, Thurcroft S66 9JA
☎ 01709 530022 📠 01709 531529
e-mail: info@consorthotel.com
web: www.consorthotel.com

Dir: *M18 junct 1, right towards Bawtry on A631. 250yds to rdbt and in further 200yds turn left then 1.5m to x-rds, hotel opposite*

Bedrooms at this modern, friendly hotel are comfortable, attractive and air conditioned, and include ten superior rooms. A wide range of dishes is served in the open-plan bar and restaurant, and there is a comfortable foyer lounge. There are good conference and function facilities, and entertainment evenings are often hosted here.

ROOMS: 27 en suite (2 fmly) (9 GF) ⊗ in 8 bedrooms
FACILITIES: STV ♫ **CONF:** Thtr 300 Class 120 Board 50 Del from £95
SERVICES: air con **PARKING:** 90 **NOTES:** ⊗ in restaurant Civ Wed 300

See advert on this page

★★★69% Best Western Elton

Main St, Bramley S66 2SF
☎ 01709 545681 📠 01709 549100
e-mail: bestwestern.eltonhotel@btinternet.com
web: www.bw-eltonhotel.co.uk

Dir: *M18 junct 1 follow A631 Rotherham, turn right to Ravenfield, hotel at end of Bramley village, follow brown signs*

Within easy reach of the M18, this welcoming, stone-built hotel is set in well-tended gardens. The Elton offers good modern accommodation, with larger rooms in the extension that are particularly comfortable and well equipped. A civil licence is held for wedding ceremonies and conference rooms are available.

ROOMS: 13 en suite 16 annexe en suite (4 fmly) (11 GF) ⊗ in 11 bedrooms s £50-£84; d £60-£90 (incl. bkfst) **LB** **FACILITIES:** STV **CONF:** Thtr 55 Class 24 Board 26 Del from £90 **PARKING:** 48 **NOTES:** ⊗ in restaurant Civ Wed 48

★★★68%
Courtyard by Marriott, Rotherham

West Bawtry Rd S60 4NA
☎ 0870 400 7235 📠 0870 400 7335
web: www.kewgreen.co.uk

Dir: *M1 junct 33, A630 towards Rotherham, hotel 0.5m on right*

Stylish and contemporary, this modern hotel is well located just

continued on p478

ROTHERHAM, continued

five minutes from the motorway. Bedrooms are spacious and boast an excellent range of facilities. Guests have the use of the leisure club with its swimming pool, spa bath and steam room.

Courtyard by Marriott, Rotherham

ROOMS: 104 en suite (10 fmly) (22 GF) ⊗ in 76 bedrooms s £59-£94; d £78-£102 (incl. bkfst) **LB** **FACILITIES: Spa** STV supervised Solarium Gym Steam room, Childrens pool **CONF:** BC Thtr 300 Class 120 Board 40 Del from £130 **SERVICES:** Lift **PARKING:** 222 **NOTES:** Civ Wed 70

★★★65% Carlton Park

102/104 Moorgate Rd S60 2BG
☎ 01709 849955 01709 368960
e-mail: reservations@carltonparkhotel.com
Dir: *M1 junct 33, onto A631, then A618. Hotel 800yds past hospital*

This modern hotel is situated in a pleasant residential area of the town, close to the District General Hospital, yet within minutes of the M1. Bedrooms and bathrooms offer very modern comfort and facilities. Three have separate sitting rooms. The restaurant and bar provide a lively atmosphere, and are popular with locals.

ROOMS: 80 en suite (14 fmly) (16 GF) ⊗ in 64 bedrooms s £50-£99; d £80-£110 (incl. bkfst) **LB** **FACILITIES:** STV Sauna Solarium Gym Jacuzzi ♫ Xmas **CONF:** Thtr 250 Class 160 Board 60 Del from £105 **SERVICES:** Lift **PARKING:** 120 **NOTES:** ⊗ in restaurant Civ Wed 100

Hotel Ibis Rotherham

Moorhead Way, Bramley S66 1YY
☎ 01709 730333 01709 730444
e-mail: H3163@accor-hotels.com
Dir: *M18 junct 1, left at rdbt & left at 1st lights. Hotel next to supermarket*

Modern, budget hotel offering comfortable accommodation in bright and practical bedrooms. Breakfast is self-service and dinner is available in the restaurant. For further details, consult the Hotel Groups page.

ROOMS: 86 en suite **CONF:** Thtr 40 Class 30 Board 30

Premier Travel Inn Rotherham

Bawtry Rd S65 3JB
☎ 08701 977222 01709 531546
web: www.premiertravelinn.com
Dir: *on A631 towards Wickersley, between M18 junct 1 & M1 junct 33*

High quality, modern budget accommodation ideal for both families and business travellers. Spacious, en suite bedrooms feature bath and shower, satellite TV and many have telephones and modem points. The adjacent family restaurant features a wide and varied menu. For further details consult the Hotel Groups page.

ROOMS: 37 en suite s £46.95-£48.95; d £46.95-£48.95

Restover Lodge

Hellaby Industrial Estate, Lowton Way, off Denby Way S66 8RY
☎ 01709 700255 01709 545169
e-mail: rotherham@envergure.co.uk
Dir: *M18 junct 1. Follow signs for Maltby off rdbt. Left at lights, 2nd on left*

This modern building offers accommodation in smart, well equipped bedrooms, all with en suite bathrooms. Refreshments may be taken at the informal Bistro.

ROOMS: 50 en suite **CONF:** Thtr 35 Class 18 Board 24

ROTHERWICK, Hampshire Map 05 SU75

Top Hotel

★★★★ Tylney Hall

RG27 9AZ
☎ 01256 764881 01256 768141
e-mail: sales@tylneyhall.com
web: www.tylneyhall.com
Dir: *M3 junct 5, A287 to Basingstoke, over junct with A30, over railway bridge, towards Newnham. Right at Newnham Green. Hotel 1m on left*

A superb Grade II listed Victorian country house, set in 66 acres of beautiful parkland. The hotel offers very high standards of comfort in relaxed yet elegant surroundings, featuring magnificently restored water gardens, which were originally laid out by famous 19th-century gardener, Gertrude Jekyll. The spacious public rooms include the Wedgwood drawing room and panelled Oak Room, which are filled with fresh flowers and warmed by log fires. The spacious bedrooms are traditionally furnished and offer a high degree of comfort.

ROOMS: 35 en suite 77 annexe en suite (1 fmly) (21 GF) s £135-£420; d £165-£450 (incl. bkfst) **LB** **FACILITIES: Spa** STV Snooker Sauna Solarium Gym Clay pigeon shooting, Archery, Falconry, Balloon rides, Laser shooting ♫ Xmas **CONF:** BC Thtr 120 Class 70 Board 40 Del from £220 **PARKING:** 120 **NOTES:** ⊗ in restaurant Civ Wed 100

ROTHLEY, Leicestershire Map 11 SK51

★★★66% Rothley Court

Westfield Ln LE7 7LG
☎ 0116 237 4141 0116 237 4483
e-mail: 6501@greeneking.co.uk
web: www.oldenglish.co.uk
Dir: *on B5328*

Mentioned in the Domesday Book, and complete with its own chapel, this historic property sits in seven acres of well-tended grounds. Public areas retain much of their original character and include an oak-panelled restaurant and a choice of function and

continued

meeting rooms. Bedrooms, some located in an adjacent stable block, are individually styled.
ROOMS: 12 en suite 18 annexe en suite (3 fmly) (6 GF) ⊗ in all bedrooms s £90; d £110-£150 (incl. bkfst) **LB FACILITIES:** STV Xmas **CONF:** BC Thtr 100 Class 35 Board 35 Del from £140 **PARKING:** 100 **NOTES:** ⊗ in restaurant Civ Wed 85

ROUSDON, Devon Map 04 SY29

★★73% Dower House
Rousdon DT7 3RB
☎ 01297 21047 01297 24748
e-mail: info@dhhotel.com
web: www.dhhotel.com
Dir: *On A3052, 3m W of Lyme Regis*
Set in its own grounds, this hotel offers traditionally decorated bedrooms, each individually styled and well equipped with modern facilities. There is a more contemporary bar/lounge with a glowing stove on cold evenings. Both the restaurants offer imaginative dishes - those in the bistro from a lighter menu and those in the fine dining restaurant having much creative flair.
ROOMS: 10 en suite (2 fmly) (1 GF) ⊗ in all bedrooms s £71-£112; d £95-£150 (incl. bkfst) **LB FACILITIES:** Xmas **CONF:** Thtr 46 Class 30 Board 18 Del from £75 **PARKING:** 35 **NOTES:** ⊗ in restaurant Civ Wed 40

ROWLAND'S CASTLE, Hampshire Map 05 SU71

Innkeeper's Lodge Portsmouth North
Whichers Gate Rd PO9 6BB
☎ 0870 243 0500 & 023 9241 3761
web: www.innkeeperslodge.com
Dir: *M3 junct 2, at rdbt, right onto the B2149 (Rowlands Castle). After 2m, left onto B2148 Whichers Gate Rd, lodge on left*
A growing concept in the travel accommodation market. Smart rooms meet essential business requirements but also have home comforts. Dining options include all-day menus plus the added advantage of breakfast, which is included in the room price. For further details consult the Hotel Groups page.
ROOMS: 21 en suite s £49.95-£52.50; d £49.95-£52.50

ROWNHAMS MOTORWAY SERVICE AREA (M27), Hampshire Map 05 SU31

Premier Travel Inn Southampton (Rownhams)
Rownhams Service Area SO16 8AP
☎ 08701 977234 023 8074 0204
web: www.premiertravelinn.com
Dir: *M27 Westbound - between junctions 3 & 4. No access from eastbound services*
High quality, modern budget accommodation ideal for both families and business travellers. Spacious, en suite bedrooms feature bath and shower, satellite TV and many have telephones and modem points. The adjacent family restaurant features a wide and varied menu. For further details consult the Hotel Groups page.
ROOMS: 39 en suite s £46.95-£49.95; d £46.95-£49.95

ROWSLEY, Derbyshire Map 16 SK26

★★★80% East Lodge Country House
DE4 2EF
☎ 01629 734474 01629 733949
e-mail: info@eastlodge.com
web: www.eastlodge.com
Dir: *A6, 3m from Bakewell, 5m from Matlock*
The hotel enjoys a romantic setting in ten acres of landscaped grounds and gardens. The stylish bedrooms are equipped with many extras such as TVs with DVD players, and most have lovely garden views. The restaurant has a popular local following and offers much produce sourced from the area. The conservatory lounge, overlooking the gardens offers afternoon teas and light meals.

ROOMS: 14 en suite (2 fmly) (1 GF) ⊗ in all bedrooms s £90-£130; d £110-£170 (incl. bkfst) **LB FACILITIES:** Xmas **CONF:** Thtr 75 Class 20 Board 22 Del from £38 **PARKING:** 40 **NOTES:** No children 7yrs ⊗ in restaurant Civ Wed 100

See advert under BAKEWELL

★★★76% The Peacock at Rowsley
Bakewell Rd DE4 2EB
☎ 01629 733518 01629 732671
e-mail: reception@thepeacockatrowsley.com
web: www.thepeacockatrowsley.com
Dir: *A6, 3m before Bakewell, 6m from Matlock towards Bakewell*

Acquired by Lord Edward Manners of nearby Haddon Hall this hotel has benefited from heavy investment. It is now a smart contemporary destination, which still retains many original features and period pieces of furniture. The menus are well balanced and feature much local produce. Dry fly fishing is a great attraction here as the hotel owns fishing rights in the area.
ROOMS: 16 en suite (5 fmly) ⊗ in 2 bedrooms s £75-£95; d £145-£175 (incl. bkfst) **FACILITIES:** STV Fishing Woodlands Fitness Centre with concessions Xmas **CONF:** Thtr 20 Class 8 Board 20 Del from £150 **PARKING:** 27 **NOTES:** ⊗ in restaurant Civ Wed 20

RUAN HIGH LANES, Cornwall & Isles of Scilly Map 02 SW93

★★75% Hundred House
TR2 5JR
☎ 01872 501336 01872 501151
e-mail: enquiries@hundredhousehotel.co.uk
Dir: *from B3287 at Tregony, left onto A3078 to St Mawes, hotel 4m on right*
This Edwardian house, now under new ownership, is set in attractive gardens and has good access to the Roseland Peninsula, which makes it an ideal base for a relaxing break or for touring

continued on p480

R

RUAN HIGH LANES, continued

the area. Bedrooms are well equipped and the lounge and bar offer a good level of comfort. Service is attentive and the staff are very much focussed on their guests' needs. Both dinner and breakfast offer freshly cooked and appetising dishes.
ROOMS: 10 en suite (1 GF) ⊕ in all bedrooms s £70-£86; d £140-£172 **LB FACILITIES:** ♨ Xmas **PARKING:** 15 **NOTES:** ✗ No children 12yrs ⊕ in restaurant

RUGBY, Warwickshire Map 11 SP57

★★★67% Corus hotel Rugby
Brownsover Ln, Old Brownsover CV21 1HU
☎ 0870 609 6104 01788 546100
▤ 01788 579241
e-mail: brownsoverhall@corushotels.com
web: www.corushotels.com
Dir: M6 junct 1, signs to Rugby A426. Dual-carriageway for 0.5m at rdbt signed "Ambulance & Brownsover Hall Hotel" turn right. Hotel 400mtrs on right

A mock-Gothic hall designed by Sir Gilbert Scott, set in seven acres of wooded parkland. Bedrooms vary in size and style, including spacious and contemporary rooms in the converted stable block. The former chapel makes a stylish restaurant, and for a less formal meal or a relaxing drink, the rugby themed bar is popular.
ROOMS: 27 en suite 20 annexe en suite (4 fmly) (12 GF) ⊕ in 38 bedrooms s £108; d £108 **LB FACILITIES:** STV Free use of Esparta Gym (0.5 mile away) Xmas **CONF:** Thtr 70 Class 36 Board 35 Del £148 **PARKING:** 100 **NOTES:** ✗ ⊕ in restaurant Civ Wed 56

★★★65% Grosvenor Hotel Rugby
81-87 Clifton Rd CV21 3QQ
☎ 01788 535686 ▤ 01788 541297
e-mail: grosvenorrugby@btconnect.com
Dir: M6 junct 1, turn right onto A426 towards Rugby centre, at 1st rdbt turn left, on to T-junct and turn right onto B5414, hotel 2m on right

Close to the town centre, this family-owned hotel is popular with
continued

both business and leisure guests. The public rooms are cosy, inviting and pleasantly furnished, and service is both friendly and attentive. Bedrooms come in a variety of styles and sizes and include several newer rooms.
ROOMS: 26 en suite (3 fmly) ⊕ in 21 bedrooms **CONF:** Thtr 100 Class 50 Board 60 **PARKING:** 50 **NOTES:** ✗ ⊕ in restaurant Civ Wed 100

★★69% Golden Lion Hotel
Easenhall CV23 0JA
☎ 01788 833577 832265 ▤ 01788 832878
e-mail: reception@goldenlioninn.co.uk
web: www.goldenlioninn.co.uk
Dir: A426 Avon Mill rdbt turn to Newbold-upon-Avon B4112, approx 2m left at Harborough Parva sign, opposite agricultural showroom, then 1m to Easenhall

This friendly, family-run 16th-century inn is situated between Rugby and Coventry, convenient for access to the M6. Bedrooms are equipped with both practical and homely items and one features a stunning Chinese bed. The beamed bar and restaurant retain many original features. New in 2005 is a development of additional bedrooms and a conference suite.
ROOMS: 17 en suite (2 fmly) (6 GF) ⊕ in all bedrooms s £52-£65; d £59-£84 (incl. bkfst) **FACILITIES:** Jacuzzi **CONF:** Thtr 60 Class 30 Board 30 Del from £120 **PARKING:** 80 **NOTES:** ✗ ⊕ in restaurant

⌂ Hotel Ibis Rugby East
Parklands NN6 7EX
☎ 01788 824331 ▤ 01788 824332
e-mail: H3588@accor-hotels.com
(For full entry see Crick)

⌂ Innkeeper's Lodge Rugby
The Green, Dunchurch CV22 6NJ
☎ 01788 810305 ▤ 01788 810931
web: www.innkeeperslodge.com
Dir: M1 junct 17/M45/A45. Follow signs for Dunchurch B4429. Lodge in village centre on x-rds of A426 and B4429
A growing concept in the travel accommodation market. Smart rooms meet essential business requirements but also have home comforts. Dining options include all-day menus plus the added advantage of breakfast, which is included in the room price. For further details consult the Hotel Groups page.
ROOMS: 16 en suite s £49.95-£59.95; d £49.95-£59.95

⌂ Premier Travel Inn Rugby
Central Park Dr, Central Park CV23 0WE
☎ 08701 977 223 ▤ 01788 565949
web: www.premiertravelinn.com
High quality, modern budget accommodation ideal for both families and business travellers. Spacious, en suite bedrooms feature bath and shower, satellite TV and many have telephones and modem points. The adjacent family restaurant features a wide and varied menu. For further details consult the Hotel Groups page.
ROOMS: 60 en suite s £46.95-£48.95; d £46.95-£48.95

RUGELEY, Staffordshire Map 10 SK01

⌂ Travelodge

Western Springs Rd WS15 2AS
☎ 08700 850 950 🖷 01889 570096
web: www.travelodge.co.uk
Dir: *on A51/B5013*
Travelodge offers good quality, good value, modern accommodation. Ideal for families, the spacious, en suite bedrooms include remote-control TV, tea and coffee-making facilities and comfortable beds. Meals can be taken at the nearby family restaurant. For further details consult the Hotel Groups page.
ROOMS: 32 en suite s fr £26; d fr £26

RUISLIP, Greater London

See LONDON SECTION plan 1 A5

★★★71% ❀❀ Barn Hotel

West End Rd HA4 6JB
☎ 01895 636057 🖷 01895 638379
e-mail: info@thebarnhotel.co.uk
web: www.thebarnhotel.co.uk
Dir: *take A4180 (Polish War Memorial) exit off A40 to Ruislip, 2m to hotel entrance off a mini-rdbt before Ruislip underground station*

Once a farm, with parts dating back to the 17th century, this impressive property sits in three acres of gardens. Bedrooms vary in style, from contemporary to traditional oak-beamed varieties. All are comfortable and well appointed. The public areas provide a high level of quality and luxury.
ROOMS: 59 en suite (3 fmly) (24 GF) ⊗ in 10 bedrooms s £95-£145; d £115-£185 (incl. bkfst) **LB** **FACILITIES:** STV Xmas **CONF:** Thtr 80 Class 50 Board 30 Del from £145 **PARKING:** 42 **NOTES:** ✕ ⊗ in restaurant Civ Wed 74

See advert under UXBRIDGE

RUNCORN, Cheshire Map 15 SJ58

★★★70% *Lawson House Hotel & Conference Centre*

Moughland Centre WA7 4SQ
☎ 01928 593300 🖷 01928 593355
e-mail: reception@lawsonhouse.co.uk
Dir: *M56 junct 12/A557 Widnes. Exit at sign for Rocksavage Weston Village & turn right at Heath mini rdbt, after church turn right into Cavendish Farm Rd, turn left at lights, hotel 200yds on left*
This hotel, conveniently located for the motorway network, road and air links, offers comfortable well-equipped accommodation. Rooms are split between the original house and a modern extension. Extensive conference and function rooms are available which are ideal for weddings or corporate entertaining. The Harewood dining room offers interesting cuisine.
ROOMS: 30 en suite **FACILITIES:** Gym **CONF:** Thtr 150 Class 80 Board 50 **PARKING:** 70 **NOTES:** ⊗ in restaurant Civ Wed 80

⌂ Campanile

Lowlands Rd WA7 5TP
☎ 01928 581771 🖷 01928 581730
e-mail: runcorn@envergure.co.uk
web: www.envergure.fr
Dir: *M56 junct 12, take A557, then follow signs for Runcorn rail station/Runcorn College*

This modern building offers accommodation in smart, well-equipped bedrooms, all with en suite bathrooms. Refreshments may be taken at the informal Bistro. For further details consult the Hotel Groups page.
ROOMS: 53 en suite s £37-£43; d £37-£43 **CONF:** Thtr 35 Class 18 Board 24

⌂ Premier Travel Inn Runcorn

Chester Rd, Preston Brook WA7 3BB
☎ 08701 977224 🖷 01928 719852
web: www.premiertravelinn.com
Dir: *1m from M56 junct 11, at Preston Brook*
High quality, modern budget accommodation ideal for both families and business travellers. Spacious, en suite bedrooms feature bath and shower, satellite TV and many have telephones and modem points. The adjacent family restaurant features a wide and varied menu. For further details consult the Hotel Groups page.
ROOMS: 40 en suite s £46.95-£48.95; d £46.95-£48.95 **CONF:** Thtr 40

RUSHDEN, Northamptonshire Map 11 SP96

⌂ Travelodge Wellingborough

Saunders Lodge NN10 9AP
☎ 08700 850 950 🖷 01933 57008
web: www.travelodge.co.uk
Dir: *on A45, eastbound*
Travelodge offers good quality, good value, modern accommodation. Ideal for families, the spacious, en suite bedrooms include remote-control TV, tea and coffee-making facilities and comfortable beds. Meals can be taken at the nearby family restaurant. For further details consult the Hotel Groups page.
ROOMS: 40 en suite s fr £26; d fr £26

RUSTINGTON, West Sussex Map 06 TQ00

⌂ Travelodge Littlehampton

Worthing Rd BN17 6LZ
☎ 08700 850 950 🖷 01903 733150
web: www.travelodge.co.uk
Dir: *on A259, 1m E of Littlehampton*
Travelodge offers good quality, good value, modern accommodation. Ideal for families, the spacious, en suite bedrooms include remote-control TV, tea and coffee-making facilities and comfortable beds. Meals can be taken at the nearby family restaurant. For further details consult the Hotel Groups page.
ROOMS: 36 en suite s fr £26; d fr £26

R

RYDE See Wight, Isle of

RYE, East Sussex — Map 07 TQ92

★★★76% Flackley Ash
TN31 6YH
☎ 01797 230651 ℻ 01797 230510
e-mail: enquiries@flackleyashhotel.co.uk
web: www.flackleyashhotel.co.uk
(For full entry see Peasmarsh)

★★★73% Rye Lodge
Hilders Cliff TN31 7LD
☎ 01797 223838 ℻ 01797 223585
e-mail: info@ryelodge.co.uk
web: www.ryelodge.co.uk
Dir: *one-way system in Rye, follow signs for town centre, through Landgate arch, hotel 100yds on right*

Standing in an elevated position, Rye Lodge has panoramic views across Romney Marshes and the Rother Estuary. Bedrooms come in a variety of sizes and styles; they are attractively decorated, tastefully furnished and thoughtfully equipped. Public rooms feature indoor leisure facilities and The Terrace Room Restaurant, where an interesting choice of home-made dishes is available.
ROOMS: 18 en suite (5 GF) ⊗ in 4 bedrooms s £70-£105; d £100-£190 (incl. bkfst) **LB** **FACILITIES: Spa** STV Sauna Aromatherapy Steam cabinet Xmas **PARKING:** 20 **NOTES:** ⊗ in restaurant

See advert on opposite page

★★★72% ❀ Mermaid Inn
Mermaid St TN31 7EY
☎ 01797 223065 & 223788 ℻ 01797 225069
e-mail: mermaidinnrye@btclick.com
web: www.mermaidinn .com
Dir: *A259, follow signs to town centre then into Mermaid St*

Situated near the top of a cobbled side street, this famous smugglers' inn is steeped in history. The charming interior has many architectural features such as attractive stone work. The bedrooms vary in size and style but are all tastefully furnished. Delightful public rooms include a choice of lounges, cosy bar and smart restaurant.
ROOMS: 31 en suite (5 fmly) s £85-£90; d £170-£220 (incl. bkfst) **LB** **FACILITIES:** Xmas **CONF:** Thtr 50 Class 40 Board 30 Del from £140 **PARKING:** 25 **NOTES:** 🐕 ⊗ in restaurant

★★★68% The Hope Anchor
Watchbell St TN31 7HA
☎ 01797 222216 ℻ 01797 223796
e-mail: info@thehopeanchor.co.uk
web: www.thehopeanchor.co.uk
Dir: *from A268, Quayside, turn right into Wishard, up Mermaid St., right into West St., right into Watchbell St., hotel at end of street.*

This historic inn sits high above the town with enviable views out over the harbour and Romney Marsh, and is accessible via delightful cobbled streets. A relaxed and friendly atmosphere prevails within the cosy public rooms, while the attractively furnished bedrooms are well equipped and many enjoy good views over the marshes.
ROOMS: 14 en suite (1 fmly) ⊗ in all bedrooms s £65-£85; d £100-£200 (incl. bkfst) **LB** **FACILITIES:** Xmas **NOTES:** 🐕 ⊗ in restaurant Closed 9 Jan-16 Jan

★★★61% The George
High St TN31 7JT
☎ 01797 222114 ℻ 01797 224065
e-mail: Stay@thegeorgeinrye.com
Situated in the centre of this popular town and surrounded by specialist shops, The George is full of character and offers comfortable public rooms including a bar, lounge and cosy restaurant which reflect the period of the building. The bedrooms have been sympathetically modernised and each one is thoughtfully equipped.
ROOMS: 22 en suite (2 fmly) (3 GF) ⊗ in all bedrooms s fr £59; d fr £89 (incl. bkfst) **LB** **FACILITIES:** Xmas **CONF:** BC Thtr 100 Class 40 Board 40 Del from £99 **PARKING:** 7 **NOTES:** ⊗ in restaurant Civ Wed 50

★★71% *Broomhill Lodge*
Rye Foreign TN31 7UN
☎ 01797 280421 ℻ 01797 280402
Dir: *1.5m N on A268*
Ideally situated just a short drive from the historic town of Rye, this charming property was built in the 1820s and is set in its own three-acre grounds. Bedrooms are individually decorated, comfortably furnished and thoughtfully equipped. Public rooms feature a choice of lounges, a smart restaurant and a small banqueting suite.
ROOMS: 12 en suite **FACILITIES:** Sauna Mini gym **CONF:** Thtr 60 Class 60 Board 30 **PARKING:** 20 **NOTES:** 🐕 ⊗ in restaurant

ST AGNES, Cornwall & Isles of Scilly Map 02 SW75

★★★72% Rose in Vale Country House

Mithian TR5 0QD
☎ 01872 552202 & 0845 1235527 📠 01872 552700
e-mail: reception@rose-in-vale-hotel.co.uk
web: www.rose-in-vale-hotel.co.uk
Dir: *A30 through Cornwall, right onto B3277 signed St Agnus. In 500yds follow hotel signs*

Peacefully located in a wooded valley this Georgian manor house has a wonderfully relaxed atmosphere and abundant charm and where guests are assured of a warm welcome. Accommodation varies in size and style; several rooms are situated on the ground floor. An imaginative fixed-price menu featuring local produce is served in the spacious restaurant.
ROOMS: 18 en suite (3 fmly) (3 GF) ⊗ in all bedrooms s £68-£145; d £120-£180 (incl. bkfst) **LB FACILITIES:** Sauna games room, table tennis, garden badminton Xmas **CONF:** Thtr 75 Class 50 Board 40 Del from £95 **PARKING:** 40 **NOTES:** ⊗ in restaurant Closed Jan-Feb Civ Wed 75

★★70% Beacon Country House Hotel

Goonvrea Rd TR5 0NW
☎ 01872 552318 📠 01872 552318
e-mail: info@beaconhotel.co.uk
web: www.beaconhotel.co.uk
Dir: *from A30 take B3277 to St Agnes. At rdbt left onto Goonvrea Rd. Hotel 0.75m on right*
Set in a quiet and attractive area away from the busy village, this relaxed, family-run hotel has splendid views over the countryside towards the sea. Guests are assured of a friendly welcome, and many return for another stay. Bedrooms are comfortable and well equipped and many benefit from the good views.
ROOMS: 11 en suite (1 fmly) (2 GF) ⊗ in all bedrooms **PARKING:** 14 **NOTES:** ⊗ in restaurant

★★70% Rosemundy House

Rosemundy Hill TR5 0UF
☎ 01872 552101 📠 01872 554000
e-mail: info@rosemundy.co.uk
Dir: *off A30 to St Agnes continue for approx 3m. On entering village take 1st right signed Rosemundy, hotel at foot of hill*
This elegant Queen Anne house has been carefully restored and extended to provide comfortable bedrooms and spacious, inviting public areas. The hotel is set in well-maintained gardens complete with an outdoor pool for warmer months. There is a choice of relaxing lounges, two restaurants and a cosy bar.
ROOMS: 46 en suite (3 fmly) (9 GF) ⊗ in 10 bedrooms s £28-£47; d £56-£94 (incl. bkfst) **LB FACILITIES:** Putt green ♫ Xmas **CONF:** Board 80 **PARKING:** 50 **NOTES:** No children 5yrs ⊗ in restaurant

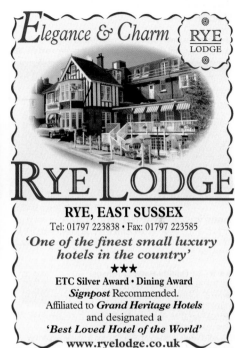

ST ALBANS, Hertfordshire Map 06 TL10

★★★★72% Sopwell House

Cottonmill Ln, Sopwell AL1 2HQ
☎ 01727 864477 📠 01727 844741/845636
e-mail: enquiries@sopwellhouse.co.uk
web: www.sopwellhouse.co.uk
Dir: *M25 junct 22, follow A1081 St Albans. At traffic lights, turn left into Mile House Lane, over mini-rdbt into Cottonmill Lane*
This imposing Georgian house retains an exclusive ambience. Bedrooms vary in style and include a number of self-contained cottages within the Sopwell Mews. Meeting and function rooms are housed in a separate section and leisure and spa facilities are particularly impressive. Dining options include the brasserie and the fine-dining Magnolia restaurant.
ROOMS: 113 en suite 16 annexe en suite (12 fmly) (11 GF) ⊗ in 109 bedrooms s £129; d £185-£275 **LB FACILITIES: Spa** STV Sauna Solarium Gym Jacuzzi Health & Beauty Spa, Hairdressing salon, 11 spa treatment room ♫ Xmas **CONF:** BC Thtr 400 Class 220 Board 120 Del from £215 **SERVICES:** Lift **PARKING:** 350 **NOTES:** ⊗ in restaurant Civ Wed 250

★★★78% St Michael's Manor

Fishpool St AL3 4RY
☎ 01727 864444 📠 01727 848909
e-mail: reservations@stmichaelsmanor.com
Dir: *from St Albans Abbey follow Fishpool Street toward St Michael's village. Hotel 0.5m on left*
Hidden from the street, adjacent to listed buildings, mills and ancient inns, this hotel is set in five acres of beautiful landscaped grounds. Inside there is a real sense of luxury, the high standard

continued on p484

S

ST ALBANS, continued

of decor and attentive service is complemented by award-winning food; the restaurant overlooks the immaculate gardens and the lake.

St Michael's Manor, St Albans

ROOMS: 30 en suite (1 fmly) (8 GF) ⊗ in 4 bedrooms s £145-£230; d £180-£310 (incl. bkfst) **LB** **FACILITIES:** STV ♫ Xmas **CONF:** Thtr 30 Class 20 Board 20 Del from £220 **SERVICES:** Lift air con **PARKING:** 70 **NOTES:** ✗ ⊗ in restaurant Civ Wed 70

★★★66% Quality Hotel St Albans

232-236 London Rd AL1 1JQ
☎ 01727 857858 🖷 01727 855666
e-mail: st.albans@quality-hotels.net
***Dir:** M25 junct 22 follow A1081 to St Albans, after 2.5m hotel on left, before overhead bridge*
This hotel offers convenient access to and from the motorway network and the railway station in the town centre. The bedrooms are well equipped and there are also conference facilities. For relaxation, there is a comfortable bar which serves light snacks, and the Grapevine Restaurant serving more substantial meals.
ROOMS: 81 en suite (7 fmly) (13 GF) ⊗ in 51 bedrooms s £49-£90; d £69-£115 (incl. bkfst) **FACILITIES:** STV supervised Sauna Gym ch fac **CONF:** Thtr 220 Class 40 Board 50 Del from £120 **SERVICES:** Lift **PARKING:** 80 **NOTES:** ✗ ⊗ in restaurant

★★69% Comfort Hotel - Ryder House

Holywell Hill AL1 1HG
☎ 01727 848849 🖷 01727 812210
e-mail: admin@gb055.u-net.com
This listed building is ideally located in the centre of the town and provides smart, comfortable accommodation. Bedrooms are spacious, stylish and well equipped. The newly refurbished public areas include a smart restaurant, a lounge bar and several meeting rooms.
ROOMS: 60 en suite (18 fmly) ⊗ in 40 bedrooms s fr £75; d fr £75 **FACILITIES:** STV **CONF:** Thtr 45 Class 30 Board 25 Del from £120 **SERVICES:** Lift **PARKING:** 60 **NOTES:** ⊗ in restaurant

ST ANNES See Lytham St Annes

ST AUSTELL, Cornwall & Isles of Scilly — Map 02 SX05

★★★★75% Carlyon Bay

Sea Rd, Carlyon Bay PL25 3RD
☎ 01726 812304 🖷 01726 814938
e-mail: reservations@carlyonbay.com
web: www.brend-hotels.co.uk
***Dir:** from St Austell, follow signs for Charlestown. Carlyon Bay signed on left, hotel at end of Sea Road*
Originally built in the 1920s, this long-established hotel lies on the clifftop in 250 acres of grounds, which include indoor and outdoor pools and a golf course. Bedrooms are well maintained, many with marvellous views across St Austell Bay. A good choice of comfortable lounges is available, whilst facilities for families include kids' clubs and entertainment.

ROOMS: 87 en suite (14 fmly) ⊗ in 14 bedrooms s £75-£100; d £140-£270 **LB** **FACILITIES: Spa** STV 18 Snooker Sauna Solarium Putt green Table tennis 9-hole approach course, Health and beauty salon ♫ ch fac Xmas **SERVICES:** Lift **PARKING:** 100 **NOTES:** ✗ ⊗ in restaurant Civ Wed 100

See advert on opposite page

★★★72% Porth Avallen

Sea Rd, Carlyon Bay PL25 3SG
☎ 01726 812802 🖷 01726 817097
e-mail: info@porthavallen.co.uk
web: www.porthavallen.co.uk
***Dir:** from A30 take A391 to St Austell. Turn right onto A390. Turn left at traffic lights and left at rdbt, then right into Sea Road*

This traditional hotel boasts panoramic views over the rugged Cornish coastline. It offers smartly appointed public areas and well-presented bedrooms, many with sea views. There is an oak-panelled lounge and conservatory; both are ideal for relaxation. Both fixed-price and carte menus are offered in the elegant restaurant.
ROOMS: 27 en suite (2 fmly) ⊗ in 17 bedrooms s £60-£100; d £80-£130 (incl. bkfst) **LB** **FACILITIES:** Xmas **CONF:** Thtr 100 Class 40 Board 40 Del from £105 **PARKING:** 50 **NOTES:** ✗ ⊗ in restaurant Civ Wed 70

See advert on opposite page

★★★70% Cliff Head

Sea Rd, Carlyon Bay PL25 3RB
☎ 01726 812345 🖷 01726 815511
e-mail: cliffheadhotel@btconnect.com
web: www.cliffheadhotel.com
***Dir:** 2m E off A390*
Set in extensive grounds and conveniently located for visiting the Eden Project, this hotel faces south and enjoys views over Carlyon

continued

Bay. A choice of lounges is provided, together with a swimming pool and solarium. 'Expressions' restaurant offers a range of menus, which feature an interesting selection of dishes.

ROOMS: 60 rms (59 en suite) (2 fmly) s £55-£65; d £100-£120 (incl. bkfst) **LB** **FACILITIES:** Sauna Solarium Gym ♫ Xmas **CONF:** Thtr 150 Class 130 Board 70 Del from £69.95 **PARKING:** 60 **NOTES:** in restaurant Civ Wed 120

★★77% *Boscundle Manor Country House*

Tregrehan PL25 3RL
☎ 01726 813557 01726 814997
e-mail: stay@boscundlemanor.co.uk
Dir: *2m E on A390, 200yds on road signed Tregrehan*

Set in beautifully maintained gardens and grounds, this handsome 18th-century stone manor house is a short distance from the Eden Project. Quality and comfort are apparent in the public areas and spacious, well-equipped bedrooms. Equally suitable for both leisure and business travellers, Boscundle Manor boasts both indoor and outdoor pools.

ROOMS: 11 en suite 3 annexe en suite (4 fmly) (4 GF) in all bedrooms **FACILITIES:** ch fac **CONF:** Thtr 40 Class 20 Board 20 **PARKING:** 15 **NOTES:** in restaurant Closed 2 Jan- 13 Feb Civ Wed 60

★★73% Pier House

Harbour Front, Charlestown PL25 3NJ
☎ 01726 67955 01726 69246
e-mail: pierhouse@btconnect.com
Dir: *follow A390 to St Austell, at Mt Charles rdbt left down Charlestown Rd*

This genuinely friendly hotel boasts a wonderful harbourside location. The unspoilt working port has been the setting for many film and television productions. Most bedrooms have sea views, and the convivial 'Harbourside Inn' is popular with locals and tourists alike. Locally caught fish features on the varied and interesting restaurant menu.

ROOMS: 26 en suite (4 fmly) in all bedrooms **PARKING:** 50 **NOTES:** in restaurant

S

ST AUSTELL, continued

★★71% Victoria Inn & Lodge
Victoria, Roche PL26 8LQ
☎ 01726 890207 📠 01726 891233
e-mail: victoriainn@smallandfriendly.co.uk
***Dir:** 6m W of Bodmin on A30. 1st left after garage, Victoria Inn approx 500yds on right*
Situated midway between Bodmin and Newquay, this establishment (now under new ownership) is a convenient choice for both the business and leisure traveller. The lodge-style bedrooms are purpose built and offer spacious, comfortable and well-equipped accommodation. A wide choice of meals is available in the convivial surroundings of the inn.
ROOMS: 42 en suite (11 fmly) (20 GF) ⊗ in all bedrooms s £46; d £46 **FACILITIES:** STV Xmas **CONF:** Thtr 30 Class 30 Board 20 **PARKING:** 100 **NOTES:** ✗ ⊗ in restaurant RS 24-26 Dec

★★71% White Hart
Church St PL25 4AT
☎ 01726 72100 📠 01726 74705
e-mail: whitehart@smallandfriendly.co.uk
Situated in the town centre, this 18th-century, stone-built inn is now under new ownership. Bedrooms offer high standards of comfort and public areas are stylish and contemporary. The light and airy restaurant is the venue for a modern menu that makes good use of local produce.
ROOMS: 17 en suite (2 fmly) ⊗ in all bedrooms s fr £50; d fr £80 (incl. bkfst) **LB** **FACILITIES:** ♫ Xmas **CONF:** Thtr 50 Board 20 **PARKING:** 13 **NOTES:** ✗ ⊗ in restaurant

ST HELENS, Merseyside — Map 15 SJ59
See also Rainhill

⌂ Premier Travel Inn St Helens North
Garswood Old Rd, East Lancs Rd WA11 7LX
☎ 0870 9906374 📠 0870 9906375
web: www.premiertravelinn.com
***Dir:** 3m from M6 junct 23, on A580 towards Liverpool*
High quality, modern budget accommodation ideal for both families and business travellers. Spacious, en suite bedrooms feature bath and shower, satellite TV and many have telephones and modem points. The adjacent family restaurant features a wide and varied menu. For further details consult the Hotel Groups page.
ROOMS: 43 en suite s £46.95-£48.95; d £46.95-£48.95 **CONF:** Thtr 85 Class 30 Board 40

⌂ Premier Travel Inn St Helens South
Mickle Head Green, Eurolink, Lea Green WA9 4TT
☎ 08701 977237 📠 01744 820531
web: www.premiertravelinn.com
***Dir:** M62 junct 7, on A570 towards St Helens*
High quality, modern budget accommodation ideal for both families and business travellers. Spacious, en suite bedrooms feature bath and shower, satellite TV and many have telephones and modem points. The adjacent family restaurant features a wide and varied menu. For further details consult the Hotel Groups page.
ROOMS: 40 en suite s £46.95-£48.95; d £46.95-£48.95

> If you wish to use a particular credit card or debit card please check with the hotel that they are happy to accept it

ST IVES, Cambridgeshire — Map 12 TL37

★★★70% Slepe Hall
Ramsey Rd PE27 5RB
☎ 01480 463122 📠 01480 300706
e-mail: mail@slepehall.co.uk
web: www.slepehall.co.uk
***Dir:** from A14 on A1096 & follow by-pass signed Huntingdon towards St Ives, left into Ramsey Rd at lights by Toyota garage, hotel on left*

A welcoming and friendly atmosphere exists within Slepe Hall, which is located close to the town centre. Bedroom types vary, with both traditional and modern styles available. A choice of dining options is provided with light meals served in the lounge and bar or more formal eating in the restaurant.
ROOMS: 16 en suite (1 fmly) **FACILITIES:** STV Guests have free access to local private leisure club **CONF:** Thtr 200 Class 80 Board 60 Del from £115 **PARKING:** 70 **NOTES:** ⊗ in restaurant Closed 24-26 Dec & 1 Jan Civ Wed 60

★★★69% ⊛ Olivers Lodge
Needingworth Rd PE27 5JP
☎ 01480 463252 📠 01480 461150
e-mail: reception@oliverslodge.co.uk
web: www.oliverslodge.co.uk
***Dir:** follow A14 towards Huntingdon/Cambridge, take B1040 to St Ives. Cross 1st rdbt, left at 2nd then 1st right. Hotel 500mtrs on right*

Olivers Lodge sits in a quiet residential area on the outskirts of the town. A popular and well-run hotel, the proprietors and staff providing a helpful and friendly service. Bedrooms are situated in the main house and adjoining wing, each room is well equipped with a good range of facilities. Public rooms include a conservatory dining area and a cosy lounge bar; function and meeting rooms are available.
ROOMS: 12 en suite 5 annexe en suite (3 fmly) (5 GF) ⊗ in 16 bedrooms s £65-£82; d £75-£90 (incl. bkfst) **LB** **FACILITIES:** STV Free use of local health club ♫ Xmas **CONF:** BC Thtr 65 Class 35 Board 28 **PARKING:** 30 **NOTES:** ⊗ in restaurant Civ Wed 85

★★★67% **Dolphin**
London Rd PE27 5EP
☎ 01480 466966 🖷 01480 495597
e-mail: enquiries@dolphinhotelcambs.co.uk
Dir: *from A14 between Huntingdon & Cambridge onto A1096 towards St Ives. Left at 1st rdbt & immediately right. Hotel on left after 0.5m*
This modern hotel sits by delightful water meadows on the banks of the River Ouse. Open-plan public rooms include a choice of bars and a pleasant restaurant offering fine river views. The bedrooms are modern and varied in style; some are in the hotel while others occupy an adjacent wing. All are comfortable and spacious. Conference and function suites are available.
ROOMS: 30 en suite 37 annexe en suite (4 fmly) (22 GF) ⊗ in 36 bedrooms s £80-£95; d £100-£120 (incl. bkfst) **LB** **FACILITIES:** STV Fishing Sauna Gym **CONF:** Thtr 150 Class 50 Board 50 Del from £100 **PARKING:** 400 **NOTES:** ✗ ⊗ in restaurant RS 24 Dec-2 Jan Civ Wed 80

ST IVES, Cornwall & Isles of Scilly Map 02 SW54

★★★74% ◎ **Carbis Bay**
Carbis Bay TR26 2NP
☎ 01736 795311 🖷 01736 797677
e-mail: carbisbayhotel@talk21.com
web: www.carbisbayhotel.co.uk
Dir: *M5 junct 31, take A30 then A3074. After 2m through Lelant, pass garage on right. Take next right (Porthreptor Rd), continue to sea*

A peaceful location with access to its own white-sand beach, this hotel offers comfortable accommodation. Attractive public areas feature a smart bar and lounge, and a sun lounge overlooking the sea. Bedrooms, many with fine views, are well equipped and spacious. Interesting cuisine and particularly enjoyable breakfasts are offered in the spacious dining room.
ROOMS: 40 en suite (16 fmly) ⊗ in 6 bedrooms s £61-£101; d £122-£202 (incl. bkfst & dinner) **LB** **FACILITIES:** Fishing Snooker Private beach ♫ **CONF:** Thtr 120 Class 80 Board 60 Del from £75 **PARKING:** 200 **NOTES:** ✗ ⊗ in restaurant Closed Xmas Civ Wed 140

See advert on this page

★★★68% **Chy-an-Albany**
Albany Ter TR26 2BS
☎ 01736 796759 🖷 01736 795584
e-mail: info@chyanalbanyhotel.com
Dir: *from A30 onto A3074 signed St Ives, hotel on left just before junct*
Conveniently located, this pleasant hotel enjoys splendid sea views. Comfortable bedrooms, some with balconies and sea views, come in a variety of sizes. Friendly staff and the relaxing environment mean that guests return on a regular basis. Freshly prepared and appetising cuisine is served in the dining room and a bar menu is also available.
ROOMS: 39 en suite (11 fmly) ⊗ in all bedrooms s £55-£76; d £110-£154 (incl. bkfst) **LB** **FACILITIES:** STV ♫ Xmas **CONF:** Thtr 80 Class 40 Board 30 Del from £59 **SERVICES:** Lift **PARKING:** 33 **NOTES:** ✗ ⊗ in restaurant Civ Wed 80

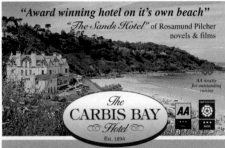

★★★67% ◎ **Garrack**
Burthallan Ln, Higher Ayr TR26 3AA
☎ 01736 796199 🖷 01736 798955
e-mail: aa@garrack.com
Dir: *turn off A30 for St Ives. Follow yellow holiday route signs on B3311. In St Ives, hotel is signed from 1st mini rdbt*

Enjoying a peaceful elevated position with splendid views across the harbour and Porthmeor Beach, the Garrack sits in its own delightful grounds and gardens. Bedrooms are comfortable and many have sea views. Public areas include a small leisure suite, a choice of lounges and an attractive restaurant.
ROOMS: 16 en suite 2 annexe en suite (2 fmly) s £68-£76; d £126-£180 (incl. bkfst) **LB** **FACILITIES:** Sauna Solarium Gym Xmas **CONF:** Thtr 30 Board 12 **PARKING:** 30 **NOTES:** ✗ ⊗ in restaurant

We have indicated only the hotels that don't accept credit or debit cards

ST IVES, continued

★★★67% Porthminster
The Terrace TR26 2BN
☎ 01736 795221 🖷 01736 797043
e-mail: reception@porthminster-hotel.co.uk
web: www.porthminster-hotel.co.uk
Dir: *on A3074*
This friendly hotel enjoys an enviable location with spectacular views of St Ives Bay. Extensive leisure facilities, a versatile function suite and a number of lounges are available. Bedrooms are comfortable and well equipped and many rooms have sea views.
ROOMS: 43 en suite (14 fmly) in 5 bedrooms s £55-£72; d £126-£160 (incl. bkfst) **LB FACILITIES: Spa** Sauna Solarium Gym Xmas **CONF:** Thtr 130 Class 20 Board 35 Del from £79 **SERVICES:** Lift **PARKING:** 43 **NOTES:** in restaurant Closed 2-12 Jan Civ Wed 130

See advert on opposite page

★★★65% Tregenna Castle Hotel
TR26 2DE
☎ 01736 795254 🖷 01736 796066
e-mail: hotel@tregenna-castle.co.uk
Dir: *A30 from Exeter to Penzance, at Lelant (W of Hayle) take A3074 to St Ives, through Carbis Bay, main entrance signed on left*
Sitting at the top of town in beautiful landscaped gardens, this popular hotel boasts spectacular views of St Ives. Many leisure facilities are available, including indoor and outdoor pools, a gym and a sauna. Families are particularly welcome. Bedrooms are generally spacious. A carte menu or carvery buffet are offered in the restaurant.
ROOMS: 81 en suite (12 fmly) (16 GF) in 49 bedrooms **FACILITIES:** STV supervised 14 Squash Sauna Solarium Gym Putt green Jacuzzi Health spa Steam room Xmas **CONF:** Thtr 250 Class 150 Board 30 Del from £90 **SERVICES:** Lift **PARKING:** 200 **NOTES:** in restaurant Civ Wed 160

★★72% *Boskerris*
Boskerris Rd, Carbis Bay TR26 2NQ
☎ 01736 795295 🖷 01736 798632
e-mail: Boskerris.Hotel@btinternet.com
Dir: *on entering Carbis Bay take 3rd right after petrol station*
This hotel, now under new ownership, enjoys a peaceful location and great views, particularly from the terraced area, which looks out over Carbis Bay and St Ives harbour. Service is friendly and attentive, and bedrooms are stylish and comfortable. Public areas provide a range of facilities including a swimming pool and attractive gardens.
ROOMS: 16 en suite (2 fmly) (2 GF) in 4 bedrooms **FACILITIES:** Table tennis **PARKING:** 20 **NOTES:** in restaurant Closed Nov-Etr

★★72% Pedn-Olva
West Porthminster Beach TR26 2EA
☎ 01736 796222 🖷 01736 797710
e-mail: pednolva@smallandfriendly.co.uk
Dir: *A30 to Hayle, then A3074 to St Ives. In St Ives turn sharp right at bus station into railway station car park, down steps to hotel*
Perched on the water's edge, this hotel is the closest thing to being aboard a ship, and the stylish public areas complement the unique location. Bedrooms combine comfort with quality and many have spectacular views across the bay. An imaginative, fixed-price menu is offered in the restaurant; during the summer, lighter meals are served on the terraces.
ROOMS: 30 en suite (5 fmly) in all bedrooms s fr £60; d fr £120 (incl. bkfst) **LB FACILITIES:** STV Xmas **PARKING:** 6 **NOTES:** in restaurant Civ Wed 60

★★67% *Cottage Hotel*
Boskerris Rd, Carbis Bay TR26 2PE
☎ 01736 795252 🖷 01736 798636
Leisureplex
e-mail: cottage.stives@alfatravel.co.uk
web: www.alfatravel.co.uk
Dir: *from A30 take A3074 to Carbis Bay. Right into Porthreptor Rd. Just before railway bridge, left through railway car park and into hotel car park*
Set in quiet, lush gardens, this pleasant hotel offers friendly and attentive service. Smart bedrooms are pleasantly spacious and many rooms enjoy splendid views. Public areas are varied and include a snooker room, a comfortable lounge and a spacious dining room with sea views over the beach and Carbis Bay.
ROOMS: 80 en suite (7 fmly) (2 GF) **FACILITIES:** Squash Snooker Sauna Gym **SERVICES:** Lift **PARKING:** 10 **NOTES:** in restaurant Closed Dec-Feb (ex Xmas) RS Nov & Mar

★★67% Hotel St Eia
Trelyon Av TR26 2AA
☎ 01736 795531 🖷 01736 793591
e-mail: hotelsteia@tinyonline.co.uk
Dir: *off A30 onto A3074, follow signs to St Ives, approaching town, hotel on right*
This smart hotel is conveniently located and enjoys spectacular views over St Ives, the harbour and Porthminster Beach. The friendly proprietors provide a relaxing environment. Bedrooms are comfortable and well equipped, some with sea views. The spacious lounge bar has a well-stocked bar and views can be enjoyed from the rooftop terrace.
ROOMS: 18 en suite (3 fmly) in all bedrooms s £29-£40; d £60-£80 (incl. bkfst) **LB PARKING:** 16 **NOTES:** in restaurant Closed Dec-Jan

ST LEONARDS-ON-SEA See Hastings & St Leonards

ST MARTIN'S See Scilly, Isles of

ST MARY CHURCH See Torquay

ST MARY'S See Scilly, Isles of

ST MAWES, Cornwall & Isles of Scilly Map 02 SW83

★★★78% Idle Rocks
Harbour Side TR2 5AN
☎ 01326 270771 🖷 01326 270062
e-mail: reception@idlerocks.co.uk
web: www.richardsonhotels.co.uk
Dir: *off A390 onto A3078, 14m to St Mawes. Hotel on left*

The Idle Rocks has splendid sea views overlooking the attractive fishing port. The lounge and bar also benefit from the views and in warmer months service is available on the terrace. Bedrooms are individually styled and tastefully furnished to a high standard.

continued

The daily-changing menu served in the restaurant features fresh, local produce in imaginative cuisine.
ROOMS: 23 en suite 10 annexe en suite (7 fmly) (2 GF) s £69-£179; d £138-£298 (incl. bkfst & dinner) **LB** **FACILITIES:** Xmas **PARKING:** 7 **NOTES:** ⊘ in restaurant

★★★76% ◉ **Rosevine**
TR2 5EW
☎ 01872 580206 📠 01872 580230
e-mail: info@rosevinehotels.co.uk
web: www.rosevine.co.uk
(For full entry see Portscatho)

★★73% ◉ **Rising Sun**
TR2 5DJ
☎ 01326 270233 📠 01326 270198
e-mail: therisingsun@btclick.com
Dir: *from A39 take A3078 signed St Mawes, hotel in village centre*
Looking out across the harbour and the Fal estuary, this smart looking hotel is a popular venue. Bedrooms are stylish and many rooms have sea views. Menus feature seafood and local produce. In the bar, which offers a large selection of ales, quality wines and malt whiskies, a range of dishes is offered. More casual dining is available in the brasserie.
ROOMS: 8 en suite (1 fmly) **PARKING:** 6 **NOTES:** ⊘ in restaurant

ST MELLION, Cornwall & Isles of Scilly — Map 03 SX36

★★★68% **St Mellion International**
PL12 6SD
☎ 01579 351351 📠 01579 350537
e-mail: stmellion@crown-golf.uk.com
web: www.st-mellion.co.uk
Dir: *from M5/A38 towards Plymouth & Saltash. St Mellion off A38 on A388 towards Callington & Launceston*
This purpose-built hotel, golfing and leisure complex is surrounded by 450 acres of land with two highly regarded 18-hole golf courses. The bedrooms generally have views over the courses and public areas include a choice of bars and eating options. Function suites are also available.
ROOMS: 39 annexe en suite (15 fmly) (8 GF) s £69-£105; d £88-£160 (incl. bkfst) **LB** **FACILITIES:** **Spa** (indoor pool) supervised ⛳ 36 Squash Snooker Sauna Solarium Gym Putt green Jacuzzi Steam room Skincare Xmas **CONF:** Thtr 350 Class 140 Board 80 Del from £115.50 **SERVICES:** Lift **PARKING:** 400 **NOTES:** (no dogs) ⊘ in restaurant Civ Wed 120

ST NEOTS, Cambridgeshire — Map 12 TL16

★★★74% **The George Hotel & Brasserie**
High St PE19 5XA
☎ 01480 812300 📠 01480 813920
e-mail: mail@thegeorgebuckden.com
web: www.thegeorgebuckden.com
Dir: *Just off A1 at Buckden 2m S of A1/A14 junct.*
Ideally situated in the heart of this historic town centre just a short drive from the A1. Public rooms feature a bustling ground floor brasserie, which offers casual dining throughout the day and evening; there is also an informal lounge bar with an open fire and comfy seating. Bedrooms are stylish, tastefully appointed and thoughtfully equipped.

continued

George Hotel, St Neots

ROOMS: 12 en suite ⊘ in all bedrooms s £70-£115; d £100-£130 (incl. bkfst) **FACILITIES:** STV Membership at local leisure centre Xmas **CONF:** Thtr 20 Class 10 Board 10 **SERVICES:** Lift **PARKING:** 25 **NOTES:** ⊘ in restaurant

★★64% **Abbotsley Golf Hotel**
Potton Rd, Eynesbury Hardwicke PE19 6XN
☎ 01480 474000 📠 01480 471018
e-mail: abbotsley@americangolf.uk.com
Dir: *A1(M) onto A428 towards Cambridge, left at Tesco rdbt, 3rd exit at 4th rdbt then 1st right & follow signs*
This purpose-built hotel caters well for its many avid golfing guests, with a 250-acre estate encompassing two courses, a golf school and leisure complex. The bedrooms are generally spacious

continued on p490

ST NEOTS, continued

and surround a pleasing courtyard garden with a putting green. Public rooms overlook the adjacent greens.
ROOMS: 42 annexe en suite (2 fmly) (13 GF) ⊗ in 10 bedrooms s £54-£58; d £78-£80 (incl. bkfst) **LB** **FACILITIES:** ⛳ 36 Squash Solarium Gym Putt green Pool tables, Clay pigeon shooting **CONF:** Thtr 40 Class 26 Board 30 Del from £90 **PARKING:** 80 **NOTES:** ⊗ in restaurant RS Closed Xmas Day

Premier Travel Inn St Neots (Colmworth Park)

Colmworth Business Park PE19 8YH
☎ 08701 977238 📠 01480 408541
web: www.premiertravelinn.com
Dir: *from A1 at southern St Neots junt. Inn at 1st rdbt (A428/B1428)*
High quality, modern budget accommodation ideal for both families and business travellers. Spacious, en suite bedrooms feature bath and shower, satellite TV and many have telephones and modem points. The adjacent family restaurant features a wide and varied menu. For further details consult the Hotel Groups page.
ROOMS: 41 en suite s £47.95-£50.95; d £47.95-£50.95

Premier Travel Inn St Neots (Eaton Socon)

Great North Rd, Eaton Socon PE19 8EN
☎ 0870 9906314 📠 0870 9906315
web: www.premiertravelinn.com
Dir: *Just off A1 at rdbt of A428 & B1428 before St.Neots, 1m from St.Neots rail station*
High quality, modern budget accommodation ideal for both families and business travellers. Spacious, en suite bedrooms feature bath and shower, satellite TV and many have telephones and modem points. The adjacent family restaurant features a wide and varied menu. For further details consult the Hotel Groups page.
ROOMS: 63 en suite s £47.95-£50.95; d £47.95-£50.95

SALCOMBE, Devon

Map 03 SX73

See also Hope Cove

★★★★73% Soar Mill Cove

Soar Mill Cove, Malborough TQ7 3DS
☎ 01548 561566 📠 01548 561223
e-mail: info@soarmillcove.co.uk
web: www.soarmillcove.co.uk
Dir: *3m W of town off A381at Malborough. Follow 'Soar' signs*
Situated amid spectacular scenery with dramatic sea views, this hotel provides a relaxing stay. Family-run, with a committed team, keen standards of hospitality and service are apparent. Bedrooms are well equipped and many rooms have private terraces. There are different seating areas where impressive cream teas are served, or, for the more active, a choice of swimming pools. Local produce is used to good effect in the restaurant.
ROOMS: 22 en suite (5 fmly) (21 GF) ⊗ in all bedrooms s £94-£174; d £188-£232 (incl. bkfst) **LB** **FACILITIES:** Sauna Putt green Table tennis, Games room, 9 hole Pitch n putt, Spa treatment suite Xmas **CONF:** BC Thtr 100 Class 50 Board 50 Del from £150 **PARKING:** 30 **NOTES:** ⊗ in restaurant Closed 2 Jan-11 Feb

★★★★72% Thurlestone Hotel

TQ7 3NN
☎ 01548 560382 📠 01548 561069
e-mail: enquiries@thurlestone.co.uk
web: www.thurlestone.co.uk
(For full entry see Thurlestone)

★★★★69% Menzies Marine

Cliff Rd TQ8 8JH
☎ 01548 844444 📠 01548 843109
e-mail: marine@menzies-hotels.co.uk
web: www.menzies-hotels.co.uk
Dir: *from A38 towards Exeter take A384 to Totnes then follow A381 to Kingsbridge & Salcombe*
Enjoying a superb position overlooking the estuary, this hotel is one of the few in the centre of town. Bedrooms, many with balconies and sea views, are spacious and comfortable and most are located at the front of the hotel. The newly appointed leisure centre boasts a good-sized indoor pool.
ROOMS: 53 en suite (10 fmly) s £130; d £130 (incl. bkfst) **LB** **FACILITIES:** STV Sauna Solarium Gym Jacuzzi Xmas **SERVICES:** Lift **PARKING:** 50 **NOTES:** ⊗ in restaurant Civ Wed 70

★★★ Buckland-Tout-Saints

Goveton TQ7 2DS
☎ 01548 853055 📠 01548 856261
e-mail: buckland@tout-saints.co.uk
web: www.tout-saints.co.uk
(For full entry see Kingsbridge)

★★★78% Tides Reach

South Sands TQ8 8LJ
☎ 01548 843466 📠 01548 843954
e-mail: enquire@tidesreach.com
web: www.tidesreach.com
Dir: *off A38 at Buckfastleigh to Totnes. Then take A381 to Salcombe, follow signs to South Sands*

Superbly situated at the water's edge, this personally run, friendly hotel has splendid views of the estuary and beach. Bedrooms, many with balconies, are spacious and comfortable. In the bar and lounge attentive service can be enjoyed along with the view, and the Garden Room restaurant serves appetising and accomplished cuisine.
ROOMS: 35 en suite (7 fmly) ⊗ in 2 bedrooms s £66-£133; d £120-£290 (incl. bkfst & dinner) **LB** **FACILITIES:** supervised Squash Snooker Sauna Solarium Gym Jacuzzi Windsurfing, Sailing, Kayaking, Scuba diving, Hair & Beauty treatment ♫ **SERVICES:** Lift **PARKING:** 100 **NOTES:** No children 8yrs ⊗ in restaurant Closed Dec-early Feb

See advert on opposite page

SALE, Greater Manchester

Map 15 SJ79

★★★★70% Belmore Hotel

143 Brooklands Rd M33 3QN
☎ 0161 973 2538 📠 0161 973 2665
e-mail: belmore_hotel@hotmail.com
Dir: *from A56 turn onto A6144. At traffic lights (Brooklands Station on right) turn right into Brooklands Rd*
This stylish hotel is set in a quiet residential area. Public rooms

continued

S

include a choice of dining options: cooking in the fine dining classic restaurant is imaginative and prepared with skill, as is the more informal menu of the downstairs brasserie. Bedrooms are tastefully furnished, spacious and well equipped.

ROOMS: 23 en suite (2 fmly) ⊗ in 13 bedrooms s £70-£110; d £100-£125 (incl. bkfst) **FACILITIES:** STV Free access to local Health Club Xmas **CONF:** Thtr 130 Class 70 Board 60 Del from £158 **PARKING:** 38 **NOTES:** ⊗ in restaurant Civ Wed 80

⌂ Premier Travel Inn Manchester (Sale)
Carrington Ln, Ashton-Upon-Mersey M33 5BL
☎ 08701 977179 🖷 0161 905 1742
web: www.premiertravelinn.com
Dir: *M60 junct 8 take A6144(M) towards Carrington. Left at 1st lights, Inn on left*
High quality, modern budget accommodation ideal for both families and business travellers. Spacious, en suite bedrooms feature bath and shower, satellite TV and many have telephones and modem points. The adjacent family restaurant features a wide and varied menu. For further details consult the Hotel Groups page.
ROOMS: 40 en suite s £47.95-£50.95; d £47.95-£50.95 **CONF:** Thtr 25

SALISBURY, Wiltshire — Map 05 SU12
See also Landford

★★★74% ❀ Red Lion
Milford St SP1 2AN
☎ 01722 323334 🖷 01722 325756
e-mail: reception@the-redlion.co.uk
web: www.the-redlion.co.uk
Dir: *in city centre close to Guildhall Square*

This 750-year-old hotel is full of character. The individual bedrooms combine contemporary comforts with historic features, including one room with a medieval fireplace dating back to 1220. Public areas are also distinctive with a bar, lounge and the elegant

continued on p492

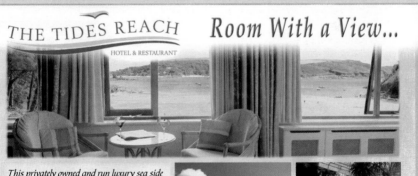

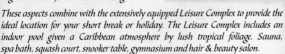

SALISBURY, continued

Vine Restaurant serving an interesting mix of modern and traditional-style dishes.
ROOMS: 51 en suite (2 fmly) ⊗ in 40 bedrooms s £97-£114; d £122-£149 (incl. bkfst) **LB** **FACILITIES:** STV Xmas **CONF:** Thtr 100 Class 50 Board 40 Del from £132 **SERVICES:** Lift **NOTES:** ⊗ in restaurant

See advert on opposite page

★★★71% Milford Hall

206 Castle St SP1 3TE
☎ 01722 417411 & 424116 🖷 01722 419444
e-mail: reception@milfordhallhotel.com
Dir: *few hundred yds from junct of Castle St, A36 ring road & A345 Amesbury Rd*

This hotel offers high standards of accommodation within easy walking distance of the city centre. There are two categories of bedroom; traditional rooms in the original Georgian house and spacious, modern rooms in a purpose built extension - all are extremely well equipped. Meals are served in the smart brasserie where a varied choice of dishes is provided.
ROOMS: 35 en suite (1 fmly) (20 GF) ⊗ in 15 bedrooms s £103-£113; d £113-£133 **LB** **FACILITIES:** STV Free facilities at local leisure centre **CONF:** Thtr 90 Class 70 Board 40 Del from £150 **PARKING:** 60 **NOTES:** ⊗ in restaurant Civ Wed 80

★★★71% The White Hart

St John St SP1 2SD
☎ 0870 400 8125 & 01722 327476
🖷 01722 412761
e-mail: whitehartsalisbury@macdonald-hotels.co.uk
web: www.macdonald-hotels.co.uk
Dir: *M3 junct 7/8 take A303 to A343 for Salisbury then A30. Follow signs for City Centre on ring road, into Exeter St, leading into St. John Street. Car park at rear.*

There has been a hotel on this site since the 16th century. Bedrooms vary between the contemporary-style rooms and those decorated in more traditional style, all of which boast a comprehensive range of facilities. The bar and lounge areas are popular with guests and locals for morning coffees and afternoon teas.
ROOMS: 68 en suite (6 fmly) ⊗ in 26 bedrooms s £90-£140; d £140-£170 (incl. bkfst) **LB** **FACILITIES:** STV Xmas **CONF:** Thtr 100 Class 40 Board 40 Del from £100 **PARKING:** 90 **NOTES:** ⊗ in restaurant Civ Wed

> Late for dinner? Quality standards mean that last orders for dinner vary according to star rating and should be no earlier than: ★★ 7.00pm ★★★ 8:00pm ★★★★ 9:00pm ★★★★★ 10:00pm

★★★67% Grasmere House Hotel

Harnhan Rd SP2 8JN
☎ 01722 338388 🖷 01722 333710
e-mail: grasmerehotel@mistral.co.uk
web: www.grasmerehotel.com
Dir: *on A3094 on S side of Salisbury next to All Saints Church in Harnham*

This popular hotel dates from 1896 and has gardens overlooking the water meadows and the cathedral. The attractive bedrooms vary in size, some offer excellent quality and comfort and some are specially equipped for less mobile guests. In summer, guests have the option of dining on the pleasant outdoor terrace.
ROOMS: 7 en suite 31 annexe en suite (16 fmly) (9 GF) ⊗ in 30 bedrooms s £85.50-£99.50; d £105.50-£135.50 (incl. bkfst) **LB** **FACILITIES:** STV Fishing Jacuzzi Xmas **CONF:** Thtr 110 Class 45 Board 45 Del from £135.50 **PARKING:** 64 **NOTES:** Civ Wed 120

See advert on opposite page

★★★60% The Rose & Crown Hotel

Harnham Rd, Harnham SP2 8JQ
☎ 0870 6096163 & 01722 399955 🖷 01722 339816
e-mail: roseandcrown@corushotels.com
web: www.corushotels.com/roseandcrown
Dir: *Just off A3094, on Harnham Rd, on S side of Salisbury*

This character hotel is situated on a quiet stretch of the River Avon, just five minutes from town. Most bedrooms are large and enjoy views of the cathedral and gardens, which reach run down to the river. Public areas are spacious and there is plenty of parking.
ROOMS: 28 en suite (5 fmly) (3 GF) ⊗ in 10 bedrooms s £116-£146; d £116-£146 **LB** **FACILITIES:** STV Fishing Xmas **CONF:** Thtr 80 Class 40 Board 40 **PARKING:** 42 **NOTES:** ⊗ in restaurant Civ Wed 90

⌂ *Kings Head Inn*

1 Bridge St SP1 2ND
☎ 01722 342050 438400 🖷 01722 326743
e-mail: salisburylodge@jdwetherspoon.co.uk
Dir: *in town centre*
Very centrally located, with some rooms overlooking the high street, this refurbished lodge offers a lively atmosphere with its

continued

popular Lloyds No 1 bar and extensive menus. The well-equipped bedrooms have a number of welcome extras. Some outdoor seating is available in the summer.
ROOMS: 32 en suite

⌂ Premier Travel Inn Salisbury

Bishopdown Retail Park, Pearce Way SP1 3YU
☎ 08701 977225 🖷 01722 337889
web: www.premiertravelinn.com
Dir: *From Salisbury Centre, follow A30 towards Marlborough for 1 mile. Inn off Hampton Park at rdbt*
High quality, modern budget accommodation ideal for both families and business travellers. Spacious, en suite bedrooms feature bath and shower, satellite TV and many have telephones and modem points. The adjacent family restaurant features a wide and varied menu. For further details consult the Hotel Groups page.
ROOMS: 60 en suite s £49.95; d £49.95

SALTASH, Cornwall & Isles of Scilly — Map 03 SX45

★★★67% China Fleet Country Club

PL12 6LJ
☎ 01752 848668 🖷 01752 848456
e-mail: sales@china-fleet.co.uk
web: www.china-fleet.co.uk
Dir: *A38 towards Plymouth/Saltash. Cross Tamar Bridge taking slip road before tunnel. Right at lights, 1st left follow signs 0.5m.*
In a convenient, quiet location, ideal for access to Plymouth and the countryside, this hotel offers an extensive range of leisure facilities including an impressive golf course. Bedrooms are all located in annexe buildings; each is equipped with its own kitchen. There is a range of dining options, and the restaurant offers interesting and imaginative choices.
ROOMS: 40 en suite (21 GF) ⊘ in 30 bedrooms s £42-£88
FACILITIES: Spa STV supervised 18 Squash Sauna Solarium Gym Putt green Jacuzzi 28 bay Floodlit driving range Health & beauty suite Hairdressers **CONF:** Thtr 80 Class 30 Board 34 **SERVICES:** Lift
PARKING: 400 **NOTES:** ⊘ in restaurant Civ Wed 80

⌂ Travelodge

Callington Rd, Carkeel PL12 6LF
☎ 08700 850 950 🖷 01752 841079
web: www.travelodge.co.uk
Dir: *on A38 Saltash bypass - 1m from Tamar Bridge*
Travelodge offers good quality, good value, modern accommodation. Ideal for families, the spacious, en suite bedrooms include remote-control TV, tea and coffee-making facilities and comfortable beds. Meals can be taken at the nearby family restaurant. For further details consult the Hotel Groups page.
ROOMS: 53 en suite s fr £26; d fr £26 **CONF:** Thtr 25 Class 15 Board 12

SALTBURN-BY-THE-SEA, North Yorkshire — Map 19 NZ62

★★★66% Rushpool Hall Hotel

Saltburn Ln TS12 1HD
☎ 01287 624111 🖷 01287 625255
A grand Victorian mansion nestling in its own grounds and woodlands. Stylish, elegant bedrooms are well equipped and spacious; many enjoy excellent sea views. The interesting public rooms are filled with charm and character, and roaring fires welcome guests in cooler months. The hotel boasts an excellent reputation as a wedding venue thanks to its superb location and experienced event management.
ROOMS: 21 en suite **FACILITIES:** STV Fishing Birdwatching Xmas
CONF: Thtr 100 Class 75 Board 60 **PARKING:** 120 **NOTES:** ⊘ in restaurant

SALTBURN-BY-THE-SEA, continued

★★67% Hunley Hall Golf Club & Hotel

Ings Ln, Brotton TS12 2QQ
☎ 01287 676216 📠 01287 678250
e-mail: enquiries@hunleyhall.co.uk
web: www.hunleyhall.co.uk
Dir: *A174 bypass take left at rdbt with monument, at T-junct turn left, pass church, turn right. 50yds turn right through housing estate, approx 0.5m*
Spectacularly situated, this hotel overlooks a 27-hole golf course and beyond to the coastline. The members' bar is licensed and serves snacks all day, and the restaurant offers a wide choice of food. Bedrooms, now refurbished, are comfortable and well equipped.
ROOMS: 8 en suite (1 fmly) (8 GF) ⊗ in all bedrooms s £47.50; d £75 (incl. bkfst) **LB** **FACILITIES:** ⛳ 27 Snooker Putt green **CONF:** Thtr 20 Class 12 Board 10 **PARKING:** 100 **NOTES:** ✗ ⊗ in restaurant RS 24 & 26 Dec

SAMPFORD PEVERELL, Devon — Map 03 ST01

★★67% Parkway House Country Hotel

EX16 7BJ
☎ 01884 820255 📠 01884 820780
e-mail: p-way@m-way.freeserve.co.uk
Dir: *M5 junct 27, follow signs for Tiverton Parkway Station. Hotel on right, on entering village*
An ideal choice for both business and leisure travellers, this hotel is located within a mile of the M5 and benefits from extensive views across the Culm Valley. The well-equipped bedrooms are comfortable and smartly presented. A popular venue for conferences and day meetings.
ROOMS: 10 en suite (2 fmly) s £40-£50; d £60-£70 (incl. bkfst) **LB** **FACILITIES:** STV Childrens Play Area **CONF:** BC Thtr 100 Class 50 Board 40 Del from £80 **PARKING:** 100 **NOTES:** ✗ ⊗ in restaurant

Travelodge Tiverton

Sampford Peverell Service Area EX16 7HD
☎ 08700 850 950 📠 01884 821087
web: www.travelodge.co.uk
Dir: *M5 junct 27*
Travelodge offers good quality, good value, modern accommodation. Ideal for families, the spacious, en suite bedrooms include remote-control TV, tea and coffee-making facilities and comfortable beds. Meals can be taken at the nearby family restaurant. For further details consult the Hotel Groups page.
ROOMS: 40 en suite s fr £26; d fr £26

AA Rosette Award for culinary excellence

SANDBACH, Cheshire — Map 15 SJ76

★★★61% The Chimney House Hotel

Congleton Rd CW11 4ST
☎ 0870 609 6164 📠 01270 768916
e-mail: chimneyhouse@corushotels.com
web: www.corushotels.com
Dir: *on A534, 1m from M6 junct 17 towards Congleton*
This conveniently positioned Tudor-style building benefits from ease of access to major motorway networks. The hotel is ideal for business meetings and functions. Bedrooms are well planned and equipped. Relax in the spacious lounge areas, or enjoy a meal in the patio restaurant overlooking the hotel gardens.

ROOMS: 48 en suite (16 fmly) (18 GF) ⊗ in 32 bedrooms s £79; d £79 **LB** **FACILITIES:** STV Sauna Putt green **CONF:** Thtr 120 Class 40 Board 40 Del £130 **PARKING:** 110 **NOTES:** ✗ ⊗ in restaurant RS Bank Holidays Civ Wed 70

Innkeeper's Lodge Sandbach

Brereton Green CW11 1RS
☎ 01477 544732
web: www.innkeeperslodge.com
Dir: *M6, junction 17, at rdbt bear left towards Holmes Chapel, follow to Brereton, lodge on left at Brereton Green*
A growing concept in the travel accommodation market. Smart rooms meet essential business requirements but also have home comforts. Dining options include all-day menus plus the added advantage of breakfast, which is included in the room price. For further details consult the Hotel Groups page.
ROOMS: 25 en suite s £45-£49.95; d £45-£49.95

SANDBANKS See Poole

SANDIWAY, Cheshire — Map 15 SJ67

★★★★79% Nunsmere Hall Country House Hotel

Tarporley Rd CW8 2ES
☎ 01606 889100 📠 01606 889055
e-mail: reservations@nunsmere.co.uk
Dir: *A54 to Chester, at x-rds with A49, turn right towards Warrington, hotel 2m on right*

In an idyllic and peaceful setting of well-kept grounds, including a 60-acre lake, this delightful house dates back to 1900. The mainly spacious bedrooms are individually styled, tastefully appointed to a very high standard and thoughtfully equipped. Guests can relax in a choice of elegant lounges, the library or the oak-panelled bar.

continued

Dining in the Crystal Restaurant is a relaxed affair and both a traditional carte and a gourmet menu are offered.
ROOMS: 36 en suite (2 GF) ⊘ in 10 bedrooms s £145-£170; d £200-£360 **LB** **FACILITIES:** Fishing Snooker Archery Air rifle, Clay pigeon shooting Falconry ♫ Xmas **CONF:** Thtr 50 Class 32 Board 26 Del £237.50 **SERVICES:** Lift **PARKING:** 80 **NOTES:** ⊘ in restaurant Civ Wed 120

SANDOWN See Wight, Isle of

SAUNTON, Devon Map 03 SS43

★★★★74% Saunton Sands

EX33 1LQ
☎ 01271 890212 01271 890145
e-mail: info@sauntonsands.com
web: www.brend-hotels.co.uk
Dir: *off A361at Braunton, signed Croyde B3231, hotel 2m on left*

Brend Hotels

Stunning sea views and direct access to five miles of sandy beach are just two of the features of this popular hotel. The majority of sea-facing rooms benefit from balconies, and splendid views can be enjoyed from all of the public areas, which include comfortable lounges. The Sands café/bar is a successful innovation and provides an informal eating option.
ROOMS: 92 en suite (39 fmly) s £72-£109; d £144-£318 **LB** **FACILITIES:** STV Squash Snooker Sauna Solarium Gym Putt green Sun Shower, Health and beauty salon, OFSTED registered nursery ♫ ch fac Xmas **SERVICES:** Lift **PARKING:** 142 **NOTES:** ⊘ in restaurant Civ Wed

See advert on this page

SAWBRIDGEWORTH, Hertfordshire Map 06 TL41

★★★72% *Manor of Groves Hotel, Golf & Country Club*

High Wych CM21 0JU
☎ 01279 600777 01279 600374
e-mail: info@manorofgroves.co.uk
web: www.manorofgroves.com
Dir: *A1184 to Sawbridgeworth, left to High Wych, right at village green & hotel 200yds left*

Delightful Georgian manor house set in 150 acres of secluded grounds and gardens, with its own 18-hole championship golf course and superb leisure facilities. Public rooms include an imposing open-plan glass atrium that features a bar, lounge area and modern restaurant. The spacious bedrooms are smartly decorated and equipped with modern facilities.
ROOMS: 80 en suite (2 fmly) (17 GF) ⊘ in 50 bedrooms **FACILITIES:** **Spa** STV supervised 18 Sauna Solarium Gym Putt green Jacuzzi Dance studio, beauty salon **CONF:** Thtr 400 Class 250 Board 50 **SERVICES:** Lift **PARKING:** 200 **NOTES:** ⊘ in restaurant RS 24 Dec-2 Jan Civ Wed 300

See advert on this page

SCARBOROUGH, North Yorkshire Map 17 TA08

★★★71% Ox Pasture Hall

Lady Edith's Dr, Raincliffe Woods YO12 5TD
☎ 01723 365295 📠 01723 355156
e-mail: oxpasturehall@btconnect.com
web: www.oxpasturehall.com
Dir: *from A171 (Scarborough to Scalby road) turn into Lady Edith's Drive*

This delightful family run country hotel is set in the quiet North Riding Forest Park and offers a very friendly atmosphere. Bedrooms are individual, stylish and comfortably equipped and are split between the main house, townhouse and the delightful courtyard. Public areas include a split-level bar, quiet lounge, and attractive restaurant. At the time of the last inspection a function room was under construction.
ROOMS: 17 en suite 6 annexe en suite (1 fmly) (14 GF) ⊗ in all bedrooms s £57.50-£67.50; d £115-£160 (incl. bkfst) **LB**
FACILITIES: Fishing ♫ Xmas **CONF:** Thtr 200 Class 100 Board 80 Del from £70 **PARKING:** 50 **NOTES:** ⊗ in restaurant

★★★70% The Crescent

2 Belvoir Ter YO11 2PP
☎ 01723 360929 📠 01723 354126
e-mail: reception@thecrescenthotel.com
web: www.thecrescenthotel.com
Dir: *From A64 towards railway station, follow signs to Brunswick Pavilion. At lights turn into hotel entrance*
This smart, Grade II listed hotel is a short distance from the town centre. The comfortable accommodation is comprehensively equipped, and there are spacious bars and lounges. There is a choice of dining areas and bars: Reflections, an elegant restaurant, serves a set-price menu and carte. A separate carvery, Cooney's, offers a less formal option. Service is caring and attentive.
ROOMS: 20 en suite ⊗ in 15 bedrooms s £49-£75; d £87.50-£125 (incl. bkfst) **LB** **CONF:** Thtr 30 Class 25 Board 25 Del from £85
SERVICES: Lift **NOTES:** ✖ No children 6yrs ⊗ in restaurant Closed 25-26 Dec

S

♫ Entertainment

★★★69% ❀ *Beiderbecke's Hotel*

1-3 The Crescent YO11 2PW
☎ 01723 365766 📠 01723 367433
e-mail: info@beiderbeckes.com
Dir: *in town centre, 200mtrs from railway station*
Situated in a Georgian crescent this hotel is close to all the main attractions. Bedrooms are very smart, well equipped and offer plenty of space and comfort. Some rooms have views over the town to the sea. Marmalade's, the hotel restaurant, offers international cuisine with a modern twist and hosts live music acts at weekends, including the resident jazz band.

continued

ROOMS: 27 en suite (1 fmly) ⊗ in 10 bedrooms **FACILITIES:** Snooker ♫ **CONF:** Thtr 35 Class 35 Board 28 **SERVICES:** Lift **PARKING:** 18 **NOTES:** ✖

★★★69% Crown

Esplanade YO11 2AG
☎ 01723 357400 📠 01723 357404
e-mail: info@ScarboroughHotel.com
web: www.scarboroughhotel.com
Dir: *on A64 follow town centre signs to lights opp railway station, turn right across Valley Bridge, then 1st left, right up Belmont Rd to cliff top*

Recent investment at this well known hotel includes refurbishment of the bedrooms and the installation of a superb new leisure and spa facility. The hotel's enviable position overlooking the harbour and South Bay means that most of the front facing bedrooms have superb views. The hotel has two restaurants and significant conference facilities.
ROOMS: 83 en suite (7 fmly) ⊗ in 20 bedrooms s £36-£75; d £54-£120 (incl. bkfst) **LB** **FACILITIES: Spa** 🏊 supervised Sauna Solarium Gym Jacuzzi Health spa ♫ Xmas **CONF:** BC Thtr 200 Class 110 Board 100 Del from £65 **SERVICES:** Lift **PARKING:** 25 **NOTES:** ⊗ in restaurant Civ Wed 160

★★★69% Royal

CLASSIC BRITISH

St Nicholas St YO11 2HE
☎ 01723 364333 & 374374 📠 01723 371780
e-mail: royalhotel@englishrosehotels.co.uk
Dir: *A64 into town. Follow town centre/South Bay signs. Hotel opp town hall*
This smart hotel enjoys a central location. Bedrooms are neatly appointed and offer a variety of styles from contemporary to traditional and include some suites. Public areas are elegant and include well-equipped conference and banqueting facilities, a leisure suite and the popular and modern Café Bliss where light snacks are served all day.
ROOMS: 118 en suite (14 fmly) ⊗ in 16 bedrooms s £60-£75; d £100-£250 (incl. bkfst) **LB** **FACILITIES:** STV 🏊 supervised Sauna Solarium Gym Jacuzzi Steam room, massage available ♫ Xmas
CONF: BC Thtr 300 Class 125 Board 75 Del from £85 **SERVICES:** Lift
NOTES: ✖ ⊗ in restaurant Civ Wed 150

See advert on opposite page

S

SCARBOROUGH, continued

★★★69% *Wrea Head Country Hotel*

Barmoor Ln, Scalby YO13 0PB
☎ 01723 378211 🖷 01723 371780
e-mail: wreahead@englishrosehotels.co.uk
web: www.englishrosehotels.co.uk
Dir: *from Scarborough follow A171 to hotel sign on left, turn into Barmoor Lane, follow road through ford & hotel entrance is immediately on left*

This elegant country house is situated in 14 acres of grounds and gardens near the road from Scarborough to Whitby. Bedrooms are individually furnished and decorated, many of them with fine views. Public rooms include the oak-panelled lounge with inglenook fireplace and a beautiful library lounge, full of books and games.
ROOMS: 20 en suite (2 fmly) (1 GF) **FACILITIES:** STV ♫ Putt green **CONF:** Thtr 30 Class 16 Board 20 **PARKING:** 50 **NOTES:** ✗ ⊗ in restaurant Civ Wed 50

See advert on page 497

★★★67% Palm Court

St Nicholas Cliff YO11 2ES
☎ 01723 368161 🖷 01723 371547
e-mail: palmcourt@scarborough.co.uk
Dir: *follow signs for Town Centre & Town Hall, hotel before Town Hall on right*

The public rooms are spacious and comfortable at this modern, town centre hotel. Traditional cooking is provided in the attractive restaurant and staff are friendly and helpful. Bedrooms are comfortable and well equipped. Extra facilities include a swimming pool and free, covered parking.
ROOMS: 43 en suite (7 fmly) **FACILITIES:** ⛾ ♫ Xmas **CONF:** Thtr 200 Class 100 Board 60 Del £75 **SERVICES:** Lift **PARKING:** 80 **NOTES:** ✗ ⊗ in restaurant

★★★66% Esplanade

Belmont Rd YO11 2AA
☎ 01723 360382 🖷 01723 376137
e-mail: enquiries@theesplanade.co.uk
Dir: *from town centre over Valley Bridge, left then immediately right onto Belmont Rd, hotel 100mtrs on right*

This large hotel enjoys a superb position overlooking South Bay and the harbour. Both the terrace, leading from the lounge bar, and the restaurant, with its striking oriel window, benefit from magnificent views. Bedrooms are comfortably furnished and are well equipped. Touring groups are also well catered for.
ROOMS: 73 en suite (9 fmly) s £51; d £96-£106 (incl. bkfst) **LB FACILITIES:** Table tennis Xmas **CONF:** Thtr 140 Class 100 Board 40 Del from £65 **SERVICES:** Lift **PARKING:** 20 **NOTES:** ⊗ in restaurant Closed 2 Jan-4 Feb

> Popped the question? Hotels with Civ wed in their entry are licensed for civil wedding ceremonies. Maximum numbers for the ceremony only are shown e.g. Civ wed 120

★★★66% Hotel St Nicholas

St Nicholas Cliff YO11 2EU
☎ 01723 364101 🖷 01723 500538
e-mail: reservations.stnicholas@crerarhotels.com
web: www.crerarhotels.com
Dir: *in town centre, railway station on right, right at lights, left at next lights, across rdbt, next right*

This attractive Victorian hotel enjoys fine views over the South Bay and is just a short walk from the town. Recent years have seen much refurbished, and the public rooms and many of the bedrooms are very smart. The hotel has a variety of seating areas, a traditional carvery restaurant and a street-side bar/bistro.

ROOMS: 138 en suite (17 fmly) ⊗ in 39 bedrooms s £55-£105; d £75-£160 (incl. bkfst) **LB FACILITIES:** STV ⛾ supervised Sauna Solarium Gym ♫ Xmas **CONF:** Thtr 400 Class 150 Board 50 Del from £95 **SERVICES:** Lift **PARKING:** 15 **NOTES:** ✗ ⊗ in restaurant Civ Wed 200

★★★63% Ambassador

Centre of the Esplanade YO11 2AY
☎ 01723 362841 🖷 01723 366166
e-mail: ask@ambassadorhotelscarborough.co.uk
web: www.ambassadorhotelscarborough.co.uk
Dir: *A64, right at 1st small rdbt opposite B&Q, right at next small rdbt, immediate left down Avenue Victoria to Cliff Top*

Standing on the South Cliff with excellent views over the bay, this friendly hotel offers well-equipped bedrooms, some of which are executive rooms. An indoor swimming pool, sauna and solarium are also available and entertainment is provided during the summer season. Public areas, including the restaurant have been refurbished.
ROOMS: 59 en suite (10 fmly) ⊗ in 10 bedrooms s £40-£100; d £50-£144 (incl. bkfst & dinner) **LB FACILITIES: Spa** STV ⛾ Sauna Solarium Steam room ♫ Xmas **CONF:** BC Thtr 140 Class 90 Board 60 Del from £100 **SERVICES:** Lift air con **NOTES:** ⊗ in restaurant

See advert on opposite page

★★73% *The Mount*

Cliff Bridge Ter, Saint Nicholas Cliff YO11 2HA
☎ 01723 360961 🖷 01723 360961

Standing in a superb, elevated position and enjoying magnificent views of the South Bay, this elegant Regency hotel is personally owned and managed to a high standard. The richly furnished and comfortable public rooms are inviting, and the well-equipped bedrooms have been attractively decorated. The deluxe rooms are mini-suites and are very spacious and comfortable.
ROOMS: 50 en suite (5 fmly) ⊗ in 2 bedrooms **FACILITIES: SERVICES:** Lift **NOTES:** Closed Jan-mid Mar

See advert on opposite page

★★68% Park Manor
Northstead Manor Dr YO12 6BB
☎ 01723 372090 🖷 01723 500480
e-mail: info@parkmanor.co.uk
web: www.parkmanor.co.uk
Dir: *off A165, next to Peasholm Park*

Enjoying a peaceful residential setting with some sea views, this smartly presented, friendly hotel provides the seaside tourist with a wide range of facilities. Bedrooms vary in size and style but all are smartly furnished and well equipped. There is a spacious lounge, smart restaurant, games room and indoor pool and steam room for relaxation.
ROOMS: 42 en suite (6 fmly) s £36-£60; d £72-£120 (incl. bkfst) **LB**
FACILITIES: Spa Pool table Steam room Table tennis Xmas
CONF: Thtr 25 Class 20 Board 20 Del from £60 **SERVICES:** Lift
PARKING: 20 **NOTES:** No children 3yrs in restaurant

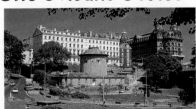

SCARBOROUGH, continued

★★67% Red Lea
Prince of Wales Ter YO11 2AJ
☎ 01723 362431 ⎙ 01723 371230
e-mail: redlea@globalnet.co.uk
web: www.redleahotel.co.uk
Dir: *follow signs for South Cliff, Prince of Wales Terrace is off Esplanade opposite cliff lift*

This friendly, family-run hotel is situated by the cliff lift. Bedrooms are well equipped and comfortably furnished, and many at the front have picturesque views of the coast. There are two large lounges and a spacious dining room in which good-value, traditional food is served.
ROOMS: 67 en suite (7 fmly) (2 GF) s £36-£40; d £72-£80 (incl. bkfst) **LB** **FACILITIES:** ⛶ Sauna Solarium Gym Xmas **CONF:** Thtr 40 Class 25 Board 25 Del from £65 **SERVICES:** Lift **NOTES:** ✗ ⊗ in restaurant

★★65% The Bedford
The Crescent YO11 2PR
☎ 01723 360084 ⎙ 01723 507374
e-mail: reception@bedfordhotel.info
Dir: *A64 to rail station, right at lights, 1st left, 1st right*
This hotel is a traditional, family owned and run seaside hotel ideally situated on this historic Crescent. The comfortable bedrooms vary in size; some are suitable for family occupancy and several have sea views. Public rooms are both spacious and comfortable, and the service is informal and friendly. Bar meals are available and the restaurant offers an interesting choice of dishes.
ROOMS: 27 en suite (8 fmly) (1 GF) s £31-£44; d £52-£78 (incl. bkfst) **LB** **FACILITIES:** ♫ Xmas **CONF:** Thtr 60 Class 40 Board 25 **NOTES:** ⊗ in restaurant

S

★★65% Bradley Court Hotel
Filey Rd, South Cliff YO11 2SE
☎ 01723 360476 ⎙ 01723 376661
e-mail: info@bradleycourthotel.co.uk
Dir: *from A64 into Scarborough, at 1st rdbt right signed Filey & South Cliff, left at next rdbt, hotel 50yds on left*
This popular hotel is only a short walk from both the town centre and the South Cliff promenade. Bedrooms are well equipped and there are spacious public rooms which include a bar lounge and a large, modern function room suitable for weddings and conferences.
ROOMS: 40 en suite (4 fmly) (8 GF) ⊗ in 30 bedrooms s £50-£60; d £60-£90 (incl. bkfst) **LB** **FACILITIES:** Xmas **CONF:** Thtr 100 Class 70 Board 60 Del from £60 **SERVICES:** Lift **PARKING:** 20 **NOTES:** ✗ ⊗ in restaurant

> Destination dining!
> 🏠 This symbol indicates a Restaurant with Rooms

★★65% *Clifton*
Queens Pde, North Cliff YO12 7HX
☎ 01723 375691 ⎙ 01723 364203
e-mail: clifton@englishrosehotels.co.uk
Dir: *on entering town centre, follow signs for North Bay*
Standing in an impressive position commanding fine views over the bay, this large holiday hotel is convenient for Peasholm Park and other local leisure attractions; tour groups are especially well catered for. Bedrooms are pleasant and entertainment is provided in the spacious public rooms during high season.
ROOMS: 71 en suite (11 fmly) **FACILITIES:** Sauna Solarium **CONF:** Thtr 120 Class 50 Board 50 **SERVICES:** Lift **PARKING:** 45 **NOTES:** ✗ ⊗ in restaurant

★★64% Manor Heath Hotel
67 Northstead Manor Dr YO12 6AF
☎ 01723 365720 ⎙ 01723 365720
e-mail: info@manorheath.co.uk
Dir: *follow signs for North Bay and Peasholm Park*
A warm welcome is offered at this pleasant, traditional, private hotel. Public areas include a comfortable lounge and a relaxing dining room. The bedrooms vary in size and style but all are bright and offer all the expected comforts. Private parking is available.
ROOMS: 14 en suite (6 fmly) ⊗ in all bedrooms s £22-£26; d £44-£52 (incl. bkfst) **PARKING:** 11 **NOTES:** ✗ ⊗ in restaurant Closed Nov-Jan

★★63% Delmont
18/19 Blenheim Ter YO12 7HE
☎ 01723 364500 ⎙ 01723 363554
e-mail: delmonthotelscar@aol.com
Dir: *Follow signs to North Bay. At seafront to top of cliff. Hotel near castle*
A friendly welcome is found at this hotel on the North Bay. Bedrooms are comfortable, and many have picturesque sea views. There are two lounges and a bar and a spacious dining room in which good-value, traditional food is served - with entertainment on most evenings.
ROOMS: 51 en suite (18 fmly) (5 GF) s £21-£37; d £42-£74 (incl. bkfst) **LB** **FACILITIES:** Games Room with Pool Table, Table Tennis, Dart Board ♫ Xmas **SERVICES:** Lift **PARKING:** 2 **NOTES:** ⊗ in restaurant

★★61% *Brooklands*
Esplanade Gardens, South Cliff YO11 2AW
☎ 01723 376576 ⎙ 01723 341093
Dir: *from A64 York, left at B&Q rdbt, right at next mini-rdbt, 1st left onto Victoria Avenue, at end turn left then 2nd left*

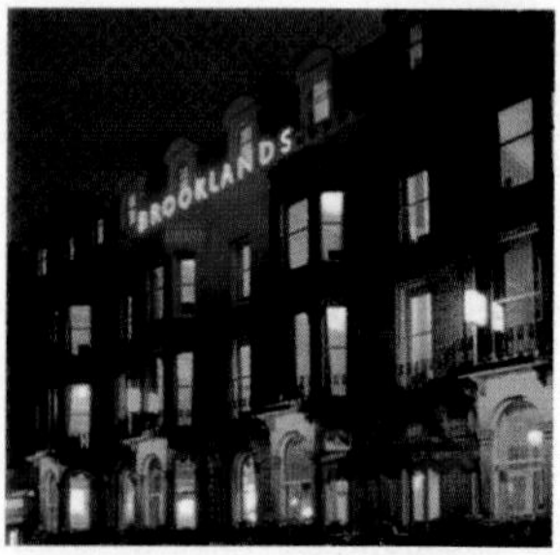

The Brooklands is a traditional, privately owned and run seaside hotel. It also caters for coach tours and offers good value for money. The hotel stands on the South Cliff overlooking Esplanade Gardens, and is within easy access of the sea. There are ample lounges to relax in and entertainment is often provided.
ROOMS: 55 en suite (11 fmly) (1 GF) ⊗ in 4 bedrooms **FACILITIES:** ♫ **CONF:** Thtr 120 Class 80 Board 30 **SERVICES:** Lift **PARKING:** 1 **NOTES:** ⊗ in restaurant Closed Jan RS Feb

SCILLY, ISLES OF

BRYHER
Map 02 SV81

Top Hotel

★★★ @@ **Hell Bay**
TR23 0PR
☎ 01720 422947 ▯ 01720 423004
e-mail: contactus@hellbay.co.uk web: www.hellbay.co.uk
Dir: *access is only by helicopter, plane or ship*
Located on the smallest of the inhabited islands on the edge of the Atlantic, this hotel makes a really special destination. The owners have filled the hotel with original works of art by artists who have connections with the islands, and the interior is decorated in cool blues and greens creating an extremely restful environment. The contemporary bedrooms are equally stylish and many have garden access and stunning sea views. Eating here is a delight, and naturally seafood features strongly on the award-winning, daily-changing menus.
ROOMS: 25 annexe en suite (3 fmly) (15 GF) ⊘ in all bedrooms d £260-£440 (incl. bkfst & dinner) **LB** **FACILITIES:** STV ⚲ ⚲ 9 Sauna Gym ⚲ Jacuzzi Boules Par 3 golf ch fac Xmas **CONF:** Thtr 36 Class 36 Board 36 Del from £200 **NOTES:** ⊘ in restaurant Closed Jan-Feb

ST MARTIN'S
Map 02 SV91

Top Hotel

★★★ @@@ **St Martin's on the Isle**
Lower Town TR25 0QW
☎ 01720 422090 & 422092 ▯ 01720 422298
e-mail: stay@stmartinshotel.co.uk
web: www.stmartinshotel.co.uk
Dir: *20-min helicopter flight to St Mary's; 20-min boat to St Martin's*
This attractive hotel, complete with its own sandy beach, enjoys an idyllic position on the waterfront overlooking Tresco and Tean. Bedrooms are brightly appointed, comfortably furnished and overlook the sea or the gardens. There is an elegant, award-winning restaurant and a lounge bar where guests can relax and enjoy the memorable view. Locally caught fish features significantly on the daily-changing menus.
ROOMS: 30 en suite (10 fmly) (14 GF) s £143-£400; d £260-£400 (incl. bkfst & dinner) **LB** **FACILITIES:** ⚲ ⚲ Snooker Clay pigeon shooting Boating Bikes Diving Snorkelling **CONF:** Thtr 50 Class 50 Board 50 **NOTES:** ⊘ in restaurant Closed Nov-Feb Civ Wed 100

ST MARY'S
Map 02 SV91

★★★73% **Tregarthens**
Hugh Town TR21 0PP
☎ 01720 422540 ▯ 01720 422089
e-mail: reception@tregarthens-hotel.co.uk
Dir: *100yds from quay*
Opened in 1848 by Captain Tregarthen this is now a well-established hotel. The impressive public areas provide wonderful views overlooking St Mary's harbour and some of the many islands, including Tresco and Bryher. The spacious bedrooms are well-equipped and neatly furnished. Traditional cuisine is served in the restaurant.
ROOMS: 31 en suite 1 annexe en suite (5 fmly) ⊘ in 4 bedrooms s £90-£120; d £180-£234 (incl. bkfst & dinner) **LB** **NOTES:** ⚲ ⊘ in restaurant Closed late Oct-mid Mar

See advert on this page

Early start?
Hotels at all star levels should provide in-room alarm clocks and/or alarm clocks

TRESCO Map 02 SV81

Top Hotel

★★★ ◎◎ **The Island**
TR24 0PU
☎ 01720 422883 🖷 01720 423008
e-mail: islandhotel@tresco.co.uk
web: www.tresco.co.uk/holidays/island_hotel.asp
Dir: *helicopter service Penzance to Tresco, hotel on NE of island*
This delightful colonial-style hotel enjoys a waterside location in its own attractive gardens. The spacious, comfortable lounges, airy restaurant and many of the bedrooms enjoy stunning sea views. All of the rooms are brightly furnished and many benefit from lounge areas, balconies or terraces. Carefully prepared, imaginative cuisine makes good use of locally caught fish.
ROOMS: 48 en suite (27 fmly) s £121-£321; d £242-£582 (incl. bkfst & dinner) **LB** **FACILITIES:** STV Fishing Boating Table tennis Bowls, boutique, internet access **CONF:** BC Thtr 80 Class 80 Board 80 Del from £200 **NOTES:** ⊗ in restaurant Closed Nov-Feb

★★77% ◎◎ **New Inn**
TR24 0QQ
☎ 01720 422844 423006 🖷 01720 423200
e-mail: newinn@tresco.co.uk
web: www.tresco.co.uk/holidays/new_inn.asp
Dir: *by New Grimsby Quay*
This friendly, popular inn enjoys a central location and offers bright, attractive, well-equipped bedrooms, many with splendid sea views. The popular bar offering real ales, serves an interesting range of snacks and meals. In addition guests may choose to dine in the airy bistro-style Pavilion or the elegant restaurant complete with its own bar.
ROOMS: 16 en suite (2 GF) s £110-£165; d £154-£218 (incl. bkfst & dinner) **LB** **FACILITIES:** Sea fishing, Bird watching, Walking Xmas **NOTES:** ⊗ in restaurant

♫ Entertainment

SCOTCH CORNER (NEAR RICHMOND), North Yorkshire Map 19 NZ20

The Scotch Corner Hotel
Scotch Corner Junction A1/A66 DL10 6NR
☎ 01748 850900 🖷 01748 825417
e-mail: enquiries@hotels-scotch-corner.com
web: www.hotels-scotch-corner.com
Dir: *at A1/A66 junct turn off towards Penrith*
At the time of going to press, the star classification for this hotel was not confirmed. Please refer to the AA internet site www.theAA.com for current information.
ROOMS: 90 en suite (5 fmly) (17 GF) ⊗ in 36 bedrooms s £39.95-£83; d £79-£93 (incl. bkfst) **LB** **FACILITIES: Spa** STV Sauna Solarium Gym Jacuzzi Hair Salon, Beautician Xmas **CONF:** Thtr 300 Class 100 Board 80 Del from £75 **SERVICES:** Lift **PARKING:** 200 **NOTES:** ⊗ in restaurant Civ Wed 200

Travelodge
Middleton Tyas Ln DL10 6PQ
☎ 08700 850 950 🖷 01325 377616
web: www.travelodge.co.uk
Dir: *A1/A66*
Travelodge offers good quality, good value, modern accommodation. Ideal for families, the spacious, en suite bedrooms include remote-control TV, tea and coffee-making facilities and comfortable beds. Meals can be taken at the nearby family restaurant. For further details consult the Hotel Groups page.
ROOMS: 50 en suite s fr £26; d fr £26

Travelodge Skeeby (Scotch Corner)
Skeeby DL10 5EQ
☎ 08700 850 950 🖷 0870 1911675
web: www.travelodge.co.uk
Dir: *0.5m S on A1*
Travelodge offers good quality, good value, modern accommodation. Ideal for families, the spacious, en suite bedrooms include remote-control TV, tea and coffee-making facilities and comfortable beds. Meals can be taken at the nearby family restaurant. For further details consult the Hotel Groups page.
ROOMS: 40 en suite s fr £26; d fr £26

SCUNTHORPE, Lincolnshire Map 17 SE81

★★★★74% ◎ **Forest Pines Hotel**
Ermine St, Broughton DN20 0AQ
☎ 01652 650770 🖷 01652 650495
e-mail: enquiries@forestpines.co.uk
web: www.forestpines.co.uk
Dir: *200yds from M180 junct 4, on Brigg-Scunthorpe rdbt*
This smart, modern hotel provides a comprehensive range of leisure facilities. Extensive conference rooms, a modern health and beauty spa, a championship golf course ensure that it is a popular choice with both corporate and leisure guests. A comfortable lounge and extensive public areas include a choice of dining options, with fine dining available in The Beech Tree Restaurant or more informal eating in the Garden Room or Mulligan's Bar. Bedrooms are modern, spacious and well equipped.
ROOMS: 114 en suite (66 fmly) (41 GF) ⊗ in 77 bedrooms s £79-£99; d £99-£129 (incl. bkfst) **LB** **FACILITIES: Spa** STV supervised 27 Sauna Gym Putt green Jacuzzi Mountain bikes Jogging track ♫ Xmas **CONF:** Thtr 375 Class 142 Board 134 Del from £149 **SERVICES:** Lift **PARKING:** 300 **NOTES:** ⊗ in restaurant Civ Wed 200

★★★67% **Wortley House**
Rowland Rd DN16 1SU
☎ 01724 842223 🖷 01724 280646
Dir: *M180 junct 3 take A18. Follow signs for Grimsby/Humberside airport, 2nd left into Brumby Wood Ln, over rdbt into Rowland Rd. Hotel 200yds on right*
A friendly hotel with good facilities for conferences, meetings, banquets and other functions. Bedrooms offer modern comfort and facilities. An extensive range of dishes is available in both the formal restaurant or the more relaxed bar setting.
ROOMS: 38 en suite (5 fmly) ⊗ in 28 bedrooms s £55-£65; d £75-£92 (incl. bkfst) **FACILITIES:** STV Xmas **CONF:** Thtr 300 Class 250 Board 50 Del from £90 **PARKING:** 100 **NOTES:** ⊗ in restaurant Civ Wed 250

continued

⌂ Premier Travel Inn Scunthorpe

Lakeside Retail Park, Lakeside Parkway DN16 3UA
☎ 08701 977226 🖷 01724 278651
web: www.premiertravelinn.com
Dir: *M180 junct 4, A18 towards Scunthorpe. At Morrisons rdbt left onto Lakeside Retail Park, Inn behind Morrisons petrol station*

High quality, modern budget accommodation ideal for both families and business travellers. Spacious, en suite bedrooms feature bath and shower, satellite TV and many have telephones and modem points. The adjacent family restaurant features a wide and varied menu. For further details consult the Hotel Groups page.

ROOMS: 40 en suite s £46.95-£48.95; d £46.95-£48.95

⌂ Travelodge Scunthorpe

Doncaster Rd, Gunness DN15 8TE
☎ 08700 850950 🖷 01724 289 391
web: www.travelodge.co.uk
Dir: *Follow M18 W to junct 5, take M180 towards Scunthorpe. 1st exit signed Scunthorpe. 1.5 m take 3rd exit at traffic island. Lodge on right.*

Travelodge offers good quality, good value, modern accommodation. Ideal for families, the spacious, en suite bedrooms include remote-control TV, tea and coffee-making facilities and comfortable beds. Meals can be taken at the nearby family restaurant. For further details consult the Hotel Groups page.

ROOMS: 40 en suite s fr £26; d fr £26

SEAHAM, Co Durham — Map 19 NZ44

Top Hotel

★★★★ ❀❀❀ Seaham Hall Hotel

Lord Byron's Walk SR7 7AG
☎ 0191 516 1400 🖷 0191 516 1410
e-mail: reservations@seaham-hall.com
web: www.seaham-hall.com
Dir: *from A19 take B1404 to Seaham. At lights straight over level crossing. Hotel approx 0.25m on right*

This imposing house was the setting for the wedding of Lord Byron and has been restored with an opulence he would have appreciated. Bedrooms, including some stunning suites, offer cutting edge technology, contemporary artwork and a real sense of style. Bathrooms are particularly lavish, with two-person baths a feature. Public rooms are equally impressive and accomplished cooking is a hallmark. The stunning Oriental Spa, accessed via an underground walkway, offers guests a wide range of treatments and a Thai brasserie.

ROOMS: 19 en suite (4 GF) ⊘ in all bedrooms s £195-£525; d £195-£525 (incl. bkfst) **LB** **FACILITIES: Spa** STV 🏊 Sauna Solarium Gym Jacuzzi Full spa Xmas **CONF:** Thtr 120 Class 48 Board 40 **SERVICES:** Lift air con **PARKING:** 122 **NOTES:** 🐕 ⊘ in restaurant Civ Wed 112

SEAHOUSES, Northumberland — Map 21 NU23

★★★67% Bamburgh Castle

NE68 7SQ
☎ 01665 720283 🖷 01665 720848
e-mail: bamburghcastlehotel@btinternet.com
web: www.bamburghcastlehotel.co.uk
Dir: *from A1 follow signs for Seahouses, car park entrance on rdbt opposite Barclays Bank, automatic barrier will rise*

This family run hotel enjoys a seafront location overlooking the harbour. There is a relaxed and friendly atmosphere with professional, friendly staff providing attentive service. Bedrooms vary in size and style with superior rooms being more spacious, all are attractively appointed. Front-facing rooms, plus the main lounge and restaurant all take advantage of the panoramic views out to sea.

ROOMS: 20 en suite (3 fmly) (3 GF) ⊘ in 16 bedrooms s £48-£58; d £84-£105 (incl. bkfst) **LB** **FACILITIES:** Putt green **CONF:** Thtr 40 Class 20 Board 25 **PARKING:** 30 **NOTES:** ⊘ in restaurant Closed 24-26 Dec & 2wks mid Jan

★★74% Olde Ship

NE68 7RD
☎ 01665 720200 🖷 01665 721383
e-mail: theoldeship@seahouses.co.uk
Dir: *lower end of main street above harbour*

Under the same ownership since 1910, this friendly hotel overlooks the harbour. Lovingly maintained, its sense of history is evident by the amount of nautical memorabilia on display. Public areas include a character bar, cosy snug and restaurant. The individual bedrooms are smartly presented. Two separate building contain executive apartments all with sea views.

ROOMS: 12 en suite 6 annexe en suite (3 GF) s £43-£50; d £86-£100 (incl. bkfst) **LB** **PARKING:** 18 **NOTES:** 🐕 No children 10yrs ⊘ in restaurant Closed Dec-Jan

SEAHOUSES, continued

★★69% *Beach House*
Sea Front NE68 7SR
☎ 01665 720337 🖷 01665 720921
e-mail: enquiries@Beachhousehotel.co.uk
web: www.beachhousehotel.co.uk
Dir: *follow signs from A1 between Alnwick & Berwick*
Enjoying a seafront location and views of the Farne Islands, this family-run hotel offers a relaxed and friendly atmosphere. Bedrooms come in a variety of sizes, but all are bright and airy. Dinner makes use of fresh produce and breakfast features local specialities. There is a well-stocked bar and comfortable lounge.
ROOMS: 14 en suite (5 fmly) ⊗ in all bedrooms **PARKING:** 16
NOTES: ✗ ⊗ in restaurant Closed Jan

SEALE, Surrey Map 06 SU84

Ramada Farnham
Hog's Back GU10 1EX
☎ 01251 782345 🖷 01251 783113
e-mail: sales.farnham@ramadajarvis.co.uk
web: www.ramadajarvis.co.uk
Dir: *on A31*
Set high on the Hog's Back Ridge, this large hotel is a popular venue for both conferences and meetings. Bedrooms are comfortably appointed for both business and leisure guests.
ROOMS: 96 en suite (6 fmly) (27 GF) ⊗ in 71 bedrooms s £99-£119; d £99-£119 **FACILITIES: Spa** STV Sauna Solarium Gym Xmas
CONF: Thtr 140 Class 60 Board 40 Del from £160 **PARKING:** 150
NOTES: ✗ ⊗ in restaurant Civ Wed 100

SEATON BURN, Tyne & Wear Map 21 NZ27

Travelodge (Newcastle North)
Front St NE13 6ED
☎ 08700 850 950 🖷 0191 217 0107
web: www.travelodge.co.uk
Dir: *A1 northbound, exit for Tyne Tunnel (A19). Lodge at 1st rdbt*
Travelodge offers good quality, good value, modern accommodation. Ideal for families, the spacious, en suite bedrooms include remote-control TV, tea and coffee-making facilities and comfortable beds. Meals can be taken at the nearby family restaurant. For further details consult the Hotel Groups page.
ROOMS: 40 en suite s fr £26; d fr £26

SEAVIEW See Wight, Isle of

SEDGEFIELD, Co Durham Map 19 NZ32

★★★75% Hardwick Hall
TS21 2EH
☎ 01740 620253 🖷 01740 622771
e-mail: info@hardwickhallhotel.co.uk
Dir: *off A1(M) junct 60 towards Sedgefield, left at 1st rdbt, hotel 400mtrs on left*
Set in extensive parkland, this 18th-century house has been transformed into a top conference and wedding venue and offers an impressive meeting and banqueting complex. There is a wing of stunning bedrooms to augment those in the original house. The atmospheric Cellar Bar and Bistro has a relaxed atmosphere.
ROOMS: 52 en suite (6 fmly) ⊗ in all bedrooms **FACILITIES:** STV
CONF: Thtr 700 Board 80 **SERVICES:** Lift **PARKING:** 200 **NOTES:** ✗ ⊗ in restaurant Civ Wed 500

Travelodge
TS21 2JX
☎ 08700 850 950 🖷 01740 623399
web: www.travelodge.co.uk
Dir: *on A689, 3m E of A1(M) junct 60*
Travelodge offers good quality, good value, modern accommodation. Ideal for families, the spacious, en suite bedrooms include remote-control TV, tea and coffee-making facilities and comfortable beds. Meals can be taken at the nearby family restaurant. For further details consult the Hotel Groups page.
ROOMS: 40 en suite s fr £26; d fr £26

SEDGEMOOR MOTORWAY SERVICE AREA (M5), Somerset Map 04 ST35

Days Inn Sedgemoor
M5 Northbound J22-21, Sedgemoor BS24 0JL
☎ 01934 750831 🖷 01934 750808
e-mail: sedgemoor.hotel@welcomebreak.co.uk
web: www.welcomebreak.co.uk
Dir: *M5 junct 21/22*
This modern building offers accommodation in smart, spacious and well-equipped bedrooms, suitable for families and business travellers, and all with en suite bathrooms. Continental breakfast is available and other refreshments may be taken at the nearby family restaurant. For further details see the Hotel Groups page.
ROOMS: 40 en suite s £45-£55; d £45-£55 **CONF:** BC

SENNEN, Cornwall & Isles of Scilly Map 02 SW32

★★66% *Old Success Inn*
Sennen Cove TR19 7DG
☎ 01736 871232 🖷 01736 871457
e-mail: oldsuccess@sennencove.fsbusiness.co.uk
Dir: *turn right off A30 approx 1m before Land's End, signed Sennen Cove. Hotel on left at bottom of hill*
This inn is romantically located at the water's edge, with spectacular views of the cove and the Atlantic Ocean. Popular with locals and visitors alike, the inn offers friendly service and a choice of dining in either the restaurant and bar; there is always a selection of fresh fish dishes.
ROOMS: 12 en suite (1 fmly) **FACILITIES:** ♫ **PARKING:** 12
NOTES: ⊗ in restaurant

⊗ No smoking

SEVENOAKS, Kent Map 06 TQ55

★★★71% Donnington Manor
London Rd, Dunton Green TN13 2TD
☎ 01732 462681 🖷 01732 458116
e-mail: reservations@donningtonmanorhotel.co.uk
web: www.donningtonmanorhotel.co.uk
Dir: *M25 junct 4, follow signs for Bromley/Orpington to rdbt. Left onto A224 (Dunton Green), left at 2nd rdbt. Left at Rose & Crown, hotel 300yds on right*
This extended 15th-century manor house is situated on the outskirts of Sevenoaks. Public rooms in the original part of the building have a wealth of character; they include an attractive

continued

oak-beamed restaurant, a comfortable lounge and a cosy bar. The purpose-built bedrooms are smartly decorated and well equipped.

ROOMS: 60 en suite (2 fmly) ⊗ in 20 bedrooms **FACILITIES:** STV ⌧ supervised Squash Sauna Gym Jacuzzi Xmas **CONF:** Thtr 180 Class 60 Board 40 Del from £125 **PARKING:** 120 **NOTES:** ⊁ ⊗ in restaurant Civ Wed 70

See advert under DARTFORD

SEVERN VIEW MOTORWAY SERVICE AREA (M4), Gloucestershire
Map 04 ST58

⌂ Travelodge
M48 Motorway, Severn Bridge BS35 4BH
☎ 08700 850 950 ▤ 01454 632482
web: www.travelodge.co.uk
Dir: M48 junct 1
Travelodge offers good quality, good value, modern accommodation. Ideal for families, the spacious, en suite bedrooms include remote-control TV, tea and coffee-making facilities and comfortable beds. Meals can be taken at the nearby family restaurant. For further details consult the Hotel Groups page.
ROOMS: 50 en suite s fr £26; d fr £26

SHAFTESBURY, Dorset
Map 04 ST82

★★★67% ◉ Royal Chase
Royal Chase Roundabout SP7 8DB
☎ 01747 853355 ▤ 01747 851969
e-mail: royalchasehotel@btinternet.com
web: www.theroyalchasehotel.co.uk
Dir: A303 to A350 signed Blandford Forum. Avoid town centre, follow road to 3rd rdbt
Equally suitable for both leisure and business guests, this well-known local landmark is situated close to the famous Gold Hill. Bedrooms come in 'standard' and 'crown' and all offer good levels of comfort and quality. In addition to the fixed-price menu in the Byzant Restaurant, guests have the option of eating more informally in the convivial bar.
ROOMS: 33 en suite (13 fmly) (6 GF) ⊗ in 10 bedrooms s £95; d £110-£120 **LB FACILITIES: Spa** STV ⌧ Turkish steam bath Xmas **CONF:** Thtr 180 Class 90 Board 50 Del £112.50 **PARKING:** 100 **NOTES:** ⊗ in restaurant Civ Wed 76

Restaurant with Rooms

🏠 ◉ La Fleur de Lys Restaurant with Rooms
Bleke St SP7 8AW
☎ 01747 853717 ▤ 01747 853130
e-mail: info@lafleurdelys.co.uk
web: www.lafleurdelys.co.uk
Dir: 0.25m off junct of A30 with A350 at Shaftesbury towards town centre
Located just a 3-minute walk from the famous Gold Hill, this

continued

restaurant with rooms combines efficient service standards with a relaxed and friendly atmosphere. Bedrooms vary for size, but all are well equipped, comfortable and include plenty of useful extras. A guest lounge and courtyard are available for afternoon tea or pre-dinner drinks.
ROOMS: 7 en suite (2 fmly) (1 GF) ⊗ in all bedrooms s £55-£65; d £85-£95 (incl. bkfst) **LB CONF:** Board 10 **PARKING:** 7 **NOTES:** ⊁ ⊗ in restaurant

SHALDON See Teignmouth

SHANKLIN See Wight, Isle of

SHAP, Cumbria
Map 18 NY51

★★★68% Shap Wells
CA10 3QU
☎ 01931 716628 ▤ 01931 716377
e-mail: manager@shapwells.com
Dir: between A6 and B6261, 4m S of Shap
This hotel, now under new ownership, occupies a wonderful secluded position amid trees and waterfalls. Extensive public areas include function and meeting rooms, a well-stocked bar, a choice of lounges and a spacious restaurant. Bedrooms vary in size and style and all are equipped with the expected facilities.
ROOMS: 91 en suite 7 annexe en suite (10 fmly) s £62; d £94 (incl. bkfst) **LB FACILITIES:** STV ⌧ Snooker Games room, walking in the 30 acre grounds Xmas **CONF:** Thtr 170 Class 80 Board 40 Del from £95 **SERVICES:** Lift **PARKING:** 200 **NOTES:** ⊗ in restaurant Civ Wed 150

SHEDFIELD, Hampshire
Map 05 SU51

★★★★66% *Marriott Meon Valley Hotel & Country Club*
Sandy Ln SO32 2HQ
☎ 01329 833455 ▤ 01329 834411
web: www.marriott.co.uk
Dir: from W, M27 junct 7 take A334 then towards Wickham and Botley. Sandy Lane is on left 2m from Botley

This modern, smartly appointed hotel and country club has extensive indoor and outdoor leisure facilities, including two golf courses. Bedrooms are spacious and well equipped, and guests have a choice of eating and drinking options. It is ideally suited for easy access to both Portsmouth and Southampton.
ROOMS: 113 en suite ⊗ in 80 bedrooms **FACILITIES:** STV ⌧ ⌧ 18 ⌧ Sauna Solarium Gym Putt green Jacuzzi Cardio-Vascular Aerobics Health & Beauty salon **CONF:** Thtr 80 Class 50 Board 32 **SERVICES:** Lift **PARKING:** 320 **NOTES:** ⊁ ⊗ in restaurant Civ Wed 96

TV dinner?
Room service at three stars and above

SHEFFIELD, South Yorkshire

Map 16 SK49

★★★★70% Sheffield Marriott Hotel

Kenwood Rd S7 1NQ
☎ 0870 400 7261 🖷 0870 400 7361
e-mail: eventorganiser.sheffield@marriotthotels.co.uk
web: www.marriott.co.uk
Dir: *follow A61 past Red Tape Studios on right , right at 2nd set of lights into St Marys Rd. At rdbt straight across, bear left into London Rd, right at lights, at top of hill straight across 1st and 2nd rdbt*

A smart, modern hotel peacefully located in a residential suburb a few miles from the city centre. Stylishly decorated bedrooms are spacious, quiet and very well equipped. The hotel also has an extensive range of leisure and meeting facilities. Drivers have the peace of mind of secure parking.

ROOMS: 114 en suite (14 fmly) (27 GF) 🚭 in 90 bedrooms **FACILITIES: Spa** STV 🏊 Fishing Sauna Solarium Gym 🏋 Jacuzzi Steam room, Health & beauty treatments ♫ **CONF:** Thtr 250 Class 100 Board 60 **SERVICES:** Lift **PARKING:** 200 **NOTES:** 🚭 in restaurant Civ Wed 200

★★★74% 🏵 Staindrop Lodge

Ln End, Chapeltown S35 3UH
☎ 0114 284 3111 🖷 0114 284 3110
e-mail: info@staindroplodge.co.uk
Dir: *M1 junct 35, take A629 for 1m, straight over 1st rdbt, right at 2nd rdbt, hotel approx 0.5m on right*

This bar, brasserie and hotel offers smart modern public areas and accommodation. An art deco theme continues throughout the open-plan public rooms and the comfortably appointed, spacious bedrooms. Service is relaxed and friendly, and all-day menus are available.

ROOMS: 32 en suite (6 fmly) (3 GF) 🚭 in 26 bedrooms s £70-£90; d £90-£130 (incl. bkfst) **LB FACILITIES:** STV **CONF:** Thtr 80 Class 60 Board 40 Del from £100 **SERVICES:** Lift air con **PARKING:** 80 **NOTES:** 🐕 🚭 in restaurant Civ Wed 80

★★★71% The Beauchief Hotel

161 Abbeydale Rd South S7 2QW
☎ 0114 262 0500 🖷 0114 235 0197
e-mail: beauchief@corushotels.com
web: www.corushotels.com
Dir: *from city centre 2m on A621 signed Bakewell*

On the southern outskirts of the city, this busy property attracts both resident and local business. The popular restaurant and Merchant's bar have an excellent reputation in the area for good food and hospitality. Bedrooms are well proportioned with many extras such as movie channels on the TV. Ample parking is a bonus.

ROOMS: 50 en suite (3 fmly) (19 GF) 🚭 in 39 bedrooms s £79; d £79 **LB FACILITIES:** STV **CONF:** Thtr 100 Class 50 Board 50 Del £120 **PARKING:** 200 **NOTES:** 🚭 in restaurant Civ Wed 95

★★★71% Whitley Hall

Elliott Ln, Grenoside S35 8NR
☎ 0114 245 4444 🖷 0114 245 5414
web: www.whitleyhall.com
Dir: *A61 past football ground, then 2m, right just before Norfolk Arms, left at bottom of hill. Hotel on left*

This 16th-century house stands in 20 acres of landscaped grounds and gardens. Public rooms are full of character and interesting architectural features, and command the best views of the gardens. Bedrooms are individually styled and furnished in keeping with this country house setting, as are the oak-panelled restaurant and bar.

ROOMS: 20 en suite (2 fmly) (1 GF) s £70-£79; d £92-£120 (incl. bkfst) **LB FACILITIES:** 🏋 ♫ **CONF:** Thtr 70 Class 50 Board 34 Del from £150 **PARKING:** 100 **NOTES:** 🐕 🚭 in restaurant Civ Wed 90

★★★67% Novotel Sheffield

50 Arundel Gate S1 2PR
☎ 0114 278 1781 🖷 0114 278 7744
e-mail: h1348@accor.com
web: www.novotel.com
Dir: *between Registry Office and Crucible/Lyceum Theatres, follow signs to Town Hall/Theatres & Hallam University*

Located in the heart of the city centre, this modern hotel is popular with both business and leisure guests. Local theatres and shops are within easy reach, while within the hotel, facilities include an indoor heated swimming pool and a range of meeting rooms. Spacious bedrooms are suitable for family occupation and yet manage to provide an equally ideal environment for business users. Novotel - AA Hotel Group of the Year 2005-6.

ROOMS: 144 en suite (40 fmly) 🚭 in 108 bedrooms s £55-£140; d £55-£140 **LB FACILITIES:** STV 🏊 Local gym facilities free for residents use Xmas **CONF:** BC Thtr 220 Class 180 Board 100 Del £130 **SERVICES:** Lift air con **PARKING:** 60 **NOTES:** Civ Wed 180

★★★66% The Garrison

Hillsborough Barracks, Penistone Rd S6 2GB
☎ 0114 249 9555 🖷 0114 249 1900
e-mail: enquiries@garrisonhotel.com
web: www.garrisonhotel.com

This unique hotel as been created from the former Hillsborough barracks and retains some of the original features. Bedrooms are modern and well equipped and a wide range of food is available in the main building. The adjacent Supertram provides easy access to the city.

ROOMS: 43 en suite (2 fmly) 🚭 in 34 bedrooms s £61.50; d £61.50 (incl. cont. bkfst) **FACILITIES:** STV Xmas **CONF:** Thtr 30 Class 30 Board 30 **PARKING:** 60 **NOTES:** 🐕 🚭 in restaurant Civ Wed 120

★★★66% Mosborough Hall

High St, Mosborough S20 5EA
☎ 0114 248 4353 🖷 0114 247 9759
e-mail: hotel@mosboroughhall.co.uk
web: www.mosboroughhall.co.uk
Dir: *M1 junct 30, take A6135 towards Sheffield, hotel 0.5m after a large set of lights, on right*

This 16th-century, Grade II listed manor house is set in gardens not far from the M1 and convenient for the city centre. Bedrooms vary in style, and some are very spacious. There is a galleried bar and conservatory lounge, and freshly prepared dishes are served in the traditional style dining room.

ROOMS: 52 en suite (1 fmly) (12 GF) 🚭 in 30 bedrooms s £52-£77; d £60-£85 (incl. bkfst) **LB CONF:** Thtr 300 Class 125 Board 70 Del £95 **PARKING:** 100 **NOTES:** 🚭 in restaurant Civ Wed 250

♫ Entertainment

★★66% Cutlers Hotel

Theatreland George St S1 2PF
☎ 0114 273 9939 🖷 0114 276 8332
e-mail: enquiries@cutlershotel.co.uk
web: www.cutlershotel.co.uk
Dir: *In retail, commerce & academic centre, 50mtrs from Crucible Theatre. Follow theatre signs*

Situated close to the Crucible Theatre in the city centre, this boutique hotel offers accommodation in well-equipped bedrooms and extras including hairdryers, trouser presses and business facilities. Public areas include a lower ground floor bistro, and room service is available if required. Small meeting rooms are also available. Discounted overnight parking is provided in the nearby public car park.

ROOMS: 45 en suite (4 fmly) ⊗ in 18 bedrooms s £40-£65; d £50-£75 (incl. bkfst) **LB** **FACILITIES:** STV Xmas **CONF:** BC Thtr 90 Class 40 Board 30 Del from £70 **SERVICES:** Lift **NOTES:** ⊗ in restaurant Civ Wed 50

⌂ *Hotel Ibis Sheffield City*

Shude Hill S1 2AR
☎ 0114 241 9600 🖷 0114 241 9610
e-mail: H2891@accor-hotels.com
Dir: *M1 junct 33, follow signs to Sheffield City Centre (A630/A57), at rdbt take 5th exit, signed Ponds Forge, for hotel*

Modern, budget hotel offering comfortable accommodation in bright and practical bedrooms. Breakfast is self-service and dinner is available in the restaurant. For further details, consult the Hotel Groups page.

ROOMS: 95 en suite

⌂ Innkeeper's Lodge Sheffield South

Hathersage Rd, Longshaw S11 7TY
☎ 01433 630374 🖷 01433 637102
web: www.innkeeperslodge.com
Dir: *8m from Sheffield city centre on A625 Sheffield Castleton Road at junction of A625 & B6051.*

A growing concept in the travel accommodation market. Smart rooms meet essential business requirements but also have home comforts. Dining options include all-day menus plus the added advantage of breakfast, which is included in the room price. For further details consult the Hotel Groups page.

ROOMS: 10 annexe en suite s £49.95; d £49.95

⌂ Premier Travel Inn Sheffield (Arena)

Attercliffe Common Rd S9 2LU
☎ 0870 238 3316 🖷 0114 242 3703
web: www.premiertravelinn.com
Dir: *M1 junct 34, follow signs to city centre. Inn opposite Arena*

High quality, modern budget accommodation ideal for both families and business travellers. Spacious, en suite bedrooms feature bath and shower, satellite TV and many have telephones and modem points. The adjacent family restaurant features a wide and varied menu. For further details consult the Hotel Groups page.

ROOMS: 61 en suite s £49.95-£52.95; d £49.95-£52.95

> The vast majority of establishments in this guide accept credit and debit cards. We indicate those that don't take any

SHEFFIELD, continued

⌂ Premier Travel Inn Sheffield (City Centre)

Angel St / Bank St Corner S3 8LN
☎ 0870 238 3324 ▤ 0870 241 9000
web: www.premiertravelinn.com
Dir: from M1 junct 33, follow signs for city centre (A630/A57). At Park Square rdbt 4th exit (A61 Barnsley). Left at 4th lights into Snig Hill then right at lights into Bank Street
High quality, modern budget accommodation ideal for both families and business travellers. Spacious, en suite bedrooms feature bath and shower, satellite TV and many have telephones and modem points. The adjacent family restaurant features a wide and varied menu. For further details consult the Hotel Groups page.
ROOMS: 160 en suite s £53.95; d £53.95

⌂ Premier Travel Inn Sheffield (Meadowhall)

Sheffield Rd, Meadowhall S9 2YL
☎ 0870 9906440 ▤ 0870 9906441
web: www.premiertravelinn.com
Dir: On A6178 approx 6m from city centre
High quality, modern budget accommodation ideal for both families and business travellers. Spacious, en suite bedrooms feature bath and shower, satellite TV and many have telephones and modem points. The adjacent family restaurant features a wide and varied menu. For further details consult the Hotel Groups page.
ROOMS: 103 en suite s £53.95; d £53.95

⌂ Travelodge

340 Prince of Wales Rd S2 1FF
☎ 08700 850 950 ▤ 0114 253 0935
web: www.travelodge.co.uk
Dir: follow A630, take exit for ring road & services
Travelodge offers good quality, good value, modern accommodation. Ideal for families, the spacious, en suite bedrooms include remote-control TV, tea and coffee-making facilities and comfortable beds. Meals can be taken at the nearby family restaurant. For further details consult the Hotel Groups page.
ROOMS: 67 en suite s fr £26; d fr £26 **CONF:** Thtr 30 Board 20

Destination dining!
🏚 This symbol indicates a Restaurant with Rooms

SHEPTON MALLET, Somerset Map 04 ST64

Top Hotel

★★★ ◉◉◉ **Charlton House**
Charlton Rd BA4 4PR
☎ 01749 342008 ▤ 01749 346362
e-mail: enquiry@charltonhouse.com
web: www.charltonhouse.com
Dir: on A361 towards Frome, 1m from town centre
Attention to detail is paramount at this wonderful hotel where the design throughout is modelled on Mulberry fabrics and furnishings. The bedrooms are decorated in individual style and all are supremely comfortable. Monty's Spa has hydrotherapy pools and spa treatment rooms for the ultimate pampering experience. Food remains a great attraction and, with Simon Crannage at the helm in the kitchen and produce
continued

from Monty-Saul's Sharpham Park organic farm, accomplished menus continue to win accolades and praise.

ROOMS: 22 en suite 4 annexe en suite (1 fmly) ⊗ in 8 bedrooms s £130-£295; d £165-£425 (incl. bkfst) **LB FACILITIES: Spa** STV ✄ Fishing Sauna Gym 🃏 Jacuzzi Archery Clay pigeon shooting Ballooning, Spa retreat programmes Xmas **CONF:** Thtr 100 Class 60 Board 40 Del from £220 **PARKING:** 72 **NOTES:** ⊗ in restaurant Civ Wed 100

★★71% **Shrubbery**
17 Commercial Rd BA4 5BU
☎ 01749 346671 ▤ 01749 346581
e-mail: reservations@shrubberyhotel17.fsnet.co.uk
Dir: off A37 at Shepton Mallet onto A371 Wells Rd, hotel 50mtrs past lights in town centre
This small hotel is located in the town centre and offers comfortable, well-equipped bedrooms, several of which are on the ground floor of a separate building. The atmosphere at the Shrubbery Hotel is relaxed and informal, and the intimate restaurant, which overlooks a delightful award-winning garden, offers a varied choice of enjoyable and well-presented dishes.
ROOMS: 6 en suite 4 annexe en suite (3 fmly) (4 GF) ⊗ in 4 bedrooms **PARKING:** 30 **NOTES:** ✖ ⊗ in restaurant

SHERBORNE, Dorset Map 04 ST61

★★★72% ◉◉ **Eastbury**
Long St DT9 3BY
☎ 01935 813131 ▤ 01935 817296
e-mail: enquiries@theeastburyhotel.co.uk
web: www.theeastburyhotel.co.uk
Dir: From A30 westbound, left into North Rd, then St Swithins, left at bottom, hotel 800yds on right
Much of the original Georgian charm and elegance is maintained at this smart, comfortable hotel. Just five minutes' stroll from the abbey and close to the town centre, the Eastbury's friendly and attentive staff ensure a relaxed and enjoyable stay. Award-winning cuisine is served in the attractive dining room that overlooks the walled garden.
ROOMS: 21 en suite (1 fmly) (3 GF) ⊗ in 10 bedrooms s £54-£62; d £98-£130 (incl. bkfst) **LB FACILITIES:** STV 🃏 Xmas **CONF:** Thtr 80 Class 40 Board 28 Del £121 **PARKING:** 30 **NOTES:** ✖ ⊗ in restaurant Civ Wed 80

★★★70% **The Grange Hotel & Restaurant**
Oborne DT9 4LA
☎ 01935 813463 ▤ 01935 817464
e-mail: reception@thegrange.co.uk
Dir: In Oborne, turn off A30 & follow signs through village
Set in beautiful gardens in a quiet hamlet, this 200-year-old, family run, country-house hotel has a wealth of charm and character. It
continued

S

offers friendly hospitality together with attentive service. Bedrooms are comfortable and tastefully appointed. Half are in the main house and the other, more contemporary, rooms are in a separate building. Public areas are elegantly furnished and the popular restaurant offers a good selection of dishes.
ROOMS: 4 en suite 6 annexe en suite (3 fmly) (4 GF) ⊗ in all bedrooms s fr £83; d £98-£138 (incl. bkfst) **LB** **FACILITIES:** Xmas **CONF:** Thtr 30 Class 20 Board 18 Del from £123.50 **PARKING:** 45 **NOTES:** ✗ ⊗ in restaurant

SHERINGHAM, Norfolk Map 13 TG14

★★★★71% Dales Country House Hotel

Lodge Hill, Upper Sheringham NR26 8TJ
☎ 01263 824555 🖷 01263 822647
e-mail: dales@mackenziehotels.com
Dir: *on B1157 1m S of Sheringham, from A148 take turning at entrance to Sheringham Park continue for 0.5m hotel on left*

Superb Grade II listed building situated in extensive landscaped grounds on the edge of Sheringham Park. The attractive public rooms are full of original character; they include a choice of lounges as well as an intimate restaurant and a cosy lounge bar. The spacious bedrooms are individually decorated, with co-ordinated soft furnishings and many thoughtful touches.
ROOMS: 17 en suite (2 GF) ⊗ in all bedrooms s £79-£128; d £118-£140 (incl. bkfst) **LB** **FACILITIES:** Xmas **CONF:** Thtr 40 Class 20 Board 27 Del from £99 **SERVICES:** Lift **PARKING:** 50 **NOTES:** ✗ No children 14yrs ⊗ in restaurant

★★72% Beaumaris

South St NR26 8LL
☎ 01263 822370 🖷 01263 821421
e-mail: beauhotel@aol.com
web: www.thebeaumarishotel.co.uk
Dir: *turn off A148, turn left at rdbt, 1st right over railway bridge, 1st left by church, 1st left into South St*

Situated in a peaceful side road a short walk from the beach, town centre and golf course. This friendly hotel has been owned and run by the same family for over 50 years and continues to provide comfortable, thoughtfully equipped accommodation throughout. Public rooms feature a smart dining room, a cosy bar and two quiet lounges.
ROOMS: 21 en suite (5 fmly) s £45-£90; d £90-£100 (incl. bkfst) **LB** **PARKING:** 25 **NOTES:** ✗ ⊗ in restaurant Closed mid Dec-1 Mar

★★72% Roman Camp Inn

Holt Rd, Aylmerton NR11 8QD
☎ 01263 838291 🖷 01263 837071
e-mail: romancampinn@lineone.net
web: www.romancampinn.co.uk
Dir: *on A148 between Sheringham and Cromer, approx 1.5m from Cromer*
A smartly presented hotel situated on the A148 that makes it ideally placed for touring the north Norfolk coastline. The property provides spacious, pleasantly decorated bedrooms with a good range of useful facilities. Public rooms include a smart conservatory-style restaurant, an comfortable, open-plan lounge with an adjacent, smart bar and a dining area.
ROOMS: 15 en suite ⊗ in 2 bedrooms s £54-£60; d £88-£100 (incl. bkfst) **LB** **CONF:** Thtr 25 Class 6 Board 12 **PARKING:** 50 **NOTES:** ✗ ⊗ in restaurant Closed 25-Dec

SHIFNAL, Shropshire Map 10 SJ70

★★★★66% Park House

Park St TF11 9BA
☎ 01952 460128 🖷 01952 461658
e-mail: parkhousehotel-shifnal@fsmail.net
Dir: *M54 junct 4 follow A464 Wolverhampton Rd for approx 2m, under railway bridge and hotel is 100yds on left*

This hotel was created from what were originally two country houses of very different architectural styles. Located on the edge of the historic market town, it offers guests easy access to motorway networks, a choice of banqueting and meeting rooms, and leisure facilities.
ROOMS: 38 en suite 16 annexe en suite (4 fmly) (8 GF) ⊗ in 16 bedrooms s £100-£150; d £110-£250 (incl. bkfst) **LB** **FACILITIES:** **Spa** STV Sauna Solarium Jacuzzi Xmas **CONF:** Thtr 180 Class 100 Board 40 Del from £125 **SERVICES:** Lift **PARKING:** 90 **NOTES:** ⊗ in restaurant Civ Wed 200

★★66% *Haughton Hall*

Haughton Ln TF11 8HG
☎ 01952 468300 🖷 01952 468313
e-mail: hotel@hostcomputers.co.uk
Dir: *M54 junct 4 take A464 into Shifnal. Turn left into Haughton Lane, hotel 600yds on left*
This listed building dates back to 1718 and stands in open parkland close to the town. It is well geared for the conference trade and also has a fine leisure club attached. Relaxing public rooms

continued on p510

S

SHIFNAL, continued

are available and the dinner menu is extensive. Bedrooms are comfortable and well equipped.

Haughton Hall, Shifnal

ROOMS: 26 en suite 6 annexe en suite (5 fmly) (3 GF) ⊗ in 26 bedrooms **FACILITIES: Spa** supervised ⛳ 9 🎾 Fishing Sauna Solarium Gym Steam Room, Therapy Room **CONF:** BC Thtr 80 Board 16 **PARKING:** 60 **NOTES:** ⊗ in restaurant Closed 25 & 31 Dec (evening) Civ Wed 70

SHIPHAM, Somerset — Map 04 ST45

★★★70% ◎◎ Daneswood House

Cuck Hill BS25 1RD
☎ 01934 843145 & 843945 📠 01934 843824
e-mail: info@daneswoodhotel.co.uk
web: www.daneswoodhotel.co.uk
Dir: *turn off A38 towards Cheddar, through village, hotel on left*

With wonderful countryside views to the Bristol Channel and Wales in the distance, this charming Edwardian house is set in its own carefully tended grounds. Each individually decorated bedroom is well equipped and the cottage suites have private lounges. Public rooms include a breakfast conservatory, comfortable lounge and inter-connecting dining areas.

ROOMS: 14 en suite 3 annexe en suite (3 fmly) ⊗ in 5 bedrooms s £75-£89.50; d £95-£105 (incl. bkfst) **LB** **CONF:** Thtr 30 Board 20 Del from £125 **PARKING:** 25 **NOTES:** 🐕 ⊗ in restaurant RS 24 Dec-6 Jan

SHIPLEY, West Yorkshire — Map 19 SE13

★★★★70% ◎ Marriott Hollins Hall Hotel & Country Club

Hollins Hill, Baildon BD17 7QW
☎ 0870 400 7227 📠 0870 400 7327
e-mail: reservations.hollinshall@marriotthotels.co.uk
web: www.marriott.co.uk
Dir: *from A650 follow signs to Salt Mill. At lights in Shipley take A6038. Hotel is 3m on left*

The hotel is located just to the north of Bradford and is easily accessible from motorway networks. Built in the 19th-century this Elizabethan-style building is set within 200 acres of grounds and offers extensive leisure facilities, including a golf course and gym. Bedrooms are attractively decorated and have a range of additional facilities.

ROOMS: 122 en suite (50 fmly) (25 GF) ⊗ in 75 bedrooms d £120-£140 (incl. bkfst) **LB** **FACILITIES: Spa** STV supervised ⛳ 18 Sauna Solarium Gym Putt green Jacuzzi Creche, Health Spa, Dance studio, Swimming lessons Xmas **CONF:** BC Thtr 175 Class 90 Board 80 Del from £150 **SERVICES:** Lift **PARKING:** 260 **NOTES:** 🐕 ⊗ in restaurant

Restaurant with Rooms

◎◎ Beeties Gallery Restaurant

7 Victoria Rd, Saltaire Village BD18 3LA
☎ 01274 595988 581718 📠 01274 582118
e-mail: jayne@beeties.co.uk

Beeties is located in the Saltaire model industrial village. The ground floor comprises a Tapas bar and bistro serving light meals and drinks at lunch and dinner, and on the first floor there is the elegant, contemporary restaurant serving imaginative, skilfully prepared dishes every evening. Bedrooms are smartly appointed and individually decorated.

ROOMS: 5 en suite (1 fmly) ⊗ in all bedrooms s fr £44 (incl. bkfst) **NOTES:** 🐕 ⊗ in restaurant Closed 25-26 Dec, 1 Jan

Hotel Ibis Bradford

Quayside, Salts Mill Rd BD18 3ST
☎ 01274 589333 📠 01274 589444
e-mail: H3158@accor-hotels.com
Dir: *follow tourist signs for Salts Mill. Follow A650 signs through & out of Bradford for approx 5m to Shipley. Hotel on Salts Mill Rd*

Modern, budget hotel offering comfortable accommodation in bright and practical bedrooms. Breakfast is self-service and dinner is available in the restaurant. For further details, consult the Hotel Groups page.

ROOMS: 78 en suite **CONF:** Thtr 30 Class 18 Board 22

SHREWSBURY, Shropshire — Map 15 SJ41

See also Church Stretton

★★★★67% Albrighton Hall

Albrighton SY4 3AG
☎ 01939 291000 📠 01939 291123
e-mail: albrighton@macdonald-hotels.co.uk
web: www.macdonald-hotels.co.uk
Dir: *from S M6 junct 10a to M54 to end. From N M6 junct 12 to M5 then M54. Follow signs Harlescott & Ellesmere to A528*

Dating back to 1630, this former ancestral home is set within 15 acres of attractive gardens. Rooms are generally spacious and the attic rooms are particularly popular. Elegant public rooms have

continued

rich oak panelling and there is a modern, well-equipped health and fitness centre.

ROOMS: 29 en suite 42 annexe en suite (18 fmly) (11 GF) ⊗ in 49 bedrooms s £90-£105; d £105-£125 (incl. bkfst) **LB** **FACILITIES: Spa** STV Squash Sauna Solarium Gym Jacuzzi Beauty treatment rooms Xmas **CONF:** Thtr 400 Class 120 Board 60 Del from £139 **SERVICES:** Lift **PARKING:** 200 **NOTES:** ⊗ in restaurant Civ Wed 350

★★★78% Albright Hussey Manor

Ellesmere Rd SY4 3AF
☎ 01939 290571 & 290523 01939 291143
e-mail: info@albrighthussey.co.uk
web: www.albrighthussey.co.uk
Dir: *2.5m N of Shrewsbury on A528, follow signs for Ellesmere*

First mentioned in the Domesday Book, this enchanting medieval manor house is complete with a moat. Bedrooms are situated in either the sumptuously appointed main house or in the more modern wing. The intimate restaurant displays an abundance of original features and there is also a comfortable cocktail bar and lounge.

ROOMS: 26 en suite (4 fmly) (8 GF) ⊗ in 16 bedrooms s £79-£95; d £90-£180 (incl. bkfst) **LB** **FACILITIES:** Jacuzzi Xmas **CONF:** BC Thtr 250 Class 180 Board 80 Del from £110 **PARKING:** 86 **NOTES:** ⊗ in restaurant Civ Wed 180

★★★77% *Rowton Castle Hotel*

Halfway House SY5 9EP
☎ 01743 884044 01743 884949
e-mail: post@rowtoncastle.com
web: www.rowtoncastle.com
Dir: *from A5 near Shrewsbury take A458 to Welshpool. Hotel 4m on right*

Standing in 17 acres of grounds where a castle has stood for nearly 800 years, this Grade II listed building dates in parts back to 1696. Many original features remain, including the oak panelling in the restaurant and a magnificent carved oak fireplace. Most bedrooms are spacious and all have modern facilities; some have four-poster beds. The hotel has a well deserved high reputation for its food and is understandably also a popular venue for weddings.

ROOMS: 19 en suite (3 fmly) **FACILITIES:** **CONF:** Thtr 80 Class 30 Board 30 **PARKING:** 100 **NOTES:** ⊗ in restaurant Civ Wed 110

★★★73% Prince Rupert

Butcher Row SY1 1UQ
☎ 01743 499955 01743 357306
e-mail: post@prince-rupert-hotel.co.uk
web: www.prince-rupert-hotel.co.uk
Dir: *follow town centre signs, over English Bridge & Wyle Cop Hill. Right into Fish St, 200yds*

Parts of this popular town centre hotel date back to medieval

continued on p512

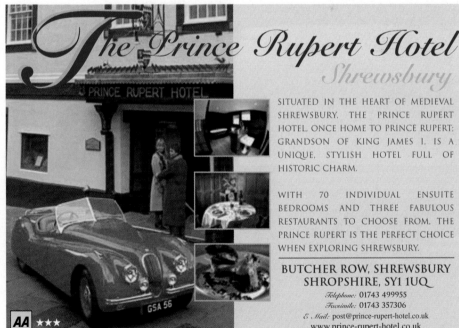

SHREWSBURY, continued

times and many bedrooms have exposed beams and other original features. Luxury suites, family rooms and rooms with four-poster beds are all available. As an alternative to the main Royalist Restaurant, diners can eat in the less formal and popular Chambers bar-bistro. The hotel's car parking service comes recommended.

Prince Rupert, Shrewsbury

ROOMS: 70 en suite (4 fmly) s £85; d £105-£175 **LB**
FACILITIES: Snooker Sauna Gym Jacuzzi Weight training room Beauty Salon Xmas **CONF:** Thtr 120 Class 80 Board 40 Del £115
SERVICES: Lift **PARKING:** 70 **NOTES:** ⊗ in restaurant

See advert on page 511

★★★70% Mytton & Mermaid

Atcham SY5 6QG
☎ 01743 761220 📠 01743 761292
e-mail: admin@myttonandmermaid.co.uk
web: www.myttonandmermaid.co.uk
Dir: *from Shrewsbury over old bridge in Atcham. Hotel opposite main entrance to Attingham Park*

Convenient for Shrewsbury, this ivy-clad former coaching inn enjoys a pleasant location beside the River Severn. Some bedrooms, including family suites, are in a converted stable block adjacent to the hotel. There is a large lounge bar, a comfortable lounge, and a brasserie that is gaining a well-deserved local reputation for the quality of its food.
ROOMS: 11 en suite 7 annexe en suite (1 fmly) ⊗ in 11 bedrooms
FACILITIES: Fishing ♫ Xmas **CONF:** BC Thtr 70 Class 24 Board 28 Del from £122.50 **PARKING:** 50 **NOTES:** ⊗ in restaurant Civ Wed 80

★★★66% Lord Hill

Abbey Foregate SY2 6AX
☎ 01743 232601 📠 01743 369734
e-mail: reservations@lordhill.u-net.com
web: www.lordhill.u-net.com
Dir: *from M54 take A5, at 1st rdbt left then 2nd rdbt take 4th exit into London Rd. At next rdbt (Lord Hill Column) take 3rd exit, hotel 300yds on left*

This pleasant, attractively appointed hotel is located close to the town centre. Most of the modern bedrooms are set in a purpose-built separate property, but those in the main building include one with a four-poster, as well as a full suite. There is also a conservatory restaurant and a large function suite.
ROOMS: 12 en suite 24 annexe en suite (2 fmly) (8 GF) ⊗ in 12 bedrooms s £60-£70; d £80-£90 (incl. bkfst) **CONF:** Thtr 250 Class 180 Board 180 Del from £85 **PARKING:** 110 **NOTES:** ⊗ in restaurant Civ Wed 70

★★★63% The Lion

Wyle Cop SY1 1UY
☎ 0870 609 6167 📠 01743 352744
e-mail: thelion@corushotels.com
web: www.corushotels.com/thelion
Dir: *from S cross English Bridge, take right fork, hotel at top of hill on left. From N to town centre, follow Castle St into Dogpole, hotel is ahead*

This 14th-century coaching inn, located in the town centre, boasts Charles Dickens amongst its previous guests. Bedrooms come in a variety of sizes, those at the rear being quieter. Public areas include the original ballroom and a bar and restaurant with oak beams and an inglenook fireplace.
ROOMS: 59 en suite (3 fmly) ⊗ in 45 bedrooms s £79; d £79 **LB**
FACILITIES: use of local gym Xmas **CONF:** Thtr 200 Class 80 Board 60 Del from £70 **SERVICES:** Lift **PARKING:** 70 **NOTES:** ⊗ in restaurant Civ Wed 200

★★65% Abbots Mead

9 St Julian's Friars SY1 1XL
☎ 01743 235281 📠 01743 369133
e-mail: res@abbotsmeadhotel.co.uk
web: www.abbotsmeadhotel.co.uk
Dir: *Entering town from south 1st left after English Bridge*

This neatly maintained Georgian town house is located in a quiet cul-de-sac, near the English Bridge and close to the River Severn and town centre. Bedrooms are compact, neatly decorated and well equipped. The hotel also has a bright dining room, overlooking the garden, and a bar featuring horse racing pictures.
ROOMS: 15 en suite (1 fmly) ⊗ in all bedrooms s £50-£55; d £65-£70 (incl. bkfst) **LB** **PARKING:** 10 **NOTES:** ⊗ in restaurant Closed Dec 24-26

Travelodge

Bayston Hill Services SY3 0DA
☎ 08700 850 950 📠 01743 874256
web: www.travelodge.co.uk
Dir: *A5/A49 junct*

Travelodge offers good quality, good value, modern accommodation. Ideal for families, the spacious, en suite bedrooms include remote-control TV, tea and coffee-making facilities and comfortable beds. Meals can be taken at the nearby family restaurant. For further details consult the Hotel Groups page.
ROOMS: 40 en suite s fr £26; d fr £26

SIDMOUTH, Devon Map 03 SY18

★★★★75% ® Victoria

The Esplanade EX10 8RY
☎ 01395 512651 📠 01395 579154
e-mail: info@victoriahotel.co.uk
web: www.brend-hotels.co.uk
Dir: *on seafront*

This imposing building, with manicured gardens, is situated overlooking the town. Wonderful sea views can be enjoyed from many of the comfortable bedrooms and elegant lounges. With indoor and outdoor leisure, the hotel caters to a year-round clientele. Carefully prepared meals are served in the refined atmosphere of the restaurant, with staff providing a professional and friendly service.
ROOMS: 61 en suite (18 fmly) s £80-£110; d £120-£270 **LB** **FACILITIES: Spa** STV Snooker Sauna Solarium Gym Putt green ♫ ch fac Xmas **CONF:** Thtr 60 **SERVICES:** Lift **PARKING:** 104 **NOTES:** in restaurant

See advert on page 513

★★★★74% ®® Riviera

The Esplanade EX10 8AY
☎ 01395 515201 📠 01395 577775
e-mail: enquiries@hotelriviera.co.uk
web: www.hotelriviera.co.uk
Dir: *M5 junct 30 & follow A3052*

Overlooking the sea and close to the town centre, the Riviera is a fine example of Regency architecture. High standards of both service and hospitality are found here, and many of the guests become regular visitors. The front-facing bedrooms benefit from wonderful sea views and many have been refurbished. The daily-changing menu places an emphasis on fresh, local produce.
ROOMS: 26 en suite (6 fmly) s £99-£150; d £198-£278 (incl. bkfst & dinner) **LB** **FACILITIES:** STV ♫ Xmas **CONF:** Thtr 85 Class 60 Board 30 **SERVICES:** Lift air con **PARKING:** 26 **NOTES:** in restaurant

See advert on opposite page

★★★★71% Belmont

The Esplanade EX10 8RX
☎ 01395 512555 📠 01395 579101
e-mail: reservations@belmont-hotel.co.uk
web: www.brend-hotels.co.uk
Dir: *on seafront*

Prominently positioned on the seafront just a few minutes' walk from the town centre, this traditional hotel has a regular following. A choice of comfortable lounges provide ample space for relaxation, and the air-conditioned restaurant has a pianist accompanying dinner. Bedrooms are attractively furnished and many have fine views over the esplanade. Leisure facilities are available at the adjacent sister hotel, the Victoria.
ROOMS: 50 en suite (4 fmly) (2 GF) s £70-£110; d £100-£180 (incl. bkfst & dinner) **LB** **FACILITIES:** STV Putt green ♫ ch fac Xmas **CONF:** Thtr 50 **SERVICES:** Lift **PARKING:** 45 **NOTES:** in restaurant Civ Wed 110

See advert on page 513

★★★80% Westcliff

Manor Rd EX10 8RU
☎ 01395 513252 & 513091 📠 01395 578203
e-mail: stay@westcliffhotel.co.uk
web: www.westcliffhotel.co.uk
Dir: *turn off A3052 to Sidmouth then to seafront and esplanade, turn right, hotel directly ahead*

This charming hotel, run by the same family for more than 38 years, is within walking distance of the promenade. Elegant lounges and the cocktail bar open onto a terrace, leading to the pool and croquet lawn. Bedrooms, several with balconies and glorious sea views, are spacious and comfortable, whilst the restaurant offers a choice of well-prepared dishes.
ROOMS: 40 en suite (4 fmly) (5 GF) in 4 bedrooms s £83-£127; d £152-£272 (incl. bkfst & dinner) **LB** **FACILITIES:** STV Gym Putt green Jacuzzi Mini tennis, Pool table, Table tennis **SERVICES:** Lift **PARKING:** 40 **NOTES:** No children 6yrs in restaurant Closed Nov-Mar

★★★73% *Sid Valley Country House*
Sidbury EX10 0QJ
☎ 01395 597274 & 597587
e-mail: sidvalleyhotel@totalise.co.uk
web: www.sidvalleyhotel.co.uk
Dir: *off A375, 2.5m from Sidmouth, hotel clearly signed*
Situated in an Area of Outstanding Natural Beauty, this family-run hotel has glorious views down the valley. Friendly, unobtrusive service is the key here. Bedrooms vary in size and are equipped with numerous thoughtful extras. Every evening an imaginative menu is served using the best of fresh, local produce. A selection of well-equipped, self-catering cottages is also available.
ROOMS: 10 en suite (2 fmly) (1 GF) ⊘ in all bedrooms
FACILITIES: STV Riding ch fac **CONF:** BC Thtr 70 Class 70 Board 70 **PARKING:** 32 **NOTES:** ⊘ in restaurant

Bad hair day?
Hairdryers in all rooms three stars and above

★★★66% Royal Glen
Glen Rd EX10 8RW
☎ 01395 513221 & 513456 📠 01395 514922
e-mail: info@royalglenhotel.co.uk
Dir: *take A303 to Honiton, A375 to Sidford, A175 to Sidmouth, follow seafront signs, right onto esplanade, right at end*
This historic 17th-century, 'cottage-orne' hotel has been owned by the same family for several generations. The connection is emphasised by the names of the comfortable bedrooms, which are furnished in period style. Guests have use of the well-maintained gardens and a heated indoor pool, and can enjoy well-prepared food in the dining room.

ROOMS: 32 en suite (4 fmly) s £35-£47; d £70-£94 (incl. bkfst) **LB**
FACILITIES: **PARKING:** 24 **NOTES:** ⊘ in restaurant Closed 2 Jan-31 Jan RS 2-31 Jan

★★★66% *Salcombe Hill House*
Beatlands Rd EX10 8JQ
☎ 01395 514697 & 514398 📠 01395 578310
e-mail: salcombehillhousehotel@eclipse.co.uk
Dir: *At Radway Cinema in town centre turn left, over bridge, turn sharp right, left into Beatlands Rd. Hotel 50yds on left*
Set in an elevated position just a short walk from the seafront, this hotel is situated in a quiet location surrounded by attractive gardens. The south-facing aspect means the lounge and patio benefit from the best of the sunshine. Bedrooms are spacious,

continued on p516

SIDMOUTH, continued

comfortable and appealing. The menu of freshly-prepared dishes on offer in the dining room changes daily.
ROOMS: 28 en suite (12 fmly) (2 GF) **FACILITIES:** Putt green Games room, Table Tennis, Darts **SERVICES:** Lift **PARKING:** 24 **NOTES:** ⊗ in restaurant

★★76% Kingswood

The Esplanade EX10 8AX
☎ 01395 516367 01395 513185
e-mail: enquiries@kingswood-hotel.co.uk
Dir: in centre of Esplanade
Super standards of hospitality are only surpassed by this hotel's prominent position on the esplanade. All bedrooms have modern facilities and some enjoy the stunning sea views. The two lounges offer comfort and space and the attractive dining room serves good traditional cooking.
ROOMS: 26 rms (25 en suite) (7 fmly) (2 GF) ⊗ in all bedrooms s £48-£75; d £48-£75 (incl. bkfst & dinner) **LB** **FACILITIES:** guests receive vouchers for local swimming pool & spectating at cricket club **SERVICES:** Lift **PARKING:** 17 **NOTES:** ⊗ in restaurant Closed 28 Dec-9 Feb

★★75% Royal York & Faulkner

The Esplanade EX10 8AZ
☎ 01395 513043 & 0800 220714 (Freephone) 01395 577472
e-mail: stay@royalyorkhotel.net
web: www.royalyorkhotel.net
Dir: from M5 take A3052, 10m to Sidmouth, hotel in centre of esplanade
This seafront hotel, owned and run by the same family for generations, maintains its Regency charm and grandeur. The attractive bedrooms vary in size; many have balconies and sea views. Staff are friendly and efficient. Public rooms are spacious, and traditional dining is offered plus Blini's café-bar offering coffees, lunches and afternoon teas.
ROOMS: 68 en suite (8 fmly) (5 GF) s £43-£69.50; d £86-£139 (incl. bkfst & dinner) **LB** **FACILITIES: Spa** STV Snooker Sauna Free swim at local indoor pool, Steam Room & Treatement Rooms ♫ Xmas **SERVICES:** Lift **PARKING:** 20 **NOTES:** ⊗ in restaurant Closed Jan

★★72% Mount Pleasant

Salcombe Rd EX10 8JA
☎ 01395 514694
Dir: turn off A3052 at Sidford x-rds after 1.25m turn left into Salcombe Rd, hotel opposite Radway Cinema
Quietly located within almost an acre of gardens, this sympathetically modernised Georgian hotel is minutes from the town centre and seafront. Bedrooms and public areas offer good levels of comfort and high quality furnishings. Guests return on a regular basis especially for the friendly, relaxed atmosphere. The daily-changing menu offers a choice of imaginative, yet traditional home-cooked dishes.
ROOMS: 16 en suite (2 fmly) (2 GF) s £40-£56; d £80-£112 (incl. bkfst & dinner) **LB** **FACILITIES:** Putt green **PARKING:** 20 **NOTES:** No children 8yrs ⊗ in restaurant Closed Dec-Jan

★★71% Devoran

Esplanade EX10 8AU
☎ 01395 513151 01395 579929
e-mail: enquiries@devoran.com
Dir: turn off B3052 at Bowd Inn follow Sidmouth sign for approx 2m turn left onto seafront, hotel 50yds at centre of Esplanade
Superbly situated, this family-run hotel, known locally as the 'pink hotel on the seafront' offers friendly, personal service. The Devoran has comfortable and attractively decorated bedrooms, some with their own balconies which benefit from the wonderful

continued

sea views. Well-maintained public rooms include a large dining room, where guests can enjoy a five-course dinner, and a comfortable lounge and bar. Guests can use the leisure facilities at the sister hotel.

ROOMS: 26 en suite (4 fmly) ⊗ in all bedrooms s £43-£51; d £86-£102 (incl. bkfst & dinner) **LB** **FACILITIES:** Fishing **SERVICES:** Lift **PARKING:** 4 **NOTES:** ⊗ in restaurant Closed mid Nov-late Feb RS Dec-Feb

★★70% Hunters Moon

Sid Rd EX10 9AA
☎ 01395 513380 01395 514270
e-mail: huntersmoon.hotel@virgin.net
Dir: from A3052 to Sidford, pass Blue Ball Pub, then next right at Fortescue, hotel 1m

Set amid three acres of attractive and well-tended grounds, this friendly, family-run hotel is peacefully located in a quiet area within walking distance of the town and esplanade. Bedrooms are comfortable and well equipped and there is a spacious lounge. Dining provides a choice of well-cooked and imaginative dishes and tea may be taken on the lawn.
ROOMS: 33 en suite (2 fmly) (12 GF) ⊗ in all bedrooms s £64-£68; d £110-£128 (incl. bkfst & dinner) **LB** **FACILITIES:** Putt green outdoor bowling green **PARKING:** 33 **NOTES:** No children 2yrs ⊗ in restaurant Closed Jan-12 Feb RS Dec & Feb

★★69% The Woodlands Hotel

Cotmaton Cross EX10 8HG
☎ 01395 513120 01395 513348
e-mail: info@woodlands-hotel.com
web: www.woodlands-hotel.com
Dir: follow signs for Sidmouth
Located in the heart of the town and ideally situated for exploring Devon, including Seaton, and Lyme Regis in Dorset. There is a spacious bar and a lounge where guests may relax. Freshly prepared dinners are enjoyed in the smart dining room. Families with children are made very welcome and may dine early.
ROOMS: 20 en suite (4 fmly) (8 GF) s £32-£53; d £64-£106 (incl. bkfst) **LB** **FACILITIES:** ch fac **PARKING:** 20 **NOTES:** ⊗ in restaurant Closed 23-29 Dec

SILCHESTER, Hampshire
Map 05 SU66

★★★72% Romans
Little London Rd RG7 2PN
☎ 0118 970 0421 📠 0118 970 0691
e-mail: romanhotel@hotmail.com
Dir: *A340 Basingstoke to Reading, hotel is signed*

This Lutyens-style manor house is in a tranquil and attractive location. Bedrooms are smartly presented and well equipped, some located in an adjacent wing. The leisure club is proud of its outdoor swimming pool, which is kept heated year round.
ROOMS: 11 en suite 14 annexe en suite (1 fmly) (11 GF) ⊗ in 5 bedrooms **FACILITIES:** STV supervised Sauna Gym Jacuzzi Xmas **CONF:** Thtr 60 Class 30 Board 24 **PARKING:** 60 **NOTES:** ⊗ in restaurant Civ Wed 65

See advert under BASINGSTOKE

SILLOTH, Cumbria
Map 18 NY15

★★★61% The Skinburness Leisure Hotel
CA7 4QY
☎ 016973 32332 📠 32549
Dir: *from Wigton take B5302 to Silloth & follow brown tourist signs to hotel*
Located on the peaceful Solway Estuary, close to sandy beaches and coastal walks, this popular hotel (now under new ownership) provides traditionally furnished bedrooms with a host of modern facilities. There is also a small leisure complex with a pool, sauna and spa. Good meals are available in the popular bar and the pleasant hotel restaurant.
ROOMS: 26 en suite (8 fmly) (1 GF) ⊗ in 4 bedrooms **FACILITIES:** Sauna Solarium Gym Jacuzzi ♫ Xmas **PARKING:** 50

★★67% Golf Hotel
Criffel St CA5 4AB
☎ 016973 31438 📠 016973 32582
e-mail: golf.hotel@virgin.net
web: www.golfhotelsilloth.co.uk
Dir: *off B5302, in Silloth at T-junct turn left, hotel overlooks the green*
This friendly, family-run hotel occupies a prime position in the centre of the historic market town and is a popular meeting place for the local community. Bedrooms are mostly well-proportioned, generally modern in style. Public areas include a spacious lounge bar, the setting for a wide range of tasty meals featuring local produce.
ROOMS: 22 en suite (4 fmly) s £39-£59; d £62-£98 (incl. bkfst) **LB** **FACILITIES:** Snooker **CONF:** Thtr 100 Class 40 Board 40 **NOTES:** Closed 25-Dec

SILVERSTONE, Northamptonshire
Map 11 SP64

Premier Travel Inn Silverstone
Brackley Hatch, Syresham NN13 5TX
☎ 0870 9906382 📠 0870 9906383
web: www.premiertravelinn.com
Dir: *On A43 near Silverstone. 13m from M40 & 11m from M1*
High quality, modern budget accommodation ideal for both families and business travellers. Spacious, en suite bedrooms feature bath and shower, satellite TV and many have telephones and modem points. The adjacent family restaurant features a wide and varied menu. For further details consult the Hotel Groups page.
ROOMS: 41 en suite s £47.95-£50.95; d £47.95-£50.95

SIMONSBATH, Somerset
Map 03 SS73

★★75% Simonsbath House
TA24 7SH
☎ 01643 831259 & 831382 📠 01643 831557
e-mail: hotel@simonsbathhouse.co.uk
web: www.simonsbathhouse.co.uk
Dir: *from Exford to Lynton, hotel on right of B3223*

This 17th-century house boasts a stunning moorland setting and its relaxed and friendly atmosphere ensures a memorable stay. Bedrooms have plenty of character, are equipped with modern facilities and offer good levels of comfort. Delightful public rooms include a choice of lounges with original features such as wood panelling and ornate fireplaces.
ROOMS: 8 en suite (1 GF) ⊗ in all bedrooms s £42.50-£60; d £85-£95 (incl. bkfst) **LB** **FACILITIES:** Fishing Mountain biking, Archery, Orienteering trails, Nature walks Xmas **CONF:** BC Thtr 50 Class 35 Board 20 **PARKING:** 25 **NOTES:** No children 12yrs ⊗ in restaurant Closed 25-26 Dec

SITTINGBOURNE, Kent
Map 07 TQ96

★★★74% Hempstead House Country Hotel
London Rd, Bapchild ME9 9PP
☎ 01795 428020 📠 01795 436362
e-mail: info@hempsteadhouse.co.uk
web: www.hempsteadhouse.co.uk
Dir: *1.5m from Sittingbourne town centre on A2 towards Canterbury*
Expect a warm welcome at this charming detached Victorian property, which is situated amidst three acres of mature landscaped gardens. Bedrooms are attractively decorated with lovely co-ordinated fabrics, tastefully furnished and equipped with many thoughtful touches. Public rooms feature a choice of

continued on p518

S

SITTINGBOURNE, continued

beautifully furnished lounges as well as a superb conservatory dining room.

Hempstead House Country Hotel, Sittingbourne

ROOMS: 27 en suite (7 fmly) (1 GF) ⊗ in all bedrooms s £75-£95; d £85-£120 (incl. bkfst) **LB FACILITIES:** STV ⁿ⁀ ♫ Xmas **CONF:** BC Thtr 150 Class 150 Board 100 Del from £138 **PARKING:** 100 **NOTES:** ⊗ in restaurant Civ Wed 150

⛫ Premier Travel Inn Sittingbourne, Kent

Bobbing Corner, Sheppy Way, Bobbing ME9 8PD
☎ 08701 977229 ■ 01795 436748
web: www.premiertravelinn.com
Dir: M2 junct 5 take A249 towards Sheerness approx 2m, 1st slip road after A2 underpass. Inn on the left
High quality, modern budget accommodation ideal for both families and business travellers. Spacious, en suite bedrooms feature bath and shower, satellite TV and many have telephones and modem points. The adjacent family restaurant features a wide and varied menu. For further details consult the Hotel Groups page.
ROOMS: 40 en suite s £46.95-£49.95; d £46.95-£49.95

SIX MILE BOTTOM, Cambridgeshire Map 12 TL55

★★★74% ⊛ Swynford Paddocks

CB8 0UE
☎ 01638 570234 ■ 01638 570283
e-mail: info@swynfordpaddocks.com
Dir: M11 junct 9, take A11 towards Newmarket, turn onto A1304 to Newmarket, hotel 0.75m on left
This smart country house is set in attractive grounds, within easy reach of Newmarket. Bedrooms are comfortably appointed, thoughtfully equipped and include some delightful four-poster rooms. Imaginative, carefully prepared food is served in the elegant restaurant; service is friendly and attentive. Meeting and conference facilities are available.
ROOMS: 15 en suite (1 fmly) s £75-£110; d £90-£135 (incl. bkfst) **LB FACILITIES:** STV ☖ ♫ Putt green **CONF:** Thtr 60 Class 40 Board 40 Del from £141 **PARKING:** 180 **NOTES:** ⊗ in restaurant Civ Wed 100

SKEGNESS, Lincolnshire Map 17 TF56

★★★67% Vine

Vine Rd, Seacroft PE25 3DB
☎ 01754 763018 & 610611 ■ 01754 769845
e-mail: info@thevinehotel.com
Dir: A52 to Skegness, S towards Gibraltar Point, turn right on to Drummond Rd, after 0.5m turn right into Vine Rd
Reputedly the second oldest building in Skegness, this traditional style hotel offers two character bars that serve excellent local beers. Freshly prepared dishes are served in both the bar and the restaurant;

continued

service is both friendly and helpful. The smart bedrooms are well equipped and comfortably appointed.

ROOMS: 24 en suite (3 fmly) ⊗ in 6 bedrooms s £50-£69; d £84-£90 (incl. bkfst) **LB FACILITIES:** STV ⌓ 18 Putt green Xmas **CONF:** Thtr 100 Class 25 Board 30 Del from £76 **PARKING:** 50 **NOTES:** ⊗ in restaurant Civ Wed 100

★★★65% Crown

Drummond Rd, Seacroft PE25 3AB
☎ 01754 610760 ■ 01754 610847
e-mail: reception@crownhotel.biz
Dir: take A52 to town centre, turn left onto Drummond Road
The Crown is ideally situated just a short walk from the seafront and town centre, close to Seacroft Village golf course and bird sanctuary. Smart bedrooms are attractively decorated and thoughtfully equipped. Public areas include a spacious bar offering a wide selection of dishes, a formal restaurant, residents' TV lounge and indoor pool; ample parking is provided.
ROOMS: 30 en suite (9 fmly) s fr £50; d fr £80 (incl. bkfst) **LB FACILITIES:** STV ☒ **CONF:** Thtr 120 Class 130 Board 120 **SERVICES:** Lift **PARKING:** 90 **NOTES:** ✖ RS 25-26 Dec Civ Wed 80

See advert on opposite page

★★67% North Shore

North Shore Rd PE25 1DN
☎ 01754 763298 ■ 01754 761902
e-mail: golf@north-shore.co.uk
web: www.north-shore.co.uk
Dir: 1m N of town centre on A52 opposite Fenland laundry

This hotel enjoys an enviable position on the beachfront, adjacent to its own championship golf course and only ten minutes from the town centre. Spacious public areas include a terrace bar serving informal meals and real ales, a formal restaurant and impressive function rooms. Bedrooms are smartly decorated and thoughtfully equipped.
ROOMS: 33 en suite 3 annexe en suite (4 fmly) s £33-£57; d £53-£79 (incl. bkfst) **LB FACILITIES:** ⌓ 18 Snooker Putt green Xmas **CONF:** Thtr 220 Class 60 Board 60 Del from £65 **PARKING:** 200 **NOTES:** ✖ ⊗ in restaurant Civ Wed 180

SKIPTON, North Yorkshire

Map 18 SD95

★★★75% The Coniston

Coniston Cold BD23 4EB
☎ 01756 748080 📠 01756 749487
e-mail: info@theconistonhotel.com
Dir: *on A65, 6m NW of Skipton*

Privately owned and situated on a 1, 400 acre estate centred around a beautiful 24-acre lake this hotel offers many exciting outdoor activities. The modern bedrooms are comfortable and most have king-size beds. MacLeod's Bar and the main restaurant offer all-day meals and fine dining in the evening. Staff are very friendly and nothing is too much trouble.
ROOMS: 40 en suite (4 fmly) (20 GF) ⊗ in 32 bedrooms s £82-£92; d £94-£104 (incl. bkfst) **LB** **FACILITIES:** STV Fishing Clay pigeon shooting, Falconry, fishing Off road Land Rover driving, Xmas **CONF:** Thtr 200 Class 80 Board 50 Del from £133.95 **PARKING:** 120 **NOTES:** ⊗ in restaurant Civ Wed 100

See advert on this page

SKIPTON, continued

★★70% Herriots Hotel

Broughton Rd BD23 1RT
☎ 01756 792781 🖷 01756 793967
e-mail: info@herriotsforleisure.co.uk
Dir: *off A59, opposite railway station*

Close to the centre of the market town, this friendly hotel offers tastefully decorated bedrooms that are well equipped. The open-plan brasserie is a relaxing place in which to dine, and has a varied menu. Meals and snacks are also available in the bar. The extension includes modern well-equipped bedrooms and a stylish conservatory lounge.
ROOMS: 23 rms (13 en suite) (3 fmly) ⊗ in 18 bedrooms s £45-£85; d £65-£115 (incl. bkfst) **LB** **FACILITIES:** Xmas **CONF:** BC Thtr 100 Class 50 Board 52 Del from £120 **SERVICES:** Lift **PARKING:** 26 **NOTES:** ⊗ in restaurant Civ Wed 80

⌂ Travelodge

Gargrave Rd BD23 1UD
☎ 08700 850 950 🖷 0870 1911676
web: www.travelodge.co.uk
Dir: *A65/A59 rdbt*
Travelodge offers good quality, good value, modern accommodation. Ideal for families, the spacious, en suite bedrooms include remote-control TV, tea and coffee-making facilities and comfortable beds. Meals can be taken at the nearby family restaurant. For further details consult the Hotel Groups page.
ROOMS: 32 en suite s fr £26; d fr £26

SLEAFORD, Lincolnshire — Map 12 TF04

★★★64% Carre Arms

1 Mareham Ln NG34 7JP
☎ 01529 303156 🖷 01529 303139
e-mail: enquiries@carrearmshotel.co.uk
web: www.carrearmshotel.co.uk
Dir: *take A153 to Sleaford, hotel on right at level crossing*
This friendly, family-run hotel is located close to the station and offers suitably appointed accommodation. Public areas include two spacious bars where a good selection of bar meals is offered and a smart Brasserie. There is also a conservatory and an old stable housing a spacious, elegant function room.
ROOMS: 13 en suite (1 fmly) s £50-£60; d £70-£80 (incl. bkfst) **CONF:** Thtr 120 Class 54 Board 40 Del from £69.50 **PARKING:** 100 **NOTES:** 🐕̸ ⊗ in restaurant

♫ Entertainment

★★★64% The Lincolnshire Oak

THE INDEPENDENTS

East Rd NG34 7EH
☎ 01529 413807 🖷 01529 413710
e-mail: reception@lincolnshire-oak.co.uk
web: www.lincolnshire-oak.co.uk
Dir: *From A17 (by-pass) exit on A153 into Sleaford. Hotel 0.75m on left*

Located on the edge of the town in well-tended grounds, this hotel has a relaxed and friendly atmosphere. A comfortable open-plan lounge bar is complemented by a cosy restaurant that looks out onto the rear garden. There are also several meeting rooms. Bedroom styles differ - all rooms are well furnished and suitably equipped; the superior rooms are more comfortably appointed.
ROOMS: 17 en suite ⊗ in 12 bedrooms s £59-£72; d £72.50-£87.50 (incl. bkfst) **LB** **FACILITIES:** STV **CONF:** Thtr 140 Class 70 Board 50 Del £80 **PARKING:** 80 **NOTES:** 🐕̸ ⊗ in restaurant Civ Wed 90

See advert on opposite page

⌂ Travelodge

Holdingham NG34 8PN
☎ 08700 850 950 🖷 01529 414752
web: www.travelodge.co.uk
Dir: *1m N, at rdbt A17/A15*
Travelodge offers good quality, good value, modern accommodation. Ideal for families, the spacious, en suite bedrooms include remote-control TV, tea and coffee-making facilities and comfortable beds. Meals can be taken at the nearby family restaurant. For further details consult the Hotel Groups page.
ROOMS: 40 en suite s fr £26; d fr £26

SLOUGH, Berkshire — Map 06 SU97

★★★★69% Copthorne Hotel Slough-Windsor

COPTHORNE

400 Cippenham Ln SL1 2YE
☎ 01753 516222 🖷 01753 516237
e-mail: sales.slough@mill-cop.com
web: www.copthorne.com/slough
Dir: *M4 junct 6 & follow A355 to Slough at next rdbt turn left & left again for hotel entrance*
Conveniently located for the motorway and for Heathrow Airport, this modern hotel offers visitors a wide range of facilities including indoor leisure and a choice of dining options. The hotel also offers discounted entrance fee to some of the attractions in the area. Air-conditioned bedrooms provide a useful range of extras including satellite TV and trouser press.
ROOMS: 219 en suite (47 fmly) ⊗ in 148 bedrooms s £58-£240; d £58-£240 **FACILITIES:** STV Sauna Gym Jacuzzi **CONF:** Thtr 250 Class 160 Board 60 Del from £155 **SERVICES:** Lift air con **PARKING:** 300 **NOTES:** 🐕̸ ⊗ in restaurant

★★★69%
Courtyard by Marriott Slough/Windsor
Church St SL1 2NH
☎ 0870 400 7215 & 07153 551551
Fax 0870 400 7315
web: www.kewgreen.co.uk
Dir: *M4 junct 6, follow A355 to rdbt, turn right, hotel approx 50yds on right*
With Heathrow Airport and the motorway networks easily accessible by car this modern hotel is in an ideal location. Spacious bedrooms feature a comprehensive range of facilities. The public areas are lively, modern and have an informal atmosphere.
ROOMS: 150 en suite (64 fmly) (6 GF) ⊗ in 113 bedrooms s £45-£145; d £45-£145 (incl. bkfst) **FACILITIES:** STV Gym Xmas **CONF:** Thtr 40 Class 16 Board 20 Del from £129 **SERVICES:** Lift air con **PARKING:** 130 **NOTES:** ✗ ⊗ in restaurant

★★★66% **Quality Hotel Heathrow**
London Rd, Brands Hill SL3 8QB
☎ 01753 684001 Fax 01753 685767
e-mail: info@qualityheathrow.com
Dir: *M4 junct 5, follow signs for Colnbrook. Hotel approx 250mtrs on right*
This stylish, modern hotel is ideally located for Heathrow Airport, and for commercial visitors to Slough. Bedrooms have good facilities, benefit from all-day room service and are smartly furnished. There is a bright and airy open-plan restaurant, bar and lounge. Transfers are available to and from the airport.
ROOMS: 128 en suite (23 fmly) (5 GF) ⊗ in 60 bedrooms s £42-£145; d £42-£145 **LB** **FACILITIES:** STV Gym **CONF:** Thtr 120 Class 50 Board 40 Del from £99 **SERVICES:** Lift **PARKING:** 100 **NOTES:** ✗

U The Pinewood Hotel
Uxbridge Rd, George Green SL3 6AP
☎ 01753 824848 Fax 01753 824282
e-mail: info@pinewoodhotel.co.uk
web: www.bespokehotels.com
Dir: *A4 N out of Slough onto A412 towards Uxbridge, hotel 3m on left*
At the time of going to press, the star classification for this hotel was not confirmed. Please refer to the AA internet site www.theAA.com for current information.
ROOMS: 33 en suite 16 annexe en suite (4 fmly) (12 GF) s £160; d £160 (incl. bkfst) **FACILITIES:** STV Xmas **CONF:** Thtr 160 Class 40 Board 24 Del £180 **SERVICES:** Lift air con **PARKING:** 40 **NOTES:** ✗ ⊗ in restaurant Closed Open from 4 July 2005 Civ Wed 50

⌂ **Innkeeper's Lodge Slough/Windsor**
399 London Rd, Langley SL3 8PS
☎ 01753 591212 Fax 01753 211362
web: www.innkeeperslodge.com
Dir: *M4 junct 5 onto London Rd, 100yds on right*
A growing concept in the travel accommodation market. Smart rooms meet essential business requirements but also have home comforts. Dining options include all-day menus plus the added advantage of breakfast, which is included in the room price. For further details consult the Hotel Groups page.
ROOMS: 57 en suite s £49.95-£69.95; d £49.95-£69.95 **CONF:** Board 15

U Star rating not confirmed

Indoor Swimming pool
Indoor Swimming pool (heated)
Outdoor Swimming pool
Outdoor Swimming pool (heated)

⌂ **Premier Travel Inn Slough**
76 Uxbridge Rd SL1 1SU
☎ 0870 9906500 Fax 0870 9906501
web: www.premiertravelinn.com
Dir: *2m from M4 junct 5, 3m from junct 6. Just off A4*
High quality, modern budget accommodation ideal for both families and business travellers. Spacious, en suite bedrooms feature bath and shower, satellite TV and many have telephones and modem points. The adjacent family restaurant features a wide and varied menu. For further details consult the Hotel Groups page.
ROOMS: 84 en suite s £49.95-£65.95; d £49.95-£65.95

⌂ **Travelodge**
Landmark Place SL1 1BZ
☎ 08700 850 950 Fax 01753 - 516897
web: www.travelodge.co.uk
Travelodge offers good quality, good value, modern accommodation. Ideal for families, the spacious, en suite bedrooms include remote-control TV, tea and coffee-making facilities and comfortable beds. Meals can be taken at the nearby family restaurant. For further details consult the Hotel Groups page.
ROOMS: 157 en suite s fr £26; d fr £26

SNETTISHAM, Norfolk
Map 12 TF63

★★71% ® **Rose & Crown**
Old Church Rd PE31 7LX
☎ 01485 541382 Fax 01485 543172
e-mail: info@roseandcrownsnettisham.co.uk
web: www.roseandcrownsnettisham.co.uk
Dir: *A149 N from King's Lynn towards Hunstanton. 10m turn into Snettisham, then into Old Church Rd. Hotel 100yds on left*
This lovely village inn provides comfortable, well equipped

continued on p522

S

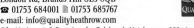

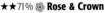

SNETTISHAM, continued

bedrooms. A range of quality meals are served in the many dining areas, while a good variety of real ales and wines is on offer. Service is friendly and a delightful atmosphere prevails. A walled garden is available on sunny days, as is a children's play area.
ROOMS: 11 en suite (3 fmly) ⊗ in all bedrooms s £50-£60; d £80-£90 (incl. bkfst) **LB** **CONF:** Del £100 **PARKING:** 70 **NOTES:** ⊗ in restaurant

---

SOLIHULL, West Midlands Map 10 SP17
See also Dorridge

★★★★70% *Renaissance Solihull*
651 Warwick Rd B91 1AT
☎ 0121 711 3000
0121 705 6629/0121 711 3963
e-mail: ed.schofield@whitbread.com
web: www.marriott.co.uk/bhxsl
Dir: *M42 junct 5, follow signs for Solihull centre. 2nd left at rdbt (Warwick Rd). Straight over 3rd sets of lights. Barley Mow pub left on approaching large rdbt. Straight ahead, hotel on right.*
With its town centre location, this modern hotel is conveniently situated for the NEC, Birmingham and many local attractions. Bedrooms are air conditioned and attractively decorated, equipped with a comprehensive range of extras. The hotel boasts extensive conference facilities, an indoor leisure facility and extensive parking.
ROOMS: 179 en suite (6 fmly) ⊗ in 87 bedrooms **FACILITIES:** STV Sauna Solarium Gym Jacuzzi Beauty therapist Large screen TV ♫ **CONF:** Thtr 700 Class 350 Board 60 **SERVICES:** Lift **PARKING:** 300 **NOTES:** Civ Wed 70

★★★68% Corus hotel Solihull
Stratford Rd, Shirley B90 4EB
☎ 0870 609 6133 0121 733 3801
e-mail: revenuemanager.solihull@corushotels.com
web: www.corushotels.com
Dir: *M42 junct 4 onto A34 cross 1st 3 rdbts, double back along dual carriageway, hotel on left*

This popular business hotel offers its guests some extra facilities such as an indoor leisure club and busy locals bar. The bedrooms are well-laid out, some modern in style and some traditional, but all comprehensively equipped.
ROOMS: 111 en suite (11 fmly) (13 GF) ⊗ in 64 bedrooms s £117-£145; d £117-£155 **LB** **FACILITIES: Spa** STV Sauna Solarium Gym Jacuzzi Steam room **CONF:** Thtr 180 Class 80 Board 60 Del £140 **SERVICES:** Lift **PARKING:** 275 **NOTES:** ⊗ in restaurant

Ramada Solihull/Birmingham
The Square B91 3RF
☎ 0121 711 2121 0121 711 3374
e-mail: sales.solihull@ramadajarvis.co.uk
web: www.ramadajarvis.co.uk
Dir: *From M42 junct 5 take A41 towards Solihull, then 1st left on slip road. Turn right at island, turn left at 2nd set of lights. Hotel on right after 600yds.*
This extensive hotel is ideally located for both the NEC and the M42. Bedrooms are comfortably appointed for both business and leisure guests.
ROOMS: 145 en suite (14 fmly) (36 GF) ⊗ in 95 bedrooms s £109-£139; d £109-£139 **FACILITIES:** Xmas **CONF:** Thtr 200 Class 80 Board 60 Del from £179 **SERVICES:** Lift **PARKING:** 180 **NOTES:** ⊗ in restaurant Civ Wed 100

Premier Travel Inn Solihull North
Stratford Rd, Shirley B90 3AG
☎ 08701 977231 0121 733 2762
web: www.premiertravelinn.com
Dir: *M42 junct 4 follow signs for Birmingham. Inn in Shirley town centre, on A34*
High quality, modern budget accommodation ideal for both families and business travellers. Spacious, en suite bedrooms feature bath and shower, satellite TV and many have telephones and modem points. The adjacent family restaurant features a wide and varied menu. For further details consult the Hotel Groups page.
ROOMS: 44 en suite s £47.95-£50.95; d £47.95-£50.95

Premier Travel Inn Solihull (Shirley)
Stratford Rd, Shirley B90 4EP
☎ 08701 977232 0121 733 7075
web: www.premiertravelinn.com
Dir: *1m from M42 junct 4 on A34, north*
High quality, modern budget accommodation ideal for both families and business travellers. Spacious, en suite bedrooms feature bath and shower, satellite TV and many have telephones and modem points. The adjacent family restaurant features a wide and varied menu. For further details consult the Hotel Groups page.
ROOMS: 51 en suite s £49.95-£52.95; d £49.95-£52.95

SONNING, Berkshire Map 05 SU77

★★★78% French Horn
RG4 6TN
☎ 0118 969 2204 0118 944 2210
e-mail: info@thefrenchhorn.co.uk
Dir: *From A4 into Sonning, follow B478 through village over bridge, hotel on right, car park on left*
This long established Thames-side restaurant with rooms has a lovely village setting and retains the traditions of classic hotel keeping. The restaurant is a particular attraction and provides attentive service. Bedrooms are spacious and comfortable, many offering stunning views over the river and include four cottage suites. A private boardroom is available for corporate guests.
ROOMS: 13 en suite 8 annexe en suite (4 GF) s £120-£165; d £150-£205 (incl. bkfst) **FACILITIES:** STV Fishing Affiliation with Nirvana Spa, complimentary 10 minute journey **CONF:** Board 16 Del £245 **SERVICES:** air con **PARKING:** 40 **NOTES:** Closed 26 Dec-30 Jan RS 1st Jan

★★★69% *The Great House at Sonning*
Thames St RG4 6UT
☎ 0118 969 2277 📠 0118 944 1296
e-mail: greathouse@btconnect.com
web: www.greathouseatsonning.co.uk
Dir: *exit A4 at rdbt with Texaco Garage & take B478 into Sonning (signed). Through village, over mini rdbt, down steep hill and bear right. Hotel on right, before bridge*

This delightful property enjoys a riverside location with a mile and a half private mooring alongside attractive terraces and lawns, making it a popular wedding venue. Comfortable, well-equipped bedrooms are situated either in the main house or set in various buildings located round an attractive courtyard. A choice of bars and restaurants is available as well as alfresco dining on the terrace.

ROOMS: 12 en suite 37 annexe en suite (11 GF) **FACILITIES:** STV ♫ ch fac **CONF:** Thtr 100 Class 50 Board 35 **PARKING:** 120 **NOTES:** RS 27 Dec -9 Jan Civ Wed 120

SOURTON, Devon — Map 03 SX59

★★75% Collaven Manor
EX20 4HH
☎ 01837 861522 📠 01837 861614
e-mail: collavenmanor@supanet.com
Dir: *off A30 onto A386 to Tavistock, hotel 2m on right*

This delightful 15th-century manor house is quietly located in five acres of well-tended grounds. The friendly proprietors provide attentive service and ensure a relaxing environment. Charming public rooms have old oak beams and granite fireplaces, and provide a range of comfortable lounges and a well stocked bar. In the restaurant, a daily-changing menu offers interesting dishes.

ROOMS: 9 en suite (1 fmly) s £59-£79; d £96-£134 (incl. bkfst) **LB** **FACILITIES:** Bowls **CONF:** Thtr 30 Class 20 Board 16 Del from £73.95 **PARKING:** 50 **NOTES:** ⊗ in restaurant Civ Wed 50

SOURTON CROSS, Devon — Map 03 SX59

Travelodge Okehampton West
EX20 4LY
☎ 08700 850 950 📠 0870 1911548
web: www.travelodge.co.uk
Dir: *4m W, at junct of A30/A386*

Travelodge offers good quality, good value, modern accommodation. Ideal for families, the spacious, en suite bedrooms include remote-control TV, tea and coffee-making facilities and comfortable beds. Meals can be taken at the nearby family restaurant. For further details consult the Hotel Groups page.

ROOMS: 42 en suite s fr £26; d fr £26

⊗ No smoking

SOUTHAMPTON, Hampshire — Map 05 SU41
See also Botley, Landford (Wilts) & Shedfield

★★★★★65% ⊛⊛ *De Vere Grand Harbour*
West Quay Rd SO15 1AG
☎ 023 8063 3033 📠 023 8063 3066
e-mail: grandharbour@devere-hotels.com
web: www.devereonline.co.uk
Dir: *M27 junct 3 follow Waterfront signs keep in left lane of dual carrriageway, then follow Heritage & Waterfront signs onto West Quay Rd*

Enjoying views of the harbour, this hotel stands alongside the medieval town walls and close to the West Quay centre. The modern design is impressive, with leisure facilities located in the dramatic glass pyramid. The spacious bedrooms are well appointed and thoughtfully equipped. For dining, guests can choose between two bars as well as fine dining within Allertons Restaurant and a more informal style within No 5 Brasserie.

ROOMS: 172 en suite (22 fmly) ⊗ in 148 bedrooms **FACILITIES: Spa** STV Snooker Sauna Solarium Gym **CONF:** BC Thtr 500 Class 200 Board 150 **SERVICES:** Lift **PARKING:** 190 **NOTES:** ⊗ in restaurant Civ Wed 310

★★★★71% ⊛⊛ *Botleigh Grange*
Hedge End SO30 2GA
☎ 01489 787700 📠 01489 788535
e-mail: enquiries@botleighgrangehotel.co.uk
Dir: *from M27 junct 7 follow A334 to Botley, hotel is 0.5m on left*

This impressive mansion, situated close to the M27, displays good quality throughout. The bedrooms are spacious with a good range of facilities. Public areas include a large conference room and a

continued on p524

SOUTHAMPTON, continued

pleasant terrace with views overlooking the gardens and lake. The restaurant offers interesting menus using fresh, local produce.

Botleigh Grange, Southampton

ROOMS: 56 en suite (8 fmly) ⊗ in 17 bedrooms **FACILITIES:** STV Fishing Putt green **CONF:** Thtr 500 Class 175 Board 60 **SERVICES:** Lift **PARKING:** 200 **NOTES:** ✗ ⊗ in restaurant Civ Wed 400

See advert on opposite page

★★★70% Chilworth Manor

CLASSIC BRITISH

SO16 7PT
☎ 023 8076 7333 ⎙ 023 8070 1743
e-mail: general@chilworth-manor.co.uk
web: www.chilworth-manor.co.uk
Dir: *1m from M3/M27 junct on A27 Romsey Rd N from Southampton. Pass Clump Inn on left, 200mtrs then left at Chilworth Science Park sign. Hotel immediately right*

Set in 12 acres of delightful grounds, this attractive Edwardian manor house is conveniently located for the nearby City of Southampton and the New Forest, now designated a National Park. Bedrooms are located in both the main house and an adjoining wing. The hotel is particularly popular as both a conference and a wedding venue.
ROOMS: 95 en suite (6 fmly) ⊗ in 75 bedrooms s £49.50-£115; d £99-£145 **LB** **FACILITIES:** STV 🎾 ♫ Trim trail walking, Giant chess, Petanque **CONF:** Thtr 160 Class 50 Board 50 Del from £165 **SERVICES:** Lift **PARKING:** 200 **NOTES:** ⊗ in restaurant Civ Wed 80

★★★69% ◉ The Woodlands Lodge

Bartley Rd, Woodlands SO40 7GN
☎ 023 8029 2257 ⎙ 023 8029 3090
e-mail: reception@woodlands-lodge.co.uk
web: www.woodlands-lodge.co.uk
Dir: *A326 towards Fawley. 2nd rdbt turn right, left after 0.25m by White Horse PH. In 1.5m cross cattle grid, hotel is 70yds on left*
An 18th-century former hunting lodge, this hotel is set in four acres of impressive and well-tended grounds on the edge of the New Forest. Well-equipped bedrooms come in varying sizes and styles and all bathrooms have a jacuzzi bath. Public areas provide

continued

a pleasant lounge and intimate cocktail bar. The dining room, with its hand-painted ceiling, serves delicious award-winning cuisine.
ROOMS: 16 en suite (1 fmly) (3 GF) ⊗ in 2 bedrooms s £72-£90; d £118-£190 (incl. bkfst) **LB** **FACILITIES:** STV ♫ Xmas **CONF:** Thtr 55 Class 14 Board 20 Del from £120 **PARKING:** 30 **NOTES:** ⊗ in restaurant Civ Wed 50

★★★67% Jury's Inn Southampton

JURYS DOYLE HOTELS

1 Charlotte Place SO14 0TB
☎ 023 8037 1111 ⎙ 023 8037 1100
web: www.jurysdoyle.com
This new hotel to Southampton is modern, stylish and is easily accessible from major road networks. Bedrooms provide good guest comfort and in-room facilities are suited to both leisure and business markets. Public areas include a number of meeting rooms, a popular bar and restaurant.
ROOMS: 270 en suite ⊗ in 206 bedrooms s £79-£99; d £79-£99 **FACILITIES:** STV Xmas **CONF:** BC Thtr 120 Class 80 Board 59 Del from £99 **SERVICES:** Lift air con **PARKING:** 160 **NOTES:** ✗ ⊗ in restaurant

★★★66% Southampton Park

Forestdale Hotels

Cumberland Place SO15 2WY
☎ 023 8034 3343 ⎙ 023 8033 2538
e-mail: southampton.park@forestdale.com
web: www.forestdale.com
Dir: *opposite Watts Park & Civic Centre*
Located in the heart of the city opposite Watts Park, this modern hotel provides well-equipped, smartly appointed bedrooms with comfortable furnishings. The public areas include a good leisure centre, a spacious bar and lounge and the lively MJ's Brasserie. Parking is available in the multi-storey behind the hotel.
ROOMS: 72 en suite (10 fmly) ⊗ in 20 bedrooms s £90-£105; d £120-£135 (incl. bkfst) **LB** **FACILITIES: Spa** STV ⛆ Sauna Solarium Gym Jacuzzi **CONF:** Thtr 200 Class 60 Board 70 Del from £125 **SERVICES:** Lift **NOTES:** ⊗ in restaurant Closed 25&26 Dec nights

★★★65% Novotel Southampton

NOVOTEL

1 West Quay Rd SO15 1RA
☎ 023 8033 0550 ⎙ 023 8022 2158
e-mail: H1073@accor-hotels.com
web: www.novotel.com
Dir: *M27 junct 3 & signs for City Centre (A33). 1m right lane for West Quay & Dock Gates 4-10. Hotel entrance on left.*
Modern purpose-built hotel situated close to the city centre, railway station, ferry terminal and major road networks. The brightly decorated bedrooms are ideal for families and business guests; four rooms have facilities for the less mobile. The open-plan public areas include the Garden brasserie, a bar and a leisure complex. Novotel - AA Hotel Group of the Year 2005-6.
ROOMS: 121 en suite (50 fmly) ⊗ in 98 bedrooms s £94-£104; d £94-£104 **LB** **FACILITIES:** STV ⛆ Sauna Gym **CONF:** Thtr 450 Class 300 Board 150 Del from £120 **SERVICES:** Lift air con **PARKING:** 300 **NOTES:** ⊗ in restaurant Civ Wed 150

★★68% Elizabeth House

42-44 The Avenue SO17 1XP
☎ 023 8022 4327 ⎙ 023 8022 4327
e-mail: enquiries@elizabethhousehotel.com
web: www.elizabethhousehotel.com
Dir: *on A33, towards S'ton on left*
The Elizabeth House is conveniently situated on The Avenue, and as such provides an ideal base for both business and leisure guests. The bedrooms are well equipped and are attractively furnished with comfort in mind. There is also a relaxing and attractive restaurant and a cosy cellar bar.
ROOMS: 18 en suite 7 annexe en suite (9 fmly) (8 GF) s fr £55; d fr £65 (incl. bkfst) **CONF:** Thtr 40 Class 24 Board 24 Del from £92 **PARKING:** 31 **NOTES:** ⊗ in restaurant

S

★★64% *Busketts Lawn*

174 Woodlands Rd, Woodlands SO40 7GL
☎ 023 8029 2272 & 8029 3417 🖷 023 8029 2487
e-mail: enquiries@buskettslawnhotel.co.uk
Dir: *A35 W of city through Ashurst, over railway bridge, sharp right into Woodlands Road*

A family run hotel on the edge of the New Forest. Bedrooms are traditionally furnished and well stocked with thoughtful additions. Leisure facilities comprise an outdoor swimming pool and croquet lawn, and there is a terrace overlooking the gardens. A small comfortable lounge and bar are also available.
ROOMS: 14 en suite (3 fmly) (1 GF) **FACILITIES:** STV Putt green Mini Football pitch **CONF:** Thtr 100 Class 60 Board 40 **PARKING:** 50 **NOTES:** in restaurant Closed Xmas Civ Wed 100

⇧ *Hotel Ibis*

West Quay Rd, Western Esplanade SO15 1RA
☎ 023 8063 4463 🖷 023 8022 3273
e-mail: H1039@accor-hotels.com
Dir: *M27 junct 3/M271. Left to city centre (A35), follow Old Town Waterfront until 4th lights, left, then left again, hotel opposite station*
Modern, budget hotel offering comfortable accommodation in bright and practical bedrooms. Breakfast is self-service and dinner is available in the restaurant. For further details, consult the Hotel Groups page.
ROOMS: 93 en suite

⇧ Premier Travel Inn Southampton Airport

Mitchell Way SO18 2XU
☎ 0870 9906436 🖷 0870 9906437
web: www.premiertravelinn.com
Dir: *Exit M27 junct 5, A335 towards Eastleigh. Right at rdbt onto Wide Ln. 1st exit at next rdbt onto Mitchell Way*
High quality, modern budget accommodation ideal for both families and business travellers. Spacious, en suite bedrooms feature bath and shower, satellite TV and many have telephones and modem points. The adjacent family restaurant features a wide and varied menu. For further details consult the Hotel Groups page.
ROOMS: 121 en suite s £55.95; d £55.95

⇧ Premier Travel Inn Southampton City Centre

New Rd SO14 0AB
☎ 0870 238 3308 🖷 023 8033 8395
web: www.premiertravelinn.com
Dir: *M27 junct 5/A335 towards city centre, at the Charlotte Place rdbt take 2nd left into East Park Terrace, then 1st left onto New Rd. Inn on right*
High quality, modern budget accommodation ideal for both families and business travellers. Spacious, en suite bedrooms feature bath and shower, satellite TV and many have telephones and modem points. The adjacent family restaurant features a wide and varied menu. For further details consult the Hotel Groups page.
ROOMS: 172 en suite

⇧ Premier Travel Inn Southampton North

Romsey Rd, Nursling SO16 0XJ
☎ 08701 977233 🖷 023 8074 0947
web: www.premiertravelinn.com
Dir: *M27 junct 3 take M271 towards Romsey. At next rdbt take 3rd exit towards Southampton (A3057) Inn 1.5m on right*
High quality, modern budget accommodation ideal for both families and business travellers. Spacious, en suite bedrooms feature bath and shower, satellite TV and many have telephones and modem points. The adjacent family restaurant features a wide and varied menu. For further details consult the Hotel Groups page.
ROOMS: 32 en suite s £50.95; d £50.95

⇧ Travelodge

Lodge Rd SO14 6QR
☎ 08700 850 950 🖷 023 8033 4569
web: www.travelodge.co.uk
Dir: *M3 junct 14, take A33 to Southampton, on left after 6th set of lights*
Travelodge offers good quality, good value, modern accommodation. Ideal for families, the spacious, en suite bedrooms include remote-control TV, tea and coffee-making facilities and comfortable beds. Meals can be taken at the nearby family restaurant. For further details consult the Hotel Groups page.
ROOMS: 59 en suite s fr £26; d fr £26

Town House Hotel
Country House Hotel
⇧ Travel Accommodation

SOUTH BRENT, Devon — Map 03 SX66

★★74% ® Glazebrook House Hotel & Restaurant

TQ10 9JE
☎ 01364 73322 📠 01364 72350
e-mail: enquiries@glazebrookhouse.com
web: www.glazebrookhouse.com
Dir: *from Exeter take Marley Head exit to South Brent. 2nd turning on right after London Inn. From Plymouth take Woodpecker exit*

Enjoying a tranquil and convenient location next to the Dartmoor National Park and set within four acres of gardens, this 18th-century former gentleman's residence offers comfortable and friendly accommodation. Bedrooms are well appointed and public areas are elegant and spacious. Cuisine offers interesting combinations of fresh, locally-sourced produce.
ROOMS: 10 en suite ⊗ in all bedrooms s £50-£55; d £75-£145 (incl. bkfst) **LB CONF:** BC Thtr 100 Class 60 Board 40 Del from £65.50 **PARKING:** 40 **NOTES:** ✈ ⊗ in restaurant Closed 1st 2 weeks in Jan Civ Wed 80

SOUTH CAVE, East Riding of Yorkshire — Map 17 SE93

⌂ Travelodge Hull

Beacon Service Area HU15 1RZ
☎ 08700 850 950 📠 01430 424455
web: www.travelodge.co.uk
Dir: *A63 eastbound, 0.5m from M62 junct 38*
Travelodge offers good quality, good value, modern accommodation. Ideal for families, the spacious, en suite bedrooms include remote-control TV, tea and coffee-making facilities and comfortable beds. Meals can be taken at the nearby family restaurant. For further details consult the Hotel Groups page.
ROOMS: 40 en suite s fr £26; d fr £26

S

> GF indicates the number of bedrooms at ground level

SOUTHEND-ON-SEA, Essex — Map 07 TQ88

★★★70% Camelia

178 Eastern Esplanade, Thorpe Bay SS1 3AA
☎ 01702 587917 📠 01702 585704
e-mail: cameliahotel@fsbdial.co.uk
web: www.cameliahotel.com
Dir: *from A13 or A127 follow signs to Southend seafront, on seafront turn left, hotel 1m east of the pier*
A smartly presented, privately owned hotel, ideally situated at the quiet end of the seafront overlooking the beach. Bedrooms are pleasantly decorated and thoughtfully equipped; many rooms have superb sea views and there are six new executive suites. The air-conditioned public areas include a cosy lounge bar, an informal restaurant and a coffee lounge.

ROOMS: 21 en suite 8 annexe en suite (7 fmly) (8 GF) ⊗ in 19 bedrooms s £55-£65; d £60-£100 (incl. bkfst) **LB FACILITIES:** STV Cycle hire and tours arranged **PARKING:** 102 **NOTES:** ✈ ⊗ in restaurant

★★★69% Roslin Hotel

Thorpe Esplanade SS1 3BG
☎ 01702 586375 📠 01702 586663
e-mail: sales@roslinhotel.com
web: www.roslinhotel.com
Dir: *A127, follow signs for Southend-on-Sea. Hotel between Walton Road and Clieveden Road, on seafront*

This friendly, family-run hotel is situated at the quiet end of the esplanade, overlooking the beach and sea. The spacious bedrooms are pleasantly decorated and thoughtfully equipped; some rooms have superb sea views. Public rooms include a large lounge bar and the attractive Mulberry restaurant, which also overlooks the sea.
ROOMS: 39 rms (35 en suite) (4 fmly) (7 GF) s £45-£77 (incl. bkfst) **LB FACILITIES:** STV Temp membership of local sports centre **CONF:** Thtr 40 Class 24 Board 24 Del from £97 **PARKING:** 36 **NOTES:** ✈ ⊗ in restaurant RS 26-Dec

See advert on opposite page

★★★68% *Westcliff*

Westcliff Pde, Westcliff-on-Sea SS0 7QW
☎ 01702 345247 📠 01702 431814
e-mail: westcliff@zolahotels.com
Dir: *M25 junct 29, A127 towards Southend, follow signs for Cliffs Pavillion when approaching town centre*
This impressive Grade II listed Victorian building is situated in an elevated position overlooking gardens and cliffs to the sea beyond. The spacious bedrooms are tastefully decorated and thoughtfully equipped; many have lovely sea views. Public rooms include a smart conservatory-style restaurant, a spacious lounge and a range of function rooms.
ROOMS: 55 en suite (2 fmly) ⊗ in 32 bedrooms **FACILITIES:** STV Jacuzzi ♫ **CONF:** Thtr 225 Class 90 Board 64 **SERVICES:** Lift **NOTES:** ✈ ⊗ in restaurant Civ Wed 60

★★★66% *Erlsmere*
24/32 Pembury Rd, Westcliff-on-Sea SS0 8DS
☎ 01702 349025 🖷 01702 337724
e-mail: erlsmerehotel@madasafish.com
Dir: *M25 junct 29 to A127 to Southend. Pass Kent Elms Corner exit at next lights to A1158 to Westbourne Grove signed seafront. At next main junct (A13) straight ahead to Chalkwell Avenue, under rail bridge left, 4th right*
Situated in a peaceful side road, just a short walk from the seafront and shops. Bedrooms come in a variety of styles but each one is pleasantly decorated and well-equipped. An interesting choice of dishes is served in the stylish new Restaurant 2432 and guests also have the use of the Patio Bar as well as a cosy lounge.
ROOMS: 30 en suite 2 annexe en suite (2 fmly) **CONF:** Thtr 120 Class 40 Board 60 **PARKING:** 12 **NOTES:** ✂

★★71% Balmoral
34 Valkyrie Rd, Westcliff-on-Sea SS0 8BU
☎ 01702 342947 🖷 01702 337828
e-mail: enq@balmoralsouthend.com
web: www.balmoralsouthend.com
Dir: *off A13*

A delightful hotel ideally situated just a short walk from the main shopping centre, railway station and seafront. The attractively decorated bedrooms are tastefully furnished and equipped with many thoughtful touches. Public rooms feature a smart open-plan bar/restaurant and further seating is provided in the reception area.
ROOMS: 29 en suite (4 fmly) (2 GF) s £55-£90; d £73-£120 (incl. bkfst) **FACILITIES:** STV Arrangement with nearby health club **PARKING:** 23 **NOTES:** ⊗ in restaurant Closed Xmas

⌂ Premier Travel Inn Southend-on-Sea
213 Eastern Esplanade SS1 3AD
☎ 0870 9906370 🖷 0870 9906371
web: www.premiertravelinn.com
Dir: *Exit M25 junct 29, A127 to Southend. Then follow signs for A1159 (A13) Shoebury onto dual carriageway. At rdbt straight across, follow signs for Thorpe Bay & seafront. At seafront turn right. Hotel on right*
High quality, modern budget accommodation ideal for both families and business travellers. Spacious, en suite bedrooms feature bath and shower, satellite TV and many have telephones and modem points. The adjacent family restaurant features a wide and varied menu. For further details consult the Hotel Groups page.
ROOMS: 42 en suite s £51.95; d £51.95

⌂ Premier Travel Inn Southend-on-Sea (West)
Thanet Grange SS2 6GB
☎ 08701 977235 🖷 01702 430838
web: www.premiertravelinn.com
Dir: *on A127 at junct with B1013*
High quality, modern budget accommodation ideal for both families and business travellers. Spacious, en suite bedrooms

continued

feature bath and shower, satellite TV and many have telephones and modem points. The adjacent family restaurant features a wide and varied menu. For further details consult the Hotel Groups page.
ROOMS: 60 en suite s £49.95; d £49.95

⌂ Travelodge (Southend-on-Sea)
Maitland House, Warrior Square, Chichester Rd SS1 2JY
☎ 08700 850950 🖷 01994 232957
web: www.travelodge.co.uk
Dir: *in town centre.*
Travelodge offers good quality, good value, modern accommodation. Ideal for families, the spacious, en suite bedrooms include remote-control TV, tea and coffee-making facilities and comfortable beds. Meals can be taken at the nearby family restaurant. For further details consult the Hotel Groups page.
ROOMS: 107 en suite s fr £26; d fr £26

SOUTH MIMMS SERVICE AREA (M25), Hertfordshire — Map 06 TL20

⌂ Days Inn South Mimms
Bignells Corner EN6 3QQ
☎ 01707 665440 🖷 01707 660189
e-mail: southmimmshotel@welcomebreak.co.uk
web: www.welcomebreak.co.uk
Dir: *M25 junct 23, at rdbt follow signs*
This modern building offers accommodation in smart, spacious and well-equipped bedrooms, suitable for families and business travellers, and all with en suite bathrooms. Continental breakfast is available and other refreshments may be taken at the nearby family restaurant. For further details see the Hotel Groups page.
ROOMS: 74 en suite s £59-£74; d £59-£74 **CONF:** Board 10

SOUTH MOLTON, Devon Map 03 SS72

★★68% The George Hotel
1 Broad St EX36 3AB
☎ 01769 572514 🖹 01769 579218
e-mail: info@georgehotelsouthmolton.co.uk
web: www.georgehotelsouthmolton.co.uk
***Dir:** off A361 at rdbt signed South Molton 1.5m to centre. Hotel in square*
Retaining many of its original features, this charming 17th-century hotel is situated in the centre of town. Providing comfortable accommodation, complemented by informal and friendly service. Regularly changing menus, featuring local produce, are offered in the restaurant and bar.
ROOMS: 9 en suite (3 fmly) ⊗ in all bedrooms s £50-£60; d £65-£75 (incl. bkfst) **LB FACILITIES:** Local Gym facilities available nearby ♫ Xmas **CONF:** Thtr 100 Class 30 Board 30 **PARKING:** 12 **NOTES:** ✗ ⊗ in restaurant RS 1st wk Jan

SOUTH NORMANTON, Derbyshire Map 16 SK45

★★★★70%
Renaissance Derby/Nottingham Hotel
Carter Ln East DE55 2EH
☎ 01773 812000 & 0870 4007262
🖹 01773 580032 & 0870 4007362
e-mail: derby@renaissancehotels.co.uk
web: www.renaissancehotels.co.uk/emabr
***Dir:** M1 junct 28, E on A38 to Mansfield*
This hotel provides comfortable bedrooms, stylishly furnished and decorated with a comprehensive range of extras provided. Public rooms include a smart leisure centre, conference facilities and Chatterley's Restaurant.
ROOMS: 158 en suite (7 fmly) (61 GF) ⊗ in 90 bedrooms s £64-£108; d £78-£128 (incl. bkfst) **LB FACILITIES:** STV supervised Sauna Gym Jacuzzi Steam room, Whirlpool Xmas **CONF:** BC Thtr 220 Class 100 Board 60 Del from £125 **PARKING:** 220 **NOTES:** ⊗ in restaurant Civ Wed 220

Premier Travel Inn Mansfield
Carter Ln East DE55 2EH
☎ 08701 977180 🖹 01773 861155
web: www.premiertravelinn.com
***Dir:** just off M1 junct 28, on A38 signed Mansfield. Entrance 200yds on left*
High quality, modern budget accommodation ideal for both families and business travellers. Spacious, en suite bedrooms feature bath and shower, satellite TV and many have telephones and modem points. The adjacent family restaurant features a wide and varied menu. For further details consult the Hotel Groups page.
ROOMS: 80 en suite s £46.95-£49.95; d £46.95-£49.95

SOUTHPORT, Merseyside Map 15 SD31
See also Formby

★★★71% Scarisbrick
Lord St PR8 1NZ
☎ 01704 543000 🖹 01704 533335
e-mail: info@scarisbrickhotel.com
web: www.scarisbrickhotel.co.uk
***Dir:** from S: M6 junct 26, M58 to Ormskirk then Southport; from N: A59 from Preston, well signed.*
Centrally located on Southport's famous Lord Street, this privately owned hotel offers a high standard of attractively furnished, thoughtfully equipped accommodation. A wide range of eating options is available, from the bistro style of Maloney's Kitchen to *continued* the more formal Knightsbridge restaurant. Extensive leisure and conference facilities are also available.
ROOMS: 88 en suite (5 fmly) ⊗ in 44 bedrooms s £35-£80; d £70-£110 (incl. bkfst) **LB FACILITIES: Spa** STV Sauna Solarium Gym Jacuzzi Use of private leisure centre, Beauty & aromatherapy studio ♫ Xmas **CONF:** BC Thtr 200 Class 100 Board 80 Del from £65 **SERVICES:** Lift **PARKING:** 68 **NOTES:** ✗ ⊗ in restaurant Civ Wed 170

★★★69% Stutelea Hotel & Leisure Club
Alexandra Rd PR9 0NB
☎ 01704 544220 🖹 01704 500232
e-mail: info@stutelea.co.uk
***Dir:** off the promenade*
This family owned and run hotel enjoys a quiet location in a residential area, a short walk from Lord Street and the Promenade. Bedrooms vary in size and style and include family suites and rooms with balconies overlooking the attractive gardens. The elegant restaurant has a cosmopolitan theme; alternatively the Garden Bar, in the leisure centre, offers light snacks throughout the day.
ROOMS: 22 en suite (4 fmly) (3 GF) ⊗ in 4 bedrooms s £70-£75; d £99-£104 (incl. bkfst) **LB FACILITIES:** STV Sauna Solarium Gym Jacuzzi Games room Keep fit classes Steam room **SERVICES:** Lift **PARKING:** 15 **NOTES:** ✗ ⊗ in restaurant

★★★66% Royal Clifton
Promenade PR8 1RB
☎ 01704 533771 🖹 01704 500657
e-mail: sales@royalclifton.co.uk
***Dir:** adjacent to Marine Lake*
This grand, traditional hotel benefits from a prime location on the promenade. Bedrooms range in size and style, but all are comfortable and thoughtfully equipped. Public areas include the lively Bar C, the elegant Pavilion Restaurant and a modern, well-equipped leisure club. Extensive conference and banqueting facilities make this hotel a popular function venue.
ROOMS: 111 en suite (22 fmly) (6 GF) ⊗ in 30 bedrooms s fr £85; d fr £115 (incl. bkfst) **LB FACILITIES: Spa** STV Sauna Solarium Gym Jacuzzi Hair & beauty Steam room, Aromatherapy ♫ Xmas **CONF:** Thtr 250 Class 100 Board 65 Del from £101 **SERVICES:** Lift **PARKING:** 60 **NOTES:** ✗ ⊗ in restaurant Civ Wed 100

★★71% Balmoral Lodge
41 Queens Rd PR9 9EX
☎ 01704 544298 & 530751 🖹 01704 501224
e-mail: balmorallg@aol.com
web: www.balmorallodge.co.uk
***Dir:** edge of town on A565 Preston road*
Situated in a quiet residential area close to Lord Street, this friendly hotel is particularly popular with golfers. Smartly appointed bedrooms are well equipped for both business and leisure guests; some benefit from private patios overlooking the attractive gardens. Stylish public areas include Oscar's restaurant and an attractive bar lounge.
ROOMS: 15 en suite (1 fmly) s £35-£45; d £70-£80 (incl. bkfst) **LB FACILITIES:** STV Sauna **PARKING:** 12 **NOTES:** ✗ ⊗ in restaurant

★★70% *Bold*
585 Lord St PR9 0BE
☎ 01704 532578 🖹 01704 532528
e-mail: info@boldhotel.com
web: www.boldhotel.com
***Dir:** M6 junct 26, M58, then A570 towards Southport. In Southport follow signs to Lord St, hotel at N end of street, on corner of Seabank Rd*
Enjoying a central location, this family hotel is just a minute's walk
continued

from the promenade and local attractions. Thoughtfully equipped, spacious bedrooms are suitable for business or leisure guests as well as for families. Public areas include a spacious bar and bistro and a large carvery that is available for parties.
ROOMS: 23 en suite (4 fmly) **FACILITIES:** Special rates for local squash club **CONF:** Thtr 40 Class 40 Board 11 **SERVICES:** air con **PARKING:** 15 **NOTES:** ✗

★★65% Metropole
Portland St PR8 1LL
☎ 01704 536836 🖷 01704 549041
e-mail: metropole.southport@btinternet.com
web: www.btinternet.com/~metropole.southport
Dir: *after Prince of Wales Hotel left off Lord St. Hotel directly behind Prince of Wales*
This family-run hotel of long standing, popular with golfers, is ideally situated just 50 yards from the famous Lord Street. Accommodation is comfortably equipped with family rooms available. In addition to the restaurant that offers a selection of freshly prepared dishes, there is a choice of lounges including a popular bar-lounge.
ROOMS: 23 en suite (4 fmly) ⊘ in 6 bedrooms s £25-£42; d £45-£72 (incl. bkfst) **LB** **FACILITIES:** Snooker Golf can be arranged at 8 local courses Xmas **PARKING:** 12 **NOTES:** ⊘ in restaurant

Premier Travel Inn Southport
Marine Dr PR8 1RY
☎ 08701 977071 🖷 08701 977704
web: www.premiertravelinn.com
Dir: *from Southport follow signs for promenade and Marine Dr. Inn at junction of Marine Pde and Marine Drive*
High quality, modern budget accommodation ideal for both families and business travellers. Spacious, en suite bedrooms feature bath and shower, satellite TV and many have telephones and modem points. The adjacent family restaurant features a wide and varied menu. For further details consult the Hotel Groups page.
ROOMS: 60 en suite s £47.95-£50.95; d £47.95-£50.95

SOUTH SHIELDS, Tyne & Wear — Map 21 NZ36

★★★66% Sea
Sea Rd NE33 2LD
☎ 0191 427 0999 🖷 0191 454 0500
e-mail: sea@bestwestern.co.uk
Dir: *A1(M) past Washington Services to A194. Then take A183 through South Shields town centre along Ocean Rd. Hotel on seafront*
Dating from the 1930s this long-established business hotel overlooks the boating lake and the Tyne estuary. Bedrooms are generally spacious and well equipped. A range of generously portioned meals is served in both the bar and restaurant.
ROOMS: 32 en suite (5 fmly) ⊘ in 8 bedrooms s £62-£67; d £72-£100 (incl. bkfst) **FACILITIES:** STV **CONF:** Thtr 200 Class 100 Board 50 Del from £92.50 **PARKING:** 70 **NOTES:** RS 26-Dec

SOUTHWAITE MOTORWAY SERVICE AREA (M6), Cumbria — Map 18 NY44

Travelodge Carlisle (Southwaite)
Broadfield Site CA4 0NT
☎ 08700 850 950 🖷 016974 75354
web: www.travelodge.co.uk
Dir: *M6 junct 41/42*
Travelodge offers good quality, good value, modern accommodation. Ideal for families, the spacious, en suite bedrooms include remote-control TV, tea and coffee-making facilities and comfortable beds. Meals can be taken at the nearby family restaurant. For further details consult the Hotel Groups page.
ROOMS: 38 en suite s fr £26; d fr £26

SOUTHWELL, Nottinghamshire — Map 17 SK65

★★★66% Saracens Head
Market Place NG25 0HE
☎ 01636 812701 🖷 01636 815408
e-mail: cc@saracensheadhotel.co.uk
web: www.saracenshead-hotel.co.uk
Dir: *from A1 to Newark turn off & follow B6386 for approx 7m*
This half-timbered inn, rich in history, is set in the centre of town and close to the Minster. There is a relaxing atmosphere within the sumptuous public areas, which include a small bar, a comfortable lounge and a large restaurant. Bedroom styles vary; all are appealing, comfortable and well equipped.
ROOMS: 27 en suite (2 fmly) ⊘ in all bedrooms s £75-£85; d £95-£150 (incl. bkfst) **LB** **FACILITIES:** STV Xmas **CONF:** BC Thtr 80 Class 60 Board 40 Del from £119 **PARKING:** 102 **NOTES:** ✗ ⊘ in restaurant

SOUTH WITHAM, Lincolnshire — Map 11 SK91

Travelodge Grantham New Fox
New Fox NG33 5LN
☎ 08700 850 950 🖷 0870 191 1576
web: www.travelodge.co.uk
Dir: *on A1, northbound*
Travelodge offers good quality, good value, modern accommodation. Ideal for families, the spacious, en suite bedrooms include remote-control TV, tea and coffee-making facilities and comfortable beds. Meals can be taken at the nearby family restaurant. For further details consult the Hotel Groups page.
ROOMS: 32 en suite s fr £26; d fr £26

SOUTHWOLD, Suffolk — Map 13 TM57

★★★76% Swan
Market Place IP18 6EG
☎ 01502 722186 🖷 01502 724800
e-mail: swan.hotel@adnams.co.uk
Dir: *take A1095 to Southwold. Hotel in town centre, parking is via archway to left of building*

A charming 17th-century coaching inn situated in the heart of this bustling town centre overlooking the market place. Public rooms feature an elegant restaurant, a comfortable drawing room, a cosy bar and a lounge where guests can enjoy afternoon tea. The spacious bedrooms are attractively decorated, tastefully furnished and thoughtfully equipped; hotel is now totally non-smoking.
ROOMS: 25 en suite 17 annexe en suite (17 GF) s £78-£88; d £136-£156 (incl. bkfst) **LB** **FACILITIES:** Xmas **CONF:** Thtr 40 Class 24 Board 12 Del from £145 **SERVICES:** Lift **PARKING:** 35 **NOTES:** ⊘ in restaurant Civ Wed 40

U Star rating not confirmed

SOUTHWOLD, continued

★★74% ◉◉ The Crown
90 High St IP18 6DP
☎ 01502 722275 🖷 01502 727263
e-mail: crown.hotel@adnams.co.uk
Dir: off A12 take A1095 to Southwold, hotel on left in High Street
A delightful old posting inn situated in the heart of the town
centre. The property combines a pub, wine bar and intimate
restaurant with superb accommodation. The tastefully decorated
bedrooms have attractive co-ordinated soft furnishings and many
thoughtful touches. Public rooms feature a back room bar serving
traditional Adnams ales as well as an elegant first floor lounge.
ROOMS: 14 rms (13 en suite) (2 fmly) s £80-£92; d £116-£168 (incl.
bkfst) **LB FACILITIES:** Xmas **PARKING:** 23 **NOTES:** ✠ ⊗ in restaurant
Closed 1st or 2nd wk Jan

★★67% The Blyth Hotel
Station Rd IP18 6AY
☎ 01502 722632 🖷 01502 724123
e-mail: accommodation@blythhotel.wanadoo.co.uk
Dir: A12 onto A1045, on entering the town Mights Bridge & at the mini
rdbt, hotel ahead
Situated just a short walk from the centre of this delightful seaside
town, this friendly, family-run hotel offers bedrooms that are
thoughtfully equipped and individually decorated with co-ordinated
soft furnishings and fabrics. Public rooms include a smart
restaurant and two different bars serving the local Adnams ales.
ROOMS: 13 en suite (5 fmly) ⊗ in all bedrooms s £65; d £95-£135 **LB**
FACILITIES: Boule pitch **PARKING:** 10 **NOTES:** ⊗ in restaurant

SOUTH ZEAL, Devon Map 03 SX69

★★68% Oxenham Arms
EX20 2JT
☎ 01837 840244 & 840577 🖷 01837 840791
e-mail: theoxenhamarms@aol.com
Dir: off A30, 4m E of Okehampton in centre of village
Dating back to the 12th century this attractive inn features original
stonework, an ancient standing stone, aged beams, flagstone
floors and interesting nooks and crannies. Now equipped with
modern facilities, the bedrooms are comfortable and spacious. A
welcoming fire crackles in the lounge during colder months and
dining options include bar meals and the relaxed dining room.
ROOMS: 8 rms (7 en suite) (3 fmly) **PARKING:** 5 **NOTES:** ⊗ in restaurant

SPALDING, Lincolnshire Map 12 TF22

★★70% ◉ Cley Hall
22 High St PE11 1TX
☎ 01775 725157 🖷 01775 710785
e-mail: cleyhall@enterprise.net
Dir: from A16/A151 rbt towards Spalding (with river on right), hotel 1.5m
on left
This Georgian house (now under new ownership) overlooks the
River Welland, with landscaped gardens to the rear. Most
bedrooms are in an adjacent building; all are smart and include
modern amenities. Dining options are popular with residents and
locals alike, particularly the fine dining menu offered within the
smart Garden Restaurant. A reception-based internet/PC
workstation with language translation facility is available.
ROOMS: 4 en suite 11 annexe en suite (4 fmly) (2 GF) ⊗ in all
bedrooms s £55-£90; d £72-£105 (incl. bkfst) **FACILITIES:** STV
competition river fishing **CONF:** Thtr 35 Class 20 Board 18
PARKING: 20 **NOTES:** ⊗ in restaurant Civ Wed 36

SPENNYMOOR, Co Durham Map 19 NZ23

★★★74%
Whitworth Hall Country Park Hotel
MEAR DL16 7QX
☎ 01388 811772 🖷 01388 818669
e-mail: enquiries@whitworthhall.co.uk
Dir: follow A690 to Crook and then follow brown signs
This hotel, peacefully situated in its own grounds in the centre of
the Deer Park, offers comfortable accommodation. Spacious
bedrooms, some with excellent views over the lake, offer stylish
and elegant decor. Public areas include a choice of restaurants and
bars, a bright conservatory and well-equipped function and
conference rooms.
ROOMS: 29 en suite (3 fmly) (17 GF) ⊗ in 25 bedrooms s £120-£140;
d £140-£160 (incl. bkfst) **LB FACILITIES:** Fishing hotel has own deer
park Xmas **CONF:** Thtr 100 Class 30 Board 30 Del £135 **PARKING:** 100
NOTES: ✠ ⊗ in restaurant Civ Wed 120

STADHAMPTON, Oxfordshire Map 05 SU69

Restaurant with Rooms

🏠 ◉◉ The Crazy Bear
Bear Ln OX44 7UR
☎ 01865 890714 🖷 01865 400481
e-mail: sales@crazybearhotel.co.uk
Dir: M40 junct 7 left at end of slip road, into Stadhampton. Over mini rdbt,
left at petrol station. Hotel is 2nd left

This popular and attractive restaurant successfully combines
modern chic with old world character. Cuisine is extensive and
varied with award-winning Thai and English restaurants (both
awarded 2 AA rosettes) under the same roof. Those choosing to
make a night of it can enjoy the concept bedrooms, all presented
and equipped to a very high standard.
ROOMS: 5 en suite 7 annexe en suite (3 fmly) (2 GF) **FACILITIES:** STV
Hairdressers, Beauty Treatments and Massages **CONF:** Thtr 30 Class 30
Board 2 **PARKING:** 50 **NOTES:** ✠ Civ Wed 50

STAFFORD, Staffordshire Map 10 SJ92

★★★★74% The Moat House

Lower Penkridge Rd, Acton Trussell ST17 0RJ
☎ 01785 712217 01785 715344
e-mail: info@moathouse.co.uk
web: www.moathouse.co.uk
Dir: *M6 junct 13 onto A449 through Acton Trussell. Hotel on right*

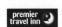

This 17th-century timbered building, with an idyllic canal-side setting, has been skilfully extended. Bedrooms are stylishly furnished, well equipped and comfortable. The bar offers a wide range of snacks and the restaurant boasts a popular fine dining option where the head chef displays his excellent skills using top quality produce.
ROOMS: 32 en suite (4 fmly) (12 GF) in 29 bedrooms s £125-£150; d £140-£165 (incl. bkfst) **LB** **FACILITIES:** STV **CONF:** Thtr 200 Class 60 Board 50 Del £115 **PARKING:** 200 **NOTES:** in restaurant Closed 25-26 Dec & 1-2 Jan

See advert on this page

★★★75% The Swan

46 Greengate St ST16 2JA
☎ 01785 258142 01785 223372
e-mail: info@theswanstafford.co.uk
Dir: *from north follow A34 access via Mill Street in town centre. From south on A449*
This former coaching inn located in the centre of town has spacious, contemporary public areas including a popular brasserie, a choice of elegant bars, a coffee shop and conference facilities. Individually styled bedrooms, many with original period features, are tastefully appointed and include two four-poster suites.
ROOMS: 31 en suite (2 fmly) in 29 bedrooms s £79-£120; d £89-£125 (incl. bkfst) **FACILITIES:** STV **SERVICES:** Lift **PARKING:** 40 **NOTES:** in restaurant Closed 25-26 Dec, 1 Jan

★★68% Abbey

65-68 Lichfield Rd ST17 4LW
☎ 01785 258531 01785 246875
Dir: *M6 junct 13 towards Stafford. Right at Esso garage to mini-rdbt, then follow Silkmore Lane to 2nd rdbt, hotel 0.25m on right*
This privately owned and personally run hotel provides well-equipped accommodation and is particularly popular with commercial visitors. Family and ground floor rooms are both available. Facilities here include a choice of smoking and non-smoking lounges. Staff throughout are friendly and keen to please.
ROOMS: 17 en suite (3 fmly) s £45-£55; d £56-£70 (incl. bkfst) **LB** **PARKING:** 25 **NOTES:** in restaurant Closed 22 Dec-7 Jan

Premier Travel Inn Stafford North (Hurricane)

1 Hurricane Close ST16 1GZ
☎ 0870 9906478 0870 9906479
web: www.premiertravelinn.com
Dir: *Exit M6 junct 14, A34 towards Stafford. Hotel approx 2m NW of town*
High quality, modern budget accommodation ideal for both families and business travellers. Spacious, en suite bedrooms feature bath and shower, satellite TV and many have telephones and modem points. The adjacent family restaurant features a wide and varied menu. For further details consult the Hotel Groups page.
ROOMS: 96 en suite s £46.95-£49.95; d £46.95-£49.95 **CONF:** Thtr 30

Premier Travel Inn Stafford North (Spitfire)

1 Spitfire Close ST16 1GX
☎ 08708 500689 08701 977 706
web: www.premiertravelinn.com
Dir: *Exit M6 junct 14, A34 north. Inn approx. 1m on left*
High quality, modern budget accommodation ideal for both families and business travellers. Spacious, en suite bedrooms feature bath and shower, satellite TV and many have telephones and modem points. The adjacent family restaurant features a wide and varied menu. For further details consult the Hotel Groups page.
ROOMS: 60 en suite s £46.95-£49.95; d £46.95-£49.95

STAFFORD MOTORWAY SERVICE AREA (M6), Staffordshire Map 10 SJ82

Premier Travel Inn Stafford (M6 Southbound)
Stafford Motorway Service Area ST15 0EU
☎ 08701 977239 📠 01785 826303
web: www.premiertravelinn.com
Dir: *M6 southbound 8m S of junct 15*
High quality, modern budget accommodation ideal for both families and business travellers. Spacious, en suite bedrooms feature bath and shower, satellite TV and many have telephones and modem points. The adjacent family restaurant features a wide and varied menu. For further details consult the Hotel Groups page.
ROOMS: 40 en suite s £46.95-£48.95; d £46.95-£48.95 **CONF:** Thtr 25 Board 15

Travelodge (Northbound only)
Moto Service Area, Eccleshall Rd ST15 0EU
☎ 08700 850 950 📠 01785 816107
web: www.travelodge.co.uk
Dir: *between M6 juncts 14 & 15 northbound only*
Travelodge offers good quality, good value, modern accommodation. Ideal for families, the spacious, en suite bedrooms include remote-control TV, tea and coffee-making facilities and comfortable beds. Meals can be taken at the nearby family restaurant. For further details consult the Hotel Groups page.
ROOMS: 49 en suite s fr £26; d fr £26

STAINES, Surrey Map 06 TQ07

★★★72% The Thames Lodge
Thames St TW18 4SF
☎ 0870 400 8121 & 01784 464433
📠 01784 454858
e-mail: sales.thameslodge@macdonald-hotels.co.uk
web: www.macdonald-hotels.co.uk
Dir: *Exit M25 junct 13. Follow signs A30 Town Centre/Bus station on right, hotel straight ahead*
Dating back to the 19th-century, this popular hotel enjoys an idyllic riverside setting. Bedrooms, many of which enjoy river views, are smartly decorated and equipped with a host of extras. Public rooms include a non-smoking lounge, a lounge/bar with outside terrace, a smart, modern brasserie and a range of function rooms.
ROOMS: 78 en suite (17 fmly) (22 GF) ⊗ in 64 bedrooms s £60-£150; d £100-£170 (incl. bkfst) **LB FACILITIES:** STV Riverside tea garden with mooring, Use of facilities at local leisure centre Xmas **CONF:** Thtr 50 Class 40 Board 40 Del from £150 **PARKING:** 40 **NOTES:** ⊗ in restaurant

Travelodge
Hale St, Two Rivers Retail Park TW18 4UW
☎ 08700 850 950 📠 01784 491 026
web: www.travelodge.co.uk
Travelodge offers good quality, good value, modern accommodation. Ideal for families, the spacious, en suite bedrooms include remote-control TV, tea and coffee-making facilities and comfortable beds. Meals can be taken at the nearby family restaurant. For further details consult the Hotel Groups page.
ROOMS: 65 en suite s fr £26; d fr £26

Popped the question? Hotels with Civ wed in their entry are licensed for civil wedding ceremonies. Maximum numbers for the ceremony only are shown e.g. Civ wed 120

STALLINGBOROUGH, Lincolnshire Map 17 TA11

★★★65% Stallingborough Grange Hotel
Riby Rd DN41 8BU
☎ 01469 561302 📠 01469 561338
e-mail: grange.hot@virgin.net
web: www.stallingborough-grange.com
Dir: *from A180 follow Stallingborough Ind Est signs, through village, from rdbt take A1173 towards Caistor, hotel 1m on left just past windmill*
This 18th-century country house has been tastefully extended to provide spacious and well-equipped bedrooms, particularly in the executive wing. This family-run hotel is popular with locals who enjoy the wide range of food offered in either the Tavern or restaurant.
ROOMS: 41 en suite (6 fmly) (9 GF) ⊗ in all bedrooms s £72-£80; d £95-£115 (incl. bkfst) **LB FACILITIES:** STV **CONF:** Thtr 60 Class 40 Board 28 **PARKING:** 100 **NOTES:** ✖ ⊗ in restaurant Civ Wed 65

STAMFORD, Lincolnshire Map 11 TF00

★★★80% The George of Stamford
71 St Martins PE9 2LB
☎ 01780 750750 & 750700 (Res) 📠 01780 750701
e-mail: reservations@georgehotelofstamford.com
web: www.georgehotelofstamford.com
Dir: *turn off A1 15m north of Peterborough onto B1081, 1m on left*
Steeped in hundreds of years of history, this delightful coaching inn provides spacious public areas that include a choice of dining options, inviting lounges, a business centre and a range of quality shops. A highlight is afternoon tea, taken in the colourful courtyard when weather permits. Bedrooms are stylishly appointed and range from traditional to contemporary in design.
ROOMS: 47 en suite (2 fmly) ⊗ in 5 bedrooms s £78-£120; d £110-£225 (incl. bkfst) **LB FACILITIES:** STV Xmas **CONF:** BC Thtr 50 Class 25 Board 25 Del from £145 **PARKING:** 120
NOTES: Civ Wed 50

★★★69% Garden House
High St, St Martins PE9 2LP
☎ 01780 763359 📠 01780 763339
e-mail: enquiries@gardenhousehotel.com
web: www.gardenhousehotel.com
Dir: *A1 to South Stamford, B1081, signed Stamford and Burghley House. Hotel on left on entering town*
Situated within a few minutes' walk of the town centre, this transformed 18th-century town house provides pleasant accommodation. Bedroom styles vary; all are well equipped and comfortably furnished. Public rooms include a charming lounge bar, conservatory restaurant and a smart breakfast room. Service is attentive and friendly throughout.
ROOMS: 20 en suite (2 fmly) (4 GF) ⊗ in 16 bedrooms s £65-£79; d £89-£95 (incl. bkfst) **LB FACILITIES:** STV ch fac Xmas **CONF:** BC Thtr 40 Class 20 Board 20 Del from £100 **PARKING:** 22 **NOTES:** ⊗ in restaurant Closed 26-30 Dec RS 1-12 Jan Civ Wed 60

★★69% Crown
All Saints Place PE9 2AG
☎ 01780 763136 📠 01780 756111
e-mail: thecrownhotel@excite.com
web: www.thecrownhotelstamford.co.uk
Dir: *off A1 onto A43, straight through town until Red Lion Sq, hotel is behind All Saints church in the square*
This small, privately owned hotel is ideally situated in the town centre. Unpretentious British food is served in the attractive restaurant and hospitality is spontaneous and sincere. The traditional bar is popular with locals. Bedrooms are mostly

continued

S

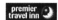

spacious and well equipped, some with four-poster beds; additional 'superior' rooms are located in a renovated Georgian town house just a short walk up the street.

ROOMS: 17 rms (16 en suite) 6 annexe rms (5 en suite) (2 fmly) (1 GF) ⊗ in all bedrooms s £75-£85; d £100-£130 (incl. bkfst) **LB** **FACILITIES:** STV Use of local health/gym club **CONF:** BC Thtr 20 Class 15 Board 15 Del from £140 **PARKING:** 21 **NOTES:** ✗ ⊗ in restaurant

STANDISH, Greater Manchester — Map 15 SD51

Premier Travel Inn Wigan North
Almond Brook Rd WN6 0SS
☎ 0870 9906474 Fax 0870 9906475
web: www.premiertravelinn.com
Dir: *Exit M6 junct 27 follow signs for Standish. Left at T-junct, then 1st right*
High quality, modern budget accommodation ideal for both families and business travellers. Spacious, en suite bedrooms feature bath and shower, satellite TV and many have telephones and modem points. The adjacent family restaurant features a wide and varied menu. For further details consult the Hotel Groups page.
ROOMS: 36 en suite s £46.95-£48.95; d £46.95-£48.95

STANSTEAD ABBOTTS, Hertfordshire — Map 06 TL31

★★★62% Briggens House
Stanstead Rd SG12 8LD
☎ 01279 829955 Fax 01279 793685
e-mail: briggenshouse@corushotels.com
web: www.corushotels.com/briggenshouse
Dir: *M11 take the A414 to Hertford, after 10th rdbt turn left signed Briggens Park*
Sitting in 80 acres of open countryside, this hotel was once a stately home and boasts a marvellous arboretum, 9-hole golf course, two all-weather tennis courts and a heated swimming pool. A number of meeting and conference rooms are available, and there is lounge seating in the traditional public rooms.
ROOMS: 54 en suite (3 fmly) (16 GF) ⊗ in 20 bedrooms s £49.50; d £49.50 **LB** **FACILITIES:** ⛳ 9 Putt green Xmas **CONF:** Thtr 100 Class 50 Board 50 Del £79 **SERVICES:** Lift **PARKING:** 100 **NOTES:** ⊗ in restaurant Civ Wed 100

STANSTED AIRPORT, Essex — Map 06 TL52
See also see also Birchanger Green Motorway Service Area (M11)

★★★70% The Stansted Manor
Birchanger Ln CM23 5ST
☎ 01279 859800 Fax 01279 467245
e-mail: info@stanstedmanor-hotel.co.uk
web: www.stanstedmanor-hotel.co.uk
Dir: *M11 junct 8 onto A120 towards Bishop's Stortford. Turn right at next major rdbt. Hotel on left*
Located just of the M11, this modern hotel is conveniently located continued for Stansted Airport, and is reached via a long drive and surrounded by landscaped grounds. Bedrooms feature modern decor, tasteful furnishings and a thoughtful range of extras, including broadband internet access. Open-plan public rooms include a comfortable lobby lounge, a lounge/bar and a conservatory restaurant. Wireless internet access is available.

ROOMS: 70 en suite (8 fmly) (23 GF) ⊗ in 31 bedrooms s £75-£120; d £75-£120 **FACILITIES:** STV **CONF:** Thtr 35 Class 16 Board 20 Del from £135 **SERVICES:** Lift **PARKING:** 100 **NOTES:** ✗ ⊗ in restaurant

Radisson SAS Hotel
Waltham Close, Stansted Airport CM24 1PP
☎ 01279 661012 Fax 01279 661013
e-mail: info.stansted@radissonsas.com
web: www.radisson.com
Dir: *directly linked to airport terminal by covered walkway*
At the time of going to press, the star classification for this hotel was not confirmed. Please refer to the AA internet site www.theAA.com for current information.
ROOMS: 500 en suite (42 fmly) ⊗ in 420 bedrooms **FACILITIES: Spa** STV Sauna Solarium Gym **CONF:** BC Thtr 400 Class 180 Board 36 Del from £145 **SERVICES:** Lift air con **PARKING:** 220 **NOTES:** ✗ Civ Wed 400

STANTON ST QUINTIN, Wiltshire — Map 04 ST97

★★★70% Stanton Manor Country House Hotel
SN14 6DQ
☎ 01666 837552 & 0870 890 02880 Fax 01666 837022
e-mail: reception@stantonmanor.co.uk
web: www.stantonmanor.co.uk
Dir: *M4 junct 17 onto A429 Malmesbury/Cirencester, within 200yds turn 1st left signed Stanton St Quintin, entrance to hotel on left just after church*

Set in seven acres of lovely gardens including a short golf course, this charming Cotswold stone manor house has easy access to the M4. The new owners here are carefully adding further to the quality and comfort of all bedrooms and bathrooms. Public areas are a delight offering both character and comfort. In the

continued on p534

S

STANTON ST QUINTIN, continued

restaurant, a short carte of imaginative dishes is supported by a selection of interesting wines.
ROOMS: 23 en suite (4 fmly) (7 GF) ⊗ in 18 bedrooms s £102.50-£135; d £135-£210 (incl. bkfst) **LB** **FACILITIES:** STV ⛳ 9 Putt green ch fac Xmas **CONF:** BC Thtr 120 Class 80 Board 40 Del from £165 **PARKING:** 60 **NOTES:** ⊗ in restaurant Civ Wed 120

STAVERTON, Devon — Map 03 SX76

★★67% *Sea Trout Inn*
TQ9 6PA
☎ 01803 762274 Fax 01803 762506
e-mail: enquiries@seatroutinn.com
web: www.seatroutinn.com
Dir: *turn off A38 onto A384 at Buckfastleigh, follow signs to Staverton*
Set in a delightful location in the Dart Valley, this 15th-century inn has bags of character. Ideal for a relaxing break, and particularly suitable for anglers with the River Dart almost on the doorstep. A range of dining options is available. An excellent choice of food is served in the bar as well as the conservatory restaurant that uses local and some organic produce.
ROOMS: 10 en suite (1 fmly) **CONF:** Board 30 **PARKING:** 48 **NOTES:** ⊗ in restaurant

STEEPLE ASTON, Oxfordshire — Map 11 SP42

★★★66% The Holt Hotel
Oxford Rd OX25 5QQ
☎ 01869 340259 Fax 01869 340865
e-mail: info@holthotel.co.uk
web: www.holthotel.co.uk
Dir: *junct of B4030/A4260*
This attractive former coaching inn has given hospitality to many over the centuries, not least to Claude Duval, a notorious 17th-century highwayman. Today guests are offered well-equipped modern bedrooms and attractive public areas, which include a relaxing bar, restaurant and a well-appointed lounge. A selection of meeting rooms is available.
ROOMS: 86 en suite (19 fmly) ⊗ in 16 bedrooms **FACILITIES:** STV Xmas **CONF:** BC Thtr 140 Class 70 Board 44 **PARKING:** 200 **NOTES:** ⊗ in restaurant Civ Wed 100

STEVENAGE, Hertfordshire — Map 12 TL22

★★★66% Novotel Stevenage
Knebworth Park SG1 2AX
☎ 01438 346100 Fax 01438 723872
e-mail: H0992@accor-hotels.com
web: www.novotel.com
Dir: *A1(M) junct 7, at entrance to Knebworth Park*
With an accessible location just off the A1(M) and a range of meeting rooms, this hotel is a popular business and conference venue. There's plenty for leisure guests too: Knebworth Park is a noteworthy neighbour and the hotel's outdoor pool and children's play area add to the appeal for families.
Novotel - AA Hotel Group of the Year 2005-6.
ROOMS: 101 en suite (20 fmly) (30 GF) ⊗ in 85 bedrooms s £99; d £99 **LB** **FACILITIES:** STV Free use of local health club **CONF:** BC Thtr 150 Class 80 Board 70 Del from £96.25 **SERVICES:** Lift **PARKING:** 80 **NOTES:** ⊗ in restaurant

> GF indicates the number of bedrooms at ground level

★★★66% The Roebuck Inn
London Rd, Broadwater SG2 8DS
☎ 0870 011 9076 Fax 0870 011 9077
e-mail: hotel@roebuckinn.com
Dir: *A1(M) junct 7, right towards Stevenage. At 2nd rdbt take 2nd exit signed Roebuck-London/Knebworth B197, hotel 1.5m*
Suitable for both the business and leisure traveller, this hotel provides spacious contemporary accommodation in well equipped bedrooms. The older part of the building, where there is a restaurant and a cosy public bar with log fire and real ales, dates back to the 15th century.
ROOMS: 54 en suite (8 fmly) ⊗ in 27 bedrooms **FACILITIES:** Xmas **CONF:** Thtr 50 Class 20 Board 30 **PARKING:** 70 **NOTES:** 🐕✗

★★★63% Corus hotel Stevenage
High St, Old Town SG1 3AZ
☎ 01438 779954 Fax 01438 742169
web: www.corushotels.com
Dir: *A1(M) junct 8. Follow signs for town centre, over 2 rdbts. Join one-way system. Turn off into Old Town. Hotel on left after mini rdbt*

Originally a farmhouse, this attractive hotel is located in the High Street of the Old Town and is easily accessible from the nearby A1(M) and mainline railway. Bedrooms vary in style between modern and more traditional. Public areas include a cosy bar/lounge and a smart, modern business centre.
ROOMS: 76 en suite (2 fmly) (15 GF) ⊗ in 33 bedrooms s £40-£95; d £50-£115 **LB** **FACILITIES:** Access to David Lloyd Gym (£5) Xmas **CONF:** BC Thtr 200 Class 50 Board 54 Del from £110 **PARKING:** 70 **NOTES:** ⊗ in restaurant Civ Wed 180

⌂ *Hotel Ibis Stevenage*
Danestrete SG1 1EJ
☎ 01438 779955 Fax 01438 741880
e-mail: H2497@accor-hotels.com
Dir: *in town centre adjacent to Tesco & Westgate Multi-Store*
Modern, budget hotel offering comfortable accommodation in bright and practical bedrooms. Breakfast is self-service and dinner is available in the restaurant. For further details, consult the Hotel Groups page.
ROOMS: 98 en suite

⌂ Premier Travel Inn Stevenage Central
Six Hills Way, Horizon Technology Park SG1 2DD
☎ 0870 990 6628
web: www.premiertravelinn.com
Dir: *Exit A1(M) junct 7 onto A602 follow signs for Stevenage, until Horizon Technology Park*
High quality, modern budget accommodation ideal for both families and business travellers. Spacious, en suite bedrooms feature bath and shower, satellite TV and many have telephones and modem points. The adjacent family restaurant features a wide and varied menu. For further details consult the Hotel Groups page.
ROOMS: 115 en suite s £50.95-£55.95; d £50.95-£55.95

⌂ Premier Travel Inn Stevenage (North)
Corey's Mill Ln SG1 4AA
☎ 08701 977240 🖷 01438 721609
web: www.premiertravelinn.com
Dir: *A1(M) junct 8, at junct of A602 Hitchin Rd & Corey's Mill Lane*
High quality, modern budget accommodation ideal for both families and business travellers. Spacious, en suite bedrooms feature bath and shower, satellite TV and many have telephones and modem points. The adjacent family restaurant features a wide and varied menu. For further details consult the Hotel Groups page.
ROOMS: 39 en suite s £47.95-£50.95; d £47.95-£50.95

STEYNING, West Sussex — Map 06 TQ11

★★★69% The Old Tollgate
The Street BN44 3WE
☎ 01903 879494 🖷 01903 813399
e-mail: info@oldtollgatehotel.com
web: www.oldtollgatehotel.com
Dir: *on A283 at Steyning rdbt, turn to Bramber, hotel approx 200yds on right*
As its name suggests, this well-presented hotel is built on the site of the old tollhouse. The spacious bedrooms are smartly designed and are furnished to a high standard. Open for both lunch and dinner, the popular carvery-style restaurant offers an extensive choice of dishes. The hotel also has adaptable function rooms for weddings and conferences.
ROOMS: 10 en suite 20 annexe en suite (5 fmly) (10 GF) ⊗ in 16 bedrooms **FACILITIES:** STV **CONF:** Thtr 50 Class 32 Board 26 Del from £98.95 **SERVICES:** Lift **PARKING:** 60 **NOTES:** 🚫🐕 ⊗ in restaurant Civ Wed 70

STILTON, Cambridgeshire — Map 12 TL18

★★★73% ❁ Bell Inn
Great North Rd PE7 3RA
☎ 01733 241066 & 242626 🖷 01733 245173
e-mail: reception@thebellstilton.co.uk
web: www.thebellstilton.co.uk
Dir: *A1(M) junct 16, follow signs for Stilton, hotel in village centre*

This delightful inn is steeped in history and retains many original features, with imaginative food served in both the character village bar and the elegant beamed first-floor restaurant; refreshments can be enjoyed in the attractive courtyard and rear gardens when weather permits. Individually designed bedrooms are stylish and equipped to a high standard.
ROOMS: 19 en suite 3 annexe en suite (1 fmly) (3 GF) ⊗ in all bedrooms s £79.50; d £99.50 (incl. bkfst) **FACILITIES:** STV **CONF:** Thtr 100 Class 46 Board 50 Del £125 **PARKING:** 30 **NOTES:** 🚫🐕 ⊗ in restaurant Closed 25 Dec RS 26 Dec Civ Wed 85

STOCK, Essex — Map 06 TQ69

★★★★70% Greenwoods Estate Hotel Spa & Retreat
Stock Rd CM4 9BE
☎ 01277 829990 🖷 01277 829899
e-mail: info@greenwoodsestate.com
Dir: *At junct 16 on A12 take B1007 signed Billericay. Hotel on right on entering village*
Grade II listed manor house situated in this picturesque village is amid landscaped grounds and surrounded by open countryside. The stylish bedrooms are tastefully furnished and thoughtfully equipped; some rooms have lovely views of the gardens. Public rooms include a choice of elegant lounges, a smart restaurant, superb leisure facilities and conference rooms.
ROOMS: 39 en suite (6 GF) ⊗ in all bedrooms s £85-£155; d £105-£240 **LB** **FACILITIES:** **Spa** STV Sauna Solarium Gym Putt green Jacuzzi Aerobic studio, therapy/relaxation rooms Xmas **CONF:** Thtr 40 Class 30 Board 24 Del from £195 **SERVICES:** Lift **PARKING:** 200 **NOTES:** 🚫🐕 No children 16yrs ⊗ in restaurant Civ Wed 50

STOCKPORT, Greater Manchester — Map 16 SJ89
See also Manchester Airport

★★★69% Bredbury Hall Hotel & Country Club
Goyt Valley SK6 2DH
☎ 0161 430 7421 🖷 0161 430 5079
e-mail: reservations@bredburyhallhotel.co.uk
Dir: *M60 junct 25 signed Bredbury, right at lights, left onto Osbourne St, hotel 500mtrs on right*
With views over open countryside, this large modern hotel is conveniently located for the M60. The stylish, well-equipped bedrooms offer space and comfort and the restaurant serves a very wide range of freshly prepared dishes. There is a popular nightclub next door to the hotel.
ROOMS: 150 en suite (2 fmly) (50 GF) s £59.50-£79.50; d £79.50-£94.50 **FACILITIES:** STV Fishing Snooker Jacuzzi Night club (Fri & Sat eve) ♫ Xmas **CONF:** Thtr 200 Class 120 Board 60 Del from £115 **PARKING:** 400 **NOTES:** 🚫🐕 Civ Wed 80

★★★66% Alma Lodge Hotel
149 Buxton Rd SK2 6EL
☎ 0161 483 4431 🖷 0161 483 1983
e-mail: reception@almalodgehotel.com
Dir: *M60 junct 1 at rdbt take 2nd exit under railway viaduct. At lights opposite Debenhams turn right onto A6, hotel approx 1.5m on left*
A large hotel, located on the main road close to the town, offering modern and well-equipped bedrooms. It is family owned and run and serves a good range of quality Italian cooking in Luigi's restaurant. Good function rooms are also available.
ROOMS: 20 en suite 32 annexe en suite (2 fmly) ⊗ in 22 bedrooms s £65 (incl. bkfst) **LB** **CONF:** Thtr 250 Class 100 Board 60 Del from £110 **PARKING:** 120 **NOTES:** 🚫🐕 RS Bank Hols Civ Wed 100

★★★61% The County Hotel
Bramhall Ln South SK7 2EB
☎ 0870 609 6148 🖷 0161 440 8071
web: www.corushotels.com/countymanchester
(For full entry see Bramhall)

❁ AA Rosette Award for culinary excellence

STOCKPORT, continued

★★69% Wycliffe
74 Edgeley Rd, Edgeley SK3 9NQ
☎ 0161 477 5395 0161 476 3219
e-mail: reception@wycliffe-hotel.com
Dir: *M60 junct 2 follow A560 for Stockport, at 1st lights turn right, hotel 0.5m on left*

This family-run, welcoming hotel provides immaculately maintained and well-equipped bedrooms. There is popular restaurant where the menu has an Italian bias, and a well stocked bar. There is ample, convenient parking.
ROOMS: 18 en suite ⊗ in all bedrooms s £55-£60; d £60-£75 (incl. bkfst) **CONF:** Thtr 30 Class 20 Board 20 **PARKING:** 46 **NOTES:** ✗ ⊗ in restaurant Closed 25-27 Dec RS BH s

★★63% Saxon Holme
230 Wellington Rd North SK4 2QN
☎ 0161 432 2335 0161 431 8076
e-mail: info@saxonholmehotel.com
Dir: *N, beside A6*
Located on the A6 a short way from the town centre this family owed and run hotel offers well equipped bedrooms, a pleasant bar lounge, a conservatory and an attractive dining room. Service is polite and friendly.
ROOMS: 33 en suite (4 fmly) (11 GF) ⊗ in 11 bedrooms s £35-£50; d £40-£60 **FACILITIES:** STV **CONF:** BC Thtr 50 Class 10 Board 20 Del from £80 **SERVICES:** Lift **PARKING:** 40 **NOTES:** ✗ ⊗ in restaurant

Innkeeper's Lodge Stockport
271 Wellington Rd, North Heaton Chapel SK4 5BP
☎ 0161 432 2753
web: www.innkeeperslodge.com
A growing concept in the travel accommodation market. Smart rooms meet essential business requirements but also have home comforts. Dining options include all-day menus plus the added advantage of breakfast, which is included in the room price. For further details consult the Hotel Groups page.
ROOMS: 22 en suite s £45-£52; d £45-£52

Premier Travel Inn Stockport East
Churchgate SK1 1YG
☎ 0870 9906544 0870 9906545
web: www.premiertravelinn.com
Dir: *Exit M60 junct 27, A626 towards Marple. Right at Spring Gardens.*
High quality, modern budget accommodation ideal for both families and business travellers. Spacious, en suite bedrooms feature bath and shower, satellite TV and many have telephones and modem points. The adjacent family restaurant features a wide and varied menu. For further details consult the Hotel Groups page.
ROOMS: 46 en suite s £47.95-£50.95; d £47.95-£50.95 **CONF:** Thtr 20 Board 20

Premier Travel Inn Stockport South
Buxton Rd SK2 6NB
☎ 08701 977242 0161 477 8320
web: www.premiertravelinn.com
Dir: *on A6, 1.5m from town centre*
High quality, modern budget accommodation ideal for both families and business travellers. Spacious, en suite bedrooms feature bath and shower, satellite TV and many have telephones and modem points. The adjacent family restaurant features a wide and varied menu. For further details consult the Hotel Groups page.
ROOMS: 40 en suite s £47.95-£50.95; d £47.95-£50.95

STOCKTON-ON-TEES, Co Durham Map 19 NZ41

★★★72% Parkmore
636 Yarm Rd, Eaglescliffe TS16 0DH
☎ 01642 786815 01642 790485
e-mail: enquiries@parkmorehotel.co.uk
web: www.parkmorehotel.co.uk
Dir: *off A19 at Crathorne, follow A67 to Yarm. Through Yarm bear right onto A135 to Stockton. Hotel 1m on left*
Set in its own gardens, this smart hotel has grown from its Victorian house origins to provide stylish public areas, as well as extensive leisure and conference facilities. The well-equipped bedrooms include studio rooms, whilst the restaurant boasts a reputation for flair and creativity. Service is friendly and obliging.
ROOMS: 55 en suite (8 fmly) (9 GF) ⊗ in 30 bedrooms s £65-£95; d £85-£108 **LB FACILITIES: Spa** STV supervised Sauna Solarium Gym Jacuzzi Beauty salon Badminton Aerobics studio **CONF:** Thtr 140 Class 40 Board 40 Del from £82 **PARKING:** 90 **NOTES:** ⊗ in restaurant Civ Wed 150

★★66% *Claireville*
519 Yarm Rd, Eaglescliffe TS16 9BG
☎ 01642 780378 01642 784109
e-mail: reception@clairevillehotel.com
Dir: *on A135 adjacent to Eaglescliffe Golf Course, between Stockton-on-Tees and Yarm*
A family-run hotel with comfortable bedrooms. There is a cosy bar/lounge and an attractive dining room that offers good value meals. The conservatory to the rear provides a relaxing garden lounge area.
ROOMS: 18 en suite (2 fmly) ⊗ in 4 bedrooms **FACILITIES:** STV **CONF:** Thtr 40 Class 20 Board 25 **PARKING:** 30 **NOTES:** ⊗ in restaurant RS Xmas & New Year

Premier Travel Inn Stockton-on-Tees
Yarm Rd TS18 3RT
☎ 08701 977243 01642 633339
web: www.premiertravelinn.com
Dir: *at junct A66/A135*
High quality, modern budget accommodation ideal for both families and business travellers. Spacious, en suite bedrooms feature bath and shower, satellite TV and many have telephones and modem points. The adjacent family restaurant features a wide and varied menu. For further details consult the Hotel Groups page.
ROOMS: 40 en suite s £46.95-£49.95; d £46.95-£49.95

Premier Travel Inn Stockton-on-Tees Middlesbrough
Whitewater Way, Thornaby TS17 6QB
☎ 08701 977244 01642 671464
web: www.premiertravelinn.com
Dir: *A19 take A66 to Stockton/Darlington. Take 1st exit, Teeside Park/Teesdale. Right at lights over viaduct bridge rdbt & Tees Barrage*
High quality, modern budget accommodation ideal for both

continued

families and business travellers. Spacious, en suite bedrooms feature bath and shower, satellite TV and many have telephones and modem points. The adjacent family restaurant features a wide and varied menu. For further details consult the Hotel Groups page.
ROOMS: 62 en suite s £46.95-£49.95; d £46.95-£49.95

STOKE D'ABERNON, Surrey — Map 06 TQ15

★★★★75% Woodlands Park

Woodlands Ln KT11 3QB
☎ 01372 843933 📠 01372 842704
e-mail: woodlandspark@handpicked.co.uk
web: www.handpicked.co.uk
Dir: *from A3 towards London, exit at Cobham. Through town centre & Stoke D'Abernon, left at garden centre into Woodlands Ln, hotel 0.5m on right*

Originally built for the Bryant family, the matchmakers, this lovely Victorian mansion enjoys an attractive parkland setting in ten and a half acres of Surrey countryside. Bedrooms in the wing are

continued

contemporary in style while those in the main house are more traditionally furnished and decorated. The hotel boasts two dining options, Quotes Bar & Brasserie and the Oak Room Restaurant.
ROOMS: 57 en suite (4 fmly) in 47 bedrooms **FACILITIES:** STV **CONF:** Thtr 150 Class 40 Board 50 **SERVICES:** Lift **PARKING:** 150
NOTES: Civ Wed 200

See advert on this page

STOKE GABRIEL, Devon — Map 03 SX85

★★★73% Gabriel Court

Stoke Hill TQ9 6SF
☎ 01803 782206 📠 01803 782333
e-mail: reservations@gabrielcourthotel.co.uk
Dir: *off A38 at Buckfastleigh onto A384 (Totnes) then A385 (Paignton). Turn right at Parkers Arms to Stoke Gabriel*

Overlooking the pretty riverside village of Stoke Gabriel, this gracious manor house stands within terraced Elizabethan gardens, surrounded by three acres of grounds. Peace and tranquillity are in abundance and there are several secluded outdoor hideaways for relaxation, or there is an elegant lounge. Bedrooms offer ample space and comfort, and many also have lovely views. The 'Churchward' restaurant serves enjoyable cuisine.
ROOMS: 16 en suite (3 fmly) s £67.50-£73.50; d £98-£125 (incl. bkfst)
LB FACILITIES: Xmas **CONF:** Thtr 12 Class 12 Board 12
PARKING: 25 **NOTES:** in restaurant

> If you wish to use a particular credit card or debit card please check with the hotel that they are happy to accept it

STOKENCHURCH, Buckinghamshire Map 05 SU79

★★★68% *The Kings Arms*
Oxford Rd HP14 3TA
☎ 01494 609090 📠 01494 484582
e-mail: kares@dhillonhotels.co.uk
Dir: *M40 junct 5, turn right over motorway bridge, hotel 600yds on left*
Located on the village green, this hotel blends traditional elegance with contemporary design. Rooms are attractively decorated and well equipped, particularly for the business guest. Public areas include a busy bar and a relaxed, informal restaurant serving a wide range of dishes throughout the day. The smart conference rooms are air conditioned.
ROOMS: 43 en suite (3 fmly) ⊗ in 22 bedrooms **FACILITIES:** STV Wycombe sports & leisure centre **CONF:** BC Thtr 200 Class 100 Board 70 **SERVICES:** Lift air con **PARKING:** 95 **NOTES:** ✗ Civ Wed 200

STOKE-ON-TRENT, Staffordshire Map 10 SJ84
See also Newcastle-under-Lyme

★★★69% Manor House
Audley Rd ST7 2QQ
☎ 01270 884000 📠 01270 882483
e-mail: mhres@compasshotels.co.uk
(For full entry see Alsager)

★★★66% ⊛ Haydon House
Haydon St, Basford ST4 6JD
☎ 01782 711311 📠 01782 717470
e-mail: enquiries@haydon-house-hotel.co.uk
Dir: *M6 junct 15, A500 to Stoke-on-Trent, onto A53 Hanley/Newcastle, at rdbt take 1st exit, up hill, take 2nd left at top of hill before lights*
A Victorian property, within easy reach of Newcastle-under-Lyme. The public rooms are furnished in a style befitting the age and character of the house and bedrooms have modern furnishings; several rooms are located in a separate house across the road. The hotel has a good reputation for its food and is popular with locals.
ROOMS: 17 en suite 6 annexe en suite (4 fmly) s £45-£70; d £60-£80 (incl. bkfst) **CONF:** Thtr 80 Class 30 Board 30 Del from £110 **PARKING:** 52 **NOTES:** ⊗ in restaurant Civ Wed 80

⇧ Innkeeper's Lodge Stoke on Trent
Longton Rd ST4 8BU
☎ 01782 644448 📠 01782 644163
web: www.innkeeperslodge.com
Dir: *M6 junct 15, follow A500 to slip road for A34 towards Stone. At rdbt take left onto A5035, lodge is 0.5m on right*
A growing concept in the travel accommodation market. Smart rooms meet essential business requirements but also have home comforts. Dining options include all-day menus plus the added advantage of breakfast, which is included in the room price. For further details consult the Hotel Groups page.
ROOMS: 30 en suite s £52.50; d £52.50

STONE, Staffordshire Map 10 SJ93

★★★70% Stone House
Stafford Rd ST15 0BQ
☎ 0870 609 6140 📠 01785 814764
e-mail: stonehouse@corushotels.com
web: www.corushotels.com
Dir: *beside A34, 0.5m S of town centre*
This former country house, set in attractive grounds, is located within easy reach of the M6. Attractive comfortable bedrooms and tastefully appointed public areas complete with leisure and conference facilities make the hotel popular with corporate and leisure guests. A light menu is offered in the bar and lounge areas or guests can choose to dine in the stylish restaurant.

ROOMS: 50 en suite (1 fmly) (15 GF) ⊗ in 33 bedrooms s fr £79; d fr £79 **LB** **FACILITIES:** STV supervised Sauna Solarium Gym **CONF:** Thtr 190 Class 80 Board 60 Del £120 **PARKING:** 120 **NOTES:** ✗ ⊗ in restaurant RS Sat Civ Wed 60

★★★66% Crown
38 High St ST15 8AS
☎ 01785 813535 📠 01785 815942
e-mail: info@stonehotels.co.uk
web: www.stonehotels.co.uk
Dir: *M6 junct 14, A34 N to Stone. M6 junct 15, A34 S to Stone*
A traditional hotel, now under new ownership, in the centre of town where the staff are helpful and friendly. The hotel has a glass-domed restaurant offering a choice of menus, and the front lounge is delightfully furnished.
ROOMS: 12 en suite 16 annexe en suite (2 fmly) (8 GF) ⊗ in 13 bedrooms s £55-£110; d £55-£120 **LB** **FACILITIES:** STV **CONF:** Thtr 150 Class 80 Board 60 **PARKING:** 100 **NOTES:** ✗ ⊗ in restaurant Civ Wed 100

STON EASTON, Somerset Map 04 ST65

U Ston Easton Park
BA3 4DF
☎ 01761 241631 📠 01761 241377
e-mail: info@stoneaston.co.uk
web: www.vonessenhotels.co.uk
Dir: *on A37*
At the time of going to press, the hotel was being extensively upgraded through a major refurbishment programme. Previous high standards of service and hospitality are not expected to be compromised during this transitional period. Please refer to the AA internet site www.theAA.com for current information.
ROOMS: 20 en suite 3 annexe en suite (2 fmly) (2 GF) ⊗ in all bedrooms s £120-£170; d £150-£195 (incl. bkfst) **LB** **FACILITIES:** Fishing Snooker By prior arrangement Archery, Clay Pigeon Shooting, Quad Bikes, Hot Air Balloon Xmas **CONF:** Thtr 120 Board 30 Del from £165 **PARKING:** 120 **NOTES:** ⊗ in restaurant Civ Wed 120

See advert on opposite page

Late for dinner? Quality standards mean that last orders for dinner vary according to star rating and should be no earlier than: ★★ 7.00pm ★★★ 8:00pm ★★★★ 9:00pm ★★★★★ 10:00pm

STONEHOUSE, Gloucestershire Map 04 SO80

Stonehouse Court
GL10 3RA
☎ 0871 871 3240 🖹 0871 871 3241
e-mail: info@stonehousecourt.co.uk
Dir: *M5 junct 13, off A419. Follow signs for Stonehouse, hotel on right 0.25m after 2nd rdbt*
At the time of going to press, the star classification for this hotel was not confirmed. Please refer to the AA internet site www.theAA.com for current information.
ROOMS: 9 en suite 27 annexe en suite (2 fmly) (2 GF) ⊗ in 6 bedrooms s £65-£77; d £80-£150 (incl. bkfst) **LB** **FACILITIES: Spa** STV Gym ♫ Xmas **CONF:** Thtr 150 Class 75 Board 70 **PARKING:** 200 **NOTES:** ⊗ in restaurant Civ Wed 150

Travelodge
A 419, Easington GL10 3SQ
☎ 08700 850 950 🖹 01453 828590
web: www.travelodge.co.uk
Dir: *M5 junct 13, onto A419*
Travelodge offers good quality, good value, modern accommodation. Ideal for families, the spacious, en suite bedrooms include remote-control TV, tea and coffee-making facilities and comfortable beds. Meals can be taken at the nearby family restaurant. For further details consult the Hotel Groups page.
ROOMS: 40 en suite s fr £26; d fr £26

Destination dining!
This symbol indicates a Restaurant with Rooms

STOURPORT-ON-SEVERN, Worcestershire Map 10 SO87

★★★★73% Menzies Stourport Manor
Hartlebury Rd DY13 9JA
☎ 01299 289955 🖹 01299 878520
e-mail: stourport@menzies-hotels.co.uk
web: www.menzies-hotels.co.uk
Dir: *M5 junct 6, follow A449 towards Kidderminster, take B4193 towards Stourport, hotel on right*
Once the home of Prime Minister Sir Stanley Baldwin, this much extended country house is set in attractive grounds. A number of bedrooms are located in the original building, although the majority are in a more modern, purpose-built section. Spacious public areas include a range of lounges, a popular brasserie, a leisure club and conference facilities.
ROOMS: 68 en suite (4 fmly) ⊗ in 25 bedrooms s £115; d £125 **LB** **FACILITIES:** STV Squash Sauna Solarium Gym Putt green Jacuzzi Xmas **CONF:** Thtr 420 Class 120 Board 80 Del from £110 **PARKING:** 200 **NOTES:** ⊗ in restaurant Civ Wed

STOWMARKET, Suffolk Map 13 TM05

★★69% Cedars
Needham Rd IP14 2AJ
☎ 01449 612668 🖹 01449 674704
e-mail: info@cedarshotel.co.uk
Dir: *from A14 junct 15 take A1120 towards Stowmarket. At junct with A1113 turn right. Hotel on right*
Expect a friendly welcome at this privately owned hotel, which is situated not far from the A14 and within easy reach of the town centre. Public rooms are full of charm and character with features

continued on p540

STOWMARKET, continued

such as exposed beams and open fireplaces. Bedrooms are pleasantly decorated and thoughtfully equipped with modern facilities.
ROOMS: 25 en suite (3 fmly) (9 GF) s fr £56; d fr £65 (incl. dinner) **LB** **CONF:** Thtr 150 Class 60 Board 40 **PARKING:** 75 **NOTES:** ⊘ in restaurant Closed 25 Dec-1 Jan Civ Wed 50

⌂ Travelodge Ipswich Stowmarket

IP14 3PY
☎ 08700 850 950 ℻ 01449 615347
web: www.travelodge.co.uk
Dir: *on A14 westbound*

Travelodge offers good quality, good value, modern accommodation. Ideal for families, the spacious, en suite bedrooms include remote-control TV, tea and coffee-making facilities and comfortable beds. Meals can be taken at the nearby family restaurant. For further details consult the Hotel Groups page.
ROOMS: 40 en suite s fr £26; d fr £26

STOW-ON-THE-WOLD, Gloucestershire Map 10 SP12

★★★★73% ✿✿ Wyck Hill House

Burford Rd GL54 1HY
☎ 01451 831936 ℻ 01451 832243
e-mail: enquiries@wyckhillhouse.com
Dir: *turn off A429. Hotel 1m on right*

This charming 18th-century house enjoys superb views across the Windrush Valley and is ideally positioned for a relaxing weekend exploring the Cotswolds. The spacious and thoughtfully equipped bedrooms provide high standards of comfort and quality and are located both in the main house and the original coach house. Elegant public rooms include the cosy bar, library and the magnificent front hall with crackling log fire. The imaginative cuisine makes effective use of local produce.
ROOMS: 16 en suite 16 annexe en suite (1 fmly) (10 GF) s £79-£123; d £79-£175 (incl. bkfst) **LB** **FACILITIES:** STV ♫ Archery Clay pigeon shooting Ballooning Honda pilots Xmas **CONF:** BC Thtr 60 Class 30 Board 24 Del from £109 **SERVICES:** Lift **PARKING:** 100 **NOTES:** ⊘ in restaurant Civ Wed 80

★★★75% ✿✿ Fosse Manor

GL54 1JX
☎ 01451 830354 ℻ 01451 832486
e-mail: enquiries@fossemanor.co.uk
web: www.fossemanor.co.uk
Dir: *1m S on A429, 300yds past junct with A424*

Deriving its name from the historic Roman Fosse Way, this popular hotel is ideally located for exploring the many delights of this picturesque area. Bedrooms, located both in the main building and the adjacent coach house, offer high standards of comfort and quality. Public areas include a comfortable lounge, elegant restaurant and convivial bar. Classy cuisine uses quality produce in imaginative dishes.

ROOMS: 11 en suite 9 annexe en suite (4 fmly) (5 GF) ⊘ in 19 bedrooms s £95-£165; d £130-£225 (incl. bkfst) **LB** **FACILITIES:** STV ♫ Xmas **CONF:** Thtr 60 Class 20 Board 26 Del £150 **PARKING:** 40 **NOTES:** ⊘ in restaurant

★★★72% ✿ Grapevine

Sheep St GL54 1AU
☎ 01451 830344 ℻ 01451 832278
e-mail: enquiries@vines.co.uk
web: www.vines.co.uk
Dir: *on A436 towards Chipping Norton. 150yds on right, facing green*

Situated in the heart of this unique market town, the Grapevine is a delightful 17th-century hotel with plenty of charm and character. Original features abound, such as stone-flagged floors. Individually styled bedrooms combine comfort and quality; each is equipped with thoughtful extras. Canopied by the ancient vine, the Conservatory Restaurant is a lovely setting for the accomplished cuisine, and alternatively, lighter meals can be enjoyed in the popular bar.
ROOMS: 12 en suite 10 annexe en suite (2 fmly) (5 GF) ⊘ in all bedrooms s £85-£95; d £140-£160 (incl. bkfst) **LB** **FACILITIES:** Xmas **CONF:** Thtr 30 Class 18 Board 20 Del £140 **PARKING:** 25 **NOTES:** 🐕 ⊘ in restaurant Civ Wed 70

★★★72% ✿✿ The Royalist

Digbeth St GL54 1BN
☎ 01451 830670 ℻ 01451 870048
e-mail: info@theroyalisthotel.co.uk
Dir: *off A429 at lights in Stow, into Sheep St & 2nd left into Digbeth St*

Verified as the oldest inn in England, this charming hotel, now under the careful guidance of new owners, has a wealth of history and character. Bedrooms and public areas have been stylishly and sympathetically decorated to ensure high levels of comfort at every turn. There are two eating options: the 947AD restaurant

continued

offers high-quality cooking and the Eagle and Child provides a more informal alternative.

ROOMS: 8 en suite (2 fmly) ⊘ in all bedrooms s £50-£90; d £240 (incl. bkfst) **FACILITIES:** Jacuzzi Discounted rates at local gym Xmas **CONF:** Thtr 46 Class 30 Board 20 Del from £139 **PARKING:** 8 **NOTES:** ⊘ in restaurant

★★★70% The Unicorn

Sheep St GL54 1HQ
☎ 01451 830257 📠 01451 831090
e-mail: reception@birchhotels.co.uk
Dir: *at junct of A429 & A436*

This attractive limestone hotel dates back to the 17th century. Individually designed bedrooms are stylish and include some delightful four-poster rooms. Spacious public areas retain much character and include a choice of inviting lounges and a traditional bar offering a good selection of bar meals and ales, as well as an attractive restaurant.
ROOMS: 20 en suite ⊘ in 8 bedrooms s £40-£80; d £50-£130 (incl. bkfst) **FACILITIES:** ♫ Xmas **CONF:** Thtr 50 Class 20 Board 28 **PARKING:** 40 **NOTES:** ⊘ in restaurant Closed May-Oct 3days RS Dates Vary Civ Wed 45

★★★69% Stow Lodge

The Square GL54 1AB
☎ 01451 830485 📠 01451 831671
e-mail: enquiries@stowlodge.com
web: www.stowlodge.com
Dir: *in town centre*
Situated in smart grounds, this non-smoking, family-run hotel has direct access to the market square and provides high standards of customer care. Bedrooms are offered both within the main building and in the converted coach house, all of which provide similar standards of homely comfort. Extensive menus and an interesting wine list make for an enjoyable dining experience.
ROOMS: 11 en suite 10 annexe en suite (1 fmly) ⊘ in all bedrooms s £60-£130; d £75-£150 (incl. bkfst) **LB** **PARKING:** 30 **NOTES:** ✗ No children 5yrs ⊘ in restaurant Closed Xmas-end Jan

★★69% Old Stocks

The Square GL54 1AF
☎ 01451 830666 📠 01451 870014
e-mail: aa@theoldstockshotel.co.uk
web: www.oldstockshotel.co.uk
Dir: *turn off A429 to town centre. Hotel facing village green*
Overlooking the old market square, this Grade II listed, mellow Cotswold-stone building is a comfortable and friendly base from which to explore this picturesque area. There is a lot of character and atmosphere with bedrooms, many now refurbished, all offering individuality and charm. Facilities include a guest lounge, restaurant and bar, whilst outside, the patio is a popular summer venue for refreshing drinks and good food.
ROOMS: 15 en suite 3 annexe en suite (5 fmly) (4 GF) ⊘ in 14 bedrooms s £35-£55; d £70-£120 (incl. bkfst) **LB** **FACILITIES:** ch fac Xmas **PARKING:** 12 **NOTES:** ⊘ in restaurant

STRATFIELD TURGIS, Hampshire — Map 05 SU65

★★★67% Wellington Arms

RG27 0AS
☎ 01256 882214 📠 01256 882934
e-mail: Wellington.Arms@virgin.net
Dir: *A33 between Basingstoke & Reading*
Situated at an entrance to the ancestral home of the Duke of Wellington. The majority of bedrooms are located in the modern Garden Wing, whereas rooms in the original building have a period feel. Public rooms include a comfortable lounge bar with log fire and a pleasant brasserie.
ROOMS: 35 en suite (2 fmly) (11 GF) ⊘ in 3 bedrooms s £95-£120; d £105-£130 (incl. bkfst) **LB** **CONF:** Thtr 160 Class 40 Board 50 Del from £152.50 **PARKING:** 150 **NOTES:** ⊘ in restaurant

STRATFORD-UPON-AVON, Warwickshire — Map 10 SP25

★★★★73% ⊛⊛ *Billesley Manor*

Billesley, Alcester B49 6NF
☎ 01789 279955 📠 01789 764145
e-mail: enquiries@billesleymanor.co.uk
web: www.furlonghotels.co.uk
Dir: *A46 towards Evesham. Over 3 rdbts, right turn for Billesley after 2m*

This 16th-century manor is set in peaceful grounds and parkland with a delightful yew topiary garden and fountain. The spacious bedrooms and suites, most in traditional country-house style, are thoughtfully designed and well equipped. Conference facilities and some of the bedrooms are found in the cedar barns. Public areas retain many original features, such as oak panelling, fireplaces and exposed stone.
ROOMS: 42 en suite 29 annexe en suite (8 fmly) (5 GF) **FACILITIES:** **Spa** STV 🏊 🎾 Sauna Solarium Gym ⛳ Steam room, Beauty treatments, Yoga studio **CONF:** Thtr 100 Class 60 Board 50 **PARKING:** 100 **NOTES:** ⊘ in restaurant Civ Wed 75

STRATFORD-UPON-AVON, continued

★★★★72% The Alveston Manor

Clopton Bridge CV37 7HP
☎ 0870 400 8181 01789 414095
e-mail: sales.alvestonmanor@macdonald-hotels.co.uk
web: www.macdonald-hotels.co.uk
Dir: *S of Clopton Bridge*

A striking red-brick and timbered façade, well-tended grounds, and a giant cedar tree all contribute to the charm of this well-established hotel, just five minutes from Stratford. The bedrooms vary in size and character - the coach house conversion offers an impressive mix of full and junior suites. The superb leisure complex offers a 20-metre swimming pool and steam room and sauna, a high-tech gym and a host of beauty treatments.

ROOMS: 113 en suite (8 fmly) (45 GF) in 46 bedrooms s fr £60; d fr £120 (incl. bkfst) **LB** **FACILITIES:** STV supervised Sauna Solarium Gym Techno-gym, Beauty treatments Xmas **CONF:** Thtr 140 Class 80 Board 40 Del from £145 **SERVICES:** air con **PARKING:** 150 **NOTES:** in restaurant Civ Wed 110

★★★★72% Menzies Welcombe Hotel & Golf Course

Warwick Rd CV37 0NR
☎ 01789 295252 01789 266336
e-mail: welcombe@menzies-hotels.co.uk
web: www.menzies-hotels.co.uk
Dir: *M40 junct 15, follow A46 towards Stratford-upon-Avon, at rdbt follow signs for A439. Hotel 3m on right.*

This Jacobean manor house is set in 157 acres of landscaped parkland. Public rooms are impressive, especially the lounge with its wood panelling and ornate marble fireplace, and the gentleman's club-style bar. Bedrooms in the original building are the stylish and gracefully proportioned; those in the garden wing are comfortable and thoughtfully equipped. The new spa development will incorporate advanced and luxurious facilities and treatments.

ROOMS: 73 en suite (5 fmly) s £170-£180; d £170-£180 (incl. bkfst) **LB** **FACILITIES:** STV 18 Putt green Xmas **CONF:** Thtr 120 Class 75 Board 30 Del £200 **PARKING:** 100 **NOTES:** in restaurant Civ Wed 120

★★★★72% Stratford Manor

Warwick Rd CV37 0PY
☎ 01789 731173 01789 731131
e-mail: stratfordmanor@marstonhotels.com
web: www.marstonhotels.com
Dir: *3m N of town centre on A439 in direction of Warwick, or leave M40 junct 15, take Stratford-upon-Avon road A439, hotel 2m on left*

Just outside Stratford, this hotel is set against a rural backdrop with lovely gardens and ample parking. Public areas include a lounge bar and a contemporary restaurant, both now re-designed. While the leisure centre boasts a large indoor pool. Service is both professional and helpful. Bedrooms are spacious and have generously proportioned beds and a range of useful facilities.

ROOMS: 104 en suite (8 fmly) in 52 bedrooms s fr £129; d fr £166 (incl. bkfst) **LB** **FACILITIES: Spa** STV Sauna Solarium Gym Beauty treatments Xmas **CONF:** Thtr 350 Class 200 Board 100 Del from £205 **SERVICES:** Lift **PARKING:** 250 **NOTES:** in restaurant Civ Wed 250

★★★★71% Stratford Victoria

Arden St CV37 6QQ
☎ 01789 271000 01789 271001
e-mail: stratfordvictoria@marstonhotels.com
web: www.marstonhotels.com
Dir: *A439 into Stratford, in town follow A3400 Birmingham, at traffic light junct turn left into Arden St, hotel 150yds on right*

Situated adjacent to the hospital, this eye-catching modern hotel with its red-brick façade is within walking distance of the town centre. Bedrooms are spacious and feature framed embroideries. The open-plan public areas include a comfortable lounge, a small atmospheric bar and spacious restaurant with exposed beams and ornately carved furniture.

ROOMS: 100 en suite (35 fmly) in 40 bedrooms s fr £103; d fr £158 (incl. bkfst) **LB** **FACILITIES: Spa** STV Gym Xmas **CONF:** Thtr 140 Class 66 Board 54 Del from £185 **SERVICES:** Lift **PARKING:** 100 **NOTES:** in restaurant Civ Wed 160

★★★★61% The Shakespeare

Chapel St CV37 6ER
☎ 0870 400 8182 01789 415411
e-mail: shakespeare@macdonald-hotels.co.uk
web: www.macdonald-hotels.co.uk
Dir: *M40 junct 15, take A46 then A439 into one-way system, left at rdbt opposite HSBC bank, hotel on left*

Dating back to the early 17th century, The Shakespeare is one of the oldest hotels in this historic town. The hotel name also represents one of the earliest exploitations of Stratford as the birthplace of one of the world's leading poets and playwrights. With exposed beams and open fires, the public rooms retain an ambience reminiscent of this era. Bedrooms have also been refurbished to an excellent standard and remain in keeping with the style of the property.

ROOMS: 63 en suite 11 annexe en suite (3 GF) in 18 bedrooms s £60-£128; d £120-£200 (incl. bkfst) **LB** **FACILITIES:** STV Use of swimming pool at sister hotel Xmas **CONF:** Thtr 80 Class 60 Board 40 Del from £140 **SERVICES:** Lift **PARKING:** 34 **NOTES:** in restaurant Civ Wed 50

> Early start?
> Hotels at all star levels should provide in-room alarm clocks and/or alarm clocks

★★★72% ❀ Salford Hall
WR11 5UT
☎ 01386 871300 & 0800 212671
Fax 01386 871301
e-mail: reception@salfordhall.co.uk
web: www.salfordhall.co.uk
(For full entry see Abbot's Salford and advert on this page)

★★★68% Grosvenor House
Warwick Rd CV37 6YT
☎ 01789 269213 Fax 01789 266087
e-mail: info@groshotelstratford.co.uk
Dir: *M40 junct 15, follow Stratford signs to A439 Warwick Rd, hotel 7m on one-way system*
This hotel is a short distance from the town centre and many of the historic attractions. Bedroom styles and sizes vary and the friendly staff offer an efficient service. Refreshments are served in the lounge all day, plus room service is available. The Garden Room restaurant offers a choice of dishes from set priced and carte menus.
ROOMS: 73 en suite (16 fmly) (25 GF) ⊗ in 25 bedrooms s £78-£125; d £96-£150 (incl. bkfst) **LB FACILITIES:** STV Xmas **CONF:** Thtr 100 Class 45 Board 50 Del from £85 **PARKING:** 46 **NOTES:** ✈ ⊗ in restaurant Civ Wed 40

★★★67% The Swan's Nest
Bridgefoot CV37 7LT
☎ 0870 400 8183 Fax 01789 414547
e-mail: sales.swansnest@macdonld-hotels.co.uk
web: www.macdonald-hotels.co.uk
Dir: *M40 junct 15, A46 for 2m, at 1st island turn left onto A439 towards Stratford. Follow one-way system, left over river bridge, hotel on right by river*
Dating back to the 17th century, this hotel is said to be one of the earliest brick-built houses in the town. The hotel occupies a prime position on the banks of the River Avon and is ideally situated for exploring the town and the Warwickshire countryside. Bedrooms, all named after birds, are appointed to a high standard.
ROOMS: 67 en suite (2 fmly) (25 GF) ⊗ in 45 bedrooms s £40-£100; d £80-£100 **FACILITIES:** Use of facilities at sister hotel Xmas **CONF:** Thtr 150 Class 80 Board 40 Del from £99 **PARKING:** 80 **NOTES:** ⊗ in restaurant Civ Wed 110

★★★65% The Falcon
Chapel St CV37 6HA
☎ 01789 279953 & 0870 609 6122
Fax 01789 414260
e-mail: thefalcon@corushotels.com
web: www.corushotels.com
Dir: *town centre-opposite Guild Chapel and Nash House*

This 16th-century inn, situated in the heart of town, provides public rooms with much original character, including a choice of bars, a brasserie-style restaurant (with tables in the conservatory

and garden), and a more formal dining option. Accommodation comes in a variety of styles; the older, beamed rooms in the original Tudor section retain much charm.
ROOMS: 84 en suite 11 annexe en suite (13 fmly) (3 GF) ⊗ in 38 bedrooms s £105; d £105 **LB FACILITIES:** Xmas **CONF:** Thtr 200 Class 110 Board 40 Del from £105 **SERVICES:** Lift **PARKING:** 124 **NOTES:** ⊗ in restaurant Civ Wed 160

★★★62% The Charlecote Pheasant Hotel
Charlecote CV35 9EW
☎ 01789 279954 Fax 01789 470222
e-mail: charlecotepheasant@corushotels.com
web: www.corushotels.com
Dir: *M40 junct 15, take A429 towards Cirencester through Barford village after 2m turn right into Charlecote, hotel opposite Charlecote Manor Park*

Located just outside Stratford, this hotel is set in extensive grounds and is a popular conference venue. Various bedroom styles are
continued on p544

STRATFORD-UPON-AVON, continued

available within the annexe wings, ranging from standard rooms to executive suites. The main building houses the restaurant and a lounge bar area.
ROOMS: 70 en suite (2 fmly) (20 GF) ⊗ in 26 bedrooms s fr £98; d £98-£120 **LB** **FACILITIES:** STV Childrens Play area Xmas **CONF:** Thtr 160 Class 90 Board 50 Del from £138 **PARKING:** 100 **NOTES:** ⊗ in restaurant Civ Wed 176

★★67% The New Inn Hotel & Restaurant
Clifford Chambers CV37 8HR
☎ 01789 293402 📠 01789 292716
e-mail: thenewinn65@aol.com
web: www.thenewinnhotel.co.uk
Dir: *off A3400 onto B4632, follow signs to Shire Horse Centre, hotel 200yds on left*
This welcoming, family-run hotel is located in the pretty village of Clifford Chambers. The bar has an open log fire and, together with the restaurant, offers a choice of dining options. Bedrooms are appealing, some rooms have four-poster beds and some are suitable for disabled guests.
ROOMS: 12 en suite (2 fmly) (3 GF) ⊗ in all bedrooms s £54-£73; d £73-£110 (incl. bkfst) **LB** **FACILITIES:** ♫ ch fac **PARKING:** 40 **NOTES:** ⊗ in restaurant Closed 23-28 Dec

STREATLEY, Berkshire — Map 05 SU58

★★★★69% The Swan at Streatley
High St RG8 9HR
☎ 01491 878800 📠 01491 872554
e-mail: sales@swan-at-streatley.co.uk
Dir: *from S right at lights in Streatley, hotel on left before bridge*
A stunning location set beside the Thames, ideal for an English summer's day. Many bedrooms enjoy the views and rooms are well appointed. The hotel offers a range of facilities including meeting rooms and leisure, the 'Streatley Belle', is moored beside the hotel and is a perfect, yet unusual meeting venue and in the leisure club guests can also enjoy the views. Cuisine is accomplished and dining here should not to be missed.
ROOMS: 46 en suite (13 GF) ⊗ in 9 bedrooms **FACILITIES:** STV Fishing Sauna Solarium Gym Jacuzzi Electric motor launches for hire **CONF:** BC Thtr 140 Class 60 Board 40 **PARKING:** 170 **NOTES:** ⊗ in restaurant Civ Wed 130

STREET, Somerset — Map 04 ST43

★★★57% Wessex
High St BA16 0EF
☎ 01458 443383 📠 01458 446589
e-mail: info@wessexhotel.com
Dir: *from A303, onto B3151 to Somerton. Then 7m, pass lights by Millfield School. Left at mini-rdbt*
This purpose-built hotel in the centre of town has plenty of parking and is only a short walk from Clarks Village. Spacious bedrooms are equipped with modern facilities. Public areas include a range of function rooms, a cosy bar and a comfortable restaurant.
ROOMS: 49 en suite (4 fmly) ⊗ in 24 bedrooms s £63-£68; d £83-£88 (incl. bkfst) **LB** **FACILITIES:** STV Xmas **CONF:** BC Thtr 250 Class 120 Board 50 **SERVICES:** Lift **PARKING:** 70 **NOTES:** ⊗ in restaurant Closed 27-29 Dec

STRENSHAM MOTORWAY SERVICE AREA (M5), Worcestershire — Map 10 SO84

Premier Travel Inn Tewkesbury (Strensham)
WR8 0BZ
☎ 08701 977252 📠 01684 273606
web: www.premiertravelinn.com
Dir: *M5 northbound junct & M5/M50 interchange (access available to southbound)*
High quality, modern budget accommodation ideal for both families and business travellers. Spacious, en suite bedrooms feature bath and shower, satellite TV and many have telephones and modem points. The adjacent family restaurant features a wide and varied menu. For further details consult the Hotel Groups page.
ROOMS: 49 en suite s £46.95-£48.95; d £46.95-£48.95 **CONF:** Thtr 22 Class 18 Board 24

STROUD, Gloucestershire — Map 04 SO80

★★★69% Burleigh Court
Burleigh, Minchinhampton GL5 2PF
☎ 01453 883804 📠 01453 886870
e-mail: info@burleighcourthotel.co.uk
Dir: *From Stroud A419 towards Cirencester. Right after 2.5m signed Burleigh & Minchinhampton. Left after 500yds signed Burleigh Court. Hotel 300yds on right*

Dating back to the 18th century, this former gentleman's manor house is in a secluded yet accessible elevated position with some wonderful countryside views. Public rooms are elegantly styled and include a wonderful oak-panelled bar for pre-dinner drinks beside a crackling fire. Combining comfort and quality, no two bedrooms are the same and some are in an adjoining coach house.
ROOMS: 18 en suite (2 fmly) (3 GF) **FACILITIES:** ch fac **CONF:** Thtr 50 Class 30 Board 30 **PARKING:** 40 **NOTES:** ⊗ in restaurant Civ Wed 50

★★★68% The Bear of Rodborough
CLASSIC BRITISH
Rodborough Common GL5 5DE
☎ 01453 878522 📠 01453 872523
e-mail: info@bearofrodborough.info
Dir: *From M5 junct 13 take A419 to Stroud. Follow signs to Rodborough. Up hill, left at top at T-junct. Hotel on right.*
This popular 17th-century coaching inn is situated high above Stroud within acres of National Trust parkland. Character abounds in the lounges, cocktail bar and Box Tree restaurant. Bedrooms offer equal measures of comfort and style with plenty of extra

continued

touches. There is also a traditional and well-patronised public bar. Cuisine is a feature where local produce is frequently utilised.
ROOMS: 46 en suite (2 fmly) ⊗ in all bedrooms s £75-£121; d £120-£237 (incl. bkfst) **LB** **FACILITIES:** Putt green Xmas **CONF:** Thtr 60 Class 35 Board 30 Del from £145 **PARKING:** 70 **NOTES:** ⊗ in restaurant Civ Wed 70

Premier Travel Inn Stroud

Stratford Lodge, Stratford Rd GL5 4AF
☎ 0870 9906378 🖷 0870 9906379
web: www.premiertravelinn.com
Dir: *Off M5 junct 13, follow A419 to town centre, then signs for leisure centre. Hotel opposite, next to Tesco superstore*
High quality, modern budget accommodation ideal for both families and business travellers. Spacious, en suite bedrooms feature bath and shower, satellite TV and many have telephones and modem points. The adjacent family restaurant features a wide and varied menu. For further details consult the Hotel Groups page.
ROOMS: 32 en suite s £46.95-£49.95; d £46.95-£49.95

STUDLAND, Dorset — Map 05 SZ08

★★68% Manor House

BH19 3AU
☎ 01929 450288 🖷 01929 452255
e-mail: themanorhousehotel@lineone.net
web: www.themanorhousehotel.com
Dir: *A338 from Bournemouth, follow signs to Sandbanks ferry, cross on ferry, then 3m to Studland*
Set in 20 acres of attractive grounds and with delightful views overlooking Studland Bay, this elegant hotel provides an impressive range of facilities. Bedrooms, many with excellent sea views, are all well equipped and many retain charming features of the original Gothic house. In the oak-panelled dining room, carefully prepared meals offer an interesting choice of dishes from the daily-changing menu.
ROOMS: 18 en suite 3 annexe en suite (9 fmly) (4 GF) s £100-£120; d £150-£236 (incl. bkfst & dinner) **LB** **FACILITIES:** Xmas **PARKING:** 80 **NOTES:** No children 5yrs ⊗ in restaurant

STURMINSTER NEWTON, Dorset — Map 04 ST71

★★★71% Plumber Manor

Hazelbury Bryan Rd DT10 2AF
☎ 01258 472507 🖷 01258 473370
e-mail: book@plumbermanor.com
web: www.plumbermanor.com
Dir: *Off A357, 1.5m SW towards Hazelbury Bryan. Follow brown tourist signs to Plumber Manor*

This 17th-century manor, set in extensive, lovingly tended grounds, is full of charm and character. Bedrooms, some set apart from the main house, are pleasantly spacious and modern in style. The public areas retain much of the style of the manor and guests can relax in the bar or lounge, or stroll in the grounds. Using fresh and local produce, the restaurant is very much the focus of the hotel.
ROOMS: 6 en suite 10 annexe en suite ⊗ in all bedrooms s £95-£110; d £110-£170 (incl. bkfst) **LB** **FACILITIES:** **CONF:** BC Thtr 25 Board 16 Del from £145 **PARKING:** 30 **NOTES:** ⊗ in restaurant Closed Feb

SUDBURY, Derbyshire — Map 10 SK13

★★★66% *The Boars Head*

Lichfield Rd DE6 5GX
☎ 01283 820344 🖷 01283 820075
e-mail: enquiries@boars-head-hotel.co.uk
web: www.boars-head-hotel.co.uk
Dir: *off A50 onto A515 towards Lichfield, hotel 1m on right*

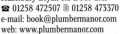

This well established popular hotel has comfortable accommodation in well-equipped bedrooms. There is a relaxed atmosphere in the public rooms, which consists of a several bars and dining options. The beamed lounge bar provides informal dining thanks to a popular carvery, while the restaurant and cocktail bar offer a more formal environment.
ROOMS: 22 en suite 1 annexe en suite (1 fmly) **FACILITIES:** STV **CONF:** Thtr 25 Class 16 Board 16 **PARKING:** 85 **NOTES:** ⊗ in restaurant

See advert under BURTON UPON TRENT

SUDBURY, Suffolk — Map 13 TL84

★★★69% Mill

Walnut Tree Ln CO10 1BD
☎ 01787 375544 🖷 01787 373027
e-mail: reservations@millhotelsuffolk.fsnet.co.uk
Dir: *from Colchester take A134 to Sudbury, follow signs for Chelmsford after town square take 2nd right*
Impressive building situated on the banks of the River Stour, overlooking open pastures on the edge of town. The hotel has its own millpond and retains many charming features such as open fires, exposed beams and a working waterwheel. Bedrooms vary in size and style; each one is thoughtfully equipped and pleasantly furnished.
ROOMS: 52 en suite (2 fmly) (9 GF) ⊗ in 45 bedrooms s £59-£129; d £89-£129 **LB** **FACILITIES:** Xmas **CONF:** Thtr 70 Class 35 Board 35 Del £85 **PARKING:** 60 **NOTES:** ⊗ in restaurant

Indoor Swimming pool
Indoor Swimming pool (heated)
Outdoor Swimming pool
Outdoor Swimming pool (heated)

SUNDERLAND, Tyne & Wear
Map 19 NZ35

★★★★69% Sunderland Marriott
Queen's Pde, Seaburn SR6 8DB
☎ 0191 529 2041 ⎙ 0191 529 4227
e-mail: sunderland.marriott@whitbread.com
web: www.marriott.co.uk
Dir: *A19, A184 (Boldon/Sunderland North), then 3m. At rdbt turn left, then right. At rdbt turn left, follow to coast. Turn right, hotel on right*

Comfortable and spacious accommodation, some with fabulous views of the North Sea and vast expanses of sandy beach, is provided in this seafront hotel. Public rooms are bright and modern and a number of meeting rooms are available. The hotel is conveniently located for access to the local visitor attractions.
ROOMS: 82 en suite (16 fmly) (4 GF) ⊗ in 55 bedrooms s £100-£120; d £100-£120 (incl. bkfst) **LB** **FACILITIES:** STV supervised Sauna Solarium Gym Jacuzzi Xmas **CONF:** Thtr 300 Class 100 Board 70 **SERVICES:** Lift **PARKING:** 120 **NOTES:** ⊗ in restaurant Civ Wed 80

★★★70% Quality Hotel Sunderland
Witney Way, Boldon NE35 9PE
☎ 0191 519 1999 ⎙ 0191 519 0655
e-mail: enquiries@hotels-sunderland.com
web: www.choicehotelseurope.com
Dir: *From Tyne Tunnel (A19) 2.5 miles south, take 1st exit rdbt junct with A184*
This modern, purpose-built hotel is within easy reach of major business and tourism amenities and is well suited to the needs of both business and leisure travellers. The bedrooms are spacious and well equipped. Public areas include a leisure centre, a variety of meeting rooms and a spacious bar and restaurant.
ROOMS: 82 en suite (10 fmly) (41 GF) ⊗ in 42 bedrooms **FACILITIES:** STV supervised Sauna Gym Jacuzzi Xmas **CONF:** Thtr 230 Class 100 Board 100 **PARKING:** 150 **NOTES:** ⊗ in restaurant Civ Wed 200

⌂ Premier Travel Inn Sunderland North West
Timber Beach Rd, Off Wessington Way, Castletown SR5 3XG
☎ 0870 9906514 ⎙ 0870 9906515
web: www.premiertravelinn.com
Dir: *Just off A1(M) junct 65. Follow A1231 towards Sunderland*
High quality, modern budget accommodation ideal for both families and business travellers. Spacious, en suite bedrooms feature bath and shower, satellite TV and many have telephones and modem points. The adjacent family restaurant features a wide and varied menu. For further details consult the Hotel Groups page.
ROOMS: 63 en suite s £46.95-£49.95; d £46.95-£49.95 **CONF:** Thtr 12 Class 12 Board 12

⌂ Premier Travel Inn Sunderland West
Wessington Way, Castletown SR5 3HR
☎ 08701 977245 ⎙ 0191 548 4044
web: www.premiertravelinn.com
Dir: *from A19 take A1231 towards Sunderland, Inn 100yds*
High quality, modern budget accommodation ideal for both families and business travellers. Spacious, en suite bedrooms feature bath and shower, satellite TV and many have telephones and modem points. The adjacent family restaurant features a wide and varied menu. For further details consult the Hotel Groups page.
ROOMS: 41 en suite s £46.95-£49.95; d £46.95-£49.95 **CONF:** Thtr 15 Board 10

⌂ Travelodge
Low Row SR1 3PT
☎ 08700 850 950 ⎙ 0191 514 3453
web: www.travelodge.co.uk
Travelodge offers good quality, good value, modern accommodation. Ideal for families, the spacious, en suite bedrooms include remote-control TV, tea and coffee-making facilities and comfortable beds. Meals can be taken at the nearby family restaurant. For further details consult the Hotel Groups page.
ROOMS: 60 en suite s fr £26; d fr £26

SUTTON, Greater London
Map 06 TQ26

★★63% *Thatched House*
135 Cheam Rd SM1 2BN
☎ 020 8642 3131 ⎙ 020 8770 0684
e-mail: thatchedhouse@btconnect.com
Dir: *M25 junct 8, A217 to London until A232, right onto A232, hotel 0.25m on right*
This family-run hotel is on a leafy road between Croydon and Epsom, within easy reach of the M25. Bedrooms are neatly presented with a good range of facilities, some of which overlook the attractive garden. Public areas include a cosy bar and a restaurant serving a good selection of dishes.
ROOMS: 32 rms (29 en suite) **CONF:** Thtr 50 Class 30 Board 26 **PARKING:** 25 **NOTES:** ⊗ in restaurant

SUTTON COLDFIELD, West Midlands
Map 10 SP19

★★★★75% *De Vere Belfry*
B76 9PR
☎ 0870 900 0066 ⎙ 01675 470256
e-mail: enquiries@thebelfry.com
web: www.devereonline.co.uk
(For full entry see Wishaw)

♫ Entertainment

★★★★68% Moor Hall Hotel & Spa
Moor Hall Dr, Four Oaks B75 6LN
☎ 0121 308 3751 ⎙ 0121 308 8974
e-mail: mail@moorhallhotel.co.uk
web: www.moorhallhotel.co.uk
Dir: *at junct of A38/A453 take A453 towards Sutton Coldfield, at traffic lights turn right into Weeford Rd, Moor Hall drive is 150yds on left*
Although only a short distance from the city centre this hotel enjoys a peaceful setting, overlooking extensive grounds and an adjacent golf course. Bedrooms are well equipped and executive rooms are particularly spacious. Public rooms include the formal

continued

Oak Room Restaurant, and the informal Country Kitchen, which offers carvery and blackboard specials.

ROOMS: 82 en suite (5 fmly) (33 GF) ⊗ in 53 bedrooms s £60-£164; d £78-£164 (incl. bkfst) **LB FACILITIES: Spa** STV 🖼 Sauna Gym Jacuzzi Steam room, 3 Spa treatment rooms **CONF:** BC Thtr 250 Class 120 Board 45 Del from £149 **SERVICES:** Lift **PARKING:** 170 **NOTES:** 🏾 ⊗ in restaurant Civ Wed 180

See advert under BIRMINGHAM

🆄 Ramada Hotel & Resort Birmingham

Penns Ln, Walmley B76 1LH
☎ 0121 351 3111 🖷 0121 313 1297
e-mail: sales.birmingham@ramadajarvis.co.uk
Dir: Take A5127 towards Sutton Coldfield for 2m, through lights, take 4th right into Penns Lane. Hotel 1m on right.
Conveniently located for both M42 and M6 this large hotel is set in private grounds overlooking a lake. Bedrooms are comfortably appointed for both business and leisure guests.
ROOMS: 170 en suite (1 fmly) ⊗ in 123 bedrooms s £99-£130; d £99-£130 **FACILITIES: Spa** 🖼 supervised Fishing Squash Sauna Solarium Gym Xmas **CONF:** Thtr 500 Class 200 Board 40 Del from £155 **SERVICES:** Lift **PARKING:** 500 **NOTES:** ⊗ in restaurant Civ Wed 150

⇧ Innkeeper's Lodge Birmingham East

Chester Rd, Streetley B73 6SP
☎ 0121 353 7785 🖷 0121 352 1443
web: www.innkeeperslodge.com
Dir: M6 junct 7 to A34 S'bound, left onto A404I. At 4th rdbt right onto A452-Chester road, lodge less 1m on right
A growing concept in the travel accommodation market. Smart rooms meet essential business requirements but also have home comforts. Dining options include all-day menus plus the added advantage of breakfast, which is included in the room price. For further details consult the Hotel Groups page.
ROOMS: 7 en suite 59 annexe en suite s £45-£49.95; d £45-£49.95 **CONF:** Thtr 40 Board 20

⇧ Innkeeper's Lodge Birmingham South

2225 Coventry Rd, Sheldon B26 3EH
☎ 0121 742 6201 🖷 0121 722 2703
web: www.innkeeperslodge.com
Dir: M42 junct 6/A45 towards Birmingham for 2m. Lodge on left (approaching overhead traffic lights)
A growing concept in the travel accommodation market. Smart rooms meet essential business requirements but also have home comforts. Dining options include all-day menus plus the added advantage of breakfast, which is included in the room price. For further details consult the Hotel Groups page.
ROOMS: 85 en suite s £45-£59.95; d £45-£59.95

⇧ Premier Travel Inn Birmingham North

Whitehouse Common Rd B75 6HD
☎ 0870 9906320 🖷 0870 9906321
web: www.premiertravelinn.com
Dir: Approx 6m from M42 junct 9. Follow A446 towards Lichfield, then A453 to Sutton Coldfield. Left into Whitehouse Common Rd, hotel on left
High quality, modern budget accommodation ideal for both families and business travellers. Spacious, en suite bedrooms feature bath and shower, satellite TV and many have telephones and modem points. The adjacent family restaurant features a wide and varied menu. For further details consult the Hotel Groups page.
ROOMS: 42 en suite s £47.95-£50.95; d £47.95-£50.95 **CONF:** Board 10

⇧ Travelodge

Boldmere Rd B73 5UP
☎ 08700 850 950 🖷 0121 355 0017
web: www.travelodge.co.uk
Dir: 2m S, on B4142
Travelodge offers good quality, good value, modern accommodation. Ideal for families, the spacious, en suite bedrooms include remote-control TV, tea and coffee-making facilities and comfortable beds. Meals can be taken at the nearby family restaurant. For further details consult the Hotel Groups page.
ROOMS: 32 en suite s fr £26; d fr £26

SUTTON ON SEA, Lincolnshire Map 17 TF58

★★★69% ◉ The Grange & Links

Sea Ln, Sandilands LN12 2RA
☎ 01507 441334 🖷 01507 443033
e-mail: grangeandlinkshotel@btconnect.com
web: www.thegrangeandlinkshotel.co.uk
Dir: A1111 to Sutton-on-Sea, follow signs to Sandilands
This friendly, family-run hotel sits in five acres of grounds, close to both the beach and its own 18-hole links golf course. Bedrooms are pleasantly appointed and are well equipped for both business and leisure guests. Public rooms include ample lounge areas, a formal restaurant and a traditional bar, serving a wide range of meals and snacks.
ROOMS: 23 en suite (10 fmly) (3 GF) ⊗ in 3 bedrooms s fr £59; d fr £78 (incl. bkfst) **LB FACILITIES:** 🗲 18 ⚲ Snooker Gym ⛳ Putt green Bowls Xmas **CONF:** Thtr 200 Board 100 Del from £75 **PARKING:** 60 **NOTES:** 🏾 Civ Wed 150

SUTTON SCOTNEY, Hampshire Map 05 SU43

⇧ Travelodge Winchester

SO21 3JY
☎ 08700 850 950 🖷 01962 761096
web: www.travelodge.co.uk
Dir: on A34 northbound
Travelodge offers good quality, good value, modern accommodation. Ideal for families, the spacious, en suite bedrooms include remote-control TV, tea and coffee-making facilities and comfortable beds. Meals can be taken at the nearby family restaurant. For further details consult the Hotel Groups page.
ROOMS: 30 en suite s fr £26; d fr £26

🏨 Town House Hotel
🏨 Country House Hotel
⇧ Travel Accommodation

SUTTON SCOTNEY, continued

Travelodge Winchester
SO21 3JY
☎ 08700 850 950 01962 761096
web: www.travelodge.co.uk
Dir: *on A34 southbound*
Travelodge offers good quality, good value, modern accommodation. Ideal for families, the spacious, en suite bedrooms include remote-control TV, tea and coffee-making facilities and comfortable beds. Meals can be taken at the nearby family restaurant. For further details consult the Hotel Groups page.
ROOMS: 40 en suite s fr £26; d fr £26

SUTTON UPON DERWENT, East Riding of Yorkshire — Map 17 SE74

★★66% Old Rectory
Sandhill Ln YO41 4BX
☎ 01904 608548 01904 608548
web: www.oldrectoryhotel.freeserve.co.uk
Dir: *off A1079 at Grimston Bar rdbt onto B1228 for Howden, through Elvington to Sutton-upon-Derwent, hotel on left opposite tennis courts*
Dating from 1854, this large country rectory on the outskirts of York stands in the village centre, overlooking the Derwent Valley and offers a very friendly welcome. The hotel is handy for the Retail Outlet, the Yorkshire Air Museum and the city. Bedrooms and public areas are spacious and comfortable, and home cooking is a speciality in the dining room.
ROOMS: 6 rms (5 en suite) (2 fmly) s £35-£45; d £56-£58 (incl. bkfst) **LB PARKING:** 30 **NOTES:** ⊗ in restaurant Closed 2wks Xmas

SWAFFHAM, Norfolk — Map 13 TF80

★★★67% George
Station Rd PE37 7LJ
☎ 01760 721238 01760 725333
e-mail: georgehotel@bestwestern.co.uk
Dir: *off A47 signed Swaffham, hotel opposite St Peter & St Paul church*

Georgian hotel situated in the heart of this bustling market town, which is ideally placed for touring north Norfolk. Bedrooms vary in size and style; each one is pleasantly decorated and well equipped. Public rooms include a cosy restaurant, a lounge and a busy bar where a range of drinks and snacks is available.
ROOMS: 29 en suite (1 fmly) ⊗ in 15 bedrooms s £75-£85; d £59-£95 (incl. bkfst) **LB FACILITIES:** STV **CONF:** Thtr 150 Class 70 Board 70 Del from £95 **PARKING:** 100 **NOTES:** ⊗ in restaurant

SWALLOWFIELD, Berkshire — Map 05 SU76

★★68% The Mill House
Old Basingstoke Rd, Swallowfield RG7 1PY
☎ 0118 988 3124 0118 988 5550
e-mail: info@themillhousehotel.co.uk
Dir: *M4 junct 11, S on A33, left at 1st rdbt onto B3349. Approx 1m after sign for Three Mile Cross & Spencer's Wood, hotel on right*
This smart Georgian house hotel enjoys a tranquil setting in its own delightful gardens, making it a popular wedding venue. Guests can enjoy fine dining in the conservatory-style restaurant or lighter meals in the cosy bar. Well-equipped bedrooms vary in size and style and include a number of spacious, well-appointed executive rooms.
ROOMS: 12 en suite (2 fmly) ⊗ in 3 bedrooms s £75-£100; d £85-£120 (incl. bkfst) **FACILITIES:** **CONF:** Thtr 250 Class 100 Board 60 Del from £125 **PARKING:** 60 **NOTES:** ⊗ in restaurant RS Sun evenings Civ Wed 125

SWANAGE, Dorset — Map 05 SZ07

★★★69% The Pines
Burlington Rd BH19 1LT
☎ 01929 425211 01929 422075
e-mail: reservations@pineshotel.co.uk
web: www.pineshotel.co.uk
Dir: *A351 to seafront, left then 2nd right. Hotel at end of road*

Enjoying a peaceful location with spectacular views over the cliffs and sea, The Pines is a pleasant place to stay. Many of the comfortable bedrooms have sea views. Guests can take tea in the lounge, enjoy appetising bar snacks in the attractive bar and interesting and accomplished cuisine in the restaurant.
ROOMS: 49 en suite (26 fmly) (6 GF) s £57-£81; d £113-£161 (incl. bkfst) **LB FACILITIES:** ♫ Xmas **CONF:** Thtr 80 Class 80 Board 80 Del from £85.60 **SERVICES:** Lift **PARKING:** 60 **NOTES:** ⊗ in restaurant

See advert on opposite page

★★★68% Purbeck House
91 High St BH19 2LZ
☎ 01929 422872 01929 421194
e-mail: reservations@purbeckhousehotel.co.uk
web: www.purbeckhousehotel.co.uk
Dir: *A351 to Swanage via Wareham, right into Shore Road, on into Institute Road, right into High Street*
Located close to the town centre, this former convent is set in well-tended grounds. The attractive bedrooms are located in the original building and also in the annexe. In addition to a very pleasant and spacious conservatory, the smartly presented public

continued

areas have some stunning features, such as painted ceilings, wood panelling and fine tiled floors.
ROOMS: 18 en suite 20 annexe en suite (5 fmly) (10 GF) ⊗ in 10 bedrooms s £69-£79; d £106-£124 (incl. bkfst) **LB** **FACILITIES:** STV ♫ Xmas **CONF:** Thtr 100 Class 36 Board 25 Del £75 **PARKING:** 50 **NOTES:** ✗ ⊗ in restaurant Civ Wed 100

See advert on this page

★★★67% Grand
Burlington Rd BH19 1LU
☎ 01929 423353 📠 01929 427068
e-mail: reservations@grandhotelswanage.com
web: www.grandhotelswanage.co.uk
Dir: *via Sandbanks Toll Ferry from Bournemouth, follow signs to Swanage, at 2nd town centre sign, 4th left into Burlington Rd*
Dating back to 1898, the Grand Hotel is located on the Isle of Purbeck and has spectacular views across Swanage Bay and Peveril Point. Bedrooms are individually decorated and well equipped; public rooms offer a number of choices from relaxing lounges to extensive leisure facilities. The hotel also has its own private beach.
ROOMS: 30 en suite (2 fmly) ⊗ in 8 bedrooms s £25-£30; d £66-£79 (incl. bkfst & dinner) **LB** **FACILITIES:** STV ⛝ supervised Fishing Sauna Solarium Gym Jacuzzi Table tennis Xmas **CONF:** Thtr 120 Class 40 Board 40 **SERVICES:** Lift **PARKING:** 15 **NOTES:** ✗ ⊗ in restaurant Closed 10 days in Jan (dates on application) Civ Wed

SWANWICK See Alfreton

Bad hair day?
Hairdryers in all rooms three stars and above

SWAVESEY, Cambridgeshire Map 12 TL36

Travelodge Cambridge (West)
Cambridge Rd CB4 5QR
☎ 08700 850 950 🖷 01954 789113
web: www.travelodge.co.uk
Dir: *on eastbound carriageway of A14*
Travelodge offers good quality, good value, modern accommodation. Ideal for families, the spacious, en suite bedrooms include remote-control TV, tea and coffee-making facilities and comfortable beds. Meals can be taken at the nearby family restaurant. For further details consult the Hotel Groups page.
ROOMS: 36 en suite s fr £26; d fr £26

SWAY, Hampshire Map 05 SZ29

★★69% Sway Manor Restaurant & Hotel
Station Rd SO41 6BA
☎ 01590 682754 🖷 01590 682955
e-mail: info@swaymanor.com
web: www.swaymanor.com
Dir: *turn off B3055 Brockenhurst/New Milton road into village centre*
Built at the turn of the 20th century, this attractive mansion is set in it own grounds, with a swimming pool, and is also conveniently located in the centre of the village. Bedrooms are well appointed and generously equipped whilst the bar and restaurant, both with views over the gardens, are popular with locals.
ROOMS: 15 en suite (3 fmly) ⊘ in 12 bedrooms s £45-£54; d £74-£108 (incl. bkfst) **LB** **FACILITIES:** Xmas **SERVICES:** Lift **PARKING:** 40 **NOTES:** ⊘ in restaurant Civ Wed 50

SWINDON, Wiltshire Map 05 SU18

★★★★74% *De Vere Swindon*
Shaw Ridge Leisure Park, Whitehill Way SN5 7DW
☎ 01793 878785 🖷 01793 877822
e-mail: dvs.sales@devere-hotels.com
web: www.devereonline.co.uk
Dir: *M4 junct 16, signs for Swindon off 1st rdbt, 2nd rdbt follow signs for Link Centre over next 2 rdbts, 2nd left at 3rd rdbt, left onto slip road*

This stylish, modern hotel is located close to the motorway network and the local business district. Day rooms are extensive and include a smart fitness centre, conference facilities and a popular restaurant. Bedrooms are very well equipped and come in a variety of sizes and styles. The staff deliver efficient service in a friendly manner.
ROOMS: 158 en suite (12 fmly) ⊘ in 119 bedrooms **FACILITIES:** STV Sauna Solarium Gym Jacuzzi Health & beauty treatment rooms **CONF:** BC Thtr 300 Class 160 Board 80 **SERVICES:** Lift **PARKING:** 170 **NOTES:** ⊘ in restaurant Civ Wed 300

★★★★71% Blunsdon House Hotel & Leisure Club
Blunsdon SN26 7AS
☎ 01793 721701 🖷 01793 721056
e-mail: info@blunsdonhouse.co.uk
web: www.blunsdonhouse.co.uk
Dir: *200 yds off A419 at Swindon, 1m N of Swindon*
Located just to the north of Swindon, Blunsdon house is set in 30 acres of well-kept grounds and offers extensive leisure facilities and spacious day rooms. The hotel has a choice of eating and drinking options; there are three bars and two restaurants. Bedrooms are comfortably furnished, and the contemporary Pavilion rooms are especially spacious.
ROOMS: 117 en suite (15 fmly) (27 GF) ⊘ in 75 bedrooms s £120-£150; d £130-£160 (incl. bkfst) **LB** **FACILITIES:** STV 9 Squash Sauna Solarium Gym Putt green Jacuzzi Beauty therapy, Woodland walk, 9 hole par 3 golf course Xmas **CONF:** Thtr 300 Class 200 Board 40 Del from £149 **SERVICES:** Lift **PARKING:** 300 **NOTES:** ⊘ in restaurant Civ Wed 200

★★★★66% Swindon Marriott Hotel
Pipers Way SN3 1SH
☎ 0870 400 7281 🖷 0870 400 7381
web: www.marriott.co.uk
Dir: *M4 junct 15, follow A419, then A4259 to Coate rdbt and B4006 signed 'Old Town'*

With convenient access to the motorway, this hotel is an easily accessible venue for meetings, and an ideal base from which to explore Wiltshire and the Cotswolds. The hotel offers a good range of public rooms, including a well-equipped leisure centre, Chats café bar and the informal, brasserie-style Mediterrano restaurant.
ROOMS: 156 en suite (42 fmly) ⊘ in 137 bedrooms s £56-£119; d £72-£119 **LB** **FACILITIES: Spa** STV Sauna Solarium Gym Jacuzzi Steam Room, Health & Beauty, Hair salon, Sports massage therapy **CONF:** Thtr 280 Class 100 Board 40 Del from £130 **SERVICES:** Lift air con **PARKING:** 185 **NOTES:** ⊘ in restaurant Civ Wed 280

★★★78% The Pear Tree at Purton
Church End SN5 4ED
☎ 01793 772100 🖷 01793 772369
e-mail: stay@peartreepurton.co.uk
(For full entry see Purton)

★★★69% Chiseldon House
New Rd, Chiseldon SN4 0NE
☎ 01793 741010 🖷 01793 741059
e-mail: info@chiseldonhousehotel.co.uk
web: www.chiseldonhousehotel.co.uk
Dir: *M4 junct 15, onto A346 signed Marlborough, at brow of hill turn right by Esso garage onto B4005 into New Rd, hotel 200yds on right*
Chiseldon is a traditional country house near Swindon that provides a peaceful location, yet is within minutes of the M4. Quiet and spacious bedrooms are tastefully decorated and include

continued

a number of thoughtful extras. Guests can relax in the comfortable lounge and enjoy the well-kept gardens.

ROOMS: 21 en suite (4 fmly) ⊗ in 15 bedrooms s £85-£105; d £105-£125 (incl. bkfst) **FACILITIES:** STV **CONF:** Thtr 50 Class 30 Board 20 Del £135 **PARKING:** 40 **NOTES:** Civ Wed 85

★★★67% *Corus hotel Swindon*

Oxford Rd, Stratton St Margaret SN3 4TL
☎ 0870 609 6150 📠 01793 831401
e-mail: reservations.madisoninn@corushotels.com
web: www.corushotels.com
Dir: *M4 junct 15, A419 to Cirencester. Over rdbt, then exit left (signed Oxford A420). Right at next 2 rdbts, hotel on left*

Conveniently located just off the M4, the hotel is ideal for touring the area. The Great Western Designer Outlet and Steam Museum are just 10 minutes' drive away. Bedrooms are large and well appointed, rooms to the rear being quieter. Facilities include four versatile conference rooms and the Olio bar and restaurant.
ROOMS: 94 en suite (3 fmly) (45 GF) ⊗ in 73 bedrooms **FACILITIES:** STV Free use of nearby gym, pool and beauty parlour **CONF:** Thtr 100 Class 50 Board 40 **PARKING:** 150 **NOTES:** ⊗ in restaurant Civ Wed 70

★★★66% Goddard Arms

High St, Old Town SN1 3EG
☎ 01793 692313 📠 01793 512984
e-mail: goddard.arms@forestdale.com
web: www.forestdale.com
Dir: *M4 junct 15, A4259 towards Swindon, onto B4006 to Old Town follow signs for PM Hospital. Hotel in High St opp Wood St next to Lloyds Bank*

Situated in the attractive Old Town area, this ivy-clad coaching inn offers bedrooms in either the main building or in a modern annexe to the rear of the property. Public areas are tastefully decorated in a traditional style; there is a lounge, Vaults bar and a popular restaurant. The conference rooms are extensive and the car park secure.
ROOMS: 18 en suite 47 annexe en suite (3 fmly) (24 GF) ⊗ in 33 bedrooms s £85-£110; d £120-£130 (incl. bkfst) **LB** **FACILITIES:** STV **CONF:** Thtr 180 Class 100 Board 40 Del from £125 **PARKING:** 90 **NOTES:** ⊗ in restaurant Civ Wed 180

SWINDON, continued

★★★66% Marsh Farm
Coped Hall SN4 8ER
☎ 01793 848044 🖷 01793 851528
e-mail: marshfarmhotel@btconnect.com
web: www.marshfarmhotel.co.uk
Dir: *from M4 junct 16 take A3102, straight on at 1st rdbt, at next rdbt (with garage on left) turn right. Hotel 200yds on left*
The stylish, well appointed bedrooms at this hotel are situated in converted barns and extensions around the original farmhouse which is set in its own grounds less than a mile from the M4. An extensive range of dishes makes up the menu offered in Reids, the smart conservatory restaurant.
ROOMS: 11 en suite 39 annexe en suite (1 fmly) ⊗ in 23 bedrooms s £55-£115; d £70-£150 (incl. bkfst) **LB** **FACILITIES:** STV Putt green Clay pigeon shooting nearby **CONF:** Thtr 120 Class 60 Board 50 Del from £120 **PARKING:** 150 **NOTES:** ✖ ⊗ in restaurant RS 26-30 Dec Civ Wed 100

See advert on page 551

★★★66% Stanton House
The Avenue, Stanton Fitzwarren SN6 7SD
☎ 01793 861777 🖷 01793 861857
e-mail: info@stantonhouse.co.uk
Dir: *off A419 onto A361 towards Highworth, pass Honda factory and turn left towards Stanton Fitzwarren about 600yds past business park, hotel on left*
Extensive grounds and superb gardens surround this Cotswold-stone manor house. Smart, well-maintained bedrooms have been equipped with modern comforts. Public areas include a games room, a lounge, a bar, conference facilities and an informal restaurant specialising in Japanese cuisine. The multi-lingual staff are friendly and a relaxed atmosphere prevails.
ROOMS: 84 en suite (31 GF) ⊗ in 35 bedrooms s £65-£143; d £109-£158 (incl. bkfst) **LB** **FACILITIES:** STV ९ Xmas **CONF:** Thtr 110 Class 70 Board 40 Del from £117.50 **SERVICES:** Lift **PARKING:** 110 **NOTES:** ✖ ⊗ in restaurant Civ Wed 110

★★★64% *Villiers Inn*
Moormead Rd, Wroughton SN4 9BY
☎ 01793 814744 🖷 01793 814119
e-mail: hotels@villiersinn.co.uk
Dir: *1m S of Swindon, on A4361, hotel 100mtrs on right*
Conveniently situated with easy access to the motorway and Swindon, this attractive period property provides well-equipped accommodation in the main building and in a purpose built extension. Public areas include a comfortable library lounge and a spacious bar. An interesting range of dishes is offered in the restaurant. Function facilities are also available.
ROOMS: 33 en suite ⊗ in 10 bedrooms **FACILITIES:** STV ch fac **CONF:** Thtr 60 Class 30 Board 32 **PARKING:** 60 **NOTES:** Civ Wed 120

★★68% The School House
Hook St, Hook, Wootton Bassett SN4 8EF
☎ 01793 851198 🖷 01793 851025
e-mail: reservations@schoolhotel.com
web: www.schoolhotel.com
Dir: *from M4 junct 16 take exit for Swindon, follow signs for Hook. At 1st rbdt turn left, next rdbt turn left, then 2-3m. Hotel at end of road on left*
This old school has been converted into a character hotel and informal restaurant. There are ten spacious bedrooms, tastefully furnished and equipped with modern facilities, and many

continued

thoughtful extras. The restaurant is comfortable, and a good choice of dishes is offered on the well-balanced menu.

ROOMS: 10 en suite (5 GF) s £55-£99; d £55-£99 (incl. bkfst) **LB** **FACILITIES:** STV **CONF:** Thtr 60 Class 30 Board 30 **PARKING:** 30 **NOTES:** ✖ ⊗ in restaurant Civ Wed

See advert on opposite page

⌂ *Hotel Ibis Swindon*
Delta Business Park, Great Western Way SN5 7XG
☎ 01793 514777 🖷 01793 514570
e-mail: H1041@accor-hotels.com
Dir: *A3102 to Swindon, straight over rdbt, slip road onto Delta Business Park , turn left*
Modern, budget hotel offering comfortable accommodation in bright and practical bedrooms. Breakfast is self-service and dinner is available in the restaurant. For further details, consult the Hotel Groups page.
ROOMS: 120 en suite **CONF:** Thtr 80 Class 40 Board 40

⌂ Premier Travel Inn Swindon North
Ermin St, Blunsdon SN26 8DJ
☎ 0870 9906356 🖷 0870 9906357
web: www.premiertravelinn.com
Dir: *N of Swindon. 5m from M4 junct 15. At junct of A419 & B4019*
High quality, modern budget accommodation ideal for both families and business travellers. Spacious, en suite bedrooms feature bath and shower, satellite TV and many have telephones and modem points. The adjacent family restaurant features a wide and varied menu. For further details consult the Hotel Groups page.
ROOMS: 60 en suite s £46.95-£49.95; d £46.95-£49.95

⌂ Premier Travel Inn Swindon West
Lydiard Way, Great Western Way SN5 8UY
☎ 08701 977247 🖷 01793 886890
web: www.premiertravelinn.com
Dir: *M4 junct 16, 3m SW of Swindon, take left lane towards Swindon, A3102*
High quality, modern budget accommodation ideal for both families and business travellers. Spacious, en suite bedrooms feature bath and shower, satellite TV and many have telephones and modem points. The adjacent family restaurant features a wide and varied menu. For further details consult the Hotel Groups page.
ROOMS: 63 en suite s £46.95-£49.95; d £46.95-£49.95

SWINTON, Greater Manchester Map 15 SD70

⌂ Premier Travel Inn Manchester West
East Lancs Rd M27 0AA
☎ 0870 9906480 🖷 0870 9906481
web: www.premiertravelinn.com
Dir: *Off M60 junct 13 (Swinton/Leigh) on A580.*
High quality, modern budget accommodation ideal for both families and business travellers. Spacious, en suite bedrooms

continued

feature bath and shower, satellite TV and many have telephones and modem points. The adjacent family restaurant features a wide and varied menu. For further details consult the Hotel Groups page.
ROOMS: 27 en suite s £47.95-£50.95; d £47.95-£50.95 **CONF:** Thtr 12 Board 12

TADCASTER, North Yorkshire — Map 16 SE44

★★★77% Hazlewood Castle

Paradise Ln, Hazlewood LS24 9NJ
☎ 01937 535353 01937 530630
e-mail: info@hazlewood-castle.co.uk
Dir: *signed off A64, W of Tadcaster & before A1/M1 link road*

Mentioned in the Domesday Book, this castle is set in 77 acres of parkland. Hospitality and service are keenly delivered and staff are only too happy to assist. Bedrooms, many of them with private sitting rooms, are split between the main house and other buildings in the courtyard. Dinner provides the highlight of any stay with eclectic, creative dishes.
ROOMS: 9 en suite 12 annexe en suite (6 fmly) (6 GF) in all bedrooms s £120-£230; d £155-£330 (incl. bkfst) **LB FACILITIES:** STV Clay pigeon shooting Xmas **CONF:** Thtr 150 Class 60 Board 36 Del from £175 **PARKING:** 150 **NOTES:** in restaurant Civ Wed 120

TADWORTH, Surrey — Map 06 TQ25

Premier Travel Inn Epsom South

Brighton Rd, Burgh Heath KT20 6BW
☎ 0870 9906442 0870 9906443
web: www.premiertravelinn.com
Dir: *Just off M25 junct 8 on A217 towards Sutton*
High quality, modern budget accommodation ideal for both families and business travellers. Spacious, en suite bedrooms feature bath and shower, satellite TV and many have telephones and modem points. The adjacent family restaurant features a wide and varied menu. For further details consult the Hotel Groups page.
ROOMS: 78 en suite s £55.95-£62.95; d £55.95-£62.95

TALKE, Staffordshire — Map 15 SJ85

Travelodge Stoke

Newcastle Rd ST7 1UP
☎ 08700 850 950 01782 777000
web: www.travelodge.co.uk
Dir: *at junct of A34/A500*
Travelodge offers good quality, good value, modern accommodation. Ideal for families, the spacious, en suite bedrooms include remote-control TV, tea and coffee-making facilities and comfortable beds. Meals can be taken at the nearby family restaurant. For further details consult the Hotel Groups page.
ROOMS: 62 en suite s fr £26; d fr £26 **CONF:** Thtr 50 Class 25 Board 32

TAMWORTH, Staffordshire — Map 10 SK20

★★74% *Drayton Court Hotel*

65 Coleshill St, Fazeley B78 3RG
☎ 01827 285805 01827 284842
e-mail: draytoncthotel@yahoo.co.uk
web: www.draytoncourthotel.co.uk
Dir: *M42 junct 9 then A446 to Litchfield, at next rdbt right onto A4091. 2m & Drayton Manor Park on left. Hotel further along on right*
Conveniently located close to the M42, this lovingly restored hotel offers elegant bedrooms that have been thoughtfully equipped to suit both business and leisure guests. Beds are particularly comfortable (a hand-made four poster is available). Public areas include a panelled bar, a relaxing lounge and an attractive restaurant.
ROOMS: 19 en suite (3 fmly) **CONF:** Board 14 **PARKING:** 23
NOTES: in restaurant Closed 24-27 Dec

Premier Travel Inn Tamworth

Bonehill Rd, Bitterscote B78 3HQ
☎ 08701 977248 01827 310420
web: www.premiertravelinn.com
Dir: *M42 junct 10 follow A5 towards Tamworth. After 3m turn left onto A51. Straight over 1st rdbt, 3rd exit off next rdbt*
High quality, modern budget accommodation ideal for both families and business travellers. Spacious, en suite bedrooms feature bath and shower, satellite TV and many have telephones and modem points. The adjacent family restaurant features a wide and varied menu. For further details consult the Hotel Groups page.
ROOMS: 58 en suite s £46.95-£49.95; d £46.95-£49.95 **CONF:** Thtr 50 Board 20

TAMWORTH, continued

⌂ Travelodge
Green Ln B77 5PS
☎ 08700 850 950 & 0800 850950 ▯ 01827 260145
web: www.travelodge.co.uk
Dir: *A5/M42 junct 10*
Travelodge offers good quality, good value, modern accommodation. Ideal for families, the spacious, en suite bedrooms include remote-control TV, tea and coffee-making facilities and comfortable beds. Meals can be taken at the nearby family restaurant. For further details consult the Hotel Groups page.
ROOMS: 62 en suite s fr £26; d fr £26

TANKERSLEY, South Yorkshire Map 16 SK39

★★★★75% Tankersley Manor
Church Ln S75 3DQ
☎ 01226 744700 ▯ 01226 745405
e-mail: tankersley@marstonhotels.com
web: www.marstonhotels.com
Dir: *M1 junct 36 take A61 Sheffield road. Hotel 0.5m on left*

High on the moors with views over the countryside, this 17th-century residence is well located for major cities, tourist attractions and motorway links. Where appropriate, bedrooms retain original features such as exposed beams or Yorkshire stone windowsills. The hotel has its own traditional country pub, complete with old beams and open fires, alongside the more formal restaurant and bar. A well-equipped leisure centre is the latest addition.
ROOMS: 99 en suite (2 fmly) ⊗ in 79 bedrooms s fr £113; d fr £166 (incl. bkfst) **LB FACILITIES: Spa** STV Sauna Gym Swimming lessons, beauty treatments Xmas **CONF:** Thtr 400 Class 200 Board 100 Del from £175 **PARKING:** 200 **NOTES:** ⊗ in restaurant Civ Wed 95

⌂ Premier Travel Inn Sheffield/Barnsley
Maple Rd S75 3DL
☎ 08701 977228 ▯ 01226 741524
web: www.premiertravelinn.com
Dir: *M1 junct 35A (northbound exit only) follow A616 for 2m. From junct 36 take A61 towards Sheffield*
High quality, modern budget accommodation ideal for both families and business travellers. Spacious, en suite bedrooms feature bath and shower, satellite TV and many have telephones and modem points. The adjacent family restaurant features a wide and varied menu. For further details consult the Hotel Groups page.
ROOMS: 42 en suite s £46.95-£48.95; d £46.95-£48.95

⊗ No smoking

TAPLOW, Buckinghamshire Map 06 SU98

Top Hotel

★★★★★ ®®® Cliveden
SL6 0JF
☎ 01628 668561 ▯ 01628 661837
e-mail: reservations@clivedenhouse.co.uk
web: www.vonessenhotels.co.uk
Dir: *M4 junct 7, follow A4 towards Maidenhead for 1.5 miles, turn onto B476 towards Taplow, 2.5 miles, hotel on left*
This wonderful stately home stands at the top of a gravelled boulevard. Visitors are treated as house-guests and staff recapture the tradition of fine hospitality. Bedrooms have individual quality and style, and reception rooms retain a timeless elegance. Both restaurants here are awarded AA rosettes - The Terrace with its delightful views has two rosettes, and Waldo's, offering innovative menus in discreet, luxurious surroundings, has three. Exceptional leisure facilities include cruises along Cliveden Reach and massages in the Pavilion.
ROOMS: 39 en suite (8 GF) ⊗ in 12 bedrooms d £225-£950 (incl. bkfst) **LB FACILITIES:** STV Squash Snooker Sauna Solarium Gym Jacuzzi Full range of beauty treatments at the Pavilion Spa, 3 vintage launches ♫ Xmas **CONF:** Thtr 40 Board 24 **SERVICES:** Lift **PARKING:** 60 **NOTES:** ⊗ in restaurant Civ Wed

★★★70% ®® Taplow House Hotel
Berry Hill SL6 0DA
☎ 01628 670056 ▯ 01628 773625
e-mail: reception@taplow.wrensgroup.com
web: www.wrensgroup.com
Dir: *off A4 onto Berry Hill, hotel 0.5m on right*

This elegant Georgian manor is set amid beautiful gardens and has been skilfully restored. Character public rooms are pleasing and include a number of air-conditioned conference rooms and

continued

an elegant restaurant. Comfortable bedrooms are individually decorated and furnished to a high standard.
ROOMS: 32 en suite (4 fmly) ⊗ in all bedrooms s £85-£135; d £95-£145 **LB FACILITIES:** STV ⓘ Putt green Xmas **CONF:** Thtr 100 Class 45 Board 40 Del from £175 **SERVICES:** air con **PARKING:** 100 **NOTES:** ✱ ⊗ in restaurant Civ Wed 80

TARPORLEY, Cheshire
Map 15 SJ56

★★★70% Swan
50 High St CW6 0AG
☎ 01829 733838 📠 01829 732932
Dir: *M56 junct 10, follow A49 signed Whitchurch*
Dating back to the 16th century, The Swan is situated in the heart of the village and is very popular with locals. Bedrooms, found in the main house and an adjacent converted coaching house, are appointed to a high standard. Public areas are full of charm and character and include a restaurant where guests can enjoy excellent cooking.
ROOMS: 10 en suite 6 annexe en suite (3 fmly) ⊗ in all bedrooms
FACILITIES: Xmas **CONF:** Thtr 65 Class 40 Board 25 **PARKING:** 26
NOTES: ⊗ in restaurant Closed 25 Dec evening

★★★68% The Wild Boar
Whitchurch Rd, Beeston CW6 9NW
☎ 01829 260309 📠 01829 261081
e-mail: wildboarpop@hotmail.com
Dir: *turn off A51 Nantwich/Chester road onto A49 to Whitchurch at Red Fox pub lights, hotel on left at brow of hill after about 1.5m*
This 17th-century, half-timbered former hunting lodge has been extended over the years to create a smart, spacious hotel with comfortable bedrooms and stylish public areas. Guests can choose between the elegant Tower Restaurant or the more informal Stables Grill. The hotel is a popular venue for meetings, functions and weddings, and offers impressive conference facilities.
ROOMS: 37 en suite (20 fmly) ⊗ in 23 bedrooms **FACILITIES:** ⬆ 18 Putt green Xmas **CONF:** Thtr 100 Class 40 Board 40 **PARKING:** 70 **NOTES:** ⊗ in restaurant Civ Wed 100

★★★68% Willington Hall
Willington CW6 0NB
☎ 01829 752321 📠 01829 752596
e-mail: enquiries@willingtonhall.co.uk
web: www.willingtonhall.co.uk
Dir: *3m NW off unclass road linking A51 & A54, at Clotton turn off A51 at Bulls Head, then follow signs*

Situated in 17 acres of parkland and built in 1829, this attractively furnished country-house hotel offers spacious bedrooms, many with views over open countryside. Service is courteous and friendly, and freshly prepared meals are offered in the dining room or adjacent bar and drawing room. A smart function suite

continued

confirms the popularity of this hotel as a premier venue for weddings and conferences.
ROOMS: 10 en suite s £70; d £110-£120 (incl. bkfst) **LB**
FACILITIES: STV Fishing Riding ⓘ **CONF:** Thtr 160 Class 80 Board 50 Del £120 **PARKING:** 60 **NOTES:** ⊗ in restaurant Closed 25 & 26 Dec Civ Wed 100

TAUNTON, Somerset
Map 04 ST22

Top Hotel

★★★ ◉◉◉ Castle
Castle Green TA1 1NF
☎ 01823 272671 📠 01823 336066
e-mail: reception@the-castle-hotel.com
web: www.the-castle-hotel.com
Dir: *from M5 junct 25/26 follow signs to town centre & hotel*
The wisteria covered Castle has been owned and run by the same family for over half a century and, with its Norman keep, is a landmark in the centre of the town. Much thought has gone into furnishing the bedrooms and public areas, ensuring guest comfort while retaining the character and endearing charm of the original building. Renowned for its interpretation of classic British dishes in the elegant restaurant, this hotel also offers a lively, modern brasserie for less formal dining.
ROOMS: 44 en suite s £129-£235; d £211-£300 (incl. bkfst) **LB**
FACILITIES: Xmas **CONF:** Thtr 100 Class 40 Board 40 Del £185
SERVICES: Lift **PARKING:** 50 **NOTES:** ⊗ in restaurant

★★★73% ◉◉ The Mount Somerset
Lower Henlade TA3 5NB
☎ 01823 442500 📠 01823 442900
e-mail: Info@mountsomersethotel.co.uk
web: www.vonessenhotels.co.uk
Dir: *M5 junct 25, take A358 towards Chard/Ilminster, at Henlade right into Stoke Rd, left at T-junct at end, then right into drive*
From its elevated and rural position, this impressive Regency house has wonderful views over Taunton Vale. Some of the well-appointed bedrooms have feature bathrooms, and the elegant public rooms are stylish with an intimate atmosphere. In addition to the daily-changing, fixed-price menu, a carefully selected seasonal carte is available in the restaurant.
ROOMS: 11 en suite (1 fmly) s £105-£120; d £135-£220 (incl. bkfst) **LB**
FACILITIES: ⓘ Xmas **CONF:** Thtr 60 Class 30 Board 20 Del from £175
SERVICES: Lift **PARKING:** 100 **NOTES:** ⊗ in restaurant Civ Wed 60

> The vast majority of establishments in this guide accept credit and debit cards. We indicate those that don't take any

TAUNTON, continued

★★★73% **Rumwell Manor**
Rumwell TA4 1EL
☎ 01823 461902 🖹 01823 254861
e-mail: reception@rumwellmanor.co.uk
Dir: *M5 junct 26 follow signs to Wellington, turn right onto A38 to Taunton, hotel is 3m on right*

A countryside location, surrounded by lovingly tended gardens, Rumwell Manor provides easy access to Taunton and the M5. Bedrooms vary in style, with those in the main house offering greater space and character. A selection of freshly prepared dishes is served in the restaurant. In addition to the cosy bar and adjacent lounge, several meeting/conference rooms are available.
ROOMS: 10 en suite 10 annexe en suite (3 fmly) (6 GF) ⊗ in 6 bedrooms s £69-£94; d £104-£124 (incl. bkfst) **LB** **FACILITIES:** Xmas **CONF:** BC Thtr 40 Class 24 Board 26 Del from £114 **PARKING:** 40 **NOTES:** ✈ ⊗ in restaurant Civ Wed 50

★★★67% ◎ ***Corner House Hotel***
Park St TA1 4DQ
☎ 01823 284683 🖹 01823 323464
e-mail: res@corner-house.co.uk
web: www.corner-house.co.uk
Dir: *0.3m from centre of Taunton. Hotel on junct of Park Street & A38 Wellington Road*
The unusual Victorian façade of the Corner House, with its turrets and stained glass windows, belies a wealth of innovation, quality and style. The contemporary bedrooms are equipped with state-of-the-art facilities but also offer traditional comforts. Informality and exceptional value for money are the hallmark of the smart public areas, which include Bistro 4DQ - a relaxed place to eat good food.
ROOMS: 28 en suite (12 fmly) (1 GF) ⊗ in 20 bedrooms **CONF:** Thtr 60 Class 10 Board 35 **PARKING:** 40 **NOTES:** ✈

Packed in a hurry? Ironing facilities should be available at all star levels, either in the rooms or on request

★★79% ◎◎ **Farthings Hotel & Restaurant**
Hatch Beauchamp TA3 6SG
☎ 01823 480664 🖹 01823 481118
e-mail: farthing1@aol.com
web: www.farthingshotel.com
Dir: *from A358, between Taunton and Ilminster turn into Hatch Beauchamp for hotel in village centre*
This delightful family run hotel, set in its own extensive gardens in a peaceful village location, offers comfortable accommodation, combined with all the character and charm of a building dating back over 200 years. The atmosphere is traditionally classic and calm. Dinner service is attentive and menus feature best quality local ingredients prepared and presented with care.

ROOMS: 10 en suite (2 fmly) (1 GF) ⊗ in all bedrooms s £75-£90; d £105-£135 (incl. bkfst) **LB** **FACILITIES:** Xmas **CONF:** BC Thtr 30 Board 20 Del £140 **PARKING:** 22 **NOTES:** ⊗ in restaurant

⌂ **Premier Travel Inn Taunton Central (North)**
Massingham Park TA2 7RX
☎ 08701 977 293 🖹 01823 422350
web: www.premiertravelinn.com
High quality, modern budget accommodation ideal for both families and business travellers. Spacious, en suite bedrooms feature bath and shower, satellite TV and many have telephones and modem points. The adjacent family restaurant features a wide and varied menu. For further details consult the Hotel Groups page.
ROOMS: 40 en suite s £49.95-£52.95; d £49.95-£52.95

⌂ **Premier Travel Inn Taunton East**
81 Bridgwater Rd TA1 2DU
☎ 08701 977249 🖹 01823 322054
web: www.premiertravelinn.com
Dir: *M5 junct 25 follow signs to Taunton over 1st rdbt & keep left at Creech Castle traffic lights, Inn 200yds on right*
High quality, modern budget accommodation ideal for both families and business travellers. Spacious, en suite bedrooms feature bath and shower, satellite TV and many have telephones and modem points. The adjacent family restaurant features a wide and varied menu. For further details consult the Hotel Groups page.
ROOMS: 40 en suite s £49.95; d £49.95

⌂ **Premier Travel Inn Taunton (Ruishton)**
Ilminster Rd, Ruishton TA3 5LU
☎ 0870 9906534 🖹 0870 9906535
web: www.premiertravelinn.com
Dir: *Just off M5 junct 25 on A38*
High quality, modern budget accommodation ideal for both families and business travellers. Spacious, en suite bedrooms feature bath and shower, satellite TV and many have telephones and modem points. The adjacent family restaurant features a wide and varied menu. For further details consult the Hotel Groups page.
ROOMS: 38 en suite s £46.95-£49.95; d £46.95-£49.95

⌂ **Travelodge**
Riverside Retail Park, Hankridge Farm TA1 2LR
☎ 08700 850 950 🖹 01823 444704
web: www.travelodge.co.uk
Dir: *M5 junct 25*
Travelodge offers good quality, good value, modern accommodation. Ideal for families, the spacious, en suite bedrooms include remote-control TV, tea and coffee-making facilities and comfortable beds. Meals can be taken at the nearby family restaurant. For further details consult the Hotel Groups page.
ROOMS: 48 en suite s fr £26; d fr £26

TAUNTON DEANE MOTORWAY SERVICE AREA (M5), Somerset — Map 04 ST12

Premier Travel Inn Taunton Deane
Trull TA3 7PF
☎ 08701 977250 📠 01823 338131
web: www.premiertravelinn.com
Dir: *M5 southbound between junct 25 & 26*
High quality, modern budget accommodation ideal for both families and business travellers. Spacious, en suite bedrooms feature bath and shower, satellite TV and many have telephones and modem points. The adjacent family restaurant features a wide and varied menu. For further details consult the Hotel Groups page.
ROOMS: 39 en suite s £46.95-£48.95; d £46.95-£48.95

TAVISTOCK, Devon — Map 03 SX47

A ★★★★ Browns Hotel, Brasserie & Wine Bar
80 West St PL19 8AQ
☎ 01822 618686 📠 01822 618646
e-mail: enquiries@brownsdevon.co.uk
web: www.brownsdevon.co.uk
Dir: *200mtrs from Pannier Market & Church*
ROOMS: 16 en suite 4 annexe en suite (1 fmly) **FACILITIES:** STV Gym Xmas **SERVICES:** Lift **PARKING:** 15 **NOTES:** No dogs; No smoking in restaurant

★★★64% Bedford
1 Plymouth Rd PL19 8BB
☎ 01822 613221 📠 01822 618034
e-mail: enquiries@bedford-hotel.co.uk
web: www.bedford-hotel.co.uk
Dir: *M5 junct 31 - Launceston/Okehampton A30. Take A386 to Tavistock, follow town centre signs. Hotel opposite church*

Built on the site of a Benedictine abbey, this impressive castellated building has been welcoming visitors for over 200 years. Very much a local landmark, the hotel offers comfortable and relaxing public areas, all reflecting charm and character throughout. Bedrooms are traditionally styled with contemporary comforts, whilst the Woburn Restaurant provides a refined setting for enjoyable cuisine.
ROOMS: 30 en suite (1 fmly) (5 GF) No smoking in 11 bedrooms s £60; d £120-£130 (incl. bkfst) **LB** **FACILITIES:** Xmas **CONF:** Thtr 70 Class 45 Board 25 Del from £120 **PARKING:** 45 **NOTES:** No smoking in restaurant

Late for dinner? Quality standards mean that last orders for dinner vary according to star rating and should be no earlier than:
★★ 7.00pm ★★★ 8:00pm ★★★★ 9:00pm ★★★★★ 10:00pm

TEBAY, Cumbria — Map 18 NY60

★★★72% Westmorland Hotel & Bretherdale Restaurant
Westmorland Place, Orton CA10 3SB
☎ 015396 24351 📠 015396 24354
e-mail: sales@westmorlandhotel.com
web: www.westmorlandhotel.com
Dir: *at N'bound service area between juncts 38 & 39 on M6. Accessible from S'bound service area*

With fine views over rugged moorland, this modern and friendly hotel is ideal for conferences and meetings. Bedrooms are spacious and comfortable, with the executive rooms particularly well equipped. Open-plan public areas provide a Tyrolean touch and include a split-level restaurant.
ROOMS: 50 en suite (18 fmly) (13 GF) No smoking in 30 bedrooms s fr £65; d fr £83 (incl. bkfst) **LB** **FACILITIES:** STV Xmas **CONF:** BC Thtr 75 Class 40 Board 30 Del from £105 **SERVICES:** Lift **PARKING:** 100 **NOTES:** No smoking in restaurant Civ Wed 80

See advert on this page

TEIGNMOUTH, Devon Map 03 SX97

★★★70% Ness House
Ness Dr, Shaldon TQ14 0HP
☎ 01626 873480
e-mail: nesshouse@talk21.com
web: www.nesshouse.co.uk
Dir: *M5 take A380 turn onto A381 to Teignmouth, cross bridge to Shaldon, hotel 0.5m on left on Torquay Rd*

Enjoying breathtaking views of the busy Teign Estuary, Ness House maintains much of its original charm. Friendly and attentive service is provided along with comfortable and well-equipped rooms; many boast balconies with sea views. A choice of dining in either the Terrace or Conservatory restaurants provides interesting dishes featuring fresh local produce and seafood from the Teign.
ROOMS: 7 en suite 5 annexe en suite (2 fmly) in all bedrooms s £60-£95; d £105-£130 (incl. bkfst) **LB** **FACILITIES:** STV **PARKING:** 20 **NOTES:** in restaurant Closed 24 & 25 Dec

TELFORD, Shropshire Map 10 SJ60
See also Worfield

★★★73% **Best Western Valley Hotel**
TF8 7DW
☎ 01952 432247 01952 432308
e-mail: info@thevalleyhotel.co.uk
Dir: *M6, M54 junct 6 onto A5223 to Ironbridge*
This privately owned hotel is situated in attractive gardens, close to the famous Iron Bridge. It was once the home of the Maws family who manufactured ceramic tiles, and fine examples of their craft are found throughout the house. Bedrooms vary in size and are split between the main house and a mews development and imaginative meals are served in the attractive Chez Maws restaurant
ROOMS: 35 en suite (2 fmly) (9 GF) in 18 bedrooms s £80-£110; d £90-£140 (incl. bkfst) **LB** **FACILITIES:** STV **CONF:** BC Thtr 200 Class 100 Board 60 Del from £110 **PARKING:** 100 **NOTES:** in restaurant RS 24 Dec-1 Jan Civ Wed 300

Early start?
Hotels at all star levels should provide in-room alarm clocks and/or alarm clocks

★★★70%
Clarion Hotel Madeley Court, Telford
Castlefields Way, Madeley TF7 5DW
☎ 01952 680068 01952 684275
e-mail: enquiries@hotels-telford.com
web: www.hotels-telford.com
Dir: *M54 junct 4, A464 onto A442, then A4169 (do not take turn for Madeley/Kidderminster A442). 1st left at rdbt on B4373*
This beautifully restored 16th-century manor house is set in extensive grounds and gardens. Bedrooms vary between character rooms and the newer annexe rooms. There are two wood-panelled lounges and the restaurant features a mix of old stone walls and modern colour themes. Facilities include a large self-contained banqueting suite and a lakeside bar.
ROOMS: 29 en suite 18 annexe en suite (1 fmly) (21 GF) in 16 bedrooms s £111; d £121 **LB** **FACILITIES:** STV Archery, Horse riding arranged Xmas **CONF:** Thtr 175 Class 100 Board 45 Del £149 **PARKING:** 180 **NOTES:** in restaurant Civ Wed 175

★★★68% **Hadley Park House**
Hadley Park TF1 6QJ
☎ 01952 677269 01952 676938
e-mail: info@hadleypark.co.uk

Located in Telford, but close to Ironbridge this elegant Georgian mansion is situated within three acres of its own grounds. Bedrooms are spacious and well equipped. There is a comfortable bar and lounge and meals are served in the attractive conservatory-style restaurant.
ROOMS: 12 en suite (3 fmly) in 5 bedrooms s £80-£100; d £95-£125 (incl. bkfst) **LB** **FACILITIES:** STV **CONF:** Thtr 90 Class 60 Board 40 Del from £115 **PARKING:** 40 **NOTES:** in restaurant Closed 24-26 Dec - 1-7 Jan Civ Wed 80

★★★66% **Telford Golf & Country Club**
Great Hay Dr, Sutton Heights TF7 4DT
☎ 01952 429977 01952 586602
e-mail: telfordcountryclub@corushotels.com
web: www.corushotels.com/telfordgolfandcountry
Dir: *M54 junct 4, A442 - Kidderminster, follow signs for Telford Golf Club*
A modern and much extended former farmhouse in an elevated situation. Comfortable bedrooms are located in several different wings, some have fine views of Ironbridge Gorge and others overlook the golf course. Guests can choose to dine in the

continued

brasserie or the more informal café. Extensive leisure facilities include the 18-hole golf course and large indoor swimming pool.

ROOMS: 95 en suite (16 fmly) (26 GF) ⊗ in 35 bedrooms s £35-£89; d £40-£89 **LB** **FACILITIES: Spa** 18 Squash Snooker Sauna Solarium Gym Putt green Jacuzzi Health & Beauty Golf driving range Xmas **CONF:** Thtr 250 Class 140 Board 60 Del from £90 **PARKING:** 200 **NOTES:** ⊗ in restaurant Civ Wed 100

Premier Travel Inn Telford

Euston Way TF3 4LY
☎ 08701 977251 01952 290742
web: www.premiertravelinn.com
Dir: *From M54 junct 5 follow signs for Central Railway Station. Inn at 2nd exit off rdbt*
High quality, modern budget accommodation ideal for both families and business travellers. Spacious, en suite bedrooms feature bath and shower, satellite TV and many have telephones and modem points. The adjacent family restaurant features a wide and varied menu. For further details consult the Hotel Groups page.
ROOMS: 60 en suite s £46.95-£49.95; d £46.95-£49.95 **CONF:** Thtr 30 Board 20

Travelodge

Whitchurch Dr, Shawbirch TF1 3QA
☎ 08700 850 950 01952 246534
web: www.travelodge.co.uk
Dir: *1m NW, on A5223 at junct of A442 & B5063*
Travelodge offers good quality, good value, modern accommodation. Ideal for families, the spacious, en suite bedrooms include remote-control TV, tea and coffee-making facilities and comfortable beds. Meals can be taken at the nearby family restaurant. For further details consult the Hotel Groups page.
ROOMS: 40 en suite s fr £26; d fr £26

TELFORD SERVICE AREA (M54), Shropshire — Map 10 SJ70

Days Inn Telford

Telford Services, Priorslee Rd TF11 8TG
☎ 01952 238400 01952 238410
e-mail: telford.hotel@welcomebreak.co.uk
web: www.welcomebreak.co.uk
Dir: *M54 junct 4*
This modern building offers accommodation in smart, spacious and well-equipped bedrooms, suitable for families and business travellers, and all with en suite bathrooms. Continental breakfast is *continued*

available and other refreshments may be taken at the nearby family restaurant. For further details see the Hotel Groups page.

ROOMS: 48 en suite s £39-£60; d £39-£60

TEMPLE SOWERBY, Cumbria — Map 18 NY62

★★★79% Temple Sowerby House Hotel & Restaurant

CA10 1RZ
☎ 017683 61578 017683 61958
e-mail: stay@templesowerby.com
web: www.templesowerby.com
Dir: *midway between Penrith and Appleby, 7m from M6 junct 40*
Set in the heart of the popular Eden Valley, this high quality hotel is perfectly located to explore both the Pennines and the Lake District. The original part of the building dates back to the 16th century and was the principal house of the village. Bedrooms are comfortable and stylish, and some include four-poster beds and ultra modern bathrooms. There is a choice of comfortable lounges and a conservatory overlooks a beautifully presented walled garden. Staff throughout are friendly and keen to please.
ROOMS: 8 en suite 4 annexe en suite (2 GF) ⊗ in all bedrooms s £80-£100; d £110-£145 (incl. bkfst) **LB** **FACILITIES:** **CONF:** Thtr 30 Class 20 Board 20 Del from £135 **PARKING:** 15 **NOTES:** No children 12yrs ⊗ in restaurant Closed 23-28 Dec Civ Wed 40

TENBURY WELLS, Worcestershire — Map 10 SO56

★★67% *Cadmore Lodge*

Berrington Green, St Michaels WR15 8TQ
☎ 01584 810044 01584 810044
e-mail: info@cadmorelodge.co.uk
web: www.cadmorelodge.co.uk
Dir: *Off A4112 for Berrington, hotel 0.75m on left*
Cadmore Lodge is situated in an idyllic rural location overlooking a private lake. On a 70-acre private estate that features a 9-hole golf course, two fishing lakes and with indoor leisure facilities, the hotel is also earning itself a well-deserved reputation for its food. The traditionally styled bedrooms have modern amenities, and a large function room with lake views is popular for weddings and special occasions.
ROOMS: 15 rms (14 en suite) (1 fmly) ⊗ in all bedrooms
FACILITIES: 9 Fishing Gym Jacuzzi Bowling green Steam room Nature reserve **CONF:** BC Thtr 100 Class 40 Board 20 **PARKING:** 100 **NOTES:** ⊗ in restaurant Civ Wed 160

T

TENBURY WELLS, continued

Restaurant with Rooms

The Peacock Inn
Worcester Rd WR15 8LL
☎ 01584 810506 🖷 01584 811236
web: www.thepeacockinn.com
Dir: *on A456 from Worcester follow A443 to Tenbury Wells. Inn 1.25m*
A warm welcome can be expected from resident proprietors at this 14th-century roadside inn, which has a wealth of original features such as wood panelling, beams and low ceilings. The atmospheric bar and restaurant are popular locally, and bedrooms are not only spacious and comfortable but are also usefully and thoughtfully equipped.
ROOMS: 4 en suite (1 fmly) (1 GF) ⊘ in all bedrooms **CONF:** Thtr 40 Class 30 Board 20 **PARKING:** 30 **NOTES:** ✗

TENTERDEN, Kent Map 07 TQ83

★★★75%
London Beach Hotel & Golf Club
Ashford Rd TN30 6HX
☎ 01580 766279 🖷 01580 763884
e-mail: enquiries@londonbeach.com
web: www.londonbeach.net
Dir: *M20 junct 9, A28 to Tenterden, right after 0.5. Hotel in 1m*
This purpose-built hotel is situated in mature grounds on the outskirts of Tenterden. The spacious bedrooms are smartly decorated, have co-ordinated soft furnishings and most rooms have balconies with superb views over the golf course. The open-plan public rooms feature a brasserie-style restaurant, where an interesting choice of dishes is served.
ROOMS: 26 en suite (2 fmly) ⊘ in 22 bedrooms s £65-£130; d £85-£135 **LB** **FACILITIES:** 9 Fishing Putt green Own 9 hole golf course Driving range Pitch 'n' putt ♫ Xmas **CONF:** Thtr 100 Class 75 Board 40 Del from £120 **SERVICES:** Lift **PARKING:** 100 **NOTES:** ✗ ⊘ in restaurant Civ Wed 100

TETBURY, Gloucestershire Map 04 ST89

Hotel of the Year
Top Hotel

★★★ **Calcot Manor**
Calcot GL8 8YJ
☎ 01666 890391 🖷 01666 890394
e-mail: reception@calcotmanor.co.uk
web: www.calcotmanor.co.uk
Dir: *3m West of Tetbury at junct A4135/A46*
Cistercian monks built the ancient barns and stables around which this lovely English farmhouse is set. No two rooms are identical, and each is beautifully decorated in a variety of styles and equipped with the contemporary comforts. Sumptuous sitting rooms, with crackling log fires in the winter, look out over immaculate gardens. There are two dining options: the elegant conservatory restaurant and the informal Gumstool Inn. There are also ample function rooms. A superb health and leisure spa includes an indoor pool, high-tech gym, massage tables, complementary therapies and much more. For children, a supervised crèche and 'playzone' are a great attraction. AA Hotel of the Year for England 2005-6.
ROOMS: 9 en suite 21 annexe en suite (10 fmly) s £160-£185; d £185-£360 (incl. bkfst) **LB** **FACILITIES: Spa** Sauna Solarium Gym Jacuzzi Clay pigeon shooting ch fac Xmas **CONF:** BC Thtr 100 Class 40 Board 35 Del £215 **PARKING:** 120 **NOTES:** ✗ ⊘ in restaurant Civ Wed 100

See advert on opposite page

★★★72% ***Close***
8 Long St GL8 8AQ
☎ 01666 502272 🖷 01666 504401
e-mail: reception@theclosehotel.co.uk
web: www.oldenglish.co.uk
Dir: *From M4 junct 17 onto A429 to Malmesbury, then follow Tetbury signs. Or M5 junct 14 onto B4509 follow signs to Tetbury*
Even with its town centre location, this charming hotel retains a country-house feel that has made this a favourite with many for years. Bedrooms are traditional and feature thoughtful touches such as home-made biscuits, fresh fruit and bottled water. The public rooms provide a choice of relaxing areas with log fires lit in the winter. In the summer, guests can enjoy the terrace in the attractive walled garden.
ROOMS: 15 en suite **FACILITIES:** STV **CONF:** Thtr 50 Board 22 **PARKING:** 22 **NOTES:** ⊘ in restaurant Civ Wed 50

★★★71% **Hare & Hounds**
Westonbirt GL8 8QL
☎ 01666 880233 & 881000 🖷 01666 880241
e-mail: reception@hareandhoundshotel.com
web: www.hareandhoundshotel.com
Dir: *2.5m SW of Tetbury on A433*

This popular hotel, set in extensive grounds, is situated close to Westonbirt Arboretum and has been run by the same family for 50 years. Staff are keen to help and public areas are charming, with polished parquet flooring, and bedrooms are traditional in style and located in both the main house and adjacent coach house. Leisure facilities include squash and tennis courts.
ROOMS: 24 en suite 7 annexe en suite (3 fmly) (5 GF) ⊘ in 12 bedrooms s £80-£88; d £100-£112 (incl. bkfst) **LB** **FACILITIES:** STV Squash Putt green Table tennis Half size snooker table ♫ Xmas **CONF:** Thtr 120 Class 80 Board 40 Del from £125 **PARKING:** 85 **NOTES:** ⊘ in restaurant Civ Wed 200

★★★70% Priory Inn Hotel
London Rd GL8 8JJ
☎ 01666 502251 ☐ 01666 503534
e-mail: info@theprioryinn.co.uk
web: www.theprioryinn.co.uk
Dir: *on A433, Cirencester/Tetbury road 200yds from High St*
A warm welcome is guaranteed at this attractive inn where friendly service is a high priority to the team. Public areas and bedrooms have a contemporary style that mixes well with more traditional features, such as an open fireplace in the cosy bar dining room. Cuisine is a highlight of any stay, with locally sourced produce skilfully prepared.
ROOMS: 14 en suite (1 fmly) (4 GF) ⊗ in 7 bedrooms s fr £59; d fr £89 (incl. bkfst) **LB FACILITIES:** STV ♫ Xmas **CONF:** Thtr 30 Class 25 Board 20 Del from £125 **PARKING:** 35 **NOTES:** ✈

★★★69% Snooty Fox
Market Place GL8 8DD
☎ 01666 502436 ☐ 01666 503479
e-mail: res@snooty-fox.co.uk
web: www.snooty-fox.co.uk
Dir: *in town centre*
Centrally situated, the Snooty Fox is a popular venue for weekend breaks, and retains many of the historic features associated with a 16th-century coaching inn. The atmosphere is relaxed and friendly, the accommodation of a high standard, and the food offered in the bar and restaurant is another good reason why many guests return.
ROOMS: 12 en suite ⊗ in 2 bedrooms s £73-£93; d £95-£139 (incl. bkfst) **LB FACILITIES:** Xmas **CONF:** Thtr 24 Class 12 Board 16 Del £112 **NOTES:** ✈ ⊗ in restaurant

★★72% Ormonds Head
23 Long St GL8 8AA
☎ 01666 505690 & 505828 ☐ 01666 505956
e-mail: reservations@ormondshead.com
web: www.ormondshead.com
Dir: *Turn off A433 from Cirencester into Long St. Hotel approx 100yds on left*

Charming, rural, pretty all describe this market town hotel. Bedrooms are fresh, with simple attractive decor and lots of character. Meals can be taken in the informal bar or in the restaurant; staff throughout are friendly and attentive.
ROOMS: 14 en suite (3 fmly) ⊗ in all bedrooms s £50-£60; d £85-£130 (incl. bkfst) **LB FACILITIES:** ♫ Xmas **CONF:** Thtr 50 Board 20 Del from £110.50 **PARKING:** 6 **NOTES:** ✈ ⊗ in restaurant

⊗ No smoking

TEWKESBURY, Gloucestershire Map 10 SO83

★★★69% The Tewkesbury Park Hotel Golf & Country Club

Lincoln Green Ln GL20 7DN
☎ 0870 609 6101 ▤ 01684 292386
e-mail: tewkesburypark@corushotels.com
web: www.corushotels.com
Dir: M5 junct 9/A438 through Tewkesbury, A38 passing Abbey on left, turn
right into Lincoln Green Lane

Only two miles from the M5, this extended 18th-century manor house boasts wonderful views across the Malvern Hills from its hilltop position. Bedrooms offer contemporary comforts and many have the added bonus of countryside views. In addition to the well-established golf course, an indoor pool, gym, sauna, squash and tennis courts are also available.

ROOMS: 80 en suite (8 fmly) (21 GF) ⊗ in 58 bedrooms s £86-£136;
d £92-£173 (incl. bkfst & dinner) **LB FACILITIES:** STV ☒ supervised ⅃
18 ♋ Squash Sauna Solarium Gym Putt green Jacuzzi Activity field, 6 hole pitch & put Xmas **CONF:** Thtr 150 Class 100 Board 50 Del £149
PARKING: 250 **NOTES:** ⊗ in restaurant Civ Wed 100

★★★60% Royal Hop Pole

Church St GL20 5RT
☎ 01684 293236 ▤ 01684 296680
e-mail: info@theroyalhoppolehotel.co.uk
web: www.theroyalhoppole.co.uk
Dir: M5 junct 9 for Tewkesbury approx 1.5m. At War Memorial rdbt,
straight across, hotel on right

This former coaching inn is within walking distance of historic Tewkesbury Abbey and has been offering a warm welcome to weary travellers since the 14th century. There is character in abundance here with many original features including age darkened beams and sloping floors. Bedrooms have great individuality some being in the main house, others in the more recent garden wing. Additional facilities include a popular bar, attractive restaurant and relaxing lounge.

ROOMS: 29 en suite (1 fmly) (5 GF) ⊗ in 20 bedrooms s £45-£55;
d £70-£100 (incl. bkfst) **FACILITIES:** Xmas **CONF:** Board 34 Del £120
PARKING: 35 **NOTES:** ⊗ in restaurant

★★65% Bell

57 Church St GL20 5SA
☎ 01684 293293 ▤ 01684 295938
e-mail: 6408@greeneking.co.uk
web: www.oldenglish.co.uk
Dir: on A38 in town centre opposite Abbey

OLD ENGLISH INNS

This 14th-century former coaching house is situated on the edge of the town, opposite the Norman abbey. The bar and lounge are

continued

the focal point of this atmospheric and friendly establishment, with a large open fire providing warmth. Bedrooms offer good levels of comfort and quality with many extra facilities provided, such as CD players.

ROOMS: 24 en suite (1 fmly) ⊗ in 5 bedrooms **CONF:** Thtr 50 Class 15 Board 20 **PARKING:** 35 **NOTES:** ⊁ ⊗ in restaurant

⌂ Premier Travel Inn Tewkesbury Central

Shannon Way, Ashchurch GL20 8RD
☎ 08708 501845
web: www.premiertravelinn.com

High quality, modern budget accommodation ideal for both families and business travellers. Spacious, en suite bedrooms feature bath and shower, satellite TV and many have telephones and modem points. The adjacent family restaurant features a wide and varied menu. For further details consult the Hotel Groups page.

ROOMS: s £46.95-£49.95; d £46.95-£49.95

⌂ Sleep Inn Tewkesbury

Off Shannon Way, Ashchurch GL20 8BL
☎ 01684 853090 & 853097 ▤ 01684 853099
e-mail: enquiries@hotels-tewkesbury.com
Dir: From M5 junct 9 take A438 to Tewkesbury. Right at 1st lights into
Shannon Way, then 1st right again

This modern, purpose built accommodation offers smartly appointed, well-equipped bedrooms, with good power showers. There is a choice of adjacent food outlets where guests may enjoy breakfast, snacks and meals.

ROOMS: 71 en suite s £62.50-£69.50; d £62-£69 **CONF:** Thtr 40 Class 16 Board 12 Del from £100

THAME, Oxfordshire Map 05 SP70

★★★74% ⊛ Spread Eagle

Cornmarket OX9 2BW
☎ 01844 213661 ▤ 01844 261380
e-mail: enquiries@spreadeaglethame.co.uk
web: www.spreadeaglethame.co.uk
Dir: on A418 Oxford to Aylesbury Road, M40 junct 6 S, junct 8 N

This former coaching inn, which is privately owned, is set on the main thoroughfare of this delightful market town. Well-equipped bedrooms vary in size and style, with some located in the extension. Public areas include a comfortable bar and the informal Fothergills Brasserie, named after the diarist and raconteur who owned the hotel in the 1920s. The hotel offers an extensive range of banqueting facilities.

ROOMS: 33 en suite (1 fmly) s £97.95-£105.95; d £112.95-£132.95 (incl. bkfst) **LB FACILITIES:** Xmas **CONF:** Thtr 250 Class 100 Board 50
PARKING: 80 **NOTES:** ⊁ ⊗ in restaurant Civ Wed 200

⌂ Travelodge
OX9 7XA
☎ 08700 850 950 🖷 01844 218740
web: www.travelodge.co.uk
Dir: *A418/B4011*

Travelodge offers good quality, good value, modern accommodation. Ideal for families, the spacious, en suite bedrooms include remote-control TV, tea and coffee-making facilities and comfortable beds. Meals can be taken at the nearby family restaurant. For further details consult the Hotel Groups page.
ROOMS: 31 en suite s fr £26; d fr £26

THAXTED, Essex — Map 12 TL63

★★69% Thaxted Hall
CM6 2RE
☎ 01371 830129 🖷 01371 830835
e-mail: reservations@thaxtedhall.co.uk
Dir: *B184/B1051 junct, 0.25m from town centre towards Saffron Walden*
Expect a warm welcome at this privately owned hotel set amid two acres of attractive landscaped grounds and within easy driving distance of Stansted Airport. Bedrooms are pleasantly decorated with co-ordinated soft furnishings and have many thoughtful touches. Public rooms include a smart lounge and a cosy breakfast room with individual tables.
ROOMS: 8 en suite (3 fmly) ⊘ in all bedrooms s £59-£79; d £69-£89 (incl. bkfst) **FACILITIES:** ch fac Xmas **CONF:** BC Thtr 150 Class 70 Board 40 **PARKING:** 50 **NOTES:** ✗ ⊘ in restaurant Civ Wed 150

THETFORD, Norfolk — Map 13 TL88

See also Brandon (Suffolk)

★★65% The Thomas Paine Hotel
White Hart St IP24 1AA
☎ 01842 755631 🖷 01842 766505
e-mail: bookings@thomaspainehotel.com
Dir: *N'bound on A11, at rdbt immediately before Thetford take A1075, hotel on right on approach to town*
This Grade II listed building is situated close to the town centre and Thetford Forest Park is just a short drive away. Public rooms include a large lounge bar and a pleasantly-appointed restaurant. Bedrooms vary in size and style; each one is attractively decorated and thoughtfully equipped.
ROOMS: 13 en suite (2 fmly) ⊘ in 5 bedrooms s £50-£55; d £60 (incl. bkfst) **LB** **FACILITIES:** Xmas **CONF:** Thtr 70 Class 35 Board 30 **PARKING:** 30 **NOTES:** ⊘ in restaurant

THIRSK, North Yorkshire — Map 19 SE48

★★75% Golden Fleece
42 Market Place YO7 1LL
☎ 01845 523108 🖷 01845 523996
e-mail: goldenfleece@bestwestern.co.uk
Dir: *off A19 to Thirsk, into town centre*
This delightful hotel began life as a coaching inn, and enjoys a central location in the market square. Bedrooms are comfortably furnished, extremely well equipped and individually styled with beautiful soft furnishings. Guests can eat in the attractive bar, or choose more formal dining in the smart restaurant where they are guaranteed friendly, attentive service.
ROOMS: 23 en suite (3 fmly) ⊘ in 4 bedrooms s £55-£65; d £70-£85 (incl. bkfst) **LB** **FACILITIES:** STV Xmas **CONF:** Thtr 75 Class 20 Board 30 Del from £95 **PARKING:** 35 **NOTES:** ⊘ in restaurant Civ Wed 70

Town House Hotel
Country House Hotel
⌂ Travel Accommodation

T

THORNBURY, Gloucestershire Map 04 ST69

Top Hotel

★★★ ®® **Thornbury Castle**
Castle St BS35 1HH
☎ 01454 281182 🖷 01454 416188
e-mail: info@thornburycastle.co.uk
web: www.vonessenhotels.co.uk
Dir: *on A38 N'bound from Bristol take 1st turn to Thornbury. At end of High St left into Castle St, follow brown sign, entrance to Castle on left behind St Marys Church*

Henry VIII ordered the first owner of this castle to be beheaded! Guests today have the opportunity of sleeping in historical surroundings fitted out with all modern amenities. Most rooms have four-poster or coronet beds and real fires. Tranquil lounges enjoy views over the gardens, while elegant, wood-panelled dining rooms make a memorable setting for a leisurely award-winning meal.

ROOMS: 25 en suite (3 fmly) (3 GF) s £80-£375; d £140-£375 (incl. bkfst) **LB** **FACILITIES:** STV Snooker Hot air ballooning, archery, helicopter ride, clay pigeon shooting Xmas **CONF:** Thtr 70 Class 40 Board 30 Del from £250 **PARKING:** 40 **NOTES:** ⊗ in restaurant Civ Wed 70

★★66% **Thornbury Golf Lodge**
Bristol Rd BS35 3XL
☎ 01454 281144 🖷 01454 281177
e-mail: info@thornburygc.co.uk
web: www.thornburygc.co.uk
Dir: *M5 junct 16 take A38 Thornbury. At traffic lights (Berkeley Vale Motors) take left. Entrance 1m on left*

The old farmhouse exterior of Thornbury Golf Lodge disguises an interior with spacious, well equipped and comfortable bedrooms. Many have pleasant views over the centre's two golf courses or towards the Severn Estuary. Meals are taken in the adjacent clubhouse which features a full bar and serves a range of hot and cold food all day.

ROOMS: 11 en suite (7 GF) s £50; d £60 **LB** **FACILITIES:** STV ⛳ 18 Putt green **CONF:** Thtr 100 Class 40 Board 40 **PARKING:** 150 **NOTES:** ✗ No children 5yrs

THORNE, South Yorkshire Map 17 SE61

★★★64% **Belmont**
Horsefair Green DN8 5EE
☎ 01405 812320 🖷 01405 740508
e-mail: belmonthotel@aol.com
Dir: *M18 junct 6 A614 signed Thorne. Hotel on right of Market Place*

This privately owned, smartly appointed hotel enjoys a prime location in the centre of town. Bedrooms vary in size and style and are all extremely well equipped for both business and leisure guests. Public areas include the popular Belmont Bar offering a good range of meals and snacks at both lunch and dinner, and the more formal restaurant and cocktail bar.

ROOMS: 23 en suite (3 fmly) (5 GF) ⊗ in 5 bedrooms s £79-£82; d £90-£115 (incl. bkfst) **LB** **FACILITIES:** STV Putt green **CONF:** Thtr 60 Class 20 Board 25 Del from £66.50 **PARKING:** 30 **NOTES:** Closed 24-28 Dec, 1 Jan

THORNHAM, Norfolk Map 12 TF74

★★69% ® **Lifeboat Inn**
Ship Ln PE36 6LT
☎ 01485 512236 🖷 01485 512323
e-mail: reception@lifeboatinn.co.uk
web: www.lifeboatinn.co.uk
Dir: *follow coast road from Hunstanton A149 for approx 6m and take 1st left after Thornham sign*

This 16th-century smugglers' alehouse enjoys superb views across open meadows to Thornham Harbour, and many of the tastefully decorated bedrooms enjoy these views. The public rooms have a wealth of character and feature open fireplaces, exposed brickwork and oak beams. The restaurant serves traditional country fare.

ROOMS: 13 en suite (3 fmly) (1 GF) ⊗ in all bedrooms s £59-£76; d £78-£112 (incl. bkfst) **LB** **FACILITIES:** Xmas **CONF:** Thtr 50 Class 30 Board 30 **PARKING:** 120 **NOTES:** ⊗ in restaurant

THORNTON HOUGH, Merseyside Map 15 SJ38

★★★★70% ®
Thornton Hall Hotel and Health Club
CLASSIC BRITISH
Neston Rd CH63 1JF
☎ 0151 336 3938 🖷 0151 336 7864
e-mail: reservations@thorntonhallhotel.com
web: www.thorntonhallhotel.com
Dir: *M53 junct 4 take B5151 Neston onto B5136 to Thornton Hough*

Dating back to the mid 1800s, this country-house hotel has been carefully extended and restored. Public areas include an impressive leisure spa boasting excellent facilities, a choice of restaurants and a spacious bar. Bedrooms vary in style and include feature rooms in the main house and more contemporary rooms in the garden wing. Delightful grounds and gardens and impressive function facilities make this a popular wedding venue.

ROOMS: 63 en suite (6 fmly) (28 GF) ⊗ in 36 bedrooms s £115; d £115 **LB** **FACILITIES: Spa** STV Sauna Solarium Gym Jacuzzi Hot tub Beauty Spa Hairdressing salon **CONF:** BC Thtr 435 Class 225 Board 80 Del £160 **PARKING:** 250 **NOTES:** ⊗ in restaurant Civ Wed 400

THORNTON WATLASS, North Yorkshire Map 19 SE28

★69% *Buck Inn*
HG4 4AH
☎ 01677 422461 📠 01677 422447
e-mail: buckwatlass@btconnect.com
Dir: *A684 towards Bedale, B6268 towards Masham, after 2m turn right at x-roads to Thornton Watlass, hotel is by Cricket Green*

This traditional country inn is situated on the edge of the village green overlooking the cricket pitch. Cricket prints and old photographs are found throughout and an open fire in the bar adds to the warm and intimate atmosphere. Wholesome lunches and dinners are served in the bar or dining room from an extensive menu. Bedrooms are brightly decorated and well equipped.
ROOMS: 7 rms (5 en suite) (1 fmly) (1 GF) **FACILITIES:** Fishing Quoits Childrens play area ♫ **CONF:** Thtr 70 Class 40 Board 30 **PARKING:** 10 **NOTES:** ⊗ in restaurant Closed 24 & 25 Dec for accommodation

THORPE (DOVEDALE), Derbyshire Map 16 SK15

★★★77% ® Izaak Walton
Dovedale DE6 2AY
☎ 01335 350555 📠 01335 350539
e-mail: reception@izaakwaltonhotel.com
web: www.izaakwalton-hotel.com
Dir: *A515 on B5054, follow road to Thorpe village, continue straight over cattle grid & 2 small bridges, take 1st right & sharp left*

This hotel is peacefully situated, with magnificent views over the valley of Dovedale to Thorpe Cloud. Many of the bedrooms have lovely views, and 'executive' rooms are particularly spacious. Meals are served in the bar area, with more formal dining in the Haddon restaurant. Staff are friendly and efficient. Fishing on the River Dove can be arranged.
ROOMS: 34 en suite (6 fmly) (7 GF) ⊗ in 28 bedrooms s £100-£110; d £135-£175 (incl. bkfst) **LB** **FACILITIES:** STV Fly fishing on nearby River Dove Xmas **CONF:** Thtr 50 Class 40 Board 30 Del from £145 **PARKING:** 80 **NOTES:** ⊗ in restaurant Civ Wed 80

See advert under ASHBOURNE

★★★67% *The Peveril of the Peak*
DE6 2AW
☎ 01335 350396 📠 01335 350507
e-mail: frontdesk@peverilofthepeak.co.uk
web: www.peverilofthepeak.co.uk
Dir: *Ashbourne A515 towards Buxton, after 1m turn left to Thorpe, approx. 4m on right just before Thorpe Village.*

Dating back to the 1830s, the hotel takes its name from one of Sir Walter Scott's heroic novels. It is set in 11 acres of grounds and surrounded by the quitessentially English countryside of the Derbyshire Dales. Most rooms overlook the gardens and many have patios. There are lounges, meeting rooms, a cosy cocktail bar and a conservatory restaurant.
ROOMS: 46 en suite (16 fmly) (6 GF) ⊗ in 30 bedrooms
FACILITIES: STV ch fac **CONF:** Thtr 70 Class 40 Board 30
PARKING: 80 **NOTES:** ⊗ in restaurant Civ Wed 60

See advert under ASHBOURNE

THORPE MARKET, Norfolk Map 13 TG23

★★74% ® Elderton Lodge Hotel & Langtry Restaurant
Gunton Park NR11 8TZ
☎ 01263 833547 📠 01263 834673
e-mail: enquiries@eldertonlodge.co.uk
web: www.eldertonlodge.co.uk
Dir: *at North Walsham take A149 towards Cromer, hotel in 3m on left, just prior to entering Thorpe Market*

Ideally placed for touring the north Norfolk coastline, this delightful former shooting lodge is set amidst six acres of mature gardens adjacent to Gunton Hall estate. The individually decorated bedrooms are tastefully furnished and thoughtfully equipped. Public rooms include a smart lounge bar, an elegant restaurant and a sunny conservatory breakfast room.
ROOMS: 11 en suite (2 fmly) (2 GF) ⊗ in all bedrooms s £60-£70; d £95-£115 (incl. bkfst) **LB** **FACILITIES:** Xmas **CONF:** BC **PARKING:** 50 **NOTES:** No children 6yrs ⊗ in restaurant

THORPE MARKET, continued

★★67% *Green Farm Restaurant & Hotel*
North Walsham Rd NR11 8TH
☎ 01263 833602 Fax 01263 833163
e-mail: grfarmh@aol.com
web: www.greenfarmhotel.co.uk
Dir: *Turn right off A140 Norwich to Cromer road at Roughton, beside fish and chip shop. 1.5m to 'Give Way' sign, turn right, hotel 200yds on left in village centre*
Attractive flint-faced, 16th-century inn situated just a short drive from Cromer. Bedrooms are located in two courtyard style wings adjacent to the main building; each one is tastefully furnished in pine and has co-ordinated fabrics. Public rooms include a popular restaurant, a comfortable lounge bar, an informal dining area and a function suite.
ROOMS: 5 en suite 9 annexe en suite (1 fmly) **CONF:** Thtr 50 Class 40 Board 100 **PARKING:** 50 **NOTES:** ⊗ in restaurant Civ Wed 50

THORPENESS, Suffolk Map 13 TM45

★★★70% Thorpeness Hotel
Lakeside Av IP16 4NH
☎ 01728 452176 Fax 01728 453868
e-mail: info@thorpeness.co.uk
web: www.thorpeness.co.uk
Dir: *A1094 towards Aldeburgh then take coast road N for 2m*

Ideally situated in an unspoilt, tranquil setting close to Aldeburgh and Snape Maltings. The extensive public rooms include a choice of lounges, a restaurant, a smart bar, a snooker room and clubhouse. The spacious bedrooms are pleasantly decorated, tastefully furnished and equipped with modern facilities. An 18-hole golf course and tennis courts are also available.
ROOMS: 30 annexe en suite (10 fmly) (10 GF) ⊗ in all bedrooms s £72-£96; d £84-£132 (incl. bkfst) **LB** **FACILITIES:** 18 Fishing Snooker Putt green Xmas **CONF:** Thtr 50 Class 30 Board 24 Del £100 **PARKING:** 60 **NOTES:** ⊗ in restaurant Civ Wed

THRAPSTON, Northamptonshire Map 11 SP97

Travelodge
Thrapston Bypass NN14 4UR
☎ 08700 850 950 Fax 01832 735199
web: www.travelodge.co.uk
Dir: *on A14 link road A1/M1*
Travelodge offers good quality, good value, modern accommodation. Ideal for families, the spacious, en suite bedrooms include remote-control TV, tea and coffee-making facilities and comfortable beds. Meals can be taken at the nearby family restaurant. For further details consult the Hotel Groups page.
ROOMS: 40 en suite s fr £26; d fr £26

THRUSSINGTON, Leicestershire Map 11 SK61

Travelodge Leicester North
LE7 8TF
☎ 08700 850 950 Fax 0870 1911584
web: www.travelodge.co.uk
Dir: *on A46, southbound*
Travelodge offers good quality, good value, modern accommodation. Ideal for families, the spacious, en suite bedrooms include remote-control TV, tea and coffee-making facilities and comfortable beds. Meals can be taken at the nearby family restaurant. For further details consult the Hotel Groups page.
ROOMS: 32 en suite s fr £26; d fr £26

THURLESTONE, Devon Map 03 SX64

★★★★72% Thurlestone
TQ7 3NN
☎ 01548 560382 Fax 01548 561069
e-mail: enquiries@thurlestone.co.uk
web: www.thurlestone.co.uk
Dir: *A38 take A384 into Totnes, A381 towards Kingsbridge, onto A379 towards Churchstow, onto B3197 turn into lane signed to Thurlestone*
This perennially popular hotel has been in the same family-ownership since 1896. A range of indoor and outdoor leisure facilities provide something for everyone and wonderful views of the south Devon coast can be enjoyed from several vantage points, including many of the bedrooms, some of which also have balconies. Elegant public rooms are styled to ensure rest and relaxation.
ROOMS: 64 en suite (23 fmly) s £65-£168; d £130-£336 (incl. bkfst & dinner) **LB** **FACILITIES: Spa** STV supervised 9 Squash Snooker Sauna Solarium Gym Putt green Jacuzzi Badminton courts, games room, toddler room. ch fac Xmas **CONF:** Thtr 150 Class 100 Board 40 Del from £165 **SERVICES:** Lift **PARKING:** 121 **NOTES:** ⊗ in restaurant Closed 1-2 wks Jan Civ Wed

TIBSHELF MOTORWAY SERVICE AREA (M1), Derbyshire Map 16 SK46

Premier Travel Inn Mansfield (Tibshelf)
Tibshelf Motorway Service Area DE55 5TZ
☎ 08701 977181 Fax 01773 876609
web: www.premiertravelinn.com
Dir: *M1 northbound between junct 28/29, access available southbound*
High quality, modern budget accommodation ideal for both families and business travellers. Spacious, en suite bedrooms feature bath and shower, satellite TV and many have telephones and modem points. The adjacent family restaurant features a wide and varied menu. For further details consult the Hotel Groups page.
ROOMS: 40 en suite s £46.95-£48.95; d £46.95-£48.95

TICEHURST, East Sussex Map 06 TQ63

★★★★75% Dale Hill Hotel & Golf Club
TN5 7DQ
☎ 01580 200112 Fax 01580 201249
e-mail: info@dalehill.co.uk
web: www.dalehill.co.uk
Dir: *M25 junct 5/A21. 5m after Lamberhurst turn right at traffic lights onto B2087 to Flimwell. Hotel 1m on the left*
This modern hotel is situated just a short drive from the village. Extensive public rooms include a lounge bar, a conservatory brasserie, a formal restaurant and the Spike Bar, which is mainly frequented by golf club members and has a lively atmosphere.

continued

T

The hotel also has a superb 18-hole golf course, swimming pool and gym.

ROOMS: 35 en suite (8 fmly) (23 GF) ⊗ in all bedrooms s £110-£130; d £120-£250 (incl. bkfst) **LB** **FACILITIES:** STV ⛝ ⛳36 Sauna Gym Putt green Covered driving range, putting green, Pool table Xmas **CONF:** Thtr 120 Class 50 Board 50 Del from £150 **SERVICES:** Lift **PARKING:** 220 **NOTES:** ✗ ⊗ in restaurant Civ Wed 150

TINTAGEL, Cornwall & Isles of Scilly — Map 02 SX08

★★66% Atlantic View

Treknow PL34 0EJ
☎ 01840 770221 📠 01840 770995
e-mail: atlantic-view@eclipse.co.uk
web: www.holidayscornwall.com
Dir: *B3263 to Tregatta, turn left into Treknow, hotel on road to Trebarwith Strand Beach*

Conveniently located for all the attractions of Tintagel, this family-run hotel has a wonderfully relaxed and welcoming atmosphere. Public areas include a bar, comfortable lounge, TV/games room and heated swimming pool. Bedrooms are generally spacious and some have the added advantage of distant sea views.

ROOMS: 9 en suite (1 fmly) ⊗ in all bedrooms s £34-£38; d £68-£76 (incl. bkfst) **LB** **FACILITIES:** ⛝ Indoor pool heated Apr-Oct **PARKING:** 10 **NOTES:** ✗ ⊗ in restaurant Closed Nov-Jan RS Feb-Mar

★★64% Bossiney House

Bossiney PL34 0AX
☎ 01840 770240 📠 01840 770501
e-mail: bossineyhh@eclipse.co.uk
web: www.bossineyhouse.co.uk
Dir: *from A39 take B3263 into Tintagel, then Boscastle Rd, 0.5m to hotel on left*

This personally run, friendly hotel is located on the outskirts of the picturesque coastal village. An attractive Scandinavian-style log cabin houses the majority of the leisure facilities, including a swimming pool. Public areas include a comfortable lounge and the convivial bar, which is a popular venue for pre-dinner drinks and a chat.

ROOMS: 19 en suite (1 fmly) s £42-£48; d £64-£74 (incl. bkfst) **LB** **FACILITIES:** ⛝ Sauna Solarium Putt green **CONF:** BC **PARKING:** 30 **NOTES:** ⊗ in restaurant Closed 25/26 Dec, 2-31 Jan

TITCHWELL, Norfolk — Map 13 TF74

★★79% ⊛⊛ Titchwell Manor

PE31 8BB
☎ 01485 210221 📠 01485 210104
e-mail: margaret@titchwellmanor.com
web: www.titchwellmanor.com
Dir: *on A149 coast road between Brancaster and Thornham*

Friendly family-run hotel ideally placed for touring the north Norfolk coastline. Bedrooms are comfortable; some in the adjacent annexe offer ground floor access. Smart public rooms include a lounge area, relaxed informal bar and a delightful conservatory restaurant, overlooking the walled garden. Imaginative menus feature quality local produce and fresh fish.

ROOMS: 8 en suite 7 annexe en suite (2 fmly) (3 GF) ⊗ in 9 bedrooms s £45-£70; d £90-£140 (incl. bkfst) **LB** **FACILITIES:** Xmas **PARKING:** 50 **NOTES:** ⊗ in restaurant

TIVERTON, Devon — Map 03 SS91

★★★70% Tiverton

Blundells Rd EX16 4DB
☎ 01884 256120 📠 01884 258101
e-mail: sales@tivertonhotel.co.uk
web: www.bw-tivertonhotel.co.uk
Dir: *M5 junct 27, onto dual carriageway A361 Devon link road, Tiverton exit 7m W. Hotel on Blundells Rd next to business park*

Conveniently situated on the outskirts of the town, with easy access to the M5, this comfortable hotel has a relaxed atmosphere. The spacious bedrooms are well equipped and decorated in a contemporary style. A formal dining option is offered in the Gallery Restaurant, and lighter snacks are served in the bar area. Room service is extensive, as is the range of conference facilities.

ROOMS: 69 en suite (10 fmly) ⊗ in 53 bedrooms s £62-£69; d £88-£97 (incl. bkfst) **LB** **FACILITIES:** STV Fishing Xmas **CONF:** Thtr 300 Class 140 Board 70 Del from £75 **PARKING:** 130 **NOTES:** ⊗ in restaurant Civ Wed 200

TODDINGTON MOTORWAY SERVICE AREA (M1), Bedfordshire — Map 11 TL02

⌂ Travelodge (Luton North)

LU5 6HR
☎ 08700 850 950 📠 01525 878452
web: www.travelodge.co.uk
Dir: *M1 between juncts 11 & 12*

Travelodge offers good quality, good value, modern accommodation. Ideal for families, the spacious, en suite bedrooms include remote-control TV, tea and coffee-making facilities and comfortable beds. Meals can be taken at the nearby family restaurant. For further details consult the Hotel Groups page.

ROOMS: 66 en suite s fr £26; d fr £26

> If you wish to use a particular credit card or debit card please check with the hotel that they are happy to accept it

T

TOLLESHUNT KNIGHTS, Essex Map 07 TL91

★★★★73% ◉◉ Five Lakes Country House
Colchester Rd CM9 8HX
☎ 01621 868888 📠 01621 869696
e-mail: enquiries@fivelakes.co.uk
web: www.fivelakes.co.uk
Dir: exit A12 at Kelvedon, follow brown signs through Tiptree to hotel
This hotel is set amidst 320 acres of open countryside, featuring two golf courses. The spacious bedrooms are furnished to a high standard and have excellent facilities. The public rooms offer a high degree of comfort and include five bars, two restaurants and a large lounge. The property also boasts extensive leisure facilities.
ROOMS: 114 en suite 80 annexe en suite (4 fmly) (40 GF) ⊗ in 118 bedrooms s £110; d £155-£225 **LB FACILITIES: Spa** STV 🏊 ⛴ 36 ⚒ Squash Snooker Sauna Solarium Gym Putt green Jacuzzi Steam room, Health & Beauty Spa, Badminton, Aerobics Studio, Hairdresser 🎵 Xmas **CONF:** Thtr 2000 Class 700 Board 60 Del from £142 **SERVICES:** Lift **PARKING:** 550 **NOTES:** ✖ ⊗ in restaurant Civ Wed 250

TOLWORTH, Greater London

⌂ Travelodge Tolworth
Tolworth Tower KT6 7EL
☎ 08700 850950
web: www.travelodge.co.uk

Dir: exit A3 at Tolworth junct. At rdbt, take 2nd exit signed London (A3), then immediate left onto Ewell Road. Travelodge is on the left.
Travelodge offers good quality, good value, modern accommodation. Ideal for families, the spacious, en suite bedrooms include remote-control TV, tea and coffee-making facilities and comfortable beds. Meals can be taken at the nearby family restaurant. For further details consult the Hotel Groups page.
ROOMS: 120 en suite s fr £26; d fr £26

Bad hair day?
Hairdryers in all rooms three stars and above

TONBRIDGE, Kent Map 06 TQ54

★★★67% Rose & Crown
125 High St TN9 1DD
☎ 01732 357966 📠 01732 357194
e-mail: rose.crown@bestwestern.co.uk
Dir: M25 junct 5 onto A21 to Hastings. At 2nd junct take B245 through Hildenborough. Continue to Tonbridge. At 1st lights right, over next set. Hotel on left

A 15th-century coaching inn situated in the town complete with its own car park and adjacent to the ruins of the old Norman castle. The hotel still retains much of its original character such as oak beams and Jacobean panelling. The bedrooms, in a variety of
continued

styles, all are well equipped. Bar meals are an option if the full restaurant dining isn't your choice.
ROOMS: 54 en suite (2 fmly) (10 GF) ⊗ in 27 bedrooms s £65-£95; d £75-£135 (incl. bkfst) **LB FACILITIES:** STV Xmas **CONF:** Thtr 80 Class 30 Board 35 **PARKING:** 39 **NOTES:** ✖ ⊗ in restaurant Civ Wed 50

★★★66% The Langley
18-20 London Rd TN10 3DA
☎ 01732 353311 📠 01732 771471
e-mail: thelangley@btconnect.com
Dir: from Tonbridge towards Hildenborough N, hotel on Tonbridge/Hildenborough border
Privately owned hotel located just a short drive from the centre of Tonbridge and ideally situated for business and leisure guests alike. Bedrooms are generally quite spacious; each one is pleasantly decorated and equipped with modern facilities. The restaurant offers a varied menu of carefully prepared fresh produce and there is a popular bar.
ROOMS: 37 en suite (3 fmly) (10 GF) ⊗ in 27 bedrooms **FACILITIES:** STV **CONF:** Thtr 150 Class 100 Board 100 **SERVICES:** Lift **PARKING:** 40 **NOTES:** ✖ ⊗ in restaurant Civ Wed 150

⌂ Premier Travel Inn Tonbridge
Pembury Rd TN11 0NA
☎ 0870 9906552 📠 0870 9906553
web: www.premiertravelinn.com
Dir: 11m from M25 junct 5. Follow A21 towards Hastings, pass A26 (Tunbridge Wells) junct. Exit at next junct, 1st exit at rdbt
High quality, modern budget accommodation ideal for both families and business travellers. Spacious, en suite bedrooms feature bath and shower, satellite TV and many have telephones and modem points. The adjacent family restaurant features a wide and varied menu. For further details consult the Hotel Groups page.
ROOMS: 38 en suite s £47.95-£50.95; d £47.95-£50.95 **CONF:** Class 14 Board 14

TOPCLIFFE, North Yorkshire Map 19 SE37

★★69% The Angel Inn
Long St YO7 3RW
☎ 01845 577237 📠 01845 578000
e-mail: info@angelinn.co.uk
Dir: turn off A168 (between A1(M) & A19). Inn in village centre

Located in the heart of Topcliffe, this attractive inn is popular for its country-style cooking using high quality local produce. Friendly staff and pleasant bars can be found along with a fine pub water garden. The very comfortable bedrooms are well equipped. A function suite is available for wedding ceremonies, meetings and functions.
ROOMS: 15 en suite (1 fmly) s £53-£57.50; d £70 (incl. bkfst) **LB FACILITIES:** STV **CONF:** BC Thtr 150 Class 60 Board 50 Del from £103.95 **PARKING:** 150 **NOTES:** ✖ ⊗ in restaurant Civ Wed 130

TORBAY See under Brixham, Paignton & Torquay

TORMARTON, Gloucestershire Map 04 ST77

★★70% Compass Inn

GL9 1JB
☎ 01454 218242 & 218577 🖷 01454 218741
e-mail: info@compass-inn.co.uk
web: www.compass-inn.co.uk
Dir: *0.5m from M4 junct 18*

Originally a coaching inn dating from the 18th century, this welcoming hostelry has grown considerably over the years. Bedrooms are spacious and well equipped, whilst public areas include a choice of bars and varied dining options. A range of conference rooms is also available, providing facilities for varied functions.

ROOMS: 26 en suite (5 fmly) (12 GF) s £70-£98; d £80-£110 **LB**
FACILITIES: French boules **CONF:** Thtr 100 Class 30 Board 34 Del from £114.95 **PARKING:** 160 **NOTES:** Closed 24-26Dec Civ Wed 100

TORQUAY, Devon Map 03 SX96

★★★★★68% The Imperial

Park Hill Rd TQ1 2DG
☎ 01803 294301 🖷 01803 298293
e-mail: imperialtorquay@paramount-hotels.co.uk
web: www.paramount-hotels.co.uk
Dir: *A380 towards the seafront. Turn left and follow road to harbour, at clocktower turn right. Hotel 300yds on right*

This hotel has an enviable location with extensive views of the coastline. Traditional in style, public areas are elegant with choice of dining including the informal TQ1 brasserie or the more formal Regatta Restaurant. Bedrooms are spacious, most with private balconies, and the hotel has an extensive range of indoor and outdoor leisure facilities.

ROOMS: 151 en suite (7 fmly) ⊗ in 26 bedrooms s £85-£100; d £170-£360 (incl. bkfst) **LB** **FACILITIES:** STV supervised Squash Snooker Sauna Solarium Gym Jacuzzi Beauty salon Hairdresser, Steam room ♫ Xmas **CONF:** Thtr 350 Class 200 Board 30 **SERVICES:** Lift **PARKING:** 140 **NOTES:** ⊗ in restaurant Civ Wed 250

★★★★68% *Palace*

Babbacombe Rd TQ1 3TG
☎ 01803 200200 🖷 01803 299899
e-mail: info@palacetorquay.co.uk
web: www.palacetorquay.co.uk
Dir: *towards harbour, left by clocktower into Babbacombe Rd, hotel on right after 1m*

Set in 25 acres of stunning, beautifully tended wooded grounds, the Palace offers a tranquil environment. Suitable for business or

continued on p570

TORQUAY, continued

leisure, the hotel boasts a huge range of well-presented indoor and outdoor facilities. Much of the original charm and grandeur has been maintained, particularly in the dining room. Many of the bedrooms enjoy views of the gardens.
ROOMS: 141 en suite (7 fmly) ⊗ in 11 bedrooms **FACILITIES:** STV supervised 9 Squash Snooker Sauna Gym Putt green Table tennis ch fac **CONF:** Thtr 1000 Class 800 Board 40 **SERVICES:** Lift **PARKING:** 140 **NOTES:** ⊗ in restaurant

See advert on page 569

★★★★66% Grand

Sea Front TQ2 6NT
☎ 01803 296677 01803 213462
e-mail: info@grandtorquay.co.uk
web: www.richardsonhotels.co.uk
Dir: *A380 to Torquay. At seafront turn right, then 1st right. Hotel on corner, entrance 1st on left*

Within level walking distance of the town, this large Edwardian hotel overlooks the bay and offers modern facilities. Many of the bedrooms, some with balconies, enjoy the best of the views; all are very well equipped. Boaters Bar also benefits from the hotel's stunning position and offers an informal alternative to the Gainsborough Restaurant.
ROOMS: 117 en suite (30 fmly) ⊗ in 20 bedrooms s £65-£100; d £130-£210 (incl. bkfst) **LB** **FACILITIES:** STV Snooker Sauna Solarium Gym Jacuzzi Hairdressers Beauty clinic ♫ Xmas **CONF:** Thtr 300 Class 130 Board 60 Del from £99 **SERVICES:** Lift **PARKING:** 45 **NOTES:** ⊗ in restaurant Civ Wed 250

See advert on opposite page

Top Hotel

★★★ Orestone Manor Hotel & Restaurant

Rockhouse Ln, Maidencombe TQ1 4SX
☎ 01803 328098 01803 328336
e-mail: enquiries@orestone.co.uk
web: www.orestone.co.uk
Dir: *off A379 coast road, Torquay-Teignmouth road (formerly B3199)*

This country-house hotel is located on the fringe of Torbay and occupies a spectacular location overlooking Lyme Bay. There is a colonial theme throughout the public areas, making a charming and comfortable environment. Bedrooms are individually styled and spacious; some have balconies. The hotel's cuisine is highly regarded and dishes, based on local ingredients, are skilfully prepared.
ROOMS: 12 en suite (3 fmly) (1 GF) s £69-£149; d £89-£225 (incl. bkfst) **LB** **FACILITIES:** STV Xmas **CONF:** Thtr 30 Class 20 Board 15 Del from £129 **PARKING:** 40 **NOTES:** ⊗ in restaurant

★★★74% Corbyn Head Hotel & Orchid Restaurant

Torquay Rd, Sea Front, Livermead TQ2 6RH
☎ 01803 213611 01803 296152
e-mail: info@corbynhead.com
web: www.corbynhead.com
Dir: *follow signs to Torquay seafront, turn right on seafront. Hotel on right with green canopies*

The Corbyn Head occupies a prime position overlooking Torbay. Well-equipped bedrooms, many with sea views and some with balconies, come in a range of sizes. Staff are friendly and attentive, and a well-stocked bar and comfortable lounge are available. Guests can enjoy fine dining in the award-winning Orchid Restaurant or more traditional dishes in the Harbour View restaurant.
ROOMS: 44 en suite (3 fmly) (9 GF) ⊗ in 15 bedrooms s £55-£150; d £110-£212 (incl. bkfst & dinner) **LB** **FACILITIES:** Squash Snooker Sauna Solarium Gym ♫ Xmas **CONF:** Thtr 50 Class 30 Board 30 Del from £80 **PARKING:** 50 **NOTES:** ⊗ in restaurant

See advert on opposite page

★★★70% Livermead House

Torbay Rd TQ2 6QJ
☎ 01803 294361 & 294363 01803 200758
e-mail: info@livermead.com
web: www.livermead.com
Dir: *from seafront turn right, follow A379 towards Paignton & Livermead, hotel opposite Institute Beach*

Having a splendid waterfront location, this hotel dates back to the 1820s and is where Charles Kingsley is said to have written *'The Water Babies'*. Bedrooms vary in size and style, excellent public rooms are popular for private parties and meetings and a range of leisure facilities is provided. Enjoyable cuisine is served in the impressive restaurant.
ROOMS: 67 en suite (6 fmly) (2 GF) ⊗ in 12 bedrooms s £65-£100; d £130-£200 (incl. bkfst & dinner) **LB** **FACILITIES:** Squash Snooker Sauna Solarium Gym ♫ Xmas **CONF:** Thtr 320 Class 175 Board 80 Del from £55 **SERVICES:** Lift **PARKING:** 131 **NOTES:** ⊗ in restaurant

See advert on page 573

T

TORQUAY, continued

★★★69% Lincombe Hall
Meadfoot Rd TQ1 2JX
☎ 01803 213361 🖷 01803 211485
e-mail: lincombe.hall@lineone.net
web: www.lincombe-hall.co.uk
Dir: *From harbour into Torwood St, at traffic lights after 100yds, turn right into Meadfoot Rd. Hotel 200yds on left*

With views over Torquay, this hotel is conveniently close to the town centre and is set in five acres of gardens and grounds. Facilities include both indoor and outdoor swimming pools. The tastefully furnished bedrooms vary in size, and the Sutherland rooms are most spacious. There are comfortable lounges and Harleys restaurant offers a comprehensive choice of dishes and wines.
ROOMS: 25 en suite 19 annexe en suite (7 fmly) (2 GF) s £35-£89; d £50-£158 (incl. bkfst & dinner) **LB** **FACILITIES:** STV Putt green Child's play area Crazy golf Pool table Table Tennis Xmas **CONF:** Thtr 30 Class 30 Board 30 **PARKING:** 44 **NOTES:** in restaurant

★★★69% Toorak Hotel
Chestnut Av TQ2 5JS
☎ 01803 400400 🖷 01803 400140
e-mail: toorak@tlh.co.uk
Dir: *opposite Riviera Conference Centre*
Forming part of a much larger complex, this hotel offers excellent leisure facilities including indoor bowls, a cyber café and a magnificent indoor swimming pool. Bedrooms have modern facilities, and both superior and standard rooms are available. The hotel also provides conference rooms and several relaxing lounges.
ROOMS: 92 en suite (29 fmly) (20 GF) in 40 bedrooms s £44-£83; d £88-£154 (incl. bkfst) **LB** **FACILITIES:** supervised Snooker Sauna Solarium Gym Jacuzzi Childrens play area, Indoor Games Arena, Swimming Pool Supervised, Internet Cafe ch fac Xmas **CONF:** Thtr 220 Class 150 Board 60 **SERVICES:** Lift **PARKING:** 90 **NOTES:** in restaurant Civ Wed 120

★★★67% Belgrave
Seafront TQ2 5HE
☎ 01803 296666 🖷 01803 211308
e-mail: info@belgrave-hotel.co.uk
web: www.belgrave-hotel.co.uk
Dir: *on A380 into Torquay continue to lights with Torre Station on right. Turn right into Avenue Rd continue to Kings Drive. Left at seafront , hotel at lights*
Enjoying an impressive position overlooking Torbay, the Belgrave offers a range of spacious and well-appointed public rooms, including comfortable lounges, the elegant restaurant and outdoor pool and patio areas. The Dickens bar is particularly stylish, and offers an innovative menu, featuring local produce. A variety of bedroom styles is available, many of which have the added bonus of stunning sea views.

ROOMS: 72 en suite (20 fmly) (18 GF) in 30 bedrooms s £58-£99; d £116-£154 (incl. bkfst) **LB** **FACILITIES:** Xmas **CONF:** BC Thtr 200 Class 100 Board 60 Del from £75 **SERVICES:** Lift **PARKING:** 90 **NOTES:** in restaurant

★★★67% The Grosvenor
Belgrave Rd TQ2 5HG
☎ 01803 294373 🖷 01803 291032
e-mail: enquiries@grosvenor-torquay.co.uk
web: www.grosvenor-torquay.co.uk
Dir: *follow signs to seafront, turn left, then 1st left into Belgrave Rd, hotel 1st on left*

Offering spacious and attractively furnished bedrooms, the Grosvenor Hotel is situated close to the seafront and the main attractions of the bay. Stylish public areas offer high levels of comfort, and guests can choose to dine in the restaurant, coffee shop or Mima's Bistro. A range of leisure facilities is available including indoor and outdoor pools, a gym and sauna.
ROOMS: 44 en suite (8 fmly) in 10 bedrooms s £41-£92; d £82-£184 (incl. bkfst) **LB** **FACILITIES: Spa** STV Sauna Solarium Gym Jacuzzi Mini snooker table Library Xmas **CONF:** Thtr 150 Class 100 Board 40 Del from £65 **PARKING:** 50 **NOTES:** in restaurant Civ Wed 300

★★★66% Livermead Cliff
Torbay Rd TQ2 6RQ
☎ 01803 299666 🖷 01803 294496
e-mail: enquiries@livermeadcliff.co.uk
web: www.livermeadcliff.co.uk
Dir: *A379/A3022 to Torquay, through town centre, turn right for Paignton. Hotel 600yds on seaward side*
Situated at the water's edge this long-established hotel offers friendly service. The splendid views can be enjoyed from the lounge, bar and dining room. Bedrooms, many with sea views and
continued

some with balconies, are comfortable and well equipped and a range of sizes is available.

ROOMS: 67 en suite (21 fmly) **FACILITIES:** supervised Fishing Solarium Sun terrace ♫ Xmas **CONF:** Thtr 80 Class 35 Board 35 Del from £60 **SERVICES:** Lift **PARKING:** 92 **NOTES:** ⊗ in restaurant

★★★64% Kistor Hotel

Belgrave Rd TQ2 5HF
☎ 01803 212632 🖷 01803 212635
e-mail: stay@kistorhotel.co.uk
Dir: *A380 to Torquay, hotel at junct of Belgrave Rd and promenade*

Within a short stroll of Torquay's many amenities and the promenade, the Kistor is conveniently located. Popular with groups, the hotel offers a relaxing and informal base for guests.

continued

Most bedrooms have sea views. In the restaurant, a fixed-price menu offers good straightforward cooking.

ROOMS: 57 en suite (4 fmly) ⊗ in all bedrooms s £30-£48; d £60-£96 (incl. bkfst) **LB** **FACILITIES: Spa** Sauna Gym Putt green Jacuzzi Games room ♫ Xmas **CONF:** Thtr 60 Class 40 Board 30 Del from £50 **SERVICES:** Lift **PARKING:** 60 **NOTES:** ⊗ in restaurant

★★★60% *Rainbow International*

Belgrave Rd TQ2 5HJ
☎ 01803 213232 🖷 01803 212925
e-mail: enquiries@rainbow-hotel.co.uk
web: www.rainbow-hotel.co.uk
Dir: *Close to harbour and marina*

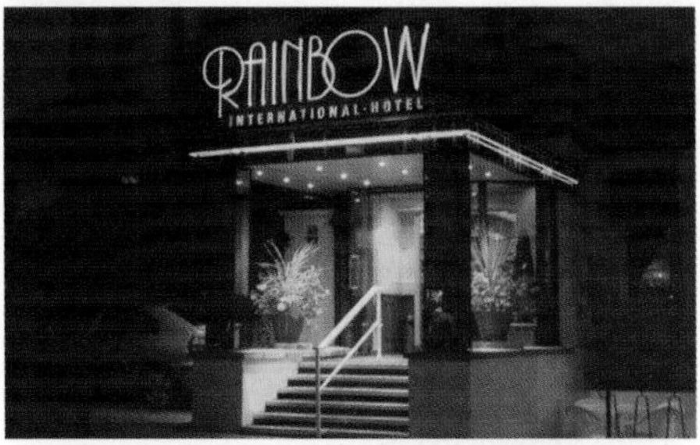

This large hotel is located within easy walking distance of the seafront. Bedrooms vary in size and shape; many family rooms are available. Entertainment is provided every evening in the

continued on p574

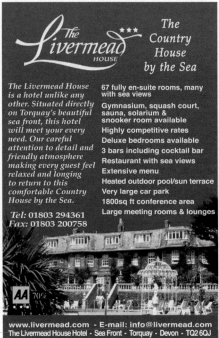

TORQUAY, continued

nightclub and the residents' ballroom. A leisure club and gym are also on offer.
ROOMS: 134 en suite (70 fmly) **FACILITIES:** Solarium Gym Table tennis Steam room ch fac **CONF:** Thtr 500 Class 250 Board 80 **SERVICES:** Lift **PARKING:** 100 **NOTES:** in restaurant

★★73% Rawlyn House

Rawlyn Rd, Chelston TQ2 6PL
☎ 01803 605208 01803 607040
e-mail: shirley@rawlynhousehotel.co.uk
web: www.rawlynhousehotel.co.uk
Dir: *A3022 to Torquay, follow sign for seafront, right at Halfords lights to Avenue Rd, at 2nd lights right to Walnut Rd, left to Old Mill Rd, Rawlyn Rd sharp right at top of hill*
Quietly located close to Cockington village and within easy reach of the centre, this friendly family-run hotel is set in well-tended grounds. Bedrooms are individual in style and offer all the expected facilities, with several rooms located on the ground floor. Dinner features freshly cooked dishes and residents can take a snack lunch around the pool or in the bar
ROOMS: 12 rms (11 en suite) (1 fmly) (2 GF) in all bedrooms s £43-£54; d £86-£108 (incl. bkfst & dinner) **LB** **FACILITIES:** Badminton Table tennis **PARKING:** 16 **NOTES:** in restaurant Closed Nov-Apr

★★72% Albaston House

27 St Marychurch Rd TQ1 3JF
☎ 01803 296758 01803 211509
e-mail: albastonhousehotel@hotmail.com
Dir: *A380 left at lights then B3199, follow signs for Plainmoor to Westhill Rd. Right at lights. Hotel 0.5m on left*
The Albaston is situated close to the town centre and is also convenient for the quieter attractions of Babbacombe. Public areas and bedrooms alike combine comfort and quality. Many guests return time after time to this hotel.
ROOMS: 13 en suite (2 fmly) in 6 bedrooms s £36-£46; d £72 (incl. bkfst) **FACILITIES:** Xmas **PARKING:** 6 **NOTES:** in restaurant

★★71% Bute Court

Belgrave Rd TQ2 5HQ
☎ 01803 293771 & 213055 01803 213429
e-mail: stay@butecourthotel.co.uk
web: www.butecourthotel.co.uk
Dir: *take A380 to Torquay, continue to lights, bear right past police station, straight across at lights, hotel 200yds on right*
This popular hotel is only a short, level walk from the seafront and resort attractions. Now refurbished, it still retains many of its Victorian features. Comfortable bedrooms offer modern facilities and many have far-reaching views. Public areas include a bar and lounges, while the attractive dining room looks across secluded gardens to the sea. Entertainment is also offered during busier periods.
ROOMS: 44 en suite (10 fmly) (13 GF) in all bedrooms s £34-£53; d £68-£106 (incl. bkfst & dinner) **LB** **FACILITIES:** Snooker Darts billiards Xmas **SERVICES:** Lift **PARKING:** 37 **NOTES:** in restaurant

★★70% Red House

Rousdown Rd, Chelston TQ2 6PB
☎ 01803 607811 01803 200592
e-mail: stay@redhouse-hotel.co.uk
web: www.redhouse-hotel.co.uk
Dir: *towards seafront/Chelston, turn into Avenue Rd, 1st lights turn right. Past shops & church, take next left. Hotel on right*
With views over Torbay, this pleasant and relaxing hotel, now under new ownership, enjoys a quiet location close to Cockington village. The comfortable bedrooms are well equipped and a good choice of bar meals are available in addition to the fixed-price menu for residents. Many guests return here on a regular basis for the excellent range of leisure facilities.
ROOMS: 9 en suite (3 fmly) s £28-£49; d £56-£74 (incl. bkfst) **FACILITIES:** **Spa** Sauna Solarium Gym Jacuzzi Xmas **CONF:** Thtr 20 Class 20 Board 16 **PARKING:** 9 **NOTES:** in restaurant

★★70% Seascape

8-10 Tor Church Rd TQ2 5UT
☎ 01803 292617 01803 299260
e-mail: stay@seascapehoteltorquay.co.uk
Dir: *A380 Torquay, at Torre station turn right, left at 2nd lights. Through lights, hotel 100yds on right*
Enjoying a convenient location, just a short stroll from the town centre, this friendly, family run hotel prides itself on genuine hospitality. Bedrooms are comfortable and well equipped, some of which have the added bonus of views across the bay. Public rooms include the convivial bar with regular live entertainment, and a sauna and solarium.
ROOMS: 60 en suite (10 fmly) in 52 bedrooms s £25-£40; d £50-£70 (incl. bkfst) **FACILITIES:** Sauna Solarium Xmas **SERVICES:** Lift **PARKING:** 13 **NOTES:** No children 12yrs in restaurant

★★70% Torcroft

28-30 Croft Rd TQ2 5UE
☎ 01803 298292 01803 291799
e-mail: enquiries@torcroft.co.uk
web: www.torcroft.co.uk
Dir: *from A390 take A3022 to Avenue Rd. Follow signs to seafront then turn left, cross lights and up Shedden Hill, 1st left into Croft Rd*
This elegant, Grade II listed Victorian property is pleasantly located in a quiet area, just a short stroll from the seafront. The delightful garden and patio are very popular with guests, ideal for a spot of sunbathing or relaxing with a good book. The comfortable bedrooms, two with balconies, are individually furnished. Pleasant, home-cooked meals are enthusiastically offered and make enjoyable dining.
ROOMS: 15 en suite (2 fmly) in all bedrooms s £27-£37; d £54-£74 (incl. bkfst) **LB** **FACILITIES:** Xmas **PARKING:** 11 **NOTES:** in restaurant

★★69% *Dunstone Hall*

Lower Warberry Rd TQ1 1QS
☎ 01803 293185 01803 201180
e-mail: info@dunstonehall.com
web: www.dunstonehall.co.uk
From its elevated position, this imposing Victorian mansion has panoramic views over the town, to Torbay in the distance. Bedrooms are comfortable and equipped with modern facilities. Public areas include a choice of lounges, a magnificent wooden staircase and gallery and the Edwardian conservatory, which provides an intimate restaurant where both dinner and the view may be enjoyed.
ROOMS: 13 en suite (3 fmly) **FACILITIES:** Arrangement with nearby Health Club ch fac **CONF:** Thtr 30 Class 30 Board 24 **PARKING:** 18 **NOTES:** in restaurant

★★69% Hotel Balmoral

Meadfoot Sea Rd TQ1 2LQ
☎ 01803 293381 & 299224 01803 299224
e-mail: barry@hotel-balmoral.co.uk
Dir: *at Torquay harbour left at clock tower towards Babbacombe. After 100yds right at lights. Follow to Meadfoot Beach. Hotel on right*
Situated a short walk from the beach, this friendly, privately-owned and personally run hotel has modern, well-equipped

continued

T

bedrooms including family rooms and a room on ground floor level. The comfortable, spacious lounge has views over the well-tended gardens and the bar is an ideal venue for a drink before home-cooked dinners in the attractive dining room.
ROOMS: 24 en suite (4 fmly) (1 GF) s £27-£31; d £54-£62 (incl. bkfst) **LB FACILITIES:** Xmas **PARKING:** 18 **NOTES:** ⊗ in restaurant

★★68% Shelley Court
29 Croft Rd TQ2 5UD
☎ 01803 295642 🖷 01803 215793
e-mail: shelleycourthotel@hotmail.com
Dir: *from B3199 up Shedden Hill Rd, 1st left into Croft Rd*
This hotel, now under new ownership, is located in a pleasant and quiet area, which overlooks the town towards Torbay. With a friendly team of staff, many guests return here time and again. Entertainment is provided most evenings in the season. Bedrooms come in a range of sizes and there is a large and comfortable lounge bar.
ROOMS: 27 en suite (2 fmly) (6 GF) **FACILITIES:** ♫ Xmas **CONF:** BC **PARKING:** 11 **NOTES:** ⊗ in restaurant Closed 5 Jan-12 Feb

★★67% Gresham Court
Babbacombe Rd TQ1 1HG
☎ 01803 293007 🖷 01803 215951
e-mail: stay@gresham-court-hotel.co.uk
web: www.gresham-court-hotel.co.uk
Dir: *along seafront, left at clock tower, passing museum on left. Hotel immediately on left on corner of Braddons Hill Road West and Babbacombe Road*
This privately owned and personally run hotel is soundly maintained and provides modern accommodation, including bedrooms on the ground floor. There is a bright and pleasant dining room, a lounge bar where live entertainment is provided, a non-smoking lounge and a games room with pool table. The hotel is a popular venue for coach tour parties.
ROOMS: 30 en suite (6 fmly) (5 GF) s £42-£48; d £64-£70 (incl. bkfst) **LB FACILITIES:** Snooker ♫ Xmas **SERVICES:** Lift **PARKING:** 4 **NOTES:** ⊗ in restaurant

★★66% *Anchorage Hotel*
Cary Park, Aveland Rd TQ1 3PT
☎ 01803 326175 🖷 01803 316439
e-mail: enquiries@anchoragehotel.co.uk

Quietly located in a residential area and providing a friendly welcome, this family-run establishment enjoys a great deal of repeat business. Bedrooms offer a range of sizes and all rooms are neatly presented. Evening entertainment is provided regularly in the large and comfortable lounge.
ROOMS: 56 en suite (5 fmly) ⊗ in all bedrooms **FACILITIES:** ♫ **SERVICES:** Lift **PARKING:** 26 **NOTES:** ⊗ in restaurant

★★66% Coppice
Babbacombe Rd TQ1 2QJ
☎ 01803 297786 🖷 01803 211085
e-mail: peter@coppicehotel.demon.co.uk
web: www.coppicehotel.co.uk
Dir: *From harbour left at clock tower for hotel 1m on left*
A friendly, comfortable and well-established hotel, The Coppice is a popular choice and provides a convenient location that is within walking distance of the beaches and shops. In addition to the indoor and outdoor swimming pools, evening entertainment is often provided in the spacious bar. Bedrooms are bright and airy with modern amenities.
ROOMS: 39 en suite (16 fmly) (22 GF) ⊗ in all bedrooms s £28-£32; d £56-£64 (incl. bkfst) **LB FACILITIES: Spa** Sauna Solarium Gym Putt green ♫ **PARKING:** 36 **NOTES:** ⊗ in restaurant Closed Dec-Jan

★★66% Elmington Hotel
St Agnes Ln, Chelston TQ2 6QE
☎ 01803 605192 🖷 01803 690488
e-mail: mail@elmington.co.uk
web: www.elmington.co.uk
Dir: *to the rear of Torquay Station*
Set in sub-tropical gardens with views over the bay, this splendid Victorian villa has been lovingly restored. The comfortable bedrooms are brightly decorated and vary in size and style. There is a spacious lounge, bar and dining room. Diners can choose from a menu of British dishes and an oriental buffet.
ROOMS: 22 rms (19 en suite) (5 fmly) (2 GF) ⊗ in all bedrooms **FACILITIES:** STV Pool table Xmas **CONF:** Thtr 40 Class 40 Board 30 **PARKING:** 22 **NOTES:** ⊗ in restaurant

★★65% Ashley Court
107 Abbey Rd TQ2 5NP
☎ 01803 292417 🖷 01803 215035
e-mail: reception@ashleycourt.co.uk
Dir: *A380 onto seafront, left to Shedden Hill to lights, hotel opposite*

Located close to the town centre and within easy strolling distance of the seafront, the Ashley Court offers a warm welcome to guests. Bedrooms are pleasantly appointed and some have sea views. The outdoor pool and patio are popular with guests wishing to soak up some sunshine. Live entertainment is provided regularly throughout the season.
ROOMS: 53 en suite (6 fmly) (8 GF) **FACILITIES:** ♫ Xmas **SERVICES:** Lift **PARKING:** 30 **NOTES:** ⊗ in restaurant Closed 3 Jan-1 Feb

TV dinner?
Room service at three stars and above

T

TORQUAY, continued

★★65% Maycliffe

St Lukes Rd North TQ2 5DP
☎ 01803 294964 📠 01803 201167
e-mail: bob.west1@virgin.net
web: www.maycliffehotel.co.uk
Dir: *left from Kings Dr, along seafront keep left lane, next lights (Belgrave Rd) up Shedden Hill, 2nd right into St Lukes Rd then 1st left*

Set in a quiet and elevated position which is convenient for the town centre and attractions, the Maycliffe is a popular venue for leisure breaks. Bedrooms are individually decorated and equipped with modern facilities, there are two rooms on the ground floor for less able guests. Guests can relax in the quiet lounge and, in the bar, cabaret is offered on some nights during the season.

ROOMS: 28 en suite (1 fmly) (2 GF) ⊗ in 12 bedrooms s £30-£38; d £50-£66 (incl. bkfst) **LB** **FACILITIES:** ♫ Xmas **SERVICES:** Lift **PARKING:** 10 **NOTES:** ✈ No children 4yrs ⊗ in restaurant Closed 2 Jan-12 Feb

★★64% Norcliffe

7 Babbacombe Downs Rd, Babbacombe TQ1 3LF
☎ 01803 328456 📠 01803 328023
e-mail: res@norcliffehotel.co.uk
Dir: *M5, take A380, after Sainsburys turn left at lights, across rdbt, next leftL at lights into Manor Rd, from Babbacombe Rd turn left*

With marvellous views across Lyme Bay, the Norcliffe is conveniently situated on the Babbacombe Downs and ideally located for visitors to St Marychurch or nearby Oddicombe Beach. Public areas are relaxing, taking advantage of the views, and include an indoor swimming pool. All bedrooms are comfortable, varying in style and size.

ROOMS: 27 en suite (3 fmly) (1 GF) s £36-£44; d £72-£88 (incl. bkfst & dinner) **LB** **FACILITIES:** 🏊 Sauna Table tennis Xmas **SERVICES:** Lift **PARKING:** 20 **NOTES:** ⊗ in restaurant

★★64% *Regina*

Victoria Pde TQ1 2BE
☎ 01803 292904 📠 01803 290270
e-mail: regina.torquay@alfatravel.co.uk
web: www.alfatravel.co.uk
Dir: *into Torquay, follow harbour signs, hotel on outer corner of harbour*

The Regina Hotel enjoys a pleasant and convenient location right on the harbour side, a short stroll from the town's attractions. Bedrooms, some with harbour views, vary in size. Entertainment is provided on most nights and there is a choice of bars.

ROOMS: 68 en suite (5 fmly) **FACILITIES:** ♫ **SERVICES:** Lift **PARKING:** 6 **NOTES:** ✈ ⊗ in restaurant Closed Jan& part Feb RS Nov-Dec (ex Xmas) & Feb-Mar

★★59% *Burlington*

462-466 Babbacombe Rd TQ1 1HN
☎ 01803 210950 📠 01803 200189
e-mail: info@burlingtontorquay.co.uk
web: www.burlingtontorquay.co.uk
Dir: *A380 follow signs to seafront, left at harbour, left at clock tower rdbt, hotel is 0.5m on right*

Popular with groups, this hotel is conveniently situated for the many attractions the area has to offer. A range of traditional dishes is served in the spacious dining room. Public areas include a games room, entertainment room, leisure facilities and a popular bar. Bedrooms are comfortable and available in a variety of sizes.

ROOMS: 55 en suite (7 fmly) **FACILITIES: Spa** 🏊 Sauna Solarium Jacuzzi ♫ **PARKING:** 20 **NOTES:** ⊗ in restaurant

TOTLAND BAY See Wight, Isle of

TOWCESTER, Northamptonshire — Map 11 SP64

⌂ Travelodge (Silverstone)

NN12 6TQ
☎ 08700 850 950 📠 01327 359105
web: www.travelodge.co.uk
Dir: *A43 East Towcester by-pass*

Travelodge offers good quality, good value, modern accommodation. Ideal for families, the spacious, en suite bedrooms include remote-control TV, tea and coffee-making facilities and comfortable beds. Meals can be taken at the nearby family restaurant. For further details consult the Hotel Groups page.

ROOMS: 55 en suite s fr £26; d fr £26

TRESCO See Scilly, Isles of

TRING, Hertfordshire — Map 06 SP91

★★★★68% ⚘ Pendley Manor

Cow Ln HP23 5QY
☎ 01442 891891 📠 01442 890687
e-mail: info@pendley-manor.co.uk
web: www.pendley-manor.co.uk
Dir: *M25 junct 20, A41 leave at Tring exit. At rdbt take exit for Berkhamsted/London. Take 1st left signed Tring Station & Pendley Manor*

This impressive Victorian mansion is set in extensive and mature landscaped grounds where peacocks roam. Spacious bedrooms, situated in the manor house or in the wing, offer a useful range of facilities. Public areas include a cosy bar, a conservatory lounge and a leisure centre and spa.

ROOMS: 74 en suite (6 fmly) ⊗ in 21 bedrooms **FACILITIES: Spa** STV 🏊 supervised ⚲ Snooker Sauna Gym Jacuzzi Steam room, Dance Studio, Internet coffee shop Xmas **CONF:** BC Thtr 230 Class 100 Board 50 **SERVICES:** Lift **PARKING:** 250 **NOTES:** ⊗ in restaurant Civ Wed 200

See advert on opposite page

★★★61% The Rose & Crown

High St HP23 5AH
☎ 01442 824071 📠 01442 890735
Dir: *off A41 between Aylesbury/Hemel Hempstead, in town centre*

This Tudor-style manor house in the centre of town, offers a great deal of charm. Bedrooms vary in size and style but all are generally well equipped. The restaurant and bar form the centre of the hotel and are popular with locals and residents. At the time of inspection the hotel was undergoing considerable refurbishment due to fire damage.

ROOMS: 27 en suite (3 fmly) ⊗ in 3 bedrooms **FACILITIES:** STV Full indoor leisure facilities available at sister hotel Xmas **CONF:** BC Thtr 80 Class 30 Board 30 **PARKING:** 60 **NOTES:** ✈ Civ Wed 100

⇧ Premier Travel Inn Tring
Tring Hill HP23 4LD
☎ 08701 977254 🖷 01442 890787
web: www.premiertravelinn.com
Dir: *M25 junct 20 take A41 towards Aylesbury, at end of Hemel Hempstead/Tring bypass straight over rdbt, Inn on right*
High quality, modern budget accommodation ideal for both families and business travellers. Spacious, en suite bedrooms feature bath and shower, satellite TV and many have telephones and modem points. The adjacent family restaurant features a wide and varied menu. For further details consult the Hotel Groups page.
ROOMS: 30 en suite s £46.95-£49.95; d £46.95-£49.95

TROUTBECK (NEAR WINDERMERE), Cumbria — Map 18 NY40

★★72% Mortal Man
LA23 1PL
☎ 01539 433193 🖷 431261
e-mail: enquiries@themortalman.co.uk
web: www.themortalman.co.uk
Dir: *2.5m N from junct of A591/A592, turn left before church into village, right at T-junct, hotel 800mtrs on right*
Dating from 1689, this traditional Lakeland inn enjoys a superb setting with stunning views towards Windermere. The owners continue to improve the hotel which offers two bar areas and a cosy lounge. A range of enjoyable meals is served in either the bars, with real fires, outside on fine days, or in the formal restaurant. Bedrooms are particularly well equipped and include a four-poster room.
ROOMS: 12 en suite ⊗ in all bedrooms **FACILITIES:** Fishing, Horse Riding, Sailing, Guided Walks, Watersports Xmas **CONF:** Thtr 30 **PARKING:** 20 **NOTES:** ⊗ in restaurant

TROWBRIDGE, Wiltshire — Map 04 ST85

★★67% Fieldways Hotel & Health Club
Hilperton Rd BA14 7JP
☎ 01225 768336 🖷 01225 753649
Dir: *Leave Trowbridge on A361 towards Melksham/Chippenham/Devizes - last property on left*
This establishment is quietly set in well-kept grounds and provides a pleasant combination of spacious, comfortably furnished bedrooms, an impressive wood-panelled dining room and a considerable range of indoor leisure facilities. 'Top to Toe' days are especially popular, and incorporate the wide range of beauty treatments on offer.
ROOMS: 8 en suite 5 annexe en suite (2 fmly) (2 GF) s £60; d £75-£85 (incl. bkfst) **LB** **FACILITIES: Spa** Sauna Solarium Gym Jacuzzi Range of beauty treatments/massage Specialists in pampering days **CONF:** Thtr 40 Class 40 Board 8 **PARKING:** 70 **NOTES:** ✗ ⊗ in restaurant

TROWELL MOTORWAY SERVICE AREA (M1), Nottinghamshire — Map 11 SK43

⇧ Travelodge Nottingham Trowell
NG9 3PL
☎ 08700 850 950 🖷 0115 944 7815
web: www.travelodge.co.uk
Dir: *M1 junct 25/26 northbound*
Travelodge offers good quality, good value, modern accommodation. Ideal for families, the spacious, en suite bedrooms include remote-control TV, tea and coffee-making facilities and comfortable beds. Meals can be taken at the nearby family restaurant. For further details consult the Hotel Groups page.
ROOMS: 35 en suite s fr £26; d fr £26

TRURO, Cornwall & Isles of Scilly — Map 02 SW84

★★★75% ❀❀ Alverton Manor
Tregolls Rd TR1 1ZQ
☎ 01872 276633 🖷 01872 222989
e-mail: reception@alvertonmanor.co.uk
Dir: *from at Carland Cross take A39 to Truro*
Formerly a convent, this impressive sandstone property stands in six acres of grounds, within walking distance of the city centre. It has a wide range of smart bedrooms, combining comfort with character. Stylish public areas include the library and the former chapel, now a striking function room. An interesting range of dishes is offered in the elegant restaurant.
ROOMS: 32 en suite (3 GF) ⊗ in 10 bedrooms **FACILITIES:** STV ⛳ 18 Xmas **CONF:** Thtr 80 Class 60 Board 40 Del from £140 **SERVICES:** Lift **PARKING:** 120 **NOTES:** ⊗ in restaurant Civ Wed 80

★★★71% Royal
Lemon St TR1 2QB
☎ 01872 270345 🖷 01872 242453
e-mail: reception@royalhotelcornwall.co.uk
web: www.royalhotelcornwall.co.uk
Dir: *follow A30 to Carland Cross then Truro. Follow brown tourists signs to hotel in city centre.*
This popular hotel is located in the heart of Truro and has a contemporary feel. Public areas offer a stylish atmosphere; the bar and restaurant are popular with locals and residents alike. Bedrooms are pleasantly appointed. A wide choice of appetising dishes is available, which feature ethnic, classical and vegetarian as well as daily specials.
ROOMS: 35 en suite 9 annexe en suite (4 fmly) (3 GF) ⊗ in 31 bedrooms s £80-£110; d £80-£150 (incl. bkfst) **LB** **FACILITIES:** STV **PARKING:** 44 **NOTES:** ✗ Closed 25 & 26 Dec

See advert on page 579

T

TRURO, continued

★★★62% *Brookdale*

Tregolls Rd TR1 1JZ
☎ 01872 273513 📠 01872 272400
e-mail: brookdale@hotelstruro.com
Dir: *from A30 onto A39, at A390 junct turn right into city centre. Hotel 600mtrs down hill*

Pleasantly situated in an elevated position close to the city centre, the Brookdale provides a range of accommodation options; all rooms are pleasantly spacious and well equipped, with some located in an adjacent annexe. Meals can be served in guests' rooms, and in the dining room a pleasant selection of dishes is available.

ROOMS: 30 en suite (2 fmly) ⊗ in 11 bedrooms **FACILITIES:** STV ch fac **CONF:** Thtr 85 Class 65 Board 25 **PARKING:** 45 **NOTES:** ⊗ in restaurant

★★68% Carlton

Falmouth Rd TR1 2HL
☎ 01872 272450 📠 01872 223938
e-mail: reception@carltonhotel.co.uk
Dir: *on A39 straight across 1st & 2nd rdbts onto bypass (Morlaix Avenue). At top of sweeping bend/hill turn right at mini rdbt into Falmouth Rd. Hotel is 100mtrs on right*

This family-run hotel is pleasantly located a short stroll from the city centre. A friendly welcome is assured and both business and leisure guests choose the Carlton on a regular basis. A smart, comfortable lounge is available, along with leisure facilities. A wide selection of home-cooked dishes is offered in the dining room.

ROOMS: 29 en suite (4 fmly) (4 GF) ⊗ in 20 bedrooms s £40-£47.50; d £57.50-£65 (incl. bkfst) **FACILITIES:** STV Sauna Jacuzzi **CONF:** Thtr 60 Class 24 Board 36 **PARKING:** 31 **NOTES:** ⊗ in restaurant Closed 21 Dec-4 Jan

Premier Travel Inn Truro

Old Carnon Hill, Carnon Downs TR3 6JT
☎ 08701 977255 📠 01872 865620
web: www.premiertravelinn.com
Dir: *on A39 (Truro to Falmouth road), 3 miles SW of Truro*

High quality, modern budget accommodation ideal for both families and business travellers. Spacious, en suite bedrooms feature bath and shower, satellite TV and many have telephones and modem points. The adjacent family restaurant features a wide and varied menu. For further details consult the Hotel Groups page.

ROOMS: 40 en suite s £49.95; d £49.95

> Popped the question? Hotels with Civ wed in their entry are licensed for civil wedding ceremonies. Maximum numbers for the ceremony only are shown e.g. Civ wed 120

TUNBRIDGE WELLS (ROYAL), Kent — Map 06 TQ53

Town House

★★★★ Hotel du Vin & Bistro

Crescent Rd TN1 2LY
☎ 01892 526455 📠 01892 512044
e-mail: reception@tunbridgewells.hotelduvin.com
web: www.hotelduvin.com
Dir: *follow town centre to main junct of Mount Pleasant Rd & Crescent Rd/Church Rd. Hotel 150yds on Crescent Rd on right just past Phillips House*

This impressive Grade II listed building dates from 1762, and as a princess, Queen Victoria often stayed here. The spacious bedrooms are available in a range of sizes, beautifully and individually appointed, and equipped with a host of thoughtful extras. Public rooms include a bistro-style restaurant, two elegant lounges and a small bar.

ROOMS: 31 en suite 4 annexe en suite ⊗ in all bedrooms s £105-£275; d £105-£275 **FACILITIES:** STV Snooker Boules court in garden **CONF:** Thtr 40 Class 30 Board 25 **SERVICES:** Lift **PARKING:** 30 **NOTES:** ⊗ in restaurant

★★★★71% The Spa

Mount Ephraim TN4 8XJ
☎ 01892 520331 📠 01892 510575
e-mail: info@spahotel.co.uk
web: www.spahotel.co.uk
Dir: *off A21 to A26, follow signs to A264 East Grinstead, hotel on right*

This imposing 18th-century country house is set in 14 acres of attractive landscaped grounds, overlooking Royal Tunbridge Wells. The spacious bedrooms are individually decorated and are tastefully furnished and thoughtfully equipped; many rooms overlook the pretty gardens. Public rooms include a comfortable lounge, a large bar, the Chandelier restaurant and excellent leisure facilities.

ROOMS: 69 en suite (10 fmly) (2 GF) s £96-£106; d £130-£140 **LB** **FACILITIES:** STV supervised Riding Sauna Gym Steam room Beauty Salon Jogging trail Xmas **CONF:** BC Thtr 300 Class 93 Board 90 Del from £135 **SERVICES:** Lift **PARKING:** 120 **NOTES:** ⊗ in restaurant Civ Wed 250

See advert on opposite page

★★65% Russell

80 London Rd TN1 1DZ
☎ 01892 544833 📠 01892 515846
e-mail: Sales@russell-hotel.com
web: www.russell-hotel.com
Dir: *at junct A26/A264 uphill onto A26, hotel on right*

This detached Victorian property is situated just a short walk from the centre of town. The generously proportioned bedrooms in the main house are pleasantly decorated and well equipped. In addition, there are several smartly appointed self-contained suites in an adjacent building. The public rooms include a lounge, a cosy bar and a restaurant.

ROOMS: 21 en suite 5 annexe en suite (5 fmly) (1 GF) ⊗ in 10 bedrooms s £70-£85; d £85-£99 (incl. bkfst) **LB** **CONF:** BC Thtr 35 Class 35 Board 35 Del from £60 **PARKING:** 15 **NOTES:**

U Ramada Tunbridge Wells

8 Tonbridge Rd, Pembury TN2 4QL
☎ 01892 823567 📠 01892 823931
e-mail: sales.tunwells@ramadajarvis.co.uk
web: www.ramadajarvis.co.uk
Dir: *From M25 junct 5 follow A21 S. Turn left at 1st rdbt signed Pembury Hospital. Hotel on left, 400yds past hospital.*

This well presented hotel is conveniently located just off the A21

continued

with easy access to the M25. Bedrooms are comfortably appointed for both business and leisure guests.
ROOMS: 84 en suite (8 fmly) (40 GF) ⊗ in 50 bedrooms s £85-£115; d £85-£115 **FACILITIES: Spa** STV ⛆ Sauna Jacuzzi Xmas **CONF:** Thtr 200 Class 80 Board 50 **PARKING:** 200 **NOTES:** ⊗ in restaurant Civ Wed 70

⌂ Innkeeper's Lodge Tunbridge
21 London Rd, Southborough TN4 0RL
☎ 01892 529292 📠 01892 510620
web: www.innkeeperslodge.com
Dir: *Off M25 onto A21, take A26 Tonbridge/Southborough turn off. Lodge on A26, opposite the cricket green.*
A growing concept in the travel accommodation market. Smart rooms meet essential business requirements but also have home comforts. Dining options include all-day menus plus the added advantage of breakfast, which is included in the room price. For further details consult the Hotel Groups page.
ROOMS: 15 en suite s £55-£59.95; d £55-£59.95

TURNERS HILL, West Sussex — Map 06 TQ33

Top Hotel

★★★ ⚘⚘ Alexander House Hotel
East St RH10 4QD
☎ 01342 714914 📠 01342 717328
e-mail: info@alexanderhouse.co.uk
web: www.alexanderhouse.co.uk
Dir: *6m from M23 junct 10 on B2110 between Turners Hill and East Grinstead*
Set in 175 acres of parklands and landscaped gardens, this delightful country house hotel dates back to the 17th century. Comfortable, stylish bedrooms have been individually designed to a high standard; all are thoughtfully equipped and benefit from superbly appointed bathrooms. Spacious, elegant public areas, furnished with antique pieces and paintings, include a choice of comfortable lounges and a stylish restaurant.
ROOMS: 32 en suite (12 fmly) (1 GF) ⊗ in all bedrooms s £125-£370; d £155-£370 **LB FACILITIES: Spa** STV ⛆ Sauna Solarium Gym Jacuzzi Clay Shooting, Archery by arrangement, Mountain bikes, Jogging Xmas **CONF:** BC Thtr 150 Del from £200 **SERVICES:** Lift **PARKING:** 100 **NOTES:** No children 7yrs ⊗ in restaurant Civ Wed 100

See advert under GATWICK AIRPORT (LONDON)

Packed in a hurry? Ironing facilities should be available at all star levels, either in the rooms or on request

TWICKENHAM, Greater London
See LONDON SECTION plan 1 B2

Premier Travel Inn Twickenham
Chertsey Rd, Whitton TW2 6LS
☎ 0870 9906416 📠 0870 9906417
web: www.premiertravelinn.com
Dir: *Exit M25 junct 12 onto M3 follow Central London signs. M3 becomes A316. In Richmond, 100yds straight over rdbt. Hotel 500yds on left*
High quality, modern budget accommodation ideal for both families and business travellers. Spacious, en suite bedrooms feature bath and shower, satellite TV and many have telephones and modem points. The adjacent family restaurant features a wide and varied menu. For further details consult the Hotel Groups page.
ROOMS: 31 en suite s £59.95-£62.95; d £59.95-£62.95

TWO BRIDGES, Devon — Map 03 SX67

★★77% Prince Hall
PL20 6SA
☎ 01822 890403 📠 01822 890676
e-mail: info@princehall.co.uk
web: www.princehall.co.uk
Dir: *on B3357 1m E of Two Bridges road junct*
Charm, peace and relaxed informality pervade at this small hotel, which has a stunning location at the heart of Dartmoor. Bedrooms, each named after a Dartmoor tor, have been equipped with thoughtful extras. The history of the house and its location are reflected throughout the public areas, which are very comfortable. The accomplished cooking is memorable here.
ROOMS: 8 en suite (1 fmly) ⊗ in all bedrooms s £85-£135; d £168-£230 (incl. bkfst & dinner) **LB FACILITIES:** Fishing Riding Guided Dartmoor Walks, Fly fishing, Garden tours **CONF:** Class 25 Board 20 Del £115 **PARKING:** 13 **NOTES:** No children 10yrs ⊗ in restaurant Closed 21 Dec-Jan

★★71% Two Bridges Hotel
PL20 6SW
☎ 01822 890581 📠 01822 892306
e-mail: enquiries@twobridges.co.uk
web: www.twobridges.co.uk
Dir: *junct of B3212 & B3357*
This wonderfully relaxing hotel is set in the heart of the Dartmoor National Park, in a beautiful riverside location. Three standards of comfortable rooms provide every modern convenience. There is a choice of lounges and fine dining is available in the restaurant, with menus featuring local game and seasonal produce.
ROOMS: 33 en suite (2 fmly) (6 GF) ⊗ in 25 bedrooms s £60-£85; d £120-£170 (incl. bkfst) **LB FACILITIES:** STV Fishing Xmas **CONF:** Thtr 130 Class 60 Board 40 Del from £110 **PARKING:** 100 **NOTES:** ⊗ in restaurant Civ Wed 130

See advert on opposite page

TYNEMOUTH, Tyne & Wear — Map 21 NZ36

★★★69% Grand
Grand Pde NE30 4ER
☎ 0191 293 6666 📠 0191 293 6665
e-mail: info@grandhotel-uk.com
web: www.grandhotel-uk.com
Dir: *A1058 for Tynemouth. At coast rdbt turn right. Hotel on right approx 0.5m*
Attracting a wide customer base, this grand Victorian building offers stunning views of the coastline. In addition to the restaurant there are two bars and an elegant and imposing staircase is the focal point. Bedrooms come in a variety of styles and are well equipped, tastefully decorated and have impressive bathrooms.
ROOMS: 40 en suite 4 annexe en suite (12 fmly) s £60-£150; d £75-£160 (incl. bkfst) **FACILITIES:** STV ♫ Xmas **CONF:** Thtr 130 Class 40 Board 40 **SERVICES:** Lift **PARKING:** 16 **NOTES:** ⊗ in restaurant RS Sun evening Civ Wed 120

TYWARDREATH, Cornwall & Isles of Scilly — Map 02 SX05

★★★78% Trenython Manor
Castle Dore Rd PL24 2TS
☎ 01726 814797 📠 01726 817030
e-mail: enquiries@trenython.co.uk
web: www.trenython.co.uk
Dir: *A390/B3269 towards Fowey, after 2m right into Castledore. Hotel 100mtrs on left*

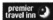

Dating from the 1800s, there is something distinctly different about Trenython, an English manor house designed by an Italian architect. Peacefully situated in extensive grounds, public areas have grace and elegance with original features, and many of the bedrooms have wonderful views. The splendour of the panelled restaurant is the venue for contemporary cuisine.
ROOMS: 24 en suite (2 fmly) ⊗ in all bedrooms s £105-£195; d £125-£225 (incl. bkfst) **LB FACILITIES: Spa** supervised Sauna Solarium Gym Jacuzzi Woodland walks, health & beauty centre Xmas **CONF:** BC Thtr 100 Class 60 Board 40 Del from £119 **PARKING:** 50 **NOTES:** ⊗ in restaurant Civ Wed 85

See advert under FOWEY

If you wish to use a particular credit card or debit card please check with the hotel that they are happy to accept it

UCKFIELD, East Sussex — Map 06 TQ42

★★★★76% Buxted Park Country House Hotel
Buxted TN22 4AY
☎ 01825 733333 📠 01825 732 990
e-mail: buxtedpark@handpicked.co.uk
web: www.handpicked.co.uk
Dir: *From A26 (Uckfield bypass) take A272 signed Buxted. Through lights, hotel 1m on right*
An attractive Grade II listed Georgian mansion dating back to the 17th century. The property is set amidst 300 acres of beautiful countryside and landscaped gardens. The stylish, thoughtfully equipped bedrooms are split between the main house and the

continued

modern Garden Wing. An interesting choice of dishes is served in the original Victorian Orangery.

ROOMS: 44 en suite (6 fmly) (16 GF) ⊗ in 22 bedrooms s £130-£180; d £130-£180 **LB** **FACILITIES:** STV Fishing Snooker Sauna Gym Putt green Beauty salon, Clay pigeon shoot, Archery, fishing, Mountain biking, Orienteering Xmas **CONF:** Thtr 130 Class 70 Board 60 Del from £225 **PARKING:** 150 **NOTES:** ⊗ in restaurant Civ Wed 130

See advert on this page

Indoor Swimming pool
Indoor Swimming pool (heated)
Outdoor Swimming pool
Outdoor Swimming pool (heated)

UCKFIELD, continued

Top Hotel

★★★ ◎◎ **Horsted Place**
Little Horsted TN22 5TS
☎ 01825 750581 🖷 01825 750459
e-mail: hotel@horstedplace.co.uk
Dir: *2m S on A26 towards Lewes*
This 17th-century property is one of Britain's finest examples of Gothic revivalist architecture. It is situated in extensive landscaped grounds, with a tennis court and croquet lawn, and is adjacent to the East Sussex National Golf Club. The spacious bedrooms are attractively decorated, tastefully furnished and equipped with many thoughtful touches such as flowers and books. Most rooms also have a separate sitting area.
ROOMS: 17 en suite 3 annexe en suite (5 fmly) (2 GF) s £130-£340; d £130-£340 (incl. bkfst) **LB** **FACILITIES:** STV ⛳ 36 🎾 ♫ Xmas **CONF:** Thtr 80 Class 50 Board 40 Del from £160 **SERVICES:** Lift **PARKING:** 32 **NOTES:** 🐕 No children 7yrs ⊘ in restaurant Civ Wed 100

ULLESTHORPE, Leicestershire Map 11 SP58

★★★70%
Ullesthorpe Court Hotel & Golf Club
Frolesworth Rd LE17 5BZ
☎ 01455 209023 🖷 01455 202537
e-mail: bookings@ullesthorpecourt.co.uk
web: www.ullesthorpecourt.co.uk
Dir: *M1 junct 20 towards Lutterworth, then follow brown tourist signs*

Complete with its own golf club, this impressively equipped hotel is within easy reach of the motorway network, NEC and Birmingham airport. Public areas include several eating options, conference and extensive leisure facilities. Bedrooms are mostly spacious and thoughtfully equipped for both the corporate or leisure guests, and a four-poster is available.
ROOMS: 38 en suite (1 fmly) (12 GF) ⊘ in 20 bedrooms s £45-£95; d £90-£120 (incl. bkfst) **LB** **FACILITIES: Spa** STV 🏊 supervised ⛳ 18 🎾 Snooker Sauna Solarium Gym Putt green Jacuzzi Beauty room, Steam Room **CONF:** Thtr 80 Class 48 Board 30 Del £120 **PARKING:** 500 **NOTES:** ⊘ in restaurant RS 25 & 26 Dec Civ Wed 120

ULLSWATER See Glenridding, Patterdale & Watermillock

ULVERSTON, Cumbria Map 18 SD27

★★70% **Lonsdale House Hotel**
11 Daltongate LA12 7BD
☎ 01229 582598 🖷 01229 581260
e-mail: info@lonsdalehousehotel.co.uk
web: www.lonsdalehousehotel.co.uk
Dir: *In Ulverston right at 2nd rdbt, follow one-way system to mini-rdbt. Left pass zebra crossing then right & 1st right*
Enjoying a town centre location, this family-run hotel was once a coaching inn. Bedrooms vary in style and size but all are extremely well equipped. Public areas include an attractive bar and restaurant, an inviting lounge and a delightful rear garden.
ROOMS: 20 en suite (2 fmly) ⊘ in 16 bedrooms s £55-£75; d £60-£120 (incl. bkfst) **LB** **FACILITIES:** STV Xmas **NOTES:** ⊘ in restaurant

UPHOLLAND, Lancashire Map 15 SD50

★★★60% **Lancashire Manor**
Prescott Rd WN8 9PU
☎ 01695 720401 🖷 01695 50953
e-mail: enquiries@hotels-skelmersdale.com
web: www.hotel-skelmersdale.com
Dir: *M6 junct 26 to M58. Exit at junct 5 for 'Pimbo'. Left at rdbt follow into Prescott Rd. Hotel on right*
Conveniently situated, this friendly hotel has attractive grounds and a magnificent Great Hall, dating back to 1580, now used primarily for banquets and weddings. The bedrooms are well equipped, and some include facilities for less mobile guests. The bare stone walls in the bar and restaurant add character to the establishment.
ROOMS: 55 en suite (3 fmly) (21 GF) ⊘ in 35 bedrooms s £50-£85; d £65-£96 **LB** **FACILITIES:** STV Xmas **CONF:** Thtr 200 Class 125 Board 70 Del £109.50 **SERVICES:** air con **PARKING:** 250 **NOTES:** ⊘ in restaurant Civ Wed 150

UPPER SLAUGHTER, Gloucestershire Map 10 SP12

Top Hotel

★★★ ◎◎◎ **Lords of the Manor**
GL54 2JD
☎ 01451 820243 🖷 01451 820696
e-mail: enquiries@lordsofthemanor.com
web: www.bespokehotels.com
Dir: *2m W of A429. Turn off A40 onto A429, take 'The Slaughters' turn. Through Lower Slaughter for 1m to Upper Slaughter. Hotel on right*
This wonderfully welcoming 17th-century manor house hotel sits in eight acres of gardens and parkland surrounded by Cotswold countryside. A relaxed atmosphere, underpinned by professional and attentive service is the hallmark here, so that guests are often reluctant to leave. The public rooms are elegant and the restaurant is the venue for consistently

continued

impressive cuisine. Bedrooms have much character and charm, combined with the extra touches expected of a hotel of this stature.

ROOMS: 27 en suite (9 GF) s £100; d £160-£310 (incl. bkfst) **LB** **FACILITIES:** STV Fishing Xmas **CONF:** Thtr 30 Class 20 Board 20 **PARKING:** 40 **NOTES:** in restaurant Civ Wed 50

UPPINGHAM, Rutland — Map 11 SP89

★★★64% Falcon

The Market Place LE15 9PY
☎ 01572 823535 01572 821620
e-mail: sales@thefalconhotel.com
web: www.thefalconhotel.com
Dir: *turn off A47 onto A6003, left at lights, hotel on right*

An attractive, 16th-century coaching inn situated in the heart of this bustling market town. Public areas feature an open-plan lounge bar, with a relaxing atmosphere and comfortable sofas. The brasserie area offers a cosmopolitan-style snack menu, while more formal meals are provided in the Garden Terrace Restaurant. Conference and meeting rooms are also available.

ROOMS: 25 en suite (4 fmly) (3 GF) s £60-£75; d £90-£125 (incl. bkfst) **LB** **FACILITIES:** STV Snooker ♫ Xmas **CONF:** Thtr 60 Class 40 Board 34 Del from £98 **PARKING:** 33 **NOTES:** in restaurant Civ Wed 150

★★73% The Lake Isle Restaurant & Town House Hotel

16 High St East LE15 9PZ
☎ 01572 822951 01572 824400
e-mail: info@lakeislehotel.com
web: www.lakeislehotel.com
Dir: *in the centre of Uppingham via Queen Street*

This attractive, town-house hotel centres round a delightful restaurant and small elegant bar. There is also an inviting and comfortable first-floor guest lounge. Bedrooms are extremely well-appointed and thoughtfully equipped and include some spacious split-level cottage suites situated across a quiet courtyard.

continued

Imaginative cooking and an extremely impressive list of wines are a highlight.

ROOMS: 9 en suite 3 annexe en suite (1 fmly) (1 GF) in all bedrooms s £55-£60; d £70-£90 (incl. bkfst) **LB** **FACILITIES:** ch fac Xmas **CONF:** Board 10 **PARKING:** 7 **NOTES:** in restaurant

UPTON UPON SEVERN, Worcestershire — Map 10 SO84

★★★69% White Lion

21 High St WR8 0HJ
☎ 01684 592551 01684 593333
e-mail: reservations@whitelionhotel.biz
Dir: *A422, A38 towards Tewkesbury. In 8m take B4104, after 1m cross bridge, turn left to hotel, past bend on left*

Famed for being the inn depicted in Henry Fielding's novel Tom Jones, this 16th-century hotel brings old England to the fore with exposed beams, wall timbers, and traditional furniture with lace table cloths and vases of fresh flowers. The White Lion has a well-deserved reputation for the quality of its food, which is complemented by friendly, attentive service.

ROOMS: 11 en suite 2 annexe en suite (2 fmly) (2 GF) s £62.50-£68; d £87.50-£98 (incl. bkfst) **LB** **CONF:** Thtr 24 Class 12 Board 12 **PARKING:** 18 **NOTES:** in restaurant Closed 01-Jan RS 25 Dec & 1 Jan

URMSTON, Greater Manchester — Map 15 SJ79

Premier Travel Inn Manchester (Trafford Centre)

premier travel inn

Trafford Boulevard M41 7JE
☎ 0870 9906310 0870 9906311
web: www.premiertravelinn.com
Dir: *Exit M6, onto M62 at junct 21a, towards Manchester. Exit M62 junct 1, M60 towards south. Exit M60 junct 10, take B5214. Hotel on left just before Ellesmere Circle*

High quality, modern budget accommodation ideal for both families and business travellers. Spacious, en suite bedrooms feature bath and shower, satellite TV and many have telephones and modem points. The adjacent family restaurant features a wide and varied menu. For further details consult the Hotel Groups page.

ROOMS: 42 en suite s £52.95; d £52.95

○ Hotel due to open in late 2005 or 2006
U Star rating not confirmed

Late for dinner? Quality standards mean that last orders for dinner vary according to star rating and should be no earlier than:
★★ 7.00pm ★★★ 8:00pm ★★★★ 9:00pm ★★★★★ 10:00pm

UTTOXETER, Staffordshire — Map 10 SK03

Restaurant with Rooms

The Riversholme Hotel & Restaurant
High St, Rocester ST14 5JU
☎ 01889 590900 📠 01889 591448
e-mail: info@riversholme.co.uk
web: www.riversholme.co.uk
Dir: *A50 exit B5030 signed Rocester. Follow to JCB Headquarters, right into village. Hotel stands back off High Street*
This delightful property is situated on the border of Derbyshire and Staffordshire, with easy access to the M6 motorway. Individually designed bedrooms boast well-appointed, beautifully tiled bathrooms and many original period features. The elegant restaurant offers imaginative modern cuisine and the attractive grounds make this an ideal and popular wedding venue.
ROOMS: 8 en suite (3 fmly) (4 GF) ⊗ in all bedrooms s £70; d £85 (incl. bkfst) **PARKING:** 20 **NOTES:** ✗ ⊗ in restaurant
Closed 25 Dec-2 Jan

Premier Travel Inn Uttoxeter
Derby Rd, (A518/A50) ST14 5AA
☎ 08701 977256 📠 01889 561801
web: www.premiertravelinn.com
Dir: *at junction of A50/A518, 1m N of town centre*
High quality, modern budget accommodation ideal for both families and business travellers. Spacious, en suite bedrooms feature bath and shower, satellite TV and many have telephones and modem points. The adjacent family restaurant features a wide and varied menu. For further details consult the Hotel Groups page.
ROOMS: 41 en suite s £49.95; d £49.95

Travelodge
Ashbourne Rd ST14 5AA
☎ 08700 850 950 📠 01889 562043
web: www.travelodge.co.uk
Dir: *on A50/B5030*
Travelodge offers good quality, good value, modern accommodation. Ideal for families, the spacious, en suite bedrooms include remote-control TV, tea and coffee-making facilities and comfortable beds. Meals can be taken at the nearby family restaurant. For further details consult the Hotel Groups page.
ROOMS: 32 en suite s fr £26; d fr £26

UXBRIDGE See advert on opposite page

VENTNOR See Wight, Isle of

VERYAN, Cornwall & Isles of Scilly — Map 02 SW93

★★★★78% *Nare*
Carne Beach TR2 5PF
☎ 01872 501111 📠 01872 501856
e-mail: office@narehotel.co.uk
web: www.narehotel.co.uk
Dir: *from Tregony follow A3078 for approx 1.5m. Left at Veryan sign, through village towards sea & hotel*
This delightful hotel offers a relaxed, country-house atmosphere in a spectacular coastal setting. Many of the bedrooms have balconies, and fresh flowers, carefully chosen artwork and antiques all contribute to the engaging individuality. A choice of dining options is available, from light snacks to superb local seafood.
ROOMS: 38 en suite (4 fmly) **FACILITIES: Spa** STV Snooker Sauna Gym Jacuzzi Health & Beauty clinic Hotel Boat Shooting, steam room ch fac **SERVICES:** Lift **PARKING:** 80 **NOTES:** ⊗ in restaurant

VIRGINIA WATER, Surrey — Map 06 TQ06

★★72% *The Wheatsheaf*
London Rd GU25 4QF
☎ 01344 842057 📠 01344 842932
e-mail: sales@wheatsheafhotel.com
web: www.wheatsheafhotel.com
Dir: *off A30, N of Sunningdale; pass Wentworth Golf Course Hotel on left at lights*

This 19th-century inn is in a prime location overlooking the lake in Great Windsor Park. Bedrooms are well proportioned and comfortable, with stylish decor and a good range of facilities. The public rooms consist of a country-style bar and restaurant which offers a substantial lunch and dinner menu. Secure parking is provided.
ROOMS: 17 en suite (2 fmly) ⊗ in 10 bedrooms **FACILITIES:** STV **CONF:** Thtr 50 Class 30 Board 25 **SERVICES:** air con **PARKING:** 100 **NOTES:** ✗ Civ Wed 60

WADEBRIDGE, Cornwall & Isles of Scilly — Map 02 SW97

★★63% Molesworth Arms
Molesworth St PL27 7DP
☎ 01208 812055 📠 01208 814254
e-mail: info@moleswortharms.co.uk
web: www.moleswortharms.co.uk
Dir: *A30 through Bodmin, then take A389 to Wadebridge. Over old bridge, right at rdbt, then 1st left*
Situated in a pedestrian area of the town, this 16th-century former coaching inn is a popular base for exploring the area. The comfortable bedrooms retain their original character and charm. In addition to the wide range of snacks and meals served in the lively bar, the Courtyard Restaurant offers a comprehensive carte with daily specials.
ROOMS: 16 rms (14 en suite) (2 fmly) s £45-£52.50; d £70-£82.50 (incl. bkfst) **LB FACILITIES:** STV **CONF:** Thtr 60 Class 50 Board 40 **PARKING:** 16 **NOTES:** ⊗ in restaurant

WAKEFIELD, West Yorkshire — Map 16 SE32

★★★★64% Cedar Court
Denby Dale Rd WF4 3QZ
☎ 01924 276310 📠 01924 280221
e-mail: sales@cedarcourthotels.co.uk
web: www.cedarcourthotels.co.uk
Dir: *adjacent to M1 junct 39*
This hotel enjoys a convenient location just off the M1. Traditionally styled bedrooms offer a good range of facilities while open-plan public areas include a busy bar and restaurant

continued

operation. Conferences and functions are extremely well catered for and a modern leisure club completes the picture.
ROOMS: 150 en suite (2 fmly) (74 GF) ⊗ in 100 bedrooms s £65-£125; d £75-£135 **LB FACILITIES: Spa** STV ☒ supervised Sauna Solarium Gym Jacuzzi Xmas **CONF:** BC Thtr 400 Class 140 Board 80 Del from £110 **SERVICES:** Lift air con **PARKING:** 350 **NOTES:** ⊗ in restaurant Civ Wed 250

★★★75% ⊛ Waterton Park
Walton Hall, The Balk, Walton WF2 6PW
☎ 01924 257911 & 249800 ▤ 01924 259686
e-mail: watertonpark@bestwestern.co.uk
Dir: 3m SE off B6378. Exit M1 junct 39 towards Wakefield. At 3rd rdbt take right for Crofton. At 2nd lights right & follow signs

A stately private house, built on an island in the centre of a lake in an idyllic setting. The main house contains many feature bedrooms, and the annexe houses more spacious rooms, all equally well equipped with modern facilities. The delightful beamed restaurant, two bars and leisure centre are located in the old hall, and there is a licence for civil weddings.
ROOMS: 25 en suite 43 annexe en suite (16 GF) ⊗ in 12 bedrooms s £80-£105; d £130-£150 (incl. bkfst) **LB FACILITIES: Spa** STV ☒ supervised ♨ 18 Fishing Sauna Solarium Gym Jacuzzi Steam room **CONF:** Thtr 150 Class 80 Board 80 Del from £125 **PARKING:** 200 **NOTES:** ✖ ⊗ in restaurant Civ Wed 130

★★★69% Hotel St Pierre
Barnsley Rd, Newmillerdam WF2 6QG THE INDEPENDENTS
☎ 01924 255596 ▤ 01924 252746
e-mail: sales@hotelstpierre.co.uk
web: www.cedarcourthotels.co.uk
Dir: M1 junct 39 take A636 to Wakefield, turn right at rdbt, on to Asdale Road to traffic lights. Turn right onto A61 towards Barnsley. Hotel just after lake
This well-furnished hotel lies south of Wakefield, close to Newmiller Dam. The interior of the modern building has comfortable and thoughtfully equipped bedrooms and smart public rooms. There is a good selection of conference rooms, a small gym and an intimate restaurant.
ROOMS: 54 en suite (3 fmly) (4 GF) ⊗ in 33 bedrooms s £49-£89; d £59-£95 (incl. bkfst) **LB FACILITIES:** STV Gym Xmas **CONF:** Thtr 120 Class 60 Board 60 Del from £70 **SERVICES:** Lift **PARKING:** 70 **NOTES:** Civ Wed 120

★★★67% Best Western Stoneleigh Hotel
Doncaster Rd WF1 5HA
☎ 01924 369461 ▤ 01924 201041
e-mail: stoneleigh@bestwestern.co.uk
Dir: A636, follow Asdale Rd then Agbrigg Rd. Hotel 1m from M1 junct 39
This hotel is a conversion of a Victorian stone terrace dating back to 1870. The modern bedrooms are located on two floors and a lift is available. The well-decorated restaurants include both
continued

The Barn Hotel
North-West London
West End Road, Ruislip, Middlesex HA4 6JB
Tel: 01895 636057 Fax: 01895 638379
Email: info@thebarnhotel.co.uk
Web Site: www.thebarnhotel.co.uk

★★★ ⊛⊛

The Barn Hotel is a unique 17th century hotel set in three acres of landscaped rose gardens and lawns. Only minutes from Heathrow Airport, Uxbridge, Harrow, with easy access to Wembley, Windsor and Central London. Five minutes from the tube station, A40 and M25. 59 bedrooms with satellite TV, all with internet/ Email data points. 5 conference rooms Licensed for civil weddings. 2 Rosette Hawtreys Restaurant and Bar.

traditional and Chinese cuisine. Guests have complementary use of a nearby health club and gym.
ROOMS: 28 en suite s £53.50-£57.50; d £63.50-£67.50 (incl. bkfst) **FACILITIES:** Xmas **CONF:** Thtr 200 Class 80 Board 60 Del from £85 **SERVICES:** Lift **PARKING:** 70 **NOTES:** ⊗ in restaurant Civ Wed 250

Ⓤ Chasley
Queen St WF1 1JU
☎ 01924 372111 ▤ 01924 383648
e-mail: admin@chasleywakefield.supanet.com
Dir: M1 junct 39 & follow signs for town centre. Queen St on left
At the time of going to press, the star classification for this hotel was not confirmed. Please refer to the AA internet site www.theAA.com for current information.
ROOMS: 64 en suite (8 fmly) ⊗ in 18 bedrooms s £65-£75; d £75-£85 (incl. bkfst) **CONF:** Thtr 250 Class 110 Board 88 Del from £65 **SERVICES:** Lift **PARKING:** 40 **NOTES:** ✖ ⊗ in restaurant Civ Wed 250

> We have indicated only the hotels that don't accept credit or debit cards

⌂ Campanile
Monckton Rd WF2 7AL Campanile
☎ 01924 201054 ▤ 01924 201055
e-mail: wakefield@envergure.co.uk
web: www.envergure.fr
Dir: M1 junct 39, A636 1m towards Wakefield, left onto Monckton Rd, hotel on left
This modern building offers accommodation in smart, well-equipped bedrooms, all with en suite bathrooms. Refreshments
continued on p586

WAKEFIELD, continued

may be taken at the informal Bistro. For further details consult the Hotel Groups page.

Campanile, Wakefield

ROOMS: 76 annexe en suite **CONF:** Thtr 35 Class 18 Board 24

⌂ Premier Travel Inn Wakefield

Thornes Park, Denby Dale Rd WF2 8DY
☎ 08701 977257 🖷 01924 373620
web: www.premiertravelinn.com
Dir: *From M1 junct 39 take A636 towards town centre. Inn on left at 3rd rdbt.*
High quality, modern budget accommodation ideal for both families and business travellers. Spacious, en suite bedrooms feature bath and shower, satellite TV and many have telephones and modem points. The adjacent family restaurant features a wide and varied menu. For further details consult the Hotel Groups page.
ROOMS: 42 en suite s £46.95-£48.95; d £46.95-£48.95 **CONF:** Thtr 54 Board 24

⌂ Travelodge Wakefield (Northbound)

M1 Service Area, West Bretton WF4 4LQ
☎ 08700 850 950 🖷 01924 830609
web: www.travelodge.co.uk
(For full entry see Woolley Edge)

WALLASEY, Merseyside — Map 15 SJ29

★★★71% Grove House

Grove Rd CH45 3HF
☎ 0151 639 3947 & 0151 630 4558 🖷 0151 639 0028
e-mail: reception@thegrovehouse.fsnet.co.uk
Dir: *M53 junct 1, A554 Wallasey New Brighton, right after church onto Harrison Drive, left after Windsors Garage onto Grove Rd.*
This is an immaculately maintained, family-owned hotel. Many of the bedrooms enjoy a view over the attractive gardens to the rear of the hotel - all are comfortably furnished and particularly well equipped. The bar lounge provides a venue to relax with drinks before dinner in the tastefully appointed oak-panelled restaurant.
ROOMS: 14 en suite (7 fmly) s £59.75; d £69.75-£79.75 **LB** **FACILITIES:** STV **CONF:** Thtr 50 Class 30 Board 50 Del £92.65 **PARKING:** 28 **NOTES:** ✗ RS Bank holidays Civ Wed 50

WALLINGFORD, Oxfordshire — Map 05 SU68

★★★72% ◎ Springs Hotel & Golf Club

Wallingford Rd, North Stoke OX10 6BE
☎ 01491 836687 🖷 01491 836877
e-mail: info@thespringshotel.com web: www.thespringshotel.com
Dir: *off A4074 (Oxford-Reading road) onto B4009 (Goring). Hotel approx 1m on right*
Set on its own golf course, this Victorian mansion has a timeless and peaceful atmosphere. The generously equipped bedrooms vary in size but many are spacious. The elegant restaurant enjoys splendid views over the spring-fed lake where a variety of wildfowl enjoy the natural surroundings. There is also a comfortable lounge with original features, and a cosy bar to relax in.

ROOMS: 32 en suite (4 fmly) (8 GF) ⊗ in 6 bedrooms s £95-£140; d £110-£155 (incl. bkfst) **LB** **FACILITIES:** STV ⛳ 18 Fishing Sauna Putt green Clay pigeon shooting ♫ Xmas **CONF:** BC Thtr 60 Class 16 Board 26 Del from £140 **PARKING:** 150 **NOTES:** ⊗ in restaurant Civ Wed 90

★★★68% The George

High St OX10 0BS
☎ 01491 836665 🖷 01491 825359
e-mail: info@george-hotel-wallingford.com
web: www.peelhotel.com
Dir: *E side of A329 on N entry to town*

Old world charm and modern facilities merge seamlessly in this former coaching inn. Bedrooms in the main house have charm and character in abundance. Those in the wing have a more contemporary style, but all are well equipped and attractively decorated. Diners can choose between the restaurant and bistro, or relax in the cosy bar.
ROOMS: 39 en suite (1 fmly) (9 GF) ⊗ in 21 bedrooms s £110-£130; d £125-£140 **LB** **FACILITIES:** STV Xmas **CONF:** Thtr 120 Class 60 Board 40 Del £139 **PARKING:** 60 **NOTES:** ✗ ⊗ in restaurant Civ Wed 100

★★★68% Shillingford Bridge

Shillingford OX10 8LZ
☎ 01865 858567 🖷 01865 858636
e-mail: shillingford.bridge@forestdale.com
web: www.forestdale.com
Dir: *M4 junct 10, A329 through Wallingford towards Thame, then B4009 through Watlington. Right on A4074 at Benson, then left at Shillingford rdbt (unclass road) Wallingford Rd*
This hotel enjoys a superb position right on the banks of the River Thames, and benefits from private moorings and a waterside open-air swimming pool. The public areas have large picture

continued

windows making the best use of the view. Bedrooms are well equipped and furnished with comfort in mind.
ROOMS: 34 en suite 8 annexe en suite (6 fmly) ⊗ in 8 bedrooms s £85-£105; d £120-£140 (incl. bkfst) **LB FACILITIES:** supervised Fishing Squash ♫ Xmas **CONF:** Thtr 80 Class 36 Board 26 Del from £125 **PARKING:** 100 **NOTES:** ⊗ in restaurant Civ Wed

WALSALL, West Midlands Map 10 SP09

★★★★65% Menzies Baron's Court
Walsall Rd, Walsall Wood WS9 9AH
☎ 01543 452020 🖹 01543 361276
e-mail: barons@menzies-hotels.co.uk
web: www.menzies-hotels.co.uk
Dir: *M6 junct 7, A34 towards Walsall, then A4148 (ring road), at rdbt right onto A461 towards Lichfield, hotel 3m on right*
This hotel prides itself on warm hospitality and is conveniently situated for business guests to this area. The lounge, bar and restaurant are modern and thoughtfully designed. Additional features include a small leisure complex and conference facilities.
ROOMS: 94 en suite (2 fmly) ⊗ in 19 bedrooms s £99; d £109 **LB FACILITIES:** STV Sauna Solarium Gym Jacuzzi ♫ Xmas **CONF:** Thtr 200 Class 100 Board 100 Del £135 **SERVICES:** Lift **PARKING:** 200 **NOTES:** ⊗ in restaurant Civ Wed

★★★76% The Fairlawns at Aldridge
178 Little Aston Rd, Aldridge WS9 0NU
☎ 01922 455122 🖹 01922 743210
e-mail: welcome@fairlawns.co.uk
web: www.fairlawns.co.uk
Dir: *off A452 towards Aldridge at x-roads with A454. Hotel 600yds on right*

In a rural location, this friendly hotel offers a wide range of facilities and modern, comfortable bedrooms. Family rooms, one with a four-poster bed, suites and even budget rooms are available. The Fairlawns Restaurant serves a wide range of award-winning seasonal dishes. The extensive leisure complex is predominantly for adult use as there is restricted availability to young people.
ROOMS: 50 en suite (8 fmly) (1 GF) ⊗ in 34 bedrooms s £75-£165; d £89.50-£122.50 (incl. bkfst) **LB FACILITIES: Spa** STV supervised Sauna Solarium Gym Jacuzzi Dance studio Beauty Salon **CONF:** BC Thtr 80 Class 40 Board 30 Del from £137.50 **PARKING:** 150 **NOTES:** ⊗ in restaurant Civ Wed 100

★★★69% Beverley
58 Lichfield Rd WS4 2DJ
☎ 01922 614967 & 622999 🖹 01922 724187
e-mail: beverleyhotel@aol.com
Dir: *1m N of Walsall town centre on A461 to Lichfield*
This privately-owned hotel dates back to 1880. Bedrooms are comfortably appointed and equipped with thoughtful extras. The tastefully decorated public areas include a relaxing guest lounge and a spacious bar combined with a conservatory. The Gallery Restaurant offers guests a choice of carefully prepared, appetising dishes.
ROOMS: 40 en suite (2 fmly) (4 GF) ⊗ in 6 bedrooms s £70-£100; d £80-£120 (incl. bkfst) **LB FACILITIES:** Games room with pool table **CONF:** BC Thtr 60 Class 30 Board 30 Del £120 **PARKING:** 68 **NOTES:** ⊗ in restaurant RS 24 Dec-2 Jan Civ Wed 50

★★★66% *Quality Hotel & Suites Walsall*
20 Wolverhampton Rd West, Bentley WS2 0BS
☎ 01922 724444 🖹 01922 723148
e-mail: enquiries@hotels-walsall.com
web: www.choicehotelseurope.com
Dir: *on rdbt at M6 junct 10*
All the accommodation at this conveniently located hotel is well equipped. It includes air-conditioned suites, which have a fax machine and a kitchen with a microwave and fridge. There is an extensive all-day menu, plus room service. Guests can also choose to dine in the carvery restaurant.
ROOMS: 154 en suite (120 fmly) (78 GF) ⊗ in 64 bedrooms **FACILITIES: Spa** STV supervised Sauna Gym Jacuzzi **CONF:** Thtr 180 Class 70 Board 80 **PARKING:** 160 **NOTES:** ⊗ in restaurant Civ Wed 150

★★★66%
Quality Hotel Birmingham North
Birmingham Rd WS5 3AB
☎ 01922 633609 🖹 01922 635727
e-mail: info@boundaryhotel.com
Dir: *M6 junct 7, A34 to Walsall. Hotel 1.5m on left*
Bedrooms at this purpose-built hotel, including some on the ground floor, are soundly furnished and well equipped. Public areas include a pleasantly appointed main restaurant (more informal meals are served in the public bar) and a cellar bar which occasionally features live music. Hotel guests also have the use of a well-maintained tennis court.
ROOMS: 96 en suite (3 fmly) (4 GF) ⊗ in 50 bedrooms s £65-£94; d £65-£94 (incl. bkfst) **LB FACILITIES:** STV Pool table ♫ Xmas **CONF:** Thtr 60 Class 30 Board 30 Del from £99 **SERVICES:** Lift **PARKING:** 250 **NOTES:** ⊗ in restaurant Civ Wed 60

Premier Travel Inn Walsall
Bentley Green, Bentley Rd North WS2 0WB
☎ 08701 977258 🖹 01922 724098
web: www.premiertravelinn.com
Dir: *M6 junct 10, A454 signed Wolverhampton & then 2nd exit (Ansons junct). Left at rdbt, 1st left at next rdbt, Inn on right*
High quality, modern budget accommodation ideal for both families and business travellers. Spacious, en suite bedrooms feature bath and shower, satellite TV and many have telephones and modem points. The adjacent family restaurant features a wide and varied menu. For further details consult the Hotel Groups page.
ROOMS: 40 en suite s £47.95-£50.95; d £47.95-£50.95

WALTERSTONE, Herefordshire Map 09 SO32

★★★68% *Allt-yr-Ynys Country House Hotel*
HR2 0DU
☎ 01873 890307 🖹 01873 890539
e-mail: allthotel@compuserve.com
(For full entry see Abergavenny (Wales))

U Star rating not confirmed

W

WALTHAM ABBEY, Essex Map 06 TL30

★★★★69% Waltham Abbey Marriott

Old Shire Ln EN9 3LX
☎ 01992 717170 01992 711841
web: www.marriott.co.uk
Dir: *M25 junct 26*

This hotel benefits from convenient access to London and the major road networks. Air-conditioned bedrooms are spacious, tastefully decorated and offer a range of facilities for the modern business traveller. The hotel also provides a range of meeting rooms, substantial car parking and a well-equipped indoor leisure centre.
ROOMS: 162 en suite (16 fmly) (80 GF) in 132 bedrooms s fr £129; d fr £129 **LB** **FACILITIES:** STV Sauna Solarium Gym Jacuzzi Steam room Xmas **CONF:** BC Thtr 280 Class 120 Board 50 Del £182 **SERVICES:** air con **PARKING:** 250 **NOTES:** in restaurant Civ Wed 200

Premier Travel Inn Waltham Abbey

The Grange, Sewardstone Rd EN9 3QF
☎ 0870 9906568 0870 9906569
web: www.premiertravelinn.com
Dir: *Exit M25 junct 26, A121 towards Waltham Abbey. Left onto A112, hotel 0.5m on left*
High quality, modern budget accommodation ideal for both families and business travellers. Spacious, en suite bedrooms feature bath and shower, satellite TV and many have telephones and modem points. The adjacent family restaurant features a wide and varied menu. For further details consult the Hotel Groups page.
ROOMS: 93 en suite s £53.95-£59.95; d £53.95-£59.95

WALTON-ON-THAMES, Surrey
See LONDON SECTION plan 1 A1

Innkeeper's Lodge Walton-on-Thames

Ashley Park Rd KT12 1JP
☎ 01932 220196 01932 220660
web: www.innkeeperslodge.com
Dir: *M25 junct 11 east towards A317 towards Weybridge, at B365 roundabout for Ashley Park, turn left then right into Station Av, left opposite station*
A growing concept in the travel accommodation market. Smart rooms meet essential business requirements but also have home comforts. Dining options include all-day menus plus the added advantage of breakfast, which is included in the room price. For further details consult the Hotel Groups page.
ROOMS: 32 en suite s £52-£79.95; d £52-£79.95 **CONF:** Thtr 60 Class 24 Board 24

No smoking

WANSFORD, Cambridgeshire Map 12 TL09

U The Haycock

PE8 6JA
☎ 01780 782223 01780 783508
e-mail: sales@thehaycock.co.uk
Dir: *from A1 follow signs for Wansford, hotel on right*
At the time of going to press, the star classification for this hotel was not confirmed. Please refer to the AA internet site www.theAA.com for current information.
ROOMS: 48 en suite (5 fmly) (14 GF) in 39 bedrooms s £80-£173; d £115-£185 (incl. bkfst) **FACILITIES:** STV Fishing Xmas **CONF:** BC Thtr 275 Class 100 Board 45 Del £160 **PARKING:** 200 **NOTES:** in restaurant Civ Wed 150

WARDLEY, Tyne & Wear Map 21 NZ36

Travelodge Newcastle Whitemare Pool

Wardley, Whitemare Pool NE10 8YB
☎ 08700 850 950 0191 469 5718
web: www.travelodge.co.uk
Dir: *from A1 S, take A184 through Gateshead towards Sunderland & South Shields. E of Gateshead take A194 towards South Shields. Hotel on left*
Travelodge offers good quality, good value, modern accommodation. Ideal for families, the spacious, en suite bedrooms include remote-control TV, tea and coffee-making facilities and comfortable beds. Meals can be taken at the nearby family restaurant. For further details consult the Hotel Groups page.
ROOMS: 71 en suite s fr £26; d fr £26

WARE, Hertfordshire Map 06 TL31

★★★★★71% *Marriott Hanbury Manor Hotel & Country Club*

SG12 0SD
☎ 01920 487722 & 0870 400 7222
01920 487692
e-mail: guestrelations.hanburymanor@marriotthotels.co.uk
web: www.marriott.co.uk
Dir: *M25 junct 25, take A10 north for 12m, hotel is on the left*

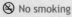

Set in 200 acres of landscaped grounds, this impressive Jacobean-style mansion boasts an enviable range of leisure facilities, including an excellent health club and championship golf course. Bedrooms are traditionally and comfortably furnished in the country-house style and have lovely marbled bathrooms. There are a number of food and drink options, including the renowned Zodiac and Oakes restaurants.
ROOMS: 134 en suite 27 annexe en suite (3 GF) in 96 bedrooms **FACILITIES: Spa** STV supervised 18 Snooker Sauna Solarium Gym Putt green Jacuzzi Health & beauty treatments, Aerobics, Yoga Dance class **CONF:** BC Thtr 120 Class 76 Board 36 **SERVICES:** Lift **PARKING:** 200 **NOTES:** Civ Wed 120

★★★68% Roebuck
Baldock St SG12 9DR
☎ 01920 409955 01920 468016
e-mail: roebuck@forestdale.com
web: www.forestdale.com
Dir: *from A10 onto B1001, left at rdbt 1st left behind Fire Station*
Close to the centre of this old market town, the hotel is convenient to major road networks connecting to major local towns and cities including Cambridge and Hertford; Stansted Airport is also a short drive away. The hotel has spacious bedrooms, a comfortable lounge, bar and conservatory restaurant. There is also a range of air-conditioned meeting rooms.
ROOMS: 50 en suite (1 fmly) (16 GF) in 16 bedrooms s £85-£110; d £120-£130 (incl. bkfst) **LB** **FACILITIES:** STV **CONF:** Thtr 200 Class 75 Board 60 Del from £125 **SERVICES:** Lift **PARKING:** 64 **NOTES:** in restaurant Civ Wed 80

WAREHAM, Dorset — Map 04 SY98

★★★68% Springfield Country Hotel & Leisure Club
Grange Rd BH20 5AL
☎ 01929 552177 01929 551862
Dir: *from Wareham take Stoborough road then 1st right in village to join by-pass. Then left, and immediately right*
Suitable for a touring base, this attractive hotel is well located in the heart of Purbeck in extensive grounds. Leisure facilities including both indoor and outdoor pools and conference and business facilities are well-patronised. Bedrooms are a good size.
ROOMS: 48 en suite (7 fmly) **FACILITIES:** Squash Snooker Sauna Gym Jacuzzi Steam room Table tennis Beauty treatment ch fac **CONF:** Thtr 200 Class 50 Board 60 **SERVICES:** Lift **PARKING:** 150 **NOTES:** in restaurant

★★★65% Worgret Manor
Worgret Rd BH20 6AB
☎ 01929 552957 01929 554804
e-mail: admin@worgretmanorhotel.co.uk
web: www.worgretmanorhotel.co.uk
Dir: *on A352 from Wareham to Wool, 0.5m from Wareham rdbt*
On the edge of Wareham, with easy access to major routes, this privately owned Georgian manor house offers a friendly, cheerful ambience. The bedrooms come in a variety of sizes. Public rooms are well presented and comprise a popular bar, a quiet lounge and an airy restaurant.
ROOMS: 12 en suite (1 fmly) (3 GF) in all bedrooms s £70-£80; d £80-£100 (incl. bkfst) **LB** **FACILITIES:** Free use of local sports centre **CONF:** Thtr 50 Del from £500 **PARKING:** 25 **NOTES:** in restaurant

★★69% Kemps Country House
East Stoke BH20 6AL
☎ 01929 462563 01929 405287
e-mail: stay@kempshotel.com
Dir: *midway between Wareham & Wool on A352*
This relaxing family-owned hotel has views to the Purbeck Hills in the distance. Bedrooms, including modern garden rooms are spacious, and there are two comfortable lounges and an adjoining bar. An extensive choice is offered from the imaginative set and carte menus; bar meals are available at lunch.
ROOMS: 5 rms (4 en suite) 10 annexe en suite (4 fmly) (8 GF) s £69-£83; d £110-£140 (incl. bkfst) **LB** **FACILITIES:** Jacuzzi Xmas **CONF:** Thtr 100 Class 50 Board 24 Del £104.95 **PARKING:** 50 **NOTES:** in restaurant

Entertainment

WARKWORTH, Northumberland — Map 21 NU20

Warkworth House Hotel
16 Bridge St NE65 0XB
☎ 01665 711276 01665 713323
e-mail: welcome@warkworthhousehotel.co.uk
web: www.warkworthhousehotel.co.uk
Dir: *From A1 take B6345 for Amble & Felton. Follow signs for Warkworth Castle. Hotel down hill from Castle*
At the time of going to press, the star classification for this hotel was not confirmed. Please refer to the AA internet site www.theAA.com for current information.
ROOMS: 15 en suite (2 GF) in 8 bedrooms s £49-£70; d £79-£125 (incl. bkfst) **LB** **FACILITIES:** Xmas **PARKING:** 14 **NOTES:** in restaurant

WARMINSTER, Wiltshire — Map 04 ST84

★★★★74% Bishopstrow House
BA12 9HH
☎ 01985 212312 01985 216769
e-mail: info@bishopstrow.co.uk
web: www.vonessenhotels.co.uk
Dir: *A303, A36, B3414, hotel 2m on right*
This is a fine example of a Georgian country home, situated in 27 acres of grounds. Public areas are traditional in style and feature antiques and open fires. Most bedrooms offer DVD players. A spa, a tennis court and several country walks ensure there is something for all guests. The restaurant serves quality contemporary cuisine.
ROOMS: 32 en suite (3 fmly) (4 GF) in 1 bedroom s fr £99; d £199-£330 (incl. bkfst) **LB** **FACILITIES: Spa** STV Fishing Sauna Gym Clay pigeon shooting Archery Cycling Xmas **CONF:** Thtr 65 Class 32 Board 36 Del from £170 **PARKING:** 100 **NOTES:** in restaurant Civ Wed 70

Travelodge
A36 Bath Rd BA12 7RU
☎ 08700 850 950 01985 214380
web: www.travelodge.co.uk
Dir: *at junct of A350/A36*
Travelodge offers good quality, good value, modern accommodation. Ideal for families, the spacious, en suite bedrooms include remote-control TV, tea and coffee-making facilities and comfortable beds. Meals can be taken at the nearby family restaurant. For further details consult the Hotel Groups page.
ROOMS: 31 en suite s fr £26; d fr £26

WARRINGTON, Cheshire — Map 15 SJ68

★★★★75% De Vere Daresbury Park
Chester Rd, Daresbury WA4 4BB
☎ 01925 267331 01925 265615
e-mail: reservations.daresbury@devere-hotels.com
web: www.devereonline.co.uk
Dir: *M56 junct 11, take 'Daresbury Park' exit at rdbt. Hotel 100mtrs*
Close to the local motorway networks and tourist attractions, this modern hotel is a very popular venue for both business and leisure travellers. Public areas are themed around 'Alice in Wonderland' in tribute to local author Lewis Carroll. These include a range of eating and drinking options, leisure facilities and extensive conference facilities.
ROOMS: 181 en suite (14 fmly) (62 GF) in 128 bedrooms **FACILITIES: Spa** STV supervised Squash Snooker Sauna Solarium Gym Jacuzzi Steam Room, Beauty salon ch fac **CONF:** BC Thtr 300 Class 200 Board 100 **SERVICES:** Lift **PARKING:** 400 **NOTES:** Civ Wed 220

W

WARRINGTON, continued

★★★★70% The Park Royal Hotel
Stretton Rd, Stretton WA4 4NS
☎ 01925 730706 📠 01925 730740
e-mail: parkroyalreservations@quintessential-hotels.co.uk
web: www.quintessential-hotels.co.uk
Dir: *M56 junct 10, A49 to Warrington, at lights turn right to Appleton Thorn, hotel 200yds on right*
This modern hotel enjoys a peaceful setting, yet is conveniently located minutes from the M56. Comfortable bedrooms are smartly appointed and thoughtfully equipped. Spacious, attractive public areas include extensive conference and function facilities, and a comprehensive leisure centre complete with outdoor tennis courts and an impressive beauty centre.
ROOMS: 142 en suite (2 fmly) (34 GF) ⊗ in 100 bedrooms s £120; d £130 **LB** **FACILITIES: Spa** STV supervised Sauna Solarium Gym Jacuzzi Xmas **CONF:** Thtr 400 Class 200 Board 90 Del from £135 **SERVICES:** Lift **PARKING:** 400 **NOTES:** ⊗ in restaurant Civ Wed

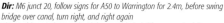

★★★72% Fir Grove
Knutsford Old Rd WA4 2LD
☎ 01925 267471 📠 01925 601092
e-mail: firgrove@bestwestern.co.uk
web: www.feathers.uk.com
Dir: *M6 junct 20, follow signs for A50 to Warrington for 2.4m, before swing bridge over canal, turn right, and right again*
Situated in a quiet residential area, this hotel is convenient for both the town centre and the motorway network. Comfortable, smart bedrooms, including spacious executive rooms, offer some excellent extra facilities such as Playstations and CD players. Public areas include a smart lounge/bar, a neatly appointed restaurant and excellent function and meeting facilities.
ROOMS: 52 en suite (3 fmly) (20 GF) ⊗ in 20 bedrooms s £45-£80; d £60-£90 (incl. bkfst) **FACILITIES:** STV Xmas **CONF:** BC Thtr 200 Class 150 Board 50 **PARKING:** 100 **NOTES:** ⊗ in restaurant Civ Wed 200

★★68% Paddington House
514 Old Manchester Rd WA1 3TZ
☎ 01925 816767 📠 01925 816651
e-mail: hotel@paddingtonhouse.co.uk
web: www.paddingtonhouse.co.uk
Dir: *1m from M6 junct 21, off A57, 2m from town centre*
This busy, friendly hotel is conveniently situated just over a mile from the M6. Bedrooms are attractively furnished, and include four-poster and ground-floor rooms. Guests can dine in the wood-panelled Padgate restaurant or in the cosy bar. Conference and function facilities are also available.
ROOMS: 37 en suite (9 fmly) (6 GF) ⊗ in 17 bedrooms s £35-£95; d £45-£95 (incl. bkfst) **LB** **FACILITIES:** STV **CONF:** Thtr 180 Class 100 Board 40 Del from £85 **SERVICES:** Lift **PARKING:** 50 **NOTES:** ⊗ in restaurant Civ Wed 150

Innkeeper's Lodge Warrington
322 Newton Rd, Lowton Village WA3 1HD
☎ 0870 243 0500 & 01942 671421 📠 01942 269692
web: www.innkeeperslodge.com
Dir: *A580 via M56 junct 23 towards Manchester, follow signs for Toby Carvery*
A growing concept in the travel accommodation market. Smart rooms meet essential business requirements but also have home comforts. Dining options include all-day menus plus the added advantage of breakfast, which is included in the room price. For further details consult the Hotel Groups page.
ROOMS: 58 en suite s £45; d £45

Premier Travel Inn Warrington Centre (South)
1430 Centre Park, Park Boulevard WA1 1QR
☎ 08701 977259 📠 01925 244259
web: www.premiertravelinn.com
Dir: *at Bridgefoot junct of A49/A50/A56 in centre of Warrington*
High quality, modern budget accommodation ideal for both families and business travellers. Spacious, en suite bedrooms feature bath and shower, satellite TV and many have telephones and modem points. The adjacent family restaurant features a wide and varied menu. For further details consult the Hotel Groups page.
ROOMS: 42 en suite s £46.95-£49.95; d £46.95-£49.95

Premier Travel Inn Warrington East
Manchester Rd, Woolston WA1 4GB
☎ 0870 9906524 📠 0870 9906525
web: www.premiertravelinn.com
Dir: *Just off M6 junct 21 on A57 to Warrington*
High quality, modern budget accommodation ideal for both families and business travellers. Spacious, en suite bedrooms feature bath and shower, satellite TV and many have telephones and modem points. The adjacent family restaurant features a wide and varied menu. For further details consult the Hotel Groups page.
ROOMS: 105 en suite s £49.95-£52.95; d £49.95-£52.95

Premier Travel Inn Warrington North East
Golborne Rd, Winwick WA2 8LF
☎ 0870 9906600 📠 0870 9906601
web: www.premiertravelinn.com
Dir: *Exit M6 junct 22. Follow signs for A573 towards Newton-le-Willows. Dual carriageway to end, take 3rd exit at rdbt. (Church opp). Hotel to right of church*
High quality, modern budget accommodation ideal for both families and business travellers. Spacious, en suite bedrooms feature bath and shower, satellite TV and many have telephones and modem points. The adjacent family restaurant features a wide and varied menu. For further details consult the Hotel Groups page.
ROOMS: 42 en suite s £46.95-£49.95; d £46.95-£49.95 **CONF:** Thtr 30 Class 20 Board 25

Premier Travel Inn Warrington North West
Woburn Rd WA2 8RN
☎ 08701 977260 📠 01925 414544
web: www.premiertravelinn.com
Dir: *M62 junct 9 towards Warrington, 100yds from junct*
High quality, modern budget accommodation ideal for both families and business travellers. Spacious, en suite bedrooms feature bath and shower, satellite TV and many have telephones and modem points. The adjacent family restaurant features a wide and varied menu. For further details consult the Hotel Groups page.
ROOMS: 40 en suite s £46.95-£49.95; d £46.95-£49.95

Premier Travel Inn Warrington South
Tarporley Rd, Stretton WA4 4NB
☎ 0870 9906526 📠 0870 9906527
web: www.premiertravelinn.com
Dir: *Just off M56 junct 10. Follow A49 to Warrington, left at 1st lights*
High quality, modern budget accommodation ideal for both families and business travellers. Spacious, en suite bedrooms feature bath and shower, satellite TV and many have telephones and modem points. The adjacent family restaurant features a wide and varied menu. For further details consult the Hotel Groups page.
ROOMS: 29 en suite s £46.95-£49.95; d £46.95-£49.95

W

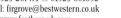

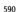

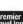

Travelodge
Kendrick/Leigh St WA1 1UZ
☎ 08700 850 950 📠 01925 639432
web: www.travelodge.co.uk
***Dir:** M6 junct 21, follow A57 towards Liverpool & Widnes to Warrington town centre, through Asda rdbt, lodge next left at lights*
Travelodge offers good quality, good value, modern accommodation. Ideal for families, the spacious, en suite bedrooms include remote-control TV, tea and coffee-making facilities and comfortable beds. Meals can be taken at the nearby family restaurant. For further details consult the Hotel Groups page.
ROOMS: 63 en suite s fr £26; d fr £26

WARWICK, Warwickshire
Map 10 SP26
See also Honiley & Leamington Spa (Royal)

★★★★74% Ardencote Manor Hotel, Country Club & Spa
Lye Green Rd CV35 8LS
☎ 01926 843111 📠 01926 842646
e-mail: hotel@ardencote.com
web: www.ardencote.com
(For full entry see Claverdon and advert on this page)

★★★64% Lord Leycester
Jury St CV34 4EJ
☎ 01926 491481 📠 01926 491561
e-mail: reception@lord-leycester.co.uk
web: www.lord-leycester.co.uk
***Dir:** M40 junct 15/A429 into town centre, past West Gate onto High St & Jury St*

This historic Grade II listed property is just a short walk from the famous castle. All the bedrooms and public rooms provide comfortable accommodation. A choice of eating options is available in either the informal Squires Buttery or the Knights Restaurant.
ROOMS: 48 en suite (3 fmly) in 25 bedrooms s £59.50-£90; d £72.50-£90 (incl. bkfst) **LB FACILITIES:** STV Xmas **CONF:** Thtr 120 Class 50 Board 40 Del from £95 **SERVICES:** Lift **PARKING:** 40
NOTES: in restaurant

See advert on this page

★★64% Warwick Arms
17 High St CV34 4AT
☎ 01926 492759 📠 01926 410587
e-mail: warwickarms@ukonline.co.uk
***Dir:** M40 junct 15, into Warwick, hotel 100yds past Lord Leycester Hospital*
A relaxed and attractive hotel in the heart of Warwick, close to the castle walls. Typical of an older building, bedrooms vary in size and style but have a good range of facilities. Bar meals are very popular and can also be taken in the smartly decorated restaurant.
ROOMS: 35 en suite (4 fmly) s fr £60; d fr £80 (incl. bkfst)
FACILITIES: Xmas **CONF:** Thtr 100 Class 30 Board 30 Del from £95
PARKING: 21

W

WARWICK MOTORWAY SERVICE AREA (M40), Warwickshire — Map 10 SP35

⌂ Days Inn Stratford upon Avon

Warwick Services, M40 Northbound junction 12-13, Banbury Rd CV35 0AA
☎ 01926 651681 ℻ 01926 651634
e-mail: warwick.north.hotel@welcomebreak.co.uk
web: www.welcomebreak.co.uk
Dir: *M40 northbound between junct 12 & 13*
This modern building offers accommodation in smart, spacious and well-equipped bedrooms, suitable for families and business travellers, and all with en suite bathrooms. Continental breakfast is available and other refreshments may be taken at the nearby family restaurant. For further details see the Hotel Groups page.
ROOMS: 54 en suite s £49-£65; d £49-£65 **CONF:** Board 10

⌂ Days Inn Stratford Upon Avon

Warwick Services, M40 Southbound, Banbury Rd CV35 0AA
☎ 01926 650168 ℻ 01926 651601
web: www.welcomebreak.co.uk
Dir: *M40 southbound between junct 14 & 12*
This modern building offers accommodation in smart, spacious and well-equipped bedrooms, suitable for families and business travellers, and all with en suite bathrooms. Continental breakfast is available and other refreshments may be taken at the nearby family restaurant. For further details see the Hotel Groups page.
ROOMS: 40 en suite s £45-£55; d £45-£55

WASHINGTON, Tyne & Wear — Map 19 NZ35

★★★67% George Washington Golf & Country Club

Stone Cellar Rd, High Usworth NE37 1PH
☎ 0191 402 9988 ℻ 0191 415 1166
e-mail: reservations@georgewashington.co.uk
web: www.georgewashington.co.uk
Dir: *Exit A1(M) junct 65 onto A194(M). Take A195 signed Washington North. Take last exit from rdbt for Washington then right at mini-rdbt. Hotel 0.5m on right*
Popular with business and leisure guests, this purpose-built hotel boasts two golf courses and a driving range. Bedrooms are being refurbished and are generally spacious and comfortably equipped. Public areas include extensive conference facilities, a business centre and fitness club.
ROOMS: 103 en suite (9 fmly) (41 GF) ⊗ in 44 bedrooms s £59-£79; d £65-£89 **LB** **FACILITIES: Spa** supervised ⛳ 18 Squash Sauna Solarium Gym Putt green Jacuzzi Golf driving range, Pitch & Putt, Pool table, Beauty salon Xmas **CONF:** BC Thtr 200 Class 80 Board 80 Del from £110 **PARKING:** 180 **NOTES:** ⊗ in restaurant Civ Wed 180

⌂ Campanile

Emerson Rd, District 5 NE37 1LE
☎ 0191 416 5010 ℻ 0191 416 5023
e-mail: washington@campanile-hotels.com
web: www.envergure.fr
Dir: *A1(M) junct 64, A195 to Washington, 1st left at rdbt into Emerson Road, Hotel 800yds on left*
This modern building offers accommodation in smart, well-equipped bedrooms, all with en suite bathrooms.

continued

Refreshments may be taken at the informal Bistro. For further details consult the Hotel Groups page.

ROOMS: 79 annexe en suite **CONF:** Thtr 35 Class 18 Board 24

WASHINGTON SERVICE AREA (A1(M)), Tyne & Wear — Map 19 NZ25

⌂ Travelodge (North)

Motorway Service Area, Portobello DH3 2SJ
☎ 08700 850 950 ℻ 0191 410 9258
web: www.travelodge.co.uk
Dir: *on northbound carriageway of A1(M)*
Travelodge offers good quality, good value, modern accommodation. Ideal for families, the spacious, en suite bedrooms include remote-control TV, tea and coffee-making facilities and comfortable beds. Meals can be taken at the nearby family restaurant. For further details consult the Hotel Groups page.
ROOMS: 31 en suite s fr £26; d fr £26

⌂ Travelodge (South)

Portobello DH3 2SJ
☎ 08700 850 950 ℻ 0191 410 0057
web: www.travelodge.co.uk
Dir: *on southbound carriageway of A1(M)*
Travelodge offers good quality, good value, modern accommodation. Ideal for families, the spacious, en suite bedrooms include remote-control TV, tea and coffee-making facilities and comfortable beds. Meals can be taken at the nearby family restaurant. For further details consult the Hotel Groups page.
ROOMS: 36 en suite s fr £26; d fr £26

WATERGATE BAY, Cornwall & Isles of Scilly — Map 02 SW86

★67% Tregurrian

TR8 4AB
☎ 01637 860280 ℻ 01637 860540
e-mail: tregurrian@holidaysincornwall.net
Dir: *Leave A30 onto A3059 towards airport, 2nd exit at rdbt, right onto B3276, left to Watergate Bay*
Located almost on the beach at this increasingly popular destination, the Tregurrian Hotel is a friendly and convenient place to stay. Bedrooms are comfortable and attractively presented, and some have sea views. In the dining room, both breakfast and dinner are served buffet-style with good use of fresh ingredients.
ROOMS: 26 en suite (8 fmly) ⊗ in all bedrooms **FACILITIES:** Sauna Jacuzzi Games room **PARKING:** 24 **NOTES:** ⊗ in restaurant Closed Nov-Feb RS Mar

Ⓤ Watergate Bay Hotel

TR8 4AA
☎ 01637 860543 🖨 01637 860333
e-mail: hotel@watergatebay.co.uk
web: www.watergatebay.co.uk
Dir: Turn off A30 onto A3059. Follow signs to airport and then Watergate Bay.
At the time of going to press, the star classification for this hotel was not confirmed. Please refer to the AA internet site www.theAA.com for current information.
ROOMS: 54 en suite 17 annexe en suite (36 fmly) s £47-£70; d £94-£140 (incl. bkfst & dinner) **LB FACILITIES: Spa** STV 🖳 ⚡ 🔍 Squash Snooker Sauna Jacuzzi Surfing, Kite Surfing, Badminton, Table Tennis, Billiards. 🎵 ch fac Xmas **CONF:** BC Thtr 150 Class 40 Board 20 Del from £100
SERVICES: Lift **PARKING:** 72 **NOTES:** ⊗ in restaurant Civ Wed 160

WATERINGBURY, Kent Map 06 TQ65

⌂ Premier Travel Inn
Maidstone (Wateringbury)

premier travel inn

103 Tonbridge Rd ME18 5NS
☎ 0870 9906346 🖨 0870 9906347
web: www.premiertravelinn.com
Dir: Exit M25 junct 3 onto M20. Exit at junct 4 onto A228 towards West Malling. Follow A26 towards Maidstone for approx 3m
High quality, modern budget accommodation ideal for both families and business travellers. Spacious, en suite bedrooms feature bath and shower, satellite TV and many have telephones and modem points. The adjacent family restaurant features a wide and varied menu. For further details consult the Hotel Groups page.
ROOMS: 40 en suite s £46.95-£49.95; d £46.95-£49.95 **CONF:** Thtr 30

WATERMILLOCK, Cumbria Map 18 NY42

★★★★73% ◉🛥 Leeming House

CA11 0JJ

MACDONALD HOTELS & RESORTS

☎ 0870 400 8131 🖨 017684 86443
e-mail: leeminghouse@macdonald-hotels.co.uk
web: www.macdonald-hotels.co.uk
Dir: M6 junct 40, take A66 to Keswick. At rdbt take A592 (Ullswater). Continue for 5m to T-junct and turn right (A592). Hotel on left (3m)
This hotel enjoys a superb location - it is set in 20 acres of mature wooded gardens in the Lake District National Park, overlooking Ullswater and towering fells. Many rooms offer views of the lake and the rugged fells beyond, with more than half having their own balcony. Public rooms include three sumptuous lounges, a cosy bar and library.
ROOMS: 41 en suite (10 GF) ⊗ in 36 bedrooms s £100-£135; d £160-£230 (incl. bkfst) **LB FACILITIES:** STV Fishing 🛥 Xmas
CONF: Thtr 24 Class 24 Board 24 Del from £130 **PARKING:** 50
NOTES: ⊗ in restaurant Civ Wed 65

Top Hotel

★★★ ◉◉◉🛥 Rampsbeck Country House

CA11 0LP
☎ 017684 86442 & 86688 🖨 017684 86688
e-mail: enquiries@rampsbeck.fsnet.co.uk
web: www.rampsbeck.fsnet.co.uk
Dir: M6 junct 40, signs for A592 to Ullswater, at T-junct with lake in front, turn right, hotel is 1.5m along lake's edge
This fine country house lies in 18 acres of parkland on the shores of Lake Ullswater and is furnished with many period and antique pieces. There are three delightful lounges, an elegant restaurant and a traditional bar. Bedrooms come in three grades; the most spacious rooms are spectacular and

continued

overlook the lake. Service is attentive and the cuisine a real highlight.

ROOMS: 19 en suite (1 GF) ⊗ in 5 bedrooms s £75-£150; d £120-£250 (incl. bkfst) **LB FACILITIES:** Fishing 🛥 Xmas
CONF: Board 15 Del from £135 **PARKING:** 30 **NOTES:** ⊗ in restaurant Closed early Jan-early Feb

WATFORD, Hertfordshire Map 06 TQ19

★★★67% The White House

Best Western

Upton Rd WD18 0JF
☎ 01923 237316 🖨 01923 233109
e-mail: info@whitehousehotel.co.uk
web: www.whitehousehotel.co.uk
Dir: from main Watford centre ring road into Exchange Rd, Upton Rd left turn off, hotel on left
This is a well located and popular commercial hotel. Bedrooms

continued on p594

BEST WESTERN

White House Hotel AA ★★★

**Upton Road, Watford
Herts WD18 0JF
Tel: 01923 237316
Fax: 01923 233109
Website: www.whitehousehotel.co.uk
Email: info@whitehousehotel.co.uk**

WILDTREE HOTELS

Watford's first luxurious town house hotel with 57 bedrooms all en suite provides the highest standard of personal service.

Located in the heart of Watford on the ring road with free parking for cars. The main motorways nearby are M1 and M25.

The hotel has air conditioned function rooms for conferences, seminars and social events, and serves international food and wine in the award winning Conservatory restaurant.

Best Western

W

WATFORD, continued

are practically furnished and decorated, and offer a good range of in-room facilities including interactive TV. The public areas are open plan in style and comprise a lounge/bar and an attractive conservatory restaurant. Functions suites are also available.

The White House, Watford

ROOMS: 57 en suite (8 GF) ⊗ in 45 bedrooms s £59-£149; d £79-£164 (incl. bkfst) **LB** **FACILITIES:** STV off site gym facilities **CONF:** Thtr 200 Class 80 Board 50 Del from £125 **SERVICES:** Lift **PARKING:** 55 **NOTES:** ⊗ in restaurant Civ Wed 120

See advert on page 593

★★★64% Watford Moat House

30-40 St Albans Rd WD17 1RN
☎ 01923 429988 01923 254638
Dir: *On A412*
Located in the heart of this busy town the hotel provides an ideal base for both corporate and leisure visitors. Bedrooms are comfortable, providing a range of useful facilities for guests. Attractive public areas offer extensive amenities including meeting rooms and a gym. Secure parking is available.
ROOMS: 90 en suite ⊗ in 68 bedrooms s £67-£89; d £67-£89 **FACILITIES:** STV Gym **CONF:** BC Thtr 300 Class 100 Board 100 Del from £110 **SERVICES:** Lift **PARKING:** 90 **NOTES:** ⊗ in restaurant Civ Wed 200

U Ramada Watford

A41, Watford Bypass WD25 8JH
☎ 020 8901 0000 020 8950 7809
e-mail: sales.watford@ramadajarvis.co.uk
web: www.ramadajarvis.co.uk
Dir: *From M1 junct 5 take A41 S to London. Straight on at island, hotel 1m on left.*
This large, modern hotel is conveniently located close to both the M1 and M25 and is a popular venue for both conferences and meetings. Bedrooms are comfortably appointed for both business and leisure guests.
ROOMS: 218 en suite (6 fmly) (80 GF) ⊗ in 120 bedrooms s £99-£119; d £99-£119 **FACILITIES: Spa** STV Sauna Solarium Gym Jacuzzi Xmas **CONF:** Thtr 200 Class 120 Board 58 Del from £170 **SERVICES:** Lift **PARKING:** 250 **NOTES:** ⊗ in restaurant Civ Wed 200

Premier Travel Inn Watford Centre (East)

Timms Meadow, Water Ln WD17 2NJ
☎ 0870 9906620 0870 9906621
web: www.premiertravelinn.com
Dir: *Exit M1 junct 5, A41 into town centre. At rdbt take 3rd exit, stay in left lane through lights. Take 1st left into Water Ln. Hotel on left*
High quality, modern budget accommodation ideal for both families and business travellers. Spacious, en suite bedrooms

continued

feature bath and shower, satellite TV and many have telephones and modem points. The adjacent family restaurant features a wide and varied menu. For further details consult the Hotel Groups page.
ROOMS: 105 en suite s £55.95-£59.95; d £55.95-£59.95

Premier Travel Inn Watford Centre West

2 Ascot Rd WD18 8AP
☎ 0870 8500328 0870 850 0343
web: www.premiertravelinn.com
High quality, modern budget accommodation ideal for both families and business travellers. Spacious, en suite bedrooms feature bath and shower, satellite TV and many have telephones and modem points. The adjacent family restaurant features a wide and varied menu. For further details consult the Hotel Groups page.
ROOMS: 120 en suite s £55.95-£59.95; d £55.95-£59.95

Premier Travel Inn Watford North

859 St Albans Rd, Garston WD25 0LH
☎ 08701 977261 01923 682164
web: www.premiertravelinn.com
Dir: *On A412 St Albans Rd, 200yds past North Orbital (A405), 0.5m S of M1 junct 6*
High quality, modern budget accommodation ideal for both families and business travellers. Spacious, en suite bedrooms feature bath and shower, satellite TV and many have telephones and modem points. The adjacent family restaurant features a wide and varied menu. For further details consult the Hotel Groups page.
ROOMS: 45 en suite s £55.95-£59.95; d £55.95-£59.95

WATFORD GAP MOTORWAY SERVICE AREA (M1), Northamptonshire — Map 11 SP66

Premier Travel Inn Daventry (Watford Gap)

NN6 7UZ
☎ 08701 977301 01327 871333
web: www.premiertravelinn.com
Dir: *M1 southbound between junct 16/17. (Access from northbound via barrier access)*
High quality, modern budget accommodation ideal for both families and business travellers. Spacious, en suite bedrooms feature bath and shower, satellite TV and many have telephones and modem points. The adjacent family restaurant features a wide and varied menu. For further details consult the Hotel Groups page.
ROOMS: 36 en suite s £46.95-£48.95; d £46.95-£48.95

WATTON, Norfolk — Map 13 TF90

★★ Broom Hall Country Hotel

Richmond Rd, Saham Toney IP25 7EX
☎ 01953 882125 01953 885325
e-mail: enquiries@broomhallhotel.co.uk
web: www.broomhallhotel.co.uk
Dir: *leave A11 at Thetford onto A1075 to Watton (12m) B1108 towards Swaffham, in 0.5m at rdbt take B1077 to Saham Toney, hotel 0.5m on the left*
ROOMS: 10 en suite 5 annexe en suite (3 fmly) (5 GF) ⊗ in all bedrooms s £65-£80; d £85-£160 (incl. bkfst) **LB** **FACILITIES:** **CONF:** Thtr 30 Class 30 Board 18 Del from £100 **PARKING:** 30 **NOTES:** ⊗ in restaurant Closed 24 Dec-4 Jan

> Popped the question? Hotels with Civ wed in their entry are licensed for civil wedding ceremonies. Maximum numbers for the ceremony only are shown e.g. Civ wed 120

WEEDON, Northamptonshire Map 11 SP64

Premier Travel Inn Daventry
High St NN7 4PX
☎ 0870 9906364 📠 0870 9906365
web: www.premiertravelinn.com
Dir: *Exit M1 junct 16 onto A45 towards Daventry. Through Upper Heyford & Flore. Hotel on left before Weedon & A5 junct*
High quality, modern budget accommodation ideal for both families and business travellers. Spacious, en suite bedrooms feature bath and shower, satellite TV and many have telephones and modem points. The adjacent family restaurant features a wide and varied menu. For further details consult the Hotel Groups page.
ROOMS: 46 en suite s £46.95-£49.95; d £46.95-£49.95 **CONF:** Thtr 70 Class 25 Board 24

WEELEY, Essex Map 07 TM12

Premier Travel Inn Clacton-On-Sea
Crown Green Roundabout, Colchester Rd, Weeley CO16 9AA
☎ 08701 977064 📠 01255 833106
web: www.premiertravelinn.com
Dir: *take A120 off A12 towards Harwich. After 4m, A133 to Clacton-on-Sea. Inn on Weeley rdbt*
High quality, modern budget accommodation ideal for both families and business travellers. Spacious, en suite bedrooms feature bath and shower, satellite TV and many have telephones and modem points. The adjacent family restaurant features a wide and varied menu. For further details consult the Hotel Groups page.
ROOMS: 40 en suite s £49.95; d £49.95

WELLESBOURNE, Warwickshire Map 10 SP25

Innkeeper's Lodge Stratford-upon-Avon East
Warwick Rd CV35 9LX
☎ 01789 840206 📠 01789 472902
web: www.innkeeperslodge.com
Dir: *M40 junct 15 S onto A429 towards Wellesbourne. Turn left at rdbt onto B4086 & lodge 300yds on right.*
A growing concept in the travel accommodation market. Smart rooms meet essential business requirements but also have home comforts. Dining options include all-day menus plus the added advantage of breakfast, which is included in the room price. For further details consult the Hotel Groups page.
ROOMS: 9 en suite s £59.95; d £59.95

WELLINGBOROUGH, Northamptonshire Map 11 SP86

★★★62% The Hind
Sheep St NN8 1BY
☎ 01933 222827 📠 01933 441921
e-mail: enquiries@thehind.co.uk
Dir: *on A509 in town centre*
Dating back to Jacobean times, this centrally located hotel provides a good base for business and leisure guests visiting the town. A good choice of dishes is available in the restaurant; alternatively the all-day coffee shop offers light snacks. Bedrooms come in a variety of styles, mostly of spacious dimensions.
ROOMS: 34 en suite (2 fmly) (5 GF) ⊗ in 20 bedrooms s £50-£65; d £65-£80 (incl. bkfst) **LB** **FACILITIES:** Pool table in public bar **CONF:** Thtr 70 Class 40 Board 40 Del from £95 **PARKING:** 17 **NOTES:** ⊗ in restaurant RS 24 Dec-2 Jan Civ Wed 70

Hotel Ibis Wellingborough
Enstone Court NN8 2DR
☎ 01933 228333 📠 01933 228444
e-mail: H3164@accor-hotels.com
Dir: *junct of A45 & A509 towards Kettering on SW edge of Wellingborough*
Modern, budget hotel offering comfortable accommodation in bright and practical bedrooms. Breakfast is self-service and dinner is available in the restaurant. For further details, consult the Hotel Groups page.
ROOMS: 78 en suite **CONF:** Thtr 20 Board 14

Premier Travel Inn Wellingborough
London Rd NN8 2DP
☎ 08701 977262 📠 01933 275947
web: www.premiertravelinn.com
Dir: *0.5m from Wellingborough town centre on A5193 near Dennington Industrial Estate*
High quality, modern budget accommodation ideal for both families and business travellers. Spacious, en suite bedrooms feature bath and shower, satellite TV and many have telephones and modem points. The adjacent family restaurant features a wide and varied menu. For further details consult the Hotel Groups page.
ROOMS: 40 en suite s £46.95-£48.95; d £46.95-£48.95

WELLINGTON See Telford (Shropshire)

WELLINGTON, Somerset Map 03 ST12

Top Hotel

★★★ ®® Bindon Country House Hotel & Restaurant
Langford Budville TA21 0RU
☎ 01823 400070 📠 01823 400071
e-mail: stay@bindon.com
web: www.bindon.com
Dir: *from Wellington B3187 to Langford Budville, through village, right towards Wiveliscombe, right at junct, pass Bindon Farm, right after 450yds*
This delightful country-house hotel is set in seven acres of formal woodland gardens. Mentioned in the Domesday Book, this tranquil retreat is the perfect antidote to stress. Bedrooms are named after battles fought by the Duke of Wellington and each is individually decorated with sumptuous fabrics and equipped with useful extras. Public rooms are elegant and stylish, and the dining room is the venue for impressive and accomplished cuisine.
ROOMS: 12 en suite (2 fmly) (1 GF) ⊗ in all bedrooms s fr £85; d £95-£195 (incl. bkfst) **FACILITIES:** Xmas **CONF:** Thtr 50 Class 25 Board 25 Del from £135 **PARKING:** 30 **NOTES:** ⊗ in restaurant Civ Wed 50

WELLINGTON, continued

★★★66% The Cleve Hotel & Country Club

Mantle St TA21 8SN
☎ 01823 662033 ⎙ 01823 660874
e-mail: reception@clevehotel.com
web: www.clevehotel.com
Dir: *M5 junct 26 follow signs to Wellington. Left before Total petrol station*
Offering comfortable bedrooms and public areas, this hotel is quietly located in an elevated position above the town. The atmosphere is relaxed and guests can enjoy Mediterranean-influenced cuisine in the stylish restaurant. Extensive leisure facilities are available including a heated indoor pool, well-equipped gym, sauna and snooker table.
ROOMS: 20 en suite (5 fmly) (3 GF) ⊗ in all bedrooms s £55-£80; d £70-£96 (incl. bkfst) **LB** **FACILITIES:** **Spa** supervised Snooker Sauna Solarium Gym Xmas **CONF:** Thtr 300 Class 130 Board 70 Del from £85 **PARKING:** 100 **NOTES:** ⊗ in restaurant Civ Wed 150

WELLS, Somerset — Map 04 ST54

★★★74% ❁ Swan

Sadler St BA5 2RX
☎ 01749 836300 ⎙ 01749 836301
e-mail: swan@bhere.co.uk
web: www.bhere.co.uk
Dir: *A39, A371, opposite cathedral*

The Swan is a former coaching inn and has a wonderful view of the west front of Wells Cathedral. The individually decorated bedrooms vary in size and style from the newer ones in an adjacent wing to the more traditionally furnished rooms including many with four-poster beds. Dinner includes a varied selection of carefully prepared dishes.
ROOMS: 50 en suite (4 fmly) (4 GF) ⊗ in all bedrooms s £89-£94; d £128-£158 (incl. bkfst) **LB** **FACILITIES:** Xmas **CONF:** Thtr 120 Class 45 Board 40 Del from £127.50 **PARKING:** 30 **NOTES:** 🐕 ⊗ in restaurant Civ Wed 90

★★72% White Hart

Sadler St BA5 2EH
☎ 01749 672056 ⎙ 01749 671074
e-mail: info@whitehart-wells.co.uk
web: www.whitehart-wells.co.uk
Dir: *Sadler St at start of one-way system. Hotel opposite cathedral*
A former coaching inn dating back to the 15th century that offers comfortable, modern accommodation; some bedrooms are in an adjoining former stable block. Public areas include a guest lounge, together with a popular restaurant and cosy bar. The restaurant serves mainly fish, plus daily specials and meat and vegetarian dishes.

ROOMS: 15 en suite (3 fmly) (2 GF) ⊗ in 5 bedrooms s £74.50-£79.50; d £94.50-£105 (incl. bkfst) **LB** **FACILITIES:** Xmas **CONF:** Thtr 150 Class 50 Board 35 Del £105 **PARKING:** 17 **NOTES:** ⊗ in restaurant Civ Wed 100

★★71% Ancient Gate House

20 Sadler St BA5 2SE
☎ 01749 672029 ⎙ 01749 670319
e-mail: info@ancientgatehouse.co.uk
Dir: *1st hotel on left on Cathedral Greenl*

Guests are treated to good old-fashioned hospitality in a friendly informal atmosphere at this charming hotel. Bedrooms, many of which boast unrivalled cathedral views and four-poster beds, are well equipped and furnished in keeping with the age and character of the building. The hotel's Rugantino Restaurant remains popular, offering typically Italian specialities and some traditional English dishes.
ROOMS: 9 en suite ⊗ in 2 bedrooms s £73-£78; d £87.50-£92.50 (incl. bkfst) **LB** **FACILITIES:** Xmas **NOTES:** ⊗ in restaurant Closed 27-29 Dec

★★70% Coxley Vineyard

Coxley BA5 1RQ
☎ 01749 670285 ⎙ 01749 679708
e-mail: max@orofino.freeserve.co.uk
Dir: *A39 from Wells signed Coxley. Village halfway between Wells & Glastonbury. Hotel off main road at end of village.*
This privately owned and personally run hotel was built in the 1980s & 90s on the site of an old cider farm. It was later part of a commercial vineyard and some of the vines are still in evidence. It provides well equipped, modern bedrooms, most situated on ground floor level. There is a comfortable bar and a spacious

continued

W

restaurant with an impressive lantern ceiling. The hotel is a popular venue for conferences and other functions.

ROOMS: 9 en suite (5 fmly) (8 GF) ⊗ in 5 bedrooms s £60-£70; d £70-£83 (incl. bkfst) **LB** **FACILITIES:** Xmas **CONF:** Thtr 90 Class 50 Board 40 Del from £99 **PARKING:** 50 **NOTES:** ⊗ in restaurant

★★67% Crown at Wells

Market Place BA5 2RP
☎ 01749 673457 📠 01749 679792
e-mail: stay@crownatwells.co.uk
web: www.crownatwells.co.uk
Dir: *in Market Place, follow signs for Hotels/Deliveries*

Retaining its original features and period charm, this historic old inn is situated in the heart of the city, just a short stroll from the cathedral. Bedrooms, all with modern facilities, vary in size and style. Public areas focus around Anton's, the popular bistro, with its bold paintings and relaxed atmosphere, and the Penn Bar, an alternative eating option.
ROOMS: 15 en suite (2 fmly) ⊗ in all bedrooms s £55-£80; d £85-£100 (incl. bkfst) **LB** **CONF:** BC **PARKING:** 15 **NOTES:** ⊗ in restaurant RS 25 Dec food not available in the evening

WELWYN, Hertfordshire — Map 06 TL21

★★★61% Quality Hotel Welwyn

The Link AL6 9XA
☎ 01438 716911 📠 01438 714065
e-mail: enquiries@hotels-welwyn.com
web: www.choicehotelseurope.com
Dir: *A1(M) junct 6 follow for A1000 Welwyn. Follow A1(M) Stevenage towards motorway again but at 3rd rdbt take first left and turn into hotel*
The clock tower of this hotel is a local landmark, ensuring that it is easily located from the motorway. This hotel is particularly popular with business guests for the range of conference and meeting rooms provided. Bedrooms are suitably appointed and feature extras such as satellite TV and Playstation games.
ROOMS: 96 en suite (3 fmly) (28 GF) ⊗ in 60 bedrooms s £91; d £113 **LB** **FACILITIES:** Xmas **CONF:** Thtr 250 Class 60 Board 50 Del from £100 **PARKING:** 150 **NOTES:** ✈ ⊗ in restaurant Civ Wed 100

WELWYN GARDEN CITY, Hertfordshire — Map 06 TL21

★★★67% The Homestead Court Hotel

Homestead Ln AL7 4LX
☎ 01707 324336 📠 01707 326447
e-mail: enquiries@homesteadcourt.co.uk
web: www.bw-homesteadcourt.co.uk
Dir: *off A1000, left at lights at Bushall Hotel. Right at rdbt into Howlands, 2nd left at Hollybush public house into Hollybush Lane. 2nd right at War Memorial into Homestead Lane*
Less than two miles from the city centre, this friendly hotel is set in a tranquil location, next to parkland. It boasts stylish, brightly decorated public areas, comfortable bedrooms and ample parking. Conference facilities are popular with local businesses.
ROOMS: 58 en suite 6 annexe en suite ⊗ in 18 bedrooms s £39-£109; d £49-£120 **LB** **FACILITIES:** STV Xmas **CONF:** BC Thtr 80 Class 40 Board 30 **SERVICES:** Lift **PARKING:** 60 **NOTES:** ✈ ⊗ in restaurant Civ Wed 80

Premier Travel Inn Welwyn Garden City

Gosling Park AL8 6DQ
☎ 08701 977263 📠 01707 393789
web: www.premiertravelinn.com
Dir: *on A6129 off A1(M) junct 4*
High quality, modern budget accommodation ideal for both families and business travellers. Spacious, en suite bedrooms feature bath and shower, satellite TV and many have telephones and modem points. The adjacent family restaurant features a wide and varied menu. For further details consult the Hotel Groups page.
ROOMS: 60 en suite s £47.95-£50.95; d £47.95-£50.95

WEMBLEY, Greater London
See LONDON SECTION plan 1 C5

★★★65% Quality Hotel, Wembley

Empire Way HA9 0NN
☎ 020 8733 9000 📠 020 8733 9001
e-mail: gm@hotels-wembley.com
Conveniently situated within walking distance of both the Arena and conference centres this modern hotel offers smart, comfortable, spacious bedrooms; many are air conditioned. All rooms offer an excellent range of amenities and some rooms offer wireless internet access. Air-conditioned public areas include a large restaurant serving a wide range of contemporary dishes.
ROOMS: 165 en suite (10 fmly) (3 GF) ⊗ in 95 bedrooms s £85-£95; d £95-£105 (incl. bkfst) **LB** **FACILITIES:** STV Xmas **CONF:** Thtr 150 Class 70 Board 70 **SERVICES:** Lift air con **PARKING:** 85 **NOTES:** ✈ Civ Wed 220

Hotel Ibis Wembley

Southway HA9 6BA
☎ 0870 609 0963
e-mail: H3141@accor-hotels.com
Dir: *From Hanger Lane on A40, follow A406 north, exit at Wembley. Follow A404 to lights at Wembley Hill Road, turn right then 1st right into Southway. Hotel 75mtrs on left.*
Modern, budget hotel offering comfortable accommodation in bright and practical bedrooms. Breakfast is self-service and dinner is available in the restaurant. For further details, consult the Hotel Groups page.
ROOMS: 210 en suite

We have indicated only the hotels that don't accept credit or debit cards

W

WEMBLEY, continued

⇧ Premier Travel Inn London Wembley

151 Wembley Park Dr HA9 8HQ
☎ 0870 9906484 📠 0870 9906485
web: www.premiertravelinn.com
Dir: *From A406 North Circular take A404 towards Wembley. 2m right into Wembley Hill Rd, keep right into Empire Way (B4565) pass Wembley Arena on right, keep right around petrol station. Hotel 200yds on left*
High quality, modern budget accommodation ideal for both families and business travellers. Spacious, en suite bedrooms feature bath and shower, satellite TV and many have telephones and modem points. The adjacent family restaurant features a wide and varied menu. For further details consult the Hotel Groups page.
ROOMS: 154 en suite s £59.95; d £59.95

WEST BAY See Bridport

WEST BEXINGTON, Dorset Map 04 SY58

★★69% The Manor

Beach Rd DT2 9DF
☎ 01308 897616 & 897785 📠 01308 897704
e-mail: themanorhotel@btconnect.com
Dir: *B3157 Weymouth/Bridport coast road, turn at Swyre, towards West Bexington*
Surrounded by scenic splendour and tranquillity, this south-facing hotel enjoys sea views. Each bedroom has its own charm and a number of thoughtful extras. The Cellar Bar provides a range of meals, and an imaginative selection of dishes is offered in the delightful restaurant.
ROOMS: 13 en suite (3 fmly) ⊘ in 1 bedroom s £70-£95; d £115-£150 (incl. bkfst) **LB** **CONF:** Thtr 40 Class 20 Board 20 **PARKING:** 40 **NOTES:** ✖ ⊘ in restaurant Civ Wed 58

WEST BROMWICH, West Midlands Map 10 SP09

★★★68% Birmingham/West Bromwich Moat House

Birmingham Rd B70 6RS
☎ 0121 609 9988 📠 0121 525 7403
e-mail: reservations.birminghamwestbromwich@moathousehotels.com
Dir: *take Birmingham Rd to West Bromich town centre, turn 1st right into Beechs Rd, take 2nd right into Europa Ave. Hotel on right*
Convenient for the M5, M42 and M6, this large, purpose-built hotel provides versatile and well-equipped accommodation. Facilities include a spacious restaurant, bright lounges, a comfortable bar and a secure car park, as well as meeting rooms and function suites. There is a modern leisure complex.
ROOMS: 168 en suite (20 fmly) ⊘ in 106 bedrooms s £46-£148; d £46-£148 **LB** **FACILITIES:** STV supervised Sauna Solarium Gym Jacuzzi Beauty treatments **CONF:** BC Thtr 475 Class 237 Board 289 Del from £99 **SERVICES:** Lift **PARKING:** 250 **NOTES:** Civ Wed 60

W

⇧ Premier Travel Inn West Bromwich

New Gas St B70 0NP
☎ 08701 977264 📠 0121 500 5670
web: www.premiertravelinn.com
Dir: *From M5 junct 1 take A41 Expressway towards Wolverhampton. At 3rd rdt, Inn on right*
High quality, modern budget accommodation ideal for both families and business travellers. Spacious, en suite bedrooms feature bath and shower, satellite TV and many have telephones and modem points. The adjacent family restaurant features a wide and varied menu. For further details consult the Hotel Groups page.
ROOMS: 40 en suite s £47.95-£50.95; d £47.95-£50.95

WESTBURY, Wiltshire Map 04 ST85

★★66% *Westbury*

The Market Place BA13 3DQ
☎ 01373 822500 📠 01373 824144
e-mail: stay@thewestburyhotel.co.uk
Dir: *turn into Market Place off main road & hotel on the corner*
Centrally located in this historic town, parts of this hotel (now under new ownership) date back to 1545. Bedrooms, some situated in property across the street, come in a variety of shapes and sizes but all are well equipped. Dinner is a highlight here with a considerable range of carefully prepared options. Guests may like to use the popular bar to relax in or dine in the quieter surroundings of the restaurant.
ROOMS: 7 en suite 4 annexe en suite (2 fmly) ⊘ in 3 bedrooms **CONF:** Thtr 30 Class 30 Board 30 **PARKING:** 20 **NOTES:** ✖ ⊘ in restaurant Closed 25 Dec-5 Jan

★★65% The Cedar

Warminster Rd BA13 3PR
☎ 01373 822753 📠 01373 858423
e-mail: cedarwestbury@aol.com
Dir: *on A350, 0.5m S of town towards Warminster*
This 18th-century hotel offers attractive accommodation in well-equipped, individually decorated bedrooms. The hotel is an ideal base for exploring Bath and the surrounding area. An interesting selection of meals is available in both the bar lounge and conservatory; the Regency restaurant is popular for more formal dining.
ROOMS: 8 en suite 12 annexe en suite (5 fmly) (10 GF) ⊘ in all bedrooms s £50-£65; d £60-£72 (incl. bkfst) **FACILITIES:** ch fac **CONF:** Thtr 35 Class 20 Board 20 **PARKING:** 30 **NOTES:** ⊘ in restaurant

WEST CHILTINGTON, West Sussex Map 06 TQ01

★★★69% Best Western Roundabout

Monkmead Ln RH20 2PF
☎ 01798 813838 📠 01798 812962
e-mail: roundabouthotelltd@btinternet.com
web: www.bw-roundabouthotel.co.uk
Dir: *A24 onto A283, right at mini rdbt in Storrington, left at hill top. Left after 1m*

Enjoying a most peaceful setting, surrounded by gardens, this well-established hotel is located deep in the Sussex countryside. Mock-Tudor in style, the hotel has plenty of character. The comfortably furnished bedrooms are well equipped, and public areas offer a spacious lounge and bar, as well as a neatly appointed restaurant serving an extensive range of dishes.
ROOMS: 23 en suite (4 fmly) (5 GF) ⊘ in 5 bedrooms s £60-£69; d £97-£124 **LB** **FACILITIES:** STV Xmas **CONF:** Thtr 60 Class 20 Board 26 Del from £94.50 **PARKING:** 46 **NOTES:** ✖ No children 3yrs ⊘ in restaurant Civ Wed 49

See advert on opposite page

WEST DRAYTON Hotels are listed under Heathrow Airport

WESTLETON, Suffolk
Map 13 TM46

★★72% ◎◎ **Westleton Crown**
IP17 3AD
☎ 01728 648777 📠 01728 648239
e-mail: reception@westletoncrown.com

A charming coaching inn, now under new ownership, situated in a peaceful village location just a few minutes from the A12. Public rooms include a smart, award-winning restaurant, comfortable lounge, and a busy bar with exposed beams and open fireplaces. The bedrooms are individually decorated and equipped with many thoughtful little extras.
ROOMS: 10 en suite 16 annexe en suite (2 fmly) (8 GF) ⊗ in all bedrooms s £75-£90; d £90-£140 (incl. bkfst) **LB FACILITIES:** Xmas
CONF: Thtr 60 Class 40 Board 30 **PARKING:** 40 **NOTES:** ⊗ in restaurant

WEST LULWORTH, Dorset
Map 04 SY88

★★66% **Cromwell House**
Lulworth Cove BH20 5RJ
☎ 01929 400253 & 400332 📠 01929 400566
e-mail: catriona@lulworthcove.co.uk
web: www.lulworthcove.co.uk
Dir: 200yds beyond end of West Lulworth village, left onto high slip road, hotel 100yds on left opposite beach car park

Built in 1881 by the Mayor of Weymouth, specifically as a guest house, this family-run hotel now provides guests with an ideal base for touring the area and for exploring the beaches and coast. Cromwell House enjoys spectacular views across the sea and countryside. Bedrooms, many with sea views, are comfortable and some have been specifically designed for family use.
ROOMS: 17 en suite (3 fmly) (1 GF) s £39-£61; d £78-£94 (incl. bkfst)
LB FACILITIES: ⚡ Access to Dorset Coastal footpath & Jurassic Coast
PARKING: 15 **NOTES:** ⊗ in restaurant Closed 22 Dec-3 Jan

BEST WESTERN AA ★★★

𝕽𝖔𝖚𝖓𝖉𝖆𝖇𝖔𝖚𝖙 𝕳𝖔𝖙𝖊𝖑

Monkmead Lane, West Chiltington
Nr Pulborough, West Sussex
Tel: West Chiltington (01798) 813838
Email: roundabouthotelltd@btinternet.com
http://www.bw-roundabouthotel.co.uk

Tucked away in beautiful countryside close to the Sussex South Downs Way, our peaceful Tudor style hotel is nowhere near a roundabout. Near to West Chiltington Golf Course.
All 23 bedrooms are individually styled with private facilities, antique oak furniture, tapestries, Satellite TV, radio, telephone and tea/coffee making facilities. Candlelit restaurant and Winter log fire, four poster and superior rooms, also six ground floor rooms available.
Special two day breaks all year round.
30 minutes drive to Brighton and 15 to Worthing. Many countrywalks and historic houses nearby.

Best Western

WESTON-ON-THE-GREEN, Oxfordshire
Map 11 SP51

★★★70% ◎◎ **Weston Manor**
OX25 3QL
☎ 01869 350621 📠 01869 350901
e-mail: reception@westonmanor.co.uk
web: www.westonmanor.co.uk
Dir: M40 junct 9, A34 towards Oxford. Turn right at rdbt (B4030), hotel 100yds on left
Character, charm and sophistication blend effortlessly in this friendly hotel set in well-tended grounds. Bedrooms are well-equipped and are located in the main house, coach house or a cottage annexe. Award-winning food can be enjoyed in the impressive vaulted restaurant, complete with original oak panelling and minstrels' gallery; other public areas include an atmospheric foyer lounge, a bar and meeting facilities.
ROOMS: 15 en suite 20 annexe en suite (5 fmly) (6 GF) ⊗ in all bedrooms s £85-£115; d £105-£154 (incl. bkfst) **LB FACILITIES:** ⚡ ↻
CONF: Thtr 60 Class 20 Board 25 Del from £150 **PARKING:** 100
NOTES: ✕ ⊗ in restaurant Civ Wed 80

WESTON-SUPER-MARE, Somerset
Map 04 ST36

★★★65% **Beachlands**
17 Uphill Rd North BS23 4NG
☎ 01934 621401 📠 01934 621966
e-mail: info@beachlandshotel.com
web: www.beachlandshotel.com
Dir: M5 junct 21, follow signs for Hospital. At Hospital rdbt follow signs for beach, hotel 300yds before beach
This popular hotel has the bonus of a 10-metre indoor pool and sauna. It is very close to the 18-hole links course and a short walk

continued on p600

WESTON-SUPER-MARE, continued

from the seafront. Elegant public areas include a bar, a choice of lounges and a bright dining room. Bedrooms vary slightly in size, but all are well equipped for both the business and leisure guest.

Beachlands, Weston-Super-Mare

ROOMS: 23 en suite (6 fmly) (11 GF) ⊗ in all bedrooms s £73-£78; d £103-£108 (incl. bkfst) **LB** **FACILITIES:** Sauna ch fac **CONF:** Thtr 60 Class 20 Board 30 Del from £93.50 **PARKING:** 28 **NOTES:** ⊗ in restaurant Closed 23 Dec-2 Jan Civ Wed 80

★★★64% *Commodore*

Beach Rd, Sand Bay, Kewstoke BS22 9UZ
☎ 01934 415778 01934 750020
e-mail: latonacom@aol.com
Dir: *From Weston-Super-Mare take Kewstoke road through Weston Woods*

Located in the pleasant village of Kewstoke by unspoilt Sand Bay, this popular hotel has direct access to the beach. There is a range of dining options, from the relaxed carvery and two-for-one specials in the beamed bar, to the more formal menu of Alice's Restaurant. Bedrooms vary in size and are split between the main hotel and two adjacent buildings.

ROOMS: 19 en suite ⊗ in 6 bedrooms **FACILITIES:** Putt green **CONF:** Thtr 90 Class 50 Board 40 **PARKING:** 70 **NOTES:** ⊗ in restaurant Civ Wed 100

★★★64% The Royal Hotel

1 South Pde BS23 1JP
☎ 01934 423100 01934 415135
e-mail: royalwsm@btopenworld.com

The Royal, which opened in 1810, was the first hotel in Weston and occupies a prime seafront position. Many of the bedrooms, including some with sea views, offer high standards of quality and comfort. Public areas include a choice of bars and the newly styled restaurant, offering a range of dishes to meet all tastes. Entertainment is provided during the season with a regular jazz slot on Sundays.

ROOMS: 37 en suite (5 fmly) ⊗ in 27 bedrooms s £62-£66; d £69-£99 (incl. bkfst) **FACILITIES:** STV ♫ **CONF:** Thtr 200 Class 100 Board 80 Del from £93 **SERVICES:** Lift **PARKING:** 152 **NOTES:** Civ Wed 200

★★72% Woodlands Country House

Hill Ln TA9 4DF
☎ 01278 760232 01278 769090
e-mail: info@woodlands-hotel.co.uk
web: www.woodlands-hotel.co.uk
(For full entry see Brent Knoll)

★★68% Battleborough Grange Country Hotel

Bristol Rd - A38 TA9 4HJ
☎ 01278 760208 01278 761950
e-mail: info@battleboroughgrangehotel.co.uk
(For full entry see Brent Knoll)

★★68% Madeira Cove Hotel

32-34 Birnbeck Rd BS23 2BX
☎ 01934 626707 01934 624882
e-mail: madeiracove@telco4u.net
Dir: *follow Western Seafront signs, then Madeira Cove sign, north towards Kewstoke & Sand Bay, pass Grand Pier, hotel on right*

Within easy walking distance of the town centre, this popular and friendly hotel enjoys an ideal location overlooking the sea. It provides comfortable and well-equipped accommodation. A good range of food is offered in the spacious restaurant and in addition to the bar, a separate upper floor lounge is available to guests.

ROOMS: 22 rms (21 en suite) 4 annexe en suite (2 fmly) ⊗ in 22 bedrooms s £35; d £70-£80 (incl. bkfst) **LB** **FACILITIES:** Xmas **CONF:** Thtr 20 **SERVICES:** Lift **NOTES:** ⊗ in restaurant

★★63% New Ocean

Madeira Cove BS23 2BS
☎ 01934 621839 01934 626474
e-mail: newoceanhotel@aol.com
web: www.newoceanhotel.co.uk
Dir: *on seafront*

Ideally positioned on the seafront, opposite the Marine Lake, several bedrooms at this family-run hotel enjoy pleasant views over Weston Bay. In the downstairs restaurant, dinner offers traditional home cooking using fresh ingredients. The smart public areas include a well-furnished bar and lounge, where entertainment is regularly provided.

ROOMS: 53 en suite (2 fmly) s £30-£35; d £60-£70 (incl. bkfst) **LB** **FACILITIES:** ♫ Xmas **SERVICES:** Lift **PARKING:** 6 **NOTES:** ⊗ in restaurant RS Jan

★★62% *Anchor Head*

19 Claremont Crescent, Birnbeck Rd BS23 2EE
☎ 01934 620880 01934 621767
e-mail: anchor.weston@alfatravel.co.uk
web: www.alfatravel.co.uk
Dir: *M5 junct 21/ A370 to Weston Seafront, right towards north end of resort past Grand Pier towards Brimbeck Pier. Hotel at end of terrace on left*

Leisureplex

Enjoying a very pleasant location with views across the bay, the Anchor Head offers a varied choice of comfortable lounges and a relaxing outdoor patio area. Bedrooms and bathrooms are traditionally furnished and include several ground-floor rooms. Dinner and breakfast are served in the spacious dining room that also benefits from sea views.

ROOMS: 52 en suite (1 fmly) (5 GF) **FACILITIES:** ♫ **SERVICES:** Lift **NOTES:** ⊗ in restaurant Closed Dec-Feb RS Mar & Nov

> Late for dinner? Quality standards mean that last orders for dinner vary according to star rating and should be no earlier than: ★★ 7.00pm ★★★ 8:00pm ★★★★ 9:00pm ★★★★★ 10:00pm

W

★68% Timbertop Aparthotel
8 Victoria Park BS23 2HZ
☎ 01934 631178 & 01934 424348 📠 01934 414716
e-mail: stay@aparthoteltimbertop.com
web: www.aparthoteltimbertop.com
Dir: *follow signs to pier, then 1st right after Winter Gardens, 1st left (Lower Church Rd). Left, then right to hotel*
Located in a leafy cul-de-sac, close to the seafront and Winter Gardens, this homely hotel offers a warm and personal welcome. Bedrooms are bright and fresh with pine furnishings and in addition to a small bar, there is a relaxing lounge. Substantial home-cooked breakfasts are provided with the emphasis on fresh ingredients.
ROOMS: 8 en suite 5 annexe en suite (2 fmly) s £27-£50; d £52-£100 (incl. bkfst) **LB** **CONF:** BC Thtr 10 Class 10 Board 10 **PARKING:** 15
NOTES: ✗ ⊗ in restaurant

⌂ Premier Travel Inn Weston-Super-Mare
Hutton Moor Rd BS22 8LY
☎ 08701 977266 📠 01934 627401
web: www.premiertravelinn.com
Dir: *From M5 junct 21, follow A370 to Weston-Super-Ware. After 3rd rdbt turn right at lights into Hutton Moor Leisure Centre. Left, follow into car park*
High quality, modern budget accommodation ideal for both families and business travellers. Spacious, en suite bedrooms feature bath and shower, satellite TV and many have telephones and modem points. The adjacent family restaurant features a wide and varied menu. For further details consult the Hotel Groups page.
ROOMS: 60 en suite s £49.95; d £49.95

WEST THURROCK, Essex — Map 06 TQ57

⌂ *Hotel Ibis London Thurrock*
Weston Av RM20 3JQ
☎ 01708 686000 📠 01708 680525
e-mail: H2176@accor-hotels.com
Dir: *M25 junct 31 to West Thurrock Services, right at 1st and 2nd rdbts then left at 3rd rdbt. Hotel on right after 500yds*
Modern, budget hotel offering comfortable accommodation in bright and practical bedrooms. Breakfast is self-service and dinner is available in the restaurant. For further details, consult the Hotel Groups page.
ROOMS: 102 en suite

⌂ Premier Travel Inn Thurrock East
Fleming Rd, Unicorn Estate, Chafford Hundred RM16 6YJ
☎ 08701 977253 📠 01375 481876
web: www.premiertravelinn.com
Dir: *from A13 follow signs for Lakeside Shopping Centre. Turn right at 1st rdbt, straight over next rdbt then 1st slip road. Turn left at next rdbt*
High quality, modern budget accommodation ideal for both families and business travellers. Spacious, en suite bedrooms feature bath and shower, satellite TV and many have telephones and modem points. The adjacent family restaurant features a wide and varied menu. For further details consult the Hotel Groups page.
ROOMS: 62 en suite s £53.95-£57.95; d £53.95-£57.95

Late for dinner? Quality standards mean that last orders for dinner vary according to star rating and should be no earlier than:
★★ 7.00pm ★★★ 8:00pm ★★★★ 9:00pm ★★★★★ 10:00pm

WEST THURROCK, continued

⌂ Premier Travel Inn Thurrock West

Stonehouse Ln RM19 1NS
☎ 0870 9906490 ⎙ 0870 9906491
web: www.premiertravelinn.com
Dir: *From N, exit M25 junct 31 follow signs for A1090 to Purfleet. Do not cross Dartford Bridge or follow signs for Lakeside. From S, exit M25 junct 31. On approach to Dartford Tunnel, bear far left signed Dagenham. After tunnel, hotel at top of slip road*
High quality, modern budget accommodation ideal for both families and business travellers. Spacious, en suite bedrooms feature bath and shower, satellite TV and many have telephones and modem points. The adjacent family restaurant features a wide and varied menu. For further details consult the Hotel Groups page.
ROOMS: 161 en suite s £53.95-£57.95; d £53.95-£57.95

⌂ Travelodge Thurrock

Arterial Rd RM16 3BG
☎ 08700 850 950 & 0800 850950 ⎙ 01708 860971
web: www.travelodge.co.uk
Dir: *off A1306 (Arterial Rd)*
Travelodge offers good quality, good value, modern accommodation. Ideal for families, the spacious, en suite bedrooms include remote-control TV, tea and coffee-making facilities and comfortable beds. Meals can be taken at the nearby family restaurant. For further details consult the Hotel Groups page.
ROOMS: 48 en suite s fr £26; d fr £26

WEST WITTON, North Yorkshire — Map 19 SE08

★★72% Wensleydale Heifer Inn

DL8 4LS
☎ 01969 622322 ⎙ 01969 624183
e-mail: info@wensleydaleheifer.co.uk
web: www.wensleydaleheifer.co.uk
Dir: *A1 to Leeming Bar junct, A684 towards Bedale for approx 10m to Leyburn, then towards Hawes 3.5m to West Witton*
Originally a 17th-century coaching inn, this sympathetically restored hotel retains much character. Bedrooms are all individual, comfortable and well equipped. Welcoming log fires await guests on chilly evenings. The beamed bar serves real ales and meals can be taken in the cosy bistro or the more formal restaurant.
ROOMS: 9 en suite (2 fmly) ⊘ in all bedrooms s £60; d £72-£98 (incl. bkfst) **LB** **FACILITIES:** Xmas **CONF:** BC Thtr 50 Class 40 Board 20 **PARKING:** 40 **NOTES:** No children 12yrs ⊘ in restaurant

WETHERBY, West Yorkshire — Map 16 SE44

★★★★76% ⊛⊛ Wood Hall

Trip Ln, Linton LS22 4JA
☎ 01937 587271 ⎙ 01937 584353
e-mail: woodhall@handpicked.co.uk
web: www.handpicked.co.uk
Dir: *from Wetherby take Harrogate Rd N (A661) for 0.5m, left to Sicklinghall & Linton. Cross bridge, left to Linton & Wood Hall. Turn right opposite Windmill Inn, 1.25m to hotel*
A striking Georgian hall sitting in 100 acres of parkland, this hotel has been extensively upgraded throughout. Spacious bedrooms are of an impressive standard and feature comprehensive facilities, including large plasma screen TVs. Public rooms reflect the same elegance and include a smart drawing room and dining room, both with fantastic views. A state-of-the art Technogym is available.

ROOMS: 14 en suite 30 annexe en suite (5 fmly) s £100-£185; d £150-£235 (incl. bkfst) **LB** **FACILITIES: Spa** STV supervised Fishing Gym Jacuzzi Beauty spa Treatment rooms Xmas **CONF:** Thtr 140 Class 70 Board 40 Del from £165 **SERVICES:** Lift **PARKING:** 200 **NOTES:** ⊘ in restaurant Civ Wed 110

See advert on opposite page

★★★72% The Bridge Hotel

Walshford LS22 5HS
☎ 01937 580115 ⎙ 01937 580556
e-mail: info@bridgeinn-bridgehotel.co.uk
web: www.walshford.co.uk
Dir: *A1 Southbound - leave A1(M) at junct 47 (York), 1st left Walshford and follow brown tourist signs*
A very conveniently located hotel close to the A1 with spacious public areas and a good range of services make this an ideal venue for business or leisure. Newly refurbished, stylish bedrooms are comfortable and well equipped. The Bridge offers a choice of bars and a large open-plan restaurant. Conference and banqueting suites are also available.
ROOMS: 30 en suite (1 fmly) s fr £65; d fr £85 (incl. bkfst) **LB** **FACILITIES:** Gym Xmas **CONF:** BC Thtr 150 Class 50 Board 50 Del £115

U Ramada Wetherby

Leeds Rd LS22 5HE
☎ 01937 583881 ⎙ 01937 580062
e-mail: sales.wetherby@ramadajarvis.o.uk
web: www.ramadajarvis.co.uk
Dir: *junct A1/A58*
This large hotel is set in open countryside, just a few minutes from the town centre. Bedrooms are comfortably appointed for both business and leisure guests.
ROOMS: 103 en suite (51 GF) ⊘ in 68 bedrooms s £76-£89; d £76-£89 **FACILITIES:** STV Xmas **CONF:** Thtr 120 Class 60 Board 45 Del from £145 **SERVICES:** Lift **PARKING:** 80 **NOTES:** ⊘ in restaurant Civ Wed 100

WEYBRIDGE, Surrey — Map 06 TQ06
See LONDON SECTION plan 1 A1

★★★★70% Oatlands Park

146 Oatlands Dr KT13 9HB
☎ 01932 847242 ⎙ 01932 842252
e-mail: info@oatlandsparkhotel.com
web: www.oatlandsparkhotel.com
Dir: *through Weybridge High Street to top of Monument Hill. Hotel on left*
Once a palace for Henry VIII, this impressive building sits in extensive grounds encompassing tennis courts, a gym and a 9-hole golf course. The spacious lounge and bar create a

continued

wonderful first impression with tall marble pillars and plush comfortable seating. Most of the bedrooms are very spacious.

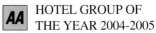

ROOMS: 144 en suite (5 fmly) (31 GF) ⊘ in 68 bedrooms
FACILITIES: STV ⛳ 9 🎾 Gym 🏌 Putt green Jogging course Fitness suite, board games ♫ Xmas **CONF:** BC Thtr 300 Class 150 Board 80
SERVICES: Lift **PARKING:** 140 **NOTES:** Civ Wed 220

★★★67% The Ship

Monument Green KT13 8BQ
☎ 01932 848364 📠 01932 857153
e-mail: recship@desbroughhotels.com
Dir: *M25 junct 11, at 3rd rdbt left into High St. Hotel 300yds on left*
A former coaching inn, The Ship retains its period charm and is now a spacious and comfortable hotel. Bedrooms, some of which overlook a delightful courtyard, are spacious and cheerfully decorated. Public areas include a lounge and cocktail bar,

continued

restaurant and a popular pub. The high street location and private car parking are a bonus.
ROOMS: 42 en suite ⊘ in 31 bedrooms s £117-£130; d £130-£160 **LB**
FACILITIES: STV **CONF:** Thtr 140 Class 70 Board 60 Del from £160
PARKING: 65 **NOTES:** ⊘ in restaurant

⌂ Innkeeper's Lodge

25 Oatlands Chase KT13 9RW
☎ 01932 253277 📠 01932 252412
e-mail: badgers.rest@bass.com
web: www.innkeeperslodge.com
Dir: *M25 junct 11, A317 towards Weybridge, at 3rd rdbt take A3050, left 1m. Turn into Oatlands Chase, lodge on right*
A growing concept in the travel accommodation market. Smart rooms meet essential business requirements but also have home comforts. Dining options include all-day menus plus the added advantage of breakfast, which is included in the room price. For further details consult the Hotel Groups page.
ROOMS: 18 en suite s £52-£79.95; d £52-£79.95

WEYMOUTH, Dorset — Map 04 SY67

★★★74% 🏵🏵 *Moonfleet Manor*

Fleet DT3 4ED
☎ 01305 786948 📠 01305 774395
Dir: *A354 to Weymouth; right on B3157 to Bridport. At Chickerell left at mini rdbt to Fleet*
This enchanting hideaway, peacefully located at the end of the village of Fleet, enjoys a wonderful sea-facing position. Children are especially welcomed throughout the hotel. Many of the well-equipped bedrooms overlook Chesil Beach and the hotel is

continued on p604

WEYMOUTH, continued

furnished with style and panache, particularly the sumptuous lounges. Accomplished cuisine is served in the beautiful restaurant.

Moonfleet Manor, Weymouth

ROOMS: 33 en suite 6 annexe en suite (26 fmly) **FACILITIES:** STV Squash Snooker Sauna Solarium Childrens nursery ch fac **CONF:** Thtr 50 Class 18 Board 26 **SERVICES:** Lift **PARKING:** 50 **NOTES:** in restaurant

★★★66% Hotel Prince Regent

139 The Esplanade DT4 7NR
☎ 01305 771313 01305 778100
e-mail: info@princeregentweymouth.co.uk
Dir: *from A354 follow seafront signs. Left at Jubilee Clock, 0.25m on seafront*

Dating back to 1855, this welcoming resort hotel boasts splendid views over Weymouth Bay from the majority of public rooms and front-facing bedrooms. It is conveniently close to the town centre, harbour and opposite the beach. The restaurant offers a choice of menus, and entertainment is regularly provided in the ballroom during the season.

ROOMS: 70 en suite (14 fmly) (5 GF) in 42 bedrooms s £49-£69; d £55-£115 (incl. bkfst & dinner) **LB** **FACILITIES:** Use of leisure facilities at sister hotel Xmas **CONF:** Thtr 180 Class 150 Board 150 Del from £69 **SERVICES:** Lift **PARKING:** 21 **NOTES:** in restaurant Civ Wed 200

★★★64% *Hotel Rex*

29 The Esplanade DT4 8DN
☎ 01305 760400 01305 760500
e-mail: rex@kingshotels.co.uk
web: www.kingshotels.co.uk
Dir: *on seafront opp Alexandra Gardens*

Originally built as the summer residence for the Duke of Clarence, this hotel benefits from its seafront location with stunning views across Weymouth Bay. Bedrooms include several sea-facing rooms and are all well equipped. A wide range of imaginative dishes is served in the popular vaulted restaurant.

ROOMS: 31 en suite (5 fmly) **FACILITIES:** STV **CONF:** Thtr 40 Class 30 Board 25 **SERVICES:** Lift **PARKING:** 6 **NOTES:** Closed Xmas

★★★62% Hotel Rembrandt

12-18 Dorchester Rd DT4 7JU
☎ 01305 764000 01305 764022
e-mail: reception@hotelrembrandt.co.uk
web: www.hotelrembrandt.co.uk
Dir: *0.75m on left after Manor rdbt on A354 from Dorchester*

Only a short distance from the seafront and town centre, this hotel is ideal for visiting local attractions. Facilities include indoor leisure, a bar and extensive meeting rooms. The hotel restaurant is open for lunch and dinner, offering an impressive carvery and carte menu.

ROOMS: 74 en suite (5 fmly) (6 GF) in 30 bedrooms s £80; d £106 (incl. bkfst) **LB** **FACILITIES:** STV Sauna Solarium Gym Steam room Xmas **CONF:** Thtr 200 Class 100 Board 50 Del £98.50 **SERVICES:** Lift **PARKING:** 80 **NOTES:** in restaurant Civ Wed 98

★★71% Glenburn

42 Preston Rd DT3 6PZ
☎ 01305 832353 01305 835610
e-mail: info@glenburnhotel.com
web: www.glenburnhotel.com
Dir: *on A353 1.5m E of town centre*

This small family-run hotel is located close to the seafront. Offering good parking and attractive gardens, including a complimentary 'Hot Tub', the Glenburn is ideal for either business or leisure guests. Bedrooms are comfortable and well equipped. Good use is made of fresh local produce to create the dishes on the daily-changing menu.

ROOMS: 13 en suite (2 fmly) in 8 bedrooms **FACILITIES:** Jacuzzi **CONF:** Thtr 20 Class 20 Board 15 **PARKING:** 15 **NOTES:** in restaurant

★★69% Acropolis

53-55 Dorchester Rd DT4 7JT
☎ 01305 784282 01305 767172
e-mail: acropolishotel@plantours.fsnet.co.uk

This friendly hotel offers comfortable, stylishly decorated and well-equipped rooms. A pleasant lounge and bar is provided and guests can relax around the pool in warmer months, where vines and olive trees create a reminder of the Mediterranean. Appetising authentic Greek cuisine and wines are served in the restaurant.

ROOMS: 10 en suite (3 fmly) in all bedrooms s £45-£80; d £80-£90 (incl. bkfst) **FACILITIES:** supervised **PARKING:** 14

U Star rating not confirmed

W

★★69% Russell
135-13 The Esplanade DT4 7NG
☎ 01305 786059 🖷 01305 775723
This hotel offers comfortable and spacious accommodation. It is situated on the seafront so many rooms benefit from magnificent views. With a sister hotel next door, banqueting facilities in a superb ballroom can be offered. Live music and entertainment are also provided.
ROOMS: 93 en suite (23 GF) ⊗ in 36 bedrooms **FACILITIES:** ♫ Xmas **SERVICES:** Lift **PARKING:** 20 **NOTES:** ✗ ⊗ in restaurant

★★66% *Crown*
51-53 St Thomas St DT4 8EQ
☎ 01305 760800 🖷 01305 760300
e-mail: crown@kingshotels.co.uk
web: www.kingshotels.co.uk
Dir: *From Dorchester, A354 to Weymouth. Follow Back Water on left & cross 2nd bridge*
This popular hotel is conveniently located adjacent to the old harbour and is ideal for shopping, local attractions or transportation links, including the ferry. Public areas include an extensive bar, ballroom and comfortable residents lounge on the first floor. Themed events, such as mock cruises, are a speciality.
ROOMS: 86 en suite (11 fmly) **FACILITIES:** STV **CONF:** Class 140 Board 80 **SERVICES:** Lift **PARKING:** 14 **NOTES:** ✗ Closed 25-26 Dec

⌂ Premier Travel Inn Weymouth
Green Hill DT4 7SX
☎ 08701 977267 🖷 01305 760589
web: www.premiertravelinn.com
Dir: *Follow signs to Weymouth, then brown signs to Lodmoor Country Park*
High quality, modern budget accommodation ideal for both families and business travellers. Spacious, en suite bedrooms feature bath and shower, satellite TV and many have telephones and modem points. The adjacent family restaurant features a wide and varied menu. For further details consult the Hotel Groups page.
ROOMS: 40 en suite s £51.95; d £51.95

WHICKHAM, Tyne & Wear — Map 21 NZ26

★★★69% Gibside
Front St NE16 4JG
☎ 0191 488 9292 🖷 0191 488 8000
e-mail: reception@gibside-hotel.co.uk
web: www.gibside-hotel.co.uk
Dir: *off A1(M) towards Whickham on B6317, onto Front St, 2m on right*
Conveniently located in the village centre, this hotel is close to the Newcastle by-pass and its elevated position affords views over the Tyne Valley. Bedrooms come in two styles, classical and contemporary. Public rooms include the Egyptian-themed Sphinx bar and a more formal restaurant. Secure garage parking is available.
ROOMS: 45 en suite (2 fmly) (13 GF) ⊗ in 10 bedrooms s £62.50-£75; d £72.50-£85 **FACILITIES:** STV Golf Academy at The Beamish Park ♫ Xmas **CONF:** Thtr 100 Class 50 Board 50 Del from £81.50 **SERVICES:** Lift **PARKING:** 28

WHITBY, North Yorkshire — Map 19 NZ81

★★★72% ◎ Dunsley Hall
Dunsley YO21 3TL
☎ 01947 893437 🖷 01947 893505
e-mail: reception@dunsleyhall.com
web: www.dunsleyhall.com
Dir: *3m N of Whitby, signed off A171*
Friendly service is found at this fine country mansion set in a quiet hamlet with coastal views north of Whitby. The house has Gothic overtones and boasts fine woodwork and panelling, no more so than in the magnificent lounge. Two lovely dining rooms offer imaginative dishes and there is also a cosy bar.

ROOMS: 18 en suite (2 fmly) (2 GF) ⊗ in all bedrooms s £82.50-£105; d £135-£177 (incl. bkfst) **LB** **FACILITIES:** Sauna Solarium Gym Putt green Xmas **CONF:** Thtr 95 Class 50 Board 40 Del from £110 **PARKING:** 30 **NOTES:** ⊗ in restaurant Civ Wed 60

★★★68% Saxonville
Ladysmith Av, Argyle Rd YO21 3HX
☎ 01947 602631 🖷 01947 820523
e-mail: newtons@saxonville.co.uk
web: www.saxonville.co.uk
Dir: *A174 on to North Promenade. Turn inland at large four towered building visible on West Cliff into Argyle Road, then 1st turning on right*
Friendly service is a feature of this long-established holiday hotel. Well maintained throughout it offers comfortable bedrooms and inviting public areas that include a well-proportioned restaurant.
ROOMS: 23 en suite (2 fmly) (1 GF) ⊗ in all bedrooms s £55-£80; d £110-£140 (incl. bkfst) **LB** **FACILITIES:** STV **CONF:** Thtr 100 Class 40 Board 40 Del from £85 **PARKING:** 20 **NOTES:** ✗ ⊗ in restaurant Closed Dec-Jan RS Feb-Mar & Nov

★★71% Cliffemount
Runswick Bay TS13 5HU
☎ 01947 840103 🖷 01947 841025
e-mail: cliffemount@runswickbay.fsnet.co.uk
web: www.cliffemounthotel.co.uk
Dir: *turn off A174 8m N of Whitby, follow road 1m to end. Hotel on clifftop*
Lying in an elevated position above the cliff-side village and with splendid views across the bay, a warm welcome awaits. The cosy bar leads to the restaurant where fish features on the interesting menus. The bedrooms, many with sea-view balconies, are well equipped and it is worth asking for one of the superb new wing rooms.
ROOMS: 19 en suite (5 GF) s £32-£55; d £69-£107.50 (incl. bkfst) **LB** **PARKING:** 30 **NOTES:** ⊗ in restaurant Closed 25-26 Dec

★★70% White House
Upgang Ln, West Cliff YO21 3JJ
☎ 01947 600469 🖷 01947 821600
e-mail: whitehousehotel@btconnect.com
Dir: *turn off A171 onto High Stakesby road, follow signs for West Cliff and Sandsend. Hotel adjacent to golf course*
Set on the cliff top overlooking the golf course and Sandsend Bay, this hotel has attractive and stylish public rooms. There are two bar areas and a dining room between, with an extensive menu available in all. Bedrooms are smartly presented and include two with balconies and four contained in a converted stone building.
ROOMS: 11 en suite 5 annexe en suite (5 fmly) (5 GF) s £39-£50; d £80-£110 (incl. bkfst) **LB** **PARKING:** 30 **NOTES:** ✗ ⊗ in restaurant

WHITBY, continued

★★64% Old West Cliff Hotel
42 Crescent Av YO21 3EQ
☎ 01947 603292 ▤ 01947 821716
e-mail: oldwestcliff@telinco.co.uk
web: www.oldwestcliff.telinco.co.uk
Dir: from A171 follow signs for West Cliff, approach spa complex. Hotel 100yds from centre off Crescent Gardens
This family owned and run hotel is close to the sea and convenient for the town centre. It provides well-equipped bedrooms, a cosy lounge and separate bar. A wide range of food is served in the cosy basement restaurant.
ROOMS: 12 en suite (6 fmly) s £51; d £62 (incl. bkfst) NOTES: ✗ ⊗ in restaurant Closed 24 Dec-31 Jan

Restaurant with Rooms

🏠 ⑧ Estbek House
East Row, Sandsend YO21 3SU
☎ 01947 893424
e-mail: reservations@estbekhouse.co.uk
Dir: on Cleveland Way, within Sandsend, next to East Beck

This listed Georgian house lies in a small coastal village north west of Whitby. A seafood restaurant with rooms, the lower ground floor contains a cosy bistro, the first floor a dining room in the period of the house, whilst the two upper floors contain individually designed bedrooms that vary in size.
ROOMS: 5 rms (4 en suite) (1 fmly) ⊗ in all bedrooms
PARKING: NOTES: ✗ ⊗ in restaurant

See advert on opposite page

WHITCHURCH, Shropshire Map 15 SJ54

★★★65% Dodington Lodge
Dodington SY13 1EN
☎ 01948 662539 ▤ 01948 667992
e-mail: info@dodingtonlodge.co.uk
web: www.dodingtonlodge.co.uk
Dir: from S approach Whitchurch via A41/A49, hotel on left of mini rdbt on outskirts of town
This family run hotel is conveniently situated close to the centre of the town, within easy reach of Chester and North Wales. Bedrooms are tastefully decorated and well equipped whilst a welcoming atmosphere prevails in the lounge bar. A choice of eating options is offered, from a light snack to a full meal. The function suite is a popular choice for weddings and meetings.
ROOMS: 10 en suite (2 fmly) s £58; d £68 (incl. bkfst) CONF: Thtr 60 Class 40 Board 25 Del from £80 PARKING: 45 NOTES: ✗ ⊗ in restaurant

WHITEHAVEN, Cumbria Map 18 NX91

⟐ Premier Travel Inn Whitehaven
Howgate CA28 6PL
☎ 08701 977268 ▤ 01946 590106
web: www.premiertravelinn.com
Dir: On outskirts of Whitehaven on A595 towards Workington
High quality, modern budget accommodation ideal for both families and business travellers. Spacious, en suite bedrooms feature bath and shower, satellite TV and many have telephones and modem points. The adjacent family restaurant features a wide and varied menu. For further details consult the Hotel Groups page.
ROOMS: 38 en suite s £46.95-£48.95; d £46.95-£48.95

WHITEWELL, Lancashire Map 18 SD64

Restaurant with Rooms

🏠 The Inn at Whitewell
Forest of Bowland, Clitheroe BB7 3AT
☎ 01200 448222 ▤ 01200 448298
This long-established culinary destination hides away in quintessential Lancashire countryside just 20 minutes from the M6. The fine dining restaurant is complemented by two historic, cosy bars, and roaring fires, real ales and slick service provide an irresistible combination. Bedrooms are richly furnished with antiques and eye-catching bijouterie, while many of the bathrooms have voluminous Victorian brass showers.
ROOMS: 13 en suite 4 annexe en suite (1 fmly) (1 GF)
FACILITIES: STV Fishing Xmas CONF: Class 60 Board 35
PARKING: 60 NOTES: Civ Wed 80

WHITLEY, Wiltshire Map 04 ST86

Restaurant with Rooms

🏠 ⑧⑧ The Pear Tree Inn
Top Ln SN12 8QX
☎ 01225 709131 ▤ 01225 702276
e-mail: enquiries@peartreeinn.co.uk

This inn boasts eight very superior bedrooms with state-of-the-art TVs and DVDs, and luxurious bathrooms. Four are situated around an attractive inner courtyard garden, complete with fountain and patio area. The restaurant draws customers from a wide area to experience the excellent food and the friendliness of the professional team.
ROOMS: 4 en suite 4 annexe en suite (2 fmly) (4 GF) ⊗ in all bedrooms s £65-£75; d £95-£120 (incl. bkfst) FACILITIES: boules pitch PARKING: 60 NOTES: ✗ ⊗ in restaurant Closed 25-26 Dec

WHITLEY BAY, Tyne & Wear — Map 21 NZ37

★★★71% **Windsor**

South Pde NE26 2RF
☎ 0191 251 8888 🖷 0191 297 0272
e-mail: info@windsorhotel-uk.com
web: www.windsorhotel-uk.com
Dir: *from A19/Tyne Tunnel follow for A1058 to Tynemouth. At coast rdbt left to Whitley Bay. After 2m left at Rex Hotel. Hotel on left*

This tastefully modernised hotel is conveniently located between the town centre and the seafront, and has lively bars that transform Thursday to Sunday nights with a carnival atmosphere. Bedrooms are very comfortably equipped and most boast superior bathrooms with bath and separate shower cubicle. Public areas are smartly presented and include the smart and stylish Bazil Brasserie.
ROOMS: 69 en suite (24 fmly) (4 GF) ⊗ in 49 bedrooms s £59-£69; d £65-£75 (incl. bkfst) **LB** **FACILITIES:** STV **CONF:** Thtr 80 Class 40 Board 40 Del from £69 **SERVICES:** Lift **PARKING:** 46 **NOTES:** ✗ ⊗ in restaurant

WHITNEY-ON-WYE, Herefordshire — Map 09 SO24

★★72% **The Rhydspence Inn**

HR3 6EU
☎ 01497 831262 🖷 01497 831751
e-mail: info@rhydspence-inn.co.uk
Dir: *1m W of Whitney-on-Wye on A438 Hereford to Brecon road*

With a history as an inn stretching back 600 years, this hotel offers the charm of yesteryear with the comforts of today and is personally run by the proprietors. Guests can expect well-equipped bedrooms and public areas with exposed beams and timber-framed walls. There is an extensive menu in the elegant restaurant and the atmospheric bar also has a blackboard menu.
ROOMS: 7 en suite s £42.50; d £85 (incl. bkfst) **LB** **PARKING:** 30 **NOTES:** ✗ ⊗ in restaurant

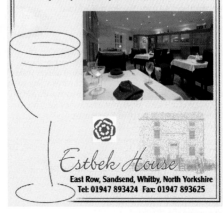

WHITSTABLE, Kent — Map 07 TR16

⌂ **Premier Travel Inn Whitstable**

Thanet Way CT5 3DB
☎ 08701 977269 🖷 01227 263151
web: www.premiertravelinn.com
Dir: *2m W of town centre on B2205*
High quality, modern budget accommodation ideal for both families and business travellers. Spacious, en suite bedrooms feature bath and shower, satellite TV and many have telephones and modem points. The adjacent family restaurant features a wide and varied menu. For further details consult the Hotel Groups page.
ROOMS: 40 en suite s £48.95; d £48.95 **CONF:** Thtr 30 Board 20

WHITTLEBURY, Northamptonshire — Map 11 SP64

★★★★79% ◎◎ **Whittlebury Hall**

NN12 8QH
☎ 01327 857857 🖷 01237 857867
e-mail: sales@whittleburyhall.co.uk
web: www.whittleburyhall.co.uk
Dir: *A43/A413 towards Buckingham, through Whittlebury turn for hotel on right (signed)*
A purpose-built, Georgian-style country house hotel with excellent spa and leisure facilities and pedestrian access to the Silverstone circuit. Grand public areas include F1 car racing memorabilia and the accommodation includes some lavishly appointed suites. Food is a strength, with a choice of various dining options. Particularly

continued on p608

WHITTLEBURY, continued

noteworthy are the afternoon teas in the spacious, comfortable lounge and the fine dining in Murray's Restaurant.
ROOMS: 211 en suite (3 fmly) in 160 bedrooms s £99-£125; d £125-£165 (incl. bkfst) **LB** **FACILITIES: Spa** STV Sauna Solarium Gym Jacuzzi Beauty treatments, Relaxation Room, Hair Studio, Heat and Ice experiences Xmas **CONF:** Thtr 500 Class 175 Board 40 **SERVICES:** Lift **PARKING:** 450 **NOTES:** in restaurant

WICKFORD, Essex — Map 06 TQ79

Innkeeper's Lodge Basildon/Wickford
Runwell Rd SS11 7QJ
☎ 01268 769671 01268 578012
web: www.innkeeperslodge.com
***Dir:** M25 junct 29/A127 Southend, leave at Basildon/Wickford, left at rdbt towards Wickford. Straight over next 2 rdbts, at 3rd rdbt take 2nd exit*
A growing concept in the travel accommodation market. Smart rooms meet essential business requirements but also have home comforts. Dining options include all-day menus plus the added advantage of breakfast, which is included in the room price. For further details consult the Hotel Groups page.
ROOMS: 24 en suite s £48; d £48

WICKHAM, Hampshire — Map 05 SU51

★★70% Old House Hotel & Restaurant
The Square PO17 5JG
☎ 01329 833049 01329 833672
e-mail: oldhousehotel@aol.com
web: www.oldhousehotel.co.uk
***Dir:** M27 junct 10, N on A32 for 2m towards Alton.*

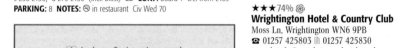

This creeper-clad former Georgian residence occupies a prime position in a charming square in the centre of town. Ongoing refurbishment is resulting in smart and comfortable public areas that include a choice of eating areas and an inviting bar and lounge. Bedrooms are well equipped although some are larger than others.
ROOMS: 8 en suite 4 annexe en suite (2 fmly) in all bedrooms s £50-£150; d £75-£150 (incl. bkfst) **LB** **CONF:** Board 1 Del from £165 **PARKING:** 8 **NOTES:** in restaurant Civ Wed 70

Indoor Swimming pool
Indoor Swimming pool (heated)
Outdoor Swimming pool
Outdoor Swimming pool (heated)

WIDNES, Cheshire — Map 15 SJ58

★★★62% The Hillcrest Hotel
75 Cronton Ln WA8 9AR
☎ 0151 424 1616 0151 495 1348
e-mail: thehillcrest@corushotels.com
web: www.corushotels.com/hillcrest
***Dir:** A5080 Cronton to lights turn right for 0.75m, right at T-junct, follow A5080 for 500yds. Hotel on right*
This comfortable hotel is located within easy reach of the motorway network. All bedrooms are comfortable and well equipped, particularly the executive rooms. Suites with four-poster or canopy beds, and spa baths are also available. Public areas include extensive conference facilities, Palms restaurant and bar, as well as Nelsons public bar.
ROOMS: 50 en suite (5 fmly) in 25 bedrooms s £35-£62; d £50-£72 **LB** **FACILITIES:** STV Xmas **CONF:** Thtr 140 Class 80 Board 40 Del from £85 **SERVICES:** Lift **PARKING:** 150 **NOTES:** Civ Wed 100

Travelodge
Fiddlers Ferry Rd WA8 2NR
☎ 08700 850 950 0151 424 8930
web: www.travelodge.co.uk
***Dir:** on A562, 3m south of Widnes*
Travelodge offers good quality, good value, modern accommodation. Ideal for families, the spacious, en suite bedrooms include remote-control TV, tea and coffee-making facilities and comfortable beds. Meals can be taken at the nearby family restaurant. For further details consult the Hotel Groups page.
ROOMS: 32 en suite s fr £26; d fr £26

WIGAN, Greater Manchester — Map 15 SD50

★★★★63% Kilhey Court
Chorley Rd, Standish WN1 2XN
☎ 01257 472100 01257 422401
e-mail: events.kilheycourt@macdonald-hotels.co.uk
web: www.macdonald-hotels.co.uk
***Dir:** M6 junct 27, A5209 Standish, over at lights, past church on right, left at T-junct, hotel on right 350yds. M61 junct 6, signed Wigan & Haigh Hall. 3m & right at T-junct. Hotel 0.5 m on right*
This hotel is peacefully situated in its own grounds yet conveniently located for the motorway network. The accommodation is comfortable and the rooms are split between the original Victorian house and a modern extension. Public areas display many original features and the split-level restaurant has views over the Worthington Lakes. This hotel is an especially popular venue for weddings.
ROOMS: 62 en suite (3 fmly) (8 GF) in 33 bedrooms s £55-£110; d £70-£125 **LB** **FACILITIES: Spa** STV Sauna Solarium Gym Jacuzzi Aerobics and yoga classes, private fishing arranged Xmas **CONF:** BC Thtr 400 Class 180 Board 60 Del from £115 **SERVICES:** Lift **PARKING:** 200 **NOTES:** in restaurant Civ Wed 300

★★★74%
Wrightington Hotel & Country Club
Moss Ln, Wrightington WN6 9PB
☎ 01257 425803 01257 425830
e-mail: info@wrightingtonhotel.co.uk
***Dir:** M6 junct 27, 0.25m W, hotel on right after church*
Situated in open countryside close to the M6 motorway, this privately owned hotel offers friendly hospitality. Accommodation is well equipped and spacious and public areas include an extensive leisure complex, Blazers Restaurant, two bars and air-conditioned

continued

W

function and banqueting facilities, along with the impressive fine dining restaurant, Simply Heathcotes.

ROOMS: 74 en suite (6 fmly) (36 GF) ⊗ in 64 bedrooms s £74-£100; d £84-£115 (incl. bkfst) **LB** **FACILITIES:** STV Squash Sauna Solarium Gym Jacuzzi Sport injury clinic, Health & beauty clinic, hairdresser **CONF:** Thtr 200 Class 120 Board 40 **SERVICES:** Lift **PARKING:** 240 **NOTES:** ⊗ in restaurant RS 24 Dec-3 Jan Civ Wed 100

★★★65% Quality Hotel Wigan

Riverway WN1 3SS
☎ 01942 826888 📠 01942 825800
e-mail: enquiries@hotels-wigan.com
web: www.choicehotelseurope.com
Dir: *from A49 take B5238 from rdbt, continue for 1.5m through lights, through 3 more sets of lights, right at 4th set, 1st left*
Close to the centre of the town this modern hotel offers spacious and well-equipped bedrooms. The open plan public areas include a comfortable lounge bar adjacent to the popular restaurant, which serves a good range of dishes. Secure parking is a bonus.
ROOMS: 88 en suite (16 GF) ⊗ in 42 bedrooms s £45-£99; d £55-£109 (incl. bkfst) **LB** **CONF:** Thtr 240 Class 90 Board 50 Del from £70 **SERVICES:** Lift **PARKING:** 100 **NOTES:** ⊗ in restaurant Civ Wed 60

★★65% Bel-Air

236 Wigan Ln WN1 2NU
☎ 01942 241410 📠 01942 243967
e-mail: belair@hotelwigan.freeserve.co.uk
web: www.belairhotel.co.uk
Dir: *M6 junct 27, follow signs for Standish. In Standish turn right at lights towards A49. Hotel 1.5m on right, towards Wigan*
This friendly, family-owned and run hotel is located just to the north of town. Accommodation varies in size and style and all rooms are well equipped. An extensive range of freshly prepared dishes is offered in the restaurant.
ROOMS: 11 en suite (1 fmly) s £35-£45; d £45-£49.50 (incl. bkfst) **CONF:** Thtr 20 Board 8 **PARKING:** 10 **NOTES:** ✗ ⊗ in restaurant

⇧ Premier Travel Inn Wigan South

53 Warrington Rd, Ashton-in-Makerfield WN4 9PJ
☎ 0870 9906582 📠 0870 9906583
web: www.premiertravelinn.com
Dir: *Just off M6 junct 23, A49 towards Wigan*
High quality, modern budget accommodation ideal for both families and business travellers. Spacious, en suite bedrooms feature bath and shower, satellite TV and many have telephones and modem points. The adjacent family restaurant features a wide and varied menu. For further details consult the Hotel Groups page.
ROOMS: 28 en suite s £46.95-£48.95; d £46.95-£48.95

⇧ Premier Travel Inn Wigan South (Marus Bridge)

Warrington Rd, Marus Bridge WN3 6XB
☎ 08701 977270 📠 01942 498679
web: www.premiertravelinn.com
Dir: *M6 junct 25 (N'bound) slip road to rdbt turn left, Inn on left*
High quality, modern budget accommodation ideal for both families and business travellers. Spacious, en suite bedrooms feature bath and shower, satellite TV and many have telephones and modem points. The adjacent family restaurant features a wide and varied menu. For further details consult the Hotel Groups page.
ROOMS: 40 en suite s £46.95-£48.95; d £46.95-£48.95

⇧ Premier Travel Inn Wigan West

Orrell Rd, Orrell WN5 8HQ
☎ 08701 977271 📠 01942 215002
web: www.premiertravelinn.com
Dir: *From M6 junct 26 follow signs for Upholland and Orrell. At first set of lights turn left. Inn on right behind Priory Wood Beefeater*
High quality, modern budget accommodation ideal for both families and business travellers. Spacious, en suite bedrooms feature bath and shower, satellite TV and many have telephones and modem points. The adjacent family restaurant features a wide and varied menu. For further details consult the Hotel Groups page.
ROOMS: 40 en suite s £46.95-£48.95; d £46.95-£48.95 **CONF:** Thtr 75 Board 40

WIGHT, ISLE OF — Map 05

BEMBRIDGE — Map 05 SZ68

★★★66% ◎ The Windmill Inn Hotel & Restaurant

1 Steyne Rd PO35 5UH
☎ 01983 872875 📠 01983 874760
e-mail: info@thewindmillhotel.co.uk
web: www.windmill-inn.com
Dir: *0.5m from town centre, towards lifeboat station*

This newly refurbished hotel offers a range of comfortably furnished public rooms where an excellent choice of freshly prepared food is available to suit virtually all tastes. Bedrooms and suites have also benefited from the refurbishment and are very well presented and thoughtfully equipped. Service is both attentive and friendly. There is an attractive garden to the rear.
ROOMS: 14 en suite (2 fmly) ⊗ in 3 bedrooms s £50-£90; d £80-£120 (incl. bkfst) **LB** **CONF:** Thtr 100 Class 100 Board 100 **PARKING:** 50 **NOTES:** ✗ ⊗ in restaurant Civ Wed 100

BONCHURCH See Ventnor

W

COWES
Map 05 SZ49

★★★68% New Holmwood
Queens Rd, Egypt Point PO31 8BW
☎ 01983 292508 🖷 01983 295020
e-mail: nholmwdh@aol.com
Dir: *from A3020 at Northwood Garage lights, left & follow road to rdbt. 1st left then sharp right into Baring Rd, 4th left into Egypt Hill. At bottom turn right, hotel on right*

Just metres from the Esplanade, this hotel has an enviable outlook. Bedrooms are comfortable and very well equipped. The light and airy, glass-fronted restaurant looks out to sea and serves a range of interesting meals. The sun terrace is delightful in the summer and there is a small pool area.
ROOMS: 26 en suite (1 fmly) (9 GF) ⊗ in all bedrooms s £79-£125; d £95-£125 (incl. bkfst) **LB** **FACILITIES: Spa** STV ⥽ Xmas **CONF:** Thtr 130 Class 60 Board 50 **PARKING:** 20 **NOTES:** ⊗ in restaurant
See advert on opposite page

★62% Duke of York
Mill Hill Rd PO31 7BT
☎ 01983 295171 🖷 01983 295047
This family-run inn is quietly situated close to the town centre. Bedrooms are divided between the main building and a nearby annexe and are neatly appointed. There is a well-stocked bar and a pleasant restaurant offering a good range of popular dishes, many featuring fish and seafood. The inn has a nautical theme enhanced by an abundance of maritime memorabilia.
ROOMS: 8 en suite 5 annexe en suite (2 fmly) (1 GF) ⊗ in 4 bedrooms s fr £40; d fr £60 (incl. bkfst) **LB** **PARKING:** 12

FRESHWATER
Map 05 SZ38

★★★68% ⊛ Farringford
Bedbury Ln PO40 9TQ
☎ 01983 752500 🖷 01983 756515
e-mail: enquiries@farringford.co.uk
web: www.farringford.co.uk
Dir: *A3054, left to Norton Green down Pixlie Hill. Left to Freshwater Bay. At bay turn right into Bedbury Ln, hotel on left*
Upon seeing Farringford, Alfred Lord Tennyson is said to have remarked "we will go no further, this must be our home" and so it was for some forty years. One hundred and fifty years later, the hotel provides bedrooms ranging in style and size, from large rooms in the main house to adjoining chalet-style rooms. The atmosphere is relaxed and dinner features fresh local produce.
ROOMS: 14 en suite 4 annexe en suite (5 fmly) (4 GF) s £33-£60; d £66-£120 (incl. bkfst) **LB** **FACILITIES:** ⥽ ⛳9 ⚲ Putt green Bowling green ♫ Xmas **CONF:** BC Thtr 120 Class 50 Board 50 Del from £60 **PARKING:** 55 **NOTES:** Civ Wed 130

⊗ No smoking

NEWPORT
Map 05 SZ58

⌂ Premier Travel Inn Isle Of Wight (Newport)
Seaclose, Fairlee Rd PO30 2DN
☎ 08701 977144 🖷 0870 241 9000
web: www.premiertravelinn.com
Dir: *From town centre take A3054 signed Ryde. After 0.75m at Seaclose lights, turn left. Inn adjacent to council offices*
High quality, modern budget accommodation ideal for both families and business travellers. Spacious, en suite bedrooms feature bath and shower, satellite TV and many have telephones and modem points. The adjacent family restaurant features a wide and varied menu. For further details consult the Hotel Groups page.
ROOMS: 42 en suite s £49.95; d £49.95

RYDE
Map 05 SZ59

★★★65% Yelf's
Union St PO33 2LG
☎ 01983 564062 🖷 01983 563937
e-mail: manager@yelfshotel.com
web: www.yelfshotel.com
Dir: *from Ryde Esplanade, turn into Union St. Hotel on right*

This former coaching inn has smart public areas including a busy bar, a separate lounge and an attractive dining room. Bedrooms are comfortably furnished and well equipped and some are located in an adjoining wing. A conservatory lounge bar and stylish terrace are ideal for relaxing.
ROOMS: 30 en suite (2 fmly) ⊗ in 5 bedrooms **FACILITIES:** STV **CONF:** Thtr 70 Class 30 Board 50 **NOTES:** ⊗ in restaurant Civ Wed 100

★★68% Appley Manor
Appley Rd PO33 1PH
☎ 01983 564777 🖷 01983 564704
e-mail: appleymanor@lineone.net
Dir: *A3055 onto B3330. Hotel 0.25m on left*
Located only five minutes from the town centre this property, which sits in peaceful surroundings, was once a Victorian manor house. The spacious bedrooms are well furnished and decorated. Dinner can be taken in the popular adjoining Manor Inn.
ROOMS: 12 en suite (2 fmly) ⊗ in 3 bedrooms s £37; d £47 **CONF:** Thtr 40 Class 40 Board 30 **PARKING:** 60 **NOTES:** 🐕

SANDOWN
Map 05 SZ58

★★68% Riviera
2 Royal St PO36 8LP
☎ 01983 402518 🖷 01983 402518
e-mail: enquiries@rivierahotel.org.uk
Dir: *pass Heights Leisure Centre and church on left. Turn 2nd right (Melville St), then 2nd right again into Royal St*
Regular guests return year after year to this friendly and
continued

welcoming family-run hotel. It is located near to the High Street and just a short stroll from the beach, pier and shops. Bedrooms, including several at ground floor level, are very well furnished and comfortably equipped. Enjoyable home-cooked meals are served in the spacious dining room.

ROOMS: 41 en suite (6 fmly) (10 GF) s £29-£32; d £58-£64 (incl. bkfst) LB **FACILITIES:** ♫ **PARKING:** 20 **NOTES:** ⊗ in restaurant Closed Nov-Mar

★★64% *Bayshore*

12-16 Pier St PO36 8JX
☎ 01983 403154 🖷 01983 406574
e-mail: bayshore.sandown@alfatravel.co.uk
web: www.alfatravel.co.uk

Leisureplex

Dir: *from the Broadway into Melville St, signed to Tourist Information Office. Across High St and bear right opposite pier. Hotel on right*

This large hotel is located on the seafront opposite the pier and offers extensive public rooms where live entertainment is provided

continued

in season. The bedrooms are well equipped and staff very friendly and helpful.

ROOMS: 78 en suite (19 fmly) **FACILITIES:** Sauna ♫ **SERVICES:** Lift **NOTES:** ✗ ⊗ in restaurant Closed Dec-Feb RS Mar & Nov

★★61% *Sandringham*

Esplanade PO36 8AH
☎ 01983 406655 🖷 01983 404395
e-mail: info@sandringhamhotel.co.uk

With a prime seafront location and splendid views, this is one of the largest hotels on the island. Comfortable public areas include a spacious lounge and a heated indoor swimming pool and Jacuzzi. Bedrooms vary in size and many sea-facing rooms have a balcony. Regular entertainment is provided in the ballroom.

ROOMS: 110 en suite (39 fmly) (6 GF) ⊗ in 3 bedrooms **FACILITIES:** Snooker Sauna Jacuzzi ♫ **SERVICES:** Lift **PARKING:** 82 **NOTES:** ✗ ⊗ in restaurant

SEAVIEW

Map 05 SZ69

★★★77% ֍֍ Priory Bay

Priory Dr PO34 5BU
☎ 01983 613146 🖷 01983 616539
e-mail: enquiries@priorybay.co.uk
web: www.priorybay.co.uk

Dir: *B3330 towards Seaview, through Nettlestone. Do not take Seaview turn, but continue 0.5m until hotel sign*

This peacefully located hotel has its own stretch of beach and a range of outdoor leisure facilities. Public areas are especially comfortable, as are the well-equipped and mostly spacious

continued on p612

SEAVIEW, continued

bedrooms. The kitchen creates interesting and imaginative dishes, using local produce as much as possible.

Priory Bay Hotel, Seaview

ROOMS: 19 en suite 12 annexe en suite (13 fmly) (2 GF) s £49-£220; d £220-£260 (incl. bkfst) **LB** **FACILITIES:** STV 6 Private beach, 70 Acres of woodland lawns and formal gardens. Xmas **CONF:** Thtr 80 Class 60 Board 40 Del from £95 **PARKING:** 100 **NOTES:** ⊗ in restaurant Civ Wed 100

★★66% *Springvale Hotel & Restaurant*

Springvale PO34 5AN
☎ 01983 612533 📠 01983 812905
e-mail: reception@springvalehotel.com
web: www.springvalehotel.com
Dir: *towards Ryde, follow A3055 onto A3330 towards Bembridge. Left at signs to Seaview, follow brown tourist signs for hotel*

A friendly hotel in a quiet beachfront location with views across the Solent. Bedrooms, which differ in shape and size, are attractive and well equipped. Public areas are traditionally furnished and include a cosy bar, dining room and small separate lounge.
ROOMS: 13 en suite (2 fmly) **FACILITIES:** Jacuzzi Sailing dinghy hire & tuition, Cruiser Charter ♫ ch fac **CONF:** Class 30 Board 20 **PARKING:** 1 **NOTES:** ⊗ in restaurant

U Seaview Hotel & Restaurant

High St PO34 5EX
☎ 01983 612711 📠 01983 613729
e-mail: reception@seaviewhotel.co.uk
Dir: *B3330 Ryde-Seaview road, turn left via Puckpool along seafront, hotel on left*

At the time of going to press, the star classification for this hotel was not confirmed. Please refer to the AA internet site www.theAA.com for current information.
ROOMS: 17 en suite (3 fmly) (3 GF) ⊗ in 13 bedrooms s £72-£177; d £89-£232 (incl. bkfst) **FACILITIES:** Arrangement with nearby sports club Xmas **PARKING:** 12 **NOTES:** 🚫🐕 ⊗ in restaurant

SHANKLIN Map 05 SZ58

★★★68% Keats Green

3 Queens Rd PO37 6AN
☎ 01983 862742 📠 01983 868572
e-mail: enquiries@keatsgreenhotel.co.uk
Dir: *on A3055 follow Old Village/Ventnor signs, avoiding town centre, hotel on left past St Saviours Church*

This well-established hotel enjoys a super location overlooking Keats Green and Sandown Bay. Bedrooms are attractively decorated in a variety of styles and many have lovely sea views. Public rooms offer a comfortable bar/lounge and a smartly appointed dining room.
ROOMS: 33 en suite (6 fmly) (3 GF) ⊗ in 1 bedroom s £42-£50; d £84-£100 (incl. bkfst) **LB** **FACILITIES:** Xmas **SERVICES:** Lift **PARKING:** 34 **NOTES:** ⊗ in restaurant Closed Jan-Mar

★★★65% Luccombe Hall

8 Luccombe Rd PO37 6RL
☎ 01983 869000 📠 01983 863082
e-mail: enquiries@luccombehall.co.uk
Dir: *take A3055 to Shanklin, through old village then 1st left into Priory Rd, left into Popham Rd, 1st right into Luccombe Rd. Hotel on left*

Appropriately described as 'the view with the hotel', this property was originally built in 1870 as a summer home for the Bishop of Portsmouth. Enjoying an impressive cliff-top location, the hotel benefits from wonderful sea views, delightful gardens and direct access to the beach. Well-equipped bedrooms are comfortably furnished and there is a range of leisure facilities.
ROOMS: 30 en suite (15 fmly) (7 GF) s £35-£55; d £70-£150 (incl. bkfst) **FACILITIES:** Squash Sauna Solarium Gym Putt green Jacuzzi Games room, Treatment room ♫ Xmas **PARKING:** 20 **NOTES:** 🚫🐕 ⊗ in restaurant

★★71% Channel View

Hope Rd PO37 6EH
☎ 01983 862309 📠 01983 868400
e-mail: enquiries@channelviewhotel.co.uk
Dir: *off A3055 at sign for esplanade & beach, hotel 250mtrs on left*

With an elevated cliff-top location overlooking Shanklin Bay,

continued

several rooms at this hotel enjoy pleasant views and all are very well decorated and furnished. The hotel is family run, and guests can enjoy efficient service, regular evening entertainment, a heated indoor swimming pool and holistic therapy.
ROOMS: 56 en suite (15 fmly) s £27-£45; d £54-£90 (incl. bkfst) **LB**
FACILITIES: Spa Sauna Solarium ♫ **SERVICES:** Lift **PARKING:** 22
NOTES: ⊘ in restaurant Closed Jan-Feb

★★70% Cliff Hall
16 Crescent Rd PO37 6DJ
☎ 01983 862828
e-mail: cliffhallhotel@btconnect.com
Dir: *A3055/A3056 to Shanklin. Right at Lake, down Lake Hill, left at Clarendon Rd, hotel at top of hill*
A privately owned hotel situated close to the beach lift and town centre. The pleasantly decorated bedrooms are generally quite spacious and have all the usual facilities; many rooms also have stunning sea views. Public areas include a lounge, bar, restaurant, coffee shop and a superb terrace with an outdoor swimming pool.
ROOMS: 28 en suite (18 fmly) (9 GF) ⊘ in all bedrooms s £31-£46; d £62-£92 (incl. bkfst & dinner) **LB FACILITIES:** Snooker 2 pool tables, table tennis ♫ Xmas **PARKING:** 30 **NOTES:** ⊘ in restaurant Closed Jan

★★67% *Somerton Lodge*
43 Victoria Av PO37 6LT
☎ 01983 862710 📠 01983 863841
e-mail: somerton@wightbiz.com
web: www.somertonlodgehotel.co.uk
Dir: *on A3020 into town*
The hotel is walking distance from the town, old village, Shanklin chine and the sea. It is situated in a peaceful tree-lined avenue within easy reach of the railway station and main bus routes. Guests can make use of the leisure facilities of the hotel next door, for a small additional charge.
ROOMS: 16 rms (13 en suite) 5 annexe en suite (2 fmly) (5 GF)
PARKING: 15 **NOTES:** No children ⊘ in restaurant

★★65% Melbourne Ardenlea
4-6 Queens Rd PO37 6AP
☎ 01983 862283 📠 01983 862865
e-mail: reservations@melbourneardenlea.co.uk
Dir: *from ferry follow A3055 to Shanklin then follow signs to Ventnor via B3328 (Queens Rd). Hotel just before end of road on right*
This quietly located hotel is within easy walking distance of the town centre and the lift down to the promenade and successfully caters for the needs of holidaymakers. Bedrooms are traditionally furnished and guests can enjoy the various spacious public areas including a welcoming bar and a large heated indoor swimming pool.
ROOMS: 54 en suite (5 fmly) (6 GF) s £35-£45; d £70-£90 (incl. bkfst)
LB FACILITIES: Snooker Sauna Jacuzzi ♫ Xmas **SERVICES:** Lift
PARKING: 26 **NOTES:** ⊘ in restaurant Closed 27 Dec-3 Jan

★★64% Malton House
8 Park Rd PO37 6AY
☎ 01983 865007 📠 01983 865576
e-mail: couvoussis@maltonhouse.freeserve.co.uk
web: www.maltonhouse.co.uk
Dir: *from Hope Road lights up hill then left into 3rd road*
A well-kept Victorian hotel set in its own gardens in a quiet area, conveniently located for cliff-top walks and the public lift down to the promenade. The bedrooms are comfortable and public rooms include a small lounge, a separate bar and a dining room where traditional homemade meals are served.
ROOMS: 15 en suite (3 fmly) s £30-£35; d £50-£56 (incl. bkfst)
PARKING: 12 **NOTES:** ⊘ in restaurant

★★64% Villa Mentone
11 Park Rd PO37 6AY
☎ 01983 862346 📠 01983 862130
e-mail: enquiry@villa-mentone.co.uk
Built in 1860, the Villa Mentone enjoys an excellent cliff-top position close to the town centre. Bedrooms vary in size but are all well equipped, and a smart conservatory extension offers views over Shanklin Bay. Enjoyable home cooking is served in the pleasant dining room, and entertainment is regularly provided in the bar.
ROOMS: 30 en suite (3 fmly) (7 GF) **FACILITIES:** STV ♫ Xmas
CONF: Thtr 45 Class 25 Board 10 **PARKING:** 10 **NOTES:** ⊘ in restaurant

U Priory Manor Hotel
Priory Rd PO37 6RJ
☎ 01983 862854 📠 01983 865321
e-mail: info@priorymanorhotel.co.uk
Dir: *next to Shanklin Chine and Rylstone Gardens*
At the time of going to press, the star classification for this hotel was not confirmed. Please refer to the AA internet site www.theAA.com for current information.
ROOMS: 38 rms (31 en suite) 6 annexe en suite (13 fmly) (8 GF) ⊘ in 38 bedrooms s £35-£40; d £60-£70 (incl. bkfst) **LB FACILITIES:** Snooker Gym Putt green ♫ Xmas **PARKING:** 40 **NOTES:** ⊘ in restaurant

The vast majority of establishments in this guide accept credit and debit cards. We indicate those that don't take any

W

TOTLAND BAY
Map 05 SZ38

★★★68% *Sentry Mead*
Madeira Rd PO39 0BJ
☎ 01983 753212 🖷 01983 753212
e-mail: julie@sentry-mead.co.uk
Dir: *off A3054 at Totland war memorial rdbt, 300yds on right*
Just two minutes' walk from the sea at Totland Bay, this well-kept Victorian villa has a comfortable lounge and separate bar, as well as a conservatory that looks out over the delightful garden. Bedrooms feature co-ordinated soft furnishings and welcome extras such as mineral water and biscuits.
ROOMS: 14 en suite (4 fmly) **PARKING:** 10 **NOTES:** ⊗ in restaurant Closed 20 Dec-4 Jan

VENTNOR
Map 05 SZ57

★★★★67% The Royal Hotel
Belgrave Rd PO38 1JJ
☎ 01983 852186 🖷 01983 855395
e-mail: enquiries@royalhoteliow.co.uk
web: www.royalhoteliow.co.uk
Dir: *A3055 into Ventnor follow one-way system, after lights left into Belgrave Road. Hotel on right*
The Royal Hotel provides good quality accommodation and the staff deliver professional service in a relaxed manner. Public areas include a sunny conservatory and restful lounge, and there is also an outdoor pool. The restaurant provides traditional surroundings in which to enjoy modern British cuisine.
ROOMS: 55 en suite (7 fmly) ⊗ in all bedrooms s £70-£106; d £120-£180 (incl. bkfst) **LB** **FACILITIES:** STV Xmas **CONF:** Thtr 100 Class 80 Board 50 Del from £110 **SERVICES:** Lift **PARKING:** 56 **NOTES:** ⊗ in restaurant Closed 1st 2 wks Jan Civ Wed 150

See advert on page 613

★★★69% Burlington
Bellevue Rd PO38 1DB
☎ 01983 852113 🖷 01983 853862
e-mail: patmctoldrige@burlingtonhotel.freeserve.co.uk
Eight of the attractively decorated bedrooms at this establishment benefit from balconies, and the three ground floor rooms have French doors that lead onto the garden. There is a cosy bar, a comfortable lounge and a dining room where home-made bread rolls accompany the five-course dinners. Service is friendly and attentive.
ROOMS: 24 en suite (8 fmly) (3 GF) ⊗ in all bedrooms s £40-£55; d £80-£110 (incl. bkfst & dinner) **LB** **FACILITIES:** **PARKING:** 20 **NOTES:** No children 3yrs ⊗ in restaurant Closed Nov-Etr

★★★68% *Ventnor Towers*
Madeira Rd PO38 1QT
☎ 01983 852277 🖷 01983 855536
e-mail: reservations@ventnortowers.com
web: www.ventnortowers.com
Dir: *1st left after Trinity church, follow Madeira Rd for 0.25m*
This mid-Victorian hotel set in spacious grounds - from which a path leads down to the shore - is high above the bay and enjoys splendid sea views. Many potted plants and fresh flowers grace the day rooms, which include two lounges and a spacious bar. Bedrooms include two four-poster rooms and some that have their own balconies.
ROOMS: 27 en suite (4 fmly) (8 GF) ⊗ in 14 bedrooms **FACILITIES:** Putt green ch fac **CONF:** Thtr 80 Class 50 Board 35 **PARKING:** 26 **NOTES:** ⊗ in restaurant Closed 21-27 Dec

★★★66% Eversley
Park Av PO38 1LB
☎ 01983 852244 & 852462 🖷 01983 856534
e-mail: eversleyhotel@yahoo.co.uk
web: www.eversleyhotel.com
Dir: *on A3055 W of Ventnor, next to Ventnor Park*
Located west of Ventnor, this hotel enjoys a quiet location and has some rooms offering garden and pool views. The spacious restaurant is sometimes used for local functions, and there is a bar, television room, lounge area and a card room as well as a jacuzzi and gym. Bedrooms are generally a good size.
ROOMS: 30 en suite (8 fmly) (2 GF) s £35-£55; d £69-£99 (incl. bkfst) **LB** **FACILITIES:** Gym Jacuzzi Pool table Xmas **CONF:** Class 40 Board 20 **PARKING:** 23 **NOTES:** ⊗ in restaurant Closed 31 Nov-22 Dec & 2 Jan-8 Feb

★★68% *Hillside Hotel*
Mitchell Av PO38 1DR
☎ 01983 852271 🖷 01983 852271
e-mail: aa@hillside-hotel.co.uk
Dir: *off A3055 onto B3327. Hotel 0.5m on right behind tennis courts*

Hillside Hotel dates back to the 19th century and enjoys a superb location overlooking Ventnor and the sea beyond. Public areas consist of a traditional lounge, a cosy bar area with an adjoining conservatory and a light, airy dining room. A welcoming and homely atmosphere is assured.
ROOMS: 12 en suite (1 fmly) (1 GF) ⊗ in all bedrooms **FACILITIES:** **PARKING:** 12 **NOTES:** No children 5yrs ⊗ in restaurant Closed Xmas

★★68% *St Maur Hotel*
Castle Rd PO38 1LG
☎ 01983 852570 & 853645 🖷 01983 852306
e-mail: sales@stmaur.co.uk
Dir: *W of Ventnor off A3055. Right at end of Park Avenue*
Guests will find a warm welcome awaits them at this hotel, which is pleasantly and quietly located overlooking the bay. The well-equipped bedrooms are traditionally decorated. In addition to a spacious lounge, the hotel benefits from a cosy residents' bar. The gardens here are a delight.
ROOMS: 12 en suite (2 fmly) ⊗ in all bedrooms **FACILITIES:** STV **PARKING:** 12 **NOTES:** No children 5yrs ⊗ in restaurant Closed Dec

Town House Hotel
Country House Hotel
Travel Accommodation

YARMOUTH Map 05 SZ38

Top Hotel

★★★ ⊛⊛⊛ George Hotel

Quay St PO41 0PE
☎ 01983 760331 📠 01983 760425
e-mail: res@thegeorge.co.uk
Dir: *between the castle and the pier*

This delightful 17th-century hotel enjoys a wonderful location at the water's edge, adjacent to the castle and the quay. Public areas include an elegant fine dining restaurant and a bright brasserie as a more informal eating option. In addition, guests can also relax in either the cosy bar or an inviting lounge. Individually styled bedrooms, with many thoughtful extras, are beautifully appointed and some benefit from spacious balconies. The hotel's motor yacht is available for hire by guests.

ROOMS: 17 en suite ⊗ in 4 bedrooms s fr £135; d £180-£245 (incl. bkfst) **FACILITIES:** STV Sailing from Yarmouth, Mountain Biking Xmas **CONF:** Thtr 30 Class 10 Board 18 Del from £185 **NOTES:** No children 10yrs Civ Wed 60

★★65% Bugle Coaching Inn

The Square PO41 0NS
☎ 01983 760272 📠 01983 760883
Dir: *200yds from Yarmouth Wightlink Ferry Terminal, in town square*

Taking pride of place in the market square, this listed 17th-century building is close to the ferry and has ample car parking. Spacious, well-furnished bedrooms are available. A selection of bars and lounges offer contemporary style and comfort. A varied range of delicious home-cooked meals is offered including daily specials.

ROOMS: 7 en suite (1 fmly) ⊗ in all bedrooms s £51-£68; d £86-£120 (incl. bkfst) **FACILITIES:** ♫ **PARKING:** 15 **NOTES:** ✗ ⊗ in restaurant

WILLERBY, East Riding of Yorkshire Map 17 TA03

★★★73% ⊛⊛ Willerby Manor

Well Ln HU10 6ER
☎ 01482 652616 📠 01482 653901
e-mail: willerbymanor@bestwestern.co.uk
web: www.willerbymanor.co.uk
Dir: *off A63, signed Humber Bridge. Follow road, right at rdbt by Waitrose. At next rdbt hotel is signed*

Set in a quiet residential area, amid well-tended gardens, this hotel was originally a private mansion; it has now been thoughtfully extended to provide very comfortable bedrooms, equipped with many useful extras. There are extensive leisure facilities and a choice of eating options in various styles, including the smart Icon Restaurant.

ROOMS: 51 en suite (6 fmly) (16 GF) ⊗ in 47 bedrooms s £50-£91.75; d £80-£120.50 (incl. bkfst) **LB** **FACILITIES:** STV ⌂ supervised Sauna Solarium Gym ♟ Jacuzzi Steam room Beauty therapist Aerobic classes **CONF:** Thtr 500 Class 200 Board 100 Del £100 **PARKING:** 300 **NOTES:** ✗ ⊗ in restaurant Closed 24-26 Dec RS 24-26 Dec Civ Wed 150

U Ramada Hull

Main St HU10 6EA
☎ 01482 656488 📠 01482 655848
e-mail: sales.hull@ramadajarvis.co.uk
web: www.ramadajarvis.co.uk
Dir: *Take A164 to Beverley signed Willerby Shopping Park. Turn left at rdbt into Grange Park Lane, hotel at end of lane.*

Situated between Hull and Beverley, this large hotel is set in 12 acres of landscaped gardens. Bedrooms are comfortably appointed for both business and leisure guests.

ROOMS: 101 en suite (8 fmly) (15 GF) ⊗ in 75 bedrooms s £82-£115; d £82-£115 **LB** **FACILITIES:** STV ⌂ Sauna Gym Jacuzzi Xmas **CONF:** Thtr 550 Class 250 Board 80 Del from £135 **SERVICES:** Lift **PARKING:** 600 **NOTES:** ⊗ in restaurant Civ Wed 80

⌂ Innkeeper's Lodge Hull

Beverley Rd HU10 6NT
☎ 01482 651518 📠 01482 658380
web: www.innkeeperslodge.com
Dir: *M62/A63, Humber Bridge exit off A63, follow signs for A164. Lodge 3m on left opposite Willerby shopping centre*

A growing concept in the travel accommodation market. Smart rooms meet essential business requirements but also have home comforts. Dining options include all-day menus plus the added advantage of breakfast, which is included in the room price. For further details consult the Hotel Groups page.

ROOMS: 32 en suite s £52; d £52

WILLITON, Somerset Map 03 ST04

★★73% ⊛⊛ *White House*

Long St TA4 4QW
☎ 01984 632306 & 632777
Dir: *on A39 in village centre*

A relaxed and easy-going atmosphere is the hallmark of this charming little Georgian hotel. Bedrooms in the main building are more spacious, and all well equipped with extra touches that make the White House a home-from-home. Delicious award-winning cooking and an impressive wine list can be found in the dining room.

ROOMS: 6 rms (5 en suite) 4 annexe en suite (1 fmly) **PARKING:** 12 **NOTES:** ⊗ in restaurant Closed 28 Oct -mid May

WILMINGTON, East Sussex Map 06 TQ50

Restaurant with Rooms

🏨 ☺☺ **Crossways**
Lewes Rd BN26 5SG
☎ 01323 482455 📠 01323 487811
e-mail: stay@crosswayshotel.co.uk
web: www.crosswayshotel.co.uk
Dir: On A27 between Lewes & Polegate, 2m E of Alfriston rdbt.
A well-established restaurant with a good local reputation is the
focus for this attractive property. Bedrooms are all individually
decorated with taste and style and superior rooms are available.
Guest comfort is paramount, and there are excellent facilities and
levels of hospitality that ensure guests return frequently.
ROOMS: 7 en suite s £62; d £95-£110 (incl. bkfst) **LB PARKING:** 30
NOTES: ✖ No children 12yrs ⊗ in restaurant Closed 24 Dec-23 Jan

WILMSLOW, Cheshire Map 16 SJ88
See also Manchester Airport

★★★★69% *De Vere Mottram Hall*
Wilmslow Rd, Mottram St Andrew, Prestbury DE VERE ● HOTELS
SK10 4QT
☎ 01625 828135 📠 01625 828950
e-mail: dmh.sales@devere-hotels.com
web: www.devereonline.co.uk
Dir: M6 junct 18 from S, M6 junct 20 from N, M56 junct 6, A538 Prestbury
Set in 272 acres of some of Cheshire's most beautiful parkland,
this 18th-century Georgian house is certainly an idyllic retreat. The
hotel boasts extensive leisure facilities, including a championship
golf course, a swimming pool and gym. Bedrooms are well
equipped and elegantly furnished, and include a number of
four-poster rooms and suites.
ROOMS: 132 en suite (44 GF) ⊗ in 64 bedrooms **FACILITIES:** STV ⊡
supervised ⌖ 18 ⚲ Squash Snooker Sauna Solarium Gym Putt green
Jacuzzi Childrens play ground ♫ **CONF:** Thtr 275 Class 140 Board 60
SERVICES: Lift **PARKING:** 300 **NOTES:** ⊗ in restaurant Civ Wed 160

⇧ Premier Travel Inn
Manchester Airport South premier travel inn
Racecourse Rd SK9 5LR
☎ 0870 9906506 📠 0870 9906507
web: www.premiertravelinn.com
*Dir: Exit M6 junct 19 to Knutsford follow Wilmslow signs. Left at 1st & 2nd
lights towards Wilmslow. Through Mobberley, left just before Bird in Hand
pub. At T-junct, right. Hotel 150yds on right*
High quality, modern budget accommodation ideal for both
families and business travellers. Spacious, en suite bedrooms
feature bath and shower, satellite TV and many have telephones
and modem points. The adjacent family restaurant features a wide
and varied menu. For further details consult the Hotel Groups page.
ROOMS: 37 en suite s £53.95-£55.95; d £53.95-£55.95

WINCANTON, Somerset Map 04 ST72

★★★76% ☺☺ *Holbrook House*
Holbrook BA9 8BS
☎ 01963 824466 📠 01963 32681
e-mail: reception@holbrookhouse.co.uk
*Dir: from A303 at Wincanton, turn left on A371 towards Castle Cary and
Shepton Mallet*
This handsome country house offers a unique blend of quality and
comfort combined with a friendly atmosphere. Set in peaceful
gardens and wooded grounds, Holbrook House is the perfect
continued

retreat. The restaurant provides a selection of innovative dishes
prepared with enthusiasm and served by a team of caring staff.

ROOMS: 16 en suite 5 annexe en suite (2 fmly) **FACILITIES:** STV ⊡ ⚲
Sauna Solarium Gym ⚏ Jacuzzi Beauty treatment ♫ ch fac
CONF: Thtr 200 Class 50 Board 55 **PARKING:** 100 **NOTES:** ✖ ⊗ in
restaurant Civ Wed 90

WINCHCOMBE, Gloucestershire Map 10 SP02

Restaurant with Rooms

🏨 ☺☺ **Wesley House**
High St GL54 5LJ
☎ 01242 602366 📠 01242 609046
e-mail: enquiries@wesleyhouse.co.uk
web: www.wesleyhouse.co.uk
Dir: on High St - B4632 between Cheltenham and Broadway
This engaging property dates back to the 15th century and is
situated in the heart of bustling Winchcombe. There are a number
of original features, such as open fires and exposed beams. The
comfortable bedrooms offer plenty of character and individuality.
The elegant restaurant is the setting for accomplished cuisine
served by friendly, attentive staff.
ROOMS: 6 en suite ⊗ in all bedrooms s £65-£90; d £75-£110 (incl.
bkfst) **LB FACILITIES:** Xmas **NOTES:** ✖ ⊗ in restaurant Closed 25-26
Dec RS Sunday nights

WINCHESTER, Hampshire Map 05 SU42

Top Hotel

★★★★ ☺☺ ♨ Lainston House
Sparsholt SO21 2LT
☎ 01962 863588 📠 01962 776672 EXCLUSIVE
e-mail: enquiries@lainstonhouse.com
web: www.exclusivehotels.co.uk
Dir: 2m NW off B3049 towards Stockbridge
This graceful example of a William and Mary House enjoys a
continued

W

countryside location amidst mature grounds and gardens. Staff provide good levels of courtesy and care with a polished, professional service. Bedrooms are tastefully appointed and include some spectacular spacious rooms with stylish handmade beds and stunning bathrooms. Public rooms include a cocktail bar built entirely from a single cedar and stocked with an impressive range of rare drinks and cigars.
ROOMS: 50 en suite (6 fmly) (18 GF) s £120-£495; d £175-£495 **LB** **FACILITIES:** STV Fishing Gym Putt green Archery, Clay pigeon shooting, Cycling Xmas **CONF:** BC Thtr 166 Class 80 Board 40 Del from £260 **PARKING:** 150 **NOTES:** ⊗ in restaurant Civ Wed 200

Town House

★★★★
Hotel du Vin & Bistro
Southgate St SO23 9EF
☎ 01962 841414 01962 842458
e-mail: info@winchester.hotelduvin.com
web: www.hotelduvin.com
Dir: *M3 junct 11 towards Winchester, follow signs. Hotel approx 2m from junct 11 on left side just past cinema*

Continuing to set high standards, this inviting hotel is best known for its high profile bistro. The individually decorated bedrooms, each sponsored by a different wine house, show considerable originality of style, and are very well equipped. The bistro serves imaginative yet simply cooked dishes from a seasonal, daily-changing menu.
ROOMS: 24 en suite (4 GF) ⊗ in all bedrooms s £115-£185; d £115-£185 **FACILITIES:** STV Xmas **CONF:** Thtr 40 Class 30 Board 20 **PARKING:** 35 **NOTES:** Civ Wed 60

★★★★63% **The Wessex**
Paternoster Row SO23 9LQ
☎ 0870 400 8126 01962 841503
e-mail: wessex@macdonald-hotels.co.uk
web: www.macdonald-hotels.co.uk
Dir: *M3, follow signs for town centre, at rdbt by King Alfred's statue past Guildhall, next left, hotel on right*

A modern hotel occupying an enviable location in the centre of this historic city and adjacent to the spectacular cathedral, yet quietly situated on a side street. Inside, the ambience is modern, restful and welcoming, with many public areas and bedrooms enjoying unrivalled views of the hotel's centuries-old neighbour.
ROOMS: 94 en suite (6 fmly) ⊗ in 61 bedrooms s £80-£120; d £120-£200 (incl. bkfst & dinner) **LB** **FACILITIES:** STV Solarium Gym Free use of local leisure centre, beauty therapy Xmas **CONF:** Thtr 100 Class 60 Board 60 Del from £140 **SERVICES:** Lift **PARKING:** 60 **NOTES:** ⊗ in restaurant Civ Wed 100

★★★70% **The Winchester Royal**
Saint Peter St SO23 8BS
☎ 01962 840840 01962 841582
web: www.forestdale.com
Dir: *M3 junct 9 to Winnal Trading Estate. Follow road to city centre, cross river, left, 1st right. Onto one-way system and 2nd right. Hotel immediately on right*

Situated in the heart of the former capital of England, this friendly hotel, now under new ownership, dates back in parts to the 16th century. The bedrooms, in various styles, are split between the main original house and the modern annexe which overlooks the attractive gardens. This hotel is ideally located for both leisure and business guests.
ROOMS: 75 en suite ⊗ in 48 bedrooms s fr £99; d fr £119 (incl. bkfst) **LB** **FACILITIES:** STV Xmas **CONF:** Thtr 120 Class 50 Board 40 Del from £175 **PARKING:** 50 **NOTES:** ⊗ in restaurant Civ Wed 110

★★★67% **Marwell**
Thompsons Ln, Colden Common, Marwell SO21 1JY
☎ 01962 777681 01962 777625
e-mail: info@marwellhotel.co.uk
web: www.bespokehotels.com
Dir: *Follow brown signs for Marwell Zoological Park, hotel adjacent*

Taking its theme from the adjacent zoo, this unusual hotel is based on the famous TreeTops safari lodge in Kenya. Bedrooms are well appointed and equipped, while the smart public areas include an airy lobby bar and an 'Out of Africa' style restaurant. There is also a selection of meeting and leisure facilities.
ROOMS: 66 en suite (10 fmly) (36 GF) ⊗ in 40 bedrooms s £89-£99; d £89-£99 (incl. bkfst) **LB** **FACILITIES:** **Spa** STV Fishing Sauna Solarium Gym Xmas **CONF:** Thtr 175 Class 60 Board 60 Del from £140 **PARKING:** 120 **NOTES:** ⊗ in restaurant Civ Wed 175

Entertainment

WINCHESTER MOTORWAY
SERVICE AREA (M3), Hampshire
Map 05 SU53

⇧ Premier Travel Inn Winchester
SO21 1PP

☎ 08701 977272 ▤ 01962 791137
web: www.premiertravelinn.com
Dir: M3 S'bound - between juncts 8 & 9. Note that distance to Inn from
Winchester is approx 26m due to location on motorway
High quality, modern budget accommodation ideal for both
families and business travellers. Spacious, en suite bedrooms
feature bath and shower, satellite TV and many have telephones
and modem points. The adjacent family restaurant features a wide
and varied menu. For further details consult the Hotel Groups page.
ROOMS: 40 en suite s £46.95-£49.95; d £46.95-£49.95

WINDERMERE, Cumbria
Map 18 SD49

★★★★66% Low Wood
LA23 1LP
☎ 015394 33338 & 0845 850 3502 ▤ 015394 34072
e-mail: lowwood@elhmail.co.uk
Dir: M6 junct 36, follow A590 then A591 to Windermere, then 3m towards
Ambleside, hotel on right

Benefiting from a lakeside location, this hotel (now under new
ownership) offers an excellent range of leisure and conference
facilities. Bedrooms, many with panoramic lake views, are
attractively furnished, and include a number of larger executive
rooms and suites. There is a choice of bars, a spacious restaurant
and the more informal Café del Lago. The Poolside bar offers
internet and e-mail access.
ROOMS: 110 en suite (13 fmly) ⊗ in 55 bedrooms s £103-£110;
d £156-£186 (incl. bkfst) **LB FACILITIES: Spa** STV ⬡ Fishing Squash
Snooker Sauna Solarium Gym Jacuzzi Water skiing Canoeing, Beauty
salon, Spa, Bungy Trampoline, Wall Climbing Xmas **CONF:** Thtr 340 Class
180 Board 150 Del from £113 **SERVICES:** Lift **PARKING:** 200
NOTES: ⊗ in restaurant Civ Wed 200

Top Hotel

★★★ ◎◎◎ **Gilpin Lodge**
Country House Hotel & Restaurant
Crook Rd LA23 3NE
☎ 015394 88818 ▤ 015394 88058
e-mail: hotel@gilpinlodge.com
web: www.gilpinlodge.com
Dir: M6 junct 36, take A590/A591 to rdbt north of Kendal, take
B5284, hotel 5m on right
This smart Victorian residence is set amidst delightful gardens
leading to the fells, and is just a short drive from the lake. The
individually styled bedrooms are stylish and a number benefit

continued

from private terraces; all are spacious and thoughtfully
equipped. The welcoming atmosphere is notable and the
attractive day rooms are perfect for relaxing, perhaps beside a
real fire. Vibrant, exciting cuisine is served in one of five
intimate dining rooms.

ROOMS: 14 en suite ⊗ in all bedrooms s fr £160; d £110-£290
(incl. bkfst & dinner) **LB FACILITIES:** ⬡ Free membership at local
Leisure Club Xmas **PARKING:** 30 **NOTES:** ✘ No children 7yrs ⊗
in restaurant

Top Hotel

★★★ ◎◎◎
Holbeck Ghyll Country House
Holbeck Ln LA23 1LU
☎ 015394 32375 ▤ 015394 34743
e-mail: stay@holbeckghyll.com
Dir: 3m N on A591, right into Holbeck Lane (signed Troutbeck), hotel
0.5m on left
With a peaceful setting in extensive grounds, this beautifully
maintained hotel enjoys breathtaking views over Lake
Windermere and the Langdale Fells. Public rooms include
luxurious, comfortable lounges and two elegant dining rooms,
where memorable meals are served. Bedrooms are
individually styled, beautifully furnished and many have
balconies or patios. Some in an adjacent, more private lodge
are less traditional in design and have superb views. The
professionalism and attentiveness of the staff is exemplary.
ROOMS: 14 en suite 6 annexe en suite (3 fmly) (3 GF) ⊗ in 6
bedrooms s £125-£175; d £220-£350 (incl. bkfst & dinner) **LB**
FACILITIES: Spa STV ⚲ Sauna Gym ⬡ Putt green Jacuzzi
Steam room, Treatment Rooms for Beauty and Massage Xmas
CONF: BC Thtr 45 Class 25 Board 25 Del from £125
PARKING: 28 **NOTES:** ⊗ in restaurant Civ Wed 65

Bad hair day?
Hairdryers in all rooms three stars and above

W

Top Hotel

★★★ ◎◎ **Linthwaite House Hotel**
Crook Rd LA23 3JA
☎ 015394 88600 📠 015394 88601
e-mail: admin@linthwaite.com
web: www.linthwaite.com
Dir: *A591 towards The Lakes for 8m to large rdbt, take 1st exit (B5284), 6m, hotel on left , 1m past Windermere golf club*
Linthwaite House is set in 14 acres of hilltop grounds and enjoys stunning views over Lake Windermere. Inviting public rooms include an attractive conservatory and adjoining lounge, a smokers' bar and an elegant restaurant. Bedrooms, which are individually decorated, combine contemporary furnishings with classical styles. All are thoughtfully equipped and include CD players. Service and hospitality are attentive and friendly.
ROOMS: 27 en suite (1 fmly) (7 GF) ⊗ in all bedrooms s £120-£149; d £198-£230 (incl. bkfst & dinner) **LB** **FACILITIES:** STV Fishing Putt green Free use of nearby leisure spa, Practice golf hole Xmas **CONF:** BC Thtr 47 Class 19 Board 25 Del from £129 **PARKING:** 40 **NOTES:** ⊗ in restaurant

See advert on this page

Top Hotel

★★★ **The Samling***
Ambleside Rd L23 1LR
☎ 015394 31922 📠 015394 30400
e-mail: info@thesamling.com
web: www.thesamling.com
Dir: *turn right off A591, 300mtrs after Low Wood Hotel*
This stylish house built in the late 1700s, is situated in 67 acres of grounds and enjoys an elevated position overlooking Lake Windermere. The spacious, beautifully furnished bedrooms and suites, some in adjacent buildings, are thoughtfully equipped and all have superb bathrooms. *At the time of going to press a new head chef had just arrived so the rosette rating has not been confirmed. Please refer to the AA internet site www.theAA.com for current information.
ROOMS: 5 en suite 6 annexe en suite s £195-£415; d £195-£415 (incl. bkfst) **FACILITIES:** STV Jacuzzi Xmas **CONF:** Thtr 60 Class 14 Board 14 Del from £260 **PARKING:** 15 **NOTES:** ⊗ in restaurant Civ Wed 100

★★★80% ◎
Lindeth Howe Country House
Lindeth Dr, Longtail Hill LA23 3JF
☎ 015394 45759 📠 015394 46368
e-mail: hotel@lindeth-howe.co.uk
web: www.lindeth-howe.co.uk
Dir: *turn off A592, 1m S of Bowness onto B5284 (Longtail Hill) signed Kendal & Lancaster, hotel last driveway on right*

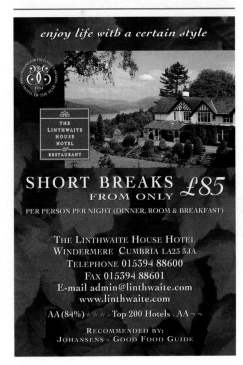

Old photographs commemorate the fact that this delightful house was once the family home of Beatrix Potter. Secluded in

continued on p620

WINDERMERE, continued

landscaped grounds, it enjoys views across the valley and Lake Windermere. Public rooms are plentiful and inviting, with the restaurant being the perfect setting for modern country-house cooking. Deluxe and superior bedrooms are spacious and smartly appointed.
ROOMS: 36 en suite (3 fmly) (2 GF) ⊗ in 30 bedrooms s £57-£97; d £114-£198 (incl. bkfst) **LB** **FACILITIES:** STV Sauna Solarium Gym Xmas **CONF:** Thtr 30 Class 20 Board 18 Del £135 **PARKING:** 50 **NOTES:** ⊗ in restaurant

★★★79% Storrs Hall
Storrs Park LA23 3LG
☎ 015394 47111 015394 47555
e-mail: storrshall@elhmail.co.uk
web: www.elh.co.uk/hotels/storrshall
Dir: *on A592 2m S of Bowness, on Newby Bridge road*

Set in 17 acres of landscaped grounds by the lakeside, this imposing Georgian mansion is delightful. There are numerous lounges to relax in, furnished with fine art and antiques. Individually styled bedrooms are generally spacious and boast impressive bathrooms. Imaginative cuisine is served in the elegant restaurant, which offers fine views across the lawn to the lake and fells beyond.
ROOMS: 29 en suite ⊗ in 10 bedrooms s £100-£140; d £150-£230 (incl. bkfst) **LB** **FACILITIES:** Fishing Use of nearby sports/beauty facilities. Xmas **CONF:** Thtr 36 Board 24 Del £150 **PARKING:** 50 **NOTES:** No children 12yrs ⊗ in restaurant Civ Wed 64

★★★74% Fayrer Garden Hotel
Lyth Valley Rd, Bowness on Windermere LA23 3JP
☎ 015394 88195 015394 45986
e-mail: lakescene@fayrergarden.com
web: www.fayrergarden.com
Dir: *on A5074 1m from Bowness Bay*

Sitting in lovely landscaped gardens, this elegant hotel enjoys spectacular views over the lake. Bedrooms come in a variety of styles and sizes, some with bathrooms of a high specification, and all are comfortably appointed. There is a choice of lounges and a stylish, conservatory restaurant. The attentive, hospitable staff ensure a relaxing stay.
ROOMS: 24 en suite 5 annexe en suite (10 GF) ⊗ in all bedrooms s £79-£119; d fr £138 (incl. bkfst & dinner) **LB** **FACILITIES:** STV Fishing Free membership of leisure club Xmas **PARKING:** 40 **NOTES:** ⊗ in restaurant Civ Wed 60

★★★74% Langdale Chase
Langdale Chase LA23 1LW
☎ 015394 32201 015394 32604
e-mail: sales@langdalechase.co.uk
web: www.langdalechase.co.uk
Dir: *2m S of Ambleside and 3m N of Windermere, on A591*

Enjoying unrivalled views of Lake Windermere, this imposing country manor has been trading as a hotel for over 70 years. Public areas feature carved fireplaces, oak panelling and a galleried staircase. Bedrooms have stylish, spacious bathrooms and outstanding views.
ROOMS: 20 en suite 7 annexe en suite (2 fmly) (1 GF) ⊗ in all bedrooms s £164; d £258 (incl. bkfst & dinner) **LB** **FACILITIES:** Fishing Putt green Sailing boats Xmas **CONF:** Thtr 30 Class 30 Board 28 **PARKING:** 50 **NOTES:** ⊗ in restaurant

★★★73%
Burn How Garden House Hotel
Back Belsfield Rd, Bowness LA23 3HH
☎ 015394 46226 015394 47000
e-mail: info@burnhow.co.uk
web: www.burnhow.co.uk
Dir: *Exit A591 at Windermere, following signs to Bowness. Pass Lake Piers on right, take 1st left to hotel entrance*
Set in its own leafy grounds, this hotel is only minutes' walk from both the lakeside and the town centre. Attractive, spacious rooms, some with four-poster beds, are situated in modern chalets or in an adjacent Victorian house. Many have private patios or terraces. Coffee can be enjoyed in the comfortable open plan lounge after taking dinner in the formal restaurant.
ROOMS: 28 annexe en suite (10 fmly) (6 GF) ⊗ in 8 bedrooms s £65-£110; d £95-£130 (incl. bkfst) **LB** **FACILITIES:** ch fac Xmas **PARKING:** 30 **NOTES:** ⊗ in restaurant

★★★71% Beech Hill
Newby Bridge Rd LA23 3LR
☎ 015394 42137 015394 43745
e-mail: reservations@beechhillhotel.co.uk
web: www.beechhillhotel.co.uk
Dir: *follow A592 from Bowness to Newby Bridge, hotel 4m on right*
This stylish, terraced hotel is set on high ground leading to the shore of Lake Windermere and has a spacious, open-plan lounge which, like the restaurant, affords splendid views across the lake.
continued

Bedrooms come in a range of styles; some have four-poster beds, and all are well equipped. Leisure facilities and a choice of conference rooms complete the package.
ROOMS: 59 en suite (4 fmly) (4 GF) ⊗ in 34 bedrooms s fr £49; d fr £98 (incl. bkfst) **LB** **FACILITIES:** Sauna Solarium ♫ Xmas **PARKING:** 70 **NOTES:** ⊗ in restaurant Civ Wed 130

See advert on this page

★★★68% Famous Wild Boar

Crook LA23 3NF
☎ 015394 45225 🖷 015394 42498
e-mail: wildboar@elhmail.co.uk
Dir: *2.5m S of Windermere on B5284. From Crook 3.5m, hotel on right*

This historic former coaching inn enjoys a peaceful rural location close to Windermere. Public areas include a cosy bar where an extensive range of wines is served by the glass, a character restaurant serving wholesome food and a welcoming lounge. Bedrooms, some with four-poster beds, vary in style and size.
ROOMS: 36 en suite (3 fmly) ⊗ in 6 bedrooms **FACILITIES:** STV Use of sports/beauty facilities at sister hotel whilst in residence Xmas **CONF:** Thtr 40 Class 20 Board 26 **PARKING:** 60 **NOTES:** ⊗ in restaurant

★★★64% The Belsfield Hotel

Kendal Rd, Bowness LA23 3EL
☎ 0870 609 6109 🖷 015394 46397
e-mail: belsfield@corushotels.com
web: www.corushotels.com
Dir: *In Bowness take 1st left after Royal Hotel*

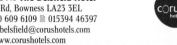

This hotel stands in six acres of gardens and has one of the best locations in the area. Bedrooms are generally spacious and well equipped, and come in a variety of styles. Views from public areas are outstanding. Main meals are taken in the spacious dining room overlooking the lake.
ROOMS: 64 en suite (6 fmly) (6 GF) ⊗ in 56 bedrooms s £105; d £105-£145 **LB** **FACILITIES:** Snooker Sauna Putt green Mini golf - Pitch & Putt 9 holes Xmas **CONF:** Thtr 130 Class 60 Board 50 Del from £120 **SERVICES:** Lift **PARKING:** 64 **NOTES:** ⊗ in restaurant Civ Wed 100

★★★63% Craig Manor

Lake Rd LA23 2JF
☎ 015394 88877 🖷 015394 88878
e-mail: info@craigmanor.co.uk
Dir: *A590, then A591 into Windermere, left at Windermere Hotel, through village, pass Magistrates' Court, hotel on left*
There are fine views to be had across the lake towards the surrounding fells from this family-run hotel. Traditionally furnished bedrooms, including family rooms and some with four-poster beds, are complemented by spacious public areas. There is a choice of comfortable lounges and a wide selection of dishes is served in the restaurant that overlooks the lake.
ROOMS: 16 en suite s £46-£90; d £64-£130 (incl. bkfst) **LB** **FACILITIES:** Use of Parklands Leisure Club Xmas **PARKING:** 70 **NOTES:** ⊗ in restaurant

> If you wish to use a particular credit card or debit card please check with the hotel that they are happy to accept it

★★★62% The Old England

Church St, Bowness LA23 3DF
☎ 0870 400 8130 🖷 015394 43432
e-mail: oldengland@macdonald-hotels.co.uk
web: www.macdonald-hotels.co.uk
Dir: *Through Windermere to Bowness. Hotel behind church*
Occupying arguably one of the best positions on Lake Windermere, this elegant Victorian mansion is tastefully furnished with period and antique pieces. Many of the stylish bedrooms have wonderful lake views, as do the restaurant, bar and lounge.

continued on p622

WINDERMERE, continued

The hotel benefits from an outdoor heated swimming pool and a private jetty. Stylish conference facilities are impressive.

The Old England, Windermere

ROOMS: 76 en suite (8 fmly) (6 GF) ⊗ in 26 bedrooms s £60-£125; d £120-£250 (incl. bkfst) **LB** **FACILITIES:** Snooker ♫ Xmas **CONF:** BC Thtr 100 Class 40 Board 26 Del from £110 **SERVICES:** Lift **PARKING:** 82 **NOTES:** ⊗ in restaurant Civ Wed 80

Top Hotel

★★ Lindeth Fell

Lyth Valley Rd, Bowness-on-Windermere LA23 3JP
☎ 015394 43286 & 44287 📠 015394 47455
e-mail: kennedy@lindethfell.co.uk
web: www.lindethfell.co.uk
Dir: *1m S of Bowness on A5074*

Enjoying delightful views, this smart Edwardian residence stands in seven acres of glorious, landscaped gardens. Bedrooms, which vary in size and style, are comfortably equipped. Skilfully prepared dinners are served in the spacious dining room that commands fine views. The resident owners and their attentive, friendly staff provide high levels of hospitality and service.

ROOMS: 14 en suite (2 fmly) (1 GF) s £65-£85; d £130-£200 (incl. bkfst & dinner) **LB** **FACILITIES:** Fishing Putt green Bowling Xmas **CONF:** Board 12 Del £130 **PARKING:** 20 **NOTES:** ⊗ in restaurant Closed 6-31 Jan

Late for dinner? Quality standards mean that last orders for dinner vary according to star rating and should be no earlier than: ★★ 7.00pm ★★★ 8:00pm ★★★★ 9:00pm ★★★★★ 10:00pm

Top Hotel

★★ Miller Howe

Rayrigg Rd LA23 1EY
☎ 015394 42536 & 44522 📠 015394 45664
e-mail: lakeview@millerhowe.com
web: www.millerhowe.com
Dir: *on A592 between Bowness & Windermere*

This long established hotel of much character enjoys a lakeside setting amidst delightful landscaped gardens. Day rooms are bright and welcoming and include sumptuous lounges, a conservatory and an opulently decorated restaurant. Imaginative dinners make use of fresh, local produce where possible and there is an extensive, well-balanced wine list. Stylish bedrooms, many with fabulous lake views, include well-equipped cottage rooms and a number with whirlpool baths.

ROOMS: 12 en suite 3 annexe en suite ⊗ in 2 bedrooms d £180-£350 (incl. bkfst & dinner) **LB** **FACILITIES:** ♫ ch fac Xmas **PARKING:** 40 **NOTES:** No children 8yrs ⊗ in restaurant Civ Wed 60

★★72% Cedar Manor Hotel & Restaurant

Ambleside Rd LA23 1AX
☎ 015394 43192 📠 015394 45970
e-mail: info@cedarmanor.co.uk
web: www.cedarmanor.co.uk
Dir: *0.25m N on A591 by St Marys Church*

Built in 1854 as country retreat this lovely old house enjoys a peaceful location that is within easy walking distance of the town centre. Bedrooms, some on the ground floor, are attractive and well equipped, with two bedrooms in the annexe. There is a comfortable lounge bar where guests can relax before enjoying dinner in the well-appointed dining room.

ROOMS: 9 en suite 2 annexe en suite (1 fmly) (2 GF) ⊗ in all bedrooms s £59-£70; d £78-£140 (incl. bkfst) **FACILITIES:** Xmas **PARKING:** 15 **NOTES:** ⊗ in restaurant

★★72% Glenburn

New Rd LA23 2EE
☎ 015394 42649 📠 015394 88998
e-mail: glen.burn@virgin.net
web: www.glenburn.uk.com
Dir: *M6 junct 36, A591, through Windermere, hotel 500yds on left*

A warm welcome awaits at this family run hotel. Smartly presented and well maintained throughout, it offers stylish accommodation in a variety of sizes that includes family rooms and a four-poster. Public areas feature an inviting residents' bar lounge and an attractive dining room where freshly prepared dinners are served from a short menu.

ROOMS: 16 en suite (2 fmly) ⊗ in all bedrooms s £47.50-£61.50; d £65-£93 (incl. bkfst) **LB** **FACILITIES:** Free use of nearby country club **PARKING:** 17 **NOTES:** No children 5yrs ⊗ in restaurant Closed 14-28 Dec

★★70% *Crag Brow Hotel & Coco's Restaurant*

Helm Rd LA23 3BU
☎ 015394 44080 📠 015394 46003
e-mail: rooms@cragbrow.com
web: www.cragbrow.com
Dir: *Leave A591 at Windermere. Follow signs for Bowness. Hotel on left on Helm Rd*

A warm welcome awaits at this family-run, conveniently located hotel with private parking. The house has been sympathetically renovated to provide very comfortable accommodation. Bedrooms are of a good size and feature both practical and homely extras with many having views to the lake. There is an attractive lounge with views over the garden; dinner is served in the stylish restaurant.

ROOMS: 11 en suite (2 fmly) ⊘ in all bedrooms **PARKING:** 20
NOTES: ⊘ in restaurant Closed 24-26 Dec

★★70% Hideaway

Phoenix Way LA23 1DB
☎ 015394 43070
e-mail: enquiries@hideaway-hotel.co.uk
web: www.hideaway-hotel co.uk
Dir: *off A591 at Ravensworth Hotel. Hotel 100yds on right*

Enjoying a secluded location, yet only a few minutes from the centre of town, hospitality is a real feature at this family-run hotel. Bedrooms, some housed in a separate building across the courtyard, are smartly appointed and individually furnished. Four-poster and family rooms are available. Dinner features tasty, home-made food and breakfasts are hearty.

ROOMS: 10 en suite 5 annexe en suite (3 fmly) s £58-£75; d £98-£170 (incl. bkfst & dinner) **LB** **FACILITIES:** Free use of nearby leisure facilities Xmas **PARKING:** 16 **NOTES:** ⊘ in restaurant Closed 3 Jan-9 Feb

★★67% Cranleigh

Kendal Rd, Bowness on Windermere LA23 3EW
☎ 015394 43293 📠 015394 47283
e-mail: mike@thecranleigh.com
Dir: *off Lake Rd opp St Martin's Church, along Kendal Rd for 150mtrs*

This friendly hotel is located just a short walk from the centre of town. Comfortable bedrooms, including a number with four-poster beds, vary in style. Guests have a choice of lounges, one with a real fire, a small bar that offers a wide range of drinks and an attractive dining room where freshly prepared meals are served.

ROOMS: 9 en suite 6 annexe en suite (3 fmly) (2 GF) ⊘ in 7 bedrooms s £41-£75; d £52-£120 (incl. bkfst) **LB** **FACILITIES:** Free membership of leisure club **PARKING:** 15 **NOTES:** ✗ ⊘ in restaurant

Late for dinner? Quality standards mean that last orders for dinner vary according to star rating and should be no earlier than:
★★ 7.00pm ★★★ 8:00pm ★★★★ 9:00pm
★★★★★ 10:00pm

WINDSOR, Berkshire

Map 06 SU97

★★★★72% *Oakley Court*

Windsor Rd, Water Oakley SL4 5UR
☎ 01753 609988 📠 01628 637011
e-mail: reservations.oakleycourt@moathousehotels.com
Dir: *M4 junct 6, towards Windsor, then right onto A308 Maidenhead. Pass racecourse & hotel is 2.5m on right*

Built in 1859 this splendid Victorian Gothic mansion is enviably situated in extensive grounds that lead down to The Thames. All rooms are spacious, beautifully furnished and many enjoy river views. Extensive public areas include a range of comfortable

continued on p624

WINDSOR, continued

lounges, the Oakleaf restaurant and comprehensive facilities, which also features a small 9-hole golf course.

Oakley Court, Windsor

ROOMS: 69 en suite 49 annexe en suite (15 fmly) (43 GF) ⊗ in 75 bedrooms **FACILITIES: Spa** STV ⛳ 9 Fishing Snooker Sauna Solarium Gym Jacuzzi Boating **CONF:** BC Thtr 170 Class 190 Board 50 **SERVICES:** air con **PARKING:** 140 **NOTES:** ⊗ in restaurant Civ Wed 120

★★★★70% ®® *Sir Christopher Wren's House Hotel & Spa*

WREN'S HOTELS

Thames St SL4 1PX
☎ 01753 861354 🖷 01753 860172
e-mail: reservations@wrensgroup.com
web: www.wrensgroup.com
Dir: *M4 junct 6, 1st exit from relief road, follow signs to Windsor, 1st major exit on left, turn left at lights*

This hotel has an enviable location right on the edge of the River Thames overlooking Eton Bridge. Diners in Stroks, the award-winning restaurant, enjoy the best views. A variety of well-appointed bedrooms are available, including several in adjacent annexes. There is also a luxury health and leisure spa.
ROOMS: 57 en suite 33 annexe en suite (11 fmly) (3 GF) ⊗ in 22 bedrooms **FACILITIES: Spa** STV Sauna Solarium Gym Jacuzzi Health & beauty club ♫ **CONF:** Thtr 120 Class 70 Board 50 **PARKING:** 15 **NOTES:** ⊗ in restaurant Civ Wed 90

★★★74% ®® The Castle

MACDONALD HOTELS & RESORTS

18 High St SL4 1LJ
☎ 0870 400 8300 🖷 01753 830244
e-mail: castle@macdonald-hotels.co.uk
web: www.macdonald-hotels.co.uk
Dir: *M4 junct 6/M25 junct 15 - follow signs to Windsor town centre and castle. Hotel at top of hill by castle opposite Guildhall*
The Castle Hotel is one of the oldest hotels in Windsor, beginning life as a coaching inn in the middle of the 16th century. Located opposite Windsor Castle, it is an ideal base from which to explore the town. Bedrooms are traditional in style and include four-poster and executive rooms. Guests have a choice of formal and informal dining options and an all-day lounge menu.

ROOMS: 38 en suite 70 annexe en suite (18 fmly) ⊗ in 86 bedrooms s fr £107; d fr £134 **LB FACILITIES:** STV Xmas **CONF:** BC Thtr 350 Class 170 Board 80 Del £285 **SERVICES:** Lift air con **PARKING:** 100 **NOTES:** ⊗ in restaurant Civ Wed 85

★★★69% Royal Adelaide

46 Kings Rd SL4 2AG
☎ 01753 863916 🖷 01753 830682
e-mail: royaladelaide@meridianleisure.com
web: www.meridianleisure.com
Dir: *M4 junct 6, A322 to Windsor. 1st left off rdbt into Clarence Rd. At 4th lights right into Sheet St and into Kings Rd. Hotel on right*

This attractive Georgian-style hotel enjoys a quiet location yet is only a short walk from the town centre; it also benefits from its own private car park. Bedrooms vary in size but all are smartly furnished and well equipped. Public areas are tastefully appointed and include a range of meeting rooms, a bar and an elegant restaurant.
ROOMS: 38 en suite 4 annexe en suite (5 fmly) (8 GF) ⊗ in 30 bedrooms s £60-£105; d £79-£129 (incl. bkfst) **LB FACILITIES:** STV 25 discount for residents at Windsor leisure centre Xmas **CONF:** Thtr 120 Class 80 Board 60 Del from £149 **SERVICES:** air con **PARKING:** 22 **NOTES:** ⊗ in restaurant Civ Wed 120

See advert on opposite page

★★★66% *Ye Harte & Garter*

High St SL4 1PH
☎ 01753 863426 🖷 01753 830527
e-mail: harte@garter.wanadoo.co.uk
Dir: *in town centre opposite front entrance to Windsor Castle*
Situated on the High Street, this hotel combines traditional style with modern comforts. Bedrooms vary in size and offer a useful range of facilities. Many have exceptional views of the castle

continued

courtyards opposite. Popular public areas include a café bar, two restaurants and a traditional pub.
ROOMS: 39 en suite 19 annexe en suite (6 fmly) ⊗ in 30 bedrooms
FACILITIES: STV ch fac **CONF:** Thtr 300 Class 150 Board 80
SERVICES: Lift **NOTES:** ✗ Civ Wed 180

See advert on this page

★★75% Aurora Garden
Bolton Av SL4 3JF
☎ 01753 868686 🖷 01753 831394
e-mail: info@aurorogarden.co.uk
web: www.auroragarden.co.uk
Dir: *M4 junct 6 onto A332 (Windsor). At 1st rdbt, 2nd exit towards Staines. At 3rd rdbt, 3rd exit for 500yds. Hotel on right*
A warm welcome is assured at this privately run hotel, located in a quiet residential area near the town. The highlights include a beautiful garden with terrace and water features, spacious rooms with extra facilities for a comfortable stay and a delightful conservatory restaurant serving a wide variety of dishes.
ROOMS: 19 en suite (7 fmly) (4 GF) s £75-£95; d £85-£105 (incl. bkfst)
LB FACILITIES: STV **CONF:** Thtr 90 Class 30 Board 25 Del from £135
PARKING: 25 **NOTES:** ✗ ⊗ in restaurant Closed 25-Dec Civ Wed 70

U Christopher Hotel
WREN'S HOTELS
110 High St, Eton SL4 6AN
☎ 01753 852359 🖷 01753 830914
e-mail: sales@thechristopher.co.uk
web: www.wrensgroup.com
Dir: *M4 junct 5 (Slough E), Colnbrook Datchet Eton (B470). At rdbt 2nd exit for Datchet. Right at mini rdbt (Eton), left into Eton Rd (3rd rdbt). Left, hotel on right*
At the time of going to press, the star classification for this hotel

continued on p626

WINDSOR, continued

was not confirmed. Please refer to the AA internet site www.theAA.com for current information.

Christopher Hotel, Windsor

ROOMS: 11 en suite 22 annexe en suite (17 GF) ⊗ in all bedrooms s £97-£130; d £108-£175 **LB** **FACILITIES:** STV Use of Health & beauty centre at nearby sister hotel 3 mins walk Xmas **PARKING:** 23 **NOTES:** ✗ ⊗ in restaurant

⌂ Innkeeper's Lodge Old Windsor

14 Straight Rd, Old Windsor SL4 2RR
☎ 01753 860769 🖷 01753 851649
web: www.innkeeperslodge.com

A growing concept in the travel accommodation market. Smart rooms meet essential business requirements but also have home comforts. Dining options include all-day menus plus the added advantage of breakfast, which is included in the room price. For further details consult the Hotel Groups page.

ROOMS: 15 en suite s £55-£79.95; d £55-£79.95

WINSCOMBE, Somerset — Map 04 ST45

⌂ Premier Travel Inn Bristol Airport

Bridgwater Rd BS25 1NN
☎ 0870 9906302 🖷 0870 9906303
web: www.premiertravelinn.com
Dir: *Between M5 junct 21 & 22 (9m from Bristol Airport). Exit onto A371 towards Banwell, Winscombe to A38. Right at lights, Hotel 300yds on left*

High quality, modern budget accommodation ideal for both families and business travellers. Spacious, en suite bedrooms feature bath and shower, satellite TV and many have telephones and modem points. The adjacent family restaurant features a wide and varied menu. For further details consult the Hotel Groups page.

ROOMS: 31 en suite s £52.95; d £52.95

WINTERINGHAM, Lincolnshire — Map 17 SE92

Top Restaurant with Rooms

⑤ Winteringham Fields

DN15 9PF
☎ 01724 733096 🖷 01724 733898
e-mail: wintfields@aol.com
web: www.winteringhamfields.com
Dir: *in the centre of the village at the crossroads*

This highly regarded restaurant with rooms, located deep in the countryside in Winteringham village, is six miles west of the Humber Bridge. Chef Germain Schwab has a hand in every skilfully crafted dish that leaves his kitchen, whilst Annie Schwab admirably leads a superb front of house team. Public rooms and bedrooms, some of which are housed in renovated barns and cottages, are delightfully cosseting, but it is the inspired cooking that remains the main draw. Germain has been awarded AA Chefs' Chef of the Year 2005-6.

ROOMS: 4 en suite 6 annexe en suite ⊗ in all bedrooms s £95-£145; d £130-£205 (incl. bkfst) **PARKING:** 17 **NOTES:** ⊗ in restaurant Closed Sun, Mon & BH/2wks Xmas/1wk Aug/1wk Mar

WISBECH, Cambridgeshire — Map 12 TF40

★★★68% Elme Hall

Elm High Rd PE14 0DQ
☎ 01945 475566 🖷 01945 475666
e-mail: elme@paktel.co.uk web: www.paktel.co.uk
Dir: *off A47 onto A1101 towards Wisbech. Hotel on right*

An imposing, Georgian-style property conveniently situated on the outskirts of the town centre just off the A47. Individually decorated bedrooms are tastefully furnished with quality reproduction pieces and equipped to a high standard. Public rooms include a choice of attractive lounges, as well as two bars, meeting rooms and a banqueting suite.

ROOMS: 7 en suite (3 fmly) ⊗ in all bedrooms s £45; d £68-£220 (incl. bkfst) **FACILITIES:** ♫ **CONF:** Thtr 350 Class 200 Board 20 **PARKING:** 200 **NOTES:** ⊗ in restaurant Civ Wed 350

★★74% Crown Lodge

Downham Rd, Outwell PE14 8SE
☎ 01945 773391 & 772206 🖷 01945 772668
e-mail: crownlodgehotel@hotmail.com
Dir: *on A1122/A1101 approx 5m from Wisbech*

This friendly, privately owned hotel enjoys a peaceful location on the banks of Well Creek in the village of Outwell, a short drive from Wisbech. The property has been carefully extended and both bedrooms and public areas are smartly appointed and well equipped. Hotel facilities include snooker, squash courts and a popular restaurant and bar.

ROOMS: 10 en suite (10 GF) ⊗ in 8 bedrooms s £63; d £79 (incl. bkfst) **LB** **FACILITIES:** Squash Solarium **CONF:** BC Thtr 80 Class 60 Board 40 **SERVICES:** air con **PARKING:** 57 **NOTES:** ⊗ in restaurant

WISHAW, Warwickshire Map 10 SP19

★★★★75% De Vere Belfry
B76 9PR
☎ 0870 900 0066 Fax 01675 470256
e-mail: enquiries@thebelfry.com
web: www.devereonline.co.uk
Dir: *M42 junct 9, A446 towards Lichfield, hotel 1m on right*
Well known as a venue for the Ryder Cup, The Belfry has three championship golf courses along with many other leisure facilities. There is a sophisticated French restaurant and cocktail bar and the spa centre boasts an impressive range of health and beauty treatments. Bedrooms vary in size, style and location; many have spectacular views.
ROOMS: 324 en suite (134 fmly) (50 GF) ⊗ in 188 bedrooms **FACILITIES: Spa** STV supervised 18 Squash Snooker Sauna Solarium Gym Putt green Jacuzzi Hair & day spa, night club ♫ ch fac **CONF:** Thtr 400 Class 260 Board 42 **SERVICES:** Lift **PARKING:** 1000 **NOTES:** ⊗ in restaurant Civ Wed 400

WITHAM, Essex Map 07 TL81

U Ramada Chelmsford
Rivenhall End CM8 3BH
☎ 01376 516969 Fax 01376 513674
e-mail: sales.chelmsford@ramadajarvis.co.uk
web: www.ramadajarvis.co.uk
Dir: *M25 junct 28 towards Chelmsford on A12, take exit for Silver End/Great Braxted. At T-junct turn right, then 1st right, hotel directly ahead.*
This modern hotel is ideally set between Chelmsford and Colchester. Bedrooms are comfortably appointed for both business and leisure guests.
ROOMS: 55 en suite (7 fmly) (43 GF) ⊗ in 38 bedrooms s £72-£85; d £72-£85 **FACILITIES:** STV Sauna Solarium Gym Jacuzzi Xmas **CONF:** Thtr 185 Class 80 Board 50 Del from £115 **PARKING:** 150 **NOTES:** ⊗ in restaurant Civ Wed 150

WITHYPOOL, Somerset Map 03 SS83

★★70% Royal Oak Inn
TA24 7QP
☎ 01643 831506 Fax 01643 831659
e-mail: enquiries@royaloakwithypool.co.uk
Dir: *7m N of Dulverton, off B3223*

For centuries this old inn (now under new ownership) has provided travellers with food, drink and shelter. Lovers of the great outdoors will find this an ideal base for exploration. Bedrooms are comfortable and each displays individuality and charm. Public areas include a choice of bars, complete with beams and crackling log fires, and the Acorn Restaurant serves cuisine with an emphasis on local produce.
ROOMS: 8 rms (7 en suite) **FACILITIES:** Riding Shooting Safaris arranged Xmas **PARKING:** 20 **NOTES:** ⊗ in restaurant

WITNEY, Oxfordshire Map 05 SP31

★★★70% Witney Four Pillars Hotel
Ducklington Ln OX28 4TJ
☎ 0800 374 692 & 01993 779777
Fax 01993 703467
e-mail: witney@four-pillars.co.uk
web: www.four-pillars.co.uk
Dir: *M40 junct 9, A34 to A40, exit A415 Witney/Abingdon. Hotel on left, 2nd exit for Witney*

This attractive modern hotel is close to Oxford and Burford and offers spacious, well-equipped bedrooms. The cosy Spinners Bar has comfortable seating areas and the popular Weavers Restaurant offers a good range of dishes. Other facilities include a swimming pool, gym, spa, sauna and live entertainment every Saturday.
ROOMS: 87 en suite (16 fmly) ⊗ in all bedrooms s £69-£108; d £79-£134 (incl. bkfst) **LB** **FACILITIES: Spa** STV Sauna Gym Whirlpool spa, steam room ♫ Xmas **CONF:** Thtr 160 Class 80 Board 46 Del £155 **SERVICES:** air con **PARKING:** 170 **NOTES:** ⊗ in restaurant Civ Wed 120

WOBURN, Bedfordshire Map 11 SP93

★★★73% The Inn at Woburn
George St MK17 9PX
☎ 01525 290441 Fax 01525 290432
e-mail: enquiries@theinnatwoburn.com
Dir: *M1 junct 13, left to Woburn, at Woburn left at T-junct, hotel in village*
This inn provides a high standard of accommodation; bedrooms are divided between the original house, a modern extension and some stunning cottage suites. Public areas include the beamed, club-style Tavistock Bar, a range of meeting rooms and an attractive restaurant with interesting dishes on offer.
ROOMS: 50 en suite 7 annexe en suite (4 fmly) (21 GF) ⊗ in 19 bedrooms **FACILITIES:** STV 54 Access to Woburn Safari Park and Woburn Abbey **CONF:** Thtr 60 Class 40 Board 40 **PARKING:** 80 **NOTES:** No children ⊗ in restaurant

WOKING, Surrey Map 06 TQ05

Innkeeper's Lodge Woking
Chobham Rd, Horsell GU21 4AL
☎ 01483 733047
web: www.innkeeperslodge.com
A growing concept in the travel accommodation market. Smart rooms meet essential business requirements but also have home comforts. Dining options include all-day menus plus the added advantage of breakfast, which is included in the room price. For further details consult the Hotel Groups page.
ROOMS: 33 en suite s £52-£79.95; d £52-£79.95

WOKING, continued

⌂ Premier Travel Inn Woking

Bridge Barn Ln GU21 6NL
☎ 08701 977276 🖷 01483 771735
web: www.premiertravelinn.com
Dir: *M25 junct 11 follow A320. Turn right at lights by Toys R Us. Take 3rd mini rbt 0.75m down Goldsworth Rd. Turn right into Bridge Barn Ln, Inn on left*
High quality, modern budget accommodation ideal for both families and business travellers. Spacious, en suite bedrooms feature bath and shower, satellite TV and many have telephones and modem points. The adjacent family restaurant features a wide and varied menu. For further details consult the Hotel Groups page.
ROOMS: 34 en suite s £57.95-£59.95; d £57.95-£59.95

WOLVERHAMPTON, West Midlands Map 10 SO99
See also Himley & Worfield

★★★67% Novotel Wolverhampton

Union St WV1 3JN
☎ 01902 871100 🖷 01902 870054
e-mail: H1188@accor.com
web: www.novotel.com
Dir: *6m from M6 junct 10. A454 to Wolverhampton. Hotel on main ring road*
This large, modern, purpose-built hotel stands close to the town centre and ring road. It provides spacious, smartly presented and well-equipped bedrooms, all of which contain convertible bed settees for family occupancy. In addition to the open-plan lounge and bar area, there is an attractive brasserie-style restaurant, which overlooks the small outdoor swimming pool.
Novotel - AA Hotel Group of the Year 2005-6.
ROOMS: 132 en suite (10 fmly) ⊗ in 88 bedrooms s £45-£115; d £45-£115 **LB** **FACILITIES:** STV ⥼ Pool table in bar area **CONF:** Thtr 200 Class 100 Board 80 Del from £110 **SERVICES:** Lift **PARKING:** 120 **NOTES:** Civ Wed 200

★★★67% Park Hall Hotel

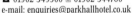

Park Dr, Goldthorn Park WV4 5AJ
☎ 01902 349500 🖷 01902 344760
e-mail: enquiries@parkhallhotel.co.uk
Dir: *off A4039 towards Penn and Wombourne, 2nd left (Ednam Rd), hotel at end of road*
This 18th-century house stands in extensive grounds and gardens, a short drive from the town centre. Bedrooms vary in style, but all are well equipped. Meals can be taken in the Terrace restaurant, which offers a carvery buffet. Conference and wedding facilities are available.
ROOMS: 74 en suite (17 GF) ⊗ in 37 bedrooms s £49-£75; d £60-£90 (incl. bkfst) **LB** **FACILITIES:** STV Leisure facilities planned for 2006 Xmas **CONF:** Thtr 700 Class 350 Board 100 Del from £90 **PARKING:** 250 **NOTES:** ⊗ in restaurant Civ Wed 700

★★★66% Quality Hotel Wolverhampton

Penn Rd WV3 0ER
☎ 01902 429216 🖷 01902 710419
e-mail: enquiries@hotels-wolverhampton.com
web: www.choicehotelseurope.com
Dir: *on A449, Wolverhampton to Kidderminster, 0.25m from ring road on right, turn onto Oaklands Rd at 1st lights*
The original Victorian house here has been considerably extended to create a large, busy and popular hotel. Ornately carved woodwork and ceilings still remain in the original building. All the bedrooms are well equipped. The pleasant public areas have a lot of character and offer a choice of bars.
ROOMS: 66 en suite 26 annexe en suite (6 fmly) (21 GF) ⊗ in 32 bedrooms s £47-£99; d £64-£125 **LB** **FACILITIES: Spa** STV ⥼ supervised Sauna Gym Steam room, Playstation, Pay movies, Big screen TV Xmas **CONF:** BC Thtr 140 Class 60 Board 40 Del from £80 **PARKING:** 124 **NOTES:** ⊗ in restaurant Civ Wed 100

★★68% Ely House

53 Tettenhall Rd WV3 9NB
☎ 01902 311311 🖷 01902 421098
e-mail: reservations@elyhousehotel.co.uk
Dir: *A41 towards Whitchurch from town centre ring road. 200yds on left after lights*
This delightful property dates back to 1742 and has been tastefully converted into a charming hotel. It provides spacious, comfortably furnished bedrooms, some of which are at ground-floor level. There is also an attractive dining room and a spacious, elegant lounge containing a bar.
ROOMS: 18 en suite (3 fmly) (4 GF) ⊗ in all bedrooms s fr £59; d fr £69 (incl. bkfst) **LB** **FACILITIES:** Xmas **CONF:** Thtr 20 Class 20 Board 20 **PARKING:** 22 **NOTES:** ✗ ⊗ in restaurant

⌂ Premier Travel Inn Wolverhampton

Wolverhampton Business Park, Stafford Rd WV10 6TA
☎ 08701 977277 🖷 01902 785260
web: www.premiertravelinn.com
Dir: *Inn off lights approx 100yds off M54 junct 2*
High quality, modern budget accommodation ideal for both families and business travellers. Spacious, en suite bedrooms feature bath and shower, satellite TV and many have telephones and modem points. The adjacent family restaurant features a wide and varied menu. For further details consult the Hotel Groups page.
ROOMS: 54 en suite s £47.95-£50.95; d £47.95-£50.95 **CONF:** Thtr 20 Board 10

WOOBURN COMMON, Buckinghamshire Map 06 SU98

★★72% ⊛ Chequers Inn

Kiln Ln, Wooburn HP10 0JQ
☎ 01628 529575 🖷 01628 850124
e-mail: info@chequers-inn.com
web: www.thechequersatwooburncommon.co.uk
Dir: *M40 junct 2 take A40 through Beaconsfield Old Town towards High Wycombe. 2m from town turn left into Broad Lane. Hotel 2.5m*

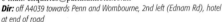

This 17th-century inn enjoys a peaceful, rural location beside the common. Bedrooms feature stripped-pine furniture, co-ordinated fabrics and an excellent range of extra facilities. The bar, with its massive oak post, beams and flagstone floor, and the restaurant,

continued

which overlooks a pretty patio, are very much focal points of the establishment.
ROOMS: 17 en suite (8 GF) s £73-£100; d £78-£108 (incl. bkfst) **LB**
FACILITIES: STV **CONF:** Thtr 50 Class 30 Board 20 Del from £130
PARKING: 60 **NOTES:** ✈ ⊗ in restaurant

WOODALL MOTORWAY SERVICE AREA (M1), South Yorkshire — Map 16 SK48

⌂ Days Inn Sheffield South
Woodall Service Area S26 7XR
☎ 0114 248 7992 🖷 0114 248 5634
e-mail: woodall.hotel@welcomebreak.co.uk
web: www.welcomebreak.co.uk
Dir: *M1 S'bound - Woodall Services - between juncts 30/31*
This modern building offers accommodation in smart, spacious and well-equipped bedrooms, suitable for families and business travellers, and all with en suite bathrooms. Continental breakfast is available and other refreshments may be taken at the nearby family restaurant. For further details see the Hotel Groups page.
ROOMS: 38 en suite s £45-£55; d £45-£55 **CONF:** Board 10

WOODBRIDGE, Suffolk — Map 13 TM24

★★★76% ⊛ Seckford Hall
IP13 6NU
☎ 01394 385678 🖷 01394 380610
e-mail: reception@seckford.co.uk
web: www.seckford.co.uk
Dir: *signed on A12. Do not follow signs for town centre*
This superb Tudor manor house is set amid lovely landscaped grounds just off the A12. The property is reputed to have been visited by Queen Elizabeth I, and retains much of its original charm and character. Public rooms include a superb panelled lounge, a cosy bar and an intimate restaurant. Bedrooms are spacious, attractively decorated, tastefully furnished and equipped with many thoughtful touches.
ROOMS: 22 en suite 10 annexe en suite (4 fmly) s £85-£130; d £130-£200 (incl. bkfst) **LB** **FACILITIES:** **Spa** ⊡ ⛳ 18 Fishing Gym Putt green Beauty Salon **CONF:** Thtr 100 Class 46 Board 40 Del from £150 **PARKING:** 200 **NOTES:** ⊗ in restaurant Closed 25-Dec Civ Wed 120

★★★72% Best Western Ufford Park Hotel Golf & Leisure
Yarmouth Rd, Ufford IP12 1QW
☎ 01394 383555 🖷 01394 383582
e-mail: mail@uffordpark.co.uk
web: www.uffordpark.co.uk
Dir: *A12 N to A1152, in Melton turn left at lights, premises 1m on right*

Modern, purpose-built hotel set in open countryside and boasting superb leisure facilities, including a challenging golf course. The

continued

spacious public rooms provide a wide choice of areas in which to relax and include a busy lounge bar, a carvery restaurant and the Vista restaurant. Bedrooms are pleasantly decorated and thoughtfully equipped; many rooms overlook the golf course.
ROOMS: 87 en suite (26 fmly) (32 GF) ⊗ in 63 bedrooms s £90-£110; d £110-£160 (incl. bkfst) **LB** **FACILITIES:** **Spa** STV ⊡ supervised ⛳ 18 Fishing Sauna Solarium Gym Putt green Jacuzzi Steam room, Golf Academy with PGA tuition, Beauty salon Xmas **CONF:** Thtr 200 Class 80 Board 80 Del from £89 **SERVICES:** Lift **PARKING:** 250 **NOTES:** ✈ ⊗ in restaurant Civ Wed 120

⊛ AA Rosette Award for culinary excellence

WOODBURY, Devon — Map 03 SY08

★★★★71% ⊛ Woodbury Park Hotel Golf & Country Club
Woodbury Castle EX5 1JJ
☎ 01395 233382 🖷 01395 233384
e-mail: enquiries@woodburypark.co.uk
web: www.woodburypark.co.uk
Dir: *M5 junct 30, A376 then A302 towards Sidmouth, onto B3180, hotel signed*
Situated in 500 acres of beautiful and unspoilt countryside, just a short drive from the M5, this hotel offers smart, well-equipped and immaculately presented accommodation with a host of leisure, sporting and banqueting facilities. Re-live the thrills and drama of Nigel Mansell's career in "The Nigel Mansell World of Racing", enjoy a game of golf on one of the two parkland courses, be

continued on p630

WOODBURY, continued

pampered in the bodyzone beauty centre and enjoy creative dishes in the Atrium Restaurant.

Woodbury Park Hotel Golf & Country Club, Woodbury

ROOMS: 57 en suite (4 fmly) ⊗ in all bedrooms **FACILITIES: Spa** STV ⛳27 Fishing Squash Snooker Sauna Gym Putt green Jacuzzi beauty salon, football pitch, driving range, 2 golf courses, hydrotherapy spa Xmas **CONF:** Thtr 250 Class 100 Board 50 Del £145 **SERVICES:** Lift **PARKING:** 400 **NOTES:** ⊗ in restaurant Civ Wed 150

WOODFORD BRIDGE, Greater London
See LONDON SECTION plan 1 H6

★★★★65% Menzies Prince Regent

Manor Rd IG8 8AE
☎ 020 8505 9966 020 8506 0807
e-mail: princeregent@menzies-hotels.co.uk
web: www.menzies-hotels.co.uk
Dir: *M25 junct 26, to Loughton and Chigwell, hotel on Manor Rd*

Situated on the edge of Woodford Bridge and Chigwell, this hotel offers easy access into London as well as the M11 & M25. There is a good range of spacious, well-equipped bedrooms, most with quiet aspects. The six conference and banqueting rooms have good facilities and are well suited to weddings and business events.

ROOMS: 61 en suite ⊗ in 10 bedrooms s £110; d £110-£130 **LB** **FACILITIES:** STV Xmas **CONF:** Thtr 500 Class 150 Board 120 Del £155 **SERVICES:** Lift **PARKING:** 60 **NOTES:** ⊗ in restaurant Civ Wed

WOODFORD GREEN, Greater London
See LONDON SECTION plan 1 G6

Innkeeper's Lodge Chigwell

735 Chigwell Rd IG8 8AS
☎ 020 84989401
web: www.innkeeperslodge.com

A growing concept in the travel accommodation market. Smart rooms meet essential business requirements but also have home comforts. Dining options include all-day menus plus the added advantage of breakfast, which is included in the room price. For further details consult the Hotel Groups page.

ROOMS: 34 en suite s £45-£49; d £45-£49

WOODHALL SPA, Lincolnshire — Map 17 TF16

★★★68% Petwood

Stixwould Rd LN10 6QF
☎ 01526 352411 01526 353473
e-mail: reception@petwood.co.uk
web: www.petwood.co.uk
Dir: *from Sleaford take A153 (signed Skegness). At Tattershall turn left on B1192. Hotel is signed from village*

This lovely Edwardian house, set in 30 acres of gardens and woodlands, is steeped in history. Built in 1905, the house was used by 617 Squadron, the famous 'Dambusters' as an officers' mess during World War II. Bedrooms and public areas are spacious, comfortable and retain many original period features. Weddings and conferences are well catered for.

ROOMS: 56 en suite (3 GF) ⊗ in 17 bedrooms s fr £90; d fr £130 (incl. bkfst) **LB** **FACILITIES:** Snooker Putt green Complimentary pass to leisure centre ♫ Xmas **CONF:** Thtr 250 Class 100 Board 50 Del from £110 **SERVICES:** Lift **PARKING:** 140 **NOTES:** ⊗ in restaurant Civ Wed 200

★★★63% Golf Hotel

The Broadway LN10 6SG
☎ 01526 353535 01526 353096
e-mail: reception@thegolf-hotel.com
web: www.thegolf-hotel.com
Dir: *from Lincoln take B1189 to Metheringham onto B1191 towards Woodhall Spa. Hotel on left approx 500yds along from rdbt*

Located near the centre of the village, this traditional hotel is ideally situated to explore the Lincolnshire countryside and coast. The adjacent golf course makes this a popular venue for golfers and gives rise to the hotel's name and much of its decorative theme. Bedrooms vary in size and include several refurbished rooms.

ROOMS: 50 en suite (4 fmly) (8 GF) ⊗ in 21 bedrooms s £65-£100; d £75-£115 (incl. bkfst) **LB** **FACILITIES:** STV Guests have use of private leisure centre 1m from hotel Xmas **CONF:** Thtr 150 Class 50 Board 50 Del £95 **SERVICES:** Lift **PARKING:** 100 **NOTES:** ⊗ in restaurant Civ Wed 150

★★65% *Eagle Lodge*

The Broadway LN10 6ST
☎ 01526 353231 01526 352797
e-mail: user@eaglelodge.fsbusiness.co.uk
Dir: *in the centre of Woodhall Spa*

This family owned hotel is located in the centre of town, close to local shops and golf courses. Spacious bedrooms are well equipped for both business and leisure guests. Public areas

continued

include a bar and brasserie in addition to a formal restaurant offering a good range of dishes to suit all tastes. Conference and meeting facilities are also available.
ROOMS: 23 en suite (2 fmly) **FACILITIES:** STV ♫ **CONF:** Thtr 100 Class 50 Board 50 **PARKING:** 70 **NOTES:** ⊗ in restaurant

WOODSTOCK, Oxfordshire — Map 11 SP41

★★★75% Feathers
Market St OX20 1SX
☎ 01993 812291 🖷 01993 813158
e-mail: enquiries@feathers.co.uk
web: www.bespokehotels.com
Dir: *from Oxford take A44 to Woodstock, 1st left after lights. Hotel on left*

This small and individual hotel enjoys a town centre location with easy access to nearby Blenheim Palace. Public areas are elegant and full of traditional character, from the cosy drawing room to the atmospheric restaurant. Individually styled bedrooms are appointed to a high standard and are furnished with attractive period and reproduction furniture.
ROOMS: 20 en suite (4 fmly) (2 GF) ⊗ in 5 bedrooms s £99-£135; d £135-£155 (incl. bkfst) **LB** **FACILITIES:** STV 1 suite has steam room Xmas **CONF:** Thtr 25 Class 20 Board 16 Del from £150 **NOTES:** ⊗ in restaurant

★★★72% ®® The Bear
Park St OX20 1SZ
☎ 0870 400 8202 & 01993 811124
🖷 01993 813380
e-mail: bear@macdonald-hotels.co.uk
web: www.macdonald-hotels.co.uk
Dir: *M40 junct 8 onto A40 to Oxford/M40 junct 9 onto A34 S to Oxford. Take A44 into Woodstock. Left to town centre hotel on left opp town hall*

With its ivy-clad façade, oak beams and open fireplaces, this 13th-century coaching inn exudes charm and cosiness. The hotel boasts bedrooms decorated in a modern style that remains sympathetic to the original character. Public rooms include a variety of function rooms, an intimate bar area and an attractive restaurant where attentive service and good food can be found.
ROOMS: 36 en suite 18 annexe en suite (1 fmly) (9 GF) ⊗ in all bedrooms s £119-£143; d £138-£198 (incl. bkfst) **LB** **FACILITIES:** STV Xmas **CONF:** Thtr 60 Class 14 Board 26 Del from £140 **PARKING:** 40 **NOTES:** ⊗ in restaurant RS 01-Jan

★★★67% Kings Arms
19 Market St OX20 1SU
☎ 01993 813636 🖷 01993 813737
e-mail: stay@kingshotelwoodstock.co.uk
web: www.kings-hotel-woodstock.co.uk
Dir: *on corner of Market St and A44 Oxford Rd in town centre*

This appealing and contemporary hotel is situated in the centre of town just a short walk from Blenheim Palace. Public areas include an attractive bistro-style restaurant and a smart bar. Bedrooms and bathrooms are comfortably furnished and equipped to a high standard.
ROOMS: 14 en suite ⊗ in all bedrooms s £70-£100; d £130-£150 (incl. bkfst) **NOTES:** No children 12yrs ⊗ in restaurant

★★ A Marlborough Arms
26 Oxford St OX20 1TS
☎ 01993 811227 🖷 01993 811657
e-mail: themarlborough@ic24.net
Dir: *200mtrs from Blenheim Palace*
ROOMS: 10 en suite (2 fmly) s £60; d £85-£95 (incl. bkfst)
CONF: Board 14 **PARKING:** 11 **NOTES:** ⊗ in restaurant

WOODY BAY, Devon — Map 03 SS64

★★66% *Woody Bay Hotel*
EX31 4QX
☎ 01598 763264 & 763563
Dir: *Signed from A39 between Blackmoor Gate & Lynton*
Popular with walkers, this hotel is perfectly situated to enjoy sweeping views over Woody Bay. Bedrooms vary in style and size; the majority have stunning views. Similarly in the restaurant, where guests have a wide choice from the imaginative fixed-price menu.
ROOMS: 10 rms (8 en suite) (1 fmly) **PARKING:** 10 **NOTES:** ⊗ in restaurant Closed Jan RS Nov, Dec & Feb

WOOLACOMBE, Devon — Map 03 SS44
See also Mortehoe

★★★81% ® Watersmeet
Mortehoe EX34 7EB
☎ 01271 870333 🖷 01271 870890
e-mail: info@watersmeethotel.co.uk
web: www.watersmeethotel.co.uk
Dir: *follow B3343 into Woolacombe, turn right onto esplanade, hotel 0.75m on left*
Offering attentive service, this popular hotel boasts magnificent

continued on p632

WOOLACOMBE, continued

views over the bay with steps leading directly to the sandy beach. Bedrooms benefit from wonderful sea views and some have the added bonus of private balconies. The public areas benefit from the hotel's stunning position, especially the attractive tiered restaurant. All tables overlook the sea where diners can admire the glorious sunsets. An imaginative and innovative range of dishes is offered each evening from a fixed-price menu.
ROOMS: 25 en suite (4 fmly) (3 GF) **FACILITIES: Spa** STV Jacuzzi Steam room, Hot tub Xmas **PARKING:** 38 **NOTES:** in restaurant Civ Wed 60

See advert on opposite page

★★★75% Woolacombe Bay
South St EX34 7BN
☎ 01271 870388 01271 870613
e-mail: woolacombe.bayhotel@btinternet.com
web: www.woolacombe-bay-hotel.co.uk
Dir: *from A361 take B3343 to Woolacombe. Hotel in centre on left*

This family-friendly hotel is adjacent to the beach and the village centre, and has a welcoming and friendly environment. The public areas are spacious and comfortable, and many of the well-equipped bedrooms have balconies with splendid views over the bay. In addition to the fixed price menu served in the stylish restaurant, Maxwell's bistro offers an informal alternative.
ROOMS: 64 en suite (27 fmly) (2 GF) in all bedrooms s £53-£147; d £106-£294 (incl. bkfst & dinner) **LB** **FACILITIES: Spa** STV 9 Squash Snooker Sauna Solarium Gym Jacuzzi Beauty salon, Creche, Childrens club, Table Tennis, Hairdresser ch fac Xmas **CONF:** Thtr 200 Class 150 Board 150 Del from £69 **SERVICES:** Lift **PARKING:** 150 **NOTES:** in restaurant Closed 3 Jan-mid Feb

WOOLER, Northumberland — Map 21 NT92

★★69% Tankerville Arms
Cottage Rd NE71 6AD
☎ 01668 281581 01668 281387
e-mail: enquiries@tankervillehotel.co.uk
web: www.tankervillehotel.co.uk
Dir: *on A697*
Dating from the 17th century, this popular inn is ideally placed for the many local attractions. The comfortable and thoughtfully equipped bedrooms come in a variety of styles and sizes. The traditional bar has an adjacent brasserie and there is a spacious restaurant. Wide-ranging menus provide a choice to suit all.
ROOMS: 16 en suite (2 fmly) s £34-£51; d £64-£96 (incl. bkfst) **LB** **CONF:** Thtr 60 Class 60 Board 30 **PARKING:** 100 **NOTES:** in restaurant Closed 22-28 Dec Civ Wed 70

WOOLLEY EDGE MOTORWAY SERVICE AREA (M1), West Yorkshire — Map 16 SE31

Travelodge Wakefield (Northbound)
M1 Service Area, West Bretton WF4 4LQ
☎ 08700 850 950 01924 830609
web: www.travelodge.co.uk
Dir: *between juncts 38 & 39 on M1, adjacent to service area*
Travelodge offers good quality, good value, modern accommodation. Ideal for families, the spacious, en suite bedrooms include remote-control TV, tea and coffee-making facilities and comfortable beds. Meals can be taken at the nearby family restaurant. For further details consult the Hotel Groups page.
ROOMS: 32 en suite s fr £26; d fr £26

Travelodge Wakefield (Southbound)
M1 Service Area Southbound, West Bretton WF4 4LQ
☎ 08700 850 950 01924 830174
web: www.travelodge.co.uk
Travelodge offers good quality, good value, modern accommodation. Ideal for families, the spacious, en suite bedrooms include remote-control TV, tea and coffee-making facilities and comfortable beds. Meals can be taken at the nearby family restaurant. For further details consult the Hotel Groups page.
ROOMS: 41 en suite s fr £26; d fr £26

WOOTTON BASSETT, Wiltshire — Map 05 SU08

★★★69% The Lodge @ Wiltshire Golf & Country Club
SN4 7PB
☎ 01793 849999 01793 849988
e-mail: thelodge@the-wiltshire.co.uk
Dir: *M4 junct 16 follow signs for Wootton Bassett. Entrance 1m S of Wootton Bassett on the left on A3102 to Lyneham*

Overlooking rolling Wiltshire countryside and set on a parkland golf course, the newly built Lodge Hotel offers contemporary bedrooms, that include purpose-designed disabled access rooms. The air-conditioned restaurant and bar open onto a large patio which overlooks the 18th green, and there are splendid leisure facilities including a techno gym and 18-meter swimming pool; beauty treatments are also on offer.
ROOMS: 58 en suite (3 fmly) (29 GF) in 27 bedrooms s fr £75; d £80-£125 (incl. bkfst) **LB** **FACILITIES: Spa** STV 18 Sauna Solarium Gym Putt green Jacuzzi Beauty Salon Steam Room Covered driving range **CONF:** Thtr 250 Class 120 Board 30 Del from £120 **SERVICES:** Lift **PARKING:** 200 **NOTES:** in restaurant Closed 24 & 25 Dec

W

WORCESTER, Worcestershire Map 10 SO85

★★★74% Pear Tree Inn & Country Hotel

Smite WR3 8SY
☎ 01905 756565 🖷 01905 756777
e-mail: thepeartreeuk@aol.com
web: www.thepeartree.co.uk
Dir: *M5 junct 6 take Droitwich road, after 300yds take 1st right into small country lane over canal bridge, up a hill, hotel on left*

This traditional English inn and country hotel has spacious bedrooms with attractive colour schemes and good facilities. Ground-floor bedrooms are available, as are suites. Guests can enjoy good food and a drink in warm and relaxed surroundings; there is also an excellent range of conference/function rooms.
ROOMS: 24 en suite (2 fmly) (12 GF) ⊗ in 12 bedrooms s £68-£85; d £88-£105 (incl. bkfst) **LB** **FACILITIES:** STV **CONF:** BC Thtr 300 Class 150 Board 30 Del from £145 **SERVICES:** Lift air con **PARKING:** 200 **NOTES:** ✗ ⊗ in restaurant Civ Wed 120

★★★70% Bank House Hotel Golf & Country Club

Bransford WR6 5JD
☎ 01886 833551 🖷 01886 832461
e-mail: info@bankhousehotel.co.uk
web: www.bw-bankhouse.co.uk
Dir: *M5 junct 7 follow signs to Worcester West, then Hereford on A4440, & A4103. Turn left, hotel approx 2m on left*

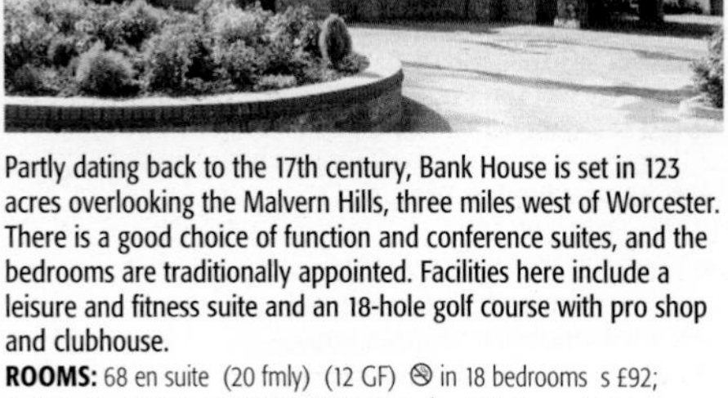

Partly dating back to the 17th century, Bank House is set in 123 acres overlooking the Malvern Hills, three miles west of Worcester. There is a good choice of function and conference suites, and the bedrooms are traditionally appointed. Facilities here include a leisure and fitness suite and an 18-hole golf course with pro shop and clubhouse.
ROOMS: 68 en suite (20 fmly) (12 GF) ⊗ in 18 bedrooms s £92; d £120 (incl. bkfst) **LB** **FACILITIES: Spa** 18 Sauna Solarium Gym Putt green Jacuzzi Xmas **CONF:** Thtr 400 Class 150 Board 70 Del £145 **PARKING:** 350 **NOTES:** ⊗ in restaurant Civ Wed 200

★★★64% Fownes

City Walls Rd WR1 2AP
☎ 01905 613151 🖷 01905 23742
e-mail: reservations@fowneshotel.co.uk
web: www.fownesgroup.co.uk/fownes
Dir: *M5 junct 7 take A44 for Worcester city centre. Turn right at 4th set of traffic lights into City Walls Rd*

On the Birmingham canal and located close to the city centre this former Victorian glove factory has been converted into an interesting-looking, modern hotel with well proportioned bedrooms. Snacks are available in the lounge bar and the King's restaurant offers an interesting carte menu. Conference and meeting facilities are available.
ROOMS: 61 en suite (10 GF) ⊗ in 28 bedrooms s £65-£98.50; d £89-£115 (incl. bkfst) **LB** **FACILITIES:** Xmas **CONF:** Thtr 100 Class 35 Board 25 **SERVICES:** Lift **PARKING:** 82 **NOTES:** ⊗ in restaurant Civ Wed 80

⇧ Premier Travel Inn Worcester

Wainwright Way, Warndon WR4 9FA
☎ 08701 977278 🖷 01905 756601
web: www.premiertravelinn.com
Dir: *M5 junct 6, at entrance of Warndon commercial development area*

High quality, modern budget accommodation ideal for both families and business travellers. Spacious, en suite bedrooms feature bath and shower, satellite TV and many have telephones and modem points. The adjacent family restaurant features a wide and varied menu. For further details consult the Hotel Groups page.
ROOMS: 60 en suite s £50.95; d £50.95 **CONF:** Thtr 8

WORFIELD, Shropshire Map 10 SO79

Top Hotel

★★★ ⊛⊛⊛ Old Vicarage Hotel and Restaurant
Worfield WV15 5JZ
☎ 01746 716497 🖷 01746 716552
e-mail: admin@the-old-vicarage.demon.co.uk
web: www.oldvicarageworfield.com
Dir: *off A454 between Bridgnorth & Wolverhampton, 5m S of Telford's southern business area*
This delightful property is set in acres of farm and woodland in a quiet and peaceful area of Shropshire and was originally an elegant Edwardian vicarage. Service is friendly and helpful, and customer care is one the many strengths of this charming small hotel. The restaurant is a joy, serving award-winning modern British cuisine in elegant surroundings. The lounge and conservatory are the perfect places to enjoy a pre-dinner drink or the complimentary afternoon tea. Bedrooms are individually appointed, thoughtfully and luxuriously furnished and well equipped.
ROOMS: 10 en suite 4 annexe en suite (1 fmly) (2 GF) ⊗ in all bedrooms s £65-£110; d £99.50-£175 (incl. bkfst) **LB** **FACILITIES: Spa** **CONF:** BC Thtr 30 Class 30 Board 20 Del £145 **PARKING:** 30 **NOTES:** ⊗ in restaurant

WORKINGTON, Cumbria Map 18 NY02

★★★80% ⊛ Washington Central
Washington St CA14 3AY
☎ 01900 65772 🖷 01900 68770
e-mail: kawildwchotel@aol.com
web: www.washingtoncentralhotelworkington.com
Dir: *M6 junct 40 towards Keswick, follow to Workington. At lights at bottom of Ramsey Brow, turn right and follow signs for hotel*

Enjoying a prominent town centre location, this modern hotel boasts memorably hospitable staff. The well-maintained and comfortable bedrooms are equipped with a range of thoughtful extras. Public areas include numerous lounges, a spacious bar, Ceasars leisure club, a smart restaurant and a popular coffee shop. The comprehensive conference facilities are ideal for meetings and weddings.
ROOMS: 46 en suite (4 fmly) ⊗ in 37 bedrooms s £77-£119.95; d £109.95-£159.95 (incl. bkfst) **LB** **FACILITIES:** STV supervised Sauna Solarium Gym Jacuzzi Free bike hire, Nightclub ♫ **CONF:** BC Thtr 300 Class 250 Board 100 Del £109.95 **SERVICES:** Lift **PARKING:** 16 **NOTES:** ⊗ in restaurant RS 25 Dec Civ Wed 300

★★★69% Hunday Manor Country House
Hunday, Winscales CA14 4JF
☎ 01900 61798 🖷 01900 601202
e-mail: info@hunday-manor-hotel.co.uk
Dir: *off A66 onto A595 towards Whitehaven, hotel is 3m on right, signed*
Delightfully situated and enjoying distant views of the Solway Firth, this charming hotel has comfortable, well-furnished rooms. The open-plan bar and foyer lounge boast welcoming open fires, and the attractive restaurant overlooks the woodland gardens. The function suite makes the hotel an excellent wedding venue.
ROOMS: 24 en suite s £59-£75; d £80-£100 (incl. bkfst) **LB** **CONF:** BC Thtr 200 Class 200 Board 200 **PARKING:** 50 **NOTES:** ⊗ in restaurant Civ Wed 250

WORKSOP, Nottinghamshire Map 16 SK57

★★★68% Lion
112 Bridge St S80 1HT
☎ 01909 477925 🖷 01909 479038
e-mail: reservations@the-lionhotel.co.uk
Dir: *A57 to town centre, turn at Walkers Garage on right and follow road to Norfolk Arms and turn left*

This former coaching inn lies on the edge of the main shopping precinct, with a car park to the rear. It has been extended to offer modern accommodation, a feature being its excellent executive rooms. A wide range of interesting dishes is offered in both the restaurant and bar.
ROOMS: 45 en suite (3 fmly) (7 GF) ⊗ in 19 bedrooms s £70-£90; d £85-£105 (incl. bkfst) **LB** **FACILITIES:** STV Xmas **CONF:** Thtr 160 Class 80 Board 70 Del from £95 **SERVICES:** Lift **PARKING:** 50 **NOTES:** ⊗ in restaurant Civ Wed 100

★★★65% Clumber Park
Clumber Park S80 3PA
☎ 01623 835333 🖷 01623 835525
e-mail: reservations@clumberparkhotel
web: www.corushotels.com/clumberpark
Dir: *M1 junct 30/31 follow signs for Worksop. A1 Fiveways rdbt onto A614, 5m NE*
Beside the A614, this hotel is situated in open countryside, edging on to Sherwood Forest and Clumber Park. Bedrooms are comfortably furnished and well equipped and public areas include

continued

a choice of formal and informal eating options. Dukes Tavern is lively and casual, while the restaurant offers a more traditional style of service.
ROOMS: 48 en suite (6 fmly) (16 GF) ⊗ in 31 bedrooms s £50-£69; d £50-£69 **LB** **FACILITIES:** STV Xmas **CONF:** Thtr 250 Class 150 Board 90 Del from £95 **PARKING:** 200 **NOTES:** ⊗ in restaurant Civ Wed 100

⌂ Travelodge
St Anne's Dr, Dukeries Dr S80 3QD
☎ 08700 850 950 ▤ 0870 191 1684
web: www.travelodge.co.uk
Dir: *on rdbt junct of A619/A57*
Travelodge offers good quality, good value, modern accommodation. Ideal for families, the spacious, en suite bedrooms include remote-control TV, tea and coffee-making facilities and comfortable beds. Meals can be taken at the nearby family restaurant. For further details consult the Hotel Groups page.
ROOMS: 40 en suite s fr £26; d fr £26

WORSLEY, Greater Manchester — Map 15 SD70

★★★63% *Novotel Manchester West*
Worsley Brow M28 2YA
☎ 0161 799 3535 ▤ 0161 703 8207
e-mail: H0907@accor-hotels.com
web: www.novotel.com
Dir: *adjacent to M60 junct 13*
Well placed for access to the Peak and Lake Districts, as well as the thriving city of Manchester, this modern hotel successfully caters for both families and business guests. Spacious bedrooms all have sofa beds and a large work area, and the hotel also boasts an outdoor swimming pool and children's play area. Novotel - AA Hotel Group of the Year 2005-6.
ROOMS: 119 en suite (4 fmly) **FACILITIES:** STV ⥾ **CONF:** Thtr 230 Class 140 Board 20 **SERVICES:** Lift **PARKING:** 140 **NOTES:** Civ Wed

WORTHING, West Sussex — Map 06 TQ10

★★★72% ⊛ *Ardington*
Steyne Gardens BN11 3DZ
☎ 01903 230451 ▤ 01903 526526
Dir: *A27 to Lancing, then to seafront. Follow signs for Worthing. Left at 1st Church into Steyne Gardens*
Overlooking the Steyne Gardens next to the seafront, this popular hotel offers well-appointed bedrooms with a good range of facilities. An elegant lounge/bar area caters for guests throughout the day and has ample seating. The restaurant has been designed in a contemporary style, and offers good standards of cuisine.
ROOMS: 45 en suite (4 fmly) ⊗ in 10 bedrooms **FACILITIES:** STV ch fac **CONF:** Thtr 140 Class 60 Board 35 **NOTES:** Closed 25 Dec-4 Jan

★★★70% Berkeley
86-95 Marine Pde BN11 3QD
☎ 01903 820000 ▤ 01903 821333
e-mail: reservations@berkelyhotel-worthing.co.uk
Dir: *follow signs to seafront; hotel 0.5m W from pier*
This hotel occupies a prime location on the seafront just a short walk from the high street. Bedrooms are modern in style and equipped with a good range of facilities; many have superb sea views. The public areas are tastefully decorated, and include a comfortable cocktail bar and a spacious restaurant.
ROOMS: 80 en suite (3 fmly) ⊗ in 29 bedrooms s £82-£98; d £105-£126 (incl. bkfst) **LB** **FACILITIES:** STV Xmas **CONF:** Thtr 100 Class 50 Board 50 Del from £99 **SERVICES:** Lift **PARKING:** 35 **NOTES:** 🐕̸ ⊗ in restaurant Civ Wed 50

★★★69% Windsor
14/20 Windsor Rd BN11 2LX
☎ 01903 239655 & 0800 9804442 ▤ 01903 210763
e-mail: reception@thewindsor.co.uk
web: www.thewindsor.co.uk
Dir: *From A27, A259. Follow hotel signs through town centre to seafront towards Brighton*
Located on a quiet road near to the seafront, this well-established hotel is popular with both business and leisure guests. Public areas include a smart lounge bar, an appealing conservatory reception and lounge area, and a popular restaurant. A choice of tastefully furnished bedrooms is available, each with a good range of facilities.
ROOMS: 30 en suite (4 fmly) (5 GF) ⊗ in 15 bedrooms s £80-£95; d £95-£130 (incl. bkfst) **LB** **FACILITIES:** STV **CONF:** Thtr 120 Class 48 Board 40 Del from £95 **SERVICES:** air con **PARKING:** 28 **NOTES:** 🐕̸ ⊗ in restaurant Closed 23-31 Dec Civ Wed 100

★★★68% Beach
Marine Pde BN11 3QJ
☎ 01903 234001 ▤ 01903 234567
e-mail: info@thebeachhotel.co.uk
web: www.thebeachhotel.co.uk
Dir: *W of town centre, approx 0.3m from pier*
With an impressive 1930's façade this well-established hotel is extremely popular with both leisure and business guests. Bedrooms, some with sea views and balconies, are comfortable and well equipped. Spacious public areas incorporate a busy restaurant serving a wide range of popular dishes. Secure parking is available.
ROOMS: 79 en suite (8 fmly) ⊗ in all bedrooms s £70-£82; d £98-£108 (incl. bkfst) **LB** **FACILITIES:** STV Xmas **CONF:** Thtr 250 Class 60 Board 60 Del from £70 **SERVICES:** Lift **PARKING:** 55 **NOTES:** 🐕̸ ⊗ in restaurant

★★★66% Kingsway
Marine Pde BN11 3QQ
☎ 01903 237542 ▤ 01903 204173
e-mail: kingsway-hotel@btconnect.com
Dir: *A27 follow signs to Worthing, then at seafront follow signs 'Hotel West'. Hotel 0.75m west of pier*
Ideally located on the seafront and close to the town centre, the Kingsway continues to provide warm hospitality. Bedrooms, which are gradually being upgraded, are comfortably furnished and equipped with modern facilities. Day rooms include two comfortable lounge areas, a bar serving snacks and a well-appointed restaurant.
ROOMS: 29 en suite 7 annexe en suite (2 fmly) (3 GF) ⊗ in 21 bedrooms s £68-£79; d £100-£138 (incl. bkfst) **LB** **FACILITIES:** STV Xmas **CONF:** Thtr 40 Class 20 Board 30 Del from £95 **SERVICES:** Lift **PARKING:** 9 **NOTES:** ⊗ in restaurant

★★★63% *Findon Manor*
High St, Findon BN14 0TA
☎ 01903 872733 ▤ 01903 877473
e-mail: hotel@findonmanor.com
web: www.findonmanor.com
Dir: *500yds off A24 between Worthing & Horsham, at the sign for Findon follow signs to Findon Manor into village*
Located in the centre of the village, Findon Manor was built as a rectory and has a beamed lounge, which doubles as the reception area. Bedrooms, several with four-poster beds, are attractively decorated in a traditional style. The cosy bar offers a very good

continued on p636

W

WORTHING, continued

range of bar food, and is popular with locals, while the restaurant overlooks a garden and offers modern and traditional dishes.

Findon Manor, Worthing

ROOMS: 11 en suite (2 fmly) **FACILITIES:** Boule **CONF:** Thtr 50 Class 18 Board 25 **PARKING:** 25 **NOTES:** No children 12yrs in restaurant RS 24-30 Dec Civ Wed 60

See advert under BRIGHTON & HOVE

★★62% Cavendish

115 Marine Pde BN11 3QG
☎ 01903 236767 01903 823840
e-mail: reservations@cavendishworthing.co.uk
web: www.cavendishworthing.co.uk
Dir: *on seafront, 600yds W of pier*

This popular, family-run hotel enjoys a prominent seafront location. Bedrooms are well equipped and soundly decorated. Guests have an extensive choice of meal options, with a varied bar menu, and carte and daily menus offered in the restaurant. Limited parking is available at the rear of the hotel.

ROOMS: 17 en suite (4 fmly) in 3 bedrooms s £40-£45; d £69-£85 (incl. bkfst) **LB** **FACILITIES:** STV **SERVICES:** air con **PARKING:** 5

WOTTON-UNDER-EDGE, Gloucestershire — Map 04 ST79

★★★★66% Tortworth Court Four Pillars

Tortworth GL12 8HH
☎ 0800 374 692 & 01454 263000
01454 263001
e-mail: tortworth@four-pillars.co.uk
web: www.four-pillars.co.uk
Dir: *M5 junct 14, B4509 pass Tortworth Visitors Centre take next right, hotel 0.5m on right*

Set within 30 acres of parkland, this Gothic mansion displays original features cleverly combined with contemporary additions. Elegant public rooms include a choice of dining options, one housed within the library, another in the atrium and the third in the orangery. Bedrooms are well equipped, and additional facilities include a host of conference rooms and a leisure centre.

ROOMS: 189 en suite in 95 bedrooms s £79-£162; d £92-£209 (incl. bkfst) **LB** **FACILITIES:** STV Sauna Gym Jacuzzi Beauty suite, Steam room Xmas **CONF:** BC Thtr 400 Class 200 Board 80 Del £195 **SERVICES:** Lift **PARKING:** 350 **NOTES:** in restaurant Civ Wed 100

Packed in a hurry? Ironing facilities should be available at all star levels, either in the rooms or on request

WREA GREEN, Lancashire — Map 18 SD33

★★★69% *Manor House*

Ribby Hall Village, Ribby Rd PR4 2PR
☎ 01772 688000 01772 688036
e-mail: themanorhousehotel@ribbyhall.co.uk
web: ww.mhhotel.co.uk
Dir: *M55 junct 33 follow A585 towards Kirkham & brown tourist signs for manor house. Straight across 3 rdbts. Ribby Hall Village 200yds on left*

This smart hotel, located in the Ribby Hall Holiday Village, overlooks an ornamental lake, complete with 50ft fountain. Accommodation consists of modern one and two-bedroom suites, some with spacious balconies. Two opulent penthouses are particularly impressive. Meals are served in the nearby restaurant. Hotel guests can make use of the extensive leisure and conference facilities.

ROOMS: 29 en suite (6 fmly) (13 GF) in all bedrooms **FACILITIES: Spa** STV supervised 9 Fishing Squash Riding Snooker Sauna Solarium Gym Jacuzzi Various other facilities available **CONF:** Thtr 350 Class 200 **SERVICES:** Lift **PARKING:** 100 **NOTES:** in restaurant Civ Wed

★★★68% Villa Country House

Moss Side Ln PR4 2PE
☎ 01772 684347 01772 687647
e-mail: info@villahotel-wreagreen.co.uk
Dir: *M55 junct 3 follow signs to Kirkham at Wrea Green follow signs to Hytham.*

This 19th-century residence stands in a peaceful location close to the village of Wrea Green. There are extensive bars and a good range of quality food is served either in the bar or the many-roomed restaurant. The modern bedrooms are very well designed and are air conditioned. The staff are friendly and helpful.

ROOMS: 25 en suite (1 fmly) (10 GF) in all bedrooms s £55-£95; d £75-£130 (incl. bkfst) **LB** **FACILITIES:** STV Xmas **CONF:** Thtr 60 Class 15 Board 14 Del from £105 **SERVICES:** Lift **PARKING:** 75 **NOTES:** in restaurant Civ Wed 60

WROTHAM, Kent — Map 06 TQ65

Premier Travel Inn Sevenoaks/Maidstone

London Rd, Wrotham Heath TN15 7RX
☎ 08701 977227 01732 870368
web: www.premiertravelinn.com
Dir: *M26 junct 2a, A20 to Wrotham Heath and West Malling. Inn past lights on right*

High quality, modern budget accommodation ideal for both families and business travellers. Spacious, en suite bedrooms

continued

feature bath and shower, satellite TV and many have telephones and modem points. The adjacent family restaurant features a wide and varied menu. For further details consult the Hotel Groups page.
ROOMS: 40 en suite s £46.95-£49.95; d £46.95-£49.95 **CONF:** Thtr 18

WROXHAM, Norfolk
Map 13 TG31

★★66% Hotel Wroxham
The Bridge NR12 8AJ
☎ 01603 782061 🖷 01603 784279
e-mail: reservations@hotelwroxham.co.uk
web: www.hotelwroxham.co.uk
Dir: *From Norwich, A1151 signed Wroxham & The Broads for approx 7m. Over bridge at Wroxham take 1st right, & sharp right again. Hotel car park on right*

Overlooking the Norfolk Broads in the heart of this bustling town centre. Bedrooms are pleasantly decorated and well equipped; some rooms have balconies with lovely views of the busy waterways. The open-plan public rooms include the lively riverside bar, a lounge, a large sun terrace and a smart restaurant serving an interesting choice of dishes.
ROOMS: 18 en suite **FACILITIES:** Fishing Boating facilities (by arrangement) ♫ Xmas **CONF:** Thtr 200 Class 50 Board 20 Del from £85 **PARKING:** 45 **NOTES:** ✗ ⊘ in restaurant

★★63% *Kings Head*
Station Rd NR12 8UR
☎ 01603 782429 🖷 01603 784622
Dir: *in centre of village*

In the heart of the bustling town centre and on the edge of the Norfolk Broads, this hotel has spacious public rooms leading out onto the river frontage and gardens. There is a popular carvery restaurant and a conservatory that overlooks the busy waterways. The well-equipped bedrooms are pleasantly furnished and simply decorated.
ROOMS: 8 en suite (2 fmly) ⊘ in all bedrooms **FACILITIES:** Fishing **PARKING:** 45 **NOTES:** ✗ ⊘ in restaurant

WYMONDHAM, Norfolk
Map 13 TG10

★★★69% Abbey
10 Church St NR18 0PH
☎ 01953 602148 🖷 01953 606247
e-mail: info@abbeyhotels.co.uk
web: www.abbeyhotels.co.uk
Dir: *from A11 follow Wymondham sign. At lights left and 1st left into one-way system. Left into Church Street*
Charming 16th-century hotel situated close to the abbey just off the main high street of this delightful market town. The spacious bedrooms are pleasantly decorated, tastefully furnished and thoughtfully equipped; five superior rooms are now available. Public rooms include a cosy lounge bar, the Benims restaurant and a further sitting room.
ROOMS: 27 en suite 1 annexe en suite (3 fmly) (6 GF) ⊘ in all bedrooms s £55-£65; d £65-£75 (incl. bkfst) **LB** **FACILITIES:** STV Xmas **SERVICES:** Lift **PARKING:** 3 **NOTES:** ✗ ⊘ in restaurant

★★73% Wymondham Consort Hotel
Best Western
28 Market St NR18 0BB
☎ 01953 606721 🖷 01953 601361
e-mail: wymondham@bestwestern.co.uk
Dir: *off A11 (M11) Thetford to Norwich road, left at lights and left again*

Privately-owned hotel situated in the centre of this bustling market town. The individually decorated bedrooms come in a variety of sizes; each one is pleasantly decorated and thoughtfully equipped. Public rooms include a cosy bar, a separate lounge, the Rendezvous wine bar and an intimate restaurant, which overlooks the busy high street.
ROOMS: 20 en suite (1 fmly) (3 GF) ⊘ in all bedrooms s £60-£75; d £75-£85 (incl. bkfst) **LB** **CONF:** Thtr 20 Board 20 **PARKING:** 16 **NOTES:** ⊘ in restaurant

♫ Entertainment

YARM, North Yorkshire Map 19 NZ41

Top Hotel

★★★ ◎◎
Judges Country House Hotel
Kirklevington Hall TS15 9LW
☎ 01642 789000 📠 01642 782878
e-mail: enquiries@judgeshotel.co.uk
web: www.judgeshotel.co.uk
Dir: *1.5m from A19. At A67 junct, follow Yarm road, hotel on left*

Formerly a lodging for local circuit judges, this gracious mansion lies in landscaped grounds through which a stream runs. Stylish bedrooms are individually decorated and come with 101 extras, including a pet goldfish! The Conservatory restaurant serves award-winning cuisine, and the genuinely caring and attentive service is equally memorable.

ROOMS: 21 en suite (3 fmly) (5 GF) ⊗ in 10 bedrooms s £139-£153; d £164-£179 (incl. bkfst) **LB** **FACILITIES:** STV Gym Boating, 4x4 hire, mountain bikes, nature trails Xmas **CONF:** BC Thtr 200 Class 120 Board 80 Del from £195 **PARKING:** 102 **NOTES:** ✗ ⊗ in restaurant Civ Wed 200

YARMOUTH See Wight, Isle of

YATELEY, Hampshire Map 05 SU86

★★★64% Casa dei Cesari Restaurant & Hotel
Handford Ln GU46 6BT
☎ 01252 873275 📠 01252 870614
e-mail: casareservations@aol.com
Dir: *M3 junct 4a, follow signs for town centre. Hotel signed approx 1.5m*

This delightful hotel where a warm welcome is guaranteed is ideally located for transportation networks. Now refurbished this hotel boasts rooms with superior quality and comfort. The

continued

Italian-themed restaurant, which is very popular locally, serves an extensive traditional menu.

ROOMS: 44 en suite (2 fmly) (11 GF) ⊗ in 11 bedrooms s £60-£93; d £65-£115 (incl. bkfst) **LB** **FACILITIES:** STV Riding Xmas **CONF:** Thtr 35 Class 30 Board 25 Del from £125 **PARKING:** 80 **NOTES:** ✗ ⊗ in restaurant Civ Wed 50

YATTENDON, Berkshire Map 05 SU57

★★72% ◎◎ *Royal Oak*
The Square RG18 0UG
☎ 01635 201325 📠 01635 201926
e-mail: oakyattendon@aol.com
Dir: *M4 junct 13, N on A34, 1st slip road right to Hermitage, left at T-junct, 2nd right signed Yattendon*

This smart country inn dates back to the 16th century and is located in a charming Berkshire village within easy reach of the M4. Bedrooms are equipped to a high standard and bathrooms are well appointed. The kitchen offers interesting dishes, available in the bar or the more formal restaurant.

ROOMS: 5 en suite ⊗ in all bedrooms **CONF:** Thtr 30 Class 18 Board 22 **NOTES:** No children 6yrs ⊗ in restaurant

YELVERTON, Devon Map 03 SX56

★★★72% Moorland Links
PL20 6DA
☎ 01822 852245 📠 01822 855004
e-mail: moorland.links@forestdale.com
web: www.forestdale.com
Dir: *A38 from Exeter to Plymouth, then A386 towards Tavistock. 5m onto open moorland, hotel 1m on left*

In Dartmoor National Park, set in nine acres of well-tended grounds, Moorland Links has spectacular views from many of the rooms across open moorland and the Tamar Valley. Bedrooms are well equipped and comfortably furnished, and some rooms have open balconies. An ideal hotel for weddings which also has ample, quiet meeting room facilities for business guests.

ROOMS: 45 en suite (4 fmly) (17 GF) ⊗ in 2 bedrooms s £85-£110; d £120-£140 (incl. bkfst) **LB** **FACILITIES:** STV Xmas **CONF:** Thtr 120 Class 60 Board 40 Del from £125 **PARKING:** 120 **NOTES:** ⊗ in restaurant

YEOVIL, Somerset Map 04 ST51
See also Martock

★★★74% ◎◎ Yeovil Court
West Coker Rd BA20 2HE
☎ 01935 863746 📠 01935 863990
e-mail: unwind@yeovilhotel.com
web: www.yeovilhotel.com
Dir: *2.5m W of town centre on A30*

This comfortable, family-run hotel benefits from a very relaxed

continued

and caring atmosphere. Bedrooms are well equipped and neatly presented; some are located in an adjacent building. Public areas consist of a smart lounge, a popular bar and an attractive restaurant. Menus combine an interesting selection including lighter options and dishes suited to special occasion dining.
ROOMS: 18 en suite 12 annexe en suite (3 fmly) (11 GF) ⊗ in 8 bedrooms s £60-£73; d £100 (incl. bkfst) **LB** **CONF:** Thtr 50 Class 18 Board 22 Del from £107 **PARKING:** 65 **NOTES:** ⊗ in restaurant RS Sat lunch, 25 Dec eve

See advert on this page

★★★72% ◎ Lanes

West Coker BA22 9AJ
☎ 01935 862555 🖷 01935 864260
Dir: *A30 between Yeovil and Crewkerne*

Re-opened in early 2005 after a major refurbishment, this former Victorian vicarage turned into a stylish, contemporary hotel where guests are assured of a relaxed and friendly stay. Additional bedrooms and a spa are due to be completed by the end of 2006. The well equipped are comfortable bedrooms, bathrooms spacious and inviting. The brasserie-style restaurant offers an imaginative range of dishes, using local produce whenever possible.
ROOMS: 10 en suite (2 fmly) s £70-£130; d £85-£130 (incl. bkfst) **LB** **FACILITIES:** Xmas **CONF:** BC Board 70 Del from £100 **PARKING:** 40 **NOTES:** ✗ ⊗ in restaurant

★★62% Preston

64 Preston Rd BA20 2DL
☎ 01935 474400 🖷 01935 410142
e-mail: prestonhotelyeo@aol.co.uk
web: www.preston-hotel.net
Dir: *A303 onto A3088, left at 1st rdbt, over 2nd rdbt & turn right at 3rd rdbt*
A relaxed and friendly atmosphere is maintained at this popular hotel. Well suited to both business and leisure guests, a spacious bar and cosy restaurant are available where home-cooked meals satisfy the heartiest of appetites.
ROOMS: 6 en suite 7 annexe en suite (1 fmly) (7 GF) ⊗ in 7 bedrooms s £50; d £58 (incl. bkfst) **CONF:** BC Class 40 Board 15 **PARKING:** 22 **NOTES:** ⊗ in restaurant

Top Hotel

★ ◎◎◎ *Little Barwick House*

Barwick Village BA22 9TD
☎ 01935 423902 🖷 01935 420908
e-mail: littlebarwick@hotmail.com
Dir: *from Yeovil on A37 towards Dorchester, left at 1st rdbt. 1st left, hotel 0.25m on left*
Situated in a quiet hamlet, this delightful listed Georgian dower house is an ideal retreat for those seeking peaceful surroundings and good food. Just one of the highlights of a stay here is a meal in the restaurant. Each of the bedrooms has its own character, charm and a range of thoughtful extras such as fresh flowers and magazines. The informal atmosphere of a private home, coupled with the facilities and comforts of a modern hotel, result in a very special combination.
ROOMS: 6 en suite **PARKING:** 30 **NOTES:** ⊗ in restaurant

YORK, North Yorkshire Map 16 SE65
See also Aldwark, Escrick, Pocklington & Sutton upon Derwent

★★★★69% York Marriott
Tadcaster Rd YO24 1QQ
☎ 01904 701000 01904 702308
e-mail: york@marriotthotels.co.uk
web: www.marriott.co.uk
***Dir:** from A64 at York 'West' onto A1036, follow signs to city centre. Approx 1.5m, hotel on right after church and lights*
Overlooking the racecourse and Knavesmire Parkland, the hotel offers modern accommodation, including family rooms, all with a comfort cooling system. Within the hotel, guests benefit from the use of extensive leisure facilities including indoor pool, putting green and tennis court. For those guests wishing to explore the historic and cultural attractions of the city there is a daily courtesy mini-bus service to the city centre, less than a mile from the hotel.
ROOMS: 151 en suite (14 fmly) (16 GF) in 60 bedrooms
FACILITIES: Spa STV Sauna Solarium Gym Putt green Jacuzzi Beauty treatment Xmas **CONF:** BC Thtr 170 Class 90 Board 40
SERVICES: Lift air con **PARKING:** 200 **NOTES:** in restaurant Civ Wed 140

See advert on opposite page

★★★★68% The Royal York
Station Rd YO24 2AA
☎ 01904 653681 01904 623503
web: www.principal-hotels.com
***Dir:** adjacent to railway station*
Situated in three acres of landscaped grounds in the very heart of the city, this newly refurbished Victorian railway hotel has views over the city and York Minster. Contemporary bedrooms are divided between those in the main hotel and the air-conditioned garden mews. There is also a leisure complex and state-of-the-art conference centre.
ROOMS: 165 en suite (10 fmly) s £80-£170; d fr £90 **LB**
FACILITIES: STV supervised Sauna Solarium Gym Jacuzzi Steam room Xmas **CONF:** BC Thtr 410 Class 250 Board 80 Del £190
SERVICES: Lift **PARKING:** 80 **NOTES:** in restaurant Civ Wed 400

Top Hotel

★★★ Middlethorpe Hall & Spa
Bishopthorpe Rd, Middlethorpe YO23 2GB
☎ 01904 641241 01904 620176
e-mail: info@middlethorpe.com
***Dir:** A1/A64 follow York West (A1036) signs. then Bishopthorpe, Middlethorpe, racecourse signs*
This fine mellow red brick house, dating from the reign of William and Mary, sits in acres of beautifully landscaped gardens. The bedrooms vary in size and are all comfortably furnished; some are in the main house, some in converted courtyard stables set and some in a cottage. Public areas, in keeping with the style of the house, include a stately drawing room, where afternoon tea is quite an event, and an oak-panelled dining room, where inventive food is served. There is also a delightful small spa in an adjacent cottage.
ROOMS: 29 en suite (10 GF) in 10 bedrooms s £115-£175; d £175-£385 (incl. cont bkfst) **LB** **FACILITIES: Spa** STV Sauna Gym Jacuzzi Health & Beauty Spa, Helipad Xmas **CONF:** Thtr 56 Class 30 Board 25 **SERVICES:** Lift **PARKING:** 70 **NOTES:** No children 8yrs in restaurant RS 25 & 31 Dec Civ Wed 56

Top Hotel

★★★ The Grange
1 Clifton YO30 6AA
☎ 01904 644744 01904 612453
e-mail: info@grangehotel.co.uk
web: www.grangehotel.co.uk
***Dir:** on A19 York/Thirsk road, approx 500yds from city centre*
This bustling Regency town house is just a few minutes' walk from the centre of York. A professional service is efficiently delivered by caring staff in a very friendly and helpful manner. Public rooms are comfortable and have been stylishly furnished; these include three dining options, the popular and informal cellar brasserie, seafood bar and The Ivy, which offers fine dining in a lavishly decorated environment. The individually designed bedrooms are comfortably appointed and have been thoughtfully equipped.
ROOMS: 30 en suite (6 GF) s £115-£260; d £135-£260 (incl. bkfst) **LB** **FACILITIES:** STV Discount at local health spa Xmas **CONF:** Thtr 50 Class 20 Board 24 Del from £157 **PARKING:** 26 **NOTES:** in restaurant Civ Wed 90

Town House Hotel
Country House Hotel
Travel Accommodation

★★★77% Dean Court
Duncombe Place YO1 7EF
☎ 01904 625082 01904 620305
e-mail: info@deancourt-york.co.uk
web: www.deancourt-york.co.uk
***Dir:** city centre opposite York Minster*
This smart hotel enjoys a central location overlooking the Minster. Public areas have an elegant, contemporary style and include the popular D.C.H. restaurant which enjoys wonderful views of the cathedral. Bedrooms are stylishly appointed. Service is particularly

continued

friendly and efficient, and light snacks are served all day in Terry's conservatory café. Valet parking is offered.

ROOMS: 37 en suite (4 fmly) ⊗ in 16 bedrooms s £80-£120; d £125-£190 (incl. bkfst) **LB FACILITIES:** Xmas **CONF:** Thtr 50 Class 10 Board 32 Del from £125 **SERVICES:** Lift **PARKING:** 30 **NOTES:** ✗ ⊗ in restaurant Civ Wed 60

★★★73% ❀ Parsonage Country House

York Rd YO19 6LF
☎ 01904 728111 🖷 01904 728151
e-mail: reservations@parsonagehotel.co.uk
web: www.parsonagehotel.co.uk
(For full entry see Escrick)

★★★71% Kilima Hotel

129 Holgate Rd YO24 4AZ
☎ 01904 625787 🖷 01904 612083
e-mail: sales@kilima.co.uk
web: www.kilima.co.uk
Dir: *on A59, on W outskirts*

Kilima is conveniently situated within easy walking distance of the city centre. There is a relaxed and friendly atmosphere in the hotel, with professional, friendly staff providing attentive service. Bedrooms are comfortable and well equipped. The hotel benefits from private parking and leisure facilities.

ROOMS: 26 en suite (2 fmly) (10 GF) ⊗ in all bedrooms s £75-£98; d £110-£140 (incl. bkfst) **LB FACILITIES:** STV Gym Leisure complex, Steam room, Fitness Suite Xmas **CONF:** Board 14 Del £120 **PARKING:** 26 **NOTES:** ✗ ⊗ in restaurant

★★★71% ❀ Mount Royale

The Mount YO24 1GU
☎ 01904 628856 🖷 01904 611171
e-mail: reservations@mountroyale.co.uk
Dir: *W on A1036, 0.5 mile after racecourse. Hotel on right after lights*

This friendly hotel offers comfortable bedrooms in a variety of styles, several leading onto the delightful gardens. Public rooms include a lounge, a meeting room and a cosy bar. There is a

continued on p642

YORK, continued

separate restaurant and cocktail lounge also overlooking the gardens called Sous le Mont where all meals and drinks can be charged to your room account. A beauty therapist is also available by appointment.
ROOMS: 24 en suite (3 fmly) (6 GF) ⊗ in all bedrooms s £85-£115; d £98-£170 (incl. bkfst) **LB** **FACILITIES:** STV supervised Sauna Solarium Jacuzzi Beauty treatment centre, Outdoor Hot-tub Xmas **CONF:** Thtr 35 Board 22 Del £135 **PARKING:** 24 **NOTES:** Closed 1-6 Jan

★★★71% York Pavilion

45 Main St, Fulford YO10 4PJ
☎ 01904 622099 📠 01904 626939
e-mail: reservations@yorkpavilionhotel.com
web: www.yorkpavilionhotel.com
Dir: *off A64 York ringroad at A19 junct towards York. Hotel 0.5m on right opposite filling station*

An attractive Georgian hotel situated in its own grounds. All the bedrooms are individually designed to a high specification; some are in the old house and some in the converted stables set around a garden terrace. There is a comfortable lounge, a conference centre and an inviting brasserie-style restaurant with a regularly changing menu.
ROOMS: 57 en suite (4 fmly) (11 GF) ⊗ in 23 bedrooms s £70-£95; d £90-£150 (incl. bkfst) **LB** **FACILITIES:** STV Xmas **CONF:** Thtr 150 Class 60 Board 45 Del from £135 **PARKING:** 40 **NOTES:** ⊗ in restaurant Civ Wed 120

See advert on opposite page

★★★70% The Gateway to York

Hull Rd, Kexby YO4 5LD
☎ 01759 388223 📠 01759 388822
e-mail: enquiry@thegatewaytoyorkhotel.co.uk
web: www.thegatewaytoyorkhotel.co.uk
Dir: *off A64 onto A1079, 3m from York, hotel on left*

Close to York's Park & Ride and the retail shopping outlet, this hotel is set in eight acres of gardens where private fishing is

continued

available for residents. Its spacious bedrooms are very comfortable and well equipped. There is a pleasant bar/lounge and a restaurant serving interesting and enjoyable dishes.
ROOMS: 30 en suite (9 fmly) ⊗ in 23 bedrooms s £55-£63; d £72-£80 (incl. bkfst) **LB** **FACILITIES:** STV Fishing Xmas **CONF:** Thtr 60 Class 40 Board 40 Del from £68 **PARKING:** 60 **NOTES:** ⊗ in restaurant Closed Jan

★★★70% *Monkbar*

Monkbar YO31 7JA
☎ 01904 638086 📠 01904 629195
e-mail: june@monkbarhotel.co.uk
Dir: *From A64 take A1079 to City, turn right at city wall, take middle lane at lights. Hotel on right*

This smart hotel enjoys a prominent position adjacent to the city walls, minutes' walk from the cathedral. Individually styled bedrooms are well-equipped for both business and leisure guests. Spacious public areas include comfortable lounges, an American-style bar, an airy restaurant and impressive meeting and training facilities.
ROOMS: 99 en suite (3 fmly) ⊗ in 45 bedrooms **FACILITIES:** STV ch fac **CONF:** Thtr 140 Class 80 Board 50 **SERVICES:** Lift **PARKING:** 70 **NOTES:** ⊗ in restaurant Civ Wed 65

★★★67% Novotel York

Fishergate YO10 4FD
☎ 01904 611660 📠 01904 610925
e-mail: H0949@accor-hotels.com
web: www.novotel.com
Dir: *A19 north to city centre, hotel set back on left*
Set just outside the ancient city walls, this modern, family-friendly hotel is conveniently located for visitors to the city. Bedrooms feature bathrooms with separate toilet, plus excellent desk space and sofa beds. Four rooms are equipped for less able guests. The hotel's facilities include indoor and outdoor children's play areas and an indoor pool. Novotel - AA Hotel Group of the Year 2005-6.
ROOMS: 124 en suite (124 fmly) ⊗ in 91 bedrooms d £80-£134 (incl. bkfst) **LB** **FACILITIES:** STV **CONF:** BC Thtr 220 Class 100 Board 120 Del from £114 **SERVICES:** Lift **PARKING:** 150

★★★66% Minster Hotel

60 Bootham YO30 7BZ
☎ 01904 621267 📠 01904 654719
e-mail: info@yorkminsterhotel.co.uk
Dir: *from York outer ringroad (A1237) exit A19 N into York Centre, hotel on right 150yds from Bootham Bar*
Now under new ownership and within easy walking distance of the Minster and the city centre, this careful conversion of two large Victorian houses provides stylish, comfortable and well-equipped bedrooms. There is a cosy bar and a bistro serving

continued

Y

imaginative dishes, and conference facilities are also available along with secure parking.
ROOMS: 31 en suite 3 annexe en suite (1 fmly) (5 GF) ⊗ in all bedrooms s £55-£130; d £69-£220 (incl. bkfst) **LB** **FACILITIES:** STV Jacuzzi Xmas **CONF:** Thtr 65 Class 45 Board 30 Del £120 **SERVICES:** Lift **PARKING:** 35 **NOTES:** ✗ ⊗ in restaurant

★★72% Knavesmire Manor

THE CIRCLE
Selected Individual Hotels
GREAT BRITAIN

302 Tadcaster Rd YO24 1HE
☎ 01904 702941 🖷 01904 709274
e-mail: knavesmire@tiscali.co.uk
web: www.knavesmire.co.uk
Dir: *A1036 into city centre. Hotel on right, overlooking racecourse*

Commanding superb views across York's famous racecourse, this former manor house offers comfortable, well-equipped bedrooms, either in the main house or the garden rooms to the rear. Comfortable day rooms are stylishly furnished, whilst the heated indoor pool provides a popular addition.
ROOMS: 11 en suite 9 annexe en suite (3 fmly) s £55-£60; d £78-£89 (incl. bkfst) **LB** **FACILITIES:** [pool] Sauna Xmas **CONF:** Thtr 40 Class 36 Board 30 Del from £85 **SERVICES:** Lift **PARKING:** 28 **NOTES:** ⊗ in restaurant Civ Wed 60

★★71% Clifton Bridge

Water End YO30 6LL
☎ 01904 610510 🖷 01904 640208
e-mail: enq@cliftonbridgehotel.co.uk
Dir: *turn off A1237 onto A19 towards city centre. Right at lights by church, hotel 50yds on left*

Standing between Clifton Green and the River Ouse, and within walking distance of the city, this hotel (now under new ownership) offers good hospitality and attentive service. The house is well furnished and features oak panelling in the public rooms. Bedrooms are attractively decorated and thoughtfully equipped. Good home cooking is served in the cosy dining room.
ROOMS: 14 en suite (1 fmly) (3 GF) ⊗ in 3 bedrooms s £45-£60; d £74-£95 (incl. bkfst) **LB** **CONF:** Board 12 Del from £60 **PARKING:** 16 **NOTES:** ✗ ⊗ in restaurant Closed 24-26 Dec

Y

YORK, continued

★★71% Heworth Court

Heworth Green YO31 7TQ
☎ 01904 425156 📠 01904 415290
e-mail: hotel@heworth.co.uk
web: www.visityork.com
Dir: *outer ring road towards Scarborough rdbt on NE side of York, exit onto A1036 Malton Rd, hotel on left*

Friendly and attentive service is provided at this family-owned hotel, conveniently located within walking distance of the city. Public rooms are comfortable and bedrooms are thoughtfully equipped and split between the hotel & Sutherland House. An extensive range of freshly prepared food is served in the Lamp Light Restaurant. Parking facilities are good.
ROOMS: 17 en suite 11 annexe en suite (2 fmly) (9 GF) ⊗ in 21 bedrooms s £54-£89.50; d £66-£119 (incl. bkfst) **LB** **FACILITIES:** STV Whisky bar Xmas **CONF:** Thtr 50 Class 24 Board 28 **PARKING:** 29 **NOTES:** 🐕 ⊗ in restaurant

See advert on opposite page

★★70% Beechwood Close

19 Shipton Rd, Clifton YO30 5RE
☎ 01904 658378 & 627093 📠 01904 647124
e-mail: bch@selcom.co.uk
web: www.beechwood-close.co.uk
Dir: *on A19 (Thirsk Road, between ring road and city centre) on right entering 30mph zone*
This long-established, comfortable hotel, personally managed by the owners, is situated just a mile north of the city centre. It offers spacious, well-equipped and well-maintained bedrooms. There is a cosy bar-lounge, and wide-ranging menus in the dining room.
ROOMS: 14 en suite (2 fmly) s £45-£52; d £68-£80 (incl. bkfst) **LB** **FACILITIES:** STV **CONF:** Thtr 50 Class 40 Board 30 Del from £72 **PARKING:** 36 **NOTES:** 🐕 Closed 25-Dec

★★69% Alhambra Court

31 St Mary's, Bootham YO30 7DD
☎ 01904 628474 📠 01904 610690
e-mail: enq@alhambracourthotel.co.uk
web: www.alhambracourthotel.co.uk
Dir: *off Bootham A19*
In a quiet side road within easy walking distance of the Minster, this attractive Georgian building is pleasantly furnished and the bedrooms are well equipped. Service is cheerful and attentive, and good home cooking is a feature.

ROOMS: 24 en suite (4 fmly) (4 GF) ⊗ in 14 bedrooms s £38-£58; d £55-£95 (incl. bkfst) **LB** **SERVICES:** Lift **PARKING:** 25 **NOTES:** 🐕 ⊗ in restaurant Closed 24-31 Dec & 1-7 Jan

★★67% Blue Bridge

Fishergate YO10 4AP
☎ 01904 621193 📠 01904 671571
e-mail: book@bluebridgehotel.co.uk
Dir: *from A64 (outer ring road) take A19 (York/Selby) S exit into York. Approx 2m, hotel on right*
Convenient for the Barbican Centre and within walking distance of the city centre, this hotel provides pine-furnished bedrooms, which include three spacious apartment rooms across the courtyard. Good value breakfast and dinner will satisfy the heartiest of appetites. Residents and diners have their own bar. Private parking is available.
ROOMS: 16 en suite (1 fmly) (1 GF) ⊗ in 19 bedrooms s £50-£100; d £60-£150 (incl. bkfst) **LB** **FACILITIES:** STV Xmas **PARKING:** 15 **NOTES:** 🐕 ⊗ in restaurant

★★67% Jacobean Lodge

Plainville Ln, Wigginton YO32 2RG
☎ 01904 762749 📠 01904 768403
e-mail: anthony.heath5@btinternet.com
Dir: *A64, A1237, B1363 signed to Wigginton. Past Wigginton & Haxby sign. Left into Corban Ln. 0.5m right at x-rds. Hotel 0.5m on right*

This comfortable inn stands in extensive lawned gardens amid open farmland along a quiet lane. The hotel provides comfortable well-equipped bedrooms. Home-cooked meals are available in the pleasant bars or the restaurant, which are well patronised by locals. Small conferences are also catered for.
ROOMS: 8 en suite **FACILITIES:** Xmas **CONF:** Thtr 35 Class 20 Board 35 **PARKING:** 40 **NOTES:** 🐕 ⊗ in restaurant

"YORK - You Deserve A Break"

YORKSHIRE BLOOM WINNER

Only twelve minutes walk to the Medieval Walled City of York, ample overnight private parking is provided for hotel guests.

WHISKY BAR

Heworth Court Hotel comes highly recommended to stay-over, wine and dine. Advance reservations are advised in the reputable oak beamed Lamplight Restaurant. Diners may unwind in the "Whisky bar" or in the

award winning stone-flagged courtyard garden, and select from an extensive menu of modern English cuisine, with a superb wine list! Treat your loved one to a beautifully

http://www.visityork.com
Email: *hotel@heworth.co.uk*

LAMPLIGHT RESTAURANT

AA ★★

appointed four-poster bedroom, a Chandelier room, or a Super King Size room. Flowers and chocolates can be arranged discretely.

FOUR-POSTER ROOMS

(01904) 425156 www.visityork.com

Y

YORK, continued

★★65% Lady Anne Middletons Hotel
Skeldergate YO1 6DS
☎ 01904 611570 📠 01904 613043
e-mail: bookings@ladyannes.co.uk
web: www.ladyannes.co.uk
Dir: *A1036 towards city centre. Right at City Walls lights, keep left, 1st left before bridge, then 1st left into Cromwell Rd. Hotel on right*
This hotel has been created from several listed buildings and is located in the centre of York. Bedrooms are comfortably equipped. Among its amenities are a bar-lounge and a dining room where a satisfying range of food is served, and an extensive fitness club. Private parking is available.
ROOMS: 37 en suite 15 annexe en suite (3 fmly) (12 GF) ⊗ in all bedrooms s £50-£85; d £80-£130 (incl. bkfst) **LB** **FACILITIES:** supervised Sauna Solarium Gym All Facilities are within Emperors Health and fitness centre available free **CONF:** Thtr 100 Class 30 Board 30 Del from £115 **PARKING:** 40 **NOTES:** ⊗ in restaurant Closed 24-29 Dec

U Ramada Abbey Park
The Mount YO24 1BN
☎ 01904 658301 📠 01904 621224
e-mail: sales.abbeypark@ramadajarvis.co.uk
web: www.ramadajarvis.co.uk
Dir: *From A1/A64 take A1036 signed City Centre, past racecourse, through 2 sets of lights, hotel on right.*
Originally a Georgian town house, this well presented hotel is just five minutes' walk from the city centre. Bedrooms are comfortably appointed for both business and leisure guests.
ROOMS: 85 en suite (14 fmly) ⊗ in 30 bedrooms s £85-£140; d £85-£140 **FACILITIES:** STV Xmas **CONF:** Thtr 120 Class 60 Board 40 Del from £143 **SERVICES:** Lift **PARKING:** 30 **NOTES:** ⊗ in restaurant

U Ramada York
Shipton Rd, Skelton YO30 1XW
☎ 01904 670222 📠 01904 670311
e-mail: sales.york@ramadajarvis.co.uk
web: www.ramadajarvis.co.uk
Dir: *From A1 exit A59 to York. At 1st rdbt turn left, left at 2nd rdbt onto A19 to Thirsk. Hotel 1m on left.*
Conveniently located on the outskirts of the city, this country-house hotel stands in six acres of private grounds. Bedrooms are comfortably appointed for both business and leisure guests.
ROOMS: 89 en suite (20 fmly) (24 GF) ⊗ in 32 bedrooms s £89-£150; d £89-£150 **FACILITIES:** STV Xmas **CONF:** Thtr 180 Class 72 Board 60 Del from £155 **SERVICES:** Lift **PARKING:** 130 **NOTES:** ⊗ in restaurant Civ Wed 100

Innkeeper's Lodge York
Hull Rd YO10 3LF
☎ 01904 411856
web: www.innkeeperslodge.com
A growing concept in the travel accommodation market. Smart rooms meet essential business requirements but also have home comforts. Dining options include all-day menus plus the added advantage of breakfast, which is included in the room price. For further details consult the Hotel Groups page.
ROOMS: 40 en suite s fr £59; d fr £59

> The vast majority of establishments in this guide accept credit and debit cards. We indicate those that don't take any

Premier Travel Inn York City Centre
20 Blossom St YO24 1AJ
☎ 0870 9906594 📠 0870 9906595
web: www.premiertravelinn.com
Dir: *12m from A1 junct 47, off A59. Close to city centre*
High quality, modern budget accommodation ideal for both families and business travellers. Spacious, en suite bedrooms feature bath and shower, satellite TV and many have telephones and modem points. The adjacent family restaurant features a wide and varied menu. For further details consult the Hotel Groups page.
ROOMS: 86 en suite s £57.95; d £57.95

Premier Travel Inn York North West
White Rose Close, York Business Park, Nether Poppleton YO26 6RL
☎ 08701 977280 📠 01904 787633
web: www.premiertravelinn.com
Dir: *on A1237 between A19 Thirsk road & A59 Harrogate road*
High quality, modern budget accommodation ideal for both families and business travellers. Spacious, en suite bedrooms feature bath and shower, satellite TV and many have telephones and modem points. The adjacent family restaurant features a wide and varied menu. For further details consult the Hotel Groups page.
ROOMS: 44 en suite s £51.95; d £51.95

Travelodge (York Central)
90 Piccadilly YO1 9NX
☎ 08700 850 950 📠 01904 652171
web: www.travelodge.co.uk
Dir: *Exit A1(M) follow A64, 3rd turn for A19, York*
Travelodge offers good quality, good value, modern accommodation. Ideal for families, the spacious, en suite bedrooms include remote-control TV, tea and coffee-making facilities and comfortable beds. Meals can be taken at the nearby family restaurant. For further details consult the Hotel Groups page.
ROOMS: 90 en suite s fr £26; d fr £26

YOXFORD, Suffolk Map 13 TM36

★★77% ®® *Satis House*
IP17 3EX
☎ 01728 668418 📠 01728 668640
e-mail: yblackmore@aol.com
Dir: *off A12 between Ipswich & Lowestoft. 9m E Alderburgh & Snape*

A charming, privately owned hotel set in landscaped grounds just off the A12. The property was once frequented by Charles Dickens, and the name Satis House features in his novel *Great Expectations.* The spacious, individually decorated bedrooms are tastefully furnished and equipped with many thoughtful touches. Public areas include an elegant lounge, smart bar and a choice of dining rooms.
ROOMS: 8 en suite (1 GF) ⊗ in 1 bedroom **FACILITIES:** Sauna Jacuzzi **CONF:** Thtr 22 Class 20 Board 14 **PARKING:** 30 **NOTES:** No children 7yrs ⊗ in restaurant Closed 26-27 Dec, 2 wks Jan RS 25 Dec

Channel Islands

Directory of establishments in alphabetical order of location.

GUERNSEY

CASTEL
Map 24

★★★70% ✿ Hotel Hougue du Pommier
Hougue du Pommier Rd GY5 7FQ
☎ 01481 256531 ℻ 01481 256260
e-mail: hotel@houguedupommier.guernsey.net
web: www.hotelhouguedupommier.com
Dir: *turn inland from Cobo Village (coast road). Turn left at first junct. Hotel 50yds on right*

Retaining much of its 18th-century character and charm, this hotel combines modern comforts with friendly yet efficient service. Bedrooms vary in size and standard, with exceptionally well-appointed and spacious deluxe rooms. An informal eating option is available in the beamed bar and the restaurant offers a carefully cooked, fixed-price menu.
ROOMS: 37 en suite 6 annexe en suite (5 fmly) ⊗ in all bedrooms s £38-£48; d £76-£114 (incl. bkfst) **LB** **FACILITIES:** STV ⥭ ⛳6 Sauna ♫ Xmas **PARKING:** 50 **NOTES:** ⊗ in restaurant

See advert on this page

COBO
Map 24

★★★72% ✿✿ *Cobo Bay*
Coast Rd GY5 7HB
☎ 01481 257102 ℻ 01481 254542
e-mail: reservations@cobobayhotel.com
web: www.cobobayhotel.com
Dir: *from airport turn right, follow road to W coast at L'Eree. Turn right onto coast road for 3m to Cobo Bay. Hotel on right*
Popular hotel situated on the seafront overlooking Cobo Bay. The well-equipped bedrooms are pleasantly decorated; many of the front rooms have balconies and there is a secluded sun terrace to the rear. Public rooms include a candlelit restaurant with stunning views of the Bay, and the Chesterfield bar with its leather sofas and armchairs.
ROOMS: 36 en suite (4 fmly) **FACILITIES:** STV Snooker Sauna Jacuzzi **CONF:** Thtr 50 Class 30 Board 20 **SERVICES:** Lift **PARKING:** 60 **NOTES:** ✗ ⊗ in restaurant Closed Jan-Feb

Packed in a hurry? Ironing facilities should be available at all star levels, either in the rooms or on request

FERMAIN BAY
Map 24

★★★69% Le Chalet
GY4 6SD
☎ 01481 235716 ℻ 01481 235718
e-mail: chalet@sarniahotels.com
Dir: *from airport left towards St Martins village. Right at filter to Sausmarez Rd, follow sign for Fermain Bay & Le Chalet Hotel*
Nestling in the wooded valley above the Fermain Bay, this family-run hotel is popular, and many guests return on a regular basis. Bedrooms vary in size and are tastefully furnished and decorated. The public areas include a panelled lounge, bar area, restaurant and a stunning sun terrace adjoining the small indoor leisure facility.
ROOMS: 40 en suite (5 fmly) s £42-£90; d £70-£109 (incl. bkfst) **LB** **FACILITIES:** Sauna Solarium Jacuzzi Spa pool **PARKING:** 35 **NOTES:** ✗ ⊗ in restaurant Closed mid Oct-mid Apr

FOREST
Map 24

★★68% Le Chene
Forest Rd GY8 0AH
☎ 01481 235566 ℻ 01481 239456
e-mail: info@lechene.co.uk
web: www.lechene.co.uk
Dir: *Between airport & St Peter Port*
This Victorian manor house is well located for guests wishing to

continued on p648

FOREST, continued

explore Guernsey's spectacular south coast. The building has been skilfully extended to house a range of well-equipped, modern bedrooms. There is a swimming pool, a cosy cellar bar and a varied range of enjoyable freshly cooked dishes at dinner.
ROOMS: 26 en suite (2 fmly) (1 GF) s £30-£52; d £60-£80 (incl. bkfst) **LB FACILITIES:** ª Library Xmas **PARKING:** 20 **NOTES:** ✗ No children 10yrs ⊗ in restaurant

PERELLE Map 24

★★★73% ◉◉ **Atlantique**
Perelle Bay GY7 9NA
☎ 01481 264056 ▤ 01481 263800
e-mail: enquiries@perellebay.com
web: www.perellebay.com
Dir: *from airport, turn right & continue to sea. Turn right & follow coast road for 1.5m*
This modern seaside hotel offers spectacular views of the sea and often, memorable sunsets. Bedrooms vary, those with sea views have balconies, and there are suites suitable for families. L'Atlantique Restaurant has an enviable reputation on the island, and the Victorian bar offers a less formal dining option.
ROOMS: 23 rms (21 en suite) (4 fmly) ⊗ in 12 bedrooms s £46-£65; d £80-£160 (incl. bkfst) **LB FACILITIES:** ª **CONF:** Thtr 40 Class 50 **PARKING:** 80 **NOTES:** ✗ ⊗ in restaurant Closed Nov-Mar

ST MARTIN Map 24

★★★75% ◉ **La Barbarie**
Saints Rd, Saints Bay GY4 6ES
☎ 01481 235217 ▤ 01481 235208
e-mail: reservations@labarbariehotel.com
web: www.labarbariehotel.com
This former priory dates back to the 17th century and retains much of its charm and style. Staff provide a most friendly and attentive environment, and the modern facilities offer guests a relaxing stay. Excellent choices and fresh local ingredients form the basis of the interesting menus in the attractive restaurant and bar.
ROOMS: 22 en suite (4 fmly) (8 GF) ⊗ in all bedrooms
FACILITIES: ª **PARKING:** 50 **NOTES:** ✗ ⊗ in restaurant Closed 30 Oct -10 Mar

★★★★74% **La Trelade**
Forest Rd GY4 6UB
☎ 01481 235454 ▤ 01481 237855
e-mail: latrelade@guernsey.net
web: www.latrelade.co.uk
Dir: *3m from St Peter Port, 1m from airport*
This hotel offers a stylish and versatile range of public areas and an impressive leisure suite. Located close to the airport, La Trelade is an ideal base from which to explore the island, and is equally suitable for business guests. Bedrooms and bathrooms are tastefully decorated and equipped to high standards with modern comforts.
ROOMS: 45 en suite (3 fmly) s £65-£75; d £90-£110 (incl. bkfst) **LB FACILITIES:** STV ⌘ Sauna Gym Xmas **CONF:** Thtr 120 Class 48 Board 40 Del from £75 **SERVICES:** Lift **PARKING:** 80 **NOTES:** ⊗ in restaurant

See advert on opposite page

★★★72% ◉ **Hotel Jerbourg**
Jerbourg Point GY4 6BJ
☎ 01481 238826 ▤ 01481 238238
e-mail: stay@hoteljerbourg.com
Dir: *from airport turn left and follow road to St Martin village, right onto filter road, straight on at lights, hotel at end of road on right*
This hotel boasts excellent sea views from its cliff-top location. Public areas are smartly appointed and include an extensive bar/lounge and bright conservatory-style restaurant. In addition to the fairly extensive carte, a daily-changing menu is available. Bedrooms are well presented and comfortable, and the luxury Bay rooms are generally more spacious.
ROOMS: 32 en suite (4 fmly) (5 GF) ⊗ in all bedrooms s £50-£80; d £75-£150 (incl. bkfst) **FACILITIES:** STV ª **PARKING:** 50 **NOTES:** ✗ ⊗ in restaurant Closed 31 Oct-18 Mar

★★★69% **Green Acres**
Les Hubits GY4 6LS
☎ 01481 235711 ▤ 01481 235978
e-mail: greenacres@guernsey.net
Dir: *from airport, take road to St Martin. Turn off road leading to parish church, continue to hotel*
Quietly located in the leafy lanes of St Martin, this pleasant hotel is ideal as a base for a relaxing break. Bedrooms are comfortable and well equipped, and staff are friendly and attentive. The public areas include a stylish lounge, which opens out onto the terrace pool area. Cuisine offers a choice of menus in different dining areas.
ROOMS: 43 en suite (3 fmly) s £30-£60; d £44-£96 (incl. bkfst) **LB FACILITIES:** ª Xmas **CONF:** Thtr 60 Class 35 Board 25 Del from £34 **PARKING:** 75 **NOTES:** ⊗ in restaurant

★★★68% **Saints Bay Hotel**
Icart Rd GY4 6JG
☎ 01481 238888 ▤ 01481 235558
e-mail: info@saintsbayhotel.com
Dir: *from St Martin village take Saints Rd and turn onto Icart Rd*

Ideally situated in an elevated position near Icart Point headland and above fisherman harbour at Saints Bay with its superb views. The spacious public rooms include a smart lounge bar, a first-floor lounge and a smart conservatory restaurant that overlooks the heated swimming pool. Bedrooms are pleasantly decorated and thoughtfully equipped.
ROOMS: 35 en suite (3 fmly) (13 GF) ⊗ in all bedrooms s £34.50-£74.50; d £48-£128 (incl. bkfst) **LB FACILITIES:** ª **PARKING:** 15 **NOTES:** ✗ ⊗ in restaurant

★★★68% La Villette
GY4 6QG
☎ 01481 235292 📠 01481 237699
e-mail: reservations@lavillettehotel.co.uk
Dir: *turn left out of airport. Follow road past La Trelade Hotel. Take next right, hotel on left*

Set in spacious grounds, this peacefully located, family-run hotel has a friendly atmosphere. The well-equipped bedrooms are spacious and comfortable. Live music is a regular feature in the large bar, while in the separate restaurant a fixed-price menu is provided. Residents have use of the excellent indoor leisure facilities.

ROOMS: 37 en suite (7 fmly) (14 GF) ⊗ in all bedrooms s £39.50-£54; d £68-£92 (incl. bkfst) **FACILITIES:** Solarium Gym Jacuzzi Steam room Petanque Leisure suite Beauty salon hair dressers Xmas **CONF:** Thtr 80 Board 40 **PARKING:** 50 **NOTES:** ⊗ in restaurant

★★74% Hotel La Michele
Les Hubits GY4 6NB
☎ 01481 238065 📠 01481 239492
e-mail: info@lamichelehotel.com
Dir: *approx 1.5m from St Peter Port*

This family-run hotel in a quiet and relaxing location provides a friendly environment and many guests return on a regular basis. Bedrooms are particularly well equipped and comfortable. Public areas include a conservatory and cosy bar, and guests can relax in the well-tended gardens or around the pool.

ROOMS: 16 en suite (3 fmly) (6 GF) ⊗ in all bedrooms s £39-£55; d £78-£110 (incl. bkfst & dinner) **LB FACILITIES:** **PARKING:** 16 **NOTES:** No children 10yrs ⊗ in restaurant Closed Nov-Mar

ST PETER PORT
Map 24

★★★★72% Old Government House Hotel & Spa
Ann's Place GY1 INW
☎ 01481 724921 📠 01481 724429
e-mail: ogh@theoghhotel.co
web: www.theoghhotel.com
Dir: *at junct of St. Julians Ave & College St.*

The affectionately known OGH is one of the island's leading hotels. Bedrooms vary in size but are comfortable and offer high-quality accommodation. The restaurant overlooks the town and neighbouring islands, and offers fine dining, while snacks are available in the Centenary bar. The varied leisure facilities, 'Beauty and The East', are well worth a visit.

ROOMS: 63 en suite (3 fmly) (1 GF) ⊗ in 30 bedrooms s £115-£245; d £125-£255 (incl. bkfst) **LB FACILITIES: Spa** STV Sauna Solarium Gym Jacuzzi Steam room, Eastern treatments, aerobics studio Xmas **CONF:** Thtr 300 Class 180 Board 90 Del from £145 **SERVICES:** Lift **PARKING:** 28 **NOTES:**

See advert on this page

ST PETER PORT, continued

★★★★67% @@ St Pierre Park
Rohais GY1 1FD
☎ 01481 728282 🖷 01481 712041
e-mail: info@stpierreparkhotel.com
Dir: *10 mins from airport. From harbour straight over rdbt, up hill through 3 sets of lights. Right at filter and continue to lights. Straight ahead, hotel 100mtrs on left*

Peacefully located on the outskirts of town amidst 45 acres of grounds featuring a 9-hole golf course. Most of the bedrooms overlook the pleasant gardens and have either a balcony or a terrace. Public areas include a choice of restaurants and a lounge bar that opens onto a spacious terrace with an elegant water feature.
ROOMS: 131 en suite (4 fmly) (20 GF) ⊘ in 17 bedrooms s £100-£150; d £130-£169 (incl. bkfst) **LB** **FACILITIES:** STV ⊠ ⛳ 9 ℚ Snooker Sauna Solarium Gym Putt green Jacuzzi Bird watching, Childrens playground, Crazy golf ♫ ch fac Xmas **CONF:** BC Thtr 300 Class 120 Board 30 Del from £120 **SERVICES:** Lift **PARKING:** 150 **NOTES:** ✗

★★★75% @@ La Fregate
Les Cotils GY1 1UT
☎ 01481 724624 🖷 01481 720443
e-mail: c.sharp@lafregatehotel.com
web: www.lafregatehotel.com
Ask for directions to this charming small hotel, which enjoys splendid views over the town and harbour from its elevated position. Bedrooms are comfortably furnished and well-equipped; many have private balconies. The restaurant is popular with both residents and locals for its carefully cooked meals and formal yet efficient service.
ROOMS: 13 en suite **CONF:** BC Thtr 40 Class 24 Board 22 **PARKING:** 25 **NOTES:** ✗

★★★73% Hotel de Havelet
Havelet GY1 1BA
☎ 01481 722199 🖷 01481 714057
e-mail: havelet@sarniahotels.com
web: www.havelet.sarniahotels.com
Dir: *from airport follow signs for St Peter Port through St. Martins. At bottom of 'Val de Terres' hill turn left into Havelet*
This extended Georgian hotel looks over the harbour to Castle Cornet. Many of the well-equipped bedrooms are set around a pretty colonial-style courtyard. Day rooms in the original building have period elegance; the restaurant and bar are on the other side of the car park in converted stables.
ROOMS: 34 en suite (4 fmly) (8 GF) ⊘ in 8 bedrooms s £48-£100; d £82-£130 (incl. bkfst) **LB** **FACILITIES:** STV ⊠ Sauna Jacuzzi Xmas **CONF:** Thtr 40 Class 24 Board 26 Del from £116 **PARKING:** 40 **NOTES:** ✗

★★★71% The Duke of Richmond
Cambridge Park GY1 1UY
☎ 01481 726221 🖷 01481 728945
e-mail: duke@guernsey.net
web: www.dukeofrichmond.com
Dir: *hotel on corner of Cambridge Park Rd and L'Hyvreuse Ave, opposite leisure centre*

Peacefully located in a predominantly residential area overlooking Cambridge Park, this hotel has comfortable, well-appointed bedrooms that vary in size. Public areas include a spacious lounge, a terrace and the unique Sausmarez Bar, with its nautical theme. The smartly uniformed team of staff provided professional standards of service.
ROOMS: 75 en suite (16 fmly) ⊘ in 35 bedrooms s £60-£75; d £85-£95 (incl. bkfst) **LB** **FACILITIES:** STV ⊰ Leisure centre close to hotel Xmas **CONF:** BC Thtr 150 Class 50 Board 36 Del from £90 **SERVICES:** Lift **PARKING:** 7 **NOTES:** ⊘ in restaurant

★★★70% Moore's
Pollet GY1 1WH
☎ 01481 724452 🖷 01481 714037
e-mail: moores@sarniahotels.com
Dir: *left at airport, follow signs to St Peter Port, Fort Road to seafront, straight on, turn right before rdbt, continue to hotel*
Elegant granite town house situated in the heart of St Peter Port amidst the shops and amenities. Public rooms feature a smart conservatory restaurant, which leads out onto a first floor terrace for alfresco dining; there is also a choice of lounges and bars as well as a patisserie. Bedrooms are pleasantly decorated and thoughtfully equipped.
ROOMS: 46 en suite 3 annexe en suite (8 fmly) ⊘ in 12 bedrooms s £43-£95; d £76-£180 (incl. bkfst) **LB** **FACILITIES:** STV Sauna Solarium Gym Jacuzzi Xmas **CONF:** Thtr 40 Class 20 Board 18 Del from £90 **SERVICES:** Lift **NOTES:** ✗

> Early start?
> Hotels at all star levels should provide in-room alarm clocks and/or alarm clocks

★★62% Duke of Normandie
Lefebvre St GY1 2JP
☎ 01481 721431 🖷 01481 711763
e-mail: dukeofnormandie@cwgsy.net
web: www.dukeofnormandie.com
Dir: *from harbour rdbt St Julians Ave, 3rd left into Anns Place, continue to right, up hill, then left into Lefebvre St, archway entrance on right*
Dating back to the 18th century, this hotel is perfectly located just a short stroll from the harbour and high street. Bedrooms tend to vary in size and comfort. The rooms surround a courtyard that

continued

S

doubles as guest parking. Public areas include the very busy bar, with beams and an open fireplace.

ROOMS: 20 en suite 17 annexe en suite (1 fmly) ⊗ in 13 bedrooms s £37-£44; d £74-£88 (incl. bkfst) **LB** **FACILITIES:** STV Xmas **CONF:** BC Thtr 40 Class 30 Board 20 Del from £62 **PARKING:** 15 **NOTES:** ✕ ⊗ in restaurant

VALE
Map 24

★★★63% Peninsula
Les Dicqs GY6 8JP
☎ 01481 248400 🖷 01481 248706
e-mail: peninsula@guernsey.net
Dir: *Coast Rd, Grand Havre Bay*
Adjacent to the sandy beach and set in five acres of grounds, this modern hotel provides comfortable accommodation. Bedrooms have an additional sofa bed to suit families and good workspace for the business traveller. Both fixed-price and carte menus are served in the restaurant, or guests can eat informally in the bar.
ROOMS: 99 en suite (99 fmly) (25 GF) ⊗ in 38 bedrooms s £55-£69; d £90-£118 (incl. bkfst) **LB** **FACILITIES:** STV ⛵ Putt green Petanque Playground ♫ Xmas **CONF:** Thtr 250 Class 140 Board 105 Del from £80 **SERVICES:** Lift **PARKING:** 120 **NOTES:** ✕ ⊗ in restaurant

Popped the question? Hotels with Civ wed in their entry are licensed for civil wedding ceremonies. Maximum numbers for the ceremony only are shown e.g. Civ wed 120

HERM
Map 24

★★★70% ® White House
GY1 3HR
☎ 01481 722159 🖷 01481 710066
e-mail: hotel@herm-island.com
web: www.herm-island.com

Enjoying a unique island setting, this attractive hotel is just a 20 minutes from Guernsey by sea. Set in well-tended gardens, the hotel offers neatly decorated bedrooms, located in either the main house or adjacent cottages; the majority of rooms have sea views. Guests can relax in one of several lounges, enjoy a drink in one of two bars and choose from two dining options.
ROOMS: 17 en suite 23 annexe en suite (23 fmly) (7 GF) s £70-£108; d £140-£210 (incl. bkfst & dinner) **LB** **FACILITIES:** no TV in bdrms ⛵ 🎾 ⛳ Fishing trips, Yacht & Motor boat charters **CONF:** Board 10 **NOTES:** ✕ ⊗ in restaurant 2 Apr-2 Oct

JERSEY

GOREY
Map 24

★★★69% Old Court House
JE3 9FS
☎ 01534 854444 🖷 01534 853587
e-mail: ochhotel@itl.net
Situated on the east of the island, a short walk from the beach, this long established hotel continues to have a loyal following for its relaxed atmosphere and friendly staff. Bedrooms are of similar standard throughout and some have balconies overlooking the gardens. Spacious public areas include a restaurant, a large bar with a dance floor and a comfortable, quiet lounge.
ROOMS: 58 en suite (4 fmly) (9 GF) s £45-£61.50; d £90-£135 (incl. bkfst) **FACILITIES:** STV ⛵ Sauna **SERVICES:** Lift **PARKING:** 40 **NOTES:** ⊗ in restaurant Closed Nov-Mar

★★★68% The Moorings
Gorey Pier JE3 6EW
☎ 01534 853633 🖷 01534 857618
e-mail: reservations@themooringshotel.com
web: www.themooringshotel.com
Dir: *at foot of Mont Orgueil Castle*
Enjoying an enviable position by the harbour, the heart of this hotel is the restaurant where a selection of menus offers an extensive choice of dishes. Other public areas include two bars and a comfortable first-floor residents' lounge. Bedrooms at the front have a fine view of the harbour; three have access to a balcony. A small sun terrace at the back of the hotel is available to guests.
ROOMS: 15 en suite s £47-£64; d £94-£128 (incl. bkfst) **LB** **FACILITIES:** STV Xmas **CONF:** Thtr 20 Class 20 Board 20 **NOTES:** ✕

ROZEL Map 24

Top Hotel

★★★ ⚜🅰🅼 **Château la Chaire**
Rozel Bay JE3 6AJ
☎ 01534 863354 🗎 01534 865137
e-mail: res@chateau-la-chaire.co.uk
web: www.chateau-la-chaire.co.uk
Dir: from St Helier on B38 turn left in village by the Rozel Bay Inn, hotel 100yds on right
Built as a gentleman's residence in 1843, Château la Chaire is a haven of peace and tranquillity, set within a secluded wooded valley. Picturesque Rozel Harbour is within easy walking distance and the house is surrounded by terraced gardens. There is a wonderful atmosphere here and the helpful staff deliver high standards of guest care. Imaginative menus, making best use of local produce, are served in the oak-panelled dining room. Bedrooms are purposely varied, with a range of different sizes and styles available.
ROOMS: 14 en suite (2 fmly) (1 GF) ⊛ in 3 bedrooms s £99-£104; d £112-£132 (incl. bkfst) LB **FACILITIES:** STV Xmas **CONF:** Thtr 20 Class 20 Board 20 Del from £145 **PARKING:** 30 **NOTES:** No children 7yrs ⊛ in restaurant Civ Wed 30

ST AUBIN Map 24

★★★74% ⚜⚜ **Somerville**
Mont du Boulevard JE3 8AD
☎ 01534 741226 🗎 01534 746621
e-mail: somerville@dolanhotels.com
web: www.dolanhotels.com
Dir: from village, follow harbour then take Mont du Boulevard and 2nd right bend

Enjoying spectacular views of St Aubin's Bay, this friendly hotel is very
continued

popular. Bedrooms vary in style and a number of superior rooms offer higher levels of luxury. Public areas are smartly presented and include a spacious bar-lounge and elegant dining room, both of which take full advantage of the hotel's enviable views.
ROOMS: 59 en suite (7 fmly) (4 GF) s £41-£70; d £82-£140 (incl. bkfst) **FACILITIES:** STV ⅂ ♫ Xmas **CONF:** Thtr 40 Class 25 Board 30 **SERVICES:** Lift **PARKING:** 26 **NOTES:** ✈ No children 4yrs ⊛ in restaurant

See advert on opposite page

ST BRELADE Map 24

Top Hotel

★★★★ ⚜⚜⚜ **The Atlantic**
Le Mont de la Pulente JE3 8HE
☎ 01534 744101 🗎 01534 744102
e-mail: info@theatlantichotel.com
Dir: from Petit Port turn right into Rue de la Sergente & right again, hotel signed
Adjoining the manicured fairways of La Moye championship golf course, this hotel enjoys a peaceful setting with breathtaking views over St Ouen's Bay. Stylish bedrooms look out over the course or the sea and offer a blend of high quality and reassuring comfort. An air of understated luxury is apparent throughout, and the attentive service achieves the perfect balance of friendliness and professionalism. The refurbished Ocean restaurant offers sophisticated, modern surroundings in which to enjoy some highly accomplished cooking.
ROOMS: 50 en suite (8 GF) s £145-£160; d £190-£225 (incl. bkfst) LB **FACILITIES:** STV ☒ supervised ⅂ ♖ Sauna Solarium Gym Jacuzzi ♫ Xmas **CONF:** Thtr 60 Class 40 Board 20 **SERVICES:** Lift **PARKING:** 60 **NOTES:** ✈ ⊛ in restaurant Closed 2 Jan-2 Feb

GF indicates the number of bedrooms at ground level

★★★★78% ⚜⚜ **Hotel L'Horizon**
St Brelade's Bay JE3 8EF
☎ 01534 743101 🗎 01534 746269
e-mail: lhorizon@handpicked.co.uk
web: www.handpicked.co.uk
Dir: 3m from airport. 6m from harbour
A combination of a truly wonderful setting on the golden sands of St Brelade's Bay, a relaxed atmosphere and excellent facilities is the winning formula here. The bedrooms have all been stylishly decorated and are equipped with modern comforts and thoughtful
continued on p654

ST BRELADE, continued

touches. Public areas are spacious and bright and include a leisure club and a choice of eating options, including the more formal Grill.

Hotel L'Horizon, St Brelade

ROOMS: 106 en suite (7 fmly) (15 GF) s £115-£155; d £230-£280 (incl. bkfst) **LB FACILITIES:** STV ☒ Sauna Gym Jacuzzi Windsurfing Water skiing Treatment rooms ♫ Xmas **CONF:** Thtr 250 Class 100 Board 50 **SERVICES:** Lift **PARKING:** 125 **NOTES:** ✲ Civ Wed

See advert on page 653

★★★★74% **St Brelade's Bay Hotel**
JE3 8EF
☎ 01534 746141 ᐧ 01534 747278
e-mail: info@stbreladesbayhotel.com
web: www.stbreladesbayhotel.com
Dir: SW corner of the island

This family hotel overlooking St Brelade's Bay has many loyal guests and members of staff. The attractive tiered gardens and grounds are ablaze with colour during summer. In addition to easy beach access and an extensive range of indoor and outdoor recreational facilities, there is a choice of pools. Most bedrooms have king-size beds, and many have a children's room within the unit. Morning and afternoon tea are included in the tariff.
ROOMS: 72 en suite (50 fmly) s £75-£114; d £110-£188 (incl. bkfst) **LB FACILITIES:** STV ⚲ supervised ⚲ Snooker Sauna Gym ♫♫ Putt green Petanque, Mini-gym, Games room, Table tennis ♫ ch fac **CONF:** Thtr 20 Board 12 Del from £125 **SERVICES:** Lift **PARKING:** 60 **NOTES:** ✲ ⊗ in restaurant Closed 3 Oct-21 Apr

★★★★66% ⊛ **Hotel La Place**
Route du Coin, La Haule JE3 8BT
☎ 01534 744261 ᐧ 01534 745164
e-mail: reservations@hotellaplacejersey.com
web: www.hotellaplacejersey.com
Dir: off main St Helier/St Aubin coast road at La Haule Manor (B25). Up hill, 2nd left (to Redhouses), 1st right. Hotel is 100mtrs on right
Developed around a 17th-century farmhouse, this friendly hotel is
continued

well placed for exploration of the island. A range of bedroom types is provided, some rooms have private patios and direct access to the sheltered pool area. The stylish cocktail bar is popular for pre-dinner drinks and a more traditional lounge is available. An interesting menu is offered, making good use of local produce.

ROOMS: 42 en suite (1 fmly) (10 GF) ⊗ in 25 bedrooms s £65-£98; d £60-£121 (incl. bkfst) **LB FACILITIES:** STV ⚲ Sauna Discount at Les Ormes Country Club, including golf, gym & indoor tennis Xmas **CONF:** Thtr 100 Class 40 Board 40 Del from £135 **PARKING:** 100 **NOTES:** ⊗ in restaurant Civ Wed 100

See advert on opposite page

★★★71% **Golden Sands**
St Brelade's Bay JE3 8EF
☎ 01534 741241 ᐧ 01534 499366
e-mail: goldensands@dolanhotels.com
web: www.dolanhotels.com
Dir: follow signs to St Brelade's Bay. Hotel on coast side of road

With direct access to the beach, this popular hotel overlooks the wonderful sandy expanse of St Brelade's Bay. Many of the comfortable bedrooms are sea-facing with balconies, where guests can relax and look out to sea. Public areas include a lounge, bar and restaurant – all have bay views.
ROOMS: 62 en suite (5 fmly) s £68-£117; d £76-£146 (incl. bkfst) **FACILITIES:** STV Childrens play room ♫ **SERVICES:** Lift **NOTES:** ✲ ⊗ in restaurant Closed Nov-mid Apr

See advert on page 653

★★72% **Beau Rivage**
St Brelade's Bay JE3 8EF
☎ 01534 745983 ᐧ 01534 747127
e-mail: beau@jerseyweb.demon.co.uk
web: www.jersey.co.uk/hotels/beau
Dir: sea side of coast road in centre of St Brelade's Bay, 1.5m S of airport
With direct access to one of Jersey's most popular beaches, residents and non-residents are welcome to this hotel's bar and terrace. Most of the well-equipped bedrooms have wonderful sea
continued

views, some the bonus of balconies. Residents have a choice of lounges, plus a sun deck exclusively for their use. Between daily set menus and an extensive carte, a range of dishes featuring English and Continental cuisine is available each evening.
ROOMS: 27 en suite (9 fmly) ⊗ in 1 bedroom s £50-£87; d £66-£140 (incl. bkfst) **LB FACILITIES:** STV Sunbathing terrace, Games Room **SERVICES:** Lift **PARKING:** 16 **NOTES:** ⊗ in restaurant RS Nov-Mar Civ Wed 80

ST HELIER Map 24

★★★★71% *De Vere Grand Jersey*

The Esplanade JE4 8WD
☎ 01534 722301 01534 737815
e-mail: grand.jersey@devere-hotels.com
web: www.devereonline.co.uk

A local landmark located on The Esplanade with the bustling streets of St Helier to the rear and pleasant views across St Aubin's Bay to the front. Bedrooms have a variety of styles, some with their own balcony. Guests can also enjoy spacious public areas, many of which look onto the bay. A full range of indoor leisure is available including pool, sauna, steam room, gym and many health and beauty treatments.
ROOMS: 118 en suite (7 GF) ⊗ in 22 bedrooms **FACILITIES: Spa** STV supervised Snooker Sauna Solarium Gym Jacuzzi Beauty therapy, Hairdressing **CONF:** Thtr 200 Class 100 Board 80 **SERVICES:** Lift **PARKING:** 27 **NOTES:** ⊗ in restaurant Civ Wed

★★★★67% Pomme d'Or

Liberation Square JE1 3UF
☎ 01534 880110 01534 737781
e-mail: enquiries@pommedorhotel.com
Dir: *opposite harbour*

This historic hotel overlooks Liberation Square and the marina and offers comfortably furnished, well-equipped bedrooms. Popular with business fraternity, a range of conference facilities and meeting rooms are available. Dining options include the traditional fine dining of the 'Petite Pomme', the smart carvery restaurant or the informal coffee shop.
ROOMS: 143 en suite (3 fmly) ⊗ in 105 bedrooms s £74-£104; d £108-£168 (incl. bkfst) **LB FACILITIES:** STV Use of Aquadome at Merton Hotel Xmas **CONF:** Thtr 220 Class 100 Board 50 Del from £125 **SERVICES:** Lift air con **NOTES:**

★★★67% Apollo

St Saviours Rd JE2 4GJ
☎ 01534 725441 01534 722120
e-mail: reservations@huggler.com
web: www.huggler.com
Dir: *on St Saviours Road at its junct with La Motte Street*

Centrally located, this popular hotel has a relaxed, informal atmosphere. Bedrooms are comfortably furnished and include

continued

useful extras. Many guests return regularly to enjoy the variety of leisure facilities including an outdoor pool with water slide. The elegant cocktail bar is an ideal place for a pre-dinner drink.

Apollo Hotel, St Helier

ROOMS: 85 en suite (5 fmly) ⊗ in 20 bedrooms d £76-£116 (incl. bkfst) **LB FACILITIES:** supervised supervised Sauna Solarium Gym Jacuzzi Xmas **CONF:** Thtr 150 Class 100 Board 80 **SERVICES:** Lift **PARKING:** 50 **NOTES:**

★★★67% Royal

David Place JE2 4TD
☎ 01534 726521 01534 811046
e-mail: enquiries@royalhoteljersey.com
web: www.royalhoteljersey.com
Dir: *follow signs for Ring Rd, pass Queen Victoria rdbt keep left, left at lights, left into Piersons Rd. Follow one-way system to Cheapside, Rouge Bouillon, at A14 turn to Midvale Rd, hotel on left*

This long established hotel is located in the centre of town and is

continued on p656

ST HELIER, continued

within easy walking distance of the business district and shops. It provides individual bedrooms and a range of public areas. The hotel has the new dining option Seasons, bar and restaurant and also boasts extensive conference facilities.

Royal Hotel, St Helier

ROOMS: 88 en suite (39 fmly) ⊘ in 16 bedrooms s £65-£87.50; d £95-£130 (incl. bkfst) **LB** **FACILITIES:** STV ♫ Xmas **CONF:** BC Thtr 400 Class 120 Board 80 Del from £125 **SERVICES:** Lift **PARKING:** 15 **NOTES:** Civ Wed 80

See advert on opposite page

★★★64% Royal Yacht

The Weighbridge JE2 3NF
☎ 01534 720511 01534 767729
e-mail: theroyalyacht@mail.com
Dir: *in town centre, opp the Marina and harbour, 0.5m from beach*

Overlooking the marina and steam clock, the Royal Yacht is thought to be the oldest established hotel on the island. Bedrooms are generally spacious, soundproofed and thoughtfully equipped. There is something for everyone here - popular bars with a disco at weekends and a choice of dining options, the traditional grill room, bar carvery, and the restaurant more quietly situated on the first floor.
ROOMS: 45 en suite **FACILITIES:** STV ♫ Xmas **CONF:** Thtr 80 Class 20 Board 20 **SERVICES:** Lift **NOTES:** Civ Wed 100

U ◎◎◎ The Club Hotel & Spa

Green St JE2 4UH
☎ 01534 876500 01534 720371
e-mail: reservations@theclubjersey.com
web: www.theclubjersey.com
Dir: *5 mins walk from main shopping centre*
At the time of going to press this newly developed town house property was due to re-open and the AA star classification had not been confirmed. The 38 guest rooms and 8 suites will include power showers and state-of-the-art technology including widescreen LCD TV, DVD and CD systems. The choice of restaurants includes Bohemia, a sophisticated eating option that continues to offer highly accomplished cooking. Please refer to the AA internet site www.theAA.com for current information.
ROOMS: 46 en suite (4 fmly) (4 GF) ⊘ in 39 bedrooms s £195; d £195-£375 (incl. bkfst) **LB** **FACILITIES: Spa** STV supervised supervised Sauna Xmas **CONF:** BC Thtr 30 Class 20 Board 14 **SERVICES:** Lift air con **PARKING:** 30 **NOTES:** ⊘ in restaurant

ST LAWRENCE

Map 24

★★★71% Hotel Cristina

Mont Feland JE3 1JA
☎ 01534 758024 01534 758028
e-mail: cristina@dolanhotels.com
web: www.dolanhotels.com
Dir: *turn off A10 onto Mont Felard, hotel on left*

This hotel has been almost totally transformed in the recent past and new bedrooms are smartly styled and comfortable. Public areas reflect a contemporary style that makes this a refreshingly different hotel, with the modern restaurant serving a range of fresh produce in a bistro-like atmosphere. The terrace is adorned with flowers and is a popular place for soaking up the sun.
ROOMS: 63 en suite (3 fmly) s £68-£99; d £76-£110 (incl. bkfst) **LB** **FACILITIES:** STV Off peak membership to Les Ormes Golf/Leisure Club ♫ **CONF:** Thtr 100 Class 70 **PARKING:** 60 **NOTES:** ⊘ in restaurant Closed Nov-Mar

See advert on page 653

ST MARY

Map 24

★★67% West View

La Grande Rue JE3 3BD
☎ 01534 481643 01534 483283
e-mail: westview@jerseymail.co.uk
web: www.westviewhoteljersey.com
Dir: *N of island, at junct of B33 & C103, rear of St Mary's village*
Located in the quiet parish of St. Mary and close to the delightful walks and cycle routes of the north coast. Bedrooms here are well equipped especially the larger, superior rooms. Entertainment is provided in the lounge bar during the summer months when guests can also enjoy a swim in the heated outdoor pool.
ROOMS: 42 en suite (3 fmly) (18 GF) s £26-£53; d £46-£82 (incl. bkfst) **FACILITIES:** Xmas **PARKING:** 38 **NOTES:** ⊘ in restaurant Closed 2 Jan-10 Mar

⊘ No smoking

ST SAVIOUR

Map 24

Top Hotel

★★★★ @@@ **Longueville Manor**

JE2 7WF
☎ 01534 725501 01534 731613
e-mail: info@longuevillemanor.com
web: www.longuevillemanor.com

Dir: *A3 E from St Helier towards Gorey. Hotel 1m on left*

Dating back to the 13th century, there is something very special about Longueville, which is why so many guests return here. It is set in 17 acres of grounds, that include woodland walks, a spectacular rose garden and a lake. Bedrooms have great style and individuality, with fresh flowers, fine embroidered bed linen and plenty of extras. The committed team of staff create a welcoming atmosphere and every effort is made to ensure a memorable stay. The accomplished cuisine is a real delight.

ROOMS: 29 en suite 1 annexe en suite (7 GF) s £175-£190; d £210-£240 (incl. bkfst) **LB** **FACILITIES:** STV Xmas **CONF:** Thtr 45 Class 30 Board 30 Del from £245 **SERVICES:** Lift **PARKING:** 40 **NOTES:** Civ Wed 40

TRINITY

Map 24

★★★72% **Highfield Country**

Route d'Ebenezer JE3 5DT
☎ 01534 862194 01534 865342
e-mail: reservations@highfieldjersey.com
web: www.highfieldjersey.com

Dir: *on A8 next to Ebenezer Chapel*

Rurally located, this family-friendly hotel offers spacious, comfortable bedrooms, some with kitchenette. Public areas are light and attractively styled, with the conservatory a popular venue for pre-dinner drinks. Leisure facilities include indoor and outdoor pools, and a sauna. A varied menu is provided at dinner, and breakfast is a self-service buffet.

ROOMS: 38 en suite (32 fmly) (1 GF) in all bedrooms s £54-£63; d £94-£114 (incl. dinner) **LB** **FACILITIES:** **Spa** Sauna Gym Petanque ch fac **SERVICES:** Lift **PARKING:** 41 **NOTES:** in restaurant Closed Dec-Mar

Destination dining!
This symbol indicates a Restaurant with Rooms

S

TRINITY, continued

★★★71% Water's Edge

Bouley Bay JE3 5AS
☎ 01534 862777 Fax 01534 863645
e-mail: www.watersedgehotel.co.je
web: mail@watersedgehotel.co.je

Set in the tranquil surroundings of Bouley Bay on Jersey's north coast, this hotel is exactly as its name conveys and offers breathtaking views. Many of the bedrooms offer especially high standards of quality and comfort. Dining options include the relaxed atmosphere of the adjoining Black Dog bar or the more formal award-winning restaurant.

ROOMS: 50 en suite (3 fmly) s £40-£61; d £80-£122 (incl. bkfst) **LB**
FACILITIES: ♫ **CONF:** Thtr 30 Class 25 Board 20 Del from £65
SERVICES: Lift **PARKING:** 20 **NOTES:** ⊗ in restaurant Closed 17 Oct-17 Apr Civ Wed 80

T

Isle of Man

Directory of establishments in alphabetical order of location.

DOUGLAS

Map 24 SC37

★★★★72% Sefton

Harris Promenade IM1 2RW
☎ 01624 645500 📠 01624 676004
e-mail: info@seftonhotel.co.im
web: www.seftonhotel.co.im
Dir: *500yds from Ferry Dock on Douglas promenade*

This Victorian hotel has been sympathetically extended and upgraded over the years. Many of the spacious and comfortably furnished bedrooms have balconies overlooking the atrium water garden, while others enjoy sweeping views across the bay. A choice of comfortable lounges is available and freshly prepared dishes are served in the informal Gallery restaurant.
ROOMS: 96 en suite ⊗ in 36 bedrooms s £80-£100; d £95-£115 (incl. bkfst) **LB** **FACILITIES: Spa** STV Sauna Solarium Gym Jacuzzi Cycle hire, Steam room, Atrium water garden, Library **CONF:** BC Thtr 100 Class 30 Board 20 Del from £150 **SERVICES:** Lift **PARKING:** 44 **NOTES:** No dogs No children ⊗ in restaurant

★★★★70% Mount Murray

Santon IM4 2HT
☎ 01624 661111 📠 01624 611116
e-mail: hotel@mountmurray.com
web: www.mountmurray.com
Dir: *4m from Douglas towards airport. Hotel signed at Santon*

This large, modern hotel and country club offers a wide range of sporting and leisure facilities, and a superb health and beauty salon. The attractively appointed public areas give a choice of bars and eating options. The spacious bedrooms are well equipped and

continued

many enjoy fine views over the 200-acre grounds and golf course. There is a very large conference suite.
ROOMS: 90 en suite (4 fmly) (28 GF) ⊗ in 12 bedrooms s £60.50-£93; d £81.50-£115.50 (incl. bkfst) **FACILITIES: Spa** STV Indoor pool Golf 18 Squash Sauna Solarium Gym Putt green Jacuzzi Bowling green, Driving range, Sports hall, Squash courts Xmas **CONF:** Thtr 300 Class 200 Board 100 Del from £125 **SERVICES:** Lift **PARKING:** 400 **NOTES:** No dogs ⊗ in restaurant

> Popped the question? Hotels with Civ wed in their entry are licensed for civil wedding ceremonies. Maximum numbers for the ceremony only are shown e.g. Civ wed 120

★★★70% *Empress*

Central Promenade IM2 4RA
☎ 01624 661155 📠 01624 673554
e-mail: empresshotel@manx.net
web: www.theempresshotel.net
This hotel is a large Victorian building on the central promenade, overlooking Douglas Bay. Well-equipped, modern bedrooms include suites, and rooms with sea views. A pianist entertains in

continued on p660

DOUGLAS, continued

the lounge bar most evenings. Other facilities available include a lounge, a sun lounge and a brasserie-style restaurant.

Empress, Douglas

ROOMS: 102 en suite ⊗ in 6 bedrooms **FACILITIES:** STV Sauna Solarium Gym Jacuzzi ♫ **CONF:** BC Thtr 200 Class 150 Board 50 **SERVICES:** Lift **NOTES:**

See advert on page 659

★★★69% Welbeck Hotel

13/15 Mona Dr IM2 4LF
☎ 01624 675663 01624 661545
e-mail: mail@welbeckhotel.com
Dir: *at crossroads of Mona & Empress Drive off Central Promenade*
The Welbeck is a privately owned and personally run hotel situated within easy reach of the seafront. It offers guests a friendly welcome and a choice of attractive accommodation, ranging from well-equipped bedrooms to six luxury apartments, each with its own lounge and small kitchen. Other facilities include two rooms for meetings and functions, plus a mini-gym and steam room.
ROOMS: 27 en suite (7 fmly) **FACILITIES:** STV Gym Steam room **CONF:** BC Thtr 50 Class 30 Board 30 Del from £50 **SERVICES:** Lift **NOTES:** ⊗ in restaurant Closed 19 Dec-5 Jan

PEEL Map 24 SC28

★★70% Ballacallin House

Dalby Village, Patrick IM5 3BT
☎ 01624 841100 01624 845055
e-mail: ballacallin@advsys.co.uk
web: www.ballacallin.com
Dir: *A27 Peel to Port Erin Rd at S end of Dalby Village*
This small, privately owned hotel situated in Dalby village is personally run and offers well-equipped, modern accommodation of a very good standard. Bedrooms with four-posters and a two-bedroom suite are available. Sea views can be enjoyed from some of the bedrooms, the bright restaurant and the spacious lounge bar.
ROOMS: 10 en suite (1 fmly) ⊗ in all bedrooms s £40-£50; d £70-£80 (incl. bkfst) **LB** **FACILITIES:** Xmas **CONF:** Thtr 30 Class 24 Board 24 Del from £89.95 **PARKING:** 70 **NOTES:** ⊗ in restaurant Closed 5-25 Jan

PORT ERIN Map 24 SC16

★★★67% Ocean Castle

The Promenade IM9 6LH
☎ 01624 836399 01624 836537
e-mail: oceancastle@btinternet.com
web: www.oceancastle.co.uk
Dir: *from airport follow signs to Port Erin, turn right following coast road. Hotel halfway up hill on right*
This hotel is set overlooking the harbour, with spacious bedrooms enjoying views over the bay. It offers a choice of restaurants at weekends, with a combination of local menus with a French twist. A large function room is ideal for conference guests as well as those enjoying a family party.
ROOMS: 40 en suite (2 fmly) s £36; d £72 (incl. bkfst) **LB** **FACILITIES:** STV Ballroom ♫ **CONF:** Thtr 200 Class 150 Board 100 **SERVICES:** Lift **NOTES:** ⊗ in restaurant Closed Nov - before Easter

★★67% Falcon's Nest

The Promenade IM9 6AF
☎ 01624 834077 01624 835370
e-mail: falconsnest@enterprise.net
web: www.falconsnesthotel.co.uk
Dir: *follow coastal road, S from airport or ferry. Hotel on seafront, immediately after steam railway station*

Situated overlooking the bay and harbour, this Victorian hotel offers generally spacious bedrooms. There is a choice of bars, one of which attracts many locals. Meals can be taken in the lounge bar, the new conservatory or in the attractively decorated main restaurant.
ROOMS: 35 en suite (9 fmly) ⊗ in 3 bedrooms d £70-£85 (incl. bkfst) **LB** **FACILITIES:** STV **CONF:** Thtr 50 Class 50 Board 50 **PARKING:** 40 **NOTES:** ⊗ in restaurant

Late for dinner? Quality standards mean that last orders for dinner vary according to star rating and should be no earlier than: ★★ 7.00pm ★★★ 8:00pm ★★★★ 9:00pm ★★★★★ 10:00pm

Scotland

Hotel of the Year for Scotland

Glenapp Castle

Ballantrae, South Ayrshire

★★★

ABERDEEN, Aberdeen City Map 23 NJ90

See also Aberdeen Airport

A

★★★★78% The Marcliffe at Pitfodels

North Deeside Rd AB15 9YA

☎ 01224 861000 ▯ 01224 868860

e-mail: enquiries@marcliffe.com

web: www.marcliffe.com

Dir: *turn off A90 onto A93 signed Braemar. 1m on right after turn at lights*

Set in attractive landscaped grounds west of the city, this impressive hotel presents a blend of styles backed by caring and attentive service. A split-level conservatory restaurant, terraces and courtyards all give a sense of the Mediterranean, whilst the elegant and sophisticated cocktail lounge is classical in style. Bedrooms are well proportioned and thoughtfully equipped.

ROOMS: 42 en suite (4 fmly) (12 GF) ⊗ in 26 bedrooms s £120-£325; d £130-£325 (incl. bkfst) **LB FACILITIES: Spa** STV Snooker Sauna Gym ⛳ Putt green No other Xmas **CONF:** BC Thtr 500 Class 300 Board 84 Del from £190 **SERVICES:** Lift **PARKING:** 222 **NOTES:** ⊗ in restaurant Civ Wed 450

See advert on opposite page

★★★★73% ® Ardoe House

South Deeside Rd, Blairs AB12 5YP

☎ 01224 860600 ▯ 01224 861283

e-mail: ardoe@macdonald-hotels.co.uk

web: www.macdonald-hotels.co.uk

Dir: *4m W of city off B9077*

From its elevated position on the banks of the River Dee, this baronial-style mansion commands excellent countryside views. Tastefully decorated, thoughtfully equipped bedrooms are located in the main house, or more modern extension. Public rooms include a spa and leisure club, a cosy lounge and cocktail bar and impressive function facilities.

ROOMS: 109 en suite (4 fmly) ⊗ in 86 bedrooms s £88-£150; d £99-£275 (incl. bkfst) **LB FACILITIES:** STV ▯ supervised ◔ Sauna Solarium Gym Jacuzzi Xmas **CONF:** Thtr 500 Class 200 Board 150 **SERVICES:** Lift **PARKING:** 250 **NOTES:** ⊗ in restaurant

★★★★70% ® Norwood Hall

Garthdee Rd, Cults AB15 9FX

☎ 01224 868951 ▯ 01224 869868

e-mail: info@norwood-hall.co.uk

web: www.norwood-hall.co.uk

Dir: *off A90, at 1st rdbt cross Bridge of Dee and turn left at rdbt onto Garthdee Rd (B&Q and Sainsbury on left) continue to hotel sign*

This imposing Victorian mansion has retained many of its features, most notably the fine oak staircase, stained glass and ornately decorated walls and ceilings. Accommodation comes in different styles. The extensive grounds ensure the hotel is a popular wedding venue.

ROOMS: 37 en suite (3 fmly) ⊗ in 15 bedrooms s £70-£145; d £90-£165 (incl. bkfst) **LB FACILITIES:** STV Xmas **CONF:** Thtr 200 Class 100 Board 70 Del from £150 **SERVICES:** Lift **PARKING:** 100 **NOTES:** ✈ ⊗ in restaurant Civ Wed 150

★★★★68% Aberdeen Patio

Beach Boulevard AB24 5EF

☎ 01224 633339 & 380000 ▯ 01224 638833

e-mail: info@patiohotels.com web: www.patiohotels.com

Dir: *from A90 follow signs for city centre, then for sea. On Beach Blvd, turn left at lights, hotel on right*

This modern, purpose-built hotel lies close to the seafront. Bedrooms come in two different styles - retro-style standard ones and spacious classical Premier Club rooms. A new building with 46 high spec bedrooms, its own bar, lounge and breakfast room opens in the autumn of 2005. The restaurant and striking Atrium bar is housed in the main building.

ROOMS: 124 en suite (8 fmly) (10 GF) ⊗ in 93 bedrooms s £48-£125; d £65-£135 (incl. bkfst) **LB FACILITIES:** STV ▯ supervised Sauna Solarium Gym Jacuzzi Steam room, Treatment Room Xmas **CONF:** Thtr 150 Class 80 Board 50 Del from £81 **SERVICES:** Lift **PARKING:** 196 **NOTES:** ⊗ in restaurant

★★★★66% ®® Copthorne Hotel Aberdeen

COPTHORNE

122 Huntly St AB10 1SU

☎ 01224 630404 ▯ 01224 640573

e-mail: reservations.aberdeen@mill-cop.com

web: www.copthorne.com/aberdeen

Dir: *W of city centre, off Union Street, up Rose Street, hotel 0.25m on right on corner with Huntly Street*

Situated just out of the city centre, this hotel offers friendly, attentive service. The smart bedrooms are well proportioned and guests will appreciate the added quality of the Connoisseur rooms. Mac's bar provides a relaxed atmosphere in which to enjoy a drink or to dine informally, whilst Poachers Restaurant offers a fine dining experience.

ROOMS: 89 en suite (15 fmly) ⊗ in 37 bedrooms s £49-£205; d £49-£205 **LB FACILITIES:** STV **CONF:** Thtr 200 Class 100 Board 70 Del from £99 **SERVICES:** Lift **PARKING:** 15 **NOTES:** RS 25-26 Dec Civ Wed 150

★★★75% **Atholl**

54 Kings Gate AB15 4YN
☎ 01224 323505 📠 01224 321555
e-mail: info@atholl-aberdeen.co.uk
web: www.atholl-aberdeen.com
Dir: *in West End 400yds from Anderson Drive, the main ring road*

A high level of hospitality and guest care are features of this hotel, set in the suburbs within easy reach of central amenities and the ring road. The stylish modern bedrooms include free broadband internet access. Guests can choose between the restaurant and bar to enjoy the dinner menu.
ROOMS: 34 en suite (1 fmly) ⊗ in all bedrooms s £50-£100; d £70-£150 (incl. bkfst) **LB** **FACILITIES:** STV **CONF:** Thtr 60 Class 25 Board 25 Del £150 **PARKING:** 60 **NOTES:** ✗ ⊗ in restaurant Closed 01-Jan

★★★71% **Queens Hotel**

51-53 Queens Rd AB15 4YP
☎ 01224 209999 📠 01224 209009
e-mail: enquiries@the-queens-hotel.com
web: www.the-queens-hotel.com
Dir: *Turn off A90 from Anderson Drive at Queens Rd, hotel is 400yds on right. From city centre take West End exit*

This well-established hotel, located a short drive from the city centre, is popular with both business travellers and for functions. Public areas include a welcoming lounge and a traditionally styled bar, where the restaurant menu is also available. The well-equipped bedrooms, many of which are spacious are in the original house and the wing.
ROOMS: 32 en suite 2 annexe en suite (6 fmly) (10 GF) ⊗ in 12 bedrooms s £45-£120; d £55-£140 (incl. bkfst) **FACILITIES:** STV **CONF:** Thtr 400 Class 150 Board 60 Del from £130 **PARKING:** 80 **NOTES:** ✗ ⊗ in restaurant Closed 25-26 Dec & 1-2 Jan

ABERDEEN, continued

★★★70% The Craighaar
Waterton Rd, Bucksburn AB21 9HS
☎ 01224 712275 🖷 01224 716362
e-mail: info@craighaar.co.uk
Dir: *turn off A96 (Airport/Inverness) onto A947, hotel signed*
Conveniently located for the airport, this welcoming hotel is a popular base for business people and tourists alike. Guests can make use of a quiet library/lounge, and enjoy meals in the bar or restaurant. Bedrooms are well equipped and a wing of luxury duplex suites provide additional comfort and facilities.
ROOMS: 55 en suite (6 fmly) (18 GF) ⊗ in 12 bedrooms s £45-£119; d £59-£129 (incl. bkfst) **LB** **FACILITIES:** STV Hotel Library **CONF:** BC Thtr 90 Class 33 Board 30 Del £110 **PARKING:** 80 **NOTES:** 🐕 Closed 26 Dec & 1-2 Jan Civ Wed 50

★★★70% The Mariner Hotel
349 Great Western Rd AB10 6NW
☎ 01224 588901 🖷 01224 571621
e-mail: info@themarinerhotel.co.uk
Dir: *E off Anderson Drive at Great Western Rd. Hotel on right on corner of Gray St*
This superbly maintained and good value hotel is conveniently located close to the city centre and forms a natural base for both business and leisure guests. The modern, spacious bedrooms are well equipped and particularly comfortable, with executive suites available. The public rooms sympathetically reflect the hotel's nautical title. The Atlantis restaurant showcases the region's reputation for excellent game and seafood.
ROOMS: 17 en suite 8 annexe en suite ⊗ in 19 bedrooms s £80-£90; d £95-£105 (incl. bkfst) **FACILITIES:** STV Xmas **PARKING:** 51 **NOTES:** 🐕

★★★68% ◉ Maryculter House Hotel
South Deeside Rd, Maryculter AB12 5GB
☎ 01224 732124 🖷 01224 733510
e-mail: info@maryculterhousehotel.com
web: www.maryculterhousehotel.com
Dir: *off A90 on S side of Aberdeen, onto B9077. Hotel 8m on right, 0.5m beyond Lower Deeside Caravan Park*

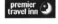

Set in grounds on the banks of the River Dee, this charming Scottish mansion dates back to medieval times and is now a popular wedding and conference venue. Exposed stonework and open fires feature in the oldest parts, which house the cocktail bar and Priory Restaurant. Lunch and breakfast are taken overlooking the river and bedrooms are equipped with business travellers in mind.
ROOMS: 23 en suite (1 fmly) (12 GF) ⊗ in 17 bedrooms s £69-£75; d £99-£110 (incl. bkfst) **LB** **FACILITIES:** STV Fishing Clay pigeon shooting, Archery Xmas **CONF:** BC Thtr 220 Class 100 Board 50 Del from £125 **PARKING:** 150 **NOTES:** ⊗ in restaurant Civ Wed 150

★★69% Dunavon House
60 Victoria St, Dyce AB21 7EE
☎ 01224 722483 🖷 01224 772721
e-mail: info@dunavonhousehotel.co.uk
Dir: *from A96 north to Inverness follow A947 into Victoria St, Dyce. Hotel 500yds on right*
Now under new ownership and within easy reach of the airport, this hotel is housed in a sympathetically converted Victorian villa. Bedrooms, many of which have now been refurbished, are generally spacious and well laid out. An extensive range of meals is served in both the lounge bar and the restaurant.
ROOMS: 18 en suite (5 GF) ⊗ in 6 bedrooms s £54-£115; d £70-£140 (incl. bkfst) **LB** **FACILITIES:** Free access to local leisure facilities **CONF:** BC **PARKING:** 26 **NOTES:** 🐕 ⊗ in restaurant

⌂ Premier Travel Inn Aberdeen Central West
North Anderson Dr AB15 6DW
☎ 0870 9906430 🖷 0870 9906431
web: www.premiertravelinn.com
Dir: *3m from city centre, 5m from Aberdeen Airport. Follow A90 towards city centre. From S, follow airport signs. Hotel 1st left after fire station*
High quality, modern budget accommodation ideal for both families and business travellers. Spacious, en suite bedrooms feature bath and shower, satellite TV and many have telephones and modem points. The adjacent family restaurant features a wide and varied menu. For further details consult the Hotel Groups page.
ROOMS: 60 en suite s £47.95-£50.95; d £47.95-£50.95

⌂ Premier Travel Inn Aberdeen City Centre
Inverlair House, West North St AB24 5AR
☎ 0870 9906300 🖷 0870 9906301
web: www.premiertravelinn.com
Dir: *From A90, follow A9013 into city centre. Turn onto A966 towards King St, then 1st left*
High quality, modern budget accommodation ideal for both families and business travellers. Spacious, en suite bedrooms feature bath and shower, satellite TV and many have telephones and modem points. The adjacent family restaurant features a wide and varied menu. For further details consult the Hotel Groups page.
ROOMS: 162 en suite s £53.95; d £53.95 **CONF:** Thtr 60

⌂ Premier Travel Inn Aberdeen North
Ellon Rd, Murcar, Bridge of Don AB23 8BP
☎ 08701 977012 🖷 01224 706869
web: www.premiertravelinn.com
Dir: *From City Centre take A90 north. At rdbt, 1m past Exhibition Centre, turn left onto B999. Inn on right*
High quality, modern budget accommodation ideal for both families and business travellers. Spacious, en suite bedrooms feature bath and shower, satellite TV and many have telephones and modem points. The adjacent family restaurant features a wide and varied menu. For further details consult the Hotel Groups page.
ROOMS: 40 en suite s £46.95-£49.95; d £46.95-£49.95

⌂ Premier Travel Inn Aberdeen South
Mains of Balquharn, Portlethen AB12 4QS
☎ 08701 977013 🖷 01224 783836
web: www.premiertravelinn.com
Dir: *on A90, exit signed Portlethen Shopping Centre & Badentoy Industrial Estate*
High quality, modern budget accommodation ideal for both families and business travellers. Spacious, en suite bedrooms

continued

feature bath and shower, satellite TV and many have telephones and modem points. The adjacent family restaurant features a wide and varied menu. For further details consult the Hotel Groups page.
ROOMS: 40 en suite s £47.95-£50.95; d £47.95-£50.95

⌂ Premier Travel Inn Aberdeen (Westhill)
Straik Rd, Westhill AB32 6HF
☎ 0870 9906348 📠 0870 9906349
web: www.premiertravelinn.com
Dir: *6m from city centre on A944*
High quality, modern budget accommodation ideal for both families and business travellers. Spacious, en suite bedrooms feature bath and shower, satellite TV and many have telephones and modem points. The adjacent family restaurant features a wide and varied menu. For further details consult the Hotel Groups page.
ROOMS: 61 en suite s £46.95-£49.95; d £46.95-£49.95

⌂ Travelodge
9 Bridge St AB11 6JL
☎ 08700 850 950 📠 01224 584587
web: www.travelodge.co.uk
Dir: *into city on A90, lodge at junct of Union St & Bridge St*
Travelodge offers good quality, good value, modern accommodation. Ideal for families, the spacious, en suite bedrooms include remote-control TV, tea and coffee-making facilities and comfortable beds. Meals can be taken at the nearby family restaurant. For further details consult the Hotel Groups page.
ROOMS: 97 en suite s fr £26; d fr £26

⌂ Travelodge (Aberdeen West)
Inverurie Rd, Bucksburn AB21 9BB
☎ 08700 850 950 📠 01224 715609
web: www.travelodge.co.uk
Dir: *west of A96 & A947 junct, towards Inverurie*
Travelodge offers good quality, good value, modern accommodation. Ideal for families, the spacious, en suite bedrooms include remote-control TV, tea and coffee-making facilities and comfortable beds. Meals can be taken at the nearby family restaurant. For further details consult the Hotel Groups page.
ROOMS: 48 en suite s fr £26; d fr £26

ABERDEEN AIRPORT, Aberdeen City — Map 23 NJ81

★★★★67% Aberdeen Marriott Hotel
Overton Circle, Dyce AB21 7AZ
☎ 01224 770011 📠 01224 722347
e-mail: reservations.scotland@marriotthotels.co.uk
web: www.marriott.co.uk
Dir: *follow A96 to Bucksburn, right at rdbt onto A947. Hotel in 2m at 2nd rdbt*
Close to the airport and conveniently located for the business district, this purpose-built hotel is a popular conference venue. The well-proportioned bedrooms come with many thoughtful extras. Public areas include an informal bar and lounge, a split-level restaurant and a leisure centre that can be accessed directly from a number of bedrooms.
ROOMS: 155 en suite (68 fmly) (61 GF) ⊗ in 124 bedrooms s £72-£115; d £72-£115 **LB** **FACILITIES: Spa** STV supervised Sauna Solarium Gym Jacuzzi Xmas **CONF:** BC Thtr 400 Class 200 Board 60 Del from £135 **SERVICES:** air con **PARKING:** 180 **NOTES:** ✈

⊗ No smoking

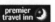

⌂ Premier Travel Inn Aberdeen Airport
Burnside Dr, off Riverside Dr, Dyce AB21 0HW
☎ 08701 977304 📠 01224 772968
web: www.premiertravelinn.com
Dir: *from Aberdeen A96 towards Inverness, turn right at rdbt onto A947, at 2nd rdbt turn right then 2nd right*
High quality, modern budget accommodation ideal for both families and business travellers. Spacious, en suite bedrooms feature bath and shower, satellite TV and many have telephones and modem points. The adjacent family restaurant features a wide and varied menu. For further details consult the Hotel Groups page.
ROOMS: 40 en suite s £46.95-£49.95; d £46.95-£49.95

ABERDOUR, Fife — Map 21 NT18

★★65% The Aberdour Hotel
38 High St KY3 0SW
☎ 01383 860325 📠 01383 860808
e-mail: reception@aberdourhotel.co.uk
web: www.aberdourhotel.co.uk
Dir: *M90 junct 1, E on A921 for 5m. Hotel in centre of village opp post office*
This small hotel has a relaxed and welcoming atmosphere. Real ales are featured in the cosy bar where good value, home-cooked meals are available, as they are in the beamed dining room. Though all are well equipped, bedrooms vary in size and style, and those in the stable block are particularly comfortable. The hotel is in easy reach of Edinburgh by train.
ROOMS: 12 en suite 4 annexe en suite (4 fmly) (2 GF) s £40-£50; d £50-£70 (incl. bkfst) **LB** **FACILITIES:** STV **PARKING:** 8 **NOTES:** ⊗ in restaurant

ABERDOUR, continued

★64% The Cedar Inn
20 Shore Rd KY3 0TR
☎ 01383 860310 🖹 01383 860004
e-mail: enquiries@cedarinn.co.uk
Dir: *in Aberdour turn right off A921 into Main St then right into Shore Rd. Hotel 100yds on left*
Situated in the heart of Aberdour this friendly hotel offers comfortable well-presented accommodation. The newly refurbished bar is very smart and is an ideal environment to relax and enjoy quality ales, after sampling the delicious meals served in the dining room.
ROOMS: 9 en suite (2 fmly) ⊗ in 5 bedrooms s £39-£45; d £60-£75 (incl. bkfst) **LB FACILITIES:** ♫ Xmas **CONF:** Del from £55 **PARKING:** 12 **NOTES:** ⊗ in restaurant

ABERFELDY, Perth & Kinross — Map 23 NN84

★★★63% Moness House Hotel & Country Club
Crieff Rd PH15 2DY
☎ 0870 443 1460 🖹 0870 443 1461
e-mail: info@moness.com web: www.moness.com
Dir: *from A9, off at A827 to Aberfeldy. Through main square, left at lights onto A826 for hotel on left after 0.25m*

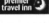

Part of a holiday ownership resort, this small hotel is set in extensive grounds. Accommodation is provided in generally spacious bedrooms a short walk away from the public rooms and leisure facilities. There is a choice of bars where meals are served in addition to the restaurant.
ROOMS: 12 en suite (1 fmly) s £43-£67; d £56-£104 (incl. bkfst) **LB FACILITIES:** Squash Snooker Solarium Putt green Jacuzzi Badminton Indoor Bowls Pool Table Tennis Steam room ♫ Xmas **CONF:** Thtr 120 Class 120 Board 50 **PARKING:** 12 **NOTES:** ⊗ in restaurant Closed 4-13 Dec Civ Wed 120

See advert on opposite page

Restaurant with Rooms

Farleyer Restaurant & Rooms
Farleyer House PH15 2JE
☎ 01887 820332 🖹 01887 829879
e-mail: info@farleyer.com
web: www.farleyer.com
Dir: *W on B846 beyond Castle Menzies*
Set in beautiful terraced gardens, a wing of this former dower house for nearby Menzies Castle has been converted to a restaurant with rooms. A contemporary bar and restaurant provide a trendy style that is not out of place in this country house, but there's always the alternative dining room. Bedrooms are spacious and comfortably equipped.
ROOMS: 6 en suite (1 fmly) (6 GF) ⊗ in 5 bedrooms
FACILITIES: Fishing rough shooting Xmas **PARKING:** 20 **NOTES:** ⊗ in restaurant Civ Wed 40

ABERFOYLE, Stirling — Map 20 NN50

★★★★66% Forest Hills
Kinlochard FK8 3TL
☎ 01877 387277 🖹 01877 387307
e-mail: forest_hills@macdonald-hotels.co.uk
web: www.macdonald-hotels.co.uk
Dir: *3m W on B829*
Situated in the heart of The Trossachs with wonderful views of Loch Ard, this popular hotel forms part of a resort complex offering a range of indoor and outdoor facilities. The main hotel has relaxing lounges and a restaurant which overlook landscaped gardens. A separate building houses the leisure centre, lounge bar and bistro.
ROOMS: 54 en suite (16 fmly) (12 GF) ⊗ in 26 bedrooms s £70-£110; d £100-£180 (incl. bkfst) **LB FACILITIES:** supervised Fishing Snooker Sauna Solarium Gym Putt green Jacuzzi Quad biking, Sailing, Canoeing, Abseiling, Archery, Mountain bikes, Guided walks ch fac Xmas **CONF:** Thtr 150 Class 60 Board 45 Del from £120 **SERVICES:** Lift **PARKING:** 80 **NOTES:** ⊗ in restaurant Civ Wed 80

ABERLOUR See Archiestown

ABINGTON MOTORWAY SERVICE AREA (M74), South Lanarkshire — Map 21 NS92

Days Inn Abington
ML12 6RG
☎ 01864 502782 🖹 01864 502759
e-mail: abington.hotel@welcomebreak.co.uk
web: www.welcomebreak.co.uk
Dir: *M74 junct 13, accessible from N'bound and S'bound carriageways*
This modern building offers accommodation in smart, spacious and well-equipped bedrooms, suitable for families and business travellers, and all with en suite bathrooms. Continental breakfast is available and other refreshments may be taken at the nearby family restaurant. For further details see the Hotel Groups page.
ROOMS: 52 en suite s £35-£55; d £35-£55 **CONF:** Board 10

ALNESS, Highland — Map 23 NH66

U Teaninch Castle
IV17 0XB
☎ 01349 883231 🖹 01349 880940
e-mail: info@teaninichcastle.com
Dir: *follow A9 N from Inverness over Cromarty Bridge, left to Alness. Follow road for 600mtrs, Castle 2nd turn on right*
At the time of going to press, the star classification for this hotel was not confirmed. Please refer to the AA internet site www.theAA.com for current information.
ROOMS: 6 en suite (1 GF) ⊗ in all bedrooms s £80-£100; d £130-£140 (incl. bkfst) **LB FACILITIES:** Gym Jacuzzi **CONF:** Thtr 30 Class 15 Board 10 **PARKING:** 20 **NOTES:** ⊗ in restaurant Civ Wed 30

ANNANDALE WATER MOTORWAY SERVICE AREA (M74), Dumfries & Galloway — Map 21 NY19

Premier Travel Inn Lockerbie (Annandale Wat)
Johnstonbridge DG11 1HD
☎ 08701 977163 🖹 01576 470644
web: www.premiertravelinn.com
Dir: *A74(M) - adjacent to junct 16. Accessible north and southbound*
High quality, modern budget accommodation ideal for both families and business travellers. Spacious, en suite bedrooms feature bath and shower, satellite TV and many have telephones and modem points. The adjacent family restaurant features a wide and varied menu. For further details consult the Hotel Groups page.
ROOMS: 42 en suite s £46.95-£48.95; d £46.95-£48.95

ARBROATH, Angus Map 21 NO64

★★65% Hotel Seaforth
Dundee Rd DD11 1QF
☎ 01241 872232 🖷 01241 877473
e-mail: hotelseaforth@ukonline.co.uk
Dir: *on southern outskirts, on A92*

This long-established commercial hotel enjoys a seafront location close to many local amenities. Family-run, a welcoming and friendly atmosphere prevails. Spacious, thoughtfully equipped bedrooms all have smart bathrooms. Public areas include a leisure centre, which includes a swimming pool and gym, a popular bar, and restaurant that serves a range of good value meals.
ROOMS: 19 en suite (4 fmly) s £50-£65; d £65-£85 (incl. bkfst) **LB** **FACILITIES:** Snooker Sauna Gym Jacuzzi Steam room Xmas **CONF:** Thtr 120 Class 60 Board 40 **PARKING:** 60 **NOTES:** ⊗ in restaurant Civ Wed 120

ARCHIESTOWN, Moray Map 23 NJ24

★★76% Archiestown
AB38 7QL
☎ 01340 810218 🖷 01340 810239
e-mail: jah@archiestownhotel.co.uk
web: www.archiestownhotel.co.uk
Dir: *A95 Craigellachie, follow B9102 to Archiestown 4m. Hotel on left of Square in centre of village*
This small, smart hotel is set in the heart of this attractive Speyside village, and is very popular with anglers and locals alike. The bedrooms are comfortable, attractive and well equipped. There is an inviting lounge complete with log fire and an attractive dining room where fresh local produce is served.
ROOMS: 11 en suite (1 fmly) ⊗ in all bedrooms s £50-£60; d fr £100 (incl. bkfst) **LB** **FACILITIES:** ⛳ **PARKING:** 20 **NOTES:** ⊗ in restaurant Closed 24-27 Dec & 1st 3 wks Jan

ARDUAINE, Argyll & Bute Map 20 NM71

★★★76% ®® Loch Melfort
PA34 4XG
☎ 01852 200233 🖷 01852 200214
e-mail: reception@lochmelfort.co.uk
web: www.lochmelfort.co.uk
Dir: *on A816, midway between Oban and Lochgilphead*
Enjoying one of the finest locations on the West Coast, this popular, family-run hotel has outstanding views across Asknish Bay towards the Islands of Jura, Scarba and Shuna. Accommodation is provided in either the balconied rooms of the

continued

Cedar wing or the more traditional rooms in the main hotel. Skilfully cooked dinners remain the highlight of any visit.

Lord Melfort, Arduane

ROOMS: 7 en suite 20 annexe en suite (2 fmly) ⊗ in 11 bedrooms s £49-£79; d £78-£158 (incl. bkfst) **LB** **FACILITIES:** Xmas **CONF:** Thtr 50 Class 35 Board 24 Del from £80 **PARKING:** 65 **NOTES:** ⊗ in restaurant Closed 4 Jan -9 Feb

ARDVASAR See Skye, Isle of

Early start?
Hotels at all star levels should provide in-room alarm clocks and/or alarm clocks

ARRAN, ISLE OF, North Ayrshire — Map 20

BLACKWATERFOOT — Map 20 NR92

★★★68% **Kinloch**
KA27 8ET
☎ 01770 860444 🖷 01770 860447
e-mail: reservations@kinlochhotel.eclipse.co.uk
Dir: Ferry from Ardrossan to Brodick, follow signs for Blackwaterfoot, hotel in centre of village

Best Western

This family-run hotel overlooks the Mull of Kintyre. Spacious public areas include a choice of lounges, bars and good leisure facilities. Bedrooms offer mixed modern appointments. The main dining room offers a well-prepared and innovative four course dinner menu, in addition to meals served in the bars.
ROOMS: 43 en suite (7 fmly) (7 GF) ⊗ in 24 bedrooms
FACILITIES: STV ⚲ Squash Snooker Sauna Gym Beauty therapy ♫
CONF: Thtr 120 Class 20 Board 40 **SERVICES:** Lift **PARKING:** 2
NOTES: ⊗ in restaurant Civ Wed 60

BRODICK — Map 20 NS03

★★★76% ⑱⑱ **Auchrannie House**
KA27 8BZ
☎ 01770 302234 🖷 01770 302812
e-mail: info@auchrannie.co.uk
Dir: turn right from Brodick Ferry terminal, through Brodick village, 2nd left after Brodick Golf Course clubhouse, 300yds to hotel
This Victorian mansion lies in landscaped grounds and provides well-equipped bedrooms. Dine in the 'Garden Restaurant' or the bistro, while a brasserie is also available in the extensive spa centre, which itself offers excellent family accommodation. Residents have their own leisure facilities but will be attracted to the superb spa set in the grounds.
ROOMS: 28 en suite (3 fmly) (4 GF) ⊗ in all bedrooms
s £55.50-£99.50; d £89-£139 (incl. bkfst) **LB FACILITIES:** Spa STV ⚲
supervised ⚲ Snooker Sauna Solarium Gym Hair salon Aromatherapy
Shiatsu Hockey Badminton Xmas **CONF:** BC Thtr 120 Class 80 Board 50
PARKING: 50 **NOTES:** ✗ ⊗ in restaurant Civ Wed 120

Top Hotel

★★ ⑱⑱⚑ *Kilmichael Country House*
Glen Cloy KA27 8BY
☎ 01770 302219 🖷 01770 302068
e-mail: enquiries@kilmichael.com
web: www.kilmichael.com
Dir: from Brodick ferry terminal follow N'bound (Lochranza) road for 1m. Left at golf course, inland between sports field & church, follow signs
Reputed to be the oldest on the island, this lovely house lies in attractive gardens in a quiet glen less than five minutes'
continued

drive from the ferry terminal. It has been lovingly restored to create a stylish, elegant country house, adorned with ornaments from around the world. There are two inviting drawing rooms and a bright dining room, serving award-winning contemporary cuisine. The delightful bedrooms are furnished in classical style; some are contained in a pretty courtyard conversion.

ROOMS: 4 en suite 3 annexe en suite (6 GF) ⊗ in all bedrooms
FACILITIES: STV Jacuzzi **PARKING:** 12 **NOTES:** No children 12yrs
⊗ in restaurant Closed Nov-Feb (ex for prior bookings)

AUCHENCAIRN, Dumfries & Galloway — Map 21 NX75

★★★76% ⑱⑱⚑ **Balcary Bay**
DG7 1QZ
☎ 01556 640217 & 640311 🖷 01556 640272
e-mail: reservations@balcary-bay-hotel.co.uk
web: www.balcary-bay-hotel.co.uk
Dir: on the A711 between Dalbeattie and Kirkcudbright, hotel on Shore road, 2m from village

SCOTLAND'S HOTELS OF DISTINCTION

Taking its name from the bay on which it lies, this hotel has lawns running down to the shore. The larger bedrooms enjoy stunning views over the bay, whilst others overlook the gardens. Comfortable public areas invite relaxation. Imaginative dishes feature at dinner, accompanied by a good wine list.
ROOMS: 20 en suite (1 fmly) (3 GF) s £63; d £118-£140 (incl. bkfst)
LB PARKING: 50 **NOTES:** ⊗ in restaurant Closed Dec-Jan

Late for dinner? Quality standards mean that last orders for dinner vary according to star rating and should be no earlier than:
★★ 7.00pm ★★★ 8:00pm ★★★★ 9:00pm
★★★★★ 10:00pm

AUCHTERARDER, Perth & Kinross Map 21 NN91

Top Hotel

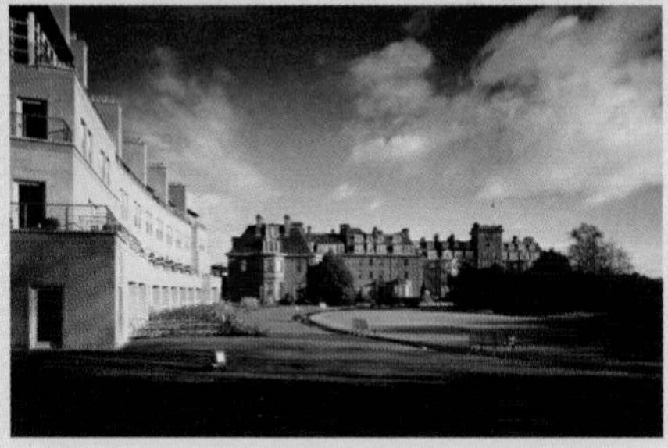

★★★★★ ◎◎◎◎ **The Gleneagles Hotel**
PH3 1NF
☎ 01764 662231 📠 01764 662134
e-mail: resort.sales@gleneagles.com
Dir: *off A9 at exit for A823 follow signs for Gleneagles Hotel*
With its international reputation for high standards, this grand hotel provides something for everyone. Set in a delightful location, Gleneagles offers a peaceful retreat, as well as many sporting activities, including the famous championship golf courses. All bedrooms are appointed to a high standard and offer both traditional and modern contemporary styles. Stylish public areas include various dining options, which include the Strathearn, with two AA rosettes, as well as some inspired cooking at Andrew Fairlie at Gleneagles, a restaurant with four rosettes. Service is always professional, staff are friendly and nothing is too much trouble.
ROOMS: 269 en suite (115 fmly) (11 GF) ⊗ in 149 bedrooms d £340-£795 (incl. bkfst) **LB** **FACILITIES: Spa** STV supervised 54 Fishing Squash Riding Snooker Sauna Solarium Gym Putt green Jacuzzi Falconry, Off road driving, Golf range, Archery, Clay target shooting ♫ Xmas **CONF:** BC Thtr 360 Class 240 Board 60 Del from £255 **SERVICES:** Lift **PARKING:** 200
NOTES: Civ Wed 360

★★76% ◎ ***Cairn Lodge***
Orchil Rd PH3 1LX
☎ 01764 662634 📠 01764 662866
e-mail: info@cairnlodge.co.uk
web: www.cairnlodge.co.uk
Dir: *leave A9 at Gleneagles exit. Turn left on A823, pass entrance to Gleneagles Hotel and take 2nd turning towards Auchterarder on Orchil Rd*
This twin turreted hotel stands in large grounds on the edge of the town. Bedrooms differ in style and size, with the newer rooms offering superb levels of quality and comfort. Public areas are smartly appointed and food can be enjoyed in either the informal atmosphere of the bar or the Capercaillie restaurant.
ROOMS: 10 en suite (6 fmly) (2 GF) **PARKING:** 30 **NOTES:** 🚭
Civ Wed 30

AYR, South Ayrshire Map 20 NS32

★★★★72% ◎◎ **Fairfield House**
12 Fairfield Rd KA7 2AR
☎ 01292 267461 📠 01292 261456
e-mail: reservations@fairfieldhotel.co.uk
Dir: *from A77 towards Ayr South (A30). Follow signs for town centre, down Miller Road and turn left then right into Fairfield Road*
Lying in a quiet street close to the esplanade, this hotel enjoys sea views towards to the Isle of Arran. Bedrooms offer either modern or classical styles, the latter featuring impressive bathrooms. Public rooms provide country house style. Enjoyable meals are served in either the brasserie or elegant restaurant.
ROOMS: 40 en suite 4 annexe en suite (3 fmly) (9 GF) ⊗ in 14 bedrooms s £103-£144; d £135-£175 (incl. bkfst) **LB** **FACILITIES:** STV supervised Sauna Solarium Gym Jacuzzi Xmas **CONF:** BC Thtr 80 Class 50 Board 40 Del from £150 **SERVICES:** Lift **PARKING:** 52
NOTES: 🚭 ⊗ in restaurant Civ Wed 100

★★★76% ◎◎ **Enterkine Country House**
Annbank KA6 5AL
☎ 01292 520580 📠 01292 521582
e-mail: mail@enterkine.com
web: www.enterkine.com
Dir: *follow A77 to Ayr, then B743 Mossblown/Mauchline for hotel on Coylton Rd on outskirts of Annbank*
This gracious country mansion dates from the 1930s and retains many original features, notably the luxurious bathroom suites. The focus is very much on dining and in country house tradition there is no bar, drinks being served in the elegant lounge and library. The well-proportioned bedrooms are furnished and equipped to high standards, many with lovely views over the countryside.
ROOMS: 6 en suite (1 fmly) s £75-£110; d £130-£150 (incl. bkfst) **LB** **FACILITIES:** STV Fishing Beauty treatments, golf, fishing, hunting Xmas **CONF:** BC Thtr 50 Class 30 Board 12 Del from £130 **SERVICES:** Lift **PARKING:** 20 **NOTES:** ⊗ in restaurant Civ Wed 80

○ Hotel due to open in late 2005 or 2006
U Star rating not confirmed

AYR, continued

★★★71% Savoy Park
16 Racecourse Rd KA7 2UT
☎ 01292 266112 📠 01292 611488
e-mail: mail@savoypark.com
Dir: *from A77 follow Holmston Road(A70) for 2m, through Parkhouse Street, turn left into Beresford Terrace, 1st right into Bellevue Rd*

This well-established hotel retains many of its traditional values including friendly, attentive service. Public rooms feature impressive panelled walls, ornate ceilings and open fires. The restaurant is reminiscent of a Highland shooting lodge and offers a wide ranging, good value menu to suit all tastes. The large superior bedrooms retain a classical elegance while others are smart and modern; all have well equipped modern bathrooms.
ROOMS: 15 en suite (3 fmly) ⊗ in all bedrooms s £70-£85; d £95-£115 (incl. bkfst) **LB** **FACILITIES:** STV ch fac Xmas **CONF:** Thtr 50 Class 40 Board 30 Del from £110 **PARKING:** 60 **NOTES:** ⊗ in restaurant Civ Wed 100 *See advert on opposite page*

★★ ⊛ *Ladyburn*
KA19 7SG
☎ 01655 740585 📠 01655 740580
e-mail: jh@ladyburn.co.uk
(For full entry see Maybole)

U Ramada Ayr
Dalblair Rd KA7 1UG
☎ 01292 269331 📠 01292 610722
e-mail: sales.ayr@ramadajarvis.co.uk
web: www.ramadajarvis.co.uk
Dir: *M27 towards Prestwick Airport, then A77 Ayr, 1st rdbt 3rd exit, 2nd rdbt straight over, left at lights, then 2nd set of lights turn left, bottom of road turn right, hotel on left.*
This modern hotel enjoys views of the Isle of Arran and Mull of Kintyre. Bedrooms are comfortably appointed for both business and leisure guests.
ROOMS: 118 en suite (8 fmly) ⊗ in 13 bedrooms s £79-£105; d £79-£105 **FACILITIES:** STV supervised Sauna Solarium Gym Jacuzzi Xmas **CONF:** Thtr 200 Class 45 Board 45 Del from £115 **SERVICES:** Lift **PARKING:** 70 **NOTES:** ⊗ in restaurant Civ Wed 60

U The Western House Hotel
2 Whitletts Rd KA8 0JE
☎ 01292 619357 & 0870 850 5666 📠 01292 262340
e-mail: cbrownlie@ayr-racecourse.co.uk
At the time of going to press, the star classification for this hotel was not confirmed. Please refer to the AA internet site www.theAA.com for current information.
ROOMS: 10 en suite 39 annexe en suite (39 fmly) s £45-£85; d £45-£185 **LB** **FACILITIES:** STV Xmas **CONF:** Thtr 1200 Class 300 Board 36 Del from £90 **SERVICES:** Lift **NOTES:** No children ⊗ in restaurant Civ Wed 180

⇧ Premier Travel Inn Ayr
Kilmarnock Rd, Monkton KA9 2RJ
☎ 08701 977020 📠 01292 678248
web: www.premiertravelinn.com
Dir: *on A77/A78 rdbt at Monkton, approx 2m from Prestwick Airport*
High quality, modern budget accommodation ideal for both families and business travellers. Spacious, en suite bedrooms feature bath and shower, satellite TV and many have telephones and modem points. The adjacent family restaurant features a wide and varied menu. For further details consult the Hotel Groups page.
ROOMS: 40 en suite s £50.95; d £50.95 **CONF:** Thtr 50 Board 20

BALLACHULISH, Highland — Map 22 NN05

★★★71% *Ballachulish Hotel*
PH49 4JY
☎ 0871 222 3415 📠 0871 222 3416
e-mail: reservations@freedomglen.co.uk
web: www.freedomglen.co.uk
Dir: *on A828, Fort William-Oban road, 3m N of Glencoe*
A relaxed atmosphere prevails at this long-established hotel, which boasts stunning views over Loch Linnhe. Bedrooms vary in size and style and all are comfortably appointed; many have superb views. Inviting public areas include a spacious and comfortable lounge, the informal Ferry Bar and a cocktail bar.
ROOMS: 54 en suite (4 fmly) **FACILITIES:** Complimentary Membership of Leisure Club at nearby sister hotel ♫ ch fac **CONF:** Thtr 100 Class 50 Board 30 **PARKING:** 50 **NOTES:** ⊗ in restaurant Closed 9-23 Dec & 5-27 Jan

BALLANTRAE, South Ayrshire — Map 20 NX08

Hotel of the Year
Top Hotel

★★★ ⊛⊛⊛ Glenapp Castle
KA26 0NZ
☎ 01465 831212 📠 831000
e-mail: enquiries@glenappcastle.com
web: www.glenappcastle.com
Dir: *1m from A77 near Ballantrae*
Friendly hospitality and attentive service prevail at this stunning Victorian castle, set in extensive private grounds to the south of the village. Impeccably furnished bedrooms are graced with antiques and period pieces and there are a number of spacious, luxurious suites. Breathtaking views of Arran and Ailsa Craig can be enjoyed from the delightful, sumptuous day rooms and from many of the bedrooms. Accomplished, imaginative cuisine using quality local ingredients is a highlight of any stay. AA Hotel of the Year for Scotland 2005-6.
ROOMS: 17 en suite (2 fmly) (7 GF) ⊗ in all bedrooms s £255-£395; d £365-£515 (incl. bkfst & dinner) **LB** **FACILITIES:** STV 30 acres of beautifully tended gardens Xmas **CONF:** Thtr 17 Class 12 Board 17 Del from £285 **SERVICES:** Lift **PARKING:** 20 **NOTES:** ⊗ in restaurant Closed Nov-Mar (Open New Year)

BALLATER, Aberdeenshire Map 23 NO39

Top Hotel

★★★ ◉◉◉ **Darroch Learg**
Braemar Rd AB35 5UX
☎ 013397 55443 📠 013397 55252
e-mail: nigel@darrochlearg.co.uk
web: www.darrochlearg.co.uk
Dir: on A93, at western side of Ballater
Set high above the road in extensive wooded grounds, this
renowned hotel offers fine views over the spectacular
countryside of Royal Deeside. Bedrooms, some with
four-poster beds, are individually styled, bright and spacious.
Food is a highlight of any visit, whether it is a freshly prepared
breakfast, a light lunch or the award-winning Scottish cuisine
served in the delightful conservatory restaurant.
ROOMS: 12 en suite 5 annexe en suite (1 GF) ⊗ in all bedrooms
CONF: Thtr 25 Board 12 **PARKING:** 25 **NOTES:** ⊗ in restaurant
Closed Xmas & Jan (ex New Year)

★★73% **Loch Kinord**
Ballater Rd, Dinnet AB34 5JY
☎ 013398 85229 📠 013397 87007
e-mail: ask@kinord.com
Dir: Between Aboyne & Ballater, on A93, in village of Dinnet

THE CIRCLE
Selected Individual Hotels
GREAT BRITAIN

Family-run, this roadside hotel lies between Aboyne and Ballater
and is well located for leisure and sporting pursuits. It has lots of
character and a friendly atmosphere. There are two bars, one
outside and a cosy one inside, plus a dining room in bold, tasteful
colour schemes. Most of the bedrooms have been stylishly
refurbished and boast smart bathrooms.
ROOMS: 21 rms (19 en suite) (3 fmly) (4 GF) ⊗ in 5 bedrooms
FACILITIES: Sauna Jacuzzi Pool table **CONF:** Thtr 40 Class 30 Board 30
PARKING: 20 **NOTES:** ⊗ in restaurant Civ Wed 50

🎵 Entertainment

Discover Ayr's leading
family run hotel where you'll
experience truly genuine hospitality
and friendly, professional service.
Relax and dream in our comfy, en suite
bedrooms. A real home from home.

16 RACECOURSE ROAD, AYR KA7 2UT
Tel 01292 266112 Fax: 01292 611488
mail@savoypark.com www.savoypark.com

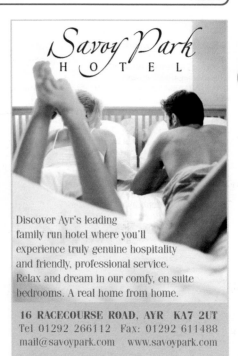

🅰 **Cambus O'May**
AB35 5SE
☎ 013397 55428 📠 013397 55428
e-mail: mckechnie@cambusomay.freeserve.co.uk
web: www.cambusomay.co.uk
Dir: from Ballater follow A93 for 4m towards Aberdeen, hotel on left
ROOMS: 12 en suite (1 fmly) s £32-£35; d £64-£70 (incl. bkfst) **LB**
PARKING: 12 **NOTES:** ★★★, No credit cards accepted ⊗ in restaurant

BALLOCH, West Dunbartonshire Map 20 NS38

★★★★★70% ◉◉◉
De Vere Cameron House
G83 8QZ
☎ 013897 55565 📠 013897 59522
e-mail: reservations@cameronhouse.co.uk
web: www.devereonline.co.uk

DE VERE ● HOTELS

Dir: M8(W) junct 30 for Erskine Bridge. Then A82 for Crainlarich. After
14m, at rdbt signed Luss straight on towards Luss, hotel on right
Enjoying an idyllic location on the banks of Loch Lomond, this
leisure orientated hotel offers spacious, well-equipped
accommodation. Bedrooms vary in size and style and many boast
wonderful views of the loch. A choice of restaurants, bars and
lounges, a host of indoor and outdoor sporting activities and a
smart spa are just some of the facilities available. Dinner in the
Georgian room is a highlight of any stay.
ROOMS: 96 en suite (9 fmly) ⊗ in all bedrooms **FACILITIES:** Spa STV
🈺 ⚓9 ✎ Fishing Squash Snooker Sauna Solarium Gym 🈺 Jacuzzi
Whole range of outdoor sports, Motor boat on Loch Lomond, Hair dressers
ch fac **CONF:** Thtr 300 Class 80 Board 80 **SERVICES:** Lift
PARKING: 200 **NOTES:** ✈ Civ Wed 200
See advert on page 673

BALLOCH, continued

Innkeeper's Lodge Loch Lomond
Balloch Rd G83 8LQ
☎ 0870 243 0500 01389 752579
web: www.innkeeperslodge.com
Dir: *M8 junct 30 onto M898. Left at Duntocher rdbt onto A82, right at rdbt (A811), left into Daluart Rd, lodge opposite*
A growing concept in the travel accommodation market. Smart rooms meet essential business requirements but also have home comforts. Dining options include all-day menus plus the added advantage of breakfast, which is included in the room price. For further details consult the Hotel Groups page.
ROOMS: 14 en suite s £59.95; d £59.95

BALQUHIDDER, Stirling Map 20 NN52

★★79% Monachyle Mhor Hotel
FK19 8PQ
☎ 01877 384622 01877 384305
e-mail: info@monachylemhor.com
web: www.monachylemhor.com
Dir: *11m N of Callander on A84, turn right at Kingshouse Hotel and under A84 towards Balquhidder, hotel 6m on right*

Often described as ' a hidden treasure' by regular guests this impressive hotel continues to provide a unique package with much style. A warm welcome and delicious food are assured here. Set in a 2000-acre estate and reached by a single-track road alongside Loch Voil, the hotel offers bedrooms that combine traditional furnishings with cutting-edge fixtures and fittings. The conservatory-style restaurant gives fine views across the glen, an ideal setting for the imaginative fixed-price menu.
ROOMS: 6 en suite 5 annexe en suite (2 GF) ⊗ in all bedrooms s fr £75; d £95-£220 (incl. bkfst) **FACILITIES:** Fishing Grouse shooting, Hill walking, Deer Stalking, Petanque Pitch Xmas **CONF:** Board 10 Del £130 **PARKING:** 20 **NOTES:** No children 12yrs ⊗ in restaurant Closed Jan Civ Wed 40

BANCHORY, Aberdeenshire Map 23 NO69

★★★78% Raemoir House
Raemoir AB31 4ED
☎ 01330 824884 01330 822171
e-mail: reservations@raemoir.com
web: www.raemoir.com
Dir: *A93 to Banchory right onto A980, to Torphins, 2m at T-junct*
This country mansion dates from the mid-18th century and retains many period features. Individually designed bedrooms vary in size and layout, though all are well equipped. Gracious public rooms include a choice of sitting rooms, a cocktail bar and a Georgian dining room. These rooms have tapestry-covered walls, open fires and fine antiques.

ROOMS: 14 en suite 6 annexe en suite (1 fmly) s £66-£85; d £95-£138 (incl. bkfst) **LB** **FACILITIES:** ⛳ 9 🎾 ♫ Putt green Shooting Stalking Xmas **CONF:** BC Thtr 45 Class 25 Board 30 Del from £115 **PARKING:** 100 **NOTES:** ⊗ in restaurant Civ Wed 40

★★★78% Tor-na-Coille
AB31 4AB
☎ 01330 822242 01330 824012
e-mail: tornacoille@btinternet.com
web: www.tornacoille.com
Dir: *on A93 (Aberdeen/Braemar road), opposite golf course*

This fine granite-stone house sits in tree-studded grounds on the west side of the town. Bedrooms come in a variety of styles and sizes, many mirroring the period charm of the house. Inviting public areas include a stylish inviting sitting room and an elegant restaurant.
ROOMS: 22 en suite (4 fmly) ⊗ in 17 bedrooms s £60-£72; d £95-£117 (incl. bkfst) **LB** **FACILITIES:** Squash ♫ ♫ **CONF:** Thtr 90 Class 60 Board 30 Del from £85 **SERVICES:** Lift **PARKING:** 130 **NOTES:** ⊗ in restaurant Closed 24-28 Dec Civ Wed 96

★★★74% Banchory Lodge
AB31 5HS
☎ 01330 822625 01330 825019
e-mail: enquiries@banchorylodge.co.uk
Dir: *off A93, 13m W of Aberdeen, hotel is off Dee Street*
This hotel enjoys a scenic setting in grounds by the River Dee. Inviting public areas include a choice of lounges, a cosy bar and a restaurant with views of the river. Bedrooms come in two distinct

continued

styles; those in the original part of the house contrasting with the newer wing rooms, which are particularly spacious.

ROOMS: 22 en suite (11 fmly) ⊗ in 10 bedrooms **FACILITIES:** Fishing Pool room Xmas **CONF:** Thtr 30 Class 30 Board 28 **PARKING:** 50 **NOTES:** ⊗ in restaurant Civ Wed 150

⊗ No smoking

★★70% Burnett Arms
25 High St AB31 5TD
☎ 01330 824944 📠 01330 825553
e-mail: theburnett@btconnect.com
Dir: *town centre on N side of A93, 18m from centre of Aberdeen*
This popular hotel is located in the heart of the town centre and gives easy access to the many attractions of Royal Deeside. Public areas include a choice of eating and drinking options, with food

continued

served in the restaurant, bar and foyer lounge. Bedrooms are thoughtfully equipped and comfortably modern.

ROOMS: 17 en suite (1 fmly) ⊗ in 7 bedrooms s £50-£67; d £71-£92 (incl. bkfst) **LB** **FACILITIES:** STV Xmas **CONF:** Thtr 100 Class 50 Board 50 Del from £91.50 **PARKING:** 40 **NOTES:** ⊗ in restaurant

See advert under ABERDEEN

BANFF, Aberdeenshire — Map 23 NJ66

★★★71% Banff Springs
Golden Knowes Rd AB45 2JE
☎ 01261 812881 📠 01261 815546
e-mail: info@banffspringshotel.co.uk
Dir: *western outskirts of town on A98 Banff to Inverness road*
Attentive service by genuinely friendly staff is a feature of this comfortable business and tourist hotel, which enjoys lovely sea views. Public areas include a smart foyer lounge and a popular bar/bistro, which provides an informal dining alternative to the

continued on p674

BANFF, continued

restaurant. The newly refurbished bedrooms are spacious and comfortable with many enjoying beach and ocean views.
ROOMS: 31 en suite s £39-£65; d £68-£97 (incl. bkfst) **LB**
FACILITIES: STV Gym Xmas **CONF:** Thtr 400 Class 100 Board 40
PARKING: 200 **NOTES:** ⊗ in restaurant Closed 25-Dec Civ Wed 200

BARRA, ISLE OF, Western Isles Map 22

TANGASDALE Map 22 NF60

★★69% Isle of Barra
Tangasdale Beach HS9 5XW
☎ 01871 810383 ▤ 01871 810385
e-mail: barrahotel@aol.com
Dir: left from ferry terminal onto A888, hotel 2m on left
It may well take the better part of a day to reach the most westerly hotel in Britain, but few journeys could be better rewarded. Overlooking the white sands of Halaman Bay and the crystal clear shallows of the Atlantic, the hotel's situation is quite breathtaking. It is comfortably furnished and most of the bedrooms enjoy the stunning views. At dinner guests can experience the finest shellfish in British waters. Staff provide warm hospitality and have a wealth of knowledge about the island.
ROOMS: 30 en suite (2 fmly) (7 GF) s £42-£48; d £72-£84 (incl. bkfst)
LB FACILITIES: STV Beach **CONF:** BC Thtr 70 Class 70 Board 60 Del from £58 **PARKING:** 50 **NOTES:** ⊗ in restaurant Closed Oct-Etr

BEARSDEN, East Dunbartonshire Map 20 NS57

⌂ Premier Travel Inn Glasgow (Bearsden)
Milngavie Rd G61 3EA
☎ 0870 9906532 ▤ 0870 9906533
web: www.premiertravelinn.com
Dir: 6m from city centre. From E, exit M8 junct 16. From W, exit M8 junct 17. Follow A81 signed Milngavie. Hotel on left
High quality, modern budget accommodation ideal for both families and business travellers. Spacious, en suite bedrooms feature bath and shower, satellite TV and many have telephones and modem points. The adjacent family restaurant features a wide and varied menu. For further details consult the Hotel Groups page.
ROOMS: 61 en suite s £46.95-£48.95; d £46.95-£48.95

BEAULY, Highland Map 23 NH54

★★★72% Priory
The Square IV4 7BX
☎ 01463 782309 ▤ 01463 782531
e-mail: reservations@priory-hotel.com
web: www.priory-hotel.com
Dir: signed from A832, into Beauly, hotel in square on left
This popular hotel occupies a central location in the town square. Standard and executive rooms are on offer, both providing a good level of comfort and range of facilities. Food is served throughout the day in the open-plan public areas, with menus offering a first rate choice.
ROOMS: 34 en suite (3 fmly) ⊗ in 9 bedrooms s £42.50-£52.50; d £85-£105 (incl. bkfst) **LB FACILITIES:** STV Snooker Xmas **CONF:** BC Thtr 40 Class 40 Board 30 Del from £72.50 **SERVICES:** Lift **PARKING:** 20 **NOTES:** ✖ ⊗ in restaurant

> If you wish to use a particular credit card or debit card please check with the hotel that they are happy to accept it

BIGGAR, South Lanarkshire Map 21 NT03

★★★73% ◎◎ ♨ Shieldhill Castle
Quothquan ML12 6NA
☎ 01899 220035 ▤ 01899 221092
e-mail: enquiries@shieldhill.co.uk web: www.shieldhill.co.uk
Dir: off A702 onto B7016 Biggar to Carnwath Rd, after 2m turn left into Shieldhill Rd. Hotel 1.5m on right

This imposing castle is set in rolling countryside and dates back almost 800 years. Public areas are atmospheric and include the high ceilinged Chancellor's restaurant and oak-panelled lounge. Bedrooms, many with oversized baths, are spacious. A friendly welcome is assured from both the enthusiastic staff and even the proprietor's dogs! Food is a highlight of any stay and uses local produce where possible.
ROOMS: 16 en suite ⊗ in all bedrooms **FACILITIES:** ᛁ Jacuzzi Cycling, Clay shoot, Hot air ballooning, laser shooting Xmas **CONF:** Thtr 500 Class 200 Board 250 **PARKING:** 50 **NOTES:** ⊗ in restaurant Civ Wed 200

BLACKWATERFOOT See Arran, Isle of

BLAIR ATHOLL, Perth & Kinross Map 23 NN86

★★74% Atholl Arms
Old North Rd PH18 5SG
☎ 01796 481205 ▤ 01796 481550
e-mail: hotel@athollarms.co.uk
web: www.athollarmshotel.co.uk
Dir: off A9 to B8079, 1m into Blair Atholl, hotel near entrance to Blair Castle

Situated close to Blair Castle and conveniently adjacent to the railway station, this stylish hotel has historically styled public rooms that include a choice of bars, and a splendid baronial-style dining room. Bedrooms vary in size and style with many rooms having been refurbished. Staff throughout are friendly and nothing is too much trouble.
ROOMS: 30 en suite (3 fmly) s £35-£60; d £50-£75 (incl. bkfst) **LB**
FACILITIES: Fishing Rough shooting ᛁ Xmas **CONF:** BC Thtr 120 Class 80 Board 60 Del from £65 **PARKING:** 130 **NOTES:** ⊗ in restaurant Civ Wed 120

★★63% *Bridge of Tilt*

Bridge of Tilt PH18 5SU
☎ 01796 481333 🖷 01796 481335
e-mail: hotels@theholidaygroup.com
Dir: *turn off A9 onto B8079, hotel 0.75m on left with wishing well in front*

Frequented by tour groups, this friendly hotel is situated close to Blair Castle. Bedrooms come in a variety of styles, with the chalet rooms being particularly popular. Public areas include a lounge, dining areas and a bar which offers live entertainment three times a week in season.

ROOMS: 20 en suite 7 annexe en suite (7 fmly) (7 GF)
FACILITIES: Jacuzzi ♫ **PARKING:** 40 **NOTES:** ⊗ in restaurant Closed Jan-Feb

BLAIRGOWRIE, Perth & Kinross — Map 21 NO14

Top Hotel

★★★ ❀❀ Kinloch House

PH10 6SG
☎ 01250 884237 🖷 01250 884333
e-mail: reception@kinlochhouse.com
Dir: *2m W of Blairgowrie on A923*

RELAIS & CHATEAUX

This is an idyllically located hotel with elegantly furnished and inviting public areas that include a choice of lounges, a conservatory bar with an impressive range of malt whiskies and a beauty and fitness centre. Spacious bedrooms are stylishly appointed and many boast opulent bathrooms. Carefully prepared meals feature high quality, local produce.

ROOMS: 18 en suite (1 fmly) (4 GF) s £95-£220; d £250-£360 (incl. bkfst & dinner) **LB** **FACILITIES:** Fishing Sauna Gym Xmas **CONF:** Thtr 16 Class 14 Board 20 Del from £172 **PARKING:** 36 **NOTES:** ⊗ in restaurant Closed 18 -29 Dec Civ Wed 50

★★★64% Angus

Wellmeadow PH10 6NH
☎ 01250 872455 🖷 01250 875615
e-mail: reservations@theangushotel.com
Dir: *20 mins north of Perth. On A93 Perth/Blairgowrie Rd overlooking Wellmeadow in town centre*

Inside this traditional town centre building is an attractive modern hotel which is popular with visiting tour groups. Bedrooms are smartly furnished and come in a variety of sizes. There is a spacious bar lounge and a restaurant offering good value meals.

ROOMS: 81 en suite (4 fmly) s £45-£55; d £90-£110 (incl. bkfst) **LB** **FACILITIES: Spa** Sauna Solarium Table tennis, playstations ♫ Xmas **CONF:** Thtr 200 Class 100 Board 50 Del from £60 **SERVICES:** Lift **PARKING:** 62 **NOTES:** ⊗ in restaurant Civ Wed 180

BOAT OF GARTEN, Highland — Map 23 NH91

★★★76% ❀❀ Boat

PH24 3BH
☎ 01479 831258 & 831696 🖷 01479 831414
e-mail: info@boathotel.co.uk
web: www.boathotel.co.uk
Dir: *off A9 N of Aviemore onto A95, follow signs to Boat of Garten*

In the heart of the Spey Valley, this delightful Victorian station hotel sits adjacent to the Strathspey Steam Railway. Bedrooms, all individually decorated, have been stylishly upgraded and many boast DVD players and modern, eye-catching bathrooms. The Capercaille Restaurant offers classic cuisine with a Scottish twist, whilst the cocktail bar has a selection of meals and specialises in a wide range of malt whiskies.

ROOMS: 22 en suite (2 fmly) ⊗ in all bedrooms s £79.50-£165; d £119-£165 (incl. bkfst) **LB** **FACILITIES:** Golf course adjacent Xmas **CONF:** Thtr 40 Class 30 Board 25 Del from £115 **PARKING:** 36 **NOTES:** ⊗ in restaurant RS 2 wks Jan

BOTHWELL, South Lanarkshire — Map 20 NS75

★★★68% Bothwell Bridge

89 Main St G71 8EU
☎ 01698 852246 🖷 01698 854686
e-mail: enquiries@bothwellbridge-hotel.com
web: www.bothwellbridge-hotel.com
Dir: *M74 junct 5 & follow signs to Uddingston, right at mini-rdbt. Hotel just past shops on left*

This red sandstone mansion house is a popular business, function and conference hotel conveniently placed for the motorway. Most bedrooms are spacious and all are well equipped. The conservatory is now a bright and comfortable restaurant serving an interesting variety of meals with an Italian influence. The lounge bar offers a comfortable seating area and is well used as a local venue for coffee.

ROOMS: 90 en suite (14 fmly) (26 GF) ⊗ in 53 bedrooms s £60-£70; d £70-£150 (incl. bkfst) **LB** **FACILITIES:** STV ♫ Xmas **CONF:** BC Thtr 200 Class 80 Board 50 **SERVICES:** Lift **PARKING:** 125 **NOTES:** Civ Wed 180

BRAE See Shetland

> Popped the question? Hotels with Civ wed in their entry are licensed for civil wedding ceremonies. Maximum numbers for the ceremony only are shown e.g. Civ wed 120

BRIDGEND OF LINTRATHEN, Angus Map 23 NO25

Restaurant with Rooms

⚘ ◉◉ Lochside Lodge & Roundhouse Restaurant
DD8 5JJ
☎ 01575 560340 ▤ 01575 560202
e-mail: enquiries@lochsidelodge.com
web: www.lochsidelodge.com
Dir: B951 from Kirriemuir towards Glenisla for 7m & take left turn to Lintrathen. Follow road over top of loch & into village. Hotel on left
This converted farmstead enjoys a rural location in the heart of Angus. The comfortable bedrooms that offer private facilities, are in the former hayloft and the original windows have been retained. Accomplished modern cuisine is served in the Roundhouse Restaurant. A spacious bar featuring agricultural implements and church pews, has a wide range of drinks including local beers.
ROOMS: 6 en suite (1 fmly) (2 GF) s £45-£60; d £70-£100 (incl. bkfst)
LB CONF: BC Class 20 Board 25 Del from £110 **PARKING:** 40
NOTES: ⊘ in restaurant Closed 1-24 Jan RS Sun, Mon & Xmas

BRIDGE OF ALLAN, Stirling Map 21 NS79

★★★68% Royal
Henderson St FK9 4HG
☎ 01786 832284 ▤ 01786 834377
e-mail: stay@royal-stirling.co.uk
web: www.royal-stirling.co.uk
Dir: M9 junct 11, turn right at rdbt for Bridge of Allan. Hotel in centre on left

This impressive Victorian building enjoys a central location in the town whilst providing quick access to the motorway network. The bedrooms (some of which are located in a smart lodge 200 yards from the main hotel) are comfortably modern in style and offer a good range of amenities. Public areas include an elegant restaurant serving innovative dishes and a bar providing a good range of bar meals.
ROOMS: 32 en suite (4 fmly) ⊘ in 10 bedrooms s £65-£100;
d £90-£130 (incl. bkfst) **LB FACILITIES:** STV Xmas **CONF:** Thtr 150
Class 60 Board 50 Del from £110 **SERVICES:** Lift **PARKING:** 40
NOTES: ⊘ in restaurant Civ Wed 80

BRODICK See Arran, Isle of

BRORA, Highland Map 23 NC90

★★★73% ◉ Royal Marine
Golf Rd KW9 6QS
☎ 01408 621252 ▤ 01408 621181
e-mail: info@highlandescape.com
web: www.highlandescape.com
Dir: off A9 in village toward beach and golf course
A distinctive Edwardian residence sympathetically extended, the
continued

Royal Marine attracts a mixed market. Its leisure centre is popular, and the restaurant, Hunters Lounge and café bar offer three contrasting eating options. A modern bedroom wing complements the original bedrooms, which retain their period style.

ROOMS: 22 en suite (1 fmly) s £79-£99; d £120-£160 (incl. bkfst) **LB**
FACILITIES: ▤ ♿ 18 ℅ Fishing Snooker Sauna Solarium Gym ♨
Putt green Jacuzzi Ice curling rink in season Xmas **CONF:** Thtr 70 Class
40 Board 40 Del from £125 **PARKING:** 40 **NOTES:** ⊘ in restaurant
Civ Wed 60

BROUGHTY FERRY, Dundee City Map 21 NO43

⌂ Premier Travel Inn Dundee East
115-117 Lawers Dr, Panmurefield Village DD5 3UP
☎ 0870 9906324 ▤ 0870 9906325
web: www.premiertravelinn.com
Dir: From N, take A92 Dundee to Arbroath. Hotel 1.5m past group of 32 lights on right. From S, follow A90 Perth to Dundee signs. At end of dual carriageway follow Dundee to Arbroath signs
High quality, modern budget accommodation ideal for both families and business travellers. Spacious, en suite bedrooms feature bath and shower, satellite TV and many have telephones and modem points. The adjacent family restaurant features a wide and varied menu. For further details consult the Hotel Groups page.
ROOMS: 60 en suite s £46.95-£48.95; d £46.95-£48.95

BURNTISLAND, Fife Map 21 NT28

★★★65% Kingswood
Kinghorn Rd KY3 9LL
☎ 01592 872329 ▤ 01592 873123
e-mail: rankin@kingswoodhotel.co.uk
web: www.kingswoodhotel.co.uk
Dir: A921 coastal road at Burntisland, right at rdbt, left at T-junct, at bottom of hill to Kingshorn road, hotel 0.5m on left

Lying east of the town, this hotel has views across the Firth of Forth to Edinburgh. Public rooms feature a range of cosy sitting areas, a spacious and attractive restaurant serving good value
continued

meals. There is also a good-size function room and multi-purpose conservatory. Bedrooms include two family suites and front-facing rooms with balconies.
ROOMS: 13 en suite (3 fmly) (1 GF) ⊗ in 2 bedrooms s £52-£66; d £85-£150 (incl. bkfst) **LB CONF:** Thtr 150 Class 20 Board 40 Del from £80 **PARKING:** 50 **NOTES:** Closed 26 Dec & 1 Jan Civ Wed 120

★★68% Inchview Hotel
65-69 Kinghorn Rd KY3 9EB
☎ 01592 872239 ▤ 01592 874866
e-mail: reception@inchview.co.uk
Dir: M90 junct 1, follow Fife Coastal Route signed Burntisland
Now under new ownership this hotel is a listed, Georgian terraced house, which looks out over the links to the Firth of Forth. Bedrooms include two family rooms housed in an adjacent building. A range of meals can be enjoyed in both the popular bar and elegant restaurant.
ROOMS: 16 en suite (1 fmly) (2 GF) ⊗ in all bedrooms s £50-£80; d £80-£120 (incl. bkfst) **FACILITIES:** ⁙ Beacon Leisure Centre 2 mins away, walled gardens **CONF:** Thtr 64 Class 64 **PARKING:** 14 **NOTES:** ⊗ in restaurant

CAIRNDOW, Argyll & Bute Map 20 NN11

★★65% Cairndow Stagecoach Inn
PA26 8BN
☎ 01499 600286 & 600252 ▤ 01499 600220
THE CIRCLE
Selected Individual Hotels
GREAT BRITAIN
e-mail: cairndowinn@aol.com
Dir: from North, either A82 to Tarbet, then A83 to Cairndown or A85 to Palmally, A819 to Inveraray and A83 to Cairndown.

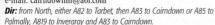

A relaxed, friendly atmosphere prevails at this 18th-century inn, overlooking the beautiful Loch Fyne. Bedrooms offer individual decor and thoughtful extras. Traditional public areas include a comfortable beamed lounge, a well-stocked bar where food is served throughout the day, and a spacious restaurant with conservatory extension.
ROOMS: 13 en suite (2 fmly) ⊗ in 3 bedrooms s £30-£55; d £60-£80 (incl. bkfst) **LB FACILITIES:** Sauna Solarium Gym Xmas **PARKING:** 32 **NOTES:** ⊗ in restaurant

CALLANDER, Stirling Map 20 NN60

★★★77% ◉◉◉ Roman Camp Country House
FK17 8BG
☎ 01877 330003 ▤ 01877 331533
e-mail: mail@roman-camp-hotel.co.uk
Dir: N on A84, left at east end of High Street. 300yds into hotel grounds
Originally a shooting lodge, this charming country house has a rich history. 20 acres of gardens and grounds lead down to the River Teith and the town centre and its attractions are only a short
continued

walk away. Food is a highlight of any stay and menus are dominated by high-quality Scottish produce that is sympathetically treated by the talented kitchen team. Real fires warm the atmospheric public areas and service is friendly yet professional.
ROOMS: 14 en suite (3 fmly) **FACILITIES:** Fishing **CONF:** Thtr 100 Class 40 Board 20 **PARKING:** 80 **NOTES:** ⊗ in restaurant

CANONBIE, Dumfries & Galloway Map 21 NY37

★★66% Cross Keys
DG14 0SY
☎ 01387 371205 371382 ▤ 371878
e-mail: enquiries@crosskeys.biz
web: www.crosskeys.biz
A former 17th-century coaching inn, this friendly hotel boasts a tastefully modern split level lounge bar offering a good selection of dishes supplemented by a carvery at weekends. Bedrooms are cheerfully decorated and come with either fine traditional pieces or stylish pine.
ROOMS: 10 rms (9 en suite) (1 fmly) s £35-£48; d £55-£58 (incl. bkfst) **PARKING:** 30 **NOTES:** ⊗ in restaurant

CARNOUSTIE, Angus Map 21 NO53

ⓤ Kinloch Arms
27-29 High St DD7 6AN
☎ 01241 853127 ▤ 01241 855183
Dir: A92 towards Arbroath, take 1st sign for Carnoustie to main street. Hotel next to library
ROOMS: 7 en suite (1 fmly) s £35-£45; d £55-£70 (incl. bkfst) **LB FACILITIES:** STV ⌕ **PARKING:** 28 **NOTES:** ★★ ⊗ in restaurant

CARRBRIDGE, Highland Map 23 NH92

★★★69% Dalrachney Lodge
PH23 3AT
☎ 01479 841252 ▤ 01479 841383
e-mail: dalrachney@aol.com
web: www.dalrachney.co.uk
Dir: follow Carrbridge signs off A9. At the N end of the village on A938
A traditional Highland lodge, Dalrachney lies in grounds by the River Dulnain on the edge of the village. Spotlessly maintained public areas include a comfortable and relaxing sitting room and a cosy well-stocked bar, which has a popular menu providing an alternative to the dining room. Bedrooms are generally spacious and furnished in period style.
ROOMS: 11 en suite (3 fmly) ⊗ in all bedrooms s £70-£140; d £95-£160 (incl. bkfst) **LB FACILITIES:** STV Fishing Xmas **PARKING:** 40 **NOTES:** ⊗ in restaurant

ⓤ Star rating not confirmed

CARRUTHERSTOWN, Dumfries & Galloway Map 21 NY17

★★★68% Hetland Hall
DG1 4JX
☎ 01387 840201 ▤ 01387 840211
e-mail: info@hetlandhallhotel.co.uk
web: www.hetlandhallhotel.co.uk
Best Western
Dir: midway between Annan & Dumfries on A75
An imposing mansion, Hetland Hall lies in attractive parkland just off the A75. It is popular for weddings and conferences and its
continued on p678

CARRUTHERSTOWN, continued

menus, available in both bar and restaurant, also draw praise. Bedrooms come in contrasting styles and sizes.

Hetland Hall, Carrutherstown

ROOMS: 14 en suite 15 annexe en suite (5 fmly) (1 GF) ⊗ in 5 bedrooms s £63-£81; d £79-£103 (incl. bkfst) **LB** **FACILITIES:** STV Sauna Gym Putt green Mini Pitch & putt, Toning tables ch fac Xmas **CONF:** Thtr 200 Class 100 Board 100 Del from £95 **PARKING:** 60 **NOTES:** ⊗ in restaurant Civ Wed 150

CASTLECARY, Falkirk Map 21 NS77

★★66% Castlecary House

Castlecary Rd G68 0HD
☎ 01324 840233 01324 841608
e-mail: enquiries@castlecaryhotel.com
web: www.castlecaryhotel.com
***Dir:** off A80 onto B816 between Glasgow and Stirling*

Close to the Forth Clyde Canal and convenient for the M80, this popular hotel provides a versatile range of accommodation, within purpose-built units in the grounds and also in an extension to the original house. The attractive and spacious restaurant serves a short carte menu and enjoyable meals are also served in the busy bars.

ROOMS: 60 rms (55 en suite) (2 fmly) s £65-£85; d £65-£85 (incl. bkfst) **CONF:** BC Thtr 200 Class 120 Board 60 Del from £120 **SERVICES:** Lift **PARKING:** 100 **NOTES:** ⊗ in restaurant

CASTLE DOUGLAS, Dumfries & Galloway Map 21 NX76

★★68% King's Arms

St Andrew's St DG7 1EL
☎ 01556 502626 01556 502097
e-mail: david@galloway-golf.co.uk
***Dir:** through main street, left at town clock, hotel on corner*

Situated a stone's throw from the town's centre, this friendly former coaching inn boasts attractive, comfortably proportioned and well equipped bedrooms. A wide range of dishes is available in all the cosy seating area - some of which have a bar - as well as in the spacious restaurant.

ROOMS: 10 rms (9 en suite) (2 fmly) ⊗ in all bedrooms s £42-£52; d £66-£70 (incl. bkfst) **LB** **CONF:** Thtr 35 Class 20 Board 25 **PARKING:** 15 **NOTES:** ⊗ in restaurant Closed 25-26 Dec & 1-2 Jan

★★67% Imperial

35 King St DG7 1AA
☎ 01556 502086 01556 503009
e-mail: david@thegolfhotel.co.uk
web: www.thegolfhotel.co.uk
***Dir:** off A75 at sign for Castle Douglas, hotel opposite town library.*

Situated in the main street, this former coaching inn, popular with golfers, offers guests well-equipped and cheerfully decorated bedrooms. There is a choice of bars and good-value meals are served either in the foyer bar or the upstairs dining room.

ROOMS: 12 en suite (1 fmly) ⊗ in all bedrooms s £42-£52; d £66-£70 (incl. bkfst) **LB** **FACILITIES:** local pool and sauna/gym 75 yds away ch fac **CONF:** Thtr 40 Class 20 Board 20 **PARKING:** 29 **NOTES:** ⊗ in restaurant Closed 23-26 Dec & 1-3 Jan

CASTLE KENNEDY, Dumfries & Galloway Map 20 NX15

★★66% The Plantings Inn

DG9 8SQ
☎ 01581 400633 01581 400637
e-mail: info@plantings.com

Convenient for Stranraer and the Irish ferries, this small hotel focuses on a pleasantly informal eating operation with a wide-ranging menu that offers hearty good-value dishes. Bedrooms are comfortable and smartly furnished; a resident's lounge is also available.

ROOMS: 5 en suite ⊗ in all bedrooms s fr £35; d fr £60 (incl. bkfst) **LB** **FACILITIES:** Xmas **CONF:** Thtr 30 Class 16 Board 16 **PARKING:** 30

CHIRNSIDE, Scottish Borders Map 21 NT85

★★★69% Chirnside Hall

TD11 3LD
☎ 01890 818219 01890 818231
e-mail: chirnsidehall@globalnet.co.uk
***Dir:** on A6105 (Berwick-on-Tweed/Duns road), approx 3m after Foulden, hotel sign on right*

At the end of a tree-lined drive this hotel is ideal for guests wishing to get away from the hustle and bustle of city life and where genuine hospitality is found. Bedrooms are spacious, many with views of the rolling Borders countryside. Real fires warm the elegantly styled lounges, and fresh local produce features on the restaurant menus.

ROOMS: 10 en suite (2 fmly) s £85-£145; d £145-£160 (incl. bkfst) **LB** **FACILITIES:** Fishing Snooker Gym Putt green Shooting Xmas **CONF:** Board 16 Del from £41.50 **PARKING:** 20 **NOTES:** ⊗ in restaurant Civ Wed 40

CLACHAN, Argyll & Bute Map 20 NR75

★★72% Balinakill Country House

PA29 6XL
☎ 01880 740206 01880 740298
e-mail: info@balinakill.com
***Dir:** access from A83, 50mtrs beyond the Thames Garage at Clachan village*

This imposing B-listed country mansion is set in grounds on the Kintyre peninsula. Graced with antiques and period pieces it boasts beautiful wood panelling and plasterwork. Many bedrooms reflect the Victorian era, with the larger ones featuring real fires. Service by hands-on owners is friendly and attentive. Meals focus on interesting menus and well-sourced produce.

ROOMS: 10 en suite (1 GF) ⊗ in all bedrooms s £45-£90; d £80-£100 (incl. bkfst) **LB** **FACILITIES:** Fishing Aromatherapy, Reflexology, Relaxing health treatments Xmas **PARKING:** 20 **NOTES:** ⊗ in restaurant

See advert on opposite page

CLACHAN-SEIL, Argyll & Bute Map 20 NM71

★★76% Willowburn

PA34 4TJ
☎ 01852 300276
e-mail: willowburn.hotel@virgin.net web: www.willowburn.co.uk
***Dir:** 0.5m from Atlantic Bridge, on left*

This welcoming small hotel enjoys a peaceful setting, with grounds

continued

stretching down to the shores of Clachan Sound. Friendly unassuming service, a relaxed atmosphere and fine food are keys to its success. Bedrooms are bright, cheerful and thoughtfully equipped. Guests can watch the wildlife from the dining room, lounge or cosy bar.
ROOMS: 7 en suite (1 GF) ⊗ in all bedrooms s £76; d £152 (incl. bkfst & dinner) **LB** **PARKING:** 20 **NOTES:** No children 8 yrs ⊗ in restaurant Closed Dec-Feb

CLUANIE INN, Highland — Map 22 NH01

★★68% Cluanie Inn

THE CIRCLE Selected Individual Hotels GREAT BRITAIN

Glenmoriston IV63 7YW
☎ 01320 340238 ▤ 01320 340293
e-mail: cluanie@ecosse.net
web: www.cluanie.co.uk
Dir: *On A87 mid-way between Loch Ness & Isle of Skye*

This delightful inn lies at the western end of Loch Cluanie and is surrounded by breathtaking Highland scenery. It's a popular base for climbers and walkers and provides the perfect stepping-stone to the Isle of Skye. Cosy bars offer roaring fires in cooler months while bedrooms are spacious and smartly furnished. Lunches are excellent value and the extensive and creative dinner menu showcases local produce from the mountains and lochs.
ROOMS: 10 en suite (2 fmly) (10 GF) ⊗ in all bedrooms s £42.50-£62.50; d £60-£116 (incl. bkfst) **LB** **FACILITIES:** Fishing Xmas **PARKING:** 20 **NOTES:** 🐕 ⊗ in restaurant RS Xmas

> Packed in a hurry? Ironing facilities should be available at all star levels, either in the rooms or on request

CLYDEBANK, West Dunbartonshire — Map 20 NS47

★★★★74% ◎◎ Beardmore

Best Western PREMIER

Beardmore St G81 4SA
☎ 0141 951 6000 ▤ 0141 951 6018
e-mail: info@beardmore.scot.nhs.uk
Dir: *M8 junct 19/A814 towards Dumbarton then follow tourist signs. Turn left onto Beardmore St & follow signs*

Attracting much business and conference custom, this stylish modern hotel lies beside the River Clyde and shares an impressive site with a hospital (although the latter does not intrude). Spacious and imposing public areas include a stylish restaurant providing innovative contemporary cooking. The café bar offers a more extensive choice of informal lighter dishes.
ROOMS: 166 en suite ⊗ in 92 bedrooms s fr £97; d fr £97 **FACILITIES: Spa** STV ▣ supervised Sauna Solarium Gym Complimentary therapies Xmas **CONF:** BC Thtr 170 Class 24 Board 26 Del from £120 **SERVICES:** Lift air con **PARKING:** 400 **NOTES:** 🐕 ⊗ in restaurant Civ Wed 170

COATBRIDGE, North Lanarkshire Map 20 NS76

Georgian Hotel
26 Lefroy St ML5 1LZ
☎ 01236 421888 📠 01236 421173
e-mail: thegeorgian@btconnect.com
Dir: *Follow brown tourist signs for Time Capsule, hotel signed on A89*
ROOMS: 8 rms (6 en suite) (1 GF) ⊗ in 4 bedrooms s £25-£40; d £40-£60 (incl. bkfst) **CONF:** BC Thtr 120 Class 70 Board 60 Del from £70 **PARKING:** 16 **NOTES:** ★★ Closed 26 Dec-1 Jan

COLBOST See Skye, Isle of

COMRIE, Perth & Kinross Map 21 NN72

★★★74% Royal
Melville Square PH6 2DN
☎ 01764 679200 📠 01764 679219
e-mail: reception@royalhotel.co.uk
web: www.royalhotel.co.uk
Dir: *off A9 on A822 to Crieff, then B827 to Comrie. Hotel in main square on A85*

A traditional façade gives little indication of the style and elegance inside this long-established hotel in the village centre. Public areas include a bar and library, a bright modern restaurant and a conservatory-style brasserie. Bedrooms are tastefully appointed and furnished with smart reproduction antiques.
ROOMS: 11 en suite s £75-£95; d £120-£160 (incl. bkfst) **LB** **FACILITIES:** STV Fishing Pool table, Fishing/shooting arranged Xmas **CONF:** Thtr 20 Class 10 Board 20 Del from £140 **PARKING:** 22 **NOTES:** ⊗ in restaurant

Early start?
Hotels at all star levels should provide in-room alarm clocks and/or alarm clocks

CONNEL, Argyll & Bute Map 20 NM93

★★72% Falls of Lora
PA37 1PB
☎ 01631 710483 📠 01631 710694
e-mail: enquiries@fallsoflora.com
web: www.fallsoflora.com
Dir: *hotel set back from A85 from Glasgow, 0.5 mile past Connel sign*
Personally run and welcoming, this long-established and thriving holiday hotel enjoys inspiring views over Loch Etive. The spacious ground floor takes in a comfortable, traditional lounge and a well-stocked bar. Guests can eat in the popular, informal bistro that caters specifically for families from 5pm onwards. Bedrooms come in a variety of styles, ranging from the standard cabin rooms to high quality, luxury rooms.

ROOMS: 30 en suite (4 fmly) (4 GF) s £39-£55; d £46-£119 (incl. bkfst) **LB** **CONF:** Thtr 45 Class 20 Board 15 **PARKING:** 40 **NOTES:** ⊗ in restaurant Closed mid Dec & Jan

See advert under OBAN

CONTIN, Highland Map 23 NH45

★★★71% Coul House
IV14 9ES
☎ 01997 421487 📠 01997 421945
e-mail: stay@coulhousehotel.com
Dir: *Turn off A9 north onto A835 (Ullapool road). Hotel on right in Contin just beyond filling station*

This imposing mansion house is set back from the road in extensive grounds. A number of the generally spacious bedrooms have superb views of the distant mountains and all are thoughtfully equipped. There is a choice of dining options available, with international cuisine served in both the elegant dining room and the less formal bistro.
ROOMS: 20 en suite (3 fmly) (4 GF) ⊗ in 7 bedrooms s £55-£75; d £90-£170 (incl. bkfst) **LB** **FACILITIES:** STV Putt green 9 hole pitch & putt Xmas **CONF:** Thtr 50 Class 30 Board 30 **PARKING:** 36 **NOTES:** ⊗ in restaurant Civ Wed 70

★★★67% Achilty
IV14 9EG
☎ 01997 421355 📠 01997 421923
e-mail: info@achiltyhotel.co.uk
web: www.achiltyhotel.co.uk
Dir: *A9 over Kessock bridge then 2nd on left at Tor rdbt onto A835, hotel on right through Contin*
Friendly owners contribute to great hospitality and a relaxed atmosphere at this roadside hotel. Public areas are full of interest; the lounges have books and games and the dining room has a musical theme. The Steading bar features exposed stone walls and

continued

offers a good selection of tasty home-cooked meals. Bedrooms are smartly furnished and cheerfully decorated.

ROOMS: 9 en suite 2 annexe en suite (3 GF) ⊗ in 9 bedrooms s £40-£66; d £61-£93 (incl. bkfst) **LB** **FACILITIES:** Xmas **CONF:** Thtr 50 Class 50 Board 20 Del from £75 **PARKING:** 100 **NOTES:** ⊗ in restaurant

CRAIGELLACHIE, Moray — Map 23 NJ24

★★★78% Craigellachie

AB38 9SR
☎ 01340 881204 📠 01340 881253
e-mail: info@craigellachie.com
web: www.craigellachie.com
Dir: *on A95 in Craigellachie, 300yds from A95/A941 junct*

This impressive and popular hotel is located in the heart of Speyside, so it is no surprise that malt whisky is a real feature with over 500 featured in the Quaich bar. Bedrooms come in various sizes, all are tastefully decorated and bathrooms are of a high specification. Creative dinners showcase local ingredients in the traditionally styled dining room.
ROOMS: 25 en suite ⊗ in all bedrooms s fr £110; d fr £140 (incl. bkfst) **LB** **FACILITIES:** STV Gym Xmas **CONF:** Thtr 60 Class 36 Board 26 Del from £122.50 **PARKING:** 50 **NOTES:** ⊗ in restaurant Civ Wed 50

CRAIGNURE See Mull, Isle of

CRAIL, Fife — Map 21 NO60

★★66% Balcomie Links

Balcomie Rd KY10 3TN
☎ 01333 450237 📠 01333 450540
e-mail: mikekadir@balcomie.fsnet.co.uk
web: www.balcomie.co.uk
Dir: *follow road to village shops, at junct of High St & Market Gate turn right. This road becomes Balcomie Rd, hotel on left*
Especially popular with visiting golfers, this family-run hotel on the east side of the village represents good value for money and has a relaxing atmosphere. Bedrooms come in a variety of sizes and styles and offer all the expected amenities. Food is served from midday in the attractive lounge bar and in the evening also in the bright cheerful dining room.
ROOMS: 15 rms (13 en suite) (2 fmly) ⊗ in all bedrooms s £55-£65; d £73-£95 (incl. bkfst) **LB** **FACILITIES:** STV Games room ♫ Xmas **PARKING:** 25 **NOTES:** ⊗ in restaurant Civ Wed 45

C

CRUDEN BAY, Aberdeenshire — Map 23 NK03

★★69% Kilmarnock Arms

Bridge St AB42 0HD
☎ 01779 812213 📠 01779 812153
e-mail: reception@kilmarnockarms.com
web: www.kilmarnockarms.com
Dir: *off A90 onto A975 N of Ellon (8m S of Peterhead). Hotel in village centre*

Lying by the riverside at the northern end of the village close to the golf course and beach, this family-run hotel offers smart, attractive modern accommodation. There is also an inviting reception lounge, plus a bar and restaurant offering a good range of popular dishes.
ROOMS: 14 en suite (1 fmly) s £40-£50; d £60-£80 (incl. bkfst) **LB** **FACILITIES:** STV Xmas **PARKING:** 10 **NOTES:** ⊗ in restaurant

★★66% *Red House*

Aulton Rd AB42 0NJ
☎ 01779 812215 📠 01779 812246
Dir: *off A952 Aberdeen/Peterhead road onto A975 (Cruden Bay), hotel opposite golf course*
Naturally popular with golfers, this welcoming small hotel overlooks the famous golf course and the sea beyond. Bedrooms are comfortably furnished, well equipped and several provide superb sea views. Guests can dine in the attractive dining room or in a choice of bars, from an extensive menu selection.
ROOMS: 6 rms (5 en suite) (1 fmly) ⊗ in all bedrooms **FACILITIES:** STV Pool tables ♫ **PARKING:** 40 **NOTES:** ⊗ in restaurant

CULLEN, Moray — Map 23 NJ56

★★★67% The Seafield Hotel

Seafield St AB56 4SG
☎ 01542 840791 📠 01542 840736
e-mail: accom@theseafieldhotel.com
web: www.theseafieldhotel.com
Dir: *in centre of town on A950*
Originally built by the Earl of Seafield as a coaching inn, this hotel was modernised in the early 70s to provide individually designed, comfortable bedrooms and is now gradually being refurbished. One of the features here is a lovely, carved wooden fireplace in

continued on p682

CULLEN, continued

the spacious lounge bar. Service is friendly and attentive with good-value and enjoyable meals served in the restaurant.

The Seafield Hotel, Cullen

ROOMS: 19 en suite (2 fmly) s £53-£65; d £80-£140 (incl. bkfst) **LB** **FACILITIES:** STV Snooker Clay pigeon shooting, Cycling, Quads, 4x4 driving, Archery Xmas **CONF:** BC Thtr 140 Class 90 Board 30 **PARKING:** 28 **NOTES:** ⊗ in restaurant Civ Wed 90

★★★66% Cullen Bay Hotel

A98 AB56 4XA
☎ 01542 840432 🖷 01542 840900
e-mail: stay@cullenbayhotel.com
web: www.cullenbayhotel.com
Dir: *on A98, 1m west of Cullen*

This family-run hotel sits on the hillside west of the town and gives lovely views of the golf course, beach and Moray Firth. The spacious restaurant, which offers a selection of fine dishes, makes the most of the view, as do many of the well-equipped bedrooms. There is a comfortable modern bar, a homely lounge and a second dining room.

ROOMS: 14 en suite (3 fmly) ⊗ in all bedrooms s £42-£50; d £68-£90 (incl. bkfst) **LB** **FACILITIES:** Xmas **CONF:** Thtr 200 Class 80 Board 80 Del from £90 **PARKING:** 100 **NOTES:** ⊗ in restaurant Civ Wed 200

CUMBERNAULD, North Lanarkshire — Map 21 NS77

★★★★69% Westerwood Hotel Golf & Country Club

1 St Andrews Dr, Westerwood G68 0EW
☎ 01236 457171 🖷 01236 738478
e-mail: westerwood@morton-hotels.com
web: www.morton-hotels.com
Dir: *A80 exit after passing Oki factory signed Wardpark/Castlecary, 2nd left at Old Inns rdbt and right at mini rdbt*

This stylish, contemporary hotel enjoys an elevated position within 400 acres at the foot of the Campsie Hills. Accommodation is provided in spacious, bright bedrooms, many with super bathrooms, and day rooms include sumptuous lounges, an airy restaurant and extensive golf, fitness and conference facilities.

ROOMS: 100 en suite (13 fmly) ⊗ in 51 bedrooms s £95-£110; d £80-£120 (incl. bkfst) **LB** **FACILITIES: Spa** STV 18 Sauna Solarium Gym Putt green Jacuzzi Beauty salon Hairdresser Xmas **CONF:** Thtr 200 Class 120 Board 60 Del from £110 **SERVICES:** Lift air con **PARKING:** 200 **NOTES:** ⊗ in restaurant Civ Wed 166

Premier Travel Inn Glasgow (Cumbernauld)

4 South Muirhead Rd G67 1AX
☎ 08701 977108 🖷 01236 736380
web: www.premiertravelinn.com
Dir: *From A80, A8011 following signs to Cumbernauld and town centre. Inn opposite Asda/McDonalds. Turn at rdbt towards Esso garage. Turn right at mini-rdbt*

High quality, modern budget accommodation ideal for both families and business travellers. Spacious, en suite bedrooms feature bath and shower, satellite TV and many have telephones and modem points. The adjacent family restaurant features a wide and varied menu. For further details consult the Hotel Groups page.

ROOMS: 37 en suite s £46.95-£48.95; d £46.95-£48.95

DALWHINNIE, Highland — Map 23 NN68

The Inn at Loch Ericht

PH19 1AG
☎ 01528 522257 🖷 01528 522270
e-mail: reservations@priory-hotel.com
Dir: *off A9 onto A886. 1m on right opposite filling station*

ROOMS: 27 en suite (2 fmly) (14 GF) ⊗ in 4 bedrooms s £33-£37; d £51-£59 (incl. bkfst) **LB** **FACILITIES:** Fishing **CONF:** Thtr 50 Class 30 Board 30 **PARKING:** 60 **NOTES:** ★

DERVAIG See Mull, Isle of

DIRLETON, East Lothian — Map 21 NT58

★★★72% *The Open Arms*

EH39 5EG
☎ 01620 850241 🖷 01620 850570
e-mail: openarms@clara.co.uk
web: www.openarmshotel.com
Dir: *from A1, follow signs for North Berwick, through Gullane, 2m on left*

Across from the picturesque village green and Dirleton Castle this long established hotel is popular with both business and leisure guests. Inviting public areas include a choice of lounges and a cosy bar. A variety of carefully prepared meals can be enjoyed in both the informal setting of Deveau's brasserie or the more intimate Library restaurant.

ROOMS: 10 en suite (1 fmly) **CONF:** Thtr 200 Class 150 Board 100 **PARKING:** 30 **NOTES:** ⊗ in restaurant Closed 4-15 Jan

DOLLAR, Clackmannanshire Map 21 NS99

★★72% Castle Campbell Hotel

11 Bridge St FK14 7DE
☎ 01259 742519 🖷 01259 743742
e-mail: bookings@castle-campbell.co.uk
web: www.castle-campbell.co.uk
Dir: *on A91 Stirling to St Andrews Rd, in the centre of Dollar, by bridge overlooking Dollar Burn & Clock Tower*

Set in the centre of a delightful country town, this hotel is popular with both local people and tourists. Accommodation ranges in size, though all rooms are thoughtfully equipped. Inviting public rooms feature a delightful lounge with real fire, a well-stocked whisky bar and a stylish restaurant.

ROOMS: 8 en suite (2 fmly) ⊗ in all bedrooms s £58-£65; d £85-£95 (incl. bkfst) **LB** **FACILITIES:** Xmas **CONF:** Thtr 80 Class 60 Board 40 Del from £75 **PARKING:** 8 **NOTES:** ⊗ in restaurant

DORNOCH, Highland Map 23 NH78

★★67% Burghfield House

IV25 3HN
☎ 01862 810212 🖷 01862 810404
e-mail: burghfield@cali.co.uk
Dir: *off A9 at Evelix junct, 1m into Dornoch. Just before War Memorial turn left and follow road up hill to tower in the trees*

Set in gardens above the town this extended Victorian mansion provides a friendly and relaxing atmosphere. Public areas, including a delightful lounge, are enhanced with antiques, fresh flowers and real fires. Bedrooms are generally well proportioned and split between the main house and the adjacent garden wing.

ROOMS: 14 rms (13 en suite) 15 annexe en suite (1 fmly) (10 GF) s £45-£65; d £80-£120 (incl. bkfst & dinner) **LB** **FACILITIES:** Putt green Xmas **CONF:** Thtr 100 Board 80 **PARKING:** 62 **NOTES:** ⊗ in restaurant Closed Jan - Feb RS Nov-Dec Civ Wed 50

U Dornoch Castle Hotel

Castle St IV25 3SD
☎ 01862 810216 🖷 01862 810981
e-mail: enquiries@dornochcastlehotel.com
web: www.dornochcastlehotel.com
Dir: *2m N of Dornoch Bridge on A9, turn right to Dornoch, Hotel in village centre on right*

At the time of going to press, the star classification for this hotel was not confirmed. Please refer to the AA internet site www.theAA.com for current information.

ROOMS: 21 en suite (3 fmly) (4 GF) ⊗ in all bedrooms s £45-£210; d £79-£220 (incl. bkfst) **LB** **CONF:** Thtr 60 Class 30 Board 30 Del from £65 **PARKING:** 16 **NOTES:** ⊗ in restaurant

DRUMNADROCHIT, Highland Map 23 NH53

A Loch Ness Lodge

IV63 6TU
☎ 01456 450342 🖷 01456 450429
e-mail: info@lochness-hotel.com
Dir: *off A82 onto A831 Cannich Rd, hotel above junction, 1m from Loch Ness*

ROOMS: 50 en suite (4 fmly) (10 GF) ⊗ in 10 bedrooms s £50-£65; d £80-£120 (incl. bkfst) **LB** **FACILITIES:** Visitors Centre, Shops, Cinema ♫ Xmas **CONF:** Thtr 50 Class 40 Board 40 Del from £78 **PARKING:** 80 **NOTES:** ★★★ ✈ Closed 5 Jan-Feb RS Mid-Jan to Mid-Feb

♫ Entertainment

DRYMEN, Stirling Map 20 NS48

★★★70% *Buchanan Arms Hotel and Leisure Club*

23 Main St G63 0BQ
☎ 01360 660588 🖷 01360 660943
e-mail: enquiries@buchananarms.co.uk
web: www.innscotland.com
Dir: *N from Glasgow on A81 then take A811, hotel at S end of Main Street*

This former coaching inn offers comfortable bedrooms in a variety of styles, with spacious public areas that include an intimate bar, a formal dining room and good function and meeting facilities as well as a fully equipped leisure centre. Teas and light meals can be served in the conservatory lounge which overlooks the gardens towards the Campsie Fells.

ROOMS: 52 en suite (3 GF) ⊗ in 6 bedrooms **FACILITIES: Spa** supervised Squash Sauna Solarium Gym Jacuzzi Bowling Green ♫ ch fac **CONF:** Thtr 180 Class 140 Board 60 **PARKING:** 100 **NOTES:** ⊗ in restaurant Civ Wed 100

★★★68% Winnock

The Square G63 0BL
☎ 01360 660245 🖷 01360 660267
e-mail: info@winnockhotel.com
Dir: *from S follow M74 onto M8 through Glasgow. Exit junct 16B, follow A809 to Aberfoyle*

Occupying a prominent position overlooking the village green, this is a popular hotel offering well-equipped bedrooms of various sizes and styles. The public rooms include a bar, a lounge and an attractive formal dining room that serves good, locally-produced food.

ROOMS: 48 en suite (12 fmly) (7 GF) ⊗ in 17 bedrooms s £59-£76; d £69-£99 (incl. bkfst) **LB** **FACILITIES:** STV Petanque ♫ ch fac Xmas **CONF:** Thtr 140 Class 60 Board 70 Del from £59 **PARKING:** 60 **NOTES:** ✈ ⊗ in restaurant Civ Wed 100

DUMBARTON, West Dunbartonshire Map 20 NS37

⌂ Travelodge

Milton G82 2TZ
☎ 08700 850 950 🖷 01389 765202
web: www.travelodge.co.uk
Dir: *2m E of Dumbarton, on A82 westbound*

Travelodge offers good quality, good value, modern accommodation. Ideal for families, the spacious, en suite bedrooms include remote-control TV, tea and coffee-making facilities and comfortable beds. Meals can be taken at the nearby family restaurant. For further details consult the Hotel Groups page.

ROOMS: 32 en suite s fr £26; d fr £26

DUMFRIES, Dumfries & Galloway Map 21 NX97
See also Carrutherstown

★★★69% ® Cairndale Hotel & Leisure Club

English St DG1 2DF
☎ 01387 254111 🖷 01387 250555
e-mail: sales@cairndale.fsnet.co.uk
web: www.cairndalehotel.co.uk
Dir: *from S turn off M6 onto A75 to Dumfries, left at 1st rdbt, cross railway bridge, continue to traffic lights, hotel 1st building on left*

Within walking distance of the town centre, this hotel provides a wide range of amenities, including leisure facilities and an impressive conference and entertainment centre. Bedrooms range from stylish suites to cosy singles. There's a choice of eating

continued on p684

DUMFRIES, continued

options in the evening. The Reivers Restaurant is smartly modern with food to match.

Cairndale Hotel & Leisure Club, Dumfries

ROOMS: 91 en suite (22 fmly) (5 GF) ⊗ in 45 bedrooms s £49.50-£89.50; d £69.50-£109.50 (incl. bkfst) **LB** **FACILITIES: Spa** STV supervised Sauna Solarium Gym Jacuzzi Steam room, air conditioned gymnasium ♫ Xmas **CONF:** BC Thtr 300 Class 150 Board 50 Del from £99 **SERVICES:** Lift **PARKING:** 120 **NOTES:** ⊗ in restaurant Civ Wed 200

See advert on opposite page

★★★69% Station
49 Lovers Walk DG1 1LT
☎ 01387 254316 🖷 01387 250388
e-mail: info@stationhotel.co.uk
web: www.stationhotel.co.uk
Dir: *A75, follow signs to Dumfries town centre, hotel opp railway station*

This hotel, sympathetically modernised in harmony with its fine Victorian features, offers well-equipped bedrooms. The Restaurant (at the time of the last inspection was about to undergo a major re-vamp) offers an extensive menu in an informal atmosphere during the evening. In addition good value meals are served in the lounge bar and conservatory during the day.
ROOMS: 32 en suite (2 fmly) ⊗ in 12 bedrooms s £55-£87; d £70-£97 (incl. bkfst) **LB** **FACILITIES:** STV Jacuzzi Use of local gym Xmas **CONF:** Thtr 60 Class 35 Board 30 Del from £85 **SERVICES:** Lift **PARKING:** 34 **NOTES:** Civ Wed 60

⌂ Premier Travel Inn Dumfries
Annan Rd, Collin DG1 3JX
☎ 08701 977078 🖷 01387 266475
web: www.premiertravelinn.com
Dir: *on main central rdbt junct of the Euroroute bypass (A75)*
High quality, modern budget accommodation ideal for both families and business travellers. Spacious, en suite bedrooms feature bath and shower, satellite TV and many have telephones and modem points. The adjacent family restaurant features a wide and varied menu. For further details consult the Hotel Groups page.
ROOMS: 40 en suite s £48.95; d £48.95

⌂ Travelodge
Annan Rd, Collin DG1 3SE
☎ 08700 850 950 🖷 01387 750658
web: www.travelodge.co.uk
Dir: *2m E of Dumfries, on A75*
Travelodge offers good quality, good value, modern accommodation. Ideal for families, the spacious, en suite bedrooms include remote-control TV, tea and coffee-making facilities and comfortable beds. Meals can be taken at the nearby family restaurant. For further details consult the Hotel Groups page.
ROOMS: 40 en suite s fr £26; d fr £26

DUNBLANE, Stirling — Map 21 NN70

Top Hotel

★★★ ◎◎ Cromlix House
Kinbuck FK15 9JT
☎ 01786 822125 🖷 01786 825450
e-mail: reservations@cromlixhouse.com
web: www.cromlixhouse.com
Dir: *off A9 N of Dunblane. Exit B8033 to Kinbuck Village then after village cross narrow bridge, drive 200yds on left*
Situated in sweeping gardens and surrounded by a 2000-acre estate, Cromlix House is an imposing Victorian mansion, boasting gracious and inviting public areas. Well-appointed bedrooms, the majority of which are suites, are spacious and elegant. The two dining rooms offer contrasting decor but both are ideal for enjoying the skilfully prepared food. Guest care is refreshingly sincere and nothing is too much trouble.
ROOMS: 14 en suite s £140-£210; d £220-£280 (incl. bkfst) **LB** **FACILITIES:** Fishing Clay pigeon shooting, Falconry, Archery Xmas **CONF:** Thtr 40 Class 24 Board 24 Del from £220 **PARKING:** 51 **NOTES:** ⊗ in restaurant Closed 2-29 Jan RS Oct-Apr Civ Wed 50

DUNDEE, Dundee City — Map 21 NO43

★★★★76% ◎◎
Apex City Quay Hotel & Spa
1 West Victoria Dock Rd DD1 3JP
☎ 01382 202404 & 0845 365 0000
🖷 01382 201401
e-mail: reservations@apexhotels.co.uk
Dir: *A85 Riverside Drive to Discovery Quay. Exit rdbt for City Quay.*
This stylish, purpose-built, modern hotel occupies an enviable position at the heart of Dundee's regenerated centre. Bedrooms,

continued

including a number of smart suites, feature the very latest in design. Warm hospitality and professional service are an integral part of the appeal. Open-plan public areas with panoramic windows and contemporary food options complete the package.

ROOMS: 153 en suite (16 fmly) ⊗ in 122 bedrooms s £70-£160; d £80-£170 (incl. bkfst) **LB** **FACILITIES: Spa** STV supervised Sauna Gym Jacuzzi Elemis treatment rooms, steam room Xmas **CONF:** BC Thtr 400 Class 180 Board 120 Del from £150 **SERVICES:** Lift **PARKING:** 150 **NOTES:** ⊗ in restaurant

★★★64% Sandford Country House Hotel

Newton Hill, Wormit DD6 8RG
☎ 01382 541802 📠 01382 542136
e-mail: sandford.hotel@btinternet.com
web: www.sandfordhotelfife.com
Dir: *off A92 at junct B946, hotel entrance 100yds from junct on left*

Built around the turn of the last century, this hotel lies in wooded grounds well off the main road. Set around a small terraced courtyard, it is a popular venue for meals, which are served in the bar or restaurant. Bedrooms come in a variety of sizes and are smart and modern in style.
ROOMS: 16 en suite (2 fmly) ⊗ in 15 bedrooms s £45-£65; d £65-£85 (incl. bkfst) **LB** **FACILITIES:** STV Adj to sports club, Cycle hire Xmas **CONF:** Thtr 45 Class 25 Board 25 Del from £95 **PARKING:** 30 **NOTES:** ⊗ in restaurant Civ Wed 40

⌂ Premier Travel Inn Dundee Centre

premier travel inn

Discovery Quay, Riverside Dr DD1 4XA
☎ 08701 977079 📠 01382 203237
web: www.premiertravelinn.com
Dir: *follow signs for Discovery Quay, situated on waterfront*
High quality, modern budget accommodation ideal for both families and business travellers. Spacious, en suite bedrooms feature bath and shower, satellite TV and many have telephones and modem points. The adjacent family restaurant features a wide and varied menu. For further details consult the Hotel Groups page.
ROOMS: 40 en suite s £55.95; d £55.95

⌂ Premier Travel Inn Dundee (Monifieth)

premier travel inn

Ethiebeaton Park, Arbroath Rd, Monifieth DD5 4HB
☎ 08701 977080 📠 01382 530468
web: www.premiertravelinn.com
Dir: *From A90 Kingsway Road follow signs for Carnoustie/Arbroath (A92)*
High quality, modern budget accommodation ideal for both families and business travellers. Spacious, en suite bedrooms feature bath and shower, satellite TV and many have telephones and modem points. The adjacent family restaurant features a wide and varied menu. For further details consult the Hotel Groups page.
ROOMS: 40 en suite s £46.95-£48.95; d £46.95-£48.95 **CONF:** Board 8

⌂ Premier Travel Inn Dundee North

premier travel inn

Dayton Dr, Camperdown Leisure Park, Kingsway DD2 3SQ
☎ 0870 9906420 📠 0870 9906421
web: www.premiertravelinn.com
Dir: *2m N of city centre on A90 at junct with A923, next to cinema & entrance to Camperdown Country Park*
High quality, modern budget accommodation ideal for both families and business travellers. Spacious, en suite bedrooms feature bath and shower, satellite TV and many have telephones and modem points. The adjacent family restaurant features a wide and varied menu. For further details consult the Hotel Groups page.
ROOMS: 78 en suite s £46.95-£48.95; d £46.95-£48.95

> The vast majority of establishments in this guide accept credit and debit cards. We indicate those that don't take any

DUNDEE, continued

⌂ Premier Travel Inn Dundee West

Kingsway West, Invergowrie DD2 5JU
☎ 08701 977081 📠 01382 568431
web: www.premiertravelinn.com
Dir: *approaching Swallow rdbt next to Technology Park rdbt take A90 towards Aberdeen, Inn on left after 250yds*
High quality, modern budget accommodation ideal for both families and business travellers. Spacious, en suite bedrooms feature bath and shower, satellite TV and many have telephones and modem points. The adjacent family restaurant features a wide and varied menu. For further details consult the Hotel Groups page.
ROOMS: 64 en suite s £46.95-£49.95; d £46.95-£49.95

⌂ Travelodge

A90 Kingsway DD2 4TD
☎ 08700 850 950 📠 01382 610488
web: www.travelodge.co.uk
Dir: *on A90*
Travelodge offers good quality, good value, modern accommodation. Ideal for families, the spacious, en suite bedrooms include remote-control TV, tea and coffee-making facilities and comfortable beds. Meals can be taken at the nearby family restaurant. For further details consult the Hotel Groups page.
ROOMS: 32 en suite s fr £26; d fr £26

DUNDONNELL, Highland Map 22 NH08

★★★70% *Dundonnell*

IV23 2QR
☎ 01854 633204 📠 01854 633366
e-mail: enquiries@dundonnellhotel.co.uk
web: www.dundonnellhotel.com
Dir: *Turn off A835 at Braemore Junction onto A832. Hotel 14 miles.*
A beautiful, isolated location at the head of Little Loch Broom is perhaps an unlikely spot for such a smart and extensively developed hotel as this. A haven of relaxation and good food, it offers a range of attractive and comfortable public areas and a choice of eating options and bars. Many of the bedrooms enjoy fine views.
ROOMS: 29 en suite 3 annexe en suite (2 fmly) (3 GF) **CONF:** Thtr 70 Class 50 Board 40 **PARKING:** 60 **NOTES:** ⊗ in restaurant

DUNFERMLINE, Fife Map 21 NT08

★★★75% Best Western Keavil House

Crossford KY12 8QW
☎ 01383 736258 📠 01383 621600
e-mail: sales@keavilhouse.co.uk
web: www.keavilhouse.co.uk
Dir: *2m W of Dunfermline on A994*

Dating from the 16th century, this former manor house is set in gardens and parkland. With a modern leisure centre and conference rooms it is suited to both business and leisure guests. Bedrooms come in a variety of sizes and occupy the original house and a modern wing. Cardoons, a contemporary conservatory restaurant, is the focal point of public rooms.
ROOMS: 47 en suite (6 fmly) (17 GF) ⊗ in 28 bedrooms
FACILITIES: Spa STV supervised Sauna Solarium Gym Jacuzzi Aerobics studio, Steam room, Beautician Xmas **CONF:** Thtr 200 Class 60 Board 50 Del from £130 **PARKING:** 150 **NOTES:** ⊗ in restaurant Civ Wed 200

★★★75% Garvock House Hotel

St John's Dr, Transy KY12 7TU
☎ 01383 621067 📠 01383 621168
e-mail: sales@garvock.co.uk
Dir: *M90 junct 3/A907 (Dunfermline). Left after football stadium (Garvock Hill), 1st right (St John's Drive), hotel on right*

A warm welcome is assured at this impeccably presented Georgian house which stands in its own beautifully landscaped gardens. Modern stylish bedrooms set high standards of quality and now include DVD players. A spacious modern function suite makes this a popular venue for weddings and conferences. Contemporary cuisine is served in the restaurant.
ROOMS: 12 en suite (1 fmly) (5 GF) ⊗ in all bedrooms s fr £79.50; d £120-£130 (incl. bkfst) **LB** **FACILITIES:** Xmas **CONF:** Thtr 70 Class 50 Board 30 **PARKING:** 70 **NOTES:** ⊗ in restaurant Civ Wed

★★★70% Pitbauchlie House

Aberdour Rd KY11 4PB
☎ 01383 722282 📠 01383 620738
e-mail: info@pitbauchlie.com
web: www.pitbauchlie.com
Dir: *M90 junct 2, onto A823, then B916. Hotel 0.5m on right*

This family hotel is set in landscaped gardens a mile south of the town centre. A stylish foyer and cocktail lounge catch the eye; the latter overlooking the garden, as does the restaurant and separate

continued

bar/bistro. The modern bedrooms are well equipped, the deluxe rooms having CD players and videos.
ROOMS: 50 en suite (3 fmly) (19 GF) ⊗ in 31 bedrooms s £88-£98; d £106-£116 (incl. bkfst) **LB** **FACILITIES:** STV Gym **CONF:** BC Thtr 150 Class 80 Board 60 Del from £134 **PARKING:** 80 **NOTES:** ⊗ in restaurant Civ Wed 150

See advert on this page

★★★65% King Malcolm

PEEL HOTELS

Queensferry Rd KY11 8DS
☎ 01383 722611 Fax 01383 730865
e-mail: info@kingmalcolm-hotel-dunfermline.com
web: www.peelhotel.com
Dir: *on A823, S of town*

Located to the south of the city, this purpose-built hotel remains popular with business clientele and is convenient for access to both Edinburgh and Fife. Public rooms include a smart foyer lounge and a conservatory bar, as well as a restaurant. Bedrooms, although not large, are well laid out and well equipped.
ROOMS: 48 en suite (2 fmly) (24 GF) ⊗ in 36 bedrooms s fr £90; d fr £120 **LB** **FACILITIES:** STV ♫ Xmas **CONF:** Thtr 150 Class 60 Board 50 Del from £95 **PARKING:** 60

⌂ Premier Travel Inn Dunfermline

premier travel inn

East Fife Retail Park, Wimbrel Place KY11 8EX
☎ 0870 6001486 Fax 0870 600 1487
web: www.premiertravelinn.com
High quality, modern budget accommodation ideal for both families and business travellers. Spacious, en suite bedrooms feature bath and shower, satellite TV and many have telephones and modem points. The adjacent family restaurant features a wide and varied menu. For further details consult the Hotel Groups page.
ROOMS: 40 en suite s £46.95-£49.95; d £46.95-£49.95

DUNKELD, Perth & Kinross — Map 21 NO04

Top Hotel

★★★ ◎◎◎ Kinnaird

RELAIS & CHATEAUX

Kinnaird Estate PH8 0LB
☎ 01796 482440 Fax 01796 482289
e-mail: enquiry@kinnairdestate.com
Dir: *from Perth, A9 towards Inverness towards Dunkeld but do not enter town, continue N for 2m then B898 on left*
An imposing Edwardian mansion set in 9, 000 acres of beautiful countryside on the west bank of the River Tay. Sitting rooms are warm and inviting with deep-cushioned sofas and open fires. Bedrooms are furnished with rich, soft, luxurious fabrics, and have marble bathrooms. Food is creative and imaginative, with abundant local produce featuring on all

continued

menus. While jacket and tie are required at dinner, the atmosphere overall is tranquil and relaxed.

ROOMS: 9 en suite (1 GF) s £195-£245; d £295-£450 (incl. bkfst) **LB** **FACILITIES:** **Spa** STV Fishing Snooker Shooting Xmas **CONF:** Thtr 25 Class 10 Board 15 Del from £225 **SERVICES:** Lift **PARKING:** 22 **NOTES:** No dogs No children 12yrs ⊗ in restaurant Civ Wed 36

DUNOON, Argyll & Bute — Map 20 NS17

★★75% Royal Marine

Hunters Quay PA23 8HJ
☎ 01369 705810 Fax 01369 702329
e-mail: rmhotel@sol.co.uk web: www.rmhotel.co.uk
Dir: *on A815 opposite Western Ferries terminal*
This welcoming privately owned hotel commands impressive views over the Firth of Clyde. The bedrooms vary in size and are

continued on p688

DUNOON, continued

modern in appointment, offering a good range of amenities. Public areas include a formal dining room where a fixed-price menu is available, a well-stocked bar and the popular Ghillies café-bar with its attractive garden area.

Royal Marine, Dunoon

ROOMS: 31 en suite 10 annexe en suite (3 fmly) (5 GF) s £51-£60; d £74-£82 (incl. bkfst) **LB** **FACILITIES:** ♫ Xmas **CONF:** Thtr 90 Class 40 Board 30 Del £64 **PARKING:** 40 **NOTES:** ✈ ⊗ in restaurant

★★66% *Selborne*

Clyde St, West Bay PA23 7HU
☎ 01369 702761 📠 01369 704032
e-mail: selborne.dunoon@alfatravel.co.uk
web: www.alfatravel.co.uk

Dir: *from Caledonian Macbrayne pier. Follow road past castle, left into Jane St and then right into Clyde St*

This holiday hotel is situated overlooking the West Bay and provides unrestricted views of the Clyde Estuary towards the Isles of Cumbrae. Tour groups are especially well catered for in this good-value establishment, which offers entertainment most nights. Bedrooms are comfortable, many having sea views.

ROOMS: 98 en suite (14 GF) **FACILITIES:** Pool table, Table tennis ♫ **SERVICES:** Lift **PARKING:** 30 **NOTES:** ✈ ⊗ in restaurant Closed Dec-Feb ex Xmas RS Nov & Mar

★★64% Esplanade Hotel

West Bay PA23 7HU
☎ 01369 704070 📠 01369 702129
e-mail: relax@ehd.co.uk

Dir: *100mtrs from Dunoon pier, 1st left after Castle House Museum*

This family-run hotel enjoys a prime location and views over the Firth of Clyde. Public areas include relaxing lounges on both the first and ground floors and a large dining room. Thoughtfully equipped bedrooms, many of which are spacious, come in a variety of styles.

ROOMS: 60 en suite 5 annexe en suite (5 fmly) (17 GF) ⊗ in 30 bedrooms s £47-£62; d £80-£110 (incl. bkfst & dinner) **LB** **FACILITIES:** STV Putt green ♫ Xmas **CONF:** Thtr 50 Class 50 Board 40 **SERVICES:** Lift **PARKING:** 23 **NOTES:** ✈ ⊗ in restaurant Closed 2 Jan-9 Apr, 17 Oct-23 Dec

EAST KILBRIDE, South Lanarkshire — Map 20 NS65

★★★★67% ®

Crutherland Country House Hotel

Strathaven Rd G75 0QZ
☎ 01355 577000 📠 01355 220855
e-mail: crutherland@macdonald-hotels.co.uk
web: www.macdonald-hotels.co.uk

Dir: *Follow A726 signed Strathaven, straight over Torrance rdbt, hotel on left after 250yds*

Extensively renovated, this mansion is set in 37 acres of landscaped grounds two miles from the town centre. Behind its Georgian façade is a very relaxing hotel with elegant public areas plus extensive banqueting and leisure facilities. The bedrooms are spacious and comfortable. Staff provide good levels of attention and enjoyable meals are served in the restaurant.

ROOMS: 75 en suite (16 fmly) (16 GF) ⊗ in 65 bedrooms s £65-£80; d £100-£120 (incl. bkfst) **FACILITIES:** STV Sauna Solarium Gym Xmas **CONF:** Thtr 500 Class 100 Board 50 Del from £135 **SERVICES:** Lift **PARKING:** 200 **NOTES:** ✈ ⊗ in restaurant Civ Wed 300

Premier Travel Inn Glasgow East Kilbride

Brunel Way, The Murray G75 0LD
☎ 08701 977110 📠 01355 230517
web: www.premiertravelinn.com

Dir: *M74 junct 5, follow signs for East Kilbride A725, then signs Paisley A726, turn left at Murray rdbt and left into Brunel Way*

High quality, modern budget accommodation ideal for both families and business travellers. Spacious, en suite bedrooms feature bath and shower, satellite TV and many have telephones and modem points. The adjacent family restaurant features a wide and varied menu. For further details consult the Hotel Groups page.

ROOMS: 40 en suite s £46.95-£49.95; d £46.95-£49.95

Premier Travel Inn Glasgow East Kilbride West

Eaglesham Rd G75 8LW
☎ 0870 9906542 📠 0870 9906543
web: www.premiertravelinn.com

Dir: *8m from M74 junct 5 on A726 at rdbt of B764*

High quality, modern budget accommodation ideal for both families and business travellers. Spacious, en suite bedrooms feature bath and shower, satellite TV and many have telephones and modem points. The adjacent family restaurant features a wide and varied menu. For further details consult the Hotel Groups page.

ROOMS: 40 en suite s £46.95-£49.95; d £46.95-£49.95

EDINBURGH, City of Edinburgh — Map 21 NT27

Top Town House

★★★★★ ®® The Scotsman

20 North Bridge EH1 1YT
☎ 0131 556 5565 📠 0131 652 3652
e-mail: reservations@thescotsmanhotelgroup.co.uk
web: www.thescotsmanhotel.co.uk

Dir: *A8 to city centre, left onto Charlotte St. Right into Queen St, right at rdbt onto Leith Street. Straight on, left onto North Bridge, hotel on right*

This stunning conversion was formerly the headquarters of The Scotsman newspaper. The classical elegance of the public

continued

areas, complete with a marble staircase, blends seamlessly with the contemporary bedrooms and their state-of-the-art technology. The superbly equipped leisure club includes a stainless steel swimming pool and large gym. Dining arrangements can be made in the funky North Bridge Brasserie, or in the opulent, award-winning Vermilion restaurant.
ROOMS: 69 en suite (4 GF) ⊗ in 25 bedrooms s £140-£890; d £180-£700 **FACILITIES: Spa** STV supervised Sauna Solarium Gym Jacuzzi Beauty treatments **CONF:** Thtr 100 Class 50 Board 40 Del from £140 **SERVICES:** Lift **NOTES:** Civ Wed 70

★★★★★71% ◎◎ Balmoral

ROCCO FORTE HOTELS

1 Princes St EH2 2EQ
☎ 0131 556 2414 📠 0131 557 3747
e-mail: reservations@thebalmoralhotel.com
web: www.roccofortehotels.com
Dir: *follow City Centre signs. Hotel at E end of Princes St, adjacent to Wavereley Station*
This elegant hotel enjoys a prestigious address at the top of Princes Street, with fine views over the city and the castle. Bedrooms and suites are stylishly furnished and decorated, all boasting a thoughtful range of extras and impressive marble bathrooms. Hotel amenities include a Roman-style health spa, extensive function facilities, a choice of bars and two very different dining options; Number One offers inspired fine dining whilst Hadrians is a bustling, informal brasserie.
ROOMS: 188 en suite (23 fmly) ⊗ in 145 bedrooms **FACILITIES: Spa** STV supervised Sauna Solarium Gym ESPA treatment rooms, steam room, exercise studio, relaxation room ♫ Xmas **CONF:** BC Thtr 350 Class 180 Board 60 Del from £265 **SERVICES:** Lift air con **PARKING:** 100 **NOTES:** ✗ Civ Wed 60

★★★★★70% ◎◎ Sheraton Grand Hotel & Spa

Sheraton HOTELS & RESORTS

1 Festival Square EH3 9SR
☎ 0131 229 9131 📠 0131 228 4510
e-mail: grandedinburgh.sheraton@sheraton.com
web: www.starwood.com
Dir: *follow City Centre signs (A8). Through Shandwick, right at lights into Lothian Rd. Right at next lights. Hotel on left at next lights*
This modern hotel has one of the best leisure centre and spas in the city - the pool is well worth a look. The spacious bedrooms are available in a variety of styles, and the suites prove very popular. There is a wide range of eating options including The Terrace, Santini's and the Grillroom that all have a loyal local following.
ROOMS: 260 en suite (25 fmly) ⊗ in 204 bedrooms s £110-£250; d £140-£290 **LB FACILITIES: Spa** STV Sauna Gym Jacuzzi Indoor/Outdoor hydropool, Thermal suite, Spa treatment rooms ♫ Xmas **CONF:** BC Thtr 485 Class 350 Board 120 Del from £190 **SERVICES:** Lift air con **PARKING:** 121 **NOTES:** ✗ ⊗ in restaurant Civ Wed 485

Top Town House

★★★★ ◎◎ Channings

CLASSIC BRITISH

15 South Learmonth Gardens EH4 1EZ
☎ 0131 332 3232 & 315 2226 📠 0131 332 9631
e-mail: reserve@channings.co.uk
web: www.channings.co.uk
Dir: *from A90 and Forth Road Bridge, follow signs for city centre*
Minutes from the city centre, this elegant town house occupies five Edwardian terraced houses. The stylish public areas include sumptuous, inviting lounges and a choice of dining options. Ochre Vita wine bar and Mediterranean

continued

restaurant offers the popular choice, but for special occasion dining try the seven-course tasting menu with wines, in the intimate Channings Restaurant. The attractive and individually designed bedrooms have a hi-tech spec for business guests.

ROOMS: 41 en suite (4 GF) ⊗ in 34 bedrooms s £95-£140; d £125-£185 (incl. bkfst) **LB FACILITIES:** STV Xmas **CONF:** Thtr 35 Board 18 Del from £140 **SERVICES:** Lift **NOTES:** ✗ ⊗ in restaurant

Top Hotel

★★★★ ◎◎ Prestonfield
Priestfield Rd EH16 5UT
☎ 0131 225 7800 📠 0131 220 4392
e-mail: reservations@prestonfield.com
web: www.prestonfield.com
Dir: *A7 towards Cameron Toll. 200mtrs beyond Royal Commonwealth Pool, into Priestfield Rd*
This centuries-old landmark has been lovingly restored and enhanced to provide deeply comfortable and dramatically furnished bedrooms. The building demands to be explored: from the tapestry lounge to the whisky room and to the restaurant, where the walls are adorned with pictures of former owners. Facilities and services are up to the minute, and carefully prepared meals are served in the Rhubarb restaurant.
ROOMS: 24 en suite (6 GF) ⊗ in 3 bedrooms s £195-£275; d £195-£275 (incl. bkfst) **LB FACILITIES:** STV ⛳ 18 Xmas **CONF:** BC Thtr 700 Class 500 Board 40 **SERVICES:** Lift **PARKING:** 250 **NOTES:** Civ Wed 350

See advert on page 691

◎ AA Rosette Award for culinary excellence

E

EDINBURGH, continued

Top Town House

★★★★ ⊛ **The Howard**
34 Great King St EH3 6QH
☎ 0131 557 3500 📠 0131 557 6515
e-mail: reserve@thehoward.com web: www.thehoward.com
Dir: *E on Queen St, 2nd left. Through 3 lights, right, hotel on left*
Quietly elegant and splendidly luxurious The Howard provides an intimate and high quality experience for the discerning traveller. It comprises three linked Georgian houses and is situated just a short walk from Princes Street. The sumptuous bedrooms, in a variety of styles, include spacious suites, well-equipped bathrooms and a host of thoughtful touches. Ornate chandeliers and lavish drapes adorn the drawing room, while the Atholl Dining Room contains unique hand-painted murals dating from the 1800s.
ROOMS: 18 en suite s £108-£145; d £180-£275 (incl. bkfst) **LB**
FACILITIES: STV Xmas **CONF:** Thtr 16 Board 14 Del £210
SERVICES: Lift **PARKING:** 10 **NOTES:** ⊗ in restaurant

★★★★78% ⊛⊛⊛ **Norton House**
Ingliston EH28 8LX
☎ 0131 333 1275 📠 0131 333 5305
e-mail: nortonhouse-cro@handpicked.co.uk
web: www.handpicked.co.uk
Dir: *off A8, 5m W of city centre*

This extended Victorian mansion, set in 55 acres of parkland, is peacefully situated just outside the city, with convenient access to the airport. Both contemporary bedrooms and more traditional and very spacious bedrooms are offered, each providing good levels of comfort. Public areas take in a choice of lounges as well as dining options, with a busy brasserie and Ushers, the intimate fine dining restaurant.
ROOMS: 47 en suite (2 fmly) (10 GF) ⊗ in 27 bedrooms s £150-£190; d £150-£190 **LB** **FACILITIES:** STV Archery, Laser, Clay pigeon shooting, Quad biking Xmas **CONF:** Thtr 300 Class 100 Board 60 Del from £155
PARKING: 200 **NOTES:** ⊗ in restaurant Civ Wed 150

See advert on this page

E

EDINBURGH, continued

★★★★72% *Marriott Dalmahoy Hotel & Country Club*

Kirknewton EH27 8EB
☎ 0870 400 7299 📠 0870 400 7399
e-mail: reservations.dalmahoy@marriotthotels.co.uk
web: www.marriott.co.uk
Dir: *Edinburgh City Bypass (A720) turn onto A71, on left*

The rolling Pentland Hills and beautifully kept parkland provide a stunning backdrop for this imposing Georgian mansion. With two championship golf courses and a health and beauty club, there is plenty here to occupy guests. Bedrooms are spacious and most have fine views, while public rooms offer a choice of formal and informal drinking and dining options.
ROOMS: 43 en suite 172 annexe en suite (59 fmly) ⊗ in 136 bedrooms **FACILITIES:** STV ⛆ ⛳ 18 Sauna Solarium Gym Putt green Jacuzzi Health & beauty treatments, Steam room, Dance studio, Driving range, Hair salon ch fac **CONF:** Thtr 300 Class 200 Board 120 **SERVICES:** Lift **PARKING:** 350 **NOTES:** ✈ ⊗ in restaurant Civ Wed 250

Town House

★★★★ The Bonham

35 Drumsheugh Gardens EH3 7RN
☎ 0131 226 6050 0131 623 9116 📠 0131 226 6080
e-mail: reserve@thebonham.com
web: www.thebonham.com
Dir: *located close to West End & Princes St*
Overlooking tree-lined gardens, this Victorian town house combines classical elegance with a contemporary style. Inviting day rooms include a reception lounge and smart restaurant. Bedrooms focus on contemporary design and include internet, video, DVD and hi-fi systems.
ROOMS: 48 en suite (1 GF) ⊗ in 24 bedrooms s £108-£145; d £146-£195 (incl. bkfst) **LB** **FACILITIES:** STV Xmas **CONF:** Thtr 50 Board 26 Del £185 **SERVICES:** Lift **PARKING:** 20 **NOTES:** ✈ ⊗ in restaurant

★★★★72% Novotel Edinburgh Centre

Lauriston Place, Lady Lawson St EH3 9DE
☎ 0131 656 3500 📠 0131 656 3510
e-mail: H3271@accor.com
web: www.novotel.com
Dir: *from Edinburgh Castle right onto George IV Bridge from Royal Mile. Follow to junct, then right onto Lauriston Pl for hotel 700mtrs on right*
One of the new generation of Novotels, this modern hotel is located in the centre of the city, close to Edinburgh Castle and five minutes from Princes Street. Public areas are contemporary in style and include a smart bar, brasserie style restaurant and indoor leisure facilities. The air-conditioned bedrooms feature a comprehensive range of extras and bathrooms with baths and separate shower cabinets. Novotel - AA Hotel Group of the Year 2005-6.
ROOMS: 180 en suite (146 fmly) ⊗ in 135 bedrooms s £79-£149; d £79-£149 **LB** **FACILITIES:** STV ⛆ Sauna Gym Jacuzzi Xmas **CONF:** BC Thtr 80 Class 50 Board 32 Del from £140 **SERVICES:** Lift air con **PARKING:** 15

★★★★71% Holyrood Hotel

Holyrood Rd EH8 8AU
☎ 0131 550 4500 📠 0131 550 4545
e-mail: holyrood@macdonald-hotels.co.uk
web: www.macdonald-hotels.co.uk
Dir: *parallel to Royal Mile, near Holyrood Palace & Dynamic Earth*

Situated just a short walk from Holyrood Palace, this impressive hotel lies next to the new Scottish Parliament building. Air-conditioned bedrooms are comfortably furnished, whilst the Club floor boasts a private lounge. Full business services complement the extensive conference suites and the spa provides an opportunity for relaxation.
ROOMS: 156 en suite ⊗ in 140 bedrooms s £89-£230; d £99-£250 **LB** **FACILITIES:** STV ⛆ Sauna Solarium Gym Beauty treatment rooms ♫ Xmas **CONF:** BC Thtr 200 Class 100 Board 80 Del from £130 **SERVICES:** Lift air con **PARKING:** 70 **NOTES:** ✈ ⊗ in restaurant Civ Wed 100

★★★★71% Carlton

North Bridge EH1 1SD
☎ 0131 472 3000 📠 0131 556 2691
e-mail: carlton@paramount-hotels.co.uk
web: www.paramount-hotels.co.uk
Dir: *on North Bridge which links Princes St to the Royal Mile*
The Carlton occupies a city centre location just off the Royal Mile; it is modern and stylish in design. Public areas include an impressive open-plan reception/lobby, modern first-floor bar and restaurant and basement leisure club. Bedrooms, many air conditioned, are generally spacious, with an excellent range of facilities.
ROOMS: 189 en suite (20 fmly) ⊗ in 140 bedrooms s £165; d £165 **LB** **FACILITIES: Spa** STV ⛆ Squash Sauna Solarium Gym Jacuzzi Table tennis, Dance studio, Creche, Exercise classes ♫ Xmas **CONF:** BC Thtr 240 Class 100 Board 60 Del £185 **SERVICES:** Lift **NOTES:** ⊗ in restaurant Civ Wed 160

★★★★70% Apex International

31/35 Grassmarket EH1 2HS
☎ 0131 300 3456 & 0845 365 0000
📠 0131 220 5345
e-mail: reservations@apexhotels.co.uk
web: www.apexhotels.co.uk
Dir: *into Lothian Rd at west end of Princes Street, then 1st left into King Stables Rd, leads into Grassmarket*
A sister to the Apex City Hotel close by, the International enjoys a superb city centre location, lying in a historic square in the

continued

shadow of Edinburgh Castle. It has a versatile business and conference centre, and the bedrooms are contemporary in style and well equipped. The fifth-floor restaurant boasts stunning views of the castle.

ROOMS: 171 en suite (99 fmly) ⊗ in 100 bedrooms s £80-£210; d £90-£220 (incl. bkfst) **LB** **FACILITIES:** STV Xmas **CONF:** Thtr 200 Class 80 Board 40 Del from £160 **SERVICES:** Lift **PARKING:** 60 **NOTES:** ✈ ⊗ in restaurant Civ Wed 200

See advert on page 697

★★★★70% Menzies Belford

69 Belford Rd EH4 3DG
☎ 0131 332 2545 📠 0131 332 3805
e-mail: belford@menzies-hotels.co.uk
web: www.menzies-hotels.co.uk
Dir: *Belford Rd off Queensferry Rd, opposite the Dean Gallery.*

This purpose-built hotel enjoys a quiet location by the Water of Leith. The bedrooms are stylishly appointed. Bright, airy public areas include a comfortable reception lounge and spacious open-plan bar and restaurant overlooking the river, as does the separate Granary bar which focuses on pub food. Conference areas have their own manned business centre.

ROOMS: 146 en suite (1 fmly) ⊗ in 56 bedrooms s £155; d £175 **LB** **FACILITIES:** Xmas **CONF:** BC Thtr 120 Class 50 Board 45 Del £170 **SERVICES:** Lift **PARKING:** 57 **NOTES:** ⊗ in restaurant Civ Wed

★★★★70% Roxburghe

38 Charlotte Square EH2 4HG
☎ 0131 240 5500 📠 0131 240 5555
e-mail: roxburghe@macdonald-hotels.co.uk
web: www.macdonald-hotels.co.uk
Dir: *on corner of Charlotte St & George St*

This long-established hotel lies in the heart of the city overlooking Charlotte Square Gardens. Public areas are inviting and include relaxing lounges, a choice of bars (in the evening) and an inner concourse that looks onto a small lawn area. Smart bedrooms come in classic or contemporary style. Secure car park.

ROOMS: 197 en suite (4 fmly) ⊗ in 167 bedrooms s £89-£230; d £99-£270 **LB** **FACILITIES: Spa** STV ⛆ Sauna Solarium Gym Dance studio, Spa treatment rooms, steam room ♫ Xmas **CONF:** Thtr 300 Class 120 Board 80 Del from £130 **SERVICES:** Lift **PARKING:** 20 **NOTES:** ✈ ⊗ in restaurant Civ Wed 280

★★★★69% Edinburgh Marriott Hotel

111 Glasgow Rd EH12 8NF
☎ 0870 400 7293 & 0131 334 9191
📠 0870 400 7393
e-mail: edinburgh@marriotthotels.co.uk
web: www.marriott.co.uk
Dir: *M8 junct 1 for Gogar, at rdbt turn right for city centre, hotel on right*

Located on the city's western edge, this purpose built hotel is convenient for the bypass, airport, showground and business park. Public areas include an attractive marbled foyer, two bars and a restaurant serving a range of international dishes alongside an attractive carvery. Air-conditioned bedrooms are spacious and equipped with a range of extras.

ROOMS: 245 en suite (76 fmly) (64 GF) ⊗ in 189 bedrooms s £112-£175; d £112-£175 **LB** **FACILITIES:** STV ⛆ Sauna Solarium Gym Jacuzzi Steam room, Massage and beauty treatment room **CONF:** BC Thtr 250 Class 120 Board 45 Del from £125 **SERVICES:** Lift air con **PARKING:** 300 **NOTES:** ✈ ⊗ in restaurant Civ Wed 80

★★★★68% George Inter-Continental

19-21 George St EH2 2PB
☎ 0131 225 1251 📠 0131 226 5644
e-mail: edinburgh@interconti.com
Dir: *Charlotte Sq, follow signs to Leith, along Queen St. Take 2nd turning on right, Hanover St, to rdbt. Left onto George St, hotel 50mtrs on right*

A long-established hotel, The George enjoys a city centre location. The splendid public areas have many original features, such as intricate plasterwork, marble-floored foyer and chandeliers. The carvery restaurant is a magnificent room and there is also Le Chambertin for a more intimate and formal meal. Bedrooms come in a mix of sizes and styles, the upper ones having fine city views.

ROOMS: 195 en suite ⊗ in 73 bedrooms s £75-£180; d £85-£240 (incl. bkfst) **LB** **FACILITIES:** STV Complimentary fitness club nearby Xmas **CONF:** BC Thtr 200 Class 80 Board 80 Del from £150 **SERVICES:** Lift **PARKING:** 20 **NOTES:** ✈ Civ Wed 200

> 🏘 Town House Hotel
> 🏡 Country House Hotel
> ⌂ Travel Accommodation

EDINBURGH, continued

★★★★65% Apex City

61 Grassmarket EH1 2JF
☎ 0131 243 3456 & 0845 365 0000
🖷 0131 225 6346
e-mail: reservations@apexhotels.co.uk
Dir: *into Lothian Rd at the west end of Princes Street, 1st left into King Stables Rd. Leads into Grassmarket*

This modern, stylish hotel is located in the heart of the city, within easy walking distance of many of Edinburgh's attractions. The spacious, design-led bedrooms are fresh and contemporary and each has artwork by Richard Dimarco. Agua bar and restaurant is a smart open-plan area in dark wood and chrome that serves a range of meals and cocktails.

ROOMS: 119 en suite ⊗ in 84 bedrooms s £90-£220; d £100-£230 (incl. bkfst) **LB** **FACILITIES:** STV Xmas **CONF:** Thtr 70 Class 24 Board 34 Del from £160 **SERVICES:** Lift **PARKING:** 10 **NOTES:** ✱ ⊗ in restaurant

See advert on page 697

★★★★65% *The Royal Terrace*

18 Royal Ter EH7 5AQ
☎ 0131 557 3222 & 524 5000 🖷 0131 557 5334
e-mail: sales@royalterracehotel.co.uk
web: www.royalterracehotel.co.uk
Dir: *A71 to city centre, follow one-way system, left into Charlotte Sq. At end right into Queens St. Left at rdbt. At next island right into London Rd, right again into Royal Terrace*

Providing the intimacy of a sophisticated town house, this stylish hotel forms part of a quiet Georgian terrace close to the city centre and main tourist attractions. Many of the bedrooms have now been refurbished in a style that successfully blends the historic architecture of the building with state-of-the-art facilities. Top floor rooms provide excellent rooftop views of the city.

ROOMS: 108 en suite (6 fmly) (5 GF) ⊗ in 30 bedrooms **FACILITIES:** STV Sauna Solarium Gym Jacuzzi Steam room **CONF:** BC Thtr 90 Class 60 Board 40 **SERVICES:** Lift **NOTES:** ✱ ⊗ in restaurant Civ Wed 80

See advert on opposite page

★★★78% ® *Malmaison*

One Tower Place EH6 7DB
☎ 0131 468 5000 🖷 0131 468 5002
e-mail: edinburgh@malmaison.com
web: www.malmaison.com
Dir: *A900 from city centre towards Leith, at end of Leith Walk , & through 3 lights, left into Tower St. Hotel on right at end of road*

Overlooking the port of Leith, this former seamen's mission is now home to the stylish Malmaison. Bedrooms have striking decor, CD players, mini-bars and a number of individual, welcoming touches. Food and drink are equally important here, with brasserie-style dining and a café bar, both of which are popular with the local clientele.

ROOMS: 101 en suite (18 fmly) ⊗ in 12 bedrooms **FACILITIES:** STV Gym **CONF:** Thtr 55 Class 30 Board 26 **SERVICES:** Lift **PARKING:** 50

★★★76% ® Best Western Bruntsfield

69/74 Bruntsfield Place EH10 4HH
☎ 0131 229 1393 🖷 0131 229 5634
e-mail: sales@thebruntsfield.co.uk
web: www.thebruntsfield.co.uk
Dir: *from S into Edinburgh on A702. Hotel 1m S of west end of Princes Street*

Overlooking Bruntsfield Links, this smart hotel has stylish public rooms including relaxing lounge areas and a lively pub. Bedrooms come in a variety of sizes and styles and are well equipped. Imaginative dinner menus and hearty Scottish breakfasts are served in the bright and modern Cardoon conservatory restaurant. Smart staff provide good levels of service and attention.

ROOMS: 73 en suite (5 fmly) ⊗ in 49 bedrooms s £89-£139; d £170-£225 (incl. bkfst) **LB** **FACILITIES:** STV Xmas **CONF:** Thtr 75 Class 30 Board 30 Del from £110 **SERVICES:** Lift **PARKING:** 25 **NOTES:** ⊗ in restaurant Closed 25 Dec Civ Wed 85

★★★75% ®®
Dalhousie Castle & Aqueous Spa

Bonnyrigg EH19 3JB
☎ 01875 820153 🖷 01875 821936
e-mail: info@dalhousiecastle.co.uk
web: www.vonessenhotels.co.uk
Dir: *A7 S from Edinburgh through Lasswade/Newtongrange, right at Shell Garage (B704), hotel 0.5m from junct*

A popular wedding venue, this imposing medieval castle sits amid lawns and parkland and even has a falconry. Bedrooms offer a mix of styles and sizes, including richly decorated themed rooms named after various historical figures. The Dungeon restaurant provides an atmospheric setting for dinner, and the less formal Orangery serves food all day.

ROOMS: 27 en suite 6 annexe en suite (3 fmly) ⊗ in all bedrooms s £120-£325; d £165-£325 (incl. bkfst) **LB** **FACILITIES: Spa** STV Fishing Sauna Solarium Jacuzzi Falconry, Clay pigeon shooting, Archery, Loch fishing Xmas **CONF:** Thtr 120 Class 60 Board 40 Del from £200 **PARKING:** 110 **NOTES:** ⊗ in restaurant Civ Wed 100

★★★71% Melville Castle

Melville Gate, Gilmerton Rd EH18 1AP
☎ 0131 654 0088 Fax 0131 654 4666
e-mail: reception@melvillecastle.com
web: www.melvillecastle.com
Dir: *from S on Bypass, exit at Gilmerton junct onto A7. Pass Dobbies Garden Centre, straight over rdbt for hotel. From N on Bypass, exit for Galashiels off Sheriff Hall rdbt. Left at next rdbt for hotel.*

A castellated mansion set in wooded grounds close to the bypass near the city's southern boundary, this hotel focuses on receptions, small conferences and corporate events. The business and leisure guest will appreciate the lovely bedrooms, including galleried suites. Meals are served in the vaulted cellar bar and brasserie.

ROOMS: 32 en suite (1 fmly) (10 GF) ⊗ in all bedrooms s £90-£135; d £130-£195 (incl. bkfst) **LB** **FACILITIES:** STV Fishing ♫ Xmas **CONF:** BC Thtr 90 Class 45 Board 45 Del from £150 **SERVICES:** Lift **PARKING:** 100 **NOTES:** ✗ ⊗ in restaurant Civ Wed 80

★★★71% Apex European

APEX HOTELS

90 Haymarket Ter EH12 5LQ
☎ 0131 474 3456 & 0845 365 0000
Fax 0131 474 3400
e-mail: reservations@apexhotels.co.uk
web: www.apexhotels.co.uk
Dir: *A8 to city centre, hotel at Haymarket just after Donaldsons School for Deaf.*

Lying just west of the city centre, close to Haymarket Station and handy for the Conference Centre, this modern hotel is popular with business travellers. Smart, stylish bedrooms offer an excellent range of facilities and have been designed with work requirements in mind. Public areas include Metro, an informal bistro. Service is friendly and pro-active.

ROOMS: 66 en suite (3 GF) ⊗ in 51 bedrooms s £70-£160; d £80-£170 (incl. bkfst) **LB** **FACILITIES:** STV Xmas **CONF:** Thtr 80 Class 30 Board 36 Del from £150 **SERVICES:** Lift **PARKING:** 17 **NOTES:** ✗ ⊗ in restaurant Closed 24-27 Dec

See advert on page 697

EDINBURGH, continued

★★★71% Best Western Edinburgh City

79 Laurieston Place EH3 9HZ
☎ 0131 622 7979 📠 0131 622 7900
e-mail: reservations@
bestwesternedinburghcity.co.uk
Dir: *follow signs for city centre A8. Onto A702, 3rd exit on left, hotel on right*

Occupying a site that was once the old maternity hospital, this tasteful conversion is located close to the city centre. Spacious bedrooms are smartly modern and well equipped to include fridges. Meals can be enjoyed in the bright contemporary restaurant and guests can relax in the cosy bar and reception lounge. Staff are friendly and obliging.

ROOMS: 52 en suite (12 fmly) (5 GF) ⊗ in 37 bedrooms s £70-£130; d £85-£190 **LB** **FACILITIES:** STV **SERVICES:** Lift **NOTES:** 🐕 ⊗ in restaurant

★★★70% *Braid Hills*

134 Braid Rd EH10 6JD
☎ 0131 447 8888 📠 0131 452 8477
e-mail: bookings@braidhillshotel.co.uk
web: www.braidhillshotel.co.uk
Dir: *2.5m S A702, opposite Braid Burn Park*

From its elevated position on the south side, this long-established hotel enjoys splendid panoramic views of the city and castle. Bedrooms are smart, stylish and well equipped. The public areas are comfortable and inviting, and guests can dine in either the restaurant or popular bistro/bar.

ROOMS: 67 en suite (6 fmly) ⊗ in 8 bedrooms **FACILITIES:** STV **CONF:** Thtr 100 Class 50 Board 30 **PARKING:** 38 **NOTES:** 🐕 ⊗ in restaurant Civ Wed 100

See advert on page 695

★★★70% Edinburgh Capital

187 Clermiston Rd EH12 6UG
☎ 0131 535 9988 📠 0131 334 9712
e-mail: manager@edinburghcapitalhotel.co.uk
Dir: *from A8 turn left into Clermiston Rd at the National Tyre Garage. Hotel is at the top of the hill.*

Attracting business, conference and leisure guests alike, this purpose-built hotel lies on the west side of the city and is convenient for the airport and the north. The conservatory restaurant provides friendly service and good value meals combined with fine views.

ROOMS: 111 en suite (6 fmly) (14 GF) ⊗ in 68 bedrooms s £49-£129; d £49-£159 **LB** **FACILITIES: Spa** STV supervised Sauna Solarium Gym Jacuzzi Beautician and sunbeds Xmas **CONF:** BC Thtr 320 Class 130 Board 80 Del from £99 **SERVICES:** Lift **PARKING:** 106 **NOTES:** ⊗ in restaurant Civ Wed 200

★★★69% Kings Manor

100 Milton Rd East EH15 2NP
☎ 0131 669 0444 & 0131 468 8003
📠 0131 669 6650
e-mail: reservations@kingsmanor.com
web: www.kingsmanor.com
Dir: *A720 E to Old Craighall junct, left into city, right att A1/A199 junct, hotel 200mtrs on right*

Lying on the eastern side of the city and convenient for the by-pass, this hotel is popular with business guests, tour groups and for conferences. It boasts a fine leisure complex and a bright modern bistro, which complements the main restaurant.

ROOMS: 67 en suite (2 fmly) (5 GF) ⊗ in 37 bedrooms s £70-£106; d £90-£155 (incl. bkfst) **LB** **FACILITIES:** STV Sauna Solarium Gym Jacuzzi Health & beauty salon , Steam room Xmas **CONF:** BC Thtr 140 Class 70 Board 50 Del from £125 **SERVICES:** Lift **PARKING:** 100 **NOTES:** Civ Wed 100

★★★66% Greens Hotel

24 Eglinton Crescent, Haymarket EH12 5BY
☎ 0131 337 1565 📠 0131 337 9405
e-mail: greens@crerarhotels.com
web: www.crerarhotels.com
Dir: *close to Haymarket Station at head of Coates Gdns off Haymarket Terrace*

Four Georgian houses have been converted to create this friendly hotel in the West End. Bedrooms are well equipped and superior rooms are particularly spacious. There is a choice of dining options that includes the Garden Restaurant and a more relaxed bar and brasserie; smart conference and meeting facilities are also available.

ROOMS: 55 en suite (6 fmly) ⊗ in 20 bedrooms s £50-£85; d £60-£140 (incl. bkfst) **LB** **FACILITIES:** Xmas **CONF:** Thtr 50 Class 24 Board 30 Del from £95 **SERVICES:** Lift **NOTES:** 🐕 ⊗ in restaurant

EDINBURGH, continued

★★★66% *Old Waverley*
43 Princes St EH2 2BY
☎ 0131 556 4648 ▤ 0131 557 6316
e-mail: reservations@oldwaverley.co.uk
web: www.oldwaverley.co.uk
Dir: *in city centre, opposite Scott Monument, Waverley Station & Jenners*
Occupying a commanding position opposite Sir Walter Scott's famous monument on Princes Street, this hotel is convenient for the station and the city centre. Public rooms are all on first floor level and along with front-facing bedrooms enjoy the fine views.
ROOMS: 66 en suite (3 fmly) ⊗ in 53 bedrooms **FACILITIES:** STV leisure facilities at sister hotel **SERVICES:** Lift **NOTES:** ✗ ⊗ in restaurant

★★★66% *Quality Hotel*
Edinburgh Airport, Ingliston EH28 8AU
☎ 0131 333 4331 ▤ 0131 333 4124
e-mail: info@qiaityhoteledinburghairport.com
Dir: *from M8, follow signs for airport.*
Just twenty minutes from the city centre, this modern hotel is convenient for Edinburgh International Airport, only two minutes away by courtesy minibus. The spacious executive bedrooms are the pick of the accommodation, and there is a café/restaurant offering a range of contemporary dishes.
ROOMS: 95 en suite ⊗ in 64 bedrooms **FACILITIES:** STV **CONF:** Thtr 70 Class 24 Board 24 **SERVICES:** Lift **PARKING:** 100 **NOTES:** ⊗ in restaurant

★★★65% Agenda
92-98 St Johns Rd EH12 8AT
☎ 0131 316 4466 ▤ 0131 334 9174
e-mail: info@agenda-edinburgh.co.uk
web: www.agenda-edinburgh.co.uk
Dir: *on A8 road into Edinburgh*
Set in the western village suburb of Corstophine this contemporary hotel is a popular venue for young, trendy bar goers, but also attracts a mixed market. A brasserie menu is available in the minimalist style all-day café bar as well as in the restaurant. Service is friendly and attentive.
ROOMS: 28 en suite ⊗ in all bedrooms s £75-£105; d £85-£140 (incl. bkfst) **LB** **FACILITIES:** STV Xmas **CONF:** Del from £95 **PARKING:** 27 **NOTES:** ✗

★★★64% Jurys Inn Edinburgh
43 Jeffrey St EH1 1DH
☎ 0131 200 3300 ▤ 0131 200 0400
e-mail: jurysinnedinburgh@jurysdoyle.com
web: www.jurysdoyle.com
Dir: *A8/M8 to City Centre, follow one-way system, across Waverley Bridge, 1st left, hotel on right.*
A smart, elegant reception lounge greets guests at this modern hotel set in the heart of the city close to Waverley Station and the Royal Mile. There is a pub and an informal restaurant serving a wide range of dishes, including a canteen-style breakfast. Bedrooms are bright and spacious.
ROOMS: 186 en suite (68 fmly) ⊗ in 121 bedrooms **FACILITIES:** STV Discounted leisure facilities at nearby hotel. ♫ **CONF:** Thtr 50 Class 35 Board 30 **SERVICES:** Lift **NOTES:** ✗ Closed 24-25 Dec

○ Hotel due to open in late 2005 or 2006
U Star rating not confirmed

Restaurant with Rooms

The Witchery by the Castle
352 Castlehill, Royal Mile EH1 2NF
☎ 0131 225 5613 ▤ 0131 220 4392
e-mail: mail@thewitchery.com
web: www.thewitchery.com
Dir: *near Edinburgh Castle gate*

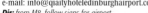

Whether staying or just dining, the Witchery is one of the most romantic and memorable of destinations. It occupies 16th-century buildings right by Edinburgh Castle. Two suites are located above the restaurant, with others across the cobbled street. All are breathtakingly furnished in lavish gothic style and superbly equipped.
ROOMS: 2 en suite 5 annexe en suite (1 GF) s fr £295; d fr £295 (incl. bkfst) **FACILITIES:** STV **NOTES:** ✗ No children 12yrs Closed 25-26 Dec

U Ramada Mount Royal
Princes St EH2 2DG
☎ 0131 225 7161 ▤ 0131 220 4671
e-mail: sales.mountroyal@ramadajarvis.co.uk
web: www.ramadajarvis.co.uk
Dir: *opposite Edinburgh Castle & Waverley Station, east end of Princes Sreet.*
This large hotel enjoys a prime city centre location with views over Princes Street Gardens and across to Edinburgh Castle. Bedrooms are comfortably appointed for both business and leisure guests.
ROOMS: 158 en suite ⊗ in 100 bedrooms s £89-£139; d £89-£139 (incl. bkfst) **FACILITIES:** STV Xmas **CONF:** Thtr 60 Class 45 Board 25 Del from £150 **SERVICES:** Lift **NOTES:** ✗ ⊗ in restaurant

⌂ *Hotel Ibis*
6 Hunter Square, (off The Royal Mile) EH1 1QW
☎ 0131 240 7000 ▤ 0131 240 7007
e-mail: H2039@accor-hotels.com
Dir: *from Queen St (M8/M9) or Waterloo Pl (A1) over North Bridge (A7) & High St, take 1st right off South Bridge, into Hunter Square*
Modern, budget hotel offering comfortable accommodation in bright and practical bedrooms. Breakfast is self-service and dinner is available in the restaurant. For further details, consult the Hotel Groups page.
ROOMS: 99 en suite

⌂ Innkeeper's Lodge Edinburgh West
114-116 St John's Rd, Corstophine EH12 8AX
☎ 0131 334 8235 ▤ 0131 316 5012
web: www.innkeeperslodge.com
Dir: *M8 junct 1, N on A720. At Gogar rdbt, right onto A8, straight over next rdbt, hotel on left just past church at St John's Rd*
A growing concept in the travel accommodation market. Smart rooms meet essential business requirements but also have home
continued

comforts. Dining options include all-day menus plus the added advantage of breakfast, which is included in the room price. For further details consult the Hotel Groups page.
ROOMS: 28 en suite s £62; d £62

Premier Travel Inn Edinburgh City Centre

1 Morrison Link EH3 8DN
☎ 0870 238 3319 Fax 0131 228 9836
web: www.premiertravelinn.com
Dir: *next to Edinburgh International Conference Centre*
High quality, modern budget accommodation ideal for both families and business travellers. Spacious, en suite bedrooms feature bath and shower, satellite TV and many have telephones and modem points. The adjacent family restaurant features a wide and varied menu. For further details consult the Hotel Groups page.
ROOMS: 281 en suite s £62.95; d £62.95

Premier Travel Inn Edinburgh East

228 Willowbrae Rd EH8 7NG
☎ 08701 977091 Fax 0131 652 2789
web: www.premiertravelinn.com
Dir: *M8 junct 1/A720, 12m, exit for A1. At ASDA rdbt turn left. 2m, Inn on left before Esso garage*
High quality, modern budget accommodation ideal for both families and business travellers. Spacious, en suite bedrooms feature bath and shower, satellite TV and many have telephones and modem points. The adjacent family restaurant features a wide and varied menu. For further details consult the Hotel Groups page.
ROOMS: 39 en suite s £52.95; d £52.95

Premier Travel Inn Edinburgh (Inveresk)

Carberry Rd, Inveresk, Musselburgh EH21 8PT
☎ 08701 977092 Fax 0131 653 2270
web: www.premiertravelinn.com
Dir: *from A1, take exit signed Dalkeith (A6094). Follow signs until rdbt, turn right, Inn 300yds on right*
High quality, modern budget accommodation ideal for both families and business travellers. Spacious, en suite bedrooms feature bath and shower, satellite TV and many have telephones and modem points. The adjacent family restaurant features a wide and varied menu. For further details consult the Hotel Groups page.
ROOMS: 40 en suite s £50.95; d £50.95 **CONF:** Thtr 80

Premier Travel Inn Edinburgh (Lauriston Place)

Lauriston Place, Lady Lawson St EH3 9HZ
☎ 0870 9906610 Fax 0870 9906611
web: www.premiertravelinn.com
Dir: *From A8 right onto A702 (Lothian Rd) to Tollcross. Left into Lauriston Place, hotel at junct with Lauriston St on left*
High quality, modern budget accommodation ideal for both families and business travellers. Spacious, en suite bedrooms feature bath and shower, satellite TV and many have telephones and modem points. The adjacent family restaurant features a wide and varied menu. For further details consult the Hotel Groups page.
ROOMS: 112 en suite s £62.95; d £62.95

Destination dining!
This symbol indicates a Restaurant with Rooms

Premier Travel Inn Edinburgh (Leith)

Pier Place, Newhaven Dicks EH6 4TX
☎ 08701 977093 Fax 0131 554 5994
web: www.premiertravelinn.com
Dir: *From A1 follow coast road through Leith. Pass Ocean Terminal, straight ahead at mini-rdbt, take 2nd exit marked Harry Ramsden's car park*
High quality, modern budget accommodation ideal for both families and business travellers. Spacious, en suite bedrooms feature bath and shower, satellite TV and many have telephones and modem points. The adjacent family restaurant features a wide and varied menu. For further details consult the Hotel Groups page.
ROOMS: 60 en suite s £50.95; d £50.95 **CONF:** Thtr 35 Board 25

Premier Travel Inn Edinburgh (Newcraighall)

91 Newcraighall Rd, Newcraighall EH21 8RX
☎ 0870 9906336 Fax 0870 9906337
web: www.premiertravelinn.com
Dir: *Close to city centre on junct of A1 & A6095 towards Musselburgh*
High quality, modern budget accommodation ideal for both families and business travellers. Spacious, en suite bedrooms feature bath and shower, satellite TV and many have telephones and modem points. The adjacent family restaurant features a wide and varied menu. For further details consult the Hotel Groups page.
ROOMS: 42 en suite s £52.95; d £52.95

Travelodge (Edinburgh Central)

33 Saint Marys St EH1 1TA
☎ 08700 850 950 Fax 0131 557 3681
web: www.travelodge.co.uk
Dir: *From A1 follow signs to city centre, after Meadow Bank stadium take left fork at lights, follow signs to Earth Museum, lodge opposite*

Travelodge offers good quality, good value, modern accommodation. Ideal for families, the spacious, en suite bedrooms include remote-control TV, tea and coffee-making facilities and comfortable beds. Meals can be taken at the nearby family restaurant. For further details consult the Hotel Groups page.
ROOMS: 193 en suite s fr £26; d fr £26

Travelodge (Edinburgh East)

Old Craighall EH21 8RE
☎ 08700 850 950 Fax 0131 653 6106
web: www.travelodge.co.uk
Dir: *off A1/A720, 2m from Edinburgh outskirts*
Travelodge offers good quality, good value, modern accommodation. Ideal for families, the spacious, en suite bedrooms include remote-control TV, tea and coffee-making facilities and comfortable beds. Meals can be taken at the nearby family restaurant. For further details consult the Hotel Groups page.
ROOMS: 45 en suite s fr £26; d fr £26

EDINBURGH, continued

⌂ Travelodge (Edinburgh South)

46 Dreghorn Link EH13 9QR
☎ 08700 850 950 Fax 0131 441 4296
web: www.travelodge.co.uk
Dir: *E'bound carriageway of A720, Edinburgh City bypass at Dreghorn/Colinton exit*
Travelodge offers good quality, good value, modern accommodation. Ideal for families, the spacious, en suite bedrooms include remote-control TV, tea and coffee-making facilities and comfortable beds. Meals can be taken at the nearby family restaurant. For further details consult the Hotel Groups page.
ROOMS: 72 en suite s fr £26; d fr £26

EDZELL, Angus — Map 23 NO66

★★★65% Glenesk

High St DD9 7TF
☎ 01356 648319 Fax 01356 647333
e-mail: gleneskhotel@btconnect.com
web: www.gleneskhotel.co.uk
Dir: *off A90 just after Brechin Bypass*
Set in gardens by the golf course, this long established hotel is popular with both leisure and business guests. Public areas are comfortable and include a leisure club with a swimming pool.
ROOMS: 24 en suite (5 fmly) s £65-£80; d fr £110 (incl. bkfst) **LB** **FACILITIES:** Snooker Sauna Gym Jacuzzi Xmas **CONF:** Thtr 120 Class 60 Board 30 **PARKING:** 80 **NOTES:** in restaurant Civ Wed 100

ELGIN, Moray — Map 23 NJ26

★★★74% Mansion House

The Haugh IV30 1AW
☎ 01343 548811 Fax 01343 547916
e-mail: reception@mhelgin.co.uk
web: www.mansionhousehotel.co.uk
Dir: *turn off A96 into Haugh Rd, then1st left*
Set in grounds by the River Lossie, this baronial mansion is popular with leisure and business guests as well as being a wedding venue. Bedrooms are spacious, many having views of the river. Extensive public areas include a choice of restaurants, with the bistro contrasting with the classical main restaurant. There is an indoor pool and a beauty and hair salon.
ROOMS: 23 en suite (5 GF) in 5 bedrooms s £90-£104; d £143-£175 (incl. bkfst) **LB** **FACILITIES: Spa** STV supervised Fishing Snooker Sauna Solarium Gym Jacuzzi Xmas **CONF:** BC Thtr 200 **PARKING:** 50 **NOTES:** in restaurant Civ Wed 160

See advert on opposite page

If you wish to use a particular credit card or debit card please check with the hotel that they are happy to accept it

★★★71% *Laichmoray*

Maisondieu Rd IV30 1QR
☎ 01343 540045 Fax 01343 540055
e-mail: enquiries@laichmorayhotel.co.uk
web: www.laichmorayhotel.co.uk
Dir: *opposite the railway station*
This popular business hotel is located close to the city centre and railway station. Warm hospitality and an informal atmosphere are real features. Bedrooms come in a variety of styles and sizes. An impressive range of meals is served in the bar, conservatory and restaurant and there is a choice of over 170 malt whiskies.

ROOMS: 35 rms (34 en suite) (4 fmly) in 8 bedrooms **FACILITIES:** Pool **CONF:** Thtr 200 Class 160 Board 40 **PARKING:** 60 **NOTES:** Closed 24-26 Dec & 31 Dec-3 Jan Civ Wed

⌂ Premier Travel Inn Elgin

1 Linkwood Way IV30 1HY
☎ 08701 977095 Fax 01343 540635
web: www.premiertravelinn.com
Dir: *on A96, 1.5m E of city centre*
High quality, modern budget accommodation ideal for both families and business travellers. Spacious, en suite bedrooms feature bath and shower, satellite TV and many have telephones and modem points. The adjacent family restaurant features a wide and varied menu. For further details consult the Hotel Groups page.
ROOMS: 40 en suite s £48.95; d £48.95 **CONF:** Thtr 24

ERISKA, Argyll & Bute — Map 20 NM94

Top Hotel

★★★★ Isle of Eriska

Eriska, Ledaig PA37 1SD
☎ 01631 720371 Fax 01631 720531
e-mail: office@eriska-hotel.co.uk
Dir: *leave A85 at Connel, onto A828, follow for 4m, then follow signs from N of Benderloch*
Situated on its own private island with delightful beaches and walking trails, this hotel offers a tranquil, personal setting for total relaxation. Spacious bedrooms are comfortable and boast some fine antique pieces. Local seafood, meats and game feature prominently on the award-winning menu, as do vegetables and herbs grown in the hotel's kitchen garden. Leisure facilities include an indoor swimming pool, gym, spa treatment rooms and a small golf course.
ROOMS: 17 en suite (2 GF) s £200; d £260-£360 (incl. bkfst) **LB** **FACILITIES: Spa** supervised 6 Fishing Sauna Gym Putt green Jacuzzi Steam room, Skeet shooting, Nature trails Xmas **CONF:** Thtr 30 Class 30 Board 30 **PARKING:** 40 **NOTES:** in restaurant Closed Jan Civ Wed 44

FALKIRK, Falkirk Map 21 NS88

★★★68% Park
Camelon Rd FK1 5RY
☎ 01324 628331 📠 01324 611593
e-mail: enquiries@parkhotelfalkirk.co.uk
web: www.parkhotelfalkirk.co.uk
Dir: *from M8 take A803 into Falkirk, hotel 1m beyond Mariner Leisure Centre, opposite Dollar Park. From M9, A803 through Falkirk, follow signs for Dollar Park*
This purpose-built, well-established hotel is popular with business travellers and easily accessible from all major transport routes. Smart contemporary public areas feature a spacious and inviting lounge and restaurant with a bar. Well-equipped bedrooms come in a variety of sizes.
ROOMS: 55 en suite (3 fmly) ⊗ in 32 bedrooms s £40-£83; d £60-£93 (incl. bkfst) **LB** **FACILITIES:** STV **CONF:** BC Thtr 300 Class 140 Board 80 Del from £85 **SERVICES:** Lift **PARKING:** 160 **NOTES:** ⊗ in restaurant Civ Wed 120

★★★66% Airth Castle Hotel
FK2 8JF
☎ 01324 831411 📠 01324 831184/831419
e-mail: reservations.stirlingshire@radissonsas.com
Dir: *M9 junct 7, M876 take 1st left A905 towards Airth. Hotel 0.5m on left*
Accommodation is provided in spacious rooms, housed in two separate buildings, one of which is an imposing castle. A popular choice for weddings, this hotel, now under new ownership, boasts excellent conference and leisure facilities. A choice of
continued
restaurants is provided, with a fine dining restaurant in the castle and a bistro-style eatery in the main building.
ROOMS: 100 en suite 23 annexe en suite (36 fmly) (33 GF) ⊗ in 65 bedrooms d £90-£130 **FACILITIES:** STV Sauna Solarium Gym Jacuzzi Steam room Xmas **CONF:** Thtr 300 Class 140 Board 60 **SERVICES:** Lift **PARKING:** 150 **NOTES:** ⊗ in restaurant Civ Wed 120

Premier Travel Inn Falkirk West
Glenbervie Business Park, Bellsdyke Rd, Larbert FK5 4EG
☎ 0870 9906550 📠 0870 9906551
web: www.premiertravelinn.com
Dir: *Just off A88. Approx 1m from M876 junct 2*
High quality, modern budget accommodation ideal for both families and business travellers. Spacious, en suite bedrooms feature bath and shower, satellite TV and many have telephones and modem points. The adjacent family restaurant features a wide and varied menu. For further details consult the Hotel Groups page.
ROOMS: 60 en suite s £46.95-£48.95; d £46.95-£48.95

FINTRY, Stirling Map 20 NS68

★★★66% Culcreuch Castle
Kippen Rd G63 0LW
☎ 01360 860555 & 860228 📠 01360 860556
e-mail: info@culcreuch.com
web: www.culcreuch.com
Dir: *on B822, 17m W of Stirling. 20m N of Glasgow*
Peacefully located in 1600 acres of parkland, this ancient castle dates back to 1296. Tastefully restored accommodation is in a mixture of individually themed castle rooms, some with four-poster beds and more modern courtyard rooms, which are suitable for
continued on p702

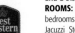

FINTRY, continued

families. Period style public rooms include a bar, serving light meals, a wood-panelled dining room and an elegant lounge.

Culcreuch Castle, Fintry

ROOMS: 10 en suite 4 annexe en suite (3 fmly) (4 GF) s £67-£112; d £84-£170 (incl. bkfst) **LB** **FACILITIES:** Fishing Xmas **CONF:** BC Thtr 140 Class 70 Del from £87.50 **PARKING:** 100 **NOTES:** ⊗ in restaurant Civ Wed 110

FORRES, Moray — Map 23 NJ05

★★★68% Ramnee

Victoria Rd IV36 3BN
☎ 01309 672410 🖷 01309 673392
e-mail: ramneehotel@btconnect.com
Dir: *off A96 at rdbt on E side of Forres, hotel 200yds on right*

Genuinely friendly staff ensure this well-established hotel remains popular with business travellers. Accommodation, including a family suite, varies in size, although all rooms are well-presented. Hearty bar food provides a less formal dining option to the imaginative restaurant menu.

ROOMS: 20 en suite (4 fmly) s £75-£85; d £90-£100 (incl. bkfst) **LB** **FACILITIES:** STV use of leisure facilities at sister hotel **CONF:** Thtr 100 Class 30 Board 45 **PARKING:** 50 **NOTES:** ⊗ in restaurant Closed 25 Dec & 1-3 Jan Civ Wed 100

⊗ No smoking

Late for dinner? Quality standards mean that last orders for dinner vary according to star rating and should be no earlier than: ★★ 7.00pm ★★★ 8:00pm ★★★★ 9:00pm ★★★★★ 10:00pm

FORT WILLIAM, Highland — Map 22 NN17

Top Hotel

★★★★ ⊛⊛⊛ Inverlochy Castle

RELAIS & CHÂTEAUX

Torlundy PH33 6SN
☎ 01397 702177 🖷 01397 702953
e-mail: info@inverlochy.co.uk
web: www.inverlochycastlehotel.com
Dir: *accessible from either A82 Glasgow-Fort William or A9 Edinburgh-Dalwhinnie. Hotel 3m N of Fort William on A82, in Torlundy*

With a backdrop of Ben Nevis, this imposing and gracious castle sits amidst extensive gardens and grounds overlooking the hotel's own loch. Lavishly appointed in classic country house style, spacious bedrooms are extremely comfortable and boast flat screen TVs and laptops with internet access. The sumptuous main hall and lounge provide the perfect setting for afternoon tea or a pre-dinner cocktail, whilst imaginative cuisine is served in one of three dining rooms. A snooker room and a DVD library are also available.

ROOMS: 17 en suite (6 fmly) ⊗ in all bedrooms s £290-£395; d £330-£550 (incl. bkfst) **LB** **FACILITIES:** STV Fishing Snooker Loch available for fishing, Massage, Riding, Hunting, Stalking, Clay Pigeon shooting ♫ Xmas **CONF:** BC Thtr 50 Class 20 Board 20 Del from £280 **PARKING:** 17 **NOTES:** ⊗ in restaurant Closed 6 Jan-01 Feb Civ Wed 50

See advert on opposite page

★★★75% ⊛ Moorings

Banavie PH33 7LY
☎ 01397 772797 🖷 01397 772441
e-mail: reservations@moorings-fortwilliam.co.uk
web: www.moorings-fortwilliam.co.uk
Dir: *A830 for 1m, cross the Caledonian Canal, 1st right*

Located on the Caledonian Canal next to a series of locks known as Neptune's Staircase, and close to Thomas Telford's house, this

continued on p704

Inverlochy Castle Hotel

Torlundy, Fort William PH33 6SN
Tel: 01397 702177 Fax: 01397 702953
www.inverlochycastlehotel.com Email: info@inverlochy.co.uk

Steeped in history Inverlochy was built in 1863 as a private residence and in 1969 was converted into a country house hotel. Nestling in the foothills of the mighty Ben Nevis and sits amidst some of Scotland's finest scenery. Visitors can reflect in the relaxed and tranquil atmosphere of a bygone era, wonderfully crafted and richly decorated, beautiful Venetian crystal chandeliers, frescoed ceiling and a handsome staircase. Each of the 17 bedrooms, all with private bathroom, have their own individual design and character, along with splendid views of the grounds and surrounding mountains. Dinner at Inverlochy is an experience to savour in any of our three dining rooms, each decorated with period and elaborate furniture presented as gifts to Inverlochy Castle from the King of Norway.

Inverlochy Castle is also the perfect location for a Highland wedding. Hotel staff can arrange everything to suit your requirements for your special day.

A wealth of sporting activities can be enjoyed in the surrounding grounds and mountains.

Four miles north of Fort William, on the A82 north towards Inverness.

F

FORT WILLIAM, continued

hotel with its dedicated, young staff offers friendly service. Accommodation comes in two distinct styles and the newer rooms are particularly appealing. Meals can be taken in the bars or the spacious dining room.
ROOMS: 28 en suite (1 fmly) (1 GF) ⊗ in 9 bedrooms s £43-£110; d £86-£130 (incl. bkfst) **LB** **FACILITIES:** STV Xmas **CONF:** Thtr 120 Class 40 Board 40 Del from £125 **PARKING:** 60 **NOTES:** ⊗ in restaurant Closed Xmas Civ Wed 120

See advert under ONICH

★★★66% Grand
Gordon Square PH33 6DX
☎ 01397 702928 📠 01397 702928
e-mail: grandhotel.scotland@virgin.net
web: www.grandhotel-scotland.co.uk
Dir: *on A82 at W end of High St*

A relaxed and welcoming atmosphere is provided at this long-established, family-run hotel, at the south end of the high street. The bedrooms are smart and modern, and there is a choice of lounges. A good range of innovative dishes is served in both the restaurant and bar.
ROOMS: 30 en suite (4 fmly) ⊗ in 15 bedrooms s £39.50-£49.50; d £59-£79 (incl. bkfst) **LB** **CONF:** Thtr 110 Class 60 Board 20 **PARKING:** 20 **NOTES:** ✈ ⊗ in restaurant Closed 30 Dec-11 Feb Civ Wed

★★71% *Imperial*
Fraser's Square PH33 6DW
☎ 01397 702040 & 703921 📠 01397 706277
e-mail: imperial@bestwestern.co.uk
Dir: *from town centre, along Middle St, approx 400mtrs from junct with A82*

Benefiting from a town centre location this hotel is popular with both business and leisure guests, and is ideally placed for many of the area's attractions. Public areas include a bar, a smart restaurant, and a lounge. Generally spacious bedrooms are comfortably appointed.
ROOMS: 34 en suite (2 fmly) ⊗ in 6 bedrooms **CONF:** Thtr 60 Class 12 Board 16 **PARKING:** 15 **NOTES:** ⊗ in restaurant

★★70% Nevis Bank
Belford Rd PH33 6BY
☎ 01397 705721 📠 01397 706275
e-mail: info@nevisbankhotel.co.uk
web: www.nevisbankhotel.co.uk
Dir: *on A82, at junct to Glen Nevis*

A warm welcome is assured at this long-established hotel. It enjoys a fine location on the outskirts of the town close to the access road for the West Highland Way and Glen Nevis.

continued

Accommodation is provided in thoughtfully equipped bedrooms of different sizes. There is a choice of bars and dining options.

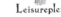

ROOMS: 31 en suite (3 fmly) (2 GF) s £25-£50; d £50-£85 (incl. bkfst) **LB** **FACILITIES:** Xmas **CONF:** BC Thtr 50 Class 30 Board 25 Del from £42.50 **PARKING:** 50 **NOTES:** ✈ ⊗ in restaurant

See advert on opposite page

★★63% *Croit Anna*
Achaintore Rd, Drimarben PH33 6RR
☎ 01397 702268 📠 01397 704099
e-mail: croitanna.fortwilliam@alfatravel.co.uk
web: www.alfatravel.co.uk
Dir: *from Glencoe on A82 into Fort William, hotel 1st on right*

Located on the edge of Loch Linnhe, just two miles out of town, this hotel offers some spacious bedrooms, many with fine views over the loch. There is a choice of two comfortable lounges and a large airy restaurant. The hotel appeals to coach parties and individual visitors alike.
ROOMS: 89 rms (79 en suite) **FACILITIES:** ♫ ch fac **PARKING:** 25 **NOTES:** ✈ ⊗ in restaurant Closed Dec-Jan RS Nov, Feb, Mar

⇧ Premier Travel Inn Fort William
Loch Iall, An Aird PH33 6AN
☎ 08701 977104 📠 01397 703618
web: www.premiertravelinn.com
Dir: *N end of Fort William Shopping Centre, just off A82 ring road*

High quality, modern budget accommodation ideal for both families and business travellers. Spacious, en suite bedrooms feature bath and shower, satellite TV and many have telephones and modem points. The adjacent family restaurant features a wide and varied menu. For further details consult the Hotel Groups page.
ROOMS: 40 en suite s £50.95; d £50.95

♫ Entertainment

GAIRLOCH, Highland
Map 22 NG87

★★69% Myrtle Bank
Low Rd IV21 2BS
☎ 01445 712004 📠 01445 712214
e-mail: myrtlebank@msn.com
web: www.myrtlebankhotel.co.uk
Dir: *A832 to Gairloch. Through village, at Mace store turn left at T-junct. Hotel 2nd on left*

A seafront location and views to the Isle of Skye are key features at this friendly, family-run hotel. The spacious bedrooms are comfortably equipped. The public areas include a smart conservatory lounge, a well-stocked bar and the sea-facing

continued

restaurant, where guests can enjoy the breathtaking sunsets of Wester Ross.

ROOMS: 12 en suite (2 fmly) s £36-£44; d £72-£88 (incl. bkfst) **LB**
PARKING: 20 **NOTES:** ⊗ in restaurant

GALASHIELS, Scottish Borders — Map 21 NT43

★★★67% Kingsknowes

Selkirk Rd TD1 3HY
☎ 01896 758375 📠 01896 750377
e-mail: enq@kingsknowes.co.uk
web: www.kingsknowes.co.uk
Dir: *off A7 at Galashiels/Selkirk rdbt*

An imposing turreted mansion, this hotel lies in attractive gardens on the outskirts of town close to the River Tweed. It boasts elegant public areas and many spacious bedrooms, some with excellent views. There is a choice of bars, one with a popular menu to supplement the restaurant.

ROOMS: 12 en suite (2 fmly) s fr £59; d fr £89 (incl. bkfst) **LB**
FACILITIES: STV **CONF:** Thtr 60 Class 40 Board 30 **PARKING:** 50
NOTES: ⊗ in restaurant Civ Wed 50

GATEHOUSE OF FLEET, Dumfries & Galloway — Map 20 NX55

★★★★73% ® Cally Palace

DG7 2DL
☎ 01557 814341 📠 01557 814522
e-mail: info@callypalace.co.uk
web: www.callypalace.co.uk
Dir: *M6 & A74, signed A75 Dumfries then Stranraer. At Gatehouse-of-Fleet turn right onto B727, left at Cally*

A resort hotel with extensive leisure facilities, this grand 18th-century building is set in 500 acres of forest and parkland that incorporates its own golf course. Bedrooms are spacious and well equipped, whilst public rooms retain a quiet elegance. The

continued on p706

GATEHOUSE OF FLEET, continued

short dinner menu focuses on freshly prepared dishes. A pianist plays most nights and jacket and tie are obligatory.
ROOMS: 55 en suite (7 fmly) s £95-£139; d £180-£204 (incl. bkfst & dinner) **LB** **FACILITIES:** STV ⛝ 18 Fishing Snooker Sauna Putt green Jacuzzi Table tennis Practice fairway Xmas **CONF:** Thtr 40 Class 40 Board 25 **SERVICES:** Lift **PARKING:** 100 **NOTES:** in restaurant Closed Jan-early Feb

See advert on opposite page

★★★68% Murray Arms
DG7 2HY
☎ 01557 814207 01557 814370
e-mail: murrayarmshotel@ukonline.co.uk
web: www.murrayarms.com
Dir: *off A75, hotel at edge of town, near clock tower*
A relaxed and welcoming atmosphere prevails at this historic coaching inn that has associations with Robert Burns. Public areas retain a comfortable, traditional feel and include a choice of sitting areas, a snug bar and an all-day restaurant serving honest and popular dishes. Bedrooms are comfortable and well presented.
ROOMS: 12 en suite (3 fmly) s £45-£55; d £90-£110 (incl. bkfst) **LB** **FACILITIES:** Xmas **CONF:** Thtr 120 Class 50 Board 30 Del from £75 **PARKING:** 50 **NOTES:** in restaurant

GLAMIS, Angus
Map 21 NO34

Top Hotel

★★★ Castleton House
Castleton of Eassie DD8 1SJ
☎ 01307 840340 01307 840506
e-mail: hotel@castletonglamis.co.uk
web: www.castletonglamis.co.uk
Dir: *on A94 midway between Forfar/Cupar Angus, 3m W of Glamis*
Set in its own grounds and with a moat, this impressive Victorian house has a relaxed and friendly atmosphere. Accommodation is provided in individually designed, spacious bedrooms. Personal service from the enthusiastic proprietors is a real feature and many guests return time and again. Accomplished cooking, utilising the best local produce, is served in the conservatory restaurant.
ROOMS: 6 en suite (2 fmly) in 1 bedroom **FACILITIES:** Putt green ch fac **CONF:** Thtr 30 Class 20 Board 20 **PARKING:** 50 **NOTES:** Civ Wed 50

GLASGOW, City of Glasgow
Map 20 NS66
See also Clydebank & Uplawmoor

Top Town House

★★★★ One Devonshire Gardens
1 Devonshire Gardens G12 0UX
☎ 0141 339 2001 0141 337 1663
e-mail: reservations@onedevonshiregardens.com
web: www.onedevonshiregardens.com
Dir: *M8 junct 17, follow signs for A82, after 1.5m turn left into Hyndland Rd, 1st right, right at mini rdbt, right at end, continue to end*
This renowned townhouse occupies four houses of a Victorian terrace in a residential area. Bedrooms, including a number of suites and four-poster rooms, are stylish, individually designed and thoughtfully equipped to a high standard. Public rooms include a choice of inviting drawing rooms, meeting and conference facilities and a smart restaurant offering imaginative cooking. Personal, attentive service is a highlight.
ROOMS: 35 en suite (4 GF) s £135-£495; d £135-£495 **FACILITIES:** STV Squash Gym Tennis facilities at nearby club **CONF:** BC Thtr 40 Class 30 Board 30 Del from £250 **NOTES:** in restaurant Civ Wed 48

★★★★77% Radisson SAS Glasgow
301 Argyle St G2 8DL
☎ 0141 204 3333 0141 204 3344
e-mail: reservations.glasgow@radissonsas.com
web: www.radisson.com
Dir: *M8 junct 19 take 1st right, continue to Argyle St. 1st left, hotel is on left opposite central station*
Located within the heart of the city centre this modern, stylish international hotel provides a high quality destination. The huge glass and wood atrium forms the central core of the hotel, leading to the lobby, bar, restaurants and the leisure centre. Spacious bedrooms feature the best in design with the focus on comfort, facilities and quality.
ROOMS: 247 en suite in 200 bedrooms s £135-£190; d £135-£190 **LB** **FACILITIES:** STV supervised Sauna Solarium Gym Jacuzzi **CONF:** BC Thtr 800 Class 360 Board 40 Del from £169 **SERVICES:** Lift air con **NOTES:** Civ Wed 240

★★★★74% Beardmore
Beardmore St G81 4SA
☎ 0141 951 6000 0141 951 6018
e-mail: info@beardmore.scot.nhs.uk
(For full entry see Clydebank)

★★★★73% ❀
Millennium Hotel Glasgow
George Square G2 1DS
☎ 0141 332 6711 📠 0141 332 4264
e-mail: reservations.glasgow@mill-cop.com
web: www.millenniumhotels.com
Dir: *M8 junct 15 follow road through 4 sets of lights, at 5th set turn left into Hanover Street. George Square directly ahead, hotel on right*
Right in the heart of the city, the Millennium has pride of place overlooking George Square. Inside, the property has a contemporary air, with a spacious reception concourse and a glass veranda overlooking the square. There is a stylish brasserie and separate wine bar, and bedrooms come in a variety of sizes.
ROOMS: 117 en suite ⊗ in 54 bedrooms s £175; d £245
FACILITIES: STV Xmas **CONF:** Thtr 40 Class 24 Board 32 Del £165
SERVICES: Lift air con **NOTES:** ✈

★★★★72% ❀❀ **Langs Hotel**
2 Port Dundas Place G2 3LD
☎ 0141 333 1500 & 352 2452 📠 0141 333 5700
e-mail: reservations@langshotels.co.uk
web: www.langshotels.co.uk
Dir: *M8 junct 16, follow signs for George Square. Hotel immediately left after Concert Square car park*
A contemporary-style city centre hotel offering a choice of restaurants for dinner. Oshi has a spacious split-level Euro fusion style, whilst Las Brisas has award-winning food in a more formal dining environment. Bedrooms, all with good facilities, offer various designs and some feature interesting duplex suites.
ROOMS: 100 en suite (4 fmly) ⊗ in 60 bedrooms s £80-£148; d £90-£148 **FACILITIES: Spa** STV Sauna Gym **CONF:** Thtr 60 Class 10 Board 12 Del £145 **SERVICES:** Lift **NOTES:** ⊗ in restaurant

★★★★70% **Menzies Glasgow Hotel**
27 Washington St G3 8AZ
☎ 0141 222 2929 & 270 2323 📠 0141 222 2626
e-mail: glasgow@menzies-hotels.co.uk
web: www.menzies-hotels.co.uk
Dir: *M8 junct 19 for SECC & follow signs for Broomielaw. Turn left at lights*
Centrally located, this modern hotel is a short drive from the airport and an even shorter walk from the centre of the city. Bedrooms are generally spacious and boast a range of facilities, including high-speed internet access. Facilities include a new Brasserie restaurant and an impressive indoor leisure facility.
ROOMS: 141 en suite (49 fmly) ⊗ in 121 bedrooms s £145; d £185 **LB**
FACILITIES: Spa STV Sauna Solarium Gym Jacuzzi Xmas
CONF: Thtr 180 Class 80 Board 50 Del £145 **SERVICES:** Lift air con
PARKING: 50 **NOTES:** ✈ ⊗ in restaurant Civ Wed 160

★★★★68% **Glasgow Marriott Hotel**
500 Argyle St, Anderston G3 8RR
☎ 0870 400 7230 📠 0870 400 7330
web: www.marriott.co.uk
Dir: *M8 junct 19, turn left at lights, then left into hotel*
Conveniently located for all major transport links and the city centre, this hotel benefits from extensive conference and banqueting facilities and a spacious car park. Public areas include an open-plan lounge/bar and a Mediterranean styled restaurant. High quality, well-equipped bedrooms benefit from air conditioning and generously sized beds; the suites are particularly comfortable.
ROOMS: 300 en suite (89 fmly) ⊗ in 212 bedrooms **FACILITIES:** STV Sauna Solarium Gym Beautician, poolside steam room **CONF:** BC Thtr 800 Class 300 Board 50 **SERVICES:** Lift air con **PARKING:** 180 **NOTES:** ✈

GLASGOW, continued

★★★★67% Glasgow Moat House
Congress Rd G3 8QT
☎ 0141 306 9988 📠 0141 221 2022
e-mail: reservations.glasgow@moathousehotels.com
Dir: M8 junct 19, follow signs for SECC, hotel adjacent to Centre
This modern building, instantly recognisable from its mirrored glass exterior, has a convenient location alongside the River Clyde. A feature of the public rooms is a huge wall mural, depicting the city's history, which looks down over the informal No 1 Dockhouse restaurant and the stylish Mariners Restaurant. Bedrooms are comfortable and well appointed and most enjoy splendid panoramic views.
ROOMS: 283 en suite (10 fmly) ⊗ in 171 bedrooms s £67-£135; d £75-£150 (incl. bkfst) **LB FACILITIES:** Spa STV ⊙ Sauna Solarium Gym Jacuzzi Beauty salon with treatments. Xmas **CONF:** Thtr 800 Class 462 Board 68 Del from £99 **SERVICES:** Lift air con **PARKING:** 300 **NOTES:** Closed 25-26 Dec, 1 Jan Civ Wed 120

★★★75% ⊛ Malmaison
278 West George St G2 4LL
☎ 0141 572 1000 📠 0141 572 1002
e-mail: glasgow@malmaison.com
web: www.malmaison.com

Malmaison

Dir: from S & E - M8 junct 18 (Charing Cross), from W & N - M8 City Centre Glasgow
Built around a former church in the historic Charing Cross area, Malmaison is a smart, contemporary hotel offering impressive levels of service and hospitality. Bedrooms are spacious and feature a host of modern facilities, such as CD players and mini bars. Dining is a treat, with French brasserie-style cuisine served in the original crypt.
ROOMS: 72 en suite (4 fmly) ⊗ in 30 bedrooms **FACILITIES:** STV Gym Cardiovascular gym **CONF:** Thtr 25 Class 20 Board 20 **SERVICES:** Lift **NOTES:** ✗

★★★73% ⊛ Holiday Inn
161 West Nile St G1 2RL
☎ 0141 352 8300 📠 0141 332 7447
e-mail: info@higlasgow.com
Dir: M8 junct 16, follow signs for Royal Concert Hall, hotel is opposite
Built on a corner site close to the Theatre Royal Concert Hall and the main shopping areas, this contemporary hotel features the popular Bonne Auberge French restaurant, a bar area and conservatory. Bedrooms are well equipped and comfortable with suites available. Staff are friendly and attentive.
ROOMS: 113 en suite (6 fmly) ⊗ in 79 bedrooms s £80-£160; d £90-£170 (incl. bkfst) **FACILITIES:** STV Mini Gym Xmas **CONF:** Thtr 120 Class 80 Board 80 **SERVICES:** Lift air con **NOTES:** ✗

★★★71% Novotel Glasgow Centre
181 Pitt St G2 4DT
☎ 0141 222 2775 📠 0141 204 5438
e-mail: H3136@accor.com
web: www.novotel.com
Dir: next to Strathclyde Police HQ. Close to the SECC, just off Sauchiehall St
Enjoying a convenient city centre location and with limited parking spaces, this hotel is ideal for both business and leisure travellers. Well-equipped bedrooms are brightly decorated and offer functional design. Modern public areas include a brasserie serving a range of meals all day and a small fitness club.
Novotel - AA Hotel Group of the Year 2005-6.
ROOMS: 139 en suite (139 fmly) ⊗ in 90 bedrooms **FACILITIES:** STV Sauna Gym Pool table, play station Xmas **CONF:** Thtr 40 Class 20 Board 20 **SERVICES:** Lift air con **PARKING:** 19

★★★69% Jurys Inn Glasgow
80 Jamaica St G1 4QE
☎ 0141 314 4800 📠 0141 314 4888
e-mail: bookings@jurysdoyle.com
web: www.jurysdoyle.com

JURYS DOYLE HOTELS

Dir: M8 junct 19 westbound. Left onto A814 Stobcross St, then left onto Oswald St, right into Midland St, right into Jamaica St. Hotel 200yds on right
This modern, stylish hotel is easily accessible from major road networks and occupies a prominent location in the city, close to the river. Bedrooms provide good guest comfort and in-room facilities are suited to both leisure and business markets. Public areas include a number of meeting rooms, a popular bar and restaurant.
ROOMS: 321 en suite (321 fmly) ⊗ in 249 bedrooms s £76; d £76 **FACILITIES:** STV Xmas **CONF:** BC Thtr 100 Class 35 Board 40 Del £120 **SERVICES:** Lift air con **NOTES:** ✗ ⊗ in restaurant Closed 25-26 Dec

★★★67% Corus hotel Glasgow
377 Argyle St G2 8LL
☎ 0870 609 6166 📠 0141 221 1014
e-mail: reservations.glasgow@corushotels.com
web: www.corushotels.com

corus hotels

Dir: from S, M8 junct 19, at pedestrian lights turn left onto Argyle St. Hotel 200yds on right

Handy for the city centre, this hotel has been designed in contemporary style. The bright modern bedrooms are not large but are well equipped and practically laid out to appeal especially to business guests. The restaurant and bar provides a wide choice of generously portioned dishes. There is also a coffee bar.
ROOMS: 121 en suite ⊗ in 79 bedrooms s £35-£89; d £35-£89 (incl. bkfst) **LB FACILITIES:** STV Xmas **CONF:** Thtr 70 Class 15 Board 20 Del from £85 **SERVICES:** Lift **NOTES:** ✗ ⊗ in restaurant

🏨 Town House Hotel
🏩 Country House Hotel
⌂ Travel Accommodation

★★★63% Bewley's Hotel Glasgow
110 Bath St G2 2EN
☎ 0141 353 0800 & 0845 234 5959
📠 0141 353 0900
e-mail: gla@bewleyshotels.com
web: www.bewleyshotels.com

BEWLEY'S HOTELS

Dir: M8 junct 18, left to Sauchiehall St & right to Birthwood St then left to West Regent St & left into Bath St.
In the heart of the city, this modern hotel is ideally suited for business and for leisure breaks. Bedrooms are comfortable and well equipped, with several enjoying impressive views over the
continued

Glasgow skyline. Loop restaurant and bar serves cosmopolitan food all day in a relaxed informal setting.

ROOMS: 103 en suite (47 fmly) 🚭 in 64 bedrooms s £69; d £69
FACILITIES: STV **SERVICES:** Lift **NOTES:** ✖ Closed 24-28 Dec

★★★63% Jurys Glasgow
Great Western Rd G12 0XP
☎ 0141 334 8161 📠 0141 334 3846
e-mail: glasgow_hotel@jurys.com
web: www.jurysdoyle.com

JURYS DOYLE HOTELS

Dir: *M8 junct 17, onto Great Western Road (A82), through 2 sets of lights, left by Gartnavel Hospital & just before Safeway. Sharp right into Shelley Rd*
This purpose-built hotel is situated on the west side of the city. Most single occupancy bedrooms provide a double bed and sofa, whilst others cater for the family/leisure market. Public areas include an Irish bar, an attractive split-level restaurant, a well-equipped leisure club and conference and banqueting facilities.
ROOMS: 137 en suite (12 fmly) 🚭 in 100 bedrooms s £40-£130; d £50-£130 **LB FACILITIES:** STV 🏊 supervised Sauna Solarium Gym Jacuzzi Xmas **CONF:** Thtr 140 Class 80 Board 40 Del from £95 **SERVICES:** Lift **PARKING:** 300 **NOTES:** 🚭 in restaurant Civ Wed 120

★★★62% Quality Hotel Glasgow
99 Gordon St G1 3SF
☎ 0141 221 9680 📠 0141 226 3948
e-mail: enquiries@quality-hotels-glasgow.com
web: www.choicehotelseurope.com

QUALITY

Dir: *M8 junct 19, left into Argyle St and left into Hope St*
A splendid Victorian railway hotel, forming part of Central Station. It retains much original charm combined with modern facilities. Public rooms are impressive and include a bar area. Bedrooms continue to be upgraded and are generally spacious and well-laid out.
ROOMS: 222 en suite (8 fmly) 🚭 in 70 bedrooms s £47-£125; d £94-£125 **LB FACILITIES:** Spa STV 🏊 supervised Sauna Solarium Gym Jacuzzi Hair & beauty salon, Steam room, Sports therapist Xmas **CONF:** BC Thtr 600 Class 160 Board 40 **SERVICES:** Lift **NOTES:** 🚭 in restaurant Civ Wed 250

★★76% 🏵🏵 Uplawmoor
Neilston Rd G78 4AF
☎ 01505 850565 📠 01505 850689
e-mail: enquiries@uplawmoor.co.uk
web: www.uplawmoor.co.uk
(For full entry see Uplawmoor)

*THE CIRCLE
Selected Individual Britain*

🆄 Arthouse
129 Bath St G2 2SZ
☎ 0141 221 6789 & 572 6000 📠 0141 221 6777
e-mail: info@arthousehotel.com
The Arthouse, opening in November 2005, will be the second Abode Hotel - a new group of individual, mid-size boutique hotels. The restaurant will be launched under the direction of the highly

continued

UPLAWMOOR
HOTEL & RESTAURANT

14 BEDROOMS
A LA CARTE
TABLE D'HOTE
BAR MEALS
REAL ALES

Eighteenth century coaching inn
situated in a peaceful village,
just thirty minutes from city & airport.
Personally managed by your hosts:
Stuart & Emma Peacock

NEILSTON ROAD, UPLAWMOOR, GLASGOW, G78 4AF
TEL: +44 (0) 1505 850565
FAX: +44 (0) 1505 850689
E-MAIL: enquiries@uplawmoor.co.uk
WEBSITE: www.uplawmoor.co.uk
AA ★★ 76% 🏵🏵 CAMRA

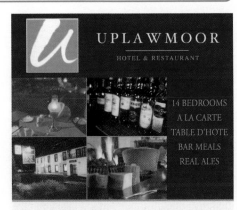

acclaimed chef Michael Caines, who is joint owner of this new venture. Please refer to the AA internet site www.theaa.com for current information.
ROOMS: 63 en suite (18 fmly) (10 GF) 🚭 in 39 bedrooms s £115-£155; d £115-£155 **FACILITIES:** Xmas **CONF:** BC Thtr 70 Class 40 Board 35 Del £155 **SERVICES:** Lift air con **NOTES:** Civ Wed 100

🆄 Ramada Glasgow City
Ingram St G1 1DQ
☎ 0141 248 4401 📠 0141 226 5149
e-mail: sales.glasgow@ramadajarvis.co.uk
web: www.ramadajarvis.co.uk

🅡 RAMADA

Dir: *M8 junct 15, straight through 4 sets of lights, left at 5th set into Hanover St, then left into George Sq and right into Frederick St. Right at 2nd set of lights into Ingram St.*
Located in the heart of the city centre, this hotel has easy access to both shopping and theatre areas. Bedrooms are comfortably appointed for both business and leisure guests.
ROOMS: 91 en suite (2 fmly) 🚭 in 61 bedrooms s £72-£92; d £72-£92 **LB FACILITIES:** STV Xmas **CONF:** Thtr 200 Class 80 Board 60 Del from £140 **SERVICES:** Lift **PARKING:** 30 **NOTES:** ✖ 🚭 in restaurant Civ Wed 40

⬆ Campanile Glasgow
10 Tunnel St G3 8HL
☎ 0141 287 7700 📠 0141 287 7701
e-mail: glasgow@envergure.co.uk
web: www.envergure.fr

Campanile

Dir: *M8 junct 19, follow signs to SECC. Hotel located next to SECC and Rotunda Casino*
This modern building offers accommodation in smart,

continued on p710

GLASGOW, continued

well-equipped bedrooms, all with en suite bathrooms. Refreshments may be taken at the informal Bistro. For further details consult the Hotel Groups page.

Campanile, Glasgow

ROOMS: 106 en suite s £49.95-£85; d £49.95-£85 **CONF:** Thtr 150 Class 60 Board 90 Del from £88

⌂ *Hotel Ibis Glasgow City Centre*

220 West Regent St G2 4DQ
☎ 0141 225 6000 🖷 0141 225 6010
e-mail: H3139@accor-hotels.com
Modern, budget hotel offering comfortable accommodation in bright and practical bedrooms. Breakfast is self-service and dinner is available in the restaurant. For further details, consult the Hotel Groups page.
ROOMS: 141 en suite

⌂ Innkeeper's Lodge Glasgow

1 Auchenkilns Park, Cumbernauld G68 9AT
☎ 01236 795861
web: www.innkeeperslodge.com
A growing concept in the travel accommodation market. Smart rooms meet essential business requirements but also have home comforts. Dining options include all-day menus plus the added advantage of breakfast, which is included in the room price. For further details consult the Hotel Groups page.
ROOMS: 57 en suite s £45-£49.95; d £45-£49.95

⌂ Premier Travel Inn Glasgow (Cambuslang)

Cambuslang G32 8EY
☎ 08701 977306 🖷 0141 778 1703
web: www.premiertravelinn.com
Dir: *on rdbt at end of M74, turn right at rdbt, at lights turn right & Inn on right*
High quality, modern budget accommodation ideal for both families and business travellers. Spacious, en suite bedrooms feature bath and shower, satellite TV and many have telephones and modem points. The adjacent family restaurant features a wide and varied menu. For further details consult the Hotel Groups page.
ROOMS: 40 en suite s £46.95-£49.95; d £46.95-£49.95

Indoor Swimming pool
Indoor Swimming pool (heated)
Outdoor Swimming pool
Outdoor Swimming pool (heated)

⌂ Premier Travel Inn Glasgow (Charing Cross)

10 Elmbank Gardens G2 4PP
☎ 0870 9906312 🖷 0870 9906313
e-mail: glasgow@premierlodge.co.uk
web: www.premiertravelinn.com
Dir: *From S, exit M8 junct 18 (right junct), through 2 sets of lights, left into Elmbank Cres. From N, exit M8 junct 18 follow city centre signs. Left at lights, left again at next. Down hill, right at lights into Elmbank St, left at BP station*
High quality, modern budget accommodation ideal for both families and business travellers. Spacious, en suite bedrooms feature bath and shower, satellite TV and many have telephones and modem points. The adjacent family restaurant features a wide and varied menu. For further details consult the Hotel Groups page.
ROOMS: 278 en suite s £49.95; d £49.95 **CONF:** Thtr 50 Class 25 Board 20

⌂ Premier Travel Inn Glasgow City Centre

Montrose House, 187 George St G1 1YU
☎ 0870 238 3320 🖷 0141 553 2719
web: www.premiertravelinn.com
Dir: *off M8 junct 15 (2 minutes walk of George Square)*
High quality, modern budget accommodation ideal for both families and business travellers. Spacious, en suite bedrooms feature bath and shower, satellite TV and many have telephones and modem points. The adjacent family restaurant features a wide and varied menu. For further details consult the Hotel Groups page.
ROOMS: 254 en suite s £53.95; d £53.95 **CONF:** Thtr 20 Board 10

⌂ Premier Travel Inn Glasgow East

601 Hamilton Rd G71 7SA
☎ 08701 977109 🖷 0141 773 8554
web: www.premiertravelinn.com
Dir: *By M73 & M74 junct 4, follow signs to Uddingston Mt. Vernon and then Zoo Park. Situated at entrance to Glasgow Zoo*
High quality, modern budget accommodation ideal for both families and business travellers. Spacious, en suite bedrooms feature bath and shower, satellite TV and many have telephones and modem points. The adjacent family restaurant features a wide and varied menu. For further details consult the Hotel Groups page.
ROOMS: 66 en suite s £46.95-£49.95; d £46.95-£49.95

⌂ Travelodge (Glasgow Central)

9 Hill St G3 6PR
☎ 08700 850 950 🖷 0141 333 1221
web: www.travelodge.co.uk
Dir: *M8 junct 17, at lights left into West Graham St. Right into Cowcaddens Rd. Right Cambridge St. Right Hill Street*
Travelodge offers good quality, good value, modern accommodation. Ideal for families, the spacious, en suite bedrooms include remote-control TV, tea and coffee-making facilities and comfortable beds. Meals can be taken at the nearby family restaurant. For further details consult the Hotel Groups page.
ROOMS: 95 en suite s fr £26; d fr £26

⌂ Travelodge Glagow Paisley Road

251 Paisley Rd G5 8RA
☎ 08700 850 950 🖷 0141 420 3884
web: www.travelodge.co.uk
Dir: *0.5m from city centre just off M8 junct 20 from S, M8 junct 21 from N. Behind Harry Ramsden's*
Travelodge offers good quality, good value, modern accommodation. Ideal for families, the spacious, en suite bedrooms include remote-control TV, tea and coffee-making facilities and comfortable beds. Meals can be taken at the nearby family restaurant. For further details consult the Hotel Groups page.
ROOMS: 75 en suite s fr £26; d fr £26

Tulip Inn Glasgow
80 Ballater St G5 0TW
☎ 0141 429 4233 🖷 0141 429 4244
e-mail: info@tulipinnglasgow.co.uk
web: www.tulipinnglasgow.co.uk
Dir: *M8 junct 21 follow East Kilbride signs, right onto Kingston St. Right onto South Portland St, left onto Norfolk St, straight through Gorbals St & onto Ballater St.*
A modern budget hotel suitable for business travellers, families and tourists. Bedrooms are bright, well proportioned and comprehensively equipped. There is a bistro, bar and small gym.
ROOMS: 114 en suite **CONF:** BC Thtr 180 Class 100 Board 60

GLASGOW AIRPORT, Renfrewshire — Map 20 NS46

★★★71% Glynhill Hotel & Leisure Club
Paisley Rd PA4 8XB
☎ 0141 886 5555 🖷 0141 885 2838
e-mail: glynhillleisurehotel@msn.com
Dir: *M8 junct 27, take A741 towards Renfrew, cross small rdbt - 300yds, hotel on right*
A smart and welcoming hotel with bedrooms ranging from spacious executive rooms to smaller standard rooms. All are tastefully appointed and have a good range of amenities. The hotel boasts a luxurious leisure complex and extensive conference facilities. The choice of contrasting bars and restaurants should suit most tastes and budgets.
ROOMS: 145 en suite (25 fmly) in 72 bedrooms **FACILITIES:** STV supervised Sauna Solarium Gym Jacuzzi **CONF:** Thtr 450 Class 240 **PARKING:** 230 **NOTES:** Civ Wed 450

★★★70% Lynnhurst
Park Rd PA5 8LS
☎ 01505 324331 & 324600 🖷 01505 324219
e-mail: enquiries@lynnhurst.co.uk
web: www.lynnhurst.co.uk
Dir: *past airport, take slip road (A737). Continue 2m, take B789 then left into Johnstone and at 1st main lights right, then 1st left and 2nd right*
Genuine hospitality together with high standards of guest care are the hallmarks of this family-run hotel, set in a quiet residential area. Bedrooms are thoughtfully equipped for both business and leisure guests. Public areas include a smart conservatory, spacious lounge bar and an impressive dining room.
ROOMS: 21 en suite (2 fmly) s £45-£55; d £80-£90 (incl. bkfst) **LB** **FACILITIES:** Arrangement with local leisure centre Xmas **CONF:** BC Thtr 160 Class 160 Board 20 Del £80 **PARKING:** 100 **NOTES:** Closed 1-3 Jan Civ Wed 100

Ramada Glasgow Airport
Marchburn Dr, Glasgow Airport Business Park PA3 2SJ ☎ 0141 840 2200 🖷 0141 889 6830
e-mail: sales.glasgowairport@ramadajarvis.co.uk
web: www.ramadajarvis.co.uk
Dir: *From M8 junct 28 follow signs for hotel.*
This brand new, purpose-built hotel is set only 500 yards from Glasgow Airport. Bedrooms are comfortably appointed for both business and leisure guests.
ROOMS: 108 en suite (108 fmly) (12 GF) in 80 bedrooms s £72-£89; d £72-£89 **FACILITIES:** STV **CONF:** Thtr 40 Class 16 Board 20 Del from £125 **SERVICES:** Lift **PARKING:** 170 **NOTES:** in restaurant

Premier Travel Inn Glasgow Airport
Whitecart Rd PA3 2TH
☎ 0870 238 3321 🖷 0141 842 1570
web: www.premiertravelinn.com
Dir: *close to airport terminal, follow signs*
High quality, modern budget accommodation ideal for both families and business travellers. Spacious, en suite bedrooms feature bath and shower, satellite TV and many have telephones and modem points. The adjacent family restaurant features a wide and varied menu. For further details consult the Hotel Groups page.
ROOMS: 104 en suite s £49.95-£52.95; d £49.95-£52.95 **CONF:** Thtr 30

Premier Travel Inn Glasgow (Paisley)
Phoenix Retail Park PA1 2BH
☎ 08701 977113 🖷 0141 887 2799
web: www.premiertravelinn.com
Dir: *M8 junct 28A, A737 signed Irvine, take 1st exit signed Linwood & turn left at 1st rdbt to Phoenix Park*
High quality, modern budget accommodation ideal for both families and business travellers. Spacious, en suite bedrooms feature bath and shower, satellite TV and many have telephones and modem points. The adjacent family restaurant features a wide and varied menu. For further details consult the Hotel Groups page.
ROOMS: 40 en suite s £46.95-£49.95; d £46.95-£49.95 **CONF:** Thtr 20 Board 15

Travelodge (Glasgow Airport)
Marchburn Dr, Glasgow Airport Business Park, Paisley PA3 2AR
☎ 08700 850 950 🖷 0141 889 0583
web: www.travelodge.co.uk
Dir: *M8 junct 28, 0.5m from Glasgow Airport*
Travelodge offers good quality, good value, modern accommodation. Ideal for families, the spacious, en suite bedrooms include remote-control TV, tea and coffee-making facilities and comfortable beds. Meals can be taken at the nearby family restaurant. For further details consult the Hotel Groups page.
ROOMS: 98 en suite s fr £26; d fr £26

GLENEAGLES See Auchterarder

GLENFINNAN, Highland — Map 22 NM98

★★75% The Prince's House
PH37 4LT
☎ 01397 722246 🖷 01397 722323
e-mail: princeshouse@glenfinnan.co.uk
web: www.glenfinnan.co.uk
Dir: *on A830, 0.5m on right past Glenfinnan Monument. 200mtrs from Glenfinnan Railway Station*
This delightful hotel enjoys a well-deserved reputation for fine food and excellent hospitality. The hotel sits close to where 'Bonnie' Prince Charlie raised the Jacobite standard and enjoys inspiring views. Comfortably appointed bedrooms offer pleasing decor and bathrooms. Excellent local game and seafood can be enjoyed in either the dining room or spacious stage house lounge bar.
ROOMS: 9 en suite (1 fmly) in all bedrooms s £45-£55; d £75-£85 (incl. bkfst) **LB** **FACILITIES:** Fishing Xmas **CONF:** Thtr 40 Class 20 **PARKING:** 18 **NOTES:** in restaurant Closed Christmas & Jan-early Feb

GLENLUCE, Dumfries & Galloway — Map 20 NX15

★★67% Kelvin House Hotel
53 Main St DG8 0PP
☎ 01581 300303 🖷 01581 300303
e-mail: mail@kelvin-house.co.uk
Dir: *off A75 signed Glenluce. Hotel in centre of village*
This small, friendly hotel lies in the centre of a village and offers bedrooms are comfortably equipped. There is a residents' lounge, and wholesome, home cooked, good-value meals are served either in the popular bar or separate restaurant overlooking the garden.
ROOMS: 6 rms (5 en suite) (3 fmly) in all bedrooms **NOTES:** in restaurant

GLENROTHES, Fife — Map 21 NO20

★★77% Rescobie House Hotel & Restaurant

6 Valley Dr, Leslie KY6 3BQ
☎ 01592 749555 01592 620231
e-mail: rescobiehotel@compuserve.com
web: www.rescobie-hotel.co.uk
Dir: *off A92 at Glenrothes onto A911, through Leslie. End of High St follow straight ahead. Take 1st left, hotel entrance 2nd left*
Hospitality and guest care are second to none at this relaxing country house, which lies secluded in gardens on the fringe of Leslie. Period architecture is enhanced by a combination of contemporary and art deco styling, a theme carried through to the bright airy bedrooms. There is an inviting lounge and an intimate restaurant serving memorable meals.
ROOMS: 10 en suite s £50-£68; d £75-£99 (incl. bkfst) **PARKING:** 12 **NOTES:** in restaurant RS None Civ Wed 24

G

Premier Travel Inn Glenrothes

Beaufort Dr KY7 4UJ
☎ 08701 977114 01592 773453
web: www.premiertravelinn.com
Dir: *From M90 junct 2a, northbound, take A92 to Glenrothes. At 2nd rdbt (Bankhead), take 3rd exit. Inn is on the left (Beaufort Drive)*
High quality, modern budget accommodation ideal for both families and business travellers. Spacious, en suite bedrooms feature bath and shower, satellite TV and many have telephones and modem points. The adjacent family restaurant features a wide and varied menu. For further details consult the Hotel Groups page.
ROOMS: 40 en suite s £48.95; d £48.95

Travelodge Glenrothes

Bankhead Park KY7 6GH
☎ 0870 850 950 01476 577500
web: www.travelodge.co.uk
Dir: *M90, A92 to junct with A910/B981(signed Glenrothes), follow to Redhouse rdbt take 2nd exit (signed Glenrothes, Tay bridge) follow to Bankhead rdbt - junct with B921.*
Travelodge offers good quality, good value, modern accommodation. Ideal for families, the spacious, en suite bedrooms include remote-control TV, tea and coffee-making facilities and comfortable beds. Meals can be taken at the nearby family restaurant. For further details consult the Hotel Groups page.
ROOMS: 50 en suite s fr £26; d fr £26

GLENSHEE (SPITTAL OF), Perth & Kinross — Map 21 NO17

★★74% *Dalmunzie House*

PH10 7QG
☎ 01250 885224 01250 885225
e-mail: reservations@dalmunzie.com web: www.dalmunzie.com
Dir: *on A93 at Spittal of Glenshee, follow signs to hotel*

This turreted mansion house enjoys a remote setting in the heart of a 6,500-acre estate, yet is within easy reach of the ski slopes of Glenshee. Accommodation ranges in style from large rooms with period furnishings to more compact rooms with modern decor. Public areas include a traditional bar, a spacious restaurant and a choice of lounges.
ROOMS: 19 rms (16 en suite) **FACILITIES:** 9 Fishing Clay pigeon shooting, Mountain bikes, Estate tours, Grouse shooting, Stalking **CONF:** Thtr 20 Class 20 Board 20 **SERVICES:** Lift **PARKING:** 33 **NOTES:** in restaurant Closed 24-27 Dec

GOUROCK, Inverclyde — Map 20 NS27

Ramada Gourock

Cloch Rd PA19 1AR
☎ 01475 634671 01475 632490
e-mail: sales.gourock@ramadajarvis.co.uk
web: www.ramadajarvis.co.uk
Dir: *A8 to Parklee rdbt, take 2nd exit, then 2nd exit at next rdbt. Through Port Glasgow. At Greenock rdbt 2nd exit signed Gourock.*
This well presented hotel is situated on the Firth of Clyde with views over the Argyll Hills. Bedrooms are comfortably appointed for both business and leisure guests.
ROOMS: 98 en suite (8 fmly) (30 GF) in 75 bedrooms s £72-£89; d £72-£89 **FACILITIES:** STV supervised Sauna Gym Jacuzzi Xmas **CONF:** Thtr 250 Class 100 Board 70 Del from £114 **SERVICES:** Lift **PARKING:** 200 **NOTES:** in restaurant Civ Wed 100

GRANGEMOUTH, Falkirk — Map 21 NS98

★★★76% The Grange Manor

Glensburgh FK3 8XJ
☎ 01324 474836 01324 665861
e-mail: info@grangemanor.co.uk
web: www.grangemanor.co.uk
Dir: *E: off M9 junct 6, hotel 200mtrs to right. W: off M9 junct 5, A905 for 2m*
Located south of town close to the M9, this stylish hotel, popular with business and corporate clientele, benefits from hands-on family ownership. It offers spacious, high quality accommodation with superb bathrooms. Public areas include a comfortable foyer area, lounge bar and smart restaurant. There is also a bar/bistro in the grounds. Staff throughout the manor are especially friendly.
ROOMS: 6 en suite 30 annexe en suite (6 fmly) (15 GF) in 22 bedrooms s £59-£99; d £80-£125 (incl. bkfst) **LB** **FACILITIES:** STV Xmas **CONF:** Thtr 190 Class 68 Board 40 Del from £125 **SERVICES:** Lift **PARKING:** 154 **NOTES:** Civ Wed 160

Popped the question? Hotels with Civ wed in their entry are licensed for civil wedding ceremonies. Maximum numbers for the ceremony only are shown e.g. Civ wed 120

GRANTOWN-ON-SPEY, Highland — Map 23 NJ03

★★★71% Muckrach Lodge

Dulnain Bridge PH26 3LY
☎ 01479 851257 01479 851325
e-mail: info@muckrach.co.uk
Dir: *from A95 Dulnain Bridge exit follow A938 towards Carrbridge. Hotel 500mtrs on right*
This former sporting lodge is set in ten acres of landscaped grounds, at the foot of the Cairngorm Mountains. Bedrooms come in a variety of sizes and styles; the larger ones are particularly well appointed. The cosy bar is popular with the sporting clientele and

continued

features a roaring log fire. Dinner can be taken in either the bistro or award-winning Finlarig restaurant.

ROOMS: 10 en suite 4 annexe en suite (3 fmly) ⊗ in all bedrooms s £60-£80; d £120-£160 (incl. bkfst) **LB** **FACILITIES:** Fishing Beauty & aroma therapy Xmas **CONF:** Thtr 30 Class 20 Board 16 Del from £135 **PARKING:** 53 **NOTES:** ⊗ in restaurant Closed 5-20 Jan RS Nov-Mar Civ Wed 50

★★79% Culdearn House

Woodlands Ter PH26 3JU
☎ 01479 872106 01479 873641
e-mail: enquiries@culdearn.com
web: www.culdearn.com
Dir: *from SW into Grantown on A95, left at 30mph sign, hotel opposite*

This immaculately maintained small hotel sits in gardens on the edge of town. The renovation of half of the bedrooms here, (with more to follow) has taken the quality to new heights. Hospitality is excellent and every effort is made to make guests feel at home. The hotel has the atmosphere of a relaxed country house.
ROOMS: 7 en suite (1 GF) ⊗ in all bedrooms s £85; d £170 (incl. bkfst & dinner) **LB** **PARKING:** 12 **NOTES:** No children 12yrs ⊗ in restaurant Closed Jan-Feb

★★79% The Pines

Woodside Av PH26 3JR
☎ 01479 872092 01479 872092
e-mail: info@thepinesgrantown.co.uk
Dir: *at lights turn onto A939, then 1st right*
This impressive Victorian house is set in well-tended gardens, a short walk from the centre of town. The delightful public areas include a choice of two lounges, both furnished with some fine period pieces and many original works of art, a library and an elegant dining room. The thoughtfully equipped bedrooms are
continued

individually styled and generally spacious; many have fine views of the lovely Speyside scenery.

ROOMS: 7 en suite (1 GF) ⊗ in all bedrooms s £85-£105; d £150-£176 (incl. bkfst & dinner) **LB** **PARKING:** 8 **NOTES:** No children 12yrs ⊗ in restaurant RS Nov-Feb

GREENOCK, Inverclyde — Map 20 NS27

Premier Travel Inn Greenock

1-3 James Watt Way PA15 2AJ
☎ 08701 977120 01475 730890
web: www.premiertravelinn.com
Dir: *Follow M8 until it becomes A8 at Langbank, straight ahead through rdbt to Greenock, turn right off A8 at 3rd rdbt, next to McDonalds*
High quality, modern budget accommodation ideal for both families and business travellers. Spacious, en suite bedrooms feature bath and shower, satellite TV and many have telephones and modem points. The adjacent family restaurant features a wide and varied menu. For further details consult the Hotel Groups page.
ROOMS: 40 en suite s £46.95-£48.95; d £46.95-£48.95

GRETNA (WITH GRETNA GREEN), Dumfries & Galloway — Map 21 NY36

★★★69% *Gretna Chase*

DG16 5JB
☎ 01461 337517 01461 337766
e-mail: enquiries@gretnachase.co.uk
Dir: *off M74 onto B7076, left at top of slip road, hotel 400yds on right*
With its colourful landscaped gardens, this hotel is a favourite venue for wedding parties. Bedrooms range from the comfortable traditional standard rooms to the impressively spacious superior and honeymoon rooms; all are well equipped. There is a foyer lounge, a spacious dining room that can accommodate functions, and a popular lounge bar serving food.
ROOMS: 19 en suite (9 fmly) ⊗ in 6 bedrooms **FACILITIES:** Jacuzzi **CONF:** Thtr 50 Class 30 Board 20 **PARKING:** 40 **NOTES:** Closed First 2 wks of Jan

★★★67% Garden House

Sarkfoot Rd DG16 5EP
☎ 01461 337621 01461 337692
e-mail: info@gardenhouse.co.uk
web: www.gardenhouse.co.uk
Dir: *just off M6 junct 45 at Gretna*
This purpose-built modern hotel lies on the edge of the village. With a focus on weddings its landscaped gardens provide an ideal setting, while inside corridor walls are adorned with photographs portraying that 'special day'. Accommodation is well presented
continued on p714

GRETNA (WITH GRETNA GREEN), continued

and there is a new wing of spacious and comfortable bedrooms, many overlooking the Japanese water gardens.

Garden House, Gretna

ROOMS: 38 en suite (11 fmly) (14 GF) **FACILITIES: Spa** STV supervised Sauna Jacuzzi Xmas **CONF:** BC Thtr 150 Class 80 Board 40 Del £71.50 **SERVICES:** Lift **PARKING:** 105 **NOTES:** in restaurant Civ Wed 150

See advert on opposite page

★★★65% Gretna Hall Hotel

CRERAR HOTELS

Gretna Green DG16 5DY
☎ 01461 338257 01461 338911
e-mail: reservations.gretna@crerarhotels.com
web: www.crerarhotels.com

Popular for weddings, conferences and banqueting, the main building dates back to 1710 and has a prime location with easy access to major road networks. The bedrooms are comfortably equipped; these come in a variety of sizes and styles from contemporary to more traditional.

ROOMS: 100 en suite (7 fmly) (25 GF) in 80 bedrooms s £65-£95; d £90-£115 (incl. bkfst) **LB** **FACILITIES:** Xmas **CONF:** BC Thtr 120 Class 80 Board 40 Del from £80 **SERVICES:** Lift **PARKING:** 80 **NOTES:** in restaurant Civ Wed 60

GRETNA SERVICE AREA (A74(M)), Dumfries & Galloway — Map 21 NY36

Days Inn Gretna

DAYS INN

Welcome Break Service Area DG16 5HQ
☎ 01461 337566 01461 337823
e-mail: gretna.hotel@welcomebreak.co.uk
web: www.welcomebreak.co.uk

***Dir:** between junct 21/22 on M74 - accessible from both N'bound & S'bound carriageway*

This modern building offers accommodation in smart, spacious and well-equipped bedrooms, suitable for families and business travellers, and all with en suite bathrooms. Continental breakfast is available and other refreshments may be taken at the nearby family restaurant. For further details see the Hotel Groups page.

ROOMS: 64 en suite s £45-£55; d £45-£55 **CONF:** Thtr 40 Board 20

Late for dinner? Quality standards mean that last orders for dinner vary according to star rating and should be no earlier than: ★★ 7.00pm ★★★ 8:00pm ★★★★ 9:00pm ★★★★★ 10:00pm

GULLANE, East Lothian — Map 21 NT48

Top Hotel

★★★ Greywalls

Muirfield EH31 2EG
☎ 01620 842144 01620 842241
e-mail: hotel@greywalls.co.uk
web: www.greywalls.co.uk

***Dir:** A198, hotel signposted at E end of village*

A dignified but relaxing Edwardian country house designed by Sir Edwin Lutyens; Greywalls overlooks the famous Muirfield Golf Course and is ideally placed just a half hours' drive from Edinburgh. Delightful public rooms look onto beautiful gardens and freshly prepared cuisine may be enjoyed in the restaurant. Stylish bedrooms, whether cosy singles or spacious master rooms, are thoughtfully equipped and many command views of the course. A gatehouse lodge is ideal for golfing parties.

ROOMS: 17 en suite 6 annexe en suite (9 GF) s £135-£255; d £230-£270 (incl. bkfst) **LB** **FACILITIES:** STV Putt green Extensive gardens **CONF:** Thtr 30 Class 20 Board 20 Del from £215 **PARKING:** 40 **NOTES:** in restaurant Closed Nov-Mar

HADDINGTON, East Lothian — Map 21 NT57

★★★64% Maitlandfield Country House

24 Sidegate EH41 4BZ
☎ 01620 826513 01620 826713
e-mail: sales@maitlandfieldhouse.co.uk
web: www.maitlandfieldhouse.co.uk

***Dir:** in Haddington follow signs to St Mary's church/Lennoxlove House on B6369 towards Gifford*

This popular hotel lies in attractive gardens looking across to the historic St Mary's Church. Public areas include an inviting lounge and a conservatory brasserie with a wide-ranging menu. Bedrooms come in a mix of sizes and are being refurbished to reflect a contemporary style complete with flat screen TVs.

ROOMS: 25 en suite (3 GF) in all bedrooms **FACILITIES:** Xmas **CONF:** BC Thtr 180 Class 100 Board 60 Del from £80 **PARKING:** 80 **NOTES:** in restaurant Civ Wed 150

HALKIRK, Highland — Map 23 ND15

★★61% *Ulbster Arms*

Bridge St KW12 6XY
☎ 01847 831206 & 831641 01847 831206
e-mail: ulbster-arms@ecosse.net

***Dir:** from A9, 3m after village of Spittal turn left*

This small hotel is located in the centre of the small village of Halkirk, close to Thurso. Attracting a mainly sporting clientele

continued

there is good fishing and shooting nearby. Bedrooms vary in size and style and public areas include a choice of eating options.
ROOMS: 10 en suite 16 annexe en suite **FACILITIES:** Fishing Shooting ♫ **CONF:** Thtr 30 Class 25 Board 20 **PARKING:** 36 **NOTES:** ⊗ in restaurant

HAMILTON MOTORWAY SERVICE AREA (M74), South Lanarkshire
Map 20 NS75

⇧ Premier Travel Inn Glasgow (Hamilton)
Hamilton Motorway Service Area ML3 6JW
☎ 08701 977124 📠 01698 891682
web: www.premiertravelinn.com

Dir: M74 northbound, 1m N of junct 6. For southbound access exit junct 6 onto A723, double back at rdbt & join M74 Glasgow exit
High quality, modern budget accommodation ideal for both families and business travellers. Spacious, en suite bedrooms feature bath and shower, satellite TV and many have telephones and modem points. The adjacent family restaurant features a wide and varied menu. For further details consult the Hotel Groups page.
ROOMS: 36 en suite s £46.95-£49.95; d £46.95-£49.95 **CONF:** Thtr 30 Board 20

HARRIS, ISLE OF, Western Isles
Map 22

SCARISTA
Map 22 NG09

Restaurant with Rooms

⛊ ◉◉ Scarista House
HS3 3HX
☎ 01859 550238 📠 01859 550277
e-mail: timandpatricia@scaristahouse.com
Dir: on A859, 15 miles south of Tarbert
A former manse, Scarista House is now a haven for food lovers who seek to explore the magnificent island of Harris. The house enjoys breathtaking views of the Atlantic and is just a short stroll from miles of golden sandy beaches. The house is run in a relaxed country-house manner by the friendly hosts. Expect wellies in the hall and masses of books and CDs in one of two lounges. Bedrooms are cosy, and delicious set dinners and memorable breakfasts are provided.
ROOMS: 3 en suite 2 annexe en suite (2 GF) ⊗ in all bedrooms s £110; d £150-£170 (incl. bkfst) **LB FACILITIES:** no TV in bdrms **CONF:** Thtr 20 Class 16 Board 16 **PARKING:** 12 **NOTES:** ⊗ in restaurant Closed Xmas RS Nov-Mar Civ Wed 40

HOWWOOD, Renfrewshire
Map 20 NS36

★★★70% ◉ Bowfield Hotel & Country Club
PA9 1DB
☎ 01505 705225 & 704225 📠 01505 705230
e-mail: enquiries@bowfieldcountryclub.co.uk
web: www.stonefieldhotels.com
Dir: M8 junct 28a/29, onto A737 for 6m, left onto B787, right after 2m, follow road for 1m to hotel
This former textile mill is a popular hotel which has become a convenient stopover for travellers using Glasgow Airport. The leisure club has been considerably expanded and offers very good facilities. Public areas have beamed ceilings, brick and white painted walls, and welcoming open fires. Bedrooms are housed in a separate wing and offer good modern comforts and facilities.
ROOMS: 23 en suite (3 fmly) (7 GF) s fr £85; d fr £130 (incl. bkfst) **LB FACILITIES: Spa** ⊠ supervised Squash Snooker Sauna Solarium Gym Jacuzzi Childrens soft play, aerobics studio, heath & beauty Xmas **CONF:** Thtr 100 Board 40 Del from £95 **PARKING:** 120 **NOTES:** ⊗ in restaurant

Garden House Hotel
★ ★ ★

Sarkfoot Road, Gretna, Dumfriesshire DG16 5EP
Tel: 01461 337621. Fax: 01461 337692

Welcome to a relaxing and enjoyable stay at the Garden House Hotel. Very centrally situated and close to romantic Gretna Green. The hotel offers a high standard of accommodation, all 21 bedrooms are en suite and individually furnished. Dining at the Garden restaurant is a pleasure, the finely prepared cultural cuisine is complemented by an extensive wine list. For the more energetic, our new Leisure Centre offers a heated Swimming Pool, Jacuzzi, Sauna, Solarium and Turkish Steam Room. Conferences, Meetings and Exhibitions are catered for with our modern air conditioned Conference Suites. Alternatively you can relax in the extensive well maintained grounds with floodlit Japanese Water Garden.

HUNTLY, Aberdeenshire
Map 23 NJ53

★★63% Gordon Arms Hotel
The Square AB54 8AF
☎ 01466 792288 📠 01466 794556
e-mail: reception@gordonarms.demon.co.uk
THE INDEPENDENTS
Dir: off A96 Aberdeen to Inverness road at Huntly. Hotel immediately on left after entering town square
This friendly family-run hotel is located in the town square and offers a good selection of tasty, well-portioned dishes served in the bar (or in the restaurant at weekends or midweek by appointment). Bedrooms come in a variety of sizes, and all are cheerfully decorated.
ROOMS: 13 en suite (3 fmly) s £35; d £48-£58 (incl. bkfst) **LB FACILITIES:** ♫ **CONF:** Thtr 160 Class 80 Board 60 Del from £45

INVERARAY, Argyll & Bute
Map 20 NN00

★★★68%
Loch Fyne Hotel & Leisure Club
PA32 8XT
☎ 01499 302148 📠 01499 302348
e-mail: lochfyne@crerarhotels.com
web: www.crerarhotels.com
CRERAR HOTELS
Dir: from A83 Loch Lomond, through town centre on A80 to Lochgilphead. Hotel in 0.5m
This popular holiday hotel overlooks Loch Fyne. Bedrooms are mainly spacious and offer comfortable modern appointments. Guests can relax in the well-stocked bar and enjoy views over the *continued on p716*

INVERARAY, continued

Loch, or enjoy a meal in the delightful restaurant. There is also a well-equipped leisure centre.

Loch Fyne Hotel & Leisure Club, Inveraray

ROOMS: 78 en suite s fr £75; d fr £125 (incl. bkfst) **LB FACILITIES:** ☜ supervised Sauna Jacuzzi Steam Room ♫ Xmas **CONF:** Thtr 50 Class 30 Board 20 Del from £95 **SERVICES:** Lift **PARKING:** 50 **NOTES:** ⊗ in restaurant

★★★67% **The Argyll**
Front St PA32 8XB
☎ 01499 302466 📠 01499 302389
e-mail: reception@the-argyll-hotel.co.uk
web: www.the-argyll-hotel.co.uk
Dir: A82 (Glasgow - Tarbet), A83 (Tarbet to Inveraray). Hotel 1st building facing loch
Located beside The Arch and enjoying super views of Loch Fyne, this hotel offers smartly furnished bedrooms that are comfortable and well equipped. Facilities include a choice of bars, foyer lounge and conservatory. The attractive restaurant features freshly prepared meals based on quality Scottish ingredients.
ROOMS: 35 en suite (7 fmly) ⊗ in 4 bedrooms s £55-£65; d £98-£108 (incl. bkfst) **LB FACILITIES:** STV Xmas **CONF:** Thtr 120 Class 80 Board 70 **PARKING:** 50 **NOTES:** ✈ ⊗ in restaurant Closed 25-26 Dec Civ Wed 120

INVERGARRY, Highland Map 22 NH30

★★★74% ◉♨ **Glengarry Castle**
PH35 4HW
☎ 01809 501254 📠 01809 501207
e-mail: castle@glengarry.net
web: www.glengarry.net
Dir: on A82 beside Loch Oich, 0.5m from A82/A87 junct

This charming country-house hotel is set in 50 acres of grounds on the shores of Loch Oich. The spacious day rooms include comfortable sitting rooms with lots to read and board games to play. The classical dining room boasts an innovative menu that

continued

showcases local Scottish produce. The smart bedrooms vary in size and style but all boast magnificent loch or woodland views.
ROOMS: 26 en suite (2 fmly) ⊗ in 10 bedrooms s £58-£90; d £86-£160 (incl. bkfst) **FACILITIES:** ॐ Fishing **PARKING:** 32 **NOTES:** ⊗ in restaurant Closed mid Nov-mid Mar

See advert on opposite page

INVERGORDON, Highland Map 23 NH76

★★★72% **Kincraig House**
IV18 0LF
☎ 01349 852587 📠 01349 852193
e-mail: info@kincraig-house-hotel.co.uk
Dir: off A9 for Invergordon & Alness. Hotel entrance on left 0.25m past Rosleen Church

This mansion house is set in well-tended grounds in an elevated position with views over the Cromarty Firth. Having undergone an extensive upgrading it offers smart, well-equipped bedrooms and inviting public areas that retain the original features of the house. However it is the friendly service and commitment to guest care that will leave a lasting impression.
ROOMS: 15 en suite (1 fmly) (1 GF) ⊗ in 12 bedrooms s £50-£65; d £90-£170 (incl. bkfst) **LB FACILITIES:** Xmas **PARKING:** 30 **NOTES:** ⊗ in restaurant

See advert on opposite page

INVERKEITHING, Fife Map 21 NT18

★★★62% **Corus hotel Edinburgh North**
St Margaret's Head, North Queensferry
KY11 1HP
☎ 0870 6096160 📠 01383 419708
e-mail: edinburghnorth@corushotels.com
web: www.corushotels.com
Dir: from N take exit after M90 junct 1 signed Park & Ride, follow signs for Deep Sea World, hotel on left. From S over Forth Road Bridge, then 1st exit then 1st left, hotel 0.5m on left

corus hotels

From its position on the north side of the river this smart, modern

continued

hotel enjoys fine views of the famous road and rail bridges. Bright, modern public areas include a comfortable foyer lounge and bar, a smart restaurant, and a good range of banqueting facilities. Bedrooms are comfortable and offer a good range of amenities.
ROOMS: 77 en suite (4 fmly) (15 GF) ⊗ in 38 bedrooms s £50-£95; d £60-£105 **LB** **FACILITIES:** STV Xmas **CONF:** Thtr 150 Class 70 Board 30 Del from £89 **SERVICES:** Lift **PARKING:** 200 **NOTES:** ⊗ in restaurant Civ Wed 200

INVERMORISTON, Highland — Map 23 NH41

★★77% Glenmoriston Arms Hotel & Restaurant
IV63 7YA
☎ 01320 351206 Fax 01320 351308
e-mail: reception@glenmoristonarms.co.uk
web: www.glenmoristonarms.co.uk
Dir: *on junct of A82 & A887 (road to Isle of Skye)*
A charming, well-maintained, small hotel, which is steeped in history, that offers a warm welcome. Inviting public areas include a cosy bar and attractive formal restaurant where fine dinners, prepared and cooked with care and dedication, are served. An alternative is offered by the Tavern bar/bistro in the grounds. The well-equipped bedrooms reflect the individuality of the house.
ROOMS: 8 en suite (1 fmly) ⊗ in 2 bedrooms **FACILITIES:** Fishing ♫ ch fac **CONF:** BC Board 8 **PARKING:** 24 **NOTES:** ⊗ in restaurant Closed 5 Jan-end Feb

INVERNESS, Highland — Map 23 NH64

★★★★71% Culloden House
Culloden IV2 7BZ
☎ 01463 790461 Fax 01463 792181
e-mail: reserv@cullodenhouse.co.uk
web: www.cullodenhouse.co.uk
Dir: *take A96 from town and turn right for Culloden. After 1m, turn left at White Church after 2nd traffic lights*
Dating from the late 1700s this impressive mansion is set in extensive grounds close to the famous Culloden battlefield. High ceilings and intricate cornices are particular features of the public rooms, including the elegant Adam dining room. Bedrooms come in a range of sizes and styles, with a number situated in a separate house.
ROOMS: 23 en suite 5 annexe en suite (1 fmly) ⊗ in 8 bedrooms s £95-£155; d £130-£210 (incl. bkfst) **LB** **FACILITIES:** STV Sauna Boules, Badminton, Golf Driving Nets, Putting Green ♫ **CONF:** Thtr 60 Class 40 Board 30 Del from £160 **PARKING:** 50 **NOTES:** No children 10yrs ⊗ in restaurant Closed 24-28 Dec Civ Wed 65

★★★★71% Inverness Marriott Hotel
Marriott HOTELS & RESORTS
Culcabock Rd IV2 3LP
☎ 01463 237166 Fax 01463 225208
e-mail: events@marriotthotels.co.uk
web: www.marriott.co.uk
Dir: *from A9 S, exit Culduthel/Kingsmills 5th exit at rdbt, 0.5m, over mini-rdbt past golf club, hotel on left after lights*
Located just one mile from the city and set in four acres, this smart, 18th-century manor hotel is easily accessed by road and rail, and is also very near the airport. Accommodation is provided in spacious, thoughtfully equipped rooms, with those in the newer wing particularly impressive. There is a choice of restaurants, a cocktail lounge bar, a leisure club and conference facilities.
ROOMS: 76 en suite 6 annexe en suite (11 fmly) (26 GF) ⊗ in 29 bedrooms **FACILITIES:** **Spa** STV Sauna Solarium Gym Putt green Hair & beauty salon Steam room **CONF:** Thtr 100 Class 35 Board 36 **SERVICES:** Lift **PARKING:** 120 **NOTES:** ⊗ in restaurant

INVERNESS, continued

★★★80% ⊛⊛ **Glenmoriston Town House Hotel**
20 Ness Bank IV2 4SF
☎ 01463 223777 📠 01463 712378
e-mail: reservations@glenmoristontownhouse.com
web: www.glenmoristontownhouse.com
Dir: on river opposite theatre, 5 mins from town centre

Bold contemporary designs blend seamlessly with the classical architecture of this stylish hotel, situated on the banks of the River Ness. Delightful day rooms include a cosy cocktail bar and a sophisticated restaurant where outstanding authentic French cuisine can be sampled. The smart, modern bedrooms have many facilities, including CD players, DVD players and flat screen TVs. Service is very friendly and attentive.
ROOMS: 30 en suite (1 fmly) (3 GF) ⊗ in 15 bedrooms s £95-£125; d £130-£180 (incl. bkfst) **LB FACILITIES:** STV Xmas **CONF:** Thtr 100 Class 50 Board 30 Del from £130 **PARKING:** 40 **NOTES:** ✗ ⊗ in restaurant

★★★74% ⊛⊛⊛ **Bunchrew House**
Bunchrew IV3 8TA
☎ 01463 234917 📠 01463 710620
e-mail: welcome@bunchrew-inverness.co.uk
web: www.bunchrew-inverness.co.uk
Dir: W on A862 along shore of Beauly Firth. Hotel 2m after canal on right

Overlooking the Beauly Firth this impressive mansion house dates from the 17th century and retains much original character. Individually styled bedrooms are spacious and tastefully furnished. A wood-panelled restaurant is the setting for artfully constructed cooking and there is a choice of comfortable lounges.
ROOMS: 16 en suite (4 fmly) (1 GF) s £95-£135; d £140-£170 (incl. bkfst) **LB FACILITIES:** Fishing **CONF:** Thtr 80 Class 30 Board 30 Del from £110 **PARKING:** 40 **NOTES:** ⊗ in restaurant Closed 24 Dec-27 Dec Civ Wed 92

★★★73% **Swallow Craigmonie Hotel & Leisure Sportif**
9 Annfield Rd IV2 3HX
☎ 01463 231649 📠 01463 233720
e-mail: swallow.craigmonie@swallowhotels.com
Dir: off A9/A96 follow signs to Hilton & Culcabock. Pass golf course to traffic lights, 1st right after lights
Set in a leafy suburb of the city, this hotel full of character dates from the 18th century. Extensive public areas include a choice of restaurants, conference facilities and a popular bar. Accommodation comes in a variety of styles, including a number of poolside suites and spacious rooms with spa baths and balconies.
ROOMS: 35 en suite s £86; d £110 (incl. bkfst) **LB FACILITIES:** STV ⊡ supervised Sauna Gym Jacuzzi **CONF:** Thtr 160 Class 70 Board 50 Del from £120 **SERVICES:** Lift **PARKING:** 60 **NOTES:** ✗ ⊗ in restaurant

★★★71% **Lochardil House**
Stratherrick Rd IV2 4LF
☎ 01463 235995 📠 01463 713394
e-mail: reservations@lochardil.co.uk
Dir: A9 Police HQ take Sir Walter Scott Drive through 2 rdbts, right onto Stratherrick Rd, 0.5m hotel on left
This hotel enjoys a peaceful location in a residential area just a mile from the town centre. Smart, comfortable bedrooms ensure a relaxed stay whilst spacious day rooms include an eye-catching conservatory restaurant, a stylish lounge bar, and a popular function suite. Staff throughout are friendly and provide a warm Highland welcome.
ROOMS: 12 en suite ⊗ in 3 bedrooms s £88-£98; d £115 (incl. bkfst) **LB FACILITIES:** STV **CONF:** Thtr 200 Class 100 Board 60 **PARKING:** 123 **NOTES:** ✗ ⊗ in restaurant Civ Wed 150

★★★69% **Columba**
7 Ness Walk IV3 5NF
☎ 01463 231391 📠 01463 715526
e-mail: thecolumba@crerarhotels.com
web: www.crerarhotels.com
Dir: from city centre towards River Ness. Hotel on river bank opposite Inverness Castle

CRERAR HOTELS

In the heart of the city and enjoying views over the River Ness, this hotel provides a contemporary, stylish destination for both leisure and business guests. It has re-opened after a complete refurbishment which is very apparent in the well-equipped and comfortable bedrooms. Spacious day rooms include a carvery restaurant and a well-stocked bar, which has folk music at weekends.
ROOMS: 76 en suite (4 fmly) ⊗ in 34 bedrooms s £65-£95; d £90-£180 (incl. bkfst) **LB FACILITIES:** ♪ Xmas **CONF:** BC Thtr 75 Class 25 Board 34 **SERVICES:** Lift **NOTES:** ⊗ in restaurant Civ Wed 60

★★★68% Royal Highland
Station Square, Academy St IV1 1LG
☎ 01463 231926 🖷 01463 710705
e-mail: info@royalhighlandhotel.co.uk
web: www.royalhighlandhotel.co.uk
Built in 1858, this hotel has the typically grand foyer of the Victorian era with comfortable seating. Adjacent to this is the ASH brasserie and bar, which offers a refreshing style for both eating and drinking throughout the day. The generally spacious bedrooms are comfortably equipped for the business traveller, with the railway station nearby.
ROOMS: 70 en suite (12 fmly) ⊗ in 40 bedrooms **FACILITIES:** STV Putt green Jacuzzi **CONF:** Thtr 200 Class 80 Board 80 **SERVICES:** Lift **PARKING:** 8 **NOTES:** ⊗ in restaurant

★★★63% Loch Ness House
Glenurquhart Rd IV3 8JL
☎ 01463 231248 🖷 01463 239327
e-mail: lnhhchris@aol.com
Dir: *1.5m from town centre, overlooking Tomnahurich Bridge on canal. From A9, left at Longman rdbt, follow signs for A82 for 2.5m*
This is a family-run hotel, lying close to the canal, which offers friendly and attentive service. Tasty meals can be chosen from a good range of dishes, available in the restaurant or the bar.
ROOMS: 21 en suite (3 fmly) ⊗ in 6 bedrooms **FACILITIES:** STV Xmas **CONF:** Thtr 150 Class 60 Board 40 **PARKING:** 60 **NOTES:** ⊗ in restaurant Civ Wed 75

U The Drumossie
Old Perth Rd IV2 5BE
☎ 01463 236451 🖷 01463 712858
e-mail: stay@drumossiehotel.co.uk
Dir: *exit from A9, follow signs for Culloden Battlefield, hotel on left after 1m*
At the time of going to press, the star classification for this hotel was not confirmed. Please refer to the AA internet site www.theAA.com for current information.
ROOMS: 44 en suite (10 fmly) (6 GF) ⊗ in all bedrooms s £90-£160; d £110-£220 (incl. bkfst) **LB** **FACILITIES:** STV Fishing Other activities by arrangement Xmas **CONF:** Thtr 500 Class 200 Board 40 Del from £125 **SERVICES:** Lift **PARKING:** 200 **NOTES:** ✈ ⊗ in restaurant Civ Wed 400

U Ramada Inverness
Church St IV1 1DX
☎ 01463 235181 🖷 01463 711206
e-mail: sales.inverness@ramadajarvis.co.uk
web: www.ramadajarvis.co.uk
Dir: *Leave A9 at Kessock Bridge, take 1st exit at rdbt, 2nd exit at next rdbt, 1st exit at 2nd rdbt, right at lights*
This large, town centre hotel is set by the River Ness and is a popular venue for both conferences and meetings. Bedrooms are comfortably appointed for both business and leisure guests.
ROOMS: 106 en suite (12 fmly) ⊗ in 42 bedrooms s £85-£119; d £85-£119 **LB** **FACILITIES:** STV Sauna Gym Jacuzzi Xmas **CONF:** Thtr 200 Class 100 Board 90 Del from £135 **SERVICES:** Lift **PARKING:** 80 **NOTES:** ⊗ in restaurant Civ Wed 70

Premier Travel Inn Inverness Centre
Millburn Rd IV2 3QX
☎ 08701 977141 🖷 01463 717826
web: www.premiertravelinn.com
Dir: *on A9 junct with A96 (Raigmore Interchange, signed Airport/Aberdeen), follow B865 towards town centre, hotel 100yds past next rdbt*
High quality, modern budget accommodation ideal for both families and business travellers. Spacious, en suite bedrooms feature bath and shower, satellite TV and many have telephones and modem points. The adjacent family restaurant features a wide and varied menu. For further details consult the Hotel Groups page.
ROOMS: 39 en suite s £57.95; d £57.95

Premier Travel Inn Inverness East
Beechwood Business Park IV2 3BW
☎ 08701 977142 🖷 01463 225233
web: www.premiertravelinn.com
Dir: *A9, left signed Hospital, Police HQ & Inshes Retail Park*
High quality, modern budget accommodation ideal for both families and business travellers. Spacious, en suite bedrooms feature bath and shower, satellite TV and many have telephones and modem points. The adjacent family restaurant features a wide and varied menu. For further details consult the Hotel Groups page.
ROOMS: 60 en suite s £51.95; d £51.95

Travelodge
Stoneyfield, A96 Inverness Rd IV2 7PA
☎ 08700 850 950 🖷 01463 718152
web: www.travelodge.co.uk
Dir: *at junct of A9/A96*
Travelodge offers good quality, good value, modern accommodation. Ideal for families, the spacious, en suite bedrooms include remote-control TV, tea and coffee-making facilities and comfortable beds. Meals can be taken at the nearby family restaurant. For further details consult the Hotel Groups page.
ROOMS: s fr £26; d fr £26

Travelodge Inverness Fairways
Castle Heather IV2 6AA
☎ 08700 880950 🖷 01463 250 703
web: www.travelodge.co.uk
Dir: *From A9 follow signs for Raigmore Hospital. At 1st rdbt take 3rd exit, follow B8082 towards Hilton/Culduthel. Approx 1.5m, pass 2 more rdbts (2nd exit/3rd exit respectively). At 4th rdbt 1st exit, hotel on left.*
Travelodge offers good quality, good value, modern accommodation. Ideal for families, the spacious, en suite bedrooms include remote-control TV, tea and coffee-making facilities and comfortable beds. Meals can be taken at the nearby family restaurant. For further details consult the Hotel Groups page.
ROOMS: 80 en suite s fr £26; d fr £26

INVERURIE, Aberdeenshire — Map 23 NJ72

★★★67% Pittodrie House
Chapel of Garioch, Pitcaple AB51 5HS
☎ 01467 681444 🖷 01467 681648
e-mail: pittodrie@macdonald-hotels.co.uk
web: www.macdonald-hotels.co.uk
Dir: *A96, Chapel of Garioch exit*
This house dates from the 15th century and retains many original features. Bedrooms come in two distinct styles; those in the original house are full of character and those in the newer wing provide more modern comfort. Public areas include a striking drawing room, restaurant and a cosy bar.
ROOMS: 27 en suite (6 fmly) ⊗ in 13 bedrooms s £85-£150; d £95-£180 (incl. bkfst) **LB** **FACILITIES:** STV Squash Snooker Clay pigeon shooting Quad biking Archery etc on estate Xmas **CONF:** Thtr 100 Class 70 Board 40 Del from £135 **PARKING:** 150 **NOTES:** ⊗ in restaurant Civ Wed 120

★★★65% Strathburn
Burghmuir Dr AB51 4GY
☎ 01467 624422 🖷 01467 625133
e-mail: strathburn@btconnect.com
web: www.strathburn-hotel.co.uk
Dir: *at Blackhall rdbt into Blackhall Rd, 100yds then into Burghmuir Drive*
Located on the western side of town, this family run hotel provides accommodation in tastefully appointed bedrooms. Public
continued on p720

INVERURIE, continued

areas include a spacious lounge with conservatory and meals can be enjoyed in both the bar and the more formal restaurant.
ROOMS: 25 en suite (2 fmly) (13 GF) ⊗ in 22 bedrooms s £55-£85; d £80-£110 (incl. bkfst) **LB** **FACILITIES:** STV **CONF:** Thtr 30 Class 24 Board 18 Del from £110 **PARKING:** 40 **NOTES:** ⊗ in restaurant Closed 25-26 Dec & 1-2 Jan

IRVINE, North Ayrshire Map 20 NS33

Gailes Lodge Restaurant and Hotel
Marine Dr, Gailes KA11 5AE
☎ 01294 204040 01294 204047
e-mail: info@gaileshotel.com web: www.gaileshotel.com
With several golf courses on its doorstep and within easy reach of Prestwick Airport, this smart modern hotel offers spacious bedrooms furnished in contemporary style. A spectacular three-bedroom penthouse suite offers something really special. A bright attractive café bar/restaurant provides food throughout the day until late. There is also an impressive conference centre.
ROOMS: 41 en suite **CONF:** BC Thtr 430 Class 100 Board 80

I

ISLE OF Placenames incorporating the words 'Isle' or 'Isle of' will be found under the actual name, eg Isle of Arran is under Arran, Isle of.

ISLAY, ISLE OF Map 20

PORT ASKAIG Map 20 NR46

★★64% Port Askaig
PA46 7RD
☎ 01496 840245 01496 840295
e-mail: hotel@portaskaig.co.uk web: www.portaskaig.co.uk
Dir: *at Ferry Terminal*

This endearing family-run hotel, set in an 18th-century building, offers comfortable bedrooms. The lounge provides fine views over the Sound of Islay to Jura and there is a choice of bars that are popular with locals. Traditional dinners are served in the bright restaurant and a full range of bar snacks and meals is also available.
ROOMS: 8 rms (6 en suite) (1 fmly) **PARKING:** 21 **NOTES:** No children 5yrs ⊗ in restaurant

ISLE ORNSAY See Skye, Isle of

TV dinner?
Room service at three stars and above

JEDBURGH, Scottish Borders Map 21 NT62

★★★77% Jedforest Hotel
Camptown TD8 6PJ
☎ 01835 840222 01835 840226
e-mail: info@jedforesthotel.com
Dir: *4 miles S of Jedburgh on the A68*
The phrase 'small is beautiful' aplly applies to this friendly and immaculately maintained country hotel (now under new ownership) set in grounds by the River Jed. Bedrooms are extremely smart, and the larger ones are particularly impressive. Inviting public rooms include two lounges and an attractive restaurant with a choice of menus.
ROOMS: 8 en suite 4 annexe en suite (1 fmly) (4 GF) ⊗ in all bedrooms s £60-£110; d £140-£190 (incl. bkfst & dinner) **FACILITIES:** Fishing Xmas **PARKING:** 25 **NOTES:** No children 12yrs ⊗ in restaurant

KELSO, Scottish Borders Map 21 NT73

★★★76% The Roxburghe Hotel & Golf Course
Heiton TD5 8JZ
☎ 01573 450331 01573 450611
e-mail: hotel@roxburghe.net
web: www.roxburghe.net
Dir: *from A68 Jedburgh join A698 to Heiton, 3m SW of Kelso*

Outdoor sporting pursuits are popular at this impressive Jacobean mansion owned by the Duke of Roxburghe and set in 500 acres of woods and parkland. Gracious public areas are the perfect settings for afternoon teas and carefully prepared meals. Bedrooms are individually designed, with some of the superior rooms having their own fires.
ROOMS: 16 en suite 6 annexe en suite (3 fmly) (3 GF) ⊗ in 1 bedroom **FACILITIES:** STV 18 Fishing Putt green Clay shooting Health & Beauty Salon Mountain bike hire, riding stables nearby Xmas **CONF:** BC Thtr 50 Class 20 Board 20 **PARKING:** 150 **NOTES:** ⊗ in restaurant Civ Wed 60

★★★71% *Ednam House*
Bridge St TD5 7HT
☎ 01573 224168 01573 226319
e-mail: contact@ednamhouse.com
Dir: *50mtrs from town square*
Overlooking a wide expanse of the River Tweed, this fine Georgian mansion has been under the Brooks family ownership for over 75 years. Accommodation styles range from standard to grand, plus a house in the grounds converted into a gracious two-bedroom apartment. Public areas include a choice of lounges and an elegant dining room which has views of the gardens.
ROOMS: 30 en suite (4 fmly) ⊗ in 3 bedrooms **FACILITIES:** Free access to Abbey Fitness Centre **CONF:** Thtr 250 Board 200 **PARKING:** 60 **NOTES:** Closed 24 Dec-06 Jan Civ Wed 100

★★★68% Cross Keys
36-37 The Square TD5 7HL
☎ 01573 223303 📠 01573 225792
e-mail: cross-keys-hotel@easynet.co.uk
web: www.cross-keys-hotel.co.uk
Dir: *follow signs for town centre. Hotel in main square*
Originally a coaching inn, but now stylishy modernised, this family-run hotel overlooks the cobbled square identified by the colourful window boxes. Bedrooms offer either superior or standard, the former ones being very well proportioned. The spacious lounge bar and restaurant are supplemented by the Oak Room bar/bistro.
ROOMS: 27 en suite (5 fmly) ⊗ in 15 bedrooms s £50-£75; d £60-£110 (incl. bkfst) **LB** **FACILITIES:** STV Xmas **CONF:** BC Thtr 220 Class 160 Board 60 **SERVICES:** Lift **NOTES:** ⊗ in restaurant Closed 25-28 Dec Civ Wed 150

KENMORE, Perth & Kinross — Map 21 NN74

★★★67% Kenmore Hotel
The Square PH15 2NU
☎ 01887 830205 📠 01887 830262
e-mail: reception@kenmorehotel.co.uk
web: www.kenmorehotel.com
Dir: *off A9 at Ballinluig onto A827, through Aberfeldy to Kenmore for hotel in village centre*
Dating back to 1572, this riverside hotel is Scotland's oldest inn and has a rich and interesting history. Bedrooms are presented in tasteful decor. Dinner can be enjoyed in the restaurant with its panoramic views of the River Tay. The choice of bars includes one with real fires.
ROOMS: 27 en suite 13 annexe en suite (4 fmly) (7 GF) ⊗ in 14 bedrooms s £50-£67; d £70-£104 (incl. bkfst) **LB** **FACILITIES:** STV 🎾 Fishing Jacuzzi Salmon fishing on River Tay for residents Xmas **CONF:** Thtr 80 Class 60 Board 50 Del from £55 **SERVICES:** Lift **PARKING:** 30 **NOTES:** ⊗ in restaurant Civ Wed 40

KILCHRENAN, Argyll & Bute — Map 20 NN02

★★★77% ◎◎ Taychreggan
PA35 1HQ
☎ 01866 833211 & 833366 📠 01866 833244
e-mail: info@taychregganhotel.co.uk
Dir: *W from Crianlarich on A85 to Taynuilt, S for 7m on B845 to Kilchrenan and Taychreggan*

Scotland's Hotels of Distinction

Surrounded by stunning Highland scenery this stylish and superbly presented hotel enjoys an idyllic setting, in 40 acres of grounds, on the shores of Loch Awe. Ground floor areas include a smart bar with adjacent Orangery and a choice of quiet lounges with deep, luxurious sofas. A fine reputation has been well earned by the kitchen for the skilfully prepared dinners that showcase the local and seasonal Scottish larder.
ROOMS: 20 en suite ⊗ in 9 bedrooms s £98; d £180-£330 (incl. bkfst & dinner) **LB** **FACILITIES:** no TV in bdrms Fishing Snooker LD Jacuzzi **CONF:** Class 15 Board 20 **PARKING:** 40 **NOTES:** No children 14yrs ⊗ in restaurant Civ Wed 70

★★★73% ◎◎ The Ardanaiseig
by Loch Awe PA35 1HE
☎ 01866 833333 📠 01866 833222
e-mail: ardanaiseig@clara.net
Dir: *turn S off A85 at Taynuilt onto B845 to Kilchrenan. Left in front of pub (road very narrow) signed 'Ardanaiseig Hotel & No Through Road'*

Set amid lovely gardens and breathtaking scenery beside the shore of Loch Awe, this peaceful country-house hotel was built in a Scottish baronial style in 1834. Many fine pieces of furniture are evident in the bedrooms and charming day rooms, which include a drawing room, a library bar, and an elegant dining room. Dinner provides the highlight of any visit with skilfully cooked dishes making excellent use of local, seasonal produce.
ROOMS: 16 en suite (4 fmly) s fr £75; d £90-£290 (incl. bkfst) **LB** **FACILITIES:** STV 🎾 Fishing Snooker LD Boating, Clay pigeon shooting, Bikes for hire Xmas **PARKING:** 20 **NOTES:** ⊗ in restaurant Closed 2 Jan-14 Feb Civ Wed 50

See advert on this page

KILLEARN, Stirling
Map 20 NS58

★★★66% Black Bull
2 The Square G63 9NG
☎ 01360 550215 01360 550143
e-mail: sales@blackbullhotel.com
web: www.blackbullhotel.com
Dir: *N from Glasgow on A81, through Blanefield just past Glengoyne Distillery, take A875 to Killearn*

This long established village inn is an ideal destination for businessmen visiting Glasgow as well as tourists wishing to enjoy the scenic splendour of the nearby Trossachs. The public areas boast a large public bar, a popular Bistro and also an elegant and spacious conservatory restaurant overlooking the attractive gardens. Accommodation is comfortable and well equipped.
ROOMS: 12 en suite (2 fmly) in all bedrooms s £65-£70; d £90-£95 (incl. bkfst) **LB** **FACILITIES:** STV ch fac Xmas **CONF:** Thtr 80 Class 32 Board 24 Del from £95 **PARKING:** 100 **NOTES:** in restaurant Civ Wed 150

KILLIECRANKIE, Perth & Kinross
Map 23 NN96

★★77% Killiecrankie House
PH16 5LG
☎ 01796 473220 01796 472451
e-mail: enquiries@killiecrankiehotel.co.uk
web: www.killiecrankiehotel.co.uk
Dir: *off A9 at Killiecrankie, hotel 3m along B8079 on right*

A long-established hotel set in mature grounds, where red squirrels are found, situated near the historic Pass of Killiecrankie. The owners Tim and Maillie Waters and their charming staff provide friendly and attentive service. Accomplished cooking can be enjoyed in the atmospheric restaurant, plus a healthy and tasty selection of dishes is offered in the bar.
ROOMS: 10 en suite (2 fmly) (2 GF) in all bedrooms s £79-£99; d £158-£198 (incl. bkfst & dinner) **LB** **FACILITIES:** Putt green Xmas **PARKING:** 20 **NOTES:** in restaurant Closed 3 Jan-Etr RS Nov & Dec Civ Wed 20

KILMARNOCK, East Ayrshire
Map 20 NS43

★★★66% Fenwick
Ayr Rd, Fenwick KA3 6AU
☎ 01560 600478 01560 600334
e-mail: fenwick@bestwestern.co.uk
web: www.fenwickhotel.com
Dir: *approx 4m N of Kilmarnock, adjacent to A77 & B751*

Best Western

Conveniently situated between Glasgow and the Ayrshire coast, this hotel is popular for its food with creative, good value menus forming the basis for its own dining club. Bedrooms are suited to the business traveller. Comfortable public rooms include a cosy fireside lounge, a brasserie-style restaurant and informal bar offering an impressive pub menu.
ROOMS: 31 en suite (2 fmly) (10 GF) in 10 bedrooms s £55-£80; d £65-£105 (incl. bkfst) **LB** **FACILITIES:** STV Putt green Clay pigeon Quad bike Xmas **CONF:** BC Thtr 160 Class 60 Board 50 Del from £62 **PARKING:** 80 **NOTES:** in restaurant Civ Wed 140

Premier Travel Inn Kilmarnock
Annadale KA1 2RS
☎ 08701 977148 01563 570536
web: www.premiertravelinn.com
Dir: *from M74 junct 8 signed Kilmarnock (A71). From M77 join A71 to Irvine. At next rdbt turn right onto B7064 signed Crosshouse Hospital. Inn on right*

premier travel inn

High quality, modern budget accommodation ideal for both families and business travellers. Spacious, en suite bedrooms feature bath and shower, satellite TV and many have telephones and modem points. The adjacent family restaurant features a wide and varied menu. For further details consult the Hotel Groups page.
ROOMS: 40 en suite s £46.95-£48.95; d £46.95-£48.95

Travelodge
Kilmarnock By Pass KA1 5LQ
☎ 08700 850 950 01563 573810
web: www.travelodge.co.uk
Dir: *at Bellfield junct just off A77*

Travelodge

Travelodge offers good quality, good value, modern accommodation. Ideal for families, the spacious, en suite bedrooms include remote-control TV, tea and coffee-making facilities and comfortable beds. Meals can be taken at the nearby family restaurant. For further details consult the Hotel Groups page.
ROOMS: 40 en suite s fr £26; d fr £26

KILWINNING, North Ayrshire
Map 20 NS34

★★★69% *Montgreenan Mansion House*
Montgreenan Estate KA13 7QZ
☎ 01294 557733 01294 850397
e-mail: enquiries@montgreenanhotel.com
web: www.montgreenanhotel.com
Dir: *hotel signs 4m N of Irvine on A736 & from Kilwinning on A737*

In a peaceful setting of 48 acres of parkland and woods, this 19th-century mansion retains many of its original features. Public areas include a splendid drawing room, a library, a club-style bar and a restaurant. Accommodation ranges from compact modern rooms to the well-proportioned classical rooms of the original house.
ROOMS: 21 en suite (1 fmly) in 16 bedrooms **FACILITIES:** STV 5 Snooker Putt green Jacuzzi in honeymoon suite, woodland walks ch fac **CONF:** Thtr 100 Class 60 Board 40 **PARKING:** 50 **NOTES:** in restaurant Civ Wed 140

♫ Entertainment

KINCARDINE, Fife | Map 21 NS98

⌂ **Premier Travel Inn Falkirk North**
Bowtrees Farm FK2 8PJ
☎ 08701 977099 📠 01324 831934
web: www.premiertravelinn.com
Dir: From north M9 junct 7 towards Kincardine Bridge, from south M876 for Kincardine Bridge. On rdbt at end of slip road
High quality, modern budget accommodation ideal for both families and business travellers. Spacious, en suite bedrooms feature bath and shower, satellite TV and many have telephones and modem points. The adjacent family restaurant features a wide and varied menu. For further details consult the Hotel Groups page.
ROOMS: 40 en suite s £46.95-£48.95; d £46.95-£48.95

KINCLAVEN, Perth & Kinross | Map 21 NO13

Top Hotel

★★★ ◎◎ ♨ **Ballathie House**
PH1 4QN
☎ 01250 883268 📠 01250 883396
e-mail: email@ballathiehousehotel.com
web: www.ballathiehousehotel.com
Dir: from A9 2m N of Perth, B9099 through Stanley & signed, or off A93 at Beech Hedge follow signs for Ballathie 2.5m
Set in delightful grounds, this splendid Scottish mansion house combines classical grandeur with modern comfort. Bedrooms range from well-proportioned master rooms to modern standard rooms and many boast antique furniture and art deco bathrooms. For the ultimate in quality, request one of the Riverside Rooms, a purpose-built development right on the banks of the river, complete with balconies and terraces. The elegant restaurant has views over the River Tay.
ROOMS: 26 en suite 16 annexe en suite (2 fmly) (10 GF) s £99-£110; d £159-£179 (incl. bkfst) **LB FACILITIES:** STV Fishing ♨ Putt green Xmas **CONF:** BC Thtr 50 Class 20 Board 30 Del from £150 **SERVICES:** Lift **PARKING:** 50 **NOTES:** ⊗ in restaurant Civ Wed 90

KINGUSSIE, Highland | Map 23 NH70

★★71% **The Scot House**
Newtonmore Rd PH21 1HE
☎ 01540 661351 📠 01540 661111
e-mail: enquiries@scothouse.com
web: www.scothouse.com
Dir: A9, take Kingussie exit, hotel approx 0.50m at S end of village Main St
This long established hotel offers comfortable accommodation in thoughtfully equipped, generally spacious rooms. The young enthusiastic team provides warm hospitality. A popular bar and

continued

restaurant are the setting for a wide range of carefully prepared meals and an excellent range of malt whiskies.
ROOMS: 9 en suite (1 fmly) ⊗ in all bedrooms s £46-£50; d £64-£98 (incl. bkfst) **LB FACILITIES:** All or the above is available within a 10m radius Xmas **PARKING:** 50 **NOTES:** ⊗ in restaurant

Top Restaurant with Rooms

🏠 ◎◎◎ **The Cross**
Tweed Mill Brae, Ardbroilach Rd PH21 1LB
☎ 01540 661166 📠 01540 661080
e-mail: relax@thecross.co.uk web: www.thecross.co.uk
Dir: from lights in Kingussie centre, along Ardbroilach Rd for 300mtrs, left into Tweed Mill Brae
This converted tweed mill in a wooded riverside setting offers comfortable bedrooms in a mix of traditional and quality pine styles. Lounges are also inviting, but it is the light and airy restaurant that is the focal point here. Refreshingly unpretentious and deceptively simple in concept, dinner showcases fine local ingredients sympathetically cooked to draw out the natural flavours. Service is attentive, backed up by a genuine feeling that guests are very welcome indeed. AA Wine Award winner for Scotland 2005-6.
ROOMS: 8 en suite (1 fmly) ⊗ in all bedrooms s £100-£210; d £150-£250 (incl. bkfst & dinner) **LB FACILITIES:** Pétanque **CONF:** Thtr 20 Class 20 Board 20 Del from £120 **PARKING:** 12 **NOTES:** ✖ ⊗ in restaurant Closed Xmas and Jan ex New Year RS Sun & Mon

KINLOCH RANNOCH, Perth & Kinross | Map 23 NN65

★★★68% ◎ **Dunalastair**
PH16 5PW
☎ 01882 632323 632218 📠 01882 632371
e-mail: robert@dunalastair.co.uk web: www.dunalastair.co.uk
Dir: A9 to Pitlochry, at northern end take B8019 to Tummel Bridge then A846 to Kinloch Rannoch

A traditional Highland hotel that is being steadily transformed.

continued on p724

KINLOCH RANNOCH, continued

Inviting public rooms are full of character - log fires, stags heads, wood panelling and an extensive selection of malt whiskies. Standard and superior bedrooms are on offer. However, it is the friendly attentive service by delightful staff, as well as first class dinners that will leave lasting impressions.
ROOMS: 28 en suite (4 fmly) (9 GF) ⊗ in 15 bedrooms s £40-£70; d £70-£150 (incl. bkfst) **LB** **FACILITIES:** STV Fishing Riding Fishing nights, 4x4 & adventure safaris, Rafting, Clay Pigeon shooting Xmas **CONF:** BC Thtr 60 Class 40 Board 40 Del from £80 **PARKING:** 33 **NOTES:** No children 8yrs ⊗ in restaurant Civ Wed 70

★★★68%
Macdonald Loch Rannoch Hotel
PH16 5PS
☎ 01882 632201 📠 01882 632203
web: www.macdonald-hotels.co.uk
Dir: *off A9 onto B847 Calvine. Follow signs to Kinloch Rannoch, hotel 1m*
Looking out across Loch Rannoch, this hotel is geared to the leisure market and provides a range of indoor and outdoor pursuits. The smart and spacious bedrooms in the new wing are worth asking for.
ROOMS: 52 en suite (25 fmly) ⊗ in all bedrooms s £65-£95; d £100-£190 (incl. bkfst & dinner) **LB** **FACILITIES:** Fishing Squash Snooker Sauna Solarium Gym Quad biking Archery Clay pigeon shooting Off road driving Bike hire Xmas **CONF:** Thtr 160 Class 80 Board 50 Del from £125 **SERVICES:** Lift **PARKING:** 52 **NOTES:** ⊗ in restaurant Civ Wed 160

KINROSS, Perth & Kinross Map 21 NO10

★★★75% **Green**
2 The Muirs KY13 8AS
☎ 01577 863467 📠 01577 863180
e-mail: reservations@green-hotel.com
web: www.green-hotel.com
Dir: *M90 junct 6 follow Kinross signs, onto A922, hotel on this road*

A long established hotel offering a wide range of indoor and outdoor activities. Public areas include a classical restaurant, a choice of bars and a well-stocked gift shop. The comfortable, well-equipped bedrooms, most of generous proportion, boast attractive colour schemes and smart modern furnishings.
ROOMS: 46 en suite (4 fmly) (14 GF) ⊗ in 12 bedrooms s £90-£110; d £160-£190 (incl. bkfst) **LB** **FACILITIES:** STV supervised 36 Fishing Squash Sauna Solarium Gym Putt green Curling in season, Petanque (French boules) Xmas **CONF:** BC Thtr 130 Class 75 Board 60 Del from £145 **PARKING:** 60 **NOTES:** ⊗ in restaurant Closed 23-28 Dec excluding Xmas day RS 25-Dec

★★★69% ***Windlestrae Hotel and Leisure Club***
The Muirs KY13 8AS
☎ 0870 609 6153 📠 01577 864733
e-mail: windlestrae@corushotels.com
web: www.corushotels.com/windlestrae
Dir: *M90 at junct 6, into Kinross, left at 2nd mini rdbt. Hotel 400yds*
This hotel is set in landscaped gardens back from the main road, yet conveniently placed for access to the town centre and many local attractions. There are impressive leisure and conference facilities and accommodation is provided in well-proportioned bedrooms. Comfortable public areas include a lounge, bar and roomy restaurant.
ROOMS: 45 en suite (5 fmly) (14 GF) ⊗ in 15 bedrooms **FACILITIES:** STV Snooker Sauna Solarium Gym Jacuzzi Beautician, Steam room, Toning tables **CONF:** Thtr 250 Class 100 Board 80 **SERVICES:** air con **PARKING:** 80 **NOTES:** ⊗ in restaurant Civ Wed 100

Travelodge
Kincardine Rd KY13 7NQ
☎ 08700 850 950 📠 01577 861641
web: www.travelodge.co.uk
Dir: *on A977, M90 junct 6, Turthills Tourist Centre*
Travelodge offers good quality, good value, modern accommodation. Ideal for families, the spacious, en suite bedrooms include remote-control TV, tea and coffee-making facilities and comfortable beds. Meals can be taken at the nearby family restaurant. For further details consult the Hotel Groups page.
ROOMS: 35 en suite s fr £26; d fr £26

KIRKBEAN, Dumfries & Galloway Map 21 NX95

★★80% **Cavens**
DG2 8AA
☎ 01387 880234 📠 01387 880467
e-mail: enquiries@cavens.com
web: www.cavens.com
Dir: *on entering Kirkbean on A710, hotel signed*
Set in parkland gardens, Cavens encapsulates all the virtues of an intimate country-house hotel. Quality is the keynote, and Angus and Jane Fordyce have spared no effort in completing a fine renovation of the house. Bedrooms are delightfully individual and very comfortably equipped, and a choice of lounges invites peaceful relaxation. A set dinner offers the best of local and home-made produce.
ROOMS: 6 en suite ⊗ in all bedrooms s £70-£100; d £80-£150 (incl. bkfst) **LB** **FACILITIES:** Shooting, Fishing, Horse Riding Xmas **CONF:** Thtr 20 Class 20 Board 20 **PARKING:** 12 **NOTES:** ⊗ in restaurant Civ Wed 100

KIRKCALDY, Fife Map 21 NT29

★★★68% **Dunnikier House Hotel**
Dunnikier Park KY1 3LP
☎ 01592 268393 📠 01592 642340
e-mail: recp@dunnikier-house-hotel.co.uk
web: www.dunnikier-house-hotel.co.uk
Dir: *off A92 at Kirkcaldy West, then 3rd exit on rdbt signed 'Hospital/Crematorium'. 1st left past school*
This imposing 18th-century manor house is set in parkland adjacent to Dunnikier Golf Course. Public areas contain many original features. Views over the park can be enjoyed from the lounge, and the bar offers a wide selection of whiskies as well as a comprehensive food menu. The Oswald restaurant provides fine meals featuring fresh, carefully prepared local produce.
ROOMS: 15 en suite (1 fmly) s £60-£67.50; d £80-£90 (incl. bkfst) **CONF:** Thtr 60 Class 20 Board 30 **PARKING:** 100 **NOTES:** ⊗ in restaurant

★★★67% Dean Park
Chapel Level KY2 6QW
☎ 01592 261635 🖹 01592 261371
e-mail: reception@deanparkhotel.co.uk
Dir: *signed from A92, Kirkcaldy West junct*
Popular with both business and leisure guests, this hotel has extensive conference and meeting facilities and ample car parking. Executive bedrooms are spacious and comfortable, and all are well equipped with modern decor and amenities. Twelve direct-access, chalet-style rooms are also available and equipped to the same specification as main bedrooms. Public areas include a choice of bars and a restaurant.
ROOMS: 34 en suite 12 annexe en suite (2 fmly) (5 GF) ⊗ in 10 bedrooms **FACILITIES:** STV ch fac **CONF:** Thtr 250 Class 125 Board 54 **SERVICES:** Lift **PARKING:** 250 **NOTES:** ✗ Civ Wed 250

KIRKCUDBRIGHT, Dumfries & Galloway — Map 20 NX65

★★67% Arden House Hotel
Tongland Rd DG6 4UU
☎ 01557 330544 🖹 01557 330742
Dir: *off A57 Euro route (Stranraer), 4m W of Castle Douglas onto A711. Signed for Kirkcudbright, crossing Telford Bridge. Hotel 400m on left*
Set well back from the main road in extensive grounds on the north-east side of town, this spotlessly maintained hotel offers attractive bedrooms, a lounge bar and adjoining conservatory serving a range of popular dishes, which are also available in the dining room. It boasts an impressive function suite in its grounds.
ROOMS: 9 rms (8 en suite) (7 fmly) s £45; d £65 (incl. bkfst) **CONF:** Thtr 175 Class 175 **PARKING:** 70 **NOTES:** No credit cards accepted

KIRRIEMUIR, Angus — Map 23 NO35

A Airlie Arms
4 St Malcolms Wynd DD8 4HB
☎ 01575 572847 🖹 01575 573055
e-mail: info@airliearms-hotel.co.uk
web: www.airliearms-hotel.co.uk
ROOMS: 10 en suite (2 fmly) (5 GF) ⊗ in 2 bedrooms s £35-£45; d £60-£80 (incl. bkfst) **LB** **FACILITIES:** STV Xmas **CONF:** Thtr 80 Class 70 Board 50 **PARKING:** 5 **NOTES:** ★★ ⊗ in restaurant

KYLE OF LOCHALSH, Highland — Map 22 NG72

★★★62% Lochalsh
Ferry Rd IV40 8AF
☎ 01599 534202 🖹 01599 534881
e-mail: mdmacrae@lochalsh-hotel.demon.co.uk
Dir: *turn off A82 onto A87*
Benefiting from lovely views over to the Isle of Skye, this hotel is set in the heart of the town close to the old ferry slip. Many of the bedrooms overlook the harbour and the contrasting aspect of the modern Skye Bridge. Meals can be enjoyed in either the relaxed atmosphere of the lounge and bar or the spacious restaurant.
ROOMS: 38 en suite (8 fmly) s £30-£75; d £80-£150 (incl. bkfst) **LB** **FACILITIES:** STV Xmas **CONF:** Thtr 20 Class 20 Board 20 **SERVICES:** Lift **PARKING:** 50 **NOTES:** ⊗ in restaurant

See advert on this page

> The vast majority of establishments in this guide accept credit and debit cards. We indicate those that don't take any

LADYBANK, Fife — Map 21 NO30

★★★61% Fernie Castle
Letham KY15 7RU
☎ 01337 810381 🖹 01337 810422
e-mail: mail@ferniecastle.demon.co.uk
Dir: *M90 junct 8 take A91 E (Tay Bridge/St Andrews) to Melville Lodges rdbt. Left onto A92 signed Tay Bridge. Hotel 1.2m on right*

An historic, turretted castle set in 17 acres of wooded grounds in the heart of Fife, which proves an extremely popular venue for weddings. Bedrooms range from King and Queen rooms, to the more standard-sized Squire and Lady rooms. The elegant Auld Alliance Restaurant presents a formal setting for dining, but guests can also eat in the bar with its impressive vaulted stone walls and ceiling.
ROOMS: 20 en suite (2 fmly) ⊗ in 15 bedrooms **FACILITIES:** ♫ Xmas **CONF:** Thtr 180 Class 120 Board 25 Del from £140 **PARKING:** 80 **NOTES:** ⊗ in restaurant Civ Wed 200

LAIRG, Highland Map 23 NC50

★★68% Overscaig House Hotel
Loch Shin IV27 4NY
☎ 01549 431203
e-mail: enquiries@overscaig.com
Dir: *N from Lairg on A836 for 3m. Turn left onto A838 towards Durness, 14m to hotel.*
Popular with fishermen and birdwatchers, this Highland hotel enjoys a lochside location amid unspoilt scenery. The dining room overlooks Loch Shin, and a bar and lounge are also available for guests. Bedrooms are modern in style and comfortably appointed. Fishing excursions can be arranged.
ROOMS: 9 en suite (2 fmly) ⊗ in all bedrooms s £49-£59; d £98-£118 (incl. bkfst & dinner) **LB** **FACILITIES:** Fishing Fishing boats Pool table **PARKING:** 10 **NOTES:** ⊗ in restaurant

LANARK, South Lanarkshire Map 21 NS84
See also Biggar

★★★66% *Cartland Bridge*
Glasgow Rd ML11 9UF
☎ 01555 664426 🖷 01555 663773
e-mail: sales@cartlandbridge.co.uk
Dir: *follow A73 through Lanark towards Carluke. Hotel 1.25m on right*
Nestling in wooded grounds on the edge of the town, this Grade I listed mansion continues to be popular with both business and leisure guests. Public areas feature wood panelling and a gallery staircase. In addition to the restaurant, food is available in the bar. Well-equipped bedrooms vary in size and style.
ROOMS: 20 rms (18 en suite) (2 fmly) ⊗ in 9 bedrooms **FACILITIES:** STV **CONF:** Thtr 250 Class 180 Board 30 **PARKING:** 120 **NOTES:** ⊗ in restaurant Civ Wed 200

LANGBANK, Renfrewshire Map 20 NS37

U Gleddoch House
PA14 6YE
☎ 01475 540711 🖷 01475 540201
e-mail: info@gleddochhouse.com
Dir: *signed from B789 at Langbank rdbt*
At the time of going to press, the star classification for this hotel was not confirmed. Please refer to the AA internet site www.theAA.com for current information.
ROOMS: 62 en suite (8 fmly) (46 GF) ⊗ in 6 bedrooms s £55-£75; d £90-£120 (incl. bkfst) **LB** **FACILITIES:** STV supervised 18 Fishing Sauna Gym Putt green Clay pigeon shooting, Offroad driving Xmas **CONF:** Thtr 150 Class 60 Board 52 **PARKING:** 200 **NOTES:** Civ Wed 100

LARGS, North Ayrshire Map 20 NS25

★★69% *Willowbank*
96 Greenock Rd KA30 8PG
☎ 01475 672311 & 675435 🖷 01475 689027
e-mail: iaincsmith@btconnect.com
Dir: *on A78*
A relaxed, friendly atmosphere prevails at this well maintained hotel where hanging baskets are feature in summer months. The nicely decorated bedrooms are, in general, spacious and offer comfortable modern appointments. The public areas include a large, well-stocked bar, a lounge and a dining room.
ROOMS: 30 en suite (4 fmly) **FACILITIES:** ♫ **CONF:** Thtr 200 Class 100 Board 40 **PARKING:** 40 **NOTES:** ⊗ in restaurant

⊗ No smoking

LAUDER, Scottish Borders Map 21 NT54

★★68% Lauderdale
1 Edinburgh Rd TD2 6TW
☎ 01578 722231 🖷 01578 718642
e-mail: enquiries@lauderdalehotel.co.uk
web: www.lauderdalehotel.co.uk
Dir: *on A68 from S, through Lauder centre, hotel on right. From Edinburgh, hotel on left at 1st bend after passing Lauder sign*
Lying on the north side of the village with spacious gardens to the side and rear, this friendly hotel is ideally placed for those wishing to stay outside of Edinburgh itself. A good range of meals is served in both the bar and the restaurant. The well-equipped bedrooms come in a variety of sizes.
ROOMS: 10 en suite (1 fmly) ⊗ in all bedrooms s £42; d £70-£80 (incl. bkfst) **FACILITIES:** STV Xmas **PARKING:** 200 **NOTES:** ⊗ in restaurant

LERWICK See Shetland

LETTERFINLAY, Highland Map 22 NN29

★★67% Letterfinlay Lodge
PH34 4DZ
☎ 01397 712622
e-mail: info@letterfinlaylodgehotel.com
web: www.letterfinlaylodgehotel.com
Dir: *7m N of Spean Bridge, on A82 beside Loch Lochy*
Boasting one of the most enviable locations in the Highlands, this long established hotel enjoys stunning views overlooking Loch Lochy. Bedrooms provide a mix of styles with loch view rooms proving popular with guests. Wide-ranging menus are available in the bar and restaurant and hearty breakfasts set guests up for the day.
ROOMS: 13 rms (11 en suite) (5 fmly) s £30-£45; d fr £60 (incl. bkfst) **LB** **FACILITIES:** Fishing **PARKING:** 100 **NOTES:** ⊗ in restaurant Closed Nov-Feb

LIVINGSTON, West Lothian Map 21 NT06

U Ramada Livingston
Almondview EH54 6QB
☎ 01506 431222 🖷 01506 434666
e-mail: sales.livingston@ramadajarvis.co.uk
web: www.ramadajarvis.co.uk
Dir: *From M8 junct 3 take A899 towards Livingston, leave at Centre Interchange, follow road and turn left at next rdbt, hotel is on left.*
This large, modern hotel is conveniently located in the town centre with easy access to the M8. Bedrooms are comfortably appointed for both business and leisure guests.
ROOMS: 120 en suite (13 fmly) (54 GF) ⊗ in 80 bedrooms s £85-£120; d £85-£120 **FACILITIES:** STV Sauna Xmas **CONF:** Thtr 100 Class 55 Board 50 Del from £145 **PARKING:** 130 **NOTES:** ⊗ in restaurant Civ Wed 80

⇧ Premier Travel Inn Livingston (Nr Edinburgh)
Deer Park Av, Knightsridge EH54 8AD
☎ 08701 977161 🖷 01506 438912
web: www.premiertravelinn.com
Dir: *on M8 junct 3. Follow road to rdbt and Inn is opposite rdbt*
High quality, modern budget accommodation ideal for both families and business travellers. Spacious, en suite bedrooms feature bath and shower, satellite TV and many have telephones and modem points. The adjacent family restaurant features a wide and varied menu. For further details consult the Hotel Groups page.
ROOMS: 83 en suite s £46.95-£48.95; d £46.95-£48.95

⌂ Travelodge (Livingston)
Almondvale Cresent EH54 7EY
☎ 08700 850 950 🖷 0121 521 6026
web: www.travelodge.co.uk
Dir: *Exit M8 junct 3 onto A899 towards Livingston. At 2nd rdbt turn right onto A779. At 2nd rdbt turn left. Lodge on left.*
Travelodge offers good quality, good value, modern accommodation. Ideal for families, the spacious, en suite bedrooms include remote-control TV, tea and coffee-making facilities and comfortable beds. Meals can be taken at the nearby family restaurant. For further details consult the Hotel Groups page.
ROOMS: 60 en suite s fr £26; d fr £26

LOCHGILPHEAD, Argyll & Bute — Map 20 NR88

★★★73% ® Cairnbaan
Crinan Canal, Cairnbaan PA31 8SJ
☎ 01546 603668 🖷 01546 606045
e-mail: info@cairnbaan.com
web: www.cairnbaan.com
Dir: *2m N, A816 from Lochgilphead, hotel off B841*
Located on the Crinan Canal, this small hotel offers relaxed hospitality in a delightful setting. Bedrooms are thoughtfully equipped, generally spacious and benefit from stylish decor. Fresh seafood is a real feature in both the formal restaurant and the comfortable bar area. Alfresco dining is popular in the warmer months.
ROOMS: 12 en suite ⊗ in all bedrooms s £72-£79; d £92.50-£145 (incl. bkfst) **LB** **FACILITIES:** Xmas **CONF:** Thtr 160 Class 100 Board 80 Del £95 **PARKING:** 53 **NOTES:** ⊗ in restaurant Civ Wed 120

★★66% Stag
47 Argyll St PA31 8NE
☎ 01546 602496 🖷 01546 603549
e-mail: reservations@staghotel.com
Dir: *on entering Lochgilphead take main mini rdbt into Argyll St for hotel at junct of Lorne St & Argyll St*
This friendly, family-run hotel benefits from a central location in this popular tourist destination. The restaurant offers a range of popular dishes at reasonable prices. The thoughtfully equipped bedrooms offer good value accommodation.
ROOMS: 18 en suite s £39-£45; d £50-£60 **FACILITIES:** **Spa** ♫ **CONF:** Thtr 40 Class 50 Board 40 **NOTES:** ✱

Destination dining!
This symbol indicates a Restaurant with Rooms

LOCHINVER, Highland — Map 22 NC02

Top Hotel

★★★ ® Inver Lodge
IV27 4LU
☎ 01571 844496 🖷 01571 844395
e-mail: stay@inverlodge.com
web: www.inverlodge.com
Dir: *A835 to Lochinver, through village, left after village hall, follow private road for 0.5m*
Genuine hospitality is a real feature at this delightful, modern hotel. Set high on the hillside above the village all bedrooms and public rooms enjoy stunning views. Public areas include a choice of lounges, a well stocked bar and a restaurant where skilled chefs make use of the abundant local produce. Accommodation is spacious, stylish and of high quality.

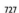

ROOMS: 20 en suite s £80; d £150 (incl. bkfst) **LB** **FACILITIES:** STV Fishing Snooker Sauna Solarium **CONF:** Thtr 30 Board 20 **PARKING:** 30 **NOTES:** ⊗ in restaurant Closed Dec-Etr

Restaurant with Rooms

®® Albannach
Baddidarrach IV27 4LP
☎ 01571 844407 🖷 01571 844285
e-mail: the.albannach@virgin.net
web: www.thealbannach.co.uk
Dir: *from Ullapool turn right over old stone bridge at foot of hill, signed Baddidarrach & Highland Stoneware Pottery. After 0.5m cross cattle grid & turn left*
Enjoying a fine reputation for its cooking and stylish accommodation, The Albannach has established itself as one of a 'must visit' destination of any gastronomic tour of Scotland. The set menu at dinner is a theatrical indulgence of fresh produce, and outstanding breakfasts showcase the local, seasonal larder. The five bedrooms are furnished with flair and enjoy stunning loch and mountain views. Guests are greeted like old friends by the professional and caring staff.
ROOMS: 4 en suite 1 annexe en suite (1 GF) ⊗ in all bedrooms s £105-£150; d £210-£250 (incl. bkfst & dinner) **FACILITIES:** STV **PARKING:** 8 **NOTES:** ✱ No children 12yrs ⊗ in restaurant Closed mid Nov-mid Mar RS mid Mar-mid Nov, excl Mon

LOCH LOMOND See Balloch Drymen & Luss

LOCKERBIE, Dumfries & Galloway — Map 21 NY18

★★★74% ® Dryfesdale
Dryfebridge DG11 2SF
☎ 01576 202427 🖷 01576 204187
e-mail: reception@dryfesdalehotel.co.uk
web: www.dryfesdalehotel.co.uk
Dir: *from M74 junct 17 take 'Lockerbie North', 3rd left at 1st rdbt, 1st exit left at 2nd rdbt, hotel is 200yds on left*
Conveniently situated for the M74, yet discreetly screened from it, this friendly hotel provides attentive service. Bedrooms, some with access to patio areas, vary in size and style, offer good levels of comfort and are well equipped. Creative, good value dinners make use of local produce and are served in the airy restaurant overlooking the manicured gardens and rolling countryside.
ROOMS: 16 en suite (4 fmly) (6 GF) ⊗ in 8 bedrooms s £50-£65; d £95-£125 (incl. bkfst) **LB** **FACILITIES:** STV Putt green Clay pigeon shooting, Fishing ♫ Xmas **CONF:** Thtr 150 Class 100 Board 100 Del from £115 **PARKING:** 60 **NOTES:** ⊗ in restaurant Civ Wed 150

LOCKERBIE, continued

★★74% *Somerton House*
35 Carlisle Rd DG11 2DR
☎ 01576 202583 & 202384 📠 01576 204218
e-mail: somerton@somertonhotel.co.uk
Dir: *off A74*
This long established Victorian mansion has been sympathetically upgraded in recent years so that original features blend seamlessly with the latest styles in eye-catching interior design. Bedrooms are well equipped and comfortable whilst day rooms include several venues for dining, the best of which is a new conservatory restaurant. Friendly proprietors and a team of long standing staff ensure the warmest of welcomes plus attentive service.
ROOMS: 7 en suite 4 annexe en suite (1 fmly) ⊗ in 7 bedrooms **CONF:** Thtr 60 Class 25 Board 25 **PARKING:** 100 **NOTES:** ⊗ in restaurant

★★70% Kings Arms Hotel
High St DG11 2JL
☎ 01576 202410 📠 01576 202410
e-mail: reception@kingsarmshotel.co.uk
web: www.kingsarmshotel.co.uk
Dir: *A74(M), 0.5m into town centre, hotel is opposite Town Hall*
Dating from the 17th century this former inn lies right in the town centre. Now a family-run hotel, it provides attractive well-equipped bedrooms. During lunch and dinner a menu ranging from snacks to full meals is served in the two cosy bars; one is non-smoking.
ROOMS: 13 en suite (2 fmly) ⊗ in 1 bedroom s fr £40; d fr £70 (incl. bkfst) **FACILITIES:** Xmas **CONF:** Thtr 80 Class 40 Board 30 Del from £45 **PARKING:** 8 **NOTES:** ⊗ in restaurant

L

★★66% Ravenshill House
12 Dumfries Rd DG11 2EF
☎ 01576 202882 📠 01576 202882
e-mail: aaenquiries@ravenshillhotellockerbie.co.uk
web: www.ravenshillhotellockerbie.co.uk
Dir: *from A74(M) Lockerbie junct onto A709. Hotel 0.5m on right*
Set in spacious gardens on the fringe of the town, this friendly, family-run hotel offers cheerful service and good value, home-cooked meals. Bedrooms are generally spacious and comfortably equipped, including an ideal two-room family unit.
ROOMS: 8 rms (7 en suite) (2 fmly) ⊗ in all bedrooms s £40-£60; d £65-£75 (incl. bkfst) **LB** **CONF:** Thtr 30 Class 20 Board 12 **PARKING:** 35 **NOTES:** ⊗ in restaurant

GF indicates the number of bedrooms at ground level

LUNDIN LINKS, Fife — Map 21 NO40

★★★78% ◎◎ Old Manor
Leven Rd KY8 6AJ
☎ 01333 320368 📠 01333 320911
e-mail: enquiries@oldmanorhotel.co.uk
web: www.oldmanorhotel.co.uk
Dir: *1m E of Leven on A915 Kirkcaldy-St Andrews road for hotel on right*
This long-established hotel lies on the edge of the village and overlooks the golf course to the Firth of Forth. Enthusiastically run, high standards are maintained throughout. Bedrooms come in a variety of styles and there is a choice of restaurants - the conservatory Terrace Brasserie and Grill with outstanding views or the more informal Coachman's Bistro within the well-tended grounds.

ROOMS: 24 en suite (2 fmly) (8 GF) ⊗ in 2 bedrooms s £97-£115; d £140-£205 (incl. bkfst) **LB** **FACILITIES:** Complimentary membership of Lundin Sports Club Xmas **CONF:** Thtr 140 Class 70 Board 50 Del from £95 **PARKING:** 100 **NOTES:** ⊗ in restaurant Civ Wed 100

LUSS, Argyll & Bute — Map 20 NS39

★★★72% ◎◎ The Lodge on Loch Lomond
G83 8PA
☎ 01436 860201 📠 01436 860203
e-mail: res@loch-lomond.co.uk
web: www.loch-lomond.co.uk
Dir: *off A82, follow sign for hotel*

This hotel is idyllically set on the shores of Loch Lomond. Public areas consist of an open-plan, split-level bar and fine dining restaurant overlooking the loch. The pine-finished bedrooms also enjoy the views and are comfortable, spacious and well equipped. All have saunas and some have DVDs/internet access. There is a stunning state-of-the-art leisure suite.
ROOMS: 29 en suite 17 annexe en suite (20 fmly) (13 GF) ⊗ in all bedrooms **FACILITIES:** **Spa** STV Sauna Jacuzzi Resident only state-of-the-art health suite & spa., fishing, boating Xmas **CONF:** Thtr 150 Class 80 Board 60 **PARKING:** 120 **NOTES:** ⊗ in restaurant Civ Wed 100

MALLAIG, Highland — Map 22 NM69

★★67% West Highland
PH41 4QZ
☎ 01687 462210 📠 01687 462130
e-mail: westhighland.hotel@virgin.net
Dir: *from Fort William turn right at rdbt then 1st right up hill, from ferry left at rdbt then 1st right uphill*
Originally the town's station hotel the original building was destroyed by fire and the current hotel built on the same site in the early 20th century. Fine views over to Skye are a real feature

continued

of the public rooms, whilst bedrooms are thoughtfully equipped and generally spacious.
ROOMS: 34 en suite (6 fmly) ⊗ in 6 bedrooms s £40; d £70-£74 (incl. bkfst) **LB** **FACILITIES:** ♫ **CONF:** Thtr 100 Class 80 Board 100 **PARKING:** 40 **NOTES:** ⊗ in restaurant Closed 16 Oct-15 Mar RS 16 Mar-1 Apr

MARKINCH, Fife — Map 21 NO20

Top Hotel

★★★★ Balbirnie House
Balbirnie Park KY7 6NE
☎ 01592 610066 01592 610529
e-mail: reservations@balbirnie.co.uk
web: www.balbirnie.co.uk
Dir: *off A92 onto B9130, entrance 0.5m on left*

The perfect venue for a business trip, wedding or romantic break, this imposing Georgian mansion lies in formal gardens and grounds amidst scenic Balbirnie Park. Delightful public room include a choice of inviting lounges as well as the Orangery Restaurant. Accommodation features some splendid well-proportioned bedrooms with the best overlooking the gardens. But even the standard rooms include little touches such as sherry, shortbread and fudge.
ROOMS: 30 en suite (9 fmly) (7 GF) ⊗ in all bedrooms s £130-£160; d £190-£250 (incl. bkfst) **LB** **FACILITIES:** STV ⛳ 18 Putt green Woodland walks Jogging trails Xmas **CONF:** Thtr 220 Class 100 Board 60 Del from £162 **PARKING:** 120 **NOTES:** ⊗ in restaurant Civ Wed 150

MAYBOLE, South Ayrshire — Map 20 NS20

Top Hotel

★★ *Ladyburn*
KA19 7SG
☎ 01655 740585 01655 740580
e-mail: jh@ladyburn.co.uk
Dir: *A77 (Glasgow/Stranraer) at Maybole turn to B7023 to Crosshill and right at War Memorial. In 2m turn left for hotel approx 1m on right*

This charming country house is the home of the Hepburn family, who take great pride in the warmth of their welcome. Sitting in open countryside with attractive gardens, it's a great place to come to relax. Classically styled bedrooms, two with four-poster beds, offer every comfort and are complemented by the library and the drawing room. Dinner comprises a *continued* carefully cooked three course set menu, and is served in a gracious candlelit setting.

ROOMS: 5 en suite ⊗ in all bedrooms **FACILITIES:** Boules **PARKING:** 12 **NOTES:** No children 16yrs ⊗ in restaurant RS 2 wks Nov-Dec, 4 wks Jan/Mar Civ Wed 50

MELROSE, Scottish Borders — Map 21 NT53

★★★71% Burt's
Market Square TD6 9PL
☎ 01896 822285 01896 822870
e-mail: burtshotel@aol.com
web: www.burtshotel.co.uk
Dir: *A6091, 2m from A68 3m S of Earlston*

Enjoying a super location in the heart of this small market town, this hotel has been under the same family ownership for over 30 years and where the genuine warmth of hospitality is notable. Food is important at Burt's and the elegant restaurant is well complemented by the range of tasty meals in the bar.
ROOMS: 20 en suite ⊗ in all bedrooms **FACILITIES:** STV Shooting Salmon Fishing **CONF:** Thtr 38 Class 20 Board 20 **PARKING:** 40 **NOTES:** ⊗ in restaurant Closed 24-26 Dec

★★★67% The Townhouse Hotel
3 Market Square TD6 9PQ
☎ 01896 822645 01896 822870
e-mail: info@thetownhousemelrose.co.uk
web: www.thetownhousemelrose.co.uk
Dir: *from A68 into Melrose*

Set in the Market Square, this hotel as the name suggests, has the style of a town house. One can dine in either the smart brasserie or more traditional restaurant (same menu); the former has a bar counter but there is not a lounge bar as such. Bedrooms vary in

continued on p730

MELROSE, continued

size but all are well equipped and it's worth requesting one of two superior rooms.

The Townhouse Hotel, Melrose

ROOMS: 11 en suite (1 fmly) (1 GF) ⊗ in all bedrooms **CONF:** Thtr 60 Class 30 Board 40 Del from £70 **NOTES:** ⊗ in restaurant Closed 26-27 Dec

MILNGAVIE, East Dunbartonshire Map 20 NS57

⌂ Premier Travel Inn Glasgow (Milngavie)

103 Main St G62 6JQ
☎ 08701 977112 📠 0141 956 7839
web: www.premiertravelinn.com
Dir: *on A81 6m N of Glasgow city centre. From M8 junct 16 follow signs A879 to Milngavie*

High quality, modern budget accommodation ideal for both families and business travellers. Spacious, en suite bedrooms feature bath and shower, satellite TV and many have telephones and modem points. The adjacent family restaurant features a wide and varied menu. For further details consult the Hotel Groups page.
ROOMS: 60 en suite s £46.95-£48.95; d £46.95-£48.95 **CONF:** Class 16 Board 16

MOFFAT, Dumfries & Galloway Map 21 NT00

★★★69% Moffat House

High St DG10 9HL
☎ 01683 220039 📠 01683 221288
e-mail: moffat@talk21.com
web: www.moffathouse.co.uk
Dir: *M74 junct 15, Beattock, take A701. hotel in 1m at end of High St*

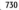

This fine Adam mansion, in its own neatly tended gardens, is set back from the main road in the centre of this popular country town. Inviting public areas include a quiet sun lounge to the rear, a comfortable lounge bar serving tasty meals and an attractive restaurant for the more formal occasion. Bedrooms present a mix of classical and modern styles.
ROOMS: 20 en suite (2 fmly) (5 GF) ⊗ in 14 bedrooms s £60-£75; d £103-£140 (incl. bkfst) **LB** **FACILITIES:** Xmas **CONF:** BC Thtr 100 Class 80 Board 60 **PARKING:** 30 **NOTES:** ⊗ in restaurant Civ Wed 110

★★68% The Star

44 High St DG10 9EF
☎ 01683 220156 📠 01683 221524
e-mail: tim@famousstarhotel.com
Dir: *M74 junct 15 signed Moffat, hotel in 2m. 1st hotel on right in High St*

This establishment claims to be the world's narrowest hotel, which makes a novel talking point. Smart, modern and well-equipped bedrooms plus a good range of food, served either in the bar or the restaurant, are just some of the virtues of this friendly hotel.
ROOMS: 8 en suite (1 fmly) s £40-£60; d £60-£75 (incl. bkfst) **LB** **FACILITIES:** STV Large screen in bar for sport **NOTES:** ✗ ⊗ in restaurant

MONTROSE, Angus Map 23 NO75

★★★74% ❀ Best Western Links Hotel

Mid Links DD10 8RL
☎ 01674 671000 📠 01674 672698
e-mail: reception@linkshotel.com
Dir: *A935 to Montrose then right at Lochside junct, left at swimming pool and right by tennis courts for hotel 200yds*

This former Edwardian town house has been stylishly refurbished and restored in recent years. Bedrooms offer a choice of attractive modern styles and are extremely well equipped to cater for business guests. Public areas include a bar, a restaurant, and a popular coffee shop where food is available all day. The hotel is also a popular venue for touring jazz and folk musicians.
ROOMS: 25 en suite (1 GF) ⊗ in 15 bedrooms s fr £59; d fr £72 (incl. bkfst) **LB** **FACILITIES:** ♫ Xmas **CONF:** Thtr 220 Class 70 Board 70 Del £126 **PARKING:** 45 **NOTES:** ⊗ in restaurant Civ Wed 120

MOTHERWELL, North Lanarkshire Map 21 NS75

⌂ Innkeeper's Lodge Glasgow/Strathclyde

Hamilton Rd ML1 3WB
☎ 01698 854715
web: www.innkeeperslodge.com

A growing concept in the travel accommodation market. Smart rooms meet essential business requirements but also have home comforts. Dining options include all-day menus plus the added advantage of breakfast, which is included in the room price. For further details consult the Hotel Groups page.
ROOMS: 28 rms s £45-£49.95; d £45-£49.95

⌂ Premier Travel Inn Glasgow (Bellshill)

Belziehill Farm, New Edinburgh Rd ML4 3HH
☎ 08701 977106 📠 01698 845969
web: www.premiertravelinn.com
Dir: *M74 junct 5 follow signs towards Coatbridge & Bellshill on A725. At 2nd exit off A725 Inn on left of rdbt*

High quality, modern budget accommodation ideal for both families and business travellers. Spacious, en suite bedrooms feature bath and shower, satellite TV and many have telephones and modem points. The adjacent family restaurant features a wide and varied menu. For further details consult the Hotel Groups page.
ROOMS: 40 en suite s £46.95-£49.95; d £46.95-£49.95

♫ Entertainment

⌂ Premier Travel Inn Glasgow (Motherwell)

Edinburgh Rd, Newhouse ML1 5SY
☎ 08701 977164 🖷 01698 861353
web: www.premiertravelinn.com

Dir: *From south M74 junct 5 onto A725 towards Coatbridge. Take A8 junct 6 towards Edinburgh, follow signs for Lanark. Inn 400yds on right*

High quality, modern budget accommodation ideal for both families and business travellers. Spacious, en suite bedrooms feature bath and shower, satellite TV and many have telephones and modem points. The adjacent family restaurant features a wide and varied menu. For further details consult the Hotel Groups page.

ROOMS: 40 en suite s £46.95-£49.95; d £46.95-£49.95 **CONF:** Thtr 40

MUIR OF ORD, Highland
Map 23 NH55

★★68% ◉⚑ Ord House
IV6 7UH
☎ 01463 870492 🖷 01463 870492
e-mail: admin@ord-house.co.uk

THE CIRCLE
Selected Individual Hotels
GREAT BRITAIN

Dir: *off A9 at Tore rdbt onto A832. Follow for 5m into Muir of Ord. Turn left outside Muir of Ord, to Ullapool. Hotel 0.5m on left*

Dating back to 1637, this country-house hotel is situated peacefully in wooded grounds and offers brightly furnished and well-proportioned accommodation. Comfortable day rooms reflect the character and charm of the house, with inviting lounges, a cosy snug bar and an elegant dining room where wide-ranging, creative menus are offered.

ROOMS: 12 en suite (3 GF) s £40-£76; d £100-£120 (incl. bkfst)
FACILITIES: no TV in bdrms ⚑ Putt green Clay pigeon shooting
PARKING: 30 **NOTES:** ⊗ in restaurant Closed Nov-Apr

MULL, ISLE OF, Argyll & Bute
Map 20

CRAIGNURE
Map 20 NM73

★★★63% Isle Of Mull Hotel
PA65 6BB
☎ 01680 812351 🖷 01680 812462
e-mail: isleofmull@british-trust-hotels.com
web: www.british-trust-hotels.com

BRITISH TRUST
━ HOTELS ━

Dir: *ferry from Oban. Turn right on main road, then right again*

This purpose-built hotel sits on the western shore of Craignure Bay, only half a mile from the ferry pier. Popular with coach tours, it has fine views across the bay to the mainland. The hotel is well appointed, with spacious lounges and bedrooms that have all the expected facilities.

ROOMS: 85 en suite (6 fmly) ⊗ in 55 bedrooms **FACILITIES:** STV ♫
CONF: Thtr 150 Class 85 Board 60 **PARKING:** 36 **NOTES:** ⊗ in restaurant

DERVAIG
Map 22 NM45

Restaurant with Rooms

🏚 ◉ Druimard Country House
PA75 6QW
☎ 01688 400345 🖷 01688 400345
e-mail: druimard.hotel@virgin.net

Dir: *from Craignure ferry terminal turn right towards Tobermory, through Salen Village. In 1.5m left to Dervaig, hotel on right before village*

A friendly home-from-home, this Victorian country house lies in an elevated position on the edge of the village looking across to the River Bellart. The intimate restaurant is the main focus, but the owner is accentuating the original character and features of the house.

ROOMS: 5 en suite 2 annexe en suite (2 fmly) (2 GF) s £60-£95;
d £100-£125 (incl. bkfst) **LB FACILITIES:** Bird watching Xmas
PARKING: 10 **NOTES:** ⊗ in restaurant Closed 4 Jan-6 Feb & 31 Oct-Nov

TOBERMORY
Map 22 NM55

★★★73% Western Isles
PA75 6PR
☎ 01688 302012 🖷 01688 302297
e-mail: wihotel@aol.com
web: www.mullhotel.com

SCOTLAND'S HOTELS
OF DISTINCTION

Dir: *from ferry follow signs to Tobermory. Over 1st mini-rdbt in Tobermory then over small bridge and immediate right & follow road to T-junct. Right again then keep left and take 1st left for hotel at top of hill on right*

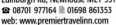

Built in 1883 and standing high above the village, this hotel enjoys spectacular views over Tobermory harbour and the Sound of Mull. Public rooms range from the classical drawing room and restaurant to the bright modern conservatory bar/bistro. Bedrooms come in a variety of styles; the impressive superior rooms include a suite complete with its own piano.

ROOMS: 28 en suite s £49-£65; d £106-£225 (incl. bkfst) **LB**
FACILITIES: Xmas **CONF:** Thtr 35 Class 20 Board 20 **PARKING:** 28
NOTES: ⊗ in restaurant Closed 17-27 Dec Civ Wed 70

M

TOBERMORY, continued

Top Hotel

★★ ◎◎ Highland Cottage

Breadalbane St PA75 6PD
☎ 01688 302030
e-mail: davidandjo@highlandcottage.co.uk
web: www.highlandcottage.co.uk
Dir: *A848 Craignure/Fishnish ferry terminal, pass Tobermory signs, straight on at mini rdbt across narrow bridge, turn right. Hotel on right opposite fire station*

Providing the highest level of natural and unassuming hospitality, this delightful little gem lies high above the island's capital. There are two inviting lounges in which to relax, one with an honesty bar and both adorned with books and magazines. The cosy dining room offers memorable dinners and splendid breakfasts. Bedrooms are individual; some have four-posters and all are comprehensively equipped to include video TVs and music centres.

ROOMS: 6 en suite (1 GF) ⊗ in all bedrooms s £95-£120; d £120-£150 (incl. bkfst) **LB** **FACILITIES:** STV **PARKING:** 6 **NOTES:** No children 10yrs ⊗ in restaurant RS Nov-Feb

★★71% ◎ Tobermory

53 Main St PA75 6NT
☎ 01688 302091 🖷 01688 302254
e-mail: tobhotel@tinyworld.co.uk
web: www.thetobermoryhotel.com
Dir: *on waterfront, overlooking Tobermory Bay*

This friendly hotel, with its pretty pink frontage, sits on the seafront amid other brightly coloured, picture-postcard buildings. There is a comfortable and homely lounge where drinks are served (there is no bar) prior to dining in the stylish restaurant. Bedrooms come in a variety of sizes; all are bright and vibrant with the superior rooms having video TVs.

ROOMS: 16 rms (15 en suite) (3 fmly) (2 GF) ⊗ in all bedrooms s £42-£52; d £84-£104 (incl. bkfst) **LB** **FACILITIES:** Xmas **NOTES:** ⊗ in restaurant Closed Xmas

NAIRN, Highland — Map 23 NH85

Top Hotel

★★ ◎◎◎ Boath House

Auldearn IV12 5TE
☎ 01667 454896 🖷 01667 455469
e-mail: wendy@boath-house.com
web: www.boath-house.com
Dir: *2m past Nairn on A96, E towards Forres, signed on main road*

Standing in its own grounds, this splendid Georgian mansion has been lovingly restored. Hospitality is first class. Owners Don and Wendy Matheson are passionate about what they do, and have an ability to establish a special relationship with their guests that will be particularly remembered. The food is also memorable here; the five-course dinners are a culinary adventure, matched only by the excellence of breakfasts. The house itself is delightful, with inviting lounges and a dining room overlooking a trout loch. Bedrooms are striking, comfortable and include many fine antique pieces. The small spa offering a number of treatments is an added attraction.

ROOMS: 6 en suite (1 fmly) (1 GF) ⊗ in all bedrooms s fr £110; d £170-£220 (incl. bkfst) **LB** **FACILITIES:** **Spa** Fishing Sauna Gym Jacuzzi Beauty salon **CONF:** Board 10 **PARKING:** 20 **NOTES:** ⊗ in restaurant Closed Xmas Civ Wed 30

★★58% Alton Burn

Alton Burn Rd IV12 5ND
☎ 01667 452051 & 453325 🖷 01667 456697
e-mail: enquiries@altonburn.co.uk
Dir: *follow signs from A96 at western boundary of Nairn*

This long-established, family-run hotel is located on the western edge of town and enjoys delightful views over the Moray Firth and adjacent golf course. Bedrooms, originally furnished in the 1950s, have been thoughtfully preserved to provide reminder of that era whilst spacious day rooms include a well-stocked bar, several comfortable lounges and a popular restaurant.

ROOMS: 23 en suite (7 GF) s fr £37.50; d fr £70 (incl. bkfst) **LB** **FACILITIES:** Putt green Table tennis, pool table, croquet **CONF:** Thtr 100 Class 50 Board 40 **PARKING:** 40 **NOTES:** ⊗ in restaurant Closed Nov-Mar

NETHY BRIDGE, Highland — Map 23 NJ02

★★★61% *Nethybridge*

PH25 3DP
☎ 01479 821203 🖷 01479 821686
e-mail: salesnethybridge@strathmorehotels.com
Dir: *Turn off A9 onto A95, then onto B970 to Nethy Bridge.*

This popular tourist and coaching hotel enjoys a central location amidst the majestic Cairngorm Mountains. Bedrooms are stylishly furnished in bold tartans whilst traditionally styled day rooms include two bars and a popular snooker room. Staff are friendly and keen to please.

ROOMS: 69 en suite (3 fmly) (7 GF) **FACILITIES:** Snooker Putt green Bowling green ♫ ch fac **SERVICES:** Lift **PARKING:** 80 **NOTES:** ⊗ in restaurant

> Packed in a hurry? Ironing facilities should be available at all star levels, either in the rooms or on request

★★72% @@ The Mountview Hotel
Grantown Rd PH25 3EB
☎ 01479 821248 🖷 01479 821515
e-mail: mviewhotel@aol.com
Dir: *from Aviemore follow signs through Boat of Garten to Nethy Bridge. On main road through village, hotel on right, 100mtrs beyond Nethy Bridge Hotel*
Aptly named, this country-house hotel enjoys stunning panoramic views from its elevated position on the edge of the village. It specialises in guided holidays and is a favoured base for bird watching and for walking groups. Public rooms include inviting lounges, while imaginative, well-prepared dinners are served in a bright and modern restaurant extension.
ROOMS: 12 rms (11 en suite) (1 GF) s £37.50-£50; d £72-£90 (incl. bkfst) **PARKING:** 20 **NOTES:** 🐕 ⊗ in restaurant

NEW LANARK, South Lanarkshire Map 21 NS84

★★★72% New Lanark Mill Hotel
Mill One, New Lanark Mills ML11 9DB
☎ 01555 667200 🖷 01555 667222
e-mail: hotel@newlanark.org web: www.newlanark.org
Dir: *signed from all major roads, M74 junct 7 & M8*
Originally a cotton mill in the 18th-century, this hotel forms part of a fully restored village, now a World Heritage Site. There's a bright modern style throughout which contrasts nicely with features from the original mill. There is a comfortable foyer-lounge with a galleried restaurant above. The hotel enjoys stunning views over the River Clyde.
ROOMS: 38 en suite (2 fmly) ⊗ in 28 bedrooms s £64; d £99 (incl. bkfst) **LB** **FACILITIES:** Fishing about 1m away Xmas **CONF:** Thtr 200 Class 60 Board 40 Del from £99 **SERVICES:** Lift **PARKING:** 75 **NOTES:** ⊗ in restaurant Civ Wed 110

NEWTON STEWART, Dumfries & Galloway Map 20 NX46

Top Hotel

★★★ @@ Kirroughtree House
Minnigaff DG8 6AN
☎ 01671 402141 🖷 01671 402425
e-mail: info@kirroughtreehouse.co.uk
web: www.kirroughtreehouse.co.uk
Dir: *from A75 take A712, New Galloway road, entrance to hotel 300yds on left*
This imposing mansion enjoys a peaceful location in eight acres of landscaped gardens near Galloway Forest Park. The inviting day rooms comprise a choice of lounges and two elegant dining rooms. Well-proportioned, individually styled bedrooms include some suites and mini-suites and many rooms enjoy fine views. Service is very friendly and attentive.
ROOMS: 17 en suite s £81-£115; d £142-£200 (incl. bkfst) **LB** **FACILITIES:** STV 9 hole pitch and putt Xmas **CONF:** Thtr 30 Class 20 Board 20 Del from £125 **SERVICES:** Lift **PARKING:** 50 **NOTES:** No children 10yrs ⊗ in restaurant Closed 4 Jan-16 Feb

NORTH BERWICK, East Lothian Map 21 NT58

★★68% Nether Abbey
20 Dirleton Av EH39 4BQ
☎ 01620 892802 🖷 01620 895298
e-mail: bookings@netherabbey.co.uk
web: www.netherabbey.co.uk
Dir: *leave A1 at junct with A198 to rdbt, take B6371 to N Berwick, hotel is 2nd on left when entering town*
Popular with golfers, this hotel has completely transformed its public areas to present stunningly contemporary open-plan reception, dining areas and bar. Upstairs, modern well-equipped bedrooms include two junior suites with CD/video players.
ROOMS: 13 en suite (4 fmly) s £35-£65; d £70-£90 (incl. bkfst) **LB** **FACILITIES:** Xmas **CONF:** Thtr 30 Class 20 Board 20 **PARKING:** 20 **NOTES:** ⊗ in restaurant

U The Marine
Cromwell Rd EH39 4LZ
MACDONALD HOTELS & RESORTS
☎ 0870 400 8129 🖷 01620 894480
e-mail: sales.marine@macdonald-hotels.co.uk
web: www.macdonald-hotels.co.uk
Dir: *from A198 turn into Hamilton Rd at lights then take 2nd right*
At the time of going to press, the star classification for this hotel was not confirmed. Please refer to the AA internet site www.theAA.com for current information.
ROOMS: 84 en suite (4 fmly) (4 GF) ⊗ in 20 bedrooms s fr £55; d fr £80 (incl. bkfst) **LB** **FACILITIES: Spa** STV supervised Sauna Solarium Gym Putt green Xmas **CONF:** Thtr 400 Class 150 Board 25 Del from £145 **SERVICES:** Lift **PARKING:** 50 **NOTES:** 🐕 ⊗ in restaurant Civ Wed 200

OBAN, Argyll & Bute Map 20 NM93

★★★72% @ Manor House
Gallanach Rd PA34 4LS
☎ 01631 562087 🖷 01631 563053
e-mail: info@manorhouseoban.com
web: www.manorhouseoban.com
Dir: *follow signs MacBrayne Ferries and pass ferry entrance for hotel on right*

Handy for the ferry terminal and with views of the bay and harbour, this elegant Georgian residence was built for the Duke of Argyll. Comfortable and attractive public rooms invite relaxation, whilst most of the well-equipped bedrooms are graced by period pieces.
ROOMS: 11 en suite ⊗ in all bedrooms **FACILITIES:** STV **PARKING:** 20 **NOTES:** No children 12yrs ⊗ in restaurant Closed 25-26 Dec

Late for dinner? Quality standards mean that last orders for dinner vary according to star rating and should be no earlier than: ★★ 7.00pm ★★★ 8:00pm ★★★★ 9:00pm ★★★★★ 10:00pm

O

OBAN, continued

★★★60% Columba
North Pier PA34 5QD
☎ 01631 562183 📠 01631 564683
e-mail: columbahotel@freeuk.com
Dir: *A85 to Oban, 1st set of lights in town and turn right*
This popular tourist hotel is located on the North Pier and many of the bedrooms overlook the bay. Public areas include a restaurant, breakfast room and a choice of contrasting bars. Guests are welcome to use the leisure facilities at the sister hotel, The Alexandra.
ROOMS: 48 en suite (6 fmly) s £49.50-£59.50; d £75-£95 (incl. bkfst) LB **FACILITIES:** ♫ Xmas **CONF:** Class 40 Board 30 **SERVICES:** Lift **PARKING:** 10 **NOTES:** ⊗ in restaurant

★★76% Willowburn
PA34 4TJ
☎ 01852 300276
e-mail: willowburn.hotel@virgin.net
web: www.willowburn.co.uk
(For full entry see Clachan-Seil)

★★72% Falls of Lora
PA37 1PB
☎ 01631 710483 📠 01631 710694
e-mail: enquiries@fallsoflora.com
web: www.fallsoflora.com
(For full entry see Connel and advert on opposite page)

OLDMELDRUM, Aberdeenshire — Map 23 NJ82

U Meldrum House Hotel Golf & Country Club
AB51 0AE
☎ 01651 872294 📠 01651 872464
e-mail: info@meldrumhouse.com
At the time of going to press, the star classification for this hotel was not confirmed. Please refer to the AA internet site www.theAA.com for current information.
ROOMS: 9 en suite (1 fmly) (1 GF) ⊗ in all bedrooms s £95-£130; d £120-£140 (incl. bkfst) **FACILITIES:** 18 Xmas **CONF:** Thtr 80 Class 20 Board 30 Del from £130 **PARKING:** 45 **NOTES:** ⊗ in restaurant Civ Wed 70

ONICH, Highland — Map 22 NN06

★★★76% Onich
PH33 6RY
☎ 01855 821214 📠 01855 821484
e-mail: enquiries@onich-fortwilliam.co.uk
web: www.onich-fortwilliam.co.uk
Dir: *beside A82, 2m N of Ballachulish Bridge*

Genuine hospitality is part of the appeal of this hotel, which lies right beside Loch Linnhe with gardens extending to shores. Nicely presented public areas include a choice of inviting lounges and contrasting bars, and views of the loch can be enjoyed from the attractive restaurant. Bedrooms, with pleasing colour schemes, are comfortably modern in appointment.
ROOMS: 25 en suite (6 fmly) ⊗ in 6 bedrooms s £43-£110; d £86-£130 (incl. bkfst) LB **FACILITIES:** STV Jacuzzi Games room Xmas **CONF:** Thtr 30 Class 20 Board 20 Del from £125 **PARKING:** 50 **NOTES:** ⊗ in restaurant Closed Xmas

★★★73% *Lodge on the Loch*
PH33 6RY
☎ 0871 222 3462 📠 0871 222 3416
e-mail: reservations@freedomglen.co.uk
web: www.freedomglen.co.uk/ll
Dir: *beside A82 in village of Onich - 5m N of Glencoe, 10m S of Fort William*
First class Highland hospitality is a real feature of this idyllically located, holiday hotel. Fine views over Loch Linnhe can be enjoyed from the public areas and many of the individually styled bedrooms. A real fire warms the cosy lounge in the cooler months and accomplished cooking features on the dinner menus.
ROOMS: 16 en suite (1 GF) ⊗ in all bedrooms **FACILITIES:** Free use of leisure facilities at sister hotel **CONF:** Thtr 40 Class 30 Board 30 **PARKING:** 25 **NOTES:** No children 16yrs ⊗ in restaurant Closed Jan-14 Feb & Nov-23 Dec RS 14 Feb - 4 April

PEAT INN, Fife — Map 21 NO40

Top Hotel

★★ Peat Inn
KY15 5LH
☎ 01334 840206 📠 01334 840530
e-mail: reception@thepeatinn.co.uk
web: www.thepeatinn.co.uk
Dir: *6m SW of St Andrews at junct B940/B941*
This 300-year-old former coaching inn enjoys a rural location yet is close to St Andrews. Accommodation, luxuriously appointed, is provided in an adjacent building and comprises split-level suites with a comfortable lounge upstairs. Food is a highlight of any visit with high quality, local produce utilised by David Wilson and his talented kitchen team.
ROOMS: 8 en suite (2 fmly) s £80-£95; d £165-£175 (incl. bkfst) LB **PARKING:** 24 **NOTES:** ⊗ in restaurant Closed Sun, Mon, 25 Dec & 1 Jan

Popped the question? Hotels with Civ wed in their entry are licensed for civil wedding ceremonies. Maximum numbers for the ceremony only are shown e.g. Civ wed 120

PEEBLES, Scottish Borders Map 21 NT24

★★★★74%
Cardrona Hotel Golf & Country Club
Cardrona Mains EH45 6LZ
☎ 01896 831144 01896 831166
e-mail: general.cardrona@macdonald-hotels.co.uk
web: www.macdonald-hotels.co.uk
Dir: *20m S of Edinburgh on A72, 3m S of Peebles.*

The rolling hills of the Scottish Borders are a stunning backdrop for this modern, purpose-built hotel. Spacious bedrooms are traditional in style, equipped with a range of extras, and most enjoy fantastic countryside views. The hotel features some impressive leisure facilities, including an 18-hole golf course, 18-metre indoor pool and state-of-the-art gym.
ROOMS: 100 en suite (23 fmly) (17 GF) in all bedrooms s £65-£120; d £80-£180 (incl. bkfst & dinner) **LB FACILITIES: Spa** STV 18 Fishing Sauna Solarium Gym Putt green Quad biking, Kayaking, Shooting, Archery, Horse riding, Bike Trail. Xmas **CONF:** Thtr 250 Class 120 Board 90 Del from £85 **SERVICES:** Lift **PARKING:** 200 **NOTES:** in restaurant Civ Wed 250

★★★★70% **Peebles Hotel Hydro**
EH45 8LX
☎ 01721 720602 01721 722999
e-mail: info@peebleshydro.com
Dir: *on A702, 0.3m from town*

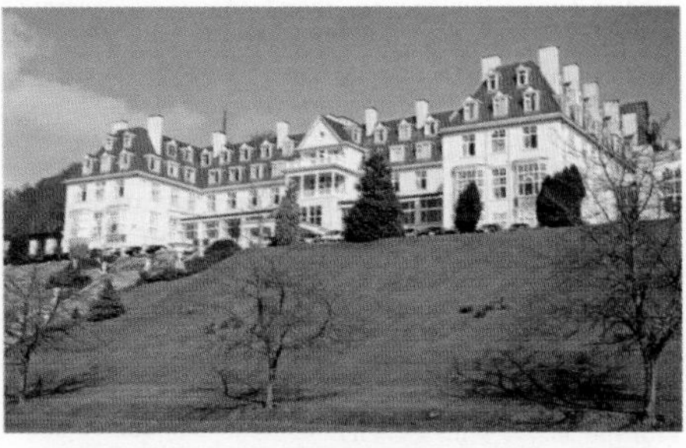

A majestic building, this resort hotel sits in grounds on the edge of the town, its elevated position giving striking views across the valley. Its range of indoor and outdoor leisure activities is second to none and makes the hotel a favourite with both families and conference delegates. Accommodation comes in a range of styles and includes a number of family rooms.
ROOMS: 128 en suite (25 fmly) (15 GF) s £126-£119; d £190-£214 (incl. bkfst & dinner) **LB FACILITIES: Spa** STV Riding Snooker Sauna Solarium Gym Putt green Badminton, Beautician, Hairdressing, Giant Chess & Draughts, Pitch & Putt ch fac Xmas **CONF:** Thtr 450 Class 200 Board 74 Del from £143 **SERVICES:** Lift **PARKING:** 200 **NOTES:** in restaurant Civ Wed 200

Top Hotel

★★★ **Cringletie House**
Edinburgh Rd EH45 8PL
☎ 01721 725750 01721 725751
e-mail: enquiries@cringletie.com
web: www.cringletie.com
Dir: *2m N on A703*
This long-established hotel is a romantic baronial mansion set in 28 acres of gardens and woodland with stunning views from all rooms. Delightful public rooms include a cocktail lounge with adjoining conservatory, whilst the first-floor restaurant is graced by a magnificent hand-painted ceiling. Bedrooms, many of them particularly spacious, are most attractively furnished.
ROOMS: 14 en suite (2 GF) in all bedrooms s £95-£120; d £115-£160 (incl. bkfst) **LB FACILITIES:** STV Putt green Xmas **CONF:** BC Thtr 45 Class 20 Board 24 Del from £160 **SERVICES:** Lift **PARKING:** 30 **NOTES:** in restaurant Closed early Jan-early Feb Civ Wed 45

PEEBLES, continued

★★★75% ◎◎ Castle Venlaw
Edinburgh Rd EH45 8QG
☎ 01721 720384 ⎙ 01721 724066
e-mail: stay@venlaw.co.uk
web: www.venlaw.co.uk
Dir: *off A703 Peebles/Edinburgh road, 0.75m from Peebles*

This 18th-century castle is set in four acres of landscaped gardens, set high above the town. Bedrooms, many with delightful views, are named after malt whiskies and include three with adjoining turrets. Well-prepared meals are served in the formal restaurant, while light meals are served in the wood-panelled library bar.
ROOMS: 12 en suite (3 fmly) ⊗ in all bedrooms s £72-£100; d £124-£200 (incl. bkfst) **LB** **FACILITIES:** Xmas **CONF:** BC Thtr 30 Class 20 Board 20 Del from £120 **PARKING:** 30 **NOTES:** ⊗ in restaurant Civ Wed 35

★★★71% Park
Innerleithen Rd EH45 8BA
☎ 01721 720451 ⎙ 01721 723510
e-mail: reserve@parkpeebles.co.uk
Dir: *in town centre opposite filling station*

The Park Hotel offers pleasant, well-equipped bedrooms of various sizes; those in the original house are particularly spacious. Public areas enjoy views of the gardens and include a tartan-clad bar, a relaxing lounge and a spacious wood-panelled restaurant. Guests can use the extensive leisure facilities on offer at the sister hotel, The Hydro.
ROOMS: 24 en suite ⊗ in 6 bedrooms s £72-£84; d £131-£193 (incl. bkfst & dinner) **LB** **FACILITIES:** Putt green Use of facilities of Peebles Hotel Hydro ♫ Xmas **SERVICES:** Lift **PARKING:** 50 **NOTES:** ⊗ in restaurant

★★★70% Tontine
High St EH45 8AJ
☎ 01721 720892 ⎙ 01721 729732
e-mail: info@tontinehotel.com
web: www.tontinehotel.com
Dir: *in town centre*

Conveniently situated in the main street, this long-established hotel offers public rooms that include an elegant Adam restaurant, inviting lounge and 'clubby' bar. Bedrooms, contained in the original house and the river-facing wing, offer a smart, classical style of accommodation. The lasting impression however, will be of the excellent level of hospitality and guest care.
ROOMS: 36 en suite (3 fmly) ⊗ in 20 bedrooms s £35-£75; d £70-£110 (incl. bkfst) **LB** **FACILITIES:** Xmas **CONF:** Thtr 40 Class 24 Board 24 Del from £90 **PARKING:** 24 **NOTES:** ⊗ in restaurant

PERTH, Perth & Kinross Map 21 NO12

★★★75% ◎◎ Murrayshall Country House Hotel & Golf Course
New Scone PH2 7PH
☎ 01738 551171 ⎙ 01738 552595
e-mail: lin.murrayshall@virgin.net
Dir: *from Perth take A94 (Coupar Angus), 1m from Perth, right to Murrayshall just before New Scone*
This imposing country house is set in 350 acres of grounds, including two golf courses, one of which is of championship standard. Bedrooms come in two distinct styles: modern suites in a purpose-built building contrast with more classic rooms in the main building. The Clubhouse bar serves a range of meals all day, whilst more accomplished cooking can be enjoyed in the Old Masters Restaurant.
ROOMS: 27 en suite 14 annexe en suite (17 fmly) (4 GF) ⊗ in 1 bedroom s £90-£130; d £130-£180 (incl. bkfst) **LB** **FACILITIES:** STV ⛳ 36 ✂ Sauna Gym Putt green Driving range Xmas **CONF:** Thtr 180 Class 60 Board 30 Del from £110 **PARKING:** 80 **NOTES:** ⊗ in restaurant Civ Wed 130

★★★74% ◎ Huntingtower
Crieff Rd PH1 3JT
☎ 01738 583771 ⎙ 01738 583777
e-mail: reservations@huntingtowerhotel.co.uk
web: www.huntingtowerhotel.co.uk
Dir: *3m W off A85*
Enjoying an idyllic country setting, this Edwardian house has been extended to offer smart, comfortable public areas and a high standard of accommodation. Comfortable lounges lead to a conservatory where lunches are served, whilst the elegant Oak

continued

Room restaurant offers skilfully prepared dinners. Bedrooms are generally spacious and provide a host of modern facilities.

ROOMS: 31 en suite 3 annexe en suite (2 fmly) (8 GF) s £99; d £179 (incl. bkfst & dinner) **LB** **FACILITIES:** STV Xmas **CONF:** BC Thtr 200 Class 140 Board 30 Del from £125 **SERVICES:** Lift **PARKING:** 150 **NOTES:** ⊗ in restaurant Civ Wed 200

★★★72% ◎ Parklands Hotel

2 St Leonards Bank PH2 8EB
☎ 01738 622451 ▤ 01738 622046
e-mail: info@theparklandshotel.com
web: www.theparklandshotel.com
Dir: *exit M90 junct 10, after 1m turn left at end of park area at traffic lights, hotel on left*

This hotel has an excellent location with views over the South Inch. The enthusiastic proprietors continue to invest heavily in the business and have given bedrooms a smart contemporary feel. Public areas include a choice of restaurants with a fine dining experience offered in Acanthus.

ROOMS: 14 en suite (3 fmly) (4 GF) ⊗ in 4 bedrooms s £79-£109; d £99-£159 (incl. bkfst) **LB** **FACILITIES:** STV **CONF:** BC Thtr 24 Class 18 Board 20 Del from £104.95 **PARKING:** 30 **NOTES:** ⊗ in restaurant RS 25-26 Dec & 31 Dec-3 Jan Civ Wed 40

★★★67% Best Western Queens Hotel

Leonard St PH2 8HB
☎ 01738 442222 ▤ 01738 638496
e-mail: email@queensperth.co.uk
Dir: *from M90 follow to 2nd lights, turn left. Hotel on right, opposite railway station*

This popular hotel benefits from a central location close to both the bus and rail stations. Bedrooms vary in size and style with top floor rooms offering extra space and excellent views of the town. Public rooms include a smart leisure centre and versatile conference space. A range of meals is served in both the bar and restaurant.

ROOMS: 50 en suite (7 fmly) ⊗ in 20 bedrooms s £55-£99; d £84-£124 (incl. bkfst) **LB** **FACILITIES: Spa** STV Sauna Gym Jacuzzi Steam room Xmas **CONF:** Thtr 200 Class 70 Board 50 Del from £120 **SERVICES:** Lift **PARKING:** 50 **NOTES:** ⊗ in restaurant Civ Wed 220

★★★67% Lovat

90 Glasgow Rd PH2 0LT
☎ 01738 636555 ▤ 01738 643123
e-mail: e-mail@lovat.co.uk
Dir: *from M90 follow Stirling signs to rdbt. Right into Glasgow Rd, hotel 1.5m on right*

This popular, long established hotel on the Glasgow road offers good function facilities and largely attracts a business clientele. Public areas include a conservatory restaurant and a well stocked bar, both offering a good range of food. Bedrooms are well appointed and thoughtfully equipped.

ROOMS: 30 en suite (1 fmly) (9 GF) ⊗ in 12 bedrooms s £68-£93; d £95-£118 (incl. bkfst) **LB** **FACILITIES:** STV Use of facilities at nearby sister hotel (indoor pool, gym, steam room, jacuzzi) Xmas **CONF:** Thtr 200 Class 60 Board 50 Del from £120 **PARKING:** 40 **NOTES:** ⊗ in restaurant Civ Wed 180

Ramada Perth

West Mill St PH1 5QP
☎ 01738 628281 ▤ 01738 643423
e-mail: sales.perth@ramadajarvis.co.uk
web: www.ramadajarvis.co.uk
Dir: *From A9 follow signs for City Centre. At 2nd lights left into Marshall Place, 4th right into King St, straight through 2 sets of lights, left into West Mill St, hotel on right.*

This well presented hotel, formerly a 15th-century water mill is conveniently situated in the centre of the town. Bedrooms are comfortably appointed for both business and leisure guests.

ROOMS: 76 en suite (2 fmly) ⊗ in 57 bedrooms s £72-£95; d £72-£95 **FACILITIES:** Xmas **CONF:** Thtr 120 Class 50 Board 40 Del from £135 **PARKING:** 50 **NOTES:** ⊗ in restaurant Civ Wed 100

Innkeeper's Lodge Perth

18 Dundee Rd PH2 7AB
☎ 01738 624471
web: www.innkeeperslodge.com

A growing concept in the travel accommodation market. Smart rooms meet essential business requirements but also have home comforts. Dining options include all-day menus plus the added advantage of breakfast, which is included in the room price. For further details consult the Hotel Groups page.

ROOMS: 41 rms s £49.95; d £49.95 **CONF:** Thtr 200 Class 120 Board 120

Travelodge

PH2 0PL
☎ 08700 850 950 ▤ 01738 444783
web: www.travelodge.co.uk

Travelodge offers good quality, good value, modern accommodation. Ideal for families, the spacious, en suite bedrooms include remote-control TV, tea and coffee-making facilities and comfortable beds. Meals can be taken at the nearby family restaurant. For further details consult the Hotel Groups page.

ROOMS: s fr £26; d fr £26

PETERHEAD, Aberdeenshire — Map 23 NK14

★★★66% Palace

Prince St AB42 1PL
☎ 01779 474821 ▤ 01779 476119
e-mail: info@palacehotel.co.uk
Dir: *A90 from Aberdeen, follow signs to Peterhead, on entering town turn into Prince St, then right into main car park*

This town centre hotel is a popular venue both for business travellers and for social functions. Bedrooms come in two styles, with the executive rooms being particularly spacious and well equipped. Public areas include a themed bar, an informal diner which is reached via a spiral staircase, and a brasserie restaurant.

ROOMS: 64 en suite (2 fmly) (14 GF) ⊗ in 44 bedrooms **FACILITIES:** STV Snooker pool table, snooker room, Gym-rates reduced for guests. ♫ Xmas **CONF:** Thtr 250 Class 120 Board 50 Del from £105 **SERVICES:** Lift **PARKING:** 90

PITLOCHRY, Perth & Kinross Map 23 NN95
See also KINLOCH RANNOCH

★★★76% ◉ ⚬ Green Park
Clunie Bridge Rd PH16 5JY
☎ 01796 473248 ▤ 01796 473520
e-mail: bookings@thegreenpark.co.uk
web: www.thegreenpark.co.uk
Dir: turn off A9 at Pitlochry, follow signs 0.25m through town, hotel on banks of Loch Faskally

Benefiting from a stunning setting on the shores of Loch Faskally, this hotel has lovely landscaped gardens, complete with interesting works of art. Thoughtfully designed bedrooms, many with fine views, are spacious and offer bright decor. Dinner utilises fresh produce, much of it grown in the kitchen garden.
ROOMS: 39 en suite (10 GF) ⊗ in all bedrooms s £56-£79; d £112-£158 (incl. bkfst & dinner) LB **FACILITIES:** Putt green Xmas **PARKING:** 45 **NOTES:** ⊗ in restaurant

See advert on opposite page

★★★74% Pine Trees
Strathview Ter PH16 5QR
☎ 01796 472121 ▤ 01796 472460
e-mail: info@pinetreeshotel.co.uk
web: www.pinetreeshotel.co.uk
Dir: along main street (Atholl Rd), into Larchwood Rd, follow hotel signs
Set in ten acres of tree-studded grounds high above the town, this fine Victorian mansion retains many fine features including wood panelling, ornate ceilings and a wonderful marble staircase. The atmosphere is refined and relaxing, with public rooms looking onto the lawns. Bedrooms come in a variety of sizes and many are well proportioned. Staff are friendly and keen to please.
ROOMS: 20 en suite (3 fmly) ⊗ in all bedrooms s £64-£88; d £112-£156 (incl. bkfst & dinner) LB **FACILITIES:** Xmas **PARKING:** 20 **NOTES:** ⊗ in restaurant Civ Wed 70

★★★71% Dundarach
Perth Rd PH16 5DJ
☎ 01796 472862 ▤ 01796 473024
e-mail: aa@pitlochryhotel.co.uk
web: www.dundarach.co.uk
Dir: S of town centre on main route
This welcoming, family-run hotel stands in mature grounds at the south end of town. Bedrooms offer a variety of styles, including a block of large purpose-built rooms that will appeal to business guests. Well-proportioned public areas feature inviting lounges and a conservatory restaurant giving fine views of the Tummel Valley.
ROOMS: 20 en suite 19 annexe en suite (7 fmly) ⊗ in 11 bedrooms s £55-£65; d £80-£92 (incl. bkfst) LB **FACILITIES:** STV Sauna **CONF:** Thtr 60 Class 40 Board 40 **PARKING:** 39 **NOTES:** ✖ ⊗ in restaurant Closed Jan RS Dec-early Feb

★★★70% Scotland's
40 Bonnethill Rd PH16 5BT
☎ 01796 472292 ▤ 01796 473284
e-mail: stay@scotlandshotel.co.uk
web: www.scotlandshotel.co.uk
Dir: follow A924 (Perth road) into town until War Memorial then take next right for hotel 200mtrs on right
Enjoying a convenient town centre location, this long-established hotel is a popular base for tourists. Bedrooms, including family rooms and some with four-poster beds, vary in size and style. A choice of restaurants and bars are offered and guests can relax in the comfortable lounges.
ROOMS: 57 en suite 15 annexe en suite (21 fmly) (8 GF) ⊗ in 20 bedrooms s £50-£85; d £80-£120 (incl. bkfst) LB **FACILITIES:** ⚬ Sauna Solarium Gym Jacuzzi Therapy treatments, Aromatherapy, Reflexology, Beauty Treatments, Sports Massage Xmas **CONF:** Thtr 200 Class 75 Board 30 Del from £95 **SERVICES:** Lift **PARKING:** 100 **NOTES:** ✖ ⊗ in restaurant

★★★66% Fisher's
75-79 Atholl Rd PH16 5BN
☎ 01796 472000 ▤ 01796 473949
e-mail: fishers@crerarhotels.com
web: www.crerarhotels.com
Dir: N'bound on A9 to Pitlochry, 3m after Ballinluig. S'bound on A9 turn left to Pitlochry, 10m after Bruar

CRERAR
HOTELS

This traditional town centre hotel is convenient for the station and an ideal base for visiting local attractions. There are several styles of bedrooms, some overlook the main street, whilst others overlook the attractive gardens and many have views of the surrounding hills. Public areas are extensive, with several dining options and two bars, including the popular Kingfisher Bar.
ROOMS: 80 en suite 51 annexe en suite (8 fmly) (22 GF) s £45-£65; d £57-£105 (incl. bkfst) LB **FACILITIES:** Putt green ♫ Xmas **CONF:** BC Thtr 230 Class 100 Board 100 Del from £65 **SERVICES:** Lift **PARKING:** 45 **NOTES:** ⊗ in restaurant

★★78% ◉ Knockendarroch House
Higher Oakfield PH16 5HT
☎ 01796 473473 ▤ 01796 474068
e-mail: info@knockendarroch.co.uk
web: www.knockendarroch.co.uk
Dir: N'bound on A9 turn off at Pitlochry sign. After rail bridge take 1st right, then 2nd left
An immaculate Victorian mansion overlooking the town and Tummel Valley. There is no bar, but guests can enjoy a drink in the delightful lounge while studying the daily menu of freshly prepared and enjoyable dishes. Bedrooms are tastefully furnished,
continued

comfortable and well equipped. Those on the top floor are smaller but are not without character and appeal.

ROOMS: 12 en suite ⊗ in all bedrooms s £77-£99; d £108-£152 (incl. bkfst & dinner) **LB** **FACILITIES:** Leisure facilities at nearby hotel **PARKING:** 30 **NOTES:** No children 10yrs ⊗ in restaurant Closed 2nd wk Nov-mid Feb

★★73% Donavourd House

PH16 5JS
☎ 01796 472100 ⎙ 01796 474455
e-mail: reservations@donavourdhousehotel.co.uk
Dir: *from A9 slip road take immediate right under railway, continue 0.5m, then left up hill. At junct take left for hotel 0.5m on left*

This attractive country house sits in its own gardens in a quiet, elevated location overlooking Strathtummel. Bedrooms are spacious and well appointed with attractive colour schemes. The public areas are in period style where the dining room has crisp linen and fine glassware that complement the sound cooking skills of the chef-patron and her kitchen brigade.
ROOMS: 9 en suite (1 fmly) (1 GF) ⊗ in all bedrooms s £55-£65; d £47-£75 (incl. bkfst) **LB** **FACILITIES:** Xmas **PARKING:** 15 **NOTES:** ⊗ in restaurant Closed 25 Dec, 5 Jan-Feb Civ Wed 100

★★72% Moulin Hotel

11-13 Kirkmichael Rd, Moulin PH16 5EW
☎ 01796 472196 ⎙ 01796 474098
e-mail: sales@moulinhotel.co.uk
web: www.moulinhotel.co.uk
Dir: *off A9 into town centre take A924 signed Braemar. Moulin village 0.75m outside Pitlochry*
Steeped in history, original parts of this friendly hotel date back to 1695. One of them, the Moulin bar, serves an excellent choice of bar meals as well as real ales from the hotel's own microbrewery.

continued

Alternatively, the comfortable restaurant overlooks the Moulin Burn. Bedrooms are well equipped.

Moulin House, Pitlochry

ROOMS: 15 en suite (3 fmly) s £45-£65; d £55-£80 (incl. bkfst) **LB** **FACILITIES:** Xmas **CONF:** Thtr 15 Class 12 Board 10 **PARKING:** 30 **NOTES:** ⊗ in restaurant

★★71% *Craigvrack*

West Moulin Rd PH16 5EQ
☎ 01796 472399 ⎙ 01796 473990
e-mail: info@craigvrack-hotel.demon.co.uk
web: www.craigvrack-hotel.demon.co.uk
Dir: *from Main St, turn into West Moulin Rd*
Enjoying an elevated position above the town, this comfortable hotel has well-presented public areas, including an attractive restaurant and comfortable bar serving a varied menu. The

continued on p740

PITLOCHRY, continued

bedrooms come in a variety of sizes and are smartly furnished, with several enjoying fine views of the countryside.

Craigvrack, Pitlochry

ROOMS: 16 en suite (2 fmly) (3 GF) ⊗ in 7 bedrooms **CONF:** Thtr 30 Class 32 Board 16 **PARKING:** 26 **NOTES:** ⊗ in restaurant

★★70% Balrobin

Higher Oakfield PH16 5HT
☎ 01796 472901 📠 01796 474200
e-mail: info@balrobin.co.uk
web: www.balrobin.co.uk
Dir: *leave A9 at Pitlochry junct, continue to town centre and follow brown tourists signs to hotel*

A welcoming atmosphere prevails at this family-run hotel which, from its position above the town, enjoys delightful countryside views. Public rooms include a relaxing lounge, a well-stocked bar and an attractive restaurant offering traditional home-cooked fare. The bedrooms are comfortable and many enjoy the fine views.
ROOMS: 14 en suite (2 fmly) (4 GF) ⊗ in all bedrooms s £40-£49; d £70-£87 (incl. bkfst) **LB** **PARKING:** 15 **NOTES:** No children 5yrs ⊗ in restaurant Closed Nov-Feb

P

PLOCKTON, Highland — Map 22 NG83

★★72% The Plockton

41 Harbour St IV52 8TN
☎ 01599 544274 📠 01599 544475
e-mail: info@plocktonhotel.co.uk
Dir: *6m from Kyle of Lochalsh and 6m from Balmacara*

This very popular hotel occupies an idyllic position on the waterfront of Loch Carron. Stylish bedrooms offer individual, pleasing decor and many have spacious balconies or panoramic views. There is a choice of three dining areas and seafood is very much a speciality. The staff and owners provide a relaxed and informal style of attentive service. In addition to the hotel a self-contained cottage is available for group bookings.
ROOMS: 11 en suite 4 annexe en suite (1 fmly) (1 GF) ⊗ in all bedrooms s £40-£60; d £60-£100 (incl. bkfst) **LB** **FACILITIES:** STV Pool table Xmas **NOTES:** 🚫🐕 ⊗ in restaurant Civ Wed 45

POLMONT, Falkirk — Map 21 NS97

★★★★69% The Inchyra Grange

Grange Rd FK2 0YB
☎ 01324 711911 📠 01324 716134
e-mail: inchyra@macdonald-hotels.co.uk
web: www.macdonald-hotels.co.uk
Dir: *just beyond BP Social Club*

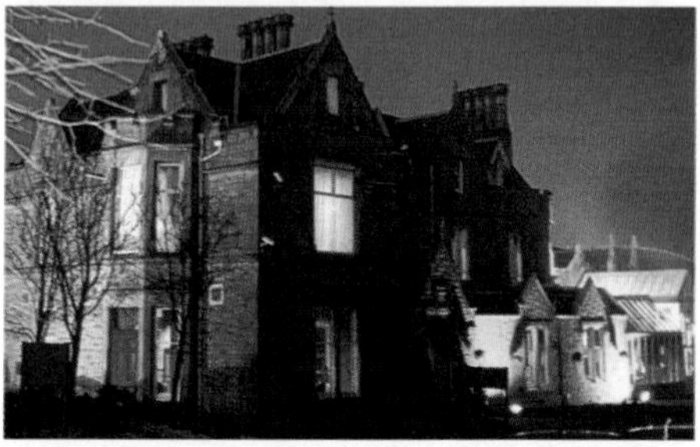

Ideally placed for the M9 and Grangemouth terminal, this former manor house has been tastefully extended. It provides extensive conference facilities and a choice of eating options: the relaxed atmosphere of the Steakhouse or the Priory Restaurant, which provides a more formal dining experience. Bedrooms are mostly spacious and comfortable.
ROOMS: 103 en suite (5 fmly) (40 GF) ⊗ in 91 bedrooms s £55-£95; d £65-£125 **LB** **FACILITIES: Spa** STV 🏊 supervised 💆 Sauna Solarium Gym Jacuzzi Steam room, Beauty therapy salons, Aromatherapist ♫ Xmas **CONF:** BC Thtr 700 Class 250 Board 80 Del from £110 **SERVICES:** Lift **PARKING:** 400 **NOTES:** ⊗ in restaurant Civ Wed 500

⌂ Premier Travel Inn Falkirk East

Beancross Rd FK2 0YS
☎ 08701 977098 📠 01324 720777
web: www.premiertravelinn.com
Dir: *M9 junct5 at rdbt take exit signed Polmont A9. Inn on left*

High quality, modern budget accommodation ideal for both families and business travellers. Spacious, en suite bedrooms feature bath and shower, satellite TV and many have telephones and modem points. The adjacent family restaurant features a wide and varied menu. For further details consult the Hotel Groups page.
ROOMS: 40 en suite s £46.95-£48.95; d £46.95-£48.95

POOLEWE, Highland — Map 22 NG88

Top Hotel

★★★ ®® Pool House Hotel

IV22 2LD
☎ 01445 781272 📠 01445 781403
e-mail: enquiries@poolhousehotel.co.uk
Dir: *6m N of Gairloch on A832. Village centre*

Set on the shores of Loch Ewe where the river meets the bay, this hotel's unassuming façade gives little hint of its splendid interior. Extensively upgraded a few years ago, it offers

continued

delightful public rooms and magnificent suites named after World War II ships, reflecting the building's former use as a military base. The hotel was amazing views and is run very much as a country house; service and hospitality by the Harrison Family are second to none, which together with the excellent food, will leave a lasting impression.

ROOMS: 5 en suite (1 fmly) ⊗ in all bedrooms
FACILITIES: Snooker Sea fishing from jetty in front of hotel
PARKING: 20 **NOTES:** ✖ No children 8yrs ⊗ in restaurant Closed Jan-Feb RS Nov & Dec

PORT APPIN, Argyll & Bute Map 20 NM94

Top Hotel

★★★ ◉◉◉ **Airds**
PA38 4DF
☎ 01631 730236 ▤ 01631 730535
e-mail: airds@airds-hotel.com
web: www.airds-hotel.com
Dir: from A828, turn at Appin signed Port Appin. Hotel 2.5m on left.
The views are stunning from this small, luxury hotel on the shores of Loch Linnhe where the staff are delightful and nothing is too much trouble. The well-equipped bedrooms provide style and luxury whilst many bathrooms are furnished in marble and have power showers. Expertly prepared dishes utilising the finest of ingredients are served in the elegant dining room. Comfortable lounges with deep sofas and roaring fires provide the ideal retreat for relaxation. A real get-away-from-it-all experience.
ROOMS: 12 en suite (2 fmly) (2 GF) ⊗ in all bedrooms s £180-£230; d £230-£280 (incl. bkfst & dinner) **LB**
FACILITIES: STV Xmas **CONF:** Thtr 16 Class 16 Board 16
PARKING: 21 **NOTES:** ⊗ in restaurant Closed 3-26 Jan & 20-28 Nov RS Nov-Feb Civ Wed 40

PORT ASKAIG See Islay, Isle of

PORTPATRICK, Dumfries & Galloway Map 20 NW95

★★★74% ◉ **Fernhill**
Heugh Rd DG9 8TD
☎ 01776 810220 ▤ 01776 810596
e-mail: info@fernhillhotel.co.uk web: www.fernhillhotel.co.uk
Dir: from Stranraer A77 to Portpatrick, 100yds past Portpatrick village sign, turn right before war memorial. Hotel is 1st on left

Set high above the village, this hotel looks out over the harbour and Irish Sea. A smart conservatory restaurant and some of the bedrooms take advantage of the views. A modern wing offers particularly spacious and well-appointed rooms - some have balconies.
ROOMS: 27 en suite 9 annexe en suite (3 fmly) (8 GF) ⊗ in 10 bedrooms s £53-£127; d £100-£204 (incl. bkfst & dinner) **LB**
FACILITIES: STV Leisure facilities available at sister hotel in Stranraer Xmas **CONF:** Thtr 24 Class 12 Board 12 Del from £95 **PARKING:** 45
NOTES: ⊗ in restaurant Closed mid-Jan - mid-Feb Civ Wed 40

Top Restaurant with Rooms

🛏 ◉◉◉ **Knockinaam Lodge**
DG9 9AD
☎ 01776 810471 ▤ 01776 810435
e-mail: reservations@knockinaamlodge.com
Dir: from A77 or A75 follow signs to Portpatrick. Through Lochans. After 2m left at signs for hotel
Any tour of Dumfries & Galloway would not be complete without a night or two at this gastronomic haven of tranquillity and relaxation. An extended Victorian house that is set back from its own pebble beach but is sheltered by majestic cliffs and woodlands. A warm welcome is assured from the proprietors and their committed team, and much emphasis is placed on providing a sophisticated but intimate home-from-home experience. The cooking here is a real treat and showcases superb local produce.
ROOMS: 9 en suite ⊗ in 2 bedrooms s £145-£335; d £250-£380 (incl. bkfst & dinner) **LB FACILITIES:** Fishing 🎯 Shooting, Walking, Sea fishing Xmas **CONF:** Thtr 30 Class 10 Board 16 Del from £160
PARKING: 20 **NOTES:** ⊗ in restaurant Civ Wed 40

PORTREE See Skye, Isle of

POWFOOT, Dumfries & Galloway — Map 21 NY16

🅰 Powfoot Golf Hotel
Links Av DG12 5PN
☎ 01461 700254 📠 01461 700288
e-mail: rooms@powfootgolfhotel.co.uk
web: www.powfootgolfhotel.co.uk
Dir: *from A75 through Annan on B721. Then take B724 for approx 3m & turn left into Powfoot*
ROOMS: 15 en suite (4 fmly) s £45-£50; d £70-£80 (incl. bkfst) **LB** **FACILITIES:** Xmas **CONF:** Thtr 120 Class 60 Board 40 Del £65 **PARKING:** 40 **NOTES:** ★★ ⊘ in restaurant Closed 25-26 Dec

PRESTWICK, South Ayrshire — Map 20 NS32

★★★70% ⊛ Parkstone
Esplanade KA9 1QN
☎ 01292 477286 📠 01292 477671
e-mail: info@parkstonehotel.co.uk
web: www.parkstonehotel.co.uk
Dir: *from Prestwick Main St (A79) turn W to seafront - hotel 600yds*

Situated on the seafront in a quiet residential area, this family-run hotel caters for business visitors as well as golfers. Bedrooms come in a variety of sizes, all being furnished in a smart contemporary style. The attractive, modern look of the bar and restaurant is matched by an equally up-to-date menu.
ROOMS: 30 en suite (2 fmly) ⊘ in all bedrooms s £47-£62; d £79-£93 (incl. bkfst) **LB** **FACILITIES:** Xmas **CONF:** Thtr 100 **PARKING:** 34 **NOTES:** ✗ ⊘ in restaurant Civ Wed 100

RENFREW For hotels see Glasgow Airport

ROSEBANK, South Lanarkshire — Map 21 NS84

★★★72% Popinjay
Best Western
Lanark Rd ML8 5QB
☎ 01555 860441 📠 01555 860204
e-mail: popinjayhotel@attglobal.net
web: www.popinjayhotel.co.uk
Dir: *on A72 between Hamilton & Lanark*
This attractive Tudor-style hotel is set in landscaped grounds leading down to the River Clyde. There is a comfortable oak-panelled bar and a light and airy restaurant; meals are served in both areas. Well-equipped bedrooms come in a variety of sizes, whilst the function suites ensures the hotel's popularity for weddings and conferences.
ROOMS: 38 en suite (2 fmly) ⊘ in 19 bedrooms **FACILITIES:** STV Fishing Xmas **CONF:** Thtr 250 Class 120 Board 60 **PARKING:** 300 **NOTES:** ⊘ in restaurant Civ Wed

See advert on opposite page

ROY BRIDGE, Highland — Map 22 NN28

★★★71% *Glenspean Lodge Hotel*
Best Western
PH31 4AW
☎ 01397 712223 📠 01397 712660
e-mail: reservations@glenspeanlodge.co.uk
web: www.glenspeanlodge.co.uk
Dir: *2m E of Roy Bridge, right off A82 at Spean Bridge onto A86*

Originally a Victorian hunting lodge, this hotel has been impressively extended and enjoys stunning views from its elevated position in the Spean Valley. Accommodation is provided in well laid out bedrooms, some suitable for families. Meals can be enjoyed in either the smart restaurant or less formal bar area.
ROOMS: 15 en suite (3 fmly) ⊘ in 10 bedrooms **FACILITIES:** STV Sauna Gym Jacuzzi snooker room, small children's play room **CONF:** Thtr 50 Class 25 Board 25 **PARKING:** 50 **NOTES:** ⊘ in restaurant Civ Wed 80

★★72% The Stronlossit Inn
PH31 4AG
☎ 01397 712253 & 0800 015 5321 📠 01397 712641
e-mail: stay@stronlossit.co.uk
web: www.stronlossit.co.uk
Dir: *off A82 at Spean Bridge onto A86, signed Roy Bridge. Hotel on left*
Boasting the quality and style of a newly refurbished hotel together with the character and hospitality of a traditional hostelry, The Stronlossit Inn is proving quite a draw for the discerning Highland tourist. The spacious bar is the focal point with a peat burning fire providing a warm welcome in cooler months; alternatively guests can eat in the attractive restaurant. Bedrooms come in a mix of sizes and styles, most being smartly modern and well equipped.
ROOMS: 10 en suite (5 GF) ⊘ in all bedrooms s £45-£55; d £66-£86 (incl. bkfst) **LB** **FACILITIES:** Free internet access Xmas **CONF:** Thtr 30 Class 18 Board 12 **PARKING:** 30 **NOTES:** ✗ No children 12yrs ⊘ in restaurant Closed 25 Nov-10 Dec Civ Wed 30

ST ANDREWS, Fife — Map 21 NO51

Top Hotel

★★★★★ ⊛⊛⊛ The Old Course Hotel, Golf Resort & Spa
KY16 9SP
☎ 01334 474371 📠 01334 477668
e-mail: reservations@oldcoursehotel.co.uk
Dir: *M90 junct 8 then A91 to St Andrews*
A haven for golfers, this internationally renowned hotel, now under new ownership, sits adjacent to the 17th hole of the championship course. Bedrooms vary in size and range from the traditional to the contemporary and stylish fairway rooms, complete with course facing balconies. Day rooms include intimate lounges, a bright conservatory, a well-equipped

continued

spa and a range of golf shops. The fine dining 'Grill', the seafood bar 'Sands' or the informal Jigger pub prove popular eating venues.

ROOMS: 146 en suite (5 fmly) ⊗ in all bedrooms s fr £250; d fr £316 (incl. bkfst) **LB** **FACILITIES: Spa** STV ⛳ 18 Sauna Solarium Gym Putt green Jacuzzi Xmas **CONF:** Thtr 300 Class 150 Board 60 **SERVICES:** Lift **PARKING:** 125 **NOTES:** ⊗ in restaurant Closed 19-28 Dec Civ Wed 130

★★★★★71% ◎◎ St Andrews Bay Golf Resort & Spa

KY16 8PN
☎ 01334 837000 🖷 01334 471115
e-mail: info@standrewsbay.com

Enjoying breathtaking coastal views, this modern hotel is flanked by its two golf courses. Spacious public areas centre round a stunning two-storey atrium. The lower floor contains an open-plan lounge and restaurant, whilst the upper floor features a plush bar and the delightful Esperante fine dining restaurant and cocktail bar. A stylish spa with full-length pool complements the extensive conference and golfing facilities.

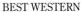

ROOMS: 209 en suite 8 annexe en suite (86 fmly) (57 GF) ⊗ in 195 bedrooms **FACILITIES: Spa** STV ⛳ 36 Sauna Gym Putt green Jacuzzi Clay pigeon shooting etc can be organised Xmas **CONF:** BC Thtr 500 Class 450 Board 168 **SERVICES:** Lift air con **NOTES:** ⊗ in restaurant Civ Wed 600

★★★★71% ◎◎ Macdonald Rusacks

MACDONALD HOTELS & RESORTS

Pilmour Links KY16 9JQ
☎ 0870 400 8128 🖷 01334 477896
e-mail: general.rusacks@macdonald-hotels.co.uk
web: www.macdonald-hotels.co.uk

Dir: *from W on A91 past golf course, through an old viaduct, hotel 200mtrs on left before rdbt*

This long-established hotel enjoys an almost unrivalled location with superb views across the famous golf course. Bedrooms are

continued on p744

comfortably appointed and well equipped. Classical public rooms include a smart restaurant - the perfect place to view golfers.
ROOMS: 68 en suite **FACILITIES:** STV Golf Mgr to organise golf Xmas **CONF:** Thtr 90 Class 40 Board 20 Del from £115 **SERVICES:** Lift **PARKING:** 21 **NOTES:** ⊗ in restaurant Civ Wed 60

Top Hotel

★★★ ⊛⊛⅊ **Rufflets Country House**
Strathkinness Low Rd KY16 9TX
☎ 01334 472594 📠 01334 478703
e-mail: reservations@rufflets.co.uk web: www.rufflets.co.uk
Dir: 1.5m W on B939
This charming property is set in extensive award-winning gardens, a few minutes' drive from the town centre. Stylish, spacious bedrooms are individually decorated and most benefit from impressive bathrooms. Public rooms include a well-stocked bar, a choice of inviting lounges and the delightful Garden Room restaurant; imaginative, carefully prepared cooking utilises produce from the hotel's own gardens whenever possible.
ROOMS: 19 en suite 5 annexe en suite (2 fmly) ⊗ in 13 bedrooms s £125-£229; d £199-£305 (incl. bkfst) **LB FACILITIES:** STV Putt green Golf driving net Xmas **CONF:** Thtr 50 Class 30 Board 25 Del from £140 **PARKING:** 52 **NOTES:** ✘ ⊗ in restaurant Civ Wed 60

Top Hotel

★★★ ⊛⊛ **St Andrews Golf**
40 The Scores KY16 9AS
☎ 01334 472611 📠 01334 472188
e-mail: reception@standrews-golf.co.uk
web: www.standrews-golf.co.uk
Dir: follow signs 'Golf Course' into Golf Place and in 200yds turn right into The Scores
A genuinely warm approach to guest care is found at this
continued

delightful, family-run hotel. In a stunning location the views of the beach, golf links and coastline can be enjoyed from the inviting day rooms. There is a choice of bars and an informal atmosphere in Ma Bell's. Bedrooms come in two distinct styles with those on the higher floors offering stylish, modern design and comfort.
ROOMS: 21 en suite d £180-£215 (incl. bkfst) **LB FACILITIES:** STV Xmas **CONF:** Thtr 200 Class 80 Board 20 Del from £120 **SERVICES:** Lift **PARKING:** 6 **NOTES:** ⊗ in restaurant Closed 26-28 Dec Civ Wed 180

★★★71% **Scores**
76 The Scores KY16 9BB
☎ 01334 472451 📠 01334 473947
e-mail: reception@scoreshotel.co.uk
web: www.scoreshotel.co.uk
Dir: on entering St Andrews follow West Sands & Sea Life Centre signs, hotel diagonally opposite Royal & Ancient Clubhouse

Enjoying views over St Andrews Bay, this smart hotel is situated only a short pitch from the first tee of the famous Old Course. Well presented throughout, it offers a choice of bars and an all-day coffee shop, and an attractive restaurant. Bedrooms are impressively furnished and come in various sizes, many quite spacious.
ROOMS: 30 en suite (1 fmly) ⊗ in 21 bedrooms s £83-£130; d £110-£172 (incl. bkfst) **LB FACILITIES:** STV Xmas **CONF:** Thtr 180 Class 60 Board 40 Del from £120 **SERVICES:** Lift **PARKING:** 10 **NOTES:** ✘ ⊗ in restaurant Civ Wed 80

★★71% ⊛ **Russell Hotel**
26 The Scores KY16 9AS
☎ 01334 473447 📠 01334 478279
e-mail: russellhotel@talk21.com
Dir: A91-St Andrews turn left at 2nd rdbt into Golf Place, turn right after 200yds into The Scores, hotel in 300yds on the left

Lying on the east bay, this friendly, family-run hotel provides well appointed bedrooms in varying sizes, some of which enjoy fine sea views. Cosy public areas include a popular bar and an
continued

intimate restaurant, both offering a good range of freshly prepared dishes.
ROOMS: 10 en suite (3 fmly) s £55-£90; d £85-£120 (incl. bkfst) **LB** **FACILITIES:** STV Xmas **NOTES:** ⊗ in restaurant Civ Wed 40

Restaurant with Rooms

The Inn at Lathones

Largoward KY9 1JE
☎ 01334 840494 01334 840694
e-mail: lathones@theinn.co.uk
web: www.theinn.co.uk
Dir: *5m S of St Andrews on A915, 0.5m before village of Largoward on left just after hidden dip*

A lovely country inn, full of character and individuality, that is 400 years old in part. The friendly staff help to create a relaxed atmosphere. Smart contemporary bedrooms are in two separate wings, both accessed from outside. The colourful, cosy restaurant is the main focus, the menu offering modern interpretations to Scottish and European dishes.
ROOMS: 13 annexe en suite (2 fmly) (11 GF) s £100-£150; d £140-£220 (incl. bkfst) **LB** **FACILITIES:** STV Xmas **CONF:** Thtr 40 Class 10 Board 20 Del from £135 **PARKING:** 35 **NOTES:** ⊗ in restaurant Closed 25-26 Dec & 3-23 Jan RS 24-Dec Civ Wed 45

ST BOSWELLS, Scottish Borders — Map 21 NT53

★★★74% Dryburgh Abbey

TD6 0RQ
☎ 01835 822261 01835 823945
e-mail: enquiries@dryburgh.co.uk
web: www.dryburgh.co.uk
Dir: *from A68 at St Boswells turn onto B6404, through village. Continue 2m, turn left B6356 Scott's View. Through Clintmains village, hotel 1.8m*

A long established hotel, this red stone baronial mansion enjoys a wonderful setting next to the Dryburgh Abbey and has fine views of the River Tweed. Comfortable and well-proportioned public areas include a choice of lounges and an elegant restaurant. Bedrooms are generally spacious and include a number of suites.
ROOMS: 37 en suite 1 annexe en suite (5 fmly) (8 GF) ⊗ in all bedrooms s £65-£155; d £130-£210 (incl. bkfst) **LB** **FACILITIES:** Fishing Putt green Xmas **CONF:** Thtr 150 Class 90 Board 70 Del from £140 **SERVICES:** Lift **PARKING:** 103 **NOTES:** ⊗ in restaurant Civ Wed 110

★★71% Buccleuch Arms

The Green TD6 0EW
☎ 01835 822243 01835 823965
e-mail: info@buccleucharmshotel.co.uk
web: www.buccleucharmshotel.co.uk
Dir: *on A68, 8m N of Jedburgh*

Formerly a coaching inn, this long-established hotel stands opposite the village green. The lounge bar is a popular eating venue and complements the attractive restaurant. Morning coffees and afternoon teas are served in the comfortable lounge with its open fire. The well-equipped bedrooms come in a variety of sizes.
ROOMS: 19 en suite (2 fmly) ⊗ in all bedrooms s £46-£50; d £77-£84 (incl. bkfst) **LB** **FACILITIES:** Xmas **CONF:** Thtr 100 Class 40 Board 30 Del from £72 **PARKING:** 50 **NOTES:** ⊗ in restaurant Closed 25-Dec Civ Wed 100

ST FILLANS, Perth & Kinross — Map 20 NN62

★★★68% The Four Seasons Hotel

Loch Earn PH6 2NF
☎ 01764 685333 01764 685444
e-mail: info@thefourseasonshotel.co.uk
web: www.thefourseasonshotel.co.uk
Dir: *on A85, towards W of village facing Loch*

Set on the edge of Loch Earn, this welcoming hotel and many of its bedrooms benefit from fine views. There is a choice of lounges, including a library, warmed by log fires during winter. Local produce is used to good effect in both the Meall Reamhar restaurant and the more informal Tarken Room.
ROOMS: 12 en suite 6 annexe en suite (7 fmly) ⊗ in 3 bedrooms s £40-£78; d £80-£126 (incl. bkfst) **LB** **FACILITIES:** ch fac Xmas **CONF:** Thtr 95 Class 45 Board 38 **PARKING:** 40 **NOTES:** ⊗ in restaurant Closed 5 Jan-end of Feb RS Nov, Dec, Mar Civ Wed 80

ST FILLANS, continued

★★72% Achray House
PH6 2NF
☎ 01764 685231 🖹 01764 685320
e-mail: info@achray-house.co.uk
Dir: *follow A85 towards Crainlarich, from Stirling follow A9 then B822 at Braco, B827 to Comrie. Turn left onto A85 to St Fillans*

A friendly holiday hotel set in gardens overlooking picturesque Loch Earn, Achray House offers smart, attractive and well-equipped bedrooms. An interesting range of freshly prepared dishes is served both in the conservatory and in the adjoining dining rooms.
ROOMS: 9 rms (8 en suite) 1 annexe en suite (2 fmly) (3 GF) ⊗ in 5 bedrooms s £60-£75; d £120-£150 (incl. bkfst & dinner) **LB** **FACILITIES:** Xmas **CONF:** Class 20 Board 20 **PARKING:** 30 **NOTES:** ⊗ in restaurant

SANQUHAR, Dumfries & Galloway — Map 21 NS70

★★67% Blackaddie House
Blackaddie Rd DG4 6JJ
☎ 01695 50270 🖹 01695 50900
e-mail: enquiries@blackaddiehotel.co.uk
Dir: *off A76 just N of Sanquhar at Burnside Service Station. Private road to hotel 300mtrs on right*
Family owned, this charming house, a former rectory, is quietly situated on the edge of the village beside the river and offers a very friendly atmosphere. As well as an inviting lounge, public areas include a cosy bar, with a real fire in the cooler months, and a conservatory restaurant giving a fine view over the neat garden to the River Nith.
ROOMS: 9 en suite (2 fmly) **PARKING:** 20 **NOTES:** ⊗ in restaurant Civ Wed 50

SCARISTA See Harris, Isle of

SCOURIE, Highland — Map 22 NC14

★★75% Scourie
IV27 4SX
☎ 01971 502396 🖹 01971 502423
e-mail: patrick@scourie-hotel.co.uk
Dir: *N'bound on A894. Hotel in village on left*
This well-established hotel is an anglers' paradise with extensive fishing rights available on a 25,000-acre estate. Public areas include a choice of comfortable lounges, a cosy bar and a smart dining room offering wholesome fare. The bedrooms are comfortable and generally spacious and the resident proprietors and their staff create a relaxed and friendly atmosphere.
ROOMS: 18 rms (17 en suite) 2 annexe en suite (2 fmly) (5 GF) ⊗ in all bedrooms s £36-£47; d £62-£82 (incl. bkfst) **LB** **FACILITIES:** no TV in bdrms Fishing Trout and Salmon fishing, Hill walking, Sea fishing **PARKING:** 30 **NOTES:** ⊗ in restaurant Closed mid Oct-end Mar Civ Wed 40

★★70% Eddrachilles
Badcall Bay IV27 4TH
☎ 01971 502080 🖹 01971 502477
e-mail: enq@eddrachilles.com
Dir: *2m S of Scourie on A894. 7m N of Kylesku Bridge*

Enjoying a peaceful location in an idyllic woodland setting beside the Badcall Bay, Eddrachilles Hotel enjoys stunning sea and island views. There are inviting lounges and a popular conservatory overlooking the bay where on occasions otters can be seen. The dining room offers careful cooking from a daily-changing menu and the well-equipped bedrooms are pleasantly decorated and furnished.
ROOMS: 11 en suite (1 fmly) (4 GF) ⊗ in all bedrooms s fr £57; d fr £84 (incl. bkfst) **FACILITIES:** Fishing Boats for hire **PARKING:** 16 **NOTES:** ✖ No children 3yrs ⊗ in restaurant Closed mid Oct-mid Mar

SHETLAND — Map 24

BRAE — Map 24 HU36

★★★69% Busta House
ZE2 9QN
☎ 01806 522506 🖹 01806 522588
e-mail: reservations@bustahouse.com
Dir: *A970 north through village, follow signs to hotel, 0.5m*
Dating back to 1724, this popular hotel boasts the reputation of being Britain's most northerly country-house hotel. Bedrooms vary in size and style but are well equipped, comfortable, and many have excellent sea views. Day rooms include the comfortable "long room" lounge; and wide-ranging menus are to be found in the Pitcairn restaurant and popular, traditional bar. The staff are friendly and keen to please.
ROOMS: 20 en suite (1 fmly) ⊗ in all bedrooms s £75; d £100-£150 (incl. bkfst) **LB** **CONF:** BC Thtr 30 Class 24 Board 24 **PARKING:** 40 **NOTES:** ⊗ in restaurant Closed 23 Dec-5 Jan Civ Wed 59

LERWICK — Map 24 HU44

★★★69% Shetland
Holmsgarth Rd ZE1 0PW
☎ 01595 695515 🖹 01595 695828
e-mail: reception@shetlandhotel.co.uk
Dir: *opposite ferry terminal, on main route N from town centre*
This purpose built hotel, situated opposite the main ferry terminal, offers spacious and comfortable bedrooms on three floors. Two dining options are available, including the informal Oasis bistro and Ninians Restaurant. Service is prompt and friendly.
ROOMS: 64 en suite (4 fmly) ⊗ in 14 bedrooms s £75; d £95 (incl. bkfst) **LB** **FACILITIES:** STV **CONF:** Thtr 300 Class 75 Board 50 **SERVICES:** Lift **PARKING:** 150 **NOTES:** ✖ Civ Wed 200

Bad hair day?
Hairdryers in all rooms three stars and above

★★★68% Lerwick
15 South Rd ZE1 0RB
☎ 01595 692166 📠 01595 694419
e-mail: reception@lerwickhotel.co.uk
web: www.shetlandhotels.com
Dir: *near town centre, on main road from airport (25m from main airport)*
Enjoying fine views across Breiwick Bay from the restaurant and some of the bedrooms, this purpose-built hotel appeals to tourists and business guests alike. Bedrooms, which vary in size and aspect, are attractively furnished and family accommodation is available. The Breiwick restaurant has fine sea views, and there is also a more informal brasserie.
ROOMS: 34 en suite (3 fmly) s fr £79; d fr £98 **LB** **FACILITIES:** STV **CONF:** BC Thtr 100 Class 40 Board 26 **PARKING:** 50 **NOTES:** 🐕 Civ Wed 100

SHIELDAIG, Highland — Map 22 NG85

Top Hotel

★ ◎◎ Tigh an Eilean
IV54 8XN
☎ 01520 755251 📠 01520 755321
e-mail: tighaneileanhotel@shieldaig.fsnet.co.uk
Dir: *off A896 onto village road signped Shieldaig, hotel in centre of village on loch front*
A superb location by the sea, with views over the bay, is the icing on the cake for this delightful small hotel. It can be a long drive to reach Sheildiag but guests remark that the journey is more than worth the effort - the genuine hospitality and excellent customer-care skills have resulted in a loyal following. Guests appreciate the superb accommodation, outstanding cooking at dinner and the polished yet intimate service. The brightly decorated bedrooms vary in size but are furnished to a high standard, though don't expect televisions.
ROOMS: 11 en suite (1 fmly) s fr £62; d fr £130 (incl. bkfst) **LB** **FACILITIES:** no TV in bdrms Bird watching, Boat available, Kayaks, Astronomy, Rock pool exploration **PARKING:** 15 **NOTES:** 🚭 in restaurant Closed late Oct-mid Mar Civ Wed 40

SKYE, ISLE OF, Highland — Map 22

ARDVASAR — Map 22 NG60

★★70% Ardvasar Hotel
Sleat IV45 8RS
☎ 01471 844223 📠 01471 844495
e-mail: richard@ardvasar-hotel.demon.co.uk
web: www.ardvasarhotel.com
Dir: *from ferry, 500mtrs & turn left*
The Isle of Skye is dotted with cosy, welcoming hotels that make touring the island easy and convenient. This hotel ranks highly

continued

amongst its peers thanks to great hospitality and a preservation of community spirit. The hotel sits less than five minutes' drive from the Mallaig ferry and provides comfortable bedrooms and a cosy bar lounge for residents. Seafood is prominent on menus, and meals can be enjoyed in either the popular bar or the attractive dining room.

ROOMS: 10 en suite (4 fmly) 🚭 in all bedrooms s £50-£80; d £80-£135 (incl. bkfst) **LB** **FACILITIES:** ♫ Xmas **CONF:** Thtr 50 Board 24 **PARKING:** 30 **NOTES:** 🚭 in restaurant

COLBOST — Map 22 NG24

Top Restaurant with Rooms

◎◎◎ Three Chimneys Restaurant & The House Over-By
IV55 8ZT
☎ 01470 511258 📠 01470 511358
e-mail: eatandstay@threechimneys.co.uk
web: www.threechimneys.co.uk
Dir: *4m W of Dunvegan village on B884 signed Glendale*
This delightful property and memorable restaurant make a trip to Skye a necessity. Shirley Spear's stunning food is the highlight of any visit. Her skilful and deft approach to cooking utilises quality local ingredients that speak for themselves. Stylish, thoughtfully equipped bedrooms in the 'House Over-By' enjoy wonderful views across Loch Dunvegan and boast spacious well appointed en suite facilities. Breakfast is an impressive event with an array of locally smoked fish and meats, local cheeses, freshly made bakery items and home-made preserves.
ROOMS: 6 en suite (1 fmly) (6 GF) 🚭 in all bedrooms d fr £240 (incl. bkfst) **LB** **FACILITIES:** STV Xmas **PARKING:** 8 **NOTES:** 🐕 🚭 in restaurant Closed 18-23 Dec, 8-27 Jan RS Sun & Nov-Mar

We have indicated only the hotels that don't accept credit or debit cards

ISLE ORNSAY Map 22 NG71

★★★74% ❀❀ ***Duisdale Country House***
IV43 8QW
☎ 01471 833202 🖷 01471 833404
e-mail: john.duisdalehotel@tiscali.co.uk
web: www.duisdale.com
Dir: *on A851 (Armadale to Broadford road), just N of village*

Warm hospitality is a real feature at this delightfully situated country house. Set in landscaped grounds a short walk from a lovely beach the location offers fine views of the Sound of Sleat and distant hills. Bedrooms come in a range of sizes and styles, all being comfortably equipped. Fresh local produce is utilised on the classically inspired menus.
ROOMS: 17 en suite (3 fmly) ⊗ in all bedrooms **FACILITIES:** STV Putt green Clay shooting **PARKING:** 20 **NOTES:** No children 6yrs ⊗ in restaurant Closed 30 Nov-28 Feb

★★76% ❀❀ ***Hotel Eilean Iarmain***
IV43 8QR
☎ 01471 833332 🖷 01471 833275
e-mail: hotel@eilean-iarmain.co.uk
Dir: *A851, A852, right to Isle Ornsay Harbour front*

THE CIRCLE
Selected Individual Hotels
GREAT BRITAIN

A hotel of charm and character, this 19th-century former inn lies by the pier and enjoys fine views across the sea lochs. Bedrooms are individual and retain a traditional style, and a stable block has been converted into four delightful suites. Public rooms are cosy and inviting, and the dining room has an attractive extension.
ROOMS: 6 en suite 10 annexe en suite (6 fmly) ⊗ in 10 bedrooms **FACILITIES:** Fishing Shooting Exibitions Whisky tasting ♫ **CONF:** Thtr 50 Class 30 Board 25 **PARKING:** 35 **NOTES:** ⊗ in restaurant

See advert on this page

⊗ No smoking

PORTREE Map 22 NG44

★★★77% ®® Cuillin Hills
IV51 9QU
☎ 01478 612003 🖷 01478 613092
e-mail: info@cuillinhills-hotel-skye.co.uk
web: www.cuillinhills-hotel-skye.co.uk
Dir: *turn right 0.25m N of Portree off A855 and follow signs for hotel*

This imposing building enjoys a superb location overlooking Portree Bay and the Cuillin Hills. Accommodation is provided in smart, well-equipped rooms that are generally spacious. Some bedrooms are found in an adjacent building. Public areas include a split-level restaurant that takes advantage of the views. Service is particularly attentive.
ROOMS: 20 en suite 7 annexe en suite (4 fmly) (8 GF) ⊗ in 13 bedrooms s £55-£75; d £110-£230 (incl. bkfst) **LB FACILITIES:** STV Xmas **CONF:** Thtr 160 Class 70 Board 40 **PARKING:** 56 **NOTES:** ⊗ in restaurant Civ Wed 70
See advert on page 749

★★★75% ®® Bosville
Bosville Ter IV51 9DG
☎ 01478 612846 🖷 01478 613434
e-mail: bosville@macleodhotels.co.uk
web: www.macleodhotels.co.uk
Dir: *A87 signed Portree, then A855 into town*
This stylish, popular hotel enjoys fine views over the harbour. Bedrooms are furnished to a high specification and have a fresh, contemporary feel. Public areas include a smart bar, bistro and the Chandlery restaurant where fantastic local produce is treated with respect and refreshing restraint.
ROOMS: 25 en suite (2 fmly) ⊗ in 10 bedrooms **FACILITIES:** Use of nearby leisure club payable Xmas **CONF:** Thtr 20 Class 20 Board 20 Del from £85 **PARKING:** 10 **NOTES:** ⊗ in restaurant Civ Wed 80
See advert on page 749

> Popped the question? Hotels with Civ wed in their entry are licensed for civil wedding ceremonies. Maximum numbers for the ceremony only are shown e.g. Civ wed 120

★★73% ® Rosedale
Beaumont Crescent IV51 9DB
☎ 01478 613131 🖷 01478 612531
e-mail: rosedalehotelsky@aol.com
web: www.rosedalehotelskye.co.uk
Dir: *follow directions to village centre & harbour. Hotel on harbour*
The atmosphere is wonderfully warm at this delightful family-run waterfront hotel. A labyrinth of stairs and corridors connects the comfortable lounges, bar and charming restaurant, which are set
continued
on different levels. The restaurant offers fine views of the bay. Modern bedrooms offer a good range of amenities.

ROOMS: 18 en suite (1 fmly) (3 GF) ⊗ in all bedrooms s £30-£50; d £60-£120 (incl. bkfst) **LB PARKING:** 2 **NOTES:** ⊗ in restaurant Closed Nov-mid Mar

SORN, East Ayrshire Map 20 NS52

Restaurant with Rooms

®® The Sorn Inn
35 Main St KA5 6HU
☎ 01290 551305 🖷 01290 553470
e-mail: craig@sorninn.com
Dir: *A70 from S or A76 from N onto B743 to Sorn*
Centrally situated in this rural village, which is convenient for many of Ayrshire's attractions, this renovated inn is now a fine dining restaurant with a cosy lounge area. There is also a popular chop house with a pub-like environment. The freshly decorated bedrooms have comfortable beds and good facilities.
ROOMS: 4 en suite (1 fmly) ⊗ in all bedrooms s £35-£50; d £70-£90 (incl. bkfst) **LB FACILITIES:** Fishing Shooting Xmas **PARKING:** 9 **NOTES:** ✈ ⊗ in restaurant

SOUTH QUEENSFERRY, City of Edinburgh Map 21 NT17

Innkeeper's Lodge South Queensferry
7 Newhalls Rd EH30 9TA
☎ 0131 331 1990 🖷 0131 331 3168
web: www.innkeeperslodge.com
Dir: *M8 follow signs for Forth Road Bridge exit at junct 2 onto M9/A8000. At rdbt take B907 follow until junction with B249. Turn right and lodge close to Forth Railway Bridge*
A growing concept in the travel accommodation market. Smart rooms meet essential business requirements but also have home comforts. Dining options include all-day menus plus the added advantage of breakfast, which is included in the room price. For further details consult the Hotel Groups page.
ROOMS: 16 en suite s £59.95; d £59.95 **CONF:** Class 18 Board 18

Premier Travel Inn (South Queensferry)
Builyeon Rd EH30 9YJ
☎ 08701 977094 🖷 0131 319 1156
web: www.premiertravelinn.com
Dir: *M8 junct 2 follow signs M9 Stirling, leave at junct 1A take A8000 towards Forth Road Bridge, at 3rd rdbt take 2nd exit into Builyeon Road, (do not go onto Forth Road Bridge)*
High quality, modern budget accommodation ideal for both families and business travellers. Spacious, en suite bedrooms feature bath and shower, satellite TV and many have telephones and modem points. The adjacent family restaurant features a wide and varied menu. For further details consult the Hotel Groups page.
ROOMS: 46 en suite s £50.95; d £50.95

SPEAN BRIDGE, Highland
Map 22 NN28

★★66% ◉ Old Pines
PH34 4EG
☎ 01397 712324 ▤ 01397 712433
e-mail: enquiries@oldpines.co.uk
Dir: 1m N of Spean Bridge on A82 next to Commando Memorial take
B8004 towards Gairlochy. Hotel 300mtrs on right
Enjoying a peaceful location just on the fringes of the village, the
Old Pines offers comfortable accommodation in a woodland
setting. Bedrooms are well appointed and well equipped. There is
a comfortable lounge and airy dining room where delicious meals
are served.
ROOMS: 8 en suite (1 fmly) (8 GF) ⊗ in all bedrooms
FACILITIES: ch fac **PARKING:** 12 **NOTES:** ⊗ in restaurant Civ Wed 30

🅰 Corriegour Lodge
Loch Lochy PH34 4EB
☎ 01397 712685 ▤ 01397 712696
e-mail: info@corriegour-lodge-hotel.com
web: www.corriegour-lodge-hotel.com
Dir: N of Fort William on A82 (south of Loch Lochy). Between Spean
Bridge & Invergarry
ROOMS: 9 en suite (3 fmly) ⊗ in all bedrooms **PARKING:** 20
NOTES: ★★★★ ✖ No children 8yrs ⊗ in restaurant Closed Dec-Jan
ex New Year RS Nov-Feb wknds only
See advert under FORT WILLIAM

STEPPS, North Lanarkshire
Map 20 NS66

★★★68% Garfield House Hotel
Cumbernauld Rd G33 6HW
☎ 0141 779 2111 ▤ 0141 779 9799
e-mail: rooms@garfieldhotel.co.uk
Dir: M8 junct 11 exit at Stepps/Queenslie, follow Stepps/A80 signs

Situated close to the A80, this considerably extended business
hotel is a popular venue for local conferences and functions.
Public areas include a welcoming reception lounge and the
popular Distillery Bar/Restaurant, an all-day eatery providing good
value meals in an informal setting. Smart, well-presented
bedrooms come in a range of sizes.
ROOMS: 45 en suite (10 fmly) (13 GF) ⊗ in 31 bedrooms s £76-£98;
d £80-£114 (incl. bkfst) **LB FACILITIES:** STV **CONF:** Thtr 100 Class 40
Board 36 Del from £120 **PARKING:** 90 **NOTES:** Closed 1-2 Jan
Civ Wed 80

Early start?
Hotels at all star levels should provide
in-room alarm clocks and/or alarm clocks

⌂ Premier Travel Inn Glasgow (Stepps)
Crowood Roundabout, Cumbernauld Rd G33 6LE
☎ 08701 977111 ▤ 0141 779 8060
web: www.premiertravelinn.com
Dir: M8 junct 13 signed M80. Exit M80 at Crowwood rdbt, take 3rd exit
signed A80 West. Inn is 1st left
High quality, modern budget accommodation ideal for both
families and business travellers. Spacious, en suite bedrooms
feature bath and shower, satellite TV and many have telephones
and modem points. The adjacent family restaurant features a wide
and varied menu. For further details consult the Hotel Groups page.
ROOMS: 80 en suite s £46.95-£48.95; d £46.95-£48.95

STIRLING, Stirling
Map 21 NS79

★★★★66% ◉ Stirling Highland
Spittal St FK8 1DU
☎ 01786 272727 ▤ 01786 272829
e-mail: stirling@paramount-hotels.co.uk
web: www.paramount-hotels.co.uk
Dir: take A84 into Stirling. Follow Stirling Castle signs as far as Albert Hall.
Left and left again, following Castle signs
Enjoying a location close to the castle and historic old town, this
atmospheric hotel was previously the High School. Public rooms
have been converted from the original classrooms and retain
many interesting features. Bedrooms are more modern in style
and comfortably equipped.
ROOMS: 96 en suite (4 fmly) ⊗ in 67 bedrooms s £85-£130;
d £115-£130 (incl. bkfst) **LB FACILITIES:** STV ▨ Squash Sauna
Solarium Gym Jacuzzi Steam room Dance Studio Beauty therapist Xmas
CONF: Thtr 100 Class 80 Board 45 Del from £135 **SERVICES:** Lift
PARKING: 96 **NOTES:** ⊗ in restaurant

⌂ Premier Travel Inn Stirling
Whins of Milton, Glasgow Rd FK7 8EX
☎ 08701 977241 ▤ 01786 816415
web: www.premiertravelinn.com
Dir: on A872, 0.25m from M9/M80 junct 9 intersection
High quality, modern budget accommodation ideal for both
families and business travellers. Spacious, en suite bedrooms
feature bath and shower, satellite TV and many have telephones
and modem points. The adjacent family restaurant features a wide
and varied menu. For further details consult the Hotel Groups page.
ROOMS: 60 en suite s £46.95-£48.95; d £46.95-£48.95

⌂ Travelodge
Pirnhall Roundabout, Snabhead FK7 8EU
☎ 08700 850 950 ▤ 01786 817646
web: www.travelodge.co.uk
Dir: junct 9, M9/M80
Travelodge offers good quality, good value, modern
accommodation. Ideal for families, the spacious, en suite
bedrooms include remote-control TV, tea and coffee-making
facilities and comfortable beds. Meals can be taken at the nearby
family restaurant. For further details consult the Hotel Groups page.
ROOMS: 37 en suite s fr £26; d fr £26

STONEHAVEN, Aberdeenshire
Map 23 NO88

★★66% County Hotel & Squash Club
Arduthie Rd AB39 2EH
☎ 01569 764386 ▤ 01569 762214
Dir: off A90, opposite railway station
This small, family-owned and operated hotel is situated close to
the railway station. Most of the traditionally decorated bedrooms
continued on p752

STONEHAVEN, continued

are spacious. It is popular for its good-value meals featuring a wide-ranging selection, served in a choice of dining rooms. The breakfast room displays a fascinating collection of theatrical photographs and posters.
ROOMS: 14 en suite (1 fmly) s £40-£46; d £55-£60 (incl. bkfst) **LB** **FACILITIES:** Squash Sauna Gym **CONF:** Thtr 150 Class 60 Board 32 **PARKING:** 40 **NOTES:** ✗

STRACHUR, Argyll & Bute — Map 20 NN00

★★★66% Creggans Inn

PA27 8BX
☎ 01369 860279 📠 01369 860637
e-mail: info@creggans-inn.co.uk
web: www.creggans-inn.co.uk
Dir: *follow A82/A83 Loch Lomond road to Arrochar. Continue on A83 then take A815 Strachur*

Benefiting from a super location on the shores of Loch Fyne, this well-established hotel is well placed for both tourists and business travellers. Many of the bedrooms have fine views and a number have high quality bathrooms. There is a choice of spacious lounges, and freshly prepared meals can be enjoyed in either the popular bar or stylish restaurant.
ROOMS: 14 en suite s £50-£90; d £100-£160 (incl. bkfst) **LB** **FACILITIES:** Fishing Xmas **CONF:** Thtr 25 Class 25 Board 25 Del from £130 **PARKING:** 50 **NOTES:** ✗ ⊗ in restaurant

STRANRAER, Dumfries & Galloway — Map 20 NX06
See also Castle Kennedy

★★★★68% North West Castle

DG9 8EH
☎ 01776 704413 📠 01776 702646
e-mail: info@northwestcastle.co.uk
web: www.northwestcastle.co.uk
Dir: *on seafront, close to Stena ferry terminal*

This long-established hotel overlooks the bay and the ferry terminal. The public areas include a classical dining room where a pianist plays during dinner and an adjoining lounge with large leather armchairs and blazing fire in season. There is a shop, leisure centre, and a curling rink that is the focus in winter. Bedrooms are comfortable and spacious.
ROOMS: 70 en suite 2 annexe en suite (22 fmly) ⊗ in 26 bedrooms s £70-£92; d £108-£152 (incl. bkfst & dinner) **LB** **FACILITIES:** STV supervised Snooker Sauna Gym Jacuzzi Curling (Oct-Apr) Games room ch fac Xmas **CONF:** Thtr 150 Class 60 Board 40 Del from £85 **SERVICES:** Lift **PARKING:** 100 **NOTES:** ⊗ in restaurant Civ Wed 130

★★★69% Corsewall Lighthouse Hotel

Corsewall Point, Kirkcolm DG9 0QG
☎ 01776 853220 📠 01776 854231
e-mail: lighthousehotel@btinternet.com
web: www.lighthousehotel.co.uk
Dir: *A718 from Stranraer to Kirkcolm (approx 8m) then follow signs to hotel for a further 4m*

Looking for something completely different? A unique hotel converted from buildings that adjoin a listed 19th-century lighthouse set on a rocky coastline. Bedrooms come in a variety of sizes, some reached by a spiral staircase, and as with the public areas, are cosy and atmospheric. Three cottage suites in the grounds offer greater space.
ROOMS: 6 en suite 3 annexe en suite (2 fmly) (5 GF) ⊗ in 6 bedrooms s £110-£250; d £130-£280 (incl. bkfst & dinner) **LB** **CONF:** Thtr 20 **PARKING:** 20 **NOTES:** ⊗ in restaurant Civ Wed 28

STRATHAVEN, South Lanarkshire — Map 20 NS74

★★★74% Strathaven

Hamilton Rd ML10 6SZ
☎ 01357 521778 📠 01357 520789
e-mail: info@strathavenhotel.com
web: www.strathavenhotel.com

Situtated in delightful gardens on the edge of town this welcoming hotel been extended with a wing of modern, stylish bedrooms, which are all well equipped. Public areas include a comfortable lounge, Lauders restaurant and a popular bar that serves a range of freshly prepared meals. Staff are friendly and keen to please.
ROOMS: 22 en suite ⊗ in 12 bedrooms s £56-£75; d £80-£100 (incl. bkfst) **LB** **FACILITIES:** STV **CONF:** Thtr 180 Class 120 Board 40 Del from £110 **PARKING:** 80 **NOTES:** ✗ ⊗ in restaurant Civ Wed 120

STRATHYRE, Stirling — Map 20 NN51

Top Hotel

★ Creagan House

FK18 8ND
☎ 01877 384638 📠 01877 384319
e-mail: eatandstay@creaganhouse.co.uk
web: www.creaganhouse.co.uk
Dir: *0.25m N of Strathyre on A84*

This delightful property dates back to the 17th century and has been sympathetically restored and upgraded to provide comfortable accommodation. Attractive bedrooms are equipped with CD players, mineral water and bathrobes, and TVs and videos are available on request. The baronial-style dining room provides a wonderful setting for imaginative

continued

cooking. Warm hospitality and attentive service are the highlight of any stay.

ROOMS: 5 en suite (1 fmly) (1 GF) ⊗ in all bedrooms s £65; d £110 (incl. bkfst) **LB** **FACILITIES:** Xmas **CONF:** Thtr 35 Class 12 Board 35 **PARKING:** 26 **NOTES:** ⊗ in restaurant Closed 22 Jan-Mar, 5-23 Nov RS 24 Nov-20 Dec

STRONTIAN, Highland Map 22 NM86

Top Hotel

★★ ◎◎ Kilcamb Lodge

PH36 4HY
☎ 01967 402257 📠 01967 402041
e-mail: enquiries@kilcamblodge.co.uk
Dir: *off A861, via Corran Ferry*

This historic house on the shores of Loch Sunart was one of the first stone buildings in the area and was used as military barracks around the time of the Jacobite uprising. Accommodation is provided in tastefully decorated rooms with high quality fabrics. Accomplished cooking, utilising much local produce, can be enjoyed in the stylish dining room. Warm hospitality is assured.

ROOMS: 12 en suite ⊗ in all bedrooms s £75-£95; d £110-£220 (incl. bkfst) **LB** **FACILITIES:** Fishing Boating Xmas **CONF:** Del £140 **PARKING:** 18 **NOTES:** No children 12yrs ⊗ in restaurant Closed 2 Jan-11 Feb Civ Wed 60

Late for dinner? Quality standards mean that last orders for dinner vary according to star rating and should be no earlier than: ★★ 7.00pm ★★★ 8:00pm ★★★★ 9:00pm ★★★★★ 10:00pm

STRUAN, Highland Map 22 NG33

U Ullinish Lodge

IV56 8FD
☎ 01470 572214 📠 01470 572341
e-mail: ullinish@theisleofskye.co.uk
web: www.theisleofskye.co.uk
Dir: *N on A863*

At the time of going to press, the star classification for this hotel was not confirmed. Please refer to the AA internet site www.theAA.com for current information.

ROOMS: 6 en suite ⊗ in all bedrooms s £90-£112; d £120-£150 **LB** **FACILITIES:** Xmas **PARKING:** 8 **NOTES:** No children 18yrs ⊗ in restaurant Closed 4-31 Jan

SWINTON, Scottish Borders Map 21 NT84

Restaurant with Rooms

◎◎ The Wheatsheaf at Swinton

Main St TD11 3JJ
☎ 01890 860257 📠 01890 860688
e-mail: reception@wheatsheaf-swinton.co.uk
Dir: *from Edinburgh turn off A697 onto B6461. From East Lothian, turn off A1 onto B6461*

Overlooking the village green, The Wheatsheaf has a country pub atmosphere. The food is the main focus however, served in a bright pine-furnished sun lounge, and when times are busy also in the cosy traditional dining room. Bedrooms are in a mix of sizes, but all are well equipped and tastefully decorated - the larger ones have luxury bathrooms.

ROOMS: 7 en suite ⊗ in all bedrooms s £65-£93; d £98-£128 (incl. bkfst) **LB** **CONF:** BC Thtr 18 Class 18 Board 12 **PARKING:** 7 **NOTES:** ⊗ in restaurant Closed 24-26 Dec RS 1 Dec-31 Jan Civ Wed 50

TAIN, Highland Map 23 NH88

★★★67% Mansfield Castle Hotel

Scotsburn Rd IV19 1PR
☎ 01862 892052 📠 01862 892260
e-mail: enquires@mansfieldcastle.co.uk
web: www.mansfieldcastle.co.uk
Dir: *A9 from S, (ignore 1st exit signed Tain) take 2nd exit signed Police Station*

Built in the 1870s, this impressive baronial-style mansion is set in pretty, landscaped grounds. The comfortably equipped bedrooms come in two distinct styles with those in the original part of the house full of character. Meals are served in both the bar and one of two stylish dining rooms.

ROOMS: 9 en suite 10 annexe en suite (3 fmly) (6 GF) ⊗ in all bedrooms s £65-£105; d £130-£190 (incl. bkfst) **LB** **FACILITIES:** STV Jacuzzi Beauty salon Xmas **CONF:** Thtr 40 Board 40 Del £110 **PARKING:** 40 **NOTES:** ⊗ in restaurant Civ Wed 45

TAIN, continued

Top Hotel

★★ ⊚⊚ ⚘ **Glenmorangie
Highland Home at Cadboll**
Cadboll, Fearn IV20 1XP
☎ 01862 871671 🖹 01862 871625
e-mail: relax@glenmorangieplc.co.uk
Dir: from A9 onto B9175 towards Nigg. Follow tourist signs
This establishment superbly balances the facilities and top class service of a nationally acclaimed hotel with the intimate customer care of an historic highland home. Evenings are dominated by the highly successful 'dinner party' where carefully selected wines and exquisite cooking combine to showcase highland hospitality and cooking at its very best. Stylish and comfortable bedrooms are divided between the traditional main house and some charming cottages in the grounds. It is an ideal base from which to enjoy world famous whisky tours.
ROOMS: 6 en suite 3 annexe en suite (4 fmly) (3 GF) ⊗ in all bedrooms s £140-£185; d £280-£370 (incl. bkfst & dinner) **LB**
FACILITIES: Fishing ⚑ Putt green Falconry, Clay pigeon shooting, Beauty treatments, Husky Sledding, Archery ♫ Xmas **CONF:** Thtr 12 Class 12 Board 12 Del from £135 **PARKING:** 20 **NOTES:** No children 14yrs ⊗ in restaurant Closed 3-31 Jan

TANGASDALE See Barra, Isle of

TARBERT LOCH FYNE, Argyll & Bute Map 20 NN30

★★★71% ⊚ **Stonefield Castle**
PA29 6YJ
☎ 01880 820836 🖹 01880 820929
e-mail: enquiries@stonefieldcastle.co.uk
Dir: off A83, 2m N of Tarbert, hotel approx 0.25m down driveway
This fine baronial castle commands a superb lochside setting amidst beautiful woodland gardens renowned for their rhododendrons - visit in late spring to see them at their best. Elegant public rooms are a feature, and the picture-window restaurant offers unrivalled views across Loch Fyne. Bedrooms are split between the main house and a purpose-built wing.
ROOMS: 33 rms (32 en suite) (10 GF) s £90-£100; d £180-£250 (incl. bkfst & dinner) **LB FACILITIES:** Fishing Snooker Xmas **CONF:** Thtr 180 Class 140 Board 40 Del £125 **SERVICES:** Lift **PARKING:** 50 **NOTES:** ⊗ in restaurant Civ Wed 120

🅄 Star rating not confirmed

TEANGUE, Highland Map 22 NG60

★★78% ⊚ **Toravaig House**
Knock Bay IV44 8RE
☎ 01471 820200 & 833231 🖹 01471 833231
e-mail: info@skyehotel.co.uk
Dir: cross Skye Bridge, turn left at Broadford onto A851, hotel 11m on left
Set in two acres and enjoying panoramic views over Sleat to the Knoydart Hills, this hotel is a haven of peace and tranquillity. Refurbishment has resulted in stylish, well-equipped and beautifully decorated bedrooms and smartly presented en suite facilities. Public areas include an inviting lounge complete with deep sofas and an elegant dining room where delicious meals are the order of the day.
ROOMS: 9 en suite ⊗ in all bedrooms s £49.50-£69.50; d £55-£65 (incl. bkfst) **LB FACILITIES:** STV Xmas **PARKING:** 20 **NOTES:** ✗ ⊗ in restaurant

THORNHILL, Dumfries & Galloway Map 21 NX89

★★75% *Trigony House*
Closeburn DG3 5EZ
☎ 01848 331211 🖹 01848 331303
e-mail: info@trigonyhotel.co.uk
web: www.trigonyhotel.co.uk
Dir: off A76 between Thornhill & Closeburn on left, clearly signed

A friendly and relaxed atmosphere prevails at this family-run, Edwardian hunting lodge, set in four acres of gardens and grounds south of the village. Bedrooms reflect the elegance and character of the house and are thoughtfully equipped. Food, which can be enjoyed either in the cosy bar or formal dining room, features fresh produce, which is organic whenever available.
ROOMS: 8 en suite **FACILITIES:** Fishing ⚑ Bicycle loan free of charge **CONF:** Thtr 30 Class 30 Board 30 **PARKING:** 20 **NOTES:** ⊗ in restaurant

THURSO, Highland Map 23 ND16
See also Halkirk

★★★60% *Royal*
Traill St KW14 8EH BRITISH TRUST
☎ 01847 893191 🖹 01847 895338 HOTELS
e-mail: royal@british-trust-hotels.com
web: www.british-trust-hotels.com
Dir: A9 to Thurso, cross Thurso Bridge at 1st lights turn right. Hotel on right
Located in the heart of the town centre this traditional hotel attracts a mixed market, being popular with both business guests and tour groups. Spacious public areas include a large bar and

continued

comfortable lounges where entertainment is a feature. High ceilinged bedrooms are generally well proportioned.

ROOMS: 102 en suite (4 fmly) **FACILITIES:** ♫ **SERVICES:** Lift
NOTES: ✈ ⊗ in restaurant

★★61% ***Ulbster Arms***
Bridge St KW12 6XY
☎ 01847 831206 & 831641 ▤ 01847 831206
e-mail: ulbster-arms@ecosse.net
(For full entry see Halkirk)

A Station Hotel & Apartments
54-58 Princes St KW14 7DH
☎ 01847 892003 ▤ 01847 891820
e-mail: stationhotel@lineone.net
web: www.stationthurso.co.uk
Dir: *from A9, in Thurso at 2nd lights turn left. Hotel at end of Sinclair St next to library (2m from ferry terminal for Orkney)*
ROOMS: 21 en suite 9 annexe en suite (8 fmly) (8 GF) ⊗ in 5 bedrooms **FACILITIES:** STV Xmas **PARKING:** 35 **NOTES:** ★★★ ⊗ in restaurant

See advert on this page

TIGHNABRUAICH, Argyll & Bute — Map 20 NR97

★★81% ⊛⊛ **The Royal at Tighnabruaich**
Shore Rd PA21 2BE
☎ 01700 811239 ▤ 01700 811300
e-mail: info@royalhotel.org.uk
web: www.royalhotel.org.uk
Dir: *from Strachur on A886 right onto A8003 to Tighnabruaich. Hotel on right at bottom of hill*
This outstanding family-run hotel continues to go from strength to strength. Set just yards from the loch shore, stunning views are guaranteed from many rooms, including the elegant restaurant and informal brasserie bar where fresh seafood and game are served. The comfortable bedrooms vary in size and style.
ROOMS: 11 en suite (1 fmly) ⊗ in all bedrooms s £60-£110; d £110 (incl. bkfst) **LB FACILITIES: Spa** sailing, fishing, windsurfing, riding, walking, bird watching Xmas **CONF:** Class 20 Board 10 **PARKING:** 20 **NOTES:** ⊗ in restaurant Closed 4 days Xmas

TOBERMORY See Mull, Isle of

Popped the question? Hotels with Civ wed in their entry are licensed for civil wedding ceremonies. Maximum numbers for the ceremony only are shown e.g. Civ wed 120

TONGUE, Highland — Map 23 NC55

★★74% ⊛ **Borgie Lodge Hotel**
Skerray KW14 7TH
☎ 01641 521332 ▤ 01641 521332
e-mail: info@borgielodgehotel.co.uk
web: www.borgielodgehotel.co.uk
Dir: *A836 between Tongue & Bettyhill, north at Borgie Bridge signed Skerray. Hotel 500yds on right*

This small outdoor-sport orientated hotel lies in a glen close to the river of the same name. Whilst fishing parties predominate, those who are not anglers are made equally welcome, and indeed the friendliness and commitment to guest care is paramount. Cosy public rooms offer a choice of lounges and an anglers' bar - they all boast welcoming log fires. The dinner menu is short but well chosen.
ROOMS: 8 rms (7 en suite) (1 GF) ⊗ in all bedrooms s £45-£65; d £80-£95 (incl. dinner) **LB FACILITIES:** Fishing Mountain bikes, Shooting, Stalking, Boating **PARKING:** 20 **NOTES:** ⊗ in restaurant

TONGUE, continued

★★72% ⊚ Ben Loyal
Main St IV27 4XE
☎ 01847 611216 📠 01847 611336
e-mail: benloyalhotel@btinternet.com
web: www.benloyal.co.uk
Dir: at junct of A838/A836. Hotel in village next to Royal Bank of Scotland
Enjoying a super location close to Ben Loyal and with views of the Kyle of Tongue, this hotel more often that not marks the welcome completion of a stunning rural drive. Bedrooms are thoughtfully equipped and brightly decorated whilst day rooms extend to a traditionally styled dining room and a cosy bar. Expertly cooked meals showcase quality local ingredients. Staff are especially friendly.
ROOMS: 11 en suite ⊗ in all bedrooms s £35; d £50-£70 (incl. bkfst)
FACILITIES: Fishing Fly fishing tuition and equipment **PARKING:** 20
NOTES: ⊗ in restaurant Closed 24 Dec-01 Mar RS Nov-Mar

TORRIDON, Highland
Map 22 NG95

Top Hotel

★★★ ⊚⊚ ♨ Loch Torridon Country House Hotel
By Achnasheen, Wester Ross IV22 2EY
☎ 01445 791242 📠 01445 712253
e-mail: stay@lochtorridonhotel.com
web: www.lochtorridonhotel.com
Dir: from A832 at Kinlochewe, take A896 towards Torridon. (Do not turn into village) continue 1m, hotel on right
Delightfully set amidst inspiring loch and mountain scenery, this elegant Victorian shooting lodge has been beautifully restored to make the most of its many original features. The attractive bedrooms are all individually furnished and most enjoy stunning Highland views. Comfortable day rooms feature fine wood panelling and roaring fires in cooler months. The whisky bar is aptly named, boasting over 300 malts and in-depth tasting notes. Outdoor activities include shooting, cycling and walking.
ROOMS: 19 en suite (2 GF) ⊗ in all bedrooms s £110-£182; d £152-£376 (incl. bkfst) **LB FACILITIES:** STV Fishing ♨ Pony trekking, Mountain biking, Archery, Clay pigeon shooting, Falconry Xmas **CONF:** Board 16 Del from £172 **SERVICES:** Lift
PARKING: 20 **NOTES:** ✗ ⊗ in restaurant Closed 3-27 Jan Civ Wed 42

TROON, South Ayrshire
Map 20 NS33

★★★★69% *Marine*
Crosbie Rd KA10 6HE
☎ 01292 314444 📠 01292 316922
e-mail: marine@paramount-hotels.co.uk
web: www.paramount-hotels.co.uk
Dir: A77 to A78, then A79 onto B749. Hotel on left after golf course
A favourite with conference and leisure guests, this hotel overlooks Royal Troon's 18th fairway. The cocktail lounge and split-level restaurant enjoy panoramic views of the Firth of Clyde across to the Isle of Arran. An impressive upgrade of bedrooms and public areas has now been completed.
ROOMS: 90 en suite (6 fmly) ⊚ in 58 bedrooms **FACILITIES:** STV ⊡ supervised Squash Sauna Solarium Gym Jacuzzi Steam room, Beauty room **CONF:** BC Thtr 220 Class 120 Board 60 **SERVICES:** Lift
PARKING: 200 **NOTES:** ⊗ in restaurant

⊕ **PARAMOUNT**
GROUP OF HOTELS

Top Hotel

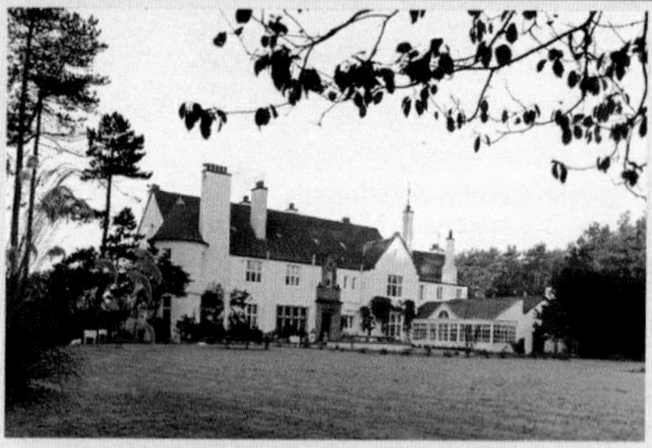

★★★ ⊚⊚⊚♨ Lochgreen House Hotel
Monktonhill Rd, Southwood KA10 7EN
☎ 01292 313343 📠 01292 318661
e-mail: lochgreen@costley-hotels.co.uk
web: www.lochgreenhouse.co.uk
Dir: from A77 follow Prestwick Airport signs. 0.5m before airport take B749 to Troon. Hotel 1m on left
Set in immaculately maintained grounds, Lochgreen House is graced by tasteful extensions which have created stunning public rooms and spacious, comfortable and elegantly furnished bedrooms. The main lounge boasts a gift boutique, and the modern brasserie is where lunch and breakfast are served. The magnificent Tapestry Restaurant provides the ideal setting for dinners that are immaculately presented.
ROOMS: 32 en suite 8 annexe en suite (18 GF) s £110; d £160 (incl. bkfst) **FACILITIES:** ⊗ Xmas **CONF:** BC Thtr 100 Class 50 Board 50 **SERVICES:** Lift **PARKING:** 50 **NOTES:** ✗ ⊗ in restaurant Civ Wed

🏠 Town House Hotel
♨ Country House Hotel
⌂ Travel Accommodation

modern luxury

your body checks in and your mind checks out

A cool summer breeze. The pure, natural light. Sand between your toes. Clear ocean views. Birds dancing overhead. Idle daydreaming. Ailsa Craig; immutable in the distance. The famous lighthouse. The 11th flag fluttering. Evening sunlight shimmering on the Spa. A lap of the pool. A drink on the terrace. Laughing, sharing the moment. Dinner by candlelight. A Heavenly Bed™. A heavenly life.

Let us reserve your stay. Call 01655 331 000. Best rates, guaranteed at westin.com/turnberry

MEMBER OF STARWOOD PREFERRED GUEST

THE WESTIN TURNBERRY RESORT
SCOTLAND

TROON, continued

★★★75% ***Piersland House***
Craigend Rd KA10 6HD
☎ 01292 314747 📠 01292 315613
e-mail: reservations@piersland.co.uk
web: www.piersland.co.uk
Dir: *just off A77 on B749 opposite Royal Troon Golf Club*
A Grade I listed building, this well presented hotel is located opposite to the famous championship golf course. Public areas retain delightful oak panelling. Bedrooms are thoughtfully equipped and include a row of 15 'cottages' each with a lounge and its own entrance, ideal for golfers. The hotel is popular both for its bar and for the good food in the restaurant.
ROOMS: 15 en suite 15 annexe en suite (15 fmly) (15 GF)
FACILITIES: STV **CONF:** Thtr 100 Class 60 Board 30 **PARKING:** 150
NOTES: ⊗ in restaurant Civ Wed 85

See advert on opposite page

TURNBERRY, South Ayrshire Map 20 NS20

Top Hotel

★★★★★ ®®
Westin Turnberry Resort
KA26 9LT
☎ 01655 331000 📠 01655 331706
e-mail: turnberry@westin.com
web: www.westin.com/turnberry
Dir: *from Glasgow take A77/M77 S towards Stranraer, 2m past Kirkoswald, follow signs for A719/Turnberry. Hotel 500mtrs on right*
This famous hotel enjoys magnificent views over to Arran, Ailsa Craig and the Mull of Kintyre. Facilities include a world-renowned golf course, the excellent Colin Montgomerie Golf Academy, a luxurious spa and a host of outdoor and country pursuits. Elegant bedrooms and suites are located in the main hotel, while adjacent lodges provide spacious, well-equipped accommodation. The Ailsa lounge, is very welcoming, and in addition to the elegant main restaurant for dining, there is a Mediterranean Terrace Brasserie and the relaxed Clubhouse.
ROOMS: 132 en suite 89 annexe en suite (9 fmly) (16 GF) ⊗ in 28 bedrooms s £175-£420; d £220-£475 (incl. bkfst) **LB**
FACILITIES: Spa STV supervised 36 Fishing Riding Snooker Sauna Gym Putt green Jacuzzi Health Spa & Leisure Club, Outdoor activity centre, Colin Montgomerie Golf Academy ♫ Xmas
CONF: BC Thtr 275 Class 145 Board 100 **SERVICES:** Lift
PARKING: 200 **NOTES:** ⊗ in restaurant Closed 12-27 Dec Civ Wed 270

See advert on page 757

★★★75% ® **Malin Court**
KA26 9PB
☎ 01655 331457 📠 01655 331072
e-mail: info@malincourt.co.uk
web: www.malincourt.co.uk
Dir: *on A74 to Ayr then take A719 to Turnberry & Maidens*

Forming part of the Malin Court Residential and Nursing Home Complex, this friendly and comfortable hotel enjoys delightful views over the Firth of Clyde and Turnberry golf courses. Standard and executive rooms are available; all are well equipped. Public areas are plentiful, with the restaurant serving high teas, dinners and light lunches.
ROOMS: 18 en suite (9 fmly) ⊗ in 9 bedrooms s £72-£82; d £104-£124 (incl. bkfst) **LB** **FACILITIES:** STV Putt green Xmas **CONF:** Thtr 200 Class 60 Board 30 **SERVICES:** Lift **PARKING:** 110 **NOTES:** ⊗ in restaurant RS Oct - Mar Civ Wed 80

UPHALL, West Lothian Map 21 NT07

★★★★68% ® **Houstoun House**
EH52 6JS
☎ 01506 853831 📠 01506 854220
e-mail: houstoun@macdonald-hotels.co.uk
web: www.macdonald-hotels.co.uk
Dir: *M8 junct 3 follow Broxburn signs, straight over rdbt then at mini-rdbt turn right towards Uphall, hotel 1m on right*
This historic 17th-century tower house lies in beautifully landscaped grounds and gardens and features a leisure club and spa, a choice of dining options, a vaulted cocktail bar and extensive conference and meeting facilities. Stylish bedrooms, some located around a courtyard, are comfortably furnished and well equipped.
ROOMS: 24 en suite 47 annexe en suite (10 GF) ⊗ in 65 bedrooms s £65-£140; d £90-£220 (incl. bkfst) **LB** **FACILITIES: Spa** STV Sauna Solarium Gym Health and beauty salon Xmas **CONF:** Thtr 400 Class 80 Board 80 Del from £140 **PARKING:** 250 **NOTES:** ⊗ in restaurant Civ Wed 200

The vast majority of establishments in this guide accept credit and debit cards. We indicate those that don't take any

If you wish to use a particular credit card or debit card please check with the hotel that they are happy to accept it

UPLAWMOOR, East Renfrewshire — Map 20 NS45

★★76% ❀❀ Uplawmoor Hotel
Neilston Rd G78 4AF
☎ 01505 850565 Fax 01505 850689
e-mail: enquiries@uplawmoor.co.uk
web: www.uplawmoor.co.uk
Dir: *M77 junct 2, A736 signed Barrhead & Irvine. Hotel 4m beyond Barrhead*

Originally an old coaching inn, this friendly hotel is set in a village off the Glasgow to Irvine road. The comfortable restaurant (with cocktail lounge adjacent) features imaginative dishes, whilst the separate lounge bar is popular for freshly prepared bar meals. The modern bedrooms are both comfortable and well equipped.
ROOMS: 14 en suite (1 fmly) ⊘ in 8 bedrooms s £39-£49; d £59-£79 (incl. bkfst) **FACILITIES:** STV **CONF:** BC Thtr 40 Class 12 Board 12 Del from £79 **PARKING:** 40 **NOTES:** ✈ ⊘ in restaurant

See advert under GLASGOW

WHITBURN, West Lothian — Map 21 NS96

★★★68% The Hilcroft
East Main St EH47 0JU
☎ 01501 740818 Fax 01501 744013
e-mail: hilcroft@bestwestern.co.uk
Dir: *M8 junct 4 follow signs for Whitburn, hotel 0.5m on left from junct*

This modern hotel features a split-level bar and restaurant offering an extensive menu throughout the day. The attractive bedrooms are well equipped, and the executive rooms are particularly spacious.
ROOMS: 32 en suite (7 fmly) (5 GF) ⊘ in 23 bedrooms s £60-£80; d £60-£95 (incl. bkfst) **LB** **FACILITIES:** STV Free use of Balbardie Sports Centre Xmas **CONF:** Thtr 200 Class 50 Board 30 Del from £75 **PARKING:** 80 **NOTES:** ✈ ⊘ in restaurant Civ Wed 180

❀ AA Rosette Award for culinary excellence

WHITEBRIDGE, Highland — Map 23 NH41

★★67% Whitebridge
IV2 6UN
☎ 01456 486226 Fax 01456 486413
e-mail: info@whitebridgehotel.co.uk
Dir: *off A9 onto B851, follow signs to Fort Augustus. Off A82 onto B862 at Fort Augustus*

Close to Loch Ness and set amid rugged mountain and moorland scenery this hotel is popular with tourists, fishermen and deerstalkers. Guests have a choice of more formal dining in the restaurant or lighter meals in the popular cosy bar. Bedrooms are thoughtfully equipped and brightly furnished.
ROOMS: 12 en suite (3 fmly) s £35-£38; d £50-£58 (incl. bkfst) **FACILITIES:** Fishing **PARKING:** 32 **NOTES:** ⊘ in restaurant Closed 11 Dec - 9 Jan

WICK, Highland — Map 23 ND35

★★70% *Mackay's*
Union St KW1 5ED
☎ 01955 602323 Fax 01955 605930
e-mail: res@mackayshotel.co.uk
Dir: *opposite Caithness General Hospital*

This well-established hotel is situated just off the town centre and overlooks the River Wick. Mackay's provides well-equipped accommodation especially suited to the business traveller. There is an attractive restaurant and a choice of bars that also offer food.
ROOMS: 27 rms (19 en suite) (4 fmly) **FACILITIES:** STV ♫ **CONF:** Thtr 100 Class 100 Board 60 **SERVICES:** Lift **NOTES:** ⊘ in restaurant Closed 1-2 Jan

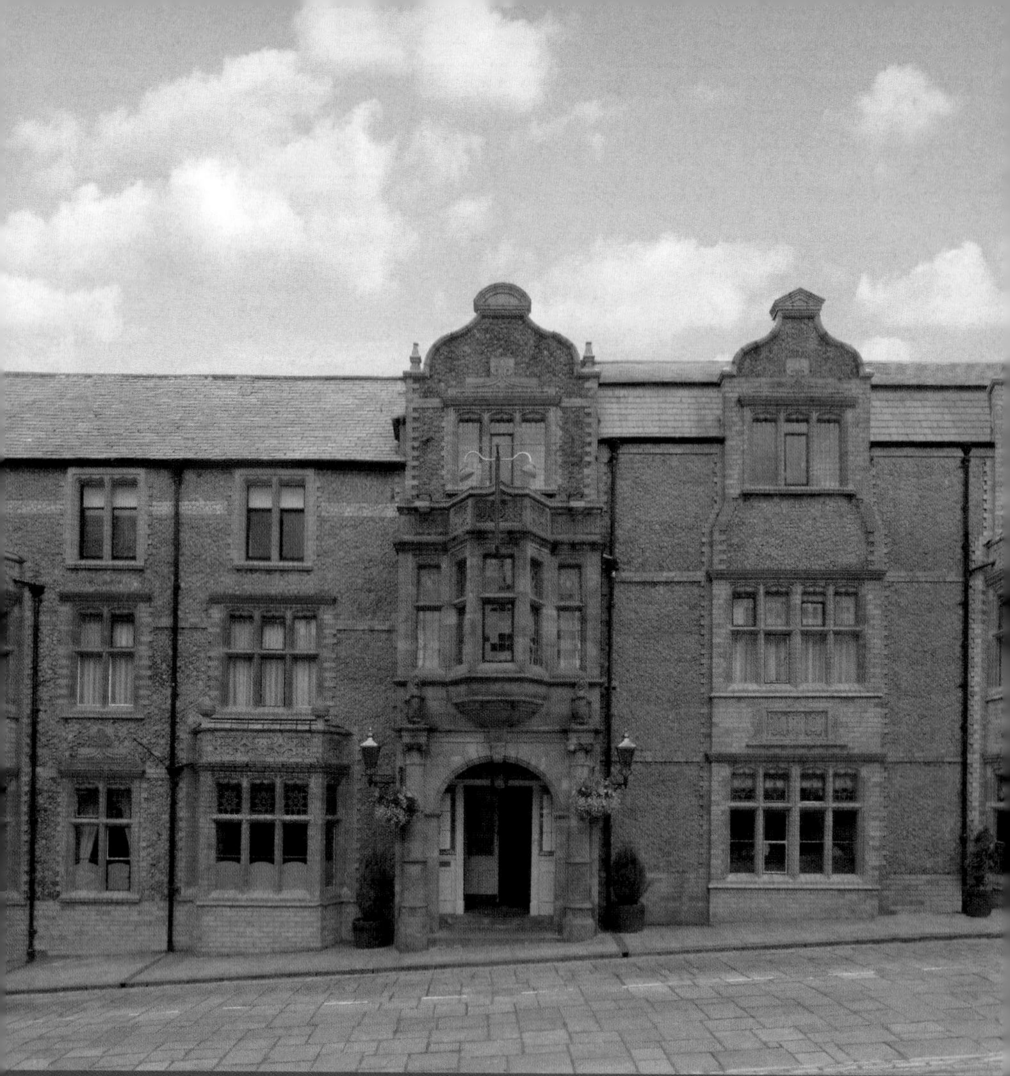

Wales

Hotel of the Year for Wales

Castle Hotel

Conwy, Conwy

★★★ ◎◎

ABERDYFI, Gwynedd Map 14 SN69

★★★75% Trefeddian

LL35 0SB
☎ 01654 767213 📠 01654 767777
e-mail: info@trefwales.com web: www.trefwales.com
Dir: *0.5m N of Aberdyfi off A493*

This large privately owned hotel in its own grounds overlooks Cardigan Bay and offers well-equipped bedrooms and bathrooms, plus some luxury rooms with balconies and sea views. Public areas include elegantly furnished lounges, a beauty salon and indoor pool. Children are welcome and recreation areas are provided. The hotel is 100-years-old, and in 2007 the Cave family will celebrate the centenary of their ownership.

ROOMS: 59 en suite (13 fmly) ⊘ in all bedrooms s £40-£80; d £80-£110 (incl. bkfst) **LB** **FACILITIES:** Snooker Solarium Putt green Table tennis, Play area, Beauty salon, internet access ch fac Xmas **SERVICES:** Lift **PARKING:** 68 **NOTES:** ⊘ in restaurant

See advert on this page

★★74% Penhelig Arms Hotel & Restaurant

LL35 0LT
☎ 01654 767215 📠 01654 767690
e-mail: info@penheligarms.com
web: www.penheligarms.com
Dir: *take A493 coastal road, hotel faces Penhelig harbour*

Situated opposite the old harbour, this delightful 18th-century hotel overlooks the Dyfi Estuary. The well-maintained bedrooms have good quality furnishings and modern facilities. Some are situated in a purpose built cliff top annexe, and a self-contained family suite is available. The public bar is much loved by locals who enjoy the real ale selections and the excellent food, with its emphasis on seafood.

ROOMS: 10 en suite 5 annexe en suite (4 fmly) ⊘ in all bedrooms s fr £49; d £78-£120 (incl. bkfst) **LB** **PARKING:** 14 **NOTES:** ⊘ in restaurant Closed 25 & 26 Dec

★★69% *Dovey Inn*

Seaview Ter LL35 0EF
☎ 01654 767332 📠 01654 767996
e-mail: info@doveyinn.com
web: www.doveyinn.com
Dir: *In village centre on A493, 9m from Machynlleth*

In the heart of Aberdyfi, this inn offers attractive rooms which are comfortable and very well equipped; most have sea views. Downstairs there are four bars where a wide range of dishes, using local produce, is available. Breakfast is served in a separate upstairs dining room.

ROOMS: 8 en suite (2 fmly) ⊘ in all bedrooms **FACILITIES:** STV Guest may use facilities at Plas Talgarth Country Club **NOTES:** ⊘ in restaurant

A

ABERGAVENNY, Monmouthshire Map 09 SO21

★★★71% ◎ Angel
15 Cross St NP7 5EN
☎ 01873 857121 🖷 01873 858059
e-mail: mail@angelhotelabergavenny.com
web: www.angelhotelabergavenny.com
Dir: *follow town centre signs from rdbt, S of Abergavenny, past rail and bus stations. Turn left by hotel*
This has long been a popular venue for both local people and visitors; the two traditional function rooms and a ballroom are in regular use. A refurbishment programme has resulted in the provision of a comfortable lounge, relaxed bar and award-winning restaurant.
ROOMS: 29 en suite (1 fmly) ⊗ in 14 bedrooms s fr £60; d £85-£120 (incl. bkfst) **LB FACILITIES:** STV ♫ Xmas **CONF:** Thtr 200 Class 120 Board 60 Del from £118 **PARKING:** 30 **NOTES:** ⊗ in restaurant Closed 25-Dec RS 24-26 Dec Civ Wed 200

★★★70% ◎◎ Llansantffraed Court
Llanvihangel Gobion NP7 9BA
☎ 01873 840678 🖷 01873 840674
e-mail: reception@llch.co.uk
web: www.llch.co.uk
Dir: *at A465/A40 Abergavenny junct take B4598 signed Usk (do not join A40). Continue towards Raglan, hotel on left in 4.5m*

In a commanding position and in its own grounds this red brick country hotel has enviable views of the Brecon Beacons. Extensive public areas include a relaxing lounge and a spacious restaurant offering imaginative and enjoyable dishes. Bedrooms are comfortably furnished and have modern facilities.
ROOMS: 21 en suite (3 fmly) ⊗ in 7 bedrooms s £80-£120; d £97-£160 (incl. bkfst) **LB FACILITIES:** STV ⚲ Fishing ⛳ Putt green Ornamental trout lake, Salmon fishing on River Usk **CONF:** BC Thtr 220 Class 120 Board 100 Del from £150 **SERVICES:** Lift **PARKING:** 250 **NOTES:** ⊗ in restaurant Civ Wed 150

★★★68% *Allt-yr-Ynys Country House Hotel*
HR2 0DU
☎ 01873 890307 🖷 01873 890539
e-mail: allthotel@compuserve.com
Dir: *take A465 N of Abergavenny. After 5m turn left at Old Pandy Inn in Pandy. After 300yds turn right, hotel on right*
Set in rolling countryside, the main house of this charming hotel dates back to 1550 and Elizabeth I is reputed to have stayed here. Most of the comfortable bedrooms are contained in separate, purpose-built buildings, located within the extensive grounds. Homely lounges, a bar with a cider mill, and an adjoining swimming pool complete the experience, together with the charming restaurant.

ROOMS: 3 en suite 18 annexe en suite (2 fmly) (18 GF) ⊗ in 6 bedrooms **FACILITIES: Spa** ⛆ Fishing Sauna Clay pigeon range **CONF:** BC Thtr 100 Class 30 Board 40 **PARKING:** 100 **NOTES:** ⊗ in restaurant Civ Wed 80

★★72% Llanwenarth
Brecon Rd NP8 1EP
☎ 01873 810550 🖷 01873 811880
e-mail: info@llanwenarthhotel.com
web: www.llanwenarthhotel.com
Dir: *A40 from Abergavenny towards Brecon. Hotel 3m past hospital on left*
Dating from the 16th century and set in magnificent scenery, this delightful hotel offers guests the chance to relax and unwind in style. Bedrooms, in a detached wing, have undergone major refurbishment and offer plenty of quality and comfort plus pleasant river views; many from their own private balcony. The airy conservatory lounge and restaurant offer a selection of carefully prepared dishes.
ROOMS: 17 en suite (3 fmly) (7 GF) ⊗ in all bedrooms s £55-£63; d £75-£85 (incl. bkfst) **FACILITIES:** Fishing & Riding Stables nearby **PARKING:** 30 **NOTES:** ✗ ⊗ in restaurant

ABERGELE, Conwy Map 14 SH97

★★★67% *Kinmel Manor*
St George's Rd LL22 9AS
☎ 01745 832014 🖷 01745 832014
e-mail: kinmelmanor@virgin.net
Dir: *exit A55 at junct 24, hotel entrance on rdbt*
Parts of this predominantly modern hotel complex date back to the 16th century and some original features are still in evidence. Set in extensive grounds, it provides well-equipped rooms and extensive leisure facilities.
ROOMS: 51 en suite (3 fmly) ⊗ in 12 bedrooms **FACILITIES: Spa** STV ⛆ Sauna Solarium Gym Steam room ch fac **CONF:** Thtr 250 Class 100 Board 100 **PARKING:** 120 **NOTES:** Civ Wed 250

ABERPORTH, Ceredigion Map 08 SN25

★★★71% Hotel Penrallt
SA43 2BS
☎ 01239 810227 & 810927 🖷 01239 811375
e-mail: info@hotelpenrallt.co.uk
Dir: *take B4333 signed Aberporth. Hotel 1m on right*
This magnificent Edwardian mansion is peacefully located in extensive grounds and offers spacious accommodation. The well-maintained public areas feature original carved ceiling beams, an impressive staircase and an eye-catching stained glass window. Guests can enjoy a relaxing atmosphere in the comfortable

continued

lounge, the popular bar and elegant restaurant. The leisure & fitness centre has a choice of swimming pools.
ROOMS: 15 en suite (2 fmly) s fr £75; d fr £110 (incl. bkfst) **LB**
FACILITIES: supervised supervised 9 Sauna Gym Putt green Jacuzzi Pool table, Golf Driving net, Table Tennis, Childrens Play Area Xmas **CONF:** Class 24 Board 20 **PARKING:** 100 **NOTES:** in restaurant Civ Wed 40

★★73% *Penbontbren Farm*
Glynarthen, Llandysul SA44 6PE
☎ 01239 810248 01239 811129
e-mail: welcome@penbontbren.com
Dir: *N on A487, 2nd right after Tan-y-Groes, signed. From south, 1st left after Salnau, signed*
Set in rolling countryside this charming hotel has been sympathetically converted from farm buildings. Bedrooms are furnished in a cottage style and are thoughtfully and extensively equipped; one is suitable for use by less able guests. There is an atmospheric restaurant, with an adjoining bar and a comfortable lounge. There is also a very pleasant garden.
ROOMS: 10 annexe en suite (6 GF) **FACILITIES:** Museum of farming ch fac **CONF:** Thtr 25 Class 25 Board 25 **PARKING:** 50 **NOTES:** in restaurant Closed Xmas

★★63% *Morlan*
SA43 2EN
☎ 01239 810611
e-mail: richardcalebs@aol.com web: www.morlanhotel.co.uk
Dir: *on B4333 2m off A487 in centre of village*
This former motel is now a small, privately owned and personally run hotel with attractively appointed accommodation. Public areas include a bar, which is popular with locals, and a games room.
ROOMS: 6 en suite (1 fmly) in all bedrooms **FACILITIES:** Jacuzzi in all bedrooms **PARKING:** 11 **NOTES:** in restaurant

ABERSOCH, Gwynedd
Map 14 SH32

★★★75% Porth Tocyn
Bwlch Tocyn LL53 7BU
☎ 01758 713303 01758 713538
e-mail: bookings@porthtocyn.fsnet.co.uk
web: www.porth-tocyn-hotel.co.uk
Dir: *2.5m S follow signs 'Porth Tocyn', after passing through hamlet of Sarnbach*

Located above Cardigan Bay with fine views over the area, Porth Tocyn is set in attractive gardens. Several elegantly furnished sitting rooms are provided and bedrooms are comfortably furnished. Children are especially welcome and have a playroom. Award-winning food is served in the restaurant.
ROOMS: 17 en suite (1 fmly) (3 GF) in all bedrooms s £62-£81; d £83-£154 (incl. bkfst) **LB** **FACILITIES:** Table Tennis **PARKING:** 50 **NOTES:** in restaurant Closed mid Nov-wk before Etr
See advert on this page

★★77% Neigwl
Lon Sarn Bach LL53 7DY
☎ 01758 712363 01758 712544
e-mail: relax@neigwl.com
web: www.neigwl.com
Dir: *on A499, through Abersoch, hotel on left*
This delightful, small hotel, now under new ownership, is conveniently located for access to the town, harbour and beach. It has a deservedly excellent reputation for its food and warm hospitality. Both the attractive restaurant and the pleasant lounge bar overlook the sea, as do several of the tastefully appointed bedrooms.
ROOMS: 9 en suite (3 fmly) (2 GF) s £95-£110; d £165-£190 (incl. bkfst & dinner) **LB** **FACILITIES:** ch fac **NOTES:** Closed January

★★66% Deucoch
LL53 7LD
☎ 01758 712680 01758 712670
e-mail: deucoch@supanet.com
web: www.deucochhotel.co.uk
Dir: *through Abersoch follow Sarn Bach signs. At x-roads in Sarn Bach (approx 1m from village centre) turn right, hotel on hill top on left*
This hotel sits in an elevated position above the village and enjoys lovely views. There is a choice of bars and food options; the regular carvery is excellent value and has a loyal following, so booking is essential. Pretty bedrooms are equipped with modern amenities and the hotel specialises in golfing packages.
ROOMS: 10 rms (9 en suite) (2 fmly) in all bedrooms s £38-£41; d £41-£44 (incl. bkfst) **LB** **FACILITIES:** Xmas **PARKING:** 30 **NOTES:** in restaurant

Entertainment

ABERYSTWYTH, Ceredigion Map 08 SN58

A

★★★75% ®® Conrah
Ffosrhydygaled, Chancery SY23 4DF
☎ 01970 617941 📠 01970 624546
e-mail: enquiries@conrah.co.uk
web: www.conrah.co.uk
Dir: *on A487, 3.5m S of Aberystwyth*

This privately owned and personally run country-house hotel stands in 22 acres of mature grounds. The elegant public rooms include a choice of comfortable lounges with welcoming open fires. Bedrooms are located in both the main house and a nearby wing and converted outbuildings. The cuisine, which is modern with international influences, achieves very high standards. Conference and leisure facilities are available.
ROOMS: 11 en suite 6 annexe en suite (1 fmly) (3 GF) s £80-£100; d £125-£155 (incl. bkfst) **LB** **FACILITIES:** Table tennis Xmas **CONF:** Thtr 40 Class 20 Board 20 Del £130 **SERVICES:** Lift **PARKING:** 50 **NOTES:** No children 5yrs ⊘ in restaurant Closed 22-30 Dec Civ Wed 50

★★★63% Belle Vue Royal
Marine Ter SY23 2BA
☎ 01970 617558 📠 01970 612190
e-mail: reception@bellevueroyalhotel.fsnet.co.uk
Dir: *on seafront, 200yds from pier*
Now under new ownership, this large hotel dates back more than 170 years and stands on the promenade which is a short walk from the shops. Family and sea-view rooms are available - all are well equipped. Public areas include extensive function rooms and a choice of bar; for dining there are bar meals or a more formal restaurant.
ROOMS: 37 rms (34 en suite) (6 fmly) (1 GF) ⊘ in 10 bedrooms s £59; d £89 (incl. bkfst) **LB** **FACILITIES:** STV Xmas **CONF:** Thtr 100 Class 30 Board 30 Del £95 **PARKING:** 14 **NOTES:** ⊘ in restaurant Civ Wed 60

> Packed in a hurry? Ironing facilities should be available at all star levels, either in the rooms or on request

★★69% Richmond
44-45 Marine Ter SY23 2BX
☎ 01970 612201 📠 01970 626706
e-mail: reservations@richmondhotel.uk.com
web: www.richmondhotel.uk.com
Dir: *on entering town follow signs for Promenade*
This privately owned and personally run, friendly hotel has good sea views from its day rooms and many of the bedrooms. The

continued

public areas and bedrooms are comfortably furnished. An attractive dining room and a comfortable lounge and bar are provided.

ROOMS: 15 en suite (6 fmly) ⊘ in all bedrooms s £55-£60; d £80-£85 (incl. bkfst) **LB** **FACILITIES:** STV **CONF:** Thtr 60 Class 22 Board 28 Del £90 **PARKING:** 22 **NOTES:** ⊘ in restaurant Closed 20 Dec-3 Jan

★★65% Marine Hotel
The Promenade SY23 2BX
☎ 01970 612444 📠 01970 617435
e-mail: marinehotel1@btconnect.com
web: www.marinehotelaberystwyth.co.uk
Dir: *from W on A44. From N or S Wales on A487. On seafront, west of pier*
The Marine is a privately owned hotel situated on the promenade overlooking Cardigan Bay. Bedrooms have been tastefully decorated, some have four-poster beds and many have sea views. The reception rooms are comfortable and relaxing, and meals are served in the elegant dining room or the bar.
ROOMS: 44 rms (43 en suite) (7 fmly) ⊘ in 1 bedroom s £45-£65; d £65-£95 (incl. bkfst) **LB** **FACILITIES: Spa** Sauna Solarium Gym Jacuzzi Xmas **CONF:** BC Thtr 220 Class 150 Board 60 Del from £75 **SERVICES:** Lift **PARKING:** 22 **NOTES:** Civ Wed 200

★★64% ® Harry's
40-46 North Pde SY23 2NF
☎ 01970 612647 📠 01970 627068
e-mail: info@harrysaberystwyth.com
Dir: *N on A487, in town centre*
Conveniently located for the shopping area and seafront, this is a friendly and popular hotel. The main attraction is the popular Harry's Restaurant, with its wide selection of dishes and specialising in local produce. Bedrooms are well equipped with modern facilities.
ROOMS: 24 en suite (2 fmly) ⊘ in 6 bedrooms s £45-£60; d £60-£80 (incl. bkfst) **CONF:** Thtr 24 Class 24 Board 40 **PARKING:** 6 **NOTES:** Closed 25-26 Dec

AMLWCH See Anglesey, Isle of

AMMANFORD, Carmarthenshire Map 08 SN61

★★69% Mill at Glynhir
Glynhir Rd, Llandybie SA18 2TE
☎ 01269 850672 📠 01269 850672
e-mail: millatglynhir@aol.com
web: www.glynhir.co.uk
Dir: *off A483 at Llandybie signed Golf Course*
This former flour mill is set peacefully on a hillside with a river at the end of the garden. There is an indoor swimming pool and a golf driving range in the extensive grounds. The bedrooms are all a good size, well equipped and most have private balconies. Public areas consist of a comfortable lounge bar and a cheerful dining room.
ROOMS: 7 en suite 3 annexe en suite s £41.50-£79; d £58-£114 (incl. bkfst) **LB** **FACILITIES: Spa** supervised 18 Fishing **PARKING:** 15 **NOTES:** No children 11yrs ⊘ in restaurant Closed 24-29 Dec

ANGLESEY, ISLE OF, Isle of Anglesey — Map 14

AMLWCH — Map 14 SH49

★★70% Lastra Farm
Penrhyd LL68 9TF
☎ 01407 830906 🖹 01407 832522
e-mail: booking@lastra-hotel.com
web: www.lastra-hotel.com
Dir: *after 'Welcome to Amlwch' sign turn left. Straight across main road, left at T-junct on to Rhosgoch Rd*
This 17th-century farmhouse offers pine-furnished, colourfully decorated bedrooms. There is also a comfortable lounge and a cosy bar. A wide range of good-value food is available either in the restaurant or Granary's Bistro. The hotel can cater for functions in a separate, purpose-built suite.
ROOMS: 5 en suite 3 annexe en suite (1 fmly) s fr £41; d fr £61 (incl. bkfst) **LB** **CONF:** Thtr 100 Class 80 Board 30 **PARKING:** 40 **NOTES:** ⊗ in restaurant Civ Wed 100

BEAUMARIS — Map 14 SH67

★★★64% The Bulkeley Hotel
Castle St LL58 8AW
☎ 01248 810415 🖹 01248 810146
e-mail: bulkeley@bestwestern.co.uk
Dir: *from M56 & M6 take A5 or A55 coast road*
A Grade I listed hotel built in 1831, the Bulkeley has fine views from many rooms. Well-equipped bedrooms are generally spacious, with pretty fabrics and wallpapers. There is a choice of bars, an all-day coffee lounge and a health club. Regular jazz evenings, a resident pianist and friendly staff create a relaxed atmosphere.
ROOMS: 43 en suite (6 fmly) ⊗ in 10 bedrooms s £77-£85; d £110-£130 (incl. bkfst) **LB** **FACILITIES: Spa** Sauna Solarium Gym Jacuzzi Hair & Beauty Salon Xmas **CONF:** Thtr 180 Class 120 Board 36 Del from £92.50 **SERVICES:** Lift **PARKING:** 30 **NOTES:** ⊗ in restaurant Civ Wed 140

★★75% ◎◎ Ye Olde Bulls Head Inn
Castle St LL58 8AP
☎ 01248 810329 🖹 01248 811294
e-mail: info@bullsheadinn.co.uk
Dir: *from Britannia road bridge follow A545, Inn in town centre*
Charles Dickens and Samuel Johnson were regular visitors to this inn which features exposed beams and antique weaponry. Richly decorated bedrooms are well equipped and there is a spacious lounge. Meetings and small functions are catered for, and food continues to attract praise in both the restaurant and brasserie.
ROOMS: 12 en suite 1 annexe en suite (2 GF) ⊗ in all bedrooms s fr £70; d fr £97 (incl. bkfst) **LB** **FACILITIES:** Leisure centre nearby **CONF:** Thtr 25 Board 16 **PARKING:** 10 **NOTES:** ✈ ⊗ in restaurant Closed 25-26 Dec & 1 Jan

★★73% ◎ Bishopsgate House
54 Castle St LL58 8BB
☎ 01248 810302 🖹 01248 810166
e-mail: hazel@johnson-ollier.freeserve.co.uk
Dir: *from Menai Bridge onto A545 to Beaumaris. Hotel on left in main street*
This immaculately maintained, privately owned and personally run small hotel dates back to 1760. It features fine examples of wood panelling and a Chinese Chippendale staircase. Thoughtfully furnished bedrooms are attractively decorated and two have four-poster beds. Quality cooking is served in the elegant restaurant and guests have a comfortable lounge and cosy bar to relax in.
ROOMS: 9 en suite s £49-£60; d £79-£92 (incl. bkfst) **LB** **PARKING:** 8 **NOTES:** ⊗ in restaurant Civ Wed 40

CEMAES BAY — Map 14 SH39

★★62% Harbour Hotel
Harbour View LL67 0NN
☎ 01407 710273 & 710977 🖹 01407 710956
e-mail: gwelforh@aol.com
Dir: *Overlooking harbour in village, take A5025 from Britannia Bridge (A55) through Benelech & Amlwch*
The Harbour Hotel has a wonderful location close to the village and overlooking Cemaes Bay. Bedrooms are comfortable and well equipped and a choice of meals are served in the bar or restaurant.
ROOMS: 17 en suite (4 fmly) s £30-£45; d £50-£60 (incl. bkfst) **LB** **FACILITIES:** STV **CONF:** Del from £45 **PARKING:** 12 **NOTES:** ⊗ in restaurant

HOLYHEAD — Map 14 SH28

★★66% Boathouse
Newry Promenade, Newry Beach LL65 1YF
☎ 01407 762094 🖹 01407 764898
e-mail: boathousehotel@supanet.com
Dir: *follow expressway into Holyhead, through yellow box, follow Marina signs. From ferry terminal right at 1st lights, right at 2nd lights, follow Marina signs. Hotel at bottom of hill*
Situated in a prominent position overlooking the harbour, this hotel makes an ideal stop for ferry travellers. Bedrooms are attractively decorated to a high standard and are well equipped. The attractive lounge bar offers a wide range of home-cooked food; there is also a separate dining room.
ROOMS: 17 en suite (1 fmly) (5 GF) ⊗ in 15 bedrooms **FACILITIES:** Painting & sketching guidance available **CONF:** BC Thtr 40 Class 30 Board 30 **PARKING:** 40 **NOTES:** ⊗ in restaurant

LLANFAIRPWLLGWYNGYLL — Map 14 SH57

★★60% Carreg Bran Country Hotel
Church Ln LL61 5YH
☎ 01248 714224 🖹 01248 716516
e-mail: info@carregbran.uk.com
web: www.carregbran.uk.com
Dir: *from Holyhead 1st junct for Llanfairpwll. Through village then 1st right before dual carriageway and bridge*
This privately owned and personally run hotel is situated close to the banks of the Menai Strait. Rooms are spacious and well equipped. The restaurant is attractive and the food is locally inspired. There is a choice of bars and a large function room, popular for weddings and business meetings.
ROOMS: 20 en suite (2 fmly) ⊗ in 5 bedrooms s fr £49; d fr £69 (incl. bkfst) **CONF:** Thtr 120 Class 60 Board 30 **PARKING:** 150 **NOTES:** ⊗ in restaurant Civ Wed 100

LLANGEFNI — Map 14 SH47

★★★76% Tre-Ysgawen Hall Country House Hotel & Spa
Capel Coch LL77 7UR
☎ 01248 750750 🖹 01248 750035
e-mail: enquiries@treysgawen-hall.co.uk
web: www.treysgawen-hall.co.uk
Dir: *From junct 6, North Wales Expressway, take B5111 from Llangefni for Amlwch/Llanerchymedd. After Rhosmeich right to Capel Coch. Hotel 1m*
Quietly located in extensive wooded grounds, this charming mansion was built in 1882 and has been extended over time. It offers a range of delightful bedrooms, with many personal touches. Public areas are elegant, spacious and comfortable. The

continued on p766

LLANGEFNI, continued

restaurant offers an interesting choice of dishes. There is a bar/bistro, a coffee shop and extensive leisure facilities.
ROOMS: 19 en suite 10 annexe en suite (2 fmly) (8 GF) ⊗ in 15 bedrooms s £99.50-£142; d £158-£220 (incl. bkfst) **LB** **FACILITIES: Spa** STV Sauna Solarium Gym Jacuzzi Steam Room, Beauty Therapy Suite, Treatment Rooms **CONF:** Thtr 200 Class 75 Board 50 Del from £150 **PARKING:** 140 **NOTES:** ⊗ in restaurant Closed 25 Dec-2 Jan Civ Wed 200

See advert on opposite page

★★★69% Bull Hotel
Bulkley Square LL77 7LR
☎ 01248 722119 📠 01248 750488
e-mail: bull@welsh-historic-inns.com
web: www.welsh-historic.inns.com
Dir: *exit A55 at Llangefni, follow town centre signs, hotel on right through one-way system*

This town centre hostelry was built in 1817 and provides well-equipped, tastefully furnished accommodation both in the main building and the annexe, including a room with a four-poster bed and a family room. Public areas offer a choice of bars, a spacious and traditional restaurant together with a comfortable, relaxing lounge.
ROOMS: 20 en suite (2 fmly) ⊗ in all bedrooms s £65-£85; d £80-£98 (incl. bkfst) **LB** **FACILITIES:** STV Xmas **CONF:** Thtr 60 Class 40 Board 30 **PARKING:** 18 **NOTES:** ⊗ in restaurant

MENAI BRIDGE
Map 14 SH57

★★67% Anglesey Arms
LL59 5EA
☎ 01248 712305 📠 01248 712076
e-mail: bookings@theangleseyarmshotel.co.uk
Dir: *1st slip road off Britannia Bridge, follow signs to Menai Bridge. Hotel on rdbt at end of Menai Bridge*
This popular hotel sits next to the Menai suspension bridge in well-maintained gardens. The hotel provides smart, well equipped accommodation. Bedrooms are attractively furnished in pine and have many thoughtful extras. There is a choice of bars and an excellent selection of meals.
ROOMS: 16 en suite (2 fmly) s £40; d £40 **FACILITIES:** Xmas **CONF:** Thtr 60 Class 40 Board 40 **PARKING:** 60 **NOTES:** ⊗ in restaurant Civ Wed 60

★★65% Victoria Hotel
Telford Rd LL59 5DR
☎ 01248 712309 📠 01248 716774
e-mail: vicmenai@barbox.net
Dir: *over Menai Bridge, take 2nd exit from rdbt continue 100yds, hotel on right*
This family-run hotel has panoramic views of the Menai Straits and Britannia Bridge. Many bedrooms have their own balconies. There are two character bars where meals are available, and also a more formal conservatory dining room. The hotel holds a civil wedding licence.
ROOMS: 14 en suite 3 annexe en suite (4 fmly) (1 GF) s £45; d £55 (incl. bkfst) **FACILITIES:** Childrens playground **CONF:** Thtr 80 Class 80 Board 50 **PARKING:** 40 **NOTES:** ⊗ in restaurant RS 25-Dec Civ Wed 85

TREARDDUR BAY
Map 14 SH27

★★★73% Trearddur Bay
LL65 2UN
☎ 01407 860301 📠 01407 861181
e-mail: enquiries@trearddurbayhotel.co.uk
Dir: *from A5 towards Holyhead left at lights in Valley onto B4545 towards Trearddur Bay, (Power garage on right), left opp garage, hotel on right*
Facilities at this fine modern hotel include extensive function and conference rooms, an indoor swimming pool and a games room. Bedrooms are well equipped, many have sea views, and suites are available. An all-day bar serves a wide range of snacks and lighter meals, supplemented by a cocktail bar and the more formal hotel restaurant.
ROOMS: 34 en suite 6 annexe en suite (7 fmly) ⊗ in 15 bedrooms s £85-£105; d £128-£150 (incl. bkfst) **LB** **FACILITIES:** STV Sailing, Shooting, Horse riding, Fishing, Diving, Golf packages ♫ Xmas **CONF:** Thtr 190 Class 100 Board 78 Del from £115 **PARKING:** 200 **NOTES:** ⊗ in restaurant

BALA, Gwynedd
Map 14 SH93

★★★79% Palé Hall Country House
Palé Estate, Llandderfel LL23 7PS
☎ 01678 530285 📠 01678 530220
e-mail: enquiries@palehall.co.uk
web: www.palehall.co.uk
Dir: *off B4401 (Corwen/Bala road) 4m from Llandrillo*
This enchanting mansion was built in 1870 and overlooks extensive grounds and beautiful woodland scenery. The fine entrance hall, with its stained glass lantern ceiling and galleried oak staircase, leads off to the library bar, two elegant lounges and the smart dining room. The standard of cooking remains high and is complemented by fine wines. The spacious bedrooms are furnished to the highest standards with many thoughtful extras.
ROOMS: 17 en suite (1 fmly) ⊗ in all bedrooms s £80-£140; d £105-£200 (incl. bkfst) **LB** **FACILITIES:** Fishing Clay pigeon/Game shooting Xmas **CONF:** Board 22 Del from £145 **PARKING:** 40 **NOTES:** No children ⊗ in restaurant

See advert on opposite page

★★65% Plas Coch
High St LL23 7AB
☎ 01678 520309 📠 01678 521135
e-mail: plascoch@tiscali.co.uk
Dir: *on A494, in town centre*
A focal point in a bustling town, this 18th-century former coaching inn is popular with locals and resident guests alike. The public areas are very attractive and bedrooms are spacious.
ROOMS: 10 en suite (4 fmly) ⊗ in all bedrooms s £39-£49; d £69 (incl. bkfst) **LB** **FACILITIES:** Windsurfing, Canoeing, Sailing, Whitewater Rafting, ch fac **CONF:** Thtr 30 Class 20 Board 20 **PARKING:** 12 **NOTES:**

Destination dining!
This symbol indicates a Restaurant with Rooms

BANGOR, Gwynedd Map 14 SH57

★★70% Garden Hotel

1 High St LL57 1DQ
☎ 01248 362189 📠 01248 371328
e-mail: reception@gardenhotelbangor.co.uk
web: www.gardenhotel.co.uk
Dir: *before rail station take 1st left, past Plaza cinema, car park on right*
This city hotel is located close to the university, hospital and railway station and makes a good base for touring Snowdonia and North Wales. The modern bedrooms are spacious and very well equipped, and the hotel also has a renowned Cantonese restaurant. A function suite is also available.
ROOMS: 11 rms (10 en suite) (1 fmly) 🚭 in all bedrooms s £40-£45; d £70-£80 (incl. bkfst) **FACILITIES:** STV Xmas **PARKING:** 6 **NOTES:** (no dogs) No children 10yrs

⌂ Premier Travel Inn Bangor

Menai Business Park LL57 4FA
☎ 08701 977023 📠 01248 679214
web: www.premiertravelinn.com
Dir: *From A55 take 3rd Bangor turn off signed Caernarfon A487, Bangor & hospital. Take 3rd exit at 1st rdbt*
High quality, modern budget accommodation ideal for both families and business travellers. Spacious, en suite bedrooms feature bath and shower, satellite TV and many have telephones and modem points. The adjacent family restaurant features a wide and varied menu. For further details consult the Hotel Groups page.
ROOMS: 40 en suite s £48.95; d £48.95

⌂ Travelodge

Llys-y-Gwynt LL57 4BG
☎ 08700 850 950 📠 0870 1911561
web: www.travelodge.co.uk
Dir: *at junct of A5/A55*
Travelodge offers good quality, good value, modern accommodation. Ideal for families, the spacious, en suite bedrooms include remote-control TV, tea and coffee-making facilities and comfortable beds. Meals can be taken at the nearby family restaurant. For further details consult the Hotel Groups page.
ROOMS: 62 en suite s fr £26; d fr £26

BARMOUTH, Gwynedd Map 14 SH61

★★★70% 🏵 Bae Abermaw

Panorama Hill LL42 1DQ
☎ 01341 280550 📠 01341 280346
e-mail: enquiries@baeabermaw.com
web: www.baeabermaw.com

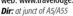

In an idyllic spot on a hillside, with striking panoramic views of the Mawddach Estuary this Victorian house has been lovingly restored to a stylish contemporary hotel. Bedrooms are spacious and well

continued on p768

BARMOUTH, continued

equipped. Popular, award-winning cuisine, based on lots of local produce, should not to be missed.
ROOMS: 14 en suite (4 fmly) ⊗ in all bedrooms **FACILITIES:** Xmas **CONF:** Thtr 100 Class 40 Board 40 Del from £160 **PARKING:** 40 **NOTES:** ✱ ⊗ in restaurant RS Mon-No Restaurant Civ Wed 100

★★71% *Wavecrest Hotel*
8 Marine Pde LL42 1NA
☎ 01341 280330 🖹 01341 280330
e-mail: thewavecrest@talk21.com
web: www.lokalink.co.uk/wavecrest.htm
Dir: *left over level-crossing, then immediately right onto Marine Parade*
There are superb views over Cardigan Bay towards the Cader Idris Mountains from many of the attractive rooms at this delightful hotel on the promenade. There is an open-plan bar and restaurant serving excellent cuisine using local and organic produce, complemented by an impressive wine list and extensive collection of malt whiskies.
ROOMS: 9 en suite (3 fmly) ⊗ in all bedrooms **NOTES:** ⊗ in restaurant Closed Nov-Mar

BARRY, Vale of Glamorgan — Map 09 ST16

★★★74% ◎ Egerton Grey Country House
Porthkerry CF62 3BZ
☎ 01446 711666 🖹 01446 711690
e-mail: info@egertongrey.co.uk
web: www.egertongrey.co.uk
Dir: *M4 junct 33 follow signs for airport, left at rdbt for Porthkerry, after 500yds turn left down lane between thatched cottages*
This former rectory enjoys a peaceful setting and views over delightful countryside with distant glimpses of the sea. The non-smoking bedrooms are spacious and individually furnished. Public areas offer charm and elegance, and include an airy lounge and restaurant, which has been sympathetically converted from the billiards room.
ROOMS: 10 en suite (4 fmly) s £85-£110; d £110-£140 (incl. bkfst) **LB FACILITIES:** Putt green 9 hole golf course 200 yds away. Xmas **CONF:** BC Thtr 30 Class 30 Board 22 Del from £140 **PARKING:** 41 **NOTES:** ⊗ in restaurant Civ Wed 40

★★★69% *Mount Sorrel*
Porthkerry Rd CF62 7XY
☎ 01446 740069 🖹 01446 746600
e-mail: reservations@mountsorrel.co.uk
Dir: *M4 junct 33 onto A4232. Follow signs for A4050 through Barry. At mini-rdbt (with church opposite) turn left, hotel 300mtrs on left*
Situated in an elevated position above the town centre, this extended Victorian property is ideally placed for exploring the nearby coast and Cardiff, and offers comfortable accommodation. The public areas include a choice of conference rooms, a restaurant and a bar, together with leisure facilities.
ROOMS: 42 en suite (3 fmly) (5 GF) ⊗ in 8 bedrooms **FACILITIES:** STV supervised Sauna Gym **CONF:** Thtr 150 Class 100 Board 50 **PARKING:** 17 **NOTES:** ⊗ in restaurant Civ Wed 150

○ *Innkeeper's Lodge Barry*
Port Rd West CF62 3BA
☎ 01446 700075
web: www.innkeeperslodge.com
Dir: *from M4 junct 33 follow signs from airport*
At the time of going to press this lodge was due to open in September 2005.
ROOMS: 14 en suite **FACILITIES:** Childrens play area ♫

BEAUMARIS See Anglesey, Isle of

BEDDGELERT, Gwynedd — Map 14 SH54

★★★70% The Royal Goat
LL55 4YE
☎ 01766 890224 🖹 01766 890422
e-mail: info@royalgoathotel.co.uk
web: www.royalgoathotel.co.uk
Dir: *On A498 at Beddgelert*
An impressive building steeped in history, the Royal Goat provides well-equipped accommodation. Attractively appointed, comfortable public areas include a choice of bars and restaurants, a residents' lounge and function rooms.
ROOMS: 32 en suite (4 fmly) ⊗ in 20 bedrooms s £53; d £90 (incl. bkfst) **LB FACILITIES:** Fishing Xmas **CONF:** Thtr 70 Class 70 Board 30 **SERVICES:** Lift **PARKING:** 100 **NOTES:** ⊗ in restaurant Closed Jan-1 Mar RS Nov-1 Jan

★★72% *Tanronnen Inn*
LL55 4YB
☎ 01766 890347 🖹 01766 890606
Dir: *in village centre*
This delightful small hotel offers comfortable, well equipped and attractively appointed accommodation, including a family room. There is also a selection of pleasant and relaxing public areas. The wide range of bar food is popular with tourists, and more formal meals are served in the restaurant.
ROOMS: 7 en suite (3 fmly) ⊗ in all bedrooms **FACILITIES:** STV **PARKING:** 15 **NOTES:** ✱

BETWS-Y-COED, Conwy — Map 14 SH75
See also Llanrwst

★★★71% ◎ Royal Oak
Holyhead Rd LL24 0AY
☎ 01690 710219 🖹 01690 710603
e-mail: royaloakmail@btopenworld.com
web: www.royaloakhotel.net
Dir: *on A5 in town centre, next to St Mary's church*

Centrally situated in the village, this fine, privately owned hotel started life as a coaching inn and now provides smart bedrooms and a wide range of public areas. The choice of eating options includes the Grill Bistro, the Stables Bar which is much frequented by locals and the more formal Llugwy Restaurant.
ROOMS: 27 en suite (3 fmly) ⊗ in 6 bedrooms s £60-£70; d £80 (incl. bkfst) **LB FACILITIES:** STV ♫ **CONF:** BC Thtr 20 Class 20 Board 20 Del from £75 **PARKING:** 90 **NOTES:** ✱ ⊗ in restaurant Closed 25-26 Dec Civ Wed 35

See advert on opposite page

★★★70% Craig-y-Dderwen Riverside Hotel

LL24 0AS
☎ 01690 710293 📠 01690 710362
e-mail: craig-y-dderwen@betws-y-coed.co.uk
web: www.snowdonia-hotel.com
Dir: *A5 to town, cross Waterloo Bridge and take 1st left*

This Victorian country-house hotel is set in well-maintained grounds alongside the River Conwy, at the end of a tree-lined drive. Very pleasant views can be enjoyed from many rooms, and two of the bedrooms have four-poster beds. There are comfortable lounges and the atmosphere is tranquil and relaxing.
ROOMS: 16 en suite (2 fmly) (1 GF) s £70-£110; d £80-£120 (incl. bkfst) **LB FACILITIES:** STV Jacuzzi Badminton, Volleyball
CONF: Thtr 50 Class 25 Board 20 Del from £118 **PARKING:** 50
NOTES: ⊗ in restaurant Closed 23-26 Dec & 30 Dec-1 Feb

★★★68% Best Western Waterloo

LL24 0AR
☎ 01690 710411 📠 01690 710666
e-mail: reservations@waterloo-hotel.info
web: www.waterloo-hotel.info
Dir: *A5, near Waterloo Bridge*

This long-established hotel, named after the nearby Waterloo Bridge, is ideally located for Snowdonia. Accommodation is split between rooms in the main hotel and modern, cottage-style rooms located in buildings to the rear. The attractive Garden Room Restaurant serves traditional Welsh specialities, and the Wellington Bar offers light meals and snacks.
ROOMS: 10 en suite 30 annexe en suite (2 fmly) (30 GF) ⊗ in 20 bedrooms s £60-£75; d £100-£120 (incl. bkfst) **LB FACILITIES:** supervised Sauna Solarium Gym Jacuzzi Steam room Xmas
CONF: Thtr 50 Class 18 Board 18 Del from £85 **PARKING:** 100
NOTES: ⊗ in restaurant Closed 25-26 Dec

Popped the question? Hotels with Civ wed in their entry are licensed for civil wedding ceremonies. Maximum numbers for the ceremony only are shown e.g. Civ wed 120

Top Hotel

★★ Tan-y-Foel Country House

Capel Garmon LL26 0RE
☎ 01690 710507 📠 01690 710681
e-mail: enquiries@tyfhotel.co.uk
web: www.tyfhotel.co.uk
Dir: *exit A5 at Betws-y-Coed onto A470, then 2m N at Capel Garmon sign on right, turn towards Capel Garmon, 1.5m, hotel sign on left*

In an idyllic hillside location with stunning views of Conwy Valley, this stylish, sophisticated hotel is a good choice for those seeking a modern, eclectic hotel. The traditional exterior reflects the hotel's 16th-century origins, while inside the design and furnishings are cutting edge. Dinner, using local organic produce whenever possible, is a highlight of any stay. Individually furnished bedrooms, which include an imaginatively converted hayloft, are designed for comfort and relaxation.
ROOMS: 4 en suite 2 annexe en suite (1 GF) ⊗ in all bedrooms s £99-£120; d £141-£155 (incl. bkfst) **LB PARKING:** 16 **NOTES:** No children 7yrs ⊗ in restaurant Closed Dec RS Jan

B

BETWS-Y-COED, continued

★★69% Park Hill
Llanrwst Rd LL24 0HD
☎ 01690 710540 📠 01690 710540
e-mail: welcome@park-hill-hotel.co.uk
web: www.park-hill-hotel.co.uk
Dir: *0.5m N of Betws-y-Coed on A470 Llanrwst road*
This friendly hotel benefits from a peaceful location overlooking the village. Comfortable bedrooms come in a wide range of sizes and are well equipped. A room with a four-poster bed and family rooms are available. There is a choice of lounges, a heated swimming pool, sauna and whirlpool bath available to residents.
ROOMS: 9 en suite s £49-£84; d £56-£84 (incl. bkfst) **LB**
FACILITIES: Sauna Jacuzzi Xmas **PARKING:** 11 **NOTES:** No children 6yrs in restaurant

★★68% Fairy Glen
LL24 0SH
☎ 01690 710269
e-mail: fairyglen@youe.fsworld.co.uk
web: www.fairyglenhotel.co.uk
Dir: *A5 onto A470 S'bound (Dolwyddelan road). Hotel 0.5m on left by Beaver Bridge*
This privately owned and personally run former coaching inn is over 300 years old. It is located near the Fairy Glen beauty spot, south of Betws-y-Coed. The modern accommodation is well equipped and service is willing, friendly and attentive. Facilities include a cosy bar and a separate comfortable lounge.
ROOMS: 8 rms (6 en suite) (1 fmly) in all bedrooms s fr £26; d fr £52 (incl. bkfst) **LB** **PARKING:** 10 **NOTES:** in restaurant Closed Nov-Jan RS Feb

BLACKWOOD, Caerphilly — Map 09 ST19

★★★68% *Maes Manor*
NP12 0AG
☎ 01495 220011 📠 01495 228217
e-mail: maesmanor@lineone.net
Dir: *A4048 to Tredega. At Pontllanfraith left at rdbt, through Blackwood High St. After 1.25m left at Rack Inn. Hotel 400yds on left*

Standing high above the town, this 19th-century manor house is set in nine acres of gardens and woodland. Bedrooms are attractively decorated with co-ordinated furnishings. As well as the popular restaurant, public rooms include a choice of bars, a lounge/lobby area and a large function room.
ROOMS: 8 en suite 14 annexe en suite (6 fmly) **CONF:** Thtr 200 Class 200 **PARKING:** 100 **NOTES:** in restaurant Closed 24-25 Dec Civ Wed 200

See advert on opposite page

BRECON, Powys — Map 09 SO02

★★★75% Nant Ddu Lodge, Bistro & Spa
Cwm Taf, Nant Ddu CF48 2HY
☎ 01685 379111 📠 01685 377088
e-mail: enquiries@nant-ddu-lodge.co.uk
web: www.nant-ddu-lodge.co.uk
(For full entry see Nant-Ddu and advert on opposite page)

★★★73% Peterstone Court
Llanhamlach LD3 7YB
☎ 01874 665387 📠 01874 665376
e-mail: info@peterstone-court.com
web: www.peterstone-court.com
Dir: *from Brecon take A40 towards Abergavenny, hotel in approx 4m, on right*

This establishment provides stunning views, standing on the edge of the Brecon Beacons and overlooking the River Usk. The style is friendly and informal, without any unnecessary fuss. No two bedrooms are alike, but all share comparable levels of comfort, quality and elegance. Public areas reflect similar standards, eclectically styled with a blend of contemporary and traditional. Quality produce is cooked with care in simple and successful dishes in the Bistro restaurant.
ROOMS: 8 en suite 4 annexe en suite (4 fmly) in 4 bedrooms
FACILITIES: Sauna Gym Jacuzzi **CONF:** Thtr 150 Class 150 Board 100 Del from £110 **PARKING:** 50 **NOTES:** in restaurant Civ Wed 100

★★70% Lansdowne Hotel & Restaurant
The Watton LD3 7EG
☎ 01874 623321 📠 01874 610438
e-mail: reception@lansdownehotel.co.uk
Dir: *off A40/A470 onto B4601*
Now a privately owned and personally run hotel, this Georgian house is conveniently located close to the town centre. The accommodation is well equipped and includes family rooms and a bedroom on ground floor level. There is a comfortable lounge and an attractive split level dining room containing a bar.
ROOMS: 9 en suite (2 fmly) (1 GF) s £38; d £55 (incl. bkfst) **LB**
NOTES: No children 5yrs in restaurant

★★67% The Castle of Brecon
Castle Square LD3 9DB
☎ 01874 624611 📠 01874 623737
e-mail: hotel@breconcastle.co.uk
web: www.breconcastle.co.uk
Dir: *A40 to Brecon, follow town centre for 2kms, left at traffic lights, right towards Cradoc, right into Castle Square*
This former coaching inn occupies an elevated position overlooking the town and River Usk. This view is shared by the restaurant and some of the bedrooms, whilst the remaining public

continued

areas are roomy and relaxed. Function and meeting rooms are available and incorporate one of the castle walls.
ROOMS: 30 en suite 12 annexe en suite (8 fmly) (2 GF) ⊗ in 12 bedrooms s £59-£89; d £69-£99 (incl. bkfst) **LB** **FACILITIES:** STV Xmas **CONF:** Thtr 160 Class 60 Board 80 Del from £90 **PARKING:** 30 **NOTES:** ⊗ in restaurant Civ Wed 120

BRIDGEND, Bridgend
Map 09 SS97

See also Porthcawl

★★★★68% Coed-y-Mwstwr
Coychurch CF35 6AF
☎ 01656 860621 🖷 01656 863122
e-mail: hotel@coed-y-mwstwr.com
web: www.coed-y-mwstwr.com
Dir: *exit A473 at Coychurch, right at petrol station. Follow signs at top of hill*
This former Victorian mansion, set in 17 acres of grounds, is an inviting retreat. Public areas are full of character featuring an impressive contemporary restaurant. Bedrooms have individual styles with a good range of extras, and include two full suites. Facilities include a large and attractive function suite with syndicate rooms, gym and outdoor swimming pool.
ROOMS: 28 en suite (2 fmly) ⊗ in 20 bedrooms s £101-£141; d £145-£175 (incl. bkfst) **LB** **FACILITIES:** STV Sauna Solarium Gym Xmas **CONF:** Thtr 180 Class 120 Board 50 **SERVICES:** Lift **PARKING:** 100 **NOTES:** ⊗ in restaurant Civ Wed 150

★★★76% *The Great House Restaurant & Hotel*
Laleston CF32 0HP
☎ 01656 657644 🖷 01656 668892
e-mail: enquiries@great-house-laleston.co.uk
web: www.great-house-laleston.co.uk
Dir: *on A473, 400yds from junct with A48*
A delightful Grade II listed building, dating back to 1550. Traditional features throughout the house add plenty of character. Leicester's restaurant offers a wide range of freshly prepared dishes; lighter snacks can be taken in the more informal bistro. The stylish, well-equipped bedrooms are located in the original building and a separate wing.
ROOMS: 8 en suite 8 annexe en suite (8 GF) ⊗ in 4 bedrooms **FACILITIES:** STV Sauna Gym Jacuzzi Health suite with sauna ch fac **CONF:** Thtr 40 Class 25 Board 20 **PARKING:** 40 **NOTES:** ⊗ in restaurant Closed 25 Dec-2 Jan Civ Wed 50

★★★69% Heronston
Ewenny Rd CF35 5AW
☎ 01656 668811 666087 🖷 01656 767391
e-mail: reservations@heronston-hotel.demon.co.uk
Dir: *M4 junct 35, follow signs for Porthcawl, at 4th rdbt turn left towards Ogmore-by-Sea (B4265) hotel 200yds on left*

Situated within easy reach of the town centre and the M4, this

continued on p772

BRIDGEND, continued

large modern hotel offers spacious well-equipped accommodation, including no-smoking bedrooms and ground floor rooms. Public areas include an open plan lounge/bar, attractive restaurant and a smart leisure & fitness club. The hotel also has a choice of function/conference rooms.
ROOMS: 69 en suite 6 annexe en suite (4 fmly) (37 GF) ⊗ in 21 bedrooms **FACILITIES:** STV supervised supervised Sauna Solarium Gym Jacuzzi Steamroom Xmas **CONF:** Thtr 250 Class 80 Board 60 Del from £90 **SERVICES:** Lift **PARKING:** 250 **NOTES:** ⊗ in restaurant Civ Wed 150

BUILTH WELLS, Powys — Map 09 SO05

★★★70% *Caer Beris Manor*

LD2 3NP
☎ 01982 552601 01982 552586
e-mail: caerberismanor@btinternet.com
web: www.caerberis.co.uk
Dir: *from town centre follow A483/Llandovery signs. Hotel on left*

THE INDEPENDENTS

With extensive landscaped grounds, guests can expect a relaxing stay at this friendly and privately owned hotel. Bedrooms are individually decorated and furnished, and retain an atmosphere of a bygone era. A spacious and comfortable lounge and a lounge bar enhance this together with the elegant restaurant, complete with 16th-century panelling.
ROOMS: 23 en suite (1 fmly) (3 GF) **FACILITIES:** STV Fishing Riding Sauna Gym Clay pigeon shooting ch fac **CONF:** BC Thtr 100 Class 75 Board 50 **PARKING:** 32 **NOTES:** ⊗ in restaurant Civ Wed 100

Restaurant with Rooms

Drawing Room

Cwmbach, Newbridge-On-Wye LD2 3RT
☎ 01982 552493
e-mail: post@the-drawing-room.co.uk
Dir: *A470 towards Rhayader, approx 3m hotel on left*

This delightful Georgian country house has been extensively and tastefully renovated by the present owners and now provides three comfortable and very well equipped bedrooms, all with luxurious en suite facilities. Public rooms include two comfortable lounges with welcoming log fires, a room for private dining and a very elegant and intimate dining room, which provides the ideal setting for enjoying the high quality cuisine.
ROOMS: 3 en suite ⊗ in all bedrooms s £85; d £120-£150 (incl. bkfst) **PARKING:** 14 **NOTES:** No children 12yrs ⊗ in restaurant Closed Sun & Mon, 2 wks in Jan & end of summer

Pencerrig Gardens

Llandrindod Wells Rd LD2 3TF
☎ 01982 553226 01982 552347
e-mail: invoices@pencerrig.co.uk
web: www.pencerrig.co.uk
Dir: *2m N on A483 towards Llandrindod Wells*

ROOMS: 10 en suite 10 annexe en suite (4 fmly) (5 GF) s £45-£60; d £70 (incl. bkfst) **LB** **FACILITIES:** ch fac **CONF:** Thtr 60 Class 30 Board 35 Del from £67.50 **PARKING:** 50 **NOTES:** ★★ ⊗ in restaurant

Late for dinner? Quality standards mean that last orders for dinner vary according to star rating and should be no earlier than:
★★ 7.00pm ★★★ 8:00pm ★★★★ 9:00pm
★★★★★ 10:00pm

CAERNARFON, Gwynedd — Map 14 SH46

Top Hotel

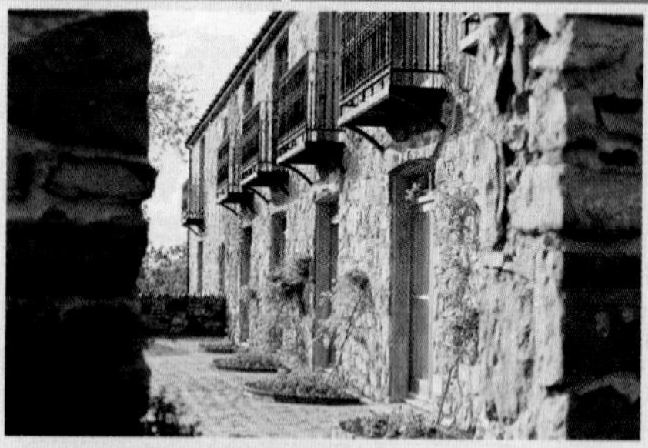

★★★ Seiont Manor

Llanrug LL55 2AQ
☎ 01286 673366 01286 672840
e-mail: seiontmanor-cro@handpicked.co.uk
web: www.handpicked.co.uk
Dir: *E on A4086, 2.5m from Caernarfon*

HandPICKED HOTELS

A splendid hotel created from authentic rural buildings, set in the tranquil countryside near Snowdonia. Bedrooms are individually decorated and well equipped, with luxurious extra touches. Public rooms are cosy and comfortable and furnished in country-house style. The kitchen team use the best of local produce to provide exciting takes on traditional dishes.
ROOMS: 28 en suite (2 fmly) (14 GF) ⊗ in 15 bedrooms s £90-£170; d £120-£200 (incl. bkfst) **LB** **FACILITIES: Spa** STV Fishing Sauna Gym Xmas **CONF:** Thtr 100 Class 40 Board 40 Del from £120 **PARKING:** 60 **NOTES:** ⊗ in restaurant Civ Wed 90

See advert on opposite page

★★★71% Celtic Royal Hotel

Bangor St LL55 1AY
☎ 01286 674477 01286 674139
e-mail: admin@celtic-royal.co.uk
web: www.celtic-royal.co.uk
Dir: *7m off A55 Expressway at Bangor. Follow A487 towards Caernarfon*

This large, impressive, privately owned hotel is situated in the town centre. It provides attractively appointed accommodation, which includes non-smoking rooms, bedrooms for less able guests and family rooms. The spacious public areas include a bar, a choice of lounges and a pleasant split-level restaurant. Guests also have the use of the impressive health club.
ROOMS: 110 en suite (12 fmly) ⊗ in 73 bedrooms s £63-£68; d £96-£106 (incl. bkfst) **LB** **FACILITIES:** STV Sauna Solarium Gym Jacuzzi Sun shower, Steam room ♫ Xmas **CONF:** BC Thtr 300 Class 120 Board 120 Del from £99 **SERVICES:** Lift **PARKING:** 180 **NOTES:** ⊗ in restaurant Civ Wed 200

★★67% *Stables*
Llanwnda LL54 5SD
☎ 01286 830711 🖷 01286 830413
Dir: *3m S of Caernarfon, on A499*
This privately owned and personally run hotel is set in 15 acres of its own land, south of Caernarfon. The bar and restaurant are located in converted stables and the bedrooms are all situated in two purpose-built, motel-style wings.
ROOMS: 22 annexe en suite (8 fmly) **FACILITIES:** Guests may bring own horse to stables **CONF:** Thtr 50 Class 30 Board 30 **PARKING:** 40

CAERPHILLY, Caerphilly — Map 09 ST18

⇧ Premier Travel Inn Caerphilly North
Corbetts Ln CF83 3HX
☎ 0870 9906368 🖷 0870 9906369
web: www.premiertravelinn.com
Dir: *4m from M4 junct 32. Follow A470, take 2nd left signed Caerphilly. At rdbt take 4th exit, at next rdbt take 2nd exit. Straight over next, and at Pwllypant rdbt, hotel on left*
High quality, modern budget accommodation ideal for both families and business travellers. Spacious, en suite bedrooms feature bath and shower, satellite TV and many have telephones and modem points. The adjacent family restaurant features a wide and varied menu. For further details consult the Hotel Groups page.
ROOMS: 40 en suite s £46.95-£48.95; d £46.95-£48.95

We have indicated only the hotels that don't accept credit or debit cards

⇧ Premier Travel Inn Caerphilly North East
Crossways Business Park, Pontypandy CF83 3NL
☎ 08701 977046 🖷 029 2086 5546
web: www.premiertravelinn.com
Dir: *M4 junct 32 take A470 towards Merthyr Tydfil. Junct 4 take A458 to Caerphilly. Stay on ring road until Crossways Business Park (5th rdbt). Inn on right of McDonald's rdbt.*
High quality, modern budget accommodation ideal for both families and business travellers. Spacious, en suite bedrooms feature bath and shower, satellite TV and many have telephones and modem points. The adjacent family restaurant features a wide and varied menu. For further details consult the Hotel Groups page.
ROOMS: 40 en suite s £46.95-£48.95; d £46.95-£48.95 **CONF:** Class 30

CAERSWS, Powys — Map 15 SO09

★★★67% *Maesmawr Hall*
SY17 5SF
☎ 01686 688255 🖷 01686 688410
e-mail: reception@maesmawr.co.uk
Dir: *6m from Newtown on A489 on right. 7m from Llanidloes A470/A489 on left*
This 16th-century timbered-framed manor house, now a privately owned and personally run hotel, is set in several acres of lawns, gardens and woodland. Many bedrooms have beamed ceilings, whilst the lounges have oak-panelled walls and carved fireplaces with cheerful log fires. It is also a popular venue for weddings and meetings.
ROOMS: 17 en suite (2 fmly) (5 GF) ⊗ in 11 bedrooms **CONF:** Thtr 120 Class 60 Board 36 **PARKING:** 60 **NOTES:** ⊗ in restaurant Closed Xmas & New Year Civ Wed 120

C

CAPEL CURIG, Conwy
Map 14 SH75

★★67% Cobdens
LL24 0EE
☎ 01690 720243 📠 01690 720354
e-mail: info@cobdens.co.uk
Dir: *on A5, 4m N of Betws-y-Coed*
In the heart of Snowdonia, this hotel has been a centre for mountaineering and other outdoor pursuits for 200 years. The bedrooms are modern and well equipped, and many enjoy lovely views. There is a bar and a wide range of meals using local produce is served in the restaurant or bar. A sauna room is also available.
ROOMS: 17 en suite (4 fmly) s £29.50-£34; d £59-£68 (incl. bkfst) **FACILITIES:** Fishing Sauna **CONF:** Thtr 50 Del £70 **PARKING:** 40 **NOTES:** ⊗ in restaurant Closed Jan RS 24-25 & 31 Dec

CARDIFF, Cardiff
Map 09 ST17
See also Barry

★★★★★70% ⊛ St David's Hotel & Spa
Havannah St CF10 5SD
☎ 029 2045 4045 📠 029 2048 7056
e-mail: reservations@thestdavidshotel.com
web: www.roccofortehotels.com
Dir: *M4 junct 33/A4232 for 9m, for Techniquest, at top exit slip road, 1st left at rdbt, 1st right*
This imposing contemporary building sits in a prime position on Cardiff Bay and has a seven-storey atrium which certainly creates a dramatic impression. Leading from this are the practically designed and comfortable bedrooms. Tides restaurant, adjacent to the stylish cocktail bar, has views across the water to Penarth, and there is a quiet first-floor lounge for guests seeking a peaceful environment. A well-equipped spa and extensive business areas complete the package.
ROOMS: 132 en suite (6 fmly) ⊗ in 108 bedrooms s £230-£550; d £260-£550 **LB** **FACILITIES: Spa** STV ⛾ supervised Sauna Gym Jacuzzi Fitness studio, 14 treatment rooms ♫ Xmas **CONF:** BC Thtr 270 Class 110 Board 60 Del from £190 **SERVICES:** Lift air con **PARKING:** 80 **NOTES:** ✗ ⊗ in restaurant Civ Wed

★★★★74% ⊛ Holland House
24/26 Newport Rd CF24 0DD
☎ 0870 122 0020 📠 029 2048 8894
e-mail: revenue.holland@macdonald-hotels.co.uk
web: www.macdonald-hotels.co.uk

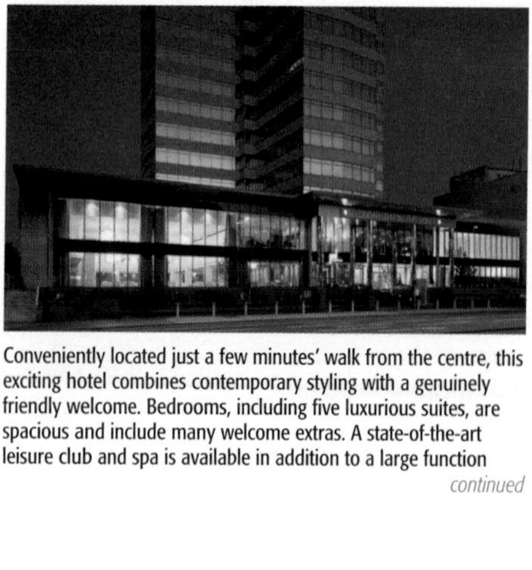

Conveniently located just a few minutes' walk from the centre, this exciting hotel combines contemporary styling with a genuinely friendly welcome. Bedrooms, including five luxurious suites, are spacious and include many welcome extras. A state-of-the-art leisure club and spa is available in addition to a large function room. An eclectic menu provides a varied range of freshly prepared, quality dishes.
ROOMS: 165 en suite (80 fmly) ⊗ in all bedrooms s £120-£215; d £140-£245 (incl. bkfst) **LB** **FACILITIES: Spa** STV ⛾ Sauna Gym Jacuzzi full leisure facilities & 14 treatment rooms ♫ **CONF:** BC Thtr 710 Class 400 Board 50 Del from £145 **SERVICES:** Lift air con **PARKING:** 80 **NOTES:** ✗ ⊗ in restaurant Civ Wed 500

★★★★70% Park Plaza Cardiff
Greyfriars Rd CF10 3AL
☎ 029 2011 1111 📠 029 2011 1112
e-mail: ppcres@parkplazahotels.co.uk
web: www.parkplaza.com
A smart, new-build hotel located in the city centre. The hotel features eye-catching, contemporary decor, a state-of-the-art indoor leisure facility, extensive conference and banqueting facilities and the spacious Laguna kitchen and bar. Bedrooms are also contemporary in style and feature a host of extras including private bar, safe and modem points.
ROOMS: 129 en suite ⊗ in 96 bedrooms s £79-£140; d £89-£180 (incl. bkfst) **LB** **FACILITIES: Spa** STV ⛾ supervised Solarium Gym Jacuzzi Dance studio **CONF:** Thtr 150 Class 80 Board 60 Del from £145 **SERVICES:** Lift air con **NOTES:** ⊗ in restaurant Civ Wed 100

★★★★68% ⊛ Copthorne Hotel Cardiff-Caerdydd
Copthorne Way, Culverhouse Cross CF5 6DH
☎ 029 2059 9100 📠 029 2059 9080
e-mail: sales.cardiff@mill-cop.com
web: www.copthorne.com/cardiff
Dir: *M4 junct 33, A4232 for 2.5m towards Cardiff West. Then A48 W to Cowbridge*
A comfortable, popular and modern hotel, conveniently located for the airport and city. Bedrooms are a good size and some have a private lounge. Public areas are smartly presented with features including a gym, pool, meeting rooms and a comfortable restaurant with views of the adjacent lake.
ROOMS: 135 en suite (14 fmly) (27 GF) ⊗ in 114 bedrooms s £75-£235.75; d £85-£251.50 (incl. bkfst) **LB** **FACILITIES:** STV ⛾ Sauna Gym Jacuzzi Steam room Xmas **CONF:** Thtr 300 Class 140 Board 80 Del from £99 **SERVICES:** Lift **PARKING:** 225 **NOTES:** ⊗ in restaurant Civ Wed 200

★★★★68% Cardiff Marriott Hotel
Mill Ln CF10 1EZ
☎ 029 2039 9944 📠 029 2039 5578
e-mail: sara.nurse@marriotthotels.co.uk
web: www.marriott.co.uk
Dir: *M4 junct 29 follow signs City Centre. Turn left into High Street opposite Castle, then 2nd left, at bottom of High St into Mill Lane*

A centrally located modern hotel, with spacious public areas and a

continued

good range of services, is ideal for business or leisure. Eating options include the informal Chats café bar and the contemporary Mediterrano restaurant. Well-equipped and newly refurbished bedrooms are comfortable and air conditioned. The leisure suite includes a gym and good sized pool.
ROOMS: 184 en suite (68 fmly) ⊗ in 146 bedrooms s £109-£295; d £109-£295 **LB** **FACILITIES:** STV Sauna Solarium Gym Jacuzzi Steam room Xmas **CONF:** Thtr 400 Class 200 Board 100 Del from £135 **SERVICES:** Lift air con **PARKING:** 110 **NOTES:** ⊗ in restaurant Civ Wed 100

★★★★68% Jurys Cardiff

JURYS DOYLE HOTELS

Mary Ann St CF10 2JH
☎ 029 2034 1441 ℻ 029 2022 3742
e-mail: info@jurysdoyle.com
web: www.jurysdoyle.com
Dir: *next to Ice Rink, opposite Cardiff International Arena*
A modern city centre hotel, located opposite the Cardiff International Arena. The hotel is built around a central atrium in which the reception, Dylan's Restaurant and Kavanagh's Irish Bar are all located. Some bedrooms overlook the atrium, while others have external views. Rooms are generally spacious, have modern decor and are equipped with a range of extras including safes.
ROOMS: 146 en suite (6 fmly) ⊗ in 109 bedrooms s £59-£325; d £59-£325 **LB** **FACILITIES:** STV **CONF:** Thtr 300 Class 120 Board 50 **SERVICES:** Lift **PARKING:** 40 **NOTES:** ⊗ in restaurant Civ Wed 150

★★★★66% Angel Hotel

PARAMOUNT GROUP OF HOTELS

Castle St CF10 1SZ
☎ 029 2064 9200 ℻ 029 2039 6212
e-mail: angelreservations@paramount-hotels.co.uk
web: www.paramount-hotels.co.uk
Dir: *opposite Cardiff Castle*
This well-established hotel is in the heart of the city overlooking the castle. All bedrooms offer air conditioning and are decorated and furnished to a high standard. Public areas include an impressive lobby, a modern restaurant and a selection of conference rooms. There is limited parking at the rear of the hotel.
ROOMS: 102 en suite (3 fmly) ⊗ in 62 bedrooms s £140-£200; d £170-£220 **LB** **FACILITIES:** Xmas **CONF:** Thtr 300 Class 180 Board 80 Del from £125 **SERVICES:** Lift air con **PARKING:** 60 **NOTES:** ⊗ in restaurant Civ Wed 200

★★★★60% Novotel Cardiff Central

NOVOTEL

Schooner Way, Atlantic Wharf CF10 4RT
☎ 029 2047 5000 ℻ 029 2048 1491
e-mail: h5982@accor.com
web: www.novotel.com
Dir: *M4 junct 33/A4232 follow Cardiff Bay signs, to Atlantic Wharf & Novotel Hotel*
Situated in the heart of the city's new development area, this hotel is equally convenient for the centre and Cardiff Bay. Bedrooms vary between standard rooms in the original wing and deluxe rooms in the more modern extension. The hotel offers good seating space in public rooms, a galleried bar and a popular leisure club. Novotel - AA Hotel Group of the Year 2005-6.
ROOMS: 143 en suite (6 fmly) ⊗ in 50 bedrooms s £59-£150; d £59-£150 **LB** **FACILITIES:** **Spa** STV supervised Sauna Solarium Gym Jacuzzi Xmas **CONF:** BC Thtr 250 Class 90 Board 65 Del from £125 **SERVICES:** Lift **PARKING:** 150 **NOTES:** ⊗ in restaurant Civ Wed 250

GF indicates the number of bedrooms at ground level

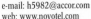

CARDIFF, continued

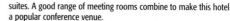

★★★72%
St Mellons Hotel & Country Club
Castleton CF3 2XR
☎ 01633 680355 📠 01633 680399
e-mail: stmellons@bestwestern.co.uk
web: www.stmellonshotel.com
Dir: *M4 junct 28 follow signs into Castleton. Through village, then sharp left at brow of hill following hotel sign into driveway*
This former Regency mansion has been tastefully converted into an elegant hotel and has an adjoining leisure complex with a strong local following. Bedrooms are spacious and smart; some are in purpose-built wings. The public areas retain their pleasing former proportions and include relaxing lounges and a restaurant.
ROOMS: 21 en suite 20 annexe en suite (9 fmly) ⊗ in 18 bedrooms s £75-£140; d £90-£150 (incl. bkfst) **LB** **FACILITIES:** STV Squash Sauna Solarium Gym Jacuzzi Beauty salon Xmas **CONF:** Thtr 220 Class 70 Board 40 Del from £139 **PARKING:** 90 **NOTES:** ⊗ in restaurant Civ Wed 160

★★★71% ⊛ **Manor Parc Country Hotel & Restaurant**
Thornhill Rd, Thornhill CF14 9UA
☎ 029 2069 3723 📠 029 2061 4624
e-mail: reception@manorparchotel.fsnet.co.uk
Dir: *on A469*
Set in open countryside on the outskirts of Cardiff, this delightful hotel retains traditional values of hospitality and service. Bedrooms, including a suite, are spacious and attractive, whilst public areas comprise a comfortable lounge and a restaurant with a magnificent lantern ceiling overlooking the well-tended grounds.
ROOMS: 21 en suite (4 fmly) (1 GF) ⊗ in all bedrooms s £65-£72; d £95-£130 (incl. bkfst) **LB** **FACILITIES:** STV **CONF:** Thtr 120 Class 80 Board 50 Del from £130 **PARKING:** 100 **NOTES:** ⊗ in restaurant Closed 26 Dec-1Jan Civ Wed 100

★★★71% ⊛ **New House Country Hotel**
Thornhill CF14 9UA
☎ 029 2052 0280 📠 029 2052 0324
e-mail: enquiries@newhousehotel.com
web: www.newhousehotel.com
Dir: *M4 junct 32, A470 towards Cardiff, then A469 to Caerphilly. Pass Thornhill Crematorium, 1m on left*
Enjoying an elevated, hilltop position, the New House enjoys unrivalled views of the city and, on clear days, across the channel to the coast of Somerset. The public areas comprise a lounge and bar, an elegant restaurant and various function suites. Accommodation is spacious and comfortable, in attractive, well-equipped rooms, many having their own balcony or terrace.
ROOMS: 36 en suite (5 fmly) (10 GF) ⊗ in 18 bedrooms s £98-£128; d £140-£190 (incl. bkfst) **LB** **FACILITIES: Spa** STV Sauna Gym Jacuzzi Xmas **CONF:** Thtr 200 Class 150 Board 200 Del from £125 **PARKING:** 100 **NOTES:** ⊗ in restaurant Civ Wed

★★★66% **Quality Hotel & Suites Cardiff**
Merthyr Rd, Tongwynlais CF15 7LD
☎ 029 2052 9988 📠 029 2052 9977
e-mail: enquiries@quality-hotels-cardiff.com
web: www.choicehotelseurope.com
Dir: *M4 junct 32, take exit for Tongwynlais A4054 off large rdbt, hotel on right*
This modern hotel is conveniently located off the M4 with easy access to Cardiff. Guests can enjoy the spacious open-plan public areas and impressive leisure facilities and relax in the well-proportioned and equipped bedrooms, which include some suites. A good range of meeting rooms combine to make this hotel a popular conference venue.
ROOMS: 95 en suite (12 fmly) (19 GF) ⊗ in 64 bedrooms s £45-£115; d £60-£145 **LB** **FACILITIES:** supervised Sauna Solarium Gym Jacuzzi Xmas **CONF:** Thtr 200 Class 140 Board 60 Del from £80 **SERVICES:** Lift air con **PARKING:** 130 **NOTES:** ⊗ in restaurant Civ Wed 180

★★66% **Sandringham**
21 St Mary St CF10 1PL
☎ 029 2023 2161 📠 029 2038 3998
e-mail: mm@sandingham-hotel.com
Dir: *M4 junct 29 follow 'City Centre' signs. Opposite the castle turn left into High Street which leads to Saint Mary Street*
This friendly, privately owned and personally run hotel is near to the Millennium Stadium and offers a convenient base for access to the city centre. Bedrooms are well equipped, and diners can relax in Café Jazz, the hotel's adjoining restaurant, where live music is provided most week nights. There is also a separate lounge/bar for residents, and an airy breakfast room.
ROOMS: 28 en suite (1 fmly) ⊗ in 16 bedrooms s £35-£100; d £45-£130 (incl. bkfst) **LB** **FACILITIES:** ♫ **CONF:** Thtr 100 Class 70 Board 60 Del from £60 **PARKING:** 10 **NOTES:** ⊗ in restaurant

Restaurant with Rooms

⊛ **The Old Post Office**
Greenwood Ln, St Fagans CF5 6EL
☎ 029 2056 5400 📠 029 2056 3400
e-mail: heiditheoldpost@aol.com
Dir: *M4 junct 33 onto A4232. Take Culverhouse Cross exit then 1st exit then left onto Michaelston Rd. Over rdbt and level crossing, then left at Castle Hill, right past church*
Located just five miles from Cardiff in the historic village of St. Fagans, this establishment offers contemporary style based on New England design. Bedrooms, like the dining room, feature striking white walls with spotlights offering a fresh, clean feel. Delicious meals include a carefully prepared selection of local produce.
ROOMS: 6 en suite (2 fmly) (6 GF) ⊗ in all bedrooms s £70; d £80 (incl. bkfst) **LB** **FACILITIES:** Outdoor chess **PARKING:** 40 **NOTES:** ⊗ in restaurant

Campanile
Caxton Place, Pentwyn CF23 8HA
☎ 029 2054 9044 📠 029 2054 9900
e-mail: cardiff@envergure.co.uk
web: www.envergure.fr
Dir: *take Pentwyn exit from A48, follow signs for Pentwyn Industrial Estate*

This modern building offers accommodation in smart, well-equipped bedrooms, all with en suite bathrooms. Refreshments may be taken at the informal Bistro. For further details consult the Hotel Groups page.
ROOMS: 47 annexe en suite **CONF:** Thtr 35 Class 18 Board 24

⌂ *Hotel Ibis Cardiff*
Churchill Way CF10 2HA
☎ 029 2064 9250 029 2920 9260
e-mail: H2936@accor-hotels.com
Dir: *M4, then A48 2nd exit A4232. Follow signs to City Centre on Newport Rd, left after railway bridge, left after Queen St station.*
Modern, budget hotel offering comfortable accommodation in bright and practical bedrooms. Breakfast is self-service and dinner is available in the restaurant. For further details, consult the Hotel Groups page.
ROOMS: 102 en suite

⌂ *Hotel Ibis Cardiff Gate*
Malthouse Av, Cardiff Gate Business Park, Pontprennau CF23 8RA
☎ 029 2073 3222 029 2073 4222
e-mail: H3159@accor-hotels.com
Dir: *M4 junct 30, take slip rd signed Cardiff Service Station. Hotel on left.*
Modern, budget hotel offering comfortable accommodation in bright and practical bedrooms. Breakfast is self-service and dinner is available in the restaurant. For further details, consult the Hotel Groups page.
ROOMS: 78 en suite **CONF:** Thtr 18 Class 12 Board 14

⌂ Innkeeper's Lodge Cardiff
Tyn-y-Parc Rd, Whitchurch CF14 6BG
☎ 029 2069 2554 029 2052 7052
web: www.innkeeperslodge.com
Dir: *M4 junct 32, southbound on A470. At 3rd set of lights turn left, inn opposite supermarket*
A growing concept in the travel accommodation market. Smart rooms meet essential business requirements but also have home comforts. Dining options include all-day menus plus the added advantage of breakfast, which is included in the room price. For further details consult the Hotel Groups page.
ROOMS: 52 en suite s £49.95; d £49.95 **CONF:** Thtr 40 Class 40 Board 20

⌂ Premier Travel Inn Cardiff Ocean Park
Keen Rd CF24 5JT
☎ 08701 977050 029 2049 0403
web: www.premiertravelinn.com
Dir: *Cardiff Docks & Bay signs from A48(M), over flyover & next 4 rdbts. At 5th rdbt, take 3rd exit. Inn 1st right & 1st right again*
High quality, modern budget accommodation ideal for both families and business travellers. Spacious, en suite bedrooms feature bath and shower, satellite TV and many have telephones and modem points. The adjacent family restaurant features a wide and varied menu. For further details consult the Hotel Groups page.
ROOMS: 73 en suite s £49.95-£52.95; d £49.95-£52.95 **CONF:** Thtr 15

⌂ Premier Travel Inn Cardiff (Roath)
David Lloyd Leisure Club, Ipswich Rd, Roath CF23 9AQ
☎ 08701 977049 029 2046 2482
web: www.premiertravelinn.com
Dir: *M4 junct 30 take A4232 to A48. 2nd exit off A48 to Cardiff East and Docks, (A4161). Follow signs for David Lloyd Leisure Club.*
High quality, modern budget accommodation ideal for both families and business travellers. Spacious, en suite bedrooms feature bath and shower, satellite TV and many have telephones and modem points. The adjacent family restaurant features a wide and varied menu. For further details consult the Hotel Groups page.
ROOMS: 70 en suite s £49.95-£52.95; d £49.95-£52.95 **CONF:** Thtr 300

♫ Entertainment

⌂ Premier Travel Inn Cardiff West
The Walston Castle, Port Road, Nantisaf, Wenvoe CF5 6DD
☎ 08701 977052 029 2059 1436
web: www.premiertravelinn.com
Dir: *From M4 junct 33 south on A4232. Take 2nd exit (signed Airport), then 3rd exit at Culverhouse Cross rdbt. Inn 0.5m on Barry Rd (A4050)*
High quality, modern budget accommodation ideal for both families and business travellers. Spacious, en suite bedrooms feature bath and shower, satellite TV and many have telephones and modem points. The adjacent family restaurant features a wide and varied menu. For further details consult the Hotel Groups page.
ROOMS: 39 en suite s £46.95-£49.95; d £46.95-£49.95 **CONF:** Thtr 12

C

⌂ Travelodge (Cardiff Central)
Imperial Gate, Saint Marys St CF10 1FA
☎ 08700 850 950 029 2039 8737
web: www.travelodge.co.uk
Dir: *M4 junct 32, A470 to city centre*
Travelodge offers good quality, good value, modern accommodation. Ideal for families, the spacious, en suite bedrooms include remote-control TV, tea and coffee-making facilities and comfortable beds. Meals can be taken at the nearby family restaurant. For further details consult the Hotel Groups page.
ROOMS: 100 en suite s fr £26; d fr £26

⌂ Travelodge (Cardiff East)
Circle Way East, Llanedeyrn CF23 9PD
☎ 08700 850 950 029 2054 9564
web: www.travelodge.co.uk
Dir: *M4 junct 30, A4232 to North Pentwyn junct. A48 & follow Cardiff East & Docks signs. 3rd exit at Llanedeyrn junct, follow Circle Way East signs*
Travelodge offers good quality, good value, modern accommodation. Ideal for families, the spacious, en suite bedrooms include remote-control TV, tea and coffee-making facilities and comfortable beds. Meals can be taken at the nearby family restaurant. For further details consult the Hotel Groups page.
ROOMS: 32 en suite s fr £26; d fr £26

⌂ Travelodge (Cardiff West)
Granada Service Area M4, Pontyclun CF72 8SA
☎ 08700 850 950 029 2089 9412
web: www.travelodge.co.uk
Dir: *M4, junct 33/A4232*
Travelodge offers good quality, good value, modern accommodation. Ideal for families, the spacious, en suite bedrooms include remote-control TV, tea and coffee-making facilities and comfortable beds. Meals can be taken at the nearby family restaurant. For further details consult the Hotel Groups page.
ROOMS: 50 en suite s fr £26; d fr £26 **CONF:** Thtr 45 Board 34

CARDIGAN See Gwbert-on-Sea

CARMARTHEN, Carmarthenshire — Map 08 SN42

★★★67% Ivy Bush Royal
Spilman St SA31 1LG
☎ 01267 235111 01267 234914
e-mail: reception@ivybushroyal.co.uk
web: www.ivybushroyal.co.uk
Dir: *M4/A48, W over 1st rdbt, 2nd rdbt turn right. Straight over next 2 rdbts. Bear left at lights. Hotel on right at top of hill.*
Now under new ownership, this hotel has been tastefully refurbished to offer guests spacious, well equipped bedrooms and bathrooms, a relaxing lounge with outdoor patio seating and a comfortable restaurant serving a varied selection of carefully

continued on p778

CARMARTHEN, continued

prepared meals. Weddings, meetings and conferences are all well catered for at this friendly, family run hotel.
ROOMS: 70 en suite (4 fmly) ⊛ in 60 bedrooms s £59-£67; d £75-£95 (incl. bkfst) **LB FACILITIES:** STV Sauna Gym Xmas **CONF:** BC Thtr 200 Class 50 Board 40 Del from £99 **SERVICES:** Lift **PARKING:** 73 **NOTES:** ⊁ ⊛ in restaurant Civ Wed 150

★★70% ◉ Falcon
Lammas St SA31 3AP
☎ 01267 234959 & 237152 ▤ 01267 221277
e-mail: reception@falconcarmarthen.co.uk
web: www.falconcarmarthen.co.uk
Dir: in town centre pass bus station turn left, hotel 200yds on left

This friendly hotel has been owned by the Exton family for over 45 years. Personally run, it is well placed in the centre of the town. Bedrooms, some with four-poster beds, are tastefully decorated with good facilities. There is a comfortable lounge with adjacent bar and the restaurant, open for lunch and dinner, has a varied selection of enjoyable dishes.
ROOMS: 16 en suite (1 fmly) s £49-£65; d £59-£75 (incl. bkfst) **LB CONF:** Thtr 80 Class 50 Board 40 Del from £80.50 **PARKING:** 36 **NOTES:** ⊛ in restaurant Closed 26 Dec RS Sun

CASTLETON, Newport Map 09 ST28

⌂ Premier Travel Inn Cardiff East
Newport Rd CF3 2UQ
☎ 08701 977051 ▤ 01633 681143
web: www.premiertravelinn.com
Dir: M4 junct 8, at rdbt take 2nd exit A48 Castleton and follow for 3m, Inn on right
High quality, modern budget accommodation ideal for both families and business travellers. Spacious, en suite bedrooms feature bath and shower, satellite TV and many have telephones and modem points. The adjacent family restaurant features a wide and varied menu. For further details consult the Hotel Groups page.
ROOMS: 49 en suite s £46.95-£49.95; d £46.95-£49.95

CEMAES BAY See Anglesey, Isle of

CHEPSTOW, Monmouthshire Map 04 ST59

★★★★70%
Marriott St Pierre Hotel & Country Club Marriott HOTELS & RESORTS
St Pierre Park NP16 6YA
☎ 01291 625261 ▤ 01291 629975
web: www.marriott.co.uk
Dir: M48 junct 2. At rdbt on slip road take A466 Chepstow. At next rdbt take 1st exit Caerwent A48. Hotel approx 2m on left
This 14th-century property offers an extensive range of leisure and
continued

conference facilities. Bedrooms are well equipped, comfortable and located in adjacent wings or in a lakeside cottage complex. The main bar, popular with golfers, overlooks the 18th green, whilst diners can choose between a traditional elegant restaurant and modern brasserie.

ROOMS: 148 en suite (16 fmly) (75 GF) ⊛ in 74 bedrooms **FACILITIES:** Spa STV ⊠ ♨ 36 ⚲ Fishing Sauna Solarium Gym ♨ Putt green Jacuzzi Health spa, Floodlit driving range, Chipping green, Short game area Xmas **CONF:** Thtr 240 Class 120 Board 90 **PARKING:** 430 **NOTES:** ⊁ ⊛ in restaurant Civ Wed 200

★★★66% Chepstow
Newport Rd NP16 5PR THE INDEPENDENTS
☎ 01291 626261 & 0845 6588700
▤ 01291 626263
e-mail: info@chepstowhotel.com web: www.chepstowhotel.com
Dir: M48 junct 2, follow Chepstow signs, A466 & A48 into town, hotel on left
This privately owned hotel is conveniently situated on the main road into town with easy access for the M4 and M48. Bedrooms vary in size and style, but all have modern equipment and facilities. The attractively appointed public areas include an air conditioned conference room and a large ballroom.
ROOMS: 31 en suite (4 fmly) ⊛ in 14 bedrooms s £55; d £65 **FACILITIES:** Xmas **CONF:** Thtr 200 Class 70 Board 50 Del £92.50 **SERVICES:** Lift **PARKING:** 100 **NOTES:** ⊛ in restaurant Civ Wed 150
See advert on opposite page

★★68% Castle View
16 Bridge St NP6 5EZ
☎ 01291 620349 ▤ 01291 627397
e-mail: dave@castview.demon.co.uk
Dir: M48 junct 2, A466 for Wye Valley, at 1st rdbt right onto A48 towards Gloucester. Follow 2nd sign to town centre, then to Chepstow Castle, hotel directly opposite
This privately owned inn is situated opposite the Norman castle. Bedrooms vary in size, and all are similarly furnished and well-equipped, with some rooms situated in separate buildings. Several family rooms are available. Public areas include a comfortable lounge, a pleasant lounge bar and a cosy restaurant offering freshly prepared cuisine.
ROOMS: 9 en suite 4 annexe en suite (7 fmly) **FACILITIES:** Xmas **NOTES:** ⊛ in restaurant
See advert on opposite page

★★63% Beaufort
Beaufort Square NP16 5EP
☎ 01291 622497 ▤ 01291 627389
e-mail: info@thebeauforthotel.co.uk
web: www.beauforthotelchepstow.com
Dir: off A48, at St Mary's church turn left and left again at end of public car park (Nelson St). Hotel car park 100yds on right
Privately owned and personally run, this 16th-century coaching inn
continued

is centrally located in town. The bedrooms vary in style and size and include two rooms on ground-floor level with direct access from the car park. The inviting and popular public areas have plenty of charm and character. They include a friendly bar and a newly refurbished restaurant that offers a varied choice of dining options. There is also a large meeting and function room.
ROOMS: 23 en suite (2 fmly) s fr £46; d fr £59 **LB** **FACILITIES:** STV **CONF:** Thtr 140 Class 70 Board 40 **PARKING:** 14 **NOTES:** ⊗ in restaurant

CHIRK, Wrexham — Map 15 SJ23

★★★66% Moreton Park Lodge

Moreton Park, Gledrid LL14 5DG
☎ 01691 776666 🖷 01691 776655
e-mail: reservations@moretonpark.com
web: www.moretonpark.com
Dir: *200yds from the rdbt of the A5 and B5070*
This privately-owned and purpose-built modern hotel is on the outskirts of Chirk. It offers well-equipped accommodation, which includes bedrooms suitable for disabled guests. Some rooms have separate lounge areas. Meals are available in the Lord Moreton pub/restaurant, and there is an indoor play area for children.
ROOMS: 46 en suite (20 fmly) (31 GF) ⊗ in 26 bedrooms s £50-£65; d £60-£75 (incl. bkfst) **LB** **FACILITIES:** STV Childrens indoor play barn **PARKING:** 400 **NOTES:** ✗ Closed 23-29 Dec

COLWYN BAY, Conwy — Map 14 SH87

★★★68% Hopeside

63-67 Princes Dr, West End LL29 8PW
☎ 01492 533244 🖷 01492 532850
e-mail: hopesidehotel@aol.com
Dir: *leave A55 at Rhos-on-Sea, turn off B5155 towards Colwyn Bay town centre. Left at next set of traffic lights into Princes Drive*
The promenade and town centre are within easy walking distance of this friendly, privately owned and personally run hotel. The bedrooms are mostly pine-furnished and all are attractively decorated. Facilities here include a small conference room, a mini gym and a sauna. At the last inspection, new owners were in the process of upgrading many areas.
ROOMS: 16 en suite (1 fmly) ⊗ in 8 bedrooms s fr £49; d fr £69 (incl. bkfst) **LB** **FACILITIES:** Sauna Gym Xmas **CONF:** Thtr 40 Class 40 Board 26 Del from £64.95 **PARKING:** 15 **NOTES:** ⊗ in restaurant Civ Wed 50

★★★66% *Norfolk House*

39 Princes Dr LL29 8PF
☎ 01492 531757 & 536466 🖷 01492 533781
e-mail: timbucknall@aol.com
web: www.norfolkhousehotel.co.uk
Dir: *A55 at Colwyn Bay, into right lane of slip road, right at lights, pass station, hotel almost opposite filling station*
Norfolk House is a privately owned and personally run hotel with a warm, friendly atmosphere. It is within easy walking distance of the seafront, town centre and railway station. The accommodation is well equipped, comfortable and relaxing. Bedrooms are attractively decorated and family suites are available. There is a choice of lounges, a small bar and conference facilities.
ROOMS: 22 en suite (4 fmly) (5 GF) **CONF:** Thtr 60 Board 30 **SERVICES:** Lift **PARKING:** 25 **NOTES:** ⊗ in restaurant

Popped the question? Hotels with Civ wed in their entry are licensed for civil wedding ceremonies. Maximum numbers for the ceremony only are shown e.g. Civ wed 120

COLWYN BAY, continued

★★66% Marine
West Promenade LL28 4BP
☎ 01492 530295 & 530883 🖷 0870 168 9400
e-mail: reservations@marinehotel.co.uk
Dir: *off A55 at Old Colwyn to seafront. Turn left, after pier left before lights, car park on corner*
This privately owned and personally run hotel stands on the promenade, overlooking the sea. The accommodation is soundly maintained and equipped to suit both commercial visitors and holidaymakers. Facilities include a small bar and a lounge.
ROOMS: 14 rms (12 en suite) (4 fmly) ⊗ in 9 bedrooms s £28-£33; d £56 (incl. bkfst) **LB** **PARKING:** 11 **NOTES:** ⊗ in restaurant Closed mid Oct-Apr

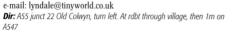

★★64% *Lyndale*
410 Abergele Rd, Old Colwyn LL29 9AB
THE INDEPENDENTS
☎ 01492 515429 🖷 01492 518805
e-mail: lyndale@tinyworld.co.uk
Dir: *A55 junct 22 Old Colwyn, turn left. At rdbt through village, then 1m on A547*
A range of accommodation is available at this friendly, family-run hotel, including suites that are suitable for family use and a four-poster bedroom. There is a cosy bar and a comfortable foyer lounge, and weddings and other functions can be catered for.
ROOMS: 14 en suite (3 fmly) ⊗ in 3 bedrooms **FACILITIES:** ch fac **CONF:** Thtr 40 Class 20 Board 20 **PARKING:** 20

CONWY, Conwy Map 14 SH77

★★★73% ◎ Groes Inn
Tyn-y-Groes LL32 8TN
☎ 01492 650545 🖷 01492 650855
web: www.groesinn.com
Dir: *A55, over Old Conwy Bridge, 1st left through Castle Walls on B5106 (Trefriw road), hotel 2m on right.*

This inn dates back in part to the 16th century and has charming features. It offers a choice of bars and has a beautifully appointed restaurant, with a conservatory extension opening on to the lovely rear garden. The comfortable, well-equipped bedrooms are contained in a separate building; some have balconies or private terraces.
ROOMS: 14 en suite (1 fmly) (4 GF) ⊗ in 6 bedrooms s £79-£120; d £95-£146 (incl. bkfst) **LB** **CONF:** Thtr 22 Class 20 Board 20 **PARKING:** 100 **NOTES:** ⊗ in restaurant Closed Xmas

Hotel of the Year

★★★72% ◎◎ Castle Hotel Conwy
High St LL32 8DB
☎ 01492 582800 🖷 01492 582300
e-mail: mail@castlewales.co.uk
web: www.castlewales.co.uk
Dir: *A55 junct 18, follow town centre signs, cross estuary (castle on left). Right then left at mini-rdbts onto one-way system. Right at Town Wall Gate, right onto Berry St then along High St on left*
This family-run, 16th-century hotel is one of Conwy's most distinguished buildings and offers a relaxed and friendly atmosphere. Bedrooms are appointed to an impressive standard including a stunning suite. Public areas include a popular modern bar and the award-winning Shakespeare's restaurant. AA Hotel of the Year for Wales 2005-6.
ROOMS: 28 en suite (2 fmly) ⊗ in 20 bedrooms s £69-£82; d £95-£300 (incl. bkfst) **LB** **FACILITIES:** STV Xmas **CONF:** Thtr 30 Class 20 Board 20 Del from £99.50 **PARKING:** 34 **NOTES:** ⊗ in restaurant

Late for dinner? Quality standards mean that last orders for dinner vary according to star rating and should be no earlier than: ★★ 7.00pm ★★★ 8:00pm ★★★★ 9:00pm ★★★★★ 10:00pm

Top Hotel

★★ ⊚⊚⊚⊪ The Old Rectory Country House

Llanrwst Rd, Llansanffraid Glan Conwy LL28 5LF
☎ 01492 580611 ▤ 01492 584555
e-mail: info@oldrectorycountryhouse.co.uk
web: www.oldrectorycountryhouse.co.uk
Dir: 0.5m S from A470/A55 junct on left, by 30mph sign

This friendly and welcoming hotel enjoys elevated views of
the Conwy Estuary and Snowdonia. Traditionally styled day
rooms are luxurious and elegant and home-baked afternoon
teas can be taken in the elegant lounge. Dinner is the
highlight of any stay and the daily-changing set menu makes
excellent use of fresh and seasonal local produce. Bedrooms
benefit from the delightful views and are furnished with
thought and care. Genuine hospitality creates a real
home-from-home atmosphere.

ROOMS: 4 en suite 2 annexe en suite ⊗ in all bedrooms
s £99-£129; d £99-£169 (incl. bkfst) **LB PARKING:** 10
NOTES: No children 5yrs ⊗ in restaurant Closed 14 Dec-15 Jan RS
Sun (ex Bank Hols)

COWBRIDGE, Vale of Glamorgan Map 09 SS97

★★★65% The Bear Hotel

63 High St CF71 7AF
☎ 01446 774814 ▤ 01446 775425
e-mail: enquiries@bearhotel.com
web: www.bearhotel.com
Dir: in town centre

Guests receive a genuinely friendly welcome at this famous
coaching inn. It is infused with character throughout and features
oak beams, real fires and a vaulted bear pit where Napoleon's
troops were apparently held. Guests have the choice of dining in
the hotel restaurant or at the modern style Oscars Bar & Grill next
door. Rooms vary in size and style and are individually decorated.
The hotel is a popular wedding venue.

ROOMS: 19 en suite 16 annexe en suite (2 fmly) (4 GF) ⊗ in 14
bedrooms s £55-£85; d £90-£115 (incl. bkfst) **LB FACILITIES:** STV Pool
table Xmas **CONF:** Thtr 100 Class 60 Board 50 Del from £105
PARKING: 70 **NOTES:** ✘ ⊗ in restaurant Civ Wed 90

🏊 Indoor Swimming pool
🏊 Indoor Swimming pool (heated)
🏊 Outdoor Swimming pool
🏊 Outdoor Swimming pool (heated)

CRICCIETH, Gwynedd Map 14 SH43

★★★77% ⊚⊪
Bron Eifion Country House

LL52 0SA
☎ 01766 522385 ▤ 01766 522003
e-mail: stay@broneifion.co.uk
web: www.broneifion.co.uk
Dir: 0.5m from Criccieth on A497 towards Pwllheli

This delightful country house built in 1883, is set in extensive
grounds to the west of Criccieth. Now a privately owned and
personally run hotel, it provides warm and very friendly hospitality
as well as attentive service. Most of the tasteful bedrooms have
period and antique furniture, and some have four-poster beds or
attractive canopies. The very impressive central hall features a
minstrels' gallery, and there is a choice of comfortable lounges.
The restaurant overlooks the gardens.

ROOMS: 19 en suite (1 fmly) (1 GF) ⊗ in 4 bedrooms s £69-£79;
d £110-£120 (incl. bkfst) **LB FACILITIES:** Xmas **CONF:** Thtr 30 Class 25
Board 25 Del from £84 **PARKING:** 50 **NOTES:** ✘ ⊗ in restaurant

★★70% Caerwylan

LL52 0HW
☎ 01766 522547
e-mail: caerwylan_hotel@plevy.fsbusiness.co.uk
Dir: near lifeboat station

Privately owned and personally run, this long established holiday
hotel commands panoramic sea views of Cardigan Bay and the
castle. Comfortably furnished lounges are available for residents
and the five-course menu changes daily. Bedrooms, including
family rooms, are smart and modern, and several have their own
private sitting areas. The friendly atmosphere ensures that many
guests return year after year.

ROOMS: 25 en suite (3 fmly) s £28-£32; d £56-£64 (incl. bkfst) **LB**
SERVICES: Lift **PARKING:** 9 **NOTES:** ⊗ in restaurant Closed Nov-Etr

★★66% Lion

Y Maes LL52 0AA
☎ 01766 522460 ▤ 01766 523075
e-mail: info@lionhotelcriccieth.co.uk
Dir: A497 on to village green north, hotel on green

This hotel lies just a short walk from the castle and seafront, with
fine views from many rooms. The bars enjoy a good local
following and staff are friendly and welcoming. Bedrooms are well
decorated and furnished, divided between the main building and
the annexe. Regular live entertainment is provided during the
summer.

ROOMS: 34 en suite 12 annexe en suite (8 fmly) ⊗ in all bedrooms
s £37-£40; d £64-£74 (incl. bkfst) **LB FACILITIES:** STV ♫ Xmas
SERVICES: Lift **PARKING:** 30 **NOTES:** ⊗ in restaurant

CRICKHOWELL, Powys

Map 09 SO21

★★★72% Gliffaes Country House Hotel

NP8 1RH
☎ 01874 730371 01874 730463
e-mail: calls@gliffaeshotel.com
web: www.gliffaeshotel.com
Dir: *1m off A40, 2.5m W of Crickhowell*

This impressive Victorian mansion, standing in 33 acres of its own gardens and wooded grounds by the River Usk, is a privately owned and personally run hotel. Public rooms retain elegance and generous proportions and include a balcony and conservatory from which to enjoy the views. Bedrooms are furnished to a high standard and offer high levels of comfort.
ROOMS: 19 en suite 3 annexe en suite in all bedrooms s fr £70; d fr £130 (incl. bkfst) **LB** **FACILITIES:** Fishing Snooker Putt green Cycling, Birdwatching, Walking, Fishing, Falconry Xmas **CONF:** Thtr 40 Class 16 Board 16 Del from £150 **PARKING:** 34 **NOTES:** in restaurant Closed 2-18 Jan Civ Wed 50

★★★71% Bear

NP8 1BW
☎ 01873 810408 01873 811696
e-mail: bearhotel@aol.com
Dir: *on A40 between Abergavenny and Brecon*
A favourite with locals as well as visitors, the character and friendliness of this 15th-century coaching inn are renowned. The bar and restaurant areas are furnished in keeping with the style and character of the building and provide a comfortable area in which to enjoy some of the finest locally-sourced ingredients. The hotel offers very popular and extensive bar food choices.
ROOMS: 13 en suite 13 annexe en suite (6 fmly) **CONF:** Thtr 40 Class 20 Board 20 Del from £130 **PARKING:** 45

Indoor Swimming pool
Indoor Swimming pool (heated)
Outdoor Swimming pool
Outdoor Swimming pool (heated)

★★★70% Manor

Brecon Rd NP8 1SE
☎ 01873 810212 01873 811938
e-mail: info@manorhotel.co.uk
web: www.manorhotel.co.uk
Dir: *on A40, Crickhowell/Brecon, 0.5m from Crickhowell*
This impressive manor house set in a stunning location was the birthplace of Sir George Everest. The bedrooms and public areas are elegant, and there are extensive leisure facilities. The restaurant, with panoramic views, is the setting for exciting modern cooking. Guests can also dine informally at the nearby Nantyffin Cider Mill, a sister operation of the hotel.

ROOMS: 22 en suite (1 fmly) in 8 bedrooms s £55-£65; d £85-£105 (incl. bkfst) **LB** **FACILITIES:** STV Sauna Solarium Gym Jacuzzi Fitness assessment Sunbed Xmas **CONF:** Thtr 400 Class 300 Board 300 Del from £100 **PARKING:** 200 **NOTES:** in restaurant Civ Wed 100

★★71% Ty Croeso

The Dardy, Llangattock NP8 1PU
☎ 01873 810573 01873 810573
e-mail: info@ty-croeso.co.uk
Dir: *A40 at Shell garage take opposite road, down hill over river bridge. Turn right, after 0.5m turn left, up hill over canal, hotel signed*
Ty Croeso, meaning 'House of Welcome' certainly lives up to its name under the careful guidance of the new owners. The newly refurbished restaurant offers carefully prepared dishes with a real emphasis on Welsh produce; a theme that continues at breakfast when Glamorgan sausages and laver bread are available. A comfortable lounge features a log fire. Bedrooms are decorated with pretty fabrics and equipped with good facilities.
ROOMS: 8 en suite (1 fmly) in all bedrooms s £40-£55; d £65-£80 (incl. bkfst) **LB** **FACILITIES:** Xmas **PARKING:** 16 **NOTES:** in restaurant

CROSS HANDS, Carmarthenshire

Map 08 SN51

Travelodge Llanelli

SA14 6NW
☎ 08700 850 950 0870 191 1729
web: www.travelodge.co.uk
Dir: *on A48, westbound*
Travelodge offers good quality, good value, modern accommodation. Ideal for families, the spacious, en suite bedrooms include remote-control TV, tea and coffee-making facilities and comfortable beds. Meals can be taken at the nearby family restaurant. For further details consult the Hotel Groups page.
ROOMS: 32 en suite s fr £26; d fr £26

CWMBRAN, Torfaen

Map 09 ST29

★★★★66% Parkway

Cwmbran Dr NP44 3UW
☎ 01633 871199 01633 869160
e-mail: enquiries@parkwayhotel.co.uk
web: www.bw-parkwayhotel.co.uk
Dir: *M4 junct 25A/26/A4051 follow signs Cwmbran-Llantarnam Park. Turn right at rdbt then right for hotel*
This hotel is purpose-built and offers comfortable bedrooms and public areas suitable for a wide range of guests. There is a sports centre and a range of conference and meeting facilities. The coffee

continued

shop offers an informal eating option during the day and there is fine dining in Ravello's Restaurant.

ROOMS: 70 en suite (4 fmly) (34 GF) ⊛ in 46 bedrooms s £65-£100; d £85-£115 **LB FACILITIES:** STV ⌨ Sauna Solarium Gym Jacuzzi Steam room, Private sun bathing terrace, Sports shop, Solaria, Relaxation area ♫ Xmas **CONF:** Thtr 500 Class 240 Board 100 Del from £83 **PARKING:** 300 **NOTES:** ⊛ in restaurant Civ Wed 100

DEVIL'S BRIDGE, Ceredigion Map 09 SN77

★★69% **Hafod Arms**
SY23 3JL
☎ 01970 890232 ▤ 01970 890394
e-mail: enquiries@hafodarms.co.uk
Dir: *leave A44 at Ponterwyd. Hotel 5m along A4120, 11m E of Aberystwyth*
This former hunting lodge dates back to the 17th century and is now a family-owned and run hotel, providing accommodation suitable for both business people and tourists. Family rooms and a four-poster room are available. In addition to the dining area and lounge, there are tea rooms and six acres of grounds.
ROOMS: 15 rms (12 en suite) s fr £42; d £65-£100 (incl. bkfst) **LB**
PARKING: 30 **NOTES:** ✖ No children 12yrs ⊛ in restaurant Closed 15 Dec-Jan RS Mid Oct-14 Dec & Feb-mid March

DOLGELLAU, Gwynedd Map 14 SH71

★★★80% ◉◉ **Penmaenuchaf Hall**
Penmaenpool LL40 1YB
☎ 01341 422129 ▤ 01341 422787
e-mail: relax@penhall.co.uk
web: www.penhall.co.uk
Dir: *off A470 onto A493 to Tywyn. Hotel approx 1m on left*

Built in 1860, this impressive hall stands in 20 acres of formal gardens, grounds and woodland and enjoys magnificent views across the River Mawddach. Careful restoration has created a
continued

Dolserau Hall
Country House Hotel
Dolgellau LL40 2AG

Dolserau Hall with Cader Idris towering above

With magnificent scenery, wonderful views, great walking country, superb traditional cuisine, comfort and a warm welcome, it is no surprise that so many of our guests keep on coming back. Special breaks all year and Christmas and New Year programme. Call us now for our comprehensive colour brochure pack.

Tel: **(01341) 422522**
email: welcome@dhh.co.uk
Website www.dhh.co.uk

AA
★★★
Rosette

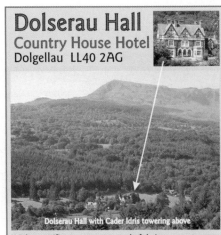

comfortable and welcoming hotel. Fresh produce cooked in modern British style is served in the panelled restaurant.
ROOMS: 14 en suite (2 fmly) (1 GF) ⊛ in 11 bedrooms s £75-£135; d £125-£185 (incl. bkfst) **LB FACILITIES:** Fishing Snooker ♪⌨ Complimentary salmon & trout fishing Xmas **CONF:** BC Thtr 50 Class 30 Board 22 Del from £155 **PARKING:** 30 **NOTES:** No children 6yrs ⊛ in restaurant Civ Wed 50

★★★74% *Plas Dolmelynllyn*
Ganllwyd LL40 2HP
☎ 01341 440273 ▤ 01341 440640
e-mail: info@dolly-hotel.co.uk
web: www.dolly-hotel.co.uk
Dir: *5m N of Dolgellau on A470*
Surrounded by three acres of mature gardens and National Trust land, this fine house dates back to the 16th century. Spacious bedrooms are attractive and offer many thoughtful extras. Carefully prepared meals are served in the comfortable dining room, adjacent to the conservatory bar.
ROOMS: 10 en suite (2 fmly) ⊛ in all bedrooms **FACILITIES:** STV Fishing Mountain walking Mountain Bike riding **CONF:** Class 15 Board 15 **PARKING:** 16 **NOTES:** ✖ ⊛ in restaurant Closed Jan

★★★73% ◉▟ **Dolserau Hall**
LL40 2AG
☎ 01341 422522 ▤ 01341 422400
e-mail: aa@dhh.co.uk
web: www.dhh.co.uk
Dir: *1.5m outside town between A494 to Bala and A470 to Dinas Mawddwy*
This privately-owned, friendly hotel lies in attractive grounds extending to the river and is surrounded by green fields. Several
continued on p784

DOLGELLAU, continued

comfortable lounges are provided and welcoming log fires are lit during cold weather. The smart bedrooms are well equipped and comfortable. A varied menu offers very competently prepared dishes.

Dolserau Hall, Dolgellau

ROOMS: 15 en suite (3 fmly) s £50-£70; d £92-£150 (incl. bkfst & dinner) **LB** **FACILITIES:** STV Xmas **SERVICES:** Lift **PARKING:** 40 **NOTES:** No children 6yrs ⊗ in restaurant Closed mid Nov-Jan (ex Xmas & New Year)

See advert on page 783

★★68% *Royal Ship*

Queens Square LL40 1AR
☎ 01341 422209 🖷 01341 421027
Dir: *in town centre*

The Royal Ship dates from 1813 when it was a coaching inn. There are three bars and several lounges, all comfortably furnished and attractively appointed. It is very much the centre of local activities and a wide range of food is available. Bedrooms are tastefully decorated.

ROOMS: 24 en suite (4 fmly) **FACILITIES:** Fishing arrangements available **CONF:** Thtr 80 Class 60 Board 60 **PARKING:** 12 **NOTES:** 🐕 ⊗ in restaurant

See advert on opposite page

★★67% Fronoleu Country Hotel

Tabor LL40 2PS
☎ 01341 422361 & 422197 🖷 01341 422023
e-mail: fronoleu@fronoleu.co.uk
web: www.fronoleu.co.uk
Dir: *A487/A470 junct, towards Tabor opposite Cross Foxes & continue for 1.25m. From Dolgellau take road for hospital & continue 1.25m up the hill*

This 16th-century farmhouse lies in the shadow of Cader Idris. Carefully extended, it retains many original features. The bar and lounge are located in the old building where there are exposed timbers and open fires, and the restaurant attracts a large local following. Most of the bedrooms are in a modern extension.

ROOMS: 11 en suite (3 fmly) ⊗ in 6 bedrooms s £40; d £67 (incl. bkfst) **LB** **FACILITIES:** Fishing Pool table, Childrens play area **CONF:** BC Thtr 150 Class 100 Board 50 Del from £64.95 **PARKING:** 60 **NOTES:** ⊗ in restaurant Civ Wed 150

★★67% *George III Hotel*

Penmaenpool LL40 1YD
☎ 01341 422525 🖷 01341 423565
e-mail: reception@george-3rd.co.uk
Dir: *2m from Dolgellau on A493*

On the banks of the Mawddach Estuary, this delightful small hotel (now under new ownership) started life as an inn and a chandlers to the local boatyard. A nearby building, now housing several bedrooms, was the local railway station. Bedrooms are well equipped and many enjoy river views. There is a choice of bars and a formal restaurant, all providing a wide range of food.

ROOMS: 6 en suite 5 annexe en suite **FACILITIES:** Fishing **CONF:** Class 32 **PARKING:** 30 **NOTES:** ⊗ in restaurant Closed 25 Dec

DOLWYDDELAN, Conwy — Map 14 SH75

★★66% Elen's Castle

LL25 0EJ
☎ 01690 750207 🖷 01690 750207
e-mail: info@elenscastlehotel.co.uk
Dir: *on A470, 5m S of Betws-y-Coed*

This small hotel is very friendly and was operated as a beer house in the 18th century. The original bar remains, complete with a slab floor and potbelly stove, and there are two cosy sitting rooms with open fires and exposed timbers. Two of the bedrooms have four-poster beds and families can be accommodated. A good range of bar and restaurant food is provided.

ROOMS: 9 rms (8 en suite) (2 fmly) ⊗ in 2 bedrooms **FACILITIES:** Coarse & fly fishing Xmas **CONF:** Thtr 30 Class 20 Board 15 **PARKING:** 40 **NOTES:** ⊗ in restaurant

EGLWYSFACH, Ceredigion — Map 14 SN69

Top Hotel

★★★ ◎◎◎◎ Ynyshir Hall

SY20 8TA
☎ 01654 781209 & 781268 🖷 01654 781366
e-mail: ynyshir@relaischateaux.com
web: www.ynyshir-hall.co.uk
Dir: *off A487, 5.5m S of Machynlleth, signed from main road*

RELAIS & CHATEAUX.

Set in beautifully landscaped grounds and surrounded by an RSBP reserve, Ynyshir Hall is a haven of calm. Lavishly styled bedrooms, each individually themed around a great painter, provide high standards of luxury and comfort. Lounge and bar

continued

have different moods, and both feature abundant fresh flowers. The dining room offers outstanding cooking using best ingredients with modern style.
ROOMS: 7 en suite 2 annexe en suite ⊗ in all bedrooms s £110-£280; d £125-£340 (incl. bkfst) **LB FACILITIES:** ♨ Xmas **CONF:** Thtr 25 Class 20 Board 18 **PARKING:** 20 **NOTES:** No children 9yrs ⊗ in restaurant Closed 5-29 Jan Civ Wed 40

EWLOE, Flintshire Map 15 SJ36

★★★★70% 🌼 *De Vere St David's Park*
St Davids Park CH5 3YB DE VERE ● HOTELS
☎ 01244 520800 ◨ 01244 520930
e-mail: reservations.stdavids@devere-hotels.com
web: www.devereonline.co.uk
Dir: A494 Queensferry to Mold for 4m, then left slip road B5127 signed Buckley, hotel visible at rdbt
This modern purpose built hotel is conveniently situated and offers a range of rooms, including four-poster suites and family rooms. Public areas include leisure and spa facilities, an all-day café, and, nearby, the hotel's own golf course. The hotel is a popular venue for conferences and other functions. Younger guests are not forgotten either and can have fun in the Dai the Dove Club.
ROOMS: 145 en suite (24 fmly) (43 GF) ⊗ in 54 bedrooms
FACILITIES: STV ⊡ supervised ॰ Snooker Sauna Solarium Gym Putt green Jacuzzi Steam bath, Beauty Therapist, Playroom **CONF:** BC Thtr 300 Class 150 Board 40 **SERVICES:** Lift **PARKING:** 240 **NOTES:** ✼ ⊗ in restaurant Civ Wed 60

FISHGUARD, Pembrokeshire Map 08 SM93

★★69% **Cartref**
15-19 High St SA65 9AW
☎ 01348 872430 ◨ 01348 873664
e-mail: cartrefhotel@btconnect.com
web: www.cartrefhotel.co.uk
Dir: on A40 in town centre
Personally run by the proprietor, this friendly hotel offers convenient access to the town centre and ferry terminal. Bedrooms are well maintained and include some family bedded rooms. There is also a cosy lounge bar and a welcoming restaurant, which looks out over the high street.
ROOMS: 10 en suite (2 fmly) s £34-£38; d £54-£60 (incl. bkfst) **LB**
PARKING: 4 **NOTES:** ⊗ in restaurant

FLINT, Flintshire Map 15 SJ27

★★★66% **Mountain Park Hotel**
Northop Rd, Flint Mountain CH6 5QG
☎ 01352 736000 & 730972 ◨ 01352 736010
e-mail: reception@mountain.co.uk
Dir: exit A55 onto A5119 for Flint , hotel 1m on left
This former farmhouse has modern, well-equipped bedrooms, many at ground-floor level with direct access to the car park. It is conveniently situated close to the A55. Facilities include the Sevens Brasserie Restaurant serving modern cuisine, a comfortable lounge bar offering a range of bar meals, and an attractively designed function/conference room. There is also a 9-hole golf course.
ROOMS: 21 annexe en suite (3 fmly) (11 GF) **FACILITIES:** STV ⅃ 9 Jacuzzi Xmas **CONF:** Thtr 150 Class 80 Board 60 Del from £70
SERVICES: air con **PARKING:** 94 **NOTES:** ✼ ⊗ in restaurant

ROYAL SHIP HOTEL★★
Queens Square, Dolgellau, Gwynedd
Telephone Dolgellau 01341 422209

• Situated in the Cader Idris mountain range
• Ideally situated in the centre of town •
Family Rooms • TV in all En-suite Rooms
• Ideally situated for touring North and Mid
Wales • Great Little Trains of Wales • Slate
Mines at Blaenau • Mountain Walking
• Cyclists Trek • Golf • Mastercard • Visa
• Eurocheque • Switch • Delta accepted
• Colour Brochure on request •

GLYN CEIRIOG, Wrexham Map 15 SJ23

★★★67% **Golden Pheasant**
Glyn Ceiriog LL20 7BB
☎ 01691 718281 ◨ 01691 718479
e-mail: goldenpheasant@micro-plus-web.net
web: www.goldenpheasanthotel.co.uk
Dir: A5/B4500 at Chirk, then 5m to Pontfadog, follow hotel signs, 1st left after Cheshire Home. Hotel at top of small hill
This 18th-century hostelry is quietly situated on the edge of the village and is surrounded by rolling hills. The bedrooms include four-poster and family rooms and there is a choice of bars, as well as a lounge and a restaurant. To the rear is an attractive courtyard with shrubs and flowerbeds.
ROOMS: 19 en suite (5 fmly) s £45-£98; d £85-£115 (incl. bkfst) **LB**
FACILITIES: Xmas **CONF:** Thtr 60 Board 20 **PARKING:** 45 **NOTES:** ⊗ in restaurant RS 25 Dec

HALKYN, Flintshire Map 15 SJ27

⌂ **Travelodge**
CH8 8RF
☎ 08700 850 950 ◨ 01352 781966
web: www.travelodge.co.uk
Dir: on A55, westbound
Travelodge offers good quality, good value, modern accommodation. Ideal for families, the spacious, en suite bedrooms include remote-control TV, tea and coffee-making facilities and comfortable beds. Meals can be taken at the nearby family restaurant. For further details consult the Hotel Groups page.
ROOMS: 31 en suite s fr £26; d fr £26

HARLECH, Gwynedd Map 14 SH53

Top Hotel

★★ ◎◎≛ **Maes y Neuadd Country House**
LL47 6YA
☎ 01766 780200 🖹 01766 780211
e-mail: maes@neuadd.com
web: www.neuadd.com
Dir: 3m NE of Harlech, signed on unclassified road, off B4573
This 14th-century hotel enjoys fine views over the mountains and across the bay to the Lleyn Peninsula. The team here is committed to highlighting and restoring some of the hidden features of the house. Bedrooms, some in an adjacent coach house, are individually furnished and many boast fine antique pieces. Public areas display a similar welcoming charm, including the restaurant, which serves locally-sourced and many home-grown ingredients.
ROOMS: 16 en suite (3 GF) ⊗ in all bedrooms s £80-£95; d £179-£270 (incl. bkfst & dinner) **LB FACILITIES:** ↓♀ clay pigeon, cooking tuition Xmas **CONF:** Thtr 20 Class 10 Board 12 Del from £185 **PARKING:** 50 **NOTES:** ⊗ in restaurant Civ Wed 65

🖪 The Castle
Castle Square LL46 2YH
☎ 01766 780529 🖹 01766 780499
Dir: directly opposite the entrance to Harlech Castle
ROOMS: 7 en suite (1 fmly) s £25-£38; d £50-£76 (incl. bkfst) **PARKING:** 30 **NOTES:** ★★ ⊁ ⊗ in restaurant

HAVERFORDWEST, Pembrokeshire Map 08 SM91

★★68% **Hotel Mariners**
Mariners Square SA61 2DU THE INDEPENDENTS
☎ 01437 763353 🖹 01437 764258
Dir: follow town centre signs, over bridge, up High St, 1st turning on right, hotel at the end
Located a few minutes' walk from the town centre, this privately owned and friendly hotel is reputed to date back to 1625. The bedrooms are equipped with modern facilities and are soundly maintained. A good range of food is offered in the popular bar, which is a focus for the town. The restaurant offers a more formal dining option. Facilities include a choice of meeting rooms.
ROOMS: 28 en suite (5 fmly) ⊗ in 16 bedrooms s £57-£66.50; d £76.50-£85 (incl. bkfst) **LB FACILITIES:** STV Short mat bowls **CONF:** Thtr 50 Class 20 Board 20 **PARKING:** 50 **NOTES:** Closed 25-27 Dec & 1 Jan

★★64% **Castle Hotel**
Castle Square SA61 2AA
☎ 01437 769322 🖹 01437 768806
Dir: from the main rdbt into Haverfordwest follow town centre signs, follow the road for approx 200yds, hotel on right
At the centre of the bustling town, this former coaching inn is very much at the heart of local activities and is a favourite with locals. A good range of wholesome food is available in both the restaurant and bar. Bedrooms have modern furnishings and facilities.
ROOMS: 9 en suite (1 fmly) **NOTES:** ⊁ ⊗ in restaurant Closed 24-25 & 31 Dec

HAY-ON-WYE, Powys Map 09 SO24

★★★70% **The Swan-at-Hay**
Church St HR3 5DQ
☎ 01497 821188 🖹 01497 821424
e-mail: info@swanathay.co.uk
Dir: from Brecon on B4350, hotel on left. From any other route follow signs for Brecon & just before leaving town hotel on right
This former coaching inn dates back to the 1800s and is only a short walk from the town centre. Bedrooms are well equipped and some are located in converted cottages across the courtyard. Spacious, relaxing public areas include a comfortable lounge, a choice of bars and a more formal restaurant. There is also a large function room and a smaller meeting room.
ROOMS: 15 en suite 4 annexe en suite (1 fmly) (2 GF) ⊗ in 16 bedrooms s £65-£125; d £90-£135 (incl. bkfst) **LB FACILITIES:** Fishing Xmas **CONF:** Thtr 140 Class 60 Board 50 Del from £115 **PARKING:** 18 **NOTES:** ⊗ in restaurant Civ Wed 50

★★73% ◎ **Old Black Lion**
26 Lion St HR3 5AD
☎ 01497 820841 🖹 01497 822960
e-mail: info@oldblacklion.co.uk
web: www.oldblacklion.co.uk
Dir: from Tourist Information car park turn right along Oxford Rd, pass Nat West bank, next left (Lion St), hotel 20yds on right
This fine old coaching inn, with a history stretching back several centuries, has a wealth of charm and character. It was occupied by Oliver Cromwell during the siege of Hay Castle. Privately owned and personally run, it provides cosy and well-equipped bedrooms, some located in an adjacent building. A wide range of well prepared food is provided, and the service is friendly.
ROOMS: 6 rms (5 en suite) 4 annexe en suite (2 GF) ⊗ in all bedrooms s £32-£65; d £80-£110 (incl. bkfst) **LB FACILITIES:** Xmas **PARKING:** 16 **NOTES:** ⊁ No children 5yrs ⊗ in restaurant

★★69% **Baskerville Arms**
Clyro HR3 5RZ
☎ 01497 820670 🖹 01497 821609
e-mail: lyn@baskervillearms.co.uk
Dir: from Hereford follow Brecon A438 into Clyro. Hotel signed
Situated near to Hay-on-Wye in the peaceful village of Clyro, this former Georgian coaching inn is personally run by its friendly and enthusiastic owners. Bedrooms are well equipped with comfort in mind, while public areas include a bar with a village inn atmosphere, a separate restaurant and a comfortable residents' lounge. There is also a large function room, plus a meeting room.
ROOMS: 13 en suite (1 fmly) ⊗ in 7 bedrooms s £35-£42; d £65-£75 (incl. bkfst) **LB FACILITIES:** Fishing **CONF:** Thtr 65 Class 40 Board 36 **PARKING:** 12 **NOTES:** ⊗ in restaurant

H

★★67% Kilverts Hotel

The Bull Ring HR3 5AG
☎ 01497 821042 ▯ 01497 821580
e-mail: info@kilverts.co.uk
Dir: *from Brecon on B4350, on entering Hay-on-Wye take 1st right after Cinema Bookshop. Then 1st left and hotel is on right after 40yds*

Situated in the centre of this fascinating town, Kilverts is a genuinely friendly and welcoming hotel. The committed staff provide attentive hospitality within a convivial atmosphere. Well-equipped bedrooms are cosy, with plenty of character. Food has an international influence, available in either the bar or stylish restaurant. The extensive gardens are ideal in the summer months.
ROOMS: 12 en suite (2 fmly) (1 GF) ⊘ in 1 bedroom s £35-£50; d £70-£100 (incl. bkfst) **LB** **CONF:** Thtr 30 Class 10 Board 16 **PARKING:** 13 **NOTES:** ⊘ in restaurant Closed 25-Dec

HENSOL, Vale of Glamorgan — Map 09 ST07

★★★★73% Vale Hotel Golf & Spa Resort

Hensol Park CF72 8JY
☎ 01443 667800 ▯ 01443 665850
e-mail: reservations@vale-hotel.com
web: www.vale-hotel.com
Dir: *M4 junct 34 towards Pendoylan, hotel signed (approx 3 mins' drive from junct)*

A wealth of leisure facilities are offered at this large and modern, purpose-built complex, including two golf courses and a driving range, extensive health spa, gym, swimming pool, squash courts and an orthopaedic clinic. Public areas are spacious and attractive, whilst bedrooms, many with balconies, are well appointed. Meeting and conference facilities are available. Guests can dine
continued
either in La Cucina which boasts a wood-fired oven, or the more traditional Lakes restaurant.
ROOMS: 29 en suite 114 annexe en suite (17 fmly) (36 GF) ⊘ in 71 bedrooms s £80-£165; d £90-£175 (incl. bkfst) **LB** **FACILITIES: Spa** STV ⛆ ⛳36 ✂ Fishing Squash Riding Sauna Solarium Gym Putt green Jacuzzi Beauty & Hydrotherapy treatments, Childrens club, Indoor training arena Xmas **CONF:** Thtr 300 Class 180 Board 60 Del from £150 **SERVICES:** Lift air con **PARKING:** 300 **NOTES:** ✖ ⊘ in restaurant Civ Wed 200

See advert under CARDIFF

HOLYHEAD See Anglesey, Isle of

HOLYWELL, Flintshire — Map 15 SJ17

★★70% Stamford Gate

Halkyn Rd CH8 7SJ
☎ 01352 712942 ▯ 01352 713309
e-mail: hotel@stamfordgate.freeserve.co.uk
Dir: *take Holywell turn off A55 on to A5026, hotel 1m on right*

This popular, friendly hotel enjoys impressive views across the Dee Estuary from its elevated position. It provides well-equipped accommodation, including a number of ground floor bedrooms. Public areas include a smart nautical themed restaurant, a stylish, spacious bar and there are meeting and function facilities.
ROOMS: 12 en suite (6 GF) **FACILITIES:** STV ♫ **CONF:** Thtr 100 Class 50 Board 30 **PARKING:** 100 **NOTES:** ✖

ISLE OF Placenames incorporating the words 'Isle' or 'Isle of' will be found under the actual name, eg Isle of Anglesey is under Anglesey, Isle of.

I

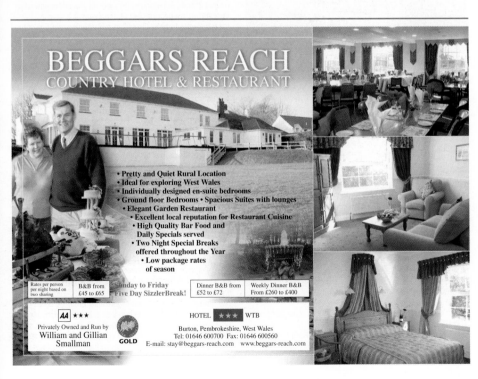

KNIGHTON, Powys Map 09 SO27

★★80% ◎◎ Milebrook House
Milebrook LD7 1LT
☎ 01547 528632 📠 01547 520509
e-mail: hotel@milebrook.kc3ltd.co.uk
web: www.milebrookhouse.co.uk
Dir: *2m E of Knighton, on A4113*
Set in three acres of grounds and gardens in the Teme Valley, this charming house dates back to 1760. Over the years since its conversion to a hotel, it has acquired a well-deserved reputation for its warm hospitality, comfortable accommodation and the quality of its food that uses local produce and home-grown vegetables.
ROOMS: 10 en suite (2 fmly) (2 GF) ⊗ in all bedrooms s £87-£91; d £147-£153 (incl. bkfst & dinner) **LB FACILITIES:** Fishing Badminton, Trout Fly Fishing Xmas **CONF:** Class 30 **PARKING:** 21 **NOTES:** No children 8yrs ⊗ in restaurant RS Mon

LAMPETER, Ceredigion Map 08 SN54

★★★74% ◎ Falcondale Mansion
SA48 7RX
☎ 01570 422910 📠 01570 423559
e-mail: info@falcondalehotel.com
web: www.falcondalehotel.com
Dir: *800yds W of High St A475 or 1.5m NW of Lampeter A482*

Built in the Italianate style, this charming Victorian property is set in extensive grounds and beautiful parkland. Bedrooms are generally spacious, well equipped and are individually and tastefully decorated. Bars and lounges are similarly well appointed with additional facilities including a conservatory and function room. Diners have a choice of either the restaurant or the less formal brasserie.
ROOMS: 20 en suite (2 fmly) ⊗ in 12 bedrooms s £95-£120; d £120-£180 (incl. bkfst) **LB FACILITIES:** Xmas **CONF:** Thtr 60 Class 30 Board 25 Del from £109 **SERVICES:** Lift **PARKING:** 60 **NOTES:** ⊗ in restaurant Civ Wed 60

LAMPHEY See Pembroke

LLANARMON DYFFRYN CEIRIOG, Wrexham Map 15 SJ13

★★76% ◎◎ West Arms
LL20 7LD
☎ 01691 600665 & 600612 📠 01691 600622
e-mail: gowestarms@aol.com
Dir: *off A483/A5 at Chirk, take B4500 to Ceiriog Valley. Llanarmon 11m at end of B4500*
Set in the beautiful Ceiriog Valley, this delightful hotel has a wealth of charm and character. There is a comfortable lounge, a room for private dining and two bars, as well as a pleasant, award-winning restaurant offering a set-price menu of freshly cooked dishes. The attractive bedrooms have a mixture of modern and period furnishings.

ROOMS: 15 en suite (2 fmly) (3 GF) **FACILITIES:** Fishing Xmas **CONF:** BC Thtr 60 Class 50 Board 50 **PARKING:** 22 **NOTES:** ⊗ in restaurant Civ Wed 50

LLANBEDR, Gwynedd Map 14 SH52

★★64% Ty Mawr
LL45 2NH
☎ 01341 241440 📠 01341 241440
e-mail: tymawrhotel@onetel.com
web: www.tymawrhotel.org.uk
Dir: *from Barmouth A496 (Harlech road). In Llanbedr turn right after bridge, hotel 50yds on left, brown tourist signs on junct*
Located in a picturesque village, this family-run hotel has a relaxed, friendly atmosphere. The pleasant grounds opposite the River Artro are a popular beer garden during fine weather. The attractive, cane-furnished bar offers a blackboard selection of food and a good choice of real ales. A more formal menu is available in the restaurant. Bedrooms are smart and brightly decorated.
ROOMS: 10 en suite (2 fmly) ⊗ in all bedrooms s £45-£50; d £70-£75 (incl. bkfst) **LB FACILITIES:** STV **CONF:** Class 25 **PARKING:** 30 **NOTES:** ⊗ in restaurant Closed 24-26 Dec

LLANBERIS, Gwynedd Map 14 SH56

Lake View Hotel & Restaurant
Tan-y-Pant LL55 4EL
☎ 01286 870422 📠 01286 872591
e-mail: reception@lakeviewhotel.co.uk
web: www.lakeviewhotel.co.uk
Dir: *1m from Llanberis on A4086 towards Caernarfon*
ROOMS: 10 rms (9 en suite) (2 fmly) ⊗ in all bedrooms s £30-£45; d £48-£68 (incl. bkfst) **LB FACILITIES:** 2 footpaths adjacent to hotel **CONF:** Del from £24 **PARKING:** 20 **NOTES:** ★★ ⊗ in restaurant RS Jan-Feb

LLANDEGLA, Denbighshire Map 15 SJ25

★★★72% ◎ Bodidris Hall
LL11 3AL
☎ 0870 7292292 & 01978 790434 📠 01978 790335
e-mail: info@bodidrishall.com
Dir: *in village take A5104 towards Chester. Hotel 2m on left, signed*
This impressive manor house is in a quiet location surrounded by ornamental gardens and mature woodlands. It has an interesting history and a wealth of charm and character, with original features such as gallery ceilinged bedrooms and inglenook fireplaces.

continued

Bedrooms have now been refurbished and many are furnished with antique pieces and some have four-poster beds.
ROOMS: 9 en suite ⊘ in 3 bedrooms s £75-£150; d £99-£199 (incl. bkfst) **LB** **FACILITIES:** Fishing Xmas **CONF:** Thtr 65 Class 20 Board 20 **PARKING:** 60 **NOTES:** ⊘ in restaurant Civ Wed 65

LLANDEILO, Carmarthenshire — Map 08 SN62

★★★70% The Plough Inn

Rhosmaen SA19 6NP
☎ 01558 823431 📠 01558 823969
e-mail: enquiries@ploughrhosmaendemon.co.uk
web: www.ploughrhosmaen.co.uk
Dir: *0.5m N of Llandeilo on A40*

This privately owned hotel has memorable views over the Towy Valley and the Black Mountains. Bedrooms, situated in a separate wing, are tastefully furnished, spacious and comfortable. The public lounge bar is popular with locals, as is the spacious restaurant where freshly prepared food can be enjoyed. Additional facilities include a sauna, gym and conference facilities.
ROOMS: 14 en suite (5 GF) ⊘ in all bedrooms s fr £55; d fr £70 (incl. bkfst) **FACILITIES:** STV Sauna Gym Xmas **CONF:** Thtr 45 Class 24 Board 24 **PARKING:** 70 **NOTES:** 🐕 ⊘ in restaurant Civ Wed 90

★★68% White Hart Inn

36 Carmarthen Rd SA19 6RS
☎ 01558 823419 📠 01558 823089
e-mail: therese@whitehartinn.fsnet.co.uk
web: www.whitehartinn.fsnet.co.uk
Dir: *off A40 onto A483, hotel 200yds on left*
This privately owned, 19th-century roadside hostelry is on the outskirts of town. The modern bedrooms are well equipped and tastefully furnished. Family rooms are available. Public areas include a choice of bars and both smoking and non-smoking dining areas, where a wide range of grill dishes is available. There are several function rooms, including a large self-contained suite.
ROOMS: 11 en suite (2 fmly) s £40; d £60 (incl. bkfst) **FACILITIES:** STV **PARKING:** 50 **NOTES:** 🐕 Civ Wed 70

LLANDOVERY, Carmarthenshire — Map 09 SN73

★★★63% Castle

King's Rd SA20 0AP
☎ 01550 720343 📠 01550 720673
e-mail: castlehotelllandovery@hotmail.com
Dir: *on A40 in town centre, between Brecon & Carmarthen*
Overlooked by the original Norman keep, the Castle Hotel is in the heart of this market town. There is a warm atmosphere, enhanced by the roaring log fires lit in the winter. There is a wide variety of

continued

bedroom styles and sizes, including rooms once occupied by George Borrow and Lord Nelson.
ROOMS: 23 en suite (4 fmly) ⊘ in 21 bedrooms s £45-£50; d £65-£80 (incl. bkfst) **FACILITIES:** STV Fishing Xmas **CONF:** BC Thtr 150 Class 150 Board 100 **PARKING:** 30 **NOTES:** ⊘ in restaurant

LLANDRINDOD WELLS, Powys — Map 09 SO06

★★★73% ❀ The Metropole

Temple St LD1 5DY
☎ 01597 823700 📠 01597 824828
e-mail: info@metropole.co.uk
web: www.metropole.co.uk
Dir: *on A483 in town centre*

The centre of this famous spa town is dominated by this large Victorian hotel, which has been personally run by the same family for well over 100 years. The lobby leads to a choice of bars and an elegant lounge. Bedrooms, many of which are non-smoking, vary

continued on p790

LLANDRINDOD WELLS, continued

in style and all are quite spacious and well equipped. Facilities here include an extensive selection conference and function rooms, as well as a leisure centre.
ROOMS: 120 en suite (7 fmly) ⊛ in 57 bedrooms s £77-£97; d £100-£120 (incl. bkfst) **LB FACILITIES:** ⊟ Sauna Solarium Gym Jacuzzi Mini-gym, Beauty and holistic treatments Xmas **CONF:** Thtr 300 Class 200 Board 80 Del from £110 **SERVICES:** Lift **PARKING:** 150 **NOTES:** ⊛ in restaurant Civ Wed 300

See advert on page 789

LLANDUDNO, Conwy

Map 14 SH78

Top Hotel

★★★★ ⊛⊛⊛ **Bodysgallen Hall & Spa**
LL30 1RS
☎ 01492 584466 📠 01492 582519
e-mail: info@bodysgallen.com web: www.bodysgallen.com
Dir: A55 junct 19, A470 towards Llandudno. Hotel 2m on right
Situated in idyllic surroundings of its own parkland and formal gardens, this 17th-century house is in an elevated position, with views towards Snowdonia and across to Conwy Castle. The lounges and dining room have fine antiques and great character. Accommodation is provided in the house, but also in delightfully converted cottages, together with a superb spa. Friendly and attentive service is discreetly offered, whilst the restaurant features fine local produce prepared with great skill.
ROOMS: 19 en suite 16 annexe en suite (3 fmly) (4 GF) ⊛ in 19 bedrooms s £135-£175; d £175-£290 (incl. bkfst) **LB**
FACILITIES: Spa STV ⊟ ⚲ Sauna Solarium Gym ⚘ Jacuzzi Beauty salons, Steam room, Club room, Relaxation Room ♫ Xmas
CONF: BC Thtr 50 Class 30 Board 24 Del from £145
PARKING: 50 **NOTES:** ✗ No children 8yrs ⊛ in restaurant
Civ Wed 45

Top Town House

★★★★ ⊛ 🏠 **Osborne House**
17 North House LL30 2LP
☎ 01492 860330 📠 01492 860791
e-mail: sales@osbornehouse.com
web: www.osbornehouse.com
Dir: exit A55 junct 19. Follow signs for Llandudno then Promenade. Continue to junct, turn right. hotel on left opposite pier entrance
Originally built in 1832, this Victorian house has been restored and converted into a luxurious townhouse by the Maddocks family. Spacious suites offer unrivalled comfort and luxury, combining antique furnishings with state-of-the-art technology and facilities. Each suite provides super views over the pier

continued

and bay. Osborne's café grill is open throughout the day and offers high quality food whilst the bar blends elegance with plasma screens, dazzling chandeliers and guilt-edged mirrors.

ROOMS: 6 en suite s £145-£220; d £145-£220 (incl. bkfst)
FACILITIES: STV use of swimming pool/sauna/jacuzzi at Empire Hotel (100 yds) Xmas **SERVICES:** air con **PARKING:** 6 **NOTES:** ✗ No children 11yrs ⊛ in restaurant Closed 19-29 Dec

★★★75% ⊛ **Empire**
Church Walks LL30 2HE
☎ 01492 860555 📠 01492 860791
e-mail: reservations@empirehotel.co.uk
web: www.empirehotel.co.uk
Dir: A55 from Chester, exit junct 19 for Llandudno. Follow town centre signs. Hotel at end facing main street

Run by the same family for over almost 60 years, the Empire offers luxuriously appointed bedrooms with every modern facility. The 'Number 72' rooms in an adjacent house are particularly sumptuous. The indoor pool is overlooked by a lounge area where snacks are served all day, and in summer an outdoor pool and roof garden are available. The Watkins restaurant offers an interesting fixed-price menu.
ROOMS: 50 en suite 8 annexe en suite (3 fmly) (2 GF) s £65-£100 (incl. bkfst) **LB FACILITIES: Spa** STV ⊟ ⚲ Sauna Full range of beauty treatments Xmas **CONF:** Thtr 25 Class 20 Board 20 Del from £87.50 **SERVICES:** Lift **PARKING:** 40 **NOTES:** ✗ ⊛ in restaurant Closed 10 days Xmas

See advert on opposite page

★★★74% ⊛ **Imperial**
The Promenade LL30 1AP
☎ 01492 877466 📠 01492 878043
e-mail: imphotel@btinternet.com
web: www.theimperial.co.uk
Dir: A470 to Llandudno
The Imperial is a large and impressive hotel, situated on the promenade, within easy reach of the town centre and other

continued

amenities. Many of the bedrooms have views over the bay and there are also several suites available. The elegant Chantrey restaurant offers a fixed-price menu which changes monthly and dishes take full advantage of local produce.

ROOMS: 100 en suite (10 fmly) ⊗ in 60 bedrooms **FACILITIES:** STV Sauna Solarium Gym Jacuzzi Beauty therapist Hairdressing ♫ Xmas **CONF:** Thtr 150 Class 50 Board 50 **SERVICES:** Lift **PARKING:** 25 **NOTES:** ⊗ in restaurant Civ Wed 150

See advert on this page

★★★69% Dunoon
Gloddaeth St LL30 2DW
☎ 01492 860787 🖷 01492 860031
e-mail: reservations@dunoonhotel.co.uk
web: www.dunoonhotel.co.uk
Dir: *exit Promenade at War Memorial by pier onto wide avenue. 200yds on right*

This smart hotel is centrally located in the town ofers a choice of attractive, well-equipped accommodation. The restaurant serves freshly prepared, tasty meals, whilst lighter snacks and afternoon tea may be taken in one of the lounges or bar.
ROOMS: 49 en suite (7 fmly) s £52-£57; d £72-£114 (incl. bkfst) **LB** **FACILITIES:** STV ♫ Xmas **CONF:** BC **SERVICES:** Lift **PARKING:** 24 **NOTES:** ⊗ in restaurant Closed 28 Dec-mid-Mar

★★★64% St George's
The Promenade LL30 2LG
☎ 01492 877544 🖷 01492 877788
e-mail: stgeorges@countrytown-hotels.co.uk
web: www.macdonald-hotels.co.uk
Dir: *A55-A470, follow to promenade, 0.25m, hotel on corner*
This popular and friendly seafront hotel was the first to be built in the town. Its many Victorian features include the splendid, ornate Wedgwood Room. The main lounges overlook the bay, are

continued on p792

LLANDUDNO, continued

comfortable, and hot and cold snacks are available all day. Several bedrooms have views over the sea, and some have balconies.

St George's, Llandudno

ROOMS: 86 en suite (6 fmly) ⊗ in 76 bedrooms s £70-£115; d £110-£150 (incl. bkfst) **LB** **FACILITIES:** STV Sauna Solarium Jacuzzi Hairdressing Health & beauty salon ch fac Xmas **CONF:** Thtr 250 Class 200 Board 45 Del from £110 **SERVICES:** Lift **PARKING:** 50 **NOTES:** ⊗ in restaurant Civ Wed 200

See advert on opposite page

★★★63% *Chatsworth House*

Central Promenade LL30 2XS
☎ 01492 860788 01492 871417
e-mail: manager@chatsworth-hotel.co.uk
web: www.chatsworth-hotel.co.uk

This traditional family-run Victorian hotel occupies a central position on the promenade and caters for many families and groups. There is an indoor swimming pool, a sauna and a solarium. Public areas are well maintained, and bedrooms are modern; some of them quite spacious.

ROOMS: 72 en suite (19 fmly) **FACILITIES:** Sauna Jacuzzi **SERVICES:** Lift **PARKING:** 9

Top Hotel

★★ St Tudno Hotel and Restaurant

The Promenade LL30 2LP
☎ 01492 874411 01492 860407
e-mail: sttudnohotel@btinternet.com
web: www.st-tudno.co.uk
Dir: *on Promenade towards pier, hotel opposite pier entrance*

A high quality family-owned hotel with friendly, attentive staff, and enjoying fine sea views. The stylish bedrooms are well equipped with mini-bars, robes, satellite TVs with videos and many other thoughtful extras. Public rooms include a lounge, a welcoming bar and a small indoor pool. The Terrace

continued

Restaurant, where seasonal and daily-changing menus are offered, has a delightful Mediterranean atmosphere. Afternoon tea is a real highlight.

ROOMS: 19 en suite (4 fmly) ⊗ in 3 bedrooms s £75-£85; d £94-£220 (incl. bkfst) **LB** **FACILITIES:** STV supervised ♫ Xmas **CONF:** Thtr 40 Class 25 Board 20 Del from £145 **SERVICES:** Lift **PARKING:** 12 **NOTES:** ⊗ in restaurant

★★73% *Tynedale*

Central Promenade LL30 2XS
☎ 01492 877426 01492 871213
e-mail: enquiries@tynedalehotel.co.uk
web: www.tynedalehotel.co.uk
Dir: *on promenade opposite bandstand*

Tour groups are well catered for at this privately owned and personally run hotel, and regular live entertainment is a feature. Public areas include good lounge facilities and an attractive patio overlooking the bay. The well maintained, no-smoking bedrooms are fresh and well equipped. Many have good views over the seafront and the Great Orme.

ROOMS: 54 en suite (4 fmly) ⊗ in all bedrooms **FACILITIES:** ♫ **SERVICES:** Lift **PARKING:** 30 **NOTES:** ⊗ in restaurant

★★72% Sunnymede

West Pde LL30 2BD
☎ 01492 877130 01492 871824
e-mail: sunnymedehotel@yahoo.co.uk
Dir: *from A55 follow Llandudno & Deganwy signs. At 1st rdbt after Deganwy take 1st exit towards sea. Left at corner, then 400yds*

Sunnymede is a friendly family-run hotel located on Llandudno's West Shore. Many rooms have views over the Conwy Estuary and Snowdonia. The modern bedrooms are attractively decorated and well equipped. Bar and lounge areas are particularly comfortable and attractive.

ROOMS: 15 en suite (3 fmly) (4 GF) ⊗ in all bedrooms s £28.50-£75; d £57-£75 (incl. bkfst) **LB** **FACILITIES:** Xmas **PARKING:** 18 **NOTES:** No children 3yrs ⊗ in restaurant Closed Jan-Feb & Nov RS Xmas period

★★72% Tan Lan

Great Orme's Rd, West Shore LL30 2AR
☎ 01492 860221 01492 870219
e-mail: info@tanlanhotel.co.uk
Dir: *off A55 junct 18 onto A546 signed Deganwy. Approx 3m, straight over mini-rdbt, hotel 50mtrs on left*

Warm and friendly hospitality is one of the many strengths at this small, well-maintained, privately owned and personally run hotel. It is located on Llandudno's West Shore, close to the Great Orme. The bedrooms, some on the ground floor, are modern and well

continued

equipped. Facilities include a pleasant dining room, lounge and bar. This is a totally no-smoking establishment.
ROOMS: 17 en suite (1 fmly) (6 GF) ⊗ in all bedrooms s £35-£40; d £50-£60 (incl. bkfst) **LB** **PARKING:** 12 **NOTES:** ✗ No children 6yrs ⊗ in restaurant Closed Nov - mid Mar

★★70% Epperstone
15 Abbey Rd LL30 2EE
☎ 01492 878746 🖹 01492 871223
e-mail: epperstonehotel@btconnect.com
Dir: *A55-A470 to Mostyn Street. Left at rdbt, 4th right into York Rd. Hotel on junct of York Rd & Abbey Rd*
This delightful hotel is located in wonderful gardens in a residential part of town, and is within easy walking distance of the seafront and shopping area. Bedrooms are attractively decorated and thoughtfully equipped. Two lounges, a comfortable non-smoking room and a Victorian-style conservatory are available. A daily changing menu is offered in the bright dining room.
ROOMS: 8 en suite (5 fmly) (1 GF) ⊗ in all bedrooms s £25-£38; d £50-£76 (incl. bkfst) **LB** **FACILITIES:** STV Xmas **PARKING:** 8 **NOTES:** No children 5yrs ⊗ in restaurant

★★68% Oak Alyn
2 Deganwy Av LL30 2YB
☎ 01492 860320 🖹 01492 860320
Dir: *in town centre, 200yds from Town Hall, opposite Catholic church*
This private hotel has been much improved by the present owners. It is close to the town centre and within a few minutes' walk of the promenade. Bedrooms have modern facilities. There is a bright and pleasant dining room with a conservatory extension, and a lounge bar.
ROOMS: 12 en suite (2 fmly) s £26-£28; d £52-£56 (incl. bkfst) **CONF:** Thtr 26 Class 30 **PARKING:** 16 **NOTES:** ✗ ⊗ in restaurant Closed 22-31 Dec

★★68% Sandringham
West Pde LL30 2BD
☎ 01492 876513 🖹 01492 877916
e-mail: enquiries@thesandringhamhotel.co.uk
web: www.thesandringhamhotel.co.uk
Dir: *enter Llandudno on A470 & follow signs for West Shore, hotel in centre of West Shore Promenade*

This pleasant and friendly hotel is privately owned and personally run. It is located at the West Shore area of Llandudno. The accommodation is well equipped and there are popular bar and restaurant operations which provide an extensive choice of wholesome food.
ROOMS: 18 en suite (3 fmly) (2 GF) ⊗ in all bedrooms s £33-£35; d £66-£70 (incl. bkfst) **LB** **FACILITIES:** STV **NOTES:** ✗ ⊗ in restaurant RS 1-14 Jan

★★68% *Somerset*
St Georges Crescent, Promenade LL30 2LF
☎ 01492 876540 🖹 01492 863700
e-mail: somerset@favroy.freeserve.co.uk
Dir: *on the Promenade*
This friendly and cheerful holiday hotel occupies an ideal location on the central promenade and affords superb views over the bay from many rooms. Regular entertainment is provided as well as a range of bar and lounge areas. Bedrooms are well decorated and modern facilities are provided.
ROOMS: 78 en suite (4 fmly) **FACILITIES:** Games room ♫ **CONF:** Thtr 70 Class 70 Board 30 **SERVICES:** Lift **PARKING:** 20 **NOTES:** ⊗ in restaurant Closed Jan-Feb

★★66% Ambassador Hotel
THE INDEPENDENTS
Grand Promenade LL30 2NR
☎ 01492 876886 🖹 01492 876347
e-mail: reception@ambasshotel.demon.co.uk
Dir: *off A55 onto A470. Take turn to Promenade, then left towards pier*
This friendly, family-run hotel is located on the seafront, close to the town centre. Bedrooms are tasteful and many have sea views. There is a choice of lounges, a patisserie, bar and restaurant.
ROOMS: 57 en suite (8 fmly) s £32-£55; d £58-£102 (incl. bkfst) **LB** **FACILITIES:** ♫ Xmas **CONF:** Thtr 45 Class 14 Board 20 **SERVICES:** Lift **PARKING:** 11 **NOTES:** ✗ ⊗ in restaurant

○ Hotel due to open in late 2005 or 2006
U Star rating not confirmed

LLANDUDNO, continued

★★66% *Hydro Hotel*

Neville Crescent LL30 1AT
☎ 01492 870101 📠 01492 870992
e-mail: hydro.llandudno@alfatravel.co.uk
web: www.alfatravel.co.uk
Dir: *follow signs for theatre to seafront, towards pier. Hotel near theatre on left*

This large hotel is situated on the promenade overlooking the sea, and offers good value-for-money, modern accommodation. Public areas are quite extensive and include a choice of lounges, a games/snooker room and a ballroom, where entertainment is provided every night. The hotel is a popular venue for coach tour parties.

ROOMS: 112 en suite (4 fmly) (8 GF) **FACILITIES:** Snooker Sauna Gym Table tennis ♫ **CONF:** Thtr 260 Class 40 **SERVICES:** Lift **PARKING:** 10 **NOTES:** 🐕 ⊘ in restaurant Closed Jan-mid Feb RS Nov-Dec & mid Feb-Mar

★★65% *Ormescliffe*

East Pde LL30 1BE
☎ 01492 877191 📠 01492 860311
e-mail: ormescliffe@clara.net
Dir: *A55 exit junct 19, A470 to promenade. Near theatre & conference centre*

A family-run hotel at the eastern end of the promenade. Bedrooms are modern and well equipped; most have superb views over the seafront and Great Orme. Comfortable bars and lounges are provided and there is a ballroom with regular entertainment.

ROOMS: 61 en suite (7 fmly) ⊘ in 6 bedrooms **FACILITIES:** Snooker Table tennis **CONF:** Thtr 120 Class 120 Board 80 **SERVICES:** Lift **PARKING:** 15 **NOTES:** ⊘ in restaurant Closed 2 Jan-2 Feb

★★64% Esplanade

Glan-y-Mor Pde, Promenade LL30 2LL
☎ 0800 318688 (freephone) & 01492 860300 📠 01492 860418
e-mail: info@esplanadehotel.co.uk
web: www.esplanadehotel.co.uk
Dir: *exit A55 at junct 19 onto A470, follow signs to promenade. Left towards Great Orme. Hotel 500yds left*

This family owned and run hotel stands on the promenade, conveniently close to the town centre and with views of the bay. Bedrooms vary in size and style, but all have modern equipment and facilities. Public areas are bright and attractively appointed, and include a room for functions and conferences. The hotel is popular with golfers.

ROOMS: 59 en suite (17 fmly) ⊘ in 36 bedrooms s £14.50-£68; d £29-£96 (incl. bkfst) **LB** **FACILITIES:** ♫ Xmas **CONF:** Thtr 80 Class 40 Board 40 Del from £55 **SERVICES:** Lift **PARKING:** 30 **NOTES:** 🐕 ⊘ in restaurant

★★63% *Royal*

Church Walks LL30 2HW
☎ 01492 876476 📠 01492 870210
e-mail: royalllandudno@aol.com
Dir: *exit A55 for A470 to Llandudno. Follow through town to T-junct, then left into Church Walks. Hotel 200yds on left, almost opposite Great Orme tram station*

Reputed to be the first hotel in Llandudno, the Royal is located on the eastern side of the Great Orme, close to the town centre and sea front. The well-equipped accommodation is particularly popular with golfers and coach tour groups.

ROOMS: 38 rms (36 en suite) (7 fmly) **FACILITIES:** Putt green **SERVICES:** Lift **PARKING:** 20 **NOTES:** 🐕 ⊘ in restaurant

★63% Min-y-Don

North Pde LL30 2LP
☎ 01492 876511 📠 01492 878169
Dir: *exit A55 junct 19 onto A470. Through Martyn St, turn right at rdbt then left into North Parade*

This cheerful family-run hotel is located under the Great Orme, opposite the pier. Bedrooms include several suitable for families and many have lovely views over the bay. Regular entertainment is held and there are comfortable lounge and bar areas.

ROOMS: 28 rms (19 en suite) (12 fmly) s £30-£32; d £58-£60 (incl. bkfst) **LB** **FACILITIES:** Xmas **SERVICES:** air con **PARKING:** 7 **NOTES:** 🐕 ⊘ in restaurant Closed Jan-Feb

LLANDUDNO JUNCTION, Conwy — Map 14 SH77

⌂ Premier Travel Inn Llandudno

Afon Conway, Llandudno Junction LL28 5LB
☎ 08701 977162 📠 01492 583614
web: www.premiertravelinn.com
Dir: *at A55 junct 19. Exit rdbt at A470 Betws-y-Coed. Inn immediately on left, opposite petrol station*

High quality, modern budget accommodation ideal for both families and business travellers. Spacious, en suite bedrooms feature bath and shower, satellite TV and many have telephones and modem points. The adjacent family restaurant features a wide and varied menu. For further details consult the Hotel Groups page.

ROOMS: 40 en suite s £48.95; d £48.95

LLANELLI, Carmarthenshire — Map 08 SN50

★★★67% Diplomat Hotel

Felinfoel SA15 3PJ
☎ 01554 756156 📠 01554 751649
e-mail: reservations@diplomat-hotel-wales.com
web: www.diplomat-hotel-wales.com
Dir: *M4 junct 48 onto A4138 then B4303 hotel in 0.75m on right*

This Victorian mansion, set in mature grounds, has been extended over the years to provide a comfortable and relaxing hotel. The well-appointed bedrooms are located in the main house and the nearby coach house. Public areas include Trubshaw's restaurant, a large function suite and a modern leisure centre.

ROOMS: 23 en suite 8 annexe en suite (2 fmly) ⊘ in 18 bedrooms s £65-£75; d £85-£95 (incl. bkfst) **LB** **FACILITIES:** **Spa** supervised Sauna Solarium Gym Jacuzzi ♫ ch fac Xmas **CONF:** Thtr 450 Class 150 Board 100 Del from £80 **SERVICES:** Lift **PARKING:** 250 **NOTES:** Civ Wed 300

See advert on opposite page

Bad hair day?
Hairdryers in all rooms three stars and above

★★★66% Stradey Park
Furnace SA15 4HA
☎ 01554 758171 📠 01554 777974
e-mail: reservations@stradeyparkhotel.com
web: www.stradeyparkhotel.com
Dir: *M4 junct 48/A484 to B4309*
The present owners continue to upgrade this large, modern complex and offer a good range of accommodation, including full suites, no-smoking bedrooms and bedrooms at ground-floor level. The spacious and attractively appointed public areas include a choice of comfortable lounges, a pleasant lounge bar and a bright brasserie-style restaurant.
ROOMS: 84 en suite (3 fmly) (19 GF) 🚭 in 40 bedrooms s £85-£110; d £110-£140 (incl. bkfst) **LB** **FACILITIES:** Xmas **CONF:** BC Thtr 300 Class 300 Board 240 Del from £91 **SERVICES:** Lift **PARKING:** 100 **NOTES:** 🐕 🚭 in restaurant

★★70% Ashburnham
Ashburnham Rd, Pembrey SA16 0TH
☎ 01554 834343 & 834455 📠 01554 834483
e-mail: info@ashburnham-hotel.co.uk
Dir: *M4 junct 48, A4138 to Llanelli, A484 West to Pembrey. Follow sign as entering village*

Amelia Earhart stayed at this friendly hotel after finishing her historic trans-Atlantic flight of 1928. Public areas include a bright bar and restaurant offering a good choice of menus, extensive function facilities and a children's outdoor play area. Bedrooms have modern furnishings and facilities. The hotel is licensed for civil wedding ceremonies and proves a popular venue.
ROOMS: 13 en suite (3 fmly) s £60; d £80 (incl. bkfst) **LB** **FACILITIES:** various within 1 mile of hotel **CONF:** Thtr 150 Class 150 Board 80 Del from £85 **PARKING:** 100 **NOTES:** 🚭 in restaurant RS 24-26Dec Civ Wed 130

★★66% Hotel Miramar
158 Station Rd SA15 1YU
☎ 01554 754726 📠 01554 772454
e-mail: miramar2002d@aol.com
Dir: *M4 junct 48 to Llanelli. Then follow rail station signs.*
This privately owned hotel is conveniently located near to the railway station and is within walking distance of the town centre. Bedrooms are well maintained and generously equipped, whilst public areas include a cheerful bar providing a good range of bar meals and a pleasantly appointed restaurant where a good choice is also available.
ROOMS: 12 en suite (2 fmly) (2 GF) s £33-£35; d £51-£54 (incl. bkfst) **FACILITIES:** Golf course and racing course nearby **PARKING:** 10 **NOTES:** 🐕 🚭 in restaurant

LLANFAIRPWLLGWYNGYLL See Anglesey, Isle of

LLANFYLLIN, Powys
Map 15 SJ11

★★67% Cain Valley
High St SY22 5AQ
☎ 01691 648366 📠 01691 648307
e-mail: info@cainvalleyhotel.co.uk
Dir: *at end of A490. Hotel in town centre, car park at rear*

This Grade II listed coaching inn has a lot of charm and character including by features such as exposed beams and a Jacobean staircase. The comfortable accommodation includes family rooms and a wide range of food is available in a choice of bars, or in the restaurant, which has a well-deserved reputation for its locally-sourced steaks.
ROOMS: 13 en suite (2 fmly) s £38-£42; d £62-£69 (incl. bkfst) **LB** **PARKING:** 10 **NOTES:** 🚭 in restaurant

LLANGAMMARCH WELLS, Powys Map 09 SN94

Top Hotel

★★★ ◎◎ **Lake Country House**

LD4 4BS

☎ 01591 620202 & 620474

🖷 01591 620457

e-mail: info@lakecountryhouse.co.uk

web: www.lakecountryhouse.co.uk

Dir: *W from Builth Wells on A483 to Garth (approx 6m). Left for Llangammarch Wells, follow hotel signs*

Expect good old fashioned values of service and hospitality at this Victorian country house hotel, which comes complete with a 9-hole, par 3 golf course, 50 acres of wooded grounds and a river. Bedrooms, including many suites, are individually decorated and have many extra comforts as standard. Traditional afternoon teas are served in the lounge in front of a log fire, and award-winning cuisine is provided in the spacious and elegant restaurant.

ROOMS: 19 en suite (2 GF) ⊗ in all bedrooms s £110-£135; d £160-£240 (incl. bkfst) **LB FACILITIES:** STV ⛳ 9 Fishing Snooker Putt green Clay pigeon shooting, horse riding, mountain biking, quad biking, archery Xmas **CONF:** BC Thtr 80 Class 30 Board 25 Del from £120 **PARKING:** 72 **NOTES:** ⊗ in restaurant Civ Wed 100

LLANGEFNI See Anglesey, Isle of

LLANGOLLEN, Denbighshire Map 15 SJ24

See also Glyn Ceiriog

★★★75% ◎ **The Wild Pheasant Hotel & Restaurant**

Berwyn Rd LL20 8AD

☎ 01978 860629 🖷 01978 861837

e-mail: wild.pheasant@talk21.com

Dir: *hotel 0.5m from town centre on left of A5 towards Betws-y-Coed/Holyhead*

This professionally run, privately owned hotel provides friendly hospitality and smart accommodation, including ground-floor, four-poster and no-smoking rooms. There is also an extension with a range of superior rooms and suites, as well as a hydro therapy pool and beauty facilities. There's a choice of eating options, either in the Cinnamon Restaurant or in the Chef's Bar for snacks. The hotel is a popular venue for weddings and conferences.

ROOMS: 46 en suite (4 fmly) (12 GF) ⊗ in 9 bedrooms s £75-£239; d £108-£248 (incl. bkfst) **LB FACILITIES: Spa** Sauna Jacuzzi Hydro pool Steam room & Beauty treatment rooms Xmas **CONF:** BC Thtr 200 Class 70 Board 50 Del from £100 **SERVICES:** Lift **PARKING:** 100 **NOTES:** ⊗ in restaurant Civ Wed 80

★★61% ***Abbey Grange Hotel***

LL20 8DD

☎ 01978 860753 🖷 01978 869070

e-mail: enquiries@abbey-grange-hotel.co.uk

web: www.abbey-grange-hotel.co.uk

Dir: *A542 signed Ruthin Abbey Grange. Hotel approx 2m on left*

This hotel, situated close to Llangollen, is a good base for exploring Offa's Dyke and the surrounding countryside. Rooms are spacious and well equipped, and some are suitable for families. Guests can dine in the restaurant or the bar, and outside there is a sun patio and a large children's play area.

ROOMS: 8 en suite (3 fmly) **PARKING:** 40

LLANRHIDIAN, Swansea Map 08 SS49

★★61% ***North Gower***

SA3 1EE

☎ 01792 390042 🖷 01792 391401

e-mail: enquiries@northgowerhotel.co.uk

web: www.northgowerhotel.co.uk

Dir: *on B4295, turn left at Llanrhidian Esso Service Station*

Situated on the Gower Peninsula with delightful views over the sea, this family-owned hotel offers guests a relaxing and comfortable stay. Bedrooms are spacious and airy, whilst public

continued

areas consist of a bar full of character, a pleasant restaurant and a choice of meeting and function rooms.
ROOMS: 18 en suite (10 fmly) (7 GF) ⊗ in 8 bedrooms **CONF:** BC Thtr 250 Class 170 Board 60 **PARKING:** 100 **NOTES:** ⊗ in restaurant

See advert on this page

LLANRWST, Conwy — Map 14 SH86
See also Betws-y-Coed

★★★66% *Maenan Abbey*

Maenan LL26 0UL
☎ 01492 660247 📠 01492 660734
e-mail: reservations@manab.co.uk
Dir: *3m N on A470*

This traditionally run private hotel was built as an abbey in 1850 on the site of a 13th-century monastery. It is now a popular venue for weddings as the grounds and magnificent galleried staircase make an ideal backdrop for photographs. Bedrooms include a large suite and are equipped with modern facilities. Meals are served in the bar and restaurant.
ROOMS: 14 en suite (2 fmly) **FACILITIES:** Fishing guided mountain walks **CONF:** BC Thtr 50 Class 30 Board 30 **PARKING:** 60 **NOTES:** ⊗ in restaurant Civ Wed 55

> Late for dinner? Quality standards mean that last orders for dinner vary according to star rating and should be no earlier than:
> ★★ 7.00pm ★★★ 8:00pm ★★★★ 9:00pm ★★★★★ 10:00pm

The North Gower Hotel

Llanrhidian, Gower, West Glamorgan SA3 1EE
Tel: 01792 390042 Fax: 01792 391401
Email: gbanchor@aol.com

The North Gower Hotel is the ideal choice for those who enjoy the tranquillity of the countryside and the easy access to the city. Guests can relax in our large public bar and restaurant overlooking the Loughor Estuary. Enjoy a meal from our extensive bar menu or special boards. Families are welcome with various room classifications available.

Visit our web site:
www.northgowerhotel.co.uk

LAKE VYRNWY HOTEL

This fine country hotel enjoys one of the best locations in Britain and lies in 26,000 acres of woodland above Lake Vyrnwy. It provides a wide range of bedrooms, most with superb views and many with four poster beds and balconies. The extensive public rooms are elegantly furnished and include a terrace, a choice of bars serving meals and the more formal dining in the restaurant. A wide range of outdoor activities - Clay & Game shooting, quad trekking, archery, fly fishing, rowing, cycling & walking.

The peace, tranquillity and remarkable views that surround this unique hotel provided the perfect setting for a relaxing stay.

Llanwddyn, Powys SY10 0LY
Tel: 01691 870692
Email: res@lakevyrnwy.com

LLANTRISANT, Monmouthshire Map 09 ST39

🅰 Greyhound Inn
NP15 1LE
☎ 01291 673447 672505 📠 01291 673255
e-mail: enquiry@greyhound-inn.com
web: www.greyhound-inn.com
Dir: *M4 junct 24, onto A449, 1st exit for Usk, 2.5m from town square, follow Llantrisant signs*
ROOMS: 10 en suite (2 fmly) (5 GF) ⊗ in all bedrooms s fr £52; d fr £72 (incl. bkfst) **LB PARKING:** 60 **NOTES:** ★★★ 🎄 Closed 25-26 Dec **RS** Sunday eve no food

LLANWDDYN, Powys Map 15 SJ01

★★★73% ◉◉🎄 Lake Vyrnwy
Lake Vyrnwy SY10 0LY
☎ 01691 870692 📠 01691 870259
e-mail: res@lakevyrnwy.com
web: www.lakevyrnwy.com
Dir: *on A4393, 200yds past dam turn sharp right into drive*

This fine country-house hotel lies in 26,000 acres of woodland above Lake Vyrnwy. It provides a wide range of bedrooms, most with superb views and many with four-poster beds and balconies. The extensive public rooms are elegantly furnished and include a terrace, a choice of bars serving meals and the more formal dining in the restaurant.
ROOMS: 35 en suite (4 fmly) s £75-£180; d £100-£205 (incl. bkfst) **LB FACILITIES:** STV ⚓ Fishing Riding Game/Clay shooting, Sailing, Cycling, Archery, Fly fishing Xmas **CONF:** Thtr 120 Class 50 Board 45 Del from £135 **PARKING:** 70 **NOTES:** ⊗ in restaurant

See advert on page 797

LLANWRTYD WELLS, Powys Map 09 SN84

★★71% ◉ Lasswade Country House Hotel
Station Rd LD5 4RW
☎ 01591 610515 📠 01591 610611
e-mail: info@lasswadehotel.co.uk
web: www.lasswadehotel.co.uk
Dir: *off A483 into Ifron Terrace, right into Station Rd, hotel 350yds on right*
This friendly hotel on the edge of the town has impressive views over the countryside. Bedrooms are comfortably furnished and well equipped, while the public areas consist of a tastefully decorated lounge, an elegant restaurant and an airy conservatory which looks out on to the neighbouring hills. The hotel is non-smoking throughout and utilises fresh, local produce to provide an enjoyable dining experience.
ROOMS: 8 en suite ⊗ in all bedrooms **FACILITIES:** ⚓ Fishing Riding Sauna Mountain biking, Trekking Xmas **CONF:** Thtr 20 Class 20 Board 16 **PARKING:** 8 **NOTES:** 🎄 ⊗ in restaurant

Restaurant with Rooms

🏨 ◉◉◉ Carlton House
Dolycoed Rd LD5 4RA
☎ 01591 610248
e-mail: info@carltonrestaurant.co.uk
web: www.carltonrestaurant.co.uk
Dir: *centre of town*
Guests are made to feel like one of the family at this character property, set amidst stunning countryside in what is reputedly the smallest rural town in Britain. Carlton House offers award-winning cuisine, complemented by a well-chosen wine list and served in an atmospheric restaurant. The themed bedrooms, like the public areas, have period furniture and are decorated in warm colours.
ROOMS: 6 rms (5 en suite) (2 fmly) s £45; d £70-£90 (incl. bkfst) **LB FACILITIES:** Pony trekking Mountain biking **NOTES:** ⊗ in restaurant Closed 15-30 Dec **RS** All year

LLYSWEN, Powys Map 09 SO13

★★★★77% ◉◉🎄 Llangoed Hall
LD3 0YP
☎ 01874 754525 📠 01874 754545
e-mail: enquiries@llangoedhall.com
web: www.llangoedhall.com
Dir: *A470 through village for 2m. Hotel drive on right*
Set against the stunning backdrop of the Black Mountains and the Wye Valley, this imposing country house is a haven of peace and quiet. The interior no less impressive, with a noteworthy art collection complementing the many antiques featured in day rooms and bedrooms. Comfortable, spacious bedrooms and suites are matched by equally inviting lounges.
ROOMS: 23 en suite s £150-£345; d £195-£385 (incl. bkfst) **LB FACILITIES:** STV ⚓ Fishing Snooker 🎱 Maze, Clay pigeon shooting 🎵 Xmas **CONF:** Thtr 60 Class 30 Board 28 Del from £187 **PARKING:** 80 **NOTES:** 🎄 No children 8yrs ⊗ in restaurant Civ Wed 80

MACHYNLLETH, Powys Map 14 SH70
See also Eglwysfach

★★70% Wynnstay
Maengwyn St SY20 8AE
☎ 01654 702941 📠 01654 703884
e-mail: info@wynnstay-hotel.com
web: www.wynnstay-hotel.com
Dir: *at junct of A487/A489, in the town centre, 25yds from the clock tower*
Long established, this former posting house lies in the centre of this historic town. Bedrooms, some with four-poster beds, have modern facilities and include no smoking and family rooms. There is a comfortable lounge bar area and a good range of food and wines is available. Guests can also dine in the new Wynnstay Pizzeria or the restaurant, which offers more formal dining.
ROOMS: 23 en suite (3 fmly) ⊗ in all bedrooms s £55-£95; d £80-£110 (incl. bkfst) **LB FACILITIES:** STV Clay shooting, Game shooting, Mountain biking Xmas **CONF:** Thtr 25 Class 12 Board 16 **PARKING:** 40 **NOTES:** ⊗ in restaurant **RS** New Years Day

MAGOR SERVICE AREA (M4), Monmouthshire Map 09 ST48

🏠 Travelodge
Magor Service Area NP26 3YL
☎ 08700 850 950 📠 01633 881896
web: www.travelodge.co.uk
Dir: *M4 junct 23a*
Travelodge offers good quality, good value, modern accommodation. Ideal for families, the spacious, en suite

continued

bedrooms include remote-control TV, tea and coffee-making facilities and comfortable beds. Meals can be taken at the nearby family restaurant. For further details consult the Hotel Groups page.
ROOMS: 43 en suite s fr £26; d fr £26

MANORBIER, Pembrokeshire Map 08 SS09

★★68% Castle Mead

SA70 7TA
☎ 01834 871358 📠 01834 871358
e-mail: castlemeadhotel@aol.com
web: www.castlemeadhotel.com
Dir: *A4139 towards Pembroke, turn onto B4585 into village & follow signs to beach & castle. Hotel on left above beach*

THE CIRCLE Selected Individual Hotels GREAT BRITAIN

Benefiting from a superb location with spectacular views of the bay, the Norman church and Manorbier Castle, this family-run hotel is friendly and welcoming. Bedrooms which include some in a converted former coach house, are generally quite spacious and have modern facilities. Public areas include a sea view restaurant, bar and residents' lounge, as well as an extensive garden.
ROOMS: 5 en suite 3 annexe en suite (2 fmly) (3 GF) ⊗ in all bedrooms s £38-£40 (incl. bkfst) **LB PARKING:** 20 **NOTES:** ⊗ in restaurant Closed Jan-Feb RS Nov/Dec/Feb

MENAI BRIDGE See Anglesey, Isle of

MERTHYR TYDFIL, Merthyr Tydfil Map 09 SO00
See also Nant-Ddu

★★★62% Bessemer

Hermon Close, Dowlais CF48 3DP
☎ 01685 350780 📠 01685 352874
e-mail: sales@bessemerhotel.co.uk

A modern hotel, with a friendly and relaxed atmosphere, that has high quality bedrooms and bathrooms. Business guests will appreciate the spacious work desks and modem points. Dinner includes the popular option of a self-service carvery, and there are three bars including one in a large function room catering for up to 160 guests.
ROOMS: 17 en suite ⊗ in 12 bedrooms s £60-£65; d £69 (incl. bkfst) **LB FACILITIES:** STV Jacuzzi **SERVICES:** Lift **PARKING:** 30 **NOTES:** 🐕

A Tregenna

Park Ter CF47 8RF
☎ 01685 723627 382055 📠 01685 721951
e-mail: reception@tregennahotel.co.uk
Dir: *M4 junct 32, onto A465 follow signs for Merthyr Tydfil signed from town centre*
ROOMS: 21 en suite (6 fmly) (7 GF) ⊗ in 4 bedrooms s £50-£55; d £65-£70 (incl. bkfst) **LB FACILITIES:** STV **PARKING:** 12 **NOTES:** ★★★ ⊗ in restaurant

⌂ Premier Travel Inn Merthyr Tydfil

Pentrebach CF48 4BD
☎ 08701 977183 📠 01443 699171
web: www.premiertravelinn.com
Dir: *M4 junct 32 follow A470 to Merthyr Tydfil. At 2nd rdbt turn right to Pentrebach, follow signs to Ind Estate*

premier travel inn

High quality, modern budget accommodation ideal for both families and business travellers. Spacious, en suite bedrooms feature bath and shower, satellite TV and many have telephones and modem points. The adjacent family restaurant features a wide and varied menu. For further details consult the Hotel Groups page.
ROOMS: 40 en suite s £46.95-£48.95; d £46.95-£48.95 **CONF:** Thtr 65 Board 30

MISKIN, Rhondda Cynon Taff Map 09 ST08

★★★★67% ◎ Miskin Manor Country Hotel

Pendoylan Rd CF72 8ND
☎ 01443 224204 📠 01443 237606
e-mail: info@miskin-manor.co.uk
web: www.miskin-manor.co.uk
Dir: *M4 junct 34, exit onto A4119, signed Llantrisant, hotel is 300yds on left*

This historic manor house is peacefully located in 20 acres of grounds yet only minutes away from the M4. Bedrooms are furnished to a high standard and include some located in converted stables and cottages. Public areas are spacious and comfortable and include a variety of function rooms. The relaxed atmosphere and the surroundings ensure this hotel remains popular for wedding functions as well as with business guests.
ROOMS: 34 en suite 9 annexe en suite (6 fmly) (6 GF) ⊗ in 11 bedrooms **FACILITIES:** STV supervised Squash Sauna Solarium Gym Jacuzzi Xmas **CONF:** Thtr 160 Class 80 Board 65 Del from £139 **PARKING:** 200 **NOTES:** ⊗ in restaurant Civ Wed 120

See advert under CARDIFF

MOLD, Flintshire Map 15 SJ26
See also Northop Hall

★★★68% Beaufort Park Hotel

Alltami Rd, New Brighton CH7 6RQ
☎ 01352 758646 📠 01352 757132
e-mail: bph@beaufortparkhotel.co.uk
web: www.beaufortparkhotel.co.uk
Dir: *A55/A494. Through Alltami lights, over mini rdbt by petrol station towards Mold, A5119. Hotel 100yds on right*

This large, modern hotel is conveniently located a short drive from the North Wales Expressway and offers various styles of spacious accommodation. There are extensive public areas, and several meeting and function rooms are available. There is a wide choice of meals in the formal restaurant and in the popular Arches bar.
ROOMS: 106 en suite (4 fmly) (33 GF) ⊗ in 25 bedrooms s £70-£95; d £85-£120 (incl. bkfst) **LB FACILITIES:** STV Squash Jacuzzi ♫ Xmas **CONF:** Thtr 250 Class 120 Board 50 Del £120 **PARKING:** 200 **NOTES:** ⊗ in restaurant Civ Wed 250

MONMOUTH, Monmouthshire
Map 10 SO51

See also Whitebrook

★★65% Riverside
Cinderhill St NP25 5EY
☎ 01600 715577 & 713236 📠 01600 712668
e-mail: info@riversidehotelmonmouth.co.uk
Dir: *exit A40 signed Rockfield & Monmouth. Hotel on left beyond garage & before rdbt*

Just a short walk from the famous 13th-century bridge, this hotel, now under new ownership, offers accommodation in a relaxed and informal atmosphere. Bedrooms are well equipped and soundly decorated. Public areas include a separate restaurant, a popular bar and a conservatory lounge at the rear of the property.

ROOMS: 17 en suite (2 fmly) (2 GF) ⊘ in 2 bedrooms s fr £46; d fr £59 **LB FACILITIES:** STV Xmas **CONF:** Thtr 150 Class 60 Board 40 Del £85 **PARKING:** 30 **NOTES:** ⊘ in restaurant

MONTGOMERY, Powys
Map 15 SO29

★★71% ⊛ Dragon
SY15 6PA
☎ 01686 668359 📠 0870 0118227
e-mail: reception@dragonhotel.com
web: www.dragonhotel.com
Dir: *behind the Town Hall*

This fine 17th-century coaching inn stands in the centre of Montgomery. Beams and timbers from the nearby castle, which was destroyed by Cromwell, are visible in the lounge and bar. A wide choice of soundly prepared, wholesome food is available in both the restaurant and bar. Bedrooms are well equipped and family rooms are available.

ROOMS: 20 en suite (6 fmly) ⊘ in 16 bedrooms s £49-£59; d £83 (incl. bkfst) **LB FACILITIES:** Sauna ♫ Xmas **CONF:** Thtr 40 Class 30 Board 25 **PARKING:** 21 **NOTES:** ⊘ in restaurant

MUMBLES (NEAR SWANSEA), Swansea
Map 08 SS68

★★★65% *St Anne's*
Western Ln SA3 4EY
☎ 01792 369147 📠 01792 360537
e-mail: info@stanneshotel-mumbles.com
web: www.stanneshotel-mumbles.com
Dir: *A483/A4067 to Mumbles. In village straight over mini-rdbt. Then take 3rd right*

This privately owned hotel stands on a steep hillside close to the town centre, and enjoys some superb views over the Swansea Bay. The accommodation is modern and the bedrooms are well equipped. No smoking bedrooms, family rooms, interconnecting rooms and bedrooms on ground floor level are all available. The bright and pleasant public areas include a spacious lounge.

ROOMS: 33 en suite (3 fmly) ⊘ in 7 bedrooms **FACILITIES:** STV **CONF:** Thtr 100 Class 50 Board 50 **PARKING:** 50 **NOTES:** ⊘ in restaurant

Restaurant with Rooms

⊛ *Patricks with Rooms*
638 Mumbles Rd SA3 4EA
☎ 01792 360199 📠 01792 369926
web: www.patrickswithrooms.com
Dir: *M4 junct 42 (sea on left) through Swansea to Mumbles. Over mini-rdbt at White Rose pub. 0.25m hotel opposite children's park on right*

A popular restaurant located on the front at Mumbles with a lively atmosphere and friendly, efficient service. Bedrooms are a real highlight here offering a choice of modern styles in a range of vibrant colours. The colonial style lounge is the perfect place to unwind with a pre- or post-dinner drink.

ROOMS: 8 en suite ⊘ in 18 bedrooms **PARKING:** 60 **NOTES:** ⊘ in restaurant Closed 3 wks Sep & 1 wk Jan

NANT-DDU (NEAR MERTHYR TYDFIL), Powys
Map 09 SO01

★★★75% ⊛ Nant Ddu Lodge
Cwm Taf, Nant Ddu CF48 2HY
☎ 01685 379111 📠 01685 377088
e-mail: enquiries@nant-ddu-lodge.co.uk
web: www.nant-ddu-lodge.co.uk
Dir: *6m N of Merthyr Tydfil, 12m S of Brecon on A470*

Close to the Brecon Beacons and stretching back 200 years, this delightful hotel has seen many improvements in the hands of the present owners. Decor throughout is contemporary and the bedrooms are thoughtfully furnished and well equipped. Meals can be taken in the modern bistro and there is a bar with a more traditional 'village inn' atmosphere. There is also a well-equipped health, beauty, leisure and fitness centre and spa.

ROOMS: 27 en suite 4 annexe en suite (5 fmly) (12 GF) s £65-£95; d £80-£125 (incl. bkfst) **FACILITIES: Spa** STV supervised Sauna Solarium Gym Jacuzzi **CONF:** BC Thtr 20 Class 20 Board 20 Del from £110 **PARKING:** 60 **NOTES:** ⊘ in restaurant RS 24-26 Dec

See advert under BRECON and on opposite page

NEATH, Neath Port Talbot
Map 09 SS79

★★★66% Castle Hotel
The Parade SA11 1RB
☎ 01639 641119 & 643581 📠 01639 641624
e-mail: info@castlehotelneath.co.uk
web: www.castlehotelneath.co.uk
Dir: *M4 junct 43, follow signs for Neath, 500yds past rail station, hotel on right. Car park 50yds further on left*

Situated in the town centre, this Georgian property, once a coaching inn, has a wealth of history and character. Lord Nelson and Lady Hamilton are reputed to have stayed here and the Welsh Rugby Union was founded here in 1881. More recently, all areas have been extensively upgraded to provide well-equipped accommodation and pleasant public areas. Bedrooms include one with a four-poster bed, non-smoking rooms and family bedded rooms. Facilities include functions and meeting rooms.

ROOMS: 29 en suite (3 fmly) ⊘ in 4 bedrooms s £45-£65; d £60-£80 (incl. bkfst) **LB FACILITIES:** STV **CONF:** Thtr 160 Class 75 Board 50 **PARKING:** 26 **NOTES:** Civ Wed 100

NEVERN, Pembrokeshire
Map 08 SN04

★★69% Trewern Arms
SA42 0NB
☎ 01239 820395 📠 01239 820173
e-mail: trewern.arms@virgin.net
Dir: *off A487 coast road - midway between Cardigan and Fishguard*

Set in a peaceful and picturesque village, this charming 16th-century inn is well positioned to offer a relaxing stay. There are many original features to be seen in the two character bars and attractive restaurant, and the spacious bedrooms are appointed to a high standard and include some family rooms.

ROOMS: 10 en suite (4 fmly) s £38; d £68 (incl. bkfst) **FACILITIES:** Fishing Riding Xmas **PARKING:** 100 **NOTES:**

TV dinner?
Room service at three stars and above

NEWPORT, Newport
Map 09 ST38

See also Cwmbran

★★★★★71% The Celtic Manor Resort
Coldra Woods NP18 1HQ
☎ 01633 413000 Fax 01633 412910
e-mail: postbox@celtic-manor.com
Dir: *M4 junct 24, take A48 towards Newport. Hotel 1st right turn past Alcatel*
This luxurious resort offers a whole host of facilities to suit any guest, whether they are conference delegates, business users or leisure guests. Three challenging golf courses are complemented by superb leisure facilities, whilst the convention centre can accommodate 1500 delegates. There is also a wide choice of dining options to tempt guests out of the deeply comfortable bedrooms and suites.
ROOMS: 330 en suite (28 fmly) in all bedrooms s £147-£225; d £147-£225 **LB** **FACILITIES: Spa** STV supervised 18 Fishing Snooker Sauna Solarium Gym Putt green Jacuzzi Golf Academy , Clay pigeon shooting, Mountain bike trail Xmas **CONF:** BC Thtr 1500 Class 300 Board 50 Del from £210 **SERVICES:** Lift air con **PARKING:** 1300 **NOTES:** in restaurant Civ Wed 100

★★★68% Newport Lodge
THE INDEPENDENTS

Bryn Bevan, Brynglas Rd NP20 5QN
☎ 01633 821818 Fax 01633 856360
e-mail: info@newportlodgehotel.co.uk
web: www.newportlodgehotel.co.uk
Dir: *M4 junct 26 follow signs Newport. Turn left after 0.5m onto Malpal Rd, up hill for 0.5m to hotel*
On the edge of the town centre and convenient for the M4, this purpose-built, friendly hotel provides comfortable and well-maintained bedrooms, with modern facilities. A room with a four-poster bed is available, as are ground floor bedrooms and no smoking rooms. The bistro-style restaurant offers a wide range of freshly prepared dishes, often using local ingredients.
ROOMS: 27 en suite (11 GF) in 8 bedrooms s £73-£90; d £91.50-£125 (incl. bkfst) **LB** **CONF:** Thtr 25 Class 20 Board 20 **PARKING:** 63 **NOTES:** No children 14yrs in restaurant

★★★66% *Kings*
High St NP20 1QU
☎ 01633 842020 Fax 01633 244667
e-mail: kingshotelswales@netscapeonline.co.uk
Dir: *from town centre take left road (not flyover) into right lane to next rdbt, take 3rd exit. Pass front of hotel then left for car park*
This large, imposing property is situated right in the town centre and helpfully has its own car park. Privately owned, it offers comfortable bedrooms including non-smoking and family rooms, and bright spacious public areas. Facilities include a choice of function rooms and a large ballroom.
ROOMS: 61 en suite (15 fmly) in 20 bedrooms **FACILITIES:** STV **CONF:** Thtr 150 Class 70 Board 50 **SERVICES:** Lift **PARKING:** 50 **NOTES:** Closed 26 Dec-4 Jan Civ Wed

See advert on this page

Premier Travel Inn Newport, South Wales
premier travel inn

Coldra Junction, Chepstow Rd NP18 2NX
☎ 08701 977193 Fax 01633 411376
web: www.premiertravelinn.com
Dir: *M4 junct 24. Take A48 to Langstone, at the next rdbt return towards junct 24. Inn on left, 50mtrs drive from the Millennium Stadium (20min)*
High quality, modern budget accommodation ideal for both families and business travellers. Spacious, en suite bedrooms

continued on p802

N

NEWPORT, continued

feature bath and shower, satellite TV and many have telephones and modem points. The adjacent family restaurant features a wide and varied menu. For further details consult the Hotel Groups page.
ROOMS: 63 en suite s £46.95-£49.95; d £46.95-£49.95

NEWPORT, Pembrokeshire Map 08 SN03

A Salutation Inn

Felindre Farchog SA41 3UY
☎ 01239 820564 🖷 01239 820355
e-mail: johndenley@aol.com
web: www.salutationcountryhotel.co.uk
Dir: *on A487 between Cardigan & Fishguard. 3m N of Newport*
ROOMS: 8 en suite (2 fmly) (8 GF) ⊗ in all bedrooms s £32-£38; d £48-£60 (incl. bkfst) **LB PARKING:** 60 **NOTES:** ★★★ ⊗ in restaurant

NEWTOWN, Powys Map 15 SO19

U *Elephant & Castle*

Broad St SY16 2BQ
☎ 01686 626271 🖷 01686 622123
e-mail: enquire@elephanthotel.fsnet.co.uk
web: www.watb.net/elephant
Dir: *A483 to town on T-junct of town centre*
At the time of going to press, the star classification for this hotel was not confirmed. Please refer to the AA internet site www.theAA.com for current information.
ROOMS: 24 en suite 11 annexe en suite (3 fmly) (4 GF) ⊗ in all bedrooms **FACILITIES: Spa** STV Fishing ♫ **CONF:** Thtr 250 Class 175 Board 175 **PARKING:** 60 **NOTES:** ✗ ⊗ in restaurant Civ Wed 40

N

NORTHOP, Flintshire Map 15 SJ26

★★★75% Soughton Hall

CH7 6AB
☎ 01352 840811 🖷 01352 840382
e-mail: info@soughtonhall.co.uk
Dir: *A55/B5126, after 500mtrs turn left for Northop, left at lights (A5119-Mold). After 0.5m follow signs*
Built as a bishop's palace in 1714, this elegant country house has magnificent grounds. Bedrooms are individually decorated and furnished with fine antiques and rich fabrics. There are several spacious day rooms furnished in keeping with the style of the house. The trendy Stables bar and restaurant offer a good range of dishes at both lunch and dinner. Understandably, the hotel is a very popular venue for weddings.
ROOMS: 14 en suite (2 fmly) (2 GF) ⊗ in all bedrooms s £100; d £130-£170 (incl. bkfst) **LB FACILITIES: Spa** Riding Jacuzzi Riding stables nearby Xmas **CONF:** BC Thtr 40 Class 40 Board 20 Del from £135 **PARKING:** 100 **NOTES:** ⊗ in restaurant Civ Wed 100

NORTHOP HALL, Flintshire Map 15 SJ26

A ★★★Northop Hall Country House

THE INDEPENDENTS

Chester Rd CH7 6HJ
☎ 01244 816181 🖷 01244 814661
e-mail: northop@hotel-chester.com
web: www.hotel-chester.com
Dir: *M56/A5117/A494. Exit Buckley/St David's Park. At rdbt, 3rd exit then 1st right to Northop Hall. After 2m, bear left at mini rdbt. Hotel entrance 200yds on left*
ROOMS: 39 en suite (16 fmly) (12 GF) ⊗ in 12 bedrooms s £55-£65; d £75.50-£115.50 **LB FACILITIES:** Childrens Play Area Xmas **CONF:** Thtr 120 Class 80 Board 70 Del from £89.50 **PARKING:** 100 **NOTES:** ✗ ⊗ in restaurant

Travelodge

Travelodge

CH7 6HB
☎ 08700 850 950 🖷 01244 816473
web: www.travelodge.co.uk
Dir: *on A55, eastbound*
Travelodge offers good quality, good value, modern accommodation. Ideal for families, the spacious, en suite bedrooms include remote-control TV, tea and coffee-making facilities and comfortable beds. Meals can be taken at the nearby family restaurant. For further details consult the Hotel Groups page.
ROOMS: 40 en suite s fr £26; d fr £26

PEMBROKE, Pembrokeshire Map 08 SM90

★★★72% Lamphey Court

Best Western

Lamphey SA71 5NT
☎ 01646 672273 🖷 01646 672480
e-mail: info@lampheycourt.co.uk
web: www.lampheycourt.co.uk
Dir: *A477 to Pembroke. Turn left at Milton village for Lamphey, hotel on right*

This former Georgian mansion is set in attractive countryside and well situated for exploring the stunning Pembrokeshire coast and beaches. Well-appointed bedrooms and family suites are situated in a converted coach house in the grounds. The elegant public areas include a leisure spa with treatment rooms, and formal and informal dining rooms that both feature dishes inspired by the local produce.
ROOMS: 26 en suite 12 annexe en suite (7 fmly) (6 GF) ⊗ in 18 bedrooms s £78-£90; d £105-£150 (incl. bkfst) **LB FACILITIES:** Sauna Solarium Gym Jacuzzi Yacht charter Xmas **CONF:** Thtr 60 Class 40 Board 30 Del from £130 **PARKING:** 50 **NOTES:** ✗ ⊗ in restaurant Civ Wed 60

See advert under TENBY

Popped the question? Hotels with Civ wed in their entry are licensed for civil wedding ceremonies. Maximum numbers for the ceremony only are shown e.g. Civ wed 120

★★★70% Beggars Reach

SA73 1PD
☎ 01646 600700 🖷 01646 600560
e-mail: stay@beggars-reach.com
web: www.beggars-reach.com
Dir: *8m S of Haverfordwest, 6m N of Pembroke, off A477*
This privately owned and personally run hotel was once a Georgian rectory. It stands in four acres of grounds peacefully located close to the village of Burton and provides modern, well-equipped accommodation; two of the bedrooms are located in former stables, which date back to the 14th century. Milford

continued

Milford Haven and the ferry terminal at Pembroke Dock are both within easy reach.

ROOMS: 15 en suite 2 annexe en suite (4 fmly) (2 GF) ⊗ in 4 bedrooms s £63-£83; d £90-£130 (incl. bkfst) **LB** **FACILITIES:** STV **CONF:** Thtr 100 Class 60 Board 60 Del £99 **PARKING:** 50 **NOTES:** ⊗ in restaurant

See advert under HAVERFORDWEST

★★75% Bethwaite's Lamphey Hall

Lamphey SA71 5NR
☎ 01646 672394 ☐ 01646 672369
e-mail: george@bethwaite.freeserve.co.uk
Dir: *from M4 follow signs for A48 towards Carmarthen, then A40 to St Clears. Follow signs for A477 & turn left at Milton Village*

Set in a delightful village, this very friendly, family-owned and run hotel offers an ideal base from which to explore the surrounding countryside. Bedrooms are well equipped, comfortably furnished and include family rooms as well as rooms on the ground floor. Diners have an extensive choice of dishes and a choice of restaurants. There is also a lounge, a bar and attractive gardens.
ROOMS: 10 en suite (1 fmly) (2 GF) ⊗ in all bedrooms **PARKING:** 32 **NOTES:** ✗ ⊗ in restaurant

★★65% Old Kings Arms

Main St SA71 4JS
☎ 01646 683611 ☐ 01646 682335
e-mail: reception@oldkingsarmshotel.freeserve.co.uk
Dir: *M4/A477 to Pembroke. Turn left for Pembroke, at rdbt follow town centre sign. Turn right onto the parade, car park is signed*

At the centre of the bustling town, this former coaching inn is very much at the heart of local activities and is a favourite with locals. The restaurant and bar have traditional stone walls, flagstone floors and roaring log fires. Both areas offer good, wholesome food.
ROOMS: 18 en suite s £38-£50; d £60 (incl. bkfst) **FACILITIES:** STV **PARKING:** 21 **NOTES:** Closed 25-26 Dec & 1 Jan

PEMBROKE DOCK, Pembrokeshire — Map 08 SM90

★★★67% Cleddau Bridge

Essex Rd SA72 6EG
☎ 01646 685961 ☐ 01646 685746
e-mail: information@cleddaubridgehotel.co.uk
Dir: *M4/A40 to St Clears. A477 to Pembroke Dock. At rdbt 2nd exit for Haverfordwest via toll bridge, left before toll bridge*

This modern, purpose-built hotel is sited adjacent to the Cleddau Bridge and affords excellent views overlooking the river. The well-equipped bedrooms are all on the ground floor, while the comfortable public areas consist of an attractive bar and restaurant, both taking advantage of the impressive views.
ROOMS: 24 en suite (2 fmly) ⊗ in 12 bedrooms s £49-£66; d £49-£85 (incl. bkfst) **LB** **FACILITIES:** STV Xmas **CONF:** Thtr 160 Class 60 Board 60 Del from £79 **PARKING:** 140 **NOTES:** ✗ ⊗ in restaurant Civ Wed 150

PENCOED, Bridgend — Map 09 SS98

★★★70% *St Mary's Hotel & Country Club*

St Marys Golf Club CF35 5EA
☎ 01656 861100 & 860280 ☐ 01656 863400
e-mail: stmarysgolfhotel@btinternet.com
Dir: *M4 junct 35, on A473*

This charming 16th-century farmhouse has been converted and extended into a modern and restful hotel, surrounded by its own two golf courses. Bedrooms are generously appointed, well-equipped and most feature whirlpool baths. Guests are offered a choice of bars, which are popular with club members, and a good range of dining options is also available.
ROOMS: 24 en suite (19 fmly) **FACILITIES:** STV ⛳ 18 Putt green Floodlit driving range **CONF:** Thtr 120 Class 60 Board 40 **PARKING:** 140 **NOTES:** ✗ Civ Wed 120

⌂ Premier Travel Inn Bridgend

Pantruthyn Farm, Pencoed CF35 5HY
☎ 08701 977041 ☐ 01656 864792
web: www.premiertravelinn.com
Dir: *off M4 junct 35, behind petrol station and McDonalds.*

High quality, modern budget accommodation ideal for both families and business travellers. Spacious, en suite bedrooms feature bath and shower, satellite TV and many have telephones and modem points. The adjacent family restaurant features a wide and varied menu. For further details consult the Hotel Groups page.
ROOMS: 40 en suite s £46.95-£48.95; d £46.95-£48.95

⌂ Travelodge

Old Mill, Felindre Rd CF3 5HU
☎ 08700 850 950 ☐ 01656 864404
web: www.travelodge.co.uk
Dir: *on A473*

Travelodge offers good quality, good value, modern accommodation. Ideal for families, the spacious, en suite bedrooms include remote-control TV, tea and coffee-making facilities and comfortable beds. Meals can be taken at the nearby family restaurant. For further details consult the Hotel Groups page.
ROOMS: 39 en suite s fr £26; d fr £26

PONTERWYD, Ceredigion — Map 09 SN78

★★66% *The George Borrow Hotel*

SY23 3AD
☎ 01970 890230 ☐ 01970 890587
e-mail: georgeborrow@lycos.co.uk
Dir: *on A44 (Aberystwyth-Llangurig road). On Aberystwyth side of village*

This family owned and personally run, friendly hotel nestles in the foothills of the Cambrian Mountains, about 12 miles from the university town of Aberystwyth. The hotel provides an ideal base for walking, fishing and bird watching (look out for red kites). Bedrooms which include family rooms, are comfortable and well equipped. There are two character bars and a restaurant. An extensive choice of food is available.
ROOMS: 9 en suite (2 fmly) ⊗ in all bedrooms **PARKING:** 30 **NOTES:** ✗ ⊗ in restaurant

> Late for dinner? Quality standards mean that last orders for dinner vary according to star rating and should be no earlier than:
> ★★ 7.00pm ★★★ 8:00pm ★★★★ 9:00pm ★★★★★ 10:00pm

PONTYPRIDD, Rhondda Cynon Taff Map 09 ST08

★★★70% Llechwen Hall

Llanfabon CF37 4HP
☎ 01443 742050 & 743020 🖷 01443 742189
e-mail: llechwen@aol.com
web: www.llechwen.com
Dir: *A470 N towards Merthyr Tydfil, then A472, then onto A4054 for Cilfynydd. After 0.25m, turn left at hotel sign & follow to top of hill*

Set on top of a hill with a stunning approach, this hotel has served a variety of uses in its 200-year history, including as a private school and as a magistrates' court. Bedrooms are individually decorated and well equipped and some are situated in the comfortable coach house nearby. The Victorian-style public areas are attractively appointed and the hotel is a popular venue for weddings.
ROOMS: 12 en suite 8 annexe en suite (11 fmly) (4 GF) ⊗ in 8 bedrooms s £55-£66; d £70-£107 (incl. bkfst) **LB** **FACILITIES:** Xmas **CONF:** Thtr 80 Class 30 Board 30 Del from £80 **PARKING:** 100 **NOTES:** ⊗ in restaurant Closed 25-28 Dec Civ Wed 60

★★★67% Heritage Park

Coed Cae Rd, Trehafod CF37 2NP
☎ 01443 687057 🖷 01443 687060
e-mail: heritageparkhotel@talk21.com
web: www.heritageparkhotel.co.uk
Dir: *off A4058, follow signs to the Rhondda Heritage Park*
This privately owned modern hotel is suitable for all types of guest. The spacious bedrooms include ground floor and interconnecting rooms, and a room equipped for less mobile guests. Meals can be taken in the attractive, wood-beamed Loft Restaurant. Facilities include a large function suite, a choice of meeting rooms and a leisure/fitness centre.
ROOMS: 44 en suite (4 fmly) (19 GF) ⊗ in 19 bedrooms s £75-£90; d £95-£100 (incl. bkfst) **LB** **FACILITIES:** STV Sauna Solarium Gym Jacuzzi Steam room **CONF:** Thtr 220 Class 40 Board 30 Del from £72.50 **PARKING:** 150 **NOTES:** ⊗ in restaurant Civ Wed 100

PORTHCAWL, Bridgend Map 09 SS87

★★★68% Atlantic

West Dr CF36 3LT
☎ 01656 785011 🖷 01656 771877
e-mail: enquiries@atlantichotelporthcawl.co.uk
Dir: *M4 junct 35/37, follow signs to Porthcawl. Then follow Seafront/Promenade signs*
This hotel is located on the seafront, a short walk from the town centre. Guests can enjoy sea views from the sun terrace, bright conservatory and some of the bedrooms, which are well equipped and tastefully decorated. A welcoming atmosphere is created here especially in the restaurant where a good selection of tempting dishes is available.
ROOMS: 18 en suite (2 fmly) **FACILITIES:** STV Xmas **CONF:** Thtr 50 Class 50 Board 25 **SERVICES:** Lift **PARKING:** 20 **NOTES:** 🐕

★★★65% Seabank

The Promenade CF36 3LU
☎ 01656 782261 🖷 01656 785363
e-mail: info@seabankhotel.co.uk
Dir: *M4 junct 37, follow A4229 to sea front, hotel on the promenade*

This large, privately owned hotel stands on the promenade. The majority of the well-equipped bedrooms enjoy panoramic sea views and several have four-poster beds. There is a spacious restaurant, a lounge bar and a choice of lounges. The hotel is a popular venue for coach tour parties, as well as weddings and conferences.
ROOMS: 67 en suite (2 fmly) ⊗ in 14 bedrooms s £40-£65; d £60-£85 (incl. bkfst) **LB** **FACILITIES:** STV Sauna Gym Jacuzzi ♫ Xmas **CONF:** Thtr 250 Class 150 Board 70 Del from £88 **SERVICES:** Lift **PARKING:** 140 **NOTES:** 🐕 Civ Wed 100

PORTHMADOG, Gwynedd Map 14 SH53

★★70% Royal Sportsman

131 High St LL49 9HB
☎ 01766 512015 🖷 01766 512490
e-mail: enquiries@royalsportsman.co.uk
Dir: *by rdbt, at A497 & A487 junct*
Ideally located in the centre of Porthmadog, this former coaching inn dates from the Victorian era and has been restored into a friendly, privately owned and personally run hotel. Rooms are tastefully decorated and well equipped, and some are in an annexe close to the hotel. There is a large comfortable lounge and a wide range of meals is served in the bar or restaurant.
ROOMS: 19 en suite 9 annexe en suite (7 fmly) (9 GF) ⊗ in all bedrooms s fr £45; d fr £68 **FACILITIES:** Xmas **CONF:** BC Thtr 50 Class 50 Board 30 **PARKING:** 18 **NOTES:** ⊗ in restaurant

PORTMEIRION, Gwynedd Map 14 SH53

★★★79% ® The Hotel Portmeirion

LL48 6ET
☎ 01766 770000 🖷 01766 771331
e-mail: hotel@portmeirion-village.com
web: www.portmeirion-village.com
Dir: *2m W, Portmeirion village is S off A487*
Saved from dereliction in the 1920s by Clough Williams-Ellis, the elegant Hotel Portmeirion enjoys one of the finest settings in Wales, located beneath the wooded slopes of the village, overlooking the sandy estuary towards Snowdonia. Many rooms have private sitting rooms and balconies with spectacular views. The mostly Welsh-speaking staff offer warm hospitality.
ROOMS: 25 en suite 26 annexe en suite (4 fmly) s fr £120; d £140-£245 **LB** **FACILITIES:** STV ⛱ 🎾 Beauty Salon Xmas **CONF:** Thtr 100 **PARKING:** 40 **NOTES:** 🐕 ⊗ in restaurant Civ Wed 100

★★★78% ® Castell Deudraeth
LL48 6EN
☎ 01766 770000 📠 01766 771771
e-mail: castell@portmeirion-village.com
Dir: *A4212 for Trawsfynydd/Porthmadog. 1.5m beyond Penrhyndeudraeth, hotel on right*
A castellated mansion that overlooks Snowdonia and the famous Italianate village featured in the 1960's cult series *'The Prisoner'*. An original concept, Castell Deudraeth combines traditional materials, such as oak and slate, with state-of-the-art technology and design. Dynamically styled bedrooms boast underfloor heating, real-flame gas fires and wide-screen TVs with DVDs and cinema surround-sound. The brasserie-themed dining room provides an informal option at dinner.
ROOMS: 11 en suite (5 fmly) s £160; d £180-£245 **LB**
FACILITIES: Spa STV ♫ Xmas **CONF:** Thtr 30 Class 18 Board 25
SERVICES: Lift air con **PARKING:** 30 **NOTES:** ⊗ in restaurant Civ Wed 30

PORT TALBOT, Neath Port Talbot — Map 09 SS78

★★★68% Aberavon Beach
SA12 6QP
☎ 01639 884949 📠 01639 897885
e-mail: sales@aberavonbeach.com
web: www.aberavonbeach.com
Dir: *M4 junct 41/A48 & follow signs for Aberavon Beach & Hollywood Park*
This friendly, purpose-built hotel enjoys a prominent position on the seafront overlooking Swansea Bay. Bedrooms, many of which have sea views, are comfortably appointed and thoughtfully equipped. Public areas include a leisure suite with swimming pool, open-plan bar and restaurant and a selection of function rooms.
ROOMS: 52 en suite (6 fmly) ⊗ in 26 bedrooms s £79-£95; d £89-£105 (incl. bkfst) **LB** **FACILITIES:** Sauna Jacuzzi All weather leisure centre ♫ Xmas **CONF:** Thtr 300 Class 200 Board 100 Del from £110
SERVICES: Lift **PARKING:** 150 **NOTES:** ⊗ in restaurant Civ Wed 300
See advert under SWANSEA

Premier Travel Inn Port Talbot
Baglan Rd, Baglan SA12 8ES
☎ 08701 977211 📠 01639 823096
web: www.premiertravelinn.com
Dir: *M4 junct 41 westbound. Follow road to rdbt. Inn just off 4th exit. junct 42 eastbound, left turn for Port Talbot. 2nd exit off 2nd rdbt.*
High quality, modern budget accommodation ideal for both families and business travellers. Spacious, en suite bedrooms feature bath and shower, satellite TV and many have telephones and modem points. The adjacent family restaurant features a wide and varied menu. For further details consult the Hotel Groups page.
ROOMS: 42 en suite s £46.95-£48.95; d £46.95-£48.95

RAGLAN, Monmouthshire — Map 09 SO40

★★74% The Beaufort Arms Coaching Inn & Restaurant
High St NP15 2DY
☎ 01291 690412 📠 01291 690935
e-mail: thebeauforthotel@hotmail.com
web: www.beaufortraglan.com
Dir: *Opposite church in Raglan. 1 min from A40 & A449 junct*
A friendly, family-run village inn dating back to the 15th century. It has historic links with nearby Raglan Castle. The bright, stylish and beautifully refurbished bedrooms are suitably equipped both for tourists and for business guests. Food is served in either the restaurant or traditional lounge and both offer friendly, relaxed service and an enjoyable selection of carefully prepared food.

ROOMS: 10 en suite 5 annexe en suite (5 GF) ⊗ in 6 bedrooms s £50-£75; d £55-£95 (incl. bkfst) **LB** **CONF:** Thtr 120 Class 60 Board 30 Del from £110 **PARKING:** 30 **NOTES:** ⊗ in restaurant Closed 1-20 Jan

Travelodge Monmouth
Granada Services A40, Nr Monmouth NP5 4BG
☎ 08700 850 950 📠 01600 740329
web: www.travelodge.co.uk
Dir: *on A40 near junct with A449*
Travelodge offers good quality, good value, modern accommodation. Ideal for families, the spacious, en suite bedrooms include remote-control TV, tea and coffee-making facilities and comfortable beds. Meals can be taken at the nearby family restaurant. For further details consult the Hotel Groups page.
ROOMS: 43 en suite s fr £26; d fr £26

REYNOLDSTON, Swansea — Map 08 SS48

Top Hotel

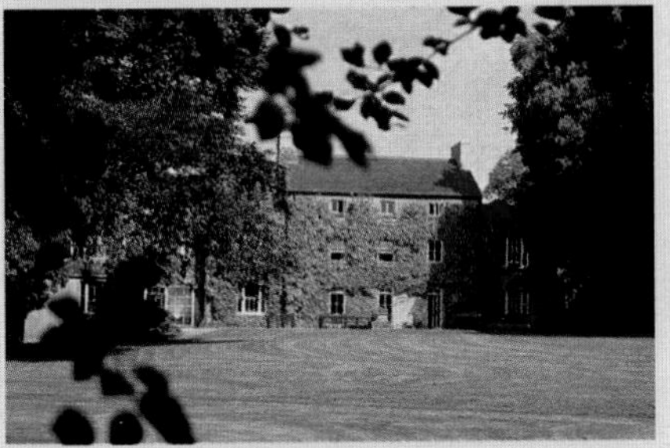

★★★ ®® Fairyhill
SA3 1BS
☎ 01792 390139 📠 01792 391358
e-mail: postbox@fairyhill.net web: www.fairyhill.net
Dir: *just outside Reynoldston off A4118*
Peace and tranquillity are never far away at this charming Georgian mansion set in the heart of the beautiful Gower peninsula. Bedrooms are furnished with care individuality and are filled with many thoughtful extras. There is also a range of comfortable seating areas with crackling log fires to choose from and a smartly appointed restaurant featuring local produce and an excellent wine list. The hotel sometimes has special wine events so do ask when you book.
ROOMS: 8 en suite s £130-£230; d £150-£250 (incl. bkfst) **LB**
FACILITIES: STV mountain bikes available **CONF:** Thtr 40 Class 20 Board 26 **PARKING:** 50 **NOTES:** No children 8yrs ⊗ in restaurant Closed 24-26 Dec & 3-21 Jan

RHAYADER, Powys
Map 09 SN96

A Elan
West St LD6 5AF
☎ 01597 810109 🖹 01597 810524
e-mail: davemackie@elanhotel.fsnet.co.uk
web: www.elanhotel.co.uk
Dir: *600mtrs from junct of A44/A470 Rhayader*
ROOMS: 10 en suite (1 fmly) ⊗ in all bedrooms s £28-£42.50; d £55-£70 (incl. bkfst) **LB** **FACILITIES:** Xmas **PARKING:** 16 **NOTES:** ★★ ⊗ in restaurant

ROSSETT, Wrexham
Map 15 SJ35

★★★73% Rossett Hall
Chester Rd LL12 0DE
☎ 01244 571000 🖹 01244 571505
e-mail: reservations@rossetthallhotel.co.uk
web: www.rossetthallhotel.co.uk
Dir: *M56/M53/A55. Take Wrexham/Chester exit towards Wrexham. Onto B5445, hotel entrance in Rossett village*
This privately owned and personally run hotel lies in several acres of mature gardens in the lovely Welsh border country. Pretty bedrooms are generally spacious and well equipped, and include ground-floor rooms and a full suite. A comfortable foyer lounge is provided and Oscar's bistro serves a wide range of skilfully prepared dishes.
ROOMS: 30 en suite (2 fmly) (10 GF) ⊗ in 20 bedrooms s fr £65; d fr £86 (incl. bkfst) **LB** **FACILITIES:** STV Xmas **CONF:** Thtr 120 Class 50 Board 50 Del from £85 **PARKING:** 120 **NOTES:** ✗ Civ Wed

★★★71% Llyndir Hall
Llyndir Ln LL12 0AY
☎ 01244 571648 🖹 01244 571258
e-mail: llyndir.hall@pageant.co.uk
Dir: *5m S of Chester on B5445 follow Pulford signs. Hotel set back*
Located on the English/Welsh border within easy reach of Chester and Wrexham, this charming manor house lies in several acres of mature grounds. The well-equipped accommodation is popular with leisure and business guests. Facilities include conference rooms, the Business Training Centre, an impressive leisure centre, a choice of comfortable lounges and a brasserie-style restaurant.
ROOMS: 48 en suite (3 fmly) ⊗ in 12 bedrooms s £61-£82.50; d £77-£98 (incl. bkfst) **LB** **FACILITIES: Spa** Sauna Solarium Gym Jacuzzi Steam room, Beauty salon. Xmas **CONF:** BC Thtr 120 Class 60 Board 40 Del £135 **PARKING:** 80 **NOTES:** ⊗ in restaurant Civ Wed 120

⊗ No smoking

RUTHIN, Denbighshire
Map 15 SJ15

★★★70% Ruthin Castle
LL15 2NU
☎ 01824 702664 🖹 01824 705978
e-mail: reservations@ruthincastle.co.uk
web: www.ruthincastle.co.uk
Dir: *A550 to Mold, A494 to Ruthin, hotel at end of Castle St just off Town Square*
Please note that this establishment has recently changed ownership. The main part of this impressive castle was built in the early 19th century, but many ruins in the impressive grounds date back much further. The elegantly panelled public areas include a restaurant and bar along with a medieval banqueting hall and

continued

there is also a tea shop. Many of the modern-equipped bedrooms are spacious and furnished with fine period pieces.

ROOMS: 58 en suite (6 fmly) ⊗ in 10 bedrooms s £59-£72.50; d £90-£120 (incl. bkfst) **LB** **FACILITIES:** Fishing Snooker Gym Beauty suites ♫ Xmas **CONF:** BC Thtr 130 Class 108 Board 48 Del from £130 **SERVICES:** Lift **PARKING:** 200 **NOTES:** ✗ Civ Wed 130

★★65% *Castle*
St Peters Square LL15 1AA
☎ 01824 702479 🖹 01824 703488
e-mail: reception@castle-hotel-ruthin.co.uk
The Castle Hotel is located in the centre of this attractive market town and is an ideal base for touring North Wales and the surrounding areas. Bedrooms are tastefully decorated and well equipped. There is a choice of bars and restaurants and functions are also catered for.
ROOMS: 18 en suite (5 fmly) (1 GF) **PARKING:** 20 **NOTES:** ⊗ in restaurant

U Woodlands Hall
Llanfwrog LL15 2AN
☎ 01824 705107 🖹 01824 704817
e-mail: info@woodlandshallhotel.co.uk
Dir: *Take B5105 out of Ruthin. Turn right at Cross Keys Inn, and continue for 0.75m.*
At the time of going to press, the star classification for this hotel was not confirmed. Please refer to the AA internet site www.theAA.com for current information.
ROOMS: 6 en suite (1 fmly) ⊗ in all bedrooms s £41-£53; d £56-£60 (incl. bkfst) **LB** **FACILITIES:** Snooker **CONF:** Thtr 30 Class 12 Board 20 Del from £80 **PARKING:** 30 **NOTES:** ⊗ in restaurant Closed 15 Feb-1Mar

ST ASAPH, Denbighshire
Map 15 SJ07

★★★72% Oriel House
Upper Denbigh Rd LL17 0LW
☎ 01745 582716 🖹 01745 585208
e-mail: reservations@orialhousehotel.com.
web: www.orielhousehotel.com
Dir: *A55 onto A525, left at cathedral, 1m on right*
Set in several acres of mature grounds south of St Asaph, Oriel House offers generally spacious, well-equipped bedrooms and has a friendly and hospitable staff. The Terrace restaurant serves imaginative food with an emphasis on local produce. Extensive function facilities cater for business meetings and weddings and the leisure club is available to guests.
ROOMS: 31 en suite (3 fmly) (9 GF) ⊗ in 26 bedrooms **FACILITIES:** STV Fishing Sauna Solarium Gym Xmas **CONF:** Thtr 250 Class 100 Board 50 **PARKING:** 200 **NOTES:** ✗ ⊗ in restaurant Civ Wed 120

★★67% Plas Elwy Hotel & Restaurant
The Roe LL17 0LT
☎ 01745 582263 & 582089 🖷 01745 583864
e-mail: plaselwy@gtleisure.co.uk
Dir: *off A55 junct 27, A525 signed Rhyl/St Asaph. On left opposite Total petrol station*
This hotel, which dates back to 1850, has retained much of its original character. Bedrooms in the purpose-built extension are spacious, and one has a four-poster bed; those in the main building are equally well equipped. Public rooms are smart and comfortably furnished and a range of food options is provided in the attractive restaurant.
ROOMS: 7 en suite 6 annexe en suite (3 fmly) (2 GF) ⊗ in 7 bedrooms s £44-£50; d £60-£70 (incl. bkfst) **PARKING:** 25 **NOTES:** ✗ ⊗ in restaurant Closed 25 Dec-4 Jan

ST CLEARS, Carmarthenshire — Map 08 SN21

⌂ Travelodge (Carmarthen)
Tenby Rd SA33 4JN
☎ 08700 850 950 🖷 01994 231227
web: www.travelodge.co.uk
Dir: *A40 westbound, before rdbt junct of A477 & A4066*
Travelodge offers good quality, good value, modern accommodation. Ideal for families, the spacious, en suite bedrooms include remote-control TV, tea and coffee-making facilities and comfortable beds. Meals can be taken at the nearby family restaurant. For further details consult the Hotel Groups page.
ROOMS: 32 en suite s fr £26; d fr £26

ST DAVID'S, Pembrokeshire — Map 08 SM72

★★★77% ®® Warpool Court
SA62 6BN
☎ 01437 720300 🖷 01437 720676
e-mail: info@warpoolcourthotel.com
web: www.warpoolcourthotel.com
Dir: *At Cross Square left by Cartref Restaurant (Goat St). Pass Farmers Arms pub, after 400mtrs left, follow hotel signs, entrance on right*

Originally the cathedral choir school, Warpool Court Hotel is set in landscaped gardens looking out to sea and is within easy walking distance of the Pembrokeshire coastal path. The lounges are spacious and comfortable and bedrooms are well furnished and equipped with modern facilities. The restaurant offers delightful cuisine.
ROOMS: 25 en suite (3 fmly) ⊗ in all bedrooms s £95-£110; d £160-£250 (incl. bkfst) **LB** **FACILITIES:** Gym Xmas **CONF:** Thtr 40 Class 25 Board 25 Del from £135 **PARKING:** 100 **NOTES:** ⊗ in restaurant Closed Jan Civ Wed 80

♫ Entertainment

★★69% Old Cross
Cross Square SA62 6SP
☎ 01437 720387 🖷 01437 720394
e-mail: enquiries@oldcrosshotel.co.uk
web: www.oldcrosshotel.co.uk
Dir: *in centre of St David's*
This friendly and comfortable hotel is situated in the centre of the town, just a short walk from the famous cathedral. Bedrooms are generally spacious and have a good range of facilities with some being suitable for families. Public areas include comfortable lounges, a popular bar and an airy restaurant where good wholesome food is offered.
ROOMS: 16 en suite 1 annexe en suite (2 fmly) ⊗ in 11 bedrooms s £38-£80; d £68-£100 (incl. bkfst) **PARKING:** 17 **NOTES:** ⊗ in restaurant Closed end Dec-last week Jan

SARN PARK MOTORWAY SERVICE AREA (M4), Bridgend — Map 09 SS98

⌂ Welcome Lodge Sarn
Sarn Park Services CF32 9RW
☎ 01656 659218 🖷 01656 768665
e-mail: sarnpark.hotel@welcomebreak.co.uk
web: www.welcomebreak.co.uk
Dir: *M4 junct 36*
This modern building offers accommodation in smart, spacious and well-equipped bedrooms, suitable for families and business travellers, and all with en suite bathrooms. Refreshments may be taken at the nearby family restaurant. For further details consult the Hotel Groups page.
ROOMS: 40 en suite s £35-£55; d £35-£55

SAUNDERSFOOT, Pembrokeshire — Map 08 SN10

★★★67% St Brides
St Brides Hill SA69 9NH
☎ 01834 812304 🖷 01834 811766
e-mail: reservations@stbrideshotel.com
web: www.stbrideshotel.com
Dir: *Exit A478 at Twy Cross rdbt, signed Saundersfoot. Hotel at bottom of hill on right*
This privately owned hotel is situated above the village and has stunning views of the harbour and coastline. The public areas are spacious and tastefully decorated, and feature exhibitions of Welsh artists' work. Bedrooms, many of which have sea views, vary in size and style.
ROOMS: 35 en suite (6 fmly) (4 GF) ⊗ in all bedrooms s £90-£145; d £120-£230 (incl. bkfst & dinner) **LB** **FACILITIES:** Xmas **CONF:** Thtr 150 Class 65 Board 46 Del from £135 **SERVICES:** Lift **PARKING:** 50 **NOTES:** ⊗ in restaurant Civ Wed 80

★★66% Merlewood
St Brides Hill SA69 9NP
☎ 01834 812421 🖷 01834 814886
e-mail: merlehotels@aol.com
Dir: *A477/A4316, hotel on other side of village on St Brides Hill*
Offering delightful views over the village and bay, and providing regular live entertainment, this hotel is a popular destination for coach parties. Bedrooms include ground floor and family rooms and there is a comfortable dining room and a large lounge bar. A pleasant outdoor swimming pool is also available for guests' use.
ROOMS: 29 en suite (8 fmly) (11 GF) ⊗ in 28 bedrooms s £34.50-£38.50; d £59-£65 (incl. bkfst) **LB** **FACILITIES:** Putt green Children's swings, Table tennis ♫ ch fac Xmas **CONF:** Thtr 60 Class 100 Board 40 **PARKING:** 34 **NOTES:** ✗ ⊗ in restaurant Closed Nov-Mar RS Xmas & New Year

S

SKENFRITH, Monmouthshire Map 09 SO42

Restaurant with Rooms

The Bell at Skenfrith

NP7 8UH
☎ 01600 750235 01600 750525
e-mail: enquiries@skenfrith.co.uk
web: www.skenfrith.co.uk
Dir: *A40/ A466 N towards Hereford. 4m turn left onto B4521, signed Abergavenny, hotel 2m on left*

The Bell is a beautifully restored, 17th-century former coaching inn that still retains much charm and character. Natural materials have been used throughout, and the bedrooms, which include full suites and rooms with four-poster beds, are stylish, luxurious and equipped with DVDs. Menus have seasonally changing dishes of traditional combinations with popular French additions. AA Wine Award winner for Wales 2005-6.

ROOMS: 8 en suite in all bedrooms s £70-£110; d £95-£170 (incl. bkfst) **FACILITIES:** Xmas **CONF:** Thtr 20 Board 16 Del from £185 **PARKING:** 36 **NOTES:** in restaurant Closed last wk Jan-1st wk Feb RS 6 Oct-Mar

SWANSEA, Swansea Map 09 SS69
See also Port Talbot

★★★★74% Grand

Ivey Place, High St SA1 1NE
☎ 01792 645898
e-mail: info@thegrandhotelswansea.co.uk
Dir: *M4 junct 42, follow signs for station.*

The Grand stands next to the railway station, offering spacious, contemporary accommodation in superbly equipped bedrooms. Choose between the informal bistro bar or the more exciting cuisine offered in the Beach restaurant. Any excess calories can be burnt up in the small but well equipped gym and leisure area.

ROOMS: 31 en suite (4 fmly) in 19 bedrooms s £95-£250; d £95-£250 (incl. bkfst) **LB FACILITIES: Spa** STV Sauna Solarium Gym Jacuzzi ♫ Xmas **SERVICES:** Lift air con **NOTES:** in restaurant

★★★★71% Morgans

Somerset Place SA1 1RR
☎ 01792 484848 01792 484849
e-mail: info@morganshotel.co.uk
Dir: *M4 junct 45 follow city centre signs. Left at 6th set of lights*

This stunning hotel now much more part of the Swansea scene, has been imaginatively developed from the Port's Authority building near the harbour side. The bedrooms are modern in design with much attention given to guest comfort including big beds, large screen TV, and DVDs. Guests have a choice of eating and drinking options.

ROOMS: 20 en suite (4 fmly) (8 GF) in all bedrooms s £100-£250; d £100-£250 (incl. bkfst) **FACILITIES:** STV **CONF:** Thtr 35 Board 26 **SERVICES:** Lift air con **PARKING:** 27 **NOTES:** in restaurant Civ Wed 100

★★★★68% Swansea Marriott Hotel

The Maritime Quarter SA1 3SS
☎ 0870 400 7282 0870 400 7382
web: www.marriott.co.uk
Dir: *M4 junct 42, A483 to city centre past Leisure Centre, then follow signs to Maritime Quarter*

Just opposite City Hall, this busy hotel enjoys fantastic views over the bay and marina. Bedrooms are spacious and equipped with a range of extras. Public rooms include a popular leisure club and Abernethy's restaurant, which overlooks the marina. It is worth noting, however, that lounge seating is limited.

ROOMS: 122 en suite (50 fmly) (11 GF) in 90 bedrooms s £77-£155; d £104-£165 (incl. bkfst) **LB FACILITIES:** STV Sauna Gym Jacuzzi **CONF:** Thtr 250 Class 120 Board 30 **SERVICES:** Lift air con **PARKING:** 122 **NOTES:** in restaurant Civ Wed 200

★★★ Fairyhill

SA3 1BS
☎ 01792 390139 01792 391358
e-mail: postbox@fairyhill.net
web: www.fairyhill.net
(For full entry see Reynoldston)

★★72% *Beaumont*

72-73 Walter Rd SA1 4QA
☎ 01792 643956 01792 643044
e-mail: info@beaumonthotel.co.uk
web: www.beaumonthotel.co.uk
Dir: *M4, towards city centre. Follow Uplands & Sketty signs. 0.5m from centre along Walter Rd, hotel on left opposite St James Church*

Situated within walking distance of the city centre, this family owned hotel offers a high level of comfort and stylish decor. Bedrooms are well equipped and thoughtfully furnished. There is a relaxing lounge bar where guests can enjoy a drink before sampling good home cooking in the Conservatory Restaurant. There is a secure car park, which is locked each evening.

ROOMS: 16 en suite (3 fmly) **CONF:** BC Class 50 Board 30 **PARKING:** 12 **NOTES:** in restaurant Closed 25-26 Dec & 31 Dec-1 Jan

★★71% *Windsor Lodge Hotel & Restaurant*

Mount Pleasant SA1 6EG
☎ 01792 642158 & 652744 01792 648996
e-mail: reservations@windsor-lodge.co.uk
web: www.windsor-lodge.co.uk
Dir: *M4 junct 42, A483, right at lights past Sainsburys, left at station, right immediately after 2nd set of lights*

This privately owned and personally run, smart and stylish hotel is just a short walk from the city centre. Bedrooms vary in size, but all are similarly well equipped. There is a choice of lounge areas and a deservedly popular restaurant.

ROOMS: 19 en suite (2 fmly) **CONF:** Thtr 30 Class 15 Board 24 **PARKING:** 25 **NOTES:** in restaurant Closed 25-26 Dec RS Sun & BH's

U Ramada Swansea

Phoenix Way, Swansea Enterprise Park SA7 9EG
☎ 01792 310330 01792 787535
e-mail: sales.swansea@ramadajarvis.co.uk
web: www.ramadajarvis.co.uk
Dir: *M44 junct 44, A48 Llansamlet, left at 3rd set of lights, right at mini rdbt, left into Phoenix Way at 2nd mini rdbt. Hotel 400yds on right.*

This large, modern hotel is conveniently situated on the outskirts

continued

of the city with easy access to the M4. Bedrooms are comfortably appointed for both business and leisure guests.
ROOMS: 119 en suite (12 fmly) (50 GF) ⊗ in 60 bedrooms s £85-£115; d £85-£115 **FACILITIES:** STV supervised Sauna Xmas **CONF:** Thtr 180 Class 80 Board 40 Del from £150 **PARKING:** 180 **NOTES:** ⊗ in restaurant Civ Wed 100

⌂ Premier Travel Inn Swansea City Centre

Salubrious Place, Salubrious Quarter, Wind St
SA1 1DP
☎ 0870 990 6562
web: www.premiertravelinn.com
Dir: *Exit M4 junct 44 take A48 onto A4217. Continue onto A483, turn into Wind St*
High quality, modern budget accommodation ideal for both families and business travellers. Spacious, en suite bedrooms feature bath and shower, satellite TV and many have telephones and modem points. The adjacent family restaurant features a wide and varied menu. For further details consult the Hotel Groups page.
ROOMS: 116 en suite s £50.95-£53.95; d £50.95-£53.95

⌂ Premier Travel Inn Swansea North

Upper Fforest Way, Morriston SA6 8WB
☎ 08701 977246 📠 01792 311929
web: www.premiertravelinn.com
Dir: *M4 junct 45/A4067 towards Swansea. At 2nd exit, after 0.5m, turn left onto Clase Rd. Inn 400yds on the left*
High quality, modern budget accommodation ideal for both families and business travellers. Spacious, en suite bedrooms feature bath and shower, satellite TV and many have telephones and modem points. The adjacent family restaurant features a wide and varied menu. For further details consult the Hotel Groups page.
ROOMS: 40 en suite s £46.95-£48.95; d £46.95-£48.95

⌂ Travelodge

Penllergaer SA4 1GT
☎ 08700 850 950 📠 01792 898972
web: www.travelodge.co.uk
Dir: *M4 junct 47*
Travelodge offers good quality, good value, modern accommodation. Ideal for families, the spacious, en suite bedrooms include remote-control TV, tea and coffee-making facilities and comfortable beds. Meals can be taken at the nearby family restaurant. For further details consult the Hotel Groups page.
ROOMS: 50 en suite s fr £26; d fr £26 **CONF:** Thtr 25 Class 32 Board 20

TALSARNAU See Harlech

TENBY, Pembrokeshire — Map 08 SN10

★★★76% ***Penally Abbey Country House***

Penally SA70 7PY
☎ 01834 843033 📠 01834 844714
e-mail: penally.abbey@btinternet.com
web: www.penally-abbey.com
Dir: *1.5m from Tenby, off A4139, near village green*
With monastic origins, this delightful country house stands in five acres of grounds with views over Carmarthen Bay. The drawing room, bar and restaurant are tastefully decorated and attractively furnished and set the scene for a relaxing stay. An impressive range of comfortable accommodation is offered. In the main hotel there are country-house style rooms or cottage-style rooms with
continued

four posters, and in the totally refurbished lodge the rooms combine classic and contemporary style.

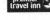

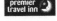

Penally Abbey Country House, Tenby

ROOMS: 8 en suite 4 annexe en suite (3 fmly) **FACILITIES:** Snooker **CONF:** Board 14 **PARKING:** 17 **NOTES:** ⊗ in restaurant Civ Wed 45

★★★75% Atlantic

The Esplanade SA70 7DU
☎ 01834 842881 & 844176 📠 01834 842881 ex 256
e-mail: enquiries@atlantic-hotel.uk.com
web: www.atlantic-hotel.uk.com
Dir: *A478 into Tenby & follow town centre signs, keep town walls on left then turn right at Esplanade, hotel half way along on right*
This privately owned and personally run, friendly hotel has an enviable position looking out over South Beach towards Caldy
continued on p810

TENBY, continued

Island. Bedrooms vary in size and style, and are well equipped and tastefully appointed. The comfortable public areas include a choice of restaurants and, in fine weather guests can also enjoy the cliff-top gardens.
ROOMS: 42 en suite (11 fmly) (4 GF) ⊗ in 4 bedrooms s £72-£76; d £96-£160 (incl. bkfst) **FACILITIES: Spa** STV Solarium Steam room **CONF:** Board 8 **SERVICES:** Lift **PARKING:** 25 **NOTES:** Closed 18 Dec-8 Jan

★★★73% Heywood Mount
Heywood Ln SA70 8DA
☎ 01834 842087 🖷 01834 842113
e-mail: reception@heywoodmount.co.uk
web: www.heywoodmount.co.uk
Dir: *A478 into Tenby, follow Heywood Mount signs then right into Serpentine Rd, turn right at T-junct into Heywood Lane, 3rd hotel on left*
This privately owned hotel is situated in a peaceful residential area, close to Tenby's beaches and town centre. The well-maintained house is surrounded by extensive gardens, and public areas include a comfortable lounge, bar, restaurant and health & fitness spa. Several of the well-appointed bedrooms are on the ground floor and the executive style rooms are particularly well equipped.
ROOMS: 28 en suite (6 fmly) (10 GF) ⊗ in all bedrooms s £45-£130; d £90-£170 (incl. bkfst) **LB FACILITIES: Spa** supervised Sauna Solarium Gym Jacuzzi Beauty therapist ♫ Xmas **CONF:** BC Thtr 80 Class 50 Board 25 Del from £75.95 **PARKING:** 28 **NOTES:** No children 3yrs ⊗ in restaurant Civ Wed 90

★★★70% Fourcroft
North Beach SA70 8AP
☎ 01834 842886 🖷 01834 842888
e-mail: staying@fourcroft-hotel.co.uk
web: www.fourcroft-hotel.co.uk
Dir: *A478, after 'Welcome to Tenby' sign left towards North Beach & Walled Town. At seafront turn sharp left. Hotel on left*
This friendly hotel has been owned and run by the same family since 1946. It offers a beach-front location, together with a number of extra facilities that make it particularly suitable for families with children. Guests have direct access to Tenby's North Beach through the hotel's cliff top gardens. Bedrooms are of a good size and have modern facilities.
ROOMS: 40 en suite (12 fmly) ⊗ in 10 bedrooms s £40-£65; d £80-£130 (incl. bkfst) **LB FACILITIES:** STV Sauna Jacuzzi Table tennis Giant chess Human Gyroscope Snooker Pool Xmas **CONF:** BC Thtr 90 Class 40 Board 50 Del from £100 **SERVICES:** Lift **PARKING:** 12 **NOTES:** ⊗ in restaurant Civ Wed 90

★★73% Panorama Hotel & Restaurant
The Esplanade SA70 7DU
☎ 01834 844976 🖷 01834 844976
e-mail: mail@panoramahotel.f9.co.uk
web: www.panoramahotel.force9.co.uk
Dir: *A478 follow 'South Beach' & 'Town Centre' signs. Sharp left under railway arches, up Greenhill Rd, onto South Pde then Esplanade*
This charming little hotel is part of a Victorian terrace, overlooking the South Beach and Caldy Island. It provides a variety of non-smoking bedrooms, all of which are well equipped. Facilities include a cosy bar and an elegant restaurant, where a good choice of skilfully prepared dishes is available.
ROOMS: 7 en suite (2 fmly) ⊗ in all bedrooms s £43; d £60-£86 (incl. bkfst) **LB NOTES:** No children 5yrs ⊗ in restaurant

THREE COCKS, Powys — Map 09 SO13

★★74% Three Cocks
LD3 0SL
☎ 01497 847215 🖷 01497 847339
e-mail: info@threecockshotel.com
web: www.threecockshotel.com
Dir: *on A438, in village centre*
This charming old country hostelry dates back to the 15th century and is set in the glorious countryside of the Beacons National Park. There is a wealth of original features and wooden beams in the comfortable lounges, and the elegant restaurant overlooks the garden. Bedrooms are tastefully decorated and a television lounge is available to guests.
ROOMS: 7 en suite (2 fmly) s £45-£60; d £70-£85 (incl. bkfst) **LB FACILITIES:** no TV in bdrms Xmas **PARKING:** 40 **NOTES:** ⊗ in restaurant

TINTERN PARVA, Monmouthshire — Map 04 SO50

★★★68% The Abbey Hotel
NP16 6SF
THE INDEPENDENTS
☎ 01291 689777 🖷 01291 689727
e-mail: info@theabbey-hotel.co.uk
web: www.theabbey-hotel.co.uk
Dir: *M48 junct 2/A466, hotel opposite the abbey ruins*

Appointed to a high standard and possessing stunning views of nearby Tintern Abbey, this friendly hotel provides modern bedrooms, including a family suite. Diners are spoilt for choice between the brasserie with its daytime carvery, the formal carte service for dinner, and the pleasant hotel bar where lighter meal options are on offer.
ROOMS: 23 en suite ⊗ in 7 bedrooms s £60-£80 (incl. bkfst) **LB FACILITIES: Spa** STV Fishing Jacuzzi ♫ Xmas **CONF:** Thtr 150 Class 60 Board 30 **PARKING:** 60 **NOTES:** ⊗ in restaurant Civ Wed 140

★★★66% *Royal George*
NP16 6SF
Best Western
☎ 01291 689205 🖷 01291 689448
e-mail: royalgeorgetintern@hotmail.com
Dir: *off M48/A466, 4m to Tintern, 2nd on left*
This privately owned and personally run hotel provides comfortable, spacious accommodation, including bedrooms with balconies overlooking the well-tended garden. There are some ground floor rooms. The public areas include a choice of bars, and a large function room. A varied and popular menu choice is available in either the bar or restaurant.
ROOMS: 2 en suite 14 annexe en suite (13 fmly) (10 GF) ⊗ in 11 bedrooms **FACILITIES:** ♫ **CONF:** Thtr 120 Class 40 Board 50 **PARKING:** 50 **NOTES:** ⊗ in restaurant Civ Wed 120

★★73% ◎ Parva Farmhouse Hotel & Restaurant

NP16 6SQ
☎ 01291 689411 & 689511 🖷 01291 689557
e-mail: parva_hotelintern@hotmail.com
Dir: *From S leave M48 junct 2, N edge of village on A466. From N, 10m S of Monmouth town & M50*

This relaxed and friendly hotel is situated on a sweep of the River Wye with far reaching views of the valley. Originally a farmhouse dating from the 17th century, many of the original features have been retained to provide a lounge full of character, which has a fire in colder months, and an atmospheric restaurant with a popular local following. Bedrooms are tastefully decorated and thoughtfully equipped.

ROOMS: 9 en suite (3 fmly) (1 GF) s fr £55; d £68-£84 (incl. bkfst) **LB** **FACILITIES:** Cycle hire ch fac **CONF:** Thtr 12 Board 12 Del from £86 **PARKING:** 10 **NOTES:** ⊗ in restaurant

TREARDDUR BAY See Anglesey, Isle of

TREFRIW, Conwy Map 14 SH76

★★73% *Hafod Country House*

LL27 0RQ
☎ 01492 640029 🖷 01492 641351
e-mail: hafod@breathemail.net
web: www.hafodhouse.co.uk
Dir: *on B5106 between A5 at Betws-y-Coed & A55 at Conwy. 2nd entrance on right entering Trefriw from south.*

This former farmhouse is a personally run and friendly hotel with a wealth of charm and character. The tasteful bedrooms feature period furnishings and thoughtful extras such as fresh fruit. There is a comfortable sitting room and a cosy bar. The fixed-price menu is imaginative and makes good use of fresh, local produce while the breakfast menu offers a wide choice.

ROOMS: 6 en suite ⊗ in all bedrooms **PARKING:** 14 **NOTES:** No children 11yrs ⊗ in restaurant Closed early Jan-mid Feb

USK, Monmouthshire Map 09 SO30

★★★73% *Glen-yr-Afon House*

Pontypool Rd NP15 1SY
☎ 01291 672302 & 673202 🖷 01291 672597
e-mail: enquiries@glen-yr-afon.co.uk
web: www.glen-yr-afon.co.uk
Dir: *A472 through High St, over river bridge, follow road to right. Hotel 200yds on left*

On the edge of this delightful old market town, Glen-yr-Afon, a unique Victorian Villa, offers all the facilities expected of a modern hotel combined with the warm atmosphere of a family home. Bedrooms are furnished to a high standard and several overlook the hotel's well-tended gardens. There is a choice of comfortable sitting areas and a stylish and spacious banqueting suite.

continued

Glen-yr-Afon House, Usk

ROOMS: 28 en suite (2 fmly) ⊗ in 14 bedrooms **FACILITIES:** STV **CONF:** Thtr 100 Class 200 Board 30 **SERVICES:** Lift **PARKING:** 101 **NOTES:** ⊗ in restaurant Civ Wed 200

★★★66% ◎ Three Salmons

Porthycarne St NP15 1RY
☎ 01291 672133 🖷 01291 673979
e-mail: threesalmons.hotel@talk21.com
web: www.3-salmons-usk.co.uk
Dir: *off A449, 1m into Usk, hotel on corner of Porthycarne St, B4598*

This 17th-century coaching inn in the heart of Usk offers spacious bedrooms that are comfortably furnished and well maintained. Both the restaurant and bar offer a wide range of carefully prepared dishes. The function room and meeting room overlook the pretty garden and courtyard to the rear.

ROOMS: 10 en suite 14 annexe en suite (2 fmly) **FACILITIES:** STV Xmas **CONF:** Thtr 100 Class 40 Board 50 Del £99 **PARKING:** 38 **NOTES:** ⊗ in restaurant Civ Wed 100

USK, continued

Restaurant with Rooms

The Newbridge
Tredunnock NP15 1LY
☎ 01633 451000 01633 451001
e-mail: thenewbridge@tinyonline.co.uk
web: www.thenewbridge.co.uk
Dir: *Turn off B4236 between Usk & Caerleon at Tredunnock sign*

This 200-year-old inn stands alongside the River Usk at Tredunnock, just four miles south of Usk. It has been renovated and converted into a spacious, traditionally furnished restaurant occupying the ground and first-floor levels. Six smart, modern and well-equipped bedrooms are located in a stone-clad, purpose-built unit adjacent to the restaurant.
ROOMS: 6 en suite (2 fmly) (4 GF) in all bedrooms s £67.50-£115; d £67.50-£130 (incl. bkfst) **LB** **FACILITIES:** Fishing Xmas **CONF:** Thtr 20 Class 10 Board 14 **PARKING:** 65 **NOTES:** Civ Wed 60

WELSHPOOL, Powys Map 15 SJ20

★★★68% **Royal Oak**
The Cross SY21 7DG
☎ 01938 552217 01938 556652
e-mail: relax@royaloakhotel.info
web: www.royaloakhotel.info
Dir: *by traffic lights at junct of A483/A458*
This traditional market town hotel dates back over 350 years. It provides well-equipped bedrooms, a choice of bars and extensive function and conference facilities. The attractively appointed restaurant is a popular venue for dining out and there is also a busy coffee shop open throughout the day. Major refurbishment is taking place from April 2005, please check website for updated information.
ROOMS: 25 en suite (2 fmly) in 12 bedrooms s £57-£64; d £84-£94 (incl. bkfst) **LB** **FACILITIES:** STV **CONF:** Thtr 150 Class 60 Board 60 Del from £90 **PARKING:** 30

TV dinner?
Room service at three stars and above

Late for dinner? Quality standards mean that last orders for dinner vary according to star rating and should be no earlier than:
★★ 7.00pm ★★★ 8:00pm ★★★★ 9:00pm ★★★★★ 10:00pm

WHITEBROOK, Monmouthshire Map 04 SO50

Restaurant with Rooms

Crown at Whitebrook
NP25 4TX
☎ 01600 860254 01600 860607
e-mail: crown@whitebrook.demon.co.uk
web: www.crownatwhitebrook.co.uk
Dir: *turn off A449, hotel 2m on right.*

Set in a delightful wooded valley, this former drover's inn dates back to the 17th century, and is now under new ownership. The lounge bar and restaurant are furnished with relaxation and comfort in mind and make an ideal partner for the cuisine, which uses quality local ingredients skilfully prepared to offer a most impressive and memorable culinary experience.
ROOMS: 10 en suite **CONF:** Board 10 **PARKING:** 20 **NOTES:** No children 12yrs in restaurant

WOLF'S CASTLE, Pembrokeshire Map 08 SM92

★★74% **Wolfscastle Country Hotel**
SA62 5LZ
☎ 01437 741688 & 741225 01437 741383
e-mail: enquiries@wolfscastle.com
web: www.wolfscastle.com
Dir: *on A40 in village at top of hill. 6m N of Haverfordwest*

This large stone house dates back to the mid-19th century and commands a regal position in the village. Now a friendly, privately owned and personally run hotel, it provides modern, well-maintained and equipped bedrooms. There is a pleasant bar and an attractive restaurant, which has a well-deserved, high reputation for its food.
ROOMS: 20 en suite 4 annexe en suite (2 fmly) in 21 bedrooms s £55-£75; d £79-£107 (incl. bkfst) **LB** **FACILITIES:** STV **CONF:** Thtr 100 Class 100 Board 30 Del from £85 **PARKING:** 60 **NOTES:** in restaurant Closed 24-26 Dec RS Sun nights

U

WREXHAM, Wrexham Map 15 SJ35

★★★68% ◉
Cross Lanes Hotel & Restaurant
Cross Lanes, Bangor Rd, Marchwiel LL13 0TF
☎ 01978 780555 📠 01978 780568
e-mail: guestservices@crosslanes.co.uk
Dir: 3m SE of Wrexham, on A525, between Marchwiel & Bangor-on-Dee

This hotel was built as a private house in 1890 and stands in over six acres of beautiful grounds. Bedrooms are well equipped and meet the needs of today's traveller, and include two with four-poster beds. A fine selection of well prepared food is available in Kagan's Brasserie.

ROOMS: 16 en suite (1 fmly) ⊗ in 6 bedrooms s £76-£88; d £92-£99
LB FACILITIES: ⬡ Putt green Xmas **CONF:** Thtr 120 Class 60 Board 40 Del from £132.50 **PARKING:** 80 **NOTES:** ✱ ⊗ in restaurant Closed 25 Dec (night) & 26 Dec Civ Wed 120

See advert under CHESTER

> If you wish to use a particular credit card or debit card please check with the hotel that they are happy to accept it

★★★68% **Llwyn Onn Hall**
Cefn Rd LL13 0NY
☎ 01978 261225 📠 01978 363233
e-mail: reception@llwynonnhallhotel.co.uk
Dir: between A525 (Wrexham-Whitchurch) & A534 (Wrexham-Nantwich). Easy access Wrexham Ind Estate, 2m off A483
Surrounded by open countryside, this fine 17th-century manor house is set in several acres of mature grounds. Exposed timbers remain and the original oak staircase is still in use. Bedrooms are equipped with modern facilities and one room has a four-poster bed which Bonnie Prince Charlie is reputed to have slept in.
ROOMS: 13 en suite (1 fmly) ⊗ in 7 bedrooms s £69-£90; d £75-£110 (incl. bkfst) **LB CONF:** Thtr 60 Class 40 Board 12 Del £105.75
PARKING: 40 **NOTES:** ✱ ⊗ in restaurant Civ Wed 60

⌂ **Premier Travel Inn Wrexham**
Chester Rd, Gresford LL12 8PW
☎ 08701 977279 📠 01978 856838
web: www.premiertravelinn.com
Dir: on B5445 just off A483 dual carriageway near village of Gresford
High quality, modern budget accommodation ideal for both families and business travellers. Spacious, en suite bedrooms feature bath and shower, satellite TV and many have telephones and modem points. The adjacent family restaurant features a wide and varied menu. For further details consult the Hotel Groups page.
ROOMS: 36 en suite s £46.95-£48.95; d £46.95-£48.95

⌂ **Travelodge**
Wrexham By Pass, Rhostyllen LL14 4EJ
☎ 08700 850 950 📠 01978 365705
web: www.travelodge.co.uk
Dir: 2m S, A483/A5152 rdbt
Travelodge offers good quality, good value, modern accommodation. Ideal for families, the spacious, en suite bedrooms include remote-control TV, tea and coffee-making facilities and comfortable beds. Meals can be taken at the nearby family restaurant. For further details consult the Hotel Groups page.
ROOMS: 32 en suite s fr £26; d fr £26

Republic of Ireland

Hotel of the Year for Republic of Ireland

Dromoland Castle

Newmarket-on-Fergus, Co Clare

★★★★★ 🏵🏵

A

Additional information for Northern Ireland & the Republic of Ireland

Licensing Regulations

Northern Ireland: Public houses open Mon-Sat 11.30-23.00 and Sun 12.30-22.00. Hotels can serve residents without restriction. Non-residents can be served 12.30-22.00 on Christmas Day. Children under 18 are not allowed in the bar area and may neither buy or consume liquor in hotels.

Republic of Ireland: General licensing hours are Mon-Sat 10.30-23.30, Friday & Saturday 12.30-00.30. Sunday 12.30-23.00. Hotels can serve residents without restriction. There is no service on Christmas Day (except for hotel residents) or Good Friday.

The Fire Services (NI) Order 1984
Covers establishments accommodating more than six people, which must have a certificate from the Northern Ireland Fire Authority. Places accommodating fewer than six persons need adequate exits. AA inspectors check emergency notices, fire-fighting equipment and fire exits here.

Republic of Ireland safety regulations are a matter for local authority regulations. For your own and others' safety, read the emergency notices and be sure you understand them.

Telephone Numbers:
Area codes for numbers in the Republic of Ireland apply only within the Republic. If dialling from outside check the telephone directory (from the UK the international dialling code is 00 353). Area codes for numbers in Britain and Northern Ireland cannot be used directly from the Republic.

For the latest information on the Republic of Ireland visit AA Ireland's website: www.aaireland.ie

ABBEYLEIX, Co Laois — Map 01 C3

★★★62% ***Abbeyleix Manor Hotel***
☎ 0502 30111 🖷 0502 30220
e-mail: info@abbeyleixmanorhotel.com
Dir: *on N8 (Dublin-Cork road) just S of Abbeyleix*
This modern hotel is situated on the N8 on the outskirts of town. Bedrooms are spacious and appointed to a high standard. Public areas are comfortable with a cosy lobby and conservatory and a themed bar where food is served all day. There are meeting and banqueting facilities and ample off street parking.
ROOMS: 23 en suite (2 fmly) **SERVICES:** air con **PARKING:** 270
NOTES: ✗ ⊘ in restaurant Closed 25-26 Dec

ACHILL ISLAND, Co Mayo — Map 01 A4

★★★61% **Achill Cliff House**
Keel
☎ 098 43400 🖷 098 43007
e-mail: info@achillcliff.com
Dir: *From Castlebar take Newport Rd, then onto Mulranny and R319 to Achill Sound. Hotel on right, in the village of Keel.*
This family run hotel is situated on Achill Island, an unspoilt place made famous by painter Paul Henry and has a lot to offer those seeking relaxation, dramatic scenery, hill walking and historic interest. Bedrooms are comfortable and the popular restaurant serves local fish and lamb dishes at reasonable prices.
ROOMS: 10 en suite (4 fmly) (2 GF) ⊘ in all bedrooms s €40-€90; d €70-€100 (incl. bkfst) **LB** **FACILITIES:** Sauna photography, painting, walking trails, Reading room **PARKING:** 20 **NOTES:** ✗ ⊘ in restaurant Closed 23-26 Dec

ADARE, Co Limerick — Map 01 B3

★★★★70% ◎◎ **Dunraven Arms**
☎ 061 396633 🖷 061 396541
e-mail: dunraven@iol.ie
This charming hotel was established in 1792 in the heart of one of Ireland's prettiest villages. It is a traditional country inn both in style and atmosphere. Comfortable lounges and bedrooms, attractive gardens, leisure and beauty facilities and good cuisine all add to enjoyable visit at the hotel. Golf and equestrian activities are specialities in Adare.
ROOMS: 75 en suite (1 fmly) **FACILITIES:** STV Fishing Riding Sauna Gym Jacuzzi Beauty salon ♫ Xmas **CONF:** Thtr 180 Class 60 Board 12 Del from €125 **SERVICES:** Lift **PARKING:** 90

★★★65%
Fitzgeralds Woodlands House Hotel
Knockanes
☎ 061 605100 🖷 061 396073
e-mail: reception@woodlands-hotel.ie
Dir: *left at Lantern Lodge rdbt on N21 S of Limerick. Hotel 0.5m on right*

Located close to Adare, this family-run hotel is friendly and welcoming. Bedrooms are well appointed. The comfortable public areas include, Woodcock bar, Timmy Mac's traditional bar and bistro and the Brennan Restaurant. There are extensive leisure and beauty facilities. Close to Limerick Racecourse, Adare and many other golf courses.
ROOMS: 92 en suite (36 fmly) **FACILITIES:** STV Sauna Solarium Gym Jacuzzi Health & beauty salon Thermal spa ♫ ch fac **CONF:** Thtr 400 Class 200 Board 50 **SERVICES:** air con **PARKING:** 290
NOTES: ✗ Closed 24-25 Dec

Packed in a hurry? Ironing facilities should be available at all star levels, either in the rooms or on request

AGHADOWEY, Co Londonderry Map 01 C6

★★70% Brown Trout Golf & Country Inn
209 Agivey Rd BT51 4AD
☎ 028 7086 8209 🖷 028 7086 8878
e-mail: bill@browntroutinn.com
Dir: *at junct of A54 & B66 junct on road to Coleraine*

IRISH COUNTRY HOTELS

Set alongside the Agivey River and featuring its own 9-hole golf course, this welcoming inn offers a choice of spacious accommodation. Comfortable and attractively furnished bedrooms are situated around a courtyard area whilst the cottage suites also have lounge areas. Home-cooked meals are served in the restaurant; lighter fare is available in the charming lounge bar.
ROOMS: 15 en suite (11 fmly) s £50-£65; d £35-£45 (incl. bkfst) **LB**
FACILITIES: ⛳ 9 Fishing Gym Putt green Game fishing ♫ Xmas
CONF: Thtr 40 Class 24 Board 28 Del from £60 **PARKING:** 80
NOTES: ⊗ in restaurant

ARKLOW, Co Wicklow Map 01 D3

★★★67% *Arklow Bay*
Ferrybank
☎ 0402 32309 🖷 0402 32300
e-mail: arklowbay@eircom.net
Dir: *off N11 at by-pass for Arklow. 1m turn left, hotel 200yds on left*

This hotel enjoys panoramic views of Arklow Bay and many of the well-appointed bedrooms take full advantage of this. The public areas are decorated in a contemporary style, and include a spacious lobby lounge and a comfortable bar where casual dining is available. For more formal dining, Howard's restaurant opens for dinner. Extensive leisure and treatment facilities are available.
ROOMS: 92 en suite (3 fmly) (27 GF) ⊗ in 20 bedrooms
FACILITIES: STV supervised Sauna Solarium Gym Jacuzzi ♫
CONF: Thtr 500 Class 200 Board 60 **SERVICES:** Lift **PARKING:** 100
NOTES: No dogs

ARMAGH, Co Armagh Map 01 C5

★★★61% Charlemont Arms Hotel
57/65 English St BT61 7LB
☎ 028 3752 2028 🖷 028 3752 6979
e-mail: info@charlemontarmshotel.com
web: www.charlemontarmshotel.com
Dir: *A3 from Partadown or A28 from Newry, into Armagh. Follow signs to Tourist Information. Hotel 100yds on right*
Centrally located for all of this historic city's principal attractions, this hotel has been under the same family ownership for almost 70 years and offers a choice of dining styles and bars. The mostly spacious bedrooms have all been appointed in a contemporary style and provide all the expected facilities.
ROOMS: 30 en suite (2 fmly) ⊗ in all bedrooms s £50-£60; d £75-£85 (incl. bkfst) **LB** **FACILITIES:** ♫ Xmas **CONF:** Thtr 150 Class 100 Board 80 **SERVICES:** Lift **PARKING:** 30 **NOTES:** No dogs Closed 25-26 Dec

ATHLONE, Co Westmeath Map 01 C4

★★★70% ⊛ Hodson Bay
Hodson Bay
☎ 090 6442000 🖷 090 6442020
e-mail: info@hodsonbayhotel.com
Dir: *from N6 take N61 to Roscommon. Turn right. Hotel 1km on Lough Rea*

On the shores of Lough Rea some not far from Athlone, this hotel has its own marina and is surrounded by the golf course. Public areas include a comfortable lounges, a carvery bar, an attractive restaurant and excellent banqueting and leisure facilities. The spacious bedrooms have been designed to take in the magnificent lake views. Further developments are due for completion early 2006.
ROOMS: 133 en suite (23 fmly) (12 GF) ⊗ in 3 bedrooms s €200; d €280 (incl. bkfst) **LB** **FACILITIES:** STV supervised ⛳ 18 Fishing Sauna Gym Steam room, play room, beauty salon ♫ Xmas **CONF:** Thtr 700 Class 250 Board 200 Del from €132.20 **SERVICES:** Lift **PARKING:** 300 **NOTES:** No dogs ⊗ in restaurant

See advert on this page

ATHLONE, continued

Restaurant with Rooms

Wineport Lodge

Glasson
☎ 090 643 9010 Fax 090 648 5471
e-mail: lodge@wineport.ie
Dir: *from N6 (Dublin/Galway road) take N55 north (Longford/Cavan exit) at Athlone. Left at Dog & Duck pub. Lodge 1m on left*
In an enviable location, three miles north of Athlone on the shores of the inner lakes of Lough Rea on the Shannon. Guests can arrive by road or water, and dine on the deck or in the attractive dining room. The cuisine is both wholesome and innovative, using the best of local produce. There are ten luxurious lakeshore bedrooms with balconies - the perfect setting for breakfast.
ROOMS: 10 en suite in all bedrooms **FACILITIES:** STV Massage, boat hire ch fac **CONF:** Thtr 50 Class 30 Board 20 **SERVICES:** air con **PARKING:** 60 **NOTES:** in restaurant Closed 24-26 Dec

U Glasson Golf Hotel & Country Club

Glasson
☎ 090 6485120 Fax 090 6485444
e-mail: info@glassongolf.ie
Dir: *6m N of Athlone on N55*
At the time of going to press, the star classification for this hotel was not confirmed. Please refer to the AA internet site www.theAA.com for current information.
ROOMS: 29 en suite (13 fmly) **FACILITIES:** STV 21 Putt green **CONF:** Thtr 120 Class 50 Board 30 **SERVICES:** Lift **PARKING:** 150 **NOTES:**

AUGHRIM, Co Wicklow — Map 01 D3

★★★65% Lawless

☎ 0402 36146 Fax 0402 36384
e-mail: info@lawlesshotel.com
IRISH COUNTRY HOTELS
Dir: *N11 to Rathnew, R752 to Rathdrun, R753 to Aughrim, hotel between bridges on outskirts of village*
Established in 1787, this family-run hotel is located in the pretty village of Aughrim. Bedrooms, some with river views, are individually decorated and well appointed, and inviting public areas include a comfortable lounge, smart restaurant and the newly decorated Thirsty Trout Bar and conservatory, which offers an imaginative menu. Golf courses and an angling park nearby.
ROOMS: 14 en suite (2 fmly) in 5 bedrooms **FACILITIES:** STV **CONF:** BC Thtr 100 Class 60 Board 40 **PARKING:** 40 **NOTES:** in restaurant Closed 23 - 26 Dec

BALLINA, Co Mayo — Map 01 B4

★★★70% Teach Iorrais

Geesala
☎ 097 86888 Fax 097 86855
e-mail: teachior@iol.ie
Located in the heart of the Erris peninsula, in Northwest Mayo, this is a warm friendly hotel offering spacious well appointed bedrooms. The public areas include a relaxing bar and a restaurant on the first floor where quality cuisine is served. A good base for golfers and anglers.

ROOMS: 31 en suite (2 fmly) (15 GF) s €56; d €92-€102 (incl. bkfst) **LB** **FACILITIES:** STV Xmas **CONF:** BC Thtr 300 Class 150 Board 80 **SERVICES:** air con **PARKING:** 85 **NOTES:** in restaurant

BALLYBOFEY, Co Donegal — Map 01 C5

★★★70% Kee's

Stranorlar
☎ 074 913 1018 Fax 074 913 1917
e-mail: info@keeshotel.ie
Dir: *2km NE on N15, in Stranorlar*
This long established hotel is now in the fourth generation of the Kee Family. Warm hospitality is one of the many features of the establishment, which enjoys a steady local custom in the Gallery Bistro. Bedrooms are well appointed and comfortable.
ROOMS: 53 en suite (10 fmly) **FACILITIES: Spa** STV supervised Sauna Solarium Gym Jacuzzi **CONF:** Thtr 250 Class 100 Board 30 **SERVICES:** Lift **PARKING:** 90 **NOTES:**

BALLYCONNELL, Co Cavan — Map 01 C4

★★★★70% Slieve Russell Hotel Golf & Country Club

☎ 049 9526444 Fax 049 9526474
e-mail: slieve-russell@quinn-hotels.com
Dir: *N3 towards Cavan. At rdbt before Cavan follow sign for Enniskillen to Belturbet. Then towards Ballyconnell, hotel approx 6m on left*
This imposing hotel stands on 300 acres, encompassing a championship golf course and a nine-hole par three course. The spacious public areas include relaxing lounges, three restaurants and extensive leisure and banqueting facilities. Bedrooms are comfortable and tastefully furnished.
ROOMS: 219 en suite (87 fmly) in 30 bedrooms s €130; d €250 (incl. bkfst) **LB** **FACILITIES: Spa** STV 18 Sauna Solarium Gym Putt green Jacuzzi Floodlit driving range, Wellness centre Xmas **CONF:** BC Thtr 1200 Class 600 Board 40 **SERVICES:** Lift **PARKING:** 600 **NOTES:** in restaurant

> Destination dining!
> This symbol indicates a Restaurant with Rooms

BALLYCOTTON, Co Cork
Map 01 C2

Top Hotel

★★★ ❀❀ Bay View

☎ 021 4646746 ▤ 021 4646075

e-mail: res@thebayviewhotel.com

Dir: *N25 Castlemartyr, turn right through Ladysbridge, Garryvoe and onto Ballycotton.*

Situated in a fishing village overlooking Ballycotton Bay, the Bay View has a very pleasant atmosphere and a stunning outlook. The public rooms and the bedrooms are very comfortable and make the most of the views, but it is the warm and friendly team that impresses most. Dinner in the Capricho Room is a delight.

ROOMS: 35 en suite (5 GF) ⊗ in 25 bedrooms **FACILITIES:** STV Fishing Riding Fishing, Pitch and putt, Sea angling **CONF:** Thtr 60 Class 30 Board 24 **SERVICES:** Lift air con **PARKING:** 40 **NOTES:** ⊗ in restaurant Closed Nov-Apr

BALLYHEIGE, Co Kerry
Map 01 A2

★★★68% The White Sands

☎ 066 7133102 ▤ 066 7133357

e-mail: whitesands@eircom.net

Dir: *18km from Tralee on coast road, hotel on main street*

Friendly staff welcome guests to this family run hotel, situated beside the beach and close to golf clubs. Attractively decorated throughout, facilities include a lounge bar, traditional pub, good restaurant and comfortable bedrooms.

ROOMS: 81 en suite (2 fmly) s €65-€79; d €104-€116 (incl. bkfst) **LB** **FACILITIES:** STV ♫ ch fac **CONF:** Class 40 Board 40 **SERVICES:** Lift air con **PARKING:** 40 **NOTES:** ✗ ⊗ in restaurant Closed Nov-Feb RS Mar-Apr & Oct

BALLYLICKEY, Co Cork
Map 01 B2

Courtesy & Care Award
Top Hotel

★★★ ❀❀ Sea View House Hotel

☎ 027 50073 & 50462 ▤ 027 51555

e-mail: info@seaviewhousehotel.com

Dir: *5km from Bantry, 11km from Glengarriff on N71*

Colourful gardens and glimpses of the sea at Bantry Bay through the mature trees frame this delightful country house. Comfort and good cuisine are the top priorities. Bedrooms are spacious and individually styled; some on the ground floor are fitted to facilitate the less able. Owner Kathleen O'Sullivan's team of staff are exceptionally pleasant and AA Ireland has awarded this hotel their Courtesy & Care Award for the Republic of Ireland 2005-6.

ROOMS: 25 en suite (3 fmly) (5 GF) s €95-€100; d €150-€180 (incl. bkfst) **LB** **FACILITIES:** STV **PARKING:** 32 **NOTES:** ⊗ in restaurant Closed mid Nov-mid Mar

BALLYMENA, Co Antrim
Map 01 D5

★★★★59% Galgorm Manor

BT42 1EA

☎ 028 2588 1001 ▤ 028 2588 0080

e-mail: mail@galgorm.com

Dir: *1m outside Ballymena on A42, between Galgorm & Cullybackey*

Standing in 85 acres of private woodland and sweeping lawns beside the River Maine, this 19th-century mansion offers spacious comfortable bedrooms. Public areas include a welcoming cocktail bar and elegant restaurant, as well as Gillies, a lively and atmospheric locals' bar. Also on the estate is an equestrian centre and a conference hall. This hotel is a popular venue for weddings.

ROOMS: 24 en suite (6 fmly) **FACILITIES:** STV Fishing Riding Clay pigeon shooting, Archery, Waterskiing ♫ **CONF:** Thtr 500 Class 200 Board 12 **PARKING:** 170 **NOTES:** ✗ RS 25-26 Dec Civ Wed 250

Late for dinner? Quality standards mean that last orders for dinner vary according to star rating and should be no earlier than: ★★ 7.00pm ★★★ 8:00pm ★★★★ 9:00pm ★★★★★ 10:00pm

BALLYVAUGHAN, Co Clare Map 01 B3

Top Hotel

★★★ ◎◎ **Gregans Castle**
☎ 065 7077005 📠 065 7077111
e-mail: stay@gregans.ie
Dir: 3.5m S of Ballyvaughan on N67

IRELAND'S BLUE BOOK

Situated in an oasis at the foot of Corkscrew Hill in the heart of the Burren, this hotel enjoys the splendid views towards Galway Bay. The area is rich in archaeological, geological and botanical interest. The Hayden family and welcoming staff offer a high level of personal service, where hospitality, good food and relaxation are the themes. Bedrooms are individually decorated, superior rooms and suites are particularly comfortable, and some of these are at ground-floor level.
ROOMS: 21 en suite (3 fmly) (7 GF) ⊗ in all bedrooms s €120-€270; d €170-€290 (incl. bkfst) **LB** **FACILITIES:** no TV in bdrms ♫ **CONF:** Thtr 25 Class 25 Board 14 Del from €150 **PARKING:** 25 **NOTES:** ⊗ in restaurant Closed Jan-6 Apr & 15 Oct-Dec

★★★67% ***Hylands Burren***
☎ 065 707 7037 📠 065 707 7131
e-mail: hylandsburren@eircom.net

IRISH COUNTRY HOTELS

This charming village hotel, dating from the 18th century, is set in the picturesque village of Ballyvaughan. In the heart of the unique Burren landscape it is ideally located for touring County Clare. Open fires burn in the traditional bar and lounges, and local seafood is a speciality in the restaurant. Bedrooms are comfortable and well appointed.
ROOMS: 29 en suite (2 fmly) ⊗ in 6 bedrooms **FACILITIES:** STV ♫ **PARKING:** 30 **NOTES:** ⊗ in restaurant Closed 22-25 Dec

BALTIMORE, Co Cork Map 01 B1

★★★67% ◎ **Baltimore Harbour Resort Hotel & Leisure Centre**
☎ 028 20361 📠 028 20466
e-mail: info@bhrhotel.ie
Dir: S from Cork take N71 to Skibbereen, then R595, 13km to Baltimore
Overlooking the natural harbour of Baltimore, this family orientated leisure hotel is perfect for a relaxing break. Bedrooms *continued* are well appointed and most have a sea view. The popular bar and sun room open out onto the patio and gardens.

ROOMS: 64 en suite (30 fmly) s €80-€104; d €120-€168 (incl. bkfst) **LB** **FACILITIES:** supervised Sauna Gym Jacuzzi Table Tennis, In-house video channel, Indoor bowls ♫ **CONF:** Thtr 120 Class 100 Board 30 **SERVICES:** Lift **PARKING:** 80 **NOTES:** ⊗ in restaurant Closed Jan RS Nov-Dec & Feb-mid Mar

★★★66% ◎ **Casey's of Baltimore**
☎ 028 20197 📠 028 20509
e-mail: info@caseysofbaltimore.com
Dir: from Cork take N71 to Skibbereen, then take R595

IRISH COUNTRY HOTELS

This relaxed family run hotel is situated in the sailing and fishing village of Baltimore. There are comfortable bedrooms, a lounge and a cosy bar with open fires and traditional music. The Casey's ensure that a variety the freshest seafood, from their own fishing trawler, is served in the restaurant. They also organise trips to the Islands.
ROOMS: 14 en suite (1 fmly) s €89-€110; d €140-€170 (incl. bkfst) **LB** **FACILITIES:** STV ♫ **CONF:** Thtr 45 Class 30 Board 25 Del from €115 **PARKING:** 50 **NOTES:** ⊗ in restaurant Closed 21-27 Dec

BANGOR, Co Down Map 01 D5

★★★78% ◎ **Clandeboye Lodge**
10 Estate Rd, Clandeboye BT19 1UR
☎ 028 9185 2500 📠 028 9185 2772
e-mail: info@clandeboyelodge.com
Dir: A2 from Belfast turn right at Blackwood Golf Centre & Hotel sign. 500yds down Ballysallagh Rd turn left into Crawfordsburn Road. Hotel 200yds on left
The hotel is located three miles west of Bangor, and sits in delightful landscaped and wooded grounds. The hotel provides high quality accommodation as well as extensive conference,
continued

banqueting and wedding facilities. Public areas also include a bright open-plan foyer bar and attractive lounge area.

ROOMS: 43 en suite (2 fmly) (13 GF) ⊗ in 20 bedrooms s £85-£95; d £95-£105 (incl. bkfst) **LB** **FACILITIES:** STV **CONF:** BC Thtr 450 Class 150 Board 50 Del £114.50 **SERVICES:** Lift **PARKING:** 250 **NOTES:** ⊗ in restaurant Closed 24-26 Dec Civ Wed 250

★★★78% *The Old Inn*

15 Main St BT19 1JH
☎ 028 9185 3255 028 9185 2775
e-mail: info@theoldinn.com
Dir: *A2, pass Belfast Airport & Holywood, 3m past Holywood sign for The Old Inn, 100yds turn left at lights, into village and hotel on left*

This delightful hotel enjoys a peaceful rural setting just a short drive from Belfast. Dating from 1614, many of the day rooms exude charm and character. Individually styled bedrooms, some with feature beds, offer comfort and modern facilities. The popular bar and intimate restaurant both offer a variety of creative menus, and staff throughout are keen to please.
ROOMS: 31 en suite 1 annexe en suite (7 fmly) (7 GF) ⊗ in 6 bedrooms **FACILITIES:** STV ♫ **CONF:** Thtr 120 Class 27 Board 40 **PARKING:** 105 **NOTES:** ⊗ in restaurant RS 25 Dec Civ Wed

★★★72% Marine Court

The Marina BT20 5ED
☎ 028 9145 1100 028 9145 1200
e-mail: marinecourt@btconnect.com
Dir: *pass Belfast city airport, follow A2 through Holywood to Bangor, down main street follow road to left for seafront*
Enjoying a delightful location overlooking the marina, this hotel offers a good range of conference and leisure facilities suited to both the business and leisure guest. Extensive public areas include the first-floor restaurant and cocktail bar. Alternatively, the popular Lord Nelson's Bistro/Bar is more relaxed and there is also the lively Bar Mocha.

ROOMS: 52 en suite (11 fmly) ⊗ in 16 bedrooms s £80-£90; d £90-£100 (incl. bkfst) **LB** **FACILITIES: Spa** STV supervised Sauna Solarium Gym Steam room Xmas **CONF:** Thtr 350 Class 150 Del from £110 **SERVICES:** Lift **PARKING:** 30 **NOTES:** ⊗ in restaurant Closed 25 Dec Civ Wed 250

★★★66% Royal

Seafront BT20 5ED
☎ 028 9127 1866 028 9146 7810
e-mail: royalhotelbangor@aol.com
web: www.royalhotelbangor.com
Dir: *A2 from Belfast. Through town centre to seafront. Turn right, hotel 300yds*

This substantial Victorian hotel enjoys a prime seafront location and overlooks the marina. Bedrooms are comfortable and practical in style. Public areas are traditional and include a choice of contrasting bars whilst traditional Irish cooking can be sampled in a popular brasserie venue.
ROOMS: 50 en suite (5 fmly) ⊗ in 10 bedrooms s £50-£68; d £60-£75 (incl. bkfst) **LB** **FACILITIES:** STV ♫ **CONF:** Thtr 120 Class 90 Board 80 Del from £95 **SERVICES:** Lift **NOTES:** Closed 25-Dec

BANTRY, Co Cork

Map 01 B2

★★★64% Westlodge

☎ 027 50360 027 50438
e-mail: reservations@westlodgehotel.ie
Dir: *N71 to West Cork*
A superb leisure centre and good children's facilities makes this hotel very popular with families. Its situation on the outskirts of

continued on p822

BANTRY, continued

the town also makes it an ideal base for touring west Cork and south Kerry. All the staff are friendly and hospitable.

Westlodge, Bantry

ROOMS: 90 en suite (20 fmly) (20 GF) ⊗ in 15 bedrooms **FACILITIES:** STV Squash Snooker Sauna Solarium Gym Putt green Jacuzzi Pitch & Putt, wooded walks ♫ **CONF:** BC Thtr 400 Class 200 Board 24 Del from €125 **SERVICES:** Lift air con **PARKING:** 400 **NOTES:** ⊗ in restaurant Closed 23-27 Dec

BELFAST Map 01 D5

★★★71% Malone Lodge
60 Eglantine Av BT9 6DY
☎ 028 9038 8000 028 9038 8088
e-mail: info@malonelodgehotel.com
web: www.malonelodgehotel.com
Dir: *at hospital rdbt exit towards Bouchar Rd, left at 1st rdbt, right at lights at top, 1st left is Eglantine Ave*
Situated in the leafy suburbs of the university area of south Belfast, this stylish hotel forms the centrepiece of an attractive row of Victorian terraced properties. The unassuming exterior belies an attractive and spacious interior with a smart lounge, popular bar and stylish Green Door restaurant. The hotel also has a small, well-equipped fitness room.
ROOMS: 51 en suite (5 fmly) (1 GF) s £95-£125; d £99-£145 (incl. bkfst) **LB** **FACILITIES:** STV Sauna Gym **CONF:** BC Thtr 150 Class 90 Board 40 Del from £109 **SERVICES:** Lift **PARKING:** 35 **NOTES:** ⊗ in restaurant Civ Wed 120

★★★70% The Crescent Townhouse
13 Lower Crescent BT7 1NR
☎ 028 9032 3349 028 9032 0646
e-mail: info@crescenttownhouse.com
Dir: *S towards Queens University, hotel on Botanic Avenue opposite Botanic Train Station*
This stylish, smartly presented Regency town house enjoys a central location close to the botanic gardens and railway station. The popular Bar Twelve and Metro Brasserie are found on the ground floor whilst a clubby lounge and well-equipped bedrooms are situated on the upper floors.
ROOMS: 17 en suite (1 fmly) ⊗ in 4 bedrooms s £55-£125; d £75-£145 (incl. bkfst) **FACILITIES:** STV ♫ **CONF:** Thtr 40 Class 20 Board 20 **NOTES:** Closed 25-27 Dec & part of Jul

★★★66% Jurys Inn Belfast
Fisherwick Place, Great Victoria St BT2 7AP
JURYS DOYLE HOTELS
☎ 028 9053 3500 028 9053 3511
e-mail: info@jurys.com web: www.jurysdoyle.com
Dir: *at junct of Grosvenor Rd & Great Victoria St, beside Opera House*
Enjoying a central location, this modern hotel is well equipped for business guests. Public areas are contemporary in style and include a foyer lounge, a bar and a smart restaurant. Spacious bedrooms provide modern facilities.
ROOMS: 190 en suite ⊗ in 76 bedrooms s £99; d £99 **FACILITIES:** STV ♫ **CONF:** Thtr 30 Class 16 Board 16 **SERVICES:** Lift **NOTES:** Closed 24-26 Dec

Travelodge
15 Brunswick St BT2 7GE
Travelodge
☎ 08700 850 950 028 9023 2999
web: www.travelodge.co.uk
Dir: *from M2 follow city centre signs to Oxford St. Turn right to May St, Brunswick St is 4th on left*

Travelodge offers good quality, good value, modern accommodation. Ideal for families, the spacious, en suite bedrooms include remote-control TV, tea and coffee-making facilities and comfortable beds. Meals can be taken at the nearby family restaurant. For further details consult the Hotel Groups page.
ROOMS: 90 en suite s fr £26; d fr £26 **CONF:** Thtr 65 Class 50 Board 34

U Malmaison Hotel
34-38 Victoria Street BT1 3GH
Malmaison
☎ 01582 792105 01582 792001
e-mail: sales.hemel@ramadajarvis.co.uk
web: www.ramadajarvis.co.uk
Dir: *City centre*
At the time of going to press, the star classification for this hotel was not confirmed. Please refer to the AA internet site www.theAA.com for current information.
ROOMS: 64 en suite

BIRR, Co Offaly Map 01 C3

★★★63% *County Arms*
☎ 0509 20791 0509 21234
e-mail: countyarmshotel@eircom.net
Dir: *N7 from Dublin to Roscrea, N62 to Birr, hotel on right before church*
The Loughnane family has run this fine Georgian House (c1810) for four generations. Authentic decor and architectural features combine well with modern comforts. Public areas include comfortable lounges, a traditional bar and conservatory, meticulously kept Victorian walled gardens, which supply the fruit, vegetables and herbs to the hotel kitchen.
ROOMS: 24 en suite (4 fmly) ⊗ in 2 bedrooms **FACILITIES:** STV Gym ♫ **CONF:** Thtr 250 Class 250 Board 25 **PARKING:** 150 **NOTES:** RS 25 Dec

Town House Hotel
Country House Hotel
Travel Accommodation

BLARNEY, Co Cork Map 01 B2

★★★67% **Blarney Castle**
The Village Green
☎ 021 4385116 🖷 021 4385542
e-mail: info@blarneycastlehotel.com
Dir: *N20 (Cork-Limerick road) onto R617 for Blarney.*

Situated in the centre of the town within walking distance of the renowned Blarney Stone, this friendly hotel has been in the same family since 1873. Many of the bedrooms are spacious and appointed to a very comfortable standard. The popular bar serves good food throughout most of the day.
ROOMS: 13 en suite ⊗ in all bedrooms s €75-€85; d €100-€120 (incl. bkfst) **LB FACILITIES:** STV **CONF:** Thtr 120 Del from €25 **SERVICES:** air con **PARKING:** 5 **NOTES:** ✈ ⊗ in restaurant Closed 25-Dec

BLESSINGTON, Co Wicklow Map 01 D3

★★★66% ◎ ***Downshire House***
☎ 045 865199 🖷 045 865335
e-mail: info@downshirehouse.com
Dir: *on N81*
This family-run Georgian house is renowned for its friendly atmosphere, comfortable lounges with open log fires and country house style cooking. Bedrooms are very attractively decorated and well appointed. The hotel is near to Blessington Lake, the Wicklow Hills, golf clubs and racecourses.
ROOMS: 14 en suite 11 annexe en suite **FACILITIES:** Table tennis **CONF:** Thtr 40 Class 20 Board 20 **PARKING:** 30 **NOTES:** ✈ Closed 22 Dec-6 Jan

BRAY, Co Wicklow Map 01 D4

★★★65% **Royal**
Main St
☎ 01 2862935 🖷 01 2867373
e-mail: royal@regencyhotels.com
Dir: *from N11, 1st exit for Bray, 2nd exit from rdbt, through 2 sets of lights, across bridge, hotel on left*
The Royal Hotel stands on the main street, close to the seafront, and within easy reach of the Dun Laoighaire ferry port. Public areas offer comfortable lounges, traditional bar and The Heritage Restaurant. Bedrooms vary in size and are well appointed. There is a well-equipped leisure centre and a supervised car park is available at the rear.
ROOMS: 98 en suite (9 fmly) ⊗ in 51 bedrooms s €74-€120; d €80-€180 (incl. bkfst) **LB FACILITIES:** supervised Sauna Solarium Gym Jacuzzi Massage and beauty clinic Therapy room Whirlpool spa, Madhatters creche ♫ Xmas **CONF:** BC Thtr 400 Class 300 Board 200 **SERVICES:** Lift **PARKING:** 60 **NOTES:** ✈ ⊗ in restaurant Civ Wed 225

BUNCLODY, Co Wexford Map 01 D3

★★★★70% ***Carlton Millrace***
☎ 054 75100
Located on the edge of the picturesque town of Bunclody, this newly built hotel offers well-appointed bedrooms and smartly presented public areas, not least of which is the rooftop Lady Lucy restaurant. Separate spa and leisure centres are also a feature. Some self-catering family suites are available.
ROOMS: 60 rms

BUNRATTY, Co Clare Map 01 B3

★★★69% **Bunratty Shannon Shamrock**
☎ 061 361177 🖷 061 471252
e-mail: reservations@dunnehotels.com
Dir: *take Bunratty by-pass, exit off Limerick/Shannon dual carriageway*
Situated in the shadow of Bunratty's famous medieval castle in a pretty village, this modern hotel is surrounded by well-maintained lawns and mature trees. Bedrooms and public areas are spacious and comfortable. There is an indoor leisure centre and impressive conference and banqueting facilities. There is a courtesy coach which transfers guests to and from Shannon International Airport.
ROOMS: 115 en suite (12 fmly) (91 GF) ⊗ in 10 bedrooms s €69-€170; d €69-€215 **LB FACILITIES: Spa** STV Sauna Solarium Gym Jacuzzi Hair & beauty salon ♫ **CONF:** BC Thtr 1200 Class 650 Board 300 Del from €172 **PARKING:** 300 **NOTES:** ✈ ⊗ in restaurant Closed 24-26 Dec

CAHERDANIEL, Co Kerry Map 01 A2

★★★66% ◎ ***Derrynane***
☎ 066 9475136 🖷 066 9475160
e-mail: info@derrynane.com
Dir: *just off main road*

Best Western

Super clifftop location overlooking Derrynane Bay with spectacular views adding a stunning dimension to this well run hotel where pleasant, efficient staff contribute to the very relaxed atmosphere. Public areas include spacious lounges, bar and restaurant, an outdoor heated pool in the garden. Bedrooms are well appointed and most enjoy the views.
ROOMS: 73 en suite (30 fmly) ⊗ in 40 bedrooms **FACILITIES:** STV supervised Sauna Solarium Gym Steam room, seaweed therapy room ♫ ch fac **SERVICES:** air con **PARKING:** 60 **NOTES:** ✈ ⊗ in restaurant Closed 4 Oct-15 Apr

The vast majority of establishments in this guide accept credit and debit cards. We indicate those that don't take any

CAHIRCIVEEN, Co Kerry — Map 01 A2

U Ring of Kerry Hotel
Valentia Rd
☎ 066 9472543 087 2306522 📠 066 9472543
e-mail: ringhotel@eircom.net
Dir: *on Ring of Kerry road*
At the time of going to press, the star classification for this hotel was not confirmed. Please refer to the AA internet site www.theAA.com for current information.
ROOMS: 24 en suite (2 fmly) ⊗ in 20 bedrooms s €55-€95; d €80-€150 (incl. bkfst) **LB** **FACILITIES:** STV ♫ **PARKING:** 24 **NOTES:** ✖ ⊗ in restaurant

CARLOW, Co Carlow — Map 01 C3

★★★70% Seven Oaks
Athy Rd
☎ 059 913 1308 📠 059 913 2155
e-mail: info@sevenoakshotel.com
IRISH COUNTRY HOTELS
Conveniently situated within walking distance of the town centre this hotel offers comfortable lounges, a traditional style bar and restaurant. Bedrooms are spacious and very well appointed. There are extensive leisure and banqueting facilities and a secure car park.
ROOMS: 59 en suite (5 fmly) **FACILITIES:** STV supervised Sauna Gym Jacuzzi Aerobic studio, Steam room ♫ **CONF:** Thtr 400 Class 150 Board 80 **SERVICES:** Lift air con **PARKING:** 200 **NOTES:** ✖ ⊗ in restaurant Closed 25-26 Dec RS Good Fri

CARNA, Co Galway — Map 01 A4

★★★63% *Carna Bay Hotel*
☎ 095 32255 📠 095 32530
Dir: *from Galway take N59 to Recess, then left onto R340 for 8-10m*
IRISH COUNTRY HOTELS
This family owned and run hotel is in the little village of Carna on the Connemara coastline and has a very friendly and relaxed atmosphere. Public areas are bright and spacious with casual meals served in the bar at lunch and in the evenings. More formal dinner is available in the restaurant where there is an emphasis on good quality local ingredients.
ROOMS: 26 en suite (1 fmly) (11 GF) ⊗ in 10 bedrooms **PARKING:** 60 **NOTES:** ⊗ in restaurant Closed 23-26 Dec

CARNLOUGH, Co Antrim — Map 01 D6

★★★68% ◎ Londonderry Arms
20 Harbour Rd BT44 0EU
☎ 028 2888 5255 📠 028 2888 5263
e-mail: lda@glensofantrim.com
Dir: *14m N from Larne on coast road, A2*
IRISH COUNTRY HOTELS
This delightful hotel was built in the mid-19th century by Lady Londonderry, whose grandson, Winston Churchill also owned it at one time. Today the hotel's Georgian architecture and rooms are still evident, and spacious bedrooms can be found in the modern extension. The hotel enjoys a prime location in this pretty fishing village overlooking the Antrim coast.
ROOMS: 35 en suite (5 fmly) s £50-£70; d £80-£100 (incl. bkfst) **LB** **FACILITIES:** Fishing ♫ Xmas **CONF:** Thtr 120 Class 60 Board 40 Del from £75 **SERVICES:** Lift **PARKING:** 50 **NOTES:** ✖ Closed Xmas

♫ Entertainment

CARRICKFERGUS, Co Antrim — Map 01 D5

★★67% Dobbins Inn
6-8 High St BT38 7AP
☎ 028 9335 1905 📠 028 9335 1905
e-mail: info@dobbinsinnhotel.co.uk
Dir: *from Belfast take M2, right at rdbt, take A2 to Carrickfergus. Left opposite castle*
Colourful window boxes adorn the front of this popular inn near the ancient castle and seafront. Public areas are furnished to a modern standard without compromising the inn's interesting, historical, character. Bedrooms vary in size and style and all provide modern comforts. Staff throughout are very friendly.
ROOMS: 15 en suite (2 fmly) **FACILITIES:** ♫ **NOTES:** Closed 25-26 Dec & 1 Jan RS Good Fri

CARRICKMACROSS, Co Monaghan — Map 01 C4

★★★★75% ◎◎ Nuremore
☎ 042 9661438 📠 042 9661853
e-mail: info@nuremore.com
Dir: *3km S of Carrickmacross, on N2 (Dublin-Derry road)*
Overlooking its own golf course and lakes, the Nuremore is a quiet retreat with excellent facilities. Public areas are spacious and include an indoor pool and gym. Ray McArdle's food in the restaurant continues to impress, with an imaginative range of dishes on offer.
ROOMS: 72 en suite (4 fmly) ⊗ in 30 bedrooms s €140-€220; d €240-€300 (incl. bkfst) **LB** **FACILITIES: Spa** STV 18 Fishing Snooker Sauna Solarium Gym Putt green Beauty treatments, Aromatherapy, Massage ♫ Xmas **CONF:** BC Thtr 250 Class 100 Board 30 Del from €190 **SERVICES:** Lift **PARKING:** 200 **NOTES:** ✖ ⊗ in restaurant

CARRICK-ON-SHANNON, Co Leitrim — Map 01 C4

★★★★60% The Landmark
☎ 071 962 2222 📠 071 962 2233
e-mail: landmarkhotel@eircom.net
Dir: *from Dublin on N4 approaching Carrick-on-Shannon, take 1st exit at rdbt, hotel on right*

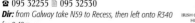

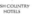

Overlooking the River Shannon, close to the Marina, this hotel offers comfortable public areas and well-equipped bedrooms and suites. Exciting developments are in place for the restaurant and bar areas. Pleasant staff will be pleased to arrange cruising, horse riding, golf and angling.
ROOMS: 50 en suite (4 fmly) ⊗ in 26 bedrooms s €125-€140; d €190-€220 (incl. bkfst) **LB** **FACILITIES:** STV ♫ Xmas **CONF:** Thtr 550 Class 210 **SERVICES:** Lift **PARKING:** 100 **NOTES:** ✖ ⊗ in restaurant Closed 24-25 Dec RS 26-Dec

CARRIGALINE, Co Cork — Map 01 B2

★★★★67% Carrigaline Court Hotel & Leisure Centre
☎ 021 4852100 ▤ 021 4371103
e-mail: reception@carrigcourt.com
*Dir: From South Link road (E from airport or W from Dublin/Lee Tunnel)
take exit for Carrigaline. Stay in right lane and onto Carrigaline*
This smart, modern hotel is situated only minutes' drive from Cork
City Airport and the Ringaskiddy Port. Bedrooms are spacious and
very well appointed. Public areas include Collins, the traditional,
themed Irish pub, The Bistro and extensive conference, leisure and
beauty facilities. Golf, sailing, angling and horse riding are
available locally.
ROOMS: 91 en suite (3 fmly) ⊗ in 39 bedrooms s £96-£120;
d £145-£185 (incl. bkfst) **LB FACILITIES:** STV ⊡ supervised Sauna
Solarium Gym Jacuzzi Beauty salon, Massage treatment rooms ♫ Xmas
CONF: Thtr 400 Class 200 Board 150 Del from £155 **SERVICES:** Lift
PARKING: 220 **NOTES:** ✖ ⊗ in restaurant Closed 25 Dec

CASHEL, Co Galway — Map 01 A4

Top Hotel

★★★ ◉◎⚑ Cashel House
☎ 095 31001 ▤ 095 31077
e-mail: info@cashel-house-hotel.com
Dir: S off N59, 1.5km W of Recess, well signed
Cashel House is a mid-19th century property standing at the
head of Cashel Bay, in the heart of Connemara. Quietly
secluded in award-winning gardens and woodland walks.
Attentive service comes with the perfect balance of friendliness
and professionalism from McEvilly family and their staff. The
comfortable lounges have turf fires and antique furnishings.
The restaurant offers local produce such as the famous
Connemara Lamb and fish from the surrounding coast.
ROOMS: 32 en suite (4 fmly) (6 GF) ⊗ in 10 bedrooms s
€85-€125; d €170-€310 (incl. bkfst) **LB FACILITIES:** ✎ Xmas
PARKING: 40 **NOTES:** No children 5yrs ⊗ in restaurant Closed 4
Jan-4 Feb

★★★77% ◉◎ Zetland Country House
Cashel Bay
☎ 095 31111 ▤ 095 31117
e-mail: zetland@iol.ie
*Dir: N59 from Galway towards Clifden, right after Recess onto R340, left
after 4m (R341), hotel 1m on right*
Standing on the edge of Cashel Bay, this former sporting lodge is
a cosy and relaxing family run hotel that exudes charm. Many of
the comfortable rooms have sea views, as has the restaurant
where very good cuisine is served. Lounge areas feature turf fires.
ROOMS: 19 en suite (10 fmly) **FACILITIES:** STV ✎ Snooker ♫
CONF: Board 20 **PARKING:** 32 **NOTES:** ⊗ in restaurant Closed Nov-9 Apr

CASHEL, Co Tipperary — Map 01 C3

★★★★73% ◉ Cashel Palace Hotel
☎ 062 62707 ▤ 062 61521
e-mail: reception@cashel-palace.ie
Dir: On N8 through town centre, hotel on main street near traffic lights

The Rock of Cashel, floodlit at night, forms a dramatic backdrop to
this fine 18th-century house. Once an Archbishop's palace, it is
elegantly furnished with antiques and fine art. The drawing room
has garden access and luxurious bedrooms in the main house are
very comfortable; those in the adjacent mews are ideal for
families.
ROOMS: 13 en suite 10 annexe en suite (8 fmly) ⊗ in 5 bedrooms
FACILITIES: STV Fishing Private path walk to the Rock of Cashel ♫
CONF: Thtr 80 Class 45 Board 40 **SERVICES:** Lift **PARKING:** 35
NOTES: ✖ Closed 2 weeks in Xmas - Jan

CASTLEBAR, Co Mayo — Map 01 B4

★★64% Welcome Inn
☎ 094 902 2288 & 902 2054 ▤ 094 902 1766
e-mail: welcomeinn@eircom.net
*Dir: take N5 to Castlebar. Hotel near town centre, via ring road & rdbts
past Church of the Holy Rosary*
This town centre hotel offers a range of modern facilities behind
its Tudor frontage, including a banqueting/conference centre.
Bedrooms are comfortable and well equipped. Enjoyable food is
served in Reynards Restaurant and there is a traditional style bar
and a nightclub with disco at weekends.
ROOMS: 40 en suite (5 fmly) **FACILITIES:** STV ♫ **CONF:** Thtr 500
Class 350 **SERVICES:** Lift **PARKING:** 100 **NOTES:** ✖ Closed 23-25 Dec

CASTLEDERMOT, Co Kildare — Map 01 C3

★★★★67% Kilkea Castle Hotel
☎ 059 914 5156 ▤ 059 914 5187
e-mail: kilkea@iol.ie
Dir: off N9 onto R418
Dating from 1180, this is reputed to be Ireland's oldest inhabited
castle. Surrounded by an 18-hole golf course, Kilkea Castle offers a
number of comfortable bars, lounges and D'Lacy's, the fine dine
restaurant. Bedrooms vary in style and well equipped. Banqueting
and conference facilities are situated in the converted stables.
ROOMS: 36 rms

Popped the question? Hotels with Civ wed
in their entry are licensed for civil wedding
ceremonies. Maximum numbers for the
ceremony only are shown e.g. Civ wed 120

CAVAN, Co Cavan Map 01 C4

★★★★72% ⊛ Cavan Crystal
Dublin Rd
☎ 049 4360600 📠 049 4360699
e-mail: info@cavancrystalhotel.com
Dir: N3 towards Cavan, at 1st rdbt onto N55 signed Athlone
Contemporary design, matched with the use of native timber, handcrafted brick and crystal chandeliers, make this a particularly distinctive hotel. This is complemented by excellent hospitality from all of the highly trained staff. Located on the southern edge of the town, the hotel also features a well-equipped health and beauty clinic and extensive banquet and conference facilities.
ROOMS: 85 en suite (2 fmly) (9 GF) **FACILITIES:** STV 📺 supervised Sauna Gym Jacuzzi 🎵 ch fac **CONF:** Thtr 500 Class 300 Board 100
SERVICES: Lift **PARKING:** 216 **NOTES:** ✘ ⊗ in restaurant Closed 24 & 25 Dec

★★★67% Kilmore
Dublin Rd
☎ 049 4332288 📠 049 4332458
e-mail: kilmore@quinn-hotels.com
Dir: approx 3km from Cavan on N3
Located on the outskirts of Cavan, easily accessible from the main N3 route, this comfortable hotel features spacious and welcoming public areas. Good food is served in the Annalee Restaurant, which is always appreciated by guests returning from nearby fishing or golf.
ROOMS: 39 en suite (17 fmly) (19 GF) s €69-€95; d €105-€148 (incl. bkfst) **LB FACILITIES:** STV free use of facilities at Slieve Russell Golf & Country Club 🎵 Xmas **CONF:** Thtr 500 Class 200 Board 60
SERVICES: air con **PARKING:** 450 **NOTES:** ✘ ⊗ in restaurant Closed 25 Dec

CLIFDEN, Co Galway Map 01 A4

★★★★69% ⊛ Abbeyglen Castle
Sky Rd
☎ 095 21201 📠 095 21797
e-mail: info@abbeyglen.ie
Dir: take N59 from Galway to Clifden. Hotel 1km from Clifden
The tranquil setting overlooking Clifden, matched with the dedication of the Hughes's father and son team and their attentive staff, combine to create a magical atmosphere here. Well-appointed rooms and very comfortable suites are available, together with a range of relaxing lounge areas.
ROOMS: 45 en suite (9 GF) ⊗ in all bedrooms s €122-€185; d €180-€263 (incl. bkfst) **LB FACILITIES:** STV 🎿 ◔ Snooker Sauna Putt green Jacuzzi 🎵 ch fac Xmas **CONF:** Thtr 100 Class 50 Board 40 Del from €213 **SERVICES:** Lift **PARKING:** 50 **NOTES:** ✘ No children ⊗ in restaurant Closed 8 Jan-3 Feb

★★★73% ⊛⊛ Ardagh
Ballyconneely Rd
☎ 095 21384 📠 095 21314
e-mail: ardaghhotel@eircom.net
Dir: N59 Galway to Clifden, signed to Ballyconneely
Situated at the head of Ardbear Bay, this family-run hotel makes full use of the spectacular scenery in the area. The restaurant is renowned for its cuisine, which is complemented by friendly and knowledgeable service. Bedrooms have large picture windows and plenty of comfort.
ROOMS: 19 en suite (2 fmly) ⊗ in all bedrooms s €102-€120; d €155-€180 (incl. bkfst) **LB FACILITIES:** Pool room 🎵 **PARKING:** 35 **NOTES:** ⊗ in restaurant Closed Nov-Mar

IRISH COUNTRY HOTELS

★★★71%
Rock Glen Country House Hotel
☎ 095 21035 📠 095 21737
e-mail: rockglen@iol.ie
Dir: N6 from Dublin to Galway, N57 from Galway to Clifden, hotel 1.5m from Clifden

MANOR HOUSE

The attractive clematis and creeper-framed façade of this house is an introduction to the comfort found inside. The hospitality of the staff makes a visit to this hotel relaxing and very pleasant. Well-appointed bedrooms and comfortable lounges here have lovely views of the gardens and the bay.
ROOMS: 26 en suite (2 fmly) (18 GF) **FACILITIES:** ◔ Snooker 🏌 Putt green 🎵 **PARKING:** 50 **NOTES:** ⊗ in restaurant Closed mid Nov-mid Feb (ex New Year)

★★★66% ⊛ Alcock & Brown Hotel
☎ 095 21206 & 21086 📠 095 21842
e-mail: alcockandbrown@eircom.net
Dir: take N59 from Galway via Oughterard, hotel in town centre
This comfortable family owned hotel is situated in the town centre. There is a cosy bar and lounge with an open fire and the restaurant offers a dinner menu of good food with many fresh local fish specialities. Bedrooms are well appointed. The friendly and attentive staff provide good service.
ROOMS: 19 en suite ⊗ in 9 bedrooms s €75-€99; d €110-€158 (incl. bkfst) **LB FACILITIES:** STV 🎵 Xmas **NOTES:** ⊗ in restaurant Closed 19-26 Dec 2005

CLONAKILTY, Co Cork Map 01 B2

★★★★75% ⊛⊛ Inchydoney Island Lodge & Spa
☎ 023 33143 📠 023 35229
e-mail: reservations@inchydoneyisland.com
Dir: follow N71 West Cork road to Clonakilty, at entry rdbt in Clonakilty take 2nd exit and follow signs to Lodge
This modern hotel is stunningly located on the coastline with steps down to two long sandy beaches. Bedrooms are decorated in warm colours and are well appointed. Diners have a choice of the

continued

third floor Gulfstream restaurant or the more casual Dunes bar and bistro.
ROOMS: 67 en suite (24 fmly) ⊗ in 17 bedrooms s fr €209; d €320-€340 (incl. bkfst) **LB** **FACILITIES: Spa** STV supervised Fishing Riding Snooker Sauna Gym Jacuzzi Thalassotherapy spa ♫ **CONF:** Thtr 300 Class 150 Board 100 Del €464 **SERVICES:** Lift **PARKING:** 200 **NOTES:** ⊗ in restaurant Closed 25-26 Dec

CLONMEL, Co Tipperary — Map 01 C2

★★★74% *Hotel Minella*

☎ 052 22388 📠 052 24381
e-mail: hotelminella@eircom.net

IRISH COUNTRY HOTELS

Dir: *Hotel S of River Suir*

This family-run hotel is set on 9 acres of well-tended gardens on the banks of the Suir River. Originating from the 1860s, the public areas include a cocktail bar and a range of lounge areas. The leisure centre in the grounds is particularly noteworthy. Two bedroom holiday homes are also available on the site.
ROOMS: 70 en suite (8 fmly) (14 GF) ⊗ in 16 bedrooms **FACILITIES:** STV Fishing Sauna Gym Jacuzzi Aerobics room **CONF:** Thtr 500 Class 300 Board 20 **SERVICES:** Lift **PARKING:** 100 **NOTES:** ⊗ in restaurant Closed 24-28 Dec

CORK, Co Cork — Map 01 B2

Top Hotel

★★★★ ◎◎ *Hayfield Manor*

Perrott Av, College Rd
☎ 021 4845900 📠 021 4316839
e-mail: enquiries@hayfieldmanor.ie
Dir: *1m W of city centre on N22 towards Killarney, turn left at University Gates off Western Rd. Turn right into College Rd, left into Perrott Ave*

As part of a grand two-acre estate with lovely walled gardens, Hayfield Manor offers luxury and seclusion, just a short distance from UCC. This fine hotel has every modern comfort and maintains an atmosphere of tranquillity, with real fires in the public areas where elegant architecture and fine furnishings are carefully combined. Bedrooms offer very high levels of comfort with many thoughtful extras. There are beauty treatments and leisure facilities available for resident guests.
ROOMS: 88 en suite ⊗ in 25 bedrooms **FACILITIES:** STV Gym Jacuzzi Steam room ♫ **CONF:** Thtr 100 Class 60 Board 40 **SERVICES:** Lift air con **PARKING:** 100 **NOTES:** ⊗ in restaurant

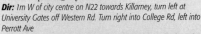

♫ Entertainment

★★★★76% *The Kingsley Hotel*

Victoria Cross
☎ 021 4800500 📠 021 4800527
e-mail: resv@kingsleyhotel.com
Dir: *off N22 opposite County Hall*

Situated on the banks of the River Lee, Ireland's tallest building is a luxury hotel that has excellent facilities. The bedrooms are spacious and feature thoughtful additional touches. The contemporary bar and restaurant have an informal atmosphere, and both the lounge and library are elegant and relaxing. Further developments are due to be completed by early 2006.
ROOMS: 69 en suite (4 fmly) ⊗ in 36 bedrooms **FACILITIES:** STV supervised Fishing Sauna Solarium Gym Jacuzzi Treatment rooms & Beautician **CONF:** Thtr 95 Class 50 Board 32 **SERVICES:** Lift air con **PARKING:** 250 **NOTES:**

See advert on this page

CORK, continued

★★★★72% Rochestown Park Hotel

Rochestown Rd, Douglas
☎ 021 4890800 📠 021 4892178
e-mail: info@rochestownpark.com
Dir: *from Lee Tunnel, 2nd exit left off dual carriageway. 400mtrs then 1st left and right at small rdbt. Hotel 600mtrs on right*

This modern hotel is situated in mature gardens on the south side of Cork. Various bedroom styles, including suites, are available; most rooms are air-conditioned and overlook Mahon Golf Club. Public areas include a traditional bar and Gallery Restaurant. There are extensive leisure, conference and exhibition facilities. Convenient for both the airport and the ferries.
ROOMS: 160 en suite (17 fmly) (23 GF) ⊘ in 120 bedrooms s €95-€320; d €140-€320 (incl. bkfst) **LB** **FACILITIES: Spa** STV ⛆ supervised Sauna Solarium Gym Jacuzzi Thalasso therapy & beauty centre Xmas **CONF:** BC Thtr 800 Class 360 Board 100 **SERVICES:** Lift **PARKING:** 300 **NOTES:** 🐕 ⊘ in restaurant Closed 25-26 Dec

★★★★71% ❀ Maryborough House

Maryborough Hill
☎ 021 4365555 📠 021 4365662
e-mail: maryboro@indigo.ie
Dir: *from Jack Lynch Tunnel take 2nd exit & slip road signed Douglas. Right at 1st rdbt & follow Rochestown Rd to fingerpost rdbt. Left, hotel on left 0.5m up hill*

Dating from 1715, Maryborough House has been renovated and extended to a fine hotel set in beautifully landscaped grounds. The suites in the main house, and the bedrooms in the wing are well appointed and comfortable. The extensive lounge is very popular for the range of food served throughout the day.
ROOMS: 79 en suite (6 fmly) ⊘ in 23 bedrooms s €145-€198; d €198-€350 (incl. bkfst) **LB** **FACILITIES:** STV ⛆ supervised Snooker Sauna Gym Jacuzzi Aromatherapy Beauty therapy Massage Reiki **CONF:** BC Thtr 500 Class 250 Board 60 Del from €225 **SERVICES:** Lift **PARKING:** 300 **NOTES:** 🐕 ⊘ in restaurant

★★★★71% Silver Springs Moran

Tivoli
☎ 021 4507533 📠 021 4507641
e-mail: silverspringsres@moranhotels.com
Dir: *N8 south Silver Springs exit and right across overpass then right for hotel on left*

The public areas of this hotel have undergone major re-development resulting in a smart, contemporary environment. Bedrooms are comfortable, many offering good views over the River Lee. Excellent conference facilities are available in a separate building, and guests have use of a nearby leisure centre.

continued

ROOMS: 109 en suite (29 fmly) ⊘ in 30 bedrooms s €100-€185; d €128-€250 (incl. bkfst) **LB** **FACILITIES: Spa** STV ⛆ supervised 🎾 Squash Snooker Sauna Solarium Gym Jacuzzi Aerobics classes ♫ Xmas **CONF:** BC Thtr 700 Class 400 Board 30 Del from €170 **SERVICES:** Lift **PARKING:** 325 **NOTES:** 🐕 ⊘ in restaurant Closed 24-26 Dec

★★★70% Ambassador

Military Hill, St Lukes
☎ 021 4551996 📠 021 4551997
e-mail: reservations@ambassadorhotel.ie
Dir: *city centre, just off Wellington Rd*

Many pleasing features distinguish this sandstone and granite building dating from the 19th century that has commanding views over the city. There is a feeling of space throughout the public areas which include a cocktail lounge, bar and restaurant. Some bedrooms have balconies, but all are very well appointed.
ROOMS: 58 en suite (8 fmly) ⊘ in 12 bedrooms s €99-€120; d €125-€150 (incl. bkfst) **LB** **FACILITIES:** STV Sauna Gym Jacuzzi ♫ Xmas **CONF:** BC Thtr 220 Class 100 Board 50 Del €125 **SERVICES:** Lift **PARKING:** 60 **NOTES:** 🐕 ⊘ in restaurant Closed 24-26 Dec

★★★69% Gresham Metropole

MacCurtain St — GRESHAM HOTELS
☎ 021 4508122 📠 021 4506450
e-mail: info@gresham-metropolehotel.com
Dir: *In city centre, opposite Merchant Quay Shopping Centre*

This long-established property is now a very comfortable city centre hotel. Bedrooms vary in size and are well equipped. Public areas include the popular Met bar and a good leisure centre. Enquire on reservation about indoor parking arrangements.
ROOMS: 113 en suite (3 fmly) ⊘ in 90 bedrooms s €95-€260; d €95-€260 (incl. bkfst) **LB** **FACILITIES:** STV ⛆ supervised Sauna Solarium Gym Jacuzzi Aerobic studio & Steam room ♫ Xmas **CONF:** Thtr 500 Class 180 Board 60 **SERVICES:** Lift **PARKING:** 240 **NOTES:** 🐕 ⊘ in restaurant

See advert on page 815

★★★69% Imperial Hotel
South Mall
☎ 021 4274040 🖷 021 4275375
e-mail: info@imperialhotelcork.ie
Dir: *in city centre business area*

This fine, long established hotel has a hospitable and welcoming atmosphere. The reception rooms are on a grand scale, especially the foyer and coffee shop. Bedrooms are appointed to a high standard. Parking, about five minutes away, is available by prior arrangement.
ROOMS: 125 en suite (4 fmly) ⊗ in 25 bedrooms s €85-€165; d €95-€180 **LB** **FACILITIES: Spa** STV Gym Jacuzzi ♫ **CONF:** BC Thtr 280 Class 150 Board 80 **SERVICES:** Lift **NOTES:** 🚫🐕 ⊗ in restaurant Closed 24-27 Dec

★★★65% Jurys Inn
Anderson's Quay
☎ 021 4276444 🖷 021 4276144
e-mail: enquiry@jurys.com web: www.jurysdoyle.com
Dir: *in city centre, on river beside eastern approach to the city from Dublin and south link road to airport*
This hotel overlooks the River Lee and is just a short walk from the main street and shopping area. Attractively decorated in a modern style. Rooms are spacious and can accommodate families. The restaurant is informal and there is also a lively pub.
ROOMS: 133 en suite ⊗ in 32 bedrooms **FACILITIES:** STV ♫ **CONF:** Thtr 35 Class 20 Board 20 **SERVICES:** Lift **PARKING:** 22 **NOTES:** 🚫🐕 Closed 24-26 Dec

★★60% *Ashley*
Coburg St
☎ 021 4501518 🖷 021 4501178
e-mail: info@ashleyhotel.com
Dir: *From N8 to 4th bridge (do not cross any bridges). Right then right at next junct*
This hotel is centrally located near the railway station and much of Cork's nightlife. Bedrooms vary in size, but are warm and comfortable. The bar is welcoming and serves food at lunch and dinner. Secure car parking is available to the rear of the hotel.
ROOMS: 27 en suite (1 fmly) ⊗ in 15 bedrooms **FACILITIES:** STV **PARKING:** 8 **NOTES:** 🚫🐕 ⊗ in restaurant Closed 22 Dec-5 Jan

⌂ Travelodge
Blackash
☎ 08700 850 950 🖷 021 4310723
web: www.travelodge.co.uk
Dir: *at rdbt junct of South Ring Road/Kinsale Rd, R600*
Travelodge offers good quality, good value, modern accommodation. Ideal for families, the spacious, en suite bedrooms include remote-control TV, tea and coffee-making facilities and comfortable beds. Meals can be taken at the nearby family restaurant. For further details consult the Hotel Groups page.
ROOMS: 60 en suite s fr €26; d fr €26

COURTOWN HARBOUR, Co Wexford — Map 01 D3

★★★60% *Bay View*
☎ 055 25307 🖷 055 25576
e-mail: bayview@iol.ie
Dir: *clearly signed to Courtown, turn left before Gorey off N11, hotel in main square*
This long-establshed comfortable hotel overlooks the marina and the Irish Sea. The McGarry family are attentive hosts as are their friendly staff. Good cuisine is served in both the restaurant and the popular bar.
ROOMS: 17 en suite (12 fmly) **FACILITIES:** Squash **PARKING:** 30 **NOTES:** 🚫🐕 ⊗ in restaurant Closed 30 Nov-14 Mar

★★★60% *Courtown*
☎ 055 25210 & 25108 🖷 055 25304
e-mail: info@courtownhotel.com
Dir: *Turn left on approach to Gorey, 5km on left*
Situated in the town centre, near to the beach and an 18-hole golf course, this family run hotel offers relaxing public areas. There is a comfortable lounge, spacious bar and an attractive restaurant and the leisure centre includes a swimming pool, gym and solarium.
ROOMS: 21 en suite (4 fmly) **FACILITIES:** supervised Squash Sauna Solarium Gym Jacuzzi Steam room, Massage, Crazy golf ♫ **PARKING:** 10 **NOTES:** 🚫🐕 Closed mid Nov - early Mar

DELGANY, Co Wicklow — Map 01 D3

★★★★64% *Glenview*
Glen O' the Downs
☎ 01 2873399 🖷 01 2877511
e-mail: glenview@iol.ie
Dir: *from Dublin city centre follow signs for N11, past Bray on southbound N11*
Set in a lovely hillside location, overlooking terraced gardens, this hotel boasts an excellent range of leisure and conference facilities. Impressive public areas include a conservatory bar, lounge and choice of dining options. Bedrooms are spacious, many enjoying great views over the valley. Championship golf, horse riding and many tourist amenities are available nearby.
ROOMS: 70 en suite (11 fmly) (16 GF) ⊗ in 11 bedrooms **FACILITIES: Spa** STV supervised Snooker Sauna Solarium Gym Jacuzzi Aerobics studio, Massage, Beauty treatment room ♫ ch fac **CONF:** Thtr 220 Class 120 Board 50 **SERVICES:** Lift **PARKING:** 200 **NOTES:** 🚫🐕 ⊗ in restaurant

DONEGAL, Co Donegal — Map 01 B5

★★★75% ❀❀ *Harvey's Point Country*
Lough Eske
☎ 074 972 2208 🖷 074 972 2352
e-mail: reservations@harveyspoint.com
Dir: *N56 from Donegal, then 1st right (Loch Eske/Harvey's Point). Hotel approx 10 mins' drive*
Situated by the lake shore, this hotel is an oasis of relaxation. Comfort, good cuisine and attentive guest care are the norm here. At the time of inspection the property's major renovation was reaching completion. There is a choice of bedroom styles available. The kitchen brigade maintain consistently high standards on the menus offered.
ROOMS: 20 en suite **FACILITIES:** STV ♫ **CONF:** Thtr 200 Class 200 Board 50 **PARKING:** 300 **NOTES:** No children 10yrs ⊗ in restaurant

❀ AA Rosette Award for culinary excellence

DONEGAL, continued

★★★70% **Mill Park**
The Mullins
☎ 074 972 2880 📠 074 972 2640

e-mail: info@millparkhotel.com
The gentle flow of the millstream and the open fires create a welcoming atmosphere at this newly built hotel that is within walking distance from the town centre. Wood and stone are incorporated with flair in the design of the public areas as in the fine dining, first-floor Granary restaurant and the less formal Café bar that serves food all day. Bedrooms are spacious and well appointed. There are extensive leisure and banqueting facilities.
ROOMS: 114 en suite (15 fmly) (44 GF) ⊗ in 35 bedrooms s £95-£150; d £150-£210 (incl. bkfst) **FACILITIES:** ⊤ supervised ⊤ Solarium Gym Jacuzzi Wellness Centre ♫ **CONF:** Thtr 500 Class 250 Board 80 Del from £110 **SERVICES:** Lift **PARKING:** 250 **NOTES:** ✗ ⊗ in restaurant Closed 24-26 Dec

DOOLIN, Co Clare　　Map 01 B3

★★★64% *Aran View House*
Coast Rd
☎ 065 7074061 & 7074420 📠 065 7074540
e-mail: bookings@aranview.com
Situated in 100 acres of rolling farmland and commanding panoramic views of the Cliffs of Moher and the Aran Islands, this family-run hotel offers comfortable accommodation. With welcoming staff and a convivial atmosphere, guests are assured of a relaxing stay. Seafood is a feature of the menu served in the attractive restaurant.
ROOMS: 13 en suite 6 annexe en suite (1 fmly) **FACILITIES:** ♫ **PARKING:** 40 **NOTES:** Closed Nov-1 Apr

DROGHEDA, Co Louth　　Map 01 D4

★★★67% **Boyne Valley Hotel & Country Club**
Stameen, Dublin Rd
☎ 041 9837737 📠 041 9839188
e-mail: admin@boyne-valley-hotel.ie
Dir: M1 towards Belfast, N of Dublin Airport on right - up Avenue before town of Drogheda
This historic mansion stands in 16 acres of gardens and woodlands on the outskirts of Drogheda. The bedrooms are very smart and provide high standards of comfort. Public areas include relaxing lounges, Terrace bar, Cellars Bistro, extensive conference and banqueting facilities and a leisure centre and hard tennis courts.
ROOMS: 73 en suite (4 fmly) (26 GF) ⊗ in 35 bedrooms s €75-€85; d €152-€160 (incl. bkfst) **LB FACILITIES: Spa** STV ⊤ supervised ⊾ Sauna Solarium Gym Jacuzzi Hot stone therapy ♫ Xmas **CONF:** BC Thtr 500 Class 350 Board 25 **SERVICES:** Lift **PARKING:** 200 **NOTES:** ✗ ⊗ in restaurant Civ Wed 300

DUBLIN, Co Dublin　　Map 01 D4
See also Portmarnock

Top Hotel
★★★★★ ⊛⊛⊛⊛ **The Merrion Hotel**
Upper Merrion St
☎ 01 6030600 📠 01 6030700
e-mail: info@merrionhotel.com
Dir: at top of Upper Merrion St on left, beyond Government buildings on right
This terrace of gracious Georgian buildings, reputed to have
continued

been the birthplace of the Duke of Wellington, embraces the character of many changes of use through over 200 years. Bedrooms and suites are spacious, offering comfort and a wide range of extra facilities. The lounges retain the charm and opulence of days gone by while the Cellar bar area is ideal for a relaxing drink. There is also a choice of dining options. Irish favourites utilise fresh and simply prepared ingredients in the Cellar Restaurant and, for that very special occasion, award-winning Restaurant Patrick Guilbaud is Dublin's finest.

ROOMS: 143 en suite ⊗ in 65 bedrooms s €370-€2200; d €390-€2200 **LB FACILITIES:** STV ⊤ Gym Steam room ♫ **CONF:** BC Thtr 60 Class 25 Board 25 Del from €250 **SERVICES:** Lift air con **PARKING:** 60 **NOTES:** ✗ ⊗ in restaurant

★★★★★64% **Berkeley Court**
Lansdowne Rd
☎ 01 665 3200 📠 01 6617238
e-mail: berkeley_court@jurysdoyle.com
web: www.jurysdoyle.com
Dir: from N11 turn right at Donnybrook Church, 1st left to bridge, right immediately then 1st left, hotel 1st on left
Located in the leafy suburb of Ballsbridge, near the rugby stadium, this modern hotel is well positioned for business and leisure visitors alike. A choice of two pleasant restaurants is available, together with lounge food in an elegant area off the spacious lobby. The hotel offers a range of well-appointed bedrooms and suites.
ROOMS: 186 en suite ⊗ in 155 bedrooms s €120-€435; d €130-€480 **LB FACILITIES:** STV Hair & Beauty salon, ♫ Xmas **CONF:** BC Thtr 450 Class 210 Board 110 **SERVICES:** Lift air con **PARKING:** 130 **NOTES:** ✗ ⊗ in restaurant

Top Hotel
★★★★ ⊛⊛ **The Clarence**
6-8 Wellington Quay D2
☎ 01 4070800 📠 01 4070820
e-mail: reservations@theclarence.ie
Dir: from O'Connell Bridge, W along Quays, through 1st lights (at Ha'penny Bridge) hotel 500mtrs
Located on the banks of the River Liffey in the city centre, The Clarence is within walking distance of the shops and visitor attractions. This is a very distinctive property, where the character of the 1850 building has been successfully combined with contemporary design of the bedrooms and
continued

suites. The friendly staff provide unobtrusive professional service.

ROOMS: 49 en suite ⊘ in 4 bedrooms s €330-€2100; d €330-€2100 **LB** **FACILITIES:** STV Gym Treatment and massage room Xmas **CONF:** Thtr 50 Class 24 Board 35 **SERVICES:** Lift **PARKING:** 15 **NOTES:** ⊘ in restaurant Closed 24-27 Dec

See advert on this page

★★★★78% The Fitzwilliam

St Stephen's Green
☎ 01 4787000 📠 01 4787878
e-mail: enq@fitzwilliamhotel.com
Dir: *in city centre, adjacent to the top of Grafton Street*
In a central position on St Stephen's Green, this friendly hotel is a pleasant blend of contemporary style with all the traditions of good hotel keeping. Bedrooms, many overlooking an internal rooftop garden, have been equipped with a wide range of thoughtful extras. There is plenty to tempt the palate - Citron offers an informal eating option while Thornton's provides a fine dining alternative.
ROOMS: 140 en suite ⊘ in 90 bedrooms s €310; d €350 **LB** **FACILITIES:** STV Gym Xmas **CONF:** BC Thtr 80 Class 50 Board 35 **SERVICES:** Lift air con **PARKING:** 85 **NOTES:** ⊘ in restaurant

★★★★77% The Herbert Park Hotel

Ballsbridge
☎ 01 6672200 📠 01 6672595
e-mail: reservations@herbertparkhotel.ie
Dir: *2m from city centre along Nassau St, Mount St over canal bridge along Northumberland Rd. Cross bridge in Ballsbridge, 1st right*
In an enviable location adjoining the lovely Park of the same name and close to the US Embassy, RDS and convenient to the city centre. Herbert Park Hotel has spacious, light-filled and very comfortable public areas. Staff are professional and very friendly. Views of the park from the Pavilion restaurant and many of the contemporary style bedrooms are delightful in any season. Secure underground parking is available.
ROOMS: 153 en suite (4 fmly) ⊘ in 60 bedrooms s €230-€350; d €275-€350 **LB** **FACILITIES:** STV Gym **CONF:** BC Thtr 120 Class 70 Board 50 Del €275 **SERVICES:** Lift air con **PARKING:** 80 **NOTES:** ⊘ in restaurant

★★★★73% Clarion Hotel Dublin IFSC

☎ 01 4338800 📠 01 4338801
e-mail: info@clarionhotelifsc.com
Dir: *N1 to city centre, at Dorset St turn left onto North Circular Rd, then to 5 Lamps-Portland Row. Right into Amiens St, left after IFSC Building/Custom House, onto North Wall Quay. Through 2 sets of lights, hotel on left*
Whether staying here for business or leisure, or eating in the restaurant, this hotel is totally focussed on providing a professional service to its guests. Located at the heart of the

continued

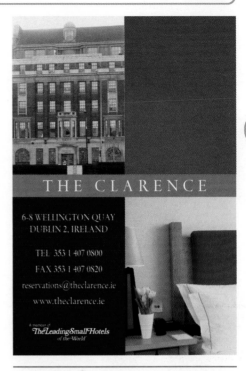

International Financial Services Centre, this well designed hotel has stylish decor, comfortable bedrooms and the staff are pleasant and attentive.
ROOMS: 147 en suite (5 fmly) ⊘ in 87 bedrooms **FACILITIES:** STV supervised Sauna Solarium Gym Jacuzzi Spinning room, treatment room, aerobics area, gym with CV equipment. **CONF:** Thtr 110 Class 42 Board 34 **SERVICES:** Lift air con **PARKING:** 55 **NOTES:** ⊘ in restaurant RS 24-26 Dec

★★★★72% *Jurys Hotel and Towers*

Pembroke Rd, Ballsbridge — JURYS DOYLE HOTELS
☎ 01 660 5000 📠 01 667 5276
e-mail: ballsbridge@jurysdoyle.com
web: www.jurysdoyle.com
Dir: *from Dun Laoghaire, follow signs for city to Merrion Rd, Ballsbridge & Pembroke Rd, hotel at junct of Pembroke Rd and Northumberland Rd*
This establishment has two identities: Jury's hotel, and the more recently opened Towers building. A wide choice of bars and restaurants along with a dedicated boardroom centre make up the spacious public areas. Bedrooms and suites are well appointed in the main hotel, while the Towers offers discreet luxury together with a separate entrance.
ROOMS: 303 en suite (13 fmly) ⊘ in 140 bedrooms **FACILITIES:** Sauna Gym Jacuzzi Hairdresser, Beauty Salon with Masseuse **CONF:** Thtr 850 Class 450 Board 40 **SERVICES:** Lift **PARKING:** 200 **NOTES:**

Indoor Swimming pool
Indoor Swimming pool (heated)
Outdoor Swimming pool
Outdoor Swimming pool (heated)

DUBLIN, continued

★★★★72% Crowne Plaza Dublin Airport

Northwood Park, Santry Demesne, Santry
☎ 01 8628888 🖷 01 8628800
e-mail: info@crowneplazadublin.ie

This smart, contemporary hotel is situated in 160 acres of parkland; it is a peaceful, country setting yet is very close to Dublin Airport. The air-conditioned bedrooms are furnished to a high standard and the clubrooms benefit from having their own lounge. Public areas are stylish with dining options and comfortable lounges. There are extensive conference facilities and a courtesy airport coach.

ROOMS: 204 en suite (17 fmly) ⊗ in 158 bedrooms s €150-€270; d €150-€300 **FACILITIES:** STV Gym The hotel is located in 120 acres of mature park land **CONF:** BC Thtr 240 Class 110 Board 45 Del from €240 **SERVICES:** Lift air con **PARKING:** 240 **NOTES:** ✗ ⊗ in restaurant RS 25 Dec

★★★★71% Gresham

O'Connell St
☎ 01 8746881 🖷 01 8787175
e-mail: info@thegresham.com
Dir: *just off M1, near GPO*

GRESHAM HOTELS

This elegant hotel enjoys a prime centre city location close to theatres, shops and museums. Excellent conference, the choice of restaurants and bars make this an ideal choice for both corporate and leisure guests. A range of bedroom options is available and the staff are very friendly. The hotel has a multi-storey car park.

ROOMS: 289 en suite (4 fmly) ⊗ in 200 bedrooms **FACILITIES:** STV Gym Xmas **CONF:** BC Thtr 350 Class 150 Board 80 **SERVICES:** Lift air con **PARKING:** 150 **NOTES:** ✗ ⊗ in restaurant

See advert on page 815

★★★★70% ◎◎ The Morrison

Lower Ormond Quay
☎ 01 8872400 🖷 01 8783185
e-mail: info@morrisonhotel.ie

This hotel was designed by the renowned John Rocha. Inside, wood, stone and natural fabrics are combined with vibrant colours to create a relaxing environment. There is a lobby lounge, café bar and the Halo Restaurant. Bedrooms and suites have a contemporary style and a dedicated, hospitable team ensures a pleasant stay. A popular club operates at weekends.

ROOMS: 138 en suite ⊗ in 69 bedrooms s €160-€285; d €160-€285 **FACILITIES:** STV Xmas **CONF:** BC Thtr 230 Class 92 Board 42 Del from €285 **SERVICES:** Lift air con **NOTES:** ✗ ⊗ in restaurant Closed 24-27 Dec

★★★★68% Burlington

Upper Leeson St
☎ 01 660 5222 🖷 01 660 8496
web: www.jurysdoyle.com
Dir: *From airport take M1 into city centre, follow signs for St. Stephens Green. From Leeson St into Upper Leeson St*

JURYS DOYLE HOTELS

Close to the city, this bustling hotel, one of Ireland's largest, features comfortable bedrooms that are well appointed; an executive floor offers additional services and a lounge area serving continental breakfast. Smart public areas include the popular Buck Mulligan pub, spacious lounges, the Sussex Room and Diplomat restaurants.

ROOMS: 500 en suite ⊗ in 245 bedrooms **FACILITIES:** STV Gym Night club Use of facilities at fitness club **CONF:** BC Thtr 1500 Class 650 Board 40 **SERVICES:** Lift **PARKING:** 700 **NOTES:** ✗ ⊗ in restaurant

★★★★67% ◎ Stillorgan Park

Stillorgan Rd
☎ 01 2881621 🖷 01 2831610
e-mail: sales@stillorganpark.com
Dir: *on N11 follow signs for Wexford, pass RTE studios on left, through next 5 sets of lights, hotel on left*

This modern hotel is attractively decorated and is situated on the southern outskirts of the city. Comfortable public areas include a spacious lobby, contemporary restaurant and inviting bar and air-conditioned banqueting and conference centre. A newly built bedroom wing, gym, spa and treatment rooms have been added.

ROOMS: 165 en suite (12 fmly) ⊗ in 25 bedrooms s €150; d €140-€195 (incl. bkfst) **LB** **FACILITIES: Spa** STV Sauna Gym Jacuzzi Beauty treatment room 8 ♫ Xmas **CONF:** BC Thtr 500 Class 220 Board 130 Del €179 **SERVICES:** Lift air con **PARKING:** 350 **NOTES:** ✗ ⊗ in restaurant RS 25 Dec Civ Wed 300

★★★★67% Red Cow Morans

Red Cow Complex, Naas Rd
☎ 01 4593650 🖷 01 4591588
e-mail: redcowres@moranhotels.com
Dir: *at junct of M50 & N7 Naas road on city side of motorway*

Located just off the M50, this hotel is 20 minutes from the airport and only minutes away from the city centre via the Luas light rail system. Classical elegance and modern design are combined throughout and the staff shows a genuine willingness to make your stay memorable. Bedrooms are well equipped and

continued

comfortable, and the public areas and conference rooms are spacious. Ample free parking is available.

ROOMS: 123 en suite (21 fmly) ⊗ in 44 bedrooms s €130-€380; d €130-€380 (incl. bkfst) **LB** **FACILITIES:** STV ♫ **CONF:** Thtr 700 Class 350 Board 150 Del from €190 **SERVICES:** Lift air con **PARKING:** 700 **NOTES:** ⊗ in restaurant Closed 24-26 Dec

★★★★62% The Plaza Hotel

Belgard Rd, Tallaght
☎ 01 4624200 01 4624600
e-mail: reservations@plazahotel.ie
web: www.plazahotel.ie
Dir: *from Dublin Airport take M50 to Tallaght sign. Turn right onto Tallaght by-pass. 1m, hotel on right*

A contemporary hotel conveniently situated just off the M50 and beside The Square Shopping Centre. Public areas are spacious and there are good corporate facilities and secure underground car parking. Bedrooms are comfortable and well equipped. The Vista Café and Olive Restaurant are on the first-floor mezzanine and enjoy views of the Dublin Mountains.

ROOMS: 122 en suite (2 fmly) ⊗ in 61 bedrooms s €99-€187; d €120-€187 **LB** **FACILITIES:** STV **CONF:** BC Thtr 200 Class 150 Board 50 **SERVICES:** Lift air con **PARKING:** 520 **NOTES:** ⊗ in restaurant Closed 24-30 Dec

★★★71% *Marine*

Sutton Cross
☎ 01 8390000 01 8390442
e-mail: sales@marinehotel.ie
Dir: *From O'Connell Bridge in city centre turn right into The Quays then left at Liberty Hall joining Amien St. Follow road through Fairview (R105) to Sutton Cross for hotel on right*

On the north shores of Dublin Bay, this hotel is situated in attractive gardens. Bedrooms are spacious and well appointed, most enjoying the spectacular views. Public areas offer comfortable lounges, an inviting restaurant, conference rooms and a leisure centre. There are five golf courses nearby.

ROOMS: 48 en suite (5 fmly) ⊗ in 12 bedrooms **FACILITIES:** STV Sauna Steam Room **CONF:** Thtr 220 Class 140 Board 40 **SERVICES:** Lift **PARKING:** 150 **NOTES:** ⊗ in restaurant Closed 25-27 Dec

★★★70% Finnstown Country House Hotel & Golf Course

Newcastle Rd, Lucan
☎ 01 6010700 01 6281088
e-mail: manager@finnstown-hotel.ie
Dir: *from M1 take 1st exit onto M50 S/bound. 1st exit after Toll Bridge. At rdbt take 3rd left (N4 W). Left at traffic lights. Over next 2 rdbts. Hotel on right*

Set in 45 acres of wooded grounds, Finnstown is a calm and peaceful country house. There is a wide choice of bedroom styles available, with the garden suites being particularly comfortable. Long stay apartments are being developed. Lounge areas are numerous with games facilities provided. Staff members are very guest-focussed.

ROOMS: 25 en suite 28 annexe en suite (6 fmly) (9 GF) ⊗ in 27 bedrooms s €60-€155; d €80-€210 (incl. bkfst) **LB** **FACILITIES:** STV Solarium Gym Putt green Turkish bath, Table tennis, Massage, Pool Table, Games Room Xmas **CONF:** BC Thtr 300 Class 60 Board 40 Del from €210 **PARKING:** 90 **NOTES:** ⊗ in restaurant

★★★70% Jurys Montrose

Stillorgan Rd
☎ 01 2693311 01 2691164
e-mail: montrose@jurysdoyle.com
web: www.jurysdoyle.com
Dir: *From city centre follow signs for N11*

Close to the University campus, this hotel offers comfortable bedrooms and smart lounges with a choice of bars and dedicated meeting rooms. Casual dining is available throughout the day, with a more formal service in the restaurant at both lunch and dinner.

ROOMS: 178 en suite ⊗ in 30 bedrooms s €93-€117; d €118-€237 **LB** **FACILITIES:** STV **CONF:** BC Thtr 80 Class 30 Board 30 **SERVICES:** Lift **PARKING:** 100 **NOTES:**

★★★70% Lynch Green Isle

Naas Rd, Newlands Cross, Naas Rd
☎ 01 4593406 01 4592178
e-mail: sales@lynchotels.com
Dir: *on N7, 10km SW of the city centre*

This hotel lies on the southern outskirts of Dublin just off the M50. All rooms are generously proportioned and at the time of inspection a further block was under construction together with a new leisure centre. Public areas include spacious conference facilities, Sorrels restaurant and Rosie O'Grady's pub, which offers a popular carvery at lunchtime.

ROOMS: 240 en suite (10 fmly) ⊗ in 144 bedrooms s €89-€276; d €104-€276 **LB** **FACILITIES: Spa** STV supervised Gym Jacuzzi Treatment rooms, Steam room ♫ **CONF:** Thtr 300 Class 100 Board 100 Del from €155 **SERVICES:** Lift **PARKING:** 350 **NOTES:** ⊗ in restaurant

★★★69% Buswells

23-25 Molesworth St
☎ 01 6146500 01 6762090
e-mail: buswells@quinn-hotels.com
Dir: *on corner of Molesworth St & Kildare St opposite Dail Eireann (Government Buildings)*

Originally a number of Georgian townhouses, Buswells is a popular meeting place for the parliamentarians from the Dail opposite. Bedrooms are comfortable and attractively decorated. The newly renovated public areas are particularly attractive, as are

continued on p834

DUBLIN, continued

the two new meeting rooms. Buswells is renowned for the friendliness of the staff.
ROOMS: 67 en suite (17 fmly) ⊗ in 33 bedrooms s €100-€175; d €140-€225 (incl. bkfst) **LB** **FACILITIES:** Gym Leisure suite **CONF:** BC Thtr 85 Class 30 Board 24 **SERVICES:** Lift **NOTES:** ✗ ⊗ in restaurant Closed 25 & 26 Dec RS 24-Dec

D

★★★68% Bewleys Hotel Leopardstown

Central Park, Leopardstown Rd
☎ 01 2935 000 ☐ 021 2935 099
e-mail: leop@bewleyshotel.com

BEWLEY'S HOTELS

Dir: *M50 junct 18, follow signs for Leopardstown, at rdbt take 2nd exit. Hotel on right.*
This hotel is conveniently situated close to the Central Business Park and Leopardstown Race Course, and serviced by the Luas light rail system and Aircoach. Contemporary in style, the open-plan public areas include a spacious lounge bar, brasserie and a selection of conference rooms. Bedrooms are well appointed. There is free underground parking.
ROOMS: 357 rms (54 fmly) ⊗ in 339 bedrooms s €89; d €89 **FACILITIES:** STV Day membership at local club 10-15mins drive **CONF:** Board 14 **SERVICES:** Lift **PARKING:** 228 **NOTES:** ✗ ⊗ in restaurant Closed 24-25 Dec

★★★68% *Camden Court*

Camden St
☎ 01 4759666 ☐ 01 4759677
e-mail: reservations@camdencourthotel.ie
Dir: *off Camden St close to St Stephens Green & Grafton St*
This hotel has a number of fine features in addition to its convenient location. These include spacious public areas, a leisure centre, well-equipped bedrooms, and the bonus of having a car park in the city centre. Conference facilities are also available.
ROOMS: 246 en suite (33 fmly) ⊗ in 13 bedrooms **FACILITIES:** Sauna Solarium Gym Jacuzzi **CONF:** Thtr 40 Class 40 Board 20 **SERVICES:** Lift **PARKING:** 96 **NOTES:** ✗ Closed Xmas/New Year

★★★68% The Carnegie Court

North St, Swords
☎ 01 8404384 ☐ 01 8404505
e-mail: info@carnegiecourt.com
Dir: *from Dublin Airport take N1 towards Belfast. At 5th rdbt take 1st exit for Swords, then sharp left for hotel*
This modern hotel has been tastefully built and is conveniently located close to Dublin Airport just off the N1 in Swords village. The air-conditioned bedrooms are well appointed, and many are particularly spacious. Public areas include a residents' lounge, contemporary Courtyard Restaurant, a dramatically designed Harp Bar and modern conference and banqueting facilities. Extensive underground parking is available.
ROOMS: 36 en suite (4 fmly) ⊗ in 7 bedrooms **FACILITIES:** STV ♫ **CONF:** Thtr 280 Class 50 Board 40 **SERVICES:** Lift air con **PARKING:** 150 **NOTES:** ✗ ⊗ in restaurant Closed 25-26 Dec

★★★68% McEniff Grand Canal Hotel

Grand Canal St
☎ 01 646 1000 ☐ 01 645 1001
e-mail: reservations@grandcanalhotel.com
This hotel is situated on the banks of the Grand Canal in Ballsbridge, close to Lansdowne Road Stadium, RDS and the city centre. Bedrooms are well appointed. The contemporary public areas are spacious and include a comfortable lounge, restaurant,

continued

Kitty O'Sheas pub and extensive conference rooms. Secure underground parking is available.
ROOMS: 142 en suite (20 fmly) (4 GF) ⊗ in 105 bedrooms s €105-€210; d €105-€210 **LB** **FACILITIES:** STV ♫ **CONF:** Thtr 140 Class 64 Board 60 **SERVICES:** Lift **PARKING:** 66 **NOTES:** ✗ ⊗ in restaurant Closed 23-28 Dec

★★★67% Bewley's Hotel Ballsbridge

Merrion Rd, Ballsbridge
☎ 01 6681111 ☐ 01 6681999
e-mail: bb@bewleyshotels.com

BEWLEY'S HOTELS

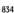

This stylish hotel is conveniently situated near the RDS Showgrounds and is close to city centre. It offers comfortable, good value accommodation. O'Connell's Restaurant and café provides food throughout the day on interesting menus. The spacious lounge is a popular meeting place. There is secure underground parking.
ROOMS: 220 en suite (25 fmly) ⊗ in 140 bedrooms s €99; d €99 **CONF:** BC Class 30 Board 14 **SERVICES:** Lift **PARKING:** 240 **NOTES:** ✗ ⊗ in restaurant Closed 24-26 Dec

★★★67% Jurys Inn Parnell Street

Parnell St
☎ 01 8784900 ☐ 01 8784999
e-mail: jurysinnparnellst.@jurysdoyle.com
Dir: *Left off O'Connell St onto Parnell St, hotel 50yds on left*
This modern, stylish hotel is prominently located in the city, close to the shopping and theatre area. Bedrooms provide good guest comfort and facilities suited to both leisure and business markets. Public areas include dedicated meeting rooms, a popular bar and restaurant on the first floor.
ROOMS: 253 en suite (116 fmly) ⊗ in 186 bedrooms s €235; d €236 **LB** **FACILITIES:** STV ch fac **CONF:** BC Thtr 50 Class 24 Board 20 Del €185 **SERVICES:** Lift air con **NOTES:** ✗ ⊗ in restaurant

★★★67% Longfield's Hotel

Fitzwilliam St Lower
☎ 01 6761367 ☐ 01 6761542
e-mail: info@longfields.ie

MANOR HOUSE HOTELS

Dir: *take Shelbourne Hotel exit from St Stephens Green, continue down Baggot St for 400mtrs, turn left at Fitzwilliam St junct and Longfields is on left*
Longfield's, a series of Georgian houses, has a very warm hospitable feel to it. Staff are all focused on guest care in an informal yet professional manner. Drinks are available in the comfortable lounge. Rooms vary in size but are well appointed and comfortable.
ROOMS: 26 en suite s €90-€130; d €120-€240 (incl. bkfst) **LB** **FACILITIES:** STV **CONF:** Thtr 20 Board 20 **SERVICES:** Lift **NOTES:** ✗ ⊗ in restaurant RS 23-27 Dec

★★★66% *Tara Towers*
Merrion Rd
☎ 01 2694666 🖷 01 2691027
e-mail: tara@jurysdoyle.com
Dir: *N11/University College follow towards Montrose Hotel. 1st left before hotel into Woodbine Rd. Left at traffic lights*
There are spectacular views over Dublin Bay from this modern hotel situated on the coast close to the city. Bedrooms are spacious and well equipped. Attractively decorated public areas include a comfortable and relaxing foyer lounge, PJ Branagans Pub and a split-level conservatory restaurant. There are extensive banqueting facilities and ample parking available.
ROOMS: 113 en suite (2 fmly) ⊗ in 20 bedrooms **FACILITIES:** STV **CONF:** Thtr 300 Class 100 Board 40 **SERVICES:** Lift **PARKING:** 100 **NOTES:** ✗

★★★65%
Bewley's Hotel Newlands Cross
BEWLEY'S HOTELS
Newlands Cross, Naas Rd
☎ 01 4640140 🖷 01 4640900
e-mail: res@BewleysHotels.com
Dir: *M50 junct 9 take N7 Naas road, hotel near N7- Belgard Rd junct at Newlands Cross*

This modern hotel is situated on the outskirts of Dublin off the N7 and close to M50. Bedrooms are well furnished and prices are competitive. The restaurant is open for casual dining all day and serves more formal meals in the evening. There is a comfortable lounge and bar and ample car parking.
ROOMS: 258 en suite (123 fmly) (63 GF) ⊗ in 183 bedrooms s €79; d €79 **FACILITIES:** STV ⚓ **CONF:** Board 12 **SERVICES:** Lift **PARKING:** 200 **NOTES:** ✗ ⊗ in restaurant Closed 24-26 Dec

★★★65% Cassidys
Cavendish Row, OConnell St Upper
☎ 01 8780555 🖷 01 8780687
e-mail: stay@cassidyshotel.com
Dir: *in city centre at north end of O'Connell St. Opposite Gate Theatre*

This family-run hotel is located at the top of O'Connell Street, on a terrace of red-brick Georgian townhouses. The warm and welcoming atmosphere of Grooms Bar lends a traditional air to Cassidy's Hotel, and Restaurant 6 is contemporary and stylish. The modern bedrooms are well appointed. Limited car parking for guests and conference facilities available.
ROOMS: 88 en suite (3 fmly) (12 GF) ⊗ in 23 bedrooms s €85-€185; d €99-€185 (incl. bkfst) **LB** **FACILITIES:** STV ♫ **CONF:** Thtr 80 Class 45 Board 45 **SERVICES:** Lift **PARKING:** 15 **NOTES:** ✗ ⊗ in restaurant Closed 24-26 Dec

★★★65% *Jurys Christchurch Inn*
JURYS DOYLE HOTELS
Christchurch Place
☎ 01 4540000 🖷 01 4540012
e-mail: info@jurysdoyle.com
web: www.jurysdoyle.com
Dir: *N7 onto Naas Rd, follow city centre signs to O'Connell St, continue past Trinity College. Right onto Dame St to Lord Edward St, hotel on left*
Centrally located opposite the 12th-century Christchurch Cathedral, this hotel is close to the Temple Bar and all the city amenities. The foyer lounge and pub are popular meeting places and there is also an informal restaurant. The bedrooms are well appointed and can accommodate families. The adjoining car park is a bonus in the city centre.
ROOMS: 182 en suite ⊗ in 114 bedrooms **SERVICES:** Lift **NOTES:** ✗ ⊗ in restaurant Closed 24-26 Dec

★★★65% Jurys Custom House Inn
JURYS DOYLE HOTELS
Custom House Quay
☎ 01 6075000 🖷 01 8290400
web: www.jurysdoyle.com
Overlooking the River Liffey and close to the International Financial Services Centre and less than ten minutes' walk away from the city's main shopping and tourist areas. Bedrooms are spacious and well equipped. Public area and contemporary in style and include facilities for business guests.
ROOMS: 239 en suite ⊗ in 145 bedrooms s €79-€225; d €79-€225 **FACILITIES:** STV **CONF:** Thtr 60 Class 30 Board 30 Del from €179 **SERVICES:** Lift **NOTES:** ✗ ⊗ in restaurant Closed 25-26 Dec

★★★65% Mount Herbert Hotel
Herbert Rd, Lansdowne Rd
☎ 01 6684321 🖷 01 6607077
e-mail: info@mountherberthotel.ie
Dir: *close to Lansdowne Road Rugby Stadium, 200mtrs from Dart Rail Station*
Located in the leafy suburb of Ballsbridge, this family-run hotel is an oasis of calm, offering true hospitality. Bedrooms are comfortable, as are the lounge areas. Good value cuisine is served in the restful restaurant overlooking the floodlit gardens.
ROOMS: 173 en suite (15 fmly) (56 GF) ⊗ in 110 bedrooms s €69-€199; d €79-€199 (incl. bkfst) **FACILITIES:** STV Childrens playground Free use of local gym **CONF:** BC Thtr 88 Class 45 Board 38 Del from €135 **SERVICES:** Lift **PARKING:** 90 **NOTES:** ✗ ⊗ in restaurant Closed 22-30 Dec

★★★63% *McEniff Skylon*
Drumcondra Rd
☎ 01 8379121 🖷 01 8372778
e-mail: reservations@skylon.org
Dir: *from Airport take M1 towards city centre. Hotel 3m on right*
In a convenient location, with easy access to the city centre and the airport, this hotel has a spacious, comfortable lobby lounge and bar where food is available all day, with more formal dining in the attractive restaurant. Bedrooms are well appointed and there is ample car parking available.
ROOMS: 88 en suite (8 fmly) ⊗ in 22 bedrooms **FACILITIES:** STV **CONF:** Thtr 35 Class 20 Board 20 **SERVICES:** Lift **NOTES:** ✗

DUBLIN, continued

★★★63% The Mercer Hotel
Mercer St Lower
☎ 01 4782179 4744120 🖷 01 4780328
e-mail: stay@mercerhotel.ie
Dir: *St Stephens Green before shopping centre turn left down York St, then right at end of road, hotel on right*
This modern hotel is situated in the city centre close to Grafton Street. Bedrooms are attractively decorated and well equipped with fridges and CD players, as well as the usual facilities. Public areas include an open-plan lounge with cocktail bar and a restaurant. Parking is available in car park next door.
ROOMS: 41 en suite ⊘ in 4 bedrooms s €110-€185; d €137-€220 (incl. dinner) LB **FACILITIES:** STV **CONF:** Thtr 100 Class 80 Board 60 **SERVICES:** air con **PARKING:** 41 **NOTES:** 🐕 ⊘ in restaurant Closed 24-26 Dec

★★★63% Temple Bar
Fleet St, Temple Bar
☎ 01 6773333 🖷 01 6773088
e-mail: reservations@tbh.ie
Dir: *from Trinity College towards O'Connell Bridge. 1st left onto Fleet St. Hotel on right*
This hotel is situated in the heart of Dublin's Temple Bar, and in close to the shops, restaurants and cultural life of the city. Bedrooms are comfortable and well equipped. Food is served throughout the day in Buskers theme bar. There is a multi storey car park nearby.
ROOMS: 129 en suite (6 fmly) ⊘ in 92 bedrooms s €100-€155; d €120-€200 (incl. bkfst) LB **FACILITIES:** STV Guest reduced rates at nearby leisure facilities **CONF:** Thtr 60 Class 40 Board 40 **SERVICES:** Lift **NOTES:** 🐕 ⊘ in restaurant Closed 23-25 Dec RS Good Friday

★★★60% *Abberley Court*
Belgard Rd, Tallaght
☎ 01 4596000 🖷 01 4621000
e-mail: abberley@iol.ie
Dir: *opposite The Square town centre at the junct of Belgard Rd and Tallaght by-pass (N81)*
Located beside an excellent complex of shops, restaurants and cinema, this hotel offers comfortable well-appointed bedrooms, the choice of two bars, a carvery and a Chinese restaurant. There are sports facilities available nearby.
ROOMS: 40 en suite (34 fmly) ⊘ in 8 bedrooms **CONF:** Thtr 40 Class 25 Board 20 **SERVICES:** Lift **PARKING:** 450 **NOTES:** 🐕 Closed 25 Dec

★★★58% *The Parliament Hotel*
Lord Edward St
☎ 01 6708777 🖷 01 6708787
e-mail: parl@regencyhotels.com
Dir: *adjacent to Dublin Castle in the Temple Bar area*
An attractive hotel, near to the Temple Bar area and Dublin Castle, offering a friendly welcome to all its guests. It provides well-furnished bedrooms, decorated in a modern style. There is also a popular bar and a separate restaurant.
ROOMS: 63 en suite (8 fmly) ⊘ in 22 bedrooms **FACILITIES:** STV **CONF:** Thtr 20 Board 10 **SERVICES:** Lift **NOTES:** 🐕 ⊘ in restaurant

★★69% *West Country Hotel*
Chapelizod
☎ 01 6264011 🖷 01 6231378
e-mail: info@westcountryhotel.ie
This family run hotel is situated just off the N4 Western Road and within walking distance of Chapelizod village. Bedrooms are well appointed. Public areas include a comfortable lobby lounge and bar where a carvery lunch is served daily and dinner in the Pine restaurant. Conference facilities are available.
ROOMS: 48 rms

U The Beacon
Beacon Court, Sandyford Business Region
☎ 01 2915000 🖷 01 2912005
e-mail: sales@thebeacon.com
Dir: *exit M50 & follow signs for Sandyford. Hotel on right after approx 2m*
At the time of going to press, the star classification for this hotel was not confirmed. Please refer to the AA internet site www.theAA.com for current information.
ROOMS: 82 en suite ⊘ in 69 bedrooms s €120-€250; d €120-€250 (incl. bkfst & dinner) LB **FACILITIES:** ♫ **CONF:** Thtr 40 Class 30 Board 25 Del from €150 **SERVICES:** Lift **PARKING:** 90 **NOTES:** 🐕 ⊘ in restaurant

U Radisson SAS St Helen's Hotel
Stillorgan Rd
☎ 01 218 6000 🖷 01 218 6010
e-mail: info.dublin@radissonsas.com
web: www.radisson.com
Dir: *from centre take N11 due S, hotel 4km on left of dual carriageway*
At the time of going to press, the star classification for this hotel was not confirmed. Please refer to the AA internet site www.theAA.com for current information.
ROOMS: 151 en suite (102 fmly) (39 GF) ⊘ in 100 bedrooms s fr €187.50; d fr €187.50 LB **FACILITIES:** STV Snooker Gym Beauty salon ♫ ch fac Xmas **CONF:** Del from €295 **SERVICES:** Lift air con **PARKING:** 220 **NOTES:** 🐕 ⊘ in restaurant

⌂ Travelodge Dublin Airport
Swords By Pass
☎ 08700 850 950 🖷 01 8409235
web: www.travelodge.co.uk
Dir: *on N1 (Dublin/Belfast road) on s'bound carriageway of Swords Rdbt*
Travelodge offers good quality, good value, modern accommodation. Ideal for families, the spacious, en suite bedrooms include remote-control TV, tea and coffee-making facilities and comfortable beds. Meals can be taken at the nearby family restaurant. For further details consult the Hotel Groups page.
ROOMS: 100 en suite s fr €26; d fr €26

⌂ Travelodge Dublin (Navan Road)
Auburn Av Roundabout, Navan Rd
☎ 08700 850 950
web: www.travelodge.co.uk
Dir: *just off M50 (Dublin ring road) at junct with Navan Rd, N3 junct 6*
Travelodge offers good quality, good value, modern accommodation. Ideal for families, the spacious, en suite bedrooms include remote-control TV, tea and coffee-making facilities and comfortable beds. Meals can be taken at the nearby family restaurant. For further details consult the Hotel Groups page.
ROOMS: 100 en suite s fr €26; d fr €26

○ *The Shelbourne*
27 St Stephen's Green
☎ 01 6634500 🖷 01 6616006
e-mail: shelbourneinfo@lemeridien.com
web: www.marriott.ie/dubbr
Closed for refurbishment. Due to open in autumn 2006.

DUNDALK, Co Louth — Map 01 D4

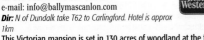

★★★73% Ballymascanlon House
☎ 042 9358200 🖷 042 9371598
e-mail: info@ballymascanlon.com
Dir: *N of Dundalk take T62 to Carlingford. Hotel is approx 1km*
This Victorian mansion is set in 130 acres of woodland at the foot of the Cooley Mountains. Elegantly designed in the original house and the modern extension. This is a very comfortable hotel with some really stylish bedrooms. Public areas include a restaurant and spacious lounge and bar, and a well equipped leisure centre.
ROOMS: 90 en suite (11 fmly) (5 GF) ⊗ in 28 bedrooms s €105-€190; d €155-€250 (incl. bkfst) **LB FACILITIES:** STV supervised 18 Sauna Gym Putt green Jacuzzi Steam room, Plunge pool, Massage ♫ Xmas **CONF:** BC Thtr 300 Class 160 Board 75 Del from €160 **SERVICES:** Lift **PARKING:** 250 **NOTES:** ⊗ in restaurant

★★★65% *Fairways Hotel*
Dublin Rd
☎ 042 9321500 🖷 042 9321511
e-mail: info@fairways.ie
Dir: *on N1 3km S of Dundalk*
Situated south of Dundalk on the Castlebellingham road, this modern hotel has been refurbished to a high standard. A wide range of food is available in the carvery/grill all day, with a more formal dinner served in Modi's restaurant. Golf can be arranged by the hotel on a choice of nearby courses.
ROOMS: 101 en suite (2 fmly) (30 GF) ⊗ in 30 bedrooms **FACILITIES: Spa** STV supervised Sauna Gym Jacuzzi ♫ **CONF:** BC Thtr 1000 Class 500 **SERVICES:** Lift **PARKING:** 700 **NOTES:** ⊗ in restaurant Closed 25 Dec

DUNDRUM, Co Tipperary — Map 01 C3

★★★72% *Dundrum House*
☎ 062 71116 🖷 062 71366
This Georgian mansion dates from 1730 and was tastefully restored by the Crowe family. Bedrooms vary in style and are comfortably furnished, rooms in the original house with antique pieces and the new rooms feature a modern theme. There are relaxing lounges with open fires and a fine dining room, with more informal food available in the golf club. The extensive facilities include a leisure centre and an 18-hole championship golf course.
ROOMS: 55 en suite (6 fmly) **FACILITIES:** no TV in bdrms Fishing Snooker ch fac **SERVICES:** Lift **PARKING:** 300 **NOTES:**

DUNFANAGHY, Co Donegal — Map 01 C6

★★★67% Arnold's
☎ 074 913 6208 🖷 074 913 6352
e-mail: arnoldshotel@eircom.net
Dir: *on N56 from Letterkenny, hotel on left entering the village*

This family run hotel is noted for its warm welcome and good food. Situated in a coastline village with sandy beaches, links golf courses and beautiful scenery. Public areas and bedrooms are comfortable, there is a traditional bar, choice of two restaurants, delightful garden, riding stables and outdoor activities available.
ROOMS: 30 en suite (10 fmly) s €89-€125; d €118-€190 (incl. bkfst) **LB FACILITIES:** STV Fishing Riding Putt green ♫ **PARKING:** 60 **NOTES:** ⊗ in restaurant Closed Nov-mid March

DUNGANNON, Co Tyrone — Map 01 C5

⌂ *Cohannon Inn*
212 Ballynakilly Rd BT71 6HJ
☎ 028 8772 4488 🖷 028 8775 2217
e-mail: enquiries@cohannon-inn.com
Dir: *400yds from M1 junct 14*
Handy for the M1, The Cohannon Inn offers competitive prices and well-maintained bedrooms, located behind the inn complex in a smart purpose-built wing. Public areas are smartly furnished and wide-ranging menus are served throughout the day.
ROOMS: 42 en suite **CONF:** Thtr 100 Class 50 Board 50

DUNGARVAN, Co Waterford — Map 01 C2

★★★61% Lawlors
☎ 058 41122 & 41056 🖷 058 41000
e-mail: info@lawlorshotel.com
Dir: *off N25*
This town centre hotel enjoys a busy local trade especially in the bar where good food is served throughout the day. The restaurant offers a particularly wide choice of menu. Many of the bedrooms are very spacious. Conference and meeting rooms are also available.
ROOMS: 89 en suite (8 fmly) **FACILITIES:** ♫ Xmas **CONF:** Thtr 420 Class 215 Board 420 **SERVICES:** Lift **NOTES:** ⊗ in restaurant Closed 25-Dec

ENFIELD, Co Meath — Map 01 C4

★★★★69% Marriott Johnstown House Hotel
☎ 046 9540000 🖹 046 9540001
e-mail: info@johnstownhouse.com
web: www.marriott.ie/dubjh
Built around a Georgian listed mansion on 80 acres of parkland and landscaped gardens, this fine hotel hi-tech conference facilities, comfortable bedrooms and suites, two restaurants and bars. The reception hall and library reflect the elegance of the 18th-century design.
ROOMS: 126 en suite (8 fmly) (41 GF) in 40 bedrooms s €100-€175; d €115-€190 (incl. bkfst) **LB** **FACILITIES: Spa** STV supervised Fishing Sauna Gym Jacuzzi Xmas **CONF:** BC Thtr 900 Class 900 Board 16 **SERVICES:** Lift **PARKING:** 350 **NOTES:** in restaurant

ENNIS, Co Clare — Map 01 B3

★★★★68% *Woodstock*
Shanaway Rd
☎ 065 684 6600 🖹 065 684 6611
e-mail: info@woodstockhotel.com
Dir: *From Ennis continue on N18 until rdbt, take N85 to Lahinch, after 1km turn left for Woodstock & continue for 1km*
This newly built hotel overlooks Woodstock 18-hole parkland Golf Course and offers privacy and seclusion on the outskirts of Ennis town. Pubic areas include an impressive lobby with comfortable lounges, which are complemented by welcoming log fires. Contemporary Irish dishes are served in Spikes Brassiere where guests enjoy spectacular views. The spacious bedrooms offer comfort and individuality in decor and furnishings. There are extensive health and leisure facilities and a choice of conference rooms available.
ROOMS: 67 en suite (20 GF) in 47 bedrooms **FACILITIES:** STV 18 Sauna Gym Jacuzzi Steam room, Swimming pool supervised **CONF:** BC Thtr 200 Class 160 Board 50 **SERVICES:** Lift air con **NOTES:** Closed 25-26 Dec

★★★67% Temple Gate
The Square
☎ 065 6823300 🖹 065 6823322
e-mail: info@templegatehotel.com
Dir: *turn off N18 onto Tulla Rd for 0.25m, hotel on left*
This smart hotel is located in the very centre of the town, accessed from the public car park at the rear. Incorporating an 19th-century Gothic-style building, the public areas are well planned and include a comfortable lounge, popular pub and JM's Bistro restaurant. Bedrooms are attractive and well equipped.
ROOMS: 70 en suite (3 fmly) (25 GF) in 11 bedrooms s €100-€220; d €140-€250 (incl. bkfst) **LB** **FACILITIES:** STV **CONF:** Thtr 220 Class 100 Board 80 Del from €135 **SERVICES:** Lift **PARKING:** 52 **NOTES:** in restaurant Closed 25 Dec & 26 Dec RS 24-Dec Civ Wed 150

ENNISCORTHY, Co Wexford — Map 01 D3

★★★64% *Treacys*
Templeshannon
☎ 054 37798 🖹 054 37733
e-mail: info@treacyshotel.com
Dir: *N11 into Enniscorthy, over bridge in left lane. Hotel on right*
This modern hotel is family run and conveniently located near the town centre. There is a choice of dining options in the Chang Thai and Begenal Harvey restaurants, with Benedict's super-pub open at weekends. Guests have complimentary use of the nearby car park and Waterfront Leisure Centre.
ROOMS: 59 rms (2 fmly) in 11 bedrooms **FACILITIES:** STV Discount at adjacent leisure complex **SERVICES:** Lift **NOTES:** Closed 23 - 25 Dec

ENNISKILLEN, Co Fermanagh — Map 01 C5

★★★★72% Killyhevlin
BT74 6RW
☎ 028 6632 3481 🖹 028 6632 4726
e-mail: info@killyhevlin.com
web: www.killyhevlin.com
Dir: *2m S, off A4*
A modern, stylish hotel nestling on the shores of Lough Erne, just south of the town. Bedrooms are particularly spacious, well equipped, and many enjoy fine views. An open-plan restaurant and informal bar complement the comfortable lounges. Staff throughout are friendly and helpful.
ROOMS: 70 en suite (42 fmly) (22 GF) in 49 bedrooms s £75-£95; d £110-£130 (incl. bkfst) **LB** **FACILITIES: Spa** STV supervised Fishing Sauna Gym Jacuzzi Leisure club **CONF:** BC Thtr 500 Class 160 Board 100 Del from £95 **PARKING:** 500 **NOTES:** Closed 25-Dec

FOXFORD, Co Mayo — Map 01 B4

★★68% Healys Restaurant & Country House Hotel
Pontoon
☎ 094 9256443 🖹 094 9256572
e-mail: info@healyspontoon.com
This attractive creeper clad former shooting lodge is now a comfortable and friendly hotel with a great view of Lough Cullen. Both the bar and restaurant serve enjoyable meals. Bedrooms are cosy and comfortable.
ROOMS: 14 en suite (1 fmly) **FACILITIES:** Fishing Xmas **PARKING:** 300 **NOTES:** in restaurant Closed 25-Dec

GALWAY, Co Galway — Map 01 B3

★★★★77% Glenlo Abbey
Bushypark
☎ 091 526666 🖹 091 527800
e-mail: info@glenloabbey.ie
Dir: *4km from Galway city centre on N59*
This cut stone Abbey was built in 1740 and has been lovingly restored to its original glory and features sculpted cornices and fine antique furniture. There is an elegant drawing room, a cocktail bar, a library, the delightful River Room restaurant and a cellar bar. The unique Orient Express Pullman Restaurant provides a second dining option. Bedrooms are in the modern wing and are spacious and well appointed.
ROOMS: 46 en suite in all bedrooms s €149-€254; d €199-€314 **LB** **FACILITIES:** STV 18 Fishing Putt green Boating, Clay pigeon shooting, Archery Xmas **CONF:** BC Thtr 180 Class 100 Board 50 Del from €245 **SERVICES:** Lift **PARKING:** 150 **NOTES:** in restaurant Closed 24-28 Dec

★★★★73% Radisson SAS Hotel & Spa
Lough Atalia Rd
☎ 091 538300 🖹 091 538380
e-mail: sales.galway@radissonsas.com
web: www.radisson.com
Dir: *take N6 into Galway City. At Hunstman Inn rdbt turn 1st left. At next lights take left fork. 0.5m, hotel at next right junct*
In a prime position on the waterfront at Lough Atalia, striking interior design and good levels of comfort and quality are the

continued

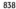

keynotes of this hotel. Bedrooms are well equipped and an executive floor has recently been added. The corporate and leisure facilities are very good.
ROOMS: 217 en suite (7 fmly) ⊗ in 177 bedrooms s €150-€530; d €150-€530 (incl. bkfst) **FACILITIES: Spa** STV supervised Sauna Solarium Gym Putt green Jacuzzi Outdoor Canadian Hot-tub Xmas **CONF:** BC Thtr 750 Class 540 Board 70 **SERVICES:** Lift air con **PARKING:** 260 **NOTES:** ⊗ in restaurant

★★★★71% Park House Hotel & Park Room Restaurant

Forster St, Eyre Square
☎ 091 564924 🖷 091 569219
e-mail: parkhousehotel@eircom.net
Dir: *city centre*

This centre city property offers well decorated and comfortable bedrooms which vary in size. The spacious restaurant has been a popular spot for the people of Galway for many years.
ROOMS: 84 en suite ⊗ in 66 bedrooms s €75-€300; d €99-€300 (incl. bkfst) **LB** **FACILITIES:** STV ♫ **CONF:** Thtr 50 Class 30 Board 30 **SERVICES:** Lift air con **PARKING:** 48 **NOTES:** ⊗ in restaurant Closed 24-26 Dec

★★★★70% Ardilaun Conference & Leisure Centre

Taylor's Hill
☎ 091 521433 🖷 091 521546
e-mail: info@ardilaunhousehotel.ie
Dir: *N6 to Galway City West, then follow signs for N59 Clifden, then N6 towards Salthill, hotel on this road*
Located on five acres of private grounds and landscaped gardens, the original Ardilaun House was built in 1840 and converted to a hotel over 40 years ago. The bedrooms have been thoughtfully equipped and pleasantly furnished. Public areas include an elegant restaurant overlooking the garden, comfortable lounges and a bar.
ROOMS: 89 en suite (7 fmly) ⊗ in 33 bedrooms s €90-€140; d €160-€280 (incl. bkfst) **LB** **FACILITIES: Spa** STV supervised Snooker Sauna Solarium Gym Jacuzzi Treatment & Analysis Rooms, Beauty salon, Spinning Room ♫ Xmas **CONF:** Thtr 400 Class 200 Board 60 Del from €180 **SERVICES:** Lift **PARKING:** 240 **NOTES:** ⊗ in restaurant Closed 22-27 Dec

★★★★70% Galway Bay Hotel Conference & Leisure Centre

The Promenade, Salthill
☎ 091 520520 🖷 091 520530
e-mail: info@galwaybayhotel.net
Dir: *follow signs to Salthill from all major roads. On promenade on coast road to Connemara.*
This smart modern hotel enjoys a most spectacular location overlooking Galway Bay and most bedrooms, lounges and the

continued

restaurant enjoy these views. There are two dining options, fine dining in the Lobster Pot and the less formal Café Lido. Conference/banqueting are impressive and there is a leisure centre and a new beauty salon.

Galway Bay Hotel, Galway

ROOMS: 153 en suite (10 fmly) (8 GF) ⊗ in 24 bedrooms s €110-€175; d €160-€280 (incl. bkfst) **LB** **FACILITIES:** STV supervised Sauna Gym Steam room, beauty salon ♫ Xmas **CONF:** BC Thtr 1100 Class 325 **SERVICES:** Lift air con **PARKING:** 300 **NOTES:** ⊗ in restaurant

See advert on this page

★★★★64% Westwood House Hotel

Dangan, Upper Newcastle
☎ 091 521442 🖷 091 521400
e-mail: reservations@westwoodhousehotel.com
Dir: *from N6 into Galway, then follow signs for Clifden (N59). House on left*
Close to the university and on the main road to Connemara, this modern hotel is well appointed with spacious public areas, and a

continued on p840

GALWAY, continued

very popular bar that serves food throughout the day. Bedrooms are comfortably equipped, as are the conference facilities.
ROOMS: 58 en suite (44 fmly) ⊗ in 17 bedrooms **FACILITIES:** STV Arrangement with local health and leisure club ♫ **CONF:** Thtr 350 Class 200 Board 70 Del from €141.50 **SERVICES:** Lift air con **PARKING:** 130 **NOTES:** ✗ ⊗ in restaurant Closed 24-25 Dec Civ Wed 275

★★★67% The Harbour

The Harbour
☎ 091 569466 🖷 091 569455
e-mail: stay@harbour.ie
Dir: *follow signs for Galway City East, at rdbt take 1st exit to Galway City, follow signs to docks, hotel approx 1m from rdbt on left*

This hotel is situated on the Galway Harbour development in the heart of the city. Contemporary in style, the ground floor includes a large lobby lounge with open fires. Krusoes café bar and restaurant offers modern cuisine. Bedrooms are smartly furnished, comfortable and well equipped. Guests have the benefit of complimentary secure car parking at the rear and there is a new leisure suite and treatment rooms available.
ROOMS: 96 en suite ⊗ in 34 bedrooms s €84-€185; d €118-€320 (incl. bkfst) **LB** **FACILITIES: Spa** STV Gym Jacuzzi ♫ Xmas **CONF:** Thtr 100 Class 80 Board 40 **SERVICES:** Lift **PARKING:** 64 **NOTES:** ✗ ⊗ in restaurant Closed 23-27 Dec

★★★65% Menlo Park Hotel

THE INDEPENDENTS

Terryland
☎ 091 761122 🖷 091 761222
e-mail: menlopkh@iol.ie
web: www.menloparkhotel.com
Dir: *at Terryland rdbt off N6 & N84 (Castlebar Rd)*
This hotel's location on the outskirts of the city makes it equally well suited to both tourists and business guests. Bedrooms are spacious, well appointed and offer a choice of standard and executive rooms. The restaurant, bar and lounge are comfortably furnished. Conference facilities and amply car parking is available.
ROOMS: 64 en suite (6 fmly) ⊗ in 10 bedrooms **FACILITIES:** STV ♫ **CONF:** Thtr 350 Class 190 Board 40 **SERVICES:** Lift air con **PARKING:** 100 **NOTES:** ✗ Closed 24-25 Dec

★★★64% Jurys Galway Inn

JURYS DOYLE HOTELS

Quay St
☎ 091 566444 🖷 091 568415
e-mail: enquiry@jurys.com
web: www.jurysdoyle.com
Dir: *N6 follow signs for Docks. At Docks take Salthill Rd*
This modern hotel stands in the heart of the city, opposite the famous Spanish Arch. The hotel has an attractive patio by the river and newly refurbished and popular contemporary bar and restaurant. The room-only rate is ideal for families and budget travellers.
ROOMS: 132 en suite (6 fmly) (12 GF) ⊗ in 111 bedrooms **FACILITIES:** STV **SERVICES:** Lift **NOTES:** ✗ ⊗ in restaurant

★★★61% Brennans Yard

Lower Merchants Rd
☎ 091 568166 🖷 091 568262
e-mail: info@brennansyardhotel.com
This friendly hotel is situated in the city centre close to the shops and business districts. All the bedrooms are individually furnished with antique pine furniture. Terry's restaurant has a wide range of dishes including Japanese dishes on some nights. The Spanish Bar offers an intimate, warm and lively atmosphere.
ROOMS: 45 en suite s €82-€89; d €105-€145 (incl. bkfst) **LB** **FACILITIES:** STV ♫ **SERVICES:** Lift **NOTES:** ✗ ⊗ in restaurant Closed 21-28 Dec

⌂ Travelodge

Travelodge

Tuam Rd
☎ 08700 850 950
web: www.travelodge.co.uk
Travelodge offers good quality, good value, modern accommodation. Ideal for families, the spacious, en suite bedrooms include remote-control TV, tea and coffee-making facilities and comfortable beds. Meals can be taken at the nearby family restaurant. For further details consult the Hotel Groups page.
ROOMS: s fr €26; d fr €26

GARRYVOE, Co Cork

Map 01 C2

★★71% ◎ Garryvoe

IRISH COUNTRY HOTELS

☎ 021 4646718 🖷 021 4646824
e-mail: res@garryvoehotel.com
Dir: *off N25 onto L72 at Castlemartyr (between Midleton & Youghal) then 6km*

A comfortable, family-run hotel with caring staff, the Garryvoe is appointed to a very high standard. It stands in a delightful position facing a sandy beach and the first-floor lounge overlooks the sea. There is a popular bar serving light meals throughout the day.
ROOMS: 48 en suite (6 fmly) ⊗ in 15 bedrooms **FACILITIES:** STV ⚲ Putt green ch fac **CONF:** BC Thtr 300 Class 150 Board 12 **SERVICES:** Lift **PARKING:** 100 **NOTES:** ✗ ⊗ in restaurant Closed 24-25 Dec

Popped the question? Hotels with Civ wed in their entry are licensed for civil wedding ceremonies. Maximum numbers for the ceremony only are shown e.g. Civ wed 120

GLENDALOUGH, Co Wicklow
Map 01 D3

★★★65% *The Glendalough*
☎ 0404 45135 📠 0404 45142
e-mail: info@glendaloughhotel.ie
Dir: *N11 to Kilmacongue, right onto R755, straight on at Caragh then right onto R756*
Mountains and forest provide the setting for this long-established hotel at the edge of the famed monastic site. Many of the well-appointed bedrooms have superb views. Food is served daily in the very popular bar while relaxing dinners are served in the charming restaurant that overlooks the river and forest.
ROOMS: 44 en suite (3 fmly) **FACILITIES:** STV Fishing ♫ **CONF:** Thtr 200 Class 150 Board 50 **SERVICES:** Lift **PARKING:** 100 **NOTES:** Closed Dec-Jan

GOREY, Co Wexford
Map 01 D3

★★★★66% Ashdown Park Hotel
The Coach Rd
☎ 055 80500 📠 055 80777
e-mail: info@ashdownparkhotel.com
Dir: *from N11, on approaching Gorey, 1st left before railway bridge, hotel on left*

Situated on an elevated position overlooking the town, this modern hotel has excellent health, leisure and banqueting facilities. There are comfortable lounges and two dining options - the popular carvery bar and first-floor fine dining restaurant. Bedrooms are spacious and well equipped. Close to golf, beaches and hill walking.
ROOMS: 80 en suite (12 fmly) (20 GF) s €105-€130; d €160-€210 (incl. bkfst) **LB** **FACILITIES:** supervised Sauna Gym Jacuzzi Steam & Therapy rooms, Beauty salon ♫ **CONF:** Thtr 800 Class 315 Board 100 Del €150 **SERVICES:** Lift **PARKING:** 150 **NOTES:** in restaurant

Top Hotel

★★★ *Marlfield House*
☎ 055 21124 📠 055 21572
e-mail: info@marlfieldhouse.ie
Dir: *1.5 hrs S of Dublin off N11, 1m outside Gorey on Courtown Road*
This Regency-style building has been sympathetically extended and developed into an excellent hotel. An atmosphere of elegance and luxury permeates every corner of the house, underpinned by truly friendly yet professional service led by the Bowe family who are always in evidence. The bedrooms are decorated in keeping with the style of the house, with some really spacious rooms and suites on the ground floor. Dinner in the restaurant is always a highlight of a stay at Marlfield.

ROOMS: 20 en suite (3 fmly) (6 GF) in all bedrooms
FACILITIES: STV Sauna **CONF:** Thtr 60 Board 20
PARKING: 50 **NOTES:** in restaurant Closed 15 Dec-30 Jan

GOUGANE BARRA, Co Cork
Map 01 B2

★★68% Gougane Barra
☎ 026 47069 📠 026 47226
e-mail: gouganbarrahotel@tinet.ie
Dir: *off N22*
Picturesquely situated on the shore of Gougane Barra Lake and at the entrance to the National Park this family run hotel offers tranquillity and very good home cooking. Bedrooms and public areas enjoy lovely views. Guests can be met from their train, boat or plane by prior arrangement.
ROOMS: 25 en suite (12 GF) in all bedrooms **FACILITIES:** STV Fishing **PARKING:** 25 **NOTES:** in restaurant Closed 10 Oct-18 Apr

HOWTH, Co Dublin
Map 01 D4

★★★67%
Deer Park Hotel & Golf Courses
☎ 01 8322624 📠 01 8392405
e-mail: sales@deerpark.iol.ie
Dir: *follow coast road from Dublin via Clontarf. Through Sutton Cross pass Offington Park. Hotel 0.5m after traffic lights on right*

This modern hotel is situated in its own parkland golf courses and overlooking Dublin Bay and Ireland's Eye. The spacious well-equipped bedrooms have spectacular views. Four Earls Restaurant is famous for fresh fish from Howth Harbour. There is a lively bar and bistro, a leisure centre, tennis courts and a choice of four golf courses. Convenient to Dublin Airport, ferry port and the DART service to the city centre.
ROOMS: 80 en suite (4 fmly) (36 GF) s €80-€120; d €150-€180 (incl. bkfst) **LB** **FACILITIES: Spa** supervised 36 Sauna Putt green **CONF:** Thtr 95 Class 60 Board 25 Del from €130 **PARKING:** 200 **NOTES:** in restaurant Closed 23-26 Dec

INNISHANNON, Co Cork
Map 01 B2

★★★63% ***Innishannon House***
☎ 021 4775121 📠 021 4775609
e-mail: info@innishannon-hotel.ie
Dir: *off N71 at east end of village, left onto Kinsale road, hotel right approx 1m*
This charming country house was built in 1720 in a beautiful location in lovely gardens that run down to the banks of the River Bandon close to Kinsale. Public areas are comfortable and there is a relaxed atmosphere. Bedrooms range from cosy and charming to large and gracious.
ROOMS: 12 en suite (4 fmly) **FACILITIES:** STV Fishing **CONF:** BC Thtr 200 Class 80 Board 50 **PARKING:** 100 **NOTES:** 🚫🐕 🚭 in restaurant Closed 22-26 Dec

IRVINESTOWN, Co Fermanagh
Map 01 C5

★★63% **Mahons**
Mill St BT94 1GS
☎ 028 6862 1656 & 6862 1657 📠 028 6862 8344
e-mail: info@mahonshotel.co.uk
Dir: *on A32 midway between Enniskillen & Omagh. By clock in town centre*
This lively hotel has been in the same family for over an amazing 137 years. At the last inspection the hotel was undergoing refurbished; the bar retains a wealth of charm and character with other public rooms taking on a more modern style. In the spacious new restaurant the menu offers a wide range of popular dishes. The new wing of bedrooms has very good standards whilst the older rooms come in a variety of sizes and styles.
ROOMS: 24 en suite (10 fmly) (1 GF) 🚭 in 2 bedrooms s £40-£45; d £75-£85 (incl. bkfst) **LB** **FACILITIES:** STV 🎾 Riding Solarium ♫ **CONF:** Thtr 400 Class 250 Board 100 Del from £39.50 **SERVICES:** air con **PARKING:** 40 **NOTES:** Closed 25 Dec

KENMARE, Co Kerry
Map 01 B2

Top Hotel

★★★★ ❀❀❀ ***Sheen Falls Lodge***
☎ 064 41600 📠 064 41386
e-mail: info@sheenfallslodge.ie
Dir: *from Kenmare take N71 to Glengarriff over suspension bridge, take 1st left*
This former fishing lodge has been developed into a beautiful hotel run by a friendly team of expertly managed staff. The cascading Sheen Falls are floodlit at night, forming a romantic backdrop to the enjoyment of award-winning cuisine in La Cascade restaurant. Bedrooms are very comfortably appointed; many of the suites are particularly spacious. The leisure centre and beauty therapy facilities offer a number of exclusive treatments.
ROOMS: 66 en suite (14 fmly) (14 GF) 🚭 in 10 bedrooms **FACILITIES:** STV 🏊 🎾 Fishing Riding Snooker Sauna Solarium Gym Jacuzzi Table tennis, steam room, clay pigeon shooting, cycling, vintage car rides, library ♫ ch fac **CONF:** BC Thtr 120 Class 65 Board 50 **SERVICES:** Lift **PARKING:** 76 **NOTES:** 🚫🐕 🚭 in restaurant Closed 2 Jan-1 Feb RS December

KILKEE, Co Clare
Map 01 B3

★★64% ***Halpin's***
Erin St
☎ 065 9056032 📠 065 9056317
e-mail: halpinstownhouse@iol.ie
Dir: *in centre of town*
The finest tradition of hotel service is offered at this family-run hotel which has a commanding view over the old Victorian town. The attractive bedrooms are comfortable.
ROOMS: 12 en suite (6 fmly) 🚭 in 4 bedrooms **FACILITIES:** STV **CONF:** Thtr 60 Class 36 Board 30 **SERVICES:** air con **PARKING:** 3 **NOTES:** 🚫🐕 Closed 16 Nov-14 Mar

KILKENNY, Co Kilkenny
Map 01 C3

★★★★71% ❀ **Kilkenny River Court Hotel**
The Bridge, John St
☎ 056 772 3388 📠 056 772 3389
e-mail: reservations@kilrivercourt.com
Dir: *at the bridge in town centre, just opposite Kilkenny Castle*
Hidden behind archways on John Street, this is a very comfortable and welcoming establishment. The restaurant, bar and many of the well-equipped bedrooms command great views of Kilkenny Castle and the River Nore. Attentive, friendly staff ensure good service in all areas. Excellent corporate and leisure facilities are provided.
ROOMS: 90 en suite (4 fmly) 🚭 in 20 bedrooms s €75-€155; d €90-€260 (incl. bkfst) **LB** **FACILITIES:** STV 🏊 supervised Sauna Gym Jacuzzi Beauty Salon ♫ Xmas **CONF:** Thtr 260 Class 110 Board 45 Del from €150 **SERVICES:** Lift **PARKING:** 84 **NOTES:** 🚫🐕 🚭 in restaurant Closed 24-26 Dec

★★★75% **Newpark**
☎ 056 776 0500 📠 056 776 0555
e-mail: info@newparkhotel.com
This hotel offers a range of well-appointed rooms, to match the impressive foyer lounge, leisure club and other public areas. Renowned for the friendliness of the staff, there is also a choice of two dining rooms, The Bistro and Gulliver's, the more formal option.
ROOMS: 130 en suite (36 fmly) 🚭 in 20 bedrooms s €130-€180; d €160-€220 (incl. bkfst) **LB** **FACILITIES:** STV 🏊 supervised Sauna Solarium Gym Jacuzzi Plunge pool ♫ Xmas **CONF:** Thtr 600 Class 300 Board 50 Del from €175 **SERVICES:** Lift **PARKING:** 350 **NOTES:** 🚫🐕 🚭 in restaurant

★★★65% **Langtons**
69 John St
☎ 056 776 5133 552 1728 📠 056 776 3693
e-mail: reservations@langtons.ie
Dir: *take N9 & N10 from Dublin follow signs for city centre at outskirts of Kilkenny turn to left Langtons 500mtrs on left after 1st set of lights*
Langton's has a long and well-founded reputation as an entertainment venue and bar. These facilities are complemented

continued on p844

KILKENNY, continued

by a range of accommodation, including some in the garden. All are very comfortably decorated and well appointed. The busy restaurant is popular with visitors and locals alike.
ROOMS: 14 en suite 16 annexe en suite (4 fmly) (8 GF) s €50-€90; d €90-€200 (incl. bkfst) **LB** **FACILITIES:** STV ♫ Xmas **CONF:** Thtr 600 Class 250 Board 50 **PARKING:** 60 **NOTES:** ✗ ⊘ in restaurant Closed Good Fri, 25 Dec

Restaurant with Rooms

Lacken House & Restaurant
Dublin Rd
☎ 056 7761085 📠 056 7762435
e-mail: info@lackenhouse.ie
Dir: *in city at start of N10 (Dublin-Carlow road)*

Located just five minutes' walk from Kilkenny City, this fine Victorian house offers comfortable accommodation in a friendly and relaxing atmosphere. The restaurant, open from Tuesday to Saturday, has an interesting menu using carefully chosen local produce. An ideal base to explore the historic sites of Kilkenny, and Mount Juliet Golf course is nearby.
ROOMS: 10 en suite (2 fmly) (4 GF) ⊘ in all bedrooms s €95-€125; d €180-€190 (incl. bkfst) **LB** **FACILITIES:** **Spa** STV **CONF:** Thtr 25 Class 20 Board 12 **PARKING:** 25 **NOTES:** ✗ ⊘ in restaurant Closed 24-26 Dec Civ Wed 40

U The Kilkenny Inn Hotel
15/15 Vicar St
☎ 056 7772828 📠 056 7761902
e-mail: info@kilkennyinn.com
Dir: *take N7/N9 from Dublin. From Rosslare take N25 to Waterford and N9 to Kilkenny*
At the time of going to press, the star classification for this hotel was not confirmed. Please refer to the AA internet site www.theAA.com for current information.
ROOMS: 30 en suite (4 fmly) ⊘ in 2 bedrooms s €40-€75; d €65-€120 (incl. bkfst) **LB** **FACILITIES:** STV ♫ Xmas **CONF:** Thtr 35 Class 25 Board 25 **SERVICES:** Lift **PARKING:** 27 **NOTES:** ✗ ⊘ in restaurant

KILL, Co Kildare — Map 01 D4

★★★59% Ambassador
☎ 045 877064 📠 045 877515
e-mail: reservations@ambassadorhotelkildare.com
Dir: *close to town centre on N7 to S and SW*
Situated south of Kill, close to Goff's Sales Complex, Mondello Park and several racecourses. A grill menu is available daily in the lounge and the Diplomat Restaurant is open Wed/Sun. Bedrooms are well equipped and comfortable, and there are conference and syndicate rooms.
ROOMS: 36 en suite (36 fmly) s €70-€150; d €125-€150 (incl. bkfst) **LB** **FACILITIES:** STV ♫ Xmas **CONF:** Thtr 350 Class 200 Board 60 **PARKING:** 150 **NOTES:** ✗ ⊘ in restaurant

KILLALOE, Co Clare — Map 01 B3

U *Kincora Hall Hotel*
☎ 061 376000 📠 061 376665
e-mail: info@kincorahall.com
IRISH COUNTRY HOTELS
At the time of going to press, the star classification for this hotel was not confirmed. Please refer to the AA internet site www.theAA.com for current information.
ROOMS: 30 en suite

KILLARNEY, Co Kerry — Map 01 B2

Top Hotel

★★★★★ ⊛ Aghadoe Heights
☎ 064 31766 📠 064 31345
e-mail: info@aghadoeheights.com
Dir: *16km S of Kerry Airport. 5km N of Killarney. Signed off N22*
The exterior of this superbly positioned hotel belies the opulence within. Overlooking Loch Lein with spectacular views of Killarney's lakes and mountains, Aghadoe Heights is appointed to the very highest standard. Friendly staff display a genuine willingness to make everyone's stay special so that happy memories are assured. Many of the bedrooms have sun decks that make the most of the panoramic scenery, and the Penthouse Suite is truly stunning. A state-of-the-art health spa has now been added.
ROOMS: 73 en suite (6 fmly) ⊘ in 10 bedrooms s €200-€280; d €230-€350 (incl. bkfst) **LB** **FACILITIES:** **Spa** STV Fishing Sauna Solarium Gym Jacuzzi The Heights spa, treatment rooms, thermal suites ♫ ch fac Xmas **CONF:** BC Thtr 120 Class 60 Board 40 **SERVICES:** Lift **PARKING:** 120 **NOTES:** ✗ ⊘ in restaurant Closed Jan-1 Mar

See advert on page 843

Top Hotel

★★★★ ⊛⊛ Killarney Park
☎ 064 35555 📠 064 35266
e-mail: info@killarneyparkhotel.ie
Dir: *N22 from Cork to Killarney. At 1st rdbt take 1st exit to town centre at 2nd rdbt take 2nd exit, 3rd rdbt take 1st exit. Hotel 2nd entrance left*
This charming hotel on the edge of the town combines elegance with comfort. It has a warm atmosphere with open fires, restful colours and friendly caring staff who ensure your

continued

stay is an enjoyable one. Bedrooms and suites are spacious and many have air conditioning and open fires. A health spa is included in the leisure facilities.

ROOMS: 72 en suite (4 fmly) ⊗ in all bedrooms s €260-€385; d €260-€385 (incl. bkfst) **LB FACILITIES: Spa** STV ⊠ supervised Snooker Sauna Gym Jacuzzi Outdoor Canadian hot-tub Plunge pool, Caldarium, Relaxation room, Bubble pool Xmas **CONF:** BC Thtr 150 Class 70 Board 35 **SERVICES:** Lift air con **PARKING:** 70 **NOTES:** ✖ ⊗ in restaurant Closed 24-26 Dec

★★★★74% Great Southern
☎ 064 38000 ▤ 064 35300
e-mail: res@killarney-gsh.com
Dating from 1854 as a railway hotel, this fine property has undergone a major refurbishment in recent years. Bedrooms vary in style and are well equipped and comfortable. Public areas are elegant, particularly the Garden room where breakfast is served. There is a choice of two restaurants for dinner, with more casual dining in the lounge and bar.
ROOMS: 171 en suite (35 fmly) **FACILITIES:** STV ⊠ ℚ Sauna Gym jacuzzi plunge pool steam room **CONF:** Thtr 1000 Class 700 Board 40 **SERVICES:** Lift **PARKING:** 200 **NOTES:** Closed 6 Jan-20 Feb

★★★★72% ◉◉ Cahernane House
Muckross Rd
☎ 064 31895 ▤ 064 34340
e-mail: cahernane@eircom.net
web: www.cahernane.com
Dir: On N22 to Killarney, take 1st exit off rdbt then left at church and 1st exit at next rdbt leading to Muckross Road

This fine country mansion, former home of the Earls of Pembroke, has a magnificent mountain backdrop and panoramic views from its lakeside setting. Elegant period furniture is complemented by more modern pieces to create a comfortable hotel offering a warm atmosphere with friendly staff.
ROOMS: 12 en suite 26 annexe en suite **FACILITIES:** ℚ Fishing ⏍ ch fac **CONF:** Thtr 15 Class 10 Board 10 **SERVICES:** Lift air con **PARKING:** 50 **NOTES:** ✖ ⊗ in restaurant Closed 21 Dec-31 Jan

★★★★72% Randles Court
Muckross Rd
☎ 064 35333 ▤ 064 35206
e-mail: info@randlescourt.com
Dir: N22 towards Muckross, turn tight at t-junct on right. From N72 take 3rd exit on 1st rdbt into town & follow signs for Muckross, hotel on left
Close to all the town's attractions, this is a friendly family-run hotel with an emphasis on customer care. Bedrooms are particularly comfortable. Checkers is the chic bistro restaurant where good food is served in the evenings, perhaps following a relaxing drink in the cosy bar. A swimming pool and other leisure facilities are also available.
ROOMS: 52 en suite **FACILITIES:** STV ⊠ Sauna Gym Putt green **CONF:** Thtr 80 Class 60 Board 40 **SERVICES:** Lift **PARKING:** 39 **NOTES:** Closed 23-27 Dec

★★★★69% Muckross Park Hotel
Muckross Village
☎ 064 31938 ▤ 064 31965
e-mail: info@muckrosspark.com
Dir: from Killarney take road to Kenmare, hotel 4km on left, adjacent to National Park, Muckross House & Gardens
Offering hospitality since 1795, this comfortable hotel is located a few kilometres from the centre of the town amid well-tended gardens. Spacious bedrooms are individually designed. Informal dining is available in the popular Molly Drake's pub throughout the day, with dinner served in GB Shaw's Restaurant.
ROOMS: 108 en suite (40 fmly) (12 GF) ⊗ in 23 bedrooms s €85-€150; d €170-€300 (incl. bkfst) **LB FACILITIES: Spa** STV Sauna Solarium Gym Jacuzzi Treatment rooms ♫ Xmas **CONF:** BC Thtr 450 Class 250 Board 200 Del from €150 **SERVICES:** Lift **PARKING:** 250 **NOTES:** ✖ ⊗ in restaurant Mar-Nov Civ Wed 300

★★★70% Gleneagle
Muckeoss Rd
☎ 064 36000 ▤ 064 32646
e-mail: info@gleneaglehotel.com
Dir: 1m outside Killarney town on N71 Kenmare road

The facilities at this large hotel are excellent and numerous. Family entertainment is a strong element of the Gleneagle experience, popular with the Irish market for almost 50 years. Comfortable rooms are matched with a range lounges, restaurants a leisure centre and INEC, one of Ireland's largest events centres.
ROOMS: 250 en suite (57 fmly) ⊗ in 20 bedrooms s €100-€180; d €150-€270 (incl. bkfst) **LB FACILITIES:** STV ⊠ supervised ℚ Squash Snooker Sauna Gym Jacuzzi Pitch & Putt Steam room Games room ♫ Xmas **CONF:** Thtr 2500 Class 1000 Board 50 Del from €70 **SERVICES:** Lift **PARKING:** 500 **NOTES:** ✖ ⊗ in restaurant

K

> **Early start?**
> Hotels at all star levels should provide in-room alarm clocks and/or alarm clocks

KILLARNEY, continued

★★★70% Lake
Muckross Rd
☎ 064 31035 📠 064 31902
e-mail: info@lakehotel.com
Dir: *on Kenmare road out of Killarney*
Set on Killarney's lakeshore this family-run hotel offers a relaxed and friendly atmosphere with views of the mountains, a former mansion it is approached by a wooded drive. Bedrooms are well appointed some with a balcony, four-poster bed and a jacuzzi. The comfortable lounges and bar have open log fires and guests can enjoy the stunning views from the attractive restaurant. The new leisure centre includes a hot tub.
ROOMS: 109 rms (105 en suite) (6 fmly) (13 GF) s €45-€360; d €90-€360 (incl. bkfst) **LB** **FACILITIES: Spa** STV Fishing Sauna Gym Jacuzzi Out door hot tub Residents Library **CONF:** BC Thtr 80 Class 60 Board 40 Del from €105 **SERVICES:** Lift air con **PARKING:** 140 **NOTES:** in restaurant Closed 18 Dec-18 Jan Civ Wed 50

See advert on opposite page

★★★69% *Castlerosse*
☎ 064 31144 📠 064 31031
e-mail: castler@iol.ie
Dir: *from Killarney town take R562 for Killorglin and The Ring of Kerry, hotel 1.5km from town on left*
A lovely location on 6,000 acres of land overlooking Lough Leane. Bedrooms are well appointed and comfortable. The restaurant enjoys panoramic views from its elevated position. Golf available on site, together with a leisure centre.
ROOMS: 121 en suite (27 fmly) in 4 bedrooms **FACILITIES:** supervised 9 Sauna Gym Jacuzzi Golfing & riding arranged **CONF:** Thtr 200 Class 100 Board 40 **SERVICES:** Lift **PARKING:** 100 **NOTES:** in restaurant Closed Dec-Feb

★★★69% *International*
East Avenue Rd
☎ 064 31816 📠 064 31837
e-mail: inter@iol.ie
Dir: *N21 from Limerick to Farranfore, then N22 to Killarney, right at 1st rdbt into Killarney follow town bypass road to hotel*
Quality bedrooms with modern comforts are on offer at this warm and friendly hotel in the heart of the town. Hannigan's bar and brasserie serves food throughout the day, with an inviting mahogany-panelled room open in the evenings. Relaxing lounge areas include a snooker room and a library.
ROOMS: 80 en suite (6 fmly) in 30 bedrooms **FACILITIES:** STV Billiards ch fac **CONF:** Thtr 200 Class 100 Board 25 **SERVICES:** Lift **NOTES:** in restaurant Closed 23-27 Dec

★★★68% Arbutus
College St
☎ 064 31037 📠 064 34033
e-mail: stay@arbutuskillarney.com
Situated in the centre of Killarney this smart hotel has been run by the Buckley family since 1926. Public areas include a comfortable foyer lounge, guest sitting room, traditional-style bar and restaurant. Staff are friendly and helpful. Many of the comfortable bedrooms are air conditioned.

continued

ROOMS: 35 en suite (4 fmly) in 25 bedrooms s €70-€160; d €130-€210 (incl. bkfst) **LB** **FACILITIES:** STV **SERVICES:** Lift **NOTES:** in restaurant Closed 12 Dec-30 Jan

See advert on opposite page

★★★66% *Killarney Royal*
College St
☎ 064 31853 📠 064 34001
e-mail: royalhot@iol.ie
Dir: *in town centre off N22*
This charming hotel is situated in the heart of Killarney and has been run by the Scally family for three generations. Bedrooms and junior suites are individually decorated with antique furniture and many thoughtful extras. Comfortable public areas include a lounge, spacious restaurant and a cosy bar.
ROOMS: 29 en suite (4 fmly) in 5 bedrooms **FACILITIES:** STV Treatment room with massage and reflexology **CONF:** BC Thtr 50 Class 30 Board 15 **SERVICES:** Lift air con **NOTES:** in restaurant Closed 23-27 Dec

★★★64% White Gates
Muckross Rd
☎ 064 31164 📠 064 34850
e-mail: whitegates@iol.ie
Dir: *1km from Killarney town on Muckross road on left*
One's eye is drawn to this hotel with its ochre and blue painted frontage. The same flair for colour is in evidence throughout the interior where bedrooms of mixed sizes are well decorated and very comfortable. There is also a light filled restaurant, with casual dining in the bar, which has a popular local trade.
ROOMS: 27 en suite (4 fmly) (4 GF) s €65-€90; d €120-€170 (incl. bkfst) **LB** **FACILITIES:** STV **CONF:** Class 50 **PARKING:** 50 **NOTES:** Closed 25-26Dec

★★★59% *Scotts Garden Hotel*
College St
☎ 064 31060 📠 064 36656
e-mail: scottskill@eircom.net
Dir: *N20, N22 to town, at Friary turn left. 500mtrs on East Avenue Rd to car park entrance*

Located in the town centre, this hotel offers pleasant bedrooms, a

continued

bar and a patio garden. Special concessions are available at the sister Gleneagles Hotel's leisure facilities.
ROOMS: 52 en suite (4 fmly) **FACILITIES:** ♫ **SERVICES:** Lift
PARKING: 60 **NOTES:** ✗ ⊘ in restaurant Closed 24-25 Dec

U The Brehon

Muckross Rd
☎ 064 30700 🖷 064 30701
e-mail: info@thebrehon.com
Dir: *1m outside Killarney on N71 Kenamre Road.*
At the time of going to press, the star classification for this hotel was not confirmed. Please refer to the AA internet site www.theAA.com for current information.

ROOMS: 125 en suite (3 fmly) ⊘ in all bedrooms s €160-€240; d €190-€290 (incl. bkfst) **LB** **FACILITIES: Spa** STV supervised Sauna Gym Putt green Jacuzzi Thai Spa inc treatments and massages. Xmas **CONF:** BC Thtr 250 Class 120 Board 60 **SERVICES:** Lift air con
PARKING: 126 **NOTES:** ✗ ⊘ in restaurant

KILLINEY, Co Dublin — Map 01 D4

★★★★69% Fitzpatrick Castle

☎ 01 2305400 🖷 01 2305430
e-mail: reservations@fitzpatricks.com
Dir: *from Dun Laoghaire port turn left, on coast road right at lights, left at next lights. Follow to Dalkey , right at McDonaghs pub, immediate left, up hill, hotel at top*
This family owned 18th-century castle has comfortable bedrooms in the modern wing and many enjoying stunning views over Dublin Bay. Facilities include a large lounge, excellent leisure centre and a choice of restaurants. A range of conference and banqueting rooms is also available.
ROOMS: 113 en suite (36 fmly) ⊘ in 50 bedrooms s €120-€180; d €140-€230 **LB** **FACILITIES:** STV supervised Sauna Solarium Gym Jacuzzi Beauty/hairdressing salon, Steam room ♫ Xmas **CONF:** BC Thtr 500 Class 250 Board 80 Del from €216 **SERVICES:** Lift **PARKING:** 300
NOTES: ✗ ⊘ in restaurant RS 25 Dec

KILMESSAN, Co Meath — Map 01 C/D4

★★★65% The Station House Hotel

☎ 046 9025239 🖷 046 9025588
e-mail: info@thestationhousehotel.com
Dir: *M50, N3 towards Navan. At Dunshaughlin turn left at end of village, follow signs*
The Station House saw its last train in 1963, and is now a comfortable, family-run hotel with a popular restaurant. The Carriage House was refurbished and bedrooms added; the Signal Box houses a suite. There is a sun terrace and conference/ banqueting suite.
ROOMS: 6 en suite 14 annexe en suite (3 fmly) (5 GF) ⊘ in 15 bedrooms s €85-€150; d €130-€260 (incl. bkfst) **LB** **FACILITIES:** ♫ Xmas **CONF:** BC Thtr 400 Class 300 Board 100 Del from €134.90
PARKING: 200 **NOTES:** ✗ ⊘ in restaurant

KILTIMAGH, Co Mayo Map 01 B4

★★★64% *Cill Aodain*
Main St
☎ 094 938 1761 🖷 094 938 1838
e-mail: cillaodain@eircom.net
Dir: *in town centre*
Situated in the heart of historic Kiltimagh, this hotel has been completely refurbished in a smart contemporary style and offers comfortable well-appointed bedrooms. Public areas include The Gallery Restaurant, Court piano bar & Bistro. Easy on and off street parking is available opposite the hotel. Close to Knock Shrine and Airport.
ROOMS: 19 en suite (4 fmly) ⊗ in 4 bedrooms **FACILITIES:** STV Riding **NOTES:** ✗

KINGSCOURT, Co Cavan Map 01 C4

★★★65% Cabra Castle Hotel
☎ 042 9667030
Rebuilt in 1808, the castle stands in 100 acres of parkland with a 9-hole golf course and is surrounded by Dun a Ri Forest Park. In addition to the bedrooms in 'The Old House' there are spacious courtyard rooms in what was formerly a granary that dates back to 1750. The main reception rooms are inviting and there is a relaxing bar, sun terrace, restaurant and banqueting faciltities.
ROOMS: 20 en suite 46 annexe en suite (5 fmly) **FACILITIES:** ⛳ 9 Riding ♫ **CONF:** Thtr 300 Class 100 Board 50 **PARKING:** 200 **NOTES:** ⊗ in restaurant Closed 25-27 Dec

K

KINSALE, Co Cork Map 01 B2

★★★73% ⊛ Actons
Pier Rd
☎ 021 4772135 🖷 021 4772231
e-mail: information@actonshotelkinsale.com
Dir: *in town centre facing harbour, 500yds from Yacht Club Marina*

Located on a site overlooking the harbour, Actons is a well established hotel with a good reputation for its friendly and courteous staff. Bedrooms are well appointed and many of them enjoy sea views, as does the restaurant where enjoyable dinners are served. The adjoining leisure centre is well equipped.
ROOMS: 76 en suite (20 fmly) s €65-€115; d €70-€140 (incl. bkfst) **LB** **FACILITIES: Spa** STV ⛆ supervised Sauna Solarium Gym Jacuzzi Aerobics studio, Outdoor hot tub, Steam room ♫ **CONF:** Thtr 300 Class 200 Board 100 Del from €95 **SERVICES:** Lift **PARKING:** 70 **NOTES:** ✗ ⊗ in restaurant Closed 24-27 Dec - Jan

GF indicates the number of bedrooms at ground level

★★★71% ⊛ *Trident*
Worlds End
☎ 021 4779300 🖷 021 4774173
e-mail: info@tridenthotel.com
Dir: *R600 from Cork to Kinsale, along Kinsale waterfront, hotel beyond pier*

Located at the harbour's edge, the Trident Hotel has its own marina with boats for hire. Many of the bedrooms have superb views and two have balconies. The restaurant and lounge both overlook the harbour and pleasant staff provide hospitable service.
ROOMS: 75 en suite (2 fmly) **FACILITIES:** Sauna Gym Jacuzzi Steam room, Deep sea angling **CONF:** Thtr 220 Class 130 Board 40 **SERVICES:** Lift **PARKING:** 60 **NOTES:** ✗ Closed 24-26 Dec

★★★67% *Blue Haven Hotel & Restaurant*
3 Pearse St
☎ 021 4772209 🖷 021 4774268
e-mail: bluhaven@iol.ie
Dir: *town centre*
In the heart of this historic town, the Blue Haven has been completely refurbished. Public areas include a welcoming lobby lounge, elegant restaurant, a lively and atmospheric bar with an open deck area and the trendy Café Blue coffee/wine bar. Bedrooms vary in size and are furnished to a high standard.
ROOMS: 17 en suite (2 fmly) ⊗ in all bedrooms **FACILITIES:** ♫ ch fac **CONF:** Thtr 50 Class 35 Board 25 **NOTES:** ✗ ⊗ in restaurant

KNOCK, Co Mayo Map 01 B4

★★★66% Knock House
Ballyhaunis Rd
☎ 094 938 8088 🖷 094 938 8044
e-mail: info@knockhousehotel.ie
Dir: *0.5km from Knock village*
Adjacent to the Marian Shrine and Basilica, this creatively designed limestone-clad building is surrounded by landscaped gardens. Facilities include comfortable lounges and bedrooms, a dispense bar, conference rooms and an attractive restaurant where lunch and dinner is served. There are six rooms adapted to facilitate wheelchair users.
ROOMS: 68 en suite (12 fmly) (40 GF) s €72-€90; d €106-€140 (incl. bkfst) **LB** **FACILITIES:** Xmas **CONF:** Thtr 150 Class 90 Board 45 **SERVICES:** Lift **PARKING:** 150 **NOTES:** ✗ ⊗ in restaurant

★★★63% Belmont
☎ 094 094 938 8122 🖷 094 938 8532
e-mail: reception@belmonthotel.ie
Dir: *on N17, Galway side of Knock. Turn right at Burke's supermarket & pub. Hotel 150yds on right*
This hotel has an Old World charm and offers lounges, a traditional bar and An Bialann Restaurant. Bedroom standards vary, all are well appointed and comfortable and there are specially adapted room for the less able. A natural health and

continued

fitness club offers a range of therapies. The hotel is close to the Marian Shrine and the Basilica.

ROOMS: 63 en suite (6 fmly) (12 GF) ⊗ in 13 bedrooms s €40-€70; d €70-€130 (incl. bkfst) **LB** **FACILITIES:** Solarium Gym Jacuzzi Steamroom Natural health therapies, hydrotherapic bath ♫ Xmas **CONF:** Thtr 500 Class 100 Board 20 **SERVICES:** Lift **PARKING:** 110 **NOTES:** ✈ ⊗ in restaurant

LEIXLIP, Co Kildare — Map 01 D4

★★★75% ❁ Leixlip House

Captains Hill
☎ 01 6242268 📠 01 6244177
e-mail: info@leixliphouse.com
Dir: *from Leixlip motorway junct continue into village. Turn right at lights and continue up hill*

This Georgian house dates back to 1772 and retains many of its original features. Overlooking Leixlip, the hotel is just eight miles from Dublin city centre. Bedrooms and public areas are furnished and decorated to a high standard. The Bradaun Restaurant offers a wide range of interesting dishes.

ROOMS: 19 en suite (2 fmly) s €140-€170; d €170-€200 (incl. bkfst) **LB** **FACILITIES:** STV **CONF:** Thtr 130 Class 60 Board 40 Del from €145 **PARKING:** 64 **NOTES:** ✈ ⊗ in restaurant

LIMAVADY, Co Londonderry — Map 01 C6

★★★★70% ❁ Radisson SAS Row Park Resort

BT49 9LB
☎ 028 7772 2222 📠 028 7772 2313
e-mail: reservations@radissonroepark.com
web: www.radisson.com
Dir: *on A2 Londonderry/Limavady road, 1m from Limavady*

This impressive, popular hotel sits centrally within its own modern golf resort. The spacious, modern bedrooms are well equipped and many have excellent views of the fairways and surrounding estate. The Greens Restaurant provides a refreshing dining experience and the Coach House brasserie offers a lighter menu. Leisure options are extensive.

ROOMS: 118 en suite (15 fmly) (37 GF) ⊗ in 76 bedrooms s £72.50-£82.50; d £95-£115 (incl. bkfst) **LB** **FACILITIES:** STV supervised ⛳ 18 Fishing Sauna Solarium Gym Putt green Jacuzzi Floodlit driving range, Outside tees, Golf training academy, Bicycle hire ♫ Xmas **CONF:** BC Thtr 450 Class 190 Board 140 Del from £115 **SERVICES:** Lift **PARKING:** 300 **NOTES:** ✈ Civ Wed 300

> We have indicated only the hotels that don't accept credit or debit cards

★★★68% Gorteen House

Deerpark, Roemill Rd BT49 9EX
☎ 028 7772 2333 📠 028 7772 2333
e-mail: info@gorteen.com
Dir: *A2 Londonderry/Coleraine. 12m from Coleraine. 0.5m from town centre on Ballyquinn road*

Situated on the outskirts of the town and popular as a function venue, this 18th-century country house has been converted and extended to provide pleasant public areas and a modern wing of bedrooms. The spacious restaurant enjoys a good local reputation for its portion sizes and value for money.

ROOMS: 26 en suite (2 fmly) (5 GF) **FACILITIES:** Snooker ♫ **CONF:** Thtr 350 Class 250 Board 100 **PARKING:** 250 **NOTES:** ✈

LIMERICK, Co Limerick — Map 01 B3

★★★★70% ❁ Castletroy Park

Dublin Rd
☎ 061 335566 📠 061 331117
e-mail: sales@castletroy-park.ie
Dir: *on N7(Dublin road), 3m from Limerick city, (25mins from Shannon Airport)*

This fine modern hotel is close to the University of Limerick. Public areas combine modern comforts with very attractive decor and include the Merry Pedler pub and the fine dining McLaughlins Restaurant, which has a splendid view of the gardens and Clare Hills. Bedrooms are very well equipped to suit both leisure and business guests. There are extensive leisure and banqueting facilities.

ROOMS: 107 en suite (78 fmly) ⊗ in 79 bedrooms s €145-€215; d €170-€250 (incl. bkfst) **LB** **FACILITIES:** STV supervised Sauna Gym Jacuzzi Running track Steam room ♫ **CONF:** BC Thtr 450 Class 270 Board 100 Del from €170 **SERVICES:** Lift **PARKING:** 160 **NOTES:** ✈ ⊗ in restaurant

★★★★69% ❁ Radisson SAS

Ennis Rd
☎ 061 326666 📠 061 327418
e-mail: reservations.limerick@radissonsas.com
Dir: *on N18 (Ennis Road), 5 mins from city centre, 15 mins from Shannon Airport*

Situated between Limerick and Shannon International Airport this smart hotel has comfortable lounge areas and a choice of dining options; the contemporary styled Porters Restaurant offers fine dining, while more casual eating can be enjoyed in Heron's Irish Pub. Bedrooms are spacious and very well appointed. There is extensive leisure and corporate facilities.

ROOMS: 154 en suite (7 fmly) ⊗ in 70 bedrooms s €115-€150; d €130-€180 (incl. bkfst) **FACILITIES: Spa** STV supervised Sauna Solarium Gym ♫ Xmas **CONF:** BC Thtr 500 Class 250 Board 50 Del from €150 **SERVICES:** Lift **PARKING:** 300 **NOTES:** ✈ ⊗ in restaurant

★★★★67% Clarion Hotel Limerick

Steamboat Quay
☎ 061 444100 📠 061 444101
e-mail: info@clarionhotellimerick.com
Dir: *From Shannon Airport take N18 W to city, follow Cork/Kerry exit on 1st rdbt. Over Shannon Bridge then 3rd exit onto Dock Rd. Hotel 1st right*

The Clarion makes an imposing silhouette on Limerick's skyline, with its height and oval shape. The same sleek design is to be found throughout this hotel, with contemporary styling in the bedrooms and public areas alike. Rooms vary in size and are all well appointed. Some two-bedded apartments are available for those staying longer than a few nights.

ROOMS: 123 en suite (14 fmly) ⊗ in 97 bedrooms **FACILITIES:** STV supervised Sauna Gym Jacuzzi Steam room **CONF:** Thtr 120 Class 70 Board 45 **SERVICES:** Lift air con **NOTES:** ✈ ⊗ in restaurant Closed 24-25 Dec RS 26-Dec

L

LIMERICK, continued

★★★65% ***Hotel Greenhills***
Caherdavin
☎ 061 453033 📠 061 453307
e-mail: info@greenhillgroup.com
Dir: *on N18, approx 2m from city centre*
Situated on the outskirts of Limerick and set amongst its own landscaped grounds, the hotel is only a short drive from Shannon International Airport. Bedrooms are attractively decorated and well appointed. There is a traditional-style bar and comfortable lounge, a restaurant and impressive leisure and conference facilities.
ROOMS: 18 rms (13 en suite) (4 fmly) **FACILITIES:** STV Sauna Solarium Gym Jacuzzi Beauty parlour Massage ♫ **CONF:** Thtr 500 Class 200 Board 50 **PARKING:** 150 **NOTES:**

★★★63% **Jurys Inn Limerick**
Lower Mallow St
JURYS DOYLE HOTELS
☎ 061 207000 📠 061 400966
e-mail: info@jurysdoyle.com
web: www.jurysdoyle.com
Dir: *from N7 follow signs for City Centre into O'Connell St, turn off at N18 (Shannon/Galway), hotel is off O'Connell St*
Conveniently situated in the shopping and business area overlooking the River Shannon this modern hotel has a spacious lobby, cosy bar, restaurant and boardroom for meetings. The 'one price' room rate and comfortable bedrooms ensure its popularity.
ROOMS: 151 en suite (108 fmly) (10 GF) ⊗ in 123 bedrooms s €55-€85; d €55-€85 **FACILITIES:** STV **CONF:** Thtr 50 Class 25 Board 18 **SERVICES:** Lift **NOTES:** ⊗ in restaurant Closed 24-26 Dec

★★★63% ***Woodfield House***
Ennis Rd
☎ 061 453022 📠 061 326755
e-mail: woodfieldhousehotel@eircom.net
Dir: *on outskirts of city on main Shannon road*
This intimate, family-run hotel is situated on the N18 a short distance from the city centre and within easy reach of Shannon Airport. The smart bedrooms are comfortable and well-appointed. Public areas include a cosy traditional-style, bar, a patio beer garden and an attractive bistro.
ROOMS: 26 en suite (3 fmly) (5 GF) **FACILITIES:** STV **CONF:** BC Thtr 130 Class 60 Board 60 **SERVICES:** air con **PARKING:** 80 **NOTES:** Closed 24-25 Dec Civ Wed

Restaurant with Rooms

Sunville Country House & Restaurant
Pallasgreen
☎ 061 384822 086 2576363 📠 061 384823
e-mail: enquiries@sunvillehouse.com
Dir: *From N24 (Limerick-Tipperary/Waterford road) turn off at sign for Pallasgreen. 1km and hotel signed*
Situated on four acres of gardens and woodland, this elegant Georgian House has been lovingly restored. Bedrooms are individually decorated and some feature four-poster beds. There is an intimate drawing room, a library and a dining room. The dinner menu includes local produce and organic vegetables from the walled garden in season. There is a conference room on the lower ground floor.
ROOMS: 6 en suite ⊗ in all bedrooms **FACILITIES:** Riding Jacuzzi ch fac **CONF:** BC Thtr 30 Class 18 Board 16 **PARKING:** 40 **NOTES:** ⊗ in restaurant

U Star rating not confirmed

LISDOONVARNA, Co Clare Map 01 B3

★★★67% ***Sheedys Country House***
MANOR HOUSE HOTELS
☎ 065 7074026 📠 065 7074555
e-mail: enquiries@sheedyscountryhouse.com
Dir: *200mtrs from The Square*
Dating in part from the 17th century and set in an unrivalled location on the edge of the Burren, this house is full of character and has an intimate atmosphere. Fine cuisine can be enjoyed in the contemporary restaurant. Bedrooms are spacious and well appointed. An ideal base for touring – close to Lahinch golf course, Doolin and the Cliffs of Moher.
ROOMS: 11 en suite (1 fmly) (5 GF) ⊗ in all bedrooms **PARKING:** 40 **NOTES:** ⊗ in restaurant Closed mid Oct-mid Mar

Restaurant with Rooms

Kincora Country House & Gallery Restaurant
☎ 065 7074300 📠 065 7074490
e-mail: kincorahotel@eircom.net
Dir: *from town centre take Doolin Rd. 200mtrs to house at 1st T-junct*
Family owned and run Kincora House has very comfortable bedrooms all with views of the garden or countryside beyond. The restaurant (which is also an art gallery) offers fine Irish cuisine.
ROOMS: 14 en suite (3 GF) ⊗ in all bedrooms **FACILITIES:** STV Art gallery **PARKING:** 15 **NOTES:** No children 10yrs ⊗ in restaurant Closed Nov-Feb

LISMORE, Co Waterford Map 01 C2

★★66% ***Ballyrafter House***
☎ 058 54002 📠 058 53050
Dir: *1km from Lismore opposite Lismore Castle*
A welcoming country house, set in its own grounds opposite Lismore Castle. Inside, most of the bedrooms are pleasantly furnished in pine. The bar and conservatory are where guests, anglers and locals meet to discuss the day's events. The hotel has its own salmon fishing on the River Blackwater.
ROOMS: 10 en suite (1 fmly) **FACILITIES:** Fishing Riding Putt green **PARKING:** 20 **NOTES:** Closed Nov-Feb

LONDONDERRY, Co Londonderry Map 01 C5

★★★★70% **Tower Hotel Derry**
The Diamond, Butcher St BT48 6HL
☎ 028 7137 1000 📠 028 7137 1234
e-mail: info@thg.ie
web: www.towerhotelderry.com
Dir: *from Craigavon Bridge into city centre. Take 2nd exit at end of bridge into Carlisle Rd then Ferryquay St. Hotel straight ahead*
This stylish hotel is popular with tourists and corporate guests alike. Modern bedrooms are furnished with flair and style and those on the upper floors enjoy superb views of the city. Minimalist day rooms include a bistro, and staff in the contemporary bar provide true Irish hospitality.
ROOMS: 93 en suite (26 fmly) ⊗ in 12 bedrooms s £57.50-£60; d £65-£110 (incl. bkfst) **LB** **FACILITIES:** STV Sauna Gym ♫ Xmas **CONF:** BC Thtr 250 Class 150 Board 50 Del from £85 **SERVICES:** Lift **PARKING:** 25 **NOTES:** Closed 24-27 Dec Civ Wed 300

★★★★64% **City Hotel**
Queens Quay BT48 7AS
☎ 028 7136 5800 📠 028 7136 5801
e-mail: res@derry-gsh.com
Dir: *Follow city centre signs. Hotel on waterfront adjacent to the Guildhall*
Occupying a central position overlooking the River Foyle, this stylish, contemporary hotel will appeal to both business and

continued

leisure guests alike. All bedrooms have excellent facilities including internet access, and the executive rooms prove a particularly good working environment. The open-plan ground floor area encourages relaxation, with the restaurant providing modern cuisine. Meeting and function facilities are extensive and there are good leisure facilities.
ROOMS: 145 en suite (16 fmly) in 112 bedrooms s £67.50-£140; d £90-£140 (incl. bkfst) **LB FACILITIES:** supervised Gym Jacuzzi Steam Room, Massage and Beauty Treatments Xmas **CONF:** BC Thtr 350 Class 150 Board 80 Del from £115 **SERVICES:** Lift air con **PARKING:** 48 **NOTES:** Closed 25 Dec Civ Wed 350

★★★73%
Beech Hill Country House Hotel
32 Ardmore Rd BT47 3QP
☎ 028 7134 9279 028 7134 5366
e-mail: info@beech-hill.com web: www.beech-hill.com
Dir: *from A6 (Londonderry-Belfast) take Faughan Bridge turn, 1m to hotel opposite Ardmore Chapel*
Dating back to 1729, Beech Hill is an impressive mansion, standing in 32 acres of glorious woodlands and gardens. Traditionally styled day rooms provide deep comfort, and ambitious cooking is served in the attractively extended dining room. The splendid bedroom wing provides spacious, well-equipped rooms in addition to the more classically designed bedrooms in the main house.
ROOMS: 17 en suite 10 annexe en suite (4 fmly) in 20 bedrooms s £70-£80; d £120-£130 (incl. bkfst) **LB FACILITIES:** Sauna Gym Jacuzzi Country walks **CONF:** Thtr 100 Class 50 Board 30 Del from £110 **SERVICES:** Lift **PARKING:** 75 **NOTES:** in restaurant Closed 24-25 Dec

★★★70% **Ramada Da Vincis Hotel**
15 Culmore Rd BT48 8JB
☎ 028 7127 9111 028 7127 9222
e-mail: info@davincishotel.com
Dir: *1m from city centre along Strand Rd, adjacent to river, onto Culmore Rd, hotel on right*
Convenient for the city centre, this stylish hotel provides well-designed, spacious and well-equipped bedrooms, most with two double beds. The public areas include the popular Da Vinci's bar and restaurant where food available ranges from light snacks to innovative meals from a carte menu.
ROOMS: 66 en suite (24 fmly) (12 GF) in 26 bedrooms s £55-£85; d £55-£100 **LB FACILITIES:** STV **CONF:** Thtr 50 Class 30 Board 30 **SERVICES:** Lift **PARKING:** 100 **NOTES:** Closed 24 & 25 Dec

★★★65% **White Horse**
68 Clooney Rd, Campsie BT47 3PA
☎ 028 7186 0606 028 7186 0371
e-mail: info@whitehorsehotel.biz web: www.whitehorsehotel.biz
Dir: *on A2 5km from city centre & 1km from Derry City Airport*

The bedrooms at this privately owned hotel, conference and leisure complex include full suites, family rooms and interconnecting rooms. All are spacious, modern and well equipped. These are complemented by bright, modern and spacious public areas. The extensive conference and function facilities together with the leisure and fitness centre are impressive.
ROOMS: 58 en suite (10 fmly) (18 GF) in 14 bedrooms s £50-£80; d £60-£90 (incl. bkfst) **LB FACILITIES: Spa** STV supervised Snooker Sauna Solarium Gym Jacuzzi Full health & leisure centre with beauty salon Xmas **CONF:** BC Thtr 500 Class 290 Board 120 Del from £75 **PARKING:** 200 **NOTES:** Civ Wed 200

Travelodge
22-24 Strand Rd BT47 2AB
☎ 08700 850 950 01287 127 1277
web: www.travelodge.co.uk
Travelodge offers good quality, good value, modern accommodation. Ideal for families, the spacious, en suite bedrooms include remote-control TV, tea and coffee-making facilities and comfortable beds. Meals can be taken at the nearby family restaurant. For further details consult the Hotel Groups page.
ROOMS: 39 en suite s fr £26; d fr £26 **CONF:** Thtr 70 Class 30 Board 25

LOUGHREA, Co Galway
Map 01 B3

★★★68% ***Meadow Court***
☎ 091 841051 091 842406
e-mail: meadowcourthotel@eircom.net
Meadow Court has had a very good reputation for many years for its food, and has added comfortable and well-equipped bedrooms to complement its other facilities. It is particularly renowned for wedding receptions. Lake fishing, golf and horse riding are all available locally.
ROOMS: 21 rms

LUCAN, Co Dublin
Map 01 D4
See also Dublin

★★★64% **Lucan Spa**
☎ 01 6280494 01 6280841
e-mail: info@lucanspahotel.ie
Dir: *on N4, approx 11km from city centre, (20mins from Dublin airport)*

Set in its own grounds off the N4 and close to the M50 the Lucan Spa is a fine Georgian house with modern extension. Bedrooms vary in size and are well equipped. There are two dining options; dinner is served in Hanora D Restaurant and The Earl Bistor for more casual dining. A conference centre is also available.
ROOMS: 71 rms (61 en suite) (15 fmly) (9 GF) in 50 bedrooms s €55-€130; d €80-€180 (incl. bkfst) **LB FACILITIES:** STV **CONF:** Thtr 600 Class 250 Board 80 **SERVICES:** Lift air con **PARKING:** 200 **NOTES:** in restaurant Closed 25 Dec

MACREDDIN, Co Wicklow Map 01 D3

★★★★76% ⊛⊛
The Brooklodge Hotel & Wells Spa
☎ 0402 36444 🖷 0402 36580
e-mail: brooklodge@macreddin.ie
Dir: *N11 to Rathnew, R752 to Rathdrum, R753 to Aughrim follow signs to Macreddin Village*

The Brooklodge is a luxurious country house hotel situated in Macreddin Village near Aughrim and is a real find, where comfort predominates among restful lounges, well-appointed bedrooms and mezzanine suites. The award-winning Strawberry Tree Restaurant is a truly romantic setting, specialising in organic and wild food. The Wells spa centre offers extensive treatments and leisure facilities.
ROOMS: 54 en suite (27 fmly) (4 GF) ⊗ in 28 bedrooms €127.50-€160 (incl. bkfst) **LB** **FACILITIES: Spa** STV Riding Snooker Sauna Gym Jacuzzi Archery Clay pigeon shooting Falconry Shiatsu Massage, Off road driving ♫ Xmas **CONF:** Thtr 300 Class 120 Board 40 Del from €160 **SERVICES:** Lift **PARKING:** 190

MACROOM, Co Cork Map 01 B2

★★★70% ⊛ **Castle**
Main St
☎ 026 41074 🖷 026 41505
e-mail: castlehotel@eircom.net
Dir: *on N22 midway between Cork & Killarney*

This town centre property is fine hotel that has just completed a very extensive redevelopment programme. Service provided by the Buckley Family and their team is excellent, where guests are made feel at home. Bedrooms are very comfortable, as are the extensive public areas. Secure parking is available to the rear.
ROOMS: 60 en suite (6 fmly) s €89-€110; d €130-€170 (incl. bkfst) **LB** **FACILITIES: Spa** STV supervised Gym Jacuzzi Steam Room ♫ **CONF:** Thtr 200 Class 80 Board 60 **SERVICES:** Lift air con **PARKING:** 30 **NOTES:** ⊗ in restaurant Closed 24-28 Dec

MAGHERA, Co Londonderry Map 01 C5

★★80% ⊛⊛ **Ardtara Country House**
8 Gorteade Rd, Upperlands BT46 5SA
☎ 028 7964 4490 🖷 028 7964 5080
e-mail: valerie@ardtara.fsbusiness.co.uk
web: www.ardtara.com
Dir: *from Maghera take A29 towards Coleraine, in 2m take B75 for Kilrea through Upperlands, pass sign Wm Clark & Sons then next left*

Ardtara is a delightful, high quality Victorian country house set in eight acres of mature gardens and woodland. The stylish public rooms include a choice of lounges and a sunroom, whilst the elegant period dining room is the perfect venue for enjoying the skilfully prepared cuisine. Bedrooms vary in style and size; all are richly furnished with fine antiques, open fires and well equipped bathrooms.
ROOMS: 8 en suite (1 fmly) s £50-£75; d £100-£150 (incl. bkfst) **LB** **FACILITIES:** Xmas **CONF:** Thtr 45 Board 20 Del from £75 **PARKING:** 40 **NOTES:** ⊗ in restaurant Closed 25-26 Dec

MALIN, Co Donegal Map 01 C6

★★65% **Malin**
Malin Town
☎ 074 937 0606 🖷 074 937 0770
e-mail: info@malinhotel.ie
Dir: *From Derry on Molville Rd, turn left at Quigleys Point to Cardonagh, then follow to Malin*
Overlooking the village green in the most northerly village in Ireland, the hotel has a friendly, welcoming atmosphere and is an ideal centre for exploring the rugged coastline and sandy beaches. Public areas include an attractive restaurant where dinner is served Wed/Sun and food is available daily in the cosy bar.
ROOMS: 14 en suite (2 fmly) ⊗ in all bedrooms s €55-€65; d €90-€110 (incl. bkfst) **LB** **FACILITIES:** Fishing Gym ♫ ch fac Xmas **CONF:** Thtr 200 Class 100 Board 60 **PARKING:** 40 **NOTES:** ⊗ in restaurant

MALLOW, Co Cork Map 01 B2

Top Hotel

★★★ ⊛⊛⊛ **Longueville House**
☎ 022 47156 & 47306 🖷 022 47459
e-mail: info@longuevillehouse.ie
Dir: *3m W of Mallow via N72 road to Killarney, right turn at Ballyclough junct, hotel entrance 200yds left*
This 18th-century Georgian mansion is set in a wooded estate on a 500-acre farm. The beautifully appointed bedrooms overlook the Backwater Valley. Two elegantly furnished sitting rooms feature fine examples of Italian plasterwork. William

continued

O'Callaghan's cuisine is served in the Presidents' Restaurant and the Victorian Turner conservatory. Most ingredients are raised or grown on the farm with fish from the river that runs through the estate.

ROOMS: 20 en suite (5 fmly) ⊗ in all bedrooms s €95-€360; d €180-€360 (incl. bkfst) **LB** **FACILITIES:** STV Fishing ♫ Xmas **CONF:** Thtr 50 Class 30 Board 30 Del from €295 **PARKING:** 30 **NOTES:** ✈ ⊗ in restaurant Closed Feb 14-23 Mar RS Nov-Mar

★★★65% Springfort Hall Country House Hotel

☎ 022 21278 ▯ 022 21557
e-mail: stay@springfort-hall.com
Dir: *on Mallow/Limerick road N20, right turn off at new Two Pot House R581, hotel 500mtrs on right sign over gate*

This 18th-century country manor is tucked away amid tranquil woodlands located just 6 kms from Mallow. There is an attractive oval dining room, drawing room and lounge bar where guests can relax. The comfortable bedrooms are in a wing and are spacious, well appointed and command suburb country views.
ROOMS: 49 en suite (4 fmly) s €75-€103; d €150-€173 (incl. bkfst) **LB** **FACILITIES:** STV ♫ **CONF:** BC Thtr 300 Class 200 Board 50 Del from €120 **PARKING:** 200 **NOTES:** ✈ ⊗ in restaurant Closed 23 Dec-2 Jan

MIDLETON, Co Cork — Map 01 C2

★★★73% *Midleton Park Hotel & Spa*

☎ 021 4631767 ▯ 021 4631605
e-mail: info@midletonparkhotel.ie
Dir: *from Cork, turn off N25 hotel on right. From Waterford, turn off N25, over bridge to T-junct, right, hotel on right*

This newly refurbished hotel is located in Midleton just off the N25. The comfortable public areas include a relaxing lobby lounge and bedrooms are spacious and attractively decorated. An interesting menu is available in the popular Park Café Bar while The Park Restaurant offers fine dining. There are extensive banqueting, private dining rooms and leisure facilities.
ROOMS: 40 en suite (12 fmly) ⊗ in 6 bedrooms **FACILITIES:** STV **CONF:** Thtr 400 Class 200 Board 40 **SERVICES:** air con **PARKING:** 500 **NOTES:** ✈ Closed 25 Dec

MONAGHAN, Co Monaghan — Map 01 C5

★★★★61% Hillgrove

Old Armagh Rd
☎ 047 4781288 ▯ 047 4784951
e-mail: info@hillgrovehotel.com
Dir: *turn off N2 at Cathedral, 400mtrs, hotel on left*

This modern hotel on the outskirts of the town offers spacious bedrooms that are well equipped and comfortable. The public

continued

areas include a split-level dining room where good food is served, and a popular local bar, serving snacks throughout the day.
ROOMS: 44 en suite (3 fmly) (9 GF) ⊗ in 7 bedrooms s €90-€105; d €170-€198 (incl. bkfst) **LB** **FACILITIES:** STV ▯ supervised Jacuzzi ♫ Xmas **CONF:** BC Thtr 1800 Class 900 Board 400 **SERVICES:** Lift air con **PARKING:** 430 **NOTES:** ✈ ⊗ in restaurant Closed 25 Dec

MULLINGAR, Co Westmeath — Map 01 C4

★★★★67% Mullingar Park

Dublin Rd
☎ 044 44446 37500 ▯ 044 35937
e-mail: info@mullingarparkhotel.com

Just 2km from Mullingar towards Dublin, this newly built hotel has much to offer. Spacious public areas, flexible banqueting suites and a well-equipped leisure centre are complemented by comfortably appointed bedrooms. The friendly staff very are guest focussed. The Terrace Restaurant is particularly popular for its lunch buffet. A themed restaurant is due to open in early 2006.
ROOMS: 95 en suite (12 fmly) ⊗ in 28 bedrooms s €80-€145; d €150-€240 (incl. bkfst) **LB** **FACILITIES: Spa** STV ▯ supervised Sauna Solarium Gym Jacuzzi Aerobic studio, children s pool, hydrotherapy pool ♫ **CONF:** Thtr 1000 Class 750 Board 40 Del from €150 **SERVICES:** Lift **PARKING:** 500 **NOTES:** ✈ ⊗ in restaurant Closed 24-25 Dec RS 26 Dec Civ Wed 500

U Bloomfield House

Belvedere
☎ 044 40894 ▯ 044 43767
e-mail: info@bloomfieldhouse.com

At the time of going to press, the star classification for this hotel was not confirmed. Please refer to the AA internet site www.theAA.com for current information.
ROOMS: 111 en suite (8 fmly) ⊗ in 24 bedrooms s €80-€110; d €140-€180 (incl. bkfst) **LB** **FACILITIES: Spa** STV ▯ supervised Sauna Solarium Gym Jacuzzi ch fac **CONF:** BC Thtr 500 Class 350 Board 12 Del from €135 **SERVICES:** Lift **PARKING:** 500 **NOTES:** ✈ ⊗ in restaurant Closed 24-26 Dec

N

NAAS, Co Kildare — Map 01 D3

★★★★70% ⊛⊛ Killashee House Hotel & Villa Spa

☎ 045 879277 ▯ 045879266
e-mail: reservations@killasheehouse.com
Dir: *N7, then straight through town on Old Kilcullen Rd (R448), hotel on left, 1.5m from centre of Naas*

This Victorian manor house, set in magnificent parkland and landscaped gardens, has been successfully converted to a large hotel with spacious public areas, very comfortable bedrooms and two dining options; fine dining in Turners, and the Nuns Kitchen and bar caters for casual dining. There are extensive banqueting and leisure facilities available.
ROOMS: 142 en suite (10 fmly) (48 GF) ⊗ in 61 bedrooms s €120-€495; d €175-€495 (incl. bkfst) **LB** **FACILITIES: Spa** STV ▯ supervised Sauna Solarium Gym ♫ Jacuzzi Archery, Biking, Clay pigeon shooting, fully equipped villa spa with upto 18 trea ♫ **CONF:** Thtr 1600 Class 144 Board 84 Del from €195 **SERVICES:** Lift **PARKING:** 600 **NOTES:** ✈ ⊗ in restaurant Closed 25-26 Dec

If you wish to use a particular credit card or debit card please check with the hotel that they are happy to accept it

NAVAN, Co Meath Map 01 C4

★★★64% Ardboyne Hotel
Dublin Rd
☎ 046 902 3119 📠 046 902 2355
e-mail: ardboyne@quinn-hotels.com
Dir: *from Dublin-N3 N through Blanchards Town to Navan, hotel on left*
This welcoming hotel is situated on the southern edge of Navan town. Bedrooms are freshly decorated and many of them overlook well maintained gardens. Public areas are smartly furnished and include a popular bar where casual food is served, and a well-appointed dining room that opens for both lunch and dinner.
ROOMS: 29 en suite (25 fmly) (14 GF) ⊗ in 10 bedrooms s €95; d €150 (incl. bkfst) **LB** **FACILITIES:** STV ♫ **CONF:** Thtr 400 Class 200 Board 150 **PARKING:** 186 **NOTES:** ✈ Closed 24-26 Dec

NEWBRIDGE, Co Kildare Map 01 C3

★★★★72% ®® Keadeen
☎ 045 431666 📠 045 434402
e-mail: keadeen@iol.ie
Dir: *M7 junct 10, (Newbridge, Curragh) at rdbt follow signs to Newbridge, hotel on left in 1km*
This family operated hotel is set in eight acres of award-winning gardens on the outskirts of the town and just off the N7. Comfortable public areas include spacious drawing rooms, an excellent leisure centre, fine dining in the Derby Restaurant and more casual fare in the bar. Ideally located for the Curragh racecourse which is nearby.
ROOMS: 75 en suite (4 fmly) ⊗ in 5 bedrooms s €147-€163; d €208-€320 (incl. bkfst) **LB** **FACILITIES:** STV supervised Sauna Solarium Gym Jacuzzi Aerobics studio Treatment room Massage ♫ **CONF:** Thtr 800 Class 300 Board 40 Del from €189 **SERVICES:** Lift **PARKING:** 200 **NOTES:** ✈ ⊗ in restaurant Closed 24 Dec-2 Jan

N

NEWCASTLE, Co Down Map 01 D5

★★65% Enniskeen House
98 Bryansford Rd BT33 0LF
☎ 028 4372 2392 📠 028 4372 4084
e-mail: info@enniskeen-hotel.demon.co.uk
Dir: *from Newcastle town centre follow signs for Tollymore Forest Park, hotel 1m on left*

Set in ten acres of grounds and in the same family ownership for over 40 years, this hotel is enhanced by its thoughtful staff. Bedrooms vary but all are well equipped and many enjoy super mountain and countryside views. The formal dining room serves traditional cuisine and the first-floor lounge makes the most of the coastal views.
ROOMS: 12 en suite (1 fmly) ⊗ in 3 bedrooms **CONF:** Thtr 60 Class 24 **SERVICES:** Lift **PARKING:** 45 **NOTES:** ✈ ⊗ in restaurant Closed 12 Nov-14 Mar

NEWMARKET-ON-FERGUS, Co Clare Map 01 B3

Hotel of the Year

Top Hotel

★★★★★ ®® Dromoland Castle
☎ 061 368144 📠 061 363355
e-mail: sales@dromoland.ie
Dir: *N18 from Shannon towards Galway, left signed 'Dromoland Interchange'*
Dromoland Castle, dating from the early 18th-century, stands on a 375-acre estate and offers extensive indoor leisure activities and outdoor pursuits. The team are wholly committed to caring for guests and demonstrate their professionalism with friendliness and enthusiasm. The thoughtfully equipped bedrooms and suites vary in style but all provide excellent levels of comfort, and the magnificent public rooms, warmed by log fires, are no less impressive. The hotel has two restaurants, the elegant fine-dining Earl of Thomond, and less formal Fig Tree in the golf clubhouse.
AA Hotel of the Year for the Republic of Ireland 2005-6.
ROOMS: 100 en suite (20 fmly) s €225-€417; d €225-€417 **LB** **FACILITIES:** STV supervised ⛳ 18 Fishing Snooker Sauna Solarium Gym Putt green Jacuzzi Beauty clinic, Archery, Clay shooting, Mountain bikes ♫ Xmas **CONF:** BC Thtr 450 Class 220 Board 80 **PARKING:** 120 **NOTES:** ✈ ⊗ in restaurant

NEW ROSS, Co Wexford

★★★67% Cedar Lodge
Carrigbyrne, Newbawn
☎ 051 428386 📠 051 428222
e-mail: cedarlodge@eircom.net
Dir: *On N25 between Wexford and New Ross*
IRISH COUNTRY HOTELS
Cedar sits in a tranquil setting beneath the slopes of Carrigbyrne Forest, just a 30-minute drive from Rosslare Port. The Martin family extend warm hospitality and provide good food in the charming conservatory restaurant with its central log fire. There are comfortable lounges, and the bedrooms, which overlook the attractive landscape gardens, are spacious and thoughtfully appointed.
ROOMS: 28 en suite (2 fmly) (10 GF) s €100-€130; d €160-€200 (incl. bkfst) **LB** **CONF:** Thtr 100 Class 60 Board 60 **PARKING:** 60 **NOTES:** ✈ ⊗ in restaurant Closed 21 Dec-31 Jan

Packed in a hurry? Ironing facilities should be available at all star levels, either in the rooms or on request

NEWTOWNMOUNTKENNEDY, Co Wicklow Map 01 D3

★★★★★72% Marriott Druids Glen Hotel & Country Club

☎ 01 2870800 📠 2870801
e-mail: mhrs.dubgs.reception@marriotthotels.com
web: www.marriottdruidsglen.com
Dir: *N11 s'bound, off at Newtownmountkennedy. Follow signs for hotel*

This fine hotel, situated between the Wicklow Mountains and the coast, has two fabulous golf courses and a range of smart indoor leisure facilities. Bedrooms have been equipped to the highest standard and service is delivered in a most professional manner and always with a smile.

ROOMS: 148 en suite ⊗ in 106 bedrooms s fr €125; d fr €150 (incl. dinner) **LB FACILITIES: Spa** STV ⛶ ⚓ 36 Sauna Gym Putt green Jacuzzi 4 Treatment Rooms, Plunge Pool ♫ Xmas **CONF:** BC Thtr 400 Class 180 Board 30 Del from €200 **SERVICES:** Lift air con **PARKING:** 350 **NOTES:** 🐕 ⊗ in restaurant

PARKNASILLA, Co Kerry Map 01 A2

★★★★75% ❀ Great Southern

☎ 064 45122 📠 064 45323
e-mail: res@parknasilla-gsh.com
Dir: *on Kenmare road 3km from Sneem village*

This delightful hotel which has been in business for over a hundred years, is a popular haven of relaxation and rejuvenation for generations of Irish families. There are many spacious lounges, that together with the restaurant and many of the bedrooms, have wonderful sea views. Service is warm and friendly, underpinned by smooth professionalism.

ROOMS: 24 en suite 59 annexe en suite (6 fmly) ⊗ in 11 bedrooms s €240-€260; d €240-€260 **LB FACILITIES: Spa** STV ⛶ supervised ⚓ 12 Fishing Riding Snooker Sauna Putt green Jacuzzi Bike hire, Windsurfing, Clay pigeon shooting, Archery ♫ Xmas **CONF:** BC Thtr 80 Class 60 Board 20 **SERVICES:** Lift **PARKING:** 60 **NOTES:** 🐕 ⊗ in restaurant

See advert on this page

PORTAFERRY, Co Down Map 01 D5

★★★69% ❀ *Portaferry*

10 The Strand BT22 1PE
☎ 028 4272 8231 📠 028 4272 8999
e-mail: info@portaferryhotel.com
web: www.portaferryhotel.com
Dir: *on Lough Shore opp ferry terminal*

This hotel, now under new ownership, enjoys a central location almost by the ferry ramp and boasts a superb panorama of Strangford Lough. Bedrooms vary in size and style. Day rooms include a cosy lounge and split-level dining room, whilst snacks can be enjoyed in the informal bar.

ROOMS: 14 en suite **FACILITIES:** STV **CONF:** Board 14 **PARKING:** 6 **NOTES:** 🐕 Closed 24-25 Dec

PORTBALLINTRAE, Co Antrim Map 01 C6

★★★70% *Bayview*

2 Bayhead Rd BT57 8RZ
☎ 028 2073 4100 📠 028 2073 4330
e-mail: info@bayviewhotelni.com
Dir: *M2 (Belfast to Ballymena) then A26 to Ballymena, onto B62 to Portrush, approx 7m right onto B17 to Bushmills. Left then immediate right to Portballintrae*

This stylish hotel commands excellent views of the ocean, beach and harbour. Bedrooms are bright, modern and well equipped and include rooms for less mobile guests and rooms for families, interconnecting rooms and non-smoking rooms. Public

continued on p856

PORTBALLINTRAE, continued

areas are airy and comfortable with a relaxing conservatory lounge at the front, with conferences and meeting rooms available.
ROOMS: 25 en suite (12 fmly) ⊗ in 2 bedrooms **FACILITIES:** ♫ **CONF:** Thtr 40 Class 30 Board 20 **SERVICES:** Lift **PARKING:** 25 **NOTES:** ✗

PORTLAOISE, Co Laoise Map 01 C3

★★★★67% The Heritage Hotel
Jessop St
☎ 0502 78588 🖷 0502 78577
e-mail: info@theheritagehotel.com
The Heritage is a newly built hotel situated in the town just off the N7. Public areas include a spacious lobby lounge, two bars and dining options, The Fitzmaurice where breakfast and dinner are served and Spago an Italian Bistro. Bedrooms are well appointed and there are extensive leisure and conference facilities, and an indoor secure car park.
ROOMS: 110 en suite (6 fmly) ⊗ in 90 bedrooms s €130-€180; d €170-€240 (incl. bkfst) **LB** **FACILITIES: Spa** STV supervised Sauna Gym Putt green Jacuzzi Health & fitness club, Beauty spa ♫ **CONF:** BC Thtr 500 Class 300 Board 50 Del from €192.50 **SERVICES:** Lift **PARKING:** 100 **NOTES:** ✗ ⊗ in restaurant Closed 23-27 Dec RS Good Friday

PORTMARNOCK, Co Dublin Map 01 D4

Top Hotel

★★★★ Portmarnock Hotel & Golf Links
Strand Rd
☎ 01 8460611 🖷 01 8462442
e-mail: sales@portmarnock.com
Dir: *Dublin Airport, N1, rdbt 1st exit, 2nd rdbt 2nd exit, next rdbt 3rd exit, T-junct turn left, over x-rds. Hotel on left past the Strand*
This 19th-century former home of the Jameson whiskey family is now a well run and smartly presented hotel, enjoys a superb location overlooking the sea and the PGA Championship Golf Links. Bedrooms are modern and equipped to high standard, public areas are spacious and very comfortable. The Osborne Restaurant comes highly recommended and a team of friendly staff goes out of their way to welcome guests.
ROOMS: 98 en suite (32 GF) ⊗ in 33 bedrooms s €143-€235; d €203-€315 (incl. bkfst) **LB** **FACILITIES: Spa** STV ⛳ 18 Sauna Gym Putt green Beauty therapist Balinotherapy Bath & treatments. Xmas **CONF:** BC Thtr 300 Class 110 Board 80 Del from €200 **SERVICES:** Lift **PARKING:** 200 **NOTES:** ✗ ⊗ in restaurant RS Christmas Eve/Day

See advert on opposite page

PORTUMNA, Co Galway Map 01 B3

★★★67% *Shannon Oaks Hotel & Country Club*
IRISH COUNTRY HOTELS
St Joseph Rd
☎ 090 974 1777 🖷 090 974 1357
e-mail: sales@shannonoaks.ie
Dir: *exiting Portumna, on left of St Josephs Rd*

Located in eight acres of parkland by Portumna National Park, this modern hotel offers very comfortable and spacious bedrooms and suites. The popular bar has food available most of the day, with more formal dining available in the Castle Gates Restaurant. Extensive conference and leisure facilities are also on site.
ROOMS: 63 en suite **FACILITIES:** STV Sauna Solarium Gym Jacuzzi ♫ **CONF:** Thtr 600 Class 320 Board 280 **SERVICES:** Lift air con **PARKING:** 360 **NOTES:** ✗

RATHMULLAN, Co Donegal Map 01 C6

★★★75% Fort Royal Hotel
MANOR HOUSE HOTELS
Fort Royal
☎ 074 9158100 🖷 074 9158103
e-mail: fortroyal@eircom.net
Dir: *take R245 from Letterkenny, through Rathmullan, hotel is signed*
On the western shores of Lough Swilly, this family-run period house stands in 18 acres of well-maintained grounds that include a 9-hole golf and tennis court. Private access is available to the secluded sandy beach. The restful lounges and inviting bar have open log fires, the fine dine restaurant overlooks the gardens and bedrooms enjoy the spectacular views.
ROOMS: 11 en suite 4 annexe en suite (1 fmly) s €77-€117; d €154-€184 (incl. bkfst) **LB** **FACILITIES:** ⛳ 9 **PARKING:** 30 **NOTES:** ⊗ in restaurant Closed Nov-Mar

RATHNEW, Co Wicklow Map 01 D3

★★★67% *Hunter's*
IRELAND'S BLUE BOOK
☎ 0404 40106 🖷 0404 40338
e-mail: reception@hunters.ie
Dir: *1.5km from village off N11*
A delightful hotel which is one of Ireland's oldest coaching inns. The comfortable bedrooms have wonderful views over prize-winning gardens bordering the River Varty. The restaurant has a good reputation for carefully prepared dishes, which make the best use of high quality local produce including fruit and vegetables from their own garden.
ROOMS: 16 en suite (2 fmly) (2 GF) **CONF:** Thtr 40 Class 40 Board 16 **PARKING:** 50 **NOTES:** ✗ ⊗ in restaurant Closed 24-26 Dec

○ Hotel due to open in late 2005 or 2006
U Star rating not confirmed

RECESS, Co Galway Map 01 A4

★★★★75% ◉◉❦ **Ballynahinch Castle**
☎ 095 31006 ▨ 095 31085
e-mail: bhinch@iol.ie
Dir: W from Galway on N59 direction Clifden. After Recess take Roundstone turn to left, hotel 4km

Open log fires and friendly professional service are just some of the delights of staying at this castle that originates from the 16th century. Set in 350 acres of woodland, rivers and lakes, this hotel has many suites and rooms with stunning views, as does the award-winning Owenmore restaurant.
ROOMS: 40 en suite ⊗ in 4 bedrooms **FACILITIES:** STV ❧ Fishing ⬐
River & Lakeside walks ♫ Xmas **CONF:** Thtr 30 Class 20 Board 20
PARKING: 55 **NOTES:** ✕ ⊗ in restaurant Closed Feb & 20-26 Dec

Top Hotel

★★★ ◉❦ *Lough Inagh Lodge*
Inagh Valley
☎ 095 34706 & 34694 ▨ 095 34708
e-mail: inagh@iol.ie
Dir: after Recess take R344 towards Kylemore through Inagh Valley
This 19th-century, former fishing lodge is a relaxing, comfortable hotel in a setting is superb. Situated in the middle of Connemara it is fronted by a good fishing lake and enjoys beautiful mountain views. Bedrooms are smartly decorated and spacious, and there is a choice of lounges and a cosy traditional bar. The delightful restaurant offers an extensive range of seafood.
ROOMS: 12 en suite (4 GF) **FACILITIES:** STV Fishing Hill walking, Fly fishing, Cycling **CONF:** Thtr 20 Class 20 Board 20
SERVICES: air con **PARKING:** 16 **NOTES:** ⊗ in restaurant Closed mid Dec-mid Mar

Portmarnock Hotel & Golf Links
Portmarnock · Dublin

Tel: 00 3531 846 0611 · Fax: 00 3531 846 2442
Once the home of the Jameson whiskey family, the hotel is in a prime location reaching down to the sea, with views over the Bernhard Langer designed 18 hole golf links. The hotel was completely renovated in 1996 but still retains the 19th century character of the ancestral home. The elegant two rosetted restaurant serves French cuisine while the Links Restaurant offers all day dining, next to the clubhouse. The luxurious bedrooms have many amenities with period furnished deluxe rooms and superior rooms available at a supplement.

RENVYLE, Co Galway Map 01 A4

★★★70% ◉ *Renvyle House Hotel*
☎ 095 43511 ▨ 095 43515
e-mail: info@renvyle.com
Dir: N59 W of Galway towards Clifden Pass through Oughterard & Maam Cross, at Recess turn right, Kylemore turn left, Letterfrack turn right, hotel 5m
This comfortable house has been operating as a hotel for over 120 years. Located on the unspoilt coast of Connemara it provides a range of outdoor leisure pursuits. The spacious lounges are comfortable with turf fires and the bedrooms are well equipped. The relaxed, friendly staff will make any visit here memorable.
ROOMS: 68 en suite (8 fmly) ⊗ in 5 bedrooms **FACILITIES:** STV ❧ ⬐
9 ❧ Fishing Riding Snooker ⬐ Putt green Clay pigeon shooting ♫ ch
fac **CONF:** Thtr 200 Class 80 Board 80 **PARKING:** 60 **NOTES:** ⊗ in restaurant Closed 6 Jan-14 Feb

ROSCOMMON, Co Roscommon Map 01 B4

★★★71% *Abbey*
Galway Rd
☎ 090 662 6240 ▨ 090 662 6021
e-mail: info@abbeyhotel.ie
Dir: on main Galway Rd
This fine manor house has been restored by the Grealy family with great care and attention to detail. The new spacious bedrooms are tastefully furnished, individually designed and overlook the magnificent gardens. The smart bar and Terrace restaurant have views of the 12th-century Dominican abbey; the
continued on p858

ROSCOMMON, continued

new carvery is very popular at lunchtime. There are extensive leisure and conference facilities.
ROOMS: 50 en suite (10 GF) ⊗ in 35 bedrooms **FACILITIES:** Sauna Solarium Gym Jacuzzi Swimming pool supervised **CONF:** Thtr 250 Class 140 Board 50 **SERVICES:** Lift **PARKING:** 100 **NOTES:** Closed 25-26 Dec

Restaurant with Rooms

Gleesons Townhouse & Restaurant
Market Square
☎ 090 6626 954 090 6627 425
e-mail: info@gleesonstownhouse.com
This 19th-century cut-limestone town house has been very tastefully restored. The bedrooms are decorated and furnished to a high standard. Dinner is served nightly in the Manse Restaurant and there is an extensive lunch and afternoon tea menu in the café or in the beautifully landscaped front courtyard. Conference facilities and secure car parking are available.
ROOMS: 19 en suite (1 fmly) ⊗ in 6 bedrooms s €55-€80; d €110-€150 (incl. bkfst) **LB** **FACILITIES:** STV Jacuzzi **CONF:** BC Thtr 80 Class 30 Board 34 Del from €100 **PARKING:** 25 **NOTES:** ⊗ in restaurant Closed Xmas & Boxing day RS Good Fri

ROSCREA, Co Tipperary — Map 01 C3

U *Racket Hall Country Golf & Conference Hotel*
Dublin Rd
☎ 0505 21748 0505 23701
e-mail: racketh@iol.ie
At the time of going to press, the star classification for this hotel was not confirmed. Please refer to the AA internet site www.theAA.com for current information.
ROOMS: 40 rms

ROSSCARBERY, Co Cork — Map 01 B2

★★★69% Celtic Ross
☎ 023 48722 023 48723
e-mail: info@celticrosshotel.com
Dir: *take N71from Cork city, through Bandon towards Clonakilty. Follow signs for Skibbereen, hotel on main road on water's edge*

The Celtic Ross Hotel is situated overlooking Rosscarbery Bay on the edge of the village. Richly textured fabrics add warmth to the polished wood of the public areas and include a 5000-year-old Bog Yew Tree sculpture and a choice of bars and restaurants. Bedrooms are comfortable and well appointed.
ROOMS: 66 en suite (30 fmly) ⊗ in 10 bedrooms s €60-€100; d €90-€180 (incl. bkfst) **LB** **FACILITIES:** STV supervised Sauna Gym Steam room, Bubble pool, Video rentals ♫ Xmas **CONF:** BC Thtr 300 Class 150 Board 60 Del from €115 **SERVICES:** Lift air con **PARKING:** 200 **NOTES:** ⊗ in restaurant Closed mid Jan-mid Feb

ROSSLARE, Co Wexford — Map 01 D2

Top Hotel

★★★★ Kelly's Resort
☎ 053 32114 053 32222
e-mail: kellyhot@iol.ie
Dir: *10m from Wexford town, turn off N25 on Rosslare/Wexford road*
Since 1895, the Kelly Family has been running this excellent hotel, where together with a dedicated team, they provide very professional and friendly service. The resort is adjacent to both the beach and Rosslare Strand. Bedrooms are thoughtfully equipped and comfortably furnished. The extensive facilities include a smart leisure club, health treatments, a children's creche and spacious gardens. La Marine Bistro offers modern cuisine and the newly refurbished Beaches restaurant serves award-winning food.
ROOMS: 118 annexe en suite (15 fmly) (20 GF) ⊗ in 110 bedrooms **FACILITIES: Spa** STV supervised Snooker Sauna Gym Jacuzzi Bowls Plunge pool Badminton Crazy golf Outdoor Canadian hot tub ♫ ch fac **CONF:** Thtr 30 Class 30 Board 20 **SERVICES:** Lift **PARKING:** 99 **NOTES:** ⊗ in restaurant Closed mid Dec-late Feb

Bad hair day?
Hairdryers in all rooms three stars and above

ROSSNOWLAGH, Co Donegal — Map 01 B5

★★★79% Sand House
☎ 071 985 1777 071 985 2100
e-mail: info@sandhouse-hotel.ie
Dir: *from Donegal on coast road to Ballyshannon. In centre of Donegal Bay*
Located on Rossnowlagh sandy beach, which is a haven for surfers. This hotel offers very comfortable lounges and restaurant, cocktail bar and Surfers bar. Bedrooms are spacious and well appointed, most enjoy the splendid sea views. Known for its

continued

hospitality, good food and service, the Sandhouse is an ideal base for touring the north west of Ireland.

ROOMS: 55 en suite (6 fmly) ◎ in 30 bedrooms s €110-€155; d €160-€180 (incl. bkfst) **LB FACILITIES: Spa** STV ◯ Sauna Solarium Jacuzzi Mini-golf Surfing Canoeing Sailing ch fac **CONF:** Thtr 60 Class 40 Board 30 Del from €145 **SERVICES:** Lift **PARKING:** 42 **NOTES:** ◎ in restaurant Closed Dec & Jan

ROUNDSTONE, Co Galway · Map 01 A4

★★70% ◉ Roundstone House Hotel
☎ 095 35864 ▤ 095 35944
e-mail: vaughanshotel@eircom.net
IRISH COUNTRY HOTELS
Dir: From Galway take N59. After Recess take 2nd left and continue for 9km.
This delightful hotel has been in operation since 1894 and owned by the Vaughan family for many years. The comfortable bedrooms enjoy the magnificent sea views and the rugged Connemara landscape. There is a relaxing residents' lounge, cosy bar and Vaughan's Restaurant which is renowned for its extensive range of seafood.
ROOMS: 12 en suite (1 fmly) **NOTES:** ✕ ◎ in restaurant Closed Oct-Etr Civ Wed

SALTHILL See Galway

SKERRIES, Co Dublin · Map 01 D4

Restaurant with Rooms

🍴 ◉ Redbank House & Restaurant
5-7 Church St ROI
☎ 01 8491005 8490439 ▤ 01 8491598
THE INDEPENDENTS
e-mail: redbank@eircom.net
Dir: N1 north past the airport & bypass Swords. 3m N at the end of dual carriageway at Esso station right towards Rush, Lusk & Skerries
Adjacent to the well-known restaurant of the same name, this comfortable double fronted period town house has two reception rooms, en suite bedrooms and a secluded garden. The restaurant is the setting for quality local produce used with an emphasis on fresh fish in imaginative cooking, served by friendly and attentive staff.
ROOMS: 7 en suite 5 annexe en suite (12 fmly) **FACILITIES:** STV **PARKING:** 4 **NOTES:** ✕ Closed 24-28 Dec

U Star rating not confirmed

SLIGO, Co Sligo · Map 01 B5

★★★71% Sligo Park
Pearse Rd
☎ 071 9190400 ▤ 071 916 9556
e-mail: sligo@leehotels.com
Dir: on N4 1m from Sligo on Dublin Road also on Galway Rd
Set on seven acres on the southern side of the town, this hotel is well positioned for touring the many attractions of the northwest and Yeats' Country. Bedrooms are spacious and newly refurbished to a high standard. There are two dining options and good leisure and banqueting facilities with ample parking available.
ROOMS: 138 en suite (5 fmly) (45 GF) ◎ in 60 bedrooms s €79-€137; d €110-€234 (incl. bkfst) **LB FACILITIES:** ◈ supervised ◯ Snooker Sauna Gym Jacuzzi Steam room, Holistic treatment centre, Plunge pool Xmas **CONF:** Thtr 520 Class 290 Board 80 Del from €155 **SERVICES:** Lift **PARKING:** 200 **NOTES:** ✕ ◎ in restaurant RS 24-26 & 31 Dec

U The Clarion Hotel Sligo
Ballinode
☎ 071 911 9000 & 911 9006 ▤ 071 911 9001
e-mail: info@clarionhotelsligo.com
Dir: On N6 off Enniskillen Rd. Hotel opposite Sligo Instiute of Technology.
At the time of going to press, the star classification for this hotel was not confirmed. Please refer to the AA internet site www.theAA.com for current information.
ROOMS: 167 en suite (91 fmly) (47 GF) ◎ in 115 bedrooms s €145-€290; d €145-€290 **LB FACILITIES: Spa** STV ◈ supervised Sauna Gym Jacuzzi Gym classes ♫ ch fac Xmas **CONF:** BC Thtr 500 Class 300 Board 80 Del from €165 **SERVICES:** Lift **PARKING:** 250 **NOTES:** ◎ in restaurant Civ Wed 250

U Radisson SAS Hotel Sligo
Rosses Point Rd, Ballincar
☎ 071 914 0008 ▤ 071 914 0005
e-mail: info.sligo@radissonsas.com
Dir: Enter Sligo on N4 to Main Bridge. Take R291 on left, Hotel 2m on right.
At the time of going to press, the star classification for this hotel was not confirmed. Please refer to the AA internet site www.theAA.com for current information.
ROOMS: 132 en suite (12 fmly) (38 GF) ◎ in 82 bedrooms s €99-€130; d €120-€200 (incl. bkfst) **LB FACILITIES: Spa** ◈ supervised Sauna Gym Jacuzzi Steam Room, Outdoor Canadian Hot Tub Xmas **CONF:** BC Thtr 950 Class 480 Board 90 **SERVICES:** Lift air con **PARKING:** 430 **NOTES:** ✕ ◎ in restaurant

SPANISH POINT, Co Clare · Map 01 B3

★★★67% Burkes Armada
☎ 065 7084110 ▤ 065 7084632
e-mail: info@burkesarmadahotel.com
IRISH COUNTRY HOTELS
Dir: N18 from Ennis take N85 Inagh, then R460 to Miltown Malbay. Follow signs for Spanish Point
Situated on the coastline, overlooking breaking waves and golden sands, this friendly, family run hotel is located in a natural, unspoiled environment. The public areas benefit from views of this stunning location, especially the contemporary restaurant. Bedrooms, many with sea views, are well equipped and brightly decorated. Good bar food menu served throughout the day.
ROOMS: 61 en suite (53 fmly) **FACILITIES:** STV Gym **CONF:** Thtr 600 Class 400 Board 60 **SERVICES:** Lift **PARKING:** 175 **NOTES:** ✕

S

STRAFFAN, Co Kildare Map 01 D4

Top Hotel

★★★★★ ◉◉◉ **The K Club**
☎ 01 6017200 📠 01 6017298
e-mail: resortsales@kclub.ie
Dir: from Dublin take N4, exit for R406, hotel on right in Straffan
The K Club, set in 700 acres of rolling woodland will host the
2006 Ryder Cup. Two magnificent championship golf courses
and a spa facility will complement the truly luxurious hotel
that is centrepiece of the resort. Public areas and bedrooms
are opulently furnished, and have views of the formal
gardens. Fine dining is served in the elegant Byerly Turk
restaurant, with more informal dining offered in Legends and
Monza restaurants in the golf pavilions.
ROOMS: 69 en suite 10 annexe en suite (10 fmly) s €245-€3800
(incl. bkfst) **LB FACILITIES: Spa** STV ◉ supervised ⌁ 36 Fishing
Snooker Sauna Solarium Gym ♨ Putt green Jacuzzi Beauty salon
Driving range Golf tuition Fishing tuition Horse riding nearby ♫ Xmas
CONF: Thtr 300 Class 300 Board 160 Del from €365
SERVICES: Lift **PARKING:** 205 **NOTES:** ✠ ⊗ in restaurant

★★★77% ◉◉ Barberstown Castle
☎ 01 6288157 📠 01 6277027
e-mail: barberstowncastle@ireland.com

With parts dating from the 13th century, the castle is now a hotel
providing the very best in standards of comfort. The inviting public
areas range from the original keep, which now is one of the two
restaurants, to the warmth of the drawing room. Bedrooms,
including some in a new wing, are elegantly appointed and named
after many of the characters that have been associated with the
property. At the time of inspection a new wing of rooms was
nearing completion.
ROOMS: 59 en suite s €150-€200; d €220-€270 (incl. bkfst) **LB**
FACILITIES: STV ♫ Xmas **CONF:** Thtr 150 Class 120 Board 30 Del
from €190 **SERVICES:** Lift **PARKING:** 200 **NOTES:** ✠ No children
12yrs ⊗ in restaurant

THOMASTOWN, Co Kilkenny Map 01 C3

Top Hotel

★★★★ ◉◉ **Mount Juliet Conrad**
☎ 056 777 3000 📠 056 777 3019
e-mail: info@mountjuliet.ie
Dir: M7 from Dublin, N9 towards Waterford then to Mount Juliet via
Carlow and Gowran
Mount Juliet Conrad is set in 1,500 acres of parkland with a
Jack Nicklaus designed golf course and an equestrian centre.
The elegant and spacious public areas retain much of the
original architectural features including ornate plasterwork
and Adam fireplaces. Bedrooms, in both the main house the
Hunters Yard annexe, are comfortable and well appointed.
Fine dining is on offer at Lady Helen, overlooking the river,
and more casual dining is available in Kendels in the Hunters
Yard, which also has a spa and health club.
ROOMS: 32 en suite 27 annexe en suite ⊗ in 1 bedroom
FACILITIES: Spa STV ◉ ⌁ 18 ⚲ Fishing Riding Snooker Sauna
Gym ♨ Putt green Spa Archery Cycling Clay pigeon shooting Golf
tuition **CONF:** Thtr 75 Class 40 Board 20 **PARKING:** 200
NOTES: ✠ ⊗ in restaurant

TIPPERARY, Co Tipperary Map 01 C3

🆄 Ramada Hotel & Suites Ballykisteen
Limerick Junction
☎ 062 33333 📠 31586
e-mail: info@ballykisteen@ramadaireland.com
Dir: On the N24 Limerick/Tipperary road.
At the time of going to press, the star classification for this hotel
was not confirmed. Please refer to the AA internet site
www.theAA.com for current information.
ROOMS: 133 en suite (45 fmly) (23 GF) ⊗ in 65 bedrooms s €75-
€140; d €79-€140 **LB FACILITIES: Spa** STV ◉ ⌁ 18 ⚲ Sauna Gym
Putt green Jacuzzi **CONF:** Thtr 350 Class 200 Board 50 Del from €167
SERVICES: Lift **PARKING:** 180 **NOTES:** ✠ ⊗ in restaurant RS Hotel
opens 20/06/2005 Civ Wed 280

TRALEE, Co Kerry Map 01 A2

★★★★70% Ballygarry House
Killarney Rd
☎ 066 7123322 📠 7127630
e-mail: info@ballygarryhouse.com
Dir: 1.5km from Tralee, on N22
Set in six acres of well-tended gardens, this fine hotel has been
family run for the last 50 years and totally renovated in recent
years to a very high standard. The elegant and stylishly decorated
bedrooms are spacious and relaxing. Good cuisine is served in the
continued

split-level restaurant. The staff are friendly and professional. Further development is due for completion in early 2006.

ROOMS: 46 en suite (10 fmly) (6 GF) ⊗ in all bedrooms **FACILITIES:** STV ♫ **CONF:** BC **SERVICES:** Lift **PARKING:** 105 **NOTES:** 🐕 ⊗ in restaurant Closed 20-26 Dec Civ Wed 350

★★★69% Meadowlands Hotel

Oakpark
☎ 066 7180444 ℻ 066 7180964
e-mail: info@meadowlands-hotel.com
Dir: *1km from Tralee town centre on N69*

This smart hotel has been extended and is within walking distance of the town centre. Bedrooms are tastefully decorated and comfortable. Johnny Frank's is the very popular pub where a wide range of food is offered throughout the day.

ROOMS: 58 en suite (1 fmly) (5 GF) ⊗ in 17 bedrooms s €80-€140; d €140-€350 (incl. bkfst) **LB** **FACILITIES:** STV ♫ **CONF:** Thtr 250 Class 110 Board 30 **SERVICES:** Lift air con **PARKING:** 200 **NOTES:** 🐕 ⊗ in restaurant Closed 24-26 Dec

★★★67% Abbey Gate

Maine St
☎ 066 7129888 ℻ 066 7129821
e-mail: info@abbeygate-hotel.com
Dir: *take N21 or N22 to town centre*

The Abbey Gate is a smart town centre hotel. The comfortable well-equipped bedrooms include some suitable for those with mobility difficulties. The bar is popular with local business people and features music at weekends. Food is served daily in the bar or in a choice of two restaurants.

ROOMS: 100 en suite (4 fmly) s €65-€160; d €130-€320 (incl. bkfst) **LB** **FACILITIES:** STV ♫ Xmas **CONF:** BC Thtr 450 Class 250 Board 40 Del from €100 **SERVICES:** Lift **PARKING:** 40 **NOTES:** 🐕 ⊗ in restaurant RS 24-26 Dec

TRAMORE, Co Waterford — Map 01 C2

★★★65% Majestic

☎ 051 381761 ℻ 051 381766
e-mail: info@majestic-hotel.ie
Dir: *turn off N25 through Waterford onto R675 to Tramore. Hotel is on right, opposite lake*

A warm welcome awaits visitors to this long established family friendly hotel in the holiday resort of Tramore. Many of the comfortable and well-equipped bedrooms have sea views.

ROOMS: 60 en suite (4 fmly) ⊗ in all bedrooms d €120-€150 (incl. bkfst) **LB** **FACILITIES:** STV Free access to Splashworld swimming pool & leisure club ♫ ch fac Xmas **SERVICES:** Lift **PARKING:** 10 **NOTES:** 🐕 ⊗ in restaurant Civ Wed 250

TULLOW, Co Carlow — Map 01 D3

★★★★72% Mount Wolseley Hilton

☎ 059 915 1674 ℻ 059 915 2123
e-mail: info@mountwolseley.ie

Located on a vast estate associated with the Wolseley family of motoring fame, this newly expanded hotel has much to offer. Public areas are very spacious and there are a range of comfortable bedrooms and suites. Leisure pursuits include golf, together with a health centre and spa facilities. The hotel offers a number of dining options.

ROOMS: 142 en suite ⊗ in 128 bedrooms s €105-€150; d €130-€190 (incl. bkfst) **FACILITIES: Spa** STV supervised ⛳ 18 Snooker Sauna Gym Putt green Jacuzzi ♫ ch fac Xmas **CONF:** BC Thtr 750 Class 288 Board 70 Del from €150 **SERVICES:** Lift air con **PARKING:** 160 **NOTES:** 🐕 ⊗ in restaurant Closed 25-26 Dec

VIRGINIA, Co Cavan — Map 01 C4

★★67% The Park

Virginia Park
☎ 049 8546100 ℻ 049 8547203
e-mail: virginiapark@eircom.net
Dir: *turn off N3 in Virginia onto R194. Hotel 500yds on left*

A charming hotel, built in 1750 as the summer retreat of the Marquis of Headford. Situated overlooking Lake Ramor on a 100-acre estate, it has a 9-hole golf course, lovely mature gardens and woodland. The Park Hotel brings together generous hospitality and a relaxed leisurely pace of life.

ROOMS: 26 en suite (1 fmly) (8 GF) **FACILITIES:** ⛳ 9 Fishing Sauna ch fac Xmas **CONF:** Thtr 70 Class 40 Board 40 **PARKING:** 50 **NOTES:** 🐕 ⊗ in restaurant Closed 25 Dec

V

WATERFORD, Co Waterford — Map 01 C2

Top Hotel

★★★★ ⚉⚉ **Waterford Castle**
The Island
☎ 051 878203 🖷 051 879316
e-mail: info@waterfordcastle.com
Dir: *from city centre, turn onto Dunmore East Rd, 1.5m, pass hospital, 0.5m left after lights, ferry at bottom of road*
This enchanting and picturesque castle dates back to Norman times and is located on a 320-acre island just a five minute journey from the mainland by chain-link ferry. The bedrooms vary but all offer high standards of comfort. Dinner is served in the oak-panelled Munster Room, with breakfast taken in the conservatory or Leinster Room. The 18-hole golf course is set in beautiful parkland where deer can be seen.
ROOMS: 19 en suite (2 fmly) ⊗ in all bedrooms **FACILITIES:** STV
⬩ 18 ⚲ ⚑ Putt green Clay pigeon shooting, archery(group) ♫
Xmas **CONF:** BC Thtr 30 Board 15 **SERVICES:** Lift **PARKING:** 50
NOTES: ⊁ ⊗ in restaurant RS 1st wk Jan-Feb

★★★★68% **Faithlegg House**
Faithlegg
☎ 051 382000 🖷 051 382010
e-mail: reservations@fhh.ie
Faithlegg House is surrounded by a championship golf course, overlooking the estuary of the River Suir. The restored house has 14 original bedrooms, with the balance in a modern block to the side. Comprehensive meeting facilities are provided together with a range of comfortable lounges. The leisure and treatment rooms are the perfect way to work off the excesses of the food offered in the Roseville Restaurant.
ROOMS: 82 rms s €180-€240; d €262-€350 (incl. bkfst) **LB**
FACILITIES: STV ⊞ supervised ⬩ 18 ⚲ Sauna Gym Putt green
Jacuzzi ♫ Xmas **CONF:** BC **SERVICES:** Lift **PARKING:** 100 **NOTES:** ⊁
⊗ in restaurant Civ Wed 130

W ★★★72% **Athenaeum House**
Christendon, Ferrybank
☎ 051 833 999 🖷 051 833 977
e-mail: info@athenaeumhousehotel.com
Dir: *N25 to Wexford, through 1st traffic lights, turn right and continue turning right into Abbey Rd. Take 1st right after bridge, hotel on right.*
Set in acres of woodland, this new hotel was originally built in the 18th century. The public rooms have been sympathetically restored in keeping with the age of the building, yet with a contemporary twist. Four bedrooms are in the main house with

continued

the others in a well-designed block on the side, accessed by a glazed link.

ROOMS: 29 en suite (5 GF) ⊗ in all bedrooms s €40-€140; d €88-€200 **LB FACILITIES:** STV ♫ Xmas **CONF:** Thtr 40 Class 35 Board 45 Del from €130 **SERVICES:** Lift **PARKING:** 35 **NOTES:** ⊁ ⊗ in restaurant Closed 24-26 Dec

★★★72% **Granville**
The Quay
☎ 051 305555 🖷 051 305566
e-mail: stay@granville-hotel.ie
Dir: *take N25 to waterfront, city centre, opposite Clock Tower*

Best Western

Centrally located on the quayside, this long established hotel has been appointed to a very high standard. The bedrooms come in a choice of standard or executive, but all are well equipped and very comfortable. Friendliness and hospitality are the hallmark of a stay here.
ROOMS: 100 en suite (5 fmly) ⊗ in 20 bedrooms s €77.50-€150; d €140-€220 (incl. bkfst) **LB FACILITIES:** STV ♫ Xmas **CONF:** Thtr 200 Class 150 Board 30 **SERVICES:** Lift **PARKING:** 300 **NOTES:** ⊁ ⊗ in restaurant Closed 25-26 Dec

★★★70% **Tower**
The Mall
☎ 051 875801 & 051 862300 🖷 051 870129
e-mail: info@thw.ie
Dir: *opp Reginald's Tower in town centre. Hotel at end of quay on N25*
An extensive refurbishment programme has given this long established hotel a new look that includes two smart restaurants, a riverside bar and upgraded bedrooms together with three river view suites. At the time of inspection the leisure centre was about to undergo further development. Good parking is provided.
ROOMS: 139 en suite (20 fmly) ⊗ in 85 bedrooms s €79-€125; d €99-€200 (incl. bkfst) **LB FACILITIES:** STV ⊞ supervised Sauna Solarium Gym Jacuzzi ♫ Xmas **CONF:** BC Thtr 500 Class 250 Board 80 Del from €90 **SERVICES:** Lift **PARKING:** 100 **NOTES:** ⊁ ⊗ in restaurant Closed 24-28 Dec

★★★67% Dooley's
30 The Quay
☎ 051 873531 📠 051 870262
e-mail: hotel@dooleys-hotel.ie
Dir: *on N25*
Situated on the Quay in Waterford overlooking the River Suir and facing a convenient public car park. This family run hotel offers friendly and relaxed atmosphere the contemporary public areas include the New Ship Restaurant, more casual dining is available in the Dry Dock Bar. Bedrooms are comfortable and well appointed.
ROOMS: 113 en suite (3 fmly) ⊘ in 75 bedrooms s €70-€130; d €120-€198 (incl. bkfst) **LB** **FACILITIES:** STV Land & water based activities ♫ **CONF:** Thtr 240 Class 150 Board 100 Del from €143 **SERVICES:** Lift **NOTES:** ✗ ⊘ in restaurant Closed 25-27 Dec

★★★67% Waterford Manor
Killotteran, Butlerstown
☎ 051 377814 📠 051 354545
e-mail: sales@waterfordmanorhotel.ie
Dir: *N25 from Waterford to Cork, right 2m after Waterford Crystal, left at end of road, hotel on right*

This manor house dates back to 1730 and is set in delightful landscaped and wooded grounds. The hotel provides high quality accommodation as well as extensive conference and banqueting facilities. Public areas include a charming drawing room and restaurant for intimate dining, and the brasserie with its own bar serves carvery lunch daily.
ROOMS: 21 en suite (3 fmly) ⊘ in all bedrooms **FACILITIES:** STV ⚲ **CONF:** BC Thtr 600 Class 300 Board 40 Del from €143 **PARKING:** 400 **NOTES:** ✗ ⊘ in restaurant RS 25-Dec

★★★64% McEniff Ard Ri Hotel
Ferrybank
☎ 051 832111 📠 051 832863
Dir: *on N25 1km from City Centre*
Overlooking the city and harbour this modern hotel enjoys spectacular views and is situated in 38 acres of grounds. Public areas are comfortable and bedrooms are spacious and well equipped. Guests can enjoy the many activities available in the extensive leisure centre.
ROOMS: 100 en suite (20 fmly) ⊘ in 4 bedrooms **FACILITIES:** ⚲ Sauna Solarium Gym Jacuzzi Steam room Plunge pool ♫ Xmas **CONF:** Thtr 700 Class 400 Board 100 Del from €105 **SERVICES:** Lift **PARKING:** 300 **NOTES:** ✗ Closed 24-27 Dec

★★★59% Bridge Hotel
1 The Quay
☎ 051 877222 📠 051 877229
e-mail: info@bridgehotelwaterford.com
Dir: *on N25, opposite Waterford City Bridge*
This busy hotel stands near the City Bridge, convenient for shopping, local amenities and the railway station. The bedrooms vary in size and are well appointed and comfortable. Public areas include a bistro, traditional lounge bar and banqueting facilities.
ROOMS: 133 en suite (20 fmly) ⊘ in 80 bedrooms s €60-€100; d €100-€140 (incl. bkfst) **LB** **FACILITIES:** STV Sauna Gym ♫ Xmas **CONF:** Thtr 400 Class 300 Board 70 **SERVICES:** Lift **PARKING:** 200 **NOTES:** ✗ ⊘ in restaurant Closed 24 & Xmas & 1st 2 wks Jan

Travelodge
Cork Rd
☎ 08700 850 950 📠 051 358890
web: www.travelodge.co.uk
Dir: *on N25, 1km from Waterford Glass Visitors Centre*
Travelodge offers good quality, good value, modern accommodation. Ideal for families, the spacious, en suite bedrooms include remote-control TV, tea and coffee-making facilities and comfortable beds. Meals can be taken at the nearby family restaurant. For further details consult the Hotel Groups page.
ROOMS: 32 en suite s fr €26; d fr €26

WATERVILLE, Co Kerry — Map 01 A2

★★★75% *Butler Arms*
☎ 066 947 4144 📠 066 947 4520
e-mail: butarms@iol.ie
Dir: *village centre on seafront. N70 Ring of Kerry*
This smartly presented hotel on the Ring of Kerry, has been in the Huggard family for four generations. A range of comfortable lounges creates a relaxing atmosphere, and excellent bar food is served in the Fisherman's bar throughout the day. More formal dining is available in the restaurant, which has commanding views of the sea and town.
ROOMS: 40 en suite (1 fmly) ⊘ in 12 bedrooms **FACILITIES:** STV ⚲ Fishing Snooker Billiards room **SERVICES:** Lift **PARKING:** 50 **NOTES:** ✗ ⊘ in restaurant Closed Nov-Apr

WESTPORT, Co Mayo — Map 01 B3

★★★★72% ® *Knockranny House Hotel*
☎ 098 28600 📠 098 28611
e-mail: info@khh.ie
Dir: *on N5 close to Westport*
Overlooking Westport with Clew Bay and Croagh Patrick in the distance, the reception rooms of this family-run hotel take full advantage of the lovely views. The luxurious furnishings create an inviting and relaxing atmosphere throughout the lounge, bar and restaurant. The spacious bedrooms are well appointed. There is a helicopter-landing pad in the well-maintained grounds and a luxury health spa is a new addition.
ROOMS: 54 en suite (4 fmly) ⊘ in 4 bedrooms **FACILITIES:** STV ⚲ Jacuzzi Full Leisure centre free to all guests, at associated hotel 3mins away ♫ **CONF:** Thtr 700 Class 400 Board 40 **SERVICES:** Lift **PARKING:** 120 **NOTES:** ✗ Closed 24-26 Dec

WESTPORT, continued

★★★76% *Hotel Westport Conference, Spa & Leisure Centre*

Newport Rd
☎ 098 25122 📠 098 26739
e-mail: reservations@hotelwestport.ie
Dir: *N5 to Westport, right at end of Castlebar St turn, 1st right, 1st left, follow to end*

Located opposite the grounds of Westport House, yet within walking distance of the town, this hotel offers welcoming public areas, a spacious restaurant and comfortable bedrooms. Leisure and business guests are both well catered for by the enthusiastic and friendly team.

ROOMS: 129 en suite (36 fmly) **FACILITIES: Spa** STV supervised Sauna Solarium Gym Jacuzzi Children's pool Jet stream Lounger pool Steam room, sauna ♫ ch fac **CONF:** Thtr 500 Class 150 Board 60 **SERVICES:** Lift **PARKING:** 220 **NOTES:** ✈ ⊗ in restaurant

★★★69% ® The Atlantic Coast Hotel

The Quay
☎ 098 29000 📠 098 29111
e-mail: info@atlanticcoasthotel.com
Dir: *N5 follow signs into Westport then Louisburgh on R335, 1m from Westport*

This distinctive hotel is in a former mill and has been renovated to a good contemporary standard with modern facilities. Many of the rooms have sea views, as has the award-winning restaurant on the fourth floor. The ground floor has comfortable lounge areas and a lively bar. Spa and treatment rooms have been added to the leisure centre.

ROOMS: 85 en suite (6 fmly) ⊗ in 28 bedrooms s €70-€155; d €120-€270 (incl. bkfst) **FACILITIES: Spa** STV supervised Sauna Solarium Gym Treatment rooms, Health & beauty spa ♫ Xmas **CONF:** BC Thtr 180 Class 100 Board 70 Del from €157.50 **SERVICES:** Lift **PARKING:** 60 **NOTES:** ✈ Closed 23-27 Dec

★★★65% The Wyatt

The Octagon
☎ 098 25027 📠 098 26316
e-mail: info@wyatthotel.com
Dir: *Follow one-way system in town. Hotel by tall monument*

This stylish, welcoming hotel is situated in the famous town centre Octagon. Bedrooms are attractively decorated and well equipped. Public areas are very comfortable with open fires and a lively contemporary bar, there are two dining options, J.W's Bar food and The Wyatt Restaurant offering fine dining.

ROOMS: 52 en suite (2 GF) s €59-€100; d €78-€160 (incl. bkfst) **LB** **FACILITIES:** STV Complimentary access to leisure park 200mtrs from hotel ♫ **CONF:** BC Thtr 300 Class 200 Board 80 **SERVICES:** Lift air con **PARKING:** 20 **NOTES:** ✈ ⊗ in restaurant Closed 25-26 Dec

W

★★74% ® The Olde Railway

The Mall
☎ 098 25166 & 25605 📠 098 25090
e-mail: railway@anu.ie
Dir: *in town centre*

Set on a tree lined mall overlooking the river; this former coaching inn has a welcoming atmosphere with blazing fires. All the bedrooms are well equipped and vary in size, with some being particularly spacious. Public areas include a cosy bar, comfortable lounge and a conservatory restaurant with access to the car park at the rear.

ROOMS: 24 en suite (2 fmly) s €75-€130; d €98-€180 (incl. bkfst) **LB** **FACILITIES:** Fishing & Shooting arranged ♫ **CONF:** Thtr 75 Class 100 **PARKING:** 34 **NOTES:** ✈ ⊗ in restaurant

U *Clew Bay Hotel*

IRISH COUNTRY HOTELS

☎ 098 28088
Dir: *at the bottom of James St, which is parallel to the main street*

At the time of going to press, the star classification for this hotel was not confirmed. Please refer to the AA internet site www.theAA.com for current information.

ROOMS: 35 en suite (3 fmly) ⊗ in 5 bedrooms **FACILITIES:** STV ♫ **NOTES:** Closed Xmas & New Year

WEXFORD, Co Wexford Map 01 D3

★★★★70% ®® Ferrycarrig

Ferrycarrig Bridge
☎ 053 20999 📠 053 20982
e-mail: ferrycarrig@ferrycarrighotel.com
Dir: *on N11 by Slaney Estuary, beside Ferrycarrig Castle*

This fine property has sweeping views of the Slaney Estuary from nearly every angle. Bedrooms are comfortable and well appointed, many of them having access to balconies. The leisure centre is particularly well equipped. The staff offer professional yet friendly service.

ROOMS: 102 en suite (10 fmly) ⊗ in all bedrooms s €80-€500; d €160-€500 (incl. bkfst) **LB** **FACILITIES:** STV supervised Sauna Solarium Gym Jacuzzi Aerobics Beauty treatments on request Hairdresser ♫ Xmas **CONF:** Thtr 400 Class 250 Board 60 **SERVICES:** Lift **PARKING:** 235 **NOTES:** ✈ ⊗ in restaurant

★★★74% Talbot

The Quay
☎ 053 22566 & 55559 📠 053 23377
e-mail: sales@talbothotel.ie
Dir: *N11 from Rosslare, follow Wexford signs, 12m, hotel on right of The Quays*

Centrally situated on the quayside, this hotel has been extensively refurbished. The well-equipped bedrooms have custom-made oak furniture and attractive decor; many have sea views. Public areas include a spacious foyer, comfortable lounges and the Ballast Quay bar serving food all day. The attractive restaurant serves interesting food, and there are good leisure facilities.
ROOMS: 109 en suite (12 fmly) ⊘ in 87 bedrooms s €75-€95; d €110-€190 (incl. bkfst) **FACILITIES: Spa** STV supervised Sauna Solarium Gym Jacuzzi Childrens room Beauty Salon ♫ Xmas **CONF:** BC Thtr 450 Class 250 Board 110 Del from €145 **SERVICES:** Lift air con **PARKING:** 160 **NOTES:** ✈ ⊘ in restaurant Closed 24-25 Dec

See advert on this page

★★★70% ❁ Whitford House Hotel Health & Leisure Club

New Line Rd
☎ 053 43444 📠 053 46399
e-mail: info@whitford.ie
web: www.whitford.ie
Dir: *from Rosslare take N25 at Duncannon Rd rdbt, right onto R733, hotel immediately left*

This is a friendly family-run hotel just 2 km from the town centre within easy reach of the Rosslare ferry. Comfortable rooms range from standard to deluxe; they are spacious and luxuriously decorated and furnished. Public areas include a choice of lounges and a popular bar where food is also served. More formal dinner is on offer in Footprints Restaurant.
ROOMS: 36 en suite (28 fmly) (18 GF) s €58-€139; d €136-€208 (incl. bkfst) **LB** **FACILITIES: Spa** STV supervised Sauna Solarium Gym Jacuzzi Childrens playground Beer garden/Adult reading room, ♫ **CONF:** Thtr 50 Class 45 Board 25 **PARKING:** 200 **NOTES:** ✈ ⊘ in restaurant RS 23 Dec-2 Jan

★★★65% River Bank House Hotel

☎ 053 23611 📠 053 23342
e-mail: river@indigo.ie
Dir: *beside Wexford Bridge on R741*

Overlooking the estuary of the Slaney River, this hotel is at the foot of the Wexford Bridge, a short distance from the town centre. Both the bar and restaurant have views of the harbour. Bedrooms are well equipped and comfortable. Impressive banqueting facilities have also been added.
ROOMS: 23 en suite (6 fmly) (7 GF) ⊘ in 8 bedrooms s €55-€110; d €90-€170 (incl. bkfst) **LB** **FACILITIES:** STV ♫ **CONF:** Thtr 350 Class 180 Board 48 Del from €90 **SERVICES:** Lift **PARKING:** 25 **NOTES:** ✈ ⊘ in restaurant Closed 24-25 Dec

Restaurant with Rooms

❁ Newbay Country House & Restaurant

Newbay, Carrick
☎ 053 42779 📠 053 46318
e-mail: newbay@newbayhouse.com

Built in the 1840s, Newbay offers a choice of two dining areas, the casual Cellar Bistro on the lower floor, or the more formal restaurant in the original house. Seafood is a passion here; indeed they have their own trawler. The very comfortable bedrooms are situated in both the house and a wing.
ROOMS: 12 en suite

WICKLOW See Rathnew

WOODENBRIDGE, Co Wicklow — Map 01 D3

★★★67% ❁ *Woodenbridge*

☎ 0402 35146 📠 0402 35573
e-mail: wbhotel@iol.ie
Dir: *between Avoca & Arklow*

Situated in the beautiful Vale of Avoca and owner-managed by the hospitable O'Brien family this smart hotel is beside the Woodenbridge Golf Club. Public areas are comfortable with open fires and good food is assured in the newly-built Italian restaurant. The new lodge bedrooms are well equipped, spacious and enjoy a peaceful riverside setting.
ROOMS: 23 en suite (13 fmly) **FACILITIES:** STV **CONF:** Thtr 200 Class 200 Board 200 **PARKING:** 100 **NOTES:** ✈ ⊘ in restaurant

♫ Entertainment

W

KEY TO ATLAS

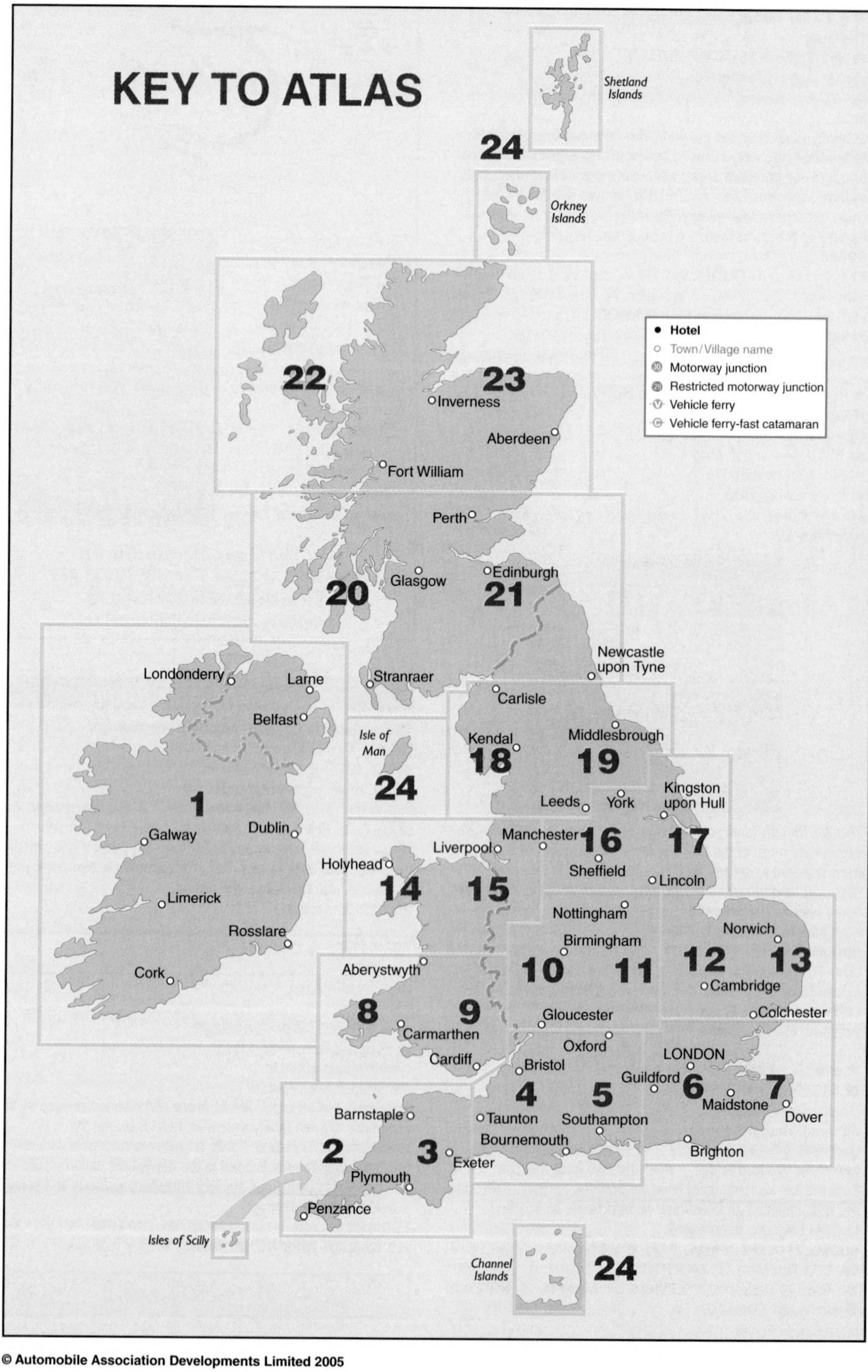

Shetland Islands
24
Orkney Islands
22
23
Inverness
Aberdeen
Fort William
Perth
Glasgow
Edinburgh
20
21
Newcastle upon Tyne
Stranraer
Carlisle
Londonderry
Larne
Belfast
Isle of Man
24
Kendal
18
Middlesbrough
19
1
Kingston upon Hull
Leeds
York
Galway
Dublin
Manchester
Liverpool
16
17
Holyhead
Sheffield
14
15
Lincoln
Limerick
Nottingham
Rosslare
Birmingham
Norwich
Cork
Aberystwyth
10
11
12
13
Cambridge
8
9
Gloucester
Colchester
Carmarthen
Oxford
Cardiff
LONDON
Bristol
Guildford
4
5
6
7
Maidstone
Barnstaple
Taunton
Southampton
Dover
Bournemouth
Brighton
2
3
Exeter
Plymouth
Penzance
Isles of Scilly
Channel Islands
24
• Hotel
○ Town/Village name
Motorway junction
Restricted motorway junction
Vehicle ferry
Vehicle ferry-fast catamaran

1
A
B
C
D
6
5
4
3
2
1
Rathlin Island
Malin Head
Malin
Portballintrae
Ballycastle
Tory Island
Dunfanaghy
Rathmullan
Limavady
Coleraine
Aghadowey
Carnlough
LONDONDERRY
Aran Island
Maghera
Larne
Strabane
Ballymena
Ballybofey
SPERRIN MTS
Carrickfergus
Bangor
NORTHERN
BELFAST
Newtownards
Donegal
Omagh
Cookstown
Dungannon
Rossnowlagh
IRELAND
Portaferry
Ballyshannon
Irvinestown
Armagh
Portadown
Donegal Bay
Enniskillen
Downpatrick
Newcastle
Newry
MOURNE MTS
Sligo
Monaghan
Bangor Erris
Ballina
OX MTS
Ballyconnell
Carrickmacross
Dundalk
Cavan
Kingscourt
Achill Island
Achill Island
Foxford
Boyle
Carrick-on-Shannon
Kiltimagh
Castlebar
Virginia
Drogheda
Knock
Castlerea
Clare Island
Westport
Longford
Kells
M1 Toll
Balbriggan
Claremorris
REPUBLIC
Navan
Inishturk
Skerries
Roscommon
Lambay
Renvyle
Kilmessan
Inishbofin
Mullingar
Portmarnock
Recess
Enfield
Leixlip
Howth
Clifden
Tuam
OF
Straffan
Lucan
DUBLIN
Roundstone
Cashel
Athlone
Oughterard
Ballinasloe
Tullamore
Newbridge
Kill
Killiney
Carna
GALWAY
Kildare
Naas
Bray
Gorumna Island
Oranmore
Loughrea
IRELAND
Delgany
Blessington
Newtownmountkennedy
Galway Bay
Rathnew
Birr
SLIEVE BLOOM MTS
Glendalough
Inishmore
Ballyvaughan
Gort
Portumna
Wicklow
Doolin
Portlaoise
Macreddin
Lisdoonvarna
Roscrea
Castledermot
WICKLOW MTS
Aughrim
Woodenbridge
Abbeyleix
Ennistymon
Carlow
Tullow
Arklow
Newmarket-on-Fergus
Nenagh
Spanish Point
Ennis
Gorey
Thurles
Kilkenny
Courtown Harbour
Killaloe
Kilkee
Bunratty
LIMERICK
Dundrum
Bunclody
Kilrush
Thomastown
Enniscorthy
Loop Head
Adare
Tipperary
Cashel
Cahir
Clonmel
Wexford
New Ross
GALTY MTS
Rosslare
Ballyheige
Abbeyfeale
KNOCKMEALDOWN MTS
WATERFORD
Charleville
Tralee
Mitchelstown
Castleisland
Lismore
Tramore
Carnsore Point
Kanturk
Mallow
Dingle
Killorglin
Fermoy
Great Blasket Island
Dungarvan
Killarney
BOGGERAGH MTS
Dingle Bay
Youghal
Midleton
Valentia Island
Caherciveen
Blarney
Garryvoe
Macroom
CORK
Parknasilla
Kenmare
Innishannon
Ballycotton
Waterville
Carrigaline
Gougane Barra
Kinsale
Caherdaniel
Ballylickey
Bantry
Clonakilty
Dursey Island
Bantry Bay
Rosscarbery
Baltimore
Mizen Head
Clear Island
N56
N13
N14
N15
A29
A26
A2
A6
M2
A36
M5
A5
M1
A32
A4
A46
N16
A1
A25
N2
N87
N17
N59
N26
N4
N5
N61
N55
N3
N52
N60
N51
N84
M50
N63
N6
M4
N62
N80
M7
M11
N81
N65
N67
N7
N11
N18
N85
N68
N78
N80
N9
N76
N8
N69
N24
N21
N20
N30
N25
N86
N72
N22
N71
N70
• Hotel
○ Town name
0
20
40 miles
0
20
40
60 kilometres

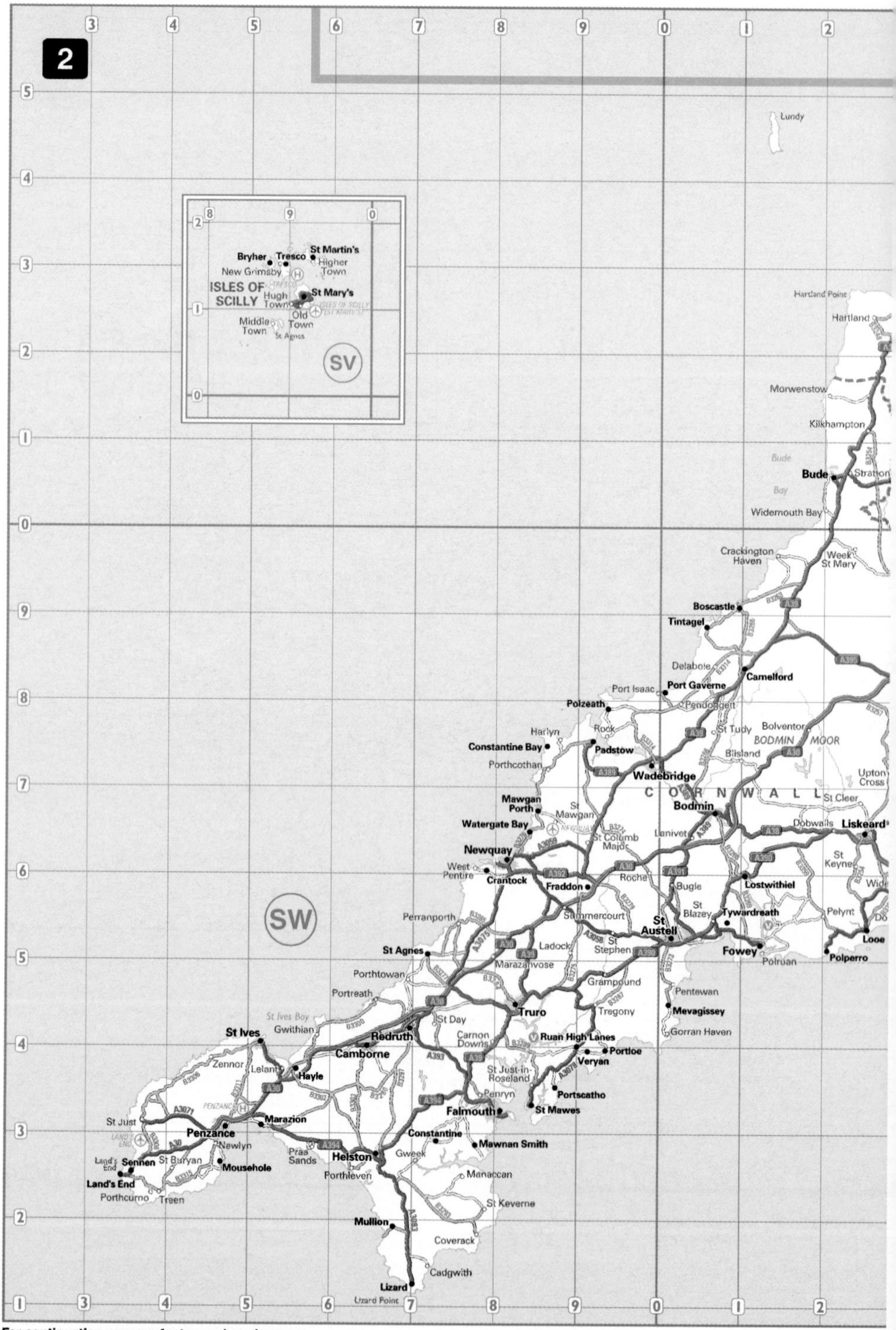

For continuation pages refer to numbered arrows

3
Bristol Channel area
Bridgwater Bay
Brent Knoll
Burnham-on-Sea
9
4
DEVON
EXMOOR FOREST
DARTMOOR FOREST
QUANTOCK HILLS
SS
ST
SX
SY
Ilfracombe
Mortehoe
Lee
Woolacombe
Georgeham
Croyde
Saunton
Braunton
Barnstaple or Bideford Bay
Combe Martin
Martinhoe
Lynton
Lynmouth
Woody Bay
Parracombe
Brendon
Porlock Weir
Porlock
Minehead
Dunster
Blue Anchor
Watchet
Wootton Courtenay
Carhampton
Challacombe
Simonsbath
Exford
Withypool
Winsford
Wheddon Cross
Brompton Regis
Bratton Fleming
Muddiford
Barnstaple
Brayford
Appledore
Instow
Northam
Westward Ho!
Bideford
Clovelly
Horns Cross
Parkham
Monkleigh
Great Torrington
Little Torrington
Stibb Cross
Merton
Dolton
Beaford
Burrington
Umberleigh
Chittlehamholt
South Molton
North Molton
Dulverton
Exebridge
Wiveliscombe
Fitzhead
Milverton
Petton
Bampton
Williton
Sampford Brett
Crowcombe
Elworthy
Kilve
Stogursey
Holford
Nether Stowey
West Huntspill
Cannington
Bridgwater
Goathurst
North Petherton
Bishops Lydeard
Taunton
Taunton Deane Services
Wellington
Sampford Arundel
Corfe
Staple Fitzpaine
Hatch Beauchamp
North Curry
Sampford Peverell
Culmstock
Hemyock
Uffculme
Willand
Halberton
Tiverton
Rackenford
Witheridge
Chulmleigh
Chawleigh
Eggesford
Lapford
Winkleigh
Bradworthy
Milton Damerel
Shebbear
Black Torrington
Sheepwash
Meeth
Chilsworthy
Holsworthy
Highampton
Hatherleigh
Halwill Junction
Clawton
Beaworthy
Ashwater
Okehampton
Bratton Clovelly
Sourton Cross
Sourton
Bridestowe
Launceston
Lewdown
Lifton
Lydford
Milton Abbot
Lamerton
Mary Tavy
Tavistock
Gulworthy
Gunnislake
Callington
Pensilva
Bere Alston
St Mellion
Pillaton
Bere Ferrers
Landrake
Saltash
Polbathic
Downderry
Portwrinkle
Crafthole
Millbrook
Cawsand
Torpoint
PLYMOUTH
Plympton
Yelverton
Horrabridge
Dousland
Princetown
Two Bridges
Shaugh Prior
Hexworthy
Postbridge
Widecombe in the Moor
Chagford
Moretonhampstead
South Zeal
Whiddon Down
Crockernwell
Dunsford
Tedburn St Mary
Crediton
Newton St Cyres
Copplestone
Morchard Bishop
Cheriton Fitzpaine
Cullompton
Bickleigh
Silverton
Stoke Canon
Broadclyst
Whimple
EXETER
Fenny Bridges
Honiton
Ottery St Mary
Wilmington
Upottery
Yarcombe
Tytherleigh
Axminster
Shute
Colyton
Colyford
Uplyme
Rousdon
Lyme Regis
Axmouth
Seaton
Beer
Branscombe
Sidmouth
Clyst St Mary
Topsham
Exminster
Woodbury
Kennford
Otterton
Budleigh Salterton
Exmouth
Kenton
Chudleigh
Bovey Tracey
Haytor Vale
Ilsington
Chudleigh Knighton
Ideford
Dawlish
Bishopsteignton
Teignmouth
Shaldon
Kingsteignton
Newton Abbot
Kingskerswell
Maidencombe
Ashburton
Holne
Buckfastleigh
Ipplepen
Staverton
Dartington
TORQUAY
Paignton
Tor Bay
Churston Ferrers
Brixham
South Brent
Cornwood
Wrangaton
Ivybridge
Totnes
Stoke Gabriel
Harbertonford
Dittisham
Ermington
Ugborough
Halwell
Kingswear
Dartmouth
Modbury
Yealmpton
Brixton
Heybrook Bay
Wembury
Holbeton
Newton Ferrers
Aveton Gifford
Stoke Fleming
Strete
Slapton
Chillington
Start Bay
Torcross
Hallsands
Start Point
Bigbury-on-Sea
Bigbury Bay
Thurlestone
Kingsbridge
Hope
Hope Cove
Malborough
Salcombe
East Prawle
M5
A30
A35
A38
A39
A361
A373
A375
A377
A379
A380
A381
A384
A385
A386
A388
A390
A396
A399
A3072
A3124
A303
A358
A3052
• Hotel
○ Town/Village name
0 10 miles
0 10 20 kilometres

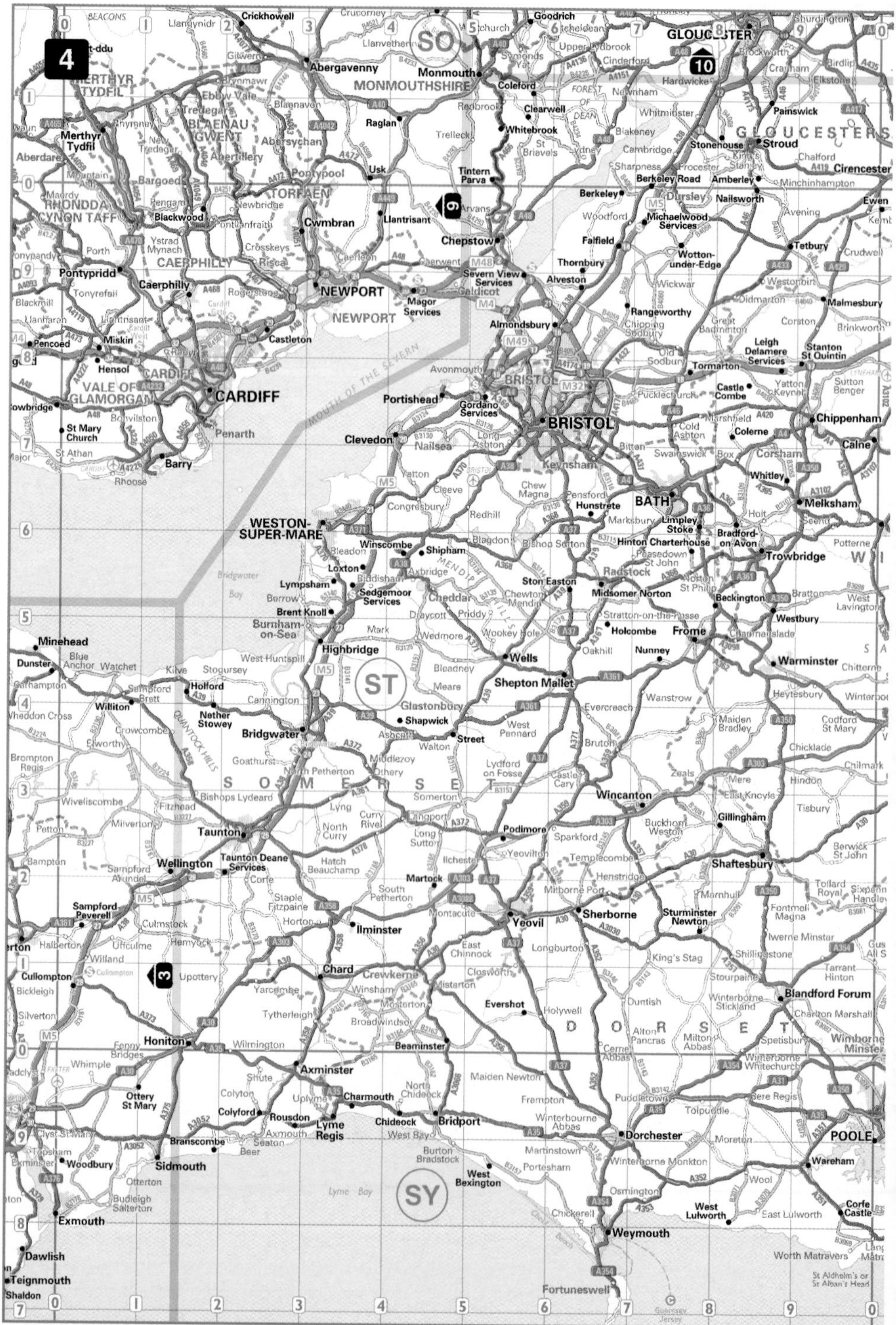

For continuation pages refer to numbered arrows

5
OXFORDSHIRE
BERKSHIRE
HAMPSHIRE
SURREY
WEST SUSSEX
ISLE OF WIGHT
NEW FOREST
SOUTH DOWNS
SP
SU
SZ
OXFORD
SWINDON
READING
BASINGSTOKE
SOUTHAMPTON
PORTSMOUTH
BOURNEMOUTH
WINCHESTER
EASTLEIGH
HAVANT
FAREHAM
WATERLOOVILLE
GOSPORT
BOGNOR REGIS
HIGH WYCOMBE
BRACKNELL
CAMBERLEY
WOKING
GUILDFORD
SLOUGH
Aylesbury
Witney
Abingdon
Didcot
Newbury
Andover
Salisbury
Romsey
Alton
Farnham
Petersfield
Midhurst
Chichester
Newport
Ryde
Cowes
Sandown
Shanklin
Ventnor
Hotel
Town/Village name
0
10 miles
0
10
20 kilometres

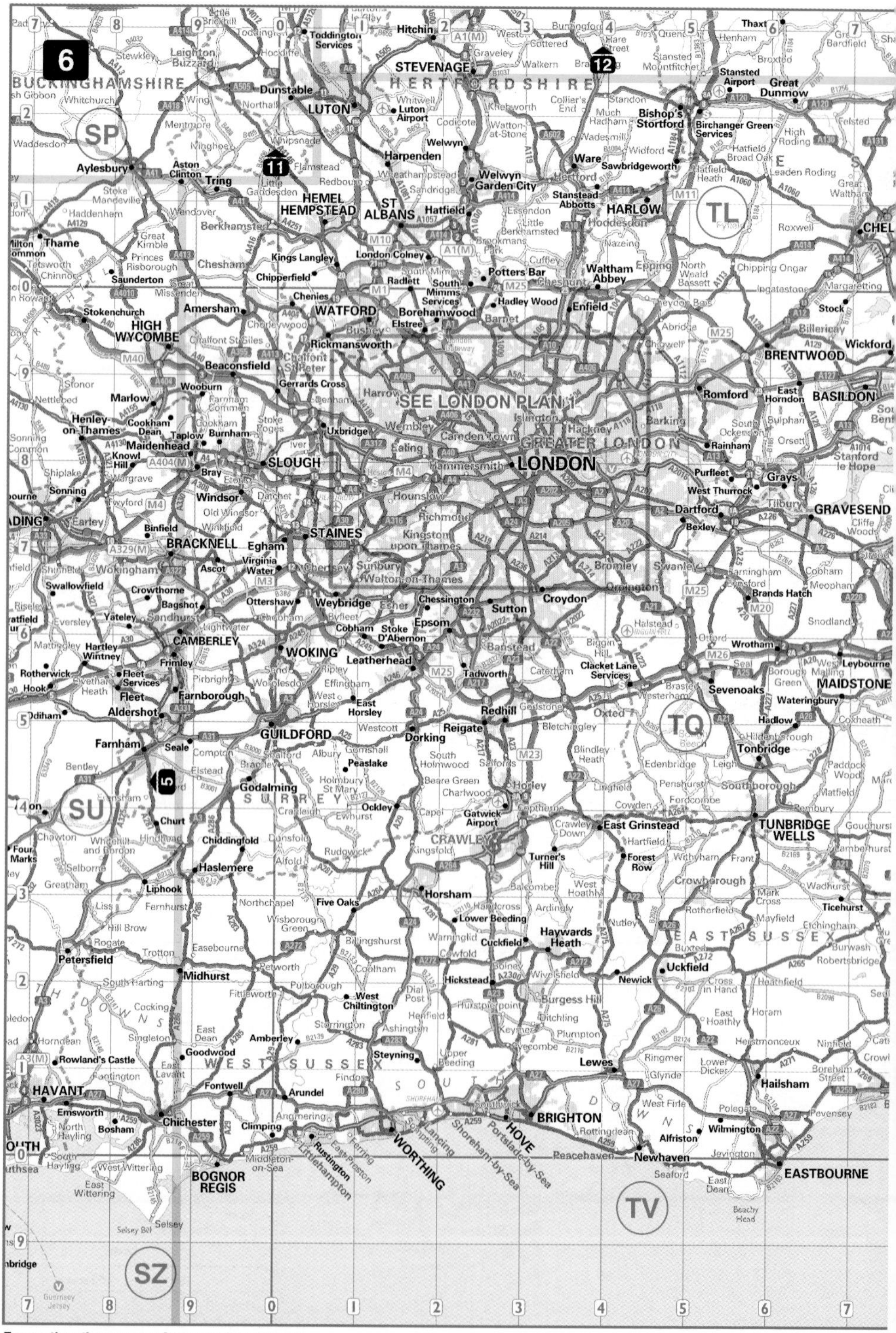

For continuation pages refer to numbered arrows

7
13
COLCHESTER
Harwich
Braintree
Earls Colne
Aldham
Marks Tey
Coggeshall
Feering
Copford Green
Wivenhoe
Elmstead Market
Ardleigh
Wix
Weeley
Thorpe-le-Soken
Walton on the Naze
Frinton-on-Sea
Little Clacton
Thorrington
Brightlingsea
St Osyth
CLACTON-ON-SEA
Silver End
Kelvedon
Tiptree
Tolleshunt Knights
Witham
Tolleshunt D'Arcy
West Mersea
Goldhanger
Tollesbury
Maldon
River Blackwater
Bradwell-on-Sea
Danbury
Steeple
Cold Norton
Latchingdon
Southminster
South Woodham Ferrers
Burnham-on-Crouch
Hockley
Rayleigh
Rochford
Great Wakering
SOUTHEND-ON-SEA
Canvey Island
Thames
TM
Grain
Sheerness
Minster
Hoo St Werburgh
Eastchurch
Leysdown-on-Sea
Isle of Sheppey
ROCHESTER
GILLINGHAM
CHATHAM
Iwade
Medway
Herne Bay
Reculver
Whitstable
MARGATE
Kingsgate
Broadstairs
Ramsgate
KENT INT
Sittingbourne
Teynham
Faversham
Ospringe
Bredhurst
Upstreet
Sarre
Minster
Blean
Sturry
Hersden
Boughton Street
Fordwich
Ash
Sandwich
Maidstone Services
Doddington
Canterbury
Wingham
Hollingbourne
Bearsted
Chilham
Chartham
Bridge
Eastry
Lenham
Charing
Challock
Aylesham
Deal
TR
Linton
Sutton Valence
KENT
Wye
Wingmore
Kingsdown
Pluckley
Headcorn
Elham
St Margaret's at Cliffe
Smarden
Staplehurst
Bethersden
Ashford
Densole
Alkham
Lyminge
DOVER
CHANNEL TUNNEL TERMINAL
Hawkinge
Biddenden
High Halden
Kingsnorth
Sellindge
Sissinghurst
Cranbrook
Woodchurch
Lympne
Hythe
FOLKESTONE
Channel Tunnel (Rail)
Benenden
Tenterden
Hamstreet
Hawkhurst
Rolvenden
Dymchurch
Wittersham
Appledore
St Mary's Bay
Bodiam
Brookland
Brenzett
Northiam
New Romney
STRAIT OF DOVER
Peasmarsh
Rye
Lydd
LYDD
Camber
Brede
Winchelsea
Dungeness
Battle
Westfield
Guestling Green
Fairlight
HASTINGS
Bexhill
• Hotel
○ Town/Village name
0
10 miles
0
10
20 kilometres

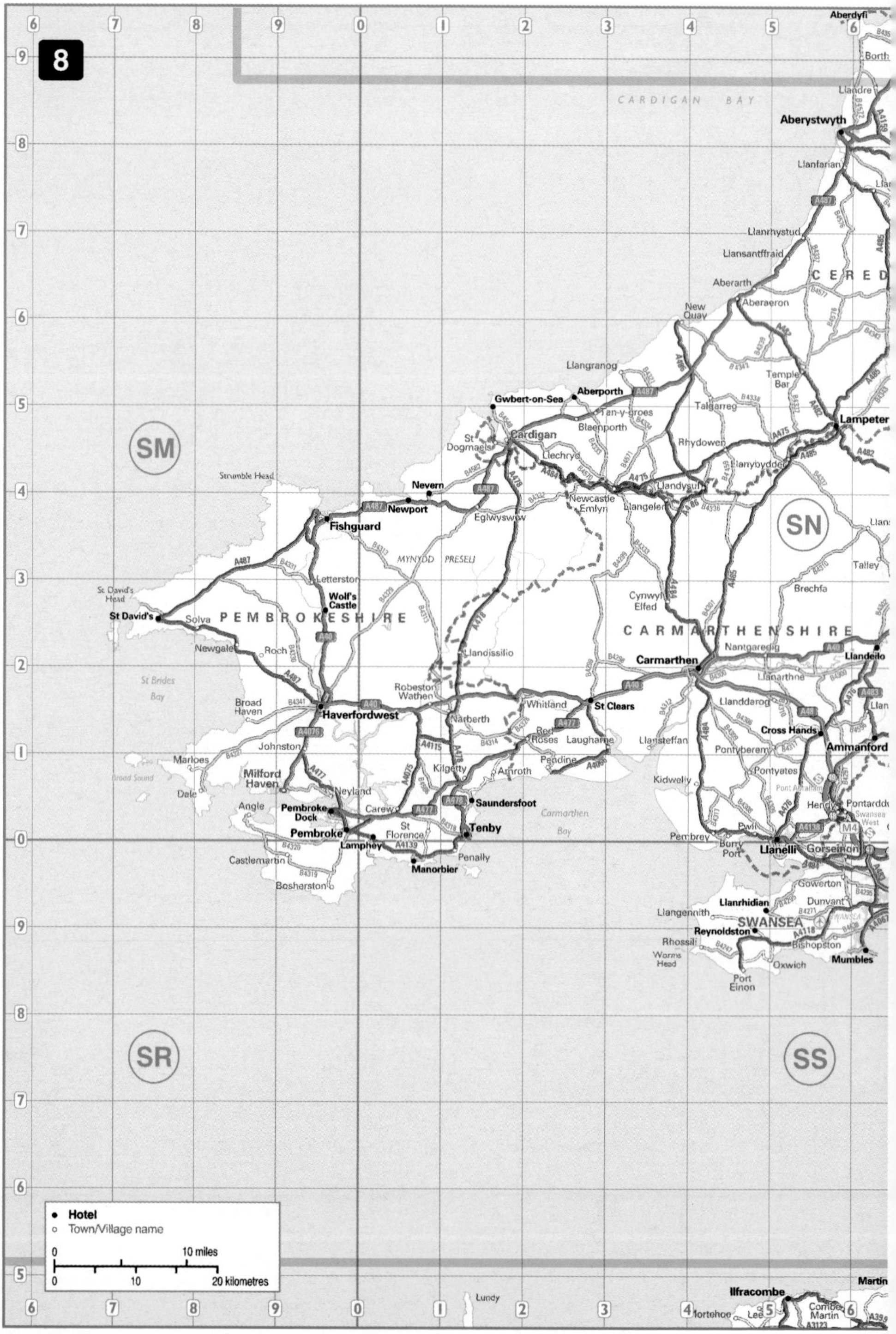

For continuation pages refer to numbered arrows

9
14
15
10
4
3
SO
ST
P O W Y S
HEREFORDSHIRE
MONMOUTHSHIRE
MERTHYR TYDFIL
BLAENAU GWENT
TORFAEN
NEATH PORT TALBOT
RHONDDA CYNON TAFF
CAERPHILLY
BRIDGEND
VALE OF GLAMORGAN
NEWPORT
BLACK MOUNTAINS
BRECON BEACONS
BLACK MOUNTAIN
MYNYDD EPPYNT
MOUTH OF THE SEVERN
MENDIP HILLS
Bridgwater Bay
Swansea Bay
Newtown
Caersws
Llanidloes
Llandinam
Kerry
Bishop's Castle
Lydham
Church Stretton
Little Stretton
Hope Bowdler
Ditton Priors
Bridgnorth
Cleobury North
Munslow
Craven Arms
Aston on Clun
Lydbury North
Clun
Bromfield
Ludlow
Leintwardine
Knighton
Cleobury Mortimer
Clows Top
Newnham
Tenbury Wells
Woofferton
Richards Castle
Presteigne
Kingsland
Leominster
Pembridge
Kington
Lyonshall
Dilwyn
Weobley
Hope under Dinmore
Bromyard
Bredenbury
Stoke Lacy
Bishop's Frome
Newtown
White Stone
Hereford
Lugwardine
Mordiford
Allensmore
Kingstone
Fownhope
Much Marcle
Much Birch
Harewood End
Ross-on-Wye
Goodrich
Whitchurch
Skenfrith
Pontrilas
Ewyas Harold
Walterstone
Grosmont
Pandy
Llanthony
Llanvihangel Crucorney
Llanvetherine
Abergavenny
Monmouth
Coleford
Symonds Yat
Cinderford
Upper Lydbrook
Clearwell
Whitebrook
St Briavels
Lydney
Trelleck
Redbrook
Raglan
Usk
Tintern Parva
Chepstow
Llantrisant
Pontypool
Abersychan
Blaenavon
Cwmbran
Ponthir
Caerleon
Newbridge
Crosskeys
Risca
Rogerstone
NEWPORT
Magor Services
Caldicot
Severn View Services
Alveston
Thornbury
Falfield
Woodford
Berkeley
Sharpness
Almondsbury
Avonmouth
Portishead
Gordano Services
BRISTOL
Keynsham
Clevedon
Nailsea
Long Ashton
Yatton
Cleeve
Congresbury
Chew Magna
Pensford
Hunstrete
Marksbury
Redhill
Blagdon
Bishop Sutton
WESTON-SUPER-MARE
Bleadon
Winscombe
Shipham
Loxton
Axbridge
Cheddar
Lympsham
Berrow
Sedgemoor Services
Brent Knoll
Draycott
Priddy
Chewton Mendip
Ston Easton
Radstock
Midsomer Norton
Holcombe
Oakhill
Wells
Wookey Hole
Wedmore
Mark
Burnham-on-Sea
Highbridge
West Huntspill
Blue Anchor
Dunster
Minehead
Porlock
Porlock Weir
Lynton
Lynmouth
Woody Bay
Parracombe
Brendon
Tal-y-bont
Ponterwyd
Goginan
Devil's Bridge
Cwmystwyth
Ysbyty Ystwyth
Pontrhydfendigaid
Tregaron
Llangurig
Pant-y-dwr
Rhayader
Elan Village
Beguildy
Llanfair Waterdine
Llanbister
Bleddfa
Whitton
Penybont
New Radnor
Walton
Llandrindod Wells
Newbridge on Wye
Beulah
Builth Wells
Garth
Llanwrtyd Wells
Llangammarch Wells
Whitney-on-Wye
Eardisley
Sarnesfield
Bredwardine
Credenhill
Clyro
Hay-on-Wye
Dorstone
Peterchurch
Erwood
Glasbury
Llyswen
Three Cocks
Bronllys
Talgarth
Pumsaint
Llandovery
Llanwrda
Llangadog
Trecastle
Sennybridge
Brecon
Llangors
Llanhamlach
Bwlch
Llangynidr
Crickhowell
Gilwern
Brynmawr
Ebbw Vale
Tredegar
Rhymney
New Tredegar
Abertillery
Glyntawe
Brynamman
Nant-ddu
Ystradgynlais
Ystalyfera
Seven Sisters
Crynant
Glyn-Neath
Hirwaun
Aberdare
Merthyr Tydfil
Pontardawe
Clydach
Resolven
Mountain Ash
Bargoed
Blackwood
Pengam
Pontllanfraith
Ystrad Mynach
Neath
Glyncorrwg
Treherbert
Maerdy
Cymer
Blaengarw
Tonypandy
Porth
Pontypridd
Caerphilly
Baglan
SWANSEA
Port Talbot
Maesteg
Llangeinor
Blackmill
Tonyrefail
Llanharan
Llantrisant
Sarn Park Services
Pencoed
Miskin
Pyle
Bridgend
Hensol
Porthcawl
Ogmore-by-Sea
Cowbridge
CARDIFF
Castleton
St Mary Church
Penarth
Llantwit Major
St Athan
Barry
Rhoose

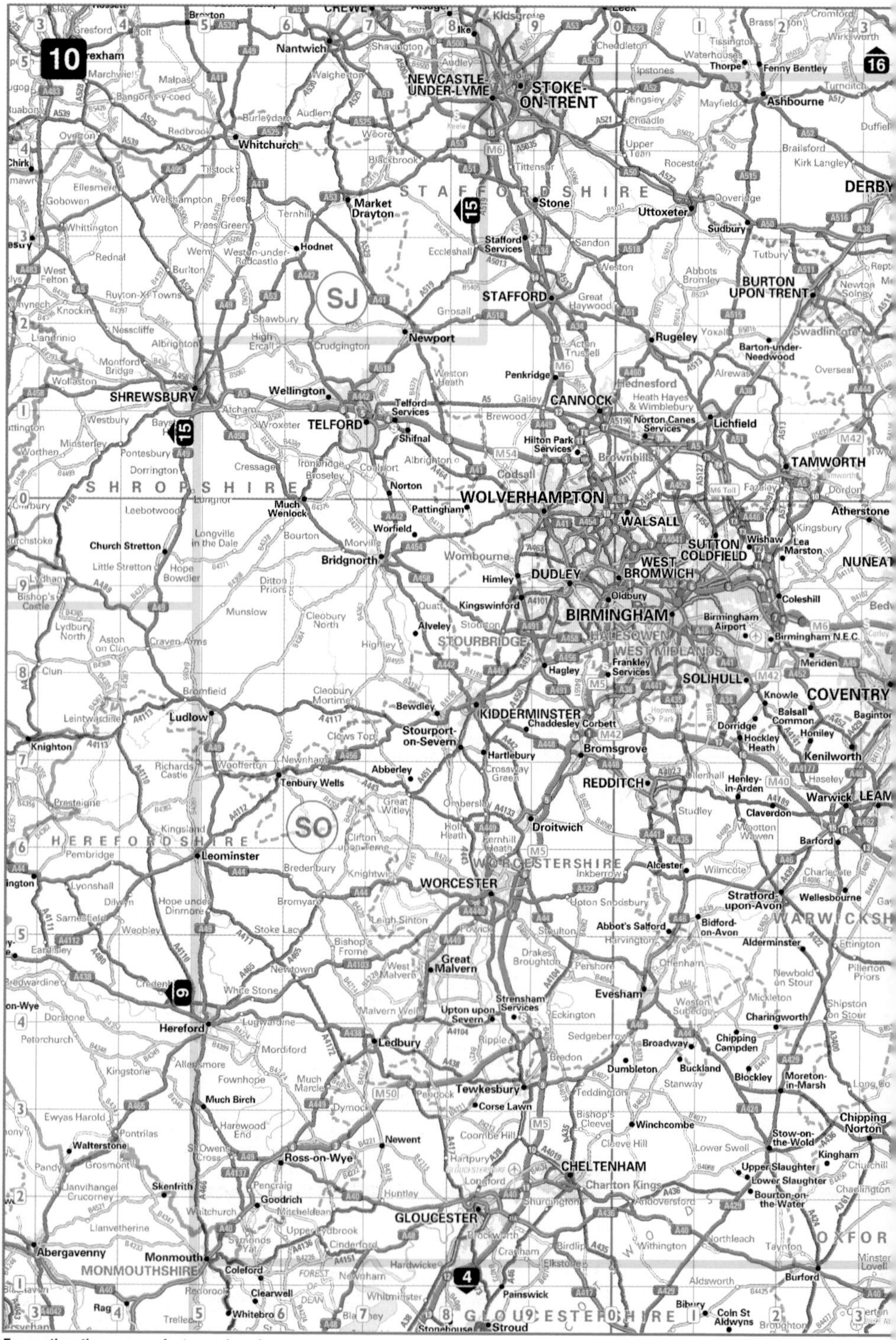

For continuation pages refer to numbered arrows

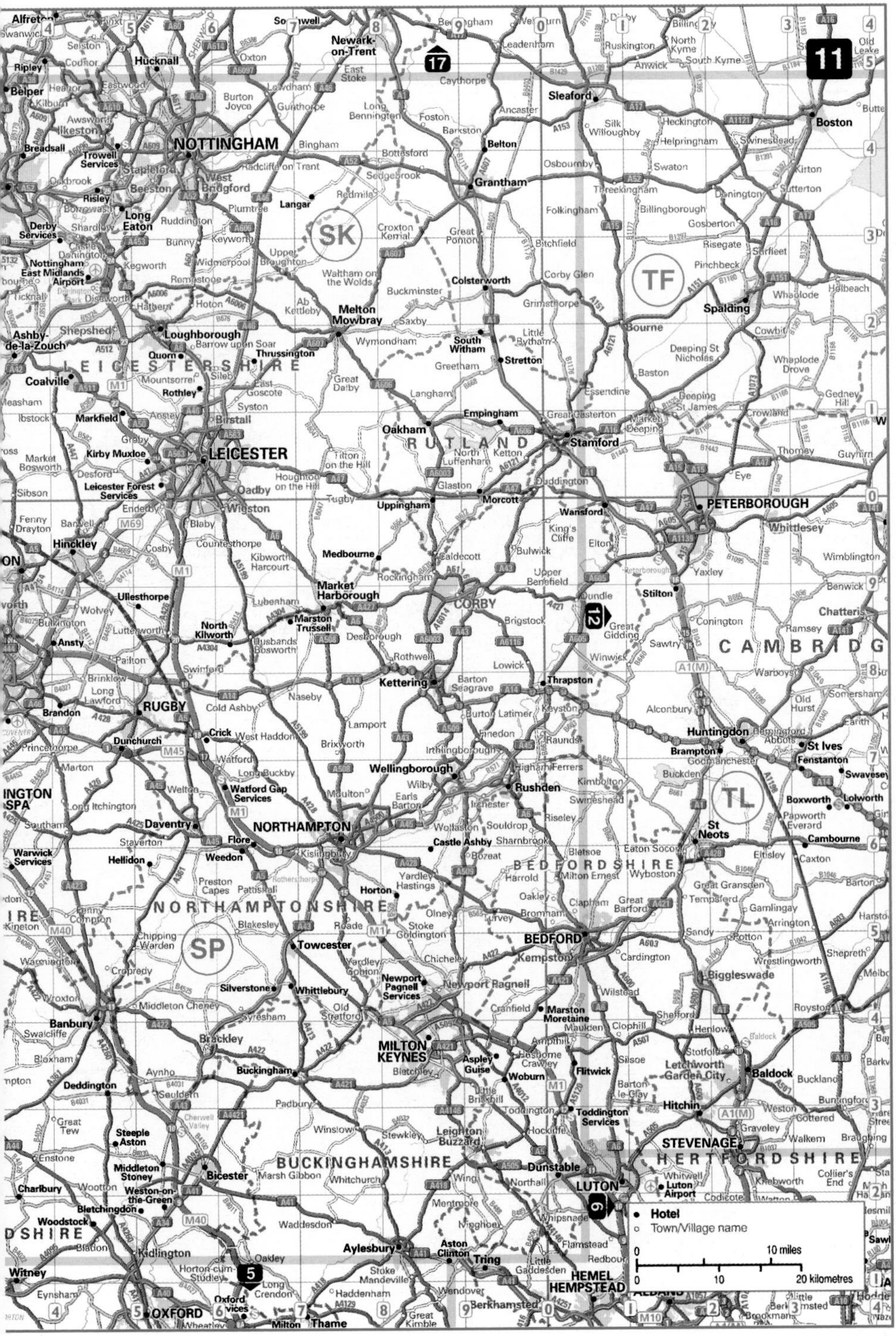
11
17
12
6
5
SK
TF
SP
TL
LEICESTERSHIRE
RUTLAND
NORTHAMPTONSHIRE
BEDFORDSHIRE
BUCKINGHAMSHIRE
HERTFORDSHIRE
CAMBRIDG
NOTTINGHAM
LEICESTER
NORTHAMPTON
PETERBOROUGH
BEDFORD
LUTON
MILTON KEYNES
OXFORD
STEVENAGE
HEMEL HEMPSTEAD
CORBY
RUGBY
Alfreton
Hucknall
Ripley
Belper
Ilkeston
Trowell Services
Stapleford
Beeston
West Bridgford
Long Eaton
Derby Services
Nottingham East Midlands Airport
Loughborough
Quorn
Coalville
Ashby-de-la-Zouch
Markfield
Kirby Muxloe
Leicester Forest Services
Rothley
Hinckley
Newark-on-Trent
Sleaford
Boston
Grantham
Belton
Langar
Melton Mowbray
Colsterworth
South Witham
Stretton
Spalding
Bourne
Stamford
Oakham
Empingham
Uppingham
Morcott
Wansford
Medbourne
Market Harborough
Marston Trussell
North Kilworth
Ullesthorpe
Ansty
Brandon
Kettering
Thrapston
Huntingdon
Brampton
St Ives
Fenstanton
Swavesey
Boxworth
Lolworth
St Neots
Cambourne
Dunchurch
Crick
Watford Gap Services
Daventry
Flore
Weedon
Hellidon
Warwick Services
Wellingborough
Rushden
Castle Ashby
Horton
Towcester
Silverstone
Whittlebury
Newport Pagnell Services
Banbury
Deddington
Buckingham
Aspley Guise
Woburn
Flitwick
Marston Moretaine
Toddington Services
Hitchin
Baldock
Steeple Aston
Middleton Stoney
Bicester
Weston-on-the-Green
Bletchingdon
Woodstock
Kidlington
Witney
Aylesbury
Aston Clinton
Tring
Dunstable
Luton Airport
Oxford Services
Milton
Thame
Berkhamsted
Hotel
Town/Village name
0
10 miles
0
10
20 kilometres

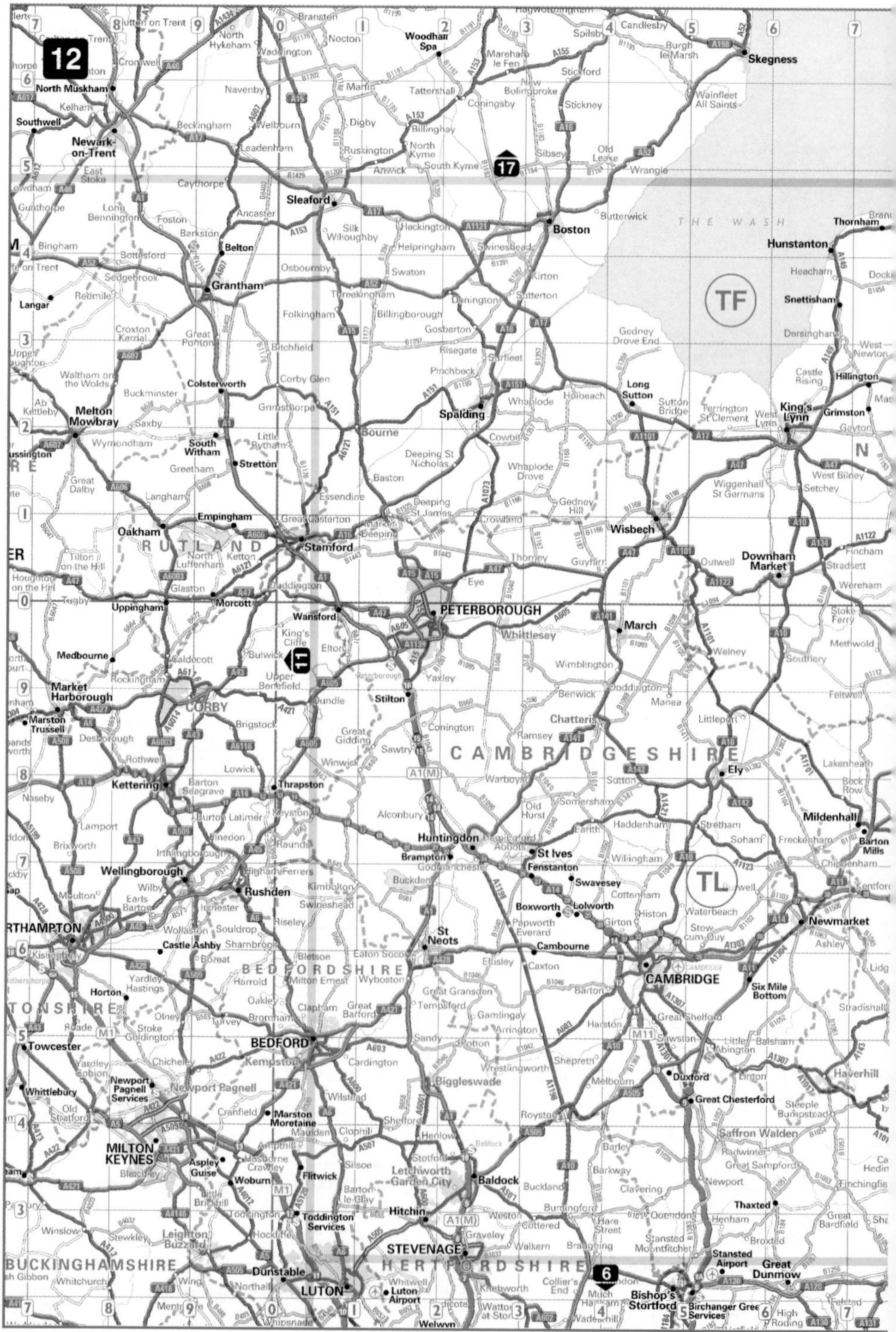

For continuation pages refer to numbered arrows

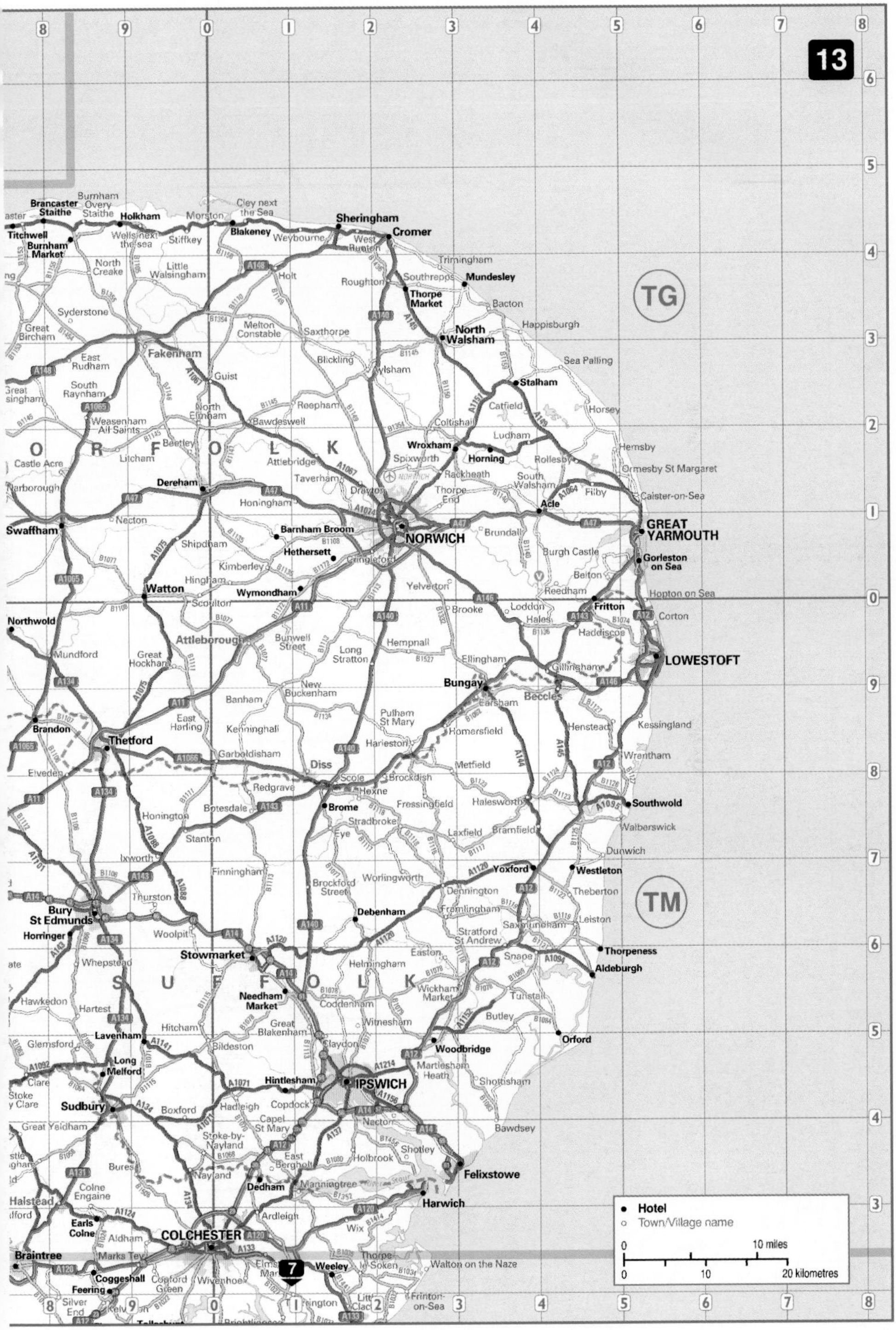
Brancaster Staithe
Burnham Overy Staithe
Holkham
Morston
Cley next the Sea
Sheringham
Cromer
Titchwell
Burnham Market
Wells next the sea
Stiffkey
Blakeney
Weybourne
West Runton
North Creake
Little Walsingham
Holt
Trimingham
Roughton
Southrepps
Mundesley
Thorpe Market
Bacton
Syderstone
Melton Constable
Saxthorpe
North Walsham
Happisburgh
TG
Great Bircham
East Rudham
Fakenham
Blickling
Aylsham
Sea Palling
Guist
Stalham
South Raynham
North Elmham
Reepham
Catfield
Horsey
Weasenham All Saints
Bawdeswell
Coltishall
Ludham
Beetley
Wroxham
Horning
Hemsby
Castle Acre
Litcham
Attlebridge
Spixworth
Rollesby
Ormesby St Margaret
Taverham
Rackheath
South Walsham
Drayton
Thorpe End
Filby
Caister-on-Sea
Dereham
Honingham
Acle
Swaffham
Necton
Barnham Broom
NORWICH
Brundall
GREAT YARMOUTH
Shipdham
Hethersett
Burgh Castle
Gorleston on Sea
Kimberley
Cringleford
Belton
Hingham
Yelverton
Reedham
Watton
Wymondham
Scoulton
Hopton on Sea
Fritton
Northwold
Brooke
Loddon
Hales
Corton
Haddiscoe
Attleborough
Bunwell Street
Long Stratton
Hempnall
LOWESTOFT
Mundford
Great Hockham
Ellingham
Gillingham
Bungay
Beccles
New Buckenham
Banham
Earsham
Brandon
East Harling
Kenninghall
Pulham St Mary
Homersfield
Henstead
Kessingland
Thetford
Harleston
Garboldisham
Wrentham
Elveden
Diss
Scole
Brockdish
Metfield
Redgrave
Hoxne
Southwold
Botesdale
Brome
Fressingfield
Halesworth
Honington
Stradbroke
Walberswick
Eye
Laxfield
Bramfield
Stanton
Dunwich
Ixworth
Finningham
Yoxford
Westleton
Brockford Street
Worlingworth
Dennington
Theberton
TM
Thurston
Bury St Edmunds
Framlingham
Debenham
Leiston
Woolpit
Saxmundham
Horringer
Stratford St Andrew
Thorpeness
Stowmarket
Easton
Whepstead
Helmingham
Snape
Aldeburgh
SUFFOLK
Wickham Market
Needham Market
Coddenham
Tunstall
Hawkedon
Hartest
Witnesham
Butley
Great Blakenham
Hitcham
Glemsford
Lavenham
Claydon
Orford
Bildeston
Woodbridge
Long Melford
Martlesham Heath
Clare
Hintlesham
IPSWICH
Shottisham
Stoke by Clare
Sudbury
Boxford
Hadleigh
Copdock
Nacton
Capel St Mary
Great Yeldham
Bawdsey
Stoke-by-Nayland
Shotley
Holbrook
East Bergholt
Bures
Nayland
Felixstowe
Colne Engaine
Dedham
Manningtree
Halstead
Harwich
Earls Colne
Ardleigh
Aldham
COLCHESTER
Wix
Braintree
Marks Tey
Thorpe-le-Soken
Weeley
Walton on the Naze
Coggeshall
Wivenhoe
Feering
Silver End
Frinton-on-Sea
Hotel
Town/Village name
0 10 miles
0 10 20 kilometres

For continuation pages refer to numbered arrows

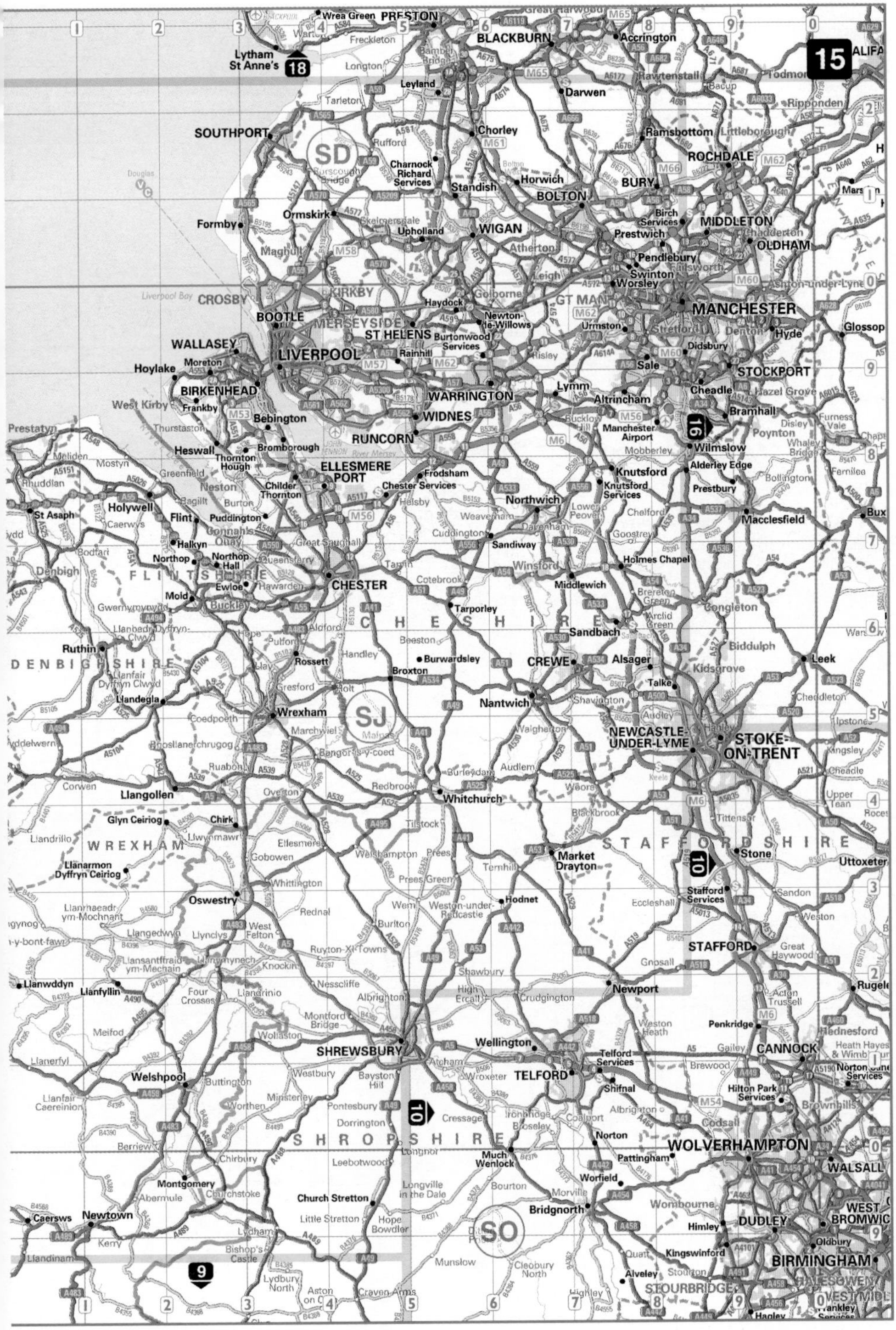

PRESTON
Wrea Green
Freckleton
Lytham St Anne's
18
Longton
BLACKBURN
Accrington
Darwen
Leyland
Tarleton
Rawtenstall
Bacup
Todmorden
Ripponden
SOUTHPORT
SD
Rufford
Chorley
Charnock Richard Services
Burscough Bridge
Horwich
Ramsbottom
Littleborough
ROCHDALE
Standish
BOLTON
BURY
Formby
Ormskirk
Birch Services
MIDDLETON
Skelmersdale
Upholland
WIGAN
Prestwich
Chadderton
OLDHAM
Maghull
Atherton
Pendlebury
Swinton
Leigh
Worsley
Ashton-under-Lyne
Liverpool Bay
CROSBY
KIRKBY
Haydock
Golborne
BOOTLE
MERSEYSIDE
Newton-le-Willows
Urmston
MANCHESTER
ST HELENS
Burtonwood Services
Stretford
Denton
Hyde
Glossop
WALLASEY
LIVERPOOL
Rainhill
Risley
Didsbury
Sale
Hoylake
Moreton
BIRKENHEAD
Lymm
STOCKPORT
WARRINGTON
Altrincham
Cheadle
Hazel Grove
West Kirby
Frankby
Bebington
WIDNES
Bramhall
Prestatyn
Thurstaston
Manchester Airport
16
Poynton
Disley
Furness Vale
Heswall
RUNCORN
Bromborough
Thornton Hough
Mobberley
Wilmslow
Whaley Bridge
Meliden
Mostyn
ELLESMERE PORT
Frodsham
Knutsford
Alderley Edge
Greenfield
Neston
Childer Thornton
Chester Services
Knutsford Services
Prestbury
Bollington
Rhuddlan
Holywell
Bagillt
Burton
Helsby
Northwich
St Asaph
Caerwys
Flint
Puddington
Connah's Quay
Weaverham
Davenham
Lower Peover
Chelford
Macclesfield
Buxton
Halkyn
Great Saughall
Cuddington
Sandiway
Goostrey
Bodfari
Northop
Northop Hall
Queensferry
Holmes Chapel
Denbigh
FLINTSHIRE
Tarvin
Winsford
Middlewich
Ewloe
Hawarden
CHESTER
Cotebrook
Mold
Buckley
Tarporley
Brereton Green
Congleton
Gwernymynydd
Arclid Green
Llanbedr Dyffryn-Clwyd
Hope
Aldford
CHESHIRE
Sandbach
Ruthin
Pulford
Beeston
Biddulph
Leek
DENBIGHSHIRE
Rossett
Handley
Burwardsley
CREWE
Alsager
Llanfair Dyffryn Clwyd
Llay
Broxton
Kidsgrove
Talke
Llandegla
Gresford
Holt
Shavington
Cheddleton
Coedpoeth
Wrexham
SJ
Nantwich
Audley
Ipstones
Marchwiel
Malpas
Wybunbury
NEWCASTLE-UNDER-LYME
STOKE-ON-TRENT
Rhosllanerchrugog
Bangor-is-y-coed
Kingsley
Ruabon
Burleydam
Audlem
Cheadle
Corwen
Llangollen
Redbrook
Overton
Whitchurch
Woore
Keele
Upper Tean
Glyn Ceiriog
Chirk
Tilstock
Blackbrook
Tittensor
Llandrillo
WREXHAM
Llwynmawr
Ellesmere
STAFFORDSHIRE
Gobowen
Whixall
Prees
Market Drayton
Stone
Uttoxeter
Llanarmon Dyffryn Ceiriog
Welshampton
Tern Hill
10
Prees Green
Whittington
Stafford Services
Sandon
Llanrhaeadr-ym-Mochnant
Oswestry
Rednal
Wem
Weston-under-Redcastle
Hodnet
Eccleshall
Weston
West Felton
Burlton
Llangedwyn
Llynclys
STAFFORD
Great Haywood
Llansantffraid-ym-Mechain
Llanymynech
Knockin
Ruyton-XI-Towns
Shawbury
Gnosall
Llanwddyn
Llanfyllin
Nesscliffe
High Ercall
Newport
Rugeley
Four Crosses
Llandrinio
Albrighton
Crudgington
Acton Trussell
Montford Bridge
Penkridge
Hednesford
Meifod
Wollaston
Weston Heath
Heath Hayes & Wimblebury
SHREWSBURY
Wellington
Gailey
CANNOCK
Llanerfyl
Atcham
Telford Services
Brewood
Norton Canes Services
Welshpool
Buttington
Westbury
Bayston Hill
Wroxeter
TELFORD
Shifnal
Hilton Park Services
Llanfair Caereinion
Minsterley
Worthen
Pontesbury
Cressage
Ironbridge
Broseley
Coalport
Albrighton
Brownhills
Dorrington
Codsall
SHROPSHIRE
Norton
Berriew
Chirbury
Longnor
Much Wenlock
WOLVERHAMPTON
Leebotwood
Pattingham
WALSALL
Montgomery
Abermule
Churchstoke
Longville in the Dale
Bourton
Worfield
Church Stretton
Morville
Wombourne
WEST BROMWICH
Caersws
Newtown
Little Stretton
Hope Bowdler
Bridgnorth
DUDLEY
Kerry
Lydham
SO
Himley
Oldbury
Bishop's Castle
Kingswinford
BIRMINGHAM
Llandinam
9
Munslow
Cleobury North
Quatt
Halesowen
Lydbury North
Aston on Clun
Craven Arms
Alveley
Stourton
Highley
STOURBRIDGE
Frankley Services
Hagley
M6
M56
M53
M54
M58
M62
M60
M61
M65
M66
M57

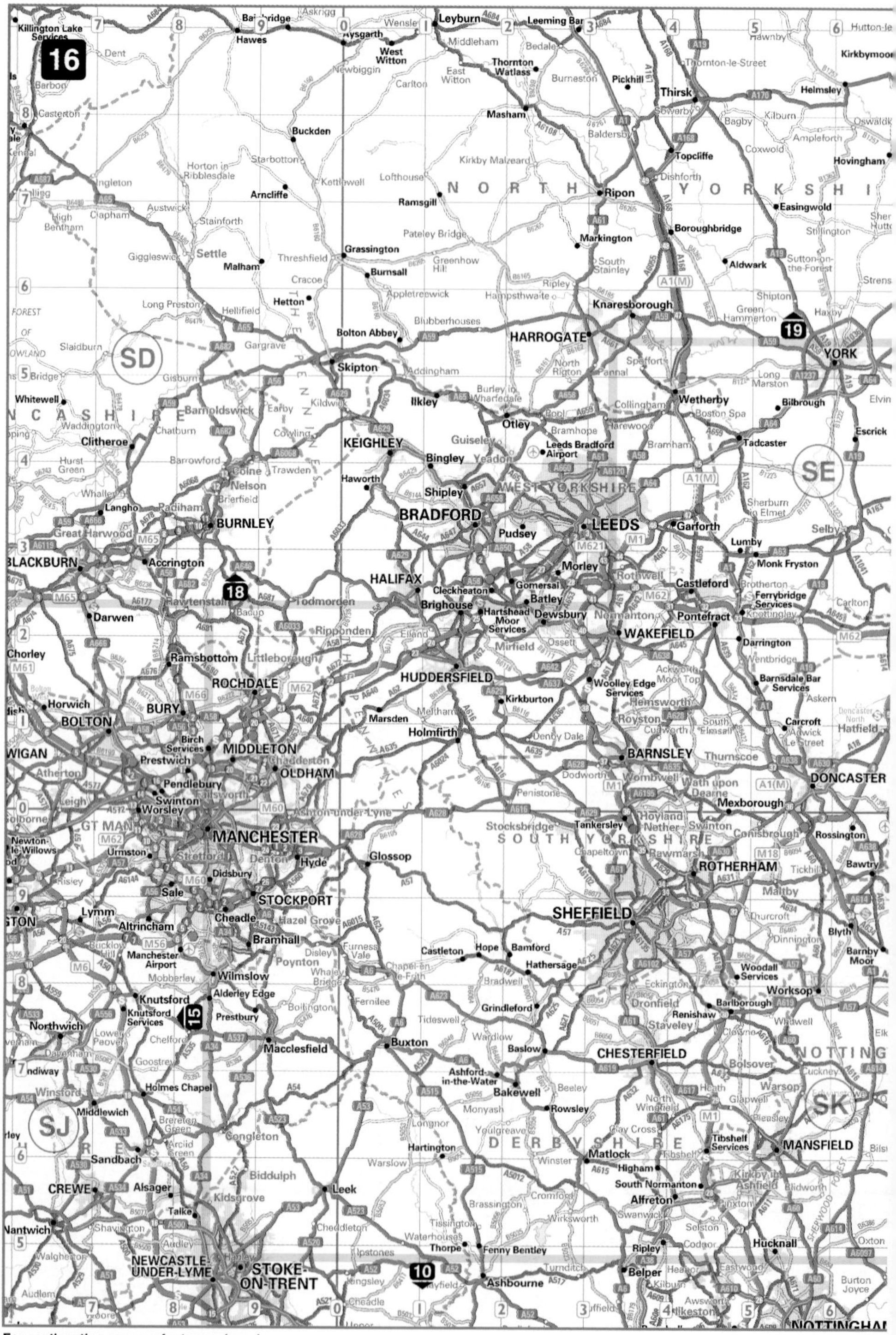

For continuation pages refer to numbered arrows

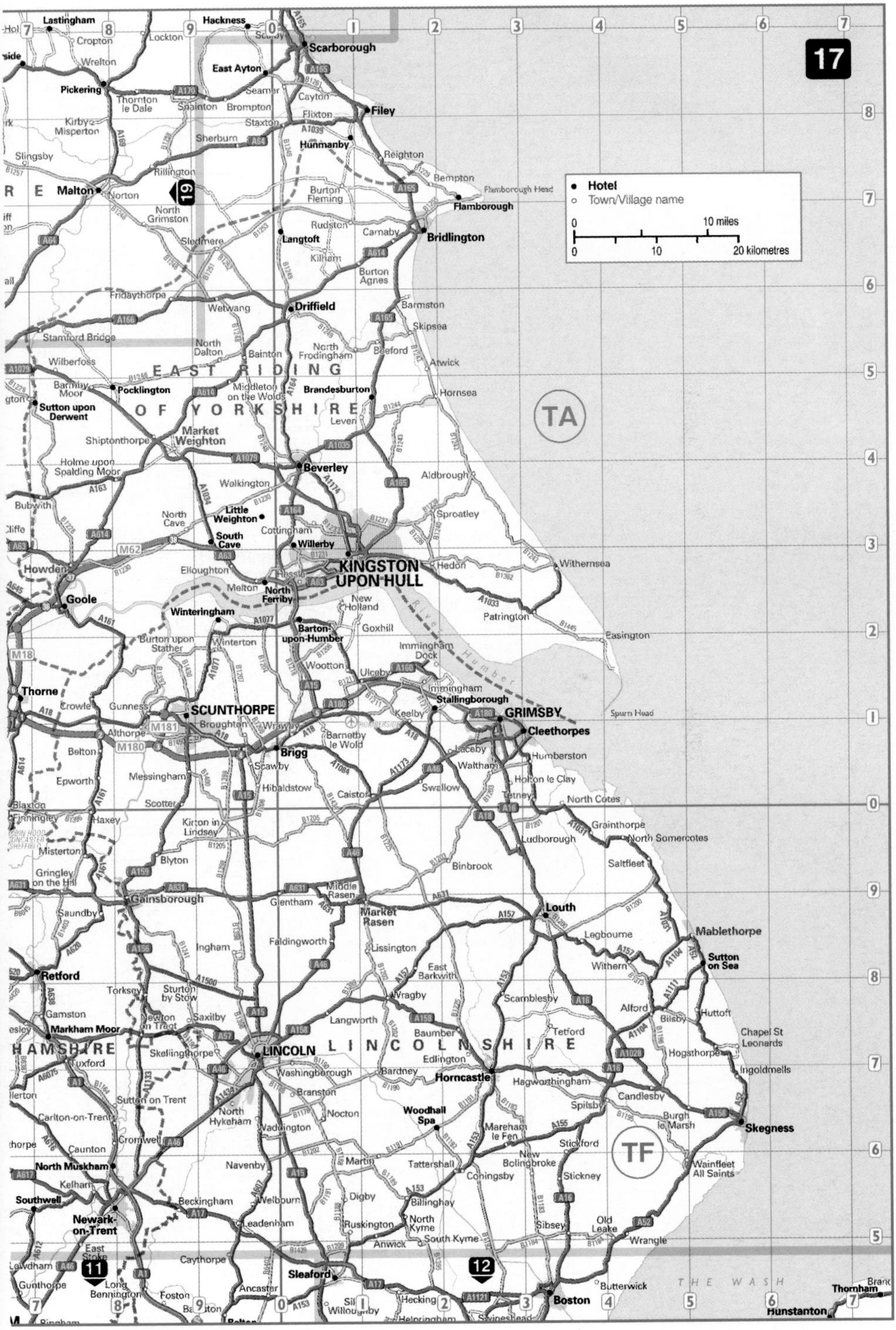
17
Hotel
Town/Village name
0
10 miles
0
10
20 kilometres
TA
TF
EAST RIDING OF YORKSHIRE
LINCOLNSHIRE
THE WASH
River Humber
Flamborough Head
Spurn Head
Lastingham
Hackness
Cropton
Lockton
Scarborough
Wrelton
East Ayton
Pickering
Thornton le Dale
Seamer
Cayton
Snainton
Brompton
Filey
Kirby Misperton
Staxton
Flixton
Sherburn
Hunmanby
Slingsby
Reighton
Rillington
Bempton
Malton
Norton
Burton Fleming
Flamborough
North Grimston
Rudston
Carnaby
Bridlington
Langtoft
Sledmere
Kilham
Burton Agnes
Fridaythorpe
Wetwang
Driffield
Barmston
Skipsea
Stamford Bridge
North Dalton
Bainton
North Frodingham
Beeford
Wilberfoss
Atwick
Barmby Moor
Pocklington
Middleton on the Wolds
Brandesburton
Hornsea
Sutton upon Derwent
Leven
Market Weighton
Shiptonthorpe
Beverley
Holme upon Spalding Moor
Walkington
Aldbrough
Bubwith
Little Weighton
Sproatley
North Cave
South Cave
Cottingham
Willerby
Howden
Elloughton
Hessle
KINGSTON UPON HULL
Hedon
Withernsea
Melton
North Ferriby
Goole
New Holland
Patrington
Winteringham
Barton-upon-Humber
Goxhill
Burton upon Stather
Winterton
Easington
Immingham Dock
Wootton
Ulceby
Thorne
Immingham
Crowle
Gunness
SCUNTHORPE
Stallingborough
GRIMSBY
Broughton
Wrawby
Keelby
Cleethorpes
Althorpe
Barnetby le Wold
Belton
Brigg
Laceby
Humberston
Scawby
Waltham
Epworth
Messingham
Holton le Clay
Hibaldstow
Caistor
Swallow
Tetney
North Cotes
Scotter
Blaxton
Finningley
Haxey
Kirton in Lindsey
Grainthorpe
North Somercotes
Ludborough
Misterton
Blyton
Binbrook
Saltfleet
Gringley on the Hill
Gainsborough
Middle Rasen
Glentham
Market Rasen
Louth
Saundby
Legbourne
Mablethorpe
Ingham
Faldingworth
Lissington
Sutton on Sea
Retford
East Barkwith
Withern
Torksey
Sturton by Stow
Scamblesby
Alford
Huttoft
Gamston
Wragby
Newton on Trent
Saxilby
Langworth
Tetford
Bilsby
Chapel St Leonards
Markham Moor
Baumber
Skellingthorpe
LINCOLN
Hogsthorpe
Tuxford
Edlington
Washingborough
Bardney
Horncastle
Ingoldmells
Hagworthingham
Branston
Candlesby
Sutton on Trent
Spilsby
North Hykeham
Nocton
Woodhall Spa
Burgh le Marsh
Carlton-on-Trent
Mareham le Fen
Skegness
Waddington
Stickford
Caunton
Cromwell
New Bolingbroke
Navenby
Martin
Tattershall
Wainfleet All Saints
North Muskham
Coningsby
Stickney
Kelham
Digby
Southwell
Beckingham
Welbourn
Billinghay
Newark-on-Trent
Leadenham
Ruskington
North Kyme
Sibsey
Old Leake
East Stoke
Anwick
South Kyme
Wrangle
Lowdham
Caythorpe
Gunthorpe
Long Bennington
Foston
Ancaster
Sleaford
Butterwick
Boston
Hunstanton
Thornham
Hecking
Willoughby
Helpringham
Swineshead
Bingham
Bottesford
11
12
19
M62
M18
M180
M181
A1
A15
A16
A18
A46
A52
A57
A63
A64
A165
A170
A180
A614
A631
A1033
A1079

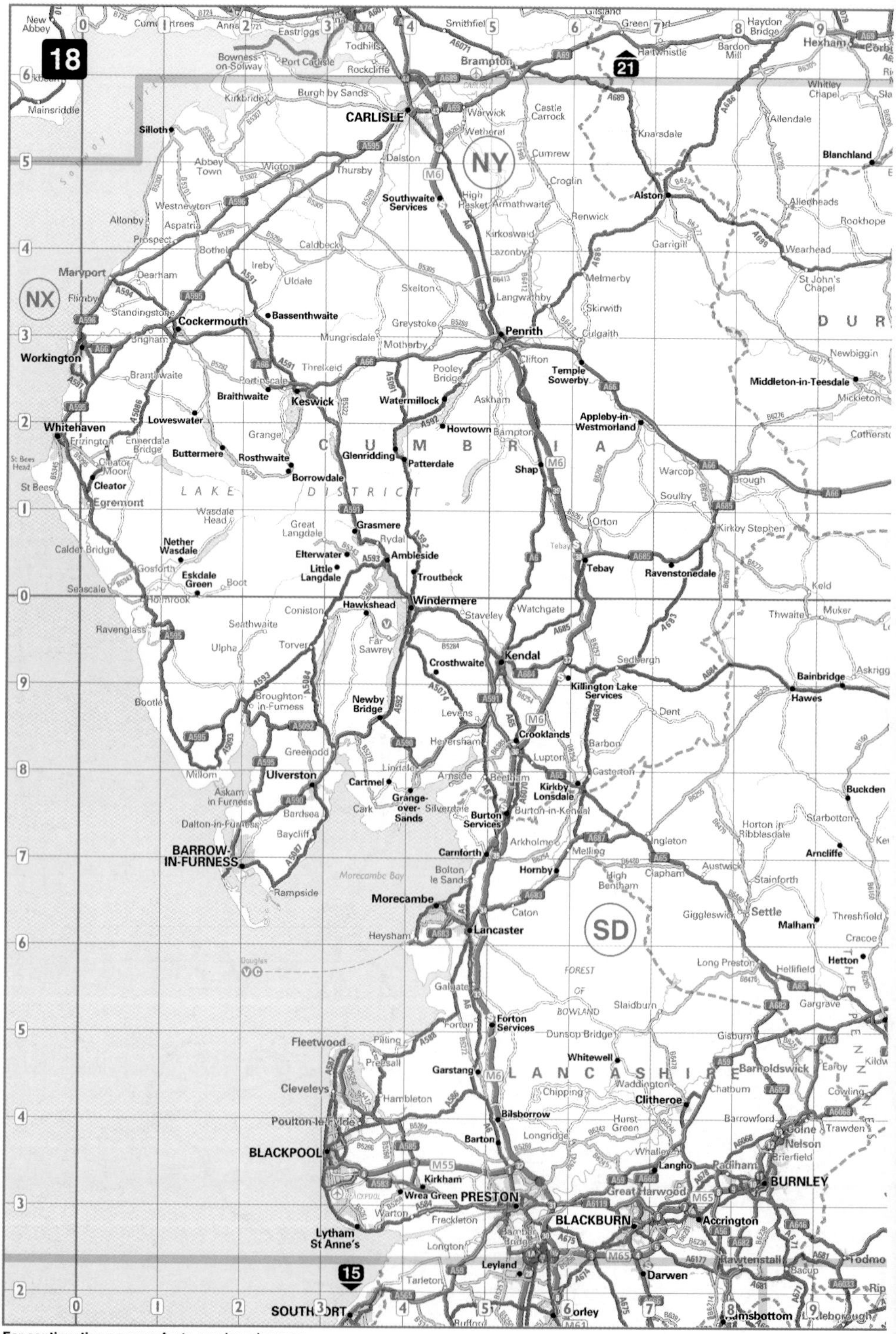

For continuation pages refer to numbered arrows

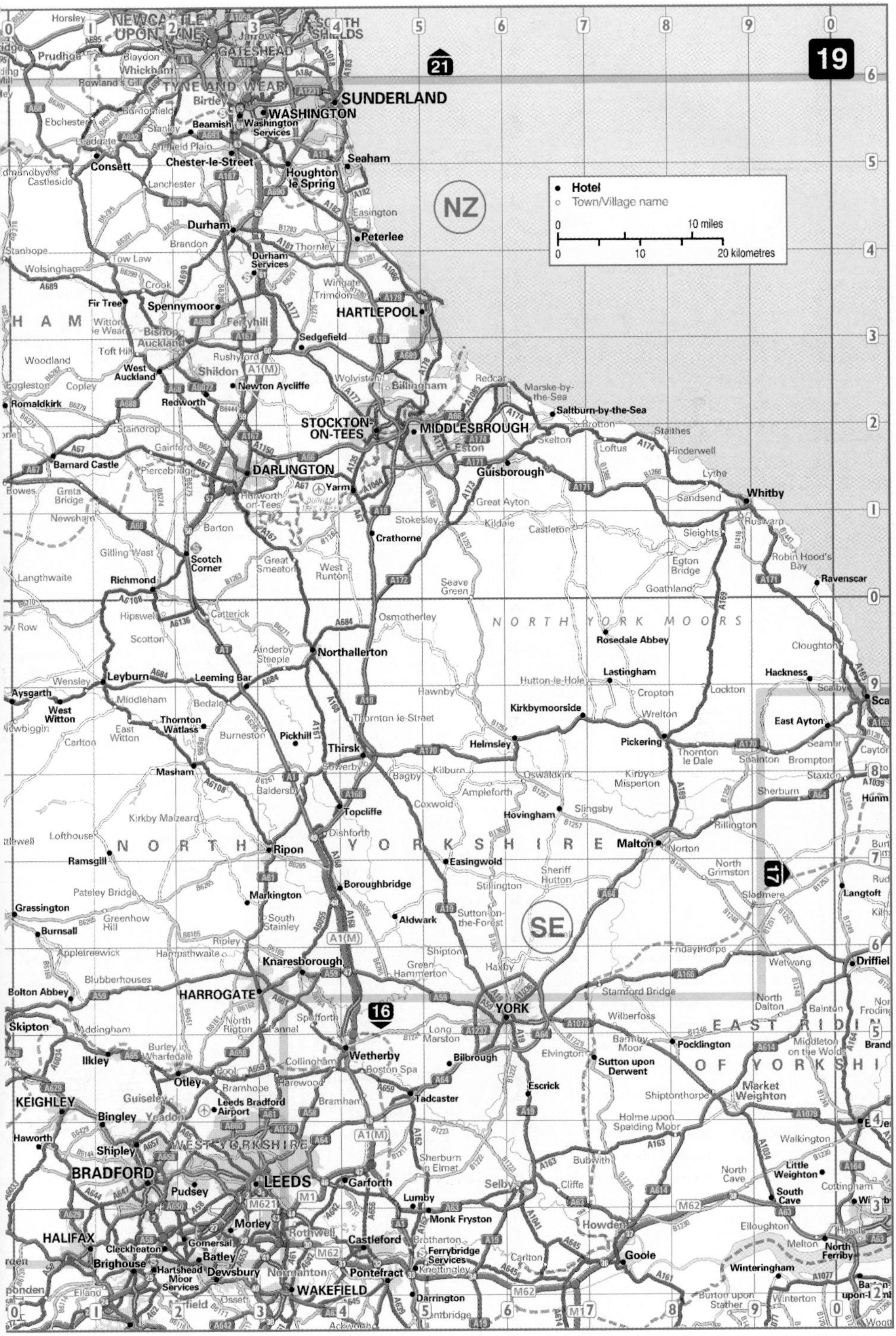
19
21
16
17
NZ
SE
Hotel
Town/Village name
0
10 miles
0
10
20 kilometres
NEWCASTLE UPON TYNE
GATESHEAD
SOUTH SHIELDS
Jarrow
Horsley
Prudhoe
Blaydon
Whickham
Rowland's Gill
TYNE AND WEAR
Birtley
Burnopfield
Ebchester
Beamish
WASHINGTON
Washington Services
SUNDERLAND
Stanley
Leadgate
Annfield Plain
Consett
Chester-le-Street
Houghton le Spring
Seaham
Edmundbyers
Castleside
Lanchester
Easington
Durham
Peterlee
Brandon
Thornley
Stanhope
Tow Law
Durham Services
Wolsingham
Wingate
Crook
Trimdon
Fir Tree
Spennymoor
HARTLEPOOL
Witton le Wear
Ferryhill
Bishop Auckland
Sedgefield
Toft Hill
Woodland
Rushyford
West Auckland
Shildon
Eggleston
Copley
Newton Aycliffe
Wolviston
Billingham
Redcar
Marske-by-the-Sea
Romaldkirk
Redworth
Saltburn-by-the-Sea
Staindrop
STOCKTON-ON-TEES
MIDDLESBROUGH
Brotton
Staithes
Gainford
Skelton
Loftus
Hinderwell
Eston
Barnard Castle
Piercebridge
DARLINGTON
Guisborough
Lythe
Bowes
Greta Bridge
Hurworth-on-Tees
Yarm
Great Ayton
Sandsend
Whitby
Newsham
Barton
Stokesley
Kildale
Castleton
Sleights
Ruswarp
Crathorne
Gilling West
Scotch Corner
Great Smeaton
West Rounton
Egton Bridge
Robin Hood's Bay
Langthwaite
Richmond
Seave Green
Goathland
Ravenscar
Catterick
Osmotherley
Hipswell
NORTH YORK MOORS
Scotton
Rosedale Abbey
Ainderby Steeple
Northallerton
Cloughton
Wensley
Leyburn
Leeming Bar
Lastingham
Hackness
Aysgarth
Middleham
Bedale
Hutton-le-Hole
Cropton
Lockton
West Witton
Hawnby
Kirkbymoorside
Wrelton
Newbiggin
Thornton Watlass
Thornton-le-Street
East Ayton
East Witton
Carlton
Burneston
Pickhill
Thirsk
Helmsley
Pickering
Thornton le Dale
Snainton
Brompton
Masham
Sowerby
Kilburn
Oswaldkirk
Kirby Misperton
Bagby
Staxton
Baldersby
Ampleforth
Coxwold
Sherburn
Kirkby Malzeard
Topcliffe
Hovingham
Slingsby
Lofthouse
Dishforth
Rillington
NORTH YORKSHIRE
Ripon
Malton
Norton
Ramsgill
Easingwold
North Grimston
Sheriff Hutton
Pateley Bridge
Boroughbridge
Stillington
Langtoft
Markington
Grassington
Sledmere
South Stainley
Aldwark
Sutton-on-the-Forest
Greenhow Hill
Burnsall
Ripley
Appletreewick
Hampsthwaite
Shipton
Fridaythorpe
Knaresborough
Green Hammerton
Haxby
Wetwang
Driffield
Blubberhouses
Bolton Abbey
HARROGATE
Stamford Bridge
North Dalton
Bainton
Spofforth
YORK
Wilberfoss
North Rigton
Pannal
Skipton
Addingham
Long Marston
EAST RIDING OF YORKSHIRE
Barmby Moor
Pocklington
Middleton on the Wolds
Burley in Wharfedale
Ilkley
Wetherby
Bilbrough
Elvington
Sutton upon Derwent
Collingham
Boston Spa
Otley
Pool
Bramhope
Harewood
Escrick
Market Weighton
Guiseley
KEIGHLEY
Leeds Bradford Airport
Tadcaster
Shiptonthorpe
Bramham
Bingley
Yeadon
Holme upon Spalding Moor
Haworth
WEST YORKSHIRE
Walkington
Shipley
Sherburn in Elmet
Bubwith
Little Weighton
BRADFORD
North Cave
LEEDS
Garforth
Selby
Cliffe
Pudsey
Cottingham
South Cave
Lumby
Monk Fryston
Morley
Howden
HALIFAX
Gomersal
Rothwell
Ellougton
Cleckheaton
Castleford
Brotherton
Melton
North Ferriby
Batley
Ferrybridge Services
Carlton
Goole
Brighouse
Hartshead Moor Services
Dewsbury
Normanton
Pontefract
Knottingley
Winteringham
Elland
WAKEFIELD
Darrington
Burton upon Stather
Winterton
Ossett
Ackworth

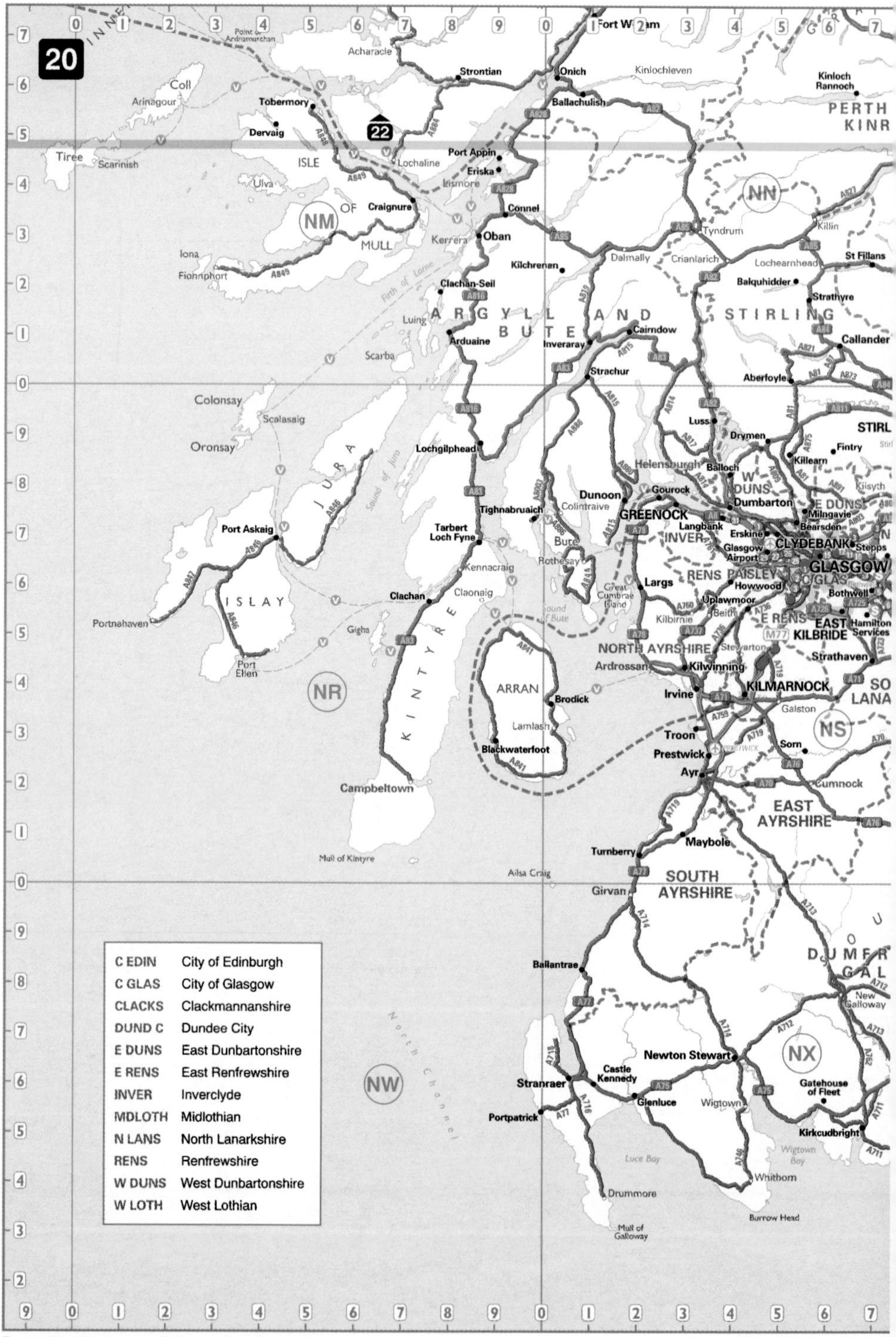

For continuation pages refer to numbered arrows

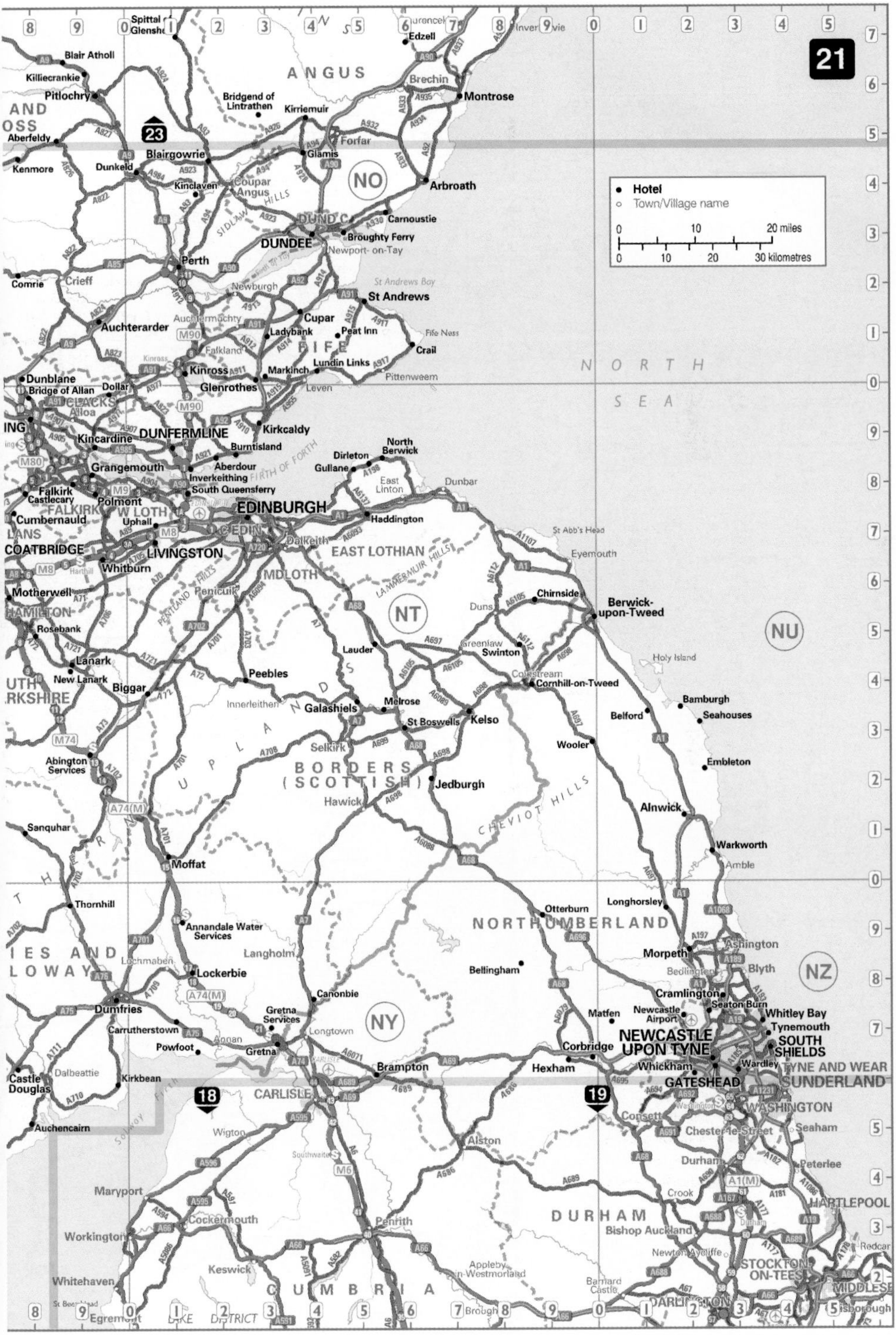
21
Hotel
Town/Village name
0 10 20 miles
0 10 20 30 kilometres
ANGUS
Blair Atholl
Killiecrankie
Pitlochry
Aberfeldy
Kenmore
Dunkeld
Blairgowrie
Bridgend of Lintrathen
Kirriemuir
Edzell
Brechin
Montrose
Forfar
Glamis
Arbroath
Carnoustie
Coupar Angus
Kinclaven
SIDLAW HILLS
DUNDEE
Broughty Ferry
Newport-on-Tay
Perth
Comrie
Crieff
Newburgh
Auchtermuchty
Auchterarder
Cupar
St Andrews Bay
St Andrews
Ladybank
Peat Inn
Fife Ness
Crail
FIFE
Falkland
Kinross
Glenrothes
Markinch
Lundin Links
Pittenweem
Leven
Dunblane
Bridge of Allan
Dollar
CLACKS
Alloa
Kincardine
DUNFERMLINE
Kirkcaldy
Burntisland
Grangemouth
Aberdour
Inverkeithing
South Queensferry
FIRTH OF FORTH
Falkirk
Castlecary
Polmont
Cumbernauld
Uphall
EDINBURGH
Dalkeith
COATBRIDGE
LIVINGSTON
Whitburn
Penicuik
PENTLAND HILLS
MIDLOTH
Motherwell
HAMILTON
Rosebank
Lanark
New Lanark
Biggar
NORTH SEA
Dirleton
North Berwick
Gullane
East Linton
Dunbar
Haddington
EAST LOTHIAN
LAMMERMUIR HILLS
St Abb's Head
Eyemouth
Chirnside
Berwick-upon-Tweed
Duns
Greenlaw
Swinton
Lauder
Coldstream
Cornhill-on-Tweed
Holy Island
Bamburgh
Seahouses
Belford
Peebles
Innerleithen
Galashiels
Melrose
St Boswells
Kelso
Wooler
Selkirk
BORDERS (SCOTTISH)
Jedburgh
Hawick
UPLANDS
Embleton
CHEVIOT HILLS
Alnwick
Warkworth
Amble
Abington Services
Sanquhar
Moffat
Thornhill
Annandale Water Services
Langholm
Lochmaben
Lockerbie
Otterburn
Longhorsley
NORTHUMBERLAND
Morpeth
Ashington
Bedlington
Blyth
Bellingham
Cramlington
Seaton Burn
Whitley Bay
Tynemouth
SOUTH SHIELDS
Newcastle Airport
Matfen
NEWCASTLE UPON TYNE
Whickham
Wardley
TYNE AND WEAR
SUNDERLAND
GATESHEAD
Canonbie
Gretna Services
Longtown
Gretna
Annan
Dumfries
Carrutherstown
Powfoot
Brampton
Hexham
Corbridge
Castle Douglas
Dalbeattie
Kirkbean
Auchencairn
CARLISLE
Wigton
Southwaite
Alston
Consett
WASHINGTON
Chester-le-Street
Seaham
Durham
Peterlee
Maryport
Cockermouth
Penrith
DURHAM
Crook
HARTLEPOOL
Bishop Auckland
Workington
Whitehaven
Keswick
Appleby-in-Westmorland
Newton Aycliffe
STOCKTON-ON-TEES
Redcar
MIDDLESBROUGH
Barnard Castle
DARLINGTON
CUMBRIA
LAKE DISTRICT
Egremont
Brough
NO
NT
NU
NY
NZ
23
18
19

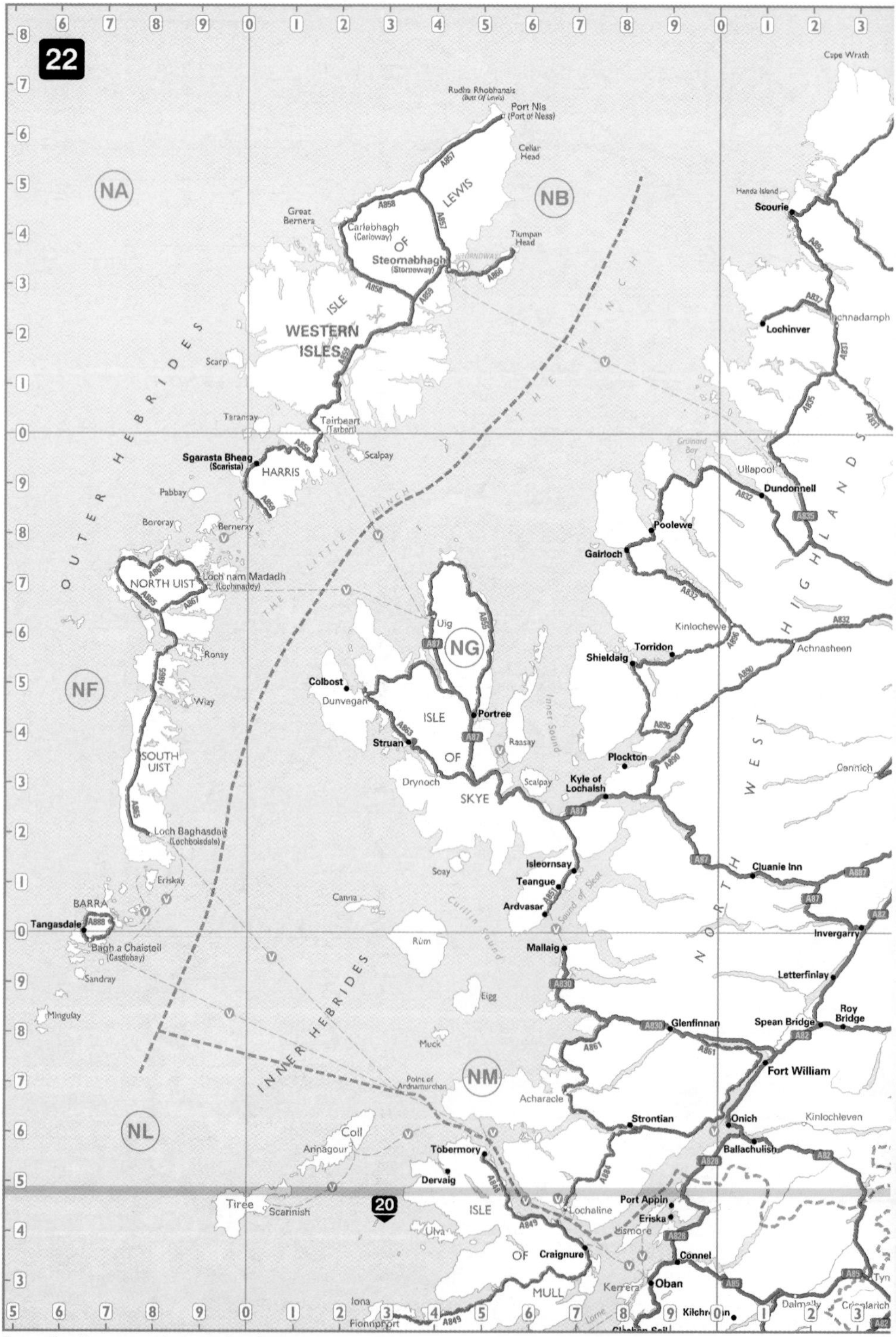

For continuation pages refer to numbered arrows

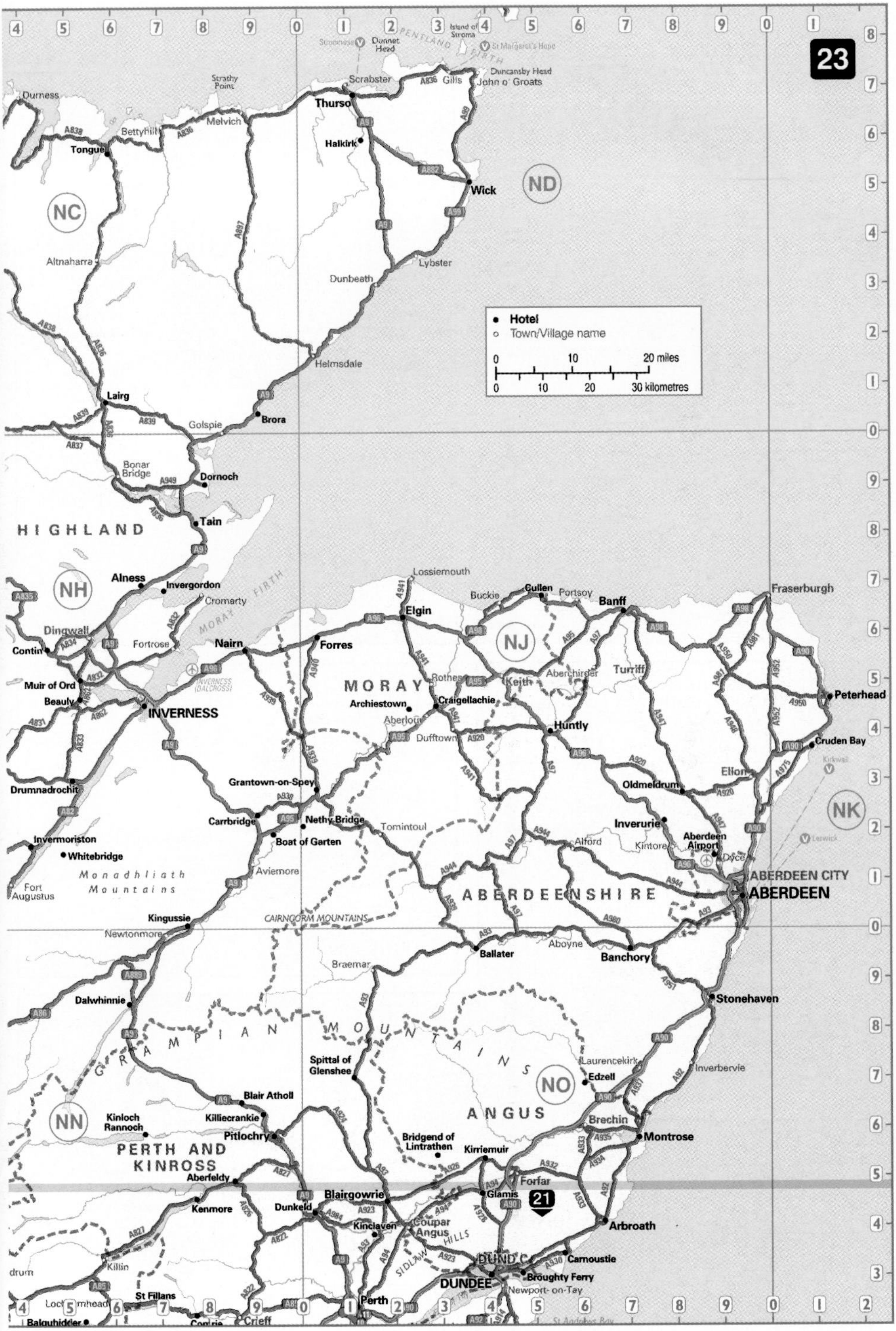

23
Hotel
Town/Village name
0 10 20 miles
0 10 20 30 kilometres
Stromness
Dunnet Head
PENTLAND FIRTH
Island of Stroma
St Margaret's Hope
Duncansby Head
John o' Groats
Strathy Point
Scrabster
Gills
Durness
Thurso
Melvich
Bettyhill
Tongue
Halkirk
Wick
ND
NC
Lybster
Altnaharra
Dunbeath
Helmsdale
Lairg
Golspie
Brora
Bonar Bridge
Dornoch
Tain
HIGHLAND
NH
Alness
Invergordon
Cromarty
MORAY FIRTH
Lossiemouth
Buckie
Cullen
Portsoy
Banff
Fraserburgh
Dingwall
Contin
Fortrose
Nairn
Forres
Elgin
NJ
Muir of Ord
Beauly
INVERNESS
INVERNESS (DALCROSS)
MORAY
Rothes
Keith
Aberchirder
Turriff
Peterhead
Archiestown
Craigellachie
Aberlour
Dufftown
Huntly
Cruden Bay
Drumnadrochit
Grantown-on-Spey
Oldmeldrum
Ellon
Kirkwall
NK
Carrbridge
Nethy Bridge
Boat of Garten
Tomintoul
Inverurie
Alford
Kintore
Aberdeen Airport
Dyce
Lerwick
Invermoriston
Whitebridge
Monadhliath Mountains
Aviemore
Fort Augustus
ABERDEEN CITY
ABERDEEN
ABERDEENSHIRE
Kingussie
Newtonmore
CAIRNGORM MOUNTAINS
Ballater
Aboyne
Banchory
Braemar
Stonehaven
Dalwhinnie
GRAMPIAN MOUNTAINS
Spittal of Glenshee
Laurencekirk
Inverbervie
Edzell
NO
Blair Atholl
NN
Kinloch Rannoch
Killiecrankie
ANGUS
Brechin
Pitlochry
PERTH AND KINROSS
Bridgend of Lintrathen
Kirriemuir
Montrose
Forfar
Aberfeldy
Blairgowrie
Glamis
21
Kenmore
Dunkeld
Coupar Angus
Kinclaven
Arbroath
SIDLAW HILLS
Killin
Carnoustie
DUNDEE
Broughty Ferry
Newport-on-Tay
Lochearnhead
St Fillans
Perth
Balquhidder
Comrie
Crieff
St Andrews Bay
A838
A836
A9
A99
A882
A897
A839
A837
A949
A835
A834
A832
A96
A862
A831
A833
A82
A939
A940
A941
A95
A920
A98
A97
A947
A950
A952
A981
A90
A975
A938
A944
A93
A980
A957
A889
A86
A92
A937
A935
A933
A934
A932
A926
A924
A827
A822
A923
A984
A94
A930
A85

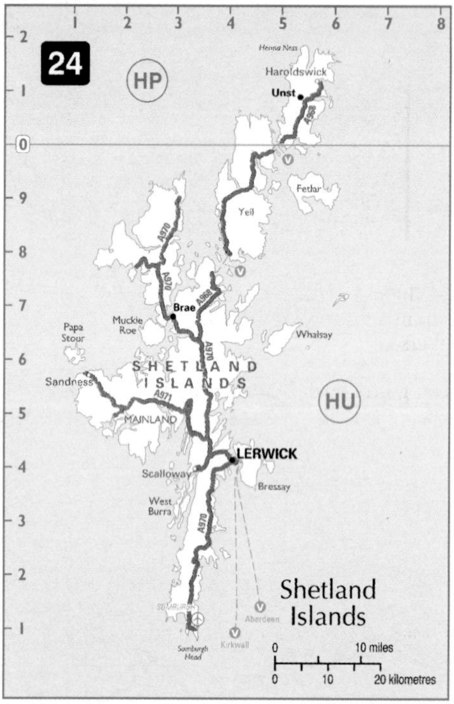
Shetland Islands
HP
HU
Herma Ness
Haroldswick
Unst
A968
Fetlar
Yell
A970
Brae
A968
Muckle Roe
Papa Stour
Whalsay
A970
SHETLAND ISLANDS
Sandness
A971
MAINLAND
LERWICK
Scalloway
Bressay
West Burra
A970
SUMBURGH
Sumburgh Head
Kirkwall
Aberdeen
0 10 miles
0 10 20 kilometres

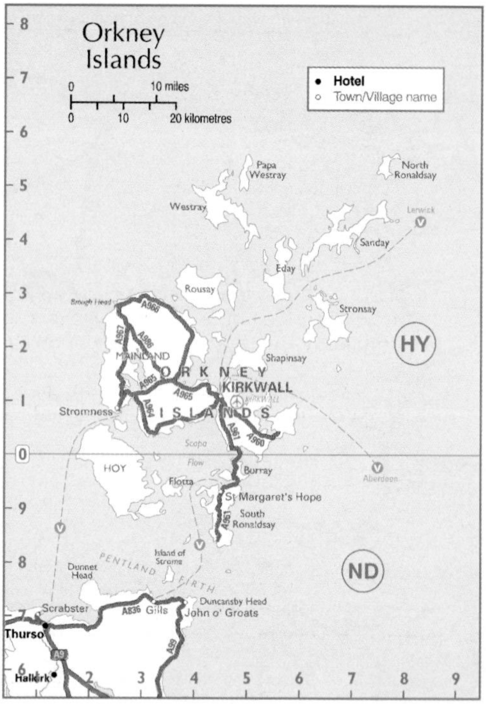
Orkney Islands
0 10 miles
0 10 20 kilometres
Hotel
Town/Village name
Papa Westray
North Ronaldsay
Westray
Lerwick
Sanday
Eday
Rousay
Brough Head
Stronsay
HY
A966
A967
A986
MAINLAND
Shapinsay
ORKNEY ISLANDS
KIRKWALL
A965
Stromness
A964
A961
A960
Scapa Flow
HOY
Flotta
Burray
Aberdeen
St Margaret's Hope
South Ronaldsay
Island of Stroma
PENTLAND FIRTH
Dunnet Head
ND
Scrabster
A836
Gills
Duncansby Head
John o' Groats
Thurso
A9
A99
Halkirk

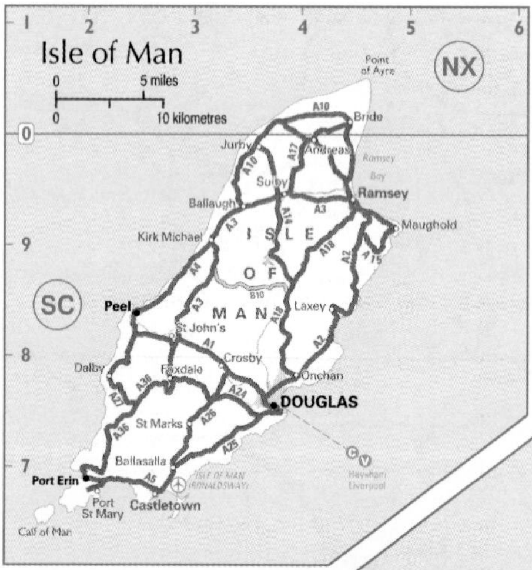
Isle of Man
0 5 miles
0 10 kilometres
NX
Point of Ayre
A10
Bride
Jurby
A17
Andreas
Ramsey Bay
Sulby
Ramsey
Ballaugh
A14
A3
Maughold
Kirk Michael
ISLE OF MAN
A18
A2
A15
A4
B10
SC
Peel
Laxey
St John's
A1
Crosby
Dalby
Foxdale
A36
Onchan
A24
DOUGLAS
A27
St Marks
A26
A25
Ballasalla
Heysham
Liverpool
Port Erin
A5
ISLE OF MAN (RONALDSWAY)
Port St Mary
Castletown
Calf of Man

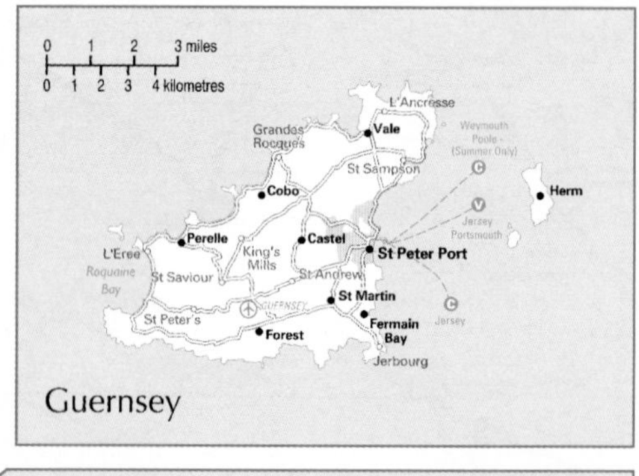
0 1 2 3 miles
0 1 2 3 4 kilometres
L'Ancresse
Grandes Rocques
Vale
Weymouth
Poole
(Summer Only)
St Sampson
Herm
Cobo
Jersey
Portsmouth
Perelle
Castel
L'Eree
King's Mills
St Peter Port
Rocquaine Bay
St Saviour
St Andrew
St Martin
GUERNSEY
St Peter's
Fermain Bay
Forest
Jerbourg
Guernsey

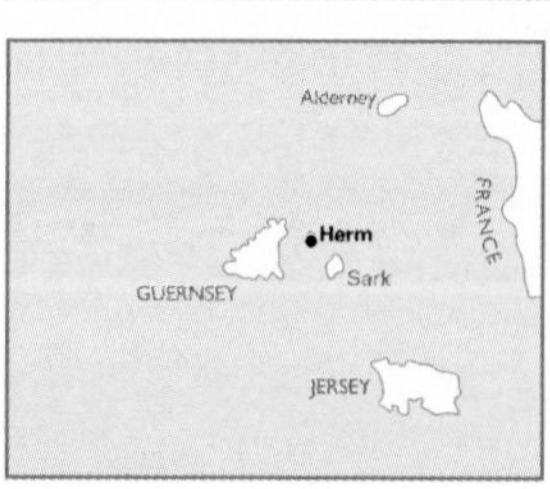
Alderney
FRANCE
Herm
Sark
GUERNSEY
JERSEY

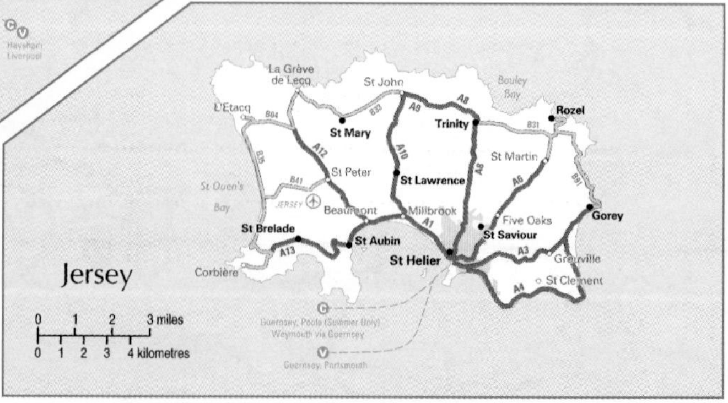
La Grève de Lecq
St John
Bouley Bay
L'Etacq
B64
B33
A9
A8
Rozel
St Mary
Trinity
B31
A12
St Martin
B35
St Peter
A10
A6
B91
B41
St Lawrence
St Ouen's Bay
JERSEY
Beaumont
Millbrook
A1
Five Oaks
Gorey
St Brelade
St Saviour
A13
St Aubin
St Helier
A3
Grouville
Corbière
A4
St Clement
Jersey
0 1 2 3 miles
0 1 2 3 4 kilometres
Guernsey, Poole (Summer Only)
Weymouth via Guernsey
Guernsey, Portsmouth

Please send this form to:
Editor, The Hotel Guide
AA Lifestyle Guides,
Fanum House,
Basingstoke RG21 4EA

or fax 01256 491647
or email lifestyleguides@theAA.com

Reader's Report form

Please use this form to recommend any hotel where you have stayed, whether it is included in the guide or not. You can also help us to improve the guide by completing the short questionnaire on the reverse.

The AA does not undertake to arbitrate between guide readers and hotels, or to obtain compensation or engage in correspondence.

Date:

Your name (block capitals)

Your address (block capitals)

....

....

....

....

email address:

Name of hotel:

Comments

....

....

....

....

....

....

....

(please attach a separate sheet if necessary)

Please tick here if you DO NOT wish to receive details of AA offers or products ☐

PTO

Have you bought this guide before? YES NO

Have you bought any other accommodation, restaurant, pub or food guides recently? If yes, which ones?

....

....

Why did you buy this guide? (circle all that apply)

holiday short break business travel special occasion

overnight stop find a venue for an event e.g. conference

other ....

How often do you stay in hotels? (circle one choice)

more than once a month once a month once in 2-3 months

once in six months once a year less than once a year

Please answer these questions to help us make improvements to the guide:

Which of these factors are most important when choosing a hotel?

Price Location Awards/ratings Service

Decor/Surroundings Previous experience Recommendation

Other (please state) ....

Do you read the editorial features in the guide?

Do you use the location atlas?

Which elements of the guide do you find the most useful when choosing somewhere to stay?

Description Photo Advertisement Star rating

Can you suggest any improvements to the guide?

....

....

....

NOTES

credits

The Automobile Association would like to thank the following for supplying photographs for this book: Hand Picked Hotels (Buxted Park 3ml, 5t, 22; Chilston Park 3mr, 19; Crathorne Hall 8; Ettington Park 1, 4, 6, 10t, 21; Hotel L'Horizon 23m; Nutfield Priory 13; The Priest House 19; Rhinefield House 20, 25; Rookery Hall 11b, 15; Wood Hall 3b, 10; Woodlands Park 3t, 12)

The remaining pictures are held in the Association's own library (AA WORLD TRAVEL LIBRARY) and were taken by: Steve Day 14, Andrew Midgley 5b